THE COMMON LAW LIBRARY

THE LAW OF CONTRACTS

VOLUME 1

GENERAL PRINCIPLES

OTHER VOLUMES IN THE COMMON LAW LIBRARY

Clerk & Lindsell on Torts

Chitty & Jacob's Queen's Bench Forms

Bullen & Leake & Jacob's Precedents of Pleadings

Charlesworth and Percy on Negligence

Bowstead and Reynolds on Agency

Gatley on Libel and Slander

McGregor on Damages

Phipson on Evidence

Benjamin's Sale of Goods

Jackson & Powell on Professional Negligence

Goff & Jones, The Law of Restitution

Arlidge, Eady & Smith on Contempt

AUSTRALIA
LBC Information Services Ltd
Sydney

CANADA and USA
Carswell
Toronto

NEW ZEALAND
Brooker's
Auckland

SINGAPORE and MALAYSIA
Sweet & Maxwell
Singapore and Kuala Lumpur

THE COMMON LAW LIBRARY

CHITTY
ON
CONTRACTS

TWENTY-EIGHTH EDITION

VOLUME 1

GENERAL PRINCIPLES

LONDON
SWEET & MAXWELL
1999

First Edition	(1826)	By Joseph Chitty, Junior
Second Edition	(1834)	” ” ”
Third Edition	(1841)	By Thompson Chitty
Fourth Edition	(1850)	By His Hon. Judge J. A. Russell, Q.C.
Fifth Edition	(1853)	” ” ”
Sixth Edition	(1857)	” ” ”
Seventh Edition	(1863)	” ” ”
Eighth Edition	(1868)	” ” ”
Ninth Edition	(1871)	” ” ”
Tenth Edition	(1876)	” ” ”
Eleventh Edition	(1881)	” ” ”
Twelfth Edition	(1890)	By J. M. Lely and Sir William Geary
Thirteenth Edition	(1896)	By J. M. Lely
Fourteenth Edition	(1904)	” ”
Fifteenth Edition	(1909)	By W. Wyatt Paine
Sixteenth Edition	(1912)	” ”
Seventeenth Edition	(1921)	” ”
Eighteenth Edition	(1930)	By W. A. MacFarlane and G. W. Wrangham
Nineteenth Edition	(1937)	General Editor: Harold Potter
Twentieth Edition	(1947)	” ” ”
Twenty-first Edition	(1955)	Under the General Editorship of John Burke and Peter Allsop
Twenty-second Edition	(1961)	General Editor: John Morris
Twenty-third Edition	(1968)	General Editor: A. G. Guest
Second Impression	(1972)	” ” ”
Twenty-fourth Edition	(1977)	” ” ”
Second Impression	(1979)	” ” ”
Third Impression	(1980)	” ” ”
Twenty-fifth Edition	(1983)	” ” ”
Twenty-sixth Edition	(1989)	” ” ”
Second Impression	(1990)	” ” ”
Third Impression	(1991)	” ” ”
Twenty-seventh Edition	(1994)	” ” ”
Second Impression	(1995)	” ” ”
Third Impression	(1997)	” ” ”
Fourth Impression	(1998)	” ” ”
Twenty-eighth Edition	(1999)	General Editor: H. G. Beale

Published by
Sweet & Maxwell Limited, of 100 Avenue Road
London NW3 3PF
http://www.smlawpub.co.uk
Computerset by
Interactive Sciences, Gloucester
and printed in Great Britain by
Clays Ltd, St Ives plc

[v]

NOTE TO READERS

Chitty on Contracts, 28th edition, consists of two volumes. Volume 1 is the *General Principles* text and Volume 2 deals with *Specific Contracts*. Customers may choose to purchase either Volume 1 alone or both Volumes together.

Please note that Volume 1 contains Chapters 1 to 31 and an Index which relates to Volume 1 only.

Volume 2 contains Chapters 32 to 44 and an Index which relates to both Volumes 1 and 2.

No natural forests were destroyed to make this product;
only farmed timber was used and replanted

A CIP catalogue record for
this book is available
from the British Library

ISBN Volume 1 0 421 691 905
ISBN Full Set 0421 647 205

PREFACE

The last edition of *Chitty on Contracts* was published in 1994 under the General Editorship of Professor A. G. Guest, Q.C., the fifth edition to be produced under his editorship. All the Editors would like to put on record their enormous appreciation of the skill, care and dedication which Professor Guest brought to the task. They in turn are committed to maintaining the very high standards which he set. They are also delighted that Professor Guest has continued to edit the chapters for which he was responsible in the previous edition.

Since the twenty-seventh edition Mr G. D. Kinley and Mr Stephen Moriarty have retired from the team responsible for Volume 2 because of their other commitments. Mr Peter MacDonald Eggers has joined the team to take over their chapters. Within the two volumes there has been some re-arrangement of responsibility, with Professor Burrows taking over Chapter 18 on Joint Obligations and Professor McKendrick Chapter 33 on Bailment.

The new edition contains two completely new chapters. In Volume 1 Dr Whittaker has written a new chapter on Unfair Terms (previously covered in the chapter on Exemption clauses) which gives a detailed account of the Unfair Terms in Consumer Contracts Regulations 1999, including discussion of the probable interpretation of the relevant Directive by the ECJ and of the view taken by the Office of Fair Trading of terms in recent use. In Volume 2 Professor John Uff Q.C. and Mr Simon Hughes have joined the team to write a new chapter on Construction Contracts.

The period since 1994 has seen a large number of important changes affecting many chapters, including significant developments in the case law and a large quantity of legislation. This has necessitated a great amount of re-writing.

Nowhere have developments in case law been more important than on the questions of concurrent liability in contract and tort following the House of Lords decision in *Henderson v. Merrett Syndicates Ltd*, and on tort liability in the contractual context in the light of cases such as *Marc Rich & Co. AG v. Bishop Rock Marine Co.*, *Spring v. Guardian Assurance plc* and *White v. Jones*, discussed in the Introduction to Volume 1. Further signs of the English judiciary accepting a general concept of good faith in contracts are also noted.

Part One contains a new section on conditional contracts in the Chapter on Agreement. Chapter 4 (Form) explains the cases interpreting Law Reform (Miscellaneous Provisions) Act 1989, section 2. Chapter 5 (Mistake) deals with *Commissioner for New Towns v. Cooper (Great Britain) Ltd* on rectification; Chapter 6 (Misrepresentation) considers the rules on damages for fraud and misrepresentation after the House of Lords decisions in *South Australia Asset Management Corp. v. York Montague Ltd* and *Smith New Court Securities Ltd v. Scrimgeour Vickers (Asset Management) Ltd*. It and Chapter 7 (Duress and Undue Influence) deal with the continuing progeny of *Barclays Bank plc v. O'Brien*, in particular the important Court of Appeal decision in *Royal Bank of Scotland v. Etridge (No. 2)* on the steps a lender should take to avoid being fixed with constructive notice; cases such as *TSB Bank plc v. Camfield* and *Dunbar Bank plc v. Nadeem* on the effect on the surety's liability if the lender is fixed with notice of misrepresentation or undue influence; and the suggestions in the Court of Appeal in *Credit Lyonnais Bank Nederland NV v. Burch* that the surety may also be given relief under the doctrine of unconscionable bargains. The sections on unconscionable bargains, on economic duress and on undue influence have been revised to give a more detailed account of these difficult topics.

In Part Two the principal development is the Local Government (Contracts Act) 1997, covered in Chapter 10.

In Part Three (The Terms of the Contract), Chapter 12 (Express Terms) has been revised to take account of the more radical approach to the interpretation of contracts advocated by Lord Hoffmann: that the meaning of words in a document, and their syntactical arrangement, must yield to what the parties using those words against the relevant background would reasonably have been understood to mean. Chapter 14 (Exemption Clauses) notes a number of new decisions on the Unfair Contract Terms Act 1977 and the proposed legislative extension of the benefit of exemption clauses to persons other than the parties to the contract (see below). Chapter 15 (Unfair Terms) is, as noted earlier, entirely new, giving much fuller coverage of the interpretation and application of the Unfair Terms in Consumer Contracts Regulations than was possible in the previous edition which appeared just after the Regulations had been passed. Chapter 16 on Arbitration Clauses has been completely re-written having regard to the enactment of the Arbitration Act 1996.

In Part Four (Illegality and Public Policy) the principal developments are the decisions of the House of Lords in *Tinsley v. Milligan* and of the Court of Appeal in *Tribe v. Tribe*. The cases on champerty and maintenance and the new arrangements on conditional fees are also considered.

In Part Five, Chapter 20 (Third Parties) anticipates the successful passage of the Contracts (Rights of Third Parties) Bill currently before Parliament, giving a detailed account of its radical impact on the existing law. The Chapter also discusses the important decisions of the Court of Appeal in *Darlington BC v. Wiltshier (Northern) Ltd* on recovery of damages by the promisee and of the House of Lords in *Marc Rich & Co. AG v. Bishop Rock Marine Co., Spring v. Guardian Assurance plc* and *White v. Jones* on liability in tort.

Part Six (Performance and Discharge) covers a number of minor yet significant developments, including in Chapter 22 (Performance) *Union Eagle Ltd v. Golden Achievement Ltd*, in Chapter 24 (Discharge by Frustration) *Gamerco SA v. ICM Fair Warning (Agency) Ltd* and in Chapter 25 (Discharge by Breach) *Vitol SA v. Norelf* and *Glencore Grain Rotterdam BV v. Lebanese Organisation for International Commerce.*

In Part Seven (Remedies) the principal developments have been in relation to Chapter 27 (Damages). This covers three major decisions in the House of Lords: *Malik v. Bank of Credit and Commerce International SA* dealing with damages for loss of reputation suffered by an employee; *Ruxley Electronics and Construction Ltd v. Forsyth* on the vexed question of whether damages for a defect in construction should be measured by the cost of re-construction or any difference in value, and suggesting a willingness to allow damages for "loss of amenity"; and the *South Australia Asset Management Corp. v. York Montague Ltd* case on the extent of liability of negligent valuers. It also explains the Late Payment of Commercial Debts (Interest) Act 1998. Chapter 28 (Specific Performance) deals with the House of Lords decision in *Co-operative Insurance Society Ltd v. Argyll Stores (Holdings) Ltd* on "keep open" covenants. In Chapter 29 (Limitation of Actions) the position relating to amendments of the claimant's statement of case after the expiration of the limitation period is now discussed in relation to the new Civil Procedure Rules.

Part Eight (Restitution) records the continuing development of this area, including the House of Lords decisions in *Kleinwort Benson Ltd v. Lincoln City Council* (payment made under mistake of law), *Banque Financière de la Cité v. Parc (Battersea) Ltd* (subrogation) and *Attorney-General v. Blake* (restitutionary damages). Part Nine (Conflict of Laws) has been revised to take account of the still relatively few reported English cases on the Rome Convention on the Law Applicable to Contractual Obligations, implemented in the United Kingdom in the Contracts (Applicable Law) Act 1990.

In Volume 2, Chapter 37 (Construction Contracts) is, as already noted, entirely new. Chapter 35 (Carriage by Air) deals with the Air Carrier Liability Order 1998 (implementing EU legislation). Chapter 36 (Carriage by Land) has been updated to take account of the fundamental changes undertaken to the railway industry as a result of the Railways Act 1993 and related European Directives. The chapter also considers the 1998 RHA Conditions and recent decisions interpreting the CMR Convention (*Laceys Footwear (Whole-sale) Ltd v. Bowler International Freight Ltd, Gefco (U.K.) Ltd v. Mason*) and issues of jurisdiction (*Réunion Européenne SA v. Spliethoffs Bevrachtingskantoor BV* and *Frans Maas Logistics (U.K.) Ltd v. CDR Trucking BV*).

Chapter 38 (Employment) deals with the major pieces of employment legislation so far enacted under the present government, namely the National Minimum Wage Act 1998, the Public Interest (Disclosure) Act 1998 and the Working Time Regulations 1998, as well as the consolidation brought about by the Employment Rights Act 1996. *Malik's* case and others on the implied term of trust and confidence are also considered.

Chapter 41 (Insurance) takes account of the many court decisions handed down recently with particular reference to effect of the duty of utmost good faith upon the presentation of a claim under an insurance policy (*The Star Sea, Insurance Corporation of the Channel Islands Limited v. McHugh, Galloway v. Guardian Royal Exchange (U.K.) Ltd*), the scope of the duty of pre-contractual disclosure (*Economides v. Commercial Union Assurance Co plc*), the nature of composite and joint insurance contracts (*State of the Netherlands v. Youell, Arab Bank Plc v. Zurich Insurance Company*), the nature of indemnity and investment insurance contracts (*Fuji Finance Inc v. Aetna Life Insurance Co Ltd*) and issues of jurisdiction (*Agnew v. Lansförsäkringsbolagens AB, Jordan Grand Prix Ltd v. Baltic Insurance Group*).

Chapter 42 on Restrictive Agreements and Competition has been extensively modified in the light of the Competition Act 1998. Chapter 43 (Sale of Goods) has been revised to take account of the major statutory amendments to the Sale of Goods Act 1979 effected by the Sale of Goods (Amendment) Act 1994, the Sale and Supply of Goods Act 1994 and the Sale of Goods (Amendment) Act 1995, and a number of important cases on the 1979 Act has been included. Chapter 44 deals with recent cases on the extent to which disclosure must be made to a surety of unusual features of the transaction guaranteed or of the risk faced by the surety (*Levett v. Barclays Bank plc; Credit Lyonnais Bank Nederland v. E.C.G.D.*).

All the remaining chapters have been updated.

In Chapter 15 it has been possible to insert references to the Unfair Terms in Consumer Contracts Regulations 1999, which were laid before Parliament on July 22, 1999; in other chapters references are to the 1994 Regulations.

The publishers have once again taken responsibility for the tables and the index. We would like to record our sincere gratitude to them for this and all their other work in producing this edition.

The law is stated as at the end of last legal year in July 1998 but it has been possible to incorporate many subsequent developments at proof stage, in particular later major decisions, references to more recent legislation and the new Civil Procedure Rules, and to anticipate the enactment of the Contracts (Rights of Third Parties) Bill.

H.G.B.

Warwick, June 7, 1999

TABLE OF CONTENTS
VOLUME 1

PART ONE

FORMATION OF CONTRACT

PART TWO

CAPACITY OF PARTIES

PART THREE

THE TERMS OF THE CONTRACT

PART FOUR

ILLEGALITY AND PUBLIC POLICY

PART FIVE

JOINT OBLIGATIONS, PRIVITY AND ASSIGNMENT

PART SIX

PERFORMANCE AND DISCHARGE

PART SEVEN

REMEDIES FOR BREACH OF CONTRACT

PART EIGHT

RESTITUTION

PART NINE

CONFLICT OF LAWS

VOLUME 2

Please note that Volume 1 is available for sale separately from Volume 2, so you will only have access to the above contents of Volume 2 if you have purchased both Volumes.

TABLE OF STATUTES

Where a reference indicates significant discussion of the statute in the text, it is in **bold**. Where a reference is to a footnote, it is *italic*.

TABLE OF STATUTORY INSTRUMENTS

Where a reference indicates significant discussion of the statutory instrument in the text, it is in **bold**. Where a reference is to a footnote, it is *italic*.

TABLE OF NON-U.K. STATUTORY MATERIAL

Where a reference indicates significant discussion of the legislation in the text, it is in **bold**. Where a reference is to a footnote, it is *italic*.

TABLE OF CASES

Where a reference indicates significant discussion of the case in the text, it is in **bold**.
Where a reference is to a footnote, it is *italic*.

TABLE OF CASES

TABLE OF EUROPEAN CASES

INTRODUCTORY

1. THE NATURE OF CONTRACT

Definitions of contract. There are two main competing definitions of a **1–001** contract in the common law. The first, which was adopted by the twenty-sixth edition of this work, defines a contract as a promise or set of promises which the law will enforce.[1] The competing view, which was taken by the second edition of this work,[2] is that a "contract is an agreement giving rise to obligations which are enforced or recognised by law."[3]

There are two main arguments in favour of the definition of contract in terms of promise. First, the idea of contracts as being based on agreement was introduced into English legal discussions only in the nineteenth century, in particular under the influence of Pothier's *Treatise on Obligations*[4] and does not accord with the raw material of the common law, in particular in relation to the requirement of consideration.[5] For English law does not in general enforce gratuitous promises, the element of non-gratuity being expressed technically by

---

[1] (26th ed.) Vol. I, § 1; Pollock, *Principles of Contract* (13th ed., 1950), p. 1; *cf. ibid.* (1st ed., 1876), p. 5. The American Law Institute's *Restatement of Contracts* (2d), § 1, adopts substantially the same definition.

[2] Chitty, *A Practical Treatise on the Law of Contracts* (1834), pp. 1–2.

[3] Treitel, *The Law of Contract* (9th ed., 1995), p. 1.

[4] Pothier, *Treatise on Obligations* (trans. Evans, 1806) and see Simpson (1975) 91 L.Q.R. 247, 257–262; Atiyah, *The Rise and Fall of Freedom of Contract* (1979), p. 399; Gordley, *The Philosophical Origins of Modern Contract Doctrine* (1991), Chap. 6.

[5] *cf.* Nicholas, *The French Law of Contract* (2nd ed., 1992), p. 144.

the requirement that some consideration must move from the promisee and in lay terms that it enforces bargains rather than agreements.[6] Moreover, it is in relation to the requirement of consideration that modern usage most readily relies on the language of promise: what is required is consideration for a party's *promise*, not consideration for the parties' *agreement*.[7] Finally, one of the justifications for the enforcement of contracts is said to lie in the moral obligation of a party to perform his promise.[8]

1–002   **Difficulties with "contract as promise".**   However, analysis of contracts in terms of an enforceable promise or sets of enforceable promises is not entirely satisfactory. First, outside the context of consideration, in general neither courts nor parties to contracts describe the relationships which they create in terms of promises, but rather in terms of agreements, and for the courts this is clearest in the context of the rules as to offer and acceptance which when satisfied form that agreement.[9] Moreover, as will be described later, the doctrine of consideration to which the "promise theory" is so closely related, is somewhat under siege: from the Law Commission, whose report on reform of privity of contract proposes legislative changes which would limit its traditional domain,[10] and from the courts, notably in the decision in *Williams v. Roffey Bros. & Nicholls (Contractors) Ltd.*[11] Secondly, definition of contracts in terms of sets of promises does not give full force to the interrelationship of the obligations of the parties which exists in many contracts,[12] an interrelationship which can be seen particularly in the availability of the remedy of rescission for substantial failure in performance, by which an injured party may terminate his own obligations by reason of the failure of the other party to perform his side of the bargain.[13]

---

[6] According to the *Restatement of Contracts op. cit.* § 3, a bargain is an agreement, whereby two or more persons exchange promises, or exchange a promise for a performance. However, the word "bargain" is seldom used in any technical sense in the law of contract, though *cf.* goods "bargained and sold" and Atiyah, *Essays on Contract* (1986), Essay 8, p. 207; and see Eisenberg (1982) 95 HLR 741. It is sometimes said that the requirement of consideration means that contracts are *exchanges*. This suggests some element of reciprocity between the parties to the contract and while this is often the case, a promise by A to do work for B can support a promise by C of payment for it: see *post*, § 3–005 According to Gordley *op. cit.* pp. 137–139, the systematisation of the doctrine of consideration took place at the same time as the acceptance of civilian theories of contract and was intended to act as a control device on the ambit of contract.

[7] See *post*, § 3–001.

[8] Goodhart, *English Law and the Moral Law* (1953), p. 101; Fried, *Contract as Promise* (1983); Harris (1983) 3 Int. Rev. Law & Econ. 69; Burrows (1985) C.L.P. 141. *cf.* Atiyah (1978) 94 L.Q.R. 193; *Promises, Morals and Law* (1981); *Essays on Contract* (1986), Essays 2 and 6; Raz in Hacker and Raz (eds.), *Law, Morality and Society* (1977), Chap. 12.

[9] See *post*, Chap. 2.

[10] The Law Commission, *Privity of Contract: Contracts for the Benefit of Third Parties*, Law Com. No. 242 (1996) §6.8 and see Contracts (Rights of Third Parties) Bill 1998 [HL Bill 5] and *post*, Chap. 18.

[11] [1991] 1 Q.B. 1 and see *post*, § 3–063.

[12] *cf.* Atiyah, *An Introduction to the Law of Contract* (5th ed., 1995), pp. 38–39.

[13] See *post*, §§ 25–033—25–045. This is not to say that the availability of this remedy cannot be expressed in terms of independent or dependent promises, but the term "promise" here is used synonymously with that of obligation and can apply to obligations imposed on a contractor by law, which are not a matter of "promise" at all. Thus, a buyer of goods can terminate the contract, and thereby extinguish his own obligation to pay the price, for breach of the term that they are of satisfactory quality, a term imposed by s.14 of the Sale of Goods Act 1979 on sellers selling goods in the course of business (and not capable of exclusion as against a buyer dealing as a consumer: Unfair Contract Terms Act 1977, s.6(2)) and see Vol. II, §§ 43–099—43–104.

Difficulties with "contract as agreement". However, an understanding of   **1–003**
modern contracts as agreements does not fit easily with two recognised types of
contract. First, in the case of an unilateral contract[14] where A promises to do
something if B does something else, the performance by B of the condition is
enough for A to be bound. Here, analysis in terms of doing something of value
in return for a promise fits more naturally than does the construction of an
acceptance by B's performance of the condition of A's promise.[15] Secondly,
promises contained in deeds[16] are enforceable by the person in whose favour they
are made, whether or not that person is aware of them[17] and so while a deed may
give contractual force to an agreement, agreement is unnecessary for the enforcement of the promises which it contains. And, for Pollock, writing in 1885, the
position of contracts under seal made it difficult for him to accept that "proposal
and acceptance [form] part of the general conception of contract."[18] For other
writers, however, it has led instead to a denial that the binding force of a promise
in a deed depends on contract at all.[19] Certainly, although it is true that the action
to enforce promises made under seal, the action of covenant, was traditionally
classified as arising *ex contractu*,[20] this classification cannot be treated as conclusive as to whether promises in deeds should be considered contractual, given
that at the time other actions which are clearly not so considered were also
included within this category (notably, actions for money had and received,
which would now be understood as restitutionary[21] and actions for detinue which
before their abolition were clearly proprietary).[22]

Actual agreement not required. Moreover, even though it is true that the   **1–004**
existence of an agreement is in the vast majority of cases a condition for the
existence of a contract not contained in a deed, this statement ought to be treated
with some caution. First, the existence of an agreement is not an issue merely of
fact, to be found by a psychological investigation of the parties at the time of its
alleged origin: English law takes an "objective" rather than a "subjective" view
of the existence of agreement[23] and so its starting-point is the manifestation of

---

[14] See *post*, § 1–036.

[15] There is some doubt as to whether an offeree of a unilateral offer must be aware of that offer on
performance of the condition for a contract to arise: see *post*, § 2–038. If the offeree need not be so
aware, then no agreement can be constructed from performance of the condition. It is clear that the
offeree of a unilateral offer does not in general have to communicate his acceptance to the offeror
before he fulfills the condition and the contract arises: *Carlill v. Carbolic Smoke Ball Co.* [1893] 1
Q.B. 256, and see *post*, § 2–042A.

[16] After the abolition by the Law of Property (Miscellaneous Provisions) Act 1989, s.1(1) of the
requirement of sealing for the validity of deeds made by individuals, it is more appropriate to refer
to promises in deeds rather than the former "promises under seal": see *post*, §§ 1–042—1–043.

[17] *Xenos v. Wickham* (1866) L.R. 2 H.L. 296, 312; *Macedo v. Stroud* [1922] 2 A.C. 330.

[18] *Principles of Contract* (4th ed.), p. 9 and *cf.* at p. 5.

[19] Treitel, *The Law of Contract* (9th ed., 1995), p. 146.

[20] Bacon, *A New Abridgment of the Law* (7th ed., 1832), Vol. I, p. 55 included debt, detinue,
account, covenant, assumpsit, *quantum meruit, quantum valebat* and annuity in his treatment of
actions *ex contractu*. *cf.* Chitty and Chitty, *A Treatise on the Parties to Actions and on Pleading* (6th
ed., 1836), pp. 98–125.

[21] See *post*, § 3–005; Birks, *An Introduction to the Law of Restitution* (1985), pp. 29–39.

[22] Technically, detinue protected the plaintiff's right to possession of personal property. For further
discussion of the classification of actions at common law, see *post*, § 1–060. Detinue was abolished
by the Torts (Interference with Goods) Act 1977, s.2.

[23] Howarth (1984) 100 L.Q.R. 265 and 528; Vorster (1987) 103 L.Q.R. 274; Goddard (1987) 7 L.S.
263; de Moor (1990) 106 L.Q.R. 632 and see *The Hannah Blumenthal* [1983] 1 A.C. 854; *The
Leonidas D.* [1985] 1 W.L.R. 925; Beatson (1986) 102 L.Q.R. 19; Atiyah (1986) 102 L.Q.R. 363 and
post, § 2–002.

mutual assent by two or more persons to one another[24]: "[a]greement is not a mental state but an act, and, as an act, is a matter of inference from conduct. The parties are to be judged, not by what is in their minds, but by what they have said or written or done."[25] Moreover, for reasons of commercial convenience, the common law regulates what is to be treated as a manifestation of assent capable of giving rise to a contract in its rules relating to offer and acceptance.[26] For example, a posted acceptance of an offer is said to conclude a contract on posting, rather than on communication to the offeror, and so an acceptance lost in the post will bind the offeror.[27] Similarly, if A sends an offer to B by post, and then changes his mind and sends a letter revoking his offer, but B posts an acceptance of the offer after A posted his letter of revocation, but before B received it, there may be a contract, though the parties were never *ad idem*.[28] Another example of common law regulation of what constitutes an agreement may be found in the general rule that silence in an offeree cannot be treated as acceptance.[29]

1–005 **Agreement and consideration not sufficient.** Secondly, the presence of an agreement supported by consideration is not always sufficient to establish the existence of a contract. This is notably the case where the parties agree in circumstances in which it is considered inappropriate for the law to impose legal obligations, for example, in a social or domestic context, and is justified on the basis that the parties cannot be considered to have intended to create a legal relationship.[30] However, the courts have used the requirement that the parties must possess an intention to create legal relations to exclude other types of non-gratuitous agreement from the domain of contract.[31] Furthermore, even if a transaction fulfils these three conditions of agreement, consideration and an intention to create legal relations, it may be defeated by the presence of other factors such as the absence of a particular form,[32] mistake,[33] misrepresentation,[34] duress,[35] undue influence,[36] incapacity[37] or illegality.[38] Some of these factors will render the contract void,[39] others voidable,[40] and others still will render it unenforceable against one or both contracting parties.[41]

1–006 **Enforcement of agreements under other rules.** Thirdly, even though contracts are in general to be defined as agreements, this does not mean that all

---

[24] *Restatement of Contracts op. cit.* § 3.

[25] Cheshire, Fifoot and Furmston's *Law of Contract* (13th ed., 1996), p. 29.

[26] See *post*, §§ 2–002—2–102.

[27] *Household Fire Insurance Co. v. Grant* (1879) 3 Ex. D. 216, overruling *British and American Telegraph Co. Ltd v. Colson* (1871) L.R. 6 Ex. 108. See *post*, § 2–043.

[28] *Byrne v. Van Tienhoven* (1880) 5 C.P.D. 344; *post*, § 2–081.

[29] *Felthouse v. Bindley* (1862) 11 C.B. (N.S.) 869, affd. (1863) 1 N.R. 401 and see *post*, §§ 2–063—2–070.

[30] See *post*, §§ 2–153—2–158.

[31] See *post*, § 2–159—2–164.

[32] See *post*, Chap. 4.

[33] See *post*, Chap. 5.

[34] See *post*, Chap. 6.

[35] See *post*, §§ 7–001—7–040.

[36] See *post*, §§ 7–041—7–074.

[37] See *post*, Chaps. 8 and 9.

[38] See *post*, Chap. 17.

[39] See *post*, § 1–037.

[40] See *post*, § 1–039.

[41] See *post*, § 1–041.

enforceable agreements (or enforceable promises) are contracts. This is particularly noticeable in relation to promissory and proprietary estoppel and constructive trust. In the case of promissory estoppel, A may be prevented from
going back on a promise not to rely on his legal rights against B, subject to the
condition that B has relied on A's promise (possibly, to B's detriment).[42] B does
not need to furnish consideration for A's promise for it to be enforceable under
this doctrine and although the requirement of reliance by B suggests some
element of acceptance on the latter's part of the benefit of the promise, there is
no need for this to be communicated to or known by A.[43] The doctrines of
proprietary estoppel and constructive trust may also enforce promises or agreements, even though these elements form merely part of the factual circumstances
which attract their application. For example, in *Crabb v. Arun District Council*,
A made an assurance to B that it would grant a right of way to B over its land
to and from B's land and B acted in reliance on this assurance.[44] B's claim for
a declaration that he was entitled to the right of access succeeded by way of
estoppel, even though apparently B could not have established the existence of
a contract on the ground of its uncertainty.[45] On the other hand, the use of the
notion of constructive trust to analyse an agreement is not usually to allow the
enforcement of an agreement between its parties which would fail as a matter of
contract, but to allow it to affect the position of third parties. For example, in
Binions v. Evans,[46] A had been given permission by B to occupy a cottage on B's
land for the rest of her life. B sold the land to C expressly subject to A's tenancy
of the cottage, but a few months later C gave A notice to quit. It was accepted
by the majority of the Court of Appeal[47] that the agreement between A and B had
contractual force, but for Lord Denning M.R. in the circumstances of the case it
would also give rise to a constructive trust so as to bind C.[48]

European definitions of contract. The definitions which we have so far **1–007**
discussed have been those which have arisen from analysis of the common law,
equitable and statutory material native to English law or the legal systems which
have developed from it. However, modern English courts now sometimes require
and will increasingly find themselves required to look to other definitions or
understandings of what is meant by a contract. For legislation of the European
Community has now had (at least *de iure*) a very considerable effect on the law
governing English contracts. This may be seen in three main areas, though others
have also been affected: first, the rules of private international law regarding both
jurisdiction and choice of law; secondly, contracts of employment and, thirdly,
consumer contracts. In all these areas, the relevant E.C. legislation, at times,
makes the application of legislation contingent on the existence of a contract, but
the question arises whether this notion should be interpreted according to the
understanding of the various Member States or instead on the basis of an
"autonomous" definition to be formulated by the European Court of Justice. It is
submitted that there is not likely to be any single answer to be given to this

---

[42] See *post*, §§ 3–120 *et seq.*
[43] See *post*, § 3–127.
[44] [1976] Ch. 179 and see *post*, § 3–132.
[45] [1976] Ch. 179, 195 and see *post*, §§ 3–133—3–134.
[46] [1972] Ch. 359.
[47] *ibid.* at 367, 371.
[48] *ibid.* at 367–368. Megaw and Stephenson L.JJ. preferred to protect A's position by holding her
to be a tenant for life within the meaning of the Settled Land Act 1925.

question. Different answers may be given according to the context of the legislation in question, these turning on a variety of considerations, but particularly on the degree of juristic integration which the European Court of Justice thinks desirable and practicable in that context. Of those areas which have already been mentioned, the European Court itself has had occasion to hold that a European and "autonomous" view should be taken of the understanding of what constitutes a contractual as opposed to an extra-contractual action for the purposes of jurisdictional rules under the Brussels Convention,[49] and this has meant that an action classified in one Member State (France) as contractual has been held extra-contractual for these purposes.[50] The European Court decided that

> the phrase "matters relating to a contract" within the meaning of Article 5(1) of the Convention should not be understood to cover a situation where there is no obligation freely entered into by one party to another. Where a sub-buyer of goods which are bought from an intermediate seller brings an action against a manufacturer for damages on the sole ground that the goods are not in conformity, it is important to observe that there is no contractual link between the sub-buyer and the manufacturer because the latter has not undertaken a contractual obligation of any kind to the former.[51]

1–008   **European definition of "worker".** As to the various legislative provisions governing contracts of employment and contracts under which "workers" act, clearly their concern is not with "contract", but rather with "employment contract" or "worker", but in this respect some of the E.C. legislation clearly invites the courts of the Member States to refer to a conception of contract drawn from their own legal system, while other provisions have attracted a European conception. So, for example, a Council Directive of 1991 which makes certain requirements as to the information to be given by employers to their employees as to the conditions of employment expressly provides that it shall apply "to every paid employee having a contract or employment relationship defined by the law in force in a Member State . . . "[52] On the other hand, the European Court of Justice had occasion to make clear as early as 1964 that "worker" for the purposes of the principle of freedom of movement of workers contained in Article 48 (new Article 39) of the E.C. Treaty must be given a European understanding[53] the fleshing out of this being the matter for a series of subsequent judgments.[54]

1–009   **"Consumer contract".** Finally, it is a question whether the notion of a "consumer contract" for the purposes of the Directive on Unfair Terms in Consumer Contracts 1993[55] will be given an autonomous European significance. If it were, then the "contractual" element of such a significance may well differ from that given by English law, notably as regards the latter's requirement of consideration, a requirement which is not shared by the other Member States except the Republic of Ireland. Furthermore, in coming to a view as to what

---

[49] Case 189/87 *Kalfelis v. Schröder* [1988] E.C.R. 5565, esp. at 5577 (Adv.-Gen. Darmon), 5585.

[50] Case C-26/91, *Jakob Handte & Co. GmbH v. Société Traitements Mécano-chimiques des Surfaces* (TMCS) [1993] I.L.Pr. 5.

[51] *ibid* at 22.

[52] 91/533/EEC art. 1(1).

[53] Case 75/63, *Hoekstra (née Unger) v. Bestuur der Bedrijfsvereniging voor Detailhandel en Ambachten* [1964] E.C.R. 177.

[54] See Craig and de Búrca, *E.C. Law*, (2nd edn., 1998) pp. 672 *et seq.*

[55] See *post*, §§ 15–015—15–020.

constitutes "a contract" for this purpose, the European Court of Justice is likely to be inspired by the work of those who have formulated or will formulate a pan-European definition of contract, such as the authors of the *Principles of European Contract Law*[56] or by the work of comparative lawyers such as Professor Kötz.[57] In formulating such a definition, the European Court may well be inspired by the famous definition to be found in the French Civil Code which states that "[a] contract is an agreement by which one or more persons undertake to one or more other persons to convey something, to do something or not to do something."[58]

Freedom of contract in the nineteenth century. In the nineteenth century, **1–010** freedom of contract was regarded by many philosophers, economists and judges as an end in itself, finding its philosophical justification in the "will theory" of contract and its economic justification in *laissez faire* liberalism.[59] Thus, the parties were to be the best judges of their own interests, and if they freely and voluntarily entered into a contract, the only function of the law was to enforce it. In particular, its validity should not be challenged on the ground that its effect was unfair or socially undesirable (as long as it was not actually illegal or immoral, the latter of which was understood in a restrictive sense)[60] and it was immaterial that one party was economically in a stronger bargaining position than the other. Nowhere can this attitude be seen more clearly than in the attitude of the courts to clauses which attempted to regulate the damages payable on breach of contract. For, the courts held that parties to a contract were able to limit or exclude liability in damages not merely for breach of contract, but also in tort.[61] The courts' attitude to freedom of contract can also be seen in their treatment of an exception to it, for while they accepted that penalty clauses were ineffective even if agreed by the parties, they did so only owing to the force of established precedent to this effect and with considerable reluctance.[62]

In modern law. Moreover, as a general principle, freedom of contract has **1–011** considerable support in the modern judiciary. For example, in 1966, Lord Reid rejected the idea that the doctrine of fundamental breach was a substantive rule of law, negativing any agreement to the contrary (and capable of being used to

---

[56] These are prepared by the Commission of European Contract Law and edited by Professors Lando and Beale. The volume on the formation of contract has yet to appear.

[57] Kötz and Flessner *European Contract Law*, (trans. Weir), Vol. I (1997) by Kötz, p. 3 and see also Chap. 4.

[58] Art. 1101 C. civ.

[59] See Dicey, *Law and Opinion in England* (2nd ed., 1914), pp. 150–158; *Printing and Numerical Registering Co. v. Sampson* (1875) L.R. 19 Eq. 462, 465, *per* Jessel M.R.; *Manchester, Sheffield and Lincolnshire Ry. v. Brown* (1883) 8 App. Cas. 703, 716–720, *per* Lord Bramwell; *Salt v. Marquis of Northampton* [1892] A.C. 1, 18–19, *per* Lord Bramwell. It is instructive to observe that Lord Bramwell, who was one of the foremost judicial champions of freedom of contract, also believed in the necessity for a real as opposed to an apparent consent: see his judgment in *British and American Telegraph Co. Ltd v. Colson* (1871) L.R. 6 Ex. 108, and his dissenting judgment in *Household Fire Insurance Co. v. Grant* (1879) 4 Ex. D. 216, 232. See further, Atiyah, *The Rise and Fall of Freedom of Contract* (1979) and *cf.* Gordley, *op. cit.* pp. 214–217.

[60] See *post*, §§ 17–001 *et seq.*, esp. at § 17–067.

[61] *Nicholson v. Willan* (1804) 5 East 507. Lord Ellenborough C.J., at 513, rejected the plaintiff's argument that the attempt of the defendant, a common carrier, to exclude his liability for the loss of goods carried beyond the value of £5 was "contrary to the policy of the common law, which has made common carriers responsible to an indefinite extent for losses not occasioned by . . . act of God [or] the King's enemies."

[62] *Ranger v. G.W. Ry. Co* (1854) 5 H.L.C. 72, 94–95, 118–119; Atiyah *op. cit.* pp. 414–415.

strike down an exemption clause)[63] on the ground, *inter alia*, that this would restrict "the general principle of English law that parties are free to contract as they may think fit."[64] In 1980, in the same context, Lord Diplock observed[65] that "[a] basic principle of the common law of contract . . . is that parties to a contract are free to determine for themselves what primary obligations they will accept."[66] Moreover, the courts have proved unwilling to strike down contracts on the ground simply that one of the parties suffered from an "inequality of bargaining power."[67] Conversely, the House of Lords has made clear that it will not *add* to the agreement which the parties have made by implying a term merely because it would be reasonable to do so, but only where it is "necessary,"[68] nor will the courts put a meaning on the words of a contract different from that which they clearly express.[69]

1-012   **Exceptions: obligations to enter contracts.** However, freedom of contract has lost much of its intellectual attraction in the late twentieth century,[70] and is subject to many exceptions in the positive law. This is reflected both as regards the freedom of a person to decide with whom or whether to contract and on what terms or with what results. Even at common law, an innkeeper or common carrier was not entitled to refuse to accommodate a would-be customer without sufficient excuse[71] and modern statutes have forbidden a person's refusal to contract in certain situations on the grounds of the sex[72] or racial group[73] of the would-be contractor.[74] Companies which supply what used to be called public utilities, such as water, gas and electricity, in some circumstances are under a statutory duty to supply the commodity in question,[75] though in this type of case the existence of the duty has led the courts to hold that the relationship so created is not contractual.[76]

---

[63] See *Suisse Atlantique Société d'Armement Maritime SA v. N.V. Rotterdamsche Kolen Centrale* [1967] 1 A.C. 361.

[64] *ibid.* at 399.

[65] *Photo Production Ltd v. Securicor Transport Ltd.* [1980] A.C. 827, 848.

[66] And see *Eurico SpA v. Philipp Brothers* [1987] 2 Lloyd's Rep. 215, 218 (term to do the impossible valid).

[67] *National Westminster Bank plc v. Morgan* [1985] 1 A.C. 686, 708, disapproving the dictum of Lord Denning M.R. in *Lloyds Bank Ltd v. Bundy* [1975] Q.B. 326, 339; and see *post* § 7–088. *cf.* 7–075 *et seq.* (unconscionable bargains).

[68] *Liverpool City Council v. Irwin* [1977] A.C. 239, 254; *Tai Hing Cotton Mill Ltd v. Liu Chong Hing Bank Ltd.* [1986] A.C. 80, 104–105; and see *post*, § 13–009.

[69] See *post*, §§ 12–041—12–060.

[70] It still has strong supporters, notably Posner, *Economic Analysis of Law* (3rd ed., 1986), Chap. 4 and *cf.* Atiyah, *An Introduction to the Law of Contract* (5th ed., 1995) pp. 27–34, who argues that from 1980 there was a swing back in favour of freedom of contract in the United Kingdom as a result of the policies of successive Conservative governments.

[71] *Clarke v. West Ham Corpn.* [1909] 2 K.B. 858, 879, 882.

[72] Sex Discrimination Act 1975, s.6(1)(c).

[73] Race Relations Act 1976, ss. 4(1)(c), 17, 20 and 21.

[74] See further, Art. 86 E.E.C. (new Art. 82 E.C.); Cases 6 and 7/73, *Instituto Chemioterpico Italiano and Commercial Solvents Corpn. v. Commission* [1974] E.C.R. 223; Vol. II, § 42–063; and see also *post*, § 1–133 which discusses the restrictions which are placed on the type of consideration to be taken into account by a public authority in deciding with whom to contract.

[75] Gas Act 1986, s.10; Electricity Act 1989, s.16; Water Act 1989, ss.45, 46. These Acts placed the supply of gas, electricity and water in the hands of private companies.

[76] *Read v. Croydon Corp.* [1938] 4 All E.R. 631; *Norweb plc v. Dixon* [1995] 1 W.L.R. 637, *cf. Oceangas (Gibraltar) Ltd v. Port of London Authority*, [1993] 2 Lloyd's Rep. 292 (no contract in respect of compulsory pilotage services).

Exceptions: restricted freedom as to terms. Moreover, even where, as in the **1–013** majority of cases, a person is free to decide whether to enter a particular contract, he is not free to determine on what terms to do so. First, many contracts, whether between two commercial parties or between such a party and a consumer, are made on the written standard terms of one of the parties in such circumstances that it is all but impossible for them to be varied,[77] a phenomenon which led French commentators to refer to such transactions as *contrats d'adhésion*. Similarly, the terms of an employee's contract of employment may be determined by agreement between his trade union and his employer,[78] or by a statutory scheme of employment.[79] However, in both the latter situations, despite the lack of real freedom of the parties to do other than accept or reject the whole package as it is offered to them, these types of transactions are still treated as contracts.[80] Secondly, although, as has been said, the courts formally state the need for a term to be "necessary" before it will be implied into a contract,[81] in fact the courts have over the years found many such implied terms, often in situations where it is difficult to see how this test is fulfilled,[82] thereby creating for many types of contracts the "legal incidents of those . . . kinds of contractual relationship."[83] According to one author, "[f]aced with a problem in contract, the Common lawyer is as likely as not to try to solve it with an implied term. [In contrast,] the Civil lawyer will probably resort to a rule, whether it be a broad and fundamental precept such as the German requirement of good faith[84] . . . or one derived from the nature of obligation or contract . . . or, finally, one derived from the nature of the particular contract in question."[85] While some judicially implied terms have been recognised by statute,[86] many remain a matter of common law, where they constitute an important part of the regulation of many contractors' relations.[87]

Thirdly, the effects of many modern contracts are regulated by statute, some- **1–014** times by way of statutory implication of an implied term,[88] but sometimes by attaching a legal consequence directly to the conclusion of a particular type of contract. This is particularly noticeable as regards some types of contracts made

---

[77] See Sales (1953) 16 M.L.R. 318. Where both parties to the contract are in business, each may attempt to impose its own conditions on the other, and this sometimes gives rise to what is known as a "battle of forms": see *post*, §§ 2–031—2–034.

[78] See Vol. II, §§ 39–040 *et seq.*

[79] *cf. Barber v. Manchester Regional Hospital Board* [1958] 1 W.L.R. 181, 196; *Roy v. Kensington & Chelsea and Westminster Family Practitioner Committee* [1992] 1 A.C. 624; *Scally v. Southern Health and Social Services Board* [1992] 1 A.C. 294, 304.

[80] *cf. post*, §§ 1–129—1–131 on the question of the availability of public law remedies in this sort of case.

[81] See *ante*, § 1–011.

[82] Treitel *op. cit.* pp. 190–194, who argues that the test of necessity is inappropriate for terms implied in law.

[83] *Mears v. Safecar Securities Ltd* [1983] Q.B. 54, 78 *per* Stephenson L.J. The learned Lord Justice specifically accepted, however, that "the obligation must be a *necessary* term; that is, required by their relationship": *ibid.*

[84] *cf. post*, § 1–019.

[85] Nicholas (1974) 48 Tulane L.R. 946, 950.

[86] See, *e.g. Jones v. Just* (1868) L.R. 3 Q.B. 197 and Sale of Goods Act 1893, s.14 (now Sale of Goods Act 1979).

[87] See, *post*, Chap. 13. The contract of employment has proved particularly fertile ground for the implication of terms: see Vol. II, §§ 39–051—39–061, 39–065—39–066.

[88] See Sale of Goods Act 1979, ss.12–15; Supply of Goods (Implied Terms) Act 1973, ss.8–11; Equal Pay Act 1970, s.1(1) as amended by the Sex Discrimination Act 1975 and the Equal Pay (Amendment) Regulations 1983 (S.I. 1983 No. 1794).

by consumers, notably contracts for the sale of goods, hire-purchase and consumer credit,[89] where the protection which the law thereby ensures is often not capable of avoidance by an expression of contrary intention.[90] Contracts of employment and between a landlord and tenant have also been subjected to considerable legislative regulation, to the extent that the voluntary aspect of the contract appears only to be whether or not to enter the contract, a decision which then triggers a set of obligations which are determined by the law.[91]

1–015   **Indirect regulation of contract.** Other statutory techniques for the regulation of contracts are less direct. For example, one aim of modern competition law is to help ensure that no company is able to impose what terms it likes on those with whom it deals because of its "dominant position" in the market.[92] This can be seen either as an intervention in the market (and therefore as interfering with the principle of freedom of contract) or as a mechanism for ensuring that the market functions properly (and therefore as enhancing freedom of contract). Another modern technique is for Parliament to set up a system of regulation for a particular type of business with an element of "self-regulation." For example, under the Financial Services Act 1986, it is an offence for a person to carry on investment business[93] without appropriate authorisation[94] and rules relating to the conduct of investment business have been made under the Act, breach of which may attract professional disciplinary sanctions on a person carrying on investment business or a statutory claim for damages by any private investor who suffers loss as a result of the contravention of these rules.[95] Clearly, this system of regulation affects the way in which contracts relating to investment business are concluded, even though breach of the rules does not affect the validity of any such contract.[96]

1–016   **The binding force of contract.** A concomitant of the doctrine of freedom of contract is the binding force of contracts,[97] a force which a classical Roman jurist compared to the binding force of the law itself.[98] English law has long recognised this principle, which suits the needs of a commercial community. However, care must be taken in interpreting what is meant by the "binding force" of contracts. Some authors argue that "[g]enerally speaking the law does not actually compel the performance of a contract, it merely gives a remedy, normally damages, for

---

[89] See Vol. II, Chaps. 38 and 43.

[90] Other contracts made with consumers, for example contracts of insurance and guarantee, were for long left unregulated in this way, but important changes were made in this respect by the Unfair Terms in Consumer Contracts Regulations 1994 (S.I. 1994 No. 3159): see *post*, §§ 15–004 *et seq.*, Vol. II, Chaps. 41, 44.

[91] Hepple (1986–1987) 36 *King's Counsel* 11.

[92] See Treaty of Rome, Arts. 85, 86 (new Arts. 81, 82 E.C.); Vol. II, Chap. 41, esp. §§ 42–003 *et seq.*

[93] As defined by the Financial Services Act 1986, s.1 and Sched. 1, Parts I–III.

[94] *ibid.* Chap. IV.

[95] *ibid.* s.62(1) as amended by Companies Act 1989, s.193, inserting a new s.62A therein; and see S.I. 1991 No. 489.

[96] *ibid.* s.62(4).

[97] This has been termed the "sanctity of contracts": see Hughes Parry, *The Sanctity of Contracts in English Law* (1959).

[98] D. 16.3.1.6; D. 50.17.23 (both attributed to Ulpian) and see French Civil Code, Art. 1134.1. Logically, this Code recognised the effectiveness of penalty clauses, whose purpose is to ensure the performance of a contract: Arts. 1152, 1226. The law relating to penalty clauses was changed in 1975, when the courts were given a discretion to modify them where otherwise their effect would be "manifestly excessive or derisory": see new art. 1152.1, C. civ.

the breach,"[99] an approach which echoes Oliver Wendell Holmes' famous statement that the law leaves a contractor "free from interference until the time for fulfilment has gone by, and therefore free to break his contract if he chooses."[1] However, four arguments can counter such an approach. First, the courts often do enforce the primary obligations of a contract: apart from the equitable remedies of specific performance and injunction, the approach to which is more liberal than formerly,[2] this is clearest in relation to the action for the agreed contract price, a remedy available at common law and as of right which enforces a party's primary contractual obligation to pay money.[3] Secondly, the purpose of many awards of damages for breach of contract, and the one which is particular to it,[4] is to put the injured party in the position as though the contract had been performed.[5] While this approach to damages is not without its restrictions[6] (notably, those imposed by the rules as to remoteness[7] and mitigation of damage[8]), where an award of damages is made on this basis, it can be seen as reflecting the idea that the obligations created by the contract *should* have been performed. Thirdly, the absence of a particular form of sanction for a breach of contract—*viz.* the threat of punishment for contempt, a sanction which exists in the contractual context only in relation to a failure to conform to a judicial order for specific performance or injunction—should not lead to a denial of the obligational effect of contracts: obligations have a normative character independent of any sanction which may arise if they are broken.[9] Fourthly, English law recognises the binding force of contracts in another way, it being a tort for a third party knowingly[10] to induce a party to a contract to break his obligations to his co-contractor.[11] While a third party may be liable in damages for such a tort of interference with a contractual relationship, its commission may also be prevented by injunction in an appropriate case.[12]

However, rather than alluding to the variety of sanctions which are available **1–017** if a contract is broken, the notion of the binding force of contracts is often used instead to draw attention to the general refusal of the courts to deny them effect on the ground of unfairness or inequality, for example where an inadequate price has been stipulated for the sale of property.[13] This refusal is also reflected in the

---

[99] Atiyah, *An Introduction to the Law of Contract* (5th ed., 1995), p. 37.

[1] *The Common Law* (1881), p. 301.

[2] See *post*, § 28–002.

[3] See *post*, § 27–008.

[4] In particular, a contrast is drawn here with the basis of awards of damages in tort: see *post*, § 1–064.

[5] See *post*, § 27–002. Such an award is sometimes said to be made to protect the injured party's "expectation interest." An award of damages may be made on other bases, in particular in order to protect what is known as the "reliance interest" of the injured party: *post*, §§ 27–058—27–067. Some authors argue that the importance in practice of the protection of the expectation interest has been overstated: see Fuller and Purdue (1937) 46 Yale L.J. 52.

[6] A practical as opposed to a legal restriction is that a claim for damages on the basis of an injured party's expectation interest may be difficult to show: see *post*, § 27–059.

[7] See *post*, §§ 27–039 *et seq.*

[8] See *post*, §§ 27–058 *et seq.*

[9] *cf.* Hart, *The Concept of Law* (1961), pp. 79–88, who distinguishes the situation where a person is under an *obligation* and where a person is *obliged.*

[10] See Markesinis and Deakin, *Tort Law* (3rd ed., 1994), p. 381.

[11] See *Lumley v. Gye* (1853) 2 E. & B. 216 and *post*, § 1–108.

[12] *e.g. Torquay Hotel Co. Ltd v. Cousins* [1969] 2 Ch. 106.

[13] This can be seen in those cases which hold that the consideration for a promise need not be adequate: *post*, §§ 3–013—3–020.

development of the law of frustration. Until 1863, the general rule was that a party who contracted in absolute terms remained liable, notwithstanding a change of circumstances between the time of making the contract and the time for performance,[14] but in that year this harsh rule was mitigated by the doctrine of frustration,[15] which for many years was reconciled with principle by the device of implying a term into the contract, to which both parties could be supposed to have agreed, and which provided for its discharge in the event of a given thing or state of things ceasing to exist. However, the doctrine came to be applied in circumstances where it was obvious that both parties would never have agreed to any such term and in *Davis Contractors Ltd v. Fareham Urban District Council*,[16] this basis for relief on frustration was firmly rejected. While some judges had relied simply on the notion of justice to justify the doctrine,[17] this decision of the House of Lords also made clear that its proper basis is the construction of the contract.[18] By so doing, reliance is again placed on what the parties agreed or rather on what they did not agree, *viz.*, to perform the contract in such radically different circumstances from those which obtained when it was made. However, even if the view were taken that the rationale for the doctrine of frustration is simply that in the circumstances the law decides that it would be unfair to keep the parties to the terms of their agreement, this does not mean that simple unfairness is the test of frustration. Again, in *Davis Contractors Ltd*[19] Lord Radcliffe made clear that the proper test for frustration is whether performance of the contract is radically different from that which was undertaken by the contract[20] and this test has been consistently upheld,[21] the courts refusing to grant relief for frustration merely because performance of the contract is more onerous than was envisaged by the parties on contract.[22]

1–018   **Limits on binding force of contracts.** Nevertheless, recognition of the principle of the binding force of contracts does not mean that contracts, or particular terms of contracts, will always be enforced. This is clearest in cases of illegal contracts,[23] but another exception to the principle exists at common law in the case of penalty clauses.[24] Furthermore, very important changes have taken place in this respect as a result of modern statutory intervention, of which the Unfair Contract Terms Act 1977 and the Unfair Terms in Consumer Contracts Regulations 1994 are particularly prominent.[25] First, the Unfair Contract Terms Act 1977 declares exemption clauses totally ineffective in certain situations, notably

---

[14] *Paradine v. Jane* (1647) Aleyn 26.

[15] *Taylor v. Caldwell* (1863) 3 B. & S. 826; see *post*, Chap. 24.

[16] [1956] A.C. 696, 720–729.

[17] *e.g. Denny, Mott & Dickson Ltd v. James B. Fraser & Co. Ltd* [1944] A.C. 265, 275; *British Movietonews v. London and District Cinemas Ltd* [1951] 1 K.B. 190, 202 (revd. [1952] A.C. 166).

[18] [1956] A.C. 696, 720–721; and see *post*, § 24–014.

[19] *Supra*.

[20] [1956] A.C. 696, 729; and see *post*, § 24–012.

[21] See *post*, § 24–013.

[22] *British Movietonews Ltd v. London and District Cinemas Ltd* [1952] A.C. 166, 185; *Davis Contractors Ltd v. Fareham UDC; Tsakiroglou & Co. Ltd v. Noblee Thorl GmbH* [1962] A.C. 93.

[23] See *post*, Chap. 17.

[24] See *post*, §§ 27–102 *et seq*. Another exception is to be found in the inability of the parties to a contract to fetter the discretion of the court in deciding whether to grant the remedy of specific performance: *Quadrant Visual Communications Ltd v. Hutchison Telephone (U.K.) Ltd* [1993] B.C.L.C. 442, 451, 452.

[25] See *post*, §§ 14–057 *et seq*. and Chap. 15.

where they attempt to exclude business liability for personal injuries caused by negligence[26] and where they attempt to exclude or limit liability for breach of the terms as to quality and fitness for purpose implied by section 14 of the Sale of Goods Act 1979 as against someone dealing as a consumer.[27] Furthermore, it gives to the courts a discretion in a wide category of other cases to deny effectiveness to an exemption clause unless it is proven to be "fair and reasonable" by the person who seeks to rely upon it.[28] Secondly, in 1994 the Unfair Terms in Consumer Contracts Regulations 1994 were issued, implementing into English law the E.C. Directive on Unfair Terms in Consumer Contracts.[29] The ambit of the system of control on the ground of unfairness which these regulations impose is not restricted to exemption, limitation and indemnity clauses, but extends to any term which has not been individually negotiated and "which contrary to the requirement of good faith causes a significant imbalance in the parties' rights and obligations under the contract to the detriment of the consumer."[30]

Good faith. The use by these Regulations of the notion of good faith raises   1–019
the question whether English law requires that a party to a contract exercise his rights in good faith, whether the right in question concerns the creation of a contract or its performance. Such a question may be expressed in a variety of ways: put negatively, it may be asked whether a party's *bad faith* should affect his exercise of rights or whether his "unconscionable conduct" in the creation of a contract should affect its validity[31] and put at its most general, whether this exercise should be recognised only if this is reasonable or fair. In 1766, in the context of recognising the duty of disclosure in contracts of insurance,[32] Lord Mansfield C.J. stated that "[t]he governing principle is applicable to all contracts and dealings. Good faith forbids either party by concealing what he privately knows, to draw the other into a bargain, from his ignorance of that fact, and his believing the contrary. But either party may be innocently silent, as to grounds open to both, to exercise their judgment upon."[33] Nevertheless, the modern view is that, in keeping with the doctrines of freedom of contract and the binding force of contracts, in English contract law good faith is in principle irrelevant.[34] As Bingham L.J. has stated:

"[i]n many civil law systems, and perhaps in most legal systems outside the common law world, the law of obligations recognises and enforces an overriding principle that in making and carrying out contracts parties should act in good faith. This does not simply mean that they should not deceive each other, a principle which any legal system must recognise; its effect is perhaps most aptly conveyed by such metaphorical colloquialisms as 'playing fair', 'coming clean' or 'putting one's cards face upwards on the

---

[26] Unfair Contract Terms Act 1977, s.2(1).
[27] *ibid.* s.6(2).
[28] *ibid.* ss.2(2), 3, 6(3) and 11; and see *post*, §§ 14–081 *et seq.*
[29] Dir. 93/13/EEC; and see *post*, §§ 15–004 *et seq.*
[30] Unfair Terms in Consumer Contracts Regulations 1994, r. 4(1).
[31] See *post*, §§ 7–075 *et seq.*
[32] See Vol. II, §§ 41–026—41–036.
[33] *Carter v. Boehm* (1766) 3 Burr. 1905, 1910.
[34] And see Atiyah, *Introduction to the Law of Contract* (5th ed., 1995), p. 212.

table.' It is in essence a principle of fair open dealing . . . English law has, character-istically, committed itself to no such overriding principle but has developed piecemeal solutions in response to demonstrated problems of unfairness."[35]

The fact that at least some English Judges are not at present attracted by the idea of a general ground for relief for unfairness is also clear from judicial treatment of Lord Denning's attempt to construct a general principle of "inequality of bargaining power" in *Lloyd's Bank Ltd v. Bundy*[36] and the House of Lords' refusal to imply a term in a "lock-out" agreement that a party to it be obliged to continue to negotiate in good faith.[37] Indeed, in that case, Lord Ackner stated that "the concept of a duty to carry on negotiations in good faith is inherently repugnant to the adversarial position of the parties when involved in negotia-tions"[38] and "unworkable in practice."[39] A very stark example of the preference of English judges for the strict application of the terms of a contract rather than tempering their effect on the grounds of fairness may be found in *Union Eagle Ltd v. Golden Achievement Ltd.*[40] There, the Privy Council refused specific performance of a contract for the sale of land to its purchaser who had paid the price ten minutes late, time having been made expressly of the essence for performance of this obligation. It rejected the argument that the courts enjoyed a discretion to relieve a party from the contractual consequences of late perform-ance (stemming from its jurisdiction to relieve from forfeitures in equity). According to Lord Hoffmann, "[t]he principle that equity will restrain the enforcement of legal rights when it would be unconscionable to insist upon them has an attractive breadth. But the reasons why the courts have rejected such generalisations are founded not merely upon authority . . . but also upon con-siderations of business. These are, in summary, that in many forms of transaction it is of great importance that if something happens for which the contract has made express provision, the parties should know with certainty that the terms of the contract will be enforced. The existence of an undefined discretion to refuse to enforce the contract on the ground that this would be 'unconscionable' is sufficient to create uncertainty"[41], though Lord Hoffmann recognised that "the same need for certainty is not present in all transactions."[42]

---

[35] *Interfoto Picture Library Ltd v. Stilletto Visual Programmes Ltd* [1989] 1 Q.B. 433, 439. Bingham L.J. gave as illustrations of these solutions equity's striking down of unconscionable bargains (see *post*, §§ 7–075 *et seq.*), statutory control of exemption clauses (see *post*, §§ 14–081 *et seq.*) and hire-purchase (see Vol. II, § 38–317 *et seq.*) and the ineffectiveness of penalty clauses (see *post*, §§ 27–102 *et seq.*).

[36] [1975] Q.B. 326, 339; and see *post*, § 7–088.

[37] *Walford v. Miles* [1992] 2 A.C. 128, 138. *cf. Little v. Courage Ltd, The Times*, January 19, 1994.

[38] [1992] 2 A.C. 128, 138. The agreement was held unenforceable on the grounds of uncertainty, and see *post*, §§ 2–126—2–127.

[39] *ibid*. In *Banque Keyser Ullmann SA v. Skandia (U.K.) Insurance Co. Ltd* [1990] 1 Q.B. 665, 772 (affd. on other grounds [1990] 2 All E.R. 947), Slade L.J. rejected Steyn J.'s formulation of the content of the ambit of the duty of disclosure on insurers based simply on the question "did good faith and fair dealing require a disclosure?" on the ground that "in the case of commercial contracts, broad concepts of honesty and fair dealing, however laudable, are a somewhat uncertain guide when determining the existence or otherwise of an obligation which may arise even in the absence of any dishonest or unfair intent."

[40] [1997] 2 All E.R. 215.

[41] *ibid*. at 218.

[42] *ibid*. at 219.

Fairness relevant: (1) construction. However, general considerations of **1–020** fairness are relevant to the way in which English courts treat the consequences of making contracts in several different ways. First, the fairness or reasonableness of the result reached is clearly relevant to the interpretation of the express terms which the parties have made. The courts have long made clear that, in general, they should look to the intention of the parties rather than the strict letter of a contract's stipulations[43] and in interpreting their intention, the courts look at the factual matrix of the contract: "modern principles of construction require the court to have regard to the commercial background, the context of the contract and the circumstances of the parties, and to consider whether, against that background and in that context, to give the words a particular or restricted meaning would lead to an apparently unreasonable and unfair result."[44] As Lord Reid earlier observed, "[t]he more unreasonable the result the more unlikely it is that the parties can have intended it."[45] Furthermore, other principles governing the relationship of the parties also find their formal source in the construction of the contract: so, for example, the courts accept that, in general, a party in default under a contract cannot take advantage of his own wrong,[46] an idea which in some other systems is put in terms of the adage *nemo auditur turpitudinem suam allegans*. Another example of English law's occasional imposition of a requirement of fairness may be found in the situation where a contract on its terms provides that a particular act of one of its parties (or their agent) will result in or affect a liability in the other: here, the courts have held that this act must be made fairly to have this effect. This result has been long established in the context of the issuing of certificates by an owner's agent (for example, his architect) in respect of building work having been properly executed: here, the certification holds good only if the agent acts fairly as between the two parties to the contract.[47] Similarly, where a charterparty provided that the ship's master's "notice of readiness" to receive cargo would, after a delay, start "notice time" running so as to allow its owner to claim demurrage, it was observed that "a notice of readiness proved to be given by the master or chief officer with knowledge that it was untrue, that is to say in the knowledge that the vessel was not then ready would be ineffective to start time running. There must by implication be a requirement of good faith."[48]

Fairness relevant: (2) implied terms. Secondly, as has been indicated,[49] the **1–021** common law often resorts to the implication of a term in a contract in a case which could otherwise be considered to be a matter of "good faith in the performance of a contract." Thus, for example, the House of Lords has accepted that a term is to be implied in contracts of employment to the effect that the "employer [will] not, without reasonable and proper cause, conduct itself in a manner likely to destroy or seriously damage the relationship of confidence and

---

[43] *e.g. Solley v. Forbes* (1820) 2 Brod. & B. 28, 48 *per* Dallas C.J.

[44] *Cargill International SA v. Bangladesh Sugar and Food Industries Corp* [1998] 1 W.L.R. 461, 468 *per* Potter L.J. and see further *Prenn v. Simmonds* [1971] 1 W.L.R. 1381 esp. at 1383–1384 and *Charter Reinsurance Co. Ltd v. Fagan* [1997] A.C. 313, esp. at 387–388.

[45] *Wickman Machine Tool Sales Ltd v. Schuler A.G.* [1974] A.C. 235, 251.

[46] *Alghussein Establishment v. Eton College* [1988] 1 W.L.R. 587.

[47] *Pawley v. Turnbull* (1861) 3 Giff. 70; *Hickman & Co. v. Roberts* [1913] A.C. 229.

[48] *Colbelfret N.V. v. Cylclades Shipping Co. Ltd (The "Linardos")* [1994] 1 Lloyd's L. Rep. 28, 32 *per* Colman J.

[49] See *ante*, § 1–013.

trust between employer and employee."[50] Sometimes, indeed, an implied term imposes a duty on an employer to act positively in the interests of the employee. So, for example, in *Scally v. Southern Health and Social Services Board*,[51] the House of Lords held that an employer who knew that its employees had a valuable right under the terms of their contracts of employment (here, relating to the enhancement of their pension rights), in a situation where it was reasonable for the employee to be unaware of that right (as it stemmed from a collective agreement), was under a duty to take reasonable steps to inform those employees of their rights. An example drawn from another context may be found in the courts' implication of a term in a contract of sale of the goodwill of a business that the seller is not entitled to solicit the business's former customers, it being "not an honest thing to pocket the price and then to recapture the subject of sale,"[52] though the courts do not go further and accept that the seller is not entitled to compete with his purchaser in the absence of express provision.[53]

1–022   **Fairness relevant: (3) duties to act in other parties' interest.** Thirdly, some particular types of contract attract rules (usually considered to be of law, though sometimes justified by reference to the implied intentions of the parties) which impose duties on one party to act other than in their own interest. This is most clearly the case in contracts under which a person assumes fiduciary duties, as is notably the case as regards agents, for a fiduciary must act honestly and must not allow his own interests to conflict with those of his principal.[54] Indeed, the Commercial Agents (Council Directive) Regulations 1993, echoing the E.C. directive which they implement, put the duties of agents to their principals expressly in terms of good faith.[55] Another example may be found in relation to mortgages. Thus, the Privy Council has recognised that a mortgagee of property must exercise his powers in good faith and for the purpose of obtaining repayment of the debt, though given this purpose these powers may be exercised in such a way that disadvantageous consequences accrue to the borrower.[56] And of course the parties to contracts of insurance owe each other duties of "the utmost good faith", the most important consequence of which is the imposition of extensive obligations of disclosure.[57]

1–023   **Fairness relevant: (4) equitable and statutory discretions.** Fourthly, general considerations of fairness are relevant to the availability of certain equitable doctrines which are significant in the contractual context, notably promissory estoppel,[58] as well as to the equitable remedies of specific performance and injunction which are sometimes available on breach.[59] To these, modern statutes

---

[50] *Malik v. Bank of Credit and Commerce International SA (in liquid.)* [1997] 3 W.L.R. 95.

[51] [1992] 1 A.C. 294.

[52] *Trego v. Hunt* [1896] A.C. 7, 25 *per* Lord Macnaghten.

[53] *ibid.* at 20.

[54] See Vol. II, §§ 32–116 *et seq.*

[55] S.I. No. 3053, r. 3(1) implementing Dir. 86/653/EEC, Art. 3(1).

[56] *Downsview Ltd v. First City Corp. Ltd* [1993] A.C. 295, 312 and see also *Albany Home Loans Ltd v. Massey* [1997] 2 All E.R. 609, 612–613.

[57] See Vol. II, § 41–026.

[58] See *post*, §§ 3–090.

[59] See *post*, §§ 28–027 *et seq.*

have added discretions given to the courts to act according to the dictates of justice, equity or reasonableness (as the case may be) in relation to the exercise of other remedies by parties to contracts, notably, in relation to rescission for misrepresentation[60] and rescission for breach in contracts of sale of goods[61] and also in relation to contracts which have been frustrated.[62]

Role of good faith disputed. It should be noted, however, that the desirability 1–024 and appropriateness of resort to the notion of good faith remains very much a matter of doctrinal dispute in English law,[63] and its present rejection of a principle of good faith of potentially general application differs from that in French and German law, in the latter of which in particular, the principle of good faith is of very great importance.[64] The position taken by English law also differs from that taken by other common law jurisdictions, in which doctrines of good faith,[65] or, conversely, unconscionable conduct,[66] have been constructed.

2. CLASSIFICATION OF CONTRACTS

The different types of classification. Contracts may be classified in a variety 1–025 of ways: according to their subject-matter[67]; according to their parties[68]; according to their form (whether contained in deeds[69] or in writing,[70] whether express or implied[71]) or according to their effect (whether bilateral or unilateral,[72] whether valid, void, voidable or unenforceable[73]).

---

[60] Misrepresentation Act 1967, s.2(2) (damages in lieu of rescission) on which see *post*, §§ 6–095—6–096.

[61] Sale of Goods Act 1979, s.15A.

[62] Law Reform (Frustrated Contracts) Act 1943 s.1(2) and s.1(3).

[63] Bridge (1984) 9 Can. Bus. L.J. 385; Collins, *The Law of Contract* (3rd ed., 1997), Chaps 13 and 15. Finn in Finn (ed.), *Essays on Contract Law* (1987), p. 104; Lüecke, *ibid*. p. 155; Steyn (1991) Denning L.J. 131; Carter and Furmston (1994) 8 J.C.L. 1; Brownsword (1994) 7 J.C.L. 197; Staughton (1994) 7 J.C.L. 193; Beatson and Friedmann, (eds.) *Good Faith and Fault in Contract Law* (1995), esp. the essays by Beatson and Friedmann, at p. 3; Cohen, at p. 25; McKendrick, at p. 305; Friedmann, at p. 399; Brownsword in Deakin and Michie (eds.), *Contracts, Co-operation and Competition* (1997), 255; Teubner, 61 (1998) M.L.R. 11.

[64] For German law, see Markesinis, Lorenz and Dannemann, *The German Law of Obligations*, Vol. I, *The Law of Contracts and Restitution: A Comparative Introduction* (1997), Chap. 7; For French Law, see Whittaker in Bell, Boyron and Whittaker, *Principles of French Law* (1998), pp. 313–316; 335–336. For a general survey of the position in the E.U., see Whittaker and Zimmermann, *Good Faith in European Contract Law* (forthcoming, 2000)

[65] See the American Law Institute's *Restatement of Contracts* (2d), § 205; U.S.A. Uniform Commercial Code, § 1–203, on which see Farnsworth, *Contracts* (1990), Vol. II, § 7.17, 7.17a; White and Summers, *Uniform Commercial Code* (4th ed., 1995), Vol. 1, Chap. 4.

[66] For the Australian position, see Carter and Harland, *Cases and Materials on Contract Law in Australia* (3rd ed., 1998), pp. 489 *et seq.*

[67] See *post*, §§ 1–026—1–030.

[68] See *post*, § 1–031.

[69] See *post*, §§ 1–033, 1–042—1–058.

[70] See Chap. 4.

[71] See *post*, § 1–034.

[72] See *post*, § 1–036.

[73] See *post*, §§ 1–037—1–041.

(a) *Classification of Contracts according to their Subject-matter*

1–026   **General.** Despite the generality of approach of English contract law,[74] the most prominent classification of contracts in the modern law divides them according to their subject-matter: thus, there are contracts of sale of goods and of land, insurance, suretyship, employment, hire, etc., and some of the more prominent of these special contracts are discussed in the second volume of this work.

1–027   **Classification for statutory purposes.** Some types of contract are statutorily defined, for example, contracts of sale of goods,[75] for the carriage of goods by sea,[76] of marine insurance,[77] and of consumer credit,[78] and the purpose of these definitions is made clear by the statute in which they are contained. However, in other cases, even where important statutory regulation applies to a particular type of contract, its definition is left to the common law, examples of this being the contracts of employment,[79] tenancy[80] or insurance.[81]

1–028   **Classification for common law purposes.** Classification of the parties' agreement as a particular type of contract may also need to be undertaken for the purposes of the common law. First, the courts have over the years found many implied terms in contracts which are not special to the particular agreement of the parties,[82] but are considered incidental to the *type* of agreement in question.[83] By attaching an implied term to a particular set of facts in this way, a court thereby either recognises an existing category of contract or creates a new one. In this respect, there is a certain tendency for the broader categories of contracts to be subdivided into smaller ones. For example, the contract of employment attracts many implied terms which are of general application,[84] but in *Sim v. Rotherham Metropolitan Borough Council*,[85] the court implied a term into a contract of employment between a local authority and a school teacher that the latter would

---

[74] Nicholas (1974) 48 Tulane L.R. 946, 948–949. This approach in English law is to be contrasted with, for example, French law. In that legal system, while the Civil Code contains provisions describing the conditions for and effects of contracts in general, it also contains much more extensive sections relating to particular *types* of contract, for example, sale, hire, mandate etc. Thus, some of the "nominate contracts" of Roman law survived into the Civil Code, though as particular examples of a general principle of contract based on agreement: Art. 1101, C. civ.

[75] Sale of Goods Act 1979, s.2(1) and see *post*, Vol. II, § 43–008.

[76] Carriage of Goods by Sea Act 1971, s.1 and Sched., art. I(b).

[77] Marine Insurance Act 1906, s.1.

[78] Consumer Credit Act 1974, s.8 and see *post*, Vol. II, § 38–002.

[79] See Vol. II, § 39–009, where it is noted that there is no comprehensive definition of the contract, the cases instead relying on a number of factors relevant to finding whether a particular contract is of service.

[80] There has been particular difficulty in distinguishing between leases and contractual licences: see *Street v. Mountford* [1985] A.C. 809; *A.G. Securities v. Vaughan* [1990] 1 A.C. 417.

[81] See Vol. II, § 41–001. For an example of the statutory significance of a contract being classified as one of insurance, see the Financial Services Act 1986, ss. 132, and 207(7), and Insurance Companies Act 1982, ss. 95, 96(1) and Vol. II, § 41–038.

[82] *cf. Ashmore v. Corpn. of Lloyd's* [1992] 2 Lloyd's Rep. 620, 630–631.

[83] See *ante*, § 1–021 and *post*, § 13–003.

[84] For example, it is an implied term in every contract of employment that the employee will not disclose any confidential information which he learns by reason of his employment: see Vol. II, § 39–059.

[85] [1987] Ch. 216.

cover for her fellow teachers in their absence if reasonably requested to do so, a term which would apply to similar contracts but not necessarily to contracts of employment beyond that context.[86] In *Scally v. Southern Health and Social Services Board*,[87] Lord Bridge felt able to imply a term in the contracts of employment between a hospital board and its employees to take reasonable steps to inform the latter of their valuable right to opt to make payments into their pension schemes. His Lordship rejected the argument that the formulation of an implied term must necessarily be too wide, holding that "this difficulty is surmounted if the category of contractual relationship in which the implication will arise is defined with sufficient precision."[88] Similarly, while some terms are implied into leases in general,[89] others apply only to particular types of lease. Thus, in *Liverpool City Council v. Irwin*[90] the House of Lords implied a term into a contract of lease, but their Lordships' speeches suggest that this term was considered incidental to a much more specific contract, namely one made by a local authority for the lease of a flat in a high-rise block.[91]

Exceptional rules. Secondly, the courts sometimes make a formal exception   **1–029** to a rule of common law which applies only to a particular type of contract. For example, although in general a breach of contract, however fundamental, does not terminate it so as to prevent the application of any exemption clause which it may contain,[92] in a contract of carriage of goods by sea, any unnecessary deviation from the agreed or customary route constitutes a breach of the contract which gives rise in the owner to a right to treat himself as discharged and this right, if exercised, does have the effect of disapplying any exemption clause from the deviating journey.[93] Similarly, although in general a person is not bound by an exemption clause in a contract to which he is not party, if for example, A sends goods for repair to B with permission to send the work out to a sub-contractor, C, A may be bound by any exemption clause in this contract of sub-bailment.[94] Again, while in general there is no pre-contractual duty of disclosure, such a duty does rest on both parties to a contract of insurance, this being said to arise from the nature of the contract itself.[95] A final example may be found in relation to restrictive covenants concerning land. These started life as a particular type of contract, or rather a particular type of contractual obligation, as they were stipulated as part of the sale of land,[96] but after *Tulk v. Moxhay*[97] in 1848, they were held capable of binding a successor in title of the purchaser of the land, despite the principle of privity of contract. While technically this is justified by saying that the making of the covenant creates an equitable (proprietary) interest

---

[86] *cf. ibid.* at 248.

[87] [1992] 1 A.C. 294.

[88] *ibid.* at 307. Lord Bridge defined the category by reference to three special circumstances.

[89] *e.g.* a landlord's implied covenant for quiet enjoyment: see Gray, *Elements of Land Law* (2nd ed., 1993), pp. 778–781.

[90] [1977] A.C. 239.

[91] See *ibid.* at 254, 258, 261. This subdivision of large categories for the purposes of the implication of terms can be seen in *Jones v. Just* (1868) L.R. 3 Q.B. 197, 202–203 in relation to sale before the Sale of Goods Act 1893.

[92] *Photo Production Ltd v. Securicor Transport Ltd* [1980] A.C. 827.

[93] See *post*, § 14–029.

[94] *Morris v. C. W. Martin & Sons Ltd* [1966] 1 Q.B. 716; *The Pioneer Container* [1994] 2 A. C. 324 and see *post*, §§ 1–121, 14–050—14–051.

[95] *Carter v. Boehm* (1766) 3 Burr. 1905, 1909 and see Vol. II, §§ 39–025 *et seq.*

[96] Lawson and Rudden, *The Law of Property* (2nd ed., 1982), p. 131.

[97] (1848) 2 Ph. 774.

in land,[98] it can equally be seen as an example of the law creating an exception to the rules of privity of contract for a particular type of term in a particular type of contract.

1–030   **Commercial practice.** Other types of contract arise from commercial practice rather than from the regulation of either statute or common law, though the practical homogeneity on which they are based easily attracts particular treatment by the courts. Very clear examples of this can be found in an area like the building industry, in which the industry offers standard forms for the conclusion of the many contracts which modern construction requires.[99] Moreover, new types of contracts in this sense are constantly arising, for example, for the supply and maintenance of information technology.[1]

(b) *Classification of Contracts according to their Parties*

1–031   **General.** Contracts are sometimes classified according to their parties and this type of classification sometimes cuts across those other types which have already been mentioned. Perhaps the most important of this type of division is between commercial and non-commercial contracts. Commercial contracts can be described as those which are made between two or more parties who are in business for the purposes of trade. "Non-commercial contracts" is a residual category and would include transactions as disparate as contracts on the dissolution of marriage, contracts under which legal claims are settled, sales between private individuals other than in the course of business as well as "consumer contracts." The latter is in the modern law an important category and may be defined as those contracts which are made between one party who is in business and one who is contracting other than for trade purposes.[2] However, the common law of contract does not recognise the categories of commercial[3] or consumer contracts and the latter category has only really become prominent as a result of modern legislation passed for the protection of consumers, in particular concerning credit agreements[4] and the effectiveness of exemption clauses[5] and other unfair contract terms.[6]

Another important distinction in the modern law is between contracts made between private persons and those where one or both parties are public bodies. This distinction will be discussed later.[7]

---

[98] Gray *op. cit.* p. 149.

[99] These are known as "RIBA/JCT standard forms": see Duncan Wallace, *Construction Contracts: Principles and Policies in Tort and Contract* (1986), p. 499 and generally, Van Deventer, *The Law of Construction* (1993).

[1] See Rennie, *Computer Contracts: precedent contracts for the computer industry worldwide* (1994).

[2] *cf.* Unfair Contract Terms Act 1977, s.12.

[3] *cf.* Goode, *Commercial Law* (2nd ed., 1995), p. 145. Some legal systems possess a commercial law code to govern at least in part the relationships of traders and which is distinct from the civil code which is of more general application: see Köndgen in Ebke and Finkin, *Introduction to German Law* (1996), Chap. 4; Bell in Bell, Boyron and Whittaker, *Principles of French Law* (1998), Chap. 11.

[4] See Vol. II, Chap. 38.

[5] Unfair Contract Terms Act 1977, see *post*, § 14–064.

[6] Unfair Terms in Consumer Contracts Regulations 1994 (S.I. 1994, No. 3159) on which see *post*, §§ 15–004 *et seq.*

[7] See *post*, §§ 1–129 *et seq.*

(c) *Classification of Contracts according to their Form*

Introduction. Contracts can also be classified according to their form and for **1–032**
this purpose, distinctions can be drawn between formal and informal contracts,
and express and implied contracts.

Formal and informal contracts. Contracts may be either formal or informal. **1–033**
Apart from the so-called contracts of record, comprising judgments and recog-
nisances, which are not properly speaking contracts at all, the only formal
contract in English law is the contract contained in a deed or specialty contract.
All others are informal contracts, or simple contracts as they are more often
termed. Such contracts may in principle be oral or in writing,[8] though particular
contracts possess different requirements as to writing.[9] The requirements of a
valid contract contained in a deed are discussed in the next section of this chapter.
The chief respect in which they differ from simple contracts is that, for historical
reasons, they are valid without the necessity for consideration.

Express and implied contracts. Contracts may be either express or implied. **1–034**
The difference is not one of legal effect but simply of the way in which the
consent of the parties is manifested. Contracts are express when their terms are
stated in words by the parties. They are often said to be implied when their terms
are not so stated, as, for example, when a passenger is permitted to board a bus:
from the conduct of the parties the law implies a promise by the passenger to pay
the fare, and a promise by the operator of the bus to carry him safely to his
destination. There may also be an implied contract when the parties make an
express contract to last for a fixed term, and continue to act as though the contract
still bound them after the term has expired. In such a case the court may infer that
the parties have agreed to renew the express contract for another term. Express
and implied contracts are both contracts in the true sense of the term, for they
both arise from the agreement of the parties, though in one case the agreement
is manifested in words and in the other case by conduct. Since, as we have seen,[10]
agreement is not a mental state but an act, an inference from conduct, and since
many of the terms of an express contract are often implied, it follows that the
distinction between express and implied contracts has very little importance,
even if it can be said to exist at all.[11]

(d) *Classification of Contracts according to their Effect*

Introduction. Contracts are sometimes classified according to their effect and **1–035**
so distinctions can be drawn between unilateral and bilateral contracts and valid,
void, voidable and unenforceable contracts. The last three terms denote varying
degrees of imperfection and are in constant use in the law of contract.

Unilateral and bilateral contracts. Contracts may be either unilateral or **1–036**
bilateral.[12] By a unilateral contract is meant a contract under which only one

---

[8] *Rann v. Hughes* (1778) 7 T.R. 350n.
[9] See *post*, Chap. 4.
[10] *Ante*, § 1–004.
[11] See Corbin, *Contracts* (1963), § 18.
[12] *Restatement of Contracts* (1932), § 12. The *Restatement of Contracts* (2d, 1981), § 45 abandons
this distinction and substitutes for unilateral contracts "option contracts."

party undertakes an obligation.[13] Bilateral (or synallagmatic) contracts, on the other hand, are those under which both parties undertake obligations. It is to be noted, though, that the unilateral nature of the contract does not (in the ordinary case) mean that there is only one party, nor that there is no need for an acceptance or the provision of consideration by the other party.[14] An example of a unilateral contract may be found in the case of an offer for a reward for the return of lost property: here, a contract is formed (at the latest) on the return of the property, this constituting the offeree's acceptance of the offer and the furnishing of consideration for the creation of the contract.[15] Bilateral contracts comprise the exchange of a promise for a promise, *e.g.* if you promise to pay me £1,000, I promise to sell you my car.

1–037   **Void contracts.** A void contract is strictly a contradiction in terms, because if an agreement is truly void it is not a contract; but the term is a useful one and well understood by lawyers. Properly speaking, a void contract should produce no legal effects whatsoever. Neither party should be able to sue the other on the contract. If goods have been delivered, they or their value should be recoverable by an action in tort, because the property will not pass. If money has been paid, it should be recoverable by an action in restitution, because the money was not due. In one situation, *i.e.* where a contract is void for mistake, these consequences would appear to follow from the fact that the contract is void.[16] But it is by no means true that all contracts termed "void" by the law necessarily produce this effect.

1–038   **"Void" contract may have effects.** For example, a contract may be void for illegality. But, although in many cases, neither party can sue on it, in other cases a party who is innocent of any illegal design may have a right of action.[17] Property may pass under an illegal contract[18] and money paid in pursuance of it is often irrecoverable.[19] Moreover, where A and B have paid money to C under an agreement under which C is empowered to pay some of the money to B, the court will not at A's request restrain C from so doing, even though the agreement is illegal and void as an unreasonable restraint of trade.[20] Other difficult questions arise in relation to the relative positions of the parties to a contract for the sale or other disposition of an interest in land which is a nullity as a result of not having been made in writing as is required by section 2 of the Law of Property (Miscellaneous Provisions) Act 1989.[21]

---

[13] See *New Zealand Shipping Co. Ltd v. A.M. Satterthwaite & Co. Ltd* [1975] A.C. 154, 167–168, 171, 177. *Quaere* whether the engagement of an estate agent is a unilateral contract: *Luxor (Eastbourne) Ltd v. Cooper* [1941] A.C. 108, 124; Murdoch (1975) 91 L.Q.R. 357; McConnell (1983) 265 E.G. 547.

[14] See *Carlill v. Carbolic Smoke Ball Co.* [1893] 1 Q.B. 256. In certain situations, a contract under which only one party undertakes an obligation may be truly one-sided, in that the other party may be dispensed from the need to provide consideration. Thus, an agreement contained in a deed under which A covenants to pay B a sum of money may be considered a unilateral contract as only A undertakes an obligation (see *post*, § 1–052).

[15] On the issue of when such a contract is formed see *post*, §§ 2–071 *et seq.*

[16] See *post*, Chap. 5.

[17] See *post*, § 17–011.

[18] See *post*, § 17–170.

[19] See *post*, § 17–176.

[20] *Boddington v. Lawton*, [1994] I.C.R. 478.

[21] See *post*, §§ 4–067—4–071.

Voidable contracts. A voidable contract is one where one or more of its   **1–039**
parties have the power, by a manifestation of election to do so, to avoid the legal
relations created by the contract; or by affirmation of the contract to extinguish
the power of avoidance.[22] In English law, contracts may be voidable, *e.g.* for
misrepresentation,[23] duress,[24] undue influence,[25] minority,[26] unsoundness of
mind,[27] drunkenness[28] or under statute.[29] If the contract is wholly executory, the
party entitled to avoid the contract can plead its voidability in an action against
him. If it has been wholly or partly executed, he can claim to have set it aside and
to be restored to his original position. But until the right of avoidance is
exercised, the contract is valid. Thus if a contract for the sale of goods is voidable
for fraud (but has not been avoided), the fraudulent party acquires a good title to
the goods which he can transfer to an innocent purchaser for value.[30] The right
of avoidance must also be exercised promptly in most cases. It is theoretically
possible for a contract to be avoidable by both parties thereto, *e.g.* if each
defrauds the other, or both are drunk; but naturally instances of this are rare.

Power to set aside on terms. It would seem that the term "voidable"   **1–040**
possesses a special meaning in relation to the effect of common fundamental
mistake of the parties in equity, as here it refers not to a power in one or other
of the parties to avoid the contract, but to a power in the court to set aside the
contract on terms.[31]

Unenforceable contracts. Unenforceable contracts are valid in all respects   **1–041**
except that one or both parties cannot be sued on the contract. Instances of
unenforceable contracts in English law are afforded by certain contracts which
are not evidenced by a signed writing as required by certain statutes[32]; contracts
in respect of which the right of action is barred by the Limitation Act 1980[33]; and
certain contracts with a foreign sovereign[34] or in breach of foreign exchange
control regulations.[35] In some cases the defect of unenforceability is curable.
Thus, if written evidence of a contract of guarantee comes into existence, the
contract becomes enforceable, though it was made orally[36]; a current period of

---

[22] See *Restatement of Contracts* (2d), § 7.
[23] See *post*, Chap. 6.
[24] See *post*, §§ 7–001—7–040.
[25] See *post*, §§ 7–041—7–074.
[26] See *post*, §§ 8–002—8–064.
[27] See *post*, §§ 8–067 *et seq.*
[28] See *post*, §§ 8–077—8–078.
[29] *e.g.* Auctions (Bidding Agreements) Act 1969, s.3(1) replacing Auctions (Bidding Agreements) Act 1927, s.2 (as amended). Consumer Credit Act 1974, ss.67–73 (cancellation of consumer credit agreements) and see *post*, Vol. II, §§ 38–084 *et seq.*
[30] See *Phillips v. Brooks Ltd* [1919] 2 K.B. 243; *Lewis v. Averay* [1972] 1 Q.B. 198; Sale of Goods Act 1979, s.23. Contrast *Cundy v. Lindsay* (1878) 3 App.Cas. 459 and *Ingram v. Little* [1961] 1 Q.B. 31, where the contract was void for mistake. See *post* § 5–045 and Vol. II, § 43–209.
[31] See *Solle v. Butcher* [1950] 1 K.B. 671, 696–697 and *post*, §§ 5–091—5–095.
[32] *e.g* consumer credit agreements: Consumer Credit Act 1974, ss.60, 61, 65 (see Vol. II, §§ 38–070, 38–080—38–081); contracts of guarantee: Statute of Frauds 1677, s.4 (see Vol. II, Chap. 32).
[33] See *post*, Chap. 29.
[34] See *post*, Chap. 11.
[35] *United City Merchants (Investments) Ltd v. Royal Bank of Canada* [1983] 1 A.C. 168, 189–190.
[36] See *post*, Vol. II, Chap. 44.

limitation may be repeatedly extended if the defendant makes a written acknowl-edgment of his indebtedness, or a part payment[37]; a foreign sovereign may waive his immunity.[38] An unenforceable contract may be indirectly enforceable by means other than bringing an action. Thus a statute-barred debt may be recover-able indirectly if the creditor has a lien on goods of the debtor which are in his possession.[39] Frequently the contract is enforceable by one party but not by the other. For example, the Financial Services Act 1986 requires that a person carrying on investment business be authorised to do so.[40] Where a person who has not been authorised enters a contract in the course of carrying on an investment business, that contract is in principle unenforceable against its other party,[41] though a court may allow the agreement to be enforced or money or property paid or transferred under it to be retained by the unauthorised person in certain circumstances.[42]

3. CONTRACTS CONTAINED IN DEEDS

(a) *Form and Delivery*

1–042   **Preliminary.** At common law, contracts under seal, or specialties, were an important example of deeds and at common law a deed was an instrument which was not merely in writing, but which was sealed by the party bound thereby, and delivered by him to or for the benefit of the person to whom the liability was incurred.[43] In no other way than by the use of this form could validity be given to executory contracts at common law in early times. At common law, all deeds were documents under seal, but not all documents under seal were and are deeds. A deed must either:

(a) effect the transference of an interest, right or property, or

(b) create an obligation binding on some person or persons, or

(c) confirm some act whereby an interest, right or property has already passed.

Many documents under seal are not deeds, for instance an arbitrator's award, a certificate of admission to a learned society, a share certificate, probate of a will[44] or a company's memorandum of association.[45]

---

[37] Limitation Act 1980, s.29 and see *post*, §§ 29–095 *et seq.*

[38] See *post*, §§ 11–016 *et seq.*

[39] See *post*, § 29–136. *Quaere* whether an action on a cheque paid in discharge of an unenforceable contract fails for total or partial failure of consideration: *Martin & Boston & Co. (a firm) v. Levy* [1982] 1 W.L.R. 1434.

[40] Financial Services Act 1986, s.3.

[41] *ibid.* s.5(1), (6).

[42] *ibid.* s.5(3).

[43] Compare *ante*, § 1–003 on the question of agreement in relation to deeds.

[44] *R. v. Morton* (1873) L.R. 2 C.C.R. 22, 27.

[45] *Re Whitley Partners Ltd* (1886) 32 Ch.D. 337, 340. But for some purposes the memorandum and articles, when registered, create obligations as if they had been signed and sealed by each member: see Companies Act 1985, s.14; Insolvency Act 1986, s.80; *Hickman v. Kent or Romney Marsh Sheep Breeders' Association* [1915] 1 Ch. 881; *Rayfield v. Hands* [1960] Ch. 1.

The general abolition of the requirement of sealing. By section 1(1)(b) of **1–043**
the Law of Property (Miscellaneous Provisions) Act 1989, the requirement of
sealing was abolished for all deeds executed by an individual.[46] The ancient
requirement of sealing[47] was replaced with new ones that the intention of the
party making a deed should make this intention clear, of signature[48] by that party
and of attestation.[49] Moreover, in the same year, the requirement of sealing for
the execution of a deed by a company incorporated under the Companies Acts
was also abolished and replaced with ones relating to the intention of the
company officers who execute it and of attestation.[50] In the case of deeds
executed by other persons, the common law requirement of sealing still
obtains.

Deeds executed by an individual. The law now requires that for an instru- **1–044**
ment made by an individual to be a deed, it must make "clear on its face that it
is intended to be a deed by the person making it or, as the case may be, by the
parties to it (whether by describing itself as a deed or expressing itself to be
executed or signed as a deed or otherwise)." It is questionable whether, while no
longer required, the affixing of a seal to an instrument would in itself be
considered sufficient to "make clear on its face" that it was intended to be a
deed.

The Law of Property (Miscellaneous Provisions) Act 1989 introduced other
requirements for the execution of a deed by an individual and preserved an
existing one. By section 1(3), for an instrument to be validly executed as a deed,
it must be "signed (i) by him in the presence of a witness who attests the
signature; or (ii) at his direction and in his presence and the presence of two
witnesses who each attest the signature." "Signature" is defined later in the
section to include making one's mark.[51] The Act specifically preserved the
common law requirement that for an instrument to be validly executed as a deed
it must be "delivered" as a deed by him or a person authorised to do so on his
behalf.[52]

Deeds executed by companies incorporated under the Companies **1–045**
Acts. By section 36A(4) of the Companies Act 1985,[53] a document signed by a
director and secretary, or by two directors, of a company incorporated under the
Act and expressed to be executed by the company has the same effect as if
executed under the common seal of the company and notwithstanding that the
company has no common seal[54] and a "document executed by a company which
makes clear on its face that it is intended by the person or persons making it to

---

[46] s.1(1)(a) and (c) also abolished respectively any rule of law which "restricts the substances on
which a deed may be written" or "requires authority by one person to another to deliver an instrument
as a deed on his behalf to be given by deed." On the common law position as to the latter, see *Phoenix
Properties Ltd v. Wimpole Street Nominees Ltd* [1992] B.C.L.C. 737. Under s.1(11) of the Act,
"nothing in this section applies in relation to instruments delivered as deeds before this section came
into force." Section 1(1)–(7) came into force on July 31, 1990 (S.I. 1990 No. 1175).
[47] Sheppard's *Touchstone of Common Assurances* (7th ed., 1820), p. 56.
[48] This requirement had been imposed by the Law of Property Act 1925, s.73.
[49] See *post*, § 1–044.
[50] Companies Act 1985, s.36A(4), (5) (as inserted by Companies Act 1989, s.130(1)).
[51] Law of Property (Miscellaneous Provisions) Act 1989, s.1(4).
[52] *ibid.* s.1(3)(b).
[53] As inserted by Companies Act 1989, s.130(1).
[54] Companies Act 1985, s.36A(3).

be a deed has effect, upon delivery, as a deed."[55] The deeds of a company must be executed in accordance with its articles of association, but in favour of a purchaser a deed is deemed to have been duly executed if its seal is affixed thereto in the presence of and attested by its secretary and a member of the board of directors[56] and a similar deeming provision applies to documents not made under the company seal, but where the document makes clear on its face that it is intended by the person or persons making it to be a deed.[57]

1–046   **Deeds executed by other persons.** Where a deed is executed by a person other than a private individual or a company incorporated under the Companies Act, the common law requirement of sealing still applies. This would apply to other corporations and to corporations sole.[58] However, this requirement has been interpreted by the courts very liberally: "to constitute a sealing neither wax nor wafer nor a piece of paper nor even an impression is necessary."[59] Pieces of green ribbon[60] or a circle printed on the document containing the letters "L.S." (*locus sigilli*)[61] or even a document bearing no indication of a seal at all[62] will suffice, if there is evidence (*e.g.* attestation) that the document was intended to be executed as a deed.[63] In the absence of such evidence, a signatory of a document expressed to have been "signed, sealed and delivered" by him may be estopped from denying that it was sealed.[64]

1–047   **Delivery.** "Where a contract is to be by deed, there must be a delivery to perfect it."[65] "Delivered," however, in this connection does not mean "handed over" to the other party. It means delivered in the old legal sense,[66] namely, an act done so as to evince an intention to be bound.[67] Any act of the party which shows that he intended to deliver the deed as an instrument binding on him is enough. He must make it his deed[68] and recognise it as presently binding on him.[69] Delivery is effective even though the grantor retains the deed in his own possession. There need be no actual transfer of possession to the other party: "the

---

[55] *ibid.* s.36A(5).

[56] Law of Property Act 1925, s.74.

[57] Companies Act 1985, s.36A(6) and *cf.* s.36C, also inserted by Companies Act 1989, s.130(1) (pre-incorporation contracts, deeds and obligations). On possible reforms of the law relating to the execution of deeds by companies, see Law Commission Consultation Paper No. 143, *The Execution of Deeds and Documents by or on behalf of Bodies Corporate* (1996).

[58] Law of Property (Miscellaneous Provisions) Act 1989, s.1(10) and see also s.1(9) which specifically reserves the requirement of sealing at common law in relation to deeds required or authorised to be made under the seals of the county palatine of Lancaster, the Duchy of Lancaster or the Duchy of Cornwall.

[59] *Ex p. Sandilands* (1871) L.R. 6 C.P. 411, 413.

[60] *Ex p. Sandilands, supra*; See also *Stromdale & Ball Ltd v. Burden* [1952] Ch. 233, 230.

[61] *First National Securities Ltd v. Jones* [1978] Ch. 109; Hoath (1980) 43 M.L.R. 415.

[62] *First National Securities Ltd v. Jones, above*; *Commercial Credit Services v. Knowles* [1978] 6 C.L. 64.

[63] *cf. National Provincial Bank v. Jackson* (1886) 33 Ch.D. 1; *Re Balkis Consolidated Ltd* (1888) 58 L.T. 300; *Re Smith* (1892) 67 L.T. 64 (these cases were explained in *First National Securities Ltd v. Jones, supra*): *cf. TCB v. Gray* [1986] 1 Ch. 621, 633.

[64] *TCB v. Gray, above. cf. Rushingdale Ltd v. Byblos Bank* (1985) P.C.C. 342, 346–347.

[65] *Xenos v. Wickham* (1863) 14 C.B.(N.S.) 435, 473; *Termes de la Ley*, s.v. Fait; Co.Litt. 171b.

[66] But see Yale [1970] C.L.J. 52.

[67] *Vincent v. Premo Enterprises Ltd* [1969] 2 Q.B. 609, 619.

[68] *Tupper v. Foulkes* (1861) 9 C.B.(N.S.) 797; *Xenos v. Wickham* (1867) L.R. 2 H.L. 296, 312; *Re Seymour* [1913] 1 Ch. 475.

[69] *Xenos v. Wickham, above.*

efficacy of a deed depends on its being sealed[70] and delivered by the maker of it, not on his ceasing to retain possession of it."[71] Where a solicitor or licensed conveyancer in the course of a transaction involving the disposition or creation of an interest in land, purports to deliver an instrument as a deed on behalf of a party to the instrument, it shall be conclusively presumed in favour of a purchaser that he is authorised so to deliver the instrument.[72]

Date. A date is not essential.[73] A deed takes effect on the date of its delivery.[74]   **1–048**

Delivery as an escrow. A party may likewise deliver a deed as an escrow, that   **1–049** is, so that it shall take effect or be his deed on certain conditions. It is in other words a limited or conditional delivery. Such delivery need not be accompanied by express words; if from all the facts attending the transaction it can reasonably be inferred that the writing was delivered so as not to take effect as a deed until a certain condition should be satisfied, it will operate as an escrow.[75] To constitute a delivery as an escrow, however, it was at one time necessary that the deed should not have been handed over to the grantee or covenantee.[76] But nowadays a deed may be delivered as an escrow by handing it to a solicitor who is acting for all the parties to it[77]; or even to the solicitor of the grantee or covenantee himself, provided it is clear upon the whole transaction that such handing over was not intended to be a delivery at that time to such grantee or covenantee.[78] In other words, evidence is admissible to show the character in which and the terms upon which the deed was delivered.[79] It is a question of fact, and depends on what the parties intended. Their intention may be ascertained either from their statements or from the surrounding circumstances prior to or simultaneous with (but not subsequent to) the delivery of the instrument.[80]

---

[70] But see *ante*, § 1–043.

[71] *Xenos v. Wickham, supra, per* Lord Cranworth at 323; *cf. per* Pigott B. at 309; *Doe* d. *Garnons v. Knight* (1826) 5 B. & C. 671; *Macedo v. Stroud* [1922] 2 A.C. 330; *Beesly v. Hallwood Estates Ltd* [1960] 1 W.L.R. 549, affd. [1961] Ch. 105; *Vincent v. Premo Enterprises Ltd* [1969] 2 Q.B. 609. Once a document has been sealed by a corporation aggregate in circumstances satisfying the requirements of s.74 of the Law of Property Act 1925, it is to be treated as executed without any need for delivery, and it is therefore a deed binding upon the corporation, either immediately or as an escrow: *D'Silva v. Lister House Development Ltd* [1971] Ch. 17 (but see (1973) 89 L.Q.R. 14).

[72] Law of Property (Miscellaneous Provisions) Act 1989, s.1(5).

[73] Bacon, *Abridgment Obligation* (C); Comyns Digest *Fait* (B3); *Goddard's Case* (1584) 2 Co.Rep. 4b.

[74] See also *post*, § 1–049 (escrow).

[75] *Murray v. Earl of Stair* (1823) 2 B. & C. 82; *Xenos v. Wickham, supra,* at 323; *Macedo v. Stroud, supra,* at 337; *Beesly v. Hallwood Estates Ltd, supra*; *Vincent v. Premo Enterprises Ltd, supra*; *D'Silva v. Lister House Development Ltd, supra*; *Kingston v. Ambrian Investment Co. Ltd* [1975] 1 W.L.R. 161; *Glessing v. Green* [1975] 1 W.L.R. 863; *Terrapin International Ltd v. I.R.C.* [1976] 1 W.L.R. 665.

[76] Co.Litt. 36a; Sheppard's *Touchstone of Common Assurances* (7th ed., 1820), p. 59.

[77] *Millership v. Brookes* (1860) 5 H. & N. 797; *Kidner v. Keith* (1863) 15 C.B.(N.S.) 35; 42. *Glessing v. Green, supra.*

[78] *Watkins v. Nash* (1875) L.R. 20 Eq. 262, 266; *Nash v. Flyn* (1844) 1 Jo. & La.T. 162, 177.

[79] *London Freehold and Leasehold Property Co. v. Suffield* [1897] 2 Ch. 608, 621–622. See *post*, § 12–103.

[80] *Bowker v. Burdekin* (1843) 11 M. & W. 128, 147; *Davis v. Jones* (1856) 17 C.B. 625, 634; *Governors, etc., of Foundling Hospital v. Crane* [1911] 2 K.B. 367, 374. *Thompson v. McCullough* [1947] K.B. 447.

1–050   **Conveyance as an escrow.** Where, in accordance with the general practice of sale of land, a conveyance is executed by the vendor and entrusted to his solicitor with a view to its being handed over to the purchaser on completion, then, in the absence of special circumstances, it is to be inferred that the conveyance is executed as an escrow conditional upon payment of the purchase price and (where appropriate) execution by the purchaser.[81] In such a case, there must be a time limit within which the implied condition of the escrow is to be performed.[82] So if the vendor by notice makes time of the essence of the contract, and the purchaser does not within the time specified in the notice perform the condition, it is no longer possible for the condition of the escrow to be performed.[83]

1–051   **Retrospective effect.** A deed, delivered as an escrow, takes effect as between grantor and grantee retrospectively from the date of its delivery, and not on the date on which the relevant conditions are satisfied.[84]

(b) *Consideration*

1–052   **No consideration required.** Generally speaking, as will be seen later in detail,[85] the law does not enforce gratuitous promises but instead requires a certain reciprocity for the creation of a "simple" contract, this requirement being expressed through the rules gathered under the heading of the doctrine of consideration. However, in contracts contained in a deed no such reciprocity is ordinarily required, the rule being that a contract contained in a deed is good even against a party standing to derive no advantage from it.[86] This means that the common law actions of debt (for a promised sum of money) or damages (for failure to perform promises more generally) are available to the person for whose benefit they are expressed. On the other hand equity never favoured voluntary transactions even though contained in a deed, and refused to grant its special remedies in cases where these were without consideration. So it has been laid down that specific performance will not be decreed of a contract contained in a deed which is entirely without consideration.[87] Knight-Bruce L.J. in *Kekewich v. Manning*[88] said, "In equity, where at least the covenantor is living, or where specific performance of such a (voluntary) covenant is sought, it stands scarcely, or not at all, on a better footing than if it were contained in an instrument unsealed."[89] And an imperfect conveyance, if voluntary, is not binding, and

---

[81] *Kingston v. Ambrian Investment Co. Ltd* [1975] 1 W.L.R. 161; *Glessing v. Green* [1975] 1 W.L.R. 863.

[82] *Glessing v. Green, supra.* Contrast *Kingston v. Ambrian Investment Co. Ltd, supra*, at 168–169.

[83] *Glessing v. Green, supra.* Contrast *Beesly v. Hallwood Estates Ltd* [1961] Ch. 105, 118, 120; *Kingston v. Ambrian Investment Co. Ltd, supra*, at 166.

[84] *Alan Estates Ltd v. W.G. Stores Ltd* [1982] Ch. 511, not following *Terrapin International Ltd v. I.R.C.* [1976] 1 W.L.R. 665; Kenny (1982) Conv. 409.

[85] See *post*, Chap. 3.

[86] See Plowd. 308; *Morley v. Boothby* (1825) 3 Bing. 107, 111–112.

[87] *Wycherley v. Wycherley* (1763) 2 Eden 175, 177. *Groves v. Groves* (1829) 3 Y. & J. 163; *Jefferys v. Jefferys* (1841) Cr. & Ph. 138. See *Fry on Specific Performance* (6th ed. 1921), p. 53; Jones and Goodhart, *Specific Performance* (1986), p. 15. Contrast *Mountford v. Scott* [1975] Ch. 258 (token payment for grant of option). See also *post*, §§ 3–020, 28–031.

[88] (1851) 1 De G.M. & G. 176, 188.

[89] But see *ante*, § 1–043.

equity will not execute it in favour of volunteers if anything remains to be done.[90] A contract contained in a deed, if made without consideration, may be impeached by third parties on similar grounds to those on which voluntary settlements can be impeached as being fraudulent as against creditors or purchasers.[91]

(c) *Other Aspects*

Benefit of person not a party. According to an ancient rule of the common **1–053** law, no one could take an immediate interest as grantee nor the benefit of a covenant as covenantee under an indenture *inter partes* (as opposed to a deed poll) unless he was named as a party thereto.[92] This was altered by section 5 of the Real Property Act 1845, which provided that under an indenture, an immediate estate or interest in any tenements or hereditaments, and the benefit of a condition or covenant respecting any tenements or hereditaments, might be taken, although the taker was not named a party to the same indenture.[93] This section was re-enacted with modifications by section 56(1) of the Law of Property Act 1925, which provides that a person may take the benefit of any covenant *or agreement* over or respecting land *or other property*, although he may not be named as a party to the conveyance or other instrument.[94] The determination of the exact scope of this provision is a matter of considerable difficulty[95]; but at any rate it is clear that it does not effect any general abrogation of the doctrine of privity of contract.[96] In *Beswick v. Beswick*,[97] a majority of the House of Lords was of the opinion that a limited meaning should be given to the word "property." Lord Guest thought it meant real property. Lord Upjohn, however, was not prepared to accept this limitation, although he considered that the application of the section was restricted to covenants contained in documents strictly *inter partes* and under seal.[98]

Non est factum. There was an ancient common law defence to actions on **1–054** specialties known as *non est factum*: if an illiterate man, to whom the provisions of a deed had been wrongly read, executed it under a mistake as to its contents, he could say that it was not his deed.[99] In modern times this doctrine has

---

[90] As in *Milroy v. Lord* (1862) 4 De G.F. & J. 264; *Richards v. Delbridge* (1874) L.R. 18 Eq. 11; *Re Kay's Settlement* [1939] Ch. 329; *Re Fry* [1946] Ch. 312. See also Law of Property Act 1925, s.173, replacing Voluntary Conveyances Act 1893.

[91] See Law of Property Act 1925, ss.172, 173.

[92] *Scudamore v. Vandenstene* (1587) 2 Co.Inst. 673; *Berkeley v. Hardy* (1826) 5 B. & C. 355; *Forster v. Elvet Colliery Co. Ltd* [1908] 1 K.B. 629, 639, affd. *sub nom. Dyson v. Forster* [1909] A.C. 98. (An "indenture" is a deed executed by more than one party, whereas a "deed poll" is one executed by only one party).

[93] See *Kelsey v. Dodd* (1881) 52 L.J.Ch.34, 39; *Forster v. Elvet Colliery Co. Ltd, supra.*

[94] "Property" is defined in s.205(1)(xx). See also Law of Property Act, s.78, re-enacting with modifications Conveyancing Act 1881, s.58.

[95] See *Beswick v. Beswick* [1968] A.C. 58; Elliott (1956) 20 Conv.(N.S.) 43, 114; Andrews (1959) 23 Conv.(N.S.) 179; Ellinger (1963) 26 M.L.R. 396; *post*, §§ 19–104—19–107.

[96] *Beswick v. Beswick, supra.*

[97] [1968] A.C. 58, 77, 81, 87.

[98] At 105–107. See also Lord Pearce at 94. The reference to sealing must be read in the light of the effect of the Law of Property (Miscellaneous Provisions) Act 1989, s.1, *ante*, § 1–043.

[99] *Thoroughgood's Case* (1584) 2 Co.Rep. 9a. But the doctrine was much older than that case: see Holdsworth, *History of English Law*, Vol. 8, p. 50.

undergone modification[1] and has been extended to cases other than those of illiteracy and to simple contracts in writing,[2] so that there is now no difference between specialty and other written contracts in this respect.

1–055   **Estoppel.** "A party who executes a deed is estopped in a Court of Law from saying that the facts stated in the deed are not truly stated."[3] The principle has been extended to statements in recitals in a deed.[4] It is a question of the construction of the deed as a whole as to which parties are estopped by a recital. When a recital is intended to be a statement which all the parties to the deed have mutually agreed to admit as true, it is an estoppel upon all. But when it is intended to be the statement of one party only, the estoppel is confined to that party: and the intention is to be gathered by construing the instrument.[5] The scope of the doctrine is extremely limited in modern law. First, it only applies between the parties to the deed and those claiming through them.[6] Secondly, it only applies when an action is brought to enforce rights arising out of the deed and not collateral to it.[7] Thirdly, it only applies if the statement is clear and unambiguous.[8] Fourthly, it does not prevent a party from relying on defences such as *non est factum*, fraud, illegality or incapacity. In such cases the facts may be pleaded in order to defeat the deed, even though they may contradict statements made on the face of the deed.[9] And so, although a party to a deed may be estopped from denying facts which are stated in it, he is not estopped from saying that, on the facts so stated, the deed is void in law.[10] Fifthly, where a deed is rectifiable (that is to say, ought to be rectified), the doctrine of estoppel by deed will not bind the parties to it.[11] In view of these limitations, there seems little point in preserving any separate category of estoppels by deed, since the basis of the estoppel appears now to be covered by estoppel by representation or by convention.[12]

1–056   **Merger.** A deed is an instrument of a higher nature than a simple contract. A security created by simple contract will be merged in and extinguished by a

---

[1] See *post*, §§ 5–054 *et seq.*

[2] See *post*, § 5–054.

[3] *Baker v. Dewey* (1823) 1 B. & C. 704, 707. See also *Hayne v. Maltby* (1789) 3 Term Rep. 438, 441; *Potts v. Nixon* (1870) I.R. 5 C.L. 45.

[4] *Lainson v. Tremere* (1834) 1 Ad. & El. 792; *Bowman v. Taylor* (1834) 2 Ad. & El. 278; *Young v. Raincock* (1849) 7 C.B. 310, 338.

[5] *Stroughill v. Buck* (1850) 14 QB 781, 787; *cf. Greer v. Kettle* [1938] A.C. 156, 168–171.

[6] *Carpenter v. Buller* (1841) 8 M. & W. 209, 212.

[7] *Carpenter v. Buller, supra* at 213; *Wiles v. Woodward* (1850) 5 Exch. 557, 563; *Ex p. Morgan* (1875) 2 Ch.D. 72.

[8] *Bensley v. Burdon* (1830) 8 L.J.(o.s.) Ch. 85, 87; *Right v. Bucknell* (1831) 2 B. & Ad. 278, 282; *Heath v. Crealock* (1874) L.R. 10 Ch.App. 22; *General Finance, etc., Co. v. Liberator, etc., Building Society* (1879) 10 Ch.D. 15; *Onward Building Society v. Smithson* [1893] 1 Ch. 1; *Poulton v. Moore* [1915] 1 K.B. 400; *cf. Trinidad Asphalte Co. v. Coryat* [1896] A.C. 587.

[9] *Collins v. Blantern* (1767) 2 Wils.K.B. 341; *Hayne v. Maltby, supra; Hill v. Manchester and Salford Waterworks Co.* (1831) 2 B. & Ad. 544.

[10] *Doe* d. *Preece v. Howells* (1831) 2 B. & Ad. 744, and see *Re A Bankruptcy Notice* [1924] 2 Ch. 76.

[11] *Greer v. Kettle* [1938] A.C. 156, 171; *Wilson v. Wilson* [1969] 1 W.L.R. 1470.

[12] *cf. Amalgamated Investment and Property Co. Ltd v. Texas Commercial International Bank Ltd* [1982] Q.B. 84.

specialty security if it secures the same obligation.[13] A simple contract may also be merged in a deed, *e.g.* a conveyance, if so intended by the parties.[14]

Variation or discharge. At common law, an attribute of a contract contained in a deed was that it could only be varied or discharged by another contract contained in a deed, and not by a contract under hand or by word of mouth[15]; but in equity such contracts could be varied or discharged by parol,[16] and the rule of equity now prevails.[17]   **1–057**

Period of limitation. The period of limitation for an action for a breach of contract is 12 years if the contract is contained in a deed, whereas it is only six years in the case of a simple contract.[18]   **1–058**

4. The Relationship between Contract and Tort

Introduction. The proper relationship between contract and tort has caused considerable difficulty in recent years and justifies some discussion of its history as well as an examination of the modern law.[19] As a matter of history, the first problem for the common law was to decide whether a particular form of action which it granted ought to be considered as founded on tort or on contract, a problem of the classification of *actions*.[20] Secondly, it is clear that there are considerable differences between the typical cases of liability in tort and contract: contractual obligations are voluntary and particular to the parties, whereas liability in tort is imposed by law as a matter of policy and affects persons generally.[21] Moreover, the distinction between the two liabilities is reflected in differences of rule which govern not merely their existence but also their incidents.[22] Thirdly, given these differences of regime between contract and tort, the question arises whether a party to a contract may choose to sue the other party in tort where the constituent elements of a tort can be made out and, if so, with   **1–059**

---

[13] See *post*, §§ 26–001 *et seq.*

[14] See *post*, § 26–003.

[15] *Kaye v. Waghorn* (1809) 1 Taunt. 428; *cf. Ex p. Morgan, supra* at 89 and see the rule recognised but infringed in *Nash v. Armstrong* (1861) 10 C.B.(N.S.) 259.

[16] *Webb v. Hewitt* (1857) 3 K. & J. 438.

[17] Supreme Court Act 1981, s.49; *Steeds v. Steeds* (1889) 22 Q.B.D. 537; *Berry v. Berry* [1929] 2 K.B. 316; *Mitas v. Hyams* [1951] 2 T.L.R. 1215; *Plymouth Corpn. v. Harvey* [1971] 1 W.L.R. 549.

[18] Limitation Act 1980, s.8(1) (but subject to s.8(2)). See, *e.g. Aiken v. Stewart Wrightson Members Agency Ltd* [1995] 1 W.L.R. 1281, 1292. See *post*, §§ 29–002, 29–003.

[19] See Prosser, *Selected Topics on the Law of Torts* (1953), p. 380; Guest (1961) 3 Univ. Malaya L.R. 191; Poulton (1966) 82 L.Q.R. 346; Fridman (1977) 93 L.Q.R. 422; Duncan Wallace (1978) L.Q.R. 60; Burrows (1983) 99 L.Q.R. 217; Smith (1984) U.B.C.L. Rev. 95; Jaffey (1985) 5 L.S. 77; Reynolds (1985) 11 N.Z. Univ. Law Rev. 215; Atiyah (1986) *Law & Contemporary Problems* 287; Cane, in Furmston (ed.), *The Law of Torts* (1986), Chap. 6; Cane, *Tort Law and Economic Interests* (1991), esp. at pp. 136–158, 326–352; McLaren (1989) 68 Can. Bar Rev. 30; Adams and Brownsword (1991) 55 Sask. L. Rev. 441. Burrows (1995) C.L.P. 103; Cane in Rose (ed.) *Consensus ad Idem* (1996) 96; Whittaker (1996) 16 O.J.L.S. 191; *idem*, (1997) 17 Legal Studies 169. For an economic analysis see Bishop (1983) 12 L.S. 241. For comparative studies see Weir, *International Encyclopedia of Comparative Law* (1976), Vol. XI, *Torts*, Chap. 12; Markesinis (1987) 103 L.Q.R. 354.

[20] See *post*, §§ 1–060—1–063.

[21] See *post*, § 1–061.

[22] See *post*, §§ 1–067—1–067.

what effects.[23] Again, where the existence of liability in tort is doubtful, the question arises whether the existence of a contract between the parties is a reason in favour of the recognition of such a tortious duty or a reason against it, a question which has arisen in particular in the context of recovery of pure economic loss in the tort of negligence.[24] Finally, the question is posed whether or to what extent the existence of a contractual obligation owed by A to B under a contract affects any liability in A to C, who is not party to that contract or, conversely, liability in C to A: do contracts affect torts beyond privity?[25]

(a) *The Classification of the Forms of Action at Common Law*

1–060   **Forms of action.** For a long time, the common law did not require formally to distinguish between actions in contract and in tort.[26] Until the late seventeenth century, only Bracton used a Roman legal framework for the treating of common law material, including the distinction between actions *ex delicto* and *ex contractu*, and even he did not make this distinction central to his exposition.[27] Moreover, while some early decisions appear to turn on such a distinction, care should be taken not to read into these cases, which turned on differences of individual writs, disputes as to a classification unfamiliar and irrelevant to contemporary legal thought[28]: indeed, the action which became the main sanction of breach of contract (*assumpsit*) and the modern torts both grew out of the action of trespass.[29] However, from the late seventeenth century, the courts did distinguish between actions in contract (*assumpsit*, covenant and account) and actions in tort (which included trespass, trover and nuisance). They did so for the purposes of rules governing transmissibility of actions on death[30] and capacity,[31] but the principal purposes were procedural and in particular the rules as to joinder of actions in the same declaration and joinder of parties to proceedings were said to turn on whether the action was in a form *ex contractu* or a form *ex delicto*.[32] Even so, it was not until the nineteenth century that this distinction was used as a general basis of exposition of the common law material,[33] though it had been mentioned in earlier works.[34] However, since the abolition in the mid-nineteenth

---

[23] See *post*, §§ 1–068 *et seq.*

[24] See *post*, §§ 1–068 *et seq.*

[25] See *post*, §§ 1–107 *et seq.*

[26] Maitland, Appendix A to Pollock, *The Law of Torts* (1st ed.), p. 467, at p. 468.

[27] *ibid.*

[28] Prosser *op.cit.* at pp. 380–381.

[29] Simpson, *A History of the Common Law of Contracts* (1975), p. 199; Milsom, *Historical Foundations of the Common Law* (2nd ed.), Chap. 12; Fridman (1977) 93 L.Q.R. 422.

[30] *Pinchon's Case* (1608) 9 Col. Rep. 86b; *Hambly v. Trott* (1776) 1 Cowp. 371.

[31] *Johnson v. Pye* (1666) 1 Sid. 258, 1 Keb. 913; *Bristow v. Eastman* (1794) 1 Esp. 172.

[32] *Denison v. Ralphson* (1682) 1 Vent. 365; *Bosun v. Sandford* (1691) 2 Salk. 440. In this respect, there was something of a dispute as to the form in which the action of detinue was properly to be classified: see Chitty, *A Practical Treatise on Pleading* (1809), Vol. 2, p. 399; *Cooper v. Chitty* (1756) 1 Burr. 20, 31; *Gledstane v. Hewitt* (1831) 1 C. & J. 566; Manning, note to *Walker v. Needham* (1841) 3 Man. & Gr. 561. This dispute appears particularly strange given the clearly proprietary function of the action.

[33] Chitty *op. cit.* Vol. I, Chaps 1 and 2.

[34] Bracton, Fol. 102; Bacon, *A New Abridgement of the Law* (1736) *Actions in General (A) Of the different Kinds of Actions*; Comyns, *A Digest of the Laws of England* (1st ed., 1762–67), Vol. 1, p. 120; Blackstone, *Commentaries*, III, Chap. VIII.

century of many of the procedural differences between the two types of action,[35] these disputes could be seen as "useless, and worse than useless learning."[36] Where, therefore, after these reforms a court has had to classify a particular *type* of claim by a plaintiff as contractual or tortious, for example for the purposes of the jurisdiction of a court of limited jurisdiction, it has done so on the basis of what it considered was the substance rather than the form of action.[37]

(b) *Differences of Substance between Contract and Tort*

General. Publication in the mid-nineteenth century of the great systematising   **1–061** textbooks of Addison,[38] Underhill,[39] and Pollock[40] saw a change in under-standing of the distinction between contract and tort from one of form to one of substance. This change resulted, not only from the sweeping away of the old procedural differences between the two types of action, but also from the acceptance by English lawyers of the "will theory" of contractual obligation,[41] a theory which pointed to the special voluntary nature of contractual obligations, in contrast to duties in tort which were not.[42] This contrast lies behind part of the generally accepted modern distinction between contract and tort. Thus, according to Winfield,[43] liability for breach of contract is distinguished from liability in tort in that:

  (i) the duties in tort are primarily fixed by the law while in contract they are fixed by the parties themselves; and

  (ii) in tort the duty is towards persons generally while in contract it is towards a specific person or persons.

---

[35] Common Law Procedure Act 1852, ss.34, 35, 41, 74.

[36] *Bryant v. Herbert* (1878) 3 C.P.D. 389, 392 *per* Bramwell L.J., referring to the problem of the classification of detinue, on which see above n. 2.

[37] *Bryant v. Herbert, supra*; *Legge v. Tucker* (1856) 1 H. & N. 500. In theory, this issue of the classification of a particular type of claim is distinct from the issue whether in cases of concurrence of actions the plaintiff may choose the basis of his claim. Thus, in *Att.-Gen. v. Canter* [1939] 1 K.B. 318 the question arose whether a claim by the Crown for a penalty imposed on a tax-payer for fraud transmitted against the latter's estate under s.1 of the Law Reform (Miscellaneous Provisions) Act 1934, and if so, whether it ought to be considered a "cause of action in tort" for the purposes of s.1(3) of the same Act which imposed time restrictions as to the accrual of such a transmitted claim. At first instance, Lawrence J. held that the claim was "one for a debt created by the statute" under which the penalty was imposed and did transmit against the estate, but was not a "cause of action in tort": *ibid.* at 321. The Court of Appeal confirmed this decision, though only the principle of transmissibility was addressed. However, the courts have also looked to the substance of a plaintiff's claim as being contract rather than tort in cases of concurrence, to prevent the plaintiff's choice of form of action from governing the procedural rule applicable: see *Legge v. Tucker, supra*, though the court denied the "independence" of the tort from the contractual duty: *ibid.* at 502; *Kelly v. Metropolitan Ry. Co.* [1895] 1 Q.B. 944; *Edwards v. Mallen* [1908] 1 K.B. 1002.

[38] *Contracts* (1st ed., 1845).

[39] *A Summary of the Law of Torts or Wrongs Independent of Contract* (1st ed., 1873).

[40] *Principles of Contract at Law and in Equity* (1st ed., 1876); *The Law of Torts* (1st ed., 1887).

[41] See Gordley, *The Philosophical Origins of Modern Contract Doctrine* (1991), Chap. 6.

[42] Atiyah, *The Rise and Fall of Freedom of Contract* (1979), p. 408.

[43] *Province of the Law of Tort* (1931), p. 380.

Both propositions still hold good, at least as a starting point. Moreover, there is a further real, general distinction: for torts can be said to make the claimant's (existing) position worse, whereas a breach of contract often consists of failing to make the claimant's position better, better, that is, from the claimant's pre-contractual position and as defined by the other party's obligations under the contract.[44] However, developments in the modern law have blurred these contrasts. First, as has already been remarked, many of the incidents of modern contracts are not fixed by the parties: the courts[45] and the legislature have regulated the relationships of many contractors. Moreover, even where this regulation is effected by the implication of a term, some terms are not susceptible to express exclusion or alteration by the parties.[46] Indeed, in some types of contracts legislative regulation has reached a level where the "voluntary element" is reduced to a simple choice whether or not to enter the relationship.[47] Furthermore, in general common law or statute, rather than the parties, specify what legal consequences arise on the failure to perform a contract, whether this is considered a matter of breach[48] or frustration.[49] It is the law itself which provides and delineates the remedies of damages, rescission for major breach of contract or specific performance, and the role of the parties' agreement here is not to create but at most to modify the rules already provided by the law.[50] Conversely, "voluntariness" can be relevant to the imposition of liability in tort: positively, where "voluntariness" or consent on the part of the *defendant* is a factor in the imposition of liability, for example, in relation to occupier's liability,[51] liability for omissions[52] or under the principle established by *Hedley Byrne & Co. Ltd v. Heller & Partners Ltd*.[53] Negatively, however, the consent of a *claimant* may prevent liability from arising in tort: thus, consent to medical treatment[54] or to a risk of injury in sport[55] may exclude liability in tort by

---

[44] *cf.* Weir, *International Encyclopedia of Comparative Law* (1976), Vol. XI, *Torts*, Chap. 12, p. 5; Whittaker (1996) 16 O.J.L.S. 191, 207 *et seq. cf. post*, § 1–073.

[45] See *ante*, § 1–014; *post*, Chap. 13.

[46] See, *e.g.* Sex Discrimination Act 1975, s.8; Sale of Goods Act 1979, s.14; Unfair Contract Terms Act 1977, s.6.

[47] Hepple (1986-1987) 36 *King's Counsel* 11 and see *ante*, § 1–013.

[48] See *post*, Chaps 25, 27, 28.

[49] See *post*, Chap. 24.

[50] For example, the law specifies what losses may be compensated by an action for damages for breach of contract: see *post*, §§ 27–069—27–071. In principle, the parties may specify the circumstances in which a right to terminate a contract on the ground of breach will arise (*post*, §§ 12–019, 25–027) or can exclude or limit a party's liability in damages, but they cannot resort to the use of "penalties": *post*, §§ 27–009—27–011.

[51] The liability of an occupier to someone on the premises for injury depends, *inter alia* on whether that person had permission to be there: see Occupiers' Liability Act 1957, s.1(2) (visitors) and Occupiers' Liability Act 1984, s.1(1) (trespassers).

[52] Thus, liability in the tort of negligence will be imposed for a negligent "pure omission" where the defendant has voluntarily accepted a duty: *Clerk & Lindsell on Torts* (17th ed., 1995), §§ 7–31, 7–36—7–37.

[53] [1964] A.C. 465. See *Spring v. Guardian Assurance Co. Ltd* [1995] 2 A.C. 296; *Henderson v. Merrett Syndicates Ltd* [1995] 2 A.C. 145; *Williams v. Natural Life Health Foods Ltd and Mistlin* [1998] 1 W.L.R. 830. *cf. Smith v. Eric. S. Bush; Harris v. Wyre Forest District Council* [1990] 1 A.C. 831, esp. at 862 and see *post*, § 1–081. See also Barker (1993) 109 L.Q.R. 461, Whittaker (1997) 17 *Legal Studies* 169.

[54] See *Sidaway v. Board of Governors of the Bethlem Royal Hospital* [1985] A.C. 871 on the more difficult issue of "informed consent" and the doctor's liability in the tort of negligence.

[55] *Condon v. Basi* [1985] 1 W.L.R. 866.

operation of the maxim *volenti non fit injuria*, as may a contractual agreement by the parties excluding liability, whether in tort or in contract.[56]

Some writers have stressed the special protection of expectations created by a contract, reflected in the nature of the damages awarded on its breach and the lack of protection of expectations by the law of torts.[57] Others have disagreed,[58] arguing that this obscures the importance of awards of damages in contract based on the claimant's "reliance interest," which is similar to that protected generally in tort.[59] Conversely, damages in tort can compensate the injured party's disappointed expectations, for example, his expectation to be able to earn a living,[60] although it has been pointed out that this expectation is general, unlike contractual expectations which are induced by making the contract.[61] On the other hand, while traditionally it could be said that recovery for non-intentional pure economic loss was generally irrecoverable in tort, while being recoverable in contract, this position has apparently been radically changed by the House of Lords' application of the principle of "assumption of responsibility" of *Hedley Byrne & Co. Ltd v. Heller & Partners*[62] to cases of the negligent performance of services.[63] **1–062**

More radical criticism of the division between contract and tort argues that it, together with other broad conceptual distinctions in the law, at times helps to obscure similarities of factual situation which cut across it and at others to group together situations which have practically nothing in common.[64] Instead, it has been suggested, private law should be reclassified according to the nature of the interest of the plaintiff to be protected.[65] However, this type of suggestion has not been generally accepted and the distinction between contract and tort has in recent years become more prominent. **1–063**

Differences of regime between contract and tort: damages. Some legal incidents of liability differ according to whether the claimant's claim is based on a breach of contract or a tort. Thus, there are important differences between the damages recoverable in contract and in tort.[66] As has been noted, the most basic difference remains that the function of damages in contract is primarily to put the injured party as far as possible in the position in which he would have been had the contract been performed,[67] whereas the function of damages in tort is to put the injured party in the position in which he would have been if the tort had not **1–064**

---

[56] See *post*, § 1–091.
[57] Burrows (1983) 99 L.Q.R. 217; Taylor (1982) 45 M.L.R. 139; Friedmann (1995) 111 L.Q.R. 628; Whittaker (1996) 16 O.J.L.S. 191, 207 *et seq. cf.* Stapleton (1997) 113 L.Q.R. 257.
[58] Atiyah, *Essays on Contract* (1986), Essay 2; Hedley (1988) 9 L.S. 137.
[59] Fuller & Purdue (1936–1937) 46 Yale L.J. 52 and 373.
[60] Atiyah, *The Rise and Fall of Freedom of Contract* (1979), pp. 762–763.
[61] Treitel, *The Law of Contract* (9th ed., 1995), p. 846.
[62] [1964] A.C. 465.
[63] See *Henderson v. Merrett Syndicates Ltd* [1995] 2 A.C. 145; *Williams v. Natural Life Health Foods Ltd and Mistlin* [1998] 1 W.L.R. 830 and *post*, §§ 1–078—1–093.
[64] Atiyah, *Essays on Contract* (1986), pp. 53–55. *cf.* Burrows (1983) 99 L.Q.R. 217.
[65] Atiyah, *ibid.* Essay 2; Hedley (1988) 8 L.S. 137.
[66] *McGregor on Damages* (16th ed., 1997), §§ 808 *et seq.* Burrows, *Remedies for Torts and Breach of Contract* (2nd ed., 1994), Chap. 2.
[67] *Robinson v. Harman* (1848) 1 Exch. 850, 855; Burrows (1983) 99 L.Q.R. 217. *cf.* Atiyah (1978) 94 L.Q.R. 193 and *Essays on Contract* (1986), Chap. 2; Owen (1984) 4 O.J.L.S. 393; Waddams (1983–84) 8 Can.Bus.L.J. 2; Friedmann (1995) 111 L.Q.R. 628.

been committed.[68] Thus, damages for breach of warranty may give the plaintiff his lost bargain,[69] whereas damages in the tort of deceit,[70] negligent misstatement[71] and under section 2 of the Misrepresentation Act 1967[72] may not, being instead restricted to what has been termed compensation of his "status quo interest."[73] The tests of remoteness of damage in contract and in tort are apparently different[74] and in general the defence of contributory negligence does not apply to claims in contract, though it is now established that the court may reduce a claimant's damages for breach of contract on this ground if his claim is based on breach of a contractual duty to take reasonable care, concurrent with liability in the tort of negligence.[75]

1–065 Other differences in the heads of damages available in contract and in tort are often to be based on circumstances other than the mere classification of the liability in issue. Thus, whereas nominal damages are always possible in an award in contract, it would appear that they are only available in tort if it is actionable *per se*.[76] Punitive or exemplary damages are sometimes said to be possible in tort, but not in contract,[77] though the exceptional circumstances in which they are permitted in tort are usually inapplicable to the contractual context.[78] Similarly, damages for injured feelings or mental distress not consequential on the claimant's own physical injury are very closely, if differently,

---

[68] *Livingstone v. Raywards Coal Co.* (1880) 5 App.Cas. 25, 39; *Lim Poh Choo v. Camden and Islington Area Health Authority* [1980] A.C. 174, 186 *et seq.*

[69] *e.g.* Sale of Goods Act 1979, s.53(3).

[70] *Peek v. Derry* (1887) 37 Ch.D. 541, 578; *Doyle v. Olby (Ironmongers) Ltd* [1969] 2 Q.B. 158, 167 and see *Smith New Court Securities v. Scrimgeour Vickers (Asset Management) Ltd*, [1994] 4 All E.R. 225. *cf. Davidson v. Tullock* (1860) 3 Macq. 783; *East v. Maurer* [1991] 1 W.L.R. 461.

[71] *Esso Petroleum Co. Ltd v. Mardon* [1976] Q.B. 801, 820–821; *Box v. Midland Bank Ltd* [1979] 2 Lloyd's Rep. 391.

[72] *André & Cie SA v. Ets Michel Blanc et Fils* [1977] 2 Lloyd's Rep. 166, 181; *McNally v. Welltrade International Ltd* [1978] I.R.L.R. 497, 499; Taylor (1982) 45 M.L.R. 139; Cartwright (1987) 51 Conv. 423; *Sharneyford Supplies Ltd v. Edge Barrington & Black* [1986] Ch. 128, [1987] Ch. 305, not following *Watts v. Spence* [1976] Ch. 16; *Royscot Trust Ltd v. Rogerson* [1991] 2 Q.B. 297.

[73] Burrows (1983) 99 L.Q.R. 217, 219–221. Damages in tort may include compensation for wasted expenditure and lost opportunities: *East v. Maurer* [1991] 1 W.L.R. 461 and see *post*, § 6–054.

[74] *Koufos v. Czarnikow Ltd* [1969] 1 A.C. 350 and see *post*, § 27–044. The principles of causation, for example in relation to the effect of supervening causes, are said sometimes to be the same in contract as in tort: *Beoco Ltd v. Alfa Laval Co. Ltd* [1995] Q.B. 137; *cf. Galoo Ltd v. Bright Grahame Murray* [1994] 1 W.L.R. 1360.

[75] Law Reform (Contributory Negligence) Act 1945, *Forsikringsaktieselskapet Vesta v. Butcher* [1989] A.C. 852; *Barclays Bank plc v. Fairclough Building Ltd* [1995] Q.B. 21; *Barclays Bank plc v. Fairclough Building Ltd (No. 2)* [1995] I.R.L.R. 605 and see *post*, § 27–037.

[76] Ogus, *The Law of Damages* (1973), p. 22 *et seq. cf. Marzetti v. Williams* (1830) 1 B. & Ad. 415.

[77] *Addis v. Gramophone Co. Ltd* [1909] A.C. 488; *Perera v. Vandiyar* [1953] 1 W.L.R. 672, see *post*, § 27–017.

[78] *Rookes v. Barnard* [1964] A.C. 1129; *Cassell & Co. Ltd v. Broome* [1972] A.C. 1027. *cf. post*, § 6–064 (fraud). The exception to this is where "the defendant's conduct had been calculated by him to make a profit for himself which may well exceed the compensation payable to the plaintiff" *Rookes v. Barnard, supra*, 1126–1127. The traditional rule is that a party injured by a breach of contract cannot on this ground alone recover against the party in breach for profits made as a consequence of that breach as distinct from losses caused by that breach: *Teacher v. Calder* [1899] A.C. 451; *Surrey C.C. v. Bredero Homes Ltd* [1993] 3 W.L.R. 1361. However, in *A.-G. v. Blake* [1998] 2 W.L.R. 805, 816–819, the Court of Appeal expressed the view that this rule, while valid in general, could be subject to exceptions in appropriate, if rare, circumstances, such a recovery of profits made by a party in breach being referred to as "restitutionary damages": on which see, *post*, §§ 27–018—27–021.

circumscribed both in tort[79] and in contract,[80] though there remains some authority which excludes them entirely from liability in contract.[81] Traditionally, it was sometimes said that damages for loss of reputation are not available in contract in contrast to tort,[82] but there were conflicting decisions on this point,[83] and some cases clearly recognised such a recovery in contract in appropriate cases, such as injury to a trader whose business reputation is affected by the breach[84] and where the contract can be said to be for the maintenance or promotion of the claimant's reputation.[85] Moreover, in *Malik v. Bank of Credit and Commerce International SA (in liq.)*,[86] the House of Lords allowed recovery by two former employees for damage to their employment prospects by breach of their employer's obligation not to damage the relationship of trust between employer and employee, seeing this as an example of the general rule allowing recovery for financial harm caused by breach of contract (as opposed to caused by the manner in which the contract was breached).[87]

Limitation of actions. Although the Limitation Act 1980,[88] provides an   **1–066** identical period of six years[89] for actions founded on simple contract or on tort, the period begins to run "from the date on which the cause of action accrued."[90] This may vary according to whether the action is framed in tort, contract or restitution.[91] For example, in contract the cause of action accrues when the breach of contract takes place, not when the damage occurs or is discovered.[92] But, in the tort of negligence, the cause of action accrues when damage occurs,

---

[79] *McGregor on Damages* (16th ed., 1997) § 90. *cf. McLoughlin v. O'Brien* [1983] 1 A.C. 785; *Alcock v. Chief Constable of South Yorkshire Police* [1992] 1 A.C. 310; *Page v. Smith* [1995] 2 W.L.R. 644; *White v. Chief Constable of South Yorkshire* [1998] 3 W.L.R. 1509.

[80] *Post*, § 27–069 and see *McGregor on Damages*, §§ 98–104; *Cook v. Swinfen* [1967] 1 W.L.R. 457; *Jarvis v. Swann Tours Ltd* [1973] 1 Q.B. 233; *Bliss v. S.E. Thames Regional Health Authority* [1985] I.R.L.R. 308; *Hayes v. James & Charles Dodd (a firm)* [1990] 2 All E.R. 815, 824; *McLeish v. Amoo-Gottfried & Co., The Times*, October 13, 1993; *Watts v. Morrow* [1991] 1 W.L.R. 1421; *Knott v. Bolton* [1995] E.G.C.S. 59; *Malik v. Bank of Credit and Commerce International SA (in liq.)* [1997] 3 W.L.R. 95.

[81] *Addis v. Gramophone Co. Ltd* [1909] A.C. 488.

[82] *Addis v. Gramophone Co. Ltd* [1909] A.C. 488; *Withers v. General Theatre Corp. Ltd* [1933] 2 K.B. 536.

[83] *cf. Withers v. General Theatre Corp. Ltd, ante,* with *Marbe v. George Edwardes (Daly's Theatre) Ltd* [1928] 1 K.B. 269.

[84] *Wilson v. United Counties Bank Ltd* [1920] A.C. 102.

[85] *Rolin v. Steward* (1854) 14 C.B. 595; *Aerial Advertising Co. v. Batchelors Peas (Manchester) Ltd* [1938] 2 All E.R. 788.

[86] [1997] 3 W.L.R. 95.

[87] *ibid.* at 114–115.

[88] ss.2, 5.

[89] But see s.11 (three years for actions in respect of personal injuries): *post* §§ 29–005 *et seq.* This provision specifically applies to actions in contract as well as in tort.

[90] A similar phrase is used in the Supreme Court Act 1981, s.35A (interest on debt and damages) which by the Administration of Justice Act 1982, s.15(1), Sched. 1, Pt. 1 replaced s.3 of the Law Reform (Miscellaneous Provisions) Act 1934.

[91] *Battley v. Faulkner* (1820) 3 B. & Ald. 288; *Beaman v. A.R.T.S. Ltd.* [1948] 2 All E.R. 89, 92 (revd. on other grounds [1949] 1 K.B. 550); *Bagot v. Stevens, Scanlan & Co. Ltd* [1966] 1 Q.B. 197; *Midland Bank Trust Co. Ltd v. Hett, Stubbs & Kemp* [1979] Ch. 384. See *post*, §§ 29–027—29–028. *Saunders v. Edwards* (1662) Sid. 95; *Bonomi v. Backhouse* (1859) E., B. & E. 646; *Gibbs v. Guild* (1881) 8 Q.B.D. 296, 302; *Chesworth v. Farrar* [1967] 1 Q.B. 407; *Pirelli General Cable Works Ltd v. Oscar Faber & Partners* [1983] 2 A.C. 1.

[92] *Battley v. Faulkner, supra; Walker v. Milner* (1866) 4 F. & F. 745; *Lynn v. Bamber* [1930] 2 K.B. 72; *Bagot v. Stevens, Scanlan & Co. Ltd, supra. cf. Shaw v. Shaw* [1954] 2 Q.B. 429; *Midland Bank Trust Co. Ltd v. Hett, Stubbs & Kemp, supra; Forster v. Outred & Co.* [1982] 1 W.L.R. 86.

and not at the time of the act or default giving rise to the claim.[93] However, the practical effect of this rule has been reduced by the provision of the Latent Damage Act 1986, which provides[94] that "actions for damages for negligence in respect of latent damage not involving personal injuries may be brought for a period of three years after the discovery of the damage by the plaintiff even if this is after six years after accrual of the cause of action." This provision has created its own distinction between claims in contract and in tort, as it has been held that the term "negligence actions" for this purpose does not include actions for breach of a contractual obligation to take reasonable care, even where this is concurrent with an action for tortious negligence.[95]

1–067 **Other differences.** A contractual right, *e.g.* a debt, can generally be assigned, but a right of action in tort generally cannot.[96] The rules of the conflict of laws are different in tort and contract[97] and so are the rules for service of claim forms outside the jurisdiction.[98] The law governing the capacity of parties is frequently different: thus, for example, a minor is in principle liable for his torts, but only to a limited extent on his contracts.[99] Statutory provisions sometimes distinguish according to rights arising out of a contract, and other rights (which would include tort) though this appears to be a diminishing practice.[1]

(c) Concurrence of Actions in Contract and Tort

1–068 **General.** Where the constituent elements of a claimant's case are capable of being put either in terms of a claim in tort or for breach of contract, the general rule is that the claimant may choose on which basis to proceed, though this rule is subject to a number of qualifications, notably where to do so would be

---

[93] *Watson v. Winget Ltd*, 1960 S.C. 92; *Cartledge v. L. Jopling & Sons Ltd* [1963] A.C. 758 (now modified by ss.11(4), 14 of the Limitation Act 1980); *Sparham-Souter v. Town and Country Developments Ltd* [1976] 1 Q.B. 858; *Anns v. Merton London Borough Council* [1978] A.C. 728; *Midland Bank Trust Co. Ltd v. Hett, Stubbs & Kemp, supra; Pirelli General Cable Works Ltd v. Oscar Faber & Partners, supra; Ketterman v. Hansel Properties Ltd* [1987] 1 A.C. 189; *London Congregational Union Inc. v. Harriss and Harriss (a firm)* [1988] 1 All E.R. 15; *D. W. Moore & Co. Ltd v. Ferrier* [1988] 1 W.L.R. 267; *Lee v. Thompson* [1989] 40 E.G. 89; McGee (1988) 104 L.Q.R. 376.
[94] New s.14A of the Limitation Act 1980.
[95] *Iron Trades Mutual Insurance Co. Ltd v. J.K. Buckenham Ltd* [1990] 1 All E.R. 808 and see *post*, § 29–092. *cf.* Consumer Protection Act 1987, s.5(5) which sets a different time of accrual for actions for damage to property against a supplier or producer under Part I of the Act from that which would exist against a contractor under the general law of limitation.
[96] See *post*, § 20–047.
[97] Tort: *Phillips v. Eyre* (1870) L.R. 6 Q.B. 1; *Boys v. Chaplin* [1971] A.C. 356. Contract: *P. & O. Steamship Co. v. Shand* (1865) 3 Moo.PC (N.S.) 272; *Lloyd v. Guibert* (1865) L.R. 1 Q.B. 115; *Mount Albert B.C. v. Australasian, etc., Life Assurance Soc.* [1938] A.C. 224; *Bonython v. Commonwealth of Australia* [1951] A.C. 201 Private International Law (Miscellaneous Provisions) Act 1995, ss.9–14; Contracts (Applicable Law) Act 1990. See Collins (1967) 16 I.C.L.Q. 103; North (1977) 26 I.C.L.Q. 214 and see *post*, Chap. 31.
[98] Convention on Jurisdiction and the Enforcement of Judgments in Civil and Commercial Matters (1968), Arts. 5(1), (3); Civil Jurisdiction and Judgments Act 1982, s.2; Civil Procedure Rules 1998, Part 50, Sched. 1, RSC Ord. 11.
[99] See *post*, §§ 8–043—8–044. See also *post*, § 9–086 (trade unions).
[1] An example may be found in ss.4 and 5 of the Business Names Act 1985. The former distinction in the Bankruptcy Act 1914, s.30(1) between demands arising by reason of contract which were provable in bankruptcy and others which were not normally so provable, is not found in the provisions which replaced it in the Insolvency Act 1985 (ss.163, 211(1), (2) and (3)).

inconsistent with the terms of the contract. This traditional position was clearly affirmed by the House of Lords in the important decision *Henderson v. Merrett Syndicates Ltd*,[2] which drew to a close the uncertainty on this point caused by a dictum of Lord Scarman in the Privy Council in 1985 in *Tai Hing Cotton Mill Ltd v. Liu Chong Hing Bank Ltd*, to the effect that "their Lordships do not believe that there is anything to the advantage of the law's development in searching for a liability in tort where the parties are in a contractual relationship."[3] This dictum appeared to favour the exclusion of claims in tort where the parties were in a contractual relationship, though the context of its acceptance by later courts was typically the denial of liability of recovery of pure economic loss in the tort of negligence.[4] However, paradoxically, the House of Lords' decision on the nature and ambit of the tortious liability to be found on the facts before it in *Henderson v. Merrett Syndicates Ltd* created new and very considerable uncertainty as regards the relationship of contractual and tortious claims between parties to a contract. For, it accepted that its own earlier decision in *Hedley Byrne & Co. Ltd v. Heller & Partners Ltd*[5] should be interpreted as establishing a "broad principle" of liability in tortious negligence based on the defendant's assumption of responsibility, an assumption which would appear to be satisfied whenever a party to a contract either possessing or holding himself out as possessing a special skill agrees to perform a service for the other party. In this respect, the courts have apparently returned to an approach similar to one taken in the earlier nineteenth century, though subsequently superseded.[6]

The present discussion will start by looking briefly at the older authorities which governed the issue of concurrence of actions in contract and tort; it will then state the modern law allowing an option, first as regards pre-contractual liability and then as regards liability for torts committed in the course of performance of a contract; as to the latter, it will discuss the breadth of the principle of "assumption of responsibility" recognised in *Henderson v. Merrett Syndicates Ltd* and the nature and ambit of the qualifications on the option and on the effects which its exercise will entail.

Older authorities. Disputes as to the availability of an action in tort against   **1–069**
one's fellow contractor are not new and before the reforms of common law procedure of the mid-nineteenth century three positions can be detected in the cases. The first was that a plaintiff could neither join a claim in tort with one in contract in the same action nor opt whether to sue in tort when there was a contract between the parties. For example, in *Orton v. Butler*,[7] Best J. refused to allow the joining of actions in trover (tort) and money had and received (contract), stating that "[t]here is a broad distinction between actions ex contractu and ex delicto. Here, it arises out of breach of a contract, and the party ought not to be allowed to proceed in the present mode of framing his count [*sci.* claim] ex delicto."[8]

---

[2] [1995] 2 A.C. 145.
[3] [1986] A.C. 80, 107.
[4] See, *e.g. Banque Keyser Ullmann SA v. Skandia (U.K.) Co. Insurance Ltd* [1990] 1 Q.B. 665, [1991] 2 A.C. 249 (affd. on other grounds; *National Bank of Greece SA v. Pinios Shipping (No. 1)* [1990] 1 A.C. 637.
[5] [1964] A.C. 465.
[6] See *post*, § 1–070.
[7] (1822) 5 B. & Ald. 652.
[8] *ibid.* at 656.

Other cases distinguished between the rules against joinder of counts in contract and tort and the question whether a plaintiff was entitled to opt on which of the two bases to put his claim,[9] some expressly recognising the validity of the option. Moreover, where they did it was acknowledged that the plaintiff's choice would affect the rules applicable to his claim. As Abbott J. observed "[t]here is nothing to compel a plaintiff to elect that form which may be most convenient to the defendant. The very notion of election imports that the plaintiff may exercise it for his own benefit."[10] At the time, those courts which allowed an option between contract and tort thereby enabled a plaintiff to avoid in particular the rules against transmissibility of actions on death which applied to actions in tort[11] or the rules of joinder of parties to litigation which applied to actions in contract.[12] However, the courts did not allow the plaintiff's option to avoid certain other rules which applied to contract, notably, those as to capacity,[13] nor the express terms of a contract, notably, limitation clauses.[14]

1–070   The third approach to the relationship between actions in contract and tort can be seen in the decision in *Brown v. Boorman*.[15] The plaintiffs retained the defendant as broker to sell their linseed oil on commission. This he did, but in breach of contract delivered it without payment and to the wrong (and later insolvent) person. The plaintiffs sued in case (*i.e.* tort), contending that the broker owed them a duty at common law to take reasonable care based on his trade or calling. The defendant countered that their proper form of action should have been *assumpsit* (*i.e.* contract). The House of Lords upheld Tindal C.J's judgment for the plaintiffs, Lord Campbell stating that "wherever there is a contract, and something to be done in the course of the employment which is the subject of that contract, if there is a breach of a duty in the course of that employment, the plaintiff may either recover in tort or in contract."[16] It is difficult not to agree with the defendant's contention that such an approach "would altogether destroy the distinction between *assumpsit* [*i.e.* contract] and tort,"[17] as it suggests that the option to plead in tort or contract exists in *all* situations of breach of contract and not merely in those where an independent cause of action exists in tort. However, this was not the fate of *Brown v. Boorman*. As Pollock stated,[18] "notwithstanding the verbal laxity of one or two passages, the House of Lords did not authorize the parties to treat the mere non-performance of a promise as a substantive tort." Instead, the decision was relied on as authority for the existence of an option for the plaintiff as to whether to sue in tort as long as a distinct and independent action in tort exists.[19]

1–071   **The modern law.** In the modern law, a distinction can usefully be drawn between a claim by a party to a contract on the basis of a pre-contractual liability

---

[9] *e.g. Brown v. Dixon* (1786) 1 T.R. 274, 276–277.
[10] *Ansell v. Waterhouse* (1817) 6 M. & S. 385, 392.
[11] *Hambly v. Trott* (1776) 1 Cowp. 371.
[12] *Govett v. Radnidge* (1802) 3 East 62.
[13] *Johnson v. Pye* (1666) 1 Sid. 258, 1 Keb. 913.
[14] *Nicholson v. Willan* (1804) 5 East 507.
[15] (1842) 3 Q.B. 511, (1844) 11 Cl. & Fin. 1, HL.
[16] (1844) 11 Cl. & Fin. 1, 44.
[17] *ibid.* at 12.
[18] *Torts* (1st ed., 1887), p. 434.
[19] *Hyman v. Nye* (1881) 6 Q.B.D. 685; *Baylis v. Lintott* (1873) L.R. 8 C.P. 345; *Esso Petroleum Co. Ltd v. Mardon* [1976] Q.B. 801; *Midland Bank Trust Co. Ltd v. Hett, Stubbs & Kemp* [1979] Ch. 384.

to be imposed on the other party and one based on a liability arising in the course of performance of the contract.

(i) Pre-contractual Liability

Representations. Even at the time when it was doubtful whether a party to a   **1–072**
contract could claim in tort against the other party in respect of matters relating to the performance of the contract, it was established that such a party could rely on established liabilities in tort arising from facts which occur in the course of the dealings of the parties before contract. A party to a contract can therefore claim damages for a pre-contractual statement which induced him to contract under various headings: in the tort of deceit, where the statement was made fraudulently[20]; in the tort of negligence,[21] if the claimant can establish the conditions for the existence of a duty of care under *Hedley Byrne & Co. Ltd v. Heller & Partners Ltd*[22] or under the provisions of the Misrepresentation Act 1967.[23] It is also clear that these rights to damages in tort may exist whether or not the misrepresentation has been incorporated into the contract, thereby giving rise to a claim for breach of contractual warranty,[24] and whether or not the claimant chooses to exercise any right of rescission of the contract on the grounds of misrepresentation.[25]

More complex, however, is the question whether the claimant's option to rely on one of these liabilities in tort enables him to avoid restrictions which exist on any claim in contract. While it is clear that a party can by contract exclude liability for negligent misstatement at common law or liability in damages for misrepresentation under the 1967 Act to the extent to which such a term satisfies the requirements of reasonableness,[26] a party to a contract cannot exclude liability in damages for his own fraud.[27] On the other hand, a party to a contract with a minor cannot avoid a defence of infancy by claiming damages in the tort of deceit against the minor on the ground that the latter fraudulently misrepresented his age, even though in general, an infant is liable for his torts,[28] because "[i]f it were in the power of a plaintiff to convert that which arises out of a

---

[20] *Pasley v. Freeman* (1789) 3 T.R. 51; *Peek v. Derry* (1887) 37 Ch.D. 541 (revd. on other grounds (1889) 14 App.Cas. 337); *Doyle v. Olby (Ironmongers) Ltd* [1969] 2 QB 158; *Archer v. Brown* [1985] 1 Q.B. 401. *cf. Jack v. Kipping* (1882) 9 Q.B.D. 113; *Tilley v. Bowman Ltd* [1910] 1 K.B. 745.

[21] *Esso Petroleum Co. Ltd v. Mardon* [1976] Q.B. 801; *Howard Marine & Dredging Co. Ltd v. A. Ogden & Sons (Excavations) Ltd* [1978] Q.B. 574; *Rust v. Abbey Life Insurance Co. Ltd* [1978] 2 Lloyd's Rep. 386; *Banque Financière de la Cité SA v. Westgate Insurance Co. Ltd* [1991] 2 A.C. 249, 275. *cf. Cemp Properties (U.K.) Ltd v. Dentsply Research & Development Corpn (No. 1)* (1989) 35 E.G. 99, 104.

[22] [1964] A.C. 465.

[23] See *post* §§ 6–067—6–089. Liability in damages under s.2(1) is treated as tortious: see *André & Cie SA v. Ets. Michel Blanc et Fils* [1977] 2 Lloyd's Rep. 166; *Royscott Trust Ltd v. Rogerson* [1991] 2 Q.B. 297 and see *post* § 6–070.

[24] *Esso Petroleum Co. Ltd v. Mardon, supra.*

[25] *Archer v. Brown* [1985] 1 Q.B. 401, 415 and see *post*, § 6–048. After the Misrepresentation Act 1967, s.1(a) a representee's right to rescind is not barred merely by the incorporation of a representation as a term of the contract. *cf.* the power of the court under s.2(2) of the Misrepresentation Act 1967 to refuse rescission of the contract and award damages in lieu; and see *post*, § 6–070.

[26] See *Hedley Byrne & Co. Ltd v. Heller & Partners Ltd, supra*; *Smith v. Eric S. Bush* [1990] 1 A.C. 831; Unfair Contract Terms Act 1977, s.2(2); Misrepresentation Act 1967, s.3 as replaced by Unfair Contract Terms Act 1977, s.8 and see *post*, §§ 6–130, 6–134.

[27] *S. Pearson & Son Ltd v. Dublin Corporation* [1907] A.C. 351, 353–354, 362.

[28] *Johnson v. Pye* (1666) 1 Sid. 258 and see *post* § 8–043.

contract into a tort, there would be an end of that protection which the law affords to infants."[29]

1–073 **Damages for misrepresentation.** Finally, although there are considerable differences between damages in tort and for breach of contract,[30] not all of these are significant in the context of pre-contractual statements. In general, an injured party can claim damages for the loss of an "expectation interest" in contract but not in tort, and in the context of pre-contractual representation the latter rule means that a claimant can recover damages for misrepresentation only so as to put him in a position as though the representation (and, therefore, it is assumed, the contract) had not been made and not damages as though the representation had been true.[31] However, in some cases where a claim is based on breach of a term which has resulted from the incorporation of a pre-contractual statement,[32] there will be no difference on this ground between the contractual and tortious measures of damages. In *Esso Petroleum Co. Ltd v. Mardon*,[33] the Court of Appeal accepted that a representation of "throughput" of petrol of a garage by Esso which later proved false, was incorporated into the contract as a warranty. However, the ability of the representee to claim for breach of contract did not affect the damages which he could recover, in particular it did not allow him to claim for the loss of profits he expected to make from taking a lease of the garage with the throughput represented, despite such claims for lost profits being typical of contract. This refusal resulted from the court's decision as to the *content* of the warranty: it was construed not as a promise that the throughput would be a certain amount, but rather that Esso had taken reasonable care in making the estimate of throughput.[34] A claim in contract can indeed put an injured party in the position as though the contract had been performed, but if Esso had performed this contractual warranty, and as a result Mardon had been given a true estimate of the throughput of the garage, then Mardon would not have entered into the contract.[35] In this way, damages in contract and in tort[36] are based on the same measure, *viz.* to put the claimant in the position as though the contract had not been made.[37] On the other hand, while it has been stated that a claimant will not recover more damages in tort than he would in contract,[38] it is clear that a claimant may indeed recover more damages where his claim is based on fraud or

---

[29] *Jennings v. Rundall* (1799) 8 T.R. 335, 336 *per* Lord Kenyon C.J. and see *post*, § 8–043.

[30] See *ante*, § 1–064.

[31] *Doyle v. Olby (Ironmongers) Ltd*; *supra*; *André & Cie SA v. Ets Michel Blanc et Fils*, *supra*; *East v. Maurer* [1991] 1 W.L.R. 461 and see *post* §§ 6–052—6–054.

[32] See Treitel, *The Law of Contract* (9th ed., 1995), pp. 326–330 and Atiyah, *Essays on Contract* (1986), Essay 10.

[33] [1976] 1 Q.B. 801.

[34] *ibid.* at 818, 823–824.

[35] *ibid.* at 820 (Lord Denning M.R.) and 834 (Shaw L.J.). This reasoning is based on two assumptions: first, that if Esso had taken reasonable care in making its statement as to throughput it would have made an accurate estimate and, secondly, that if Mardon had been given an accurate estimate he would not have entered the contract or perhaps, would not have entered it on the same terms. Ormrod L.J. expressed no view on the claim for loss of profits as it was "virtually incapable of proof": *ibid.* at 829.

[36] The Court of Appeal based its decision in tort on *Hedley Byrne & Co. Ltd v. Heller & Partners Ltd* [1964] A.C. 465.

[37] The Court of Appeal did allow Mardon damages for loss of his "general expectations," *i.e.* what he would have expected to have earned if he had not spent his time running the garage: [1976] 1 Q.B. 801, 821.

[38] *Chinery v. Viall* (1860) 5 H. & N. 28, 29 L.J. Ex. 180; *Johnson v. Stear* (1863) 33 L.J.C.P. 130 (both conversion).

for negligent misrepresentation under the 1967 Act,[39] as the test of remoteness of damage applicable to these claims is more generous than the test which applies to claims for breach of contract.[40] Furthermore, it is possible (if unlikely) that someone suing for fraud may be able to recover punitive damages,[41] whereas these are not available for claims for breach of contract.[42]

Liability for non-disclosure. As will be seen, the courts draw a clear line   **1–074** between cases of misrepresentation and of non-disclosure for the purposes of deciding the availability of rescission for the other party.[43] While in general the courts have echoed this distinction in the context of liability in damages, they have accepted that in principle a contractor may be liable in the tort of negligence for a failure to speak,[44] but the modern approach has been to restrict liability in these circumstances to cases where the defendant has "voluntarily accepted responsibility."[45] Indeed, even in a case where the law exceptionally imposes a duty of pre-contractual disclosure on a party to a contract, the courts have refused to impose liability in damages in tort to sanction its breach.[46] While this result was reached before the House of Lords in *Henderson v. Merrett Syndicates Ltd*[47] had disapproved the idea that the existence of a contract between the parties is in itself a reason for denying a claim in tort, it may well be that a future court would hold that a person cannot be said to "assume responsibility" for a matter in relation to which he owes a legal duty. Moreover, the idea that the law of tort should not be allowed to "cut across the principles of contract law" could be considered as a consideration of policy arguing against the existence of a duty of care in the tort of negligence, even where this was based on an "assumption of responsibility."[48]

Duress. Duress, whether by means of physical or economic threats, exercised   **1–075** by A against B with the view to making B enter a contract with A, may in certain circumstances give rise to a right in B to avoid that contract.[49] While the circumstances which give rise to this right of avoidance will not necessarily give

---

[39] *Royscott Trust Ltd v. Rogerson* [1991] 2 Q.B. 297, in which the Court of Appeal rejected the proposition that a claim for damages under s.2(1) of the Misrepresentation Act 1967 possesses the same test of remoteness of damage as applies generally to claims in the tort of negligence; and see *post* § 6–070.

[40] See *post*, §§ 27–039 *et seq.*

[41] *Mafo v. Adams* [1970] 1 Q.B. 548; *Cassell & Co. Ltd v. Broome* [1972] A.C. 1027, 1076; *Archer v. Brown* [1985] 1 Q.B. 401, 418–421 and see *post*, § 6–064.

[42] See *post*, § 27–017.

[43] See *post*, §§ 6–013 *et seq.*

[44] *Rust v. Abbey Life Assurance Co. Ltd* [1978] 2 Lloyd's Rep. 386; *Cornish v. Midland Bank plc* [1985] 3 All E.R. 513, 522–523; *Al-Kandari v. J.R. Brown & Co.* [1988] Q.B. 665, 672; *Banque Keyser Ullmann SA v. Skandia (U.K.) Co. Insurance Ltd* [1990] 1 Q.B. 665, 794. *Cf. Argy Trading Developments Ltd v. Lapid Developments Ltd* [1977] 1 W.L.R. 444, 461; *Barclays Bank plc v. Khaira* [1992] 1 W.L.R. 623; *Ashmore v. Corpn of Lloyd's* [1992] 2 Lloyd's Rep. 1, 5 (and see [1992] 2 Lloyd's Rep. 620.).

[45] *Banque Keyser Ullmann SA v. Skandia (U.K.) Insurance Co. Ltd, supra*, at 794, *per* Slade L.J. *cf. post* §§ 1–081—1–084 concerning the significance more generally of a "voluntary assumption of responsibility" for liability for pure economic loss in the tort of negligence.

[46] *Banque Keyser Ullmann SA v. Skandia (U.K.) Insurance Co. Ltd, supra.*

[47] [1995] 1 A.C. 145.

[48] For the relevance of considerations of policy in this context, see *post*, §§ 1–082 *et seq.*

[49] See *post*, §§ 7–001 *et seq.*

rise to a right to damages,[50] in contrast to the position as regards fraud,[51] they may give rise to the conditions of liability under the tort of intimidation.[52] This tort is usually applied to cases where A forces B to do or to refrain from doing something to the prejudice of C ("three-party intimidation"), but there is high authority for the proposition that it also applies to cases where A forces B to do something for A's intended benefit ("two-party intimidation").[53] In circumstances where the conditions for the existence of the tort exist, it would seem that it can be relied on by one party to a contract as against the other, although it is more controversial whether this right remains after the coerced party has affirmed the contract.[54] While the proper ambit of the doctrine of economic duress as a vitiating element in contract remains controversial,[55] some argue that its ambit should be co-terminous and not wider than any liability which would exist under the tort of intimidation.[56]

1–076   **"Culpa in contrahendo."** Some legal systems consider that cases of fraud or duress are merely examples of a wider category of "fault in the formation of contract," a category famously termed *culpa in contrahendo* by the German jurist, Ihering.[57] In French law, despite its general rule against allowing delict to intrude between contractors (a rule known as *non-cumul*),[58] pre-contractual fault can give rise to a claim for damages in delict,[59] there being a very general principle of delictual liability based on fault.[60] However, English law possesses no such general principle and so no claims for damages in tort based on a party's "pre-contractual fault" can be brought in the absence of proof of an established tort. This had led to an occasional temptation in the courts to resort to the law of contract to found a claim for damages in this type of situation. This was clearest in relation to claims for damages for innocent (*i.e.* non-fraudulent) misrepresentation before the Misrepresentation Act 1967, where the courts allowed some claims for damages for false pre-contractual statements by way of contractual warranty.[61] More recently, in *Blackpool and Fylde Aero Club v. Blackpool Borough Council*,[62] the defendant local authority had invited sealed tenders from a limited number of persons for licences to use a local airport, to arrive at their premises by a certain date. The plaintiff delivered such a tender by the stipulated time, but owing to the failure of the defendant's staff, it did not

---

[50] *Universe Tankships Inc. of Monrovia v. International Transport Workers Federation* [1983] 1 A.C. 366, 385, *cf.* at 400; *Banque Keyser Ullmann SA v. Skandia (U.K.) Insurance Co. Ltd, supra,* at 780; and see *post,* § 7–040.

[51] See *ante,* § 1–073 and *post,* § 6–045.

[52] See *Clerk & Lindsell on Torts* (17th ed., 1995), 23–38—23–55. Where the defendant's conduct threatens physical injury to the plaintiff, the latter may possess an action of assault: *ibid.* at 12–12—12–13.

[53] *Rookes v. Barnard* [1964] A.C. 1129, 1205, 1209 and see *Clerk and Lindsell* § 23–54.

[54] See *post,* § 7–040.

[55] See *post,* §§ 7–010 *et seq.*

[56] *Clerk and Lindsell op. cit.* § 23–54.

[57] On the German position see Markesinis, *The German Law of Obligations,* Vol. I, *The Law of Contracts and Restitution: a Comparative Introduction* (1997) by Markesinis, Lorenz and Dannemann, pp. 64 *et seq.*

[58] *Bell v. Peter Browne & Co.* [1990] 2 Q.B. 495, 511. The full term for the rule is *non-cumul des responsabilités contractuelle et délictuelle* and see Whittaker in Bell, Boyron and Whittaker, *Principles of French Law,* (1998) pp. 331–332.

[59] Whittaker, *ibid.* pp. 313–314.

[60] *i.e.* Arts. 1382–1383 C. civ. and see Whittaker, *ibid.* p. 357 *et seq.*

[61] *Esso Petroleum Co. Ltd v. Mardon* [1976] QB 801, 817.

[62] [1990] 1 W.L.R. 1195.

consider the plaintiff's tender and failed therefore to award it a licence. The plaintiff's claim for damages for breach of contract was upheld by the Court of Appeal[63] on the basis that the defendant local authority's express request for tenders to be made in a particular form by a particular date,[64] coupled with the limited number of persons invited to tender,[65] gave rise to an implied contract to consider conforming tenders[66] and therefore the court found it unnecessary to consider whether the plaintiff could have succeeded in the tort of negligence.[67] Overall, however, it cannot be said that English courts evince any desire to develop a general principle of liability in damages for pre-contractual fault, whether this is put in terms of tort or contract, any more than they wish to recognise a general principle of pre-contractual good faith to which such a liability would be closely related.[68]

(ii) *Torts Committed in the Course of Performance of a Contract*

General. As Greer L.J. observed in 1936, "where the breach of duty alleged   **1–077** arises out of a liability independent of the personal obligation undertaken by contract, it is tort, and it may be tort even though there may happen to be a contract between the parties, if the duty in fact arises independently of the contract."[69] In the modern law, it may be stated that a party to a contract may choose to base his claim on an established and independent tort against the other party, but this choice will not be allowed to subvert the contract's express[70] or implied terms[71] nor any legal immunity attaching to the other party *qua* contractor.[72] On the other hand, where the contract is silent as to the issue to which a tort relates, in principle this is no reason for denying the existence of that tort, though an exception may properly be made where the tort is based on the defendant's "assumption of responsibility."[73] In general,[74] though, the choice whether to sue in tort or contract does allow a plaintiff to gain the benefit of any incidental rules of the regime of liability applicable,[75] though the modern tendency has been to reduce the differences between these two regimes in cases of concurrence.[76]

Henderson v. Merrett Syndicates Ltd. As has been noted, in *Henderson v.*   **1–078** *Merrett Syndicates Ltd*[77] (*"Henderson"*) the House of Lords held that a party to a contract may rely on a tort committed by the other party, as long as doing so is not inconsistent with the express or implied terms of the contract. However, in

---

[63] The case came to the court by way of a preliminary issue as to the existence of liability.

[64] [1990] 1 W.L.R. 1195, 1204.

[65] *ibid.* at 1202.

[66] The public character of the defendant was also relied on by the plaintiff as support for the existence of the contract as it had as a matter of public law a duty to comply with its standing orders (to consider tenders) and a fiduciary duty to ratepayers to act with reasonable prudence in managing its financial affairs: *ibid.* at 1201.

[67] *ibid.* at 1204.

[68] See *ante*, § 1–019.

[69] *Jarvis v. Moy, Davies, Smith, Vandervell & Co.* [1936] 1 K.B. 399, 405.

[70] See *post*, §§ 1–087, 1–091—1092.

[71] See *post*, § 1–087.

[72] See *post*, § 1–094.

[73] See *post*, §§ 1–095—1–099.

[74] The notable exception is in the case of contractual capacity: *post*, § 1–101.

[75] See *post*, § 1–100.

[76] See *post*, §§ 1–100 *et seq.*

[77] [1995] 2 A.C. 145.

finding a duty of care on which to base the plaintiffs' claim in tort, Lord Goff of Chieveley relied on *Hedley Byrne* as establishing a very broad principle of liability based on an "assumption of responsibility" and this principle suggests a very considerable overlap between the tort of negligence and liability in contract between parties to contracts.[78] As will be seen, moreover, the basis of a finding of an "assumption of responsibility" is so closely related to the finding of an agreement in respect of the same matter that the claim to true independence of the tortious liability thereby established is open to question.

1–079　　In *Henderson*, the plaintiffs were all Lloyd's "Names" who had agreed to take unlimited liability in respect of certain proportions of risks to be underwritten in the insurance market, but who had done so through different forms of arrangement. In the case of "direct Names,"[79] those persons who acted as their members' agents also acted as their managing agents (being known sometimes as "combined agents", though being termed "managing agents" here) and therefore any claim for negligence in respect of their claims was within privity of contract. The issue which came before the House of Lords was whether the "direct Names" could opt to sue their managing agents in the tort of negligence in respect of the management of the underwriting, the limitation period for their action for breach of contract having expired. In this respect, Lord Goff of Chieveley, who gave the leading speech and with whom Lords Keith of Kinkel, Browne-Wilkinson, Mustill and Nolan concurred, held that prima facie the managing agents did owe a duty of care in the tort of negligence to the "Names". Such a duty was, according to Lord Goff, to be based on a broad principle found in *Hedley Byrne & Co. Ltd v. Heller & Partners Ltd*,[80] according to which a person possessed of special skill or knowledge may owe a duty of care in tort by assuming a responsibility to another person within a relationship (whether special or particular to a transaction and whether contractual or not): the principle was not, therefore, restricted to cases of statements.[81] The House of Lords further held that, on the facts of the case, there was no reason why the "Names" should not opt to sue on the breach of such a duty of care in the tort of negligence rather than for breach of an implied term in their contract with the managing agents. Lord Goff considered that there was "no sound basis for a rule which automatically restricts the claimant to either a tortious or a contractual remedy,"[82] though he added that this general right of option was "subject only to ascertaining whether the tortious duty is so inconsistent with the applicable contract that, in accordance with ordinary principle, the parties must be taken to have agreed that the tortious remedy is to be limited or excluded".[83]

1–080　　**Contract inconsistent with liability in tort.** This decision therefore affirms the general availability of an option to sue in either tort or contract where the constituent elements allow, the exception being where the contract is inconsistent with a claim in tort. While Lord Goff's discussion of the "inconsistency of the contract" did not go beyond reference to its express or implied terms (on the facts there was no reason for it to do so), it is submitted that neither the decision itself

---

[78] Burrows (1995) C.L.P. 103, 118 *et seq.*; Whittaker (1997) 17 Legal Studies 169.
[79] For the position of "indirect Names" see *post*, § 1–117.
[80] [1964] A.C. 465.
[81] [1995] 2 A.C. 145, 180–181.
[82] *ibid.* at 193–194.
[83] *ibid.* at 194.

in *Henderson* nor Lord Goff's speech casts doubt on the proposition that such an "inconsistency" may be found in other features of the contract, notably the existence of a certain contractual immunity enjoyed by the party to the contract against whom the claim in tort is brought.[83a]

Assumption of responsibility. However, with respect, Lord Goff's approach   **1–081**
in *Henderson* to the existence of a duty of care in tort on which a party to a contract may choose to rely is more problematic. As has been noted, this approach rested on a broad principle of assumption of responsibility drawn from the speeches of the members of the House of Lords in *Hedley Byrne*.[84] While the notion of "assumption of responsibility" is clearly present in those speeches, they also contained various other elements on which the imposition of a duty of care was to be based, including the special skill and knowledge of the defendant and his or her "special relationship" with the plaintiff. During the period from its decision in 1963 to the mid-1990s,[85] the courts either combined these various elements or emphasised one or more of them as the facts of the case or their own preference suggested,[86] but *Hedley Byrne* was not, in general, used to expand liability for pure economic loss beyond the situation of liability for negligent *misstatements*.[87] This restriction on the ambit of the "broad principle of assumption of responsibility" was, however, firmly rejected by Lord Goff in *Henderson*[88] and it seems that the principle will apply where: (i) the defendant has agreed to perform a service or otherwise to do something for the claimant, whether under a contract or not[89]; (ii) the defendant possessed or held himself out as possessing special skill or knowledge in relation to these services or this task[90] and (iii) some evidence of reliance by the claimant can be made out. As regards the last of these conditions, in cases of negligent misstatement the claimant's reliance provides the causal link between the defendant's statement and the claimant's loss.[91] However, outside this type of case and as between parties to a contract, the element of "reliance" by the claimant may be found in the claimant's entering the contract under which the services, etc. are agreed to be done by the defendant.[92] This basis of liability in tort is not merely "equivalent to contract"; it is likely in very many cases to be parasitic on it.

Fair, just and reasonable. Finally, according to Lord Goff, where an alleged   **1–082**
duty of care is based on the doctrine of assumption of responsiblity there is no need to enter the question of whether it is "fair, just and reasonable" to impose

---

[83a] See post § 1–087 *et seq.*

[84] *Hedley Byrne & Co. Ltd v. Heller & Partners Ltd* [1964] A.C. 465.

[85] It would seem that the speech of Lord Goff in *Spring v. Guardian Assurance plc* [1995] 2 A.C. 296 marked the turning-point.

[86] *e.g. Caparo Industries v. Dickman* [1990] 2 A.C. 605; *Smith v. Eric S. Bush* [1990] 1 A.C. 831.

[87] An exception could be found in the decision of the House of Lords in *Junior Books Ltd v. Veitchi Co. Ltd* [1983] 1 A.C. 520, but this decision has not been followed but has been distinguished on various grounds: see *post*, §§ 1–113—1–114.

[88] [1995] 2 A.C. 145, 178–181.

[89] See esp. *White v. Jones* [1995] 2 A.C. 207, 273–274 (Lord Browne-Wilkinson, referring to "assumption of responsibility for the task not the assumption of legal liability"), 280, 288 (Lord Mustill). See also *Barclays Bank plc v. Fairclough Building Ltd (No. 2)* [1995] I.R.L.R. 605, *post*, § 1–083.

[90] *Henderson* [1995] 2 A.C. 145, 180 (*per* Lord Goff of Chieveley).

[91] *Henderson* [1995] 2 A.C. 145, 180.

[92] *Henderson* [1995] 2 A.C. 145, 180, 182.

such a duty, even in cases where the claimant's loss is purely economic: "the concept [of assumption of responsibility] provides its own explanation why there is no problem in cases of this kind about liability for economic loss; for if a person assumes responsibility to another in respect of certain services, there is no reason why he should not be liable in damages for [*sic*, to] that other in respect of economic loss which flows from the negligent performance of those services."[93] It may be argued in support of this proposition that where a claimant has satisfied the conditions for the application of the "broad principle", there is no need for an inquiry as to the desirability as a matter of policy of the imposition of liability *for pure economic loss* as the principle itself contains the requisite factors—such as "special skill or knowledge" and "reliance"—which balance the justice of its imposition.[94] However, in the dictum quoted above Lord Goff may be thought to go further: for it appears to suggest, if not that a person who "assumes responsibility" does so *for* economic loss (a position which gives to "assumption of responsibility" the meaning of agreeing *to be liable* which was clearly rejected by the House of Lords), then at least that such a person is to be held liable for a type of loss which flows from the nature of his agreement (to perform a certain type of service) which he has made. If so, this surely expresses no more than the idea that in these circumstances pure economic loss is a natural and probable (or indeed forseeable) type of harm arising from the breach of his agreement. And if this is so, then it is at most an argument in favour of recovery for pure economic loss, rather than a unaswerable reason for it. With the greatest respect, Lord Goff's suggestion that there "should be no need" to inquire into the "fairness, justice and reasonableness" of imposition of a duty of care should not be interpreted to mean that, apart from the issue of liability for pure economic loss, questions of policy are incapable of acting to negative a prima facie duty arising from an assumption of responsibility. Such an interpretation would, it is submitted, be inconsistent with the decision in *Rondel v. Worsley*,[95] where the House of Lords held that a barrister should not owe a duty of care in respect of the conduct and management of work in court under *Hedley Byrne*[96] or otherwise as this would be contrary to the public interest in the proper administration of justice.[97] Moreover, in *Marc Rich & Co. AG v. Bishop Rock Marine Co.*,[98] the House of Lords confirmed that the mere fact that a defendant's conduct has caused damage to property of a forseeable type does not rule out an inquiry as to the "justice and reasonableness" of the imposition of a duty of care in the tort of negligence. It would be indeed a paradox if the courts were to inquire into the

---

[93] *Henderson* [1995] 2 A.C. 145, 181. This proposition was treated as established by *Henderson* by Lord Steyn in *Williams v. Natural Life Health Foods Ltd and Mistlin* [1998] 1 W.L.R. 830, 834.

[94] *cf.* the approach of Lord Steyn to the question of "justice and reasonableness" in *Marc Rich & Co. AG v. Bishop Rock Marine Co.* [1996] 1 A.C. 221 at 236 *et seq.*, where he weighs various factors for and against the imposition of a duty of care on the facts.

[95] [1969] 1 A.C. 191.

[96] See especially at 260–261, 263–265 (*per* Lord Pearce), 281 (*per* Lord Upjohn) and 289 (*per* Lord Pearson).

[97] This approach may be supported by reference to the views expressed by Ward L.J. in *Welton v. North Cornwall D.C.* [1997] 1 W.L.R. 570, 583 though *cf.* at 580–581, *per* Rose L.J. who doubted the relevance of policy considerations (and with whom Judge L.J. agreed). *cf.* also *Stanton v. Callaghan* [1998] 4 All E.R. 961, in which the CA upheld a certain immunity from liability in negligence for expert witnesses on the grounds of public policy.

[98] [1996] 1 A.C. 211.

justice and reasonableness of imposing liability for forseeable damage to property caused by negligence, but not into the justice and reasonableness of imposing liability for albeit forseeable pure economic loss.

Effect of broad liability in tort. One effect of judicial acceptance of such a   **1–083**
very broad principle of "assumption of responsibility" may be seen to be the creation of a very wide means of circumventing the doctrine of consideration: for as long as a defendant is possessed of special skill or knowledge, his agreement with the claimant to perform a service within that skill or pertaining to that knowledge will give rise to a cause of action in tort based on the negligent performance of those services, whether they were to be paid for or not. A second type of effect may be the disapplication of other established rules of contract law. For example, in *Barclays Bank plc v. Fairclough Building Ltd (No. 2)*[99], building sub-contractors had engaged cleaning contractors to clean an asbestos cement roof, but in doing so negligently the cleaners created a danger from the asbestos which required considerable expenditure by the owner of the building to make it safe.[1] The Court of Appeal upheld the builders' claim for an indemnity against the cleaners in respect of their own liabilities, but reduced the award on the basis of their contributory negligence in failing to take steps to inform themselves of the problems involved in the cleaning of the asbestos cement in the way intended. The Court of Appeal accepted that contributory negligence is a defence to a claim for breach of contract only where it is concurrent with the existence of a liability in tort based on negligence,[2] but found such a liability in the cleaners in their breach of a duty of care based on their "assumption of responsibility," the latter arising simply from their contractual undertaking to do a job which required special skill and which they held themselves out as capable of doing, coupled with the roofing contractors' reliance on this, as evidenced by their entering into the same contract. In the result, the cleaners were entitled to rely on their own duty of care in tort to allow them to reduce by one half their own liability for breach of contract. Clearly, then, while in some cases, notably those turning on issues of limitation of actions such as *Henderson* itself, judicial acceptance of such a wide basis for establishing a duty of care in tort will benefit claimants, allowing them to avoid disadvantageous incidental rules applicable to actions in contract, paradoxically in others, it will instead benefit defendants.

The following discussion will look first at the question whether a threatened   **1–084**
breach of contract gives rise to liability in the tort of intimidation, before turning to examine the qualifications on the general rule allowing a claimant to opt whether to sue in contract or in tort and at how such an option affects the regime of liability applicable to the plaintiff's claim.

Threatened breach of contract as a tort. While some dicta in *Brown v.*   **1–085**
Boorman[3] suggest that any breach of contract gives rise to liability in tort,[4] such a broad interpretation of that case does not reflect the modern law: a breach of

---

[99] [1995] I.R.L.R. 605.
[1] *cf. Barclays Bank plc v. Fairclough Building Ltd* [1995] Q.B. 214 which concerned the claim by the owner of the buildings against the main building contractors.
[2] *Forsikringsaktieselskapet Vesta v. Butcher* [1989] A.C. 852 and see § 27–037.
[3] (1842) 3 Q.B. 511; (1844) 11 Cl. & Fin. 1, HL.
[4] See *ante*, § 1–070.

contract may be linked historically to tort, but does not itself constitute one.[5] However, it would seem that the tort of intimidation could allow at least *threatened* breaches of contract to give rise to liability in tort. This tort is committed, *inter alia*, where A uses "unlawful means" to force B to do something to his prejudice and although there is some uncertainty as to the full significance of "unlawful means" for this purpose, it is clear that it includes a threatened breach of contract[6] and it appears that this applies to "two-party" intimidation as much as to "three-party" intimidation.[7] Thus, according to *Clerk and Lindsell on Torts*, intimidation extends to a threat of breach of contract or at least to a threat of *some* breaches of contract,[8] despite the fact that the victim of such a threat may also have an action for anticipatory breach of contract.[9]

1–086   If so, then it would appear that rules which govern claims in contract, for example ruling out punitive damages or relating to remoteness of damage, could be avoided.[10] Indeed, the same authors add that it is not clear whether a party who has affirmed the contract after a threatened breach is thereby prevented from relying on the tort of intimidation.[11] However, if a claimant who was the victim of such a threat were allowed to rely on this tort rather than on the contract, it would be odd to deny him the same option where the other party had not merely threatened to break the contract, but had carried out this threat.[12] If this situation were allowed to give rise to liability in the tort of intimidation, then the law would be fast approaching the recognition of a distinction based on whether or not a defendant's breach of contract was "wilful" or "intended to injure." While American courts have moved in this direction,[13] there is no reason to think that English courts are inclined to do so.[14] It is submitted that there is no convincing reason for allowing a party to a contract to avoid the restrictions which the law already has decided should apply to that party's claim simply by claiming in tort. For this reason, the view that "two-party" and "three-party" intimidation should

---

[5] But compare § 1–083, *ante.*

[6] *Rookes v. Barnard* [1964] A.C. 1129.

[7] For example, where A threatens B, his creditor, that he will not pay a debt owed unless B accepts a smaller sum in full satisfaction, A may be liable to B in the tort of intimidation: *D. & C. Builders Ltd v. Rees* [1966] 2 Q.B. 617, 625.

[8] (17th ed., 1995), §§ 23–50—23–51. In *Morgan v. Fry* [1968] 2 Q.B. 710, 737, Russell L.J.'s judgment suggests that not every threat to break a contract of employment would be sufficient to constitute the tort of intimidation. *Clerk and Lindsell on Torts op. cit.* § 23–51, text at n. 80, suggest that this view "may depend upon absence of proof that the threat of a minor breach could cause damage. For damage is, of course, essential to the cause of action and the plaintiff must prove that his damage was caused by the coercive threat."

[9] See *post*, § 25–020.

[10] *Clerk and Lindsell on Torts op. cit.* at § 23–54, esp. at n. 9, referring to *Kenny v. Preen* [1963] 1 Q.B. 499 in which the Court of Appeal refused to award punitive damages where the claim was only for breach of contract and see *ante*, § 1–065 and *post*, § 27–017.

[11] *Clerk and Lindsell on Torts op. cit.* § 23–54, n.13.

[12] Cane, *Tort Law and Economic Interests* (1991), p. 137.

[13] Farnsworth, *Contracts* (1990), Vol. 3, § 17a.

[14] *cf. Kenny v. Preen, supra; McCall v. Abelesz* [1976] Q.B. 585, 594 and see *post*, § 27–017 and *cf.* the refusal of English courts to distinguish between deliberate and other breaches of contract for the purposes of the validity of exemption clauses, *post*, § 14–016 and see Unfair Contract Terms Act 1977, s.1(4). In *Bank of Nova Scotia v. Hellenic Mutual War Risks Association (Bermuda) Ltd* [1990] 1 Q.B. 818, 894 May L.J. observed that "a deliberate contract breaker is guilty of no more than breach of contract."

be treated differently where breach of contract is relied on as the unlawful means is to be preferred.[15] Thus, while a threatened breach of contract may constitute the tort of intimidation, the threatened breach should not in itself be considered sufficient "unlawful means" for the purposes of that tort; other *independent* "unlawful" elements should be required, for example, tortious means.

Contractual standards of care: can tort be stricter? It is clear that where   **1–087** either the express or implied terms of the contract or the law itself governs the standard of care owed by the defendant to the claimant, the latter cannot seek to impose a higher standard by claiming in tort, notably the tort of negligence.[16] Where a contract expressly restricts a party's standard of care, it would seem that ordinary principles of construction apply, rather than construction *contra proferentum* which applies to exemption clauses proper, *i.e.* those clauses which intend to restrict or exclude a party's *liability.*[17] In the case of implied terms, those which relate to the safety of a person or of his property often impose either reasonable care[18] or some stricter duty on the contractor,[19] and so any liability in tort in the latter would not impose any higher standard than in contract. However, implied terms whose breach gives rise to economic loss in the other party sometimes impose a more restricted standard of care than that imposed by the general law, and here the courts have refused to allow the other party to circumvent this contractual standard by claiming in tort. This was the particular issue in *Tai Hing Cotton Mill Ltd v. Liu Chong Hing Bank Ltd*[20] which gave rise to Lord Scarman's dictum advising against the intervention of tort between parties to a contract,[21] and this was the basis on which the decision of the Privy Council in that case which denied a claim in tort was explained by the House of Lords in *Henderson v. Merrett Syndicates Ltd*[22] *Tai Hing Cotton Mill Ltd* itself concerned a claim by a bank against its customer for economic loss caused by the latter's alleged negligence in the running of its own account. The Privy Council held that as a matter of authority a bank customer owed only a duty to act honestly in relation to the conduct of his own account under its contract with the bank and should not, therefore, be held to a duty to take reasonable care whether

---

[15] *Winfield and Jolowicz on Tort* (15th ed., 1998), pp. 639–640.

[16] An exception to this rule is found in the case of personal fraud in a contractor liability for which cannot be excluded by contract: *S. Pearson & Son Ltd v. Dublin Corporation* [1907] A.C. 351, 353–354, 362. Fraud may occur in the course of performance of a contract as well at the pre-contractual stage, for example, where a solicitor's clerk acts fraudulently in relation to his commission: see *Lloyd v. Grace, Smith & Co.* [1912] A.C. 716, where a solicitor's employee's fraud was held to give rise to liability in both tort and contract in the solicitor. Of course, in many situations the standard of care owed by a contractor is the same in tort and in contract, notably where the tort is one of negligence and the relevant contractual obligation is one of reasonable care: see *post*, §§ 13–014, 13–028.

[17] *cf. Trade and Transport Inc. v. Iino Kaiun Kaisha Ltd* [1973] 1 W.L.R. 210, 230–231 and see *post*, § 14–009 but *cf.* Unfair Contract Terms Act 1977, s.13(1), *post*, § 14–061.

[18] *e.g. Readhead v. Midland Ry. Co.* (1867) L.R. 2 Q.B. 412, (1869) L.R. 4 Q.B. 379 (carriage of persons); *Davie v. New Merton Board Mills* [1959] A.C. 604 (employment); Occupiers' Liability Act 1957, s.5(1); *Thake v. Maurice* [1986] 1 Q.B. 644 (medical liability).

[19] *e.g. Samuels v. Davis* [1943] 1 K.B. 526 (dentist who designed and constructed prothesis liable strictly to patient) and see Sale of Goods Act 1979, s.14.

[20] [1986] A.C. 80.

[21] [1986] A.C. 80, 107.

[22] [1995] 2 A.C. 145 see esp. at 186.

by way of implied term or of breach of an alleged duty of care in the tort of negligence.[23]

1–088   **Contractual standards and equitable principles.** The courts have taken a similar approach where the relationship between the parties is contractual, but where it has traditionally been subject to regulation by equitable principle. Thus, in *Parker-Tweedale v. Dunbar Bank plc*[24] Nourse L.J. stated that any duty of a mortgagee to a mortgagor or of a creditor to a guarantor in respect of the property or debt respectively arose in equity out of that particular relationship, it being "both unnecessary and confusing for the duties owed by a mortgagee to the mortgagor and the surety, if there is one, to be expressed in terms of the tort of negligence."[25] Similarly, Lord Templeman, giving judgment on behalf of the Privy Council, has stated that where a creditor was "not obliged to do anything" for the benefit of a surety under these equitable principles, for example in relation to the recovery of the debt, no duty of care in the tort of negligence can arise.[26]

1–089   **Contractual standard stricter.**   In certain types of case, the courts have refused to construe a contract or imply a term in it so as to circumvent the traditional standard of care or scope of liability applied to the type of case in question, even where this has usually been put as a matter of tort. For example, in *Thake v. Maurice*,[27] a majority of the Court of Appeal refused to interpret a contract to perform a vasectomy as importing an obligation that the patient would be rendered sterile as a result, holding that it contained only one of reasonable care in warning the latter of the possibility of future fertility. Although not put in these terms by the court, it could be said that the established standard of care in tort was applied to the claim in contract despite persuasive factual considerations which would lead in a different direction.[28] However, in many other situations the courts have accepted that the standard of care owed by a defendant in contract by reason of an implied term is higher than the reasonable care which would be imposed in the tort of negligence.[29] A recent example may be found in the decision of the Privy Council in *Wong Mee Wan v. Kwan Kin Travel Services Ltd*.[30] There a travel agent was held liable for the death of one of its customers on the basis of the negligence of one of its agents, even though there was no

---

[23] *cf. Blackwood v. Robertson* 1984 S.L.T. 68 (lesser standard of care between partners).

[24] [1991] Ch. 12 (and see *Shamji v. Johnson Matthey Bankers Ltd* [1986] B.C.L.C. 278).

[25] *ibid.* at 18 (and *cf.* at 24–25, Purchas L.J.), thereby disapproving Salmon L.J.'s dictum in *Cuckmere Brick Co. Ltd v. Mutual Finance Ltd* [1971] Ch. 949, 966 which talks of a duty of care in the context of the liability of a mortgagee; and see *Downsview Nominees Ltd v. First City Corpn Ltd* [1993] A.C. 295, 315 and *AIB Finance Ltd v. Debtors* [1998] 2 All E.R. 929, 937.

[26] *China and South Seas Bank v. Tan* [1990] 1 A.C. 536, 543–544.

[27] [1986] 1 Q.B. 644. Peter Pain J. at first instance and Kerr L.J. on appeal took the opposite view on this issue from the majority in the Court of Appeal and see *post*, § 1–102.

[28] *cf. Readhead v. Midland Ry. Co.* (1867) L.R. 2 Q.B. 412, (1869) L.R. 4 Q.B. 379, in which the court held that a passenger injured while travelling on a railway could sue the company only on the basis of breach of a duty to take reasonable care, rejecting the plaintiff's contention that the company owed an obligation to provide a carriage fit for its purpose, by analogy with cases on sale of goods.

[29] The stricter type of contractual term was implied by the courts in the context of sale of goods: *Jones v. Just* (1868) L.R. 3 Q.B. 197 (see now Sale of Goods Act 1979, s.14). See further *Samuels v. Davis* [1943] 1 K.B. 526 (liability of dentist in respect of manufacture and supply of dental prothesis) and *post*, § 13–028.

[30] [1996] 1 W.L.R. 38.

negligence on its own part, on the basis that the contract included an obligation that the services which the travel agent had engaged to perform *would be carried out* with reasonable care.

Stricter contractual standard does not affect tort. Finally, in *Aiken v.* **1–090** *Stewart Wrightson Members Agency Ltd*[31] the question arose whether the fact that the defendant owed a contractual duty *more onerous* than one of reasonable care could and should affect the standard of care owed in the tort of negligence. The case concerned a claim by Lloyd's "indirect Names" against their "members' agents", *i.e.* their agents who had contracted with them to advise them on their choice of syndicates and to place them on any syndicate once chosen, leaving the placing of the insurance to "managing agents". It was conceded by the members' agents that they owed the plaintiff "Names" a contractual duty that "the actual underwriting would be carried out with reasonable care and skill so that the members' agent remains directly responsible to its Names for any failure to exercise reasonable care and skill by the managing agent of any syndicate to whom such underwriting has been delegated."[32] The "Names" contended that the members' agents also owed them a duty of care in the tort of negligence of the same content, a "parallel and *co-extensive* duty of care in tort", arguing that it was inherent in Lord Goff's view expressed in *Henderson v. Merrett Syndicates Ltd*[33] that any liability in tort should not be inconsistent with the terms of the contract that the latter "ought in logic and in law to be definitive also of the nature and extent of their duty in tort."[34] However, Potter J rejected this argument both as a matter of authority[35] and principle. The latter he considered well expressed in a dictum of Le Dain J. in *Central Trust Co. v. Refuse*[36]: "[a] claim cannot be said to be in tort if it depends for the nature and scope of the asserted duty of care on the manner in which an obligation or duty has been expressly and specifically defined by a contract." Potter J. therefore concluded that on the facts before him the "common law duty of care . . . falls short of the specific obligation or duty imposed by the express terms of the contract, unless that common law duty of care can be shown to be non-delegable in character for the purposes of the law of tort", a proviso which was not satisfied in the case itself.[37]

Contractual exclusion of liability in tort. The law has taken a similar but not **1–091** identical approach to cases where a contract term excludes or limits *liability* of one contractor to another. Since at least the early nineteenth century, exemption clauses have been held capable of excluding or limiting liability in tort,[38] though it should be noted that where the clause limits liability, a (limited) claim in tort may still exist.[39] While at times the interpretation of exemption clauses *contra proferentum* has led to the courts distinguishing between the two types of liability, holding that a particular clause covered a strict contractual liability but

---

[31] [1995] 1 W.L.R. 1281.
[32] *ibid.* at 1290.
[33] [1995] 2 A.C. 145, 194 and see *ante*, §§ 1–078—1–079.
[34] [1995] 1 W.L.R. 1281 at 1294.
[35] *ibid.* at 1295. Notably, *Tai Hing Cotton Mill Ltd v. Liu Chong Hing Bank Ltd, supra.*
[36] (1986) 31 D.L.R. (4th) 481, 521–522.
[37] [1995] 1 W.L.R. 1281, 1301, 1305.
[38] *Nicholson v. Willan* (1804) 5 East 507 and see *post*, §§ 14–001 *et seq.*
[39] *White v. John Warwick & Co. Ltd* [1953] 1 W.L.R. 1285.

did not cover liability for negligence in tort,[40] there would appear to be no real reason to characterise a contractor's liability for negligence in these circumstances as tortious rather than contractual and in other cases the courts have simply inquired whether a particular clause should be construed to cover cases of negligence as well as any stricter liability.[41] Of course, in many situations, the effectiveness of such a term will be subject to the provisions of section 2 of the Unfair Contract Terms Act 1977, which applies to cases of tortious as well as to contractual negligence.[42]

1–092   **Incompatibility of express term and liability in tort.** *Johnstone v. Bloomsbury Health Authority*[43] concerned an alleged incompatibility between an express term of a contract and the existence of an established liability in the tort of negligence in a rather unusual way. The plaintiff was a junior hospital doctor who worked under a contract of employment which stipulated a working week of 40 hours and provided for a possible 48 additional hours availability for work. He claimed that in compliance with this contract he had sometimes worked in excess of 88 hours per week and had become ill as a result. The issue before the Court of Appeal was whether his claim for a declaration that he should not be required to work more than a 72-hour week should be struck out. The plaintiff relied on his employer's duty, which exists both as a matter of contract and the tort of negligence,[44] to take reasonable care as to his health at work, but the defendant countered that the express provision in the contract as to his hours of work limited the impact of this implied term and that no wider tortious duty could be imposed, relying on Lord Scarman's dictum in *Tai Hing Cotton Mill Ltd v. Liu Chong Hing Bank Ltd.*[45] The majority of the Court of Appeal refused to strike out the plaintiff's claim, but for different reasons. Stuart-Smith L.J. considered that while it was quite possible for an express term to exclude an implied one, the express term in question had not attempted to do so.[46] Sir Nicolas Browne-Wilkinson V.-C. agreed with Stuart-Smith L.J.'s decision on this point, but on more restricted grounds. The Vice-Chancellor considered that the approach of the Privy Council in *Tai Hing Cotton Mill Ltd* "shows that where there is a contractual relationship between the parties their respective rights and duties have to be analysed wholly in contractual terms and not a mixture of duties in tort and contract. It necessarily follows that the scope of the duties owed by one party to the other will be defined by the terms of the contract between them."[47] However, the Vice-Chancellor held that the clause in question did not on its terms impose an absolute obligation on the doctor to work the extra hours, but merely gave the defendant a discretion as to the number of hours extra that were to be worked and that this right should be considered subject to their ordinary duty not

---

[40] *White v. John Warwick & Co. Ltd, supra,* at 1294 where Denning L.J. held that the plaintiff "can avoid the exemption clause by framing his claim in tort."

[41] *e.g. Hollier v. Rambler Motors (A.M.C.) Ltd* [1972] 2 Q.B. 71.

[42] Unfair Contract Terms Act 1977, s.1(1) and see *post,* § 14–059. Such an attempted exclusion may also fall within the controls of the Unfair Terms in Consumer Contracts Regulations 1994 (S.I. 1994, No. 3159), *post,* §§ 15–004 *et seq.*

[43] [1992] Q.B. 334.

[44] See *Davie v. New Merton Board Mills* [1959] A.C. 604 (negligence); *Matthews v. Kuwait Bechtel Cpn.* [1959] 2 Q.B. 57 (contract).

[45] [1986] A.C. 80, 107; see *ante,* § 1–068.

[46] *ibid.*

[47] *ibid.* at 350.

to injure the plaintiff.[48] Leggatt L.J., dissenting, considered that the express term on the facts did indeed cut down the impact of the employer's implied term as to the safety of its employee and, following *Tai Hing Cotton Mill Ltd*, no tortious obligation could be any greater.[49] It is submitted that the approach of all members of the Court of Appeal in *Johnstone v. Bloomsbury Health Authority* to these issues is consistent with that adopted subsequently by the House of Lords in *Henderson v. Merrett Syndicates Ltd*,[50] since the latter confirmed that no concurrent liability in tort would be allowed where this would be inconsistent with the terms of the contract between the parties.[51] However, the decisions of the majority in *Johnstone* also shows that judges will be slow to interpret a contract as incompatible with an established liability in tort, perhaps particularly where this relates to personal injuries.

Contract removing condition of or giving rise to a defence to liability in tort.   1-093   A contract's terms can affect liability in tort in another way as it may remove one of the conditions for its existence or give rise to the existence of a defence, and this is particularly clear where the consent of an injured party excludes liability. Thus, in cases concerning medical treatment involving physical contact with the patient, the contact is prima facie a battery unless the claimant has consented to the treatment,[52] but where a person is able to and has consented, this will exclude liability in tort as well as contract.[53] Similarly, a contractual licence given by an owner of land prevents any liability arising in the licensee in the tort of trespass as long as the latter does not act beyond the permission.[54] A contractual consent can also allow the application of the defence of *volenti non fit injuria*. For example, in *Chapman v. Ellesmere*,[55] a racing steward who acted under a licence from the Jockey Club was held unable to sue members of a committee appointed under that club's rules in the tort of defamation in respect of the publication of a report on his role in a particular race, because on accepting his licence he had agreed to rules under which publication of such a report was specifically permitted.

Legal immunities for contractors.   1-094   Where the law itself rather than a contractual term grants a party to a contract a certain immunity from liability, the courts have looked to the reason for this immunity and decided whether it applies equally to a claim in tort as to the one in contract. For example, there is no doubt that a solicitor's immunity from liability for negligence in relation to the conduct and management of a case in court and of pre-trial work intimately connected with it, which is granted on grounds of public policy, applies both to tort and

---

[48] *ibid.* at 350–351.
[49] *ibid.* at 349.
[50] [1995] 2 A.C. 145.
[51] See *ante*, §§ 1–078—1–080.
[52] *Chatterton v. Gerson* [1981] 1 Q.B. 432, 442–443. For the extent to which the consent needs to be "informed" see *Sidaway v. Governors of the Bethlem Royal Hospital* [1985] A.C. 871. That the consent of the plaintiff goes to the existence of the tort of battery rather than being merely an example of *volenti non fit injuria* is supported by the fact that the claimant must show his own lack of consent: *Freeman v. Home Office (No. 2)* [1984] Q.B. 524, 539.
[53] *Sidaway v. Governors of the Bethlem Royal Hospital, supra*, at 904–905.
[54] There is no need for such a licence to be contractual for the defence to arise. See *Clerk and Lindsell on Torts op. cit.* § 17–46.
[55] [1932] 2 K.B. 431.

contract.[56] However, the approach of the courts to the very wide[57] immunity from liability at common law[58] of landlords to their tenants has been very different. In *Rimmer v. Liverpool City Council*,[59] while the Court of Appeal did not consider itself able as a matter of authority to impose a duty of care in the tort of negligence on a landlord as to the safety of the premises at the time of letting, it did impose a duty of care on a landlord *qua* designer of the premises let as to the reasonable safety of their design to the tenant *qua* person who might reasonably be expected to be affected.[60] As Stephenson L.J. noted, *Cavalier v. Pope*,[61] the leading authority which supported the landlord's immunity, should be restrictively interpreted[62] for at the time it was decided, "contractual duties were regarded as excluding delictual duties and a contractual relationship determined completely the rights and obligations of the related parties, as well as the rights of third parties."[63] In this context, and as regards liability for personal injuries, the courts showed themselves willing to allow the tort of negligence to develop in order to circumvent an immunity attaching to a particular contract where that immunity was no longer considered justified as a matter of policy, but which was supported by superior authority.

The decision of the Court of Appeal in *Bank of Nova Scotia v. Hellenic Mutual War Risks Association (Bermuda) Ltd, (The Good Luck)*[64] concerned a situation in which a legal rule (as opposed to the terms of the contract) provided one party to a contract with a remedy based on breach of a duty in the other, but where that breach of duty had not previously been held to give rise to liability in damages. One issue before the court was whether breach by an insurer of its duty to disclose matters to the assured during the course of the contract could give rise to liability in damages as well as the possibility of rescission of the contract by the assured.[65] Having held that it should not imply a relevant term as to disclosure into the contract either on the basis of the "bystander test"[66] or the "test of necessity,"[67] the court considered that, whatever the degree of proximity of the parties or the fairness and reasonableness of recognising a duty of care in tort, it should still apply the "principle established in *Tai Hing Cotton Mill Ltd v. Lui Chong Hing Bank Ltd.*"[68] According to May L.J. "the [insurer] was

---

[56] As a matter of history, this immunity from liability in negligence arose first as regards barristers, who do not act under contracts with their clients and so whose liability to the latter could only be tortious: *Rondel v. Worsley* [1969] A.C. 191; *Saif Ali v. Sydney Mitchell & Co.* [1980] A.C. 198. In the latter case, the House of Lords considered that this immunity applied equally to a solicitor acting as an advocate in court: *ibid.* at 224, 227 and see *Somasundaram v. M. Julius Melchoir & Co.* [1988] 1 W.L.R. 1394. The immunity from liability for negligence of barristers at common law is expressly stated to apply to any liability for negligence or for breach of contract by a solicitor by the Courts and Legal Services Act 1990, s.62. *cf.* the immunity of arbitrators: *Sutcliffe v. Thackrah* [1974] A.C. 727; *Arenson v. Arenson* [1977] A.C. 405.

[57] The immunity extended to positive acts of malfeasance as well as to non-feasance and to claims for personal injuries: *Travers v. Gloucester Corpn* [1947] 1 K.B. 71.

[58] *Cavalier v. Pope* [1906] A.C. 428. See now Defective Premises Act 1972, ss.3, 4.

[59] [1985] 1 Q.B. 1.

[60] *ibid.* at 13.

[61] [1906] A.C. 428.

[62] *Rimmer v. Liverpool City Council, supra,* at 9.

[63] *ibid.* at 11.

[64] [1990] 1 Q.B. 818 (revd. on other grounds [1992] 1 A.C. 233).

[65] *cf. Banque Keyser Ullmann SA v. Sakandia (U.K.) Co. Insurance Ltd* [1990] 1 Q.B. 655 (aff'd on other grounds [1991] 2 A.C. 249).

[66] [1990] 1 Q.B. 818. *ibid.* at 897–898 and see *post,* § 13–007.

[67] *ibid.* at 898–899 and see *post,* §§ 13–005, 13–009.

[68] [1990] 1 Q.B. 818, at 901, *per* May L.J.

entitled . . . to look to the contract between the parties to discover what was the obligation of the [insurer] with regard to reporting to the [assured]".[69] Thus, legal recognition of a *limited* remedy for a party to a contract for breach of a particular legal duty imposed on the other party, was seen by the court as a reason for refusing to impose a duty of care in the tort of negligence so as to give an *additional* remedy.

It should be noted, however, that *Bank of Nova Scotia v. Hellenic Mutual War Risks Association (Bermuda) Ltd (The Good Luck)* was decided before the decision of the House of Lords in *Henderson v. Merrett Syndicates Ltd*[70] and therefore at a time when *Tai Hing Cotton Mill Ltd v. Liu Chong Hing Bank Ltd*[71] was still seen as an authority against allowing a liability in tort (at least for economic loss) to be relied on by one party to a contract against the other and some of these dicta should be seen in this light.[72] While it would be open to a future court simply to distinguish the decision on this basis, it is submitted that it is more likely that the latter will be interpreted as an illustration of the proposition that new or doubtful liabilities in tort should not be imposed between parties to a contract where to do so would subvert the policy of the law of contract as reflected in its grant of a more limited remedy than recognition of the tort would entail. Such a proposition could be seen as the reflection of the idea that any liability in tort between the parties to a contract should not be inconsistent with that contract or, more directly, as constituting a consideration of policy arguing for the rejection of a duty of care in tort.[73]

Contractual silence. In the preceding situations, either the contract's terms or the law itself has regulated the obligation or liability imposed on the defendant. More difficult has been the case where the contract is silent as to an issue which is allegedly governed by a tort, for silence is ambiguous: where the parties have not provided for a certain issue, this can mean either that they did not address that issue, even implicitly, or it can mean that they consciously chose *not* to provide for that issue.[74] The typical case in which this problem has arisen has been where a contract has been held not to contain a relevant implied term and so the plaintiff has sued instead in the tort of negligence. Clearly, the choice for a court is whether to hold that the contract's silence excludes the recognition of any liability in tort, or, conversely, that it has no effect on the recognition of any liability in tort, which arises or does not arise according to its own rules. The acceptance by the House of Lords in *Henderson v. Merrett Syndicates Ltd* of the general rule that a party to a contract may rely on a tort committed by the other party even in the course of performance of the contract would appear at first sight to have settled this question in favour of the latter position, but, as been already noted, that same decision's acceptance of the "broad principle" of assumption of   **1–095**

---

[69] *ibid.* at 902.

[70] [1995] 2 A.C. 145.

[71] [1986] A.C. 80.

[72] See *ante,* § 1–068.

[73] On this role of policy in recognition of the duty of care in the tort of negligence, see esp. *Marc Rich & Co. AG v. Bishop Rock Marine Co.* [1996] 1 A.C. 211. For the significance of considerations of policy in relation to liability in the tort of negligence based on an "assumption of responsibility," see *ante,* § 1–082.

[74] *cf. Ali v. Christian Salvesen Food Services Ltd* [1997] 1 All E.R. 721, esp. at 726 in which the Court of Appeal refused to imply a term in a collective agreement which represented "a carefully negotiated compromise between two potentially conflicting objectives" and which was "wholly silent" as to the issue about which it was argued a term should be implied.

responsibility drawn from *Hedley Byrne* re-introduces the question in this particular context. The following will, therefore, look first at the general position and
then at the approach taken by the courts to the question of tortious "assumptions
of responsibility" between parties to a contract which is silent as to the issue on
which the assumption is alleged to have been made.

1–096　　**The general position.** In *Henderson v. Merrett Syndicates Ltd* it was held,
inter alia, that a party to a contract may rely on a tort committed by the other
party, as long as doing so is not inconsistent with its express or implied terms:
contract does not necessarily exclude tort. While *Henderson* itself concerned a
case where the defendant owed a contractual duty *concurrent* with the alleged
tortious duty, it could be argued that a contract's silence is by its nature not
inconsistent with the existence of any liability in tort. In support of this interpretation, it can be noted that to allow a person's mere entering into a contract
with another to have the effect of excluding the latter's liability in tort would
mean that the law allowed by *implication* (the implication that by their silence the
parties had intended that the issue in question should not be regulated) what it
traditionally allowed only by a very clear contractual *expression*,[75] a paradox
which would only be heightened by the fact that such an express exemption
clause would, in many cases, be subject to legislative control.[76] In general,
therefore, a contract's silence should not be interpreted as a choice to oust the
general law of tort.

1–097　　**Contractual silence and "assumption of responsibility".** However, more
difficulty arises in relation to cases of recovery of pure economic loss in the tort
of negligence based on the idea of "assumption of responsibility" drawn from
the speeches of the members of the House of Lords in *Hedley Byrne*. Certainly,
until the decision of the House of Lords in *Henderson v. Merrett Syndicates Ltd*[77]
the courts on more than one occasion refused to recognise a duty of care in the
tort of negligence in respect of pure economic loss based on an "assumption of
responsibility" of one party to a contract to the other where that contract was
silent as to the issue in question. For example, in *Reid v. Rush & Tompkins Group
plc*[78] the plaintiff was injured in a car accident in Ethiopia in the course of his
employment for his English employer, but as he could not recover compensation
there from the person responsible, he sued his employer, arguing that the latter
owed him an obligation either to insure him against this type of accident or to
advise him that he ought himself to take out appropriate insurance. However,
having refused to find an implied term in his contract of employment either as to
insurance or advising him of his position,[79] the Court of Appeal rejected his
claim for pure economic loss in the tort of negligence, refusing to accept his
argument that the defendant had voluntarily accepted this responsibility. According to Ralph Gibson L.J., "[w]here there is a contract between the parties, and
any 'voluntary assumption of responsibility' occurred, if at all, at the time of

---

[75] See *post*, §§ 14–005 *et seq.* and *cf. Smith v. Charles Baker & Sons* [1891] A.C. 325 (mere entry
of contract with knowledge of risk not sufficient for defence of *volenti non fit injuria*).

[76] This would be the case notably as regards "business liability for negligence" under the Unfair
Contract Terms Act 1977, s.2.

[77] [1995] 2 A.C. 145.

[78] [1990] 1 W.L.R. 212 and see also *Van Oppen v. Clerk to the Bedford Charity Trustees* [1990] 1
W.L.R. 235.

[79] *Liverpool City Council v. Irwin* [1977] A.C. 239 and see *post* § 13–008.

making and by reason of the contract, it seems unreal to me to try to separate a duty of care arising from the relationship created by the contract from one 'voluntarily assumed' but not specifically assumed by a term of the contract itself."[80] Having cited with approval Lord Scarman's dictum in *Tai Hing Cotton Ltd v. Liu Chong Hing Bank Ltd*[81] the learned Lord Justice added that "it is not open to this court to extend the duty of care owed by this defendant to the plaintiff by imposing a duty in tort which . . . is not contained in any express or implied term of the contract.[82] Similarly, in *National Bank of Greece SA v. Pinios Shipping Co. No. 1, The Maira,*[83] while Lloyd L.J. accepted that "in a large class of cases it was always, and maybe still is, possible for the plaintiff to sue either in contract or in tort"[84] he considered that "it has never been the law that a plaintiff who has the choice of suing in contract or tort can fail in contract yet nevertheless succeed in tort; and if it ever was the law, it has ceased to be the law since *Tai Hing Cotton Ltd.*"[85] Here, again, therefore, the silence of the contract prevented the imposition of a duty of care in tort.[86]

However, as this brief discussion makes clear, this approach to the imposition   **1–098** of a duty of care based on an assumption of responsibility in the context of contractual silence was heavily influenced by the general judicial disfavour with which *any* liability in tort between the parties to a contract was viewed, and such an approach was thoroughly disapproved by the House of Lords in *Henderson v. Merrett Syndicates Ltd.*[87] However, even after the latter decision a logical difficulty remains with the imposition of liability in tort based on an assumption of responsibility where the contract is silent. As has been seen, the current meaning given to the notion of "assumption of responsibility" by the courts is that the defendant agreed to undertake a task or perform some service for the plaintiff. In cases of "contractual silence", *ex hypothesi,*[88] the court has already decided that a defendant did not make any relevant agreement (as a matter of the express or implied construction of the contract). How then can a court hold that a defendant did not agree for one legal purpose, but did do so for another? It would be understandable if a court should consider it illogical to find the existence of such a duty of care owed by one contractor to another having already decided that there has been no *contractual* assumption of responsibility.

However, in *Holt v. Payne Skillington,*[89] the Court of Appeal took a rather   **1–099** different view of this matter. In this case the plaintiffs had indicated to the defendant estate agents that they wished to purchase a property in London with the view to letting it on "holiday lets", a use which they made clear they required

---

[80] [1990] 1 W.L.R. 212 at 229.

[81] [1986] A.C. 80, 107.

[82] [1990] 1 W.L.R. 212, 232.

[83] [1990] 1 A.C. 637.

[84] *ibid.* at 650.

[85] *ibid.* If given a general application, this statement would clearly prevent a plaintiff from suing in tort after the expiry of a limitation period applicable to a contractual action, on which see *post,* § 1–105.

[86] See similarly, *Bank of Nova Scotia v. Hellenic War Risks Association (Bermuda) Ltd, ante,* and see *ante* § 1–094 and *Greater Nottingham Co-Operative Society Ltd v. Cementation Piling & Foundations Ltd* [1989] Q.B. 71.

[87] *Ante,* §§ 1–078 *et seq.*

[88] On the assumption that the implied term is put before the court for its consideration.

[89] [1995] 49 Con. L.R. 99.

so as to benefit from tax relief in respect of a capital gain they had already made.[90] One of the estate agents' employees had, at some time before any retainer, assured them that he knew about the local planning requirements which would need to be satisfied to allow the plaintiffs to use whatever property they bought for this purpose. In the result, however, the property which the estate agents put forward and which the plaintiffs bought could not be used for holiday lets under the relevant planning rules. At first instance, the judge held the estate agents liable in the tort of negligence, but *not* liable for breach of contract on the basis that there was no express term of the retainer agreement (nor of a second "valuation agreement") between the parties that the agents should investigate the planning issue. The estate agents appealed against this decision as to their liability in tort, but no appeal was made by the plaintiffs on the decision made against them in contract. Before the Court of Appeal, therefore, the estate agents argued that any duty of care in tort which they might have owed to the plaintiffs could not be wider than the express and implied terms of the contract between them and contended that the judge's decision on the terms of their contracts meant that they could not be liable in tort. Hirst L.J., however, rejected this argument, relying on a passage of Lord Goff of Chieveley's speech in *Henderson v. Merrett Syndicates Ltd*[91] and stating that:

> "[T]here is no reason in principle why a *Hedley Byrne* type of duty of care cannot arise in an overall set of circumstances where, by reference to certain limited aspects of those circumstances, the same parties enter into a contractual relationship involving more limited obligations than those imposed by the duty of care in tort. In such circumstances, the duty of care in tort and the duties imposed by the contract will be concurrent but not coextensive."[92]

The Court of Appeal held, therefore, that the judge below was entitled to rely on a factual context wider than the contractual agreements between the parties to establish a duty of care in tort. This approach clearly accords with the general position taken in *Henderson v. Merrett Syndicates Ltd* in favour of allowing tort to apply between parties to a contract, but it appears to ignore the thrust of the "logical argument" outlined in the previous paragraph against finding a tortious assumption of responsibility in a case of contractual silence. In this regard, however, there is, with respect, a particular difficulty with the decision in *Holt*: for while Hirst L.J. based the estate agents' liability in tort on the principle of assumption of responsibility,[93] he found (as he had been invited to by *both* parties) the "essential characteristics of a situation giving rise to a cause of action in negligence based on a duty of case of the *Hedley Byrne* type" in a passage of Lord Oliver's speech in *Caparo Industries plc v. Dickman*,[94] which looks to the defendant's giving of advice to a person who he knows is likely to rely on it, rather than to any agreement to do a task by the defendant.[95] This approach to the *Hedley Byrne* principle was entirely understandable on the facts, since it was clearly the bad or inadequate advice which the plaintiffs were given by the estate

---

[90] The plaintiffs also claimed against their solicitors, but no issue relating to the latters' liability arose before the Court of Appeal.

[91] [1995] 2 A.C. 145, 193.

[92] [1995] 49 Con. L.R. 99, 114.

[93] This can be seen Hirst L.J.'s reliance on passages from Lord Goff's speech in *Henderson v. Merrett Syndicates Ltd* notably, [1995] 2 A.C. 145, 178 & 193–194.

[94] [1990] 2 A.C. 605, 638.

[95] [1996] 49 Con. L.R. 99, 114.

agents' employee which formed the basis of any imposition of liability in tort. Certainly, where liability under *Hedley Byrne* is put in terms of a negligent misstatement given by a person who can foresee that it will be relied on rather than in the broader terms of an "assumption of responsibility" in the sense of an agreement to perform a service for the other party, then there is nothing inconsistent in finding a duty of care under *Hedley Byrne* but no express or implied duty of care in contract. By contrast, however, to the extent to which a defendant's having "assumed responsibility" for doing something is to mean that he "agreed to do it", then it is submitted that it is much more difficult to hold that a party "agreed to do it" for the purposes of the tort but did not "agree to do it" for the purposes of the contract.[96]

The contractual regime. Both common law and legislation attach particular   **1–100** legal consequences to the classification of a claim as contractual and together these consequences can be considered to form the "contractual regime." As has been noted, some rules of this regime are significantly different from their counterparts in the law of torts, particularly in the context of rules as to capacity, damages, limitation of actions and the conflict of laws.[97] It is clear from the decision of the House of Lords in *Henderson v. Merrett Syndicates Ltd*[98] that, in principle, the option of party to a contract to sue in tort rather than in contract attracts the application to his claim of those rules incidental to tort, since on the facts of that case proceeding in tort allowed the plaintiffs to avoid the expiry of the limitation period for their action for breach of contract. However, the general terms of the acceptance by the House of Lords of a party's option to sue in tort (if one is established on the facts) rather than in contract supports the converse of this proposition, so that a party who could sue in tort, but chooses instead to sue in contract, thereby gains whatever advantages may be had from those rules which are incidental to claims in contract. However, it is submitted that these general effects of an option will not be universally followed by the courts (as the example of contractual capacity will show) and, perhaps more importantly, where (even before *Henderson v. Merrett Syndicates Ltd*) the courts have accepted a plaintiff's option, they have sometimes reduced the practical differences between the rules incidental to one or other basis of liability, so that the choice of legal basis does not affect the outcome of the case.

Capacity. A party's capacity to make a contract and to commit a tort are very   **1–101** different.[99] However, as has been seen, a party to a contract with a minor cannot in general avoid a minor's contractual incapacity by suing in tort where to do so would subvert the policy of the common law in protecting minors from making unfavourable contracts.[1] This approach is particularly clear in the context of a fraudulent misrepresentation by a minor as to his age,[2] but has been applied to other torts.[3] However, the courts have allowed a person who has contracted with a minor to sue the latter in tort, but only if the minor's tort can be considered as

---

[96] *cf. Tesco Stores Ltd v. The Norman Hitchcox Partnership Ltd* [1998] 56 Con. L.R. 52, 163–165.

[97] See *ante*, §§ 1–064—1–067.

[98] [1995] 2 A.C. 145.

[99] See *post*, § 8–043.

[1] See *ante*, § 1–039.

[2] *Johnson v. Pye* (1665) 1 Sid. 258.

[3] See *post*, § 8–043.

arising *independently* of the contract.[4] For example, in one case a minor who hired a mare "merely for a ride" and was warned at the hiring that she was unfit for jumping, having lent her to a friend who killed her by that act, was held liable in the tort of trespass which was "wholly independent of any contract."[5] Here, it cannot be said that the tort was unrelated to the contract: the tort consisted in permitting something to be done which the minor had been expressly forbidden by the contract to do.[6] In this type of case, the courts are concerned to limit the protection which the rules of contractual capacity give to a minor where this policy is considered to be outweighed by the tort's appeal for sanction and this is the case where a contractual permission for use of property by the minor is exceeded.[7]

1–102   **Damages.** There are important differences in the rules under which damages are awarded for breach of contract and in tort.[8] However, in cases of concurrence of liability in contract and tort, in many cases the courts have found means to prevent a claimant recovering more damages merely by the way in which his claim is put.

Thus, although a claim for breach of contract can compensate the claimant for loss of his "expectation interest," whereas a claim in tort can compensate only his "status quo interest,"[9] in cases of concurrence of liability the courts are slow to allow the claimant to recover damages based on the former measure merely because the claim can be classified as contractual, and instead award damages for loss of his "general expectations."[10] In this type of case, indeed, the significant distinction appears to be between cases where the content of the contractual obligation is to take reasonable care and where it is stricter, a "guarantee" that something is the case or will occur.[11]

This has already been seen in relation to pre-contractual statements which are held to have been incorporated into the contract,[12] but that the proper distinction in these cases turns on the content of the defendant's obligation, rather than on the mere classification of his liability can be supported by other cases which concern professional negligence, whether contractual or tortious. In *Ford v. White & Co.*[13] a firm of solicitors was sued for contractual[14] negligence by the plaintiffs who had been advised that a particular restrictive covenant did not affect a plot of land which they were intending to purchase (whereas it did).[15] The plaintiffs' claim for the difference between the value of the property with and without the restriction was rejected by the court. Although Pennycuick J.

---

[4] See *post*, § 8–044.

[5] *Burnard v. Haggis* (1863) 32 L.J.N.S. 189, 191 *per* Keating J. This passage does not appear in the other report at (1863) 14 C.B.(N.S.) 45.

[6] (1863) 14 C.B. (N.S.) 45, 53; (1863) 32 L.J.N.S. 189, 191.

[7] See also *Ballett v. Mingay* [1943] K.B. 281.

[8] See *ante*, § 1–064.

[9] See *ante*, § 1–064 and *post* §§ 6–052, 27–001.

[10] See *ante*, § 1–064.

[11] And *cf.* Cane, *Tort Law and Economic Interests* (2nd ed., 1996), pp. 142–145 and Whittaker (1996) 16 O.J.L.S. 191, 207 *et seq.*

[12] See *ante*, § 1–073.

[13] [1964] 1 W.L.R. 885.

[14] *ibid.* at 891.

[15] And *cf. County Personnel (Employment Agency) Ltd v. Alan R. Pulver & Co.* [1987] 1 W.L.R. 916, where the court did not generally feel it necessary to classify the claim beyond that it was for negligence, though the test of remoteness applied was found in *Hadley v. Baxendale* (1854) 9 Exch. 341: *ibid.* at 926.

accepted that in general damages for breach of contract should put the injured party in "as good a situation as if the contract had been performed,"[16] this did not mean that the plaintiffs should be put in a better position than if the defendant solicitors had performed their duty, as though the latter had warranted that their view of the restrictive covenant was right.[17] A similar view was taken recently by the House of Lords in relation to a claim by a finance company against a valuer of a house intended as security for a loan.[18] Their Lordships held that the finance company could recover damages for the negligence of the valuer representing the difference in what the secured property could make if sold (less the expenses of this) and the amount which they had lent in reliance on the valuation. The House of Lords rejected the finance company's claim that it could recover the interest which it had hoped to charge the borrower on the transaction (but had not been able to), accepting the valuer's argument that this would put them in a position as if he had warranted performance of the loan contract by the borrower,[19] rather than the proper damages for the valuer's negligence.[20] *Thake v. Maurice*[21] supplies an example of this difference in the context of medical negligence. At first instance, Peter Pain J. had found on the facts that the defendant surgeon had warranted to his patient that a vasectomy operation would be successful,[22] but the majority of the Court of Appeal disagreed,[23] holding that the defendant could be held bound only to take reasonable care in the giving of information as to the effect of the operation and finding it unnecessary to distinguish for this purpose between claims of contractual or tortious negligence, referring to this as the "negligence claim."[24] However, Kerr L.J. disagreed with the majority's interpretation of the contract and would have upheld the existence of a contractual warranty as to the success of the operation (the "contractual claim").[25] If this approach had been accepted, he considered that it would affect the damages recoverable by the plaintiffs, as damages in tort (*i.e.* the negligence claim) would be lower than those in contract.[26] In tort, damages for pain and suffering caused by the pregnancy should be reduced to take into account the distress of having to undergo an abortion (which *would* have been the case even if the patient had been properly advised as to the risk of pregnancy after the operation), but this was not the case in contract,[27] where if the defendant's warranty had not been broken the plaintiff's wife would not have become pregnant and so would not have suffered either proceeding. It is clear, however, that though put in terms of a contrast between tort and contract, the contrast which Kerr L.J. was intending to draw was

---

[16] [1964] 1 W.L.R. 885, 887, citing Lord Haldane in *British Westinghouse Electric & Manufacturing Co. Ltd v. Underground Electric Rlys. Co. of London Ltd* [1912] A.C. 673, 689.

[17] *ibid.* at 888. As the property with the restriction was worth the price which they paid, the plaintiffs' loss was held to be nil: *ibid.* at 891. *cf. Murray v. Lloyd* [1989] 1 W.L.R. 1260.

[18] *Swingcastle Ltd v. Alistair Gibson* [1991] 2 A.C. 223. *cf. Banque Bruxelles Lambert SA v. Eagle Star Insurance Co. Ltd sub nom. South Australia Asset Management Corpn v. York Montague Ltd* [1997] A.C. 191 esp. at 216–217, and see *post*, § 27–065.

[19] [1991] 2 A.C. 223, 225.

[20] *ibid.* at 238. While the House of Lords noted that the action before it was founded in tort, it did not consider the principles applicable to be any different from those in contract: *ibid.*

[21] [1986] 1 Q.B. 644.

[22] *ibid.* at 658.

[23] *ibid.* at 685, 688.

[24] *ibid.* at 679 (Kerr L.J.), with whom Neill and Nourse L.JJ. agreed on this point: *ibid.*, at 684, 685.

[25] *ibid.* at 678.

[26] *ibid.* at 683. This point had been agreed by the parties.

[27] *ibid.*

between a duty to take reasonable care whether in tort or contract and a contractual duty to see that a particular result occurs.

1–103   **Remoteness of damage.** Another important difference between claims in tort and contract is said to be found in relation to the applicable tests of remoteness of damage.[28] In contract, the court asks whether the kind of loss is within the reasonable contemplation of the parties,[29] whereas in the tort of negligence, it asks whether the type of harm is reasonably foreseeable.[30] Although the difference between these has been termed "semantic, not substantial,"[31] members of the House of Lords in *The Heron II*[32] considered, and some authors agree,[33] that a real difference in the two tests exists in relation to the degree of probability required, the position in contract being less generous than that in tort. However, where a case concerns concurrent liability in tort and contract, the courts are unwilling to allow the way in which the claimant puts his claim to affect the quantum of damages recoverable. Thus, in the Court of Appeal's decision in *H. Parsons (Livestock) Ltd v. Uttley Ingham & Co. Ltd*[34] which was such a case, Scarman L.J., with whom Orr L.J. agreed, assimilated the tests of remoteness in tort and in contract.[35] On the other hand, the "foreseeability test" of remoteness of damage[36] does not apply to claims for damages in the tort of deceit, where the plaintiff can recover all the damage directly flowing from the tortious act,[37] and the Court of Appeal has made clear that the latter test also applies to claims for damages under section 2(1) of the Misrepresentation Act 1967, whose imposition rests on a fiction of fraud.[38] This suggests that in some cases a representee will have an advantage in claiming damages for misrepresentation, rather than for breach of a contractual warranty which results from the incorporation of a statement into the contract,[39] as the former allows recovery of all losses flowing from the misrepresentation even if unforeseeable, "provided that they [are] not otherwise too remote."[40]

---

[28] And see Cane *op. cit.* pp. 137–142, for a discussion of the different treatment in tort and contract of damages for "lost chances."

[29] See *post*, §§ 27–039 *et seq.*

[30] *Overseas Tankship (U.K.) Ltd v. Morts Dock & Engineering Co. Ltd, The Wagon Mound (No. 1)* [1961] A.C. 388.

[31] *H. Parsons (Livestock) Ltd v. Uttley Ingham & Co. Ltd* [1978] Q.B. 791, 807. See similarly *Banque Bruxelles Lambert SA v. Eagle Star Insurance Co. Ltd* [1995] Q.B. 375, 405 *per* Sir Thomas Bingham M.R. (though the decision of the Court of Appeal was reversed on other grounds *sub nom. South Australia Asset Management Corp. v. York Montague Ltd* [1997] A.C. 191.

[32] *Koufos v. C. Czarnikow Ltd* [1969] 1 A.C. 350, 385–386, 422–423 and *cf.* at 413 and see *post*, § 27–044.

[33] See Harris, *Remedies in Contract and Tort* (1988), pp. 225–227; Cane *op. cit.* p. 145.

[34] [1978] Q.B. 791.

[35] *ibid.* at 806–807. Lord Denning M.R. agreed with the result of the majority, but justified it by drawing a distinction between claims for physical damage and ones for economic loss: *ibid.* at 802–804. For further discussion of this decision, see Burrows, *Remedies for Torts and Breach of Contract* (2nd ed., 1994), p. 47 *et seq.*; Cane *op. cit.* 146–147. *cf. Galoo Ltd v. Bright Grahame Murray* [1994] 1 W.L.R. 1360, 1369 where Glidewell L.J. adopted an approach to causation which he considered applicable to a claim for breach of contract and to one in "tort in a situation analogous to a breach of contract."

[36] *The Wagon Mound (No. 1), supra.*

[37] *Doyle v. Olby (Ironmongers) Ltd* [1969] 2 Q.B. 158.

[38] *Royscott Trust Ltd v. Rogerson* [1991] 2 Q.B. 297; and see *post*, § 6–070.

[39] See *ante*, § 1–073.

[40] *Royscott Trust Ltd v. Rogerson, supra*, at 307, *per* Balcombe L.J.

Contributory negligence. In *Forsikringsaktieselskapet Vesta v. Butcher*,[41] the   **1–104**
Court of Appeal took a very similar approach to the defence of contributory
negligence as it had done in *H. Parsons (Livestock) Ltd v. Uttley Ingham & Co.
Ltd*[42] to remoteness of damage, and held that while section 1 of the Law Reform
(Contributory Negligence) Act 1945 does not in general apply to claims for
breach of contract so as to allow a court to reduce any award of damages on the
ground of contributory negligence, it does apply to claims based on the breach of
a contractual obligation to take reasonable care ("contractual negligence") as
long as this is concurrent with liability for breach of a duty of care in tort.[43] This
approach leads to the paradox that a court's recognition of a duty of care in the
tort of negligence in *addition* to and concurrent with a contractual obligation to
take reasonable care owed to a claimant may lead to the *reduction* of the latter's
damages on the ground of contributory negligence, whereas its refusal to do so
would rule out such a reduction.[44]

Limitation of actions. As has been seen, differences as to the rules of   **1–105**
limitation of actions exist according to whether the claim is brought in tort or
contract[45] and this has often been a reason for a plaintiff to put a claim in tort
rather for breach of contract. Traditionally, the courts allowed a claimant's choice
whether to sue for breach of contract or in tort to determine which of the two
regimes of limitation will apply and this practice was confirmed in *Henderson v.
Merrett Syndicates Ltd.*[46] However, although the general rule is that an action in
contract accrues on its breach, whereas an action in tort accrues only on damage
being suffered by the claimant,[47] in those cases where the courts accept that the
claimant would have had[48] a claim for pure economic loss in the tort of
negligence concurrent with a claim in contract, their approach has been to
assimilate the two rules as to accrual, by finding that the claimant suffered
damage for the purposes of the rule in tort at the same date as the breach of

---

[41] [1989] A.C. 852, 858.

[42] [1978] QB 791.

[43] And see *Gran Gelato Ltd v. Richcliff (Group) Ltd* [1992] Ch. 560; *Youell v. Bland Welch & Co.
Ltd (No. 2)* [1990] 2 Lloyd's Rep. 431; *Barclays Bank plc v. Fairclough Building Ltd* [1995] Q.B.
214; *Barclays Bank plc v. Fairclough Building Ltd (No. 2)* [1995] I.R.L.R. 605 on which see *ante*,
§ 1–083 and *post*, § 27–027.

[44] *Barclays Bank plc v. Fairclough Building Ltd (No. 2)*, *supra*.

[45] In particular, in principle, accrual of actions for breach of contract occurs on breach, whereas
accrual for actions in tort occurs when the damage is suffered. The latter rule has caused not
inconsiderable difficulty in cases for negligently caused economic loss: see *D.W. Moore & Co. Ltd
v. Ferrier* [1988] 1 W.L.R. 267, 279–280; *Iron Trades Mutual Insurance Co. Ltd v. J.K. Buckenham
Ltd*, [1990] 1 All E.R. 808; *Bell v. Peter Browne & Co.* [1990] 2 Q.B. 495; *F.G. Whitley & Sons Co.
Ltd v. Thomas Bickerton* (1993) 07 E.G. 100 and see *ante*, § 1–066.

[46] [1995] 2 A.C. 145. In *Midland Bank Trust Co. Ltd v. Hett, Stubbs & Kemp* [1979] Ch. 384, it
was held that a claim in tort could exist even if the claim in contract was statute-barred, though the
contract claim still existed on the facts. In *Pirelli General Cable Works Ltd v. Oscar Faber &
Partners* [1983] 2 A.C. 1, a case in which the plaintiff's claim in contract was statute-barred, the
House of Lords had to decide when a claim in tort accrued, on the plaintiff's suffering of the damage
or on its discovery: *ibid.* at 12. This discussion would have been pointless if the expiry of the
contractual limitation period had been thought to have prevented any concurrent claim in tort even
if the latter's limitation period had not expired.

[47] *Pirelli General Cable Works Ltd v. Oscar Faber & Partners*, *supra*, at 19 and see *ante*
§ 1–066.

[48] *i.e.* apart from the question whether the claim is statute-barred.

contract.[49] On the other hand, rather than reducing differences of rule as to limitation of actions in contract and in tort, the Latent Damage Act 1986 added a further one, as its provision according to which "negligence actions" for latent damage can accrue on the latter's discovery rather than on its occurrence, has been held to apply only to actions based on negligence in *tort*.[50]

1–106   **The conflict of laws.** It was clearly established at common law that in cases with a foreign element where English law allows a person alternative claims in contract and in tort, his election between them brings with it the appropriate rules both of jurisdiction and choice of law.[51] Thus, in *Matthews v. Kuwait Bechtel Corpn.*[52] the plaintiff, who was injured at work abroad, was allowed to take advantage of the jurisdictional rules applicable to actions for breach of contract, it being held that an action by an employee against his employer for negligently caused personal injuries while at work lay either in tort or contract.[53] Conversely, in *Coupland v. Arabian Gulf Oil Co.*[54] the plaintiff, who had also been injured at work abroad, was held able to rely on the choice of law rules applicable to actions in tort,[55] the Court of Appeal rejecting the defendant's contention that his claim in tort should not be allowed to proceed without first looking at the position as regards the law applicable to the contract. However, where a person seeks to establish jurisdiction under the Brussels Convention[56] in a case where English municipal law would allow him a choice whether to put his claim in terms of contract or of tort, it appears that the European Court of Justice would regard such a claim as contractual for this purpose and outside the scope of the jurisdictional rule for tort,[57] the classification of a claim as contractual or tortious for these purposes being in principle a matter for European Community law as these concepts should have an "autonomous" interpretation.[58] This view of the position was taken by the Court of Appeal in *Source Ltd v. TUV Rheinland Holding AG.*[59] In that case, the plaintiffs claimed that the English courts had jurisdiction to hear their claim in tortious negligence against the defendants, a claim which arose out of and was concurrent with a claim against them for breach of their contractual obligation to exercise reasonable care and skill in presenting a report following the inspection of goods which they (the plaintiffs) had wished to import from China and Taiwan. The Court of Appeal noticed that the European

---

[49] See *D.W. Moore & Co. Ltd v. Ferrier* [1988] 1 W.L.R. 267, 280; *Iron Trades Mutual Insurance Co. Ltd v. J.K. Buckenham Ltd, supra*, at pp. 820–821; *Bell v. Peter Browne & Co.* [1990] 2 Q.B. 495, 501–504; *Lee v. Thompson* [1989] 40 E.G. 89. *cf. Forster v. Outred & Co.* [1982] 1 W.L.R. 86; *F.G. Whitley & Sons Co. Ltd v. Thomas Bickerton supra* at 108 and see Cane *op. cit.* pp. 34–136

[50] *Iron Trades Mutual Insurance Co. Ltd v. J.K.Buckenham* [1990] 1 All E.R. 808, see *ante*, § 1–066.

[51] See *Dicey and Morris on The Conflict of Laws* (11th ed., 1987), Vol. 1, pp. 328, 329, 345.

[52] [1959] 2 Q.B. 57.

[53] *cf. ante* § 1–092.

[54] [1983] 1 W.L.R. 1136. See also Carter (1983) 54 B.Y.B.I.L. 301; Morse (1984) 33 I.C.L.Q. 449. *cf. Johnson v. Coventry Churchill International Ltd* [1992] 3 All E.R. 14.

[55] See *Boys v. Chaplin* [1971] A.C. 356.

[56] Convention on Jurisdiction and the Enforcement of Judgments in Civil and Commercial Matters 1968, the Civil Jurisdiction and Judgments Act 1987.

[57] Case 189/87 *Kalfelis v. Schröder* [1988] E.C.R. 5565, esp. at 5577 (Adv.-Gen. Darmon), 5585 and see *Dicey and Morris on the Conflict of Laws* (12th ed., 1993), pp. 361–362.

[58] Case 814/79, *Netherlands State v. Rüffer* [1980] E.C.R. 3807, 3832–3833, 3836; Case 189/87 *Kalfelis v. Schröder, supra*; Case C–26/91, *Jakob Handte & Co. GmbH v. Société Traitements Mécano-chimiques des Surfaces (TMCS)* [1993] I.L.Pr. 5 and see *Dicey and Morris op. cit.* p. 361.

[59] [1998] Q.B. 54.

Court of Justice in *Kalfelis v. Schröder*,[60] had held that the phrase "matters relating to tort" in article 5(3) of the Brussels Convention refers to "all actions which seek to establish the liability of a defendant and which are not related to a 'contract' within the meaning of article 5(1)".[61] For Staughton L.J., with whom Waite and Aldous L.JJ. agreed, this means that a claim which may be brought under a contract or independently of a contract on the same facts, save that a contract does not need to be established, is excluded from article 5(3) by the European Court's words "which are not related to a 'contract' within the meaning of article 5(1)."[62] In the result, therefore, both the contractual and tortious claims of the plaintiffs "related to a contract" and they could not by relying on article 5(3) bring the tortious claim before the English courts. On the other hand, though the matter is not free from doubt, it would seem that there is nothing in the Rome Convention[63] to prevent such a person from framing his claim in tort so as to attract the choice of law rules applicable to that basis of liability, rather than in contract whose applicable law would be determined by that Convention.[64] The European Court of Justice has also taken the view that the notion of contract for the purposes of the Rome Convention must be understood "autonomously."[65] Even if a claimant is allowed to claim in tort rather than in contract so as generally to avoid the law applicable to the contract, the latter may be relevant, for example, if its contract law grants a defence to the defendant.[66]

(d) *The Influence of Contract on Tort beyond Privity*

Introduction. One of the most basic characteristics of liability in tort is that   **1–107** it can exist in the absence of any contractual relationship existing between the parties: there is in general no need for any voluntary element on the part of someone on whom duties or liabilities in tort are imposed.[67] However, a contract may affect liabilities in tort beyond its parties either positively or negatively. Positively, in certain circumstances someone not party to a contract, C, may be liable in tort for behaviour which interferes with the performance of B's contract with A (the tort of interference with contractual relations)[68] and, secondly, A may be liable to C for threatening B that he will break his contract with B (so-called "three-party" intimidation).[69] A contract may have a negative effect on torts

---

[60] Case 189/87 [1988] E.C.R. 5565.

[61] *ibid* at 5585.

[62] [1998] Q.B. 54, 63.

[63] Rome Convention on the Law Applicable to Contractual Obligations, Contracts (Applicable Law) Act 1990 and see generally, *post* §§ 31–016 *et seq.*

[64] *Dicey and Morris op. cit.* pp. 1198, 1315–1316 and see *post*, §§ 31–019, 31–103.

[65] *Dicey and Morris op. cit.* pp. 1197–1198 and see *post*, §§ 31–019, 31–103.

[66] *Dicey and Morris op. cit.* pp. 1315–1316, relying on *Sayers v. International Drilling Co.* [1971] 1 W.L.R. 1176; *Coupland v. Arabian Gulf Oil Co., supra.*

[67] See *ante*, § 1–061. *cf. post*, §§ 1–116—1–119 on liability in the tort of negligence beyond privity on the basis of an "assumption of responsibility".

[68] See *post*, § 1–108.

[69] See *post*, § 1–109. Contracts may have other consequences for the incidence of liability in tort. For example, where A has sold goods to B, who has resold them to C, the question whether the contract between A and B is void for mistake or merely voidable for fraud determines whether title to the property has passed to B and therefore whether C is liable to A in the tort of conversion: see *Ingram v. Little* [1961] 1 Q.B. 31; *Lewis v. Averay* [1973] 1 W.L.R. 510; *post*, §§ 5–045 *et seq.*

involving third parties in two ways. First, in certain circumstances the fact that A and B are parties to a contract has sometimes been seen as a reason for refusing to impose or for modifying any liability in tort in A to C. This idea, long derided as the "contract fallacy", enjoyed during the later 1980s and early 1990s a resurgence of judicial popularity in the context of liability for pure economic loss in the tort of negligence, and to a much lesser extent, in the context of liability in the same tort for damage to property.[70] However, since 1994 the courts have taken rather different approaches to these questions, in general coralling liability in negligence for pure economic loss within the doctrine of "assumption of responsibility" and treating the disruption of contractual arrangements as a possible reason of policy for refusing to accept a novel duty of care. Secondly, the existence of a contract between A and B may be a reason for refusing to impose liability on C to either A or B, depending on the terms of the contract between A and B. This issue arises clearly in the context of the question whether A and B can by contract ensure that a third party, C, enjoys the benefit of an exemption clause so as to be protected from liability to A or B, whether or not C is in privity of contract with that person. These situations will be examined in turn.

1–108   **Interference with contractual relations.** It was clearly established in *Lumley v. Gye*[71] in 1853 that if A intentionally induces B to break her contract with C, then A can be liable in damages for any harmful consequences that this causes C[72] or restrained by injunction from continuing such interference with C's contractual rights.[73] Moreover, the courts accept that in this way C may be able to recover more damages against A than he would be able to against B, this being seen as a reason for imposing the liability in tort, rather than for denying it.[74] While this liability in tort is often termed "procuring breach of contract," it can extend to cases where A's interference with C's rights does not give rise to liability in B, for example where the latter is protected by an exemption clause from this consequence of breach.[75] However, liability under this tort does not extend to interference with remedies arising out of a broken contract. Thus, where A has received shares from B in breach of B's contractual obligations to C, while A may be ordered to retransfer the shares to B and may be restrained by injunction from retransferring them to D, it is no *tort* in A to retransfer them nor in D to receive them.[76]

---

[70] See *post*, §§ 1–114 *et seq.*

[71] (1853) 2 E. & B. 216.

[72] As was the case in *Lumley v. Gye, supra,* itself.

[73] As was the case in *Torquay Hotel Co. Ltd v. Cousins* [1969] 2 Ch. 106 and see generally, *Clerk and Lindsell op. cit.* § 23–09 *et seq.*

[74] *Lumley v. Gye, supra,* at 234.

[75] *Torquay Hotel Co. Ltd v. Cousins* [1969] 2 Ch. 106 and see *Clerk and Lindsell op. cit.* § 23–015. The question whether liability extends to cases of "interference" with contractual relations which results in no breach of a primary obligation of the contract is less clear: see *Merkur Island Shipping Corpn v. Laughton* [1983] 2 A.C. 570, 607–610 and Markesinis and Deakin, *Tort Law* (3rd ed., 1994), pp. 385–387 but *cf. Clerk and Lindsell op. cit.* §§23–13—23–18, which distinguishes between a tort of "procuring breach of contract" and a tort of "indirect procurement of interference with business and contractual relations" in which liability requires the existence of "unlawful means."

[76] *Law Debenture Trust Corporation plc v. Ural Caspian Oil Corporation Ltd*, [1994] 3 W.L.R. 1221, esp. at 1231–1232.

"Three-party intimidation." The tort of intimidation is committed, *inter* **1–109**
alia,[77] where A threatens B that he will commit an act, or use means, unlawful
as against B, as a result of which B does or refrains from doing some act which
he is entitled to do, thereby causing damage to C.[78] In *Rookes v. Barnard*,[79] the
House of Lords recognised the existence of this tort and further held that a
threatened breach of contract by A can constitute unlawful means for this
purpose. In the Court of Appeal the view had been expressed that to extend the
tort to threats of breach of contract "would overturn or outflank some elementary
principles of contract law,"[80] notably, privity of contract.[81] However, for the
House of Lords the two causes of action (for breach of contract and for the tort
of intimidation) are "quite independent,"[82] "the vice of [C's] argument is the
threat to break and not the breach itself."[83] Thus, it is the independence of
liability in tort which allows its extension into what had previously been an
exclusively contractual domain.[84]

A contractor's liability beyond privity and independent torts. Where A's **1–110**
failure to perform an obligation owed under a contract to B causes harm to C, the
principle of privity of contract prevents such a breach of contract in A giving rise
to an action in C in contract, even in circumstances where this was intended by
A and B.[85] But can C sue A in tort? First, it is clear that the mere breach of a
contract by A does not in itself give rise to liability in tort to C. As Pollock stated
in 1887[86]:

> "there is a certain tendency to hold that facts which constitute a contract cannot have
> any other legal effect. We think we have shown that such is not really the law ... the
> authorities commonly relied on for this proposition[87] really prove something different
> and much more rational, namely that if A breaks his contract with B ... that is not of
> itself sufficient to make A liable to C, a stranger to the contract, for consequential
> damage."

Secondly, therefore, where the facts which constitute a breach of contract in A to
B also constitute the grounds of an *independent* liability in tort in A to C, the
existence of that contract does not in itself prevent liability in A to C.[88] Thus, as
has been seen, where A *threatens* to break his contract with B, this may give rise

---

[77] The proposition in the text describes liability in a case of "three-party" intimidation. For "two-party" intimidation see *ante*, § 1–000 and *Clerk and Lindsell op. cit.* § 23–54.

[78] See *ibid.* § 23–38.

[79] [1964] A.C. 1129.

[80] [1963] 1 Q.B. 623, 695, *per* Pearson L.J.

[81] *ibid.*

[82] [1964] A.C. 1129, 1207, *per* Lord Devlin.

[83] *ibid.* at 1200–1201, *per* Lord Hodson and see also *ibid.* at 1168, 1234–1235.

[84] *cf.* Wedderburn (1964) 27 M.L.R. 257 at 263–267.

[85] See *post*, § 19–001. The Law Commission has recommended that the law of privity of contract be reformed by statute so as to grant to a third party a right to enforce a contract in circumstances where the contract contains an express term to this effect for where it purports to confer a benefit on that third party, as long as (in the latter case) on its proper construction it does not appear that the parties did not intend the contract to be enforceable by the third party: Law Commission, *Privity of Contract: Contracts for the Benefit of Third Parties* (1996), Law Com. No. 242. These recommendations have resulted in the Contracts (Rights of Third Parties) Bill 1998, HL 5. See *post*, §§ 19–075 *et seq.*

[86] *The Law of Torts* (1st ed.), pp. 448–449.

[87] Notably *Winterbottom v. Wright* (1842) 10 M. & W. 109 and see *post*, § 1–111.

[88] Pollock *op. cit.* at 450.

to an action in C in the tort of intimidation[89] and this tort may also apply to cases of actual as opposed to threatened breach of contract.[90] Similarly, where a tenant, A, commits an act which constitutes a breach of the terms of his lease with his landlord, B, this does not prevent his neighbour, C, from suing A in private nuisance for any harm which he suffers as a result as long as the conditions for the existence of that tort are fulfilled.[91] "If it is the tenant who has undertaken the repair [*sci.* of the premises], of course he is liable, but his liability is based on the fact that he is the occupier of the premises; any additional obligation which he may have undertaken by contract with the landlord cannot affect his liability in tort to third parties."[92] On the other hand, where the landlord has undertaken to the tenant to repair, he can be liable in nuisance to a third party based on the control which this gives him despite not being an occupier[93] in addition to his liability to the tenant.[94] Finally, where an agent publishes defamatory material concerning the plaintiff, the fact that this publication also constitutes a breach of his contract actionable at the suit of his principal[95] does not prevent the plaintiff from suing the agent in the tort of defamation.[96]

1–111   **Privity of contract and the tort of negligence.**[97] At two stages in the development of the tort of negligence, it has been argued that A's breach of contract to B should not be considered capable of giving rise to liability in this tort for harm caused to C. The leading nineteenth century authority was *Winterbottom v. Wright*,[98] in which the plaintiff was employed to drive a mail-coach by one Atkinson, who had been engaged to carry mail by the Postmaster-General. The latter had hired a coach from the defendant, who had undertaken to him that it would be kept in a fit, proper, safe and secure state. The plaintiff's claim for damages in respect of injuries suffered when the coach broke down on a journey owing to its dangerous state was rejected by the court, which accepted the defendant's contention that "wherever a wrong arises merely out of the breach of a contract . . . whether the form in which the action is conceived be *ex contractu* or *ex delicto*, the party who made the contract alone can sue."[99] However, this

---

[89] See *ante*, § 1–109.

[90] *cf. ante*, § 1–085. In either case, this tort is clearly restricted to situations where A has acted intentionally to injure C: *Rookes v. Barnard* [1964] A.C. 1129, 1183 and see *Clerk and Lindsell on Torts op. cit.* § 23–38.

[91] *Winfield and Jolowicz on Tort* (13th ed., 1989), pp. 404–405.

[92] *ibid.* and see *Russell v. Shenton* (1842) 3 Q.B. 449, 457.

[93] *Payne v. Rogers* (1794) 2 H.Bl. 350, 351; *Wringe v. Cohen* [1940] 1 K.B. 229.

[94] *St. Anne's Well Brewery Co. v. Roberts* (1929) 140 L.T. 1, 8. *cf.* Defective Premises Act 1972, ss. 1, 4; and see Spencer (1974) C.L.J. 307, (1975) C.L.J. 48 and *Andrews v. Schooling* [1991] 1 W.L.R. 783.

[95] It has been held to be a breach of contract for an agent to disclose a document which is libellous: *Weld-Blundell v. Stephens* [1920] A.C. 956.

[96] In *Weld-Blundell v. Stephens, supra*, the principal had been held liable in libel personally for publishing the defamatory statement, which had then been republished by the agent.

[97] See *post*, § 19–023 *et seq.*

[98] (1842) 10 M. & W. 109.

[99] *ibid.* at 111, 114. See also *Tollit v. Sherstone* (1839) 5 M. & W. 283, 289 where Maule B. considered it "clear that an action of contract cannot be maintained by a person who is not a party to the contract; and the same principle extends to an action of tort arising out of a contract." Pollock *op. cit.* p. 449 supported the *decision* in *Winterbottom v. Wright* on the ground that no bad faith or negligence in the defendant had been shown and *cf. Donoghue v. Stevenson* [1932] A.C. 562, 589. *cf.* also Atiyah, *The Rise and Fall of Freedom of Contract* (1979), pp. 501–505.

approach[1] was of course rejected by the House of Lords in *Donoghue v. Stevenson*.[2] As Lord Macmillan put it, "there is no reason why the same set of facts should not give one person a right of action in contract and another person a right of action in tort."[3] The approach in *Winterbottom v. Wright*[4] came to be derided as the "contract fallacy."[5]

Liability for pure economic loss. While the courts were still willing to **1–112** extend liability in the tort of negligence, the "contractual environment" of a claim in the tort of negligence was even considered a ground for the imposition of a duty of care, rather than a reason for rejecting one. Thus, in *Hedley Byrne & Co. Ltd v. Heller & Partners Ltd*[6] one of the circumstances on which the House of Lords relied for finding the existence of a "special relationship" so as to give rise to liability for economic loss caused by a negligent misstatement was that the relationship of the parties was "equivalent to contract".[7] While Lord Devlin considered that the reason that the plaintiff's claim could not be considered contractual was the absence of consideration for the defendants' undertaking,[8] on the facts there was also no obvious privity between the parties.[9]

The Junior Books case. The courts' recognition of liability for negligently **1–113** caused pure economic loss was taken one stage further in 1982 in the decision of the House of Lords in *Junior Books Ltd v. Veitchi Co. Ltd.*,[10] where it held that a specialist flooring sub-contractor who had built a defective but not dangerous floor could owe a duty of care to the owner of the building who had to replace it as a result.[11] Clearly, there was no privity of contract between the parties, but the majority of their Lordships found that there was a "special relationship" between them, which again rested on a variety of factors, of which one was the fact that it fell "only just short of a direct contractual relationship."[12] At the time of its decision, *Junior Books* appeared to mark a radical departure, for it allowed recovery of pure economic loss beyond privity of contract other than where it was consequential on the defendant's negligent misstatement. However, the fate of *Junior Books* was not a happy one, its approach to liability for pure economic

---

[1] The approach was not universal: see *Payne v. Rogers, supra* (landlord liable to third party injured on highway owing to poor state of repair of premises as long as landlord had covenanted to repair) and *Gladwell v. Steggall* (1839) 5 Bing. (N.C.) 733 (medical practitioner liable to patient where fees had been paid by patient's father).

[2] [1932] A.C. 562. *cf.* the dissent of Lord Buckmaster on this ground at 568, 577–578 and see *Grant v. Australian Knitting Mills Ltd* [1936] A.C. 85, 101–102.

[3] [1932] A.C. 562, 610.

[4] *Supra.*

[5] See *Greene v. Chelsea Borough Council* [1954] 2 Q.B. 127, 138 and see as late as 1983, *Rimmer v. Liverpool City Council* [1985] Q.B. 1, 11.

[6] [1964] A.C. 465.

[7] *ibid.* at 525–526, 529 and *cf.* at 538.

[8] *ibid.* at 529.

[9] The statement in question had been made by A (the defendants) to B at the latter's request (who had in turn been asked to do so by C), A knowing that the statement would be passed on to B's customer, C (the plaintiff). In these circumstances, A could only be considered in privity with C if B were treated as C's agent for this purpose.

[10] [1983] 1 A.C. 520 and see *post*, §§ 19–024.

[11] As the case came to the House of Lords by way of a preliminary issue, it was not necessary to consider what damages would be recoverable nor whether the sub-contractor was negligent.

[12] [1983] 1 A.C. 520, 533 *per* Lord Fraser of Tullybelton and *cf. ibid.* at 542.

loss not being followed by subsequent courts.[13] While the courts gave many reasons in the many cases in which recovery for pure economic loss in the tort of negligence has been denied,[14] in some cases the presence of a contract or contracts has proven particularly important. In *Junior Books* itself, Lord Roskill noted that any exclusion clause in the main contract[15] may exclude or modify the liability in the sub-contractor directly to the building owner,[16] and Lord Fraser of Tullybelton considered that the terms of the sub-contract may have a similar effect.[17] However, later courts considered the *possibility* that the imposition of a duty of care will upset contractual standards or allocations of risk as itself a reason for refusing to impose one, thereby preferring Lord Brandon's approach in his dissenting speech in *Junior Books*.[18]

1–114 **"Contractual structure" and liability in tort.** Thus, the existence of a "contractual structure" of which the parties to the litigation are members but according to which they are not in privity of contract was relied on as a reason for refusing to impose liability for economic loss in the tort of negligence. For example, in *Balsamo v. Medici*[19] Walton J. refused to allow a claim in the tort of negligence by a principal against an unauthorised sub-agent on the ground that otherwise the *Anns* principle[20] of the tort of negligence "will come perilously close to abrogating completely the concept of privity of contract."[21] In 1987 in *Simaan General Contracting Co. v. Pilkington Glass Ltd (No. 2)*,[22] there was a chain of contracts, consisting of a building owner (A), a main building contractor (B), a sub-contractor (C) and a manufacturer of glass which had been incorporated into a building (D). The glass had failed to come up to specification and B, who had settled with A, claimed damages in the tort of negligence against D for

---

[13] See *Governors of the Peabody Donation Fund v. Sir Lindsay Parkinson & Co. Ltd* [1985] A.C. 210; *Leigh & Sillavan Ltd v. Aliakmon Shipping Co. Ltd* [1986] A.C. 785; *Candlewood Navigation Corpn Ltd v. Mitsui O.S.K. Lines Ltd* [1986] A.C. 1; *Muirhead v. Industrial Tank Specialities Ltd* [1986] Q.B. 507; *D. & F. Estates Ltd v. Church Commissioners for England* [1989] A.C. 177; *Simaan General Contracting Co. v. Pilkington Glass Ltd (No. 2)* [1988] Q.B. 758; *Yuen Kun Yeu v. Att.-Gen. of Hong Kong* [1988] A.C. 175; *Business Computers International Ltd v. Registrar of Companies and Alex Lawrie Factors* [1988] Ch. 229; *Pacific Associates v. Baxter* [1990] 1 Q.B. 993; *Parker-Tweedale v. Dunbar Bank plc* [1991] Ch. 12; *Murphy v. Brentwood District Council* [1991] 1 A.C. 398; *Dept. of Environment v. Thomas Bates & Son Ltd* [1991] 1 A.C. 499; *Punjab National Bank v. De Boinville* [1992] 3 All E.R. 104; *Saipem SpA v. Dredging VO2 BV* [1993] 2 Lloyd's Rep. 315.

[14] See Stapleton (1991) 107 L.Q.R. 249.

[15] The relevant terms of neither this contract nor the subcontract were presented to the House of Lords: [1983] 1 A.C. 520, 538.

[16] *ibid.* at 546.

[17] *ibid.* at 533–534.

[18] [1983] A.C. 520, 550–552 and see *Greater Nottingham Co-operative Society Ltd v. Cementation Piling & Foundations Ltd* [1989] QB 71, 96 where Purchas L.J. noted that Lord Brandon's speech had subsequently achieved greater significance. This approach avoids the difficult question whether *liability* arising on breach of a recognised duty of care in respect of pure economic loss may be modified or excluded by either (i) an exemption clause in A's contract with B restricting A's liability to C (*Simaan General Contracting Co. v. Pilkington Glass Ltd (No. 2)* [1988] Q.B. 758, 782–783; 785–786) or (ii) an exemption clause in A's contract with B which attempts to exclude C's liability to A (*Southern Water Authority v. Carey* [1985] 2 All E.R. 1077, 1093–1094) and see *post*, §§ 1–120, 14–052 *et seq.*

[19] [1984] 1 W.L.R. 951 and see Whittaker (1985) 48 M.L.R. 86.

[20] This is to be found in Lord Wilberforce's speech in *Anns v. Merton London Borough Council* [1978] A.C. 728, 751–752. This principle itself has been subject to considerable judicial reservation: see *Governors of the Peabody Donation Fund v. Sir Lindsay Parkinson & Co. Ltd, supra*, at 240–241.

[21] [1984] 1 W.L.R. 951, 959–960.

[22] [1988] Q.B. 758. *cf. Muirhead v. Industrial Tank Specialities Ltd* [1986] Q.B. 507.

the economic loss which it had thereby been caused. The Court of Appeal rejected this claim. According to Bingham L.J., "[j]ust as equity remedied the inadequacies of the common law, so has the law of torts filled gaps left by other causes of action where the interests of justice so required. I see no such gap here, because there is no reason why the claims beginning with [A] should not be pursued down the contractual chain."[23] Thus the courts treated the fact that A owes a duty under a contract to B to be an important factor in denying liability to C for negligently caused pure economic loss[24] and considered that where B owes a contractual duty to C, there is no good reason for adding an additional duty of care in A for C's benefit.[25]

Nevertheless, at least in some situations the existence of a contractual duty in   **1–115** A to B was not allowed to rule out the existence of a duty of care in respect of pure economic loss owed by A to C concerning the same issue. This was the position in the decision of the House of Lords in *Smith v. Eric S. Bush*,[26] in which a valuer had been engaged by a mortgagee to report on a property of modest value to be bought by the plaintiff. The plaintiff bought the property in reliance on the report and suffered economic loss as a result. The House of Lords unanimously held that the valuer owed the plaintiff a duty of care in the circumstances, which included the fact that the valuer knew that the plaintiff would be told of their advice and that he would act in reliance on it. The House of Lords further held that a contractual disclaimer under which the valuer worked did not prevent the duty of care in tort from arising on the basis that it was incompatible with any "voluntary assumption of responsibility," but was to be treated as an exemption clause and subjected to the reasonableness test imposed by the Unfair Contract Terms Act 1977.[27] Moreover, Lord Griffiths disapproved the notion of "assumption of responsibility" as a test for the imposition of a duty of care in the tort of negligence, considering it "not a helpful or realistic test of liability."[28]

Recent cases. However, since 1994 the House of Lords has taken a very   **1–116** different approach to the imposition of liability for pure economic loss in the tort of negligence and by so doing has allowed liability to be imposed on one party to a contract beyond privity. The basis on which it has chosen to rely for the

---

[23] [1988] Q.B. 758, 782 and *cf. Greater Nottingham Co-operative Society Ltd v. Cementation Piling & Foundations Ltd* [1989] Q.B. 7, 99 and *Pacific Associates v. Baxter* [1990] 1 Q.B. 993.

[24] *Pacific Associates v. Baxter, supra*, at 1023. And see *Duncan Stevenson Macmillan v. A.W. Knott Becker Scott supra*, at 110–111; *Parker-Tweedale v. Dunbar Bank plc (No. 1)* [1991] Ch. 12 (no duty of care in tort owed by mortgagor to beneficiary under trust of property subject to mortgage); *Verderame v. Commercial Union Assurance Co. plc, The Times*, April 2, 1992 (no duty of care owed by insurance brokers employed by a company to the directors of that company); *Hemmens v. Wilson Browne* [1994] 2 W.L.R. 323, 334–335 (no duty of care owed by solicitor to beneficiary of ineffective *inter vivos* transaction where the situation was not irremediable).

[25] *Gran Gelato Ltd v. Richcliff (Group) Ltd* [1992] Ch. 560, 570–571, in which the court held that there is in normal conveyancing transactions no duty of care in the solicitor of a vendor of land to the buyer in respect of misstatements. On the facts, the court accepted that the duty owed by A, the vendor, to B, the buyer could be put equally in terms of contract or the tort of negligence: *ibid.* at 569, relying on *Esso Petroleum Co. Ltd v. Mardon* [1976] Q.B. 801.

[26] Joined with the decision in *Harris v. Wyre Forest District Council* [1990] 1 A.C. 831. *cf. Preston v. Torfaen Borough Council* [1993] N.P.C. 111.

[27] s.2(2).

[28] [1990] 1 A.C. 831 at 862. *cf. ibid.* 846 *per* Lord Templeman.

imposition of liability has been an "assumption of responsibility" in the defendant to the plaintiff, this idea being drawn from the Lords' earlier decision in *Hedley Byrne & Co. Ltd v. Heller & Partners Ltd*[29] but its application being extended beyond the context of negligent misstatement. This "broad principle of *Hedley Byrne*" or of "assumption of responsibility" has already been seen in relation to liability in the tort of negligence between the parties to a contract, but now its impact beyond the parties will be assessed. In this respect, three cases are of particular importance.[30]

1–117   *Henderson v. Merrett Syndicates Ltd.* The first and most important is *Henderson v. Merrett Syndicates Ltd.*[31] This case concerned claims in the tort of negligence by various underwriting members of Lloyd's ("Names") against the underwriting agents who had acted for them. In the case of the "indirect Names", with whom we are now concerned, they had entered agreements with underwriting agents, known as "members' agents", who advised "Names", *inter alia*, on their choice of syndicates and placed them on a syndicate once chosen, but who entrusted the placing of the insurance to others, "managing agents" for the syndicate which they had chosen. The claims of the "indirect Names" therefore bypassed two contracts: the first being the agency contract between themselves and the members' agents and the second being the sub-agency contract between the members' agents and the managing agents. Despite this, however, the House of Lords found no difficulty in finding a duty of care owed by the managing agents directly to the "indirect Names". Lord Goff of Chieveley, who gave the leading speech and with whom Lords Keith of Kinkel, Browne-Wilkinson, Mustill and Nolan concurred, based this decision on a finding of an assumption of responsibility by the managing agents to the "indirect Names", this being found in the managing agents' agreement to undertake the commission for the indirect Names, coupled with the formers' special skill. However, the significance of this decision is far from clear. Lord Goff "strongly suspect[ed] that the situation . . . [was] most unusual; and that in many cases in which a contractual chain comparable to that in the present case is constructed it may well prove to be inconsistent with an assumption of responsibility which has the effect of, so to speak, short circuiting the contractual structure so put in place by the parties."[32] With the greatest respect, no very clear indication was given as to what was special about the facts of *Henderson* for this purpose: the managing agents had agreed to take on their commission and were aware of the position of their ultimate principals, but then so are many other sub-agents. Clearly, the context of the Lloyd's insurance market may have played some part, but the

---

[29] [1964] A.C. 465.

[30] The doctrine of "assumption of responsibility" was relied on by Lord Goff in *Spring v. Guardian Assurance plc* [1995] 2 A.C. 296, 324 but it had not been argued before the House and his fellow judges chose to rely on other grounds for their decisions. For other cases discussing "assumption of responsibility" as a basis for imposing a duty of care on a party to a contract beyond privity, see *Woodward v. Wolferstans (a Firm) The Times*, April 8, 1997; *Carr-Glynn v. Frearsons (a Firm)* [1997] 2 All E.R. 614; *Bank of Credit and Commerce International (Overseas) Ltd (in liquid.) v. Price Waterhouse, The Times*, March 4 1998. For cases discussing "assumption of responsibility" outside a contractual context, see *Goodwill v. British Pregnancy Advisory Service* [1996] 1 W.L.R. 1397; *Capital and Counties plc. v. Hampshire C.C.* [1997] 2 All E.R. 865, esp. at 883 *et seq.*; *Harris v. Evans* [1998] 1 W.L.R. 1285; *Kapfunde v. Abbey National plc* [1991] I.C.R. 1; *Costello v. Chief Constable of the Northumbria Police* [1999] 1 All E.R. 550. For cases discussing "assumption of responsibility" between parties to a contract, see *ante*, §§ 1–081 *et seq.*

[31] [1995] 2 A.C. 145 and see Whittaker (1996) 16 O.J.L.S. 191, esp. 204–205, 219 *et seq.*

[32] *ibid.* at 195.

precise nature of its role does not appear from the speeches. On the other hand, Lord Goff did see the case of a claim by a building owner against his sub-contractor in respect of a failure to conform to the required standard as an example of where "ordinarily" such an assumption of responsibility would be inconsistent with a contractual structure.[33] Clearly, then, it was not intended that any doubt should be thrown on the decision of the House in *Murphy v. Brentwood District Council*.[34]

White v. Jones. The second important decision is *White v. Jones*,[35] in which   **1–118** a majority of the House of Lords held that a solicitor who had negligently failed to execute a testament before the decease of the testator owed a duty of care in the tort of negligence to the would-be legatee under that testament. The House of Lords considered whether the legatee should be able to sue in contract, rather than in tort, the contract in question being between the testator and the defendant solicitor. While Lord Goff of Chieveley considered this attractive, he thought that it "would be open to criticism as an illegitimate circumvention of [the] long-established doctrines" of privity and consideration.[36] Instead, he preferred to hold the defendant liable in tort on the basis that his "assumption of responsibil-ity... should be held in law to extend" to the plaintiff, though the contract between the testator and the solicitor remained significant in that its terms set the content of the duty of care in tort.[37] Lord Nolan also relied on the defendant's "assumption of responsibility", though apparently seeing this as real rather than (as with Lord Goff) deemed.[38] Lord Browne-Wilkinson preferred to consider the facts before him as justifying the imposition of a duty of care as a matter of "justice and reasonableness" as an "extension of the principle of assumption of responsibility."[39] By contrast, Lords Mustill and Keith of Kinkel dissented, finding no special reason why a special exception should be made in the circumstances, the latter expressing the view that the principle of privity of contract should not be circumvented by extending the law of tort.[40] This decision of the majority is clearly a remarkable example of the willingness of our judges to find legal justifications for the imposition of a duty where they find it necessary in the interests of justice and, as both their own and the minority's speeches make clear, despite established principle, whether tortious or contractual. However, the speeches of their lordships in the case itself and subsequent judicial discussions of it have made clear that the situation in *White v. Jones* was exceptional[41] and it is, therefore, less likely to serve as the benchmark for subsequent judicial developments than is *Henderson v. Merrett Syndicates Ltd*.[42]

Williams v. Natural Life Health Foods Ltd and Mistlin. The importance of   **1–119** *Henderson v. Merrett Syndicates Ltd*, and more particularly, the significance of

---

[33] *ibid.* at 196.

[34] [1991] 1 A.C. 398.

[35] [1995] 2 A.C. 207.

[36] *ibid.* at 266.

[37] *ibid.* at 268.

[38] *ibid.* at 294.

[39] *ibid.* at 270, 275–276.

[40] *ibid.* at 251.

[41] See, notably, *Williams v. Natural Life Health Foods Ltd and Mistlin* [1998] 1 W.L.R. 830, 837 *per* Lord Steyn.

[42] *cf.* the approach of the High Court of Australia in *R.F. Hill & Associates v. Van Erp* [1997] 14 A.L.R. 687.

Lord Goff's exposition there of the principle of "assumption of responsibility" can be seen in the decision of the House of Lords in 1998 in *Williams v. Natural Life Health Foods Ltd and Mistlin*.[43] In that case, the second defendant, M, who had worked in the health food trade for several years, formed a company, the first defendant, to franchise the concept of health food shops. M was the company's managing director and principal shareholder, having only two employees. The plaintiffs approached the company with the view to acquiring a franchise, dealing with one of the employees, but also relying on a brochure produced by the company which advertised M's experience in the trade. The plaintiffs entered a franchise agreement with the company, but the turnover of the shop was substantially less than predicted by the company and they traded for only 18 months and at a loss. The question before the House of Lords was whether M owed the plaintiffs a duty of care so as to allow him to be liable personally in damages for the loss caused by their entering the contract of franchise. According to Lord Steyn, who gave judgment on behalf of the House, the governing principles for the case were to be found in the "extended *Hedley Byrne* principle" to be found Lord Goff's speech in *Henderson v. Merrett Syndicates Ltd*, which Lord Steyn saw as a "rationalisation or technique adopted by English law to provide a remedy for the recovery of damages in respect of economic loss caused by the negligent performance of services."[44] He noted that the test of "assumption of responsibility" is an objective one and this means that the primary focus of the courts should be on what was said or done by the defendant or on his behalf in dealings with the plaintiff. This meant that the question for the House was "whether the director, or anybody on his behalf, conveyed directly or indirectly to the prospective franchisees that the director assumed personal responsibility towards the prospective franchisees."[45] However, applying this principle to the facts, Lord Steyn held that there was not enough to show a personal assumption of responsibility in M to the plaintiffs: while the brochure produced by the company made clear that its expertise came from M's experience, in the absence of more and in particular of personal dealings with the plaintiffs, no duty of care arose.[46]

Lord Steyn in *Williams v. Natural Life Health Foods Ltd and Mistlin* accepted the view expressed by Lord Goff in *Henderson* that once a court finds that a defendant has "accepted responsibility" towards the plaintiff in the relevant sense, there is no need to investigate whether it is "just, fair and reasonable" to impose liability for pure economic loss.[47] This aspect of Lord Goff's views has already been discussed,[48] but here a striking contrast can be noted with Lord Steyn's own approach to the imposition of a duty of care *not* based on an "assumption of responsibility" taken earlier in *Marc Rich & Co. AG v. Bishop Rock Marine Co.*[49] In the latter case, the plaintiffs were cargo owners whose property was lost when the vessel in which it was carried sank. They claimed damages against the shipowners on the basis that the sinking had been caused by the latters' failure to act with due diligence in relation to the seaworthiness of the vessel at the beginning of the voyage, but they also claimed damages from a

---

[43] [1998] 1 W.L.R. 830.
[44] *ibid.* at 834.
[45] *ibid.* at 836.
[46] *ibid.* at 837–838.
[47] [1998] 1 W.L.R. 830, 834. For Lord Goff's position, see *ante*, § 1–082.
[48] See *ante*, § 1–082.
[49] [1996] 1 A.C. 211.

classification society, one of whose surveyors had inspected the vessel during its voyage and had recommended that its voyage should continue. Lord Steyn,[50] considered that since *Dorset Yacht Co Ltd v. Home Office*[51] it had been settled law that considerations of fairness, justice and reasonableness as well as the elements of foreseeability and proximity are relevant to the imposition of a duty of care in the tort of negligence, whatever the nature of the harm sustained by the plaintiff and, therefore, including the situation where the plaintiff has sustained damage to property.[52] On the facts before the House in *Marc Rich*, Lord Steyn considered that the property damage suffered by the cargo owners was only indirect as it was the shipowners rather than the classification society which were primary responsible for the vessel's sailing in an seaworthy condition nor was there any direct contact between the plaintiffs and the classification society and therefore no element of reliance so as to give rise to an assumption of responsibility in the sense explained by Lord Goff in *Henderson v. Merrett Syndicates Ltd.*[53] Even so, Lord Steyn was prepared to assume that there was sufficient proximity between the cargo owners and the classification society, but considered that it was not "fair, just and reasonable" to impose a duty of care. First, such a duty would outflank the bargain between the shipowners and the cargo-owners. He stated:

> "The dealings between shipowners and cargo owners are based on a contractual structure, the Hague Rules, and tonnage limitation on which the insurance of international trade depends . . . Underlying it is the system of double or overlapping insurance of the cargo. Shipowners take out liability risks insurance in respect of breaches of their duties of care in respect of the cargo. The insurance system is structured on the basis that the potential liability of shipowners to cargo owners is limited under the Hague Rules and by virtue of tonnage limitation provisions. And insurance premiums payable by owners obviously reflect such limitations on the shipowners' exposure".[54]

While Lord Steyn found various other policy factors which argued against imposing a duty of care, including the non-profit-making nature of the defendant, the scale of the classification society's potential liability and the added complication to the settlement of proceedings concerning lost or damaged cargo of such societies' involvement, clearly the limited nature of the rights of A (the cargo owners) under a contract with B (the shipowners) was significant in the House of Lords' decision not to impose a duty of care in the tort of negligence on C to A, even in respect of damage to property.

The effect of contractual terms on established torts beyond privity. In **1–120** general, a term in a contract between A and B will not affect liability in A to C under an established tort since to allow it to do so would contravene the principle of privity of contract.[55] However, the courts have allowed exceptions to be developed to this general rule and these are particularly clear where the term in

---

[50] Lords Keith of Kinkel, Jauncey of Tullichettle and Browne-Wilkinson agreed; Lord Lloyd of Berwick dissented.

[51] [1970] A.C. 1004.

[52] [1996] 1 A.C. 211, 235.

[53] *ibid.* at 237–238.

[54] [1996] 1 A.C. 211, 239.

[55] *Post*, §§ 14–039 *et seq.*

question expressly allocates the risk of some event, often by way of an exemption clause. Two situations ought to be distinguished.

1-121   **Clauses in contract between tortfeasor and another.** First, although in general A's contractual exclusion of liability to B will not affect A's liability to C,[56] it has been held to do so in certain circumstances. Thus, where a court relies on a defendant's "voluntary assumption of responsibility" for the imposition of a duty of care, any disclaimer of liability will apparently affect any third party who wishes to rely on it,[57] though in the case of liability for negligent misstatements, it appears that such a clause will only be effective if notice of it has come to the third party.[58] So too, where an owner of property entrusts it to a bailee and expressly or implicitly consents to the latter sub-contracting work to a sub-bailee subject to certain exemption conditions, the owner will not be able to sue that sub-bailee in tort except subject to these conditions.[59]

1-122   **Clauses in contract between victim and another.** Secondly, if A contracts with B on terms that A will not be able to sue C, the courts have found various ways to give effect to this agreement despite privity of contract. In *New Zealand Shipping Co. Ltd v. A.M. Satterthwaite & Co. Ltd (The Eurymedon)*[60] the Privy Council found that a stevedore engaged to unload goods by a carrier was protected from liability to their shipper in the tort of negligence for damage to the goods by a clause in the contract between the shipper and the carrier which was expressed to exempt the stevedore from liability and to be made by the carrier as his agent. Here, then, an exemption clause was given effect by the finding of a collateral contract between A and C, through the agency of B. However, on occasion the courts have instead refused to recognise the *existence* of a duty of care in the tort of negligence where to do so would disrupt the "contractual structure" in which the parties worked, not only in the context of a claim for pure economic loss,[61] but also in one of physical damage to the plaintiff's property. In *Norwich City Council v. Harvey*,[62] the plaintiff owned a building, which it wished to have extended and it employed building contractors to do so on standard terms according to which the "existing structures" should be at its own risk as regards loss or damage by fire while the works were in progress and should be insured against these risks. The building contractors engaged sub-contractors to undertake the roofing of the extension on this basis and owing to the negligence of one of the latter's employees, a fire was started which spread to and damaged the plaintiff's existing building. The Court of Appeal rejected the plaintiff's claim for this damage to its property, refusing to recognise the existence of a duty of care

---

[56] See *Haseldine v. C.A. Daw & Son Ltd* [1941] 2 K.B. 343, 397 and see *post*, § 14–040.

[57] *Pacific Associates v. Baxter* [1990] 1 Q.B. 993, 1022–1023, 1033. *White v. Jones* [1995] 2 A.C. 207, 268.

[58] In *Smith v. Eric S. Bush, Harris v. Wyre Forest District Council* [1990] 1 A.C. 831, the House of Lords considered the validity of such a clause under the Unfair Contract Terms Act 1977, s.2(2) which concerns the effect of contractual terms and *notices*.

[59] *Morris v. C.W. Martin & Sons Ltd* [1966] 1 Q.B. 716, 729 and see also *Johnson Matthey Co. Ltd v. Constantine Terminals Ltd* [1976] 2 Lloyd's Rep. 215; *The Pioneer Container* [1994] 2 A.C. 324 and *post*, § 14–050.

[60] [1975] A.C. 154 and see *post* §§ 14–043—14–045.

[61] See *ante* § 1–114.

[62] [1989] 1 W.L.R. 828.

in these circumstances. "On the basis of what is just and reasonable"[63] May L.J. did not think that "the mere fact that there is no strict privity between the employer and the subcontractor should prevent the latter from relying on the clear basis on which all the parties contracted in relation to damage to the employer's building caused by fire, even when due to the negligence of the contractors or sub-contractors."[64] In a Canadian decision, both the approach in the *The Eurymedon*[65] and the one based on the "justice and reasonableness" of imposing a duty of care in *Norwich City Council v. Harvey* were relied on by the court so as to allow an exemption clause in a contract between A and B to protect B's *employees* from liability to A in tort for negligence in respect of damage to A's property.[66] However, some writers suggest that a *contractual* approach to these types of problems is more appropriate[67] and if the Law Commission's recommendations as to the reform of privity of contract are put into law,[68] it will be possible for A and B by contract to grant rights to C, including rights of immunity against A.[69]

5. CONTRACT AND OTHER LEGAL CATEGORIES

Contract and trust. It is sometimes important to distinguish a contract,   **1–123** which creates rights *in personam*, from a trust which creates equitable rights indistinguishable in practice from rights *in rem*.[70] Thus if A agrees with B to pay money to C in return for valuable consideration furnished by B, C cannot in his own right sue A for failure to pay the money, because he is not a party to the contract[71]; but he can do so if he establishes that a trust was created in his favour.[72] Again, if A, the owner of a chattel, first agrees that B shall have the right to use it, and then, during the currency of the agreement, sells or charges it to C, who takes with notice of B's rights, B can sue A for breach of contract if C refuses to honour the agreement, and he may be able to recover damages from C for the tort of knowingly inducing a breach of contract. The question whether B is able to restrain C by injunction from using the chattel in such a way as to

---

[63] The phrase " just and reasonable" is a reference to the approach recommended to the finding of a duty of care by Lord Keith of Kinkel in *Governors of Peabody Donation Fund v. Sir Lindsay Parkinson & Co. Ltd* [1985] A.C. 210, 240–241, which May L.J. had previously quoted.

[64] [1989] 1 W.L.R. 828, 837 *per* May L.J. and *cf.* the approach of the House of Lords in *Marc Rich & Co. AG v. Bishop Rock Marine Co.* [1996] 1 A.C. 211, *ante*, § 1–119.

[65] *Supra.*

[66] *London Drugs Ltd v. Kuehne and Nagel International Ltd* [1990] 4 W.W.R. 289 (B.C.C.A.); *cf. Muller Martini Canada Inc. v. Kuehne & Nagel International Ltd* (1990) 73 D.L.R. (4th) 315 and see Adams and Brownsword (1991) 55 Sask. L. Rev. 441.

[67] Markesinis (1990) 106 L.Q.R. 556; Adams and Brownsword [1990] L.S. 12; Beyleveld and Brownsword (1991) 54 M.L.R. 48; Lorenz and Markesinis (1993) 56 M.L.R. 558.

[68] *Privity of Contract: Contracts for the Benefit of Third Parties*, Law Commission Report No. 242 (1996) and see Contracts (Rights of Third Parties) Bill 1998 H.L. 5 and post, §§ 19–075 *et seq.*

[69] *ibid.* at 16–24.

[70] This is the generally accepted view, despite Maitland's opinion to the contrary: *Equity* (1909), Lect. IX. See Scott (1917) 17 Col.L.R. 269; Winfield, *Province of the Law of Tort* (1931), pp. 108–112. See also *Binions v. Evans* [1972] Ch. 359; *Re Sharpe* [1980] 1 W.L.R. 219; *Tinsley v. Milligan* [1993] 3 W.L.R. 126, 147–148. See also the cases cited in § 13–026, n. 30, *post.*

[71] *Tweddle v. Atkinson* (1861) 1 B. & S. 393; *Dunlop Pneumatic Tyre Co. Ltd v. Selfridge & Co. Ltd* [1915] A.C. 847 (although B can obtain an order for specific performance in favour of C: *Beswick v. Beswick* [1968] A.C. 58); and see *post*, Chap. 19.

[72] See *post*, §§ 19–065 *et seq.*

prevent A from performing his contractual obligations is more difficult. The better view appears to be that there are three bases on which to ground such an injunction. The first is found in the equitable doctrine in *De Mattos v. Gibson*,[73] and the second in the tort of interference with contract.[74] The third basis is for B to establish an equitable interest in or charge over the chattel or that C is in the position of constructive trustee.[75]

1–124   Moreover, in some cases the courts have found a trust relationship between the parties in parallel to their established contractual one.[76] Thus, for example, in *Barclays Bank Ltd v. Quistclose Investments Ltd*,[77] A Ltd loaned a sum of money to B Ltd on condition that it would be used to pay the latter's share dividends. The money was paid into a separate account specially opened for this purpose with and to the knowledge of a bank, C Ltd. On B Ltd's voluntary liquidation, the House of Lords held A Ltd entitled to the money held by C Ltd and not paid out as dividend: the loan arrangements showed a clear intention "to create a secondary trust for the benefit of the lender, to arise if the primary trust, to pay the dividend could not be carried out."[78] On the other hand, more recently, the Court of Appeal accepted an approach to the relationship between contract and trust which echoes that already examined in relation to contract and tort.[79] In *Lipkin Gorman v. Karpnale Ltd*[80] a partner in a firm of solicitors drew cheques on a client account and then gambled away the proceeds. The solicitors sued, *inter alia*,[81] the bank, claiming that the latter was liable under a constructive trust. The Court of Appeal took the view that a bank would be subject to a constructive trust to its customer in respect of the running of an account only in circumstances where the bank would also be in breach of its contractual duty of care.[82] Moreover, the content of this duty had to be set in the context of the bank's primary contractual duty which was to honour its customer's cheques in accordance with its mandate[83] and so should be limited to cases where there is a

---

[73] (1858) 4 De G. & J. 276, 282; and see *Lord Strathcona Steamship Co. Ltd v. Dominion Coal Co. Ltd* [1926] A.C. 108; *Port Line Ltd v. Ben Line Steamers Ltd* [1958] 2 Q.B. 146; *Swiss Bank Cpn v. Lloyds Bank Ltd* [1979] Ch. 548; [1982] A.C. 584. See also *post*, §§ 19–020—19–021.

[74] Gardner (1982) 98 L.Q.R. 279; Tettenborn (1982) 41 C.L.J. 58, 82. *cf. Swiss Bank Cpn v. Lloyds Bank Ltd* [1979] Ch. 548, 573 where the court considered that the law in *De Mattos v. Gibson, supra*, is to be understood merely as the "equitable counterpart of the tort of interference with contract."

[75] *Swiss Bank Cpn v. Lloyds Bank Ltd, supra.*

[76] For example, where a solicitor is employed by a mortgagee lending a sum to a mortgagor for the purchase of property and pays the mortgage money which he has received before his authority to do so, he is liable for breach of trust in respect of that money unless he can justify this action: *Target Holdings Ltd v. Redferns* [1996] 1 A.C. 421; *cf.* also *Tinsley v. Milligan* [1993] 3 W.L.R. 126 and see generally McKendrick (ed.), *Commercial Aspects of Trusts and Fiduciary Obligations* (1992).

[77] [1970] A.C. 567. *cf. Re E. Dibbens & Sons Ltd* [1990] B.C.L.C. 577.

[78] [1970] A.C. 567, 582. See also *Re Kayford* [1975] 1 W.L.R. 279; Goodhart and Jones (1980) 43 M.L.R. 489; *Swiss Bank Cpn v. Lloyds Bank Ltd, supra* and *cf. Clough Mill Ltd v. Martin* [1985] 1 W.L.R. 111, 120 and *Swain v. The Law Society* [1983] 1 A.C. 598.

[79] See *ante*, §§ 1–078 *et seq.*

[80] [1989] 1 W.L.R. 1340. The claim against the bank was not pursued in the House of Lords: [1991] 2 A.C. 548.

[81] The solicitors also claimed against the casino where the money was lost: see *Lipkin Gorman v. Karpnale Ltd* [1991] 2 A.C. 548.

[82] [1989] 1 W.L.R. 1340, 1373. This point had been conceded by the solicitors early in argument: *ibid.* at 1349.

[83] *ibid.* at 1356.

"serious or real possibility, albeit not amounting to a probability, that its customer might be being defrauded."[84] *Lipkin Gorman v. Karpnale Ltd* therefore concerned the requisite degree of knowledge for liability in a third party "accessory" to a breach of trust and is to be distinguished from *Barclays Bank Ltd v. Quistclose Investments Ltd* where the bank (C Ltd) had *received* the money in respect of which the constructive trust was imposed and had actual notice of the purpose for which it was intended.

In other situations, the courts have used a contractual rather than a trust **1–125** analysis, for example, to solve issues relating to the distribution of assets held by unincorporated associations.[85]

Contract and conveyance. A contract, which creates rights *in personam*, **1–126** must be distinguished from a conveyance of property, which creates rights *in rem*. Yet sometimes a contract operates, to some extent at any rate, as a conveyance of property. For instance, a specifically enforceable contract for the sale of land constitutes the vendor a trustee of the property for the purchaser, and thus conveys equitable rights which are scarcely distinguishable in practice from rights *in rem*. Again, a contract for the sale of goods passes the property in the goods to the buyer under section 18 of the Sale of Goods Act 1979. But in both cases the vendor has a lien on the property for unpaid purchase-money; and in the case of goods, as the rubric to the group of sections containing section 18 indicates, the property passes only as between the seller and the buyer: as regards third parties the seller in possession has powers of disposition which may defeat the buyer's title, notwithstanding the maxim *nemo dat quod non habet*.[86]

Contract and restitution. "The law of restitution is the law relating to all **1–127** claims, quasi-contractual or otherwise, which are founded upon the principle of unjust enrichment."[87] Such claims are not dependent upon the existence of any contract, express or implied, between the person enriched and the person at whose expense the enrichment has occurred. From the seventeenth century, the same form of action, *indebitatus assumpsit*, was used to remedy breaches of contract and to enforce claims which we would nowadays consider to be claims in restitution, *e.g.* for money had and received, for money paid to the use of another, and on a *quantum meruit*. In these cases the obligation to make restitution was deemed to arise on an implied promise or implied contract (*quasi ex contractu*) in order to render them enforceable by a court in *indebitatus assumpsit*. This fiction can now be disregarded. Further, although the boundaries of the law of restitution are not, and have no need to be, settled, restitutionary claims extend beyond those previously classified as "quasi-contractual."

---

[84] *ibid.* at 1378, *per* Parker L.J. and *cf. ibid.* at 1356 and see Birks (1989) 105 L.Q.R. 352, 355. *Modern Equity* (15th ed., 1997), pp. 237–240;

[85] Hanbury and Martin *op. cit.* pp. 241–244; *Re Bucks Constabulary Fund (No. 2)* [1979] 1 W.L.R. 936. *cf. Davis v. Richards & Wallington Industries Ltd* [1990] 1 W.L.R. 1511.

[86] See Vol. II, §§ 43–213 *et seq.*

[87] Goff and Jones, *The Law of Restitution* (5th ed., 1998), p. 3. See *Lipkin Gorman v. Karpnale Ltd* [1991] 2 A.C. 548, 578; *Woolwich Equitable Building Society v. I.R.C.* [1993] A.C. 70; Birks, *An Introduction to the Law of Restitution* (1985), pp. 44–48; [1983] C.L.P. 141; *cf.* Atiyah, *The Rise and Fall of Freedom of Contract* (1979), p. 768; *Essays on Contract* (1986), pp. 47–52. See also *post*, Chap. 30.

1–128   The fact that the benefit conferred by one person upon another has been conferred in pursuance of a valid contract may preclude the claim that the recipient has been "unjustly" enriched.[88]

1–129   **Contract and public law.** The distinction between public and private law has since the early 1980s become particularly prominent.[89] In particular, the House of Lords has made clear that the procedure for judicial review under RSC, Ord. 53 is an exclusive one.[90] Thus, if a plaintiff's case is a matter of "private right" he cannot proceed by way of judicial review,[91] whereas if it is a matter of "public right" this is the only appropriate way of commencing proceedings.[92]

1–130   It is clear that the mere existence of a contractual relationship between an applicant for judicial review and the respondent does not make the case a matter of private law, nor conversely are all issues arising from a public authority's contracts matters of public law.[93] The courts have used a range of criteria to determine where to draw the line between private and public law,[94] but in the employment context, the *source* of the power or duty challenged was for some time prominent. Thus, in one leading case the applicant was a nurse who had been dismissed on grounds of misconduct.[95] His claim under Ord. 53 argued that his dismissal was *ultra vires* and decided upon in breach of natural justice. To support this, he alleged a breach of particular conditions of his employment which had been incorporated into his contract in compliance with regulations made under statute. However, this statutory background was not enough to give him "public law rights." According to the Court of Appeal, these would only arise if Parliament had directly restricted his employer's freedom to dismiss him, rather than requiring his employer to contract on particular terms, otherwise his claim was purely contractual.[96] The applicant was therefore left to his private law remedies for unfair dismissal and breach of contract.[97] By contrast, in a later case, the applicant, who had been a prison officer, based his application for the judicial review of his dismissal on the failure to observe a code of discipline of

---

[88] Goff and Jones *op. cit.* pp. 46, 48 *et seq.*
[89] Samuels (1983) 46 M.L.R. 558; Wade (1985) 101 L.Q.R. 153 & 180; Woolf (1986) P.L. 220; Beatson (1987) 103 L.Q.R. 34; Wade and Forsyth, *Administrative Law* (7th ed., 1994), Chap. 18 and see *post*, Chap. 10.
[90] *O'Reilly v. Mackman* [1983] 2 A.C. 237; *Cocks v. Thanet District Council* [1983] 2 A.C. 286. The terms of RSC Ord. 53 were retained by the Civil Procedure Rules 1998, Part 50, Sched. 1, r. 53.
[91] *R. v. East Berkshire Health Authority, ex p. Walsh* [1985] Q.B. 152. In *Council of Civil Service Trade Unions v. Minister for the Civil Service* [1985] A.C. 374, Crown service was held susceptible to judicial review, although the contractual issues involved were not argued before the House of Lords: see Wade (1985) 101 L.Q.R. 180, 194–197 and *cf.* Fredman and Morris (1988) P.L. 58.
[92] *O'Reilly v. Mackman, supra*; *Cocks v. Thanet District Council, supra*.
[93] *cf.* Wade and Forsyth, *op. cit.* pp. 689 *et seq.* Beatson (1987) 103 L.Q.R. 34, 48. On the contractual capacity of public authorities see *post*, §§ 10–022 *et seq.*
[94] Beatson (1987) 103 L.Q.R. 34.
[95] *R. v. East Berkshire Health Authority, ex p. Walsh* [1985] Q.B. 152.
[96] *ibid.* at 165. *cf. R. v. Crown Prosecution Service, ex p. Hogg* (1994) 6 Admin. L.R. 778.
[97] Employment Rights Act 1996, Part X, as amended. In some employment cases the courts have considered issues typical of public law, such as the reasonableness of the exercise of a discretion and relating to observance of natural justice, as a matter of contract law and in the course of private law proceedings: *R. v. British Broadcasting Corporation, ex p. Lavelle* [1983] 1 W.L.R. 23; *Dietman v. Brent London Borough Council* [1987] I.C.R. 737, 752; *Hughes v. London Borough of Southwark* [1988] I.R.L.R. 55.

prison officers in the Prison Rules, themselves made under a statutory power.[98] The court held that this basis gave his claim "sufficient statutory under-pinning" for it to be properly a matter of public law,[99] although the lack of any other remedy in the context appeared to weigh in the applicant's favour.[1]

On the other hand, a rather different approach was taken to the resolution of **1-131** this type of procedural dispute by the House of Lords in *Roy v. Kensington & Chelsea and Westminster Family Practitioner Committee*.[2] In that case, a doctor who worked for the defendant committee as a general practitioner under a statutory scheme claimed by writ sums allegedly owing to him which had been denied him because the Committee had come to the view that he had not devoted a "substantial amount of time to general practice" within the meaning of the relevant regulations. The Committee claimed that his action should be struck out as an abuse of the process of the court, arguing that his proper recourse was by judicial review alone. The House of Lords rejected this argument, holding that, whether or not the doctor worked under a contract for the committee, his claim for payment was a matter of "private right." According to Lord Bridge, "where a litigant asserts his entitlement to a subsisting right in private law, whether by way of claim or defence,[3] the circumstance that the existence and extent of the private right asserted may incidentally involve the examination of a public law issue cannot prevent the litigant from seeking to establish his right by action commenced by writ or originating summons, any more than it can prevent him from setting up his private right in proceedings brought against him."[4] Moreover, Lord Lowry noticed that Lord Diplock in *O'Reilly v. Mackman*[5] had acknowledged that there may be exceptions to the principle that cases involving public law issues should proceed only by way of judicial review, "particularly where the invalidity of the decision arises as a collateral issue in a claim for infringement of a right of the plaintiff arising under private law."[6] Lord Lowry recommended that a "liberal attitude" be taken to the ambit of such exceptions,[7] and approved a broad approach according to which judicial review would be reserved for cases where private rights were not at stake.[8] Clearly, the House of Lords intended to mould the distinction between private and public law according to the appropriateness of the different procedures in a particular case (for example, whether the case required oral evidence and discovery[9]), rather than according to the formal source of the plaintiff's claim. However, the decision by no means answers all the questions which arise at the borderline between private and public law in cases with "contractual echoes"[10]: if, as the House of Lords was content

---

[98] *R. v. Secretary of State for the Home Department, ex p. Benwell* [1984] 3 All E.R. 854.

[99] [1984] 3 All E.R. 854, 867.

[1] [1984] 3 All E.R. 854, 866, 868.

[2] [1992] 1 A.C. 624 and see Cane (1992) P.L. 193.

[3] See *Wandsworth London Borough Council v. Winder* [1985] A.C. 461.

[4] [1992] 1 A.C. 624, 628–629.

[5] *Supra.*

[6] [1983] 2 A.C. 237, 285, quoted in [1992] 1 A.C. 624, 642.

[7] [1992] 1 A.C. 624, 654.

[8] *ibid.* at 653. Lord Lowry was content to take a narrower view of the availability of recourse by action for the purposes of the appeal.

[9] [1992] 1 A.C. 624 at 647, *per* Lord Lowry, approving the approach of Woolf L.J. in *R. v. Derbyshire County Council, ex p. Noble* [1990] I.C.R. 808, 813.

[10] *ibid.* at 649, *per* Lord Lowry.

to assume, the plaintiff's claim did not rest on contract, it rested on statute and it is surely not the case to hold that all statutory rights are "private."[11]

The approach of the House of Lords in *Roy v. Kensington & Chelsea and Westminster Family Practitioner Committee* was followed by the Court of Appeal in *Trustees of the Dennis Rye Pension Fund v. Sheffield City Council.*[12] In the latter case, the plaintiffs had been served with an improvement notice by the defendant local authority in respect of the premises of which they were landlords and they had afterwards applied for an improvement grant from the same authority. The latter accepted the application, but later refused to pay the grants on the ground that the improvements had not been effected to its satisfaction. The plaintiffs claimed the grants by private law action, to which the defendants countered that the correct procedure was judicial review. In dealing with this issue, Lord Woolf M.R. noticed that "a very substantial volume of resources of the parties and the courts are still being consumed to little or no purpose over largely tactical issues as to whether the correct procedure has been adopted."[13] The Court of Appeal then held that the plaintiffs were entitled to proceed in their action, as once a person became entitled to the benefit of an improvement grant by fulfilling the relevant statutory conditions, there was no reason why he or she should not proceed to recover it by way of ordinary action: "[j]udicial review was not intended to be used for debt collecting."[14]

1–132 **Challenges to domestic tribunals.** The courts have also refused to allow the use of the public law procedure to challenge the decisions of certain types of domestic tribunal, in part on the ground that the relationship between the association and its members was "wholly contractual."[15] However, a decision of the Take-Over and Mergers Panel has been held susceptible to judicial review despite the self-regulatory and private form of its control, because *inter alia* it operated as an integral part of a governmental framework for the regulation of financial activity.[16]

1–133 **Contracts made by public bodies.** There are also circumstances in which the public nature of a party's contractual capacity (or contract-making power) affects the substantive rules applicable.[17] For example, the general rule, based on the principle of freedom of contract, is that a person can choose with whom to contract and with whom not to contract.[18] However,[19] a local authority's decision not to contract with a company which had indirect trading links with South Africa was successfully challenged by way of judicial review: although the

---

[11] Cane (1992) P.L. 193, 197.

[12] [1997] 4 All E.R. 747.

[13] *ibid.* at 749.

[14] *ibid.* at 752, *per* Lord Woolf M.R.

[15] *Law v. National Greyhound Racing Club Ltd* [1983] 1 W.L.R. 1302, following *R. v. Criminal Injuries Compensation Board, ex p. Lain* [1967] 2 Q.B. 864; *R. v. British Broadcasting Corporation, ex p. Lavelle* [1983] 1 W.L.R. 23 and see *R. v. Fernhill Manor School, ex p. A.* [1993] 1 F.L.R. 620; *R. v. Disciplinary Committee of the Jockey Club, ex parte Aga Khan* [1993] 2 All E.R. 853.

[16] *R. v. Panel of Take-Overs and Mergers, ex p. Datafin plc* [1987] 1 Q.B. 815 and see *R. v. East Berkshire Authority, ex p. Walsh, supra* and *Wandsworth London Borough Council v. Winder* [1985] A.C. 461.

[17] And see Freedland (1994) P.L. 86.

[18] See *ante* §§ 1–010—1–012.

[19] *R. v. Lewisham London Borough Council, ex p. Shell U.K. Ltd* [1988] 1 All E.R. 938, applying *Wheeler v. Leicester City Council* [1985] A.C. 1054 and see Local Government Act 1988, ss.17–23 and *post,* § 10–034.

policy was not itself unreasonable, it had been adopted partly in order to penalise the company in question and not solely in order to further racial harmony within the borough.[20] Moreover, a public authority must not discriminate against the nationals or products of the Member States of the European Union in awarding major contracts.[21] Another example of difference in substantive rule may be found in *Swain v. The Law Society*[22] in which the rules as to accountability of an agent were held inapplicable to the Society's arrangement of liability insurance on behalf of its members. The insurance scheme was made under statutory powers and the Society and its Council acted thereby "in a public capacity and what they do in that capacity is governed by public law."[23]

---

[20] This was the purpose of the statutory power relied upon by the local authority in its defence: Race Relations Act 1976, s.71.

[21] See Public Works Contracts Regulations 1991 (S.I. 1991 No. 2060); Public Supply Contracts Regulations (S.I. 1991 No. 2679); Utility Supply and Works Contracts Regulations 1992 (S.I. 1996 No. 2911) and see *post*, § 10–029.

[22] [1983] 1 A.C. 598.

[23] *ibid.* at 608.

Part One
FORMATION OF CONTRACT

CHAPTER 2

THE AGREEMENT

1. INTRODUCTION

General principles. There may be said to be three basic essentials to the **2–001** creation of a contract: agreement, contractual intention and consideration. The first two form the subject-matter of this chapter. The third, consideration, is discussed in Chapter 3.

The normal test for determining whether the parties have reached agreement is to ask whether an offer has been made by one party and accepted by the other.[1] Even where an agreement has been reached, it may fail to give rise to a binding contract because it is incomplete,[2] or not sufficiently certain.[3]

In deciding whether the parties have reached agreement, the courts normally apply the objective test,[4] which is further discussed in § 2–002 below. Under this test, once the parties have to all outward appearances agreed in the same terms

---

[1] The analysis of agreement into offer and acceptance gives rise to difficulties in a number of situations to be discussed in § 2–101 *post*.

[2] *Post* §§ 2–103—2–127.

[3] *Post* §§ 2–128—2–133.

[4] Howarth (1984) 100 L.Q.R. 12 at 265; Vorster (1987) 103 L.Q.R. at 286; De Moor (1990) 106 L.Q.R. 632.

on the same subject-matter,[5] then neither can, generally,[6] rely on some unexpressed qualification or reservation to show that he had not in fact agreed to the terms to which he had appeared to agree. Such subjective reservations of one party therefore do not prevent the formation of a contract.[7]

2. THE OFFER

2–002   **Offer defined.** The offer is an expression of willingness to contract made with the intention (actual or apparent) that it is to become binding on the person making it as soon as it is accepted by the person to whom it is addressed.[8] Under the objective test of agreement,[9] an apparent intention to be bound may suffice, *i.e.* the alleged offeror (A) may be bound if his words or conduct[10] are such as to induce a reasonable person to believe that he intends to be bound, even though in fact he has no such intention. This was, for example, held to be the case where a university had made an offer of a place to an intending student as a result of a clerical error;[11] and where a solicitor who had been instructed by his client to settle a claim for $155,000 by mistake offered to settle it for the higher sum of £150,000.[12] Similarly, if A offers to sell a book to B for £10 and B accepts the offer, A cannot escape liability merely by showing that his actual intention was to offer the book to B for £20, or that he intended the offer to relate to a book different from that specified in the offer.[13]

2–003   **State of mind of alleged offeree.** Whether A is actually bound by an acceptance of his apparent offer depends on the state of mind of the alleged offeree (B); to this extent, the test is not purely objective.[14] With regard to B's state of mind, there are three possibilities. First, B actually believes that A has the requisite

---

[5] See *Falck v. Williams* [1900] A.C. 176; *cf. Thake v. Maurice* [1986] Q.B. 644 and *Eyre v. Measday* [1986] 1 All E.R. 488 (applying the objective test for the purpose of determining the contents of an admitted contract).

[6] The rule stated in the text does not apply where one party knows that the other does not assent to the terms proposed: *e.g.* where an offer is expressed in a language which the offeree, to the offeror's knowledge, does not understand. See *Geier v. Kujawa, Weston and Warne Bros. (Transport) Ltd* [1970] 1 Lloyd's Rep. 364; and *cf. post* § 2–021. The rule is further subject to defences such as mistake, misrepresentation, duress and undue influence.

[7] See, for example, *Thoresen Car Ferries Ltd v. Weymouth Portland B.C.* [1977] 2 Lloyd's Rep. 614.

[8] *e.g. Storer v. Manchester C.C.* [1974] 1 W.L.R. 1403; *First Energy (U.K.) Ltd v. Hungarian International Bank Ltd* [1993] 2 Lloyd's Rep. 195, 201; contrast *André & Cie v. Cook Industries Inc.* [1987] 2 Lloyd's Rep. 463; *Schuldenfrei v. Hilton (Inspector of Taxes, The Times,* February 25, 1998 (statement that something *had* been done not an offer).

[9] *Ante,* § 2–001; *Ignazio Messina & Co. v. Polskie Linie Oceaniczne* [1995] 2 Lloyd's Rep. 566, 571; *Bowerman v. ABTA Ltd* [1995] N.L.J. 1815.

[10] For offers made by conduct, see *infra,* at nn. 20 *et seq.*; *The Aramis* [1989] 1 Lloyd's Rep. 213 (where the objective test was not satisfied); *G. Percy Trentham Ltd v. Archital Luxfer Ltd* [1993] 1 Lloyd's Rep. 25, 27.

[11] *Moran v. University College Salford (No. 2), The Times,* November 23, 1993.

[12] *O.T. Africa Line Ltd v. Vickers plc* [1996] 1 Lloyd's Rep. 700.

[13] *cf. Centrovincial Estates plc v. Merchant Investors Assurance Co. Ltd* [1983] Com.L.R. 158; cited with approval in *Whittaker v. Campbell* [1984] Q.B. 318, 327, in *Food Corp. of India v. Antclizo Shipping Corp. (The Antclizo)* [1987] 2 Lloyd's Rep. 130, 146, affd. [1988] 1 W.L.R. 603 and in *O.T. Africa Lines Ltd v. Vickers plc* [1996] 1 Lloyd's Rep. 700, 702.

[14] *Paal Wilson & Co. A/S v. Partenreederei; Hannah Blumenthal (The Hannah Blumenthal)* [1983] 1 A.C. 854, 924.

intention: here the objective test is satisfied so that B can hold A to his apparent offer even though A did not, subjectively, have the requisite intention.[15] The general view is that there is no further requirement that A must also be aware of B's state of mind.[16] Secondly, B knows that, in spite of the objective appearance, A does not have the requisite intention: here A is not bound; the objective test does not apply in favour of B as he knows the truth about A's actual intention.[17] Thirdly, B has simply not addressed his mind to the question of A's intention, so that B neither believes that A has the requisite intention nor knows that A does not have this intention: this situation has given rise to a conflict of judicial opinion. One view is that A is not bound: in other words, the objective test is satisfied only if A's conduct is such as to induce a reasonable person to believe that A had the requisite intention *and* if B actually held that belief.[18] The opposing view is that (in our third situation) A is bound: in other words, the objective test is satisfied if A's words or conduct would induce a reasonable person to believe that A had the requisite intention, so long as B does not actually know that A does *not* have any such intention.[19] This latter view no doubt facilitates proof of agreement, but it is hard to see why B should be protected in the situation to which it refers. Where B has no positive belief in A's (apparent) intention to be bound, he cannot be prejudiced by acting in reliance on it; and the purpose of the objective test is simply to protect B from the risk of suffering such prejudice. The test embodies a principle of convenience; it is not based on any inherent superiority of objective over subjective criteria. It is therefore submitted that the objective test should not apply to our third situation since in it there is, by reason of B's state of mind, no risk of his suffering any prejudice as a result of the objective appearance of A's intention. For this purpose, it should make no difference whether B's state of mind amounts to knowledge of, or merely to indifference to, the truth.

---

[15] *André & Cie SA v. Marine Transocean Ltd (The Splendid Sun)* [1981] 1 Q.B. 694, as explained in *The Hannah Blumenthal, supra; Challoner v. Bower* (1984) 269 E.G. 725; *Tankrederei Ahrentzeil GmbH v. Frahuil SA (The Multibank Holsatia)* 2 Lloyd's Rep. 486, 493 ("subjective understanding").

[16] The suggestion that A must be aware of B's state of mind was made by Lord Diplock in *The Hannah Blumenthal* [1983] 1 A.C. 854, 916, but Lord Brightman's contrary view, expressed *ibid.* 924 has been generally preferred: see *The Multibank Holsatia, supra*, 492.

[17] *Ignazio Messina & Co. v. Polskie Linie Oceaniczna* [1995] 2 Lloyd's Rep. 566, 571; *O.T. Africa Line Ltd v. Vickers plc* [1996] 1 Lloyd's Rep. 700, 703; and see the authorities cited in n. 19, *infra*.

[18] *The Hannah Blumenthal, supra*, as interpreted in *Allied Marine Transport v. Vale de Rio Doce Navegaçeo SA (The Leonidas D.)* [1985] 1 W.L.R. 925; Beatson (1986) 102 L.Q.R. 1; Atiyah, *ibid.* 363; *Gebr. van Weelde Sheepvaart Kantoor BV v. Homeric Marine Services (The Agrabele)* [1987] 2 Lloyd's Rep. 223, esp. at 235; *cf. Cie Française d'Importation, etc., SA v. Deutsche Continental Handelsgesellschaft* [1985] 2 Lloyd's Rep. 592, 597; *Amherst v. James Walker Goldsmith and Silversmith Ltd* [1983] Ch. 305.

[19] *Excomm Ltd v. Guan Guan Shipping (Pte) Ltd (The Golden Bear)* [1987] 1 Lloyd's Rep. 330, 341 (doubted on another point in § 2–064, n. 48 *post*, and see infra n. 29); this view was approved in *The Antclizo* [1987] 2 Lloyd's Rep. 130, 143 but doubted *ibid.* 147 (affd. [1988] 1 W.L.R. 603 without reference to the point); and *semble* in *Floating Dock Ltd v. Hong Kong and Shanghai Bank Ltd* [1986] 1 Lloyd's Rep. 65, 77; *The Multibank Holsatia* [1988] 2 Lloyd's Rep. 486, 492 ("at least did not conflict with [B's] subjective understanding"); *Tai-Europe Tapioca Service Ltd v. Seine Navigation Inc. (The Maritime Winner)* [1989] 2 Lloyd's Rep. 506, 515 (using similar language). A dictum in *Furness Withy (Australia) Pty Ltd v. Metal Distribution (U.K.) Ltd (The Amazonia)* [1990] 1 Lloyd's Rep. 236, 242 goes even further in suggesting that there may be a contract even though "*neither* [party] intended to make a contract."

2–004 **Conduct as offer.** An offer may be addressed either to an individual or to a specified group of persons or to the world at large; and it may be made expressly (by words) or by conduct. At common law, a person who had contracted to sell goods and tendered different goods (or a different quantity) might be considered to make an offer by conduct to sell the goods which he had tendered.[20] It seems that an offer to sell can still be made in this way, though by statute the dispatch of goods "without any prior request" may amount to a gift to the recipient, rather than to an offer to sell.[21]

2–005 **Inactivity as an offer.** A number of cases raise the further question whether the "conduct" from which an offer may be inferred can take the form of inactivity. The issue in these cases was whether an agreement to submit a dispute to arbitration could be said to have been "abandoned" by long delay, where, over a long period of time, neither party had taken any steps in the arbitration proceedings. In cases of "inordinate and inexcusable delay" of this kind, arbitrators now have a statutory power to dismiss the claim for want of prosecution[22] and it is also open to the parties expressly to provide for "lapse" of the claim if steps in the proceedings are not taken within a specified period.[23] Conversely, however, the statutory power to dismiss the claim for want of prosecution may be excluded by agreement,[24] and where it is so excluded the question of abandonment can still arise in the present context. Such a question could also arise in the context of the alleged abandonment of some other type of right or remedy,[25] to which no similar legislative provision extends. The arbitration cases indicate that, on the objective test, inactivity may amount to an offer of abandonment when combined with other circumstances (such as the destruction of relevant files),[26] even though those circumstances would not, of themselves, constitute sufficient evidence from which an offer could be inferred. But mere inactivity by one party is unlikely,[27] when standing alone, to have this effect, for it is equivocal and

---

[20] *Hart v. Mills* (1846) 15 L.J.Ex. 200; *cf. Steven v. Bromley & Son* [1919] 2 K.B. 722; *cf. Greenmast Shipping Co. S.A. v. Jean Lion et Cie. SA (The Saronikos)* [1986] 2 Lloyd's Rep. 277.

[21] Unsolicited Goods and Services Act 1971, ss.1, 6. Normally this statutory rule would not apply where goods were dispatched in response to the buyer's order, even if they were not in accordance with the order; but it might apply where the qualitative or quantitative difference between what was ordered and what was sent was extreme.

[22] Arbitration Act 1996, s.41(3), replacing Arbitration Act 1950, s.13A. Under s.13A, it had been held that the court could take into account delay occurring before the section came into force: *Yamashita-Shinnihon SS. Co. Ltd v. L'Office Cherifien des Phosphate (The Boucraa)* [1994] 1 A.C. 486, and that the court would *(mutatis mutandis)* apply the same principles to the power to dismiss arbitration proceedings as those which govern the dismissal of an action for want of prosecution: *James Lazenby & Co. v. McNicholas Construction Co. Ltd* [1995] 1 W.L.R. 615.

[23] See the GAFTA arbitration rules referred to in *Cargill SpA v. Kadinopoulos SA* [1992] 1 Lloyd's Rep. 1.

[24] Arbitration Act 1996, s.41(2) so provides.

[25] *cf. Amherst Ltd v. James Walker Goldsmith & Silversmith Ltd* [1983] Ch. 305; *Collin v. Duke of Westminster* [1985] Q.B. 581; *M.S.C. Mediterranean Shipping SA v. B.R.E. Metro Ltd* [1985] 2 Lloyd's Rep. 239; *Fenton Inns. Ltd v. Gothaer Versicherungsbank VVaG* [1991] 1 Lloyd's Rep. 172, 180.

[26] *The Splendid Sun* [1981] Q.B. 694, as explained in *The Hannah Blumenthal* [1983] 1 A.C. 854 (though this explanation was doubted in *Cie. Française d'Importation, etc., SA v. Deutsche Conti Handelsgesellschaft* [1985] 2 Lloyd's Rep. 592, 599); *Tracomin SA v. Anton C. Nielsen* [1984] 2 Lloyd's Rep. 195 (as to which see *post*, § 2–069, n. 76); *The Multibank Holsatia* [1988] 2 Lloyd's Rep. 486; for the question whether such an offer can be *accepted* by inactivity, see *post*, § 2–063.

[27] *Unisys International Services Ltd v. Eastern Countries Newspaper Group Ltd* [1991] 1 Lloyd's Rep. 538, 553 suggests that the possibility cannot be wholly ruled out; *cf. The Boucraa* [1994] 1 A.C. 486, 521 (describing the "abandonment" approach as "largely useless in practice").

generally explicable on other grounds, such as inertia or forgetfulness, or the tactical consideration that the party alleged to have made the offer does not wish to reactivate his opponent's counter-claims.[28] Consequently, it will not normally suffice to induce a reasonable person in the position of the other party to believe that an offer is being made[29]; and the mere fact that the other party nevertheless had this belief cannot suffice to turn the former party's inactivity into such an offer.[30]

Offer and invitation to treat. When parties negotiate with a view to making a contract, many preliminary communications may pass between them before a definite offer is made. One party may simply ask, or respond to a request, for information, or he may invite the other to make an offer. For example, in *Harvey v. Facey*[31] the claimants telegraphed to the defendants, "Will you sell us Bumper Hall Pen? Telegraph lowest cash price." The defendants replied, "Lowest cash price for Bumper Hall Pen £900." The claimants then telegraphed, "We agree to buy Bumper Hall Pen for £900 asked for by you." The Judicial Committee of the Privy Council held that the defendants' telegram was not an offer but merely a statement as to price; the claimants' second telegram was in fact an offer to buy, but as this had never been accepted by the defendants, there was no contract. Similarly, in *Gibson v. Manchester City Council*[32] it was held that a letter in which a local authority stated (in reply to an enquiry from the tenant of a council house) that it "may be prepared to sell" the house to him at a specified price was not an offer to sell the house: its purpose was simply to invite the making of a "formal application," amounting to an offer, from the tenant. On the same principle, a telephoned request for the supply of goods suitable for a prospective customer's purpose has been held to be only a "preliminary enquiry,"[33] the offer being made by conduct, when the supplier subsequently despatched the goods. **2–006**

A communication by which a party is invited to make an offer is commonly called an invitation to treat. It is distinguishable from an offer primarily on the ground that it is not made with the intention that it is to become binding as soon as the person to whom it is addressed simply communicates his assent to its terms. A statement is clearly not an offer if it expressly provides that the person who makes it is *not* to be bound merely by the other party's notification of assent but only when he himself has signed the document in which the statement is contained.[34] Apart from this type of case, the wording of the statement is not conclusive: it may be an invitation to treat although it contains the word **2–007**

---

[28] *Unisys* case, *supra* n. 27 at 553.

[29] *The Leonidas D.* [1985] 1 W.L.R. 925; *Cie Française d'Importation, etc., SA v. Deutsche Conti Handelsgesellschaft* [1985] 2 Lloyd's Rep. 592; *The Antclizo* [1988] 1 W.L.R. 603; *The Agrabele* [1987] 2 Lloyd's Rep. 223; *The Maritime Winner* [1989] 2 Lloyd's Rep. 506; *contra, The Golden Bear* [1987] 1 Lloyd's Rep. 330 (*sed quaere*: the decision was in part based on the decision at first instance in *The Agrabele* [1985] 2 Lloyd's Rep. 496, but this was reversed on appeal: [1987] 2 Lloyd's Rep. 223); *Ulysses Compania Naviera SA v. Huntington Petroleum Services (The Ermoupolis)* [1990] 1 Lloyd's Rep. 161, 166 see also *post*, § 2–064, n. 48); *Unisys* case, *supra* n. 27.

[30] *The Antclizo, supra*; Davenport (1988) 104 L.Q.R. 493.

[31] [1893] A.C. 552. See also *Clifton v. Palumbo* [1944] 2 All E.R. 497; *Scancarriers A/S v. Aotearoa International Ltd (The Barranduna)* [1985] 2 Lloyd's Rep. 419 (quotation of freight rates not an offer). But see *Philip & Co. v. Knoblauch*, 1907 S.C. 994 (*Harvey v. Facey* distinguished).

[32] [1979] 1 W.L.R. 294.

[33] *Interfoto Picture Library Ltd v. Stiletto Visual Programmes Ltd* [1989] 1 Q.B. 433, 436.

[34] *Financings Ltd v. Stimson* [1962] 1 W.L.R. 1184.

"offer"[35]; while a statement may *be* an offer although it is expressed as an "acceptance,"[36] or although it requests the person to whom it is addressed to make an "offer."[37]

2–008 **Distinction between offer and invitation to treat.** The distinction between offer and invitation to treat is often hard to draw, as it depends primarily on the elusive criterion of the intention of the person making the statement. But it does not depend entirely on this criterion. In certain stereotyped situations, the distinction is determined, at least prima facie, by rules of law. It may be that such rules can be displaced by evidence of contrary intention; but in the absence of such evidence they will determine the distinction between offer and invitation to treat, and they will do so without reference to the intention (actual or even objectively ascertained) of the maker of the statement. This is true, for example, in the cases of auction sales and shop window displays. These and other illustrations of the distinction will be discussed in §§ 2–009 to 2–021 below.

2–009 **Auctions.** At an auction sale the general rule is that the auctioneer's request for bids is not an offer which can be accepted by the highest bidder.[38] Instead it is a bid that constitutes an offer, and this the auctioneer may accept or reject. Accordingly the Sale of Goods Act 1979[39] provides that a sale by auction is completed when the auctioneer announces its completion by the fall of the hammer, or in other customary manner; and that until then any bid may be withdrawn. Similarly, the auctioneer can generally withdraw the lot before he accepts the bid. It seems, moreover, that the offer made by each bidder lapses[40] as soon as a higher bid is made. Thus if a higher bid is made and then withdrawn, the auctioneer can no longer accept the next highest.

2–010 **Auctions with and without reserve.** When property is put up for auction subject to a reserve price, there is no contract if the auctioneer by mistake purports to accept a bid lower than the reserve price.[41] Where the auction is without reserve, there is no contract *of sale* between the highest bidder and the *owner* of the property if the auctioneer refuses to accept the highest bid. But it has been held that the *auctioneer* is in such a case liable on a separate contract between him and the highest bidder that the sale will be without reserve.[42] Although a mere advertisement of an auction is not an offer to hold it,[43] the actual request for bids at the auction itself seems to be an offer by the auctioneer that he will on the owner's behalf accept the highest bid; and this offer is accepted by

---

[35] *Spencer v. Harding* (1870) L.R. 5 C.P. 561; *Clifton v. Palumbo, ante,* § 2–006, n. 31.

[36] *Bigg v. Boyd Gibbins Ltd* [1971] 1 W.L.R. 913; (1987) 87 L.Q.R. 307.

[37] *Harvela Investments Ltd v. Royal Trust Co. of Canada (C.I.) Ltd* [1986] A.C. 207.

[38] *Payne v. Cave* (1789) 3 T.R. 148; *British Car Auctions v. Wright* [1972] 1 W.L.R. 1519; (1973) 89 L.Q.R. 7.

[39] s.57(2).

[40] *Post,* § 2–088.

[41] *McManus v. Fortescue* [1907] 2 K.B. 1; on a sale of land, it must be expressly stated whether the sale is with reserve or not: Sale of Land by Auction Act 1867, s.5.

[42] *Warlow v. Harrison* (1859) 1 E. & E. 309; *cf. Johnston v. Boyes* [1899] 2 Ch. 73, 77. *Contra, Fenwick v. Macdonald, Fraser & Co. Ltd* (1904) 6 F. (Ct. of Sess.) 850; Slade (1952) 68 L.Q.R. 238; Gower, *ibid.* 457; Slade (1953) 69 L.Q.R. 21. Under the American Uniform Commercial Code (hereinafter referred to as U.C.C.) the goods may not be withdrawn once they have been put up, if the auction is without reserve: s.2–328(3).

[43] *Harris v. Nickerson* (1873) L.R. 8 Q.B. 286.

bidding. The question whether there is any consideration for such a contract between auctioneer and highest bidder is discussed in Chapter 3.[44]

Provision for resale in case of dispute. An auction sale may be conducted   **2–011** subject to the express stipulation that, "if any dispute[45] arises between two or more bidders, the lot in dispute shall be immediately put up again and resold." If the dispute arises after the lot has been knocked down to one bidder, it seems that there is a contract with him, subject to the condition subsequent that the sale may be annulled if a dispute immediately breaks out between two or more bidders.

Display of goods for sale. As a general rule, a display of goods at a fixed   **2–012** price in a shop window[46] or on a shelf in a self-service store[47] is an invitation to treat and not an offer; an offer may be made by a prospective buyer and this the retailer may accept or reject. The same is true of an indication of the price at which petrol is to be sold at a filling station[48]: the offer to buy is made by the customer and may be accepted by the seller's conduct in putting petrol into the tank.[49] The position may be different where the station operates a self-service system[50] and the customer has actually put petrol into his tank, for in such a case the seller has no effective choice of refusing to deal when payment is later tendered. The general rule applies to normal shop window or shelf displays; but it seems that it can be excluded by special circumstances: *e.g.* if the retailer has stated unequivocally that he will sell to the first customer who tenders the required price. The distinction between an offer and an invitation to treat depends, in the last resort, on the intention of the maker of the statement; and where his intention to be bound immediately on acceptance is sufficiently clear it is submitted that a shop window or shelf display may be an offer: thus a notice in a shop window stating that "We will beat any TV . . . price by £20 on the spot" has been described as "a continuing offer."[51] The customer may, indeed, still lose his bargain since the offer can be withdrawn at any time before it is accepted[52]; but if it is so withdrawn the person displaying the notice may incur criminal liability under legislation passed for the protection of consumers.[53] In the case of a self-service shop, acceptance of any offer which might be made by the terms

---

[44] *Post*, § 3–162.

[45] See *Richards v. Phillips* [1969] 1 Ch. 39.

[46] *Timothy v. Simpson* (1834) 6 C. & P. 499, 500; *Fisher v. Bell* [1961] 1 Q.B. 394 (actual decision reversed by Restriction of Offensive Weapons Act 1961, s.1; contrast Criminal Justice Act 1988, s.14A(1), as inserted by Offensive Weapons Act 1996, s.6: this refers only to selling). Dicta in *Wiles v. Maddison* [1943] 1 All E.R. 315, 317 may perhaps suggest that a shop window display is an offer. See also Winfield (1939) 55 L.Q.R. 499, 516–518.

[47] *Pharmaceutical Society of Great Britain v. Boots Cash Chemists (Southern) Ltd* [1953] 1 Q.B. 410; *cf. Lacis v. Cashmarts Ltd* [1969] 2 Q.B. 400; *Davies v. Leighton* [1978] Crim.L.R. 575. For the contrary view, see Ellison Kahn (1955) 72 S.A.L.J. 246, 250–253; *Lasky v. Economic Grocery Stores*, 319 Mass. 224, 65 N.E. 2d 305 (1946).

[48] *Esso Petroleum Ltd v. Commissioners of Customs & Excise* [1976] 1 W.L.R. 1, 5, 6, 11; *Richardson v. Worrall* [1985] S.T.C. 693, 717.

[49] *Re Charge Card Services* [1989] Ch. 417, 512; for acceptance by conduct, see *post* § 2–027.

[50] *cf. post*, § 2–013 at n. 56.

[51] *R. v. Warwickshire C.C., ex p. Johnson* [1993] A.C. 583, 588.

[52] *Post* § 2–080.

[53] Consumer Protection Act 1987, s.20(1): see *R. v. Warwickshire C.C., ex p. Johnson, supra*. The section applies also to misleading price indications relating to the supply of services, accommodation and other facilities. Such misleading indications could also conceivably amount to deceit. And see *post*, § 2–017.

of the display would not normally take place when the customer took the goods off the shelf, but only when he did some less equivocal act, such as presenting them for payment.[54]

2–013   **Other displays.** The principles stated in § 2–012 above also apply to other displays. Thus where a menu is displayed outside a restaurant, or handed to a customer, it seems that the proprietor only makes an invitation to treat,[55] the offer coming from the customer. On the other hand, a notice at the entrance to an automatic car-park may be an offer which can be accepted by driving in[56]; and a display of deck-chairs for *hire* has been held to be an offer.[57] There is no perfectly general answer to the question whether such displays are offers or invitations to treat; the answer depends in each case on the intention with which the display was made.[58]

2–014   **Advertisements of bilateral contracts.** Such advertisements are not often held to be offers. Thus a newspaper advertisement that goods are for sale is not generally an offer[59]; an advertisement that a scholarship examination will be held is not an offer to a candidate[60]; and the circulation of a price-list by a wine merchant has been held only to be an invitation to treat.[61] It has been said that, if such statements were offers, a merchant could be liable to everyone who purported to accept his offer even though his stocks were insufficient to meet the requirements of all the "acceptors."[62] But this result would not necessarily follow even if the advertisement were an offer; for it could be construed as one which expired as soon as the merchant's stock was exhausted. There is, again, no absolute rule determining the character of advertisements of bilateral contracts: they are normally invitations to treat, but they may be offers if the advertiser's intention to be bound immediately on acceptance is sufficiently clear.[63]

2–015   **Advertisements of unilateral contracts.** There are probably two reasons why advertisements of bilateral contracts are not commonly regarded as offers. First, such advertisements often lead to further bargaining, *e.g.* where a house is advertised for sale. Secondly, the advertiser may legitimately wish, before becoming bound, to assure himself that the other party is able (financially or otherwise) to perform his obligations under any contract which may result. Neither of these reasons applies in the case of a unilateral contract; and advertisements of such contracts are therefore commonly held to be offers. In the leading

---

[54] See *Lasky v. Economic Grocery Stores*, *supra*, n. 47. An alternative possibility is that the acceptance may take place before such presentation of the goods but be subject until then to the customer's power to cancel: see *Gillespie v. Great Atlantic & Pacific Stores*, 187 S.E. 3d 441 (1972); *Sheeskin v. Giant Food Inc.*, 318 A 2d 874 (1974). *cf. R. v. Morris* [1984] A.C. 320 where taking goods off the shelf of a self-service store *and changing the price-labels* was held to be an "appropriation" within Theft Act 1968, s.3(1); but it does not follow that at this stage there would for the purpose of the law of contract be an acceptance even if the shelf-display amounted to an offer: see *ibid.* 334.

[55] *cf. Guildford v. Lockyer* [1975] Crim.L.R. 235.

[56] *Thornton v. Shoe Lane Parking Ltd* [1971] 2 Q.B. 163, 169.

[57] *Chapelton v. Barry U.D.C.* [1940] 1 K.B. 532.

[58] *cf.* the cases discussed in § 2–018, *post.*

[59] *Partridge v. Crittenden* [1968] 1 W.L.R. 1204; contrast *Lefkowitz v. Great Minneapolis Surplus Stores*, 86 N.W. 2d. 689 (1957).

[60] *Rooke v. Dawson* [1895] 1 Ch. 480.

[61] *Grainger & Son v. Gough* [1896] A.C. 325.

[62] *ibid.* at 334.

[63] *cf.* the cases discussed in § 2–018, *post.*

case of *Carlill v. Carbolic Smoke Ball Co. Ltd*,[64] for example, the defendants issued an advertisement promising to pay £100 to any person who used a carbolic smoke ball made by them, in accordance with certain directions, and then caught influenza. This was held to be an offer, the defendants' intention to be bound[65] being made particularly clear by their statement that they had deposited £1,000 with their bankers "shewing our sincerity in the matter." A case nearer the borderline was *Bowerman v. Association of British Travel Agents Ltd*[66] where a package holiday had been booked with a tour operator who was a member of the defendant association (ABTA). A notice displayed on the tour operator's premises stated, *inter alia*, that in the event of the financial failure of an ABTA member before commencement of the holiday, "ABTA arranges for you to be reimbursed the money you have paid for your holiday." A majority of the Court of Appeal held that these words constituted an offer since, on the objective test,[67] they would reasonably be regarded as such by a member of the public booking a holiday with an ABTA member.

Rewards. Advertisements of rewards for the return of lost or stolen property, **2–016** or for information leading to the capture or conviction of a criminal, are commonly regarded as offers.[68] Some difficulty arises if, in cases of this kind, the information is given by several persons in succession. In one case it was held that the first person to give the information was alone entitled to the reward[69] as the offeror did not intend to pay more than once. This is no doubt the most likely construction; but an advertisement could be so worded as to impose a more extensive liability. The defendants' liability in *Carlill's* case would not have been limited to 10 persons merely because the advertisement stated that they had deposited only £1,000.

Other liability in connection with advertisements. A person who issues an **2–017** advertisement may be under some form of liability even though the advertisement does not amount to an offer. For example, a person who indicates by such an advertisement that he intends to sell goods when he in fact has no such intention might be liable in deceit to someone who suffered loss by acting in reliance on the statement; and he might incur criminal liability under legislation passed for the protection of consumers.[70] He may also be liable for false statements in advertisements relating to the characteristics of the subject-matter, or to the terms on which it is to be supplied.[71]

Timetables and passenger tickets. There is a remarkable diversity of views **2–018** on the question just when a contract of carriage is concluded between a carrier

---

[64] [1893] 1 Q.B. 256.

[65] Contrast *Lambert v. Lewis* [1982] A.C. 225, 262, *per* Stephenson L.J., affd. without reference to the point [1982] A.C. 271, *post*, § 2–151.

[66] [1995] N.L.J. 1815.

[67] *Ante*, §§ 2–001, 2–002.

[68] *e.g. Gibbons v. Proctor* (1891) 64 L.T. 594; *Williams v. Carwardine* (1833) 5 C. & P. 566; 4 B. & Ad. 621.

[69] *Lancaster v. Walsh* (1838) 4 M. & W. 16. Where two persons *together* supply the information, they may share a single reward: *Lockhart v. Barnard* (1845) 14 M. & W. 674.

[70] *e.g.* under Trade Descriptions Act 1968, s.14(1)(b): see *R. v. Thomson Holidays Ltd* [1974] Q.B. 592. See also Consumer Credit Act 1974, ss.45, 46; Consumer Protection Act 1987, s.20: *R. v. Warwickshire C.C., ex p. Johnson* [1993] A.C. 583; conceivably, an order might also be made under Pt. II of the Fair Trading Act 1973.

[71] *Post*, Chap. 6.

and an intending passenger. It has been said that railway carriers made offers by issuing advertisements stating the times at and conditions under which trains would run[72]; and that a road carrier made offers to intending passengers by the act of running buses.[73] Such offers could be accepted by an indication on the part of the passenger that he wished to travel: *e.g.* by applying for a ticket or getting on the bus. Another view is that the carrier makes the offer at a later stage, by issuing the ticket; and that this offer is accepted by the passenger's retention of the ticket without objection,[74] or even later, when he claims the accommodation offered in the ticket.[75] On this view, the passenger makes no more than an invitation to treat when he asks for a ticket to be issued to him; and the offer contained in the ticket may be made to, and accepted by, the passenger even though the fare is paid by a third party (*e.g.* the passenger's employer).[76] Where the booking is made in advance, through a travel agent, yet a third view has been expressed: that the contract is concluded when the carrier indicates, even before issuing the ticket, that he "accepts" booking,[77] or when he issues the ticket[78]: on this view, it is the passenger who makes the offer. The authorities yield no single rule; one can only say that the exact time of contracting depends in each case on the wording of the relevant document and on the circumstances in which it was issued.

2–019   **Tenders.** At common law, a statement that goods are to be sold by tender is not normally an offer to sell to the person making the highest tender[79]; it merely indicates a readiness to receive offers. Similarly, an invitation for tenders for the supply of goods or for the execution of works is, generally, not an offer,[80] even though the preparation of the tender may involve very considerable expense. The offer comes from the person who submits the tender and there is no contract until the person asking for the tenders accepts one of them. These rules may, however, be excluded by evidence of contrary intention: *e.g.* where the person who invites the tenders states in the invitation that he binds himself to accept the highest offer to buy[81] (or, as the case may be, the lowest offer to sell or to provide the specified services).[82] In such cases, the invitation for tenders may be regarded *either* as

---

[72] *Denton v. G.N. Ry.* (1856) 5 E. & B. 860; *Thompson v. L.M.S. Ry.* [1930] 1 K.B. 41, 47; perhaps because such companies could not refuse to carry? See now Railways Act 1993, s.123.

[73] *Wilkie v. L.P.T.B.* [1947] 1 All E.R. 258, 259.

[74] *Thornton v. Shoe Lane Parking Ltd* [1971] 2 Q.B. 163, 169; *Cockerton v. Naviera Aznar SA* [1960] 2 Lloyd's Rep. 450; the acceptance in such cases would be by conduct rather than by "silence": *cf. post*, § 2–069.

[75] *MacRobertson-Miller Airline Services v. Commissioner of State Taxation* [1975] A.L.R. 131; the principle resembles that stated in *Heskell v. Continental Express Ltd* [1950] 1 All E.R. 1033, 1037 in relation to the time of formation of a contract for the carriage of goods by sea.

[76] *Hobbs v. L. & S.W. Ry.* (1875) L.R. 10 Q.B. 111, 119, as explained in the *MacRobertson-Miller* case, *supra*, at 147; consideration for the promises of both parties would be provided on the principle of *Gore v. Van der Lann* [1967] 2 Q.B. 31, *post*, § 3–168.

[77] *Hollingworth v. Southern Ferries Ltd (The Eagle)* [1977] 2 Lloyd's Rep. 70; *Daly v. Gen. Steam Navigation Co. Ltd (The Dragon)* [1980] 2 Lloyd's Rep. 415 affg. [1979] 1 Lloyd's Rep. 257; *Oceanic Sun Line Special Shipping Co. v. Fay* (1988) 165 C.L.R. 97; *cf.* (in cases of carriage of goods by sea) *Gulf Steel Co. Ltd v. Al Khalifa Shipping Co. (The Anwar al Sabar)* [1980] 2 Lloyd's Rep. 261, 263. See also *British Airways Board v. Taylor* [1976] 1 W.L.R. 13.

[78] *Dillon v. Baltic Shipping Co. (The Mikhail Lermontov)* [1991] 2 Lloyd's Rep. 155, 159, *revsd.* on other grounds (1993) 176 C.L.R. 344.

[79] *Spencer v. Harding* (1870) L.R. 5 C.P. 561.

[80] *ibid.* at 564.

[81] *ibid.* at 563.

[82] See *William Lacey (Hounslow) Ltd v. Davis* [1957] 1 W.L.R. 932, 939.

itself an offer *or* as an invitation to submit offers coupled with an undertaking to accept the highest (or, as the case may be, the lowest) offer; and the contract is concluded as soon as the highest offer to buy (or lowest offer to sell, etc.) is communicated.[83] There is also an intermediate possibility. This is illustrated by a case[84] in which an invitation to submit tenders was sent by a local authority to seven selected parties; the invitation stated that tenders submitted after a specified deadline would not be considered. It was held that the authority was contractually bound to consider (though not to accept) a tender submitted before the deadline.

Public procurement. The common law position stated above is modified by   **2–020**
legislation, for example, by Regulations[85] which give effect to European Community Directives, the object of which is to prevent discrimination in the award of major contracts for public works, supplies and services in one member state against nationals of another member state. These Regulations restrict the freedom of the body seeking tenders to decide which tender it will accept and provide a remedy in damages for a person who has made a tender and is prejudiced by breach of the Regulations. A more detailed account of the topic is given in Chapter 10.[86]

Share offers. A company which, in commercial language,[87] makes an "offer   **2–021**
to the public" of new shares does not in law "offer" to allot the shares. It invites members of the public to apply for them, reserving the right to decide how many, if any, to allot to any particular applicant.[88] On the other hand a letter informing an existing shareholder of his entitlement under a "rights" issue of new shares is regarded as an offer.[89] This type of communication will set out the precise rights of the persons to whom it is addressed, so that it may be inferred that the company intends to be bound in relation to any shareholder who takes up his rights.

Place of making an offer. It may, for a variety of purposes, be important to   **2–022**
know exactly *where* an offer has been made: for example, in order to determine whether a contract can be sued on in a particular court.[90] For this purpose it has been held that an offer sent through the post had been made where it was

---

[83] *Harvela Investments Ltd v. Royal Trust of Canada (C.I.) Ltd* [1986] A.C. 207, 224–225.

[84] *Blackpool and Fylde Aero Club Ltd v. Blackpool B.C.* [1990] 1 W.L.R. 25. No decision was reached on the quantum of damages. See also *Fairclough Building v. Port Talbot B.C.* (1992) 62 B.L.R. 82.

[85] S.I. 1991 No. 2679; S.I. 1991 No. 2680, applied *R. v. Portsmouth C.C., ex p. Coles, The Times,* November 13, 1996; S.I. 1992 No. 3279; S.I. 1993 No. 3228, applied in *R. v. S of S for the Environment, ex p. Harrow L.B.C.* [1996] E.G.C.S. 2; Craig in (ed. Rose) *Consensus ad Idem, Essays in the Law of Contract in Honour of Guenter Treitel,* 148–151. See also Environmental Protection Act 1990, Sched. 2, Pt.II, applied in *R. v. Avon C.C., ex p. Terry Adams Ltd., The Times,* January 20, 1994.

[86] *Post,* § 10–029.

[87] And, indeed, in the terminology of Companies Act 1985, ss.59, 80(1) and 744 and of Financial Services Act 1986, s.158(4).

[88] *e.g. Hebb's Case* (1867) L.R. 4 Eq. 9; *Harris' Case* (1872) L.R. 7 Ch.App. 587; *Wall's Case* (1872) 42 L.J.Ch. 372; *cf. Wallace's Case* [1900] 2 Ch. 671; *National Westminster Bank plc v. I.R.C.* [1995] 1 A.C. 119, 126; *cf. Rust v. Abbey Life Ins. Co.* [1979] 2 Lloyd's Rep. 335 (property bonds).

[89] *Jackson v. Turquand* (1869) L.R. 4 H.L. 305.

[90] *Taylor v. Jones* (1875) 1 C.P.D. 87; *cf.* in criminal law, *Treacy v. D.P.P.* [1971] A.C. 537 (blackmail); contrast *R. v. Baxter* [1972] 1 Q.B. 1 (attempt to obtain by deception).

posted.[91] Since requirements of this kind are generally imposed by legislation, it is unsafe to lay down any general rule. The question where an offer was made must, in the last resort, turn on the construction of the relevant legislation.

2–023   **Time of making an offer.** Since an offer may expire by lapse of time,[92] the question *when* it was made may also be of importance, especially if there has been some delay in its transmission. In *Adams v. Lindsell*[93] an offer to sell wool was made in a letter which was misdirected by the offerors and consequently delayed by two days. On receipt of the letter, the offeree immediately posted an acceptance. It was held that there was a binding contract as the delay arose "entirely from the mistake of the" offerors. On the other hand, if the delay had been of such length as to make it clear to the offeree that the offer was "stale," it seems unlikely that the offeree could still have accepted. The emphasis placed in *Adams v. Lindsell* on the fault of the offerors also makes it possible to argue that a different rule might apply where the delay is due to some other factor, *e.g.* to an accident in the post. In such a case the time within which the offer could be accepted might more appropriately run from the moment at which the offer would, but for the accident, have been communicated[94] to the offeree.

3. The Acceptance

(a) *Definition*

2–024   **Acceptance defined.** An acceptance is a final and unqualified expression of assent to the terms of an offer. The objective test of agreement applies to an acceptance no less than to an offer.[95] On this test, a mere acknowledgement of an offer would not be an acceptance; nor is there an acceptance where a person who has received an offer to sell goods merely replies that it is his "intention to place an order."[96] Where the offer is made in alternative terms, the acceptance must make it clear to which set of terms the assent is directed. In *Peter Lind & Co. Ltd v. Mersey Docks & Harbour Board*[97] an offer to build a freight terminal was made by a tender quoting in the alternative a fixed, and a "cost-plus," price. The offeree purported to accept "your tender," and it was held that there was no contract.

2–025   **Continuing negotiations.** When parties carry on lengthy negotiations, it may be hard to say exactly when an offer has been made and accepted. As negotiations progress, each party may make concessions or new demands and the parties may in the end disagree as to whether they had ever agreed at all. The court must then look at the whole correspondence and decide whether, on its true construction, the parties had agreed to the same terms. If so, there is a contract even though both parties, or one of them, had reservations not expressed in the

---

[91] *Taylor v. Jones, supra.*
[92] *Post,* §§ 2–087—2–089.
[93] (1818) 1 B. & Ald. 681; Winfield (1939) 55 L.Q.R. at 499, 503–504.
[94] As to the meaning of "communicated" *cf. post,* §§ 2–041, 2–083.
[95] *Ante,* § 2–002.
[96] *O.T.M. Ltd v. Hydranautics* [1981] 2 Lloyd's Rep. 211, 214.
[97] [1972] 2 Lloyd's Rep. 234.

correspondence.[98] The court will be particularly anxious to hold that continuing negotiations have resulted in a contract where the performance which was the subject-matter of the negotiations has actually been rendered. In one such case a building sub-contract was held to have come into existence, even though agreement had not been reached when the work was begun, because during its progress outstanding matters were resolved by further negotiations[99]; and this contract may then be given retrospective effect to cover work done before its conclusion.[1]

Negotiation after apparent agreement. Businessmen do not, any more than   **2–026** the courts, find it easy to say precisely when they have reached agreement, and may sometimes continue to negotiate after they appear to have agreed to the same terms. The court will then look at the entire course of negotiations to decide whether an apparently unqualified acceptance did in fact conclude the agreement.[2] If it did, the fact that the parties continued negotiations after this point does not affect the existence of the contract between them,[3] unless the continued correspondence can be construed as an agreement to rescind the contract. *A fortiori*, the binding force of an oral contract is not affected or altered merely by the fact that, after its conclusion, one party sends to the other a document containing terms significantly different from those which had been orally agreed.[4]

Acceptance by conduct. An offer may be accepted by conduct. For example,   **2–027** an offer to buy goods can be accepted by supplying them[5]; an offer to sell goods, made by sending them to the offeree, can be accepted by using them,[6] and an offer contained in a request for services can be accepted by beginning to render

---

[98] *Kennedy v. Lee* (1817) 3 Mer. 441; *cf. Cie de Commerce, etc.* v. *Parkinson Stove Co.* [1953] 2 Lloyd's Rep. 487; B.S.E., 17 M.L.R. 476; *Port Sudan Cotton Co. v. Govindaswamy Chettiar & Sons* [1977] 2 Lloyd's Rep. 5; *Thoresen Car Ferries Ltd v. Weymouth Portland B.C.* [1977] 2 Lloyd's Rep. 614; *O.T.M. Ltd v. Hydranautics* [1981] 2 Lloyd's Rep. 211, 215.

[99] *G. Percy Trentham Ltd v. Archital Luxfer Ltd* [1993] 1 Lloyd's Rep. 25. *Peter Lind's* case (*supra*, n. 97) shows that the factor of performance of work is not decisive, though it may (as in that case) give the performing party a restitutionary claim.

[1] *G. Percy Trentham Ltd v. Archital Luxfer Ltd*, *supra* at n. 99.

[2] *Hussey v. Horne-Payne* (1878) 4 App.Cas. 311; *Bristol, Cardiff & Swansea Aerated Bread Co. v. Maggs* (1890) 44 Ch.D. 616; *British Guiana Credit Corporation v. Da Silva* [1965] 1 W.L.R. 248; *Container Transport International Inc. v. Oceanus Mutual, etc., Association* [1984] 1 Lloyd's Rep. 476; *Asty Maritime Co. Ltd v. Rocco Guiseppe & Figli (The Astyanax)* [1985] 2 Lloyd's Rep. 109, 112; *Hofflinghouse & Co. Ltd v. C. Trade SA (The Intra Transporter)* [1986] 2 Lloyd's Rep. 132; *Pagnan SpA v. Granaria B.V.* [1986] 1 Lloyd's Rep. 547; *Pagnan SpA v. Feed Products Ltd* [1987] 2 Lloyd's Rep. 601, 619; *Ignazio Messina & Co. v. Polskie Linie Oceaniczne* [1995] 2 Lloyd's Rep. 566 (no contract); *Frota Oceanica Brasileira SA v. Steamship Mutual Underwriting Association (The Frotanorte)* [1996] 2 Lloyd's Rep. 461 (no contract as matters of substance remained unresolved).

[3] *Perry v. Suffields Ltd* [1916] 2 Ch. 187; *Davies v. Sweet* [1962] 2 Q.B. 300; *Cranleigh Precision Engineering Ltd* v. *Bryant* [1965] 1 W.L.R. 1293; *Harmony Shipping Co. SA v. Saudi-Europe Line Ltd (The Good Helmsman)* [1981] 1 Lloyd's Rep. 377, 409, 416.

[4] *Jayaar Impex Ltd v. Toaken Group Ltd* [1996] 2 Lloyd's Rep. 437.

[5] *Harvey v. Johnson* (1848) 6 C.B. 305; *cf. Steven v. Bromley & Son* [1919] 2 K.B. 722, 728; *Greenmast Shipping Co. SA v. Jean Lion et Cie (The Saronikos)* [1986] 2 Lloyd's Rep. 277; *cf. Interfoto Picture Library Ltd v. Stiletto Visual Programmes Ltd* [1989] Q.B. 433, 436; *Re Charge Card Services* [1989] Ch. 417 (*ante* § 2–012); contrast *Capital Finance Co. Ltd v. Bray* [1964] 1 W.L.R. 323. As to counter-offers, see *post*, §§ 2–084, 2–085.

[6] *Weatherby v. Banham* (1832) 5 C. & P. 228; *Brogden v. Metropolitan Ry.* (1877) 2 App.Cas. 666, *infra*, at n. 14; *cf. Hart v. Mills* (1846) 15 L.J.Ex. 200. It is assumed that the goods are not "unsolicited" within Unsolicited Goods and Services Act 1971, ss.1, 6 (*ante*, § 2–004).

them.[7] But conduct will only amount to acceptance if it is clear that the offeree did the act with the intention (actual or apparent) of accepting the offer. Thus a buyer's taking delivery of goods after the conclusion of an oral contract of sale will not amount to his acceptance of written terms which differ significantly from those orally agreed and which are sent to him by the seller after the making of that contract but before taking delivery.[8] That conduct is then referable to the oral contract rather than to the attempted later variation. Nor is a company's offer to insure a car accepted by taking the car out on the road, if there is evidence that the driver intended to insure with another company.[9] A fortiori, there is no acceptance where the offeree's conduct clearly indicates an intention to reject the offer. This was the position in a Scottish case where a notice on a package containing computer software stated that opening the package would indicate acceptance of the terms on which the supply was made, and the customer returned the package unopened.[10]

2-028   **Establishing the terms of contracts made by conduct.** Where an offer or an acceptance or both are alleged to have been made by conduct, the terms of the agreement are obviously more difficult to ascertain than where the agreement was negotiated by express words. The difficulty may be so great as to force the court to conclude that no agreement was reached at all.[11] But sometimes the court can resolve the uncertainty by applying the standard of reasonableness[12] or by reference to another contract (whether between the same parties or between one of them and a third party[13]), or even to a draft agreement between them which had never matured into a contract. For example, in *Brogden v. Metropolitan Ry.*[14] a railway company submitted to a merchant a draft agreement for the supply of coal. He returned it marked "approved" but also made a number of alterations to it, to which the railway company did not expressly assent; but the company accepted deliveries of coal under the draft agreement for two years. It was held that once the company began to accept these deliveries there was a contract on the terms of the draft agreement.[15]

2-029   **Correspondence between acceptance and offer.** A communication may fail to take effect as an acceptance because it attempts to vary the terms of the offer. Thus an offer to sell 1,200 tons of iron is not accepted by a reply asking for 800

---

[7] *Smit International Singapore Pte Ltd v. Kurnia Dewi Shipping SA (The Kurnia Dewi)* [1997] 1 Lloyd's Rep. 553.

[8] *Jayaar Impex Ltd v. Toaken Group Ltd* [1996] 2 Lloyd's Rep. 437.

[9] *Taylor v. Allon* [1966] 1 Q.B. 304. The objective principle (*supra*, §§ 2–001, 2–002) clearly could not apply in this case, as the conduct alleged to constitute the acceptance had never come to the notice of the offeror. *cf.*, in another context, *Re Leyland Daf Ltd* [1994] 4 All E.R. 300, *affd. sub nom. Powdrill v. Watson* [1995] 2 A.C. 394.

[10] *Beta Computers (Europe) v. Adobe Systems (Europe)* 1996 S.L.T. 604; even opening the package would not necessarily have an acceptance so as to incorporate the printed terms: see Tapper in (ed. Rose) *Consensus ad Idem, Essays in the Law of Contract in Honour of Guenter Treitel*, 287–288.

[11] *Capital Finance Co. Ltd v. Bray* [1964] 1 W.L.R. 323.

[12] Sale of Goods Act 1979, s.8(2); Supply of Goods and Services Act 1982, s.15(1); *cf. Steven v. Bromley & Son* [1919] 2 K.B. 722.

[13] *e.g. Pyrene Co. Ltd v. Scindia Navigation Co. Ltd* [1954] 2 Q.B. 402.

[14] (1877) 2 App.Cas. 666; see also *Jones v. Daniel* [1894] 2 Ch. 332; *Port Sudan Cotton Co. v. Govindaswamy Chettiar & Sons* [1977] 2 Lloyd's Rep. 5; contrast *D. & M. Trailers (Halifax) Ltd v. Stirling* [1978] R.T.R. 468. *U.K. Safety Group Ltd v. Heane* [1998] 2 B.C.L.C. 208.

[15] Contrast *Jayaar Impex Ltd v. Toaken Group Ltd* [1996] 2 Lloyd's Rep. 437, where the conduct of the buyer was referable, not to the draft sent by the seller, but to the earlier oral agreement (*supra* n. 8) between the parties.

tons[16]; an offer to pay a *fixed* price for building work cannot be accepted by a promise to do the work for a *variable* price[17]; an offer to *supply* goods cannot be accepted by an "order" for their "*supply and installation.*"[18] Nor, generally, can an offer be accepted by a reply which varies one of its other terms (*e.g.* that specifying the time of performance),[19] or by a reply which introduces an entirely new term.[20] Such a reply is not an acceptance; but it may, on the contrary, be a counter-offer,[21] which the original offeror can then accept or reject. On the other hand, statements which are not intended to vary the terms of the offer, or to add new terms, do not vitiate the acceptance, even where they do not precisely match the words of the offer.[22] It is, moreover, submitted that, if the new term merely makes express what would otherwise be implied, it does not destroy the effectiveness of the acceptance.[23] Nor will it have this effect if it is merely a declaration by the acceptor that he is prepared to grant some indulgence to the offeror, *e.g.* to condone late payment in return for specified interest.[24] Similarly, it is submitted, that an acceptance which asks for some indulgence to the offeree is, nevertheless, effective, so long as it is clear that the offeree is prepared to perform even if the indulgence is not granted: *e.g.* to buy for cash if his request for credit is refused. The test in each case is whether the offeror reasonably regarded the purported acceptance "as introducing a new term into the bargain and not as a clear acceptance of the offer."[25] It is also possible for a communication which contains new terms to amount: (1) to an acceptance of the offer, and (2) to a new offer to enter into a further contract. In such a case, there will be a contract on the terms of the original offer, but none on the terms of the new offer, unless that, in turn, is accepted.[26]

Subsequent formal document inaccurate. After parties have reached agreement, the offer and acceptance may be set out in formal documents. The purpose of such documents may be to record the agreed terms[27]; and where one of the documents performs this function accurately while the other fails to do so, the discrepancy between the offer and the acceptance will not prevent the formation of a contract. In such a case, the court can rectify the document which fails to   **2–030**

---

[16] *Tinn v. Hoffman & Co.* (1873) 29 L.T. 271; *cf. Holland v. Eyre* (1825) 2 Sim. & St. 194; *Jordan v. Norton* (1838) 4 M. & W. 155; *Harrison v. Battye* [1975] 1 W.L.R. 58.

[17] *North West Leicestershire DC v. East Midlands Housing Association* [1981] 1 W.L.R. 1396.

[18] *Butler Machine Tool Co. Ltd v. Ex-Cell-O Corp. (England) Ltd* [1979] 1 W.L.R. 401.

[19] *ibid.*; *North West Leicestershire DC v. East Midlands Housing Association* [1981] 1 W.L.R. 1396; *cf. Brinkibon Ltd v. Stahag Stahl und Stahlwarenhandelsgesellschaft mbH* [1983] 2 A.C. 34.

[20] *Jackson v. Turquand* (1869) L.R. 4 H.L. 305; *Jones v. Daniel* [1894] 2 Ch. 332; *Von Hatzfeldt-Wildenburg v. Alexander* [1912] 1 Ch. 284; *Love & Stewart Ltd v. S. Instone & Co. Ltd* (1917) 33 T.L.R. 475; *Northland Airliners v. Dennis Ferranti Meters Ltd* (1970) 114 S.J. 845; *Lark v. Outhwaite* [1991] 2 Lloyd's Rep. 132, 139.

[21] *Post*, § 2–084.

[22] *Clive v. Beaumont* (1847) 1 De G. & Sm. 397; *Simpson v. Hughes* (1897) 66 L.J.Ch. 334; *Butler Machine Tool Co. Ltd v. Ex-Cell-O Corporation (England) Ltd* [1979] 1 W.L.R. 401.

[23] *Lark v. Outhwaite* [1991] 2 Lloyd's Rep. 132, 139. For another qualification of the requirement of exact correspondence between offer and acceptance, see Vienna Convention on Contracts for the International Sale of Goods (*post* § 2–057), Art. 19(2).

[24] *Harris's Case* (1872) L.R. 7 Ch.App. 587.

[25] *Global Tankers Inc. v. Amercoat Europa N.V.* [1975] 1 Lloyd's Rep. 666, 671; *cf. G. Percy Trentham Ltd v. Archital Luxfer Ltd* [1993] 1 Lloyd's Rep. 25, 28.

[26] *Monrovia Motorship Corp. v. Keppel Shipyard (Private) Ltd (The Master Stelios)* [1983] 1 Lloyd's Rep. 356.

[27] *e.g. O.T.M. Ltd v. Hydranautics* [1981] 2 Lloyd's Rep. 211, 215; *cf. post*, § 2–106.

record the agreed terms, and a contract will be concluded on those agreed terms.[28]

2–031 **The "battle of forms."** The rule that offer and acceptance must correspond gives rise to problems where one or both of the parties wish to contract by reference to a "standard form" contractual document. Two situations call for discussion.

2–032 **One party's "usual conditions".** First, A may make an offer to B by asking for a supply of goods or services. B may reply that he is willing to supply the goods or services on his "usual conditions." Prima facie, B's statement is a counter-offer which A is free to accept or reject, and he may accept it by accepting the goods or services. If he does so, there is a contract between A and B, though the question whether B's "usual conditions" actually form part of it may depend on a number of further factors which will be discussed in Chapter 12.[29]

2–033 **Each party refers to own conditions.** Secondly, *each* party may purport to contract with reference to his own set of standard terms and these terms may conflict. In *B.R.S. v. Arthur V. Crutchley Ltd*[30] the claimants delivered a consignment of whisky to the defendants for storage. Their driver handed the defendants a delivery note purporting to incorporate the claimants' "conditions of carriage." The note was stamped by the defendants: "Received under [the defendants'] conditions." It was held that this amounted to a counter-offer which the claimants had accepted by handing over the goods, and that the contract therefore incorporated the defendants' and not the claimants' conditions.

2–034 **"Last shot" doctrine.** This case gave some support to the so-called "last shot" doctrine: *i.e.* to the view that, where conflicting communications are exchanged, each is a counter-offer, so that if a contract results at all (*e.g.* from an acceptance by conduct) it must be on the terms of the final document in the series leading to the conclusion of the contract.[31] But this view requires some modification in the light of *Butler Machine Tool Co. Ltd v. Ex-Cell-O Corporation (England) Ltd.*[32] In that case sellers offered to supply a machine for a specified sum. The offer was expressed to be subject to certain terms and conditions, including a "price escalation clause" by which the amount actually payable by the buyers was to depend on "prices ruling upon date of delivery." In reply the buyers placed an order for the machinery on a form setting out their own terms and conditions, which differed from those of the sellers in containing no price-escalation clause and also in various other respects.[33] It also contained a tear-off

---

[28] *Domb v. Isoz* [1980] Ch. 548, 559.

[29] *Post*, §§ 12–008—12–018. If the test of reasonable notice or signature is satisfied, the contract will be on B's conditions.

[30] [1968] 1 All E.R. 811; *cf. A. Davies & Co. (Shopfitters) v. William Old* (1969) 113 S.J. 262; *O.T.M. Ltd v. Hydranautics* (1981) 2 Lloyd's Rep. 211; *Muirhead v. Industrial Tank Specialities Ltd* [1986] Q.B. 507, 530; *Souter Automation v. Goodman Mechanical Services* (1984) 34 Build.L.R. 81.

[31] As in *Zambia Steel & Building Supplies v. James Clark & Eaton Ltd* [1986] 2 Lloyd's Rep. 225.

[32] [1979] 1 W.L.R. 401, especially at 405; Adams (1979) 94 L.Q.R. 481; Rawlings (1979) 42 M.L.R. 715.

[33] *Ante*, § 2–029 at nn. 18 and 19.

slip to be signed by the sellers and returned to the buyers, stating that the sellers accepted the order "on the terms and conditions stated therein." The sellers did sign the slip and returned it with a letter saying that they were "entering" the order "in accordance with" the offer. This communication from the sellers was held to be an acceptance of the buyers' counter-offer[34] so that the resulting contract was on the buyer's terms, and the sellers were not entitled to the benefit of the price escalation clause. The sellers' reply to the buyers' order did not prevail (though it was the "last shot" in the series) because the reference in it to the original offer was not made for the purpose of re-iterating all its terms, but only for the purpose of identifying the subject-matter. It would, however, have been possible for the sellers to have turned their final communication into a counter-offer by explicitly referring in it not only to the subject-matter of the original offer, but also to all its other terms. In that case no contract would have been concluded, since the buyers had made it clear before the machine was delivered that they did not agree to the "price escalation" clause.[35] Thus it is possible by careful draftsmanship to avoid losing the battle of forms, but not (if the other party is equally careful) to win it. In the *Butler Machine Tool* case, for example, sellers' conditions included one by which their terms were to "prevail over any terms and conditions in Buyer's order"; but this failed (in consequence of the terms of the buyers' counter-offer) to produce the effect desired by the sellers.[36] The most that the draftsman can be certain of achieving is the stalemate situation in which there is no contract at all. Such a conclusion will often be inconvenient,[37] though where the goods are nevertheless delivered it will presumably lead to a liability on the part of the buyers to pay a reasonable price.[38]

Documents sent after contract made. The above discussion is concerned with the effect of the submission of a document or documents containing terms *before* the alleged contract is made. The submission of such a document by one party *after* the making of the contract will not affect the existence of the contract[39]; nor will the terms of the document form part of the contract unless they are, in turn, accepted as variations of the contract, either expressly or by conduct. **2–035**

Acceptance of tenders. We have seen that the submission of a tender normally amounts to an offer[40]; and the effect of an "acceptance" of such a tender turns on the construction of the acceptance and the tender in each case. Where a tender is submitted, *e.g.* for the erection of a building, a binding contract will normally arise from acceptance of the tender, unless it is expressly stipulated that **2–036**

---

[34] *Per* Lawton and Buckley L.JJ.; Lord Denning M.R. also uses this analysis, but prefers the alternative approach of considering "the documents ... as a whole": see 405 and *cf. ante*, § 2–025.

[35] At 406, *per* Lawton L.J.

[36] *cf. Matter of Doughboy Industries Inc.*, 233 N.Y.S. 2d 488, 490 (1962): "The buyer and seller accomplished a legal equivalent to the irresistible force colliding with the immoveable object."

[37] It seems to have been rejected for this reason in *Johnson Matthey Bankers Ltd v. State Trading Corp. of India* [1984] 1 Lloyd's Rep. 427.

[38] *cf. Peter Lind & Co. Ltd v. Mersey Docks & Harbour Board* [1972] 2 Lloyd's Rep. 234, *ante*, § 2–024; McKendrick (1988) 8 O.J.L.S.197.

[39] *Jayaar Impex Ltd v. Toaken Group Ltd* [1996] 2 Lloyd's Rep. 437; *cf. post*, § 2–106.

[40] *Ante*, § 2–019.

there is to be no contract until certain formal documents have been executed.[41] But greater difficulty arises in construing an "acceptance" of a tender to supply, for example, "such quantities (not exceeding a specified amount) as you may order." The person to whom such a tender is submitted does not incur any liability merely by "accepting" it: he becomes liable only when he places an order for goods,[42] and he would not be bound to place any order at all[43] unless he had (expressly or by necessary implication[44]) indicated in his invitation for tenders that he would do so.[45] The party submitting the tender also becomes bound, once a definite order has been placed, to fulfil it.[46] Whether he can withdraw before this point, or avoid liability with respect to future orders, depends on the interpretation of the tender. He can do so if the tender means: "I will supply such quantities as you may order."[47] But he will not be entitled to withdraw if the tender means "I hereby bind myself to execute orders which you may place," and if this promise is supported by some consideration.[48]

2–037   **Acceptance by tender.** There are exceptional cases in which an invitation for tenders may amount to an offer, *e.g.* where the person issuing the invitation binds himself to accept the highest or, as the case may be, the lowest tender.[49] The acceptance then takes the form of the submission of a tender; but difficulties can arise where several tenders are made and one (or more) of them takes the form of a so-called "referential bid." In *Harvela Investments Ltd v. Royal Trust Co. of Canada (C.I.) Ltd*[50] an invitation for the submission of "offers" for the purchase of shares was addressed to two persons; it stated that the prospective sellers bound themselves to accept the "highest offer." One of the persons to whom the invitation was addressed made a bid of a fixed sum while the other submitted a "referential bid" undertaking to pay either a fixed sum or a specified amount in excess of the bid made by the other, whichever was the higher amount. It was held that the submission of the fixed bid concluded the contract and that the "referential bid" was ineffective. In reaching this conclusion, the House of Lords stressed that the bids were, by the terms of the invitation, to be confidential, so that neither bidder would know the amount bid by the other. In these circumstances the object of the invitation, which was to ascertain the highest amount that each of the persons to whom it was addressed was willing to pay, would have been defeated by allowing it to be accepted by a "referential bid."

2–038   **Acceptance in ignorance of offer: unilateral contracts** If services are performed so that the terms of an offer to pay for them are in fact satisfied, but the performer is not aware that the offer has been made, can he claim payment when

---

[41] *Post*, § 2–106.
[42] *Percival Ltd v. L.C.C. Asylums, etc., Committee* (1918) 87 L.J.K.B. 677.
[43] *cf. Churchward v. R.* (1865) L.R. 1 Q.B. 173; *R. v. Demers* [1900] A.C. 103.
[44] *e.g. Sylvan Crest Sand & Gravel Co. v. U.S.*, 150 F.2d 642 (1945).
[45] *cf. Harvela Investments Ltd v. Royal Trust Co. of Canada (C.I.) Ltd* [1986] A.C. 207.
[46] *Great Northern Ry. v. Witham* (1873) L.R. 9 C.P. 16; *cf.* the similar rule applied to "declarations" under an "open cover" insurance in *Citadel Insurance Co. v. Atlantic Union Insurance Co.* [1982] 2 Lloyd's Rep. 543.
[47] *G.N. Ry. v. Witham* (1873) L.R. C.P. 16, 19.
[48] *Percival Ltd v. L.C.C. Asylums, etc., Committee* (1918) 87 L.J.K.B. 677, 678; *Miller v. F. A. Sadd & Son Ltd* [1981] 3 All E.R. 265. For an exception to the requirement of consideration in the law of insurance, see the *Citadel* case, *supra*, n. 46 at 546; *post*, § 3–161.
[49] *Ante*, § 2–019.
[50] [1986] A.C. 207.

he becomes aware of the offer? In some jurisdictions it has been held that a person who gives information for which a reward has been offered cannot claim the reward unless he knew of the offer at the time of giving the information[51]; and the position has been said to be the same where that person once knew of the offer but had, at the time of the alleged acceptance, forgotten it.[52] The English case of *Gibbons v. Proctor*[53] is sometimes thought to support the contrary view, but the actual decision can probably be explained on the ground that the plaintiff did know of the offer of reward by the time the information was given on his behalf to the person named in the advertisement.[54] To allow recovery where the plaintiff did *not* know of the offer when he gave the information may raise doctrinal difficulties but it is hard to see that it prejudices any legitimate interest of the promisor.

Acceptance in ignorance of offer: bilateral contracts. Different considera-   **2–039**
tions may apply where a person who does acts amounting to acceptance of an offer of a bilateral contract does these acts in ignorance of the offer. For in that case the actor may (if the acts amount to an acceptance) not only acquire rights but also incur liabilities under the contract, and it may be unfair to subject him to these if at the time of the alleged acceptance he was not aware of the fact that an offer had been made to him; and thus had no intention of entering into a contract. In *Upton R.D.C. v. Powell*[55] the defendant, whose house was on fire, telephoned the Upton police and asked for "the fire brigade." He was entitled to the services of the Pershore fire brigade free of charge as he lived in its district; but the police called the Upton fire brigade, in the belief that the defendant lived in that district. The Upton fire brigade for a time shared this belief and thought "that they were rendering gratuitous services in their own area."[56] It was held that the defendant was contractually bound to pay for these services. But even if the defendant's telephone call was an offer, it is hard to see how the Upton fire brigade's services, given with no thought of reward, could be an acceptance. It would have been better to give the claimants a restitutionary remedy than to hold that there was a contract. The case was concerned only with the rights of the fire brigade, but, if there was a contract, the fire brigade also owed more extensive duties than they would have owed, had they been volunteers. It may well be hard to subject a person who thinks he is a volunteer to the more stringent duties of a contractor.[57] Similar reasoning applies where the effect of an alleged bilateral contract is not to impose liabilities on a party but simply to deprive him of rights.

---

[51] *Bloom v. American Swiss Watch Co.* (1915) App.Div. 100 (S. Afr.); American authorities are divided: see Corbin, *Contracts*, § 59.

[52] *R. v. Clarke* (1927) 40 C.L.R. 277, 241.

[53] (1891) 64 L.T. 594; 55 J.P. 616; *cf. Neville v. Kelly* (1862) 12 C.B.(N.S.) 740.

[54] "The information ultimately reached Penn at a time when the plaintiff knew that the reward had been offered": 55 J.P. 616.

[55] [1942] 1 All E.R. 220; Mitchell, (1997) 12 J.C.L. 78; for the extent of the fire brigade's duty apart from contract, see *John Monroe (Acrylics) Ltd v. London Fire & Civil Defence Authority* [1997] 2 Lloyd's Rep. 161.

[56] At 221.

[57] *cf. B.S.C. v. Cleveland Bridge & Engineering Co. Ltd* [1984] 1 All E.R. 504, 510. *Quaere* what the position should be where one party thinks that he is giving or getting a gratuitous service while the other thinks that he is contracting; *i.e.* if the fire brigade had intended from the beginning to charge for their services.

It has accordingly been held that an alleged offer to abandon arbitration proceedings cannot be accepted unless the persons claiming to have accepted it understood or believed at the time of the alleged acceptance that such an offer was being made.[58]

2–039   **Motive for the acceptance.** A person who knows of the offer may do the required act of acceptance with some motive other than that of accepting the offer. In *Williams v. Carwardine*[59] the defendant offered a reward of £20 to anyone who gave information leading to the conviction of the murderers of Walter Carwardine. The plaintiff knew of the offer, and, thinking that she had not long to live, signed a "voluntary statement to ease my conscience, and in hopes of forgiveness hereafter." This statement resulted in the conviction of the murderers. It was held that the plaintiff had brought herself within the terms of the offer and was entitled to the reward. Patteson J. added: "We cannot go into the plaintiff's motives."[60] Similarly, in *Carlill v. Carbolic Smoke Ball Co.*,[61] the claimant recovered the £100, although her predominant motive in using the smoke ball was (presumably) to avoid catching influenza. But in the Australian case of *R. v. Clarke*[62] a reward had been offered for information leading to the arrest and conviction of the murderers of two police officers. Clarke, who knew of the offer and was himself suspected of the crime, gave information leading to the conviction of the culprits. He admitted that he gave the information to clear himself of the charge, and with no thought of claiming the reward. His claim for the reward failed as he had not given the information "in exchange for the offer."[63] It seems that an act which is *wholly* motivated by factors other than the existence of the offer cannot amount to an acceptance[64]; but if the existence of the offer plays some part, however small, in inducing a person to do the required act, there is a valid acceptance of the offer.

2–040   **Cross-offers.** It seems that there is generally no contract if two persons make identical cross-offers, neither knowing of the other's offer when he made his own: *e.g.* if A writes to B offering to sell B his car for £5,000 and B simultaneously writes to A offering to buy the car for £5,000. The most natural reaction to letters which cross in this way would be for one of the parties to communicate with the other to make sure that there was indeed an agreement between them. To hold that there was a contract without some such further communication might cause considerable surprise to one of the parties, or possibly to both. The view that "cross-offers are not an acceptance of each other"[65] can therefore be supported not only on the theoretical ground that the requirements of offer and

---

[58] *Tracomin SA v. Anton C. Nielsen* [1984] 2 Lloyd's Rep. 195, 203; and see *ante* § 2–005, *post* § 2–064.

[59] (1833) 5 C. & P. 566; 4 B. & Ad. 621; it must be assumed that the claimant knew of the offer; *Carlill v. Carbolic Smoke Ball Co. Ltd* [1892] 2 Q.B. 484, 489, n. 2. See also *England v. Davidson* (1840) 11 A. & E. 856; *Smith v. Moore* (1845) 1 C.B. 438; and *cf. Bent v. Wakefield Bank* (1878) 4 C.P.D. 1; *Fallick v. Barber* (1813) 1 M. & S. 108. See also Theft Act 1968, s.23, penalising advertisements of rewards for stolen goods which state that no questions will be asked, etc.

[60] (1833) 4 B. & Ad. at 623.

[61] [1893] 1 Q.B. 256; *ante*, § 2–015.

[62] (1927) 40 C.L.R. 227; contrast *Simonds v. U.S.*, 308 F. 2d 160 (1962).

[63] (1927) 40 C.L.R. 227, 233; *Tracomin SA v. Anton C. Nielsen* [1984] 2 Lloyd's Rep. 195, 203.

[64] *Lark v. Outhwaite* [1991] 2 Lloyd's Rep. 132, 140.

[65] *Tinn v. Hoffman & Co.* (1873) 29 L.T. 271, 278.

acceptance are not satisfied, but also on the practical ground that it accords with normal commercial expectations and that it promotes certainty.

(b) *Communication of Acceptance*

General requirement of communication. The general rule is that an accep-   **2–041**
tance must be communicated to the offeror.[66] Accordingly, there is no contract where a person writes an acceptance on a piece of paper which he simply keeps[67]; where a company resolves to accept an application for shares but does not communicate the resolution to the applicant[68]; where a person decides to accept an offer to sell goods to him and instructs his bank to pay the offeror but neither he nor the bank gives notice of this fact to the offeror[69]; and where a person communicates the acceptance only to his own agent.[70] The main reason for the rule is that it could cause hardship to the offeror to be bound without knowing that his offer had been accepted. It follows that, so long as the offeror knows of the acceptance, there can be a contract even though the acceptance was not brought to his notice *by the offeree*.[71] However, there will be no contract if the communication is made by a third party without the authority of the offeree in circumstances indicating that the offeree's decision to accept was not yet regarded by him as irrevocable.[72]

What amounts to communication. For an acceptance to be "communi-   **2–042**
cated" it must normally be brought to the notice of the offeror. Thus there is no contract if the words of acceptance are "drowned by an aircraft flying overhead"; or if they are spoken into a telephone after the line has gone dead or become so indistinct that the offeror does not hear them.[73] The requirement of "communica-tion" may, however, in some circumstances be satisfied even though the accep-tance has not actually come to the notice of the offeror: *e.g.* where a written notice of acceptance is left by the offeree at the offeror's address.[74]

Exceptions to requirement of communication of acceptance. In the follow-   **2–042A**
ing cases an acceptance is, or may be, effective although it is not communicated to the offeror.
   (1) Waiver. First, the offer may expressly or impliedly waive the requirement of communication of acceptance. One situation in which this may be the case is

---

[66] *McIver v. Richardson* (1813) 1 M. & S. 557; *Mozley v. Tinkler* (1835) 1 C.M. & R. 692; *Ex p. Stark* [1897] 1 Ch. 575; *Holwell Securities Ltd v. Hughes* [1974] 1 W.L.R. 155, 157; *Allied Marine Transport Ltd v. Vale do Rio Doce Navegaçao SA (The Leonidas D.)* [1985] 1 W.L.R. 925, 937.
[67] *Kennedy v. Thomassen* [1929] 1 Ch. 426; *Brogden v. Metropolitan Ry.* (1877) 2 App. Cas. 666, 692.
[68] *Best's Case* (1865) 2 D.J. & S. 650; *cf. Gunn's Case* (1867) L.R. 3 Ch.App. 40.
[69] *Brinkibon Ltd v. Stahag Stahl und Stahlwarenhandelsgesellschaft mbH* [1983] 2 A.C. 34.
[70] *Hebb's Case* (1867) L.R. 4 Eq. 9; *Kennedy v. Thomassen* [1929] 1 Ch. 426.
[71] *Bloxham's Case* (1864) 33 Beav. 529; (1864) 4 D.J. & S. 447; *Levita's Case* (1867) L.R. 3 Ch.App. 36.
[72] This appears to be the best explanation of *Powell v. Lee* (1908) 99 L.T. 284.
[73] *Entores Ltd v. Miles Far East Corp.* [1955] 2 Q.B. 327, 332.
[74] *cf. post* § 2–083.

that in which an offer invites acceptance by conduct. For example, where an offer
to supply goods is made by sending them to the offeree it may be accepted by
simply using[75-76] them; and where an offer to buy goods is made by ordering
them, it may sometimes be accepted by simply despatching them.[77] And a tenant
can accept an offer of a new tenancy by simply staying on the premises.[78] Where
the contract is unilateral, the requirement of communication is almost always
waived. Performance of the required act is sufficient without any previous
intimation of acceptance.[79] Thus in *Carlill v. Carbolic Smoke Ball Co.*[80] the court
rejected the argument that the claimant should have notified the defendants of her
acceptance of their offer. The contract which arises[81] between a bank which has
issued a credit card to one of its customers and the retailer to whom the customer
presents the card has similarly been described as unilateral,[82] so that it can be
accepted by the retailer's dealing with the customer without any need for the
retailer's acceptance to be communicated to the bank.[83]

(2) *"Fault" of offeror.* The offeror may be precluded from denying that the
acceptance was communicated if it was "his own fault that he did not get it"; *e.g.*
"if the listener on the telephone does not catch the words of acceptance but
nevertheless does not . . . ask for them to be repeated"[84]; or if the acceptance is
sent during business hours by telex but is simply not read by anyone in the
offeror's office when it is there transcribed on his machine.[85] If such a message
is received out of business hours, it probably takes effect at the beginning of the
next business day.[86]

(3) *Communication to agent.* The acceptance may be communicated, not to the
offeror personally, but to his agent. The effect of such a communication depends
on the agent's authority.[87] It concludes a contract if the agent is authorised to
receive the acceptance, but not if he is authorised only to *transmit* it to the
offeror: *e.g.* if a written acceptance is handed to a messenger. In the latter case
the acceptance takes effect only when it is communicated to the offeror (unless
the case falls within one of the other exceptions to the general rule requiring the
acceptance to be communicated to the offeror).

[75-76] *Weatherby v. Banham* (1832) 5 C. & P. 228; *cf. Minories Finance Ltd v. Afribank Nigeria Ltd*
[1995] 1 Lloyd's Rep. 134, 140; it is assumed that the goods are not "unsolicited" within Unsolicited
Goods and Services Act 1971, ss.1, 6 (*ante*, § 2–004).

[77] *Port Huron Machinery Co. v. Wohlers*, 207 Iowa 826, 221 N.W. 843 (1928); *cf.* U.C.C.,
s.2–206(1); *Smit International Singapore Pte. Ltd v. Kurnia Dewi Shipping S.A. (The Kurnia Dewi)*
[1997] 1 Lloyd's Rep. 553, 559.

[78] *Roberts v. Hayward* (1828) 3 C. & P. 432; but not if the tenant disclaims the intention to accept:
Glossop v. Ashley [1921] 2 K.B. 451.

[79] *Shipton v. Cardiff Corp.* (1917) 87 L.J.K.B. 51; *Davies v. Rhondda U.D.C.* (1917) 87 L.J.K.B.
166.

[80] [1893] 1 Q.B. 256, *ante*, § 2–015.

[81] *Post*, §§ 3–037, 19–007.

[82] *First Sport Ltd v. Barclays Bank plc* [1993] 1 W.L.R. 1228, 1234 (where the card had been stolen
and been presented to the retailer by the thief).

[83] *ibid.* at 1234–1235.

[84] *Entores Ltd v. Miles Far East Corp.* [1955] 2 Q.B. 327, 333.

[85] *cf. Tenax Steamship Co. Ltd v. The Brimnes (Owners) (The Brimnes)* [1975] Q.B. 929; and see
post § 2–083.

[86] *Schelde Delta Shipping B.V. v. Astarte Shipping Ltd (The Pamela)* [1995] 2 Lloyd's Rep. 249,
252; *Galaxy Energy International Ltd v. Novorossiyk Shipping Co. (The Peter Schmidt)* [1998] 2
Lloyd's Rep. 1.

[87] *Henthorn v. Fraser* [1892] 2 Ch. 27, 33.

(4) Acceptance sent by post. An acceptance sent by post often takes effect before it is communicated. The exact effects of such an acceptance are discussed in the following paragraphs.

(c) *Posted Acceptance*

The posting rule.[88] What is usually regarded as the general rule[89] is that a   **2–043**
postal acceptance takes effect when the letter of acceptance is posted.[90] A letter is "posted" for this purpose when it is put in the control of the Post Office or of one of its employees authorised to *receive* letters. Handing letters to a postman authorised to *deliver* letters is not posting.[91] An acceptance by telegram similarly takes effect when the telegram is communicated to a person authorised to receive it for transmission to the addressee[92]; and it seems that this rule would apply to telemessages, which have replaced inland telegrams. The "posting" rule is probably best explained as one of convenience; it generally favours the offeree for the reasons stated in §§ 2–048 to 2–052 below.

Conditions of applicability. The posting rule applies only if it is reasonable   **2–044**
to use the post. This will normally be the case if the offer itself is made by post. It may be reasonable to use the post even though the offer was made orally if immediate acceptance was not contemplated and the parties lived at a distance.[93] On the other hand it would not normally be reasonable to attempt to reply by a posted letter of acceptance to an offer made by telex[94] or by telephone, fax or e-mail. Nor would it be reasonable to accept by post if the postal service was, to the acceptor's knowledge, disrupted.[95]

Instantaneous communications. The posting rule does not apply to accep-   **2–045**
tances made by some "instantaneous" mode of communication, *e.g.* by telephone or by telex.[96] The reason why the rule does not apply in such cases is that the acceptor will often know at once that his attempt to communicate was unsuccessful, so that he has the opportunity of making a proper communication.[97] A person who accepts by a letter which goes astray, on the other hand, may not know of the loss or delay until it is too late to make another communication. Such

---

[88] Winfield (1939) 55 L.Q.R. 499; Nussbaum (1926) 36 Col.L.Rev. 920; Ellison Kahn (1955) 72 S.A.L.J. 246; Evans (1966) 15 I.C.L.Q. 553; Gardner (1992) 12 O.J.L.S. 170.

[89] But see *post*, §§ 2–048 *et seq.*

[90] *Henthorn v. Fraser* [1892] 2 Ch. 27, 33; *Adams v. Lindsell* (1818) 1 B. & Ald. 681; *Potter v. Sanders* (1846) 6 Hare 1; *Harris' Case* (1872) L.R. 7 Ch.App. 587.

[91] *Re London & Northern Bank* [1900] 1 Ch. 220.

[92] *Bruner v. Moore* [1904] 1 Ch. 305; *cf. Stevenson Jacques & Co. v. McLean* (1880) 5 Q.B.D. 346. See also *Cowan v. O'Connor* (1888) 20 Q.B.D. 640 (place of acceptance).

[93] *e.g.* in *Henthorn v. Fraser* [1892] 2 Ch. 27. Such a written acceptance of an oral offer does not, however, create a "contract by correspondence" within Law of Property Act 1925, s.46: *Stearn v. Twitchell* [1985] 1 All E.R. 631.

[94] *cf. Quenerduaine v. Cole* (1883) 32 W.R. 185 (telegram).

[95] *Bal v. Van Staden* [1902] T.S. 128.

[96] *Entores Ltd v. Miles Far East Corp.* [1955] 2 Q.B. 327; *Brinkibon Ltd v. Stahag Stahl und Stahlwarengesellschaft mbH* [1983] 2 A.C. 34; *cf. N.V. Stoomv Maats "De Maas" v. Nippon Yusen Kaisha (The Pendrecht)* [1980] 2 Lloyd's Rep. 56, 66; *Gill & Duffus Landauer Ltd v. London Export Corp. GmbH* [1982] 2 Lloyd's Rep. 627; *cf. Schelde Delta Shipping B.V. v. Astarte Shipping Ltd (The Pamela)* [1995] 2 Lloyd's Rep. 249, 252 (telexed notice withdrawing ship from charterparty); and (in tort) *Diamond v. Bank of London & Montreal* [1979] Q.B. 333.

[97] See the *Entores* case, *supra*, at 333 and the *Brinkibon* case, *supra*, at 43.

instantaneous communications are therefore governed by the general rule[98] that an acceptance must be actually communicated, subject to the other exceptions to that rule stated in § 2–042 above.

2–046   **Dictated telegrams, telemessages, faxes and e-mails.** There is no authority on the question whether an acceptance by telegram or telemessage dictated over the telephone takes effect when the message is dictated by the sender or when it is communicated to the addressee. It is submitted that such an acceptance should, in accordance with the above reasoning,[99] take effect as soon as it is dictated[1]; for if it later goes astray, the acceptor is unlikely to have any means of knowing this fact until it is too late to make a further communication. Fax messages seem to occupy an intermediate position. The sender will know at once if his message has not been received at all, and where this is the position the message should not amount to an effective acceptance. But if the message is received in such a form that it is wholly or partly illegible, the sender is unlikely to know this at once, and it is suggested that an acceptance sent by fax might well be effective in such circumstances. The same principles should apply to other forms of instantaneous communication such as e-mail: here again the effects of unsuccessful attempts to communicate should depend on whether the sender of the message knows (or has the means of knowing) at once of any failure in communication.

2–047   **Terms of the offer.** The posting rule can be excluded by the terms of the offer. For this purpose, it is not necessary to say expressly that the acceptance will take effect only when it has been actually communicated. In *Holwell Securities Ltd v. Hughes*[2] an offer to sell a house was made in the form of an option "to be exercisable by notice in writing to the Intending Vendor." Such a notice was posted but did not arrive. It was held that there was no contract of sale as the offer, on its true construction, required actual communication of acceptance.

2–048   **Operation of the posting rule.** The posting rule is essentially one of convenience.[3] The English authorities support its application in three situations discussed in §§ 2–049 to 2–052 below. It should not, however, be thought that the rule will be mechanically applied to all situations which it might, by a process of apparently logical deduction, be thought to govern. It has been said that the rule will not be applied where it would lead to "manifest inconvenience and absurdity"[4]; so that the question of its application to a further group of cases discussed in §§ 2–053 to 2–056 below depends on practical considerations and on the balance of convenience.

2–049   **Posted acceptance preceded by uncommunicated withdrawal.** A posted acceptance prevails over a withdrawal of an offer which was posted before the acceptance but which had not yet reached the offeree when the acceptance was

---

[98] *Ante,* § 2–042.
[99] At n. 97, *supra.*
[1] Treitel, *The Law of Contract* (10th ed., 1991), pp. 25–26; *contra* Winfield (1939) 55 L.Q.R. 499, 515.
[2] [1974] 1 W.L.R. 155; *cf. New Hart Builders Ltd v. Brindley* [1975] Ch. 342.
[3] *Brinkibon* case (*supra,* n. 96 at 41; *Gill & Duffus Landauer* case (*supra* n. 96 at 631).
[4] *Holwell Securities Ltd v. Hughes* [1974] 1 W.L.R. 157, 161.

posted.[5] In practice, this is probably the most important application of the rule. It can be justified on the ground that, if the acceptance did not prevail, reliance could not be placed on a posted offer. It also operates as a restriction on the otherwise unfettered power[6] of the offeror to withdraw his offer.

Acceptance lost or delayed in the post. A posted acceptance takes effect **2–050** even though it never reaches the offeror because it is lost through an accident in the post[7]; and the same rule probably applies where the acceptance is merely delayed through an accident in the post,[8] *i.e.* the contract is concluded at the time of posting of the acceptance. In *Household Fire Insurance Co. Ltd v. Grant*,[9] for example, the defendant had applied for shares in a company: this application amounted to an offer by him to subscribe for the shares.[10] An acceptance, in the form of a letter of allotment, was posted to him but never received. Some three years later, the company went into liquidation, and it was held that the defendant was a shareholder and so liable for calls on the shares. The case has certain unusual features: namely that the initial deposit on application for the shares was not actually paid, the defendant being instead credited with an equivalent sum due to him from the company; and that dividends declared by the company were not actually paid out to the defendant but simply credited to his account with the company. But for these circumstances the defendant would necessarily have become aware (long before the end of the three years) of the fact that he was regarded by the company as a shareholder.

The decision in *Household Fire Insurance Co. Ltd v. Grant* was reached only **2–051** by a majority and involved the overruling of a previous contrary decision.[11] This indicates that the arguments of convenience for and against applying the posting rule to such a situation are finely balanced. On the one hand, it may be hard to hold an offeror liable on an acceptance which, through no fault of his own, was never received by him; on the other it may be equally hard to deprive the offeree of the benefit of an acceptance if he had taken all reasonable steps to communicate it. Moreover, each party may act in reliance on his (perfectly reasonable) view of the situation: the offeror may enter into other contracts, believing that his offer had not been accepted, while the offeree may refrain from doing so, believing that he had effectively accepted the offer. In this situation, English law favours the offeree on the grounds that it is the offeror who "trusts to the post"[12] and that the offeror can safeguard himself by stipulating in the offer that the acceptance must be actually communicated to him.[13] These arguments may be generally valid but they are not wholly convincing. The offer may be a counter-offer, in which case it will be the ultimate offeree who originally trusted to the

---

[5] *Harris' Case* (1872) L.R. 7 Ch.App. 587; *Byrne & Co. v. Leon van Tienhoven* (1880) 5 C.P.D. 344; *Henthorn v. Fraser* [1892] 2 Ch. 27; *Re London & Northern Bank* [1900] 1 Ch. 200.

[6] *Post*, §§ 2–080, 3–160.

[7] *Household Fire Insurance Co. Ltd v. Grant* (1879) 4 Ex.D. 216.

[8] See *Dunlop v. Higgins* (1848) 1 H.L.C. 381, which would probably be followed in England though it is expressly restricted (at 402) to Scots law.

[9] (1879) 4 Ex.D. 216.

[10] *Ante*, § 2–021.

[11] *British & American Telegraph Co. v. Colson* (1871) L.R.Ex. 108.

[12] (1879) 4 Ex.D. 216, 223.

[13] *ibid.*

post. Or the offer may be made on a form prepared by the offeree, in which case he and not the offeror will, for practical purposes, be in control of its terms.

2–052 **Priorities.** A contract is taken to be made at the time when the acceptance was posted, so as to take priority over another contract affecting the same subject-matter made after the posting of the first acceptance.[14] This application of the posting rule can perhaps be explained as a reward for the superior diligence of the first acceptor.

2–053 **Misdirected letter of acceptance.** A letter of acceptance may be lost or delayed because it bears a wrong or an incomplete address, or because it is not properly stamped. Normally such defects will be due to the carelessness of the offeree; and, although there is no English authority precisely in point,[15] it is submitted that the posting rule should not apply to such cases. Although an offeror may have to take the risk of accidents in the post, it would be unreasonable to impose on him the further risk of the acceptor's carelessness. These arguments do not apply where the misdirection is due to the fault of the *offeror—e.g.* where his own address is incompletely or illegibly given in the offer itself.[16] In such a case, the offeror should not be allowed to rely on the fact that the acceptance was misdirected (except perhaps where his error in stating his own address was obvious to the offeree; for in such a case the offeror's fault would not be the effective cause of the misdirection of the acceptance). It is submitted that a misdirected acceptance should take effect (if at all) at the time which is least favourable to the party responsible for the misdirection.

2–054 **Garbled telegram or telemessage of acceptance.** In *Henkel v. Pape*[17] the claimant invited the defendant to make an offer to buy 50 rifles; and the defendant, not wanting this number, telegraphed "send *three* rifles." The telegram reached the claimant in the form "send *the* rifles" and the claimant despatched 50. It was held that the defendant was not bound to accept more than three. Here the garbled telegram was an offer, but such a communication could also be an acceptance: for example where, in response to an offer to sell 50, the buyer despatches a telemessage saying "send *the* rifles." It is submitted that this would be a valid acceptance (so long as it was reasonable for the buyer to accept by telemessage) even if the telemessage arrived in the form "send *three* rifles." If the offeror has to take the risk of loss or delay in the post, there seems to be no good reason why he should not also take the risk of errors in the transmission of a telemessage; for in each case the offeree will have no means of knowing that something has gone wrong until it is too late to make another, proper, communication.[18]

2–055 **Revocation of posted acceptance.** There is no English authority on the question whether a posted acceptance can be revoked by a later communication

---

[14] *Potter v. Sanders* (1846) 6 Hare 1.

[15] See, by way of analogy, *Getreide-Import Gesellschaft v. Contimar* [1953] 1 W.L.R. 207 and *ibid.* 793.

[16] *cf. Townsend's Case* (1871) L.R. 13 Eq. 148 (the actual reasoning of which is obsolete since *Household Fire Insurance Co. Ltd v. Grant* (1879) 4 Ex.D. 216).

[17] (1870) 6 Ex. 7.

[18] *cf. ante* § 2–045.

(such as a telex) which reaches the offeror before, or at the same time as, the acceptance. One view is that the revocation has no effect since, once a contract has been concluded by the posting of the acceptance, it cannot be dissolved by the act of one party.[19] But this apparently "logical" deduction from the "posting rule" overlooks the fundamental point that that rule is only one of convenience.[20] Hence the issue is whether the offeror could be unjustly prejudiced by allowing the offeree to rely on the subsequent revocation. On the one hand, it can be argued that the offeror cannot be prejudiced since he was not entitled to have his offer accepted and cannot have relied on its having been accepted if he did not yet know of the acceptance. On the other hand it can be argued that, once the acceptance has been posted, the offeror can no longer withdraw his offer,[21] and that reciprocity demands that the offeree should likewise not be allowed to withdraw his acceptance. For if the offeree were allowed to do this he could speculate, without risk to himself, at the offeror's expense. He could post an acceptance and hold the offeror bound if the market moved in his own favour, but retract the acceptance by an overtaking communication if the market moved against him, while the offeror had no similar freedom of action. It has been suggested that the offeror should take the risk of such a revocation, just as he takes the risk of loss or delay[22]; but while the offeror may take the risks of accidents in the post, it is submitted that he should not have to bear risks due entirely to the conduct of the offeree.[23]

So far it has been assumed that the offeror wants to hold the offeree to the **2–056** contract notwithstanding the revocation. It is also possible for the offeror to have acted in reliance on the revocation; *e.g.* by selling the subject-matter of the original offer to a third party. In such a case it is submitted that the offeree should not be entitled to change his mind yet again and rely on his letter of acceptance with the object of claiming damages from the offeror. The offeree's subsequent purported revocation could in such a case be regarded as an offer to rescind the contract, accepted by the offeror's conduct in relation to subject-matter; communication of such acceptance could be deemed to have been waived. Alternatively, the purported revocation could be regarded as repudiation in breach of contract, giving the offeror the power to put an end to his obligations under the contract by "accepting" the breach.[24]

---

[19] This view is sometimes said to be supported by *Wenkheim v. Arndt* (N.Z.) 1 J.R. 73 (1873), where the defendant by letter accepted an offer of marriage: *her mother* sent a telegram purporting to cancel the acceptance. The actual decision was that the mother had no authority to act on behalf of her daughter in this way, so that the claimant recovered damages of one farthing. The view stated in the text is supported by *Morrison v. Thoelke*, 155 So. 2d 889 (1963) and by *A to Z Bazaars (Pty.) Ltd v. Minister of Agriculture* (1974) (4) S.A. 392 (c) (discussed by Turpin [1975] C.L.J. 25); but contradicted by *Dick v. U.S.*, 82 F.Supp. 326 (1949). It is also sometimes said to be contradicted by *Dunmore v. Alexander* (1830) 9 Shaw 190, but there the first letter was probably an offer; only the dissenting judge regarded it as an acceptance. See generally Hudson (1966) 82 L.Q.R. 169. *cf. Kinch v. Bullard* [1998] 4 All E.R. 650 (notice which, by virtue of Law of Property Act 1925 s.196(3), had taken effect on being left at a person's place of abode, but without having been actually communicated to him, could not thereafter be withdrawn by sender).

[20] *Ante*, § 2–043.

[21] *Ante*, § 2–049.

[22] Hudson, *supra*, n. 19.

[23] *cf. ante* § 2–053.

[24] *post*, § 25–001.

2–057   **International sales.** The Vienna Convention on Contracts for the International Sale of Goods[25] (which has not yet been ratified by the United Kingdom) governs not only the rights and duties of the parties to, but also the formation of, such contracts. Under the Convention an offer takes effect when it "reaches" the offeree[26] and an acceptance when it "reaches" the offeror,[27] *i.e.* (in both cases) when it is communicated to the addressee or delivered to his address.[28] Thus there is no contract if the acceptance is lost in the post; but if the acceptance is delayed in transmission, it is effective, unless the offeror informs the offeree promptly on its receipt that he regards the offer as having lapsed.[29] Once an offer has become effective, it cannot be revoked after the offeree has dispatched his acceptance[30]: this again preserves the English position that a posted acceptance prevails over a previously posted withdrawal (referred to in the Convention as a revocation). An acceptance may be withdrawn by a communication which reaches the offeror before (or at the same time as) the acceptance would have become effective[31] if there had been no such withdrawal.

(d) *Prescribed Mode of Acceptance*

2–058   **Method must generally be complied with.** An offer which requires the acceptance to be expressed or communicated in a specified way can generally be accepted only in that way. Thus if the offeror asks for the acceptance to be sent to a particular place one sent elsewhere will not bind him[32]; nor will he be bound by an oral acceptance if he has asked for one to be expressed in writing.[33] This rule is particularly strict where the offer is contained in an option.[34]

2–059   **Purported acceptance as counter-offer.** It is sometimes possible for a purported acceptance which does not comply with the prescribed method to be regarded as a counter-offer and for a contract to come into existence when that counter-offer is in turn accepted.[35] Since such acceptance may be effected by conduct,[36] the contract may be concluded without any further communication between the parties after the original, ineffective, acceptance.

2–060   **Other equally efficacious mode.** Stipulations as to the mode of acceptance are usually made by the offeror with some particular object in view, *e.g.* to obtain a speedy acceptance, or one expressed (for the sake of certainty) in a particular

---

[25] Honnold, *Uniform Law for International Sales* (2nd ed., 1988); Bianca and Bonnell (eds.), *Commentary on the International Sales Law* (1987); Schlechtriem (ed.), *Commentary on the UN Convention on International Sale of Goods* (1998); Mullis, *Vienna Convention on Contracts for the International Sale of Goods* (1998); Feltham [1981] J.B.L. 346; Nicholas (1989) 105 L.Q.R. 201.

[26] Art. 15(1).

[27] Art. 18(2).

[28] Art. 24.

[29] Art. 21(2).

[30] Art. 16(1); "dispatch" is not defined.

[31] Art. 22.

[32] *Frank v. Knight* (1937) O.P.D. 113; *cf. Eliason v. Henshaw* (1819) 4 Wheat. 225; *Walker v. Glass* [1979] N.I. 129.

[33] *Financings Ltd v. Stimson* [1962] 1 W.L.R. 1184.

[34] *Holwell Securities Ltd v. Hughes* [1974] 1 W.L.R. 157.

[35] *Wettern Electricity Ltd v. Welsh Development Agency* [1983] Q.B. 796.

[36] As in the *Wettern Electricity* case, *supra*; provided, however, that such conduct is accompanied by the requisite contractual intention: see *Harvela Investments Ltd v. Royal Trust Co. of Canada (C.I.) Ltd* [1986] A.C. 207 and *post*, § 2–147; for counter-offers, see *ante* § 2–029; *post* § 2–084.

form. It seems that an acceptance which accomplishes that object just as well as, or better than, the stipulated method may bind the offeror. For this purpose, the court must first decide, as a matter of construction, what object it was that the offeror had in view. For example, a requirement that the acceptance must be sent by letter by return of post may "fix the time for acceptance and not the manner of accepting."[37] In that case an acceptance by telex would suffice. But such an acceptance would not be effective if the offeror's object (on the true construction of the offer) was to have a full and signed record of the acceptance.

Method of acceptance waived. Even if the prescribed method of acceptance is not complied with, the offeror would no doubt be bound if he had acquiesced in a different mode of acceptance and had so waived the stipulated mode.   2–061

Terms of offer drawn up by offeree. The rules relating to failure to use a prescribed mode of acceptance are traditionally based on two assumptions: that the offer was drawn up by the offeror; and that stipulations as to the mode of acceptance were made by him for his own benefit. It is, however, becoming increasingly common for the offer to be made on a form drawn up by the offeree: *e.g.* where a customer submits a proposal to enter into a hire-purchase agreement; or where an offer is made by tender on a form of tender issued by the offeree. Stipulations as to the mode of acceptance in such documents are usually intended for the benefit and protection of the *offeree*. If the offeree accepts in some other way, this will often be evidence that he has waived the stipulation; and it is submitted that the acceptance ought to be treated as effective unless it can be shown that failure to use the stipulated mode has prejudiced the offeror.[38]   2–062

(e) *Silence*

Offeree generally not bound. As a general rule, an offeree who does nothing in response to an offer is not bound by its terms. This is so even though the offer provides that it can be accepted by silence. Thus in *Felthouse v. Bindley*[39] an uncle offered to buy a horse from his nephew for £30 15s., adding "If I hear no more about him I shall consider the horse is mine at £30 15s." The uncle brought an action for conversion against an auctioneer who had sold the horse by mistake after having been informed by the nephew that it had already been sold to the uncle. It was held that, as the nephew's intention to accept the offer had never been communicated to the uncle, there was no contract of sale, and that accordingly the horse did not belong to the uncle at the time of the auction. Where the offeree does not wish to accept the offer, it is generally undesirable to put him to the trouble and expense of refusing the offer. In *Felthouse v. Bindley*, however, the nephew did intend to accept the offer; and the terms of the uncle's offer seem to amount to a waiver of the requirement of communicating the acceptance.[40]   2–063

---

[37] *Tinn v. Hoffman & Co.* (1873) 29 L.T. 271, 278; *cf. Manchester Diocesan Council for Education v. Commercial & General Investments Ltd* [1970] 1 W.L.R. 242; *Edmond Murray v. P.S.B. International Foundations* (1992) 33 Con.L.R. 1.

[38] See *Robophone Facilities v. Blank* [1966] 1 W.L.R. 1428 and *cf.* the *Manchester Diocesan* case, *supra*, n. 37; from this point of view these cases are, it is submitted, to be preferred to *Financings Ltd v. Stimson* [1962] 1 W.L.R. 1184.

[39] (1862) 11 C.B.(N.S.) 869; affd. (1863) 1 N.R. 401; Miller (1972) 35 M.L.R. 489; *cf. Financial Techniques (Planning Services) v. Hughes* [1981] I.R.L.R. 32.

[40] *Ante*, § 2–042.

The actual decision is, in view of these facts, hard to support, but this is no criticism of the general rule laid down in the case.

2–064   The question whether silence may amount to an acceptance binding the offeree has also arisen in the arbitration cases (discussed in § 2–005 above) in which the issue was whether an agreement to abandon an earlier agreement to submit a claim to arbitration could be inferred from inactivity in the form of long delay in prosecuting the claim. Such a delay is now in certain circumstances a statutory ground for dismissing the claim for want of prosecution[41]; but the statutory power to dismiss claims on this ground can be excluded by contrary agreement[42]; and similar questions of agreement to abandon *other* types of claim could still be governed by the common law principles developed in the arbitration cases. In these cases, it had been held that, even if one party's inactivity could be regarded as an offer to abandon the arbitration,[43] the mere silence or inactivity of the other did not normally amount to an acceptance. For one thing, such inactivity was often[44] equivocal,[45] being explicable on other grounds (such as forgetfulness or delay on the part of the offeree's solicitors).[46] For another, acceptance could not, as a matter of law, be inferred from silence alone[47] "save in the most exceptional circumstances."[48]

2–065   **Can offeree exceptionally be bound?** As the above reference to "exceptional circumstances" suggests, there may be exceptions to the general rule that an offeree is not bound by silence. If the offer has been solicited by the offeree, the argument that he should not be put to the trouble of repudiating it loses much of its force,[49] especially if the offer is made on a form provided by the offeree[50] and that form stipulates that silence may amount to acceptance.[51] Again, if there is a course of dealing between the parties, the offeror may be led to suppose that silence amounts to acceptance: *e.g.* where his offers to buy goods have in the past been accepted as a matter of course by the despatch of the goods in question.[52]

---

[41] Arbitration Act 1996 s.41(3).

[42] *ibid.* s.41(2).

[43] *Ante*, § 2–005.

[44] But not always: see § 2–065 at n. 53.

[45] *e.g. Jayaar Impex Ltd v. Toaken Group Ltd* [1996] 2 Lloyd's Rep. 437, 445.

[46] For acceptance by silence and conduct, see *post*, § 2–069.

[47] *Allied Marine Transport Ltd v. Vale do Rio Doce Navegaçao SA (The Leonidas D.)* [1985] 1 W.L.R. 925, 927; *Rafsanjan Pistachio Producers Co-operative v. Bank Leumi (U.K.) plc* [1992] 1 Lloyd's Rep. 513, 542; *Exmar N.V. v. BP Shipping Ltd (The Gas Enterprise)* [1993] 2 Lloyd's Rep. 352, 357, affd. without reference to this point *ibid.* at 364; *Vitol SA v. Norelf Ltd* [1996] A.C. 800, 812. Such "exceptional circumstances" may be illustrated by *André & Cie SA v. Marine Transocean Ltd (The Splendid Sun)* [1981] Q.B. 694 (where the acceptance may have been by conduct: *post*, § 2–069, n. 76), though it has been said that this case is hard to reconcile with *The Leonidas D, supra*: see *Food Corp. of India v. Antclizo Shipping Corp. (The Antclizo)* [1987] 2 Lloyd's Rep. 130, 149, affd. [1988] 1 W.L.R. 607.

[48] *The Leonidas D., supra*, n. 47; *Cie Française d'Importation, etc. v. Deutsche Continental Handelsgesellschaft* [1985] 2 Lloyd's Rep. 592, 598; *Gebr. van Weelde Sheepvaartkantoor B.V. v. Compania Naviera Orient SA (The Agrabele)* [1987] 2 Lloyd's Rep. 223, 234–235. *Excomm Ltd v. Guan Guan Shipping (Pte) Ltd (The Golden Bear)* [1987] 1 Lloyd's Rep. 330 is hard to reconcile with these cases and was apparently doubted in *The Antclizo, supra* n. 47, [1987] 2 Lloyd's Rep. at 147.

[49] *cf. Rust v. Abbey Life Ins. Co.* [1979] 2 Lloyd's Rep. 335, *post*, § 2–070.

[50] *cf. ante*, § 2–062.

[51] As in *Alexander Hamilton Institute v. Jones* 234 Ill.App. 444 (1924).

[52] As in *Cole-McIntyre-Norfleet Co. v. Holloway* 141 Tenn. 679, 214 S.W. 87 (1919) .

In such a case it may not be unreasonable to impose on the offeree an obligation to give notice of his rejection of the offer, especially if the offeror, in reliance on his belief that the goods would be delivered in the usual way, had forborne from seeking an alternative supply. On a somewhat similar principle, one party's wrongful repudiation of a contract may be accepted by the other party's failure to take such further steps in the performance of that contract as he would have been expected to take, if he were treating the contract as still in force.[53] There may also be "an express undertaking or implied obligation to speak"[54] arising out of the course of negotiations between the parties, e.g. "where the offeree himself indicates that an offer is to be taken as accepted if he does not indicate the contrary by an ascertainable time."[55] Failure to perform such an "obligation to speak" could be held to amount to an acceptance by silence. There is also the possibility that silence may constitute an acceptance by virtue of the custom of the trade or business in question.[56]

Where the offeree is under a "duty to speak," his failure to perform that duty may thus enable the *offeror* to treat that failure as an acceptance by silence. But it is not normally open to the *offeree* in such cases to treat his own silence (in breach of his duty to speak) as an acceptance.[57] This course would be open to him only in situations such as that in *Felthouse v. Bindley*,[58] in which the offeror had indicated (usually in the terms of the offer) that he would treat silence as an acceptance.

Liability based on estoppel? Even where silence of the offeree does not **2–066** amount to an acceptance, it is arguable that he might be liable on a different basis. In *Spiro v. Lintern* it was said that: "If A sees B acting in the mistaken belief that A is under some binding obligation to him and in a manner consistent only with such an obligation, which would be to B's disadvantage if A were thereafter to deny the obligation, A is under a duty to B to disclose the non-existence of the supposed obligation."[59] Although this statement was made with reference to wholly different circumstances, it could also be applied to certain cases in which an offeror had, to the offeree's knowledge,[60] acted in reliance on the belief that his offer had been accepted by silence. The liability of the offeree would then be based on a kind of estoppel.[61] But the application of this doctrine to cases of alleged acceptance by silence gives rise to the difficulty that such an estoppel can

---

[53] *Vitol S.A. v. Norelf Ltd* [1996] A.C. 800.

[54] *Gebr. van Weelde Scheepvaartkantor B.V. v. Compania Naviera Orient SA (The Agrabele)* [1985] 2 Lloyd's Rep. 496, 509, *per* Evans J., whose statement of the relevant principles was approved on appeal though the actual decision was reversed on the facts: [1987] 2 Lloyd's Rep. 223, 225. The case concerned an alleged "abandonment" by delay of an agreement to submit a claim to arbitration and would now be governed by Arbitration Act 1996 s.41(3) (*ante*, § 2–005).

[55] *Re Selectmove* [1995] 1 W.L.R. 474, 478 (where the point was left open).

[56] *Minories Finance Ltd v. Afribank Nigeria Ltd* [1995] 1 Lloyd's Rep. 134 (where a contract between two banks for the collection of drafts and remittance of their proceeds arose in this way).

[57] *Yona International Ltd v. La Réunion Française, etc.* [1996] 2 Lloyd's Rep. 84, 110.

[58] *Ante*, § 2–063; further discussed in § 2–068 *post*.

[59] [1973] 1 W.L.R. 1002, 1011.

[60] See *Yona International Ltd v. Law Réunion Française, etc.* [1996] 2 Lloyd's Rep. 84, 107 (where this requirement of knowledge was not satisfied).

[61] *Post*, § 3–095; and *cf. The Stolt Loyalty* [1993] 2 Lloyd's Rep. 281, 289–291 (*affd.*, without reference to this point, [1995] 1 Lloyd's Rep. 598). The case would not be one of estoppel by convention (*post*, § 3–100); for such estoppel is based on an *agreed* assumption of fact, while in cases of the present kind the question is whether there was any agreement.

only arise out of a "clear and unequivocal"[62] representation. For this purpose, mere inactivity is not generally sufficient,[63] so that silence in response to an offer will not normally give rise to an estoppel. It is likely to do so only in cases of the kind discussed above,[64] in which there are special circumstances which give rise to a "duty to speak," and in which it would be unconscionable for the party under that duty to deny that a contract had come into existence.

2–067   **Performance by offeror benefiting offeree.** It is finally possible that the offeree may be bound by silence if the offeror to the offeree's knowledge actually performs in accordance with his offer and so confers a benefit on the offeree; though the better solution in this type of case would be to make the offeree restore the benefit rather than to hold him to an obligation to perform his part of a contract to which he had never agreed.

2–068   **Can offeror be bound?** There is some authority for saying that the offeror cannot, any more than the offeree, be bound where the offeree simply remains silent in response to an offer,[65] and the case is not one of the exceptional ones, discussed in § 2–065 above, in which an offer can be accepted by silence. But it is submitted that the general rule in *Felthouse v. Bindley*[66] does not lead necessarily to such a conclusion. For the object of this rule is to protect the *offeree* from having to incur the trouble and expense of rejecting the offer so as to avoid being bound. No similar argument can be advanced for protecting the offeror. He may, indeed, be left in doubt on the point whether his offer has been accepted; but this is a matter about which he cannot legitimately complain where he has drawn his offer so as to permit (and even to encourage) acceptance by silence.[67] Thus it is submitted that the uncle in *Felthouse v. Bindley* might have been bound if the nephew had resolved to accept the offer and had, in reliance on its terms, forborne from attempting to dispose of the horse elsewhere. This possibility has, indeed, been doubted[68]; but in the case in which the doubt was expressed there was no express stipulation in the offer that silence would be regarded as acceptance. Where the offer does contain such a stipulation, it is submitted that silence in response to it by the offeree should be capable of binding the offeror.

2–069   **Silence and conduct.** The general rule that there can be no acceptance by silence does not mean that an acceptance always has to be given in so many words. An offer can be accepted by conduct; and this is never thought to give rise to any difficulty where the conduct takes the form of a positive act.[69] In principle, conduct can also take the form of a forbearance: for example, a debtor's offer to give additional security for a debt can be accepted by the creditor's forbearing to sue for the debt.[70] Similarly, a tenant can accept an offer of a new tenancy by simply not vacating the premises. In one such case it was said that the offer had

---

[62] *Post*, § 3–085.
[63] *Post*, § 3–087.
[64] *Supra*, at n. 84.
[65] *Fairline Shipping Corp. v. Anderson* [1975] Q.B. 180, 189.
[66] *Ante*, § 2–063.
[67] This argument would, however, not apply where the terms of the offer had been drafted by the offeree: *cf. ante*, § 2–062.
[68] *Fairline Shipping Corp. v. Anderson, supra*, n. 65.
[69] *cf. ante*, § 2–027.
[70] *Post*, § 3–045.

been accepted by "silence"[71]; but it seems better to say that it was accepted by conduct and that the landlord had waived notice of acceptance. Similarly an offer made *to* a landowner to occupy land under a licence containing specified terms may be accepted by the landowner's permitting the offeror to occupy the land.[72] The possibility of acceptance by conduct is, yet again, illustrated by the arbitration cases already mentioned, in which an agreement to abandon the proceedings was alleged to have arisen from delay in prosecuting them. As already noted, legislation has now dealt with the practical problems which used to arise from delay in the pursuit of arbitration claims,[73] but the reasoning of the arbitration cases could still apply where the legislative provisions have been excluded by agreement[74] or where it was alleged that some other type of claim or remedy had been abandoned by tacit agreement. According to those cases, an offer of abandonment can be accepted by reacting to it, not merely by inactivity,[75] but also by some further conduct: *e.g.* by closing, or disposing of, the relevant files.[76]

In *Rust v. Abbey Life Ins. Co.*[77] the plaintiff applied and paid for a "property   **2–070** bond" which was allocated to her on the terms of the defendants' usual policy of insurance. After having retained this document for some seven months, she claimed the return of her payment, alleging that no contract had been concluded. The claim was rejected on the ground that her application was an offer which had been accepted by issue of the policy.[78] But it was further held that, even if the policy constituted a counter-offer, that counter-offer had been accepted by "the conduct of the plaintiff in doing and saying nothing for seven months . . . ".[79] Thus mere inaction was said to be sufficient to constitute acceptance; but it is submitted that this conclusion may be justified by reference to the special circumstances of the case. The negotiations had been started by the plaintiff (the counter-offeree)[80] and, in view of this fact, it was reasonable for the defendants to infer from her silence over a long period that she had accepted the terms of the policy which had been sent to her and which she must be "taken to have examined."[81] The case thus falls within one of the suggested exceptions[82] to the general rule that an offeree is not bound by silence where this alone is alleged to amount to an acceptance.

---

[71] *Roberts v. Hayward* (1828) 3 C. & P. 432.

[72] *Wettern Electric Ltd v. Welsh Development Agency* [1983] Q.B. 796.

[73] Arbitration Act 1996 s.41(3); *ante*, § 2–005.

[74] *ibid.* s.41(2).

[75] *cf. Collin v. Duke of Westminster* [1985] Q.B. 581.

[76] See *André & Cie v. Marine Transocean Ltd (The Splendid Sun)* [1981] Q.B. 694, 712, 713 ("closed their file"); *cf. ibid.* 706 ("did so act"). *Tracomin SA v. Anton C. Nielsen A/S* [1984] 2 Lloyd's Rep. 195 can be supported on the same ground even though it was in part based on the decision at first instance in *Allied Marine Transport Ltd v. Vale do Rio Doce Navegaçao SA (The Leonidas D.)* which was reversed on appeal [1985] 1 W.L.R. 925; *ante* § 2–047; *cf. Tankrederei Ahrenkeil GmGH v. Frahuil SA (The Multibank Holsatia)* [1988] 2 Lloyd's Rep. 486, 493 (where the offeree had destroyed relevant files, so that the case was not one of mere inaction). There seems to have been no "conduct" amounting to an acceptance in *Excomm Ltd v. Guan Guan Shipping (Pte) Ltd (The Golden Bear)* [1988] 1 Lloyd's Rep. 330.

[77] [1979] 2 Lloyd's Rep. 355.

[78] *cf. ante*, § 2–021.

[79] [1979] 2 Lloyd's Rep. 335, 340, affg. [1978] 2 Lloyd's Rep. 386, 393.

[80] *cf. ante*, § 2–062 and *Vitol S.A. v. Norelf Ltd* [1996] A.C. 800 (*ante*, § 2–065).

[81] *Yona International Ltd v. La Réunion Française, etc.* [1996] 2 Lloyd's Rep. 84, 110 (where no inference of assent was drawn from silence).

[82] *Ante*, § 2–065.

(f) *Unilateral Contracts*

2–071   **In general.** The time at which an offer is accepted in the case of a unilateral contract has given rise to some difficulty: for instance, where an offer is made to pay a reward for the return of an article of lost property, or to pay a sum of money to the offeree if he refrains from smoking until he reaches the age of 21. In such cases, the offeror is no doubt liable once the required act or forbearance has been fully performed[83]; and it is also clear that the offeree can accept by simply performing, without giving advance notice of his acceptance to the offeror.[84] But it is less clear whether the offer can still be revoked when the offeree has partly performed: *e.g.* when he has found the lost property and is about to return it; when he has refrained from smoking until he is almost 21; or as Brett J. said in *Great Northern Ry. v. Witham*,[85] if one person promises another £100 if he will go to York, can the offer be revoked when the offeree has almost completed his journey?

2–072   One possible view is that the offer in each of these cases is revocable until the required act or forbearance has been actually completed, because it is only entire performance of that act or forbearance which constitutes acceptance. This view may be correct where it is the intention of both parties that the offeror should have a *locus poenitentiae* until this stage is reached. But in most cases the offeree will not intend to expose himself to the risk of withdrawal when he has partly performed[86] and intends to complete performance. It is now generally accepted that a distinction, originally put forward by Sir Frederick Pollock,[87] is to be drawn between the acceptance of an offer and the conditions which have to be satisfied before the offeree can enforce the promise contained in the offer. In a unilateral contract the offeree is not entitled to enforce the promise until the performance is complete. But the acceptance generally takes effect as soon as the offeree has made an unequivocal beginning of the requested performance, so that thereafter the offeror cannot revoke.[88] Of course it may be difficult in fact to tell when performance has begun, particularly where the offer amounts to a promise in return for an abstention. But if the conduct of the offeree goes beyond mere

---

[83] See *Daulia Ltd v. Four Millbank Nominees Ltd* [1978] Ch. 231, 238; *Harvela Investments Ltd v. Royal Trust of Canada (C.I.) Ltd* [1986] A.C. 207, 229.

[84] *Carlill v. Carbolic Smoke Ball Co.* [1893] 1 Q.B. 256; *Bowerman v. Association of British Travel Agents* [1995] N.L.J. 1815.

[85] (1873) L.R. 9 C.P. 16, 19.

[86] Lord Diplock in *Harvela Investments Ltd v. Royal Trust of Canada (C.I.) Ltd* [1986] A.C. 207, 224 can be read as depriving the offeror of the power to withdraw as soon as his offer is *communicated* (*i.e.* before any performance); but in that case the offeree had completely performed the required act by making the requested bid.

[87] *Principles of Contract* (13th ed.), p. 19.

[88] So long as performance remains within his power: see *Morrison SS. Co. v. The Crown* (1924) 20 Ll.L.Rep. 283 (where the House of Lords held that the offer could be withdrawn, in spite of the fact that the offeree had taken steps towards performance, as the acts of foreign governments had made it impossible for the offeree to complete performance). *cf.* also the American Law Institute's *Restatement of the Law*, Contracts (hereinafter called Restatement, *Contracts*), § 45, and *Restatement of the Law*, 2d, Contracts (hereinafter called Restatement, 2d, *Contracts*), § 45. The Restatement, 2d, *Contracts* § 12 abandons the distinction between bilateral and unilateral contracts, and in § 45 substitutes "option contract" where formerly "unilateral contract" had been used. See also *post*, § 3–011.

preparation to perform, and amounts to actual part performance, then the offeror cannot, as a general rule, withdraw.

Support for this view is to be found in *Errington v. Errington*,[89] where a father **2–073** bought a house, subject to a mortgage, allowed his son and daughter-in-law to live in it, and told them that if they paid the mortgage instalments the house would be theirs when the mortgage was paid off. The couple started to live in the house and paid some of the mortgage instalments; but they did not bind themselves to go on making the payments. It was held that the arrangement amounted to a contract which could not, after the father's death, be revoked by his personal representatives. Denning L.J. said: "The father's promise was a unilateral contract—a promise of the house in return for their act of paying the instalments. It could not be revoked by him once the couple entered on the performance of the act, but it would cease to bind him if they left it incomplete and unperformed."[90]

Continuing guarantees. The view that part performance of a unilateral con- **2–074** tract can amount to an acceptance, and so deprive the offeror of the power to withdraw, is also supported by the law relating to continuing guarantees. These may be divisible, where each advance constitutes a separate transaction; or indivisible, *e.g.* where, on A's admission to an association, B guarantees all liabilities which A may incur as a member of the association.[91] If the guarantee is divisible, it can be revoked at any time with regard to future advances,[92] but an indivisible guarantee cannot be revoked once the creditor has begun to act on it by giving credit to the principal debtor.[93] This rule applies even though the contract of guarantee is unilateral, in the sense that the creditor has not made any promise to the guarantor (in return for the guarantee) to give credit to the principal debtor.

Bankers' irrevocable credits. The issue (or confirmation) by a bank of an **2–075** irrevocable credit amounts to a promise to pay to the beneficiary a sum of money on certain conditions, usually if the beneficiary will present certain specified documents to the bank.[94] Often the beneficiary is a seller of goods who will have done some act of part performance, *e.g.* in manufacturing or shipping the goods. As he makes no promise *to the bank*, its liability to him might at first sight seem to be based on a unilateral contract between them. But the bank's promise is regarded as binding as soon as it is communicated to the seller, *i.e.* before he has done any act of part performance or indeed done any other act of acceptance. The binding force of the promise is therefore not explicable in terms of acceptance of an offer of a unilateral contract.[95]

---

[89] [1952] 1 K.B. 290; doubted on other points in *National Provincial Bank Ltd v. Ainsworth* [1965] A.C. 1175, 1239–1240, 1251–1252 and in *Ashburn Anstalt v. Arnold* [1989] Ch. 1, 17 (overruled on another ground in *Prudential Assurance Co. Ltd v. London Residuary Body* [1992] A.C. 386). For another possible illustration, see *Beaton v. McDivitt* (1988) 13 N.S.W.L.R. 162, 175.

[90] [1952] 1 K.B. 290, 295. *cf. Daulia Ltd v. Four Millbank Nominees Ltd* [1978] Ch. 231, 239.

[91] As in *Lloyd's v. Harper* (1880) 16 Ch.D. 290.

[92] As in *Offord v. Davies* (1862) 12 C.B.(N.S.) 748. An obscure passage in the argument at 753 is inconclusive on the general question of acceptance in unilateral contracts; *cf. infra*, n. 98.

[93] *Lloyd's v. Harper* (1880) 16 Ch.D. 290.

[94] See *post*, Vol. II, § 32–145.

[95] *ibid.* § 34–443.

2–076 **Unilateral contract becoming bilateral.** A contract may be in its inception unilateral but become bilateral in the course of its performance.[96] In the examples given in § 2–071 above, a bilateral contract would not indeed arise merely because the promiser had promised to perform the stipulated act or abstention (*e.g.* to walk to York). This is because the promisor has not bargained for a counter-promise, so that his offer cannot be accepted by promising to perform but only by actually performing (or by beginning to do so). But if A promises to pay B a sum of money in return for some service to be rendered to B (such as repainting A's house) it is possible that B may, by beginning to render the service (*e.g.*, by stripping off the old paint), impliedly promise[97] to complete it.[98] In such a case, the contract would at this stage become bilateral, so that neither party could withdraw with impunity.

2–077 **Estate agents' contracts.** A unilateral contract may arise where an estate agent is engaged to negotiate the sale of a house. In one case of this kind it was said that "No obligation is imposed on the agent to do anything."[99] If he succeeds in negotiating a sale, his claim for the agreed commission could be regarded as a claim based on a unilateral contract. However, it is well settled that the client may revoke his instructions, or sell through another agent, or without any agent, in spite of the fact that the first agent has made considerable efforts to find a purchaser.[1] It could be argued that this line of cases supports the view that the offeror (i.e., the client) can withdraw after part performance; but the better explanation is that this is one of the exceptional types of case in which, on the true construction of the promise, a *locus poenitentiae* is intended to be reserved to the client even after part performance by the agent.

2–078 **Estate agents appointed "sole agents"** There is a further group of cases in which persons appointed "sole agents" have been held entitled to damages when the client sold through another agent.[2] However, these have been treated as cases of bilateral contracts, on the ground that the agents promised to use their best

---

[96] *cf. New Zealand Shipping Co. Ltd v. A.N. Satterthwaite Ltd (The Eurymedon)* [1975] A.C. 154, 167–168 ("a bargain initially unilateral but capable of becoming mutual"); contrast *The Mahkutai* [1996] 2 A.C. 650, 664, treating the contract in *The Eurymedon* as "nowadays bilateral" (but *quaere* whether the offeree in that case would have intended to be bound before even beginning performance).

[97] It has, indeed, been suggested that it is "impossible to imply terms (. . . which impose legal obligations . . . into a unilateral contract" (*Little v. Courage* (1995) 70 P. & C.R. 469, 474). The reason for this view seems to be that such an implication would destroy the unilateral character of the contract by imposing an obligation on the promisee. But there is, it is submitted, no good reason why an intention to undertake such an obligation should not be inferred from the conduct of the promisee *after* the unilateral contract has come into existence. This possibility is recognised in the dictum from *The Eurymedon* cited in n. 96 *supra* and by the example given in the text to this note.

[98] See *The Unique Mariner* [1979] 2 Lloyd's Rep. 37, 51–2; *Smit International Singapore Pte Ltd v. Kurnia Dewi Shipping SA (The Kurnia Dewi)* [1997] 1 Lloyd's Rep. 553, 559; contrast *B.S.C. v. Cleveland Bridge & Engineering Co. Ltd* [1984] 1 All E.R. 504, 510–511, where such an implied promise was negatived by the fact that the terms of a bilateral contract were still under negotiation and were never agreed. It is not clear whether the situation discussed in *Offord v. Davies* (1862) 12 C.B.N.S. 748, 753 falls into the category of a unilateral or into that of a bilateral contract.

[99] *Luxor (Eastbourne) Ltd v. Cooper* [1941] A.C. 108, 124. But in fact he may promise to do something: see *infra*, at nn. 3 and 4; *cf.* Murdoch (1975) 91 L.Q.R. 357.

[1] *Post*, Vol. II, §§ 32–135, 32–145.

[2] *Hampton & Sons v. George* [1939] 3 All E.R. 627; *Christopher v. Essig* [1958] W.N. 461; and see *post*, Vol. II, § 32–145.

endeavours to effect a sale,[3] or to bear advertising expenses.[4] Such promises may be (and, it seems, commonly are) made by agents who are not sole agents at all, though the question whether a promise to use best endeavours is sufficiently certain to have any legal effect may still be as an open one.[5] The rules as to the revocability of the client's promise would, it seems, apply whether the contract is regarded as a unilateral or as a bilateral one and accordingly it is doubtful whether the estate agency cases shed any light on the problems of acceptance in unilateral contracts.

4. TERMINATION OF THE OFFER

Introductory. An offer may be terminated by withdrawal, rejection, lapse of time, occurrence of a condition, death and supervening incapacity. These methods of termination will be discussed in the paragraphs that follow. **2–079**

(a) *Withdrawal*

General rule. The general rule is that an offer may be withdrawn at any time before it is accepted.[6] The rule applies even though the offeror has promised to keep the offer open for a specified time,[7] for such a promise is unsupported by consideration[8] and is therefore not binding. Thus in *Routledge v. Grant*[9] the defendant offered to buy a house, giving the offeree six weeks for a definite answer; it was held that the defendant was free to withdraw at any time before acceptance even though the six weeks had not expired. Conversely, in *Dickinson v. Dodds*[10] the defendant offered to sell his house to the offeree and said that the offer was to be "left over till Friday." It was held that he could nevertheless withdraw before Friday. **2–080**

Communication of withdrawal generally required. An offer cannot be withdrawn merely by acting inconsistently with it: for example, an offer to sell goods to A is not withdrawn by selling them to B.[11] If A accepts the offer before he has notice of the subsequent sale, he will be entitled to damages (though not **2–081**

---

[3] *Christopher v. Essig, supra*, n. 83; *John McCann & Co. v. Pow* [1974] 1 W.L.R. 1643, 1647. In *Wood v. Lucy, Lady Duff-Gordon* (1917) 222 N.Y. 88, 118 N.E. 214 it was held that such a promise could be implied.

[4] *cf. Bentall, Horsley & Baldry v. Vicary* [1931] 1 K.B. 253 (where it was held that the owner committed no breach of a "sole agency" agreement by selling it without the intervention of a second agent).

[5] *Post*, §§ 2–127.

[6] See, *e.g. Payne v. Cave* (1789) 3 T.R. 148; *Routledge v. Grant* (1828) 4 Bing. 653; *Offord v. Davies* (1862) 12 C.B.(N.S.) 748; *Hebb's Case* (1867) L.R. 4 Eq. 9; *Tuck v. Baker* [1990] 2 E.G.L.R. 195; *cf.* Defamation Act 1996, s.2(6). For a statutory exception, see Companies Act 1985, s.82(7); see also Vienna Convention on Contracts for the International Sale of Goods (*ante*, § 2–057), Art. 16(2).

[7] It is assumed that the offer is to be open for a reasonable time if nothing is said to limit it: see *Ramsgate Victoria Hotel Co. Ltd v. Montefiore* (1866) L.R. 1 Ex. 109; *post* § 2–088.

[8] *Post*, § 3–160.

[9] (1828) 4 Bing. 653. See also *Cooke v. Oxley* (1790) 3 T.R. 653.

[10] (1876) 2 Ch.D. 463.

[11] *Adams v. Lindsell* (1818) 1 B. & Ald. 681; *Stevenson, Jacques & Co. v. Maclean* (1880) 5 Q.B.D. 346; it is submitted that contrary dicta in *Dickinson v. Dodds* (1876) 2 Ch.D. 463, 472 would no longer be followed.

to the goods themselves). To be effective in law, a withdrawal must, in general, be communicated to the offeree: that is, notice of the withdrawal must actually reach the offeree.[12] This requirement of communication applies to withdrawals sent through the post and by telegram as well as to those sent by other methods. In *Byrne & Co. v. Van Tienhoven*[13] the defendants in Cardiff on October 1 posted a letter to the offerees in New York offering to sell goods. The offerees received the letter on October 11 and accepted by telegram on the same day, which they confirmed by letter posted on the 15th. Meanwhile, however, the defendants had posted a letter withdrawing their offer on October 8; this letter reached the offerees on the 20th. It was held that this withdrawal did not take effect on posting: it could only take effect when it reached the offerees. As the acceptance had been posted before this happened, there was a binding contract.[14] The result was that a contract came into existence even though the parties were demonstrably never in agreement; for when the offerees first learnt of the defendants' offer the defendants had already ceased to intend to deal with the offerees. The rule is based on convenience; for no reliance could be placed on a posted offer if it could be effectively withdrawn by a letter posted by the offeror but not yet received by the offeree.

2–082   **Method of communication.** Although the withdrawal of an offer must, in general, be communicated *to the offeree*, the communication need not come *from the offeror*: it is sufficient if the offeree knows from any reliable source that the offeror no longer intends to deal with him. In *Dickinson v. Dodds*[15] it was accordingly held that an offer to sell land could not be accepted after the offeror had, to the offeree's knowledge, decided to sell the land to a third party. The judgments stress the fact that there is, in such circumstances, no agreement between the parties; but this would also be true if the offeree had no knowledge at all of the offeror's change of mind. Yet where this is the case there can be a contract, as *Byrne & Co. v. Van Tienhoven*[16] shows. The rule that communication of withdrawal need not come from the offeror can be a source of uncertainty, making it hard for the offeree to tell at exactly which point of time it becomes impossible for him to accept the offer.

2–083   **Exceptions to the requirement of communication.** If the general rule means that notice of withdrawal must actually be "brought to the mind of"[17] the offeree, convenience clearly requires its qualification in a number of situations.

(1) Letter reaches commercial organisation. In the first place, where the offer has been made to a commercial organisation, the requirement cannot be taken quite literally in the sense of requiring the withdrawal to be brought to the actual notice of the officer responsible for the matter. It seems probable that the offer would be withdrawn when the letter of revocation "was opened in the ordinary

---

[12] For a statutory exception to the rule stated in the text, see Consumer Credit Act 1974, s.69(1)(ii) and (7).

[13] (1880) 5 C.P.D. 44. See also *Stevenson v. McLean* (1880) 5 Q.B.D. 346; *Henthorn v. Fraser* [1892] 2 Ch. 27; *Raeburn & Verel v. Burness & Son* (1895) 1 Com.Cas. 22.

[14] The same result would be reached under Vienna Convention on Contracts for the International Sale of Goods, Art. 16(1) (see *ante*, § 2–057), even though under Arts. 18(2) and 24 the contract would not be made until the acceptance was communicated to the offeror or delivered to his address.

[15] (1876) 2 Ch.D. 463; *cf. Cartwright v. Hoogstoel* (1911) 105 L.T. 628.

[16] (1880) 5 C.P.D. 344; *ante*, § 2–081.

[17] *Henthorn v. Fraser* [1892] 2 Ch. 27, 32.

course of business or would have been so opened if the ordinary course of business was followed."[18]

(2) Offeree's conduct displaces general rule. Secondly, the concluding words of the passage just quoted suggest that the general rule may be displaced by the conduct of the offeree. For example, a withdrawal which was delivered to the offeree's last known address could be effective if he had moved without notifying the offeror. Similarly, a withdrawal which had reached the offeree could be effective even though he had simply failed to read it after it had reached him: this would be the position where a withdrawal by telex was typed out on the offeree's machine during business hours[19] even though it was not actually read by the offeree or by any of his staff till the next day.[20] Of course the withdrawal would not be effective, in such a case, if it had been sent to the offeree at a time when he and all responsible members of his staff were, to the offeror's knowledge, away on holiday or on other business.[21]

(3) Withdrawal of offers to the public. A third exception to the requirement that a withdrawal must be actually communicated relates to offers made to the public, *e.g.* of rewards for information leading to the arrest of the perpetrator of a crime. As it is impossible for the offeror to ensure that the notice of withdrawal comes to the attention of everyone who knew of the offer, it seems to be enough for him to take reasonable steps to bring the withdrawal to the attention of such persons, even though it does not in fact come to the attention of them all.[22]

(b) *Rejection*

What amounts to rejection; counter-offers. A rejection terminates an offer, so that it can no longer be accepted.[23] For this purpose, an attempt to accept an offer on new terms (not contained in the offer) may be a rejection accompanied by a counter-offer.[24] Thus in *Hyde v. Wrench*[25] the defendant offered to sell a farm for £1,000. The offeree replied offering to buy for £950, and when that counter-offer was rejected, purported to accept the defendant's original offer to sell for £1,000. It was held that there was no contract as the offeree had, by making a counter-offer of £950, rejected, and so terminated, the original offer. 2–084

Inquiries and requests for information. A communication from the offeree *may* be construed as a counter-offer (and hence as a rejection) even though it takes the form of a question as to the offeror's willingness to vary the terms of the offer.[26] But such a communication is not *necessarily* a counter-offer: it may 2–085

---

[18] *Eaglehill Ltd v. J. Needham (Builders) Ltd* [1973] A.C. 992, 1011, discussing notice of dishonour of a cheque; *cf. Curtice v. London, etc., Bank* [1908] 1 K.B. 291, 300–301 (notice to countermand a cheque); *Schelde Delta Shipping B.V. v. Astarte Shipping Ltd (The Pamela)* [1995] 2 Lloyd's Rep. 249, 252; contrast *N.V. Stoomv Maats "De Maas" v. Nippon Yusen Kaisha (The Pendrecht)* [1980] 2 Lloyd's Rep. 56, 66 (telex notice of arbitration).

[19] For the effect of such messages when sent *out* of business hours, see *ante*, § 2–042.

[20] *cf. Tenax Steamship Co. Ltd v. Brimnes (Owners), The Brimnes* [1975] 5 Q.B. 929 (notice withdrawing ship from charterparty).

[21] *Brinkibon Ltd v. Stahag Stahl und Stahlwarenhandelsgesellschaft mbH* [1983] 2 A.C. 34, 42.

[22] *Shuey v. U.S.* (1875) 92 U.S. 73.

[23] *Tinn v. Hoffmann & Co.* (1873) 29 L.T. 271, 278.

[24] *Ante* § 2–029; for an exception see Vienna Convention on Contracts for the International Sale of Goods *(ante* § 2–057), Art. 19(2).

[25] (1840) 3 Beav. 334; *cf. O.T.M. Ltd v. Hydranautics* [1981] 2 Lloyd's Rep. 211, 214.

[26] See the treatment in *Tinn v. Hoffmann* (1873) 29 L.T. 271, 278 of the claimant's letter of November 27.

be a mere inquiry or request for information made without any intention of rejecting the terms of the offer.[27] Whether the communication is a counter-offer or a request for information depends on the intention, objectively ascertained,[28] with which it was made. In *Stevenson, Jacques & Co. v. McLean*[29] an offer was made to sell iron to offerees who asked by telegram whether they might take delivery over a period of four months. It was held that this telegram was not a counter-offer but only a request for information as it was "meant . . . only as an inquiry" and as the offeror "ought to have regarded it" in that sense.[30] Similarly, if an offer is made for the sale of a house at a specified price, an inquiry whether the intending vendor is prepared to reduce that price will not amount to a rejection of the offer if the inquiry is "merely exploratory."[31]

2–086   **Communication of rejection.** A rejection takes effect when it is communicated to the offeree. There is no ground of convenience for holding that it should terminate the offer as soon as it is posted. The offeree will not act in reliance on it as he derives no rights or liabilities from it; and the offeror will not know that he is free from the offer until the rejection is actually communicated to him. Hence if the rejection is overtaken by a subsequently despatched acceptance which reaches the offeror first, the latter should take effect. If, however, the rejection has reached the offeror, it is submitted that he would not be bound by an acceptance posted after the rejection and also reaching the offeror after the rejection. To apply the "posted acceptance" rule[32] here merely because at the time of posting the rejection had not reached the offeror could cause serious inconvenience to the offeror particularly where he had acted on the rejection, *e.g.* by disposing of the subject-matter elsewhere. An offeree who has posted a rejection and then wishes, after all, to accept the offer should ensure that that acceptance comes to the notice of the offeror before the latter has received the rejection.

(c) *Lapse of time*

2–087   **Specified time.** An offer which expressly states that it will last for a specified time only cannot be accepted after that time. The most common application of this rule is to offers taking the form of options, which obviously cannot be accepted after the expiry of the period during which the option is expressed to be exercisable. On a similar principle, an offer which stipulates for acceptance "by return of post" must be accepted either in the specified way or by some other no less expeditious method.[33]

2–088   **Reasonable time.** Where the duration of an offer is not limited by its express terms, the offer comes to an end after the lapse of a reasonable time.[34] What is

---

[27] *cf. ante,* § 2–029.

[28] *Ante* §§ 2–001, 2–002.

[29] (1880) 5 Q.B.D. 346.

[30] *ibid.* at 349–350; in fact the offeror did not so regard it but sold the iron to a third party.

[31] *Gibson v. Manchester C.C.* [1979] 1 W.L.R. 294, 302.

[32] *Ante* § 2–043.

[33] *cf. ante,* §§ 2–058, 2–060.

[34] *Ramsgate Victoria Hotel Co. v. Montefiore* (1866) L.R. 1 Ex. 109; see also *Reynolds v. Atherton* (1922) 127 L.T. 189; *Chem Co. Leasing SpA v. Rediffusion* [1987] 1 F.T.L.R. 201. *Semble,* the offeror could waive the delay. See also Vienna Convention on Contracts for the International Sale of Goods (*ante,* § 2–057), Art. 21(1).

a reasonable time depends on all the circumstances: for example on the nature of the subject-matter and on the means used to communicate the offer. An offer to sell a perishable thing, or a thing subject to violent price fluctuations, would terminate after a relatively short time; and this would often also be true of an offer made by telex or by telegram[35] or by other equally speedy means of communication such as telex or fax.

Conduct of offeree known to offeror. The period which would normally   **2–089**
constitute a reasonable time for acceptance may be extended if the conduct of the offeree within that period indicates an intention to accept and this is known to the offeror. Often on such facts there would be an acceptance by conduct, but this possibility may be ruled out by the terms of the offer, which may require the acceptance to be by written notice sent to a specified address.[36] In such a case the offeree's conduct, though it could not *amount* to an acceptance, could nevertheless prolong the time for giving a proper notice of acceptance. For the offeree's conduct to have this effect, it must be known to the offeror; for if this were not the case the offeror might reasonably suppose that the offer had not been accepted within the normal period of lapse, and act in reliance on that belief: *e.g.* by disposing elsewhere of the subject-matter.

(d) *Occurrence of Condition*

Offer subject to express or implied condition. An offer which expressly   **2–090**
provides that it is to determine on the occurrence of some condition cannot be accepted after that condition has occurred; and a similar provision for determination may be implied. If an offer to buy, or hire-purchase, goods is made after the offeror has examined them, it may be subject to the implied condition that the goods shall remain in substantially the same state as that in which they were when the offer was made. Such an offer could not be accepted after the goods had been seriously damaged.[37] Similarly, an offer to insure the life of a person cannot be accepted after he has suffered serious injuries by falling over a cliff.[38] On the same principle, it is submitted that the offer which is made by bidding at an auction impliedly provides that it is to lapse as soon as a higher bid is made.[39]

(e) *Death*

In general. It has been suggested that the death of either party terminates the   **2–091**
offer as it makes it impossible for the parties to reach agreement.[40] But there may be a contract in spite of a demonstrable lack of agreement, if this result is required by considerations of convenience[41]: and such considerations might in

---

[35] *Quenerduaine v. Cole* (1883) 32 W.R. 185.

[36] As in *Manchester Diocesan Council for Education v. Commercial and General Investments Ltd* [1970] 1 W.L.R. 241.

[37] *Financings Ltd v. Stimson* [1962] 1 W.L.R. 1184.

[38] *Canning v. Farquhar* (1885) 16 Q.B.D. 727; *Looker v. Law Union Insurance Co. Ltd* [1928] 1 K.B. 554.

[39] *Ante* § 2–009.

[40] *Dickinson v. Dodds* (1876) 2 Ch.D. 463, 475.

[41] As, for example, in *Byrne & Co. v. Van Tienhoven* (1880) 5 C.P.D. 344 (*ante*, § 2–081), where the offeree did not know that the offeror intended to contract with him until after the offeror had ceased to have any such intention.

some circumstances support the view that an offer should be capable of acceptance after the death of one party. This would, in particular, be the case where one party was ignorant of the other's death at the relevant time; or where a person who had validly contracted not to revoke an offer for a fixed period died during that time. More generally, it may be doubted whether there are any grounds of convenience for holding that the death of either party should of itself terminate an offer, except where the offer is one to enter into a contract which, because of its "personal" nature, would be determined by the death of either party.[42]

2–092 **Death of the offeror.** The effect of the death of the offeror has been considered in a number of cases concerning continuing guarantees. Such a guarantee (*e.g.* of a bank overdraft) is, in general divisible: it is a continuing offer, accepted from time to time as the bank makes further loans to its customer. It seems that a guarantee of this kind is not determined merely by the death of the guarantor.[43] But it is determined if the creditor knows that the guarantor is dead and that his personal representatives have no power under his will to continue the guarantee[44]; or if for some other reason it is inequitable to charge the guarantor's estate.[45] If the guarantee expressly provides that it can only be determined by notice given by the guarantor or his personal representatives, the death of the guarantor (even if known to the creditor) will not determine the guarantee; only express notice will have this effect.[46] In so far as any general statement can be based on this highly special group of cases, it seems that the death of the offeror determines an offer only if the offer on its true construction so provides.

2–093 **Death of the offeree.** Two cases have some bearing on the effect of the death of the offeree. In *Reynolds v. Atherton*[47] an offer to sell shares was made in 1911 to "the directors of" a company. An attempt to accept the offer was made in 1919 by the survivors of the persons who were directors in 1911 and by the personal representatives of those who had since died. The purported acceptance was held to be ineffective; and Warrington L.J. said: "The offer having been made to a living person who ceases to be a living person before the offer is accepted, there is no longer an offer at all. The offer is not intended to be made to a dead person or to his executors, and the offer ceases to be an offer capable of acceptance." The actual ground for the decision, however, was that the offer had, on its true construction, been made to the directors of the company for the time being, and not to those who had happened to hold office in 1911. In *Kennedy v. Thomassen*[48] acceptance by solicitors of the offeree in ignorance of her death was held ineffective on the grounds that their authority to act on her behalf had been revoked by her death[49] and that they had acted under a mistake. Neither case

---

[42] *Post*, §§ 21–006, 24–036. Even in such cases the legal effects of saying that the offer was determined, so that there was never any contract, would be likely to differ from those of saying that there had been a contract which had been determined: *e.g.* the Law Reform (Frustrated Contracts) Act 1943 could apply to the latter, but not to the former, situation.
[43] *Bradbury v. Morgan* (1862) 1 H. & C. 249; *Harriss v. Fawcett* (1873) L.R. 8 Ch.App. 866, 869; *Coulthart v. Clementson* (1879) 5 Q.B.D. 42, 46.
[44] *Coulthart v. Clementson, supra.*
[45] *Harriss v. Fawcett* (1873) L.R. 8 Ch.App. 866.
[46] *Re Silvester* [1895] 1 Ch. 573.
[47] (1921) 125 L.T. 690, 695; affd. (1922) 127 L.T. 189; *cf. Somerville v. N.C.B.*, 1963 S.L.T. 334.
[48] [1929] 1 Ch. 426.
[49] *Post*, Vol. II, § 32–160.

supports the view that an offer can never be accepted after the death of the offeree. It is submitted that, where an offer related to a contract which was not "personal,"[50] it might, on its true construction, be held to have been made to the offeree or to his executors, and that such an offer could be accepted after the death of the original offeree.

(f) *Supervening Personal Incapacity*

Mental patients. If an offeror became a mental patient he would not be bound 2–094 by an acceptance made after this fact had become known to the offeree, or after the patient's property had been made subject to the control of the court. But the patient could hold the other party to the acceptance; and an offer made to a person who later became a mental patient could be accepted so as to bind the other party. These rules can readily be deduced from the law as to contracts with mental patients.[51]

(g) *Supervening Corporate Incapacity*

Supervening corporate incapacity. In discussing the effect on an offer of 2–095 supervening corporate incapacity, a distinction must be drawn between companies incorporated under the Companies Acts (and now governed by the Companies Act 1985) and other companies.

Companies incorporated under the Companies Acts. Such a company may 2–096 lose its capacity to do an act by altering its memorandum of association. If the company nevertheless entered into transactions after depriving itself of the capacity to do so, those transactions were formerly *ultra vires* and void.[52] Now the general rule[53] is that acts done by the company can no longer be called into question on the ground that the company lacked capacity to do them by reason of anything in its memorandum[54]; and that, in favour of a person dealing with the company in good faith, the power of the board of directors to bind the company, or to authorise others to do so, is deemed to be free of any limitation under the company's constitution.[55] But a member of the company may bring proceedings to restrain the doing of acts beyond the company's capacity, or beyond the powers of the directors, except where such acts are done in fulfilment of legal obligations arising from previous acts of the company.[56] The effect of these provisions must be considered on offers made *to* and *by* the company.

Company as offeree. A company may receive an offer to enter into a contract 2–097 and then alter its memorandum and so deprive itself of the capacity to enter into that contract. If it nevertheless accepts the offer, the acceptance is effective in favour of a person who deals with the company in good faith; but before the

---

[50] "Personal" is here used in the same sense as in the law relating to termination of a contract by the death of a party: see n. 42, *supra*.
[51] *Post*, §§ 8–067, 8–076.
[52] *Post*, § 9–020.
[53] See generally *post*, §§ 9–027, 9–036.
[54] Companies Act 1985, s.35(1) (as substituted by Companies Act 1989, s.108).
[55] *ibid.* s.35A(1).
[56] *ibid.* ss.35(2), 35A(4).

company has accepted the offer, it can be restrained from doing so in proceedings brought by one of its members.

2–098 **Company as offeror.** A company may make an offer to enter into a contract and then alter its memorandum and so deprive itself of the capacity to enter into that contract. An acceptance of that offer is nevertheless effective in favour of a person dealing with the company in good faith; but it is not entirely clear whether in this situation a member of the company could take proceedings to prevent the conclusion of the contract. Such proceedings only lie to restrain "the doing of an act"[57] by the company and since the relevant act on the company's part (*i.e.* the making of the offer) would already have been done when the company still had capacity to do it, there seems to be nothing for the member of restrain, unless holding the offer open could be described as a continuing act.

2–099 Of course, the company itself could normally withdraw the offer and would be likely to do so in pursuance of the policy which had led it to change its memorandum. But this possibility would not be open to the company where it had bound itself not to withdraw the offer, *i.e.* where it had granted a legally enforceable option[58]; and in such a case it is clear that a member could not take proceedings to prevent the conclusion of the contract since such proceedings cannot be taken "in respect of an act to be done in fulfilment of a legal obligation arising from a previous act of the company"[59]: *i.e.* in the case put, from the grant of the option.

2–100 **Other corporations.** Companies may also be incorporated by Royal Charter or by special legislation. Charter corporations have the legal capacity of a natural person so that an alteration of the charter would not affect the validity of an offer or acceptance made by the corporation.[60] The legal capacity of corporations incorporated by special statute is governed by the statute, and acts not within that capacity are *ultra vires* and void.[61] An alteration of the statute could therefore prevent the corporation from accepting an offer made to it, and from being bound by the acceptance of an offer made by it, where the offer was made before the alteration came into effect. In practice, the problem is likely to be dealt with in the statute which changes the capacity of the corporation.

5. SPECIAL CASES

2–101 **Difficulty of offer and acceptance analysis in certain cases.** The analysis of the process of reaching agreement into the elements of offer and acceptance gives rise, in a number of situations, to considerable difficulties. One such situation arises where participants in a competition address their entries to the organiser. It is hard to say whether a particular entry constitutes an offer or an acceptance (or both), or whether two entry forms put into the post by different competitors

---

[57] *ibid.*

[58] For legally enforceable options, see *post* § 3–160, n. 79.

[59] Companies Act 1985, ss.35(2), 35A(3) (as substituted by Companies Act 1989, s.108).

[60] *Post*, § 9–003; but a member of the corporation could bring proceedings to restrain the conclusion of the contract: *ibid.*

[61] Subject to mitigations provided for, in the case of contracts with "local authorities", by Local Government Contracts Act 1996.

at the same time constituted cross-offers. Yet in spite of such difficulties it has been held that the competitors enter into contracts with each other to observe the rules of the competition.[62] It is, again, hard to apply the analysis of offer and acceptance where a contract is made through a single broker acting for both parties who eventually obtains their consent to the same terms[63]; where negotiations have reached deadlock and the parties simultaneously agree to a solution proposed by a third party whom they have asked to resolve their differences[64]; and in a number of other cases.[65]

The difficulties described above have given rise to the view that the analysis **2–102** in terms of offer and acceptance is "out of date"[66] and that "you should look at the correspondence as a whole and at the conduct of the parties and see therefrom whether the parties have come to an agreement."[67] But such an outright rejection of the traditional analysis is open to the objection that it provides too little guidance for the courts (or for the parties or for their legal advisers) in determining whether an agreement has been reached. For this reason the cases described above are best regarded as exceptions[68] to a general requirement of offer and acceptance. This approach is supported by cases in which it has been held that there was no contract precisely because there was no offer and acceptance[69]; and by those in which the terms of the contact have been held to depend on the analysis of the negotiations into offer, counter-offer and acceptance.[70]

6. INCOMPLETE AGREEMENT

Agreement in principle only.[71] Parties may reach agreement on essential **2–103** matters of principle, but leave important points unsettled so that their agreement is incomplete. It has, for example, been held that there was no contract where an agreement for a lease failed to specify the date on which the term was to commence[72]; and that an agreement for sale of land by instalments was not a

---

[62] *The Satanita* [1895] P. 248, affd. *sub nom. Clarke v. Dunraven* [1897] A.C. 59; Phillips, 92 L.Q.R. 499.

[63] *Pagnan SpA v. Feed Products Ltd* [1987] 2 Lloyd's Rep. 601, 616.

[64] See Pollock, *Principles of Contract* (13th ed.), p. 5.

[65] *e.g. A. N. Satterthwaite & Co. Ltd v. New Zealand Shipping Co. Ltd (The Eurymedon)* [1975] A.C. 154, 167; *Commission for the New Towns v. Cooper (G.B.) Ltd* [1995] Ch. 259 (*post*, § 2–109) and see *infra* nn. 66 and 67.

[66] *Butler Machine Tool Co. Ltd v. Ex-Cell-O Corp. (England) Ltd* [1979] 1 W.L.R. 401, 404; *cf. Port Sudan Cotton Co. v. Govindaswamy Chettiar & Sons* [1977] 2 Lloyd's Rep. 5, 10; *Tankrederei Ahrenkeil GmbH v. Frahuil SA (The Multibank Holsatia)* [1988] 2 Lloyd's Rep. 486, 491–492; *Interfoto Picture Library Ltd v. Stiletto Visual Programmes Ltd* [1989] Ch. 433, 443.

[67] *Gibson v. Manchester C.C.* [1978] 1 W.L.R. 520, 523, revd. [1979] 1 W.L.R. 294.

[68] *Gibson v. Manchester C.C.* [1979] 1 W.L.R. 294, 297; *cf. Harmony Shipping Co. SA v. Saudi-Europe Line Ltd (The Good Helmsman)* [1981] 1 Lloyd's Rep. 377, 409; *G. Percy Trentham Ltd v. Archital Luxfer Ltd* [1993] 1 Lloyd's Rep. 27, 29–30.

[69] *Hispanica de Petroleos SA v. Vencedora Oceanica Navegacion SA (The Kapetan Markos N.L.)* [1987] 2 Lloyd's Rep. 323, 331 ("What was the mechanism of offer and acceptance?"); *The Aramis* [1989] 1 Lloyd's Rep. 213; Treitel [1989] L.M.C.L.Q. 162; *Taylor v. Dickens* [1998] FLR 806, 818. The "offer and acceptance" analysis is also used in many of the arbitration cases discussed in §§ 2–005, 2–069 *ante*, though it is viewed with scepticism in *The Multibank Holsatia, supra* n. 66, at 91 and in *Thai-Europe Tapioca Service Ltd v. Seine Navigation Inc. (The Maritime Winner)* [1989] 2 Lloyd's Rep. 506, 515.

[70] *e.g.* the "battle of forms" cases discussed in § 2–031, *ante*.

[71] Lücke (1967) 3 Adelaide L.Rev. 46.

[72] *Harvey v. Pratt* [1965] 1 W.L.R. 1025; and see *Re Day's Will Trusts* [1962] 1 W.L.R. 1419.

binding contract where it provided for conveyance of "a proportionate part" as each instalment of the price was paid, but failed to specify which part is to be conveyed on each payment.[73]

2–104   **Agreement complete despite lack of detail.** On the other hand, an agreement may be complete although it is not worked out in meticulous detail.[74] Thus an agreement for the sale of goods may be complete as soon as the parties have agreed to buy and sell, where the remaining details can be determined by the standard of reasonableness or by law. Even an agreement as to the price is not necessary in such a case. Section 8(2) of the Sale of Goods Act 1979 provides that, if no price is determined by the contract, a reasonable price must be paid. Under section 15(1) of the Supply of Goods and Services Act 1982, a reasonable sum must similarly be paid where a contract for the supply of services fails to fix the remuneration to be paid for them.[75] These statutory provisions assume that the agreement amounts to a contract in spite of its failure to fix the price or remuneration. The very fact that the parties have not reached agreement on this vital point may indicate that there is *no* contract, *e.g.* because the price or remuneration is to be fixed by further agreement.[76] In such a case, the statutory provisions for payment of a reasonable sum do not apply. There may, however, be a claim for payment of such a sum at common law: for example, where work is done in the belief that there was a contract or in the expectation that the negotiations between the parties would result in the conclusion of a contract.[77] Such liability is based on restitutionary principles and arises in spite of the fact that there was *no* contract. It follows that the party doing the work, though he is entitled to a reasonable sum, is not liable in damages, *e.g.* for failing to do the work within a reasonable time.[78] If the claim were made under a contract by virtue of section 15(1) of the 1982 Act, the party doing the work would be both entitled and liable.

2–105   Even an agreement for sale of land dealing only with the barest essentials may be regarded as complete if that was the clear intention of the parties. Thus in *Perry v. Suffields Ltd*[79] an offer to sell a public-house with vacant possession for £7,000 was accepted without qualification. It was held that there was a binding contract even though many important points, *e.g.* the date for completion[80] and the question of paying a deposit, were left open. In another case[81] a buyer and seller of corn feed pellets had reached agreement on the "cardinal terms of the deal: product, price, quantity, period of shipment, range of loading ports and

---

[73] *Bushwall Properties Ltd v. Vortex Properties* [1976] 1 W.L.R. 591; *cf. Hillreed Land v. Beautridge* [1994] E.G.C.S. 55; *Avintar v. Avill* 1995 S.C.L.R. 1012.

[74] *First Energy (UK) Ltd v. Hungarian International Bank Ltd* [1993] 2 Lloyd's Rep. 195, 205.

[75] *cf.*, at common law, *Way v. Latilla* [1937] 3 All E.R. 759; and see, as to agents' commissions, *British Bank of Foreign Trade v. Novinex* [1949] 1 K.B. 623; *Powell v. Braun* [1954] 1 W.L.R. 401.

[76] *e.g. May & Butcher v. R.* [1934] 2 K.B. 17n, *post,* § 2–116; *Courtney & Fairbairn Ltd v. Tolaini Bros. (Hotels) Ltd* [1975] 1 W.L.R. 297; *Dugdale and Lowe* [1976] J.B.L. 312; *Chamberlain v. Boodle & King* [1982] 1 W.L.R. 1443n; *Pagnan SpA v. Granaria B.V.* [1986] 2 Lloyd's Rep. 547; *Russell Bros. (Paddington) Ltd v. John Elliott Management Ltd* (1995) 11 Const. L.J. 377; *Southwark L.B.C. v. Logan* (1996) 8 Admin. L.R. 315.

[77] *Post,* § 30–185.

[78] *B.S.C. v. Cleveland Bridge & Engineering Co. Ltd* [1984] 1 All E.R. 504.

[79] [1916] 2 Ch. 187; *cf. Elias v. George Sahely & Co. (Barbados) Ltd* [1982] 3 All E.R. 801.

[80] *cf. Storer v. Manchester C.C.* [1974] 1 W.L.R. 1403.

[81] *Pagnan SpA v. Feed Products Ltd* [1987] 2 Lloyd's Rep. 601.

governing contract terms."[82] The agreement was held to have contractual force even though the parties had not yet reached agreement on a number of other important points, such as the loading port,[83] the rate of loading and certain payments (other than the price) which might in certain events become payable under the contract. And a publisher's oral commitment to publish a book has been held to amount to a binding contract, even though no details were specified in the agreement and nothing more precise was said about the author's remuneration than that he was to be paid a royalty to be agreed, or in default of agreement a fair one.[84] In all these cases, the courts took the view that the parties intended to be bound at once in spite of the fact that further significant terms were to be agreed later and that even their failure to reach such agreement would not invalidate the contract unless without such agreement it was unworkable or too uncertain[85] to be enforced.

Stipulation for the execution of a formal document. The effect of a stipulation that an agreement is to be embodied in a formal written document depends on its purpose.[86] One possibility is that the agreement is regarded by the parties as incomplete, or as not intended to be legally binding,[87] until the terms of the formal document are agreed and the document is duly executed in accordance with the terms of the preliminary agreement (*e.g.* by signature).[88] A second possibility is that such a document is intended only as a solemn record of an already complete and binding agreement.[89] Yet a third possibility is that the main contract is not concluded for want of execution of the formal document but that **2–106**

---

[82] *ibid.* at 611.

[83] *cf. post,* § 2–132.

[84] *Malcolm v. Chancellor, Masters and Scholars of the University of Oxford, The Times,* December 19, 1990, revg. *The Times,* March 23, 1990.

[85] *Post* § 2–099.

[86] *Von Hatzfeldt-Wildenburg v. Alexander* [1912] 1 Ch. 284, 288–289.

[87] *B.S.C. v. Cleveland Bridge & Engineering Co. Ltd* [1984] 1 All E.R. 504.

[88] *Okura & Co. Ltd v. Navara Shipping Corp. SA* [1982] 2 Lloyd's Rep. 537; *cf. R. v. Sevenoaks DC, ex p. Terry* [1985] 3 All E.R. 226; *Samos Shipping Enterprises Ltd v. Eckhart & Co. K.G. (The Nissos Samos)* [1985] 1 Lloyd's Rep. 378; *Hofflinghouse & Co. Ltd v. C. Trade SA (The Intra Transporter)* [1985] 2 Lloyd's Rep. 159, 163, affd. [1986] 2 Lloyd's Rep. 132; Debattista [1985] L.M.C.L.Q. 241; *Star Steamship Society v. Beogradska Plovidba (The Junior K.)* [1988] 2 Lloyd's Rep. 583; Debattista [1988] L.M.C.L.Q. 441; *Atlantic Marine Transport Corp. v. Coscol Petroleum Corp. (The Pina)* [1992] 2 Lloyd's Rep. 103, 107; *New England Reinsurance Corp. v. Messaghios Insurance Co. SA* [1992] 2 Lloyd's Rep. 251; *CPC Consolidated Pool Carriers GmbH v. CTM Cia Transmediterranea SA (The CPC Gallia)* [1994] 1 Lloyd's Rep. 68; *Ignazio Messina & Co. v. Polskie Linie Oceaniczne* [1995] 2 Lloyd's Rep. 566; *Drake Scull Engineering Ltd v. Higgs & Hill (Northern) Ltd* (1995) 11 Const. L.J. 214; *Regalian Properties plc v. London Dockland Development Corp.* [1995] 1 W.L.R. 212; *Enfield L.B.C. v. Arajah* [1995] E.G.C.S. 164; contrast *Prudential Assurance Co. Ltd v. Mount Eden Land Co. Ltd* [1997] 1 E.G.L.R. 37 (consent to alterations given by landlord "subject to licence" held effective as the consent was a unilateral act, so that no question of agreement arose).

[89] *Rossiter v. Miller* (1878) 3 App.Cas. 1124 (*post,* § 2–113); *Filby v. Hounsell* [1896] 2 Ch. 737; *Branca v. Cobarro* [1947] K.B. 854 (*post,* § 2–113); *E.R. Ives Investments Ltd v. High* [1967] 2 Q.B. 379; *Elias v. George Sahely & Co. (Barbados) Ltd* [1982] 3 All E.R. 801; *Damon Cie Naviera SA v. Hapag-Lloyd International SA (The Blankenstein)* [1985] 1 W.L.R. 435; *Clipper Maritime Ltd v. Shirlstar Container Transport Ltd (The Anemone)* [1987] 1 Lloyd's Rep. 547; *Malcolm v. Chancellor, Masters and Scholars of the University of Oxford, The Times,* December 19, 1990; *Ateni Maritime Corp. v. Great Marine Ltd (The Great Marine) (No. 2)* [1990] 2 Lloyd's Rep. 250, affd. (without reference to this point) [1991] 1 Lloyd's Rep. 421; *Jayaar Impex Ltd v. Toaken Group Ltd* [1996] 2 Lloyd's Rep. 437; *The Kurnia Dewi, infra.* n. 90, at 559; *cf. Crowden v. Aldridge* [1993] 1 W.L.R. 433, applying the same principle to a document which was not a contract but a direction by beneficiaries to executors.

nevertheless a separate preliminary contract comes into existence at an earlier stage, *e.g.* when one party begins to render services requested by the other, so that under this contract the former party will be entitled to a reasonable remuneration for those services.[90] The first two of these possibilities are further illustrated in the following paragraphs.

2–107　　**Insurance.** A contract of insurance is generally regarded as complete as soon as the insurer initials a slip setting out the main terms of the contract. This is so even though the execution of a formal policy is contemplated[91] and even though the contract, if it is one of marine insurance, is "inadmissible in evidence" unless it is embodied in a policy signed by the insurer and containing particulars specified by statute.[92]

2–108　　**Agreement "subject to contract."** Agreements for the sale of land by private treaty are usually[93] made "subject to contract." Such agreements are normally[94] regarded as incomplete until the terms of a formal contract have been settled and approved by the parties. Thus in *Winn v. Bull*[95] the defendant agreed to take a lease of a house for a specified time at a stated rent, "subject to the preparation and approval of a formal contract." It was held that there was no enforceable contract and Jessel M.R. said,[96] "It comes, therefore, to this, that where you have a proposal or agreement made in writing expressed to be subject to a formal contract being prepared, it means what it says; it is subject to and is dependent upon a formal contract being prepared." Other examples where it has been held that the parties have made the operation of their contract conditional on the execution of a further document are an agreement to purchase freehold land "subject to a proper contract to be prepared by the vendor's solicitors"[97]; an agreement to take a flat "subject to suitable agreements being arranged between your solicitors and mine"[98]; an agreement to grant a lease "subject to the terms of a lease" (because this meant "subject to the terms to be contained in a lease executed by the lessor"[99]); and an agreement to purchase a house "subject to formal contract to be prepared by the vendors' solicitors if the vendors shall so require."[1] In each of these cases the court held that the agreement gave rise to no

---

[90] *Smit International Singapore Pte Ltd v. Kurnia Dewi Shipping SA (The Kurnia Dewi)* [1997] 1 Lloyd's Rep. 553.

[91] *Ionides v. Pacific Insurance Co.* (1871) L.R. 6 Q.B. 674, 684; *Cory v. Patton* (1872) L.R. 7 Q.B. 304; *General Reinsurance Corp. v. Forsakringsaktiebolaget Fennia Patria* [1983] Q.B. 856; *Haden-fayre Ltd v. British National Insurance Soc. Ltd* [1984] 2 Lloyd's Rep. 393; *G.A.F.L.A.C. v. Tanter (The Zephyr)* [1984] 1 Lloyd's Rep. 56, 69–70 (revd. in part on other grounds [1985] 2 Lloyd's Rep. 529); *Youell v. Bland Welch & Co. Ltd* [1992] 2 Lloyd's Rep. 127, 140–141. Under an "open cover" arrangement, it is not the initialling of the slip but the declaration of the insured, which creates the obligation of the insurer: *Citadel Insurance Co. v. Atlantic Union Insurance Co.* [1985] 2 Lloyd's Rep. 543.

[92] See Marine Insurance Act 1906, ss.22, 23 and 24.

[93] Not always: see *Storer v. Manchester C.C.* [1974] 1 W.L.R. 1403; *Tweddell v. Henderson* [1975] 1 W.L.R. 1496, 1501–1502; *Elias v. Group Sahely & Co. (Barbados) Ltd* [1982] 3 All E.R. 801.

[94] See *infra* at n. 4.

[95] (1877) 7 Ch.D. 29. See also *Santa Fé Land Co. v. Forestal Land Co.* (1910) 26 T.L.R. 534.

[96] (1877) 7 Ch.D. 29, 32.

[97] *Chillingworth v. Esche* [1924] 1 Ch. 97.

[98] *Lockett v. Norman-Wright* [1925] Ch. 56.

[99] *Raingold v. Bromley* [1931] 2 Ch. 307. See also *Berry Ltd v. Brighton and Sussex Building Society* [1939] 3 All E.R. 217.

[1] *Riley v. Troll* [1953] 1 All E.R. 966.

legal liability.[2] On the same principle, it has been held that an agreement to pay a fee to an estate agent was not legally binding where it was expressed to be "subject to contract."[3]

General requirement of "exchange of contracts." Even after the terms of 2–109 the formal contract have been agreed, there is, where the agreement is subject to contract, no binding contract until there has been an "exchange of contracts."[4] It is also necessary (though not sufficient) for the formal requirements for contracts for the sale of land (which are described in Chapter 4) to be satisfied.[5] The formal requirement in cases of the present kind is that each party must sign a document containing all the terms which have been expressly agreed[6]; and the requirement of exchange prima facie refers to the handing over by each party to the other of one of these documents, or to their despatch by post; if the latter method is adopted, the process is completed on the receipt of the second of the posted documents.[7] Before the "exchange," neither party intends to be legally bound.[8] Such an exchange may be effected by telephone or by telex.[9] It has been held in Australia that, once an exchange has taken place, there can be a binding contract even though the two parts do not match precisely (unless it is clear that the parties only intended to be bound by an exchange of precisely corresponding parts).[10] The discrepancy can then be remedied by rectification.

Mitigations of the requirement of "exchange of contracts." The rules 2–110 stated in §§ 2–108 to 2–109 above enable either party to a concluded agreement to go back on it with impunity. This position has been described as "a social and moral blot on our law"[11] and there are indications that the courts are prepared to mitigate the former strictness of the requirement of "exchange of contracts." Thus it has been held that certain technical slips in the process of exchange may be disregarded[12]; and that exchange is not necessary where both parties use the

---

[2] Other authorities are *Kingston-upon-Hull (Governors) v. Petch* (1854) 10 Ex. 610; *Chinnock v. Marchioness of Ely* (1865) 4 De G.J. & S. 638; *Harvey v. Barnard's Inn* (1881) 50 L.J.Ch. 750; *May v. Thomson* (1882) 20 Ch.D. 705; *Hawkesworth v. Chaffey* (1886) 55 L.J.Ch. 335; *Von Hatzfeldt-Wildenburgh v. Alexander* [1912] 1 Ch. 284 (disapproving *North v. Percival* [1898] 2 Ch. 128); *Rossdale v. Denny* [1921] 1 Ch. 57; *Looker v. Law Union Insurance Co. Ltd* [1928] 1 K.B. 554; *Brilliant v. Michaels* [1945] 1 All E.R. 121; *Lowis v. Wilson* [1949] Ir.R. 347; *Graham & Scott (Southgate) Ltd v. Oxlade* [1950] 2 K.B. 257; *Bennett, Walden & Co. v. Wood* [1950] 2 All E.R. 134; *Christie, Owen and Davies Ltd v. Stockton* [1953] 1 W.L.R. 1353.
[3] *Ronald Preston & Partners v. Markheath Securities* [1988] 2 E.G.L.R. 23.
[4] *Eccles v. Bryant & Pollock* [1948] Ch. 93; *Sante Fé Land Co. Ltd v. Forestal Land Co. Ltd* (1910) 26 T.L.R. 534; *cf. Coope v. Ridout* [1921] 1 Ch. 291; *Chillingworth v. Esche* [1924] 1 Ch. 97; *Raingold v. Bromley* [1931] 2 Ch. 307; *Cohen v. Nessdale* [1982] 2 All E.R. 97.
[5] *post* § 4–047. A document setting out all the terms expressly agreed and signed by both parties would satisfy the *formal* requirements; but if it were expressed to be "subject to contract" it would not give rise to a contract till "exchange" had taken place.
[6] Law of Property (Miscellaneous Provisions) Act 1989, ss.2(1), (3).
[7] See *Commission for the New Towns v. Cooper (Great Britain) Ltd* [1995] Ch. 259, 285, 289; *cf. ibid.* at 293, 295.
[8] *Post*, § 2–149.
[9] *Domb v. Izoz* [1980] Ch. 548. This relaxation refers only to the process of exchange; the formal requirements referred to at n. 5 *supra* must also be satisfied.
[10] *Sindel v. Georgiou* (1984) 154 C.L.R. 661.
[11] *Cohen v. Nessdale* [1981] 3 All E.R. 118, 128, affd. [1982] 2 All E.R. 97; *cf.* Law Commission Paper Nos. 65 and 91.
[12] *Harrison v. Battye* [1975] 1 W.L.R. 53.

same solicitor.[13] The parties may also create a binding contract by a subsequent agreement to remove the effect of the words "subject to contract," thus indicating their intention henceforth to be legally bound.[14] Subsequent conduct may also give rise to liability on other grounds: where one party to the agreement encourages the other to believe that he will not withdraw, and the other acts to his detriment in reliance on that belief, the former may be liable on the basis of "proprietary estoppel."[15] In "a very strong and exceptional context"[16] the court may infer that the parties had such an intention when executing the original document, even though it is expressed to be "subject to contract." This was held to be the position where a document containing these words laid down an elaborate time-table, imposed a duty on the purchaser to approve the draft contract (subject only to reasonable amendments) and required him then to exchange contracts.[17] In these exceptional circumstances, the words "subject to contract" were taken merely to mean that the parties had not yet settled all the details of the transaction and therefore not to negative the intention to be bound.

2–111   **Collateral contracts and "lock out" agreements.** There is also the possibility that the freedom of action of the parties may be restricted by a collateral contract. For example a vendor who has agreed to sell land "subject to contract" may, either at the same time or subsequently, undertake not to negotiate for the sale of the land with a third party. Such a collateral agreement (sometimes called a "lock-out" agreement) must itself satisfy the requirement of certainty[18] and in *Walford v. Miles*[19] it was held that this requirement had not been satisfied where the agreement failed to specify the time for which the vendor's freedom to negotiate with third parties was to be restricted. But in a later case[20] it was held that a vendor's promise not to negotiate with third parties *for two weeks* was sufficiently certain, and that the purchaser had provided consideration for it by in turn promising to complete with that time.

2–112   **Exceptions to requirement of execution and exchange of formal contracts.** Agreements for the sale of land by auction or by tender are not normally made "subject to contract." The intention of the parties in such cases is to enter into a binding contract as soon as an offer has been accepted; and the terms of

---

[13] *Smith v. Mansi* [1963] 1 W.L.R. 26; exchange is also unnecessary in the case of a deed which takes effect as soon as it has been executed: *Vincent v. Premo Enterprises Ltd* [1969] 2 Q.B. 609; *D'Silva v. Lister House Development Ltd* [1971] Ch. 17.

[14] *Law v. Jones* [1974] Ch. 112, as explained in *Daulia v. Four Millbank Nominees* [1978] Ch. 231, 250; *Cohen v. Nessdale* [1981] 3 All E.R. 118, 127; [1982] 2 All E.R. 97, 104; see also *Tiverton Estates Ltd v. Wearwell* [1975] Ch. 146. The subsequent agreement would now have to satisfy more stringent requirements, imposed by Law of Property (Miscellaneous Provisions) Act 1989, s.2 (*post*, § 4–049) than those which were in force at the time of the decisions cited in this note, though these requirements would not apply if the subsequent agreement could take effect as a collateral contract.

[15] See the discussion at § 3–135 *post* of *Att.-Gen. of Hong Kong v. Humphreys Estate (Queen's Gardens) Ltd* [1987] A.C. 114.

[16] *Alpenstow Ltd v. Regalian Properties Ltd* [1985] 1 W.L.R. 721, 730; Harpum [1986] C.L.J. at 356.

[17] *Alpenstow Ltd v. Regalian Properties Ltd, supra.*

[18] *Post*, § 2–128.

[19] [1992] 2 A.C. 128. See further § 2–126.

[20] *Pitt v. PHH Asset Management Ltd* [1994] 1 W.L.R. 327; *cf. Tye v. House* [1997] 2 E.G.L.R. 171.

that contract are usually set out, or referred to, in a document signed to provide a written record of the fact of agreement. In one case of this kind,[21] however, the words "subject to contract" were, by a clerical error, added to the acceptance. It was held that there was nevertheless a binding contract since the tender documents set out in full the description of the property and the terms of the transaction. In these highly exceptional[22] circumstances, the words "subject to contract" were treated as meaningless and disregarded.[23] Presumably this reasoning could also apply where the sale was by auction. The same reasoning has also been applied where a notice exercising an option to purchase land was expressed to be "subject to contract": this phrase was again held to be meaningless as the notice was clearly intended to give rise to a binding contract.[24]

Binding provisional agreements. Even in the case of an ordinary sale of land **2–113** by private treaty, the agreement is not invariably made "subject to contract,"[25] and the court may on construction find that the parties have made an immediately binding agreement, even though this is later to be superseded by a formal contract. Thus in *Rossiter v. Miller*[26] the defendant offered to purchase land and was informed that he must purchase subject to certain conditions; his offer remained open and was accepted "subject to the conditions and stipulations printed on the plan." It was held by the House of Lords that there was a completed contract and Lord Blackburn said,[27] " . . . the mere fact that the parties have expressly stipulated that there shall be a formal agreement prepared . . . does not, by itself, show that they continue merely in negotiation." And in *Branca v. Cobarro*[28] the defendant agreed to sell a farm; the agreement contained the following clause, "This is a provisional agreement until a fully legalised agreement, drawn up by a solicitor and embodying all the conditions herewith stated, is signed." The Court of Appeal held that the provisional agreement was binding until it was superseded when the formal agreement was drawn up and signed; execution of the formal agreement was not a condition which had to be fulfilled before the parties were bound.

Acting on agreement subsequently completed. The parties may begin to act **2–114** on the terms of an agreement before a contract between them is actually concluded. That contract may then, if it expressly or by implication so provides, have retrospective effect so as to apply to work done or goods supplied before it was actually made.[29]

---

[21] *Michael Richards Properties Ltd v. St. Saviour's* [1975] 3 All E.R. 416; Emery [1976] C.L.J. 28.

[22] See *Munton v. G.L.C.* [1976] 1 W.L.R. 649.

[23] *cf. post,* § 2–133.

[24] *Westway Homes v. Moore* (1991) 63 P. & C.R. 480.

[25] *Storer v. Manchester C.C.* [1974] 1 W.L.R. 1403; *Tweddell v. Henderson* [1975] 1 W.L.R. 1496, 1501–1502; *Elias v. George Sahely & Co. (Barbados) Ltd* [1982] 3 All E.R. 801.

[26] (1878) 3 App.Cas. 1124. For other examples of a completed agreement, see *Lewis v. Brass* (1877) 3 Q.B.D. 667; *Bonnewell v. Jenkins* (1878) 8 Ch.D. 70; *Bolton Partners v. Lambert* (1888) 41 Ch.D. 295; *Gray v. Smith* (1889) 43 Ch.D. 208; *Filby v. Hounsell* [1896] 2 Ch. 737; *Lever v. Koffler* [1901] 1 Ch. 543; *E.R. Ives Investments Ltd v. High* [1967] 2 Q.B. 379; *cf. Willis v. Baggs and Salt* (1925) 41 T.L.R. 453; *Morton v. Morton* [1942] 1 All E.R. 273; *Cranleigh Precision Engineering Ltd v. Bryant* [1965] 1 W.L.R. 1293.

[27] (1878) 3 App.Cas. 1124, 1151.

[28] [1947] K.B. 854.

[29] *Trollope & Colls Ltd v. Atomic Power Construction Ltd* [1963] 1 W.L.R. 333.

2–115 **Letters of intent; letters of comfort.**[30] There is as yet no clear authority on the legal effect of the practice whereby the parties to a transaction exchange "letters of intent" on which they act pending the preparation of formal contracts. The terms of such letters may, of course, negative contractual intention.[31] This was, for example, held to be the case where a company issued a "letter of comfort" to a lender in respect of a loan to one of the company's subsidiaries: it was held that the company had not undertaken any contractual responsibility to the lender.[32] The letter stated that "it is our policy that [the subsidiary] is at all times in a position to meet its liabilities" in respect of the loan. This was interpreted to be no more than a statement of the present policy of the company: it was not an undertaking that the policy would not be changed, since the parties had not intended the statement to take effect as a contractual promise. On the other hand, where the language of such a document does not negative contractual intention, it is open to the courts to hold the parties bound by the document; and they will, in particular, be inclined to do so where the parties have acted on the document for a long period of time or have expended considerable sums of money in reliance on it.[33] The fact that the parties envisage that the letter is to be superseded by a later, more formal, contractual document does not, of itself, prevent it from taking effect as a contract.[34]

2–116 **Terms "to be agreed."** The parties to an agreement may be reluctant to commit themselves to a rigid long-term arrangement, particularly when prices and other economic conditions are likely to fluctuate. They sometimes attempt to introduce an element of flexibility by providing that certain terms are to be agreed later, or from time to time. The result of such a provision may be to make the agreement so uncertain that it cannot be enforced. In *May & Butcher v. R.*[35] an agreement for the sale of tentage provided that the price, dates of payment and manner of delivery should be agreed from time to time. The House of Lords held that the agreement was incomplete as it left vital matters to be settled. Had the agreement simply been silent on these points, they could perhaps have been settled in accordance with the provisions of the Sale of Goods Act 1979[36] or by the standard of reasonableness; but the parties showed that this was not their intention by providing that such points were to be settled by further agreement between them. Similarly, a lease at "a rent to be agreed" is not a binding

---

[30] Lake (and Draetta, *Letters of Intent* (2d ed (1994); Furmston, Poole and Norinado, *Contract Formation and Letters of Intent* (1997).

[31] *Post*, § 2–165; *cf. Snelling v. John G. Snelling Ltd* [1973] 1 Q.B. 87.

[32] *Kleinwort Benson Ltd v. Malaysian Mining Corp.* [1989] 1 All E.R. 785. Reynolds 104 L.Q.R. 353 (1988); Davenport [1988] L.M.C.L.Q. 290; Prentice (1989) 105 L.Q.R. 346; Ayres and Moore [1989] L.M.C.L.Q. 281; Tyree (1989) 2 J.C.L. 279, *cf. Chemco Leasing SpA v. Rediffusion* [1987] 1 F.T.L.R. 201 (where such a letter was held to be an offer but to have lapsed before acceptance); *cf. Monk Construction v. Norwich Union Life Insurance Society* (1992) 62 B.L.R. 107.

[33] *cf. Turriff Construction Ltd v. Regalia Knitting Mills* (1971) 22 E.G. 169 (letter of intent held to be a collateral contract for preliminary work); *Wilson Smithett & Cape (Sugar) Ltd v. Bangladesh Sugar Industries Ltd* [1986] 1 Lloyd's Rep. 378 (letter of intent held to be an acceptance); *Chemco Leasing SpA v. Rediffusion* [1987] 1 F.T.L.R. 201 (letter of intent held to be an offer but to have lapsed before acceptance).

[34] *Ante*, § 2–106.

[35] [1934] 2 K.B. 17n.; *cf. British Homophone Ltd v. Kunz* (1935) 152 L.T. 589; *Mmecen SA v. Inter Ro-Ro SA (The Shamah)* [1981] 1 Lloyd's Rep. 40, 43; *Harmony Shipping Co. SA v. Saudi-Europe Line Ltd (The Good Helmsman)* [1981] 1 Lloyd's Rep. 377, 409; *Pancommerce SA v. Veecheema BV* [1983] 2 Lloyd's Rep. 304, 307; *Cedar Trading Co. Ltd v. Transworld Oil Ltd (The Gudermes)* [1985] 2 Lloyd's Rep. 623.

[36] *Ante*, § 2–104; *cf.* Supply of Goods and Services Act 1982, s.15(1).

contract.[37] In the above cases, the most natural inference to be drawn from the fact that the parties left such an important matter as the price to be settled by further agreement was that they did not intend to be bound until they had agreed on the price. Even where the points left outstanding are of relatively minor importance, there will be no contract if it appears from the words used or other circumstances that the parties did not intend to be bound until agreement on these points had been reached.[38] *A fortiori* parties are not bound by a term requiring outstanding points to be agreed if that term forms part of an agreement which is itself not binding because it was made without any intention of entering into contractual relations.[39]

Options and rights of pre-emption. It follows from the principle stated in **2–117** § 2–116 above that an option to sell land "at a price to be agreed" is not a binding contract[40]; but such an option must be distinguished from a "right of pre-emption" by which a landowner agrees to give the purchaser the right to buy "at a figure to be agreed" should the landowner wish to sell.[41] An *option* has at least some of the characteristics of an offer[42] which becomes a contract of sale when the purchaser accepts it by exercising the option; and it cannot have this effect where it fails to specify the price. A *right of pre-emption* is not itself an offer but an undertaking to make an offer in certain specified future circumstances.[43] An agreement conferring such a right is, therefore, not void for uncertainty merely because it fails to specify the price. It obliges the land-owner to offer the land to the purchaser at a price at which he is in fact prepared to sell; and if the purchaser accepts that offer there is no uncertainty as to price.[44] This is so even though the parties have described the right as an "option" when its true legal nature is that of a right of pre-emption.[45]

Agreement not incomplete merely because further agreement is requir- **2–118** **ed.** Because the courts are "reluctant to hold void for uncertainty any provision that was intended to have legal effect,"[46] they may sometimes give effect even to an agreement which provides for further terms "to be agreed." This was the position in *Foley v. Classique Coaches Ltd.*[47] The claimant owned a petrol-filling

---

[37] *King's Motors (Oxford) Ltd v. Lax* [1970] 1 W.L.R. 426; *cf. King v. King* (1981) 41 P. & C.R. 311 (rent review clause).

[38] *Metal Scrap Trade Corporation v. Kate Shipping Co. Ltd (The Gladys)* [1994] 2 Lloyd's Rep. 402; *Ignazio Messina & Co. v. Polskie Linie Oceaniczne* [1995] 2 Lloyd's Rep. 566.

[39] *Orion Insurance plc v. Sphere Drake Insurance plc* [1992] 1 Lloyd's Rep. 239.

[40] This is assumed in *Brown v. Gould* [1972] Ch. 53, where, however, the option was upheld as it specified criteria for determining the price: see § 2–120, *post.*

[41] *Pritchard v. Briggs* [1980] Ch. 339. For the purposes of Landlord and Tenant (Covenants) Act 1995, "option" includes "a right of first refusal": s.1(6).

[42] *Post*, § 3–160, n. 79.

[43] Similarly, a "lock-out" agreement (*ante*, § 2–111) does not bind the promisor to sell to the promisee; it merely restricts his freedom to sell to someone else: see *Tye v. House* [1997] 2 E.G.L.R. 171.

[44] *Smith v. Morgan* [1971] 1 W.L.R. 803; *cf. Snelling v. John G. Snelling Ltd* [1973] 1 Q.B. 87, 93; *Fraser v. Thames Television Ltd* [1984] Q.B. 44, 57; *Miller v. Lakefield Estates Ltd, The Times*, May 16, 1988.

[45] See *Fraser v. Thames Television Ltd* [1984] Q.B. 44.

[46] *Brown v. Gould* [1972] Ch. 53, 57–58; *cf. Smith v. Morgan* [1971] 1 W.L.R. 803, 807; *Snelling v. John G. Snelling Ltd* [1973] 1 Q.B. 87, 93; *Queensland Electricity Generating Board v. New Hope Collieries Pty. Ltd* [1989] 1 Lloyd's Rep. 205, 210; *Global Container Lines Ltd v. State Black Sea Shipping Co.* [1999] 1 Lloyd's Rep. 127, 155.

[47] [1934] 2 K.B. 1.

station and adjoining land. He sold the land to the defendants on condition that they should enter into an agreement to buy petrol for the purpose of their motor-coach business exclusively from him. This agreement was duly executed, but the defendants broke it, and argued that it was incomplete because it provided that the petrol should be bought "at a price to be agreed by the parties from time to time." The Court of Appeal rejected this argument and held that, in default of agreement, a reasonable price must be paid.[48] *May & Butcher v. R.*[49] was distinguished on a number of grounds: the agreement in *Foley's* case was contained in a stamped document; it was believed by both parties to be binding and had been acted upon for a number of years; it contained an arbitration clause in a somewhat unusual form which was construed to apply "to any failure to agree as to the price"[50]; and it formed part of a larger bargain under which the defendants had acquired the land at a price which was no doubt based on the assumption that they would be bound to buy all their petrol from the claimant.[51] While none of these factors in itself is conclusive,[52] their cumulative effect seems to be sufficient to distinguish the two cases.[53]

2–119   Thus an agreement is not incomplete *merely* because it calls for some further agreement between the parties. Even the parties' later failure to agree on the matters left outstanding will vitiate the contract only if it makes it "unworkable or void for uncertainty."[54] Often, the failure will not have this effect, for it may be possible to resolve the uncertainty in one of the ways already discussed, *e.g.* by applying the standard of reasonableness[55]; or the matter to be negotiated may be of such subsidiary importance[56] as not to negative the intention of the parties to be bound by the more significant terms to which they have agreed. Thus in *Nelson v. Stewart*[57] a contract for the sale of shares provided that part of the price payable by the buyer was to be lent back to him and to a third party on repayment terms to be negotiated after one year. The House of Lords held that there was nevertheless a binding contract for the sale of the shares as the parties had not

---

[48] *cf. British Bank for Foreign Trade v. Novinex* [1949] 1 K.B. 623; *Beer v. Bowden* [1981] 1 W.L.R. 522; *Thomas Bates & Son Ltd v. Wyndham's (Lingerie) Ltd* [1981] 1 W.L.R. 505; 518–519; *Tropwood A.G. of Zug v. Jade Enterprises (The Tropwind)* [1982] 2 Lloyd's Rep. 233, 236; *Pagnan SpA v. Feed Products Ltd* [1987] 2 Lloyd's Rep. 601; *Granit SA v. Benship International SA* [1994] 1 Lloyd's Rep. 526; *Mitsui Babcock Engineering Ltd v. John Brown Engineering Ltd* (1996) 51 Const. L.R. 129.

[49] *Ante*, § 2–116.

[50] [1934] 2 K.B. 1, 10; the clause covered disputes as to "the *subject-matter or* construction of this agreement," while the arbitration clause in *May & Butcher v. R.* covered "disputes with reference to or arising out of this agreement." For the distinction between the two forms of clause, see *Heyman v. Darwins* [1942] A.C. 356, 385, 392. *cf.* also *Sykes (Wessex) Ltd v. Fine Fare Ltd* [1967] 1 Lloyd's Rep. 53; *Voest Alpine Intertrading GmbH v. Chevron International Oil Co. Ltd* [1985] 2 Lloyd's Rep. 547; and see *Vosper Thorneycroft Ltd v. Ministry of Defence* [1976] 1 Lloyd's Rep. 58 where the existence of a contract was admitted and the arbitration clause referred to "any dispute *or differ-ence*. . . . "

[51] Scrutton L.J. said at 7 that he was glad to decide in favour of the claimant "because I do not regard the appellants' [defendants'] contention as an honest one."

[52] R.S.T.C. (1933) 49 L.Q.R. at 316.

[53] *Foley's* case was approved by the House of Lords in *G. Scammell & Nephew Ltd v. Ouston* [1941] A.C. 251.

[54] *Pagnan SpA v. Feed Products Ltd* [1987] 2 Lloyd's Rep. 601, 619.

[55] *Ante*, § 2–104; *post*, § 2–131; or by imposing on one party the duty to resolve the uncertainty: *post*, § 2–132; *Pagnan SpA v. Feed Products Ltd, supra.*

[56] Though this point is not decisive: see *ante*, § 2–116 at n. 38.

[57] (1991) S.L.R. 523.

intended the validity of this contract to depend on the outcome of the negotiations as to the repayment of the loan.

There can be no doubt as to the commercial convenience of the judicial approach just described. Businessmen often intend to make agreements binding in principle without being able at the time precisely to settle all the details. For example, contracts of insurance may be made "at a premium to be arranged" when immediate cover is required but there is no time to go into all the details at once: such agreements are perfectly valid and a reasonable premium must be paid.[58] All this is not to say that the courts will hold parties bound when they have not yet reached substantial agreement,[59] but once they have reached such agreement it is not fatal that some points remain to be settled by further negotiation.[60]

Criteria laid down in the agreement. The courts have less difficulty in **2–120** upholding agreements which lay down *criteria* for determining matters which are left open. For example, in *Hillas & Co. Ltd v. Arcos Ltd*[61] an option to buy timber was held binding even though it did not specify the price, since it provided for the price to be calculated by reference to the official price list. Similarly, an option to renew a lease "at a rent to be fixed having regard to the market value of the premises" has been held binding as it provided a criterion (though not a very precise one) for resolving the uncertainty.[62] Even a provision that hire under a charterparty was in certain specified events to be "equitably decreased by an amount to be mutually agreed" has been held (by reason of its reference to what was equitable) "to provide a sufficient criterion to enable the appropriate reduction . . . to be determined."[63]

Machinery laid down in the agreement. Alternatively, the agreement may **2–121** provide *machinery* for resolving matters originally left open. Perhaps the most striking illustration of this possibility is provided by cases in which such matters are to be resolved by the decision of one party: for example a term, by which interest rates are expressed to be variable on notification by the creditor, is perfectly valid.[64] Similarly, an arbitration clause can validly provide for the arbitration to take place at one of two or more places to be selected by one of the parties.[65] Agreements are *a fortiori* not incomplete merely because they provide

---

[58] *Glicksten & Son Ltd v. State Assurance Co.* (1922) 10 Ll.L.Rep. 604; *cf.* Marine Insurance Act 1906, s.31(2); contrast *American Airline Inc. v. Hope* [1973] 1 Lloyd's Rep. 233 affd. [1974] 2 Lloyd's Rep. 301 ("at an additional premium *and geographical area* to be agreed").

[59] *e.g. Shakleford's Case* (1866) L.R. 1 Ch.App. 567; *Bertel v. Neveux* (1878) 39 L.T. 257; *Loftus v. Roberts* (1902) 18 T.L.R. 532; *Hofflinghouse SpA v. C-Trade SA (The Intra Transporter)* [1986] 2 Lloyd's Rep. 132; *Pagnan SpA v. Granaria B.V.* [1986] 2 Lloyd's Rep. 547.

[60] *Voest Alpine Intertrading GmbH v. Chevron International Oil Co. Ltd* [1987] 2 Lloyd's Rep. 547.

[61] (1932) 147 L.T. 503; *cf. Miller v. F.A. Sadd & Son Ltd* [1981] 3 All E.R. 265.

[62] *Brown v. Gould* [1972] Ch. 53.

[63] *Didymi Corp. v. Atlantic Lines & Navigation Co. Inc.* [1987] 2 Lloyd's Rep. 166, 169; Reynolds (1988) 104 L.Q.R. 353; affd. [1988] 2 Lloyd's Rep. 108; *cf. post*, § 2–131.

[64] *Lombard Tricity Finance Ltd v. Paton* [1989] 1 All E.R. 918. This position is preserved by Unfair Terms in Consumer Contracts Regulations 1994 (S.I. 1994 No. 3159) Reg. 4(4) and Sched. 3, para. 2(b).

[65] *Star Shipping AS v. China National Foreign Trade Transportation Corp. (The Star Texas)* [1993] 2 Lloyd's Rep. 445.

that outstanding points shall be determined by arbitration[66] or by the decision of a third party; though the Sale of Goods Act 1979 provides that if the third party "cannot or does not make the valuation, the agreement is avoided."[67] An agreement is not, however, ineffective merely because such machinery fails to work. Thus in *Sudbrook Trading Estate Ltd v. Eggleton*[68] a lease gave a tenant an option to purchase the premises "at such price as may be agreed upon by two valuers, one to be nominated by" each party. The landlord having refused to appoint a valuer, the House of Lords held that the option did not fail for uncertainty. It amounted, on its true construction, to an agreement to sell at a reasonable price to be determined by valuers. The stipulation that each party should nominate one of the valuers was merely "subsidiary and inessential"[69]; and where the agreed machinery is of this character,[70] the court can, on its failure to operate, substitute other machinery: for example, the court can itself fix the price with the aid of expert evidence. This is so not only where the agreed machinery fails because of one party's refusal to operate it,[71] but also where it fails for some other reason, such as the refusal of a designated valuer to make the valuation.[72]

2–122   **Rent review clauses.** Problems of the kind discussed in §§ 2–116 to 2–121 have in a number of cases arisen in connection with rent review clauses in leases. A provision in a lease that, after an initial period for which the rent is specified, the tenant shall pay "such rent as may be agreed" is prima facie ineffective.[73] It does not follow that the lease is, or becomes, void on failure to agree the new rent; indeed, it is unlikely that the court would so hold where the parties had acted during the initial period in the belief that the lease was binding for its full term; nor is it likely that the court would hold that, in default of agreement, no rent at all need be paid.[74] Failure to agree a new rent will therefore lead to one of two results: that the old rent continues[75] or that a reasonable rent must be paid. The first of these conclusions is open to the objection that it makes the rent review clause inoperative since under it the party in whose interest it was to maintain the old rent would have no incentive to agree to a new one.[76] The better view, therefore, is that a reasonable rent must be paid.[77] The lease may, of course, contain an express provision to this effect,[78] or provide for the rent to be determined by arbitration or by a valuer.[79] The original rent may, however, continue to govern for some *other* reason than the fact that the clause provides

---

[66] *Arcos Ltd v. Aronson* (1930) 36 Ll.L.Rep. 108; *cf. Campbell v. Edwards* [1976] 1 W.L.R. 403; *Buber v. Kenwood Mfg. Co. Ltd* [1978] 1 Lloyd's Rep. 175; *Queensland Electricity Generating Board v. New Hope Collieries Pty Ltd* [1989] 1 Lloyd's Rep. 205.

[67] Sale of Goods Act 1979, s.9(1); *cf. Pym v. Campbell* (1856) 6 E. & B. 370.

[68] [1982] 1 A.C. 493; Robertshaw (1982) 46 M.L.R. at 493.

[69] *Re Malpas* [1985] Ch. 42, 50; *cf. Tito v. Waddell (No. 2)* [1877] Ch. 106, 314; *Didymi Corp. v. Atlantic Lines & Navigation Co. Ltd* [1988] 2 Lloyd's Rep. 108, 115.

[70] *i.e.* not if it is "essential."

[71] As in *Sudbrook Trading Estate Ltd v. Eggleton* [1982] 1 A.C. 493.

[72] As in *Re Malpas, supra; cf. Royal Bank of Scotland v. Jennings* [1996] E.G.C.S. 168.

[73] *King v. King* (1981) 41 P. & C.R. 311.

[74] See *Beer v. Bowden* [1981] 1 W.L.R. 522, 525.

[75] *King v. King, supra.*

[76] *Beer v. Bowden, supra.*

[77] *Beer v. Bowden, supra; Thomas Bates & Son Ltd v. Wyndham's (Lingerie) Ltd* [1981] 1 W.L.R. 505.

[78] See *Brown v. Gould* [1972] Ch. 53.

[79] In *Thomas Bates & Sons Ltd v. Wyndham's (Lingerie) Ltd, supra,* the lease was rectified to include such a term.

that the new rent is to be agreed or to be fixed by a third party: for example, because the party who wishes to vary it has not complied with the conditions laid down by the contract as a prerequisite to the operation of the rent review clause.[80]

Facts to be ascertained. An agreement is not ineffective for uncertainty merely because the facts on which its operation is to depend are not known when it is made. The requirement of certainty will be satisfied if those facts become ascertainable and are ascertained, without the need for further negotiation, after the making of the agreement. Thus a finance agreement which depended on the merchantability of goods dealt with under it was held not to be invalid for uncertainty merely because it was not known, when the agreement was made, whether the goods were in fact merchantable.[81]   **2–123**

Contract to make a contract. In some cases of incomplete agreements it is said that there is a "contract to make a contract."[82] This expression may refer to a number of different situations.   **2–124**

Contract to execute a document incorporating terms previously agreed. One possibility is that the parties may agree to execute a formal document incorporating terms on which they have previously agreed. Such a "contract to make a contract" is perfectly binding.[83] For example, in *Morton v. Morton*[84] an agreement to "enter into a separation deed containing the following clauses" was held to be a binding contract. The grant of an option to purchase can similarly be described as a contract by which one party binds himself to enter into a further contract if the other so elects; and neither of these contracts is void for uncertainty.[85]   **2–125**

Agreement to negotiate. A further possibility is that the parties have simply agreed to negotiate. In spite of dicta to the contrary,[86] it has been held that a mere agreement to negotiate is not a contract "because it is too uncertain to have any binding force."[87] It therefore does not impose any obligations to negotiate, or to use best endeavours to reach agreement[88] or to accept proposals that "with   **2–126**

---

[80] *Weller v. Akehurst* [1981] 3 All E.R. 411 (where the rent review clause was invoked too late and time was expressly made of the essence of the contract: *cf. post*, § 21–011; contrast *Metroland's Investment Ltd v. J.H. Dewhurst Ltd* [1986] 3 All E.R. 659 (where time was not of the essence).

[81] *Welsh Development Agency v. Export Finance Co. Ltd*, [1992] B.C.L.C. 148.

[82] *Von Hatzfeld-Wildenburg v. Alexander* [1912] 1 Ch. 284, 284, 288–289 ("contract to enter into a contract").

[83] Subject to statutory exceptions: see Consumer Credit Act 1974, s.59.

[84] [1942] 1 All E.R. 273.

[85] See *The Messiniaki Bergen* [1983] 1 Lloyd's Rep. 424, 426. *cf. post*, § 3–160, n. 79 for the nature of an option.

[86] *Chillingworth v. Esche* [1924] 1 Ch. 91, 113; *Hillas & Co. Ltd v. Arcos Ltd* (1932) 147 L.T. 503, 515. See F.P. (1932) 48 L.Q.R. 141; F.W.M.C. *ibid.* 310; Williams (1943) 6 M.L.R. 81.

[87] *Courtney & Fairbairn Ltd v. Tolaini Bros. (Hotels) Ltd* [1975] 1 W.L.R. 297, 301; *cf. Von Hatzfeldt-Wildenburg v. Alexander* [1912] 1 Ch. 284, 249; *Malozzi v. Carapelli SpA* [1976] 1 Lloyd's Rep. 407; *Scandinavian Trading Tanker Co. A.B. v. Flota Petrolera Ecuatoriana (The Scaptrade)* [1981] 2 Lloyd's Rep. 425, 432 (affd. without reference to this point [1983] 2 A.C. 694); *Nile Co. for the Export of Agricultural Crops v. H. & J. M. Bennett (Commodities) Ltd* [1986] 1 Lloyd's Rep. 555, 587; *Paul Smith Ltd v. H. & S. International Holdings* [1991] 2 Lloyd's Rep. 127, 131.

[88] *The Scaptrade, supra*, at 432; *Star Steamship Society v. Beogradska Plovidba (The Junior K.)* [1988] 2 Lloyd's Rep. 583. Contrast, in the United States, *Hoffman v. Red Owl Stores Inc.*, 133 N.W. 2d 267 (1965).

hindsight appear to be reasonable."[89] Nor, where an agreement fails to satisfy the requirement of certainty, can this defect be cured by *implying* into it a term to the effect that the parties must continue to negotiate in good faith. In *Walford v. Miles*,[90] a "lock-out" agreement collateral to negotiations for the sale of a business lacked sufficient certainty because it failed to specify the time during which the vendors were not to negotiate with third parties[91]; and the House of Lords unanimously rejected the argument that a term should be implied requiring the vendors to continue to negotiate in good faith with the purchaser for as long as the vendors continued to desire to sell, since such a term was itself too uncertain to be enforced. The uncertainty lay in the fact that the alleged duty was "inherently inconsistent position of a negotiating party"[92] who must be free to advance his own interests during the negotiations. The point is well illustrated by the facts of *Walford v. Miles* itself, where the defendants had agreed subject to contract to sell a property to the purchasers for £2m and had (in breach of the ineffective "lock-out" agreement) sold it to a third party for exactly that sum, and the purchasers then claimed damages of £1m on the basis that the property was (by reason of facts known to them but not to the defendants) worth £3m. If a duty to negotiate in good faith exists, it must be equally incumbent on both parties, so that it can hardly require a vendor to agree to sell a valuable property for only two thirds of its true value when the facts affecting that value are known to the purchaser and not disclosed (as good faith would seem to require) to the vendor. The actual result in *Walford v. Miles* (in which the purchasers recovered the sum of £700 in respect of their wasted expenses as damages for misrepresentation,[93] but not the £1m which they claimed as damages for breach of contract[94]) seems, with respect, to be entirely appropriate on the facts, especially because the vendors reasonably believed themselves to be protected from liability in the principal negotiation by the phrase "subject to contract."

2–127 In *Walford v. Miles* Lord Ackner, with whom all the other members of the House agreed, described as "unsustainable" the view expressed in an American case[95] "that an agreement to negotiate in good faith is synonymous with an agreement to use best endeavours and, as the latter is enforceable so is the former."[96] He went on to say that "the reason why an agreement to negotiate, like an agreement to agree, is unenforceable is simply because it lacks the necessary certainty. The same does not apply to an agreement to use best endeavours."[97] This passage gives rise to a number of difficulties. The first arises from dictum in an English case[98] (which is cited with approval in *Walford v. Miles*[99]) to the

---

[89] *Pagnan SpA v. Granaria B.V.* [1985] 1 Lloyd's Rep. 256, 270; affd. [1986] 2 Lloyd's Rep. 547.

[90] [1992] 2 A.C. 128; Neill (1992) 108 L.Q.R. 405.

[91] *Ante*, § 2–111.

[92] [1992] 2 A.C. 128, 138; *cf. Surrey C.C. v. Bredero Homes Ltd* [1993] 1 W.L.R. 1361, 1368.

[93] See [1992] 2 A.C. 128, 136.

[94] *ibid.* at 135.

[95] *Channel Home Centers Division of Grace Retail Corp. v. Grossman* (1986) 795 F. 2d 291.

[96] [1992] 2 A.C. 128, 138.

[97] *ibid.*

[98] *Scandanavian Trading Co. A.B. v. Fluta Petrolera Ecuatoriana (The Scaptrade)* [1981] 2 Lloyd's Rep. 425, 432 (and see *supra* n. 87); *cf. Star Steamships Society v. Beogradska Plovidba (The Junior K.)* [1988] 2 Lloyd's Rep. 583; *Little v. Courage* (1995) 70 P. & C.R. 469, 475. A duty to negotiate may, however, be imposed by statute: *e.g.* Railways Act 1993, s.33(1).

[99] [1992] 2 A.C. 128, 137.

effect that an agreement to negotiate does not impose any obligation to use best endeavours to reach agreement; and this dictum certainly supports the view that an agreement to negotiate contains no *implied* term to use best endeavours. It may be that Lord Ackner's reference was to an *express* term to use best endeavours, or that he was simply prepared to assume (without deciding) that an agreement (express or implied) to use best endeavours might be legally enforceable and that he was concerned only to make the point that, even on that assumption, the same was not true of an agreement to negotiate in good faith. That explanation of Lord Ackner's statement in turn gives rise to the difficulty of distinguishing between the two types of agreement. One possibility is that an agreement to negotiate in good faith refers to the *formation* and one to use best endeavours to the *performance* of a contract, *e.g.* where an admitted contract between A and B requries A to use his best endeavours to procure C to enter into a contract with B. There is no doubt that such a term can impose a legal obligation on A.[1] Another possibility is that, while an agreement to use best endeavours could be interpreted as referring to the *machinery* of negotiation, one to negotiate in good faith is more plausibly interpreted as referring to its *substance*. A promise to use best endeavours might, for example, oblige a party to make himself available for negotiations, or at least not (*e.g.* by deliberately failing to pick up his telephone) to prevent the other from communicating with him.[2] A promise to negotiate in good faith, on the other hand, would oblige a party not to take unreasonable or exorbitant positions during the negotiations; and it is the difficulty of giving precise content to this obligation, while maintaining each party's freedom to pursue his own interests, that makes such a promise too uncertain to be enforced.

In *Walford v. Miles* the principal agreement was not legally binding because it was subject to contract, and the lock-out agreement was not legally binding for the reason given above. The case does not exclude the possibility that a different conclusion may be reached where the parties have reached agreement on all essential points so as to show that they do intend to be legally bound by the agreement, but have left other points open. The court may then imply a term that they are to negotiate in good faith so as to settle outstanding details which are to be incorporated in the formal document setting out the full terms of the contract between them.[3]

7. CERTAINTY OF TERMS

The terms of the contract must be certain. An agreement may be so vague **2–128** or uncertain that it cannot give rise to a binding contract. This principle is

---

[1] *e.g.* in the cases discussed in § 2–078 *ante*; *cf. Lambert v. HTV Cymru (Wales) Ltd, The Times,* March 17, 1998.

[2] Example based on *Nissho Iwai Petroleum Co. Inc. v. Cargill International SA* [1993] 1 Lloyd's Rep. 80, where such conduct was held to amount to a breach of a party's duty to co-operate in the *performance* (not in the *formation*) of a contract.

[3] *Donwin Productions Ltd v. E.M.I. Films Ltd, The Times,* March 9, 1984 (not cited in *Walford v. Miles* [1992] 2 A.C. 128).

illustrated by *G. Scammell & Nephew Ltd v. Ouston*,[4] where the House of Lords held that an agreement to acquire goods "on hire-purchase" was too vague since there were many kinds of hire-purchase agreements in widely different terms, so that it was impossible to specify the terms on which the parties had agreed. Similar reasoning is sometimes applied where the agreement is expressed so as to be subject to a condition depending on the satisfaction of one of the parties.[5] The problems arising from such provisions are discussed in § 2–141 below.

2–129   **Qualifications of the requirement of certainty.** The courts do not expect commercial documents to be drafted with strict legal precision. The cases provide many examples of judicial awareness of the danger that too strict an application of the requirement of certainty could result in the striking down of agreements intended by businessmen to have binding force. The courts are reluctant to reach such a conclusion, particularly where the parties have acted on the agreement.[6] As Lord Wright said in *Hillas & Co. Ltd v. Arcos Ltd*[7]:

> "Businessmen often record the most important agreements in crude and summary fashion; modes of expression sufficient and clear to them in the course of their business may appear to those unfamiliar with the business far from complete or precise. It is accordingly the duty of the court to construe such documents fairly and broadly, without being too astute or subtle in finding defects; but, on the contrary, the court should seek to apply the old maxim of English law, *verba ita sunt intelligenda ut res magis valeat quam pereat.* That maxim, however, does not mean that the court is to make a contract for the parties, or to go outside the words they have used, except in so far as they are appropriate implications of law."

In accordance with these principles, the courts have developed a number of qualifications to the requirement of certainty; these qualifications are stated in §§ 2–130 to 2–133 below.

2–130   **Custom and trade usage.** Apparent vagueness may be resolved by custom. For example, a contract to load coal at Grimsby "on the terms of the usual colliery guarantee" was upheld on proof of the terms usually contained in such

---

[4] [1941] A.C. 251 see also *Davies v. Davies* (1887) 36 Ch.D. 359; *Kingsley & Keith Ltd v. Glynn Bros. (Chemicals) Ltd* [1953] 1 Lloyd's Rep. 211.

[5] *e.g. Montreal Gas Co. v. Vasey* [1900] A.C. 595; *Hofflinghouse & Co. Ltd v. C. Trade SA (The Intra Transporter)* [1986] 2 Lloyd's Rep. 132; *Shipping Enterprises Ltd v. Eckhart & Co. K G (The Nissos Samos)* [1985] 1 Lloyd's Rep. 378, 385.

[6] *Brown v. Gould* [1977] Ch. 53, 57–58; *Tito v. Waddell (No. 2)* [1977] Ch. 106, 314; *Sudbrook Trading Estate Ltd v. Eggleton* [1983] 1 A.C. 444; *Clement v. Gibb* [1996] C.L.Y. 1209; *Hanjin Shipping Co. Ltd v. Zenith Chartering Corp. (The Mercedes Envoy)* [1995] 2 Lloyd's Rep. 559, 564.

[7] (1932) 147 L.T. 503, 514; *cf. Rahcassi Shipping Co. v. Blue Star Line* [1969] 1 Q.B. 176 (agreement for arbitration "by commercial men and not lawyers" upheld); *Nea Agrex SA v. Baltic Shipping Co. Ltd* [1976] Q.B. 933; *Tropwood A.G. of Zug v. Jade Enterprises Inc. (The Tropwind)* [1981] 1 Lloyd's Rep. 232; *Deutsche Schachtbau und Tiefbohrgesellschaft mbH v. Ras Al Khaimah National Oil Co.* [1990] 1 A.C. 295, 306 (revd. on other grounds, *ibid.* 329 *et seq.*); *Grace Shipping Inc. v. C.F. Sharpe (Malaysia) Pte.* [1987] 1 Lloyd's Rep. 207; *Didymi Corp. v. Atlantic Lines & Navigation Co. Inc.* [1987] 2 Lloyd's Rep. 166, affd. [1988] 2 Lloyd's Rep. 108 (*ante*, § 2–120); *Anangel Atlas Compania Naviera SA v. Ishikawajima Harima Heavy Industries Corp. (No. 2)* [1990] 2 Lloyd's Rep. 526, 546; *Star Shipping A.S. v. China National Foreign Trade Transportation Corp. (The Star Texas)* [1993] 2 Lloyd's Rep. 445, 455. See also Fridman (1960) 76 L.Q.R. 521.

guarantees at Grimsby.[8] An undertaking to grant a lease of a shop "in prime position" has similarly been held not to be too uncertain to be enforced since the phrase was commonly used by persons dealing with shop property, so that its meaning could be determined by expert evidence.[9] On the other hand, agreements "subject to war clause,"[10] "subject to strike and lock-out clause,"[11] and "subject to *force majeure* conditions,"[12] have been held too vague, as there was no evidence in any of the cases of any customary or usual form of such clauses or conditions.

Reasonableness. In *Hillas & Co. Ltd v. Arcos Ltd*[13] an agreement for the sale **2–131** of timber "of fair specification" was made between persons well acquainted with the timber trade. The agreement was held binding since in these circumstances the standard of reasonableness could be applied to give sufficient certainty to an otherwise vague phrase.

Duty to resolve uncertainty. An agreement containing a vague phrase may **2–132** be binding because one party is under a duty to resolve the uncertainty. In one case an agreement to sell goods provided for delivery "free on board . . . good Danish port." It was held that the agreement was not too vague: it amounted to a contract under which the buyer was bound to select the port of shipment.[14]

Meaningless and self-contradictory terms. The court will make consider- **2–133** able efforts to give meaning to an apparently meaningless phrase[15]; but even where these efforts yield no result, such phrases do not necessarily vitiate the agreement. In *Nicolene Ltd v. Simmonds*[16] steel bars were bought on terms which were perfectly clear except for a clause which provided that the sale was subject to "the usual conditions of acceptance." There were, in fact, no usual conditions of acceptance. It was held that the phrase was meaningless, but that this did not vitiate the whole contract: the phrase was severable and could be ignored. The same possibility exists where a clause is self-contradictory. Thus where an arbitration clause provided for arbitration of "any dispute" in London and of "any other dispute" in Moscow the court disregarded the clause and determined

---

[8] *Shamrock SS. Co. v. Storey & Co.* (1899) 81 L.T. 413; *cf. Hart v. Hart* (1881) 18 Ch.D. 670; *Bayham v. Phillips Electronics (U.K.) Ltd, The Times,* July 19, 1995 where uncertainty in a long-term health insurance agreement was resolved by reference to circumstances existing at the time of its formation.

[9] *Ashburn Anstalt v. Arnold* [1989] Ch. 1, 27, overruled, on another ground, in *Prudential Assurance Co. Ltd v. London Residuary Body* [1992] A.C. 386.

[10] *Bishop & Baxter Ltd v. Anglo-Eastern Trading Co.* [1944] K.B. 12.

[11] *Love & Stewart Ltd v. S. Instone Ltd* (1917) 33 T.L.R. 475.

[12] *British Electrical, etc., Industries v. Patley Pressings Ltd* [1953] 1 W.L.R. 280.

[13] (1932) 147 L.T. 503 (and see *ante,* § 2–120); *Sweet & Maxwell Ltd v. Universal News Services Ltd* [1964] 2 Q.B. 699; *cf. G.L.C. v. Connolly* [1970] 2 Q.B. 100; *Finchbourne v. Rodriguez* [1976] 3 All E.R. 581; *Pagnan SpA v. Feed Products Ltd* [1987] 2 Lloyd's Rep. 601; *Malcolm v. Chancellor, Masters and Scholars of the University of Oxford, The Times,* December 19, 1990; *Carmichael v. National Power plc* [1998] I.R.L.R. 301; contrast the position where the terms of the agreement are such as to negative contractual intention: *post,* § 2–159.

[14] *David T. Boyd & Co. v. Louis Louca* [1973] 1 Lloyd's Rep. 209; *cf. Siew Soon Wah v. Yong Tong Hong* [1973] A.C. 836; contrast *Bushwall Properties Ltd v. Vortex Properties Ltd* [1976] 1 W.L.R. 591, *ante,* § 2–103.

[15] *Tropwood A.G. of Zug v. Jade Enterprises Inc. (The Tropwind)* [1982] 1 Lloyd's Rep. 232.

[16] [1953] 1 Q.B. 543; discussed in *Heisler v. Anglo-Dal Ltd* [1954] 1 W.L.R. 1273 and applied in *Michael Richards Properties Ltd v. St. Saviour's* [1975] 3 All E.R. 416; see also *Slater v. Raw, The Times,* October 15, 1977.

the dispute itself.[17] Such cases show that the question whether the inclusion of a meaningless clause vitiates the contract, or can be ignored, depends on the importance which the parties may be considered to have attached to it. If it is simply verbiage, not intended to add anything to an otherwise complete agreement, or if it relates to a matter of relatively minor importance, it can be ignored. But if the parties intend it to govern some vital aspect of their relationship its vagueness will vitiate the entire agreement.

8. CONDITIONAL AGREEMENTS

2–134   **Introductory.** An agreement is conditional if its operation depends on an event which is not certain to occur. Discussions of this topic are made difficult by the fact that in the law of contract the word "condition" bears many senses: it is "a chameleon-like word which takes on its meaning from its surroundings."[18] At this stage, we are concerned with only one of these meanings; but to clear the ground it is necessary to draw a number of preliminary distinctions.

2–135   **Contingent and promissory conditions.** The word "condition" may refer either to an *event*, or to a *term* of a contract (as in the phrase "conditions of sale"[19]). Where "condition" refers to an event, that event may be either an occurrence which neither party undertakes to bring about, or the performance by one party of his undertaking. The first possibility is illustrated by a contract by which A is to work for B, and B is to pay A £50, "if it rains tomorrow." Here the obligations of both parties are contingent on the happening of the specified event which may be described as a *contingent* condition. The second possibility is illustrated by the ordinary case in which A agrees to work for B at a weekly wage payable at the end of the week. Here the contract is immediately binding on both parties, but B is not liable to pay until A has performed his promise to work. Such performance is a condition of B's liability, and, as A has promised to render it, the condition may be described as *promissory*.[20] Our concern here is with contingent conditions.

2–136   **Conditions precedent and subsequent.** Contingent conditions may be precedent or subsequent.[21] A condition is precedent if it provides that the contract is not to be binding until the specified event occurs. It is subsequent if it provides

---

[17] *E. J. R. Lovelock v. Exportles* [1968] 1 Lloyd's Rep. 163. Contrast *Star Shipping A/S v. China National Foreign Trade Transportation Corp. (The Star Texas)* [1993] 2 Lloyd's Rep. 445 where a clause for "arbitration in Beijing or London *in defendant's option*" was upheld.

[18] *Skips A/S Nordheim v. Petrofina S.A. (The Varenna)* [1984] Q.B. 599, 618.

[19] *Property and Bloodstock Ltd v. Emerton* [1968] Ch. 94, 118.

[20] For the distinction between *promissory* and *contingent* condition see Chalmers, *Sale of Goods* (18th ed.) Appendix 2, Note A; *Roadworks (1952) Ltd v. Charman* [1994] 2 Lloyd's Rep. 99, 103. *Total Gas Marketing Ltd v. Arco British Ltd* [1998] 2 Lloyd's Rep. 209, 215, 218.

[21] Conditions precedent are also sometimes called "suspensive," and conditions subsequent "resolutive," conditions: see Treitel, *Remedies for Breach of Contract*, (1988) 262–263. In *Ignazio Messina & Co. v. Polskie Linie Oceaniczne* [1995] 2 Lloyd's Rep. 566, 580 a condition there under discussion was said to be "a true condition subsequent or suspensive condition." "Subsequent" here seems to be a misprint for "precedent".

that a previously binding contract is to determine on the occurrence of the event: *e.g.* where A contracts to pay an allowance to B until B marries.[22]

Effects of agreements subject to contingent conditions precedent: in general. Where an agreement is subject to a contingent condition precedent, there is, before the occurrence of the condition, no duty on either party to render the principal performance promised by him: for example, a seller is not bound to deliver and a buyer is not bound to pay. Nor, in such a case, does either party undertake that the condition will occur. But an agreement subject to such a condition may impose some degree of obligation on the parties or on one of them. Whether it has this effect, and if so what degree of obligation is imposed, depends on the true construction of the term specifying condition.[23] Various possible degrees of obligation are discussed in §§ 2–138 to 2–142 below. **2–137**

Unrestricted right to withdraw. One possibility is that, before the event occurs, each party is free to withdraw from the agreement. In *Pym v. Campbell*[24] an agreement for the sale of a patent was executed, but the parties at the same time agreed that it should not "be the agreement" unless a third party approved of the invention. He did not approve, and it was held that the buyer was not liable for refusing to perform. The written agreement was "not an agreement at all."[25] If this is taken literally, either party could have withdrawn even before the third party had given his opinion. **2–138**

Restricted right to withdraw. A second possibility is that, before the event occurs, the main obligations have not accrued; but that, so long as the event can still occur, one (or both) of the parties cannot withdraw. This in *Smith v. Butler*[26] A bought land from B on condition that a loan to B (secured by a mortgage on the premises) would be transferred to A.[27] It was held that A could not withdraw before the time fixed for completion: he was bound to wait until then to see whether B could arrange the transfer. However, if it becomes clear that the condition has not occurred, or that it can no longer occur, within the time specified in the contract, the parties will be under no further obligations under the contract. In such a case, the effect of the non-occurrence of the condition is that the parties are "no longer bound"[28] by the contract, or that the contract is **2–139**

---

[22] *cf. Brown v. Knowsley B.C.* [1986] I.R.L.R. 102 (appointment to "last only as long as sufficient funds were provided" from specified sources); (*semble*) *Gyllenhammar & Partners International v. Sour Brodogradevna Industria* [1989] 2 Lloyd's Rep. 403 (contract to "become null and void" if certain consents were not obtained) and *Jameson v. CEGB* [1999] 1 All E.R. 193, 207 (settlement of tort claim immediately binding but subject to implied resolutive condition that it was to become void if the agreed amount was not paid). The distinction between conditions precedent and subsequent was criticised by Holmes (*The Common Law* (1881), 371); for discussion of this criticism, see Treitel, *Remedies for Breach of Contract* (1988), 263–264. English authority recognises that the distinction is by no means always clear cut: see *infra* at n. 30.

[23] For special difficulties where the condition precedent is implied, see *Bentworth Finance Ltd v. Lubert* [1968] 1 Q.B. 680; Carnegie 31 M.L.R. 78.

[24] (1856) 6 E. & B. 370.

[25] *ibid.* at 374.

[26] [1900] 1 Q.B. 694, *cf. Flexistowe Dock & Ry. Co. v. British Transport Docks Bd.* [1976] 2 Lloyd's Rep. 656; *Alan Estates Ltd v. W. G. Stores Ltd* [1982] Ch. 511, 520.

[27] On agreements "subject to finance," see Coote, 40 Conv. (N.S.) 37; Furmston, 3 O.J.L.S. 438, discussing *Meehan v. Jones* (1982) 149 C.L.R. 571.

[28] *North Sea Energy Holdings NV v. Petroleum Authority of Thailand* [1997] 2 Lloyd's Rep. 418, 428–429 (affd. [1999] 1 Lloyd's Rep. 483). *Total Gas Marketing Ltd v. Arco British Ltd* [1998] 2 Lloyd's Rep. 209, 215.

"discharged."[29] What the parties have called a "condition precedent" can thus operate, or have the effect of, a condition subsequent.[30]

2–140   **Duty not to prevent occurrence of the event.** A third possibility is that, before the event occurs, the main obligations have not accrued; but that in the meantime neither party must do anything to prevent the occurrence of that event. Thus in *Mackay v. Dick*[31] an excavating machine was sold on condition that it could excavate at a specified rate on the buyer's property. The buyer's refusal to provide facilities for a proper trial was held to be a breach. Similarly, the seller would have been in breach, had he refused to subject the machine to the proper test. The same principle is illustrated by a case[32] in which a professional footballer was transferred for a fee, part of which was to be paid only after he had scored 20 goals. Before he had done so, the new club dropped him from their first team, and they were held to be in breach as they had not given the player a reasonable opportunity to score the 20 goals. The duty not to prevent the occurrence of the condition has been explained as resting on an implied term and this explanation limits the scope of the duty in a number of ways. For example, the implied term may be only to the effect that a party will not *deliberately* prevent the occurrence of the condition[33]; or (even more narrowly) that he will not *wrongfully* do so.[34] The latter type of implication may allow a party to engage in certain kinds of deliberate prevention but not in others: for example, it may allow a company which has promised an employee the opportunity of earning a bonus to deprive him of that opportunity by going out of business, but not by simply dismissing him, before the bonus has become due.[35]

2–141   **Condition of "satisfaction".** The implied term can also be excluded by an express contrary provision[36] and, in particular, by a provision making the operation of a contract depend on the "satisfaction" of one of the parties with the subject-matter or other aspects relating to the other's performance. Thus it has been held that there was no contract where a house was bought "subject to satisfactory mortgage"[37]; and where a boat was bought "subject to satisfactory survey"[38] it was held that the buyer was not bound if he expressed his dissatisfaction,[39] in spite of the fact that such expression was a deliberate act on his part which prevented the occurrence of the condition. The same is true where goods

---

[29] *ibid.* at 218.

[30] *ibid.* at 221, 224. And see n. 31 *infra*.

[31] (1881) 6 App.Cas. 251. The condition is described as subsequent in *Colley v. Overseas Exporters* [1921] 3 K.B. 302, 308. *cf.* also *Shipping Corp. of India v. Naviera Letasa* [1976] 1 Lloyd's Rep. 132 and *C.I.A. Barca de Panama S.A. v. George Wimpey & Co. Ltd* [1980] 1 Lloyd's Rep. 598; *South West Trains Ltd v. Wightman, The Times*, January 14, 1998.

[32] *Bournemouth & Boscombe Athletic F.C. v. Manchester United F.C., The Times*, May 22, 1980.

[33] See *Blake & Co. v. Sohn* [1969] 1 W.L.R. 1412.

[34] See *Thompson v. ASDA-MFI Group plc* [1988] Ch. 241.

[35] Example based on *Thompson v. ASDA-MFI Group plc, supra*.

[36] See *Micklefield v. S.A.C. Technology Ltd* [1990] 1 W.L.R. 1002.

[37] *Lee-Parker v. Izett (No. 2)* [1975] 1 W.L.R. 775; distinguished in *Janmohammed v. Hassam, The Times*, June 10, 1976.

[38] *Astra Trust Ltd v. Adams & Wiliams* [1969] 1 Lloyd's Rep. 81 doubted in *Varverakis v. Compagnia de Navegacion Artico SA (The Merak)* [1976] 2 Lloyd's Rep. 250, 254 and in *Ee v. Kahar* (1979) 40 P. & C.R. 223 (as to which see below, n. 43).

[39] But if the buyer declared his satisfaction the seller would be bound even though the survey was not objectively satisfactory: *Graham v. Pitkin* [1992] 1 W.L.R. 403, 405.

are bought on approval and the buyer does not approve them,[40] and where an offer of employment is made "subject to satisfactory references," and the prospective employer does not regard the references as satisfactory.[41] But sometimes the courts do restrict the freedom of action of the party on whose satisfaction the operation of the contract depends. Thus where a ship was sold "subject to satisfactory completion of two trial voyages" it was said that such a stipulation was to be construed as "subject to bona fides"[42]; and it has also been held that the party on whose satisfaction the operation of the contract depends must at least provide facilities for, or not impede, the inspection referred to in the agreement.[43] Of course if the result of the inspection is unsatisfactory, the principal obligation of the contract will not take effect.[44]

Duty of reasonable diligence to bring about the event. A fourth possibility **2–142** is that, before the event occurs, the main obligations have not accrued but that one of the parties undertakes to use reasonable efforts to bring the event about (without absolutely undertaking that his efforts will succeed). This construction was applied, for instance, where land was sold subject to the condition that the purchaser should obtain planning permission to use the land as a transport depot: he was bound to make reasonable efforts to obtain the permission, but he was free from liability when those efforts failed.[45] Similarly, where goods are sold "subject to export (or import) licence," the party whose duty it is to obtain the licence[46] does not prima facie promise absolutely that a licence will be obtained[47]; but only undertakes to make reasonable efforts to that end.[48] The

---

[40] *cf.* Sale of Goods Act 1979, s.18, rule 4.

[41] *Wishart v. National Association of Citizens' Advice Bureaux* [1990] I.C.R. 794.

[42] *Albion Sugar Co. v. William Tankers (The John S. Darbyshire)* [1977] 2 Lloyd's Rep. 457, 464; *cf. BV Oliehandel Jongkind v. Coastal International Ltd* [1983] 2 Lloyd's Rep. 463; *The Nissos Samos* [1985] 1 Lloyd's Rep. 378, 385; contrast *Star Steamship Society v. Beogradska Plovidba (The Junior K)* [1988] 2 Lloyd's Rep. 583, 589 (where the words were held to negative contractual intention). See also *El Awadi v. Bank of Credit & Commerce International SA* [1990] 1 Q.B. 606, 619; and, in an analogous context, *Abu Dhabi National Tanker Co. v. Product Star Shipping Co. (The Product Star (No. 2))* [1993] 1 Lloyd's Rep. 397, 404.

[43] *Varverakis v. Compagnia de Navegacion Artico SA (The Merak)* [1976] 2 Lloyd's Rep. 250; *cf. Ee v. Kahar* (1979) 40 P. & C.R. 223 (where the sale was simply "subject to survey"—omitting the word "satisfactory"—thus falling, it is submitted, within the principle of *Mackay v. Dick, supra* n. 31).

[44] As in *Albion Sugar Co. v. Williams Tankers (The John S. Darbyshire)* [1977] 2 Lloyd's Rep. 457.

[45] *Hargreaves Transport Ltd v. Lynch* [1969] 1 W.L.R. 215 (condition not satisfied); *Richard West & Partners (Inverness) Ltd v. Dick* [1969] 2 Ch. 424 (similar condition satisfied); *cf. Fisher v. Tomatousos* [1991] 2 E.G.L.R. 204. Contrast *Tesco Stores Ltd v. Gibson* (1970) 214 E.G. 835 (no obligation on purchaser to apply for planning permission).

[46] As to which party has this duty, see *H. O. Brandt & Co. v. H. N. Morris & Co.* [1917] 2 K.B. 784; *A. V. Pound & Co. v. M. W. Hardy & Co.* [1956] A.C. 588; *Benjamin's Sale of Goods* (5th ed., (1997) §§ 18–248 to 18–250.

[47] The prima facie rule may be excluded by express words which do, on their true construction, impose an absolute duty; *e.g. Peter Cassidy Seed Co. Ltd v. Osuustukkukauppa* [1957] 1 W.L.R. 273; *C. Czarnikow Ltd v. Centrale Handlu Zagranicznego "Rolimpex"* [1979] A.C. 351, 371; *Congimex Companhia Geral, etc., S.A.R.L. v. Tradax Export S.A.* [1983] 1 Lloyd's Rep. 250; *Pagnan S.p.A. v. Tradax Ocean Transport S.A.* [1987] 3 All E.R. 565; Yates and Carter, 1 J.C.L. 57.

[48] *Re Anglo-Russian Merchant Traders and John Batt & Co. (London) Ltd* [1917] 2 K.B. 679; *Coloniale Import-Export v. Loumidis & Sons* [1978] 2 Lloyd's Rep. 560; *Overseas Buyers Ltd v. Granadex S.A.* [1980] 2 Lloyd's Rep. 608; *Gamerco S.A. v. I.C.M./Fair Warning (Agency) Ltd* [1995] 1 W.L.R. 1226, 1231. Where the contract is expressly subject to the approval of a public authority, there may not even be a duty to make reasonable efforts to secure that approval: see *Gyllenhammar*

principal obligations to buy and sell will not take effect if no licence is obtained[49]; but if the party who should have made reasonable efforts has failed to do so he will be liable in damages,[50] unless he can show that any such efforts, which he should have made would (if made) have necessarily been unsuccessful.[51] The same principles have been applied where an agreement was made "subject to the approval of the court"; and where an agreement was made to assign a lease which could only be assigned with the consent of the landlord. In such cases the requisite approval or consent must be sought; but the main obligations do not accrue until the approval or consent is given,[52] and if it is refused the principal obligation will not take effect.[53]

2–143   **Principal and subsidiary obligations.** It will be seen that in cases falling within categories discussed in §§ 2–139 to 2–142 above, a distinction must be drawn between two types of obligation: the principal obligation of each party (*e.g.* to buy and sell) and a subsidiary obligation, *i.e.* one not to withdraw, not to prevent occurrence of the condition, or to make reasonable efforts to bring it about. One view is that the party who fails to perform the subsidiary obligation is to be treated as if the condition had occurred; and that he is then liable on the principal obligation. Thus in *Mackay v. Dick*[54] the buyer was held liable *for the price*; but there was no discussion as to the remedy. In principle it seems wrong to hold him so liable, for such a result ignores the possibility that the machine might have failed to come up to the standard required by the contract, even if proper facilities for trial had been provided. It is submitted that the correct result in cases of this kind is to award *damages* for breach of the subsidiary obligation: in assessing such damages, the court can take into account the possibility that the condition might not have occurred, even if there had been no such breach.[55] To hold the party in breach liable for the full performance promised by him, on the fiction that the condition had occurred, seems to introduce into this branch of the law a punitive element that is inappropriate to a contractual action. The most recent authority rightly holds that such a doctrine of "fictional fulfilment" of a condition does not form part of English law.[56–57]

Partners International v. Sour Brodegradevna Industria [1989] 2 Lloyd's Rep. 403. For the standard of duty, see generally *Benjamin's Sale of Goods* (5th ed., 1997) §§ 18–252 to 18–257.

[49] *Charles H. Windschuegl Ltd v. Alexander Pickering & Co. Ltd* (1950) 84 Ll.L.Rep. 89, 92–93; *Brauer & Co. (Great Britain) Ltd v. James Clark (Brush Materials) Ltd* [1952] 2 All E.R. 497, 501; *cf.* the cases on sales of goods "to arrive" discussed in Benjamin's *Sale of Goods* (5th ed., 1997), §§ 21–022 to 21–027.

[50] *e.g. Malik v. C.E.T.A.* [1974] 1 Lloyd's Rep. 279; *Agroexport v. Cie. Européenne de Céréales* [1974] 1 Lloyd's Rep. 499.

[51] See Benjamin's *Sale of Goods* (5th ed., 1997), § 18–267; *Overseas Buyers Ltd v. Granadex S.A.*, *supra*, at 612.

[52] *Smallman v. Smallman* [1972] Fam. 25.

[53] *Shires v. Brock* (1977) 247 E.G. 127.

[54] (1881) 6 App.Cas. 251, *ante*, § 2–140.

[55] *Bournemouth & Boscombe Athletic F.C. v. Manchester United F.C., The Times*, May 22, 1980; *cf. The Blankenstein* [1985] 1 W.L.R. 435; *Alpha Trading Ltd v. Dunshaw-Patten Ltd* [1981] Q.B. 290; *George Moundreas & Co. S.A. v. Navimpex Centrala Navala* [1985] 2 Lloyd's Rep. 515; *Orient Overseas Management & Finance Ltd v. File Shipping Co. Ltd (The Energy Progress)* [1993] 1 Lloyd's Rep. 355, 358.

[56–57] *Thompson v. ASDA-MFI Group plc* [1988] Ch. 241, 266 (where the condition was said at 251 to be subsequent). *Little v. Courage Ltd* (1995) 70 P. & C.R. 469, 474.

Waiver of condition. Where a condition is inserted entirely for the benefit of   2–144
one party, that party may waive the condition. He can then sue[58] and be sued[59]
on the contract as if the condition had occurred. Obviously this rule does not
apply to cases falling within the first of the categories discussed above, in which
there is no contract at all before the condition occurs.

9. CONTRACTUAL INTENTION

General. In a number of situations to be discussed in § 2–146 to 2–169 below,   2–145
it has been held that an agreement, though supported by consideration,[60] was not
binding as a contract[61] because it was made without any intention of creating
legal relations.[62]

Burden of proof: express agreements. In the case of ordinary commercial   2–146
transactions it is not normally necessary to prove that the parties to an express
contract in fact intended to create legal relations.[63] The onus of proving that there
was no such intention "is on the party who asserts that no legal effect is intended,
and the onus is a heavy one."[64] In deciding whether the onus has been discharged, the courts will be influenced by the importance of the agreement to the
parties, and by the fact that one of them acted in reliance on it.[65]

Burden of proof: agreements inferred from conduct. The rule as to burden   2–147
of proof stated above applies where the parties had entered into an *express*
agreement; but claims or defences are sometimes based on the allegation that
parties between whom there was no express agreement had so conducted themselves in relation to each other that an implied contract was to be inferred from

---

[58] *Wood Preservation Ltd v. Prior* [1969] 1 W.L.R. 1077; contrast *Heron Garages Properties Ltd v. Moss* [1974] 1 W.L.R. 148.

[59] *McKillop v. McMullan* [1979] N.I. 85.

[60] *R. v. Civil Service Appeal Board, ex p. Bruce* [1988] 3 All E.R. 686, 693, 698; *cf. Re Beaumont* [1980] Ch. 444, 453: consideration may be provided "under a contract *or otherwise.*"

[61] For enforcement on other grounds, see *John Fox v. Bannister King & Rigbeys* [1988] Q.B. 925, 928 (court's jurisdiction to enforce honourable conduct on the part of solicitors); *Xydhias v. Xydhias* [1999] 2 All E.R. 386, 394 (compromise of claim for ancillary relief in divorce proceedings).

[62] See also *Zakhem International Construction Ltd v. Nippon Kohan KK* [1987] 2 Lloyd's Rep. 596. For a denial of the requirement, see Williston, *Contracts*, § 21; *cf.* Tuck, 21 Can. Bar Rev. 123 (1943); Shatwell (1954) 1 Sydney L.R. at 293; Unger (1956) 19 M.L.R. 96; Hepple [1970] C.L.J. 122; Hedley (1985) 50 J.L.S. 391. There is also said to be a requirement of "mutuality": see *Simpkins v. Pays* [1955] 1 W.L.R. 975, 979; *Rajbenback v. Mamon* [1955] 1 Q.B. 283, 286; but this expression refers to consideration rather than to contractual intention: see *Lees v. Whitcombe* (1828) 5 Bing. 34; *Sykes v. Dixon* (1839) 9 Ad. & El. 693; *Westhead v. Sproson* (1861) 6 H. & N. 728; Treitel (1961) 77 L.Q.R. 83.

[63] Certain regulated agreements under the Consumer Credit Act 1974 must contain a signature in a "signature box" warning the signer to sign the agreement "only if you want to be legally bound by its terms": Consumer Credit (Agreements) Regulations 1983 (S.I. 1983 No. 1553).

[64] *Edwards v. Skyways Ltd* [1964] 1 W.L.R. 349, 355; *Bahamas Oil Refining Co. v. Kristiansands Tankrederei A/S (The Polyduke)* [1978] 1 Lloyd's Rep. 211; *Financial Techniques (Planning Serv-ices) Ltd v. Hughes* [1981] I.R.L.R. 32; *G.A.F.L.A.C. v. Tanter (The Zephyr)* [1985] 2 Lloyd's Rep. 529, 537 (disapproving [1984] 1 Lloyd's Rep. 58, 63–64); *Yani Haryanto v. E.D. & F. Man (Sugar) Ltd* [1986] 2 Lloyd's Rep. 44; *Orion Insurance plc v. Sphere Drake Insurance plc* [1992] 1 Lloyd's Rep. 132, 141; *cf. Coastal Bermuda Petroleum Ltd v. VTT Vulcan Petroleum S.A. (The Marine Star) (No. 2)* [1994] 2 Lloyd's Rep. 629, 632, revsd. on other grounds [1996] 2 Lloyd's Rep. 383.

[65] *cf. ante*, § 2–129; *Kingswood Estate Co. v. Anderson* [1963] 2 Q.B. 169; *South West Water Authority v. Palmer* (1982) 263 E.G. 438.

their conduct; and in a number of cases of this kind the allegation has been rejected on the ground that there was no contractual intention.[66] Such cases illustrate the judicial attitude that "contracts are not lightly to be implied" and that the courts must (in case of this kind) be able "to conclude with confidence that . . . the parties intended to create contractual relations."[67] The burden of proof on this issue appears, in cases of this kind, to be on the proponent of the contract, contrary to the rule which applies to express agreements regulating commercial relationships.

2–148   **Intention judged objectively.** In deciding issues of contractual intention, the courts normally apply an objective test[68]: for example, where the sale of a house is *not* "subject to contract,"[69] both parties are likely to be bound even though one of them subjectively believed that he would not be bound until the usual exchange of contracts had taken place.[70] But the objective test is here (as elsewhere)[71] subject to the limitation that it does not apply in favour of a party who knows the truth. Thus in the example just given the party who did not intend to be bound would not be bound if his state of mind was actually known to the other party.[72] Nor could a party who did not in fact intend to be bound invoke the objective test so as to hold the other party to the contract[73]: to apply that test in such a case would pervert its purpose, which is to protect a party who has relied on the objective appearance of consent from the prejudice which he would suffer if the *other* party could escape liability on the ground that he had no real intention to be bound. Nor does the objective test apply where the parties have expressed their actual intention in the document alleged to constitute the contract: the question whether they intended the document to have contractual force then becomes one of construction. The objective test, in other words, merely prevents a party from relying on his *uncommunicated* belief as to the binding force of the agreement. "Where such a belief is expressed in the documents, it must be a question of construction of the documents as a whole what effect is to be given to such a statement."[74] In the absence of such an expression of intention, however, the legal *effects* of an agreement which is clearly intended to give rise to some legal relations is similarly not determined by the subjective intentions of the parties or of one of them: for example, an agreement may take effect as a

---

[66] *Hispanica de Petroleos SA v. Vencedora Oceana Navegaceon SA (The Kapetan Markos N.L.) (No. 2)* [1987] 2 Lloyd's Rep. 323; *The Aramis* [1989] 1 Lloyd's Rep. 213; *Mitsui & Co. Ltd v. Novorossiysk Shipping Co. (The Gudermes)* [1993] 1 Lloyd's Rep. 311; in some of these cases rights and liabilities under the shipping documents would now arise by virtue of Carriage of Goods by Sea Act 1992, ss.2 and 3.

[67] *Blackpool and Fylde Aero Club v. Blackpool B.C.* [1990] 1 W.L.R. 1195, 1202.

[68] See *Carlill v. Carbolic Smoke Ball Co.* [1893] 1 Q.B. 256; *Ignazio Messina & Co. v. Polskie Linie Oceaniczne* [1995] 2 Lloyd's Rep. 566, 579; *Bowerman v. Association of British Travel Agents* [1995] N.L.J. 1815. *cf. Crowden v. Aldridge* [1993] 1 W.L.R. 433, applying the objective test of intention to produce legal consequences to a non-contractual direction to executors in favour of a third party. *Quaere* whether, in the absence of reliance on the direction, the policy which justifies the objective test in a contractual context extends to the situation which arose in this case.

[69] *Ante*, § 2–108.

[70] *Tweddell v. Henderson* [1975] 1 W.L.R. 1496; *Storer v. Manchester C.C.* [1974] 1 W.L.R. 1403, 1408.

[71] *Ante*, § 2–002.

[72] *Pateman v. Pay* (1974) 263 E.G. 467.

[73] *Lark v. Outhwaite* [1991] 2 Lloyd's Rep. 132, 141.

[74] *R. v. Lord Chancellor's Department, ex p. Nangle* [1991] I.C.R. 743, 751.

lease even though it is intended by the lessor to take effect only as a licence.[75]

Intention expressly negatived. The clearest illustration of the requirement of contractual intention is to be found in cases where the agreement contains an express provision negativing the intention.[76] For example, in *Rose & Frank Co. v. J.R. Crompton & Bros. Ltd*[77] an agency agreement provided: "This arrangement is not entered into, nor is this memorandum written, as a formal or legal agreement . . . but it is only a definite expression and record of the purpose and intention of the . . . parties concerned, to which they each honourably pledge themselves." It was held that this "honour clause" negatived contractual intention. Similarly agreements for the sale of land are generally made "subject to contract." These words negative contractual intention, so that the parties are not normally bound until formal contracts are exchanged.[78] It is a crucial part of this process of "exchange" that the parties should intend by it to bring a legally binding contract into existence.[79] Football pool coupons also commonly contain words expressly negativing contractual intention.[80]
    2–149

Whether a particular phrase has this effect is a question of construction.[81] In *Edwards v. Skyways Ltd*[82] employers promised to make a dismissed employee an "*ex gratia* payment." It was held that these words did not negative contractual intention but amounted merely to a denial of a pre-existing legal liability to make the payment. Contractual intention was, similarly, not negatived where an arbitration clause in a reinsurance contract provided that "this treaty shall be *interpreted as* an honourable engagement rather than as a legal obligation . . . " The contract as a whole was clearly intended to be binding; and the purpose of the words quoted was merely to free the arbitrator "to some extent from strict legal rules"[83] in interpreting the agreement. Again, in *The Mercedes Envoy*[84] a shipowner during negotiations for a charterparty said: "we are fixed in good faith." It was held that the words "in good faith" did not negative contractual intention: if they had any effect, it amounted merely to a "collateral understanding"[85] that account
    2–150

---

[75] *Street v. Mountford* [1985] A.C. 809; *A. G. Securities v. Vaughan* [1990 1 A.C. 417; contrast *Ogwr B.C. v. Dykes* [1989] 1 W.L.R. 295; *Monmouth B.C. v. Marlog, The Times*, May 4, 1994 (where there was no intention to enter into *any* legal relationship); *Bruton v. Quadrant Housing Trust* [1997] N.L.J. 1385.

[76] e.g. *W. v. Essex CC* [1998] 3 All E.R. 111, 128.

[77] [1925] A.C. 445, affg. [1923] 2 K.B. 261; *County Ltd v. Girozentrale Securities* [1996] 3 All E.R. 834.

[78] *Ante*, §§ 2–108, 2–109; *Rose & Frank Co. v. J.R. Crompton & Bros. Ltd* [1923] 2 K.B. 261, 294; *Ali v. Ahmed* (1996) 71 P. & C.R. D39.

[79] *Commission for the New Towns v. Cooper (G.B.) Ltd* [1995] Ch. 259, 295.

[80] See *Jones v. Vernons Pools Ltd* [1938] 2 All E.R. 626; *Appleson v. Littlewood Ltd* [1939] 1 All E.R. 464; *Guest v. Empire Pools* (1964) 108 S.J. 98. In Scotland, it has been argued that such honour clauses in football coupons may be unreasonable and hence ineffective: *Ferguson v. Littlewoods Pools* 1997 S.L.T. 309, 314–315.

[81] *R. v. Lord Chancellor's Department, ex p. Nangle* [1991] I.C.R. 743.

[82] [1964] 1 W.L.R. 349. It was admitted that there was consideration moving from the employee.

[83] *Home Insurance Co. Ltd v. Administratia Asigurarilor* [1983] 2 Lloyd's Rep. 674, 677; *Home and Overseas Insurance Co. Ltd v. Mentor Insurance Co. (U.K.) Ltd* [1989] 1 Lloyd's Rep. 473.

[84] *Hanjin Shipping Co. Ltd v. Zenith Chartering Corp. (The Mercedes Envoy)* [1995] 2 Lloyd's Rep. 559.

[85] *ibid.* at 564.

should be taken of damage to the vessel, of which both shipowner and charterer were aware.

2–151   **Statements inducing a contract.** A statement inducing a contract may be a "mere puff" if the court considers that it was not seriously meant and that this should have been obvious to the person to whom it was made. In *Weeks v. Tybald*,[86] for example, the defendant "affirmed and published that he would give £100 to him that should marry his daughter with his consent." The court held that it was "not reasonable that the defendant should be bound by such general words spoken to excite suitors." Similarly, in *Lambert v. Lewis*,[87] a manufacturer stated in promotional literature that his product was "foolproof" and that it "required no maintenance." These statements did not give rise to a contract between the manufacturer and a dealer (who had bought the product from an intermediary) as they were "not intended to be, nor were they, acted on as being express warranties."[88]

2–152   Other statements which induce persons to enter into contracts have some effect in law, but exactly what that effect is often turns on whether they are "mere representations" or have contractual force. The distinction between these categories turns on the test of contractual intention. In cases concerning the effect of such statements, the test of intention generally determines the *contents* of a contract, the *existence* of which is not in doubt. But where the inducing statement for some reason cannot take effect as a term of the main contract it may, nevertheless, amount to a collateral contract; and whether it has this effect again depends on the test of contractual intention. For example, in *Heilbut, Symons & Co. v. Buckleton*[89] the claimant applied for shares in a company after a conversation with the defendants' manager, which led the claimant to believe that the company (which the defendants were "bringing out") was a rubber company. It was not a rubber company, and the claimant alleged that the defendants had warranted that it was a rubber company. It was held that nothing said by the manager was intended to have the effect of a collateral contract. Lord Moulton said: "Not only the terms of such contracts but the existence of an *animus contrahendi* on the part of all the parties to them must be clearly shewn."[90]

2–153   **Social agreements.** Many social arrangements do not amount to contracts because they are not intended to be legally binding. "The ordinary example is where two parties agree to take a walk together, or where there is an offer and an acceptance of hospitality."[91] Similarly it has been held that the winner of a

---

[86] (1605) Noy 11; *cf. Dalrymple v. Dalrymple* (1811) 2 Hag.Con. 54, 105.

[87] [1982] A.C. 225 affd. so far as the manufacturer's liability was concerned, but on other grounds *ibid.* at 271.

[88] [1982] A.C. 225, 262; contrast *Carlill v. Carbolic Smoke Ball Co. Ltd* [1893] 1 Q.B. 256 and *Bowerman v. Association of British Travel Agents* [1995] N.L.J. 1815, *ante*, § 2–015.

[89] [1913] A.C. 30 criticised by Atiyah in *The Rise and Fall of Freedom of Contract*, p. 772; but followed by the House of Lords in *I.B.A. v. E.M.I. Electronics Ltd* (1980) 14 Build.L.R. 1; *cf. Strover v. Harrington* [1988] Ch. 390, 410; *Ignazio Messina & Co. v. Polskie Linie Oceaniczne* [1995] 2 Lloyd's Rep. 566, 581.

[90] [1913] A.C. 30, 47; *Unit Construction Co. Ltd v. Liverpool Corp.* (1972) 221 E.G. 459; *Hispanica de Petroleos SA v. Vencedora Oceanica Navegacion SA (The Kapetan Markos NL)* [1987] 2 Lloyd's Rep. 323, 332.

[91] *Balfour v. Balfour* [1919] 2 K.B. 571, 578; *Rose & Frank Co. v. J.R. Crompton & Bros. Ltd* [1923] 2 K.B. 261, 293; *Wyatt v. Kreglinger & Fernau* [1933] 1 K.B. 793, 806.

competition held by a golf club could not sue for his prize where "no one concerned with that competition ever intended that there should be any legal results flowing from the conditions posted and the acceptance by the competitor of those conditions"[92]; that the rules of a competition organised by a "jalopy club" for charitable purposes did not have contractual force[93]; that "car pool" and similar arrangements between friends or neighbours did not amount to contracts even though one party contributed to the running costs of the other's vehicle[94]; and that the provision of free residential accommodation for close friends did not amount to a contract as it was an act of bounty, done without any intention to enter into legal relations.[95]

Domestic agreements. Many domestic arrangements are not intended to be **2–154** legally binding. In *Balfour v. Balfour*[96] a husband who worked abroad promised to pay an allowance of £30 per month to his wife, who had to stay in England on medical grounds. The wife's attempt to enforce this promise by action failed for two reasons: she had not provided any consideration, and the parties did not intend the arrangement to be legally binding. On the second ground alone, most domestic arrangements between husband and wife are not contracts. Atkin L.J. said: "Those agreements, or many of them, do not result in contracts at all . . . even though there may be what as between other parties would constitute consideration for the agreement. . . . They are not contracts . . . because the parties did not intend that they should be attended by legal consequences. . . . Agreements such as these are outside the realm of contracts altogether."[97] It has been said that the facts of *Balfour v. Balfour* "stretched the doctrine to its limits"[98]; but the doctrine itself has not been judicially questioned and the cases provide many other instances of its application.[99]

The doctrine does not, of course, prevent a husband from making a binding **2–155** contract with his wife. For example, a husband can be his wife's tenant.[1] Binding separation agreements are often made when husband and wife agree to live

---

[92] *Lens v. Devonshire Club, The Times*, December 4, 1914; referred to in *Wyatt's* case, *supra* n. 91 from which the quotation in the text is taken.

[93] *White v. Blackmore* [1972] 2 Q.B. 651.

[94] *Coward v. M.I.B.* [1963] 1 Q.B. 259; overruled, but not on the issue of contractual intention, in *Albert v. M.I.B.* [1972] A.C. 301; *Buckpitt v. Oates* [1968] 1 All E.R. 1145, criticised on this point by Karsten (1969) 32 M.L.R. 88. The actual decisions are obsolete by reason of Road Traffic Act 1988, ss.145, 149; *cf.* also s.150. But an issue of contractual intention might still arise if one party to such an arrangement simply failed to turn up at the agreed time. For another context in which sharing of expenses did not give rise to an inference of contractual intention, see *Monmouth C.C. v. Marlog, The Times*, May 4, 1994.

[95] *Heslop v. Burns* [1974] 1 W.L.R. 1241; contrast *Horrocks v. Forray* [1976] 1 W.L.R. 230.

[96] [1919] 2 K.B. 571.

[97] *ibid.* at 578: it would clearly be undesirable to enforce such agreements in accordance with their original terms, however much the position of the parties had changed.

[98] *Pettitt v. Pettitt* [1970] A.C. 777, 816; *cf. Gould v. Gould* [1970] 1 Q.B. 275, where there was a division of opinion on the issue of contractual intention, the majority holding that there was no such intention where a husband on leaving his wife promised to pay her £15 per week so long as he could manage it. And see generally Ingman [1970] J.B.L. 109.

[99] *e.g. Gage v. King* [1961] 1 Q.B. 188; *Spellman v. Spellman* [1961] 1 W.L.R. 921; *cf. Re Beaumont (decd.)* [1980] Ch. 444, 453; *cf. Lloyds Bank plc v. Rosset* [1991] A.C. 107.

[1] *Pearce v. Merriman* [1904] 1 K.B. 80; contrast *Morris v. Tarrant* [1971] 2 Q.B. 143.

apart.[2] And where a man before marriage promised his future wife to leave her a house if she married him she was able to enforce the promise although it was made informally and in affectionate terms.[3] Similarly, the requirement of contractual intention may be satisfied where a man and a woman make an agreement with regard to a house in which they live together as husband and wife without being married. In one such case, it was said to be "part of the bargain between the parties expressed or to be implied that the [woman] should contribute her labour towards the reparation of the house in which she was to have some beneficial interest."[4] This "bargain" was enforceable, either by way of contract[5] or by way of constructive trust.[6] Formal requirements (imposed in 1989) for contracts for the creation of interests in land[7] make it unlikely[8] that such an arrangement could now take effect as such a contract, but they would not prevent it from taking effect by way of constructive trust.[9] Even where the woman did nothing to increase the value of the house (and so had no "proprietary interest in the property")[10] the man's promise that the house should continue to be available for her and the couple's children was held to be enforceable as a contractual licence as she had moved out of her rent-controlled flat in reliance on the promise.[11] But in another case,[12] in which there was no such element of reliance, it was held that the provision by a married man of a house for his mistress did not give rise to a legally binding promise that she should be allowed to stay in the house. Even when such a promise can be established, it would (whether the parties were married or not) be more difficult to show that some less important promise, *e.g.* as to the amount of money to be provided by way of a dress or housekeeping allowance, was intended to have contractual effect.

2–156   Similar issues of contractual intention can arise from promises between parents and children. An informal promise by a parent to pay a child an allowance during study is not normally a contract, though it may become one if, for example it is part of a bargain made to induce the child to give up some occupation so as to enter on some particular course of study.[13] Similarly, there is not normally a contract where a mother agrees to nurse her child who has fallen ill or been

---

[2] *e.g. Merritt v. Merritt* [1970] 1 W.L.R. 1211; *cf. Tanner v. Tanner* [1975] 1 W.L.R. 1346 as explained in *Horrocks v. Forray* [1976] 1 W.L.R. 230; *Re Windle* [1975] 1 W.L.R. 1628 (doubted in *Re Kumar* [1993] 1 W.L.R. 224); contrast *Vaughan v. Vaughan* [1953] 1 Q.B. 762 (*post*, § 2–165).

[3] *Synge v. Synge* [1894] 1 Q.B. 466, *cf. Jennings v. Brown* (1842) 9 M. & W. 496 (promise to discarded mistress).

[4] *Eves v. Eves* [1975] 1 W.L.R. 1338, 1345.

[5] *ibid. per* Browne L.J. and Brightman J.

[6] *ibid.* at 1342, *per* Lord Denning M.R.; for this basis of liability, see *Grant v. Edwards* [1986] Ch. 638; *cf. Lloyds Bank plc v. Rosset* [1991] A.C. 107, 129, contrast *Burns v. Burns* [1984] Ch. 317; Lowe and Smith (1984) 47 M.L.R. 341; Dewar, *ibid.* 735.

[7] Law of Property (Miscellaneous Provisions) Act 1989, s.2; *post*, § 4–047.

[8] *e.g. Taylor v. Dickens* [1998] FLR 806, 819; s.2(1) of the 1989 Act (*supra*, n. 7) requires the contract to be made in writing by incorporating all its "expressly agreed" terms in a document (or documents, where contracts are exchanged), and if the promise in *Eves v. Eves* (*supra*, at n. 4) was indeed implied, it could be argued that there were no "expressly agreed" terms.

[9] The formal requirements imposed by the 1989 Act (*supra* n. 7) do not apply to "the creation or operation of . . . construction trusts": s.2(5).

[10] *Tanner v. Tanner* [1975] 1 W.L.R. 1346, 1351.

[11] *Tanner v. Tanner, supra.*

[12] *Horrocks v. Forray* [1976] 1 W.L.R. 320; *cf. Coombes v. Smith* [1986] 1 W.L.R. 808; *Windeler v. Whitehall* [1990] 2 FLR 505.

[13] See *Jones v. Padavatton* [1969] 1 W.L.R. 328, 333; *cf. Shadwell v. Shadwell* (1860) 9 C.B.(N.S.) 159; *post*, § 3–068.

injured, even though she has to give up her work to do so.[14] Conversely, it has been held that the gift of a flat by a mother to her daughter on condition that the daughter should look after the mother there did not amount to a contract because it was not intended to have contractual force.[15] On the other hand, where a mother bought a house as a residence for her son and daughter-in-law on the terms that they should pay her £7 per week to pay off the purchase price, this was held to amount to a contractual licence which the mother could not revoke so long as either of the young couple kept up the payments.[16]

Where adult members of a family (other than husband and wife or persons **2–157** living together as such) share a common household, the financial terms on which they do so may well be intended to have contractual effect. This was for example held to be the position where a young couple were induced to sell their house, and to move in with their elderly relations, by the latters' promise to leave them a share of the proposed joint home. The argument that this promise was not intended to be legally binding was rejected as the young people would not have taken the important step of selling their own house on the faith of a merely social arrangement.[17] But while the common household was a going concern the parties must have made many arrangements about its day-to-day management which were not intended to be legally binding. In cases of this kind, it may often be clear that there is some contract, but the terms of the arrangement may be so imprecise that it is hard to say just what obligation it imposes. For example, in *Hussey v. Palmer*[18] a lady spent £600 on having a room added to her son-in-law's house, on the understanding that she could live there for the rest of her life. When she left voluntarily, about a year later, it was held that there was no contract of loan in respect of the £600[19]; but it seems likely that there was a contract to allow her to live in the room for the rest of her life.

An agreement between persons who share a common household may be a **2–158** contract if it has nothing to do with the routine management of the household. Thus in *Simpkins v. Pays*[20] three ladies who lived in the same house took part in a fashion competition run by a newspaper. They agreed to send in their entries on one coupon and to share the prize which any entry might win. The court rejected the contention that the agreement to share was not intended to be legally binding.

---

[14] If there is very clear evidence of contractual intention there may be a binding contract, as in *Haggar v. de Placido* [1972] 1 W.L.R. 716. But in practice such "contracts" were only made as a device to enable the value of the mother's services to be recovered from a tortfeasor who had injured the child, and for this purpose they are now unnecessary: *Donelly v. Joyce* [1974] Q.B. 454.

[15] *Ellis v. Chief Adjudication Officer* [1998] 1 FLR 184, 188.

[16] *Hardwick v. Johnson* [1978] 1 W.L.R. 683, *per* Roskill and Browne L.JJ.; Lord Denning M.R. thought that there was no contract but reached the same conclusion on other grounds; *cf. Collier v. Hollingshead* (1984) 272 E.G. 941.

[17] *Parker v. Clark* [1960] 1 W.L.R. 286; *cf. Schaefer v. Schuhman* [1972] A.C. 572; Lee (1972) 88 L.Q.R. 320; *Tanner v. Tanner* [1975] 1 W.L.R. 1346; *Nunn v. Dalrymple, The Times*, August 3, 1989.

[18] [1972] 1 W.L.R. 1286.

[19] But she recovered the £600 on equitable grounds; *post,* § 3–131; *cf. Re Sharpe* [1980] 1 W.L.R. 219, where there was both a loan and an equitable right in the lender; *Briggs v. Rowan* [1991] E.G.C.S. 6.

[20] [1955] 1 W.L.R. 975.

2–159   **Agreements giving discretion to one party whether to perform.** An agreement may consist of mutual promises one of which gives a very wide discretion to one party. In such a case the discretionary promise may be too vague to constitute consideration for the other party's promise which may therefore be unenforceable.[21] But if the other party has actually performed (so that there can be no question that *he* has provided consideration), the further question may arise whether the discretionary promise can be enforced; and this raises an issue of contractual intention. In *Taylor v. Brewer*[22] the claimant agreed to do work for a committee who resolved that he should receive "such remuneration . . . as should be deemed right." His claim for a reasonable remuneration for work done failed: the promise to pay was "merely an engagement of honour."[23] This case is now more often distinguished than followed,[24] but its reasoning would still be followed if the wording made it clear that the promise was not intended to be legally binding.[25]

2–160   **Agreements giving discretion to rescind.** An agreement may give one party a discretion to rescind. That party will not be bound if his promise means "I will only perform if I do not change my mind." But the power to rescind may only be inserted as a safeguard in certain eventualities which are not exhaustively stated, for example, where a contract for the sale of land entitles the vendor to rescind if the purchaser persists in some requisition or objection which the vendor is "unable *or unwilling* to satisfy." In such a case there is a contract and the court will control the exercise of the power to rescind by insisting that the vendor must not rescind "arbitrarily, or capriciously, or unreasonably. Much less, can he act in bad faith."[26]

2–161   **Collective agreements.** The terms of collective agreements between trade unions and employers (or employers' associations) may be incorporated in individual employment contracts and so become binding on the parties to those contracts.[27] But the general common law view was that such collective agreements were not legally binding between the parties to them[28]; and in 1969 this view was upheld in *Ford Motor Co. Ltd v. A.E.F.*[29] The Trade Union and Labour Relations (Consolidation) Act 1992 goes further in providing that a collective

---

[21] *Post*, § 3–024.

[22] (1813) 1 M. & S. 290; *cf. Shallcross v. Wright* (1850) 12 Beav. 558; *Roberts v. Smith* (1859) 28 L.J.Ex. 164.

[23] (1813) 1 M. & S. 290, 291.

[24] *Post*, Vol. II, § 39–071; *cf. Re Brand's Estate* [1936] 3 All E.R. 374.

[25] *cf. Re Richmond Gate Property Co. Ltd* [1965] 1 W.L.R. 335.

[26] *Selkirk v. Romar Investments Ltd* [1963] 1 W.L.R. 1415, 1422; *cf.* the authorities on agreements subject to a condition depending on the "satisfaction" of one party, discussed in § 2–141, *ante*. A contract term giving a wide discretion to one party may be subject to the requirement of reasonableness under Unfair Contract Terms Act 1977, s.3(2)(b)(ii), or may not be binding on a consumer under Unfair Terms in Consumer Contracts Regulations 1994 (S.I. 1994 No. 3159), especially Sched. 3, para 1(c).

[27] *Robertson v. British Gas Corp.* [1983] I.C.R. 351; *Marley v. Forward Trust Group* [1986] I.C.R. 891; contrast *N.C.B. v. N.U.M.* [1986] I.C.R. 736; and see *post*, § 13–019, Vol. II, § 39–042.

[28] Kahn-Freund in Flanders and Clegg (eds.), *The System of Industrial Relations in Great Britain*, Chap. 2; and in Ginsberg (ed.), *Law and Opinion in England in the 20th Century*, p. 215; Grunfeld, *Modern Trade Union Law*, pp. 219–220; Wedderburn, *The Worker and the Law* (3rd ed.), pp. 318–322; Report of the Royal Commission on Trade Unions and Employers Associations, Cmnd. 3623 (1968), §§ 470–471.

[29] [1969] 2 Q.B. 303; Selwyn (1969) 32 M.L.R. 377; Hepple [1970] C.L.J. 122.

agreement[30] is "conclusively presumed not to have been intended by the parties to be a legally enforceable contract" unless it is in writing and expressly provides the contrary (in which case the agreement is conclusively presumed to have been intended by the parties to be a legally enforceable contract).[31] To displace the presumption that a collective agreement is not intended to be a legally binding contract, the agreement must provide that it was intended to be *legally* binding. The presumption is not displaced by a statement that the parties shall be "bound by the agreement" for this may mean that they are bound in honour only.[32]

Free travel passes. There are conflicting decisions on the question whether **2–162** the issue and acceptance of a free travel pass amounts to a contract. In *Wilkie v. L.P.T.B.*[33] it was held that such a pass issued by a transport undertaking to one of its own employees did not amount to a contract. But the contrary conclusion was reached in *Gore v. Van der Lann*[34] where the pass was issued to an old age pensioner. This conclusion was based on the ground that an application for the pass had been made on a form couched in contractual language; and *Wilkie's* case was distinguished on the ground that the pass there was issued to the employee "as a matter of course . . . as one of the privileges attaching to his employment."[35] But as the pass in *Gore's* case was issued expressly on the "understanding" that it only constituted a licence subject to conditions, the distinction seems, with respect, to be a tenuous one.

Statements of governmental policy. In a case[36] arising out of the First World **2–163** War a statement was made, during the war, on behalf of the Government, to the effect that a certain neutral ship would be allowed to leave a British port if specified conditions were met. It was held that the statement did not amount to a contract: it was "merely an expression of intention to act in a particular way in a certain event."[37]

Other cases. The cases in which there is no intention to create legal relations **2–164** cannot be exhaustively classified. Contractual intention may, for example, be negatived by evidence that "the agreement was a good will agreement . . . made without any intention of creating legal relations,"[38] that it was a sham, made with "no intention . . . to create bona fide legal relations,"[39] and by many other

---

[30] As defined by s.178(1) and (2) of the 1992 Act.
[31] s.179(1) and (2); *Universe Tankships Inc. v. International Transport Workers' Federation (The Universe Sentinel)* [1983] A.C. 366, 380; *Monterosso Shipping Co. Ltd v. International Transport Workers' Federation (The Rosso)* [1982] 2 Lloyd's Rep. 120; *N.C.B. v. N.U.M.* [1986] I.C.R. 736; *cf. Cheall v. A.P.E.X.* [1983] A.C. 180, 189 (inter-union agreement); provisions making collective agreements legally binding seem to be very rare: see *Commission of the European Communities v. United Kingdom* [1984] I.C.R. 192, 195.
[32] *N.C.B. v. N.U.M.* [1986] I.C.R. 736.
[33] [1947] 1 All E.R. 258.
[34] [1967] 2 Q.B. 31; Odgers (1970) 86 L.Q.R. 69.
[35] *ibid.* at 41.
[36] *Rederiaktiebolaget Amphitrite v. R.* [1921] 3 K.B. 500.
[37] *ibid.* at 503; see further §§ 10–007 to 10–009, *post.*
[38] *Orion Ins. Co. plc v. Sphere Drake Ins. plc* [1990] 1 Lloyd's Rep. 465, 505, affd. (by a majority) [1990] 1 Lloyd's Rep. 239; *Mitsui & Co. Ltd v. Novorossiysk Shipping Co. (The Gudermes)* [1993] 1 Lloyd's Rep. 311; *cf. County Ltd v. Girozentrale Securities Ltd* [1996] 3 All E.R. 834, 837 (*post,* § 3–129).
[39] *Glatzer & Warwick Shipping Co. v. Bradstone Ltd. (The Ocean Enterprise)* [1997] 1 Lloyd's Rep. 449, 484.

disparate factors. For example, where an agreement was made that a landlord would not enforce an order for possession against a tenant who had fallen into arrears with her rent, it was held that this agreement did not create a new tenancy as the parties "plainly did not [so] intend"[40]: the agreement merely had the effect of turning the tenant into a "tolerated trespasser."[41] A number of cases support the view that an arrangement which is believed simply to give effect to pre-existing rights is not a contract because the parties had no intention to enter into a *new* contract.[42] But other cases show that contractual intention is not negatived where the conduct of the parties makes it clear that they intended not merely to give effect to their earlier contract but also to enter into a new contract containing additional terms[43]; or merely because the conduct of one party to the alleged new contract consisted of his performance of a contract between him and a third party.[44] The context in which an agreement is made may negative contractual intention. For example, in *President of the Methodist Conference v. Parfitt*[45] it was held that the appointment of a person as a Minister of the Methodist Church did not give rise to a contract as the relationship was not one "in which the parties intended to create legal relations between themselves so as to make the agreement . . . enforceable in the courts."[46] At one time, it was thought that the relationship between the Crown and one of its civil servants was not contractual because the Crown did not, when the relationship was entered into, have the necessary contractual intention.[47] But in one of the cases which supported that view it was said that there was evidence that the Crown was reconsidering its position on the point[48]; and more recently it has been held[49] that the requirement of contractual intention was satisfied in spite of the fact that the terms of appointment stated that "a civil servant does not have a contract of employment" but rather "a letter of appointment." These words were not sufficient to turn a relationship which, apart from them, had all the characteristics of a contract into one which was binding in honour only.

2–165   **Vague agreements.** Another relevant factor is the degree of precision with which the agreement is expressed. In one case it was held that a husband's

---

[40] *Burrows v. Brent L.B.C.* [1996] 1 W.L.R. 1448, 1454.

[41] *ibid.* at 1455.

[42] *Beesly v. Hallwood Estates Ltd* [1960] 1 W.L.R. 549, 558, affd. on other grounds [1961] Ch. 105; *cf. Harvela Investments Ltd v. Royal Trust of Canada (C.I.) Ltd* [1986] A.C. 207; *The Aramis* [1989] 1 Lloyd's Rep. 213; Treitel; [1989] L.M.C.L.Q. 162; *Mitsui & Co. Ltd v. Novorossiysk Shipping Co. (The Gudermes)* [1993] 1 Lloyd's Rep. 311.

[43] *Furness Withy (Australia) Pty. Ltd v. Metal Distributors (U.K.) Ltd (The Amazonia)* [1990] 1 Lloyd's Rep. 238, 241–242. *GF Sharp & Co Ltd v. McMillan* [1998] I.R.L.R. 632.

[44] *Pyrene v. Scindia Navigation Co. Ltd* [1954] 2 Q.B. 402; *A.M. Satterthwaite & Co. Ltd v. New Zealand Shipping Co. Ltd (The Eurymedon)* [1975] A.C. 514; *Companie Portorafti Commerciale SA v. Ultramar Panama Inc. (The Captain Gregos) (No. 2)* [1990] 2 Lloyd's Rep. 395 (so far as it relates to BP's claim). *cf. Halifax Building Society v. Edell* [1992] Ch. 436, discussed *post*, § 19–014.

[45] [1984] Q.B. 368.

[46] *ibid.* at 378; approved in *Davies v. Presbyterian Church of Wales* [1986] 1 W.L.R. 323 (no contract of employment between pastor and Presbyterian church); Woolman (1986) 102 L.Q.R. at 356; *Santok Sing v. Guru Nanak Gurdwara* [1990] I.C.R. 309; *Birmingham Mosque Trust v. Alawi* [1992] I.C.R. 435; *Diocese of Southwark v. Coker* [1998] I.C.R. 140.

[47] *R. v. Civil Service Appeal Board, ex p. Bruce* [1988] I.C.R. 649, affd. on other grounds [1989] I.C.R. 171; *Mclaren v. Home Office, The Times*, May 18, 1989.

[48] *R. v. Civil Service Appeal Board, ex p. Bruce, supra*, at 659.

[49] *R. v. Lord Chancellor's Department, ex p. Nangle* [1991] I.C.R. 743; *cf.* Trade Union and Labour Relations (Consolidation) Act 1992, ss.62(7), 245: "deemed [for certain purposes] to constitute a contract."

promise to let his deserted wife stay in the matrimonial home had no contractual force because it was not "intended by him, or understood by her, to have any contractual basis or effect."[50] The promise was too vague: it did not state for how long or on what terms the wife could stay in the house.[51] So, too, the use of deliberately vague language was held to negative contractual intention where a property developer reached an "understanding" with a firm of solicitors to employ them in connection with a proposed development, but neither side entered into a definite commitment.[52] For the same reason, "letters of intent"[53] may lack the force of legally binding contracts.[54] The assumption in all these cases was that the parties had reached agreement, and in them lack of contractual intention prevented that agreement from having legal effect. No such issue of contractual intention can arise where vagueness has the more fundamental effect of showing that the parties had never reached agreement at all.[55]

Statements made in jest or anger. Contractual intention may, again, be **2–166** negatived by the fact that the statement is made in jest or anger, at least if this fact is obvious to the person to whom the statement is made.[56] Thus in *Licences Insurance Corporation v. Lawson*[57] the defendant was a director of Company A and of Company B. Company A held shares in Company B and resolved, in the defendant's absence, to sell them. At a later meeting this resolution was rescinded after a heated discussion, during which the defendant said that he would make good any loss which Company A might suffer if it kept the shares. It was held that the defendant was not liable on this undertaking. Nobody at the meeting regarded it as a contract; it was not recorded as such in the minute book; and the defendant's fellow-directors at most thought that he was bound in honour.

The cases on this topic,[58] and in particular those discussed in §§ 2–164 to **2–167** 2–166 above, show that the question of contractual intention is, in the last resort, one of fact[59]; and in doubtful cases its resolution depends, in particular, on the incidence of the burden of proof and on the objective test which generally determines the issue. These points have already been discussed,[60] they help to

---

[50] *Vaughan v. Vaughan* [1953] 1 Q.B. 762, 765; *cf. Booker v. Palmer* [1942] 2 All E.R. 674; *Horrocks v. Forray* [1976] 1 W.L.R. 230; *Windeler v. Whitehall* [1990] 2 FLR 505.

[51] *cf. Jones v. Padavatton* [1969] 1 W.L.R. 328; and see *Gould v. Gould* [1970] 1 Q.B. 275; *Layton v. Morris, The Times*, December 11, 1985.

[52] *J.H. Milner & Son v. Percy Bilton Ltd* [1966] 1 W.L.R. 1582.

[53] *Ante*, § 2–115.

[54] *cf. Snelling v. John G. Snelling Ltd* [1973] 1 Q.B. 87, 93; *cf. Montreal Gas Co. v. Vasey* [1900] A.C. 595; *B.S.C. v. Cleveland Bridge & Engineering Co. Ltd* [1984] 1 All E.R. 504; contrast *Turiff Construction Ltd v. Regalia Knitting Mills* (1971) 222 E.G. 169 (letter of intent held to be a collateral contract to pay for preliminary work); *Wilson Smithett & Cope (Sugar) Ltd v. Bangladesh Sugar Industries Ltd* [1986] 1 Lloyd's Rep. 378 (letter of intent held to be an acceptance); *Kleinwort Benson Ltd v. Malaysian Mining Corp.* [1989] 1 W.L.R. 379 ("letters of comfort").

[55] See *Re Goodchild* [1997] 1 W.L.R. 1216 where it is said at 1226 that one of the parties to alleged mutual wills "regarded the arrangement as irrevocable, but . . . [the other] did not"; *cf. Taylor v. Dickens* [1998] 1 FLR 806.

[56] So that he cannot rely on the objective test: see *ante*, § 2–148.

[57] (1896) 12 T.L.R. 501.

[58] *Ante*, §§ 2–149 *et seq.*

[59] See *Zakhem International Construction Ltd v. Nippon Kohan KK* [1987] 2 Lloyd's Rep. 596.

[60] *Ante*, §§ 2–146—2–148.

explain two controversial decisions, in each of which there was a difference of opinion on the issue of contractual intention.

2-168   The first is *Esso Petroleum Ltd v. Commissioners of Customs and Excise.*[61] Esso supplied garages with tokens called "World Cup coins," instructing them to give away one coin with every four gallons of petrol sold. The scheme was advertised by Esso and also on posters displayed by garages. By a majority of four to one, the House of Lords held that there was no "sale" of the coins; but that majority was equally divided on the question whether there was any contract at all with regard to the coins. Those who thought that there was a contract[62] relied on the incidence of the burden of proof, and on the argument that "Esso envisaged a bargain of some sort between the garage proprietor and the motorist."[63] But this argument relates rather to the intention of Esso than to that of the alleged contracting parties. With regard to their intention, it is submitted that the more realistic view is that of Lords Dilhorne and Russell, who relied on the language of the advertisements (in which the coins were said to be "going free"), and on the minimal value of the coins, as negativing contractual intention.

2-169   The second case is *J. Evans & Son (Portsmouth) Ltd v. Andrea Merzario Ltd.*[64] The representative of a firm of forwarding agents told a customer (with whom the firm had long dealt) that his goods would henceforth be packed in containers, and that these would be carried under deck. About a year later, one such container was carried on deck and lost. At first instance,[65] Kerr J. held that the promise was not intended to be legally binding since it was made in the course of a courtesy call, not related to any particular transaction, and indefinite with regard to its future duration. The Court of Appeal, however, held[66] that the promise did have contractual force, relying principally on the importance attached by the customer to the carriage of his goods under deck, and on the fact that he would not have agreed to the new mode of carriage but for the promise. The case is no doubt a borderline one, but it is submitted that Kerr J.'s view accords more closely with the objective test of contractual intention. In most cases, that test prevents the promisor from relying on his subjective intention not to enter into a contractual undertaking; but it should equally prevent the promisee's subjective intention (if not known to the promisor) from being decisive. The Court of Appeal appears with respect to have attached too much weight to the customer's subjective intention, and too little weight to the circumstances in which the promise was made.

---

[61] [1976] 1 W.L.R. 1; Atiyah (1976) 39 M.L.R. 335.
[62] Lords Simon and Wilberforce. Lord Fraser, who dissented on the main issue, took the same view.
[63] [1976] 1 W.L.R. 1, 6.
[64] [1976] 1 W.L.R. 1078; Adams (1977) 40 M.L.R. 227.
[65] [1975] 1 Lloyd's Rep. 162.
[66] [1976] 1 W.L.R. 1078.

CHAPTER 3

CONSIDERATION[1]

1. INTRODUCTION

General. In English law, a promise is not, as a general rule, binding as a **3–001**
contract unless it is either made in a deed or supported by some "consideration."
The purpose of the doctrine of consideration is to put some legal limits on the
enforceability of agreements even where they are intended to be legally binding
and are not vitiated by some factor such as mistake, misrepresentation, duress or
illegality. The existence of such limits is not a peculiarity of English law: for
example, in some civil law countries certain promises which in England are not
binding for "want of consideration" cannot be enforced unless they are made in
some special form, *e.g.* by a notarised writing.[2] The view was, indeed, at one time

---

[1] Sutton, *Consideration Reconsidered* (1974); Shatwell (1955) 1 *Sydney Law Review* 289.
[2] See generally von Mehren (1959) 72 Harv.L.Rev. 1009.

put forward that consideration was only evidence of the intention of the parties to be bound, and that (at any rate in the case of certain commercial contracts), such evidence could equally well be furnished by writing.[3] But the view that agreements (other than those contained in deeds) were binding without consideration merely because they were in writing was rejected over 200 years ago,[4] though it has been revived as a proposal for law reform.[5] The present position therefore is that English law limits the enforceability of agreements (not in deeds) by reference to a complex and multifarious body of rules known as "the doctrine of consideration."

3–002   **Informal gratuitous promises.** The basic feature of that doctrine is that "something of value in the eye of the law"[6] must be given for a promise in order to make it enforceable as a contract. It follows that an informal gratuitous promise does not amount to a contract.[7] A person or body to whom a promise of a gift is made from purely charitable or sentimental motives gives nothing for the promise; and the claims of such a promisee are regarded as less compelling than those of a person who has provided (or promised) some return for the promise.[8] The invalidity of informal gratuitous promises of this kind can also be supported on the ground that their enforcement could prejudice third parties such as creditors of the promisor.[9] Such promises, too, may be rashly made[10]; and the requirements of executing a deed or giving value provide at least some protection against this danger.

3–003   **Other promises without consideration.** The doctrine of consideration however, also struck at many promises which were not "gratuitous" in any ordinary or commercial sense. These applications of the doctrine were brought within its scope by stressing that consideration must be not merely "something of value," but "something of value *in the eye of the law.*"[11] The law in certain cases refused to recognise the "value" of acts or promises even though they would, or might, be regarded as valuable by a layman. This refusal was based on many disparate policies; so that "promises without consideration" included many different kinds of transactions which, at first sight, had little in common.[12] It is this fact which is the cause of the very great complexity of the doctrine; and which has also led to its occasional unwarranted extensions and hence to demands for reform of the law.[13]

---

[3] *Pillans v. Van Mierop* (1765) 3 Burr. 1663.

[4] *Rann v. Hughes* (1778) 7 T.R. 350n; 4 Bro.P.C. 27.

[5] Law Revision Committee, 6th Interim Report, Cmnd. 5449 (1937), para. 29; for comments on this and other proposals in the Report, see Lord Wright, *Legal Essays and Addresses*, p. 287; Hamson (1938) 54 L.Q.R. 233; Hays (1941) 41 Col.L.Rev. 849; Chloros (1968) 17 I.C.L.Q. 137; Beatson [1992] C.L.P. 1.

[6] *Thomas v. Thomas* (1842) 2 Q.B. 851, 859.

[7] *Re Hudson* (1885) 54 L.J.Ch. 811; *Re Cory* (1912) 29 T.L.R. 18; *Williams v. Roffey Bros & Nicholls (Contractors) Ltd* [1991] 1 Q.B. 1, 19.

[8] *cf.* Eisenberg, 85 Cal.L.Rev. 821 (1997).

[9] *Eastwood v. Kenyon* (1840) 11 Ad. & E. 438, 451.

[10] It is often easier to promise to make a gift than actually to make one.

[11] *Supra*, at n. 6.

[12] *cf.* Corbin, *Contracts*, Vol. I, p. 489: "The doctrine of consideration is many doctrines."

[13] See *supra*, n. 5.

2. Definitions

Benefit and detriment. The traditional definition of consideration concen-   **3–004**
trates on the requirement that "something of value" must be given and accordingly states that consideration is either some detriment to the promisee (in that he
may give value) or some benefit to the promisor (in that he may receive value).[14]
Usually, this detriment and benefit are merely the same thing looked at from
different points of view. Thus payment by a buyer is consideration for the seller's
promise to deliver and can be described either as a detriment to the buyer or as
a benefit to the seller; and conversely delivery by a seller is consideration for the
buyer's promise to pay and can be described either as a detriment to the seller or
as a benefit to the buyer. It should be emphasised that these statements relate to
the consideration *for each promise* looked at separately. For example, the seller
suffers a "detriment" when he delivers the goods and this enables him to enforce
the buyer's promise to pay the price. It is quite irrelevant that the seller has made
a good bargain and so gets a benefit from the performance of the contract. What
the law is concerned with is the consideration *for a promise*—not the consideration *for a contract*.

Either sufficient. Under the traditional definition, it is sufficient if there is   **3–005**
either a detriment to the promisee or a benefit to the promisor. Thus detriment to
the promisee suffices even though the promisor does not benefit[15]: for example
where A guarantees B's bank overdraft and the promisee bank suffers detriment
by advancing money to B.[16] The view of Sir William Holdsworth, indeed, was
that "Detriment to the promisee is of the essence of the doctrine, and benefit to
the promisor is, when it exists, merely an accident."[17] But in a number of cases
promises have been enforced in spite of the fact that there was no apparent
detriment to the promisee[18]; and these cases support the view that benefit to the
promisor is sufficient to satisfy the requirement of consideration.

Benefit and detriment may be factual or legal. The traditional definition of   **3–006**
consideration lacks precision because the key notions of "benefit" and "detriment" are used in at least two senses. They may mean, first any act,[19] which is
of some value, or secondly, only such acts, the performance of which is not
already legally due from the promisee. In the first sense, there is consideration if
a benefit or detriment is *in fact* obtained or suffered. When the words are used in
the second sense this factual benefit or detriment is disregarded, and a notion of

---

[14] *Currie v. Misa* (1875) L.R. 10 Ex. 153, 162. See also *Barber v. Fox* (1670) 2 Wms.Saund. 134,
n. (e); *Cooke v. Oxley* (1790) 3 T.R. 653, 654; *Jones v. Ashburnham* (1804) 4 East 455; *Bainbridge
v. Firmstone* (1838) 8 A. & E. 743, 744; *Thomas v. Thomas* (1842) 2 Q.B. 851, 859; *Bolton v. Madden*
(1873) L.R. 9 Q.B. 55, 56; *Gore v. Van der Lann* [1967] 2 Q.B. 31, 42; *Argy Trading Development
Co. Ltd v. Lapid Developments Ltd* [1977] Lloyd's Rep. 67, 75; *Midland Bank & Trust Co. Ltd v.
Green* [1981] A.C. 513, 531; *R. v. Braithwaite* [1983] 1 W.L.R. 383, 391; *Johnsey Estates Ltd v. Lewis
Manley (Engineering) Ltd* [1987] 2 E.G.L.R. 69, 70; *Guiness Mahon & Co. Ltd v. Kensington &
Chelsea Royal B.C.* [1998] 2 All E.R. 272, 290.
[15] *O'Sullivan v. Management Agency & Music Ltd* [1985] Q.B. 428, 459; *Re Dale* [1994] Ch. 31,
38.
[16] *cf. post*, § 3–037.
[17] *History of English Law*, Vol. 8, p. 11.
[18] *e.g. post*, §§ 3–036, 3–037, 3–017.
[19] Or forbearance, or promise to do or to forbear. For the sake of simplicity, references in the text
are confined to the doing of an act.

what may be called legal benefit or detriment is substituted. Under this notion, the promisee may provide consideration by doing anything that he was not legally bound to do, whether or not it actually occasions a detriment to him or confers a benefit on the promisor; while conversely he may provide no consideration by doing only what he was legally bound to do, however much this may in fact occasion a detriment to him or confer a benefit on the promisor. The English courts have not consistently adopted either of these senses of the words "benefit" and "detriment." In some of the cases to be discussed in this chapter, factual benefit is stressed[20] even though legal detriment may also have been present; while in others the absence of legal detriment or benefit has in the past been regarded as decisive.[21] One modern authority[22] regards factual benefit to the promisor as sufficient, even in the absence of a legal benefit to him or of a legal detriment to the promisee; and it is possible (though far from certain) that this approach may spread to at least some[23] of the situations in which the courts have in the past insisted on legal benefit or detriment.

3–007   **Other definitions.** The traditional definition of consideration in terms of benefit and detriment is sometimes felt to be unsatisfactory. One cause of dissatisfaction is that it is thought to be wrong to talk of benefit and detriment when both parties expect to, and actually may, benefit from the contract. But this reasoning falls, with respect, into the error of looking at the subject-matter of the definition as the consideration *for a contract*,[24] when the definition is actually concerned with the consideration *for a promise*.[25] Another cause of dissatisfaction is the artificial reasoning that is sometimes necessary to accommodate the cases within the traditional definition. Sir Frederick Pollock has, accordingly, described consideration simply as "the price for which the promise is bought."[26] This statement has been approved in the House of Lords[27]; but if it is to be regarded as a definition of consideration it is defective in being so vague as to give no help in determining whether consideration exists on a given set of facts. A view which leads to even more uncertainty is that consideration "*means* a reason for the enforcement of promises"[28]—that reason being simply "the justice of the case."[29] But "the justice of the case" is in almost all the decided cases highly debatable, so that the suggested definition provides no basis at all for

---

[20] *e.g.* in *Bolton v. Madden* (1873) L.R. 9 Q.B. 55, *post*, § 3–037.

[21] *e.g.* in some of the existing duty cases discussed in §§ 3–063, 3–068, 3–070, *post*.

[22] *Williams v. Roffey Bros & Nicholls (Contractors) Ltd* [1991] 1 Q.B. 1.

[23] *e.g.* to the variation cases discussed in §§ 3–074—3–075; but probably not to the forebearance to sue cases discussed in §§ 3–049—3–052.

[24] There are traces of this approach in *Williams v. Roffey Bros. & Nicholls (Contractors) Ltd* [1991] 1 Q.B. 1, 23: "If both parties benefit from an agreement it is not necessary that each also suffered a detriment."

[25] *Ante*, § 3–004.

[26] *Principles of Contract* (13th ed.), p. 133.

[27] *Dunlop Pneumatic Tyre Co. Ltd v. Selfridge Ltd* [1915] A.C. 847, 855.

[28] Atiyah, *Consideration in Contracts: A Fundamental Restatement*, Canberra, 1971, p. 60. For an earlier, similar statement, see Llewellyn (1931) 40 Yale L.J. at p. 741—"any sufficient justification for court enforcement"; but no attempt is made to suggest that this actually is the law. For further criticism of Atiyah's views, see Treitel (1976) 50 A.L.J. 439. *cf. Colonia Versicherung A.G. v. Amoco Oil Co.* [1995] 1 Lloyd's Rep. 570, 577 (affd. without reference to this point [1997] 1 Lloyd's Rep. 261) where the words "(a) the reason for and (b) ample consideration for" a payment clearly treat these concepts as distinct.

[29] Atiyah, *loc. cit.* pp. 52, 58.

formulating a coherent legal doctrine.[30] A modification of the suggested definition, describing consideration as "a reason for the recognition of an obligation"[31] is open to the same objection. Of course the traditional definition does not provide complete (or even a very high degree of) certainty. But it does state the doctrine in a way that is broadly consistent with the case law on the subject and that gives some basis for predicting the course of future decisions. The traditional definition also has more support in the authorities than any other definition. For these reasons it will be used in this chapter.

Invented consideration. Normally, a party enters into a contract with a view   **3–008** to obtaining the consideration promised by the other: for example, the buyer wants the goods and the seller the price. In the United States it has been said that this is essential, and that "Nothing is consideration that is not regarded as such by both parties."[32] But English courts do not insist on this requirement and often regard an act or forbearance as the consideration for a promise even though it was not the object of the promisor to secure it.[33] They may also regard the possibility of some prejudice to the promisee as a detriment without regard to the question whether it has in fact been suffered.[34] These practices may be called "inventing" consideration,[35] and the temptation to adopt one or the other of them is particularly strong when the act or forbearance which was actually bargained for cannot be regarded as consideration for some reason which is thought to be technical and without merit. In such cases the practice of inventing consideration may help to make the operation of the doctrine of consideration more acceptable; but the practice may also be criticised[36] on the ground that it gives the courts a wide discretion to hold promises binding or not as they please. Thus the argument that the promisee *might* have suffered prejudice by acting in reliance on a

---

[30] *cf.* the description of a similar concept as "potentially very confusing": *Guiness Mahon & Co. Ltd v. Kensington & Chelsea Royal B.C.* [1998] 2 All E.R. 272, 280.

[31] Atiyah, *Essays on Contracts*, pp. 179, 183.

[32] *Philpot v. Gruninger* (1872) 14 Wall. 570, 577; Restatement, *Contracts*, § 75(1): "bargained for and given in exchange for the promise"; Restatement 2d, *Contracts*, § 75(1) and (2); Williston, *Contracts* (rev.ed.), Vol. 1, p. 320; Corbin, *Contracts*, § 172, is more sceptical. The Restatement 2d, § 72 also supports the converse proposition that "any performance which is bargained for is consideration," even though there may be no element of benefit or detriment; but this is subject to important exceptions, especially where the performance bargained for is the settlement of an invalid claim and the performance of an existing duty: see §§ 73 and 74; as to these topics, see *post*, §§ 3–049—3–070.

[33] See, for example, *post*, §§ 3–012, 3–015, 3–068, 3–164 and *infra.* at n. 37; and *cf. Pollwaty Ltd v. Abdullah* [1974] 1 W.L.R. 493, discussed by Zuckerman (1975) 38 M.L.R. 384 and Thornely [1975] C.L.J. 26; *cf. Vantage Navigation Corp. v. Sahail and Saud Building Materials Co. LLC (The Alev)* [1989] 1 Lloyd's Rep. 138, 147; *Moran v. University College Salford (No. 2), The Times,* November 23, 1993.

[34] *e.g. infra,* n. 37.

[35] Atiyah, *loc. cit.* n. 28 *supra,* accuses the present editor of having "invented the concept of invented consideration;" but all that the editor can claim to have invented is a phrase for describing what the courts sometimes actually do. The phrase does not imply approval of the practice: see *infra* after n. 36. Nor does the phrase necessarily imply inconsistency between decisions, as Atiyah suggests *ibid.*: courts could *consistently* hold that an act or forbearance was consideration although it was not the promisor's object to secure it. In fact, the decisions on the point are not perfectly consistent with each other: see *infra* at nn. 37 and 38; but that is hardly unusual in a common law system.

[36] For criticism, see Holmes, *The Common Law*, p. 292. In the United States there is less need for "inventing" consideration because of the existence of a broad doctrine of promissory estoppel: see Restatement, *Contracts*, § 90, and Restatement 2d, *Contracts*, § 90 and *post* § 3–099.

promise is in some cases made a basis of decision,[37] while in others precisely the same argument is rejected.[38] The practice of "inventing" consideration is, therefore, a source of considerable uncertainty in this branch of the law.

3–009   **Motive and consideration.** In *Thomas v. Thomas*[39] a testator shortly before his death expressed a desire that his widow should during her life have the house in which he lived, or £100. After his death, his executors "in consideration of such desire" promised to convey the house to the widow during her life or for so long as she should continue a widow, "provided nevertheless and it is hereby further agreed" that she should pay £1 per annum towards the ground rent, and keep the house in repair. In an action by the widow for breach of this agreement, the consideration for the executors' promise was stated to be the widow's promise to pay and repair. An objection that the declaration omitted to state part of the consideration, *viz.* the testator's desire, was rejected. Patteson J. said: "Motive is not the same thing with consideration. Consideration means something which is of value in the eye of the law moving from the plaintiff."[40] This remark should not be misunderstood: a common motive for making a promise is of course the desire to obtain the consideration; and an act or forbearance on the part of the promisee may (unless the court is prepared to "invent"[41] a consideration) fail to constitute consideration precisely because it was not the promisor's motive to secure it. What Patteson J. meant was that a motive for promising did not amount to consideration unless two further conditions were satisfied, *viz.*: (i) that the thing secured in exchange for the promise was "of some value in the eye of the law"; and (ii) that it moved from the plaintiff.[42] Consideration and motive are not opposites; the former concept is a subdivision of the latter. The consideration for a promise is (unless the consideration is nominal or invented)[43] always a motive for promising; but a motive for making a promise is not necessarily consideration for it in law. Thus the testator's desire in *Thomas v. Thomas* was a motive for the executors' promise but not part of the consideration for it. The widow's promise to pay and repair was another motive for the executors' promise and did constitute the consideration for that promise.

3–010   **Consideration and condition.** *Thomas v. Thomas* also illustrates the difference between consideration and condition: the plaintiff's remaining a widow was not part of the consideration but a condition of her entitlement to enforce the executor's promise. On the other hand, in *Re Soames*[44] A promised £3,000 to B if B would set up a school in the running of which A was to have an active part. It was held that, by establishing the school, B had provided consideration for A's

---

[37] *Shadwell v. Shadwell* (1860) 9 C.B.(N.S.) 159, 174: the consideration was said by Erle C.J. to consist of the possibility that the promisor "*may* have made a most material change in his position. . . . "

[38] In *Offord v. Davies* (1862) 12 C.B.(N.S.) 748: the argument of counsel (at 750) that "the plaintiff *might* have altered his position in consequence of the guarantie" was rejected. Erle C.J. being again a member of the court. *cf.* also *post*, § 3–015 n. 73 and at n. 80 for refusal to "invent" consideration.

[39] (1842) 2 Q.B. 851.

[40] At 859.

[41] *Ante*, § 3–008.

[42] Discussion of these requirements forms the bulk of this chapter.

[43] In *Thomas v. Thomas* the consideration may not have been adequate, but it was not nominal; *cf. Westminster City Council v. Duke of Westminster* [1991] 4 All E.R. 136 (*revsd.* in part on other grounds (1992) 24 H.L.R. 572); *post*, § 3–019.

[44] (1897) 13 T.L.R. 439; *cf. post*, § 3–158.

promise. It seems that the distinction between consideration and condition depends, in such cases, on whether " a reasonable man would or would not understand that the performance of the condition was requested as the price or exchange for the promise."[45] In *Thomas v. Thomas* the executors had not requested the plaintiff to remain a widow; while in *Re Soames* a request that B should establish the school could be inferred from A's expressed intention to participate in its management. The distinction is further illustrated by *Carlill v. Carbolic Smoke Ball Co.*[46] where the claimant provided consideration for the defendants' promise by using the smoke-ball; but her catching influenza was a condition of her entitlement to enforce that promise.[47]

Executed and executory consideration. It is common to distinguish between **3–011** executed and executory consideration. The former consists of the performance of an act or forbearance in return for a promise. Illustrations of executed consideration may be found in offers of rewards.[48] Where, for instance, the owner of a lost article promises a reward to a person who finds it and returns it to him, the finder by returning the article both accepts the offer and provides the consideration for the promise.[49] Executory consideration, on the other hand, consists of mutual promises. The rule that such promises can amount to consideration for each other has long been settled.[50] Hence if a seller promises to deliver goods in six months' time and the buyer to pay for them on delivery, there is an immediately binding contract from which neither party can withdraw, though, of course, performance cannot be claimed till the appointed time. An implied, no less than an express, promise is capable of constituting consideration.[51] A promise can, however, only be regarded as consideration for a counter-promise if the performance of the promise would have been so regarded.[52] It is, for example, settled that part payment of a debt by the debtor on or after the due day does not amount to consideration for a promise by the creditor to forgo the balance,[53] and the position would be exactly the same if the debtor, instead of actually making such a payment, simply promised to do so. Similarly, a promise to make a gift of £100

---

[45] Williston, *Contracts* (3rd ed.), § 112; *cf. Dickenson v. Abel* [1969] 1 W.L.R. 295 (where A had made no request to B to perform the condition); see also *Ellis v. Chief Adjudication Officer* [1998] 1 FLR 184 where performance of the condition was no doubt requested but the actual decision was that an executed gift of a flat failed because the condition (that the donee should look after her mother there) had not been performed. The agreement in that case lacked contractual force for want of contractual intention: *ante*, § 2–156.

[46] [1893] 1 Q.B. 256; stated *ante*, § 2–155.

[47] For the purpose of assessing VAT, a wider test (laid down by European Community Law), requiring only a "direct link" between performance and counterperformance, suffices: see *Rosgill Group Ltd v. Customs & Excise Commissioners* [1997] 3 All E.R. 1012, though in that case the English test for what constitutes consideration was also said at 1020 to have been satisfied.

[48] See also *Carlill v. Carbolic Smoke Ball Co.* [1892] 2 Q.B. 484; *Budgett v. Stratford Co-operative and Industrial Society Ltd* (1916) 32 T.L.R. 378.

[49] He may accept and provide consideration at an earlier stage: see *ante*, § 2–071 and *post*, § 3–158.

[50] See, *e.g. Pecke v. Redman* (1555) 1 Dyer 113a; *Joscelin v. Shelton* (1557) 3 Leon. 4; *Manwood v. Burston* (1586) 2 Leon. 203; *Harrison v. Cage* (1698) 12 Mod. 214; Simpson, *A History of the Common Law of Contract*, pp. 459–470; Baker (1980) 43 M.L.R. 467, 468 (reviewing Atiyah, *The Rise and Fall of Freedom of Contract*). But a mere proposal falling short of a promise does not suffice: *The Kaliningrad and Nadezhda Krupskaya* [1997] 2 Lloyd's Rep. 35, 39.

[51] *Thoresen Car Ferries Ltd v. Weymouth Portland B.C.* [1977] 2 Lloyd's Rep. 614, 619.

[52] *Re Dale* [1994] Ch. 31, 38.

[53] *Post*, § 3–107.

could not be made binding by a counter-promise to accept it since performance of the counter-promise could not conceivably amount to a benefit to the original promisor or to a detriment to the original promisee. Such benefit or detriment can only arise if the subject-matter of the promised gift is onerous property and the donee makes a counter-promise to discharge the obligations attached to it: *e.g.* to perform the covenants in a lease,[54] or to pay outstanding mortgage instalments[55] or to pay calls on shares.[56] Of course if the property is worth more than the obligations attached to it there will be an element of gift in such a transaction; and special safeguards are provided by law to ensure that certain categories of third parties (such as creditors of the promisor) are not prejudiced by this aspect of the transaction.[57]

3–012　**Certain limited effects of promises without consideration.** A promise that is not supported by consideration may nevertheless give rise to certain legal effects. In particular, English law places certain restrictions on the revocability of a promise where the promisee has acted on it in a way that was intended and could have been anticipated (without having been requested) by the promisor; and it may give a remedy against a promisor who would be unjustly enriched if he were allowed freely to revoke a promise after such action in reliance on it by the promisee. These limited legal effects of promises without consideration are discussed later in this chapter.[58] Here it is only necessary to emphasise that these legal effects do not give such promises the full consequences of a binding contract. Thus the restriction on revocability may be only temporary[59]; breach of the promise may not entitle the injured party to the full loss of bargain damages normally awarded for breach of contract,[60] or may not entitle him to them as of right.[61] Only a promise supported by consideration or made in a deed has these full contractual effects. "Contract" does not exhaust the category of promises having *some* legal effect; it refers, more narrowly, to those promises or agreements leading to the full degree of enforceability accorded by the law to a contractual promise. Moreover, while promises without consideration may have some legal effects, the promisee can still gain a number of important practical advantages by showing that he provided consideration. If the promise was supported by consideration, the promisee will not need to show action by him in reliance on the promise or unjust enrichment of the promisor; the promise will not be revocable but enforceable according to its terms; and the promisee will be entitled to full loss of bargain damages as of right. The limited legal effects of promises without consideration may have mitigated some of the rigours of the

---

[54] *Price v. Jenkins* (1877) 5 Ch.D. 619. In so far as *Thomas v. Thomas* (1842) 2 Q.B. 851 (*ante,* § 3–009) is *contra*, it seems to be inconsistent with *Price v. Jenkins* (where the "case which is not reported" mentioned at p. 620 closely resembles *Thomas v. Thomas*); *cf. Johnsey Estates v. Lewis & Manley* [1987] 2 E.G.L.R. 69; *Westminster City Council v. Duke of Westminster* [1991] 4 All E.R. 136 (*revsd.* in part on other grounds (1992) 24 H.L.R. 572).

[55] *Merritt v. Merritt* [1970] 1 W.L.R. 1211.

[56] *Cheale v. Kenward* (1858) 3 D. & J. 27.

[57] Insolvency Act 1986, ss.238, 339; and see *post*, § 3–017 n. 89; *Re Kumar* [1993] 1 W.L.R. 224.

[58] *Post*, §§ 3–076—3–099, 3–120—3–152.

[59] *Post*, §§ 3–091, 3–121, 3–140.

[60] *Post*, § 3–145—3–146.

[61] *Post*, § 3–145.

strict doctrine; but they have not eliminated consideration as an essential requirement of a binding contract.[62]

3. ADEQUACY OF CONSIDERATION

Courts generally will not judge adequacy. Under the doctrine of considera-   **3–013**
tion, a promise has no contractual force unless *some* value has been given for it.
But as a general rule[63] the courts do not concern themselves with the question
whether "adequate" value has been given,[64] or whether the agreement is harsh or
one-sided.[65] The fact that a person pays "too much" or "too little" for a thing
may be evidence of fraud[66] or mistake, or it may induce the court to imply a term
as to the quality of the subject-matter or be relevant to the question whether a
contract has been frustrated. But it does not of itself affect the validity of the
contract. This rule is subject to a number of exceptions discussed elsewhere in
this book.[67] These indicate that the courts are (even where the legislature has not
intervened) by no means insensitive to the problems raised by unequal or unfair
bargains; but in none of them is a promise held invalid merely because adequate
value for it has not been given. Some additional factor is required to bring a case
within one of the exceptions: for example, the existence of a relationship in
which one party is able to take an unfair advantage of the other. In the absence
of some such factor, the general rule applies that the courts will enforce a promise
so long as *some* value for it has been given: "no bargain will be upset which is
the result of the ordinary interplay of forces."[68]

Illustrations. It follows from the principles stated in § 3–013 above that acts   **3–014**
or omissions of very small value can be consideration. Thus it has been said that
there was consideration for a promise to give a man £50 "if you will come to my
house"[69]; that the act of executing a deed could be consideration for a promise
to pay money although the deed was void[70]; that the execution of a will can be
consideration (for a promise to make, and not to revoke, a similar will) even

---

[62] See further, *post*, §§ 3–098, 3–152.

[63] For exceptional cases, see *post*, §§ 3–075, 3–088, 28–030.

[64] *Haigh v. Brooks* (1839) 10 A. & E. 309, 320; *Moss v. Hall* (1850) 5 Exch. 46, 49–50; *Westlake v. Adams* (1858) 5 C.B.(N.S.) 248, 265; *Gravely v. Barnard* (1874) L.R. 18 Eq. 518; *Wild v. Tucker* [1914] 3 K.B. 36, 39; *Midland Bank & Trust Co. Ltd v. Green* [1981] A.C. 513, 532; *cf. Ball v. National and Grindley's Bank* [1973] Ch. 127, 139; *Langdale v. Danby* [1982] 1 W.L.R. 1123; *CCC Films (London) Ltd v. Impact Quadrant Films Ltd* [1985] QB 16, 27; *Brady v. Brady* [1989] A.C. 755, 775; *Normid Housing Association Ltd v. R. John Ralphs* [1989] 1 Lloyd's Rep. 265, 272; *cf.* Barton (1987) 103 L.Q.R. 118. The principle is recognised and preserved by Unfair Terms in Consumer Contracts Regulations 1994 (S.I. 1994 No. 3159) Reg. 3(2)(b), giving effect to the E.C. Directive on Unfair Terms in Consumer Contracts (93/13/EEC), Art. 4(2).

[65] *Gaumont-British Pictures Corp. v. Alexander* [1936] 2 All E.R. 1686. On such facts, the Regulations cited in the previous note would not apply: see Reg. 3(1) and Sched. 1, para. (a).

[66] *Tennent v. Tennents* (1870) L.R. 2 Sc. & Div. 6, 9. See also *Rice v. Gordon* (1847) 11 Beav. 265; *Cockell v. Taylor* (1851) 15 Beav. 103.

[67] See *supra*, n. 63; Waddams (1976) 39 M.L.R. 393; Tiplady (1983) 46 M.L.R. 601.

[68] *Lloyd's Bank Ltd v. Bundy* [1975] Q.B. 326, 336, *per* Lord Denning M.R.

[69] *Gilbert v. Ruddeard* (1608) 3 Dy. 272b (n); *cf. Denton v. G.N. Ry.* (1856) 5 E. & B. 860.

[70] *Westlake v. Adams* (1858) 5 C.B.(N.S.) 248; perhaps there was also an element of compromise in this case.

though the will is in its nature revocable[71]; that to give up a piece of paper without reference to its contents was consideration,[72] and even that to show a person a document was consideration.[73]

3–015   **Objects of trifling value.** In *Chappell & Co. Ltd v. Nestlé Co. Ltd*,[74] chocolate manufacturers sold gramophone records for 1s. 6d. plus three wrappers of their 6d. bars of chocolate. It was held that the delivery of the wrappers formed part of the consideration, though the wrappers were of little value to the buyer and were in fact thrown away by the seller. If the delivery of the wrappers formed part of the consideration it could, presumably, have formed the whole of the consideration, so that a promise to deliver records for wrappers alone would have been binding. This case should be contrasted with *Lipkin Gorman v. Karpnale Ltd*,[75] where gaming chips supplied by a gaming club to one of its members (and then lost by the member in the course of the gaming) were held not to constitute consideration for the money which the member had paid for them. One reason for this view appears to have been that "the chips themselves were worthless"[76]; but this is equally true of the wrappers in the *Chappel* case. Another seems to have been that the chips "remained the property of the club"[77]; but this again would not of itself be decisive, for the transfer of possession (no less than that of ownership) is clearly capable of constituting consideration.[78] A third reason for the view that the chips were not consideration for the money may be that the parties did not so regard the transaction: they regarded the chips as merely "a convenient mechanism for facilitating gambling,"[79] and the case can be regarded as one in which the court refused in "invent" consideration[80] (by regarding something as consideration which was not so regarded by the parties) even though this course was technically open to it. This refusal appears to have been based on the context in which the question arose. The issue was not whether the club could sue the member on any promise made by him: it arose because the money paid by the member to the club had been stolen; and the club, which had received the money in good faith, argued that it had given valuable consideration for it, so as to defeat the true owner's claim for the return of the money. This explanation of the case derives some support from Lord Goff's discussion of a hypothetical case of tokens supplied by a department store in exchange for cash: he said that "by receiving the money in these circumstances the store does not *for present purposes* give valuable consideration for it."[81] Yet he also accepted that (in the store example) "an independent contract is made for the chips when the

---

[71] *Re Dale* [1994] Ch. 31. Contrast *Re Goodchild* [1997] 1 W.L.R. 1216 where a mere "common understanding" (as opposed to definite mutual promises) did not suffice to make B's promise irrevocable, but some effect to it was given by an order in favour of the intended beneficiary under the Inheritance (Provision for Dependants) Act 1975; *cf. Taylor v. Dickens* [1998] 1 FLR 806.

[72] *Haigh v. Brooks* (1839) 10 A. & E. 309, 334; contrast *Foster v. Dawber* (1861) 6 Ex. 839.

[73] *Sturlyn v. Albany* (1587) Cro.Eliz. 67; *March v. Culpepper* (1628) Cro.Car.70; contrast *Re Charge Card Services* [1987] Ch. 150, 164, affd. [1989] Ch. 487 (production of charge card and signature of voucher not consideration for a supply of goods, evidently because such "consideration" would be blatantly "invented": *cf. ante*, § 3–008).

[74] [1960] A.C. 87.

[75] [1991] 2 A.C. 548.

[76] *ibid.* at 561.

[77] *ibid.*; and see 575.

[78] *Bainbridge v. Firmstone* (1838) 8 A. & E. 743.

[79] *Lipkin Gorman's* case at 575.

[80] *Ante*, § 3–008.

[81] *Lipkin Gorman's* case at 577; italics supplied; *cf. post*, § 3–030.

customer originally obtains them at the cash desk."[82] The question whether a party has provided consideration may thus receive one answer when it arises for the purpose of determining the enforceability of a promise, and a different and narrower one when it arises for the purpose of determining whether a transaction has adversely affected the rights of a third party.[83] It was the desire to protect the victim of the theft which led the House of Lords in the *Lipkin Gorman* case to reject the, no doubt somewhat technical, argument that the chips constituted consideration for the money.

The *Lipkin Gorman* case gives rise to further difficulty because the chips were **3–016** supplied on the terms that they could be used, not only for gaming, but also to purchase refreshments at the club. There was no evidence of their having been used for this purpose,[84] but Lord Templeman said that "neither the power to buy refreshments nor the exercise of that power could constitute consideration for the receipt [by the club] of £154,693."[85] One possible interpretation of this passage is that the supply of refreshments could not constitute consideration for £154,693 (the sum lost by the member of the club) since the disparity in value was too great; but this would be inconsistent with the principle that consideration need not be adequate. It is submitted that the preferable explanation of Lord Templeman's statement is that the chips were simply "treated as currency"[86] in the club and could be used for a variety of transactions. The reason why the supply of refreshments was no consideration for the amount lost at play was simply that these transactions were entirely separate ones.

Nominal consideration. The rule that consideration need not be adequate **3–017** makes it possible to evade the doctrine of consideration in the sense that a gratuitous promise can be made binding by giving a nominal consideration, *e.g.* £1 for the promise of valuable property, or a peppercorn for a substantial sum of money. Such cases are merely extreme examples of the rule that the courts will not judge the adequacy of consideration.[87] If, however, it appears on the face of the agreement that the consideration must as a matter of arithmetic be worth less than the performance of the counter-promise, there would seem to be no contract: for example, where A promised to pay B £100 in return for £1 to be simultaneously paid by B. It is assumed in the example that both sums are simply to be paid in legal tender. An agreement to exchange a specific coin or coins of a particular description for a sum of money greater than their face value (*e.g.* 20 shilling pieces bearing the date 1900 for £100) would be a good contract. The same would be true of an agreement to pay a sum in one currency in exchange for one payable in another, and of an agreement to pay a larger sum tomorrow in exchange for a smaller sum paid today.

---

[82] *Lipkin Gorman's* case at 576.
[83] *Ante*, § 3–002.
[84] *Lipkin Gorman's* case at 569.
[85] *ibid.* at 567.
[86] *ibid.* at 561.
[87] Atiyah, *Essays on Contracts*, p. 194 argues that there is no logical connection between the two rules, relying on the fact that in many of the United States the courts recognise the principle that consideration need not be adequate, while rejecting the device of nominal consideration. The answer to this argument lies in Holmes' aphorism (*The Common Law*, p. 1) that "life of the law has not been logic: it has been experience:" American courts which reject the device of nominal consideration do so on policy grounds which have nothing to do with logic.

3–018   Where an agreement is legally binding on the ground that it is supported by nominal consideration, the doctrine of consideration does not serve its main purpose, of distinguishing between gratuitous and onerous promises. But the law has no settled policy against enforcing all gratuitous promises. It only refuses to enforce *informal* gratuitous promises; and the deliberate use of a nominal consideration can be regarded as a form to make a gratuitous promise binding. In some cases it may, indeed, be undesirable to give promises supported by nominal consideration the same legal effect as promises supported by substantial consideration; but these cases are best dealt with by special rules.[88] Such rules are particularly necessary where the promise can cause prejudice to third parties. For example, the danger that promoters of companies might use the device of nominal consideration to the prejudice of shareholders is avoided by imposing fiduciary duties on the promoters.[89]

3–019   **Nominal distinguished from inadequate consideration.** It is not normally necessary to distinguish between "nominal" and "inadequate" consideration, since both equally suffice to make a promise binding. The need to draw the distinction may, however, arise where rules of law treat promises or conveyances supported only by nominal consideration differently from those supported by consideration which is substantial or "valuable" even though it may be inadequate.[90] One view is that a nominal consideration is one that is of only token value,[91] while an inadequate consideration is one that has substantial value even though it is manifestly less than that of the performance promised or rendered in return. A second view is that " 'Nominal consideration' and 'nominal sum' appear . . . , as terms of art, to refer to a sum or consideration which can be mentioned as consideration but is not necessarily paid."[92] This view was expressed by Lord Wilberforce (in a speech with which all the other members of the House of Lords concurred) in *Midland Bank & Trust Co. Ltd v. Green*.[93] In that case a husband sold a farm, said to be worth £40,000, to his wife for £500. It was held that the wife was, for the purposes of section 13(2) of the Land Charges Act 1925, a "purchaser for money or money's worth" so that the sale to her prevailed over an unregistered option to purchase the land, which had been granted to one of the couple's children.[94] It was not necessary to decide whether the consideration for the sale was nominal but Lord Wilberforce said that he would have had "great difficulty" in so holding; and that "To equate 'nominal' with 'inadequate' or even 'grossly inadequate' consideration would embark the

---

[88] Thus a nominal consideration was disregarded in *Milroy v. Lord* (1862) 4 D.F. & J. 264, discussed *post*, § 20–034 specific performance will not be ordered of a promise supported by only nominal consideration (*post*, § 28–031) and for the purposes of the Law of Property Act 1925, "valuable consideration does not include a nominal consideration in money": s.205(1)(xxi).

[89] *Post*, § 9–058. For other ways of protecting third parties from being prejudiced by promises made for inadequate consideration, see Trustee Act 1925, s.13; Law of Property Act 1925, ss.172, 173; Inheritance (Provision for Family and Dependants) Act 1975, ss.10(2)(b), 10(5)(b), 11(2)(c); Insolvency Act 1986, ss.238, 239, 423 (applied in *Barclays Bank plc v. Eustice* [1995] 1 W.L.R. 1238; *Agricultural Mortgage Corp. plc v. Woodward* [1995] B.C.L.C. 1); *cf.* Companies Act 1985, ss.103, 320.

[90] *Ante*, § 3–017 at nn. 88 and 89.

[91] This seems to be the sense in which 10 shillings was described as "nominal" consideration (for the assignment of a debt) in *Turner v. Forwood* [1951] 1 All E.R. 746.

[92] *Midland Bank & Trustee Co. Ltd v. Green* [1981] A.C. 513, 532.

[93] *Supra.*

[94] For later successful proceedings by that child against the parents for conspiracy, see [1982] Ch. 529.

law on inquiries which I cannot think were ever intended by Parliament."[95] On the facts of the case the £500 was in fact paid and was more than a mere token, so that the consideration was not nominal on either of the two views stated above. But if the stated consideration had been only £1, or a peppercorn, it is submitted that it would have been nominal even if it had been paid, or delivered, in accordance with the intention of the parties. So to hold would not lead to inquiries as to inadequacy of consideration; for the distinction between a consideration that is a mere token and one that is inadequate (or even grossly inadequate) is, it is submitted, clear as a matter of common sense. Thus where the question was whether a lease amounted to a "disposition . . . for a nominal consideration"[96] it was said that "Any substantial value—that is, a value of more than, say, £5 . . . will prevent [the] disposition from being for a nominal consideration."[97] Such an approach certainly gives rise to no more difficulty than the concept of a consideration which is "mentioned as a consideration but . . . not necessarily paid." This test would presumably make the question whether consideration was nominal turn on the intention of the parties; and in the present context this would be an even more than usually elusive criterion since no guidance could be obtained from the terms of the contract, those terms being in cases of this kind often deliberately drafted so as to conceal the true nature of the transaction.

Attitude of equity. Even in equity the validity of a contract could not **3–020** generally be challenged on the ground that the consideration provided for one party's promise was inadequate.[98] But the equitable remedy of specific performance may be refused on this ground[99] (at least if coupled with certain other factors); and in exceptional cases gross undervalue may even be a ground for more radical forms of equitable relief, such as setting a contract aside or reopening it.[1] Equity also refuses to aid a "volunteer"—so that its remedy of specific performance is not available to a person who has given no substantial consideration but who can nevertheless bring an action on the promise because it is under seal or supported by nominal consideration.[2]

4. REALITY OF CONSIDERATION

Consideration must be real. Although consideration need not be adequate, it **3–021** must be real, that is, capable of estimation in terms of value, "of some value in the eye of the law."[3] This is one reason why there is no consideration for a

---

[95] [1981] A.C. 513, 532. In other legislative contexts such an inquiry may be intended: *e.g.* by use of the phrase "full and valuable consideration" in the Inheritance (Provisions for Family and Dependants) Act 1975, s.1(3).

[96] Within Law of Property Act 1925, s.84(7).

[97] *Westminster City Council v. Duke of Westminster* [1991] 4 All E.R. 136, 146 (*revsd.* in part on another ground (1992) 24 H.L.R. 572).

[98] See, *e.g. Cheale v. Kenward* (1858) 3 De G. & J. 27; *Townsend v. Toker* (1866) L.R. 1 Ch.App. 446.

[99] *Post*, § 28–030.

[1] *Post*; § 7–077; *Pennell v. Miller* (1857) 23 Beav. 172; *Butler v. Miller* (1867) L.R. 1 Eq. 195, 210; *Tennent v. Tennents* (1870) L.R. 2 Sc. & Div. 6, 9.

[2] *Jefferys v. Jefferys* (1841) Cr. & Ph. 138; *post*, § 28–031.

[3] *Thomas v. Thomas* (1842) 2 Q.B. 851, 859.

promise made "in consideration of natural love and affection,"[4] and why in *Thomas v. Thomas*[5] the testator's desire that his widow should live in his house was not part of the consideration for the executors' promise that she might do so. The same reasoning probably explains the decision in *White v. Bluett*[6] that a son does not provide consideration for his father's promise to release him from a debt by promising in return not to bore his father with complaints. But in *Ward v. Byham*[7] a promise by the mother of an illegitimate child to make it happy appears to have been regarded as part of the consideration for the father's promise to pay her an allowance. It is by no means clear why the mother's promise in the latter case was, while the son's promise in the former was not, thought to have "value in the eye of the law."[8]

3–022   **Impossible and illusory consideration.** A contract may be void for mistake if at the time of the agreement its performance is, unknown to either party, physically impossible.[9] In such a case there may nevertheless be consideration, *e.g.* in the mutual promises of the parties. But if the performance of one party's promise is known by both to be impossible to perform, it is arguable that the consideration is only illusory and not real. For example, a promise by A to pay B £100 for all the wine in B's cellar would probably be regarded as gratuitous if at the time when it was made both A and B knew[10] that there was no wine in the cellar. The position would be different if B's promise was to deliver the *future* contents of the cellar. In that case, A would be buying the chance of the cellar's containing wine[11]; and the value of that chance would be illusory only if the question whether any wine was put into the cellar had been left entirely to B's discretion.[12]

3–023   **Promisee would have performed anyway.** Consideration may also be said to be illusory where it is clear that the promisee would have accomplished the act of forbearance anyway, even if the promise had not been made. This would be the position if A promised B, who had religious objections to smoking, £10 if B did not smoke for a week. Since "it is no consideration to refrain from a course of conduct which it was never intended to pursue,"[13] B's forbearance from smoking would not constitute consideration for A's promise. But where the promise provided *an* inducement for the act or forbearance, the requirement of

---

[4] *Bret v. J.S.* (1600) Cr.Eliz. 755; *Tweddle v. Atkinson* (1861) 1 B. & S. 393, disapproving of *Dutton v. Poole* (1677) 2 Lev. 211; *cf. Horrocks v. Forray* [1976] 1 W.L.R. 230; *Mansukhani v. Sharkey, The Times*, April 17, 1992.

[5] (1842) 2 Q.B. 851; *ante*, § 3–009.

[6] (1853) 23 L.J.Ex. 36.

[7] [1956] 1 W.L.R. 496; *post*, § 3–059.

[8] *White v. Bluett, supra*, can perhaps be explained that the father, in spite of his promise, retained the note.

[9] *Post*, Chap. 5.

[10] There could be a good contract if the parties were in doubt on this point: see *Smith v. Harrison* (1857) 26 L.J.Ch. 412.

[11] *cf. Brady v. Brady* [1989] A.C. 755, 774 ("at the date of the promise").

[12] *Post*, § 3–024.

[13] *Arrale v. Costain Civil Engineering Ltd* [1976] 1 Lloyd's Rep. 98, 106; *cf. Colchester B.C. v. Smith* [1991] Ch. 448, 489, affd. without reference to this point [1992] Ch. 421; *Beaton v. McDivitt* (1988) 13 N.S.W.L.R. 162. *Semble* the burden of proof on this issue is on the promisor: *cf. post*, § 3–138.

consideration is satisfied even though there were also other inducements operating on the promisee's mind.[14]

Discretionary promise. Consideration would again be illusory where it was alleged to consist of a promise the terms of which left performance entirely to the discretion of the promisor.[15] A person does not provide consideration by promising to do something "if I feel like it," or "unless I change my mind." Promises are not often made in this form; but the same principle may apply in analogous cases. Thus a promise may be illusory if it is accompanied by a clause effectively[16] excluding all liability of the promisor for breach.[17] And a promise to pay for "so much coal as I may decide to order" would be an illusory consideration for the seller's counter-promise to deliver, which would therefore not be enforced.[18] On the other hand, if the promise were one to buy "so much of the coal that I require as I may order from you," the court could give reality to the promise by implying a term into it to the effect that at least a reasonable part of any requirements which the promisor actually turned out to have must be ordered from the promisee.[19] Equally the buyer would provide consideration by promising to buy "*all* the coal I require"; for in such a case, even if the buyer does not promise to have any requirements, he does at least give a definite undertaking not to deal with anybody else.[20] This promise may, it is true, be illegal as being in restraint of trade; but if this makes the whole contract invalid, such invalidity probably rests on grounds of public policy and not on lack of consideration.[21] Similarly, a promise which is subject to cancellation by A may nevertheless constitute consideration for a counter-promise from B where A's power to cancel is limited by the express terms of the promise: *e.g.* where it can be exercised only within a specified time. Such a limitation on the power to cancel may also be implied, so that (for example) A could not cancel after B had begun to perform his counter-promise. A's promise would then constitute consideration, so that B would be liable if he failed to complete the performance. Finally, the objection that a promise amounts only to illusory consideration on the grounds here discussed can be removed if the promise is performed: such actual performance can constitute consideration even though the person who has rendered it was not legally obliged to render it.[22]

3–024

---

[14] *Brikom Investments Ltd v. Carr* [1979] Q.B. 467, 490.

[15] For another problem arising out of such promises, see *ante*, § 2–159.

[16] See *post*, Chap. 14. If the clause were ineffective (e.g. under Unfair Terms in Consumer Contracts Regulations 1994, S.I. 1994 No. 3159, Sched. 3, paras 1(c) and 1(f)), this fact would give reality to an otherwise illusory promise.

[17] *Firestone Tyre & Rubber Co. Ltd v. Vokins* [1951] 1 Lloyd's Rep. 32, 39; *cf.* the discussion of *The Cap Palos* [1921] P. 458, in the *Suisse Atlantique* case [1967] 1 A.C. 361, 432.

[18] See *Wickham & Burton Coal Co. v. Farmer's Lumber Co.* (1923) 189 Iowa 1183, 179 N.W. 417. For an exception, see *Citadel Insurance Co. v. Atlantic Union Insurance Co.* [1982] 2 Lloyd's Rep. 543, *post* § 3–161.

[19] *cf. Carmichael v. National Power plc* [1998] I.R.L.R. 301.

[20] The validity of "requirement" contracts is assumed in such cases as *Metropolitan Electric Supply Co. v. Ginder* [1901] 2 Ch. 799 and *Dominion Coal Co. Ltd v. Dominion Steel & Iron Co. Ltd* [1901] A.C. 293. Similarly, a contract by a manufacturer to sell his entire output to a particular buyer is binding even though he does not bind himself to have any output: see, for example, *Donnell v. Bennett* (1883) 22 Ch.D. 835 and *cf.* Howard (1967) 2 U. of Tas.L.R. 446; Adams (1978) 94 L.Q.R. 173.

[21] *Post*, § 3–153.

[22] *Cambridge Nutrition Ltd v. B.B.C.* [1990] 3 All E.R. 523, 528.

5. PAST CONSIDERATION

3–025   **Past consideration is no consideration.** The consideration for a promise must be given in return for the promise. If the act or forbearance alleged to constitute the consideration has already been done before, and independently of, the giving of the promise, it is said to amount to "past consideration"; and such past acts or forbearances do not in law amount to consideration for the promise.[23] If, for example, a thing is guaranteed by a seller *after* it has been sold, the buyer cannot sue on the guarantee as the consideration for it is past.[24] Similarly a promise to make a payment in respect of past services is not contractually binding unless the conditions specified in § 3–028 below are satisfied or some other consideration is provided. For example, a promise to pay money may be made to an employee after his retirement or to an agent after the termination of the agency. If the sole consideration for the promise is the service previously rendered by the former employee or agent, it will be past consideration, so that the promise will not be contractually binding.[25] It will be so binding only if some consideration other than the past service has been provided by the promisee. Such other consideration may consist in his giving up rights which are outstanding (or are in good faith believed to be outstanding) under the original contract,[26] or in his promising or performing some other act or forbearance not due from him under the original contract: for example, in his validly promising not to compete with the promisor.[27]

3–026   **When consideration is past.** In determining whether consideration is past, the courts are not, it is submitted, bound to apply a strictly chronological test. If the giving of the consideration and the making of the promise are substantially one transaction, the exact order in which these events occur is not decisive.[28] A manufacturer's "guarantee" is sometimes given to a customer after he has bought the goods. But it is submitted that the consideration for such a guarantee is not, merely on that ground, past, for the sale and the giving of the "guarantee" will often in substance be a single transaction. Similarly, where a contract to erect buildings on land and to grant a lease of that land are substantially one transaction, the expenditure of money on the buildings would not be past consideration for the execution of the lease, even though the lease was not executed until after completion of the buildings.[29]

---

[23] *Dent v. Bennett* (1839) 4 My. & Cr. 269; *Eastwood v. Kenyon* (1840) 11 A. & E. 438.

[24] *Thorner v. Field* (1612) 1 Bulst. 120; *Roscorla v. Thomas* (1842) 3 Q.B. 234. In the latter case an oral warranty was in fact given at the time of sale (see (1842) 11 L.J.Q.B. 214 and 6 Jur. 929) but this was presumably considered at the time to be "void" for want of written evidence: *cf. post*, § 4–036.

[25] See the facts of *Simpson v. John Reynolds* [1975] 1 W.L.R. 617, where such a payment was held to be voluntary for tax purposes and *cf. Murray v. Goodhews* [1978] 1 W.L.R. 499.

[26] *e.g. Bell v. Lever Bros. Ltd* [1932] A.C. 1616 (where the value of the rights given up in return for the payment was uncertain in amount since it included not only future salary but also possible future commission).

[27] *cf. Wyatt v. Kreglinger and Fernau* [1933] 1 K.B. 793—where the ex-employee's claim would have succeeded if the restraint undertaken by him had not been invalid (*post*, § 17–102).

[28] *Thornton v. Jenkyns* (1840) 1 M. & G. 166; *Tanner v. Moore* (1846) 9 Q.B. 1; *cf.* the discussion of *Halifax B.S. v. Edell* [1992] Ch. 436, *post*, § 19–014.

[29] *Westminster City Council v. Duke of Westminster* [1991] 4 All E.R. 136, 145 (*revsd.* in part on another ground (1992) 24 H.L.R. 572).

Terms of promise not decisive. The question whether consideration is past is one of fact: the wording of the promise is not decisive. Thus in *Re McArdle*[30] a promise made "in consideration of your carrying out" certain work was held to be gratuitous on the ground that the work had already been done. Conversely, a promise made "in consideration of your having today advanced . . . £750" has been held to be binding on proof that the advance was made at the same time as the promise.[31]   **3–027**

Past act done at promisor's request. Even an act done before the promise was made can be consideration for the promise if three conditions are satisfied. First, the act must have been done at the request of the promisor[32]; secondly, it must have been understood that payment would be made; and thirdly, the payment, if it had been promised in advance, must have been legally recoverable.[33] In such a case the promisee is, quite apart from the subsequent promise, entitled to a *quantum meruit* for his services. The promise can be regarded either as fixing the amount of that *quantum meruit*[34] or as being given in consideration of the promisee's releasing his *quantum meruit* claim. On the other hand, a past service for which payment was not expected, or one for which payment, though expected, is not legally recoverable, is no consideration for a subsequent promise to pay for it.[35]   **3–028**

Past promise given at promisor's request. The principle stated in § 3–028 above can apply not only where the consideration for A's promise consists of a past *act* done by B at A's request, but also where it consists of an earlier *promise* made by B at A's request. Thus in *Pao On v. Lau Yiu Long*[36] the claimants had entered into a contract with the X Co. for the sale to that company of their shares in another company. Under that contract, the claimants were to be paid by an allotment of shares in the X Co., and they also promised not to sell 60 per cent of these shares for one year. This promise had been made at the request of the defendants, who held most of the shares in the X Co. and who were anxious that the value of their holding should not be depressed by a sudden sale of all the shares allotted to the claimants. Later, the defendants gave the claimants a guarantee in which they promised to indemnify the claimants against any loss which they might suffer as a result of a fall in the value during the year of the shares in the X Co.[37] The Privy Council rejected the argument that the consideration for the guarantee was past.[38] The claimants' promise not to sell the shares in   **3–029**

---

[30] [1951] Ch. 669.

[31] *Goldshede v. Swan* (1847) 1 Ex. 154. In such cases, the burden of proving that the consideration is not past lies on the person seeking to enforce the promise: *Savage v. Uwechia* [1961] 1 W.L.R. 455.

[32] See *Southwark L.B.C. v. Logan* (1996) 8 Admin.L.R. 292 (where this requirement was not satisfied).

[33] *Re Casey's Patents* [1892] 1 Ch. 104, 115–116; *cf. Lampleigh v. Brathwait* (1615) Hob. 105.

[34] *Kennedy v. Brown* (1863) 13 C.B.(N.S.) 677, 740; *Rondel v. Worsley* [1969] 1 A.C. 191, 236, 278, 287.

[35] See the authorities cited in the preceding note: promise to pay barrister for past professional services not binding since he could not sue for his fees; see now Courts and Legal Services Act 1990, s.61.

[36] [1980] A.C. 614.

[37] This guarantee replaced an earlier agreement (made at the time of the principal sale but subsidiary to it) which was less favourable to the claimants.

[38] For the further argument that the consideration was no more than the promise to perform an existing contractual duty, see *post*, § 3–070.

the X Co. was good consideration for the guarantee; for although that promise had been made before the guarantee was given, it had been made at the defendants' request and on the understanding that the claimants were, in return for making it, to receive some form of protection against the risk (to which the promise exposed them) of a fall in the value of the X Co.'s shares.

3–030   **Antecedent debt.** In a number of cases it has been held that the mere existence of an antecedent debt does not constitute "value" for a transfer since it amounts only to past consideration. Accordingly, in *Roger v. Comptoir d'Escompte de Paris*[39] it was held that a transfer of a bill of lading by a buyer in consideration of a debt already due from him to the transferee did not deprive the seller of his right of stoppage *in transit*[40]; in *Re Barker's Estate*[41] a mortgage executed as security for an antecedent debt and not communicated to the creditor was held to be voluntary and hence a fraudulent conveyance in bankruptcy; and in *Wigan v. English & Scottish Law Life Assurance Society*[42] an assignment of an insurance policy which was made as security for an antecedent debt and had not been communicated to the creditor was held not to have been made "for valuable consideration" within a clause of the policy protecting the rights of such an assignee on the death of the assured by his own hand. These cases are not directly concerned with the enforceability of promises between promisor and promisee: indeed, in *Wigan's* case such enforceability at common law could hardly have been disputed since the assignment was under seal. The cases may, however, be relevant by analogy to the enforceability of promises; and, in principle, it seems that where the only possible consideration for a promise is an antecedent debt owed by the promisor to the promisee, such consideration is past, so that the promise is not contractually binding.[43] In practice, however, the creditor (*i.e.* the promisee) will often be held to have provided consideration for such a promise if, on the strength of it, he forbears to sue for the debt.[44]

3–031   **"Moral" obligation.** In the eighteenth and early nineteenth centuries, an attempt was made (originally by Lord Mansfield) to define consideration so as to include certain pre-existing "moral" obligations. In accordance with this theory it was held that an executor was personally liable on a promise to pay a legacy if he had sufficient assets of the deceased in his hands to pay his debts and legacies[45]; that a promise by a discharged bankrupt to pay a debt contracted before the discharge was binding[46]; and that a promise to pay a statute-barred debt[47] or one contracted during minority[48] was binding. In some of these cases, the consideration for the promise was said to be the "moral" obligation of the

---

[39] (1869) L.R. 2 P.C. 393.
[40] *Post*, Vol. II, § 43–324.
[41] (1875) 44 L.J.Ch. 487.
[42] [1909] 1 Ch. 291.
[43] *e.g. Hopkinson v. Logan* (1839) 5 M. & W. 241.
[44] *Post*, §§ 3–045, 3–047.
[45] *Atkins v. Hill* (1775) 1 Cowp. 284; *Hawkes v. Saunders* (1782) 1 Cowp. 289; an alternative ground for the decision given by Buller J. was that the defendant's equitable (as opposed to "moral") obligation to pay the legacy was consideration for the promise.
[46] *Trueman v. Fenton* (1777) 2 Cowp. 544.
[47] *Hyeling v. Hastings* (1699) 1 Ld.Raym. 389.
[48] *Post*, § 8–041, *cf. Lee v. Muggeridge* (1813) 5 Taunt. 36 (promise by a woman after her husband's death to pay debt incurred during marriage); for attempts to restrict or define the doctrine, see *Littlefield v. Shee* (1831) 2 B. & Ad. 811; *Meyer v. Haworth* (1838) 8 A. & E. 467.

promisor to pay the debt. In this context, the term "moral obligation" was used in a narrow sense. It was restricted to cases in which the promisor's previous obligation was not legally enforceable (or, at any rate, not enforceable in the particular court in which the action on the promise was brought[49]) because it suffered from some specific legal defect. It did not follow that any "moral obligation," such as one which might be said to arise from the receipt of a past benefit, constituted consideration. Thus in *Eastwood v. Kenyon*[50] the guardian of a young girl had raised a loan to pay for her maintenance and education, and to improve her estate. She subsequently came of age and married; and her husband promised the guardian to pay the amount of the loan. In dismissing the guardian's action on this promise, the court rejected the argument that the defendant's promise was binding merely because he was under a moral obligation to perform it. Lord Denman C.J. said that this argument would "annihilate the necessity for any consideration at all, inasmuch as the mere fact of giving a promise creates a moral obligation to perform it."[51] The case also shows that the mere existence of an antecedent moral obligation (in the ordinary sense of the phrase) to reimburse the guardian did not amount to consideration for the husband's promise. From this point of view, the case provides the classic illustration of the requirement that the consideration for a promise must not be past.

Defective obligations as consideration: present position. Many of the cases 3–032 in which promises were held binding under the old "moral obligation" theory would now go the other way. For example, an executor who has assets of the deceased in his hands is no longer personally liable on a promise to pay legacies[52]; a promise by a discharged bankrupt to pay in full debts incurred before his discharge is only binding if supported by fresh consideration[53]; and the same is true of a promise to pay a debt after it has become statute-barred.[54] There is Australian authority in favour of the same rule where a company renewed a note that was originally *ultra vires* after it had been validated by subsequent legislation.[55] On the other hand, a promise by an adult to pay a debt (or to perform some other obligation) contracted during minority is enforceable[56]; and *Eastwood v. Kenyon*[57] did not purport to overrule the "moral obligation" theory in its original narrow sense, that a promise to discharge an earlier obligation which suffered from some specific legal defect might be binding. In this sense the theory was again recognised in *Flight v. Reed*.[58] That case supports the view that a promise made after the repeal of the legislation against usury was not invalid for want of consideration merely because the original loan was usurious. Of course an action on such a promise might, under the modern view of past

---

[49] As in *Hawkes v. Saunders, supra*, n. 45.

[50] (1840) 11 A. & E. 438.

[51] *ibid.* at 450.

[52] *Williams, Mortimer and Sunnucks on Executors, Administrators and Probate* (17th ed., 1993), p. 714.

[53] *Jakeman v. Cook* (1878) 4 Ex.D. 26; *Re Bonacina* [1912] 2 Ch. 394; *Wild v. Tucker* [1914] 3 K.B. 36.

[54] Limitation Act 1980, s.29(7) (*post* § 3–034); *cf.*, as to time bars imposed by contract, *Nippon Yusen Kaisha v. Pacifica Navegaceon SA (The Ion)* [1980] 2 Lloyd's Rep. 245, 249.

[55] *Sharp v. Ellis* (1971) 20 F.L.R. 199.

[56] Minors' Contracts Act 1987, ss.1 and 4, repealing Infants Relief Act 1874, s.2 and Betting and Loans (Infants) Act 1892, s.5.

[57] (1840) 11 A. & E. 438.

[58] (1863) 1 H. & C. 703; mentioned with approval in *J. Evans & Co. v. Heathcote* [1918] 1 K.B. 418, 437.

consideration, fail because the loan was an antecedent debt; but this objection would be overcome if the promisee's forbearance to enforce the loan could be regarded as consideration for the promise in accordance with the requirements stated in §§ 3–045 and 3–047 below.

3–033 **Bills of exchange.** Under section 27(1)(b) of the Bills of Exchange Act 1882, an "antecedent debt or liability" constitutes valuable consideration for a bill of exchange.[59] In many cases, such a consideration would not be past: it could be said to consist in the forbearance of the creditor to sue for the debt or in his treating the bill as conditional payment.[60] But the provision would apply even though, for some reason, this analysis were not possible; and in such cases it would constitute an exception to the rule that past consideration is no consideration.

3–034 **Acknowledgments of statute-barred debts.** A further qualification of the past consideration rule is contained in section 29(5) of the Limitation Act 1980. This provides (*inter alia*) that, where a debtor in a writing signed by him[61] "acknowledges" a debt, it shall be deemed to have accrued on and not before the date of the acknowledgment. An "acknowledgment" need not take the form of a promise[62]; but if it does take this form the promise can extend the period of limitation even though the only consideration for it was the antecedent debt, and thus past. Further acknowledgments made within such an extended period or periods have the same effect.[63] But once the debt has become statute-barred the right to sue for it cannot be revived by any subsequent acknowledgment[64]: to this extent, the old "moral obligation" theory as applied to statute-barred debts[65] has been reversed.

6. Consideration Must Move from the Promisee

3–035 **Promisee must provide consideration.** The rule that "consideration must move from the promisee"[66] means that a person can enforce a promise only if he himself provided consideration for it. Thus if A promises B to pay a sum of money to B if C will do a certain act, B cannot enforce the promise (unless, of course, he procured, or expressly or impliedly undertook to procure, C to do the

---

[59] *Post*, Vol. II, § 34–062.

[60] See *Currie v. Misa* (1875) L.R. 10 Ex. 153 and *cf. post*, §§ 3–045—3–048.

[61] Limitation Act 1980, s.30(1).

[62] An admission of liability suffices: *Surrendra Overseas Ltd v. Government of Sri Lanka* [1977] 1 W.L.R. 481; *cf. Re Overmark Smith Warden Ltd* [1982] 1 W.L.R. 1195 ("statement of affairs" by insolvent company).

[63] Limitation Act 1980, s.29(7).

[64] *ibid.*

[65] *Ante*, § 3–031.

[66] *Barber v. Fox* (1670) 2 Wms.Saund. 134, n. (*e*); *Thomas v. Thomas* (1842) 2 Q.B. 851, 859; *Tweddle v. Atkinson* (1861) 1 B. & S. 393, 399; *Pollway v. Abdullah* [1974] 1 W.L.R. 493, 497; *cf. Dickinson v. Abel* [1969] 1 W.L.R. 295, and (for VAT purposes) *Customs and Excise Commissioners v. Telemed* [1992] S.T.C. 89. For criticism of a possibly contrary dictum, see *post*, § 3–042 at n. 47.

act). It is, however, not necessary for the promisee to provide the whole consideration for the promise: thus he can enforce a promise part of the consideration for which was provided by his agent or partner or by some other co-promisee.[67-68]

Benefit to promisor sufficient. The requirement that consideration must move from the promisee is most generally satisfied where some detriment is suffered by him: *e.g.* where he parts with money or goods, or renders services, in exchange for the promise. But the requirement may equally well be satisfied where the promisee confers a benefit on the promisor without suffering any detriment. This point is illustrated by two rules to be discussed later in this chapter. The first is that performance of an existing contractual duty (or a promise to perform such a duty) can constitute consideration if it benefits the promisor[69]: this benefit "moves" from the promisee in that it is conferred by him, even though it may cause him no detriment[70] in the sense that he was already bound to do the acts in question. The second is that a composition agreement between a debtor and his creditors is binding[71] because it benefits the creditors; and this benefit can be said to "move" from the debtor in that his co-operation is essential to the making and performance of the composition agreement. It could be said that the debtor suffers a legal detriment by signing the agreement when he is not bound to do so. But the rule in question is not in fact based on this invented consideration.[72] It is based on benefit to the promisors.[73] **3–036**

Consideration need not move to the promisor. While consideration must move from the promisee, it need not move to the promisor.[74] It follows that the requirement of consideration may be satisfied where the promisee suffers some detriment at the promisor's request, but confers no corresponding benefit on the promisor. Thus the promisee may provide consideration by giving up a job[75] or the tenancy of a flat,[76] even though no direct benefit results to the promisor from these acts. It also follows that the promisee may provide consideration by conferring a benefit on a third party at the promisor's request: *e.g.* by entering **3–037**

[67-68] *Jones v. Robinson* (1847) 1 Ex.454; *Fleming v. Bank of New Zealand* [1900] A.C. 577. For the position where the *whole* consideration is provided by a co-promisee, see *post*, §§ 3–039—3–042.

[69] *Post*, § 3–063.

[70] *Williams v. Roffey Bros. & Nicholls (Contractors) Ltd* [1991] 1 Q.B. 1, 16.

[71] *Post*, § 3–117; the application of this rule in *West York Darracq Agency Ltd v. Coleridge* [1911] 2 K.B. 326 is hard to support, since there the creditors got nothing and so received no benefit. The consideration was said at 329 to be benefit to the debtor, but he was the person *to* whom the promise was made, and benefit to the promisee is obviously no consideration. If it were, there would be consideration for every gratuitous promise.

[72] *Ante*, § 3–008. The creditors do not bargain for the debtor's signature but for a dividend. If the debtor's signature were regarded as the consideration it could equally well be so regarded in a composition with a single creditor, *i.e.* in a case such as *Foakes v. Beer* (1884) 9 App.Cas. 605, *post*, § 3–107, where it was held that the agreement was not binding.

[73] *Post*, § 3–117.

[74] *Re Wyvern Developments Ltd* [1974] 1 W.L.R. 1097; *cf. International Petroleum Refining & Supply Ltd v. Caleb Brett & Sons Ltd* [1980] 1 Lloyd's Rep. 569, 594 (*post*, § 19–008); *Barclays Bank plc v. Weeks, Legg & Dean* [1998] 3 All E.R. 213, 220–221.

[75] *Jones v. Padavatton* [1969] 1 W.L.R. 628.

[76] *Tanner v. Tanner* [1975] 1 W.L.R. 1346; contrast *Horrocks v. Forray* [1976] 1 W.L.R. 230 where there was no such (nor any other) consideration and no contract, partly for this reason and partly for lack of contractual intention: *ante*, § 2–154; and see *Coombes v. Smith* [1986] 1 W.L.R. 808.

into a contract with the third party.[77] This possibility is illustrated by the case in which goods are bought and paid for by the use of a cheque card or credit card. The issuer of the card makes a promise to the supplier of the goods that the cheque will be honoured or that the supplier will be paid; and the supplier provides consideration for this promise by supplying the goods to the customer.[78] In the case of a credit card transaction there is also consideration in the form of the discount allowed by the supplier of the goods or services to the issuer of the card[79]: this is both a detriment to the supplier and a benefit to the issuer of the card.

3-038   In the last example, there was detriment to the supplier; but the rule that consideration need not move to the promisor equally applies where the consideration consists simply in a benefit conferred by the promisee without loss to himself. Here the requirement of consideration is satisfied if a benefit is conferred either on the promisor or on a third person at his request. For example, in *Bolton v. Madden*[80] the claimant and defendant were subscribers to a charity and entitled to vote on the disposition of its funds. The claimant promised to vote at one meeting for a person whom the defendant wished to benefit, and the defendant promised in return to vote at the next meeting for a person whom the claimant wished to benefit. In an action to enforce the defendant's promise, it was argued that there was no consideration for it as the claimant "incurred neither trouble nor prejudice,"[81] but the court rejected this argument and held the agreement binding. Consideration moved from the claimant simply because he had at the defendant's request conferred a benefit on a third party. It could, of course, be argued that the claimant had suffered a legal detriment[82] by voting in accordance with his promise as he was not previously bound to do so. But this was not the basis of the decision.

3-039   **More than one promisee.**[83] Where a promise is made to more than one person, it is clear that it can be enforced by any of the promisees even though he provided only part of the consideration.[84] But the further question may arise whether the promise can be enforced by one of the promisees even though he provided no part of the consideration, the whole being provided by the other or others. There is no clear answer in the present law to this question; but it is submitted that the position depends on the following distinctions.

3-040   **Joint promisees.** Where a promise is made to A and B *jointly*, it can be enforced by both of them, even though the whole consideration was provided by

---

[77] See *International Petroleum Refining Supply Ltd v. Caleb Brett & Son Ltd* [1980] 1 Lloyd's Rep. 569, 594, where the promisor benefited indirectly since promisor and third party were associated companies. *cf. Pearl Carriers Inc. v. Japan Lines Ltd (The Chemical Venture)* [1993] 1 Lloyd's Rep. 509, 522 (payments made by charterers of ship to the crew regarded as consideration for promise by shipowners to charterers).

[78] *R. v. Lambie* [1982] A.C. 449; *Re Charge Card Services* [1987] Ch. 150, affd. [1989] Ch. 497.

[79] *Customs & Excise Commissioners v. Diners Club Ltd* [1989] 1 W.L.R. 1196, 1207.

[80] (1873) L.R. 9 Q.B. 55.

[81] At 57.

[82] *Ante,* § 3–006.

[83] Cullity (1969) 85 L.Q.R. 530; Winterton (1970) 47 Can.Bar Rev. 483.

[84] *Ante,* § 3–035, at n. 68.

A.[85] If this were not so, the promise could not be enforced at all; for, if A tried to sue alone, he would be defeated by the rule that all the creditors must be parties to the action.[86] It follows from the doctrine of survivorship (which applies between joint promisees)[87] that B would be entitled to the entire benefit of the promise after A's death.

Several promisees. None of the above reasoning applies where a promise is made to A and B *severally*.[88] Hence it seems that each promisee must provide consideration for what is in theory a separate promise to him.   **3–041**

Joint and several promisees. It is, however, uncertain which of the above rules applies to the intermediate case of a promise made to two persons *jointly and severally*. Such a promise may be made under section 81 of the Law of Property Act 1925[89]; but that section appears to contemplate only promises under seal,[90] so that no question of consideration can arise. The common law originally did not recognise the possibility that a promise *to* a number of persons[91] could be joint and several[92]; but the possibility came to be recognised late in the nineteenth century.[93] It may be illustrated by *McEvoy v. Belfast Banking Co.*,[94] where a father, A, deposited £10,000 in a bank and the deposit receipt stated that this amount had been received from him and his son, B, and that it was payable "to either or the survivor." With reference to these facts, Lord Atkin said *obiter* that the contract was not by the bank with A for the benefit of B[95] but "with A and B, and I think with them jointly and severally. A purports to make the contract on behalf of B as well as himself and the consideration supports such a contract."[96] Of course after A's death (which in *McEvoy's* case had occurred) B would be entitled to sue on any joint promise under the doctrine of survivorship. But it is harder to see how he could sue on any several promise, for this is *ex hypothesi* an independent promise and on the facts stated no consideration for it moved from B.[97] Indeed, the more probable view of such facts is that the bank   **3–042**

---

[85] This proposition seems to have been accepted in *Coulls v. Bagot's Executor and Trustee Co. Ltd* [1967] A.L.R. 385; though the majority of the court held that no joint promise had in fact been made: *post*, § 19–061.

[86] *Jell v. Douglas* (1821) 4 B. & Ald. 374; *Sorsbie v. Park* (1843) 12 M. & W. 146; *Thompson v. Hakewill* (1865) 9 C.B.(N.S.) 713.

[87] *Anderson v. Martindale* (1801) 1 East 497.

[88] In such cases it is not necessary to join all the creditors to the action: *James v. Emery* (1818) 5 Price 529; *Keightley v. Watson* (1849) 3 Ex. 716; *Palmer v. Mallett* (1887) 36 Ch.D. 411; nor did the doctrine of survivorship apply: *Withers v. Bircham* (1824) 3 B. & C. 254.

[89] Re-enacting, with some changes, the Conveyancing Act 1881, s.60. Section 81 of the 1925 Act does not affect the law relating to joint *debtors*: *Johnson v. Davies* [1998] 2 All E.R. 649, 656; but our present concern is with the case in which there is more than one *creditor*.

[90] See now Law of Property (Miscellaneous Provisions) Act 1989, s.1(7).

[91] For promises made *by* a number of persons, see Chap. 18, *post*.

[92] *Slingsby's Case* (1588) 5 Co.Rep. 186; *Anderson v. Martindale* (1801) 1 East 487; *Bradburne v. Batfield* (1845) 14 M. & W. 559, 573; *Keighley v. Watson* (1849) 3 Ex. 716, 723 (criticising the rule).

[93] *Thompson v. Hakewill* (1865) 19 C.B.(N.S.) 713, 726; *Palmer v. Mallett* (1887) 36 Ch.D. 410, 421.

[94] [1935] A.C. 24.

[95] Hence such a case will not be affected by the coming into force of the Contracts (Rights of Third Parties) Bill 1998, *post*, §§ 19–075 *et seq.* there being in this case (and in the other cases discussed in this paragraph) no intention of the contracting parties that B should be entitled to enforce the contract.

[96] At 43.

[97] S.J.B. (1935) 51 L.Q.R. 419.

makes no promise at all to B but only has authority to pay him. Hence it is discharged by paying B but it is not liable to him.[98] The bank would not, however, be discharged by such payment if it was *not* authorised by its contract with A to pay B. This possibility is illustrated by *Thavorn v. Bank of Credit & Commerce SA*[99] where A opened a bank account in the name of her nephew B (who was under age), stipulating that only A should operate the account. It was held that B was a mere nominee and that the bank was not discharged by (or was liable in damages for) paying B at the sole request of B and without any instructions from A. There were two reasons why B could not have sued the bank: no promise by the bank had been made to him, and no consideration had moved from him.

3–043   **Contracts (Rights of Third Parties) Bill 1998.** After this Bill has come into force, a term in a contract between A (the promisor) and B (the promisee) will, in certain specified conditions, be enforceable by a third party, C, against A. The Bill is more fully discussed in Chapter 19[1]; the only points to be made here are that C is not prevented from enforcing the term by the fact that no consideration for A's promise moved from him,[2] and that his right to enforce that promise can be described as a quasi-exception to the rule that consideration must move from the promiser.[3] It is not a true exception to the rule since in the case put the promisee is B, who must provide consideration for A's promise.

7. Forbearance to Sue

(a) *In General*

3–044   **Promise not to sue on a valid claim.** A creditor's promise not to enforce a valid claim may be good consideration for a promise given in return.[4] For example, a creditor to whom a sum of money has become due may promise to give the debtor extra time to pay, in return for the debtor's promise to give additional security or to pay higher interest. In such a case, there is good consideration for the debtor's promise: the creditor suffers a detriment in that he is, at least for a time, kept out of his money, while the debtor benefits by getting extra time to pay.[5] In the case put (of a creditor giving his debtor extra time to pay) there is such detriment and benefit even though the creditor has promised to forbear only for a limited time[6]; if no time is specified in the promise, it will be

---

[98] See *Coulls v. Bagot's Executor and Trustee Co. Ltd* [1967] A.L.R. 385; *post,* § 19–061.

[99] [1985] 1 Lloyd's Rep. 529.

[1] *Post,* § 19–075 *et seq.*

[2] Law Com. No. 242 (on which the Bill is based), § 6.8.

[3] *Post,* § 19–082.

[4] See *Pullin v. Stokes* (1794) 2 H.Bl. 312; *Smith v. Algar* (1830) 1 B. & Ad. 603; *Morton v. Burn* (1837) 7 A. & E. 19; *Coles v. Pack* (1869) L.R. 5 C.P. 65; *Crears v. Hunter* (1887) 19 Q.B.D. 341; *Greene v. Church Commissioners for England* [1974] Ch. 467. See also *Oliver v. Davis* [1949] 2 K.B. 727, especially at 743; *Centrovincial Estates plc v. Merchant Investors Assurance Co. Ltd, The Times,* March 8, 1983 (as to which see *ante* § 2–002, n. 13); *G.N. Angelakis Co. SA v. Cie Algérienne de Navigation (The Attika Hope)* [1988] 1 Lloyd's Rep. 439.

[5] *Crowther v. Farrer* (1850) 15 Q.B. 677. It seems to be immaterial whether the proceedings have been commenced or not: see *Wade v. Simeon* (1846) 2 C.B. 548, 565, 567.

[6] *Willatts v. Kennedy* (1831) 8 Bing. 5; *Morton v. Burn* (1837) A. & E. 19; *Board v. Hoey* (1949) 65 T.L.R. 43.

construed as one to forbear for a reasonable time.[7] *A fortiori*, the creditor will provide consideration where he promises absolutely not to sue on the claim[8]: this is the position where a valid claim is settled by agreement between the parties. The principles just stated apply not only to a promise not to enforce a claim but also to one to abandon a good defence[9]; and to one to abandon a particular remedy: *e.g.* to one to abandon arbitration proceedings.[10]

Two further possibilities call for discussion. The first is that the creditor may not make any promise to forbear, but simply *forbear in fact* from pursuing his claim; and the second is that his claim may be *invalid or doubtful*. These possibilities are considered in §§ 3–045 to 3–053 below.

(b) *Actual Forbearance*

Actual forbearance may be consideration. A creditor who, without making   **3–045** any express promise, simply forbears from enforcing a debt or other claim may be held to have impliedly promised to forbear.[11] For example, the acceptance of a cheque in payment of a debt may be evidence of a promise not to sue the debtor so long as the cheque is not dishonoured, or at least for a reasonable time.[12] An actual forbearance may, moreover constitute consideration even though the creditor has not made any express or implied promise to forbear. In *Alliance Bank v. Broom*[13] the defendant owed £22,000 to his bank, who pressed him to give security. He promised to do so but the bank made no counter-promise not to sue him. It was held that there was consideration for the defendant's promise as the bank had given, and the defendant received, "some degree of forbearance."[14] On the other hand, in *Miles v. New Zealand Alford Estate Co.*[15] a company had bought land and then became dissatisfied with the purchase. The vendor later promised to make certain payments to the company, and it was alleged that the consideration for this promise was the company's forbearance to take proceedings to rescind the contract. A majority of the Court of Appeal held that there was no consideration for the vendor's promise as no proceedings to rescind were ever intended; and Cotton L.J. added that "it must be shown that there was something which would bind the company not to institute proceedings."[16] Bowen L.J. dissented from his proposition,[17] relying on *Alliance Bank v. Broom*; but it may be possible to reconcile the cases by reference to the types of claim forborne. A bank to which £22,000 is owed is virtually certain to take steps to enforce its claim, but a dissatisfied purchaser of land is much less certain to take proceedings

---

[7] *Payne v. Wilson* (1827) 7 B. & C. 423; *Oldershaw v. King* (1857) 2 H. & N. 517; *Fullerton v. Provincial Bank of Ireland* [1903] A.C. 309, 313.

[8] *Mapes v. Sidney* (1624) Cro.Jac. 683.

[9] See *Banque de l'Indochine v. J. H. Rayner (Mincing Lane) Ltd* [1983] Q.B. 711.

[10] *Allied Marine Transport Ltd v. Vale do Rio Doce Navegaçao SA (The Leonidas D.)* [1985] 1 W.L.R. 925, 933.

[11] *Re Wyvern Developments Ltd* [1974] 1 W.L.R. 1097.

[12] *Baker v. Walker* (1845) 14 M. & W. 465; *Elkington v. Cooke-Hill* (1914) 30 T.L.R. 670; contrast *Hasan v. Wilson* [1977] 1 Lloyd's Rep. 431, where the debt in respect of which the cheque was given was that of a third party.

[13] (1864) 2 Dr. & Sm. 289.

[14] At 292.

[15] (1886) 32 Ch.D. 267; *cf. Hunter v. Bradford Property Trust Ltd*, 1970 S.L.T. 173.

[16] (1886) 32 Ch.D. at 267.

[17] *ibid.* at 291; his view was approved by Lord Macnaghten in *Fullerton v. Provincial Bank of Ireland* [1903] A.C. 309, 314.

for rescission. It may, therefore, be reasonable to say that mere forbearance will amount to consideration in relation to the former type of claim, but that a promise to forbear is necessary where it is problematical whether the claim will ever be enforced at all. A promise to forbear is also, of course, necessary where that is what the debtor bargains for.

3–046   **Time for which creditor must forbear.** Where the consideration consists of a promise to forbear which specifies no time the creditor must forbear for a reasonable time.[18] There is no such requirement where the consideration consists of actual forbearance: here it is enough that the debtor had "a certain amount of forbearance."[19]

3–047   **Relation between actual forbearance and the promise made in return for it.** Where the consideration is alleged to consist of an actual forbearance, that forbearance must be causally connected with the debtor's promise. A creditor does not give consideration[20] merely by forbearing to enforce an antecedent debt.[21] In *Wigan v. English & Scottish Law Life Assurance Society*[22] a debtor executed an assignment by way of mortgage of an insurance policy in favour of his creditor. Parker J. held that the creditor, who knew nothing of the mortgage, had given no consideration for it[23]; but he added that the creditor would have provided consideration if he had been told of the mortgage and if, "on the strength of" it, he had actually forborne to sue for the debt.

3–048   **Express or implied request of debtor necessary.** The crucial question, therefore, is whether the creditor has forborne "on the strength of" the debtor's promise. He will clearly have done so where the debtor has *expressly* requested the forbearance.[24] But such an express request is not necessary. In *Alliance Bank v. Broom*[25] the bank's forbearance was held to constitute consideration even though the defendant had not expressly requested it. Lord Macnaghten later explained the case on the ground that the debtor had impliedly requested forbearance.[26] It seems that an actual forbearance which is not induced by either the express or the implied request of the debtor is no consideration. In *Combe v. Combe*[27] a husband during divorce proceedings promised to pay his wife an annual allowance. In an action to enforce this promise, the wife argued, *inter alia*, that she had given consideration for it by forbearing to apply to the court for a maintenance order. But it was held that there was no consideration as the wife had not forborne at the husband's request.[28]

---

[18] *Ante*, § 3–044.
[19] *Alliance Bank v. Broom* (1864) 2 Dr. & Sm. 289, 292.
[20] Or, which comes to the same thing, only gives past consideration.
[21] *Ante*, § 3–030.
[22] [1909] 1 Ch. 291; *cf. Hopkins v. Logan* (1839) 5 M. & W. 241.
[23] *Ante*, § 3–030.
[24] *Crears v. Hunter* (1887) 19 Q.B.D. 341, 344.
[25] (1864) 2 Dr. & Sm. 289.
[26] *Fullerton v. Provincial Bank of Ireland* [1903] A.C. 309, 313.
[27] [1951] 2 K.B. 215.
[28] *Quaere* whether such a request should not have been implied. On the question whether a "request" is necessary, see A.L.G. (1951) 67 L.Q.R. 456; Smith (1953) 69 L.Q.R. 99. It seems that in the present type of case, involving a forbearance to sue, a request is necessary, whether or not this is true of unilateral contracts generally. As to this, see *Australian Woollen Mills Pty. Ltd v. The Commonwealth* (1954) 92 C.L.R. 424, especially at 457–460.

(c) *Invalid or Doubtful Claims*

Claims known to be invalid. A promise is not binding if the sole[29] considera- **3–049**
tion for it is a forbearance to enforce (or a promise to forbear from enforcing) a
claim which is invalid and which is either known by the party forbearing to be
invalid or not believed by him to be valid. As Tindal C.J. said in *Wade v.
Simeon*[30]: "It is almost *contra bonos mores* and certainly contrary to all the
principles of natural justice that a man should institute proceedings against
another when he is conscious that he has no good cause of action." Thus a
promise by a bookmaker not to sue a client for the amount of lost bets is no
consideration for a promise made in return by the client.[31]

Claims which are doubtful. If, however, the validity of the claim is doubtful, **3–050**
forbearance to enforce it can be good consideration: for example, in *Haigh v.
Brooks*[32] it was held that the promisee had provided consideration by giving up
a guarantee containing "an ambiguity that might be explained . . . so as to make
it a valid contract."[33]

Claims in law invalid but made in good faith. It has, further, been held that **3–051**
the same rule applies even if the claim is clearly invalid in law, so long as it was
a "reasonable claim"[34] (*i.e.* one made on reasonable grounds) which was in good
faith believed by the party forbearing to have at any rate a fair chance of success.
Thus in *Callisher v. Bischoffsheim*[35] the claimant alleged that money was due to
him and was about to take proceedings to enforce his claim; the defendant then
promised to deliver certain securities to the claimant in consideration of the
claimant's taking no proceedings for an agreed time. The court held that the
defendant was bound by his promise. Cockburn C.J. said[36]: "Every day a
compromise is effected on the ground that the party making it has a chance of
succeeding in it, and if he bona fide believes he has a fair chance of success, he
has a reasonable ground for suing, and his forbearance to sue will constitute a
good consideration. . . . It would be another matter if a person made a claim
which he knew to be unfounded, and, by a compromise, derived an advantage

---

[29] The position is different if there is also *other* consideration for the promise; see *The Siboen and
the Sibotre* [1976] 1 Lloyd's Rep. 293, 334.
[30] (1846) 2 C.B. 548, 564. See also *Edwards v. Baugh* (1843) 11 M. & W. 641, especially at
646.
[31] *Hyams v. Coombes* (1912) 28 T.L.R. 413; *Burrell & Son v. Leven* (1926) 42 T.L.R. 407;
Poteliakhoff v. Teakle [1938] 2 K.B. 816; *Goodson v. Baker* (1908) 98 L.T. 415 (*contra*) seems wrong;
see generally Vol. II, § 40–024.
[32] (1839) 10 A. & E. 309; for the earlier, contrary view see *Stone v. Wythipol* (1588) Cro.Eliz. 126;
Jones v. Ashburnham (1804) 4 East 455 and dicta in *Ex p. Banner* (1881) 17 Ch.D. 480, 490 (these
dicta being disapproved in *Miles v. New Zealand Alford Estate Co.* (1885) 32 Ch.D. 266).
[33] (1839) 10 A. & E. 309, 334; *cf. Colchester B.C. v. Smith* [1992] Ch. 421; *Colonia Versicherung
A.G. v. Amoco Oil Co.* [1995] 1 Lloyd's Rep. 570, 577 (affd. without reference to this point [1997]
1 Lloyd's Rep. 261).
[34] *Cook v. Wright* (1861) 1 B. & S. 559, 569.
[35] (1870) L.R. 5 Q.B. 449. See also *Longridge v. Dorville* (1821) 5 B. & Ad. 117; *Cooper v. Parker*
(1855) 15 C.B. 822; *Cook v. Wright* (1861) 1 B. & S. 559; *Ockford v. Barelli* (1871) 20 W.R. 116;
Holsworthy U.D.C. v. Holsworthy R.D.C. [1907] 2 Ch. 62; *Re Cole* [1931] 2 Ch. 174; *Freedman v.
Union Group plc* [1997] E.G.C.S. 28. For a discussion of the English decisions on a Scottish appeal,
see *Hunter v. Bradford Property Trust*, 1970 S.L.T. 173. Scots law does not require promises to be
supported by consideration but distinguishes for certain purposes between gratuitous and onerous
promises.
[36] (1870) L.R. 5 Q.B. at 452.

under it: in that case his conduct would be fraudulent." And in *Miles v. New Zealand Alford Estate Co.*[37] Bowen L.J. said: "It seems to me that if an intending litigant bona fide forbears a right to litigate a question of law or fact which is not vexatious or frivolous to litigate, he does give up something of value. It is a mistake to suppose it is not an advantage, which a suitor is capable of appreciating, to be able to litigate his claim, even if it turns out to be wrong."

3–052   Two further conditions must be satisfied by a party who relies on his forbearance to enforce an invalid claim as the consideration for a promise made to him. He must not deliberately conceal from the other party (*i.e.* the promisor) facts which, if known to the latter, would enable him to defeat the claim.[38] And he must show that he seriously intended to pursue the claim.[39]

3–053   **Claims on disputed facts.** The cases considered in § 3–051 and 3–052 all concern claims the validity of which is doubtful in law. It seems that the same principles can apply where the validity of a claim is in doubt because of a dispute about the facts. Where the settlement of a dispute is based on a simple *mistake* of fact shared by both parties, it may be void for mistake.[40] But this would not be the case where both parties knowingly take the risk that the facts may turn out to be different from the facts as they were alleged or supposed to be. A negotiation of a settlement on disputed facts always takes such an element of risk into account.

3–054   **Void forbearances.** The forbearance itself (as opposed to the claim forborne) may be void on grounds of public policy, or by statute: for example, where a wife promises her husband not to apply for maintenance in matrimonial proceedings.[41] In such cases the promise to forbear cannot of course be enforced; but, unless the promise is illegal, it may nevertheless constitute consideration for a counter-promise to make a payment in return for it.[42] A *fortiori* the performance of the promise to forbear may (if the promise was not illegal) be good consideration for a counter-promise[43] even though the promise could not have been enforced.

3–055   **Executed compromises.** The discussion in §§ 3–049 to 3–054 is concerned with the enforceability of an agreement to compromise a claim. Different problems can arise after such an agreement has been *performed*, generally by payment of the amount which one party agreed to pay under the compromise. Even if there was, under the rules discussed above, no consideration for that party's promise, he will not be entitled to the return of the payment if it was made

---

[37] (1885) 32 Ch.D. 266, 291; *cf. Pitt v. P.H.H. Asset Management Ltd* [1994] 1 W.L.R. 327, 322 but in this case it was not clear that the party forbearing in fact believed in the validity of his claim.

[38] *Miles v. New Zealand Alford Estate Co., supra,* at 284; *Colchester B.C. v. Smith* [1992] Ch. 421, 435. Contrast *Bank of Credit and Commerce International v. Ali* [1999] 2 All E.R. 1005 (compromise of a *valid* claim).

[39] *Cook v. Wright* (1861) 1 B. & S. 559, 569; *Syros Shipping Co. SA v. Elaghill Trading Co. (The Proodos C)* [1980] 2 Lloyd's Rep. 390, 392.

[40] *Grains & Fourrages SA v. Huyton* [1997] 1 Lloyd's Rep. 628, where there was no compromise since both parties wished from the start to achieve the same result but were mistaken only as to the effect of the steps they had taken to achieve it.

[41] Matrimonial Causes Act 1973, s.34, re-enacting Maintenance Agreements Act 1957, s.1, *post,* § 17–044.

[42] *Post,* § 3–154.

[43] *Post,* § 3–155.

"to close the transaction"[44]; in such a case the payment is treated as if it were an executed gift.[45] To give rise to a claim for repayment, it will be necessary to establish other circumstances, such as that the payment was made under duress.[46]

8. EXISTING DUTIES AS CONSIDERATION[47]

General. Much difficulty arises in determining whether a person who does, or promises to do, what he is already in law bound to do thereby provides consideration for a promise made to him. One possible view is that, as he was already bound to do the thing in question, his doing, or promising to do, it has no "value in the eye of the law": hence it cannot amount to a legal detriment to him, or to a legal benefit[48] to the person already entitled to performance. On the other hand the actual performance of the legal duty may amount to a factual detriment or benefit: it may be a detriment to the party performing the duty since actual performance may be more troublesome to him than the payment of (or the risk of being sued for) damages; while the other party may benefit in the sense of finding his legal remedy for breach of the duty less beneficial than its actual performance. Denning L.J. has therefore said that the performance of an existing duty, or the promise to perform it, was always good consideration.[49] This radical view has not been accepted; but the requirement of consideration in this group of cases has been mitigated by recognising that it can be satisfied where the promisee has conferred a factual (as opposed to a legal) benefit on the promisor.[50]

3–056

(a) *Public Duty*

Where the promisee is under a public duty. It has been held that a person cannot recover money promised to him in return for his performance of, or promise to perform, a duty imposed by law. In *Collins v. Godefroy*,[51] an attorney had been subpoenaed to give evidence on the defendant's behalf and alleged that the defendant had promised to pay him a guinea a day for his loss of time incurred in such attendance. It was held that, as the promisee was under a duty imposed by law to attend, the defendant's promise was given "without consideration." Other authorities on the point can, however, be more readily explained on grounds of public policy: it has, for example, been held that a public officer cannot enforce a promise by a private citizen to pay him money for doing his

3–057

[44] *Woolwich Equitable B.S. v. IRC* [1993] A.C. 70, 165.

[45] *ibid.* citing *Maskell v. Horner* [1915] 3 K.B. 106, 120.

[46] *Post*, Chap. 7.

[47] Reynolds and Treitel (1965) 7 Malaya L.Rev. 1; Aivazian, Trebilcock & Penny (1984) 22 Osgoode Hall L.J. 173; Hooley [1991] J.B.L. 195; Halson (1991) 107 L.Q.R. 649.

[48] *Ante*, § 3–006.

[49] *Ward v. Byham* [1956] 1 W.L.R. 496, 498; *Williams v. Williams* [1957] 1 W.L.R. 148, 151.

[50] *Post*, § 3–063.

[51] (1831) 1 B. & Ad. 950. See also *Willis v. Peckham* (1820) 1 Br. & B. 515; *Thoresen Car Ferries Ltd v. Weymouth Portland B.C.* [1977] 2 Lloyd's Rep. 614, 619.

public duty[52] and that a person cannot enforce a promise made in consideration of his forbearing to engage in a course of conduct that is criminal.[53] To uphold such promises would encourage extortion; and this, rather than want of consideration, accounts for most of the authorities which establish the present rule. It is arguable that, when there are no such grounds of public policy against enforcing the promise, an action on it will not fail for want of consideration merely because the performance rendered in return was already due under a public duty from the promisee. Before 1968 a person who knew that a felony had been committed and had information which might lead to the arrest of the felon was bound to communicate the information to the police: if he failed to do so he was guilty of misprision of felony.[54] Yet promises to pay rewards for such information could be enforced, even by police officers giving the information.[55] Public policy was not offended by such offers, as they might induce people to look for the information and so promote the interests of justice. The term "felony" is now obsolete[56] and the mere failure to disclose information which might lead to the arrest of a criminal is no longer an offence[57] or a breach of a duty imposed by law. But the old reward cases show that an act may constitute consideration even though there is a public duty to do it.

3–058   **Promisee doing more than public duty.** A person who is under a public duty can provide consideration for a promise by doing (or promising to do) more than he was by law obliged to do. In *Glasbrook Brothers Ltd v. Glamorgan County Council*[58] the owners of a coal mine, who feared violence from strikers, asked the police for a greater degree of protection than the police reasonably thought necessary. It was held that the police had provided consideration for this promise by providing the extra protection, and that accordingly the promise was enforceable. The position in cases of this kind is now regulated by statute. Section 25(1) of the Police Act 1996 provides that payment can be claimed for "special police services" rendered at the "request" of the person requiring them. Such a request can be implied from conduct: *e.g.* where a person organises an event which cannot safely take place without such services. On this reasoning, a football club has been held liable to the police authority for the cost of policing matches played on its ground.[59] Such liability arises irrespective of contract.

---

[52] *Wathen v. Sandys* (1811) 2 Camp. 640; *Morris v. Burdett* (1808) 1 Camp. 218; *Bilke v. Havelock* (1813) 3 Camp. 374; *cf. Morgan v. Palmer* (1824) 2 B. & C. 729, 736 (where the actual decision was that money paid to the official was recoverable by the payee as having been extorted from him *colore officii*: see *Woolwich Equitable B.S. v. I.R.C.* [1993] A.C. 70, 155, 165, 181, 198).

[53] *Brown v. Brine* (1875) L.R. 1 Ex.D. 5 (forbearance to commit criminal libel).

[54] *Sykes v. D.P.P.* [1962] A.C. 528.

[55] *England v. Davidson* (1840) 11 A. & E. 856; *Smith v. Moore* (1845) 1 C.B. 438; *Neville v. Kelly* (1862) 12 C.B.(N.S.) 740; *Bent v. Wakefield and Barnsley Union Bank* (1878) 4 C.P.D. 1. Contrast *Maryland Casualty Co. v. Matthews* (1962) 209 F.Supp. 822 where a similar claim by a detective failed on grounds of public policy.

[56] Criminal Law Act 1967, s.1.

[57] The offence of concealing an arrestable offence created by s.5(1) of the Criminal Law Act 1967 is much narrower in scope than the former offence of misprision of felony; the statutory offence is committed only if the person withholding the information accepts or agrees to accept some consideration (other than making good the loss) for not disclosing it. For the definition of "arrestable offence," see now Police and Criminal Evidence Act 1984, s.24.

[58] [1925] A.C. 270. *cf. Thoresen Car Ferries v. Weymouth Portland B.C.* [1997] 2 Lloyd's Rep. 614 (A's promise to *make use* of B's services for which he was under a legal duty to *pay* held to constitute consideration for B's counterpromise).

[59] *Harris v. Sheffield United F.C. Ltd* [1988] Q.B. 77.

In *Ward v. Byham*[60] the father of an illegitimate child wrote to its mother, from   **3–059**
whom he was separated, saying that she could have the child and an allowance
of £1 a week if she proved that the child was "well looked after and happy and
also that she is allowed to decide for herself whether or not she wishes to come
and live with you." The father refused to continue the payments after the
marriage of the mother to another man. It was held that the mother was entitled
to enforce the father's promise even though she was under a statutory duty to
maintain the child. One ground for the decision is that the mother had provided
consideration by showing that she had made the child happy, etc.: in this way, she
could be said to have done more than she was required by law to do,[61] and to
have conferred a factual benefit on the father[62] or on the child,[63] even though she
may not have suffered any detriment. But if a son's promise not to bore his father
is not good consideration, it is hard to see why a mother's promise to make her
child happy should, for the present purpose, stand on a different footing.[64] There
is, with respect, force in Denning L.J.'s view that the mother provided consideration by merely performing her legal duty to support the child. There was certainly
no ground of public policy for refusing to enforce the promise.

(b) *Duty Imposed by Contract with Promisor*

Contractual duty to promisor. When A was bound by contract with B to do,   **3–060**
or to forbear from doing, something, the law at one time took the view that A's
performance of that duty (or his promise to perform it) was no consideration for
a new promise by B. Later authority has qualified that view, but the extent of the
qualification is uncertain. The cases fall into three groups.

Cases in which there was no consideration. The view that there was no   **3–061**
consideration for B's new promise is usually traced back to *Stilk Myrick*.[65] In that
case some of the crew of a ship had deserted during the voyage for which they
had contracted to serve and the master promised to divide the wages of the
deserters amongst the remaining crew members if they would work the ship
home short-handed. The court rejected a claim brought by one of the promisees
against the master for a share of the extra wages promised by the master.
According to one of the reports,[66] the claim was rejected on grounds of public
policy stated in an earlier similar case,[67] *viz.* that the enforcement of such
promises might lead sailors to refuse to perform their contracts unless they were
promised extra pay; and that it would encourage undesirable forms of pressure
amounting to extortion. According to the other report[68] (which has been said to

---

[60] [1956] 1 W.L.R. 496.
[61] This may be what Morris and Parker L.JJ. had in mind when saying at 499 that the mother had
provided "ample consideration" for the promise.
[62] See *Williams v. Roffey Bros. & Nicholls (Contractors) Ltd* [1991] 1 Q.B. 1, 13.
[63] Consideration need not move to the promisor: *ante* § 3–037.
[64] *Ante*, § 3–021.
[65] (1809) 2 Camp. 317; 6 Esp. 129. See also *Harris v. Carter* (1854) 3 E. & B. 559; *Sanderson v.
Workington Borough Council* (1918) 34 T.L.R. 386; *Swain v. West (Butchers) Ltd* [1936] 1 All E.R.
224.
[66] (1809) 6 Esp. 129.
[67] *Harris v. Watson* (1791) Peake 102.
[68] (1809) 2 Camp. 317; in *Harris v. Carter* (1854) 3 E. & B. 559, both public policy and want of
consideration are relied on to explain the rule.

have "the better reputation")[69] the decision was based on the ground that the promisees had provided no consideration as they were already bound by their contracts to work the ship home; and it is on this ground that the case is now generally explained.[70] On the same principle, a promise to pay extra freight for the carriage of goods to the agreed destination cannot be enforced by the carrier[71]; and, where a debt is already due in full, a promise by the debtor to pay it in stated instalments is no consideration for the creditor's promise not to take bankruptcy proceedings in respect of the debt.[72]

3–062   **Bases of the rule.** The view that the new promises in cases of the kind discussed in § 3–061 above should not be enforced seems to be based on two related lines of reasoning.

(1) Protection from extortion. The first rests on the need to protect the party to whom the duty is owed from extortion, in the shape of the other party's refusal to perform unless he is promised extra pay. But this argument is much reduced in importance now that such a refusal may constitute duress.[73] Where the refusal *does* amount to duress, a promise induced by it can be avoided (and money paid in pursuance of it be recovered back) on that ground.[74] This is true even where the promise *is* supported by consideration: for example, where the promisee has undertaken not merely to perform his duties under the original contract, but also to render some relatively small additional service.[75] If, on the other hand, the promisee's refusal to perform the original contract does *not* amount to duress, the promise cannot be impugned merely on the ground that the refusal amounted to an abuse by the promisee of a dominant bargaining position.[76] To allow a promise to be invalidated on this ground even though there was *no* duress would introduce an intermediate category of promises unfairly obtained; and this would (in the words of Lord Scarman) "be unhelpful because it would render the law uncertain."[77]

(2) Absence of legal detriment or benefit. The second reason for the view that the new promise should not be enforced was that the promisee suffered no legal

---

[69] *North Ocean Shipping Co. Ltd v. Hyundai Construction Co. Ltd (The Atlantic Baron)* [1979] Q.B. 705, 712, where the rule in *Stilk v. Myrick* was recognised as being still good law, though held inapplicable for reasons stated in § 3–065, *post*; Coote [1980] C.L.J. 40.

[70] *Harrison v. Dodd* (1914) 111 L.T. 47; *Swain v. West (Butchers) Ltd* [1936] 3 All E.R. 261; *North Ocean Shipping Co. Ltd v. Hyundai Construction Co. Ltd (The Atlantic Baron)* [1979] Q.B. 705, 712; *Pao On v. Lau Yiu Long* [1980] A.C. 614, 633; *Sybron Corp. v. Rochem Ltd* [1983] I.C.R. 801, 817; *Vantage Navigation Corp. v. Suhail and Saud Building Materials LLC (The Alev)* [1989] 1 Lloyd's Rep. 138, 147.

[71] *Syros Shipping Co. SA v. Elaghill Trading Co. Ltd (The Proodos C)* [1980] 2 Lloyd's Rep. 390; *Atlas Express Ltd v. Kafco (Importers and Distributors) Ltd* [1989] 1 Q.B. 833.

[72] *Vanbergen v. St. Edmunds Properties Ltd* [1933] 2 K.B. 223.

[73] *Post*, Chap. 7; *Atlas Express Ltd v. Kafco (Importers and Distributors) Ltd* [1989] 1 Q.B. 833.

[74] This would have been the result in *North Ocean Shipping Co. Ltd v. Hyundai Construction Co. Ltd (The Atlantic Baron)*, *supra* n. 69, if the victim of the duress had not affirmed the contract. For cases in which recovery was allowed on this ground, see *Universe Tankships Inc. v. International Transport Workers' Federation (The Universe Sentinel)* [1983] 1 A.C. 366; *B. & S. Contracts & Designs v. Victor Green Publications Ltd* [1984] I.C.R. 449; and *T. A. Sundell & Sons Pty. Ltd v. Emm Yannoulatos (Overseas) Pty. Ltd* [1956] 56 S.R. (N.S.W.) 323.

[75] *e.g. North Ocean Shipping Co. Ltd v. Hyundai Construction Co. Ltd (The Atlantic Baron)* [1979] Q.B. 705; *post*, § 3–065; *Vantage Navigation Corp. v. Sahail and Saud Building Materials LLC (The Alev)* [1989] 1 Lloyd's Rep. 138, 147.

[76] *Pao On v. Lau Yiu Long* [1980] A.C. 614, 632.

[77] *ibid.* at 634. This statement was made in a case involving three parties, but is of general application: *Williams v. Roffey Bros. & Nicholls (Contractors) Ltd* [1991] 1 Q.B. 1, 15.

detriment[78] in performing what was already due from him, nor did the promisor receive any legal benefit in receiving what was already due to him. But this reasoning takes no account of the fact that the promisee may in fact suffer a detriment: for example, the wages which a seaman could earn elsewhere might exceed those due under the original contract together with the damages which he would have to pay for breaking it. Conversely the promisor may in fact benefit from the performance which he receives in consequence of the new promise: in *Stilk v. Myrick* the master got his ship home, and this may well have been worth more to him than any damages that he could have recovered from the crew.

Factual benefit to promisor. The forgoing discussion shows that a new   **3–063** promise by B in consideration of A's performing his duty to B under an earlier contract between them is not necessarily obtained by duress; and that A's performance of the duty may in fact benefit B. Where both these conditions are satisfied, it has been held that A can enforce B's new promise. In *Williams v. Roffey Bros. & Nicholls (Contractors) Ltd*[79] B had engaged A as carpentry sub-contractor, for the purpose of performing a contract between B and X to refurbish a number of flats. The amount payable by B to A under the subcontract was £20,000 but B later promised to make extra payments to A, who undertook no additional obligation in return.[80] B made this new promise because B's own surveyor recognised that the originally agreed sum of £20,000 was too low, and because B feared that A (who was in financial difficulties) would not be able to complete his work on time, and so expose B to penalties for delay under his contract with X. It was held that B's promise to make the extra payments to A was supported by consideration in the shape of the "practical benefits"[81] obtained by B from A's performance of his duties under the original contract between them.[82] Since no allegation of duress on A's part had been made by B, the new promise by B to pay extra could not be avoided on this ground. There had been no threat by A to break his original contract; indeed, the initiative for the agreement containing the promise of extra pay seems to have come from B.

The consideration for B's promise in the *Williams* case appears to have been   **3–064** the factual benefit obtained by B from A's actual performance of his earlier contract with B. This element of factual benefit has been regarded as considera-tion where a person performs or (promises to perform) a contractual duty owed to a third party[83]; and the *Williams* case is to be welcomed in bringing the two-party cases in line with those involving three parties.[84] But it is by no means clear

---

[78] *Ante*, § 3–006.

[79] [1991] 1 Q.B. 1; Adams and Brownsword (1991) 53 M.L.R. 536; Chen-Wishart (1991) 14 N.Z.U.L.R. 270; Hird and Blair, [1996] J.B.L. 254.

[80] The payments under the original contract were found to be due in unspecified instalments while those under the new promise were due as each flat was completed, but no attempt was made to argue that this change in the times when payment was due *might* have been to A's disadvantage and therefore provided consideration. There is perhaps a hint to this effect in Russell L.J.'s judgment at 19.

[81] [1991] 1 Q.B. at 11; *cf. ibid.* at 19, 23, followed in *Anangel Atlas Compania Naviera SA v. Ishikawajima Harima Heavy Industries Co. Ltd (No. 2)* [1990] 2 Lloyd's Rep. 526, where "prom-isor" and "promisee" appear to have been transposed in a passage at 545.

[82] In fact, B did not secure the whole of this benefit, but this was because B's wrongful failure to make the extra payments justified A's refusal to continue with the work.

[83] *Post*, § 3–070.

[84] See *post*, § 3–069.

how the case is, from this point of view, to be reconciled with *Stilk v. Myrick* and the line of more recent decisions which have followed that case.[85] As has been suggested above, the master in *Stilk v. Myrick* also obtained a factual benefit (in getting his ship home); and such a factual benefit will very often be obtained by B where he secures actual performance from A (as opposed to having to sue him for non-performance of the original contract). In the *Williams* case, *Stilk v. Myrick* was not overruled; indeed Purchas L.J. described it as a "pillarstone of the law of contract."[86] But he added that the case might be differently decided today[87]; while Glidewell L.J. said that the present decision did not "contravene" but did "refine and limit"[88] the principle of the earlier case; and Russell L.J. said that the "rigid approach" to consideration in *Stilk v. Myrick* was "no longer necessary or desirable."[89] The conclusion which may tentatively be drawn from these statements is that the factual benefit to B in securing A's performance of the earlier contract will normally suffice to constitute consideration. The insistence in the earlier cases on the stricter requirement of legal benefit or detriment is no longer justified by the need to guard against extortion, now that this risk is more satisfactorily dealt with by the expanding concept of duress.

3–065   **Other consideration.** The promisee may provide other consideration for the new promise by doing, or promising, more than he was bound by the original contract to do. Thus in one case[90] a seaman was promoted during the course of the voyage and undertook additional duties: these were held to constitute consideration for a promise to pay him extra wages. The same principle was applied where shipbuilders claimed an increase in the agreed price for a supertanker on the ground that the currency in which that price was to be paid had been devalued. The contract provided for the giving by the builders of a performance guarantee, and it was held that they had provided consideration for the prospective owners' promise to pay the price-increase by making corresponding increase in their performance guarantee.[91]

3–066   The promisee similarly provides other consideration where, before the new promise was made, circumstances have arisen which justify the promisee's refusal to perform the original contract. Thus in *Hartley v. Ponsonby*,[92] a ship during the course of a voyage became so short-handed that it was dangerous to proceed with the reduced crew. It was held that this was sufficient to discharge the crew from their original contract; in consequence they were free to enter into

---

[85] *Ante*, § 3–063.
[86] [1991] 1 Q.B. 1, 20.
[87] *ibid.* at 21. But he was not prepared to accept *Watkins v. Carrig* 21 A. 2d 591 (1941), where a contractor who had agreed to do excavating work unexpectedly struck hard rock and was held entitled to enforce a promise to pay nine times the originally agreed sum. The case was said not to represent English law in *North Ocean Shipping Co. Ltd v. Hyundai Construction Co. Ltd (The Atlantic Baron)* [1979] Q.B. 705, 714; *cf.* also *Finland SS. Co. Ltd v. Felixstowe Dock & Ry. Co.* [1980] 2 Lloyd's Rep. 390.
[88] [1991] 1 Q.B. 1, 16.
[89] *ibid.* at 18.
[90] *Hanson v. Royden* (1867) L.R. 3 C.P. 47; *cf. Turner v. Owen* (1862) 3 F. & F. 176. *Semble*, such extra pay is recoverable notwithstanding failure to comply with the formal requirements now prescribed by Merchant Shipping Act 1995, s.25.
[91] *North Ocean Shipping Co. Ltd v. Hyundai Construction Co. Ltd (The Atlantic Baron)* [1979] Q.B. 705.
[92] (1857) 7 E. & B. 872. See also *O'Neil v. Armstrong Mitchell & Co.* [1895] 2 Q.B. 418; *Palace Shipping Co. v. Caine* [1907] A.C. 386; *Liston v. SS. Carpathian (Owners)* [1915] 2 K.B. 42.

a new contract, and a promise by the captain of additional wages in return for their taking the ship to the next port was held to be enforceable. The same principle applies if the original contract is determined for other reasons: for example, by lapse of time or by notice or by mutual consent. Thus the parties to a contract could rescind it and then make a new agreement providing for the payment of higher wages; though in practice this would be hard to distinguish from a simple promise to pay higher wages under the original contract. If the original contract is void, or voidable at the option of the promisee, or unenforceable against him, performance of the work specified in it would, it seems, be consideration for a promise of extra pay; and if the original contract was in fact good but was believed to be defective, the new promise might still be binding on the analogy of the rule that forbearance to litigate an invalid claim may amount to consideration.[93] A further possibility is that the original contract might, expressly or impliedly, provide for revision of pay scales[94]; in which case a promise to pay higher wages made during the currency of the contract would be binding at common law even if it was not matched by a promise of higher productivity.[95]

(c) *Contractual Duty Owed to a Third Party*

Introductory.[96] Two problems arise under this heading. The first is whether, **3–067** if A is under a contractual duty to B, the *performance* of this duty can constitute consideration for a promise made to A by C. The second is whether A's *promise* to perform his contractual duty to B can constitute consideration for a counter-promise made to A by C.

Performance of the duty. It is now generally accepted that actual perform- **3–068** ance of a contractual duty owed to a third party can constitute consideration.[97] Two mid-nineteenth century cases which support this view are not wholly conclusive, since in each of them the promisee did, or may have done, more than he was bound under the earlier contract to do, and so have provided additional consideration.[98] But it is harder to find any such additional consideration in *Shadwell v. Shadwell*.[99] An uncle wrote to his nephew: "I am glad to hear of your

---

[93] *Ante,* § 3–051; *E. Hulton & Co. v. Chadwick Taylor Ltd* (1918) 34 T.L.R. 230, 231.

[94] *cf. Lombard Tricity Finance Ltd v. Paton* [1989] 1 All E.R. 918 (contract providing for increase in interest rates to be made by lender).

[95] *e.g. Pepper & Hope v. Daish* [1980] I.R.L.R. 13. Perhaps it was for this reason that the argument of want of consideration was not raised in *Universe Tankships Inc. v. International Transport Workers' Federation (The Universe Sentinel)* [1983] 1 A.C. 366.

[96] See A. G. Davis (1937) 6 Camb.L.J. 202.

[97] For the contrary view, see *McDevitt v. Stokes* 192 S.W. (1917). In *Pfizer Corp. v. Ministry of Health* [1965] A.C. 512 Lord Reid said that there was no contract where a chemist supplied drugs to a patient under the National Health Service in return for a prescription charge, because the chemist is "bound by his contract with the appropriate authority to supply the drug . . . " (at 536). But it seems from the context that Lord Reid was considering whether the relationship was consensual and was not thinking of the problem of consideration.

[98] *Scotson v. Peg* (1861) 6 H. & N. 295; *Chichester v. Cobb* (1866) 14 L.T. 433. The question in these cases was whether A provided consideration for C's promise by performing a contractual duty owed by A to B. There is no doubt that C's promise to perform a duty owed by B to A (or the performance of such a promise) can constitute consideration for a promise (express or implied) by A to C: see, *e.g. Brandt v. Liverpool, etc. S.N. Co.* [1924] 1 K.B. 575; *The Aramis* [1989] 1 Lloyd's Rep. 213, 225 (where C's claim failed for want of contractual intention: *ante* § 2–164).

[99] (1860) 9 C.B.(N.S.) 159.

intended marriage with Ellen Nicholl; and as I promised to assist you at starting, I am happy to tell you that I will pay you £150 yearly during my life. . . . " A majority of the Court of Common Pleas held that the nephew had provided consideration for the uncle's promise by marrying Ellen Nicholl. It was said that there was a detriment to the nephew in that he "may have made a most material change in his position, and induced the object of his affection to do the same, and may have incurred pecuniary liabilities resulting in embarrassments"[1]; and that there was a benefit to the uncle in that the marriage was "an object of interest to a near relative."[2] This reasoning simply ignores the nephew's previous con-tractual obligation[3] to marry Ellen Nicholl, under which he was legally bound to suffer the alleged detriment. It could perhaps be argued that he forbore from trying to persuade his fiancée to postpone the wedding or to put an end to the engagement[4]; but it is doubtful whether his forbearance to attempt to persuade her to do this can be regarded as consideration in the absence of any suggestion that he contemplated the possibility.[5] The argument that the uncle benefited fares little better, for the benefit described by the court was a purely sentimental one. It is, moreover, very doubtful whether, on the true construction of the uncle's letter, the nephew's marriage to Ellen Nicholl was intended to be the considera-tion for the uncle's promise, or only a condition.[6] Byles J., who dissented, treated it as a condition and also thought that the uncle's promise was not made with any contractual intent. His view was subsequently approved,[7] so that the correctness of the actual decision in *Shadwell v. Shadwell* is very much in doubt. But for what the decision is worth, it does support the view that the performance of a contractual duty owed to a third party can be good consideration for a promise. More recent authorities also support that view. In *The Eurymedon*,[8] A (a firm of stevedores) had unloaded goods from B's ship. Some of these belonged to C who, for present purposes,[9] may be taken to have promised A not to sue him for damaging the goods. It was held that A had provided consideration for this promise by unloading the goods even if he was already bound by a contract with B to unload them.

3–069   **Comparison of two- and three-party cases.** The view that performance of a contractual duty owed to a third party can constitute good consideration thus appears to be established by the authorities discussed in § 3–068 above; and the cases which support it must be contrasted with those discussed in § 3–061 above, in which the performance of a contractual duty owed to the promisor himself was held not to constitute consideration. The distinction between the two types of cases can perhaps be explained on the theoretical ground that, in the three-

---

[1] *ibid.* at 174.

[2] *ibid.*

[3] If the facts recurred now, there would be no such obligation: Law Reform (Miscellaneous Provisions) Act 1970, s.1.

[4] *cf. De Cicco v. Schweitzer* (1917) 221 N.Y. 413, 117 N.E. 807.

[5] *Ante,* § 3–023.

[6] *cf. ante,* § 3–010.

[7] *Jones v. Padavatton* [1969] 1 W.L.R. 328, 333.

[8] *New Zealand Shipping Co. Ltd v. A.M. Satterthwaite & Co. Ltd (The Eurymedon)* [1975] A.C. 154, 168; followed in *Port Jackson Stevedoring Pty. Ltd v. Salmond and Spraggon (Australia) Pty. Ltd (The New York Star)* [1981] 1 W.L.R. 138 and *Glebe Island Terminals Pty. Ltd v. Continental Seagram Pty. Ltd (The Antwerpen)* [1994] 1 Lloyd's Rep. 213; *The Mahkutai* [1996] A.C. 650, 664.

[9] See further § 14–044, *post.*

party cases *the promisor* was not entitled to the performance, and that he may thus gain a legal as well as a factual benefit from the transaction.[10] As a matter of policy, it can also be argued that improper pressure is less likely to be exerted on the promisor in three-party than in two-party cases[11] but this is not invariably true. Sailors in a case like *Stilk v. Myrick*[12] could bring improper pressure to bear on the captain whether their original contract was with him or with a third party.[13] It is now recognised that, in both types of case, the performance of a contractual duty can be good consideration if there is in fact a benefit to the promisor.[14] Adequate safeguards against extortion or other forms of pressure recognised as undesirable by law are now provided by the expanding concept of duress.[15]

Promise of performance. There was formerly some support for the view that **3–070** a promise to perform a contractual duty owed to a third party (as opposed to the actual performance of the duty) could not constitute consideration for a counter-promise. Thus in *Jones v. Waite*[16] it was said that a promise by A to C that A would pay a debt which he owed to B was no consideration for a promise made by C to A. This view seems to be based on the idea that A suffers no (legal) detriment by promising to pay a debt that he was already bound to pay; nor did it appear that C gained any benefit as a result of the promise. But C may gain such a benefit: for example, where B is a company in which C has an interest. This was the position in *Pao On v. Lau Yiu Long*[17] where the claimants, having entered into a contract with a company, refused to perform it unless the defendants, who were shareholders in the company, guaranteed them against loss which might be incurred as a result of the performance of one of the terms of that contract. The guarantee was given in consideration of the claimants' promise to perform their pre-existing contractual obligations to the company; and was held binding[18] on the ground that "A promise to perform, or the performance of, a pre-existing contractual obligation to a third party can be valid consideration."[19] This view seems, with respect, to be preferable to that expressed in *Waite v.*

---

[10] See *ante*, § 3–006.

[11] Goodhart (1956) 72 L.Q.R. 490.

[12] *Ante*, § 3–061.

[13] In *Stilk v. Myrick* the distinction between two- and three-party cases was ignored; no one asked whether the original contract was with the captain (the promisor) or the shipowner, if these were separate persons. The report in 6 Esp. 129 makes it clear that the *action* was against the captain. *cf.* also *Turner v. Owen* (1862) 3 F. & F. 176, where improper pressure may have been the ground for the jury's verdict; and *B. & S. Contractors & Designs v. Victor Green Publications Ltd* [1984] I.C.R. 419.

[14] *Ante*, §§ 3–063, 3–070.

[15] *Ante*, § 3–062, *post*, Chap. 7.

[16] (1839) 5 Bing.N.C. 341 affd. without reference to this point (1842) 9 Cl. & F. 101. A dictum in *Pfizer Corp. v. Ministry of Health* [1965] A.C. 512, 536 could be interpreted to support the same view but appears (from the context) to be based on lack of contractual intention: see *ante*, § 3–068, n. 97.

[17] [1980] A.C. 614.

[18] For rejection of the argument that the consideration was past, see *ante*, § 3–029.

[19] [1980] A.C. 614, 632. In *The Eurymedon, supra*, n. 8, it was said at 168 that a promise to perform a contractual duty owed by a third party was consideration because it was a *benefit to the promisee*. This is at first sight puzzling, since consideration must be a detriment to the promisee or a benefit to the promisor. The reference, however, was to a case in which A's promise to C was said to be consideration for C's *counter-promise* to A and it was the consideration for that counter-promise which was in issue. In relation to that counter-promise, C was the promisor and the benefit that C got from A's promise satisfied the orthodox test of consideration for C's counter-promise. *cf. ante* § 3–004.

Jones; for, where a shareholder makes a promise to induce a person to perform a contract with the company, the promise is certainly not gratuitous in a commercial sense. It will, of course, be open to the promisor to avoid liability if he can show that the promisee's refusal to perform the contract with the company amounted to duress[20] not merely with regard to the company, but also with regard to the promisor himself.

9. Discharge and Variation of Contractual Duties[21]

3–071   **Introduction.** The parties to a contract may agree to rescind it or to vary its terms. This subject is discussed in Chapter 23, but it is necessary in the present chapter to say something of the problems of consideration to which such agreements give rise. Indeed one aspect of the matter has already been discussed, for cases such as *Stilk v. Myrick*[22] and *Williams v. Roffey Bros. & Nicholls (Contractors) Ltd*[23] raise a problem of consideration arising from the variation of an existing contract. In those cases, the question was whether the performance by A of his obligations under the old contract could be consideration for a new promise from B. Our present problem is whether there is consideration for a promise by B to accept, in discharge of A's obligations, some performance other than that originally undertaken by A, or to grant A a total release from his obligations under the original contract. Even if there is no such consideration, B's subsequent promise may, nevertheless, have some limited legal effect.[24]

(a) Rescission

3–072   **Agreements to rescind where each party has outstanding rights.** The parties of a contract may agree to rescind it at a time when each has outstanding rights under the contract against the other. In such a case each party generally provides consideration for the other's promise to release him by giving up his own rights under the contract.[25] It is, of course, essential that *each* party should promise to give up his rights. If only one party does so, the other making no counter-promise, the former party's promise will be "entirely unilateral and unsupported by any consideration."[26]

3–073   **Agreements to rescind where only one party has outstanding rights.** An agreement to rescind a contract may also be unsupported by consideration (and so lack contractual force) where only one party has outstanding rights under the contract. This will often be the position where the contract has been wholly executed by that party (A) alone and he then promises to release the other party (B) from his obligations. In such a case there is prima facie no consideration for A's promise since A gets no benefit and B suffers no detriment from the arrangement. To make it binding, B must provide some separate consideration

---

[20] *cf. ante*, § 3–062.
[21] Wilken and Villiers, *Waiver, Variation and Estoppel.*
[22] (1809) 2 Camp. 317; 6 Esp. 129; *ante*, § 3–061.
[23] [1991] 1 Q.B. 1, *ante*, § 3–063.
[24] *Post*, §§ 3–076—3–094, 3–120—3–128.
[25] *Foster v. Dawber* (1851) 6 Ex.839, 850; *cf. Marseille Fret SA v. D. Oltman Schiffahrts GmbH & Co. (The Trado)* [1982] 1 Lloyd's Rep. 157.
[26] *Collin v. Duke of Westminster* [1985] Q.B. 581, 588.

(usually in the shape of some additional performance or promise). There must, in the traditional terminology, be not merely accord but also satisfaction. The "accord" here refers to the agreement and the "satisfaction" to the consideration for it.[27]

(b) *Variation*

(i) *Requirement of Consideration*

Agreements to vary contracts. Four situations call for discussion.   **3–074**

(1) Rescission followed by new contract. First, the parties may agree to rescind an existing contract and to enter into a new one, on different terms, in relation to the same subject-matter. The question whether there is consideration for the rescission depends on the tests stated in § 3–072 to 3–073. If these are satisfied, there will also generally be consideration for the promises of both parties made under the new contract. "The same consideration which existed for the old agreement is imported into the new agreement which is substituted for it."[28]

(2) Variation which can prejudice or benefit either party. Secondly, the parties may agree to vary the contract in a way that can prejudice or benefit either party. Here the possible detriment or benefit suffices to provide consideration for the promise of each party. This situation may be illustrated by an agreement to vary the currency in which a future payment under a contract of sale is to be made.[29] The seller's promise to accept payment in the new currency is supported by consideration since it *may* benefit him and prejudice the buyer as it is possible for the new currency to appreciate in relation to the old between the time of the variation and the time of payment. This possibility of benefit and detriment is sufficient. It is immaterial for the purpose of the requirement of consideration that the new currency in fact depreciates in relation to the old, or even that at the time of the variation it was highly probable that it would so depreciate. If a variation is, taken as a whole, capable of benefiting either party, the requirement of consideration will be satisfied even though a particular term of the variation is for the sole benefit of one.[30] However, it has been held that there is no consideration for a variation which, though capable of benefiting either party, is in fact made wholly for the benefit of one. For example, a variation as to the place at which a debt is to be paid is capable of benefiting either party; but where such a variation was introduced solely for the benefit of the debtor there was held to be no consideration for a promise by the creditor: *e.g.* for one to accept part payment in full settlement if the debtor made such payment at the different place.[31]

(3) Variation which can benefit only one party. Thirdly, the parties may agree   **3–075** to vary the contract in a way that is considered to be capable of conferring a legal benefit on one party only: *e.g.* where one party agrees to pay more for the

---

[27] *Post*, § 3–107. For an exception to the requirement, see Bills of Exchange Act 1882, s.62, *post*, Vol. II, § 34–140. For the time at which the accord takes effect, see *Johnson v. CEGB* [1999] 1 All E.R. 193, 207.

[28] *Stead v. Dawber* (1839) 10 A. & E. 57, 66.

[29] *W. J. Alan & Co. Ltd v. El Nasr Export & Import Co.* [1972] 2 Q.B. 189; *Woodhouse A.C. Israel Cocoa Ltd SA v. Nigerian Produce Marketing Co.* [1972] A.C. 741.

[30] *Ficom SA v. Sociedad Cadex Ltd* [1980] 2 Lloyd's Rep. 118, 132.

[31] *Vanbergen v. St. Edmunds Properties Ltd* [1933] 2 K.B. 233; *cf. Continental Grain Export Corp. v. S.T.M. Grain Ltd* [1979] 2 Lloyd's Rep. 460, 476.

performance of the other party's original obligation, or to accept less than the other party had originally undertaken without any corresponding variation (that could benefit him) of his own obligation. In some situations of this kind, it is settled that there is no consideration. Where, for example, after a debt has fallen due, the creditor promises to accept part payment of it in full settlement, the mere part payment does not constitute consideration for the variation,[32] though the creditor's promise may have a limited effect as a waiver, or in equity.[33] Consideration for the creditor's promise could be provided by some further variation which could benefit the creditor: *e.g.* by the debtor's promise to make the payment *before* the day when the debt becomes due. In other situations falling within the present group, it is arguable[34] that the variation may be supported by consideration if, though capable of conferring a legal benefit on only one party, it can also confer a factual benefit[35] on the other: *e.g.* where a buyer's promise to pay more than the originally agreed price secures eventual delivery of goods when strict insistence on the original contract would have led to nothing but litigation.

(4) "Variation" before conclusion of contract. Fourthly, there is the apparently paradoxical possibility that the parties may agree to vary a contract even before that contract has been concluded. This may be the position where A and B negotiate on the basis of formal documents and A represents that the proposed contract will be on terms less favourable to himself than those set out in the documents. If the documents are nevertheless executed without alteration, the representation may then be enforceable as a collateral contract. The consideration for the promise contained in A's representation is provided by B when he executes the documents, and so enters into the principal contract, at the request of A and in reliance on the representation. This was the position in *Brikom Investments Ltd v. Carr*,[36] where the landlords of blocks of flats negotiated with their tenants for the sale of long leases of the flats on terms requiring the tenants to contribute to the cost of (*inter alia*) roof maintenance. At the time of the negotiations, the roof was in need of repairs, and the landlords promised to execute these "at our own cost." It was held that one of the tenants had provided consideration for this promise by executing the agreement for the lease, and the lease itself; and that the promise was accordingly binding as a collateral contract. It followed that the landlords could not enforce the term in the lease under which the tenant would (but for the collateral contract) have been liable to contribute to the cost of the roof repair.[37] Greater difficulty would have arisen if the tenant had already entered into the agreement to take the lease *before* the landlord's promise had been made,[38] for in that case the execution of the documents would have

---

[32] *Post*, § 3–107.

[33] *Post*, §§ 3–120—3–128.

[34] On the analogy of the reasoning of *Williams v. Roffey Bros. & Nicholls (Contractors) Ltd* [1991] 1 Q.B. 1, *ante*, § 3–063.

[35] *Ante*, § 3–006.

[36] [1979] Q.B. 467.

[37] This was agreed by all members of the Court of Appeal. For other grounds for the decision, see *post*, §§ 3–119, 3–125.

[38] From the grounds of appeal as stated on pp. 472–473 of the report, it seems that reliance was placed on pre-contract promises or representations; *cf.* the statement at 490 that the landlord's promise was made "at the time when the leases were granted." According to Lord Denning M.R. at 480 "some of the tenants" had already signed agreements for leases when the representations were made; but that does not seem to have been the position with regard to any of the cases before the court.

been past consideration.[39] The tenants could, however, have succeeded, even in such a case, on an alternative ground. The landlords had been guilty of unreasonable delay in executing the repairs, and the tenants would, by forbearing to take proceedings in respect of that breach,[40] have provided consideration for the landlords' promise to bear the cost of the repairs.

(ii) *Common Law Mitigations*

Waiver[41] or forbearance at common law. A variation which is not con-   3–076
tractually binding (*e.g.* for want of consideration) may nevertheless have certain limited legal effects. These are sometimes said to arise because the promise by a party to relinquish some or all of his rights under a contract amounts to a "waiver" of those rights. Unfortunately, however, "the word 'waiver' . . . covers a variety of situations different in their legal nature. . . . "[42] It is, for example, sometimes used to refer to the variation of a contract which is supported by consideration and therefore binding as a contract.[43] To distinguish between such variations and those which are not supported by consideration, the latter will in the following discussion be referred to as "forbearances." A forbearance in this sense may in certain circumstances limit the right of the party granting it to enforce his rights under the contract. The exact effects of such a forbearance are discussed in Chapter 23; but something must be said here about the distinction between a forbearance and a variation.

Forbearance generally revocable. The effect of a forbearance of the kind   3–077
mentioned in the preceding paragraph differs from that of a binding variation which is supported by consideration in that it does not *irrevocably* alter the rights of the parties under the original contract. The party granting the forbearance *can generally retract it*, provided that he gives reasonable notice of his intention to do so to the other party.[44] Thus in *Charles Rickards Ltd v. Oppenhaim*[45] a contract for the sale of a car provided for delivery on March 20. The car was not delivered on that day but the buyer continued to press for delivery and finally told

---

[39] *Ante*, § 3–025.

[40] See [1979] Q.B. 467, 490; *cf. ante*, § 3–045. Delay in *executing* the repairs was a breach irrespective of the question of who was to *pay* for them.

[41] Ewart, *Waiver Distributed*; Cheshire and Fifoot (1947) 63 L.Q.R. 283; Stoljar (1958) 35 Can. Bar Rev. 485; Dugdale and Yates (1976) 39 M.L.R. 680.

[42] *Mardorf Peach & Co. Ltd v. Attica Sea Carriers Corp. of Liberia (The Laconia)* [1977] A.C. 850, 871; *cf. Kammins Ballrooms Co. Ltd v. Zenith Investments (Torquay) Ltd* [1971] A.C. 850, 882–883; *Telfair Shipping Corp. v. Athos Shipping Corp. (The Athos)* [1981] 2 Lloyd's Rep. 74, 87 (a passage approved on appeal: [1983] 1 Lloyd's Rep. 127, 134); *Scandinavian Trading Tanker Co. A.B. v. Flota Petrolera Ecuatoriana (The Scaptrade)* [1981] 2 Lloyd's Rep. 425, 430, affd. [1983] 2 A.C. 694; *Motor Oil Hellas (Corinth) Refineries SA v. Shipping Corp. of India (The Kanchenjunga)* [1990] 1 Lloyd's Rep. 391, 397.

[43] *e.g.* in *Hickman v. Haynes* (1875) L.R. 10 C.P. 598, 604; and (*semble*) by Roskill and Cumming-Bruce L.JJ. in *Brikom Investments Ltd v. Carr* [1979] Q.B. 467; *cf. Shamsher Jute Mills v. Sethia (London) Ltd* [1987] 1 Lloyd's Rep. 388, 392. In *Royal Bosakalis Westminster NV v. Mountain* [1997] 2 All E.R. 929 "waiver" is similarly used to refer to a variation which would have been contractually binding if it had not been vitiated by duress and illegality. Only Phillips L.J. took the view that there was no "meaningful" consideration. "Meaningful" here seems to mean no more than "adequate;" for it appears from the facts stated at 934 and 958–959 that in the subsequent agreement each party gave up rights existing under the original contract.

[44] *Banning v. Wright* [1972] 1 W.L.R. 972, 981; *Ficom SA v. Sociedad Cadex Ltda.* [1980] 2 Lloyd's Rep. 118, 131.

[45] [1950] 1 K.B. 616; *cf. State Trading Corp. of India v. Cie Française d'Importation et de Distribution* [1983] 2 Lloyd's Rep. 679, 681.

the seller on June 29 that he must have the car by July 25 at the latest. It was held that the buyer could not have refused peremptorily to accept the car merely because the original delivery date had gone by, as he had continued to press for delivery; but that he could refuse on the seller's failure to comply with a notice to deliver within a reasonable time. Here the notice did give the seller a reasonable time to deliver, so that the buyer was justified in refusing to take the car after July 25. *A fortiori*, the buyer could have refused to take delivery if the original delivery date had been extended only for a fixed time and if delivery had not been made by the end of that time.[46]

3–078　　**Forbearance may become irrevocable.** A forbearance may, however, become irrevocable as a result of subsequent events: for example if a buyer indicates that he is willing to accept goods of a different quality from those contracted for, and the seller, in reliance on that assurance, so conducts himself as to put it out of his power to supply goods of the contract quality within the contract period.[47]

3–079　　**Basis of distinction between variation and forbearance.** The question whether a subsequent agreement amounted to a contractual variation or to a forbearance is sometimes said to depend on the intention of the parties.[48] It seems that a statement should be a forbearance if the party making it intended to reserve a power to retract, and a variation if he intended it permanently to affect his rights. In practice, however, neither this nor any other explanation of the distinction provides any very sound basis for distinguishing the authorities on this subject. The explanation is also open to the objection that it leads to the paradoxical result that, the more a party tried to bind himself by a subsequent agreement, the less he was likely to succeed. An attempt to abandon a right altogether would be classified as a variation, and so be invalid without consideration; while an attempt merely to suspend a right would have at least a limited effect as a waiver. The courts were, however anxious to avoid the injustice which could result from holding that a variation was not binding for want of consideration. Accordingly, they were inclined to interpret the subsequent agreement as a forbearance, so as to give it at least some legal effects.

(iii) *Equitable Mitigations*

3–080　　**Forbearance in equity.** Equity developed a more satisfactory approach to the problem by concentrating, not on the intention of the party granting the forbearance, but on the conduct of that party and on its effect on the position of the other party. The leading case is *Hughes v. Metropolitan Ry.*[49] where a landlord gave his tenant notice requiring him to do repairs within six months. During the six months he began to negotiate with the tenant for the purchase of his lease. When the negotiations broke down, he immediately claimed to forfeit the lease on the ground that the tenant had not done the repairs. The claim was rejected. Lord Cairns said that if one party leads the other "to suppose that the strict rights

---

[46] *cf. Nichimen Corp. v. Gatoil Overseas Inc.* [1987] 2 Lloyd's Rep. 46, where similar fixed-term extensions were granted by a seller.

[47] *Toepfer v. Warinco A.G.* [1978] 2 Lloyd's Rep. 569, 576; *cf. Leather Cloth Co. v. Hieronimus* (1875) L.R. 10 Q.B. 140 (goods lost while on altered route).

[48] *Stead v. Dawber* (1839) 10 A. & E. 57, 64.

[49] (1877) 2 App.Cas. 439.

arising under the contract will not be enforced, or will be kept in suspense, or held in abeyance, the person who otherwise might have enforced those rights will not be allowed to enforce them where it would be inequitable having regard to the dealings which have thus taken place between the parties."[50] The landlord had by his conduct during the negotiations led the tenant to suppose that he would not enforce his right to forfeit. Hence he could not forfeit immediately the negotiations broke down; he was bound to give the tenant a reasonable time from that date to do the repairs. This equitable doctrine can now be applied to arrangements which might formerly have been regarded as variations ineffective at common law for want of consideration.[51] For reasons to be discussed in § 3–095 below, the doctrine is often (if rather misleadingly) referred to as "promissory" or "equitable" estoppel.

Requirements. For the equitable doctrine to operate there must be a legal   **3–081** relationship giving rise to rights and duties between the parties; a promise or a representation by one party that he will not enforce against the other his strict legal rights arising out of that relationship; an intention on the part of the former party that the latter will rely on the representation; and such reliance by the latter party.[52] Even if these requirements are satisfied, the operation of the doctrine may be excluded if it is, nevertheless, not "inequitable" for the first party to go back on his promise. The doctrine most commonly applies to promises not to enforce contractual rights, but it also extends to certain other relationships. These points will be discussed in the following paragraphs.

Relationships within the doctrine. The legal rights which the promisor or   **3–082** representor is prevented by the equitable doctrine from enforcing normally arise out of a contract between him and the other party. But the doctrine can also apply where the relationship giving rise to rights and correlative duties is non-contractual: *e.g.* to prevent the enforcement of a liability imposed by statute on a company director for signing a bill of exchange on which the company's name is not correctly given[53]; or to prevent a man from ejecting a woman, with whom he has been cohabiting, from the family home.[54] On the other hand, it has been said that the doctrine has "no application as between landlord and trespasser."[55] Hence the mere fact that a landowner has for some time failed or neglected to enforce his rights against a trespasser does not prevent him from subsequently doing so without notice.

---

[50] *ibid.* at 448.

[51] *e.g. Charles Rickards Ltd v. Oppenhaim* [1950] K.B. 616 (where both common law and equitable principles were applied). The principle in *Hughes v. Metropolitan Ry.* was said in *Brikom Investments Ltd v. Carr* [1979] Q.B. 467, 489 to be "an illustration of *contractual* variation of strict contractual rights." This description was apt on the facts of that case, where the promise not to enforce such rights was supported by consideration: *ante*, § 3–075. But the principle stated in *Hughes v. Metropolitan Ry.* applies even in the absence of such consideration: *cf. post*, § 3–124.

[52] *B.P. Exploration (Libya) v. Hunt (No. 2)* [1979] 1 W.L.R. 783, 812, affd. (without reference to the point) [1983] 2 A.C. 352; *Nippon Yusen Kaisha v. Pacifica Navegacion SA (The Ion)* [1980] 2 Lloyd's Rep. 245, 250.

[53] *Durham Fancy Goods Ltd v. Michael Jackson (Fancy Goods) Ltd* [1968] 2 Q.B. 839. A statement may also prevent the representor from denying the existence of a statutory liability, as in *Robertson v. Minister of Pensions* [1949] 1 K.B. 227, as to which see also § 3–095, n. 37 *post*.

[54] *Maharaj v. Chand* [1986] A.C. 898.

[55] *Morris v. Tarrant* [1971] 2 Q.B. 143, 160. *cf. Burrows v. Brent London Borough Council* [1996] 1 W.L.R. 1448, 1455, where no attempt was made to invoke the doctrine in favour of a "tolerated trespasser".

3–083   **Requirement of pre-existing legal relationship.** It has, indeed, been suggested that the doctrine can apply where, before the making of the promise or representation, there is no legal relationship giving rise to rights and duties between the parties,[56] or where there is only a putative contract between them: *e.g.* where the promisee is induced to believe that a contract into which he had undoubtedly entered was between him and the promisor, when in fact it was between the promisee and another person.[57] But it is submitted that these suggestions mistake the nature of the doctrine, which is to restrict the enforcement by the promisor of previously existing rights against the promisee. Such rights can arise only out of a legal relationship existing between these parties before the making of the promise or representation. To apply doctrine where there was no such relationship would contravene the rule (to be discussed in § 3–093 below) that the doctrine creates no new rights.

3–084   **A promise or representation.** There must, next, be a promise (or an assurance or representation in the nature of a promise[58]) which is intended to affect the legal relationship between the parties[59] and which indicates that the promisor will not insist on his strict legal rights,[60] arising out of that relationship, against the promisee. Here, as elsewhere, the law applies an objective test. It is enough if the promise induces the promisee reasonably to believe that the other party will not insist on his strict legal rights.[61] A mere threat to do something is not sufficient, nor, probably, is a representation or promise by a person that he *will* enforce a legal right: thus the doctrine does not apply where A tells B that he will exercise his right to cancel a contract between them unless by a specified date B has paid sums due under the contract to A.[62]

3–085   **The promise or representation must be "clear" or "unequivocal".** The promise or representation must be "clear" or "unequivocal," or "precise and unambiguous." This requirement seems to have originated in the law relating to estoppel by representation[63]; and it is now frequently stated in relation to

---

[56] *Evenden v. Guildford City F.C.* [1975] Q.B. 917, 924, 926 (actual decision overruled in *Secretary of State for Employment v. Globe Elastic Thread Co. Ltd* [1980] A.C. 506); *cf.*, in Australia, *Waltons Stores (Interstate) Ltd v. Maher* (1988) 164 C.L.R. 387.

[57] *Pacol Ltd v. Trade Lines Ltd (The Henrik Sif)* [1982] 1 Lloyd's Rep. 456, 466. Some doubt as to the correctness of this case is expressed by Webster J. (who decided it) in *Shearson Lehman Hutton Inc. v. MacLaine Watson & Co. Ltd* [1989] 2 Lloyd's Rep. 570, 596, 604 though the decision was approved on another point in *The Stolt Loyalty* [1993] 2 Lloyd's Rep. 281, 289–290, 291, affd. without reference to this point [1995] 1 Lloyd's Rep. 599; see also *Orion Finance Ltd v. J. D. Williams & Co Ltd* [1997] C.L.Y. 986.

[58] *James v. Heim Galleries* (1980) 256 E.G. 819, 821; *Collin v. Duke of Westminster* [1985] Q.B. 581, 595.

[59] *Spence v. Shell* (1980) 256 E.G. 55, 63.

[60] Or that he will not rely on an available defence: *post* § 3–095.

[61] *Bremer Handelsgesellschaft mbH v. Vanden Avenne-Izegem P.V.B.A.* [1978] 2 Lloyd's Rep. 109, 126; *Bremer Handelsgesellschaft mbH v. C. Mackprang Jr.* [1979] 1 Lloyd's Rep. 221 (both these cases concerned "waiver"); *cf. infra*, n. 64.

[62] *Drexel Burnham Lambert International NV v. El Nasr* [1986] 1 Lloyd's Rep. 357.

[63] *Low v. Bouverie* [1891] 3 Ch. 82, 106; *Woodhouse A.C. Israel Cocoa Ltd SA v. Nigerian Produce Marketing Co. Ltd* [1972] A.C. 741; *The Shackleford* [1978] 2 Lloyd's Rep. 155, 159; *Channel Island Ferries Ltd v. Sealink U.K. Ltd* [1987] 1 Lloyd's Rep. 559, 580, affd. without reference to this point [1988] 1 Lloyd's Rep. 323.

"waiver"[64] and "promissory estoppel."[65] It does not mean that the promise or representation must be express[66]; it may equally well be implied. For example, in *Hughes v. Metropolitan Ry.*[67] itself the landlord made no express promise that he would not enforce his right to forfeit the lease; but an implication of such a promise fairly arose from the course of the negotiations between the parties. There is some support for the view that the promise must have the same degree of certainty as would be needed to give it contractual effect if it were supported by consideration.[68] Thus if the statement could not take effect as a contract because it was too vague,[69] or if it was insufficiently precise to amount to an offer,[70] it will not bring the equitable doctrine into operation.[71]

The purpose of the requirement that the promise or representation must be **3–086** "clear" or "unequivocal" is to prevent a party from losing his legal rights under a contract merely because he has granted some indulgence by failing to insist throughout on strict performance of the contract[72]; or because he has offered some concession in the course of negotiations for the settlement of a dispute arising out of the contract.[73] Thus the requirement was not satisfied where one of

---

[64] *Finagrain SA Geneva v. P. Kruse Hamburg* [1976] 2 Lloyd's Rep. 508, 534; *Mardorf Peach & Co. Ltd v. Attica Sea Carriers Corp. of Liberia (The Laconia)* [1977] A.C. 850, 871; *Bremer Handelsgesellschaft mbH v. Vanden Avenne-Izegem P.V.B.A.* [1978] 2 Lloyd's Rep. 109, 126; *China National Foreign Trade Transportation Corp. v. Evoglia Shipping Co. of Panama SA (The Mihalios Xilas)* [1979] 1 W.L.R. 1018, 1024; *Avimex SA v. Dewulf & Cie.* [1979] 2 Lloyd's Rep. 57, 67; *Bremer Handelsgesellschaft mbH v. Westzucker GmbH* [1981] 1 Lloyd's Rep. 207, 212; *Bremer Handelsgesellschaft mbH v. Finagrain Cie. Commercial Agricole & Financière SA* [1981] 2 Lloyd's Rep, 259, 266; *Scandinavian Tanker Co. A.B. v. Flota Petrolera Ecuatoriana (The Scaptrade)* [1981] 2 Lloyd's Rep. 425, 431; (affd. [1983] 2 A.C. 694) *Italmare Shipping Co. v. Ocean Tanker Co. Inc. (The Rio Sun)* [1981] 2 Lloyd's Rep. 489 and [1982] 1 Lloyd's Rep. 404; *Telfair Shipping Corp. v. Athos Shipping Corp. (The Athos)* [1983] 1 Lloyd's Rep. 127, 134–135; *Bremer Handelsgesellschaft mbH v. Deutsche-Conti Handelsgesellschaft mbH* [1983] 1 Lloyd's Rep. 689; for the analogy between waiver and the equitable doctrine here under discussion, see *ante*, § 3–080; *post*, § 3–097.

[65] *B.P. Exploration Co. (Libya) Ltd v. Hunt (No. 2)* [1979] 1 W.L.R. 783, 812 (affd. without reference to this point [1983] 2 A.C. 352; *Spence v. Shell* (1980) 256 E.G. 55, 63; *James v. Heim Galleries* (1980) 256 E.G. 819, 821; *Société Italo-Belge pour le Commerce et l'Industrie v. Palm & Vegetable Oils (Malaysia) Sdn. Bhd. (The Post Chaser)* [1981] 2 Lloyd's Rep. 695, 700; *Goldsworthy v. Bricknell* (1987) Ch. 378, 410; *Hiscox v. Outhwaite (No. 3)* [1991] 2 Lloyd's Rep. 523, 524, 535.

[66] *Spence v. Shell* (1980) 256 E.G. 55, 63.

[67] (1877) 2 App.Cas. 439; *cf. The Post Chaser, supra*, n. 65, at 700.

[68] *China-Pacific SA v. The Food Corp. of India (The Winson)* [1980] 2 Lloyd's Rep. 213, 222; reversed on other grounds [1982] A.C. 939; *Food Corp. of India v. Antclizo Shipping Corp. (The Antclizo)* [1988] 2 Lloyd's Rep. 130, 142, affd. [1988] 1 W.L.R. 603; *Youell v. Bland Welch & Co. Ltd (The Superhulls Cover Case) (No. 2)* [1990] 2 Lloyd's Rep. 431, 452; *Rafsanjan Pistachio Producers Co-operative v. Bank Leumi (U.K.) plc* [1992] 1 Lloyd's Rep. 513, 542.

[69] *Ante*, §§ 2–128—2–133.

[70] *Ante*, § 2–002.

[71] *China-Pacific SA v. The Food Corp. of India (The Winson)* [1980] 2 Lloyd's Rep. 213, 223; revd. on other grounds [1982] A.C. 939; *Drexel Burnham Lambert International NV v. El Nasr* [1986] 1 Lloyd's Rep. 357.

[72] *Scandinavian Trading Tanker Co. A.B. v. Flora Petrolera Ecuatoriana (The Scaptrade)* [1981] 2 Lloyd's Rep. 425, 431, distinguishing *Tankexpress AS v. Cie. Financière Belge des Petroles SA* [1949] A.C. 76 on the ground that there the creditor's conduct had resulted in a change in the "accepted method of payments"; *The Scaptrade, supra* was affd. without reference to the present point [1983] 2 A.C. 694; *cf. Cape Asbestos Ltd v. Lloyd's Bank Ltd* [1921] W.N. 274, 276; *Bunge SA v. Compagnie Européenne de Céréales* [1982] 1 Lloyd's Rep. 306; *Bremer Handelsgesellschaft mbH v. Raiffeisen Hauptgenossenschaft E.G.* [1982] 2 Lloyd's Rep. 599; *Bremer Handelsgesellschaft mbH v. Bunge Corp.* [1983] 1 Lloyd's Rep. 476.

[73] *cf. London & Clydebank Properties v. H.M. Investment Co.* [1993] E.G.C.S. 63.

the parties to such a negotiation throughout insisted on strict compliance with the terms of the contract[74]; where he accepted less than that to which he was entitled but did so subject to an express reservation of his rights[75]; and where an admission that he was liable for certain expenses was made by his solicitor, expressly "without prejudice."[76] Failure, in the course of negotiations of this kind, to object to a defect or deficiency in performance is likewise insufficient if the injured party did not know and could not reasonably have known of it[77] or if full performance remained possible and continued to be demanded by that party.[78] On the other hand, failure to object to a known defect or deficiency within a reasonable time of its discovery[79] may be regarded as an unequivocal indication of the injured party's intention not to insist on his strict legal rights.[80] The position seems to be the same where the defect or deficiency, though not actually known to the injured party, was obvious or could have been discovered by him, if he had taken reasonable steps.[81] But where more than one matter is in dispute between the parties, "emphatic reliance upon some important disputed point does not by itself . . . imply any unequivocal representation that compliance with other parts of the bargain is thereby waived."[82]

3–087   **Inactivity.** Although a promise or representation may be made by conduct, mere inactivity will not normally suffice for the present purpose since "it is difficult to imagine how silence and inaction can be anything but equivocal."[83] Unless the law took this view, mere failure to assert a contractual right could lead to its loss; and the courts have on a number of occasions rejected this clearly undesirable conclusion. Thus it has been held that there is "no ground for saying

---

[74] *V. Berg & Son Ltd v. Vanden Avenne-Izegem P.V.B.A.* [1977] 1 Lloyd's Rep. 500; *cf. Edm. J. M. Mertens & Co. P.V.B.A. v. Veevoeder Import Export Vimex B.V.* [1979] 2 Lloyd's Rep. 372.

[75] *Finagrain SA Geneva v. P. Kruse Hamburg* [1976] 2 Lloyd's Rep. 508; *cf. Cook Industries Inc. v. Meunerie Liegeois SA* [1981] 1 Lloyd's Rep. 359, 368; *Peter Cremer v. Granaria B.V.* [1981] 2 Lloyd's Rep. 583; *Bremer Handelsgesellschaft mbH v. Deutsche Conti-Handelsgesellschaft mbH* [1983] 2 Lloyd's Rep. 476.

[76] *China-Pacific SA v. The Food Corp. of India (The Winson)* [1980] 2 Lloyd's Rep. 213 (revd. on other grounds [1982] A.C. 399.

[77] *Avimex SA v. Dewulf & Cie* [1979] 2 Lloyd's Rep. 57.

[78] *China National Foreign Trade Transportation Corp. v. Evoglia Shipping Co. SA of Panama (The Mihalios Xilas)* [1979] 1 W.L.R. 1018; *Bremer Handelsgesellschaft mbH v. Westzucker GmbH* [1981] 1 Lloyd's Rep. 207, 212–213; *Bremer Handelsgesellschaft mbH v. C. Mackprang Jr.* [1981] 1 Lloyd's Rep. 292, 299; *Peter Cremer v. Granaria B.V.* [1981] 2 Lloyd's Rep. 583; *The Post Chaser, supra,* n. 65 at 700.

[79] See *Mardorf Peach & Co. Ltd v. Attica Sea Carriers Corp. of Liberia (The Laconia)* [1977] A.C. 850 (where retention of an under-payment accepted without authority by the payee's bank was held not to amount to a waiver).

[80] *e.g. Bremer Handelsgesellschaft mbH v. Vanden Avenne-Izegem P.V.B.A.* [1978] 2 Lloyd's Rep. 109.

[81] See *Bremer Handelsgesellschaft mbH v. C. Mackprang Jr.* [1979] 1 Lloyd's Rep. 221, where there was a division of opinion on the point in the Court of Appeal.

[82] *Telfair Shipping Corp. v. Athos Shipping Corp. (The Athos)* [1983] 1 Lloyd's Rep. 127, 135.

[83] *Allied Marine Transport v. Vale do Rio Doce Navegaçao SA (The Leonidas D.)* [1985] 1 W.L.R. 925, 937; *cf. Cook Industries v. Tradax Export SA* [1983] 1 Lloyd's Rep. 327, 332 ([1985] 2 Lloyd's Rep. 454); *K. Lokumal & Sons (London) Ltd v. Lotte Shipping Co. Pte. Ltd (The August P. Leonhardt)* [1985] 2 Lloyd's Rep. 28, 33; *M.S.C. Mediterranean Shipping Co. SA v. B.R.E. Metro Ltd* [1985] 2 Lloyd's Rep. 239; *Cie Française d'Importation, etc., SA v. Deutsche Continental Handelsgesellschaft* [1985] 2 Lloyd's Rep. 592, 598; *Food Corp. of India v. Antclizo Shipping Corp. (The Antclizo)* [1986] 1 Lloyd's Rep. 181, 187, affd. 1 W.L.R. 603; *Youell v. Bland Welch & Co. Ltd (The Superhulls Cover Case) (No. 2)* [1990] 2 Lloyd's Rep. 431, 452. *cf. Tankerederei Ahrenkeil GmbH v. Frahuil SA (The Multibank Holstia)* [1988] 2 Lloyd's Rep. 486, 493 (no estoppel as no action in reliance).

that mere delay, however lengthy, destroys the contractual rights"[84]; and that the mere failure to prosecute a claim regarded by both parties as hopeless did not amount to a promise to abandon it.[85] The only circumstances in which "silence and inaction" can have this effect are the exceptional ones (discussed elsewhere in this book[86]) in which the law imposes a duty to disclose facts or to clarify a legal relationship and the party under the duty fails to perform it.

Reliance. The first requirement to be discussed under this heading is that the **3–088** promise or representation must in some way have influenced the conduct of the party to whom it was made. Although the promise need not form the sole inducement,[87] it must (it is submitted) be *some* inducement. Hence the present requirement would not be satisfied if it could be shown that the other party's conduct was not influenced by the promise[88] so that he was not in any way prejudiced by it.[89] But if this is a matter of "mere speculation,"[90] or if the promise or representation "was one of the factors . . . relied upon,"[91] it would form a sufficient inducement. In other words, where the conduct intended by the promisor has followed the making of the promise, it will be up to the promisor to establish that the conduct was not induced by the promise.[92]

Whether "detriment" required. There is sometimes said to be a further **3–089** requirement, namely that the promisee must have suffered "detriment" by acting in reliance on the promise.[93] This may mean that the promisee must have done something that he was not previously bound to do and as a result suffered loss: for example, by incurring some expenditure in reliance on the promise. This alleged requirement of "detriment" is based on the analogy of the doctrine of

---

[84] *Amherst v. James Walker Goldsmith & Silversmith Ltd* [1983] Ch. 305, 315; *cf.*, in another context, *Agip SpA v. Navigazione Alta Italia SpA (The Nai Genova)* [1984] 1 Lloyd's Rep. 353, 365.

[85] *Collin v. Duke of Westminster* [1985] Q.B. 581.

[86] *Ante*, § 2–065; *post*, §§ 6–135—6–153; see, for example, *Tradax Export SA v. Dorada Compania Naviera SA (The Lutetian)* [1982] 2 Lloyd's Rep. 140, 158; *The Stolt Loyalty* [1993] 2 Lloyd's Rep. 281, 289–291, affd. (without reference to the point here under discussion) [1995] 1 Lloyd's Rep. 559; and see *Petrotrade Inc. v. Stinnes Handel GmbH* [1995] 1 Lloyd's Rep. 142, 151, where the statement that there may be a representation by "conduct (including silence)" evidently refers to the exceptional situations described in the text above.

[87] *cf.* post, § 6–039.

[88] See *Fontana N.V. v. Mautner* (1979) 254 E.G. 199; *Raiffeisen Hauptgenossenschaft v. Louis Dreyfus & Co.* [1981] 1 Lloyd's Rep. 345, 352; *Cook Industries Ltd v. Meunerie Liegeois SA* [1981] 1 Lloyd's Rep. 359, 368; *Scandinavian Trading Tanker Co. A.B. v. Flota Petrolera Ecuatoriana (The Scaptrade)* [1983] 1 All E.R. 301, affd. without reference to this point [1983] 2 A.C. 694; *Bremer Handelsgesellschaft mbH v. Bunge Corp.* [1983] 1 Lloyd's Rep. 476; *Bremer Handelsgesellschaft mbH v. Deutsche Conti-Handelsgesellschaft mbH* [1983] 1 Lloyd's Rep. 689; *Lark v. Outhwaite* [1991] 2 Lloyd's Rep. 132, 142; *The Nerano* [1996] 1 Lloyd's Rep. 1.

[89] *Ets. Soules & Cie v. International Trade Development Co. Ltd* [1980] 1 Lloyd's Rep. 129; *Tankredlrei Ahrenkeil GmbH v. Frahuil SA (The Multibank Holsatia)* [1988] 2 Lloyd's Rep. 486, 493.

[90] *Brikom Investments Ltd v. Carr* [1979] Q.B. 467, 482.

[91] *ibid.* at 490 (*per* Cumming-Bruce L.J., whose decision was based on the different ground discussed in § 3–075, *ante*).

[92] *cf.* the similar rule in cases of "proprietary estoppel" stated in § 3–138, *post*.

[93] *e.g.* in *Fontana N.V. v. Mautner* (1979) 254 E.G. 199; *Meng Long Development Pte. Ltd v. Jip Hong Trading Co. Pte. Ltd* [1985] A.C. 511, 524; *cf.* Wilson (1951) 67 L.Q.R. 344.

estoppel,[94] to be discussed in § 3–095 below. But the equitable doctrine may be applied even though there is no "detriment" in this sense. It is enough if the promisee has altered his position in reliance on the promise so that it would be inequitable to allow the promisor to act inconsistently with it[95]: for example, if the promisee has forborne from taking steps that he would otherwise have taken to safeguard his legal position (as in *Hughes v. Metropolitan Ry.*[96] itself); or if he has performed, or made efforts to perform the altered obligation (for example, where a seller after being promised extra time for delivery has continued his efforts to perform after the originally agreed delivery date had gone by). On the other hand, the fact that the promisee has not suffered any prejudice by acting in reliance on the promise may be relevant for the purpose of the requirement to be discussed in § 3–090 below; for in such circumstances it may not be "inequitable" for the promisor to go back on his promise.[97]

3–090   **Inequitable.** It must be "inequitable" for the promisor to go back on the promise. This requirement cannot be defined with anything approaching precision, but the basic idea is that the promisee must have acted in reliance on the promise in one of the ways just described, so that he cannot be restored to the position in which he was before he took such action.[98] If the promisee can be restored to that position, it will not be inequitable for the promisor to go back on the promise. In one case[99] the promisor reasserted his strict legal rights only two days after the promise had been made. It was held that this was not "inequitable" since the promisee had not, in this short period, suffered any prejudice by acting in reliance on the promise. Sometimes, moreover, extraneous circumstances may justify the promisor in going back on the promise even without giving reasonable notice of his intention to do so.[1] In *Williams v. Stern*[2] the plaintiff gave the defendant a bill of sale of furniture as security for a loan; the bill entitled the defendant to seize the furniture if the plaintiff defaulted in making payments under it. When the fourteenth instalment became due, the plaintiff asked for extra time, and the defendant said that he "would not look to a week." Three days later he seized the furniture because he had heard that the plaintiff's landlord intended to distrain it for arrears of rent. It was held that the defendant's seizure was justified. The defendant's promise to give time was not binding contractually as the plaintiff had given no consideration for it; nor did it, in the circumstances,

---

[94] For the requirement of detriment in cases of estoppel, see *Carr v. L. & N.W. Ry.* (1875) L.R. 10 C.P. 310, 317.

[95] *James v. Heim Galleries* (1980) 256 E.G. 819, 825; *Société Italo-Belge pour le Commerce et l'Industrie v. Palm & Vegetable Oils (Malaysia) Sdn. Bhd. (The Post Chaser)* [1981] 2 Lloyd's Rep. 695, 701. *Youell v. Bland Welch & Co. Ltd (The Superhulls Cover Case) (No. 2)* [1990] 2 Lloyd's Rep. 431, 454.

[96] (1877) 2 App.Cas. 439.

[97] *Société Italo-Belge pour le Commerce et l'Industrie v. Palm & Vegetable Oils (Malaysia) Sdn. Bhd. (The Post Chaser)* [1981] 2 Lloyd's Rep. 695.

[98] *Maharaj v. Chand* [1986] A.C. 898.

[99] *Société Italo-Belge pour le Commerce et l'Industrie v. Vegetable Oils (Malaysia) Sdn. Bhd. (The Post Chaser)* [1981] 2 Lloyd's Rep. 695; *cf. Bremer Handelsgesellschaft mbH v. Bunge Corp.* [1983] 1 Lloyd's Rep. 476, 484; *Marseille Fret SA v. D. Ottman Schiffahrts GmbH & Co. K.G. (The Trado)* [1982] 1 Lloyd's Rep. 157, 160; *Bremer Handelsgesellschaft mbH v. Deutsche Conti-Handelsgesellschaft mbH* [1983] 1 Lloyd's Rep. 689; *Banner Industrial & Commercial Properties Ltd v. Clark Paterson Ltd* [1990] 2 E.G.L.R. 139; *Transatlantica de Commercio SA v. Incrobasa Industrial & Commercio Brazileira SA* [1995] 1 Lloyd's Rep. 214, 219.

[1] See *post*, § 3–091 and *cf. ante*, § 3–077 for this requirement.

[2] (1879) 5 Q.B.D. 409.

bring the equitable doctrine into operation. Brett L.J. said: "Has there been any misconduct on the part of the defendant? I think not: it appears that a distress by the plaintiff's landlord has been threatened; and under these circumstances I do not blame the defendant for changing his mind."[3] It is also arguable that a promisor does not act "inequitably" by going back on a promise improperly obtained, *e.g.* by extortion.[4]

Effect of the doctrine generally suspensive. The equitable doctrine, like the   3–091
common law doctrine of waiver, generally does not extinguish, but only suspends rights. The landlord in *Hughes v. Metropolitan Ry.*[5] was not permanently debarred from enforcing the covenant to repair. He could have enforced it by giving reasonable notice to the tenant requiring him to repair.[6] The reason for the general rule is that equity confers a discretion on the court to give such remedy as is just and equitable in all the circumstances[7]; and in cases such as *Hughes v. Metropolitan Ry.* it would be neither equitable nor in accordance with the intention of the parties to treat the promisor's rights as having been wholly extinguished.[8]

Extinctive effect in exceptional cases. Subsequent events may, however,   3–092
give the doctrine an extinctive effect, by way of exception to the general rule stated in § 3–091 above.[9] They can most obviously have this effect where they make it impossible for the promisee to perform his original obligation. For example, in *Birmingham & District Land Co. v. L. & N.W. Ry.*[10] a building lease bound the tenant to build by 1885. The lessor agreed to suspend this obligation; but in 1886, while the suspension was still in force, the land was compulsorily acquired by a railway company, so that performance of the tenant's obligation became impossible. The tenant recovered statutory compensation from the railway company on the footing that the building lease was still binding; but clearly his obligation to build was utterly extinguished. Even where performance of the original obligation has not actually become impossible, the doctrine may sometimes have an extinctive effect. For example, where a vendor of land on August 15 indicated that he would not insist on the contractual completion date of August 30, it was held that no question of reinstating that date could arise

---

[3] *ibid.* at 413; *cf.* also *Southwark L.B.C. v. Logan* (1996) 8 Admin.L.R. 315.

[4] *cf. ante*, § 3–062 and *D. & C. Builders Ltd v. Rees* [1966] 2 Q.B. 617.

[5] (1877) 2 App.Cas. 439.

[6] *cf. Tool Metal Manufacturing Co. Ltd v. Tungsten Electric Co. Ltd* [1955] 1 W.L.R. 761; (*post*, § 3–123) *Banning v. Wright* [1972] 1 W.L.R. 972, 981; *Brikom Investments Ltd v. Seaford* [1981] 1 W.L.R. 863, 869; *Société Italo-Belge v. Palm & Vegetable Oils (The Post Chaser)* [1981] 2 Lloyd's Rep. 695, 701; *Meng Long Development Pte. Ltd v. Jip Hong Trading Co. Ltd* [1985] A.C. 511, 524; *Motor Oil Hellas (Corinth) Refineries SA v. Shipping Corp. of India (The Kanchenjunga)* [1987] 2 Lloyd's Rep. 509, 518 affd. [1989] 1 Lloyd's Rep. 354.

[7] [1994] A.C. 224, 234.

[8] This is also true of cases such as *Tool Metal Manufacturing Co. Ltd v. Tungsten Electric Co. Ltd* [1955] 1 W.L.R. 761 and *Ajayi v. R. T. Briscoe (Nig.) Ltd* [1964] 1 W.L.R. 1236, discussed in §§ 3–122 and 3–123 *post*.

[9] *cf. post*, § 3–124.

[10] (1888) 40 Ch.D. 268; *cf. W. J. Alan & Co. Ltd v. El Nasr Export & Import Co.* [1972] 2 Q.B. 189, where the actual decision was that there was a contractually binding variation: see *ante*, § 3–074.

"because the time was far too short."[11] And where a shipowner represented to a charterer that he would not rely, by way of defence to claims under the charter-party, on a one-year time bar (which had expired) it was held that he could not, after nearly another year had gone by, go back on the representation, since it would by then have been too late to restore the charterer to his original position.[12] In all these cases the doctrine has an extinctive effect because subsequent events or the passage of time, though not making performance of the original obligation impossible, have made it highly inequitable to require such performance, even after reasonable notice.[13]

3–093   **Defensive nature of the doctrine.** The equitable doctrine makes it possible for a party to rely on a promise for which there was no consideration, so as to excuse his non-performance of an existing obligation. It does not create an entirely new obligation or extend the scope of an existing one. For a promise to have this effect, it must still be supported by consideration, which "remains a cardinal necessity of the formation of a contract, though not of its discharge."[14] The point was decided in *Combe v. Combe*[15] where a husband, during divorce proceedings, promised to pay £100 per annum to his wife, who in reliance on the husband's promise, forbore from applying to the court for maintenance. It was held that the equitable doctrine did not enable her to enforce the husband's promise since that doctrine did not "create new causes of action where none existed before."[16] The scope of the equitable doctrine is limited in this way because it would (in the words of Roskill L.J.) "be wrong to extend the doctrine of promissory estoppel, whatever its precise limits at the present day, to the extent of abolishing in this back-handed way the doctrine of consideration."[17] The view that the equitable doctrine does not create new causes of action seems to have been doubted[18] or ignored[19] by dicta in later cases; but the promises in these cases created new rights on the perfectly orthodox ground that they were, in fact, supported by consideration.[20] *Combe v. Combe* therefore still stands as the leading English[21] authority for the proposition that the equitable doctrine

---

[11] *Ogilvie v. Hope-Davies* [1976] 1 All E.R. 683, 696; *cf. Voest Alpine International GmbH v. Chevron International Oil Co. Ltd* [1987] 2 Lloyd's Rep. 547, 560.

[12] *Nippon Yusen Kaisha v. Pacifica Navegacion SA (The Ion)* [1980] 2 Lloyd's Rep. 245.

[13] See *Maharaj v. Chand* [1986] A.C. 898; *cf. W. J. Alan & Co. Ltd v. El Nasr Export & Import Co.* [1972] 2 Q.B. 189 (where the actual decision was that there was a variation supported by consideration).

[14] *Combe v. Combe* [1951] 2 K.B. 215, 220.

[15] [1951] 2 K.B. 215.

[16] *ibid.* at 219.

[17] *Brikom Investments Ltd v. Carr* [1979] Q.B. 467, 486; *cf. Combe v. Combe* [1951] 2 K.B. 215, 219–220; *Tool Metal Manufacturing Co. Ltd v. Tungsten Electric Co. Ltd* [1955] 1 W.L.R. 761, 764; *Beesly v. Hallwood Estates Ltd* [1960] 1 W.L.R. 549, 561; *Drexel Burnham Lambert International N.V. v. El Nasr* [1986] 1 Lloyd's Rep. 357, 365. Contrast *Vaughan v. Vaughan* [1953] Q.B. 762, 768; Denning (1952) 15 M.L.R. 1.

[18] *Re Wyvern Developments Ltd* [1974] 1 W.L.R. 1097, 1104–1105; Atiyah (1974) 38 M.L.R. 65; and see Allan (1963) 79 L.Q.R. 238; the point was left open in *Pacol Ltd v. Trade Lines Ltd (The Henrik Sif)* [1982] 1 Lloyd's Rep. 456, 466–468 (as to which see *ante* § 3–083, n. 57).

[19] *Evenden v. Guildford City F.C.* [1975] Q.B. 917, 924, 926; Napier [1976] C.L.J. 38; and see next note.

[20] See *Secretary of State for Employment v. Globe Elastic Thread Co. Ltd* [1980] A.C. 506, overruling *Evenden's* case, *supra.* Lord Wilberforce remarked at 518 that "To convert this [contract] into an estoppel is to turn the doctrine of promissory estoppel . . . upside down."

[21] For the position in other common law jurisdictions, see § 3–099, *post.*

creates no new rights[22]; and this proposition has been reaffirmed in a number of later cases.[23] It follows that the equitable doctrine would not enable employees in a case like *Stilk v. Myrick*[24] to recover the extra pay which they had been promised. It could, indeed, be argued[25] that in such a case the cause of action was the original contract of employment and that the subsequent agreement fell within the principle stated by Denning L.J. in *Combe v. Combe* that consideration was not necessary for the "modification or discharge"[26] of a contract where the conditions required for the operation of the equitable doctrine were otherwise satisfied. But it is submitted that in this phrase Denning L.J. had in mind a modification which *reduced* a party's obligations[27]; for to apply it to a case in which it had the effect of *increasing* them necessarily amounts to giving the other party new rights of action as a result of a promise for which he has not provided any consideration; and *Combe v. Combe* decides that this is not the effect of the equitable doctrine here under discussion. A cause of action on a promise unsupported by consideration may, however, arise under other equitable doctrines: *e.g.* under the doctrine of "proprietary estoppel," discussed later in this chapter.[28]

"Shield and not a sword". The essentially defensive nature of the equitable **3–094** doctrine here under discussion is sometimes expressed by saying that it operates as a shield and not as a sword.[29] This is true in most cases: usually it protects a promisee from being sued on the original obligation. But the essential point is that the doctrine excuses (at least temporarily) the performance of the original obligation; and such an excuse may benefit a claimant no less than a defendant. For example, if the creditor's conduct in *Williams v. Stern*[30] (discussed in § 3–090 above) had been "inequitable" the debtor could no doubt have restrained a *threatened* seizure of his property by injunction. Similarly, a seller may tender delivery after the originally agreed date in reliance on the buyer's promise to accept such delivery. If the buyer then refuses to accept the delivery, the seller can claim damages.[31]

Doctrine may deprive promisor of certain defences. The equitable doctrine **3–095** can also assist the promisee as claimant in that it may prevent the promisor from relying on a defence that would, but for the promise, have been available to him: *e.g.* the defence that a claim which the promisee has made against him is time-

---

[22] *cf.* the position in cases of estoppel by representation, *post*, § 3–095.

[23] *Argy Trading Development Co. Ltd v. Lapid Developments Ltd* [1977] 1 W.L.R. 444, 457; *Aquaflite Ltd v. Jaymar International Freight Consultants Ltd* [1980] 1 Lloyd's Rep. 36; *Syros Shipping Co. SA v. Elaghill Trading Co. (The Proodos C)* [1980] 2 Lloyd's Rep. 390, 391; *James v. Heim Galleries* (1980) 256 E.G. 819, 821; *Brikom Investments Ltd v. Seaford* [1981] 1 W.L.R. 863; *cf. Taylors Fashions Ltd v. Liverpool Victoria Trustee Co. Ltd* [1982] Q.B. 133, 152.

[24] (1809) 2 Camp. 317; 6 Esp. 129; *ante*, § 3–061.

[25] See *Hiscox v. Outhwaite (No. 3)* [1991] 2 Lloyd's Rep. 524, 535.

[26] [1951] 2 K.B. 215, 219.

[27] As in *Central London Property Trust Ltd v. High Trees House Ltd* [1947] K.B. 130, *post* § 3–120, this case being under discussion in *Combe v. Combe, supra.*

[28] *Post*, §§ 3–129—3–152, especially § 3–142.

[29] *Combe v. Combe* [1951] 2 K.B. 215, 224; *Lark v. Outhwaite* [1991] 2 Lloyd's Rep. 132, 142; *Hiscox v. Outhwaite (No. 3)* [1991] 2 Lloyd's Rep. 524, 535.

[30] (1879) 5 Q.B.D. 409.

[31] *cf. Hartley v. Hymans* [1920] 3 K.B. 475, applying the corresponding common law doctrine: *ante*, § 3–076. And see Jackson (1965) 81 L.Q.R. 223.

barred,[32] or that the claim has been satisfied.[33] In such cases, the doctrine will, once again, enable the promisee to win an action which, but for the doctrine, he would have lost. But it must be stressed that, in cases of this kind, the promisee's cause of action will have arisen independently of the promise which brought the equitable doctrine into operation: the effect of the doctrine is merely to prevent the promisor from relying on some circumstance which would, if the promise had not been made, *have destroyed the promisee's original cause of action*. This situation must be distinguished from that in which the promisor's "defence" is that (apart from the promise) the promisee's alleged *cause of action never existed at all*. It is submitted that the equitable doctrine should not prevent the promisor from relying on a "defence" of this kind. To allow the doctrine to operate in this way would amount to giving the promisee a new cause of action based on the promise though it was unsupported by consideration; and such a result would be inconsistent with the essentially defensive nature of the equitable doctrine.[34]

3–096 **Analogy with estoppel.** The equitable doctrine is sometimes compared with the doctrine of estoppel by representation and the two have, indeed, certain features in common. Each is based on a representation followed by reliance, and the nature of each is defensive in the sense that neither is capable of giving rise to new rights. On the other hand, there are many significant differences between the two, even though the word "estoppel" is now often used to refer to the equitable doctrine.[35] These differences are reflected in the statement of Millett L.J. that "the attempt . . . to demonstrate that all estoppels . . . are now subsumed in the single and all-embracing estoppel by representation and that they are all governed by the same principle" has "never won general acceptance."[36] The most important difference between the two doctrines here under discussion relates to the types of representations required to bring them into operation. For the purpose of true estoppel by representation, there must be representation of *existing fact*.[37] The equitable doctrine, by contrast, can apply where there is no

---

[32] See *Nippon Yusen Kaisha v. Pacifica Navegacion SA (The Ion)* [1980] 2 Lloyd's Rep. 245, *ante*, § 3–092; the Australian case of *Commonwealth of Australia v. Verwayen* (1990) 170 C.L.R. 394 (discussed by Spence (1991) 107 L.Q.R. 221) could, in England, be decided on the same ground though it was actually based on the wider Australian principle referred to in § 3–099, *post*.

[33] *cf.* in cases of estoppel by representation, *Burrowes v. Lock* (1805) Ves. 470, as explained in *Low v. Bouverie* [1891] 3 Ch. 82.

[34] *cf.* the criticism (*ante*, § 3–083) of *Pacol Ltd v. Trade Lines Ltd (The Henrik Sif)* [1982] 1 Lloyd's Rep. 456. For the position in relation to estoppel by convention see *post*, § 00–000.

[35] *Infra*, n. 38.

[36] *First National Bank plc v. Thomson* [1996] Ch. 231, 236.

[37] *Jordan v. Money* (1854) 5 H.L.C. 195, criticised by Jackson (1965) 81 L.Q.R. 84; *cf.* Halliwell, 5 L.S. 15. Atiyah (*op. cit., ante*, § 3–007, n. 28, pp. 53–57) suggests that the case does not support the proposition for which it is usually cited, but that there *was* a contract, which was unenforceable for want of written evidence. But the claimant alleged no such contract: as Lord Cranworth said at p. 215, "it is put entirely on the ground of misrepresentation." The orthodox view is also supported by Lord Selborne (who was counsel in *Jordan v. Money*) in his speech in *Maddison v. Alderson* (1883) 8 App.Cas. 467, 473. For recent statements of the rule that estoppel can only be based on a representation of *existing fact*, see *Argy Trading Development Co. Ltd v. Lapid Developments Ltd* [1977] 1 Lloyd's Rep. 67, 76; *China-Pacific SA v. The Food Corp. of India (The Winson)* [1980] 2 Lloyd's Rep. 213, 222 (revd. on other grounds [1982] A.C. 939); *Spence v. Shell* (1980) 256 E.G. 55, 63; *T.C.B. Ltd v. Gray* [1986] Ch. 621, 634 (affd. [1988] 1 All E.R. 108); *Roebuck v. Mungovin* [1994] 2 A.C. 224, 235; *cf. Janred Properties v. Ente Nazionale per il Turismo* [1987] F.L.R. 179 (implied representation that approval *had* been given). So-called "estoppel by convention" is similarly based on a common assumption of *fact* or "law": see *post*, § 3–103, n. 85. In *Robertson v. Minister of Pensions* [1949] 1 K.B. 227, the equitable doctrine was mentioned though the representation was a statement of fact rather than a promise.

such representation, but only one of intention as to the promisor's future conduct, or a promise. For this reason, and because the doctrine was developed in equity, the doctrine is sometimes called "promissory" or "equitable" estoppel.[38] The latter description is, however, misleading as the requirement of a representation of existing fact for the purposes of estoppel by representation was recognised in equity[39] no less than at common law.[40] There are, moreover, other significant differences between the two doctrines. The equitable doctrine may operate even though there is no such "detriment" as is required to bring the doctrine of estoppel by representation into play.[41] And the equitable doctrine is suspensive in nature,[42] while estoppel by representation, where it operates, has a permanent effect.

Analogy with waiver. It is submitted that the characteristics of the equitable   3–097
doctrine mentioned in § 3–096 above indicate that the equitable doctrine is not truly analogous to estoppel by representation. As Denning J. (a leading proponent of the modern equitable doctrine) has pointed out, the authorities which support that doctrine, "although they are said to be cases of estoppel, are not really such".[43] The doctrine has closer affinities with the common law rules of waiver, in the sense of forbearance[44]: both are based on promises, or representations of intention; and both are suspensive (rather than extinctive) in nature. The main difference between them is that the equitable doctrine avoids the difficulties encountered at common law in distinguishing between a variation and a forbearance.[45]

There is now much judicial support for these submissions. Thus Lord Pearson in *Woodhouse A.C. Israel Cocoa Ltd v. Nigerian Produce Marketing Co. Ltd* said that "promissory estoppel" was "far removed from the familiar estoppel by

---

[38] *e.g. Woodhouse A.C. Israel Cocoa Ltd v. Nigerian Produce Marketing Co. Ltd* [1972] A.C. 741, 758; *Ogilvy v. Hope-Davies* [1976] 1 All E.R. 683, 689; *B.P. Exploration Co. (Libya) Ltd v. Hunt (No. 2)* [1979] 1 W.L.R. 783, 812 (affd. [1983] 2 A.C. 352, without reference to this point); *China-Pacific SA v. The Food Corp. Of India (The Winson)* [1980] 2 Lloyd's Rep. 213, 222 (revd. on other grounds [1982] A.C. 939); *Ets. Soules & Cie v. International Trade Development Co. Ltd* [1980] 1 Lloyd's Rep. 129, 133; *Nippon Yusen Kaisha v. Pacifica Navegacion SA (The Ion)* [1980] 1 Lloyd's Rep. 245, 259; *Peter Cremer v. Granaria B.V.* [1981] 2 Lloyd's Rep. 583, 587; *Société Italo-Belge pour le Commerce et l'Industrie v. Palm & Vegetable Oils (Malaysia) Sdn. Bhd. (The Post Chaser)* [1981] 2 Lloyd's Rep. 695, 700; *Roebuck v. Mungovin* [1994] 2 A.C. 224, 235; contrast *Brikom Investments Ltd v. Carr* [1979] Q.B. 467, 485, 489, where Roskill L.J. prefers to refer simply to the principle of *Hughes v. Metropolitan Ry.* (1877) 2 App.Cas. 439. *Amherst v. James Walker Goldsmiths & Silversmiths Ltd* [1983] Ch. 305, 316 somewhat puzzlingly seems to distinguish between "promissory" and "equitable" estoppel. Terminological difficulty is compounded by occasional use of the phrase "equitable estoppel" to refer to true estoppel by representation: see *infra* n. 40.
[39] *Jordan v. Money, ante*, was itself an appeal from the Court of Appeal in Chancery. See also *Pigott v. Stratton* (1859) 1 D.F. & J. 33, 51; *Citizens' Bank of Louisiana v. First National Bank of New Orleans* (1873) L.R. 6 HL 352, 360; *Maddison v. Alderson* (1883) 8 App.Cas. 467, 473; *Chadwick v. Manning* [1896] A.C. 231, 238.
[40] Estoppel by representation of fact was recognised at common law at least as long ago as *Freeman v. Cooke* (1848) 2 Ex. 654; but sometimes this form of estoppel is (confusingly) referred to as "equitable estoppel:" *e.g.* in *Lombard North Central plc v. Stobart* [1990] Tr.L.R. 105, 107. In that case, an estoppel arose from a finance company's statement that no more than £1003 was due under a conditional sale, when the actual sum due was nearly five times as much. This statement was clearly a representation of *fact* rather than a *promise*.
[41] *Ante*, § 3–089.
[42] *Ante*, § 3–091.
[43] *Central London Property Trust v. High Trees House Ltd* [1947] K.B. 130, 134.
[44] *Ante*, § 3–076. For other senses of "waiver" see *post*, §§ 23–039—23–045.
[45] *Ante* § 3–079.

representation of fact and seems, at any rate in a case of this kind, to be more like a waiver of contractual rights."[46] In a number of later cases, "waiver" and "promissory estoppel" (or the rule in *Hughes v. Metropolitan Ry.*)[47] are treated as substantially similar doctrines,[48] the requirements and effects of the one being stated in terms equally applicable to the other.[49] Indeed, the expressions "waiver" and "promissory estoppel" have been judicially described as "two ways of saying exactly the same thing,"[50] and the courts often use them interchangeably when discussing situations in which it is alleged that one party to a legal relationship has indicated that he will not enforce his strict legal rights against the other.[51] This usage further supports the view that the equitable doctrine is more closely akin to waiver (in the sense of forbearance) than to true estoppel by representation of fact.

3–098   **Distinguished from promises supported by consideration.** Under the equitable doctrine, certain limited effects are given to a promise without consideration. But it is nevertheless in the interests of the promisee to show, if he can, that he did provide consideration so that the promise amounted to a contractually binding variation. Such proof will free him from the many rules that restrict the scope of the equitable doctrine: he need not then show that he has in any way

---

[46] [1972] A.C. 741, 762.

[47] (1877) 2 App.Cas. 439; *ante*, § 3–080.

[48] *e.g. Ogilvy v. Hope-Davies* [1976] 1 All E.R. 683, 688–689; *Finagrain SA Geneva v. P. Kruse Hamburg* [1976] 2 Lloyd's Rep. 508, 534; *Bremer Handelsgesellschaft mbH v. C. Mackprang Jr.* [1979] 1 Lloyd's Rep. 221, 226; *Prosper Homes v. Hambro's Bank Executor & Trustee Co.* (1979) 39 R. & C.R. 395, 401; *Brikom Investments Ltd v. Carr* [1979] Q.B. 467, 488, 489, 490; *Scandinavian Trading Tanker Co. A.B. v. Flota Petrolera Ecuatoriana (The Scaptrade)* [1981] 2 Lloyd's Rep. 425, 430 (affd. without reference to this point [1983] 2 A.C. 694) *Procter & Gamble Philippine Manufacturing Corp. v. Peter Cremer GmbH & Co. (The Manila)* [1988] 3 All E.R. 843, 853; *cf. Bremer Handelsgesellschaft mbH v. Finagrain Cie. Commercial Agricole & Financière* [1981] 2 Lloyd's Rep. 259, where Lord Denning M.R. refers at 263 to "the principle . . . in *Hughes v. Metropolitan Railway*" while Fox L.J. refers at 266 to "waiver"; *Bremer Handelsgesellschaft mbH v. C. Mackprang Jr.* [1981] 1 Lloyd's Rep. 292, 298; *Bremer Handelsgesellschaft mbH v. Bunge Corp.* [1983] 1 Lloyd's Rep. 476, 484; *BICC Ltd v. Burndy Corp.* [1985] Ch. 232, 253; *Pearl Carriers Inc. v. Japan Lines Ltd (The Chemical Venture)* [1993] 1 Lloyd's Rep. 509, 521. In *W. J. Alan & Co. Ltd v. El Nasr Export & Import Co.* [1972] 2 Q.B. 189, 212 waiver is described as an instance of the principle of *Hughes v. Metropolitan Ry.* (*supra*), which, however, is said to be of "wider" scope; *cf. Nippon Yusen Kaisha v. Pacifica Navegacion SA (The Ion)* [1980] 2 Lloyd's Rep. 245 where an agreement not to plead a contractual time bar was held not to take effect as a "waiver" (at 249) but to give rise to an "equitable or promissory estoppel" (at 250). In *Brikom Investments Ltd v. Carr* [1979] Q.B. 467, 485, 489 the principle of *Hughes v. Metropolitan Ry.* (*supra*) is, unusually, regarded as distinct from "promissory estoppel" but rather as an illustration of "waiver," thus suggesting a difference between these two concepts—perhaps because in the *Brikom* case the waiver amounted to a contractual variation supported by consideration: *cf. post*, § 3–125. In *Youell v. Bland Welch & Co. Ltd (The Superhulls Cover Case) (No. 2)* [1990] 2 Lloyd's Rep. 431, 449 "waiver" is distinguished from "equitable estoppel" on the ground that the former doctrine requires the party who is alleged to have lost his rights to know the material facts, while the latter is not subject to any such requirements. But when "waiver" is said to be subject to this requirement, the reference is to "waiver" in the sense of election between remedies (*post*, § 25–006) and not to the "waiver" in the sense of relinquishing rights; and it is this latter type of waiver which is here under discussion. The reference in *Union Eagle Ltd v. Golden Achievement Ltd* [1997] A.C. 514, 518 to "waiver or estoppel" is likewise to election between remedies rather than to the relinquishing of rights which is under discussion in the present Chapter.

[49] *e.g. Bremer Handelsgesellschaft mbH v. Westzucker GmbH* [1981] 1 Lloyd's Rep. 207, 212–213.

[50] *Prosper Homes v. Hambro's Bank Executor Trustee Co.* (1979) P. & C.R. 395, 401; *cf. The Nerano* [1996] 1 Lloyd's Rep. 1, 6 ("really one and the same thing").

[51] See the authorities cited in nn. 48 and 49, *supra*.

"relied" on the promise, or that it would be "inequitable" for the other party to go back on it; the variation will permanently affect the rights of the promisor and not merely suspend them (unless it is expressed so as to have only a temporary effect); and a contractual variation can not only reduce or extinguish existing rights but also create new ones. Where parties agree to modify an existing contract, the equitable doctrine and its common law counterpart may have reduced, but they have by no means eliminated, the practical importance of the doctrine of consideration.

Other jurisdictions. The English view that the doctrine of promissory estop-   **3–099**
pel gives rise to no cause of action has not been followed in other jurisdictions. In the United States, a similar doctrine has long been regarded as being capable of creating new rights, though both the existence and the content of the resulting rights are matters for the discretion of the courts.[52] A line of Australian cases likewise supports the view that promises or representations which, for want of consideration or of contractual intention, lack contractual force can nevertheless be enforced as if they were binding contracts. The leading Australian case is *Waltons Stores (Interstate) Ltd v. Maher*,[53] where a prospective lessor of business premises did demolition and building work on the premises while the agreement for the lease lacked contractual force because it was still subject to contract[54]; he had done so to meet the prospective lessee's requirements and on the assumption, of which the prospective lessee must have known, that a binding contract would come into existence. The prospective lessee withdrew from the agreement (relying on his solicitor's advice that he was not bound by it); and it was held that he was estopped from denying that a contract had come into existence and that the agreement for the lease was therefore specifically enforceable against him. The reasoning of the High Court is complex, but the basis of the decision appears to be that the prospective lessee had knowingly induced the prospective lessor to believe that a binding contract would come into existence by exchange of contracts[55] and to act in reasonable reliance on that belief. In English law, such reliance is, in appropriate circumstances, capable of giving rise to a variety of remedies, even where the promise or representation which induces it lacks contractual force. Sometimes the remedy may be the enforcement of the promise according to its terms, as in cases of proprietary estoppel (to be discussed later in this Chapter)[56]; sometimes it may be an award of the reasonable value of work done in the belief that a contract had, or would, come into existence.[57] Neither of these remedies would have been available in the *Waltons Stores* case since proprietary estoppel does not arise where work is done on the promisee's (rather than on the promisor's) land[58] and a claim for the reasonable value of the

---

[52] *Restatement, Contracts* § 90 and *Restatement 2d*, Contracts § 90. In English law, the need to use the doctrine to give rise to a cause of action is less acute than in the United States, where the courts are less ready than the English courts to "invent" consideration (*ante* § 3–008).

[53] (1988) 164 C.L.R. 387; Duthie 104 L.Q.R. 362; Sutton 1 J.C.L. 205.

[54] *Ante*, § 2–108.

[55] For this requirement, see *ante*, § 2–109.

[56] *e.g.*, in *Dillwyn v. Llewelyn* (1862) 4 D.F. & G. 517 *post*, §§ 3–131, 3–142.

[57] *e.g.*, in *William Lacey (Hounslow) Ltd v. Davis* [1954] 1 Q.B. 428.

[58] *Post*, § 3–136; proprietary estoppel would also probably have been excluded on the ground that the prospective lessor had no belief that a right had been or would be created in his favour while the agreement remained "subject to contract": see *Att.-Gen of Hong Kong v. Humphreys Estates (Queens Gardens)* [1987] 1 A.C. 114; this obstacle could be overcome one party induces the other to believe that he will not withdraw: see *ibid.* at 124; but this qualification can scarcely enable the party *by* whom the interest in property is to be created to rely on proprietary estoppel.

claimant's work is not available where he is aware of the fact that no binding agreement has come into existence and so takes the risk that the negotiations may fail.[59] Even where the second of these objections can be overcome (*e.g.* on the ground that the work was done at the request of the promisor or as a result of his assurance that an exchange of contracts would take place) it does not follow that the appropriate remedy is enforcement of the contract in its terms: if the basis of "Australian estoppel"[60] is reliance induced by the promisor, compensation for reliance loss would appear to be the more appropriate remedy. The Australian doctrine also gives rise to the difficulties that there appear to be no clear limits to its scope, and that this lack of clarity is a regrettable source of uncertainty. The doctrine is, moreover, hard to reconcile with a number of fundamental principles of English law, such as the non-enforceability of informal gratuitous promises (even if relied on)[61] and the rule that there is no right to damages for a wholly innocent non-contractual misrepresentation.[62] While on the facts of some of the cases in which the Australian doctrine has been applied the same conclusions would probably be reached in English law on other grounds,[63] the broad doctrine remains, in the present context, inconsistent with the view that the English doctrine of promissory estoppel (like that of estoppel by representation)[64] does not give rise to a cause of action in the sense of entitling the promisee to enforce a promise in its terms, even though it was unsupported by consideration. It is true that other forms of estoppel, such as proprietary estoppel, may produce this result; but the scope of that doctrine is limited in many important ways[65] and the law would present an incongruous appearance if those limits could be outflanked simply by invoking the broader doctrine of "Australian estoppel."

3–100   **Distinguished from estoppel by convention.** Estoppel by convention may arise where both[66] parties to a transaction "act on assumed state of facts or law, the assumption being either shared by both or acquiesced in by the other."[67] The parties are then precluded from denying the truth of that assumption, if it would be unjust or unconscionable[68] to allow them (or one of them) to go back on it.[69]

---

[59] *Regalian Properties plc v. London Dockland Development Corp.* [1995] 1 W.L.R. 212.

[60] A phrase borrowed from the title of a thesis for the degree of D.Phil. at Oxford University by M. J. Spence, in which the Australian cases are fully discussed and compared with English and other common law authorities. See further Spence, *Protecting Reliance* (1999).

[61] *Ante*, § 3–002.

[62] *e.g. Oscar Chess Ltd v. Williams* [1957] 1 W.L.R. 370.

[63] See, for example, *Commonwealth of Australia v. Verwayen* (1990) 179 C.L.R. 394, which could be explained in English law on the ground stated in § 3–095 at n. 32.

[64] *Low v. Bouverie* [1891] 3 Ch. 82; *Clipper Maritime Ltd v. Shirlstar Container Transport Ltd (The Anemone)* [1987] 1 Lloyd's Rep. 547, 557.

[65] *e.g.* by the requirements that the promisee must believe that legal rights have been, or will be, created in his favour, and that these are rights in or over the promisor's land: see *post*, § 3–116, n. 55.

[66] There can be no such estoppel where one party is not yet in existence: see *Rover International Ltd v. Cannon Film Sales Ltd* (1987) 3 B.C.C. 369, revsd. in part on other grounds [1989] 1 W.L.R. 912 (company not yet formed).

[67] *Republic of India v. Indian Steamship Co. (The Indian Endurance) (No. 2)* [1998] A.C. 878, 913; and see *Norwegian American Cruises A/S v. Paul Mundy Ltd (The Vistafjord)* [1988] 2 Lloyd's Rep. 343, 351; *Shearson Lehman Hutton Inc. v. Maclaine Watson & Co. Ltd* [1989] 2 Lloyd's Rep. 570, 596; Spencer Bower and Turner, *Estoppel by Representation*, (3rd ed., 1977) p. 157; Dawson (1989) L.S. 16.

[68] *Crédit Suisse v. Borough Council of Allerdale* [1995] 2 Lloyd's Rep. 315, 367–370 (where this requirement was not satisfied); affd. on other grounds [1997] Q.B. 362.

[69] *Norwegian American Cruises A/S v. Paul Mundy Ltd (The Vistafjord)* [1988] 2 Lloyd's Rep. 343, 352; *Hiscox v. Outhwaite (No. 1)* [1992] 1 A.C. 562, affd. on other grounds *ibid.* at 585; *The Indian*

Such an estoppel differs from estoppel by representation and from promissory estoppel[70] in that it does not depend on any "clear and unequivocal" representation or promise[71]: it can arise where the assumption was based on a mistake spontaneously made by the party relying on it, and acquiesced in by the other party. Estoppel by convention has also been said to arise out of an express agreement by which the parties had compromised a disputed claim[72]; but where such a compromise is supported by consideration (in accordance with the principles discussed earlier in this Chapter[73]) it is binding as a contract,[74] so that there is, it is submitted, no need to rely on estoppel by convention in order to determine the legal effects of the agreement.

Requirements of estoppel by convention. This kind of estoppel was dis-   **3–101** cussed in *Amalgamated Investment & Property Co. Ltd v. Texas Commerce International Bank Ltd.*[75] In that case, A Co. negotiated with X Bank for a loan to B Co. (one of A Co.'s subsidiaries) for the purpose of acquiring and developing a property in the Bahamas. It was agreed that the loan was to be secured by a mortgage on that property and also by a guarantee from A Co. In the guarantee, A Co. promised X Bank, in consideration of the Bank's giving credit to B Co., to "pay you . . . all moneys . . . due *to you*" from B Co. This was an inappropriate form of words since the loan to B Co. was not made directly by X Bank but by one of its subsidiaries, Y Bank, with money provided by X Bank: hence, if the guarantee were read literally, it would not apply to the loan since no money was due from B Co. to X Bank. The Court of Appeal, however, took the view that this literal interpretation would defeat the intention of the parties, and held that, on its true construction, the guarantee applied to the loan made by Y Bank.[76] But even if the guarantee did not, on its true construction, produce this result, A Co. was estopped from denying that the guarantee covered the loan by Y Bank, since, when negotiating the loan, both A Co. and X Bank had assumed that the guarantee did cover it; and since X Bank continued subsequently to act on that assumption[77] in granting various indulgences to A Co. in respect of the loan to B Co. and of another loan made directly by X Bank to A Co. It made no difference that the assumption was not induced by any representation[78] made by A Co. but originated in X Bank's own mistake: the estoppel was not one by

---

Endurance (No. 2), supra, at 913; in *Commercial Union Assurance plc v. Sun Alliance Assurance Group plc* [1992] 1 Lloyd's Rep. 474, 481 estoppel by convention was rejected on the ground that the evidence did not "clearly and unequivocally establish the agreement of the parties on the relevant conventional interpretation"; but this statement seems to relate to quantum of proof rather than to the definition of the facts to be proved.

[70] *cf.* the dictum from *First National Bank plc v. Thomson* [1996] Ch. 231, 236 cited in § 3–096, n. 36 *ante*.

[71] *Troop v. Gibson* (1986) 277 E.G. 1134.

[72] *Colchester B.C. v. Smith* [1992] Ch. 421, 434.

[73] *Ante*, §§ 3–044 *et seq.*

[74] *Colchester B.C. v. Smith, supra,* at 435.

[75] [1982] Q.B. 84. See also *Astilleros Canarios SA v. Cape Hatteras Shipping Co. SA* [1982] 1 Lloyd's Rep. 518, 527.

[76] *cf.* on the issue of construction, *TCB Ltd v. Gray* [1988] 1 All E.R. 108; *Bank of Scotland v. Wright* [1990] B.C.C. 663.

[77] Contrast *Crédit Suisse v. Borough Council of Allerdale* [1996] 2 Lloyd's Rep. 315, 367, where this requirement was not satisfied as the conduct of the party alleged to be estopped had not "influenced the mind" of the other party; affd. on other grounds [1997] Q.B. 362.

[78] A dictum in the *Crédit Suisse* case, *supra* at 367 which appears to treat representation as a requirement of estoppel by convention is, with respect, inconsistent with the treatment of that doctrine in the *Amalgamated Investment* case.

representation but by convention.[79] The same principle was applied in *The Vistafjord*[80] where an agreement for the charter of a cruise ship had been negotiated by agents on behalf of the owners. Both the agents and the owners believed throughout that commission on this transaction would be payable under an earlier agreement, but on its true construction this agreement gave no such rights to the agents. It was held that estoppel by convention precluded the owners from relying on the true construction of the earlier agreement, so that the agents were justified in retaining the amount of the commission out of sums received by them from the charterers.

3–102   **"Communication" passing "across the line".** To give rise to an estoppel by convention, the mistaken assumption of the party claiming the benefit of the estoppel must, however, have been shared or acquiesced in by the party alleged to be estopped; and both parties must have conducted themselves on the basis of such a shared assumption[81]: the estoppel "requires communications to pass across the line between the parties. It is not enough that each of two parties acts on an assumption not communicated to the other."[82] Such communication may be effected by the conduct of one party, known to the other.[83] But no estoppel by convention arose where each party spontaneously made a different mistake and there was no subsequent conduct by the party alleged to be estopped from which any acquiescence in the other party's mistaken assumption could be inferred.[84]

3–103   **Effects of estoppel by convention.** The effect of this form of estoppel is to preclude a party from denying the agreed or common assumption.[85] One such assumption may be that a particular promise has been made[86]: thus it is possible

---

[79] cf. *Government of Swaziland Central Transport Administration v. Leila Maritime Co. Ltd (The Leila)* [1985] 2 Lloyd's Rep. 172; and see *infra*, n. 84.

[80] *Norwegian American Cruises A/S v. Paul Mundy Ltd (The Vistafjord)* [1988] 2 Lloyd's Rep. 343. cf. also *Kenneth Allison Ltd v. A. E. Limehouse & Co.* [1992] 2 A.C. 105, 127 per Lord Goff. The other members of the House of Lords took the view that there was an actual agreement (to accept service of a writ) which was legally effective even though the requirements of the Rules of the Supreme Court (with regard to personal service) had not been complied with.

[81] *Empresa Lineas Maritimas Argentinas v. The Oceanus Mutual Underwriting Association (Bermuda) Ltd* [1984] 2 Lloyd's Rep. 517 (where neither of these requirements was satisfied); *Astilleros Canarios SA v. Cape Hatteras Shipping Co. SA* [1982] 1 Lloyd's Rep. 518, 527; *Heinrich Hanno & Co. B.V. v. Fairlight Shipping Co. (The Kostas K.)* [1985] 1 Lloyd's Rep. 231, 237; *The Vistafjord*, *supra* n. 80.

[82] *Compania Portorafti Commerciale SA v. Ultramar Panama Inc. (The Captain Gregos) (No. 2)* [1990] 2 Lloyd's Rep. 395, 405, following *K. Lokumal & Sons (London) Ltd v. Lotte Shipping Co. Pty. Ltd (The August P. Leonhardt)* [1985] 2 Lloyd's Rep. 28, 35; *Hiscox v. Outhwaite (No. 3)* [1991] 2 Lloyd's Rep. 524, 533; *The Indian Endurance*, *supra*, at 913.

[83] As in *The Vistafjord* [1988] 2 Lloyd's Rep. 343, 351 ("very clear conduct crossing the line . . . of which the other party was fully cognisant").

[84] *K. Lokumal & Sons (London) Ltd v. Lotte Shipping Co. Pty. Ltd (The August P. Leonhardt)* [1985] 2 Lloyd's Rep. 28, revg. [1984] 1 Lloyd's Rep. 332, which had been followed in *The Leila*, *supra* n. 79. The present status of *The Leila* therefore remains in some doubt but the two cases can be reconciled on the ground that in *The Leila* there was, while in *The August P. Leonhardt* there was not, conduct by the party alleged to be estopped from which acquiescence in the other party's mistaken belief could be inferred.

[85] *Amalgamated Investment & Property* case [1982] Q.B. 84, 126, 130; it is often said that the assumption may be one of "fact or law"; see *ibid.* at 122 cf. *The Vistafjord* [1988] 2 Lloyd's Rep. 343, 351; *Shearson Lehman Hutton Inc. v. Maclaine Watson & Co. Ltd* [1989] 2 Lloyd's Rep. 570, 596; and *ante*, § 3–100, *semble*, the reference to law is intended to meet the objection that the construction of a document is often said to be a matter of "law." Such an assumption of "law" could be described as one of private right: cf. *post*, § 6–011.

[86] Such a representation is one of fact (and not as to the future): *post*, § 6–010.

to describe the result in *Amalgamated Investment & Property Co. Ltd v. Texas Commerce International Bank Ltd* by saying that A Co. was estopped from denying that it had promised X Bank to repay any sum left unpaid by B Co. to Y bank. But, although estoppel by convention may thus take effect in relation to a promise, it is quite different in nature from promissory estoppel. In cases of promissory estoppel, the promisor or representor is not estopped from denying that the promise or representation *has been made*: on the contrary, this must be proved to establish that kind of estoppel. The doctrine of promissory estoppel is concerned with the *legal effects* of a promise that has been shown to exist. Estoppel by convention, on the other hand, may operate so as to prevent a party from denying that a promise *has been made* or from disputing its terms: it does not specify the *legal effects* of the assumed promise. Hence it has been said that the effect of estoppel by convention is not to give rise to an enforceable contract without consideration: "Estoppel by convention is not dependent on contract but on a common assumption."[87] In *Amalgamated Investment & Property Co. Ltd v. Texas Commerce International Bank Ltd*, once A Co. was estopped from denying the *existence* of the promise described above, no question arose as to its legal *validity*. There could be no doubt that that promise was supported by consideration[88]: this was provided by X Bank in making funds available to Y Bank to enable it to make a loan to B Co., and in inducing Y Bank to make that loan. This aspect of the case provides a simple illustration of the rule that consideration need only move from the promisee (X Bank) but need not move to the promisor (A Co.)[89]

3–104 Where the assumed promise is one that would, if actually made, have been unsupported by consideration, both types of estoppel can, however, operate in the same case: estoppel by convention to establish the existence of the promise, and promissory estoppel to determine its legal effect.[90]

3–105 **Whether estoppel by convention creates new rights.** We have seen that promissory estoppel does not "create new causes of action where none existed before"[91]; and we shall see that the same principle applies to estoppel by representation.[92] Estoppel by convention resembles estoppel by representation in that it can prevent a party from denying *existing facts*, and one would therefore expect estoppel by convention to operate only where its effect was defensive in substance. The question whether estoppel by convention is so limited was discussed in the *Amalgamated Investment & Property* case[93] where, however, it was not necessary to decide the point. This action was brought because X Bank had sought to apply money due from it to A Co. under another transaction in discharge of A Co.'s alleged liability under its guarantee of B Co.'s debt. Hence the effect of the estoppel was to provide X Bank with a defence to A Co.'s claim

---

[87] *The Vistafjord* [1988] 2 Lloyd's Rep. 343, 351. For this reason the citation in *Williams v. Roffey Bros & Nicholls (Contractors) Ltd* [1991] 1 Q.B. 1, 17–18 of the *Amalgamated Investment & Property* case (*ante*, § 3–101) seems, with respect, to be of doubtful relevance. In the *Williams* case there was no doubt that the promise had been made; and the actual decision was that it was supported by consideration and thus binding contractually: *ante*, § 3–063.

[88] This was also true in *The Vistafjord*, *supra*, § 3–101.

[89] *Ante*, §§ 3–037 *et seq.*

[90] *e.g.* (apparently) *Troop v. Gibson* (1986) 277 E.G. 1134.

[91] *Combe v. Combe* [1951] 2 K.B. 215, 219; *ante*, § 3–093.

[92] *Post*, § 6–094.

[93] [1982] Q.B. 84; *ante*, § 3–101.

for a declaration that it was not entitled to apply the money in that way. Eveleigh L.J. said: "I do not think that the bank could have succeeded in a claim on the guarantee itself."[94] Brandon L.J. seems to have taken the view that the bank could have sued on the guarantee, but to have based that view on the ground that the loan agreement between A Co. and X Bank imposed an obligation on A Co. to give the guarantee: hence it was that agreement, and not the estoppel, which would have given rise to X Bank's cause of action, if it had sued on the guarantee.[95] Lord Denning M.R. seems to have expressed the principle of estoppel by convention in such a way as to enable it to give rise to a cause of action[96] but he was alone in stating the principle so broadly.[97] In *The Vistafjord*[98] the estoppel similarly operated defensively. This factor was not stressed in the judgments, but there is no suggestion in them that in this respect estoppel by convention differs from estoppel by representation, which does not, of itself, give rise to a cause of action.[99] It is indeed, possible for estoppel by convention (as it is for promissory estoppel[1]) to deprive the defendant of a *defence*, and so to enable the claimant to win an action which otherwise he would have lost[2]; but even in such cases the estoppel does not create the cause of action, for the *facts giving rise to the cause of action* exist independently of the estoppel. No other authority squarely supports the view that estoppel by convention can, of itself, create a new cause of action; and the present position seems to be that it cannot, any more than promissory estoppel or estoppel by representation, produce this effect.[3]

3–106   **Invalidity of assumed term.** A party is not liable on the basis of estoppel by convention where the alleged agreement would, if concluded, have been ineffective for want of contractual intention,[4] or where the term in respect of which such an estoppel is alleged to operate would, if actually incorporated in the contract, have been invalid (*e.g.* because it amounted to an attempt to deprive a tenant of statutory security of tenure which could not be excluded by contract)[5]; nor does

---

[94] [1982] Q.B. 84, 126.

[95] *ibid.* at 132.

[96] *ibid.* at 122.

[97] *Keen v. Holland* [1984] 1 W.L.R. 251, 261–262. In *Wilson Bowden Properties Ltd v. Milner and Bardon* [1996] C.L.Y. 1229 the cause of action arose out of the undisputed contract and not out of the estoppel.

[98] [1988] 2 Lloyd's Rep. 343; *ante*, § 3–101. In *Shearson Lehman Hutton Inc. v. Maclaine Watson & Co. Ltd* [1989] 2 Lloyd's Rep. 570, the estoppel would likewise (if supported on the facts) have operated defensively; *cf.* also *Mitsui Babcock Energy Ltd v. John Brown Energy Ltd* (1996) 51 Const. L.R. 129, 185–186 where the effect of the estoppel would (if the contract in question had not existed) again have been to *restrict* the plaintiff's rights by reference to the terms of the (in that event non-existent) contract.

[99] *Post*, § 6–094.

[1] *Ante*, § 3–095.

[2] This was the effect of the estoppel in *Furness Withy (Australia) Ltd v. Metal Distrubutors (U.K.) Ltd, (The Amazonia)* [1990] 1 Lloyd's Rep. 238, where it operated to prevent a party from relying on facts giving rise to a mistake of both parties alleged to make the contract void (*post*, § 5–034) and where the effect of allowing him to rely on those facts would have been to bar the other party's claim by lapse of time.

[3] *cf. Russell Brothers (Paddington) Ltd v. John Elliott Management Ltd* (1995) 1 Const. L.J. 377, denying that estoppel by convention can be used as a sword.

[4] *Orion Insurance plc v. Sphere Drake Insurance* [1922] 1 Lloyd's Rep. 239.

[5] See *Keen v. Holland* [1984] 1 W.L.R. 251; contrast *Furness Withy (Australia) Pty Ltd v. Metal Distributors (U.K.) Ltd (The Amazonia)* [1989] 1 Lloyd's Rep. 403 (illegality under foreign statute); *Godden v. Merthyr Tydfil Housing Association* (1997) 74 P.& C.R. D1.

such an estoppel prevent a party from relying on the true legal effect (as opposed to the meaning[6]) of an admitted contract merely because the parties have entered into it under a mistaken view as to that effect.[7]

10. PART PAYMENT OF A DEBT

(a) *General Rule*

General common law rule. At common law, the general rule is that a creditor   **3–107** is not bound by a promise to accept part payment in full settlement of a debt. A debt can only be discharged by accord and satisfaction.[8] A promise by the debtor to pay only part of the debt provides no consideration for the accord, as it is merely a promise to perform part of an existing duty owed to the creditor. And the actual payment is no satisfaction under the rule in *Pinnel's Case* that "Payment of a lesser sum on the day in satisfaction of a greater sum cannot be any satisfaction for the whole."[9] This rule was finally approved by the House of Lords in *Foakes v. Beer*.[10] Mrs Beer had obtained a judgment against Dr Foakes for £2,090 19s. Sixteen months later, Dr Foakes asked for time to pay. A written agreement[11] was made whereby Mrs Beer undertook not to take "any proceedings whatsoever" on the judgment, in consideration of an immediate payment by Dr Foakes of £500 and on condition of his paying specified instalments "until the whole of the said sum of £2,090 19s. shall have been paid and satisfied." Some five years later, when Dr Foakes had paid £2,090 19s., Mrs Beer claimed £360[12] for interest on the judgment debt. The House of Lords upheld her claim and the actual result does not appear to be unjust; for it seems that in making the agreement Mrs Beer intended only to give Dr Foakes time to pay and not to forgive interest.[13]

Effects of the rule. The rule established in *Foakes v. Beer* may sometimes   **3–108** have performed the useful function of protecting a creditor against a debtor who too ruthlessly exploited the tactical advantage of being a potential defendant in

---

[6] *Supra*, n. 85.

[7] *Keen v. Holland, supra*, n. 5; *Hamed El Chiaty & Co. (T/A Travco Nile Cruise Lines) v. Thomas Cook Group (The Nile Rhapsody)* [1992] 2 Lloyd's Rep. 399, 408, where, however, the court treated the contract as rectified so as to correct the mistake; affd. [1994] 1 Lloyd's Rep. 382, without reference to estoppel by convention.

[8] *Commissioners of Stamp Duties v. Bone* [1977] A.C. 511, 519 ("A debt can only be truly released by agreement for valuable consideration or under seal.") This principle appears to have been overlooked in a dictum in *Brikom Investments Ltd v. Carr* [1979] Q.B. 467, 488, according to which a "waiver" of instalments of rent would bind the landlord. The actual promise of the landlord in that case was supported by consideration: *ante*, § 3–075; *post*, § 3–125.

[9] (1602) 5 Co.Rep. 117a; *Cumber v. Wane* (1721) 1 Stra. 426; *McManus v. Bark* (1870) L.R. 5 Ex. 65; *Underwood v. Underwood* [1894] P. 204; *Re Broderick* [1986] N.I.J.B. 36, 49–55; *Tilney Engineering v. Admods Knitting Machinery* [1987] C.L.Y. 412; contrast *Bagge v. Slade* (1616) 3 Bulst. 162.

[10] (1884) 9 App.Cas. 605.

[11] Drawn up by Dr Foakes' solicitor: (1884) 9 App.Cas. at 625.

[12] *Beer v. Foakes* (1883) 11 Q.B.D. 221, 222.

[13] Lords Fitzgerald and Watson thought that the agreement did not, on its true construction, cover interest. Lords Selborne and Blackburn sympathised with this view but felt unable to adopt it as the operative part of the document was too "clear" to be controlled by the recitals. See (1884) 9 App.Cas. at 610, 614, 615.

litigation. This aspect of the matter is well illustrated by *D. & C. Builders Ltd v. Rees*.[14] The defendant owed £482 to a firm of builders. Six months after payment had first been demanded, the defendant's wife (acting on his behalf) offered the builders £300 in full settlement. The builders accepted this offer as they were in desperate straits financially and there was some evidence that the defendant's wife knew this.[15] It was held that they were nevertheless entitled to the balance; and the majority[16] of the Court of Appeal based their decision to this effect on the rule in *Foakes v. Beer*.

3–109   On the other hand, it is arguable that the function of protecting the creditor in such a situation is now more satisfactorily performed by the expanding concept of duress[17] than by the rule in *Pinnel's Case*; and that the rule therefore no longer serves any useful purpose. In some circumstances, an agreement to accept part payment of a debt in full settlement may be a perfectly fair and reasonable transaction.[18] Moreover, in *Foakes v. Beer* the rule was criticised[19] on the ground that part payment was often in fact more beneficial to the creditor than strict insistence on his legal rights. A factual benefit[20] of a similar kind has been accepted as sufficient consideration for a promise to make an extra payment for the performance of an existing contractual duty owed by the promisee to the promisor[21]; and the law would be more consistent, as well as more satisfactory in its practical operation, if it adopted the same approach to cases of part payment of a debt. Agreements of the kind here under discussion would then be binding unless they had been made under duress. But the rule in *Foakes v. Beer* is open to challenge only in the House of Lords.[22] In the meantime, its operation is mitigated by limitations on its scope at common law and in equity. These are discussed in the following paragraphs.

(b) *Limitations at Common Law*

3–110   **Disputed claims.** The rule stated in § 3–107 above does not apply where the creditor's claim (or its amount) is disputed in good faith.[23] In such a case, the value of the creditor's claim is doubtful and the debtor therefore provides consideration by paying something, even though it is less than the amount claimed. It is irrelevant that the amount paid is small in relation to the amount

---

[14] [1966] 2 Q.B. 617; Chorley (1966) 29 M.L.R. 165; Cornish (1966) 29 M.L.R. 428; and see *post*, § 3–128.

[15] [1966] 2 Q.B. at 625.

[16] Lord Denning M.R. based his decision on a different ground: *post*, § 3–128.

[17] *cf. ante*, § 3–062. A debtor who by any deception dishonestly induces the creditor to accept part payment of a debt in full settlement may also be guilty of an offence under the Theft Act 1978, s.2.

[18] *e.g.* on the facts of *Central London Property Trust Ltd v. High Trees House Ltd* [1947] K.B. 130; *post*, § 3–120.

[19] Especially by Lord Blackburn: (1884) 9 App.Cas. at 617–622; see also Lord Selborne at 613 and *Couldery v. Bartrum* (1881) 19 Ch.D. 394, 399, where Jessel M.R. called the rule "a most extraordinary peculiarity of English law."

[20] *Ante*, § 3–096.

[21] *Williams v. Roffey Bros. & Nicholls (Contractors) Ltd* [1991] 1 Q.B. 1, *ante* § 3–063.

[22] *Re Selectmove* [1995] 1 W.L.R. 474, where the Court of Appeal refused to apply the principle of the *Williams* case, *supra* n. 21, in the present context; Peel, (1994) 110 L.Q.R. 353.

[23] *Cooper v. Parker* (1855) 15 C.B. 822; *Re Warren* (1884) 53 L.J.Ch. 1016; *Anangel Atlas Compania Naviera SA v. Ishikawajima Harima Heavy Industries Co. Ltd (No. 2)* [1990] 2 Lloyd's Rep. 526, 544; for other consideration in this case, see *ibid.* at 545 and *post*, § 3–115.

claimed, or that the creditor has a good chance of succeeding on the claim; for the law will not generally investigate the adequacy of consideration.[24] However, where the defendant admits liability for less than the amount claimed, payment of the smaller sum is no consideration for the claimant's promise to accept that payment in full settlement of the larger claim. The rule in *Foakes v. Beer* applies since, once a binding admission has been made to pay the smaller sum, the payment of it amounts to no more than the performance of what, at that stage, is legally due from the defendant.[25]

Unliquidated claims. For similar reasons the general rule applies only if the   **3–111**
original claim is a "liquidated" one, *i.e.* a claim for a fixed sum of money, such as one for money lent or for the agreed price of goods[26] or services. It does not apply where the creditor's claim is an unliquidated one,[27] such as a claim for damages or for a reasonable remuneration (where none is fixed by the contract). The value of such a claim is again uncertain; and even if the overwhelming probability is that it is worth more than the sum paid, the possibility that it may be worth less suffices to satisfy the requirement of consideration.

Unliquidated claims becoming liquidated. An originally unliquidated claim   **3–112**
may subsequently become liquidated by act of the parties. This appears to have happened in *D. & C. Builders v. Rees*,[28] where it does not seem that the contract specified the amount to be paid to the builders. When they presented their account they had only an unliquidated claim; and if they had at this stage accepted the £300 in full settlement they would not have been protected by the rule in *Foakes v. Beer*.[29] That rule became applicable only because the defendant had, by retaining the account without objection, impliedly agreed that it correctly stated the sum due, and so turned the plaintiffs' claim into a liquidated one.[30]

Claim partly liquidated and partly unliquidated. A creditor may have two   **3–113**
claims against the same debtor, one of them liquidated and the other unliqui-
dated; or a single claim which is partly liquidated and partly unliquidated. If the debtor pays no more than the liquidated amount, and if his liability to pay this amount was undisputed, the payment of it will not constitute consideration for a promise by the creditor to accept that payment in full settlement of the *whole* of the claim or claims in question. In *Arrale v. Costain Civil Engineering Ltd*[31] an employee was injured at work. Legislation in force at the place of work gave him

---

[24] *Ante*, § 3–013. But the fact that the sum received is much smaller than that claimed may be evidence that the recipient has not accepted it in full settlement: *Rustenburg Platinum Mines Ltd v. Pan Am* [1979] 1 Lloyd's Rep. 19.

[25] *Ferguson v. Davies* [1997] 1 All E.R. 315 *per* Henry L.J.; Evans L.J.'s judgment is based on the ground that, as a matter of construction, the claimant had not accepted the smaller sum in full settlement. Aldous L.J. agreed with both the other judgments.

[26] A claim may be "liquidated" even though it is disputed and even though the dispute relates to its amount: *e.g.* where it is for the price of goods and the buyer alleges short delivery: *Aectra Refining and Manufacturing Inc. v. Exmar N.V. (The New Vanguard)* [1994] 1 W.L.R. 1634.

[27] *Wilkinson v. Byers* (1834) 1 A. & E. 106; *Ibberson v. Neck* (1886) 2 T.L.R. 427.

[28] [1966] 2 Q.B. 617; *ante*, § 3–108.

[29] (1884) 9 App.Cas. 605; *ante*, § 3–107.

[30] *cf. Amantilla v. Telefusion* (1987) 9 Con.L.R. 139, where a builder's *quantum meruit* claim, which had not been disputed, was treated as "liquidated" for the purpose of Limitation Act 1980, s.29(5)(a).

[31] [1976] 1 Lloyd's Rep. 98; *cf. Rustenburg Platinum Mines Ltd v. Pan Am* [1979] 1 Lloyd's Rep. 19, 24.

a right against the employers to a fixed lump sum of £490, for which the employers did not dispute liability; and it was assumed that he also had a common law right to sue the employers in tort for unliquidated damages. It was held that any promise which he might have made not to pursue the common law claim was not made binding by the employers' payment of the £490. The employers had provided no consideration for such a promise since in making the payment, they merely did what they were already bound to do.[32]

3–114   **Variation in the debtor's performance.** Consideration for a creditor's promise to accept part payment of a debt in full settlement can be provided by the debtor's doing some act that he was not previously bound by the contract to do.[33] For example, payment of a smaller sum at the creditor's request before the due day is good consideration for a promise to forgo the balance, since it is a benefit to the creditor to be paid before he was entitled to payment, and a corresponding detriment to the debtor to pay early.[34] The same applies, *mutatis mutandis*, where payment of a smaller sum is made at the creditor's request at a place different from that originally fixed for payment,[35] or in a different currency.[36] Again, payment of a smaller sum accompanied at the creditor's request by the delivery of a chattel is good consideration for a promise to forgo the balance: "The gift of a horse, hawk or robe, etc. in satisfaction is goods. For it shall be intended that a horse, hawk or robe, etc., might be more beneficial than the money. . . . "[37]

3–115   **Other benefit to creditor.** We have seen that a promise to pay a supplier of services more than the agreed sum for performing his part of the contract can be supported by consideration in the form of a benefit in fact obtained by the other party as a result of his obtaining the promised performance.[38] Conversely, a promise by the supplier to accept less than the agreed sum may be supported by a similar consideration. The mere receipt of the smaller sum cannot, indeed, constitute the consideration: that possibility is precluded by *Foakes v. Beer.*[39] But the performance by the debtor of *other* obligations under the contract may confer such a benefit on the creditor and so satisfy the requirement of consideration. This possibility is illustrated by the *Anangel Atlas*[40] case, where a shipbuilder's promise to reduce the agreed price was held to have been supported by consideration, and one reason for this conclusion was that the buyers to whom the reduction was promised had provided consideration by accepting delivery on the day fixed for such acceptance. Even if the buyers were already bound to take delivery on that day, they had conferred a benefit on the shipbuilder by so doing

---

[32] *Per* Stephenson and Geoffrey Lane L.JJ.; Lord Denning M.R. based his decision on a different ground: *post*, § 3–128, n. 6.

[33] *e.g. Re William Porter & Co.* [1937] 2 All E.R. 261; *Ledingham v. Bermejo Estancia Co. Ltd* [1947] 2 All E.R. 748.

[34] *Pinnel's Case, ante,* § 3–107.

[35] *ibid.*

[36] *cf. ante,* § 3–074.

[37] *Pinnel's Case, ante,* § 3–107. Many cases formerly supported the view that part payment by a negotiable instrument, made at the request of the creditor and accepted by him in full settlement, discharged the debt. But these cases were overruled in *D. & C. Builders Ltd v. Rees* [1966] 2 Q.B. 617.

[38] *Williams v. Roffey Bros & Nicholls (Contractors) Ltd* [1991] 1 Q.B. 1, *ante,* § 3–063.

[39] (1884) 9 App. Cas. 605, *ante,* § 3–112.

[40] *Anangel Atlas Compania Naviera SA v. Ishikawajima Harima Heavy Industries Co. Ltd (No. 2)* [1990] 2 Lloyd's Rep. 526. For other consideration in that case, in the form of reducing "a previously ill-defined understanding to 'precise terms,' and so settling a potential dispute", see *ibid.* 544.

since they were "core customers"[41] and their refusal to take delivery might have led other actual or potential customers to cancel (or not to place) orders.

Forbearance to enforce cross-claims. A debtor may provide consideration **3–116** for the creditor's promise not only by doing an *act* that he was not previously bound to do, but also by a *forbearance*. Thus, where the debtor has a claim against the creditor, the debtor's forbearance to enforce that claim can constitute consideration for the creditor's promise not to claim part of the debt. For example, where a landlord promises to accept part payment of rent in full settlement, the tenant may provide consideration for this promise by forbearing to sue the landlord for breach of the latter's obligation to keep the premises in repair.[42]

Composition with creditors. The doctrine of consideration gives rise to some **3–117** difficulty in relation to composition agreements by which a debtor who cannot pay all his creditors in full induces them to agree with himself and with each other to accept part payment in full settlement of their claims.[43] The binding force of such agreements is well established,[44] in spite of the rule in *Foakes v. Beer*.[45] One possible reason for the validity of such agreements is that it would be a fraud on the other parties for a creditor who had accepted a composition to claim the balance of his original debt.[46] An alternative view is that the consideration for the creditor's promise is to be found in the promise of every other creditor to forgo part of his own debt[47]; but this consideration does not move from the promisee (*i.e.* the debtor) unless he also joins in the agreement.[48] In that event there may be consideration in the shape of a benefit to each creditor[49]: he is certain of some payment, while in the scramble for priorities which might take place if there were no composition agreement he might get nothing at all.

---

[41] *ibid.* at 544.

[42] *Brikom Investments Ltd v. Carr* [1979] Q.B. 467, as explained in § 3–075, *ante.*

[43] Provision for publicity and substantial agreement among creditors is made by Deeds of Arrangement Act 1914 (repealed in part by Insolvency Act 1985, s.235 and Sched. 10, Pt. III, and amended by Insolvency Act 1986, s.439(2)). *Oral* agreements are not caught by the 1914 Act: *Hughes & Falconer v. Newton* [1939] 3 All E.R. 869. "Voluntary arrangements" under Insolvency Act 1986, Pts. I and VIII can, by virtue of ss.5(2) and 260(2), bind even a creditor who did not attend the meeting, or dissented from the proposal, "as if he were a party to the arrangement:" see *Johnson v. Davies* [1998] 2 All E.R. 649, 665; *cf. Re Cancol Ltd* [1997] 1 All E.R. 921. *cf. Re a Debtor (No. 259 of 1990)* [1992] 1 W.L.R. 226.

[44] *Good v. Cheesman* (1831) 2 B. & Ad. 328; *Boyd v. Hind* (1857) 1 H. & N. 938; an *agreement* to pay a dividend may, if the parties so intend, operate as satisfaction: *Bradley v. Gregory* (1810) 2 Camp. 383.

[45] (1894) 9 App.Cas. 605; *ante,* § 3–107.

[46] *Wood v. Roberts* (1818) 2 Stark. 417; *Cook v. Lister* (1863) 13 C.B.(N.S.) 543, 595.

[47] *Boothbey v. Snowden* (1812) 3 Camp. 175.

[48] As in *Good v. Cheesman* (1831) 2 B. & Ad. 328 where the debtor also made an assignment for the benefit of his creditors.

[49] In *West Yorkshire Darracq Agency Ltd v. Coleridge* [1911] 2 K.B. 326, the same principle was applied although the creditors got nothing; but it is hard to see how this application of the rule can be justified: *ante,* § 3–037, n. 71. Even in such a case, the debtor may get the benefit of the agreement if, when he is sued by one creditor, the other (or others) can intervene to stay the action: see *Snelling v. John G. Snelling* [1973] 1 Q.B. 87, *post,* § 19–058. The debtor will not, however, be able to avoid the requirement of consideration by relying on the Contracts (Rights of Third Parties) Bill 1998 since this applies only in favour of "a person who is *not* a party" to the contract (subsection 1(1)); and in the case of a composition agreement the debtor typically *will* be a party.

3–118   **Part payment of debt by a third party.** In *Welby v. Drake*[50] a creditor sued a son, after having accepted from his father in full satisfaction half the amount owed by the son. In refusing to allow the claim for the balance, Abbott C.J. said, " ... by suing the son he commits fraud on the father, whom he induced to advance money on the faith of such advance being a discharge of his son from further liability." In *Hirachand Punamchand v. Temple*[51] the debtor's father sent the creditor in full settlement of his son's debt a draft for an amount less than that of the debt; the creditor cashed the draft. The court relied on the statement of Willes J. in *Cook v. Lister*[52] that "if a stranger pays part of a debt in discharge of the whole, the debt is gone because it would be a fraud on the stranger to proceed"; and held that, as the creditor had accepted the sum offered by the father in settlement of the claim, he could not maintain an action against the debtor for the balance. The view that this result is based on fraud on the third party rather than on contract[53] between debtor and creditor is generally accepted. But "fraud" is not used here in its strict common law sense, for the fraud in question is a breach of promise and not a misstatement of fact. Alternatively, it can be said that the court will not help the creditor to break his contract with the third party by allowing him to obtain a judgment against the debtor. On the contrary, it has been held that where A (the creditor) expressly contracts with B (the third party) not to sue C (the debtor) and A nevertheless does sue C, B can intervene so as to obtain a stay of the action.[54] This possibility would extend to the case where the consideration provided by B was a *promise* by B to pay A: it thus goes beyond the cases discussed in this paragraph, in which B had *actually paid* A. After the coming into force of the Contracts (Rights of Third Parties) Bill 1998, the debtor may also, if the requirements of the Bill are satisfied,[54a] be able to take the benefit of any term in the contract between the creditor and the person making the payment, which may exclude the debtor's liability for the balance; and he will be able to do so without having to show that he provided any consideration for the creditor's promise to accept the part payment in full settlement.[54b]

3–119   **Collateral contract.** An agreement to accept part payment of a debt may take effect as a collateral contract if the requirements of contractual intention and consideration are satisfied. This was the position in *Brikom Investments Ltd v. Carr*[55] where a tenant's liability to contribute to the maintenance costs of a block of flats was held to have been reduced by a collateral contract under which the landlord undertook to execute certain roof repairs at his own expense.[56] The landlord's claim for contribution in this case was probably unliquidated; but the

---

[50] (1825) 1 C. & P. 557.
[51] [1911] 2 K.B. 330.
[52] (1863) 13 C.B.(N.S.) 543.
[53] In *Hirachand Punamchand v. Temple, supra*, n. 51, no promise was made to the debtor and no consideration moved from him, so that there was clearly no contract with him.
[54] See *Snelling v. John G. Snelling Ltd* [1973] 1 Q.B. 87 (*post*, § 19–058), distinguishing *Gore v. Van der Lann* [1967] 2 Q.B. 31 where no promise was made not to sue C. *cf.*, in cases of joint debts, *Johnson v. Davies* [1998] 2 All E.R. 649, 658.
[54a] *Post*, §§ 19–075 *et seq.*
[54b] *Ante*, § 3–043, *post* § 19–082. For the purposes of the Bill it is the debtor who is the "third party".
[55] [1979] Q.B. 467.
[56] For the consideration supporting this promise, see *ante*, § 3–075; for other grounds for the decision, see *post*, § 3–125.

principle seems to be equally applicable where a creditor enters into a collateral contract to accept part payment in full settlement of a liquidated claim.

(c) *Limitations in Equity*

Equitable forbearance. Under the rule in *Hughes v. Metropolitan Ry.*[57] a   **3–120** promise by a contracting party not to enforce his strict legal rights has (even where it is not supported by consideration) at least a limited effect in equity. Before 1947, this rule had not been applied to a creditor's promise to accept part payment of a debt in full settlement: indeed such an extension of the rule seemed to be barred by *Foakes v. Beer.*[58] The possibility of making the extension was, however, suggested in 1947 in *Central London Property Trust Ltd v. High Trees House Ltd.*[59] In that case a block of flats had been leased to the defendants in 1937 at a rent of £2,500 a year. In January 1940 the landlords agreed to reduce this rent to £1,250 a year because of wartime conditions as a result of which only a few of the flats were let. By the beginning of 1945 all the flats were let again but the defendants were still paying the reduced rent. The landlords claimed the full rent, and tested their claim by suing for rent at the original rate for the last two quarters of 1945. The claim was upheld on the ground that, as a matter of construction, the agreement of 1940 was intended to apply only while the war-time difficulties of sub-letting lasted, and that it had therefore ceased to operate in the early part of 1945. But Denning J. also said that the landlords could not have recovered the full rent for a period which *was* covered by the agreement of 1940. There was, indeed, no consideration for the landlords' promise to reduce the rent; and the doctrine of estoppel by representation would not have assisted the defendants because the landlords' representation related to the future and not to an existing fact.[60] But the defendants could have relied on the rule in *Hughes v. Metropolitan Ry.*,[61] on the basis of which Denning J. in the *High Trees* case formulated the principle that a promise intended to be binding, intended to be acted on, and in fact acted on should be binding.[62] He added: "The logical consequence no doubt is that a promise to accept a smaller sum in discharge of a larger sum, if acted upon, is binding notwithstanding the absence of consideration."

Suspensive nature of the doctrine. The statement just quoted is, at first sight,   **3–121** in direct conflict with the decision of the House of Lords in *Foakes v. Beer.*[63] One possible reconciliation between this case and the *High Trees*[64] case is to say that the former case was decided on purely common law principles, without reference

---

[57] (1877) 2 App.Cas. 439; *ante*, § 3–080.

[58] (1884) 9 App.Cas. 605.

[59] [1947] K.B. 130; Denning (1952) 15 M.L.R. 1; Wilson (1951) 67 L.Q.R. 330; Sheridan (1952) 15 M.L.R. 325; Bennion (1953) 16 M.L.R. 441; Guest (1955) 30 A.L.J. 187; Turner (1964) 1 N.Z.U.L.Rev. 185; Campbell, *ibid.* 232.

[60] *Jordan v. Money* (1854) 5 H.L.C. 185; *ante*, § 3–096.

[61] (1877) 2 App.Cas. 439. See also *Birmingham and District Land Co. v. L.N.W. Ry.* (1888) 49 Ch.D. 268; *Panoutsos v. Raymond Hadley Corporation* [1917] 2 K.B. 473; *Salisbury v. Gilmore* [1942] 2 K.B. 38.

[62] [1947] K.B. 130, 134.

[63] (1884) 9 App.Cas. 605; *ante*, § 3–107.

[64] [1947] K.B. 130; *ante*, § 3–120.

to equity,[65] and is therefore "no longer valid"[66]; but this is unsatisfactory as the rule in *Pinnel's Case*[67] (on which *Foakes v. Beer* was based) was recognised in equity no less than at common law.[68] Another possibility is to say that *Hughes v. Metropolitan Ry.* was simply not discussed in *Foakes v. Beer.*[69] The third possibility, and the one which does least violence to the authorities, is to say that the creditor's right to the balance of his debt is (save in exceptional cases[70]) not extinguished but only suspended.[71] This is generally the sole effect of the rule in *Hughes v. Metropolitan Ry.*[72] and in the present context it would give effect to the intention of the parties where the purpose of the arrangement was to give the debtor extra time to pay,[73] rather than to extinguish the debt. Of course where the intention is to extinguish, and not merely to suspend, the creditor's right to the balance, the suggestion that he is permanently bound by his promise to accept part payment in full settlement[74] may seem to be an attractive one.[75] But such an extension of the principle of *Hughes v. Metropolitan Ry.* would require the overruling of *Foakes v. Beer.* It is, no doubt, with such difficulties in mind that Lord Hailsham L.C. has said that the *High Trees* principle "may need to be reviewed and reduced to a coherent body of doctrine by the courts."[76]

3–122   **Continuing obligations.** For the present, the better view is that the principle is only suspensive; but the meaning of this statement is not entirely clear where the promisee is under a continuing obligation to make a series of payments, *e.g.* of rent under a lease,[77] of royalties under a licence to use a patent,[78] or of instalments under a hire-purchase agreement.[79] In such cases the statement may mean one of two things: first, that the creditor is entitled to payment in full only of amounts which fall due after the expiry of a reasonable notice of the retraction of the promise,[80] or, secondly, that he is then entitled, not only to future payments in full, but also to the balance of past ones. Of course the latter interpretation of the rule might sometimes be at variance with the intention of the parties at the

---

[65] *High Trees* case, *supra*, at 133.

[66] *Arrale v. Costain Civil Engineering Ltd* [1976] 1 Lloyd's Rep. 806, 830.

[67] (1602) Co.Rep. 117a; *ante*, § 3–107.

[68] *Re Warren* (1884) 53 L.J.Ch. 1016; *Bidder v. Bridges* (1887) 37 Ch.D. 406.

[69] See *High Trees* case, *supra* § 3–120, at 133 ("That aspect was not considered in *Foakes v. Beer*"); *cf. Arrale v. Costain Civil Engineering Ltd* [1976] 1 Lloyd's Rep. 98, 102.

[70] *Post*, § 3–124.

[71] *Ajayi v. R.T. Briscoe (Nig.) Ltd* [1964] 1 W.L.R. 1326, 1330; Unger (1965) 28 M.L.R. 231; *cf. Re Venning* [1947] W.N. 196. Gordon [1963] C.L.J. 222 objects to giving the creditors' promise even this limited effect, arguing that the equitable principle is limited to relief against forfeiture. But though *Hughes v. Metropolitan Ry.* was a case of this kind, the equitable principle had developed since 1877 and is no longer restricted to such cases: see Wilson [1965] C.L.J. 93.

[72] *Ante*, § 3–091.

[73] *e.g.* in *Ajayi v. R.T. Briscoe (Nig.) Ltd* [1964] 1 W.L.R. 1326: see *post*, § 3–122, n. 81.

[74] Originally made by Lord Denning in the *High Trees* case at 134 and repeated by him in *D. & C. Builders Ltd v. Rees* [1966] 2 Q.B. 617, 624; *cf. W.J. Alan & Co. Ltd v. El Nasr Export & Import Co.* [1972] 2 Q.B. 189, 213; *cf. ibid.* at 218, 220; but in that case there was consideration: *ante*, § 3–074.

[75] Provided, at any rate, that there were no circumstances of oppression: *cf. ante*, § 3–108.

[76] *Woodhouse A.C. Israel Cocoa Ltd v. Nigerian Produce Marketing Co.* [1972] A.C. 741, 758.

[77] As in the *High Trees* case, *supra*, § 3–120.

[78] As in the *Tool Metal* case [1955] 1 W.L.R. 761, discussed *infra*, at n. 83.

[79] As in *Ajayi v. R.T. Briscoe (Nig.) Ltd* [1964] 1 W.L.R. 1326.

[80] *Banning v. Wright* [1972] 1 W.L.R. 972, 981; *cf. W.J. Alan & Co. Ltd v. El Nasr Export & Import Co.* [1972] 2 Q.B. 189, 213.

time of the promise.[81] On the other hand it is hard to see why a debtor whose liability accrues from time to time should, for the purpose of the present rule, be in a more favourable position than one whose liability is to pay a single lump sum; nor is it clear which of the two possible rules should apply where a debtor who owed a lump sum promised to pay it off in instalments and the creditor first made, and then gave reasonable notice revoking, a promise to accept reduced instalments. In such a case, it is at least arguable that the intention of the creditor is only to give extra time for payment. Hence the total debt remains due, and the only effect of the promise is to extend the period over which it is to be repaid.[82]

In *Tool Metal Manufacturing Co. Ltd v. Tungsten Electric Co. Ltd*[83] a licence   **3–123** for the use of a patent provided that the licensees should pay "compensation" if they manufactured more than a stated number of articles incorporating the patent. The owners of the patent agreed in 1942 to suspend the obligation to pay compensation until a new agreement was made. No such agreement had been made by 1944, when disputes arose between the parties. In 1945 the owners claimed to have revoked their suspension and to be entitled to compensation as from June 1, 1945. This claim failed, the Court of Appeal holding that the arrangement to suspend claims for compensation was binding until proper notice of its termination had been given; and that no such notice had been given. The owners then brought the present action claiming compensation as from January 1, 1947. The House of Lords upheld the claim on the ground that, by then, a sufficient notice had been given of the ending of the suspension period. It seems to have been assumed that the defendants were no longer liable to pay the sums which would, under the original contract, have fallen due during the suspension period. But this point was not directly considered by the House of Lords; so that the case does not conclusively determine the precise results that flow, in cases of continuing obligations, from the suspensive nature of the doctrine.

Extinctive effects in exceptional cases. There are, however, exceptional   **3–124** situations in which the creditor's promise may wholly extinguish his rights. We have seen that, under the rule in *Hughes v. Metropolitan Ry.*,[84] a promise cannot be retracted where subsequent events make it impossible to perform the original obligation.[85] That principle cannot, as such, be applied to cases of part payment of a debt, since performance of the original obligation, being one to pay money, can never become literally impossible. But there is also support for the view that a forbearance cannot be retracted where it would, even after reasonable notice, be highly inequitable to require performance of the original obligation[86]; and this

---

[81] This would be so in cases like the *High Trees* case and the *Tool Metal* case (*infra*, at n. 83) but probably not in a case like *Ajayi v. R.T. Briscoe (Nig.) Ltd* [1964] 1 W.L.R. 1326, as the promise there "was not intended to be irrevocable:" *Meng Long Development Pte. Ltd v. Jip Hong Trading Pte. Ltd* [1985] A.C. 511, 524. *J.T. Sydenham & Co. Ltd v. Enichem Elastometers Ltd* [1989] E.G.L.R. 257, 260 (discussed by Cartwright [1990] C.L.J. 13) purports to give the "estoppel" an extinctive effect; but the amount of rent due in that case was in dispute, so that the actual decision is explicable on the ground stated in § 3–110, *ante*.

[82] *Hardwick v. Johnson* [1978] 1 W.L.R. 683 (where the creditor was said at 691 to have agreed to "postpone" the debtor's obligation to pay instalments).

[83] [1955] 1 W.L.R. 761; Smith (1955) 18 M.L.R. 609.

[84] (1877) 2 App.Cas. 439; *ante* § 3–080.

[85] *Ante* § 3–092.

[86] *ibid.*

aspect of the principle could be applied to cases of the present kind, with the result that the promise becomes "final and irrevocable if the promisee cannot resume his position."[87] Thus the creditor's right to the balance of a debt might be extinguished if in reliance on his promise the debtor had undertaken new commitments in relation to the subject-matter: if, for example, the tenant in the *High Trees* case had used the rebate to modernise the flats.[88]

3–125   In *Brikom Investments Ltd v. Carr*[89] long leases of flats obliged the tenants to pay, not only rent and a maintenance charge, but also contributions in respect of certain "excess expenses" incurred by the landlords in keeping the structure in repair. In the course of the negotiations leading to the execution of the leases, the landlords had promised to put the roof into repair "at our own cost." This was held to amount to a collateral contract[90] with one of the original tenants, precluding the landlords from enforcing against her the provision in the lease requiring her to contribute to the cost of the roof repairs. It was further held that claims for contributions to the cost of those repairs could not be made against assignees and sub-assignees of original tenants, even though there was no collateral contract with these persons. Lord Denning M.R. based this conclusion on the *High Trees* principle which, in his view, was available not only between the original parties, but also in favour of and against their assigns.[91] The extinctive effect of the principle in these circumstances can perhaps be supported on the ground that the original tenants, the assignees and the sub-assignees had all, in reliance on the landlords' promise, undertaken fresh commitments by entering into long leases of the flats. Roskill and Cumming-Bruce L.JJ., on the other hand, treated the case, not as one of "promissory estoppel,"[92] but as one of "waiver."[93] It seems that the latter expression here refers to a variation supported by consideration,[94] for the consideration provided by the tenants[95] could equally support the landlords' promise whether that promise was regarded as a collateral contract or as a variation. On this interpretation of the case, there is no difficulty in accounting for the extinctive effect of the landlords' promise. It amounted to a variation supported by consideration, so that the liability of the original tenants to contribute to the cost of the repairs in question was extinguished; and once it had been so extinguished it was not revived on assignment of the leases.

3–126   **Requirements.** Granted that the equitable principle can apply to cases of part payment of a debt, it is in this context subject to the usual requirements on which

---

[87] *Ajayi v. R.T. Briscoe (Nig.) Ltd* [1964] 1 W.L.R. 1326, 1330.

[88] *cf.* Mitchell (1951) Univ. of W. Australia Law Rev. 245, 251. The principle is somewhat similar to that which underlies the defence of "change of position" in an action for the recovery of money paid; for recognition of this defence, see *Lipkin Gorman v. Karpnale Ltd* [1991] 2 A.C. 548; *post* § 30–114.

[89] [1979] Q.B. 467.

[90] *Ante*, § 3–075.

[91] [1979] Q.B. 467, 484–485.

[92] *ibid.* at 485, 490.

[93] *ibid.* at 488, 490.

[94] *cf. ante*, § 3–076.

[95] *Ante*, § 3–075. Roskill L.J. at 489 refers to *Hughes v. Metropolitan Ry.* (1877) 2 App.Cas. 439 (*ante*, § 3–080) as stating a principle of "contractual variation of strict contractual rights." It is respectfully submitted that this phrase should be interpreted to refer simply to *variations of contracts*, rather than to *contractually binding variations*; for the principle clearly applies to variations which are not contractually binding (but revocable on reasonable notice) because they are not supported by consideration.

its operation depends. These have already been considered[96] but two of them call for further discussion at this point.

Whether detriment necessary. The equitable principle is sometimes said to **3–127** be analogous to the doctrine of estoppel by representation.[97] According to this analogy the principle would operate only in favour of a person who had suffered some "detriment" in the sense in which that word is used in that branch of the law.[98] A tenant who pays only half the agreed rent suffers no such "detriment"; and although ingenious attempts have been made to find some other "detriment" in the *High Trees* case,[99] the better view is that "detriment" of the kind required for the purpose of estoppel by representation is not an essential requirement of the operation of the equitable principle.[1] This is the position under the rule in *Hughes v. Metropolitan Ry.*[2] on which the *High Trees* case is based. All that is necessary is that the promisee should have acted in reliance on the promise in such a way as to make it inequitable to allow the promisor to act inconsistently with it.[3] This requirement was satisfied on the facts of the *High Trees* case, no less than on those of *Hughes v. Metropolitan Ry.*

Inequitable. By making the part payment, the debtor acts in reliance on the **3–128** creditor's promise, and so normally makes it "inequitable" for the creditor peremptorily to go back on his promise. But other circumstances may lead to the conclusion that it would not be "inequitable" for the creditor to reassert his claim for the full amount[4]: this would, for example, be the position where the debtor had failed to perform his promise to pay the smaller amount.[5] This possibility may be illustrated by further reference to *D. & C. Builders Ltd v. Rees.*[6] Lord Denning M.R. there stressed the fact that the builders' promise to accept £300 in full settlement of their claim for £482 had been obtained by taking undue advantage of their desperate financial position. In these circumstances it was not "inequitable" for the builders to go back on their promise, so that the *High Trees* principle did not apply. The difficulty with this reasoning is that most debtors who offer part payment in full settlement try to exert some kind of "pressure" against their creditors. The law now recognises that it is possible for such "pressure" to amount to duress,[7] and where it has this effect, a promise obtained as a result of it should clearly not bring the *High Trees* principle into effect. Where, on the other hand, there is no duress, the *High Trees* principle should not be excluded merely because it could be said that the promise has been "improperly obtained." Such an intermediate category between promises obtained by

---

[96] *Ante*, §§ 3–081 *et seq.*

[97] *Ante*, § 3–095.

[98] *cf. ante*, § 3–089.

[99] Wilson (1951) 67 L.Q.R. 330, 344.

[1] *cf.* Denning (1952) 15 M.L.R. 1, 6–8.

[2] (1877) 2 App.Cas. 439.

[3] *Ante*, § 3–090; *Tool Metal* case [1955] 1 W.L.R. 761, 764; *Beesly v. Hallwood Estates Ltd* [1960] 1 W.L.R. 548, 560; affd. [1961] Ch. 105; *Ajayi v. R.T. Briscoe (Nig.) Ltd* [1964] 1 W.L.R. 1326, 1330.

[4] *cf. ante*, § 3–092.

[5] *Re Selectmove* [1995] 1 W.L.R. 474, 481, where the debtor's promise was not to pay *less* but to pay *late*; *cf. Burrows v. Brent L.B.C.* [1996] 1 W.L.R. 1448, where decision was based on lack of contractual intention so that neither consideration or the equitable doctrine was discussed.

[6] [1966] 2 Q.B. 617; *ante* § 3–108; Winder (1966) 82 L.Q.R. 165; *cf. Arrale v. Costain Civil Engineering Ltd* [1976] 1 Lloyd's Rep. 98, 102.

[7] *Post*, § 7–010.

duress and those not so obtained should here, as elsewhere,[8] be rejected as "unhelpful because it would render the law uncertain."[9]

11. Proprietary Estoppel

(a) *Nature of the Doctrine*

3–129　　**Introductory.** Proprietary estoppel is said to arise in certain situations in which a person has done acts in reliance on the belief that he has, or that he will acquire, rights in or over another's land. Usually, but not invariably, these acts consist of erecting buildings on, or making other improvements to, the land in question. Where the requirements of proprietary estoppel are satisfied, the land-owner is precluded from denying the existence of the rights in question, and may indeed be compelled to grant them. Because the estoppel precludes him from denying the existence of rights in property, it has come to be known as "proprie-tary estoppel."[10] It is distinct[11] from promissory estoppel, both in the conditions which must be satisfied before it comes into operation and in its effects. But under both doctrines some legal effects are given to promises which are not contractually binding for want of consideration; and it is this aspect[12] of proprie-tary estoppel which calls for discussion in the present chapter.

3–130　　**Scope of proprietary estoppel.** Proprietary estoppel operates in a variety of cases so disparate that it has been described as "an amalgam of doubtful utility."[13] The cases can be divided broadly into two categories. In the first, one person acts under a mistake as to the existence or as to the extent of his rights in or over another's land. Even though the mistake was in no way induced by the landowner, he might be prevented from taking advantage of it, particularly if he "stood by" knowing of the mistake, or actively encouraged the mistaken party to act in reliance on his mistaken belief.[14] These cases of so-called "acquies-cence"[15] do not raise any questions as to the enforceability of promises and therefore do not call for further discussion in this chapter.[16] In the second situation, there is not merely "acquiescence" by the landowner, but "encourage-ment:"[17] that is, conduct by the landowner, or a representation by him, from

---

[8] *Ante*, § 3–062.

[9] *Pao On v. Lau Yiu Long* [1980] A.C. 614, 634.

[10] *Jones v. Jones* [1977] 1 W.L.R. 438, 442; *Pascoe v. Turner* [1979] 1 W.L.R. 431, 436; *Re Sharpe* [1980] 1 W.L.R. 219, 233; *Greasley v. Cooke* [1980] 1 W.L.R. 1306, 1311; *cf. Midland Bank plc v. Cooke* [1995] 4 All E.R. 564, 573 ("equities in the nature of an estoppel").

[11] *Fontana N.V. v. Mautner* (1980) 254 E.G. 199, 207; and see *post*, §§ 3–148—3–151.

[12] For wider discussions see Davies (1979) 8 Sydney L.Rev. 200 and (1980) 7 Adelaide L.Rev. 200; Moriarty (1984) 100 L.Q.R. 376; Smith in (ed. Rose) *Consensus ad Idem: Essays in the Law of Contract in Honour of Guenter Treitel*, p. 235 (1996).

[13] *Amalgamated Investment & Property Co. Ltd v. Texas Commerce International Bank Ltd* [1982] Q.B. 84, 103.

[14] *Wilmott v. Barber* (1880) 15 Ch.D. 96; *cf. Taylors Fashions Ltd v. Liverpool Victoria Trustee Co. Ltd* [1982] Q.B. 133 note; *Coombes v. Smith* [1986] 1 W.L.R. 808; *Matharu v. Matharu, The Times,* May 13, 1994.

[15] *Wilmott v. Barber* (1880) 15 Ch.D. 96, 105.

[16] See *post*, § 30–108.

[17] *Ramsden v. Dyson* (1866) L.R. 1 H.L. 129, 170; *cf. Att.-Gen. of Hong Kong v. Humphreys Estates (Queen's Gardens)* [1987] 1 A.C. 114 (where this requirement was not satisfied: *post*, § 3–135).

which a promise to the other party (the promisee) can be inferred[18] to the effect
that the promisee has a legally enforceable[19] interest in the land or that one will
be created in his favour. If the other party acts in reliance on such a promise, the
question will arise to what extent the promise can be enforced, even though it
may not be supported by consideration, or fail to satisfy the other requirements
(such as certainty) of a binding contract.

(b) *Bases of Liability*

Expenditure on another's land in reliance on a promise. In *Dillwyn v.*   **3–131**
Llewelyn[20] a father executed a memorandum "presenting" a named estate to his
son "for the purpose of furnishing himself with a dwelling house." The son spent
£14,000 in building a house on the land; and it was held (after the father's death)
that he was entitled to have the fee simple of the estate conveyed to him. Many
later cases similarly give some degree of legal enforceability to a promise by a
landowner in reliance on which the promisee has spent money on making
improvements to the promisor's land: for example, where A built a bungalow on
B's land in reliance on B's promise that A could stay there for the rest of his
life[21]; where B purported to make a gift of a cottage to her son A "provided he
did it up" and A incurred considerable expense in doing so[22]; where A spent
money on extending or improving B's house in reliance on a similar promise by
B[23]; where, in reliance on such a promise, A actually did the work of improvement him- or herself[24]; and where a tenant, whose lease had been terminated,
spent money on improving the premises in reliance on the landlord's promise to
grant him a new lease.[25] Cases of this kind can be explained on the basis of unjust
enrichment: in all of them, the landowner would benefit unjustly if he were
allowed to disregard his promise and to take back the land after he had induced
the promisee to make improvements to it. This explanation is, perhaps, reflected
in statements found in some modern cases that the liability is based on "an
implied or constructive trust."[26] But the unjust enrichment explanation will not
account for cases in which the doctrine has been applied even though the
promisee's expenditure on another's land did not result in any benefit at all to the
owner of that land.[27] It follows that, although unjust enrichment of the promisor

---

[18] See *Lloyd's Bank plc v. Rosset* [1991] 1 A.C. 107 (where this requirement was not satisfied).
[19] *Coombes v. Smith* [1986] 1 W.L.R. 808 (where there was no belief in the existence of a *legally enforceable* right); and *cf. Brinand v. Ewens* (1987) 19 H.L.R. 415.
[20] (1862) 4 D.F. & G. 517.
[21] *Inwards v. Baker* [1965] 2 Q.B. 507.
[22] *Voyce v. Voyce* (1991) 62 P. & C.R. 290.
[23] *Hussey v. Palmer* [1972] 1 W.L.R. 1286; *Pascoe v. Turner* [1979] 1 W.L.R. 431; *Durrant v. Heritage* [1994] E.G.C.S. 134; *semble* spending money on mere maintenance would not suffice: *Griffiths v. Williams* [1978] E.G.D. 919. *cf. Maharaj v. Chand* [1986] A.C. 898 (where, because of local legislation, proprietary estoppel was not argued).
[24] *Eves v. Eves* [1975] 1 W.L.R. 1338; *Jones v. Jones* [1977] 1 W.L.R. 438; *Ungurian v. Lesnoff* [1990] Ch. 206; *Clough v. Kelly* (1996) 72 P. & C.R. D22 (where the claimant had also spent money on the premises).
[25] *J.T. Developments v. Quinn* (1991) 62 P. & C.R. 33.
[26] *Sen v. Headley* [1991] Ch. 425, 440; *Re Dale* [1994] Ch. 31, 47; *Lloyd's Bank plc v. Carrick* [1996] 4 All E.R. 632, 640; *cf. Drake v. Whipp* (1996) 28 H.L.R. 531.
[27] *Canadian Pacific Railway v. The King* [1931] A.C. 414; *Armstrong v. Sheppard & Short* [1959] 2 Q.B. 384.

may be the most obvious basis of proprietary estoppel, it cannot provide complete explanation of the doctrine.

3–132   **Other acts done in reliance on the promise.** The operation of proprietary estoppel is not confined to cases in which the promisee has incurred expenditure on, or done work to, the promisor's land. It can also apply where the promisee has conferred some other benefit on the promisor[28]; and even where no work has been done on the promisor's land and he has not received any other benefit. This indeed appears from one of the illustrations given by Lord Westbury in *Dillwyn v. Llewelyn*: if "A gives a house to B, but makes no formal conveyance, and the house is afterwards included, with the knowledge of A, in the marriage settlement of B, A would be bound to complete the title of the parties claiming under the settlement."[29] Similarly, the doctrine operated in the absence of any expenditure on the promisor's land in *Crabb v. Arun DC*[30] In that case A (a local authority) by its conduct represented to B that B had a right of way from his land over adjoining land owned by A. In reliance on that representation, B sold part of his own land, so that the only access from the remainder to the nearest public highway was by means of the right of way across A's land. It was held that B had a right to cross A's land for the purpose of access to his retained land. Detrimental reliance by the promisee can therefore give rise to a proprietary estoppel even though no benefit is conferred on the promisor.[31]

3–133   **Alternative explanation: contract.** In *Dillwyn v. Llewelyn* Lord Westbury, while referring to the parties of the transaction as "donor" and "donee" also said that the son's expenditure "supplied a valuable consideration originally wanting"[32]; and in discussing a hypothetical example similar to the facts of the case before him he concluded "that the donee acquires a right from the subsequent transaction to call upon the donor to perform that contract and to complete the imperfect donation."[33] These passages may suggest that he regarded the memorandum as a kind of unilateral contract by which the father promised to convey the land if the son built a house on it. The terms of the memorandum make it improbable that a modern court would so regard it; it is more likely that these terms would now be regarded as negativing contractual intention.[34] However, in

---

[28] *e.g. Tanner v. Tanner* [1975] 1 W.L.R. 1346 (services rendered to promisor in managing his property); *Greasley v. Cooke* [1980] 1 W.L.R. 1306 (personal and nursing services); *Wayling v. Jones* (1993) 69 P. & C.R. 170 (services rendered to promisor for virtually no pay); *cf. Plimmer v. Mayor of Wellington* (1884) 9 App.Cas. 699 and *E.R. Ives Investments Ltd v. High* [1967] 2 Q.B. 379 (where the landowner benefited from improvements to his land but also—and more significantly—in other ways); *cf. Grant v. Edwards* [1986] Ch. 638, 657; contrast *Howard v. Jones* (1988) 19 Fam. Law 231 (contribution to running costs of *another* property insufficient).

[29] (1862) 4 D.F. & G. 517, 521.

[30] [1976] Ch. 179. The case was described in *Amalgamated Investment & Property Co. Ltd v. Texas Commerce International Bank Ltd* [1982] Q.B. 84, 121 as one of "estoppel by convention"; but this would require a dealing between A and B on the basis of a common assumption (*ante*, §§ 3–101, 3–102, while in *Crabb's* case the dealing was between B and the purchaser from him. In *Waltons Stores (Interstate) Ltd v. Maher* (1988) 164 C.L.R. 387, 403, *Crabb's* case was described as one of "promissory estoppel" (see *ante*, § 3–080); but the requirements of that doctrine (in particular, the requirement of a pre-existing legal relationship: *ante*, § 3–083) were not satisfied in *Crabb's* case, and the effect of the estoppel differed from promissory estoppel in giving rise to a new right: *cf. ante*, § 3–093.

[31] *cf. Hammersmith & Fulham B.C. v. Top Shop Centres Ltd* [1990] Ch. 237.

[32] (1862) 4 D. F. & G. 517, 521.

[33] *ibid.* at 522.

[34] *Ante*, § 2–154.

a number of later cases the rights of a person who has expended money on the property of another have been explained as being based on contract[35]; and often such an explanation is sufficiently plausible to make reliance on a doctrine of proprietary estoppel unnecessary.[36] A unilateral contract to transfer an interest in land has been held to arise out of a promise to make the transfer if the promisee would pay instalments due under a mortgage on the house[37]; it can equally arise out of a promise to make the transfer if the promisee will make improvements to the land, or indeed do any other act.[38]

But there are, it is submitted, obstacles to treating all cases of proprietary   **3–134**
estoppel as depending on contract. One, already mentioned, is that the promises in cases of this kind are often made in a family context, without contractual intention. Another is that the promise may lack consideration because the party relying on the estoppel made no counter-promise and so incurred no obligation, and that the arrangement was one in which it would not be in accordance with the intention of the parties to treat it as a unilateral contract.[39] A third is that the terms of the alleged contract are often too vague to satisfy the requirement of certainty.[40] This difficulty accounts for the view of the Court of Appeal that there was no contract in *Crabb v. Arun DC*[41]: there may have been an implied promise to grant the claimant some right of way across the defendant's land, but no financial or other terms were specified in that promise, so that it would not (even if supported by consideration) have been sufficiently certain to give rise to a contract. Finally, many arrangements which can give rise to proprietary estoppel are made without any attempt to comply with the stringent formal requirements now imposed on the making of contracts for the disposition of interests in land.[42] Failure to comply with these requirements will not prevent such arrangements from giving rise to a proprietary estoppel,[43] but it will prevent them from taking effect as contracts. The possibility of explaining proprietary estoppel on the basis

---

[35] *e.g. Plimmer v. Mayor of Wellington* (1884) 9 App.Cas. 699 as explained in *Canadian Pacific Railway v. The King* [1931] A.C. 414, 428; *Eves v. Eves* [1975] 1 W.L.R. 1338; *Tanner v. Tanner* [1975] 1 W.L.R. 1346; *cf. Re Sharpe* [1980] 1 W.L.R. 219, 224; and see *E.R. Ives Investments Ltd v. High* [1967] 2 Q.B. 379 (where there was a contract between the defendant and the claimant's predecessor in title).

[36] See *Lloyd's Bank plc v. Carrick* [1996] 4 All E.R. 632, where the existence of a contract of sale precluded reliance by the purchaser on proprietary estoppel, even though that contract was, as against a bank to which the property had been charged as security, void for non-registration.

[37] *Errington v. Errington* [1952] 1 Q.B. 290; *ante,* § 2–073.

[38] *e.g. Tanner v. Tanner* [1975] 1 W.L.R. 1346; merely to maintain the house in repair could be sufficient for the present purpose, even if it did not suffice to raise a proprietary estoppel: see *supra,* n. 00.

[39] *J.T. Developments v. Quinn* (1991) 62 P. & C.R. 33; *Gillett v. Holt* [1998] 3 All E.R. 917, 929–930.

[40] *Ante,* § 3–132.

[41] [1976] Ch. 179; Atiyah (1974) 92 L.Q.R. 174 criticises the view that there was no contract but the argument is based on the fallacy that, merely because a promise has *some* legal effects, it must necessarily have *all* the effects of a contract: *cf. ante,* §§ 3–012, 3–098 and *post,* § 3–152. The alleged contract in *Crabb's* case would, quite apart from lacking consideration, be impossibly vague: see *ante,* § 2–128 and *cf.* Millett (1976) 92 L.Q.R. 342; Duncanson (1976) 39 M.L.R. 268.

[42] Law of Property (Miscellaneous Provisions) Act 1989, s.2(1)–(3). Previously the contract could be *made* informally, but Law of Property Act 1925, s.40 (replacing part of Statute of Frauds 1677, s.4, and now repealed) had required either a note or memorandum in writing as evidence of the contract, or "part performance" of the contract. The latter requirement was often satisfied by the conduct of the promisee giving rise to proprietary estoppel. *cf.* the reference to "part performance" in *Dillwyn v. Llewelyn* (1862) 4 D.F. & G. 517, 521.

[43] *cf.* Law Com. No. 164 (1987) § 5.5.

of contract is therefore in practice likely to be restricted to cases where the arrangement does *not* purport to dispose of an interest in land: *e.g.* where it amounts to no more than a promise to grant a licence to occupy the land.[44]

(c) *Conditions giving rise to Liability*

3–135 **Kinds of promises capable of giving rise to a proprietary estoppel.** A promise may give rise to a proprietary estoppel even though it is not express but is implied: for example, from the fact that the parties acted on the common assumption that one of them was to have the right to reside on the other's property.[45] The promise must be of such a kind that it is reasonable for the promisee to rely on it; the promisor must have been aware of the fact that the promisee would so rely on it[46]; and it must induce the promisee to believe that a legal right has been, or will be, created in his favour. It follows that a promise will not give rise to proprietary estoppel if it expressly disclaims legal effect: for example, in one case[47] it was held that no proprietary estoppel arose out of an agreement for the transfer of a number of flats "subject to contract," it being well known that the effect of these words was to negative the intention to be legally bound.[48] The promisee may have formed "the confident and not unreasonable hope"[49] that the promise would not be withdrawn; but no *belief* to this effect had been encouraged[50] by the promisor or relied on by the promisee. It seems that a proprietary estoppel could arise out of such an agreement if one of the parties *did* encourage such a belief in the other and the other acted to his detriment in reliance on that belief.[51] Similar reasoning applies where the promise in terms reserves a right to the promisor wholly to revoke the promise. Thus where a landowner promised her part-time gardener to leave him her house in her will but told him "not to count his chickens before they were hatched", it was held that no proprietary estoppel arose when, after having made a will in his favour, she then revoked it and made another leaving the property to someone else.[52] The position is the same where the promise, even though it does not in terms reserve

---

[44] The earlier legislation referred to in n. 42, *supra* did not apply to a licence to occupy land: *Wright v. Stavert* (1860) 2 E. & E. 721; *cf. Taylor v. Waters* (1816) 7 Taunt. 374 (licence to use opera box). The position seems to be the same under Law of Property (Miscellaneous Provisions) Act 1989, s.2(6).

[45] *e.g. Re Sharpe* [1980] 1 W.L.R. 219.

[46] *Gillett v. Holt* [1998] 3 All E.R. 917, 930.

[47] *Att.-Gen. of Hong Kong v. Humphreys Estates (Queen's Gardens)* [1987] 1 A.C. 114; the case was said in *Waltons Stores (Interstate) Ltd v. Maher* (1988) 164 C.L.R. 387, 404 to be "not a case of proprietary estoppel" but (apparently) one of *promissory* estoppel. But most of the authorities relied on in the *Humphreys Estates* case were cases of proprietary estoppel; the leading cases on promissory estoppel were not cited; and if the requirements of encouragement and reliance had been satisfied the estoppel would have created a new right, which in English law is not the effect of promissory estoppel: *ante* § 3–093. *cf. Saloman v. Akiens* [1993] 1 E.G.L.R. 101 (no proprietary estoppel arising from agreement "subject to lease"); *Pridean Ltd v. Forest Taverns* (1998) 75 P. & C.R. 447 (no proprietary estoppel arising from work done during negotiations which failed to lead to a contract).

[48] *Ante,* § 2–108.

[49] [1987] 1 A.C. 114, 124.

[50] *cf. ante* § 3–130; *Brinnand v. Ewens* (1987) 19 H.L.R. 415; and (in a different context) *Kelly v. Liverpool Maritime Terminals* [1988] I.R.L.R. 310, where authorities on proprietary estoppel are cited in a case unconnected with property).

[51] This is assumed in *Att.-Gen. of Hong Kong v. Humphreys Estate (Queen's Gardens),* n. 49, *supra*, where the Privy Council at 124 stresses that there had been *no* such encouragement.

[52] *Taylor v. Dickens* [1998] FLR 806.

a power of revocation, is in its nature irrevocable: thus the mere statement by A that he has made or that he will make a will in favour of B does not suffice to give rise to a proprietary estoppel since it is well known that wills are revocable and that testamentary intentions are liable to change.[53] A proprietary estoppel would arise out of a statement of this kind only if it went beyond a mere statement of such intention and could reasonably be regarded as an irrevocable promise by A as to the way in which he was going to dispose by will of his property.[54]

Promise must generally be to create rights in or over promisor's prop-   3–136
erty. The right which the promisee believes to have been created must, as a general rule, be rights in or over the property of the promisor. Thus a representation by a planning authority to the effect that a landowner does not need permission to carry out development on his *own* land is not capable of giving rise to a proprietary estoppel.[55] The promisor may, however, make two promises, of which the first relates to the promisor's land while the second relates to that of the promisee; and the two promises may be so closely linked as to form in substance a single transaction. If the doctrine of proprietary estoppel applies to that transaction as a whole, then it can provide the promisee with a remedy in respect of the second promise even though that promise, standing alone, could not have given rise to proprietary estoppel because it related only to the promisee's land. In one case,[56] for example, A promised B (1) to sell Blackacre to B to enable B to build on it, and (2) to buy Whiteacre from B so that B could pay for the building operations on Blackacre. B carried out the building work envisaged in the first of A's promises and it was held that the doctrine of proprietary estoppel provided B with a remedy in respect of the second promise (which had no contractual force), even though that promise related only to B's land. But it was recognised that the doctrine could not have applied to the second promise if it had stood alone and not formed part of a transaction also relating to A's land.[57] It could not, for example, have applied if A had simply made a non-contractual promise to B to buy Whiteacre from B, knowing that B intended to use the proceeds of the sale to buy shares from C, and if B had then entered into a contract to that effect with C. Normally, the doctrine applies to promises to *grant* rights in land *to* the promisee; it only applies to promises to *acquire* such rights *from* him where they are inextricably linked with promises of the former kind.

Subject-matter of the promise. In the cases to which the doctrine has so far   3–137
been applied, the subject-matter of the promise has always been (or at least included[58]) land. The question whether a promise can give rise to proprietary estoppel where its subject-matter is property of some other kind remains an open one.[59] Even if the doctrine is extended to such promises, its scope will in one

---

[53] *Gillett v. Holt* [1998] 3 All E.R. 917.
[54] *ibid.* 930.
[55] *Western Fish Products Ltd v. Penwith DC* [1981] 2 All E.R. 204 (decided in 1978); *cf. Lloyd's Bank plc v. Carrick* [1996] 4 All E.R. 632 (no proprietary estoppel in favour of a purchaser of land as by virtue of the contract he had become equitable owner of the land).
[56] *Salvation Army Trustee Co. v. West Yorks Metropolitan C.C.* (1981) 41 P. & C.R. 179.
[57] *ibid.* at 191; the case was approved but distinguished in *Att.-Gen. of Hong Kong v. Humphreys Estates (Queen's Gardens)* [1987] A.C. 114, 126–127.
[58] *Re Basham* [1987] 1 W.L.R. 1498.
[59] *Western Fish case, supra,* n. 55 at 217; *cf.* the reference *ibid.* at 218, and in *Crabb v. Arun DC* [1976] Ch. 179, 187, to the decision of the Court of Appeal in *Moorgate Mercantile Co. v. Twitchings* [1976] Q.B. 225; that decision was reversed by the House of Lords: [1977] A.C. 890.

respect remain narrower than that of so-called promissory estoppel[60]: it is essential that the promisee should be induced to believe that he will acquire an interest in the property that is the subject-matter of the promise. It is not enough that the promise should merely (in some other way) relate to property: for example, the doctrine of proprietary estoppel would not apply on the facts of *Central London Property Trust v. High Trees House Ltd.*[61]

3–138   **Detrimental reliance.** The promisee must have relied on the promise or representation to his detriment.[62] The requirement has been doubted[63]; but in the absence of any such reliance it is hard to see why failure to perform a merely gratuitous promise should be regarded as giving rise to any legal liability. The existence of the requirement is also supported by the rules (to be discussed in § 3–140 below) as to the revocability of the promise. Where a promise has been made which is capable of inducing detrimental reliance, and which is in fact followed by such reliance, the question may arise whether the reliance was actually induced by the promise. The burden on this issue is on the promisor: that is, it is up to the promisor, in order to escape liability, to show that the promisee would have done the acts in question anyway (even if the promise had not been made).[64] The position appears to be different where a proprietary estoppel arises because both parties have acted under a mistake as to their rights in the land.[65] Here it seems to be up to the party relying on the proprietary estoppel to show that his conduct in relation to the property was in fact induced by his belief that he had an interest in it.[66]

3–139   **Whether reliance must relate to specific property.** The authorities are divided on the further question whether, to give rise to a proprietary estoppel, the reliance must relate to identifiable property. According to one case, the promisee's conduct must relate to "some specific asset" in which an interest is claimed; so that proprietary estoppel did not arise merely because B rendered services to A in the expectation of receiving some indeterminate benefit under A's will.[67] But in another case reliance on a similar expectation (induced by A's promise) was held sufficient even though it did not relate to any "particular property."[68] The latter case can perhaps be explained on the ground that the promise did to

---

[60] See *ante*, §§ 3–080, 3–095, 3–120.

[61] [1947] K.B. 130; *ante*, § 3–120.

[62] This was the view of the majority of the Court of Appeal in *Greasley v. Cooke* [1980] 1 W.L.R. 1306; the requirement is assumed to exist in *Taylors Fashions Ltd v. Liverpool Victoria Trustee Co. Ltd* [1982] Q.B. 133n, and stated in *Grant v. Edwards* [1986] Ch. 638, 657; *cf. Lloyds Bank plc v. Rosset* [1991] 1 A.C. 107, 132; *Hammond v. Mitchell* [1991] 1 W.L.R. 1127. The fact that there was no such reliance was one reason why the claim based on proprietary estoppel failed in *Western Fish Products Ltd v. Penwith DC* [1981] 2 All E.R. 204, see 217; in *Coombes v. Smith* [1986] 1 W.L.R. 808; and in *Att.-Gen. of Hong Kong v. Humphreys Estates (Queen's Gardens)* [1987] A.C. 114; *cf. Mecca Leisure v. The London Residuary Body* [1988] C.L.Y. 1375; *Jones v. Stones, The Times*, June 3, 1999.

[63] By Lord Denning M.R. in *Greasley v. Cooke, supra* at 1311.

[64] *Greasley v. Cooke, supra; Grant v. Edwards* [1986] Ch. 638, 657; *Re Basham* [1986] 1 W.L.R. 1498; *Hammersmith & Fulham B.C. v. Top Shop Centres Ltd* [1990] Ch. 237; *Wayling v. Jones* (1993) 69 P. & C.R. 170, 172.

[65] *Ante*, § 3–130.

[66] *Taylors Fashions Ltd v. Liverpool Victoria Trustee Co. Ltd* [1982] Q.B. 133 note; *cf. Coombes v. Smith* [1986] 1 W.L.R. 808.

[67] *Layton v. Martin* [1986] 2 F.L.R. 277.

[68] *Re Basham* [1986] 1 W.L.R. 1498, 1508; *cf. Gillett v. Holt* [1998] 3 All E.R. 917, 920, leaving open the question whether proprietary estoppel can arise out of a simple promise to leave a person the promisor's residuary estate.

some extent identify the property.[69] It is submitted that the view that the promise must relate to identified or identifiable property is to be preferred; for without some such limitation on the scope of proprietary estoppel the doctrine could extend to any gift promise on which the promisee had relied to his detriment. Such a very broad doctrine would be fundamentally inconsistent with the doctrine of consideration[70] and, indeed, with the rule that the doctrine of promissory estoppel gives rise to no new rights.[71]

(d) *Effects of the Doctrine*

Revocability. We have seen that proprietary estoppel will not arise at all **3–140** where the promise to confer a benefit on the promisee is revocable in the sense that it reserves a power to the promisor wholly to deprive the promisee of that benefit.[72] But even where the promise does not allow the promisor do this, and so is capable of giving rise to a proprietary estoppel, the extent of the promisee's rights under the estoppel may be limited by terms of the promise giving the promisor a power of putting an end to those rights. Thus if the landowner promises to allow the promisee to stay on the land "until I decide to sell," then the promisee cannot, merely by spending money on improvements to the land, acquire any right to stay there for a longer period.[73] Even where the promise is not expressed to be revocable, it can be revoked before the promisee has acted on it. Thus in *Dillwyn v. Llewelyn*[74] it seems that the father could have revoked his promise before the son had started to build on the land[75]; and in *Crabb v. Arun DC*[76] the promise to grant a right of way could have been revoked before the promisee, by selling off part of his land, had made it impossible for himself to obtain access to the retained land except by means of the promised right of way. In this respect proprietary estoppel resembles so-called promissory estoppel (under which promises are similarly revocable[77]) and differs from contractually binding promises which are not revocable unless they expressly, or impliedly, so provide. The cases on proprietary estoppel assume that, once the promisee has acted on the representation, he cannot be restored to his original position. Where he has made improvements to land, this will generally be the case. Where a restoration of the status quo is physically possible, it seems that a promise giving rise to a proprietary estoppel could be revoked, even after the promisee had acted on it, provided that the promisor in fact restored the promisee to the position in which he was before he had acted in reliance on the promise.

A promise which has given rise to proprietary estoppel may also be none the less revocable, because the court considers it appropriate in this way to limit the effect to be given to the promise. The situation is discussed in § 3–142 below.[78]

---

[69] By referring to the promisor's cottage.

[70] *e.g. ante*, §§ 3–002, 3–025.

[71] *Ante*, § 3–093.

[72] *Ante*, § 3–135.

[73] *E. & L. Berg Homes v. Gray* (1979) 253 E.G. 473.

[74] (1862) D. F. & G. 517; *ante*, § 3–131.

[75] *cf. Pascoe v. Turner* [1979] 1 W.L.R. 431, 435 (where before the promisee's action in reliance on the promise she was said to be only a licensee at will).

[76] [1976] Ch. 179; *ante*, § 3–132.

[77] *Ante*, § 3–091.

[78] At n. 86.

3–141   **Operation of a proprietary estoppel.** Granted that the conditions required to give rise to a proprietary estoppel have been satisfied, the effect of the doctrine is said to be to confer an "equity" on the promisee. Two further questions then arise: namely, what is the extent of that "equity," and what are the remedies for its enforcement.[79] In practice these questions tend to merge into each other; but an attempt to discuss them in turn will be made in §§ 3–142 to 3–144 and 3–145 to 3–147 below.

3–142   **Extent of the equity.** At one extreme, the promisee may be entitled to conveyance of the fee simple in the property which is the subject-matter of the promise, as in *Dillwyn v. Llewelyn.*[80] On the other hand, in *Inwards v. Baker,*[81] where a son had also built a house for himself at his father's suggestion on the latter's land, the result of the estoppel was only to entitle the son to occupy the house for life. Similar results were reached in a number of later cases in which the promisee made improvements to the promisor's property (or otherwise acted to his detriment) in reliance on a promise, or common understanding, that the promisee would be able to reside in the property for as long as he or she wished to do so[82]; or for some shorter period: *e.g.* until her children had left school[83]; or that a lease of the premises would be granted to him.[84] Such cases can be reconciled with *Dillwyn v. Llewelyn* by reference to the terms of the respective promises: in the former case, the promise was expressed in terms of a gift of the property, while in the latter cases it amounted to no more than an assurance that the promisee would be entitled to reside in the property for the specified period. Another way of giving effect to a promise of the latter kind is by the grant of a long, non-assignable lease at a nominal rent, on terms that ensured that the right of occupation was personal to the promisee.[85] In other cases, not concerned with rights of personal occupation but with the right to keep and use structures on promisor's land, the promisee has been held entitled only to a revocable licence.[86]

3–143   **Estoppel available against third party donee.** Where the circumstances are such as to give rise to an estoppel against the landowner, the estoppel is equally available against a third party who claims later to have obtained title to the land by way of gift from the landowner.[87]

3–144   **Estoppel may operate conditionally.** The estoppel may operate conditionally where the promisee has acted in reliance on the promise but it is clear from the terms of the promise that the promisor did not intend to give up his title to the land gratuitously. This was the position in *Lim Teng Huan v. Ang Swee*

---

[79] *Crabb v. Arun DC* [1976] Ch. 179, 193, *per* Scarman L.J.
[80] (1862) D. F. & G. 517; *ante,* § 3–131 or, in the exceptional cases discussed in § 3–136, n. 56, to an order requiring the promisor to *acquire* the promisee's land.
[81] [1965] 2 Q.B. 507; *ante,* § 3–131, n. 21.
[82] *Jones v. Jones* [1977] 1 W.L.R. 438; *Re Sharpe* [1980] 1 W.L.R. 219; *Greasley v. Cooke* [1980] 1 W.L.R. 1306.
[83] *Tanner v. Tanner* [1975] 1 W.L.R. 1346 (where there was a contract: *cf. ante,* § 3–133).
[84] *J.T. Developments v. Quinn* (1991) 62 P. & C.R. 33.
[85] *Griffiths v. Williams* [1978] E.G.D. 919; *cf. Jones v. Jones* [1977] 1 W.L.R. 438.
[86] *Canadian Pacific Railway v. The King* [1931] A.C. 414; *Armstrong v. Sheppard & Short* [1959] Q.B. 384.
[87] *Voyce v. Voyce* (1991) 62 P. & C.R. 290.

Chuan[88] where A built a house on land jointly owned by him and L, who had agreed that he was to have no title to the house and would exchange his share in the land for other land. The arrangement had no contractual force as the other land was not identified with sufficient certainty; and it was held that L was estopped from asserting title to the house but that he was entitled to be compensated for the loss of his share in the land. Similarly, where the promise is one to allow the promisee access to his own land over that of the promisor, the effect of the proprietary estoppel will be to entitle the promisee to an easement or licence on terms.[89] Such terms, if not agreed between the parties, may be imposed by the court: they can specify the extent of the permitted user as well as any payment that the promisee may be required to make for the exercise of the right.[90] However, an order for such payment may not be appropriate where the promisor has already obtained other benefits under the agreement.[91] It may also be inappropriate for other reasons to be discussed in the following paragraph.

Remedy. In deciding what remedy to grant to the promisee, the court can take **3–145** a wide variety of factors into account to reach a result that is equitable in all the circumstances.[92] Thus it may take into account not only the terms of the promise and the extent of the promisee's reliance on it, but also the conduct of the promisor after the occurrence of the facts giving rise to the proprietary estoppel. Thus in *Crabb v. Arun DC*[93] the defendants had acted without warning in blocking the claimant's access to his land. In view of this "high-handedness"[94] and the resulting loss to the claimant, he was not required to make the payment that would otherwise have been a condition of the exercise of the right of way. Similarly, in *Pascoe v. Turner*[95] a proprietary estoppel arose when a man told a woman with whom he had formerly cohabited that the house in which they had lived was hers, and she later spent some £230 of her limited resources on repairs and improvements to it. The Court of Appeal relied on the man's "ruthlessness"[96] in seeking to evict the promisee as a ground for ordering him to convey the fee simple to her. The submission that she should have no more than a licence to occupy the house was rejected since this would not protect her against a bona fide purchaser from the promisor. The result seems, with respect, unduly punitive; and intermediate possibilities (such as granting the promisee a long lease[97]) were not put before the court.

Compensation in money. *Pascoe v. Turner* illustrates a situation in which the **3–146** grant of an irrevocable licence to remain on the property may constitute an unsatisfactory remedy because it will not adequately secure the promisee's possession. It may also be unsatisfactory on account of its inflexibility: thus in *Inwards v. Baker*[98] the promisee would have had no remedy in respect of his expenditure, had he wanted to move elsewhere; nor would his dependants have

---

[88] [1991] 1 W.L.R. 113.
[89] *E.R. Ives Investments Ltd v. High* [1967] 2 Q.B. 379; *Crabb v. Arun DC* [1976] Ch. 179.
[90] *Crabb v. Arun DC, supra,* at 199.
[91] As in *E.R. Ives Investments Ltd v. High* [1967] 2 Q.B. 379.
[92] *Roebuck v. Mungorin* [1994] 2 A.C. 244, 235.
[93] [1976] Ch. 179; *ante,* § 3–132.
[94] [1976] Ch. at 199; *cf. ibid.* at 189.
[95] [1979] 1 W.L.R. 431.
[96] *ibid.* at 439.
[97] As in *Griffiths v. Williams* [1978] E.G. 919; *ante,* § 3–142.
[98] [1965] 2 Q.B. 507; *ante,* § 3–131.

had any remedy, had he died shortly after completing the house. In such cases a remedy by way of compensation in money would be more satisfactory for the promisee; and it would also have the advantage for the promisor that he would not be impeded in dealing with the property for an indefinite time.[99] Such a remedy was granted in *Dodsworth v. Dodsworth*[1] where the promisees spent £700 on improvements to the promisor's bungalow in reliance on an implied promise (not intended to have contractual force) that the promisee and his wife could live there as if it were their home. The Court of Appeal held that to give the promisees a right of occupation for an indefinite time would confer on them a greater interest than had been contemplated by the parties; and that the most appropriate remedy was to repay them their outlay on improvements. Compensation in money will also be the more appropriate remedy where, as a practical matter, the promise which gave rise to the estoppel cannot be specifically enforced: for example, where its performance would involve joint occupation of premises by, and co-operation between, members of a family who later quarrel,[2] or between a couple whose relationship has broken down.[3] Where there is evidence that the improved property has increased in value by reason of market fluctuations, it is submitted that the amount recoverable by the promisee should be increased correspondingly; conversely, it should be reduced where the market value of the property has declined.[4]

3–147   In *Dodsworth v. Dodsworth*[5] the court awarded compensation even though, when the action was brought, the promisee was still in possession of the improved property. More commonly this form of remedy is granted where the promisee is no longer in possession, having either left voluntarily[6] or been lawfully ejected as a result of legal proceedings.[7] Where the promisee has been wrongly ordered to give up possession, compensation in money is similarly available,[8] though in such a case the court may alternatively order the promisee to be put back into possession of the premises.[9] The compensation has been assessed in a variety of ways: at the cost of improvements made with the promisee's money[10]; at a proportionate interest in the property[11]; or at the reasonable value of the right of occupation, based (presumably) on the cost to the promisee of equivalent alternative accommodation.[12]

The court may, finally, deny the promisee a remedy where, on balance, greater injustice would be produced by giving effect to the promise than by allowing the promisor to go back on it. This was the position in *Sledmore v. Dalby*,[13] where

---

[99] *cf.* criticisms of the law by Browne-Wilkinson J. in *Re Sharpe* [1980] 1 W.L.R. 219, 226.

[1] [1973] E.G.D. 233; to the extent that the reasoning is based on the provisions of Settled Land Act 1925, s.1, it is criticised in *Griffiths v. Williams* [1978] E.G.D. 919.

[2] *Burrows and Burrows v. Sharp* (1991) 23 H.L.R. 82; *cf. Baker v. Baker* (1993) 25 H.L.R. 408 (when the action was for damages).

[3] *Clough v. Kelly* (1996) 72 P. & C.R. D22.

[4] *cf.*, in a case of undue influence. *Cheese v. Thomas* [1994] 1 W.L.R. 129.

[5] *Supra*, n. 1.

[6] As in *Hussey v. Palmer* [1972] 1 W.L.R. 1286 and *Eves v. Eves* [1975] 1 W.L.R. 1328.

[7] As in *Plimmer v. Mayor of Wellington* (1884) 9 App.Cas. 699.

[8] *Tanner v. Tanner* [1975] 1 W.L.R. 1346 (where there was a contract).

[9] *ibid.*

[10] *Hussey v. Palmer* [1972] 1 W.L.R. 1286; *Burrows and Burrows v. Sharp* (1991) 23 H.L.R. 82.

[11] *Eves v. Eves* [1975] 1 W.L.R. 1338.

[12] *Tanner v. Tanner* [1975] 1 W.L.R. 1346; *Baker v. Baker* (1993) 25 H.L.R. 408.

[13] (1996) 72 P. & C.R. 196.

the promisee had contributed to major improvements to the property but at the time of the proceedings had already enjoyed 20 years' rent-free occupation and was gainfully employed, while the promisor was a widow living on social security benefits. The promisee's claim to be entitled to a licence for life to stay in the house was in these circumstances rejected and the promisor was held entitled to possession.

(e) *Comparison with other Doctrines*

Proprietary and promissory estoppels. Proprietary and promissory estop- **3–148** pels have a number of points in common. Both can arise from promises[14]; consideration is not, while action in reliance is, a necessary condition for their operation[15]; and both are, within limits, revocable.[16] But there are also many important points of difference between the two doctrines.

Proprietary estoppel in some respects narrower than promissory estop- **3–149** **pel.** The scope of proprietary is in two respects narrower than that of promissory estoppel. First, proprietary estoppel is restricted to situations in which one party acts under the belief that he has or will be granted an interest in or over the property (generally the land) of another. A promissory estoppel may, on the other hand, arise (if other necessary conditions are satisfied[17]) out of *any* promise that strict legal rights will not be enforced: there is no need for those rights to relate to land or other property. Secondly, proprietary estoppel requires the promisee to have acted to his detriment,[18] while promissory estoppel may operate even though the promisee merely performs a pre-existing duty and so suffers no detriment in the sense of doing something that he was not previously bound to do.[19] This difference between the two doctrines follows from the fact that promissory estoppel is (unlike proprietary estoppel) concerned only with the variation of rights arising out of a pre-existing legal relationship between promisor and promisee.

Proprietary estoppel in other respects wider than promissory estop- **3–150** **pel.** On the other hand, the scope of proprietary is in two respects wider than that of promissory estoppel. First, promissory estoppel arises only out of a representation or promise that is "clear" or "precise and unambiguous."[20] There is no such requirement in the case of a proprietary estoppel: this can arise where there is no actual promise: for example, where one party makes improvements to another's land under a mistake and the other either knows of the mistake[21] or seeks to take unconscionable advantage of it.[22] Secondly (and most importantly), while promissory estoppel is essentially defensive in nature,[23] proprietary estoppel can give

---

[14] *Ante,* §§ 3–084, 3–130. For use of the expression "promissory estoppel" see *ante,* § 3–096.
[15] *Ante,* §§ 3–088, 3–131.
[16] *Ante,* §§ 3–091, 3–140.
[17] *Ante,* §§ 3–081—3–090.
[18] *Ante,* § 3–138.
[19] *Ante,* § 3–089.
[20] *Ante,* § 3–085.
[21] *Wilmott v. Barber* (1880) 15 Ch.D. 96, 105 (the claim in that case failed as the party against whom it was made did not know of the extent of his own rights or of the other party's mistake).
[22] *Taylors Fashions Ltd v. Liverpool Victoria Trustee Co. Ltd* [1982] Q.B. 133.
[23] *Ante,* § 3–093.

rise to a cause of action.[24] The promisee is not merely entitled to raise the estoppel as a defence to an action of trespass or to a claim for possession: the court can make an order for the land to be conveyed to him,[25] or for compensation[26] or for such other remedy as it regards as appropriate.[27] Although the authorities support this second distinction between the two kinds of estoppel, they do not make any attempt to explain or justify it. It is submitted that the explanation is in part historical and terminological. In the early cases, proprietary estoppel was explained in terms of *acquiescence*[28] or *encouragement*.[29] Hence no conflict with the requirement that *promises* must be supported by consideration was perceived; or where it was perceived the facts were said to give rise to a contract.[30] Promissory estoppel, on the other hand, dealt principally with the renegotiation of contracts; it obviously depended on giving binding effect to promises, and did so in the context of releases and variations, in which the common law requirement of consideration had long been established.[31] The rule that promissory estoppel gives rise to no cause of action was evolved to prevent what would otherwise have been an obvious conflict between promissory estoppel and consideration. In cases of proprietary estoppel there was no such conflict where liability was based on "acquiescence"; and where it was based on "encouragement" the conflict, though sometimes real enough, was at least less obvious. There are, moreover, two aspects of proprietary estoppel which help to justify the distinction. These are that the acts done by the promisee are not ones which he was under any previous legal obligation to perform; and that generally their effect would be unjustly to enrich the promisor if he were allowed to go back on his promise.[32] In these respects, the facts on which proprietary estoppel is based provide more compelling grounds for relief[33] than those commonly found in cases of promissory estoppel.

3–151   **Bases of proprietary and promissory estoppel.** While the two doctrines are in the above respects distinct it can also be argued that they have a common basis, *viz.* that it would be unconscionable for the promisor to go back on his promise after the promisee has acted on it to his detriment; and that the precise labels to be attached to them are "immaterial."[34] It is perhaps for these reasons that the distinction between the two kinds of estoppel was described as "not . . . helpful" by Scarman L.J. in *Crabb v. Arun DC*.[35] That decision was, in a later case, said

---

[24] *Crabb v. Arun DC* [1976] Ch. 179, 187; *Taylors Fashions Ltd v. Liverpool Victoria Trustee Co. Ltd* [1982] Q.B. 133, 148.

[25] *e.g. Dillwyn v. Llewelyn* (1862) 4 D. F. & G. 517.

[26] *e.g. Eves v. Eves* [1975] 1 W.L.R. 1338.

[27] See *ante*, § 3–130.

[28] *Wilmott v. Barber* (1880) 15 Ch.D. 96, 105.

[29] *Ramsden v. Dyson* (1866) L.R. 1 HL 129, 170.

[30] *Dillwyn v. Llewelyn* (1862) 4 D. F. & G. 517, 522; *ante*, § 3–133.

[31] *Ante*, §§ 3–072—3–075.

[32] See the reference to the landowner's "profit" in *Ramsden v. Dyson* (1866) L.R. 1 HL 129, 141 and *cf. ante*, § 3–131.

[33] See Fuller and Eisenberg, *Basic Contract Law* (3rd ed.), p. 70; "Unjust enrichment presents a more urgent case for judicial intervention than losses through reliance which do not benefit the defendant." *cf.* Fuller and Perdue (1936) 46 Yale L.J. 52, 56.

[34] *Taylors Fashions Ltd v. Liverpool Victoria Trustee Co. Ltd* [1982] Q.B. 133, 153, where, however, a distinction is also drawn between "promissory estoppel" and the principle in *Ramsden v. Dyson* (1866) L.R. 1 H.L. 129 (*i.e.* proprietary estoppel).

[35] [1976] Ch. 179, 193.

to illustrate "a virtual equation of promissory and proprietary estoppel,"[36] perhaps because it extended the operation of proprietary estoppel beyond the situations originally within its scope, *viz.* those in which the promisor would be unjustly enriched by the work done by the promisee on his land unless some legal effect were given to the promise. Nevertheless it is submitted that the doctrines are distinct in the respects stated above.[37] Attempts to unite them by posing "simply" the question whether it would be "unconscionable"[38] for the promisor to go back on his promise are, it is submitted, unhelpful.[39] They tend (as has been said in the context of two other kinds of estoppel) "to blur the necessarily separate requirements, and distinct terrain of application"[40] of different types of estoppel; and they provide no basis on which a legal doctrine capable of yielding predictable results can be developed.

Proprietary estoppel and contract contrasted. We have seen that some 　3–152
cases which have been said to support the doctrine of proprietary estoppel have been explained on the alternative basis that there was a contract between the parties.[41] But often no such explanation is possible; for proprietary estoppel can operate even though the conditions required for the creation of a contract are not satisfied. The need to discuss the doctrine in this chapter arises precisely because a promise can give rise to a proprietary estoppel even though it is not supported by consideration; and it can also have this effect even though it cannot take effect as a contract because it is not sufficiently certain or because it fails to comply with formal requirements. Moreover, the effect of a proprietary estoppel differs from that of a contract. Sometimes, indeed, the result of a proprietary estoppel is to give effect to the promise in the terms in which it was made[42]; but such a result does not follow as of right. We have seen that the extent of the promisee's rights may depend, not only on the terms of the promise and the extent to which the promisee has acted on it, but also on the subsequent conduct of the promisor. Thus in *Crabb v. Arun DC* the promisee would have had to make some payment for the right of way but for the "high-handedness"[43] of the promisor; and in *Pascoe v. Turner* the promisee would not have been entitled to the fee simple of the house (but only to an irrevocable licence for life) if the promisor had not shown a "ruthless"[44] determination to evict her. The rights arising under a binding contract are fixed at its formation and not subject to such variation in the

---

[36] *Taylors Fashions Ltd v. Liverpool Victoria Trustee Co. Ltd* [1982] Q.B. 133, 153; the use of "promissory estoppel" to describe a typical proprietary estoppel situation in *Griffiths v. Williams* [1978] E.G.D. 919, 921 may well be a misprint.

[37] At §§ 3–149 and 3–150; *cf. ante*, § 3–138.

[38] *Taylors Fashions Ltd v. Liverpool Victoria Trustee Co. Ltd* [1982] Q.B. 133, 155; *cf. Habib Bank Ltd v. Habib Bank A.G. Zurich* [1981] 1 W.L.R. 1265, 1285; *Amalgamated Investment & Property Co. Ltd v. Texas Commerce International Bank* [1982] Q.B. 84, 104, 122.

[39] *cf. Haslemere Estates Ltd v. Baker* [1982] 1 W.L.R. 1009, 1119 where Megarry V.-C., rejecting the argument that proprietary estoppel arises "whenever justice and good conscience requires it," said "I do not think that the subject is as wide and indefinite as that." Dicta emphasising flexibility of the *remedy* (*ante*, § 3–145) should not be read as referring equally to *conditions of liability.*

[40] *Republic of India v. Indian Steamship Co. (The Indian Endurance) (No. 2)* [1998] A.C. 878, 914, distinguishing between estoppels by convention and by acquiescence; *cf.* the rejection by Millett L.J. in *First National Bank v. Thomson* [1996] Ch. 231, 236 of the view that estoppels are "all governed by the same requirements."

[41] *Ante*, § 3–133.

[42] *e.g. Dillwyn v. Llewelyn* (1862) 4 D. F. & G. 517.

[43] [1976] Ch. 179, 199.

[44] [1979] 1 W.L.R. 431, 438.

light of the court's approval or disapproval of the subsequent conduct of one of the parties. For this reason, and because proprietary estoppel may be revocable,[45] it will generally be more advantageous to a party to show the existence of a binding contract than to rely on a proprietary estoppel.

12. Special Cases

3–153   **Defective promises.**[46] Mutual promises are generally consideration for each other,[47] but difficulty is sometimes felt in treating a promise as consideration for another if the former is legally defective. The law on this topic is based on expediency rather than on any supposedly logical deductions which might be drawn from the doctrine of consideration. The question whether a defective promise can constitute consideration for a counter-promise depends on the policy of the rule of law making the former promise defective.

3–154   **Policy considerations.** One group of cases concerns contracts made between persons, one of whom lacks contractual capacity. A minor can enforce a promise made to him under such a contract even though the only consideration for it is his own promise, which does not bind him by reason of his minority.[48] The same rule applies to contracts with mental patients.[49] The reason for these rules is that it is the policy of the law to protect the person under the incapacity, and not the other party, who is therefore not allowed to rely on that incapacity. A contrasting group of cases concerns contracts which are illegal. Obviously the illegal promise cannot be enforced and if both promises are illegal the consequence that neither can be enforced follows from the policy of the invalidating rule rather than from the fact that an illegal promise cannot constitute consideration.[50] But in some cases of illegal contracts only one of the promises is illegal: this is, for example, often the position where the contract is in restraint of trade. In such a case, the party who makes the illegal promise (*e.g.* not to compete) cannot enforce the counter-promise (*e.g.* to pay a sum of money) if the illegal promise constitutes the sole consideration for the counter-promise.[51] Indeed, where one of the two promises is illegal, the counter-promise cannot be enforced even if there was *some* other consideration for it, but the *main* consideration for it was the illegal promise. The reason for this rule lies in the policy of the law to discourage illegal bargains.[52]

3–155   **Performance of defective promises.** Where a defective *promise* did not constitute consideration, the *performance* of it was nevertheless sometimes held to provide consideration for the counter-promise.[53] A similar principle applies

---

[45] *Ante*, § 3–140.
[46] Treitel (1961) 77 L.Q.R. 83.
[47] *Ante*, § 3–011.
[48] *Holt v. Ward Clarencieux* (1732) Stra. 937; *post* § 8–039.
[49] *Post*, § 8–067.
[50] As suggested in *Nerot v. Wallace* (1789) 3 T.R. 17, 23.
[51] *e.g. Wyatt v. Kreglinger & Fernau* [1933] 1 K.B. 793.
[52] See *Goodinson v. Goodinson* [1954] 2 Q.B. 118 (the actual decision is obsolete in view of Matrimonial Causes Act 1973, s.34, *post*, § 3–156).
[53] See *Fishmonger's Corp. v. Robertson* (1843) 5 Man. & G. 131 (unsealed contract by company: so long as such a contract was executory, the company's promise was no consideration: *Kidderminster Corp. v. Hardwick* (1873) L.R. 9 Ex. 13. The requirement of sealing was abolished by Corporated Bodies' Contracts Act 1960); *Re Dale* [1994] Ch. 31, 38.

where a victim of fraud, misrepresentation, duress or undue influence can sue but not be sued: by suing, he affirms the contract, makes his own promise binding, and so supplies consideration. But where the promise of one party is illegal even its performance does not entitle that party to enforce the counter-promise,[54] for the law must not give him any incentive to perform the illegal promise.

Promise defective by statute. Where one of the promises is defective by   **3–156** statute, the statute may expressly solve the problem whether the person giving the defective promise can sue on the counter-promise.[55] Thus a party who gives a promise which is defective under section 4 of the Statute of Frauds 1677, or under section 34 of the Matrimonial Causes Act 1973 may be entitled to sue although he (or she) is not bound[56] and this may be so even though for other purposes (such as the validity of a disposition) his or her promise, precisely because it is void, cannot constitute consideration.[57] Where a statute invalidates a promise but does not provide for the effect of its invalidity on the other party's promise, the general rule seems to be that the invalid promise is not good consideration[58]; but, unless the promise is illegal, the party giving it can sue on the counter-promise if he actually performs his promise.[59]

Both promises defective by statute. A statute may also invalidate *both*   **3–157** promises: this is the position with regard to wagering contracts which are "null and void" under section 18 of the Gaming Act 1845.[60] Performance of one such promise clearly would not make the other enforceable[61] but the question whether performance of the void promise could constitute consideration might also arise in another context, for example in the context of the question whether the performance amounted to consideration for the purpose of a rule of law by which a transfer or disposition of property was effective only if made for valuable consideration. This was the question which arose in *Lipkin Gorman v. Karpnale Ltd*,[62] where stolen money was used by the thief for gambling at a club of which he was a member, and it was held that the club had not received the money for valuable consideration so as to be entitled, as against the owner of the money, to retain it. We have already noted that the club did not provide consideration for the payment by exchanging the money for gaming chips.[63] The present point is that the club did not provide consideration for the payments made to it by the member by allowing him to gamble and promising to pay, or actually paying him, in respect of any bets which he had won. The club's promise to pay did not amount to consideration since it was void under section 18 of the 1845 Act. Nor did performance of that promise constitute consideration; for, even though the club

---

[54] *e.g. Wyatt v. Kreglinger & Fernau* [1933] 1 K.B. 793.

[55] See *Laythoarp v. Bryant* (1836) 2 Bing.N.C. 735.

[56] *Post*, § 17–044. For more elaborate provisions of this kind, see Financial Services Act 1986, ss.5, 6, 56, 57, 131 and 132.

[57] *Re Kumar* [1993] 1 W.L.R. 224, where the void promise was held not to constitute consideration for the purpose of Insolvency Act 1986, s.339.

[58] *Clayton v. Jennings* (1760) 2 W.Bl. 706.

[59] *Rajbenback v. Mamon* [1955] 1 Q.B. 283 as explained in (1961) 77 L.Q.R. 83, 95; contrast Unger (1956) 19 M.L.R. 99.

[60] *Post*, Vol. II, § 40–018.

[61] *Ante* § 3–155.

[62] [1991] 2 A.C. 548; *post*, Vol. II, § 40–081.

[63] *Ante*, § 3–015.

was not entitled to the return of any payment so made to one of its members,[64] such a payment was said by Lords Templeman and Goff to be treated in law as a completed voluntary gift to the winner.[65] To treat the payment of losses as gifts may not be easy to reconcile with the "common sense approach"[66] used in the same case to rebut the argument that the club had provided consideration for the payments by supplying the member with gaming chips. Indeed, in another part of his speech Lord Goff said that "the practical business position is that if the casino does not pay winnings when they are due it will simply go out of business. So the obligation in honour to pay winnings is an obligation which, in business terms, the casino has to comply with."[67] Conversely, a member who did not pay losses when due would no doubt be excluded from the club. It is scarcely realistic to describe payments made under such pressures as voluntary gifts. But the view that the club did not provide consideration by paying bets which it had lost can be explained by reference to the context in which it arose: it helped to protect the victim of the theft,[68] or at least formed the first step in a line of reasoning which enabled the House of Lords to split the loss between the victim of the theft and the equally innocent recipient of the money.[69]

3–158   **Unilateral contracts.** In the case of a unilateral contract, the promisee clearly provides consideration if he completes the stipulated act or forbearance (such as walking to York, or not smoking for a year).[70] This amounts in law to a detriment to the promisee; and the promisor may also obtain a benefit: *e.g.* where he promises a reward for the return of lost property and it is actually returned to him. It was suggested in Chapter 2 that commencement of performance can amount to acceptance of an offer of a unilateral contract[71]; and it is submitted that such commencement can also amount to consideration; for it may be a detriment to the promisee to walk only part of the way to York, or to refrain from smoking for part of the year. Difficult questions of fact may, indeed, arise in determining whether performance has actually begun and whether such a beginning was made "on the strength of"[72] the promise. This is particularly true where the stipulated perform-ance was a forbearance; but if an actual forbearance to sue can constitute good consideration,[73] it must in principle be possible to tell when a forbearance has begun. Thus commencement of performance (whether of an act or of a for-bearance) may provide both an acceptance and consideration, and may accord-ingly deprive the promisor of his right to revoke the promise.[74] Of course, the promisor's liability to pay the amount promised (*e.g.* the £100 for walking to York) does not accrue before the promisee has fully performed the required act

---

[64] *Post*, Vol. II, § 40–027.
[65] [1991] 2 A.C. 548, 562, 565, 577.
[66] *ibid.* at 576.
[67] *ibid.* at 581.
[68] *Post*, Vol. II §§ 40–081—40–083.
[69] *Post*, Vol. II § 40–085.
[70] See *Daulia Ltd v. Four Millbank Nominees Ltd* [1978] Ch. 231, 238.
[71] *Ante*, § 2–072.
[72] *Wigan v. English & Scottish Law Life Assurance Association* [1909] 1 Ch. 291, 298; *ante*, § 3–047.
[73] See *ante*, § 3–045.
[74] For the contrary view see Wormser in *Selected Readings on the Law of Contracts*, p. 307—but he recanted in (1956) 3 *Journal of Legal Education* 146.

or forbearance. The present point is merely that, after part performance by the promisee, the promisor cannot withdraw with impunity.

The further suggestion has been made that a unilateral contract may be made **3–159** as soon as the offer is received by the offeree[75]; and this could be interpreted to mean that the contract was binding even before the offeree has acted on it in any way. But at this stage the offeree has clearly not provided any consideration, and in the case in which the suggestion was made no problem of consideration arose as the offeree had in fact completed the required act[76] before any attempt to withdraw the offer was made. Except in the case of bankers' irrevocable credits,[77] the better view is that an offer of a unilateral contract is not binding on receipt, but only when the offeree has begun to render the required performance.

Firm offers. By a "firm" offer is meant one containing a promise not to **3–160** revoke it for a specified time. The mere fact that such a promise has been made does not prevent the offeror from revoking the offer within that period since normally the promise will be unsupported by consideration.[78] Most obviously such consideration will be provided if the offeree pays (or promises to pay) a sum of money for the promise and so buys an option.[79] Consideration may also be provided by some other promise: for example, in the case of an offer to sell a house, the offeree may provide consideration for the offeror's promise to hold the offer open by promising to apply for a mortgage on the house; and, in the case of an offer to buy shares, the offeree may provide consideration for the offeror's promise not to revoke the offer for a specified time by promising not to dispose of those shares elsewhere during that time. The performance of the offeree's promise in such cases could likewise provide consideration for the offeror's promise to keep the offer open. In one case a vendor of land entered into a so-called "lock-out" agreement[80] by which he promised a prospective purchaser not to consider other offers if that purchaser would exchange contracts within two weeks; and it was said that "the promise by the [purchaser] to get on by limiting himself to just two weeks"[81] constituted consideration for the vendor's promise not to consider other offers. The case is not strictly one of a firm offer since the vendor's promise would not in terms have prevented him from simply deciding not to sell at all; but the practical effect of a binding "lock-out"

---

[75] *Harvela Investments Ltd v. Royal Trust Co. of Canada (C.I.) Ltd* [1986] 1 A.C. 207, 224 ("when the invitation was received").

[76] By submitting the requested bid: *cf. ante* § 2–037.

[77] *Post* § 3–169.

[78] *Cooke v. Oxley* (1790) 3 T.R. 653; *Routledge v. Grant* (1828) 4 Bing. 653; *Head v. Diggon* (1828) 3 M. & Ry. 97; *Dickinson v. Dodds* (1876) 2 Ch.D. 463; *ante*, § 2–080.

[79] The legal characteristics of such an option have been variously described: (1) as a contract: *Greene v. Church Commissioners for England* [1947] Ch. 467, 476, 478 (disapproving a dictum in *Beesly v. Hallwood Estates Ltd* [1960] 1 W.L.R. 549, 555, actual decision affirmed [1961] Ch. 549); though not one of sale: *Chippenham Golf Club v. North Wilts. R.D.C.* (1992) 64 P. & C.R. 527; (2) as a transaction which, even though it is not a contract, gives rise to an interest in property: *Re Button Lease* [1964] Ch. 263, 270–271; *Armstrong & Holmes Ltd v. Holmes* [1994] 1 All E.R. 826; (3) as a unilateral contract: *United Scientific Holdings Ltd v. Burnley B.C.* [1978] A.C. 904, 945; *Little v. Courage* (1995) 70 P. & C.R. 469, 474; and (4) as being *sui generis*: *Spiro v. Glencrown Properties* [1991] Ch. 537, 544. And see Mowbray, 74 L.Q.R. 242; Lücke, 3 Adelaide L.Rev. 200.

[80] *Ante*, § 2–111.

[81] *Pitt v. P.H.H. Asset Management Ltd* [1994] 1 W.L.R. 327, 332; for other consideration in this case, see *ante*. § 3–051; *Tye v. House* [1997] 2 E.G.L.R. 171.

agreement may be to prevent the vendor from withdrawing his offer; and the reasoning quoted above could apply to the case of a firm offer. The reasoning gives rise to some difficulty in that it does not appear that the purchaser made any promise to exchange contracts within two weeks. It seems more plausible to say that the vendor's promise had become binding as a unilateral contract under which the purchaser had provided consideration by actually making efforts to meet the deadline, even though he had not promised to do so. Similar reasoning can apply if a seller of land promises to keep an offer open for a month, asking the buyer during that period to make efforts to raise the necessary money. If the buyer makes such efforts (without promising to do so), it is arguable that he has by part performance accepted the seller's offer of a unilateral contract to keep the principal offer open. Similarly, it is possible for a person, to whom a promise not to revoke an offer for the sale of a house has been made, to provide consideration for that promise by incurring the expense of a survey.[82] On the other hand, the equitable principle applied in *Hughes v. Metropolitan Ry.*[83] and in the *High Trees* case[84] will not avail the offeree since it only operates defensively and does not create new causes of action where none existed before.[85] Nor does it seem probable that the offeree will be able to claim damages in tort[86] under the principles laid down in *Hedley Byrne & Co. Ltd v. Heller & Partners Ltd.*[87]

3–161   **Exceptions.** The general rule that a promise to keep an offer open is not binding has been criticised[88]; indeed, there are some situations in which it has been said that "the market would disdain to take"[89] the point that such a promise was not binding. The rule does not, of course, apply if the promise is made in a deed; and it is rejected by the Vienna Convention on Contracts for the International Sale of Goods.[90] It is also subject to a common law exception in the law of insurance where an underwriter who initials a slip under an "open cover" arrangement is regarded as making a "standing offer" which the insured can accept from time to time by making "declarations" under it. The underwriter's commitment is regarded as binding even though there is no consideration for his implied promise not to revoke the "standing offer."[91] But even with these mitigations, the rule can still cause hardship to an offeree who has acted in

---

[82] *cf. Ee v. Kakar* (1979) 40 P. & C.R. 223 (a case not concerned with a "firm" offer).

[83] (1877) 2 App.Cas. 439; *ante*, § 3–080.

[84] [1947] K.B. 130; *ante*, § 3–120.

[85] *Ante*, § 3–093.

[86] *cf. Holman Construction Ltd v. Delta Timber Co. Ltd* [1972] N.Z.L.R. 1081; and see *Blackpool and Fylde Aero Club v. Blackpool B.C.* [1990] 1 W.L.R. 1195, 1202.

[87] [1964] A.C. 465; *post*, § 6–067.

[88] Law Revision Committee, 6th Interim Report, Cmd. 5449 (1937), para. 38; Law Commission Working Paper No. 60 (1975).

[89] *Jaglom v. Excess Insurance Ltd* [1972] 2 Q.B. 250, 258; *cf. County Ltd v. Girozentrale Securities* [1996] 3 All E.R. 834 where an "offer to subscribe" for shares was described at 837 as "not legally binding but regarded by City convention as binding in honour unless some unforeseen exceptional circumstances supervened." It seems that the "commitment" (*ibid.*) was given not to the company but to the underwriter, or by prospective investors to each other, so that the principles discussed in § 2–021 *ante* did not apply. For the view that the statement in question in the *Jaglom* case was not an offer at all, but an acceptance (and binding as such) see *General Reinsurance Corporation v. Forsakringsaktiebolaget Fennia Patria* [1983] Q.B. 856, 863–864.

[90] *Ante*, § 2–057; Art. 16(2).

[91] *Citadel Insurance Co. v. Atlantic Union Insurance Co.* [1982] 2 Lloyd's Rep. 543, 546.

reliance on the promise to keep the offer open[92]; and further legislation, limiting the right to withdraw firm offers, seems to be desirable.[93]

Auction sales without reserve. Where goods are put up for auction without **3–162** reserve, there is no contract *of sale* if the auctioneer refuses to knock the goods down to the highest bidder; but the auctioneer is liable to the highest bidder on a separate promise that the auction will be without reserve.[94] It can be argued that there is no consideration for this promise as the bidder is not bound by his unaccepted bid.[95] But the better view is that there is both a detriment to the bidder, since he runs the risk of being bound, and a benefit to the auctioneer, as the bidding is driven up. Hence there is consideration for the auctioneer's separate promise, and it makes no difference to the auctioneer's liability *on this promise* that he would not be liable if he did not put the goods up for sale at all (since an advertisement of an auction is not an offer to hold it),[96] or that there was no contract of sale because of his refusal to accept the highest bid.[97]

Novation of partnership debts. When the composition of a partnership **3–163** changes, it is usual to arrange that liability for the debts owed by the existing partners should be transferred by novation[98] to the new partners. Two situations may be considered.

(1) A and B are in partnership; A retires and C is admitted as a new partner; it is agreed between A, B and C, and the creditors of the old firm of A and B, that A shall cease to be liable for the firm's debts, and that C shall undertake such liability. The result is that the creditors can sue C and can no longer sue A. They provide good consideration for C's promise to pay by abandoning their claim against A; and A provides good consideration for their promise to release him by procuring a substitute debtor, C.

(2) A and B are in partnership; A retires; it is agreed between A, B and the creditors of the firm that A shall cease to be liable and that B shall be solely liable. It seems that the creditors cannot sue A, but it is hard to see what consideration moves from him. In one case it was said that there was consideration in that a remedy against a single debtor might be easier to enforce than one against several, all of whom were solvent[99]; thus the creditors benefit by the release of A. This is possible, if invented,[1] consideration.

Gratuitous bailments. A gratuitous bailment may be for the benefit of the **3–164** bailee or for the benefit of the bailor.

---

[92] *e.g.* where a builder enters into a contract in reliance of offers from sub-contractors to supply services or materials and expressed to be "firm" for a fixed period. For conflicting American authorities, see *James Baird Co. v. Gimbel Bros.*, 64 F. 2d. 344 (1933); *Drennan v. Star Paving Co.* 51 Cal. 2d. 409, 333 P. 2d. 757 (1958); for a review of Canadian authorities, see *Northern Construction Co. v. Gloge Heating & Plumbing* (1984) 6 D.L.R. (4th) 450 (holding the sub-contractor bound by his offer).

[93] For proposals for reform, see *supra* n. 88.

[94] *Warlow v. Harrison* (1859) 1 E. & E. 309; *Harris v. Nickerson* (1873) L.R. 8 Q.B. 286, 288; *Johnson v. Boyes* [1899] 2 Ch. 73, 77.

[95] For discussion of the point, see Slade (1952) 68 L.Q.R. 238; Gower, *ibid.* at 457; Slade (1953) 69 L.Q.R. 21.

[96] *Harris v. Nickerson* (1873) L.R. 8 Q.B. 286; *ante* § 2–010.

[97] *ibid.*

[98] *Post*, § 20–084; Partnership Act 1890, s.17(3).

[99] *Lyth v. Ault* (1852) 7 Ex. 669; *Thompson v. Percival* (1834) 5 B. & Ad. 925 is based on reasoning which is obsolete after *D. & C. Builders Ltd v. Rees* [1967] 2 Q.B. 617; *ante*, § 3–114, n. 37.

[1] *Ante*, § 3–008.

(1) For benefit of bailee. The first possibility is illustrated by *Bainbridge v. Firmstone*[2] where the defendant asked for and received permission from the plaintiff to weigh two boilers belonging to the plaintiff. In performing this operation, the defendant damaged the boilers, and the plaintiff claimed damages for breach of the defendant's promise to return the boilers in good condition. The defendant argued that, as he was not paid to weigh or look after the boilers, no consideration for his promise had been provided by the plaintiff; but the court rejected this argument. Patteson J. said: "I suppose the defendant thought he had some benefit; at any rate, there is a detriment to the plaintiff from his parting with the possession for even so short a time."[3] This consideration would also support some other promise by the defendant, *e.g.* a promise to repair the boilers. It is more doubtful whether there would be any consideration moving from the defendant for any promise by the plaintiff to allow the defendant to have possession of the boilers. A mere promise to return the boilers might not suffice on the ground that it was no more than a promise to perform a duty imposed by law on all bailees; but a promise to look after the boilers for a fixed time would probably be regarded as consideration moving from the defendant.[4]

(2) For benefit of bailor. The second possibility would, for example, arise where a thing was deposited by A with B, not for use but for safe-keeping, without reward. In such a case parting with the possession is hardly a detriment to A. B's duty to look after the thing[5] does not arise out of contract but is imposed by the general law.[6] It follows that B's *only* duty is that imposed by law. Thus B is under no obligation before he actually receives the thing; and if he promised to do anything which went beyond the duty imposed by law (for example, to keep the property in repair) he would be bound by his promise only if A had provided some consideration for it apart from the delivery of the chattel.[7] To constitute such consideration, it is not necessary to show that A profited from the transaction: thus it is enough if B reimburses (or promises to reimburse) A for any expenses that A has incurred for the purpose of performing his promise.[8] This follows from the rule that the law generally does not inquire into the adequacy of consideration.[9]

3–165   **Gratuitous services.** A promise to render services without reward is not supported by consideration and is therefore not binding contractually. For example, where A gratuitously promises to insure B's property but fails to do so, A is not liable to B for breach of contract if the property is destroyed or damaged.[10] Occasionally, it may be possible to find consideration in the indirect financial

---

[2] (1838) 8 A. & E. 743.

[3] At 744.

[4] *cf. Verral v. Farnes* [1966] 1 W.L.R. 1254, a case relating to land; followed in *Milton v. Farrow* (1980) 255 E.G. 449.

[5] See *Coggs v. Bernard* (1703) 2 Ld. Raym. 909; *Mitchell v. Ealing London Borough Council* [1979] Q.B. 1; *Port Swettenham Authority v. T.W. Wu & Co.* [1979] A.C. 580, 590.

[6] *Morris v. C.W. Martin Ltd* [1966] 1 Q.B. 716, 731; *Compania Continental del Peru v. Evelpis Shipping Corp. (The Agia Skepi)* [1992] 2 Lloyd's Rep. 467, 472.

[7] *cf. Charnock v. Liverpool Corporation* [1968] 1 W.L.R. 1498; *post*, § 19–008.

[8] *C.C.C. Films (London) Ltd v. Impact Quadrant Films Ltd* [1985] Q.B. 16, 27.

[9] *Ante*, § 3–013.

[10] *Argy Trading & Development Co. Ltd v. Lapid Developments Ltd* [1977] 1 W.L.R. 444; *cf.* the New York case of *Thorn v. Deas*, 4 Johns. 84 (1809); later American authorities are divided: Corbin, *Contracts*, § 205, n. 54.

benefit which the promisor obtains from the arrangement e.g., in the form of favourable publicity.[11]

Liability in tort for negligent performance. Even where the promise is not   **3–166** supported by consideration, the promisor may be liable in tort for negligence if he actually renders the gratuitous services but fails to perform a duty to exercise due care in rendering them and so causes loss. A banker giving a negligent reference or an accountant giving a negligent report on the financial position of a company could be liable on this ground, even though he made no charge to the person to whom the information was given.[12] Similarly, where A gratuitously promised to insure B's property but did so negligently, with the result that the policy did not cover the loss which occurred, A was held liable to B in tort.[13] In one case, a person was even held liable in damages for negligently giving free advice to a friend in connection with the purchase of a second-hand car which turned out to be seriously defective.[14]

Non-feasance and misfeasance. The most important distinction between the   **3–167** two groups of cases discussed at §§ 3–165 and 3–166 is that between non-feasance and misfeasance in the performance of a promise to render gratuitous service. For this purpose, non-feasance means complete failure to pursue a *promised course of action*, while misfeasance means carelessness in the pursuit of that course of action, leading to failure to achieve a *promised result*. The first group of cases shows that non-feasance gives rise (in the absence of consideration) to no liability in contract, while the second shows that misfeasance can give rise to liability in tort. There is no liability in tort for simply doing nothing after having promised to render services gratuitously; for to impose such liability would amount to holding "that the law of England recognises the enforceability of a gratuitous promise. On the face of it, this would be inconsistent with fundamental principle."[15] In cases of pure non-feasance, the promisee will therefore have a remedy only if he can show that he provided consideration for

---

[11] cf. *De la Bere v. Pearson* [1908] 1 K.B. 280, 287.

[12] *Hedley Byrne & Co. Ltd v. Heller & Partners Ltd* [1964] A.C. 465; cf. *post*, § 6–067.

[13] *Wilkinson v. Coverdale* (1793) 1 Esp. 75.

[14] *Chaudhry v. Prabhakar* [1989] 1 W.L.R. 29; the defendant conceded that he owed a duty of care to the claimant and two members of the Court of Appeal seem to have regarded this concession as correct; Brown [1989] L.M.C.L.Q. 148. Contrast *Henderson v. Merrett Syndicates Ltd* [1995] 2 A.C. 145, 181, suggesting that there may be no liability in respect of services rendered on "an informal occasion."

[15] *G.A.F.L.A.C. v. Tanter (The Zephyr)* [1985] 2 Lloyd's Rep. 529, 538, disapproving the contrary view expressed at first instance [1984] 1 Lloyd's Rep. 58, 85 and there based on authorities which were all cases of misfeasance. *The Zephyr* itself was also such a case: [1984] 1 Lloyd's Rep. at 79, 86 ("he was making the position steadily worse"). *A fortiori*, there is no liability in tort for pure omission where *no* promise has been made: see *Reid v. Rush & Tompkins Group plc* [1990] 1 W.L.R. 212 and *Van Oppen v. Clerk to the Bedford Charity Trustees* [1990] 1 W.L.R. 235 though in the latter case it was said at 260 that a voluntary assumption of responsibility by one party followed by reliance on it by the other might in exceptional cases give rise to such liability. The nature of the exceptions is not clear; in the last two cases it was held that there was *no* duty on respectively an employer and a school to advise an employee or the parents of a pupil to insure against foreseeable risks of injury. See also *White v. Jones* [1995] 2 A.C. 207, 261, 266 (*post* § 19–037) for liability in tort for pure omission where there is a "duty to act"; but it is submitted that no such duty would be imposed by merely making gratuitous promise.

the promise. If he can show this he may also be in a better position with regard to damages even in cases of misfeasance.[16]

3–168   In *Gore v. Van der Lann*[17] a corporation issued a free travel pass to the claimant who "in consideration of my being granted a free pass" undertook that the use of the pass by her should be subject to certain conditions. One of these was that she would not sue the corporation or its servants for loss or injury suffered while she was boarding, alighting from, or being carried in, the corporation's vehicles. The claimant was injured while boarding a corporation bus; and it was held that the issue and acceptance of the free pass amounted to a contract.[18] Willmer L.J. said that "Each party gave good consideration by accepting a detriment in return for the advantages gained."[19] The parties were, as a result of the issue of the pass, brought into a relationship of passenger and carrier which gave rise to duties quite independently of contract; and it was the promise not to enforce these obligations which constituted the consideration moving from the claimant. In the absence of such a relationship, the person to whom the gratuitous service was promised would not provide consideration for that promise merely by making a counter-promise not to sue for loss or damage caused by the defective perform-ance of the services. It follows that, if in *Gore v. Van der Lann* the pass had been issued for a specified period of time but had been withdrawn before the end of that period, then the holder would have had no claim in contract in respect of that premature withdrawal.

3–169   **Bankers' irrevocable credits.** Where a banker issues (or confirms) an irrevo-cable credit, the generally held commercial view is that the banker's promise to the beneficiary is binding as soon as it is communicated to the beneficiary, and before the latter has acted on it in any way.[20] If, as seems probable, this view also represents the law, it constitutes a clear exception to the doctrine of consideration.[21]

---

[16] Because he will then be able to recover damages for loss of bargain.

[17] [1967] 2 Q.B. 31; Harris (1967) 30 M.L.R. 584; Odgers (1970) 86 L.Q.R. 69; and see *ante*, § 2–162 on the issue of contractual intention.

[18] This contract was void, so far as it purported to exclude liability for personal injury, by virtue of s.151 of the Road Traffic Act 1960 (now Public Passenger Vehicles Act 1981, s.29); *post*, § 14–107.

[19] [1967] 2 Q.B. 31, 42.

[20] *Post*, Vol. II, § 34–434.

[21] For explicit recognition of such an exception in the United States, see U.C.C., s.5–105; *cf. United City Merchants Ltd v. Royal Bank of Canada (The American Accord)* [1982] Q.B. 208, 225, revd. on other grounds [1983] 1 A.C. 168. After the coming into force of the Contracts (Rights of Third Parties) Bill 1998 (*post*, §§ 19–075 *et seq.*) the beneficiary might have a claim against the bank under the Bill as a third party identified in the contract between the bank and its customer. But his rights under the Bill would be less secure than his common law rights in two respects. First, they would be subject under subsection 3(2) to any defences which the bank might have against its customer. And, secondly they could be defeated or diminished by recission or variation of the contract by subsequent agreement between the bank and its customer before the seller had *either* communi-cated his assent to the bank *or* relied on the credit, and the bank either was aware of, or reasonably should have foreseen such reliance: see subsection 2(1).

FORM

1. In General

The general rule. The general rule of English law is that contracts can be made quite informally: no writing or other form is necessary. At common law there was only one exception to this rule: a corporation had to contract under seal until the last vestiges of this rule were abolished in 1960.[1] At present, all formal requirements in the law of contract are contained in statutes which deal with specific contracts. There are four main purposes for making such formal requirements.[2] First, they may serve as clear evidence of a transaction and of its terms. Secondly, they may have a cautionary effect, thereby deterring hasty, premature or ill-considered contracts being made. Thirdly, they may have a "channelling" function, offering "a legal framework into which a party may fit his actions."[3] Thus, formalities may mark off transactions from one another and create a standardised form of transaction.[4] Fourthly, formal requirements may be used as a device to protect the weaker parties to contracts. There has been an increasing tendency to impose such requirements with this last purpose in view: for example, in the cases of tenants, employees, debtors and sureties under consumer

4–001

---

[1] Corporate Bodies' Contracts Act 1960.
[2] Fuller (1941) 41 Col.L.Rev. 799; Law Commission No. 164 (1987), pp. 6–7.
[3] Fuller *op. cit.* at p. 801.
[4] Law Com. No. 164 (1987), p. 7.

credit agreements[5] as consumers of certain classes of services, such as package holidays[6] or "timeshare" accommodation.[7]

Formal requirements are discussed in relation to a number of specific contracts in Volume II of this work.[8] In the present Volume, which deals with general principles, there would be no point in attempting to make an exhaustive list of contracts for which formal requirements are imposed by statute. But two general points may be mentioned here. These are discussed in the next two paragraphs.

4–002 **Types of formal requirement.** Statutory requirements of form differ widely from one another. In a few cases, contracts are required to be made by deed: this is true, for example, of a lease for more than three years.[9] More frequently the requirement is that certain contracts must be in, or evidenced in, writing; but even requirements of this kind vary a good deal in stringency. Some statutes simply require, in general terms, that the contract must be in writing, or that there must be a note or memorandum in writing.[10] Others set out the formal requirements in great detail and even specify the size of the lettering and the colour of the print and paper.[11] Yet others do not require the contract to be, or to be evidenced in, writing at all, but only require one party to give the other written notice of specified terms of the contract.[12]

A further type of formal requirement may be found in the Timeshare Act 1992 which requires that those offering timeshare rights in respect of immovable property inform their would-be customers in writing of various matters relating to the contract, such as the services to which the customer would have access and the common facilities.[13]

The form of a contract may also affect the regulation which it attracts, rather than going to its validity. Thus, for example, the scheme of rules governing "construction contracts" under Part II of the Housing Grants, Construction and Regeneration Act 1996 applies only "where the construction contract is in writing", any other agreement between the parties being "effective for the purposes of this Part only if in writing".[14]

---

[5] Landlord and Tenant Act 1985, s.4; Consumer Credit Act 1974, ss.60, 61, 105; Consumer Credit (Agreements) Regulations (S.I. 1983 No. 1553), Sched. 5 as amended by S.I. 1984 No. 1600, S.I. 1985 No. 666, S.I. 1988 No. 2047.

[6] The Package Travel, Package Holidays and Package Tours Regulations 1992 (S.I. 1992 No. 3288), reg. 9.

[7] The Timeshare Regulations 1997, (S.I. 1997 No. 1081) reg. 6, amending the Timeshare Act 1992.

[8] See Vol. II, Chaps. 34, 38, 39, and 41.

[9] Law of Property Act 1925, ss.52, 54, as amended by Law of Property (Miscellaneous Provisions) Act 1989, s.1(8), Sched. 1, para. 2.

[10] *e.g.* Law of Property Act 1925, s.40, discussed *post*, §§ 4–005 *et seq.*

[11] *e.g.* Regulations made or to be made by the Secretary of State under the Hire-Purchase Act 1965, under the Consumer Credit Act 1974, s.60, or under the Unsolicited Goods and Services Act 1971, s.3A (inserted by the Unsolicited Goods and Services (Amendment) Act 1975, s.1). See S.I. 1965 No. 1646, S.I. 1975 No. 731, S.I. 1975 No. 732, and see regulations *cit. ante* n. 5.

[12] *e.g.* Landlord and Tenant Act 1962, s.1; Employment Rights Act 1996, ss.1–2, 4–6 (as amended); Estate Agents Act 1979, s.18.

[13] Timeshare Act 1992, s.1A(1) and Sched. 1 as inserted by Timeshare Regulations 1997, S.I. 1997 No. 1081, reg. 3.

[14] Housing Grants, Construction and Regeneration Act 1996, s.107 (which defines what is meant by agreement in writing for this purpose).

Effect of non-compliance. Non-compliance with such statutory requirements may produce various effects. It may make the contract void,[15] or unenforceable,[16] or unenforceable by one party[17] or enforceable only on an order of the court.[18] It may simply deprive the transaction of certain effects which it would have had, if the formal requirement had been observed, without generally impairing its validity or enforceability; this would be the case, for example, if a lease for more than three years were not made by deed[19]; if an assignment of a chose in action were made orally[20]; or if the sort of promise which is normally contained in a bill of exchange or promissory note were made orally. Failure to comply with formal requirements may also be a criminal offence, and in some cases this is the sole consequence of failure which is actually specified in the relevant statute.[21] The civil consequences of failure to comply with a statutory requirement of form in such a case would presumably depend on the court's view of the objects which the legislature sought to achieve in imposing the requirement. If the requirement was imposed to protect one of the parties to a contract, that party would probably be able to enforce the contract notwithstanding the formal defect; whether the other party could enforce it would depend on principles discussed elsewhere in this book.[22]

4–003

2. CONTRACTS FOR THE SALE OR OTHER DISPOSITION OF AN INTEREST IN LAND

Legislative history. The Statute of Frauds was passed in 1677 and in sections 4 and 17 it required that six classes of contracts must be supported by written evidence. Its object was to prevent fraudulent claims based on false evidence; but in practice it worked badly as it enabled contracting parties to rely on what were considered to be technical defences. Hence the statute was, whenever possible, whittled down by judicial construction; and it was largely repealed by the Law Reform (Enforcement of Contracts) Act 1954. Nevertheless, the statute still applies to contracts of guarantee[23] and its provisions were re-enacted in section 40 of the Law of Property Act 1925, which applies to contracts for the disposition of interests in land made on or before 26 September 1989.[24] However, by the Law of Property (Miscellaneous Provisions) Act 1989, s.2, section 40 of the Law of Property Act 1925 was itself repealed and new requirements were enacted which apply to all contracts for the sale or other disposition of interests in land made on or after September 27, 1989. The present edition of this work retains

4–004

---

[15] Bills of Sale Act (1878) Amendment Act 1882, s.9; Law of Property (Miscellaneous Provisions) Act 1989, s.2.

[16] *e.g.* Law of Property Act 1925, s.40: for the distinction between "void" and "unenforceable" contracts, see *ante*, §§ 1–037, 1–041.

[17] Consumer Credit Act 1974, s.65; Timeshare Act 1992, ss.5(2), 5A (as inserted by Timeshare Regulations 1997, S.I. 1997 No. 1081, reg. 9.

[18] Consumer Credit Act 1974, s.127.

[19] Law of Property Act 1925, s.52 ("void for the purpose of conveying or creating a legal estate"); and see s.54, as amended by the Law of Property (Miscellaneous Provisions) Act 1989, s.1 and Sched. 1, para. 2.

[20] *Post*, §§ 20–006, 20–015, 20–034.

[21] *e.g.* Landlord and Tenant Act 1962, s.1; *Shaw v. Groom* [1970] 2 Q.B. 504 (*post*, § 17–146).

[22] *i.e.* on the principles stated in *St. John Shipping Corp. v. Joseph Rank Ltd* [1957] 1 Q.B. 267; *post*, §§ 17–145 *et seq.*

[23] See Vol. II, Chap. 43.

[24] See *post*, §§ 4–005—4–046.

discussion of the old law (in the present tense) as it still governs contracts made before that date. While the old law may at times be of help in interpreting the new, this may not always be appropriate. As Peter Gibson L.J. observed in *Firstpost Homes Ltd v. Johnson*[25] "the Act of 1989 seems to me to have a new and different philosophy from that which the Statute of Frauds 1677 and section 40 of the Act of 1925 had. Oral contracts are no longer permitted. To my mind it is clear that Parliament intended that questions as to whether there was a contract, and what were the terms of the contract, should be readily ascertained by looking at the single document said to constitute the contract."

(a) *The Old Law: Contracts made on or before September 26, 1989*

4–005   **Law of Property Act 1925, s.40.** By section 40(1) of the Law of Property Act 1925,

> "No action may be brought upon any contract for the sale[26] or other disposition of land or any interest in land, unless the agreement upon which such action is brought, or some memorandum or note thereof, is in writing, and signed by the party to be charged or by some other person thereunto by him lawfully authorised."[27]

The section replaced, and was intended to give effect to the construction judicially placed upon, that portion of section 4 of the Statute of Frauds which related to interests in land. The section applies to contracts whether made before or after the commencement of the year 1926[28] and on or before September 26, 1989[29] and does not affect the law relating to part performance and sales by the court.[30]

(i) *Contracts within Section 40 of the Law of Property Act 1925*

4–006   **Contracts within the section.** The words "or other disposition" are widely defined[31] and include, *inter alia*, a mortgage, charge, lease, release and disclaimer; and an "interest in land" includes an undivided share, although this is now converted into an equivalent share in the proceeds of sale.[32] Similarly, section 4 of the Statute of Frauds applied to many contracts that concerned land although they were not contracts of sale.[33] Thus an agreement to convey an equity of redemption in land was within the statute, for a court of equity treated the equity of redemption as the land itself, or at all events as an interest in land.[34]

---

[25] [1995] 1 W.L.R. 1567 at 1576 and see *McCausland v. Duncan Lawrie Ltd* [1996] 4 All E.R. 995, 1001.

[26] A "sale" means the exchanging of property for money. An agreement to extinguish an existing debt if land is transferred is not a sale, see *Simpson v. Connolly* [1953] 1 W.L.R. 911.

[27] As to the contents and signature of the memorandum or note in writing, see *post*, §§ 4–017 *et seq.*; and see *Shardlow v. Cotterell* (1881) 20 Ch.D. 90; *Studds v. Watson* (1884) 28 Ch.D. 305; *Auerbach v. Nelson* [1919] 2 Ch. 383; *Lord Cloncurry v. Laffan* [1924] 1 Ir.R. 78.

[28] The date at which the Law of Property Act 1925 came into operation.

[29] The day before the Law of Property (Miscellaneous Provisions) Act 1989, s.2 came into operation.

[30] s.40(2); *post*, §§ 4–037—4–045.

[31] s.205(1)(ii).

[32] See *Cooper v. Critchley* [1955] Ch. 431, 439. *cf. Irani Finance Ltd v. Singh* [1971] 1 Ch. 59, 79.

[33] *McManus v. Cooke* (1887) 35 Ch.D. 681, 687–690, and cases there cited.

[34] *Massey v. Johnson* (1847) 1 Exch. 241, 255.

Contracts for the disposition of an interest in land within the meaning of the statute have been held to include the following: an agreement that if the plaintiff, the tenant of a farm, would surrender her tenancy to her landlord, and would prevail on her landlord to accept the defendant as his tenant in place of the plaintiff, the defendant would pay the plaintiff £100[35]; an agreement by the defendant, the landlord of a house, to put certain furniture into the house in consideration that the plaintiff would become tenant thereof[36]; an agreement to grant a lease of furnished premises[37]; and an agreement by the plaintiff to let a house to the defendant, to sell him furniture and fixtures therein, and to make alterations and improvements in the house, the defendant agreeing to take the house, and to pay for the furniture, fixtures and alterations.[38] An agreement to extend the time for acceptance, or an agreement that an acceptance which is out of time shall be treated as valid so as to create a contract, is not an agreement which the statute requires to be evidenced in writing, provided that the note or memorandum contained in the signed offer is otherwise sufficient.[39] Furthermore, it has been held that an agreement which compromised an action arising out of claims for land between cohabitants was not a contract for the disposition of land, but rather related to accounting for the proceeds of sale of the properties.[40]

An agreement to sell a debt, secured by bond and also by a mortgage of land,[41] **4–007** or to sell debentures of a company possessed of land charging all its property whatsoever and wheresoever,[42] is within the section. So is an agreement between two persons to become partners in working a colliery owned by one of them[43]; but a contract for a partnership is not within the section merely because the acquisition of land is necessary for carrying on the business.[44] An agreement by A, who had borrowed a sum of money from his bankers in July, to repay the loan out of the rent of a farm to become due to him at the Michaelmas following,[45] has been held within the section; so also has an agreement for regulating the height of a party wall, which was to be pulled down and rebuilt, and the position and shape of skylights on either side of it.[46] It seems that the contract may be within the section although the party agreeing to confer the interest does not, at the time, possess any interest in the land in question, as was held in an action against a

---

[35] *Cocking v. Ward* (1845) 1 C.B. 858, 867; followed in *Kelly v. Webster* (1852) 12 C.B. 283. (In both these cases there was a "part performance," but this could not assist the plaintiffs in courts of common law before the Judicature Acts.)

[36] *Mechelen v. Wallace* (1837) 7 A. & E. 49.

[37] *Inman v. Stamp* (1815) 1 Stark. 12; *Edge v. Strafford* (1831) 1 Cr. & J. 391; *Thursby v. Eccles* (1900) 17 T.L.R. 130.

[38] *Vaughan v. Hancock* (1846) 3 C.B. 766.

[39] *Morrell v. Studd and Millington* [1913] 2 Ch. 648, 658.

[40] *Simmons v. Simmons*, FAFMF 95/0485/F, [1996] C.L.Y. 2874 (decided under Law of Property (Miscellaneous Provisions) Act, s.2 which specifies that "disposition" bears the same meaning as under the Law of Property Act 1925, s.40).

[41] *Toppin v. Lomas* (1855) 16 C.B. 145.

[42] *Driver v. Broad* [1893] 1 Q.B. 744.

[43] *Caddick v. Skidmore* (1857) 2 De G. & J. 52.

[44] *Forster v. Hale* (1800) 5 Ves. 308; *Dale v. Hamilton* (1846) 5 Hare 369; *Gray v. Smith* (1890) 43 Ch.D. 208; *cf. Re De Nicols (No. 2)* [1900] 2 Ch. 410.

[45] *Ex p. Hall* (1879) 10 Ch.D. 615.

[46] *McManus v. Cooke* (1887) 35 Ch.D. 681.

public-house broker for breach of a contract to procure a lease of a public-house to be transferred by the lessee to the plaintiff.[47]

4–008   It has been held that a right of option in respect of land, as opposed to a mere right of pre-emption, is an interest in land for the purposes of binding third parties.[48] It is not settled, however, whether this distinction holds good in the context of the requirements of section 40.[49] Similarly, licences to occupy land may create "interests in land" in order to bind third parties, sometimes by way of proprietory estoppel and sometimes by way of imposing a constructive trust.[50] There is no requirement of written evidence in the case of the *creation* of a constructive trust,[51] but it appears that any *disposition* of an interest arising thereby would fall within section 53(1)(*c*) of the Law of Property Act.[52] A similar distinction may well apply to any interest arising under the doctrine of proprietary estoppel.

4–009   It is established that any transfer of an interest occurring as a result of compulsory purchase does not require the observance of section 40.[53] And where an equitable mortgage secures a guarantee, it appears that it is subject to the formal requirements of section 4 of the Statute of Frauds which applies to guarantees[54] rather than those of section 40 of the Law of Property Act 1925.[55]

4–010   **Variations.** In *Morall v. Krause*[56] the Court of Appeal held that any variation of a contract for the sale or other disposition of land must also satisfy the formal requirements of section 40 of the Law of Property Act 1925. In the absence of either a written memorandum or of part performance, any oral variation of such a contract can have no effect.

4–011   **Collateral agreements.**[57] If a collateral agreement, not involving the acquisition of land, is entered into at or before the time of making a written contract

---

[47] *Horsey v. Graham* (1869) L.R. 5 C.P. 9.

[48] *Pritchard v. Briggs* [1980] Ch. 388, 418 (for the purposes of the Land Charges Act 1925, s.10), followed in *Kling v. Keston Properties Ltd* [1985] P. & C.R. 212 (for the purposes of s.70(1) Land Registration Act 1925).

[49] *Emmett on Title* (1993), § 2.039 citing *National Provincial Bank Ltd v. Moore* (1967) 111 S.J. 357 and *cf. Cooper v. Critchley* [1955] Ch. 431 and *Irani Finance Ltd v. Singh* [1971] 1 Ch. 59 which establish that an undivided share in land is an "interest in land" for the purposes of s.40 Law of Property Act 1925 but *not* for the purposes of registration under the Land Charges Act 1925 or Land Registration Act 1925.

[50] Megarry and Wade, *The Law of Real Property* (5th ed., 1984), pp. 798 *et seq. cf.* Gray, *Elements of Land Law* (2nd ed., 1993), pp. 901 *et seq. cf. Wright v. Stavert* (1860) 3 E. & E. 721 where a "mere contractual licence" was held not subject to the Statute of Frauds, s.4.

[51] Law of Property Act 1925, s.53(2).

[52] Hanbury and Martin, *Modern Equity* (15th ed., 1997), pp. 78 *et seq. Oughtred v. I.R.C.* [1960] A.C. 206. It could be argued that the transfer of such an interest is part of the *operation* of a constructive trust within s.53(2) but *cf.* Law Com. No. 164 (1987), § 4.4 which recommended that the disposition of equitable interests in land, even those created informally, should be subject to formal requirements and see *post,* § 4–047.

[53] *Munton v. G.L.C.* [1976] 1 W.L.R. 649, 653.

[54] See Vol. II, §§ 44–038 *et seq.*

[55] *Deutsche Bank A.G. v. Ibrahim, Financial Times,* December 13, 1991 and January 15, 1992; Baughen [1992] Conv. 330; and see *post,* § 4–052.

[56] [1994] E.G.C.S. 177.

[57] Wedderburn [1959] Camb.L.J. 58, *cf.* Law Com. No. 164 (1987), pp. 20–21; and see *post,* § 4–063.

concerning land, the collateral agreement does not require to be evidenced in writing.[58] So, on the purchase of land an oral promise by the vendor to make up the road leading to the premises sold is not a contract for an interest in land apart from a conveyance of the highway.[59] Any such collateral agreement must be clearly proved.[60] Where, however, a collateral agreement is established, damages for breach of it can be recovered after conveyance of the land, as, for example, where the contract was to complete the building of a house on the land conveyed.[61]

Entire agreement clauses. No oral collateral agreement may arise if the **4–012** written contract, for example, of sale of an interest in land, is expressed to constitute the entire contract between the parties, variable only in writing.[62]

Sale of growing crops. A contract conferring an exclusive right to enter land **4–013** in order to mow and take away a crop of grass has been held to be within the statute.[63] It is difficult to reconcile all the decisions and dicta on the subject of simple sales of growing crops (conferring no right to enter the land).[64] A distinction is commonly drawn between *fructus industriales* and *fructus naturales*. The former are crops which are produced by annual cultivation and are not within the section. The latter are things which grow without any or with very little cultivation, trees being *fructus naturales* because "the labour employed in their planting bears so small a proportion to their natural growth."[65] It seems that a contract for the sale of *fructus naturales*, such as trees, is a contract for the sale of an interest in land if the trees are to remain in the land; but if they are to be immediately severed by the vendor[66] or if the contract requires the purchaser to sever them at once, the contract is not one for the sale of an interest in land.[67]

Other things to be detached from land. The section has been applied to **4–014** other things to be detached from land, such as gravel[68] and the building materials to accrue on the demolition of a house.[69] Such things are now within the definition of "goods" given in section 61 of the Sale of Goods Act 1979; but it may equally well be that such things are goods for the purpose of the Sale of

---

[58] *Angell v. Duke* (1875) L.R. 10 Q.B. 174 (in which *Cocking v. Ward* (1845) 1 C.B. 858 and *Mechelen v. Wallace* (1837) 7 A. & E. 49 were distinguished); *Boston v. Boston* [1904] 1 K.B. 124. See also *Pullbrook v. Laws* (1876) 1 Q.B.D. 284.

[59] *Jameson v. Kinmell Bay Land Co. Ltd* (1931) 47 T.L.R. 593; following *Erskine v. Adeane* (1873) L.R. 8 Ch.App. 756.

[60] *Hodges v. Jones* [1935] Ch. 657.

[61] *Lawrence v. Cassell* [1930] 2 K.B. 83.

[62] *McGrath v. Shah, The Times*, October 22, 1987 and see *Britain v. Rossiter* (1883) 11 Q.B.D. 123, 127.

[63] *Crosby v. Wadsworth* (1805) 6 East 602; and see *Wood v. Leadbitter* (1845) 13 M. & W. 838.

[64] See, *e.g. Marshall v. Green* (1875) 1 C.P.D. 35, 38 *et seq.*; and *Lavery v. Pursell* (1888) 39 Ch.D. 508.

[65] *Marshall v. Green* (1875) 1 C.P.D. 35, 40.

[66] *Smith v. Surman* (1829) 9 B. & C. 561; *Washbourn v. Burrows* (1847) 1 Exch. 107, 115.

[67] *Marshall v. Green, supra; Kauri Timber Co. Ltd v. Commissioner of Taxes* [1913] A.C. 771, 778.

[68] *Morgan v. Russell & Sons* [1909] 1 K.B. 357, 365.

[69] *Lavery v. Pursell* (1888) 39 Ch.D. 508.

Goods Act and land or interests in land for the purpose of section 40 of the Law of Property Act 1925.[70]

4–015   **Fixtures.** Fixtures are normally an interest in land. But a sale by a tenant of fixtures which he is entitled to remove is not within the section. He is considered to have sold neither goods nor an interest in land but to have assigned his right to sever.[71]

4–016   **Shooting rights.** A grant of a right to shoot over land and to take away a part of the game killed is a grant of an interest in land, and consequently within the statute.[72]

(ii) *Formal Requirements*

4–017   **General.** Section 40 does not specify the matters which the memorandum is to contain. These have been left to judicial interpretation and the courts have laid down the following rules as to the contents and nature of the memorandum.

4–018   **Parties.** The memorandum must identify the parties and the capacity in which each of them contracts: it must name or describe them[73] and state which is (for example) buyer and which is seller.[74] It may sufficiently describe the parties without actually naming them. Thus a vendor of land may be adequately described as "proprietor,"[75] or as "trustee selling under a trust for sale"[76] or even as "legal personal representative."[77] But it is not sufficient to describe a party as "vendor"[78] or "landlord."[79] A pronoun may be sufficient if there is evidence to show to whom it refers.[80]

4–019   **Subject-matter.** The memorandum must describe the subject-matter,[81] but may sufficiently describe it even though the description has to be supplemented by extrinsic evidence. Thus a memorandum recording the sale of "24 acres of land, freehold . . . at Totmonslow" was held sufficient on proof that the vendor had no other land there.[82] If the land is subject to incumbrances the memorandum need not state them all.[83]

---

[70] *Benjamin's Sale of Goods* (5th ed., 1997), § 1.091. See also Blackburn, *Contract of Sale* (3rd ed. 1910), pp. 7–16.

[71] *Hallen v. Runder* (1834) 1 Cr.M. & R. 266; *Lee v. Gaskell* (1876) 1 Q.B.D. 700.

[72] *Webber v. Lee* (1882) 9 Q.B.D. 315; *R. v. Surrey County Court Judge* [1910] 2 K.B. 410.

[73] See *Williams v. Jordan* (1877) 6 Ch.D. 517 ("Sir" insufficient); *Re Lindrea* (1913) 109 L.T. 623 (Christian name sufficient); *E. Goldsmith (Sicklesmere) Ltd v. Baxter* [1970] Ch. 85 (company misdescribed but identifiable) and see *Perrylease Ltd v. Imecar A.G.* [1988] 1 W.L.R. 463, 468–469.

[74] *Vandenbergh v. Spooner* (1866) L.R. 1 Ex. 316; *Newell v. Radford* (1867) L.R. 3 C.P. 52; *Stockwell v. Niven* (1889) 61 L.T. 18; *Dewar v. Mintoft* [1912] 2 K.B. 373.

[75] *Sale v. Lambert* (1874) L.R. 18 Eq. 1; *Rossiter v. Miller* (1878) 3 App.Cas. 1125, 1140–1141.

[76] *Catling v. King* (1877) 5 Ch.D. 660, 664.

[77] *Fay v. Miller, Wilkins & Co.* [1941] Ch. 360.

[78] *Potter v. Duffield* (1874) L.R. 18 Eq. 4; *Thomas v. Brown* (1876) 1 Q.B.D. 714; *cf. Jarrett v. Hunter* (1886) 34 Ch.D. 182.

[79] *Coombs v. Wilks* [1891] 3 Ch. 77.

[80] *Carr v. Lynch* [1900] 1 Ch. 613; *cf. Stokes v. Whicher* [1920] 1 Ch. 411, 419–422.

[81] Description of part is insufficient: *Burgess v. Cox* [1951] Ch. 383.

[82] *Plant v. Bourne* [1897] 2 Ch. 281 and see *Perrylease Ltd v. Imecar A.G., supra* at 469–473.

[83] *Timmins v. Moreland Street Property Co.* [1958] Ch. 110.

Consideration. The memorandum of a contract for the disposition of an **4–020** interest in land must state the consideration provided by the purchaser.[84]

Terms. The memorandum must contain a statement of the material[85] terms of **4–021** the contract. Thus the memorandum of an agreement for a lease must state the beginning and duration of the term.[86] If on a sale separate prices are to be paid for separate lots,[87] or if the price is agreed to be paid by instalments,[88] or if chattels are to be included as well as land for an indivisible price,[89] the memorandum must not omit such terms, otherwise it will not satisfy the statute. The reason for these rules is that "the very object of the Statute of Frauds was to prevent parol evidence being gone into to elucidate that which the parties failed to make distinct by reducing it into writing."[90] There is, however, authority[91] for the view that if a material term has been omitted from the memorandum, the plaintiff may waive such a term where it is solely for his benefit[92] and not of a major importance, and enforce the contract without the term in question. Conversely, a party may cure the omission of a term to his detriment by consenting to perform it.[93] Finally, an express term which is identical to a term implied by law, for example, a term that vacant possession is to be given on completion, need not be included in the memorandum.[94]

Memorandum need not be prepared as such. The memorandum need not **4–022** be prepared for the purpose of satisfying the statutory requirement of written evidence. Any writing which contains the requisite particulars will suffice so long as it comes into existence before an action is brought on the contract.[95] Thus a recital in a will,[96] a receipt given by an auctioneer before receiving the purchaser's deposit,[97] a letter written by one of the parties to his own agent,[98] an entry in the minute book of a company[99] and pleadings in a previous action between different parties[1] have been held sufficient. A letter repudiating liability is sufficient if it admits the terms of the contract but disputes the construction put

---

[84] *Blagden v. Bradbear* (1806) 12 Ves. 466, 471; *Laythoarp v. Bryant* (1836) 2 Bing.N.C. 735, 742; *Burgess v. Cox* [1951] Ch. 383 (disapproved on other grounds in *Scott v. Bradley* [1971] Ch. 850). *cf. Sudbrook Trading Estate Ltd v. Eggleton* [1983] 1 A.C. 444.

[85] *Hawkins v. Price* [1947] Ch. 645; *cf. Beckett v. Nurse* [1948] 1 K.B. 535.

[86] *Marshall v. Berridge* (1881) 19 Ch.D. 233; *Edwards v. Jones* (1921) 124 L.T. 740.

[87] *Smith v. MacGowan* (1938) 159 L.T. 278.

[88] *Tweddell v. Henderson* [1975] 1 W.L.R. 1496.

[89] *Ram Narayan s/o Shankar v. Rishad Hussain Shah s/o Tusaduq Hussain Shah* [1979] 1 W.L.R. 1349.

[90] *Caddick v. Skidmore* (1857) 2 De G. & J. 52, 56.

[91] *Morrell v. Studd and Millington* [1913] 2 Ch. 648, 660; *North v. Loomes* [1919] 1 Ch. 378, 385–386; *Beckett v. Nurse* [1948] 1 K.B. 535; *Turner v. Hatton* [1952] 1 T.L.R. 1184; *Ram Narayan s/o Shankar v. Rishad Hussain Shah s/o Tusaduq Hussain Shah, supra,* at 1351.

[92] *cf. Hawkins v. Price* [1947] Ch. 645, 657–658.

[93] *Martin v. Pycroft* (1852) 2 De G.M. & G. 785; Megarry (1951) 67 L.Q.R. 300; *Scott v. Bradley* [1971] Ch. 850. Contrast *Burgess v. Cox* [1951] Ch. 383, 391.

[94] *Farrell v. Green* (1974) 232 E.G. 587.

[95] See *Lucas v. Dixon* (1889) 22 Q.B.D. 357; *cf. Farr, Smith & Co. Ltd v. Messers Ltd* [1928] 1 K.B. 397; *Daniels v. Trefusis* [1914] 1 K.B. 788.

[96] *Re Hoyle* [1893] 1 Ch. 84.

[97] *Phillips v. Butler* [1945] Ch. 358.

[98] *Gibson v. Holland* (1865) L.R. 1 C.P. 1; *Law v. Robert Roberts & Co.* [1964] I.R. 292.

[99] *Jones v. Victoria Graving Dock Co.* (1877) 2 Q.B.D. 314.

[1] *Grindell v. Bass* [1920] 2 Ch. 487; *cf. Hardy v. Elphick* [1974] Ch. 65 (action between same parties).

upon them by the other party; but not if it denies that a contract was ever made on the terms alleged.[2] Apart from the exceptional case of a written offer signed by one party and accepted orally by the other,[3] the writing must acknowledge the existence of a contract. It is now settled, after some hesitation, that a letter expressed to be "subject to contract" is not in itself a sufficient memorandum to satisfy the statute.[4]

4–023   **Agreement contained in several documents.** Where no single document fully records the transaction, it may be possible to produce a sufficient memorandum by joining together two or more documents. This may be done where the document which is signed by the party to be charged expressly or by implication refers to another existing document.[5] Thus where a signed document, which does not contain the terms of the agreement, refers to an unsigned document which does, parol evidence may be given for the purpose of identifying the latter as being the document referred to in the former.[6] But such express reference is not absolutely necessary: it is enough if "you can spell out of the document a reference in it to some other transaction."[7] So in *Stokes v. Whicher*[8] the defendant's agent signed for him, as "vendor," a carbon copy of a typewritten contract not containing a purchaser's name. The plaintiff had signed the original document, of which the carbon copy was a duplicate, and had given a cheque for the deposit, a receipt for it signed by the defendant's agent being put on the carbon copy. The court held that a sufficient memorandum had been constituted by (a) incorporating the cheque into the carbon copy, (b) connecting the carbon copy with the original, and (c) identifying the person who paid the deposit as the plaintiff. A similar decision was reached where a house was sold by auction and the name of the vendor did not appear in the memorandum signed by the purchaser. The latter, however, by the memorandum acknowledged that she

---

[2] *Dobell v. Hutchinson* (1835) 3 A. & E. 355; *Bailey v. Sweeting* (1861) 9 C.B.(N.S.) 843; *Wilkinson v. Evans* (1866) L.R. 1 C.P. 407; *Buxton v. Rust* (1872) L.R. 7 Ex. 279; *Thirkell v. Cambi* [1919] 2 K.B. 591.

[3] *Smith v. Neale* (1857) 2 C.B.(N.S.) 67, 88; *Reuss v. Picksley* (1866) L.R. 1 Ex. 342; *Lever v. Koffler* [1901] 1 Ch. 543; *Parker v. Clark* [1960] 1 W.L.R. 286. But *cf. Re New Eberhardt Co.* (1889) 43 Ch.D. 118, 129.

[4] *Tiverton Estates Ltd v. Wearwell Ltd* [1975] Ch. 146; *Sherbrooke v. Dipple* (1980) 255 E.G. 1203; *Cohen v. Nessdale Ltd* [1981] 3 All E.R. 118, [1982] 2 All E.R. 97; *Clipper Maritime Ltd v. Shirlstar Container Transport Ltd* [1987] 1 Lloyd's Rep. 546 (guarantee). *cf. Griffiths v. Young* [1970] Ch. 675. *Law v. Jones* [1974] Ch. 112 was not followed in *Tiverton Estates Ltd v. Wearwell Ltd, supra: cf. Daulia Ltd v. Four Millbank Nominees Ltd* [1978] Ch. 231, 249–251 and *cf.* Law Com. No. 164 (1987), § 1.4.

[5] *Ridgway v. Wharton* (1857) 6 H.L.C. 238; *Long v. Millar* (1879) 4 C.P.D. 450; *Studds v. Watson* (1884) 28 Ch.D. 305; *Wylson v. Dunn* (1887) 34 Ch.D. 569; *cf. Reading Trust Ltd v. Spero* [1930] 1 K.B. 492; *Hill v. Hill* [1947] Ch. 231; *Fowler v. Bratt* [1950] 2 K.B. 96; *Burgess v. Cox* [1951] Ch. 383; *Timmins v. Moreland Street Property Co. Ltd* [1958] Ch. 110, 130; *Elias v. George Sahely & Co. (Barbados) Ltd* [1983] 1 A.C. 646. See also *Re Danish Bacon Co. Ltd Staff Pension Fund Trusts* [1971] 1 W.L.R. 248 (on s.53(1)(c) of the Law of Property Act 1925; *post*, § 20–025). The document must be in existence: *Turnley v. Hartley* (1848) 3 New Pr. Cas. 96; *Timmins v. Moreland Street Property Co. Ltd, supra*, at 123, 133.

[6] See *Ridgway v. Wharton* (1857) 6 H.L.C. 238, 257; *Jones v. Victoria Graving Dock Co.* (1877) 2 Q.B.D. 314; *Oliver v. Hunting* (1890) 44 Ch.D. 205; *Smith-Bird v. Blower* [1939] 2 All E.R. 406; *Re Danish Bacon Co. Ltd Staff Pension Fund Trusts, supra*.

[7] *Stokes v. Whicher* [1920] 1 Ch. 411, 418.

[8] [1920] 1 Ch. 411. *cf. Cave v. Hastings* (1881) 7 Q.B.D. 125; *Franco-British Ship Store Co. v. Compagnie des Chargeurs Française* (1926) 42 T.L.R. 735; *Jacobs v. Batavia & General Plantations Trust Ltd* [1924] 1 Ch. 287 (a case not involving the statute); contrast *Coombs v. Quinney* (1916) 142 L.T.J. 23.

bought the property "subject to the conditions of sale," the contents of which sufficiently identified the vendor. The memorandum was therefore sufficient to satisfy the statute.[9] Similarly, a letter which admits the existence of an oral agreement may be joined with an earlier letter written "subject to contract," to which the latter letter refers, for the purpose of ascertaining the terms of the admitted agreement.[10] Also a letter beginning "Dear Sir" and signed by the defendant can be joined with the envelope in which it was sent (so as to identify the addressee)[11] since "the existence of a letter sent by post presupposes the existence of an envelope containing it."[12] And it has been held that two documents can be joined (even if they do not refer to each other) if on placing them side by side it becomes obvious without the aid of parol evidence that they are connected.[13]

Documents which cannot be connected by parol evidence. Parol evidence **4–024** to identify references has been frequently admitted.[14] But parol evidence cannot be admitted to connect two or more writings which contain no reference express or implied to each other. Thus, where the defendant signed a book, headed "Shakespeare Subscribers, their Signatures," and a printed prospectus which contained the terms of the agreement was delivered to him at the time, but this prospectus was not referred to in the book signed by the defendant, the contract was unenforceable because the connection between the book containing the signature and the prospectus could be established only by parol evidence.[15] So where, at a sale of goods by auction, the auctioneer signed the purchaser's name in the catalogue, but the conditions of sale were not annexed to the catalogue or referred to therein, it was held that there was not a sufficient memorandum of the contract within section 40.[16] An entry in the auctioneer's book cannot be used to prove a contract within the statute, unless the entry comprises such a reference to the conditions of sale as will identify them upon production as being the conditions mentioned in the entry.[17] In *Timmins v. Moreland Street Property Co. Ltd*,[18] prospective purchasers gave a cheque payable to the vendors' solicitors as the deposit on the purchase and the vendors in return gave a receipt incorporating

---

[9] *Fay v. Miller, Wilkins & Co.* [1941] Ch. 360. See also *Albert (Men's Wear) v. Prevezer* (1949) 154 E.G. 424.

[10] *Griffiths v. Young* [1970] Ch. 675, as interpreted in *Tiverton Estates Ltd v. Wearwell Ltd* [1975] Ch. 146. See also *Law v. Jones* [1974] Ch. 112 as interpreted in *Daulia Ltd v. Four Millbank Nominees Ltd* [1978] Ch. 231; *Elias v. George Sahely & Co. (Barbados) Ltd, supra,* at 655.

[11] *Pearce v. Gardner* [1897] 1 Q.B. 688.

[12] *Stokes v. Whicher* [1920] 1 Ch. 411, 418. See also *Last v. Hucklesby* (1914) 58 S.J. 431 (lost envelope).

[13] *Studds v. Watson* [1884] 28 Ch.D. 305, 308–309; *Sheers v. Thimbleby* (1897) 13 T.L.R. 451; *Stokes v. Whicher, supra,* at 419. *cf. Burgess v. Cox* [1951] Ch. 383 (disapproved on other grounds by *Scott v. Bradley* [1971] Ch. 850).

[14] See *Cave v. Hastings* (1881) 7 Q.B.D. 125, 128, and the cases there cited; *Oliver v. Hunting, supra; Shardlow v. Cottrell* (1881) 20 Ch.D. 90; *Studds v. Watson* (1884) 28 Ch.D. 305; *Filby v. Hounsell* (1896) 2 Ch. 737; *Auerbach v. Nelson* [1919] 2 Ch. 383; *Elliott v. Pierson* [1948] Ch. 452, 455.

[15] *Boydell v. Drummond* (1809) 11 East 142, 158; *cf. Peirce v. Corf* (1874) L.R. 9 Q.B. 210; *Kronheim v. Johnson* (1877) 7 Ch.D. 60.

[16] *Kenworthy v. Schofield* (1824) 2 B. & C. 945; *Rishton v. Whatmore* (1878) 8 Ch.D. 467.

[17] *Rishton v. Whatmore, supra* at 468; *M'Meekin v. Stevenson* [1917] 1 Ir.R. 348.

[18] [1958] Ch. 110. See Megarry (1958) 74 L.Q.R. 22.

the terms of the contract. It was held that there could not be spelled out of the cheque any reference, express or implied, to any other document or to any transaction other than the order to pay a sum of money constituted by the cheque itself.

4–025   **Lost memorandum.** If it is proved that the memorandum has been lost or destroyed a copy not signed by the party to be charged may be admitted as secondary evidence.[19]

4–026   **Signature.** The Law of Property Act 1925, s.40, requires that the document should be "signed by the party to be charged," and it is sufficient if it is signed by the party to be charged without being signed by the other party.[20] The interpretation of this provision well illustrates the reluctance of the courts to enforce the full rigour of the statute, as will be seen from the following paragraphs.

4–027   **Position of signature.** The signature need not be at the foot of the matter written, but may be either in the body or at the beginning of it[21]; it may be in any part of the document provided that it authenticates every material clause.[22] If it is at the foot of the matter written, it is to be taken to apply to the whole, unless there is something expressly to rebut that presumption: and if it is not at the foot it may apply to the whole if upon the evidence it is found that the party signing so intended.[23] Accordingly it has been held that if a party draws up an agreement in his own handwriting, beginning: "I, AB, agree, etc.," this is a sufficient signature, although he does not subscribe his name at the bottom.[24] So, a memorandum in the buyer's handwriting beginning, "Sold J.D." (*i.e. to* him) and signed by the seller's agent, was held to bind the buyer.[25] But if a memorandum is headed "Articles of Agreement between A and B" and concludes "As witness our hands . . . " the parties must actually subscribe: the mention of their names at the beginning is clearly not intended as a signature.[26] And it is clear that, if the memorandum which contains the name of the party to be charged is written by someone else, the fact of his name being written in the body of it will not avail as a signature within the statute unless there is evidence that the person who wrote the instrument had the authority of that party to do so.[27] When an auctioneer filled in the defendant's name as vendor in a document purporting to be an agreement for sale and presented it to the plaintiff purchaser for signature,

---

[19] *Barber v. Rowe* [1948] 2 All E.R. 1050.

[20] *Laythoarp v. Bryant* (1836) 2 Bing.N.C. 735; *Buxton v. Rust* (1872) L.R. 7 Ex. 279. *cf. post,* § 4–061.

[21] *Schneider v. Norris* (1814) 2 M. & S. 286 (bill-head); *Caton v. Caton* (1867) L.R. 2 H.L. 127; *Evans v. Hoare* [1892] 1 Q.B. 593.

[22] *Caton v. Caton, supra*; *Kronheim v. Johnson* (1877) 7 Ch.D. 60, 67; *Cohen v. Roche* [1927] 1 K.B. 169, 174–176; *Behnke v. Bede Shipping Co. Ltd* [1927] 1 K.B. 649, 660; *Hill v. Hill* [1947] 1 Ch. 231, 240.

[23] *Foster v. Mentor Life Assurance Co.* (1854) 3 E. & B. 48, 71; and see *Lobb v. Stanley* (1844) 5 Q.B. 574.

[24] *Knight v. Crockford* (1794) 1 Esp. 190.

[25] *Johnson v. Dodgson* (1837) 2 M. & W. 653; *Durrell v. Evans* (1862) 1 H. & C. 174.

[26] *Hubert v. Treherne* (1842) 3 Man. & G. 743, 754.

[27] *Hubert v. Treherne, supra*; *Hucklesbury v. Hook* (1900) 82 L.T. 117, 118.

the document was a valid memorandum, although neither auctioneer nor vendor had signed it in the ordinary sense of the word.[28]

Signature intended to authenticate document. The signature must be **4–028** affixed with the intention of authenticating the whole document. Thus where one party or his agent merely adds his signature to the document as witness of the signature of the other, the former is not bound by the signature.[29] But the use of the term "witness" is not conclusive to show that the signature was added for the purpose of witnessing, especially if the document did not require attestation.[30]

Form of signature. Where the name of the vendor was printed in the heading **4–029** of an invoice sent by him to the buyer, and which contained the particulars, quantities and prices of the goods sold, the printed name was held to be a sufficient signature to bind the vendor.[31] But there must be circumstances which show a recognition of the printed signature as his own by the party to be charged in order that the document to which it is affixed may bind him. Where a purchaser took up a sheet of paper bearing the printed name and address of the vendor, wrote in his own address and the name of the vendor, but the paper was not signed by the latter or dictated by him, it was held not to be a sufficient memorandum to bind the vendor.[32]

Signature by pencil is clearly sufficient,[33] and so is the signature on a telegraph form,[34] or by mark,[35] or by initials.[36]

Alteration in memorandum. Where a memorandum is altered after it has **4–030** been signed either in order to correct a mistake in the written statement of an existing contract[37] or before the parties are contractually bound at all,[38] parol evidence is admissible to show that the signature was intended to apply to the memorandum as altered.[39] But such signature cannot authenticate subsequent alterations which effect a variation of a contract concluded and binding on the parties at some time previous to the alterations.[40] And an alteration of the

---

[28] *Leeman v. Stocks* [1951] Ch. 941, applying *Schneider v. Norris* (1814) 2 M. & S. 286 and *Evans v. Hoare* [1892] 1 Q.B. 593; distinguishing *Hubert v. Treherne, supra.*

[29] *Gosbell v. Archer* (1835) 2 A. & E. 500; *Kerns v. Manning* [1935] I.R. 869.

[30] *Wallace v. Roe* [1903] 1 I.R. 32.

[31] *Saunderson v. Jackson* (1800) 2 B. & P. 238; *Schneider v. Norris* (1814) 2 M. & S. 286; *Sweet v. Lee* (1841) 3 Man. & G. 452; and see *Durrell v. Evans* (1862) 1 H. & C. 174; *Tourret v. Cripps* (1879) 48 L.J.Ch. 567; *Cohen v. Roche* [1927] 1 K.B. 169.

[32] *Hucklesby v. Hook* (1900) 82 L.T. 117; *Cohen v. Roche, supra; cf. Evans v. Hoare* [1892] 1 Q.B. 593; *Behnke v. Bede Shipping Co. Ltd, supra* at 660; *Decouvreur v. Jordan, The Times,* May 25, 1987.

[33] See *Geary v. Physic* (1826) 5 B. & C. 234 (indorsement of promissory note).

[34] *Godwin v. Francis* (1870) L.R. 5 C.P. 295; *McBlain v. Cross* (1872) 25 L.T. 804; *R. v. Riley* [1896] 1 Q.B. 309, 313.

[35] See *Baker v. Dening* (1838) 8 A. & E. 94 (signature of will); *Dyas v. Stafford* (1881) 7 L.R.Ir. 590.

[36] *In the Goods of Blewitt* (1879) 5 P.D. 116 (signature of will); see *Phillimore v. Barry* (1818) 1 Camp. 513; *Chichester v. Cobb* (1866) 14 L.T. 433; *Hill v. Hill* [1947] Ch. 231, 240.

[37] *Black v. Gompertz* (1852) 7 Exch. 862.

[38] *Stewart v. Eddowes* (1874) L.R. 9 C.P. 311; *Koenigsblatt v. Sweet* [1923] 2 Ch. 314.

[39] *New Hart Builders Ltd v. Brindley* [1975] Ch. 342.

[40] *ibid.,* although the court considered that there was no logical ground for this distinction, at 352.

memorandum in a material particular subsequent to the signature without the consent of both parties destroys the rights of the party making such alteration.[41]

4–031   **Signature by agent.** A memorandum in writing within the statute may be signed by the party to be charged or "by some other person thereunto by him lawfully authorised." The authority of the agent need not be in writing[42]; and the principal may be undisclosed[43] or unnamed.[44] In order to satisfy the statute the memorandum so signed need not be one which the principal has authorised the agent to sign for the purpose of a contract: thus where the chairman of a limited company signed minutes containing the contract there was a sufficient memorandum.[45] Any letter written by an agent within the scope of his authority which refers to and recognises an unsigned document as containing the terms of a contract made by his principal is a sufficient memorandum and it is not necessary that the principal should have authorised the agent to sign the letter as a record of the contract.[46] A solicitor who is employed to prepare a draft contract has no authority to state the heads of the agreement to be embodied in the formal contract in such a way as to bind his client,[47] nor, if he is instructed by his client to deny the existence of a contract, has he any authority to admit it[48]; but counsel employed to draft pleadings in an action[49] and a solicitor authorised to complete a contract[50] have been held to be lawfully authorised to sign a memorandum.[51] In *Smith v. MacGowan*[52] the defendant's solicitors purchased on his account three lots of freehold land at an auction. The three lots were combined in one memorandum, but the solicitors had no authority so to combine the lots; there ought to have been a separate memorandum for each lot. In an action for specific performance, it was held that the memorandum was not a proper memorandum of any of the contracts shown to have been entered into and did not satisfy the statute.

4–032   **Estate agents.** In general, the function of an estate agent is to introduce a purchaser for property which it is desired to sell to a would-be vendor. Ordinarily, therefore, he has no authority to enter into or sign a contract on behalf of the

---

[41] *Davidson v. Cooper* (1844) M. & W. 343 (guarantee). As to what is a material particular see *Adsetts v. Hives* (1863) 33 Beav. 52; and see *post*, § 26–019.

[42] *Emmerson v. Heelis* (1809) 2 Taunt. 38, 46; *Graham v. Musson* (1839) 5 Bing.N.C. 603; *Heard v. Pilley* (1869) L.R. 4 Ch.App. 548; *Daniels v. Trefusis* [1914] 1 Ch. 788.

[43] *Filby v. Hounsell* [1896] 2 Ch. 737.

[44] *Davies v. Sweet* [1962] 2 Q.B. 300.

[45] *Jones v. Victoria Graving Dock Co.* (1877) 2 Q.B.D. 314; *cf. John Griffiths Cycle Corporation Ltd v. Humber & Co. Ltd* [1899] 2 Q.B. 414, 417; *Daniels v. Trefusis* [1914] 1 Ch. 788; *North v. Loomes* [1919] 1 Ch. 378.

[46] *John Griffiths Cycle Corporation Ltd v. Humber & Co. Ltd, supra*; *Horner v. Walker* [1923] 2 Ch. 218.

[47] *Smith v. Webster* (1876) 3 Ch.D. 49.

[48] *Thirkell v. Cambi* [1919] 2 K.B. 590. *cf. Daniels v. Trefusis, supra.*

[49] *Grindell v. Bass* [1920] 2 Ch. 487; *Farr, Smith & Co. Ltd v. Messers Ltd* [1928] 1 K.B. 397.

[50] *North v. Loomes* [1919] 1 Ch. 378; *Gavaghan v. Edwards* [1961] 2 Q.B. 220; *Smith v. Mansi* [1963] 1 W.L.R. 26, 34.

[51] Legal professional privilege may attach to such documents so as to prevent disclosure of a memorandum for the purposes of s.40: *Balabel v. Air India* [1988] Ch. 317, 330.

[52] [1938] 3 All E.R. 447.

vendor, although this may be conferred upon him expressly.[53] A vendor may, however, be estopped from asserting the want of authority of his agent.[54]

Agent for both parties. The same person may be agent for both parties.[55] **4-033** Thus, by the usage of a business, a broker may be the agent of both buyer and seller, so that his signature of the contract binds both parties within the statute.[56] A sale by auction is within the section and the auctioneer, who is primarily the agent of the vendor, becomes at the fall of the hammer the agent of the highest bidder also; he is authorised to sign the highest bidder's name as purchaser and so may sign the contract for both parties.[57] Thus he is entitled to sign in the name and on behalf of the purchaser a memorandum sufficient to satisfy the provisions of the statute,[58] provided that he does so at the time of the auction.[59] The authority of the auctioneer does not extend to his clerk[60] unless the bidder by word or sign or otherwise confers such authority on the clerk[61] but a licensed auctioneer employed by a firm of auctioneers to conduct the auction can sign on behalf of the buyer even though the buyer has not specifically conferred authority on him.[62]

Agent must be a third person. The memorandum cannot be signed by one **4-034** contracting party as agent of the other.[63] Nor, generally speaking, will one contracting party be bound by the signature of an employee of the other party[64]; but he may be bound by such signature if the employee in question has, for the purpose of the transaction, authority to sign on behalf of both parties.[65]

Deeds. It was formerly doubtful whether the requirement of writing applied to **4-035** deeds, the subject-matter of which was within the statute, so as to require them, as was usual and desirable, to be signed as well as sealed[66]; but in the case of

---

[53] *Davies v. Sweet, supra* at 305; *Wragg v. Lovett* [1948] 2 All E.R. 968, 969. *cf. Rosenbaum v. Belson* [1900] 2 Ch. 267.

[54] *Worboys v. Carter* (1987) 283 E.G. 307.

[55] *Durrell v. Evans* (1862) 1 H. & C. 174; *Murphy v. Boese* (1875) L.R. 10 Ex. 126; *Gavaghan v. Edwards* [1961] 2 Q.B. 220.

[56] *Rucker v. Cammeyer* (1794) 1 Esp. 105; *Parton v. Crofts* (1864) 16 C.B.(N.S.) 11; *Trueman v. Loder* (1840) 11 A. & E. 589; and see *Pike Sons & Co. v. Ongley* (1887) 18 Q.B.D. 708; *Thompson v. Gardiner* (1876) 1 C.P.D. 777.

[57] *Kenworthy v. Schofield* (1824) 2 B. & C. 945, 947; *Bartlett v. Purnell* (1836) 4 A. & E. 792; *Phillips v. Butler* [1945] Ch. 358.

[58] *Emmerson v. Heelis* (1809) 2 Taunt. 38; *White v. Procter* (1811) 4 Taunt. 209; *Sims v. Landray* [1894] 2 Ch. 318, 320; see *Van Praagh v. Everidge* [1903] 1 Ch. 434; *Dewar v. Mintoft* [1912] 2 K.B. 373, doubted in *Cohen v. Roche* [1927] 1 K.B. 169; *Phillips v. Butler* [1945] Ch. 358; Fry, *Specific Performance* (6th ed., 1921), §§ 529–531.

[59] *Peirce v. Corf* (1874) L.R. 9 Q.B. 210; *Chaney v. Maclow* [1929] 1 Ch. 461; the auctioneer's signature need not be appended before he leaves the saleroom but must fairly form "part of the transaction of sale." *M'Meekin v. Stevenson* [1917] 1 Ir.R. 348, 354; *Sakhas v. Donford Ltd* (1983) 46 P. & C.R. 290.

[60] *Bell v. Balls* [1897] 1 Ch. 663.

[61] As in *Bird v. Boulter* (1833) 4 B. & Ad. 443; *Sims v. Landray* [1894] 2 Ch. 318, 320.

[62] *Wilson & Sons v. Pike* [1949] 1 K.B. 176. The distinctions drawn in the text above are supported by authority but appear to have little (if any) merit.

[63] *Farebrother v. Simmons* (1822) 5 B. & Ad. 333; *Sharman v. Brandt* (1871) L.R. 6 Q.B. 720.

[64] *Dixon v. Broomfield* (1814) 2 Chit. 205 (guarantee); *cf. Graham v. Musson* (1839) 5 Bing.N.C. 603.

[65] *Wilson & Sons v. Pike* [1949] 1 K.B. 176.

[66] See *Aveline v. Whisson* (1842) 4 Man. & G. 801; *Cooch v. Goodman* (1842) 2 Q.B. 580; *Cherry v. Hemming* (1849) 4 Exch. 631, 636; but see *Pitman v. Woodbury* (1848) 3 Exch. 4, 11; Black. Com.ii. 306.

deeds executed on or after January 1, 1926, it is provided by section 73 of the Law of Property Act 1925 that where an individual executes a deed he shall either sign or place his mark upon the same and sealing alone shall not be deemed sufficient.[67] Moreover, with effect from July 31, 1990, the requirement of sealing for deeds executed by individuals[68] and by companies within the meaning of the Companies Act 1985[69] has been abolished and replaced with new requirements of intention, signature and attestation.[70]

(iii) *The Effect of Failure to Comply with the Formal Requirements*

4–036 **At law: contract unenforceable.** A contract which fails to comply with the statutory formalities imposed by section 40 is not void but only unenforceable.[71] No action can be brought to enforce it directly. Nor can it be indirectly enforced by suing on some other cause of action. Thus if A orally agrees to allow B to dig for gravel on A's land and later turns B and his machinery off the land, B cannot sue A in trespass.[72] But as the contract is not void, it can sometimes be relied upon as a defence.[73] Thus in the above example B does not commit a trespass by entering on the land and digging for the gravel: the oral contract operates as a licence and excuses the trespass.[74] Once, however, A withdraws the licence B will become a trespasser if he does not leave within a reasonable time; and if A then sues B for possession B cannot, in this action, rely on the oral contract as a defence.[75] *A fortiori* A is entitled to turn B out or to sue for possession if he withdraws the licence before B enters but B nonetheless makes a clandestine entry.[76]

As the contract is not void, money or property transferred under it cannot be recovered back: thus, if a purchaser pays a deposit under an oral contract, the vendor can retain the deposit if the purchaser defaults.[77] And a security given for the performance of the oral contract is not void for want of consideration merely because the oral contract is unenforceable: thus an action can be brought on a cheque given in payment of a deposit under the oral contract.[78]

4–037 **In equity: the doctrine of part performance.** Where the claimant has partly performed an oral contract required by the statute to be evidenced in writing, in

---

[67] See *ante*, § 1–043.

[68] Law of Property (Miscellaneous Provisions) Act 1989, s.1.

[69] Companies Act 1985, s.36A (as inserted by Companies Act 1989, s.130(1)).

[70] See *ante*, §§ 1–043 *et seq.*

[71] *Leroux v. Brown* (1852) 12 C.B. 801; *Elias v. George Sahely & Co. (Barbados) Ltd* [1983] A.C. 646, at 650.

[72] *Carrington v. Roots* (1837) 2 M. & W. 248; the actual decision is still law though dicta at 255, 257 that failure to comply with the statute makes the contract void are not.

[73] Williams (1934) 50 L.Q.R. 532. *cf. Take Harvest Ltd v. Liu* [1993] A.C. 532.

[74] *Carrington v. Roots, supra,* at 255.

[75] *cf. Sidebotham v. Holland* [1895] 1 Q.B. 378. It is assumed that the licence is revocable.

[76] *Delany v. T. P. Smith Ltd* [1946] K.B. 393; *cf. Maddison v. Alderson* (1883) 8 App.Cas. 467 (title deeds wrongfully obtained).

[77] *Thomas v. Brown* (1876) 1 Q.B.D. 714; *Monnickendam v. Leanse* (1923) 39 T.L.R. 445. After the decision of the House of Lords in *Kleinwort Benson v. Lincoln City Council* [1998] 3 W.L.R. 1095 a person who has paid money under a contract of sale etc. of an interest in land thought by that person to be valid, but in law unenforceable for want of formality, may be able to recover it on the ground of this mistake of law, see *post*, §§ 4–069 and 13–038 *et seq.* Of course, if the vendor repudiates, the purchaser can recover the deposit on the ground of failure of consideration: *Pulbrook v. Lawes* (1876) 1 Q.B.D. 284. See also Law of Property Act 1925, s.49(2) and Goff and Jones, *The Law of Restitution* (3rd ed. 1986), pp. 395–400.

[78] *Low v. Fry* (1935) 152 L.T. 585.

the expectation that the defendant would perform the rest of the contract, the court will not allow the defendant to escape from his contract upon the strength of the statute,[79] but may order specific performance of the oral contract. The principle is that the defendant may not set up the statute where the claimant has been induced, or allowed, by the defendant to alter his position on the faith of the contract, so that it would be fraud on the part of the defendant to rely on the statute.[80] The doctrine of part performance was expressly preserved by sections 40(2) and 55(d) of the Law of Property Act 1925.

Scope of the doctrine. There was formerly some conflict of judicial opinion **4–038** as to the types of contract within the doctrine,[81] but it is now applicable only to contracts affecting interests in land within the meaning of section 40(1) of the Law of Property Act 1925. There must, however, be a definite contract in existence of which the court would order specific performance, since part performance cannot of itself determine material terms of the contract.[82] Nor will part performance substantiate a claim for damages unless the contract is specifically enforceable, in which case damages may be awarded in lieu of specific performance.[83]

Acts by the person seeking to enforce the contract. The acts of part **4–039** performance relied on must have been done by the person seeking to enforce the contract, or on his behalf.[84] It is not therefore in general possible to rely on acts done by the person against whom the contract is sought to be enforced. However, in *United Bank of Kuwait plc v. Sahib*[85] the court accepted that, by way of exception to this rule, a deposit of deeds with the intention of creating an equitable mortgage avoids the need to satisfy the formal requirements of section 40, even though the deposit (and therefore the act of part performance) is made by the mortgagor and, therefore, not by the person seeking to enforce the contract.

Acts must point to the existence of a contract. The acts of part performance **4–040** relied on must be such as to be referable to some contract, and may be referred to the alleged one; they must prove the existence of some contract, and be consistent with the contract alleged.[86] In *Maddison v. Alderson*,[87] the House of Lords held that an oral contract between an intestate and a woman, that he should devise to her a life estate in land, in return for her promise to serve him as his housekeeper without wages, could not be enforced merely because the woman

---

[79] *Mundy v. Jolliffe* (1839) 5 My. & Cr. 167, 177; *Ungley v. Ungley* (1877) 5 Ch.D. 887; *Dickinson v. Barrow* [1904] 2 Ch. 339; *Rawlinson v. Ames* [1925] Ch. 96.

[80] See *Caton v. Caton* (1865) L.R. 1 Ch.App. 137, 148, affd. (1867) L.R. 2 H.L. 127.

[81] See *Britain v. Rossiter* (1879) 11 Q.B.D. 123, 129; *Maddison v. Alderson, supra*, at 474; *McManus v. Cooke* (1887) 35 Ch.D. 681. *cf.* Spry, *Equitable Remedies* (3rd ed., 1984), p. 252.

[82] *Stimson v. Gray* [1929] 1 Ch. 629, 643–644.

[83] *Britain v. Rossiter* (1879) 11 Q.B.D. 123; *Lavery v. Pursell* (1888) 39 Ch.D. 508; *Stimson v. Gray, supra*.

[84] *Caton v. Caton* (1865) L.R. 1 Ch.App. 137, 148, affd. (1867) L.R. 2 H.L. 127; *Maddison v. Alderson* (1883) 8 App.Cas. 467, 475; *Rawlinson v. Ames* [1925] Ch. 96, 108.

[85] [1995] 2 W.L.R. 94, 108, 110. Compare the position under the 1989 Act, *post*, § 4–052.

[86] Fry, *Specific Performance* (6th ed., 1921), p. 278, cited with approval in *Kingswood Estate Co. Ltd v. Anderson* [1963] 2 Q.B. 169, 189; *Wakeham v. Mackenzie* [1968] 1 W.L.R. 1175, 1181; *Steadman v. Steadman* [1976] A.C. 536.

[87] (1883) 8 App.Cas. 467. See also *Re Gonin* [1979] Ch. 16. Contrast *Wakeham v. Mackenzie, supra*.

had served without wages for many years up to his death, since her service might have been for reasons other than the alleged contract. In his work on specific performance Fry L.J. further stated that the acts of part performance must be referable to "no other title" than the alleged contract[88]; but this view "has long been exploded."[89] If the obvious explanation of the acts is that they were done with reference to a contract, the doctrine of part performance applies although some ingenious alternative explanation for them can be suggested.[90] It is only necessary that the acts relied on should, on the balance of probabilities, point to their having been done in pursuance of[91] some contract, and either show the nature of or be consistent with the oral contract alleged.[92] It is not necessary for the acts of part performance to show the precise terms of the oral contract.[93]

4–041 **Act relating to land.** It is not clear from the decision of the House of Lords in *Steadman v. Steadman*[94] whether the acts of part performance need to be referable to the disposition of an interest in land. In that case, the payment by a husband to his wife of £100 arrears of maintenance was held to be on the facts a sufficient act of part performance of an oral agreement for the transfer by the wife of an interest in the matrimonial home. Lord Reid and Viscount Dilhorne considered that the acts of part performance need not relate to land, whereas Lord Salmon and Lord Morris of Borth-y-Gest (dissenting) considered that they did.[95] Lord Simon of Glaisdale found it unnecessary to determine the issue as he found a sufficient act relating to land on the facts.[96] Walton J. subsequently considered that he was entitled to follow the traditional view which requires that the act relates to land.[97] It has been suggested, however, that acts of part performance which have reference to any term of an indivisible contract will be acceptable as sufficient to allow the doctrine to be applied when this is necessary to prevent injustice.[98] Such a suggestion may be supported by reference to Lord Reid's observation in *Steadman v. Steadman* that the doctrine of part performance is "an invention of the Court of Chancery and in deciding any case not clearly covered by authority . . . the equitable nature of the remedy must be kept in mind."[99]

4–042 **Acts held sufficient.** A sufficient act of part performance has been found where one party (previously a stranger to the possession) has taken possession of premises with the consent of the other party[1]; where one party has instructed solicitors to prepare a transfer, paid costs and disbursements including those of

---

[88] (6th ed., 1921), p. 277.

[89] *Kingswood Estate Co. Ltd v. Anderson, supra,* at 189.

[90] *Broughton v. Snook* [1938] Ch. 505, 515.

[91] *Elsden v. Pick* [1980] 1 W.L.R. 898, 905.

[92] *Steadman v. Steadman, supra.*

[93] *Kingswood Estate Co. Ltd v. Anderson, supra,* cited with approval in *Steadman v. Steadman, supra* at 542, 546.

[94] [1976] A.C. 536. See also *Liddell v. Hopkinson* (1974) 233 E.G. 513, and Wade (1974) 90 L.Q.R. 433.

[95] *ibid.* at 542, 554, 568–570 and 547 respectively.

[96] *ibid.* at 563.

[97] *Re Gonin, supra* at 31 and see *Sutton v. Sutton* [1984] Ch. 184; Thompson (1984) 48 Conv. 152.

[98] Hanbury and Maudsley, *Modern Equity* (12th ed., 1985), p. 669.

[99] [1976] A.C. 536, 540.

[1] *Morphett v. Jones* (1818) 1 Swanst. 172; *Ungley v. Ungley* (1877) 5 Ch.D. 887; *Brough v. Nettleton* [1921] 2 Ch. 25; *Kingswood Estate Co. Ltd v. Anderson* [1963] 2 Q.B. 169; *Lloyds Bank plc v. Carrick, The Times,* March 13, 1996.

mortgagees, and entered into covenants with mortgagees[2]; where alterations have been done on the premises by one party at the request of and under the supervision of the other (the purchaser)[3]; where one party has given notice to weekly tenants at the other's (the purchaser's) request[4]; and where a third party was let into possession, it appearing that the contract was made for that party's benefit.[5] Where an oral agreement for a lease provided for an option to purchase and the proposed lessee took possession, it was held that the lessee could exercise the option.[6]

On the other hand, acts in contemplation of or preparatory to performance,[7] **4–043** such as viewing the land or having it valued,[8] are not sufficient, nor is the attendance of one party at the other party's premises at an appointed time with a banker's draft for the deposit, and his part of the written contract of sale duly signed and engrossed, which is then and there tendered.[9] The mere continued possession of a tenant at will, or from year to year, in expectation of a lease is not part performance,[10] for possession is not sufficient if it is explicable without reference to a contract.[11] The payment of one quarter's rent at an increased figure orally stipulated for has been held to be such part performance of a contract for a lease by a tenant as to entitle him to enforce the contract.[12] Any act which is referable to the grant of a new tenancy is sufficient. Thus while expenditure on a farm in the ordinary course of husbandry will not suffice,[13] expenditure on such things as alterations, new buildings, or repairs, will entitle the tenant to a decree.[14] An application for planning permission has been held insufficient.[15]

Payment of money. It was previously believed that part payment of the **4–044** purchase price[16] or of rent in advance[17] was not part performance, for "the payment of money is an equivocal act, not (in itself) . . . indicative of a contract concerning land."[18] But since the decision of the House of Lords in *Steadman v. Steadman*,[19] there is no general rule that the payment of money cannot constitute an act of part performance.[20]

---

[2] *Re Windle* [1975] 1 W.L.R. 1628, 1635–1636.

[3] *Dickinson v. Barrow* [1904] 2 Ch. 339; *Rawlinson v. Ames* [1925] Ch. 96; *Broughton v. Snook* [1938] Ch. 505.

[4] *Daniels v. Trefusis* [1914] 1 Ch. 788, 799.

[5] *Hohler v. Aston* [1920] 2 Ch. 420.

[6] *Brough v. Nettleton, supra.*

[7] Fry *op. cit.* p. 295.

[8] *Clerk v. Wright* (1737) 1 Atk. 12, 13; *Cooth v. Jackson* (1801) 6 Ves. 12, 41; *Elsden v. Pick* [1980] 1 W.L.R. 898, 905. *cf. Re Windle, supra.*

[9] *Daulia Ltd v. Four Millbank Nominees Ltd* [1978] Ch. 231.

[10] *Faulkner v. Llewellin* (1862) 31 L.J.Ch. 549.

[11] *Wills v. Stradling* (1797) 3 Ves. 378; *Kingswood Estate Co. Ltd v. Anderson* [1963] 2 Q.B. 169, 181.

[12] *Nunn v. Fabian* (1865) L.R. 1 Ch.App. 35; *Miller and Aldworth Ltd v. Sharp* [1899] 1 Ch. 622.

[13] *Brennan v. Bolton* (1842) 2 Dr. & War. 349; *Conner v. Fitzgerald* (1883) 11 L.R.Ir. 106, 113.

[14] *Lester v. Foxcroft* (1701) 1 Colles PC 108; *Williams v. Evans* (1875) L.R. 19 Eq. 547; *Broughton v. Snook* [1938] Ch. 505.

[15] *New Hart Builders Ltd v. Brindley* [1975] Ch. 342.

[16] *Britain v. Rossiter* (1879) 11 Q.B.D. 123, 130.

[17] *Chapronière v. Lambert* [1917] 2 Ch. 356.

[18] *Maddison v. Alderson* (1883) 8 App.Cas. 467, 479.

[19] [1976] A.C. 536.

[20] *Steadman v. Steadman, supra; Re Gonin* [1979] Ch. 16, 30; *Cohen v. Nessdale Ltd* [1981] 3 All E.R. 118 affd. on other grounds [1982] 2 All E.R. 97. *cf. Re Windle* [1975] 1 W.L.R. 1628, 1635.

4–045   **Effect of an act of part performance.** The effect of a sufficient act of part performance is to enable evidence to be given of all the terms of the contract and not only of the terms related to the act of part performance.[21] It does not, however, enable evidence to be given of independent contracts, even though made between the same parties and on the same occasion.[22]

4–046   **Proprietary estoppel.** A substantive equitable right of property may also be conferred by the operation of "proprietary estoppel"[23] in cases of acquiescence or encouragement, without any need for a written memorandum or agreement.

(b) The New Law: Contracts made on or after September 27, 1989

4–047   **Law of Property (Miscellaneous Provisions) Act 1989, s.2.** The law relating to the formal requirements of contracts for the sale or other disposition of an interest in land were significantly changed by the Law of Property (Miscellaneous Provisions) Act 1989, s.2. This provision, which puts into law the recommendations of the Law Commission in its report, *Formalities for Contracts for Sale etc. of Land*[24] supersedes section 40 of the Law of Property Act, 1925[25] in relation to contracts made on or after September 27, 1989.[26] Section 2(1) states:

> "A contract for the sale or other disposition of an interest in land can only be made in writing and only by incorporating all the terms which the parties have expressly agreed in one document or, where contracts are exchanged, in each."

This change was prompted by a concern to settle the uncertainty surrounding section 40, in particular as regards the status of letters made "subject to contract" as memoranda for the purposes of that section[27] and the ambit of the doctrine of part performance after the decision of the House of Lords in *Steadman v. Steadman*.[28] Section 2 makes a strict formal requirement whose effect is to preclude the existence of any contract for the sale or other disposition of land unless it is *made* in writing. Unlike the position under the old law, written evidence by way of a memorandum or note of the contract is clearly not enough. Moreover, the doctrine of part performance, at least in its normal form, is abolished.[29]

4–048   **Agreements made "subject to contract".** In *Enfield L.B.C. v. Arajah*[30] the Court of Appeal held that, quite apart from the question whether the formal requirements contained in section 2 of the 1989 Act had been satisfied, a letter which was headed "subject to contract" and which was relied on by a tenant as creating a new tenancy, clearly envisaged that a new lease would be completed

---

[21] *Sutherland v. Briggs* (1841) 1 Hare 26, 32; *Brough v. Nettleton* [1921] 2 Ch. 25.
[22] *Buckmaster v. Harrop* (1807) 13 Ves. 456, 474.
[23] See *ante*, §§ 3–129 *et seq.*
[24] Law Com. No. 164 (1987).
[25] Law of Property (Miscellaneous Provisions) Act 1989, s.2(8).
[26] *ibid.* s.5(3), (4).
[27] Law Com. No. 164 (1987), §§ 1.4–1.6 and *cf. ante*, § 4–022, n. 4.
[28] [1976] A.C. 563 and see Law Com. No. 164, § 1.9 and *cf. ante*, § 4–041.
[29] This paragraph of § 4–047 was quoted with approval by Simon Brown L.J. in *Godden v. Merthyr Tydfil Housing Association* [1997] 1 N.P.C. 1.
[30] [1995] E.G.C.S. 164.

before the parties were bound, with the result that, while this qualification was in force, the relationship did not become binding on either party unless and until there was an exchange of lease and counterpart.

(i) *Contracts within Section 2 of the Law of Property (Miscellaneous Provisions) Act 1989*

General. The new formal requirements apply to contracts[31] for the "sale or other disposition of an interest in land."[32] Section 2(6) of the 1989 Act specifies that "disposition" has the same meaning for this purpose as for the Law of Property Act 1925 and reference should be made to the earlier discussion of this term in that context.[33] The 1989 Act, however, itself defines the term "interest in land" for the purposes of these new formal requirements as "any estate, interest or charge in or over land or in or over the proceeds of sale of land."[34] It has been held that section 2 of the 1989 Act applies equally to an executory agreement, that is in this context, an agreement which was made at a time when neither of its parties possessed any proprietary interest in the property in question.[35]   **4–049**

Variations. In *McCausland v. Duncan Lawrie Ltd*[36] the Court of Appeal held that material variations of contracts of sale, etc. of an interest in land also have to fulfill the formal requirements contained in section 2 of the 1989 Act. According to the court this means that the contract as varied has to be in writing and incorporated in one document, or each document if contracts were exchanged, and signed by or on behalf of each party to the contract.[37] On the facts of *McCausland*, the variation was held to be material as it attempted to advance the contractual date for completion and therefore the time when either party might make time of the essence by service of a notice to complete.   **4–050**

Options. In *Spiro v. Glencrown Properties Ltd*[38] the question arose whether an option granted by a vendor of land is a "contract for the sale or other disposition of an interest in land" within the meaning of section 2(1) of the 1989 Act.[39] Hoffmann J. held that it was, but that the notice by which the option was   **4–051**

---

[31] Jenkins [1993] Conv. 13, 18 *et seq.* contends that the term "contract" for the purposes of s.2 of the 1989 Act does not include "arrangements" effected by deed. However, it is difficult to see why a court should wish to allow avoidance of the special formal requirements imposed on contracts for the sale etc. of interests in land contained in s.2, simply because such a contract is contained in a deed. The historical differences between covenant and *assumpsit* on which Jenkins relies should not be permitted to defeat the clear purpose of s.2 which was to make one set of clear requirements in relation to this type of contract in the interests of certainty.

[32] Law of Property (Miscellaneous Provisions) Act 1989, s.2(1).

[33] See *ante*, §§ 4–006 *et seq.*

[34] Law of Property (Miscellaneous Provisions) Act 1989, s.2(6). This definition made clear that the term includes an agreement to assign an undivided share in land, that is a share in the proceeds of sale of land subject to a trust for sale, but this has become unnecessary since the amendments made by the Trusts of Land and Appointment of Trustees Act 1996: *Emmett on Title* (1998) § 2–039.

[35] *Singh v. Beggs* (1996) 71 P. & C.R. 120.

[36] [1997] 1 W.L.R. 38. *cf. Morall v. Krause* [1994] E.G.C.S. 177 (decided under the Law of Property Act 1925, s.40) *ante*, § 0–000.

[37] The Court of Appeal thereby followed the approach of the House of Lords in *Morris v. Baron & Co.* [1918] A.C. 1, 31 and 29 and Willes J. in *Noble v. Ward* (1867) L.R. 2 Ex. 135, 137, though in relation to different formal requirements.

[38] [1991] Ch. 537; and see Jenkins [1993] Conv. 13.

[39] As Scott L.J. remarked in a later case "[i]t is evident that the draftsman of this section did not take account of options": *Trustees of the Chippenham Golf Club v. North Wiltshire District Council* (1991) 64 P. & C.R. 527, 530.

exercised was not: the section "was intended to prevent disputes over whether the parties had entered into a binding agreement or over what terms they had agreed. It prescribes the formalities for recording their mutual consent. But only the grant of the option depends upon consent. The exercise of the option is a unilateral act. It would destroy the very purpose of the option if the purchaser had to obtain the vendor's countersignature to the notice by which it was exercised."[40] As Scott L.J. observed in a later case, the alternative view which Hoffmann J. rejected, and according to which the exercise of options are subject to the section's formal requirements, would mean that it "had by an unintended side wind destroyed the enforceability of options."[41]

4–052   **Equitable mortgages.** In *United Bank of Kuwait plc v. Sahib*,[42] the Court of Appeal held that equitable mortgages or charges arising out of a deposit of documents of title found their basis in an implied contract and that such a contract could exist only if the rigorous formal requirements of section 2 of the Law of Property (Miscellaneous Provisions) Act 1989 are satisfied. But it is less clear whether this provision applies where the equitable mortgage secures a guarantee which would attract the less rigorous requirements of section 4 of the Statute of Frauds.[43] In *Deutsche Bank A.G. v. Ibrahim*,[44] which was decided under the old law,[45] the plaintiff bank sought a declaration that a deposit of documents of title by the defendants created an enforceable equitable mortgage in its favour. However, the court accepted the defendants' argument that where a third party pledges property with a creditor for the purposes of providing security for the liability of a debtor, that third party is a guarantor up to the value of the pledged property and the transaction is therefore governed by the formal requirements contained in section 4 of the Statute of Frauds rather than section 40 of the Law of Property Act 1925, and therefore held that the doctrine of part performance was inapplicable.[46] However, as one commentator has noted, there was no clear reason given by the court for giving priority to section 4 of the Statute of Frauds in this way, particularly given that the plaintiff had relied on the equitable mortgage rather than on the guarantee.[47] It may be thought instead that where two analyses of a transaction exist in parallel, each with their own formal requirements, the more demanding set of requirements should prevail, and, if this were accepted, then section 2 of the 1989 Act would apply to cases like *Deutsche Bank A.G. v. Ibrahim*. It is submitted, however, that a better view would be to apply those formal requirements which apply to the analysis of the transaction on which the claimant is relying before the court. Thus, where a claimant seeks a remedy such as foreclosure which can only be justified by treating the transaction as an equitable mortgage, section 2 of the 1989 Act should apply.[48]

---

[40] [1991] Ch. 537, 541, *per* Hoffmann J.
[41] *Trustees of the Chippenham Golf Club v. North Wiltshire District Council, supra,* at 530; and see further *Tootal Clothing Ltd v. Guinea Properties Ltd* (1991) 64 P. & C.R. 452, 455.
[42] [1997] Ch. 107.
[43] See *post*, Vol. II, §§ 44–038 *et seq.*
[44] *Financial Times*, December 13, 1991 and January 15, 1992, noted by Baughen [1992] Conv. 330.
[45] See *ante*, §§ 4–005—4–046.
[46] *cf. ante.*
[47] Baughen *op. cit.* p. 332.
[48] *ibid.*

Equitable leases. Under the old law, a lease which was required to be made 4–053
by deed[49] but which had been merely put in writing could take effect in equity
as a contract to create a legal lease as the writing would satisfy the formal
requirements of section 40 of the Law of Property Act 1925.[50] However, this
equitable relief depended on the availability of specific enforcement of a contract
to create the lease and this would clearly not be available if this contract were a
nullity owing to its failure to comply with the formal requirements of section 2.[51]
While under the old law a purely oral contract to create a lease could be
enforceable as long as there existed sufficient part performance, with the exception of short leases,[52] such an oral contract for a lease would also fall foul of
section 2.

"Lock-out agreements." Where a prospective vendor of land agrees with a 4–054
prospective purchaser for a clear specified period not to deal with any other
purchaser and this agreement is supported by consideration,[53] this agreement is
in principle enforceable and is commonly known as a "lock-out agreement."[54]
Although such an agreement clearly relates to the sale of land, the Court of
Appeal has confirmed that its negative nature means that it is not a contract for
the sale of any interest in land and is not therefore subject to the requirements of
section 2 of the 1989 Act.[55]

Compromises. In *Payne v. Zafiropoyloy*[56] the Eastbourne County Court held 4–055
that a compromise of a dispute over the parties' respective interests in a property
which were the subject of legal proceedings did not constitute a contract for the
sale or other disposition of an interest in land for the purposes of section 2 of the
Law of Property (Miscellaneous Provisions) Act 1989.

Composite agreements. Where a larger agreement between two parties 4–056
includes within it one relating to the sale or other disposition of an interest in
land, the formal requirements of section 2 apply only to that part of their
composite agreement. So, according to Scott L.J. "[i]f parties choose to hive off
part of the terms of their composite bargain into a separate contract distinct from
the written land contract that incorporates the rest of the terms, I can see nothing
in section 2 that provides an answer to an action for enforcement of the land
contract, on the one hand, or of the separate contract on the other hand. Each has
become, by the contractual choice of the parties, a separate contract."[57] Where
the land contract otherwise fulfils the formal requirements of section 2, it will not
fail to do so simply because it does not incorporate other elements from the

---

[49] The Law of Property (Miscellaneous Provisions) Act 1989, s.1 changed the law relating to the
formal requirements for deeds, abolishing the requirement of sealing and replacing it with requirements of a clear intention as to the making of a deed, of signature and of attestation: see *ante*,
§§ 1–043 *et seq.*

[50] Gray *op. cit.* p. 744.

[51] Howell [1990] Conv. 441, 443.

[52] See *post*, § 4–057.

[53] Such an agreement would be valid in the absence of consideration if contained in a deed, but this
would possess its own formal requirements: see *ante*, §§ 1–042 *et seq.*

[54] *Walford v. Miles* [1992] 2 A.C. 128, 139.

[55] *Pitt v. P.H.H. Asset Management Ltd* [1994] 1 W.L.R. 322.

[56] [1994] C.L.Y. 3513. *cf. Simmons v. Simmons* FAFMF 95/0485/F [1996] C.L.Y. 2874 and *ante*,
§ 4–006.

[57] *Tootal Clothing Ltd v. Guinea Properties Ltd* (1991) 64 P. & C.R. 452, 456; *Simmons v.
Simmons, supra.*

composite agreement.[58] On the other hand, in *Godden v. Merthyr Tydfil Housing Association*[59] the parties had made an agreement under which the defendants undertook to purchase from the plaintiff land which he was to acquire, prepare and develop to their order. The Court of Appeal held that this agreement constituted a single scheme and could not be divided into two discrete agreements, one involving the disposition of land and another not.

4–057   **Excluded contracts.** Section 2(5) of the 1989 Act excludes from the new formal requirements contracts to grant short leases,[60] contracts regulated by the Financial Services Act 1986, and those made in the course of a public auction. The last of these exclusions represents a change, as such contracts were subject to a requirement of a written memorandum under the previous law.[61] The Law Commission considered that the retention of this requirement fulfilled no cautionary or protective purpose as the practice is that the auctioneer may sign as agent for both the purchaser and vendor.[62]

(ii) *Formal Requirements*

4–058   **"Made in writing."** As has been noted, the most important change is that contracts for the sale etc. of an interest in land "can only be made in writing and only by incorporating all the terms which the parties have expressly agreed in one document, or where contracts are exchanged, in each."[63] It is explained that "[t]he terms may be incorporated in a document either by being set out in it or by reference to some other document."[64] No longer is a note or memorandum which may serve as evidence of the contract enough.

4–059   **"All the terms which the parties have expressly agreed in one document" and rectification.** At first sight, the omission of an express term of an oral agreement would seem to have the effect of rendering the whole contract a nullity as one can "only be made . . . by incorporating all the terms . . . expressly agreed."[65] However, section 2(4) of the Act recognises the power of the court to order the rectification of a written document so as to conform with the express terms of the oral agreement which it records and provides that where a written document relating to the sale of land has been so rectified, "the contract shall come into being, or be deemed to have come into being, at such a time as may be specified in the order."

In *Firstpost Homes Ltd v. Johnson*,[66] the Court of Appeal explained what is meant by the requirement that the contract be made in one document. There, an owner of certain farm property had agreed orally with a director of a company to sell the property to it at a cost of £1,000 per acre. The director had then typed a letter purporting to come from the owner agreeing to sell the land at this price, with a place for her signature and with an enclosed plan, which showed the land

---

[58] *cf. post*, § 4–059.
[59] [1997] 1 N.P.C. 1.
[60] Under the Law of Property Act 1925, s.54(2).
[61] See *ante*, § 4–033.
[62] Law Com. No. 164 (1987), § 4.11. For another exclusion from the ambit of s.2, see Channel Tunnel Rail Link Act 1996, ss.41(1) and 56(1).
[63] Law of Property (Miscellaneous Provisions) Act 1989, s.2(1).
[64] *ibid.* s.2(2).
[65] *ibid.* s.2(1).
[66] [1995] 1 W.L.R. 1567.

in question outlined in colour and which was signed by the director. The Court of Appeal held that, on these facts, the requirements of section 2 of the 1989 Act had not been fulfilled, as the letter and the plan constituted two documents (the former referring to the latter as being enclosed with it), but the letter (which allegedly contained the contract) had not been signed by the director on behalf of the company as was required.[67] However, the court also noted that while on its terms the letter contained no commitment by the company to purchase the property, the company could have applied to the court to rectify the letter so as to reflect the oral agreement.[68] In *Robert Leonard (Developments) Ltd v. Wright*, the Court of Appeal exercised its power to order rectification of the terms of documents exchanged by the parties' solicitors by telephone so as to include reference to the sale of the chattels which had been included in the parties' previous oral contract, and the court also ordered that this rectified contract should be deemed to come into being from the date of the exchange of documents.[69] The Court of Appeal recognised that allowing rectification detracted from the legislative purpose of section 2 which was to prevent disputes either as to whether the parties had entered into a binding agreement or as to what terms they had agreed, but the availability of rectification showed that "it was clearly the intention of the Act that the all terms requirement should not be so inflexible as to cause hardship or unfairness where there has been a mistake resulting in a venial non-compliance with the Act."[70]

"Exchange of contracts." In *Commission for the New Towns v. Cooper*   **4–060**
(Great Britain) Ltd,[71] the Court of Appeal explained the significance of the alternative formal requirement in section 2 of the Law of Property (Miscellaneous Provisions) Act 1989 that all the terms of the contract which the parties have expressly agreed be incorporated "where contracts are exchanged, in each [document]". According to Stuart-Smith L.J.[72] the expression "exchange of contracts", even if not a term of art, possesses the following features.

1. Each party draws up or is given a document which incorporates all the terms which they have agreed, and which is intended to record their proposed contract. The terms that have been agreed may have been agreed either orally or in writing or partly orally or [*sci*: and] partly in writing.
2. The documents are referred to as "contracts" or "parts of contract", although they need not be so entitled. They are intended to take effect as formal documents of title and must be capable on their face of being fairly described as contracts having that effect.
3. Each party signs his part in the expectation that the other party has also executed or will execute a corresponding part incorporating the same terms.
4. At the time of execution neither party is bound by the terms of the document which he has executed, it being their mutual intention that neither will be bound until the executed parts are exchanged.

---

[67] See *post*, § 4–061.
[68] [1995] 1 W.L.R. 1567 at 1576, 1577.
[69] [1994] N.P.C. 49. *cf. Enfield L.B.C. v. Arajah* [1995] E.G.C.S. 164 (where apparently the possibility of rectification was not raised).
[70] Lexis transcript, at 10 *per* Henry L.J.
[71] [1995] Ch. 259.
[72] *ibid.* at 285.

5. The act of exchange is a formal delivery by each party of its part into the actual or constructive possession of the other with the intention that the parties will become actually bound when exchange occurs, but not before.

6. The manner of exchange may be agreed and determined by the parties . . .

As a result, the Court of Appeal held (through strictly *obiter*) that this requirement was not satisfied by the mere exchange of a signed letter of offer and a signed letter of acceptance, even if each had contained the (same) express terms of the contract as alleged.[73]

4–061 **Signature.** Section 2(3) requires that "[t]he document incorporating the terms or, where contracts are exchanged, one of the documents incorporating them (but not necessarily the same one) must be signed by or on behalf of each party to the contract." This provision requires both parties to the contract to sign,[74] though it recognises the possibility of valid signature by the agent of either vendor or purchaser. As one leading work has noted, however, a solicitor is not necessarily authorised to sign the writing on behalf of his client merely as a result of the solicitor-client relationship and so express authority should be given by the client where it is intended that the solicitor is to sign.[75]

In *Firstpost Homes Ltd v. Johnson*,[76] the Court of Appeal held that "signature" in section 2 of the 1989 Act should be given its ordinary linguistic meaning, with the result that the section requires that the parties must write their names with their own hands upon the document. The court thereby rejected the applicability of earlier authorities on the meaning of "signature" for the purposes of the Statute of Frauds 1677 and section 40 of the Law of Property Act 925.[77] As Balcombe L.J. observed, "the clear policy of [section 2] is to avoid the possibility that one or other party may be able to go behind the document and introduce extrinsic evidence to establish a contract, which was undoubtedly a problem under the old law".[78]

On the other hand, in the same case, Peter Gibson L.J. accepted that the principle laid down by the House of Lords in *Caton v. Caton*[79] in relation to the Statute of Frauds 1677 to the effect that the party's signature must be inserted in such a way as to authenticate the whole instrument[80] applies equally to the requirement of signature made by section 2 of the 1989 Act. Thus, where a letter in which A agrees to sell a piece of land to B refers to a plan of the land in question and the court considers that the letter and the plans constitute a single

---

[73] The Court of Appeal distinguished its earlier unreported decision in *Hooper v. Sherman*, November 30, 1994 which took a different position adding that it had been made on the basis of a wrong concession by counsel: [1995] Ch. 259, 289, 295.

[74] Under s.40 of the Law of Property Act 1925, signature is necessary only for "the party to be charged": see *ante*, § 4–026.

[75] *Emmett on Title* (1998), § 2–048 and see *ante*, § 4–031.

[76] [1995] 1 W.L.R. 1567.

[77] Notably *Evans v. Hoare* [1892] 1 Q.B. 550, 561 and *cf. ante*, § 4–000: see [1995] 1 W.L.R. 1567, 1574–1577.

[78] [1995] 1 W.L.R. 1567, 1577.

[79] (1867) L.R. 2 H.L. 127.

[80] See *ante*, § 4–027.

document, B's signature of the plan may well not constitute authentication of the whole.[81]

(iii) *The Effect of Failure to Comply with the Formal Requirements*

Effect of non-compliance. Unlike section 40 of the Law of Property Act   **4–062**
1925, which makes unenforceable those contracts which do not comply with its requirements,[82] any agreement not complying with the requirements contained in section 2 of the 1989 Act is a nullity,[83] as a contract governed by the section "can only be made in writing." The Law Commission considered that the principal effect of this would be to exclude the operation of the doctrine of part perform-ance[84]: "[w]ithout writing there will be no contract for either party to perform."[85] Certainly, the courts could hardly use the doctrine of part performance as such to enforce an oral agreement. However, the doctrine is itself merely part of a wider equitable principle, *viz.*, that equity will not allow a statute to be used as an engine of fraud[86] and this principle is left untouched by the Act: indeed, it is difficult to see how the operation of such a principle could be excluded by the legislature.[87] In *Singh v. Beggs*[88] Neill L.J. doubted the view that section 2 of the 1989 Act had "abolished" the doctrine of part performance, observing (if *obiter*) that

It is true that it is provided by section 2(8) of the 1989 Act, that section 40 of the Law of Property Act 1925 will cease to have effect, but the doctrine [of part performance] is an equitable doctrine, and it may be that in certain circumstances the doctrine could be relied on.[89]

The Law Commission itself recognised that circumstances may arise in which justice would be denied if a strict requirement of writing were universally upheld. Its view, reflected in section 2(5) of the 1989 Act,[90] was that any potential injustice could be avoided by judicial use of the techniques of collateral contracts, constructive trust or equitable estoppel.

Collateral contracts.[91] In *Record v. Bell*,[92] the question arose whether the   **4–063**
formal requirements contained in section 2 of the 1989 Act had been satisfied where a contract in two parts had been duly signed by the respective parties and was awaiting exchange and then some term was orally agreed immediately prior to exchange and was confirmed by the exchange of letters. On the facts, the vendor had made an undertaking as to the state of his title in order to induce the

---

[81] [1995] 1 W.L.R. 1567, 1573 (though on the facts the Court of Appeal held that the letter and plan before them constituted *two* documents: see *ante*, § 4–059.
[82] See *ante*, § 4–036.
[83] Gray, *Elements of Land Law* (2nd ed., 1993), p. 257 ("utterly void and ineffective").
[84] See *ante*, §§ 4–037 *et seq.*
[85] Law Com. No. 164 (1987), § 4.13.
[86] *Lincoln v. Wright* (1859) 4 De G. & J. 16; *Maddison v. Alderson* (1883) 8 App.Cas. 467.
[87] See Goff & Jones, *The Law of Restitution* (5th ed., 1998), p. 580.
[88] (1996) 71 P. & C.R. 120.
[89] *ibid.* at 122.
[90] "[N]othing in this section affects the creation or operation of resulting, implied or constructive trusts."
[91] *cf. ante*, § 4–011.
[92] [1991] 1 W.L.R. 853. See Harpum [1991] C.L.J. 399.

buyer to exchange contracts.[93] The court held that it resulted from section 2 of the 1989 Act that such a term would only be incorporated into the contract of sale if the latter referred to it.[94] However, the court felt able to construe the oral agreement as to the new term as an independent collateral contract, which was valid so long as it was itself not a sale of an interest in land.[95] Thus, the requirements of section 2 had been fulfilled. As Judge Paul Baker Q.C. observed, "[i]t would be unfortunate if common transactions of this nature should nevertheless cause the contracts to be avoided. It may, of course, lead to a greater use of the concept of collateral warranties than has hitherto been necessary."[96]

4–064   **Proprietary estoppel.**[97] Proprietary estoppel was considered particularly attractive by the Law Commission as a technique for the avoidance of injustice caused by a rigid adherence to the new formality rules because, unlike the doctrine of part performance, it does not simply enforce the underlying agreement but allows a flexible remedy which can vary according to the particular circumstances.[98] While it is somewhat elusive of definition,[99] for one author "the doctrine of proprietary estoppel is applicable where some action is taken by a person . . . in reliance on a mistaken belief as to his rights in or over land, or in reliance on expectations relating to land, where the landowner stands by or encourages the action in such circumstances that it would be unconscionable for him later to seek to enforce his strict legal rights."[1] Thus, even if adopted by a court in a case where an agreement for the sale of land did not satisfy the formal requirements of section 2, it would apply only so as to give a remedy to a would-be purchaser[2]: any claim by a would-be vendor would not be for a right to land nor indeed for a specific asset, but for a sum of money, a simple claim for a debt.[3] Even though there is no precise correlation between the application of the old doctrine of part performance and the likely application of proprietary estoppel to this context,[4] to the extent that the courts will have recourse to proprietary estoppel to remedy unfairness caused by the new formalities of section 2, the new law's claim to introduce a new clarity and certainty to this area of the law must be doubted.

    An example of the application of proprietary estoppel in this context may be found in *Wayling v. Jones*.[5] In that case, A had promised his companion of some ten years, B, that he would bequeath B the business in which he worked at very low wages, but died without having done so. The Court of Appeal held that B was entitled to rely on a proprietary estoppel against A's executors and therefore ordered them to pay the proceeds of sale of the business to B. If, by contrast, B had alleged that he had *contracted* with A that the latter would bequeath him the

---

[93] [1991] 1 W.L.R. 853 at 862.
[94] *ibid.* at 860.
[95] *ibid.*
[96] *ibid.* at 862.
[97] See *ante*, §§ 3–129—3–152.
[98] Law Com. No. 164 (1987), § 5.5.
[99] Gray *op. cit.* pp. 313–314.
[1] Davis (1993) 13 O.J.L.S. 101, 103.
[2] *ibid.*
[3] *ibid.* at 104 and see *Godden v. Merthyr Tydfil Housing Association* (1997) 74 P. & C.R. D1.
[4] *ibid.* at 111.
[5] [1995] 2 FLR 1029.

business in return for working for low wages, his claim would have failed for lack of fulfilling the formal requirements in section 2 of the 1989 Act.

Other types of estoppel. Contrasting approaches to the application of other **4–065** types of estoppel in this context have been taken by the Court of Appeal. In *McCausland v. Duncan Lawrie Ltd.*[6] Neill L.J. considered that the "doctrine of estoppel" (without further specification) was "plainly arguable" to give some effect to the agreement underlying a variation of a contract for the sale etc. of an interest in land, the variation itself being void for informality.[7] Morritt L.J. observed that

> "Section 2 does not give rise to any illegality if its terms are not observed and the need for an estoppel arises in just those circumstances where there is no enforceable contract. For my part I would not place weight on the contention that an estoppel such as the vendor would advance is impossible as a matter of law but it still has to be made out as a matter of fact."[8]

The issue could not, therefore, be determined in an application to strike out a plaintiff's claim.

A very different approach to the application of estoppel (and specifically, **4–066** estoppel by convention) in the context of section 2 of the 1989 Act was taken by a differently constituted Court of Appeal in *Godden v. Merthyr Tydfil Housing Association.*[9] This case concerned a claim for damages by a building contractor for breach of an oral agreement with a Housing Association, under which he had agreed to purchase a particular site, obtain planning permission for the building of seven houses and prepare the site for development, the Housing Association agreeing to reimburse him for the costs of this acquisition and work and that it would enter a contract with him for the construction of the houses. In response to the Housing Association's claim that this agreement failed the formal requirements of section 2 of the 1989 Act, the builder argued that since both parties had contracted in ignorance of this provision, the Housing Association was precluded by the doctrine of estoppel by convention from relying on this provision so as to deny that there was indeed an agreement reached between the parties. According to Simon Brown L.J., with whom Thorpe L.J. and Sir John Balcombe agreed, this submission

> "necessarily involves saying that, although Parliament has dictated that a contract involving the disposition of land made otherwise than in compliance with s.2 is void, the defendants are not allowed to say so. That, to my mind, is an impossible argument. . . . [I]f it were soundly made, it is difficult to see why it should not operate to escape the intended constraints of s.2 in virtually all cases."[10]

In Simon Brown L.J.'s view, the doctrine of estoppel may not be invoked to render valid a transaction which the legislature has, on grounds of general public policy, enacted is to be invalid.[11] With the greatest respect to the views expressed

---

[6] [1997] 1 W.L.R. 38.
[7] *ibid.* at 45.
[8] *ibid.* at 50. Tucker L.J. agreed. *cf. King v. Jackson* [1998] 03 E.G. 138.
[9] (1997) 74 P. & C.R. D1. On estoppel by convention generally, see *ante*, §§ 3–100—3–106.
[10] *ibid.* at D3 (quoted in full by Lexis transcript).
[11] Simon Brown L.J. thereby approved the statement found in *Halsbury's Laws of England*, Vol. 16 (4th ed.), § 962.

in *McCausland v. Duncan Lawrie Ltd* (views which were tentatively expressed and made in the context of a striking-out application), the position adopted by the Court of Appeal in *Godden v. Merthyr Tydfil Housing Association* is to be preferred as regards estoppel by convention: as Sir John Balcombe observed in that case, to allow estoppel to apply "would drive a coach and horses though a recent Act of Parliament enacted for very specific reasons of public policy."[12] The position adopted by the Court of Appeal in *Godden v. Merthyr Tydfil Housing Association* leaves the possibility of reliance by the *purchaser*, etc. of an interest in land on the doctrine of proprietary estoppel.[13] As regards the doctrine of promissory estoppel (or 'forbearance in equity"), in the present context it would not improve a vendor's position owing to its essentially defensive nature,[14] for promissory estoppel cannot create a new cause of action in substitution for the contractual action denied for want of formality.

4–067   **Restitution: recovery of money paid by purchaser on a failure of consideration.** The availability of restitution of money paid under an agreement which fails to comply with section 40 of the Law of Property Act 1925 depends on whether the vendor or purchaser defaults. The general rule is that if the vendor defaults, the purchaser may recover his deposit on the ground of total failure of consideration.[15] It is, however, possible that, even here, consideration for the payment will not have failed if the vendor has done acts of part performance of the contract and these acts benefited the purchaser.[16] If, on the other hand, the purchaser defaults, he may not recover a deposit paid on the ground of failure of consideration as the consideration for the payment cannot be said to have failed,[17] and this position remains unaltered under the new law.[18]

4–068   Nevertheless, failure to fulfil the requirements of section 2 of the 1989 Act may lead to different restitutionary effects. In the case of a vendor in default, if the notion of consideration were understood as the basis on which the payment was made,[19] then this basis would be the existence of the contract of sale. Under the new requirements, failure to comply with the formalities would nullify the contract rather than simply make it unenforceable: thus, consideration for the payment will always fail if the formal requirements are not fulfilled. If, on the other hand, the receipt of any benefit by the purchaser (such as, for example, by entering possession) were to be taken as preventing the failure of consideration even under this non-existent contract, then recovery would be denied. The former interpretation of the notion of failure of consideration has the attraction in the present context of tending to further the protective purpose of the new formal requirements: a purchaser who pays a deposit under an informal sale of land should not be discouraged from claiming the benefit of the statutory invalidity by the threat of losing his deposit, even if he can be said to have benefited in some

---

[12] Lexis transcript.

[13] See generally, *ante*, § 4–064.

[14] See generally, *ante*, § 3–093.

[15] See *ante*, § 4–036 and *post*, §§ 30–048 *et seq.*

[16] *cf.* Goff and Jones, *The Law of Restitution* (5th ed., 1998), pp. 42–43. Of course, if the acts of part performance are sufficient to satisfy the doctrine of part performance, then the contract may be enforced in equity: see *ante*, §§ 4–037 *et seq.*

[17] *Thomas v. Brown* [1878] 1 Q.B.D. 714, subject to the discretion granted to the court under the Law of Property Act 1925, s.49(2).

[18] *cf.* Burrows, *The Law of Restitution* (1993), pp. 257, 304.

[19] Birks, *An Introduction to the Law of Restitution* (1985), pp. 219–221.

way from the transaction. However, where a buyer has paid the full price and entered into possession of the land for a period, it is submitted that it would be unjust to allow him to rely on the statutory invalidity in order to claim back the price, leaving the seller to any possible counter-claim in restitution on the ground of the buyer's unjust enrichment in enjoying the property during the period.[20] Therefore, this type of case makes more attractive an understanding of the notion of failure of consideration in terms, not of the existence of the underlying contract, but of the absence of any benefit received under it by the party claiming restitution.[20a]

Restitution: recovery of money paid by purchaser under a mistake of law. As the previous paragraph indicates, the traditional ground for recovery of money paid under a contract for the sale etc. of an interest of land has been a total failure of consideration. However, in *Kleinwort Benson v. Lincoln City Council*[21] the House of Lords allowed a party to a contract void under the ultra vires doctrine to recover payments made under it on the ground that at the time of payment it laboured under a mistake of law as to the validity of the contract: restitution for mistaken payments applies in principle to mistakes of law as to mistakes of fact.[22] While, therefore, this decision was not made in the context of a contract which failed to comply with the formal requirements of section 2 of the 1989 Act, the abolition of the mistake of law rule was put in very general terms and it could well be argued that where a purchaser of land pays money under an agreement for the sale etc. of an interest in land thinking it to be a valid contract, but which as a matter of law is void for want of formality, then that purchaser should be able to recover the money on the ground of this mistake of law, whether or not consideration for the payment can be said to have failed. However, such a reopening of executed *land* transactions may be thought undesirable by future courts. In this respect, it is to be recalled that in *Tootal Clothing Ltd v. Guinea Properties Ltd* (which was not cited to the House of Lords in *Kleinwort Benson v. Lincoln City Council*), Scott L.J. expressed the view that "section 2 [of the 1989 Act] is of relevance only to executory contracts. It has no relevance to contracts which have been completed. If parties choose to complete an oral land contract or a land contract that does not in some respect or other comply with section 2, they are at liberty to do so. Once they have done so, it becomes irrelevant that the contract they have completed may not have been in accordance with section 2."[23] While in *Kleinwort Benson v. Lincoln City Council* Lord Goff of Chieveley (with whom Lord Browne-Wilkinson, Lord Lloyd of Berwick, Lord Hoffman and Lord Hope of Craighead agreed on this point) rejected a restriction on the ambit of restitution on the ground of mistake of law for the case where a transaction is completed,[24] he did so by reference to the cause of the voidness of the contracts before him, *i.e.* interest rate swap transactions. These had been held void on the ground that they were ultra vires the local authorities which had

4–069

---

[20] *cf.* Goff and Jones *op. cit.* p. 581.

[20a] *cf.* Burrows *op.cit.* pp. 259–261 who argues that the law ought to recognise a partial failure of consideration as a ground of restitutionary liability and see *Westdeutsche Landesbank Girozentrale v. Islington L.B.C.* [1996] A.C. 669; *Goss v. Chilcott* [1996] A.C. 788; *Stocznia Gdanska SA v. Latvian S.S. Co.* [1998] 1 All E.R. 882, 898 and *post*, §§ 30–048 *et seq.*

[21] [1998] 3 W.L.R. 1095.

[22] See further, *post*, §§ 30–038—30–043.

[23] (1991) 64 P. & C.R. 452, 455.

[24] [1998] 3 W.L.R. 1095, 1125–1127. Lord Goff thereby rejected an argument to this effect found in Birks (1993) 23 U.W.A.L.R. 195, 230.

entered them and, as Lord Goff concluded, "it is incompatible with the ultra vires rule that an ultra vires transaction should become binding on a local authority simply on the ground that it has been completed."[25] According to Lord Hope, "the purpose of the ultra vires doctrine is to protect the public" and therefore "it would be unsatisfactory if restitution were to be possible only in the case of uncompleted transactions,"[26] though he put his rejection of the restriction in very general terms.[27] It is submitted that a future court could take the view that the policy underlying the invalidity of informal transactions relating to land may not be defeated by a rule which prevented the restitution of monies paid under them where they are wholly executed. For, while the formalities required by the 1989 Act may to a degree serve a protective purpose of would-be purchasers, the main reason for the requirements is the need for certainty in transactions and where a transaction had been completed there should be no concern on this ground.[28] On the other hand, a court could instead take a position similar to that taken by the Court of Appeal in *Godden v. Merthyr Tydfil Housing Association* in relation to the application of the doctrine of estoppel by convention to a land transaction void for informality, where it held that a court should not uphold a transaction declared invalid on grounds of general public policy.[29] If it did, or if otherwise the full force of restitution on the ground of mistake of law is not otherwise restrained, then any payments made under a transaction which was thought valid by the payer, but was void for informality may be recovered.

4–070 **Restitution: benefits conferred other than money.** Under the Law of Property Act 1925, section 40, a *purchaser* of an interest in land under a contract unenforceable under that provision may recover on a *quantum meruit* for improvements to the land if the vendor has allowed him to go on to effect them, but then repudiates the contract, as the permission to enter may be taken as acquiescence in the work being done.[30] Similarly, in *Deglman v. Guaranty Trust Co. of Canada and Constantineau*,[31] the defendants' predecessor in title had promised to bequeath a house to the plaintiff, her nephew, if he performed various household tasks. He performed the tasks, but she did not leave the house to him in her will. The Supreme Court of Canada held his acts were not sufficient to satisfy the doctrine of part performance and thus to avoid the effect of the Statute of Frauds, but further held that the plaintiff was entitled to recover on a *quantum meruit* for the work he had done in the expectation of some remuneration and at his aunt's request. This law would also apply under section 2 of the 1989 Act.[32]

4–071 On the other hand, if the *vendor* of an interest in land improves it at the request of the purchaser and in anticipation of the contract going ahead, it is not clear whether the purchaser will be liable on a *quantum meruit* in respect of the work, because although he has requested the work done, he has not benefited from its

---

[25] *ibid.* 1126–1127.
[26] *ibid.* 1152.
[27] *ibid.* 1153–1154 and see Burrows [1995] R.L.R. 15, 18–19.
[28] See *Firstpost Homes Ltd v. Johnson* [1995] 1 W.L.R. 1567, 1576, *per* Peter Gibson L.J., quoted *supra*, 4–004.
[29] (1997) 74 P. & C.R. D1 at D3. *cf. McCausland v. Duncan Lawrie Ltd* [1997] 1 W.L.R. 38, 45, 50 and see *ante*, § 4–066.
[30] Goff and Jones, *op. cit.*, p. 581.
[31] [1954] 3 D.L.R. 78 and *cf. post*, § 30–184.
[32] *cf.* Bentley & Coughlan [1989] 10 L.S. 325.

execution.[33] Dicta in the decision of the Court of Appeal in *Brewer Street Investments Ltd v. Barclays Woollen Co. Ltd*[34] suggest that a vendor should not recover where a contract has failed to materialise owing to his own fault, but only where it is owing to the purchaser's fault, or perhaps, circumstances beyond either's control. However, the case concerned an agreement made expressly "subject to contract" which failed to proceed further and it is submitted that, whatever the position under section 40 of the Law of Property Act 1925, a distinction based on the respective fault of the parties is inappropriate to recovery in respect of benefits conferred under a contract nullified under the 1989 Act: a party could not be described as "at fault" merely by relying on the statutory invalidity of an agreement which he has made—an invalidity part of whose purpose was his own protection.[35] On the other hand, if a purchaser is allowed to enter possession under a contract void for failing to fulfill the requirements of section 2 of the 1989 Act, a vendor should be able to recover on a *quantum meruit* for the purchaser's enjoyment of the property, this clearly counting as a benefit for this purpose.[36]

---

[33] *cf.* Goff and Jones, *The Law of Restitution* (5th ed., 1998), pp. 666 *et seq.*
[34] [1954] 1 Q.B. 428, 434, 437, 438.
[35] See Law Com. No. 164 (1987), § 2.9.
[36] Goff and Jones, *op. cit.*, p. 581.

CHAPTER 5

MISTAKE[1]

1. INTRODUCTION

Types of mistake and their effects. Mistake in the law of contract deals with **5–001** two rather different situations. In the first, the parties are agreed on the terms of the contract but have entered it under a mutual (or shared[2]) and fundamental misapprehension as to the facts.[3] In the second, there is some mistake or misunderstanding in the communications between the parties which prevents there being an effective agreement: for instance, the parties misunderstand each other, or one party in an offer states terms which the other party knows the first party does not intend. The first type of mistake is sometimes said to operate so as to nullify consent, the second so as to negative it.[4] In either case, if the mistake is operative the contract is said to be void *ab initio*.[5] The rules of equity cut across this distinction. For example, in equity either type of mistake may be a defence in an action for specific performance.[6] Either a shared or a unilateral mistake may entitle a party to the contract to have it rectified if it has been reduced to writing but is not expressed in accordance with the parties' true

---

[1] See generally Cheshire (1944) 60 L.Q.R. 175; Tylor (1948) 11 M.L.R. 257; Slade (1954) 70 L.Q.R. 385; Stoljar (1965) 28 M.L.R. 265; Stoljar, *Mistake and Misrepresentation: A Study in Contractual Principles* (1968); Smith (1994) 110 L.Q.R. 400.

[2] Modern works sometimes refer to this type of mistake as "common mistake" (*e.g.* Cheshire, Fifoot and Furmston, *Law of Contract* (13th ed.), Chap. 8. Here the phrase "mutual mistake" is retained, following the terminology used by Lord Atkin in *Bell v. Lever Bros.* [1932] A.C. 161; but care must be taken not to confuse mutual mistake with what is termed here "mutual misunderstanding" (where the parties are at cross-purposes as to the terms of the contract): see *post*, § 5–033.

[3] Or possibly law: see *post*, § 5–018.

[4] *Bell v. Lever Brothers Ltd* [1932] A.C. 161, 217.

[5] See, however, *post*, §§ 5–005, 5–037 *et seq.*

[6] See *post*, §§ 5–039—5–040.

intention.[7] In contrast, mistake seems to be a ground for rescission in equity only if it is mutual.[8]

5–002   **Money paid under mistake of fact.** Mistake may also entitle a party who has paid money under the mistake to recover it back in an action for money had and received to his use.[9] The subject of the recovery of money paid under a mistake is principally dealt with in Chapter 30 of this work. The other effects of mistake are treated in the present chapter under (1) Mistake at Common Law, and (2) Mistake in Equity.

2. MISTAKE AT COMMON LAW

5–003   **Generally.** The operation of common law mistake is very narrowly confined. The cases in which the courts have pronounced a contract void fall into the two categories mentioned at § 5–001. The first comprises "cases in which the parties, though genuinely agreed, have both contracted in the mistaken belief that some fact which lies at the root of the contract is true."[10] This category is often referred to as "mutual" mistake, for both parties have contracted under the same mis-apprehension. The second is "where, although to all outward appearances the parties are agreed, there is in fact no genuine agreement between them, and the law therefore does not regard a contract as having come into existence."[11] This category of mistake can be referred to as unilateral mistake, where only one of the parties is mistaken, or of misunderstanding, where each is mistaken as to the other's intentions. It appears that mistakes in this category will only operate to negative consent where the mistake is about the terms of the contract.[12] Thus there are situations which may loosely be called cases of "mistake" in which the contract will nonetheless be binding at common law. Suppose I buy a ring mistakenly thinking it is a gold ring. Nothing is said by the vendor as to the quality of the ring; he knows that it is not gold. Even if he knows that I think the ring to be of gold, I cannot avoid the contract on the ground of mistake, though I would never have entered into it had I known the true position. The mistake may be fundamental but it is not shared; nor does it relate to the terms of the contract, which are simply to sell and buy the specific ring. There are, of course, many circumstances in which liability may be imposed on a party for the consequences of unknown facts by the implication of appropriate terms, or otherwise by the normal process of construction. But subject to this, mere silence as regards a material fact which the one party is not bound to disclose to the other is not a ground of invalidity, for the principle of *caveat emptor* is of general application in the English law of contract.[13] As Lord Atkin said[14]: "It is of

---

[7] See *post*, §§ 5–065—5–086.
[8] See *post*, §§ 5–087—5–095; though Australian authority differs on this point: *infra* § 5–089, n. 25.
[9] See *post*, §§ 30–026 *et seq.*
[10] *Anson's Law of Contract* (27th ed., by Beatson, 1998), p. 296. On the question of terminology see *ante*, § 5–001 at n. 2.
[11] *Anson's Law of Contract* (27th ed., by Beatson, 1988), p. 296.
[12] See *post*, § 5–036.
[13] *Bell v. Lever Brothers Ltd* [1932] A.C. 161, 227; *Keates v. Lord Cadogan* (1851) 10 C.B. 591; *Turner v. Green* [1895] 2 Ch. 203.
[14] *Bell v. Lever Brothers Ltd* [1932] A.C. 161, 224.

paramount importance that contracts should be observed, and that if parties honestly comply with the essentials of the formation of contracts—*i.e.* agree in the same terms on the same subject-matter—they are bound, and must rely on the stipulations of the contract for protection from the effect of facts unknown to them."

Non est factum. There is, however, one type of mistake which, for conven- **5–004** ience, will be placed in a separate category; it is peculiar to the law of written contracts, and it allows a party who has executed a document under a funda- mental misapprehension as to its nature to plead that it is "not his deed." This is the defence of *non est factum*.[14a]

Effect of mistake at common law. In all three cases of mistake it is usually **5–005** said that the effect of the mistake is that the apparent contract is void.[15] This is certainly correct in cases of mutual mistake at common law,[16] cases of mutual misunderstanding[17] and in some cases of unilateral mistake.[18] Thus a unilateral mistake as to the identity of the other party may prevent the formation of a contract, so that if the subject matter of the contract consists of goods, no property in the goods will pass under the contract, and they may be recovered by the true owner even from a bona fide purchaser for value.[19] However, it is not clear that this is the result in all cases of unilateral mistake; rather, there may be a contract on the terms actually intended by the mistaken party.[20] Further, in cases of common mistake it may happen that the contract is void but the parties have acted on the assumption that it was valid. If it would now be unconscionable for either party to deny the existence of the contract because, knowingly or unknowingly, he has allowed the other to act on it to the latter's detriment, estoppel by convention will apply.[21]

(a) *Mutual Mistake*[22]

Mutual mistake. Where the mistake is mutual, that is shared by both **5–006** parties, there is *consensus ad idem*, but the law may nullify this consent if the parties are mistaken as to some fact or point of law which lies at the basis of the contract. While, on the authorities, a doctrine of mutual mistake appears to exist in English law, the situation is complicated by the fact that there are three possible conceptual routes which have been employed in considering whether a fundamental mistake has prevented the formation of an effective contract: that there has been a total failure of consideration, that the contract was subject to an

---

[14a] See *post*, §§ 5–054—5–059.
[15] See *post*, §§ 5–006, 5–032 and 5–054.
[16] *Post*, § 5–006.
[17] *Post*, § 5–033.
[18] *Post*, §§ 5–037 *et seq.*
[19] *Hardman v. Booth* (1863) 1 H. & C. 803; *Cundy v. Lindsay* (1878) 3 App.Cas. 459; *Ingram v. Little* [1961] 1 Q.B. 31.
[20] See *post*, § 5–037.
[21] *Furness Withy (Australia) Pty. Ltd v. Metal Distributors (U.K.) Ltd (The Amazonia)* [1990] 1 Lloyd's Rep. 236. See *ante*, §§ 3–100—3–106.
[22] See Cheshire (1944) 60 L.Q.R. 175, 177; Tylor (1948) 11 M.L.R. 257, 262; Slade (1954) 70 L.Q.R. 385, 396; Bamford (1955) 32 S.A.L.J. 166; Atiyah (1957) 73 L.Q.R. 340; Atiyah and Bennion (1961) 24 M.L.R. 421; McTurnan (1963) 41 Can. Bar Rev. 1; Stoljar (1965) 28 M.L.R. 265, 275.

express or implied condition that the facts were as the parties believed them to be and through a separate doctrine of mistake. In the paragraphs that follow, the first explanation will be rejected, but it will be suggested that the second and third overlap to such an extent that there is room for doubt as to whether there is really room in English law for an independent doctrine of mutual mistake.

5–007   **Total failure of consideration.** In *Kennedy v. Panama, New Zealand and Australian Royal Mail Co.*[23] the prospectus of a company offering shares stated that fresh capital was required in order to fulfil a lucrative mail contract with the Postmaster of New Zealand. The contract proved to be beyond the Postmaster's authority to make and the plaintiff, who had purchased shares in reliance on the prospectus, claimed to repudiate the transaction on the ground that there had been a total failure of consideration. The Court of Queen's Bench refused to allow him to do so. In deciding whether or not that had been a total failure of consideration so as to entitle the buyer to get his money back, Blackburn J. referred to the Roman law on mistake and its distinction between mistakes as to substance, which in Roman law would invalidate the contract, and mistakes as to quality, which would not; and held that as the misunderstanding about the shares went only to quality, there was no total failure of consideration. It is easy to see how this might be interpreted as saying that a mistake as to substance might make the contract void in English law. It is not clear that this was what was meant; and in any event, the fact that a mistake has led to there being a total failure of consideration cannot lead straight to the conclusion that the contract is void, since it might be that the seller is liable for non-performance.[24] In other words, while cases of total failure of consideration may have played a historical role in the development of a doctrine of mistake in English law, total failure is not an independent ground on which a contract may be held void: rather, it is the basis of an action for the recovery of money when the contract is void. There will equally be a total failure of consideration when one party has simply failed to perform.[25]

5–008   **Express or implied condition precedent.** We shall see that the courts have sometimes found that a contract was concluded subject to an express or implied condition precedent that a particular state of affairs exists; so that if it does not, the contract is ineffective.[26] The difficulty here is that it is not at all clear what scope this leaves for an independent doctrine of mistake; and it may be that the doctrine of mistake at common law is no more than an alternative way of expressing the idea that the contract may be dependent on such a condition precedent, but a way of putting it which will give more guidance as to when such a condition will be implied. However, in a recent leading decision condition precedent and mutual mistake were treated as alternative grounds for the decision that the contract was void.[27] The point is discussed below.

---

[23] (1867) L.R. 2 Q.B. 580.
[24] See also *Couturier v. Hastie* (1856) 5 H.L.C. 673, discussed *post*, § 5–021.
[25] See *post*, §§ 30–048 *et seq.*
[26] *Post*, §§ 5–012 and 5–016.
[27] *Associated Japanese Bank International Ltd v. Crédit du Nord SA* [1989] 1 W.L.R. 255. Steyn J. based his decision on the first ground but stated that he would have found the contract void for mistake.

The doctrine of mutual mistake. It is not wholly clear when a separate   **5–009** doctrine of mutual mistake emerged in English law,[28] though it seems to have been accepted in relation to goods which have perished by the draftsman of the Sale of Goods Act 1893.[29] The leading case on this topic is that of *Bell v. Lever Brothers Ltd.*[30] There an action was brought by Lever Brothers for the recovery of money paid to the two defendants under the following circumstances. Lever Brothers had large interests in Africa and set up a subsidiary company, called the Niger Company, to control them there. The defendants were members of the board of the Niger Company and received large salaries in respect of their service agreements with Lever Brothers. One of the conditions of their service agreements was that they were not to make any private profit for themselves by doing business on their own account while serving the company. The defendants did in fact make such profits, unknown to Lever Brothers and undisclosed by the defendants. Lever Brothers, having made other arrangements for their interests in Africa, desired to terminate the service agreements with the defendants before their expiry, and accordingly entered into compensation agreements with them whereby the defendants consented to terminate their service agreements in consideration of the payment to them of large sums of money. After the money had been paid, Lever Brothers discovered the breaches of their service agreements committed by the defendants, which would have entitled the company to dismiss them summarily without notice or compensation. They therefore claimed to recover the sums which they had paid on the ground, *inter alia*, that they had entered into the compensation agreements under the mistaken assumption that the service contracts could only have been determined by them with the consent of the defendants.

At the trial of the action, the jury found that there was no evidence of fraud on   **5–010** the part of the defendants, and that when they entered into the compensation agreements they had not directed their minds to their previous breaches of duty. The case was therefore one of mutual mistake, as both parties had made the same mistaken assumption. Wright J. held that this assumption that a state of facts existed which entitled the defendants to compensation was essential to the agreement; consequently there could be no binding contract, and Lever Brothers were therefore entitled to recover the money paid. This decision was unanimously affirmed by the Court of Appeal. In the House of Lords, however, an appeal by the defendants was allowed by a majority of three to two. Lord Blanesburgh,[31] one of the majority, based his opinion largely on the fact that mutual mistake had not been originally pleaded. The other two majority opinions, those of Lord Atkin[32] and Lord Thankerton,[33] both rested on the ground that the mistake was not sufficiently fundamental to avoid the contract, although they

---

[28] See the judgment of Steyn J. in *Associated Japanese Bank International Ltd v. Crédit du Nord SA* [1989] 1 W.L.R. 255, 264–265.

[29] See *post*, § 5–022.

[30] [1932] A.C. 161; [1931] 1 K.B. 574, CA; [1931] 1 K.B. 557 (Wright J.); the case was distinguished in *Magee v. Pennine Insurance Co. Ltd* [1969] 2 Q.B. 507, *infra*, § 5–092.

[31] [1932] A.C. 161, 167. Lord Blanesburgh also held that the payments were irrecoverable as (i) the defendants' service contracts were made with the Niger Company and not with the plaintiffs, and (ii) the payments were in part voluntary, since they greatly exceeded in value the unexpired portion of the service agreements: see *post*, §§ 30–062 *et seq.*

[32] At 210.

[33] At 229.

reached this conclusion by somewhat different paths. Lord Warrington of Clyffe (with whom Lord Hailsham agreed) dissented.[34]

5–011   **Varying interpretations.** As a result of these differences of opinion within the highest tribunal, it is extremely difficult to discover the precise interpretation to be put on this decision. Varying interpretations have been advanced. First, it has been said that this case establishes that there is no general rule of English law that a fundamental mutual mistake makes the contract void.[35] Yet it is assumed throughout by each of their Lordships that mistakes of some kind will avoid a transaction. Secondly, it has been asserted that a contract will only be void for mutual mistake if a term can be implied that, unless the facts are or are not of a particular nature, or unless an event has or has not happened, the contract is not to take effect.[36] This is discussed in the following paragraphs. For a third interpretation, that the contract will be void only "if there is nothing to contract about," see *post*, § 5–17.

5–012   **Risk.** The question of the effect of mutual mistake in the law of contract is basically one of the allocation of risk as to the facts being as assumed.[37] In most situations one or other of the parties will be considered to have assumed the risk of the ordinary uncertainties which exist when an agreement is concluded. Where contracts of sale of goods are concerned, for example, the seller will normally be held to have assumed the risk that the goods may be defective under express or implied terms, except insofar as the usual conditions are validly excluded, or may in the particular circumstances be inapplicable. Thus it has been said that one must first determine whether the contract itself, by express or implied condition (promissory or non-promissory) or otherwise, provides who bears the risk of the relevant mistake. Only if the contract is silent on the point is there scope for invoking the doctrine of mistake.[38] However, it has been pointed out that if the enquiry whether the construction of the contract is only as to whether one party or the other bears the risk, and the answer is that neither does, that does not preclude a second enquiry as to the effect of the mistake; but if it includes asking whether, if neither bears the risk, the contract is as a matter of construction subject to an implied condition precedent that the facts assumed existed, there seems to be no scope for asking whether the contract is void for mistake.[39] In other words, there is no room for an independent doctrine of mistake.[40] This is a formidable argument.

5–013   **Implied condition.** The argument that there is no room for an independent doctrine of mistake might seem to gain support from the fact that in *Bell v. Lever*

---

[34] At 200.

[35] Slade (1954) 70 L.Q.R. 385; Shatwell (1955) 33 Can. Bar Rev. 164.

[36] Slade (1954) 70 L.Q.R. 385; Atiyah (1957) 73 L.Q.R. 340.

[37] *Amalgamated Investment & Property Co. Ltd v. John Walker & Sons Ltd* [1977] 1 W.L.R. 164; McTurnan (1963) 41 Can. Bar Rev. 1; Swan, "The Allocation of Risk in the Analysis of Mistake and Frustration," in Reiter and Swan, *Studies in Contract Law* (1980); American Law Institute's *Restatement of Contracts* (2d), § 152.

[38] *Associated Japanese Bank International Ltd v. Credit du Nord SA* [1989] 1 W.L.R. 255, 268. See also *William Sindall plc v. Cambridgeshire County Council* [1994] 1 W.L.R. 1016, 1035; *Grains & Fourriers SA v. Huyton* [1997] 1 Lloyd's Rep. 628; *Bank of Credit and Commerce International SA (in liquidation) v. Ali* [1992] 2 All E.R. 1005, 1020.

[39] Smith, (1994) 110 L.Q.R. 400, 407.

[40] *ibid.* p. 419. See also Denning L.J.'s explanation of the cases in which goods have perished at the time of sale as being "void by reason of an implied condition precedent": *Solle v. Butcher* [1950] 1 K.B. 671, 691; *post*, § 5–091.

Bros. Ltd Lord Atkin accepted a proposition formulated by counsel for the respondents: "Whenever it is to be inferred from the terms of a contract or its surrounding circumstances that the consensus has been reached upon the basis of a particular contractual assumption, and that assumption is not true, the contract is avoided; *i.e.* it is void *ab initio* if the assumption is of present fact and it ceases to bind if the assumption is of future fact."[41] It is submitted, however, that Lord Atkin considered the "condition precedent" argument as "an alternative way of expressing the result of a mutual mistake"; but one which gives little guidance as to when a condition should be implied that the facts are as the parties believed them to be.

> " . . . if the contract expressly or impliedly contains a term that a particular assumption is a condition of the contract, the contract is avoided if the assumption is not true. But we have not advanced far on the inquiry whether the contract does contain such a condition . . . The implications to be made are to be no more than are 'necessary' for giving business efficacy to the transaction; and it appears to me that as to both existing and future[42] facts a condition should not be implied unless the new state of facts makes the contract something different in kind from the contract in the original state of facts . . . We therefore get a common standard for mutual mistake and implied conditions . . . ".[43]

Thus it seems that Lord Atkin viewed saying that the contract was subject to an implied condition precedent and saying that it was void for mutual mistake as an alternative way of putting the same thing, though he seems to have regarded the latter as having more explanatory power as to when the contract will fail.

Thus it is submitted that the first question the court should ask is whether, **5–014** under the express or implied terms of the contract, the risk of the relevant mistake is allocated to one or other of the parties. If it is not allocated to either, the question must be asked whether the contract is subject to an *express* condition precedent that the facts should be as the parties believed them to be. If the answer to this is negative, it may then be asked whether the matter to which the mistake relates was sufficiently fundamental that the contract should be treated as subject to an *implied* condition precedent, or whether it should be treated as void for mutual mistake. The last is better viewed as a separate question but, it is submitted, cases in which it is held that the contract is not subject to an implied condition precedent yet is void for mutual mistake will be rare. In *Associated Japanese Bank International Ltd v. Credit du Nord SA*[44] the two approaches led to the same result. The plaintiffs had entered a sale and lease-back agreement with B and the defendants had guaranteed the performance of B's obligations under the lease. It was then discovered that the machines purportedly sold and leased back did not exist and the arrangement was a fraud perpetrated by B. Steyn J. held that the defendants were not liable on the guarantee, which was expressly or by necessary implication subject to a condition precedent that the machines leased existed. He then went on to say that in his view the guarantee was also void for common mistake.

---

[41] [1932] A.C. 161, 225.
[42] This is presumably a reference to the doctrine of frustration, *post*, Chap. 24.
[43] [1932] A.C. 161, 224–225.
[44] [1989] 1 W.L.R. 255.

5–015 **Mistake should have been known to one party.** The linking of the doctrine of mutual mistake and implied conditions explains why a very serious mutual mistake may not result in the contract being void, because one party should have known the true facts. As suggested earlier, the court will first ask whether, under the express or implied terms of the contract the risk of what happened was allocated to one or other of the parties; and only if this was not the case will it consider whether the contract was subject to an implied condition that the facts were as the parties believed them to be.[45] It would not be appropriate to imply such a condition when one party ought to have known the true state of affairs as it seems most unlikely that the other party would have agreed to such a term. We will see when we consider sales of non-existent goods that just this approach was taken by the High Court of Australia in a case in which the seller should have known that the goods had never existed; the seller was held liable for breach of contract.[46] Equally it has been said that the common law doctrine of mutual mistake cannot be invoked by a party who had no reasonable grounds for his belief.[47]

5–016 **Implied condition where mistake not fundamental.** It does not follow that a condition will only be implied when the contract would be held void for mutual mistake. The court may, on the particular facts of the case, decide that a contract was conditional upon the existence of certain facts although the absence of those facts does not seem to make the subject-matter of the contract essentially different. In *Financings Ltd v. Stimson*[48] the defendant offered to take a car on hire-purchase, his offer acknowledging that he had examined the car and had satisfied himself that it was in good condition. Before his offer had been accepted the car was stolen and damaged. It was held that his offer was subject to the implied condition that the car remained in substantially the same condition as when he saw it, so that the offer could no longer be accepted.[49]

5–017 **Doctrine not limited to absence of res.** Finally, the opinion has been put forward that *Bell v. Lever Bros* lays down the rule that "a contract will be void only if there is nothing to contract about, . . . and the ground of such a nullity is not the mistake but the absence of a *res*."[50] It is submitted, however, that the operation of mutual mistake in English law is somewhat wider than this view would indicate; and in the *Associated Japanese Bank case*[51] it was said that that case decided that a mistake might render a contract void provided it rendered the subject-matter essentially and radically different from what the parties believed to exist. It is submitted also that the absence of a *res* does not necessarily render the contract void.[51a]

---

[45] *Ante*, § 5–012.

[46] *McRae v. Commonwealth Disposals Commission* (1950) 84 C.L.R. 377, 408; *post*, § 5–022.

[47] *Associated Japanese Bank International Ltd v. Credit du Nord SA* [1989] 1 W.L.R. 255, 268.

[48] [1962] 1 W.L.R. 1184.

[49] See further Atiyah, *Essays in Contract* (1986), Chap. 10.

[50] Cheshire & Fifoot, *Law of Contract* (11th ed.), p. 228. In the 13th ed., p. 246, the editor notes that this view was not followed in the *Associated Japanese Bank* case.

[51] *Associated Japanese Bank International Ltd v. Credit du Nord SA* [1989] 1 W.L.R. 255, 266–267, 268.

[51a] See *post*, § 5–022.

Mistakes as to law. Until recently it has been established that, for a mutual   **5–018**
mistake to be operative at common law,[52] it must be a mistake as to fact and not
one as to law. This seems likely to have been based on the rule that only a mistake
of fact would entitle a party to claim restitution on the grounds of mistake.[53] The
House of Lords has recently held that the latter rule is not part of English law.[54]
Whether this will affect the law of mutual mistake is not entirely clear. The
grounds on which a payment made by mistake may be recovered are wider than
those on which a contract may be void (or voidable in equity[55]) for mutual
mistake.[56] This is said to be because of the policy favouring finality of contracts.[57] Thus a mistaken payment may be recovered without showing that the
mistake was fundamental or that the recipient shared the payer's mistake.[58]
However, it does not seem that any policy of finality of contract would be
assisted by maintaining the distinction between a mistake of fact and a mistake
of law as a ground on which a contract may be void. It is therefore submitted that
a fundamental mistake may now render a contract void even though the mistake
is one of law. (In any event, a question of foreign law is a question of fact.[59])

Factual situations. No test of universal validity can be laid down to deter-   **5–019**
mine whether there is a sufficient disparity between the facts as they actually
were and as they were assumed to be such that the contract is nullified on the
ground of mutual mistake. But as in the case of the operation of the analogous
doctrine of frustration,[60] a number of factual situations have been considered by
the courts and these may be conveniently marshalled into several categories.

Existence of the subject-matter of the contract. Mistake as to the existence   **5–020**
of the subject-matter of the contract may render a contract void. In *Bell v. Lever
Brothers Ltd*, Lord Atkin said[61]: "So the agreement of A and B to purchase a
specific article is void if in fact the article had perished before the date of sale.
In this case, though the parties in fact were agreed about the subject-matter, yet
a consent to transfer or take delivery of something not existent is deemed useless,
the consent is nullified." It is also enacted in section 6 of the Sale of Goods Act
1979[62] that where there is a contract for the sale of specific goods and the goods
without the knowledge of the seller have perished at the time when the contract
was made, the contract is void. So in *Barrow, Lane & Ballard Ltd v. Phillip
Phillips & Co.*,[63] A agreed to buy and B to sell 700 specific bags of nuts lying
in a particular warehouse. Unknown to both parties, 109 bags had been stolen

---

[52] The position in equity appears to have been more flexible: *post*, § 5–062.
[53] *e.g. Bilbie v. Lumley* (1802) 2 East 469: see below, §§ 30–038 *et seq.*
[54] *Kleinwort Benson Ltd v. Lincoln City Council* [1999] 1 A.C. 153; *post*, § 30–041.
[55] See *post*, §§ 5–087 *et seq.*
[56] *Post*, § 30–030.
[57] See the authors cited in § 30–030, n. 46.
[58] See § 30–030, nn. 48–52.
[59] *Furness Withy (Australia) Pty. Ltd v. Metal Distributors (U.K.) Ltd (The Amazonia)* [1990] 1
Lloyd's Rep. 236.
[60] *Bank Line Ltd v. A. Capel & Co.* [1919] A.C. 435, 445; *Bell v. Lever Bros. Ltd* [1932] A.C. 161,
226. Contrast *Joseph Constantine SS. Line Ltd v. Imperial Smelting Cpn. Ltd* [1942] A.C. 154, 186;
Bell v. Lever Bros. Ltd, supra, at 237.
[61] At 217.
[62] See also s.7 of the Act, and Vol. II, §§ 43–031—43–036.
[63] [1929] 1 K.B. 574.

prior to the sale. The contract was held void.[64] Lord Atkin's statement and section 6 refer strictly to those cases where the subject-matter of the contract has once been in existence, but has subsequently perished before the contract is made. One question is whether the fact that the subject matter of the contract has perished always renders the contract void; another, whether the same principles apply where the subject-matter of the contract has never been in existence at all.[65] These questions will be considered in the next two paragraphs.

5–021   Where money has been paid by one party to the other in pursuance of a contract, the subject-matter of which was not in existence at the time that the contract was made, it can be recovered in an action for money had and received, for the consideration for the contract has totally failed.[66] Thus the purchaser of an annuity on the life of a man who was, unknown to both parties, already dead, was able to recover the purchase price from the vendor as the annuity had ceased to exist at the time of the contract for sale.[67] By the same token, money which has not yet been paid cannot lawfully be demanded for the contract is incapable of performance. In *Couturier v. Hastie*[68] there was a sale of a cargo of corn which was believed to be in transit from Salonica to the United Kingdom. Unknown to both parties the cargo had deteriorated and had already been sold by the master of the ship. The liability of the purchaser to pay the price depended upon the construction of the contract. If the contract was a contract for the sale of that specific cargo of corn, then the consideration for the contract had totally failed and the seller was not entitled to the price. If, however, as the seller contended, it was a contract for the sale of the adventure, the seller had performed his side of the contract by offering to deliver the shipping documents and the purchaser was liable to pay the purchase price. The House of Lords held that the contract was for the sale of a cargo and therefore the purchaser was not bound to pay. This case has been cited in support of the proposition that a mistake as to the existence of the subject-matter of the contract renders the contract inexorably void.[69] But it must be admitted that the crucial question of the invalidity of the contract was never directly in issue. There was a total failure of consideration and so it did not matter whether the contract was valid or void. The purchaser could not be compelled to pay for what he had never received.

5–022   **Implied condition that exists.** An alternative approach to contracts concerning non-existent subject-matter was offered by Denning L.J. in *Solle v. Butcher*,[70] where he said: "The cases where goods have perished at the time of sale . . . are really contracts which are not void for mistake but are void by reason of an implied condition precedent because the contract proceeded on the basic assumption that it was possible of performance." If this statement correctly represents

---

[64] But it should be noted that the surviving bags were delivered and paid for; the action was brought by the sellers for the price of the missing bags.

[65] *cf.* Atiyah (1957) 83 L.Q.R. 340, 348; Sale of Goods Act 1979, s.55.

[66] *Hitchcock v. Giddings* (1817) 4 Price 135; *Gompertz v. Bartlett* (1853) 2 E. & B. 849; *Gurney v. Womersley* (1854) 4 E. & B. 133; *Pritchard v. Merchants' and Tradesmen's Life Assurance Soc.* (1858) 3 C.B.(N.S.) 622, 645; *Cochrane v. Willis* (1865) L.R. 1 Ch.App. 58; *Norwich Union Fire Insurance Ltd v. W. H. Price Ltd* [1934] A.C. 455. See *post*, §§ 30–030 *et seq.*

[67] *Strickland v. Turner* (1852) 7 Exch. 208.

[68] (1856) 5 H.L.R. 673, H.L.; (1853) 9 Exch. 102 (Ex.Ch.); (1852) 8 Exch. 40.

[69] Cheshire & Fifoot, *Law of Contract* (13th ed.), pp. 238–239, citing *Pritchard v. Merchants' and Tradesmen's Life Assurance Soc.*, *supra*.

[70] [1950] 1 K.B. 671, 691. In *Associated Japanese Bank International Ltd v. Credit du Nord SA* [1989] 1 W.L.R. 255, 266, this was described as Lord Denning's "own view."

the law, or if, as suggested earlier, a contract will seldom be held void on the ground of mutual mistake unless a condition can be implied that the contract should not be effective unless the goods exist,[71] then invalidity is not a necessary consequence of such a mistake. The court may refuse to imply such a condition where it would be inappropriate. In *McRae v. Commonwealth Disposals Commission*[72] the defendants sold to the plaintiffs an oil tanker said to be lying on a certain reef off New Guinea. The plaintiffs thereupon fitted out a salvage expedition, but found that there was no tanker at the place indicated, nor even any such reef. They brought an action against the defendants claiming damages for breach of contract. The High Court of Australia held that the plaintiffs were entitled to succeed. No condition could be implied into the contract that it was to be void if the tanker was not in existence, for the defendants had contracted that it did exist at the place specified; they should have known that it did not exist.[73] In reliance upon this decision, it has been suggested that a contract concerning non-existent subject-matter is always valid and binding unless a condition can be implied to the contrary.[74] It is submitted, however, that a mistake of which neither party should have been aware as to the existence of the subject-matter usually justifies the inference that neither party assumed the risk of such mischance[75] and that such a contract is prima facie void. The question is really one of the construction of the contract.[76] Normally the parties must be taken to have contracted on the basis that the subject-matter of their agreement was in existence. Prima facie, therefore, the contract will be void. But if (as was argued in *Couturier v. Hastie*[77]) one of the parties contracts to purchase an adventure, he binds himself to pay in any event; or if the other party either expressly or impliedly assumes responsibility that the subject-matter of the contract is in existence, he will be liable in damages if in fact it is non-existent.[78] Where, however, the case is one of the sale of goods which have perished before the contract was made, section 6 of the Sale of Goods Act 1979 may preclude such a result, since it provides that the contract will be void. It does not seem that the parties can vary this rule by contrary agreement.[79]

---

[71] See *ante*, § 5–014.

[72] (1951) 84 C.L.R. 377; *Tommey v. Finextra* (1962) 106 S.J. 1012.

[73] *cf. ante*, § 5–015.

[74] *Svanosio v. McNamara* (1956) 96 C.L.R. 186; Slade (1954) 70 L.Q.R. 385; Shatwell (1955) 33 Can. Bar Rev. 164; Atiyah (1957) 73 L.Q.R. 340.

[75] *Couturier v. Hastie* (1856) 5 H.L.C. 673, 681; *Barrow, Lane & Ballard Ltd v. Phillip Phillips & Co.* [1929] 1 K.B. 574, 582; Anson's Law of Contract (27th ed., by Beatson, 1998), p. 301; Treitel, *The Law of Contract* (9th ed., 1995), pp. 262–263; Corbin, *Contracts* (1960) Vol. 3, § 600; American Law Institute's *Restatement of Contracts* (1932), §§ 456, 460 and *Restatement of Contracts* (2d), § 263; Uniform Commercial Code, s. 2–613. It is possible that the attitude of the court may differ between an executed transaction (as in *Bell v. Lever Bros. Ltd, supra*) and an executory transaction (as in *Magee v. Pennine Insurance Co. Ltd* [1969] 2 Q.B. 507).

[76] See *ante*, § 5–012; *post*, § 24–014.

[77] (1856) 5 H.L.C. 673, *supra*.

[78] *McRae v. Commonwealth Disposals Commission* (1951) 84 C.L.R. 377.

[79] See Treitel, *The Law of Contract* (9th ed., 1995), p. 273; contrast Atiyah, *Sale of Goods* (9th ed., 1995), pp. 70–71. Alternatively, it might be held that he was liable for breach of a collateral warranty (see *post*, § 12–004) or in tort for damages for negligent misstatement, if such should exist, under the principle stated in *Hedley Byrne & Co. v. Heller & Partners* [1964] A.C. 465. It is doubtful whether he could be liable under Misrepresentation Act 1967, s.2(1), as that subsection applies "where a person has entered a contract . . . " and thus may not apply when the contract is void for mistake. See further, *post*, §§ 6–067—6–076.

5–023   **Mistake as to title** Where a man enters into a contract believing that the subject-matter of the contract is the property of the other party, whereas it is in fact his own, the contract is again prima facie void. In *Bell v. Lever Brothers Ltd*,[80] Lord Atkin said: "Corresponding to mistake as to the existence of the subject-matter is mistake as to title in cases where, unknown to the parties, the buyer is already the owner of that which the seller purports to sell to him. The parties intend to effect a transfer of ownership; such a transfer is impossible; the stipulation is *naturali ratione inutilis*." In support, he cited the case of *Cooper v. Phibbs*.[81] There A agreed to take a lease of a fishery in Ireland from B, though contrary to the belief of both parties at the time A was himself tenant in tail of the fishery. The lease was set aside. The proceedings were brought in equity, but it seems that the transaction would also have been completely void at common law.[82]

5–024   **Mistake as to quality of subject-matter.** This category gives rise to the most difficult problems in this branch of the law of contract. As Lord Atkin said in *Bell v. Lever Brothers Ltd*[83]: "mistake as to quality of the thing contracted for raises more difficult questions. In such a case a mistake will not affect assent unless it is the mistake of both parties, and is as to the existence of some quality which makes the thing without the quality essentially different from the thing as it was believed to be." In the light of this statement it has been suggested that a distinction should be drawn between a mistake as to the substance of the thing contracted for, which will avoid the contract, and mistake as to its qualities, which will be without effect.[84] In *Kennedy v. Panama, New Zealand and Australian Royal Mail Co.*,[85] the prospectus of a company offering shares stated that fresh capital was required in order to fulfil a lucrative mail contract with the Postmaster of New Zealand. This contract proved to be beyond the Postmaster's authority to make, and the plaintiff, who had purchased shares in reliance upon the prospectus, claimed to recover what he had paid on the ground that the shares were different in substance from those contracted for. The Court of Queen's Bench refused to allow him to do so. They recognised the validity of the distinction between substance and quality, but held that, in this case, the shares bought under this misapprehension as to the existence of the mail contract were not substantially different from the shares described in the prospectus and applied for on the faith of that description. There could therefore be no relief in the absence of fraud, or of a definite warranty.[86] It is submitted, however, that a simple distinction between substance and quality cannot be supported.

5–025   It is true that a number of cases illustrate that a mistake as to quality in contracts of sale is normally without effect, for either the buyer or the seller will be held to have assumed the risk. "A buys B's horse; he thinks the horse is sound and he pays the price of a sound horse; he would certainly not have bought the horse if he had known as the fact is that the horse is unsound. If B has made no

---

[80] [1932] A.C. 161, 218.
[81] (1867) L.R. 2 H.L. 149. See *post*, § 5–088.
[82] *Bell v. Lever Brothers Ltd* [1932] A.C. 161, 218, 235; but see Slade, 70 L.Q.R. 385, 406 and Matthews, 105 L.Q.R. 599.
[83] *ibid.* at 218.
[84] Tylor (1948) 11 M.L.R. 257.
[85] (1867) L.R. 2 Q.B. 580. See also *Scott v. Littledale* (1858) 8 E. & B. 815; *Smith v. Hughes* (1871) L.R. 6 Q.B. 597.
[86] This was a case decided at common law before the Judicature Act 1873, so no remedy was available for innocent misrepresentation.

representation as to soundness and has not contracted that the horse is sound, A is bound and cannot recover back the price. . . . A agrees to take on lease or to buy from B an unfurnished dwelling-house. The house is in fact uninhabitable. A would never have entered into the bargain if he had known the fact. A has no remedy . . . ".[87] So where both parties entered into a contract for the sale of a picture, erroneously believing the picture to have been painted by Constable,[88] where they believed a particular brand of kapok to be pure kapok, whereas it contained an admixture of brush cotton and was a commercially inferior product,[89] and where a 1939 car was purchased in mistake for a 1948 car,[90] the validity of the contract was unaffected. But it should be remembered that Lord Atkin stated that a mutual mistake as to the quality of the thing may affect assent if "it is the mistake of both parties and is to the existence of some quality which makes the thing without the quality essentially different from the thing as it was believed to be."[91]

Care must be taken not to assume that because a defect in quality in a contract **5-026** of sale of goods does not invalidate the contract, therefore the buyer has no remedy. The buyer is today normally so well protected by implied terms in such a contract[92] that there is virtually no room for holding the contract void for mistake. The converse possibility, *viz.* that the seller may claim the contract to be void on the ground that the goods were of far higher quality than believed, though equally rare, is perhaps less likely to be ruled out by statutory implied terms.[93] In less common types of contract, it may be more difficult to determine which party has assumed the relevant risks, but an allocation of the risks to one party or the other (especially where the contract is substantially executed), is a more probable outcome than a holding that the contract is void.[94]

Even a mistake as to the substance of the thing contracted for does not **5-027** necessarily render the contract void. In *Solle v. Butcher*[95] both parties entered into a lease of a flat under the mutual apprehension that certain alterations which had been made to the flat had so altered its identity as to make it a "new" dwelling-house and so outside the Rent Acts. Yet the contract was still valid at common law.[96] Also in *Frederick E. Rose (London) Ltd v. William H. Pim Junior & Co. Ltd*[97] parties entered into a contract for the sale of horse-beans, thinking that these would be the "feveroles" the buyer needed to fulfil an order from a customer. "Horse-bean" is in fact a generic category comprising several types of bean and the type supplied, "feves," were quite different from "feveroles." The

---

[87] *Bell v. Lever Brothers Ltd* [1932] A.C. 161, *per* Lord Atkin at 224.

[88] *ibid.* at 224; *Leaf v. International Galleries* [1950] 2 K.B. 86. It has been doubted whether this example, though given by Lord Atkin, is correct if the parties were primarily concerned with the authenticity rather than the subject-matter of the painting: Treitel, *The Law of Contract* (9th ed., 1995), pp. 268–269. Mistake was not argued in *Harlingdon and Leinster Enterprises Ltd v. Christopher Hull Fine Art Ltd* [1991] 1 Q.B. 564, nor in *Naughton v. O'Callaghan* [1990] 3 All E.R. 191 (misrepresentation as to pedigree of horse).

[89] *Harrison & Jones Ltd v. Bunten and Lancaster Ltd* [1953] 1 Q.B. 646.

[90] *Oscar Chess Ltd v. Williams* [1957] 1 W.L.R. 370.

[91] See *supra*, n. 83.

[92] See Vol. II, §§ 43–058—43–098.

[93] See *Sherwood v. Walker* (1887) 33 N.W. 919; *cf. Wood v. Boynton* (1885) 25 N.W. 42.

[94] See, *e.g.* A. L. *Gullison & Sons Ltd v. Corey* (1980) 29 N.B.R. (2d) 86.

[95] [1950] 1 K.B. 671.

[96] Though it was set aside in equity: *post*, § 5–091.

[97] [1953] 2 Q.B. 450. *cf.* Denning L.J. at 460.

contract was not void. It would seem that there must be a difference so complete that, if the contract were enforced in the actual circumstances which have unexpectedly emerged, this would involve an obligation fundamentally different from that which the parties believed they were undertaking.[98] In the words of Lord Atkin[99]: "Does the state of the new facts destroy the identity of the subject-matter as it was in the original state of facts?" Or in the words of Lord Thankerton[1] the error must be such that "it either appeared on the face of the contract that the matter as to which the mistake existed was an essential and integral element of the subject-matter of the contract, or was an inevitable inference from the nature of the contract that all the parties so regarded it."

5–028   **False and fundamental assumption.**   "Whenever it is to be inferred from the terms of the contract or its surrounding circumstances that the *consensus* has been reached upon the basis of a particular contractual assumption, and that assumption is not true, the contract is avoided."[2] This proposition was formulated for the assistance of their Lordships in *Bell v. Lever Brothers Ltd*[3] by counsel for the respondents. It was accepted by both sides of the House, with the additional rider that the assumption must have been fundamental to the validity of the contract, or a foundation essential to its existence.[4] In the case of *Bell v. Lever Brothers Ltd* the House of Lords divided as to whether or not the assumption was sufficiently fundamental, but the principle applied was quite clear. In *Magee v. Pennine Insurance Co. Ltd*[5] it was held by a majority of the Court of Appeal that an agreement by an insurance company to pay £385 on the occurrence of the risk insured against was invalidated because the policy was voidable though this was only discovered later.[6] In *Scott v. Coulson*[7] a contract for the sale of a life insurance policy was avoided at the suit of the vendor because at the time that the contract was made the person whose life was assured was already dead. The vendor could recover the policy and the money payable under it. In *Griffith v. Brymer*[8] an agreement to hire a room for the purpose of viewing the coronation procession of King Edward VII was held void because, at the time the contract was entered into, the procession had already been cancelled. In *Galloway v. Galloway*[9] a separation deed was pronounced void on the ground that both the husband and wife had entered into it under the belief that they were married at the time, whereas this was not the case. And in *Associated*

---

[98] For example, see *Bell v. Lever Brothers Ltd* [1932] A.C. 161, 222; *Gompertz v. Bartlett* (1853) 2 E. & B. 849; *Frazer v. Dalgety & Co. Ltd* [1953] N.Z.L.R. 126. See also *Nicholson and Venn v. Smith-Marriott* (1947) 177 L.T. 189 (which was said to have been wrongly decided on this point in *Solle v. Butcher* [1950] 1 K.B. 671, 692) and *Financings Ltd v. Stimson* [1962] 1 W.L.R. 1184 (*ante*, §§ 2–090 and 5–016).

[99] [1932] A.C. 161, 227.

[1] *ibid.* at 236.

[2] *Bell v. Lever Brothers Ltd* [1932] A.C. 161, *per* Sir John Simon K.C. *arguendo.*

[3] At 225.

[4] At 225, 226, 236.

[5] [1969] 2 Q.B. 507. See also *Toronto Dominion Bank v. Fortin* (1978) 88 D.L.R. (3d) 232.

[6] But there was no majority decision as to whether the contract was void. Only Fenton Atkinson L.J. held that it was; he approved the opening statements in this para. (then in the 23rd ed.); Lord Denning M.R. based his decision on equitable grounds, see *post*, § 5–092. As to whether the insurer could have recovered his money if it had actually been paid, see, *post*, § 30–034 and American cases cited in Goff and Jones, *The Law of Restitution* (5th ed., 1998), pp. 198–199.

[7] [1903] 2 Ch. 249.

[8] (1903) 19 T.L.R. 434; *Clark v. Lindsay* (1903) 19 T.L.R. 202.

[9] (1914) 30 T.L.R. 531.

Japanese Bank International Ltd v. Credit du Nord SA[10] a guarantee of a lease of a machine was said to be void when it transpired that the machine did not exist and the lease was invalid; the machine was the prime security to which the guarantors looked.

An important case on this point is that of *Sheikh Brothers Ltd v. Ochsner*[11]   **5–029** which was decided by the Judicial Committee of the Privy Council on appeal from the Court of Appeal for Eastern Africa. The appellants granted to the respondent a licence to enter and cut sisal growing on a certain estate in their possession, and in return for this concession the respondent paid to the appellants a sum of money and promised to deliver to them for processing a minimum of 50 tons per month of the sisal cut. The estate was, unknown to both parties, incapable of producing this amount of sisal. The Indian Contract Act 1872, s.20, enacts that where both the parties to an agreement are under a mistake as to a matter of fact essential to the agreement, the agreement is void. The English authorities on the law of mistake were expressly cited to the board, and they held that the contract was void. In this case, however, there was nothing to indicate that the respondent undertook the risk that the estate would not yield so much sisal, and the decision would be otherwise where the terms and circumstances of the contract show that he agreed to pay in any event.[12]

Mutual mistake and frustration. There is a close analogy between the   **5–030** question of whether a contract is void for some pre-existing mutual mistake, or whether it is frustrated as a result of some subsequent event.[13] Most of the "coronation cases," as is well known, were treated as frustration cases because the announcement of the postponement of the coronation occurred after the contracts were made.[14] But there were also some cases in which the contracts were made in ignorance of the fact that the announcement had already been made.[15] In these cases the contracts were held void for mistake. In some cases it is clearly difficult to determine whether the event is more properly classified as a pre-existing fact or as a subsequent event; for instance, in the coronation cases, the King's illness (rather than the official announcement of the postponement of the coronation) might have been regarded as the relevant event, and it might then have been difficult to decide precisely when the event occurred, and hence whether any particular contract was made before or after the event. A similar problem arose in *Amalgamated Investment and Property Co. Ltd v. John Walker & Sons Ltd*[16] where the plaintiffs contracted to buy a valuable property from the

---

[10] [1989] 1 W.L.R. 255, 269; see *ante*, § 5–014. In *Re Cleveland Trust plc* [1991] B.C.L.C. 424 the common law of mistake was applied to a bonus issue of shares which was held to be void when a subsidiary's dividend, which was to pay for the issue, was held to be *ultra vires*. In *Grains & Fourriers SA v. Huyton* [1997] 1 Lloyd's Rep. 628 the parties believed the results in two certificates of analysis to have been transposed. An agreement to rectify them was void when it was discovered that there had been no transposition, so the rectification would produce the very result it was supposed to avoid.

[11] [1957] A.C. 136. See also *Clifford v. Watts* (1870) L.R. 5 C.P. 577; *R. v. Ontario Flue-Cured Tobacco Growers' Marketing Board* (1965) 51 D.L.R. (2d) 7.

[12] *Marquis of Bute v. Thompson* (1844) 13 M. & W. 487; *Mellers v. Duke of Devonshire* (1852) 16 Beav. 252; *Haywood v. Cope* (1858) 25 Beav. 140; *Jefferys v. Fairs* (1876) 4 Ch.D. 448.

[13] On frustration generally, see *post*, Chap. 24.

[14] On the "coronation cases," see *post*, §§ 24–032—24–033.

[15] *Griffith v. Brymer* (1903) 19 T.L.R. 434; *Clark v. Lindsay* (1903) 19 T.L.R. 202, *ante*, § 5–028.

[16] [1977] 1 W.L.R. 164.

defendants, and very shortly after the contract was made the building was "listed" by the authorities under the Town and Country Planning Act 1971, as a result of which its value was greatly reduced. The plaintiffs sought to argue that the contract was void for mistake on the ground that the relevant event was the internal decision of the authorities to "list" the building, and this had taken place before the contract was made. The Court of Appeal rejected this argument, holding that the relevant event was the official act of "listing" the building which only occurred after the contract was made.

5–031   In many borderline cases of this nature, it is reasonably clear that the result will be the same whether the case is regarded as one of mutual mistake or of frustration; and there is the authority of Lord Atkin in *Bell v. Lever Bros. Ltd*[17] for saying that the test for the application of the doctrines is the same. But there may be some circumstances in which the principles governing the two doctrines do not operate identically, for example, because the risks arising from pre-existing facts are more easily allocated to the parties than are the risks of frustrating events; this is because parties can usually be expected to be aware of existing risks when they contract, while future events are less easily anticipated. In such circumstances it may be necessary to decide, as in the *John Walker* case, *supra*, precisely what is the relevant event to be considered.

(b) *Mistakes as to the Terms of the Contract*[18]

5–032   **Mistake may prevent agreement.** No contract can be formed if there is no correspondence between the offer and the acceptance.[19] If, therefore, one party makes to the other an offer which the other party accepts in a fundamentally different sense from that intended by the offeror, the contract may be void. The intention of the parties is, as a general rule, to be construed objectively. The language used by one party, whatever his real intention may be, is to be construed in the sense in which it would be reasonably understood by the other.[20–21] Nevertheless cases may occur in which the terms of the offer and acceptance suffer from such latent ambiguity that it is impossible reasonably to impute any agreement between them; or it may happen that one party knowingly accepts a promise in different terms from those intended by the other. In such circumstances, the mistake may render the contract void or have some other effect.[22]

(i) *Mutual Misunderstanding*

5–033   **Parties at cross-purposes.** In most cases the application of the objective test will preclude a party who has entered into a contract under a mistake from setting up his mistake as a defence to an action against him for breach of contract. If a reasonable man would have understood the contract in a certain sense, then,

---

[17] [1932] A.C. 161, 226–227. See also *William Sindall plc v. Cambridgeshire County Council* [1994] 1 WLR 1016, 1039, *per* Evans L.J.

[18] See Cheshire (1944) 60 L.Q.R. 175, 178, 180; Tylor (1948) 11 M.L.R. 257, 259; Slade (1954) 70 L.Q.R. 385, 386; Stoljar (1965) 28 M.L.R. 265, 266.

[19] See *ante*, § 2–029.

[20–21] *Cornish v. Abington* (1859) 4 H. & N. 549, 556; *Fowkes v. Manchester and London Assurance Association* (1863) 3 B. & S. 917, 929; *Smith v. Hughes* (1871) L.R. 6 Q.B. 597, 607; *Woodhouse A.C. Israel Cocoa Ltd SA v. Nigerian Products Marketing Co. Ltd* [1972] A.C. 741; *McInerny v. Lloyds Bank* [1974] 1 Lloyd's Rep. 246.

[22] See *post*, § 5–037.

despite his mistake, the court will hold that the mistaken party is bound.[23] But where parties are genuinely at cross-purposes as to the subject-matter of the contract and the terms of the offer and acceptance are so ambiguous that it is not possible to point to one or other of the interpretations as the more probable, the court must necessarily hold that no contract exists.[24] In the case of *Scriven v. Hindley*,[25] an auctioneer acting for the plaintiff put up for sale lots of hemp and tow. The auction catalogue did not indicate the difference in their content. A lot of tow was put up, and the defendant bid for it thinking it was hemp. The bid was accepted. The jury found that the auctioneer intended to sell tow, while the defendant intended to bid for hemp, and that the former had merely thought that an overvalue had been placed by the defendant on the tow. It was held that, as the parties were never *ad idem* as to the subject-matter of the contract, there was no binding contract of sale; the decision probably turned on the misleading nature of the catalogue, because in the ordinary way an auctioneer is entitled to assume that a bidder knows what he is bidding for, and acceptance of a bid will create a binding contract. In *Raffles v. Wichelhaus*[26] the defendants contracted to buy a cargo of cotton to arrive *"ex Peerless* from Bombay."* There were two ships of that name and both sailed from Bombay, but one left in October and the other in December. The description of the goods pointed equally to either cargo. To an action for refusal to accept goods from the December shipment, the defendant pleaded that the agreement referred to the other one. The plaintiff demurred, but the court gave judgment for the defendants, apparently taking the view that it was open to the latter to adduce parol evidence as to which ship was meant. The judgment does not indicate what the position would be if the parol evidence failed to point to one cargo rather than the other, but the court did not express any disagreement with counsel's proposition that, if the defendant meant one *Peerless* and the plaintiff the other, there would be no contract. It is unlikely that in a modern case of a similar character the facts proved would be so sparse as not to give some ground for adopting one interpretation of the contract rather than the other.

(ii) *Unilateral Mistake as to Terms*

Mistake known to the other party. A mistake as to the terms of the contract, **5–034** *if known to the other party*, may avoid the contract. In this case, the normal rule of objective interpretation is displaced in favour of admitting evidence of subjective intention.[27] In *Hartog v. Colin and Shields*[28] the defendants offered for

---

[23] *Scott v. Littledale* (1858) 8 E. & B. 815; *Wood v. Scarth* (1855) 1 F. & F. 293; *Smith v. Hughes* (1871) L.R. 6 Q.B. 597.

[24] *Thornton v. Kempster* (1814) 5 Taunt. 786; *Henkel v. Pape* (1870) L.R. 6 Ex. 7; *Smidt v. Tiden* (1874) L.R. 9 Q.B. 446; *Hickman v. Berens* [1895] 2 Ch. 638; *Falck v. Williams* [1900] A.C. 176; *Van Praagh v. Everidge* [1903] 1 Ch. 434; *cf. Marwood v. Charter Credit Corporation* (1971) 20 D.L.R. (3d) 563. However, it seems possible that the mistake must relate to a point which is of some importance. If the misunderstanding is as to some unimportant point the court might simply disregard the relevant term and uphold the rest of the contract. *cf. Nicolene Ltd v. Simmonds* [1953] 1 Q.B. 543.

[25] [1913] 3 K.B. 564.

[26] (1864) 2 H. & C. 906. See further as to this case, Grant Gilmore, *The Death of Contract* (1974), pp. 35–41; Simpson (1975) 91 L.Q.R. 247, 268.

[27] Contrast *L.C.C. v. Henry Boot & Sons Ltd* [1959] 1 W.L.R. 1069, criticised by Goodhart (1960) 76 L.Q.R. 32.

[28] [1939] 3 All E.R. 566, followed in *McMaster University v. Wilcher Construction Ltd* (1971) 22 D.L.R. (3d) 9.

sale to the plaintiffs some Argentine hare skins, but by mistake offered them at so much per pound instead of so much per piece. The previous negotiations between the parties had proceeded on the basis that the price was to be assessed at so much per piece as was usual in the trade. But the plaintiffs purported to accept the offer and sued for damages for non-delivery. The court held that the plaintiffs must have known that the offer did not express the true intention of the defendants and that the contract was therefore void.[29] On the same principle, it has been held in Canada[30] that an offer contained in a tender cannot be accepted when it is apparent that the tender is based upon a serious mistake in calculating the totals.

5–035   **Mistakes which ought to have been apparent.** It is not clear whether for the mistake to be operative it must actually be known to the other party, or whether it is enough that it ought to have been apparent to any reasonable man. In Canada the latter suffices.[31] In *Centrovincial Estates plc v. Merchant Investors Assurance Co. Ltd*[32] the Court of Appeal appeared to consider that the plaintiff might be able to negate any binding agreement by showing that the defendant ought to have known that the plaintiff's offer contained an error; and in *O.T. Africa Line Ltd v. Vickers Plc*[33] Mance J. said that the objective principle would be displaced if a party knew or ought to have known of the mistake. The latter situation would include cases in which the party refrained from making enquiries or failed to make enquiries when these were reasonably called for,[34] but first there must be a real reason to suspect a mistake. Such an approach would be consistent with the recent decision of the House of Lords on mistakes in contractual notices. In *Mannai Investment Co. Ltd v. Eagle Star Life Assurance Co. Ltd*[35] the House held that a contractual notice to determine a lease was effective although it did not comply exactly with the break clause in the contract, provided that the notice given would convey the lessee's intention to exercise its rights under the clause unambiguously to a reasonable recipient. The majority held that the relevant test was whether the intention of the party giving the notice was, in its context, obvious to a reasonable recipient[35a]; if it was, it was immaterial that it contained a minor error. To require literal compliance with the clause in all cases would be to confuse the meaning of words with the question of what meaning in the

---

[29] See also *Watkin v. Watson-Smith, The Times*, July 3, 1986. In *Taylor v. Johnson* (1983) 45 A.L.R. 265 the High Court held that where one party knew that the other was mistaken as to a term in a formal written contract, the contract was voidable rather than void; *sed quaere*. Part of the majority judgment of the High Court was adopted by the Court of Appeal in *Commission for New Towns v. Cooper (Great Britain) Ltd* [1995] 2 Ch. 259, a case of rectification, without discussion of the majority's view on this point. See further, *post*, § 5–024. In *Deputy Commissioner of Taxation (N.S.W.) v. Chamberlain* (1990) 93 A.L.R. 729 (Federal Ct., General Division) a taxpayer was not permitted to take advantage of a typing error he had noticed in a writ issued against him.

[30] *Bell River Community Arena Inc. v. Kaufmann Co. Ltd* (1978) 87 D.L.R. (3d) 761; to the same effect is *U.S. v. Braunstein* (1948) 168 F. 2d 749.

[31] See case cited in n.28 *ante*.

[32] [1983] Com.L.R. 158. In this case it was said that if the other party did not know and had no reason to know of the mistake, he is entitled to hold the mistaken party to the terms of the contract in their objective sense; it is immaterial that he has not changed his position or relied upon the contract.

[33] [1996] 1 Lloyd's Rep. 700.

[34] See *post* § 5–073.

[35] [1997] A.C. 749, reversing the Court of Appeal [1995] 1 W.L.R. 1508. The *Mannai* case was applied in *Garston v. Scottish Widows' Fund and Life Assurance Society* [1998] 3 All E.R. 596.

[35a] [1997] A.C. 749, 767, 780, 782. Lord Clyde said that the actual understanding of the recipient would be relevant only if some question of estoppel arose (at 782).

particular setting the use of words was intended to convey, and the notice would be effective if, as here, the reasonable recipient was left in no doubt that the tenant intended to determine the lease and to do so from the date permitted by the clause. The principle was stated[36] to be applicable to contractual notices generally, though a more restricted approach is to be applied to documents such as bankers' commercial credits where the same document might "have different meanings to different people according to their knowledge of the background". However, in modern times issues of unilateral mistake often arise in connection with claims for the rectification of written documents, and here it seems that relief will be given only if the mistake was actually known to the party against whom rectification is sought. Reference should be made to the sections dealing with that topic.[37]

Mistake as to the terms of the contract. It is not sufficient that one party   **5–036** knows the other has entered the contract under a mistake of some kind. The mistake must relate to the terms of the contract. If it relates, for example, merely to the quality or the substance of the thing contracted for, it will be an error in motive and it is well established that an error in motive will not avoid a contract.[38] In *Smith v. Hughes*[39] the defendant purchased from the plaintiff a quantity of oats in the belief that they were old oats, whereas in fact they were new oats and quite unsuitable for the purpose for which he wanted them. On discovering his mistake, he refused to accept them and was sued by the plaintiff for the price. The judge asked the jury whether the plaintiff believed the defendant to believe, or to be under the impression, that he was contracting for the purchase of old oats. If so, they were to return a verdict for the defendant. On a motion for a new trial, the Court of Queen's Bench considered that this direction would not sufficiently distinguish between a mistake on the part of the defendant that the oats were old oats, and a mistake that they were being offered to him as old oats. In the former case, the contract would be valid, as the error would be one of motive; in the latter, the mistake would be as to the terms of the contract, and, if known to the plaintiff, would provide a defence to the action. A new trial was ordered. It is not clear whether the defendant would, on the latter hypothesis, have been free from liability on the ground that the contract was void, or on the ground that the seller was in breach by delivering new oats.[40] As the buyer had been given a sample of the oats it is difficult to see how, on similar facts occurring today, any sort of a defence could be made out.

Effect of mistake as to terms. In both *Hartog v. Colin and Shields*[41] and   **5–037** *Smith v. Hughes*[42] it was said that the effect of a mistake by one party as to the

---

[36] [1997] A.C. 749 at 768 and 789–790.

[37] See *post*, §§ 5–065—5–086.

[38] *Balfour v. Sea Fire and Life Assurance Co.* (1857) 3 C.B.(N.S.) 300; *Scrivener v. Pask* (1866) L.R. 1 C.P. 715; *Pope v. Buenos Ayres New Gas Co.* (1892) 8 T.L.R. 758; *cf. Gill v. M'Dowell* [1903] 2 Ir.Rep. 463. In *G & S Fashions v. B & Q plc* [1995] 1 W.L.R. 1088 it was held that, if a landlord purports to forfeit a lease in the mistaken belief that the tenant is in breach of covenant, the fact that the tenant knows of the landlord's mistake does not prevent it accepting the forfeiture. See also *Bank of Credit and Commerce International SA (in liquidation) v. Ali* [1999] 2 All E.R. 1005, 1019. See further *ante*, § 5–003.

[39] (1871) L.R. 6 Q.B. 597.

[40] See *Roberts & Co. Ltd v. Leicestershire C.C.* [1961] Ch. 555 (rectification).

[41] [1939] 3 All E.R. 566; *supra* § 5–034.

[42] *Supra*, n. 39.

terms of the contract would, if it were known to the other party, make the contract void. However in both cases the only question was whether the party who had made the mistake could be held to the objective meaning of his words. The *apparent* contract was void, but it was not decided that neither party had any contractual rights against the other. When the actual intentions of the mistaken party are known to the other, it is possible that the mistaken party can enforce the contract in those terms. Thus it may be that in *Hartog v. Colin and Shields* the seller could have enforced the contract at so much per piece (the figure the seller actually intended) against the buyer.[43] The buyer, having accepted an offer which he knew was meant to read so much per piece, could be said to be bound by it. A number of arguments may be adduced to support this submission.

5–038   **Mistakes in contractual notices.** First, it is consistent with a recent House of Lords decision on the effect of a mistake in a contractual notice. In *Mannai Investment Co. Ltd v. Eagle Star Life Assurance Co. Ltd*[44] the House of Lords held that a contractual notice to determine a lease was effective although it did not comply exactly with the break clause in the contract, provided that the notice given would convey the lessee's intention to exercise its rights under the clause unambiguously to a reasonable recipient. By analogy, an offeree who must have known what the offeror meant despite a mistake in the offer and who purports to accept the offer should be bound by what the offeror really intended.

5–039   **Estoppel.** Second, it has been said that if one party knows the other has made a mistake and fails to point it out when the reasonable person would expect him to do so were he acting honestly and reasonably, an estoppel by silence or acquiescence may arise and result in liability where there would otherwise be none.[45]

5–040   **Rectification cases.** Third, this interpretation is consistent with the cases granting rectification in cases of unilateral mistake.[46] There it is said that if the party against whom rectification is sought knew that the documents did not represent the true intention of the party seeking relief, the documents will be rectified to show what the party seeking relief actually intended. This presupposes the existence of a valid contract despite the mistake.

5–041   **Effect of mistake where true intention not known to other party.** A more difficult case would be where one party knows that the other does not intend what he has said or written in his offer, but does not know what the offer was supposed to say. If the first party were to purport to accept the apparent offer, it might be argued that he was estopped from denying that he had accepted whatever the offeror can prove he actually meant; but as this would leave the first party in great uncertainty, it seems more likely that the court would hold that no contract had resulted.

---

[43] See also Anson, *Law of Contract* (27th ed., by Beatson, 1998), p. 311; compare Treitel, *Law of Contract* (9th ed., 1995), pp. 285–286 (possibly seller could have held buyer to contract on the stated terms had he wished to do so).

[44] [1997] A.C. 749; *ante*, § 5–035.

[45] *Pacol Ltd v. Trade Lines Ltd, The Henryk Sif* [1982] 1 Lloyd's Rep. 456, 465; *The Stolt Loyalty* [1993] 2 Lloyd's Rep. 281, 290; *Republic of India v. Indian Steamship Co., The Indian Grace (No. 2)* [1994] 2 Lloyd's Rep. 331, 344. See *ante*, § 2–073.

[46] See *post*, §§ 2–065 and 3–087.

Comparison to effect where document signed in error. It may be noted that 5–042
there is a difference between the treatment of oral and written contracts which
have been entered into as the result of a mistake as to the terms by one party
which was apparent to the other. As just suggested, with an oral contract or one
made by exchange of written communications the result appears to be either that
the contract is void or, if the submission above[47] is correct, that there is a contract
on the terms actually intended by the mistaken party. As was just mentioned,[48]
a party who has signed a written agreement under a mistake may, if the mistake
was known to the other party, claim to have the document rectified. However, the
right to rectification may be lost, so that it is the ostensible agreement which will
stand.[49]

Where the mistake should have been known to the other party. It was 5–043
submitted earlier that, at present, English law gives relief for a unilateral mistake
if the mistake was known to the other party; but there are suggestions in some of
the cases that relief should also be given if the other party ought to have known
of it.[50] If it were decided to give relief in these circumstances, what should
the effect on the contract be? In this situation it might seem inappropriate to hold
the second party to what the first party actually meant when that was unknown
to the second party, and therefore to be more appropriate to hold that there is no
contract.[51] On the other hand, it can be argued that he will not be in a worse
position than a party who finds that the correct interpretation of the contract is
very different to what he had mistakenly understood by it.

Parties aware of disagreement over meaning of clause. It has been held that 5–044
there may be a valid contract despite the fact that the parties know that they are
not agreed as to the meaning of one of its terms. Provided there is evidence that
the parties intended to make a binding agreement, the contract will be valid and
the parties are treated as having left it to the court to determine its correct
meaning.[52]

(iii) *Mistaken Identity*

Mistaken identity. A number of cases have raised the question whether a 5–045
mistake by one party as to the identity of the person with whom he appears to be
contracting will render the contract void. The question arises in a recurrent
situation typified by the facts of *Cundy v. Lindsay*.[53] A fraudulent person named
Blenkarn wrote to the plaintiffs offering to buy certain goods, and so contrived
his signature to resemble that of Blenkiron & Co., a prosperous firm carrying on

---

[47] See § 5–037, *ante*.

[48] See § 5–040, *ante*.

[49] See *post*, § 5–082. In *Taylor v. Johnson* (1983) 45 A.L.R. 265 the Australian High Court held
that where one party knew that the other was probably mistaken as to the terms of a formal written
contract, and tried to prevent her discovering the mistake, the contract was voidable rather than void.
This is an attractive solution but seems to go beyond English authority in allowing recission of
unilateral mistake: see *post*, § 5–089.

[50] See § 5–035, *ante*.

[51] In Canada, in the analogous situation in which the mistaken party seeks rectification, the other
party is given the option of submitting to rectification or to rescission, see *post*, § 5–075. It does not
seem easy to reach a parallel conclusion in the case of an oral agreement while it remains the law that
the effect of a mistake is to make the contract void rather than voidable.

[52] *London County Council v. Henry Boot & Sons Ltd* [1959] 1 W.L.R. 1069.

[53] (1878) 3 App. Cas. 459; see *post*, § 5–048.

business in the same street and with whom the plaintiffs had previously dealt. The plaintiffs despatched the goods in the belief that they were dealing with Blenkiron & Co. and the goods eventually came into the hands of an innocent purchaser, the defendant. If the contract between the plaintiffs and Blenkarn was void for mistake, no property in the goods had passed under the contract, and the plaintiffs were entitled to recover them. But otherwise the contract was merely voidable for fraud, and the defendant would have acquired a good title.[54]

5–046   **Mistake as to the person.**[55] The identity of the person with whom one is contracting or proposing to contract is often immaterial. It is usually of no importance to a shopkeeper to whom he sells goods across the counter for cash[56]; and an auctioneer who accepts a bid at a public auction is not normally concerned with the identity of the person who makes the bid.[57] Sometimes, however, and for special reasons, the identity of the person is material and in such a case there may be no contract if a mistake has been made as to this.

5–047   **Offer to B cannot be accepted by C.** Assuming the identity of the other party to be material, we may start with the general proposition that, if A offers to make a contract with B, C cannot give himself any rights under the offer. "A person cannot constitute himself a contracting party with one whom he knows or ought to know has no intention of contracting with him. An offer can be accepted only by the person to whom it is addressed."[58] In *Boulton v. Jones*[59] the defendant had been used to deal with one Brocklehurst, against whom he had a set-off. He sent Brocklehurst a written order for some goods. On the very day that the order was sent, Brocklehurst had transferred his business to his foreman, the plaintiff. The plaintiff thereupon dispatched the goods without informing the defendant of the change of ownership. The defendant refused to pay for the goods, and the court held that he was not liable to do so as the plaintiff could not accept an offer which was not addressed to him. Nevertheless the test is not entirely a subjective one. The question is not simply "With whom did the offeror intend to contract?" but also "How would the offer have been understood by a reasonable man in the position of the offeree?" If A makes an offer to B in mistake for C, and B accepts the offer reasonably believing it to have been intended for him, A will be bound despite the mistake.[60] In *Boulton v. Jones* the circumstances were such that a reasonable man would not have believed the offer to have been addressed to him. The business had only just changed hands, and the plaintiff either knew of[61] or could easily have discovered the existence of the set-off. But where such

---

[54] The owner who has parted with possession of the goods to the rogue is not estopped from reclaiming them from the innocent third party to whom the rogue sells them; contrast the case where a party has mistakenly signed a document which is relied on by an innocent third party, *post*, § 5–055.

[55] See Goodhart (1941) 57 L.Q.R. 228; Cheshire (1944) 60 L.Q.R. 175, 183; Williams (1945) 23 Can. Bar Rev. 271; Tylor (1948) 11 M.L.R. 257, 259; Slade (1954) 70 L.Q.R. 385, 390; Wilson (1954) 17 M.L.R. 515; Unger (1955) 18 M.L.R. 259; Hall [1961] Camb.L.J. 86; Stoljar (1965) 28 M.L.R. 265, 280.

[56] *Ingram v. Little* [1961] 1 Q.B. 31, 57.

[57] *Dennant v. Skinner* [1948] 2 K.B. 164. See also *Smith v. Wheatcroft* (1878) 9 Ch.D. 223.

[58] Anson, *Law of Contract* (27th ed., by Beatson, 1998), p. 311.

[59] (1857) 2 H. & N. 564.

[60] Goodhart (1941) 57 L.Q.R. 228, 241–244; Cheshire (1944) 60 L.Q.R. 175, 186–187. See also *Upton-on-Severn R.D.C. v. Powell* [1942] 1 All E.R. 220.

[61] See the report in (1857) 6 W.R. 107.

knowledge or means of knowledge is lacking, the offeror will be bound. More-over, the growth of companies and the increasing depersonalisation of commerce may mean that nineteenth-century cases on questions of this kind are not very reliable as authorities. In 1857 a buyer of goods from a shop may well have regarded the identity of the seller as a matter of importance; in the day of the supermarket this is less likely to be the case.

Mistake must be as to identity. For a mistake to be operative, it must normally be a mistake as to the identity of the person with whom the contract is made. A mistake as to attributes—for example, as to character, solvency, or social position—will normally be insufficient.[62] In *Cundy v. Lindsay*[63] (the facts of which were stated in § 5–045, *ante*) the House of Lords held that the mistake was one as to the identity of the other contracting party and the contract was void. On the other hand, in *King's Norton Metal Co. v. Edridge, Merrett & Co. Ltd*[64] the plaintiffs had despatched goods to one Wallis, who had written to them posing as a member of a mythical firm named "Hallam & Co." Wallis subse-quently sold the goods so obtained to the defendants, who took in good faith and for value. The Court of Appeal held that the plaintiffs had intended to contract with the writer of the letter, although they had invested him with the attributes of solvency and respectability. If there had been a separate entity called Hallam & Co. the case might have been within *Cundy v. Lindsay*. On the facts there was no mistake as to identity, and so they could not recover the goods. It is possible that in exceptional circumstances a mistake as to attribute may prevent a contract coming into existence, if a person is for the purpose identified by some attribute. An offer made only to members of the University of Warwick could not be accepted by someone who was not a member of the University.[65]   5–048

Mistake *inter praesentes*. Where the contract is in writing, prima facie the persons named in the writing are the parties to the contract.[66] More difficult problems arise where the offer and acceptance are made by the parties in each other's presence. There will be no contract if it is shown that "there was no objective agreement, *e.g.* that the offer was, objectively speaking, made to one person and (perhaps as the result of fraud) objectively speaking, accepted by another."[67] But in face-to-face dealings the offeror must be taken prima facie to have intended to contract with the person in front of him, and with no one else. In *Phillips v. Brooks*[68] one North entered the plaintiff's shop and selected several pieces of jewellery. He then wrote out a cheque for the price, saying "I am Sir George Bullough"—a person known by reputation to the plaintiff. He took away some of the jewellery and pledged it with the defendant who received it in good faith. In an action by the plaintiff to recover the jewellery pledged, it was held that the plaintiff intended to contract with the person in the shop. There was   5–049

---

[62] A mistake as to whether a person is contracting as agent for another or as principal may be relevant, as in *Hardman v. Booth* (1863) 1 H. & C. 803; but not a mistake as to the identity of a mere messenger: *Midland Bank plc v. Brown Shipley & Co. Ltd* [1991] 1 Lloyd's Rep. 576.

[63] (1878) 3 App.Cas. 459; *Baillie's Case* [1898] 1 Ch. 110.

[64] (1897) 14 T.L.R. 98.

[65] See Treitel, *The Law of Contract* (9th ed., 1995), p. 278.

[66] *Hector v. Lyons* (1989) 58 P. & C.R. 156.

[67] Robert Goff L.J. in *Whittaker v. Campbell* [1984] Q.B. 318, 327.

[68] [1919] 2 K.B. 243, criticised by Goodhart (1941) 57 L.Q.R. 228 at 241, and by Gresson P. in *Fawcett v. Star Car Sales* [1960] N.Z.L.R. 406. See also *Dennant v. Skinner* [1948] 2 K.B. 164; *Barclays Bank Ltd v. Okenarhe* [1966] 2 Lloyd's Rep. 87.

therefore no operative mistake and the property in the jewellery passed. This case was distinguished in *Lake v. Simmons*[69] where it was pointed out[70] that the misrepresentation of his identity by North had not occurred until after the sale had been concluded and the property had passed. Circumstances may therefore be present, even in a contract *inter praesentes*, which will indicate that the offeror intended to contract with an entirely different person from the one in front of him.[71]

5–050   Perhaps the most cogent factor tending to this conclusion will be proof by the mistaken party that he had personal knowledge of the existence of the person with whom he supposed himself to be contracting.[72] But such knowledge is not an essential requirement of invalidity. There may be other circumstances which are almost as compelling. In *Ingram v. Little*[73] the plaintiffs advertised their car for sale. A rogue who called himself Hutchinson offered to buy the car and to pay for it with a cheque. This offer was rejected. "Hutchinson" then gave his initials and address, describing himself as a respectable business man living in Caterham. The plaintiffs had never heard of this man but one of the plaintiffs ascertained from the telephone directory that such a person lived at that address. Relying on this information, they accepted the cheque which was dishonoured on presentation. The rogue sold the car, which subsequently came into the hands of the defendant, a bona fide purchaser for value. In an action by the plaintiffs to recover the car, or its value, from the defendant, the Court of Appeal held that the contract between the plaintiffs and the rogue was void for mistake as to identity, and that they were entitled to judgment since the car was still their property. The circumstances (particularly the investigation of the telephone directory) indicated that it was with Hutchinson that the plaintiffs intended to deal and not with the rogue who was physically present before them. However, this decision was criticised and not followed in *Lewis v. Averay*[74] where the facts were very similar but judgment was given for the bona fide purchaser. The court here emphasised that each of these cases must be decided on its own facts but that there is a strong presumption against holding a contract to be totally void where it is entered into *inter praesentes*.

5–051   **Mistake and third parties.** It is not clear whether a person can intervene and allege that a contract is void for mistake as to the person when the contracting parties themselves are unwilling to assert its invalidity. In *Fawcett v. Saint Merat (Star Car Sales Ltd, Claimant)*[75] Hardie Boys J. in the Supreme Court of New Zealand held that a third party could not raise "in the name of one of the contracting parties" the question of mistake as to the person; but his view did not form part of the reasoning of the decision on appeal.[76] At first sight it might seem that a third party should be allowed to rely on the invalidity of the transaction for

---

[69] [1927] A.C. 487; distinguished in *J. Rigby (Haulage) Ltd v. Reliance Marine Insurance Co. Ltd* [1956] 2 Q.B. 468 and in *Ingram v. Little* [1961] 1 Q.B. 31, *per* Devlin L.J. (dissenting) at 71.

[70] [1927] A.C. 487, 502.

[71] *Hardman v. Booth* (1863) 1 H. & C. 803 (agency); *Lake v. Simmons* [1927] A.C. 487, 500.

[72] *Hardman v. Booth, supra*; *Cundy v. Lindsay* (1878) 3 App.Cas. 459. Contrast *Fawcett v. Star Car Sales* [1960] N.Z.L.R. 406.

[73] [1961] 1 Q.B. 31 (Devlin L.J. dissenting).

[74] [1972] 1 Q.B. 198.

[75] [1959] N.Z.L.R. 952.

[76] [1960] N.Z.L.R. 406, *sub nom. Fawcett v. Star Car Sales*. The majority of the court make no reference to this point, and Gresson P. (dissenting) expressly rejects it.

the contract is not voidable at the parties' option but void *ab initio*. But in practice some strange consequences would follow from permitting such intervention. If the buyer in *Boulton v. Jones*[77] had waived his objections to the identity of the seller and paid for the goods could it really be contended by a third party that the property did not thereby pass to the buyer?

No third person. A further refinement must be noted in this branch of the law   **5–052** of mistake. In the cases of operative mistake previously cited, there has been in the mind of the offeror a third and identifiable person with whom he alleged he intended to contract. It would appear to be unnecessary that this third person should actually be alive and physically in existence. A mistake as to identity could well arise even though the offeror erroneously believed in the existence of a third person with whom he intended to contract.[78] Provided it can be established by evidence that A made an offer to B believing himself to be contracting with C (whether in existence or not) and that this fact was known, either actually or inferentially, to B, no contract will arise. But suppose that A makes an offer to B merely in the belief that B is not B? The position is then very different. The offer has been made to B even though A would never have made it had he known B's true identity. B can therefore accept the offer whether or not he knows of the mistake. The contract may be voidable for fraud, but it is not a nullity from the beginning.[79] It is only if a term can be implied into the contract that B is not B, and it is proved that this was known to the other party, that the contract will be void *ab initio*.[80] In such a case there is a mistake as to the terms of the contract known to the other party, and, as we have seen,[81] this may invalidate the agreement.

Proposal for reform. In its Twelfth Report,[82] the Law Reform Committee   **5–053** recommended that, in the case of mistake as to the person, the distinction between void and voidable contracts should be abrogated so far as the acquisition of title by innocent parties is concerned. However, the Report was never implemented.

(c) *Non est Factum*

Definition. This category of mistake is derived from a small group of cases   **5–054** most of them of modern times, although the doctrine existed at least as early as 1584.[83] The general rule is that a man is estopped by his deed, and although there is no such estoppel in the case of ordinary signed documents, a party of full age

---

[77] (1857) 2 H. & N. 564, *ante*, § 5–047.

[78] *Lake v. Simmons* [1927] A.C. 487; *cf. Newborne v. Sensolid (Great Britain) Ltd* [1954] 1 Q.B. 45.

[79] *Ingram v. Little* [1961] 1 Q.B. 31, 54; Goodhart (1941) 57 L.Q.R. 228; Unger (1955) 18 M.L.R. 259. See also *Dyster v. Randall & Sons* [1926] Ch. 932. Contrast *Gordon v. Street* [1899] 2 Q.B. 641; *Sowler v. Potter* [1940] 1 K.B. 271, which may perhaps now be taken to have been overruled, see *Solle v. Butcher* [1950] 1 K.B. 671, 691; *Gallie v. Lee* [1969] 2 Ch. 17, 33, 41, 45, affd. *sub nom. Saunders v. Anglia Building Society* [1971] A.C. 1004; *Lewis v. Averay* [1972] 1 Q.B. 198, 206; and Wilson (1954) 17 M.L.R. 515.

[80] *Said v. Butt* [1920] 3 K.B. 497 (a case of agency); see Vol. II, § 32–065.

[81] See *ante*, § 5–037.

[82] Cmnd. 2958 (1966), § 15.

[83] *Thoroughgood's Case* (1584) 2 Co.Rep. 9a. The doctrine was probably much older than that case: see Holdsworth, *History of English Law*, Vol. 8, p. 50.

and understanding is normally bound by his signature to a document, whether he reads or understands it or not. If, however, a party has been misled into executing a deed or signing a document essentially different from that which he intended to execute or sign, he can plead *non est factum* in an action against him. The deed or writing is completely void in whosesoever hands it may come. In most of the cases in which *non est factum* has been successfully pleaded, the mistake has been induced by fraud. But the presence of fraud is probably not a necessary factor. As Byles J. said in *Foster v. Mackinnon*,[84] "it is invalid not merely on the ground of fraud, where fraud exists, but on the ground that the mind of the signor did not accompany the signature; in other words, that he never intended to sign, and therefore in contemplation of law never did sign, the contract to which his name is appended."

5–055   **Importance of doctrine.** The defence of *non est factum* is most obviously important in two situations. The first is where a party has signed the supposed contract as the result of the fraud of a third party and the other party to it has no knowledge, actual or constructive, of the fraud.[85] For example, in *United Dominions Trust Ltd v. Western*[86] the defendant signed a blank hire-purchase proposal form and the dealer filled in incorrect figures before dispatching it to the finance company. The second is where the fraud has been committed by the other party to the alleged contract or deed and a third party has then relied on the document. In *Saunders v. Anglia Building Society*[87] an elderly lady signed what she believed to be a deed of gift to her house to her nephew but which was in fact an assignment on sale to a third party who mortgaged the house to the defendants and kept the proceeds. If the case is one of fraud or misrepresentation by the other party to the contract, with no third party involved, the majority in the Court of Appeal in *Lloyds Bank plc v. Waterhouse*[88] said that the case should be dealt with as one of misrepresentation. Alternatively, where the other party knew that the document did not represent the intention of the party signing it, the latter may have a remedy for unilateral mistake.[89]

5–056   **Nature of mistake necessary to invalidate transaction.** The plea of *non est factum* was formerly held to be available only if the mistake was as to the very nature of the transaction. In *Foster v. Mackinnon*[90] the defendant was induced to indorse a bill of exchange on the false representation that it was a guarantee similar to one he had signed on a previous occasion. He was held not liable when

---

[84] (1869) L.R. 4 C.P. 704, 711. See also *Bank of Ireland v. M'Manamy* [1916] 2 I.R. 161. *cf. Hasham v. Zenab* [1960] A.C. 316; *Mercantile Credit Co. Ltd v. Hamblin* [1965] 2 Q.B. 242, 268, 280 (misrepresentation).

[85] On notice of fraud or misrepresentation by a third party, see *post*, §§ 6–018—6–031.

[86] [1976] Q.B. 513.

[87] [1971] A.C. 1004.

[88] (1991) 10 Tr.L.R. 161.

[89] See the judgment of Sir Edward Eveleigh in *Lloyds Bank plc v. Waterhouse*, *supra*. Although a contract entered under an operative mistake is usually said to be void, *ante*, § 5–037, it appears that this cannot be raised by the mistaken party against a third party who in good faith and without notice of the mistake has relied on the signed document. The signer is estopped and can only succeed against the third party if he can show *non est factum*: *ibid*. Contrast the "mistaken identity" cases, *ante*, § 5–045, where the mistaken party is not estopped simply by entrusting possession of his property to the rogue who sells it to the third party.

[90] (1869) L.R. 4 C.P. 704; *cf. National Provincial Bank of England v. Jackson* (1886) 33 Ch.D. 1; *Carlisle and Cumberland Banking Co. v. Bragg* [1911] 1 K.B. 489; *Muskham Finance Ltd v. Howard* [1963] 1 Q.B. 904. See also *Bagot v. Chapman* [1907] 2 Ch. 222.

sued by an innocent indorsee of the bill. In *Lewis v. Clay*[91] the result was the same. The defendant was induced by a friend of long standing to sign a document, which was covered by a paper with four openings in it, under the representation that he was witnessing it. The defendant had in fact signed two promissory notes and two letters authorising the plaintiff to pay the proceeds of the notes to the friend. The defendant was held not liable because his mind never went with the transaction. On the other hand, mistake as to the contents of a deed or document was held not sufficient. An extreme case was that of *Howatson v. Webb*,[92] where the defendant was fraudulently induced by one Hooper to execute a mortgage relating to certain property. The defendant executed the mortgage without reading the deed; he knew that it disposed in some way of the land in question, but was induced to believe that it was a conveyance rather than a mortgage. The plaintiff became transferee of the mortgage in good faith and sued the defendant on a covenant therein to repay £1,000. The defendant's plea of *non est factum* did not succeed as the deed in question was not of a wholly different class and character from that which the defendant believed it to be. It purported to be a transfer of property, and the defendant was merely mistaken as to its contents.

Distinction between nature and contents of document rejected. The law on   5-057
this subject was completely reviewed and restated by the House of Lords in *Saunders v. Anglia Building Society*[93] and the distinction between the character and nature of a document and the contents of the document was rejected as unsatisfactory. It was stressed that the defence of *non est factum* was not lightly to be allowed where a person of full age and capacity had signed a written document embodying contractual terms. But it was nevertheless held that in exceptional circumstances the plea was available so long as the person signing the document had made a fundamental mistake as to the character or effect of the document. Their Lordships appear to have concentrated on the disparity between the effect of the document actually signed, and the document as it was believed to be (rather than on the nature of the mistake) stressing that the disparity must be "radical," "essential," "fundamental," or "very substantial."[94]

Documents signed in blank. The plea of *non est factum* is likewise poten-   5-058
tially applicable where one person signs a document in blank and hands it to another, leaving him to fill in the details and complete the transaction.[95] However, where erroneous details are inserted which are not in accord with the instructions of the person executing the document, he may yet be liable if the transaction which the document purports to effect is not essentially different in substance or in kind from the transaction intended.[96] Moreover, the onus is on the

---

[91] (1898) 67 L.J.Q.B. 224.

[92] [1907] 1 Ch. 537, affd. [1908] 1 Ch. 1; *cf. Mercantile Credit Co. Ltd v. Hamblin* [1965] 2 Q.B. 242.

[93] [1971] A.C. 1004; see Stone (1972) 88 L.Q.R. 190.

[94] [1971] A.C. 1004, at 1017, 1022, 1026. In *Lloyds Bank plc v. Waterhouse* (1991) 10 Tr.L.R. 161 it was held that an "all monies" guarantee was fundamentally different to one of liability under a particular transaction for the purchase of land. *cf. Hambros Bank Ltd v. British Historic Buildings Trust and Din* [1995] N.P.C. 179.

[95] *United Dominions Trust v. Western* [1976] Q.B. 513. *cf. Mercantile Credit Co. Ltd v. Hamblin, supra,* at 279–280.

[96] *United Dominions Trust Ltd v. Western, supra,* disapproving *Campbell Discount Ltd v. Gall* [1961] 1 Q.B. 431; see also Bills of Exchange Act 1882, s.20. *cf. Unity Finance Ltd v. Hammond* (1965) 109 S.J. 70.

person signing the document to show that he has acted carefully,[97] and if he fails to discharge that onus he will be bound.[98]

5–059   **Negligence.** A person who signs a document may not be permitted to raise the defence of *non est factum* where he has been guilty of negligence in appending his signature. It was formerly held in a number of cases, of which the leading one was *Carlisle and Cumberland Banking Co. v. Bragg*[99] that negligence was only material where the document actually signed was a negotiable instrument, for there was not otherwise any duty of care owed by the person executing the document to an innocent third party who acted in reliance on it. But these cases were much criticised, both by the courts[1] and by writers,[2] and they were eventually reconsidered by the House of Lords in *Saunders v. Anglia Building Society, supra. Bragg's* case was overruled, and it was held that no matter what class of document was in question, negligence or carelessness on the part of the person signing the document would exclude the defence of *non est factum*. This does not depend on the principle of estoppel but on the principle that no man can take advantage of his own wrong.[3]

3. MISTAKE IN EQUITY

5–060   **Equity and common law.** Considerable difficulty may arise with regard to the relationship between the rules of equity and those of common law.[4] Before the Judicature Act 1873, the courts of equity and common law seem each to have followed their own distinct principles.[5] But now it is necessary to consider cases of mistake in the light of their joint effect. Much, of course, will depend upon the nature of the relief claimed in each individual case. One approach may be for the court to consider first whether the contract is valid or void at common law. If—but only if—the mistake is not sufficient to avoid the agreement, the court may then go on to consider whether grounds exist for relief in equity.[6] But there are some cases in which the courts appear to be moving towards a genuine fusion of legal and equitable principles.[7] Thus it is arguable that (for instance) rectification is only possible where, even as a matter of law, the true construction of the contract is what the contract would say if it were rectified. And it is also arguable

---

[97] See *post*, § 5–059 (same principles applicable).
[98] See also *British Ry. Traffic and Electric Co. Ltd v. Roper* (1939) 162 L.T. 217; *Eastern Distributors Ltd v. Goldring* [1957] 2 Q.B. 600.
[99] [1911] 1 K.B. 489; *Campbell Discount Co. Ltd v. Gall, supra*; *Wilson and Meeson v. Pickering* [1946] K.B. 422, 425.
[1] *Muskham Finance Ltd v. Howard* [1963] 1 Q.B. 904, 913; *Mercantile Credit Co. Ltd v. Hamblin, supra*, at 278.
[2] Anson (1912) 28 L.Q.R. 190; Guest (1963) 79 L.Q.R. 346.
[3] [1971] A.C. 1004, at 1019, 1038. In the Australian case of *Petelin v. Cullen* (1975) 132 C.L.R. 355 the High Court held that where no innocent third party is involved the question of negligence is not relevant. But in England it has been held that such a case should be dealt with as one of misrepresentation or unilateral mistake, not as *non est factum*, *ante*, § 5–055. Negligence was one ground for failure of the plea in *Hambros Bank Ltd v. British Historic Buildings Trust and Din* [1995] N.P.C. 179.
[4] See Grunfeld (1952) 15 M.L.R. 297.
[5] See for example *Wood v. Scarth* (1855) 2 K. & J. 33 (equity); (1858) 1 F. & F. 293 (law).
[6] *Solle v. Butcher, post*, § 5–091, but *cf. ibid.* at 692, 694; *Grist v. Bailey, post*, § 5–091; *Ivanochko v. Sych, post*, § 5–091.
[7] See, *e.g. Riverlate Properties Ltd v. Paul* [1975] Ch. 133, *post*, § 5–075.

that rescission in equity is not available except where the contract would anyhow be void at law; but in fact relief in equity has been given in cases of mutual mistake,[8] as will be explained later (*post* § 5–087 *et seq.*)

As a general rule, equity follows the law in its attitude towards mistake.[9] If the   **5–061** contract is void at common law, equity will also treat it as a nullity from the beginning. In certain exceptional cases, however, equity will intervene so as to relieve one of the parties from the effects of a mistake, even though the mistake would not be operative at common law. This relief may take the form of (i) the refusal of an order for specific performance; or (ii) the rectification of a written agreement; or (iii) rescission of the contract. But in such cases, the contract will not be pronounced void *ab initio*. The contract is at the most voidable and not void.

Mistake of law. There was some authority for saying that a contract entered   **5–062** into as the result of a mistake of law might give ground for relief in equity,[10] and this certainly seemed to be the case when the error resulted in a mistake as to private rights which led to a party attempting to buy his own property.[11] On the other hand, in *Solle v. Butcher*,[12] the Court of Appeal assumed that no relief could be given where the mistake was one of law. It is submitted that relief may now be given in equity and at common law as the result of the decision by the House of Lords that payments made under a mistake of law may be recoverable.[13]

(a) *Refusal of Specific Performance*

Mistake as a defence. Specific performance is a discretionary remedy, and, in   **5–063** the exercise of its discretion, a court may refuse an order for specific performance on the ground of a mistake by the defendant.[14] Courts of Chancery and Equity judges have adopted differing approaches over the years to the possibility of refusing specific performance on the ground of a mistake not sufficient to invalidate a contract. On the one hand it has been held that specific performance will not be refused for a mistake as to the legal effect of the contract.[15] On the other hand, in *Barrow v. Scammell*[16] Bacon V.-C. said:

> "It cannot be disputed that courts of equity have at all times relieved against honest mistakes in contracts, where the literal effect and the specific performance of them

---

[8] Following the views of Lord Denning in *Solle v. Butcher, post,* § 5–091, *Frederick E. Rose (London) Ltd v. W.H. Pim & Co. Ltd* [1953] 2 Q.B. 450, 460–461, and *Oscar Chess Ltd v. Williams* [1957] 1 W.L.R. 370, 373–374; see also *Robert A. Munro & Co. Ltd v. Meyer* [1930] 2 K.B. 312, 333–335.

[9] The relationship of the equitable doctrine to that at common law is not precisely settled. See *post,* §§ 5–092 *et seq.*

[10] *Stone v. Godfrey* (1854) 5 De G.M. & G. 76, 90; *Rogers v. Ingham* (1876) 3 Ch.D. 351, 357; *Alcard v. Walker* [1896] 2 Ch. 369, 375; *Re Diplock* [1948] Ch. 465 (affd. *sub nom. Ministry of Health v. Simpson* [1951] A.C. 251); *Whiteside v. Whiteside* [1950] Ch. 65, 74; see *post,* § 30–045.

[11] *Cooper v. Phibbs* (1867) L.R. 2 H.L. 149.

[12] [1950] 1 K.B. 671.

[13] *Kleinwort Benson Ltd v. Lincoln City Council* [1999] 1 A.C. 153, discussed *ante,* § 5–018 and *post,* § 30–041.

[14] *Townshend v. Stangroom* (1801) 6 Ves. 328.

[15] *Powell v. Smith* (1872) L.R. 14 Eq. 85; *Hart v. Hart* (1881) 18 Ch.D. 670.

[16] (1881) 19 Ch.D. 175, 182. See also *Preston v. Luck* (1884) 27 Ch.D. 497, 506; *Stewart v. Kennedy* (1890) 15 App.Cas. 75, 105.

would be to impose a burden not contemplated, and which it would be against all reason and justice to fix, upon the person who, without the imputation of fraud, has inadvertently committed an accidental mistake; and also where not to correct the mistake would be to give an unconscionable advantage to the other party."

It has been held that specific performance may be refused if it would cause the defendant "a hardship amounting to injustice"[17] although he may still be liable to an action for damages at law.[18] It has also been held against conscience for one man to take advantage of the mistake of another, so that an offeree who knowingly accepts an offer made to him in a different sense than that intended by the offeror will be refused specific performance.[19] Mistake will also be a defence if the plaintiff has in some way contributed, even unwittingly, to the mistake.[20] But a mistake which is entirely the product of the defendant's own carelessness will afford no ground for relief[21] unless (perhaps) the case is one of considerable harshness or hardship.[22] It is not yet clear whether the modern tendency[23] to cut down defences of unilateral mistake as grounds for invalidating a contract, or rectifying a contract, will extend also to cases where the defendant seeks to be excused from specific performance.

5–064   **Identity of party.** Unless personal qualifications possessed by one party form a material ingredient to the contract, the other party cannot resist a claim for specific performance on the ground that, through non-disclosure, he was unaware of the true identity, or attributes, of the person with whom he has in fact contracted.[24]

(b) *Rectification of Written Agreements*

5–065   **Common mistake.** Rectification naturally only applies to contracts which have been reduced to writing. It has long been an established rule of equity that where a contract has by reason of a mistake common[25] to the contracting parties been drawn up so as to militate against the intentions of both as revealed in their previous oral understanding, the court will rectify the contract so as to carry out such intentions[26] so long as there is an issue between the parties as to their legal rights *inter se*. If there is no such issue or if no substantive relief is sought and

---

[17] *Tamplin v. James* (1880) 15 Ch.D. 215, 221.

[18] *Webster v. Cecil* (1861) 30 Beav. 62, 64.

[19] *ibid.* But see, at common law, *ante*, § 5–034.

[20] *Baskomb v. Beckwith* (1869) L.R. 8 Eq. 100; *Denny v. Hancock* (1870) L.R. 6 Ch.App. 1; *Wilding v. Sanderson* [1897] 2 Ch. 534.

[21] *Tamplin v. James, supra.*

[22] *Manser v. Back* (1848) 6 Hare 443; *Malins v. Freeman* (1837) 2 Keen 25; *Van Praagh v. Everidge* [1903] 1 Ch. 434.

[23] See, *post*, §§ 5–075—5–076.

[24] *Dyster v. Randall* [1926] Ch. 932; *Smith v. Wheatcroft* (1878) 9 Ch.D. 223; *Nash v. Dix* (1898) 78 L.T. 445; *cf. Said v. Butt* [1920] 3 K.B. 497.

[25] *Murray v. Parker* (1854) 19 Beav. 305.

[26] *Burroughs v. Abbott* [1922] 1 Ch. 86; *Constantinidi v. Ralli* [1935] Ch. 427; *Jervis v. Howle and Talke Colliery Co. Ltd* [1937] Ch. 67. As regards past transactions, the court may give effect to a "defence" of rectification without actually ordering rectification: *The Nile Rhapsody* [1992] 2 Lloyd's Rep. 399, 408. A claimant may also invoke rectification on the same basis; *ibid.* at 409.

no practical purpose will be achieved rectification may be refused.[27] It will also be refused if a written agreement fails to mention a matter because the parties simply overlooked it, having no intention on the point at all.[28] In such a case the written agreement must be construed as it stands.[29]

Mistake of fact. It was the general rule that in cases where a contract was sought to be rectified the mistake must be one of fact, not law.[30] This rule did not apply to mistakes as to private rights of property,[31] and in any event it may need to be reconsidered in the light of the decision that a payment made under a mistake of law may be grounds for restitution.[32] **5–066**

Parol evidence. Where it is sought to construe a document, parol evidence **5–067** may not be admissible to add to or vary the terms of the written agreement.[33] But where it is sought to rectify a document, this rule does not apply.[34] In *Murray v. Parker*[35] Lord Romilly M.R. said:

"In matters of mistake the court undoubtedly has jurisdiction, and though this jurisdiction is to be exercised with great caution and care, still it is to be exercised, in all cases, where a deed, as executed, is not according to the real agreement between the parties. In all cases the real agreement must be established by evidence, whether parol or written . . . If there be a previous agreement in writing which is unambiguous, the deed will be reformed accordingly: if ambiguous, parol evidence may be used to explain it, in the same manner as in other cases where parol evidence is admitted to explain ambiguities in a written instrument."

Even where the contract is one which is required to be in writing under section 2(1) of the Law of Property (Miscellaneous Provisions) Act 1989[36] or under section 4 of the Statute of Frauds 1677[37] parol evidence is admissible, for the jurisdiction of the court to rectify is outside the prohibition of the statute.[38]

---

[27] *Whiteside v. Whiteside* [1950] Ch. 65; *cf. Re Colebrook's Conveyances* [1972] 1 W.L.R. 1397; *Etablissements Georges et Paul Levy v. Adderley Navigation Co. SA* [1980] 2 Lloyd's Rep. 67. Provided that there is an issue capable of being contested by the parties it is no bar to rectification that both sides wish the document to be rectified so as to reduce one party's tax liability: *Lake v. Lake* [1989] S.T.C. 895; *Racal v. Ashmore* [1995] S.T.C. 1151.

[28] *Harlow Development Corporation v. Kingsgate (Clothing Productions)* (1973) 226 E.G. 1960; *Olympia Sauna Shipping Co. SA v. Shinwa Kaiun Kaisha Ltd (The Ypatia Halcoussi)* [1985] 2 Lloyd's Rep. 364.

[29] *ibid.*

[30] *Midland G.W. Ry. of Ireland v. Johnson* (1858) 6 H.L.R. 798, 811. But see *Burroughs v. Abbott* [1922] 1 Ch. 86; *Jervis v. Howle and Talke Colliery Co. Ltd* [1937] Ch. 67; and *ante*, § 5–062.

[31] *Cooper v. Phibbs* (1867) L.R. 2 H.L. 149; *Earl of Beauchamp v. Winn* (1872) L.R. 6 H.L. 223, 234.

[32] *Kleinwort Benson Ltd v. Lincoln City Council* [1999] 1 A.C. 153, discussed *ante*, § 5–018 and *post*, § 30–041.

[33] See *post*, §§ 12–094 *et seq.*

[34] *Lovell and Christmas Ltd v. Wall* (1911) 104 L.T. 85. In *J.J. Huber (Investments) Ltd v. Private DIY Co. Ltd* [1995] N.P.C. 102, (Ch.D.) it was held that the presence on an "entire agreement" clause in the contract does not prevent rectification.

[35] (1854) 19 Beav. 305, 308.

[36] See *ante*, §§ 4–049 *et seq.*

[37] See Vol. II, Chap. 44 (contracts of suretyship).

[38] *Cowen v. Truefitt Ltd* [1899] 2 Ch. 309; *Johnson v. Bragge* [1901] 1 Ch. 28; *Thompson v. Hickman* [1907] 1 Ch. 550; *Craddock Bros. v. Hunt* [1923] Ch. 136; *USA v. Motor Trucks Ltd* [1924] A.C. 196. cf. § 4–059.

5–068   **Concluded agreement.** It was formerly thought that a plaintiff must show that there was an antecedent concluded contract, which was inaccurately represented by the instrument purporting to be made in pursuance of it. "Courts of equity do not rectify contracts; they may and do rectify instruments purporting to have been made in pursuance of the terms of contracts."[39] Where, therefore, a builder entered into a contract with an urban authority, the contract being sealed in accordance with section 174 of the Public Health Act 1875, it was held that it could not subsequently be rectified, for until the seal was affixed to the formal contract (*i.e.* the instrument sought to be rectified) there was no contract at all between the parties, and also because the effect of rectification, if allowed, would have been to bind the corporation to a contract which required a seal for its validity but which they had never sealed.[40] But although there was a strong body of judicial opinion in favour of this view,[41] Clauson J. in *Shipley U.D.C. v. Bradford Corporation*[42] refused to accept that "the jurisdiction of the court cannot be exercised even in cases of clear mutual mistakes in the attempt to embody in the instrument the concurrent intentions of the parties existing at the moment of the execution of the instrument unless a previously existing contract can be proved." This view was confirmed by a unanimous Court of Appeal in *Joscelyne v. Nissen*.[43] The parties had negotiated an agreement but no concluded contract was made until execution of a formal legal document. It was held that the court had power to rectify the agreement so long as there was a continuing common intention in regard to a particular provision down to the execution of the written contract. It is unnecessary to show that there was a binding agreement prior to the execution of the written document, but there must have been an "outward expression of accord."[44] It is not necessary, however, that the parties had formulated their intention into words at the time provided they had a common intention as to the substance.[45]

5–069   **Proof of mistake.** The burden of proof is on the party seeking rectification.[46] He must produce "convincing proof"[47] not only that the document to be rectified was not in accordance with the parties' true intentions at the time of its execution,

---

[39] *Mackenzie v. Coulson* (1869) L.R. 8 Eq. 368, 375.

[40] *W. Higgins Ltd v. Northampton Cpn.* [1927] 1 Ch. 128.

[41] *Mackenzie v. Coulson* (1869) L.R. 8 Eq. 368; *Faraday v. Tamworth Union* (1916) 86 L.J.Ch. 436, 438; *W. Higgins Ltd v. Northampton Cpn.* [1927] 1 Ch. 128, 136; *U.S.A. v. Motor Trucks Ltd* [1924] A.C. 196, 200; *Lovell & Christmas Ltd v. Wall* (1911) 104 L.T. 85.

[42] [1936] Ch. 375. See also *Frederick E. Rose (London) Ltd v. William H. Pim Jnr. & Co. Ltd* [1953] 2 Q.B. 450, 461; *Crane v. Hegemann-Harris Co. Inc.* [1939] 1 All E.R. 662, affd. [1939] 4 All E.R. 68 (now more fully reported in [1971] 1 W.L.R. 1390n.); *Monaghan C.C. v. Vaughan* [1948] Ir.R. 306; *Carlton Contractors v. Bexley Cpn.* (1962) 106 S.J. 391; *Kent v. Hartley* (1966) 200 E.G. 1027.

[43] [1970] 2 Q.B. 86.

[44] Use of this phrase is criticised by Bromley in (1971) 87 L.Q.R. 532.

[45] *Grand Metropolitan plc v. William Hill Group Ltd* [1997] 1 B.C.L.C. 390. In *Mangistaumunaigaz Oil Production Association v. United World Trading Inc.* [1995] 1 Lloyd's Rep. 617 no prior agreement was shown and rectification was refused.

[46] *Tucker v. Bennett* (1887) 38 Ch.D. 1, 9.

[47] This was the expression preferred by the Court of Appeal in *Joscelyne v. Nissen, supra.* See also *Ernest Scragg & Sons Ltd v. Perseverance Banking and Trust Co. Ltd* [1973] 2 Lloyd's Rep. 101; *Thomas Bates & Son v. Wyndhams Ltd* [1981] 1 W.L.R. 505; compare *Atlantic Maritime Transport Corporation v. Coscol Petroleum Corpn., The Pina* [1991] 1 Lloyd's Rep. 246, 250 ("proof to the criminal standard").

but also that the document in its proposed form does accord with their intentions.[48] It is essential that the extent of the rectification should be clearly ascertained and defined by evidence contemporaneous with or anterior to the contract.[49] The denial of one of the parties that the deed as it stands is contrary to his intention ought to have considerable weight,[50] and unless the other party can convince the court that the document does not represent both parties' intentions at the time of execution, rectification will only exceptionally be ordered.[51] Indeed, it has been said that it is not sufficient that the written contract does not represent the true intention of the parties; it must be shown that the written contract was actually *contrary* to the intention of the parties.[52] Where it is sought to rectify a document in accordance with a prior agreement between the parties, it must be shown that the intention of the parties continued unaltered up to the time of the execution of the document.[53]

Literal disparity. There must be a literal disparity between the terms of the   5–070
prior agreement and those of the document which it is sought to rectify. In *Frederick E. Rose (London) Ltd v. William H. Pim Junior & Co. Ltd*,[54] Denning L.J. said:

> "Rectification is concerned with contracts and documents, not with intentions. In order to get rectification it is necessary to show that the parties were in complete agreement on the terms of their contract, but by an error wrote them down wrongly; and in this regard, in order to ascertain the terms of the contract, you do not look into the inner minds of the parties—into their intentions—any more than you do in the formation of any other contract."

In this case, the parties entered into an oral agreement for the purchase of horsebeans, in the belief that they were "feveroles," and a subsequent written agreement embodied the same terms. The Court of Appeal refused rectification as both the oral and written contracts were for horse-beans; there was no literal disparity between them. However, in *London Weekend Television v. Paris and Griffith*[55] Megaw J. held that, where two persons expressly agree with one another what is the meaning of a particular phrase used in a written contract, the contract can be rectified to make it clear that the phrase bears the meaning agreed.

Specific performance. Before the Judicature Act 1873, it was generally held   5–071
that the court would not grant rectification of the contract to comply with its

---

[48] *Fowler v. Fowler* (1859) 4 De G. & J. 250, 265; *Constantinidi v. Ralli* [1935] Ch. 427. But provided that the true agreement is clear, it is sufficient if it is merely doubtful whether the document accurately records this agreement: *Re Walton's Settlement* [1922] 2 Ch. 509.

[49] *Earl of Bradford v. Earl of Romney* (1862) 30 Beav. 431; *Harris v. Pepperell* (1867) L.R. 5 Eq. 1, 4; *Stait v. Fenner* [1912] 2 Ch. 504.

[50] *Fowler v. Fowler* (1859) 4 De G. & J. 250, 265; *Wollaston v. Tribe* (1869) L.R. 9 Eq. 44; *Cook v. Fearn* (1878) 48 L.J.Ch. 63; *Hanley v. Pearson* (1879) 13 Ch.D. 545. *cf. Tucker v. Bennett* (1887) 38 Ch.D. 1; *Bonhote v. Henderson* [1895] 1 Ch. 742, affd. [1895] 2 Ch. 202; *Re Walton's Settlement* [1922] 2 Ch. 509.

[51] *W. Higgins Ltd v. Northampton Cpn.* [1927] 1 Ch. 128. See *post*, § 5–073.

[52] *Lloyd v. Stanbury* [1971] 1 W.L.R. 535. It is not enough that there has been confusion between the parties as to what was being agreed: *Cambro Contractors Ltd v. John Kennelly Sales Ltd, The Times*, April 14, 1994.

[53] *Fowler v. Fowler* (1859) 4 De G. & J. 250.

[54] [1953] 2 Q.B. 450, 461.

[55] (1969) 113 S.J. 222; see also *Re Butlin's Settlement Trusts* [1976] Ch. 251.

proper terms and then grant specific performance of the contract so rectified, at least in the same action.[56] But the Judicature Act 1925, s.43, requires the court to grant to the parties in one action all the relief to which they are entitled, and this has been held to confer upon the court the power to order rectification and specific performance in the same action, even though the mistake has been proved by parol evidence.[57]

5–072   **Effect of negligence.** The fact that one party's negligence has caused the mistake appears to be irrelevant where rectification is sought on the ground of a mistake common to both parties.[58]

5–073   **Unilateral mistake.** Where the mistake is unilateral, that is of one party only, it was formerly thought that rectification would not be granted unless a case of fraud or misrepresentation,[59] or unfair dealing,[60] or estoppel[61] or perhaps sharp practice, could be shown. But the Court of Appeal has rejected these limits on the availability of the remedy of rectification.[62] Where one party is mistaken as to the incorporation of the agreement in the document, and the other knows of the mistake, and does not draw it to the attention of the first party, it suffices that it would be inequitable to allow the second party to insist on the binding force of the document, either because this would benefit him or because it would be detrimental to the mistaken party.[63] However, even though sharp practice may not be required, unilateral mistake is not by itself a ground for rescinding or rectifying a contract unless the other party knew of the mistake.[64] It appears that the knowledge must be actual knowledge.[65] It is not enough that the party against whom rectification is sought may have suspected that a mistake had been made[66]; but if a party wilfully shuts its eyes to the obvious, or wilfully and recklessly fails to make such inquiries as an honest and reasonable man would make, that will count as actual knowledge.[67] It has been suggested that it is not sufficient that he

---

[56] *Woollam v. Hearn* (1802) 7 Ves. 211; *Martin v. Pycroft* (1852) 3 De G.M. & G. 785; *cf. Thomas v. Davis* (1757) 1 Dick. 301.

[57] *Olley v. Fisher* (1886) 34 Ch.D. 367; *Craddock Bros. v. Hunt* [1923] 2 Ch. 136; *USA v. Motor Trucks Ltd* [1924] A.C. 196, not following *May v. Platt* [1900] 1 Ch. 616. See now Supreme Court Act 1981, s.49.

[58] *Kent v. Hartley* (1966) 200 E.G. 1027; *Weeds v. Blaney, The Times*, March 18, 1976.

[59] *Wood v. Scarth* (1855) 2 K. & J. 33, 41; *May v. Platt* [1900] 1 Ch. 616.

[60] *Hoblyn v. Hoblyn* (1889) 41 Ch.D. 200; *McCausland v. Young* [1949] N.I. 49; *Solle v. Butcher* [1950] 1 K.B. 671, 692.

[61] *Roberts & Co. Ltd v. Leicestershire C.C.* [1961] Ch. 555.

[62] *Thomas Bates & Son v. Wyndhams Ltd* [1981] 1 W.L.R. 505.

[63] Differing views were expressed by the members of the Court of Appeal in *Thomas Bates & Son v. Wyndhams Ltd, supra*, as to the effect of detriment in this situation.

[64] *Riverlate Properties Ltd v. Paul* [1975] Ch. 133, *post*, § 5–075; *Kemp v. Neptune Concrete* (1989) 57 P. & C.R. 369.

[65] *Agip SpA v. Navigazione Alta Italia SpA (The Nai Genova and the Nai Superba)* [1984] 1 Lloyd's Rep. 353; *Commission for New Towns v. Cooper (Great Britain)* [1993] N.P.C. 115. *cf. ante*, § 5–035.

[66] *Olympia Sauna Shipping Co. SA v. Shinwa Kaiun Kaisha Ltd (The Ypatia Halcoussi)* [1985] 2 Lloyd's Rep. 364, 371.

[67] *cf. Commission for New Towns v. Cooper (Great Britain) Ltd* [1995] 2 Ch. 259, applying the analysis of various forms of knowledge made by Peter Gibson J. in *Baden v. Société Générale pour Favouriser le Développement du Commerce et de l'Industrie en France SA* [1993] 1 W.L.R. 509 and adopted by Millett J. in *Agip (Africa) Ltd v. Jackson* [1990] Ch. 265, see further *post*, Vol. II, §§ 34–270 *et seq.*

contributed to the mistake unless he did so knowingly,[68] though if a party puts forward a draft document in such a way that he makes a representation that it is in accordance with an earlier accord of the parties, and the other party foreseeably relies on this, an estoppel may arise.[69] If A intends B to be mistaken as to the terms of the agreement, so conducts himself that he diverts B's attention from discovering the mistake and B in fact makes the very mistake that A intends, rectification to bring the document into accordance with B's understanding may be granted without proof of actual knowledge on A's part or of misrepresentation by A. In the Australian case of *Taylor v. Johnson*[70] the High Court had held that this sort of unconscionable conduct on A's part would suffice for the contract to be rescinded on the ground of mistake.[71] The same principle does not necessarily apply to cases of rectification, since the court is not simply undoing the bargain but also imposing a different bargain on A. However, it is not unjust to insist that the contract be performed according to B's understanding where that was the very meaning that A intended B to put on it, and rectification may be granted.[72] If it is reasonable to expect the other party to check the draft, there will be no relief.[73] In cases of pure unilateral mistake unknown to the other party the remedy (if any, and there will often be none), is refusal of an order of specific performance[74] or, possibly, rescission.[75]

Cancellation with option of rectification. In a small group of cases, how-   **5–074** ever, a middle course between refusing and granting rectification was adopted. These cases are *Garrard v. Frankel*,[76] *Harris v. Pepperell*,[77] *Bloomer v. Spittle*[78] and *Paget v. Marshall*.[79] The course adopted was to order cancellation with an option to the defendant to accept rectification instead. They are all cases of unilateral mistake. In *Garrard v. Frankel*[80] the defendant agreed to take from the plaintiff a lease of a house at the rent of £230, and in the lease drawn up in pursuance of the agreement the rent was stated to be £130. Lord Romilly M.R. considered that the error was the plaintiff's but that the defendant must have perceived it, and held that though the plaintiff was not entitled to have the lease rectified, the lessee ought to be put to his election whether to have the lease rectified or to reject it. In *Harris v. Pepperell*[81] the vendor had executed a conveyance including a piece of land he had not intended to sell but which the defendant alleged he had intended to buy. Lord Romilly, following his previous decision in *Garrard v. Frankel*, gave the defendant the option "of having the whole contract annulled or else of taking it in the form which the plaintiff

---

[68] *Agip SpA v. Navigazione Alta Italia SpA (The Nai Genova and the Nai Superba)* [1983] 2 Lloyd's Rep. 333, 344. The point was not discussed directly on appeal but appears to be consistent with the Court of Appeal's insistence on actual knowledge: [1984] 1 Lloyd's Rep. 353.

[69] *ibid.* [1984] 1 Lloyd's Rep. 353, 365.

[70] (1983) 45 A.L.R. 265; see *ante*, § 5–042, n. 49 and *post*, § 5–089, n. 25.

[71] See *ante*, § 5–034.

[72] *Commission for New Towns v. Cooper (Great Britain) Ltd* [1995] 2 Ch. 259.

[73] *Taylor Barnard v. Tozer* (1984) 269 E.G. 225.

[74] See *ante*, § 5–063.

[75] See *post*, § 5–089.

[76] (1862) 30 Beav. 445.

[77] (1867) L.R. 5 Eq. 1.

[78] (1872) L.R. 13 Eq. 427.

[79] (1884) 28 Ch.D. 255.

[80] *Ante*, n. 76.

[81] *Ante*, n. 77.

intended." In *Bloomer v. Spittle*[82] a conveyance of land reserved to the vendor the right to minerals. The purchaser alleged that the reservation had been inserted by mistake, but the vendor denied that this was so. The vendor died before he could be cross-examined on this point. In an action by the purchaser for rectification of the conveyance, it was held that this relief could not be granted after a long lapse of time and in the face of the vendor's denial. Nevertheless the personal representatives of the vendor were to choose whether to have the conveyance set aside or rectified. In *Paget v. Marshall*[83] the plaintiff by mistake had offered and demised to the defendant four floors of three houses, whereas he had intended to reserve for his own use the first floor of one of the houses. Again the defendant had to elect whether to submit to rectification or have the lease cancelled.

5–075   This group of cases has, however, been critically re-examined by the Court of Appeal. In *Riverlate Properties Ltd v. Paul*[84] the court expressed serious doubts about the authority of these cases and was specially critical of *Garrard v. Frankel*.[85] Although they did not expressly overrule this case they left little doubt that in their view it was wrongly decided. They emphasised that if the defendant neither knows of, nor contributes to nor shares the mistake, but bona fide assumes that the written document correctly represents the common intention, there is no ground for rescission or rectification. If, on the other hand, the defendant does know of the claimant's mistake, the claimant is today entitled to rectification, and there is no reason why the defendant should be offered the option of rescission. It seems that the cases referred to in § 5–074 must be explained on the ground that they were decided before it became clear that rectification could be ordered even for a unilateral mistake if known to (or, perhaps, if contributed to) by the defendant.[86]

5–076   **Corrections of clerical errors.** Reference is made elsewhere to a series of cases in which the courts of common law have corrected clerical errors[87]; and also to cases in which parol evidence has been admitted to explain latent ambiguities.[88]

5–077   **Other instances of rectification.** The court has rectified a bill of exchange,[89] a marine insurance policy,[90] a transfer of shares wrongly numbered,[91] a bill of quantities,[92] and bought and sold notes by inserting therein a clause customary in a particular trade,[93] and very frequently conveyances of land.[94]

---

[82] (1872) L.R. 13 Eq. 427. This decision was said by Neville J. in *Beale v. Kyte* [1907] 1 Ch. 564, 565 to be "unintelligible as reported."

[83] *Ante*, n. 79.

[84] *Supra*, n. 64.

[85] *Supra*, n. 76.

[86] In *Stepps Investments Ltd v. Security Capital Corp. Ltd* (1976) 73 D.L.R. (3d) 351 the Ontario High Court held that an order for rectification or rescission at the defendant's option could be granted where the defendant did not actually know of the mistake but should have known of it.

[87] See *post*, §§ 12–070—12–078.

[88] See *post*, §§ 12–115—12–124.

[89] *Druiff v. Lord Parker* (1868) L.R. 5 Eq. 131.

[90] *Spalding v. Crocker* (1897) 2 Com.Cas. 189.

[91] *Re International Contract Co.* (1872) L.R. 7 Ch.App. 485.

[92] *Neill v. Midland Ry.* (1869) 17 W.R. 871.

[93] *Caraman Rowley & May v. Aperghis* (1923) 40 T.L.R. 124.

[94] *Beale v. Kyte* [1907] 1 Ch. 564; *Craddock Bros. v. Hunt* [1923] 2 Ch. 136.

Marriage settlements. The court has used its jurisdiction in order to rectify 5–078 marriage settlements.[95] If both the marriage articles and the settlement are executed before the marriage takes place, rectification will not be ordered so as to bring the settlement into line with the articles unless the settlement is expressly or impliedly executed in pursuance of the articles. But if the settlement is made after the marriage, it will be rectified so as to make it correspond with the articles.[96] It also seems that the court will readily admit evidence on behalf of the settlor alone that the settlement does not conform with his intention.[97]

Articles of association. The court has no jurisdiction to rectify the articles of 5–079 association of a company on the ground that they do not accord with the proved intention of the signatories at the moment of signature. Any power of alteration in this respect is purely statutory and there is no hint in the Companies Act of any power in the court to rectify.[98]

Voluntary settlements. A voluntary deed cannot be rectified except with the 5–080 consent of the donor,[99] and the court will hesitate to rectify such a deed at the suit of the settlor merely on his own evidence as to his intention unsupported by other evidence such as written instructions.[1] Nevertheless, the unilateral mistake of the settlor will suffice, in certain circumstances, to justify rectification of a settlement.[2] If it is clearly shown that the settlement as executed does not express the true intentions of the settlor, and if the settlement was not executed by trustees or other parties as the result of a contract or bargain, rectification can be ordered. If the trustees object, however, the court may, in its discretion, refuse an order for rectification.[3]

Part performance. Part performance of a subsequent oral agreement incon- 5–081 sistent with the terms of an antecedent written contract constitutes no ground for rectification of the instrument.[4]

Parties must be restored to former position. Rectification will be refused if 5–082 the parties cannot be restored to the same position which they occupied prior to the contract sought to be rectified; but this rule will not be applied so strictly as to require an exact restoration where such is difficult or impossible.[5]

Payment of money under judgment. Mere lapse of time is no bar if the 5–083 mistake is clearly proved[6] but after money had been paid under a judgment founded on the construction of an agreement, an action to rectify the agreement

---

[95] *Johnson v. Bragge* [1901] 1 Ch. 28.
[96] *Cogan v. Duffield* (1876) 2 Ch.D. 44.
[97] *Hanley v. Pearson* (1879) 13 Ch.D. 545; *cf. Tucker v. Bennett* (1887) 38 Ch.D. 1.
[98] *Evans v. Chapman* (1902) 86 L.T. 381; *Scott v. Frank F. Scott (London) Ltd* [1940] Ch. 217, 794.
[99] *Phillipson v. Kerry* (1863) 32 Beav. 628.
[1] *Bonhote v. Henderson* [1895] 1 Ch. 742, affd. [1895] 2 Ch. 202; *Van der Linde v. Van der Linde* [1947] Ch. 306, 311.
[2] *Re Butlin's Settlement Trusts* [1976] Ch. 251.
[3] *ibid.*
[4] *Conway Bridge Commissioners v. Jones* (1910) 102 L.T. 92.
[5] *Earl of Beauchamp v. Winn* (1873) L.R. 6 H.L. 223.
[6] *Millar v. Craig* (1843) 6 Beav. 433; *Re Garnett* (1885) 31 Ch.D. 1; *cf. Beale v. Kyte* [1907] 1 Ch. 564 (laches).

on the ground that this construction was contrary to the intention of all parties was refused by the Court of Appeal. There was no question of *res judicata*, but the agreement had been worked out and a fund distributed on that footing.[7]

5–084   **Third parties.** Rectification may be granted against third parties[8] but a conveyance will not be rectified as against a purchaser for value of a legal or equitable interest claiming under the deed in good faith and without notice of the mistake.[9] It may, however, be granted after the death of one of the parties.[10]

5–085   **Procedure.** Actions for rectification, setting aside or cancellation of deeds or other written instruments are by section 61 of and Schedule 1 to the Supreme Court Act 1981 assigned to the Chancery Division of the High Court, but a counterclaim for rectification or cancellation is not infrequently entertained by the Queen's Bench Division.[11]

5–086   **Jurisdiction of the county court.** By sections 23 and 147(1) of the County Courts Act 1984,[12] a county court may exercise all the powers of the High Court in proceedings for the rectification, delivery up or cancellation of any agreement for the sale, purchase or lease of any property where, in the case of a sale or purchase, the purchase money, or, in the case of a lease, the value of the property, does not exceed £30,000 and also in proceedings for relief against fraud or mistake, where the damage sustained or the estate or fund in respect of which relief is sought does not exceed in amount or value £30,000.[13] The same limit applies to actions for the specific performance of such contracts.[14]

(c) *Rescission*

5–087   **Generally.** The equitable remedy of rescission is one which is available in a number of different instances where equitable relief is called for.[15] A contract which is void for mistake at common law is void *ab initio*; but a contract which may be rescinded is voidable and not void. It is valid unless and until it is set aside. Any property transferred under the contract will not be recoverable from a bona fide purchaser for value. The advantages of this situation may in some cases have fostered a desire to extend the equitable at the expense of the legal remedy[16]; but the cases tend to show that, although specific performance is not infrequently refused on the ground of mistake[17] the court is more reluctant to rescind a contract on the same ground.

---

[7] *Caird v. Moss* (1886) 33 Ch.D. 22.

[8] *Leuty v. Hillas* (1858) 2 De G. & J. 110; *Craddock Bros. v. Hunt* [1923] 2 Ch. 136.

[9] *Bell v. Cundall* (1750) Amb. 101; *Smith v. Jones* [1954] 1 W.L.R. 1089; *Lyme Valley Squash Club Ltd v. Newcastle-under-Lyme B.C.* [1985] 2 All E.R. 405, 413.

[10] *Johnson v. Bragge* [1901] 1 Ch. 28.

[11] *Mostyn v. West Mostyn Coal & Iron Co. Ltd* (1876) 1 C.P.D. 145; *Storey v. Waddle* (1879) 4 Q.B.D. 289; but see *Leslie v. Clifford* (1884) 50 L.T. 690 (partnership accounts transferred to Chancery Division).

[12] See County Courts Jurisdiction Order 1981 (S.I. 1981 No. 1123).

[13] *R. v. Judge Whitethorne* [1904] 1 K.B. 827 and *Angel v. Jay* [1911] 1 K.B. 666.

[14] See *post*, Chap. 28; but see also *Bourne v. Macdonald* [1950] 2 K.B. 422 and ss.21 and 38 of the Act.

[15] See *post*, §§ 7–039, 7–041, 7–075.

[16] *Solle v. Butcher* [1950] 1 K.B. 671; see *post*, § 5–091.

[17] See *ante*, § 5–063.

Mutual mistake. At common law, where an agreement is entered into for the **5–088** purchase of land, and the purchaser pays over the purchase money to the vendor, the purchaser can recover the money if it turns out that the vendor has no title to the land.[18] But where the land has actually been conveyed to him, he cannot recover the price unless he has protected himself by taking a covenant as to title from the vendor. A mutual mistake as to title is therefore, at law, no ground for upsetting a conveyance, and in this respect equity follows the law.[19] If, however, a purchaser agrees to buy land which, unknown to himself and the vendor, is his own already, the contract will be set aside[20] even though it may have been completed by conveyance.[21] The mistake, although strictly one of law, is one as to private rights, and equity will grant relief.[22] In *Cooper v. Phibbs*[23] the petitioner agreed to take from the respondents the lease of a fishery of which he was, unknown to both parties, already tenant in tail. Although the proceedings were brought in equity, it has been said that the contract was void at common law.[24] The House of Lords ordered that the agreement should be set aside. However the respondents had a lien on the fishery for the money they had spent on its improvement.

Unilateral mistake. A contract which is otherwise valid at common law will **5–089** very rarely, if ever, be rescinded on the ground of unilateral mistake.[25] If there has been a misrepresentation, whether fraudulent or otherwise, it may be rescinded[26]; but in the absence of such a misrepresentation it seems that the defendant must have in some way contributed to the mistake, and it must be inequitable for him to avail himself of the legal advantage so obtained.[27]

Consent orders. Except in matrimonial cases,[28] a judgment given or an order **5–090** made by consent, being founded on the agreement of the parties, may be set aside if it was entered into under a mutual mistake of fact[29] or in ignorance of a

---

[18] *Johnson v. Johnson* (1802) 3 B. & P. 162.

[19] *Brownlie v. Campbell* (1880) 5 App.Cas. 925; *Soper v. Arnold* (1887) 37 Ch.D. 96; *Debenham v. Sawbridge* [1901] 2 Ch. 98.

[20] *Cooper v. Phibbs* (1867) L.R. 2 H.L. 149; *Earl of Beauchamp v. Winn* (1873) L.R. 6 H.L. 223.

[21] *Bingham v. Bingham* (1748) 1 Ves.Sen. 126.

[22] *Cooper v. Phibbs* (1867) L.R. 2 H.L. 149, 170.

[23] (1867) L.R. 2 H.L. 149; see *ante*, § 5–023.

[24] See *ante*, § 5–023.

[25] In the Australian case of *Taylor v. Johnson* (1983) 45 A.L.R. 265 the High Court adopted the view that a unilateral mistake by one party as to the terms of a formal, written contract will, if the mistake was known to the other, make the contract voidable rather than void. This does not appear to represent English law, at least where the other party knows that mistake has been made. However, the analogy to cases of rectification is plain (see *ante*, § 5–042); and the court left open the question of cases involving oral contracts or mistaken identity (at 270). See §§ 5–034 and 5–037 *ante*.

[26] See *post*, §§ 6–101 *et seq.*

[27] *Cocking v. Pratt* (1749) 1 Ves.Sen. 400; *Torrance v. Boulton* (1872) L.R. 8 Ch.App. 118, 124; *Riverlate Properties Ltd v. Paul* [1975] Ch. 133; *Thomas Bates & Son v. Wyndhams Ltd* [1981] 1 W.L.R. 505, *ante*, § 5–073. Contrast *Imperial Glass Ltd v. Imperial Supplies Ltd* (1960) 22 D.L.R. (2d) 759.

[28] As to which see *de Lasala v. de Lasala* [1980] A.C. 546, 560 and *Thwaite v. Thwaite* [1982] Fam. 1, 7–8.

[29] *Huddersfield Banking Co. Ltd v. Henry Lister & Son Ltd* [1895] 2 Ch. 273; *Wilding v. Sanderson* [1897] 2 Ch. 534.

material fact[30] if the mistake would justify the setting aside of an agreement on the same grounds.[31] In *Huddersfield Banking Co. Ltd v. Henry Lister & Son Ltd*[32] the mortgagees of certain factory premises allowed the defendants to sell, under a consent order, trade machinery on the premises in the belief, shared by both parties, that the machinery was affixed to the realty. It subsequently appeared that it had been unlawfully detached, and so properly belonged to the mortgagees. The order was set aside. But a consent order cannot be set aside on the ground of a mistake where the mistake would not suffice to impeach the agreement on which the order was based.[33]

5–091   **Extension of equitable principle.**[34] At least so far as mutual mistake is concerned, the equitable principle of rescission was considerably extended by the Court of Appeal in the case of *Solle v. Butcher*.[35] Drawing upon the various cases in which contracts have been set aside on the ground of mistake, together with those in which the defendant has been given the option to rescind or accept rectification,[36] the Court of Appeal enunciated a new doctrine of mistake in equity: that the courts have a discretionary jurisdiction to grant such relief as in the circumstances seems just, including setting aside the contract on terms. In that case, the defendant leased to the plaintiff a dwelling-house which both parties erroneously believed to have been so altered in structure that it had become a "new" dwelling-house and fell outside the restrictions imposed by the Rent Acts. The controlled rent of the house was £140 per annum, but the rent inserted in the lease was £250 per annum. The plaintiff claimed to recover the money overpaid, and, in his defence, the defendant counter-claimed for rescission of the lease on the ground of mutual mistake. The majority of the Court of Appeal[37] considered that there had been a mutual mistake of fact. They ordered that the lease should be rescinded, but on the terms that the plaintiff should choose whether to accept the rescission or claim a new lease at the full rent of £250 per annum. In his judgment Denning L.J. said[38]:

> "It is now clear that a contract will be set aside if the mistake of one party has been induced by the material misrepresentation of the other, even though it was not fraudulent or fundamental; or if one party, knowing that the other is mistaken about the terms of an offer, or the identity of the person by whom it is made, lets him remain under his delusion and concludes a contract on the mistaken terms instead of pointing out the mistake. . . . A contract is also liable in equity to be set aside if the parties were under a common misapprehension either as to facts or as to their relative or respective rights, provided that the misapprehension was fundamental, and that the party seeking to set it aside was not himself at fault."

---

[30] *Furnival v. Bogle* (1827) 4 Russ. 142; *Dietz v. Lennig Chemicals Ltd* [1969] 1 A.C. 170.

[31] *Att.-Gen. v. Tomline* (1877) 7 Ch.D. 388. See also *Hickman v. Berens* [1895] 2 Ch. 638; *Allcard v. Walker* [1896] 2 Ch. 369; *Wilding v. Sanderson* [1897] 2 Ch. 534.

[32] [1895] 2 Ch. 273.

[33] *Purcell v. F.C. Trigell Ltd* [1971] 1 Q.B. 358; *cf. Chanel Ltd v. F.W. Woolworth & Co. Ltd* [1981] 1 W.L.R. 485.

[34] See Cartwright (1987) 103 L.Q.R. 594; Goff & Jones, *Law of Restitution* (5th ed., 1998), pp. 288–297.

[35] [1950] 1 K.B. 671.

[36] See *ante*, §§ 5–074—5–075.

[37] Denning and Bucknill L.JJ. (Jenkins L.J. dissenting).

[38] At 692.

Parts of this statement, especially those relating to the effect of a mistake as to the promise or of a mistake as to the person, would not find universal acceptance[39]; but the application of these principles to the facts of the case would seem to indicate a more extensive operation of equitable remedies in the sphere of mutual mistake in English law.[40] In *Associated Japanese Bank International Ltd v. Credit du Nord SA* Steyn J. said that he would have been prepared to set the contract aside even if he had not found it to be void at common law.[41]

Scope of equitable jurisdiction. Even if it is accepted that there is an **5–092** equitable jurisdiction to set aside a contract on terms on the ground of a mutual mistake, there remains doubt about how the jurisdiction is to be exercised. First, it was suggested above that the common law doctrine will not apply if the risk is one which the contract expressly or by implication puts on one of the parties. Given the general importance of upholding agreements and the agreed allocation of risk,[42] it would be surprising if relief were given in equity in these circumstances. However, the only explicit limitation upon the equitable doctrine is that the party seeking relief should not be at fault, and it has to be said that relief has sometimes been given when the normal allocation of risk would suggest that it should be denied. In *Grist v. Bailey*[43] a vendor sold property subject to an existing tenancy which both parties thought was protected, when in fact both the protected tenant and her husband were dead. Although neither the vendor nor her solicitor were personally at fault, it seems more natural to put the risk of this kind of mistake occurring on the vendor; yet the contract was set aside.[44] Perhaps it was relevant that if it had been upheld the purchaser would have received a considerable windfall at the vendor's expense.[45]

Secondly, it seems that there must be some difference between common law **5–093** and equity in the seriousness of the mistake which is necessary for the doctrine to operate, or it is hard to see why the contract in *Solle v. Butcher* was not void at common law. However, it is not easy to see the difference between a mistake rendering the thing contracted for essentially different from what it was believed to be (the test at common law[46]) and a fundamental mistake (the test in equity[47]).

---

[39] See the principles enunciated *ante*, §§ 5–032 *et seq*. The application of the equitable remedies was considered, but refused, in the case of *Harrison & Jones Ltd v. Bunten and Lancaster Ltd* [1953] 1 Q.B. 647, *ante*, § 5–025.

[40] See *Peters v. Batchelor* (1950) 100 L.J. News. 718; *Grist v. Bailey* [1967] Ch. 532; *Magee v. Pennine Insurance Co. Ltd* [1969] 2 Q.B. 507, *ante*, § 5–028; *Laurence v. Lexcourt Holdings Ltd* [1978] 1 W.L.R. 1128 (*sed quaere* if this case is not inconsistent with *Amalgamated Investment & Property Co. Ltd v. John Walker & Sons Ltd* [1977] 1 W.L.R. 164); *London Borough of Redbridge v. Robinson Rentals* (1969) 211 E.G. 1125; *Ivanochko v. Sych* (1967) 60 D.L.R. (2d) 474. Contrast *Svanoso v. McNamara* (1956) 96 C.L.R. 186; Slade (1954) 70 L.Q.R. 385, 407; Shatwell (1955) 33 Can. Bar Rev. 164; Atiyah and Bennion (1961) 24 M.L.R. 421, 439.

[41] [1989] 1 W.L.R. 255, 270. See *ante*, § 5–014.

[42] See *ante*, §§ 5–003, 5–012.

[43] [1967] Ch. 532.

[44] *Magee's* case (*ante*, n. 00) has also been criticised on this ground: Atiyah, *Introduction to the Law of Contract* (5th ed.) p. 226. In *William Sindall plc v. Cambridgeshire County Council* [1994] 1 W.L.R. 1016, 1035, Hoffman L.J. suggested that this case and *Laurence v. Lexcourt Holdings Ltd* [1978] 1 W.L.R. 1128 might have been decided differently if the judges at first instance had adverted to the question of the contractual allocation of risk.

[45] It is not clear that *Magee's* case can be explained in this way; the insured could probably have obtained insurance without making the misrepresentation for which the policy was voidable.

[46] See *ante*, § 5–024.

[47] See *ante*, § 5–091.

In the *Associated Japanese Bank case*[48] Steyn J. merely remarked that the equitable doctrine "will give relief against mistake in cases where the common law will not." In *William Sindall plc v. Cambridgeshire County Council*[49] Evans L.J. said "the difference may be that the common law rule is limited to mistakes with regard to the subject matter, whilst equity can have regard to a wider and perhaps unlimited category of 'fundamental' mistake".

5–094   If relief is to be given more readily in equity than at common law, and particularly if the normal allocation of risks is not to be a determining factor, it is hard to resist the conclusion that *Solle v. Butcher* and the cases following it represent a shift in policy towards granting relief where the outcome of a contract may be considered unfair but there was no procedural impropriety (such as misrepresentation, duress, undue influence or unconscionable behaviour) when the contract was made. This shift does not seem consistent with recent decisions in other areas.[50] It seems that the relationship between law and equity in this area has not yet been finally settled.

5–095   **Loss of right to rescind.** Presumably the right to rescind on the ground of mutual mistake may be lost in similar ways to the right to rescind for misrepresentation, as to which see Chapter 6, *post*.[51]

---

[48] *Ante*, n. 41 at 270.
[49] [1994] 1 W.L.R. 1016, 1035.
[50] Cartwright (1987) 103 L.Q.R. 594.
[51] §§ 6–112—6–128. Treitel, *The Law of Contract* (9th ed., 1995), p. 297 notes that the rules governing loss of the right to rescind for mistake and for misrepresentation may be different: in *Re Garnett* (1885) 31 Ch.D. 1 the right to rescind was not lost after 20 years, whereas this lapse of time would bar rescission for misrepresentation, see *post*, § 6–123. But *Re Garnett* was a case in which a deed without consideration was being set aside and the rules on setting aside gifts for mistake may be more generous to the mistaken party than the rules on contracts: see Goff & Jones, *The Law of Restitution* (5th ed., 1998), pp. 188–191. It is not clear that the same rule would be applied to a contract.

Chapter 6

MISREPRESENTATION[1]

1. In General

Preliminary. The modern law relating to misrepresentation is a somewhat **6–001** complex amalgam of rules of common law, equity and (since the coming into force of the Misrepresentation Act 1967)[2] statute law. It is also complicated by the fact that misrepresentation may constitute an actionable tort in certain circumstances, as well as providing grounds for relief in the law of contract. Prior to the enactment of the Misrepresentation Act 1967, the position broadly speaking was that a misrepresentation which induced a person to enter into a contract gave the representee the right to rescind the contract, subject to certain conditions, but generally gave him no right to damages unless the misrepresentation was fraudulent, or, in some cases, negligent, or unless the misrepresentation had contractual force. Since the coming into force of the Misrepresentation Act the representee will always be able to claim damages for negligent misrepresentation in circumstances in which he could have recovered damages had the misrepresentation been fraudulent. In addition the Act gives the court a discretion to refuse to permit a representee to rescind a contract, but to award him damages in lieu of rescission, if the misrepresentation is negligent or wholly innocent; but it leaves the representee with an absolute right to rescind where the misrepresentation is fraudulent. The Act of 1967 does not, however, alter the rules as to what constitutes an effective misrepresentation.

---

[1] See Allen, *Misrepresentation* (1988); Cartwright, *Unequal Bargaining* (1991), chap. 3.

[2] The Act was based on the recommendations in the Law Reform Committee's Tenth Report, Cmnd. 1782, (1962) but with one important change, as to which see *post*, § 6–128. For a full appraisal of the Act, see Atiyah and Treitel, "Misrepresentation Act 1967" (1967) 30 M.L.R. 369.

6–002   **Misrepresentation and contractual terms.** Before the Misrepresentation Act was passed, the law relating to misrepresentation was generally concerned solely with misrepresentations made before the contract was entered into, and not to misrepresentations which actually constituted contractual terms. Although the word "misrepresentation" is literally applicable to a contractual term which consists of a false statement of fact (as opposed to a promise of future conduct), the term was commonly confined to misrepresentations which did not constitute contractual terms, simply because the law relating to contractual terms (whether promises as to future conduct or misrepresentations of fact) differed from the law relating to misrepresentations which were not contractual terms. Moreover, there was also some authority for the proposition that if a misrepresentation was made before a contract was entered into, and the misrepresentation was subsequently incorporated into the contract as a contractual term, the law relating to misrepresentation was not applicable, and the case had to be dealt with as one involving a contractual term and nothing else.[3] Since the passing of the Act of 1967 this is no longer the case, and it will often be necessary in any one situation to inquire carefully as to the effect of a misrepresentation both as a pre-contractual statement, *and* as a contractual term. Where these effects differ (as they often do) it is in some cases a matter of considerable difficulty to determine with any certainty the effect of the Misrepresentation Act on the law relating to contractual misstatement.[4]

6–003   **Terminology.** For many years it was usual to divide misrepresentations into two categories, fraudulent and innocent misrepresentation. The latter category included negligent misrepresentations, for, at least until the decision of the House of Lords in *Hedley Byrne & Co. Ltd v. Heller and Partners Ltd*,[5] it was thought that there was generally no difference between a negligent and a completely innocent misrepresentation. But since that decision, and the passing of the Misrepresentation Act, which also distinguishes in some respects between negligent and completely innocent misrepresentations, it has clearly become necessary to recognise that there are now three categories of misrepresentations. It seems better, therefore, to reserve the term "innocent misrepresentation" for representations which are neither fraudulent nor negligent, though it must be appreciated that there are many cases in which the term has been used to include negligent misrepresentation.

2. WHAT CONSTITUTES EFFECTIVE MISREPRESENTATION

(a) *Statement of Fact*

6–004   **Statements of opinion and intention.** The traditional rule is that a representation must be a statement of fact, past or present, as distinct from a statement of opinion, or of intention, or of law. A mere statement of opinion, which proves to have been unfounded, will not be treated as a misrepresentation,[6] nor will a

---

[3] *Pennsylvania Shipping Co. v. Compagnie Nationale de Navigation* [1936] 2 All E.R. 1167, 1171; *Leaf v. International Galleries* [1950] 2 K.B. 86.

[4] *Post*, §§ 6–105—6–106, 6–132.

[5] [1964] A.C. 465.

[6] This passage was cited with approval in *Hummingbird Motors Ltd v. Hobbs* [1986] R.T.R. 276.

simple statement of intention which is not put into effect; for as a general rule these cannot be regarded as representations of fact, except in so far as they show that the opinion or intention is held by the person expressing it.[6a]

Statement of opinion may amount to statement of fact. However, in certain circumstances a statement of opinion or of intention may be regarded as a statement of fact, and therefore as a ground for avoiding a contract if the statement is false. Thus, if it can be proved that the person who expressed the opinion did not hold it, or could not, as a reasonable man having his knowledge of the facts, honestly have held it, the statement may be regarded as a statement of fact.[7]   **6–005**

Opinion not honestly held. If a person states as his opinion something which he does not in fact believe, or which given the facts known to him, he could not honestly hold, he makes a false statement of fact. So where, at a sale of property, the vendor described the occupier as "a most desirable tenant," while in fact he knew that the rent was considerably in arrear, this was held to entitle the purchaser to rescind the contract.[8]   **6–006**

Statement of opinion may carry implication that grounds for belief. In *Brown v. Raphael*,[9] the purchaser of an absolute reversion in a trust fund expectant on the death of an annuitant was likewise held entitled to rescind: the particulars of sale stated that estate duty would be payable on the death of the annuitant, "who is believed to have no aggregable estate"; the vendor's solicitors honestly believed this to be true but had no reasonable grounds for this belief. The Court of Appeal held that as the vendor was in a far stronger position than the purchaser to ascertain the facts, there must be implied a further representation that the former had reasonable grounds for his belief.[10] If, on the other hand, it is clear that the person who expressed the opinion had no real way of knowing whether or not it was correct, no such implication can be made.[11] In *Economides v. Commercial Union Assurance Co. plc*[12] it was held that a statement by an insured, a private person with no specialist knowledge, of the value of the   **6–007**

[6a] See *Strachan & Henshaw Ltd v. Stein Industrie (U.K.) Ltd (No. 2)* (1997) 87 B.L.R. 52.

[7] The sentences in this paragraph were cited with approval in *Economides v. Commercial Union Assurance Co. plc* [1998] Q.B. 587, by Simon Brown L.J. at 645 (who considered that *Brown v. Raphael, infra* § 6–007, rested on a different principle) and Sir Iain Glidewell (who considered that the statement summarised that case accurately also), 655.

[8] *Smith v. Land and House Property Corporation* (1884) 28 Ch.D. 7.

[9] [1958] Ch. 636; *Credit Lyonnais Bank Nederland v. Export Credit Guarantee Department* [1996] 1 Lloyd's Rep. 200 (bank's statement that a management was "respectable and trustworthy" a misrepresentation as it was contrary to the bank's actual experience of the management). See also *Patterson v. Landsberg & Son* (1905) 7 F. 675.

[10] It is possible that *Smith v. Land House Property Corporation, supra,* was also decided on the basis that the vendor was impliedly representing that he had reasonable grounds for his belief, or at least that he knew of nothing which might be inconsistent with it: Bennett (1998) 61 M.L.R. 886, 888. See also *Highland Insurance Co. v. Continental Insurance Co.* [1987] 1 Lloyd's Rep. 109; *Credit Lyonnais Bank Nederland v. Export Credit Guarantee Department* [1996] 1 Lloyd's Rep. 200.

[11] *Hummingbird Motors Ltd v. Hobbs* [1986] R.T.R. 276.

[12] [1998] Q.B. 587. Simon Brown and Peter Gibson LJJ expressed the view that under the Marine Insurance Act 1906, s.20(5), which states that a representation as to a matter of expectation or belief is true if it be made in good faith, there is no room for such an implication, doubting a dictum to the contrary by Steyn J. in *Highlands Insurance Co. v. Continental Insurance Co.* [1987] 1 Lloyd's Rep. 109, 112–113. Sir Iain Glidewell preferred to leave the matter open. But see Bennett (1998) 61 M.L.R. 886. See further below, §§ 6–010 and 41–030.

contents of a flat which contained his parents' belongings as well as his own, did not carry an implication that he had an objectively reasonable basis for the value stated. Thus a statement of the value which the insured made honestly was not a misrepresentation even though it was inaccurate. Mere "puffs" or commendatory statements do not amount to representations[13] and subject to the principle illustrated by *Brown v. Raphael*,[14] an opinion expressed in good faith is not to be held to be a misrepresentation merely because it turns out to be incorrect.[15] But a statement of opinion which is published as if it were a fact may be regarded as a statement of fact.[16]

6–008   **Statement of intention not honestly held.** With regard to a statement of intention, this may be looked upon as a misrepresentation of existing fact if, at the time when it was made, there was not the will or the ability to put the intention into effect; for the promisor's state of mind was not what he led the other party to believe it to be.[17] Thus, where a man ordered goods having at the time the intention not to pay for them, he was held to have made a fraudulent misrepresentation.[18] There is no doubt that a statement as to the intentions of a third party is a statement of fact and can constitute a misrepresentation in the ordinary way.[19]

6–009   **Implied representations.** *Brown v. Raphael, supra,* could be regarded as a case of an implied representation; there are a number of other cases which can also be regarded as instances of implied representations, though this category overlaps with that of representations by conduct.[20] In the criminal law the concept of an implied representation is widely relied upon in prosecutions under the Theft Act; for instance, it has been held[21] that a minicab driver who solicited a customer at a London airport, saying, "Yes, I am an airport taxi," and subsequently assured the customer that £27.50 was the "correct fare" was guilty of representing that he was an officially licensed taxi driver and that the fare was somehow at an officially approved rate. Other criminal cases of implied representations are referred to below in the section on representations by conduct.[22] There does not seem to be any difference between the principles of the criminal and the civil law with regard to this question. For instance, it has been held that a description of premises as "offices" may amount to an implied representation as to the availability of the appropriate planning consents.[23]

---

[13] *Dimmock v. Hallett* (1866) L.R. 7 Ch.App. 21, 27. See also, for an analogous criminal law case, *West Yorkshire Metropolitan County Council v. M.F.I. Furniture Centre* [1983] 1 W.L.R. 1175; *Chartered Trust v. Davies* [1997] 2 E.G.L.R. 83, 86 ("prestigious retail development").

[14] [1958] Ch. 636; *supra.*

[15] *New Brunswick and Canada Ry. and Land Co. v. Conybeare* (1862) 9 H.L.C. 711; *Anderson v. Pacific Insurance Co.* (1872) L.R. 7 C.P. 65; *Bisset v. Wilkinson* [1927] A.C. 177; *Sanders v. Gall* [1952] *Current Property Law* 343.

[16] See *Reese River Silver Mining Co. Ltd v. Smith* (1869) L.R. 4 H.L. 64.

[17] See *Edgington v. Fitzmaurice* (1885) 29 Ch.D. 459; *Angus v. Clifford* [1891] 2 Ch. 449, 470; *Goff v. Gauthier* (1991) P. & C.R. 388.

[18] *Re Shackleton, ex p. Whittaker* (1875) L.R. 10 Ch.App. 446; *Ray v. Sempers* [1974] A.C. 370; *Re Gerald Cooper Chemicals Ltd* [1978] Ch. 262.

[19] *Smelter Corpn. of Ireland Ltd v. O'Driscoll* [1977] I.R. 305.

[20] See *post,* § 6–015.

[21] *R. v. Banaster* [1979] R.T.R. 113.

[22] See *post,* § 6–015.

[23] *Laurence v. Lexcourt Holdings Ltd* [1978] 1 W.L.R. 1128.

Reasonable reliance on statements of opinion or statements as to the **6–010**
future. It is submitted that no simple distinction between statements of fact and
statements of opinion or intention will sufficiently take account of the different
varieties of possible statements which may be made in pre-contractual negotiations. For example, statements as to the future are not always mere statements of
intention; and statements of opinion may range from casual, unconsidered
remarks, to considered judgments, based on well-studied evidence. Cases have
occurred, for instance, which suggest the need for a more careful differentiation
between types of statements of opinion, and statements as to the future. For
instance, in *Esso Petroleum Co. v. Mardon*[24] an action for damages for negligent
misrepresentation succeeded where a petrol company, negotiating with a prospective tenant about a lease of a filling station, had offered a forecast of the
probable sales potential of the filling station. In *McNally v. Welltrade International Ltd*[25] an employment agency was held liable to an employee for implied
representations as to the plaintiff's suitability for a job from which he was
dismissed. And in *Box v. Midland Bank Ltd*[26] it was said that the distinction
between fact and opinion had become much less important since *Esso Petroleum
Ltd v. Mardon*. It is suggested that the fundamental principle which underlies the
cases is not so much that statements as to the future, or statements of opinion,
cannot be misrepresentations; but rather that statements are not to be treated as
representations where, having regard to all the circumstances, it is unreasonable
of the representee to rely on the representor's statements rather than on his own
judgment.[27] In general this seems to be the reason why statements as to the future
and statements of opinion have been held not to ground relief; in dealing with
statements of this nature it has usually been felt that the representee ought not to
have relied on the representor. It has been recognised that sometimes a statement
which was on its face a statement of fact was really only one of opinion because
it was apparent that the maker had no real knowledge or was simply passing on
information for what it was worth.[28] On the other hand there are circumstances
in which it is perfectly reasonable for the representee to rely on the representor's
statements even where those statements are matters of opinion, or statements as
to the future, and where this is the case, it is thought that the statement should be
treated as a representation in the relevant sense. However, there are some cases
under the Trade Descriptions Act in which the courts have continued to apply the
traditional distinctions drawn in the contractual cases between statements as to
the future and statements of fact.[29]

Statements of law. It is commonly said that a statement of law cannot be   **6–011**
treated as a misrepresentation.[30] But the truth of this proposition is questionable.

---

[24] [1976] Q.B. 801, *post*, § 6–085.

[25] [1978] I.R.L.R. 497.

[26] [1979] 2 Lloyd's Rep. 391; in the Court of Appeal (on costs only) [1981] 1 Lloyd's Rep.
434.

[27] cf. *Harlingdon and Leinster Enterprises Ltd v. Christopher Hull Fine Art Ltd* [1991] 1 Q.B. 564,
post, Vol. II, § 41–030.

[28] *Bisset v. Wilkinson* [1927] A.C. 177; *Highland Insurance Co. v. Continental Insurance Co.*
[1987] 1 Lloyd's Rep. 109; and the cases cited in § 6–007, *ante*. But see *Sirius International
Insurance Corp. v. Oriental Insurance Corp.* [1999] 1 All E.R. (Comm.) 699.

[29] *R. v. Sunair Holidays Ltd* [1973] 1 W.L.R. 1105; *Kensington and Chelsea B.C. v. Riley* [1973]
R.T.R. 122; *Robertson v. Diciccio* [1972] R.T.R. 431; *Beckett v. Cohen* [1972] 1 W.L.R. 1593; *British
Airways Board v. Taylor* [1976] 1 W.L.R. 13.

[30] *Beattie v. Ebury* (1872) L.R. 7 Ch.App. 777, 802; *Beesly v. Hallwood Estates Ltd* [1960] 1
W.L.R. 549, 560.

First, a statement of law is a statement of opinion, and just as a statement of opinion may be a representation of fact, so too a statement of law may amount to a representation, or misrepresentation, as the case may be. So a wilful misstatement of law would always amount to a misrepresentation[31] and even an innocent misstatement of law may do so where it carries an implication of fact which is itself untrue. Secondly, the question whether a statement is one of law or fact gives rise to no small difficulty,[32] especially as statements of law and of fact are so frequently intermingled. It has been said that the dichotomy between statements of fact and statements of law is too neat, and is apt to mislead.[33] It seems that the courts tend to regard statements of mixed law and fact, and statements capable of having either meaning, as statements of fact,[34] and therefore as representations; that they also regard statements as to the purport, effect and objects of documents as representations[35]; and in *Cooper v. Phibbs*,[36] a statement as to private rights, as distinct from the general law, was regarded as a statement of fact.[37] So a representation that planning permission exists for a particular use is a representation of fact, and not of law[38]; similarly with a representation by a landlord that he accepts liability for repairs under a lease.[39] On the other hand a statement of law made separately from a statement of fact has been held not to be a misrepresentation.[40] This seems to rest on a distinction between a statement of an abstract proposition of law, which was not regarded as a misrepresentation, and a statement applying the law to the facts of a particular situation which, at least in some circumstances, may constitute a misrepresentation.[41] But thirdly, in the law of restitution the distinction between a payment made under a mistake of fact and one made under a mistake of law has recently been held by the House of Lords not to be part of English law.[42] This suggests that for the purposes of the law of misrepresentation also, the distinction between statements of law and statements of fact is no longer maintainable and that even an incorrect statement of an abstract proposition of law may amount to a misrepresentation unless it is apparent that all that is being offered is an opinion without implication that the speaker has reasonable grounds for that opinion.[43] It is submitted that the underlying principle here is the same as that suggested in the previous paragraph, *viz.* that even a statement as to the law may be a misrepresentation if it was reasonable, in all the circumstances, for the representee

---

[31] *West London Commercial Bank v. Kitson* (1884) 13 Q.B.D. 360, 362–363; *Oudaille v. Lawson* [1922] N.Z.L.R. 259.

[32] See *Solle v. Butcher* [1950] 1 K.B. 671.

[33] *Brikom Investments Ltd v. Seaford* [1981] 1 W.L.R. 863.

[34] *Reynell v. Sprye* (1852) 1 De G.M. & G. 660; *West London Commercial Bank v. Kitson, supra*; *Hughes v. Liverpool Victoria Legal Friendly Society* [1916] 2 K.B. 482.

[35] *Hirshfeld v. L.B. & S.C. Ry.* (1876) 2 Q.B.D. 1; *De Tchihatchef v. Salerni Coupling Ltd* [1932] 1 Ch. 330.

[36] (1867) L.R. 2 H.L. 149.

[37] At 170.

[38] *Laurence v. Lexcourt Holdings Ltd* [1977] 1 W.L.R. 1128.

[39] *Brikom Investments Ltd v. Seaford, supra.* But *cf., China Pacific SA v. Food Corpn. of India* [1981] Q.B. 403, 429 (revd. on different grounds [1982] A.C. 939) where an admission of liability was said to be a representation of law.

[40] *Rashdall v. Ford* (1866) L.R. 2 Eq. 750; *Harse v. Pearl Life Assurance Co.* [1904] 1 K.B. 558.

[41] See also, *post*, §§ 30–044—30–047.

[42] *Kleinwort Benson Ltd v. Lincoln City Council* [1999] 1 A.C. 153. See *post*, § 30–041.

[43] *cf.* § 6–007, *ante*.

to rely upon it. In any event a statement of foreign law is here (as elsewhere in the law) treated as a statement of fact.[44]

Advice distinguished from misrepresentation. The suggestions made in the 6–012 last two paragraphs as to the need for a more extensive treatment of the definition of a representation are, at present, somewhat speculative, but it is necessary to bear in mind that an action in tort may sometimes lie for negligent advice. This form of liability is considered later,[45] but it is mentioned here in order to stress that in an action in tort it is not necessary to show that the statement complained of was a representation in the sense which this term has traditionally borne in the law of contract. Thus, where there is a sufficient "special relationship" to give rise to liability in tort under *Hedley Byrne & Co. Ltd v. Heller & Partners Ltd*,[46] it would seem immaterial that the statement consists of mere opinion or even of a proposition of abstract law.[47] Similarly, in certain circumstances a mere non-disclosure may ground liability under the *Hedley Byrne* principle,[48] although non-disclosure does not generally constitute a misrepresentation.

Non-disclosure. The general rule is that mere non-disclosure does not con- 6–013 stitute misrepresentation, for there is, in general, no duty on the parties to a contract to disclose material facts to each other, however dishonest such non-disclosure may be in particular circumstances.[49] So, for example, in *Percival v. Wright*,[50] a company director who had inside information about certain facts likely to enhance the value of the company's shares was held to be under no duty to disclose this fact to a shareholder from whom he bought some shares. For the same reason it is not possible to set up an estoppel on the basis of an omission to disclose unless a duty to disclose can be established in the particular circumstances of the case.[51] Tacit acquiescence in another's self-deception does not itself amount to a misrepresentation, provided that it has not previously been caused by a positive misrepresentation.[52] But there are exceptions to the general rule that there is no duty to disclose, namely, where the contract is within the class of contracts *uberrimae fidei*,[53] where there is a fiduciary relationship between the parties,[54] and where failure to disclose some fact distorts a positive representation. It is also possible for a person to be guilty of misrepresentation by

---

[44] *André & Cie SA v. Ets Michel Blanc & Fils* [1977] 2 Lloyd's Rep. 166.

[45] *Post*, §§ 6–078—6–089.

[46] [1964] A.C. 465; *post*, § 6–081.

[47] *Esso Petroleum Co. Ltd v. Mardon, ante*, § 6–010 and *post*, § 6–085.

[48] See *post*, § 6–135.

[49] *Ward v. Hobbs* (1878) 4 App.Cas. 13, but doubts have been cast on this case by the House of Lords in *Hurley v. Dyke* [1979] R.T.R. 265. Certain statutes may impose duties of disclosure in particular circumstances: *e.g.* Housing and Planning Act 1986 (as am.), s.125(4A): see *Payne v. Barnet L.B.C.* (1998) 30 H.L.R. 295 (no duty at common law should be superimposed on statutory scheme).

[50] [1902] 2 Ch. 421; *cf. Coleman v. Myers* [1977] 2 N.Z.L.R. 225, and see also *Gething v. Kilner* [1972] 1 W.L.R. 237; *Prudential Insurance Co. Ltd v. Newman Industries Ltd* [1981] Ch. 257, 295. Such conduct could constitute an offence under the Criminal Justice Act 1993, s.52, but s.63(2) provides that no contract shall be void or unenforceable by reason only of s.52.

[51] *Moorgate Mercantile Co. Ltd v. Twitchings* [1977] A.C. 890.

[52] See *Keates v. Cadogan* (1851) 10 C.B. 591; *New Brunswick and Canada Ry. and Land Co. v. Conybeare* (1862) 9 H.L.C. 711; *Smith v. Hughes* (1871) L.R. 6 Q.B. 597; *Turner v. Green* [1895] 2 Ch. 205; see also *Jewson & Son Ltd v. Arcos Ltd* (1933) 39 Com.Cas. 59; *Wales v. Wadham* [1977] 1 W.L.R. 199.

[53] See *post*, §§ 6–135—6–153.

[54] See *post*, §§ 6–079—6–080.

conduct.[55] The first two of these classes of cases are dealt with later; the third and fourth require examination here.

6–014   **Misrepresentation by conduct.** As previously mentioned, a person may be guilty of misrepresentation by conduct. In the simplest case, conduct may be intended to convey information in precisely the same way as the written or spoken word. Thus a person who goes into a shop in a university town wearing cap and gown may (if such costume is still customary) be representing that he is an undergraduate,[56] a person who sits down in a restaurant and orders a meal impliedly represents that he has the means to pay,[57] and more generally it has been said in a well-known dictum that "a nod or a wink or a shake of the head or a smile"[58] may amount to a representation if it is intended to induce the other party to believe in a certain state of facts. It is well established that a mere ordering of goods in the course of business carries a representation that the buyer is not aware that he will be unable to pay for them[59]; a mere payment of money by A to B may in appropriate circumstances (*e.g.* where A is B's employer) amount to a representation by A that B is entitled to the money so paid[60]; and it has been held in a criminal case that tendering of obsolete foreign bank notes to a currency dealer is a representation that the notes are current tender of some value.[61] Other important criminal cases concerning representations by conduct relate to the use of bank (cheque) cards and credit cards. In *R. v. Charles*[62] the House of Lords held that use of a cheque card amounts to a representation that the user has authority, as between himself and his bank, to use his card. Thus, even though payment of the cheque may be guaranteed by the bank, and may in fact be made by the bank, the use of the card will amount to a false representation if it is, in the circumstances, unauthorised by the bank. In *R. v. Lambie*[63] the House of Lords likewise held that use of a credit card to purchase goods amounts to a representation that the user has the authority of the credit card company to use the card. So even if the credit card company has a previous contract with the seller whereby it undertakes to pay for goods acquired with the use of the card, irrespective of amount, there will be a false representation if the user exceeds the limits agreed between him and the credit card company. The importance of these decisions for the civil law is that they justify the seller or supplier in rescinding the contract of sale and reclaiming the goods in the event of the fraud being discovered while the goods are still in the possession of the buyer.

6–015   **Conduct intended to conceal facts.** But there is also another class of case where conduct may amount to a representation, and that is where the conduct is not so much intended to convey information as to conceal facts from the other party. There does not appear to be any modern authority illustrating this type of

---

[55] In certain circumstances failing to disclose information may be a criminal offence, *e.g.* Timeshare Act 1992, s.1A (inserted by Timeshare Regulations 1997 (S.I. 1997 No. 1081)).

[56] *R. v. Barnard* (1837) 7 C. & P. 784.

[57] *Ray v. Sempers* [1974] A.C. 370.

[58] *Walters v. Morgan* (1861) 3 De G.F. & J. 718, 723. See also *Gill v. M'Dowel* [1903] 2 Ir.R. 463.

[59] *Re Shackleton, ex p. Whittaker* (1875) L.R. 10 Ch.App. 446; *Re Gerald Cooper Chemicals Ltd* [1978] Ch. 262; *Ray v. Sempers, supra.*

[60] *Avon County Council v. Howlett* [1981] I.R.L.R. 447.

[61] *R. v. Williams* [1980] Crim.L.R. 589.

[62] [1977] A.C. 177.

[63] [1982] A.C. 449.

misrepresentation, but there are some nineteenth-century cases in which a seller of goods was held guilty of misrepresentation where it was shown that he had deliberately concealed defects in the goods being sold, as, for instance, by nailing down planks and closing the seams of a rotten ship,[64] or by plugging a hole in a gun with soft metal.[65] This principle has not been fully developed by the courts, and it is uncertain whether it would extend to conduct which is not intended solely to conceal defects; it is, for instance, not clear whether the vendor of a house could be held guilty of misrepresentation if he papered a room, partly to hide the defective state of the plaster, but partly because it needed decorating in any event.

Partial non-disclosure.[66] Although total non-disclosure does not amount to a   **6–016** misrepresentation, a partial non-disclosure may do so. This may happen in a number of different ways. For example, a statement may be made which is true at that time but which subsequently ceases to be true to the knowledge of the representor before the contract is entered into. In such circumstances a failure to inform the representee of the change in circumstances will itself amount to a misrepresentation.[67] So also a statement may be a misrepresentation even though it is literally true if it implies certain additional facts which are themselves false. A striking instance of this possibility is *Goldsmith v. Rodger*[68] in which the defendant who was negotiating for the purchase of the plaintiff's yacht informed the plaintiff, after paying a visit to the yacht, that she had rot in her keel. The Court of Appeal held that this statement implied that the defendant had actually examined the keel, and as he had not done so, this was itself a misrepresentation, whether or not the yacht did have rot in her keel. Again, a statement may amount to a misrepresentation if facts are omitted which render that which has actually been stated false or misleading in the context in which it is made.[69] So, for example, where a shop assistant told a customer that a receipt for the cleaning of a dress which she was required to sign excluded liability for damage to beads and sequins, and in fact the receipt excluded all liability, this was held to be a misrepresentation.[70] It will be observed that these cases of partial non-disclosure can either be explained as cases of actual misrepresentation, or as cases in which there is a duty to disclose certain facts by reason of the facts actually stated. Until

---

[64] *Baglehole v. Walters* (1811) 3 Camp. 154; *Schneider v. Heath* (1813) 3 Camp. 506. For a case under the Trade Descriptions Act 1968, see *Cottee v. Douglas Seaton (Used Cars) Ltd* [1972] 1 W.L.R. 1408. In *Taittinger v. Allbev* (1993) 12 Tr.L.R. 165, a passing-off case, it was held that the labelling and "get-up" of a bottle constituted a false representation.

[65] *Horsfall v. Thomas* (1862) 1 H. & C. 90, but it was held in this case that as the buyer had not examined the gun he had not been influenced by the misrepresentation. See also *post*, § 6–034.

[66] See Hudson (1969) 85 L.Q.R. 524.

[67] *Traill v. Baring* (1864) 33 L.J.Ch. 521; *With v. O'Flanagan* [1936] Ch. 575; *Ray v. Sempers* [1974] A.C. 370; *cf. Wales v. Wadham* [1977] 1 W.L.R. 199 (see *post*, § 6–147, n. 93). It has been said that if a person who has made a representation of fact which, before the contract is made, he discovers to be untrue, he is not faudulent in failing to correct the representation, as he will not be dishonest: *Thomas Witter Ltd v. TBP Industries Ltd* [1994] Tr.L.R. 145. It is submitted that there may still be fraud if the person knows that he should tell the other party but fails to do so; see (1995) 111 L.Q.R. 385.

[68] [1962] 2 Lloyd's Rep. 249.

[69] *Oakes v. Turquand* (1867) L.R. 2 H.L. 325; *Barwick v. English Joint Stock Bank* (1867) L.R. 2 Ex. 259; *Peek v. Gurney* (1873) L.R. 6 H.L. 377, 403; *Arkwright v. Newbold* (1881) 17 Ch.D. 301, 318; *R. v. Kylsant* [1932] 1 K.B. 442; *Jewson & Sons Ltd v. Arcos Ltd* (1933) 39 Com.Cas. 59; *R. v. Bishirgian* [1936] 1 All E.R. 586.

[70] *Curtis v. Chemical Cleaning and Dyeing Co. Ltd* [1951] 1 K.B. 805; see *post*, § 14–121.

the passing of the Misrepresentation Act 1967, it was immaterial which explanation was adopted since the effect of an actual misrepresentation and the breach of a duty to disclose (where such a duty exists) were generally the same. But since the passing of this Act this is no longer the case as the Act applies to misrepresentations, but not to the breach of duties of disclosure. It is thought that cases of partial non-disclosure will normally be treated as cases of actual misrepresentation falling within the Act, but it has been held that cases of complete non-disclosure will not.[71]

6–017 **Continuity of representations.** Representations are treated for many purposes as continuing in their effect until the contract between the parties is actually concluded. This is one reason why a statement which is true when made, but which ceases to be true to the knowledge of the representor before the contract is concluded, is treated as a misrepresentation unless the representor informs the representee of the change in circumstances.[72] This principle may have other effects as well. For example, if a representation is made innocently but falsely, and facts later come to the knowledge of the representor which show that the statement was false, a failure to inform the representee of the truth may convert what was originally an innocent misrepresentation into a fraudulent one.[73] Again, if a man truthfully states that he intends to do something but changes his mind at a later stage he may come under a duty to disclose that change.[74] The principle is also recognised by section 2(1) of the Misrepresentation Act which extends the right to damages for negligent misrepresentation,[75] for a misrepresentation falls within this subsection unless the representor had reasonable grounds to believe and did believe *up to the time the contract was made* that the facts represented were true.[76] Another consequence of the principle that representations are continuous in their effect is that if a representation is made by an agent who is acting without authority, and he subsequently obtains the authority of his principal to continue the negotiations, the principal will become responsible for the representations previously made by the agent.[77] There are some circumstances in which a contract may be treated as commercially binding before it becomes legally binding, and in such a case it seems that the principle of continuity of representations does not operate beyond the time when the contract becomes commercially binding. So, for instance, an insured was held not to be obliged (despite the general duty of disclosure in insurance contracts[78]) to disclose facts coming to his notice after the insurer had initialled a slip indicating that he was at risk, although there was no binding legal contract until a policy was issued later.[79]

---

[71] *Banque Keyser Ullman SA v. Skandia (U.K.) Insurance Co. Ltd* [1990] 1 Q.B. 665, 787–789, affd. on other grounds [1991] 2 A.C. 249; *cf.* Hudson (1969) 85 L.Q.R. 524.

[72] *Ante*, § 6–018.

[73] *Davies v. London Provincial Marine Insurance Co.* (1878) 8 Ch.D. 469.

[74] *Ray v. Sempers* [1974] A.C. 370. But contrast *Wales v. Wadham* [1977] 1 W.L.R. 199, 211 (wife not obliged to reveal charge of intention not to marry; overruled on another ground but apparent approval given to the decision on this point, *Livesey v. Jenkins* [1985] A.C. 424, 439); see Cartwright, *Unequal Bargaining*, pp. 84–88.

[75] This is dealt with fully, *post*, §§ 6–068 *et seq.*

[76] *Corner v. Munday* [1987] C.L.Y. 479.

[77] *Briess v. Woolley* [1954] A.C. 333.

[78] *Post*, § 6–136.

[79] *Cory v. Patton* (1872) L.R. 7 Q.B. 304; *cf. Berger and Light Diffusers Pty. Ltd v. Pollock* [1973] 2 Lloyd's Rep. 442, 460–461.

(b) *Statement By or Known to Other Party*

The representor. In order to ground relief to a person who has entered into a   **6–018**
contract as a result of a misrepresentation, it is normally necessary that the misrepresentation should have been made either by the other party to the contract,[80]
or by his agent acting within the scope of his authority,[81] or that the other party
had notice of the misrepresentation.[82] A person who has been induced to enter
into a contract with A as a result of a misrepresentation made to him by B and
of which A had no notice has no ground of relief against A unless B were A's
agent.[83] It is, however, not necessary to show that the misrepresentor was the
agent of the other contracting party for the purpose of concluding the contract, or
even for the purpose of conducting negotiations; it is sufficient if the misrepresentor was the agent of the other contracting party simply for the purpose of
passing on the misrepresentation to the misrepresentee.[84]

Third party representor may be liable in damages. Although, apart from   **6–019**
cases of notice or of agency, a misrepresentation made by one person will not
found relief against another, nevertheless where the representee has been induced
to enter into a contract with a third party, the representor may himself be liable
in damages to the representee, either in tort, if the misrepresentation was fraudulent or, in some cases, negligent[85] or on the grounds of a collateral contract
between the representor and the representee.[86]

Constructive notice. In a number of cases a recurring situation has arisen. A   **6–020**
husband has wanted to borrow money from a creditor which has refused to
proceed without having a guarantee secured by a charge over the matrimonial
home, or similarly a charge without a guarantee, from the wife. The wife's
consent has been secured by misrepresentation[87] or undue influence[88] by the
husband.[89] Can the creditor enforce the guarantee? In a number of cases it was
held that if the creditor had "left it to the husband" to get the wife's signature,
the husband was acting as agent for the creditor[90] and it was therefore responsible
for his misconduct.

---

[80] *Hasan v. Willson* [1977] 1 Lloyd's Rep. 431.

[81] But an agent who seeks to enforce in his own name a contract made by him as such is affected
by a misrepresentation made by his principal: *Garnac Grain Co. Inc. v. H.M. Faure & Fairclough Ltd*
[1966] 1 Q.B. 650, revd. on the facts [1966] 1 Q.B. 658 and [1968] A.C. 1130n. See also *U.B.A.F.
Ltd v. European American Banking Corp.* [1984] Q.B. 713.

[82] *Barclays Bank plc v. O'Brien* [1994] 1 A.C. 180; *Bank of Credit and Commerce International
SA v. Aboody* [1990] 1 Q.B. 923, 973 (undue influence: see *post*, § 7–070).

[83] For an extreme example, see *Foote v. Hayne* (1824) 1 C. & P. 545 (defendant liable for breach
of promise of marriage despite fraud of plaintiff's father with respect to plaintiff's illegitimate
child).

[84] *Pilmore v. Hood* (1838) 5 Bing.N.C. 97.

[85] That is, if the case falls within the principle in *Hedley Byrne & Co. Ltd v. Heller & Partners Ltd*
[1964] A.C. 465, *post*, § 6–081.

[86] See, *e.g. Wells (Merstham) Ltd v. Buckland Sand & Silica Co. Ltd* [1965] 2 Q.B. 170, *post*,
§ 12–006.

[87] *Kings North Trust Ltd v. Bell* [1961] 1 W.L.R. 119.

[88] *e.g. CIBC Mortgages plc v. Pitt* [1994] 1 A.C. 200. See further *post*, § 7–070, n. 24.

[89] For a wide ranging study of the problem, see Fehlberg, *Sexually Transmitted Debt* (1997).

[90] See *Coldunell Ltd v. Gallon* [1986] Q.B. 1184.

6–021   **Agency "artificial"; wife's "special equity".** In *Barclays Bank plc v. O'Brien*, a case where the husband had secured his wife's signature by misrepresentation, the Court of Appeal[91] expressed the view that this approach was often artificial on the facts. It held that it was not just in cases in which the debtor was acting as the agent of the creditor in the true sense that the creditor would be unable to enforce the guarantee if the debtor had procured the surety's signature by misrepresentation. If the relationship between the debtor and a surety who charged property to secure the debt was one in which influence by the debtor over the surety and reliance on the debtor by the surety were natural and probable features, as in the case of husband and wife, and this was known to the creditor, a special rule applied. If the debtor procured the surety's consent by misrepresentation or undue influence, or the surety lacked an adequate understanding of the nature and effect of the transaction, and the creditor, whether by leaving it to the debtor to deal with the surety or otherwise, failed to take reasonable steps to try to ensure that the surety entered the transaction with adequate understanding and that the consent was a true and informed one, the creditor may not enforce the security given by the surety.[92]

6–022   In the House of Lords[93] this approach was rejected: there is no special theory in equity to protect wives.[94] However the appeal of the Bank was dismissed on the ground that it had constructive notice of the husband's misrepresentation that the change was to secure only £60,000, when it was in fact unlimited, and that the liability would be released in a short time when the matrimonial home was unmortgaged. There is a substantial risk that when the transaction is not to the wife's advantage she may have agreed to act as surety or to the charge because of some legal or equitable wrong by the husband. Where the creditor is aware that the debtor and the surety are husband and wife, and the transaction is on its face not one which is to the financial advantage of the surety as well as of the debtor, the creditor will be fixed with constructive notice of any undue influence, misrepresentation or other legal wrong by the debtor unless it has taken reasonable steps to satisfy itself that the surety has entered into the obligation freely and with knowledge of the true facts.[95] The surety cannot set aside the transaction simply on the ground that she did not fully understand it.[96] However the creditor should explain to the surety the amount of her potential liability and of the risks involved, and advise her to seek independent legal advice before entering the guarantee[97]; and this should be done in a personal interview, as written warnings are often not read and are sometimes intercepted by the debtor.[98] The interview

---

[91] [1993] Q.B. 109.

[92] Considerable reliance was placed on *Turnbull & Co. v. Dural* [1902] A.C. 429, PC.

[93] [1994] 1 A.C. 180. In Scotland a similar result has been reached but via the different route of recognising a duty of good faith by the creditor towards the cautioner: *Smith v. Bank of Scotland* 1997 S.L.T. 1061. In Australia, the problem has been approached through the doctrine of unconscionability (post, § 7–080): see Tjio (1997) 113 L.Q.R. 13.

[94] *Turnbull's* case was doubted.

[95] *ibid.* at 429. In *CIBC Mortgages plc v. Pitt* [1994] 1 A.C. 200, which was heard with *O'Brien's* case, the loan appeared to be a normal loan for the joint benefit of husband and wife and therefore the creditor was not fixed with constructive notice of the undue influence used by the husband to secure the wife's agreement.

[96] *ibid.* at 197.

[97] This much is required by the Code of Banking Practice adopted by banks and building societies in March 1992 and revised in 1994 and 1997. The code also provides that unlimited guarantees or security will not be taken.

[98] [1994] 1 A.C. 180, 198.

should not be attended by the husband. As in this case the bank's clerk, in disregard of her instructions, had not warned the wife of the risks involved nor recommended her to take legal advice before getting her to sign the documents charging the matrimonial home, the bank could not enforce the charge. If the bank has notice of facts rendering misrepresentation or undue influence not just possible but probable it must insist that the wife actually is separately advised.[99]

Relationships giving rise to notice. In *Barclays Bank v. O'Brien*[99a] it was held that, even though the relationship of husband and wife does not give rise to a presumption of undue influence,[1] where the transaction was not on its face advantageous to the wife, that and the fact that the parties were known to be husband and wife was sufficient to put the bank on notice. The same principles apply when the creditor knows that the debtor and surety are cohabitees and in other cases where the creditor is aware that the surety reposes trust and confidence in the debtor in relation to financial affairs, for instance vulnerable elderly parents providing security for the debts of their adult son[2] or if the parties are in the kind of relationship which gives rise to a presumption of undue influence.[3] The bank may also be put on notice if the transaction is so improvident that it is inexplicable unless there has been some impropriety in the debtor's behaviour towards the surety.[4] It has justly been pointed out that a transaction which might actually be advantageous to a wife may be inexplicable in the case of someone else with little or nothing to gain from it.[5] Thus it seems conceivable that simply the terms of the transaction might put a creditor on notice even when it is not aware of any relationship between the parties.[6]

6–023

Transaction not on its face to the advantage of the surety. The creditor is not put on notice unless the transaction is on its face disadvantageous to the surety. The fact that the loan appears to be a joint one to husband and wife may, as in *CIBC Mortgages Ltd v. Pitt*,[7] mean that the creditor is not put on enquiry; but the mere fact that the loan is joint will not have this effect. Thus in *Allied Irish Bank plc v. Byrne*[8] the Bank knew that the loan was primarily for the benefit of the husband and it was made as a joint loan to husband and wife at the Bank's suggestion; the Bank was put on notice. The creditor must look at the substance of the matter so far as this is apparent to it. In *Goode Durant Administration v. Biddulph*[9] a loan was made to a property company, the husband and the wife

6–024

---

[99] *ibid.* 197.

[99a] [1994] A.C. 180.

[1] See *post*, § 7–058.

[2] *Avon Finance Co. Ltd v. Bridger* (1979) [1985] 2 All E.R. 281; *Barclays Bank plc v. O'Brien, supra*, at p.198. There may also be cases in which the creditor is responsible for the husband's actions because it can be said, "without artificiality," that the husband was acting as agent of the creditor, but "such cases will be of very rare occurrence."

[3] *Royal Bank of Scotland v. Etridge (No. 2)* [1998] 4 All E.R. 705, 719.

[4] *ibid.*, referring to *Credit Lyonnais Bank Nederland SA v. Burch* [1997] 1 All E.R. 144; see *post*, § 7–077.

[5] *Royal Bank of Scotland v. Etridge (No. 2)* [1998] 4 All E.R. 705, 719.

[6] But in such an extreme case the bank may anyway be taking unconscionable advantage, see *post*, § 7–077.

[7] [1994] 1 A.C. 200.

[8] [1995] 2 FLR 325.

[9] [1995] 1 FLR 196. See also *Bank of Cyprus (London) Ltd v. Markou* [1999] 2 All E.R. 707, 720.

jointly. The creditor knew that the company was a new vehicle for the business schemes of the husband and that the wife owned only 2.5 per cent of the shares. Again, the creditor was put on enquiry. However, in *Royal Bank of Scotland v. Etridge (No. 2)*,[10] Stuart Smith L.J., delivering the judgment of the court, pointed out that where a wife is asked to give a guarantee or charge over the matrimonial home to support her husband's indebtedness, the transaction is not necessarily to her disadvantage: "if the marriage is secure and the indebtedness which has been incurred by the business which provides the husband's livelihood and on which the prosperity of his wife and family depends, there is no real conflict between the interests of the husband and the wife."[11] However, this was said in the context of explaining what advice a solicitor might properly give the wife and it should not be taken that the creditor is not put on notice just because it takes the view, for this or similar reasons, that the transaction is in fact for the wife's benefit.[11a]

6–025   **Facts known to solicitor.** If the loan is on the face of it for the joint benefit of husband and wife, the fact that a solicitor who is acting for both the borrowers and the creditor knows that the loan is actually to be used to pay the husband's business debts does not fix the creditor with notice of that purpose. The creditor is not affected by anything discovered by the solicitor unless the solicitor was acting as the creditor's solicitor at the time.[12] The solicitor is under a duty to the borrower not to disclose the relevant facts and, when a conflict of interest emerges he should notify the lender that he can no longer act for it, rather than revealing the information that has come to him as solicitor for the borrower; this being so, his knowledge will not be imputed to the lender.[13]

6–026   **Reasonable steps.** There has been a large number of cases since *Barclays Bank v. O'Brien* on the question of what steps the creditor must take in order to avoid being fixed with constructive notice of any misrepresentation (or, in most of the cases, undue influence) by the debtor.[14] In *O'Brien's* case, Lord Browne-Wilkinson said that, to avoid being fixed with constructive notice, the creditor should insist that "the wife attend a private meeting (in the absence of the husband) with a representative of the creditor at which she is told of the extent of her liability as surety, warned of the risk she is running and urged to take independent legal advice." In many of the subsequent cases (the facts of many of which occurred before the House of Lords' decision in *O'Brien*), the creditor had not itself advised the wife[15] but had relied on a certificate from a third party, typically a solicitor employed by the husband or by the creditor itself, that the

---

[10] [1998] 4 All E.R. 705.

[11] *ibid.* at 716.

[11a] But see *Society of Lloyds v. Khan* [1998] 3 F.C.R. 93 (Lloyds not put on notice when wife agreed to be a Name, which enabled her to undertake a risk in return for reward).

[12] Law of Property Act 1925, s.199(i)(ii)(b).

[13] *Halifax Mortgage Services Ltd. v. Stepsky* [1995] 3 W.L.R. 701. See also *National Westminster Bank plc v. Beaton* (1998) 30 H.L.R. 99.

[14] See Fehlberg (1996) 59 M.L.R. 675.

[15] In *Royal Bank of Scotland v. Etridge (No. 2)* [1998] 4 All E.R. 705, 720, Stuart-Smith L.J. doubted if banks would be willing to do this even after *O'Brien's* case, as it "is likely to expose the bank to greater risks than those from which it wishes to be protected".

wife had been given some explanation.[16] The position in such cases was summarised recently by the Court of Appeal in *Royal Bank of Scotland v. Etridge (No. 2)*.[17]

"(1) Where the wife deals with the bank through a solicitor, whether acting for her alone or for her and her husband, the bank is not ordinarily put on inquiry. The bank is entitled to assume that the solicitor has considered whether there is a sufficient conflict of interest to make it necessary for him to advise her to obtain independent legal advice. It is not necessary for the bank to ask the solicitor to carry out his professional obligation to give proper advice to the wife or to confirm that he has done so. The bank is ordinarily not required to take any steps at all.[18]

(2) Where the wife does not approach the bank through a solicitor, it is normally sufficient if the bank has urged her to obtain independent legal advice before entering into the transaction.[19] This is especially the case if the solicitor provides confirmation that he has explained the transaction to the wife and that she appears to understand it.[20]

(3) When giving advice to the wife the solicitor is acting exclusively as her solicitor.[21] It makes no difference whether he is unconnected with the husband or the wife[22] or is also the husband's solicitor[23] or that he has agreed to act in a ministerial capacity as the bank's agent at completion.[24] Whoever introduces the solicitor to the wife and asks him to advise her, and whoever is responsible for his fees, the bank is entitled to expect the solicitor to regard himself as owing a duty to the wife alone when giving her advice.[25] If the solicitor accepts the bank's instructions to advise the wife, he still acts as her solicitor and not the bank's solicitor when he interviews her.[26]

(4) It follows that the bank is not fixed with imputed notice of what the solicitor learns in the course of advising the wife even if he is also the bank's solicitor. Such knowledge does not come to him in his capacity as the bank's solicitor.[27]

(5) The bank is entitled to rely on the fact that the solicitor undertook the task of explaining the transaction to the wife as showing that he considered himself to be sufficiently independent for this purpose.[28] The bank is not required to question the solicitor's independence, even if it knows that he is also the husband's solicitor.[29]

---

[16] Which Stuart-Smith L.J. points out, *ibid.*, goes beyond what *O'Brien* required for the normal case in that the bank insists that the wife actually receives advice.

[17] [1998] 4 All E.R. 705, 721 (references are shown as footnotes).

[18] *Bank of Baroda v. Rayarel* [1995] 2 F.C.R. 631.

[19] *ibid.* and *Massey v. Midland Bank plc* [1995] 1 All E.R. 929.

[20] *Bank of Baroda v. Rayarel* [1995] 2 F.C.R. 631.

[21] *Midland Bank plc v. Serter* [1995] 3 F.C.R. 711; *Barclays Bank plc v. Thomson* [1997] 4 All E.R. 816.

[22] *Barclays Bank plc v. Thomson* [1997] 4 All E.R. 816.

[23] *Midland Bank plc v. Serter* [1995] 3 F.C.R. 711; *Massey v. Midland Bank plc* [1995] 1 All E.R. 929; *Banco Exterior v. Mann* [1995] 1 All E.R. 936.

[24] *Midland Bank v. Serter* [1995] 3 F.C.R. 711; *Halifax Mortgage Services Ltd v. Stepsky* [1995] 3 W.L.R. 701.

[25] *Barclays Bank plc v. Thomson* [1997] 4 All E.R. 816.

[26] *ibid.*

[27] *Halifax Mortgage Services Ltd v. Stepsky* [1995] 3 W.L.R. 701.

[28] *Banco Exterior Internacional v. Mann* [1995] 1 All E.R. 936; *Bank of Baroda v. Rayarel* [1995] 2 F.C.R. 631.

[29] *Massey v. Midland Bank plc* [1995] 1 All E.R. 929; *Bank of Baroda v. Rayarel* [1995] 2 F.C.R. 631.

(6) The bank is not concerned to question the sufficiency of the advice, and is not put on further inquiry by the fact that the solicitor was asked only to explain the transaction to the wife and ensure that she understood it and not to see that she was sufficiently independent of her husband. Nor is the bank put on inquiry by the fact that the confirmation provided by the solicitor is similarly limited."[30]

The Court refused to follow the earlier Court of Appeal decision in *Royal Bank of Scotland v. Etridge*[31] at the interlocutory stage, which held that when a solicitor who had been instructed by the bank to "act on our behalf in completion of the security" and who had certified that he had explained the charge to the wife, had, she alleged, failed to do so, the bank had delegated its task to its own solicitor and thus would be responsible for the solicitor discharging that duty, so the wife had an arguable defence.

6-027   It seems that where the bank has asked a solicitor to explain the transaction to the wife, it must obtain a certificate that he has done so, so that it is not protected if the solicitor fails to confirm[32] nor if it receives a written confirmation that advice would be given by an unnamed solicitor[33] and in fact the wife has not been advised.[34]

6-028   **Application to cases of misrepresentation.** Many of the cases cited above were of alleged undue influence and the application of these rules to that situation will be considered in Chapter 7. As far as cases of misrepresentation are concerned, it should be noted that the Court of Appeal has stated that the bank cannot rely on a solicitor to give advice if it has material information which is not available to the solicitor. Where there has been a misrepresentation by the husband of the kind which occurred in *O'Brien's* case (as to the extent and duration of the guarantee), this should pose no problem, as presumably the solicitor will always have a copy of the guarantee or charge. What may be more problematic is if there has been some misrepresentation by the husband as to some other matter, such as the state of his business affairs.[35] The creditor does not normally have any duty to disclose to a surety any unusual risks relating to the debtor,[36] let alone normal ones. However, it has been said that in order for the solicitor to advise the wife properly, he will normally have to ask for information:

"[It] will usually be necessary for the solicitor to inform himself of the indebtedness and of the new advance, and of the reasons for the new advance or the bank's request for additional security."[37]

---

[30] *Passim.*

[31] [1997] 3 All E.R. 628.

[32] *Royal Bank of Scotland v. Etridge (No. 2)* [1998] 4 All E.R. 705, 722; *Cooke v. National Westminster Bank plc, The Times*, July 27 1998.

[33] *Bank Melli Iran v. Samadi-Rad* [1995] 1 F.C.R. 465; though see an apparently contrary suggestion by Nourse L.J. in *TSB Bank plc v. Camfield* [1995] 1 W.L.R. 430 (in which the point was not argued).

[34] *Royal Bank of Scotland v. Etridge (No. 2)* [1998] 4 All E.R. 705, 722. On the other hand, the bank may rely on a confirmation by one solicitor that the wife has been advised even though the confirmation was based on what the first solicitor had been told by the other: *Virdee v. Scottish Equitable Life plc, The Independent*, November 30, 1998, CS.

[35] cf. *Massey v. Midland Bank plc* [1995] 1 All E.R. 929.

[36] *Credit Lyonnais Bank Nederland v. Export Credit Guarantee Department* [1996] 1 Lloyd's Rep. 200; *post*, § 7–077. See also *Bank of Baroda v. Rayarel* [1995] 2 F.C.R. 631.

[37] *Royal Bank of Scotland v. Etridge (No. 2)* [1998] 4 All E.R. 705, 717.

It is submitted that the creditor should not be able to rely on the wife having sufficiently accurate information through the husband: the whole point of the rule on constructive notice is that there is a real danger that the husband may have secured his wife's consent by misrepresentation.[38] Thus it may be that if the creditor knows that this information has not been disclosed to either the wife or the solicitor who has purportedly advised her, it will not be able to rely on the fact that she has been told to get independent advice or has actually seen a solicitor as being reasonably sufficient to allay suspicion of misrepresentation.[39]

Effect of constructive notice. After *O'Brien's* case there was some uncer- **6–029** tainty as to the position when, as in that case, the husband had misrepresented the extent of the charge and the bank had constructive notice of the misrepresenta- tion. Is the charge completely unenforceable against the wife or enforceable to the extent she was given to believe? (In *O'Brien's* case it seems that £60,000, the sum which the wife had been led to believe was the limit of her liability, had been paid before the final decision, which did not mention discuss its fate.) In *TSB Bank plc v. Camfield*[40] the Court of Appeal held on similar facts that the charge was completely unenforceable. As against the husband the wife would have the right to set aside the whole charge.[41] The bank took subject to the equity in favour of the wife and could not be in a better position. However, in that case the wife had not received any benefit under the agreement. If she had done so, her right to rescind would have been conditional on her making counter-restitution of the benefit received.[42] Where a later security is enforceable by reason of undue influence, that may still leave an earlier, untainted one in force.[43]

Need the party who made the misrepresentation be a party to the **6–030** **transaction?** In *TSB Bank plc v. Camfield*[44] the bank was treated as having constructive notice of the wife's right to set aside the charge as against the husband. What would be the position if the husband were not a party to the charge? As a matter of principle, it seems that a party to a contract who has actual notice that the other party has entered the contract as the result of a mis- representation by a third party should be unable to enforce it, and it is submitted that the same should apply in cases of constructive notice. In *Banco Exterior Internacional SA v. Thomas*[45] (a case of alleged undue influence) Sir Richard Scott V-C expressed the view that it could not have made a difference if in *O'Brien's* case the wife had been sole owner of the home, but the case was

---

[38] See *ante*, § 6–020. For the same reason it is submitted that it would normally be unsafe for the solicitor to rely on information given by the wife without checking it with the creditor, and this even when the wife assures the solicitor that she believes the information her husband has given her. Particularly where the solicitor also acts for the husband, the wife may be reluctant to reveal her doubts for fear that it may "get back" to the husband that she has been questioning his word.

[39] *cf. Credit Lyonnais Bank Nederland NV v. Burch* [1997] 1 All E.R. 144, 151–152, 155–157.

[40] [1995] 1 W.L.R. 430.

[41] This was said to be implicit in Misrepresentation Act 1967, s.2(2), which also implies that the court had no discretion save under that sub-section. The sub-section does not apply as between a misrepresentee and a third party.

[42] *Dunbar Bank plc v. Nadeem* [1998] 3 All E.R. 876; *Midland Bank plc v. Greene* (1995) 27 H.L.R. 350. See further below, § 7–064.

[43] *Barclays Bank plc v. Caplan* [1998] 1 F.L.R. 532.

[44] [1995] 1 W.L.R. 430.

[45] [1997] 1 W.L.R. 221.

decided on other grounds, Roch LJ reserving this question. More recent authority treats the two situations in the same way.[46]

6–031   **Procedure.** A party who wishes to rely on the defence against the creditor of constructive notice of wrongdoing by the debtor need only state the relevant facts and need not plead constructive notice in so many words.[47]

(c) *Other Requirements*

6–032   **The representee.** In order to be entitled to relief in respect of misrepresentation, the person seeking relief must be able to demonstrate that he is a representee; for, subject to the transmission by operation of law of claims on death, bankruptcy and assignment, the person or persons who in law come within the category of representees are alone entitled to a remedy. There may be said to be three types of representees[48]: first, persons to whom the representation is directly made and their principals; secondly, persons to whom the representor intended or expected the representation to be passed on[49]; and thirdly, members of a class at which the representation was directed: the class may amount to the public at large,[50] for if a representation is made to the public generally with the intention that it should be acted upon, any member of the public may be a representee, though it does not follow that a legal remedy exists in respect of it.[51] But if the representation is directed at a particular class of persons, the alleged representee must be able to bring himself within that class. *Peek v. Gurney*[52] illustrates this point: the plaintiffs bought shares in the market in reliance on the terms of a fraudulent prospectus issued by the promoters. The House of Lords held that the plaintiffs could not recover from the promoters: the purpose of issuing a prospectus was said to be to induce people to apply for shares, and not to induce them to buy in the market shares already issued; therefore the function of the prospectus was exhausted with the allotment, and the plaintiffs could not show that they came within the class of persons at which it was directed.[53] Similarly, in *Gross v. Lewis Hillman Ltd*[54] it was held that the right of a purchaser of certain land to rescind the contract for misrepresentation did not "run with the land" so

---

[46] *Royal Bank of Scotland v. Etridge (No. 2)* [1998] 4 All E.R. 705, 717–718. See also Proksch [1997] R.L.R. 71.

[47] *Barclays Bank plc v. Boutler* [1998] 1 W.L.R. 1.

[48] See *Swift v. Winterbotham* (1873) L.R. 8 Q.B. 244, 253; the rule there stated was applied in *Richardson v. Silvester* (1873) L.R. 9 Q.B. 34, 36; see also *Commercial Banking Co. of Sydney Ltd v. R.H. Brown & Co.* (1972) 126 C.L.R. 13, *post*, § 6–042.

[49] This category includes third persons to whom the original representee passes on the representation to the knowledge of the representor (see *Pilmore v. Hood* (1838) 5 Bing.N.C. 97; *Yianni v. Edwin Evans & Sons* [1982] Q.B. 438), but excludes persons to whom the representor does not intend any communication to be made (see *Peek v. Gurney* (1873) L.R. 6 H.L. 377), unless (*semble*) he ought to foresee such communication, see *infra*.

[50] *R. v. Silverlock* [1984] 2 Q.B. 766.

[51] Particularly in cases of negligence, where (even if any member of the public is a representee) the absence of a duty of care may be fatal to a claim for damages, *post*, §§ 6–081—6–085.

[52] (1873) L.R. 6 H.L. 377.

[53] It might be thought that the actual decision in this case is no longer law because a prospectus today is intended to be addressed to would-be purchasers in the market just as much as to purchasers from the company. However, it was applied in a case of alleged negligent misstatement: *Al Nakib Investments Ltd v. Longcroft* [1990] 1 W.L.R. 1390; see Gower's, *Principles of Modern Company Law* (6th ed., 1997), pp. 438–439, 555–556.

[54] [1970] Ch. 445.

as to be available to a subsequent purchaser; the subsequent purchaser was not himself a representee of the original vendor. On the other hand, where a person makes a false statement in a document (such as a bill of lading) which he knows is going to be passed on to other people and relied on by them, any person who does in fact rely on the document will be a representee.[55] Nor is it always necessary that the actual representation should reach the representee. If a person asks an agent to find some property for him, and the agent, relying on the fraudulent inducements of the vendor, recommends the vendor's property, the buyer will be entitled to relief for misrepresentation even though the agent did not actually pass on the fraudulent statements.[56]

Tort actions for misrepresentation. In tort actions, based on negligent mis- **6–033** representation, there seems to be a tendency to apply rules which may be somewhat more favourable to a party claiming to be a representee. This is because in such actions the defendant's liability turns on whether he owed a duty of care to the claimant, and that in turn may depend largely upon whether he ought to have foreseen that the statement would be acted upon by the claimant. In *Yianni v. Edwin Evans & Sons*[57] the plaintiffs purchased a property with the aid of a loan from a building society. The building society had obtained a valuation on the property from the defendants, who were surveyors. The plaintiffs, as is customary, paid the defendants' fee, though through the building society, and not directly to the defendants. The plaintiffs did not themselves see the defendants' report which was sent to the building society, but Park J. held that the plaintiffs had acted in reliance on the valuation in the sense that they believed that it confirmed the value of the house to be at least equal to the loan the building society was prepared to make on the strength of the valuation. It seems clear that the defendants did not intend that their report should be made available to the plaintiffs (though they knew that it was being sought in connection with a purchase to be made by them); the building society's booklet told the plaintiffs that the surveyor's report was confidential and exclusively for the use of the building society. Nevertheless it was held that the defendants did owe a duty of care to the plaintiffs because they ought to have foreseen (as the evidence showed) that the plaintiffs, in common with most house purchasers, would not have an independent survey, but would rely on the defendants' survey. This decision was approved by the House of Lords in *Harris v. Wyre Forest DC*.[58] Lord Griffiths said that sufficient proximity to ground a duty of care in tort would arise if the surveyor knew it was probable that the purchaser would rely on the valuation.[59]

Inducement. It is essential if the misrepresentation is to have legal effect that **6–034** it should have operated on the mind of the representee. It follows that if the misrepresentation did not affect the representee's mind, because he was unaware

---

[55] See, *e.g. Brown, Jenkinson & Co. Ltd v. Percy Dalton (London) Ltd* [1957] 2 Q.B. 621.

[56] *Gross v. Hillman Ltd* [1970] Ch. 445, 461.

[57] [1982] Q.B. 438; *Standard Chartered Bank v. Pakistan National Shipping Corp.* [1995] 2 Lloyd's Rep. 365.

[58] Heard with *Smith v. Eric S. Bush* [1990] 1 A.C. 831 (in *Smith's* case it was known that the report would be passed to the plaintiff).

[59] *ibid.* at 865. Compare *McCullagh v. Lane Fox and Partners Ltd* [1996] 1 E.G.L.R. 35, where at the time the information was given the surveyor did not know that the purchaser would act without getting his own survey, and by the time the surveyor did know he had issued a disclaimer.

that it had been made,[60] or because he was not influenced by it,[61] or because he would have entered into the contract even had he known the true facts,[62] or because he knew that it was false,[63] he has no remedy. Thus in *Horsfall v. Thomas*[64] a seller delivered to a buyer a gun which was defective, for after being fired it exploded, and the buyer was injured; the buyer had not examined the gun, but he alleged that the sale had been procured by fraudulent misrepresentation and that the defect had been concealed. The court rejected his claim because, as the buyer had never examined the gun, an attempt to conceal the defect, if such an attempt had been made, had had no effect on his mind. An action for breach of the implied terms as to quality and fitness would probably lie in such circumstances today.[65] Where an estate agent's particulars misrepresented the size of a garage, and the buyer had examined the whole property thoroughly on two separate occasions, it was held that the misrepresentation had had no effect.[66] However, once it is proved that a false statement was made which was likely to induce the contract, and that the representee entered the contract, it is a fair inference of fact (though not an inference of law) that he was influenced by the statement.[67] Even if the misrepresentation was not likely to influence a reasonable person, the representee may rescind if he can show that he was induced by it to enter into the contract.[68]

6–035   **Burden of proof.** The burden of proving that the claimant had actual knowledge of the truth, and therefore was not deceived by the misrepresentation, lies on the defendant; if established, knowledge on the part of the representee is of course a complete defence, because he is then unable to show that he was misled

---

[60] *Horsfall v. Thomas* (1862) 1 H. & C. 90.

[61] *Attwood v. Small* (1838) 6 Cl. & F. 232; *Jennings v. Broughton* (1853) 5 De G.M. & G. 126; *Smith v. Chadwick* (1884) 9 App.Cas. 187; *Holmes v. Jones* (1907) 4 C.L.R. 1692.

[62] *Industrial Properties Ltd v. Associated Electrical Industries Ltd* [1977] Q.B. 580; *J.E.B. Fasteners Ltd v. Marks, Bloom & Co.* [1981] 3 All E.R. 289, [1983] 1 All E.R. 583. In *Pan Atlantic Insurance Co. Ltd v. Pine Top Insurance Co. Ltd* [1995] 1 A.C. 501, the House of Lords held that, for both marine insurance under Marine Insurance Act 1906, s.18(2) and non-marine insurance, a misrepresentation or non-disclosure must actually have induced the making of the policy for the policy to be voidable. See also *St. Paul Fire and Marine Insurance Co. Ltd v. McConnell Dowell Constructors Ltd* [1996] 1 All E.R. 96.

[63] *Cooper v. Tamms* [1988] 1 E.G.L.R. 257.

[64] (1862) 1 H. & C. 90. The judgment of Bramwell B. was criticised in *Smith v. Hughes* (1871) L.R. 6 Q.B. 597, 605 by Cockburn C.J.

[65] See Vol. II, §§ 43–077—43–095.

[66] *Hartlelid v. Sawyer & McClockin Real Estate Ltd* [1977] 5 W.W.R. 481.

[67] *Smith v. Chadwick* (1884) 9 App.Cas. 187, 196; also (1882) 20 Ch.D. 27, 44–45; *Pan Atlantic Insurance Co. Ltd v. Pine Top Insurance Co. Ltd* [1992] 1 Lloyd's Rep. 101, 112–113 (affd. without reference to this point, [1993] 1 Lloyd's Rep. 496, and by the House of Lords, where Lord Mustill refers to the "presumption of inducement" in the case of fraud, but he does not deny that there may be a similar presumption in other cases of positive misrepresentation: [1995] 1 A.C. 501, 542.) There is not unanimity as to the weight of any presumption. The following passage from Halsbury's *Laws of England*, (4th ed., Vol 31, para. 1067): "Inducement cannot be inferred in law from proved materiality, although there may be cases where the materiality is so obvious as to justify an inference of fact that the representee was actually induced, but, even in such exceptional cases, the inference is only a prima facie one and may be rebutted by counter-evidence", was approved in *St. Paul Fire and Marine Insurance Co. Ltd v. McConnell Dowell Costructors Ltd* [1996] 1 All E.R. 96, 112; but the same case refers simply to a "presumption". See Bennett (1996) 112 L.Q.R. 405. A material respresentation was said to create a presumption in *Strachan & Henshaw Ltd v. Stein Industrie (U.K.) Ltd* (1997) 13 Const.L.J. 418.

[68] *Museprime Properties Ltd v. Adhill Properties Ltd* [1990] 2 E.G.L.R. 196.

by the misrepresentation.[69] It has also been held that a defence is made out if the truth was known to the agent of the claimant, at least where the facts had deliberately been communicated to the agent.[70]

Representee could have discovered truth: rescission. If the representee did 6–036
not know that the representation was false, it is no defence to an action for rescission that the representee might have discovered its falsity by the exercise of reasonable care.[71] It has been argued that the rule that a misrepresentee's failure to take advantage of an opportunity to discover the truth is no bar to rescission may require re-consideration in the light of indications in cases of claims for damages for negligent mistatement to the effect that buyers of expensive or commercial properties would be expected to have their own survey done, and thus would fail in a claim for negligent misrepresentation against a surveyor employed by the lender[72]; it is suggested that the rule should be limited to cases in which it was reasonable not to take the opportunity.[73] It is not clear, however, that the same approach should apply as between contracting parties, when the misrepresentee is seeking to rescind, as is taken when a party claims damages for a negligent misstatement by a person with whom he is not in a contractual relationship. When the misstatement leads to a contract with the misrepresentor, there is at least the possibility that the misrepresentor will have benefited from his mistatement, for example by obtaining a better price for the property he is selling. The fact that he was innocent, and the other party careless of his own interests, does not necessarily justify allowing the misrepresentor to retain the advantage gained.[74]

Representee could have discovered truth: damages. As will be seen later, 6–037
the victim of a fraudulent or negligent misrepresentation may have a claim for damages. Can these be reduced on the ground that the representee might have discovered the truth? Contributory negligence is not a defence to an action of deceit and the Law Reform (Contributory Negligence) Act 1945[75] does not apply.[76] It has been held that damages for negligent misrepresentation under the Misrepresentation Act 1967, s.2(1)[77] may be reduced if the loss was partly the fault of the representee, at least when there is concurrent liability under that section and in tort for negligent misrepresentation under the principle of *Hedley Byrne v. Heller*[78]; but it would not be just and equitable to reduce the damages when the representor had intended, or should be taken as having intended, that

---

[69] *Dyer v. Hargrave* (1805) 10 Ves. 505; *Attwood v. Small* (1838) 6 Cl. & F. 232; *Vigers v. Pike* (1842) 8 Cl. & F. 562, 650.

[70] *Strover v. Harrington* [1988] Ch. 390; compare *Markappa Inc. v. N.W. Spratt & Son Ltd* [1985] 1 Lloyd's Rep. 534. However, the information must be received by a person authorised and able to appreciate its significance: *Malhi v. Abbey Life Assurance Co. Ltd* [1996] L.R.L.R. 237.

[71] *Dyer v. Hargrave* (1805) 10 Ves. 505; *Dobell v. Stevens* (1825) 3 B. & C. 623; *Reynell v. Sprye* (1852) 1 De G.M. & G. 660; *Central Ry. of Venezuela v. Kisch* (1867) L.R. 2 H.L. 99, 120; *Redgrave v. Hurd* (1881) 20 Ch.D. 1; *Nocton v. Ashburton* [1914] A.C. 932, 962; *Laurence v. Lexcourt Holdings Ltd* [1977] 1 W.L.R. 1128.

[72] *Smith v. Eric S. Bush* [1990] 1 A.C. 831, 854, 872.

[73] Treitel, *The Law of Contract* (9th ed., 1995) p. 316.

[74] See Jessel M.R. in *Redgrave v. Hurd* (1881) 20 Ch.D. 1, 13.

[75] See *post*, § 6–074.

[76] *Alliance and Leicester Building Society v. Edgestop Ltd* [1994] 1 All E.R. 38.

[77] See *post*, § 6–074.

[78] See *post*, § 6–081.

the representee should act in reliance on the answers which had been given to his questions.[79]

6–038   **Unforeseeable reliance.** A person may be entitled to rescind a contract into which he entered as a result of a fraudulent misrepresentation even though one would not have expected a reasonable person to enter the contract at that stage because, for example, he has not yet secured finance for the transaction.[80] It is not clear whether the same would apply if the party unforeseeably entered into a transaction as the result of an innocent or negligent misrepresentation, rather than a fraudulent one which was intended to induce the other to act quickly.

6–039   **Need not be sole inducement.** It is not necessary that the misrepresentation should be the sole cause which induced the representee to make the contract. It is sufficient if it can be shown to have been one of the inducing causes.[81] Thus in *Edgington v. Fitzmaurice*[82] the plaintiff was induced to take debentures in a company partly because of a misrepresentation in the prospectus, but also because of a mistaken belief of his own that the debentures conferred a charge on the company's property. He was held to be entitled to have the contract rescinded, and Cotton L.J. said, "It is not necessary to show that the misstatement was the sole cause of his acting as he did."[83] In other words, where a person seeks to rescind a contract on the ground of misrepresentation, it is not necessary for him to prove that if the misrepresentation had not been made, he would not have made the contract[84]; it is sufficient if there is evidence to show that he was materially influenced by the misrepresentation.

6–040   **Materiality.** It is sometimes said that a misrepresentation will not be effective to ground relief in law unless it was material, in the sense that a reasonable man would have been influenced by it in deciding whether to enter into the contract.[85] It is true that courts have sometimes used language which would support this contention[86] and it is also true that if the representation is not material in this sense, the representee may have considerable difficulty in satisfying the court that he was in fact influenced by it. But there is no clear authority denying relief to a representee who has in fact been influenced by a misrepresentation which would not have influenced a reasonable man, although this may be one reason

---

[79] *Gran Gelato Ltd v. Richcliff (Group) Ltd* [1992] Ch. 560. See further *post*, § 6–074. In *Smith v. Eric S. Bush* [1990] 1 A.C. 831 (where there was no contract between plaintiff and defendant) the plaintiff recovered although she might have had her own survey of the house she bought; but it was not reasonable to expect her to have her own survey of a modest property. Had the property been more expensive it might have been different and a disclaimer of liability might have been reasonable: *ibid.* at 854, 872. See *ante*, § 1–115 and *post*, § 14–088.

[80] *Goff v. Gauthier* (1991) 62 P. & C.R. 388.

[81] *Western Bank of Scotland v. Addie* (1867) L.R. 1 Sc. & Div. 145, 158.

[82] (1885) 29 Ch.D. 459; see also *Arnison v. Smith* (1889) 41 Ch.D. 348.

[83] At 481.

[84] See *Re Leeds Bank* (1887) 56 L.J.Ch. 321. But *cf.* § 6–034, *ante*.

[85] Treitel, *Law of Contract* (9th ed., 1995), p. 313.

[86] *Jennings v. Broughton* (1854) 5 De G.M. & G. 126, 130; *Smith v. Chadwick* (1884) 9 App.Cas. 187. The Marine Insurance Act 1906, s.20(2), incorporates the requirement of materiality, and it has been said that this represents the general law: *Locker & Woolf Ltd v. Western Australian Insurance Co. Ltd* [1936] 1 K.B. 408, 414. But a requirement of materiality is a necessary part of a rule requiring disclosure; it is not a necessary part of a rule affording relief for active misrepresentation. Note the recent definition of materiality in relation to non-disclosure in insurance: *Pan Atlantic Insurance Co. Ltd v. Pine Top Insurance Co. Ltd* [1995] 1 A.C. 501, *post*, § 6–137.

why a mere "puff" or sales talk does not ground relief.[87] It is submitted that, at least where the representor knows or ought to know that the representee is likely to act on the misrepresentation, relief will not be denied merely because a reasonable man would not have been influenced by it.[88] It may be that the position is otherwise where the representor has no reason to know that the representee regards some fact as material which is not material in this objective sense.

The above paragraph was quoted with apparent approval and applied in *Goff* **6–041** *v. Gauthier*.[89] In *Museprime Properties Ltd v. Adhill Properties Ltd*[90] it was said that materiality was really a question of the burden of proof: if the statement would not have influenced a reasonable person, the burden of proving that it did induce the contract will be on the representee, but relief may still be obtained if the burden is discharged. But in neither case was the question whether the substance of the misrepresentation was material, but rather whether in the circumstances the representee was likely to act on it, in other words a question of whether reliance has to be reasonable.[91]

Intention. It is also sometimes said that a misrepresentation will not be **6–042** effective to ground relief unless it was intended to be acted on by the representee.[92] If this means no more than that the representee cannot complain unless the misrepresentation was addressed to him, or to a class of persons of whom he was one, the statement is doubtless correct. This point has been dealt with earlier.[93] But if the statement that the representor must have intended the representee to act on the representation is to be understood literally it seems contrary to authority. In *Cullen v. Thomson*[94] three company directors were responsible for reading a report to a shareholders' meeting which contained a completely fraudulent account of the company's condition. It seems probable that the report was merely intended to conceal the company's financial condition from the shareholders, but the plaintiff, himself a shareholder, purchased additional shares in reliance on this report. It was held that the directors were liable for their fraudulent misrepresentations if they were made "with the real intent to cause the [representee] to act on that representation, or under such circumstances as they must have supposed would probably induce a person in the situation of the [representee] to act upon it."[95] So, also, in *Hedley Byrne & Co. Ltd v. Heller and Partners Ltd*[96] a case of negligent misrepresentation in tort, the plaintiffs asked their bankers to obtain a reference from the defendants, who were also bankers, about a client with whom the plaintiffs were proposing to do business. Although the action failed on other grounds, it was held that it was no defence that the defendants did not know anything about the plaintiffs personally, for it was

---

[87] *Ante*, § 6–004.

[88] It has been so held in Australia: *Nicholas v. Thompson* [1924] V.L.R. 554.

[89] (1991) 62 P. & C.R. 388.

[90] [1990] 2 E.G.L.R. 196, approving a passage to that effect in Goff & Jones, *Law of Restitution* (3rd ed., 1986), p.168; see now 5th ed., 1998, p. 272.

[91] See Treitel, *The Law of Contract* (9th ed., 1995), p.313 and *ante*, § 6–038.

[92] Anson, *Law of Contract* (22nd ed.), p. 211; *cf.* Beatson, *Anson Law of Contact* (27th ed., 1998), p. 233.

[93] *Ante*, § 6–032.

[94] (1862) 6 L.T. 870.

[95] At 874.

[96] [1964] A.C. 465.

enough that they must have realised that the reference was wanted by some customer of the bank who would most probably act upon it. And the Australian High Court has held that a bank giving a reference to another bank must have known that the reference would be passed on to the second bank's client even though it was prefaced with the words "This opinion is confidential and for your private use."[97]

6–043   In *Smith v. Eric S. Bush*[98] a surveyor instructed by a building society to value a house for mortgage purposes knew that the prospective purchaser, who had in effect paid for the valuation, would probably rely on it in deciding whether or not to purchase. The surveyor was liable in tort to the purchaser even though the purchaser's application form for the mortgage contained a disclaimer of responsibility on the part of the surveyor towards the purchaser; the clause was held not to be fair and reasonable under the Unfair Contract Terms Act 1977.[99] It would seem, therefore, that it is sufficient if the representor either intends the representee to act on the statement or at least should have realised that he would probably do so. On the other hand, in *Caparo Industries plc v. Dickman*[1] it was held that there will be no liability in tort for negligent misrepresentation unless the maker of the statement knew that the statement would be communicated to the person relying on it, either as an individual or as a member of a specified class, specifically in connection with a particular transaction or a transaction of a particular kind.[2] In relation to misrepresentation as between contracting parties, the second requirement appears to mean that the misrepresentation must have been made in connection with the contract in respect of which relief is sought, or at least that reliance on the representation in connection with the contract was likely.

3. Damages for Misrepresentation

6–044   **Preliminary.** Damages are always recoverable for a fraudulent misrepresentation.[3] Under section 2(1) of the Misrepresentation Act 1967 damages are now always recoverable for a negligent misrepresentation if they would have been so recoverable in fraud, where the representee enters into a contract with the representor as a result of the misrepresentation.[4] Damages for negligent misrepresentation are also recoverable in some circumstances at common law, quite apart from the Act of 1967.[5] Damages are not generally recoverable for innocent misrepresentation unless the representation is, or becomes, a contractual term, but there are a number of important exceptions to this principle.[6]

---

[97] *Commercial Banking Co. of Sydney Ltd v. R.H. Brown & Co.* (1972) 126 C.L.R. 13. See also *Yianni v. Edwin Evans & Sons* [1982] Q.B. 438 and *supra*, § 6–032.

[98] [1990] 1 A.C. 831.

[99] s.2(2); see *post*, § 14–068.

[1] [1990] 2 A.C. 605.

[2] Compare *Morgan Crucible Co. plc v. Hill Samuel Bank Ltd* [1991] Ch. 295; *Galoo Ltd (in liquidation) v. Bright Grahame Murray* [1994] 1 W.L.R. 1360.

[3] *Post*, §§ 6–045—6–066.

[4] *Post*, §§ 6–068—6–077. Whether it is strictly correct to refer to the statutory liability as a liability for negligent misrepresentation may be open to argument, see *post*, § 6–068, n. 76.

[5] *Post*, §§ 6–078—6–089.

[6] *Post*, §§ 6–093—6–100.

(a) *Fraudulent Misrepresentation*

Claims for damages for fraud. Where a person has been induced to enter **6–045** into a contract as a result of a fraudulent misrepresentation by the other contracting party, he may rescind the contract, or claim damages, or both.[7] Rescission is dealt with in the next section,[8] but it should be noted here that, as a result of the Misrepresentation Act 1967, claims for damages by a person who has been induced to enter into a contract by the misrepresentation of another party thereto may now be based either on fraud or on negligence. As will be seen in detail below,[9] section 2(1) of this Act allows a person who has been induced to enter into a contract by a misrepresentation to make a claim for damages as of right, as though the representation had been fraudulent, unless the representor "proves that he had reasonable ground to believe and did believe up to the time the contract was made that the facts represented were true." In an action under this subsection, it is for the representor to disprove negligence, whereas in an action in fraud it is for the representee affirmatively to prove the fraud—and the burden is no light one.[10] However, claims for damages against a representor who does not subsequently enter into a contract with the representee may have to be brought in fraud, for although even here negligence may sometimes suffice, it will not always do so.[11] Further, as will be seen below, the Misrepresentation Act has created a new distinction of some importance between fraudulent and other misrepresentations in connection with rescission.[12]

Definition of fraud. The common law relating to fraud was established by the **6–046** House of Lords in *Derry v. Peek*.[13] It was there decided that in order for fraud to be established, it is necessary to prove the absence of an honest belief in the truth of that which has been stated; in the words of Lord Herschell, "fraud is proved when it is shown that a false representation has been made (1) knowingly, or (2) without belief in its truth, or (3) recklessly, careless whether it be true or false."[14] The converse of this is that however negligent a person may be, he cannot be liable for fraud, provided that his belief is honest; mere carelessness is not sufficient, although gross carelessness may justify an inference that he was not honest.

Absence of honest belief. That the claimant who alleges fraud must prove the **6–047** absence of an honest belief is demonstrated by *Derry v. Peek* itself. A company issued a prospectus stating that it was entitled to use steam power to run trams; the respondents obtained shares on the strength of this representation, which was in fact false, although at the time the company had reason to believe that permission would be granted by the Board of Trade as a matter of course. Permission to use steam power was, however, not granted and the company was wound up; in an action for deceit the House of Lords held that the directors were

---

[7] *Archer v. Brown* [1985] Q.B. 401.
[8] *Post*, §§ 6–101—6–128.
[9] *Post*, §§ 6–068 *et seq.*
[10] Strictly, the burden is the same as that in other civil proceedings, namely, proof on the balance of probabilities (*Hornal v. Neuberger Properties Ltd* [1957] 1 Q.B. 247), but it is well known that the burden of proof of fraud is not easily discharged in practice.
[11] *Post*, § 6–087.
[12] *Post*, § 6–105.
[13] (1889) 14 App.Cas. 337.
[14] At 374.

not liable in damages for fraudulent misrepresentation. The decisive factor, in Lord Herschell's words, was that "they honestly believed that what they asserted was true."[15]

6–048 **Defendant's knowledge of falsity of statement.** The requirement of proof of the absence of honest belief does not, however, mean that the claimant must prove the defendant's knowledge of the falsity of the statement. It is enough to establish that the latter suspected that his statement might be inaccurate, or that he neglected to inquire into its accuracy, without proving that he actually knew that it was false. Thus where directors issued a prospectus setting out the advantages of working a particular mine, without having ascertained the truth of these representations, they were held to have committed a fraud.[16] Lord Cairns expressed the principle as follows: "If persons take upon themselves to make assertions as to which they are ignorant whether they are true or untrue, they must, in a civil point of view, be held as responsible as if they had asserted that which they know to be untrue."[17]

6–049 **Motive irrelevant.** Further, it is not necessary to establish that the defendant's motive was dishonest.[18]

6–050 **Ambiguity.** If the statement is ambiguous, the representee must first prove that he understood the statement in a sense in which it is in fact false.[19] If the representor intended the statement to be understood in that sense, he will be guilty of fraud. But a person who makes a statement honestly believing it to be true in the sense which he understands it to bear is not guilty of fraud merely because the representee understands it in a different sense which is false to the knowledge of the representor.[20] And this is still the case even though the court may agree that the sense in which the representee understands the statement is the meaning which, on its true construction, it ought to bear.[21] To hold a person guilty of fraud it must be shown that he intended, or at least was willing, that the representation should be understood in a sense which is false.[22]

6–051 **Principal and agent.** Much difficulty has arisen in dealing with cases where responsibility for a statement is divided between principal and agent, or between several agents of one principal. It has been held that the law does not recognise any conception of "composite fraud," *i.e.* an action in fraud will not lie where a statement is made by an agent who honestly believes it to be true, merely because the principal, or another agent, knew the statement to be false.[23] But a principal is vicariously liable for the fraud of an agent, so that if an agent makes a

---

[15] At 379.

[16] *Reese River Silver Mining Co. Ltd v. Smith* (1869) L.R. 4 H.L. 64. See also *Taylor v. Ashton* (1843) 11 M. & W. 401, 415; *Evans v. Edmonds* (1853) 13 C.B. 777, 786.

[17] (1869) L.R. 4 H.L. 64, 79–80.

[18] See *Polhill v. Walter* (1832) 3 B. & Ad. 114; *Denton v. G.N. Ry.* (1856) 5 E. & B. 860; *Brown Jenkinson & Co. Ltd v. Percy Dalton (London) Ltd* [1957] 2 Q.B. 621; *Standard Chartered Bank v. Pakistan National Shipping Corp.* [1995] 2 Lloyd's Rep. 365.

[19] *Smith v. Chadwick* (1884) 9 App.Cas. 187.

[20] *Akerhielm v. De Mare* [1959] A.C. 789; *John McGrath Motors (Canberra) Pty Ltd v. Applebee* (1964) 110 C.L.R. 656.

[21] *Akerhielm v. De Mare, supra.*

[22] *Gross v. Lewis Hillman Ltd* [1970] Ch. 445.

[23] *Cornfoot v. Fowke* (1840) 6 M. & W. 358; *Armstrong v. Strain* [1952] 1 K.B. 232.

statement in the scope of his authority, and the agent is himself fraudulent, the principal will be liable.[24] And if one agent makes a fraudulent statement to another agent, intending the latter to pass the statement on to a third party, and this is done, the principal will again be liable; for in these circumstances, the first agent is guilty of the complete tort of fraudulent misrepresentation, the second agent being his innocent agent.[25] Again, if one agent makes a statement honestly believing it to be true, but another agent or the principal himself knows that it is not true, knows that the statement will be or has been made, and deliberately abstains from intervening, the principal will be liable.[26] In these circumstances the party with the guilty knowledge can himself be treated as being guilty of fraud.

Measure of damages for fraudulent misrepresentation. The proper measure of damages for fraudulent misrepresentation was discussed by the Court of Appeal in *Doyle v. Olby (Ironmongers) Ltd.*[27] It was here held that damages for fraud were not the same as damages for breach of contract in that they were not designed to place the innocent party in the position he would have been in if the representation had been true; but to put him in the position he would have been in if the representation had not been made. The presumption seems to be that if the misrepresentation had not been made, the claimant would not have entered into the contract.[28] So the plaintiff ought to be awarded such damages as will put him back in the financial position he was in before the contract was made. This means that where a person is induced by fraud to buy some property, the proper measure of damages is prima facie the difference between the price paid and the fair value of the property.[29] In *Doyle v. Olby (Ironmongers) Ltd*, it was held that in cases of fraud the plaintiff was entitled to damages for any such loss which flowed from the defendants' fraud, even if the loss could not have been foreseen by the latter. Thus the claimant may recover not only the difference between the price paid and the value of what he received[30] but also expenditure wasted in reliance on the contract and compensation for other opportunities passed over in reliance on it.   6–052

In *Smith New Court Securities Ltd v. Scrimgeour Vickers (Asset Management) Ltd*[31] Lord Browne-Wilkinson described *Doyle v. Olby (Ironmongers) Ltd* as re-stating the law correctly. He stated the principles applicable in assessing damages where a party has been induced by a fraudulent misrepresentation to buy property as follows: 6–053

---

[24] *Lloyd v. Grace, Smith & Co.* [1912] A.C. 716; *Briess v. Woolley* [1954] A.C. 333.

[25] *London County Freehold & Leasehold Properties Ltd v. Berkeley Property & Investment Co. Ltd* [1936] 2 All E.R. 1039, as explained in *Armstrong v. Strain, supra.*

[26] *Ludgater v. Love* (1881) 44 L.T. 694; *Occidental Worldwide Investment Corpn. v. Skibs A/S Avanti* [1976] 1 Lloyd's Rep. 293, 320–321 (where this sentence in the text was cited with approval).

[27] [1969] 2 Q.B. 158, noted (1969) in 32 M.L.R. 556; see also *New Zealand Refrigerating Co. v. Scott* [1969] N.Z.L.R. 30; *Parma v. G. & S. Properties* (1969) 5 D.L.R. (3d) 315.

[28] See *Esso Petroleum Ltd v. Mardon* [1976] Q.B. 801, 820, 828, 833.

[29] *Newark Engineering (N.Z.) Ltd v. Jenkin* [1980] N.Z.L.R. 504; *Smith Kline & French Laboratories Ltd v. Long* [1989] 1 W.L.R. 1.

[30] When there is no evidence as to values, the cost of making good the representation may be taken to represent the difference in value: *Jacovides v. Constantinou, The Times,* October 27, 1986.

[31] [1997] A.C. 254, 263.

"(1)   The defendant is bound to make reparation for all the damage directly flowing from the transaction;

(2)   although such damage need not have been foreseeable, it must have been directly caused by the transaction;

(3)   in assessing such damage, the plaintiff is entitled to recover by way of damages the full price paid by him, but he must give credit for any benefits which he has received as a result of the transaction;

(4)   as a general rule, the benefits received by him include the market value of the property acquired at the date of the transaction; but such general rule is not to be inflexibly applied where to do so would prevent him obtaining full compensation for the wrong suffered;

(5)   although the circumstances in which the general rule should not apply cannot be comprehensively stated, it will normally not apply where either (a) the misrepresentation has continued to operate after the date of the acquisition of the asset so as to induce the plaintiff to retain the asset or (b) the circumstances of the case are such that the plaintiff is, by reason of the fraud, locked into the property;

(6)   in addition, the plaintiff is entitled to recover consequential losses caused by the transaction;

(7)   the plaintiff must take all reasonable steps to mitigate his loss once he has discovered the fraud." [32]

6–054   **Lost opportunity but not loss of bargain.** The points that damages for fraud will not compensate the claimant for loss of bargain but may cover loss caused by passing up other profitable opportunities are well illustrated by *East v. Maurer.*[33] The plaintiffs bought a hairdressing business in reliance on a false representation that the defendant had no intention of working regularly at a second hairdressing business he owned in the same town. In fact he continued to work at the second business and the plaintiffs were forced to resell the business they had bought at a substantial loss. They were awarded damages for the difference between the price they had paid and the price they received on resale, plus expenditure wasted in attempting to improve the business and in other ways. They were also awarded the sum they could have expected to make as profit had they bought another similar business in the same area.[34] However they were not entitled to the higher amount they might have earned from the actual business bought had the defendant kept to his stated intention; he had not warranted that they would keep all his old customers or that he would not compete. Thus in many cases the measure of damages for breach of contract will be higher, as it

---

[32] [1997] A.C. 254, 267. Lord Mustill said that the judgment of Lord Denning in *Doyle v. Olby (Ironmongers) Ltd* was in some respects too broad-brush; the case had not been fully argued (apparently a reference to the fact mentioned by Lord Browne-Wilkinson that certain nineteenth century cases on the date of valuation had not been cited). He considered that, in future, courts would do well to be guided by Lord Browne-Wilkinson's seven propositions: *ibid.* at 269. On the duty to mitigate, see *Standard Chartered Bank v. Pakistan National Shipping Corp.* [1999] 1 All E.R. (Comm.) 417.

[33] [1991] 1 W.L.R. 461. Similar damages for wasted expenditure and loss of other opportunities were awarded in *Esso Petroleum Ltd v. Mardon* [1976] Q.B. 801. But compare *Davis v. Churchward*, unreported, May 6, 1993, noted in (1994) 110 L.Q.R. 35. See also *Smith Kline & French Laboratories Ltd v. Long* [1989] 1 W.L.R. 1, in which sellers, who had been tricked into supplying goods to a buyer who was unable to pay, recovered the normal wholesale price of the goods, not just the cost of producing them.

[34] The award in *East v. Maurer* based on a hypothetical profitable business in which the plaintiff would have engaged but for the deceit has been described by Lord Steyn as "classic consequential loss": *Smith New Court Securities Ltd v. Scrimgeour Vickers (Asset Management) Ltd* [1997] A.C. 254, 282.

will include the profit that would have been made on the contract in question had the representation been true. If as a result of a fraudulent misrepresentation the claimant has bought a property, but the property appears to be worth the price paid for it and there is no wasted expenditure or loss of a more valuable opportunity, the claimant damages according to the tort measure would appear to be nil.[35]

Property worth less than paid for it. While the claimant in an action for 6–055 fraud cannot claim to be put into the position he would have been in if the fact represented were true, a claimant who has made a bad bargain, in the sense that even if what he had been told were true, at the time the contract is made the property he is induced to buy would have been worth less than he has agreed to pay for it, he will be better off under the tortious measure than the contractual one.[36]

Subsequent falls in value of property. As Lord Browne-Wilkinson's fourth 6–056 proposition indicates, the damages are normally to be calculated according to the difference between the contract price and the value of the property at the time of the contract.[37] This seems to follow from the rule that the loss must flow directly from the transaction.[38] But this is only a prima facie rule; as Lord Steyn put it,[39] the date of transaction rule is simply a second-order rule applicable only if the valuation method is followed, and the court is entitled to assess the loss flowing directly from the fraud without any reference to the date of the transaction or indeed any particular date. In some situations, the claimant may recover the difference between the contract price and the value of the property at a later date. This is so when the fall in value is due to the discovery of the defendant's fraud, which has also deceived others in the market.[40] However, it may also apply even if the reduction of value is not the result of the fraud.

"Already flawed assets." One such case is where, as the result of the fraud, 6–057 the claimant has bought an "already flawed asset", the value of which falls when the flaw is discovered, but the fraud did not relate to the flaw. In *Smith New Court Securities Ltd v. Scrimgeour Vickers (Asset Management) Ltd*,[41] SNC had bought

---

[35] In the United States, some jurisdictions allow recovery of damages for loss of bargain in actions for fraud, *e.g. Beardmore v. T.D. Burgess Co.* 226 A. 2d 329 (1967); *cf. Uncle Ben's Tartan Holdings Ltd v. North West Sport Enterprises Ltd* (1974) 46 D.L.R. (3d) 280. Loss of bargain damages did appear to be recoverable in English law where there had been fraud by a vendor of land who knew that he had no good title and would be unable to make one, with the result that the rule in *Bain v. Fothergill* (1874) L.R. 7 H.L. 158, *post* § 27–075 did not apply; but this was not a true exception: the fraud simply lifted a restriction on recovery of damages for breach of contract that would otherwise apply. Mere negligence was not enough: see the disapproval of *Watts v. Spence* [1976] Ch. 165 in *Sharneyford Supplies Ltd v. Edge* at first instance [1986] Ch. 128, 149 and by Balcombe L.J. in the Court of Appeal [1987] Ch. 305, 323. In any event the rule has been abolished as regards all contracts made after September 27, 1989.

[36] *Smith New Court Securities Ltd v. Scrimgeour Vickers (Asset Management) Ltd* [1997] A.C. 254, 281–282, *per* Lord Steyn, approving the statement by Treitel (1969) 32 M.L.R. 558–559.

[37] See the speech of Lord Steyn in *Smith New Court Securities Ltd v. Scrimgeour Vickers (Asset Management) Ltd* [1997] A.C. 254, 284; *McGregor on Damages* (16th ed., 1997) § 1971.

[38] See the speech of Lord Steyn at 281–284.

[39] [1997] A.C. 254, 284.

[40] [1997] A.C. 254, 262 and 265; *McGregor on Damages* (16th ed., 1997) § 1972. A rather similar explanation may underlie *Naughton v. O'Callaghan* [1990] 3 All E.R. 191, a case under Misrepresentation Act, s.2(1), in which the purchaser did not realise that the pedigree of the horse had been misrepresented until it had been very unsuccessful, by which time its value had fallen. See *McGregor on Damages* (16th ed., 1997) § 2008.

[41] [1997] A.C. 254.

shares in Ferranti as the result of fraudulent misrepresentations by the defendants. SNC intended to keep the shares for a period of time. Their value fell drastically when it was discovered that Ferranti had been the victim of another fraud by a third party. The House of Lords, reversing the Court of Appeal,[42] held that SNC were not limited to recovering the difference between the contract price and the market value of the shares at the date of the transaction; they could recover the difference between the contract price and the prices obtained for the shares when they were sold after the discovery of the fraud. As stated in the fourth and fifth propositions of Lord Browne-Wilkinson quoted above (see § 6–053), the date of transaction rule will not be applied if it would prevent the claimant obtaining full compensation, for example if the claimant is locked into the transaction. In this case, as SNC had intended to keep the shares and it was not commercially feasible to re-sell them immediately, it was locked into the property.

6–058   It is not wholly clear whether the purchaser who has bought a "flawed asset", which falls in value after the date of the transaction because the flaw is discovered, can recover for this further loss if it was not clearly the purchaser's purpose to retain the property. In *Twycross v. Grant*,[43] Cockburn C.J. gave the example of a person who is induced by fraud to buy a racehorse. If the horse has already contracted some disease from which it dies when he gets it home, the buyer may recover the entire price paid. In the *Smith New Court Securities* case Lord Steyn refers to this example with apparent approval.[44] It may suffice that it was to be expected that the claimant would keep the property for at least the time that it took the flaw to emerge.

6–059   **Loss caused by fall in market.** Secondly, as the result of the fraud, the claimant may have acquired a property which, had it known the truth, it would not have acquired, and that property may have fallen because of a subsequent fall in the general value of property of the kind in question. It is possible that in an appropriate case, damages for fraud may include such losses. In *South Australia Asset Management Corp. v. York Montague Ltd*[45] the House of Lords held that in a case of negligent valuation, recovery of such losses may be "capped", but it left open the question in cases of fraud.[46] In *Downs v. Chappell*[47] the plaintiffs had bought a business as the result of the defendant's fraudulent statements; they recovered the difference between the price paid and the value of the business when the fraud was discovered, even though the difference may have been increased by a general fall in property prices. In that case, Hobhouse L.J. said that only losses flowing from the tort would be recoverable, and as a means of testing whether the loss was caused by the tort and of preventing over-compensation, proposed comparing "the loss to consequent upon entering the transaction that which what would have been the position had the represented, or supposed, state of affairs actually existed." This last aspect of the case was disapproved by the House of Lords in *Smith New Court Securities Ltd v. Scrimgeour Vickers (Asset Management) Ltd.*[48] Thus it appears that in a fraud

---

[42] [1994] 1 W.L.R. 1271.
[43] (1877) 2 C.P.D. 469, 544–545.
[44] [1997] A.C. 254, 279.
[45] [1997] A.C. 191. See *post*, §§ 27–078—27–080.
[46] At 215.
[47] [1997] 1 W.L.R. 426.
[48] [1997] A.C. 254.

case the claimant can recover the full fall in value of the property, at least up to the date of discovery of the fraud, where the claimant was "locked into the transaction." Lord Steyn justified a special rule for cases of deceit by considerations of morality and deterrence.[49]

Other cases. Where the asset bought is not "already flawed" and the claimant **6–060** is not locked into the transaction, nor is the fraud continuing to operate to induce him to retain the property (so that Lord Browne-Wilkinson's fifth proposition does not apply), it appears that the damages will still be assessed by the value of the property at the date of the transaction. In *Twycross v. Grant*,[50] Cockburn C.J. also gave the example of a person who is induced by fraud to buy a racehorse which subsequently catches a disease and dies; the buyer may only recover the difference between the price paid and the real value at the time of the transaction. In *Smith New Court Securities Ltd v. Scrimgeour Vickers (Asset Management) Ltd* Lord Steyn gave this as an example of a case in which there would not be a sufficient causal link between the fraud and the loss.[51] But it seems that the claimant will be treated as locked into the transaction where the other party knew that the claimant was purchasing the property for a purpose that would require him to retain it.

Claimant would have entered another losing transaction. As mentioned **6–061** earlier, in fraud cases it is presumed that had it not been for the fraud, the claimant would not have entered the contract.[52] In *Downs v. Chappell*[53] it was said that a party who has been induced to enter a contract by fraud and who seeks damages need not show that, but for the misrepresentation, he would not have entered the transaction. He need only show that he was induced to enter the contract by a material misrepresentation and the loss that flowed from entering it. Where the misrepresentee claims to rescind the contract, it is irrelevant that he might have entered a contract with the misrepresentor even if the misrepresentation had not been made: it need only have been one of the factors which influenced him.[54] But what the misrepresentee would have done may be relevant to a claim for damages, since he must show a causal connection between the misrepresentation and the loss claimed. Thus in *South Australia Asset Management Corp. v. York Montague Ltd* Lord Hoffman pointed out that it might be shown that, had the valuer not been negligent, the lender would have lent a lesser amount to the same borrower on the same security, or "would have used his money in some altogether different, but equally disastrous venture".[55] But it seems that this may not apply in cases of fraud. Here, according to Lord Steyn's speech in the *Smith New Court Securities* case, the rules of causation are applied

---

[49] At 280. *McGregor on Damages* (16th ed., 1997), § 1975 appears to take the view that the plaintiff may only be compensated for a subsequent fall in value when the asset was already flawed.

[50] See *supra*, n. 43.

[51] [1997] A.C. 254, 285.

[52] See *ante*, § 6–034, n. 67.

[53] [1997] 1 W.L.R. 426.

[54] See § 6–039, *ante*.

[55] [1997] A.C. 191, 218. The decision in *Downs v. Chappell* [1997] 1 W.L.R. 426, as far as the vendor's accountants were concerned, may have been interpreted in *Bristol and West Building Society v. Mothew* [1998] Ch. 1 as applying the same measure in cases of negligence, but Hobhouse L.J., who delivered the only full judgment in *Downs*, has said that this is not an accurate account of the decision: *Swindle v. Harrison* [1997] 4 All E.R. 705, 728.

differently[56] and "it is not necessary for the judge to embark on a hypothetical reconstruction of what the parties would have agreed had the deceit not occurred."[57]

6–062   **Mitigation.** Finally it should be noted that Lord Browne-Wilkinson's final proposition is that once the fraud is discovered, the plaintiff must take all reasonable steps to mitigate his loss.[58]

6–063   **No account of profits.** The victim of fraud may not obtain an account of profits made by the fraudulent party, at least where the victim has affirmed the contract and has suffered no loss.[59]

6–064   **Exemplary damages.** It is not yet wholly clear if exemplary damages can be awarded for fraud.[60] However this now seems very unlikely. Even if it could be brought within the second of Lord Devlin's three categories in *Rookes v. Barnard*,[61] the interpretation of and explanation of those categories by the House of Lords in *Cassell & Co. Ltd v. Broome*[62] and by the Court of Appeal in *AB v. South West Water Services Ltd*[63] require that for exemplary damages to be awarded the tort must be one in respect of which such an award had been made prior to 1964. In *Cassell & Co. Ltd v. Broome*, Lord Hailsham L.C. gave deceit as a specific example of an action in which there was no previous authority for the award of exemplary or aggravated damages and to which Lord Devlin cannot have intended that such damages should be extended.[64] Even if it is still open to a court to hold that exemplary damages may be awarded in an action for deceit (even if the defendant has not succeeded in making any profit from his deceit) it is wrong to do so where the defendant has already been convicted and imprisoned for the same fraud.[65] This would infringe the basic principle that a man should not be punished twice for the same offence. But damages for worry and inconvenience,[66] and for mental and physical suffering[67] have been awarded in actions based on fraud.

6–065   **Contributory negligence.** Contributory negligence is not a defence to an action of deceit and the Law Reform (Contributory Negligence) Act 1945[68] does not apply.[69]

---

[56] [1997] A.C. 254, 284–285.

[57] *ibid.*, 283. But a different view is taken by *McGregor on Damages* (16th ed., 1997), § 1970 n. 36.

[58] For an application of the mitigation rule in a fraud case see *Downs v. Chappell* [1997] 1 W.L.R. 426.

[59] *Halifax B.S. v. Thomas* [1996] Ch. 217; *post,* § 30–092.

[60] See *Mafo v. Adams* [1970] 1 Q.B. 548, *Cassell & Co. Ltd v. Broome* [1972] A.C. 1027 and *Archer v. Brown* [1985] 1 Q.B. 401, 418–421.

[61] [1964] A.C. 1129.

[62] *Supra; Mafo v. Adams* was criticised at [1972] A.C. 1076.

[63] [1993] Q.B. 507.

[64] [1972] A.C. 1027, 1076. See also Law Commission, *Aggravated, Exemplary and Restitutionary Damages* (Report No. 247, HC 346, 1997), para. 4.25.

[65] *Archer v. Brown* [1985] Q.B. 401.

[66] *McNally v. Welltrade International Ltd* [1978] I.R.L.R. 497; *Jones v. Emerton-Court* [1983] C.L.Y. 982.

[67] *Shelley v. Paddock* [1980] Q.B. 348; *Archer v. Brown* [1985] Q.B. 401.

[68] See *post,* § 6–074.

[69] *Alliance and Leicester Building Society v. Edgestop Ltd* [1993] 1 W.L.R. 1462; see also *Corporation Nacional del Cobre de Chile v. Sogemin Metals Ltd* [1997] 2 All E.R. 917, 921–923.

Illegality. It has been held that payments made under a contract which was illegal (though not to the knowledge of the plaintiff) could be recovered in an action of fraud,[70] though the contract itself could not be sued upon because of the illegality. Further, damages for fraud may be recovered even where the contract was known by the plaintiffs to be illegal, if the fraud and the illegality were quite unconnected.[71] In *Hughes v. Clewley, The Siben (No. 2)*[72] the misrepresentee was permitted to claim damages for fraud although part of the business transferred to him was used for immoral purposes, as it was said that he did not have to rely on the illegal contract. Moreover, in calculating the value of what he had received for the purposes of damages, the value of this part of the business was disregarded.

6–066

(b) *Negligent Misrepresentation*

Preliminary. A negligent misrepresentation is one which is made carelessly, or without reasonable grounds for believing it to be true. Apart from statute, a misrepresentation could not be regarded as negligent unless the representor owed a duty to be careful to the representee, and the law relating to the existence of such a duty of care has undergone some quite remarkable fluctuations since the case of *Derry v. Peek*.[73] That case was at one time thought to lay down that there could never be a duty to take care in the making of statements unless the duty arose out of a contract itself, but the House of Lords has rejected this view in two leading cases in this country. In *Nocton v. Ashburton*[74] it was decided that such a duty to take care could arise out of a fiduciary relationship, and in *Hedley Byrne & Co. Ltd v. Heller and Partners Ltd*[75] the law was greatly widened by the decision that a duty to take care in making statements could arise out of many other "special relationships." But the enactment of the Misrepresentation Act 1967 has somewhat reduced the importance of these cases so far as the law of contract is concerned.

6–067

Misrepresentation Act, s.2(1). This subsection reads as follows:

6–068

"Where a person has entered into a contract after a misrepresentation has been made to him by another party thereto and as a result thereof he has suffered loss, then, if the person making the misrepresentation would be liable to damages in respect thereof had the misrepresentation been made fraudulently, that person shall be so liable notwith-standing that the misrepresentation was not made fraudulently, unless he proves that he had reasonable ground to believe and did believe up to the time the contract was made that the facts represented were true."

Thus, where a person is induced to enter into a contract as a result of a misrepresentation, this subsection does away with the need to establish any duty of care as between the representor and the representee. In any circumstances in which this section applies, the representee will have an action for damages under the Act. In *Howard Marine and Dredging Co. Ltd v. A. Ogden & Sons (Excavations) Ltd*[76] the plaintiffs misrepresented to the defendants the carrying capacity

---

[70] *ibid.*
[71] *Saunders v. Edwards* [1987] 1 W.L.R. 1116.
[72] [1996] 1 Lloyd's Rep. 35.
[73] (1889) 14 App.Cas. 337; *ante*, §§ 6–046—6–048.
[74] [1914] A.C. 932.
[75] [1964] A.C. 465.
[76] [1978] Q.B. 574, noted (1978) 94 L.Q.R. 334.

of two barges which the defendants wished to hire for carrying large quantities of clay out to sea and then dumping. The defendants entered into the contract in reliance on this misrepresentation and used the barges for some time after which they discovered the true facts and returned the barges. It was said by a majority of the Court of Appeal that the plaintiffs were probably not under a duty of care at common law, but a differently-constituted majority held that the defendants were entitled to damages for a breach of section 2(1) of the 1967 Act. It was also stressed that the question was, strictly speaking, not one of negligence, but that the Act imposed an absolute obligation not to state facts which the representor cannot prove he had reasonable grounds to believe. No doubt it is correct to say that it is not a question of negligence, as at common law, where a duty of care is in issue; and it is possible that circumstances may exist in which a person may make a statement without having reasonable ground to believe it, yet in which it would be held that he was not (having regard to all the circumstances) negligent. Nevertheless, for most practical purposes it will usually be correct to equate liability under section 2(1) of the Act with liability for negligence, and the statutory liability is referred to in this chapter, for the sake of convenience, as a liability for negligence.

6–069 **Effect of section 2(1).** It will be noted that the gist of the subsection is to confer a right to damages for negligent misrepresentation in circumstances in which such a right would exist if the misrepresentation has been fraudulent. A number of consequences seem to follow from this. First, the rules relating to what constitutes a misrepresentation,[77] and the principle that the representation must have been one of the inducements influencing the mind of the representee,[78] will apply to an action under the subsection as they apply to an action in fraud. Secondly, it is now settled that the measure of damages under the subsection is the same as the measure of damages for fraud.[79] This follows from the wording of the subsection.[80] In any event it would be highly anomalous if the measure of damages for negligent misrepresentation under the Act were different from the normal measure of damages for common law negligent misrepresentation. This means that generally damages will be awarded to put the representee in the position in which he would have been if he had never entered into the contract, and not to put him in the position in which he would have been if the misrepresentation had been true.[81]

6–070 **Application of rules on damages for fraud.** It has been shown that damages for fraud are governed by somewhat different rules to damages for negligent

---

[77] *Ante,* §§ 6–004 *et seq.*

[78] *Ante,* §§ 6–034 *et seq.* See the *Howard Marine* case, *supra.*

[79] *Royscott Trust Ltd v. Rogerson* [1991] 2 Q.B. 297. See also *F. & H. Entertainments Ltd v. Leisure Enterprises Ltd* (1976) 120 S.J. 331; *André & Cie SA v. Ets Michel Blanc & Fils* [1977] 2 Lloyd's Rep. 166; *McNally v. Welltrade International Ltd* [1978] I.R.L.R. 497; *Chesnau v. Interhomes* (1983) 134 New.L.J. 341; *Heineman v. Cooper* (1987) 19 H.L.R. 262 (apparently an action under s.2(1)); *Cooper v. Tamms* [1988] 1 E.G.L.R. 257.

[80] *Royscott Trust Ltd v. Rogerson, supra.* Note that actual fraud still has to be proved if it becomes relevant for other purposes: *Garden Neptune Shipping Ltd v. Occidental World Wide Investment Ltd* [1990] 1 Lloyd's Rep. 330.

[81] But see *Jarvis v. Swan Tours Ltd* [1973] Q.B. 233, 237. See also *Davis & Co. (Wines) Ltd v. Afa-Minerva (E.M.I.) Ltd* [1974] 2 Lloyd's Rep. 27; *Esso Petroleum Co. Ltd v. Mardon* [1976] Q.B. 801. *Watts v. Spence* [1976] Ch. 165, which suggested that damages under s.2(1) might be on a loss of bargain basis, has been disapproved: see *ante,* n. 35.

misrepresentation at common law: losses may be recoverable even though they were not of a foreseeable kind[82] and, in some circumstances, consequential losses may include compensation for falls in the value of the property acquired which were unrelated to the fraudulent statement.[83] It is not clear whether these rules, which appear to be justified by considerations of morality and deterrence,[84] are applicable to damages claimed under s.2(1). In the 26th edition of this work it was suggested[85] that the first rule did not apply, but this was rejected by the Court of Appeal in *Royscot Trust Ltd v. Rogerson*[86] on the ground that this interpretation "is to ignore the plain words of the subsection".[87] In *Smith New Court Securities Ltd v. Scrimgeour Vickers (Asset Management) Ltd*[88] both Lords Browne-Wilkinson and Steyn declined to comment on the correctness of the *Royscot* case. If the interpretation of section 2(1) taken in *Royscot* is correct, however, it would presumably follow that damages under section 2(1) can also include compensation for loss of value caused by a fall in the market, at least where the claimant has acquired an "already flawed asset",[89] and that contributory negligence will not necessarily be a defence or lead to a reduction in the claimant's damages.[90]

Fraud rules on knowledge. Further, a possible consequence of the decision in *Royscot Trust Ltd v. Rogerson*[91] is that the difficulties which arise in cases of fraud where the misrepresentation is made by one person, but the guilty knowledge is that of another, seem to apply equally to an action for negligence under the subsection.[92] If, for example, the representee contracts with a company as a result of a misrepresentation made to him by one of the company's employees or agents, and that employee or agent did have reasonable grounds for believing the statement to be true, the representee will have no action under the subsection merely because another employee or agent of the company knew that the representation was untrue, or knew that there were no reasonable grounds for believing it to be true.[93] However, in practice this type of case may not prove so troublesome in cases of negligence as it has been in cases of fraud. Although a court will not impute fraud to an employee or agent merely because his principal (or another employee or agent) knows that the statement he has made is untrue, a court might be much more ready to hold that the person making the statement in these circumstances did not have reasonable grounds for believing that the facts stated were true; and it would also be possible to find negligence at common law as a result of a failure of one employee to inform another of the true facts.[94]

6–071

---

[82] *Ante*, § 6–052.

[83] *Ante*, §§ 6–056—6–060.

[84] See the words of Lord Steyn in *Smith New Court Securities Ltd v. Scrimgeour Vickers (Asset Management) Ltd* [1997] A.C. 254, 280, referred to earlier, § 6–059.

[85] 26th ed., Chap. 6, § 439, referring to Treitel, *Law of Contract* (7th ed.), p. 278.

[86] [1991] 2 Q.B. 297. See the criticisms of that case in (1991) 107 L.Q.R. 547.

[87] [1991] 2 Q.B. 297 at 307 and 309.

[88] [1997] A.C. 254 at 267 and 283.

[89] *Ante*, §§ 6–056—6–060.

[90] See *ante*, § 6–065 and *post*, § 6–074.

[91] *Supra*.

[92] *Ante*, § 6–051.

[93] *cf. Armstrong v. Strain* [1952] 1 K.B. 232.

[94] See, *e.g. W.B. Anderson & Sons Ltd v. Rhodes (Liverpool) Ltd* [1967] 2 All E.R. 850.

Damages have been awarded under this subsection against a vendor of land because of the misrepresentations of his estate agent.[95]

6–072 **Rescission and damages.** There is nothing in the subsection to prevent the representee from both rescinding the contract and claiming damages,[96] though (as will be seen below)[97] the court now has a discretion to refuse to allow rescission, except in cases of fraud, under section 2(2) of the Act. If the representee does rescind he was, even before the passing of the Act, entitled to an "indemnity"[98] against liabilities incurred as a result of the contract, and it seems clear that he cannot claim both an indemnity and damages under section 2(1) in respect of the same loss.

6–073 The section does not give rise to liability in damages for failure to disclose, even when there is a duty to disclose material facts.[99] Silence as to material facts which should be disclosed is not an implicit representation that there is nothing to be disclosed, nor does it constitute a "misrepresentation made" within section 2(1).[1]

6–074 **Contributory negligence.** It was held in *Gran Gelato Ltd v. Richcliff (Group) Ltd*[2] that damages for negligent misrepresentation under section 2(1) of the Misrepresentation Act 1967 may be reduced under section 1 of the Law Reform (Contributory Negligence) Act 1945[3] if the loss was partly the fault of the representee. Liability under section 2(1) applies unless the representor "had reasonable grounds to believe and did believe . . . that the facts represented were true" and thus is "essentially founded on negligence." However it would not be just and equitable to reduce the damages when the representor had intended, or should be taken as having intended, that the representee should act in reliance on the answers which had been given to his questions.[4] The decision was based on the fact that there was concurrent liability under section 2(1) and in tort for negligent misrepresentation under the principle of *Hedley Byrne & Co. Ltd v. Heller & Partners Ltd.*[5] It may happen that a defendant is liable under s.2(1) without being concurrently liable in tort for negligent misrepresentation, for instance because the court considers that there was on the facts no undertaking of responsibility towards the claimant.[6] In such a case it seems that the claimant's damages could not be reduced on account of any contributory negligence. This is because section 2(1) makes the misrepresentor who cannot prove reasonable grounds liable as if the statement had been fraudulent. Section 1(1) of the Law Reform (Contributory Negligence) Act 1945 applies "When any person suffers damage as the result partly of his own fault and partly of the fault of any other

---

[95] *Gosling v. Anderson* [1972] C.L.Y. 492.
[96] See *F. & H. Entertainments Ltd v. Leisure Enterprises Ltd, supra.*
[97] *Post,* § 6–095.
[98] *Post,* § 6–117—6–118.
[99] See *post,* §§ 6–135—6–137.
[1] *Banque Keyser Ullman SA v. Skandia (UK) Insurance Co. Ltd* [1990] 1 Q.B. 665, 787–789, approved by the House of Lords [1991] 2 A.C. 249, 268, 280, 281.
[2] [1992] Ch. 560.
[3] See *post,* § 27–037.
[4] [1992] Ch. 560, 574.
[5] [1964] A.C. 465.
[6] See the views of the majority in the *Howard Marine* case [1978] Q.B. 574, *post,* § 6–085, n. 48.

person . . . " Section 4 defines "fault" as "negligence, breach of statutory duty or other act or omission which gives rise to liability in tort or would, apart from this Act, give rise to the defence of contributory negligence." Thus for the Act to apply, the claimant's conduct must either be an act giving rise to liability to the defendant in tort or be one which at common law would have given rise to the defence of contributory negligence.[7] It has been held that at common law contributory negligence is not a defence to fraud and that therefore the Law Reform (Contributory Negligence) Act does not apply to fraud.[8] Because the misrepresentor is to be liable under the Misrepresentation Act 1967, section 2(1), "as if the representation had been fraudulent",[9] the Law Reform (Contributory Negligence) Act seems not to apply to claims under section 2(1) where there is no concurrent liability in tort for negligent misrepresentation.

Burden of proof. Once the representee proves that the statement was in fact **6–075** false, the burden under the subsection shifts to the representor to prove that he had reasonable ground to believe and did believe up to the time the contract was made that the facts represented were true. Where the negotiations for a contract have continued over a substantial time, and the misrepresentation was made some while before the contract was finally entered into, this burden may indeed prove a heavy one. It will not be sufficient for the representor to prove that he had reasonable grounds to believe the statement was true when made; he will have to go on to prove that he had reasonable grounds to believe and did believe the statement was true when the contract was made.[10]

Parties liable under the subsection. The subsection only applies where the **6–076** representee has entered into a contract after a misrepresentation was made to him by another party to the contract. Presumably, ordinary principles of agency will still apply, so that an action will lie under the subsection where the misrepresentation has been made by an agent of the other contracting party, acting within the scope of his authority.[11] But an agent who makes a misrepresentation which is within his actual or ostensible authority is not personally liable under the subsection, despite the fact that the subsection, having referred to a misrepresentation having been made by a *party* to the contract (*i.e.* the principal via the agent) then goes on to refer to the liability of the *person* making the representation.[12] The agent may, of course, be liable for negligence at common law but only if he has assumed personal responsibility towards the claimant.[13] If the agent seeks to enforce the contract in his own name, the misrepresentation may be set up as a defence against him whether or not it is attributable to him rather than his principal.[14]

---

[7] *Forsikringaktieselskapet Vesta v. Butcher (No. 1)* [1989] A.C. 852 at 862 *et seq.*

[8] *Alliance and Leicester Building Society v. Edgestop Ltd* [1993] 1 W.L.R. 1462, *ante*, § 6–065.

[9] *Royscot Trust Ltd v. Rogerson* [1991] 2 Q.B. 297, *ante*, § 6–071.

[10] *Cooper v. Tamms* [1988] 1 E.G.L.R. 257. Perhaps the burden would also have been discharged in *Oscar Chess Ltd v. Williams* [1957] 1 W.L.R. 370.

[11] See *Gosling v. Anderson* [1972] C.L.Y. 492.

[12] *Resolute Maritime Inc. v. Nippon Kaiji Kyokai (The Skopas)* [1983] 1 W.L.R. 857, disapproving a suggestion in earlier editions of this work.

[13] *Williams v. Natural Life Health Foods Ltd* [1998] 1 W.L.R. 830; see further *post*, § 6–000.

[14] *Garnac Grain Co. v. H.M. Faure & Fairclough Ltd* [1966] 1 Q.B. 650, reversed on facts, *ibid.* 658 and [1968] A.C. 1130n.

6–077   **Misrepresentation by third person.** The subsection has no application where the representor is neither himself the other contracting party nor the agent of the other contracting party. Thus where B is induced to enter into a contract with C as a result of a misrepresentation made by A, and A is not C's agent,[15] B will have no right of action against A under the subsection. He may, however, have a remedy in damages against A on some other ground. There is, of course, no doubt that A would be liable to B in tort for fraud if fraud were proved, and in these circumstances, he might also be liable on the ground of a collateral contract or warranty (which requires neither fraud nor negligence to support it).[16] Further, an action may lie for negligent misrepresentation quite apart from section 2(1) of the Misrepresentation Act.

6–078   **Liability for negligence at common law.** It would be beyond the scope of this work to examine this kind of liability in detail[17] since it is not strictly contractual in its nature, and in any event, its importance has been greatly diminished by section 2(1) of the Misrepresentation Act which has been discussed in the preceding paragraphs.[18] But some account of this kind of liability is not out of place even in a work on the law of contract, since cases may arise in which a person is induced to enter into a contract as a result of a misrepresentation by a third party, and in these circumstances it is obviously desirable to consider the remedies available to the representee as a whole. This kind of liability may sometimes also arise where parties are negotiating for a contract but no contract is ever concluded, and loss is caused to one party as a result of a negligent statement by the other. Since the decisions in *Nocton v. Ashburton*[19] and *Hedley Byrne & Co. Ltd v. Heller and Partners Ltd*[20] it is clear that an action will lie in tort for negligent misrepresentation causing loss to the representee where the relationship of the parties is such as to give rise to a duty of care. The former case establishes that such a duty may arise (even apart from contract) out of a fiduciary relationship, such as that of solicitor and client, principal and agent, or trustee and beneficiary; the latter case establishes that such a duty may also arise in other circumstances.[21]

6–079   **Nocton v. Ashburton.** In this case a mortgagee sued his solicitor, alleging that by improper advice the latter had induced him to release part of his security, whereby the security had become insufficient; it was further alleged that the solicitor knew that the security would be rendered insufficient, and that his advice was given in order that he himself might benefit. The House of Lords held that fraud in the sense of *Derry v. Peek*[22] had not been proved, but that the mortgagee was entitled to relief for the breach of a duty imposed on the solicitor by the relationship in which he stood to his client.

---

[15] As happened, *e.g.* in *Hedley Byrne & Co. Ltd v. Heller and Partners Ltd* [1964] A.C. 465. For rescission in such circumstances see *ante*, §§ 6–018 *et seq.*

[16] See *Wells (Merstham) Ltd v. Buckland Sand & Silica Co. Ltd* [1965] 2 Q.B. 170; *post*, § 12–006.

[17] For a full account see *Clerk & Lindsell on Torts* (17th ed., 1995), §§ 7–61—7–77.

[18] But the existence of concurrent liability under s.2(1) and at common law may be important if a question of contributory negligence arises; see *ante*, § 6–074.

[19] [1914] A.C. 932.

[20] [1964] A.C. 465.

[21] The plaintiff may be required to specify the nature of the duty in his pleadings: *Selangor United Rubber Estates Co. Ltd v. Cradock* [1965] Ch. 896.

[22] (1889) 14 App.Cas. 337; *ante*, § 6–046.

What is a fiduciary relationship. The fiduciary or confidential relationship   **6–080**
necessary to bring this doctrine into operation extends to certain obvious ties,
such as those between trustee and *cestui que trust*, solicitor and client, and parent
and child. But the courts have not fettered their jurisdiction by defining its limits,
and are ready to interfere in order to protect the person who is under the influence
of another. The principle was stated in *Tate v. Williamson*[23]:

> "Wherever two persons stand in such a relation that, while it continues, confidence is
> necessarily reposed by one, and the influence which naturally grows out of that
> confidence is possessed by the other, and this confidence is abused, or the influence is
> exerted to obtain an advantage at the expense of the confiding party, the person so
> availing himself of his position will not be permitted to retain the advantage, although
> the transaction could not have been impeached if no such confidential relation had
> existed."[24]

Cases relating to fiduciary relationships are generally dealt with as part of the
doctrine of "undue influence,"[25] but it is not wholly clear whether every relationship which would justify rescission of a contract for undue influence would also
give rise to a duty of care which would support an action for damages for
negligence.[26]

Hedley Byrne & Co. Ltd v. Heller and Partners Ltd. Until the decision of   **6–081**
the House of Lords in the *Hedley Byrne*[27] case in 1964, it was thought that a duty
to take care in the making of statements could only arise in the case of fiduciary
(or, of course, contractual) relationships, but that decision has shown that the law
is very much wider than this. Although the House made it clear that misrepresentations made in the course of a mere social relationship would not
ground liability in tort, they also made it clear that many "special relationships"
would suffice. In particular, it is clear that professional relationships, even where
there is no contract between the parties, will normally give rise to a duty of care
wherever it can be said that the representor knew or ought reasonably to have
known that the representee was likely to act on the representation.[28] So, for
example, if a company's auditor gives negligent advice to a person who invests
money in the company on the strength of the advice, and it can be shown that the
auditor ought to have realised that the representee would act on the advice, an

---

[23] (1866) L.R. 2 Ch.App. 55.
[24] At 61.
[25] *Post*, §§ 7–041 *et seq.*
[26] It is perhaps not strictly accurate to refer to an action for "damages" for negligence in breach
of a fiduciary relationship, for this was an equitable remedy and equity did not award damages. In
Nocton v. Ashburton [1914] A.C. 932 the House of Lords spoke of an action for "compensation" and
it may be that the measure of damages which they had in mind as appropriate in that case would have
been lower than the usual tort measure. But today it is at least clear that a fiduciary relationship
arising out of a professional relationship will ordinarily support a duty of care in tort for which
ordinary tort damages will be recoverable, see, *e.g. Arenson v. Arenson* [1977] A.C. 405, *Midland
Bank v. Hett, Stubbs and Kemp* [1979] Ch. 384.
[27] *Supra.* On the facts the defendants could not be liable because they had coupled their statement
with a disclaimer of responsibility. Such a disclaimer is subject to Unfair Contract Terms Act 1977,
s.2(2): *Smith v. Eric S. Bush* and *Harris v. Wyre Forest DC* [1990] 1 A.C. 831.
[28] It seems that an explicit voluntary assumption of responsibility by the defendant may not always
be needed, at least when the defendant should know that the plaintiff will reasonably rely on the
defendant's statement: see further *post*, § 6–083.

action for negligent misrepresentation will lie against the auditor.[29] Again advice given "in a business connection" about the creditworthiness of a third party may give rise to a duty of care even where the adviser is not acting in a professional capacity,[30] provided he has some financial interest in the transaction.[31] On the other hand, the question whether a banker owes a duty to take care in giving references about his customers was left open by the House of Lords in the *Hedley Byrne* case, since it was thought that such a liability might be too onerous. It was, however, said that a "duty to be honest" is at least owed in such circumstances, though it is far from clear whether this is the same thing as the duty merely to abstain from fraud.[32] If the "duty to be honest" goes beyond liability in fraud, it would seem necessary to recognise a new form of liability midway between fraud and negligence, but it is submitted that this is a confusing and unnecessary conception. Since the duty of care means a duty to take such care as is reasonable in all circumstances of the case, the law of negligence is already sufficiently flexible to cater for different degrees of care. There is, for instance, no reason why a court should not hold that a banker giving references about a customer does owe a duty of care to the representee, while at the same time recognising that this duty does not require the banker to compile an exhaustive dossier on the customer's activities over a period of many years.[33]

6–082   **Statement in connection with particular transaction.** In *Caparo Industries plc v. Dickman*[34] it was held that there will be no liability in tort for negligent misrepresentation unless the maker of the statement knew that the statement would be communicated to the person relying on it specifically in connection with a particular transaction or a transaction of a particular kind. In relation to misrepresentation as between contracting parties,[35] this appears to mean that the misrepresentation must have been made in connection with the contract in respect of which relief is sought, or at least that reliance on the representation in connection with the contract was likely.

6–083   **Voluntary assumption of responsibility.** In *Hedley Byrne*, considerable emphasis was placed on whether the defendants had voluntarily assumed responsibility towards the plaintiffs[36]; and the defendants' disclaimer of responsibility prevented them from being liable in that case. The meaning of assumption of responsibility is not wholly clear. In *Smith v. Eric S. Bush*,[37] in which the plaintiff had purchased a house on the strength of a valuation made by surveyors

---

[29] See, *e.g. Candler v. Crane, Christmas & Co.* [1951] 2 K.B. 164, the majority decision in which was overruled in the *Hedley Byrne* case, *supra*; *J.E.B. Fasteners Ltd v. Marks, Bloom & Co.* [1981] 3 All E.R. 289, [1983] 1 All E.R. 583. But note the restriction described in § 6–082, *post*.

[30] *W.B. Anderson & Sons Ltd v. Rhodes (Liverpool) Ltd* [1967] 2 All E.R. 850.

[31] See *post*, § 6–084.

[32] Honoré, "Hedley Byrne & Co. Ltd v. Heller and Partners Ltd" (1965), 8 *Journal of the Society of Public Teachers of Law* (N.S.) 284.

[33] For Commonwealth cases on the *Hedley Byrne* principle, see *Clerk & Lindsell on Tort* (17th ed., 1995) §§ 7–061—7–077.

[34] [1990] 2 A.C. 605. Compare *Morgan Crucible Co. plc v. Hill Samuel Bank Ltd* [1991] Ch. 295. In *Galoo Ltd (in liquidation) v. Bright Grahame Murray* [1994] 1 W.L.R. 1360, it was held that an auditor of a company's accounts may owe a duty of care to a take-over bidder if he has expressly been informed that the bidder will rely on the accounts for the purpose of deciding whether to make an increased bid and intends that the bidder should so rely. See also *Possfund Custodian Trustee Ltd v. Diamond* [1996] 1 W.L.R. 1351.

[35] See *post*, § 6–085.

[36] *e.g.* by Lord Reid and Lord Devlin, [1964] A.C. 465 at 487 and 529 respectively.

[37] [1990] 1 A.C. 831.

employed by the building society from whom the plaintiff borrowed to finance the purchase, the application form signed by the plaintiff stated that the defendant valuer's report would be "supplied without acceptance of responsibility on their part to me." Similarly, in the joined case of *Harris v. Wyre Forest DC*, in which the survey was carried out by an employee of the lender, the application form stated that the lender took "no responsibility . . . for the value or condition of the property". It was held by the House of Lords that the defendants were responsible nonetheless; the clauses were subject to Unfair Contract Terms Act 1977, s.2(2) and had not been shown to be reasonable. Lord Griffiths stated that he did not find that "voluntary assumption of responsibility is a helpful or realistic test for liability".[38] However, more recent authority in the House of Lords has again stressed that liability for economic loss, including in cases of negligent misstatement, is based on an "assumption of responsibility"[39] However, Lord Goff has explained that:

" . . . especially in a context concerned with a liability which may arise under a contract or in a situation 'equivalent to contract', it must be expected that an objective test will be applied when asking the question whether, in a particular case, responsibility should be held to have been assumed by the defendant to the plaintiff . . . "[40]

Thus the existence of a disclaimer will not necessarily negate an assumption of liability if the defendant knows that there is a strong probability that the plaintiff will nonetheless rely on the information given.[41] The defendant will be protected only if he shows that the disclaimer is satisfies the requirement of reasonableness under the Unfair Contract Terms Act 1977.[42]

Statements not made in course of business. The principle of the *Hedley*   **6–084**
Byrne case was somewhat limited by the majority decision of the Privy Council in *Mutual Life and Citizen's Assurance Co. Ltd v. Evatt*[43] where it was held that in general there is no duty to take care in the making of statements unless the maker has held himself out as having some special skill or competence in the matter in question. In general, it was held, the duty will only arise where the statement is made in the course of a business though in some cases other factors may be sufficient to impose a duty, for example that the person making the statement has a financial interest in the transaction on which he has given advice.[44] However, it seems unlikely that this decision will now be followed. It was only decided by a bare majority and several judges have felt free to indicate their preference for the minority judgments of Lord Reid and Lord Morris.[45]

---

[38] *ibid.* at 862.

[39] See *Henderson v. Merrett Syndicates Ltd* [1995] 2 A.C. 145; *White v. Jones* [1995] 2 A.C. 207; *Williams v. Natural Life Health Foods Ltd* [1998] 1 W.L.R. 830. All three cases are discussed in more detail *ante*, §§ 1–117—1–119.

[40] *Henderson v. Merrett Syndicates Ltd* [1995] 2 A.C. 145, 181. See also the speech of Lord Steyn in *Williams v. Natural Life Health Foods Ltd, supra.*

[41] See, *e.g.* the judgments of Lords Templeman and Griffiths in *Smith v. Eric S. Bush* [1990] 1 A.C. 831, at 852 and 865 respectively.

[42] Ss.2(2), 11(5) and 13.

[43] [1971] A.C. 793, noted (1971) 87 L.Q.R. 147.

[44] See *W.B. Anderson & Sons Ltd v. Rhodes (Liverpool) Ltd, supra.*

[45] In *Esso Petroleum Co. Ltd v. Mardon* [1975] Q.B. 819 and [1976] Q.B. 801, *post*, § 6–085, and also in the *Howard Marine* case [1978] Q.B. 574, *ante*, § 6–068. The Australian High Court has also refused to follow the majority judgments in the *Evatt* case: see *L. Shaddock & Associates Pty. Ltd v. Parramatta City Council* (1981) 55 A.L.J.R. 713.

6–085   **Special relationship between parties negotiating contract.** It has now become clear that a special relationship, giving rise to a duty of care, may subsist between parties negotiating a contract if information is given in connection with the contract.[46] In *Esso Petroleum Co. Ltd v. Mardon*[47] it was held that a petroleum company, negotiating a lease of a filling station, was liable to the tenant for negligently giving him over-optimistic estimates of the sales potential of the filling station. It should be noted that this was not a casual observation made between parties each of whom was in the same position to judge the accuracy of the estimate. The information was based on a detailed evaluation of the position by the petroleum company and the tenant was clearly not in as good a position as they were to make such an estimate.[48] Similarly, it has been held that a special relationship existed between a landlord and a tenant as a result of pre-contractual discussion during which the landlord assured the tenant that he would keep the premises insured[49]; but it was also held in this case that the duty was only a duty not to give misleading information, and did not extend to requiring the landlord to exercise care not to allow the insurance to expire unrenewed without informing the tenant.[50] On the other hand, it has been held that a special relationship existed between an astute and experienced business woman and an insurance company with whom she was contemplating investing over £90,000 in a property bond; and in this case it was held that the consequential duty of care required the defendants' agent to give the plaintiff an adequate explanation of the nature of property bonds, and was not merely a duty to avoid misrepresentation.[51] An estate agent may be liable to a customer who purchases a house in reliance on a negligent misrepresentation.[52] A Canadian case has held that a builder who provided an estimate as to the cost of building a house was under a duty to take care to see that the client realised that his estimate did not include his 15 per cent. mark-up.[53] Sometimes even a failure to disclose may give rise to liability, but this will only be so if there has been a voluntary assumption of responsibility to disclose and the claimant has relied on it. There is no liability under the *Hedley Byrne* principle simply because the contract was *uberrimae fidei* and thus could be avoided for non-disclosure of a material fact.[54]

6–086   **Relationship between manufacturer and purchaser of goods.** In *Lambert v. Lewis*[55] it was held by the Court of Appeal that a person who purchases goods

---

[46] See *ante*, § 6–082.

[47] See *ante*, n. 45; also *McInerny v. Lloyds Bank Ltd* [1974] 2 Lloyd's Rep. 246, 253–254; *Cornish v. Midland Bank plc* [1985] 3 All E.R. 513; *Gran Gelato Ltd v. Richcliff (Group) Ltd* [1992] Ch. 560.

[48] Contrast the *Howard Marine* case [1978] Q.B. 574, where the majority seems to have considered that the casual nature of the answer precluded a duty of care.

[49] *Argy Trading Development Co. Ltd v. Lapid Developments Ltd* [1977] 1 W.L.R. 444.

[50] *ibid.*

[51] *Rust v. Abbey Life Insurance Co. Ltd* [1978] 2 Lloyd's Rep. 386.

[52] *Computastaff Ltd v. Ingledew Brown Bennison & Garrett* (1983) 268 E.G. 598.

[53] *A.L. Gullison & Sons Ltd v. Corey* (1980) 29 N.B.R. (2d) 86.

[54] *La Banque Financière de la Cité SA v. Westgate Insurance Co. Ltd. Banque Keyser Ullman SA v. Skandia (U.K.) Insurance Co. Ltd* [1990] 1 Q.B. 665, 791, 794–795, 799, 802–803, affd. on other grounds [1991] 2 A.C. 249. On contracts *uberrimae fidei* see *post*, §§ 6–135—6–153. It is possible that there might be an implicit assumption of responsibility if the defendant should have known that the plaintiff was reasonably relying on the defendant to disclose certain facts: *cf. Smith v. Eric S. Bush* [1990] 1 A.C. 831, *ante*, § 6–083.

[55] [1982] A.C. 225; this issue was not discussed on appeal to the House of Lords, *ibid.*

in reliance on statements in a manufacturer's promotional literature is not, for that reason alone, entitled to claim that a special relationship exists as a result of which the manufacturer may be held liable for negligent statements in the literature. The mere making of a serious statement with the intent that it should be relied upon was not enough, said the court, to create a special relationship. It may seem regrettable that a manufacturer is under no duty of care with respect to statements made in his brochures and advertising leaflets which are plainly designed to influence buyers. However, the decision itself seems consistent with the later decision in *Caparo Industries plc v. Dickman*[56] that there will be no liability in tort for negligent misrepresentation unless the maker of the statement knew that the statement would be communicated to the person relying on it either as an individual or as a member of a specified class, specifically in connection with a particular transaction or a transaction of a particular kind. In most cases a manufacturer will not know the purchaser's identity other than as a member of a very broad class and will know the purchaser's purposes only in general terms. If the manufacturer knows both the purchaser's identity and his purposes it is submitted that there may be a special relationship.[57] There is authority for saying that in such circumstances information given by the manufacturer may constitute a contractual warranty.[58] There is some ground for suggesting that even in the absence of direct contact between manufacturer and purchaser, statements in the manufacturer's literature should be treated as warranties, rendering the manufacturer strictly liable, and not merely liable for negligence: this is certainly the position in American law,[59] but in English law such statements are said not to be warranties unless there is an intent to warrant.[60]

Where negotiations do not lead to contract. In principle there seems no   **6-087** reason why a special relationship should not be held to exist between parties negotiating a contract even where the negotiations break down so that no contract is ultimately made. Indeed, this seems to have been the basis of the decision in *Box v. Midland Bank Ltd*[61] where the plaintiff sought a large loan from his bankers. His bank manager told him that the loan would need approval from head office but gave the plaintiff to think that this was a formality; in the meantime, the plaintiff was permitted overdraft facilities. The loan application was refused by head office and the plaintiff claimed that he had suffered loss through being led to believe that the loan would be forthcoming. This claim was, in part, upheld by Lloyd J. on the basis that the bank manager owed a duty not to mislead the plaintiff by careless advice as to the probable outcome of his loan application.

Special relationship between parties already in contractual relation-   **6-088** **ship.** It is now clear that one party to a contractual relationship may owe duties in tort to the other; these duties may overlap with contractual duties, and where this is the case the claimant may have alternative causes of action in contract and

---

[56] [1990] 2 A.C. 605, *ante*, § 6–082.

[57] *cf. Independent Broadcasting Authority v. EMI Electronics and BICC Construction Ltd* (1980) 14 Build. L.R. 1, a case of a post-contractual representation.

[58] *Shanklin Pier v. Detel Products Ltd* [1951] 2 K.B. 854; *Wells (Merstham) Ltd v. Buckland Sand and Silica Co. Ltd* [1965] 2 Q.B. 170.

[59] See, *e.g. Greenman v. Yuba Power Products*, 377 P. 2d 897 (1963), and many other cases cited in White & Summers, *Uniform Commercial Code* (3rd ed., 1988), pp. 467–468.

[60] See *Lambert v. Lewis* itself, and see also *post*, § 12–003.

[61] [1979] 2 Lloyd's Rep. 391, on appeal (as to costs only) [1981] 1 Lloyd's Rep. 434.

in tort.[62] It has also been held that damages may be obtainable for misrepresentations made in the course of renegotiating a contract already in existence, under the Misrepresentation Act,[63] and there seems no reason to doubt that in an appropriate case liability could also arise under the *Hedley Byrne* principle in such a situation.

6-089   **Damages at common law.** Damages for negligent misrepresentation at common law will naturally be on the tortious measure[64]; but the usual rules on remoteness[65] and contributory negligence[66] will apply. So will the restrictions on a negligent valuer's liability for subsequent falls in the value of the property set down in *South Australia Asset Management Corp. v. York Montague Ltd.*[67]

6-090   **Other statutory provisions creating liability for negligent misrepresentations: financial services.** There are a number of other statutory provisions creating a liability in damages for negligent misrepresentation, for example, section 150 of the Financial Services Act 1986.[68] This makes persons responsible for the listing particulars of securities for admission to the Official List liable to pay compensation to any person who has acquired any of the securities and has suffered a loss as the result of any untrue or misleading statement in the particulars; but section 151 provides a defence, *inter alia*, if the persons responsible reasonably believed, having made such inquiries (if any) as were reasonable, that the statement was true and not misleading, and continued in that belief until the time the securities were acquired.[69] It is also possible that a civil action may lie for a breach of section 35 of the Banking Act 1987, though this section only provides in terms for a penal remedy. The section concerns fraudulent or reckless statements made in an invitation to the public to deposit money with a person. In applying to reckless statements, the section probably extends beyond cases of fraud at law since it extends to recklessness whether it is dishonest or not,[70] though it plainly requires something more than a mere failure to take care.[71] On the other hand, it also goes beyond the traditional principles of the ordinary law relating to misrepresentation since it extends to fraudulent and reckless promises and forecasts, as well as to statements of fact; but, as previously noted, some common law cases are now moving in the same direction. Section 47 of the Financial Services Act 1986, which replaces section 13(1) of the Prevention of Fraud (Investments) Act 1958 and which concerns fraudulent statements made in circulars inviting the public to invest, is in similar terms; but

---

[62] *Henderson v. Merrett Syndicates Ltd* [1995] 2 A.C. 145; *ante*, §§ 1–068 *et seq.*

[63] *André & Cie SA v. Ets Michel Blanc & Fils* [1977] 2 Lloyd's Rep. 166.

[64] See *ante*, § 6–052.

[65] *Ante*, § 6–052.

[66] *Ante*, § 6–074.

[67] [1997] A.C. 191; *ante*, § 6–059 and *post*, §§ 27–078—27–080.

[68] These provisions stem from the Directors Liability Act 1890, which was passed to reverse the effect of *Derry v. Peek* (1889) 14 App.Cas. 337, so far as it applied to prospectuses. For the possible impact of the *Hedley Byrne* case, *ante*, § 6–081, and of the Misrepresentation Act 1967 on liability for misstatements in prospectuses and particulars of securities, see Boyle & Birds, *Company Law* (3rd ed.), § 5.19; *Gower's Principles of Modern Company Law* (6th ed., 1997), pp. 435–439.

[69] For unlisted securities see Public Offers of Securities Regulations 1995, S.I. 1995 No. 1537; *Gower, op. cit.*, pp. 428 *et seq.*

[70] The words "dishonestly or otherwise" appear in s.35(1) of the Banking Act 1987. See also *M.F.I. Warehouses Ltd v. Nattrass* [1973] 1 W.L.R. 307.

[71] See *R. v. Russell* [1953] 1 W.L.R. 77 and *R. v. Grunwald* [1963] 1 Q.B. 935.

it seems that no action for breach of statutory duty will lie.[72] The court may, however, on the application of the Secretary of State, make a restitution order in favour of persons who have entered a transaction with the person responsible and have suffered loss as a result of the false statement.[73]

Property Misdescriptions Act. Under section 1 of the Property Misdescrip- **6–091**
tions Act 1991, the making of a false or misleading statement about a prescribed matter[74] in the course of an estate agency business or a property development business may constitute a criminal offence, unless all reasonable steps and due diligence had been used to avoid committing the offence.[75] However no contract is void or unenforceable and no right of action in civil proceedings will arise by reason only of the commission of an offence under the section.[76]

Package travel, etc. Under the Package Travel, Package Holidays and Pack- **6–092**
age Tours Regulations 1992,[77] organisers or retailers of such packages must not supply any descriptive matter concerning a package, the price of a package or any other conditions applying to the contract which contains misleading information. If a consumer suffers loss as a result of a breach of this requirement the organiser or retailer is liable to pay compensation.[78] As liability appears to be strict it may be better regarded as contractual than for misrepresentation. The measure of damages is not stated.

(c) Innocent Misrepresentation

No damages for innocent misrepresentation. The term "innocent misrep- **6–093**
resentation" is here used to mean a representation which is neither fraudulent nor negligent, and the general rule remains what it has always been, namely, that no action for damages lies for a mere innocent misrepresentation in this sense.[79] But it must be stressed that a misrepresentation will found a claim for damages if it can be construed as a contractual promise, and is either part of a wider contract, or is itself supported by consideration. This may happen in two principal types of case. First, where the representor and representee themselves enter into a contract after the misrepresentation was made. Here, if the misrepresentation becomes a term of the contract, an action for damages will lie, whether the

---

[72] *Norwich Union Life Insurance Society v. Qureshi*, 8 June 1998 (unrep.). s.62 (now qualified by s.62A, inserted by Companies Act 1989, s.193) creates an action for breach of statutory duty in favour of private investors for breaches of other provisions of that Part of the Act, thereby seeming to exclude an action for breach of s.47: see *Norwich Union Life Insurance Society v. Qureshi* [1998] C.L.C. 1605; but in *Aldrich v. Norwich Union Life Insurance Co. Ltd* (November 23, 1998, unreported) the Court of Appeal considered the point to be arguable. Nor will civil liability arise to investors or other persons affected by a failure to comply with a statement of principle issued by the Secretary of State under Financial Services Act 1986, s.47A (inserted by Companies Act 1989, s.192).
[73] s.61, applied in *Securities and Investments Board Ltd v. Pantell SA (No. 2)* [1993] Ch. 256. See generally Boyle & Birds, *Company Law* (3rd ed., § 5.19); Gower's *Principles of Modern Company Law* (6th ed., 1997) pp. 433–435.
[74] See Property Misdescriptions (Specified Matters) Order (S.I. 1992 No. 2834).
[75] s.2. See *Enfield L.B.C. v. Castles Estate Agents Ltd* (1997) 73 P & CR 343.
[76] s.1(4).
[77] S.I. 1992 No. 3288, implementing EEC Council Directive 90/314. See *post*, § 13–033.
[78] reg. 4.
[79] *Heilbut, Symonds & Co. v. Buckleton* [1913] A.C. 30; *Gilchester Properties Ltd v. Gomm* [1948] 1 All E.R. 493.

misrepresentation was fraudulent, negligent or innocent.[80] Secondly, the representee may enter into a contract with a third party as a result of the misrepresentation. Even in this situation, it is often possible to construe the misrepresentation as a collateral contract, the consideration for which is supplied by the fact that the representee enters into the contract with the third party.[81] A familiar illustration of the principle of the collateral contract can be seen in an agent's liability for breach of warranty of authority.[82]

6–094   **Estoppel.** Circumstances may arise in which damages are recoverable for a completely innocent misrepresentation, through the assistance of the doctrine of estoppel. For example, if a person agrees to buy shares in a company on the strength of a share certificate issued to the seller stating that he is the registered owner of the shares, the company may be estopped from denying that the seller was in truth the owner of the shares. The purchaser is, in these circumstances, entitled to demand that the company register him as the owner of the shares, or to claim damages in lieu.[83] The purchaser does not claim damages directly for the misrepresentation, but the net effect is very much the same. For the doctrine of estoppel to apply the usual requirements of an estoppel must be satisfied; in particular the statement relied on must be precise, unambiguous and unqualified.[84] An estoppel may in exceptional circumstances arise out of non-disclosure, but a duty to disclose must then be shown.[85] It is also necessary that some independent cause of action be shown, apart from the misrepresentation itself.[86] This cause of action will normally be a claim to some form of property to which the representee would be entitled if the representation were true, and the truth of which the representor is not entitled to deny, for example, money which would be due to the representee as assignee,[87] or goods which the representor has acknowledged that he holds on behalf of the representee.[88]

6–095   **Misrepresentation Act, s.2(2).** This subsection reads as follows:

> "Where a person has entered into a contract after a misrepresentation has been made to him otherwise than fraudulently, and he would be entitled, by reason of the misrepresentation, to rescind the contract, then, if it is claimed, in any proceedings arising out of the contract, that the contract ought to be or has been rescinded, the court or arbitrator may declare the contract subsisting and award damages in lieu of rescission, if of opinion that it would be equitable to do so, having regard to the nature of the

---

[80] See, *e.g. Dick Bentley Productions Ltd v. Harold Smith (Motors) Ltd* [1965] 1 W.L.R. 623, *post*, § 12–003.

[81] *Post*, § 12–006.

[82] See Vol. II, §§ 32–099—32–106.

[83] *Re Bahia and San Francisco Ry.* (1868) L.R. 3 Q.B. 584; *Balkis Consolidated Co. v. Tomkinson* [1893] A.C. 396.

[84] *Low v. Bouverie* [1891] 3 Ch. 82; *Woodhouse A.C. Israel Cocoa Ltd v. Nigerian Produce Marketing Co. Ltd* [1972] A.C. 741; *China-Pacific SA v. Food Corpn. of India* [1981] Q.B. 403, revd. on different grounds [1982] A.C. 939.

[85] *Greenwood v. Martin's Bank* [1933] A.C. 51; *Moorgate Mercantile Co. Ltd v. Twitchings* [1977] A.C. 890; *Banque Keyser Ullman SA v. Skandia (U.K.) Insurance Co. Ltd* [1990] 1 Q.B. 665, affd. on other grounds [1991] 2 A.C. 249.

[86] *ibid.* But *cf. Brikom Investments Ltd v. Seaford* [1981] 1 W.L.R. 863; *Re Wyvern Developments Ltd* [1974] 1 W.L.R. 1097. In cases based on "proprietary estoppel" it seems that no independent cause of action need be shown, but the authorities in this area of the law are still developing. See *ante*, §§ 3–093—3–099 and 3–129—3–152.

[87] *Burrows v. Lock* (1805) 10 Ves. 470.

[88] *Seton, Laing & Co. v. Lafone* (1887) 19 Q.B.D. 68.

misrepresentation and the loss that would be caused by it if the contract were upheld, as well as to the loss that rescission would cause to the other party."

It will be seen that this subsection does not give a representee any *right* to claim damages, but it enables the court, in its discretion, to grant damages to the representee in lieu of rescinding the contract.[89] It seems probable that the subsection was intended principally for the benefit of the representor, so that a contract need not be rescinded where the court feels that the representee can be adequately compensated in damages.[90] But cases may well occur in which damages would be the preferable remedy for the representee. In this event there seems nothing to prevent the representee from suing for rescission, and then inviting the court to award damages in lieu. Nor does there seem to be anything which would prevent the court from taking this course over the protests of the representor, who may prefer rescission to an award of damages.

Damages only in lieu of rescission. But it is important to note two limitations   6–096
on the power to award damages under this subsection. First, damages can only be awarded *in lieu* of rescission. In the case of a fraudulent misrepresentation, to which the subsection does not apply, the representee can both rescind and claim damages as of right.[91] Rescission for fraud is rescission *ab initio*, and damages for breach of contract cannot be recovered after such rescission, but damages for fraud are recovered in tort and there is no reason why this remedy should not survive rescission of the contract. In the case of a negligent misrepresentation, the representee can claim both rescission and damages, but whereas his claim to damages is as of right under section 2(1) his claim to rescission is now subject to the discretion of the court under section 2(2).[92] But in the case of an innocent misrepresentation, the representee cannot get both rescission and damages,[93] nor can he claim either remedy as of right.

Rescission barred. A second possible limitation contained in the subsection   6–097
is that the power to grant damages may only be available where the remedy of rescission would still be available at the time of the court's order. It must be said, however, that the words of the subsection are far from clear, for the court may award damages in lieu of rescission wherever the representee "would be entitled . . . to rescind the contract." The question is whether this means: "would be entitled at the time of the court's order," or: "would have been entitled after the representation was made."[94] Purely linguistic considerations suggest that the

---

[89] It is apparent from subs. (3) that this subsection also applies where the misrepresentation was negligent, but clearly a representee who wants damages rather than rescission will claim under subs. (1).

[90] See §§ 11 and 12 of the Tenth Report of the Law Reform Committee, Cmnd. 1782 (1962) on which s.2 was based.

[91] *Attwood v. Small* (1838) 6 Cl. & F. 232, 444; *Newbigging v. Adam* (1886) 34 Ch.D. 582, 592. There is nothing inconsistent with this in *Johnson v. Agnew* [1980] A.C. 367. See *post*, §§ 6–104 and 25–046.

[92] For a case in which damages and rescission were permitted under the Act, see *F. & H. Entertainments Ltd v. Leisure Enterprises Ltd* (1976) 120 S.J. 331.

[93] Except in those exceptional cases in which damages are recoverable for innocent misrepresentation, *ante* §§ 6–093—6–094. Note also that, on rescission, the representee is entitled to an indemnity for burdens assumed under the contract, but this is much narrower than the right to damages, *post*, §§ 6–117—6–118.

[94] *cf.* the similar problems over the interpretation of the words "would, if sued, have been liable" in s.6(1)(c) of the Law Reform (Married Women and Tortfeasors) Act 1935 (now repealed); *George Wimpey & Co. Ltd v. B.O.A.C.* [1955] A.C. 169; *Harvey v. R.G. O'Dell Ltd* [1958] 2 Q.B. 78.

former meaning is the correct one and in *Atlantic Lines & Navigation Co. Inc. v. Hallam Ltd (The Lucy)*[95] Mustill J. accepted it. But his remarks on section 2(2) did not form part of the *ratio* of the case, and the matter cannot be regarded as free from doubt, particularly as the results of adopting the "time of the court's order" construction would be so unsatisfactory that the other construction seems preferable. If the former construction were adopted the court would have no power to award damages to a representee under this subsection where he has affirmed the contract,[96] or where third parties have acquired rights in the subject-matter of the contract,[97] or where there has been unreasonable delay,[98] or where *restitutio in integrum* is impossible.[99] These are strange results for the circumstances which deprive a representee of his right of rescission would, in many situations, have no relevance to the question whether damages should be awarded. For example, if a person buys a car as a result of an innocent misrepresentation as to its age he will generally lose his right to rescind the contract once he himself has resold the car,[1] and the result of this construction of subsection (2) is that the court's power to award damages for the misrepresentation would cease at the same time. The position could be even stranger if the representee were so ill advised as to affirm the contract, while reserving any right to claim damages, for the very act of affirmation would, on this view of subsection (2), debar him from relief under the subsection. It is therefore submitted that the alternative construction of the subsection, if permissible, would produce preferable results, so that damages for innocent misrepresentation could be awarded in the discretion of the court even though rescission is no longer possible at the date of the order. In *Thomas Witter Ltd v. TBP Industries Ltd*[2] Jacob J. expressed the view that damages could have been awarded under section 2(2) even though the misrepresentee had lost the right to rescind. He considered the section to be ambiguous and referred to a statement of the Solicitor-General during a debate on the Misrepresentation Bill. The statement itself lends some support to this view but further investigation of the legislative history throws some doubt on it.[3]

6–098   **Measure of damages.** It is possible that the measure of damages which may be awarded under subsection (2) is intended to be lower than the measure of damages for fraudulent misrepresentation which, as seen above, is now also applicable to negligent misrepresentation under section 2(1). This possibility is suggested by subsection (3) of the same section which provides that damages may be awarded under subsection (2) whether or not the representor is liable to damages under subsection (1) (*i.e.* whether or not he has been negligent), but goes on to provide that any damages awarded under subsection (2) shall be taken into account in assessing liability under subsection (1). This seems to indicate that the damages awarded under subsection (2) may be lower than the damages awarded under subsection (1), and there might be something to be said for this since the representor may be wholly innocent in a case under subsection (2). But

---

[95] [1983] 1 Lloyd's Rep. 188.
[96] *Post*, § 6–120.
[97] *Post*, § 6–125.
[98] *Post*, § 6–123.
[99] *Post*, §§ 6–112—6–118.
[1] See, *e.g. Oscar Chess Ltd v. Williams* [1957] 1 W.L.R. 370.
[2] [1996] 2 All E.R. 573.
[3] See (1995) 111 L.Q.R. 385.

the Act gives little clue as to how damages are to be assessed under this subsection if they are not to be assessed in the same way as under subsection (1). It has already been seen that damages under subsection (1) are tortious rather than contractual.[4] It would seem *a fortiori* that damages under subsection (2) would not be at the contractual level. The alternatives then would seem to be to award either the tort measure or a special measure designed to compensate the representee for the loss resulting from his inability to obtain rescission. There seem to be two reasons to interpret section 2(2) as applying a special measure. The first relates to consequential loss. Suppose the vendor of a house has made an innocent misrepresentation about the state of the drains and as a result the purchaser has suffered personal injury and property damage. Rescission, even with an indemnity, would not compensate the purchaser for these losses[5] and it is arguable that they should not be compensated under section 2(2), which refers to damages "in lieu of rescission."[6] But it has been held that consequential damages may be recovered under this subsection,[7] though without averting to these questions.

Bad bargains. The second relates to cases where the misrepresentee has **6–099** made a bad bargain in the sense that, quite apart from the misrepresentation, the property is worth less than he has paid for it. In such a case the court might well exercise its discretion to declare the contract subsisting. Were the damages in lieu of rescission to be on the tortious measure as applied in actions for fraud,[8] or were the damages to be calculated so as to indemnify the misrepresentee fully against the consequences of rescission being refused, the damages might include loss suffered by the misrepresentor through the general fall in value of the property. The Court of Appeal in *William Sindall plc v. Cambridgeshire County Council*[9] said that this would not be appropriate in a case like the one outlined since the result would be to defeat the object of declaring the contract subsisting; the loss caused by the general fall in value would once again be put onto the misrepresentor. Evans L.J.[10] said that in such a case the contract measure—the difference in value between the property with and without the "defect" to which the misrepresentation related, or the cost of correcting the defect—would be appropriate. With respect, this solution will not always be attractive; even without the defect, the property might be worth as much as the misrepresentee

---

[4] *Ante,* § 6–069.

[5] *Whittington v. Seale-Hayne* (1900) 82 L.T. 49, *post*, § 6–118.

[6] In favour of this alternative is the literal interpretation given to s.2(1) by the Court of Appeal in *Royscott Trust Ltd v. Rogerson* [1991] 2 Q.B. 297. Against it is the analogy of damages under Lord Cairns' Act 1858 *in lieu* of an award of specific performance where (it seems) the damages are to be assessed as at common law, and not in accordance with some special measure: *Johnson v. Agnew* [1980] A.C. 367, 400.

[7] *Davis & Co. (Wines) Ltd v. Afa-Minerva (E.M.I.) Ltd* [1974] 2 Lloyd's Rep. 27. In *William Sindall plc v. Cambridgeshire County Council* [1994] 1 W.L.R. 1016, 1044 Evans L.J. said that in his view a plaintiff under s.2(2) should recover the same additional compensation as was permitted in *Cemp Properties (U.K.) Ltd v. Dentsply Research and Development Corpn*, [1991] 2 E.G.L.R. 197, a case under s.2(1) in which the plaintiffs recovered for wasted expenditure. See generally *McGregor, on Damages,* (16th ed., 1997) §§ 2013 *et seq.*

[8] See *ante,* § 6–052 *et seq.*

[9] [1994] 1 W.L.R. 1016: held that there were no grounds for rescission.

[10] *ibid.* at 1045. At 1037 Hoffmann L.J. remarked that while s.2(1) is concerned with damage flowing from the plaintiff having entered the contract, s.2(2) is concerned with damage caused by the property not being what it was supposed to be.

had paid for it. In such circumstances and provided that there is no consequential loss, damages for misrepresentation will be nil.[11] However, since the *Sindall* case was decided it has become clear that in a claim at common law against a negligent valuer, the valuer will not necessarily be liable for the losses caused by the fall in property prices generally, even though the lender would not have taken the property as security had a correct valuation been given. The damages are limited to the difference between the valuation negligently provided and the correct property value at the time.[12] By analogy, it is submitted that damages under Misrepresentation Act 1967, s.2(2) should be limited to any difference between the contract price and the actual value of the property taking account the misrepresentation but not taking into account the general fall in the value of the property. This was canvassed as an alternative approach by Evans L.J. in *Sindall's* case[13] and it does not seem inconsistent with the words of the statute. It would, in effect, reverse any unjust enrichment of the defendant.[14]

6–100   **Exercise of court's discretion.** The court's discretion under section 2(2) is a wide one. In particular, it is to be noted that the court is not confined to a consideration of whether damages would be an adequate remedy to the representee. The court is also required to consider the loss that would be caused to the representor by rescission. Thus even where damages would not be an adequate remedy for the representee, the court may feel that it would be more equitable to award damages where it is shown that great loss would be caused to the representor by rescinding the whole contract, for instance because the market value of the services to be rendered has fallen dramatically.[15] A court is unlikely to exercise its power to declare the contract subsisting under section 2(2) when an award of damages against the misrepresentor will be an empty remedy.[16] However, it has been said that it would not be appropriate to refuse rescission of a reinsurance contract for misrepresentation by the reinsured, as avoidance of the contract performs an important policing function.[17]

4. Rescission for Misrepresentation

(a) *General*

6–101   **Preliminary.** Before the passing of the Misrepresentation Act 1967, the position with regard to rescission was, broadly speaking, as follows: where a person was induced to enter into a contract as a result of a misrepresentation by

---

[11] See *McGregor On Damages* (16th ed., 1997), §§ 2017 *et seq.*

[12] *South Australia Asset Management Corp. v. York Montague Ltd* [1997] A.C. 191; see *post*, §§ 27–078—27–080.

[13] [1994] 1 W.L.R. 1016, 1046.

[14] See Birks [1997] R.L.R. 72, who argues that this is what Parliament intended despite use of the word "damages".

[15] *Atlantic Lines & Navigation Co. Inc. v. Hallam Ltd* [1983] 1 Lloyd's Rep. 188; and see *William Sindell plc v. Cambridgeshire County Council*, discussed in the previous paragraph.

[16] *TSB Bank plc v. Camfield* [1995] 1 W.L.R. 430, 439.

[17] *Highland Insurance Co. v. Continental Insurance Co.* [1987] 1 Lloyd's. Rep. 109.

the other party to the contract, and the misrepresentation never became incorporated as a contractual term, the representee was entitled to rescind the contract, whether the misrepresentation was fraudulent, negligent or wholly innocent. At common law, the right to rescind was confined to cases in which the misrepresentation was fraudulent or in which there was a total failure of consideration,[18] but in equity there was a right to rescind even for innocent misrepresentation.[19] Since the Act of 1967 this right of rescission is qualified (except in cases of fraud) by the court's power to refuse rescission and award damages in lieu,[20] and there remain certain bars to rescission in all cases, which are discussed below.[21] But it still remains a general proposition that the remedy for misrepresentation is rescission of the contract.

Misrepresentation incorporated as contractual term. Where the misrep- **6–102** resentation was later incorporated into the contract as a contractual term, the position was in some respects uncertain before the Act of 1967. In cases of fraud, the subsequent incorporation of the misrepresentation into the contract made no difference to the representee's right to rescind, but in cases of innocent misrepresentation (including, for this purpose, negligent misrepresentation) the position was different. For in this case there was some authority for saying that the equitable right to rescind did not arise, and the representee's right to rescind (if any) depended entirely on the effect of the misrepresentation as a contractual term.[22] That is to say, if the term was a condition or an innominate term, breach might justify rescission (or, as it would now be more appropriately put,[23] termination of the representee's outstanding obligations) whereas if the term was a warranty, breach would not justify rescission at all.[24] Thus the somewhat strange result followed that a misrepresentation which would have justified rescission as of right by the representee if it had remained a representation pure and simple, might cease to have this effect if it later became incorporated into the contract as a warranty.[25]

Misrepresentation Act, s.1(a). Section 1(a) of the Act of 1967 provides that **6–103** a person is not to be deprived of the right to rescind for misrepresentation merely because the representation has become a term of the contract. Thus a misrepresentation which is subsequently incorporated into the contract as a warranty will now remain a ground for rescission, whereas breach of a warranty which has never been a misrepresentation will never ground rescission. But it is not easy to see how, in fact, a misrepresentation could ever be a term of the contract except

---

[18] *Kennedy v. Panama, etc., Royal Mail Co. Ltd* (1867) L.R. 2 Q.B. 580.
[19] *Lamare v. Dixon* (1873) L.R. 6 H.L. 414. The generalisation of this remedy was largely a post-Judicature Act development, stemming principally from *Redgrave v. Hurd* (1881) 20 Ch.D. 1 and *Adam v. Newbigging* (1888) 13 App.Cas. 308.
[20] *Ante,* §§ 6–095 *et seq.*
[21] *Post,* §§ 6–112—6–128.
[22] *Pennsylvania Shipping Co. v. Compagnie Nationale de Navigation* [1936] 2 All E.R. 1167, 1171; *Leaf v. International Galleries* [1950] 2 K.B. 86; *cf. Compagnie Française de Chemins de Fer Paris-Orleans v. Leeston Shipping Co. Ltd* (1919) 1 Ll.L.Rep. 235, 237–238.
[23] See *Johnson v. Agnew* [1980] A.C. 367.
[24] See *post,* §§ 12–019—12–040.
[25] However, this "somewhat strange result" was held not to be law in *Academy of Health and Fitness Pty. Ltd v. Power* [1973] V.R. 254, a case arising in a jurisdiction not governed by the Misrepresentation Act 1967.

where the term had previously been a representation,[26] though a warranty might, of course, be a promise as to future conduct which would not be a misrepresentation in any event (unless fraudulent).

6–104   **Rescission and termination.** Since the decision of the House of Lords in *Johnson v. Agnew*[27] a much clearer and sharper distinction has been drawn between rescission of a contract *ab initio* and termination of the contract for subsequent breach. The former generally has retrospective effect, while the latter does not; indeed, termination usually affects only some of the obligations under the contract and it is strictly incorrect to speak of the contract ceasing to exist through termination. It is clear from *Johnson v. Agnew* itself that rescission for fraud is rescission *ab initio*, and will therefore prima facie have retrospective effect, though it has already been submitted[28] that such rescission will not deprive the representee of a right to damages for fraud, because that right arises in tort, and not out of the contract. Where section 1(a) of the Act of 1967 applies, it seems that the representee retains his right to rescind *ab initio*, but may in addition have a right to terminate for breach of the one-time representation, now become a term of the contract. Problems may well arise in deciding whether a refusal to continue with the contract in such circumstances amounts to a rescission or only a termination. It has been held that where a variation of a contract has been induced by fraud, the innocent party may rescind the variation *ab initio*, with the effect that the original contract is retrospectively revived.[29]

6–105   **Present position.** The right to rescind for fraudulent misrepresentation is unimpaired by the Misrepresentation Act, but there is no longer any absolute right to rescind for negligent or innocent misrepresentation. Section 2(2) of the Act (which has been set out above)[30] provides that the court now has a discretion to award damages in lieu of rescission wherever it is of the opinion that it would be equitable to do so, having regard to the nature of the misrepresentation and the loss that would be caused by it if the contract were upheld, as well as to the loss that rescission would cause the other party. It has already been observed that this is a wide discretion, and the court is not confined to a consideration of whether damages would be an adequate remedy to the representee.[31]

6–106   **Effect on right to terminate for breach.** There is one point of possible difficulty on the construction of section 2(2) of the Act. As mentioned above, it is clear from section 1(a) of the Act that (subject to the court's discretion under section 2(2)) there is now a right to rescind for any misrepresentation made before the contract was entered into, notwithstanding that the misrepresentation has become a term of the contract. But what is not wholly clear is whether, when this happens, any right to terminate for breach of contract also becomes subject to the discretion of the court under subsection (2). There are many circumstances

---

[26] If the representee did not know of the representation before the contract was made (as, *e.g.* where he simply signed a written agreement) it would not in any event be an effective misrepresentation, *ante*, § 6–034. But it is possible, though in practice unlikely, for a person to warrant the truth of a fact without making any representation at all, *e.g.* where he expressly agrees to take the risk, however the facts may turn out.

[27] [1980] A.C. 367.

[28] See *ante*, § 6–096.

[29] *Occidental Worldwide Investment Corpn. v. Skibs A/S Avanti* [1976] 1 Lloyd's Rep. 293.

[30] *Ante*, § 6–095.

[31] *Ante*, § 6–100.

in which a person has a right to terminate a contract for breach of condition, in which no loss has in fact been incurred by him, and a case could be made for saying that, where the term is a representation of fact, the court now has a discretion to refuse to permit repudiation, but to award damages in lieu—indeed, the damages might well be nominal.[32] On the other hand, it is unlikely that the subsection was intended to have this effect, and it could be argued that the words: "Where a person . . . would be entitled by reason of the misrepresentation, to rescind the contract" would exclude the case under discussion since the right to rescind then arises from breach of the contractual term.[33] But whatever the answer to this point may be, it is at least clear that subsection (2) would not affect a right to treat the contract as terminated for breach of a contractual term which was a promise of future conduct; nor for a breach of a contractual term which was an undertaking as to fact but which was never made before the contract was entered into.

Misrepresentation as defence to proceedings. There is no doubt that a **6–107** misrepresentation which would justify rescission of a contract may also be used as a defence to an action brought by the representor against the representee. The use of misrepresentation as a defence has sometimes been distinguished from its use as a ground for rescission,[34] and it is possible that the principles governing the two situations are not in all respects identical[35] but generally speaking they appear to be the same. Indeed, the courts have sometimes treated the setting up of a misrepresentation as a defence as though this were in itself one way of rescinding the contract.[36] Accordingly, it is thought that although section 2(2) of the 1967 Act speaks of rescission, its provisions would apply equally to a case in which the misrepresentation is set up by way of defence.

Rescission normally requires notice. The general rule is that, in order to **6–108** rescind the contract, the representee must communicate his intention to do so to the representor.[37] But in *Car & Universal Finance Co. Ltd v. Caldwell*[38] it was held by the Court of Appeal that this was not an inflexible rule. In this case a person was induced to sell his car by fraud to a purchaser who paid with a bad cheque, and promptly disappeared. When the seller discovered the fraud he informed the police and the Automobile Association, but was, of course, unable

---

[32] See, *e.g. Re Moore & Co. Ltd and Landauer Co.* [1921] 2 K.B. 519 (although the term here may well have been a promise rather than a statement of fact). This argument is also applicable to insurance contracts in which the insured may warrant some fact which is untrue, but the fact in question may have no bearing on the risk which occurs. Hitherto, it has always been clear that the insurer may repudiate liability in these circumstances, *post*, § 6–144.

[33] Yet the term is, *ex hypothesi*, a misrepresentation itself.

[34] Treitel, *The Law of Contract* (9th ed., 1995), pp. 344–345.

[35] Treitel, *loc. cit.* points to the rule that an insurer who uses fraud as a defence may repudiate liability and keep the premiums: see *post*, Vol. II, § 41–048. Further, he suggests that in cases of criminal fraud a representee who sets the fraud up by way of defence need not return money received under the contract (*Berg v. Sadler & Moore* [1937] 2 K.B. 158), whereas if he sues for rescission he must do so (*Spence v. Crawford* [1939] 3 All E.R. 271). *Berg v. Sadler & Moore* is contrary to dicta of the Exchequer Chamber in *Clough v. L. & N.W. Ry.* (1871) L.R. 7 Ex. 26, 37 which do not seem to have been cited.

[36] *Clough v. L. & N.W. Ry.* (1871) L.R. 7 Ex. 26; *Academy of Health and Fitness Pty. Ltd v. Power* [1973] V.R. 254.

[37] *Car & Universal Finance Co. Ltd v. Caldwell* [1961] 1 Q.B. 525.

[38] *Supra*; see also *Newtons of Wembley Ltd v. Williams* [1965] 1 Q.B. 560.

to notify the fraudulent purchaser. It was held that the seller had done sufficient to rescind the contract, and that accordingly a subsequent purchaser from the fraudulent party had acquired no title to the car, as the title had revested in the seller on rescission. The actual *ratio* of the decision seems confined to circumstances in which communication of the representee's desire to rescind is not possible because the representor is deliberately keeping out of the way, and the court left open the question whether the decision would apply to a case where the impossibility of communication did not arise from the representor's deliberate fraud.

6–109   **Court order not required.** Although it is common to speak of a court "setting aside" or rescinding a contract for misrepresentation, it seems clear from this and other cases[39] that the remedy is not necessarily a judicial one. A representee is entitled to rescind for misrepresentation without invoking the assistance of the court at all, although the court now has (as seen above) a discretion to refuse to allow rescission in some cases.[40] It may well be, as a purely practical matter, that the representee will require the assistance of the court in some cases, *e.g.* where rescission of an executed conveyance is sought[41]; but "the process of rescission is essentially the act of the party rescinding, and not of the court."[42]

6–110   **Rescission not available except against contracting party.** It seems clear that rescission is prima facie a remedy which is only available against the other party to the contract. In *Northern Bank Finance Corp. Ltd v. Charlton*[43] this principle was affirmed by a bare majority of the Supreme Court of Eire in a case in which the plaintiff had been induced by the fraud of a bank to pay various sums to the bank in order that these sums should be used by the bank to purchase various properties on behalf of the plaintiff. The properties were in fact so purchased from third parties. The plaintiff claimed rescission of the contracts of purchase but the majority of the court held that rescission was not available as against the bank since the properties were not bought from the bank itself. Rescission would in fact have amounted to a sort of compulsory subrogation

---

[39] *Abram SS. Co. Ltd v. Westville Shipping Co. Ltd* [1923] A.C. 773. In Australia, the High Court has taken a different approach, holding that even in a case of fraud equity does more than recognise rescission effected by the action of the innocent party. It may impose terms to achieve observance of the requirements of good conscience and practical justice and this enables it to grant partial rescission. Thus it could set aside the part of a contract of guarantee to which the fraud related (previous supplies) but leave the rest (as to future supplies) intact: *Vadasz v. Pioneer Concrete (S.A.) Pty. Ltd* (1995) 184 C.L.R. 102, noted (1997) 113 L.Q.R. 16; Proksch [1996] R.L.R. 71.

[40] Thus the court may, in effect, annul a rescission previously effected by self-help: see *Atlantic Lines & Navigation Co. Inc. v. Hallam Ltd* [1983] 1 Lloyd's Rep. 188, 202. The conferral of a discretion on the court by s.2(2) has been said to imply that, apart from that section, there is no power to declare the contract subsisting; the right to rescind is that of the representee, not that of the court, which merely has to decide whether the rescission was lawful: *TSB Bank plc v. Camfield* [1995] 1 W.L.R. 430, 439.

[41] In *Hughes v. Clewley, The Siben (No. 2)* [1996] 1 Lloyd's Rep. 35 it was held that rescission will not be ordered [sic] if the effect would be to transfer a business being used for unlawful purposes from one party to the other. The case was one of fraud, so there was no power to declare the contract subsisting under s.2(2). See further below.

[42] *Horsler v. Zorro* [1975] Ch. 302, 310.

[43] [1979] I.R. 149.

under which the bank would have taken over the properties and refunded the purchase price to the plaintiff.

Misrepresentation inducing consent order. Where proceedings are compro- **6–111**
mised by agreement, and the compromise is made the subject of a consent order,
the court may set aside the consent order if it is shown to have been based on an
agreement induced by misrepresentation.[44]

(b) *Restitutio in Integrum*

Restitutio in integrum. The purpose of rescission is to restore the *status quo* **6–112**
ante, and it was said by Bowen L.J. in *Newbigging v. Adam*[45] that "there
ought . . . to be a giving back and a taking back on both sides." Thus the
traditional view is that the remedy will not lie if the parties are not in a position
to make *restitutio in integrum*. In *Clarke v. Dickson*[46] Crompton J. said that when
a party "exercises his option to rescind the contract, he must be in a state to
rescind; that is he must be in such a situation as to be able to put the parties into
their original state before the contract."

Common law and equity. Common law put a strict interpretation on the **6–113**
requirement of restitution, and consequently restricted the field within which
rescission could operate. Further, there was no machinery for taking accounts, or
for balancing set-offs against each other, or for making allowances. As a result
the injured party was often relegated to his remedy in damages, if any. In contrast
equity offered two advantages to the litigant. As at common law the parties to an
action for rescission were required to make restitution, but equity did not insist
that this should be precise. It was content to do practical justice between the
parties. Secondly, the greater flexibility of the machinery at its disposal enabled
equity to direct accounts to be taken and balances to be struck and adjustments
to be made which were impossible at common law. Both of these points were
emphasised by Lord Blackburn in *Erlanger v. New Sombrero Phosphate Co.*[47]:

> "It [a court of equity] can take account of profits and make allowance for deterioration.
> And I think the practice has always been for a court of equity to give this relief
> whenever, by the exercise of its powers, it can do what is practically just, though it
> cannot restore the parties precisely to the state they were in before the contract."

The present position seems to be that in contracts where the benefits received are
in their nature returnable, such as contracts of sale, while an ability to make
restitution is an essential to an action for rescission, the courts require that this

---

[44] *Dietz v. Lennig Chemicals Ltd* [1969] 1 A.C. 170. The consent order had not been drawn up in
this case, but that seems immaterial. Except in matrimonial cases, a consent order derives its force
and effect from the contract underlying it, and if the contract can be set aside, so can the order: *Purcell
v. F.C. Trigell Ltd* [1971] 1 Q.B. 358. See further *ante*, § 5–090.
[45] (1886) 34 Ch.D. 582, 595.
[46] (1858) E.B. & E. 148, 154.
[47] (1878) 3 App.Cas. 1218, 1278–1279. See also *O'Sullivan v. Management Agency Ltd* [1985]
Q.B. 428, *post*, § 7–066.

should be substantial rather than precise.[48] In other words, the equitable approach to this requirement has prevailed over that of the common law. Further, it has been suggested that a contract for services, which in their nature cannot be restored, may be rescinded despite part performance of the services by the misrepresentor.[49]

6–114   **Alteration of subject-matter.** Clearly, it is impossible to make substantial restitution of property transferred under the contract if it has altered its character. Thus in *Clarke v. Dickson*[50] rescission was refused where a partnership, in which the representee had been induced to take shares, had been converted into a limited liability company, for the existing shares were wholly different from those which he originally received. Other examples of alteration in the subject-matter of the contract sufficient to disentitle the representee to rescission are the working out of mines[51]; the conversion of an unincorporated banking company into an incorporated joint stock company[52]; a material change in the position of both parties in relation to the patents and business in question[53]; the commencement of winding-up proceedings[54] and, when completion was a bar to rescission of a contract for the sale of land,[55] part performance of a single contract.[56] On the other hand, if property has retained its substantial identity, restitution may be ordered even though it has deteriorated or depreciated or cannot be restored in its original state.[57] Thus in *Adam v. Newbigging*[58] the respondent was induced by an innocent misrepresentation to become a partner in a business which was insolvent and which subsequently failed. He was held to be entitled to rescind and to have his capital repaid although the business to be restored was worthless. Two further comments may be useful: first, in appropriate cases the court may order the plaintiff to pay compensation on account of any deterioration that has occurred, in accordance with the principle that this is preferable to allowing the defendant to retain all the advantages of property transferred under the contract.[59] The point was put by Roche J. as follows: "The principle of *restitutio in integrum*

---

[48] In *Smith New Court Securities Ltd v. Scrimgeour Vickers (Asset Management) Ltd* in the Court of Appeal it had been accepted that rescission was no longer possible because the plaintiffs had disposed of the shares they had brought. Nourse L.J. referred to this rule as harsh in relation to fungible assets: [1994] 1 W.L.R. 1271, 1280. In the House of Lords, Lord Browne-Wilkinson remarked that, if a sale of shares cannot be rescinded once the specific shares purchased have sold, "the law will need to be looked at closely hereafter": [1997] A.C. 254, 262. See Halson [1997] R.L.R. 89.

[49] *Atlantic Lines & Navigation Co. Inc. v. Hallam Ltd* [1983] 1 Lloyd's Rep. 188, 202. See further *post.* § 6–115.

[50] (1858) E.B. & E. 148. Some dicta in this case were disapproved in *Armstrong v. Jackson* [1917] 2 K.B. 822, 829. A Name at Lloyds cannot rescind membership because the benefits received are not in their nature returnable: *Lloyds of London v. Leigh* [1997] CA Transcript 1416; *Society of Lloyds v. Khan* [1998] 3 F.C.R. 93).

[51] *Vigers v. Pike* (1842) 8 Cl. & F. 562.

[52] *Western Bank of Scotland v. Addie* (1867) L.R. 1 Sc. & Div. 145, 159–160.

[53] *Sheffield Nickel Co. v. Unwin* (1877) 2 Q.B.D. 214; see also *Lagunas Nitrate Co. v. Lagunas Syndicate* [1899] 2 Ch. 392.

[54] *Oakes v. Turquand* (1867) L.R. 2 H.L. 325.

[55] See now *post*, § 6–128.

[56] *Thorpe v. Fasey* [1949] Ch. 649; *cf. Kupchak v. Dayson Holdings Co. Ltd* (1965) 53 D.L.R. (2d) 482.

[57] *Armstrong v. Jackson* [1917] 2 K.B. 822.

[58] (1888) 13 App.Cas. 308.

[59] *Lagunas Nitrate Co. v. Lagunas Syndicate* [1899] 2 Ch. 392, 456, 457. See also *O'Sullivan v. Management Agency Ltd* [1985] Q.B. 428, *post*, § 7–066.

did not require that a person should be put back into the same position as before; it meant that he should be put into as good a position as before."[60] Secondly, it seems that the courts are more willing to exercise their discretionary powers and to order restitution in a case of fraud than in a case of innocent misrepresentation.[61] Thus in *Hulton v. Hulton*[62] the court rescinded a separation deed obtained by the husband by fraudulent misrepresentation, and refused to order the wife to repay the sums that she had received under the deed because the husband had received corresponding benefits, such as freedom from molestation and from proceedings by the wife for restitution of conjugal rights.

Services. The suggestion[63] that a partly performed contract for services may   **6–115**
be rescinded is attractive but raises difficulties. One view might be that the contract is rescinded for the future, leaving the services already rendered unaffected, but this would be inconsistent with the normal view that rescission for misrepresentation is rescission *ab initio*.[64] It might also result in the party who has rendered the services going without payment for them if the contract was entire and the payment due on completion.[65] Rather the suggestion seems to be that the contract is rescinded *ab initio* but the misrepresentee must make an allowance for the services received.[66] That seems a workable proposition but it would leave an anomaly when the services had been performed by the misrepresentee: it would be rather hard if he were permitted to rescind only at the price of forgoing payment for what he had done, but unless the contract was severable it is not clear what remedy he would have to claim payment. The adjustments and allowances which a court may make in a claim for rescission may not include the allowance of a *quantum meruit*. This is suggested by *Boyd and Forrest v. Glasgow Railway*[67]: during the negotiations for a contract for constructing a railway, an innocent misrepresentation was made about the nature of the subsoil; the contractors claimed to rescind the contract, and sued on a *quantum meruit* for the difference between the contract price, which they had received, and the increased cost of the work which was due to the misrepresentation. The House of Lords, reversing the Scottish courts, rejected the claim on the ground that, if allowed, it would be equivalent to an award of damages to the contractors.

A more flexible approach? In the *Boyd and Forrest* case[68] the work had   **6–116**
actually been completed, so it was clearly too late for the contractor to "rescind", and it is to be hoped that a modern court might see its way to granting a *quantum meruit* to the misrepresentee in a case in which he only discovers that an innocent misrepresentation has been made after he has performed some of the services

---

[60] *Compagnie Chemin de Fer Paris-Orleans v. Leeston Shipping Co.* (1919) 36 T.L.R. 68, 69; *cf. Wiebe v. Butchart's Motors* [1949] 4 D.L.R. 838 (contract for sale of car rescinded subject to allowance for depreciation during use).

[61] *Spence v. Crawford* [1939] 3 All E.R. 271, 288. The effect of negligent misrepresentation in this respect is an open question.

[62] [1917] 1 K.B. 813.

[63] *Ante*, § 6–113, n. 49.

[64] *Ante*, § 6–112. These two sentences were endorsed by the Court of Appeal in *Society of Lloyds v. Lyon*, August 11, 1997 (unreported).

[65] See *post*, § 25–053.

[66] [1983] 1 Lloyd's Rep. 188, 202.

[67] 1915 S.C. (H.L.) 20.

[68] *Supra.*

required of him.[69] It has been argued that the courts should adopt a still more flexible approach to the requirement of *restitutio in integrum* where third party rights are not in question,[70] allowing restitution to be made in the form of money.[71] This, despite recent endorsement by the Court of Appeal of the difficulties alluded to earlier,[72] seems a sensible development and one which is in line with a recent decision in a case of undue influence to award "equitable compensation" when the property transferred could no longer be returned.[73]

6–117   **Indemnity distinguished from damages.** Assuming that a claimant who wishes to rescind is in a position to make *restitutio in integrum*, the present position seems to be that he may expect the restoration of benefits and resumption of burdens which have passed under the contract. Thus, if property has been delivered, it must be restored, and the claimant likewise must make restitution of any property delivered to him; and if obligations have passed to the claimant, these must be resumed by the defendant so that the restoration of the *status quo ante* may be achieved. In practical terms this means that the defendant must indemnify the claimant against obligations which he has discharged or will become liable to discharge. One problem arises: how is the rule requiring the defendant to indemnify the claimant for obligations assumed by him reconciled with the rule that damages cannot be recovered for an innocent misrepresentation which has not become a term of the contract? The traditional answer has been that the defendant must indemnify the claimant against obligations necessarily created by the contract, *i.e.* against liabilities to third parties which the contract required the claimant to incur or payments to third parties which it required him to make, but against these only. Thus the court is enabled to stop short of making an award which could be classified as damages.[74]

6–118   The practical operation of the distinction between indemnity and damages is illustrated by *Whittington v. Seale-Hayne*.[75] The plaintiffs took a lease of certain premises on the strength of the defendant's innocent misrepresentation that they were in a sanitary condition and they erected certain poultry sheds thereon. As a result of the insanitary state of the premises the manager of the plaintiffs' poultry farm became ill, and the poultry died; the local council ordered the plaintiffs to renew the drains, and the plaintiffs were obliged to remove their sheds. In an action for rescission and for an indemnity against the consequences of having entered into the contract, it was held that the plaintiffs were entitled to an indemnity against the obligations to pay rates and to effect repairs, for these were necessarily assumed under the contract. But they were not entitled to recover

---

[69] If the misrepresentation had been fraudulent or negligent the problem could be avoided since the victim could claim the cost of performing as part of the damages. In the loosely analogous situation where a contract is terminated for breach after the victim has performed part of the services required, the victim may opt to abandon his remedies on the contract and claim a *quantum meruit: Planché v. Colburn* (1831) 8 Bing. 14; see *post*, § 30–178.

[70] *cf. post*, § 7–065 *et seq.*

[71] Burrows, *Law of Restitution* (1993), pp. 133–136; Birks [1997] R.L.R.

[72] See *supra*, n. 49.

[73] *Mahoney v. Purnell* [1996] 3 All E.R. 61, discussed *post*, § 7–067.

[74] *Newbigging v. Adam* (1886) 34 Ch.D. 582, 594, *per* Bowen L.J. Cotton and Fry L.JJ. interpreted "indemnity" more widely, but their view was not followed in *Whittington v. Seale-Hayne* (1900) 82 L.T. 49, *post. cf. Horsler v. Zorro* [1975] Ch. 302 where it was held that, on termination for *breach of contract* the innocent party was entitled to recover expenses thrown away.

[75] *Supra*.

anything in respect of medical expenses or loss of poultry, or the removal of the sheds, for these were in effect claims for damages, and therefore not admissible in an action based on innocent misrepresentation.

(c) *Other Bars to Remedy of Rescission*

Restrictions on the right to rescind. The ability to make restitution is an **6–119** essential to the rescission of a contract, but it does not follow that because restitution is possible, rescission must result. For (apart altogether from the court's discretionary power to refuse rescission in cases of innocent or negligent misrepresentation)[76] the plaintiff may find his claim barred by one of three restrictions on the right to rescind, namely, affirmation of the contract, lapse of time or the acquisition by a third party of rights in the subject-matter of the contract. Until the passing of the Misrepresentation Act there was also a fourth bar to rescission in cases of innocent misrepresentation, namely, the execution of the contract; this has now been abrogated.[77]

Affirmation of the contract. If the representee, having discovered the mis- **6–120** representation, either expressly declares his intention to proceed with the contract, or does some act inconsistent with an intention to rescind the contract, he is bound by his affirmation.[78] Thus a shareholder's right to claim rescission of a contract to take shares, made on the strength of a misrepresentation in the prospectus, may be lost if, after discovering the facts, he carries on the business of which the shares give him control,[79] or if he attends a shareholders' meeting[80] or tries to sell the shares[81]; for by such acts he is taken to have affirmed the contract. But, where rescission cannot in fact be made without the co-operation of the representor, affirmation is not to be inferred merely because the representee continues to enjoy the fruits of the contract. So where purchasers of shares in a motel company continued to occupy the motel and manage the company after discovering that they had been induced to buy by fraud, this was held insufficient evidence of affirmation[82]; the purchasers in fact took prompt proceedings for rescission, and they could not have rescinded out of court without the co-operation of the vendors. And a representee who became suspicious of the truth of representations which induced her to buy a share in a partnership was held not to have affirmed merely because she continued to act as a partner while she took steps to verify her suspicions.[83] Each case is decided on its own facts, and the courts pay particular attention to the nature of the contract, to any lapse of time which may have occurred, and to the question whether the representor

---

[76] *Ante*, §§ 6–095 *et seq.*

[77] In *Hughes v. Clewley, The Siben (No. 2)* [1996] 1 Lloyd's Rep. 35 it was held that rescission will not be ordered (*sic*: see § 6–109 *ante*) if the effect would be to transfer a business being used for unlawful purposes from one party to the other. (This was a case of fraud, so there was no power to declare the contract subsisting under s.2(2).) This might seem to constitute a new bar to rescission.

[78] *Ormes v. Beadel* (1860) 2 De G.F. & J. 333; *Clough v. L. & N.W. Ry.* (1871) L.R. 7 Ex. 26, 34; *Sharpley v. Louth and East Coast Ry.* (1876) 2 Ch.D. 663.

[79] *Seddon v. North Eastern Salt Co.* [1905] 1 Ch. 326. As to the wider grounds for this decision, see *post*, § 6–128.

[80] *Sharpley v. Louth and East Coast Ry., supra.*

[81] *Re Hop and Malt Exchange and Warehouse Co., ex p. Briggs* (1866) L.R. 1 Eq. 483.

[82] *Kupchak v. Dayson Holdings Co. Ltd* (1965) 53 D.L.R. (2d) 482.

[83] *Senenayake v. Cheng* [1966] A.C. 63.

has changed his position in reliance on the absence of a protest by the representee, or whether third parties have been affected by this.[84]

6–121   **Affirmation requires knowledge.** In contracts for the sale of goods, it has
been said that the right to rescind for innocent misrepresentation will be lost
when, had the statement been a condition, the right to reject for breach of
condition would have been lost.[85] In most circumstances an act which constitutes
an acceptance of the goods within section 35 of the Sale of Goods Act, and so
bars the right to reject the goods for breach of condition, would doubtless also
constitute an affirmation of the contract and would also bar the right to rescind.
But there may be some cases in which this is not so, because a person can
"accept" goods within section 35 without knowing of his right to reject them,[86]
whereas there can be no affirmation without knowledge of the facts. In *Peyman
v. Lanjani*,[87] after a full review of the authorities, the Court of Appeal concluded
that a party entitled to rescind or avoid a contract will not be held to have
affirmed it unless he knows the facts, and also is aware that he has a right to
rescind or avoid. Such an affirmation, where there is such knowledge, is conclusive evidence of the party's election, whether or not it is acted upon, and
whether or not there is any change of position by the other party.

6–122   **Estoppel.** A party may, however, be held estopped from rescinding or avoiding the contract even where he does not know the facts or his rights, but in this
event, he must have led the other to believe, by unequivocal statements or
actions, that he does intend to affirm the contract, and the other party must show
that he has acted on the statement or conduct to his prejudice.[88]

6–123   **Lapse of time.** Lapse of time may be evidence of affirmation.[89] In *Clough v.
L. & N.W. Ry.*[90] it was said that "when the lapse of time is great it probably would
be treated in practice as conclusive evidence" of a decision to proceed with the
contract. This is especially true of contracts for the sale or allotment of shares in
companies, where the utmost promptness is required.[91] In such a case a delay of

---

[84] See *Clough v. L. & N.W. Ry.* (1871) L.R. 7 Ex. 26, 34, 35; *Bank of Credit and Commerce
International SA (in liquidation) v. Ali* [1999] 2 All E.R. 1005, 1023.

[85] *Leaf v. International Galleries* [1950] 2 K.B. 86 (lapse of time). See also *Long v. Lloyd* [1958]
1 W.L.R. 753. Sale and delivery to a sub-purchaser also amounts to acceptance (though only after he
has had a reasonable opportunity to examine the goods: Sale of Goods Act 1979, (as am.), s.35), but
if the sub-purchaser rejects the goods the right to rescind for misrepresentation can probably still be
exercised, *cf.* § 6–127, *post.* It should make no difference to the right to rescind for misrepresentation
that the representation has become a term of the contract: Misrepresentation Act 1967, s.1(a). On loss
of the right to reject, see *post*, Vol. II, §§ 43–272 *et seq.*

[86] *e.g. Leaf v. International Galleries, supra.*

[87] [1985] Ch. 457.

[88] *ibid.* See also *Container Transport International Inc. v. Oceanus Mutual Underwriting Association (Bermuda) Ltd* [1984] 1 Lloyd's Rep. 476; *Motor Oil Hellas (Corinth Refineries SA v. Shipping
Corp. of India (The Kanchenjunga)* [1990] 1 Lloyd's Rep. 391, 397–399.

[89] *Lindsay Petroleum Co. v. Hurd* (1874) L.R. 5 P.C. 221; *Erlanger v. New Sombrero Phosphate
Co.* (1878) 3 App.Cas. 1218; *Clough v. L. & N.W. Ry.* (1871) L.R. 7 Ex. 26, 35; *Oelkers v. Ellis* [1914]
2 K.B. 139; *Armstrong v. Jackson* [1917] 2 K.B. 822; *Leaf v. International Galleries* [1950] 2 K.B.
86.

[90] (1871) L.R. 7 Ex. 26, 34, 35.

[91] *Taite's Case* (1867) L.R. 3 Eq. 795; *Sharpley v. Louth and East Coast Ry.* (1876) 2 Ch.D. 663;
Re Scottish Petroleum Co. (1883) 23 Ch.D. 413; *Aaron's Reefs Ltd v. Twiss* [1896] A.C. 273, 294;
Taylor v. Oil and Ozokerite Co. (1913) 29 T.L.R. 515; *First National Reinsurance Co. Ltd v.
Greenfield* [1921] 2 K.B. 260.

even a few weeks after discovery of the misrepresentation is usually fatal, and there cannot, in any event, be rescission of an allotment after the company has gone into liquidation.[92] But there can normally be no affirmation where the representee is ignorant of the truth and therefore of his right to rescind,[93] and the inference of affirmation from lapse of time should therefore be rebuttable by proof of lack of knowledge of the untruth. Yet in *Leaf v. International Galleries*[94] the right to rescind was held barred by five years' delay despite the fact that the representee only discovered the truth shortly before the proceedings. It seems, therefore, that mere lapse of time may itself bar rescission in cases of completely innocent misrepresentation, but this will not be so in cases of fraud, nor where there has been breach of a fiduciary duty.[95]

Effect on representee. In considering whether the representee has lost his **6–124** right to rescind by lapse of time, it may be important to inquire if the representee has been adversely affected by the delay.[96] Thus in *Morrison v. Universal Marine Insurance Co.*[97] it was said that rescission of a contract of marine insurance, the policy of which was voidable for non-disclosure of a material fact, would have been refused if there had been any evidence that the failure of the underwriters to avoid the contract after they had become aware of the defect had led the insured party to refrain from insuring elsewhere. But the fact that the representor has changed his position is not by itself a bar to rescission, so, *e.g.* a contract of guarantee can be rescinded by the guarantor notwithstanding that money has been lent by the representor in reliance on the guarantee.[98] But prompt action would doubtless be required once the representee knows the truth in a case of this nature.

Third-party rights. The intervention of a third party may prevent rescission. **6–125** This is one of the risks run by the injured party if he delays in taking action, for if a third party acquires an interest in the subject-matter of the contract before the contract has been avoided a claim for rescission will not lie,[99] provided that the third party acted in good faith and gave consideration.[1] Thus, although there may be no duty to act within a prescribed time, it is in the representee's interest to act promptly, for the longer the delay, the greater the possibility of a third party acquiring rights in the subject-matter of the contract. This rule does not apply to

---

[92] *Oakes v. Turquand* (1867) L.R. 2 H.L. 325.

[93] *Aaron's Reefs Ltd v. Twiss* [1896] A.C. 273, 287; *Armstrong v. Jackson* [1917] 2 K.B. 822; and see *ante*, § 6–121.

[94] [1950] 2 K.B. 86.

[95] *Armstrong v. Jackson, supra.* Nor where there has been a breach of condition: *Allen v. Robles* [1969] 1 W.L.R. 1193 (delay no bar unless so long that evidence of waiver).

[96] See *Clough v. L. & N.W. Ry.* (1871) L.R. 7 Ex. 26, 34, 35; *Morrison v. Universal Marine Insurance Co.* (1873) L.R. 8 Ex. 197, 205; *Erlanger v. New Sombrero Phosphate Co.* (1878) 3 App.Cas. 1218, 1278. See also *Re Cape Breton Co.* (1885) 29 Ch.D. 795 and *Ladywell Mining Co. v. Brookes* (1887) 35 Ch.D. 400. In *Leaf v. International Galleries, supra*, Denning L.J. and Lord Evershed M.R. said that the right rescind for innocent misrepresentation must be barred if a right to reject for breach of condition would be barred by acceptance, *sed quaere*: the latter may be lost by acceptance after a reasonable time has passed, which may be after a matter of weeks: *Bernstein v. Pamson Motors (Golders Green) Ltd* [1987] 2 All E.R. 220. It is not clear that a similar rule applies to rescission for innocent misrepresentation.

[97] (1873) L.R. 8 Ex. 197.

[98] *Mackenzie v. Royal Bank of Canada* [1934] A.C. 468.

[99] *White v. Garden* (1851) 10 C.B. 919; *Babcock v. Lawson* (1880) 5 Q.B.D. 284; *Re L.G. Clarke* [1967] Ch. 1121.

[1] *Scholefield v. Templer* (1859) 4 De G. & J. 429, 433–434.

void contracts, for in such cases the transferee has no title to pass to the third party[2]; it does apply to voidable contracts, for here the transferee has a good title until the contract is avoided.[3] Thus the rule may operate in all cases of misrepresentation (whether innocent, negligent or fraudulent) unless the effect of the misrepresentation is to make the contract void for mistake.[4] The effect on third parties, in this case insured persons, may also prevent a Name at Lloyd's from rescinding her agreement to become a Name.[4a]

6–126 **Assignments "subject to equities".** But this principle only applies to a transfer of goods and not to an assignment of contractual rights. If A is induced to sell goods to B by the fraud of B, and B resells the goods to C who takes in good faith and for value, C acquires a good title to the goods. But if A is induced to buy goods from B by the fraud of B, and B assigns the right to receive the purchase price to C, the rule that assignments are "subject to equities"[5] means that C gets no better right than B.

6–127 **Rescission by sub-buyer.** If a contract is induced by an innocent misrepresentation and that same innocent misrepresentation is passed on to a sub-buyer and in turn induces a subcontract, the sub-buyer may rescind the subcontract; if he does so, there is nothing to prevent the first representee from rescinding the original contract.[6]

6–128 **Executed contracts.** Until the passing of the Misrepresentation Act 1967 there was a further bar to rescission in certain cases of innocent misrepresentation, namely, the execution of the contract. This rule, often known as the rule in *Seddon v. North Eastern Salt Co. Ltd*[7] did not apply to cases of fraud, nor to cases of breach of fiduciary relationships,[8] and its application to particular types of contract was much disputed. The rule was, however, completely abrogated by section 1(b) of the Misrepresentation Act which provides that the performance of the contract shall be no bar to rescission for any misrepresentation where it would not have barred rescission for fraud. Although the Law Reform Committee (on whose Report the Act was based) had recommended that this rule should be retained for contracts for the sale of an interest in land, except for leases not exceeding three years,[9] the Act contains no special provision for such contracts. And despite the fact that the word "performed" is perhaps not wholly appropriate to contracts for the sale of an interest in land, it is thought that there can be no doubt that rescission of such contracts is now possible after execution of a conveyance or other grant in all cases of misrepresentation. Of course, the

---

[2] *Hardman v. Booth* (1863) 1 H. & C. 803; *Cundy v. Lindsay* (1878) 3 App.Cas. 459; *Ingram v. Little* [1961] 1 Q.B. 31.

[3] Sale of Goods Act 1979, s.23.

[4] As, for example, in *Cundy v. Lindsay, supra,* and *Ingram v. Little, supra.* The rule that intervention of third party rights prevents rescission is normally invoked where a third party has acquired rights over the property transferred; but it can also apply where liability to third parties has been incurred before rescission is claimed and rescission would cause detriment to them: *Society of Lloyd's v. Lyon,* August 11, 1997 (unreported).

[4a] *Society of Lloyds v. Khan* [1998] 3 F.C.R. 93.

[5] *Post,* § 20–068.

[6] *Abram SS. Co. v. Westville Shipping Co.* [1923] A.C. 773.

[7] [1905] 1 Ch. 326. See also *Senenayake v. Cheng* [1966] A.C. 63, decided shortly before the 1967 Act was passed.

[8] *Armstrong v. Jackson* [1917] 2 K.B. 822.

[9] Tenth Report, Cmnd. 1782 (1962), §§ 6 and 7.

execution of the contract may still be a bar to rescission on other grounds, for example, because it is evidence of affirmation,[10] or because *restitutio in integrum* is no longer possible.[11] Moreover, it is to be anticipated that a court might be more ready to exercise its discretion under section 2(2) of the Act of 1967 to award damages in lieu of rescission in cases where the contract has been executed.[12] But execution of the contract will no longer in itself be an absolute bar to rescission.

5. EXCLUSION OF LIABILITY FOR MISREPRESENTATION

Position at common law. At common law a person could not contract out of   **6–129** liability for fraud inducing the making of a contract with him, at least where the fraud was his own.[13] It is, however, possible that he could do so where the fraud was that of his employees,[14] and there seems no doubt that it was possible, by a provision of the contract itself, to exclude or modify the normal consequences of innocent or negligent misrepresentation.[15] Such clauses were, however, subject to the normal principles of construction common to all exemption clauses.[16]

Misrepresentation Act, s.3. Section 3 of the Act of 1967 limits the freedom   **6–130** of the parties to contract out of the effect of the Act in certain respects. The original section 3 was replaced by section 8 of the Unfair Contract Terms Act 1977, and the new section 3 is now as follows:

"If a contract contains a term which would exclude or restrict—
(a) any liability to which a party to a contract may be subject by reason of any misrepresentation made by him before the contract was made; or
(b) any remedy available to another party to the contract by reason of such a misrepresentation,
that term shall be of no effect except in so far as it satisfies the requirement of reasonableness as stated in section 11(1) of the Unfair Contract Terms Act 1977; and it is for those claiming that the term satisfies that requirement to show that it does."

The main change of substance between the new and the original section 3 is that under the original section it was *reliance* on the exempting provision which had to be shown to be reasonable; under the new section 3, it is the exempting term

---

[10] *Ante*, § 6–120.
[11] *Ante*, §§ 6–112—6–118.
[12] *Ante*, § 6–100.
[13] *S. Pearson & Son Ltd v. Dublin Corpn.* [1907] A.C. 351.
[14] See *John Carter (Fine Worsteds) Ltd v. Hanson Haulage (Leeds) Ltd* [1965] 2 Q.B. 495.
[15] *Boyd and Forrest v. Glasgow Ry.*, 1915 S.C. (HL) 20, 36. A properly worded clause which excludes a right of avoidance will be effective (assuming it is not affected by Misrepresentation Act 1967, s.3, see next para.) notwithstanding a purported rescission of the contract as a whole by the misrepresentee: *Toomey v. Eagle Star Insurance Co. Ltd (No. 2)* [1995] 2 Lloyd's Rep. 88.
[16] *Post*, Chap. 14. Thus a clause stating that a contract of re-insurance was "neither cancellable nor voidable by either party" was held to apply only to cases of innocent misrepresentation or non-disclosure, and not to alleged negligence, nor to exclude the right to damages under Misrepresentation Act 1967, s.2(1): *Toomey v. Eagle Star Insurance Co. Ltd (No. 2)* [1995] 2 Lloyd's Rep. 88. A disclaimer "without responsibility" does not prevent rescission on the ground of misrepresentation: *Credit Lyonnais Bank Nederland v. Export Credit Guarantee Department* [1996] 1 Lloyd's Rep. 1. However, a clause applying to "rights, obligations and liabilities arising . . . in connection with this contract" may apply to a claim for misrepresentation, *Strachan & Henshaw Ltd v. Stein Industrie (U.K.) Ltd (No. 2)* (1997) 87 B.L.R. 52.

itself which has to be shown to be reasonable. Thus a very wide exempting term may be held unreasonable under the new section 3 while reliance on it might have been reasonable under the old section 3[17]; equally, a term may now be held reasonable where reliance on it in particular circumstances might formerly have been held unreasonable. A further change is that the new section 3 makes it clear that the onus is on a person claiming to rely upon an exempting term to show that it is reasonable under the relevant section of the Unfair Contract Terms Act. The requirement of reasonableness is now stated in section 11(1) of the Unfair Contract Terms Act 1977 as a requirement that the term in question "shall have been a fair and reasonable one to be included having regard to the circumstances which were, or ought reasonably to have been, known to or in the contemplation of the parties when the contract was made." Reasonableness under the Act is discussed *post* (§§ 14–081—14–094).[18]

6–131   The following points about this section should be noted. First, the terms "any liability" and "any remedy" are presumably wide enough to cover provisions which would exclude or restrict a claim to damages, or the right to rescind, or the right to set up the misrepresentation by way of defence to an action.[19] Secondly, the section applies not merely to provisions totally excluding the normal consequences of misrepresentation, but also to provisions which restrict any liability or remedy arising from a misrepresentation. This means, for instance, that a provision barring rescission but allowing claims for damages would fall within the section, as also would a provision limiting the amount of damages or the time within which a claim may be made. It has, however, been held that the section does not prevent a principal from limiting the authority of his agent even though the effect is to exclude or restrict a liability to which the principal would otherwise be subject.[20] Nor does it apply to clauses stating that the written document constitutes the entire contract and that particulars given do not constitute an offer or contract.[21] Thirdly, it seems that the court must consider the reasonableness of the provision as a whole.[22] A clause may be invalid because, taken as a whole, it is too wide, even though it would not necessarily be unreasonable to exclude or restrict liability on the facts which have occurred. Thus a clause which purports to exclude liability for misrepresentation of any

---

[17] In the *Howard Marine* case [1978] Q.B. 554 (*ante*, § 6–068) Lord Denning M.R. was prepared to uphold reliance on an exempting clause under the old s.3 as reasonable; the majority of the court disagreed without giving reasons.

[18] It has been held that condition 17 of the National Conditions of Sale (19th edition) was invalid as unreasonable under the new section 3 of the Misrepresentation Act: *Walker v. Boyle* [1982] 1 W.L.R. 495. Condition 17 stated that replies to questions by the vendor or his agents do not obviate the need for the buyer to make his own inquiries and inspections, and are not to be treated as representations. See also *Southwestern General Property Co. Ltd v. Marton* (1982) 263 E.G. 1090; *White Cross Equipment Ltd v. Farrell* (1982) 2 Tr.L.R. 21; *Cooper v. Tamms* [1988] 1 E.G.L.R. 257; *Goff v. Gauthier* [1991] 62 P. & C.R. 388.

[19] A right of set-off is a remedy for this purpose: *Skipskredittforeningen v. Emperor Navigation* [1998] 1 Lloyd's Rep. 66, not following *Society of Lloyd's v. Wilkinson (No. 2)* [1997] 6 Re L.R. 214 on this point. See also *WRM Group Ltd v. Wood* [1998] C.L.C. 189. But a term that purchasers of a lease would be permitted to enter into possession before completion "at their own risk" was held not to be within the section (though unreasonable if it was): *F. & H. Entertainments Ltd v. Leisure Enterprises Ltd* (1976) 120 S.J. 331.

[20] *Overbrooke Estates Ltd v. Glencombe Properties Ltd* [1974] 1 W.L.R. 1335, approved by the Court of Appeal in *Museprime Properties Ltd v. Adhill Properties Ltd* [1990] 2 E.G.L.R. 196, 200.

[21] *McGrath v. Shah* (1989) 57 P. & C.R. 452.

[22] See *post*, § 14–091. *cf. R. W. Green Ltd v. Cade Bros.* [1978] 1 Lloyd's Rep. 602.

kind will be unreasonable, since it is not reasonable to exclude liability for fraud, and the clause as a whole will be invalid.[23] The court should not, however, hold a clause unreasonable because it might extend to some situation which is unlikely to occur.[24] But if the clause is too wide, the court cannot rewrite the clause in a reasonable fashion and, as the test under section 11(1) of the Unfair Contract Terms Act 1977 is whether the term was "a fair and reasonable one to be included," it seems that the court could not allow the misrepresentor to rely on it so far as seems reasonable.[25] Thus it cannot uphold a provision in so far as it would bar rescission, but reject it in so far as it would bar a claim for damages. However, it is possible that a clause which is in distinct parts might be severed and the reasonable parts upheld.

Clauses covering breach. The section does not seem to apply to a provision   **6–132** which excludes or restricts liability arising solely from breach of a contractual term, whether the term is a promise or a representation of fact. But, read literally, the section would appear to apply to a provision which excludes or restricts liabilities or remedies arising both from misrepresentations as such, and from misrepresentations as contractual terms.[26]

Effect of contractual term that representee not to rely on statements. In   **6–133** certain types of contract, *e.g.* building contracts, it is common for information to be given by one party to the other, but for express terms to be included in the contract documents, or the contract itself, stating that the representee is not to rely upon the statements of the representor, but is to satisfy himself as to their truth or accuracy. The effect of such a term was discussed in *Cremdean Properties Ltd v. Nash*[27] where the defendants invited tenders for the construction of certain buildings. The invitation to tender contained various particulars as to the dimensions of the premises which were to be built, and the amount of lettable office space they would contain. Some of these particulars were false. The invitation also contained a notice declaring that tenderers were to satisfy themselves as to the correctness of all statements in the documents, and were not to rely thereon. The tenderers sought rescission for misrepresentation, and the owners relied on the notice by way of defence. It was held that section 3 of the 1967 Act (in its original form)[28] could not be used to settle the issue as a pure question of law. The question was whether a misrepresentation was made; if it was, section 3 necessarily applied, and its effect could not be excluded. But the notice might, in conjunction with the rest of the evidence, negative any actual misrepresentation; in effect the notice might be taken to mean that the statements complained of were not being asserted or represented as facts at all, but (for

---

[23] *Thomas Witter Ltd v. TBP Industries Ltd* [1992] All E.R. 573. *cf. Stewart Gill Ltd v. Horatio Myer & Co. Ltd* [1992] Q.B. 600; *post*, § 14–091. In *Skipskredittforeningen v. Emperor Navigation* [1998] 1 Lloyd's Rep. 66 it was held not to be unreasonable to include in a loan agreement a no-set off clause which might apply even in cases of fraud.

[24] *Skipskredittforeningen v. Emperor Navigation* [1998] 1 Lloyd's Rep. 66, 75–76.

[25] Compare the formulation used by the original version of s.3 before amendment by the 1977 Act: " . . . that provision shall be of no effect except to the extent that . . . the court or arbitrator may allow reliance on it as being fair and reasonable in the circumstances of the case."

[26] As already seen (*ante*, § 6–103) s.1(a) of the 1967 Act provides that a misrepresentation continues to be effective as such even if it becomes a term of the contract. See also *post*, § 14–105.

[27] (1977) 241 E.G. 837.

[28] But nothing in the new s.3 affects this point.

instance) merely proffered as matters of opinion; alternatively the evidence may show, taken as a whole, that the representee did not rely on the misrepresentation. The decision in this case appears to use a test for the application of section 3 which is close to that used by the courts in deciding whether a disclaimer is effective under the Trade Descriptions Act 1968, and cases under that Act may therefore be relevant to this issue.[29]

6–134   **Other statutory provisions affecting disclaimers.** A clause aimed at preventing liability arising in tort under *Hedley Byrne & Co. Ltd v. Heller & Partners Ltd*[30] on the part of a business will be valid under the Unfair Contract Terms Act 1977, s.2(2) only if it satisfies the requirement of reasonableness under that Act.[31] The Unfair Terms in Consumer Contracts Regulations 1994[32] also affect clauses in consumer contracts which unfairly exclude or restrict the consumer's remedies for misrepresentation. For the most part it seems likely that the test of unfairness under the Regulations will produce substantially similar results to the reasonableness test of section 11 of the Unfair Contract Terms Act 1977. Any clause excluding or limiting liability for misrepresentation, however it is worded, will be within the Regulations provided that it is "in a contract concluded between a seller or supplier and a consumer" and "has not been individually negotiated".[33] Thus clauses limiting the authority of agents or defining the terms of the contract, which are not caught by section 3 of the Misrepresentation Act 1967,[34] will be covered.

6. CONTRACTS *UBERRIMAE FIDEI*

6–135   **Non-disclosure.** Mere non-disclosure of fact, material or not, does not ordinarily amount to misrepresentation, and the general rule is that in order to be actionable a representation must take an active form.[35] But in certain cases a stricter rule is enforced. The most important of these are the contracts *uberrimae fidei*[36] in which knowledge of the material facts generally lies with one party alone; that party is under a duty to make a full disclosure of these facts, and failure to do so makes the contract voidable. However, even if the non-disclosure is negligent, it does not give rise to liability in damages under Misrepresentation Act 1967, section 2(1) or, without more, at common law.[37] The duty varies in its extent from one type of contract to another. Contracts of insurance of every kind form the main group of contracts *uberrimae fidei*. Other examples generally included, though these are probably not all *uberrimae fidei* in the strict sense, are

---

[29] See in particular *R. v. Hammerton Cars Ltd* [1976] 1 W.L.R. 1243; *Waltham Forest L.B.C. v. T. G. Wheatley* [1978] R.T.R. 157; *R. v. Southwood* [1987] 1 W.L.R. 1361.

[30] [1964] A.C. 465; *ante*, § 6–081.

[31] *Smith v. Eric S. Bush* [1990] 1 A.C. 831; see *ante*, § 6–083 and *post*, § 14–088.

[32] S.I. 1994, No. 3159; see *post*, Chap. 15.

[33] Reg. 3(1).

[34] See *ante*, § 6–131.

[35] See *ante*, § 6–013.

[36] For the others, see *ante*, §§ 6–013—6–017.

[37] *Banque Keyser Ullman SA v. Skandia (U.K.) Insurance Co. Ltd* [1990] 1 Q.B. 665, 787–789, 790–805, affd. on other grounds [1991] 2 A.C. 249. See *ante*, § 1–074.

contracts to subscribe for shares in a company,[38] family settlements,[39] contracts for the sale of land,[40] contracts for suretyship,[41] and partnerships. Contracts of service are not *uberrimae fidei*[42] nor are contracts of sale of goods.[43]

Contracts of insurance.[44] All of these are *uberrimae fidei*, whatever their **6–136** subject-matter, that is whether they relate to marine, fire, life or burglary insurance, or to any other risk. Marine insurance is governed by the Marine Insurance Act 1906, which codified the existing law. Non-marine insurance is subject to the common law. It is thought to be contrary to good faith to withhold material facts from the insurer.[45] Such facts are generally known only to the assured, and he is therefore under a duty to disclose them.[46]

Materiality. A circumstance is material if it "would influence the judgment **6–137** of a prudent insurer in fixing the premium, or determining whether he will take the risk." This is the definition given in the Marine Insurance Act 1906, s.18(2), and it was held in *Locker and Woolf Ltd v. Western Australian Insurance Co. Ltd*[47] that the definition applies to all forms of insurance. In *Pan Atlantic Insurance Co. Ltd v. Pine Top Insurance Co. Ltd*[48] the House of Lords held that, for both marine insurance under Marine Insurance Act 1906, section 18(2) and non-marine insurance, the test of materiality is not whether the matter would have had a decisive effect on the prudent insurer's decision whether to accept the risk or at what premium, but whether it would have an effect on the mind of the prudent insurer in weighing up the risk.[49] In *St. Paul Fire and Marine Insurance Co. Ltd v. McConnell Dowell Constructors Ltd*[50] it was held that a matter did not necessarily have to lead to an increase in the risk in order to be material; it was sufficient that the risk was different.[51] But in the *Pan Atlantic* case the House of Lords held that, in addition to being material, a misrepresentation or non-disclosure must have induced the making of the policy.[52] In this respect, the law

---

[38] *Post*, § 6–145.

[39] *Post*, § 6–147.

[40] *Post*, § 6–148.

[41] *Post*, § 6–150.

[42] *Bell v. Lever Bros. Ltd* [1932] A.C. 161, 227.

[43] *Jewson & Sons Ltd v. Arcos Ltd* (1932) 39 Com.Cas. 59.

[44] See Hasson (1969) 32 M.L.R. 615 and Vol. II, §§ 41–026 *et seq.* Proposals for reform of the law were made by the Law Commission, see Law Com. No. 104, Cmnd. 8064 (1980).

[45] See *Carter v. Boehm* (1766) 3 Burr. 1905, 1909; *London Assurance Co. v. Mansel* (1879) 11 Ch.D. 363, 367.

[46] A contract of marine insurance appears to be based on an implied condition that there is no misrepresentation or concealment: *Blackburn v. Vigors* (1886) 17 Q.B.D. 552, 561, 562; *Pickersgill v. London and Provincial Marine and General Insurance Co.* [1912] 3 K.B. 614, 621. The duty of disclosure in non-marine insurance, on the other hand, is said to rest on a common law, and not on a contractual duty: *Joel v. Law Union and Crown Insurance Co.* [1908] 2 K.B. 863, 886; *Merchants and Manufacturers Insurance Co. v. Hunt and Thorne* [1941] 1 K.B. 295, 313. But see *Moens v. Hayworth* (1842) 10 M. & W. 147, 157. It is otherwise of course if the common law obligation is superseded by a term in the contract itself.

[47] [1936] 1 K.B. 408, 415. This was also the test applied in *Lambert v. Co-operative Insurance Society Ltd* [1975] 2 Lloyd's Rep. 485.

[48] [1995] 1 A.C. 501.

[49] See further *post*, Vol. II, § 49–027.

[50] [1996] 1 All E.R. 96.

[51] *ibid.* at 107.

[52] [1995] 1 A.C. 501, 549–550.

on insurance contracts is parallel to the general law on positive misrepresenta-tion.[53] Lord Mustill[54] refers to "a presumption in favour of causative effect", as there is in the case of a positive misrepresentation.[55]

6–138   **Duty on insurer also.** The obligation to disclose material facts is mutual and a duty also rests on the insurer to disclose all facts known to him which are material either to the nature of the risk sought to be covered or to the recover-ability of a claim under the policy.[56] In this case the test of materiality is whether the fact not disclosed would be taken into account by a prudent insured in deciding whether to place the risk with that insurer.[57]

6–139   The following have been held to be material facts and their non-disclosure made the contract in question voidable: that goods were insured upon a voyage for an amount in excess of their value[58]; that the vessel itself was over-insured[59]; that (in the particular circumstances of the case) the insured under a policy of burglary insurance was an alien[60]; that the insured had been convicted of robbery 12 years previously[61]; that in relation to an insurance comparable to that sought previous claims had been made.[62] On the other hand, certain details may on construction be held to be irrelevant,[63] such as the place where a lorry was to be garaged.[64] A circumstance that is material for one type of insurance is not necessarily material for another; for example, the fact that the risk has been refused by another company is material in life, fire, accident and burglary insurance, but not in marine insurance.[65] Whether a particular circumstance is material is a question of fact, and the opinion of the assured on its materiality is irrelevant.[66]

6–140   In marine insurance the duty to disclose is defined as follows:

"Subject to the provisions of this section, the assured must disclose to the insurer,

---

[53] See *ante*, § 6–034.

[54] [1995] 1 A.C. 501, 542.

[55] See *ante*, § 6–034, n. 67; and also *St. Paul Fire and Marine Insurance Co. Ltd v. McConnell Dowell Constructors Ltd* [1996] 1 All E.R. 96, 112.

[56] *Carter v. Boehm* (1766) 3 Burr. 1905; *Banque Keyser Ullman SA v. Skandia (U.K.) Insurance Co. Ltd* [1990] 1 Q.B. 665, 770–772, affd. on other grounds but without disapproval of this statement of principle, [1991] 2 A.C. 249.

[57] *ibid.* [1990] 1 Q.B. 665, 772.

[58] *Ionides v. Pender* (1874) L.R. 9 Q.B. 531; *Gooding v. White* (1913) 29 T.L.R. 312.

[59] *Thames and Mersey Marine Insurance Co. v. Gunford Ship Co. Ltd* [1911] A.C. 529.

[60] *Horne v. Poland* [1922] 2 K.B. 364. But *cf. Associated Oil Carriers Ltd v. Union Insurance Society* [1917] 2 K.B. 184.

[61] *Woolcott v. Sun Alliance & London Insurance Ltd* [1978] 1 W.L.R. 493; contrast *Reynolds and Anderson v. Phoenix Assurance Co. Ltd* [1978] 2 Lloyd's Rep. 440 (mere allegation of fraud need not be disclosed). Note the effect of the Rehabilitation of Offenders Act 1974 on cases of this kind, see s.4(2) and (3).

[62] *Farra v. Hetherington* (1931) 47 T.L.R. 465.

[63] *Perrins v. Marine Insurance Society* (1859) 2 E. & E. 317.

[64] *Dawsons Ltd v. Bonnin* [1922] 2 A.C. 413.

[65] *London Assurance Co. v. Mansel* (1879) 11 Ch.D. 363; *Yager v. Guardian Assurance Co.* (1912) 29 T.L.R. 53; *Glicksman v. Lancashire and General Assurance Co.* [1927] A.C. 139; *Holts' Motors v. South East Lancashire Insurance Co.* (1930) 35 Com.Cas. 281; *Locker and Woolf Ltd v. Western Australian Insurance Co.* [1936] 1 K.B. 408.

[66] *Lindenau v. Desborough* (1828) 8 B. & C. 586, 592; *London Assurance Co. v. Mansel* (1879) 11 Ch.D. 363; *Joel v. Law Union and Crown Insurance Co.* [1908] 2 K.B. 863, 884; *Godfrey v. Britannic Assurance Co. Ltd* [1963] 2 Lloyd's Rep. 515; *Lambert v. Co-operative Insurance Society Ltd* [1975] 2 Lloyd's Rep. 485.

before the contract is concluded, every material circumstance which is known to the assured and the assured is deemed to know every circumstance which, in the ordinary course of business, ought to be known by him."[67]

In non-marine insurance the duty may extend only to facts actually known to the assured.[68] If so, he is under no duty to disclose facts of which he is ignorant. A statement which is expressed to depend on the assured's state of mind will not be untrue simply because he was unaware of the true facts, provided that his statement of belief was genuine. For instance, a statement by the assured that he is in good health in relation to a proposed life policy will generally be construed to mean in good health to his own knowledge, and the contract cannot be rescinded on proof that at the time of the contract the assured's state of health was not what he believed it to be.[69] If, however, he is aware of a fact which a reasonable or prudent insurer might treat as material, he must disclose it; the test is not whether a reasonable man would think it material.[70]

"Basis of the contract". But the duty to disclose may be enlarged by the terms of the contract, and insurers commonly provide that the declarations of the assured shall form the basis of the contract. In effect this means that the assured guarantees that the information which he supplies is correct, the penalty for inaccuracy being the avoidance of the contract by the insurer. Thus a contract may be avoided if the assured fails to disclose even a non-material fact,[71] or a fact never within his knowledge, or if he gives what has proved to be an inaccurate statement on a matter of opinion.[72] Where an attempt is made to enlarge the duty by the terms of the contract, the courts put a strict burden of proof upon the insurer.[73] But this has not prevented the courts from holding that even disclosure to a representative of the insurer is insufficient, if (as has in the past commonly been the case with some forms of insurance) the proposal form declares that any person filling in the form is deemed to be the agent of the insured, and not of the insurer.[74] More recently, however, it has been held that if the representative is   **6–141**

---

[67] Marine Insurance Act 1906, s.18(1). On the interpretation of this section see *PCW Syndicates v. PCW Reinsurers* [1996] 1 W.L.R. 1136.

[68] *Blackburn, Low & Co. v. Vigors* (1887) 12 App.Cas. 531 (a marine insurance case before the Marine Insurance Act 1906); *Joel v. Law Union and Crown Insurance Co.* [1908] 2 K.B. 863, 884–885. In the *Economides v. Commercial Union Assurance Co. plc* [1998] Q.B. 587 it was held that an insured who is not acting in the course of business has only to disclose material facts actually known to him; provided that he did not wilfully shut his eyes to the truth (so-called "Nelsonian blindness"), he is not under a duty to inquire further, for example by checking that his honest belief in the value of the property is in fact accurate. But see Vol. II, § 41–032.

[69] *Wheelton v. Hardisty* (1857) 8 E. & B. 232. But see *Macdonald v. Law Union Insurance Co.* (1874) L.R. 9 Q.B. 328.

[70] *Lambert v. Co-operative Insurance Society Ltd* [1975] 2 Lloyd's Rep. 485.

[71] *Anderson v. Fitzgerald* (1853) 4 H.L.C. 484; *Condogianis v. Guardian Assurance Co.* [1921] 2 A.C. 125; *Dawsons Ltd v. Bonnin* [1922] 2 A.C. 413. See Vol. II, § 41–035.

[72] For the insurance industry's Statement of Insurance Practice which relates to non-disclosure of matters not known to the insured, see Law Com. No. 104, para. 31.26 and *infra*, § 41–036.

[73] *Anderson v. Fitzgerald* (1853) 4 H.L.C. 484; *Joel v. Law Union and Crown Insurance Co.* [1908] 2 K.B. 863; *Anstey v. British National Premium Life Association Ltd* (1908) 99 L.T. 765.

[74] *Newsholme Brothers v. Road Transport and General Insurance Co. Ltd* [1929] 2 K.B. 356; *Facer v. Vehicle & General Insurance Co. Ltd* [1965] 1 Lloyd's Rep. 113. *Contra, Bawden v. London, Edinburgh and Glasgow Assurance Co. Ltd* [1892] 2 Q.B. 534; this case was treated as virtually overruled by the *Newsholme Bros.* case, *supra*, in the *Facer* case, *supra*, but now seems to have been rehabilitated by *Stone v. Reliance Mutual Insurance Society Ltd* [1972] 1 Lloyd's Rep. 469. Such a clause might well be caught by Unfair Terms in Consumer Contracts Regulations, 1994: see *post*, § 15–066.

authorised by the insurer to fill in the forms and then secure the proposer's signature thereto, he may be held to be the agent of the insurer.[75]

6–142 **Burden of proof.** With regard to the burden of proof generally, the insurer must produce evidence to show non-disclosure, unless there is prima facie evidence of concealment. In that case the burden is on the assured to prove disclosure.[76]

6–143 **Continuing duty.** The duty to disclose continues until the contract is concluded. Thus if before the acceptance of the proposal a new material fact arises, or a fact thought to be non-material becomes material, this must be disclosed.[77]

6–144 **Effect of Misrepresentation Act on insurance contracts.** It has been seen above that the Act of 1967 has no application to cases of pure non-disclosure,[78] but most insurance contracts in effect convert what would be a non-disclosure into a positive misrepresentation constituting a term of the contract. It has also been seen above[79] that it is not clear whether section 2(2) of the Misrepresentation Act enables a court to refuse to allow rescission for misrepresentation where the statement in question was later incorporated as a term of the contract. If it did have this effect, the totally unexpected result might follow, that an insurer might no longer be able to repudiate liability for an immaterial misrepresentation, or even for a material misrepresentation which had no bearing on the risk which has occurred. But this is not generally thought to be the result of the 1967 Act[80]; and in any event it is very unlikely that the court would exercise its jurisdiction to prevent an insurer rescinding on the ground of misrepresentation by the insured.[81]

6–145 **Companies.** Contracts to take shares in companies may be classified as *uberrimae fidei* because again the knowledge of the material facts lies with one party alone, namely, the promoters, directors and others responsible for the issue of the prospectus. It was long ago recognised that invitations to invest, made through a prospectus, could lead to much enrichment of individuals at the public expense, and at least from promoters the utmost good faith was required.[82] In time the legislature intervened to protect the public and to supplement the common law. The present position is largely governed by the Financial Services Act 1986. Sections 146 and 147, applying to particulars of listed securities, and Public Offers of Securities Regulations 1995,[83] applying to prospectuses for unlisted securities, require the disclosure of specified matters. Although it seems

---

[75] *Stone v. Reliance Mutual Insurance Society Ltd, supra*; see also *Maye v. Colonial Mutual Life Assurance Society Ltd* (1924) 35 C.L.R. 14.

[76] *Glicksman v. Lancashire and General Assurance Co.* [1925] 2 K.B. 593; [1927] A.C. 139.

[77] *Allis Chalmers Co. v. Maryland Fidelity and Deposit Co.* (1916) 114 L.T. 433; *Looker v. Law Union and Rock Insurance Co.* [1928] 1 K.B. 554; *cf. Blackley v. National Mutual Life Association of Australasia Ltd* [1972] N.Z.L.R. 1038. See Vol. II, § 41–029.

[78] *Ante,* § 6–016.

[79] *Ante,* § 6–106.

[80] See Hudson (1969) 85 L.Q.R. 524 and Vol. II, § 41–033, n. 41.

[81] See *ante,* § 6–100.

[82] *Erlanger v. New Sombrero Phosphate Co.* (1878) 3 App.Cas. 1218.

[83] S.I. 1995, No. 1537.

to render those responsible liable in damages,[84] mere non-disclosure does not *per se* give a right to rescission. It is this fact which provokes the doubt as to whether contracts to take shares in companies are properly classified as contracts *uberrimae fidei*. However, if failure to disclose makes the prospectus misleading by falsifying that which is stated, there is a remedy as for positive misrepresentation.[85] With regard to misrepresentations as distinct from non-disclosures, an untrue statement in the prospectus which has induced a person to subscribe for shares does of course give that person the right to rescind the contract, provided that he acts promptly and before winding-up proceedings have begun.[86]

The position of the promoters is also regulated by the common law. They have **6–146** a fiduciary relationship with the company, and the rule is that they must not make a secret profit at its expense.[87] They are under a duty to disclose either to an independent board of directors, or to the intended shareholders, for instance by making a disclosure in the prospectus, any profit made by them on a sale of property to the company. A breach of this duty entitles the company to sue the promoters for damages, or to recover the profit,[88] or to rescind the contract.[89]

Family settlements. In these and in negotiations for these there must not only **6–147** be an absence of misrepresentation but a full communication of all material facts known to the parties. Any failure to disclose may be a ground for setting aside the settlement, and it is immaterial that information was withheld because of a mistaken opinion as to its accuracy or importance. In *Gordon v. Gordon*[90] a division of property, based on the assumption that the eldest son was illegitimate, was set aside after 19 years on proof that the younger son had withheld knowledge of a marriage ceremony that had taken place between his parents before the birth of his brother. Lord Eldon said that "whether the omission of disclosure originated in design, or in honest opinion of the invalidity of the ceremony,"[91] the agreement could not stand. On the other hand, in *Wales v. Wadham*[92] it was held that a wife was under no duty to disclose to her husband, when they were negotiating for a financial settlement to be embodied in a consent order after divorce, that she intended to remarry. In the particular circumstances of the case, the parties had been negotiating a compromise on the basis that neither party was required to make a full disclosure. However, *Wales v. Wadham* was overruled so far as it related to disclosure in proceedings for financial relief by the House of Lords in *Livesey v. Jenkins*.[93] This held that the relevant statutory provisions required a court exercising jurisdiction to make financial provision or property

---

[84] See *Gower's Principles of Modern Company Law* (6th ed., 1997), pp 426–433.

[85] See *Central Ry. of Venezuela v. Kisch* (1867) L.R. 2 H.L. 99.

[86] Further, a shareholder may rescind if misrepresentations are made in a document issued by the promoters before the company is formed: *Karberg's Case* [1892] 3 Ch. 1.

[87] *Erlanger v. New Phosphate Co.* (1878) 3 App.Cas. 1218; *Lagunas Nitrate Co. v. Lagunas Syndicate* [1899] 2 Ch. 392; *Re Leeds and Hanley Theatre of Varieties* [1902] 2 Ch. 809; see also *post*, § 9–058.

[88] *Gluckstein v. Barnes* [1900] A.C. 240.

[89] *Erlanger v. New Sombrero Phosphate Co.* (1878) 3 App.Cas. 1218 (provided of course that *restitutio in integrum* is still possible).

[90] (1816–19) 3 Swans. 400; see also *Fane v. Fane* (1875) L.R. 20 Eq. 698.

[91] At 477.

[92] [1977] 1 W.L.R. 199.

[93] [1985] A.C. 424. See *ante*, § 6–017, n. 74.

adjustment between spouses to be placed in full possession of the facts, so that each side must make full disclosure.[94] These decisions leave it uncertain whether the common law today recognises family settlements as contracts *uberrimae fidei*.

6–148 **Sales of land.** Contracts for the sale of land are not *uberrimae fidei* in the sense that the vendor has to make to the purchaser a full disclosure of all material facts. In the absence of actual misrepresentation[95] the general rule is *caveat emptor*. But certain qualifications must be made because the vendor is under a duty to disclose defects relating to title. Every material defect in the vendor's title must be disclosed, because if the title is in fact defective the vendor will be unable to perform his contract in the absence of a condition that the purchaser should accept a defective title. In consequence, if any such defect is not disclosed the purchaser may rescind the contract or resist a suit for specific performance. But it has been persuasively argued that there is in addition a duty on the vendor to disclose all latent defects in his title, since if an undisclosed latent defect appears the purchaser may apparently terminate the contract without waiting to see whether the vendor will be able to remove the defect before the date for completion.[96] However, as it appears that all defects must be revealed whether known to the vendor or not, and that if a latent defect is not revealed the purchaser may recover damages for breach of contract, it seems that the duty must be based on an implied term of the contract.[97]

6–149 It seems that any fact which will prevent the purchaser from obtaining such a title as he was led to expect may constitute a defect in title.[98] So where the subject of the sale was a leasehold interest, and the lease contained onerous and unusual covenants which were not disclosed by the vendor, the purchaser was held to be entitled to rescind the contract.[99] It has also been suggested that a tenant who is selling his leasehold interest is bound to disclose receipt of notice from his landlord of an intention to proceed under a rent review clause.[1] A purchaser may, of course, contract to accept a defective title, but even an express agreement to this effect will not (it seems) save the vendor where he fails to disclose defects known to him.[2] A purchaser is not obliged to disclose any information he may have which may affect the value of the property; but it has been held that a purchaser who applies for planning permission in the name of the vendor prior to the exchange of contracts is acting as a self-appointed agent, and may thereby come under fiduciary duties to the vendor.[3]

---

[94] Matrimonial Causes Act 1973, s.25, now replaced by Matrimonial and Family Proceedings Act 1984, s.3.

[95] See *Dyster v. Randall* [1926] Ch. 932.

[96] Harpum (1992) 108 L.Q.R. 208, relying on, *inter alia*, *Carlish v. Salt* [1906] 1 Ch. 355 and *Reeve v. Berridge* (1888) 20 Q.B.D. 423. The existence of such a duty was accepted by at least the majority of the Court of Appeal in *Peyman v. Lanjani* [1985] Ch. 457, 482, 496–497.

[97] Harpum, *op. cit.* pp. 332–333.

[98] But see *Re Flynn and Newman's Contract* [1948] Ir.R. 104.

[99] *Molyneux v. Hawtrey* [1903] 2 K.B. 487.

[1] *F. & H. Entertainments Ltd v. Leisure Enterprises Ltd* (1976) 120 S.J. 331.

[2] *Becker v. Partridge* [1966] 2 Q.B. 155.

[3] *English v. Dedham Vale Properties Ltd* [1978] 1 W.L.R. 93; *Rignall Developments Ltd v. Halil* [1988] Ch. 190.

Suretyship.[4] It seems that contracts of suretyship are not contracts *uberrimae* **6–150**
fidei properly so-called, although they are sometimes said to bear certain characteristics of that class. One difficulty is that it may be a matter for doubt whether
a given contract is one of suretyship or of insurance. In *Seaton v. Heath*[5] Romer
L.J. said that many contracts may with equal propriety be called contracts of
insurance or contracts of suretyship, and that whether a contract requires *uber-
rima fides* or not depends not upon what it is called, but upon its substantial
character and how it came to be effected. Sureties are generally persons who
know the risk they undertake without it being explained to them, and who if they
do not know it, would make inquiry on the subject; in contracts of insurance, on
the other hand, the person desiring to be insured has means of knowledge of the
risk which the insurer does not possess, and he puts the risk before the insurer as
a business proposition.

The position seems to be that while a contract of insurance requires a full **6–151**
disclosure of all material facts, a contract of suretyship does not.[6] Thus it has
been held that a bank was under no duty to disclose to the guarantor of a
customer's overdrawn account suspicions that the customer was defrauding him.[7]
On the other hand, it seems that there is a limited duty of disclosure even in
contracts of suretyship, though the nature and scope of this limited duty are hard
to define. In *Levett v. Barclays Bank plc*[8] it was held that there is a duty to
disclose to the surety any unusual feature of the contract between the principal
debtor and the creditor which makes it materially different in a potentially
disadvantageous respect from what the surety might naturally expect. In *Credit
Lyonnais Bank Nederland v. Export Credit Guarantee Department*[9] it was held
that any duty to disclose unusual features only applied to unusual features of the
transaction itself, not to unusual features of the risk; and it did not extend to
matters of which the bank had no knowledge, even if what it knew might have
led it to make further enquiries. However, where a person guaranteed the honesty
of a servant to an employer, who knew but did not disclose the fact that the
servant had previously been dishonest while in his employment, the bond was
held to be unenforceable when the servant subsequently committed a further act
of dishonesty.[10]

Binding authority to issue insurance. It has been suggested that an obliga- **6–152**
tion to point out unusual facts, similar to that which appears to apply to
suretyship,[11] may apply to a binding authority to issue insurance, so that unusual
features of the coverholder to whom the authority is to be given should be
pointed out.[12]

---

[4] See Vol. II, Chap. 44.
[5] [1899] 1 Q.B. 782, 792–793.
[6] *North British Insurance Co. v. Lloyd* (1854) 10 Ex. 523; *Lee v. Jones* (1864) 17 C.B.(N.S.)
482.
[7] *National Provincial Bank v. Glanusk* [1913] 3 K.B. 335; see also *Royal Bank of Scotland v.
Greenshields*, 1914 S.C. 259; *Cooper v. National Provincial Bank* [1946] K.B. 1.
[8] [1995] 1 W.L.R. 1260.
[9] [1996] 1 Lloyd's Rep. 200.
[10] *London General Omnibus Co. v. Holloway* [1912] 2 K.B. 72; see also *Phillips v. Foxall* (1872)
L.R. 7 Q.B. 666. For further discussion of these points see *post*, Vol. II, § 44–032.
[11] See previous paragraph.
[12] *Pryke v. Gibbs Hartley Cooper Ltd* [1991] 1 Lloyd's Rep. 602, 616.

6–153   **Partnership.** The fundamental duty of every partner is to show the utmost good faith in his dealings with the other partners. This applies not only during the continuance of the partnership, but also during the negotiations leading to its formation and during the winding up after dissolution.[13] The duties of partners are regulated for the most part, in the absence of agreement to the contrary, by the Partnership Act 1890; and although the principle requiring the utmost good faith is not expressly enunciated by the Act, it is embodied in sections 28, 29 and 30. Thus a partner must account for any private profit made by him; so for instance, if a partner is buying from or selling to the firm, he cannot do either at a profit to himself.[14]

---

[13] *Fawcett v. Whitehouse* (1829) 1 Russ. & M. 132.
[14] *Bentley v. Craven* (1853) 18 Beav. 75; *Dunne v. English* (1874) L.R. 18 Eq. 524.

1. DURESS

(a) *Introduction*

Introductory. A contract which has been entered as the result of duress may **7–001**
be avoided by the party who was threatened. It has long been recognised that a
threat to the victim's person may amount to duress[2]; it is now established that the
same is true of wrongful threats to his property, including threats to seize his
goods,[3] and of wrongful or illegitimate threats to his economic interests,[4] where
the victim has no practical alternative but to submit.[5] In each case, the wrongful
or illegitimate threat must have caused him to enter the contract, but the causal
requirements may differ between the various kinds of duress.[6]

(b) *Nature of Duress*

Basis of law relating to duress. It was at one time common to treat the legal **7–002**
rules relating to duress (and frequently also the equitable rules relating to undue
influence) as resting on the absence of consent. A party who was subject to

---

[1] See Cartwright, *Unequal Bargaining* (1991), Part III.
[2] *Post,* § 7–008.
[3] *Post,* § 7–009.
[4] *Post,* § 7–010.
[5] *Post,* § 7–019.
[6] *Post,* §§ 7–015—7–018.

duress, or even undue influence, was often said to have had his will "overborne" so that he was incapable of making a free choice, or even of acting voluntarily. Most of the older cases cited in this chapter rest on this assumption; and even many modern decisions use the same kind of language.[7] But the basis of the law relating to these topics has been reconsidered in light of the speeches in the House of Lords in *Lynch v. D.P.P. of Northern Ireland*.[8] This case was concerned with the defence of duress in the criminal law, and there are no doubt important differences between the civil and the criminal law on what can constitute duress; but the case contains by far the most extensive analysis of the juridical nature of duress in the law reports, and on this question, there appears to be no difference between the criminal and the civil law. Indeed, two of their Lordships in this case specifically relied upon the analogy of the law of contract.[9] All five members of the House of Lords in *Lynch's* case rejected the notion that duress deprives a person of his free choice, or makes his acts non-voluntary.[10] Duress does not "overbear" the will, nor destroy it; it "deflects" it.[11] Duress does not literally deprive the person affected of all choice; it leaves him with a choice between evils.[12] A person acting under duress intends to do what he does; but does so unwillingly.[13] Lord Wilberforce specifically stated that "duress does not destroy the will, for example, to enter into a contract, but prevents the law from accepting what has happened as a contract valid in law."[14] Similarly, Lord Simon of Glaisdale said that in the law of contract "Duress again deflects without destroying, the will of one of the contracting parties. There is still an intention on his part to contract in the apparently consensual terms; but there is *coactus volui* on his side. The contrast is with *non est factum*. The contract procured by duress is therefore not void: it is voidable—at the discretion of the party subject to duress."[15]

7–003   Notwithstanding these clear declarations of principle, in several important decisions relating to economic duress which post-date the *Lynch* decision the judges spoke of duress as negativing true consent and rendering the coerced party's actions non-voluntary.[16] For example, in *Pao On v. Lau Yiu Long*[17] it was accepted by the Privy Council that economic duress might be recognised in principle by the law, but it was insisted that "the basis of such recognition is that it must amount to a coercion of will, which vitiates consent. It must be shown that

---

[7] Even in *Barton v. Armstrong* [1976] A.C. 104, 121, the dissenting speech of Lord Wilberforce and Lord Simon refers to the defence of duress as resting on the absence of true consent; and in several other modern cases courts have continued to use the same kind of language, see Atiyah (1982) 98 L.Q.R. 197.

[8] [1975] A.C. 653.

[9] The same analysis of the nature of duress is almost universally adhered to in America. For an early example, see Holmes J. in *Union Pacific Ry. Co. v. Public Service Commission of Missouri* (1918) 248 U.S. 67, 70.

[10] See Lord Morris of Borth-y-Gest at 670, 675; Lord Wilberforce at 680; Lord Simon of Glaisdale at 690–691, 695; Lord Kilbrandon at 703; and Lord Edmund-Davies at 709–711.

[11] Lord Simon, *ibid.* at 695.

[12] *ibid.* at 690–691.

[13] Lord Morris at 670.

[14] *ibid.* at 680.

[15] *ibid.* at 695.

[16] See *Occidental Worldwide Investment Corpn. v. Skibs A/S Avanti* [1976] 1 Lloyd's Rep. 293; *North Ocean Shipping Co. Ltd v. Hyundai Construction Co. Ltd* [1979] Q.B. 705; *Pao On v. Lau Yiu Long* [1980] A.C. 614; *Universe Tankships of Monrovia Inc. v. I.T.W.F.* [1983] 1 A.C. 366; see also *Syros Shipping Co. v. Elaghill Trading Co.* [1981] 3 All E.R. 189.

[17] *Supra*, and see *post*, § 7–012.

the payment made or the contract entered into was not a voluntary act."[18] However in *Universe Tankships of Monrovia v. I.T.W.F.* Lord Diplock said that the rationale was that the party's consent was induced by pressure which the law does not regard as legitimate with the consequence that the consent is treated in law as revocable.[19] Similarly Lord Scarman, though dissenting in the result, agreed that the real issue is whether there has been illegitimate pressure, the practical effect of which is compulsion or absence of choice. "The classic case of duress is, however, not the lack of will to submit but the victim's intentional submission arising from the realisation that there is no practical choice open to him."[20] Subsequent decisions have for the most part applied the test of whether the victim had a practical choice.[21]

Importance of basis of duress. No doubt in many circumstances the precise   7–004
basis of duress will be immaterial; but in other circumstances it will be a matter of the greatest importance. For, so long as the doctrine of duress is treated as resting on an absence of consent, or of a voluntary act, it would seem immaterial what has caused the absence of consent, or the act to be involuntary. Duress would be a question of fact, and not of law. Further, absence of consent would logically render a contract void and not voidable. It is clear from *Lynch's* case that all these propositions are inconsistent with the analysis of the nature of duress in the speeches in the House of Lords. Because duress does not destroy the will or the consent of the putative contracting parties, it is not possible to treat the issue as one of pure fact, nor is it immaterial what caused the will to be deflected, or the consent to be distorted. So, also, because duress does not truly deprive a party of all choice, but only presents him with a choice between evils, it is not possible to inquire simply whether the party relying on duress had "no choice"; the inquiry must necessarily be as to the nature of the choices he was presented with, and in what respect the choices differed from those ordinarily available in the market—where a person also has to choose, between paying the market price and going without. The question whether the doctrine rests on the absence of consent or on the use of illegitimate pressure may also affect questions of causation: on the latter approach, it may not be necessary to show that the threat was an overwhelming cause of the victim entering the contract.[22]

Analogy with fraud and mistake. Both in *Lynch's* case and in *Barton v.*   7–005
Armstrong[23] the analogy with fraud and mistake has been relied upon by the courts. Thus (as shown by the quotation from Lord Simon's speech in *Lynch's* case, *supra*, § 7–002) duress renders a contract voidable rather than void; and in

---

[18] [1980] A.C. 614, 636.
[19] [1983] 1 A.C. 366, 384.
[20] *ibid.* at 400.
[21] *e.g. B. & S. Contracts & Design Ltd v. Victor Green Publications Ltd* [1984] I.C.R. 419; *Vantage Navigation Corp. v. Suhail and Saud Bahwan Building Materials, The Alev* [1989] 1 Lloyd's Rep. 138. See Beatson, *The Use and Abuse of Unjust Enrichment* (1991), pp. 109–117; and the remarks of Lord Goff in *Dimskal Shipping Co. SA v. ITWF* [1992] 2 A.C. 152, 166, agreeing with McHugh JA in *Crescendo Management Pty Ltd v. Westpac Banking Corp.* (1988) 19 N.S.W.L.R. 40, 45–46, that the "overbearing of the will" test is unhelpful.
[22] See *post*, §§ 7–015—7–018.
[23] [1976] A.C. 104.

this respect it operates like fraud, and not like *non est factum*.[24] No doubt there will be extreme cases of duress, as there are extreme cases of fraud or mistake, in which *non est factum* is available as a plea and in which there is a total absence of consent; the gunman who actually helps himself to his victim's wallet is stealing it against his victim's consent, and in no sense obtaining it by means of a coerced contract. But (artificial though the distinction may seem in such a case) the gunman who *demands and is given* the wallet by the victim, is obtaining it by duress. As is mentioned below, § 7–016, the analogy with fraud was also used in *Barton v. Armstrong* to justify the view that even a contract entered into under duress will stand if it can be shown that the duress was not a causal inducement acting on the mind of the party coerced, and that he would have entered into the contract in any event.[25]

7–006   **Pressure and threats.** Once it is accepted that the basis of duress does not depend upon the absence of consent, but on the combination of pressure and absence of practical choice,[26] it follows that it is the nature of the pressure or the threats which becomes all-important.[27] Clearly, not all pressure is illegitimate, nor even are all threats illegitimate. In ordinary commercial activity, pressure and even threats are both commonplace and often perfectly proper. Indeed, in one sense, all contracts are made under pressure: every offeror "threatens" that unless the offeree accepts the terms offered, he will not get the benefit of whatever goods or services are on offer. Nor can it even be said that the force or weight of the pressure or the threats is the decisive factor, "for in life, including the life of commerce and finance, many acts are done under pressure, sometimes overwhelming pressure, so that one can say that the actor had no choice but to act."[28] It therefore becomes essential to distinguish between legitimate and illegitimate forms of pressure.

7–007   **Types of illegitimate pressure.** Violence to the person, and threats of such violence, have long been recognised as illegitimate forms of pressure. The law therefore allows a party to avoid any promise extorted from him by terror or violence, whether on the part of the person to whom the promise is made or that of his agent.[29] Contracts made under such circumstances are said to be made under *duress*,[30] a term derived from the common law, which took a narrow view as to the facts which would establish (as was then thought) the absence of free consent. At common law, duress consisted of actual or threatened violence or imprisonment.[31] Courts of equity, however, administered the wider doctrine of

---

[24] As to the defence *non est factum*, see *ante*, §§ 5–054—5–059. In *Barton v. Armstrong* [1976] A.C. 104 Lord Cross, speaking for the majority, referred to the deeds as void (at 120), but he had previously referred to "setting aside a disposition for duress" (at 118). The dissenting minority seemed to consider that duress renders a contract voidable.

[25] There may, of course, be some issues on which the analogy with fraud would be inappropriate and inapplicable, *e.g.* duress is not necessarily tortious: *post*, § 7–040.

[26] See further *post*, § 7–019.

[27] See *Universe Tankships of Monrovia Inc. v. I.T.W.F.* [1983] 1 A.C. 366, at 384, 391, 400.

[28] *Barton v. Armstrong* [1976] A.C. 104, 121, *per* Lord Wilberforce and Lord Simon dissenting, but not on this point.

[29] For the parallel doctrine in cases concerning marriage, see *Scott v. Sebright* (1886) 12 P.D. 21; *Griffith v. Griffith* [1944] I.R. 35; *H. v. H.* [1954] P. 258; *Szechter v. Szechter* [1971] P. 286; *Singh v. Singh* [1971] P. 226; Davies (1972) 88 L.Q.R. 549; Matrimonial Causes Act 1973, s.12. See also *Re Roberts (deceased)* [1978] 1 W.L.R. 653; *Hirani v. Hirani* (1983) 4 F.L.R. 232.

[30] See generally Beatson [1974] C.L.J. 97.

[31] 1 Roll.Abr. 687; Coke 2 Inst. 482.

undue influence[32] which was applied chiefly to cases where some fiduciary relation existed between the parties, but was not in any way limited to them. Equity might therefore grant relief where the compulsion complained of was something less than that required by the common law. Since the Judicature Act 1873 it has been the duty of all courts to administer both doctrines concurrently and cases of coercion must be dealt with in the light of their combined effect. In recent years the courts have recognised that other forms of duress may be grounds for avoiding a contract: firstly, where there was a wrongful threat to seize the claimant's goods and secondly, where there was "economic duress". The latter may blur the traditional distinction between duress and undue influence.[33]

(c) *Duress of the Person*

Form of duress. Duress of the person may consist in violence to the person, or threats of violence, or in imprisonment whether actual or threatened.[34] It is submitted that the threat of violence need not be directed at the claimant: a threat of violence against a spouse or near relation must also suffice[35] and it is suggested that a threat against even a stranger should be enough if the claimant genuinely believed that submission was the only way to prevent the stranger from being injured or worse.   7–008

(d) *Duress of Goods*

Duress of goods. Until recently the traditional view has been that duress of goods, that is to say, the unlawful detention or threatened detention of a person's goods, is not duress which will at common law avoid an agreement obtained by it.[36] It used to be said that the distinction between duress of the person and duress of goods was that "the former is a constraining force, which not only takes away the free agency, but may leave no room for appeal to the law for a remedy . . . ; but the fear that goods may be taken or injured does not deprive anyone of his free agency who possesses that ordinary degree of firmness which the law requires all to exert."[37] There is no evidence of any wider equitable rule concerning duress of goods, although it has for many years been well established that money paid in order to get possession of goods wrongfully detained, or to avoid their wrongful detention, may be recovered in an action for money had and received.[38] So in *Maskell v. Horner*[39] tolls were levied on the plaintiff under a   7–009

---

[32] See *post*, §§ 7–041 *et seq.*

[33] See *post*, § 7–033.

[34] For modern examples, see *Friedeberg-Seeley v. Klass* (1957) 101 S.J. 275; *Barton v. Armstrong* [1976] A.C. 104.

[35] *cf. Williams v. Bayley* (1866) L.R. 1 H.L. 200. See Goff & Jones, *Law of Restitution* (5th ed., 1998), p. 311. See further *post*, § 7–033.

[36] It has been said that a threat to destroy or damage property could amount to duress: *Occidental Worldwide Investment Corp. v. Skibs A/S Avanti* [1976] 1 Lloyd's Rep. 293, 335.

[37] *Skeate v. Beale* (1840) 11 A. & E. 983, 990; *The Unitas* [1948] P. 205, affd. *sub nom. Lever Bros. & Unilever N.V. v. H.M. Procurator General* [1950] A.C. 536.

[38] *Astley v. Reynolds* (1731) 2 Str. 915; *Atlee v. Backhouse* (1838) 3 M. & W. 633; *Wakefield v. Newbon* (1844) 6 Q.B. 276; *Oates v. Hudson* (1851) 6 Exch. 346. Money paid to recover goods in the custody of the law is not paid under duress and cannot be recovered: *Liverpool Marine Credit Co. v. Hunter* (1868) L.R. 3 Ch.App. 479. See generally *post*, §§ 30–071 *et seq.*

[39] [1915] 3 K.B. 106; *post*, § 30–071.

threat of seizure of goods. The tolls were in fact unlawfully demanded. Their payment was held to be recoverable as it had been made to avoid seizure of the goods and the plaintiff was entitled to recover the payments he had made under the illegal demand. Lord Reading C.J. said, "If a person pays money, which he is not bound to pay, under the compulsion of urgent and pressing necessity or of seizure, actual or threatened, of his goods, he can recover it as money had and received."[40] It is nevertheless somewhat difficult to reconcile this rule with the traditional rule that duress of goods would not avoid a contract. A possible solution may be that money paid in this way can only be recovered if it has been paid under protest, without any binding agreement[41]; otherwise the absurd result must ensue that, although an agreement to pay money under duress of goods can be enforced, any money so paid will be recoverable by the person paying it as money had and received to his use. But there are cases inconsistent with the notion that duress can only be relied upon by someone who acted under protest[42]; and an alternative view which is receiving increasing support[43] is that the rule that duress of goods does not invalidate a contract only applies where the duress is in purported execution of legal process such as distress or execution. Where this is the case, an agreement made to secure the release of the goods is a form of submission to legal process, and seizure of goods under legal process can scarcely be regarded as an illegitimate form of pressure. This argument thus opened the door to a broad concept of duress of goods as a ground of relief in contract law, and recent cases lend strong support to this possibility; indeed, the courts have now endorsed both duress of goods and the broader concept of "economic duress."[44]

(e) *Economic Duress*

7–010   **Recognition of economic duress.** Three English cases, and one important Privy Council appeal, first recognised the possibility of the concept of economic duress. In substance this amounts to recognising that certain threats or forms of pressure, not associated with threats to the person, nor limited to the seizure or withholding of goods, may give grounds for relief to a party who enters into a contract as a result of the threats or the pressure. In *Occidental Worldwide Investment Corpn. v. Skibs A/S Avanti*,[45] the charterers of two ships secured a renegotiation of the rate of hire, after a slump in market rates, by threatening the owners that they (the charterers) had no substantial assets, and that they would

---

[40] *ibid.* at 118.

[41] *Atlee v. Backhouse, supra,* at 650; *Parker v. Bristol & Exeter Ry.* (1851) 6 Exch. 702, 705.

[42] See, *e.g. Spanish Government v. North of England SS. Ltd* (1938) 54 T.L.R. 852; *T.A. Sundell & Sons Pty. Ltd v. Emm Yannoulatos (Overseas) Pty. Ltd* (1956) 56 S.R. (N.S.W.) 323; *Universe Tankships of Monrovia Inc. v. I.T.W.F.* [1983] 1 A.C. 366, 400.

[43] See especially *Wakefield v. Newbon, supra; Occidental Worldwide Investment Corpn. v. Skibs A/S Avanti* [1976] 1 Lloyd's Rep. 293; *North Ocean Shipping Co. Ltd v. Hyundai Construction Co. Ltd* [1979] Q.B. 705; Goff & Jones, *Law of Restitution* (5th ed., 1998), pp. 312–313, 316–320. The older cases denying relief are probably best explained as cases in which the claim was voluntarily compromised by the plaintiff: see Beatson, *The Use and Abuse of Unjust Enrichment* (1991), pp. 105–106; *North Ocean Shipping, supra,* at 719. On voluntary settlements see further *post,* § 7–020.

[44] *Dimskal Shipping Co. Ltd v. I.T.W.F.* [1992] 2 A.C. 152, 165 (limitation to duress of the person now discarded). *The Alev* [1989] 1 Lloyd's Rep. 138 was in fact a case of duress of goods but it appears to have been decided on the basis of economic duress.

[45] [1976] 1 Lloyd's Rep. 293, noted (1976) 92 L.Q.R. 496.

go bankrupt if the rates were not lowered. This threat was strongly coercive because, given the slump in the market, the owners would have had to lay up the tankers if the charterers had returned them, and would then have been unable to pay mortgage charges on the ships—all these facts being well known to the charterers. In fact the charterers' allegations, or threats, that they had no substantial assets and would go bankrupt if the rate of hire were not lowered, were false and fraudulent, and Kerr J. held that the owners were therefore entitled to avoid the renegotiated terms, and withdraw the ships on the ground of fraud; but he recognised that the economic pressure of the threats might also have given rise to relief on the ground of duress, at least in principle. In the event, however, he denied relief on this ground because the owners' consent or will was not vitiated by the pressures, which were only normal commercial pressures. In light of the discussion of *Lynch's* case, *supra*, § 7–002, this ground of decision seems dubious; the question which the learned judge ought to have asked himself was not whether the owners' consent was negatived by the pressure, but whether the pressure was permissible pressure to exert.[46] Given his finding that the pressure was based on fraud, it would seem that duress should have been a further ground for relief, although in the circumstances it would have been immaterial, given that relief was available for fraud anyhow.

In *North Ocean Shipping Co. Ltd v. Hyundai Construction Co. Ltd*[47] ship-   **7–011** builders who were building a ship under a contract for the plaintiffs, threatened, without any legal justification, to terminate the contract unless the plaintiffs agreed (within a few days) to increase the price by 10 per cent. The owners had chartered the vessel to Shell at very favourable rates and feared that they would lose the charter if the vessel were delivered late, so they reluctantly acquiesced in this demand, but under protest, and without prejudice to their rights. Mocatta J. held[48] that this amounted to a case of economic duress, and that the plaintiffs would have been entitled, on that ground, to have refused payment of the additional 10 per cent. But he went on to hold that the owners had, by implication, affirmed the contract, or waived their right to avoid it for duress, even though they had not intended to do so; the basis for this part of his decision was that the owners had failed to raise the matter at any further stage, paying the extra instalments, and taking delivery of the ship in due course, and so giving the builders grounds for belief that the owners had affirmed the variation in price.

The Privy Council case is *Pao On v. Lau Yiu Long*[49] in which again the   **7–012** allegation was made that a party had secured an amendment to a prior commercial transaction of some complexity, as a result of a threat to break his contract. Here also the Privy Council conceded that economic duress could be recognised in principle, but held that the plea was not made out on the facts. The speech of Lord Scarman emphasised that the defendant in this case had carefully considered his position when faced with the threatened breach of contract, and had

---

[46] It might, however, be said that his finding that consent was not negatived was tantamount to finding that the pressure was not of sufficient *weight* to constitute duress, see *post*, § 7–021.

[47] [1979] Q.B. 705.

[48] Relying, *inter alia*, on *Parker v. G.W.R.* (1844) 7 M. & G. 253; *G.W.R. v. Sutton* (1869) L.R. 4 H.L. 226; *Close v. Phipps* (1844) 7 M. & G. 586; *Fernley v. Branson* (1851) 20 L.J.Q.B. 178; *Nixon v. Furphy* (1925) 25 S.R. (N.S.W.) 151; *Smith v. William Charlick* (1924) 34 C.L.R. 38, 56; and *D. & C. Builders Ltd v. Rees* [1966] 2 Q.B. 617, as to which see *post*, § 7–014.

[49] [1980] A.C. 614.

concluded that it was in his interests to grant the concession demanded rather than to sue on the original contract. In determining the validity of the plea of duress in such circumstances, Lord Scarman said that "it is material to inquire whether the person alleged to have been coerced did or did not protest; whether, at the time he was allegedly coerced into making the contract, he did or did not have an alternative course open to him such as an adequate legal remedy; whether he was independently advised; and whether after entering the contract he took steps to avoid it."[50] Lord Scarman did, however, draw attention to American case law which stressed the effectiveness of alternative remedies available to the party allegedly coerced; and it seems clear that it would no longer be regarded as an adequate answer to a plea of duress that the party coerced had a legal remedy which he could in due course have pursued in the courts. The all-important question is whether, having regard to all the circumstances, that remedy is a practical and effective one.

7-013   The fourth case is *Universe Tankships of Monrovia v. International Transport Workers Federation*[51] in which the defendant trade union had "blacked" the plaintiffs' ship in port, and refused to release her except on payment of a large sum of money; most of the money was claimed as back pay on behalf of seamen on the ship, but a part of it was a payment for the union's welfare fund. The Court of Appeal, affirming Parker J., held that the union's actions constituted duress which would prima facie have justified the shipowners in recovering the money, because the coercive nature of the threat was so powerful, and at common law involved unlawful pressure on various third parties to break their contracts. But the Court of Appeal went on to hold that the union's conduct was protected by the statutory immunities in the Trade Union and Labour Relations Act 1974, because it was in the course of, or in furtherance of, a trade dispute under that Act. The "trade dispute" defence was disallowed in the House of Lords where the finding of economic duress was not challenged. The decision involves rejection of the defendants' argument that a plea of duress requires the party guilty of the duress to appreciate that the other party is acting under duress. In effect, this was an attempt to revive, in a slightly different form, the argument that payments made under duress are only recoverable if they are paid under protest; as already seen (*supra*, § 7–009) this view has been rejected in a number of previous cases.

7-013A   The doctrine of economic duress is therefore now clearly established[52] and it has been applied in a number of other cases.[53] For example, in *B. & S. Contracts & Design Ltd v. Victor Green Publications Ltd*[54] the plaintiffs had contracted to

---

[50] At 635.

[51] [1981] I.C.R. 129, revd. [1983] A.C. 366.

[52] See the judgment of Lord Goff in *Dimskal Shipping Co. SA v. I.T.W.F.* [1992] 2 A.C. 152, 165.

[53] *B. & S. Contracts & Design Ltd v. Victor Green Publications Ltd* [1984] I.C.R. 419; *Atlas Express Ltd v. Kafco (Importers and Distributors) Ltd* [1989] Q.B. 833 (carrier refused to perform without extra payment after miscalculating number of cartons it could carry per load); *The Alev* [1989] 1 Lloyd's Rep. 138 (owner demanded "financial assistance" from consignee before it would deliver goods under freight pre-paid bills when charterer had failed to pay hire). See also *Alec Lobb Ltd v. Total Oil G.B. Ltd* [1983] 1 W.L.R. 87 (varied on other points, [1985] 1 W.L.R. 173); *Dimskal Shipping Co. Ltd v. I.T.W.F.* [1992] 2 A.C. 152; *CTN Cash and Carry Ltd v. Gallaher Ltd* [1994] 4 All E.R. 714 (*post*, § 7–031); *Finance Ltd v. Bank of New Zealand* (1993) 32 N.S.W.L.R. 50 (CA, N.S.W.).

[54] [1984] I.C.R. 419.

erect an exhibition stand for the defendants at Olympia, but their workmen went on strike. To get the work done the defendants agreed to contribute £4,500 to pay off the workmen's claims. It was held by the Court of Appeal that this promise was made under duress as the defendants had no realistic alternative[55] but to promise to pay, given the serious threat to their economic interests.

Relationship between doctrine of consideration and economic duress. In **7–014** the first three cases cited in §§ 7–010—7–012, the parties were already in a contractual relationship; in these circumstances, a variation of the contract secured by one party as a result of threats to break the contract might until recently have been viewed as invalid on the ground of lack of consideration, irrespective of any issue of economic duress. Thus in *D. & C. Builders Ltd v. Rees*[56] the defendants, who owed the plaintiffs some £482, refused to pay anything unless the plaintiffs would accept £300 in full satisfaction of the claim; the plaintiffs (as the defendants knew) were in desperate financial straits, so that recourse to law was not a practicable remedy, and they accepted the £300, giving a receipt in full satisfaction. It was held that this was not a valid surrender of their claim to the balance because of the absence of consideration.[57] The case could, it is submitted, now be supported on the ground of economic duress. In contrast, in cases in which a promise is made to pay an additional sum to the promisee if the latter will perform its existing contractual duty, but where there is no duress, the law has recently undergone a marked change. In *Williams v. Roffey Bros. & Nicholls (Contractors) Ltd*[58] a carpentry subcontractor which had underpriced work on a number of flats was having difficulty in completing it on time. The contractor promised an additional payment for each flat finished. It was held that this promise was enforceable although the subcontractor was only performing its existing obligation; in the absence of duress the "practical benefit" to the contractor, that if the work was finished on time it would avoid liability for liquidated damages under the main contract, constituted consideration. Although in this case the subcontractor made no threat,[59] the decision suggests that not every case in which a party agrees to make an extra payment in order to obtain the performance originally promised is one of duress, nor perhaps will every agreement secured by a threat to break a contract be voidable. As will be seen later (*post*, § 7–018) a threat to break a contract will only amount to duress where it is particularly coercive having regard to all the circumstances. Where some trifling consideration is present, it seems that the gross inadequacy of the consideration may be relevant in establishing that the variation of the contract has been secured by improper pressure.

(f) *Causation*

Causation in general. In all cases of duress it is necessary that the victim's **7–015** agreement was caused by the duress.[60] However, it is not clear that the causal requirements are the same for all types of duress.

---

[55] On the question of absence of choice see *post*, § 7–019.
[56] [1966] 2 Q.B. 716; see also *T.A. Sundell & Sons Pty. Ltd v. Emm Yannoulatos (Overseas) Ltd* (1956) 56 S.R. (N.S.W.) 323.
[57] See *ante*, § 3–108.
[58] [1991] 1 Q.B. 1. See *ante*, § 3–063.
[59] See further *post*, § 7–025.
[60] See the speech of Lord Goff in *Dimskal Shipping Co. SA v. I.T.W.F.* [1992] 2 A.C. 152, 165.

7–016   **Duress to the person.** In *Barton v. Armstrong*[61] the Privy Council, relying on the analogy of fraud,[62] held that it was sufficient that the threat was a reason for the victim entering the contract: not only it did not have to be the predominant reason, but the victim was entitled to relief even if he had not shown that he would not have entered the contract without the threat. It would be up to the party who made the threat to show that it had not influenced the victim in any way.[63]

7–017   **Duress to goods.** In cases of duress to goods, it seems that the threatened seizure must have been a significant cause[64] of the victim's agreeing to the contract or payment. Thus the victim will not be entitled to avoid the contract if he had an effective alternative remedy, for example to obtain an injunction to prevent the seizure, though it is recognised that a legal remedy may be of no avail if the victim has an urgent need for the goods.[65] The victim will also be unable to avoid the contract if it was a "voluntary settlement" of the other party's claim. The meaning of this is not wholly clear[66] but it appears that relief will be denied if the threat was not the reason for the victim agreeing to the other party's demand. On the other hand, it seems unlikely that the victim will have the benefit of the reversed burden of proof in the same way as the victim of duress to the person.[67]

7–018   **Economic duress.** As mentioned earlier,[68] some cases of economic duress applied the test of whether the victim's will was overborne so that he did not consent to the contract. This suggested that relief was only possible if the threat was the overwhelming reason for the victim's decision. Now that the "overborne will" test has been abandoned,[69] it is submitted that it is not necessary for the victim to show that the threat was the predominant cause. On the other hand, it seems unlikely that the victim will have the benefit of the reversed burden of proof in the same way as the victim of duress to the person.[70] It may be that, while the victim's will need not be overborne, in the sense that he deliberately chooses to submit to the demands made on him, and while the threat of the breach of contract need only play a "significant" causal role, relief will only be given on the ground of economic duress if the combination of the threat and the victim's situation was "particularly coercive" to the claimant in his particular circumstances. This seems consistent with the approach of Kerr J. in *Occidental Worldwide Investment Corpn. v. Skibs A/S Avanti*,[71] where the plea of duress was rejected on the basis that the owners were subjected only to "normal commercial pressures", and with the tests suggested by Lord Scarman in *Pao On v. Lau Liu*

---

[61] [1976] A.C. 104, *ante*, § 7–005.

[62] *cf. ante*, § 7–005.

[63] [1976] A.C. 104, 120.

[64] See the speech of Lord Goff in *Dimskal Shipping Co. SA v. I.T.W.F.* [1992] 2 A.C. 152, 165.

[65] *Astley v. Reynolds* (1731) 2 Stra. 915, 916.

[66] See Burrows, *Law of Restitution* (1993), p. 162.

[67] *cf. ante*, § 7–016.

[68] *Ante*, § 7–003.

[69] *Ante*, § 7–003.

[70] Burrows, *Law of Restitution* (1993), p. 177 (noting the contrary authority of *Crescendo Management Pty Ltd v. Westpac Banking Corp.* (1988) 19 N.S.W.L.R. 40); *Huyten SA v. Peter Cremer GmbH & Co.* [1999] 1 Lloyd's Rep. 620, 636, 639.

[71] [1976] 1 Lloyd's Rep. 293; *ante*, § 7–010.

Long,[72] which relate to the claimant's behaviour. However, a causal test of this kind would be difficult to apply[73]; and it is not consistent with other high authority. In *Dimskal Shipping Co. SA v. I.T.W.F.*[74] Lord Goff said that there may be duress where "the economic pressure . . . has constituted a significant cause", which suggests that even the combination of threat and other pressures need not be overwhelming. Thus it is submitted that any causal test is satisfied by the victim showing that he was influenced by the combination of threat and pressure of circumstances. There are a number of factors which must be taken into account, which are explored in the following paragraphs. It will then be suggested that other factors may explain the slowness of the courts to find economic duress; in particular, not every threatened of breach of contract may be regarded as illegitimate.[75]

Reasonable alternative. It is relevant whether or not the victim had a reason-   7–019
able alternative.[76] It is not clear whether this is a prerequisite or merely evidential[77]; but it seems that if the victim had a reasonable alternative to submitting to the other party's demand, he will not obtain relief; and this is sometimes to be explained on causal grounds. Thus a refusal, in breach of contract, to supply goods unless some extra consideration is supplied by the buyer, may lack genuine coercive force where alternative supplies are available in the market. Similarly, where the party claiming relief had adequate time to claim redress at law, and there is no reason to think that this would not protect or compensate him, submission to the threat may simply reflect that party's belief that his best interests would be served by such submission rather than by resort to the courts. This may have been relevant in the *Pao On*[78] decision itself: Lord Scarman referred in general terms to American case law stressing the importance of examining the alternatives available to the party claiming relief.[79]

Voluntary submission. Equally, it seems that relief will be denied if the   7–020
principal reason for the victim's agreement was that he was prepared to pay it anyway. This may have been relevant in the *Pao On* case,[80] where the actual decision seems to have rested on the fact that the defendants thought that they would lose very little by granting the amendment sought.[81]

Gravity of threat. For similar reasons it is likely that the threat must normally   7–021
be one of some gravity. This is to some extent implicit in the factors to which attention must be had, as specified by Lord Scarman in the *Pao On* case.[82] For if attention must be paid to the alternative remedies available to the threatened party (and their effectiveness), it is evident that minor threats, even if unlawful

---

[72] [1980] A.C. 614; *ante*, § 7–012.
[73] Birks, *Introduction to the Law of Restitution* (1985), p. 183; compare Burrows, *op. cit.* p. 176.
[74] [1992] 2 A.C. 152, 165.
[75] *Post*, §§ 7–024—7–029.
[76] *Pao On v. Lau Liu Long* [1980] A.C. 614, 635. See also Halson (1991) 107 L.Q.R. 649.
[77] See Beatson, *op. cit.* pp. 122–126.
[78] [1980] A.C. 614.
[79] For examples, see *Tristate Roofing Co. of Uniontown v. Simon* (1958) A.2d. 333, 335; *Gallagher Switchboard Corp. v. Heckler Electric Co.* (1962) 229 N.Y.S. 2d. 623, 630.
[80] *Supra*.
[81] [1980] A.C. 614, 635.
[82] *Supra*.

or improper, can normally give no redress in contract law: the party threatened ought to pursue his other remedies. How serious the threats must be in order to constitute duress may depend on the physical and mental condition of the person threatened. Weakness of intellect or fear, whether reasonably entertained or not, may be relevant factors which should be taken into account.[83]

7–022   **"Legitimacy" of the demand.** It may also be relevant that the victim some-how recognised either that the demand was in some way justified, for example because (as in most of the decided cases), what was being demanded was a re-negotiation of an existing contract and the victim conceded that the original contract was rather one-sided. Again this might go to showing that he was not really influenced by the threat. However, these matters may also go to the question of whether the threat made is illegitimate.[84]

(g) *Nature of Threats Amounting to Duress*[85]

7–023   **Threat to commit an unlawful act.** As already indicated, it is clear that not all threats can be regarded as improper or illegitimate, and it is necessary in the law of duress to distinguish between legitimate and other forms of pressure or threats. Prima facie it is thought to be clear that a threat to commit an unlawful act will constitute an improper threat for the purposes of the law of duress.[86] Certainly a threat to commit a crime or a tort as a means of inducing the coerced party to enter into some contract must prima facie be improper.[87]

7–024   **Threat to break a contract.** It is now recognised that in cases of economic duress, the question is not whether the victim's will is overborne but whether the other party had used illegitimate pressure, the practical effect of which is that the victim had no choice. It does not seem, however, that the victim will necessarily be entitled to relief because his decision was influenced by a threatened breach of contract and was the only way to avoid the threatened action. The decisions in *Occidental Worldwide Investment Corpn v. Skibs A/S Avanti*[88] and *Pao On v. Lau Liu Long*[89] suggest that something more than this is required. In *B. & S. Contracts & Design Ltd v. Victor Green Publications Ltd*[90] the Court of Appeal stressed that it is not "on every occasion when one party unwillingly agrees to a variation of a contract, that the law would consider that he had acted by reason

---

[83] *Scott v. Sebright* (1866) 12 P.D. 21.

[84] *Post*, §§ 7–024—7–029.

[85] See Beatson, *The Use and Abuse of Unjust Enrichment* (1991), pp. 117–129; Burrows, *Law of Restitution* (1993), esp. at pp. 174–182.

[86] In *Dimskal Shipping Co. SA v. ITWF, The Evia Luck* [1992] 2 A.C. 152 the House of Lords held that the question of whether economic pressure amounted to duress was prima facie a matter for the proper law of the contract, so that whether the conduct was lawful or not fell to be determined by the proper law of the contract rather than by that of the place where the threat was made. In *Royal Boskalis Westminster Nv v. Mountain* [1998] 2 W.L.R. 538, 552, 590 it was said that, nonetheless, counsel had been correct to concede, in the light of *Kaufman v. Gerson* [1904] 1 K.B. 591, that some forms of duress are so shocking that English law would not enforce a contract made under such duress irrespective of whether the threat would be acceptable and the contract valid under the governing law. See *post*, § 31–161.

[87] See the American *Restatement of Contract*, 2d, § 176(1).

[88] [1976] 1 Lloyd's Rep. 293; *ante*, § 7–010.

[89] [1980] A.C. 614; *ante*, § 7–012.

[90] [1984] I.C.R. 419, 425.

of duress." There are at least two types of situation in which it would seem inappropriate to treat a threat to break a contract as amounting to unlawful pressure or duress. First, there are circumstances in which the party claiming relief was not in fact coerced by the threat. Here the claim will fail on causal grounds.[91] Secondly, the cases just cited suggest that claim of economic duress may fail even though the threat and pressure clearly had some influence. If it is correct (as submitted earlier) that the decisions should not be explained on the ground that the threat must have been the overwhelming cause of the victim's agreement, they suggest that not every threatened breach of contract, even if it has had some "significant effect", will amount to duress. A possible explanation is that some threats of breach of contract may be regarded as not illegitimate. This possibility is suggested by American cases. Where unexpected difficulties arise in the performance of a contract (even if they do not amount to frustrating circumstances) it is often commercially reasonable for one party to claim extra remuneration, or some other extra-contractual concession, as the price of his continuing with performance. In these circumstances, a threat to break the contract unless the extra consideration is forthcoming may well be regarded as a legitimate form of commercial pressure,[92] if the threatening party acts in the bona fide belief that he is entitled to some extra payment, or particularly where the unanticipated difficulty means that he is genuinely unable to perform without an extra payment.[93] This point might have been significant in *Williams v. Roffey Bros. & Nicholls (Contractors) Ltd*[94] had the subcontractor demanded extra payment. On the facts there was no duress because no threat was made: the initiative for the extra payment came from the contractors.[95] If, however, the subcontractors had said that without extra payment, they would be unable to perform, and the main contractors had then promised the extra payment, it seems unlikely that the main contractors could have avoided the promise to pay extra on the ground of duress. There are a number of ways in which this result could be explained.

Threat or statement of the inevitable? One is that a party who truthfully   **7–025** states that, without the extra payment or concession demanded, he will be unable to perform is not making a threat; he is simply stating a fact.[96] This raises the difficult borderline between threats and warnings[97] and might lead to nice distinctions over the terms in which the demand was made.

Bad faith. Another approach is to say that a demand made in bad faith is   **7–026** illegitimate and may amount to duress.[98] It seems correct to say that a party who exploits the other's position to demand a payment which is unrelated to the

---

[91] See *ante*, § 7–015.

[92] See, *e.g. Goebel v. Linn* (1882) 11 N.W. 284; *Linz v. Schuck* (1907) 67 A. 286. There is a sense in which the *Pao On* case also resembles these cases inasmuch as the variation obtained by the alleged duress was needed to put right what was an obvious commercial omission or mistake in the original contract.

[93] Posner (1977) 6 J.L.S. 411 makes the telling point that if a party will become bankrupt unless he is promised extra, it is very much in the promisor's interest to be able to make a binding promise to pay the extra amount in order to get the work finished, even though the promisor has no practical choice. On the use of bad faith as a test of duress, see Birks [1990] L.M.C.L.Q. 342, 347.

[94] [1991] 1 Q.B. 1; *ante*, § 7–014.

[95] But see further *post*, § 7–028.

[96] Birks, *An Introduction to the Law of Restitution* (1985), p. 183.

[97] See *post*, § 7–036.

[98] Birks, *op. cit.*, p. 183; also [1990] L.M.C.L.Q. 342, 347.

contract and which he knows he has no right to is guilty of economic duress.[99] To this extent the bad faith test is acceptable, but there would be difficulties in applying it when a party makes a demand which is related to the contract. One interpretation is that a party is in bad faith unless he honestly believes that his demand is legally justified.[1] Certainly, such a belief would suggest that the claim was not illegitimate, but should every claim which is known not to have a legal basis be treated as one in bad faith? A party may have encountered some difficulty he did not expect and feel morally justified in demanding an extra payment, yet be aware that his demand has no legal basis. If the difficulty related to the contract and was not of the party's own making, it seems plausible to argue that the demand is made in good faith; but on existing authorities it seems that good faith in this sense does not preclude a finding of economic duress.[2] Similar circumstances may have obtained in the *North Ocean Shipping* case,[3] yet it was held that there was economic duress.

7-027　　**Knowledge of the victim's predicament.** Bad faith also suggests deliberate exploitation of the victim, by taking advantage of his predicament. Again, it is not clear on the existing authorities that this is necessary: it appears that in the *North Ocean Shipping* case[4] the builders did not know of the charter to Shell.

7-028　　**Fairness of the demand.** In the cases, some of the demands appear to have been made in order to rectify an apparent imbalance in the existing contract; others appear to have been unrelated to any such factor. Where the demand is recognised by the "victim" as fair, that may lead to the conclusion that he was not really influenced by the threat so much as by a desire to help out the other party, and thus the necessary causal link will be missing.[5] But if it is clear that the threat did have a significant influence, it does not seem that the fact that the demand might rectify an imbalance in the contract will make the demand legitimate. In *Atlas Express Ltd v. Kafco (Importers and Distributors) Ltd*[6] the plaintiffs miscalculated the number of cartons of the defendants' goods that they could carry on a trailer load for delivery to a retail chain and, when they discovered the truth, stated that they would not carry any more cartons without an extra payment. The defendants were heavily reliant on the contract with the retail chain and were unable to find an alternative carrier, so they agreed; but later they refused to pay the extra charges. Tucker J. held that their consent had been vitiated by duress.[7] Although the mistake was the plaintiffs' and unknown to the defendant, it seems likely that the latter did get the benefit of cheaper rates than

---

[99] Compare *B & S Contracts and Design Ltd v. Victor Green Publications Ltd* [1984] I.C.R. 419, where the difficulty faced by the threatening party (a strike by its workers) was not related to the contract and may have been one it should have dealt with.

[1] But compare Goff & Jones, *Law of Restitution* (5th ed., 1998), pp. 346–7.

[2] See Birks and Chin in Beatson & Friedmann (eds.), *Good Faith and Fault in Contract Law* (1995), pp. 57–97, 62. See also *Huyten SA v. Peter Cremer GmbH & Co.* [1999] 1 Lloyd's Rep. 620, 637.

[3] [1979] Q.B. 705; *supra*, § 7–011.

[4] [1979] Q.B. 705; *supra*, § 7–011.

[5] The attitude of the main contractors in *Williams v. Roffey* may be explained by the fact that the subcontractors appear to have under-priced the job.

[6] [1989] Q.B. 833.

[7] He also held that there was no consideration for the payment; but after the decision in *Williams v. Roffey & Nicholls (Contractors) Ltd* [1991] 1 Q.B. 1, the presence or absence of consideration may depend on whether or not there was duress: see *ante*, § 3–063.

normal for the goods to be carried. Nor would an evaluation of the "fairness" of the changed contract be consistent with the courts' normal approach.[8]

Conclusion. It is thus difficult to state with confidence whether a threat of a   **7–029**
breach of contract will ever be regarded as legitimate and, if so, in what circumstances. It is submitted that deliberate exploitation of the victim's position with a view to gaining some advantage unrelated to the contract and to which the threatening party knows he is not entitled is clearly illegitimate. Conversely, an apparent threat should not be treated as illegitimate if it was really no more than a true statement that, unless the demand is met, the party making it will be unable to perform; nor if the party has a genuine belief that he is legally entitled to the amount demanded. It is suggested that a demand made in good faith, in the sense that the party demanding has a genuine belief in the moral strength of his claim—for example, because he has encountered serious and unexpected difficulties in performing and will suffer considerable hardship if his demand is not met; or to correct an acknowledged imbalance in the existing contract—might in some circumstances also be treated as legitimate. Here the behaviour of the victim, for example whether he protests, will be relevant. First, it will go to causation: if the victim pays without protest, that may be evidence that he was not influenced by the threat. But secondly, payment without protest may leave the demanding party believing that the justice of his demand is admitted, whereas it will be harder for him to prove that he was acting in good faith if he ignores the victim's protests.

Threat to commit otherwise lawful act. Threatening to carry out something   **7–030**
perfectly within one's rights will not normally amount to duress; for instance, a party who relies on his existing contractual rights to drive a hard bargain is not, on that ground alone, guilty of economic duress.[9] There can be no doubt that even a threat to commit what would otherwise be a perfectly lawful act may be improper if the threat is coupled with a demand which goes substantially beyond what is normal or legitimate in commercial arrangements. It was at one time suggested that it could not be unlawful to threaten to exercise one's legal rights, no matter what the motive.[10] But such a principle is too widely stated. There are, for example, many cases where a man who has a "right," in the sense of a liberty or capacity of doing an act which is not unlawful, but which is calculated seriously to injure another, will be liable to a charge of blackmail if he demands money from that other as the price of abstaining, *e.g.* from disclosing discreditable incidents in the victim's life.[11] Although it is, in general, true to say that a contract is not rendered voidable by reason of the fact that pressure has been lawfully applied so as to compel the promisor to accept its terms,[12] it is unlikely

---

[8] For a helpful discussion of "fairness" in this context, see Burrows, *op. cit.*, pp. 180–181.

[9] *Alec Lobb Ltd v. Total Oil G.B. Ltd* [1983] 1 W.L.R. 87 (varied on other points, [1985] 1 W.L.R. 173).

[10] *Allen v. Flood* [1898] A.C. 1; *Ware and De Freville v. Motor Trade Association* [1921] 3 K.B. 40; *Hardie and Lane Ltd v. Chilton* [1928] 2 K.B. 306; *Chapman v. Honig* [1963] 2 Q.B. 502; *cf. Quinn v. Leathem* [1901] A.C. 495.

[11] *Thorne v. Motor Trade Association* [1937] A.C. 797, 822; *Universe Tankships of Monrovia Inc. v. I.T.W.F.* [1983] 1 A.C. 366, 401.

[12] *Hardie and Lane Ltd v. Chilton, supra*; *Eric Gnapp Ltd v. Petroleum Board* [1949] 1 All E.R. 980.

that a court would refuse to entertain an action at the suit of one who had paid money under a threat amounting to blackmail, or to set aside any agreement entered into as the result of such a threat.[13] In American law there are many illustrations of other threats to commit acts lawful in themselves which have been held to amount to duress when coupled with unreasonable demands.[14] For instance, a threat (lawfully) to dismiss an injured employee unless he accepted a manifestly low settlement for his injuries has been held to be unlawful duress.[15] It seems probable that a similar decision would be reached on such facts by an English court. On the other hand, care must be taken in treating threats lawful in themselves as amounting to duress, for otherwise threats commonly used in business (*e.g.* of lawful strikes[16]) would fall into the category of economic duress.

7–031   In *CTN Cash and Carry Ltd v. Gallaher Ltd*[17] the plaintiffs had ordered goods from the defendants, who delivered them by mistake to the wrong warehouse, from which they were stolen. The defendants, honestly but wrongly believing that the goods were at the plaintiffs' risk, invoiced them. The plaintiffs refused to pay until the defendants threatened to withdraw the plaintiffs' credit facilities, which, it was said, would seriously jeopardise the plaintiffs' business. The defendants had the right to withdraw credit facilities at any time. The plaintiffs later sought repayment. The Court of Appeal upheld the trial judge's decision that no case of economic duress had been made out. Steyn L.J., with whom the other members of the Court agreed, said that the combination of the facts that (i) the defendants were entitled to refuse to enter into any future contracts with the plaintiffs for any reason and (ii), critically, that the defendants bona fide thought that the plaintiffs owed the sum in question, was sufficient to distinguish cases in which a plea of economic duress had succeeded. The fact that the defendants were in a sense in a monopoly position was irrelevant, the control of monopolies being as matter for Parliament. Although there are cases in which the courts have accepted that a threat of a lawful action coupled with a demand for payment may be illegitimate,[18] it would be a relatively rare case in which "lawful act duress" could be established in a commercial context.

7–032   **Threat not to contract.** It is not clear whether a threat not to enter into a contract unless the threatener's terms are met could ever amount to improper pressure, for example where the threatener's terms are extortionate. There are a number of salvage cases in which extortionate demands have been made to rescue a vessel (or those on board) and the contracts so entered into have been

---

[13] *Norreys v. Zeffert* [1939] 2 All E.R. 187; *United Australia Ltd v. Barclays Bank Ltd* [1941] A.C. 1, 29; *Universe Tankships of Monrovia Inc. v. I.T.W.F.* [1983] A.C. 366, 401.

[14] And see *Restatement of Contracts* 2d, § 176(2).

[15] *Mitchell v. C.C. Sanitation Co.* (1968) 430 S.W. 2d. 933; *cf.* the somewhat similar facts in *Arrale v. Costain Engineering Ltd* [1976] 2 Lloyd's Rep. 98, though there was no real duress in this case.

[16] Threats of unlawful strikes are usually protected by the statutory immunities governing acts done in the course of furtherance of a trade dispute: see Trade Union and Labour Relations Consolidation Act 1992. But coercive threats falling outside these immunities will often constitute unlawful duress, see, *e.g. Universe Tankships of Monrovia Inc. v. I.T.W.F.* [1983] A.C. 366, *ante*, § 7–013.

[17] [1994] 4 All E.R. 715.

[18] *e.g. Thorne v. Motor Trade Association* [1937] A.C. 797.

set aside, or refused enforcement.[19] But these cases may rest upon the principle of maritime law that a duty to rescue human life is imposed on putative rescuers, so that the threat not to rescue may be unlawful. Other cases can be put in which a threat not to act, or not to contract, may be lawful in itself, and yet may be strongly coercive, for example where the threatener is in a monopoly position. However, there are Commonwealth authorities which hold that a person who is under no duty to enter into a contract with another is entitled to set his own terms, even though these may seem extortionate and the other party may have little choice but to comply.[20]

Threat to prosecute. A threat to prosecute may itself be an unlawful threat if **7–033** the charge is known to be false and the threat is made for malice or other improper motive. Such a threat would amount to a threat to commit the tort of malicious prosecution.[21] Consequently, a contract made as a result of such a threat would, it seems, be a clear case of a contract entered into as a result of duress, and if the other conditions are satisfied, would be voidable for that reason. Even at common law such action could constitute duress as to the person because the result of the prosecution could be the imprisonment of the threatened party, and this was sufficient to constitute duress as to the person[22]; in equity, an even broader view was taken, though most of the equitable cases are dealt with as instances of undue influence.[23] Further, a threat to prosecute, even when perfectly proper in itself, in the sense that a prosecution would be justified, may amount to an improper threat for the purposes of the law, if it is coupled with a demand for restitution or for a promise of restitution or other contractual undertaking.[24] In *Mutual Finance Co. Ltd v. John Wetton & Sons Ltd*[25] a guarantee was obtained from a family company under an implied threat to prosecute a member of the family for the alleged forgery of a previous guarantee. The persons seeking to enforce the guarantee knew that at the time it was given the father of the alleged forger was so ill that the shock of the prosecution of his son was likely to endanger his life. The guarantee was held to be invalid on the basis of actual undue influence. It is submitted that today the wider equitable rule will prevail,

---

[19] See *Akerblom v. Price* (1881) 7 Q.B.D. 129; *The Rialto* [1891] P. 175; *The Port Caledonia and the Anna* [1903] P. 184; *The Crusader* [1907] P. 196. See now Merchant Shipping Act 1995, s.224, which provides for the Salvage Convention 1989 (contained in Schedule 11 to the Act) to have the force of law. The Convention provides in Article 7:

"Annulment and modification of contracts

A contract or any terms thereof may be annulled or modified if—
  (a) the contract has been entered into under undue influence or the influence of danger and its terms are inequitable; or
  (b) the payment under the contract is in an excessive degree too large or too small for the services actually rendered."

Article 13 sets out criteria for fixing the proper reward.

[20] See, *e.g. Smith v. William Charlick Ltd* (1924) 34 C.L.R. 38; *Morton Construction v. City of Hamilton* (1961) 31 D.L.R. (2d) 323. See Goff & Jones, *Law of Restitution* (5th ed., 1998), pp. 344–345.

[21] *Duke Cadaval v. Collins* (1836) 4 A. & E. 858; *Flower v. Sadler* (1882) 10 Q.B.D. 572.

[22] *Smith v. Monteith* (1844) 13 M. & W. 427; *Mutual Finance Co. Ltd v. John Wetton & Sons Ltd* [1937] 2 K.B. 389, 395.

[23] See *Williams v. Bayley* (1866) L.R. 1 H.L. 200; *post,* § 7–046.

[24] *Kaufman v. Gerson* [1904] 1 K.B. 591.

[25] [1937] 2 K.B. 389.

so that a contract will be voidable if obtained by a threat of criminal prosecution or other lawful imprisonment, if the threat amounts to the use of illegitimate pressure.

7–034   **Stifling a prosecution.** An agreement obtained by threats to prosecute for a criminal offence may also be invalid on the ground that it involves the stifling of a prosecution for the offence.[26] In such a case, it is not sufficient for the party seeking to avoid the contract to show that his promise induced the other party to abstain from criminal proceedings.[27] He must go further and show that it was an express or implied term of the contract that there should be no prosecution.[28] An agreement of this nature is not only voidable on the ground of duress, but may be void as being contrary to public policy.[29] Money paid in pursuance of an illegal agreement is ordinarily irrecoverable; but the presence of duress may enable the party threatened to plead that he was not *in pari delicto*, and so he may recover his money by an action for money had and received.[30] The law will permit the compromise of a claim for damages, though made the subject of a criminal prosecution, in certain limited circumstances.[31] It is, however, submitted that a plea of duress might still be admitted to an action on a compromise of this nature if it were shown that it was arrived at by an illegitimate threat of a criminal prosecution. The modern trend seems to be to discourage the making of such contracts whenever serious crime is involved. If a contract is made without the matter being reported to the police there is a strong probability that the transaction will be held to amount to the stifling of a prosecution. And if the contract is made after the matter is reported to the police then there is a danger that it will amount to a conspiracy to pervert the course of justice.[32] To make a valid contract in such circumstances, it should be made absolutely clear that the innocent party is only compromising his *civil* claim for damages, and is neither threatening to report the matter to the police, nor to prosecute, nor offering not to do so.

7–035   **Threat to institute civil proceedings.** Since recourse to law is the remedy for redress provided by the law itself, it is obvious that prima facie a threat to enforce one's legal rights by instituting civil proceedings cannot be an unlawful or wrongful threat. Consequently a contract which is obtained by means of such a threat must prima facie be valid, and cannot be impeached on grounds of duress.[33] So an ordinary bona fide compromise is clearly a valid contract even though exacted under threats to bring (or defend) legal proceedings, or to appeal

---

[26] *Williams v. Bayley* (1866) L.R. 1 H.L. 200; *Windhill Local Board v. Vint* (1890) 45 Ch.D. 351; *Jones v. Merionethshire Permanent Benefit Building Society* [1892] 1 Ch. 173; see also Criminal Law Act 1967, s.5(1), (5) and *post*, §§ 17–036—17–037.

[27] *Flower v. Sadler* (1882) 10 Q.B.D. 572; *Barnes v. Richards* (1902) 71 L.J.K.B. 341.

[28] *Jones v. Merionethshire Permanent Benefit Building Society, supra,* but the modern trend seems somewhat against this restricted view: see *R. v. Panayiotou* [1973] 1 W.L.R. 1032.

[29] See *post*, § 17–035; *Keir v. Leeman* (1846) 9 Q.B. 371.

[30] *Smith v. Cuff* (1817) 6 M. &. S. 160; *Davies v. London and Provincial Marine Insurance Co.* (1878) 8 Ch.D. 469. The same is generally true of fraud: *Atkinson v. Denby* (1862) 7 H. & N. 934; *Shelley v. Puddock* [1980] Q.B. 348.

[31] *Keir v. Leeman, supra,* at 395; *Fisher & Co. v. Apollinaris Co.* (1875) L.R. 10 Ch.App. 297; see also Criminal Law Act 1967, s.5(1), (5), and *post*, §§ 17–036—17–037. See also Hudson (1980) 43 M.L.R. 532.

[32] See *R. v. Panayiotou, supra.*

[33] *Powell v. Hoyland* (1851) 6 Exch. 67; *Ex p. Hall* (1882) 19 Ch.D. 580.

from a judgment already given. Even a threat to bring proceedings where there is no ground of action in law is prima facie not an unlawful threat, at least where the threat is made bona fide, and is not manifestly frivolous or vexatious.[34] On the other hand, the malicious institution of some forms of legal process or other civil proceedings is, at least in limited circumstances, a tort,[35] and a threat to institute proceedings which would constitute a tort will therefore prima facie constitute a threat to do something unlawful; consequently a contract entered into as a result of such a threat may be voidable on grounds of duress. It is not clear whether a threat to institute civil proceedings which is not unlawful in itself could ever constitute duress for present purposes, if it is coupled (for instance) with a wholly unjustified demand, or if it is made in special circumstances (for instance) in which the defendant has a particular fear of the publicity which may follow from a claim. In principle there seems no reason why such a threat should not amount to duress in appropriate circumstances, but for obvious reasons these are likely to be rare.

Threats and warnings. At common law, it was formerly held necessary to distinguish a threat from a simple warning—although the dividing line was not easy to draw. In *Biffin v. Bignell*,[36] for example, it was held to be no duress to warn the promisor that the probable consequence of her failure to agree would be her continued detention in a lunatic asylum. On the other hand, in *Cumming v. Ince*,[37] where the plaintiff had been taken to a lunatic asylum and confined there, a commission in lunacy was sued out against her by the defendants and an inquisition was held. Before any verdict was reached, an agreement was entered into by counsel acting on her behalf whereby she would deposit certain deeds in consideration for her immediate release from detention. On an issue to try the right to possession of the deeds surrendered, it was held that the agreement was not binding upon her; for either the inquisition was properly brought, in which case she was incompetent to contract or to appoint counsel to act for her, or it was improperly brought, in which case "she was induced to resign [the deeds] by fear of personal suffering brought upon her by her confinement in a lunatic asylum by the act of the defendants." In equity, however, where an agreement is entered into through fear of prosecution, "not only is no direct threat necessary, but no promise need be given to abstain from a prosecution. It is enough if the undertaking were given to prevent a prosecution and that desire were known to those to whom the undertaking was given."[38] Thus in *Williams v. Bayley*,[39] a father executed a mortgage to a banker, who insisted on this course as he had it in his power to prosecute the father's son for forgery. There was no direct threat of a prosecution, but the mortgage was executed in return for the delivery up of

7-036

---

[34] Decisions upholding the validity of compromises in such cases usually turn on the existence of consideration and have been dealt with above (*ante*, §§ 3-044 *et seq.*); although the presence of consideration is not conclusive that there is no duress (see *ante*, § 7-014) it seems clear that a bona fide compromise could not be attacked on grounds of duress any more than on grounds of want of consideration.

[35] See, *e.g. Roy v. Prior* [1971] A.C. 470.

[36] (1862) 7 H. & N. 877.

[37] (1847) 11 Q.B. 112.

[38] *Mutual Finance Co. Ltd v. John Wetton & Sons Ltd* [1937] 2 K.B. 389, 395.

[39] (1866) L.R. 1 H.L. 200.

the documents forged. It was held that the mortgage was unenforceable in equity as the father was not a free and voluntary agent since he knew that unless he undertook the liability his son would be prosecuted. It is submitted that for the purposes of the modern law both of duress and undue influence, this is the correct approach; the distinction between a threat and a warning is untenable, at least where a demand is coupled with the threat or warning.[40] A "veiled threat" has been held to constitute duress.[41]

(h) *Parties to Duress*

7–037   **By whom suffered.** It was at one time said that the duress must be suffered by the party who enters into the contract, so that duress against a principal debtor would be no defence to an action on a bond against a surety.[42] But there is no modern authority to this effect, and it does not seem likely that a surety would be held liable on a transaction entered into by the principal debtor under manifestly illegal threats of violence.[43] Similarly, if an agent enters into a contract for his principal, from the same fear of the inconvenience which may arise to the principal from the latter being kept in confinement as would affect the mind of the principal himself, such a contract will be voidable on the ground of duress.[44] So, too, duress to a wife will avoid a contract given under its influence by her husband,[45] duress to a parent will avoid a contract obtained by means thereof from a child,[46] and even duress to a more remote relative will suffice if a contract is entered into under its influence.[47] Duress to a stranger was formerly thought to be ineffective,[48] and would no doubt be exceedingly rare. But if A takes B as a hostage and threatens to shoot him unless C signs a written agreement placed in front of him by A, it does not seem likely that the agreement would be held binding merely because B is a stranger to C. There are old cases holding that a contract made by a person in consideration of the discharge of a third party from illegal arrest is unenforceable as a mere *nudum pactum*.[49] In modern times it is, perhaps, more likely that a court would find consideration in such circumstances (for the promisor would not have made the promise unless he regarded the release of the third party as a benefit to him) but would hold the promise voidable for duress.

7–038   **Duress exercised by third party.** Where it is sought to avoid a contract on the ground of duress exercised, not by the party seeking to enforce the agreement, but by some third person, the party seeking to avoid the contract must prove that

---

[40] See Birks [1990] L.M.C.L.Q. 342, 346.
[41] *B. & S. Contracts & Design Ltd* v.*Victor Green Publications Ltd* [1984] I.C.R. 419.
[42] Roll.Abr. 687, pl. 7; Bacon Abr. *Duress* (B); *Huscombe v. Standing* (1607) Cro.Jac. 187. And see Vol. II, § 44–028.
[43] *cf. ante*, § 7–008.
[44] *Cumming v. Ince* (1847) 11 Q.B. 112.
[45] *Kaufman v. Gerson* [1904] 1 K.B. 591.
[46] *Williams v. Bayley* (1866) L.R. 1 H.L. 200.
[47] *Seear v. Cohen* (1881) 45 L.T. 589; *Jones v. Merionethshire Permanent Benefit Building Society* [1892] 1 Ch. 173.
[48] 1 Roll.Abr. 687, pl. 6.
[49] *Smith v. Monteith* (1844) 13 M. & W. 427; *Pole v. Harrobin* (1782) 9 East. 416n.

the other party knew of the duress,[50] or had constructive notice of it or had procured the making of the contract through the agency of the party who exercised the duress.[51]

(i) General Effect of Duress

Contract under duress is voidable. Despite earlier doubts,[52] it now seems **7–039** clearly established that a contract entered into under duress is voidable and not void[53]; consequently a person who has entered into a contract under duress may either affirm or avoid such contract after the duress has ceased[54]; and if he has voluntarily acted under it with a full knowledge of all the circumstances he may be held bound on the ground of ratification,[55] or if, after escaping from the duress, he takes no steps to set aside the transaction, he may be found to have affirmed it.[56]

Damages for duress. As previously stated,[56a] modern authorities have relied **7–040** upon the analogy of fraud in adumbrating the law relating to duress. In particular, it now seems clear that a person may affirm a contract which would have been voidable for duress. In these circumstances it may be a matter of some importance to consider whether duress may constitute a tort, like fraud, so that damages may be obtained, either in addition to, or in lieu of, rescission of a contract entered into as a result of the duress. The leading authority on the tort of intimidation (or duress) is *Rookes v. Barnard*[57] where the defendants conspired together to threaten to break their contracts of employment with the plaintiff's employer if he did not terminate the plaintiff's contract of employment. They were held liable to the plaintiff on the ground that a threat to break a contract was a sufficient unlawful act for the purpose of the tort of intimidation, at least where the intimidation is of a third party. Since it now appears clear that a threat to break a contract may, in appropriate circumstances, constitute unlawful duress in

---

[50] *Kesarmal s/o Letchman Das v. Valliappa Chettiar (N.K.V.) s/o Nagappa Chettiar* [1954] 1 W.L.R. 380. In the case of a bill of exchange, the onus of proof is shifted by s.30(2) of the Bills of Exchange Act 1882, but this has been held not to apply where the holder seeking to enforce the instrument is the person to whom it was originally delivered and in whose possession it remains: *Talbot v. Von Boris* [1911] 1 K.B. 854; *Hasan v. Willson* [1977] 1 Lloyd's Rep. 431 (fraud). See also *post,* § 7–070.

[51] These propositions are based on the cases of misrepresentation and undue influence, see *ante,* §§ 6–018 *et seq.* and *post,* §§ 7–070 *et seq.*

[52] Lanham (1966) 29 M.L.R. 615. In *Barton v. Armstrong, supra,* at 120, the majority of the Privy Council spoke of the contract as being void "so far as concerns" the plaintiff, but they were not adverting to this point. Indeed, the analogy with fraud which was relied upon by the majority supports the view stated in the text. See *ante,* § 7–005, n. 18.

[53] See *Lynch v. D.P.P. of Northern Ireland* [1975] A.C. 653, 695; *North Ocean Shipping Co. Ltd v. Hyundai Construction Co. Ltd* [1979] Q.B. 705.

[54] *ibid.* See also *Pao On v. Lau Yiu Long* [1980] A.C. 614.

[55] *Ormes v. Beadel* (1860) 2 De G.F. & J. 333.

[56] As in *North Ocean Shipping Co. Ltd v. Hyundai Construction Ltd* [1979] Q.B. 705, in which this passage was cited. See further *post,* § 7–063. In *Royal Boskalis Westminster NV v. Mountain* [1998] 2 W.L.R. 538, 591, Phillips L.J. expressed some difficulty in saying that a contract has been avoided on the grounds of duress if it is governed by a foreign law which would afford no right of avoidance but where the duress was so unconscionable that English law would override the proper law of the contract (see *ante,* § 7–023). However, he considered that English law would not recognise the effects of the contract (at 592).

[56a] *Ante,* § 7–005.

[57] [1964] A.C. 1129.

the law of contract, so that a variation of the contract thereby obtained may be voidable as a matter of contract law, it would seem that the doctrines of duress and intimidation are based on similar principles.[58] (It is, of course, also clear that a threat to commit a crime or a tort may equally constitute both duress in contract law, and intimidation in tort law.) If this is correct, it may be that, even where a person has affirmed a contract which is voidable for duress, damages could still be recovered in tort. In *Universe Tankships of Monrovia v. I.T.W.F.*[59] Lords Diplock and Scarman expressed differing views on the point. The question was not considered in *North Ocean Shipping Co. Ltd v. Hyundai Construction Co. Ltd*,[60] even though this case is a firm authority for holding that duress renders a contract voidable and not void. Yet it is arguable that this conclusion makes it all the more necessary to recognise that damages may be recovered for duress; for otherwise (as indeed was held in this case) the plaintiff who has lost his right to avoid will be left without any remedy for a wrongful act.

2. UNDUE INFLUENCE

(a) *Introduction*

7–041   **Equitable doctrine of undue influence.** The equitable doctrine of undue influence is a comprehensive phrase covering cases of undue influence in particular relations and also cases of coercion, domination, or pressure outside those special relations. As was said by Lord Chelmsford L.C.: "The courts have always been careful not to fetter this useful jurisdiction by defining the exact limits of its exercise."[61] Although most of the cases in which undue influence has been successfully pleaded relate to gifts, the same principles apply to purchases at an undervalue or sales at an excessive price.[62] The difference between a gift and a manifestly disadvantageous contract is for this purpose only a matter of degree.[63] The rules may also apply to contracts which are not manifestly disadvantageous, at least where actual undue influence is shown.[64]

7–042   **Basis of doctrine.** At common law, the presence of duress was (as has been seen) traditionally justified on the ground that the duress prevented the party constrained from forming a full and independent resolution to contract. In equity, however, the application of the doctrine of undue influence was intended rather

---

[58] See *Universe Tankships of Monrovia Inc. v. I.T.W.F.* [1983] 1 A.C. 366, 385, 400. But *cf.* Lord Reid in *J. T. Stratford & Son Ltd v. Lindley* [1965] A.C. 269, 325, where some doubt is thrown on the possible assimilation of two-party duress cases (where A coerces B) with three-party cases (where A coerces B who acts so as to cause loss to C). The reason for Lord Reid's doubts is that in the two-party case, unlike the three-party case, the plaintiff has a choice not to submit to the coercion, but to pursue his legal remedies. But this doubt seems to be disposed of by Lord Scarman's judgment in *Pao On v. Lau Yin Long* [1980] A.C. 614, (*supra*, § 7–012), where it is stressed that the question turns on the effectiveness of the remedy which the coerced party has.

[59] [1983] A.C. 366, 385, 400. See Carty and Evans [1983] J.B.L. 218, 223–225. In *Dimskal Shipping Co. SA v. I.T.W.F.* [1992] 2 A.C. 152, Lord Goff followed Lord Diplock's analysis that economic duress is not a tort *per se.*

[60] [1979] Q.B. 705, *ante*, § 7–011.

[61] *Tate v. Williamson* (1866) L.R. 2 Ch.App. 55, 61. See also Winder (1940) 3 M.L.R. 97.

[62] *Tufton v. Sperni* [1952] 2 T.L.R. 516, 526.

[63] *Wright v. Carter* [1903] 1 Ch. 27, 52.

[64] *Post*, § 7–044.

to ensure that no person should be allowed to retain the benefit of his own fraud or wrongful act. The equity view was well expressed in *Allcard v. Skinner*[65]: "This is not a limitation placed on the action of the donor; it is a fetter placed upon the conscience of the recipient of the gift, and one which arises out of public policy and fair play." Equity therefore acts on the conscience of the donee, not primarily on want of a true consent on the part of the donor. As a result, the equitable doctrine extends not only to cases of coercion (as previously referred to), but to all cases "where influence is acquired and abused, where confidence is reposed and betrayed,"[66] and to cases in which there is a danger that there may have been influence but proof of it is likely to be difficult[67]; in the latter type of case undue influence is presumed but the presumption may be rebutted on the facts.[68] But "the question is not whether [the party influenced] knew what she was doing, had done or was proposing to do, but how the intention was produced".[69] In a recent House of Lords case, actual undue influence was described as "a species of fraud" and from this was drawn the conclusion that the complainant need not show that she was manifestly disadvantaged by the transaction concerned.[70] The analogy with fraud may also be relevant to causal issues.[71] However, it should be stressed that, except with certain types of actual undue influence, it is not necessary to show unconscientious behaviour on the part of the defendant.[72] This is clear in cases of presumed undue influence, where the presumption may not have been rebutted even though it is accepted that the defendant acted with propriety[73]; and in many cases of actual undue influence the complaint is merely that the defendant made the decision for the claimant, without allowing the latter to make her own decision. The defendant's intention may have been to benefit the claimant.[74] In either type of case it is immaterial that the person to whom the gift or promise is made derives no personal benefit from it.[75]

Classes of undue influence. In *Allcard v. Skinner* Cotton L.J. classified the **7–043** cases into two:

"First, where the court has been satisfied that the gift was the result of influence expressly used by the donee for the purpose; second, where the relations between the donor and donee have at or shortly before the execution of the gift been such as to raise a presumption that the donee had influence over the donor. In such a case the court sets aside the voluntary gift, unless it is proved that in fact the gift was the spontaneous act

---

[65] (1887) 35 Ch.D. 145, 190.

[66] *Smith v. Kay* (1859) 7 H.L.C. 750, 779.

[67] Lindley L.J. in *Allcard v. Skinner, supra*, at 183.

[68] See *post*, § 7–059.

[69] Lord Eldon L.C. in *Huguenin v. Baseley* (1807) 14 Ves. 273, 300.

[70] Lord Browne-Wilkinson in *CIBC Mortgages Ltd v. Pitt* [1994] 1 A.C. 200, 209. See further *post*, § 7–044.

[71] See further *post*, § 7–052.

[72] This has led for a call for undue influence cases to be re-classified as "plaintiff-sided", the core of the doctrine being that the complainant's dependency led to the impairment of her decision, rather than that the defendant took advantage. See Birks and Chin in Beatson & Friedmann (eds.), *Good Faith and Fault in Contract Law* (1995) pp. 57–97, who at 59 cite dicta by the Australian High court in *Commercial Bank of Australia Ltd v. Amadio* (1983) 151 C.L.R. 447, 461, 474 to similar effect.

[73] *e.g. Cheese v. Thomas* [1994] 1 W.L.R. 173; Chen-Wishart (1994) 110 L.Q.R. 173, 175.

[74] *Dunbar Bank plc v. Nadeem* [1998] 3 All E.R. 876.

[75] *Ellis v. Barker* (1871) L.R. 7 Ch.App. 104; *Allcard v. Skinner, supra*; *Bullock v. Lloyds Bank Ltd* [1955] Ch. 317.

of the donor acting under circumstances which enabled him to exercise an independent will and which justify the court in holding that the gift was the result of a free exercise of the donor's will. The first class of cases may be considered as depending on the principle that no one shall be allowed to retain any benefit arising from his own fraud or wrongful act. In the second class of cases the court interferes, not on the ground that any wrongful act has in fact been committed by the donee, but on the ground of public policy, and to prevent the relations which existed between the parties and the influence arising therefrom being abused."[76]

More recently Lord Browne-Wilkinson[77] adopted a classification previously set out by the Court of Appeal[78]:

"Class 1: Actual undue influence

In these cases it is necessary for the claimant to prove affirmatively that the wrongdoer exerted undue influence on the complainant to enter into the particular transaction which is impugned.

Class 2: Presumed undue influence

In these cases the complainant only has to show, in the first instance, that there was a relationship of trust and confidence between the complainant and the wrongdoer of such a nature that it is fair to presume that the wrongdoer abused that relationship in procuring the complainant to enter into the impugned transaction. In Class 2 cases therefore there is no need to produce evidence that actual undue influence was exerted in relation to the particular transaction impugned: once a confidential relationship has been proved, the burden then shifts to the wrongdoer to prove that the complainant entered into the impugned transaction freely, for example by showing that the complainant had independent advice. Such a confidential relationship can be established in two ways, *viz.*:

Class 2(A)

Certain relationships (for example solicitor and client, medical advisor and patient) as a matter of law raise the presumption that undue influence has been exercised.

Class 2(B)

Even if there is no relationship falling within Class 2(A), if the complainant proves the de facto existence of a relationship under which the complainant generally reposed trust and confidence in the wrongdoer, the existence of such relationship raises the presumption of undue influence. In a Class 2(B) case therefore, in the absence of evidence disproving due influence, the complainant will succeed in setting aside the impugned transaction merely by proof that the complainant reposed trust and confidence in the wrongdoer without having to prove that the wrongdoer exerted actual undue influence or otherwise abused such trust and confidence in relation to the particular transaction impugned."

7–044   **Manifest disadvantage.** In cases where actual undue influence has been shown, the party influenced is entitled to a remedy[79] unless the right to rescind has been lost.[80] But in Class 2 cases, it is not sufficient for the complaining party

---

[76] *Allcard v. Skinner* (1887) 36 Ch.D. 145, 171.
[77] In *Barclays Bank plc v. O'Brien* [1994] 1 A.C. 180, 189–190.
[78] In *Bank of Credit and Commerce International SA v. Aboody* [1990] 1 Q.B. 923, 953.
[79] *CIBC Mortgages Ltd v. Pitt* [1994] 1 A.C. 200.
[80] See *post*, §§ 7–063 *et seq.*

to show the existence of a confidential relationship for the presumption of undue influence to arise. In *National Westminster Bank plc v. Morgan* Lord Scarman, giving the only full speech in the House of Lords, stated that relief for undue influence rests "not on some vague 'public policy' but specifically the victim-isation of one party by the other."[81] The House, reversing the Court of Appeal,[82] held that the presumption that undue influence was used only arises if the transaction is "manifestly disadvantageous" to the person influenced.[83] As Nourse L.J. put it in a later case, "the presumption is not perfected and remains inoperative until the party who has ceded the trust and confidence makes a gift so large, or enters a transaction so improvident, as not to be reasonably accounted for on the ground of friendship, relationship, charity or other ordinary motives on which men act. Although influence might have been presumed beforehand, it is only then that it is presumed to have been undue."[84]

Although most of the transactions which have been set aside were obviously **7–044A** one-sided,[85] this decision seems to represent a narrowing of the doctrine. For instance, in the Court of Appeal in *National Westminster Bank Ltd v. Morgan* there had been some discussion of the position of the client who is induced by his solicitor to sell his house to the solicitor at a fair price but who regrets the sale for other reasons.[86] In a later case in the Court of Appeal it was pointed out that even if undue influence would not be a ground for upsetting such a transaction, the client might be able to obtain relief on the more limited ground of abuse of confidence.[87] This applies only between solicitor and client, principal and agent, trustee and beneficiary and persons in similar positions.[88] In these cases it is not necessary for the party seeking relief to show that the transaction is manifestly disadvantageous to him. In a leading case Lord Parmoor, delivering the judgment of the Privy Council, said that relief will be given "unless the person claiming to enforce the contract can prove, affirmatively, that the person standing in such a confidential position has disclosed, without reservation, all the information in his possession and can further show that the transaction was, in itself, a fair one."[89] The existence of cases in which relief was given on the basis of abuse of confidence, and to which the House of Lords in *Morgan* were apparently not referred, seems to have led to that decision being the subject of some doubt in the most recent House of Lords decision. The actual decision in *CIBC Mortgages plc v. Pitt*[90] was that manifest disadvantage need not be shown in cases of actual undue influence (*i.e.* in Class 1 cases[91]). But Lord Browne-Wilkinson, in a judgment with which the other members of the House agreed, pointed out the difficulty of reconciling *Morgan* with the abuse of confidence cases, which are

---

[81] [1985] A.C. 686, 705.

[82] [1983] 3 All E.R. 85.

[83] [1985] A.C. 686, 704, relying on a Privy Council decision on the Indian Contracts Act, *Poosathurai v. Kannappa Chettiar* (1919) L.R. 47 Ind.App. 1.

[84] *Goldsworthy v. Brickell* [1987] Ch. 378, 401.

[85] In *Allcard v. Skinner* (1887) 36 Ch.D. 145, 185 Lindley L.J. had said that no presumption would arise unless a gift were large enough "not reasonably to be accounted for on the ground of friendship, relationship, charity or other ordinary motives on which ordinary men act".

[86] [1983] 3 All E.R. 85, 90.

[87] *Bank of Credit & Commerce International SA v. Aboody* [1990] 1 Q.B. 923, 943. See *Snell's Principles of Equity* (29th ed., 1991), p. 558.

[88] *Aboody's case, supra* 943.

[89] *Demara Bauxite Co. Ltd v. Hubbard* [1923] A.C. 673, 681–682.

[90] [1994] 1 A.C. 200. See *post*, § 7–049.

[91] *Ante*, § 7–043.

"founded on considerations of general public policy, *viz.* that in order to protect those to whom fiduciaries owe duties *as a class* from exploitation by fiduciaries *as a class*, the law imposes a heavy duty on fiduciaries to show the righteousness of the transactions . . . ."[92] He stated that "the exact limits of *Morgan* may have to be examined in the future."[93]

7–045   In the context of contracts as opposed to gifts, it is not easy to say what will constitute manifest disadvantage for the purposes of establishing the presumption of undue influence in classes 2A and 2B.[94] Certainly, a sale at undervalue will be manifestly disadvantageous[95]; and so will a transaction which brings the weaker party significant benefits if the benefit is obviously outweighed by the risks involved.[96] In cases in which the complainant is induced to guarantee or execute a charge to secure the other party's business debts, there is manifest disadvantage if the complainant is merely an employee with no stake in the business[97]; indeed some such transactions have been so one-sided that they "shock the conscience of the court" and may be set aside as unconscionable bargains.[98] A charge executed by a wife to secure her husband's business debts may be manifestly disadvantageous, even though she would benefit if the business were to thrive.[99] In *Barclays Bank plc v. O'Brien*[1] Lord Browne-Wilkinson said quite simply that the charge to secure the husband's business debts was on the face of it "not to her financial advantage" because she had no direct pecuniary interest in the business, but there the question was whether the creditor was put on constructive notice of possible misrepresentation or undue influence and it seems that, as between the stronger and weaker party, more must be shown in order to raise the presumption of undue influence.[2] In *Bank of Credit and Commerce International SA v. Aboody* the Court of Appeal held that the question

" . . . must depend on two factors, namely (a) the seriousness of the risk of enforcement to the giver, in practical terms, and (b) the benefits gained by the giver in accepting the risk."[3]

The Court of Appeal refused to interfere with the trial judge's findings that, as the wife would receive substantial benefits if the business survived, and at the relevant times it had "more than an equal chance" or "at least a reasonably good

---

[92] [1994] 1 A.C. 200, 209.

[93] *ibid.* For criticism of the requirement see Goff & Jones, *Law of Restitution* (5th ed., 1998), p. 362, Capper (1998) 114 L.Q.R. 479, 487 and numerous further comments cited, *ibid.* at note 44.

[94] Goff & Jones, *Law of Restitution* (5th ed., 1998), p. 362.

[95] *Mahoney v. Purnell* [1996] 3 All E.R. 61.

[96] *Cheese v. Thomas* [1994] 1 W.L.R. 129. It has been argued that a transaction under which the complainant parted with property at full market value may still be manifestly disadvantageous if it was not one that a party in similar situation would ordinarily be expected to have made, such as to sell the family land: Birks and Chin in Beatson & Friedmann (eds.), *Good Faith and Fault in Contract Law* (1995) 57–97, at 83; but *cf.* § 7–044A *ante.*

[97] *Steeples v. Lea* [1998] 1 F.L.R. 138.

[98] *Crédit Lyonnais Bank Nederland NV v. Burch* [1997] 1 All E.R. 144, 152; *Royal Bank of Scotland v. Etridge (No. 2)* [1998] 4 All E.R. 705, 713. See further, *post,* § 7–077.

[99] *Turner v. Barclays Bank plc* [1997] 2 F.C.R. 151, 165.

[1] [1994] 1 A.C. 180, 199.

[2] But see *Royal Bank of Scotland v. Etridge (No. 2)*, *supra,* at 727. The question should be considered as between the parties, *Bank of Cyprus (London) Ltd v. Markou* [1999] 2 All E.R. 707, 717. Compare the disadvantage sufficient to put a third party creditor on notice, *ante,* § 6–024.

[3] [1990] 1 Q.B. 923, 965. In *National Westminster Bank plc v. Morgan* [1985] A.C. 686 the charge was not manifestly disadvantageous as it was the only way to save the matrimonial home from repossession by another creditor.

chance of surviving", the transactions were not manifestly disadvantageous to the wife. Conversely, if the chances of the business surviving are not good or if the marriage is already in difficulties and were it to founder the wife would be left without her only substantial asset, the transaction may be manifestly disadvantageous.[4] But the disadvantage must "be obvious as such to any independent and reasonable persons who considered the transactions at the time with knowledge of all the relevant facts."[5]

(b) Actual Undue Influence

Express influence. If there is no special relationship, of the kind to be **7–046** mentioned below, between the parties, the onus is upon the person seeking to avoid the transaction to establish that undue influence existed.[6] This may be done by showing that there was actual coercion by the donee; these cases are probably now better viewed as cases of illegitimate pressure[7] and, accordingly, they were treated in the previous section. Actual undue influence may also be shown by proving that the stronger party exercised such a degree of domination or control over the mind of the weaker party that the latter's independence of decision was substantially undermined.[8] In *Bank of Credit and Commerce International SA v. Aboody* Slade L.J., delivering the judgment of the Court of Appeal, said:

> "[W]e think that a person relying on a plea of actual undue influence must show that (a) the other party to the transaction . . . had the capacity to influence the complainant; (b) the influence was exercised; (c) its exercise was undue; (d) that its exercise brought about the transaction."[9]

Many of the cases on this point have concerned spiritual "advisers," who have used their expert knowledge of the next world to obtain advantages in this.[10] In *Morley v. Loughnan*[11] executors recovered from the defendant large sums of money obtained by him from their testator during the last seven years of his life, on the ground that they had been obtained by undue influence in the guise of religion, it being held unnecessary to decide whether there was a fiduciary or confidential relationship between the defendant and the testator. There have also been cases where an employee obtained complete control over an employer of weak understanding,[12] and where an older man acquired a strong influence over

---

[4] *Royal Bank of Scotland v. Etridge (No. 2), supra,* at 716.

[5] *Bank of Credit and Commerce International SA v. Aboody, supra,* at 965.

[6] *Allcard v. Skinner* (1887) 36 Ch.D. 145, 181.

[7] Birks and Chin in Beatson & Friedmann (eds.), *Good Faith and Fault in Contract Law* (1995), pp. 57–97, at pp. 63–65; Capper (1998) 114 L.Q.R. 479, 484, 493.

[8] *Smith v. Kay* (1859) 7 H.L.C. 750; *Bank of Montreal v. Stuart* [1911] A.C. 120. See also *Coldunell Ltd v. Gallon* [1985] Q.B. 429.

[9] [1990] 1 Q.B. 923, 967.

[10] *Norton v. Relly* (1764) 2 Eden 286; *Nottidge v. Prince* (1860) 2 Giff. 246; *Lyon v. Home* (1868) L.R. 6 Eq. 655.

[11] [1893] 1 Ch. 736.

[12] *Bridgeman v. Green* (1755) 2 Ves.Sen. 627; *Re Craig* [1971] Ch. 95. Whether there was actual influence depends on the individual involved, not on whether a normal person would be influenced: *Re Brocklehurst's Estate* [1978] Ch. 14, 40.

a younger one, inducing him to execute securities for debts contracted by them in their career of mutual dissipation.[13] The transactions were set aside.

7–047   The critical question is whether the complainant was allowed to exercise an independent and informed judgment; "importunity and pressure . . . [are] neither always necessary nor sufficient".[14] In *Aboody's* case itself, the wife trusted her husband in business matters and signed documents he put before her without question. Although there was also evidence that he bullied her and that she signed because she wanted peace, the Court of Appeal did not rely on these; it considered that if the husband had intentionally exploited her trust to get the wife to sign manifestly disadvantageous documents without explaining them to her, that would constitute undue influence. On the facts, it did not consider the transactions to be manifestly disadvantageous, and, as it held that manifest disadvantage was essential to a plea of actual undue influence, it refused relief. On the latter point the case has been reversed: in cases of actual undue influence it is not necessary to prove that the transaction was manifestly disadvantageous in order to obtain relief.[15] It therefore seems that a party who exploits another's trust to get them to enter transactions without proper consideration or explanation will be held to be exercising actual undue influence, even if the transactions are not manifestly disadvantageous; the influenced party's mind is still "a mere channel through which the will of [the influencing party] operates",[16] and manifest disadvantage is merely powerful evidence of undue influence has been exercised.[17] In *Bank of Montreal v. Stuart* the wife succeeded in establishing undue influence even though he had put no pressure on her because none was needed as "she had no will of her own . . . she was ready to sign and do anything he told her to do".[18]

7–048   Actual undue influence may be shown more readily when the complainant really did not exercise any choice than when she did so but under pressure. As stated earlier, "importunity and pressure . . . [are] neither always necessary nor sufficient".[19] When a wife, for example, understands what is at stake in signing a charge over the matrimonial home, the fact that she is under legitimate pressure from the husband's creditors coupled with pressure from family loyalty will not amount to undue influence "unless they go beyond what is permissible and lead the complainant to execute the charge not because, however reluctantly, she is persuaded that it is the right thing to do, but because the wrongdoer's importunity

---

[13] *Smith v. Kay* (1859) 7 H.L.C. 750.

[14] *Royal Bank of Scotland v. Etridge (No. 2)* [1998] 4 All E.R. 705, 712. See also *Dunbar Bank plc v. Nadeem* [1998] 3 All E.R. 876, 883.

[15] *CIBC Mortgages plc v. Pitt* [1994] 1 A.C. 200, overruling *Bank of Credit & Commerce International SA v. Aboody* [1990] 1 Q.B. 923.

[16] *Bank of Credit and Commerce International SA v. Aboody* [1990] 1 Q.B. 923, 969, referring to the observations of Jenkins and Morris L.JJ. in *Tufton v. Sperni* [1952] 2 T.L.R. 516, 530, 532.

[17] *Royal Bank of Scotland v. Etridge (No. 2)* [1998] 4 All E.R. 705, 713.

[18] [1911] A.C. 120, 136–137. In *Royal Bank of Scotland v. Etridge (No. 2) supra*, at 712, Stuart-Smith L.J. said that this would today be more readily classed as a Class 2B case. If there is a sufficient relationship for Class 2B (*post*, § 7–057) and also manifest disadvantage, it will be in the weaker party's interest to plead the case as Class 2B as it then is up to the other party to rebut the presumption of undue influence; but actual undue influence remains an attractive alternative if there is doubt about the nature of the relationship or the existence of manifest disadvantage.

[19] *Royal Bank of Scotland v. Etridge (No. 2)* [1998] 4 All E.R. 705, 712.

has left her with no will of her own."[20] Lesser pressure is not, in the words used by the Court of Appeal in *Aboody's* case,[21] "undue".[22]

In a case in which the wife simply signed whatever her husband put in front **7–049** of her, it was said that the husband's influence was not "undue" because the transaction appeared at the time to be to her advantage: the husband was seeking to obtain for her an interest in a property which at the time was worth more than the amount charged as he "was getting on". "The court of equity is a court of conscience. It sets aside transactions obtained by the exercise of undue influence because such conduct is unconscionable . . . ".[23] With respect, this interpretation is doubtful. In *CIBC Mortgages plc v. Pitt*[24] Lord Browne-Wilkinson said that actual undue influence was a species of fraud, and the victim is entitled to have the transaction set aside as of right. He continued:

"No case decided before [*National Westminster Bank plc v. Morgan*[25]] was cited (nor am I aware of any) in which a transaction proved to have been obtained by actual undue influence has been upheld nor is there any case in which a court has even considered whether the transaction was, or was not, advantageous."

It is submitted that in the context of parties who trust the other to the extent that they sign without question, the fact that they are deprived of the opportunity to make an independent and informed judgment in itself makes the influence undue. It may be true that the other party was not dishonest in the sense of intending to harm the complainant's interests; but in fraud cases it is no defence that there was no intent to injure; it suffices that the statement was known to be untrue or was made recklessly.[26] A parallel rule appears to apply in cases in which the complainant was deprived of the opportunity to make up his or her own mind as to the risk and benefits involved.

Causation. As in cases of fraud, the fraud must have induced the contract, so **7–050** actual undue influence must have influenced the contract.[27] However, the analogies with fraud and duress suggest that the undue influence need only be "a significant reason" for the complainant entering the contract[28]; and it is possible that the same presumption applies as in fraud so that it will be for the stronger party to show that the undue influence made no difference to the complainant's decision.[29]

---

[20] *ibid.* at 713.

[21] See *ante*, § 7–045 at n. 3.

[22] For an example, see *Lloyds Bank plc v. Lucken*, heard with the *Etridge (No. 2)* case, [1998] 4 All E.R. 705, 738, 746. It is only in cases of actual undue influence through pressure that the question of legitimacy of the pressure arises: Birks and Chin in Beatson & Friedmann (ed.), *Good Faith and Fault in Contract Law* (1995), p. 57–97, at p. 88.

[23] *Dunbar Bank plc v. Nadeem* [1998] 3 All E.R. 876, 883–884, *per* Millett L.J. The other members of the court did not consider the question.

[24] [1994] 1 A.C. 200, 209.

[25] [1985] A.C. 686; *ante*, § 7–044.

[26] *Ante*, § 6–046.

[27] See *supra*, § 6–034.

[28] See *supra*, § 7–018, n. 74.

[29] In *Bank of Credit and Commerce International SA v. Aboody* [1990] 1 Q.B. 923 it was said (at 971) that it would not be appropriate for the court to exercise its jurisdiction to set aside the contract "where the evidence establishes that on the balance of probabilities the complainant would have entered the contract in any event."

(c) *Presumed Undue Influence*

7–051   **Presumption from certain relationships.** If the parties were at the time of the transaction in one of certain types of confidential relationship with each other, influence is presumed.[30] Once the transaction has been shown to be disadvantageous, the onus is on the party taking the benefit to justify that it was free from undue influence. In *Powell v. Powell*,[31] a voluntary settlement was executed by a daughter under the influence of her stepmother in favour of the stepmother's children. Farwell J. said: "The mere existence of the fiduciary relation raises the presumption, and must be rebutted by the donee."[32] The relationships which give rise to this presumption are described below.[33] But even outside these recognised relationships, if the plaintiff proves that at the time of the disadvantageous transaction a confidential relationship in fact existed between the parties, the presumption of undue influence will arise.[34] The classic statement is that of Lord Chelmsford in *Tate v. Williamson*[35]:

> "Wherever two persons stand in such a relation that, while it continues, confidence is necessarily reposed by one, and the influence which naturally grows out of that confidence is possessed by the other, and this confidence is abused, or the influence is exerted to obtain an advantage at the expense of the confiding party, the person so availing himself of his position will not be permitted to retain the advantage, although the transaction could not have been impeached if no such confidential relationship existed."

Nevertheless, the presumption of undue influence does not arise merely because the relationship between the parties can be described as fiduciary (as, for instance, that of principal and agent). It arises only where the fiduciary relationship is of a particular kind which, in the opinion of equity judges, is such as to raise the presumption.[36] For example, the relationship of bank manager and customer is not normally a confidential one in the relevant sense[37]; but when an elderly farmer, without consulting his solicitor, charged his property to his bank by way of guarantee of the debts of his son's company, and it was obvious that he was relying upon the bank manager for advice, a confidential relationship arose. As the manager neither explained the company's position fully nor suggested that the farmer get independent advice, the charge was set aside.[38]

7–052   **Dominating influence unnecessary.** Despite the fact that in *Morgan* Lord Scarman had referred to a "dominating influence,"[39] in Class 2 cases it is

---

[30] *Allcard v. Skinner* (1887) 36 Ch.D. 145, 181. These are now referred to as "Class 2(A)" cases, see *ante*, § 7–043.

[31] [1900] 1 Ch. 243.

[32] *ibid.* at 246.

[33] *Post*, §§ 7–053—7–056.

[34] *Tufton v. Sperni* [1952] 2 T.L.R. 516, 522; *Lloyds Bank Ltd v. Bundy* [1975] Q.B. 326. These are now referred to as Class 2(B) cases: see *ante*, § 7–043.

[35] (1866) L.R. 2 Ch.App. 55, 61.

[36] *Smith v. Kay* (1859) 7 H.L.C. 750, 771; *Re Coomber* [1911] Ch. 723.

[37] *National Westminster Bank plc v. Morgan* [1985] A.C. 686. If a bank takes it upon itself to explain the nature or effect of a guarantee to a customer, it will be liable for negligently misstating that nature or effect; and it was suggested that in some circumstances a bank might be under a duty to explain the nature of a guarantee to a guarantor before it is executed: *Cornish v. Midland Bank plc* [1985] 3 All E.R. 513.

[38] *Lloyds Bank Ltd v. Bundy* [1975] Q.B. 326. See also *Re Craig* [1971] Ch. 95; *Horry v. Tate & Lyle* [1982] 2 Lloyds Rep. 416. See further *post*, § 7–057.

[39] [1985] A.C. 686, 707.

immaterial whether one party has acquired a dominating influence over the mind of the other party.[40] "It is enough to show that the party in whom the trust and confidence is reposed is in a position to exert influence over him who reposes it."[41] These cases depend "on the concept that once the special relationship has been shown to exist, no benefit can be retained from the transaction unless it has been positively established that the duty of fiduciary care has been entirely fulfilled."[42]

Parent and child. In the earliest cases in which benefits conferred by children   7–053
upon their parents were set aside, the relief seems to have been extended on the ground of actual fraud.[43] Now, however, it is well established that such transactions are presumed to have been carried out as a result of undue influence,[44] even though the child may have attained his majority not long before.[45] If a gift is made to a parent shortly after the child reaches the age of majority, the parent will be required to show that the child was acting independently of his influence.[46] This presumption can continue even after marriage,[47] although the duration of the presumption is a question of fact and degree in the circumstances of each particular case. Family arrangements, however, are treated more leniently. "Transactions between parent and child may proceed upon arrangements between them for the settlement of property, and of their rights in property in which they are interested. In such cases the court regards the transactions with favour."[48] But even so, if the parent gets a disproportionate advantage, the arrangement is likely to be set aside.[49] Where an adult child acquires a position of dominance over elderly or senile parents, it is possible to establish a case of undue influence on the facts,[50] although no presumption arises either way.

Guardian and ward. The presumption also applies to dealings between   7–054
guardian and ward,[51] and the fact that the guardianship has legally terminated will not necessarily mean that the influence ceases, provided that there is still some control over the ward's property or actions.[52] Persons *in loco parentis* are also subject to the same surveillance by the court, such as uncle and niece,[53] stepfather and stepdaughter,[54] stepmother and stepdaughter,[55] elder and younger

---

[40] *Lloyds Bank Ltd v. Bundy* [1975] Q.B. 326.

[41] *Goldsworthy v. Brickell* [1987] Ch. 378, 404.

[42] *Lloyds Bank Ltd v. Bundy, supra, per* Sir Eric Sachs at 346.

[43] *Glissen v. Ogden* (1731), cited 2 Atk. 258; *Young v. Peachy* (1741) 2 Atk. 254; *Cocking v. Pratt* (1749) 1 Ves.Sen. 400.

[44] *Wright v. Vanderplank* (1855) 2 K. & J. 1.

[45] *Archer v. Hudson* (1844) 7 Beav. 551; *Berdoe v. Dawson* (1865) 34 Beav. 603; *Powell v. Powell* [1900] 1 Ch. 243; *London and Westminster Loan & Discount Ltd v. Bilton* (1911) 27 T.L.R. 184.

[46] *Bainbridge v. Browne* (1881) 18 Ch.D. 188; *Bullock v. Lloyds Bank Ltd* [1955] Ch. 317; *Re Pauling's Settlement Trusts* [1964] Ch. 303, 336.

[47] *Lancashire Loans Ltd v. Black* [1934] 1 K.B. 380.

[48] *Baker v. Bradley* (1855) 7 De G.M. & G. 597, 620; *Hartopp v. Hartopp* (1855) 21 Beav. 259; *Jenner v. Jenner* (1860) 2 De G.F. & J. 359; *Hoblyn v. Hoblyn* (1889) 41 Ch.D. 200. cf. *Bullock v. Lloyds Bank Ltd* [1955] Ch. 317.

[49] *Hoghton v. Hoghton* (1852) 15 Beav. 278; *Turner v. Collins* (1871) L.R. 7 Ch.App. 329.

[50] *Avon Finance Co. Ltd v. Bridger* [1985] 2 All E.R. 281.

[51] *Hylton v. Hylton* (1754) 2 Ves.Sen. 547; *Taylor v. Johnston* (1882) 19 Ch.D. 603.

[52] *Hatch v. Hatch* (1804) 9 Ves. 292.

[53] *Archer v. Hudson* (1844) 7 Beav. 551.

[54] *Kempson v. Ashbel* (1874) L.R. 10 Ch.App. 15.

[55] *Powell v. Powell* [1900] 1 Ch. 243.

brother,[56] and even an executor and beneficiary,[57] where the relationship confers a power analogous to that of parental control.

7–055   **Solicitor and client.** Any gift or sale by a client to his solicitor will be regarded with considerable suspicion by the court.[58] The relationship between solicitor and client is not only sufficient to raise a presumption of undue influence should the client enter a manifestly disadvantageous transaction with the solicitor; as mentioned earlier, the solicitor is subject to the stricter regime of abuse of confidence.[59] The solicitor must show the utmost good faith in his dealings with his client,[60] and must not make any benefit for himself at his client's expense.[61] Even if the benefit is an indirect one, as where a gift is made to the solicitor's wife[62] or son,[63] and even if the relationship of solicitor and client has technically ceased,[64] the presumption will apply where the influence still continues between them.

7–056   **Other instances possibly within Class 2(A).** The presumption applies to certain transactions between fiancé and fiancée.[65] It also applies to the relationship of medical man and patient,[66] trustee and *cestui que trust*,[67] and to a religious adviser and a person to whom he gives advice.[68]

7–057   **Confidential relationship shown on facts.** As stated earlier, a presumption of undue influence may also arise if on the facts it is shown that the parties were in a confidential relationship although one would not be presumed to exist as a matter of law: the cases now referred to as falling within Class 2(B).[69] A confidential relationship may arise in "all the variety of relations, in which dominion is exercised by one person over another",[70] or where the complaint proves that he or she reposed trust and confidence in the wrongdoer. Thus while there is normally no confidential relationship of the relevant kind between bank manager and customer, the position is different if the bank manager must have

---

[56] *Sercombe v. Sanders* (1865) 34 Beav. 382; *cf. Glover v. Glover* [1951] 1 D.L.R. 657.

[57] *Grosvenor v. Sherratt* (1860) 28 Beav. 659.

[58] For the analogous principles governing testamentary dispositions to solicitors, see *Wintle v. Nye* [1959] 1 W.L.R. 284.

[59] *Ante*, § 7–044A.

[60] See *ante*, §§ 6–079—6–080; *Moody v. Cox and Hatt* [1917] 2 Ch. 71.

[61] *Turrell v. Bank of London* (1862) 10 H.L.C. 26; *Wright v. Carter* [1903] 1 Ch. 27.

[62] *Liles v. Terry* [1895] 2 Q.B. 679.

[63] *Barron v. Willis* [1902] A.C. 271.

[64] *Demerara Bauxite Co. Ltd v. Hubbard* [1923] A.C. 673; *McMaster v. Byrne* [1952] 1 All E.R. 1362.

[65] *Cobbett v. Brock* (1855) 20 Beav. 524; *Lovesy v. Smith* (1880) 15 Ch.D. 655; *Re Lloyds Bank Ltd* [1931] 1 Ch. 289. Contrast *Zamet v. Hyman* [1961] 1 W.L.R. 1442. Gifts between engaged couples may now also be set aside, if the marriage does not take place, under the Law Reform (Miscellaneous Provisions) Act 1970.

[66] *Mitchell v. Homfray* (1881) 8 Q.B.D. 587; *Radcliffe v. Price* (1902) 18 T.L.R. 466.

[67] *Ellis v. Barker* (1871) L.R. 7 Ch.App. 104; *Beningfield v. Baxter* (1866) 12 App.Cas. 167.

[68] *Huguenin v. Baseley* (1807) 14 Ves. 273; *Lyon v. Home* (1868) L.R. 6 Eq. 655; *Allcard v. Skinner* (1887) 36 Ch.D. 145. It has been rightly pointed out that it is dangerous to assume that every relationship of this type, or of the other types just listed, will give rise to the presumption, as the relationship between the parties may not be confidential: Cartwright, *Unequal Bargaining* (1991), p. 178.

[69] See *ante*, § 7–043.

[70] *Huguenin v. Baseley, supra*, at 286, *per* Sir S. Romilly *arguendo*; *Smith v. Kay* (1859) 7 H.L.C. 750, 779; *Lloyds Bank Ltd v. Bundy* [1975] Q.B. 326.

known that the customer was in need of advice and was looking to the manager to give it.[71] Moreover, the existence of a relationship of trust and confidence may be inferred from the fact that one party has entered an excessively onerous transaction at the request of the other (in the case in question, a junior employee with no stake in the business had at her employer's request given a second charge over her flat and an unlimited all monies guarantee of the employer's business debts).[72] But in such an extreme case the plaintiff may be able to set aside the transaction on the basis of unconscionability.[73] So, too, where a young man in financial difficulties sought the advice of a more experienced relative, who himself purchased the young man's property at a third of its proper price,[74] where a young woman granted a mining lease to her uncle and to the son of her father's executor, being advised to do so by the executor in whom she placed "the greatest confidence,"[75] and where a member of a committee set up to establish a Moslem cultural centre in London was induced by a fellow member to buy the latter's house from him for the purpose at a price which greatly exceeded its market value,[76] the transactions were set aside on the ground that the defendants had failed to rebut the presumption of undue influence.

Husband and wife. The presumption does not apply between husband and wife[77]; but the House of Lords has recognised "a special tenderness of treatment afforded to wives" because in many cases "the wife demonstrates that she placed trust and confidence in her husband in relation to her financial affairs[78] and therefore raises a presumption of undue influence" and because "sexual and emotional ties . . . provide a ready weapon for undue influence."[79]   **7–058**

Rebutting the presumption. In order to rebut the presumption of undue influence, evidence must be adduced to satisfy the court "that the donor was acting independently of any influence from the donee and with the full appreciation of what he was doing."[80] The most usual, though not the only, way of rebutting the presumption is to prove that the claimant had competent and independent advice,[81] and the position of the defendant is stronger if the claimant's action was taken in accordance with, than if it was taken in spite of, such advice. But circumstances may establish the fact that the claimant's will was   **7–059**

---

[71] See ante, § 7–051; *National Westminster Bank plc v. Morgan* [1985] A.C. 686; *Lloyds Bank Ltd v. Bundy, supra*.

[72] *Crédit Lyonnais Bank Nederland NV v. Burch* [1997] 1 All E.R. 144, esp. at 154 and 158. See Chen-Wishart [1997] C.L.J. 60, 65–66.

[73] See post, § 7–075.

[74] *Tate v. Williamson* (1866) L.R. 2 Ch.App. 55.

[75] *Grosvenor v. Sherratt* (1860) 28 Beav. 659.

[76] *Tufton v. Sperni* [1952] 2 T.L.R. 516. See also ante, § 7–029.

[77] *Hoes v. Bishop* [1909] 2 K.B. 390. See also *Grigby v. Cox* (1750) 1 Ves.Sen. 517; *Nedby v. Nedby* (1852) 5 De G. & Sm. 377; *Barron v. Willis* [1899] 2 Ch. 578, 585; *Mackenzie v. Royal Bank of Canada* [1934] A.C. 468; *Midland Bank plc v. Shephard* [1988] 3 All E.R. 17. But *cf. Cresswell v. Potter* [1978] 1 W.L.R. 255n. and *Backhouse v. Backhouse* [1978] 1 W.L.R. 243, post, § 7–077.

[78] Compare *Society of Lloyd's v. Khan* [1998] 3 F.C.R. 93.

[79] *Barclays Bank plc v. O'Brien* [1994] 1 A.C. 180, 190. In *Barclays Bank plc v. Rivett* (1997) 29 H.L.R. 893 it was the wife who had influence over the husband.

[80] *Inche Noriah v. Shaik Allie Bin Omar* [1929] A.C. 127, 135.

[81] *Morley v. Loughnan* [1893] 1 Ch. 736, 752; *Re Coomber* [1911] 1 Ch. 723; *Inche Noriah v. Shaik Allie Bin Omar* [1929] A.C. 127.

freely exercised although no independent advice was given or although such advice was disregarded.[82]

7–060   **Duty of confidence.** In cases falling within the second of the two categories referred to in *Allcard v. Skinner*[83] it is not to the point to attempt to "rebut the presumption" of undue influence by evidence that the donor's will was exercised free of domination. In cases of this kind what needs to be established is that the duty of confidence has been fulfilled. What constitutes fulfilment of that duty depends on the facts of the particular case, but in general the duty requires that the person liable to be influenced should be enabled to form an independent and informed judgment.[84] Where the case involves the giving of advice by a legal or other confidential adviser this no doubt means that the advice must be fairly and disinterestedly offered, and must also be reasonable and adequate advice in the circumstances. In other cases the question may not be so much as to any advice given by the defendant, but as to the availability of advice from other sources. In some cases, such a duty may be held to require disclosure of material facts, and no real question arises of undue influence in the literal sense.[85]

7–061   **Independent advice.** Independent advice is not the only way in which the presumption may be rebutted and the complainant be shown to have acted with an independent will, but where there are no other circumstances it may be the only way.[86] On the subject of independent advice there have been varying statements of judicial opinion. In *Re Coomber*,[87] it was said that it is sufficient if an independent adviser sees that the donor understands what he is doing and intends to do it; he need not advise him to do it or not to do it. On the other hand, in *Powell v. Powell*,[88] it was said: "The solicitor does not discharge his duty by satisfying himself simply that the donor understands and wishes to carry out the particular transaction. He must also satisfy himself that the gift is one which it is right and proper for the donor to make under all the circumstances, and if he is not so satisfied, his duty is to advise his client not to go on with the transaction, and to refuse to act further for him if he persists." It has been said that in this event the solicitor should inform the other parties (including a creditor in whose favour the party advised is proposing to give a guarantee or charge) that he has seen his client and has given him certain advice and as a result has declined to act further for him.[89] He should also tell the client that he is not bound to enter the transaction of the terms offered or at all.[90]

7–062   **Adequacy of advice.** It has been said that the independent adviser should ensure that the party entering the transaction understands it even where there has been no misrepresentation by the other party. In particular, where a wife is asked

---

[82] *Inche Noriah v. Shaik Allie Bin Omar, supra,* at 135; *Re Estate of Brocklehurst* [1978] Ch. 141.

[83] See *ante,* § 7–043.

[84] *Lloyds Bank Ltd v. Bundy* [1975] Q.B. 326, 342.

[85] *English v. Dedham Vale Properties Ltd* [1978] 1 W.L.R. 93.

[86] *Inche Noriah v. Shaik Allie Bin Omar* [1929] A.C. 127, PC. The fact that the complainant had the possibility of taking advice will not suffice at least if it is evident that he has not taken it: *Claughton v. Price* (1998) 30 H.L.R. 396.

[87] [1911] 1 Ch. 723.

[88] [1900] 1 Ch. 243, 247; *Barron v. Willis* [1902] A.C. 271; *Wright v. Carter* [1903] 1 Ch. 27.

[89] *Royal Bank of Scotland v. Etridge (No. 2)* [1998] 4 All E.R. 705, 715.

[90] *ibid.*; *Credit Lyonnais Bank Nederland NV v. Burch* [1997] 1 All E.R. 144.

by her husband to give an unlimited guarantee, the adviser should make sure the wife has understood that the liability will not be limited to the advance the husband is seeking.[91] Advising the wife and deciding whether the transaction is one that the wife could properly be advised to enter will be difficult as the possible benefits to the wife must be considered:

> "[It] will usually be necessary for the solicitor to inform himself of the existing indebtedness and of the new advance, and of the reasons for the new advance or the bank's reasons for additional security. He may also need to probe the stability of the marriage. This would need to be done with sensitivity; but the wife should at least be warned that by entering into the transaction she could be putting at risk the one substantial asset which she could rely on should the marriage come to grief".[92]

It appears that if the solicitor does not have the relevant information or ask the relevant questions, the advice may be treated as inadequate and the presumption will not be rebutted. The Judicial Committee of the Privy Council considered this question in *Inche Noriah v. Shaik Allie Bin Omar*,[93] where there was a gift of almost the whole of her property by an aged Malay widow to her nephew. The Board was of the opinion that independent advice might be effective even though it was not shown that the advice was taken; but then it must be given "with a knowledge of all relevant circumstances and must be such as a competent and honest adviser would give if acting solely in the interests of the donor."[94] In the instant case, the gift was set aside, for although the widow had received independent advice from a solicitor, he did not know at the time that the gift comprised almost all of her property, nor did he advise her that she could equally well have benefited her nephew by will.[95]

Affirmation. A transaction entered into as the result of undue influence is **7–063** voidable and not void. The right to rescind on the ground of undue influence may be lost either by express affirmation of the transaction by the victim,[96] by estoppel or by delay amounting to proof of acquiescence.[97] Although there can normally be no affirmation until the party knows he has the right to rescind, it has been doubted whether this is a hard and fast rule: "the whole of the circumstances must be looked at to see whether it is just that the complaining beneficiary should succeed."[98] Estoppel requires a clear and unequivocal representation that the claimant would not seek to set the agreement aside, intended to be acted on and in fact acted on by the other party to his detriment or in such a way that it would be inequitable to allow the claimant to go back on his representation.[99]

---

[91] *Royal Bank of Scotland v. Etridge (No. 2)* [1998] 4 All E.R. 705, 715. Stuart-Smith L.J. noted (at 716) that such problems should be much rarer in future because of the provision in the 1997 version of the Code of Banking Practice that unlimited guarantees or security will not be taken. However it should be stressed that the Code is only voluntary and not all lenders adhere to it.

[92] *ibid.* at 717.

[93] [1929] A.C. 127.

[94] [1929] A.C. 127, 136.

[95] *cf. post*, § 7–071.

[96] *Mitchell v. Homfray* (1881) 8 Q.B.D. 587; *Morse v. Royal* (1806) 12 Ves. 355.

[97] *Allcard v. Skinner* (1887) 36 Ch.D. 145; *Turner v. Collins* (1871) L.R. 7 Ch.App. 329. See *post*, §§ 29–139—29–145.

[98] *Goldsworthy v. Brickell* [1987] Ch. 378, 412 (Nourse L.J.) and 416 (Parker L.J.). Nourse L.J. considered that the defence might have succeeded on the basis that by the time of the alleged act of affirmation, the complainant had consulted solicitors. *cf. Lloyds Bank plc v. Lucken*, heard with the *Etridge (No. 2)* case, [1998] 4 All E.R. 705, 738, 751.

[99] *Goldsworthy v. Brickell* [1987] Ch. 378, 410–411.

In either case, to be of any value, the affirmation must take place after the influence has ceased. "The right to property acquired by such means cannot be confirmed in this court unless there be full knowledge of all the facts, full knowledge of the equitable rights arising out of those facts, and an absolute release from the undue influence by means of which the frauds were practised."[1] Lapse of time in itself does not seem to constitute a bar to relief,[2] but it will provide evidence of acquiescence if the victim fails to take any steps to set aside the transaction within a reasonable time after he is freed from the undue influence.[3] And where he has himself failed to commence proceedings in this way during his lifetime, his personal representatives cannot do so after his death.[4]

7–064   **Restitution.** A complainant who has received no benefit under the contract may simply have it set aside.[5] If the complainant has received a benefit[6] and rescinds, she must make restitution[7] and it has been said that her right to rescission is "conditional on her making counter-restitution."[8]

7–065   **Impossibility of restitution not necessarily a bar.** It is thought that, as between the parties, the fact that property transferred can no longer be returned as such to the complainant (for example, because an innocent third party has acquired rights over it) is not necessarily a bar to rescission on the grounds of undue influence. Instead, the defendant may be required to make counter-restitution by a monetary equivalent.[9] This is suggested by the cases discussed in the next two paragraphs.

7–066   **Account of profits.** A transaction entered into as a result of undue influence can be rescinded even though it has been fully executed, and even though *restitutio in integrum* is no longer fully possible, so long as the court can do substantial justice. Where a series of contracts between a young singer and his manager and agent was set aside after the singer had achieved world-wide success, it was held that the defendant could be made liable to account for all the profit made from the contracts, but subject to a reasonable allowance for his work under the transactions in question. This allowance could include a reasonable element of profit, but not so much as might have been obtained by the defendant if the plaintiff had been properly advised by independent advisers at the outset.[10]

---

[1] *Moxon v. Payne* (1873) L.R. 8 Ch.App. 881, 885.
[2] *Hatch v. Hatch* (1804) 9 Ves. 292; *Re Pauling's Settlement Trusts* [1964] Ch. 303.
[3] *Allcard v. Skinner* (1887) 36 Ch.D. 145; *cf. Bullock v. Lloyds Bank Ltd* [1955] Ch. 317.
[4] *Wright v. Vanderplank* (1855) 2 K. & J. 1; *Mitchell v. Homfray* (1881) 8 Q.B.D. 587.
[5] *cf. TSB Bank plc v. Camfield* [1995] 1 W.L.R. 430 (misrepresentation), *ante*, § 6–030.
[6] It seems likely that in this context "benefit" refers to something received directly under the contract to be set aside or one inextricably linked with it (as in the case cited in the next note) rather than to, *e.g.* a benefit received by a wife through the successful operation of her husband's business for a period before the creditor sought to enforce the charge in question given by the wife.
[7] *Dunbar Bank plc v. Nadeem* [1998] 3 All E.R. 876; see also *Midland Bank plc v. Greene* [1994] 2 F.L.R. 827.
[8] *Dunbar Bank plc v. Nadeem, supra* at 884.
[9] Burrows, *Law of Restitution* (1993), pp. 191–192.
[10] *O'Sullivan v. Management Agency Ltd* [1985] Q.B. 428, following the authorities relating to setting aside contracts for misrepresentation, *ante*, §§ 6–112—6–118.

Equitable compensation. It has been held that if *restitutio in integrum* is no   **7–067**
longer possible, and the defendant does not retain any profits for which he may
be made to account, the claimant may still be given "compensation in equity".
In *Mahoney v. Purnell*[11] May J. held that equitable compensation under *Nocton
v. Lord Ashburton*[12] is also available in such circumstances and the plaintiff could
recover the value of what he had transferred, giving credit for what he had
received. The judge described this as the practical equivalent of awarding
damages, though it should be noted that equitable compensation will not include
compensation for consequential losses.[13] Doubt has been expressed whether
equitable compensation is available in every case of undue influence, or only
those in which there is a fiduciary relationship of a narrower sort, such as
between solicitor and client or beneficiary and trustee.[14] In *Bank of Credit and
Commerce International SA v. Aboody*[15] Slade L.J. treated such cases as different
to normal cases of undue influence[16] and said that cases such as *Tate v. Williamson*[17] did not draw a sufficiently clear distinction between the two types of case;
but there is no sign that May J. saw the case before him to be anything other than
one of Class 2B undue influence. However, it has been argued persuasively that
"equitable compensation" in this context should be understood as referring to
pecuniary restitution of any unjust enrichment, which is appropriate in cases of
undue influence. The case shows not that equitable compensation may be given
when restitution is impossible so much as that rescission need not be prevented
by the fact that property cannot be returned *in specie*; as between the parties it
may be effected in money.[18]

Sharing of loss. Conversely, where as the result of undue influence the   **7–068**
claimant has contributed to the purchase of property which as a result of
the transaction being set aside has to be sold, and the property does not fetch the
price paid for it, the claimant is not entitled to the return of the full contribution
he made. The principle is to prevent unjust enrichment of the other party and the
sum obtained on sale of the property should be shared in the same proportions as
the parties' original contributions to the purchase.[19]

Change of position. It has been noted that the decision described in the last   **7–069**
paragraph might be viewed as a form of change of position defence to even
monetary restitution; and that in *Allcard v. Skinner*[20] the possibility of such a
defence was recognised by all three Lords Justice, in that they considered that the
complainant would have been able, had she taken steps in time, to recover from
the religious order to which she had made her gifts only such sums as remained
unspent in its hands.[21]

---

[11] [1996] 3 All E.R. 61.
[12] [1914] A.C. 932 (a case of a mortgagee suing his solicitor, see § 6–079).
[13] See § 6–080, n. 26.
[14] See Heydon (1997) 113 L.Q.R. 8, 9 and § 6–080.
[15] [1990] 1 Q.B. 923, 943.
[16] See § 7–044A at nn. 87 and 92.
[17] (1866) LR 2 Ch. App. 55.
[18] Birks [1997] R.L.R. 72. But compare Goff & Jones, *Law of Restitution* (5th ed., 1998), p. 369.
See also *ante*, § 6–116.
[19] *Cheese v. Thomas* [1994] 1 W.L.R. 129.
[20] (1887) 36 Ch. D. 145.
[21] Chen-Wishart (1994) 110 L.Q.R. 173, 177–178; *Allcard v. Skinner* (1887) 36 Ch. D. 145, 164,
171, 186.

(d) *Undue Influence by a Third Party*

7-070   **Undue influence by spouses.** Where one party seeks to avoid a contract on the ground of undue influence by a third person, it must appear either that the third person was acting as the other party's agent, or that the other party had actual or constructive notice of the undue influence. In *Barclays Bank plc v. O'Brien*,[22] a case where the husband had by misrepresentation secured his wife's signature to a charge over the matrimonial home to secure the debts of his business, the bank was prevented from enforcing the charge on the ground that it had constructive notice of the husband's misrepresentation even though it had no actual knowledge of it. Lord Browne-Wilkinson, delivering the only full speech in the House of Lords, pointed out that there is a substantial risk that the wife may act as surety when the transaction is not to her advantage because of some legal or equitable wrong by the husband. Where the creditor is aware that the debtor and the surety are husband and wife, and the transaction is on its face not to the financial advantage of the surety as well as of the debtor, the creditor will be fixed with constructive notice of any undue influence, misrepresentation or other legal wrong by the debtor unless it has taken reasonable steps to satisfy itself that the surety has entered into the obligation freely and with knowledge of the true facts.[23] It is the combination of the fact that the parties are husband and wife and that the transaction is on its face not to the wife's advantage that should put the creditor on notice. In contrast, in *CIBC Mortgages plc v. Pitt*,[24] which was heard with *O'Brien's* case, the loan appeared on its face to be a normal one for the joint benefit of husband and wife and therefore the creditor was not fixed with constructive notice of the undue influence used by the husband to secure the wife's agreement.

7-071   **Steps to avoid constructive notice.** The steps that the creditor should take to avoid being fixed with constructive notice of any undue influence by the debtor are set out in Chapter 6.[25] It will be noted that in most cases the creditor will be protected if the wife is already dealing with the bank through a solicitor or the bank has either advised the wife to take independent advice or (as has more usually been the case in the reported cases) it has received a letter from a solicitor confirming that he has seen the wife, explained the transaction and made sure she understood it. Although, as Hobson L.J. put it, the problem in cases of undue influence is not that the wife does not understand the transaction but that she has no independence,[26] the bank can expect the solicitor to act professionally; and this includes satisfying himself that his client is acting freely from improper influence. As already stated,[27] if the solicitor is not so satisfied and the client, against his advice, persists in going ahead, the solicitor should refuse to act. Further, if the transaction is particularly disadvantageous, or the suspicion of undue influence particularly strong, the creditor cannot rely on telling the wife to get independent advice but must see that she gets it.[28] It has been said that if the

---

[22] [1994] 1 A.C. 180; see *ante*, §§ 6–021—6–031.

[23] *ibid.* at 196. The steps the House of Lords suggested the creditor should take are set out *ante*, § 6–022.

[24] [1994] 1 A.C. 200.

[25] *Ante*, §§ 6–026—6–027.

[26] In his dissenting judgment in *Banco Exterior Internacional v. Mann* [1995] 1 All E.R. 936, 947. See also *Crédit Lyonnais Bank Nederland NV v. Burch* [1997] 1 All E.R. 144, 156.

[27] *Ante*, § 7–061.

[28] *Crédit Lyonnais Bank Nederland NV v. Burch* [1997] 1 All E.R. 144.

transaction is so one-sided that no competent solicitor could advise her to enter it, even a solicitor's letter to the effect that the wife has been advised will not protect the bank; the steps taken cannot reasonably allay the suspicion of undue influence.[29]

Other relationships. The same principles apply when the creditor knows that   **7–072**
the debtor and surety are cohabitees and in other cases where the creditor is aware that the surety reposes trust and confidence in the debtor in relation to financial affairs, for instance vulnerable elderly parents providing security for the debts of their adult son.[30] A bank was also held to be put on notice of undue influence between an employer and a junior employee when the transaction was so manifestly disadvantageous to the latter that it could hardly be explained except as being the result of some such overreaching.[31] As Millett L.J. remarked, for a junior employee with no stake in a company to give an unlimited all-monies guarantee of its debts is even less explicable than for a wife to do so, as the wife might consider it was in her financial interest that the business should prosper, or give the guarantee to avoid putting the marriage at risk.[32] Thus it appears that the *Barclays Bank plc v. O'Brien* principle[33] may apply even when the creditor is not aware of any particular relationship which gives rise to a risk of undue influence, provided that the transaction is sufficiently one-sided and there is nothing in the relationship between the parties which would explain it in some other way, for example, when the guarantee is given to a young person by an older and wealthier friend.

Other cases. This doctrine of constructive notice should avoid the need for   **7–073**
the somewhat strained approach used in a number of earlier cases to the effect that the creditor, by "leaving it to the debtor" to get the surety's signature, was appointing the debtor as its agent and was therefore in no better position than the debtor would have been.[34] There may still be cases in which the creditor is responsible for the husband's actions because it can be said, "without artificiality," that the husband was acting as agent of the creditor, but "such cases will be of very rare occurrence."[35] In *O'Sullivan v. Management Agency Ltd*[36] it was held that where a person in a fiduciary relationship procures by undue influence contracts to be entered into with companies under his control and direction, the companies will be affected by the doctrine of undue influence even though they themselves were not in fiduciary relationships. In such a case it is immaterial that the undue influence is exercised in order to obtain a benefit for third parties rather than for the person himself exercising the undue influence.

---

[29] *ibid.* especially at 155–157 (Millett L.J.) Such a one-sided transaction is probably avoidable also on the ground of unconscionability, *ibid.*: see further *post*, § 7–077.

[30] *Avon Finance Co. Ltd v. Bridger* (1979) [1985] 2 All E.R. 281; *Barclays Bank plc v. O'Brien, supra*, at 198.

[31] *Crédit Lyonnais Bank Nederland NV v. Burch* [1997] 1 All E.R. 144. See Chen-Wishart [1997] C.L.J. 60, 71.

[32] *ibid.* at 155.

[33] *Ante*, § 7–070.

[34] The first case appears to have been *Avon Finance Co. Ltd v. Bridger, supra*; see also *King's North Trust Ltd v. Bell* [1986] 1 W.L.R. 119. These cases had been criticised by the Court of Appeal in *O'Brien's* case as "lending an air of unreality to the arguments": [1993] Q.B. 109, 113.

[35] *Barclays Bank plc v. O'Brien, supra*, at 195.

[36] [1985] Q.B. 428.

7-074   **Volunteers.** Alternatively, it may suffice to set aside the contract if the person against whom relief is sought gave no consideration, *i.e.* he was merely a volunteer.[37] It is not possible to avoid the contract as against a bona fide purchaser for value without notice.[38] It is clear that a gift made to a person who has exercised no influence will not be set aside because there is in the same instrument a gift to a person within the suspect relationships, unless the instrument as a whole can be said to have been executed as a result of undue influence.[39]

3. UNCONSCIONABLE BARGAINS AND INEQUALITY OF BARGAINING POWER

7-075   **Equitable relief against unconscionable bargains.** There are a number of well-established areas of the law where equitable relief is available against harsh or unconscionable bargains, such as in the law relating to penalties,[40] forfeitures[41] and mortgages; there are also many legislative interferences with freedom of contract designed to protect those who enter into harsh or unconscionable bargains.[42] But it remains doubtful in modern law to what extent there is any general equitable principle entitling the courts to interfere with freedom of contract on the ground that the contract (or a part of it) is, in all the circumstances of the case, a harsh and unconscionable bargain.[43] Until recent years, the legacy of nineteenth-century ideology in favour of freedom of contract has restricted the development of possible residuary principles of unconscionability, but there were for a time some signs of a possible resurgence of a broader equitable approach to unconscionable bargains.[44] More recently, however, the cases have shown a determination to adhere firmly to principles of freedom of contract, particularly in commercial contracts between businessmen.[45] However, it is clear that relief is possible in certain cases of unconscionable advantage taking and the real question is the scope of the principles involved, particularly that of relief against unconscionable bargains with persons suffering from some form of bargaining disadvantage.[46]

---

[37] *Bridgeman v. Green* (1755) Wilm. 58, 65; *Huguenin v. Baseley* (1807) 14 Ves. 273.

[38] *Cobbett v. Brock* (1855) 20 Beav. 524, 528; *O'Sullivan v. Management Agency Ltd* [1985] Q.B. 428.

[39] *Wright v. Carter* [1903] 1 Ch. 27.

[40] See *post*, §§ 27–102 *et seq.*

[41] See *post*, §§ 27–121—27–123.

[42] See in particular the Unfair Contract Terms Act 1977, *post*, §§ 14–057 *et seq.* Unfair Terms in Consumer Contracts Regulations 1994, *post* Chap. 15 and Consumer Credit Act 1974, ss.137–140, Vol. II, §§ 38–191—38–205.

[43] See Waddams (1976) 39 M.L.R. 369; Reiter (1981) 1 O.J.L.S. 347.

[44] See, *e.g.* dicta of Lord Simon of Glaisdale in *Shiloh Spinners Ltd v. Harding* [1973] A.C. 691, 726; Lord Diplock in *A. Schroeder Music Publishing Co. v. Macaulay* [1974] 1 W.L.R. 1308, 1315; *Burmah Oil Co. v. Bank of England, The Times*, July 4, 1981 (no relief for mere unfair bargain—there must be an unconscionable bargain—a bargain whose very terms reveal conduct which shocks the conscience of the court); and *Alec Lobb (Garages) Ltd v. Total Oil (Great Britain) Ltd* [1985] 1 W.L.R. 173, in which the Court of Appeal did not rule out a broad doctrine of unconscionability, though it held that no unconscientious conduct had occurred. See also cases cited *post*, § 7–077.

[45] See, *e.g. Photo Productions Ltd v. Securicor Transport Ltd* [1980] A.C. 827; *The Chikuma* [1981] 1 W.L.R. 314; *Multiservice Bookbinding Ltd v. Marden* [1979] Ch. 84; for a slightly earlier dictum to the same effect, see Lord Radcliffe in *Bridge v. Campbell Discount Co. Ltd* [1962] A.C. 600, 626; and, in the particular context of unconscionability, *post*, § 7–088.

[46] See *post*, §§ 7–078 *et seq.*

Salvage cases. Reference has been made above (§ 7–032) to the power of the   **7–076**
court to set aside unconscionable contracts for salvage services rendered to a
vessel in distress. These cases could perhaps be treated as illustrations of the
modern principle of economic duress,[47] but they antedate the recognition of any
such principle in the law, so when they were first decided they may have been
based upon some broader principle permitting the overriding of unconscionable
contracts.

Unconscionable bargains with poor and ignorant persons.[48] Another prin-   **7–077**
ciple of equity which can be traced back to the old equitable rules permitting
intervention for the protection of expectant heirs[49] has been used in modern times
to justify a substantial broadening of this jurisdiction. The old equitable principle
was reviewed and restated in *Fry v. Lane*[50] where it was held that the court could
set aside a purchase at a considerable undervalue from "a poor and ignorant
man" who had received no independent advice. Here the property being sold
consisted of reversionary rights, so the case fell squarely within the old principles
about expectant heirs, but little stress was laid upon the nature of the property in
the judgment in this case; indeed it was expressly said that the principle extended
to a sale of property in possession. In two more modern decisions, on somewhat
similar facts, it has been held that the court could set aside a contract by a
separated wife by which she gave up her rights in the matrimonial home in
consideration of an indemnity against liability on the mortgage. In the first of
these cases[51] Megarry J. held that the requirements of "poverty" and "ignorance" referred to in *Fry v. Lane* were satisfied because the wife was a "member
of the lower income group" and "less highly educated" (than whom, does not
appear). In the second,[52] Balcombe J. was willing to follow Megarry J.'s
decision, though the question did not strictly arise, where the wife "was certainly
not wealthy," and was also not "ignorant," but in fact "an intelligent woman."
These generous interpretations of the meaning of vague words like "poverty"
and "ignorance" appear, on their face, to open the door to the possibility of relief
in a substantial number of contracts where the terms are exorbitant or unconscionable, and the party aggrieved did not have independent advice. and since
there have been a number of cases in which relief on the ground of unconscionability has been considered[53] and some in which it has been granted. Thus
the Privy Council has set aside the renewal of a lease, on very unfavourable
terms, granted by a plaintiff who was "somewhat slow" and who was put under
pressure by the lessee while the plaintiff's usual advisor was away.[54] Most

---

[47] See *ante*, §§ 7–010—7–014.
[48] Bamforth [1995] L.M.C.L.Q. 538.
[49] *e.g. Aylesford v. Morris* (1873) L.R. 3 Ch.App. 484. See Treitel, *Law of Contract* (9th ed., 1995),
pp. 370–371.
[50] (1888) 40 Ch.D. 312. See also *Wood v. Abrey* (1818) 3 Madd. 417; *Longmate v. Ledger* (1860)
2 Giff. 157; *Clark v. Malpas* (1862) 4 De G.F. & J. 401; *Baker v. Monk* (1864) 4 De G.J. & S. 388;
Prees v. Coke (1870) L.R. 6 Ch.App. 645; *James v. Kerr* (1888) 40 Ch.D. 449; *Rees v. De Bernardy*
(1896) 2 Ch. 437; *cf. Harrison v. Guest* (1860) 8 H.L.C. 481.
[51] *Cresswell v. Potter* [1978] 1 W.L.R. 255n. (decided in 1968).
[52] *Backhouse v. Backhouse* [1978] 1 W.L.R. 243.
[53] See *Multiservice Bookbinding Ltd v. Marden* [1979] Ch. 84; *Alec Lobb (Garages) Ltd v. Total
Oil (Great Britain) Ltd* [1983] 1 W.L.R. 87; *Hart v. O'Connor* [1985] A.C. 1000. Unconscionability
was not found on the facts in *Pye v. Ambrose* [1994] N.P.C. 53. The *Multiservice* and *Alec Lobb* cases
draw on a line of authority relating to mortgages: see Bamforth [1995] L.M.C.L.Q. 538, 546.
[54] (1995) 69 P. & C.R. 298; see also *Watkin v. Watson-Smith, The Times,* July 3, 1986.

recently, in *Credit Lyonnais Bank Nederland NV v. Burch*[55] the defendant had given a guarantee and charged her flat to secure the borrowings of her employer's company, in circumstances in which the transaction was manifestly disadvantageous to her. The case was decided on the ground that the bank had constructive notice of undue influence by the employer, but both Nourse and Millett LJ.J. suggested that it might have been argued that she had a direct right, as against the bank, to set aside the transaction on the grounds of unconscionability. The bank had only explained the nature of the transaction without giving the defendant adequate information as to the risks and should have known she had not taken independent advice.[56]

7–078　　**Scope of the doctrine.** The doctrine of unconscionable bargains seems to be limited in three ways. The first is that the bargain must be oppressive to the complainant in overall terms; the second that it may only apply when the complainant was suffering from certain types of bargaining weakness; and the third that the other party must have acted unconscionably in the sense of having knowingly taken advantage of the complainant. These points will be discussed in turn.

7–079　　**An oppressive bargain.** The modern cases in which relief has been granted or said to be available have all involved transactions which were substantively unfair in that the complainant was parting with property for much less than it was worth,[57] or getting nothing out of the transaction.[58] "The resulting transaction has been, not merely hard or improvident, but overreaching and oppressive" so that its terms, together with the conduct of the stronger party, "shock the conscience of the court".[59] In *Boustany v. Piggott*[60] the original lease had reserved a rent of $833 per month and imposed an obligation of repair on the lessee; the new lease which was set aside imposed no such obligation; the rent was fixed at $1,000 per month for a 10-year period. Thus it is doubtful whether English courts would follow dicta in Australia[61] to the effect that inadequacy of consideration is not essential.[62] It is equally doubtful whether the doctrine would be applied as it has

---

[55] [1997] 1 All E.R. 144, noted Chen-Wishart [1997] C.L.J. 60; Hooley and O'Sullivan [1997] L.M.C.L.Q. 17; Tijo (1997) 113 L.Q.R. 10.

[56] [1997] 1 All E.R. 144, 151, 152–153.

[57] *Cresswell v. Potter* [1978] 1 W.L.R. 255n.; *Backhouse v. Backhouse* [1978] 1 W.L.R. 243; *Watkin v. Watson-Smith, The Times,* July 3, 1986; *Boustany v. Piggott* (1995) 69 P. & C.R. 298.

[58] *Crédit Lyonnais Bank Nederland NV v. Burch* [1997] 1 All E.R. 144.

[59] *Alec Lobb Ltd v. Total Oil (Great Britain) Ltd* [1983] 1 W.L.R. 87, 94–95, *per* Peter Millett Q.C. sitting as a Deputy High Court Judge (reversed in part [1985] 1 W.L.R. 173); see also *Crédit Lyonnais Bank Nederland NV v. Burch* [1997] 1 All E.R. 144, 152–153.

[60] (1995) 69 P. & C.R. 298.

[61] *Blomley v. Ryan* (1956) 99 C.L.R. 362, 405; *Commonwealth Bank of Australia v. Amadio* (1983) 151 C.L.R. 447, 475. But in the latter case (which was one of a guarantee, so that the complainant would not expect to receive anything) Deane J. said that the transaction might be unfair, unreasonable and unjust although there was no inadequacy of consideration: *ibid.*

[62] *cf.* the suggestion in *Langton v. Langton* [1995] 2 FLR 890 that the jurisdiction to set aside contracts on the ground of unconscionability does not extend to gifts, as this would mean that in the case of all gifts by poor and ignorant persons without independent advice, an onus would be placed on the recipient to show that the gift was fair, just and reasonable. Note that Capper (1998) 114 L.Q.R. 479 argues that "transactional imbalance" is not a precondition of relief but only evidential (at 491). He thus argues that unconscionability and undue influence can be assimilated.

been in the United States[63] to a single harsh term such as a limitation of liability clause, unless the contract was oppressive overall.[64]

The complainant's circumstances. As noted earlier,[65] the traditional require-   **7–080** ment that the complainant be "poor and ignorant"[66] received a broad interpretation in some of the modern cases; and in the most recent case[67] the majority of the Court of Appeal were prepared to say that relief could have been given to a young employee who had charged her flat to secure her employer's debts without discussing the requirement.[68] Commonwealth cases have allowed relief in a broad variety of "disabling" circumstances. In *Blomley v. Ryan*[69] Fullagar J. listed as examples:

> "[P]overty or need of any kind, sickness, age, sex, infirmity of body or mind, drunkenness, illiteracy or lack of education, lack of assistance or explanation where assistance or explanation is necessary."

and in *Commercial Bank of Australia v. Amadio*[70] Deane J. said that the jurisdiction is established

> "as extending generally to circumstances in which . . . a party to a transaction was under a special disability in dealing with the other party with the consequences that there was an absence of any reasonable degree of equality between them."

It is submitted that English law can give relief in an equally wide range of circumstances, provided that "one party has been at a serious disadvantage to the other, whether through poverty, or ignorance, or lack of advice, *or otherwise*, so that circumstances existed of which unfair advantage could be taken."[71]

Unconscionable conduct. A contract will not be set aside merely because the   **7–081** aggrieved party did not have independent advice and the consideration was inadequate. It must also be shown that the other party engaged in unconscionable conduct or an unconscientious use of power.[72] He must have behaved "in a morally reprehensible manner . . . which affects his conscience . . . . The classic example of an unconscionable bargain is where advantage has been taken of a young, inexperienced or ignorant person to introduce a term which no sensible, well-advised . . . person would have accepted."[73] If there has been no equitable fraud, victimisation, taking advantage, overreaching or other unconscionable

---

[63] See *post*, § 7–085.
[64] *cf. Multiservice Bookbinding Ltd v. Marden* [1979] Ch. 84.
[65] *Ante*, § 7–077.
[66] *e.g. Fry v. Lane* (1888) 40 Ch. D. 312.
[67] *Crédit Lyonnais Bank Nederland NV v. Burch* [1997] 1 All E.R. 144.
[68] See Hooley and O'Sullivan [1997] L.M.C.L.Q. 17, 23.
[69] (1956) 99 C.L.R. 362, 405.
[70] (1983) 151 C.L.R. 447, 474. In that case the complainants were elderly immigrants with limited knowledge of written English.
[71] *Alec Lobb Ltd v. Total Oil (Great Britain) Ltd* [1983] 1 W.L.R. 87, 94–95, *per* Peter Millett Q.C. sitting as a Deputy High Court Judge (reversed in part [1985] 1 W.L.R. 173) (emphasis supplied). In *Barclays Bank plc v. Schwartz, The Times*, August 2, 1995 Millett L.J. observed that a person whose illiteracy or inability to speak English is taken advantage of may, in an appropriate case, be able to have the contract set aside on the grounds of unconscionability. See *post*, § 8–001.
[72] *Alec Lobb (Garages) Ltd v. Total Oil (Great Britain) Ltd* [1985] 1 W.L.R. 173, 182.
[73] *Multiservice Bookbinding Ltd v. Marden* [1979] Ch. 84, 110.

conduct, relief will not be granted.[74] Thus in *Hart v. O'Connor*[75] the vendor was of unsound mind, but this was not apparent to the purchaser and the vendor appeared to be advised by a solicitor who had proposed the terms of the bargain. The Privy Council held that the contract could not be set aside on the grounds of insanity unless the vendor's incapacity was known to the purchaser,[76] nor as unconscionable because the purchaser had acted with complete innocence. In the words of Lord Brightman, there must be "procedural unfairness" as well as "contractual imbalance," though "contractual imbalance may be so extreme as to raise a presumption of procedural unfairness, such as undue influence or some other form of victimisation."[77] In *Boustany v. Piggott*[78] Lord Templeman, delivering the judgment of the Privy Council, agreed in general terms with the submissions of counsel for the appellant: (1) there must be unconscionability in the sense that objectionable terms have been imposed on the weaker party in a reprehensible manner; (2) "unconscionability" refers not only to the unreasonable terms but to the behaviour of the stronger party, which must be morally culpable or reprehensible; (3) unequal bargaining power or objectively unreasonable terms are no basis for interference in equity in the absence of unconscionable or extortionate abuse where, exceptionally and as a matter of common fairness, "it is unfair that the strong should be allowed to push the weak to the wall"; (4) a contract will not be set aside as unconscionable in the absence of actual or constructive fraud or other unconscionable conduct; and (5) the weaker party must show unconscionable conduct, in that the stronger party took unconscientious advantage of the weaker party's disabling condition or circumstances.

7–082   **Unconscionable conduct may be inferred.** In *Crédit Lyonnais Bank Nederland NV v. Burch*[79] Millett L.J. pointed out that it would be necessary to show that the bank had imposed the objectionable terms in a morally objectionable manner, but said that impropriety might be inferred from the terms of the transaction itself in the absence of an innocent explanation.[80]

7–083   **Absence of independent advice.** The traditional statements of the rule on unconscionable bargains also state that the complainant must have acted without independent advice. However, it is submitted that the absence of such advice is not essential. In *Crédit Lyonnais Bank Nederland NV v. Burch*[81] Millett L.J. said that the fact that the complainant had been offered independent advice would not necessarily save a transaction which was so harsh that no competent advisor could have recommended it. In *Boustany v. Piggott*[82] a lawyer called on to

---

[74] *Hart v. O'Connor* [1985] A.C. 1000; *Boustany v. Pigott* [1993] N.P.C. 75, PC.

[75] *Supra.*

[76] Overruling *Archer v. Cutler* [1980] 1 N.Z.L.R. 386; *post*, § 8–067. But the New Zealand court has rejected this approach to unconscionability: *Nichols v. Jessup (No. 2)* [1986] 1 N.Z.L.R. 237; see Bamforth [1995] L.M.C.L.Q. 538, 550.

[77] [1985] A.C. 1000 at 1018. Lord Brightman's language seems to reflect American terminology, *post*, § 7–085. It is interesting to contrast the justification offered in *Redgrave v. Hurd* (1881) 20 Ch.D. 1, 13, for rescission for innocent misrepresentation; it is moral fraud to insist on keeping the contract now you know the representation is false. *cf. Rooney v. Conway* [1982] 5 N.I.J.B.

[78] (1995) 69 P. & C.R. 298, 303.

[79] [1997] 1 All E.R. 144.

[80] At 153, referring to *Multiservice Bookbinding Ltd v. Marden* [1979] Ch. 84, 110 and *Alec Lobb (Garages) Ltd v. Total Oil (Great Britain) Ltd* [1983] 1 W.L.R. 87, 95.

[81] *Supra.*

[82] (1995) 69 P. & C.R. 298.

prepare the documents had pointed out that their terms were disadvantageous but did not refuse to proceed with execution of the document; the Privy Council refused to interfere with the trial judge's finding that the transaction was unconscionable. It may be suggested that an oppressive transaction will only be saved by independent advice if the advisor explains fully to the complainant why the transaction is so disadvantageous and that she is under no obligation to agree to it, or to agree to the terms offered; and (where relevant) refuses to act on her behalf if she persists in going ahead.[83]

Burden of showing fair, just and reasonable. Once the conditions for relief   **7–084** are met, the burden shifts to the stronger party to show that the transactions are fair, just and reasonable.[84] In practice, this will mean showing either that, in the particular circumstances, the transaction was not in fact oppressive; or that the complainant was fully aware of what she was doing. This will normally come back to the question of whether she had received proper independent advice.

Commonwealth and American developments. It has already been stated   **7–085** that Commonwealth courts appear to be more in favour of a possible general doctrine of unconscionability.[85] There is a good deal of Canadian authority,[86] and in Australia the courts seem prepared to give relief in a wide range of circumstances provided that advantage has been taken,[87] and to apply the criteria liberally.[88] In America an even broader doctrine of unconscionability is now a well-established principle of the law entitling courts to refuse to enforce contracts, or contractual clauses, which are harsh, exorbitant or unconscionable. The principle is partly statutory, deriving from § 2–302 of the Uniform Commercial Code, but is widely applied by American courts as a matter of common law where the Code is inapplicable. A distinction is generally drawn in American law between "procedural unconscionability" and "substantive unconscionability."[89] The former can be invoked where some element of oppression or wrongdoing (in a broad sense) has occurred in the process of making the contract: this enables courts to use doctrines like duress and undue influence as merely illustrative of a broader principle requiring that undue advantage or surprise should not be taken of a party; so matters like illiteracy, lack of knowledge of the English language, general inability to comprehend a complicated document, etc., may be treated as matters of procedural unconscionability. Substantive unconscionability, by contrast, goes to the actual substance of the contract and its terms. In practice substantive unconscionability covers excessively wide exclusion clauses on the one side, and grossly exorbitant or excessive prices, on the other. The leading commentary on the Uniform Commercial Code states that "Most parties who assert 2–302 [*sci.* the Code section dealing with unconscionability] and most of those who have used it successfully in reported cases have been consumers.

---

[83] *cf. ante*, § 7–061.

[84] *Aylesford v. Morris* (1873) 8 Ch. App. 484, 490–491.

[85] See generally Bamforth [1995] L.M.C.L.Q. 538, *passim*.

[86] See, *e.g. Black v. Wilcox* (1976) 30 D.L.R. (3d) 192; *Paris v. Machnik* (1972) 30 D.L.R. (3d) 723; *Morrison v. Coast Finance* (1965) 55 D.L.R. (2d) 710; and other cases cited in Waddams, *Law of Contracts* (3rd ed.), § 511 and Enman (1987) 16 Anglo-Am.L.R. 191.

[87] *Blomley v. Ryan* (1956) 99 C.L.R. 362.

[88] *Commonwealth Bank of Australia v. Amadio* (1983) 57 A.L.J.R. 358; Hardingham (1984) 4 O.J.L.S. 275.

[89] Leff (1967) 115 Un. Pennsylvania L.R. 485.

Most of these successful consumer litigants have been poor or otherwise disadvantaged. . . . The courts have not generally been receptive to pleas of unconscionability by one merchant against another."[90]

7–086   **Unfair terms in consumer contracts.** With the implementation of Council Directive 93/13/EEC on Unfair Terms in Consumer Contracts,[91] English law may move slightly closer to the concept of "substantive unconscionability" since Article 3 of the Directive defines a contractual term which has not been individually negotiated as unfair (and therefore not binding on the consumer), "if, contrary to the requirements of good faith, it causes a significant imbalance in the parties' rights and obligations arising under the contract, to the detriment of the consumer." Thus the Regulations[92] implementing the Directive apply to harsh clauses in standard form consumer contracts.[93] But it will not cover the cases of sales at undervalue which have formed the core of unconscionable bargain cases in England since under the Directive and the Regulations the adequacy of the price cannot be reviewed.[94]

7–087   **Statutory provisions.** Under the Consumer Credit Act 1974, a credit bargain which is extortionate may be re-opened.[95] There is some disagreement as to whether the principles of unconscionability apply to this jurisdiction.[96]

7–088   **Inequality of bargaining power.** A possible principle which is closely related to the broad idea of unconscionability, but slightly narrower in scope, is that of inequality of bargaining power. In *Lloyds Bank Ltd v. Bundy*,[97] Lord Denning M.R. stated the single general principle, which, in his view, underlay many of the cases discussed in this chapter. He considered that the thread running through the cases was the concept of "inequality of bargaining power." "By virtue of it, the English law gives relief to one who, without independent advice, enters into a contract upon terms which are very unfair or transfers property for a consideration which is grossly inadequate, when his bargaining power is grievously impaired by reason of his own needs or desires, or by his own ignorance or infirmity, coupled with undue influences or pressures brought to bear on him by or for the benefit of the other."[98] In *National Westminster Bank plc v. Morgan* Lord Scarman questioned (the other Law Lords all concurring) whether there was any need in the modern law to erect a general principle of relief against equality of bargaining power."[99] It is certainly unlikely that mere

---

[90] White & Summers, *Uniform Commercial Code* (3rd ed., 1990), § 4–2, though see also § 4–9.

[91] See *post*, Chap. 15.

[92] Unfair Terms in Consumer Contracts Regulations 1994, S.I. 1994 No. 3159.

[93] *e.g.* the "add-on" clause in *Williams v. Walker Thomas Furniture* Co., 121 U.S. App.D.C. 315, 350 F.2d 445 (1965).

[94] Art. 4(2) and reg. 3(2), *post* §§ 15–025—15–027.

[95] Ss.137–140; see *post*, Vol. II, §§ 38–191—38–205.

[96] Compare *Davies v. Directloans Ltd* [1986] 1 W.L.R. 823, 831 and *Shahabina v. Gyachi* (1989) unreported, cited in Bamforth [1995] L.M.C.L.Q. 538, 559.

[97] [1975] Q.B. 326; see too *Arrale v. Costain Engineering Ltd* [1976] 2 Lloyd's Rep. 98; *Levison v. Patent Steam Carpet Cleaning Co. Ltd* [1978] Q.B. 69, 78–79; *Langdale v. Danby, The Times*, November 24, 1981.

[98] *ibid.* at 339. See also *A. Schroeder Music Publishing Co. v. Macaulay* [1974] 1 W.L.R. 1308, 1315.

[99] [1985] A.C. 686, 708. With respect, the question is not so much whether there is any need for a principle of this character as whether there may not be a need for a residuary principle to catch cases which may otherwise slip through the various statutory protections.

inequality of bargaining power, even when this leads to the exertion of considerable pressure, will be recognised as a ground for setting aside a contract. Even Lord Denning would not have given relief when the pressure was "the result of the ordinary interplay of forces."[1] And unless and until a general doctrine along the lines suggested by Lord Denning is recognised, it seems that a contract will only be set aside if it falls within one of the recognised categories of "victimisation" such as duress, undue influence or unconscionable advantage taking.

---

[1] [1975] Q.B. 326, 336.

Part Two
CAPACITY OF PARTIES

CHAPTER 8

PERSONAL INCAPACITY

1. IN GENERAL

Contractual incapacity. The incapacity of one or more of the contracting **8–001** parties may defeat an otherwise valid contract. Prima facie, however, the law presumes that everyone has a capacity to contract; so that, where exemption from liability to fulfil an obligation is claimed by reason of want of capacity, this fact must be strictly established on the part of the person who claims the exemption. In English law, four classes of individuals are subject to some degree of personal contractual incapacity. These are minors,[1] married women (although little or no vestige of their contractual incapacity remains),[2] mentally disordered persons,[3] and drunken persons.[4] Abnormal weakness of mind short of such mental disorder as prevents a person understanding the nature of the transaction, or immaturity of reason in one who has attained full age, or the mere absence of skill upon the subject of the particular contract, affords *per se* no ground for relief at law or in equity,[5] although in certain cases, undue influence[6] or unconscionable dealing by the other party[7] or (perhaps) inequality of bargaining power may permit the

---

[1] See *post*, §§ 8–002 *et seq.*
[2] See *post*, §§ 8–065—8–066.
[3] See *post*, §§ 8–067 *et seq.*
[4] See *post*, §§ 8–077—8–078.
[5] *Osmond v. Fitzroy* (1731) 3 P.Wms. 129; *Lewis v. Pead* (1789) 1 Ves.Jun. 19 and see Barton (1987) 103 L.Q.R. 118.
[6] See *ante*, §§ 7–041 *et seq.*
[7] See *ante*, § 7–075.

transaction to be set aside as inequitable.[8] Moreover, illiteracy and unfamiliarity with the English language are not to be equated with disabilities like mental incapacity or drunkenness. According to Millett L.J. in *Barclays Bank plc v. Schwartz*,[9] although all four conditions are disabilities which may prevent the sufferer from possessing a full understanding of a transaction into which he enters, "mental incapacity and drunkenness [may] not only deprive the sufferer of understanding the transaction, but also deprive him of the awareness that he [does] not understand it", which is not the case as regards an illiterate or a person unfamiliar with English. Again, however, such a person may in an appropriate case claim that the transaction be set aside as a harsh and unconscionable bargain.[10]

2. Minors[11]

(a) *Generally*

8–002   **Definition of minors.** The age of capacity, for the purposes of the law of contract (as for most other legal purposes) which was 21 at common law, was reduced to 18 by section 1 of the Family Law Reform Act 1969. Section 9 of the same Act also abolished the common law rule under which a person attained his majority on the day preceding the relevant anniversary of the birth.[12] Under this section a person is deemed to attain the age of 18 at the commencement of the eighteenth anniversary of his birthday. The Act also declares that a person who is not of full age may be described as a "minor" instead of an "infant."

8–003   **Very young children.** The cases at common law concerning the capacity of a minor to make contracts generally concern older children.[13] However, it has been doubted whether a very young child has the mental capacity to enter a contract, even where the contract is of a type which would normally be held valid, though voidable at common law. In *R. v. Oldham Metropolitan Borough Council, ex p. Garlick*,[14] Scott L.J. observed that "[i]f a minor is to enter into a contract with the limited efficacy that the law allows, the minor must at least be old enough to understand the nature of the transaction and, if the transaction involves obligations on the minor of a continuing nature, the nature of those obligations."[15] Thus, while he considered that a child well under the age of ten

---

[8] See *ante*, § 7–088.

[9] *The Times*, August 2, 1995.

[10] *Ante*, § 7–075.

[11] The Report of the Committee on the Age of Majority, Cmnd. 3342 (1967) contained proposals for fundamental changes in the law relating to minors' contracts but the only recommendation which was implemented was the reduction of the age of majority to 18. Many other proposals for reform are canvassed in the Law Commission Working Paper No. 81 on *Minors' Contracts* (1982), including a possible further reduction in the age of contractual capacity to 16. The Law Commission's *Report on Minors' Contracts* (1984) Law Com. No. 134 led to the Minors' Contracts Act 1987, on which see *post*, §§ 8–005, 8–042, 8–051—8–054.

[12] *Re Shurey, Savory v. Shurey* [1918] 1 Ch. 263.

[13] At common law the age of majority was 21 years: see *ante*, § 8–002.

[14] [1993] 1 FLR 645. The decision of the Court of Appeal was affirmed by the House of Lords: [1993] A.C. 509.

[15] *ibid.* at 662.

years could purchase sweets, a four-year-old could not contract for the occupation of residential premises.[16] This approach to the position of very young children can be related to that taken by the common law to incapacity by reason of mental disorder.[17]

Contracts binding on a minor. The only contracts which are binding on a **8–004** minor are contracts for necessaries. There is, however, in the cases, a diversity of meanings given to the word "necessaries." In one sense, the term is confined to necessary goods and services supplied to the minor.[18] In another, it extends to contracts for the minor's benefit and in particular to contracts of apprenticeship, education and service.[19] It has long been customary for a distinction to be drawn between these two classes of contract, but it is doubtful whether any practical importance still attaches to the distinction, although it is convenient to retain it purely for purposes of exposition.

Voidable contracts. Apart from contracts for necessaries and contracts of **8–005** apprenticeship, education and service, the general rule at common law is that a minor's contracts are voidable at his option, *i.e.* not binding on the minor but binding on the other party.[20] Of these voidable contracts there are two classes:

(a) contracts which are binding on the minor unless he repudiates them during minority, or within a reasonable time of attaining his majority[21];

(b) contracts which are not binding on him unless and until he ratifies them after attaining his majority.[22]

Prior to the passing of the Minors' Contracts Act 1987, the second of these classes was partially governed by the Infants Relief Act 1874, which also introduced a fourth category of minors' contracts, namely those declared by section 1 to be "absolutely void." By section 1 of the 1987 Act, however, both these changes have been abolished and the position returned to the common law.[23]

Deeds. In general a minor is bound by a deed to the same extent that he would **8–006** be bound if the promise contained in the deed were parol. He is, therefore, liable on a deed which contains a promise to pay for necessaries.[24]

---

[16] *ibid.* The context of these observations was the challenge by two four-year-old boys of a local authority's refusal to accept their application for accommodation under the Housing Act 1985, s.62.

[17] See *post*, §§ 8–067—8–069.

[18] *Wharton v. Mackenzie* (1844) 5 Q.B. 606; *Peters v. Fleming* (1840) 6 M. & W. 42, 46; *Cowern v. Nield* [1912] 2 K.B. 419, 422.

[19] *Walter v. Everard* [1891] 2 Q.B. 369; *Roberts v. Gray* [1913] 1 K.B. 520, 525, 528, 529; *Shears v. Mendeloff* (1914) 30 T.L.R. 342.

[20] In many old cases certain types of minors' contracts were often said to be "void" but normally where the word "void" was used "voidable" was intended: *Williams v. Moor* (1843) 11 M. & W. 256, 263–264.

[21] See *post*, §§ 8–029 *et seq.*

[22] See *post*, §§ 8–039 *et seq.*

[23] For the position obtaining under the Infants Relief Act 1874 governing contracts made before June 9, 1987 see the 25th edition of the present work, Vol. I §§ 569–574.

[24] *Walter v. Everard* [1891] 2 Q.B. 369. As to the effect of a disposition of property by deed, see *post*, §§ 8–062—8–064.

(b) *Contracts Binding on a Minor*

(i) *Liability for Necessaries*

8–007   **Liability for necessaries.** Executed contracts for "necessary" goods and services were binding on a minor at common law,[25] though this does not mean that the minor will be liable for the price of the goods or services as stipulated.[26] The common law was codified (or partially codified) in relation to the sale and delivery of necessary goods by the Sale of Goods Act 1893.[27] Less clear is the position of executory contracts for necessaries.[28] The meaning of "necessaries" is an extended one for this purpose, by no means being confined to "necessities" in the ordinary sense.

8–008   **Meaning of necessaries.** Such things as relate immediately to the person of the minor, as his necessary food, drink, clothing, lodging and medicine, are clearly necessaries for which he is liable. But the term is not confined to such matters only as are positively essential to the minor's personal subsistence or support; it is also employed to denote articles purchased for real use, so long as they are not merely ornamental, or are used as matters of comfort or convenience only, and it is a relative term to be construed with reference to the minor's age and station in life.[29] The burden of showing that the goods supplied are necessaries is always on the supplier. "Having shewn that the goods were suitable to the condition in life of the infant, he [the tradesman] must then go on to show that they were suitable to his actual requirements at the time of the sale and delivery."[30] Thus the fact that the minor was already sufficiently supplied with the goods in question will defeat any claim against him[31] even though this fact was unknown to the supplier.[32]

8–009   **Contracts for necessaries must be beneficial.** Even a contract for necessaries will not be binding on the minor if it contains harsh and oppressive terms so that the contract, taken as a whole, cannot be said to be for the minor's benefit.[33] So, for instance, in *Flower v. London & North Western Ry Co.*[34] it was held that a contract of carriage (though clearly a necessary in the circumstances) was void as against the minor because it contained a clause exempting the defendants from liability for injury to the minor even if caused by negligence.

8–010   **Liability for goods "sold and delivered."** Section 3 of the Sale of Goods Act 1979 (replacing section 2 of the 1893 Act) provides that where necessaries

---

[25] *Peter v. Fleming* (1840) 6 M. & W. 42; *Ryder v. Wombwell* (1868) L.R. 4 Ex. 32. See *post*, § 8–011 as to the position of executory contracts for necessaries.

[26] *Post*, § 8–010.

[27] s.2 (now Sale of Goods Act 1979, s.3).

[28] See *post*, § 8–011.

[29] *Peters v. Flemming* (1840) 6 M. & W. 42; *Ryder v. Wombwell* (1869) L.R. 4 Ex. 32; *Nash v. Inman* [1908] 2 K.B. 1.

[30] *Nash v. Inman, supra*, at 5 *per* Cozens-Hardy M.R., *Maddox v. Miller* (1813) 1 M. & S. 738; *Harrison v. Fane* (1840) 1 M. & G. 550; *Brooker v. Scott* (1843) 11 M. & W. 67; *Ryder v. Wombwell, supra*.

[31] *Barnes & Co. v. Toye* (1884) 13 Q.B.D. 410; *Johnstone v. Marks* (1887) 19 Q.B.D. 509; *Nash v. Inman* [1908] 2 K.B. 1.

[32] *Barnes & Co. v. Toye, supra; Johnstone v. Marks, supra*. See also *Bainbridge v. Pickering* (1780) 2 W.Bl. 1325; *Brayshaw v. Eaton* (1839) 7 Scott 183; *Foster v. Redgrave* (1867) L.R. 4 Ex. 35n.

[33] *Fawcett v. Smethurst* (1914) 84 L.J.K.B. 473.

[34] [1894] 2 Q.B. 65. See also *Buckpitt v. Oates* [1968] 1 All E.R. 1145, 1147–1148.

are sold and delivered to a minor he must pay a reasonable price for them. "Necessaries" are defined by section 3(3) as goods suitable to the condition in life of the minor and to his actual requirements at the time of the sale and delivery. There are two difficult points arising out of the impact of this section on the common law which have not yet been resolved. First, it is uncertain whether a minor can be held liable on an executory contract for the purchase of necessaries; and, secondly, where such a contract is executed by the delivery of the goods to the minor, it is uncertain whether the goods must be necessary for the minor at the time of sale as well as at the time of delivery.

Executory contracts for necessary goods. Section 3 of the Sale of Goods **8–011** Act 1979 deals only with the case of necessary goods *sold and delivered*; it does not in terms deal with the case of necessaries sold but not delivered to a minor, and such a case may, therefore, still be governed by the common law. But even at common law it is uncertain whether a minor could be liable on an executory contract for the purchase of necessary goods.[35] Whether a minor is so liable may depend on the view taken of the basis of the minor's liability, though this seems to restate the problem rather than to solve it. On the one hand it is argued that the minor is liable on such a contract quite apart from the Act, for a contract for necessaries is one which, despite his lack of age, a minor may make.[36] This may be supported by more recent authority which has recognised that a minor may give a valid consent, notably, to medical treatment,[37] and by analogy with decisions which have held a minor liable on an executory contract for education and training.[38] On the other hand it is said that a minor's obligation to pay for goods supplied to him is not contractual at all but is restitutionary, arising *quasi ex contractu*.[39] Delivery would, therefore, be necessary, for without it the minor could not be said to be unjustly enriched at the seller's expense. The supporters of this view buttress their argument by pointing to the fact that the minor is bound to pay only a reasonable price for the goods, rather than the contractual price.[40] This, they say, does not suggest a consensual liability.[41] Moreover, if section 3 of the Sale of Goods Act 1979 were treated as superseding the common law, this would suggest that a minor would not be liable except where the goods were "sold and delivered."[42]

Goods necessary when delivered, but not when sold, and vice versa. The **8–012** second problem is, to some extent, tied up with the first. At common law there seems to be no doubt that the crucial question was always whether the goods were necessary when delivered[43] and it was immaterial whether or not they were

---

[35] Miles (1927) 43 L.Q.R. 389.

[36] *Nash v. Inman* [1908] 2 K.B. 1, 12.

[37] *Gillick v. West Norfolk Area Health Authority* [1986] A.C. 112, 169. *cf. R. v. D.* [1984] A.C. 778, 806 (consent to kidnapping).

[38] *Roberts v. Gray* [1913] 1 K.B. 520; *Hamilton v. Bennett* (1930) 94 J.P.N. 136; *Doyle v. White City Stadium Ltd* [1935] 1 K.B. 110. See *post*, § 8–026.

[39] *Nash v. Inman, supra* at 8; *Elkington & Co. Ltd v. Amery* [1936] 2 All E.R. 86, 88; Birks, *An Introduction to the Law of Restitution* (1985), p. 436. As to mentally disordered persons, see *Re Rhodes* (1890) 44 Ch.D. 94, 105, and *Re J.* [1909] 1 Ch. 574, 577, and *post*, §§ 8–067—8–071. But the analogy between these cases and cases of minors is imperfect: Treitel, *The Law of Contract* (9th ed., 1995), p. 497.

[40] Sale of Goods Act 1979, s.3(2) and see Birks *op. cit.* p. 436.

[41] *Pontypridd Union v. Drew* [1927] 1 K.B. 214, 220.

[42] See *post*, § 8–013.

[43] Winfield (1942) 58 L.Q.R. 82.

necessary when the contract was made. This again would seem to support the theory that the minor's liability is restitutionary rather than contractual, for if it were contractual it would be hard to see why a change of circumstances between the time of sale and the time of delivery should affect the liability of the minor. But whatever the position may have been at common law it is possible that section 3 of the Sale of Goods Act has resolved both questions. In *Nash v. Inman*[44] the Court of Appeal appears to have treated this section as completely superseding the common law on the liability of a minor for necessary goods, and the wording of the section appears to support the view that the goods must be necessary both when sold and when delivered. If this is indeed the effect of the section it can hardly be supposed that a minor could today be held liable on a purely executory contract.[45]

8–013   **Necessary services.** Services as well as goods may be necessaries. So, for example, a contract for legal[46] or medical services[47] may be a contract for necessaries. It has also been held that a contract by a widow (who was a minor) to pay for her husband's funeral was binding as for a necessary.[48] Unlike the uncertain position in respect of contracts to supply necessary goods, it is clear that executory contracts for necessary services may be enforced against a minor, at least in the context of apprenticeship or contracts for education. Thus, a minor's promise to pay part of the premium for his apprenticeship on gaining his majority has been enforced[49] and his (reasonable) restrictive covenant against competing with his master after service is concluded has been enforced by injunction after gaining his majority.[50] In *Roberts v. Gray*, the Court of Appeal held a minor who had entered a contract to go on a tour with a professional billiard player liable in damages for failing to proceed with the tour.[51] The court considered that once it had been decided that a contract is one for necessaries not qualified by unreasonable terms, then it was binding on the minor, so as to allow the other contracting party all such remedies as were appropriate on breach.[52] The reasoning of these decisions runs counter to that which argues for a non-contractual basis of an infant's liability for necessaries.[53] The question whether the services must be necessary only when rendered or whether they must also be necessary when ordered seems never to have been considered.

8–014   **Fact and law.** Whether the particular goods or services are necessaries has for many years been treated as a question of fact in each case, subject to there being

---

[44] [1908] 2 K.B. 1, 7, 9.

[45] It is, however, arguable that the words of s.3 of the Sale of Goods Act "at the time of the sale and delivery" appear to contemplate one time only. See also Treitel, *The Law of Contract* (9th edn., 1995), p. 497. If a minor is liable on an executory contract it would have to be decided whether the goods must be necessary when sold, or at the time when they ought to have been delivered, or perhaps even when the minor refuses to take delivery.

[46] *Helps v. Clayton* (1864) 17 C.B.(N.S.) 553; *De Stacpoole v. De Stacpoole* (1887) 37 Ch.D. 139; *Re Jones, an Infant* (1883) 48 L.T. 188.

[47] *Huggins v. Wiseman* (1690) Carth. 110. But *quaere* whether this is still so having regard to the National Health Service.

[48] *Chapple v. Cooper* (1844) 13 M. & W. 252.

[49] *Walter v. Everard* [1891] 2 Q.B. 369.

[50] *Gadd v. Thompson* [1911] 1 K.B. 304.

[51] [1913] 1 K.B. 520. *cf.* Mathews (1982) 33 N.Ir.L.Q. 150, 154–155.

[52] [1913] 1 K.B. 520, 530.

[53] *cf. ante* § 8–011.

some evidence on which they might properly be so found.[54] Today, however, it would seem that, while it is still a pure question of fact whether the minor is already well supplied with the goods or services in question, it is really a question of mixed fact and law or a matter of evaluating the facts whether the goods or services can be treated as necessaries in themselves.[55]

Contracts for both necessaries and non-necessaries. If a minor buys a   **8–015**
quantity of goods, some of which may be necessaries, but a substantial number of which cannot be necessaries, it has been said that the minor will not be liable at all if the contract is one entire contract.[56] On the other hand the courts have sometimes allowed a plaintiff to recover for necessaries while disallowing a claim for non-necessaries without adverting to the question whether the contract was an entire contract.[57] Since the minor is not bound to pay the contract price but only a reasonable price, there seems no reason why this course should not always be followed.[58]

Examples. The following have been held to be necessaries (although it must   **8–016**
be remembered that the usages of society change and articles which once were necessaries may no longer be held to be so and vice versa): engagement and wedding rings,[59] regimental uniform (for an enlisted solider),[60] presents for a fiancée,[61] a racing bicycle for a youth earning (in 1898) 21s. a week,[62] the hire of horses[63] and for work done for them,[64] and the hire of a car to fetch luggage from a station six miles away.[65] On the other hand, the following have been held not to be necessaries: 11 fancy waistcoats for a Cambridge undergraduate already sufficiently supplied with clothing,[66] expensive dinners with fruit and confectionery for another undergraduate,[67] jewelled solitaire sleeve-links for the son of a deceased baronet,[68] a large quantity of tobacco for an army officer,[69] lessons in flying for a law student,[70] a vanity-bag worth (in 1936) £20 10s. bought by the son of an ex-cabinet minister for his fiancée,[71] a hunter for an impecunious cavalry officer[72] and a collection of snuff-boxes and curios.[73]

---

[54] *Ryder v. Wombwell* (1868) L.R. 3 Ex. 90.
[55] *cf. Benmax v. Austin Motor Co. Ltd* [1955] A.C. 370.
[56] *Stocks v. Wilson* [1913] 2 K.B. 235, 241–242. As to entire contracts, see *post*, § 00–000.
[57] See, *e.g. Ryder v. Wombwell* (1868) L.R. 3 Ex. 90.
[58] Certainly this would be the right course if the minor's liability is restitutionary; see *ante*, § 8–013.
[59] *Elkington & Co. Ltd v. Amery* [1936] 2 All E.R. 86.
[60] *Coates v. Wilson* (1804) 5 Esp. 152.
[61] *Jenner v. Walker* (1868) 19 L.T. 398; *cf. Hewlings v. Graham* (1901) 70 L.J. Ch. 568; *Elkington & Co. Ltd v. Amery, supra.*
[62] *Clyde Cycle Co. v. Hargreaves* (1898) 78 L.T. 296.
[63] *Hart v. Prater* (1837) 1 Jur. 623; *cf. Harrison v. Fane* (1840) 1 M. & G. 550.
[64] *Clowes v. Brook* (1739) 2 Str. 1101.
[65] *Fawcett v. Smethurst* (1914) 84 L.J.K.B. 473.
[66] *Nash v. Inman* [1908] 2 K.B. 1.
[67] *Wharton v. Mackenzie* (1844) 5 Q.B. 606.
[68] *Ryder v. Wombwell* (1869) L.R. 4 Ex. 32.
[69] *Bryant v. Richardson* (1866) L.R. 3 Ex. 93.
[70] *Hamilton v. Bennett* (1930) 94 J.P.N. 136.
[71] *Elkington & Co. Ltd v. Amery* [1936] 2 All E.R. 86.
[72] *Re Mead* [1916] 2 I.R. 285.
[73] *Stocks v. Wilson* [1913] 2 K.B. 235.

8–017   **Trading contracts.** A minor's trading contracts are not contracts for necessaries.[74] While there is no precise definition of a trading contract for this purpose, it has been held that a minor will not be liable in contract upon an agreement for services performed for him to enable him to carry on his trade,[75] or for goods supplied to him for the purposes of his trade,[76] or where he fails to deliver goods to a purchaser who has paid for them.[77] However, if the contract can be considered to be one by which the minor gains proficiency in a certain trade (as in a contract of service or apprenticeship) it will be binding on him if, viewed as a whole, it is for his benefit.[78]

8–018   Where a minor's contract is a "trading contract" the minor cannot be adjudicated bankrupt on this basis for he is not a debtor at law,[79] though he may be liable for (and be made bankrupt on account of) a tax debt.[80] It has even been held that a minor is not liable in restitution for the recovery of the price of goods sold by him but not delivered,[81] but the authority of this decision is open to doubt since it dates from a time when a restitutionary claim was thought to be founded on an "implied contract," and it has been persuasively argued that it "allows an antiquated and now discredited pleading fiction to influence substantive rights."[82] Moreover, the court now possesses a discretion to order the minor to transfer money, or property representing it, to the other contracting party under section 3(1) of the Minors' Contracts Act 1987.[83]

8–019   **Necessaries for wife or children.** There have been some extensions of the doctrine of minors' necessaries. Necessaries for a minor's wife are necessaries for him,[84] though he is not liable on contracts made by his wife unless he has authorised them or she has authority to pledge his credit. There seems no reason why a minor husband should not be liable for household necessaries purchased by his wife on the ground that she has authority to pledge his credit[85] and either spouse is bound by a contract to pay for the funeral of the other where he or she dies leaving no sufficient estate.[86]

8–020   **Loans for necessaries.** A minor cannot be made liable on a loan advanced to enable him to purchase necessaries.[87] If, however, the loan is actually expended

---

[74] *Lowe v. Griffith* (1835) 1 Scott 458.

[75] *Re Jones, ex p. Jones* (1881) 18 Ch.D. 109.

[76] *Mercantile Union Guarantee Cpn. Ltd v. Ball* [1937] 2 K.B. 498. But where a minor used goods (supplied to him in his trade) for household purposes he was held liable: *Turberville v. Whitehouse* (1823) 1 C. & P. 94.

[77] *Cowern v. Nield* [1912] 2 K.B. 419.

[78] *Roberts v. Gray* [1913] 1 K.B. 520; *Doyle v. White City Stadium Ltd* [1935] 1 K.B. 110. *cf. Shears v. Mendeloff* (1914) 30 T.L.R. 342; *post,* §§ 8–021—8–028.

[79] *Re Jones, ex p. Jones* (1881) 18 Ch.D. 109, 120; *Re Davenport* [1963] 1 W.L.R. 817.

[80] *Re a Debtor (No. 564 of 1949)* [1950] Ch. 282.

[81] *Cowern v. Nield* [1912] 2 K.B. 419.

[82] Goff & Jones, *Law of Restitution* (5th ed., 1998), p. 645 and see *post,* § 30–015.

[83] See *post,* §§ 8–051—8–054.

[84] *Rainsford v. Fenwick* (1671) Carter 215; *Turner v. Trisby* (1719) 1 Stra. 168.

[85] See Vol. II, § 32–049. The wife's agency of necessity was abolished by s.41 of the Matrimonial Proceedings and Property Act 1970.

[86] *Chapple v. Cooper* (1844) 13 M. & W. 252. It was doubted whether a minor would be bound by a contract to pay for the funeral of a parent or other relative: *ibid.* at 260. The common law rule that a husband is always bound to pay for his wife's funeral no longer obtains: *Rees v. Hughes* [1946] K.B. 517.

[87] *Darby v. Boucher* (1694) 1 Salk. 279.

on necessaries, the lender can recover the amount spent thereon under the equitable principle of subrogation laid down in *Marlow v. Pitfield*.[88] A person who purchased necessaries for a minor at his request was held at common law to be entitled to sue the minor for money paid to his use.[89] It would seem that today such an action could be maintained either by treating the purchaser as a lender and entitled to invoke the principle of subrogation, or by treating the purchaser as the minor's agent.[90] Any security given in respect of a loan is unenforceable even though the money was required for necessaries[91] and an account stated is voidable despite the fact that some of the items in the account consist of necessaries.[92] A bill of exchange or promissory note is void both as against the minor and any third person although given in payment of necessaries.[93] But the person who supplied the necessaries can, of course, disregard the account stated or the security and sue for a reasonable price.[94]

(ii) *Apprenticeship, Service and other Beneficial Contracts*

Beneficial contracts. Since it is of obvious advantage to a minor that he **8–021** should be able to fit himself for his future trade or profession and to obtain a livelihood, he may enter into contracts of apprenticeship, service, education and instruction, provided that these are beneficial to him. As was said by Kay L.J. in *Clements v. London and North Western Ry. Co.*,[95] "It has been clearly held that contracts of apprenticeship and with regard to labour are not contracts to an action on which the plea of infancy is a complete defence, and the question has always been, both at law and in equity, whether the contract, when carefully examined in all its terms, is for the benefit of the infant. If it is so, the court before which the question comes will not allow the infant to repudiate it."

Apprenticeship. A minor may bind himself apprentice to an employer, and **8–022** after the employer's death to his executors provided that they carry on the same trade in the same place.[96] The validity of such a contract depends on whether the contract is as a whole, beneficial to the minor at the time when it is entered into.[97] If the contract of apprenticeship imposes onerous terms[98] such as a penalty clause,[99] or a provision that his wages are to depend on the will of his employer,[1]

---

[88] (1719) 1 P.Wms. 558; *Re National Permanent Benefit Building Society* (1869) L.R. 5 Ch.App. 309, 313; *Martin v. Gale* (1876) 4 Ch.D. 428; *Lewis v. Alleyne* (1888) 4 T.L.R. 560; Birks, *An Introduction to the Law of Restitution* (1985), p. 398. For a similar principle in a different context, see *The Mogileff* (1921) 6 Ll.L.Rep. 528; *The Fairport (No. 5)* [1967] 2 Lloyd's Rep. 162.
[89] *Ellis* v. *Ellis* (1689) Comb. 482; *Earle v. Peale* (1712) 10 Mod. 67.
[90] See *post*, § 8–055.
[91] *Martin v. Gale, supra.*
[92] *Williams v. Moor* (1843) 11 M. & W. 256. An account stated may be ratified at common law by the minor on reaching majority: *ibid.* at 266. The Infants Relief Act 1874, s.1, which made void all accounts stated with infants was repealed by the Minors' Contracts Act 1987, s.1.
[93] *Re Soltykoff, ex p. Margrett* [1891] 1 Q.B. 413; *cf.* Bills of Exchange Act 1882, s.22(2).
[94] *Re Soltykoff, ex p. Margrett, supra*; *Walter v. Everard* [1891] 2 Q.B. 369.
[95] [1894] 2 Q.B. 482, 491.
[96] *Cooper v. Simmons* (1862) 7 H. & N. 707.
[97] *De Francesco v. Barnum* (1890) 45 Ch.D. 430; *Dillingham v. Harrison* [1917] W.N. 305; *Mackinlay v. Bathurst* (1919) 36 T.L.R. 31; *Chaplin v. Leslie Frewin (Publishers) Ltd* [1966] Ch. 71.
[98] *Meakin v. Morris* (1884) 12 Q.B.D. 352; *De Francesco v. Barnum, supra.*
[99] *De Francesco v. Barnum, supra*, at 439.
[1] *R. v. Lord* (1850) 12 Q.B. 757; *Corn v. Matthews* [1893] 1 Q.B. 310; *Meakin v. Morris, supra; cf. Green v. Thompson* [1899] 2 Q.B. 1.

or if it places the minor virtually in a position of entire subservience to his employer,[2] it will be unenforceable. The question of fairness will depend upon whether the clause was common to labour contracts at the time, or accorded with the current conditions of trade, so that the employer was reasonably justified in imposing it in protection to himself.[3]

A contract of apprenticeship must be made in writing[4] and it is usually made by deed under which the minor promises faithfully to serve his employer and the employer to provide proper instruction for the minor and to pay him wages. Although a minor may by contract bind himself apprentice, during the period of apprenticeship no action is maintainable against him on his covenant to serve in such a contract,[5] nor can an injunction be obtained to enforce a negative covenant in the contract.[6] Accordingly, it is customary for the minor's father or mother to execute the contract so as to covenant for his due performance of the agreement.[7] After his apprenticeship has ceased, however, a restrictive covenant in such a contract may be enforced provided that the contract as a whole is for the minor's benefit.[8]

8–023   **Rescission of contracts of apprenticeship.** It has been held that a minor cannot validly agree to rescind a binding contract of apprenticeship unless its rescission would be beneficial and this will not normally be so, since if the contract is beneficial to him its dissolution cannot normally be beneficial.[9] In a later case this rule was held to mean that a master cannot terminate a contract of apprenticeship made with a minor on the ground of the latter's breach of his covenants to serve, etc. since the minor cannot by breaking his covenants do indirectly what he may not do directly.[10] However, in the same case it was noted that earlier authorities on the relationship of master and apprentice dated from a time when the master possessed real and considerable powers of domestic chastisement,[11] and that (in 1922) these powers no longer existed and that this social change justified an exception to be made to the master's inability to terminate for breach where "there is habitual and systematic conduct, arising out of the character of the apprentice, which renders it impossible that the work of service and of teaching should continue."[12]

8–024   **Contracts of employment** A contract of employment entered into by a minor is dealt with by the law in the same manner as a contract of apprenticeship. A

---

[2] *De Francesco v. Barnum, supra.*
[3] *Leslie v. Fitzpatrick* (1877) 3 Q.B.D. 229, 232.
[4] *Kirkby v. Taylor* [1910] 1 K.B. 529; *MacDonald v. John Twiname Ltd* [1953] 2 Q.B. 304; Apprentices Act 1814, s.2.
[5] *De Francesco v. Barnum* (1889) 43 Ch.D. 165, 171, where it was noted that the master might correct him in service or complain to a justice of the peace to have the apprentice punished under the statute 5 Eliz. c.4.
[6] *ibid.*
[7] Where a child is being "looked after" by a local authority within the meaning of the Children Act 1989, s.22 or is a person qualifying for advice and assistance within the meaning of *ibid.* s.24(2), the authority may undertake any obligation by way of guarantee under any deed of apprenticeship or articles of clerkship which he enters into: *ibid.* s.23(9), Sched. 2, para. 18(1).
[8] *Cornwall v. Hawkins* (1872) 41 L.J.Ch. 435; *Fellows v. Wood* (1888) 59 L.T. 513; *Evans v. Ware* [1892] 3 Ch. 502; *Gadd v. Thompson* [1911] 1 K.B. 304; *cf. Brown v. Harper* (1893) 68 L.T. 488.
[9] *R. v. Great Wigston (Inhabitants)* (1824) 3 B. & C. 484.
[10] *Waterman v. Fryer* [1922] 1 K.B. 499.
[11] *ibid.* at 506.
[12] *ibid.* at 507, *per* Shearman J. citing *Learoyd v. Brook* [1891] 1 Q.B. 431 as an example.

contract of employment may be binding even if the minor gives up certain rights available under the general law, at least if he gets something equally advantageous in return,[13] and an agreement to submit disputes to arbitration may also be binding if it forms part of a binding contract of employment.[14] But a contract containing a term by which his work and wages depend on the will of his employer[15] or by which, in consideration of special terms, he contracts to waive all claims for compensation for accident[16] is not binding on him. There are many statutory restrictions on the employment of minors under which it is in general unlawful to employ a person under the age of 13, and the employment of persons between 13 and 16 is subject to many restrictions.[17] An agreement in breach of these provisions would presumably be unenforceable against the minor.

Covenants in restraint of trade. If a minor enters into a contract of employ- **8–025** ment or apprenticeship containing a covenant restraining his freedom to compete after the termination of the contract, it must first be decided whether this provision would have been valid against an adult.[18] But a covenant of this kind may be void against a minor even where it would have been upheld against an adult.[19] Whether, if the covenant is void, it invalidates the whole contract of employment or apprenticeship may be a difficult question. It seems that in deciding this question regard must be had to the covenant only in so far as it would have been valid against an adult. If, therefore, the covenant is severable according to the ordinary principles governing severence,[20] the question is whether the enforceable part of the covenant (and not the whole covenant) is so unfair or oppressive as to render the whole contract not beneficial.[21] It seems to follow that if the whole covenant is void quite apart from the defence of want of age it should be disregarded altogether in deciding whether the remainder of the contract is beneficial to the minor. Where, on the other hand, the covenant is itself valid and does not render the whole contract void, it may be enforced against the minor by injunction in the usual way.[22]

Education. At common law a minor could bind himself by a contract for **8–026** instruction and education, on the same ground as other contracts for necessaries. Having regard to modern statutory provisions for compulsory and free schooling it is doubtful if it could still be regarded as necessary for a minor to contract for ordinary schooling below the school-leaving age except perhaps in very special circumstances.[23] But a minor can doubtless still bind himself with regard to other forms of education or instruction, and a minor has been held liable under a contract for singing lessons to be paid for by commission on his earnings as a

---

[13] *Clements v. L. & N.W. Ry.* [1894] 2 Q.B. 482.

[14] *Slade v. Metrodent Ltd* [1953] 2 Q.B. 112.

[15] *R. v. Lord* (1848) 12 Q.B. 757.

[16] *Flower v. London & N.W. Ry. Co.* [1894] 2 Q.B. 65; *Butterfield v. Sibbitt* [1950] 4 D.L.R. 302; *Buckpitt v. Oates* [1968] 1 All E.R. 1145.

[17] See Children and Young Persons Act 1933 s.18(1), as substituted by Children Act 1972, s.1(2); *ibid.*, s.18(3), as amended by Employment of Children Act 1973, s.1(3).

[18] See *post*, §§ 17–101—17–113.

[19] *Sir W.C. Leng & Co. Ltd v. Andrews* [1909] 1 Ch. 763; *Gadd v. Thompson* [1911] 1 K.B. 304; *Express Dairy Co. v. Jackson* (1930) 99 L.J.K.B. 181, 183.

[20] See *post*, §§ 17–185 *et seq.*

[21] *Bromley v. Smith* [1909] 2 K.B. 235.

[22] See cases cited above, n. 19.

[23] *cf. Practice Direction (Minor: School Fees)* [1980] 1 W.L.R. 1441; *Practice Direction (Minor: Payment of School Fees)* [1983] 1 W.L.R. 800; *Sherdley v. Sherdley* [1988] A.C. 213, 225.

singer.[24] That the contract is executory appears to be immaterial.[25] On the other hand, not every form of instruction or education is appropriate to the status and position of a particular minor, and a contract for unnecessary education is no more binding than a contract for unnecessary goods.[26]

8-027   **Other beneficial contracts.** The principle that contracts beneficial to a minor are binding on him is not confined to contracts for necessaries and contracts of employment, apprenticeship or education in a strict sense. It extends also to other contracts which in a broad sense may be treated as analogous to contracts of service, apprenticeship or education.[27] So, for instance, a contract by a minor (who was a professional boxer) with the British Boxing Board of Control whereby he agreed to adhere to the rules of the Board was held binding on him because he could not have earned his living as a boxer without entering into the agreement.[28] Similarly, it has been held that an agreement between a minor and a publisher for the publication of the minor's biography which was to be written by a "ghost writer" was binding on the minor.[29] So also, a contract between a group of under-age musicians (known as "The Kinks") whereby they appointed a company as their manager and agent was held binding as analogous to a contract of employment.[30] On the other hand there is no general principle to the effect that *any* contract beneficial to a minor is binding on him.[31] So a minor's trading contracts are not binding on him, even if beneficial.[32]

8-028   **Benefit.** Where the contract contains terms, some of which are beneficial to the minor and others not, the question is whether, taken as a whole, it is to his advantage. If it is, he is bound.[33] One stipulation may be so unfair to the minor that it affects the validity of the whole contract[34]; but if the agreement as a whole is for his benefit, he cannot pick and choose and adopt those terms while rejecting those terms which are not beneficial or not clearly beneficial.[35]

(c) *Contracts Binding on a Minor unless Repudiated*

8-029   **Contracts for an interest of a permanent nature.** When a minor enters into a contract which involves the acquisition of an interest in property of a permanent

---

[24] *Mackinlay v. Bathurst* (1919) 36 T.L.R. 31.

[25] *cf. ante*, § 8–011.

[26] *Hamilton v. Bennett* (1930) 94 J.P.N. 136.

[27] *Roberts v. Gray* [1913] 1 K.B. 525.

[28] *Doyle v. White City Stadium Ltd* [1935] 1 K.B. 110.

[29] *Chaplin v. Leslie Frewin (Publishers) Ltd* [1966] Ch. 71.

[30] *Denmark Productions Ltd v. Boscobel Productions Ltd* (1967) 111 S.J. 715 reversed on other grounds [1969] 1 Q.B. 699; *cf. Shears v. Mendeloff* (1914) 30 T.L.R. 342 where the contract contained oppressive terms and was void.

[31] *Martin v. Gale* (1876) 4 Ch.D. 428, 431; *Mercantile Union Guarantee Corpn. Ltd v. Ball* [1937] 2 K.B. 498; *Bojczuk v. Gregorcewicz* [1961] S.A.S.R. 128; *Sellin v. Scott* (1901) 1 S.R.(N.S.W.) Eq. 64; but *cf. Slade v. Metrodent Ltd* [1953] 2 Q.B. 112, 115.

[32] *Cowern v. Nield* [1912] 2 K.B. 419, *supra*, § 8–017.

[33] *De Francesco v. Barnum* (1890) 45 Ch.D. 430, 439; *Clements v. London & N.W. Ry.* [1894] 2 Q.B. 482; *Roberts v. Gray* [1913] 1 K.B. 520; *Doyle v. White City Stadium Ltd* [1935] 1 K.B. 110; *I.R.C. v. Mills* [1975] A.C. 38, 53.

[34] *R. v. Lord* (1848) 12 Q.B. 757; *Meakin v. Morris* (1884) 12 Q.B.D. 352; *Corn v. Matthews* [1893] 1 Q.B. 310; *Flower v. London & N.W. Ry. Co.* [1894] 2 Q.B. 65; *Stephens v. Dudbridge Ironworks Co.* [1904] 2 K.B. 225; *Express Dairy Co. v. Jackson* (1930) 99 L.J.K.B. 181.

[35] *Slade v. Metrodent Ltd* [1935] 2 Q.B. 112.

nature, with continuing obligations attached to it, he may avoid it at his option either before, or within a reasonable time after, attaining his majority.[36] But until he does so avoid it, he is bound to carry out the obligations as they become due; and if he waits until attaining his majority before avoiding the contract, he must then act promptly and clearly, or he will be bound by the contract for its full term. The reason for this was explained by Parke B. in *North Western Ry. Co. v. M'Michael*,[37] a case where a minor was sued for a call on railway shares. The learned Baron, after referring to various cases[38] in which it had been held that minor shareholders in railway companies were liable for calls on their shares whilst they were minors, continued, "They have been treated, therefore, as persons in a different situation from mere contractors, for then they would have been exempt; but in truth they are purchasers who have acquired an interest, not in a mere chattel, but in a subject of a permanent nature ... and with certain obligations attached to it, which they were bound to discharge, and having been thereby placed in a situation analogous to an infant purchaser of real estate, who has taken possession, and thereby becomes liable to all the obligations attached to the estate, or instance, to pay rent in the case of a lease rendering rent ... unless they have elected to waive or disagree to the purchase altogether, either during infancy or after full age, at either of which times it is competent for an infant to do so. ... "[39]

Despite this explanation there does not seem to be any general principle to the effect that *any* contract conferring an interest in a subject-matter of a permanent nature is valid until repudiated. There appear to be four types of case which fall within this category though it is not clear whether these are exhaustive. These are contracts to lease or purchase land, marriage settlements, contracts to subscribe for or to purchase shares, and partnerships. On the other hand, a contract of hire or of hire-purchase entered into by a minor as hirer is either valid (if for necessaries) or unenforceable against the minor without a need for repudiation.[40]

Benefit. There is old authority for the view that the underlying principle is one of benefit to the minor—that is, if the contract were beneficial to the minor, he could not avoid it at all,[41] whereas if it were not beneficial, he was not bound at all.[42] But since the mid-nineteenth century it has been established that even if the contract is not beneficial, the minor is bound if he takes possession of the property, but only until he disclaims within the time stated.[43]   8–030

Contracts to lease or purchase land. At common law a lease to a minor was voidable only,[44] but even during his minority he was liable for accrued rent, if he had gone into occupation.[45] If he continued in occupation after attaining his   8–031

---

[36] Presumably the minor could not affirm and then repudiate the transaction, even if he acted within a reasonable time. *cf.* the principle stated in § 8–032, *post*.

[37] (1850) 5 Exch. 114, 123, 124, 127, 128.

[38] *Cork and Bandon Ry. v. Cazenove* (1847) 10 Q.B. 935; *Leeds & Thirsk Ry. Co. v. Fearnley* (1849) 4 Exch. 26.

[39] (1850) 5 Exch. 114, 123–124.

[40] See *Mercantile Union Guarantee Corpn. v. Ball* [1937] 2 K.B. 498.

[41] *Maddon v. White* (1787) 2 Term R. 159.

[42] *Ketsey's Case* (1614) Cro.Jac. 320; Brownlow 120 (*Kirton v. Elliott*, 2 Bulst. 69).

[43] *North Western Ry. Co. v. M'Michael* (1850) 5 Exch. 114, 128.

[44] *Davies v. Beynon-Harris* (1931) 47 T.L.R. 424.

[45] *Blake v. Concannon* (1870) 4 Ir.Rep.C.L. 323; *Kelly v. Coote* (1856) 5 Ir.C.L.R. 469.

majority he was liable for rent which had accrued prior to that date.[46] He was entitled to repudiate the lease either during his minority or within a reasonable time of attaining full age.[47] It seems that a contract by a minor to purchase freehold land is also in this category, *i.e.* the contract is binding unless and until repudiated by the minor,[48] at all events where there are outstanding obligations on the minor after completion. If there are no such obligations outstanding the question is really academic for even if the minor can repudiate the contract after completion he cannot recover the purchase price.[49]

8–032   **Conveyances to minors.** Since 1926, a minor has not been able to acquire or hold any legal estate,[50] nor has a minor been able to be a tenant for life or exercise the powers of a tenant for life.[51] A conveyance or lease to a minor has taken effect only as an agreement for valuable consideration to execute a settlement in his favour, and in the meantime to hold the land in trust for him.[52] The 1925 property legislation did not, however, affect a minor's beneficial interest, or prevent his holding an equitable interest in settled land.[53] However, this position was altered by the Trusts of Land and Appointment of Trustees Act 1996 as the latter repealed the provisions of the earlier legislation regarding the effect of conveyance or lease to a minor,[54] and instead provided that after its commencement a conveyance of a legal estate to a minor will take effect as a declaration of trust and that, where immediately before its commencement a conveyance is operating as an agreement to execute a settlement in favour of a minor, the agreement ceases to have effect and subsequently operates instead as a declaration that the land is held in trust for the minor.[55] In effect, therefore, the common law rule with regard to leases to minors is preserved. Equity will not allow a minor who has had the benefit of the statutory trusts to affirm them upon his majority and afterwards to say that he is not liable upon their obligations.[56]

8–033   **Marriage settlements.** Further instances of contracts of this class are to be found in marriage settlements and agreements for marriage settlements. They can be avoided by the minor within a reasonable time of coming of age.[57] But he must accept or reject them in their entirety. He cannot take the benefit and refuse to accept a burden.[58] If he elects to avoid the settlement, any interest taken by the

---

[46] *Blake v. Concannon, supra.*

[47] *Holmes v. Blogg* (1818) 8 Taunt. 508.

[48] *Thurston v. Nottingham Permanent Benefit Building Society* [1902] 1 Ch. 1, 9, affd. [1903] A.C. 6; *Whittingham v. Murdy* (1889) 60 L.T. 956.

[49] *Steinberg v. Scala (Leeds) Ltd* [1923] 2 Ch. 452, a case dealing with the purchase of shares.

[50] Law of Property Act 1925, s.1(6).

[51] Settled Land Act 1925, ss.19, 20.

[52] Law of Property Act 1925, s.19; Settled Land Act 1925, s.27(1).

[53] Law of Property Act 1925, s.19; Settled Land Act 1925, ss.26, 27.

[54] s.25(2), Sched. 4, repealing Law of Property Act 1925, s.19; Settled Land Act 1925, s.27.

[55] Trusts of Land and Appointment of Trustees Act 1996, s.2, Sched. 1, s.1(1) & 1(3). The Act came into force on January 1, 1997: Trusts of Land and Appointment of Trustees Act 1996 (Commencement) Order 1996, S.I. 1996 No. 2974.

[56] *Davies v. Beynon-Harris* (1931) 47 T.R.R. 424.

[57] *Burnaby v. Equitable Revisionary Interest Society* (1885) 28 Ch.D. 416; *Cooper v. Cooper* (1888) 13 App.Cas. 88; *Duncan v. Dixon* (1890) 44 Ch.D. 211; *Edwards v. Carter* [1893] A.C. 360. *Kingsman v. Kingsman* (1880) 6 Q.B.D. 122, which appears to suggest that such a contract is void rather than voidable, can no longer be relied on.

[58] *Codrington v. Codrington* (1875) L.R. 7 H.L. 854; *Hamilton v. Hamilton* [1892] 1 Ch. 396. *cf. Re Vardon's Trusts* (1885) 31 Ch.D. 275 as to which see *Re Hargrove* [1915] 1 Ch. 398.

minor in property brought into the settlement by the other party may be taken away to make up to the beneficiaries the loss which they have sustained because of the avoidance.[59]

Shareholder under age. A minor may be a shareholder in a company regu- **8–034** lated by the Companies Clauses Consolidation Act 1845,[60] or by the Companies Act 1985, or in any corporation formed under a statute which authorises, either expressly or by implication, the membership of minors, or which by its nature does not prohibit their membership.[61] A contract by a minor to subscribe for shares in the company may be repudiated either while he is under age or within a reasonable time of attaining full age,[62] but until he does so he is liable for calls made even while he is under age.[63] If he wishes to avoid the contract after coming of age he must do so promptly or he will be bound by acquiescence.[64]

Purchase of shares. If a minor purchases shares in the market and thereafter **8–035** becomes registered as a shareholder there are two contracts whose validity may come into question, *viz.* that between the minor and the company, and that between the minor and the vendor. In the nineteenth century there were a number of decisions concerning the validity of a transfer of partly paid-up shares to a minor, and the liability of the transferor to pay calls or to contribute in a winding up.[65] In these cases it was held that the transferor generally remained liable for calls notwithstanding that the minor had been registered as a shareholder. But although it was said in these cases that a transfer of shares to a minor was voidable none of them actually raised any question as to the validity of the contracts made between the minor on the one hand and the vendor or the company on the other. So far as the contract with the company is concerned the question is largely academic for the only liability likely to be enforceable against the shareholders is the obligation to pay calls, and partly paid-up shares are rarely met with today. But if the question were raised it would seem that the position must be the same as in the case of shares applied for by the minor and allotted to him by the company itself, *i.e.* the contract would be binding unless and until repudiated.[66] As to the contract between the minor and the vendor of the shares it is uncertain whether the contract is unenforceable against the minor, or whether it is voidable in the sense that it is binding until repudiated. It is submitted that

---

[59] *Hamilton v. Hamilton, supra; Carter v. Silber* [1891] 3 Ch. 553.

[60] s.79.

[61] *Seymour v. Royal Naval School* [1910] 1 Ch. 806.

[62] *Newry and Enniskillen Ry. Co. v. Coombe* (1849) 3 Exch. 565; *North Western Ry. Co. v. M'Michael* (1850) 5 Exch. 114; *Hamilton v. Vaughan-Sherrin Electrical Engineering Co.* [1894] 3 Ch. 589; *Re Alexandra Park Co.* (1868) L.R. 6 Eq. 512.

[63] *Leeds and Thirsk Ry. v. Fearnley* (1849) 4 Exch. 26; *Birkenhead, etc., Ry. v. Pilcher* (1850) 5 Exch. 121; *North Western Ry. Co. v. M'Michael, supra; Dublin and Wicklow Ry. v. Black* (1852) 8 Exch. 181. Unless perhaps he has derived no advantage from the shares and is still a minor: *Newry and Enniskillen Ry. v. Coombe, supra.*

[64] *Cork and Bandon Ry. Co. v. Cazenove* (1847) 10 Q.B. 935; *Dublin and Wicklow Ry. Co. v. Black, supra.*

[65] *Gooch's Case* (1872) L.R. 8 Ch.App. 266; *Capper's Case* (1868) L.R. 3 Ch.App. 458; *Merry v. Nickalls* (1872) L.R. 7 Ch.App. 733; *Lumsden's Case* (1868) L.R. 4 Ch.App. 31; *Curtis's Case* (1868) L.R. 6 Eq. 455; *Re Crenver and Wheal Abraham United Mining Co.* (1872) L.R. 8 Ch.App. 45.

[66] *Steinberg v. Scala (Leeds) Ltd* [1923] 2 Ch. 452, a case of allotment and not purchase in the market; and see *Capper's Case, supra,* at 461.

such a contract would be unenforceable against the minor, but any price paid by him would be irrecoverable unless there was a total failure of consideration.[67]

8–036   **Partnerships.** A minor who becomes a member of a partnership is, as between himself and his partners, bound by the contract unless and until he repudiates it.[68] He does not become liable to partnership creditors for debts or liabilities incurred while he is a minor,[69] but if he repudiates the partnership agreement while still a minor or within a reasonable time of coming of age, his co-partners may insist on all partnership debts being paid and liabilities being met before the minor can draw any profits or capital from the firm.[70] It seems that the creditors may also avail themselves of this right of the minor's partners in appropriate proceedings.[71] Furthermore, even if the minor repudiates before attaining his majority he may still become liable for partnership debts subsequently incurred on the holding-out principle, by which a person who holds himself out as being a partner is bound to those who deal with the firm upon the faith of that supposed partnership.[72]

8–037   **Effect of avoidance.** In all contracts of this class, namely, contracts involving the acquisition of an interest in property of a permanent nature with continuing obligations attached to it, the effect of avoidance by the minor is that he escapes from liability to perform obligations which have not accrued at the time of avoidance. He has, however, to meet obligations which have already accrued[73]; moreover, he can recover nothing which he has paid under the contract unless there has been a total failure of consideration. So, where a minor paid a premium to the defendant on taking a lease from him, and entered upon and used and enjoyed the premises for a short period before he came of age, he could not recover the premium.[74] And where a minor applied for and was allotted shares in a company and paid the amounts due on allotment and on the first call, it was held that upon subsequently repudiating while still under age she could not recover back what she had paid, for although she had received no dividends she had received "the very consideration for which she bargained."[75]

8–038   **Time of avoidance.** What is a reasonable time after attaining majority will depend upon the circumstances of each particular case.[76] A minor cannot plead ignorance of his right to repudiate as an excuse for his failure to exercise that right within a reasonable time[77] nor even that the property had not yet come into

---

[67] *Steinberg v. Scala (Leeds) Ltd, supra,* at 458. *cf. Hamilton v. Vaughan-Sherrin Electrical Engineering Co., supra. cf. post,* §§ 30–038 *et seq.* on recovery of money paid under a mistake of law.

[68] *Goode v. Harrison* (1821) 5 B. & Ald. 147.

[69] *Lovell & Christmas v. Beauchamp* [1894] A.C. 607.

[70] *ibid.*

[71] *ibid.* at 611.

[72] *Goode v. Harrison, supra* at 157; see Vol. II, §§ 32–057 *et seq.*

[73] *Cork & Bandon Ry. Co. v. Cazenove* (1847) 10 Q.B. 935. *cf. North Western Ry. Co. v. M'Michael* (1850) 5 Exch. 114, 125; *Newry and Enniskillen Ry. Co. v. Coombe* (1849) 3 Exch. 565.

[74] *Holmes v. Blogg* (1818) 8 Taunt. 508; *cf. Re Burrows* (1856) 8 De G.M. & G. 254.

[75] *Steinberg v. Scala (Leeds) Ltd* [1923] 2 Ch. 452. Insofar as *Hamilton v. Vaughan-Sherrin Engineering Co.* [1894] 3 Ch. 589 decides to the contrary, it must be taken to have been overruled. *cf. post* §§ 30–038 *et seq.* on recovery of payments made under a mistake of law.

[76] See *Carter v. Silber* [1892] 2 Ch. 278, affd. *sub nom. Edwards v. Carter* [1893] A.C. 360; *Carnell v. Harrison* [1916] 1 Ch. 328 (disapproving *Re Jones* [1893] 2 Ch. 461).

[77] *Carnell v. Harrison, supra.*

possession, so that there was nothing certain on which the repudiation could operate.[78]

(d) *Contracts Unenforceable against a Minor unless Ratified*

Contracts not binding until ratified. The largest class of minor's contracts are enforceable by the minor,[79] but are not binding upon him unless he expressly ratifies them upon coming of age. It is in this sense that general propositions as to minors' incapacity should be understood. Indeed, were it otherwise, the minor's incapacity, instead of being an advantage to him might in many cases turn greatly to his disadvantage.[80] The class includes all contracts other than those for necessaries, beneficial contracts of employment and contracts for the acquisition of a permanent interest in property which are valid unless expressly avoided.[81] Thus, a minor may sue but may not be sued upon an account stated[82] or upon a contract for the sale of goods (other than necessaries) or any other simple contract. It was also held, for example, (before the abolition of actions for breach of promise of marriage) that a minor could sue an adult for breach of promise of marriage,[83] although the adult could not sue the minor on such a promise.[84] And a minor can maintain an action for money had and received against an attorney for damages recovered by his next friend in an action brought on his behalf.[85] A minor cannot, however, obtain specific performance of a contract because the remedy would not be mutual,[86] at any rate not unless he has himself performed his side of the agreement.[87]

8–039

Examples. The general rule that a minor's contracts are not binding on him unless ratified on attaining his majority has the consequence that a minor is not, at common law, liable on a warranty of goods or chattels sold by him[88] even where the warranty is fraudulent.[89] Nor is he liable on the custom of the realm as an innkeeper.[90] He is not bound by an agreement to refer a dispute to

8–040

---

[78] *Edwards v. Carter, supra.*

[79] See *post*, § 8–042.

[80] *Warwick v. Bruce* (1813) 2 M. & S. 205; *Shannon v. Bradstreet* (1803) 1 Sch. & Lcf. 52, 58; *Re Smith's Trusts* (1890) 25 L.R.Ir. 439, 443.

[81] See *ante*, §§ 8–007, 8–029.

[82] *Williams v. Moor* (1843) 11 M. & W. 256.

[83] *Holt v. Ward* (1732) 2 Str. 937, 939.

[84] *Hale v. Ruthven* (1869) 20 L.T. 404.

[85] *Collins v. Brook* (1860) 5 H. & N. 700.

[86] *Flight v. Bolland* (1828) 4 Russ. 298. By the same token, specific performance cannot be obtained against an adult who is co-defendant with a minor: *Lumley v. Ravenscroft* [1895] 1 Q.B. 683, commented on in *Basma v. Weekes* [1950] A.C. 441, 456.

[87] See *post* § 28–041.

[88] *Howlett v. Haswell* (1814) 4 Camp. 118.

[89] *Green v. Greenbank* (1816) 2 Marsh. 485.

[90] *Williams v. Harrison* (1691) Carth. 160; 1 Roll.Abr. *Action sur Case*, D (3).

arbitration[91]; nor by the recitals in a deed made during infancy[92]; nor by a release of a legal claim[93]; nor by a contract of guarantee.[94]

8–041   **Ratification after full age.** At common law, the general rule in this class of contract is that if, on attaining his majority, a minor ratifies a contract made by him during his minority, it will bind him although there may be no consideration for the new promise.[95] Formerly, this rule was replaced by section 20 of the Infants Relief Act 1874 which provided that debts contracted during infancy were made incapable of becoming binding by ratification by the minor on majority, unless new consideration for such ratification was provided.[96] This provision itself has been repealed,[97] returning the law relating to ratification to the position at common law. Ratification after reaching majority may be express or implied from the former minor's conduct.[98]

(e) *Third Parties and Incapacity*

8–042   **Third parties.** In general, lack of capacity of a minor is a personal privilege and does not prevent the other party being bound. However, there are circumstances where a third party has taken advantage of the invalidity of a minor's contract. Thus, for example, in one case an impresario employed an infant who had entered an unreasonable deed of apprenticeship with the plaintiff. The latter's action against the impresario for enticement was rejected by the court as the contract of apprenticeship was invalid as between its parties.[99] Another example used to be found in the liability of the guarantor of an infant's debts. By section 1 of the Infants Relief Act 1874, a loan to an infant was made absolutely void and there was authority that this meant that any guarantors of the loan were not bound by their guarantee.[1] However, section 2 of the Minors' Contracts Act 1987 expressly[2] provides that where a guarantee is given in respect of an obligation of a party to a contract made after its commencement and that obligation is unenforceable against him (or he repudiates the contract) on the grounds of minority, then the guarantee is not unenforceable for that reason alone.[3] The extent to which a minor may give title to property, which may have consequences for third parties, is discussed below.[4]

---

[91] Unless it forms one term of an otherwise beneficial contract of service, etc.: *Slade v. Metrodent Ltd* [1953] 2 Q.B. 112.

[92] *Milner v. Lord Harewood* (1810) 18 Ves. 259, 274; *Field v. Moore* (1854) 7 De G.M. & G. 691.

[93] *Overton v. Bannister* (1844) 3 Ha. 503; *Mattei v. Vautro* (1898) 78 L.T. 682. But see now Civil Procedure Rules 1998, r. 21.10(2), which enables the court to sanction a compromise by a minor even where no proceedings are otherwise contemplated.

[94] *Re Davenport* [1963] 1 W.L.R. 817.

[95] *Southerton v. Whitlock* (1726) 2 Str. 690; *Williams v. Moor* (1843) 11 M. & W. 256, 298.

[96] See for its effect the 25th ed. of the present work §§ 569–570.

[97] Minors' Contracts Act 1987, s.1.

[98] *cf. Brown v. Harper* (1893) 68 L.T. 488.

[99] *De Francesco v. Barnum* (1890) 45 Ch.D. 430, 438 and 443.

[1] *Coutts & Co. v. Browne-Lecky* [1947] K.B. 104.

[2] As s.1 of the Minors' Contracts Act 1987 repeals s.1 of the 1874 Act, it would have been arguable that a guarantor of an unenforceable (as opposed to a void) loan should be liable.

[3] See also s.113(7) of the Consumer Credit Act 1974, as amended by the Minors' Contracts Act 1987, s.4.

[4] See *post* §§ 8–062—8–064.

(f) *Liability of Minor in Tort and Contract*

Liability for tort. A minor is liable for a tort[5] but if the claim arises out of a   **8–043**
contract upon which the minor is not liable, a party may not charge the minor, by
treating the breach of that contract as a tort and suing accordingly. "If one
delivers goods to an infant on a contract, knowing him to be a minor, he shall not
be charged for them in trover or conversion."[6] Therefore, where a minor, having
hired a horse, injured it by riding it too hard, it was held that he was not liable
in an action for the tort,[7] and where a minor obtained a loan by falsely misrepresenting his age he could not be made liable in damages for deceit.[8] In
Fawcett v. Smethurst[9] a minor hired a car to fetch his bag from the station six
miles away. He met a friend with whom he drove on further. The car caught fire
and was damaged on the extra journey without the negligence of the minor. It
was held that he was not liable in tort, as the extra journey did not take his actions
outside the scope of the contract, nor in contract, as the hiring did not render him
liable for loss arising without fault on his part. Although the hiring itself might
have been necessary, the contract would not have been binding on him had its
effect been to render him liable without fault.

On the other hand, if the tort may properly be considered as arising independ-   **8–044**
ently of the contract or outside its ambit altogether, the minor can be made liable.
So a minor who hired a mare "merely for a ride" and was warned at the hiring
that she was unfit for jumping, having lent her to a friend who killed her by that
act, was held to be guilty of a bare trespass, not within the object of the hiring,
and to be consequently liable.[10] A minor who embezzled money belonging to his
employer was held liable in an action for money had and received, because he
would have been liable in trover,[11] and one who hired a microphone and
improperly parted with it to a friend was held liable in an action of detinue.[12] It
is generally assumed that a minor who buys non-necessary goods cannot be sued
in conversion even where he fails to pay the price and keeps the goods.[13] But it
has been held that a bailee under age who refuses to return goods delivered to
him by the bailor may be sued in detinue,[14] and that non-necessary goods sold to
a minor can be recovered, when he refuses to pay for them, though the minor is

---

[5] *Bristow v. Eastman* (1794) 1 Esp. 172; *Defries v. Davis* (1835) 1 Scott 594. *cf. ante*, § 1–067.

[6] *Manby v. Scott* (1659) 1 Sid. 109, 129; *cf. R. v. McDonald* (1885) 15 Q.B.D. 323, 327.

[7] *Jennings v. Rundall* (1799) 8 Term R. 335.

[8] *Johnson v. Pye* (1665) 1 Sid. 258; *Stikeman v. Dawson* (1847) 1 De G. & Sm. 90; *R. Leslie Ltd
v. Sheill* [1914] 3 K.B. 607, 612.

[9] (1915) 84 L.J.K.B. 473.

[10] *Burnard v. Haggis* (1863) 14 C.B.(N.S.) 45. See also *Walley v. Holt* (1876) 35 L.T. 631.

[11] *Bristow v. Eastman* (1794) 1 Esp. 172; *Re Seager* (1889) 60 L.T. 665. *cf. Cowern v. Nield* [1912]
2 K.B. 419.

[12] *Ballett v. Mingay* [1943] K.B. 281.

[13] Atiyah (1959) 22 M.L.R. 273, 281. The view that the minor is not liable is supported by the
generally accepted opinion that property in non-necessary goods may pass to the minor: *Stocks v.
Wilson* [1913] 2 K.B. 235, 246 and see Treitel, *The Law of Contract*, (9th ed., 1995), pp. 505–506.
cf. Minors' Contracts Act 1987, s.3(1) which refers to "property acquired" by the minor and to the
power of the court to order him to "transfer" such property.

[14] *Mills v. Graham* (1804) 1 B. & P.N.R. 140 (minor refusing to return skins delivered for
finishing). Detinue was abolished by s.2(1) of the Torts (Interference with Goods) Act 1977, and
replaced by liability in conversion. See also *R. v. McDonald* (1885) 15 Q.B.D. 323; *Robinson's Motor
Vehicles Ltd v. Graham* [1956] N.Z.L.R. 545.

not liable to damages for conversion.[15] It is more likely, however, that a court will exercise its discretion under section 3 of the Minors' Contracts Act 1987 to require a minor to transfer to the claimant any property acquired by the defendant under the contract, or any property representing it.[16]

(g) Liability of Minor to make Restitution[17]

8–045   **Generally.** In general a minor cannot be sued on his contracts, but this rule leaves open the question whether he may be made to make restitution to the other party for benefits conferred on him under the contract. Such benefits may consist of the receipt of money, goods, interests in land or services. Common law, equity and statute have different answers to this question of a minor's liability in restitution.

8–046   **At common law.** The common law rule is that a minor is not liable to restore benefits conferred on him under a contract which is unenforceable against him, even if the contract results from his fraudulent misrepresentation of majority.[18] Despite this rule, however, three possible routes may exist to recovery. The first route is for the other contracting party to rely on an independent tort which the minor has committed, for example, conversion or deceit, damages for which may compensate him for the loss which he has suffered by the minor's retention of the benefit, even though this may not always be the same as the minor's gain.[19] The second route is for the other contracting party to find such an independent tort, "waive" it and sue for any money had and received in respect of property conferred on the minor.[20] The third possible route to recovery at common law would be to claim restitution of money paid under an unenforceable contract to a minor based on a total failure of consideration, but this route has been rejected by the courts.[21] It has, however, been convincingly argued that a distinction should be drawn for this purpose between the situation where the restitutionary claim in effect enforces the contract, as, for example, with a loan to a minor,[22] and where it does not do so, but merely restores the parties to the *status quo ante*.[23] In the latter situation, a restitutionary claim ought to be available. Similar considerations apply to the denial of quasi-contractual claims for the value of non-necessary goods and services supplied to a minor who has failed to pay the contractual price; for holding a minor even to a reasonable price would undermine his protection.[24] Thus in *Lemprière v. Lange*, for example, a lease which a minor had taken was set aside and possession by him given up, but the court

---

[15] *Re Henderson* (1916) 12 Tas.L.R. 40; *cf. Hall v. Wells* [1962] Tas.S.R. 122, 128–129.

[16] See *post* §§ 8–051 *et seq.*

[17] See Goff & Jones, *The Law of Restitution* (5th ed., 1998), pp. 644 *et seq.*

[18] *Johnson v. Pye* (1665) 1 Sid. 258; *Liverpool Adelphi Loan Assoc. v. Fairhurst* (1854) 9 Exch. 422.

[19] See *ante*, §§ 8–043—8–044.

[20] *Bristow v. Eastman* (1794) 1 Esp. 172 and see Goff & Jones *op. cit.* p. 644, n. 61.

[21] *Cowern v. Nield* [1912] 2 K.B. 491; *R. Leslie Ltd v. Sheill* [1914] 3 K.B. 607. *cf. Thavorn v. Bank of Credit & Commerce International SA* [1985] 1 Lloyd's Rep. 259 (where it was held that a minor was not liable to make restitution for monies received under a mistake of fact.)

[22] *R. Leslie Ltd v. Sheill, supra.*

[23] Goff & Jones *op. cit.* pp. 645–646.

[24] *ibid.* at p. 645.

refused to award a sum to the lessor as damages for use and occupation of the land on the ground that the two remedies were incompatible.[25]

In equity. It is no answer at law to a plea of incapacity based on lack of age   **8–047** that the defendant at the time of entering into the contract fraudulently repre- sented himself to be of full age, and that the other party believing this representa- tion and on the faith of it contracted with him[26] nor did these facts before the Judicature Act form the subject of a good replication on equitable grounds to a plea of infancy.[27] But in certain cases equity will grant relief against the minor, not on the ground of enforcing the contract, or recovering the debt, but of an equitable liability resulting from the fraud. He will be compelled to restore his ill- gotten gains, or to release the party deceived from obligations or acts in law induced by the fraud.[28] This obligation is, however, strictly limited in extent.

Restoration of gains. [29] If a minor has obtained property by fraudulently   **8–048** misrepresenting his age,[30] he can be compelled to restore it; if he has obtained money, he can be compelled to refund it.[31] This remedy is an equitable one and arises quite independently of the contract.[32] It lasts, however, only so long as the minor retains the property or money or, perhaps, the proceeds of the property or money. If he has sold the goods or spent the money, he cannot be compelled through a personal judgment to pay an equivalent sum out of his present or future resources, for this would be nothing but enforcing an unenforceable contract.[33] "Restitution stopped where repayment began."[34] In *Stocks v. Wilson*,[35] however, a minor who had obtained non-necessary goods by fraudulently misrepresenting his age was held bound to account for the proceeds of their sale. This decision was criticised, although not expressly overruled by the Court of Appeal in *R. Leslie Ltd v. Sheill*.[36] Sir Frederick Pollock[37] considered the decision to be correct on the principle of following the property (*i.e.* as represented by the money) and not otherwise. His view is supported by other textbook writers[38] and it is suggested that a fraudulent misrepresentation of full age by a minor will

---

[25] (1879) 12 Ch.D. 675 and see *post* § 8–050.

[26] *Johnson v. Pye* (1665) 1 Sid. 258; *Liverpool Adelphi Loan Assocn. v. Fairhurst* (1854) 9 Exch. 422, 430; *Inman v. Inman* (1873) L.R. 15 Eq. 260; *Levene v. Brougham* (1909) 25 T.L.R. 265 (no estoppel).

[27] *Bartlett v. Wells* (1862) 1 B. & S. 836; *De Roo v. Foster* (1862) 12 C.B.(n.s.) 272.

[28] See Atiyah (1959) 22 M.L.R. 273.

[29] See generally Goff & Jones, *Law of Restitution* (5th ed., 1998), pp. 646 *et seq.* and *post* Chap. 30.

[30] The representation must be explicit and not inferential: *Stikeman v. Dawson* (1847) 1 De G. & Sm. 90; *Maclean v. Dummett* (1869) 22 L.T. 710; *Re Jones, ex p. Jones* (1881) 18 Ch.D. 109, 120–121. See also *Nelson v. Stocker* (1859) 4 De G. & J. 458.

[31] *Stocks v. Wilson* [1913] 2 K.B. 235.

[32] *Re King, ex p. Unity Joint Stock Mutual Banking Association* (1858) 3 De G. & J. 63; *Re Jones, ex p. Jones, supra*; *Stocks v. Wilson, supra.*

[33] *Leslie v. Sheill* [1914] 3 K.B. 607 at 618.

[34] *ibid.*

[35] [1913] 2 K.B. 235, 247.

[36] [1914] 3 K.B. 607.

[37] Pollock, *Principles of Contract* (13th ed., 1950), p. 64.

[38] *Anson's Law of Contract* (27th ed., 1998) by Beatson, pp. 222–224; Treitel, *The Law of Contract* (9th ed., 1995), pp. 510–511. *cf.* Cheshire, Fifoot and Furmston's, *Law of Contract* (13th ed., 1996), p. 454–455.

allow the person deceived to trace his property in equity by an action *in rem* similar to that possessed by a beneficiary in respect of trust property.[39]

8–049   **"Bankruptcy Debt".** Under the Insolvency Act 1986, section 382, a "bankruptcy debt" means any debt or liability to which a bankrupt is subject either at the commencement of the bankruptcy or to which he may become subject after the bankruptcy by reason of any obligation incurred before the commencement of the bankruptcy and for this purpose "liability" includes "a liability to pay money, . . . any liability in contract . . . and any liability arising out of an obligation to make restitution."[40] Thus, while a person who has loaned money to a minor may not prove this as a debt in the latter's bankruptcy, there being no enforceable liability against the minor,[41] if that person was induced to make the loan by the minor's fraudulent misrepresentation of age, then any equitable liability in the minor arising from the fraud may be proved as a "bankruptcy debt."[42]

8–050   **Release from obligations.** A party who has been induced to enter into an obligation or to perform some act in law by the fraudulent misrepresentation of a minor that he is of full age will be released from that obligation and restored, where possible, to his former position. In *Clarke v. Cobley*[43] the defendant, a minor, by such a misrepresentation, induced the plaintiff to accept a bond for the amount of two promissory notes drawn by the defendant's wife before her marriage. The plaintiff accordingly gave up the notes. When the plaintiff discovered the fact of the defendant's incapacity he filed a bill after the defendant had attained majority, praying that the defendant might be ordered to execute a fresh bond, or to pay the money secured, or deliver back the notes to him. The court ordered this last and also that the defendant should not plead limitation to any action brought upon them or set up any other plea open to him when the bond was executed, but refused to decree payment of the money, holding that the court could do no more than see that the parties were restored to the same situation in which they were at the date of the bond. And where a minor obtained a lease by fraudulently misrepresenting that he was of full age, the court set it aside and ordered him to give up possession and to pay his costs.[44]

8–051   **Minors' Contracts Act 1987, s.3.** The most important means by which a minor may be ordered to make restitution of benefits obtained under a contract unenforceable against him is found in section 3 of the Minors' Contracts Act 1987, which provides that:

---

[39] *cf.* Goff & Jones *op. cit.* pp. 650–651; Atiyah (1959) 22 M.L.R. 273. See *post*, §§ 30–097 *et seq.*

[40] Insolvency Act 1986, s.382(4).

[41] *Re Jones, ex p. Jones* (1881) 18 Ch.D. 109 (decided under the old law) and *cf.* the position of debts of a bankrupt barred by the Limitation Acts: *Muir Hunter on Personal Insolvency*, § 3–388/8. For the position as to loans for necessaries, see *ante*, § 8–020.

[42] Re *King, ex p. Unity Joint-Stock Mutual Banking Association* (1858) 3 De G. & J. 63; *Stocks v. Wilson, supra,* at 246 and see *ante*, §§ 8–047—8–048.

[43] (1789) 2 Cox. 173 (fraud must be presumed though not appearing specifically in the report).

[44] *Lemprière v. Lange* (1879) 12 Ch.D. 675. A claim by the lessor for damages for use and occupation was held inconsistent with this relief and dismissed. See also *Cory v. Gertcken* (1816) 2 Madd. 40; *Overton v. Banister* (1844) 3 Ha. 503; *Woolf v. Woolf* [1899] 1 Ch. 343.

"the court may, if it is just and equitable to do so, require the defendant [minor] to transfer to the plaintiff [other contracting party] any property acquired by the defendant under the contract, or any property representing it."

This provision gives a considerable discretion to the court to order restitution of property acquired by a minor under a contract, unless it is one for necessaries and therefore binding on him.[45] It is wider than the equitable remedy already described which is only available where fraud on the part of the minor is established.[46]

"Property." Only property acquired by a minor under the contract is **8–052** included: thus any property acquired by way of inducement to enter the contract falls outside the section. "Property" itself is not defined by the Act. Clearly, it includes chattels and it is submitted that it should be taken to include interests in land to the extent that a minor is permitted by law to hold them.[47] More difficult is the question whether "property" includes money. Although there is some authority in the context of the equitable relief against fraud for recovery of money representing the proceeds of sale of goods transferred,[48] this was subject to criticism.[49] The better view, it is submitted, is that money should be included within the statutory definition of property.[50] The concern to prevent indirect enforcement of a minor's contract which led to the refusal of recovery of monies in equity as at common law may be fully taken into account as a factor in the discretion which section 3 confers.

"Any property representing it." This phrase gives the court power to order **8–053** the transfer, not only of property acquired by a minor, but also the product of its exchange, and, assuming money is included within the provision,[51] its proceeds on sale. This will give rise to a process of statutory tracing, for which cases at common law and in equity may, though in different contexts, serve as illustrations.[52] However, it has been suggested that certain difficulties encountered in these cases, for example the identification of the exchange product of proceeds in a mixed fund, may go to the discretion of the court to make an award under section 3.[53] For example, if a minor has sold non-necessary goods acquired under a contract of sale and placed the money in a bank account together with other monies, the court should hesitate to apply the rules as to tracing of money through accounts in equity which were constructed for and are appropriate to the context of trustees or fiduciaries.[54] In the minor's context, the effect of the award should not be, or even, perhaps, risk being, the payment out of his present or future resources of a sum equivalent to that owed under a contractual obligation.

Discretion. It is submitted that a court should look in deciding whether to **8–054** make an order under section 3 at the general fairness of the contract which the

---

[45] See *ante* § 8–007.
[46] See *ante* § 8–047.
[47] See *ante* § 8–037.
[48] *Stocks v. Wilson* [1913] 2 K.B. 235.
[49] *R. Leslie Ltd v. Sheill* [1914] 3 K.B. 607.
[50] Treitel, *The Law of Contract* (9th ed., 1995), pp. 508–509.
[51] See *ante*, § 8–052.
[52] See Goff & Jones, *The Law of Restitution* (5th ed., 1998), Chap. 2.
[53] Treitel *op. cit.* p. 509.
[54] Goff & Jones *op. cit.* pp. 79 *et seq.*

minor has made. In particular, if the other contracting party took advantage of the minor's inexperience or tricked him, then the latter should not be held liable to restore property acquired. Clearly, the question whether a minor appears or does not appear to be of full capacity, even in the absence of misrepresentation as to full age, will be relevant to the exercise of the discretion. The most important issue in this exercise will be the balance between the need to preserve the minor's protection which is the basis of his contractual incapacity and the interests of the other contracting party in recovery of benefits conferred by him on the minor.

(h) Agency and Membership of Societies

8–055   **Minor as principal.** A minor cannot execute a valid power of attorney,[55] but he is bound by a contract made by his agent with his authority, where the circumstances are such that he would have been bound if he had himself made the contract.[56] A minor may validly appoint an agent where he earns his living in a manner which necessitates this.[57] And it seems that if a minor authorises an agent to purchase necessaries for him, and the agent pays for them, the minor can be compelled to reimburse the agent.[58]

8–056   **Minor as agent.** A minor can act as agent or as the donee of a power of attorney[59] but is not personally liable on the contracts entered into on behalf of his principal.[60]

8–057   **Membership of societies.** Subject to certain conditions, a minor may become a member of a friendly society,[61] an industrial and provident society,[62] a trade union,[63] or a building society.[64]

(i) Liability of Parent or Guardian

8–058   **Parent not liable for minor's debts.** A parent may be ordered to provide financial relief for the benefit of his or her child,[65] but apart from agency[66] or

---

[55] *Zouch v. Parsons* (1765) 3 Burr. 1794; *Olliver v. Woodroffe* (1839) 4 M. & W. 650; *Doe d. Thomas v. Roberts* (1847) 16 M. & W. 778, 780. An act done by an agent under a void power of attorney is itself void: *Doe d. Thomas v. Roberts, supra.*

[56] See Vol. II, § 32–037; Megarry (1953) 69 L.Q.R. 446; Webb (1955) 18 M.L.R. 461. *cf. Shepherd v. Cartwright* [1953] Ch. 728, 755, and see *G.(A.) v. G.(T.)* [1970] 3 All E.R. 546, 549.

[57] *Denmark Productions Ltd v. Boscobel Productions Ltd* (1967) 111 S.J. 715.

[58] See *ante*, § 8–020.

[59] *Watkins v. Vince* (1818) 2 Stark 368; *Re D'Angibau* (1880) 15 Ch.D. 228, 246.

[60] *Smally v. Smally* (1700) 1 Eq.Cas.Abr. 283.

[61] Friendly Societies Act 1974, s.60.

[62] Industrial and Provident Societies Act 1965, s.20 (as amended).

[63] Explicit provision to this effect was formerly found in the Trade Union Act Amendment Act 1876, s.9 but this Act was repealed by the Industrial Relations Act 1971 and the right of a minor to be a member of a trade union seems now to depend on inference. *cf.* Trade Union and Labour Relations (Consolidation) Act 1992, s.174.

[64] Building Societies Act 1986, Sched. 2, para. 5(3).

[65] Children Act 1989, s.15(1), Sched. 1, para. 1. See also Social Security Administration Act 1992, ss.104–108.

[66] *e.g.* where a parent expressly or impliedly authorises the minor to contract on his behalf or where his wife or some other person, such as his servant, has authority to pledge his credit: *Cooper v. Phillips* (1831) 4 C. & P. 581; *Bazeley v. Forder* (1868) L.R. 3 Q.B. 559; *Collins v. Cory* (1901) 17 T.L.R. 242. *cf. Fluck v. Tollemache* (1823) 1 C. & P. 5; *Urmston v. Newcomen* (1836) 4 A. & E. 899; *Ruttinger v. Temple* (1863) 4 B. & S. 491.

personal contract, he is no more liable to pay a debt contracted by the child with a third party (even for necessaries) than a mere stranger would be.[67] The same principles apply in the case of a guardian and ward.

(j) *Procedure in Actions*

Procedure. Formerly, under the Rules of the Supreme Court and the County Court Rules, a minor sued by his next friend and defended by his guardian *ad litem*.[68] However, since the coming into effect of the Civil Procedure Rules 1998, proceedings involving minors (termed by these rules, "children") are governed by a uniform set of rules[69] under which "a child must have a litigation friend to conduct proceedings on his behalf" unless the court otherwise orders, and the former distinction between next friends and guardians *ad litem* is therefore no longer drawn.[70] Under these rules, special provision is made for the assessment of costs of proceedings where the claimant is a child and where money is ordered to paid to him or for his benefit or where money is ordered to be paid by him or on his behalf.[71] No settlement, compromise or payment and no acceptance of money paid into court shall be valid, so far as it relates to the claim by a child without the approval of the court.[72] As regards the exercise of this power of approval, it has been held (under the former procedural rules which made similar provision[73]) that the court has no power to compel a compromise against the opinion of the minor's advisers[74] and that a compromise will not be sanctioned, although made in good faith, if not for the minor's benefit.[75]

8–059

Joint obligations. Where one of two joint contracting parties is a minor whose promise is voidable or unenforceable against him, there is no need to join him as a party to the action and the action may be maintained against the adult only; but if both are sued and the minor pleads his want of age, the plaintiff may still recover against the adult defendant.[76] Moreover, in contrast with the position at common law,[77] since 1987 where a contract is entered by a minor and the latter's obligations are guaranteed by an adult, the unenforceability of those obligations against the minor shall not alone render the guarantee unenforceable.[78]

8–060

---

[67] *Fluck v. Tollemache, supra*; *Shelton v. Springett* (1851) 11 C.B. 452; *Mortimore v. Wright* (1840) 6 M. & W. 482. *cf. Hesketh v. Gowing* (1804) 5 Esp. 131; *Gore v. Hawsey* (1862) 3 F. & F. 509 (illegitimate children recognised by father); *Greenspan v. Slate* (1953) 97 A. 2d. 390 (parent liable for cost of emergency medical treatment to child though he had refused to authorise it); and see Goff & Jones, *The Law of Restitution* (5th ed., 1998), pp. 479–480.

[68] RSC Ord. 80, rr. 1 & 2; County Court Rules, Ord. 10, r. 1.

[69] Civil Procedure Rules 1998, part 21 (which also governs litigation involving mental patients). These rules came into force on April 26, 1999.

[70] CPR r. 21.1(2).

[71] CPR r. 48.5.

[72] CPR r. 21.10.

[73] RSC Ord. 80, rr. 10, 11; County Court Rules, Ord. 10, r. 10.

[74] *Re Birchall* (1880) 16 Ch.D. 41; *Norman v. Strains* (1880) 6 P.D. 219. See also *Re Taylor's Application* [1972] 2 Q.B. 369.

[75] *Rhodes v. Swithenbank* (1889) 22 Q.B.D. 577; *Mattei v. Vautro* (1898) 78 L.T. 682.

[76] See, *e.g. Burgess v. Merrill* (1812) 4 Taunt. 468; *Gillow v. Lillie* (1835) 1 Scott 597; *Lovell and Christmas v. Beauchamp* [1894] A.C. 607; *Wauthier v. Wilson* (1912) 28 T.L.R. 239. See *post*, § 18–005.

[77] *Coutts v. Browne-Lecky* [1947] K.B. 104.

[78] Minors' Contract Act 1987, s.2(1) and see Vol. II, § 44–036.

8–061   **Defence of minority.** Under the Civil Procedure Rules 1998, where a defendant denies an allegation in the claimant's particulars of claim, he must state his reasons for doing so[79] and so a child who intends to rely on a defence of minority to a claim for the enforcement of a contract should make this clear in the defence which he files.

(k) Disposition of Property by Minors

8–062   **Disposition of property by delivery.** A minor can clearly dispose of property under a contract which is binding on him, but there are also cases in which a minor can effectively dispose of property belonging to him under a contract which is not binding on him. So, for instance, it has been held that a gift of a chattel by a minor is irrevocable after delivery.[80] And money paid by a minor under a contract which is voidable or unenforceable against him cannot be recovered by him unless there is a total failure of consideration,[81] although if the minor paid it under a mistake as to the voidable nature or unenforceability of the contract, he may be able to recover it on the basis of this mistake of law.[82]

8–063   **Disposition of property by grant.** A disposition of property not accompanied by delivery is, in general, ineffective against a minor.[83] So, for instance, an assignment of an interest in a trust fund by way of security (at least if it is intended to secure an unenforceable obligation) is, it seems, ineffective to pass any interest as against a grantor who is a minor.[84] And a mortgage granted by a minor to secure an unenforceable loan is itself unenforceable.[85] On the other hand, in *Chaplin v. Leslie Frewin (Publishers) Ltd*,[86] it was held that a contract whereby a minor assigned the copyright in a written work to a publisher was effective to pass the copyright and that even if the contract was voidable the minor could not revoke the contract so as to restore the copyright to himself.

8–064   **Dispositions relating to land.** A minor cannot grant a legal estate in land. But a minor may convey an equitable interest in land, whether by way of outright sale or by way of lease only. So long as the transfer is executory only it seems that

---

[79] CPR 16.5.

[80] *Taylor v. Johnston* (1882) 19 Ch.D. 603, 608 and see *Pearce v. Brain* [1929] 2 K.B. 310, (where it was held that a minor who delivers a chattel belonging to him under a contract "absolutely void" under s.1 of the Infants' Relief Act 1874 cannot recover it unless there has been a total failure of consideration). *cf.* Halsbury, *Laws of England* (4th ed.) Vol. 20, § 10 and see *G.(A.) v. G.(T.)* [1970] 3 All E.R. 546, 549.

[81] *Wilson v. Kearse* (1800) Peake Add.Cas. 196; *Corpe v. Overton* (1833) 10 Bing. 252, 259; *Re Burrows* (1856) 8 De G.M. & G. 254, 256; *Valentini v. Canali* (1889) 24 Q.B.D. 166; *Steinberg v. Scala (Leeds) Ltd* [1923] 2 Ch. 452.

[82] *cf. Kleinwort Benson v. Lincoln City Council* [1998] 3 W.L.R. 1095, on which see *post*, § 30–038 *et seq.*

[83] *Zouch v. Parsons* (1765) 3 Burr. 1794, 1807, 1808.

[84] *Inman v. Inman* (1873) 15 Eq. 260. See also *Martin v. Gale* (1876) 4 Ch.D. 428.

[85] *Nottingham Permanent Benefit Building Society v. Thurston* [1903] A.C. 6, which was decided under the Infants' Relief Act 1874 and held that a mortgage to secure a void loan was itself void.

[86] [1966] Ch. 71. There are dicta in this case (at 94) which appear to suggest that a minor can never, by repudiating a voidable contract, recover property which has passed to the other party. This may be true (at least if there is no total failure of consideration) where the contract is voidable in the normal sense of the word, but it is doubtful if this is correct where the contract is void as against the minor, rather than voidable. *cf. ibid* at 96.

the minor would not be bound by it,[87] but the position may be different after the grantee has gone into possession.

3. MARRIED WOMEN

Power to contract. At common law a married woman could not, as a general 8–065 rule, enter into any contract on her own account either with her husband or with a third party.[88] Successive statutes from 1857 to 1949 progressively removed this incapacity, so that a married woman is now subject to the requirements and obligations of the ordinary law of contracts. Nevertheless, mutual promises made between husband and wife in the ordinary course of domestic relationship do not necessarily give rise to any actionable obligation, as there may be no intention to affect legal relations.[89] Also there remains one outstanding problem in relation to ante-nuptial contracts between husband and wife.

Ante-nuptial contracts. The effect of marriage between the two contracting 8–066 parties was at common law to extinguish any ante-nuptial contract between them, unless made on the occasion and in consideration of the marriage, so that, thenceforward, by reason of the coverture, it could not be sued upon.[90] In *Butler v. Butler*[91] the question at issue was whether the passing of the Married Women's Property Act 1882 had so affected the position as to enable a husband to sue his wife in respect of a debt contracted by her before the marriage. Wills J. held that it had not, and that in respect of the ante-nuptial liabilities of a wife to her husband (although not of a husband to his wife) no action could be maintained.[92] This case was decided before the passing of the Law Reform (Married Women and Tortfeasors) Act 1935, which enacts that "a married woman shall . . . be capable of suing and being sued, either in tort or in contract or otherwise . . . in all respects as if she were a *feme sole*."[93] This enactment does not, however, deal in specific terms with ante-nuptial contracts, and makes no such alterations in the Act of 1882 as would affect the reasoning of Wills J. in *Butler v. Butler*.[94] Nevertheless, it is submitted, both on the words and intention of the Act of 1935, that it applies to actions between husband and wife, and so to ante-nuptial contracts, with the result that both husband and wife are enabled to sue one

---

[87] *Zouch v. Parsons, supra.*

[88] *Cahill v. Cahill* (1883) 8 App.Cas. 420. See also Morrison in *A Century of Family Law* (1957), Chap. 6.

[89] *Balfour v. Balfour* [1919] 2 K.B. 571; *Hoddinott v. Hoddinott* [1949] 2 K.B. 406; see *ante*, §§ 2–154—2–155.

[90] *Post v. Nedham* (1611) 8 Co.Rep. 135a.

[91] (1885) 14 Q.B.D. 831 affirmed on appeal on a different point (1885) 16 Q.B.D. 374.

[92] He reasoned that (i) s.12 of the Act gave the wife full civil remedies for the protection of her separate property but did not give the husband correlative rights against his wife; (ii) s.13 of the Act made the wife liable in respect of her ante-nuptial contracts with strangers, but had to be restrictively construed so as to exclude claims by the husband against the wife; (iii) s.1(2) of the Act which enacted that "a married woman shall be capable of suing and of being sued either in contract or in tort or otherwise in all respects as if she were a *feme sole*" was confined to procedure and did not affect substantive rights and liabilities. These narrow interpretations have been much criticised. See generally, Kahn-Freund (1952) 15 M.L.R. 138–140, and *cf. Re Kendrew* [1953] Ch. 291.

[93] s.1(a).

[94] See nn. 91 and 92, *supra*.

another upon ante-nuptial contracts in the same way as if they had remained unmarried. But the point awaits definite decision.[95]

4. Mentally Disordered Persons

8–067   **Liability generally.** In the case of contracts other than for necessaries, the general rule is that a mentally disordered person is bound by his contract unless he can show that owing to his mental condition he did not understand what he was doing, and further that the other party was aware of this incapacity.[96] But if these two conditions are satisfied, the contract is voidable at his option.[97] This rule was laid down in *Imperial Loan Co. Ltd v. Stone*[98] where Lord Esher M.R. said:

> "When a person enters into a contract, and afterwards alleges that he was so insane at the time that he did not know what he was doing, and proves the allegation, the contract is as binding on him in every respect, whether it is executory or executed, as if he had been sane when he made it, unless he can prove further that the person with whom he contracted knew him to be so insane as not to be capable of understanding what he was about."

8–068   **Ratification.** It would appear that a mentally disordered person may be bound by a voidable contract if he ratifies it subsequently after recovery or during a lucid interval.[99]

8–069   **Nature of understanding required.** The understanding and competence required to uphold the validity of a transaction depend on the nature of the transaction.[1] There is no fixed standard of sanity which is requisite for all transactions.[2] What is required in relation to each particular matter or piece of

---

[95] The argument in the contrary sense is that, if it had been intended to deal with ante-nuptial contracts, more specific words would have been used, and s.13 of the Act of 1882, which has been held not to confer any right of action upon the husband, would have been repealed on the reasoning of Wills J. in *Butler v. Butler*. (But s.1 of the Act of 1935 deals with something more than mere procedure, and it is plainly contemplated that it affects, or may affect, the position between husband and wife, as otherwise the saving for actions of tort would be necessary. If it was not intended to change the law as to ante-nuptial contracts it is curious that no saving clause to this effect should have been added.)

s.4(2)(c) provides that nothing in the Act shall prevent husband and wife from suing and being sued either in tort or in contract or otherwise, in like manner as if they were not married: but, as this provision does not purport to alter the existing law, it does not affect the position upon this point.

[96] *Brown v. Jodrell* (1827) M. & M. 105; *Niell v. Morley* (1804) 9 Ves. 478; *Molton v. Camroux* (1849) 4 Exch. 17; *Beavan v. M'Donnell* (1854) 9 Exch. 309; *Jacobs v. Richards* (1854) 18 Beav. 300; *York Glass Co. v. Jubb* (1925) 42 T.L.R. 1; *Hart v. O'Connor* [1985] A.C. 1000, disapproving *Archer v. Cutler* [1980] 1 N.Z.L.R. 386, noted Beatson (1981) 1 O.J.L.S 426. See Goudy (1901) 17 L.Q.R. 147; Wilson (1902) 18 L.Q.R. 21; Hudson (1984) 48 Conv. 32; (1986) 50 Conv. 178. *cf. Re F.* [1990] 2 A.C. 1 (medical treatment where inability to consent).

[97] *Manches v. Trimborn* (1946) 115 L.J.K.B. 305; *Gibbons v. Wright* (1954) 91 C.L.R. 423.

[98] [1892] 1 Q.B. 599, 601.

[99] *Matthews v. Baxter* (1873) L.R. 8 Ex. 132 (drunken person).

[1] *Manches v. Trimborn, supra. cf. In the Estate of Park* [1954] P. 112 and see Fridman (1963) 79 L.Q.R. 502, 518–519.

[2] *Gibbons v. Wright, supra.*

business transacted, is that the party in question should have an understanding of the general nature of what he is doing.[3]

Evidence of mental disorder. If the party was sane when the contract was **8–070** made, evidence of previous or subsequent mental disorder is not material.[4] But in a doubtful case such evidence might create a suspicion that he was mentally disordered at the time of making the contract.[5] The mere existence of a delusion in the mind of a person making a contract is not conclusive of his inability to understand it, even though the delusion is connected with the subject-matter of the contract.[6] And evidence that he is well known in the neighbourhood to be mentally disordered is not admissible to prove that the other party knew of the insanity.[7] It is probable that treatment for mental disorder under the Mental Health Act 1983 or a finding of a judge of the Court of Protection that the contracting party was incapable of managing and administering his property and affairs would constitute prima facie evidence of mental disorder. But the absence of any such treatment or finding could hardly be treated as even prima facie evidence of capacity where there is any evidence of mental disorder.

Liability for necessaries. By section 3 of the Sale of Goods Act 1979 it is **8–071** provided that where necessaries are sold and delivered to a person who by reason of mental incapacity is incompetent to contract, he must pay a reasonable price for them; and further that "necessaries" in this section mean goods suitable to the condition in life of such a person, and to his actual requirements at the time of the sale and delivery. There seems little doubt that this liability is restitutionary[8] and that the necessaries must have been supplied with the intention of claiming payment.[9] The estate of a husband who is mentally disordered is also liable at common law for necessaries supplied to his wife[10] and one who supplies money for the purchase of necessaries for a mentally disordered person is entitled in equity to be repaid, although without interest.[11]

Deeds. A deed executed by a mentally disordered person is valid if at the time **8–072** of execution he is capable of understanding its effect.[12] Thus deeds executed during a lucid interval are valid.[13] But although good in law they are subject, like

---

[3] *In the Estate of Park, supra*; *Bennett v. Bennett* [1969] 1 W.L.R. 430; *Re Roberts* [1978] 1 W.L.R. 653 (capacity to marry); *Mason v. Mason* [1972] Fam. 302 (consent to decree of divorce). *cf. Clarke v. Prus* [1995] N.P.C. 41 in relation to gifts.

[4] *Hall v. Warren* (1804) 9 Ves.Jun. 605.

[5] *M'Adam v. Walker* (1813) 1 Dow. 148, 177, HL.

[6] *Jenkins v. Morris* (1880) 14 Ch.D. 674.

[7] *Greenslade v. Dare* (1855) 20 Beav. 284, 290.

[8] *Re Rhodes* (1890) 44 Ch.D. 94; *Re J.* [1909] Ch. 574. See *ante*, § 8–011. But it may well be that *some* element of consent is necessary for liability, for a person can hardly force goods (even necessaries) on a mentally disordered person and then claim payment. The goods must be "sold." In most cases the consent will be that of an agent acting for the mentally disordered person. *cf.* Mathews (1982) 33 N.Ir.L.Q. 148.

[9] *Re Rhodes, supra*, at 107.

[10] *Read v. Legard* (1851) 6 Exch. 636. See Vol. II, § 32–049.

[11] *Re Beavan* [1912] 1 Ch. 196; *Re E.G.* [1914] 1 Ch. 927; *Pontypridd Union v. Drew* [1927] 1 K.B. 214; Mental Health Act 1983, s.96. See also Social Security Administration Act, ss.105–108.

[12] *Elliott v. Ince* (1857) 7 De G.M. & G. 475; *Re Beaney* [1978] 1 W.L.R. 770. But see *post*, § 8–075.

[13] *Hall v. Warren* (1804) 9 Ves. 605; *Selby v. Jackson* (1844) 6 Beav. 192; *Birkin v. Wing* (1890) 63 L.T. 80; *Re Beaney* [1978] 1 W.L.R. 770. *cf. Daily Telegraph Newspaper Co. Ltd v. McLaughlin* [1904] A.C. 776.

all other contracts, to be set aside on equitable grounds, such as that the party dealing with the mentally disordered person took advantage of his weakness of mind, even though that weakness did not amount to insanity.[14]

8–073   **Effect upon agency.** As between the principal and the agent, the insanity of either revokes the agency.[15] In some cases a principal who has become insane may be liable on contracts subsequently made by his agent, and an agent may be liable for breach of an implied warranty of authority.[16]

8–074   **The Mental Health Acts 1959 and 1983.** The Mental Health Act 1959, which repealed previously existing enactments and set out comprehensively the law relating to persons suffering from mental disorder, was itself the subject of considerable repeal and replacement by the Mental Health Act 1983. Under Part VII of the 1983 Act, wide discretionary powers are conferred upon a judge of the Court of Protection where, after considering medical evidence, he is satisfied that a person is incapable, by reason of mental disorder, of managing and administering his property and affairs.[17] A person as to whom the judge is so satisfied is referred to as a "patient" for the purposes of this part of the Act. The judge is empowered *inter alia* to make orders or give directions or authority for the sale, exchange, charging or other disposition of or dealing with the property of the patient; the acquisition of any property in the name or on behalf of the patient; the carrying on by a suitable person of any profession, trade or business of the patient; the dissolution of a partnership of which the patient is a member; the carrying out of any contract entered into by the patient; the conduct of legal proceedings in the name of the patient or on his behalf; and the reimbursement out of the property of the patient of money applied by any person in payment of the patient's debts or for the maintenance or other benefit of the patient or a member of his family.[18] He may also by order appoint a receiver to manage the patient's property and affairs.[19]

8–075   **Mentally disordered persons under court's control.** Under the Lunacy and Mental Treatment Acts 1890 to 1930 a person might be found to be of unsound mind by inquisition, and if so found was held to be incapable of making a valid disposition of property by deed even during a lucid interval.[20] Whether the validity of ordinary contracts was similarly affected is not clear. The reason for imposing this incapacity on mental patients was that the statutory purpose of protecting and administering the property of such a person would be frustrated if he remained capable of disposing of it by contract.

The Lunacy and Mental Treatment Acts have been repealed[21] but the question still remains whether a patient who has been found by a judge (under the 1983 Act) to be incapable by reason of mental disorder of managing and administering

---

[14] See *ante* §§ 7–041 *et seq.*, §§ 7–077 *et seq.*
[15] *Drew v. Nunn* (1879) 4 Q.B.D. 661, 666–667.
[16] *Drew v. Nunn, supra; Yonge v. Toynbee* [1910] 1 K.B. 215. For further details on this point, see Vol. II, § 32–160.
[17] See Hoggett, *Mental Health Law* (4th ed., 1996), pp. 237 *et seq.*
[18] ss.92–113.
[19] s.99.
[20] *Re Walker* [1905] 1 Ch. 160; *Re Marshall* [1920] 1 Ch. 284. *cf. In the Estate of Walker* (1912) 28 T.L.R. 466 (disposition by will).
[21] Mental Health Act 1959, Sched. 8.

his property and affairs,[22] or one in respect of whose property a receiver has been appointed,[23] can execute a valid deed or enter into a valid contract. The general opinion would seem to be that he cannot,[24] although the point awaits authoritative decision.

Property legislation. By section 22(1) of the Law of Property Act 1925 (as amended), where a legal estate in land (whether settled or not) is vested in a person suffering from mental disorder, his receiver or (if no receiver is acting for him) any person authorised in that behalf shall, under an order of the authority having jurisdiction under Part VII of the Mental Health Act 1983, or of the court, or under any statutory power, make all requisite dispositions for conveying or creating a legal estate in his name, or on his behalf.[25] And by section 22(2), if land held on trust for sale is vested in a person who is incapable, by reason of mental disorder, of exercising his functions as trustee, a new trustee must be appointed in his place, or he must be otherwise discharged from the trust, before the legal estate is dealt with.[26] Also under section 96 of the Mental Health Act 1983, the judge may order a settlement of any property of the patient, and he may exercise any power (including a power to contract) vested in the patient, whether beneficially or as guardian or trustee or otherwise.[27]

8–076

5. DRUNKEN PERSONS

Effect of drunkenness. In *Pitt v. Smith*[28] in 1811, Lord Ellenborough held that a person in a state of complete intoxication has "no agreeing mind"; and later, in an action for work and labour, held that proof that the plaintiff was drunk when he signed what the defendant insisted was an agreement, dispensed with the necessity of producing it, the instrument being a nullity.[29] It was at one time thought that the test of incapacity by reason of drunkenness was the same as that for mentally disordered persons, *viz.* whether the person alleged to be incapable was so drunk as not to understand what he was doing, and whether the other party knew of his condition.[30] A contract made in such circumstances was said to be voidable at the drunken person's option, and could accordingly be ratified by him when sober.[31] But other authorities suggest that equity has a wider jurisdiction to set aside an unfair or unconscionable transaction entered into by a person

8–077

---

[22] *ibid.* s.96.
[23] *ibid.* s.99.
[24] Heywood and Massey, *Court of Protection Practice* (12th ed., 1991), p. 227; Treitel, *The Law of Contract* (9th ed., 1995), p. 514 (at least as regards contracts which potentially may interfere with the court's control over the property). Fridman (1963) 79 L.Q.R. 501, and see Court of Protection Rules 1984 (S.I. 1984 No. 2035). However the court has power under s.96(1)(h) of the Mental Health Act 1983 to make such orders as it thinks fit for "the carrying out of any contract entered into by the patient"; and the legislative history of this provision suggests that it applies to contracts entered into after the patient became incapable; and see Mathews (1982) 33 N.Ir.L.Q. 150, 158 *et seq.*
[25] Mental Health Act 1959, Sched. 7.
[26] *ibid.* Sched. 7.
[27] s.28 of the Settled Land Act 1925 and s.171 of the Law of Property Act 1925 were repealed by the Mental Health Act 1959, Sched. 8.
[28] (1811) 3 Camp. 33.
[29] *Fenton v. Holloway* (1815) 1 Stark. 126.
[30] *Gore v. Gibson* (1845) 13 M. & W. 623; *Molton v. Camroux* (1849) 4 Exch. 17; *Imperial Loan Co. v. Stone* [1892] 1 Q.B. 599; *Hart v. O'Connor* [1985] A.C. 1000.
[31] *Matthews v. Baxter* (1873) L.R. 8 Ex. 132.

affected by drink.[32] It would seem that a similar approach would be taken to a contract made under the influence of intoxicating substances other than alcohol, notably drugs. In *Barclays Bank plc v. Schwartz*,[33] Millett L.J. accepted that the reason for drunkenness of a party to a contract affecting its validity is that like mental incapacity it deprives a person not only of a full understanding of a transaction, but also of the awareness that he does not understand it.

8–078   **Liability for necessaries.** For necessaries sold and delivered, the liability of a drunken person is, by section 3 of the Sale of Goods Act 1979,[34] similar to that of a mentally disordered person.

---

[32] *Cory v. Cory* (1747) 1 Ves.Sen. 19; *Cooke v. Clayworth* (1811) 18 Ves. 12; *Butler v. Mulvihill* (1823) 1 Bligh 137; *Wiltshire v. Marshall* (1866) 14 L.T.(N.S.) 396; *Blomley v. Ryan* (1956) 99 C.L.R. 362.

[33] *The Times*, August 2, 1995.

[34] See *ante*, § 8–071.

CHAPTER 9

CORPORATIONS AND UNINCORPORATED ASSOCIATIONS

1. CORPORATIONS

(a) *Kinds of Corporations*

Kinds of corporations. Corporations, which are legal *personae* just as much **9–001**
as are individuals,[1] are either sole or aggregate. They may also be classified as
ecclesiastical and lay, or as statutory and non-statutory. Lay corporations may be
either trading or non-trading.[2]

Corporations sole and aggregate. A corporation sole consists of a single **9–002**
person and his successors in office, such as the Crown, an archbishop, bishop or
parson, the Treasury Solicitor,[3] or the Public Trustee.[4] It would seem that the
benefit[5] and burden[6] of contracts made with a corporation sole pass, on the death
of the holder of the office, to his successor in office; and contracts purportedly
made with the corporation during a vacancy in the office take effect on the
vacancy being filled, subject to a right of disclaimer by the successor in office.[7]
A corporation aggregate is a legal person composed of individual members, but

---

[1] *Re Sheffield, etc., Building Society* (1889) 22 Q.B.D. 470, 476.
[2] There is also the European Economic Interest Grouping (EEIG) which is an entity distinct from
its members: see [1985] O.J. L199/1; the European Economic Interest Grouping Regulations 1989
(S.I. 1989 No. 638).
[3] Treasury Solicitor Act 1876, s.1.
[4] Public Trustee Act 1906, s.1.
[5] Law of Property Act 1925, ss.180(1) and 205(1)(xx), reversing the common law rule in *Howley
v. Knight* (1849) 14 Q.B. 240, 255.
[6] See Co.Litt. 144b, n. 2.
[7] Law of Property Act 1925, s.180(3).

with a continuous identity distinct from that of the members composing it.[8] It follows that it can hold property in its own right, that its rights and liabilities are unaffected by changes in its membership and that, generally speaking, its property but not that of its members is available to satisfy its liabilities.

(b) *Corporations in General*

9–003 **Corporation created by charter.** A corporation created by charter can, unless prevented by some statute regulating its proceedings,[9] contract and deal with its property in the same way as an individual.[10] Contracts made by it outside the terms of its charter are valid, but by making them the corporation renders itself liable to the revocation of its charter.[11] But a member may obtain an injunction to restrain a chartered company from acting on regulations which would materially change the character of the company and which could not have been contemplated at the date of its incorporation.[12] But he cannot restrain the corporation, acting on the wishes of a majority of its members, from applying to the Crown for an alteration of the charter.[13]

9–004 **Corporation created by statute.** The powers of a corporation, whether sole or aggregate, created by statute are confined to those given expressly or by reasonable inference by the statute concerned.[14] If the subject-matter of a contract made by such a corporation is outside the scope of its constitution as defined by the statute, the contract is *ultra vires* and void.[15] This principle applies to all statutory corporations and not only to companies incorporated under the Companies Act.[16] However, the *ultra vires* rule is substantially modified (though not completely abrogated) by section 35 of the Companies Act 1985,[17] the overall purpose of this provision being to guarantee security of transactions between companies and persons with whom they deal.

9–005 **Corporations regulated by legislation.** Certain corporations, although not created by statute, are regulated by legislation. Thus, the powers of ecclesiastical

---

[8] As to the juristic nature of corporations, see Wolff (1938) 54 L.Q.R. 494; Hart (1954) 70 L.Q.R. 37; *Gower's Principles of Modern Company Law* (6th ed., 1997), Chap. 5; *Rayner (Mincing Lane) Ltd v. D.T.I.* [1990] 2 A.C. 418; *Adams v. Cape Industries plc* [1990] Ch. 433.

[9] See *Att.-Gen. v. Manchester Corporation* [1906] 1 Ch. 643.

[10] *Sutton's Hospital Case* (1612) 10 Co.Rep. 23a; *Baroness Wenlock v. River Dee Co.* (1887) 36 Ch.D. 674, 685n.; *Bonanza Creek Gold Mining Co. Ltd v. R.* [1916] 1 A.C. 566, 583–584; *Institution of Mechanical Engineers v. Cane* [1961] A.C. 696, 724–725; *Pharmaceutical Society of Great Britain v. Dickson* [1970] A.C. 403. See the Companies Act 1985, s.718 and Sched. 22.

[11] See n. 9, *ante*; and see *British South Africa Co. v. De Beers Consolidated Mines Ltd* [1910] 1 Ch. 354, 374–376; revd. on other grounds [1912] A.C. 52. *cf. Att.-Gen., New Brunswick v. St. John* [1948] 3 D.L.R. 693.

[12] *Jenkin v. Pharmaceutical Society of Great Britain* [1921] 1 Ch. 392. A similar action lies if the alteration is in restraint of trade. See the *Pharmaceutical Society* case, *supra*, n. 10.

[13] *Gray v. Trinity College, Dublin* [1910] 1 Ir.R. 370.

[14] For local authorities see *Hazell v. Hammersmith and Fulham London Borough Council* [1992] A.C. 1.

[15] *Ashbury Ry. Carriage and Iron Co. v. Riche* (1875) L.R. 7 H.L. 653.

[16] *Baroness Wenlock v. River Dee Co.* (1885) 10 App.Cas. 354. The doctrine of *ultra vires* is discussed further at *post*, §§ 9–020 *et seq*. As to the application of this principle to overseas companies, see *Dicey and Morris on the Conflict of Laws* (12th ed., 1993), pp. 1111–1116; *Janred Properties Ltd v. Ente National Per Il Turismo (No. 2)* [1986] 1 F.T.L.R. 246.

[17] *Post*, §§ 9–027 *et seq*.

corporations, sole and aggregate, are limited by particular statutory provisions[18]; and most charitable corporations[19] are subject to the control of the Charity Commissioners under the Charities Act 1993.[20]

(c) Attribution of acts to a company

It is a trite observation that a company can only act through the instrumentability **9–006** of individuals to, for example, enter into contracts. The question arises as to which individuals will bind the company so that it is liable under a contract. The answer to this question is provided by the rules of attribution whereby the acts of certain individuals are attributed to the company. The principles of attribution were analysed by Lord Hoffmann in *Meridian Global Funds Management Ltd v. Securities Commission.*[21] First, there are the company's primary rules of attribution which are to be found normally in the company's constitution (the articles and memorandum of association) and which will determine who or which organ of the company can enter into transactions on behalf of the company.[22] The primary rules of attribution may also be provided by the rules of company law, for example, the principle that the unanimous decision of all the shareholders of a solvent company, even though given informally, constitutes a decision of the company.[23] Coupled with the company's primary rules of attribution are general rules of attribution, namely, the principles of agency and vicarious liability.[24] There will be situations, however, where the primary and secondary rules of attribution do not provide an answer and in these situations the court will have to determine who, if anyone, for the particular matter under consideration is intended to count as the person whose acts are attributed to the company.

Company's name.[25] The Business Names Act 1985 regulates the names **9–007** under which individuals, partnerships and companies may carry on business. The 1985 Act provides that where a company[26] carries on business under a name which "does not consist of its corporate name without any addition other than one so permitted"[27] it must take steps to ensure that its corporate name appears on a wide range of written instruments connected with the carrying on of its business. In particular, the corporate name must appear on all business letters, written orders for goods or services, invoices and receipts and written demands for payments of debts.[28] Also, the company's name must appear in a prominent

---

[18] Ecclesiastical Leasing Acts 1842 and 1858; Ecclesiastical Leases Acts 1861, 1862 and 1865.

[19] On the nature of charitable companies see *Liverpool and District Hospital for Diseases of the Heart v. Att.-Gen.* [1981] Ch.D. 193.

[20] See also §§ 9–027 *et seq., post* dealing with the application of the ultra vires doctrine to companies.

[21] [1995] A.C. 500, PC.

[22] See, *e.g.* art. 70 of Table A Companies (Tables A-F) Regulations 1985, S.I. 1984 No. 805.

[23] *Multinational Gas and Petrochemical Co. v. Multinational Gas and Petrochemical Services Ltd* [1983] Ch. 258.

[24] See *New Zealand Guardian Trust Co. Ltd v. Brooks* [1995] 1 W.L.R. 96.

[25] There are other provisions regulating the use of names by companies but these are not of relevance to the present discussion: see Companies Act 1985, ss.25–34; *Cotronic (U.K.) Ltd v. Dezonie* [1991] B.C.L.C. 721.

[26] Defined as a company capable of being wound up under the Companies Act 1985: see Business Names Act 1985, s.1(1)(c).

[27] s.1(1)(c). For permitted additions see s.1(2).

[28] s.4(1)(a). For the situation where the transaction is oral or partly oral see s.4(2).

position in any premises in which the company's business is carried on and to which its customers or suppliers have access.[29] In the event of the failure to disclose the company's name as required, any legal proceedings arising out of a right to enforce a contract may be dismissed if the defendant shows that he has a claim arising out of that contract which he has been unable to pursue because of the failure,[30] or he has suffered some financial loss because of the failure.[31] It is important to note that the prohibition extends to enforcing a right "arising out of a contract" and not merely to an action to enforce the contract itself. The court before which the proceedings are brought may however permit them to continue where it is satisfied that it is just and equitable to do so.

9–008   **Personal liability: estoppel.** A director, manager or secretary of a company may be personally liable if he signs, or authorises the signature of certain documents (a bill of exchange, promissory note, cheque, or order for money or goods) wherein the name of the company is not fully and accurately stated.[32] A director who authorises the signing of the relevant document falling within section 349 is only liable if he authorises that it be signed in a way that the name of the company does not properly appear.[33] The court will not rectify a document falling within section 349 on which the name of the company does not properly appear as this would undermine the section.[34] In *Durham Fancy Goods Ltd v. Michael Jackson (Fancy Goods) Ltd*[35] Donaldson J. held that the plaintiff company, which drew a bill of exchange on the defendant company which misstated the latter's name, was estopped from invoking the equivalent of section 349 in the 1948 Act against the directors of the defendant company. In *Blum v. OCP Repartition SA*[36] May L.J. reserved his position as far as this case was concerned. It is submitted that the *Durham Fancy Goods* case should be treated with caution. The obligation to comply with section 349 is the primary responsibility of the directors of the company and it is difficult to see how the conduct of persons dealing with the company could operate by way of estoppel to prevent liability from arising where there had been breach of the section.[37] Such conduct could not, for example, preclude liability from arising under section 349(4) which imposes criminal liability for misstating the company's name. If there is any scope for the operation of the doctrine it would operate in favour of the

---

[29] s.4(1)(b).

[30] s.5(1)(a).

[31] s.5(1)(b). For criminal penalties see s.7.

[32] Companies Act 1985, s.349 and s.744 (definition of officer). See *Atkins & Co. v. Wardle* (1889) 61 L.T. 23; 5 T.L.R. 734; *F. Stacey & Co. v. Wallis* (1912) 106 L.T. 544; *Banque de L'Indochine et de Suez SA v. Euroseas Group Finance Co. Ltd* [1981] 3 All E.R. 198; *Lindholst & Co. A/S v. Fowler* [1988] B.C.L.C. 166; *Jenice Ltd v. Dan* [1993] B.C.L.C. 1349; *Chalmers and Guest on Bills of Exchange* (15th ed.), pp. 149–151.

[33] *John Wilkes Ltd v. Lee International (Footwear) Ltd* [1985] B.C.L.C. 444. There must, however, be a signature before there can be any liability: see *Oshkosh B'Gosh Incorporated v. Dan Marbel Incorporated Ltd* [1988] B.C.L.C. 507.

[34] *Blum v. OCP Repartition SA* [1988] B.C.L.C. 170.

[35] [1968] 2 Q.B. 839.

[36] [1988] B.C.L.C. 170. The principle in the *Durham Fancy Goods Ltd* case would not apply where the words of acceptance of a bill of exchange were not dictated by the plaintiff so that there would be no grounds on which the doctrine of estoppel could operate: *Lindholst A/S v. Fowler* [1988] B.C.L.C. 166, 169a. See also *Rafsanjan Pistachio Producers Co-operative v. Keiss* [1990] B.C.L.C. 352.

[37] In this context it is important to note that the courts have emphasised the importance of this section in forewarning persons that they are dealing with a limited liability company: see *Atkins & Co. v. Wardle* (1889) 5 T.L.R. 734.

company and not in favour of its directors. Where a person dealing with the company has been guilty of some fraudulent practice then no doubt he would be precluded from relying on the section but this would be because of the principle that a statute should not itself be used as an instrument of fraud.[38]

Abolition of old rule requiring seal: other formalities. The contracts of a   **9–009**
corporation sole were never required to be made under seal.[39] But the old common law rule was that a corporation aggregate could contract only under seal.[40] The scope of this rule had been greatly restricted by numerous statutory, common law and equitable exceptions; it did not apply to companies incorporated under the Companies Act[41] and it was finally abolished altogether by the Corporate Bodies Contracts Act 1960.

Deeds. Section 1(2) of the Law of Property (Miscellaneous Provisions) Act   **9–010**
1989, which defines what constitutes a deed, applies to companies. How a deed is to be executed by a company is set out in section 36A of the Companies Act 1985.[42] This section also dispenses with the need for a company to have a common seal in order to execute an instrument as a deed.

(d) *Registered Companies*[43]

Registered companies. This section is principally concerned with companies   **9–011**
registered under the Companies Acts, but many of the principles herein discussed also apply to corporations created by particular private or public Acts.

(i) *Contracts between Companies and Third Parties*

Pre-incorporation contracts. Contracts entered into before a company is   **9–012**
registered can, prima facie, bind or confer rights only on the actual makers of the contract and not the company,[44] the reason for this being that a company could not be bound by a contract entered into when it was non-existent.[45] At common law such contracts could even be completely null and void if the persons purporting to sign on behalf of the company were not the real principals.[46]

---

[38] The principle in *Durham Fancy Goods* would not surely be applicable where the company unknown to the person drawing the bill of exchange has changed its name. See also n.30.

[39] Bl. Comm. Vol. I, at 475.

[40] *Yarborough v. Bank of England* (1812) 16 East 6; *Ludlow Corporation v. Charlton* (1840) 6 M. & W. 815; *A.R. Wright & Son Ltd v. Romford B.C.* [1957] 1 Q.B. 431.

[41] See now, Companies Act 1985, s.36 (substituted by the Companies Act 1989, s.130(1), the Secretary of State has power to extend this section to companies incorporated outside Great Britain: Companies Act 1989, s.130(6) (S.I. 1994 No. 950).

[42] Introduced by s.130(1) of the Companies Act 1989. See *The Execution of Deeds and Documents By or On Behalf of Bodies Corporate* (Law Commission, No. 253, Cm. 4026, 1998); *Johnsey Estates (1990) Ltd v. Newport Market World Ltd* (May 10, 1990, unreported).

[43] This is not a summary of company law, but only of the law applicable to the contracts of companies.

[44] *Kelner v. Baxter* (1866) L.R. 2 C.P. 174; *Scott v. Lord Ebury* (1867) L.R. 2 C.P. 255; *Wilson & Co. v. Baker, Lees & Co.* (1901) 17 T.L.R. 473; *King v. David Allen & Sons Billposting Ltd* [1916] 2 A.C. 54; *Gross* (1971) 87 L.Q.R. 367.

[45] On the likely effect were the Contracts (Rights of Third Parties) Bill to be enacted see Law Commission, *Privity of Contract: Contracts for the Benefit of Third Parties* (Report No. 242), §§ 8.9–8.16.

[46] *Newborne v. Sensolid (Great Britain) Ltd* [1954] 1 Q.B. 45; *Black v. Smallwood* (1965–66) 117 C.L.R. 52. See also Vol. II, § 32–028.

However, the courts are strongly disposed to give effect to pre-incorporation contracts and, acting on the maxim *ut res magis valeat quam pereat*, the agent more likely than not will be personally bound on the contract particularly where both parties were aware at the time of contracting of the non-existence of the company.[47] It must be emphasised, however, that at common law there was no general rule that a person acting for a non-existent principal would be automatically bound by the contract; in the final analysis the agent's liability turns on the intention of the parties.[48] The common law was significantly modified by the need to implement Article 7 of the First Directive on Company Law which deals with pre-incorporation contracts.[49] Article 7 was first implemented by section 9(2) of the European Communities Act 1972, was consolidated into section 36(4) of the Companies Act 1985 and is now to be found in section 36C of the 1985 Act.[50] Commenting on section 36(4) Oliver L.J. in *Phonogram Ltd v. Lane*[51] stated that it swept away the "subtle distinctions" of the common law so that "where a person purports to contract on behalf of a company not yet formed, then however he expresses his signature he himself is personally liable on the contract."[52] *Phonogram Ltd v. Lane* was the first case[53] to interpret section 36(4), and the Court of Appeal rejected attempts to construe narrowly the effect of the section. In particular, it rejected the argument that the phrase "subject to any agreement to the contrary" should be interpreted to relieve a person of liability where he signs the contract as agent, in that this could be taken as evincing an agreement that the person acting for the company was not to be personally liable.[54] A person acting for an unformed company could only avoid liability under section 36C where there was an "express agreement"[55] that he was not to be liable. Section 36C makes a person acting for an unformed company "liable on the contract" and it does not confer on him any independent rights of enforcement.[56]

9–013   Section 36C does not affect the company itself, and it remains the law that a company is not entitled to the benefits of, or bound by the liabilities in, a contract entered into before it was incorporated. But in some circumstances a company may acquire rights or incur liabilities at law or equity in respect of a transaction originally entered into before the incorporation of the company. Broadly speaking, for a company to be so liable it must enter into a new contract after it has

---

[47] *Kelner v. Baxter* (1866) L.R. 2 C.P. 174.

[48] *Hawkes Bay Milk Corp. v. Watson* [1974] 2 N.Z.L.R. 236. Note also the possible liability of the putative agent for breach of warranty of authority: see *Bowstead on Agency* (16th ed., 1996), Art. 112.

[49] Article 7 of the First Directive (68/151/EEC) provides that: "If, before a company being formed has acquired legal personality, action has been carried out in its name and the company does not assume the obligations arising from such action, the persons who acted shall, without limit, be jointly and severally liable therefore, unless otherwise agreed."

[50] This was inserted by s.130(4) of the 1989 Act. The wording of s.36C is different from that of its predecessors.

[51] [1982] 1 Q.B. 938, 946.

[52] *ibid.* at 944, *per* Lord Denning M.R.

[53] For other cases dealing with s.36(4) of the 1985 Act see: *Rover International Ltd v. Cannon Film Sales Ltd* [1987] B.C.L.C. 540 (the subsection, as would be the case with s.36C, does not affect foreign companies); *Oshkosh B'Gosh Inc. v. Dan Marbel Ltd* [1989] B.C.L.C. 507; *Cotronic (U.K.) Ltd v. Dezonie* [1991] B.C.L.C. 721; *Badgerhill Properties Ltd v. Cottrell* [1991] B.C.L.C. 805.

[54] *e.g.* as in *Newborne v. Sensolid (Great Britain) Ltd* [1954] 1 Q.B. 45. See generally Prentice (1973) 89 L.Q.R. 518, 530–533.

[55] *Phonogram Ltd v. Lane, supra,* at 940.

[56] *Cotronic (U.K.) Ltd v. Dezonie* [1991] B.C.L.C. 721.

been incorporated, but it is arguable (as will be seen later) that a company can be liable in other circumstances.

At law. A company cannot ratify or adopt a contract made ostensibly on its **9–014** behalf before its incorporation, since a person cannot by a subsequent ratification make himself liable as a principal where he was not in existence at the time of the original contract.[57] Before a company is bound it must enter into a new contract. If promoters purport to enter into a contract on behalf of a company before its incorporation, the facts may show that a new contract is made with the company after its incorporation on the terms of the old. But the circumstances relied on for this purpose must be necessarily referable to, or must necessarily imply, a new contract between the company and the other contracting party.[58] This is a question of fact.[59] Where the company's conduct is attributable to its mistaken belief that it was bound by the original contract[60] or is attributable to the performance by the company of a contract between it and, for example the promoters,[61] it will be difficult, if not impossible, to show that the company's conduct is necessarily referable to a new contract with the other contracting party. In *Rover International Ltd v. Cannon Film Sales Ltd*[62] Harman J. rejected the argument that the doctrine of estoppel by convention could operate to preclude the company from claiming that it was not bound by a pre-incorporation contract if both parties to the contract had, after the company's incorporation, acted as though it were bound.[63] He reasoned that where estoppel by convention operates it must relate to an "assumption of agreed facts . . . (existing) before the contract or dealing is made or agreed" and as the company did not exist at the time the contract was entered into there was accordingly no basis on which the estoppel could operate. Admittedly, in *Amalagamated Investment and Property Co. Ltd v. Texas Commerce International Bank Ltd*[64] the facts on which the estoppel was based existed at the time the purported contract was entered into, but it is submitted that it is an unnecessarily narrow reading of the estoppel doctrine to confine it to facts that existed at the time the contract was entered into. There is, however, no reason in principle why the estoppel should not date from the time the company is incorporated. The estoppel point was not pursued on appeal in the *Rover International* case,[65] but the court allowed a *quantum meruit* claim with respect to services rendered by the company after it had been incorporated. Where the company, after its incorporation, has taken possession of property belonging to the other contracting party, in pursuance to the agreement,[66] or has

---

[57] *Kelner v. Baxter* (1866) L.R. 2 C.P. 174; *Melhado v. Porto Alegre Ry.* (1874) L.R. 9 C.P. 503; *North Sydney Investment & Tramway Co. v. Higgins* [1899] A.C. 263; *Scott v. Lord Ebury* (1867) L.R. 2 C.P. 255, 267.

[58] *Natal Land, etc., Co. v. Pauline Colliery Syndicate* [1904] A.C. 120.

[59] *Howard v. Patent Ivory Manufacturing Co.* (1888) 38 Ch.D. 156.

[60] *Re Northumberland Avenue Hotel Co.* (1886) 33 Ch.D. 16; *Bagot Pneumatic Tyre Co. v. Clipper Pneumatic Tyre Co.* [1901] 1 Ch. 196, 203.

[61] *Howard v. Patent Ivory Manufacturing Co.* (1888) 38 Ch.D. 156, 164–168.

[62] [1987] W.L.R. 1597 (Harman J.); [1989] 1 W.L.R. 912. For other proceedings involving the parties see *Films Rover International Ltd v. Cannon Film Sales Ltd* [1987] 1 W.L.R. 670 where Hoffmann J. stated that it "would be a blot on English jurisprudence if this contract, acted on by both sides, had now to be held null and void" (at 679).

[63] This argument was advanced in the 25th edition of this text at p. 334.

[64] [1982] Q.B. 84.

[65] [1989] 1 W.L.R. 912; noted (1989) 105 L.Q.R. 179 (Beatson). For other aspects of this case see § 9–017.

[66] See n. 61.

agreed to modify the terms of the original contract,[67] it will be easier to infer the making of a new contract.

9–015   **In equity.** Equity also will not assist (in the sense of enforcing a contract) a person who has entered into a contract for the benefit of a corporation which, at the time of the making of the contract, did not exist, and it will not, it would seem, enforce such contracts unless they are enforceable at law.[68] It is true that there are certain late nineteenth-century decisions in which courts of equity did enforce such contracts on the ground that the company had "adopted" the promoters' contract[69]; but the distinction between ratification and adoption was never clear[70] and they can no longer be relied upon.[71] Another attempt to enforce pre-incorporation contracts against companies sought to utilise the device of the trust; thus where a promoter had contracted with third parties that a company not yet in existence should pay the third parties £2,000 in consideration for certain services by the third parties, and the promoter was in a position to sue the company for that remuneration, the promoter was held to be a trustee for the third parties of his right of action, and the third parties, being *cestuis que trustent*, could sue the company.[72] But the courts are increasingly reluctant to imply a trust in such circumstances,[73] and, in any event, as later decisions show, the promoter will not have any right of action to hold in trust for the benefit of a third party unless the company, *after its incorporation*, makes a contract with him.[74]

9–016   **Pre-incorporation benefits.** A company is under no liability, either at law or in equity, to pay for benefits rendered to it prior to its incorporation.[75] So, for instance, a company is not bound to reimburse a promoter in respect of the expense of incorporation[76] unless after it has been formed it enters into a binding contract to do so. Similarly, a company is not bound by any agreement made by

---

[67] *Howard v. Patent Ivory Manufacturing Co. ibid.* at 166.

[68] In some nineteenth-century cases there are dicta that persons who perform services for an unformed company will have a claim in equity for payment on the grounds that it is "inequitable for a man not to pay for services of which he has taken the benefit," *per* James L.J., *Re Empress Engineering Co.* (1880) 16 Ch.D. 125, 130. See also *Hereford South Wales Waggon & Engineering Co.* (1876) 2 Ch.D. 621; Buckley, *The Companies Acts* (14th ed.), p. 26. These dicta are of doubtful authority: no case actually turns on their application; they are often cited in the context of a company having purportedly "adopted" the contract, a phrase used with no great clarity; they are scarcely compatible with subsequent authority and were rejected in *Re English and Colonial Produce Co. Ltd* [1906] 2 Ch. 435, 442.

[69] *Spiller v. Paris Skating Rink Co.* (1878) 7 Ch.D. 368. The question of "adoption" was often bound up with the problem of part performance in connection with the Statute of Frauds (see *ante* §§ 4–036—4–046) and it was sometimes suggested that part performance was itself a ground of liability in equity even in the absence of a binding contract (see *Wilson v. West Hartlepool Ry.* (1865) 2 De G.J. & S. 475) but it is clear today that this is not so: *Hunt v. Wimbledon Local Board* (1878) 4 C.P.D. 48, 61.

[70] *Falcke v. Scottish Imperial Insurance Co.* (1886) 34 Ch.D. 234, 249–250.

[71] *Re Empress Engineering Co.* (1880) 16 Ch.D. 125, 130; *Natal Land, etc., Co. v. Pauline Colliery Syndicate* [1904] A.C. 120.

[72] *Touche v. Metropolitan Ry. Warehousing Co.* (1871) L.R. 6 Ch.App. 671 (it is important to note that the court found that there was a trust of the company's promise to the promoter, although how the trust was actually constituted is not clear from the facts).

[73] *Re Empress Engineering Co., supra*; and see *post*, §§ 19–065—19–066.

[74] *Re National Motor Mail Coach Co., Clinton's Claim* [1908] 2 Ch. 515.

[75] *Re English & Colonial Produce Co. Ltd* [1906] 2 Ch. 435, disapproving dicta in *Re Hereford & South Wales Waggon, etc., Co.* (1876) 2 Ch.D. 621; see also n. 68.

[76] *ibid.*

its promoters that it will, when formed, pay something to a third party who has agreed not to oppose the formation of the company in consideration of such a payment.[77] There are some nineteenth-century cases concerning the incorporation of railway companies by private Acts of Parliament which suggest that the court will not allow such a company to exercise its statutory powers without performing undertakings contained in a contract made by the promoters with a third party, in consideration of which that party agreed not to oppose the formation of the company.[78] But equity will not interfere even to this extent unless the original contract would have been *intra vires* of the company if originally made by the company.[79]

Post-incorporation benefits. It may be that a company will benefit in a **9–017** tangible way from acts arising under a pre-incorporation contract which does not give rise to any contractual claim by the other party to the contract. With the recognition of unjust enrichment as a ground for granting restitutionary remedies,[80] there are now a range of doctrines that can be invoked by the party providing the tangible benefit to obtain restitution for the benefit conferred. Where property or money has been transferred to a company pursuant to a pre-incorporation contract, the property or money may be recovered on the basis that the transfer or payment was made under a mistake of fact.[81] Alternatively, recovery may be available on the grounds of failure of consideration in the sense that the plaintiff has not received any part of the consideration bargained for under the purported contract.[82] In *Westdeutsche Landesbank Girozentrale v. The Council of the London Borough of Islington*[83] it was held that there was a general principle that moneys, paid under an *ultra vires* contract that was void *ab initio*, were recoverable on the grounds of total failure of consideration, or on equitable principles entitling a transferor to recover property that in equity belonged to him. Since a pre-incorporation contract is, like an *ultra vires* contract, void, these principles could also be applied to moneys paid to a company pursuant to a pre-incorporation contract.[84] Where benefits are conferred on a company on the basis

---

[77] *Earl of Lindsey v. Great Northern Ry.* (1853) 10 Hare 664; *Earl of Shrewsbury v. North Staffordshire Ry.* (1865) L.R. 1 Eq. 593.

[78] *ibid.* These cases, decided before the consequences of the entity doctrine were fully appreciated, were considered to have been seriously "shaken" by the development of this doctrine: see Hodges, *A Law of Railways* (7th ed.), pp. 141–152. There is much substance to this view which is not significantly undermined by a more relaxed doctrine of privity, as to hold the company bound would for all intents and purposes sweep away the learning on pre-incorporation contracts, something which is scarcely likely to happen. The promoters who gave the assurance may, of course, be liable if there is deceit or, perhaps, for negligent misrepresentation or breach of warranty of authority.

[79] *Earl of Shrewsbury v. North Staffordshire Ry.*, supra, n. 71. See *Westdeutsche Landesbank Girozentrale v. Islington L.B.C.* [1996] A.C 669. The effect (if any) of s.35 of the Companies Act 1985 on this type of case is uncertain. For the categories of company covered by s.35, see s.735.

[80] See Chap. 30.

[81] *Rover International Ltd v. Cannon Film Sales Ltd* [1989] 1 W.L.R. 912. See Burrows, *The Law of Restitution* (1993), pp.103–104; Goff and Jones, *The Law of Restitution* (5th ed., 1998), pp. 660–662.

[82] *Rover International Ltd v. Cannon Sales Ltd* [1989] 1 W.L.R. 912; Burrows *op. cit.* at pp. 253–257.

[83] *Supra*; see also *Kleinwort Benson Ltd v. The South Tyneside M.B.C.* [1994] 4 All E.R. 972.

[84] Moneys paid on behalf of a company before it is has been formed could not be recoverable by the company, the company has lost nothing. see *Rover International Ltd v. Cannon Film Sales Ltd* [1989] 1 W.L.R. 912.

of a pre-incorporation contract, the party providing the benefit will be entitled to a *quantum meruit*.[85]

9–018   It is submitted that money in the hands of a company can be "traced" no less when it has come into the company's hands as the result of a pre-incorporation contract than when it has done so as the result of an *ultra vires* contract,[86] and that the ordinary rules of equity also apply where a company has stood by and allowed another to expend money on its property in the mistaken belief, based on a pre-incorporation contract and known to the company, that he has some interest in that property.[87]

9–019   **Public companies: trading certificate.** A company which is registered as a public company shall not do business or exercise its borrowing powers unless it obtains a certificate from the registrar of companies.[88] Broadly speaking, the registrar is obliged to issue such a certificate once he has been satisfied that the company possesses the necessary authorised minimum share capital.[89] Failure to obtain a certificate can give rise to criminal and civil consequences.[90] In particular, if a public company trades without a certificate and fails to obtain one within 21 days from being called upon to do so, the directors of the company shall be jointly and severally liable to indemnify the other party to the transaction in respect of any loss or damage suffered by him by reason of the failure of the company to comply with those obligations.[91]

9–020   **Ultra vires contracts.** Before examining the reform of the doctrine of *ultra vires*,[92] it is necessary, as a background for understanding that reform, to set out the nature and evolution of the doctrine. A company which owes its corporate existence to statute has not the inherent common law powers of chartered corporations.[93] Indeed, it has only capacity to enter into contracts authorised by the objects clause in its memorandum of association, or, in the case of companies not registered under the Companies Act 1985, by the terms of its special Act. Thus, it was held in *Ashbury Railway Carriage & Iron Co. v. Riche*[94] that any contract outside the scope of the objects clause is *ultra vires* of the company and void, even if the whole body of shareholders in the company assent to it.[95] A

---

[85] *Rover International Ltd v. Cannon Film Sales Ltd* [1989] 1 W.L.R. 912; *Cotronic (U.K.) Ltd v. Dezonie* [1991] B.C.L.C. 721. In the latter case, the court held that s.34 of the 1985 Act did not preclude recovery.

[86] See *post*, § 9–026.

[87] See *Hunt* v. *Wimbledon Local Board* (1878) 4 C.P.D. 48, 61; and see *post*, § 00–000. The same rules will apply where it is the company which has expended the money on another's property.

[88] Companies Act 1985, s.117.

[89] *ibid.* ss.117(2), 117(3).

[90] See Prentice, *Companies Act 1980*, pp. 6–7 (dealing with the provisions of the Companies Act 1980 from which s.117 is derived).

[91] Companies Act 1985, s.117(8).

[92] See *post*, §§ 9–027 *et seq.*

[93] See *ante*, § 9–004.

[94] (1875) L.R. 7 H.L. 653; and see *Att.-Gen.* v. *Great Eastern Ry.* (1880) 5 App.Cas. 473; *Wenlock (Baroness) v. River Dee Co.* (1885) 10 App.Cas. 354; *L.C.C. v. Att.-Gen.* [1902] A.C. 165; *Att.-Gen. v. Mersey Ry.* [1907] 1 Ch. 81; [1907] A.C. 415; *Re Jon Beauforte (London) Ltd* [1953] Ch. 131; *Parke v. Daily News Ltd* [1962] Ch. 927.

[95] "An *ultra vires* agreement cannot become *intra vires* by means of estoppel, lapse of time, ratification, acquiescence, or delay": *York Corporation v. Henry Leetham & Sons Ltd* [1924] 1 Ch. 557, 573; see also § 9–024.

member of a company[96] is entitled to an injunction to restrain the company and its directors[97] from entering into an *ultra vires* contract or otherwise acting outside the powers of the company, *e.g.* criminally.[98] Although sections 35–35C of the Companies Act 1985 (originally section 9(1) of the European Communities Act 1972) has greatly reduced the importance of the *ultra vires* doctrine, it does not abrogate the doctrine, and there may be some situations (although these will be rare) where the common law doctrine will have relevance. More importantly, as stated earlier, some knowledge of the common law is needed in order to understand fully the statutory modifications of the *ultra vires* doctrine. Accordingly, the common law position is discussed in the next six paragraphs, and section 35 is then considered.[99] At this point it must be emphasised that the development of the *ultra vires* doctrine since the *Riche* decision has witnessed judicial attempts, on the whole successful, to attenuate the doctrine so that a person dealing with a company will not be prejudiced by the latter's lack of capacity except in exceptional circumstances.

Scope of the rule. The phrase *ultra vires* "should be restricted to those cases **9–021** where the transaction is beyond the capacity of the company and therefore wholly void."[1] The question whether the making of a particular contract is or is not *ultra vires* of the company depends upon the terms of the company's memorandum of association, which must state the company's objects.[2] Explaining the rule Lord Wrenbury[3] said:

"The purpose, I apprehend, is twofold. The first is that the intending corporator who contemplates the investment of his capital shall know within what field it is to be put at risk. The second is that anyone who shall deal with the company shall know without reasonable doubt whether the contractual relationship into which he contemplates entering with the company is one relating to a matter within its corporate objects."

As was stated by Browne-Wilkinson L.J. in *Rolled Steel Products (Holdings) Ltd v. British Steel Corporation*,[4] "The question whether a transaction is outside

---

[96] But not, in general, a creditor: *Mills v. Northern Ry. of Buenos Aires Co.* (1870) L.R. 5 Ch.App. 621; *Cross v. Imperial Continental Gas Association* [1923] 2 Ch. 553; *Lawrence v. W. Somerset Mineral Ry. Co.* [1918] 2 Ch. 250; contrast *Maunsell v. Midland G.W. (Ireland) Ry.* (1863) 1 Hem. & M. 130. See also *Charles Roberts & Co. Ltd v. British Railways Board* [1965] 1 W.L.R. 396 (action for declaration by business competitor of a nationalised industry); and as to relator actions, see *Att.-Gen. v. Crayford U.D.C.* [1962] Ch. 575.

[97] *Hoole v. G.W. Ry.* (1867) L.R. 3 Ch.App. 262. The right to restrain prospective *ultra vires* acts is based on the contract constituted by s.14 of the Companies Act 1985. A shareholder's standing to complain of past *ultra vires* acts gives rise to more complex problems: see *Smith v. Croft (No. 2)* [1988] Ch. 114.

[98] See Buckley, *The Companies Acts* (14th ed.), pp. 199–200.

[99] Proposals for the reform of the *ultra vires* doctrine were put forward in a DTI consultative document: *Reform of the Ultra Vires Rule: A Consultative Report* (1986). These were partly implemented by ss.108–109 of the Companies Act 1989.

[1] *Rolled Steel Products (Holdings) Ltd v. British Steel Corporation* [1986] 1 Ch. 246, 303, *per* Browne-Wilkinson L.J. (see also Slade L.J. 297) The phrase should not therefore be used to refer to situations where directors abuse or exceed their authority or where the transaction is illegal.

[2] s. 2(1)(c). It has been said that a wider construction ought to be given to the memorandum of association of a commercial company than to the statute creating a company with special powers: *Att.-Gen. v. Mersey Ry.* [1907] 1 Ch. 81, 106 (revd. [1907] A.C. 415), but see *Charles Roberts & Co. Ltd v. British Railways Board, supra,* at 400.

[3] *Cotman v. Brougham* [1918] A.C. 514, 522; *Hazell v. Hammersmith and Fulham L.B.C.* [1992] 2 A.C. 1, 36–37; *Westdeutsche case, supra,* n. 79.

[4] [1986] Ch. 246, 306.

the capacity of the company depends solely upon whether, on the true construction of its memorandum of association, the transaction is capable of falling within the objects of the company. . . . " At common law the doctrine is not dependent on the person dealing with the company having notice of the company's lack of capacity; it operates regardless of the third party's state of knowledge as regards the contents of the company's objects clause.[5] In a number of cases it was held that where a company exercised a power which it undoubtedly possessed but for a *purpose* which was *ultra vires*, and this purpose was known to the party dealing with the company, the contract would be *ultra vires* in the sense of being outside the capacity of the company and hence void.[6] However, in the *Rolled Steel* decision the Court of Appeal considered that these cases should be treated as cases dealing with an abuse of the company's powers, not with corporate capacity, with the result that the transactions in these cases would be enforceable against the company unless the party dealing with it had notice (actual or constructive) that the transaction was in excess of or an abuse of the company's powers.[7] Normally a transaction falling within a company's objects clause will be within the *vires* of a company. However, in certain situations a provision in the objects clause may not be capable as existing as an object and may be merely an ancillary power; for example, the power to borrow.[8] Formerly parties dealing with companies were deemed to have notice of companies' memoranda of association[9] but this rule has now been abrogated.[10]

9–022 **What contracts are ultra vires.** It has been repeatedly asserted that the *ultra vires* doctrine must be reasonably applied, and that any contract made by a company which may fairly be regarded as incidental to or consequential upon those things which are authorised by the memorandum is not, unless expressly prohibited, to be held *ultra vires*.[11] This depends on the circumstances of each case. Thus a trading corporation has implied power to borrow money either upon security or otherwise,[12] to sell its property,[13] to purchase the subject matter of its business,[14] or to compromise claims made by or against it.[15] Wide powers given by general words in the memorandum of association may be construed as only

---

[5] *ibid.* 304. See also *Freeman & Lockyer v. Buckhurst Park Properties (Mangal) Ltd* [1964] 2 Q.B. 480, 504.

[6] See, *e.g. Re Lee, Behrens & Co.* [1932] 2 Ch. 46; *Re Jon Beauforte (London) Ltd* [1953] Ch. 131. *cf.* Insolvency Act 1986, s.238(5); *Westdeutsche Landesbank Girozentrale v. Islington L.B.C.* [1996] A.C. 669.

[7] Where third party has knowledge the contract would appear to be void ([1986] 1 Ch. 246, 306–307). *Quaere* if the contract is enforceable by the company and therefore only voidable.

[8] [1986] Ch. 246, 305.

[9] *ibid.*; *Ernest v. Nicholls* (1857) 6 H.L.Cas. 401. Copies of all a company's public documents are available for inspection: Companies Act 1985, s.709.

[10] See *post* §9–034.

[11] *Att.-Gen. v. Great Eastern Ry.* (1880) 5 App.Cas. 473, 478; *Peel v. L. & N.W. Ry.* [1907] 1 Ch. 5; *S. Pearson & Sons Ltd v. Dublin & S.E. Ry.* [1909] A.C. 217, 220; *Dundee Harbour Trustees v. Nicol* [1915] A.C. 550; *Municipal Mutual Insurance Ltd v. Pontefract Corpn.* (1917) 116 L.T. 671; *Evans v. Brunner, Mond & Co.* [1921] 1 Ch. 359; *Deuchar v. Gas Light & Coke Co.* [1925] A.C. 691; *Wimbledon & Putney Commons Conservators v. Tuely* [1931] 1 Ch. 190; *City of Winnipeg v. C.P.R. Co.* [1953] A.C. 618.

[12] *General Auction Estate & Monetary Co. v. Smith* [1891] 3 Ch. 432.

[13] *Re Kingsbury Collieries Ltd and Moore's Contract* [1907] 2 Ch. 259; *Re Thomas (William) & Co. Ltd* [1915] 1 Ch. 325.

[14] *Leifchild's Case* (1865) L.R. 1 Eq. 231.

[15] *Dixon v. Evans* (1872) L.R. 5 H.L. 606; *Bath's Case* (1878) 8 Ch.D. 334.

ancillary to the company's main objects[16]; but this rule of construction may be excluded by the wording of the memorandum.[17] Not all the activities stated in a company's objects clause are necessarily objects in the strict sense, and "some of them may only be capable of existing as, or on their true construction are, ancillary powers."[18] Thus, for example, (as was stated earlier) a provision in a company's objects clause relating to borrowing will normally be treated as a power and not an independent object.[19] The courts have strained to interpret objects clauses liberally so as to validate transactions. In *Re New Finance & Mortgage Co. Ltd*[20] the operation of a petrol station was held to fall within the terms of an objects clause authorising the company to carry on the business of "merchants generally." Goulding J., in the course of his judgment opined that the company's entire "objects clause is too loosely drawn to be of any real value to subscribers or persons dealing with the company."[21]

Opinion of the directors. Whether a contract is *ultra vires* or not depends in **9–023** principle on whether the memorandum does in fact authorise the transaction in question, and not on whether the directors think that it does.[22] But where a memorandum states that the company can carry on any business which, in the opinion of the board of directors, can be advantageously carried on in connection with, or as ancillary to, its authorised business, the position is different. In such circumstances the bona fide opinion of the directors that a business can be advantageously carried on in connection with, or as ancillary to, the company's principal business will suffice to render the former business *intra vires*.[23] The memorandum of a company may contain a statement that the powers of the company, or a particular power, must be exercised for "purposes of the company." Normally the court will construe this as being a limitation on the powers of the directors and *not* as a "condition limiting the company's corporate capacity."[24]

No ratification or estoppel. An *ultra vires* contract is not capable of ratifica- **9–024** tion by a company[25]; nor can the company be estopped by deed[26] or otherwise[27]

---

[16] *Re German Date Coffee Co.* (1882) 20 Ch.D. 169, 188. This case dealt with a petition to wind up a company on the grounds that its substratum had disappeared, a doctrine which although having a strong resemblance to that of *ultra vires* is not the same: *Cotman v. Brougham* [1918] A.C. 514; *Re Tivoli Freeholds* [1972] V.R. 445.

[17] *Cotman v. Brougham op. cit.; Anglo-Overseas Agencies Ltd v. Green* [1961] 1 Q.B. 1.

[18] *Rolled Steel Products (Holdings) Ltd v. British Steel Corporation* [1986] Ch. 246, 305.

[19] *ibid.* Normally it will not be possible to elevate this power into an object by a provision in a company's objects clause requiring all the objects to be interpreted independently of each other, although in other situations the courts have given full effect to such a clause: see *Cotman v. Brougham* [1918] A.C. 514.

[20] [1975] 1 Ch. 420. See also *Newstead v. Frost* [1980] 1 W.L.R. 135.

[21] *ibid.* at 425.

[22] *Tinkler v. Wandsworth D.B.W.* (1858) 2 De G. & J. 261, 274 (directors cannot confer power on a statutory company by asserting that something falls within the spirit of the Act).

[23] *Bell Houses Ltd v. City Wall Properties Ltd* [1966] 2 Q.B. 656. Although the statement to this effect in *Bell* was technically *obiter*, the Court of Appeal found the contract to be *intra vires*, it is generally considered to be correct: see *American Home Assurance Co. v. Tjmond Properties Ltd* [1986] B.C.L.C. 181 (N.Z.C.A.).

[24] *Rolled Steel Products (Holdings) Ltd v. British Steel Corporation* [1986] Ch. 246, 295.

[25] *Ashbury Railway Carriage & Iron Co. v. Riche* (1875) L.R. 7 HL 653; see now § 9–028.

[26] *Ex p. Watson* (1888) 21 Q.B.D. 301.

[27] *Great N.-W. Central Ry. v. Charlebois* [1899] A.C. 114; *York Corpn. v. Henry Leetham & Sons Ltd* [1924] 1 Ch. 557; see also n. 95, *supra; cf. Islington Vestry v. Hornsey U.D.C.* [1900] 1 Ch. 695.

from showing that they had no power to do that which they profess to have done.[28]

9–025   **Effect of ultra vires borrowing.** A loan contracted by persons on behalf of a company which has no power to borrow does not create an indebtedness on the part of the company either at law or in equity.[29] Securities deposited by the company to secure such a loan can be recovered by it from the lender.[30] The money borrowed cannot be recovered from the company upon an implied promise to repay, as money had and received by the company to the use of the lender.[31] But if any part of the money which has been borrowed has been applied in discharging the company's debts, the lender is entitled to have that part of the loan treated as valid.[32] However, the lender is not subrogated to any securities or priorities enjoyed by the creditors who are paid by means of his money, the reason for this being that the *ultra vires* unsecured creditors should not be put in a better position than the company's unsecured creditors.[33] Money which is in the company's hands as the result of an *ultra vires* loan is treated as money belonging to the purported lender. So long therefore as that money is identifiable or traceable the lender is entitled to recover it or to a charge on the fund of which it forms part.[34]

9–026   **Recovery of property of money under ultra vires transaction.**[35] Where money or property is transferred under an *ultra vires* contract it can be recovered on the ground that since the contract was wholly void there was an inadequacy of consideration.[36] However, this right or recovery would not be available if the defendant could invoke the defence of change of position, that is, the recipient of the money had so changed his position that it would be inequitable to compel him to make restitution or to make restitution in full.[37]

---

[28] For the present statutory provision see *post* §§ 9–027 *et seq.*

[29] *Baroness Wenlock v. River Dee Co.* (1885) 10 App.Cas. 354; see generally Vann, (1978) 52 A.L.J. 490.

[30] *Cunliffe Brooks & Co. v. Blackburn Benefit Building Society* (1882) 22 Ch.D. 61; (1884) 9 App.Cas. 857.

[31] *Sinclair v. Brougham* [1914] A.C. 398. See § 9–026. For criticisms of *Sinclair v. Brougham* see *Westdeutsche Landesbank Girozentrale v. Islington L.B.C.* [1996] A.C. 669, 709–714.

[32] *Re Cork and Youghal Ry.* (1869) L.R. 4 Ch.App. 748; *Cunliffe Brooks & Co. v. Blackburn Benefit Building Society, supra; B. Liggett (Liverpool) Ltd v. Barclays Bank Ltd* [1928] 1 K.B. 48; *Re Airedale Co-operative Worsted Manufacturing Society Ltd* [1933] Ch. 639. The onus is on the person claiming the money to establish the necessary factual connection: see *Westdeutsche Landesbank Girozentrale v. Islington L.B.C.*, [1996] A.C. 689.

[33] *Re Wrexham Mold and Connah's Quay Ry.* [1899] 1 Ch. 440; Goff and Jones, *The Law of Restitution* (5th ed., 1998), pp. 153–158. On the limits of subrogation where the contract is illegal see *Orakpo v. Manson Investments Ltd* [1978] A.C. 95.

[34] *Sinclair v. Brougham* [1914] A.C. 398, where the principle of *Re Hallett's Estate* (1880) 13 Ch.D. 696 as to the tracing and identification of blended money was explained and the method adopted in *Re Guardian Permanent Benefit Building Society (Crace Calvert's Case)* (1882) 23 Ch.D. 440 was criticised. See also *Re Diplock* [1948] Ch. 465, 518–519 (affd. *sub nom Ministry of Health v. Simpson* [1951] A.C. 251). For other consequences of an *ultra vires* transaction see Goff and Jones, *The Law of Restitution* (5th ed., 1998), at pp. 652–662.

[35] See *post* §§ 30–048 *et seq.*

[36] Title to money or property can be transferred under an *ultra vires* contract: see *Ayres v. South Australian Banking Corp.* (1871) L.R. 3 PC 548; *Westdeutsche Landesbank Girozentrale v. Islington L.B.C.* [1996] A.C. 669, 689–690.

[37] *Lipkin Gorman v. Karpnale* [1991] 2 A.C. 548; see also *post* §§ 30–062 *et seq.*

Sections 35–35C of the Companies Act 1985. Article 9 of the First Directive   **9-027**
on Company Law[38] requires member states to introduce legislation abrogating
the doctrine of *ultra vires* so as to ensure security of transactions between
companies and those with whom they contract. This aspect of the Directive was
first implemented by section 9(1) of the European Communities Act 1972[39]
which became section 35 of the 1985 Act. Section 35 was amended by section
108 of the Companies Act 1989 which inserted sections 35–35B into the 1985
Act.[40]

Corporate capacity. In reforming the doctrine of *ultra vires* so as to ensure   **9-028**
security of transactions between companies and those with whom they deal, it is
necessary to ensure that the validity of the transaction cannot be called into
question on the grounds of the company's want of capacity. This is clearly done
by section 35(1) of the 1985 Act which provides that the "validity of an act done
by a company" shall not be called into question by reason of anything in the
company's memorandum. Since a company's objects clause both confers
capacity and restricts it, this means that the restriction, implicit by stating objects
in the memorandum, does not affect the validity of any act entered into by
the company. It is important to note that the section refers to an "act" of the
company, a word that is of the widest import. The common law rule that a
company could not ratify an *ultra vires* transaction has also been modified so as
to allow a company to ratify an *ultra vires* transaction.[41] Given the breadth of
section 35(1) it is difficult to envisage many situations where such ratification
would be needed and it may be that such ratification will only be of use as a
means of reassuring the nervous. Where a contract can be avoided, for example,
because of a conflict of interest of a director who is a party to the contract, the
European Court of Justice has held that this does not constitute a breach of
Article 9(1) of the First Directive.[42]

Ultra vires **and shareholder rights.** Under section 14 of the 1985 Act the   **9-029**
articles and memorandum constitute a contract between the members and the
company. If nothing were done to restrict the scope of this section, the effects of
ultra vires could be introduced through the backdoor by a suit by a shareholder
to prevent the company from performing a contract which is not authorised by
the company's objects clause.[43] Section 35(2) addresses this problem. It provides
that a member of the company may bring an action to restrain anything that is
outside the capacity of the company but that no such action can be brought "in
respect of an act to be done in fulfilment of a legal obligation arising from the
previous act of the company." Thus no action may be brought to restrain the
performance of an act which is made legally binding by section 35(1). A
shareholder is only prevented from bringing an action where the company is

---

[38] 68/151: [1968] J.O. L65/7.

[39] See Prentice (1973) 89 L.Q.R. 518; Collier and Sealy (1973) C.L.J. 1.

[40] These provisions were brought into effect on February 4, 1991. These reforms were based in part
on a consultative report, *Reform of the Ultra Vires Rule* (D.T.I., 1986) see also "Modern Company
Law—The Strategic Framework", Company Law Review Steering Committee (February 1999),
Chap. 5.3.

[41] s.35(3).

[42] *Co-operative Rabobank Vecht en Plassgebied BA v. Minderland (Case C–104/96)* [1997] All
E.R. (D) 114.

[43] See, for example, *Taylor v. National Union of Mineworkers (Derbyshire Area)* [1985] B.C.L.C.
237.

legally obliged to perform an act and thus this would not cover a situation where the company has an option which relates to an *ultra vires* transaction but which the company is not obliged to exercise.

9–030   **Ultra vires and director's duties.** It is a breach of duty for directors to enter into an *ultra vires* transaction since as fiduciaries they must keep within the limit of their powers arising from the limit on their principal's capacity.[44] The reform of *ultra vires* so as to ensure security of transactions, does not require that a director's duty to the company to act within its objects should in any way be modified. Accordingly, section 35(3) provides that it remains the duty of directors to observe any limitation on their powers flowing from the company's memorandum of association. If the company ratifies an *ultra vires* transaction such a vote does not affect any liability of the directors for breach of duty. The relief of directors for breach of duty for entering into an *ultra vires* transaction must be agreed to by a separate special resolution.[45]

9–031   **Ultra vires and director's authority.** The authority of directors entering into contracts binding on a company is also constrained by the *ultra vires* doctrine since directors either individually or collectively could not possess any greater authority than their principal. If the doctrine of *ultra vires* is to be successfully abrogated it is also necessary to deal with this aspect of the problem. Section 35A(1) provides that in "favour of a person dealing with a company in good faith" the power of the board shall be deemed to be free of any limitation flowing from the company's constitution; the same applies to the power of the directors to authorise others to act on behalf of the company.[46] Critical to the operation of this provision are the concepts of "dealing with" and "good faith." Both are defined in section 35A(2). Section 35A(2)(*a*) provides that if a person deals with a company he is a party to any act or transaction to which the company is a party. This would cover not only commercial transactions but also transactions which are gratuitous.[47]

9–032   The definition of "good faith" is more tortuous and indirect. Section 35A(2)(b) provides that a person shall not be treated as acting in bad faith by reason of his knowing that the act or transaction is "beyond the powers of the directors under the company's constitution." This is not a definition of "good faith" but rather the singling out of a particular act as not constituting "bad faith." The reason for this is to be found in Article 9(2) of the First Directive. This provides that the "limits on the powers of the organs of the company, arising under the statutes or from a decision of the competent organs, may never be relied on as against third parties, even if they have been disclosed." This provision only deals with

---

[44] *Re Faure Electric Accumulator Co.* (1889) 40 Ch.D 141; *Ferguson v. Wilson* (1866) L.R. 2 Ch. 77; *Northern Counties Securities Ltd v. Jackson & Steeple Ltd* [1974] 1 W.L.R. 1133; *Bowstead and Reynolds on Agency* (16th ed., 1996), pp. 172–175.

[45] s.35(3).

[46] Note that this covers all limitations flowing from the company's constitution. Limitations on the directors' powers flowing from a resolution of any meeting or a class meeting of shareholders or any agreement of the members are covered: see s.35A(3). On this type of constitutional limitation see, *e.g. Cane v. Jones* [1980] 1 W.L.R. 1451.

[47] As, *e.g.* in *Parke v. Daily News Ltd* [1962] Ch. 927; *Simmonds v. Heffer* [1983] B.C.L.C. 298.

restrictions on the scope of an agent's or organ's[48] authority and not with the abuse of authority. Although the provision does not contain any "good faith" limitation it is clear from the debates on the implementation of the Directive that it was not designed to protect persons who were acting in bad faith,[49] for example, entering into a transaction which they knew the directors were entering into not in the interests of the company but in their own interests.[50] This position has been implicitly adopted by the ECJ.[51] Thus section 35A(2)(b) attempts to steer between actions which are in excess of authority as opposed to acts which constitute an abuse of authority—the dividing line between these situations will often be wafer thin in that a failure by directors to observe the limitations of a company's objects clause may often be indicative of a failure to act in the interests of the company. Good faith should not be interpreted as "reasonableness"[52] and failure to understand a company's objects should not be taken as evidence of bad faith,[53] but the more implausible the interpretation the easier it will be for the company to show an absence of good faith.[54] There is a presumption that a person has dealt with the company in good faith and the onus is on the company to prove the contrary.[55]

Limitations on director's authority and shareholder rights. As we have already seen when discussing corporate capacity,[56] a member of a company has the right to compel the company to observe the company's articles and memorandum of association. If this right were not curtailed then, similarly with the abrogation of the *ultra vires* doctrine, it would be possible for shareholders by asserting this right to enforce indirectly limitations on the powers of directors against third parties. To prevent this from happening, section 35A(4) provides that no proceedings by a member shall lie to enjoin a company from entering into a transaction in fulfilment of a legal obligation arising out of a previous act of the company and this would cover legal obligations arising because of section 35A.[57]   9–033

Constructive notice. As previously stated,[58] it was a principle of company law that a person dealing with a company was deemed to have constructive notice of the company's public documents and, while there was some uncertainty as to what exactly fell within the category of public document for this purpose,   9–034

---

[48] The concept of organ does not fit neatly into English company law but would at least include the board and the shareholders in general meeting, including it is submitted, a class meeting of shareholders.

[49] See Stein, *Harmonization of European Company Law* (1970), p.294.

[50] See, *e.g. Rolled Steel Products (Holdings) Ltd v. British Steel Corporation* [1986] Ch. 246.

[51] *Co-operative Rabobank 'Vecht en Plassengebied BA v. Minderhoud* (Case C–104/96) [1997] 4 All E.R. (D) 114.

[52] *Barclays Bank Ltd v. TOSG Trustfund* [1984] B.C.L.C. 1, 18 ("reasonableness is not a necessary ingredient of good faith" *per* Nourse J. at first instance); *cf.* Bills of Exchange Act 1882, s.90. Paget, *The Law of Banking* (11th ed.), p. 383. See also *International Sales and Agencies Ltd v. Marcus* [1982] 3 All E.R. 551, 559.

[53] For example, if the person dealing with the company reads but misinterprets the articles: see *Re Introductions Ltd* [1970] Ch. 199.

[54] See, *e.g.* the bank in *Re Introductions Ltd* [1970] Ch. 199.

[55] s.35A(2)(c).

[56] See §9–024.

[57] It remains a breach of duty for directors to enter into a transaction which is not authorised by the company's constitution: see s.35A(5).

[58] See §9–021.

it undoubtedly covered the company's memorandum and articles of association.[59] It is obviously a necessary corollary to the abrogation of the doctrine of *ultra vires* that this doctrine be also substantially repealed. This has been principally achieved by section 35B which provides that a person dealing with a company is not bound to enquire as to whether the transaction is permitted by the company's memorandum or whether there is any limitation on the power of the directors to enter into it.[60]

9–035　*Ultra vires* **contracts involving directors.** It was not felt proper that a director should benefit from section 35A in the case of contracts in which the director was personally involved. Where a director of the company or of it's holding company or any person connected with such a director is a party to a transaction which exceeds any limitation on the powers of the directors, such transaction is voidable.[61] Also, irrespective of whether it is avoided, the director will be obliged to account to the company for any profit or to indemnify it for any loss.[62] Where a person who is a party to a contract along with a director to whom this provision applies, that person may petition the court to have the contract affirmed, severed or set aside on such terms as the court thinks fit.[63]

9–036　**General commercial company.** The practice of drafting prolix objects clauses has meant that their very length is an impediment to understanding.[64] Coupled with this, there is an argument that the ease with which subsidiaries can be formed, and the modern conglomerate structure, has meant that objects clauses are in many situations something of an anomaly. To deal with this the 1989 Act introduced the "general commercial company."[65] Where the memorandum states that "the" object of the company is to carry on business as a general commercial company such company will have the object of carrying on any trade or business whatsoever and shall have all the powers that are necessary or conducive to the carrying on of such trade or business. There are two drawbacks with this company. First, on one interpretation the general commercial company is restricted to having the one object set out in section 3A and no other object may be joined.[66] This narrow interpretation requires the phrase "the object" to be interpreted as the "only" object. Such a restrictive interpretation, although achieving the purpose of restricting the verbosity of objects clauses, would greatly minimise the usefulness of this type of company form. For this reason, "the object" should be interpreted to mean "one of the" and not "the only." Secondly, the uncertainty of what constitutes something that is necessary and conducive to the carrying on of a company's trade or business (for example, the

---

[59] *Irvine v. Union Bank of Australia* (1877) 2 App. Cas. 399 PC, *Re London and New York Investment Corp.* [1895] 2 Ch. 860.

[60] Also of relevance is s.711A which abolishes any doctrine of deemed constructive notice (this section has not as yet been brought into effect).

[61] s.322A(1), (2). Bars to avoidance of the contract: s.322A(5). See also § 9–060.

[62] s.322A(3). *Quaere* if the liability under this subsection can be waived by the company. Other parties to the transaction can also be liable in the same way as directors but they are provided with a defence in s.322A(6).

[63] s.322A(7).

[64] See § 9–022.

[65] s.110(1) (the (1) is omitted from the HMSO version) inserts a new s.3A into the 1985 Act.

[66] If other objects were added and the registrar granted a certificate of incorporation then this would bring into operation s.13 of the 1985 Act (presumption that the company has been validly incorporated).

power to make political contributions or to execute group guarantees) may prove to be substantial disincentive to the use of this type of company. Also, of course, this provision is unsuitable for companies that are not carrying on a business.

Charitable companies. Section 111 of the 1989 Act introduced special provisions into the Charities Act 1960[67] as regards the application of the statutory reforms of *ultra vires* to charitable companies. These provisions are now to be found in sections 65–68 of the Charities Act 1993.[68] Sections 35 and 35A do not apply to the acts of a company which is a charity except in favour of a person (i) who gives full consideration in money or money's worth, (ii) does not know that the act is not permitted or that it is beyond the powers of the directors, or (iii) does not know that at the time the relevant act was done that the company was a charity.[69] There is added protection for persons who acquire an interest in or over property acquired from a charitable company.[70] **9–037**

Whether ultra vires contract enforceable by the company. Since the purpose of the *ultra vires* doctrine is to protect creditors and shareholders of the company it was argued, prior to the statutory reforms of the doctrine, that it should not be available to defeat an action brought by the company itself.[71] But in *Bell Houses Ltd v. City Wall Properties Ltd*[72] this argument was rejected by Mocatta J. on the ground that an *ultra vires* contract "is void and in the eyes of the law non-existent." The learned judge went on to hold that it was immaterial that the contract had been carried out by the company, though he intimated that in such a case the company might be able to sue on a *quantum meruit*[73] or for money had and received. The decision in this case was reversed by the Court of Appeal[74] but only on the ground that the contract in question was not *ultra vires*. The Court of Appeal expressed no opinion on the question decided by Mocatta J., though Salmon L.J. found the result "strange."[75] Section 35(1) of the 1985 Act makes it abundantly clear that a transaction beyond the company's capacity is valid both as regards the company's rights and it's obligations. **9–038**

Other applications of ultra vires principle. The *ultra vires* doctrine has sometimes been invoked to explain the invalidity of certain types of contracts entered into by companies, though in truth these appear to have little to do with the contractual capacity of companies. For example, prior to the Companies Act **9–039**

---

[67] ss.30–30C.

[68] Although the First Directive applies to all companies (Article 1), charitable companies can be excluded because Article 58 of the Treaty of the European Community, under which the Directive was enacted, excludes non-profit making companies from the right of establishment.

[69] s.65(1). Various business correspondence of the company must indicate that the company is a charity: s.68. The onus of showing that the person dealing with a company knew that it was a charitable company is on the person so asserting it; the same burden applies to showing that a person knew that the act was beyond the capacity of the company or that it was beyond the powers of the director: see s.65(3).

[70] s.65(2).

[71] Furmston (1961) 24 M.L.R. 715.

[72] [1966] 1 Q.B. 207.

[73] See *post*, §§ 30–062 *et seq.* (restitutionary remedies).

[74] [1966] 2 Q.B. 656.

[75] See also *Re K.L. Tractors Ltd* (1961) 106 C.L.R. 318; *Breckenridge Speedway Ltd v. R.* (1969) 9 D.L.R. (3d) 142. It may be that the courts will draw a distinction between executory and executed contracts and at least where the company has executed its part of the bargain it will be able to enforce the contract: *Triggs v. Staines U.D.C.* [1969] 1 Ch. 10, 20.

1981, a contract by a company to purchase its own shares was void,[76] and a contract by a company to provide financial assistance in connection with the purchase of its own shares was illegal and unenforceable.[77] Again, a contract entered into by a company will not be binding on it if its directors have not been acting bona fide in the interests of the company in making the contract and this is known to the other party to the contract.[78] But cases of this kind do not appear to involve questions of capacity and are explicable on other grounds[79] (e.g. illegality or agency) which do not properly fall within the scope of this chapter.

9–040 **Ratification of unauthorised act of officer.** If a contract is *intra vires* of the company but beyond the powers of the officer of the company by whom it was effected, it may be ratified by the company so as to become binding upon it.[80] So, assuming that the transaction is not valid under section 35A of the 1985 Act, where the directors merely exceed their authority the shareholders may ratify their act[81] or they may by acquiescence in the act of the directors be estopped from objecting to its validity.[82] The test of acquiescence in such cases is whether the shareholders had notice of the way in which the affairs of the company were being conducted and were content not to oppose those acts which they knew were being done.[83] So, where everything that is done by the directors is known to and acquiesced in by a sole beneficial shareholder,[84] or by all shareholders with a right to attend and vote at a general meeting,[85] the company will be bound by the directors' acts whatever the articles of association or memorandum may say unless those acts are illegal. Where a corporation actually takes the benefit of a contract made in an irregular manner, though not *ultra vires* of the company

---

[76] This was the old rule in *Trevor v. Whitworth* (1887) 12 App.Cas. 409. Companies may now purchase their own shares provided certain statutory pre-conditions are satisfied: see Companies Act 1985, Chapter VIII; see also *Precision Dippings Ltd v. Precision Dippings Marketing Ltd* [1986] Ch. 447 (the transaction in that case would have been more appropriately classified as illegal rather than *ultra vires*).

[77] *Victor Battery Co. v. Curry's Ltd* [1946] Ch. 242; *South Western Mineral Water Co. Ltd v. Ashmore* [1967] 1 W.L.R. 1110; *Armour Hick Northern Ltd v. Whitehouse* [1980] 1 W.L.R. 1520 interpreting the Companies Act 1948, s.54. On financial assistance by a company in the purchase of its own shares see now the Companies Act 1985, Chapter VI; *Brady v. Brady* [1989] A.C. 755.

[78] For a recent example, see *Re R.W. Roith Ltd* [1967] 1 W.L.R. 432. Where the contract is with a third party who has no notice of the director's want of good faith, the contract will be enforceable: *Rolled Steel Products (Holdings) Ltd v. British Steel Corp.* [1986] Ch. 246.

[79] See Gower, *Principles of Modern Company Law* (6th ed., 1997), p. 205; see also *Charterbridge Corpn. Ltd v. Lloyds Bank* [1970] Ch. 62; *Heald v. O'Connor* [1971] 1 W.L.R. 497.

[80] *Reuter v. Electric Telegraph Co.* (1856) 6 E. & B. 341, 348; *Allard v. Bourne* (1863) 15 C.B.(N.S.) 468; *Rolled Steel Products (Holdings) Ltd v. British Steel Corporation* [1986] Ch. 246 clearly distinguishes the issues of corporate capacity and director's duties.

[81] *Irvine v. Union Bank of Australia* (1877) 2 App.Cas. 366; *Grant v. United Kingdom Switchback Ry.* (1888) 40 Ch.D. 135; *Boschoek Proprietory Co. Ltd v. Fuke* [1906] 1 Ch. 148. But an attempt to confer authority on directors with respect to future transactions would be treated as an attempt to alter the articles of association for which a special resolution would be necessary: *Grant v. U.K. Switchbank Ry.* (1888) 40 Ch.D. 135.

[82] *Re Magdalena Steam Navigation Co.* (1860) Johns. 690.

[83] *Evans v. Smallcombe* (1868) L.R. 3 H.L. 249, 256; and see *Phosphate of Lime Co. Ltd v. Green* (1871) L.R. 7 C.P. 43; *London Financial Association v. Kelk* (1884) 26 Ch.D. 107; *Re Bailey Hay & Co. Ltd* [1971] 1 W.L.R. 1357.

[84] *Personal Service Laundry Ltd v. National Bank Ltd* [1964] I.R. 49; *Walton v. Bank of Nova Scotia* (1965) 52 D.L.R. (2d) 506.

[85] *Re Duomatic Ltd* [1969] 2 Ch. 365.

itself, the adoption will amount to ratification.[86] Where the contract is *ultra vires* then despite section 35 it is strongly arguable that this doctrine does not apply in so far as it could be taken to exonerate the directors for breach of duty.[87] This is because of the requirement in section 35(3), which requires any ratification of the act of the directors entering into a transaction which is beyond the capacity of the company to be given by special resolution.[88] However, given the scope of section 35(1), this is not a matter which could ever foreseeably cause prejudice to a third party dealing with a company in a transaction which is beyond the company's capacity. Also, it would appear that the agreement of all the shareholders although evidenced informally will bind the company as though it were a resolution of a properly summoned shareholders' meeting so that no question of ratification or adoption will arise.[89]

The liability of directors for ultra vires acts. When the doctrine of *ultra*   **9–041**
vires was fully operable, there was authority for the proposition that directors who entered into *ultra vires* contracts on behalf of a company might become liable to the person with whom they contract for breach of warranty of authority. They were liable if what was involved amounted to a misrepresentation of fact and not one of law. Thus directors of a company incorporated by special act of parliament were held not to be liable for breach of warranty of authority where they entered into a contract which exceeded the company's capacity as this was a misrepresentation of law and not of fact.[90] Where what was involved constituted a misrepresentation of fact, for example, that the company could issue debenture stock after its power to do so had been exhausted, then directors were liable for breach of warranty of authority.[91] However, in the light of section 35(1) of the 1985 Act it is difficult to see when the doctrine of breach of warranty of authority could ever apply. Transactions beyond the capacity of the company will normally be validated by that provision and therefore there will be no basis for invoking the doctrine of breach of warranty of authority since the person dealing with the company will be able to enforce the transaction against the company.

Royal British Bank v. Turquand. Where an officer of a company (in partic-   **9–042**
ular a director) enters into a transaction which is beyond his authority but within the company's capacity and the company declines to ratify it, the difficult question then arises whether or not the company is bound. The company may be bound either by the ordinary rules of agency or by virtue of the rule in *Royal British Bank v. Turquand*.[92] The latter has been variously described as part of the

---

[86] *Smith v. Hull Glass Co.* (1852) 11 C.B. 897; *Re Bonelli's Telegraph Co., Collie's Claim* (1871) L.R. 12 Eq. 246, 259.
[87] On when the ratification of an act by the shareholders can be taken to exonerate the directors see *Re D'Jan of London Ltd* [1993] B.C.C. 646.
[88] The informal consents of all the shareholders can be treated as a special resolution: see *Cane v. Jones* [1980] 1 W.L.R. 1451.
[89] *Cane v. Jones, supra*; *Multinational Gas and Petrochemical Co. v. Multinational Gas and Petrochemical Services Ltd* [1983] Ch. 258. This is also implicit from s.35A(3)(b).
[90] *Beattie v. Lord Ebury* (1872) L.R. 7 Ch.App. 777. *cf. Kleinwort Benson Ltd v. Lincoln City Council* [1998] 3 W.L.R. 1095.
[91] *Firbank's Executors v. Humphreys* (1886) 18 Q.B.D. 54 (in this case the directors acted innocently in that they failed to appreciate that they were making an over-issue of debenture stock).
[92] (1856) 6 E. & B. 327. See generally, Campbell, 75 L.Q.R. 469, 76 L.Q.R. 115 (1959–60).

law of agency,[93] and as distinct from it,[94] but more recently authority has strongly favoured the first line of reasoning.[95] But it is generally agreed that this branch of the law presents exceptional difficulties although many of these have been reduced by section 36A of the 1985 Act. The general rule is that a stranger is entitled to assume that matters of internal management have been regularly carried out and that the formalities (if any) necessary to enable the company's officers to exercise their powers have been duly performed. But one who has notice that an agent of a company is contracting in excess of his authority cannot enforce that contract against the company.[96] Formerly notice of the memorandum and articles of association was imputed to every person having dealings with the company,[97] but this rule is effectively abrogated by section 35B of the 1985 Act. The result of this seems to be that, whatever its original significance, the rule in *Turquand's* case now falls to be treated in most cases as part of the ordinary law of agency. Previous authorities holding that a third party could not rely on the apparent authority of the directors because of some provision, unknown to him, in the articles of association, must now be treated as obsolete.[98] The section has thus made no longer applicable cases holding (for example) that where directors have, by the articles, a power to borrow only up to a certain amount, any loan beyond that amount will be beyond the authority of the directors and therefore not binding on the company.[99]

9-043   The rule in *Turquand's* case,[1] however, does not apply where the circumstances are such as to put the third party on inquiry, as for example, where a bank negligently paid the cheques of a company signed by only one director,[2] or where the company's cheques were paid into a director's private account[3]; these decisions appear to be unaffected by section 35B of the Companies Act 1985 because they do not depend on any limitations on the powers of the directors to bind the company arising from the memorandum or articles of association.[4] Another restriction on the operation of the rule at common law was that it could not apply to protect a third party who contracted with the company if, in some

---

[93] *Gower's Principles of Modern Company Law* (6th ed., 1996), Chap. 10.

[94] Pennington, *Company Law* (7th ed., 1995), p. 138.

[95] *Freeman & Lockyer v. Buckhurst Park Properties Mangal Ltd* [1964] 2 Q.B. 480; Nock (1966) Conv.(N.S.) 123, 163. *cf. Northside Developments Pty. Ltd v. Registrar-General* (1990) 64 A.L.J.R. 427.

[96] *Rolled Steel Products (Holdings) Ltd v. British Steel Corporation* [1986] Ch. 246, 283 (*per* Slade L.J.), 304 (*per* Browne-Wilkinson L.J.)

[97] See *Fountaine v. Carmarthen Ry.* (1868) L.R. 5 Eq. 316; *Crampton v. Varnay Ry.* (1872) L.R. 7 Ch.App. 562, 568; *Mahony v. East Holyford Mining Co.* (1875) L.R. 7 H.L. 869, 893; *County of Gloucester Bank v. Rudry Merthyr Steam & House Coal Colliery Co.* [1895] 1 Ch. 629.

[98] If the articles restrict the authority of a company's secretary, s.35B would also apply to this. On the secretary's usual authority see *Panorama Developments (Guildford) Ltd v. Fidelis Furnishing Fabrics Ltd* [1971] 2 Q.B. 711.

[99] *Irvine v. Union Bank of Australia* (1877) 2 App.Cas. 366. A case which arguably was decided on a wrong application of the *Turquand* rule. In that case, Sir Barnes Pollock considered that the resolution authorising the director to borrow above the stipulated limit would have had to be registered under the Companies Act 1862, s.53, so that a person dealing with the company would have had notice of it. This in fact was not so, and the ordinary resolution increasing the directors' borrowing powers did not have to be registered.

[1] (1856) 6 E. & B. 327.

[2] *B. Liggett (Liverpool) Ltd v. Barclays Ltd* [1928] 1 K.B. 48; *cf. South London Greyhound Racecourses Ltd v. Wake* [1931] 1 Ch. 496; *Houghton & Co. v. Nothard, Lowe & Wills* [1927] 1 K.B. 246, affd. [1928] A.C. 1.

[3] *A.L. Underwood Ltd v. Bank of Liverpool & Martins* [1924] 1 K.B. 775.

[4] *International Sales and Agencies Ltd v. Marcus* [1982] 3 All E.R. 551.

different capacity, *e.g.* as a director, he also acted on behalf of the company in making the contract.[5] These cases would now need to be interpreted in the light of section 322A of the 1985 Act which applies to a contract where the parties include a "director" irrespective of the capacity in which he enters into it.[6]

The rule cannot itself confer apparent authority. The rule in *Turquand's* **9–044** case was often treated as an application of estoppel and it followed that an outsider who had not in fact examined the company's public documents could not assert the existence of an apparent authority merely because of some provision in those documents. This aspect of the rule is unaffected by sections 35 to 35B of the 1985 Act. On the other hand, this in no way prevents an outsider from setting up an apparent authority on ordinary principles of agency where the company holds a person out as having authority otherwise than by provisions in its articles. Thus if the articles of a company provide that the powers, or certain of the powers, of the board of directors may be delegated to a managing director, and one director acts as a managing director to the knowledge of the board, then even though he has never been formally appointed as such, an outsider is entitled to assume that the director has in fact the authority which a managing director would normally have.[7] Where, however, the director enters into some transaction which would not normally be within the powers of a managing director and there is no holding out so as to make section 35A of the 1985 Act applicable, it may be that an outsider cannot rely on any apparent authority unless he has examined the articles, and the articles themselves show that a properly appointed managing director would have such authority.[8]

In *Freeman and Lockyer v. Buckhurst Park Properties (Mangal) Ltd*,[9] where **9–045** the authorities on this difficult question were reviewed by the Court of Appeal,

---

[5] *Morris v. Kanssen* [1946] A.C. 459; *cf. Hely-Hutchinson v. Brayhead Ltd* [1968] 1 Q.B. 549, affd. on different grounds, *ibid.* at 573; see also *John v. Rees* [1970] Ch. 345.

[6] See § 9–035.

[7] *Freeman and Lockyer v. Buckhurst Park Properties (Mangal) Ltd* [1964] 2 Q.B. 480. All the earlier authorities must now be read in the light of this case, see, *e.g. Biggerstaff v. Rowatt's Wharf Ltd* [1896] 2 Ch. 93; *Dey v. Pullinger Engineering Co.* [1921] 1 K.B. 77; *Houghton & Co. v. Nothard, Lowe & Wills Ltd* [1927] 1 K.B. 246; *Kreditbank Cassel GmbH v. Schenkers Ltd* [1927] 1 K.B. 826; *British Thomson-Houston Co. Ltd v. Federated European Bank Ltd* [1932] 2 K.B. 176; *South London Greyhound Racecourses Ltd v. Wake* [1931] 1 Ch. 496; *Rama Corporation v. Proved Tin & General Investments Ltd* [1952] 2 Q.B. 147; *British Bank of the Middle East v. Sun Life Assurance Co. of Canada (U.K.) Ltd* [1983] 2 Lloyd's Rep. 9; *Rhoddian River Shipping Co. SA v. Halla Maritime Corp.* [1984] 1 Lloyd's Rep. 373. See also Vol. II, § 32–058.

[8] In the *Freeman and Lockyer* case this was held to be the correct explanation of the *Houghton* case, *supra*, the *Schenkers* case, *supra*, and the *Rama* case, *supra*. As a matter of principle it is difficult to see how mere knowledge of the articles could operate to confer an apparent authority on a director: see *Houghton & Co. v. Nothard Lowe & Wills Ltd* [1927] 1 K.B. 246, 266.

[9] *Supra.* See also *Hely-Hutchinson v. Brayhead Ltd, supra.* As to the authority of: (1) a company's secretary, see *Panorama Develoments (Guildford) Ltd v. Fidelis Furnishing Fabrics Ltd* [1971] 2 Q.B. 711; (2) the individual director, see Leigh, *The Criminal Liability of Companies in English Law* (1969), pp. 94–95. There is controversy as to whether being chairman of the board confers authority on the holder of this position greater than that of the ordinary director. Although there is some authority that it does (*British Thomson-Houston Co. Ltd v. Federated European Bank* [1932] 2 K.B. 176; *Clay Hill Brick Co. Ltd v. Rawlings* [1938] 4 All E.R. 100), it is difficult to appreciate why being appointed chairman should confer this additional authority; see generally *Gower's Principles of Modern Company Law* (6th ed., 1996), pp. 225–226. The implementation of the Cadbury Report (*The Financial Aspects of Corporate Governance*) for listed companies may in the long run have implications for the authority of a board chairman. See now, *The Combined Code—Principles of Corporate Governance Code of Best Practice (The Stock Exchange Listing Rules).*

Diplock L.J. stated the following four conditions which must be satisfied to entitle a contractor to enforce a contract entered into on behalf of a company by an agent without actual authority.

"It must be shown: (1) that a representation that the agent had authority to enter on behalf of the company into a contract of the kind sought to be enforced was made to the contractor; (2) that such representation was made by a person or persons who had 'actual' authority[10] to manage the business of the company either generally or in respect of those matters to which the contract relates; (3) that he (the contractor) was induced by such representation to enter into the contract, that is, that he in fact relied on it; and (4) that under its memorandum or articles of association the company was not deprived of the capacity either to enter into a contract of the kind sought to be enforced or to delegate authority to enter into a contract of that kind to the agent."[11]

It is important to note how these principles have been affected by sections 35–35B of the 1985 Act. Principle (4) has been abrogated by the combined effect of sections 35(1), 35A(1) and 35B. More importantly, principle (2) has also been virtually abrogated by section 35A since where that section applies the company will be bound by a transaction outside the authority of the directors even though no holding out was made by a person with actual authority to make one.

9–046　　**Section 285 of the Companies Act 1985.** In some circumstances section 285 of the Companies Act 1985 may also apply. That section provides that "the acts of a director or manager shall be valid notwithstanding any defect that may afterwards be discovered in his appointment or qualification."[12] As stated in Buckley,[13] "Endangering accuracy for the sake of brevity, it may be said that the effect of this section is that, as between the company and persons having no notice to the contrary, directors, etc., *de facto* are as good as directors, etc., *de iure.*" In some ways the section is wider than the rule in *Turquand's* case[14] in that it may be relied upon not only by outsiders, but also by directors of the company and by the company itself; on the other hand, unlike the rule in *Turquand's* case,

---

[10] There was, however, a difference of opinion in the Court of Appeal on this point. Pearson L.J. took the view that a director acting as the *alter ego* of a company may hold *himself* out *qua* agent as having the necessary authority: [1964] 2 Q.B. 480, 499, citing Greer L.J. in the *British Thomson-Houston* case [1932] 2 K.B. 176, 182, although the judgment of Greer L.J. provides scant support for this proposition. The *British Thomson-Houston* case was cited with approval by Browne-Wilkinson L.J. in *Egyptian International Foreign Trading Co. v. Soplex Wholesale Supplies Ltd and P.S. Refson & Co. Ltd* [1985] 2 Lloyd's Rep 36, 43, but Kerr L.J. in the latter case, "as at present advised," considered that an agent's assurance as to his authority could not vest him with wider authority than he already possessed (at p.46). For dicta which on the whole support Kerr L.J. see *Armagas Ltd v. Mundogas SA* [1985] 1 Lloyd's Rep. 1, 37 and 67–68, [1986] A.C. 717, 733–735, 749. See also Diplock L.J. in *Freeman*: a "contractor cannot rely on the agent's own representation as to his actual authority" (at 505). These somewhat conflicting dicta were reconciled in *First Energy (U.K.) Ltd v. Hungarian International Bank Ltd* [1993] B.C.L.C. 1409 on the grounds that while an agent, without actual authority or apparent authority, cannot enlarge his appearance of authority by his own representation, he may nevertheless have apparent authority to communicate decisions of the company, for example, that the board of directors have approved of a particular transaction.

[11] [1964] 2 Q.B. 480, 504–505.

[12] s.285 now expressly overrides s.292(2). See also Companies (Table A–F) Regulations 1985 (S.I. 1985 No. 805), reg. 92.

[13] *The Companies Acts* (14th ed.), p. 432.

[14] (1856) 6 E. & B. 327.

section 285 will not apply unless there has been an "appointment," albeit a defective appointment.[15] Neither the rule nor the section can be called in aid by a third party who knew or should have known of the defect.[16]

Forgeries. It has been said that the rule in *Turquand's* case[17] does not apply **9–047** where the document upon which it is sought to make the company responsible is a forgery.[18] But the three cases in which this question has arisen can all be explained on the ground either that the forged document was not put forward as genuine by an official acting within his actual or apparent authority, or that the outsider was put on inquiry.[19] This was the view taken by the High Court of Australia in *Northside Developments Pty. Ltd v. Registrar-General*[20] where the court stated that a company would be bound by a "forgery" where it was "estopped from denying the authority of the persons affixing the genuine seal and writing the genuine signature to it."[21] It is submitted therefore that where a document is made by an officer of a company who has apparent authority to do so, the rule can be applied and the company may be bound by the document even though the officer forged it for some purpose of his own.

Registration of charges. [22] A contract entered into by a company which **9–048** involves a charge on its assets may require registration with the Registrar of Companies under sections 395 and 396 of the Companies Act 1985. The most important types of charge covered by this section are charges to secure an issue of debentures; charges created by an instrument which, if executed by an individual, would require registration as a bill of sale; charges on land or any interest therein; charges on book debts; and floating charges on the undertaking or property of the company. Prescribed particulars of a charge covered by section 395 must be delivered to the Registrar within 21 days after its creation. Failure to deliver particulars of a charge[23] renders the charge void against a liquidator

---

[15] *Morris v. Kanssen* [1946] A.C. 459, 471.

[16] *Kanssen v. Rialto (West End) Ltd* [1944] Ch. 346; affd. *sub nom. Morris v. Kanssen, supra.*

[17] See n. 14, *ante.*

[18] *Ruben v. Great Fingall Consolidated Co.* [1906] A.C. 439, 443; *Kreditbank Cassel GmbH v. Schenkers Ltd* [1927] 1 K.B. 826, 844; *South London Greyhound Racecourses Ltd v. Wake* [1931] 1 Ch. 496.

[19] See *Gower's Principles of Modern Company Law* (6th ed., 1996), p. 228. Campbell, (1960) 76 L.Q.R. 115, 130 *et seq.*

[20] (1990) 64 A.L.J.R. 427.

[21] *ibid.* at 443. See also *Lonsdale Nominee Pty. Ltd v. Southern Cross Airlines Ltd* (1993) 10 A.C.S.R. 739. Where there is a forgery in the strict sense of the word, *i.e.* the name of a person is falsely appended to a document, then this would obviously not be binding on the company.

[22] For details, see Buckley, *The Companies Acts* (14th ed.), pp. 238 *et seq.*; Gough, *Company Charges* (2nd ed., 1998). As to the conclusiveness of the Registrar's certificate of registration, see Companies Act 1985, s.401(2)(b); [1971] Ch. 442; *R. v. Registrar of Companies, ex p. Esal Commodities Ltd* [1986] Q.B. 1114.

[23] It is important to note that it is delivery of the particulars of the charge rather than registration which saves it from invalidity; see *N.V. Slavenburg's Bank v. Intercontinental Natural Resources Ltd* [1980] 1 W.L.R. 1076. The Companies Act 1989 (Pt. IV) makes extensive modifications to the provisions relating to the registration of charges but have not as yet been brought into effect. They have been subjected to criticism and the DTI have conducted consultations to determine whether or not they should be brought into effect. The outcome is that Part XII will not be brought into effect in its present form: see *Company Law Review: Proposals for Reform of Part XII of the Companies Act 1985* (DTI, A Consultative Document, Nov. 1994).

and any creditor of the company, and also renders any debt secured by the charge immediately repayable. The court has power under section 404 of the Companies Act 1985 to extend the time for registration in various circumstances.

9–049   **Effect of winding up on company's contracts.** A compulsory winding up automatically brings the powers of a director to an end[24] and publication of the winding up order discharges all persons employed by the company, giving them a right to damages for wrongful dismissal.[25] The liquidator may waive the dismissal brought about by publication of the winding up order, and where he does so the old contract of employment continues.[26] Where the winding up is voluntary the powers of the directors likewise cease, except that the company in general meeting or the liquidator may sanction their continuance[27]; the passing of a resolution for voluntary winding up may, but does not necessarily, terminate general contracts of employment with the company so as to give the company's employees a right to damages for wrongful dismissal.[28] It may do so where the circumstances are such that the employee knows that the company cannot continue to fulfil its obligations,[29] or where, on the facts, the company has ceased to carry on business and there is no implied term in the contract of employment that the contract is subject to the continuance of business by the company.[30] Where an order is made by the court under section 427 of the Companies Act 1985 for the amalgamation of two companies, a contract of employment between a worker and the transferor company does not automatically become a contract of employment between the worker and the transferee company.[31]

9–050   **Winding up not a repudiation.** On the other hand, the winding up of a company is not by itself a repudiation of the contractual obligations of the company unless the personality of the company goes to the root of the contract,[32]

---

[24] *Re Oriental Inland Steam Co.* (1874) 9 Ch.App. 557, 560; *Fowler v. Broad's Patent Night Light Co.* [1893] 1 Ch. 724; *Gosling v. Gaskell* [1897] A.C. 575, 587; *Measures Brothers v. Measures* [1910] 2 Ch. 248, 256. In the case of a voluntary winding up, see Insolvency Act 1986, ss.91(2), 103. On whether or not the office of director ceases, see McPherson, *The Law of Company Liquidation* (3rd ed., 1987), pp. 171–172.

[25] *Re General Rolling Stock Co., Chapman's Case* (1866) L.R. 1 Eq. 346; *Ex p. Maclure* (1870) L.R. 5 Ch. 737; *Re R.S. Newman Ltd* [1916] 2 Ch. 309; *Re Oriental Bank Corporation, MacDowall's Case* (1886) 32 Ch.D. 366. An employee's right to damages is not affected by the fact that he may, as a shareholder, have supported the resolution for voluntary winding up: *Fowler v. Commercial Timber Co.* [1930] 2 K.B. 1. See Graham (1952) 15 M.L.R. 48; Freedland, *The Contract of Employment* (1975), pp. 332–347.

[26] *Re English Joint Stock Bank, ex p. Harding* (1867) 3 Eq. 341.

[27] Insolvency Act 1986, ss.91(2), 103.

[28] *Midland Counties District Bank Ltd v. Attwood* [1905] 1 Ch. 357; *Fox Bros. (Clothes) Ltd v. Bryant* [1979] I.C.R. 64; Graham (1952) 15 M.L.R. 48; McPherson *op. cit.* at p. 175.

[29] *Reigate v. Union Manufacturing Co. (Ramsbottom) Ltd* [1918] 1 K.B. 592.

[30] *Reigate v. Union Manufacturing Co. (Ramsbottom) Ltd, ibid.; Fowler v. Commercial Timber Co.* [1930] 2 K.B. 1, 6.

[31] *Nokes v. Doncaster Amalgamated Collieries Ltd* [1940] A.C. 1014. See now the Transfer of Undertakings (Protection of Employment) Regulations 1981 (S.I. 1981 No. 1794) and *cf.* Employment Protection (Consolidation) Act 1978, Sched. 13, para. 17 which operates for purposes of that Act and the Redundancy Payments Act 1965.

[32] *British Waggon Co. v. Lea* (1880) 5 Q.B.D. 149; *cf. Tolhurst v. Associated Portland Cement Manufacturers Ltd* [1903] A.C. 414, commented on in *Nokes v. Doncaster Amalgamated Collieries Ltd, supra,* at 1019–1020; and see §§ 20–052—20–055.

though there are statutory provisions for the disclaimer of leases or other onerous or unprofitable contracts.[33] The liquidator has certain statutory powers to deal with the company's property some of which can only be exercised with the sanction of the court, the liquidation committee, or, in the case of a members' voluntary winding up, the members.[34] Where a liquidator, appointed by the court, performs a contract of the company without disclaimer or where he purports to make a new contract on its behalf, he acts as agent for the company[35] and there is no presumption that he does so in a personal capacity.[36]

Dispositions of property in winding up. In a winding up by the court any **9–051** disposition of the property of the company, including things in action, and any transfer of shares, or alteration in the status of members of the company, made after the commencement of the winding up, is, unless the court otherwise orders, void.[37] The court has a wide discretion in this respect which will be exercised having regard to what is fair and just in all the circumstances, particular attention being paid to the question of good faith and the principle that a company's free assets should be distributed *pro rata* among the company's unsecured creditors.[38] The court will readily validate transactions entered into bona fide in the course of trade and completed before the date of the winding-up order[39]; but the court will not validate the payment of a debt by the company to a debtor who has notice of the presentation of a winding-up petition[40] unless it is a "necessary part of a transaction which as a whole is beneficial to the general body of unsecured creditors."[41] The court will also normally validate the sale of an asset at its full market value as this does not dissipate the company's assets.[42] Further, the court can only validate a disposition of property; a contract for the sale of goods by a

---

[33] See Insolvency Act 1986, s.178. This is a change from the old law: see *Re Hans Place Ltd* [1993] B.C.L.C. 768; *Re Morrish* (1882) 22 Ch.D. 410; *Re A.B.C. Coupler and Engineering Co. Ltd (No. 3)* [1970] 1 W.L.R. 702; *Warnford Investments Ltd v. Duckworth* [1979] Ch. 127; *Re A.E. Realisations (1986) Ltd* [1987] B.C.L.C. 486. Such disclaimer does not release a guarantor of the rents from his guarantee: *Hindcastle Ltd v. Barbara Attenborough Associates Ltd* [1997] A.C. 70. See also *Re Park Air Services Plc* [1999] 2 W.L.R. 396.

[34] Insolvency Act 1986, ss.165–167; see *Bateman v. Ball* (1887) 56 L.J.Q.B. 291; *Hire Purchase Furnishing Co. v. Richens* (1887) 20 Q.B.D. 387.

[35] *Re Anglo-Moravian Co.* (1875) 1 Ch.D. 130.

[36] *Stead Hazel & Co. v. Cooper* [1933] 1 K.B. 840. Representative language was not used in this case although it is always prudent for a liquidator to contract clearly in a representative capacity.

[37] Insolvency Act 1986, s.127; *Mond v. Hammond Suddards* [1996] 2 B.C.L.C. 470.

[38] *Re Steane's (Bournemouth) Ltd* [1950] 1 All E.R. 21; *Re T.W. Construction Ltd* [1954] 1 W.L.R. 540; *Re Clifton Place Garage Ltd* [1970] Ch. 477; *Re Operator Control Cabs Ltd* [1970] 3 All E.R. 657n.; *Re Argentum Reductions (U.K.)* [1975] 1 W.L.R. 186; *Re Gray's Inn Construction Co. Ltd* [1890] 1 W.L.R. 711; *Re Tramway Building and Construction Co. Ltd* [1987] B.C.L.C. 632; *Re Webb Electric Ltd* [1988] B.C.L.C. 382; *Denney v. John Hudson & Co. Ltd* [1992] B.C.L.C. 901.

[39] *Re Wiltshire Iron Co.* (1868) L.R. 3 Ch.App. 443; *Re Park Ward & Co.* [1926] Ch. 828; *Re French's (Wine Bar) Ltd* [1987] B.C.L.C. 437.

[40] *Re Civil Service & General Store Ltd* (1887) 57 L.J.Ch. 119; *cf. Re T.W. Construction Ltd* [1954] 1 W.L.R. 540.

[41] *Re Gray's Inn Construction Co. Ltd* [1980] 1 W.L.R. 711, 719. See also *Denney v. John Hudson & Co. Ltd* [1992] B.C.L.C. 901.

[42] *ibid.* In the case of a solvent company, the court will validate a disposition under s.127 provided that an intelligent and honest board of directors could reasonably take the view that the arrangements were in the best interests of the company. Only where bad faith or other exceptional circumstances are proved will the court decline to act under s.127; *Re Burton and Deakin Ltd* [1977] 1 W.L.R. 390.

company is not a disposition of property which can be validated by the court unless the property in the goods has passed to the purchaser.[43]

9–052 **Appointment of a receiver or manager.**[44] The appointment of a receiver and manager by the court operates to discharge the company's employees.[45] But the appointment of a receiver and manager out of court by debenture holders, so that he becomes an agent of the company, does not normally operate to discharge the company's employees.[46] At common law such an appointment will, however, operate to discharge the company's employees if the appointment is accompanied by a sale of the company's business,[47] or if the appointment is accompanied by or followed by a new agreement with the company's employees,[48] and probably only if the new contract is inconsistent with the old,[49] or if the company's employees occupy positions which would be inconsistent with the position of the receiver.[50] Section 44(1)(a) of the Insolvency Act 1986 makes an administrative receiver of the assets of a company the company's agent, a device that is primarily designed to avoid the security holder who appointed him from being treated as a mortgagee in possession. An administrative receiver is also made personally liable on any contract entered into by him.[51] Such liability can be excluded and almost invariably is. The 1986 Act also makes an administrative receiver personally liable "on any contract of employment adopted by him in carrying out" his functions, but that he is not to be "taken to have adopted a contract of employment by anything done or omitted to be done within 14 days after his appointment."[52] Initially, there was considerable uncertainty as to what this section means and, in particular, whether mere acquiescence in the continuation of contracts of employment can constitute an adoption.[53]

9–053 However, in *Powdrill v. Watson*[54] the House of Lords held that a receiver will be taken to have adopted a contract of employment where he treats the continued contract as giving rise to a separate liability in the receivership. The House also decided that the receiver could not reject some of the terms of the contract but

---

[43] *Re Oriental Bank Corporation, ex p. Guillemin* (1883) 28 Ch.D. 634; *Re Wiltshire Iron Co., supra.*

[44] For the definition of receiver see Insolvency Act 1986, s.29. In particular note the definition of administrative receiver a term first introduced by the Insolvency Act 1986: see also s.251 of the 1986 Act.

[45] *Reid v. Explosives Co.* (1887) 19 Q.B.D. 264 (note, however, the reservations of Fry L.J.); *Re Mack Trucks (Britain) Ltd* [1967] 1 W.L.R. 780; *Griffiths v. Secretary of State for Social Services* [1974] Q.B. 468. This principle has not been followed in Australia: see *Spidad Holding v. Popovic* (1995) 19 A.C.S.R. 108.

[46] *Griffiths v. Secretary of State for Social Services, supra*; *Deaway Trading Ltd v. Calverley* [1973] I.C.R. 546.

[47] *Re Foster Clark Ltd's Indenture Trusts* [1966] 1 W.L.R. 125. The position has now been substantially modified by the Transfer of Undertakings (Protection of Employment) Regulations 1981 (S.I. 1981 No. 1794). See Vol. II, §§ 39–156 *et seq.*

[48] *Re Mack Trucks (Britain) Ltd, supra.*

[49] *Griffiths v. Secretary of State for Social Services* [1974] Q.B. 468, 486.

[50] *Griffiths v. Secretary of State for Social Services, ibid.*; see Freedland, *The Contract of Employment* (1975), p. 339.

[51] s.44(1)(b). On the nature of the administrative receiver's liability see *Re Atlantic Computer Systems plc (No. 1)* [1992] Ch. 505, 526.

[52] s.44(1)(b), (2). This was designed to overcome the decision in *Nicoll v. Cutts* [1985] B.C.L.C. 322.

[53] Stewart, *Administrative Receivers and Administrators*, pp. 96–99.

[54] [1995] 2 A.C. 394.

accept others, but that his liability could be limited to liabilities arising during the period when he was in office.[55]

The appointment of a receiver does not amount to a repudiation of the trading **9–054** contracts of the company, except in special circumstances.[56] It is often claimed that the receiver is in a better position than the company in that he need not observe existing contracts and, in addition, such contracts cannot be specifically enforced against him.[57] To permit contracts to be enforced against the company, or to require the receiver to comply with them would reverse the order of priorities in that it would oblige the receiver to prefer the interests of unsecured creditors over the interests of the security holder that appointed him. It is for this reason that the receiver is in a better position than the company as regards the obligation to observe existing contracts.[58] Where a receiver and manager, appointed by the court, orders goods for the purpose of the business of the company, the inference is that he pledges his personal credit for the goods, looking for indemnity to the assets of the company; he is therefore not necessarily the agent of the company[59] though he may be in particular circumstances.[60] The same is true of receivers appointed out of court.[61] The authority of a receiver is terminated by the winding up of the company whether it is voluntary[62] or by the court.[63] Although the authority of a receiver to act on behalf of the company is prima facie terminated by a winding-up order, this does not mean that a receiver appointed by debenture holders can no longer sell or convey property charged to the debenture holders, in respect of which a power of sale exists.[64] He can still exercise the *in rem* rights that his appointor has against the company's property.

Receivers and the tort of inducing a breach of contract. The question has **9–055** arisen in a number of cases as to whether a receiver who does not observe a contract which the company has entered into before his appointment can be liable for the tort of inducing a breach of contract.[65] It has been held (not without

---

[55] In the lower courts it was held that the receiver who adopted the contract would be liable for all outstanding liabilities: see [1995] A.C. 394 where the judgment of Lightman J. is reported. Because of the threat of liability this resulted in receivers, and more importantly administrators who are similarly liable under s.19 of the 1986 Act, in terminating contracts of employment. S.44 and s.19 have been modified by the Insolvency Act 1994 so that receivers and administrators will only be liable for services on a contract of employment rendered during the administration or receivership after the adoption of the contract of employment (referred to as "qualifying liabilities").

[56] *Airlines Airspaces Ltd v. Handley Page Ltd* [1970] Ch. 193. *cf. Rother Iron Works Ltd v. Canterbury Precision Engineers* [1974] Q.B. 1; *George Barker (Transport) Ltd v. Eynon* [1974] 1 W.L.R. 462.

[57] See, however, *Ash & Newman Ltd v. Creative Devices Research Ltd* [1991] B.C.L.C. 403 where an injunction was granted to protect a pre-emption right of the plaintiff but the facts were exceptional in that the injunction did not prejudice the interests of the security holder.

[58] *Hill (Edwin) & Partners v. First National Finance Corporation plc* [1989] B.C.L.C. 89; *Astor Chemicals Ltd v. Synthetic Technology Ltd* [1990] B.C.L.C. 1, 11.

[59] *Burt, Boulton & Hayward v. Bull* [1895] 1 Q.B. 276, 279. On the right of a court appointed receiver to be remunerated see *Mellor v. Mellor* [1993] B.C.L.C. 30.

[60] *Lawson v. Hosemaster Co. Ltd* [1966] 1 W.L.R. 1300.

[61] Insolvency Act 1986, s.44(1)(b).

[62] *Thomas v. Todd* [1926] 2 K.B. 571.

[63] *Gosling v. Gaskell* [1897] A.C. 575; *Re S. Brown & Co. etc., Ltd* [1940] Ch. 961; see also *Bacal Contracting Ltd v. Modern Engineering (Bristol) Ltd* [1980] 2 All E.R. 655, 658.

[64] *Sowman v. David Samuel Trust Ltd* [1978] 1 W.L.R. 22.

[65] The authorities are collected in *Welsh Development Agency v. Export Finance Co. Ltd* [1992] B.C.L.C. 148.

misgivings) that a receiver cannot be held so liable in that the receiver as agent of the company is the alter ego of the company, the other party to the contract, and accordingly no possible action could lie against a person for procuring himself to induce a breach of contract.[66]

9–056 **Administrators.** Part II of the Insolvency Act 1986 enables a court to appoint an administrator. Such an order can be made where the court is "satisfied that the company is or is likely to become unable to pay its debts" and the appointment of the administrator would (inter alia) be "likely to achieve" the "survival of the company" or a more advantageous realisation of its assets than would be effected on a winding up.[67] Such an appointment cannot be made if an administrative receiver has been appointed.[68] Once such an appointment is made no proceedings may be brought against the company and no steps may be taken to enforce any security against the company or to repossess goods in possession of the company under a hire-purchase contract.[69] The administrator (who is an officer of the court) is given extensive powers to manage the affairs of the company[70] and in carrying out his duties he is made the agent of the company.[71] However, a person dealing with an administrator in good faith and for value is "not concerned to inquire whether the administrator is acting within his powers."[72]

9–057 **Administrators and existing contracts.** Where an administration order is granted then it imposes a moratorium on the enforcement of contracts against the company or the taking of any steps to enforce security.[73] This does not prevent a person from serving a notice making time of the essence or of accepting a repudiatory breach by the company.[74] Unlike receivers, administrators are bound by existing contracts of the company and specific relief can be granted to enforce such contracts.[75]

(ii) *Contracts between Companies and Promoters or Directors*

9–058 **Promoters.** Promoters are the persons who procure the formation of a company and its "flotation."[76] The term "promoter" is not a legal term but depends upon the function being carried out with respect to the formation of the company.

---

[66] *ibid.* at 171–173.

[67] Insolvency Act 1986, s.8; for a more comprehensive treatment of this topic see Stewart *op. cit.* Part III.

[68] Insolvency Act 1986, s.9(3).

[69] s.11(3) (see s.10(4) which defines hire-purchase agreement).

[70] s.14(1) and Sched. 1.

[71] s.14(5).

[72] s.14(6). *Quaere* if this is compatible with art. 9(2) of the First Directive.

[73] s.11(3)(c) and (d) of the Insolvency Act 1986.

[74] *Re Olympia & York Canary Wharf Ltd* [1993] B.C.L.C. 453.

[75] *Astor Chemicals Ltd v. Synthetic Technology Ltd* [1990] B.C.L.C. 1; *Re Hartlebury Printers Ltd* [1993] 1 All E.R. 470; [1993] B.C.L.C. 902. Leave to commence such proceedings would need to be given by the court or the administrator: Insolvency Act 1986, s.11.

[76] Flotation in this sense does not, of course, require that the company's securities be offered to the public; *Gifford v. Willoughby's Mashonaland Expedition Co.* (1899) 16 T.L.R. 24; *Torva Exploring Syndicate v. Kelly* [1900] A.C. 612.

A promoter stands in a fiduciary relationship to the company both before and after its formation.[77] While, therefore, promoter may make a profit out of the sale of his property to the company,[78] that profit must be disclosed to an independent board of directors or to the shareholders[79]; he may not take a secret commission from a person selling to the company,[80] and if he does so, the company may rescind the contract[81] or claim to recover the secret profit from the promoter,[82] or (at any rate in some cases) sue him for damages.[83] Where promoters acquired property before they began to promote and thereafter sold to the company without disclosing that they were the vendors, it was held that rescission was the only right open to the company, as the promoters were not at the time of their purchase in a fiduciary position to the company.[84] If disclosure is relied on, it must be a genuine disclosure, that is to say, either a disclosure to a board of directors independent of the promoters,[85] or a communication to all the share-holders,[86] or a plain indication in the prospectus that the board of directors are acting for the promoters.[87]

Directors. Directors also owe fiduciary obligations to the company and may **9–059** not make any secret profit by virtue of their office.[88] But directors are in a more responsible position than promoters and neither they nor companies in which they are interested[89] can make an enforceable contract with the company, unless so authorised by the articles of association.[90] Such authorisation is in practice almost universally included in the articles of association,[91] but even where it is given the interested director has a statutory obligation to disclose his interest fully.[92] In the absence of the necessary authority in the articles, or in the event of

---

[77] *Erlanger v. New Sombrero Phosphate Co.* (1878) 3 App.Cas. 1218; *Emma Silver Mining Co. v. Lewis* (1879) 4 C.P.D. 396; *Lagunas Nitrate Co. v. Lagunas Syndicate* [1899] 2 Ch. 392, 428; *Gluckstein v. Barnes* [1900] A.C. 240.

[78] *Omnium Electric Palaces Ltd v. Baines* [1914] 1 Ch. 332.

[79] *Gluckstein v. Barnes* [1900] A.C. 240; *Re Leeds & Hanley Theatres of Varieties Ltd* [1902] 2 Ch. 809; *Jubilee Cotton Mills Ltd v. Lewis* [1924] A.C. 958.

[80] *Lydney & Wigpool Iron Co. v. Bird* (1886) 33 Ch.D. 85.

[81] See n. 77, *ante.*

[82] See n. 79, *ante.*

[83] *Re Leeds & Hanley Theatres of Varieties Ltd* [1902] 2 Ch. 809; *Jacobus Marler Estates v. Marler* (1913) L.J.P.C. 167n.

[84] *Ladywell Mining Co. v. Brookes* (1887) 35 Ch.D. 400; *cf. Burland v. Earle* [1902] A.C. 83. For liability with respect to defective prospectuses see Financial Services Act 1986, s.150; Public Offering of Securities Regulations 1995, S.I 1995 No. 1537, paragraph 14.

[85] *Gluckstein v. Barnes, supra; Burland v. Earle, supra.*

[86] *Salomon v. Salomon & Co.* [1897] A.C. 22; *Att.-Gen for Canada v. Standard Trust Co. of New York* [1911] A.C. 498.

[87] *Lagunas Nitrate Co. v. Lagunas Syndicate* [1899] 2 Ch. 392.

[88] *Imperial Mercantile Credit Association v. Coleman* (1873) L.R. 6 H.L. 189; *Parker v. McKenna* (1874) L.R. 10 Ch.App. 96; *Kaye v. Croydon Tramways Co.* [1898] 1 Ch. 358; *Tiessen v. Henderson* [1899] 1 Ch. 861; *Clarkson v. Davies* [1923] A.C. 100; *Regal (Hastings) Ltd v. Gulliver* [1942] 1 All E.R. 378; [1967] 2 A.C. 134n.; *Industrial Development Consultants Ltd v. Cooley* [1972] 1 W.L.R. 443.

[89] *Flanagan v. Great Western Ry.* (1868) L.R. 7 Eq. 116; *Transvaal Lands Co. v. New Belgium Land Co.* [1914] 2 Ch. 488.

[90] *Costa Rica Railroad Co. v. Forwood* [1901] 1 Ch. 746; *Re Republic of Bolivia Exploration Syndicate Ltd* [1914] 1 Ch. 139.

[91] See Companies (Table A–F) Regulations 1985 (S.I. 1985 No. 805), regs. 84–86.

[92] Companies Act 1985, s.317. Failure to comply with the section does not render the contract void or voidable: *Hely-Hutchinson v. Brayhead Ltd* [1968] 1 Q.B. 549; *Guinness plc v. Saunders* [1990] 2 A.C. 663. It would also appear that breach of s.317 does not vest in the company any right of action for damages for breach of statutory duty: *Castlereagh Motels Ltd v. Davies-Roe* (1966) 67 S.R.

a failure to disclose an interest where there is such authority, the contracts will be voidable by the company.[93] It may be affirmed by the shareholders in general meeting[94] or (probably) by an independent board of directors,[95] or alternatively the company may rescind the contract if *restitutio in integrum* is still possible. The company cannot, however, claim both to affirm the contract and an account of profits unless actual fraud or breach of trust can be proved, as, for example, where a director has sold to the company property which he already held as trustee (expressly or constructively) for the company.[96] Where the director is guilty merely of non-disclosure, having, for example, acquired his interest in the property which he sold to the company before he became a director, the company may either affirm the sale and pay the price agreed or rescind the transaction altogether, but, unless the transaction falls within section 320 of the Companies Act 1985,[97] it cannot claim to affirm and yet to recover the profit made by the director.[98]

9–060   **Companies Acts and directors' contracts.** The Companies Acts contain extensive provisions designed to regulate transactions between directors and their companies, the overall purpose of these provisions being to prevent overreaching by directors and to compel disclosure to the members of the details of the transactions. Some types of transaction are prohibited (*e.g.* loans),[99] others must be disclosed and approved in advance (*e.g.* payments made in connection with the loss of office),[1] while others merely have to be disclosed (*e.g.* emoluments).[2] These provisions are much too technical and extensive to be dealt with here and specialist texts on Company Law should be referred to. Of greater significance with respect to contracts between directors and their companies is section 317 of the Companies Act 1985,[3] which requires a director who has a direct or indirect interest in a proposed contract with his company to make disclosure of his interest in the way set out in the section. This provision is extended by section 317(8) to shadow directors, and by section 317(6) to cover transactions other than contracts between a director and his company. There are also special provisions dealing with contracts which include as one of the parties a director

---

(N.S.W.) 279. See also *Lee Panavision Ltd v. Lee Lighting Ltd* [1992] B.C.L.C. 575; *Runciman v. Walter Runciman plc* [1992] B.C.L.C. 1084.

[93] *Transvaal Lands Company v. New Belgium (Transvaal) Land and Development Company* [1914] 2 Ch. 488.

[94] *North West Transportation Co. v. Beatty* (1887) 12 App.Cas. 589. The interested director may vote for ratification of the contract in his capacity as shareholder: *ibid.*

[95] *Queensland Mines Ltd v. Hudson* (1978) 52 A.L.J.R. 399, PC; noted (1979) 42 M.L.R. 711. It is important to note that in this case the shareholders were all aware of the director's conduct: see *Cane v. Jones* [1980] 1 W.L.R. 1451 and *ante* § 9–040.

[96] *Re Leeds and Hanley Theatres of Varieties Ltd* [1902] 2 Ch. 809.

[97] Where the transaction is a substantial property transaction as defined in s.320 of the Companies Act 1985, and that section is not complied with, the director must account for any gain and are liable to indemnify the company for all losses (s.322); see *Joint Receivers and Managers of Niltan Carson Ltd v. Hawthorne* [1988] B.C.L.C. 298; *Duckwari Plc v. Offerventure Ltd (No. 2)* [1998] 3 W.L.R. 913; [1999] 1 B.C.L.C. 168).

[98] *Re Cape Breton Co.* (1884) 26 Ch.D. 221; 29 Ch.D. 795; *Burland v. Earle* [1902] A.C. 83.

[99] Companies Act 1985, s.330.

[1] *ibid.* ss.312–316; see *Company Directors: Regulating Conflicts of Interest and Formulating a Statement of Duties* (Law Commission, Consultation Paper No. 153).

[2] *ibid.* s.318.

[3] See also nn. 93 and 94, *ante.*

of the company and with respect to that contract the board exceeds limitations on its powers under the company's constitution.[4] Such contracts are (subject to limitations) made voidable at the option of the company.[5]

Managing directors. The appointment of a managing director does not nec- **9–061** essarily constitute a contract between the holder of that office and the company and in the absence of a contract he is removable according to the regulations in the articles.[6] Even where a person is appointed as a managing director pursuant to a contract to that effect the company can lawfully terminate the appointment at any time in accordance with the articles of association if the appointment is not made for a specific term, though reasonable notice may be required in this event. A person appointed managing director cannot, in the absence of an agreement to that effect, claim to be entitled to continue as such so long as he remains a director.[7]

Contract for term of years. A managing director may, however, be **9–062** employed in that capacity by a company under a contract for a term of years,[8] and if so his appointment cannot be lawfully revoked by the company before the expiration of that time by removing him from his directorship in accordance with the articles of association or section 303 of the Companies Act 1985.[9] Although the company's power to remove a director under section 303 cannot be taken away by contract,[10] the exercise of the power may be a breach of contract because a managing director who is removed from his position as a director will necessarily lose his post as managing director,[11] and the company will then be in breach of its contract to employ him as such. Even if remuneration is attached to the office and there is a contract, the contract may exceptionally (particularly where it is an informal parol agreement) be treated as being subject to the provisions of the articles. In this event removal of the managing director in accordance with the articles will not be a breach of contract.[12]

Improper appointment. If a managing director is improperly appointed, fees **9–063** received by him as such may be recovered from him by the company.[13]

---

[4] s.322A. The purpose of this provision is to deny to directors the full protection of ss.35–35B. See § 9–035.

[5] *ibid.*

[6] An appointment without remuneration will normally mean that there is no contract: *Foster v. Foster* [1916] 1 Ch. 532.

[7] *Foster v. Foster, supra.*

[8] Special provision is made with respect to contracts of service of all directors of longer than five years' duration: see Companies Act 1985, s.318.

[9] *Southern Foundries Ltd v. Shirlaw* [1940] A.C. 701; *Shindler v. Northern Raincoat Co. Ltd* [1960] 1 W.L.R. 1038; *Cumbrian Newspapers Group Ltd v. Cumberland and Westmoreland Newspaper and Printing Co. Ltd* [1987] Ch. 10.

[10] See, however, *Bushell v. Faith* [1970] A.C. 1099.

[11] *Re Alexander's Timber Co.* (1901) 70 L.J.Ch. 767; *Bluett v. Stutchbury's Ltd* (1908) 24 T.L.R. 469.

[12] *Read v. Astoria Garage (Streatham) Ltd* [1952] Ch. 637; contrast *Shindler v. Northern Raincoat Co. Ltd* [1960] 1 W.L.R. 1038. This gives rise to difficult conceptual problems: see Trebilcock (1967) 31 Conv.(N.S.) 95; *Carrier Australia Ltd v. Hunt* (1935) 61 C.L.R. 534.

[13] *Brown & Green v. Hays* (1920) 36 T.L.R. 330; *Kerr v. Marine Products* (1928) 44 T.L.R. 292; *cf. Craven Ellis v. Canons Ltd* [1936] 2 K.B. 403.

(iii) *Contracts between Companies and their Members*

9–064   **Purchase and allotment.** The contract between a company and a shareholder may be made in a number of ways. By section 22 of the Companies Act 1985, the subscribers to the memorandum of association are deemed to have agreed to become members of the company. The phrase "agrees to become a member" in section 22 does not require a binding contract and this requirement is satisfied where the name of a person is entered in the register of members with his consent.[14] However, in most cases,[15] the contract between the shareholder and the company will either be preceded by a purchase of shares from a third party or will be made by application to the company followed by allotment. In the former case the contract is probably made by the application of the prospective shareholder to be entered in the register followed by his being so entered. In the latter case the contract is constituted by an application to take shares, accepted by the company by a notification that shares have been allotted.[16] Notice of allotment must be given within a reasonable time or the application lapses.[17] It was held in *Houldsworth v. City of Glasgow Bank*[18] that a person who had applied for and been allotted shares in a company could not, while he remained a member of the company, sue the company for damages for breach of his contract of membership,[19] or for damages for fraudulently inducing him to enter into it.[20] The only remedy used to be that of rescission of the contract and rectification of the register of members.

9–065   The position has now been altered by the Financial Services Act 1986[21] and section 111A of the 1985 Act.[22] Rescission will normally be ordered if the applicant succeeds in showing that he has been induced to take the shares by a material misrepresentation of fact on the part of the company. A misrepresentation made by a person acting on behalf of the company within the scope of his authority[23] or contained in a document which is, to the knowledge of the company, the basis of the contract to take shares,[24] is a good ground for rescission.[25] In most cases the representations complained of are contained in a prospectus issued by the company, and inasmuch as the offer to take shares is an

---

[14] *Re Nuneaton Borough Association Football Club Ltd* [1989] B.C.L.C. 454.

[15] *cf. Mackley's Case* (1875) 1 Ch.D. 247.

[16] For the statutory rules relating to allotment and the effects of irregular allotment, see Companies Act 1985, ss.82–86 repealed in part by Financial Services Act 1986, Sched. 17, settling the law left uncertain in *Jubilee Cotton Mills Ltd v. Lewis* [1924] A.C. 958; *Re James Burton & Son Ltd* [1927] 2 Ch. 132.

[17] *Ramsgate Victoria Hotel Co. v. Montefiore* (1866) L.R. 1 Ex. 109.

[18] (1880) 5 App.Cas. 317; *Soden v. British and Commonwealth Holdings Plc* [1997] 2 B.C.L.C. 501.

[19] *Re Addlestone Linoleum Co.* (1887) 37 Ch.D. 191.

[20] *Western Bank of Scotland v. Addie* (1867) L.R. 1 Sc. & Div. 145; *Houldsworth v. City of Glasgow Bank* (1880) 5 App.Cas. 317.

[21] s.150 gives a right of compensation for damages suffered because of misstatements in listing particulars and s.166 provides a remedy for damages suffered because of misstatements in prospectuses. The latter section has not as yet been brought into effect.

[22] s.111A was introduced by s.131 of the Companies Act 1989. Note also the Misrepresentation Act 1967.

[23] *Lydney v. Anglo-Italian Hemp Spinning Co.* [1896] 1 Ch. 178; *cf. Lagunas Nitrate Co. v. Lagunas Syndicate* [1899] 2 Ch. 392.

[24] *Karberg's Case* [1892] 3 Ch. 1; *Collins v. Associated Greyhound Racecourses* [1930] 1 Ch. 1.

[25] See *ante*, Chap. 6.

offer to take them on the terms of the prospectus, the materiality of the statements contained in the prospectus will in most cases be beyond dispute.[26] If the shareholder does not rescind the contract and take steps to have the register rectified within a reasonable time,[27] and in any event before the commencement of the winding up of the company,[28] he loses his right of rescission; but this rule does not apply to a shareholder whose shares have been forfeited by the company and who has done nothing to affirm the contract, for he has ceased to be a shareholder and has become a debtor to the company.[29]

Effect of articles. The terms of the contract of membership of a company are 9–066 contained in the memorandum and articles of association. The articles are subordinate to the memorandum and, in the case of inconsistency between them, the memorandum prevails.[30] The extent to which the articles of association form an enforceable contract between the company and its individual members is determined by section 14 of the Companies Act 1985 which provides that the memorandum and articles shall, when registered, bind the company and the members thereof to the same extent as if they had been signed and sealed by each member and contained covenants on the part of each member to observe all the provisions of the memorandum and articles. In *Hickman v. Kent or Romney Marsh Sheep-Breeders' Association*,[31] Astbury J. made an elaborate examination of the cases, some of which decided that the articles of association created no contract between the company and its members and others that a company was entitled as against its members to enforce and restrain breaches of its regulations; he concluded "It is difficult to reconcile these two classes of decisions and the judicial opinions therein expressed," but he went on to formulate the following rules:

(1) No article can constitute a contract between the company and a third person.[32]
(2) No right purporting to be given by an article to a person, whether a member or not, in a capacity other than that of a member, as, for instance, a solicitor,[33] promoter[34] or director,[35] can be enforced against the company.

---

[26] See *Karberg's Case* [1892] 3 Ch. 1; *Mair v. Rio Grande Rubber Estates* [1913] A.C. 853; *Re Pacaya Rubber & Produce Co.* [1914] 1 Ch. 542. The public distribution of securities is now regulated by Pt. IV of the Financial Services Act 1986 Public Offering of Securities Regulations 1995; (S.I. 1995 No. 1537); see also §§ 6–033—6–036.

[27] *First National Reinsurance Co. v. Greenfield* [1921] 2 K.B. 260.

[28] *Oakes v. Turquand* (1867) L.R. 2 HL 325; *Reese River Silver Mining Co. v. Smith* (1869) L.R. 4 H.L. 64.

[29] *Aaron's Reefs v. Twiss* [1896] A.C. 273.

[30] *Ashbury v. Watson* (1885) 30 Ch.D. 376; *Rayfield v. Hands* [1960] Ch. 1.

[31] [1915] 1 Ch. 881, 900; approved *Beattie v. Beattie Ltd* [1938] Ch. 708. See also *Mutual Life Insurance Co. of New York v. The Rank Organisation Ltd* [1985] B.C.L.C. 11 (the contract constituted by the articles does not import the requirement that there be parity of treatment of shareholders of the same class); *Bratton Seymour Service Co. Ltd v. Oxborough* [1992] B.C.L.C. 693.

[32] *Melhado v. Porto Alegre Ry.* (1874) L.R. 9 C.P. 503; *Re Greene* [1949] Ch. 333.

[33] *Eley v. Positive Life Assurance Co.* (1876) 1 Ex.D. 88; *cf. Cumbrian Newspapers Group Ltd v. Cumberland and Westmoreland Herald Newspaper & Printing Co. Ltd* [1987] Ch. 1, 16.

[34] *Pritchard's Case* (1873) L.R. 8 Ch. 956.

[35] *Browne v. La Trinidad* (1887) 37 Ch.D. 1; *Beattie v. Beattie Ltd* [1938] Ch. 708; contrast *Rayfield v. Hands* [1960] Ch. 1, on which see Gower (1958) 21 M.L.R. 401, 465.

(3) Articles regulating the rights and obligations of the members generally as such do create rights and obligations between them and the company respectively.

The articles also constitute a contract been the members *inter se.*[36]

(iv) *Contracts between Companies and their Auditors*

9–067 **Appointment and removal of auditors.** Although the first auditors may be appointed by the directors,[37] auditors are normally elected at the general meeting at which the company's accounts are considered[38] and the terms of the auditor's remuneration will also be determined at this meeting.[39] The auditor's term of office must run from the conclusion of that meeting to the conclusion of the next such meeting,[40] and although an auditor may resign he must follow certain stipulated procedures.[41] By virtue of the Companies Act 1985, s.391, a company may by ordinary resolution remove its auditor from office, notwithstanding any agreement to the contrary; but by virtue of section 391(3) of the Act, any such removal is without prejudice to any claim for damages for breach of contract.

9–068 **Rules of industrial societies.** It would appear that the rules of a society registered under the Industrial and Provident Societies Act 1965 (or earlier Acts replaced by that Act) bind the members of such a society to the same extent as the articles of association bind the shareholders.[42]

2. Unincorporated Associations

(a) *Generally*

9–069 **Liability of unincorporated associations.** An unincorporated association is not a legal person and therefore cannot sue or be sued[43] unless such a course is authorised by express or implied statutory provisions as in the case of a trade union[44] and a trustee savings bank.[45] Nor can a contract be made so as to bind

---

[36] *Rayfields v. Hands, supra.* See also *Re Royal Institution of Chartered Surveyors' Application* [1985] I.C.R. 330, 345–347 (relationship between members of a body corporate incorporated by Royal Charter). It has been argued that a member also has the right to compel a company to observe all of the provisions in the company's articles of association, a proposition which if accurate would provide a means for enforcing indirectly outsider rights. Although some cases recognise such a right, it has not constituted the basis of any decision and its status remains very uncertain. See generally, Wedderburn (1957) C.L.J. 194; [1958] C.L.J. 93.

[37] Companies Act 1985, s.385(3).

[38] *ibid.* s.384(1) and s.385(2).

[39] *ibid.* s.390A.

[40] *ibid.* s.385(2).

[41] *ibid.* ss.392, 392A, 394.

[42] *Biddulph & District Agricultural Society v. Agricultural Wholesale Society* [1925] Ch. 769; [1927] A.C. 76.

[43] *London Association for Protection of Trade v. Greenlands Ltd* [1916] 2 A.C. 15, 20, 38; *Steele v. Gourley* (1886) 3 T.L.R. 118, 119; affd. (1887) 3 T.L.R. 772. See, generally, Ford, *Unincorporated Non-Profit Associations*, 1959; Keeler (1971) 34 M.L.R. 615.

[44] Trade Union and Labour Relations (Consolidation) Act 1992, s.10; *British Association of Advisers and Lecturers in Physical Education v. National Union of Teachers* [1986] I.R.L.R. 497, CA, see generally *Gower's Principles of Modern Company Law* (5th ed., 1992), at pp. 80–81; *E.E.T.P.U. v. Times Newspapers Ltd* [1980] Q.B. 585.

[45] *Knight and Searle v. Dove* [1964] 2 Q.B. 631. See Wedderburn (1965) 28 M.L.R. 62.

all persons who from time to time become members of such an association.[46] But a contract purportedly made by or with an incorporated association is not necessarily a nullity.[47] If the person or persons who actually made the contract had no authority to contract on behalf of the members they may be held to have contracted personally.[48] On the other hand, if they had the authority, express or implied, of all or some of the members of the association to contract on their behalf, the contract can be enforced by or against those members as co-principals to the contract by the ordinary rules of agency.[49]

Representative action. By the rules of agency, therefore, a large number of **9–070** members of an association may find themselves parties to a contract. In practice it would be impossible in such a case to join all the members as plaintiffs or defendants, and therefore recourse must be had to the device of a representative action. Ord. 15, r. 12, of the Rules of the Supreme Court (which is preserved by the Civil Procedure Rules, Sched. 1) provides that where there are numerous persons having the same interest in any proceedings,[50] the proceedings may be begun and, unless the court otherwise orders, continued by or against any one or more of them as representing all or as representing all except one or more of them. The attitude of the courts is to interpret the open textured language of Ord. 15, r. 12, in a liberal manner. Its language, according to Megarry V.-C., is wide and permissive and the rule should be used as "a flexible tool of convenience in the administration of justice."[51]

Requirements for representative action. In *Prudential Assurance Co. Ltd v.* **9–071** *Newman Industries Ltd*[52] Vinelott J. reviewed the authorities relating to representative actions and formulated the following principles with respect to the bringing of such actions.

Not if would confer new right of action. First, a representative action may **9–072** not be brought if the effect of so doing is "to confer a right of action on a member of the class represented who would not otherwise have been able to assert such a right in separate proceedings, or to bar a defence which might otherwise be available to the defendant, in such separate proceedings."[53] From this Vinelott J. reasoned that the plaintiff in a representative action will normally be only entitled to declaratory relief, although he may join with the representative action a claim for personal damages. Although this is the normal rule, in exceptional circumstances the court may grant damages in favour of the plaintiff in an action commenced in representative form.[54] Also, it may be that the contractual

---

[46] See *Walker v. Sur* [1914] 2 K.B. 930; *Jarrott v. Ackerley* (1915) 85 L.J.Ch. 135.

[47] As to associations of persons who, because of the size of their membership and their objects, should be registered under s.716 of the Companies Act 1985, see Calvert (1962) 26 Conv.(N.S.) 253.

[48] *Bradley Egg Farm v. Clifford* [1943] 2 All E.R. 378.

[49] See Vol. II, Chap. 32.

[50] *Barker v. Allanson* [1937] 1 K.B. 463; *London Association for Protection of Trade v. Greenlands Ltd* [1916] 2 A.C. 15, 39; *Janson v. Property Insurance Co.* (1913) 30 T.L.R. 49.

[51] *John v. Rees* [1970] Ch. 345, 370.

[52] [1981] Ch. 229; *CBS/SONY Hong Kong Ltd v. Television Broadcasts Ltd* [1987] F.S.R. 262.

[53] *ibid.* at 254.

[54] *E.M.I. Records Ltd v. Riley* [1981] 1 W.L.R. 923.

arrangements between the parties make it appropriate that there be an action in representative form.[55] An action of libel cannot be instituted under the rule where some of the members of the association might not have authorised the publication of the alleged libel, or might be out of the country.[56] Similarly, it was refused where an order was sought against the members at the date of the proceedings and the members had changed since the cause of action had arisen,[57] and, in an action for breach of a contract for the carriage of goods by sea, where the shippers in a general ship held different bills of lading and different defences might have been raised against them.[58]

9–073 **Not to enforce a personal liability.** Nor can representative proceedings under this rule be used in an action in which a personal liability, such as a judgment for money due or for damages, is sought to be enforced against the individual members of the association.[59] In *Lord Churchill v. Whetnall*,[60] where three subscribers to a fund brought an action for misrepresentation in the circular inviting subscriptions to the fund on behalf of themselves and the other 200 subscribers, it was held that there could be no representative action to establish the right of numerous persons to recover damages, each in his own several right, where the only right claimed was the right to recover such damages: before a subscriber could recover he would have to show that he had been induced by the representation and this could only be done in separate proceedings.[61] But where the association is possessed of funds in the hands of trustees, a plaintiff may sue proper persons as representatives of the association for a declaration of his right against the property belonging to the association, and, by adding the trustees as defendants, may obtain an order charging the funds which are in their hands and of which they are the legal owners.[62]

9–074 **Common interest.** The second requirement laid down in the *Prudential Assurance* case for the bringing of a representative action is that there must be an "interest" shared by all the members: "there must be a common ingredient in the

---

[55] *Irish Shipping Ltd v. Commercial Union Assurance Co. plc* [1991] 2 Q.B. 206 (action in representative form against the lead underwriter of an insurance contract).

[56] *Mercantile Marine Service Association v. Toms* [1916] 2 K.B. 243; *E.E.T.P.U. v. Times Newspapers Ltd* [1980] Q.B. 585.

[57] *Barker v. Allanson* [1937] 1 K.B. 463; *Roche v. Sherrington* [1982] 2 All E.R. 426; *cf. Campbell v. Thompson* [1953] 1 Q.B. 445. There is no reason why a representative action should not be instituted against those persons who were members when the cause of action arose, but in this event no order could be made affecting the assets of the association.

[58] *Markt & Co. v. Knight SS. Co.* [1910] 2 K.B. 1021.

[59] *Walker v. Sur* [1914] 2 K.B. 930; *Hardie and Lane v. Chiltern* [1928] 1 K.B. 663. See, however, *Morrison SS. Co. Ltd v. Greystoke Castle (Cargo Owners)* [1947] A.C. 265. It may also be noted that the new Ord. 15, r. 12 is in wider terms than the old Ord. 16, r. 9, and it is perhaps arguable that the cases denying the use of this procedure in an action for damages should not now be followed. But see the *Prudential Assurance* case, *supra*, at 244; *The Supreme Court Practice 1993*, 15/12/2; *Roche v. Sherrington* [1982] 2 All E.R. 426.

[60] (1918) 87 L.J.Ch. 524; *Wing v. Burn* (1928) 44 T.L.R. 258; *Markt & Co. v. Knight SS. Co.* [1910] 2 K.B. 1021, 1035.

[61] See the *Prudential Assurance* case, *supra*, at 251.

[62] *Wood v. McCarthy* [1893] 1 Q.B. 775; *Taff Vale Ry. v. Amalgamated Society of Railway Servants* [1901] A.C. 426, 443; *Linaker v. Pilcher* (1901) 17 T.L.R. 256; *Ideal Films v. Richards* [1927] 1 K.B. 374, 381.

cause of action of each member of the class."[63] This to a large extent is nothing more than a rephrasing of the first requirement.

For benefit of class. The third, and related requirement, is that it is for the   9-075
benefit of the class that the representative action be brought.[64] This, among other things, will require that all evidence relating to the claim is adduced to avoid any unfairness to members of the class who will be bound by the outcome of the litigation.

Relation of unincorporated association to its members. Inasmuch as unin-   9-076
corporated associations are generally not legal persons, but mere collective names for all their members, a contract made by one member with some person or persons on behalf of the association is a contract by a man with himself and others; and as no man can be both covenantor and covenantee upon a contract, it must be construed as a contract between the member and the other members.[65] If that contract is broken the injured member can sue and recover damages from those who have broken it,[66] though he cannot sue the association except where statutory authorisation for such a course can be found. But he may be faced with the difficulty that the wrongful act was committed by an agent of the association on behalf of its members, including himself. In that case it is possible that he may be unable to recover from his fellow members, whose responsibility, in the circumstances, will be no greater than his own. But the other members, in order to rely on such a defence, must show that the agent was really acting on behalf of the injured member; and, at any rate where the injury is a wrongful expulsion in breach of the rules, that will not be so.[67]

(b) *Clubs*[68]

Kinds of clubs. The principal bodies with regard to which these questions   9-077
arise are clubs and trade unions. Clubs are unincorporated associations and may be formed for any purpose for which associations may be lawfully constituted. There are two principal types of club: members' clubs and proprietary clubs.[69]

(i) *Members' Clubs*

Members' liability. The question whether contracts purporting to have been   9-078
made on behalf of an association bind all the members or only some (*e.g.* the

---

[63] *Prudential Assurance Co. Ltd v. Newman Industries Ltd, supra*, at 255. Vinelott J. cited *Markt & Co. v. Knight SS. Co.* [1910] 2 K.B. 1021 and *Lord Churchill v. Whitnell* [1918] 87 L.J.Ch. as two cases where this requirement was not satisfied.

[64] *Prudential Assurance Co. Ltd v. Newman Industries Ltd, supra*, at 255.

[65] Law of Property Act 1925, s.82. See also *John v. Matthews* [1970] 2 Q.B. 443; *Reel v. Holder* [1981] 1 W.L.R. 1226.

[66] See *Abbott v. Sullivan* [1952] 1 K.B. 189, 193, 219; *Lee v. Showmen's Guild of Great Britain* [1952] 2 Q.B. 329, 341.

[67] *Bonsor v. Musicians' Union* [1956] A.C. 104, 148–149, 153.

[68] See Josling and Alexander, *The Law of Clubs* (6th ed., 1987).

[69] The Friendly Societies Act 1974, s.7(2)(d) recognised the "working men's clubs" but this definition is not repeated in the Friendly Societies Act 1992. However, the social and philanthropic purposes that could be carried out by working men's clubs as defined in 1974 Act could be carried out by a body registered as a Friendly Society under the 1992 Act: see Sched. 2, Pt. D as amplified by s.7(2)(b) and s.10 of the 1992 Act.

committee) is one which turns on the general law of agency.[70] Thus, no member of a members' club is liable for the debts of the club except to the extent that he has expressly or impliedly authorised some official of the club to pledge his personal credit.[71] Clubs are not partnerships[72] and the "law, which was at one time uncertain, is now settled, that no member of a club is liable to a creditor except, so far as he has assented to the contract in respect of which such liability has arisen."[73] Unless the rules expressly so provide,[74] the committee of a club has no authority to pledge the credit of the members by borrowing on debentures,[75] or by ordering work to be done for or goods to be supplied to the club[76]; but a member may make himself liable by ratifying the order.[77] Members of the committee of a club are liable in respect of contracts made by them on behalf of the club,[78] but not in respect of contracts made by officials of the club which they have not themselves authorised.[79] Where one committee man has paid out money under a contract on which another committee man also could have been sued, the former has a right of contribution against the latter in respect of such payment,[80] but he has no right of indemnity against the members of the club.[81]

9–079   **Relation of club to its members.** The relations between the members of a club are governed by a contract between the members which may be express or implied and which is usually found in the rules of the club[82]; membership of a club may also confer proprietary rights on members which will be of significance where the club is being dissolved.[83] In *Lee v. Showmen's Guild of Great Britain*[84] Denning L.J. said: "It was once said by Sir George Jessel M.R. that the courts only intervened in these cases to protect rights of property: see *Rigby v. Connol*[85]; and other judges have often said the same thing: see, for instance, *Cookson v. Harewood*.[86] But Fletcher Moulton L.J. denied that there was any such limitation on the power of the courts: see *Osborne v. Amalgamated Society of Railway Servants*[87]; and it has now become clear that he was right: see the cornporters' case, *Abbott v. Sullivan*.[88] That case shows that the power of this court to

---

[70] See Vol. II, Chap. 31: *Lascelles v. Rathbun* (1919) 35 T.L.R. 347; *Shore v. Ministry of Works* [1950] 2 All E.R. 228; *Prole v. Allen* [1950] 1 All E.R. 476; *cf. Moshenan v. Segar* [1917] 2 K.B. 325 dealing with proprietary clubs.
[71] *Steele v. Gourley* (1887) 3 T.L.R. 772; *Wise v. Perpetual Trustee Co.* [1903] A.C. 139.
[72] *ibid.*
[73] *Re St. James' Club* (1852) 2 De G.M. & G. 383, 387.
[74] *Cockerell v. Aucompte* (1857) 2 C.B.(N.S.) 440.
[75] *Re St. James' Club* (1852) 2 De G.M. & G. 383.
[76] *Flemyng v. Hector* (1836) 2 M. & W. 172; *Hawke v. Cole* (1890) 62 L.T. 658; *Draper v. Earl Manvers* (1892) 9 T.L.R. 73.
[77] *Delauney v. Strickland* (1818) 2 Stark. 416.
[78] *Lee v. Bissett* (1856) 4 W.R. 233; *Re London Marine Insurance Association* (1869) L.R. 8 Eq. 176; *Duke of Queensbury v. Cullen* (1787) 1 Bro.P.C. 396.
[79] *Todd v. Emly* (1841) 7 M. & W. 427; 8 M. & W. 505.
[80] *Earl of Mountcashell v. Barber* (1853) 14 C.B. 53.
[81] *Wise v. Perpetual Trustee Co.* [1903] A.C. 139.
[82] *Harington v. Sendall* [1903] 1 Ch. 921; *Lee v. Showmen's Guild of Great Britain* [1952] 2 Q.B. 329. On the liability of a club or its officers to its members in tort: see *Robertson v. Ridley* [1988] 2 All E.R. 474.
[83] *Re Sick and Funeral Society of St. John's Sunday School, Golcar* [1973] Ch. 51.
[84] [1952] 2 Q.B. 329, 341–342.
[85] (1880) 14 Ch.D. 482, 487.
[86] [1932] 2 K.B. 478, 481, 488.
[87] [1911] 1 Ch. 540, 562.
[88] [1952] 1 K.B. 189.

intervene is founded on its jurisdiction to protect rights of contract.[89] If a member is expelled by a committee in breach of contract, this court will grant a declaration that their action is *ultra vires*. It will also grant an injunction to prevent his expulsion, if that is necessary to protect a proprietary right of his; or to protect him in his right to earn his livelihood: see *Amalgamated Society of Carpenters, etc. v. Braithwaite*[90]; but it will not grant an injunction to give a member the right to enter a social club, unless there are proprietary rights attached to it, because it is too personal to be specifically enforced: see *Baird v. Wells*.[91] That is, I think, the only relevance of rights of property in this connection. It goes to the form of remedy, not to the right." But the absence of property rights may, in certain circumstances, be some evidence that the members did not intend that their club membership should create legal relations between them.[92] As a result of the contractual nature of the rules the court will interfere to prevent them being altered,[93] unless they are altered in accordance with a procedure prescribed therein[94] or with the consent of every member.

Expulsion of members.[95] The court will not restrain the exercise by a club of **9–080** a power, contained in its rules, to expel members unless it is shown that what has been done is, in fact, contrary to the rules or has been done in bad faith[96] or, at least where some sort of inquiry is contemplated, where the rules of natural justice have been infringed.[97] It has been said that to give one reason for expelling a member and to act upon another is evidence of bad faith.[98] In a case of expulsion it was held that the issues were whether the rules of the club had been observed, whether the committee had given the member a fair hearing and whether it had acted in good faith.[99] Every member of the committee must be summoned to the meeting or the proceedings may be invalidated.[1] Notice must be given to the member of the charge made against him and he must have a proper opportunity of being heard in his own defence[2]; a rule purporting to

---

[89] See, however, *Nagle v. Feilden* [1966] 2 Q.B. 633, which suggests that in the case of associations which control entry to a trade or profession (such as the Jockey Club, the Stock Exchange or the Inns of Court) the court's power to grant redress is not confined to cases of contract. See also *R. v. Jockey Club, ex p. RAM Racecourses Ltd* [1993] 2 All E.R. 225, 247–248. Detailed consideration of this question falls outside the scope of this work, but see *post*, § 9–088, n. 39, as to trade unions and §§ 17–134—17–138 as to the doctrine of restraint of trade. *cf. Goring v. British Actors Equity Association* [1987] I.R.L.R. 122, 127–128.

[90] [1922] 2 A.C. 440.

[91] (1890) 44 Ch.D. 661, 675–676. But a right to vote may be protected by injunction: *Woodford v. Smith* [1970] 1 W.L.R. 806.

[92] See *Rigby v. Connol* (1880) 14 Ch.D. 482, 487 (this was based on the discredited theory that court intervention in the affairs of an association was only justified to protect rights of property).

[93] *Harington v. Sendall* [1903] 1 Ch. 921.

[94] *Thellusson v. Viscount Valentia* [1907] 2 Ch. 1.

[95] See Lloyd (1957) 10 C.L.P. 36; Robson, *Justice and Administrative Law* (3rd ed.), Chap. 4; *de Smith's Judicial Review of Administrative Action* (5th ed., 1995), § 7–012, §§ 7037–7039.

[96] *Hopkinson v. Marquis of Exeter* (1867) L.R. 5 Eq. 63; *Richardson-Gardner v. Fremantle* (1870) 24 L.T. 81; *Dawkins v. Antrobus* (1879) 17 Ch.D. 615; *Lambert v. Addison* (1882) 46 L.T. 20. See Lloyd (1952) 15 M.L.R. 413.

[97] *Russell v. Duke of Norfolk* [1949] 1 All E.R. 109; *Lawlor v. Union of Post Office Workers* [1965] Ch. 712. *cf. Gaiman v. National Association of Mental Health* [1971] Ch. 317.

[98] *D'Arcy v. Adamson* (1913) 29 T.L.R. 367.

[99] *Lamberton v. Thorpe* (1929) 141 L.T. 638, following *Maclean v. Workers' Union* [1929] 1 Ch. 602.

[1] *Young v. Ladies' Imperial Club Ltd* [1920] 2 K.B. 523.

[2] *Labouchere v. Earl Wharncliffe* (1879) 13 Ch.D. 346; *Fisher v. Keane* (1878) 11 Ch.D. 353; *Gray v. Allison* (1909) 25 T.L.R. 531.

deprive him of this right would probably be invalid as contrary to public policy.[3] If a decision of a committee, based on the opinion of the committee, is challenged, the court will only interfere if there was no evidence upon which to base the opinion, in which case it will declare the decision *ultra vires*. The club cannot oust the jurisdiction of the courts by making the committee the final arbiter on questions of law; and the construction of the rules is always a question of law.[4]

9–081 **Election.** Generally speaking, a person who is refused membership of an unincorporated association has no ground for legal redress.[5] It has, however, been suggested that if the grounds for such refusal are unlawful as being in restraint of trade, redress may be available.[6] But refusal to admit a person to membership of a *social* club could hardly be in restraint of trade.[7] A refusal to admit a person to membership of a club on the grounds of colour, race or ethnic or national origins may constitute a breach of section 25 of the Race Relations Act 1976.[8]

9–082 **Re-election.** Where the rules of an unincorporated association provide for re-election at stated intervals by the committee, the committee (somewhat surprisingly in the light of the rules relating to expulsion) is not bound to give a member notice of any objection to his re-election,[9] and provided that they act neither arbitrarily nor capriciously but in the honest exercise of their discretion, which in the absence of evidence to the contrary will be presumed, their decision cannot be questioned.[10]

9–083 **Resignation.** A member of a club may unilaterally resign his membership even in the absence of any provision in the club's rules, and such resignation may be inferred from long-continued non-payment of dues.[11]

9–084 **Officers' mess.** For goods supplied to an officers' mess neither an individual member of the mess[12] nor the commanding officer[13] can be made liable without evidence that he authorised his credit to be pledged and that he was the person to whom the seller gave credit.

(ii) *Proprietary Clubs*

9–085 **Proprietary clubs.** In a proprietary club the property and funds of the club belong to the proprietor who regulates the use of the property by the members in

---

[3] *Lee v. Showmen's Guild of Great Britain* [1952] 2 Q.B. 329, 342; *Faramus v. Film Artistes' Federation* [1964] A.C. 925, 941; *John v. Rees* [1970] Ch. 345; *Enderby Town Football Club Ltd v. Football Association Ltd* [1971] Ch. 591.

[4] *Lee v. Showmen's Guild of Great Britain, supra*; followed in *Barker v. Jones* [1954] 1 W.L.R. 1005.

[5] *Faramus v. Film Artistes' Association* [1964] A.C. 925, 947.

[6] *Nagle v. Feilden* [1966] 2 Q.B. 633; *Reg v. Disciplinary Committee of The Jockey Club* [1993] 1 W.L.R. 909, 933; *Bunbury v. Lautro Ltd* [1996] C.L.C. 1273.

[7] *ibid.* at 644, 653.

[8] The law on this is complicated and it is necessary to refer to specialist texts: see Feldman, *Civil Liberties & Human Rights* (1993).

[9] *Cassel v. Inglis* [1916] 2 Ch. 211.

[10] *Weinberger v. Inglis* [1919] A.C. 606; *cf. Nagle v. Fielden, supra*.

[11] *Re Sick and Funeral Society of St. John's Sunday School, Golcar* [1973] Ch. 51.

[12] *Hawke v. Cole* (1890) 62 L.T. 658.

[13] *Lascelles v. Rathbun* (1919) 35 T.L.R. 347.

return for their subscriptions. The management is generally in the hands of a committee of members. Although it was formerly thought that the only remedy of a member of a proprietary club which had itself no property was against the proprietor,[14] it is now clear that this is not so.[15] But since members have no right of property in the case of a proprietary club, one who has been expelled by the committee cannot obtain relief by way of injunction, even though the proceedings were irregular, but will be left to obtain it in damages.[16]

(c) *Trade Unions*

Contractual capacity of trade unions. The law relating to the contractual   **9–086** capacity of trade unions has undergone some remarkable vicissitudes since the beginning of this century. Under the nineteenth-century statutes governing trade unions there was no express provision for incorporation, but the *Taff Vale* case,[17] which held that registered unions could be sued in their own name, resulted in a limited contractual capacity being conferred upon them.[18] Legislation on trade unions in the twentieth century has tended to confer some type of "corporate" status on trade unions.[19] The present position is to be found in section 10 of the Trade Union and Labour Relations (Consolidation) Act 1992 which provides that a trade union is not nor is it to be treated as a "body corporate."[20] However, despite this statutory denial of corporate status a trade union, so far as the capacity to enter into contracts is concerned, is treated as if it were a body corporate since it is expressly provided that a trade union is capable of entering into contracts[21] and that it can sue or be sued in its own name.[22] Any judgment or order made against a trade union is enforceable against any property held in trust[23] for it is as though it were a body corporate.[24] The agreements of a trade union are not void or voidable because they may be in restraint of trade.[25] Thus for most practical purposes in connection with contracts with third parties the position of a trade union has been equated with that of a body corporate.

Contracts between trade unions and their members. The relationship   **9–087** between a member of a trade union and the union itself is contractual, and the terms of the contract are to be found in the rules of the union.[26] A member of a trade union has in general the right to take proceedings to enforce compliance

---

[14] *Lyttleton v. Blackburne* (1875) 45 L.J.Ch. 219; *Baird v. Wells* (1890) 44 Ch.D. 661.

[15] *Lee v. Showmen's Guild of Great Britain* [1952] 2 Q.B. 329.

[16] *Baird v. Wells* (1890) 44 Ch.D. 661. cf. *Millennium Productions Ltd v. Winter Garden Theatre (London) Ltd* [1946] W.N. 151; revd. *sub nom. Winter Garden Theatre (London) Ltd v. Millennium Productions Ltd* [1948] A.C. 173.

[17] [1901] A.C. 426.

[18] See the 23rd ed. of this work, §§ 520–524.

[19] See, for example, s.2 of the Trade Union and Labour Relations Act 1974 (now repealed).

[20] s.10(1) and (2). A trade union is not affected by s.35 of the Companies Act 1985 since that section only applies to bodies corporate as defined in the 1985 Act and a trade union cannot be registered under that act (s.10(3)(a) of the Trade Union and Labour Relations Consolidation Act 1992).

[21] s.10(1)(a).

[22] s.10(1)(b).

[23] s.12(1) provides that all the property of a trade union must be vested in trustees to be held on trust for it.

[24] s.12(2).

[25] s.11.

[26] *Bonsor v. Musicians' Union* [1956] A.C. 104.

with the union's own rules in relation to matters such as election of officers and other internal regulations.[27] In general the court has no power to declare provisions of a trade union's rules to be void as unreasonable any more than it has with the provisions of any other contract.[28] However, in *Edwards v. SOGAT*[29] the Court of Appeal, prior to the 1974 Act, struck down a union rule permitting capricious and arbitrary expulsion of a member, apparently on the ground that such a rule is contrary to public policy in so far as it permits such expulsion.[30] Section 46 of the Trade Union and Labour Relations (Consolidation) Act 1992 imposes a statutory duty on a trade union to ensure that it's officers[31] are elected by secret ballot.[32] Re-elections for such offices must take place at intervals of not more than five years.[33]

9–088   **Expulsion and exclusion from a trade union.** Prior to the Industrial Relations Act 1971 the courts had protected members of a union against unlawful expulsion where it could be shown that the union had violated the procedure laid down in its own rules, and was thus in breach of its contract with its member. It was originally thought that the only remedy was by injunction but it was eventually held by the House of Lords that damages could also be awarded against the union.[34] It was also well established that a union, like any other domestic tribunal, must in general observe the rules of natural justice,[35] and it also seemed that the rules of the union could not validly exclude the rules of natural justice.[36] Where the rules of natural justice applied, a trade union, like the committee of a club,[37] was required to give a man notice of the charge against him and a reasonable opportunity of meeting it.[38] A trade union could not in any case oust the jurisdiction of the court and could not be made the final arbiter on questions of law[39]; and if it acted without evidence, the courts would interfere.[40] But the courts did not claim to act as courts of appeal from domestic tribunals and would not disturb a decision which was on a matter of opinion only.[41]

9–089   **Refusal of membership.** No attempt to protect a worker from arbitrary or unreasonable refusal of membership could (it is thought) have succeeded at

---

[27] See *Taylor v. N.U.M. (Derbyshire Area)* [1985] B.C.L.C. 237 (on right of members to sue with respect to *ultra vires* disbursements of union assets.)

[28] *Faramus v. Film Artistes' Federation* [1964] A.C. 925, 943.

[29] [1971] Ch. 354.

[30] See generally, Rideout, *Principles of Labour Law* (5th ed., 1989), pp. 395–432.

[31] These are defined in s.4(2).

[32] The voting procedures are set out in ss.47–52.

[33] s.46(1)(b).

[34] *Bonsor v. Musicians' Union, supra.* On the availability of an interlocutory injunction, see *Porter v. N.U.J.* [1980] 1 I.R.L.R. 404.

[35] *Lee v. Showmen's Guild of Great Britain* [1952] 2 Q.B. 329; Kidner, *Trade Union Law* (2nd ed.), Chap. 3.

[36] *Russell v. Duke of Norfolk* [1949] 1 All E.R. 109; *Lawler v. Union of Post Office Workers* [1965] Ch. 712; *Taylor v. National Union of Seamen* [1967] 1 W.L.R. 532; *Lee v. Showmen's Guild of Great Britain, supra: Faramus v. Film Artistes' Federation, supra.*

[37] See § 9–080.

[38] *Annamunthodo v. Oilfield Workers' Trade Union* [1961] A.C. 945; *Breen v. Amalgamated Engineering Union* [1971] 2 Q.B. 175.

[39] *Luby v. Warwickshire Miners' Association* [1912] 2 Ch. 371; *Burn v. National Amalgamated Labourers' Union* [1920] 2 Ch. 364; *Leigh v. National Union of Railwaymen* [1970] Ch. 326; and see *Australian Workers' Union v. Brown* (1948) 77 C.L.R. 601; *White v. Kuzych* [1951] A.C. 585.

[40] *Lee v. Showmen's Guild of Great Britain, supra,* at 340.

[41] *ibid.*

common law since no contractual relation could, *ex hypothesi*, be established between a would-be member and the union.[42]

Statutory protection of member's rights. Of greater importance than the common law in protecting a trade union member's rights are the statutory protections accorded to trade union members to prevent them from being excluded, expelled or disciplined on grounds that the statute treats as being unjustifiable.[43]

9–090

---

[42] In *Nagle v. Feilden* [1966] 2 Q.B. 633, it was suggested that in some circumstances the court's power to intervene might extend beyond cases of contract, but in so far as this decision was based on the invalidity of an unreasonable restraint of trade it could have no application anyhow to a trade union by reason of s.3 of the Trade Union Act 1871, now replaced by s.11 of the Trade Union and Labour Relations (Consolidation) Act 1992. Indeed the wording of s.11 is more clearly calculated to exclude the argument suggested in *Nagle* v. *Feilden*. See *Greig v. Insole* [1978] 1 W.L.R. 302, 363; *Goring v. Bristol Actors' Equity Association* [1987] I.R.L.R. 122, 127–128.

[43] The major statutory protections are to be found in Chapter V of the Trade Union and Labour Relations (Consolidation) Act 1992 as amended by ss.15 and 16 of the Trade Union Reform and Employment Rights Act 1993; ss.174–177 of the 1992 Act were replaced by s.14 of the 1993 Act.

CHAPTER 10

THE CROWN, PUBLIC AUTHORITIES[1] AND THE EUROPEAN COMMUNITY

1. THE CROWN

Contracts between Crown and subject. The Crown may contract with a **10–001** subject, and the Attorney-General, suing on its behalf, has always been able to enforce against a subject a contract so made.[2] But until the Crown Proceedings Act 1947 actions could not generally be brought against the Crown or government departments. The only remedy against the Crown was, with the *fiat* of the Sovereign, by petition of right.[3] This remedy was not available in tort,[4] but did lie to recover debts,[5] and damages for breach of contract.[6] It also lay to enforce some quasi-contractual claims, *e.g. quantum meruit* claims,[7] and claims for money paid under a mistake[8] although the scope of the remedy in quasi-contract was never precisely determined.[9] There was, moreover, some authority for the

---

[1] See generally Arrowsmith, *Civil Liability and Public Authorities* (1992), pp. 6–18, Chaps. 2–4; Hogg, *Liability of the Crown* (1971), Chaps. 5, 6; Mitchell, *The Contracts of Public Authorities* (1954); Street, *Governmental Liability* (1953), Chap. 3; Arrowsmith, *The Law of Public and Utilities Procurement* (1996); Turpin, *Government Procurement and Contracts* (1989).

[2] Proceedings by the Crown are now to be taken in accordance with the Crown Proceedings Act 1947. The Crown's special methods of enforcing its claims have been abolished by the Act (Sched. 1 and s.33), except in respect of certain debts (s.26).

[3] Procedure was regulated by the Petitions of Right Act 1860 (now repealed). For an exceptional case in which it was necessary to use the old common law form of Petition of Right (because the alleged liability arose "otherwise than in respect of [Her] Majesty's Government in the United Kingdom" within the Crown Proceedings Act 1947, s.40(2)(b)), see *Franklin v. Att.-Gen.* [1974] Q.B. 185; *Franklin v. The Queen* [1974] Q.B. 202; *Franklin v. The Queen (No. 2)* [1974] Q.B. 205; *Barclays Bank Ltd v. The Queen* [1974] Q.B. 823; contrast *Tito v. Waddell (No. 2)* [1977] Ch. 106, 252–256.

[4] *Viscount Canterbury v. Att.-Gen.* (1843) 4 St.Tr.(N.S.) 767.

[5] *Bankers' Case* (1699) Skin. 601.

[6] *Thomas v. R.* (1874) L.R. 10 Q.B. 31.

[7] *R. v. Doutre* (1884) 9 App.Cas. 745.

[8] *Malkin v. R.* [1906] 2 K.B. 886; for mistake of law, see *William Whiteley v. R.* (1909) 101 L.T. 741; *National Pari-Mutuel Assoc. Ltd v. R.* (1930) 47 T.L.R. 110; *cf. Mason v. New South Wales* (1985) 102 C.L.R. 108 *post,* § 30–075. A petition of right lay to recover overpayments of tax: *Re Nathan* (1884) 12 Q.B.D. 461; and *semble* for money received to the use of the suppliant: *Bucknall v. R.* (1930) 46 T.L.R. 449.

[9] See *Brocklebank Ltd v. The King* [1925] 1 K.B. 52; *Anglo-Saxon Petroleum Ltd v. Admiralty* [1947] K.B. 794 and see Williams, *Crown Proceedings* (1948), pp. 12–15. For the recovery of *ultra vires* receipts by the Crown in modern law see *Woolwich Equitable B.S. v. I.R.C.* [1993] A.C. 70; *post* § 30–080.

view that certain incorporated government departments could be sued by ordinary action in contract[10]; and contractual actions could also be maintained against departments which, by statute, could "sue and be sued."[11] Besides the petition of right a declaration could and still can sometimes be issued against the Attorney-General in civil proceedings in matters affecting the rights of the Crown.[12]

10–002   **Crown Proceedings Act.** Section 1 of the Crown Proceedings Act 1947 provides:

"Where any person has a claim against the Crown after the commencement of this Act,[13] and, if this Act had not been passed, the claim might have been enforced, subject to the grant of His Majesty's fiat, by petition of right, or might have been enforced by a proceeding provided by any statutory provision repealed by this Act,[14] then, subject to the provisions of this Act, the claim may be enforced as of right, and without the fiat of His Majesty, by proceedings taken against the Crown for that purpose in accordance with the provisions of this Act."

By section 13 of the Act, but subject to its provisions, proceedings by way of petition of right are abolished, and all civil proceedings by or against the Crown in the High Court are to be instituted and proceeded with in accordance with rules of court.[15] By section 15 any civil proceedings against the Crown may be instituted in a county court in accordance with county court rules.[16] It is also provided[17] that the Treasury shall publish a list specifying the government departments authorised to institute or defend proceedings by or against the Crown, but if no appropriate department exists, or in case of doubt, proceedings should be instituted against the Attorney-General. The Act does not apply to proceedings by or against the Sovereign in her private capacity.[18]

10–003   **Incidence of Crown privilege.** As a result of the Crown Proceedings Act, proceedings by or against the Crown in contract are, for the most part, governed by the same rules of procedure as proceedings between subjects. But the substantive law of contract to be administered in those proceedings is subject to the same reservations of liability on the part of the Crown which existed before the Act. Moreover the Act itself prohibits the grant of certain kinds of relief against

---

[10] *Graham v. Commissioners of Public Works* [1901] 2 K.B. 781.

[11] *Minister of Supply v. British Thomson-Houston Co.* [1943] K.B. 478.

[12] *Dyson v. Att.-Gen.* [1912] 1 K.B. 410; *cf. Bombay and Persia Steam Navigation Co. v. Maclay* [1920] 3 K.B. 402, 408; Crown Proceedings Act 1947, s.21(1); *Tito v. Waddell (No. 2)* [1977] Ch. 106, 256–260; *Tranwick v. Lennox* [1985] 1 W.L.R. 532, 549; and see Zamir and Woolf, *The Declaratory Judgment* (2nd ed., 1993), pp. 26–29, 243–249; Young, *Declaratory Orders* (1975), §§ 103, 108, 609, 809.

[13] January 1, 1948: see S.R. & O. 1947 No. 2527.

[14] Crown Proceedings Act 1947, s.39(1) and Sched. 2.

[15] See generally RSC, Ord. 77, which remains in force under the Civil Procedure Rules, Sched. 1.

[16] See CCR, 1981, Ord. 42 which remains in force; and see County Courts Act 1984, s.46(1)(2), for proceedings brought *by* the Crown.

[17] s.17. For the most recent list, see *The Supreme Court Practice 1999*, Vol. II, para. 212–237.

[18] s.40(1); County Courts Act 1984, s.46(3). The former remedy by petition of right presumably remains available in cases of actions against the Sovereign in her private capacity, but it is uncertain whether such proceedings would still be governed by the Petitions of Right Act 1860 or by the previous rules of common law: Williams, *Crown Proceedings* (1948), p. 8; Wade & Forsyth, *Administrative Law* (7th ed. 1994) p. 822.

the Crown in civil proceedings.[19] In view of these limitations, it is still necessary to consider who is entitled to Crown privilege. On this point, the Act itself gives little guidance: "Civil proceedings by or against the Crown" are to be construed as including a reference to civil proceedings to which the Attorney-General, or any government department, or any officer of the Crown as such, is a party[20] but have been held not to include proceedings by way of an application for judicial review.[21] Two questions which may arise in a contractual context are left open by this definition. First, which public corporations (or unincorporated statutory bodies) can be regarded as government departments or agents of the Crown for the purpose of entitlement to Crown privilege?[22] Probably the test is the same as that which determines whether such bodies are, for other purposes, servants or agents of the Crown: in the absence of an express provision to that effect in the statute (if any) setting up the body in question, this appears to depend on the degree of control exercised over the body by a Minister of the Crown.[23] Secondly, does a person who is admittedly an officer of the Crown always act "as such" when performing public functions imposed, for instance, on a Minister by statute? The view that he will be regarded as so acting unless the relevant statute expressly or by necessary implication provides the contrary[24] has been said to be incorrect insofar as it suggested that a Minister when acting in an official capacity could not be sued personally and an injunction granted against him.[25] In judicial review proceedings it has been held that a Minister of the Crown does not always act "as such" when performing public functions.[26]

Pre-contractual procedures. Where a person or body invites tenders to be   **10–004**
submitted for a contract and prescribes a clear, orderly and familiar procedure, an

---

[19] See *post*, § 10–019.

[20] s.38(4). See also s.38(2).

[21] See *post*, § 10–019.

[22] Next Steps Agencies, which now employ about 60 per cent of civil servants, are not legal entities. See Goldsworthy, *Setting Up Next Steps* (HMSO 1991). By the National Health Service and Community Care Act 1990, s.60, no health service body shall be regarded as the servant or agent of the Crown or as enjoying any Crown privilege. See also Deregulation and Contracting Out Act 1994, ss.69–70 for the extension of the principle in *Carltona Ltd v. Commissioners of Works* [1943] 2 All E.R. 560 to non-departmental bodies. Part II of the Housing Grants, Construction and Regeneration Act 1996 applies to the Crown: s.117.

[23] *Cannon Brewery Co. Ltd v. Central Land Board* [1919] A.C. 744; *International Railway Co. v. Niagara Parks Commission* [1941] A.C. 328; *Territorial Forces Association v. Philpot* [1947] 2 All E.R. 376; *Territorial and Auxiliary Forces Association of London v. Nichols* [1949] 1 K.B. 35; *Tamlin v. Hannaford* [1950] 1 K.B. 18; *Bank voor Handel en Scheepvaart v. Administrator of Hungarian Property* [1954] A.C. 584; *Hills (Patents) Ltd v. University College Hospital Board of Governors* [1956] 1 Q.B. 90; *Glasgow Corporation v. Central Land Board* (1956) S.C. 1; *Pfizer Corpn. v. Ministry of Health* [1964] Ch. 614, affd. [1965] A.C. 512; *B.B.C. v. Johns* [1965] Ch. 32; *Mellenger v. New Brunswick Development Corporation* [1971] 1 W.L.R. 604; *cf. Moukataff v. B.O.A.C.* [1967] 1 Lloyd's Rep. 396, and see Griffith (1952) 9 Univ. of Toronto L.J. 169; Treitel [1957] P.L. 321, 327; Wade and Forsyth, *op. cit.*, pp. 172, 176–177.

[24] *Merricks v. Heathcoat-Amory* [1955] Ch. 567, 575–576; *Town Investments Ltd v. Department of Environment* [1978] A.C. 359; *cf. Att.-Gen. for the Straits Settlements v. Pang Ah Yew* [1925] A.C. 555.

[25] *M. v. Home Office* [1994] 1 A.C. 377, HL, reviewing the earlier authorities in which *Merricks v. Heathcoat-Amory* was doubted. See also *Pearce v. Secretary of State for Defence* [1988] A.C. 755, 790 (*Town Investments* said not to cover the meaning of "The Crown").

[26] *ibid.*; *Padfield v. Minister of Agriculture, Fisheries and Food* [1968] A.C. 997 (statutory duties imposed upon "the Minister" enforceable by mandamus, a remedy not available against the Crown).

obligation to consider conforming tenders and to adhere to the specified requirements may be implied.[27] The tendering procedures used by the Crown and central
government departments will often give rise to such an implied obligation. They
are also subject to the procurement procedures and remedies required by European Community law discussed *post*, §§ 10–029—10–030.

10–005   **Source of power to contract.** As a non-statutory corporation sole the contracts of the Crown are not subject to the *ultra vires* doctrine. In certain cases the
powers of individual Ministers have been defined by statute[28] or statutory
instruments made under the Ministers of the Crown Act 1975.[29] These may limit
the capacity of the Crown itself,[30] or the scope of authority possessed by Crown
agents.[31] Apart from such statutory restrictions, the Crown has the power to
contract without the need for any specific statutory authority. It has been suggested that this may be the case only for contracts which are incidental to the
ordinary and well-recognised functions of government[32] although there appears
to be no reason in principle for this limitation.[33]

10–006   **Parliamentary funds.** However, it has often been said that obligations undertaken by the Crown to pay money are subject to the implied condition that the
funds necessary to satisfy the obligation shall be made available by Parliament.[34]
The precise legal effect of this principle seems at one time to have been
misunderstood. In *Churchward v. The Queen*[35] the Admiralty covenanted to pay
the plaintiff £18,000 per annum for the carriage of cross-Channel mail. The
appropriation for this contract was expressly and deliberately withheld by Act of
Parliament. The plaintiff sued for the promised sum. He failed on the ground that
the contract provided for payment "out of moneys provided by Parliament," and
no such moneys were ever provided. Shee J. went further and said: "I am of
opinion that the providing of funds by Parliament is a condition precedent to [the
covenant] attaching."[36] But in *New South Wales v. Bardolph*,[37] the High Court of
Australia held that it was no answer to a suit against the Crown upon a contract
that the moneys necessary to answer the liability had not, up to the time of the
suit, been provided by Parliament. The provision of funds by Parliament was
simply a condition which must be fulfilled before actual payment by the Crown,

---

[27] *R. v. Lord Chancellor, ex p. Hibbit and Saunders* [1993] C.O.D. 326; *Blackpool and Fylde Aero Club v. Blackpool B.C.* [1990] 1 W.L.R. 1195; *Fairclough Building Ltd v. Port Talbot B.C.* [1992] C.I.L.L. 779; and see the discussion *ante*, § 2–019.
[28] *e.g.* Supply Powers Act 1975, s.1.
[29] This replaced the Ministers of the Crown (Transfer of Functions) Act 1946. See also Government Trading Funds Act 1973. For a list of statutory instruments, see *Halsbury's Statutory Instruments*, Vol. 5, pp. 23–24. See also, *ibid.* pp. 25 *et seq.*
[30] *Cugden Rutile (No. 2) Ltd v. Chalk* [1975] A.C. 520.
[31] Daintith (1979) 32 C.L.P. 41, 42–45; see *post*, § 10–016.
[32] *New South Wales v. Bardolph* (1934) 52 C.L.R. 455, 474–496, 502–503, 508, 518; *A. v. Hayden (No. 2)* (1985) 59 A.L.J.R. 6, 27.
[33] *Verreault & Fils Ltée v. Att.-Gen. for Quebec* (1975) 57 D.L.R. (3d) 403 (Supt.Ct. of Canada); *Skywest Airlines Pty. Ltd v. Northern Territory* (1987) 87 F.L.R. 312, 326; Campbell (1970) 44 A.L.J. 14; Hogg, *Liability of the Crown* (1971), pp. 120–121; Turpin, *Government Procurement and Contracts* (1989), p. 84.
[34] *Macbeath v. Haldimand* (1786) 1 T.R. 172, 176; *Mackay v. Att.-Gen. for British Columbia* [1922] 1 A.C. 457, 461; *Auckland Harbour Board v. The King* [1924] A.C. 318; *Att.-Gen. v. Great Southern and Western Ry. of Ireland* [1925] A.C. 754, 773.
[35] (1865) L.R. 1 Q.B. 173.
[36] At 209–210.
[37] (1934) 52 C.L.R. 455.

and did not go to the formation, legality or validity of the contract.[38] Moreover it seems that an express appropriation is not required; it is sufficient if provision has been made for a class of transaction to which the contract belongs.[39] It is submitted that the interpretation of the rule adopted by the Australian case is to be preferred to that of Shee J. in *Churchward v. The Queen*.[40]

Future executive action. The power of the Crown (like that of other public **10–007** authorities[41]) to fetter itself by contract from exercising its discretion is limited, but it is difficult to state the extent and effect of the non-fettering principle with precision. In *The Amphitrite*,[42] Rowlatt J. said that "it is not competent for the Government to fetter its future executive action which must necessarily be determined by the needs of the community when the question arises. It cannot by contract hamper its freedom of action in matters which concern the welfare of the State."[43] This statement has been criticised[44] for its width. Three issues must be separated; the validity of the contract *ab initio*, the question whether, assuming the contract is valid, the Government is thereafter under a duty to exercise its powers in a manner consistent with it and, thirdly, the question whether, assuming there is no valid contract, the Crown is nevertheless precluded from exercising its discretion in a particular way by an estoppel or the application of the emerging principle of legitimate expectation.[45]

Validity of the contract *ab initio* As far as the first issue is concerned, the **10–008** vast majority of government contracts are commercial contracts for goods or services and it is generally accepted that the Government can bind itself by a commercial contract.[46] However, *The Amphitrite* was not such a case. There, the Swedish owners of a steamship obtained an undertaking from the British Legation in Stockholm that if they sent her to this country with a designated cargo she would not be detained as a result of the Government's measures for the wartime blockade of Germany. The ship was dispatched, but the Government nevertheless refused her clearance. The shipowners, after the end of the war, unsuccessfully brought a petition of right, claiming damages for breach of contract. Rowlatt J. held that the undertaking was not a contract but merely an expression of intention

---

[38] This view as based on the statements of Cockburn C.J. in *Churchward's* case, *supra*, at 200. See also *R. v. Fisher* [1903] A.C. 158; *Kidman v. Commonwealth* (1926) 32 Argus L.R. 2; *A. v. Hayden (No. 2)* (1985) 59 A.L.J.R. 6, 27. A contract may be subject to a specific parliamentary appropriation of funds by express words (as in *Churchward's* case), by statute (as by s.8(8), Industry Act 1972), or possibly by constitutional practice: *Commercial Cable Co. v. Government of Newfoundland* [1916] 2 A.C. 610; *New South Wales v. Bardolph, supra*, at 502 (Starke J.); *cf.* Dixon J. at 510.

[39] *cf. New South Wales v. Bardolph, supra*, at 474.

[40] (1865) L.R. 1 Q.B. 173.

[41] Mitchell, *The Contracts of Public Authorities* (1954), pp. 57–65. See also *Commissioners of Crown Lands v. Page* [1960] 2 Q.B. 274, 287, 291; *Ansett Transport Industries (Operations) Pty. Ltd v. Commonwealth* (1977) 17 A.L.R. 513 where the analogue was recognised, although see *Page's* case, at 292, for its limits.

[42] *Rederiaktiebolaget Amphitrite v. The King* [1921] 3 K.B. 500.

[43] *ibid.* at 503.

[44] *Robertson v. Minister of Pensions* [1949] 1 K.B. 227, 231; *Ansett Transport Industries (Operations) Pty. Ltd v. Commonwealth* (1977) 17 A.L.R. 513, 530, 562; *A. v. Hayden (No. 2)* (1985) 59 A.L.J.R. 6, 8; Holdsworth (1929) 45 L.Q.R. 166; Mitchell, *op. cit.* pp. 27–32, 52–57; *cf. Howell v. Falmouth Boat Construction Co. Ltd* [1951] A.C. 837.

[45] On which see, *post*, § 10–038.

[46] Rowlatt J. conceded this: [1921] 3 K.B. 500, 503. Estoppels may arise in such circumstances: see *Att.-Gen. of Hong Kong v. Humphreys Estate (Queen's Gardens)* [1987] 1 A.C. 114, 127–128.

to act in a particular way in a certain event because the Crown could not bind itself to fetter its future executive action. The distinction between "commercial" and "non-commercial" contracts has been criticised,[47] but Rowlatt J.'s view that there was no contract may be justified on the ground that the *only* consideration moving from the Crown was the undertaking to exercise its powers in a particular way[48] or that there was no *animus contrahendi*.[49]

10–009   **Exercise of discretionary power in relation to a valid contract.** Where a Crown contract has been validly entered into, it is necessary to consider the extent of the Crown's obligations. The freedom to exercise discretionary powers (whether statutory or prerogative) for the public good will not, as a matter of construction, be impliedly excluded by the contract.[50] "No one can imagine, for example, that when the Crown makes a contract which could not be fulfilled in time of war, it is pledging itself not to declare war for so long as the contract lasts."[51] Thus it has been held that an implied covenant for quiet enjoyment in a Crown lease did not prevent the Crown from requisitioning the premises.[52] The position of an express and specific undertaking is less clear and largely depends on the formulation of the non-fettering rule in *The Amphitrite*. That rule is based on the general principle that a contract will not be enforced "in any case where some essential governmental activity would be thereby rendered impossible or seriously impeded."[53] In applying this principle to Crown contracts the courts have to bear in mind the nature of the contract and the type of executive power involved. But it should also be remembered that specific relief is not available against the Crown in civil proceedings[54] and that an award of damages is much less likely than specific relief would be to impede an essential government activity or to render it impossible.[55] In practice the rule stated in the *Amphitrite* case does not often have to be applied since many contracts falling within its

---

[47] *Ansett Transport Industries (Operations) Pty. Ltd v. Commonwealth* (1977) 17 A.L.R. 513, 562; Holdsworth *op. cit.*; Mitchell *op. cit.* p. 62.

[48] *Cameron v. Lord Advocate*, 1952 S.C. 165, 173; See also *Commissioners of Crown Lands v. Page* [1960] 2 Q.B. 274, 293. This justification is unlikely to survive the recognitition of practical benefit as consideration (*Williams v. Roffey Bros. & Nicholls (Contractors) Ltd* [1991] 1 Q.B. 1), *ante*, §3–063.

[49] *Robertson v. Minister of Pensions* [1949] 1 K.B. 227; *ante*, § 2–163.

[50] *Board of Trade v. Temperley Steam Shipping Co. Ltd* (1926) 26 Ll.L.Rep. 76, affd. (1927) 27 Ll.L.Rep. 230; *Commissioners of Crown Lands v. Page* [1960] 2 Q.B. 274; *Ansett Transport Industries (Operations) Pty. Ltd v. Commonwealth* (1977) 17 A.L.R. 513.

[51] *Commissioners of Crown Lands v. Page, supra*, at 292.

[52] *ibid.* In the cases cited above, the term the Crown was allegedly in breach of was an implied term. In *Page's* case Devlin L.J. thought nothing turned on this (at 292), but Evershed M.R. and Ormrod L.J. reserved their position. Devlin L.J.'s view is inferentially supported in *Ansett Transport Industries (Operations) Pty. Ltd v. Commonwealth* (1977) A.L.R. 513. See also *post*, § 10–033.

[53] Mitchell, *The Contracts of Public Authorities* (1954), p. 7; (1950) 13 M.L.R. 318, 455; 63 *Juridical Review* 60 (1951). See *Ansett Transport Industries (Operations) Pty. Ltd v. Commonwealth* (1977) 17 A.L.R. 513 for a possible example of an agreement limiting executive power which is not an improper fetter. See also, *post*, § 10–031.

[54] *Post*, § 10–019.

[55] *cf.* Hogg, *Liability of the Crown* (1971), pp. 136–139, who argues that awarding damages always "adjusts the conflict between public purposes and private interests quite satisfactorily." See *Sutling v. Director-General of Education* [1985] 3 N.S.W.L.R. 427, 446–447. But this would not be so where one aim of the executive action is to save money; *e.g.* by reducing a retirement age, as was done in *Hughes v. D.H.S.S.* [1985] A.C. 776 (but not necessarily with that aim).

scope contain cancellation clauses which usually make provision for compensation.[56]

Crown employees: dismissibility. The general rule is that persons in Crown   **10–010** employment hold office during the pleasure of the Crown.[57] This rule may of course be varied by statute, *e.g.* by the statutory provision under which judges of the High Court and Court of Appeal hold office during good behaviour,[58] but subject to a retirement age.[59] It is more doubtful whether the rule can be varied by contract or by the terms of appointment where these are not prescribed, or given binding effect, by legislation. In the case of members of the armed forces, it is established that the terms of appointment cannot oust the general rule of dismissibility at pleasure.[60] In the case of other persons in Crown employment, the general rule is not ousted *merely* because the terms of appointment provide that the appointment is to last for a fixed period.[61] A dictum in *Reilly v. R.*[62] is sometimes taken to mean that the general rule may be ousted if the terms of appointment prescribe a fixed period *and* provide for power to determine "for cause"[63]; but the dictum may refer only to cases where (as in *Reilly's* case) the terms of appointment are prescribed by legislation.[64] Where such terms do not have legislative backing, there is at least one clear decision to the effect that they do not oust the general rule of dismissibility at pleasure.[65] There may, however, be a distinction between, on the one hand, persons whose relations to the Crown are much the same as those between ordinary employer and employee, and, on the other hand, persons such as established civil servants, whose employment has been said not to depend on contract but on appointment to an office by the Crown[66]; and it may be that where "the Crown appoints to an office on the terms that it is to be held during good behaviour or that the holder is only to be removed

---

[56] See, for example, Turpin *op. cit.* at pp. 243–246.

[57] *Shenton v. Smith* [1895] A.C. 229; *Gould v. Stewart* [1896] A.C. 575; *Fisher v. Steward* (1920) 36 T.L.R. 395; *Rodwell v. Thomas* [1944] K.B. 596; *I.R.C. v. Hambrook* [1956] 2 Q.B. 641, 653; *Riordan v. War Office* [1959] 1 W.L.R. 1047 (affd. [1961] 1 W.L.R. 210); *Att.-Gen. for Guyana v. Nobrega* [1969] 3 All E.R. 1604; *Kodeeswaran v. Att.-Gen. of Ceylon* [1970] A.C. 1111; *Thomas v. Att.-Gen. of Trinidad and Tobago* [1982] A.C. 113; *Minister for Civil Service v. C.C.S.U.* [1985] 1 A.C. 374, 419; *R. v. Civil Service Appeal Board, ex p. Bruce* [1988] I.C.R. 649; affd. [1989] I.C.R. 171. See Griffith (1956) 19 M.L.R. 701. For the opposing Scots view, see *Cameron v. Lord Advocate*, 1952 S.C. 165, where some of the English cases are discussed.

[58] Supreme Court Act 1981, s.11(3). These provisions do not apply to colonial judges: *Terrell v. Secretary of State for the Colonies* [1953] 2 Q.B. 482. Circuit judges appointed under the Courts Act 1971 may be removed by the Lord Chancellor "on the ground of incapacity or misbehaviour" (s.17(4)). If a subsequent statute alters or abrogates the terms of service prescribed by statute, the employee has no redress at common law: *Reilly v. R.* [1934] A.C. 176, though a discretionary payment may be made to him, *e.g.* under s.2(2) of the Superannuation Act 1972.

[59] Judicial Pensions and Retirement Act 1993.

[60] *Re Tufnell* (1876) 3 Ch.D. 164; *Grant v. Secretary of State for India* (1877) 2 C.P.D. 445; *De Dohsé v. R.* (1886) 3 T.L.R. 114; *cf. Kynaston v. Att.-Gen.* (1933) 49 T.L.R. 300.

[61] *Dunn v. R.* [1896] 1 Q.B. 116; *cf. Terrell v. Secretary of State for the Colonies* [1953] 2 Q.B. 482; *Riordan v. War Office* [1959] 1 W.L.R. 1047 (affd. [1961] 1 W.L.R. 210); *Sutling v. Director-General of Education* [1985] 3 N.S.W.L.R. 427; Nettheim (1975) 34 C.L.J. 253.

[62] [1934] A.C. 176, 179.

[63] *e.g.* in *Robertson v. Minister of Pensions* [1949] 1 K.B. 227, 231.

[64] *Terrell v. Secretary of State for the Colonies* [1953] 2 Q.B. 482, 498–499; Mitchell, *The Contracts of Public Authorities*, p. 44; Nettheim (1975) 34 C.L.J. 253, 275–276.

[65] *Denning v. Secretary of State for India* (1920) 37 T.L.R. 138; *cf. Rodwell v. Thomas* [1944] K.B. 596.

[66] *I.R.C. v. Hambrook* [1956] 2 Q.B. 641, 654.

'for cause' . . . he would be entitled . . . to bring an action if he were removed without cause."[67]

10–011   **Status or contract?** It has been suggested that the relationship between the Crown and its employees is one of status and not truly contractual[68]; but this may in fact reflect the absence of an intention to contract on the part of the Crown and it has been said that there is "nothing unconstitutional about civil servants being employed by the Crown pursuant to contracts of service."[69] However, there are conflicting decisions as to whether the use of language of obligation or even of the word "contract" suffices to indicate an intention by the Crown to depart from the non-contractual relationship expressed in the Civil Service Pay and Conditions Service Code.[70] Even if the relationship is one of status, little light is shed on the question to what extent the terms of that relationship are legally enforceable at common law. The weight of English authority favours the view that dismissal in breach of the terms of appointment gives rise to no cause of action at common law.[71] If the relationship is not contractual then, whether the power to dismiss is statutory, prerogative or derived from the common law, such dismissal may be susceptible to the public law remedy of judicial review where it is *ultra vires*, an abuse of discretion or where the principles of procedural fairness have not been observed.[72] Remedies by way of judicial review are, however, discretionary and may not be granted where an alternative remedy is available.[73]

10–012   **Regulations, agreements and statutory protection.** In practice the conditions of Crown employment are generally governed by regulations and agreements which are observed even though they may not be legally binding either as contracts or as delegated legislation.[74] Moreover the Employment Rights Act 1996[75] extends to Crown employees[76] the remedies available for unfair dis-

---

[67] *Terrell v. Secretary of State for the Colonies* [1953] 2 Q.B. 482, 499–500; contrast *ibid.* at 497–498: "Once it is established that the Crown has power to dismiss at pleasure, that right cannot be taken away by any contractual arrangement made by an executive officer or department of State."

[68] Blair (1958) 21 M.L.R. 265; Blair [1958] P.L. 32; Fredman and Morris [1988] P.L. 58. The distinction is central to the question of whether relief by way of judicial review is available; see *post*, n. 73.

[69] *R. v. Civil Service Appeal Board, ex p. Bruce* [1988] I.C.R. 649; affd. [1989] I.C.R. 171 (*per* May L.J.).

[70] *cf. McClaren v. Home Office* [1990] I.C.R. 84 (no contract) and *R. v. Derbyshire CC, ex p. Noble* [1990] I.C.R. 808; *R. v. Lord Chancellor's Dept., ex p. Nangle* [1991] I.C.R. 743 (contract).

[71] See nn. 57, 60 and 65, *ante*.

[72] *R. v. Secretary of State for the Home Department, ex p. Benwell* [1985] Q.B. 554 (dismissal of prison officer in breach of code quashed); *Council of Civil Service Unions v. Minister for the Civil Service* [1985] 1 A.C. 374. For the grounds of judicial review, see Wade *op. cit.* Parts III–V.

[73] *R. v. East Berkshire Health Authority, ex p. Walsh* [1985] Q.B. 152; *R. v. Civil Service Appeal Board, ex p. Bruce, supra* (judicial review not available where individual seeking to enforce rights under contract of employment and probably not where industrial tribunal has jurisdiction); *ante*, §§ 1–129—1–131. On the availability of judicial review, see Walsh [1989] P.L. 131; Fredman and Morris (1991) 107 L.Q.R. 298; [1991] P.L. 485.

[74] See, for example, *Riordan v. War Office* [1959] 1 W.L.R. 1047; *Department of Health and Social Security v. Randall* [1981] I.C.R. 100; *cf. Cresswell v. Board of Inland Revenue* [1984] I.C.R. 508 (conditions of service treated as legally enforceable).

[75] s.191. See also Trade Union and Labour Relations (Consolidation) Act 1992, ss.152, 273 (dismissals on ground of trade union membership and activities or non-membership) and Vol. II, § 39–031.

[76] Including members of the armed forces: s.192(1), as inserted by the Trade Union Reform and Employment Rights Act 1993, s.31 (*Robinson v. County of London Territorial and Auxiliary Forces*

missal,[77] so that, to this extent, the power of the Crown to dismiss at pleasure, without payment of compensation, has been limited by statute. Employees of the Crown do not, however, enjoy all the statutory rights given to other employees.[78] In particular they are not entitled to minimum periods of notice[79] or to redundancy payments.[80] As, however, the terms of appointment of Crown employees may expressly give the Crown the right to change conditions of service[81] or remit issues to the discretion of the employer, the exercise of which is subject to changes in administrative policy,[82] in practice the remedies available to Crown employees will be limited whatever the nature of the relationship.

Crown employees: arrears of pay. Members of the armed forces cannot sue 10–013 for arrears of pay.[83] In *Lucas v. Lucas*[84] Pilcher J. held that the same rule applied to other Crown employees; but this view has been convincingly criticised[85] and the actual decision can be explained on the ground that the pay of a civil servant could not (and still cannot)[86] be attached by garnishee proceedings. A number of earlier authorities appear to assume that civil servants can recover arrears of pay[87]; and this view is supported by dicta in two later cases.[88] In *Kodeeswaran v. Att.-Gen. of Ceylon*,[89] on appeal from Ceylon, the Privy Council held that a person in Crown employment could sue the Crown for arrears of pay in respect of services rendered as a civil servant, and Lord Diplock said that the Crown's right to terminate at will "cannot affect any right to salary already earned under the terms of his existing contract before its termination."[90] It is submitted that the reasoning of *Lucas v. Lucas* would not now be followed and that civil servants are entitled to recover arrears of pay. This may even be the case where the civil servant is in breach of the conditions of service. Provided the requisite intention

---

Assocn. [1967] I.T.R. 652) but not prison officers whose status is that of constable (*Home Office v. Robinson* [1981] I.R.L.R. 524; *R. v Secretary of State for the Home Department, ex p. Benwell* [1985] Q.B. 554, 571–572) or where a Minister certifies that exemption in respect of a particular employment is required by national security (this was done in relation to staff at Government Communications Headquarters, for example).

[77] They are also entitled to a written statement of reasons for dismissal: ss.92, 191(2), 192(1).

[78] House of Commons and House of Lords staff are entitled to most rights: Employment Rights Act 1996, ss.194–195.

[79] Pt. IV of the Employment Rights Act 1996 does not apply to Crown employment: s.191(2).

[80] *ibid.* s.191(6). But see s.171(3). Public officers are also excluded from this: s.159(a). See Vol. II, § 37–029.

[81] *Cresswell v. Board of Inland Revenue* [1984] I.C.R. 508, 521. See also *Council of Civil Service Unions v. Minister for the Civil Service* [1985] 1 A.C. 374 (change of regulations governing union membership); *Hughes v. D.H.S.S.* [1985] A.C. 776, *post* § 10–038.

[82] *Hughes v. D.H.S.S.* [1985] A.C. 776 (change of policy about the normal retiring age). See also *Council of Civil Service Unions v. Minister for the Civil Service, supra.* But the doctrine of legitimate expectation may afford protection against unannounced changes of policy: *post,* § 10–038.

[83] *Mitchell v. R.* [1896] 1 Q.B. 121n.; *Leaman v. R.* [1920] 3 K.B. 663; *cf. Smith v. Lord Advocate* (1897) 25 R. 112.

[84] [1943] P. 68; the Scots decision to the same effect in *Mulvenna v. The Admiralty*, 1926 S.C. 842 was disapproved in *Cameron v. Lord Advocate*, 1952 S.C. 165.

[85] Logan (1945) 61 L.Q.R. 240.

[86] Crown Proceedings Act 1947, s.27(1)(a).

[87] *Sutton v. Att.-Gen.* (1923) 39 T.L.R. 295; *Pidduck v. R.* (1924) 41 T.L.R. 51; *Brandy v. Owners of SS. Raphael* [1911] A.C. 413; *cf. R. v. Fisher* [1903] A.C. 158.

[88] *Terrell v. Secretary of State for the Colonies* [1953] 2 Q.B. 482, 499; *I.R.C. v. Hambrook* [1956] 2 Q.B. 641, 654, where it is added that "He would claim on a *quantum meruit.*" But it seems to be envisaged that he would recover the stipulated sum ("his salary").

[89] [1970] A.C. 1111.

[90] *ibid.* at 1123.

to contract exists the Crown's liability will be contractual. Otherwise, as where the terms of the appointment show that there is no intention to contract, it may be possible to bring a restitutionary action provided the contract has been terminated and the Crown has not made it clear that only full contractual performance would be acceptable.[91] An action may also be brought against the Crown to recover either a reasonable or (probably) the agreed remuneration due for professional services.[92]

10–014   **Crown employees: liability.** Although there is no authority on the question whether the Crown can sue its employees for breach of contract[93] it is submitted that such an action should lie. This is certainly so if an intention to contract can be established and the relationship between the Crown and its employees is therefore contractual but subject to the Crown's right to dismiss at pleasure. The rule entitling the Crown to dismiss its employees at pleasure exists for the protection of the Crown and the policy of the rule does not require reciprocal protection to be given to Crown employees. In principle, therefore, remedies should be available against Crown employees who are in breach of their terms of appointment.[94] Even where the relationship between the Crown and its employees is not contractual a remedy may be available against the employee in certain circumstances such as breach of confidence.[95] Furthermore, by statute,[96] the terms of Crown employment are deemed to constitute a contract of employment for the purpose of the torts of inducing breach of (or interfering with) contract and intimidation. Thus, unless their actions are in contemplation or furtherance of a trade dispute and fall within the statutory immunity,[97] third parties who induce Crown employees to break their engagements with the Crown will be liable in tort.[98]

10–015   **Agents of Crown: liability of agent.** The general rule is that an employee or agent of the Crown who contracts on behalf of the Crown cannot himself be sued

---

[91] *Wiluszynski v. Tower Hamlets L.B.C.* [1989] I.C.R. 493; *Cresswell v. Board of Inland Revenue* [1984] I.C.R. 508, *post*, §§ 30–178—30–180; *cf. Miles v. Wakefield M.B.C.* [1987] A.C. 539.

[92] *R. v. Doutre* (1884) 9 App.Cas. 745.

[93] Although see *Fisher v. Steward* (1920) 36 T.L.R. 395.

[94] While employers rarely sue their employees for breach of contract one example of such an action is to enforce obligations of confidence. See *Schering Chemicals Ltd v. Falkman Ltd* [1982] 1 Q.B. 18. For other duties see Vol. II, §§ 39–059—39–061.

[95] *Att.-Gen. v. Guardian Newspapers (No. 2)* [1990] 1 A.C. 109; *Att.-Gen. v. Blake* [1998] 1 All E.R. 833 (*post*, § 30–096); *Snepp v. U.S.*, 100 S.Ct. 763 (1980). But *cf.* Fredman and Morris [1988] P.L. 58, 70–71 (equitable remedy may be less far-reaching than one based on contract); *A. v. Hayden (No. 2)* (1985) 59 A.L.J.R. 6, 27 (*Crown's* obligation of confidence not enforceable).

[96] Trade Union and Labour Relations (Consolidation) Act 1992, s.245.

[97] *ibid.* s.219, as amended by the Trade Union Reform and Employment Rights Act 1993, Sched. 8, para. 32. See Vol. II, § 39–069.

[98] Indeed, such third parties may commit an offence if the employee is a member of the armed forces (Incitement to Mutiny Act 1797; Incitement to Disaffection Act 1934, s.1) or the police (Police Act 1996, s.91).

on the contract[99] or be made liable for breach of warranty of authority.[1] A public officer is only liable where he *expressly* pledges his personal credit.[2]

Crown contracting through agents. The Crown generally contracts through **10–016** agents; but the ordinary principles of agency may apply to such cases with some modification. The Crown is liable where the agent acts within his actual or ostensible authority[3]; but in accordance with the ordinary principles of agency[4] ostensible authority cannot arise merely from a representation by the agent that he has authority: there must be a holding out by the principal,[5] or by someone authorised by him. A private principal is also liable, even though there has been no holding out, for acts which are in fact unauthorised but are "within the authority usually confided to an agent of . . . [the] character"[6] in question. It is doubtful whether the Crown would be liable in such a case.[7]

Estoppel.[8] The Crown may not be bound by estoppels by deed,[9] but it may be **10–017** bound by estoppels by conduct.[10] In *Robertson v. Minister of Pensions*[11] the plaintiff was assured by the War Office that, for the purposes of a pension, his disability had been accepted as attributable to military service. Relying on this assurance he forbore to obtain an independent medical opinion. But the officer who made the assurance had no authority to make it since the administration of certain disablement claims (including the plaintiff's) had been transferred from the War Office to the Ministry of Pensions. It was held that the Minister of Pensions could not deny that the plaintiff's injury was attributable to service. The decision could be regarded as an application to the Crown of the ordinary principles of estoppel. Denning J. also stated the wider principle that "if a government department in its dealings with a subject takes upon itself to assume authority upon a matter with which he is concerned, he is entitled to rely on it having the authority which it assumes."[12] But this proposition, if taken literally, could validate a contract which was *ultra vires*[13] or legalise an otherwise illegal

---

[99] *Macbeath v. Haldimand* (1786) 1 T.R. 172; *Unwin v. Wolseley* (1787) 1 T.R. 674; *Myrtle v. Beaver* (1800) 1 East 135; *Rice v. Chute* (1801) 1 East 579; *Auty v. Hutchinson* (1848) 6 C.B. 266, 271; *Palmer v. Hutchinson* (1881) 6 App.Cas. 619. This rule cannot be evaded by suing the Crown employee for a declaration: *Hosier Bros. v. Earl of Derby* [1918] 2 K.B. 671.

[1] *Dunn v. Macdonald* [1897] 1 Q.B. 555 applied in *The Prometheus* (1949) 82 Ll.L.Rep. 859; criticised by Street, *Government Liability* (1953), p. 93.

[2] *Prosser v. Allen* (1819) Gow 117; *Clutterbuck v. Coffin* (1842) 3 M. & G. 842; *Samuel Bros. v. Whetherly* [1908] 1 K.B. 184; *cf. Graham v. Public Works Commissioners* [1901] 2 K.B. 781.

[3] *Att.-Gen. for Ceylon v. A. D. Silva* [1953] A.C. 461, 479; Craig, *Administrative Law* (3rd ed., 1994), pp. 654–655.

[4] See Vol. II, Chap. 32.

[5] *Att.-Gen. for Ceylon v. A. D. Silva, supra*, at 479.

[6] *Watteau v. Fenwick* [1893] 1 Q.B. 346, 348–349. But *cf.* Vol. II, § 32–046.

[7] See *Robertson v. Minister of Pensions* [1949] 1 K.B. 227; *Att.-Gen. for Ceylon v. Silva* [1953] A.C. 461; Treitel [1957] P.L. 321, 335–339. But *cf. Meates v. Att.-Gen.* [1979] 1 N.Z.L.R. 415, 462; [1983] N.Z.L.R. 308, 377.

[8] The authorities make no sharp difference between the position of the Crown and that of other public authorities. See *post*, § 10–037.

[9] *Coke's Case* (1623) Godb. 289, 299; *cf. Farrer* (1933) 49 L.Q.R. 511.

[10] *Att.-Gen. to Prince of Wales v. Collom* [1916] 2 K.B. 193, 204; *Att.-Gen. for Hong Kong v. Humphreys Estate (Queen's Gardens)* [1987] 1 A.C. 114.

[11] [1949] 1 K.B. 227. See also *Re 56 Denton Road, Twickenham* [1953] Ch. 51; *Wells v. Minister of Housing and Local Govt.* [1967] 1 W.L.R. 1000; *Re L. (An Infant)* [1971] 3 All E.R. 743.

[12] [1949] 1 K.B. 227, 232.

[13] See *Minister of Agriculture and Fisheries v. Matthews* [1950] 1 K.B. 148; and see *ante*, § 10–004, *post*, § 10–037.

agreement.[14] In these contexts the principle has been repudiated by the House of Lords.[15] But the actual decision in *Robertson's* case was not overruled and it has been followed.[16] Furthermore, under the public law principle of legitimate expectation, it has been held that where a Minister's conduct is equivalent to a breach of contract or breach of representation it might be subject to judicial review for unfairness amounting to abuse of power.[17] It is, however, generally recognised that "estoppel cannot be allowed to hinder the formation of government policy"[18] and an estoppel will not arise where the person dealing with the government body has behaved inequitably, for instance by not making full disclosure of all the material facts known to him when seeking a ruling.[19] Finally, it should be remembered that a negligent misstatement by the Crown might give rise to liability in tort.[20]

10–018   **Postal packets.** No action can be brought in contract against the Crown for loss of or damage to any postal packet since the relationship between the Crown and the sender is not contractual.[21] But a special statutory cause of action has been created in respect of the loss of or damage to a registered inland postal packet.[22]

10–019   **Types of remedy available against the Crown.** The normal remedies and relief available to a litigant in an action between subject and subject are available against the Crown, but no injunction or order of specific performance, or order for the recovery of land or delivery of property, can be granted or made against the Crown in "civil proceedings."[23] Instead the court makes an order declaratory of the rights of the parties.[24] Also no injunction or order can be granted or made against an officer of the Crown in such proceedings if its effect would be to give any relief against the Crown which would not have been available in proceedings

---

[14] See *Howell v. Falmouth Boat Construction Co. Ltd* [1951] A.C. 837.

[15] *Howell v. Falmouth Boat Construction Co. Ltd, supra,* at 844, 845. But see *Re L. (An Infant), supra*; Craig, *Administrative Law* (3rd ed., 1994), Chap. 18 and see the doubts expressed in *Gowa v. Att.-Gen.* [1985] 1 W.L.R. 1003, 1005, 1009. For the view that the assurance in *Robertson's* case was *ultra vires* see Ganz [1965] P.L. 237, 244–245.

[16] *Re L. (An Infant), supra.*

[17] *R. v. Secretary of State for the Home Department, ex p. Khan* [1984] 1 W.L.R. 1337; *R. v. Secretary of State for the Home Department, ex p. Ruddock* [1987] 1 W.L.R. 1482; *Re Preston* [1985] A.C. 835, 867. See also *Council for Civil Service Unions v. Minister for the Civil Service* [1985] A.C. 374, 408.

[18] *Laker Airways Ltd v. Department of Trade* [1977] Q.B. 643, 680–682, 707, 709, 728; *Hughes v. D.H.S.S.* [1985] A.C. 776.

[19] *R. v. Board of Inland Revenue, ex p. MFK Underwriting Agencies Ltd* [1990] 1 W.L.R. 1545.

[20] *Minister of Housing and Local Government v. Sharp* [1970] 2 Q.B. 223. *cf. Yuen Kun Yeu v. Att.-Gen. of Hong Kong* [1988] A.C. 175.

[21] *Triefus v. Post Office* [1957] 2 Q.B. 352, relying on *Lane v. Cotton* (1701) Ld. Raym. 646; *Whitfield v. Lord Le Despencer* (1778) 2 Cowp. 754. Actions in tort are barred by s.29 of the Post Office Act 1969. The protection extends to a carrier employed as an independent contractor by the Post Office for the carriage of mail: *American Express v. British Airways Board* [1983] 1 All E.R. 557; *cf. Moukataff v. B.O.A.C.* [1967] 1 Lloyd's Rep. 396.

[22] Post Office Act 1969, s.30, as amended by s.70 of the British Telecommunications Act 1981. For damages under the corresponding repealed section (s.9(2)) of the Crown Proceedings Act 1947, see *Building and Civil Engineering Holidays Scheme Management Ltd v. Post Office* [1966] 1 Q.B. 247. But see s.30(3) of the 1969 Act.

[23] *ibid.* s.38(2), *ante,* § 10–004.

[24] Crown Proceedings Act 1947, s.21(1). This does not empower interim declarations to be made against the Crown in civil proceedings: *I.R.C. v. Rossminster* [1980] A.C. 952; but *cf. M. v. Home Office* [1994] 1 A.C. 377, 422–423 and *Yotvin v. The State of Israel* 1980 P.D. (2) 344, translated in Zamir and Woolf, *The Declaratory Judgment* (2nd ed., 1993).

against the Crown.[25] However, it has been held that proceedings by way of judicial review are not "civil proceedings," and that injunctive relief, including interim relief, may be given against Ministers of the Crown acting in their official capacity in judicial review proceedings.[26] The Crown may be required to make discovery of documents, produce documents for inspection and answer interrogatories, but (subject to scrutiny of its claim by the court) it may claim public interest immunity for the withholding of any document or the refusal to answer any question on the ground that the disclosure of the document or the answering of the question would be injurious to the public interest.[27] No execution or attachment can be issued against the Crown for enforcing payment of debts, damages or costs against the Crown[28] and proceedings *in rem* cannot be brought against the Crown or Crown property.[29] However, where a Minister has disregarded an injunction made against him in judicial review proceedings, the court has jurisdiction to make a finding of contempt against him or his department.[30]

Injunctions at the suit of the Crown. Since the Crown Proceedings Act **10–020** 1947, the former rule or practice[31] whereby the Crown was not required to give an undertaking in damages as a condition of being granted an interim injunction cannot be justified[32]; but in a case where the Crown seeks by the injunction to enforce what is prima facie the law of the land, as opposed to its proprietary rights, the person against whom the injunction is sought is required to show very good reason why the Crown should be obliged to give the undertaking as a condition of being granted the injunction.[33]

Arbitration. The Crown is bound by the terms of a written agreement to **10–021** arbitrate, and Part I of the Arbitration Act 1996 applies to the Crown.[34]

2. PUBLIC AUTHORITIES

Nature of public authorities. Until 1954, it was necessary to define the term **10–022** "public authority" since a body falling within the definition could rely on the

---

[25] *ibid.* s.21(2); *Harper v. Home Secretary* [1955] Ch. 238; *Merricks v. Heathcoat-Amory* [1955] Ch. 567.

[26] *M. v. Home Office* [1994] 1 A.C. 377; *R. v. Secretary of State for Transport, ex p. Factortame Ltd (No. 2) (Case C213–89)* [1991] 1 A.C. 603, 644. For the principles on which interim relief is granted see *post*, § 10–039; *R. v. Secretary of State for Transport, ex p. Factortame, supra*, at 674; *Scotia Pharmaceuticals International Ltd v. Department of Health* [1993] C.O.D. 408; *R. v. Secretary of State for the National Heritage, ex p. Continental Television BV10* [1993] C.O.D. 421; *R. v. H.M. Treasury, ex p. British Telecommunications plc* [1996] Q.B. 615; *R. v. Secretary of State for Health, ex p. Macrae Seafoods* [1995] C.O.D. 369.

[27] Crown Proceedings Act 1947, s.28(1). See generally CPR, r. 31.19; *Conway v. Rimmer* [1968] A.C. 910; *Burmah Oil Ltd v. Bank of England* [1980] A.C. 1090; *Air Canada v. British Airports Authority* [1983] 2 A.C. 394; *R. v. Chief Constable of West Midlands, ex p. Wiley* [1995] 1 A.C. 274; *Attorney General's Guidelines* (February 4, 1998).

[28] Crown Proceedings Act 1947, ss.24, 25.

[29] *ibid.* s.29 (including liens).

[30] *M. v. Home Office* [1994] 1 A.C. 377.

[31] *Att.-Gen. v. Albany Hotel Co.* [1896] 2 Ch. 696.

[32] *F. Hoffmann-La Roche & Co. A.G. v. Secretary of State for Trade and Industry* [1975] A.C. 295.

[33] *ibid.*

[34] s.106.

special periods of limitation provided by the Public Authorities Protection Act 1893 and by section 21 of the Limitation Act 1939. These special periods of limitation were abolished in 1954[35] and the term "public authority" no longer seems to require precise legal definition.[36] In the remaining part of this chapter the term is used to refer to local government bodies,[37] and to bodies which have been set up by Parliament to regulate privatised utilities,[38] to provide social services,[39] or to implement the policy of some particular statute.[40] The term may also include certain other bodies which have not been set up by Parliament but which are exclusively engaged in the performance of public functions and duties. The term is commonly used to refer to bodies even though they are not departments or agencies of the Crown.[41] For certain purposes, for instance the procurement regime for public works, supplies and services contracts and refusal to contract,[42] private sector companies providing certain utilities services are treated in a similar way to public authorities.

10–023   **Ultra vires rule.** Public authorities whose powers are defined by statute are subject to the *ultra vires* rule.[43] Local authorities in England and Wales now exercise their functions under the Local Government Act 1972 and under the London Government Act 1963, as amended by the 1972 Act. The contracts of local authorities will therefore be void[44] unless they relate to functions which the authority is authorised, expressly or impliedly, to perform, or unless the acts done are calculated to facilitate, or are conducive or incidental to, the discharge of those functions.[45] "Functions" covers all the activities Parliament has expressly or impliedly entrusted to a local authority.[46] However, it does not include all associated activities. For instance, while the consideration and determination of planning applications is a function of a local authority, the giving of pre-application advice is not, even though it is conducive or incidental to its planning

---

[35] Law Reform (Limitation of Actions, etc.) Act 1954. But see *Arnold v. Central Electricity Generating Board* [1988] A.C. 228 (restriction on retrospective effect).

[36] But see *R. v. Manners* [1978] A.C. 43; *R. v. Hirst & McNamee* (1975) 64 Cr.App.R. 151 ("public body"); Employment Rights Act 1996, s.159(a) ("public office"); Local Government Act 1988, s.1 and Sched. 2, *post*, § 10–028.

[37] *Post*, § 10–026.

[38] *e.g.* by the Gas Act 1986, ss.1, 4; Electricity Act 1989, ss.3, 6.

[39] *e.g.* by the National Health Service Act 1977, ss.8, 13 (as amended). Note that the National Health Service and Community Care Act 1990, ss.4(1) and (3) (as amended by the Health Authorities Act 1995) provide that Hospital Trusts "contract" with District Health Authorities but that no enforceable rights arise under such contracts.

[40] *e.g.* by the Broadcasting Act 1990, s.1.

[41] *e.g.* to local authorities. It might not be improper to call the British Broadcasting Corporation a "public authority" even though it is not a Crown department: *ante*, § 10–003, text to n. 23.

[42] *Post*, §§ 10–029, 10–030.

[43] *Ante*, §§ 9–004, 9–021, 9–022.

[44] *L.C.C. v. Att.-Gen.* [1902] A.C. 165; *Att.-Gen. v. Manchester Corp.* [1906] 1 Ch. 643; *Att.-Gen. v. Fulham Corp.* [1921] 1 Ch. 440; *Rhyl U.D.C. v. Rhyl Amusements Ltd* [1959] 1 W.L.R. 465; *Hazell v. Hammersmith & Fulham L.B.C.* [1992] 2 A.C. 1. But see s.137 of the Local Government Act 1972, as amended, (limited power to incur expenditure for certain purposes not otherwise authorised). *cf. ibid.* s.161.

[45] Local Government Act 1972, s.111; Local Government (Contracts) Act 1997, s.1. See also *Att.-Gen. v. Leeds Corp.* [1929] 2 Ch. 291; *Att.-Gen. v. Smethwick Corp.* [1932] 1 Ch. 562; *Att.-Gen. v. Crayford U.D.C.* [1962] Ch. 575; *R. v. G.L.C., ex p. Burgess* [1978] I.C.R. 991, 994.

[46] *Hazell v. Hammersmith and Fulham L.B.C.* [1992] 2 A.C. 1, 29, 45; *R. v. Richmond L.B.C., ex p. McCarthy and Stone* [1992] 2 A.C. 48, 69–70.

functions.[47] So contracts between local authorities and banks, which participated in housing or recreational schemes by local authorities either as joint venturer or as guarantor, were held to be *ultra vires*.[48] In determining whether a contract is conducive or incidental to the discharge of a Council's functions, regard is had to any statutory regulation and limitation of that function. Thus, the existence of a statutory code defining and limiting the borrowing powers of local authorities has been held to be inconsistent with any incidental power to enter into interests swap contracts.[49]

Charter Corporations. The *ultra vires* rule does not apply to charter corpora- **10–024** tions.[50] But the grant of a charter to a district council,[51] or the retention by a parish or community council of city or borough status,[52] will not, it is submitted, validate a contract entered into in excess of the council's powers.[53]

Modification of ultra vires rule. The rule has been modified by statute in the **10–025** case of contracts by local authorities for the purposes of or in connection with the discharge of any functions which are intended to operate for at least five years. Section 2 of the Local Government (Contracts) Act 1997 provides that where a local authority has issued a certificate stating that it has power to enter into the contract and containing information about the statutory provisions conferring the power and the purpose of the contract, the contract has effect "as if the local authority had had power to enter into it (and exercised that power properly in entering into it)".[54] The purpose of the legislation is to render contracts enforceable, and it will still be possible to challenge the power of an authority to enter a contract in judicial review proceedings or an audit of the authority's activities.[55] But the 1997 Act will protect those who, in good faith, enter a contract of the specified type with a local authority. First, even where a court holds in judicial review proceedings that the contract is *ultra vires*, there is discretion to allow it to have effect if the consequences for the financial provision of the authority and the provision of services would otherwise be severe.[56] Secondly, where the contract is not allowed to have effect, the Act provides for special discharge terms to ensure the contractor is compensated for loss incurred or loss of profits, and for an adjustment of rights and liabilities relating to assets or goods provided or made available under the contract.[57]

Local authorities. The Local Government Act 1972[58] provides for the incor- **10–026** poration and regulation of county and district councils,[59] and (in England) parish

---

[47] *R. v. Richmond L.B.C., ex p. McCarthy and Stone* [1992] 2 A.C. 48, 70. Charging for preapplication advice was not therefore authorised under s.111.

[48] *Crédit Suisse v. Allerdale DC*; *Crédit Suisse v. Waltham Forest L.B.C.* [1997] Q.B. 306, 362.

[49] *Hazell v. Hammersmith and Fulham L.B.C.* [1992] 2 A.C. 1, 29, 31–34, 45.

[50] See *Att.-Gen. v. Leicester Corp.* [1943] Ch. 86.

[51] Local Government Act 1972, s.245.

[52] *ibid.* s.246.

[53] *Att.-Gen. v. Manchester Corp., supra.* But it is arguable that the "charter trustees" constituted by s.246(4) of the Local Government Act 1972 are not so limited.

[54] By s.4 the certificate is presumed to be lawful if it purports to meet the certification requirements in s.3.

[55] Local Government (Contracts) Act 1997, s.5.

[56] *ibid.* s.5(3).

[57] *ibid.* ss.6, 7. *cf.* Law Reform (Frustrated Contracts) Act 1943, ss.1(2), 1(3) *post* § 24–072.

[58] See also London Government Act 1963; Local Government Act 1974; Local Government Act 1985 (as amended); Local Government (Wales) Act 1994.

[59] ss.2(3), 21(3).

councils[60] and parish trustees,[61] and (in Wales) community councils.[62] The Act empowers local authorities to make standing orders with respect to the making of contracts by them or on their behalf,[63] and, in the case of contracts for the supply of goods or materials or for the execution of works, requires such standing orders to be made.[64] But a person entering into a contract with a local authority is not bound to inquire whether the standing orders have been complied with, and the contract is valid whether or not they have been complied with.[65]

10–027   **Pre-contractual duties.** Although there is no requirement under section 135 of the Local Government Act 1972 to award the contract to the party offering the best value, the overall position of local authorities depends on other controls which may have this effect.[66] An invitation by an authority for tenders to be submitted may give rise to an implied obligation to consider conforming tenders and to adhere to specified requirements.[67]

10–028   **Statutory control: U.K. legislation.** The Local Government Act 1988 restricts the contracting power of local and many other authorities in two respects. First, when drawing up approved lists of contractors, including or excluding contractors from an invitation to tender, selecting contractors, and terminating contracts for public works or supply contracts, authorities subject to Part II of the Act[68] are required to exercise their functions without reference to "non-commercial matters."[69] It has been held that an authority subject to the 1988 Act may not require those contracting with it to comply with statutory requirements for the health, safety and welfare of the contractors' employees.[70] A limited exception, however, permits account to be taken of the need to eliminate unlawful racial discrimination and promote equality of opportunity.[71] An authority is under a duty to notify persons of any decision regulated by the

---

[60] s.14(2).

[61] s.13(3).

[62] s.33(2).

[63] s.135(1).

[64] s.135(2), (3). For the disclosure of interest by members of local authorities, members of committees and officers, see Local Government Act 1972, ss.94–98, 105, 117. See also *R. v. Hendon U.D.C., ex p. Chorley* [1933] 2 K.B. 696.

[65] s.135(4). But see *R. v. Hereford Corp.* [1970] 1 W.L.R. 1424; *North West Leicestershire DC v. East Midlands Housing Association Ltd* [1981] 1 W.L.R. 1396. See also Local Authorities (Goods and Services) Act 1970; Local Authorities (Goods and Services) (Public Bodies) Order 1972 (S.I. 1972 No. 853); Local Authorities (Goods and Services) (Public Bodies) Order (S.I. 1975 No. 193); Local Authorities (Goods and Services) (Public Bodies) Order (S.I. 1981 No. 1049).

[66] *Post,* §§ 10–029—10–030.

[67] *Blackpool and Fylde Aero Club v. Blackpool B.C.* [1990] 1 W.L.R. 1195; *R. v. Lord Chancellor's Department, ex p. Hibbit & Saunders* [1993] C.O.D. 326; and see *ante,* § 2–019.

[68] s.17(2) and Sched. 2. Other statutes contain tendering requirements, see *e.g.* Environmental Protection Act 1990, s.51 (*R. v. Cardiff C.C., ex p. Gooding Investments Ltd* [1996] C.O.D. 129).

[69] s.17. Non-commercial matters are defined by s.17(5) and include the terms and conditions upon which contractors employ workers, the composition of and arrangements for the promotion, transfer or training of workforces, involvement of the contractor's business with irrelevant fields of Government policy (such as defence and foreign policy), the conduct of contractors or workers in industrial disputes, the country or territory of origin of supplies to or the location in any country of contractors' business interests, the contractors' political, industrial or sectarian affiliations or interests, the contractors' financial support or lack of support for any institution to which the authority gives or withholds support.

[70] *R. v. Islington L.B.C., ex p. Building Employers Confederation* [1989] I.R.L.R. 383.

[71] s.18. There is no such exception in respect of discrimination on the ground of sex. See *R. v. Islington L.B.C., ex p. Building Employers Confederation, supra.*

statute and, if requested, to provide a written statement of the reasons for it.[72] Secondly, it provides that authorities subject to Part II of the Act[73] may not enter into a contract to carry out defined work, such as refuse collection, cleaning and catering, unless a competitive tendering process has been satisfied.[74] There is, however, no damages remedy for breach of the Act.[75]

Statutory control: European Community law.[76] European Community law   **10–029** seeks to ensure that there is no discrimination against nationals of other member states or products from other states in the award of government contracts.[77] Discrimination in procurement against contractors and products from other states is outlawed under general provisions of the Community Treaties, and in addition a number of directives have been adopted to regulate award procedures for major contracts, to ensure publicity for contracts across the E.C. and to ensure procedures are followed which give contractors from other member states a fair opportunity to bid, and make it difficult to disguise discriminatory decisions. Broadly speaking the Directives and implementing regulations apply to major contracts made by national and local government authorities, and bodies governed by public law.[78] Where they do apply, publicity in the form of Community-wide advertising of contracts is required. Contracting authorities are also required to use non-discriminatory European Community specifications and standards or implementing national standards wherever these exist. Authorities must choose between one of three specified procedures: the open procedure permitting all interested suppliers to tender, the restricted procedure permitting

---

[72] s.20. See *R. v. Enfield L.B.C., ex p. T.F. Unwin (Roydon) Ltd,* [1989] C.O.D. 466 (fairness required some reasons even where a police investigation was taking place).

[73] s.1.

[74] s.4. It is, however, *ultra vires* for the Secretary of State to make an order under s.14 of the Act that authorities seek his consent before allocating a contractual task to a direct labour organisation: *R. v. Secretary of State for the Environment, ex p. Knowlsey M.B.C., The Times,* May 28, 1991. See further Arrowsmith, *The Law of Public and Utilities Procurement* (1996). Chap. 12.

[75] But note that where there has been knowing or malicious breach an authority may be liable: *Bourgoin SA v. Minister of Agriculture, Fisheries and Food* [1986] Q.B. 716; *Jones v. Swansea C.C.* [1990] 1 W.L.R. 1453.

[76] See generally Arrowsmith, *The Law of Public and Utilities Procurement* (1996); Lee, *Public Procurement* (1992); Trepe and Geddes, *Public Procurement: A Practical Guide* (1993); Digings and Bennett, *E.C. Public Procurement: Law and Practice* (looseleaf), p. 51; Weiss, *Public Procurement in European Community Law* (1993); *Halsbury's Laws of England* (4th ed.), para. 11.74 (and supplement). The relevant Directives were consolidated in 1993: see 93/36, 93/37, 93/38 EEC [1993] O.J. L 199/1, 54, 84. The rules on public sector contracts have been implemented in the U.K. by the Public Works Contracts Regulations 1991 (S.I. 1991 No. 2680); Public Supply Contracts Regulations 1992 (S.I. 1992 No. 3228); Public Supply Contracts Regulations 1995 (S.I. 1995 No. 201). The Utilities Directive 93/38 extends to certain nationalised industries and private sector companies providing utility services concerning energy, telecommunications, transport and water which have been granted special or exclusive rights: see the Utility Supply and Works Contracts Regulations 1992 (S.I. 1992 No. 3279); Utilities Contracts Regulations 1996 (S.I. 1996 No. 2911). See *General Building & Maintenance v. Greenwich L.B.C.* [1993] I.R.L.R. 535; Case C–331/92 *Gestion Hotelera Internacional SA v. Communidad Autonoma de Canarias* [1994] E.C.R. I–1329; Case C–324/93 *R. v. Home Secretary, ex p. Evans Medical Ltd* [1996] 1 C.M.L.R. 53.

[77] For the financial thresholds, see S.I. 1991 No. 2679, r. 7; S.I. 1991 No. 2680, r. 7; S.I. 1992 No. 3279, r. 9; S.I. 1995 No. 201, r. 7.

[78] The regulations list of bodies includes bodies financed or controlled by the state or another public body, established for the specific purpose of meeting needs in the general interest but not having a commercial or industrial nature: see S.I. 1991 No. 2679, r. 3(1)(r); S.I. 1991 No. 2680, r. 3(1)(r); S.I. 1995 No. 201, r. 3(1)(r). Where government subsidises building work for hospitals, sports, leisure facilities, educational and administrative buildings, or road bridges or railways engineering or construction projects by more than 50 per cent the rules apply.

suppliers invited to participate by the contracting authority to tender and the negotiated procedure under which direct discussions and negotiations take place between the authority and one or more suppliers of its choice.[79] Once a call for competition has been advertised, an authority must proceed with the procedure it has chosen within specified time limits which vary according to the procedure used.[80] The Directives and regulations also regulate the procedure for excluding suppliers who lack financial and economic standing or technical capacity.[81] Finally, the Directives require authorities deciding which tender to accept to apply one of two criteria: either the lowest price or the "most economically advantageous" tender.[82] In the case of the latter criterion the authority is required to specify in advance the factors on which it intends to make its decision, if possible in descending order of importance.[83]

10–030   **European Community law: remedies.** Where there is an infringement of the rules on procurement it is generally open to the Commission to commence proceedings in the European Court of Justice against the relevant member state, under Article 226 (formerly Article 169) of the EEC Treaty. Apart from this, the Directives leave the fate of a contract made in breach of the rules to national law.[84] The United Kingdom's implementing regulations provide that the court shall not have power to order any remedy other than an award of damages if the contract in relation to which the breach occurred has been entered into.[85] Concluded contracts cannot therefore be set aside on the application of a third party (normally a disappointed tenderer). Therefore, remedies, whether by way of judicial review such as certiorari and mandamus, or injunctions in ordinary proceedings, will only be of assistance where the person complaining of breach invokes the assistance of the court before the award of the contract and can persuade the court to grant interim relief. In other cases the only remedy will be monetary compensation by way of damages under the regulations.[86]

10–031   **Contracts incompatible with powers or duties.** "If a person or public body is entrusted by the legislature with certain powers and duties expressly or impliedly for public purposes, those persons or bodies cannot divest themselves of those powers and duties. They cannot enter into any contract or take any action

---

[79] While the Utilities Directive permits a free choice of procedure, the other Directives only permit the negotiated procedure to be used in certain specified circumstances.

[80] *e.g.* in the case of open procedures: (a) public works, public services and utilities contracts, a minimum of 52 days from dispatch of notice of the *Official Journal* or 36 days if a prior information notice has been published; (b) public supply contracts, a minimum of 52 days from the date of dispatch of the tender notice or 40 days for bodies governed by the GATT agreement.

[81] S.I. No. 2679, rr. 8, 15; S.I. No. 2680, rr. 8, 15; S.I. No. 3279, r. 11; S.I. 1995 No. 201, rr. 11(7), 13(7) and 14–19.

[82] S.I. 1991 No. 2679, r. 20; S.I. 1991 No. 2680, r. 20; S.I. 1992 No. 3279, r. 20; S.I. 1995 No. 201, r. 21(1). See *R. v. Portsmouth C.C., ex p. Coles, The Times*, November 13, 1996 (effect of breach of reg. 20).

[83] S.I. 1991 No. 2679, r. 20(3); S.I. No. 2680, r. 20(3); S.I. 1992 No. 3279, r. 20(3); S.I. 1995 No. 201. In the case of abnormally low tenders the authority is required to seek an explanation from the tenderer and is not permitted to reject the tender if the price quoted can be justified: see S.I. 1991 No. 2679, rr. 20(4)–(5); S.I. 1991 No. 2680, rr. 20(5)–(7); S.I. 1992 No. 3279, rr. 20(6)–(8); S.I. 1995 No. 201, r. 20(7)–(8).

[84] Compliance Directive [1989] O.J. L395/33, Art. 2(6).

[85] S.I. 1991 No. 2679, r. 26(6); S.I. 1991 No. 2680, r. 31(7); S.I. 1992 No. 3279, r. 30(6); S.I. 1995 No. 201, r. 30(6).

[86] For the United Kingdom provisions, see S.I. 1991 No. 2679, r. 26(2), (5)(b); S.I. 1991 No. 2680, r. 31(3), (6)(b); S.I. 1992 No. 3279, r. 30(1), (5)(b)(ii).

incompatible with the due exercise of their powers or the discharge of their duties."[87] In *York Corporation v. Henry Leetham & Sons*,[88] the York Corporation was entrusted by statute with the control and management of two rivers with power to levy tolls, within certain limits, in order to make them navigable for the public benefit. The corporation entered into a covenant with the defendants to allow them to use the rivers in consideration of an annual payment of £800 in place of the authorised tolls. It was held that this covenant was *ultra vires* as it prevented the corporation from increasing the tolls to the level which might be necessary in order to perform its statutory duty. On the other hand, in *Birkdale District Electric Supply Co. v. Southport Corporation*[89] the defendants, an electric supply company, were sued by the Southport Corporation on an agreement whereby they had covenanted not to charge higher prices for electricity than those charged in the borough of Southport. They had begun to charge higher prices, contending that the agreement was *ultra vires* on the ground that it was incompatible with their statutory duties to supply electricity to the public within a given area. But the House of Lords held that the agreement was not incompatible and that the defendants were bound by it. Their Lordships' reasons for distinguishing the *York Corporation* case are neither uniform nor clear, and it may be that the cases cannot easily be reconciled.[90] But it is submitted that the decision in the *Birkdale* case at least established that the contractual stipulations must be clearly proved to be incompatible with the full observance of the terms and the full attainment of the purposes for which the statutory powers have been granted.[91] If the incompetence of the public authority is only an incompetence *sub modo*, beyond which the powers necessary to its operation may be freely exercised,[92] the contract will stand.

An arrangement with a public authority which does not constitute a contract **10–032** because of the non-fettering principle may, however, have some effect in the sense that later action inconsistent with it might be judicially reviewed for unfairness amounting to an abuse of power.[93]

Exercise of discretionary power in relation to a valid contract. As with the **10–033** Crown,[94] where the contract of a public authority is valid, it will not be construed so as impliedly to exclude the authority's freedom to exercise discretionary powers.[95] Thus in *Dowty Boulton Paul Ltd v. Wolverhampton Corporation*

---

[87] *Birkdale District Electric Supply Co. v. Southport Corp.* [1926] A.C. 355, 364.

[88] [1924] 1 Ch. 557. See also *Att.-Gen. v. Plymouth Corp.* (1845) 9 Beav. 67; *Ayr Harbour Trustees v. Oswald* (1883) 8 App.Cas. 623; *Re S.E. Ry. Co. and Wiffin's Contract* [1907] 2 Ch. 366; *Salford Guardians v. Dewhurst* [1926] A.C. 619; *Nixon v. Att.-Gen.* [1931] A.C. 184; *Powell v. Sheffield Corp.* [1936] 1 K.B. 680; *Riach v. Lord Advocate*, 1932 S.C. 138; *Re Heywood's Conveyance* [1938] 2 All E.R. 230; *William Cory & Son Ltd v. London Corp.* [1951] 2 K.B. 476; *Triggs v. Staines U.D.C.* [1969] 1 Ch. 10.

[89] [1926] A.C. 355. See also *Stourcliffe Estates Co. Ltd v. Bournemouth Corp.* [1910] 2 Ch. 12; *R. v. Liverpool Corp.* [1972] 2 Q.B. 299; *Earl of Leicester v. Wells-next-the-sea U.D.C.* [1973] Ch. 110.

[90] [1926] A.C. 355, 366, 374. See Mitchell (1950) 13 M.L.R. 318 and 455, 461.

[91] [1926] A.C. 355, 369; *British Transport Commission v. Westmoreland County Council* [1958] A.C. 126. See also *ante*, §§ 10–007—10–009.

[92] [1926] A.C. 355, at 370.

[93] *H.T.V. v. Price Commission* [1976] I.C.R. 170. See also *ante*, § 10–017 and *post*, § 10–038.

[94] *Ante*, § 10–009.

[95] *William Cory & Co. Ltd v. London Corp.* [1951] 2 K.B. 476.

(No. 2)[96] it was held that a local authority's statutory power to close an airfield and build houses on the site was not precluded because, in a lease of adjoining land to the plaintiff, it had covenanted to allow the plaintiff to use the airfield. But, subject to this, the exercise of contractual powers (*e.g.* to terminate a contract) by a public authority is in principle reviewable although probably only for fraud, corruption or bad faith.[97]

10–034   **Refusal to contract.** Although the general rule, based upon the principle of freedom of contract, is that a person can choose with whom to contract and with whom not to contract, in the case of public authorities this freedom is limited. Both legislation, such as the Local Government Act 1988 and the regulations implementing E.C. directives on public sector contracts,[98] and general principles governing the exercise of discretionary powers may invalidate refusals to contract at all or only on particular terms. Such refusals may be based on a policy which amounts to an improper fetter on an authority's discretion or be "unfair" in the light of an individual's legitimate expectations.[99] Thus, a decision not to contract with a company in part motivated by the wish to procure the company's ceasing its trade with South Africa was held to be *ultra vires*.[1] However, the courts may be reluctant to exercise this supervisory jurisdiction where they regard an authority's powers as managerial[2] although, where an authority has not complied with the requirements of procedural fairness, such as the statutory duty to give reasons under the Local Government Act 1988, it will be reviewed.[3]

10–035   **Public officers: tenure of office.** The terms on which public officers may be appointed are to a considerable extent governed by legislation. In the past it was customary to provide that local government officers held office at the pleasure or will of the local authority. It was decided that such a provision rendered *ultra vires* a term that the appointment was to be for a fixed period[4]; and that a statutory provision that an authority "may remove" an officer had the same effect.[5] Section 112 of the Local Government Act 1972 now simply provides that an officer appointed by a local authority shall hold office on such "reasonable terms and conditions" as the authority appointing him thinks fit. A public officer may be appointed to hold office during pleasure.[6] But there are many other forms of legislative regulation of the tenure of public offices. One common formula provides that the person in question "shall hold and vacate office in accordance

---

[96] [1976] Ch. 13; *cf. ibid.* [1971] 1 W.L.R. 204; *Windsor and Maidenhead Royal Borough Council v. Brandrose Investments Ltd* [1983] 1 W.L.R. 509; *R. v. Hammersmith and Fulham L.B.C., ex p. Beddowes* [1987] Q.B. 1050.

[97] *Mercury Ltd v. Electricity Corp.* [1994] 1 W.L.R. 521.

[98] See *ante*, §§ 10–028—10–030.

[99] See *post*, § 10–038, *ante*, § 10–028.

[1] *R. v. Lewisham L.B.C., ex p. Shell U.K. Ltd* [1988] 1 All E.R. 938. See now Local Government Act 1988, s.17, *ante*, § 10–028; *R. v. Islington L.B.C., ex p. Building Employers Confederation*, [1989] I.R.L.R. 383.

[2] *R. v. National Coal Board, ex p. N.U.M.* [1986] I.C.R. 791.

[3] *R. v. Enfield L.B.C., ex p. T.F. Unwin (Roydon) Ltd* [1989] C.O.D. 466; *R. v. Wear Valley, ex p. Binks* [1985] 2 All E.R. 699.

[4] *Brown v. Dagenham U.D.C.* [1929] 1 K.B. 737.

[5] *McManus v. Bowes* [1938] 1 K.B. 98.

[6] *e.g.* Friendly Societies Act 1974, s.2(4).

with the terms of his appointment."[7] Some of the relevant legislative provisions
in addition prescribe the maximum term of appointment,[8] or specify grounds or
procedure for dismissal.[9] Another common technique is to give the relevant
Minister power to make regulations with respect to the appointment, tenure and
vacation of the office in question.[10] It seems that all such provisions make the
terms of appointment legally enforceable,[11] and reflect the view that there is no
ground of policy which requires all public officers to be dismissible at pleasure.
Indeed, in some cases policy demands that public officers should be protected to
some extent against arbitrary dismissal by those who appoint them. Some statutes
contain express provisions to this end,[12] which is also served by the rule of
common law that dismissal from a public office is in some cases ineffective, as
opposed to merely wrongful.[13]

Agency. A public authority is bound, in the same way as the Crown,[14] by a   **10–036**
contract made on its behalf by its agent acting within his actual or ostensible
authority.[15] There is no decision as to whether the servants or agents of a public
authority are personally liable on contracts entered into by them on behalf of a
public authority, but the same rule probably applies as in the case of Crown
employees or agents, *viz.* that they incur no personal liability on the contract
unless they expressly pledge their personal credit[16] and that they are not liable for
breach of warranty of authority.

Estoppel. A public authority cannot be estopped by its previous conduct so as   **10–037**
to hinder its obligation to carry out its statutory powers or duties[17] nor will such
conduct prevent it from putting an end to an *ultra vires* situation.[18] On the other
hand, in *Wells v. Minister of Housing and Local Government*,[19] Lord Denning
M.R. said: "I take the law to be that a defect in procedure can be cured, and an
irregularity can be waived, even by a public authority, so as to render valid that
which would otherwise be invalid." Such a waiver lies within the powers of a
public authority. So, if an officer, acting within the scope of his ostensible

---

[7] *e.g.* Race Relations Act 1976, Sched. 1, para. 3; Agriculture Act 1967, Sched. I, Pt. II, para. 4(1);
Tribunals and Inquiries Act 1992, s.3(1); Fair Trading Act 1973, s.1(4); Nature Conservancy Council
Act 1973, Sched. 3, para. 3; National Heritage Act 1980, Sched. 1, para. 4(1); Civil Aviation Act
1982, Sched. 1, para. 2.

[8] *e.g.* Law Commissions Act 1965, ss.1(3), 2(3); Broadcasting Act 1980, Sched. 3, para. 3(2); Fair
Trading Act 1973, s.1(2); Broadcasting Act 1990, Sched. 1, para. 3(2); Banking Act 1987, Sched. 1,
para. 1.

[9] *e.g.* New Towns Act 1965, Sched. 9, para. 2; Fair Trading Act 1973, s.1(3).

[10] *e.g.* Town and Country Planning Act 1990; National Health Service Act 1977, s.7(2).

[11] See *McClelland v. Northern Ireland General Health Services Board* [1957] 1 W.L.R. 594.

[12] *e.g.* Rent Act 1977, s.63(2)(b) (rent officers cannot be dismissed by the appointing authority
without consent of the Minister).

[13] *Ridge v. Baldwin* [1964] A.C. 40.

[14] *Ante*, § 10–016.

[15] See Local Government Act 1972, s.135(4), Sched. 13, para. 20.

[16] See *ante*, § 10–015.

[17] *York Corp. v. Henry Leetham & Sons* [1924] 1 Ch. 557; *Sunderland Corp. v. Priestman* [1927]
2 Ch. 107; *Stockwell v. Southgate Corp.* [1936] 2 All E.R. 1343; *Maritime Electric Co. v. General
Dairies Ltd* [1937] A.C. 610; *Rhyl U.D.C. v. Rhyl Amusements Ltd* [1959] 1 W.L.R. 465; *Southend
Corp. v. Hodgson (Wickford) Ltd* [1962] 1 Q.B. 416; *Co-operative Retail Services Ltd v. Taff-Ely B.C.*
(1979) 39 P. & C.R. 223.

[18] *Islington Vestry v. Hornsey U.D.C.* [1900] 1 Ch. 695.

[19] [1967] 1 W.L.R. 1000, 1007.

authority, purports to make such a waiver on which another person acts, the public authority may be bound by it.[20]

10–038 **Legitimate expectation.** A public authority may be under a public law duty to act consistently with an arrangement which does not give rise to a contract or an estoppel because of the principle that discretionary powers may not be fettered where the arrangement gives the person dealing with the public authority a legitimate expectation that a benefit will be granted or continue to be enjoyed. Where this is so later action inconsistent with the arrangement may be an abuse of power and judicially reviewed on the ground of unfairness.[21] Inconsistency is not, however, necessarily unfair[22] and the courts will not let an arrangement that has given rise to a legitimate expectation hinder the formation of policy. They recognise that administrative policies may change with changing circumstances.[23] For example, an authority that has received and resolved to accept a tender from its own workforce might choose to abandon the project or seek fresh tenders.[24] Even where inconsistency is prima facie unfair, a court exercising supervisory jurisdiction by way of judicial review will take into account the wider public interest and may refuse relief in the exercise of its discretion.[25]

10–039 **Local Authority injunctions.** Injunctive relief may be given against local authorities both in civil proceedings and in proceedings by way of judicial review. In cases where an injunction is sought to restrain a public authority from acting on an apparently valid regulation or public law decision, the ordinary test[26] is modified. First, as public authorities are not generally liable in damages in respect of *ultra vires* acts, this element of the test does not provide much assistance in such cases. Secondly, in considering the balance of convenience the court has to look more widely, taking account of the public in general to whom a public authority owed duties.[27] A similar approach is taken in judicial review proceedings where interim relief is sought against a Minister.[28]

---

[20] *Wells v. Minister of Housing and Local Govt.* [1967] 1 W.L.R. 1000; *Lever (Finance) Ltd v. Westminster Corp.* [1971] 1 Q.B. 222; *Re L. (An Infant)* [1971] 3 All E.R. 743; *Norfolk C.C. v. Sec. of State for the Environment* [1973] 1 W.L.R. 1400; *Western Fish Products Ltd v. Penwith DC* [1981] 2 All E.R. 204; *Rootkin v. Kent C.C.* [1981] 1 W.L.R. 1186. See also *Algar v. Middlesex C.C.* [1945] 2 All E.R. 243; and *ante*, § 10–017.

[21] *Re Preston* [1985] A.C. 835, 867; *Council for Civil Service Unions v. Minister for the Civil Service* [1985] A.C. 374, 408. See also, *ante*, § 10–017 n. 17; § 10–034.

[22] *Re Preston* [1985] A.C. 835, 867; *H.T.V. v. Price Commission* [1976] I.C.R. 170, 192; *Hughes v. D.H.S.S.* [1985] A.C. 776.

[23] *Hughes v. D.H.S.S.* [1985] A.C. 776, 788; *Re Findlay* [1985] A.C. 318; *R. v. Home Secretary, ex p. Hargreaves* [1997] 1 All E.R. 397.

[24] *R. v. Walsall M.B.C., ex p. Yapp* [1994] I.C.R. 528.

[25] Woolf L.J. (extra-judicially) [1987] P.L. 220, 227. *Ante*, § 10–011 n. 73.

[26] *American Cyanamid v. Ethicon Ltd* [1975] A.C. 396.

[27] *Smith v. I.L.E.A.* [1978] 1 All E.R. 411; *Meade v Haringey L.B.C.* [1979] 1 W.L.R. 637; *R. v. Inspectorate of Pollution, ex p. Greenpeace Ltd* [1994] 1 W.L.R. 570, 573–4, 576–7.

[28] *R. v. Secretary of State for Transport, ex p. Factortame Ltd* [1991] 1 A.C. 603, 674 (an interim injunction to restrain the enforcement of an apparently authentic law should not be given unless the court is satisfied that the challenge is prima facie so firmly based as to justify so exceptional a course being taken); *R. v. Secretary of State for the Environment, ex p. R.S.P.B.* (1995) 5 Admin. L.R. 434, 443; *R. v. Secretary of State for Health, ex p. Generics (U.K.) Ltd* (1997) 40 B.M.L.R. 90. See *ante*, § 10–019.

3. THE EUROPEAN COMMUNITY

Capacity of Community to contract. The European Community has legal   **10–040**
personality.[29] By virtue of Article 282 (formerly Article 211) of the European
Community Treaty,[30] the Community enjoys in the United Kingdom "the most
extensive legal capacity accorded to legal persons" under the laws of the United
Kingdom, and may, in particular, acquire or dispose of movable and immovable
property, and may be a party to legal proceedings. To this end, the Community
is to be represented by the Commission. There can be little doubt that the
Community can enter into contracts and be subject to contractual obligations.
The Treaty does not attempt to create a Community law of contract and the
contractual liability of the Community is governed by the law applicable to the
contract in question.[31] Whether or not there are any limits to this liability remains
to be seen, but it would appear that the Community could bind itself by contract
as to the manner in which it will exercise its powers.[32]

Jurisdiction of national courts. In principle, a contract to which the Commu-   **10–041**
nity is a party is subject to the jurisdiction of national courts. Article 240
(formerly Article 183) of the European Community Treaty[33] provides that, save
where jurisdiction is conferred on the Court of Justice by the Treaty,[34] disputes
to which the Community is a party shall not on that ground be excluded from the
jurisdiction of the courts or tribunals of Member States.

---

[29] E.C. Treaty, Art. 281 (formerly Art. 210). See also the ECSC Treaty, Art. 6.

[30] See also ECSC Treaty, Art. 6; Euratom Treaty, Arts. 101–106.

[31] E.C. Treaty, Art. 288(1) (formerly Art. 215(1)). See also the Euratom Treaty, Art. 188; Case 23/76, *Luigi Pellegrini & C.S.A.S. v. Commission of the EEC* [1976] E.C.R. 1807; [1977] 2 C.M.L.R. 77.

[32] Case 81/72, *Commissioner of the EEC v. Council of the EEC* [1973] E.C.R. 575; [1973] C.M.L.R. 639; *cf. ante*, §§ 10–007, 10–009, 10–023.

[33] See also the ECSC Treaty, Art. 40; Euratom Treaty, Art. 155.

[34] *e.g.* by virtue of Art. 235 (formerly Art. 178), where the dispute relates to compensation for damage provided for in the second para. of E.C. Treaty, Art. 288. See also Art. 181 (arbitration clauses), Art. 236 (disputes with Commission staff), and the ECSC Treaty, Arts. 40, 42; Euratom Treaty, Arts. 151, 153.

CHAPTER 11

POLITICAL AND PROFESSIONAL IMMUNITY AND INCAPACITY

1. FOREIGN STATES, SOVEREIGNS, AMBASSADORS AND INTERNATIONAL
ORGANISATIONS

Foreign states and sovereigns: the common law rule. The rule at common **11–001**
law was that no independent foreign state or foreign sovereign could be sued in
an English court without consent.[1] This immunity was derived from rules of
public international law which had become part of English law.[2] The immunity
extended both to direct actions against the state or sovereign and to indirect
actions against its property. Formerly, foreign states were afforded immunity not
only with regard to governmental activities but also with regard to their purely
commercial activities.[3] This absolute theory was abandoned by the courts in
favour of the more restricted approach under which immunity did not apply
either to an action, whether *in rem*[4] or *in personam*,[5] against a ship belonging to
a sovereign state, or one of its organs, if the ship was being operated as an
ordinary trading ship, nor indeed to actions *in personam* generally in relation to
ordinary commercial activities[6]; but did extend to governmental acts, *acta iure
imperii*, of the sovereign state.[7]

---

[1] *Duke of Brunswick v. King of Hanover* (1844) 6 Beav. 1; (1848) 2 H.L.C. 1.
[2] *The Christina* [1938] A.C. 485, 490; *Thai-Europe Tapioca Services Ltd v. Government of
Pakistan* [1975] 1 W.L.R. 1485.
[3] *The Porto Alexandre* [1920] P. 30; *The Christina* [1938] A.C. 485, 490; *Kahan v. Pakistan
Federation* [1951] 2 K.B. 1003; *Baccus S.R.L. v. Servicio Nacional del Trigo* [1957] 1 Q.B. 438.
[4] *The Phillippine Admiral* [1977] A.C. 373.
[5] *I Congreso del Partido* [1983] 1 A.C. 244, 261.
[6] *Trendtex Trading Corp. v. Central Bank of Nigeria* [1977] Q.B. 529; *Hispano Americana
Mercantil SA v. Central Bank of Nigeria* [1979] 2 Lloyd's Rep. 277; *Planmount Ltd v. Republic of
Zaire* [1981] 1 All E.R. 1110; *I Congreso del Partido* [1983] 1 A.C. 244, 261–262; *Alcom Ltd v.
Republic of Columbia* [1984] A.C. 580, 598–599.
[7] *I Congreso del Partido* [1983] 1 A.C. 244, 262, 272, 276; *Sengupta v. Republic of India* [1983]
I.C.R. 221; *Littrell v. Government of the United States (No. 2)* [1995] 1 W.L.R. 82. For discussion of
the changes, see *J.H. Rayner (Mincing Lane) Ltd v. Dept. of Trade and Industry* [1989] Ch. 72, affd.
without reference to these points, [1990] 2 A.C. 418.

11–002   **State Immunity Act 1978.** The law of sovereign immunity was placed on a statutory basis by the State Immunity Act 1978,[8] though the Act is not retrospective in effect.[9] The Act applies both to cases where the question of the immunity of a foreign state arises directly in the proceedings as where the state is named as a defendant, and also to the common case of "indirect impleading," as where an action between two other parties puts the title to the state's goods in issue.[10] The basic principle of the Act is that a foreign state is immune from the jurisdiction of the English courts whether or not it appears in the proceedings,[11] and the issue of immunity must be decided as a preliminary issue before the substantive action can proceed.[12] This immunity applies to any foreign or Commonwealth state, other than the United Kingdom, to the sovereign or other head of state in his public capacity and to the government or any department of that state.[13] It also applies to a "separate entity," such as a state corporation, not being a department of the state, where proceedings relate to something done by the separate entity in the exercise of sovereign authority and the state itself would have been immune.[14] It will be for the courts to develop criteria for determining what constitutes a separate entity. It is suggested, however, that the notion of separate entity does not extend to any agent of a foreign state. Rather, it should be regarded as limited to an entity owned or controlled by the foreign state since it is only if such ownership or control exists that an entity can realistically be regarded as capable of doing something in the exercise of sovereign authority.[15]

11–003   To the general principle of immunity there are several important and wide-ranging exceptions. The most important is that there is no immunity for a state's commercial transactions,[16] thus confirming the judicial developments confining the common law rule to *acta iure imperii*, though it may still be difficult to determine in any particular case the dividing line between commercial and

---

[8] Implementing the 1972 European Convention on State Immunity: Cmnd. 5081, though the Act is more extensive in scope. For discussion and references to relevant literature (which is copious) see *Dicey and Morris on the Conflict of Laws* (12th ed., 1993), pp. 241–257: Cheshire and North, *Private International Law* (12th ed., 1992), pp. 265–271.

[9] It only applies to matters which occurred after it came into force (November 1978): s.23(3); and see *Planmount Ltd v. Republic of Zaire* [1981] 1 All E.R. 1110; *Sengupta v. Republic of India* [1983] I.C.R. 221.

[10] *e.g. The Parlement Belge* (1880) L.R. 5 P.D. 197; *United States of America and Republic of France v. Dollfus Mieg et Cie SA and Bank of England* [1952] A.C. 582. On the scope of the Act in respect of immunity from taxation, see *R. v. I.R.C., ex p. Camacq Corporation* [1990] 1 W.L.R. 191 and *post*, § 11–003.

[11] 1978 Act, s.1. See *United Arab Emirates v. Abdelghafar* [1995] I.C.R. 65; *Malaysian Industrial Development Authority v. Jeyasingham* [1998] I.C.R. 307.

[12] *J.H. Rayner (Mincing Lane) Ltd v. Dept. of Trade and Industry* [1989] Ch. 72, 194–195, 252, affd. without reference to this point, [1990] 2 A.C. 418: *A. Co. Ltd v. Republic of X.* [1990] 2 Lloyd's Rep. 520, 525.

[13] *ibid.* s.14. See *Propend Finance Pty Ltd v. Sing, The Times*, May 2, 1997; *Bank of Credit and Commerce International (Overseas) Ltd v. Price Waterhouse* [1997] 4 All E.R. 108.

[14] *ibid.* See *Kuwait Airways Corp. v. Iraqi Airways Co.* [1995] 1 W.L.R. 1147; *Propend Finance Pty Ltd v. Sing, The Times*, May 2, 1997.

[15] *Dicey and Morris on the Conflict of Laws* (12th ed., 1993), pp. 233–234. See also *Re Rafidain Bank* [1992] B.C.L.C. 301; *Kuwait Airways Corp. v. Iraqi Airways Co.* [1995] 1 W.L.R. 1147; *Propend Finance Pty Ltd v. Sing, The Times*, May 2, 1997.

[16] *ibid.* s.3(1)(a): see *Re Rafidain Bank* [1992] B.C.L.C. 301.

governmental activity.[17] The funds in the bank account of a state's London embassy have been considered not to be used for commercial purposes.[18] There is no immunity for contractual obligations (whether arising out of a commercial transaction or not) to be performed in the United Kingdom[19]; or in the case of contracts of employment made or to be performed in the United Kingdom[20]; or as to claims for personal injury or damage to property caused by misconduct in the United Kingdom[21]; or in proceedings relating to immovables in the United Kingdom[22] or to an interest in other property by way of succession, gift or *bona vacantia*[23]; or in the case of proceedings relating to various forms of intellectual property[24]; or the administration of estates or trusts, or insolvency, even though a state may claim an interest in the property[25]; or where a state is a member of a corporate or unincorporate body constituted under United Kingdom law or controlled from the United Kingdom[26]; or in relation to various tax claims[27]; or as to claims arising from use of ships for commercial purposes[28] (again confirming an important common law development); or, finally, where the state has submitted to the jurisdiction of our courts.[29]

The 1978 Act also deals with a variety of procedural matters, such as service of process on a foreign state.[30] Power is given to restrict or extend the Act's immunities and privileges by Order in Council in relation to individual foreign

---

[17] *I Congreso del Partido* [1983] 1 A.C. 244, where the House of Lords divided 3–2 on this issue. Section 3(3) of the 1978 Act defines a "commercial transaction" as any contract and any guarantee or indemnity in respect of such a transaction or other financial obligation, or any other transaction or activity into which a State enters (apart from a contract of employment between a State and an individual) otherwise than in the exercise of sovereign authority. On this provision, see *Alcom Ltd v. Republic of Colombia* [1984] A.C. 580; *Amalgamated Metal Trading Ltd v. Dept. of Trade and Industry, The Times*, March 21, 1989; *Kuwait Airways Corp. v. Iraqi Airways Co.* [1995] 1 W.L.R. 1147; Staker (1995) 66 B.Y.I.L. 496; Fox (1996) 112 L.Q.R. 186. See also *Littrell v. Government of the United States (No. 2)* [1995] 1 W.L.R. 82; *Holland v. Lampen–Wolfe* [1999] 1 W.L.R. 188.

[18] *Alcom Ltd v. Republic of Columbia, supra.*

[19] 1978 Act, s.3(1)(b), though note the limitation, *ibid.* s.3(2). See *J.H. Rayner (Mincing Lane) Ltd v. Dept. of Trade and Industry* [1989] Ch. 72, 194–195, 222, 252, affd. without reference to the point, [1990] 2 A.C. 418.

[20] *ibid.* s.4. This section does not apply to proceedings concerning the employment of the members of a mission within the meaning of the Convention scheduled to the Diplomatic Privileges Act 1964 or of the members of a consular post within the meaning of the Convention scheduled to the Consular Relations Act 1968: s.16(1)(a). See *Sengupta v. Republic of India* [1983] I.C.R. 221; *United Arab Emirates v. Abdelghafar* [1995] I.C.R. 65; *Arab Republic of Egypt v. Gamal-Eldin* [1996] I.C.R. 13; *Ahmed v. Government of the Kingdom of Saudi Arabia* [1996] I.C.R. 25; *Malaysian Industrial Development Authority v. Jeyasingham* [1998] I.C.R. 307; Garnett (1997) 46 I.C.L.Q. 81.

[21] *ibid.* s.5.

[22] As with proceedings for breach of covenants in a lease: *Intpro Properties (U.K.) Ltd v. Sauvel* [1983] Q.B. 1019.

[23] 1978 Act, s.6.

[24] *ibid.* s.7.

[25] *ibid.* s.6(3). See *Re Rafidain Bank* [1992] B.C.L.C. 301.

[26] *ibid.* s.8. See *Maclaine, Watson & Co. Ltd v. International Tin Council* [1989] Ch. 253, 282–283, affd. on other grounds, [1990] 2 A.C. 418.

[27] *ibid.* s.11.

[28] *ibid.* s.10.

[29] *ibid.* s.2; see *A. Co. Ltd v. Republic of X.* [1990] 2 Lloyd's Rep. 520; *Kuwait Airways Corp. v. Iraqi Airways Co.* [1995] 1 W.L.R. 1147; see s.9 on submission in arbitration proceedings.

[30] *ibid.* ss.12–14; see *Alcom Ltd v. Republic of Colombia* [1984] A.C. 580; *Westminster City Council v. Government of the Islamic Republic of Iran* [1986] 1 W.L.R. 979; *Kuwait Airways Corp. v. Iraqi Airways Co.* [1995] 1 W.L.R. 1147; *Crescent Oil and Shipping Services Ltd v. Importang UEE* [1997] 3 All E.R. 428. And see *Soleh Boneh International Ltd v. Government of the Republic of Uganda* [1993] 2 Lloyd's Rep. 208, 213.

states[31]; and provision is also made for the recognition here of foreign judgments involving the United Kingdom as a foreign state.[32] A certificate from the Secretary of State is conclusive evidence on the question as to whether for the purposes of the Act any country is a state, is part of a federal state and as to the person or persons to be regarded as the head or government of a state.[33]

11–004   **Acts of sovereign states.** In addition to the law relating to the immunity of foreign states or sovereigns, there are other circumstances in which an English court will decline to entertain proceedings involving sovereign states.[34] Under the "act of state" doctrine, the courts have no jurisdiction to investigate the propriety of an act of the Crown[35] performed in the course of its relations with a foreign state[36] and the concept of "act of state" may extend to cover acts authorised or ratified by the Crown in the exercise of sovereign power.[37] Furthermore, English courts have no jurisdiction, it appears, to investigate the propriety of the acts of a foreign sovereign state recognised by Her Majesty's Government, where the act is performed on the territory of that state.[38] Indeed, there is now established a general principle that "the courts will not adjudicate upon the transactions of foreign sovereign states"—a principle which calls in such cases for "judicial restraint or abstention."[39]

11–005   **Foreign heads of state, ambassadors and their staffs.** The immunity from suit of foreign ambassadors and members of their staffs is conferred by the Diplomatic Privileges Act 1964,[40] which enacts as part of the law of the United Kingdom certain articles of the Vienna Convention on Diplomatic Relations (1961). These articles are set out in Schedule 1 to the Act. Where a foreign sovereign or other head of a recognised state acts in his public capacity, effectively as the embodiment of the state, he is entitled to all the immunities which the state has under the State Immunity Act 1978.[41] When acting in a private

---

[31] *ibid.* s.15.

[32] *ibid.* ss.18–19.

[33] *ibid.* s.21(a).

[34] See *Dicey and Morris on the Conflict of Laws* (12th ed., 1993), pp. 108–111.

[35] The position of the Crown generally is discussed in Chap. 10.

[36] *e.g. Secretary of State in Council of India v. Kamachee Boye Sahaba* (1859) 13 Moo.P.C. 22, 75; *Salaman v. Secretary of State of India* [1906] 1 K.B. 613.

[37] *e.g. Buron v. Denman* (1848) 2 Exch. 167; *Nissan v. Att.-Gen.* [1970] A.C. 179.

[38] *Duke of Brunswick v. King of Hanover* (1844) 6 Beav. 1, 57–58; (1848) 2 H.L.C. 1, 21–22, 26–27; *Carr v. Fracis Times* [1902] A.C. 179–180; *Johnstone v. Pedlar* [1921] 2 A.C. 262, 291; *Empresa Exportadora de Acuzar v. Industria Azacurera Nacional SA* [1983] 2 Lloyd's Rep. 171, 194.

[39] *Buttes Gas and Oil Co. v. Hammer (No. 3)* [1982] A.C. 888, 931; and see *J.H. Rayner (Mincing Lane) Ltd v. Dept. of Trade and Industry* [1990] 2 A.C. 418; *Arab Monetary Fund v. Hashim (No. 3)* [1991] 2 A.C. 114; *Kuwait Airways Corp. v. Iraqi Airways Co.* [1995] 1 W.L.R. 1147; *Arab Monetary Fund v. Hashim* [1993] 1 Lloyd's Rep. 543, 572, affd. on this point [1996] 1 Lloyd's Rep. 589; *Philipp Brothers v. Republic of Sierra Leone* [1995] 1 Lloyd's Rep. 289; *Westland Helicopters Ltd v. Arab Organisation for Industrialisation* [1995] Q.B. 282. *cf. Kuwait Airways Corp. v. Iraqi Airways Co., The Times,* May 12, 1998.

[40] The 1964 Act has been amended, mainly in minor respects, by the Diplomatic and other Privileges Act 1971, the State Immunity Act 1978, the Diplomatic and Consular Premises Act 1987 and the Arms Control and Disarmament (Privileges and Immunities) Act 1988.

[41] State Immunity Act 1978, s.14; *Bank of Credit and Commerce International (Overseas) Ltd v. Price Waterhouse* [1997] 4 All E.R. 108. On the immunity of a former head of state in the context of criminal liability, see *R. v. Bow Street Metropolitan Stipendiary Magistrate, ex p. Pinochet Ugarte (No. 3)* [1999] 2 W.L.R. 827. On heads of state, see generally, Watts (1994) 224 *Recueil des Cours,* III, 9.

capacity, however, such a foreign sovereign or other head of a recognised state is entitled to the immunities, with certain appropriate modifications, which are conferred by the Diplomatic Privileges Act 1964, since the 1978 Act extends those immunities to such persons.[42]

The immunity from suit of the chief representatives in the United Kingdom of countries of the Commonwealth and of the Republic of Ireland, and of members of their staffs, formerly depended on section 1(1) of the Diplomatic Immunities (Commonwealth Countries and Republic of Ireland) Act 1952. But that subsection has now been repealed[43] and such immunity now depends on the Diplomatic Privileges Act 1964, *i.e.* on the Vienna Convention.[44]

Categories of persons entitled to diplomatic immunity. The Convention   **11–006** divides persons entitled to diplomatic immunity into three categories[45]: (1) "diplomatic agents," namely, the head of the mission and members of his diplomatic staff; (2) "members of the administrative and technical staff," *e.g.* persons employed in secretarial, clerical, communications and public relations duties; and (3) "members of the service staff," namely, members of the staff of the mission in its domestic service.

Diplomatic agents. Diplomatic agents enjoy immunity from criminal, civil[46]   **11–007** and administrative jurisdiction and from execution, except in three cases: (a) a real action relating to private immovable property situated in the United Kingdom (unless the property is held for the purposes of the mission,[47] and this does not include a diplomatic agent's private residence)[48]; (b) an action relating to succession in which the diplomatic agent is involved as executor, administrator or beneficiary as a private person; and (c) an action relating to any professional or commercial activity exercised by the diplomatic agent outside his official functions.[49] A like immunity is conferred on the members of the family of a diplomatic agent forming part of his household.[50]

Diplomatic premises. The actual premises of a diplomatic (or consular mis-   **11–008** sion) are inviolable,[51] as is the private residence of a diplomatic agent,[52] despite the fact that a diplomatic agent may not enjoy immunity from suit in respect of

---

[42] State Immunity Act 1978, s.20; *Bank of Credit and Commerce International (Overseas) Ltd v. Price Waterhouse* [1997] 4 All E.R. 108; *R. v. Bow Street Metropolitan Stipendiary Magistrate, ex p. Pinochet Ugarte (No. 3)* [1999] 2 W.L.R. 827. The immunities extend to members of the family of the foreign sovereign or other head of a recognised state who form part of his household and to his private servants: 1978 Act, s.20(1).

[43] Diplomatic Privileges Act 1964, s.8(4) and Sched. 2.

[44] *Empson v. Smith* [1966] 1 Q.B. 426; *Omerri v. Uganda High Commission* [1973] I.T.R. 14; *cf. Sengupta v. Republic of India* [1983] I.C.R. 221, 226.

[45] Diplomatic Privileges Act 1964, Sched. 1, art. 1.

[46] Including a divorce petition: *Shaw v. Shaw* [1979] Fam. 62. For the position in relation to proceedings under the Child Abduction and Custody Act 1985, see *P v. P (Diplomatic immunity: Jurisdiction)*, [1998] 1 FLR 1026.

[47] *Alcom Ltd v. Republic of Colombia* [1984] A.C. 580.

[48] *Intpro Properties (U.K.) Ltd v. Sauvel* [1983] Q.B. 1019, 1032–1033.

[49] Art. 31.

[50] Art. 37(1).

[51] Art. 22.

[52] Art. 30; *cf. Agbor v. Metropolitan Police Commissioner* [1969] 1 W.L.R. 703.

it.[53] However, the inviolability of diplomatic premises only applies to ones which are currently so used[54]; and the Diplomatic and Consular Premises Act 1987 gives the Secretary of State power to determine whether land has diplomatic or consular status.

11–009   **Administrative, technical and service staff.** The members of the administrative and technical staff of the mission, together with their families forming part of their respective households, and the members of the service staff of the mission, enjoy a like immunity, but with the important qualification that the immunity does not extend to acts performed outside the course of their duties.[55]

11–010   **Period of immunity.** Every person entitled to immunity from jurisdiction enjoys it from the moment he enters the United Kingdom to take up his post or, if he is already there, from the moment when his appointment is notified to the department of the Secretary of State concerned.[56] In the former case it would not seem necessary, in addition, that his appointment be notified to, or accepted by, the department of the Secretary of State concerned.[57] He can claim the immunity even if he only became entitled to it after the issue of the claim form.[58] When his functions come to an end, his immunity normally ceases at the moment when he leaves the country, or on the expiry of a reasonable period in which to do so[59]; but it continues to subsist in the case of acts performed in the exercise of his functions.[60] If a claim form is issued before immunity has ceased, then provided it has not been struck out, the proceedings may continue once the immunity has come to an end.[61] If he dies, the members of his family continue to enjoy the immunity to which they were entitled until the expiry of a reasonable period in which to leave the country.[62] The running of the Statute of Limitations is suspended during such time as the defendant enjoys diplomatic immunity.[63]

11–011   **Certificate of entitlement.** If in any proceedings any question arises whether or not any person is entitled to diplomatic immunity, a certificate issued by or

---

[53] *Intpro Properties (U.K.) Ltd v. Sauvel* [1983] Q.B. 1019, 1033–1034.
[54] *Westminster City Council v. Government of the Islamic Republic of Iran* [1986] 1 W.L.R. 979, 984–985.
[55] Art. 37(2), (3).
[56] Art. 39(1) and s.2(2) of the Act.
[57] *R. v. Secretary of State for the Home Department, ex p. Bagga* [1991] 1 Q.B. 485 in which the Court of Appeal, albeit in an immigration context, doubted the correctness of *R. v. Governor of Pentonville Prison, ex p. Teja* [1971] 2 Q.B. 274, *R. v. Lambeth Justices, ex p. Yusufu* [1985] Crim.L.R. 510 and *R. v. Governor of Pentonville Prison, ex p. Osman (No. 2)* [1989] C.O.D. 446 which appear to suggest that such notification and acceptance is necessary. *Ex p. Bagga, supra,* was followed by the Court of Appeal in the context of the State Immunity Act 1978, s.16(1) in *Ahmed v. Government of the Kingdom of Saudi Arabia* [1996] I.C.R. 25. See *Dicey and Morris on the Conflict of Laws* (12th ed., 1993), p. 261; *cf. Cheshire and North, Private International Law* (12th ed., 1992), pp. 271–272.
[58] *Ghosh v. D'Rozario* [1963] 1 Q.B. 106.
[59] *Re Regina and Palacios* (1984) 45 O.R. (2d) 269.
[60] Art. 39(2); *Propend Finance Pty Ltd v. Sing, The Times,* May 2, 1997. *cf. Musurus Bey v. Gadban* [1894] 2 Q.B. 352; *Zoernsch v. Waldock* [1964] 1 W.L.R. 675.
[61] *Shaw v. Shaw* [1979] Fam. 62.
[62] Art. 39(3).
[63] *Musurus Bey v. Gadban, supra.*

under the authority of the Secretary of State stating any fact relating to the question is conclusive evidence of that fact.[64]

British citizens. Diplomatic immunity is restricted if the person entitled to it **11–012** is a British citizen, a British Dependent Territories citizen or a British Overseas citizen.[65] Diplomatic agents who are such citizens or are permanently resident in the United Kingdom only enjoy immunity from jurisdiction in respect of official acts performed in the exercise of their functions, except in so far as additional immunities may be granted by the receiving state.[66] Other members of the staff of the mission and private servants of members of the mission who are such citizens or are permanently resident in the United Kingdom enjoy immunities only to the extent admitted by the receiving state.[67] The "extent admitted by the receiving state" and the "additional immunities" here referred to mean such as may be specified by Order in Council.[68] Members of the family of diplomatic agents or of members of the administrative or technical staff, or members of the service staff of the mission, enjoy no immunity from jurisdiction if they are British, British Dependent Territories or British Overseas citizens or are permanently resident in the United Kingdom.[69]

Consular immunity. The regulation of consular immunity so far as foreign **11–013** consuls and their staffs are concerned is governed by the Consular Relations Act 1968[70] giving effect to certain articles of the Vienna Convention on Consular Relations 1963. In the case of civil proceedings, consular officers, who are defined as "any person, including the head of a consular post, entrusted in that capacity with the exercise of consular functions,"[71] and consular employees, who are any persons "employed in the administrative or technical service of a consular post,"[72] shall not be amenable to the jurisdiction of the courts of this country in respect of acts performed in the exercise of consular functions. This immunity shall not apply, in the case of a contractual action, where such officer or employee did not contract expressly or impliedly as an agent of his sending state or in the case of an action by a third party for damage arising from an accident in the United Kingdom caused by a vessel, vehicle or aircraft.[73] Special provision is made for the fact that immunity from civil jurisdiction shall not be accorded to consular employees who carry on private gainful occupation in the United Kingdom.[74] The position of officers from the Commonwealth and the Republic of Ireland who perform duties substantially similar to those performed by consular officers from foreign countries is governed by the Diplomatic Immunities (Commonwealth Countries and Republic of Ireland) Act 1952[75] until

---

[64] Diplomatic Privileges Act 1964, s.4; and see *Engelke v. Musmann* [1928] A.C. 433; *R. v. Governor of Pentonville Prison, ex p. Teja* [1971] 2 Q.B. 274. *cf. Re P (Children Act: Diplomatic Immunity)* [1998] 1 F.L.R. 625, 626.

[65] See British Nationality Act 1981, s.51(3).

[66] Art. 38(1) and s.2(2) of the Act.

[67] Art. 38(2) and s.2(2) of the Act.

[68] s.2(6) of the Act.

[69] Art. 37 and s.2(2) of the Act.

[70] As amended by the Diplomatic and other Privileges Act 1971 and the Diplomatic and Consular Premises Act 1987.

[71] Consular Relations Act 1968, Sched. I, art. 1.

[72] *ibid.*

[73] Art. 43.

[74] Art. 57.

[75] s.1(2).

such time as the provisions of the Consular Relations Act 1968[76] are applied to them by Order in Council.

11-014 **International organisations.** The International Organisations Acts 1968[77] and 1981, which replaced the International Organisations (Immunities and Privileges) Act 1950, empower the Crown by Order in Council to confer complete immunity from suit and legal process[78] upon any international organisation of which the United Kingdom and any other Sovereign power are members,[79] and to confer the like immunity from suit and legal process as is accorded to the head of a diplomatic mission upon representatives of the organisation or representatives of a member of any organs or committees of the organisation, and upon specified high officers of the organisation and persons employed by or serving on the organisation as experts or as persons engaged on missions for the organisation.[80] Similar immunity extends to the members of the official staff of such representatives, provided they are recognised as holding a rank equivalent to that of diplomatic agent,[81] and to the members of the family forming part of the household of such representatives, high officers and members of their official staffs holding diplomatic rank.[82] A limited immunity from suit extending only to things done or omitted to be done in the course of the performance of official duties is conferred upon specified subordinate officers and servants of the organisation[83] and upon members of the administrative or technical service of the representative[84] and members of their families forming part of their households.[85] However, no such immunities may be conferred on any person as the representative of the United Kingdom or as a member of his staff.[86]

11-015 **Other persons entitled to immunity.** Special provision is made in the Acts of 1968 and 1981 for conferring immunity on officers of specialised agencies of the United Nations,[87] and on other organisations of which the United Kingdom

---

[76] s.12 as substituted by the Diplomatic and other Privileges Act 1971, Sched.

[77] As amended by the Diplomatic and other Privileges Act 1971.

[78] Including winding up: *Re International Tin Council* [1989] Ch. 309. For further litigation involving the Tin Council and its immunities under the 1968 Act, see *J.H. Rayner (Mincing Lane) Ltd v. Dept. of Trade and Industry* [1989] Ch. 72 affd. [1990] 2 A.C. 418; *Standard Chartered Bank v. International Tin Council* [1987] 1 W.L.R. 641; *Shearson Lehman Bros. Inc. v. Maclaine, Watson & Co. Ltd* [1988] 1 W.L.R. 16, H.L.; *Maclaine, Watson & Co. Ltd v. International Tin Council* [1989] Ch. 253; *Maclaine, Watson & Co. Ltd v. International Tin Council (No. 2)* [1989] Ch. 286. In *Mukoro v. European Bank for Reconstruction and Development* [1994] I.C.R. 897 it was held that immunity extended to proceedings in an industrial tribunal under the Race Relations Act 1976 by an individual whose application for a post with the organisation had been rejected. The making of an Order in Council in relation to an organisation may lead to the conclusion that that organisation is thereby clothed with such legal personality as to be capable of entering into valid contracts: *J.H. Rayner (Mincing Lane) Ltd v. Dept. of Trade and Industry* [1990] 2 A.C. 415.

[79] s.1(1), (2)(b) and Sched. 1, Pt. I, para. 1. The immunities conferred by s.1 may be extended to include representatives at conferences of the organisation in the United Kingdom: s.5A.

[80] s.1(2)(c), (3), and Sched. 1, Pt. II, para. 9.

[81] s.1(4) and Sched. 1, Pt. IV, para. 20.

[82] s.1(4) and Sched. 1, Pt. IV, para. 23.

[83] s.1(2)(d) and Sched. 1, Pt. III, para. 14.

[84] s.1(4) and Sched. 1, Pt. IV, para. 21.

[85] s.1(4) and Sched. 1, Pt. IV, para. 23(4).

[86] s.1(6)(b). This is subject to s.4 of the International Organisations Act 1981.

[87] s.2(1).

is not a member,[88] including international commodity organisations.[89] The Acts further provide for the grant of immunity from suit to the judges and registrars of any international tribunal and to parties to any proceedings before any such tribunal and to their agents, advisers or advocates and to any witnesses in or assessors for the purposes of any proceedings before any international tribunal,[90] and for the grant of similar immunity to the representatives of foreign states and their official staffs attending conferences in the United Kingdom.[91] (The Diplomatic Immunities (Conferences with Commonwealth Countries and the Republic of Ireland) Act 1961[92] makes similar provision for representatives of the Commonwealth and of the Republic of Ireland and their official staff attending conferences in the United Kingdom.) Orders in Council have been made applying the Acts of 1950, 1968 and 1981 to a large number of organisations and (in most cases) to their representatives, officers, etc.[93] Any Order in Council made under the 1950 Act in force at the time of the passage of the 1968 Act shall continue to have effect, notwithstanding the repeal of the 1950 Act, until revoked or varied.[94] Special statutes or Orders in Council made thereunder confer immunity from suit on a number of international organisations and their representatives in the United Kingdom.[95] The immunities of major international organisations of which the United Kingdom is a member, such as the United Nations, the European Economic Community[96] and the Council of Europe, and of persons employed by or connected with such organisations, are provided for in a variety of separate international agreements.[97]

Waiver of immunity: common law. At common law, both sovereign[98] and **11–016** diplomatic[99] immunity could be waived by or on behalf of the foreign state

---

[88] s.4. In *Arab Monetary Fund v. Hashim (No. 3)* [1991] 2 A.C. 114 (see F.A. Mann (1991) 107 L.Q.R. 357; Marston (1991) C.L.J. 218) it was held that an international organisation of which the United Kingdom was not a member and which had been given legal personality under the law of the United Arab Emirates, where its headquarters were situated, had capacity to sue in England even though no legal capacity had been conferred upon it by English law. Attribution of legal personality by the law of the Emirates created a corporation capable of being recognised in England. Although the organisation was not entitled to immunity under the English Acts, it has been held that it may be entitled to immunity, in respect of official acts, under customary international law, that such immunity may be recognised by the English courts and, further, that the immunity may extend to senior officials of the organisation: *Arab Monetary Fund v. Hashim* [1993] 1 Lloyd's Rep. 543, 573–574. As to waiver of this immunity, see *post* § 11–016.

[89] s.4A (added to the 1968 Act by s.2 of the International Organisations Act 1981) and representatives at conferences organised by them in the United Kingdom: s.5A.

[90] s.5.

[91] s.6.

[92] s.1, as amended by the Diplomatic Privileges Act 1964, s.8(4) and Sched. 2.

[93] See Halsbury's *Laws of England* (4th ed.), Vol. 18, para. 1598.

[94] 1968 Act, s.12(5).

[95] See, *e.g.* Commonwealth Secretariat Act 1966, s.1(2) and Sched.; Arbitration (International Investment Disputes) Act 1966, s.4 and Sched.; International Monetary Fund Act 1979, s.5(1); Overseas Development and Co-operation Act 1980, s.9; Multilateral Investment Guarantee Agency Act 1988, s.3.

[96] The E.E.C. cannot claim sovereign immunity *J.H. Rayner (Mincing Lane) Ltd v. Dept. of Trade and Industry* [1989] Ch. 72, 196–203, 252–253, CA., affd. on other grounds, [1990] 2 A.C. 418.

[97] For a list of such agreements, see Halsbury's *Laws of England* (4th ed.), Vol. 18, paras. 1595–1596. See also, *J.H. Rayner (Mincing Lane) Ltd v. Dept. of Trade and Industry* [1989] Ch. 72, 203–205.

[98] *Duke of Brunswick v. King of Hanover* (1844) 6 Beav. 1, 37, 38; *Sultan of Johore v. Bendahar* [1952] A.C. 318.

[99] *Taylor v. Best* (1854) 14 C.B. 487; *Re Suarez* [1918] 1 Ch. 176; *Dickinson v. Del Solar* [1930] 1 K.B. 376; *R. v. A.B.* [1941] 1 K.B. 454.

concerned. But the doctrine was confined within narrow limits. In the first place, there could be no waiver except with full knowledge of the right and with the authority of the foreign sovereign or ambassador.[1] Secondly, waiver had to take place at the time when the court was asked to exercise jurisdiction[2]: it could not be inferred from a prior contract to submit to the jurisdiction of the court,[3] nor from the agreement to submit to arbitration,[4] nor even from an application to the court to set aside an arbitration award,[5] nor (*semble*) could it take place after judgment had been pronounced.[6]

11–017   **Submission to jurisdiction.** The State Immunity Act 1978 now makes express provision for a state to submit to the jurisdiction of the court and thereby waive its state immunity, but such waiver does not exclude the assertion of absolute privilege[7] nor does submission to the adjudicative jurisdiction of the courts necessarily imply submission to the enforcement jurisdiction of the courts.[8] There are detailed rules as to what constitutes submission[9] but one of their main effects is to free the doctrine of waiver from its narrow common law limits. Submission may, under the Act, be by prior written agreement and is permitted after a dispute has arisen.[10] A state is also deemed to submit if it institutes the proceedings[11] or if it intervenes, or takes any step, in proceedings unless it does so in reasonable ignorance of facts entitling it to immunity and immunity is then claimed as soon as reasonably practicable.[12] However, inter-vention merely to claim immunity or to assert an interest in property in circum-stances where the state would have been entitled to immunity in any proceedings brought against it does not constitute submission[13]; nor is submission to be deduced from a choice of law clause.[14] Submission extends to any appeal, but not to any counterclaim unless it arises out of the same legal relationship or facts as

---

[1] *Re Republic of Bolivia Exploration Syndicate Ltd* [1914] 1 Ch. 139; *Baccus S.R.L. v. Servicio Nacional del Trigo* [1957] 1 Q.B. 438; *R. v. Madan* [1961] 2 Q.B. 1.

[2] *Mighell v. Sultan of Johore* [1894] 1 Q.B. 149, 159, 161, 162–164; *Duff Development Co. v. Government of Kelantan* [1924] A.C. 797; *Kahan v. Pakistan Federation* [1951] 2 K.B. 1003; *The Philippine Admiral* [1974] 2 Lloyd's Rep. 568, 586–587, affd. [1977] A.C. 373.

[3] *Kahan v. Pakistan Federation, supra; Baccus S.R.L. v. Servicio Nacional del Trigo, supra.*

[4] *Duff Development Co. v. Government of Kelantan, supra.* Where a state has agreed in writing to submit a dispute which has arisen, or may arise, to arbitration, the state cannot then claim immunity as respects proceedings in the courts of the United Kingdom which relate to the arbitration, unless there is a contrary provision in the agreement or the arbitration agreement is between states: State Immunity Act 1978, s.9. The provision probably does not extend to enforcement of an award: *ibid.* s.13(2)(b); *Dicey and Morris on the Conflict of Laws* (12th ed., 1993), p. 256.

[5] *ibid.* See n. 3, *ante.*

[6] *R. v. Madan* [1961] 2 Q.B. 1.

[7] *Fayed v. Al Tajir* [1988] Q.B. 712.

[8] 1978 Act, s.13(2); *Alcom Ltd v. Republic of Colombia* [1983] A.C. 580.

[9] 1978 Act, s.2.

[10] *ibid.* s.2(2). See *A. Co. Ltd v. Republic of X.* [1990] 2 Lloyd's Rep. 520.

[11] *ibid.* s.2(3)(a). See *Ahmed v. Government of the Kingdom of Saudi Arabia* [1996] I.C.R. 25 (meaning of "written agreement"); *Propend Finance Pty Ltd v. Sing, The Times,* May 2, 1997.

[12] *ibid.* s.2(3)(b), (5). See *Kuwait Airways Corp. v. Iraqi Airways Co.* [1995] 1 Lloyd's Rep. 25, CA, rvsd., in part, on other grounds, [1995] 1 W.L.R. 1147, HL; *London Branch of the Nigerian Universities Commission v. Bastians* [1995] I.C.R. 358; *Arab Republic of Egypt v. Gamal-Eldin* [1996] I.C.R. 13; *Malaysian Industrial Development Authority v. Jeyasingham* [1998] I.C.R. 307.

[13] *ibid.* s.2(3), (4).

[14] *ibid.* s.2(2).

the claim.[15] The head of a state's diplomatic mission is deemed to have authority to submit on behalf of the state,[16] as is any person who entered into a contract on behalf of the state in respect of proceedings arising out of the contract.[17] Submission to the jurisdiction is not submission to execution, though such process may be issued with the written consent of the state.[18]

Waiver of diplomatic or consular immunity. The Diplomatic Privileges Act **11–018** 1964[19] and the Consular Relations Act 1968[20] provide that diplomatic and consular immunity may be waived by the sending state; and both Acts provide that a waiver by the head or acting head of the mission is deemed to be a waiver by that state.[21] Waiver must always be express, except that the initiating of proceedings precludes the plaintiff from invoking immunity from jurisdiction in respect of any counterclaim directly connected with the principal claim. But though waiver must be express, there is no requirement under the Acts (as there was at common law[22]) that it must take place at the time when the court is asked to exercise jurisdiction. The better view, it is submitted, is that there is no such requirement since although waiver is not defined, the term in both Acts is derived from international conventions and should not, therefore, be given the narrow interpretation attributed to it at common law.[23] Unfortunately, however, it has been held that diplomatic immunity cannot be waived by contract *inter partes* but only by an undertaking or consent, given when the court is asked to exercise jurisdiction,[24] a regressive view which, it is submitted, should not be followed.[25] Waiver of immunity from jurisdiction in civil or administrative proceedings does not imply waiver of immunity in respect of the execution of the judgment, for which a separate waiver is required.[26]

Waiver of other statutory immunities. The possibility of waiver of the **11–019** immunity is specifically provided for in Orders in Council made under the

---

[15] *ibid.* s.2(6). See *Propend Finance Pty Ltd v. Sing, The Times,* May 2, 1997. *cf. Sultan of Johore v. Bendahar* [1952] A.C. 318 (appeal); *High Commissioner for India v. Ghosh* [1960] 1 Q.B. 134 (counterclaim).

[16] *ibid.* s.2(7). See *Ahmed v. Government of the Kingdom of Saudi Arabia* [1996] I.C.R. 25; *Arab Republic of Egypt v. Gamal-Eldin* [1996] I.C.R. 13; *Propend Finance Pty Ltd v. Sing, The Times,* May 2, 1997; *Malaysian Industrial Development Authority v. Jeyasingham* [1998] I.C.R. 307. On the method of waiver or submission, see *Fayed v. Al Tajir* [1988] Q.B. 712, 733, 736–737.

[17] 1978 Act, s.2(7). See *Ahmed v. Government of the Kingdom of Saudi Arabia* [1996] I.C.R. 25.

[18] *ibid.* s.13(3); *cf. Re Suarez* [1917] 2 Ch. 131; *Duff Development Co. v. Government of Kelantan* [1923] 1 Ch. 385; [1924] A.C. 797, 810, 821, 830.

[19] Sched. 1, art. 32.

[20] Sched. 1, art. 45.

[21] 1964 Act, s.2(3); see *Propend Finance Pty Ltd v. Sing, The Times,* May 2, 1997; 1968 Act, s.1(5).

[22] *Mighell v. Sultan of Johore* [1894] 1 Q.B. 149; *Duff Development Co. v. Government of Kelantan* [1924] A.C. 797; *Kahan v. Pakistan Federation* [1951] 2 K.B. 1003.

[23] See *Dicey and Morris on the Conflict of Laws* (12th ed., 1993), p. 283; Cohn (1958) 34 B.Y.I.L. 360; F.A. Mann (1991) 107 L.Q.R. 362.

[24] *A. Co. Ltd v. Republic of X.* [1990] 2 Lloyd's Rep. 520, cogently criticised by F.A. Mann, *ibid.*

[25] F.A. Mann, *ibid.*

[26] Which waiver must also be given by an undertaking or consent given to the court when it is asked to exercise jurisdiction: *A. Co. Ltd v. Republic of X.* [1990] 2 Lloyd's Rep. 520.

International Organisations Act 1968,[27] and in the Commonwealth Secretariat Act 1966,[28] and the Arbitration (International Investments Disputes) Act 1966.[29]

2. Alien Enemies[30]

11–020   **Who is an alien enemy.** At common law, the term "alien enemy" means any person irrespective of nationality who voluntarily[31] resides or who carries on business in any enemy or enemy-occupied country during a war in which the United Kingdom is engaged.[32] As will be seen,[33] an enemy subject who resides or carries on business in the United Kingdom or in a neutral or allied country is nearly always treated as an alien friend. Hence the test of enemy character at common law is a territorial and not a national one. It is an objective test and depends on facts, not on the prejudices, passions or patriotism of the individual concerned.[34] So during the Second World War a company incorporated in Holland and having its principal place of business in Rotterdam was held to be an alien enemy after the German occupation of Holland.[35]

11–021   **Companies.** A company registered in an enemy or enemy-occupied country is an alien enemy,[36] unless the control of its affairs is shifted to a country not occupied by the enemy.[37] But a company registered in the United Kingdom and carrying on business here may acquire enemy character by reason of the hostile residence or activities of its agents or other persons in *de facto* control of its affairs.[38] Thus where all the shares except one in an English company were held

---

[27] See, *e.g. Standard Chartered Bank v. International Tin Council* [1987] 1 W.L.R. 641. A senior official of an international organisation which is entitled to immunity under customary international law (see *ante*, § 11–015, n. 88) may also be entitled to immunity, as a matter of customary international law, from legal process in respect of official acts, but since the immunity is granted to the official for the benefit of the organisation, rather than the individual official, then the immunity may be waived by the organisation, and, if it is so waived, there is no further bar to proceedings against the official: *Arab Monetary Fund v. Hashim* [1993] 1 Lloyd's Rep. 543, 574.

[28] s.1(2) and Sched., para. 8.

[29] Sched. 1, arts. 20, 21.

[30] The leading modern authorities on the procedural incapacity of alien enemies are the judgment of the full Court of Appeal in *Porter v. Freudenberg* [1915] 1 K.B. 857; the dissenting judgment of Lord Sumner in *Rodriguez v. Speyer Brothers* [1919] A.C. 59; and the judgment of Lord Wright in *Sovfracht (V/O) v. Van Udens Scheepvaart en Agentuur Maatschappij (N.V. Gebr)* [1943] A.C. 203. See also McNair, *Legal Effects of War* (4th ed., 1966), Chap. 3.

[31] *e.g.* not as a prisoner of war: *Vandyke v. Adams* [1942] Ch. 155, a case under the Trading with the Enemy Act 1939. Contrast *Scotland v. South African Territories Ltd* (1917) 33 T.L.R. 255.

[32] *Porter v. Freudenberg* [1915] 1 K.B. 857; *Sovfracht (V/O) v. Van Udens* [1943] A.C. 203; *cf. The Hoop* (1799) 1 C.Rob. 196; *McConnell v. Hector* (1802) 3 Bros. & P. 113; *O'Mealey v. Wilson* (1808) 1 Camp. 482; *Roberts v. Hardy* (1815) 3 M. & S. 533; *Janson v. Driefontein Consolidated Mines* [1902] A.C. 484, 505.

[33] *Post*, § 11–023.

[34] *Sovfracht (V/O) v. Van Udens* [1943] 203, 219.

[35] *Sovfracht (V/O) v. Van Udens, supra.* Contrast *The Pamia* [1943] 1 All E.R. 269, where a Belgian company moved its head office from Antwerp to Pittsburgh shortly after the German occupation of Belgium and so was held not to be an alien enemy.

[36] *Janson v. Driefontein Consolidated Mines* [1902] A.C. 484; *Sovfracht (V/O) v. Van Udens, supra.*

[37] *The Pamia, supra.*

[38] *Daimler Co. Ltd v. Continental Tyre and Rubber Co. Ltd* [1916] 2 A.C. 307, 344. But it does not cease to be an English company and is therefore not immune from the Trading with the Enemy Act 1939: *Kuenigl v. Donnersmarck* [1955] 1 Q.B. 515.

by Germans resident in Germany, and all its directors were Germans so resident, the company was treated as an alien enemy.[39] In that case it was said that a company registered in the United Kingdom but carrying on business in an enemy country is to be regarded as an alien enemy.[40] But that proposition is too widely stated, for the contrary has since been held.[41]

Trading with the Enemy Act 1939. The Trading with the Enemy Act 1939[42]   **11–022** contains a statutory definition of an "enemy." But this definition is limited to the purposes of the Act and does not affect the common law rule with regard to the separate question of an alien enemy's capacity to sue,[43] with which alone this section is concerned.

Alien enemy as claimant. An alien enemy cannot sue in the Queen's courts   **11–023** or take up the position of an *actor* in British litigation[44] save under royal licence.[45] The fact that the action was commenced before the outbreak of war does not enable an alien enemy to continue his action during the war,[46] nor can he appeal against a judgment given against him before the war.[47] He cannot appear as claimant in an interpleader issue.[48] The royal licence necessary to cure the claimant's incapacity to sue may be either express,[49] or inferred from the fact of his presence here with the knowledge and tacit approval of the Crown, *e.g.* if he registered under the Aliens Restriction Act 1914 and orders made thereunder.[50] Such a licence can be revoked,[51] but it is not revoked merely by the internment of the alien,[52] at any rate if the internment was an act of general policy adopted for the safety of the realm and was not due to a hostile act or attitude on the alien's part. The effect of a licence is to place the alien enemy under the protection of the Crown, with the result that in all respects except perhaps one[53] he is treated as an alien friend for procedural purposes.

---

[39] *Daimler Co. Ltd v. Continental Tyre and Rubber Co. Ltd, supra.*

[40] *Daimler Co. Ltd v. Continental Tyre and Rubber Co. Ltd, supra,* at 346.

[41] *Re Hicks* [1917] 1 K.B. 48.

[42] s.2, as amended by the Emergency Laws (Miscellaneous Provisions) Act 1953, s.2 and Sched. II, para. 3.

[43] *Sovfracht (V/O) v. Van Udens* [1943] A.C. 203, 219, approving the view of the Court of Appeal on this point.

[44] *Porter v. Freudenberg* [1915] 1 K.B. 857; *Sovfracht (V/O) v. Van Udens, supra,* at 209.

[45] *Wells v. Wiliams* (1697) 1 Ld.Raym. 282; *The Hoop* (1799) 1 C.Rob. 196, 201.

[46] See McNair *op. cit.* pp. 84–86; *Le Bret v. Papillon* (1804) 4 East 502; *Alcenius v. Nigren* (1854) 1 E. & B. 217. See also *Geiringer v. Swiss Bank Corporation* [1940] 1 All E.R. 406; *Eichengruen v. Mond* [1940] Ch. 785.

[47] *Porter v. Freudenberg* [1915] 1 K.B. 857, 884.

[48] *Geiringer v. Swiss Bank Corporation, supra.*

[49] See, *e.g. Fibrosa v. Fairbairn* [1943] A.C. 32, 35, 39–40, and comments thereon in *Sovfracht v. Van Udens* [1943] A.C. 203, 208; *The Brighton* [1951] 2 Lloyd's Rep. 65.

[50] *Princess Thurn and Taxis v. Moffitt* [1915] 1 Ch. 58, approved in *Porter v. Freudenberg, supra,* at 874; *Vokl v. Rotuna Hospital* [1914] 2 I.R. 549; *cf. Re Mary, Duchess of Sutherland* (1915) 31 T.L.R. 248, 394 (enemy national resident in a neutral country may sue). The Aliens Restriction Act 1914 was repealed by the Immigration Act 1971, s.34(1), Sched. 6.

[51] *Netz v. Ede* [1946] Ch. 224.

[52] *Schaffenius v. Goldberg* [1916] 1 K.B. 284; *cf. Sparenburgh v. Bannatyne* (1797) 1 Bos. & P. 163, where an enemy prisoner of war was allowed to sue.

[53] He may be unable to apply for a writ of habeas corpus: *The Three Spanish Sailors* (1779) 2 W.Bl. 1324; *Ex p. Liebmann* [1916] 1 K.B. 268; *R. v. Bottrill* [1947] K.B. 41; but see Sharpe, *The Law of Habeas Corpus* (1976), pp. 112–114.

11–024   The rule which debars an alien enemy from suing is an ancient rule of the common law which is based on public policy.[54] It is immaterial that Emergency Regulations made under the Trading with the Enemy Act 1939 would prevent the claimant from transmitting abroad the sum recovered until the end of the war, because he might more easily raise a loan from neutral sources on the security of a judgment debt than he could on the security of a simple contract debt, and so help to furnish the enemy country with the sinews of war.[55]

11–025   **Exceptions.** There are two or possibly three exceptions to the rule:

(1) In *Rodriguez v. Speyer Brothers*[56] it was held by a bare majority of the House of Lords (against powerful dissent by Lords Atkinson and Sumner) that an alien enemy could be joined as co-plaintiff in an action by a firm of partners of which he was formerly a member to recover a pre-war debt due to the firm, on the somewhat specious grounds that the rule should not be applied if to do so would inflict hardship not on the enemy but on British or neutral partners.[57] Lord Wright has said that this decision must be limited to its special facts.[58]

(2) An alien enemy can be heard without a licence in the Prize Court if his claim is based on an international treaty or convention, but not otherwise.[59]

(3) There is ancient authority for the proposition that an alien enemy can sue *en autre droit*, e.g. as executor or administrator of a deceased person.[60] It is, however, an open question whether this authority would be followed at the present day.[61]

11–026   **Alien enemy as defendant.** There is no rule of common law which prevents an alien enemy from being sued if service or substituted service can be effected.[62] There may be difficulties about service,[63] but in time of war it is usual for the rules as to substituted service to be relaxed under statutory authority.[64] If he is sued, an alien enemy can appear and be heard in his defence and may take all such steps as may be deemed necessary for the proper presentation of his defence, and may appeal against any judgment given against him, for to hold otherwise would be contrary to natural justice.[65] He may plead a set-off, but he

---

[54] *Porter v. Freudenberg* [1915] 1 K.B. 857, 880; *Rodriguez v. Speyer Brothers* [1919] A.C. 59, 66, 124; *Sovfracht (V/O) v. Van Udens* [1943] A.C. 203, 213.

[55] *Rodriguez v. Speyer Brothers, supra,* at 114; *Sovfracht (V/O) v. Van Udens, supra,* at 212, 236, 252.

[56] [1919] A.C. 59.

[57] *ibid.* at 71.

[58] *Sovfracht (V/O) v. Van Udens, supra,* at 233; *cf.* McNair *op. cit.* p. 83, n. 4: "The House of Lords have in the *Sovfracht* case substantially repaired the damage done by the majority speeches in *Rodriguez v. Speyer Brothers.*"

[59] *The Möwe* [1915] P. 1; *The Glenroy* [1943] P. 109.

[60] *Brocks v. Phillips* (1599) Cro.Eliz. 683; *Richfield v. Udell* (1667) Carter 191; *Villa v. Dimock* (1694) Skin. 370.

[61] See *Rodriguez v. Speyer Brothers* [1919] A.C. 59, 70, 102, 118, 137; and see McNair *op. cit.* p. 86.

[62] *Robinson & Co. v. Continental Insurance Co. of Mannheim* [1915] 1 K.B. 155; *Porter v. Freudenberg* [1915] 1 K.B. 857, 880 *et seq.*

[63] These were discussed in *Porter v. Freudenberg, supra,* at 886–890, and *Churchill & Co. v. Lonberg* [1914] 3 All E.R. 137.

[64] See, *e.g.* Legal Proceedings against Alien Enemies Act 1915 (repealed in 1927); RSC, Ord. 9, r. 14(b) (added in 1941 and repealed in 1964).

[65] *Porter v. Freudenberg, supra,* at 883–884.

may not counterclaim,[66] nor take third party proceedings,[67] nor execute a judgment for costs during the war,[68] because in doing any of these things he would become an *actor.* He may be made bankrupt[69] and may prove in the bankruptcy of another,[70] but if his proof is rejected he may not take proceedings or challenge the trustee's decision, for in doing so he would become an *actor.*[71]

Limitation of actions. The Limitation (Enemies and War Prisoners) Act   **11–027**
1945[72] suspended the running of any period of limitation for the bringing of any action in which any person who would have been a necessary party was an enemy or was detained in enemy territory until he ceased to be so and for 12 months thereafter.

Illegal contracts with alien enemies. The rule which has been considered in   **11–028**
this Section, that an alien enemy has no *persona standi in judicio*, must be carefully distinguished from the rule that contracts involving trading or other intercourse with the enemy are illegal at common law as well as by statute. The two rules are often confused, but they differ fundamentally in that the former merely creates a procedural incapacity which lasts only so long as the war lasts, while the latter destroys the cause of action once and for all.[73] The latter rule has nothing to do with capacity, and is therefore considered elsewhere in this work.[74]

3. PROFESSIONAL PERSONS

Barristers: right to fees. A barrister has no legal right to fees for his services   **11–029**
and cannot recover them by action either from the solicitor[75] or from the client.[76]
The rule is not confined to litigation but extends to all work done by a barrister as a barrister, even if the work is done by an English barrister in a foreign country by whose law advocates can recover their fees by action.[77] But it does not extend to work which does not involve any relationship of counsel and client, *e.g.* acting

---

[66] *Re Stahlwerk Becker A/G's Patent* [1917] 2 Ch. 272, 276.
[67] *Halsey v. Lowenfeld* [1916] 2 K.B. 707.
[68] *Robinson & Co. v. Continental Insurance Co. of Mannheim, supra*, at 162.
[69] *Re Hilckes* [1917] 1 K.B. 48.
[70] *Ex p. Boussmaker* (1806) 13 Ves. 71.
[71] *Re Wilson and Wilson, ex p. Marum* (1915) 84 L.J.K.B. 1893.
[72] As amended. See *The Atlantic Scout* [1950] P. 266; Franks, *Limitation of Actions* (1959), Appendix II. For limitation generally, see *post*, Chap. 29.
[73] See *Schmitz v. Van der Veen & Co.* (1915) 84 L.J.K.B. 861, 864; *Rodriguez v. Speyer Brothers* [1919] A.C. 59, 122.
[74] See *post*, 17–026—17–034.
[75] *Re May* (1858) 4 Jur.(N.S.) 1169; *Re Le Brasseur and Oakley* [1896] 2 Ch. 487, 493–494, 495–496; *Wells v. Wells* [1914] P. 157. See also *Turner v. Philipps* (1792) Peake 166. These cases were based on a rule which prevented a barrister from entering into a contract for the provision of services as a barrister. This rule was abolished by the Courts and Legal Services Act 1990, s.61(1), subject to the right of the General Council of the Bar to make rules in whatever form to prohibit or restrict barristers from entering into contracts: *ibid.* s.61(2). The relevant rules of professional conduct which have been made and which have effect, in this context, by virtue of s.61(2) effectively preclude a barrister from entering into a contract to secure payment of fees: see *Code of Conduct of the Bar of England and Wales* (1990), Appendix D, paras. 25–27.
[76] *Kennedy v. Broun* (1863) 13 C.B.(N.S.) 677.
[77] *R. v. Doutre* (1884) 9 App.Cas. 745, 752.

as arbitrator[78] or as returning officer in an election.[79] Even if a solicitor receives counsel's fees from his client, counsel cannot recover them by action against the solicitor.[80]

11–030   **Barristers' immunity.** A barrister is not liable for negligence in conducting litigation.[81] This immunity, which is grounded in public policy,[82] clearly extends to the conduct of a case in court.[83] Generally, the immunity "exists only where the particular work is so intimately connected with the conduct of the cause in court that it can fairly be said to be a preliminary decision affecting the way the cause is to be conducted when it comes to a hearing. The protection should not be given any wider application than is absolutely necessary in the interests of the administration of justice . . . "[84] This formula leaves a certain margin of appreciation in its application in particular cases.[85] Thus, for example, a majority of the Court of Appeal has held that on the basis of this formula, immunity attaches to advice given in relation to a settlement reached at the door of the court.[86] It is also

---

[78] *Hoggins v. Gordon* (1842) 3 Q.B. 466.

[79] *Egan v. Guardians of Kensington Union* (1841) 3 Q.B. 935n.

[80] *Hobart v. Butler* (1859) 9 Ir.C.L.R. 127; *Re Angell* (1860) 29 L.J.C.P. 227; *Wells v. Wells* [1914] P. 157; *Re Sandiford (No. 2)* [1935] Ch. 681.

[81] *Rondel v. Worsley* [1969] 1 A.C. 191. The immunity of a barrister is recognised by statute: see Courts and Legal Services Act 1990, s.62(1). See generally on this immunity *Jackson and Powell on Professional Negligence* (4th ed., 1997), §§ 5–07–5–18, 5–18, 5–25–5–36. A barrister may now be liable to pay the costs of his lay client or those of the opposing side which have been wasted as a result of his default: Courts and Legal Services Act 1990, s.4. For the relevant guidelines as to wasted costs orders (which may be made against all legal representatives), see *Re A Barrister (Wasted Costs Order) (No. 1 of 1991)* [1993] Q.B. 293 (criminal cases); *Ridehalgh v. Horsefield* [1994] Ch. 205 (civil cases). On the exercise of this jurisdiction see *e.g. R. v. Secretary of State for the Home Department, ex p. Abassi, The Times,* April 6, 1992; *Re A Barrister (Wasted Costs Order) (No. 4 of 1992), The Times,* March 15, 1994; *Filmlab Systems International Ltd v. Pennington* [1995] 1 W.L.R. 673; *Re A Barrister (Wasted Costs Order) (No. 4 of 1993), The Times,* December 4, 1995; Jackson and Powell *op. cit.* §§ 4–102–4–107, 5–20–5–24.

[82] *Rondel v. Worsley* [1969] 1 A.C. 191, 227–229, 230, 247, 249–251, 272, 274–276, 281–283; *Saif Ali v. Sydney Mitchell & Co.* [1980] A.C. 198, 219–220, 221, 222–223, 235–236; *Kelley v. Corston* [1998] 3 W.L.R. 246. For approval, see Report of the Royal Commission on Legal Services, Cmnd. 7648 (1979), Chap. 24. For criticism, see Zander, *Legal Services for the Community* (1978), Chap. 4; Veljanowski and Whelan (1983) 46 M.L.R. 700; Evans, *Lawyers' Liabilities* (1996), Chap. 4.

[83] *Rondel v. Worsley* [1969] 1 A.C. 191.

[84] *Rees v. Sinclair* [1974] 1 N.Z.L.R. 180, 187, adopted by a majority of the House of Lords in *Saif Ali v. Sydney Mitchell & Co.* [1980] A.C. 198, 215, 224, 231; *Kelley v. Corston* [1998] Q.B. 686.

[85] See *Jackson and Powell on Professional Negligence op.cit.* § 5–18.

[86] *Kelley v. Corston* [1998] Q.B. 686, *per* Pill and Butler-Sloss L.JJ. Judge L.J. held that immunity attached on the narrower ground that the settlement required approval of the court. *B v. Miller & Co.* [1996] 2 F.L.R. 23 was overruled in this case. The earlier decision of Holland J. in *Landall v. Dennis Faulkner & Alsop* [1994] 5 Med. L.R. 268 was approved. *cf. Swinfen v. Lord Chelmsford* (1860) 5 H. & N. 890 (counsel immune in compromising action without authority of client); *Donnellan v. Watson* (1990) 21 N.S.W.L.R. 713 (counsel not immune in failing to carry out compromise authorised by client and agreeing instead to less advantageous terms announced in court).

likely that immunity will extend to some pre-trial work,[87] but not, apparently, to failing to plead a cause of action.[88]

Solicitors. [89] A solicitor can recover his fees by action provided his certificate **11–031** was in force when the work was done[90] and also provided he does not bring his action until the expiration of one month from the time when he delivered a signed bill of costs.[91] A solicitor may be liable to his client both in contract and in tort for negligence in failing to exercise a reasonable amount of skill, diligence and knowledge,[92] but not for the consequences of a mistake on a doubtful point of law or a nice point of practice.[93] Whilst a solicitor acting as an advocate in court enjoys the same immunity as a barrister,[94] this immunity does not necessarily extend to advice as to plea.[95]

Physicians. A Fellow of the Royal College of Physicians is admitted only on **11–032** the condition that he does not sue for his fees.

---

[87] *Somasundaram v. M. Julius Melchoir* [1988] 1 W.L.R. 1394 (counsel immune in respect of advice given to client as to plea in criminal proceedings); *McFarlane v. Wilkinson* [1996] 1 Lloyd's Rep 406, rvsd. without reference to this point, [1997] 2 Lloyd's Rep. 259. (counsel immune in respect of advice not to amend pleadings between decision on preliminary issue and appeal on that issue); *Atwell v. Michael Perry & Co.*, [1998] 4 All E.R. 65 (counsel immune when ignorant of authority crucial to client's case and accordingly failed to plead an unanswerable defence on client's behalf and failed to serve witness summonses on important witnesses with the consequence that the client lost his case, but *not* immune for failure to advise that client had good grounds for appeal); *Connolly-Martin v. D, The Times*, August 17, 1998 (counsel not immune for giving undertaking without express authority of lay client and for wrongly advising that client was not bound by that undertaking) rvsd., but not on this point, *The Times*, June 8, 1999, CA.

[88] *McFarlane v. Wilkinson* [1997] 2 Lloyd's Rep 259, but counsel will only be liable for omitting to plead a cause of action where no other reasonably competent counsel, acting with ordinary care, would have failed to plead the cause of action. See too *Saif Ali v. Sydney Mitchell & Co.* [1980] A.C. 198 (counsel not immune in failing to advise that person should be joined as defendant) *cf. Atwell v. Michael Perry & Co.*, *supra*.

[89] See *Cordery on Solicitors* (8th ed.), Chaps. 5–6.

[90] Solicitors Act 1974, s.25; see *Hudgell Yeates & Co. v. Watson* [1978] Q.B. 451.

[91] *ibid.* s.69. See *Re A Debtor (No. 88 of 1991)* [1993] Ch. 286.

[92] *Midland Bank Trust Co. Ltd v. Hett, Stubbs & Kemp* [1979] Ch. 384; *Henderson v. Merrett Syndicates Ltd* [1995] 2 A.C. 145, 181–182. For a solicitor's liability in tort to a third party, see *Ross v. Caunters* [1980] Ch. 297; *Al-Kandari v. J. R. Brown & Co.* [1988] Q.B. 665; *Clarke v. Bruce Lance & Co.* [1988] 1 W.L.R. 881; *Gran Gelato Ltd v. Richcliff (Group) Ltd* [1992] Ch. 560; *White v. Jones* [1995] 2 A.C. 207; *Hemmens v. Wilson Browne* [1995] Ch. 223; *Woodward v. Wolferstans, The Times*, April 8, 1997; *Carr-Glynn v. Frearsons* [1997] 2 All E.R. 614; *Penn v. Bristol and West Building Society* [1997] 1 W.L.R. 1356. See generally, *Jackson and Powell on Professional Negligence op. cit.* §§ 4–23 *et seq.*

[93] *Godefroy v. Dalton* (1830) 6 Bing. 460; *Kemp v. Burt* (1833) 4 B. & Ad. 424; *Faithfull v. Kesteven* (1910) 103 L.T. 56. *cf. Walpole v. Patridge & Wilson* [1994] Q.B. 106 (failure to prosecute appeal), doubting *Palmer v. Durnford Ford* [1992] Q.B. 483.

[94] *Rondel v. Worsley, supra*, at 232, 243–244, 267, 284–285; *Saif Ali v. Sydney Mitchell & Co., supra*, at 215, 224, 227; *Acton v. Graham Pearce & Co.* [1997] 3 All E.R. 909; *Kelley v. Corston* [1998] Q.B. 686. The same immunity as that accorded to barristers is given to any person who lawfully provides legal services in relation to any proceedings. See Courts and Legal Services Act 1990, s.62(1). The immunity extends to an action in contract if such contract exists: *ibid.* s.62(2).

[95] *Somasundaram v. M. Julius Melchior* [1988] 1 W.L.R. 1394 (immunity attaches to advice as to plea where solicitor acts as advocate, but is not available to solicitor where barrister is engaged to advise).

Part Three
THE TERMS OF THE CONTRACT

CHAPTER 12

EXPRESS TERMS

Generally. Assuming that a contract has been validly created, it is necessary **12–001** to consider the extent of the obligations imposed on the parties by the contract. In order to do this, the exact terms of the contract must be determined[1] and their comparative importance evaluated.[2] There may be some doubt about the interpretation of the contract, and resort will then have to be made to the rules of construction which have been laid down by the courts,[3] and also to those which govern the admissibility of evidence extrinsic to a written agreement.[4]

1. Proof of Terms

Proof of terms. Where the agreement of the parties has been reduced to **12–002** writing and the document containing the agreement has been signed by one or both of them, it is well established that the party signing will ordinarily be bound by the terms of the written agreement whether or not he has read them and

---

[1] See *post*, §§ 12–002 *et seq.*
[2] See *post*, §§ 12–019 *et seq.*
[3] See *post*, §§ 12–041 *et seq.*
[4] See *post*, §§ 12–093 *et seq.*

whether or not he is ignorant of their precise legal effect.[5] But it by no means follows that the document will contain all the terms of the contract: it may be partly oral, and partly in writing.[6] Further, many contracts are made solely by word of mouth[7] or are contained in or evidenced by documents which have not been signed by the party affected. In such cases, it will be necessary to prove which statements, or stipulations, were intended to be incorporated as terms of the contract or to have contractual effect.

(a) *Contractual Undertakings and Representations*

12–003   **Terms and representations.** During the course of negotiations leading to the conclusion of a valid and binding contract, a number of statements may be made, some of which may, and others may not, be intended to have contractual force. Some statements may be considered to be mere representations, intended to induce the other party to enter into the contract, but not imposing liability for breach of contract.[8] Others may be considered to be terms of the contract, for the breach of which an action for damages will lie.[9] The question whether any particular statement is a mere representation or a term of the contract is frequently a difficult one for the court. In reaching a conclusion it will take into account the following considerations: the importance of the truth of the statement[10]; the time which elapsed between the making of the statement and the final manifestation of *consensus*[11]; whether the party making the statement was, *vis-à-vis* the other party, in a better position to ascertain the truth of the statement[12]; and whether the statement was subsequently omitted when the agreement was embodied in a more formal contract in writing.[13] But none of these criteria is conclusive[14] and the true test would seem to be whether there is "evidence of an intention by one or both parties that there should be contractual liability in

---

[5] *Parker v. South Eastern Ry.* (1877) 2 C.P.D. 416, 421; *Howatson v. Webb* [1908] 1 Ch. 1; *The Luna* [1920] P. 22; *L'Estrange v. Graucob Ltd* [1934] 2 K.B. 394; *McCutcheon v. David MacBrayne Ltd* [1964] 1 W.L.R. 125, 132–134; *Bahamas Oil Refining Co. v. Kristiansands Tank-rederie A/S* [1978] 1 Lloyd's Rep. 211; *Charlotte Thirty Ltd v. Croker Ltd* (1990) 24 Const. L.R. 46. But see *Jaques v. Lloyd D. George & Partners Ltd* [1968] 1 W.L.R. 625, 630; *Tilden Rent-a-Car Co. v. Clendenning* (1978) 83 D.L.R. (3d) 400; *Crocker v. Sundance Northwest Resorts Ltd* (1988) 51 D.L.R. (4th) 321; Spencer [1978] C.L.J. 104; and *ante*, §§ 5–054—5–059; *post*, §§ 14–121 *et seq.*

[6] See *post*, §§ 12–094—12–097.

[7] See *ante*, § 4–001.

[8] *Hopkins v. Tanqueray* (1854) 15 C.B. 130; *Heilbut, Symons & Co. v. Buckleton* [1913] A.C. 30; *Routledge v. McKay* [1954] 1 W.L.R. 615; *Oscar Chess Ltd v. Williams* [1957] 1 W.L.R. 370. See also *ante*, § 6–002.

[9] *Bannerman v. White* (1861) 10 C.B.(N.S.) 844; *De Lassalle v. Guildford* [1901] 2 K.B. 215; *Schawel v. Reade* [1913] 2 I.R. 64; *Dick Bentley Productions Ltd v. Harold Smith (Motors) Ltd* [1965] 1 W.L.R. 623; and see the cases cited in nn. 22–24, *post*.

[10] *Bannerman v. White, supra. cf. Oscar Chess Ltd v. Williams, supra.*

[11] *Routledge v. McKay, supra.* See also *Pasley v. Freeman* (1789) 3 Term Rep. 51, 57; *Schawel v. Read, supra; Mahon v. Ainscough* [1952] 1 All E.R. 337.

[12] *Dick Bentley Productions Ltd v. Harold Smith (Motors) Ltd* [1965] 1 W.L.R. 623; *Esso Petroleum Co. Ltd v. Mardon* [1976] Q.B. 801. Contrast *Heilbut, Symons & Co. v. Buckleton, supra; Gilchester Properties Ltd v. Gomm* [1948] 1 All E.R. 493.

[13] *Heilbut, Symons & Co. v. Buckleton, supra*, at 50; *Gilchester Properties Ltd v. Gomm, supra. cf. Miller v. Cannon Hill Estates Ltd* [1931] 2 K.B. 113.

[14] *Heilbut, Symons & Co. v. Buckleton, supra*, at 50.

respect of the accuracy of the statement."[15] In *Oscar Chess Ltd v. Williams*[16] a statement made to a motor dealer by a private vendor of a motor-car, based on a previous alteration of the car log-book by an unknown person, that the car was "a 1948 model," whereas in fact it had been first registered in 1939, was held by the Court of Appeal to be a mere representation. But in *Dick Bentley Productions Ltd v. Harold Smith (Motors) Ltd*[17] a statement made by a motor dealer to a private purchaser, based on a reading of the mileometer, that it had done only 20,000 miles, whereas in fact it had done approximately 100,000, was held to be a warranty. The *Oscar Chess* case was distinguished on the ground that the vendor "honestly believed and on reasonable grounds that [the statement] was true," whereas the motor dealer in the latter case "stated a fact that should be within his own knowledge. He had jumped to a conclusion and stated it as a fact."[18] Such cases show that, in this area of contract, the circumstances of each case must be individually considered to ascertain the intention of the parties and that the criteria stated above furnish no decisive tests in law. "The intention of the parties can only be deduced from the totality of the evidence, and no secondary principles of such a kind can be universally true."[19]

Collateral contracts.[20] It may be difficult to treat a statement made in the course of negotiations for a contract as a term of the contract itself, either because the statement was clearly prior to or outside the contract or because the existence of the parol evidence rule[21] prevents its inclusion. Nevertheless, the courts are prepared in some circumstances to treat a statement intended to have contractual effect as a separate contract or warranty, collateral to the main transaction.[22] In particular, they will do so where one party refuses to enter into the contract unless the other gives him an assurance on a certain point[23] or unless the other promises not to enforce a term of the written agreement.[24] Thus in *De Lassalle v. Guildford*[25] the plaintiff and the defendant negotiated for the lease of a house. The terms of the lease were arranged, but the plaintiff (the prospective tenant) **12–004**

---

[15] *ibid.* at 51 (and see 38, 42); *Pasley v. Freeman* (1789) 3 T.R. 51, 57; *Oscar Chess Ltd v. Williams, supra,* at 374; *Dick Bentley Productions Ltd v. Harold Smith (Motors) Ltd, supra,* at 629; *Esso Petroleum Co. Ltd v. Mardon, supra.* See also *J.J. Savage & Sons Pty Ltd v. Blackney* (1970) 119 C.L.R. 435.

[16] [1957] 1 W.L.R. 370. See also *Routledge v. McKay* [1954] 1 W.L.R. 615; *Dawson v. Yeoward* [1961] 1 Lloyd's Rep. 431. *cf. Turner v. Anquetil* [1953] N.Z.L.R. 952; *Beale v. Taylor* [1967] 1 W.L.R. 1193.

[17] [1965] 1 W.L.R. 623.

[18] *ibid.* at 628, 629.

[19] *Heilbut, Symons & Co. v. Buckleton, supra,* at 51.

[20] See Paterson, *Collateral Warranties Explained* (1991).

[21] See *post,* §§ 12–094—12–103.

[22] *Lindley v. Lacey* (1864) 17 C.B.(N.S.) 578; *Mann v. Nunn* (1874) 30 L.T. 526; *Spicer v. Martin* (1888) 14 App.Cas. 12; *Jacobs v. Batavia & General Plantations Trust Ltd* [1924] 1 Ch. 287; *Jameson v. Kinmell Bay Land Co. Ltd* (1931) 47 T.L.R. 593; *Miller v. Cannon Hill Estates Ltd* [1931] 2 K.B. 113; *Birch v. Paramount Estates* (1956) 167 E.G. 396; *Frisby v. B.B.C.* [1967] Ch. 932; *Quickmaid Rental Services v. Reece* (1970) 114 S.J. 372, CA; *J. Evans & Son (Portsmouth) Ltd v. Andrea Merzario Ltd* [1976] 1 W.L.R. 1078; *Esso Petroleum Co. Ltd v. Mardon* [1976] Q.B. 801; *Record v. Bell* [1991] 1 W.L.R. 853; *Wake v. Renault (U.K.) Ltd* (1996) 15 Tr. L.R. 514; Wedderburn [1959] C.L.J. 58; Greig (1971) 87 L.Q.R. 179.

[23] *Morgan v. Griffith* (1871) L.R. 6 Ex. 70; *Erskine v. Adeane* (1873) L.R. 8 Ch.App. 756; *Newman v. Gatti* (1907) 24 T.L.R. 18, 20; *Heilbut, Symons & Co. v. Buckleton, supra,* at 47.

[24] *Couchman v. Hill* [1947] K.B. 554; *Webster v. Higgin* [1948] 2 All E.R. 127; *Harling v. Eddy* [1951] 2 K.B. 739; *City of Westminster Properties (1934) Ltd v. Mudd* [1959] Ch. 129; *Brikom Investments Ltd v. Carr* [1979] Q.B. 467.

[25] [1901] 2 K.B. 215.

refused to hand over the counterpart of the lease which he had signed unless the defendant assured him that the drains were in good order. The defendant gave this assurance, and the counterpart lease was thereupon handed to him. The drains were not in fact, in good order, and the plaintiff sued the defendant on his assurance, no reference to drains having been made in the lease itself. The Court of Appeal held that the assurance constituted a contract collateral to the lease on which the defendant was liable. However, in *Heilbut Symons & Co. v. Buckleton*,[26] Lord Moulton said: "Such collateral contracts, the sole effect of which is to vary or add to the terms of the written contract, are therefore viewed with suspicion by the law . . . Not only the terms of such contracts but the existence of an *animus contrahendi* on the part of all the parties to them must be strictly shown." But more recently Lord Denning M.R. has stated[27] that "much of what was said in that case is entirely out of date."

12–005 It is undoubtedly true that the courts are nowadays much more willing to accept that a pre-contractual assurance gives rise to a collateral contract,[28] so that such collateral contracts are no longer rare. Where the assurance consists of a statement of present or past fact, there may be less need to infer a collateral contract, since a remedy in damages may be available under the Misrepresentation Act 1967[29] for a representation of fact. But where the assurance is as to the future, the Act does not apply[30] and in such a case the plaintiff must prove a collateral contract or fail completely. Lord Denning M.R. has said[31]: "When a person gives a promise or an assurance to another, intending that he should act on it by entering into a contract, and he does act on it by entering into the contract, we hold that it is binding."

12–006 Consideration for the collateral contract is normally provided by entering into the main contract,[32] but a collateral contract may also be actionable even if the main contract is unenforceable, *e.g.* for illegality.[33] Breach of the collateral contract will give rise to an action for damages for its breach, but not as a general rule to a right to treat the main contract as repudiated. However, the effect of a collateral contract may be to vary the terms of the main contract[34] or to estop a party from acting inconsistently with it if it would be inequitable for him to do so.[35]

12–007 **Third parties.** A collateral contract may also be found to exist where the main contract is not between the claimant and the defendant, but between the

---

[26] [1913] A.C. 30, 47.

[27] *J. Evans & Son (Portsmouth) Ltd v. Andrea Merzario Ltd* [1976] 1 W.L.R. 1078, 1081; *Howard Marine & Dredging Co. Ltd v. A. Ogden & Sons (Excavations) Ltd* [1978] Q.B. 574, 590. See also *Esso Petroleum Co. Ltd v. Mardon* [1978] Q.B. 801, 817.

[28] *Esso Petroleum Co. Ltd v. Mardon, supra.* But compare *Howard Marine & Dredging Co. Ltd v. A. Ogden & Sons (Excavations) Ltd, supra.*

[29] s.2(1); see *ante*, § 6–068.

[30] See *ante*, § 6–004.

[31] *J. Evans & Son (Portsmouth) Ltd v. Andrea Merzario Ltd, supra*, at 1081. But see *Heilbut Symons & Co. v. Buckleton* [1913] A.C. 30, 38, 42, 47, 49–50.

[32] *cf. De Lassalle v. Guildford* [1901] 2 K.B. 215; *Hill v. Harris* [1965] Q.B. 601.

[33] See *post*, § 17–168.

[34] *Wake v. Renault (U.K.) Ltd* (1996) 15 Tr. L.R. 514.

[35] *Brikom Investments Ltd v. Carr* [1979] Q.B. 467; but see *ante*, § 3–119.

claimant and a third party. In *Shanklin Pier Ltd v. Detel Products Ltd*,[36] the plaintiffs, owners of Shanklin Pier, wished to have their pier painted with suitable paint. They asked the defendants, a firm of paint manufacturers, whether their paint was suitable for this purpose, and were assured that it was. The plaintiffs therefore caused to be inserted in a contract made between them and the contractors who were to paint the pier a stipulation that the defendants' paint should be used. The paint was entirely unsuitable, and the plaintiffs sued the defendants on their assurance. It was held that the assurance constituted a contract, collateral to the contract for painting the pier, the consideration for which was the plaintiffs' entry into the contract containing the stipulation that the defendants' paint should be used. Similarly a collateral contract may exist where the main contract is between the defendant and a third party, as in *Charnock v. Liverpool Corporation*,[37] where the main contract to repair a car was between the repairer and an insurance company, but there was also a collateral contract between the repairer and the owner of the car that the repairer should do the repairs within a reasonable time.

(b) *Standard Form Contracts*

Contracts in standard form. A different problem may arise in proving the　**12–008** terms of the agreement where it is sought to show that they are contained in a contract in standard form, *i.e.* in some ticket, receipt, or standard form document. If a party signs a contractual document,[38] he will normally be bound by its terms.[39] More often, however, the document is simply handed to him at the time of making the contract, and the question will then arise whether the printed conditions which it contains have become terms of the contract.[40] The party receiving the document will probably not trouble to read it, and may even be ignorant that it contains any conditions at all. Yet standard form contracts very frequently embody clauses which purport to impose obligations on him or to exclude or restrict the liability of the person supplying the document.[41] Thus it becomes important to determine whether these clauses should be given contractual effect.

Contractual document. The document must be of a class which either the　**12–009** party receiving it knows, or which a reasonable man would expect, to contain contractual conditions. Thus a cheque book,[42] a ticket for a deck chair,[43] a ticket

---

[36] [1951] 2 K.B. 854. See *Brown v. Sheen & Richmond Car Sales Ltd* [1950] 1 All E.R. 1102; *Andrews v. Hopkinson* [1957] 1 Q.B. 229; *Smith v. Spurling Motor Bodies Ltd* (1961) 105 S.J. 967; *Yeoman Credit Ltd v. Odgers* [1962] 1 W.L.R. 215; *Wells (Merstham) Ltd v. Buckland Sand & Silica Ltd* [1965] 2 Q.B. 170. *cf. Drury v. Victor Buckland Ltd* [1941] 1 All E.R. 269; *Independent Broadcasting Authority v. E.M.I. Electronics* (1980) 14 Build. L.R. 1; *Lambert v. Lewis* [1982] A.C. 225; *Law Debenture Trust Corpn. v. Ural Caspian Oil Corpn. Ltd* [1993] 1 W.L.R. 138 (revd. on other grounds, [1995] Ch. 132). See *post*, § 19–005.
[37] [1968] 1 W.L.R. 1498. *cf. Brown and Davis Ltd v. Galbraith* [1972] 1 W.L.R. 997. See *post*, § 19–008.
[38] *cf. Grogan v. Robin Meredith Plant Hire* (1996) 15 Tr. L.R. 371 (non-contractual document).
[39] See the cases cited in §§ 12–002, n. 5, *ante*.
[40] See Sales (1953) 16 M.L.R. 318; Clarke [1976] C.L.J. 51.
[41] See *post*, Chap. 14.
[42] *Burnett v. Westminster Bank* [1966] 1 Q.B. 742.
[43] *Chapelton v. Barry U.D.C.* [1940] 1 K.B. 532.

handed to a person at a public bath house[44] and a parking ticket issued by an automatic machine[45] have been held to be cases "where it would be quite reasonable that the party receiving it should assume that the writing contained no condition and should put it in his pocket unread."[46] On the other hand, a railway[47] or ship[48] ticket or a receipt for goods deposited[49] has been held to be a contractual document.

12–010   **Time of notice.** The conditions must be brought to the notice[50] of the party to be bound before or at the time when the contract is made. If they are not communicated to him until after the contract is concluded, they will be of no effect. In *Olley v. Marlborough Court Ltd*[51] certain property of the plaintiff was stolen from his hotel bedroom owing to the negligence of the hotel management. On arrival at the hotel he had signed the hotel register which contained no mention of any exemption clauses, but in the bedroom there was a notice disclaiming liability for articles lost or stolen. It was held that the notice was ineffective as he had not been made aware of it until after the contract was made.

12–011   **Course of dealing.** Conditions will not necessarily be incorporated into a contract by reason of the fact that the parties have, on previous occasions, dealt with each other subject to those conditions.[52] But they may be incorporated by a "course of dealing" between the parties where each party has led the other reasonably to believe that he intended that their rights and liabilities should be ascertained by reference to the terms of a document which had been consistently used by them in previous transactions.[53]

---

[44] *Taylor v. Glasgow Corp.*, 1952 S.C. 440.

[45] *Thornton v. Shoe Lane Parking Ltd* [1971] 2 Q.B. 163.

[46] *Parker v. South Eastern Ry.* (1877) 2 C.P.D. 416, 422.

[47] *Thompson v. L.M. & S. Ry.* [1930] 1 K.B. 41.

[48] *Hood v. Anchor Line (Henderson Bros.) Ltd* [1918] A.C. 837; *Cockerton v. Naviera Aznar SA* [1960] 2 Lloyd's Rep. 451.

[49] *Parker v. South Eastern Ry., supra*; *Alexander v. Ry. Executive* [1951] 2 K.B. 882.

[50] For the meaning of notice, see *post*, § 12–013.

[51] [1949] 1 K.B. 532. See also *Thornton v. Shoe Lane Parking Ltd* [1971] 2 Q.B. 163 (ticket proffered by automatic machine); *Hollingworth v. Southern Ferries Ltd* [1977] 2 Lloyd's Rep. 70; *Daly v. General Steam Navigation Co. Ltd* [1979] 1 Lloyd's Rep. 257; *Dillon v. Baltic Shipping Co.* [1991] 2 Lloyd's Rep. 155 (ship tickets); *Metaalhandel JA Magnus B.V. v. Ardfields Transport Ltd* [1988] 1 Lloyd's Rep. 197, 204 (conditions in invoice). *cf. Cockerton v. Naviera Aznar SA* [1960] 2 Lloyd's Rep. 451.

[52] *McCutcheon v. David Macbrayne Ltd* [1964] 1 W.L.R. 125, HL (no consistent course of dealing); *Hollier v. Rambler Motors (A.M.C.) Ltd* [1972] 2 Q.B. 71 (only three or four times in five years).

[53] *J. Spurling Ltd v. Bradshaw* [1956] 1 W.L.R. 461, 467; *Cockerton v. Naviera Aznar SA* [1960] 2 Lloyd's Rep. 451; *Henry Kendall & Sons v. William Lillico & Sons Ltd* [1969] 2 A.C. 31, 90, 91, 104, 105, 130; *Transmotors Ltd v. Robertson Buckley & Co. Ltd* [1970] 1 Lloyd's Rep. 224; *Eastman Chemical International A.G. v. N.M.T. Trading Ltd* [1972] 2 Lloyd's Rep. 25; *Gillespie Bros. & Co. Ltd v. Roy Bowles Transport Ltd* [1973] Q.B. 400; *S.I.A.T. di del Ferro v. Tradax Overseas SA* [1978] 2 Lloyd's Rep. 470; *Lamport & Holt Lines Ltd v. Coubro & Scrutton (M. & I.) Ltd* [1981] 2 Lloyd's Rep. 659 (affd. [1982] 2 Lloyd's Rep. 42); *McCrone v. Boots Farm Sales Ltd*, 1981 S.L.T. 103; *George Mitchell (Chesterhall) Ltd v. Finney Lock Seeds Ltd* [1983] Q.B. 284, 295 (affd. [1983] 2 A.C. 803); *Johnson Matthey Bankers Ltd v. State Trading Corpn. of India Ltd* [1984] 1 Lloyd's Rep. 427; *Circle Freight International Ltd v. Medeast Gulf Exports Ltd* [1988] 2 Lloyd's Rep. 427; *cf. Banque Paribas v. Cargill International SA* [1992] 1 Lloyd's Rep. 96, 98; see Hoggett (1970) 33 M.L.R. 518.

Usual trade conditions. Conditions usual in a particular trade may likewise **12–012** be incorporated where both parties are in the trade and are aware that conditions are habitually imposed and of the substance of those conditions, even if they are not referred to at the time of contracting.[54]

Meaning of notice. It is not necessary that the conditions contained in the **12–013** standard form document should have been read by the person receiving it, or that he should have been made subjectively aware of their import or effect. The rules which have been laid down by the courts[55] regarding notice in such circumstances are three in number:

(1) If the person receiving the document did not know that there was writing or printing on it, he is not bound.

(2) If he knew that the writing or printing contained or referred to conditions, he is bound.

(3) If the party tendering the document did what was reasonably sufficient to give the other party notice of the conditions, and if the other party knew that there was writing or printing on the document, but did not know it contained conditions, then the conditions will become the terms of the contract between them.

Reasonable sufficiency of notice. It is the third of these rules which has most **12–014** often to be considered by the courts. The question whether the party tendering the document has done all that was reasonably sufficient to give the other notice of the conditions is a question of fact in each case, in answering which the tribunal must look at all the circumstances and the situation of the parties.[56] But it is for the court, as a matter of law, to decide whether there is evidence for holding that the notice is reasonably sufficient.[57] Cases in which the notice has been held to be insufficient have been those where the conditions were printed on the back of the document, without any reference, or any adequate reference, on its face, such as, "For conditions, see back,"[58] where, on documents sent by fax, reference was made to conditions stated on the back, but those conditions were not in fact stated on the back or otherwise communicated,[59] or where the conditions were obliterated by a printed stamp.[60] In many situations, however, the tender of printed

---

[54] *British Crane Hire Corp. Ltd v. Ipswich Plant Hire Ltd* [1975] Q.B. 303; *Chevron International Oil Co. Ltd v. A/S Sea Team* [1983] 2 Lloyd's Rep. 256; *Laceys Footwear (Wholesale) Ltd v. Bowler International Freight Ltd* [1997] 2 Lloyd's Rep. 369, 378. *cf. Salsi v. Jetspread Air Services Ltd* [1977] 2 Lloyd's Rep. 57; *Neptune Orient Lines Ltd v. J.V.C. (U.K.) Ltd* [1983] 2 Lloyd's Rep. 438; *Shipbuilders Ltd v. Benson* [1992] 3 N.Z.L.R. 349; *Grogan v. Robin Meredith Plant Hire* (1996) 15 Tr. L.R. 371.

[55] *Parker v. South Eastern Ry.* (1877) 2 C.P.D. 416, 421, 423; *Richardson, Spence & Co. v. Rowntree* [1894] A.C. 217; *Hood v. Anchor Line (Henderson Bros.) Ltd* [1918] A.C. 837; *McCutcheon v. David Macbrayne Ltd* [1964] 1 W.L.R. 125; *Burnett v. Westminster Bank* [1966] 1 Q.B. 742; *Thornton v. Shoe Lane Parking Ltd* [1971] 2 Q.B. 163. See Clarke [1976] C.L.J. 51.

[56] *Parker v. South Eastern Ry., supra; Richardson, Spence & Co. v. Rowntree, supra; Hood v. Anchor Line (Henderson Bros.) Ltd, supra,* at 844, 847.

[57] *Thompson v. L.M. & S. Ry.* [1930] 1 K.B. 41.

[58] *Henderson v. Stevenson* (1875) L.R. 2 H.L.(Sc.) 470; *Sugar v. L.M. & S. Ry.* [1941] 1 All E.R. 172; *White v. Blackmore* [1972] 2 Q.B. 651, 664.

[59] *Poseidon Freight Forwarding Co. Ltd v. Davies Turner Southern Ltd* [1996] 2 Lloyd's Rep. 388.

[60] *Richardson, Spence & Co. v. Rowntree, supra.* On small and illegible print, see *Paterson Zochonis & Co. Ltd v. Elder, Dempster & Co. Ltd* [1923] 1 K.B. 420, 441. *cf. P.S. Chellaram & Co. Ltd v. China Ocean Shipping Co.* [1991] 1 Lloyd's Rep. 493, 519.

conditions will in itself be sufficient.[61] It is not necessary that the conditions themselves should be set out in the document tendered: they may be incorporated by reference, provided that reasonable notice of them has been given.[62]

12–015   **Onerous or unusual terms.** Although the party receiving the document knows it contains conditions, if the particular condition relied on is one which is a particularly onerous or unusual term, or is one which involves the abrogation of a right given by statute, the party tendering the document must show that it has been brought fairly and reasonably to the other's attention.[63] "Some clauses which I have seen," said Denning L.J.,[64] "would need to be printed in red ink on the face of the document with a red hand pointing to it before the notice could be held to be sufficient."

12–016   **Personal disability.** It is immaterial that the party receiving the document is under some personal, but non-legal, disability, such as blindness, illiteracy, or an inability to read our language.[65] Provided the notice is reasonably sufficient for the class of persons to which the party belongs (*e.g.* passengers on a ship or railway) he will be bound by the conditions.

12–017   **Printed notices.** Where printed notices are exhibited, it may be sufficient if the party to be bound has, before or at the time of making the contract, had his attention drawn to the notices,[66] or received a printed document which refers him to the notices,[67] in circumstances which make it clear to him that the contract is subject to the conditions contained in the notices.[68] The reference may be circuitous provided it is clear.[69] It has, however, been stated by Denning L.J. that: "The party who is liable at law cannot escape liability by simply putting up a printed notice, or issuing a printed catalogue, containing exempting conditions. He must go further and show affirmatively that it is a contractual document and

---

[61] *Parker v. South Eastern Ry., supra; Hood v. Anchor Line (Henderson Bros). Ltd, supra; Cockerton v. Naviera Aznar SA* [1960] 2 Lloyd's Rep. 451; *Budd v. P. & O. Steam Navigation Co.* [1969] 2 Lloyd's Rep. 262. *cf. Union Steamships v. Barnes* (1956) 5 D.L.R. (2d) 535.

[62] *Circle Freight International Ltd v. Medeast Gulf Exports Ltd* [1988] 2 Lloyd's Rep. 427; *Shearson Lehman Hutton Inc. v. Maclaine Watson & Co. Ltd* [1989] 2 Lloyd's Rep. 570, 613; *Crédit Suisse Financial Products v. Société Generale d'Enterprises* (1996) 5 Bank. L.R. 220.

[63] *Parker v. South Eastern Ry.* (1877) 2 C.P.D. 416, 428; *Thornton v. Shoe Lane Parking Ltd* [1971] 2 Q.B. 163; *Hollingworth v. Southern Ferries Ltd* [1977] 2 Lloyd's Rep. 70; *Interfoto Picture Library Ltd v. Stiletto Visual Programmes Ltd* [1989] Q.B. 433; *Dillon v. Baltic Shipping Co.* [1991] 2 Lloyd's Rep. 155; *Laceys Footwear v. Bowler International Freight (Wholesale) Ltd* [1997] 2 Lloyd's Rep. 369, 384–385. For the extension of this principle to signed documents, see *Tilden Rent-a-Car Co. v. Clendenning* (1978) 83 D.L.R. (3d) 400. *cf. Shearson Lehman Hutton Inc. v. Maclaine Watson & Co. Ltd, supra,* at 612.

[64] *J. Spurling Ltd v. Bradshaw* [1956] 1 W.L.R. 461, 466.

[65] *Thompson v. L.M. & S. Ry.* [1930] 1 K.B. 41. *cf. Firchuk and Firchuk v. Waterfront Cartage Division, etc., Ltd* [1969] 2 Lloyd's Rep. 533, 534. *Quaere* if the disability is known to the other contracting party: see *Geier v. Kujawa Weston and Warne Bros. (Transport) Ltd* [1970] 1 Lloyd's Rep. 364.

[66] *Birch v. Thomas* [1972] 1 W.L.R. 294.

[67] *Watkins v. Rymill* (1883) 10 Q.B.D. 178.

[68] *cf. Hollingworth v. Southern Ferries Ltd* [1977] 2 Lloyd's Rep. 70.

[69] *Wyndham Rather Ltd v. Eagle Star and British Dominions Insurance Co. Ltd* (1925) 21 Ll.L. Rep. 214; *Thompson v. L.M. & S. Ry., supra; Goodyear Tyre & Rubber Co. v. Lancashire Batteries* [1958] 1 W.L.R. 857.

accepted as such by the party affected."[70] In many situations it will be sufficient to display a prominent public notice which can be plainly seen at the time of making the contract.[71] But the issue of a catalogue or brochure which states that the contract to be concluded will be subject to exempting conditions may not be sufficient to make the conditions terms of the contract if further steps to incorporate the conditions are not taken at the time the contract is concluded.[72]

Statute. Certain additional requirements of form have been imposed by statute on some classes of contract; for example, by the Carriers Act 1830, s.4, common carriers cannot limit their liability by publication of notices alone, but only by special contract.[73]   **12–018**

2. CLASSIFICATION OF TERMS

Conditions and warranties. Once it has been established that a certain   **12–019**
stipulation is indeed a term of the contract, the question arises as to its comparative importance and effect. Traditionally, in English law, the terms of a contract have been classified as being either *conditions* or *warranties*, the difference between them being that any breach of a condition entitles the innocent party, if he so chooses, to treat himself as discharged from further performance under the contract,[74] and in any event to claim damages for loss sustained by the breach. A breach of warranty, on the other hand, does not entitle him to treat himself as discharged, but to claim damages only.

Intermediate terms. The dichotomy between conditions and warranties is   **12–020**
not, however, exhaustive. The "more modern doctrine"[75] is that there exists a third category of "intermediate" terms, the failure to perform which may or may not entitle the innocent party to treat himself as discharged, depending on the nature and consequences of the breach.[76]

Fundamental terms. There is some support for the view that, in addition to   **12–021**
conditions, warranties and intermediate terms, the law recognises yet a fourth category of term, the "fundamental term."[77] The fundamental term has been described as part of the "core" of the contract,[78] the non-performance of which destroys the very substance of the agreement. It has been distinguished by

---

[70] *Harling v. Eddy* [1951] 2 K.B. 739, 748. See also *Olley v. Marlborough Court Ltd* [1949] 1 K.B. 532, 549; *Adams (Durham) Ltd v. Trust Houses Ltd* [1960] 1 Lloyd's Rep. 380; *Mendelssohn v. Normand Ltd* [1970] 1 Q.B. 177, 182.

[71] *Olley v. Marlborough Court Ltd, supra,* at p. 549; *Ashdown v. Samuel Williams & Sons Ltd* [1957] 1 Q.B. 409; *Thornton v. Shoe Lane Parking Ltd* [1970] 1 Q.B. 177; *White v. Blackmore* [1972] 2 Q.B. 651. Contrast *McCutcheon v. David Macbrayne Ltd* [1964] 1 W.L.R. 125, H.L.; *Smith v. Taylor* [1966] 2 Lloyd's Rep. 231; *Burnett v. British Waterways Board* [1973] 1 W.L.R. 700.

[72] *Hollingworth v. Southern Ferries Ltd, supra.*

[73] See Vol. II, § 36–040.

[74] See *post,* § 25–037.

[75] *Reardon Smith Line Ltd v. Yngvar Hansen-Tangen* [1976] 1 W.L.R. 989, 998.

[76] See *post,* § 12–024.

[77] See *post,* §§ 14–020, 14–024. See also Guest (1961) 77 L.Q.R. 98, 327; Montrose [1964] C.L.J. 60, 254; Reynolds (1963) 79 L.Q.R. 534; Lord Devlin [1966] C.L.J. 192; Jenkins [1969] C.L.J. 251.

[78] *Alderslade v. Hendon Laundry Ltd* [1945] K.B. 189, 192.

Devlin J.[79] as being "something narrower than a condition of the contract" and as "something which underlies the whole contract so that, if it is not complied with, the performance becomes totally different from that which the contract contemplates." Examples usually cited are those where a seller delivers goods wholly different from the agreed contract goods or delivers goods which are so seriously defective as to render them in substance not the goods contracted for: *e.g.* the delivery of beans instead of peas,[80] of pinewood logs instead of mahogany logs,[81] or of a vehicle which is incapable or barely capable of self-propulsion instead of a motor car.[82] In each case, so it is said, there is a breach of the fundamental term, that is to say, of the "core" obligation to deliver the essential goods which are the subject-matter of the contract of sale.

12–022   The concept of the fundamental term has most often been employed in relation to exemption clauses. At one time it was asserted that, even though liability for a breach of condition might be excluded by an appropriately drafted exemption clause, no such clause could exonerate a party from failure to perform the fundamental term of an agreement. The House of Lords, however, has since held that there is no rule of law that an exemption clause is inapplicable in the case of a "fundamental" or "total" breach.[83] The question is now whether the clause, on its true construction, applies to the breach which has occurred. No doubt, as a matter of construction, a court will be reluctant to ascribe to an exemption clause so wide an ambit as in effect to deprive one party's stipulations of all contractual force.[84] But, for the purpose of ascertaining the intention of the parties in this respect, it seems unnecessary to predicate the existence of a fundamental term, *i.e.* in considering whether an exemption clause covers the delivery of beans instead of peas, to say that the contract contains a "fundamental term" to deliver peas. There may also be difficulties in identifying the "core" of the particular contract: Is it to supply "peas" or "leguminous vegetables" or "agricultural produce"?[85] The quest for the fundamental term may well deflect the court from its proper task of ascertaining the true construction of the exemption clause into a barren enquiry as to whether the essential object of the contract has not been fulfilled at all or whether it has been fulfilled, but not in a way that the contract requires.

12–023   Whether any further consequences follow from the categorisation of a particular contractual obligation as a fundamental term is even more doubtful. It is

---

[79] *Smeaton Hanscomb & Co. Ltd v. Sassoon I. Setty Son & Co.* [1953] 1 W.L.R. 1468, 1470.
[80] *Chanter v. Hopkins* (1838) 4 M. & W. 399, 404.
[81] *Smeaton Hanscomb & Co. Ltd v. Sassoon I. Setty Son & Co.*, *supra*, at 1470.
[82] *Karsales (Harrow) Ltd v. Wallis* [1956] 1 W.L.R. 17; *Yeoman Credit Ltd v. Apps* [1962] 2 Q.B. 508; *Farnworth Finance Facilities Ltd v. Attryde* [1970] 1 W.L.R. 1053.
[83] *Suisse Atlantique Société d'Armement Maritime SA v. N.V. Rotterdamsche Kolen Centrale* [1967] 1 A.C. 361; *Photo Production Ltd v. Securicor Transport Ltd* [1980] A.C. 827; *Ailsa Craig Fishing Co. Ltd v. Malvern Fishing Co. Ltd* [1983] 1 W.L.R. 964, 971; *George Mitchell (Chesterhall) Ltd v. Finney Lock Seeds Ltd* [1983] 2 A.C. 803; see *post*, § 14–020.
[84] *Suisse Atlantique Société d'Armement Maritime SA v. N.V. Rotterdamsche Kolen Centrale*, *supra*, at 432. See also *Tor Line A.B. v. Alltrans Group of Canada Ltd* [1984] 1 W.L.R. 48, 58–59. See *post*, § 14–007.
[85] See, *e.g. George Mitchell (Chesterhall) Ltd v. Finney Lock Seeds Ltd*, n. 83, *supra*; Lord Devlin [1966] C.L.J. 192, 212.

possible to contend that section 11(4) of the Sale of Goods Act 1979,[86] which in certain circumstances precludes a buyer who has accepted the goods from subsequently rejecting them and treating the contract as repudiated, does not apply to the breach of a fundamental term.[87] This seems to be only an *ex-post facto* rationalisation of an independent principle (if such exists) that, for the purposes of section 35 of the 1979 Act, a buyer will not be deemed to have accepted goods that are wholly different from those agreed to be sold. It is also possible to assert that the breach of a fundamental term gives rise, not merely to a claim for damages, but to recover all money paid as upon a consideration which has totally failed.[88] But it seems better to regard the question whether or not there has been a total failure of consideration as dependent upon the facts of the case, rather than upon the breach of a "fundamental term."

In conclusion it is submitted that it is neither necessary nor desirable to create   **12–024** yet a fourth category of contractual term—the "fundamental term"—in addition to conditions, warranties and intermediate terms. In *Suisse Atlantique Société d'Armement Maritime SA v. N.V. Rotterdamsche Kolen Centrale*,[89] Lord Upjohn defined the expression "fundamental term" in language which clearly indicated that he regarded it as an alternative way of referring to a condition, *i.e.* a term which went to the root of the contract so that any breach of it entitled the innocent party to be discharged. There is therefore strong ground for the view that English law does not recognise any category of "fundamental terms" distinct from conditions.

(a) *Conditions*

Differing terminology. The word "condition" is sometimes used, even in   **12–025** legal documents, to mean simply "a stipulation, a provision" and not to connote a condition in the technical sense of that word.[90] Even within the sphere of the technical meaning attached to the word "condition," the terminology employed is, unfortunately, not uniform.[91] There may, for example, be conditions, the failure of which gives no right of action, but which merely suspends the rights and obligations of the parties.[92] The most commonly used sense of the word "condition" is that of an essential stipulation of the contract which one party guarantees is true or promises will be fulfilled. Any breach of such a stipulation entitles the innocent party, if he so chooses, to treat himself as discharged from further performance of the contract, and notwithstanding that he has suffered no prejudice by the breach. He can also claim damages for any loss suffered.

---

[86] Formerly s.11(1)(c) of the Sale of Goods Act 1893.

[87] See Vol. II, § 43–053.

[88] *Rowland v. Divall* [1923] 2 K.B. 500; *Karflex Ltd v. Poole* [1933] 2 K.B. 251; *Warman v. Southern Counties Car Finance Corp. Ltd* [1949] 2 K.B. 576; *Butterworth v. Kingsway Motors Ltd* [1954] 1 W.L.R. 1286; *Karsales (Harrow) Ltd v. Wallis* [1956] 1 W.L.R. 936. See also *Hain SS. Co. v. Tate & Lyle Ltd* (1936) 41 Com.Cas. 350, 368, 369, and Vol. II, §§ 38–349, 43–052, 43–107.

[89] [1967] 1 A.C. 361, 422; see *post*, § 14–021.

[90] *L.G. Schuler A.G. v. Wickman Machine Tool Sales Ltd* [1974] A.C. 235. *cf. Skips A/S Nordheim v. Syrian Petroleum Ltd* [1984] Q.B. 509.

[91] See Stoljar (1953) L.Q.R. 485.

[92] See *post*, § 12–027.

12–026 **Conditions and other contract terms.** The use of the word "condition" in this sense appears to have originated in the seventeenth century[93]: a stipulation might be regarded as so vital to the contract that its complete and exact performance by one party was a condition precedent to the obligation of the other party to perform his part.[94] In the modern law, the reason why a breach of a condition entitles the innocent party to treat himself as discharged has been said to be that conditions "go so directly to the substance of the contract or, in other words, are so essential to its very nature that their non-performance may fairly be considered by the other party as a substantial failure to perform the contract at all."[95] And the reason why *any* breach of condition has this effect has been put on the ground that the parties are to be regarded as having agreed that any failure of performance, irrespective of the gravity of the event that has in fact resulted from the breach, should entitle the other party to elect to put an end to all primary obligations of both parties remaining unperformed.[96] The parties may, by express words[97] or by implication of law,[98] agree that a particular stipulation is to be a condition of their contract. But they may also be held to have done so by necessary implication arising from the nature, purpose and circumstances of the contract,[99] and in this respect "There is no way of deciding that question except by looking at the contract in the light of the surrounding circumstances, and then making up one's mind whether the intention of the parties, as gathered from the instrument itself, will best be carried out by treating the promise as a warranty sounding only in damages, or as a condition precedent by the failure to perform which the other party is relieved of his liability."[1]

12–027 **Promissory and contingent conditions.** A condition in the sense mentioned above may conveniently be termed a "promissory" condition, being a promise or assurance for the non-performance of which a right of action accrues to the

---

[93] See *Pordage v. Cole* (1669) 1 Wms.Saund. 319; *Kingston v. Preston* (1773) 2 Doug. 689, 691; *Boone v. Eyre* (1777) 1 H.Bl. 273n.; *Cutter v. Powell* (1795) 6 Term.R. 320; *Hongkong Fir Shipping Co. Ltd v. Kawasaki Kisen Kaisha* [1962] 2 Q.B. 26, 65; *Cehave N.V. v. Bremer Handelsgesellschaft mbH* [1976] Q.B. 44, 57, 72. See also Chalmers, *Sale of Goods* (2nd ed.), p. 164; Dawson [1981] C.L.J. 83, 87; and *post*, § 25–036.

[94] See also (marine insurance) Marine Insurance Act 1906, ss.33–41; *Bank of Nova Scotia v. Hellenic Mutual War Risks Association (Bermuda) Ltd* [1992] 1 A.C. 233.

[95] *Wallis, Son & Wells v. Pratt & Haynes* [1910] 2 K.B. 1003, 1012, *per* Fletcher Moulton J. (dissenting): approved [1911] A.C. 394; *L.G. Schuler A.G. v. Wickman Machine Tool Sales Ltd* [1974] A.C. 235, 264, 272; *State Trading Corpn. of India Ltd v. M. Golodetz Ltd* [1989] 2 Lloyd's Rep. 277, 282.

[96] *Photo Production Ltd v. Securicor Transport Ltd* [1980] A.C. 827, 849. See also *Bunge Cpn. v. Tradax Export SA* [1981] 1 W.L.R. 711; *State Trading Corpn. of India Ltd v. M. Golodetz Ltd*, *supra*.

[97] *Dawsons Ltd v. Bonnin* [1922] 2 A.C. 413; *Lombard North Central plc v. Butterworth* [1987] Q.B. 527. But the terminology used may not be decisive: Sale of Goods Act 1979, s.11(3).

[98] *e.g.* Sale of Goods Act 1979, ss.11(3), 12(5A), 13(1A), 14(6), 15(3).

[99] *Bunge Cpn. v. Tradax Export SA, supra*. See also the cases cited in § 12–037 *post* (mercantile contracts).

[1] *Bentsen v. Taylor, Sons & Co.* [1893] 2 Q.B. 274, 281. See also *Glaholm v. Hays* (1841) 2 M. & G. 257, 266; *Re Comptoir Commercial Anversois and Power, Son & Co.* [1920] 1 K.B. 868, 899; *Hongkong Fir Shipping Co. Ltd v. Kawasaki Kisen Kaisha* [1962] 2 Q.B. 26, 60; *Astley Industrial Trust Ltd v. Grimley* [1963] 1 W.L.R. 584, 590; *L.G. Schuler A.G. v. Wickman Machine Tool Sales Ltd* [1974] A.C. 235; *Bunge Cpn. v. Tradax Export SA, supra*, at 719, 725; *State Trading Corpn. of India Ltd v. M. Golodetz Ltd* [1989] 2 Lloyd's Rep. 277, 282; *Compagnie Commerciale Sucres et Denrees v. Czarnikow Ltd* [1990] 1 W.L.R. 1337, 1347; *Torvald Klaveness A/S v. Arni Maritime Corpn.* [1994] 1 W.L.R. 1465, 1475–1476; Sale of Goods Act 1979, ss.11(3), 61(1).

innocent party.[2] This sense must be carefully distinguished from that of a "contingent" condition, *i.e.* a provision that on the happening of some uncertain event an obligation shall come into force, or that an obligation shall not come into force until such an event happens.[3] In this latter case, the non-fulfilment of the condition gives no right of action for breach[4]; it simply suspends the obligations of one or both parties.[5] In *Trans Trust S.P.R.L. v. Danubian Trading Co. Ltd*,[6] Denning L.J. considered a condition in a contract for the sale of goods whereby the buyer was to open a confirmed credit in favour of the seller, and said:

"What is the legal position of such a stipulation? Sometimes it is a condition precedent to the formation of a contract, that is, it is a condition which must be fulfilled before any contract is concluded at all. In those cases the stipulation 'subject to the opening of a credit' is rather like a stipulation 'subject to contract.' If no credit is provided, there is no contract between the parties.[7] In other cases, a contract is concluded and the stipulation for a credit is a condition which is an essential term of the contract. In those cases the provision of the credit is a condition precedent, not to the formation of the contract, but to the obligation of the seller to deliver the goods. If the buyer fails to provide the credit, the seller can treat himself as discharged from any further performance of the contract and can sue the buyer for damages for not providing the credit."

The first of these instances provided by Denning L.J. is that of a contingent, and the second of a promissory, condition.

Conditions precedent. The liability of one or both of the contracting parties 12–028 may become effective only if certain facts are ascertained to exist or upon the occurrence or non-occurrence of some further event. In such a case the contract is said to be subject to a condition precedent.[8] The failure of a condition precedent may have one of a number of effects.[9] It may, in the first place, suspend

---

[2] Stoljar (1953) 69 L.Q.R. 485.

[3] *London Passenger Transport Board v. Moscrop* [1942] A.C. 332, 341; *Panoutsos v. Raymond Hadley Cpn. of New York* [1917] 2 K.B. 473; *Aberfoyle Plantations Ltd v. Cheng* [1960] A.C. 115; *Banque Keyser Ullmann SA v. Skandia (U.K.) Insurance Co. Ltd* [1990] 1 Q.B. 665, (affd. on other grounds [1991] 2 A.C. 249); *Total Gas Marketing Ltd v. Arco British Ltd* [1998] 2 Lloyd's Rep. 209. In *Damon Compania Naviera SA v. Hapag-Lloyd International SA* [1985] 1 W.L.R. 435, it was held that a provision for payment of a deposit on signing a memorandum of agreement was not a condition precedent (*i.e.* contingent condition) to the formation of the contract, but was a fundamental term (*i.e.* promissory condition) of a concluded contract.

[4] Unless one party himself deliberately procures the non-fulfilment of the condition in certain circumstances: see *post*, §§ 12–080, 13–012.

[5] See *post*, § 12–028.

[6] [1952] 2 Q.B. 297, 304.

[7] The analogy is not, however, an exact one, for in the case of a stipulation "subject to contract" no contract will usually come into existence at all (see *ante*, § 2–108) whereas in the case of a contingent condition relating to the opening of a credit a contract normally comes into existence, though certain rights and obligations of the parties are suspended until the condition is fulfilled (see *post*, § 12–028).

[8] For the other use of the term "condition precedent" to mean a promissory condition, see *ante*, § 12–026, *post*, § 25–037.

[9] See the analyses, *e.g.* in *Property and Bloodstock Ltd v. Emerton* [1967] 2 All E.R. 839, affd. [1968] Ch. 94; *United Dominions Trust (Commercial) Ltd v. Eagle Aircraft Services Ltd* [1968] 1 W.L.R. 74, 82; *Wood Preservation Ltd v. Prior* [1969] 1 W.L.R. 1077; *L.G. Schuler A.G. v. Wickman Machine Tool Sales Ltd* [1972] 1 W.L.R. 840, 850, 854, 859, CA; affd. [1974] A.C. 235, 250–251, 256, HL; *North Sea Energy Holdings NV v. Petroleum Authority of Thailand* [1997] 2 Lloyd's Rep. 418, 429.

the rights and obligations of both parties, as, for instance, where the parties enter into an agreement on the express understanding that it is not to become binding on either of them unless the condition is fulfilled.[10] Secondly, one party may assume an immediate unilateral binding obligation, subject to a condition. From this he cannot withdraw[11]; but no bilateral contract, binding on both parties, comes into existence until the condition is fulfilled.[12] Thirdly, the parties may enter into an immediate binding contract, but subject to a condition, which suspends all or some of the obligations of one or both parties pending fulfilment of the condition.[13] These conditions precedent are, however, normally contingent and not promissory, and in such a case neither party will be liable to the other if the condition is not fulfilled.

12–029 **Concurrent conditions.** The word "condition" has also been employed in the case of "concurrent conditions." Where the promises made by each party are to be fulfilled at the same time, or, at any rate, where each party's obligation is to depend on the readiness and willingness of the other to perform at that time, the promises are termed concurrent conditions. For example, in a contract of sale of goods, delivery of the goods and payment of the price are in the absence of a contrary intention concurrent conditions, that is to say, the seller must be ready and willing to give possession of the goods to the buyer in exchange for the price and the buyer must be ready and willing to pay the price in exchange for possession of the goods.[14] Similarly, when freight is payable on delivery of cargo, payment of the freight and delivery of the cargo are normally concurrent conditions.[15]

12–030 **Conditions subsequent.** The obligation of one or both parties may be made subject to a condition that it is to be immediately binding, but if certain facts are ascertained to exist or upon the occurrence or non-occurrence of some further event, then either the contract is to cease to bind or one or both parties are to have the right to avoid the contract or bring it to an end.[16] In such a case the contract is said to be subject to a condition subsequent. An example is provided by the case of *Head v. Tattersall*[17] where A bought a horse from B which B warranted to have been hunted with the Bicester hounds. If it did not answer its description, A was to have the right to return it by a certain day. The horse did not answer its

---

[10] *Pym v. Campbell* (1856) 6 E. & B. 370; *Aberfoyle Plantations Ltd v. Cheng* [1960] A.C. 115; *William Cory & Son Ltd v. I.R.C.* [1965] A.C. 1088; *Haslemere Estates Ltd v. Baker* [1982] 1 W.L.R. 1109.

[11] *Smith v. Butler* [1900] 1 Q.B. 694.

[12] *United Dominions Trust (Commercial) Ltd v. Eagle Aircraft Services Ltd, supra*; *Wood Preservation Ltd v. Prior, supra. cf. Eastham v. Leigh, London & Provincial Properties Ltd* [1971] Ch. 871.

[13] *Worsley v. Wood* (1796) 6 Term Rep. 710; *Clarke v. Watson* (1865) 18 C.B.(N.S.) 278; *Re Sandwell Park Colliery Co.* [1929] 1 Ch. 277; *Parway Estates Ltd v. I.R.C.* (1958) 45 T.C. 135; *Smallman v. Smallman* [1972] Fam. 25; *North Sea Energy Holdings NV v. Petroleum Authority of Thailand, supra. cf. Total Gas Marketing Ltd v. Arco British Ltd* [1998] 2 Lloyd's Rep. 209.

[14] Sale of Goods Act 1979, s.28. See Vol. II, § 43–235.

[15] *Paynter v. James* (1867) L.R. 2 C.P. 348; *Duthie v. Hilton* (1868) L.R. 4 C.P. 138; *Vogeman v. Bisley* (1897) 13 T.L.R. 172.

[16] *Total Gas Marketing Ltd v. Arco British Ltd* [1998] 2 Lloyd's Rep. 209. Examples can also be found in the "excepted risks" clauses of charterparties (*Atlantic Maritime Co. Inc. v. Gibbon* [1954] 1 Q.B. 88), and the power given to a landlord to re-enter in cases of breach of covenant (*Bashir v. Commissioner of Lands* [1960] A.C. 44). The former are contingent conditions; the latter, promissory.

[17] (1871) L.R. 7 Ex. 7.

description and A accordingly returned it before the day. In the meantime, however, the horse had been injured without A's fault. It was held that the injury did not cause A to lose his right to return the horse and he could recover the purchase price paid.[18]

(b) *Warranties*

Warranties. The word "warranty" has been described as "one of the most ill-used expressions in the legal dictionary."[19] In many older cases, it was used in the sense of "condition"[20] and today it is very frequently used simply in the sense of a contractual undertaking or promise. In its most technical sense, however, it is to be understood as meaning a term of the contract, the breach of which may give rise to a claim for damages but not to a right to treat the contract as repudiated.[21] The use of the word "warranty" in this sense is reserved for the less important terms of a contract, or those which are collateral to the main purpose of the contract,[22] the breach of which by one party does not entitle the other to treat his obligations as discharged. But the emergence of the new category of "intermediate" terms seems likely to have reduced the number of occasions when a term will be classified as a warranty in this sense almost to vanishing point,[23] save in the very exceptional circumstances where a term has been specifically so classified by statute.[24]   **12–031**

"Warranty" upon election. Upon the occurrence of a breach of condition, the injured party may elect to treat the breach of condition as a breach of warranty only and not as a ground for treating the contract as repudiated[25]; or he may be compelled to do so where he goes on with the contract and takes some benefit under it.[26] In such a case he is sometimes said to sue on a "warranty *ex post facto*," although this expression is somewhat misleading since the breach is still that of a condition of the contract.[27]   **12–032**

Collateral warranties. Undertakings may be given that are collateral to another contract.[28] They may be considered to be independent of that other   **12–033**

---

[18] But Cleasby J. held (at 13, 14) that, since the property in the horse had reverted to B, B had to bear the risk of loss which had occurred without A's fault in the meantime.

[19] *Finnegan v. Allen* [1943] 1 K.B. 425, 430.

[20] *Behn v. Burness* (1863) 3 B. & S. 751. In marine insurance, a promissory "warranty" is used to signify a condition precedent, the breach of which discharges the insurer from liability as from the date of breach: Marine Insurance Act 1906, ss.33–41; *Thomson v. Weems* (1884) 9 App.Cas. 671, 684; *Bank of Nova Scotia v. Hellenic Mutual War Risks Association (Bermuda) Ltd* [1992] 1 A.C. 233.

[21] *Hongkong Fir Shipping Co. Ltd v. Kawasaki Kisen Kaisha Ltd* [1962] 2 Q.B. 26, 70; Sale of Goods Act 1979, ss.11(3), 61(1).

[22] Sale of Goods Act 1979, s.61(1).

[23] But see *Palmco Shipping Inc. v. Continental Ore Cpn.* [1970] 2 Lloyd's Rep. 21; *Anglia Commercial Properties v. North East Essex Building Co.* (1983) 266 E.G. 1096.

[24] Sale of Goods Act 1979, ss.11(3), 12(5A). See also Supply of Goods (Implied Terms) Act 1973, s.8(3).

[25] Sale of Goods Act 1979, s.11(2).

[26] *ibid.* s.11(4).

[27] *Wallis, Son & Wells v. Pratt & Haynes* [1911] A.C. 394.

[28] See *ante*, § 12–004; Wedderburn [1959] Camb.L.J. 58.

contract either because they cannot fairly be regarded as having been incorporated therein,[29] or because rules of evidence hinder their incorporation,[30] or because the main contract is defective in some way[31] or is subject to certain requirements of form[32] or is made between parties other than those by or to whom the undertaking is given.[33] Such undertakings are often referred to as collateral contracts, or "collateral warranties."

(c) *Intermediate Terms*

12–034   **Intermediate terms.** The advantage that arises from the classification of a particular term as a condition is that of certainty[34]: the party affected by the breach of such a term knows at once where he stands, *i.e.* that he is immediately and unequivocally entitled to treat the contract as repudiated and, for example in a contract of sale of goods, to reject the goods.[35] On the other hand, since *any* breach of condition gives rise to this right, it may be exercised irrespective of the gravity of the breach or of the consequences resulting from the breach. The innocent party may have suffered no, or only trifling, loss or damage by reason of the breach, but is nevertheless entitled to refuse further performance of the contract. In recent years, the courts have therefore curtailed the right of discharge which follows from the classification of a term as a condition by the creation of a new category of terms, adopting a more flexible approach to the consequences of breach and tending to encourage, rather than discourage, performance of the contract.[36] In *Hongkong Fir Shipping Co. Ltd v. Kawasaki Kisen Kaisha Ltd*,[37] the Court of Appeal refused to ascribe to the shipowner's obligation to deliver a seaworthy vessel the character of a condition, and Diplock L.J. said[38]:

> "There are, however, many contractual undertakings of a more complex character which cannot be categorised as being 'conditions' or 'warranties' . . . Of such undertakings all that can be predicated is that some breaches will and others will not give rise to an event which will deprive the party not in default of substantially the whole benefit which it was intended he should obtain from the contract; and the legal consequences of a breach of such undertaking, unless provided for expressly[39] in the contract, depend upon the nature of the event to which the breach gives rise and do not follow automatically from a prior classification of the undertaking, as a 'condition' or a 'warranty.' "

---

[29] *Esso Petroleum Ltd v. Mardon* [1976] Q.B. 801.

[30] See *post*, § 12–093.

[31] *e.g.* for illegality: see *post*, § 17–168.

[32] *Record v. Bell* [1991] 1 W.L.R. 853.

[33] See *ante*, § 12–007.

[34] *A/S Awilco of Oslo v. Fulvia Spa (The Chikuma)* [1981] 1 W.L.R. 314, 322; *Bunge Corporation v. Tradax Export SA* [1981] 1 W.L.R. 711, 715, 718, 720, 725; *Compagnie Commerciale Sucres et Denrees v. Czarnikow Ltd* [1990] 1 W.L.R. 1337, 1348; *Richco International Ltd v. Bunge & Co. Ltd* [1991] 2 Lloyd's Rep. 93, 99.

[35] Sale of Goods Act 1979, ss.11(3), 12(5A), 13(1A), 14(6), 15(3). But see the modification of remedies for breach of condition in non-consumer sales contained in s.15A of the 1979 Act; Vol. II, § 43–055.

[36] *Cehave N.V. v. Bremer Handelsgesellschaft mbH* [1976] Q.B. 44, 70; *Bunge Cpn. v. Tradax Export SA* [1981] 1 W.L.R. 711, 715, 179.

[37] [1962] 2 Q.B. 26.

[38] At 70.

[39] Or impliedly: see *Bunge Corporation v. Tradax Export SA* [1981] 1 W.L.R. 711 and *post*, § 12–040.

The description that has been applied to such terms is that of "intermediate" or "innominate" terms.[40] Breach of such a term entitles the party not in default to treat the contract as repudiated only if the other party has thereby renounced his obligations under the contract,[41] or rendered them impossible of performance,[42] in some essential respect or if the consequences of the breach are so serious as to deprive the innocent party of substantially the whole benefit which it was intended that he should obtain from the contract.[43]

Instances of classification. A term is most likely to be classified as inter- **12–035** mediate if it is capable of being broken either in a manner that is trivial and capable of remedy by an award of damages or in a way that is so fundamental as to undermine the whole contract. Thus, for example, a shipowner's obligation in a charterparty to provide a seaworthy vessel,[44] to load containers without any stability problem[45] or to commence and carry out the voyage agreed on with reasonable despatch,[46] or a clause by which the master of the ship was to act under the charterer's orders,[47] have been classified as intermediate terms, the breach of which does not entitle discharge unless the consequences are such as to deprive the charterer of substantially the whole benefit of the contract or to frustrate the object of the charterer in chartering the ship.[48]

Classification of terms in sale of goods contracts. The Sale of Goods Act **12–036** 1979 and the Supply of Goods (Implied Terms) Act 1973 expressly define certain implied terms in contracts of sale of goods or hire-purchase as being "conditions" or "warranties."[49] There can be no doubt that such classification is binding. But in *Cehave N.V. v. Bremer Handelsgesellschaft mbH*[50] it was argued that section 11(1) of the Sale of Goods Act 1893 created a statutory dichotomy which divided all terms in contracts for the sale of goods into conditions and warranties. The Court of Appeal rejected that argument and held that an express term "shipment to be made in good condition" was an intermediate term the breach of which had to be so serious as to go to the root of the contract in order to entitle the buyer to reject the goods. In *Reardon Smith Line Ltd v. Yngvar*

---

[40] *Cehave N.V. v. Bremer Handelsgesellschaft mbH* [1976] Q.B. 44, 60; *Bremer Handelsgesellschaft mbH v. Vanden Avenne-Izegem P.V.B.A.* [1978] 2 Lloyd's Rep. 109, 113; *Bunge Corporation v. Tradax Export SA, supra*, at 714, 717, 719, 724; *Aktion Maritime Corpn. of Liberia v. S. Kasmas & Brothers Ltd* [1987] 1 Lloyd's Rep. 283; *Phibro Energy A.G. v. Nissho Iwai Corpn.* [1990] 1 Lloyd's Rep. 38, 58–59.

[41] See *post*, § 25–017.

[42] See *post*, § 25–027.

[43] See *post*, § 25–039.

[44] *Hongkong Fir Shipping Co. Ltd v. Kawasaki Kisen Kaisha Ltd* [1962] 2 Q.B. 26; *Nitrate Cpn. of Chile Ltd v. Pansuiza Compania de Navegacion SA* [1980] 1 Lloyd's Rep. 638.

[45] *Compagnie Generale Maritime v. Diakan Spirit SA* [1982] 2 Lloyd's Rep. 574.

[46] *Freeman v. Taylor* (1831) 8 Bing. 124; *Clipsham v. Vertue* (1843) 5 Q.B. 565; *MacAndrew v. Chapple* (1866) L.R. 1 C.P. 643.

[47] *Federal Commerce & Navigation Co. Ltd v. Molena Alpha Inc.* [1979] A.C. 757.

[48] *MacAndrew v. Chapple, supra*, at 648.

[49] See Vol. II, §§ 43–042, 43–058—43–098.

[50] [1976] Q.B. 44. See also *Tradax International SA v. Goldschmidt* [1977] 2 Lloyd's Rep. 604 (provision as to impurities); *Aktion Maritime Corpn. of Liberia v. S. Kasmas & Brothers Ltd* [1987] 1 Lloyd's Rep. 283 (condition of vessel on delivery); *Total International Ltd v. Addax BV* [1996] 2 Lloyd's Rep. 333 (provision as to quality). Contrast *Tradax Export SA v. European Grain & Shipping Co.* [1983] 2 Lloyd's Rep. 100.

Hansen-Tangen[51] two charterparties were entered into in similar terms for the charter of a ship "to be built by the Osaka Shipbuilding Co. Ltd and known as Hull No. 354." Owing to her size, the ship was built at a new yard by Oshima Shipbuilding Co. Ltd (a company in which Osaka had a 50 per cent. interest) and bore the yard or hull number Oshima 004, although she was still referred to in external documents as "called Osaka 354." The charterers sought to reject the vessel on the ground that, by analogy with contracts of sale of goods, the description of the ship was a condition of the contract, any departure from which justified rejection. The House of Lords held that they were not entitled to do so. On the other hand, terms, for example, in contracts of sale of goods that the goods contracted to be sold are afloat or already shipped,[52] or on board a ship "now at Rangoon"[53] or on a ship that will sail direct to the port of destination,[54] or that they are "under deck,"[55] or as to the date of shipment,[56] have been held to be part of the description of the goods, and conditions. Also, a stipulation as to the place of delivery in an f.o.b. contract[57] and a stipulation "linerterms Rotterdam" in a c.i.f. contract[58] have been held to be conditions.

12–037   **Classification of time stipulations.** A number of cases have arisen relating to the question whether contractual stipulations as to the time of performance should be construed as making time of the essence of the contract (*i.e.* as conditions) or as intermediate terms. At common law, stipulations as to the time of performance were normally regarded as being of the essence of a contract.[59] But in equity they were not generally so regarded,[60] in particular in relation to contracts for the sale of land, and today the equitable rule prevails.[61] The relationship between the common law and equitable rules was considered by the House of Lords in *United Scientific Holdings Ltd v. Burnley Borough Council*,[62] where it was held that the time-table specified in rent review clauses for the completion of the various steps for determining the rent payable in respect of the period following the review was not of the essence. It is, however, clear that, although stipulations as to time will not ordinarily be construed as being of the essence, they will be so construed if expressly stated to be such[63] or if the court infers from the nature of the subject-matter of the contract or the surrounding circumstances that the parties intended them to have that effect.[64] In mercantile contracts, where it is of importance that the parties should know precisely what

---

[51] [1976] 1 W.L.R. 989. See also *Sanko Steamship Co. Ltd v. Kano Trading Ltd* [1978] 1 Lloyd's Rep. 156.

[52] *Benabu & Co. v. Produce Brokers Co. Ltd* (1921) 37 T.L.R. 609, 851; *Macpherson Train & Co. Ltd v. Howard Ross & Co. Ltd* [1955] 1 W.L.R. 640, 642.

[53] *Oppenheimer v. Fraser* (1876) 34 L.T. 524.

[54] *Bergerco U.S.A. v. Vegoil Ltd* [1984] 1 Lloyd's Rep. 440.

[55] *Montagu L. Meyer Ltd v. Travaru A/B; H Cornelius of Gambleby* (1930) 46 T.L.R. 553; *Messers Ltd v. Morrison's Export Co. Ltd* [1939] 1 All E.R. 92.

[56] *Bowes v. Shand* (1877) 2 App.Cas. 455.

[57] *Petrotrade Inc. v. Stinnes Handel GmbH* [1995] 1 Lloyd's Rep. 142.

[58] *Soon Hua Seng Co. Ltd v. Glencore Grain Co. Ltd* [1996] 1 Lloyd's Rep. 398.

[59] See *post*, § 22–011.

[60] See *post*, § 22–011.

[61] Law of Property Act 1925, s.41; *post*, § 22–012.

[62] [1978] A.C. 904 (esp. at 928); *post*, § 22–012.

[63] *Steadman v. Drunkle* [1916] 1 A.C. 275, 279; *Financings Ltd v. Baldock* [1963] 2 Q.B. 104, 120; *Bunge Corpn. v. Tradax Export SA* [1980] 1 Lloyd's Rep. 294, 305, 307, 309, 310 (affd. [1981] 1 W.L.R. 711); *Lombard North Central plc v. Butterworth* [1987] Q.B. 527.

[64] [1978] A.C. 904, 937, 941, 944, 950, 958; *Bunge Cpn. v. Tradax Export SA* [1981] 1 W.L.R. 711.

their obligations are and be able to act with confidence in the legal results of their actions, the courts will readily construe a stipulation as to time as a condition of the contract.[65] Thus stipulations, for example, as to the time within which a ship must be nominated[66] or is expected ready to load under a charterparty,[67] goods must be delivered under a contract of sale,[68] the loading port must be nominated,[69] the vessel provided,[70] notice of readiness to load must be given[71] and the goods must be ready to be delivered[72] under an f.o.b. contract, goods must be shipped,[73] documents tendered[74] and notice of appropriation given[75] under a c.i.f. contract, a letter of credit must be opened,[76] or hire paid under a time charter[77] have been held to be conditions, entitling the innocent party in the event of default in punctual performance to treat himself as discharged. But there is no presumption of fact or rule of law that time is of the essence in mercantile contracts[78] and a stipulation as to time in such a contract, may on its true construction, be found to be merely an intermediate term.[79]

Effect of failure to perform on time. Where one party to a contract fails to   **12–038** perform an obligation by the date fixed by the contract, the other party may be entitled, in certain circumstances, immediately to serve notice that he will treat the contract as discharged if the obligation is not performed within a reasonable time as stipulated in the notice. This matter is discussed in Chapter 22 (Performance) later in this work[80]; but it is to be noted that, as a general rule, where the original stipulation as to the time of performance was merely an intermediate

---

[65] *Bunge Cpn. v. Tradax Export SA, supra,* at 716.

[66] *Greenwich Marine Inc. v. Federal Commerce and Navigation Co. Inc.* [1985] 1 Lloyd's Rep. 580.

[67] *The Mihalis Angelos* [1971] 1 Q.B. 164. See also *Behn v. Burness* (1863) 3 B. & S. 751; *Compania de Naviera Nedelka SA v. Tradax Internacional S.A.* [1974] Q.B. 264.

[68] *Hartley v. Hymans* [1920] 3 K.B. 475, 484; *Scandinavian Trading Co. A/B v. Zodiac Petroleum SA* [1981] 1 Lloyd's Rep. 81.

[69] *Gill & Duffus SA v. Société pour l'Exportation des Sucres* [1986] 1 Lloyd's Rep. 322.

[70] *Olearia Tirrena SpA v. N.V. Algemeene Oliehandel* [1973] 2 Lloyd's Rep. 86.

[71] *Bunge Cpn. v. Tradax Export SA, supra.*

[72] *Compagnie Commerciale Sucres et Denrees v. Czarnikow Ltd* [1990] 1 W.L.R. 1337.

[73] *Bowes v. Shand* (1877) 2 App.Cas. 455.

[74] *Toepfer v. Lenersan-Poortman N.V.* [1980] 1 Lloyd's Rep. 143; *Cerealmangimi SpA v. Toepfer* [1981] 1 Lloyd's Rep. 337.

[75] *Reuter v. Sala* (1879) 4 C.P.D. 239; *Bunge GmbH v. Landbouwbelang G.A.* [1980] 1 Lloyd's Rep. 458. See also *Société Italo-Belge pour le Commerce et L'Industrie SA v. Palm and Vegetable Oils (Malaysia) Sdn. Bhd.* [1981] 2 Lloyd's Rep. 695 (notice of shipment).

[76] *Pavia & Co. SpA v. Thurmann-Nielsen* [1952] 1 Lloyd's Rep. 153; *Ian Stach Ltd v. Baker Bosley Ltd* [1958] 2 Q.B. 130; *Nichimen Corpn. v. Gatoil Overseas Inc.* [1987] 2 Lloyd's Rep. 46; *Transpetrol Ltd v. Transol Olieprodukten B.V.* [1989] 1 Lloyd's Rep. 309. See also *Warde v. Feedex International Inc.* [1985] 2 Lloyd's Rep. 289 (nomination of bank). Contrast *State Trading Corpn. of India Ltd v. M. Golodetz Ltd* [1989] 2 Lloyd's Rep. 277 (opening of counter-trade guarantee).

[77] *Mardorf Peach & Co. Ltd v. Attica Sea Carriers Cpn. of Liberia* [1977] A.C. 850; *A/S Awilco of Oslo v. Fulvia Spa (The Chikuma)* [1981] 1 W.L.R. 314.

[78] *Bunge Corpn. v. Tradax Export SA, supra,* at 719; *State Trading Corpn. of India Ltd v. M. Golodetz Ltd* [1989] 2 Lloyd's Rep. 277; *Compagnie Commerciale Sucres et Denrees v. Czarnikow Ltd, supra,* at 1347; *Phibro Energy A.G. v. Nissho Iwai Corpn.* [1991] 1 Lloyd's Rep. 38, 45, 48.

[79] See, for example, *State Trading Corpn. of India Ltd v. M. Golodetz Ltd, supra* (opening of counter trade guarantee); *Re Olympia & York Canary Wharf Ltd (No. 2)* [1993] B.C.C. 159 (indemnity clause); *Torvald Klaveness A/S v. Arni Maritime Corpn.* [1994] 1 W.L.R. 1465 (charterer's re-delivery of ship).

[80] *Post,* §§ 22–014—22–017.

term, failure to perform the obligation within the time limited by the notice does not, in itself, constitute a repudiation irrespective of the consequences of the breach.[81]

12–039   **Force majeure clauses.** A clause in a contract of sale excusing delivery, or permitting the seller to postpone or suspend delivery upon the happening of events beyond his control (a *force majeure* clause)[82] may require that certain procedures are to be followed or notices given to the buyer before the seller is entitled to rely on the clause. Such measures may be a condition precedent on which the availability of the protection provided by the clause depends, or merely an intermediate term, the non-compliance with which does not necessarily deprive the seller of his right to rely on the clause. The classification depends, as Lord Wilberforce said in *Bremer Handelsgesellschaft v. Vanden Avenne-Izegem P.V.B.A.*[83] on "(i) the form of the clause itself, (ii) the relation of the clause to the contract as a whole, (iii) general considerations of law." In that case, the House of Lords had to consider two such provisions. The first was a prohibition of export clause which required the sellers to advise the buyers "without delay" of impossibility of shipment by reason of such prohibition.[84] This was held to be an intermediate term, since it did not establish any definite time limit within which the advice was to be given. The second provision, which took effect upon a number of events of *force majeure*, established a time-table of fixed periods within which the occurrence was to be notified, an extension of the shipping period claimed, and the buyers were to have the option of cancelling the contract. The stipulation as to time for claiming an extension was held to be a condition, punctual compliance with which was required as part of a "complete regulatory code." It was further held that a requirement of this second provision that the sellers should notify the buyers of the port or ports of loading from which it was intended to ship in consequence of the event of *force majeure* had to be precisely complied with.[85]

12–040   **Conclusion.** The conclusion to be drawn from these cases is that a term of a contract will be held to be a condition:

     (i) if it is expressly so provided by statute;

     (ii) if it has been so categorised as the result of previous judicial decision (although it has been said that some of the decisions on this matter are excessively technical and are open to re-examination by the House of Lords)[86];

---

[81] See *Eshun v. Moorgate Mercantile Co. Ltd* [1971] 1 W.L.R. 722, 726; *Behzadi v. Shaftesbury Hotels Ltd* [1992] Ch. 1, 12; *Re Olympia & York Canary Wharf Ltd (No. 2), supra; post,* § 22–017.

[82] See *post,* § 14–126.

[83] [1978] 2 Lloyd's Rep. 109, 113.

[84] The clause is not accurately set out in the headnote.

[85] See also *Tradax Export SA v. André & Cie SA* [1976] 1 Lloyd's Rep. 416; *Berg (V.) & Son Ltd v. Vanden Avenne-Izegem P.V.B.A.* [1977] 1 Lloyd's Rep. 499; *Toepfer v. Schwarze* [1980] 1 Lloyd's Rep. 385.

[86] *Reardon Smith Line Ltd v. Yngvar Hansen-Tangen* [1976] 1 W.L.R. 989, 998.

(iii) if it is so designated in the contract[87] or if the consequences of its breach, that is, the right of the innocent party to treat himself as discharged, are provided for expressly in the contract[88]; or

(iv) if the nature of the contract or the subject-matter or the circumstances of the case lead to the conclusion that the parties must, by necessary implication, have intended that the innocent party would be discharged from further performance of his obligations in the event that the term was not fully and precisely complied with.[89]

Otherwise a term of a contract will be considered to be an intermediate term.[90] Failure to perform such a term will ordinarily entitle the party not in default to treat himself as discharged only if the effect of breach of the term deprives him of substantially the whole benefit which it was intended that he should obtain from the contract.[91]

3. CONSTRUCTION OF TERMS[92]

(a) *General Rules of Construction*

Construction. The word "construction" refers to the process by which a   **12–041**
court determines the meaning and legal effect of a contract. As such, it will embrace oral contracts as well as those in writing and implied terms as well as those that are expressed. In this chapter, however, the "rules of construction" discussed in the following paragraphs have mainly been developed in relation to written documents, and in this context "construction" denotes the process (sometimes referred to as *interpretation*) by which a court arrives at the meaning to be given to the language used by the parties in the express terms of a written agreement.

---

[87] *Bettini v. Gye* (1876) 1 Q.B.D. 183, 187; *Financings Ltd v. Baldock* [1963] 2 Q.B. 104, 120; *Bunge Cpn. v. Tradax Export SA* [1980] 1 Lloyd's Rep. 294, 305, 307, 309, 310 (affd. [1981] 1 W.L.R. 711); *Lombard North Central Plc v. Butterworth* [1987] Q.B. 527. *cf. L.G. Schuler A.G. v. Wickman Machine Tool Sales Ltd* [1974] A.C. 235; *Antaios Compania Naviera SA v. Salen Rederierna A.B.* [1985] A.C. 191.

[88] *Hongkong Fir Shipping Co. Ltd v. Kawasaki Kisen Kaisha Ltd* [1962] 2 Q.B. 26, 70; *United Scientific Holdings Ltd v. Burnley B.C.* [1978] A.C. 904, 937, 941, 944, 950, 958; *Bremer Handelsgesellschaft mbH v. Vanden Avenne-Izegem P.V.B.A.* [1978] 2 Lloyd's Rep. 109, 113; *Photo Production Ltd v. Securicor Transport Ltd* [1980] A.C. 827, 849; *Bunge Cpn. v. Tradax Export SA* [1981] 1 W.L.R. 711.

[89] *United Scientific Holdings Ltd v. Burnley B.C., supra,* at 937, 941, 944, 950, 958; *Bremer Handelsgesellschaft mbH v. Vanden Avenne-Izegem P.V.B.A., supra,* at 113, 116; *Bunge Cpn. v. Tradax Export SA, supra,* at 716, 717, 720, 729; *State Trading Corpn. of India Ltd v. M. Golodetz Ltd* [1989] 2 Lloyd's Rep. 277, 283; *Barber v. NWS Bank plc* [1996] 1 W.L.R. 641.

[90] *Hongkong Fir Shipping Co. Ltd v. Kawasaki Kisen Kaisha Ltd, supra; Cehave M.V. v. Bremer Handelsgesellschaft mbH* [1976] Q.B. 44; *United Scientific Holdings Ltd v. Burnley B.C., supra,* at 928; *Bremer Handelsgesellschaft mbH v. Vanden Avenne-Izegem P.V.B.A., supra,* at 113, 121, 128, 130; *Bunge Cpn. v. Tradax Export SA, supra,* at 715–716, 717, 719, 724; *Phibro Energy A.G. v. Nissho Iwai Corpn.* [1990] 1 Lloyd's Rep. 38, 45, 58–59.

[91] See *post,* § 25–039.

[92] See generally, Odgers, *Construction of Deeds and Statutes* (5th ed.); *Norton on Deeds* (2nd ed.), Lewison, *Interpretation of Contracts* (2nd ed.).

12–042   **Object of construction.** The object of all construction of the terms of a written agreement is to discover therefrom the intention of the parties to the agreement.[93] The rules which govern the construction of contracts are the same at law and in equity,[94] for simple contracts and for specialties.[95]

12–043   **Intention of the parties.** The task of ascertaining the intention of the parties must be approached objectively[96]: the question is not what one or other of the parties meant or understood by the words used, but "the meaning which the document would convey to a reasonable person having all the background knowledge which would reasonably have been available to the parties in the situation in which they were at the time of the contract".[97] The cardinal presumption is that the parties have intended what they have in fact said, so that their words must be construed as they stand.[98] That is to say the meaning of the document or of a particular part of it is to be sought *in the document itself.* "One must consider the meaning of the words used, not what one may guess to be the intention of the parties".[99] However, this is not to say that the meaning of the words in a written document must be ascertained by reference to the words of the document alone. In the modern law, the courts will, in principle, look at all the circumstances surrounding the making of the contract which would assist in determining how the language of the document would have been understood by a reasonable man.[1]

12–044   Further it has long been accepted that the courts will not approach the task of construction with too nice a concentration upon individual words.

> "The common and universal principle ought to be applied: namely, that [an agreement] ought to receive that construction which its language will admit, and which will best effectuate the intention of the parties, to be collected from the whole of the agreement, and that greater regard is to be had to the clear intention of the parties than to any particular words which they may have used in the expression of their intent."[2]

12–045   **Rules of construction.** Certain rules of construction have been formulated by the courts. Previously, these rules were applied somewhat rigidly and adhered to tenaciously (even though the application of one rule in preference to another

---

[93] *Marquis of Cholmondeley v. Clinton* (1820) 2 Jac. & W. 1, 91.

[94] *Hotham v. East India Co.* (1787) Doug. 272, 277; *Eaton v. Lyon* (1798) 3 Ves. 690, 692; *Re Terry and White's Contract* (1886) 32 Ch.D. 14, 21.

[95] *Seddon v. Senate* (1810) 13 East. 63, 74; *Total Transport Cpn. v. Arcadia Petroleum Ltd* [1998] 1 Lloyd's Rep. 351, 362.

[96] *Mannai Investment Co. Ltd v. Eagle Star Life Assurance Co. Ltd* [1997] A.C. 749, 767, 775, 782; *Investors Compensation Scheme Ltd v. West Bromwich Building Society* [1998] 1 W.L.R. 896, 912–913. See also *Guardian Ocean Cargoes Ltd v. Banco do Brasil SA* [1994] 2 Lloyd's Rep. 152.

[97] *Investors Compensation Scheme Ltd v. West Bromwich Building Society, supra,* at 912.

[98] *I.R.C. v. Raphael* [1935] A.C. 96, 142; *British Movietonews v. London and District Cinemas* [1952] A.C. 166.

[99] *Smith v. Lucas* (1881) 18 Ch.D. 531, 542. See also *Prenn v. Simmonds* [1971] 1 W.L.R. 1381, 1385, H.L.; *Hyundai Merchant Marine Co. Ltd v. Gesuri Chartering Co. Ltd* [1991] 1 Lloyd's Rep. 100, 103.

[1] See *post,* § 12–116. McMeel [1999] L.M.C.L.Q. 382.

[2] *Ford v. Beech* (1848) 11 Q.B. 852, 866. See also *Smith v. Packhurst* (1742) 3 Atk. 135, 136; *Lloyd v. Lloyd* (1837) 2 My. & Cr. 192, 202; *SA Maritime et Commerciale of Geneva v. Anglo-Iranian Oil Co. Ltd* [1953] 1 W.L.R. 1379; affd. [1954] 1 W.L.R. 496.

might lead to an opposite result). However, it has been pointed out[3] that the modern approach to construction is "to assimilate the way in which [contractual] documents are interpreted by judges to the common-sense principles by which any serious utterance would be interpreted in ordinary life". As a result, most rules of construction are nowadays better regarded merely as guidelines or assumptions as to what the court may regard as the normal use of language and which assist judges to arrive at a reasonable interpretation of the parties' intentions, though subject to examination of the relevant circumstances surrounding the transaction. Some rules, on the other hand, such as the *contra proferentem* rule,[4] are of a different nature in that they are less obviously designed to ascertain the intentions of the parties and are more closely assimilated to "rules" in the traditional sense.

Law and fact. The construction of written instruments is a question of mixed   **12–046** law and fact. The expression "construction" as applied to a document includes two things, first, the meaning of the words; and, secondly, their legal effect, or the effect which is to be given to them.[5] Construction becomes a question of law as soon as the true meaning of the words in which an instrument has been expressed and the surrounding circumstances, if any, have been ascertained as facts.[6] However, the meaning of an ordinary English word,[7] of technical or commercial terms[8] and of latent ambiguities,[9] and the discovery of the surrounding circumstances (when they are relevant) are questions of fact.[10]

Construction of contract not wholly in writing. Where the contract does not   **12–047** depend solely on written documents, the question as to the character of the contract is properly one of fact.[11] But if a document is lost, so that secondary evidence of its contents is admissible, the construction of its terms is still a question of law and not of fact.[12]

Computerised "documents". It is submitted that an agreement which is   **12–048** concluded by electronic means, the terms of which are recorded electronically in a computer or on disc and which are capable of being retrieved and converted into readable form, should be regarded as a written agreement for the purposes of the application of rules of construction and the admissibility of extrinsic evidence.[13]

---

[3] By Lord Hoffmann in *Investors Compensation Scheme Ltd v. West Bromwich Building Society* [1998] 1 W.L.R. 896, 912. See also *Don King Productions Ltd v. Warren* [1998] 2 Lloyd's Rep. 176, 188; [1999] 1 Lloyd's Rep. 588.

[4] See *post*, § 12–081.

[5] *Chatenay v. Brazilian Submarine Telegraph Co. Ltd* [1891] 1 Q.B. 79, 85.

[6] *Bowes v. Shand* (1877) 2 App.Cas. 455, 462. See also *Neilson v. Harford* (1841) 8 M. & W. 806, 823; *Stephens v. The Queen* (1978) 139 C.L.R. 315; *R. v. Spens* [1991] 1 W.L.R. 624, 631. *cf. R. v. Adams, The Times*, January 28, 1993.

[7] *Cozens v. Brutus* [1973] A.C. 854, 861; *Belgravia Navigation Co. SA v. Cannor Shipping Ltd* [1988] 2 Lloyd's Rep. 423.

[8] *Hill v. Evans* (1862) 4 De G.F. & J. 288, 295.

[9] *Robinson v. Great Western Ry.* (1865) 35 L.J.C.P. 123.

[10] *Simpson v. Margitson* (1847) 11 Q.B. 23.

[11] *Moore v. Garwood* (1849) 4 Exch. 681; *Brook v. Hook* (1871) L.R. 6 Ex. 89; *Maskelyne v. Stollery* (1899) 16 T.L.R. 97.

[12] *Berwick v. Horsfall* (1858) 4 C.B.(N.S.) 450.

[13] *Derby & Co. Ltd v. Weldon (No. 9)* [1991] 1 W.L.R. 652.

(b) *Ordinary Meaning to be Adopted*

12–049   **Meaning of words.**[14] Judges differ widely in their belief in the reliability of
language and in the inherent meaning of words. In 1997 in *Mannai Investment
Co. Ltd v. Eagle Star Life Assurance Co. Ltd*[15] Lord Hoffmann said[16]:

> "It is of course true that the law is not concerned with the speaker's subjective
> intentions. But the notion that the law's concern is therefore with the 'meaning of his
> words' conceals an important ambiguity. The ambiguity lies in a failure to distinguish
> between the meanings of words and the question of what would be understood as the
> meaning of a person who uses words. The meaning of words, as they would appear in
> a dictionary, and the effect of their syntactical arrangement, as it would appear in a
> grammar, is part of the material which we use to understand a speaker's utterance. But
> it is only a part; another part is our knowledge of the background against which the
> utterance was made. It is that background which enables us, not only to choose the
> intended meaning when a word has more than one dictionary meaning but also . . . to
> understand a speaker's meaning, often without ambiguity, when he has used the wrong
> words".

Again in 1998, in *Investors Compensation Scheme Ltd v. West Bromwich Building Society*,[17] he said: "The meaning which a document (or any other utterance)
would convey to a reasonable man is not the same thing as the meaning of its
words. The meaning of words is a matter of dictionaries and grammars; the
meaning of the document is what the parties using those words against the
relevant background would reasonably have been understood to mean".[18] Some
eighty years earlier Holmes J. had similarly commented "A word is not a crystal,
transparent and unchanged, it is the skin of a living thought and may vary greatly
in colour and content according to the circumstances and the time in which it is
used".[19] It would be unduly pessimistic to accept that human language is such
that no sensible meaning can ever be given to the words in a document without
reference to the circumstances in which those words came to be used. But even
the "plain" and "obvious" meaning may, on this view, take on a different
meaning in the light of the circumstances prevailing when the document was
made.[20] On the other hand the actual language used by the parties undoubtedly
does impose constraints on the court's willingness to depart from the plain and
obvious meaning. If the meaning of the words is clear and unambiguous, why
should the court not assume that it was what the parties intended?[21] Moreover, an
examination of all the factual circumstances which might point to an interpretation which differs from the one which the words themselves convey may
lead to an unnecessary protraction of the judicial process. A balance has therefore
to be struck. As Corbin remarked[22]: "The more bizarre and unusual an asserted
interpretation is, the more convincing must be the testimony that supports it. At
what point the court should cease listening to testimony that white is black and

---

[14] See Farnsworth (1967) 76 Yale L.J. 939.
[15] [1997] A.C. 749.
[16] At 775.
[17] [1998] 1 W.L.R. 896.
[18] At 913.
[19] *Towne v. Eisner* (1918) 245 U.S. 416, 425.
[20] See *post*, § 12–116.
[21] *Melanesian Mission Trust Board v. Australian Mutual Provident Society* [1997] 1 N.Z.L.R. 391,
394 (Lord Hope).
[22] (1944) 53 Yale L.J. 603, 623.

that a dollar is fifty cents is a matter for sound judicial discretion and common sense".

Adoption of the ordinary meaning of words. The starting point in constru- **12–050** ing a contract is that words are to be given their ordinary and natural meaning. This is not necessarily the dictionary meaning of the word, but that in which it is generally understood. The courts assume that the parties have used language in the way that reasonable persons ordinarily do. So terms are "to be understood in their plain, ordinary, and popular sense, unless they have generally in respect to the subject-matter, as by the known usage of trade, or the like, acquired a peculiar sense distinct from the popular sense of the same words; or unless the context evidently points out that they must in the particular instance, and in order to effectuate the immediate intention of the parties to that contract, be understood in some other special and peculiar sense."[23]

Technical words. Prima facie the rule is that technical words must have their **12–051** technical meaning given to them unless something can be found in the context to exclude it,[24] for if a word is of a technical or scientific character, then its primary meaning is its technical and scientific meaning.[25] But "when it is clear from the context of an instrument in what sense words are used in that instrument, the sound rule of construction is to attribute to them that meaning, even though the words be technical and have technically a different meaning; for it is only so that you can effectuate the intention. . . . "[26] Also, "where it can be ascertained that a particular vernacular meaning is attributed to words under circumstances similar to those in which the [scientific] expression to be construed is found, the vernacular meaning must prevail over the scientific."[27] Thus "petroleum" in a reservation in a conveyance was construed according to the vernacular, and not the scientific, meaning, and so was held to include gas in solution in the liquid as it existed in the earth.[28] Yet even this distinction is not a rigid one to be applied without regard to the circumstances of the case.[29]

Established judicial construction. Where the same words or contractual **12–052** provisions have for many years received a judicial construction, the court will

---

[23] *Robertson v. French* (1803) 4 East 130, 135. See also *Shore v. Wilson* (1842) 9 Cl. & Fin. 355, 527; *Mallan v. May* (1844) 12 M. & W. 511, 517; *Tielens v. Hooper* (1850) 5 Exch. 830; *Grey v. Pearson* (1857) 6 H.L. Cas. 61, 78, 106; *Beard v. Moira Colliery Co.* [1915] 1 Ch. 257, 268; *Royal Greek Govt. v. Minister of Transport* [1949] 1 K.B. 525, 528; *Melanesian Mission Trust Board v. Australian Mutual Provident Society* [1997] 1 N.Z.L.R. 391, 394, PC. Contrast *Staffordshire A.H.A. v. South Staffordshire Waterworks Co.* [1978] 1 W.L.R. 1387, 1394.

[24] *Laird v. Briggs* (1881) 19 Ch.D. 22, 34; *Monypenny v. Monypenny* (1858) 4 K. & J. 174, 182; *Roddy v. Fitzgerald* (1858) 6 H.L.C. 823, 877.

[25] *Holt & Co. v. Collyer* (1881) 16 Ch.D. 718, 720.

[26] *Graham v. Ewart* (1856) 1 H. & N. 550, 562; *Musgrave v. Forster* (1871) L.R. 6 Q.B. 590, 596.

[27] *Michael Borys v. Canadian Pacific Ry.* [1953] A.C. 217, 223; *Lord Provost and Magistrates of Glasgow v. Farie* (1888) 13 App.Cas. 657, 669; *Luigi Monta of Genoa v. Cechofracht Co. Ltd* [1956] 2 Q.B. 552.

[28] *Michael Borys v. Canadian Pacific Ry., supra.* See also *Lovell and Christmas Ltd v. Wall* (1911) 103 L.T. 588; *Tester v. Bisley* (1948) 64 T.L.R. 184. *cf. Earl of Lonsdale v. Att.-Gen.* [1982] 1 W.L.R. 887.

[29] *Michael Borys v. Canadian Pacific Ry., supra,* at 223.

suppose that the parties have contracted upon the belief that their words will be understood in the accepted legal sense.[30]

12–053   **Absurdity, inconsistency, etc.** In *Investors Compensation Scheme Ltd v. West Bromwich Building Society*[31] Lord Hoffmann said[32]:

> "The 'rule' that words should be given their 'natural and ordinary meaning' reflects the common sense proposition that we do not easily accept that people have made linguistic mistakes, particularly in formal documents. On the other hand, if one would nevertheless conclude from the background that something must have gone wrong with the language, the law does not require judges to attribute to the parties an intention which they plainly could not have had."

So, the rule that words must be construed in their ordinary sense is liable to be departed from where that meaning would involve an absurdity[33] or would create some inconsistency with the rest of the instrument.[34] It may also not be applied where, if the words were construed in their ordinary sense, they would lead to a very unreasonable result or impose upon the contractor a responsibility which it could not reasonably be supposed he meant to assume.[35] In *Wickman Machine Tools Sales Ltd v. L. G. Schuler AG*[36] Lord Reid said: "The fact that a particular construction leads to a very unreasonable result must be a relevant consideration. The more unreasonable the result, the more unlikely it is that the parties can have intended it, and if they do intend it the more necessary it is that they shall make their intention abundantly clear".[37]

---

[30] *Thames and Mersey Marine Insurance Co. v. Hamilton, Fraser & Co.* (1887) 12 App. Cas. 484, 490; *Skips A/S Nordheim v. Syrian Petroleum Co. Ltd* [1983] 2 Lloyd's Rep. 592, 597; *Navrom v. Callitsis Ship Management SA* [1987] 2 Lloyd's Rep. 276, 278 (affd. [1988] 2 Lloyd's Rep. 416); *Marc Rich & Co. Ltd v. Tourloti Compania Naviera SA* [1988] 2 Lloyd's Rep. 101, 105; *Chiswell Shipping Ltd v. National Iranian Tanker Co.* [1991] 2 Lloyd's Rep. 251, 257. But contrast *Wickman Machine Tool Sales Ltd v. L.G. Schuler A.G.* [1974] A.C. 235; *Macedonia Maritime Co. v. Austin & Pickersgill Ltd* [1989] 1 Lloyd's Rep. 73.

[31] [1998] 1 W.L.R. 896.

[32] At 913.

[33] *Grey v. Pearson* (1857) 6 H.L.C. 61, 106; *Abbott v. Middleton* (1858) 7 H.L.C. 68, 114; *Thelluson v. Rendlesham* (1859) 7 H.L.C. 429, 519; *Caledonian Ry. v. North British Ry.* (1881) 6 App.Cas. 114, 130. *cf. Charter Reinsurance Co. Ltd v. Fagan* [1997] A.C. 313, 387.

[34] Words prima facie synonymous should be construed in the same sense throughout the instrument; *Re Birks* [1900] 1 Ch. 417, 418, but there is no rule of general application to compel this: *Watson v. Haggitt* [1928] A.C. 127.

[35] *Re Levy, ex p. Walton* (1881) 17 Ch.D. 746, 751; *Baumwoll Manufactur von Scheibler v. Furness* [1893] A.C. 8, 15; *Dodd v. Churton* [1897] 1 Q.B. 562, 566; *Miramar Maritime Corpn. v. Holborn Oil Trading Ltd* [1984] A.C. 676, 682; *Antaios Compania Naviera SA v. Salen Rederierna A.B.* [1985] A.C. 191, 200–201. Contrast *Jones v. St. John's College, Oxford* (1870) L.R. 6 Q.B. 115; *The Raven* [1980] 2 Lloyd's Rep. 266, 269; *Lakeport Navigation Co. Panama SA v. Anonima Petroli Italiana* [1982] 2 Lloyd's Rep. 205; *Pera Shipping Corpn. v. Petroship SA* [1985] 2 Lloyd's Rep. 103, 107; *Eurico SpA v. Phillipp Bros.* [1987] 2 Lloyd's Rep. 215; *Benjamin Developments Ltd v. Robt. Jones (Pacific) Ltd* [1994] 3 N.Z.L.R. 189.

[36] [1974] A.C. 235.

[37] At 251. This dictum was cited with approval in *Wace v. Pan Atlantic Group Ltd* [1981] 2 Lloyd's Rep. 339, 343; *Forsikringsaktieselskapet Vesta v. J.N.E. Butcher Bain Dawes Ltd* [1989] 1 Lloyd's Rep. 330, 346; *Macedonia Maritime Co. v. Austin & Pickersgill Ltd* [1989] 2 Lloyd's Rep. 73, 81; *Niobe Maritime Corpn. v. Tradax Ocean Transportation SA* [1995] 1 Lloyd's Rep. 579; *International Fina Services AG v. Katrina Shipping Ltd* [1995] 2 Lloyd's Rep. 344, 350; *Charter Reinsurance Co. Ltd v. Fagan* [1997] A.C. 313, 355.

Badly drafted contracts. In *Mitsui Construction Co. Ltd v. Att.-Gen. of Hong*   **12–054**
Kong[38] Lord Bridge said (of a building contract) that the fact that the contract
was badly drafted,

> "affords no reason to depart from the fundamental rule of construction of contractual
> documents that the intention of the parties must be ascertained from the language they
> have used interpreted in the light of the relevant factual situation in which the contract
> was made. But the poorer the quality of the drafting, the less willing any court should
> be to be driven by semantic niceties to attribute to the parties an improbable and
> unbusinesslike intention, if the language used, whatever it may lack in precision, is
> reasonably capable of an interpretation which attributes to the parties an intention to
> make provision for contingencies inherent in the work contracted for on a sensible and
> businesslike basis."

Mercantile contracts. Although it has been stated that there is not in law any   **12–055**
difference of construction between mercantile contracts and other instruments,[39]
commercial documents "must be construed in a business fashion"[40] and "there
must be ascribed to the words a meaning that would make good commercial
sense."[41] Indeed, in *The Antaios*[42] Lord Diplock said that "if detailed semantic
and syntactical analysis of words in a commercial contract is going to lead to a
conclusion that flouts business commonsense, it must yield to business commonsense." Moreover, in mercantile contracts, the words employed may have
acquired a special meaning,[43] and this may be a different meaning from their
natural one.[44] Hence it is that mercantile contracts are to be construed according
to the usage and custom of merchants,[45] provided that the custom is not inconsistent with the agreement.[46] When such contracts contain peculiar expressions
which have in particular places or trades a known meaning attached to them, the
meaning of these expressions is a question of fact, although the meaning of the
contract still remains a question of law.[47] Also "the custom of trade, which is a
matter of evidence, may be used to annex incidents to all written contracts,
commercial or agricultural, and others, which do not by their terms exclude it,

---

[38] (1986) 33 Build.L.R. 1, 14, PC.

[39] *Southwell v. Bowditch* (1876) 1 C.P.D. 374, 376.

[40] *Southland Frozen Meat and Produce Export Co. Ltd v. Nelson Brothers Ltd* [1898] A.C. 442,
444. See also *Menth & Co. v. Ropner & Co.* [1913] 1 K.B. 27, 32 ("must be understood in a business
and practical sense").

[41] *Miramar Maritime Corpn. v. Holborn Oil Trading Ltd* [1984] A.C. 676, 682; *International Fina
Services AG v. Katrina Shipping Ltd* [1995] 2 Lloyd's Rep. 344, 350.

[42] *Antaios Compania Naviera SA v. Salen Rederierna A.B.* [1984] A.C. 191, 201. See also *Shipping
Corpn. of India Ltd v. NBB Niederelke Schiffartsgesellschaft mbH & Co.* [1991] 1 Lloyd's Rep. 77,
80; *Bankers Trust Co. v. State Bank of India* [1991] 2 Lloyd's Rep. 443, 456; *International Fina
Services AG v. Katrina Shipping Ltd, supra*, at 350; *Charter Reinsurance Co. Ltd v. Fagan* [1997]
A.C. 313, 355; but *cf. ibid.*, at 387.

[43] See, *e.g. Care Shipping Corpn. v. Itex Itagrani Export SA* [1993] Q.B. 1 ("sub-freights").

[44] See *e.g. Seacrystal Shipping Ltd v. Bulk Transport Group Shipping Co. Ltd* [1989] 1 Lloyd's
Rep. 1, 6 ("whether in berth or not").

[45] *Re Walkers, Winser & Hamm and Shaw, Son & Co.* [1904] 2 K.B. 152; *Upjohn v. Hitchens*
[1918] 2 K.B. 48; see *post*, § 12–130.

[46] *Gibbon v. Young* (1818) 8 Taunt. 254; *Hayton v. Irwin* (1879) 5 C.P.D. 130; *The Alhambra* (1881)
6 P.D. 68; *Re L. Sutro & Co. and Heilbut, Symons & Co.* [1917] 2 K.B. 348; *Westacott v. Hahn* [1918]
1 K.B. 495; *Palgrave, Brown & Sons v. SS. Turid* [1922] 1 A.C. 397; see *post*, § 12–126.

[47] *Hutchinson v. Bowker* (1839) 5 M. & W. 535; *Hill v. Evans* (1862) 4 De G.F. & J. 288; see *ante*,
§ 12–046.

upon the presumption that the parties have contracted with reference to such usage, if it is applicable."[48]

12–056   **Custom of particular place.** There are also cases in which regard must be had to the usage or custom of the place where the contract was made or to which it had reference, in order to discover the meaning and intention of the parties. Where, therefore, it appeared that, in the place where a contract concerning a sale of cider was made, the word meant the juice of apples as soon as the juice was expressed, it was held that the contract must be construed to have been for the sale of cider in that sense of the word.[49] And so where a lease was granted of a warren in Suffolk, and the landlord covenanted to pay £60 per thousand rabbits which the tenant was bound to leave on the premises, and it appeared by custom in Suffolk in such cases that 1,000 rabbits meant 1,200, it was held that the landlord was only bound to pay for rabbits reckoned at that rate.[50]

12–057   On the other hand, there are occasions when the courts have refused to modify the natural meaning of a word in the light of custom, *e.g.* to attribute to the word "alongside" in contracts of affreightment a peculiar meaning derived from the custom of a port so as to increase the shipowner's obligation.[51] Moreover it is a question of fact in each case whether or not a contract containing terms which have a peculiar meaning owing to some usage or custom was in fact made with reference to that usage or custom, and the mere fact that such a custom exists in the district covered by the contract does not raise a conclusion in law that the meaning of the contract is to be governed by the custom.[52]

12–058   **Special meaning.** Although a contract must normally be construed in accord with the ordinary meaning of the expressions contained in it, by considering the circumstances and situation of the parties at the time, and the subject-matter of the agreement, the court may be enabled to ascertain a special meaning placed upon the words[53] and such special meaning then takes the place of the ordinary meaning for the purpose of construing the contract. Also words in ancient documents are to be interpreted according to the meaning which they bore at the date of the document.[54]

12–059   **Law of Property Act, s.61.** By section 61 of the Law of Property Act 1925, in all deeds, contracts, wills, orders, and other instruments executed, made, or coming into operation after December 31, 1925, unless the context otherwise requires:

---

[48] *Gibson v. Small* (1853) 4 H.L.C. 353, 397.

[49] *Studdy v. Sanders* (1826) 5 B. & C. 628.

[50] *Smith v. Wilson* (1832) 3 B. & Ad. 728. See *post*, § 12–128.

[51] *Palgrave, Brown & Sons v. SS. Turid* [1922] 1 A.C. 397; *Aktieselskabet Dampsskibsselskabet Primula v. Horsley* (1923) 40 T.L.R. 11; *Hillas & Co. v. Rederiaktiebolaget Aeolus* (1926) 32 Com.Cas. 169. *cf. Aktieselskab Helios v. Ekman* [1872] 2 Q.B.D. 83; *Smith, Hogg & Co. v. Louis Bamberger & Sons* [1929] 1 K.B. 150.

[52] *Clayton v. Gregson* (1836) 5 A. & E. 302.

[53] *Shore v. Wilson* (1842) 9 Cl. & F. 355, 555; *Smith v. Doe* (1821) 2 B. & B. 473, 550, 602; *Payne v. Haine* (1847) 16 M. & W. 541; *Myers v. Sarl* (1860) 3 E. & E. 306; *Perrin v. Morgan* [1943] A.C. 399, 421; *Levermore v. Jobey* [1956] 1 W.L.R. 697; *cf. Hospital for Sick Children v. Walt Disney Productions Inc.* [1968] Ch. 52.

[54] *Shore v. Wilson, supra,* at 566; *North British Ry. Co. v. Budhill Coal and Sandstone Co.* [1910] A.C. 116, 128; *Earl of Lonsdale v. Att.-Gen.* [1982] 1 W.L.R. 887, 924–928. See *post*, § 12–119.

(a) "month" means calendar month[55];

(b) "person" includes a corporation;

(c) the singular includes the plural and vice versa[56];

(d) the masculine includes the feminine and vice versa.

Construction of general words. The rule as to the construction of general   **12–060**
words is that they are restricted according to the nature of the circumstances or
of the person.[57] Thus where a railway company agreed *efficiently* to work and
repair the railway and works demised, it was held that the word "efficiently" had
to be construed according to the resources and powers of the particular
company.[58]

(c) *Whole Contract to be Considered*[59]

The whole contract is to be considered. Every contract is to be construed   **12–061**
with reference to its object and the whole of its terms,[60] and accordingly, the
whole context must be considered in endeavouring to collect the intention of the
parties, even though the immediate object of inquiry is the meaning of an isolated
word or clause.[61] "It is a true rule of construction that the sense and meaning of
the parties in any particular part of an instrument may be collected *ex antecedentibus et consequentibus*; every part of it may be brought into action in order
to collect from the whole one uniform and consistent sense, if that may be
done."[62] And so Lord Davey said in *N.E. Railway v. Hastings*,[63] quoting Lord

---

[55] Prior to 1926, the general rule was that "month" meant lunar month, but the rule was fortunately almost destroyed by exceptions. The word always meant calendar month in ecclesiastical law, in mercantile transactions, mortgages and statutes (since 1850), or where the meaning required it from the context: see *Schiller v. Petersen* [1924] 1 Ch. 394, 417; Sale of Goods Act 1979, s.10(3).

A calendar month ends on the day of the next following month having the same number as that on which computation began, *e.g.* March 30 to April 30; but if the next month has no day of the same number, the calendar month ends on the last day of the next month, *e.g.* January 30 to February 28 or 29 (in leap year): *Dodds v. Walker* [1981] 1 W.L.R. 1027, see also *post,* 22–026.

See also the Interpretation Act 1978, s.5 and Sched. 1; *Wilkie v. I.R.C.* [1952] 1 Ch. 153.

[56] *cf. Re a Solicitor's Arbitration* [1962] 1 W.L.R. 353.

[57] *Verba generalia restringuntur ad habilitatem rei vel aptitudinem personae* (Bac.Max. 10). See *post,* § 12–121.

[58] *West London Ry. v. London and N.W. Ry.* (1853) 11 C.B. 327, 356. See also *Burges v. Wickham* (1863) 3 B. & S. 669, 698; *Booth v. Alcock* (1873) L.R. 8 Ch.App. 663, 667; *Thames and Mersey Marine Insurance Co. v. Hamilton, Fraser & Co.* (1887) 12 App.Cas. 484, 490; *Shell Tankers (U.K.) Ltd v. Astro Comino Armadora SA* [1981] 2 Lloyd's Rep. 40.

[59] *Ex antecedentibus et consequentibus fit optima interpretatio* (2 Co.Inst. 317).

[60] *Throcmerton v. Tracey* (1585) 1 Plow. 145, 161; *Hume v. Rundell* (1824) 2 S. & S. 174, 177; *Richards v. Bluck* (1848) 6 C.B. 437, 441; *Reid v. Fairbanks* (1853) 13 C.B. 692, 730; *Re Strand Music Hall Co. Ltd* (1865) 35 Beav. 153, 159; *Miller v. Borner* [1900] 1 Q.B. 691.

[61] *Smith v. Packhurst* (1742) 3 Atk. 135, 136; *Browning v. Wright* (1799) 2 B. & P. 13; *Stavers v. Curling* (1836) 3 Scott 740; *Turner v. Evans* (1853) 2 E. & B. 512; *Glynn v. Margetson* [1893] A.C. 351; *Midland Ry. of Western Australia v. State of Western Australia* [1956] 1 W.L.R. 1037; *Nereide SpA di Navigazione v. Bulk Oil International Ltd* [1982] 1 Lloyd's Rep. 1; *Abu Dhabi National Tanker Co. v. Product Star Shipping Ltd* [1991] 2 Lloyd's Rep. 468, 478; *Cementation Piling and Foundations Ltd v. Aegon Insurance Co. Ltd* [1995] 1 Lloyd's Rep. 97, 101; *International Fina Services AG v. Katrina Shipping Ltd* [1995] 2 Lloyd's Rep. 344, 350.

[62] *Barton v. Fitzgerald* (1812) 15 East 529, 541; *Coles v. Hulme* (1828) 8 B. & C. 568. See also *Trenchard v. Hoskins* (1625) Winch. 93.

[63] [1900] A.C. 260, 267.

Watson[64]: "The deed must be read as a whole in order to ascertain the true meaning of its several clauses, and the words of each clause should be interpreted as to bring them into harmony with the other provisions of the deed if that interpretation does no violence to the meaning of which they are naturally susceptible."

12–062   In the case of a bond with a condition, the condition may be read in order to explain the obligatory part of the instrument, *e.g.* where no species of money was mentioned, but the debtor was bound for 7,700[65]; and in determining the meaning of words which are used for the purpose of designating periods of time, such as the words "from" and "until,"[66] the whole contract is to be taken into consideration.[67] Also, when the meaning of a contract for services is ambiguous, the court will take into consideration even the price agreed to be paid for those services for the purpose of enabling them to determine the extent of the service to be rendered under the contract.[68]

12–063   **Intention unequivocally expressed.** On the other hand, where, even by the use of general words, the intention of the parties is clearly and unequivocally expressed, the court is bound by it, however capricious it may be, unless it is plainly controlled by other parts of the instrument.[69] So in *Barton v. Fitzgerald*[70] it was held that the generality of a covenant for title in an assignment of a lease was not limited by other covenants which went only to provide for or against acts of the assignor himself or those who claimed under him. There was no intention disclosed to limit the general words.

12–064   **Control by recitals.** When the words in the operative part of an instrument are ambiguous, the recitals and other parts of the instrument may be used to discover the intention of the parties and to fix the true meaning of those words.[71] But clear words in the operative part of an instrument cannot be controlled by recitals.[72]

12–065   **Several instruments.** Several instruments made to effect one object may be construed as one instrument, and be read together, but so that each shall have its

---

[64] *Chamber Colliery Co. v. Twyerould* (1893) reported [1915] 1 Ch. 268n., 272. See also *Sir Lindsay Parkinson & Co. v. Commissioners of H.M. Works and Public Buildings* [1949] 2 K.B. 632, 662.

[65] *Coles v. Hulme* (1828) 2 B. & C. 568.

[66] See *post*, 22–023.

[67] *R. v. Stevens* (1804) 5 East 244; *Wilkinson v. Gaston* (1846) 9 Q.B. 137.

[68] *Allen v. Cameron* (1833) 1 C. & M. 832, 840.

[69] *Lloyd v. Lloyd* (1837) 2 My. & Cr. 192, 202.

[70] (1812) 15 East 530. See also *Worthington v. Warrington* (1848) 5 C.B. 635; 8 C.B. 134. *cf. Young v. Raincock* (1849) 7 C.B. 310, 340; *Strouhill v. Buck* (1850) 14 Q.B. 781, 787.

[71] *Hesse v. Albert* (1828) 3 M. & Ry. 406; *Walsh v. Trevanion* (1850) 15 Q.B. 733, 751; *Re Mitchell's Trusts* (1878) 9 Ch.D. 5, 9; *Leggott v. Barrett* (1880) 15 Ch. D. 306, 311; *Re Moon, ex p. Dawes* (1886) 17 Q.B.D. 275, 286; *Orr v. Mitchell* [1893] A.C. 238, 253, 254; *Crouch v. Crouch* [1912] 1 K.B. 378.

[72] *Leggott v. Barrett, supra*, at 311; *Re Moon, ex p. Dawes, supra*, at 286. See also *Young v. Smith* (1865) L.R. 1 Eq. 180, 183; *Dawes v. Tredwell* (1881) 18 Ch.D. 354, 358; *Foakes v. Beer* (1884) 9 App.Cas. 605; *Australian Joint Stock Bank v. Bailey* [1899] A.C. 396; *Royal Insurance Co. Ltd v. G. & S. Assured Investments Co. Ltd* [1972] 1 Lloyd's Rep. 267, 274.

distinct effect in carrying out the main design.[73] Thus, a lease and counterpart are two documents relating to one transaction and a palpable mistake in the lease may be corrected by reference to the counterpart, just as it might be by reference to other parts of the lease itself.[74] "Where several deeds form part of one transaction and are contemporaneously executed they have the same effect for all purposes such as are relevant to the case as if they were one deed."[75] Yet although the words "contemporaneously executed" have been used, there is no doubt that this is not essential, so long as the court, having regard to the circumstances, comes to the conclusion that the series of documents represents a single transaction between the same parties.[76] So the articles of association of a company may be read to explain the memorandum[77] and a prospectus which invited applications for deposit notes on certain terms could be read together with a deposit note from which one of those terms had been omitted.[78]

Supplemental instruments. Under section 58 of the Law of Property Act 1925, any instrument expressed to be supplemental to a previous instrument shall, as far as may be, be read and have effect as if the supplemental instrument contained a full recital of the previous instrument. **12–066**

Alterations and deletions. Evidence of prior negotiations is normally not admissible to construe a written contract[79] and drafts will not be admitted either to alter the language of the contract or to help in its interpretation.[80] So, where an instrument appears to have been altered while the parties were negotiating, the court cannot look at it as it originally stood compared with the alterations which were made in it, to see whether those alterations will throw any light upon the question of intention.[81] However, when the parties use a printed form, and delete parts of it, there is some authority for the view that regard may be paid to what has been deleted as part of the surrounding circumstances in the light of which the meaning of the words which they chose to leave in is to be ascertained.[82] But **12–067**

---

[73] *Duke of Bolton v. Williams* (1793) 2 Ves. 138; *Harrison v. Mexican Rail Co.* (1875) L.R. 19 Eq. 358; *Stott v. Shaw* [1928] 2 K.B. 26.

[74] *Burchell v. Clark* (1876) 2 C.P.D. 88; *Matthews v. Smallwood* [1910] 1 Ch. 777.

[75] *Manks v. Whiteley* [1912] 1 Ch. 735, 754 (revd. on other grounds *sub nom. Whiteley v. Delaney* [1914] A.C. 132); *Fowler v. Hunter* (1829) 3 Y. & J. 506.

[76] *Smith v. Chadwick* (1882) 20 Ch.D. 27, 63; *Ford v. Stuart* (1852) 15 Beav. 493; *Whitbread v. Smith* (1854) 3 De G.M. & G. 727.

[77] *Re Capital Fire Insurance Association* (1882) 21 Ch.D. 209, 212.

[78] *Jacobs v. Batavia and General Plantations Trusts Ltd* [1924] 2 Ch. 329. cf. *Smith v. Chadwick, supra.*

[79] See *post*, § 12–117.

[80] *ibid.*

[81] *Inglis v. Buttery* (1878) 3 App.Cas. 552, 558, 569, 576; *Channel Islands Ferries Ltd v. Sealink U.K. Ltd* [1987] 1 Lloyd's Rep. 559, 577 (affd. [1988] 1 Lloyd's Rep. 323).

[82] *Baumwoll Manufactur von Scheibler v. Gilchrest & Co.* [1892] 1 Q.B. 253, 256 cf. [1893] A.C. 8, 15; *Gray v. Carr* (1871) L.R. 6 Q.B. 522, 524, 529; *Stanton v. Richardson* (1874) L.R. 9 C.P. 390; *Glynn v. Margetson* [1893] A.C. 351, 357; *Caffin v. Aldridge* [1895] 2 Q.B. 648, 650; *Santay & Co. v. Cox, McEllen & Co.* (1921) 10 Ll.L.Rep. 459, 460; *Bailey Sons & Co. v. Ross, Smythe & Co.* [1940] 3 All E.R. 60; *Louis Dreyfus et Cie v. Parnaso Compania Naviera SA, infra*; *London & Overseas Freighters Ltd v. Timber Shipping Co SA* [1972] A.C. 1, 15; *Mottram Consultants Ltd v. Bernard Sunley Ltd* [1975] 2 Lloyd's Rep. 197, 209; *Punjab National Bank v. De Boinville* [1992] 1 W.L.R. 1138, 1148.

there is weighty authority to the contrary.[83] In any event, it is doubtful whether the court can look at the words deleted except to resolve an ambiguity in the words retained.[84] The position may nevertheless be different where alterations are made to an already concluded agreement. In *Punjab National Bank v. De Boinville*[85] Staughton L.J. said: " . . . if the parties to a concluded agreement subsequently agree in express terms that some words in it are to be replaced by others, one can have regard to all aspects of the subsequent agreement in construing the contract, including the deletions, even in a case which is not, or not wholly, concerned with a printed form." Also where a one-off contract has been drafted by reference to a standard form contract which formed the basis for its drafting, the court can taken into account the omission from the one-off contract of words that appear in the standard form contract in order to resolve an ambiguity in the former document.[86]

12–068   **Printed and written clauses.** Where the contract is contained in a printed form with writing superadded, the written words, if there should be any reasonable doubt about the sense and meaning of the whole, are to have greater effect attributed to them than the printed words, inasmuch as the written words are the immediate language and terms selected by the parties themselves for the expression of their meaning, and the printed words are a general formula adapted equally to their case and that of all other contracting parties upon similar occasions and subjects.[87] Nevertheless, it is open to the parties to stipulate in their printed conditions of contract that written provisions appended to the printed form are not to override, modify or affect in any way the application or interpretation of that which is contained in the printed conditions, and effect must then be given to such a stipulation even though this is contrary to the ordinary rule.[88]

12–069   **Discrepancy between words and figures.** In the event of a difference between words and figures, the written words normally prevail.[89]

---

[83] *Ambatielos v. Jurgens* [1923] A.C. 175, 185; *Sassoon v. International Banking Cpn.* [1927] A.C. 711, 721; *City & Westminster Properties (1934) Ltd v. Mudd* [1959] Ch. 129; *Finzel, Berry & Co. v. Eastcheap Dried Fruit Co.* [1962] 1 Lloyd's Rep. 370, affd. [1962] 2 Lloyd's Rep. 11; *Compania Naviera Termar SA v. Tradax Export SA* [1965] 1 Lloyd's Rep. 198, 204; *Borthwick (Thomas) (Glasgow) Ltd v. Bunge & Co. Ltd* [1969] 1 Lloyd's Rep. 17; *Tradax Export v. Volkswagenwerk* [1969] 2 Q.B. 599, 607; *Ben Shipping Co. (Pte) Ltd v. An-Board Bainne* [1986] 2 Lloyd's Rep. 285, 291; *Wates Construction (London) Ltd v. Franthom Property Ltd* (1991) 7 Const.L.J. 243.

[84] *Louis Dreyfus et Cie v. Parnaso Cia. Naviera SA* [1959] 1 Q.B. 498, revd. on other grounds [1960] 2 Q.B. 49.

[85] [1992] 1 W.L.R. 1138, 1149. See also *Centrepoint Custodians Pty. Ltd v. Lidgerwood Investments Pty. Ltd* [1990] V.R. 411; *Trasimex Holdings SA v. Addax BV* [1997] 1 Lloyd's Rep. 610, 614.

[86] *Team Services v. Kier Management and Design* (1994) 63 Build. L.R. 76.

[87] *Robertson v. French* (1803) 4 East 130, 136; *Re L. Sutro & Co. and Heilbut, Symons & Co.* [1917] 2 K.B. 348, 358, 361; *Hadjipateras v. Weigall & Co.* (1918) 34 T.L.R. 360; *Société d'Avances Commerciales (London) Ltd v. A. Besse & Co. Ltd* [1952] 1 T.L.R. 644; *The Brabant* [1967] 1 Q.B. 588; *Kum v. Wah Tat Bank Ltd* [1971] 1 Lloyd's Rep. 439, 445; *Naviera Amazonica Peruana SA v. Compania Internacional de Seguros del Peru* [1988] 1 Lloyd's Rep. 116, 121. *cf. T. W. Thomas & Co. v. Portsea Steamship Co. Ltd* [1912] A.C. 1; *Evergos Naftiki Eteria v. Cargill plc* [1997] 1 Lloyd's Rep. 35, 38.

[88] *Gold v. Patman & Fotheringham Ltd* [1958] 1 W.L.R. 697, 701; *North West Metropolitan Regional Hospital Board v. T. A. Bickerton & Son Ltd* [1970] 1 W.L.R. 607, 617; *English Industrial Estates Corpn. v. George Wimpey & Co. Ltd* [1973] 1 Lloyd's Rep. 118. But the written provisions may be looked at "to follow exactly what was going on," *ibid.* at 126, 128.

[89] *Saunderson v. Piper* (1839) 5 Bing.N.C. 425; Bills of Exchange Act 1882, s.9(2).

(d) *Effecting the Intention of the Parties*

Parties' intention. It is not open to the court to revise the words used by the   **12–070**
parties, or to put upon them a meaning other than that which they ordinarily bear,
in order to bring them into line with what the court may think the parties really
intended or ought to have intended.[90] But if, from the document itself and the
admissible background,[91] the intention of the parties can reasonably be discerned, then the court will give effect to that intention even though this involves
departing from or qualifying particular words used. So the court will be prepared
to restrict, transpose, modify, supply or reject words or terms in the document,
provided the intention of the parties is plain in spite of the words. The duty of the
court in this respect was summed up by Kelly C.B. in *Gwyn v. Neath Canal Co.*[92]:
"The result of all the authorities is, that when a court of law can clearly collect
from the language within the four corners of a deed, or instrument in writing, the
real intentions of the parties, they are bound to give effect to it by supplying
anything necessarily to be inferred from the terms used, and by rejecting as
superfluous whatever is repugnant to the intention so discerned." Some examples
of these expedients are discussed in the paragraphs which follow.

Restricting. Where some of the words in a printed form of charterparty were   **12–071**
left in by oversight, instead of being struck out, the House of Lords restricted the
printed words to those applicable to the particular agreement.[93] Also in *Glynn v.
Margetson*[94] there was a wide deviation clause in a bill of lading for the carriage
of oranges from Malaga to Liverpool. The ship left Malaga for a port not on the
way to Liverpool, and the oranges were damaged by the delay. The House of
Lords held that the deviation clause must be restricted to conform with the
intention of a voyage from Malaga to Liverpool with a perishable cargo; to hold
otherwise would defeat the object and intent of the contract.

Transposing. "Words shall be transposed to support the intent of the par-   **12–072**
ties."[95] "The law is not nice in grants, and therefore it doth often transpose words
contrary to their order to bring them to the intent of the parties."[96] In a marriage
settlement the words "Such younger child or children" were made to include
both sons and daughters by transposing a clause creating a power to make
provision "for such younger children" and that containing a limitation to
daughters.[97]

Modifying. It has already been noted that the grammatical or ordinary sense   **12–073**
of the words of a contract may be modified if this would lead to some absurdity

---

[90] See *ante*, § 12–042.
[91] See *post*, § 12–116.
[92] (1865) L.R. 3 Ex. 209, 215, cited with approval by Lord Lowry in *Forsikringsaktieselskapet
Vesta v. J. N. E. Butcher, Bain Dawes Ltd* [1989] 1 Lloyd's Rep. 331, 345. See also *Indian Oil Corpn.
v. Vanol Inc.* [1991] 2 Lloyd's Rep. 634, 636.
[93] *Baumwoll Manufactur von Scheibler v. Gilchrest & Co.* [1893] A.C. 8, 15. See also *Dudgeon v.
Pembroke* (1877) 2 App.Cas. 284.
[94] [1893] A.C. 351, 357. See also *Davy Offshore Ltd v. Emerald Field Contracting Ltd* [1992] 2
Lloyd's Rep. 142, 155. *cf. G.H. Renton & Co. Ltd v. Palmyra Trading Corpn. of Panama* [1957] A.C.
149; *Sudatlantica Navegacion SA v. Devamar Shipping Corpn.* [1985] 2 Lloyd's Rep. 271, 274. See
post, § 14–029.
[95] Comyns' Digest, art. "Parols," A.21.
[96] *Parkhurst v. Smith* (1742) Wiles 327, 332. *cf. Magrath v. McGeany* [1938] Ir.R. 309.
[97] *Fenton v. Fenton* (1837) 1 Dr. & W. 66.

or inconsistency with the rest of the instrument.[98] It is also open to the court to correct a misnomer or mistaken designation in a contract: *Falsa demonstratio non nocet cum de corpore constat.*[99] So where the parties to a charterparty attached thereto a typed paramount clause which stated that "this *bill of lading* shall have effect subject to the provisions of the Carriage by Sea Act of the United States . . . which shall be deemed to be incorporated herein," it was held that the erroneous description of the charterparty as a bill of lading did not defeat the intention of the parties that the document should be subject to the Act.[1] However, the court will not be inclined to engage in a "verbal manipulation" of a designation in a contract if the actual words used make perfectly good sense without any modification.[2]

12–074   **Supplying.** A bill of sale was executed to secure an advance of £70 and interest. Principal and interest were to be repaid by instalments of "seven" on a certain day each month. The court held the bill of sale valid and inserted "pounds" or "£" after or before the word "seven."[3] So the omission of the word "pounds" in the body of a bill of exchange may be aided by the proper subscription of the sum on the face of the instrument.[4] So in deeds the name of the grantor,[5] the obligor[6] and the grantee[7] have been supplied, and in a charterparty such words as are required to make commercial sense of a clause.[8]

12–075   **Rejecting.** It might be thought to be a sensible rule of construction that an interpretation which leaves part of the language of a document useless or creates surplusage is to be avoided. But this presumption has often been said to be of little value in the construction of commercial documents.[9] If there is in a contract a word or phrase to which no sensible meaning can be given[10] or which is mere

---

[98] See *ante*, § 12–053.

[99] *Llewellyn v. Jersey* (1843) 11 M. & W. 183, 189; *Morrell v. Fisher* (1849) 4 Exch. 591, 604; *Cowen v. Truefitt Ltd* [1899] 2 Ch. 309; *Eastwood v. Ashton* [1915] A.C. 900, 914; *Whittam v. W.J. Daniel & Co. Ltd* [1962] 1 Q.B. 271, 277; *F. Goldsmith (Sicklesmere) Ltd v. Baxter* [1970] Ch. 85; *Modern Buildings Wales Ltd v. Limmer and Trinidad Co. Ltd* [1975] 1 W.L.R. 1281; *Nittan v. Solent Steel Fabrication Ltd* [1981] 1 Lloyd's Rep. 633; *Lamport & Holt Lines Ltd v. Coubro & Scrutton (M. & I.) Ltd* [1981] 2 Lloyd's Rep. 659 (affd. [1982] 2 Lloyd's Rep. 42); *Mohammed bin Abdul Rahman Orri v. Seawind Navigation Co. SA* [1986] 1 Lloyd's Rep. 36; *Coral (U.K.) Ltd v. Rechtman* [1996] 1 Lloyd's Rep. 235.

[1] *Adamastos Shipping Co. Ltd v. Anglo-Saxon Petroleum Co. Ltd* [1959] A.C. 133. In the Court of Appeal, it had been held that the paramount clause was meaningless and to be rejected: [1957] 2 Q.B. 233.

[2] *Miramar Maritime Corpn. v. Holborn Oil Trading Ltd* [1984] A.C. 676. But see *Mannai Investment Co. Ltd v. Eagle Star Life Assurance Ltd* [1997] A.C. 749.

[3] *Mourmand v. Le Clair* [1903] 2 K.B. 216; *Coles v. Hulme* (1828) 8 B. & C. 568.

[4] *Elliott's case* (1777) 2 East P.C. 951; 1 Leach 175.

[5] *Lord Say and Seal's Case* (1711) 10 Mod. 41, 45.

[6] *Dobson v. Keys* (1610) Cro.Jac. 261.

[7] Co.Litt. 7a.

[8] *Tropwood A.G. of Zug v. Jade Enterprises Ltd* [1982] 1 Lloyd's Rep. 282. *cf. Petroleo Brasileiro SA v. Elounda Shipping Co.* [1985] 2 Lloyd's Rep. 154.

[9] *Royal Greek Government v. Minister of Transport* (1949) 83 Ll.L.Rep. 228, 235; *Chandris v. Isbrandtsen-Moller Inc.* [1951] 1 K.B. 385, 392; *Total Transport Corpn. v. Arcadia Petroleum Ltd* [1998] 1 Lloyd's Rep. 351, 357.

[10] *Smith v. Packhurst* (1742) 3 Atk. 135, 136; *Stone v. Yeovil Corpn.* (1876) 1 C.P.D. 691, 701; *Nicolene v. Simmonds* [1953] 1 Q.B. 543. Contrast *British Electrical and Associated Industries (Cardiff) Ltd v. Patley Pressings Ltd* [1953] 1 W.L.R. 280; *Tropwood A.G. of Zug v. Jade Enterprises Ltd, supra; Commercial Union Assurance Co. v. Sun Alliance Insurance Group plc.* [1992] 1 Lloyd's Rep. 475, 480.

surplusage,[11] it may be rejected to carry out the intention of the parties. Inconsistent or repugnant words or expressions, if they cannot be harmonised, must similarly be rejected.

Inconsistent or repugnant clauses. Where the different parts of an instru- 12–076 ment are inconsistent, effect must be given to that part which is calculated to carry into effect the real intention of the parties as gathered from the instrument as a whole, and that part which would defeat it must be rejected.[12] The old rule was, in such a case, that the earlier clause was to be received and the later rejected[13]; but this rule was a mere rule of thumb, totally unscientific, and out of keeping with the modern construction of documents. To be inconsistent a term must contradict another term or be in conflict with it, such that effect cannot fairly be given to both clauses.[14] A term may also be rejected if it is repugnant to the intention of the parties as it appears from the document.[15] However, an effort should be made to give effect to every clause in the agreement and not to reject a clause unless it is manifestly inconsistent with or repugnant to the rest of the agreement.[16] Thus, if there is a personal covenant and a proviso that the covenantor shall not be personally liable under the covenant, the proviso is inconsistent and void.[17] But if a clause merely limits or qualifies without destroying altogether the obligation created by another clause, the two are to be read together and effect is to be given to the intention of the parties as disclosed by the instrument as a whole.[18]

Clauses incorporated by reference. If clauses are incorporated by reference 12–077 into a written agreement, and those clauses conflict with the clauses of the agreement, then, in the ordinary way,[19] the clauses of the written agreement will prevail.[20] Moreover, the incorporating provision may be so general or wide as to

---

[11] *Waugh v. Bussell* (1814) 5 Taunt. 707, 711; *Gray v. Carr* (1871) L.R. 6 Q.B. 522, 536, 550, 557; *Burrell & Sons v. F. Green & Co.* [1914] 1 K.B. 293, 303; *Chandris v. Isbrandtsen-Moller Co. Inc.* [1951] 1 K.B. 240, 245; *Carga del Sur Compania Naviera SA v. Ross T. Smyth & Co. Ltd* [1962] 2 Lloyd's Rep. 147, 154; *The Merak* [1965] P. 223; *Pera Shipping Corpn. v. Petroship SA* [1985] 2 Lloyd's Rep. 103, 106–107; *Mangistaumunaigaz Oil Production Association v. United World Trade Inc.* [1995] 1 Lloyd's Rep. 617; *Total Transport Corpn. v. Arcadia Petroleum Ltd*, *supra*, at pp. 357–358.

[12] *Walker v. Giles* (1848) 6 C.B. 662, 702; *Love v. Rowtor Steamship Co. Ltd* [1916] 2 A.C. 527, 535; *Sabah Flour and Feedmills Sdn. Bhd. v. Comfez Ltd* [1988] 2 Lloyd's Rep. 18.

[13] Shep.Touch. 88; *Doe d. Leicester v. Biggs* (1809) 2 Taunt. 109, 113; *Forbes v. Git* [1922] 1 A.C. 256, 259.

[14] *Pagnan SpA v. Tradax Ocean Transportation SA* [1987] 2 Lloyd's Rep. 342, 350.

[15] *Adamastos Shipping Co. Ltd v. Anglo-Saxon Petroleum Co. Ltd* [1959] A.C. 133.

[16] *Barton v. Fitzgerald* (1812) 15 East 529, 541; *Bush v. Watkins* (1851) 14 Beav. 425, 432; *Société Co-operative Suisse des Céréales et Matières Fourrageres v. La Plata Cereal Co. SA* (1947) 80 Ll.L.Rep. 530, 537; *Bremer Handelsgesellschaft mbH v. J.H. Rayner & Co. Ltd* [1979] 2 Lloyd's Rep. 216; *Sudatlantica Navegacion SA v. Devamar Shipping Corpn.* [1985] 2 Lloyd's Rep. 271; *Pagnan SpA v. Tradax Ocean Transportation SA, supra*, at 349.

[17] *Furnivall v. Coombes* (1843) 5 M. & G. 736. See also *Watling v. Lewis* [1911] 1 Ch. 414; *Re Tewkesbury Gas Co.* [1911] 2 Ch. 279 (affd. [1912] 1 Ch. 1).

[18] *Williams v. Hathaway* (1877) 6 Ch.D. 544; *Forbes v. Git* [1922] 1 A.C. 256, 259; *Walton (Grain & Shipping) Ltd v. British Italian Trading Co. Ltd* [1959] 1 Lloyd's Rep. 223, 227; *Pagnan SpA v. Tradax Ocean Transportation SA, supra*, at 351.

[19] *cf. Sabah Flour and Feedmills Sdn. Bhd. v. Comfez Ltd* [1988] 2 Lloyd's Rep. 18.

[20] *Adamastos Shipping Co. Ltd v. Anglo-Saxon Petroleum Co. Ltd* [1959] A.C. 133, 155, 178–179; *Modern Buildings Wales Ltd v. Limmer and Trinidad Co. Ltd* [1975] 1 W.L.R. 1281, 1289; *Sabah Flour and Feedmills Sdn. Bhd. v. Comfez Ltd, supra*, at 20; *Metalfer Corpn. v. Pan Ocean Shipping Co. Ltd* [1998] 2 Lloyd's Rep. 632, 637; *Finagra (U.K.) Ltd v. O.T. Africa Line Ltd* [1998] 2 Lloyd's Rep. 622, 627.

have the effect of incorporating more than can make any sense in the context of the agreement, in which case the surplus may be rejected as insensible or inconsistent, or disregarded as "mere surplusage."[21]

12–078 **Grammatical errors.** Errors of syntax are a particularly frequent source of disputes in relation to written contracts. However plain the syntax of a sentence may be, if it is clear from the content of the instrument and the admissible background[22] that the apparent grammatical construction cannot be the true one, then that which upon the whole is the true meaning prevails, in spite of the syntax of such particular sentence. So, in *Ewing v. Ewing*,[23] a deed of partnership provided that the capital of a deceased partner should be paid out as at the last balance by certain regular instalments "with interest thereon from the date of the last balance." The word "thereon" was held to refer not to the last instalment but was intended to be payable on the balance of the capital remaining unpaid. In *Investors Compensation Scheme Ltd v. West Bromwich Building Society*[24] a majority of the House of Lords held that an exception from an assignment of "Any claim (whether sounding in rescission for undue influence or otherwise)" should be construed to read "Any claim sounding in rescission (whether for undue influence or otherwise)", thus limiting the exception. The background circumstances and the terms of related non-contractual documents showed, it was said, that the apparent syntax did not convey the intended meaning.

12–079 **Saving the document.** If the words used in an agreement are susceptible of two meanings, one of which would validate the instrument or the particular clause in the instrument, and the other render it void, ineffective or meaningless, the former sense is to be adopted. This rule is often expressed in the phrase *ut res magis valeat cum pereat*.[25] Thus, if by a particular construction the agreement would be rendered ineffectual and the apparent object of the contract would be frustrated, but another construction, though *per se* less appropriate looking to the words only, would produce a different effect, the latter interpretation is to be applied, if it can possibly be supported by anything in the contract.[26] So, where the words of a guarantee were capable of expressing either a past or a concurrent consideration, the court adopted the latter construction, because the former would render the instrument void.[27] If one construction makes the contract lawful and the other unlawful, the former is to be preferred. Thus a bond conditioned "to assign all offices" will be construed to apply to such offices as are by law assignable.[28]

---

[21] *Skips A/S Nordheim v. Syrian Petroleum Co. Ltd* [1983] 2 Lloyd's Rep. 592, 594. *cf. Miramar Maritime Corpn. v. Holborn Oil Trading Ltd* [1984] A.C. 676, 683; *Balli Trading Ltd v. Afalona Shipping Co. Ltd* [1993] 1 Lloyd's Rep. 1, 6.

[22] See *post*, § 12–116.

[23] (1882) 8 App.Cas. 822. See also *Wills v. Wright* (1677) 2 Mod. 285; *Waugh v. Middleton* (1853) 8 Exch. 352, 356.

[24] [1998] 1 W.L.R. 896.

[25] *Verba ita sunt intelligenda ut res magis valeat cum pereat*: Bac. Max. 3; Noy. Max. 50.

[26] *Solly v. Forbes* (1820) 2 B. & B. 38, 48. See also Co.Litt. 42a; *Mills v. Dunham* [1891] 1 Ch. 576, 590.

[27] *Haigh v. Brooks* (1839) 10 A. & E. 309; *Goldshede v. Swan* (1847) 1 Exch. 154; *Steele v. Hoe* (1849) 14 Q.B. 431; *Broom v. Batchelor* (1856) 1 H. & N. 255.

[28] *Harrington v. Kloprogge* (1785) 2 B. & B. 678, note (a). See also *Lewis v. Davison* (1839) 4 M. & W. 654. The same principle applies to the performance of a contract: if a payment is made in performance of a contract partly legal and partly illegal it is presumed that it is made in performance of the legal part of the contract: *A. Smith & Son (Bognor Regis) Ltd v. Walker* [1952] 2 Q.B. 319.

Party cannot rely on his own breach. It has been said that, as a matter of **12–080** construction, unless the contract clearly provides to the contrary[29] it will be presumed that it was not the intention of the parties that either should be entitled to rely on his own breach of duty to avoid the contract or bring it to an end or to obtain a benefit under it.[30] This presumption applies only to acts or omissions which constitute a breach by that party of an express or implied contractual obligation,[31] or (possibly) of a non-contractual duty,[32] owed by him to the other party. Breach of a duty, whether contractual or non-contractual, owed to a stranger to the contract will not suffice.[33] However, such a "rule of construction" appears to be somewhat different in nature from those discussed above. It may therefore be that it is better regarded as depending on an implied term of the contract in question[34] or as one illustration of a more general principle that "A man cannot be permitted to take advantage of his own wrong."[35]

(e) *Construction against Grantor*

Construction against grantor. Another rule of construction is that a deed or **12–081** other instrument shall be construed more strongly against the grantor or maker thereof.[36] This rule is often misinterpreted. It is only to be applied in cases of ambiguity[37] and where other rules of construction fail.[38] Nevertheless, despite

---

[29] *Micklefield v. S.A.C. Technology Ltd* [1990] 1 W.L.R. 1002. See also *Richco International Ltd v. Alfred C. Toepfer International GmbH* [1991] 1 Lloyd's Rep. 136.

[30] *Alghussein Establishment v. Eton College* [1988] 1 W.L.R. 587, HL. See also *Doe d. Bryan v. Bancks* (1821) 4 B. & Ald. 401, 406; *Malins v. Freeman* (1838) 4 Bing. N.C. 395, 399; *New Zealand Shipping Co. v. Société des Ateliers et Chantiers de France* [1919] A.C. 1, 6, 8, 9, 15; *Quesnel Forks Gold Mining Co. Ltd v. Ward* [1920] A.C. 222, 227; *Amalgamated Building Contractors Ltd v. Waltham Holy Cross U.D.C.* [1952] 2 All E.R. 452, 455; *Cheall v. Assn. of Professional Executive and Computer Staff* [1983] 2 A.C. 180, 189; *Ackerman v. Protim Services* [1988] 2 E.G.L.R. 259; *Gyllenhammar & Partners International Ltd v. Saur Brodogradevna Industrija* [1989] 2 Lloyd's Rep. 403, 412; *Micklefield v. S.A.C. Technology Ltd, supra*, at 1007; *Richco International Ltd v. Alfred C. Toepfer International GmbH, supra*, at 144; *Cerium Investments v. Evans* [1991] C.L.Y 1870, CA. The breach may be deliberate or inadvertent: *Cheall v. Assn. of Professional Executive and Computer Staff, supra*.

[31] *Cheall v. Assn. of Professional Executive and Computer Staff, supra*; *Alghussein Establishment v. Eton College, supra*; *Gyllenhammar & Partners International Ltd v. Saur Brodogradevna Industrija, supra*; *J. Lauritzen A.S. v. Wijsmuller B.V.* [1950] 1 W.L.R. 1, 13; *Antclizo Shipping Corpn. v. Food Corpn. of India (The Antclizo) (No. 2)* [1992] 1 Lloyd's Rep. 558, 567–568.

[32] *Cheall v. Assn. of Professional Executive and Computer Staff, supra*; *Ackerman v. Protim Services, supra*; *J. Lauritzen A.S. v. Wijsmuller B.V., supra*, at 13; *Antclizo Shipping Corpn. v. Food Corpn. of India (The Antclizo) (No. 2), supra*, at 568.

[33] *Cheall v. Assn. of Professional Executive and Computer Staff, supra*.

[34] *Richco International Ltd v. Alfred C. Toepfer International GmbH* [1991] 1 Lloyd's Rep. 136. See also *Bulk Shipping A.G. v. Ipco Trading SA* [1992] 1 Lloyd's Rep. 39, 43, and *post*, § 13–012.

[35] See, *e.g. Rede v. Farr* (1817) 6 M. & S. 121, 124; *Doe d. Bryan v. Bancks* (1821) 4 B. & Ald. 401, 409; *Roberts v. Bury Commissioners* (1870) L.R. 4 C.P. 755; *Alfred C. Toepfer v. Peter Cremer* [1975] 2 Lloyd's Rep. 118, 124; *Total Transport Corpn. v. Amoco Trading Co.* [1985] 1 Lloyd's Rep. 423, 426. But that principle is not absolute: *Cheall v. Assn. of Professional Executive and Computer Staff* [1983] 2 A.C. 180, 189; *Alghussein Establishment v. Eton College* [1988] 1 W.L.R. 587, 595; *Micklefield v. S.A.C. Technology Ltd* [1990] 1 W.L.R. 1002; *Richco International Ltd v. Alfred C. Toepfer International GmbH, supra*. See also *post*, § 13–012.

[36] *Verba cartarum fortius accipiuntur contra proferentem* (Bac. Max. 3).

[37] *Borradaile v. Hunter* (1843) 5 M. & G. 639; *Birrell v. Dryer* (1884) 9 App.Cas. 345, 350; *Cornish v. Accident Insurance Company* (1889) 23 Q.B.D. 453, 456; *London & Lancashire Insurance v. Bolands Ltd* [1924] A.C. 836, 848; *Houghton v. Trafalgar Insurance Co.* [1954] 1 Q.B. 247; *Lakeport Navigation Co. Panama SA v. Anonima Petroli Italiana* [1982] 2 Lloyd's Rep. 205, 208.

[38] *Lindus v. Melrose* (1858) 3 H. & N. 177, 182.

certain doubts which have been cast upon it from time to time,[39] the rule has been constantly cited as a rule of construction from Coke's time to the present day.[40] For instance, Coke says[41]: "It is a maxim in law that every man's grant shall be taken by construction of law most forcibly against himself"; and in 1949, Evershed M.R. said:

> "We are presented with two alternative readings of this document and the reading which one should adopt is to be determined, among other things, by a consideration of the fact that the defendants put forward the document. They have put forward a clause which is by no means free from obscurity and have contended . . . that it has a remarkably, if not an extravagantly, wide scope, and I think that the rule *contra proferentem* should be applied. . . . "[42]

12–082   The justification for the rule has been said to be that "a person who puts forward the wording of a proposed agreement may be assumed to have looked after his own interests so that if the words leave room for doubt about whether he is intended to have a particular benefit there is reason to suppose that he is not."[43]

12–083   So, in the case of a guarantee, if the party who drafts it uses ambiguous language, such ambiguity will be taken more strongly against himself.[44] If a carrier gives two notices, limiting his responsibility in cases of loss of goods, he is bound by that which is least beneficial to himself.[45] A notice under which a party claims a general lien is to be construed against him.[46] And if an instrument is made in terms so ambiguous as to make it doubtful whether it is a bill or note, the holder may, as against the maker of the instrument, treat it as either at his election.[47] Important applications of this rule arise in the case of the excepted perils in insurance policies[48] and in the case of time-bar[49] and exemption clauses,[50] for it is usually the party who has drafted the document who is seeking to rely on the protection of its provisions.[51]

---

[39] *Taylor v. St. Helens Corporation* (1877) 6 Ch.D. 264, 270, *per* Jessel M.R., but the cases on which he relies turned upon the construction of wills.

[40] *Manchester College v. Trafford* (1679) 2 Show. 31; *Johnson v. Edgware, etc., Ry.* (1866) 35 Beav. 480, 484; *Neill v. Duke of Devonshire* (1882) 8 App.Cas. 135, 149.

[41] Co.Litt. 36a, 183a, 183b.

[42] *John Lee & Son (Grantham) Ltd v. Railway Executive* [1949] 2 All E.R. 581, 583.

[43] *Tam Wing Chuen v. Bank of Credit and Commerce Hong Kong Ltd* [1996] 2 B.C.L.C. 69, 77 (Lord Mustill).

[44] *Hargreave v. Smee* (1829) 6 Bing. 244, 248; *Adams v. Richardson & Starling Ltd* [1969] 1 W.L.R. 1645, 1653.

[45] *Munn v. Baker* (1817) 2 Stark. 255.

[46] *Crumpston v. Haigh* (1836) 2 Scott 684.

[47] *Edis v. Bury* (1827) 6 B. & C. 433; *Lloyd v. Oliver* (1852) 18 Q.B. 471.

[48] *Blackett v. Royal Exchange Assurance Co.* (1832) 2 Cr. & J. 244; *Petros M. Nomikos Ltd v. Robertson* (1939) 64 Ll.L.Rep. 45.

[49] *Board of Trade (Minister of Materials) v. Steel Bus. & Co. Ltd* [1952] 1 Lloyd's Rep. 87; *Pera Shipping Corpn. v. Petroship SA* [1985] 2 Lloyd's Rep. 103.

[50] See *post*, § 14–009.

[51] It has, however, been pointed out by Staughton L.J. in *Pera Shipping Corpn. v. Petroship SA* [1984] 2 Lloyd's Rep. 363, 365, and in *Youell v. Bland Welch & Co. Ltd* [1992] 2 Lloyd's Rep. 127, 134, in relation to the application of the maxim, that the *proferens* is sometimes regarded as the draftsman of the document and sometimes as the party who seeks to rely on the protection of its provisions. These may not coincide.

Crown contracts. "The King's grant is taken most strongly against the   **12–084**
grantee, and most favourably for the King, although the thing which he grants
came to the King by purchase or descent."[52] This ancient rule is still applicable
to grants of land or of an interest in land,[53] but it no longer applies to commercial
contracts with the Crown.[54] In any event, it does not in any way override other
rules of construction.[55]

(f) *Ejusdem Generis Rule*

Ejusdem generis rule. The rule which is laid down with reference to the   **12–085**
construction of statutes, namely, that where several words preceding a general
word point to a confined meaning the general word shall not extend in its effect
beyond subjects *ejusdem generis* (of the same class),[56] applies to the construction
of contracts.[57] The rule depends on the assumed intention of the framer of the
instrument, *i.e.* that the general words were only intended to guard against some
accidental omission in the objects of the kind mentioned and were not intended
to extend to objects of a wholly different kind. Indeed, this rule follows as a
corollary of the rule that the whole contract is to be considered,[58] being simply
that every word shall be taken in conjunction with the words that accompany it.[59]
Therefore the words "all the perils" in the ordinary form of marine insurance
policy include only perils of the sea or perils *ejusdem generis* therewith, because
their meaning is restricted by the subject-matter, *i.e.* marine risks, and by the
genus of perils mentioned specifically in the policy.[60] General words such as
"other accidents beyond the charterer's control" occurring at the end of a list of
specific exceptions in a charterparty are construed to cover only accidents similar
to those expressly mentioned.[61] Where a lease contained a proviso for an
abatement of rent in case the demised premises should at any time during the
term "be destroyed or damaged by fire, flood, storm, tempest, or other inevitable
accident," it was held that the words "inevitable accident" must be construed by
the rule of *ejusdem generis*, that is, they must be taken to mean accident of a
similar kind to "fire, flood, storm, or tempest," and not to include accidents
occasioned by the acts or defaults of the contracting parties.[62]

---

[52] *Willion v. Berkley* (1562) 1 Plow. 223, 243; *Att.-Gen. v. Ewelme Hospital* (1853) 17 Beav. 366,
385; *Feather v. The Queen* (1865) 6 B. & S. 257, 283, 284; *Viscountess Rhondda's Claim* [1922] A.C.
359, 353; *Earl of Lonsdale v. Att.-Gen.*, [1982] 1 W.L.R. 887, 901.

[53] *Earl of Lonsdale v. Att.-Gen.*, *supra.*

[54] *Lonrho Exports Ltd v. Export Credit Guarantee Department* [1998] 3 W.L.R. 394.

[55] *Att.-Gen. v. Ewelme Hospital, supra*, at 386.

[56] *Sandiman v. Breach* (1827) 7 B. & C. 96, 100; *R. v. Nevill* (1846) 8 Q.B. 452; *Re Stockport
Ragged Schools* [1898] 2 Ch. 687; *Att.-Gen. v. Brown* [1920] 1 K.B. 773.

[57] *Cullen v. Butler* (1816) 5 M. & S. 461; *Harrison v. Blackburn* (1864) 17 C.B.(N.S.) 678.

[58] See *ante*, §§ 12–061—12–069.

[59] The maxim is *noscitur a sociis*: *Newby v. Sharpe* (1878) 8 Ch.D. 39, 52.

[60] *Thames and Mersey Marine Insurance Co. v. Hamilton, Fraser & Co.* (1887) 12 App. Cas. 494,
490; *Bolivia Republic v. Indemnity Mutual Marine Assurance Co.* [1909] 1 K.B. 785; *Stott (Baltic)
Steamers v. Marten* [1916] 1 A.C. 304; Marine Insurance Act 1906, Sched. I, r. 12.

[61] *Fenwick v. Schmalz* (1868) L.R. 3 C.P. 313; *Re Richardsons and Samuel* [1898] 1 Q.B. 261;
Mudie v. Strick (1909) 100 L.T. 701; *Thorman v. Dowgate Steamship Co.* [1910] 1 K.B. 410;
Hadjipateras v. S. Weigall & Co. (1918) 34 T.L.R. 360; *Aktieselskabet Frank v. Namague Copper Co.*
(1920) 25 Com.Cas. 212; *Jones v. Oceanic Steam Navigation Co.* [1924] 2 K.B. 730 (passage ticket).
But see the cases on *force majeure* clauses in commercial contracts cited *post*, § 12–087, n. 68.

[62] *Saner v. Bilton* (1878) 7 Ch.D. 815; *Manchester Bonded Warehouse Co. v. Carr* (1880) 5 C.P.D.
507; *Barking and Dagenham L.B.C. v. Stamford Asphalt Co. Ltd, The Times*, April 10, 1997.

12–086   **No common category.** The *ejusdem generis* rule cannot, however, be applied unless there is a genus to which the general words can be restricted. Therefore, where the matters specifically referred to are so various that they fall into no common category the meaning of subsequent general words is not limited by relation to them. For instance, liability was repudiated in the event of "deficiency of men or owner's stores, breakdown of machinery, or damage to hull *or other accident.*" It was held that the matters specifically referred to made up no common category, so that the general words "or other accident" extended to delay caused by stranding.[63] The genus need not be definable with logical or scientific exactitude, provided it is reasonably clear what it includes and what it excludes; for example, "war and disturbance" sufficiently indicate a genus that excludes damage from ice.[64] It has been held that where only one matter is specifically referred to, the rule cannot be applied, because a single species cannot constitute a genus[65]; but there is no reason why in such a case the general words should not be limited with respect to the subject-matter in relation to which they are used.[66] In a commercial contract, if a genus cannot be found, that is one factor indicating that the parties did not intend to restrict the meaning of the words; but it is not universally true that, whenever a genus cannot be found, the words must have been intended to have their literal meaning, whatever other indications there may be to the contrary.[67]

12–087   **Canon of construction.** The *ejusdem generis* rule is not a rigid technical rule, but a mere canon of construction. It has been held that, in a commercial contract, where general words follow an enumeration of particular things, those words are prima facie to be construed as having their natural and larger meaning, and are not to be restricted to things *ejusdem generis* with those previously enumerated, unless there is something in the instrument which shows an intention so to restrict them.[68] Also where a charterparty contained an exemption from liability arising from "frost, flood, strikes . . . and any other unavoidable accidents or hindrances of what kind soever beyond their control delaying the loading of the cargo," it was held that the parties, by inserting the words, "of what kind soever," intended to exclude the *ejusdem generis* rule, and that the contract was to be construed so as to exclude delays caused by a block of other shipping at the loading port.[69] On the other hand, the words "or otherwise" may be subject to the *ejusdem generis* principle.[70]

---

[63] *SS. Magnhild v. McIntyre Bros. & Co.* [1920] 3 K.B. 321; [1921] 2 K.B. 97; *Tillmanns v. SS. Knutsford* [1908] 2 K.B. 385, 395, 403, 409; affd. [1908] A.C. 406.

[64] *Tillmanns v. SS. Knutsford, supra*; *Thorman v. Dowgate Steamship Co.* [1910] 1 K.B. 410; *Re Richardsons and Samuel* [1898] 1 Q.B. 261.

[65] *R. v. Special Commissioners* [1923] 1 K.B. 393; *Re Ellwood* [1927] 1 Ch. 455.

[66] See *ante*, § 12–060; *Newby v. Sharpe* (1878) 8 Ch.D. 39, 52.

[67] *Chandris v. Isbrandtsen-Moller Co. Inc.* [1951] 1 K.B. 240, 246.

[68] *Andersen v. Andersen* [1895] 1 Q.B. 749; *Chandris v. Isbrandtsen-Moller Co. Inc., ante*; *P.J. Vander Zijden Wildhandel N.V. v. Tucker & Cross Ltd* [1975] 2 Lloyd's Rep. 240. Contrast *Tillmanns Co. v. SS. Knutsford, supra*; *Crompton v. Jarratt* (1885) 30 Ch.D. 298 where the contrary presumption is said to be correct.

[69] *Larson v. Sylvester* [1908] A.C. 295; *Earl of Jersey v. Neath Poor Law Union* (1889) 22 Q.B.D. 555; *Belcore Maritime Corpn. v. Filli Moretti Cereali SpA* [1983] 2 Lloyd's Rep. 66, 68; *CA Venezolana de Navegacion v. BankLine* [1987] 2 Lloyd's Rep. 498, 507; see also *Archbishop of Canterbury's Case* (1596) 2 Co.Rep. 46a (general words following particular words will not be taken to include anything of a superior class to that to which the particular words belong).

[70] *Re Kershaw, Whittaker v. Kershaw* (1890) 45 Ch.D. *cf. Keeble v. Keeble* [1956] 1 W.L.R. 94.

Where specific words follow general words instead of preceding them, the **12–088**
House of Lords has held that, as a general rule, the generality of the earlier should
not be restricted by the insertion of the subsequent words, which may be regarded
simply as examples of what was meant by the general words.[71] Similarly, even
if the specific words precede the general words, they may be regarded as
examples of what is comprehended in the general words.[72]

(g) Restriction by Express Provisions

Expressio unius. The express mention in an instrument of a particular person, **12–089**
power or thing may show an intention to exclude any other person, power or
thing: *expressio unius est exclusio alterius.*[73] Thus, where a deed conveyed to a
mortgagee an iron foundry and two dwelling-houses, and the appurtenances,
together with the fixtures in and about the said houses, it was held that the
specification of the fixtures in the dwelling-houses showed that those in the foundry were not intended to pass, although they would have passed had the other not
been mentioned.[74] This maxim has been said to be a valuable servant but a bad
master in the construction of documents. Failure to complete the *expressio* may
be accidental[75] and the maxim can only be applied if the instrument can be
considered to contain all the terms agreed upon by the parties.[76]

Expressum facit cessare tacitum. Where there is an express covenant in an **12–090**
instrument on a particular matter, no implication of any other covenant on the
same subject-matter can be raised.[77] "Where the parties have entered into written
engagements with expressed stipulations, it is manifestly not desirable to extend
them by any implications; the presumption is that, having expressed some, they
have expressed all the conditions by which they intend to be bound under that
instrument."[78]

(h) Stipulations as to Time

Time in contracts. Generally, the words "till" and "until" are considered to **12–091**
be ambiguous and may be either exclusive or inclusive, according to the subject-
matter and context[79]; "from" may be taken to be either inclusive or exclusive,[80]

---

[71] *Ambatielos v. Anton Jurgens Margarine Works* [1923] A.C. 175. *cf. Herman v. Morris* (1919) 35
T.L.R. 328; affd. (1919) 35 T.L.R. 574.
[72] *Stornvaart Maatschappij Sophie H. v. Merchants' Marine Insurance Co. Ltd* (1919) 89 L.J.K.B.
834, HL.
[73] Co.Litt. 210a; *Blackburn v. Flavelle* (1881) 6 App.Cas. 628, 634.
[74] *Hare v. Horton* (1833) 5 B. & Ad. 715. See also *Wood v. Rowcliffe* (1851) 6 Exch. 407; *Miller
v. Emcer Products Ltd* [1956] Ch. 304.
[75] *Colquhoun v. Brooks* (1887) 19 Q.B.D. 400, 406; affd. (1889) 14 App.Cas. 493.
[76] *Devonald v. Rosser & Sons* [1906] 2 K.B. 728, 745.
[77] Co.Litt. 183, 210a; *Mathew v. Blackmore* (1857) 1 H. & N. 762, 772.
[78] *Aspdin v. Austin* (1844) 5 Q.B. 671, 684.
[79] *R. v. Stevens* (1804) 5 East 244; *Dakins v. Wagner* (1835) 3 Dowl. 535, 536; *Kerr v. Jeston*
(1842) 1 Dowl.(N.S.) 538, 539; *Startup v. Macdonald* (1843) 6 M. & G. 593; *Rogers v. Davis* (1845)
8 Ir.L.R. 399, 400; *Bellhouse v. Mellor, Proudman & Mellor* (1859) 4 H. & N. 116, 123; *Isaacs v.
Royal Insurance Co.* (1870) L.R. 5 Ex. 296; *Heinrich Hirdes GmbH v. Edmund* [1991] 2 Lloyd's Rep.
546.
[80] *Lester v. Garland* (1808) 15 Ves.Jun. 248, 258; *Wilkinson v. Gaston* (1846) 9 Q.B. 137, 145; *Re
North* [1895] 2 Q.B. 264, 269; *Sheffield Corp. v. Sheffield Electric Light Co.* [1898] 1 Ch. 203, 209;
Scottish Metropolitan Assurance Co. v. Stewart (1923) 14 Ll.L.Rep. 55; *Carapanayoti & Co. Ltd v.
Comptoir Commercial André & Cie SA* [1972] 1 Lloyd's Rep. 139.

although the general rule is that the day of the date, act or event is to be excluded in the computation.[81] This rule, however, is not an absolute one, and the wording of the contract or the intention of the parties may indicate a contrary construction.[82]

12–092 "On" or "upon" may mean either before the act done to which it relates, or simultaneously with the act done, or after the act done, according as reason and good sense require the interpretation with reference to the context, and the subject-matter of the agreement.[83]

4. ADMISSIBILITY OF EXTRINSIC EVIDENCE

12–093 **Written documents.** Where the parties appear to have embodied their agreement in a written document,[84] the question arises whether extrinsic evidence, that is to say, evidence of matters outside the document, is admissible so as to affect its content. Two issues are involved: first, whether it is permissible to adduce extrinsic evidence of terms other than those included, expressly or by reference, in the document; secondly, whether extrinsic evidence may be admitted to explain or interpret the words used in the document.

(a) *The Parol Evidence Rule*

12–094 **Whether document conclusive.** It is often said to be a rule of law that "If there be a contract which has been reduced to writing, verbal evidence is not allowed to be given . . . so as to add to or subtract from, or in any manner to vary or qualify the written contract."[85] Indeed, in 1897, Lord Morris[86] accepted that

---

[81] *Lester v. Garland, supra; Ackland v. Lutley* (1839) 9 A. & E. 879, 894; *South Staffordshire Tramways Co. v. Sickness and Accident Assn.* [1891] 1 Q.B. 402; *Radcliffe v. Bartholomew* [1892] 1 Q.B. 161; *Goldsmiths' Co. v. West Metropolitan Ry.* [1904] 1 K.B. 1, 5; *Stewart v. Chapman* [1951] 2 K.B. 792; *Cartwright v. MacCormack* [1963] 1 W.L.R. 18; *Re Figgis* [1969] Ch. 123; *London and Overseas Freighters Ltd v. Timber Shipping Co. SA* [1972] A.C. 1; *Alma Shipping Cpn. of Monrovia v. Mantovani* [1975] 1 Lloyd's Rep. 115; *Dodds v. Walker* [1981] 1 W.L.R. 1027, HL. See also the "clear day" principle: *Young v. Higgon* (1840) 6 M. & W. 49; *Thompson v. Stimpson* [1961] 1 Q.B. 195; *Carapanayoti & Co. Ltd v. Comptoir Commercial André & Cie SA, supra.* See also *post,* § 22–024.

[82] *Pugh v. Duke of Leeds* (1777) 2 Cowp. 714; *Cornfoot v. Royal Exchange Assurance Corp.* [1904] 1 K.B. 40; *English v. Cliff* [1914] 2 Ch. 376; *Hare v. Gocher* [1962] 2 Q.B. 641; *Trow v. Ind Coope (West Midlands) Ltd* [1967] 2 Q.B. 299; *Bevan Ashford v. Malin* [1995] I.R.L.R. 360.

[83] *R. v. Humphery* (1839) 10 A. & E. 335, 370; *R. v. Arkwright* (1848) 12 Q.B. 960, 970; *Paynter v. James* (1867) L.R. 2 C.P. 348, 354; *Wm. Cory & Son Ltd v. I.R.C.* [1964] 1 W.L.R. 529 (affd. [1965] A.C. 1088); *Kuratau Land Co. Ltd v. Kahu Te Kuru* [1966] N.Z.L.R. 544, 547; *Air New Zealand Ltd v. Nippon Credit Bank Ltd* [1997] 1 N.Z.L.R. 218, 221–222.

[84] For computerised "documents," see *ante,* § 12–048.

[85] *Goss v. Lord Nugent* (1833) 5 B. & Ad. 58, 64. See also *Countess of Rutland's Case* (1602) 5 Co.Rep. 25b, 26a; *Meres v. Ansell* (1771) 3 Wils. 275; *Smith v. Doe d. Jersey* (1821) 2 Brod. & Bing. 473, 541; *Smith v. Jeffryes* (1846) 15 M. & W. 561; *Hitchin v. Groom* (1848) 5 C.B. 515; *Evans v. Roe* (1872) L.R. 7 C.P. 138; *Mercantile Agency Co. Ltd v. Flitwick Chalybeate Co.* (1897) 14 T.L.R. 90; *Newman v. Gatti* (1907) 24 T.L.R. 18; *Reliance Marine Insurance v. Duder* [1913] 1 K.B. 256, 273; *Hitchings & Coulthurst Co. v. Northern Leather Co. of America and Doushkess* [1914] 3 K.B. 907; *Jacobs v. Batavia and General Plantations Trust Ltd* [1924] 1 Ch. 287, 295; *Tsang Chuen v. Li Po Kwai* [1932] A.C. 713, 727; *O'Connor v. Hume* [1954] 1 W.L.R. 824, 830; *Rabin v. Gerson Berger Association Ltd* [1986] 1 W.L.R. 526, 530; *Edwards v. O'Connor* [1991] 2 N.Z.L.R. 542.

[86] *Bank of Australasia v. Palmer* [1897] A.C. 540, 545 (cited in *National Westminster Bank Ltd v. Halesowen Presswork & Assemblies Ltd* [1972] A.C. 785, 818–819).

"[p]arol testimony cannot be received to contradict, vary, add to or subtract from the terms of a written contract, or the terms in which the parties have deliberately agreed to record any part of their contract." This rule is usually known as the "parol evidence" rule. Its operation is not confined to oral evidence: it has been taken to exclude extrinsic matter in writing, such as drafts,[87] preliminary agreements,[88] and letters of negotiation.[89] The rule has been justified on the ground that it upholds the value of written proof,[90] effectuates the finality intended by the parties in recording their contract in written form,[91] and eliminates "great inconvenience and troublesome litigation in many instances."[92]

However, the parol evidence rule is and has long been subject to a number of **12–095** exceptions.[93] In particular, since the nineteenth century, the courts have been prepared to admit extrinsic evidence of terms additional to those contained in the written document if it is shown that the document was not intended to express the entire agreement between the parties.[94] So, for example, if the parties intend their contract to be partly oral and partly in writing, extrinsic evidence is admissible to prove the oral part of the agreement.[95] In *Gillespie Bros. & Co. v. Cheney, Eggar & Co.*,[96] Lord Russell C.J. stated

" . . . although when the parties arrive at a definite written contract the implication or presumption is very strong that such contract is intended to contain all the terms of their bargain, it is a presumption only, and it is open to either of the parties to allege that there was, in addition to what appears in the written agreement, an antecedent express stipulation not intended by the parties to be excluded, but intended to continue in force with the express written agreement."

It cannot therefore be asserted that, in modern times, the mere production of a written agreement, however complete it may look, will as a matter of law render inadmissible evidence of other terms not included expressly or by reference in the document. "The court is entitled to look at and should look at all the evidence from start to finish in order to see what the bargain was that was struck between the parties."[97]

Scope of the rule. It follows that the scope of the parol evidence rule is much **12–096** narrower than at first sight appears. It has no application until it is first determined that the terms of the parties' agreement are wholly contained in the written document. The rule "only applies where the parties to an agreement reduce it to

---

[87] *Miller v. Travers* (1832) 8 Bing. 244; *Inglis v. Buttery* (1878) 3 App.Cas. 552; *National Bank of Australasia v. Falkingham & Sons* [1902] A.C. 585.

[88] *Evans v. Roe, supra; Leggott v. Barrett* (1880) 15 Ch.D. 306, 309, 311; *Henderson v. Arthur* [1907] 1 K.B. 10; *Newman v. Gatti, supra; Hitchings & Coulthurst Co. v. Northern Leather Co. of America and Doushkess, supra; Hutton v. Watling* [1948] Ch. 398; *Youell v. Bland Welch & Co. Ltd* [1992] 2 Lloyd's Rep. 127.

[89] *Mercantile Bank of Sydney v. Taylor* [1893] A.C. 317.

[90] *Pickering v. Dowson* (1813) 4 Taunt. 779, 784.

[91] *Inglis v. Buttery, supra,* at 577.

[92] *Mercantile Agency Co. Ltd v. Flitwick Chalybeate Co., supra,* at 90.

[93] See *post,* § 12–104 *et seq.*

[94] *Mercantile Bank of Sydney v. Taylor* [1893] A.C. 317, 321.

[95] *Harris v. Rickett* (1859) 4 H. & N. 1; *Malpas v. L. & S.W. Ry.* (1866) L.R. 1 C.P. 336; *Gillespie Bros. v. Cheney Eggar & Co.* [1896] 2 Q.B. 59; *J. Evans & Son (Portsmouth) Ltd v. Andrea Merzario Ltd* [1976] 1 W.L.R. 1078; *Yani Haryanto v. E.D. & F. Man (Sugar) Ltd* [1986] 2 Lloyd's Rep. 44, 46–47.

[96] [1896] 2 Q.B. 59, 62.

[97] *J. Evans & Son (Portsmouth) Ltd v. Andrea Merzario Ltd, supra,* at 1083.

writing, and agree or intend that the writing shall be their agreement."[98] Whether the parties did so agree or intend is a matter to be decided by the court upon consideration of all the evidence relevant to this issue. It is therefore always open to a party to adduce extrinsic evidence to prove that the document is not a complete record of the contract. If, on that evidence, the court finds that terms additional to those in the document were agreed and intended by the parties to form part of the contract, then the court will have found that the contract consists partly of the terms contained in the document and partly of the terms agreed outside of it. The parol evidence rule will not apply. If, on the other hand, the court finds that the document is a complete record of the contract, then it will reject the evidence of additional terms. But it will do so, not because it is required to ignore the additional terms or the evidence said to prove them, but because such evidence is inconsistent with its finding that the document does contain the whole terms of the parties' agreement.[99] No doubt, in practice, where a document is produced which appears to be a complete contract, a party will experience considerable difficulty in proving, on the balance of probabilities, that further contractual terms were agreed outside the written terms of the document. But extrinsic evidence of such terms is not *ipso facto* excluded.

12–097   **Law Commission Report.** In 1986, the Law Commission considered[1] whether it should recommend that the parol evidence rule be abolished or amended by statute. For this purpose, it was necessary for the Commission to analyse the rule in detail as to its applicability, width and effect. The Commission expressed the opinion[2] that:

> " . . . although a proposition of law can be stated which can be described as the 'parol evidence' rule it is not a rule of law which, correctly applied, could lead to evidence being unjustly excluded. Rather, it is a proposition of law which is no more than a circular statement: [W]hen it is proved or admitted that the parties to a contract intended that all the express terms of their agreement should be as recorded in a particular document or documents, evidence will be inadmissible (because irrelevant) if it is tendered only for the purpose of adding to, varying, subtracting from or contradicting the express terms of that contract."

The general conclusion[3] reached by the Commission was "that there is no *rule of law* that evidence is rendered inadmissible or is to be ignored solely because a document exists which looks like a complete contract. Whether it is a complete contract depends upon the intention of the parties, objectively judged, and not on any rule of law." It is submitted that this general conclusion is correct.[4]

12–098   **Extrinsic evidence to contradict document.** Where it appears that the parties did not intend to record all the terms of their agreement in a particular

---

[98] *Harris v. Rickett* (1859) 4 H. & N. 1, 7; *Turner v. Forwood* [1951] 1 All E.R. 746, 749; *Air Great Lakes Pty. Ltd v. K.S. Easter (Holdings) Pty. Ltd* (1985) 2 N.S.W.L.R. 309, 337; *State Rail Authority of New South Wales v. Heath Outdoor Pty. Ltd* (1986) 7 N.S.W.L.R. 170, 191.

[99] *Wild v. Civil Aviation Authority*, unreported, September 25, 1987, CA.

[1] Law Com. 154, Cmnd. 9700 (1986). See Marston [1986] C.L.J. 192.

[2] Para. 2.7.

[3] Para. 2.17.

[4] The Commission's Report was referred to with approval in *Wild v. Civil Aviation Authority*, unreported, September 25, 1987, CA and in *State Rail Authority of New South Wales v. Heath Outdoor Pty. Ltd* (1986) 7 N.S.W.L.R. 170, 192. See also *Yani Haryanto v. E.D. & F. Man (Sugar) Ltd* [1986] 2 Lloyd's Rep. 44, 46; *Youell v. Bland Welch & Co. Ltd* [1992] 2 Lloyd's Rep. 127, 140.

document, then on the same analysis extrinsic evidence might possibly be admissible to prove other terms even if they varied or contradicted those in the document.[5] Thus if the terms of a document stipulated that payment should be made on a certain day, evidence would be admissible of a contemporaneous agreement outside the document that payment was to be deferred until a later day.[6] Or if the terms of the document provided that one party was to have the unqualified right to terminate the contract upon one month's notice in writing, evidence would be admissible to prove a contractual agreement outside the document that the contract should only determine by effluxion of time.[7] If there is an inconsistency, that is, if effect cannot fairly be given to both terms, then the court might reject that term which defeats the object and intent of the parties as expressed in the whole of their agreement.[8] Of such a situation the Law Commission said[9]: "[it] is no different in principle from that in which the parties agree two inconsistent terms both of which are set out in the same document. The court will have to decide which of the inconsistent terms more nearly represents the intention of the parties." However, the difficulty of proving that the written document did not express the true agreement of the parties may lead the party who alleges a promise or assurance inconsistent with the document to seek to establish a collateral contract or warranty[10] or (in appropriate cases) to seek rectification of the document on the ground that it did not express the concurrent intentions of the parties at the time of its execution.[11]

Contracts required to be in or evidenced by writing. Certain contracts are **12–099** required by law to be in writing.[12] The effect of this requirement will be to exclude *oral* evidence which is offered for no other purpose than to contradict, vary, add to or subtract from the contract as contained in writing. In particular, the contracts of the various parties to a bill of exchange or promissory note must be in writing.[13] It is well established that, even as between immediate parties to a bill or note, evidence will not be admitted to prove an oral agreement to qualify the absolute undertaking of a party on the instrument, for example, to show that his liability is to be enforceable against him only in certain contingencies or that it is to be postponed to a time later than that expressed on the face of the instrument.[14] But "a written agreement on a distinct paper, to renew, or in other

---

[5] But see, *e.g. Angell v. Duke* (1875) 32 L.T. 320; *Henderson v. Arthur* [1907] 1 K.B. 10.

[6] *Young v. Austen* (1869) L.R. 4 C.P. 553; *Maillard v. Page* (1870) L.R. 5 Ex. 312 (in these cases the extrinsic agreement was in writing, as the contract was required to be in writing: see *post*, § 12–099).

[7] *cf. State Rail Authority of New South Wales v. Heath Outdoor Pty. Ltd* (1986) 7 N.S.W.L.R. 170, 191–192.

[8] See *ante*, § 12–076.

[9] Law Com. 154, Cmnd. 9700 (1986), para. 2.16.

[10] See *post*, § 12–101.

[11] See *ante*, § 5–065.

[12] See *ante*, § 4–001.

[13] Bills of Exchange Act 1882, s.3(1) (drawer), s.17(1) (acceptor), s.32(1) (indorser), s.83(1) (maker).

[14] *Hoare v. Graham* (1811) 3 Camp. 57; *Free v. Hawkins* (1817) 8 Taunt. 92; *Woodbridge v. Spooner* (1819) 3 B. & Ald. 233; *Campbell v. Hodgson* (1819) Gow 74; *Moseley v. Hanford* (1830) 10 B. & C. 729; *Foster v. Jolly* (1835) 1 C.M. & R. 703; *Adams v. Wordley* (1836) 1 M. & W. 374; *Besant v. Cross* (1851) 10 C.B. 895; *Drain v. Harvey* (1855) 17 C.B. 257; *Abrey v. Crux* (1869) L.R. 6 C.P. 37; *Young v. Austen* (1869) L.R. 4 C.P. 553, 556; *Maillard v. Page* (1870) L.R. 5 Exch. 312, 319; *Stott v. Fairlamb* (1883) 52 L.J.Q.B. 420; *New London Credit Syndicate v. Neale* [1898] 2 Q.B. 487; *Hitchings and Coulthurst Co. v. Northern Leather Co. of America and Doushkess* [1914] 3 K.B. 907.

respects to qualify, the liability of the maker or acceptor, is good as between the original parties."[15] Indeed it would seem that, as between immediate parties, evidence may always be given of a contemporaneous *written* agreement to vary the effect of the instrument and regulate their rights between themselves.[16] However, in the case of a contract for the sale or other disposition of an interest in land which is required by the Law of Property (Miscellaneous Provisions) Act 1989[17] to be made in writing and signed by or on behalf of each party to the contract, all the terms which the parties have expressly agreed must be incorporated in one document (or, where contracts are exchanged, in each).[18] Terms may be incorporated in a document either by being set out in it or by reference to some other document.[19] But, in the absence of such a reference in the signed document, evidence will not be admissible to prove that other terms were agreed in writing in addition to those set out in the document,[20] except to show that the document does not satisfy the statutory requirements.[21]

12–100   Where the contract is one which by statute must be evidenced by a note or memorandum in writing signed by the party to be charged or his agent, as in the case of a contract of guarantee,[22] the memorandum must contain a statement of the material terms of the contract.[23] Extrinsic evidence is not admissible to prove that the parties orally agreed material terms which ought to have been, but were not, included in the memorandum, since the admission of such evidence would plainly not satisfy the statute.[24] Parol evidence is, however, admissible to connect two or more documents, provided that the document which is signed by the party to be charged expressly or by implication refers to the other document or documents,[25] but not otherwise.[26]

12–101   **Collateral contracts.** Even though the parties intended to express the whole of their agreement in a particular document, extrinsic evidence may nevertheless be admitted to prove a contract or warranty collateral to that agreement.[27] The reason is that "The parol agreement neither alters nor adds to the written one, but is an independent agreement."[28] Such evidence is certainly admissible in respect of a matter on which the written contract is silent.[29] In a number of older cases

---

[15] *Byles on Bills of Exchange* (26th ed.) p. 401.

[16] *Bowerbank v. Monteiro* (1813) 4 Taunt. 844; *Young v. Austen* (1869) L.R. 4 C.P. 553; *Maillard v. Page* (1870) L.R. 5 Exch. 312, 319. But the written agreement must be supported by valuable consideration (*Bowerbank v. Monteiro, supra*; *McManus v. Bark* (1870) L.R. 5 Exch. 65) and be between the same parties (*Salmon v. Webb* (1852) 3 H.L.C. 310).

[17] See *ante*, § 4–049.

[18] s. 2(1).

[19] s. 2(2).

[20] But such terms may have effect as a collateral contract or warranty: see *post*, § 12–101.

[21] But see s.2(4) (rectification); *ante* § 4–059.

[22] Statute of Frauds 1677, s.4; see Vol. II, § 44–038.

[23] *Holmes v. Mitchell* (1859) 7 C.B., N.S. 361. But *cf.* Mercantile Law Amendment Act 1856 (consideration need not be stated).

[24] *Holmes v. Mitchell, supra*; *Sheers v. Thimbleby & Son* (1897) 76 L.T. 709, 711. But extrinsic evidence will be admitted to show that, by reason of the omission, the memorandum does *not* satisfy the statute: see, *e.g. Beckett v. Nurse* [1948] 1 K.B. 535, (on Law of Property Act 1925, s.40).

[25] *Timmins v. Moreland Street Property Co. Ltd* [1958] Ch. 110; *Elias v. George Sahely & Co. (Barbados) Ltd* [1983] A.C. 646; see *ante*, § 4–023.

[26] But *cf. Sheers v. Thimbleby & Son, supra*.

[27] See *ante*, §§ 12–004—12–006, 12–033; Wedderburn [1959] C.L.J. 58, 71.

[28] *Mann v. Nunn* (1874) 30 L.T. 526, 527.

[29] See, *e.g. De Lassalle v. Guildford* [1901] 2 K.B. 515.

it was stated that evidence of such a contract or warranty must not contradict the express terms of the written contract.[30] However, more recently, the courts have admitted evidence to prove an overriding oral warranty[31] or to prove an oral promise that the written contract will not be enforced in accordance with its terms.[32] Thus in *City of Westminster Properties (1934) Ltd v. Mudd*[33] the draft of a new lease presented to a tenant contained a covenant that he would use the premises for business purposes only and not as sleeping quarters. The tenant objected to this covenant, and the landlords gave him an oral assurance that, if he signed the lease, they would not enforce it against him. The tenant signed the lease, but later the landlords sought to forfeit the lease for breach of this covenant. Harman J. held that the oral assurance constituted a separate collateral contract from which the landlords would not be permitted to resile. The collateral contract or warranty may be oral or informal[34] even though the main contract is one which is required by law to be in or evidenced by writing.[35]

"Entire agreement" clauses. The practice has developed[36] of including in **12–102** written agreements of a formal character an "entire agreement" clause, for example:

"This Agreement contains the entire and only agreement between the parties and supersedes all previous agreements between the parties respecting the subject-matter hereof; each party acknowledges that in entering into this Agreement it has not relied on any representation or undertaking, whether oral or in writing, save such as are expressly incorporated herein."

The purpose of such a clause is to achieve, by a somewhat roundabout route, the exclusion of liability for statements other than those set out in the written contract. The effect of the clause will necessarily depend upon its precise wording. But it is submitted that, in principle, an "entire agreement" clause will render inadmissible extrinsic evidence to prove terms other than those in the

---

[30] *Lindley v. Lacey* (1864) 17 C.B.(N.S.) 578, 586, 587; *Morgan v. Griffith* (1871) L.R. 6 Ex. 70, 73; *Erskine v. Adeane* (1873) L.R. 8 Ch.App. 756, 766; *Angell v. Duke* (1875) 32 L.T. 320; *Leggott v. Barrett* (1880) 15 Ch.D. 306, 314; *Newman v. Gatti* (1907) 24 T.L.R. 18; *Henderson v. Arthur* [1907] 1 K.B. 10; *Goldfoot v. Welch* [1914] 1 Ch. 213, 218. See also *Maybury v. Atlantic Union Oil Co. Ltd* (1953) 89 C.L.R. 507, 518; *Donovan v. Northlea Farms Ltd* [1976] 1 N.Z.L.R. 180 (where the other view was adopted).

[31] *Couchman v. Hill* [1947] K.B. 554; *Webster v. Higgin* [1948] 2 All E.R. 127; *Harling v. Eddy* [1951] 2 K.B. 739; *Mendelssohn v. Normand Ltd* [1970] 1 Q.B. 177, 184; *J. Evans & Son (Portsmouth) Ltd v. Andrea Merzario Ltd* [1976] 1 W.L.R. 1078.

[32] *City and Westminster Properties (1934) Ltd v. Mudd* [1959] Ch. 129. See also *Brikom Investments Ltd v. Carr* [1979] Q.B. 467.

[33] [1959] Ch. 129. This case was referred to with approval in *Frisby v. B.B.C.* [1967] Ch. 932, 945; *Lee-Parker v. Izzett (No. 2)* [1972] 1 W.L.R. 775, 779; *Atlantic Lines and Navigation Co. Inc. v. Hallam Ltd* [1983] 1 Lloyd's Rep. 188, 197. It might be thought that the same result could be reached by application of the principle of promissory estoppel (see *ante*, § 3–080), but it would appear that that principle may not extend to pre-contractual negotiations: see *Secretary of State for Employment v. Globe Elastic Thread Co. Ltd* [1980] A.C. 506. Contrast, however, *Bank Negara Indonesia v. Philip Hoalim* [1973] 2 M.L.J. 3, PC; *Brikom Investments Ltd v. Carr* [1979] Q.B. 467, 484–485; *State Rail Authority of New South Wales v. Heath Outdoor Pty. Ltd* (1986) 7 N.S.W.L.R. 171.

[34] Unless its subject-matter is such that it is itself required to be in or evidenced by writing: *Daulia Ltd v. Four Millbank Nominees Ltd* [1978] Ch. 231.

[35] See, *e.g. Angell v. Duke* (1875) L.R. 10 Q.B. 174 (but such evidence was later rejected: (1875) 32 L.T. 320); *Record v. Bell* [1991] 1 W.L.R. 853.

[36] The practice probably originated in the United States: see Uniform Commercial Code, § 2–202.

written contract, since the parties have by the clause expressed their intention that the document is to contain all the terms of their agreement.[37] However, the language of the clause may not be apt to exclude representations[38] even if it excludes claims arising out of a collateral contract or warranty.[39]

12–103   **Extrinsic evidence admissible.** There are, in any event, a number of situations in which the written instrument is not conclusive evidence of the contract alleged to be embodied in it. These situations may be regarded either as exceptions to the parol evidence rule or simply as cases falling outside the rule.[40] They will now be discussed.

(b) *Evidence as to the Validity or Effectiveness of the Written Agreement*

12–104   **No contract.** Extrinsic evidence is admissible to show that what appears to be a valid and binding contract is in fact no contract at all. Thus evidence may be admitted to show that one or both parties contracted under a mistake,[41] or that a person who signed the document was under a misapprehension as to the real nature of the transaction into which he had entered so that it was "not his deed" in law.[42] Also it may be shown that the writing was not intended by the parties to give rise to contractual obligations[43] or that the contract is void for non-compliance with a statute.[44]

12–105   **Documents that are not contracts.** The parol evidence rule applies only to an instrument which is intended itself to be the formal and conclusive expression by the parties of their agreement.[45] If the document in question is not such an instrument, then extrinsic evidence is admissible to ascertain or interpret the intentions of the parties. Thus if a document is intended to be merely an informal memorandum of an agreement previously concluded, extrinsic evidence may be

---

[37] See *McGrath v. Shah* (1989) 57 P. & C.R. 452. Contrast the view expressed by the Law Commission, Law Com. 154, Cmnd. 9700 (1986), para. 2.15: "It may have a strong persuasive effect but if it were proved that, notwithstanding the clause, the parties actually intended some additional term to be of contractual effect, the court would give effect to that term because such was the intention of the parties."

[38] *Alman and Benson v. Associated Newspapers Group Ltd*, unreported, June 20, 1980 (Lexis); *Thomas Witter Ltd v. T.B.P. Industries Ltd* [1996] 2 All E.R. 573; *Deepak Fertilisers and Petrochemicals Corpn. v. ICI* [1999] 1 Lloyd's Rep. 387, 395. See *ante*, § 6–131. If the statement sought to be excluded is a misrepresentation, then the clause may in any event be ineffective under s.3 of the Misrepresentation Act 1967 (as amended by s.8 of the Unfair Contract Terms Act 1977). See also ss.11, 13 of the 1977 Act, and *post*, § 14–061, n. 28, 15–063.

[39] *Deepak Fertilisers and Petrochemicals Corpn. v. ICI, supra*, at 395. But, except by way of estoppel, a party cannot be made to acknowledge or "agree" that which is in fact untrue: *Lowe v. Lombank Ltd* [1960] 1 W.L.R. 196.

[40] See the Report of the Law Commission, Law Com. 154, Cmnd. 9700 (1986), paras. 2.30, 2.31.

[41] *Pym v. Campbell* (1856) 6 E. & B. 370, 374; *Raffles v. Wichelhaus* (1864) 2 H. & C. 906. See *ante*, § 5–001.

[42] See, *e.g. Foster v. Mackinnon* (1869) L.R. 4 C.P. 704; *Lewis v. Clay* (1898) 67 L.J.Q.B. 224; *Roe v. R.A. Naylor Ltd* (1918) 87 L.J.K.B. 958, 964. Direct evidence of intention is always admissible where the *factum* of the instrument is impugned. See *ante*, § 5–054.

[43] *Bowes v. Foster* (1858) 2 H. & N. 779; *Rogers v. Hadley* (1863) 2 H. & C. 227; *Pattle v. Hornibrook* [1897] 1 Ch. 25, *Orion Insurance Co. Plc v. Sphere Drake Insurance Plc* [1992] 1 Lloyd's Rep. 239, 273, 301.

[44] *Lockett v. Nicklin* (1848) 2 Exch. 93; *Campbell Discount Co. Ltd v. Gall* [1961] 1 Q.B. 431.

[45] Or, in the case of a unilateral instrument such as a deed, the formal and conclusive expression of the intentions of the maker: *Rabin v. Gerson Berger Assn. Ltd* [1986] 1 W.L.R. 526.

admitted to show that this informal memorandum does not embody the terms contained in the previous agreement.[46] A receipt,[47] an invoice,[48] a payment instruction[49] and even bills of lading,[50] have been held to come within this exception.

Consideration. Consideration is a necessary requirement for the formation of **12–106** all contracts which are not made by deed.[51] Extrinsic evidence may therefore be admitted to show want of or failure of the consideration stated to have been given in a written instrument.[52] Thus the words in a bill of exchange "for value received" do not preclude the court from finding that no consideration has in fact been given.[53] Extrinsic evidence is also admissible to prove the true consideration where no consideration, or a nominal consideration, has been stated,[54] where the expressed consideration is in general terms or ambiguously stated,[55] or where the consideration is inaccurately recorded.[56] Also an additional consideration may be proved, provided it does not contradict the stated consideration.[57]

> "The rule is that, where there is one consideration stated in a deed, you may prove any other consideration which existed, not in contradiction to the instrument; and it is not in contradiction to the instrument to prove a larger consideration than that which is stated."[58]

Conditional contracts. Extrinsic evidence is admissible to show that, at the **12–107** time a document was signed by the parties, they were agreed that it was not to take effect as a contract except on the fulfilment of a certain condition,[59] *e.g.* in the case of deeds, evidence of an escrow.[60]

---

[46] *Orion Insurance Co. Plc v. Sphere Drake Insurance Plc* [1992] 1 Lloyd's Rep. 239. *cf. Hutton v. Watling* [1948] Ch. 398.

[47] *Graves v. Key* (1832) 3 B. & Ad. 313; *Allen v. Pink* (1838) 4 M. & W. 140; *Lee v. L. & Y. Ry.* (1871) L.R. 6 Ch.App. 527; *Beckett v. Nurse* [1948] 1 K.B. 535.

[48] *Holding v. Elliott* (1860) 5 H. & N. 117.

[49] *Guardian Ocean Cargoes Ltd v. Banco do Brasil SA* [1991] 2 Lloyd's Rep. 68.

[50] *Crooks v. Allan* (1879) 5 Q.B.D. 38; *Moss Steamship Co. v. Whinney* [1912] A.C. 254, 264; *The Ardennes* [1951] 1 K.B. 55.

[51] See *ante*, Chap. 3.

[52] *Abbott v. Hendrix* (1840) 1 M. & G. 791, 794, 796; *Young v. Austen* (1869) L.R. 4 C.P. 553, 556; *Abrey v. Crux* (1869) L.R. 5 C.P. 37, 45; *Equitable Office v. Ching* [1907] A.C. 96; Law of Property Act 1925, s.67. But *cf. Roberts v. Security Co.* [1897] 1 Q.B. 111; Law of Property Act 1925, s.68.

[53] *Solly v. Hinde* (1834) 2 Cr. & M. 516; *Abbott v. Hendrix, supra*, at 795.

[54] *Gale v. Williamson* (1841) 8 M. & W. 405; *Clifford v. Turrell* (1845) 1 Y. & C.C.C. 138; *Pott v. Todhunter* (1845) 2 Coll. 76; *Re Holland* [1902] 2 Ch. 360, 388.

[55] *Goldshede v. Swan* (1847) 1 Exch. 154; *Hoad v. Grace* (1861) 7 H. & N. 494.

[56] *Booker v. Seddon* (1858) 1 F. & F. 196. It is a moot point whether extrinsic evidence is admissible to prove a real (*e.g.* smaller) consideration inconsistent with that expressed in the instrument. See *Ridout v. Bristow* (1830) 9 Exch. 48; *Abbott v. Hendrix, supra*, at 796; *Turner v. Forwood* [1951] 1 All E.R. 746. The views of Lord Hardwicke in *Peacock v. Monk* (1748) 1 Ves.Sen. 127, 128 must now be read with caution. See also *Woods v. Wise* [1955] 2 Q.B. 29; *Peffer v. Rigg* [1977] 1 W.L.R. 285, 293.

[57] *Leifchild's Case* (1865) L.R. 1 Eq. 231; *Townend v. Toker* (1866) L.R. 1 Ch.App. 446, 459; *Frith v. Frith* [1906] A.C. 254; *Turner v. Forwood, supra*; *Pao On v. Lau Yiu Long* [1980] A.C. 614.

[58] *Clifford v. Turrell, supra* at 149.

[59] *Pym v. Campbell* (1856) 6 E. & B. 370; *Wallis v. Littell* (1861) 11 C.B.(N.S.) 369; *Lindley v. Lacey* (1864) 17 C.B.(N.S.) 578; *Pattle v. Hornibrook* [1897] 1 Ch. 25. *cf. Smith v. Mansi* [1963] 1 W.L.R. 26.

[60] *London Freehold and Leasehold Property v. Lord Suffield* [1897] 2 Ch. 608, 622. See *ante*, § 1–049.

12–108   **Evidence of date.** Extrinsic evidence is also admitted to prove the actual date of delivery of a deed,[61] or the date of execution of a written instrument,[62] in contradiction of the date stated therein; and also, where it has no date, to show from what time a written instrument was intended to operate.[63]

12–109   **Subsequent variation or discharge.** The rule regarding the admissibility of extrinsic evidence applies merely to the discovery of the original intention of the parties as expressed in the instrument, and has no application to the variation[64] or discharge[65] of the contract by a subsequent agreement.

12–110   **Fraud, illegality, etc.** Extrinsic evidence will always be admitted to defeat a deed or written contract on the ground of fraud,[66] illegality,[67] misrepresentation,[68] mistake[69] or duress.[70] Also in the application of equitable remedies such as specific performance or the refusal thereof,[71] rectification,[72] or rescission,[73] extrinsic evidence will be admitted to prove the grounds upon which relief is sought.

(c) *Evidence as to the True Nature of the Agreement*

12–111   **True nature of the agreement.** Extrinsic evidence is admissible to prove the true nature of the agreement, or the legal relationship of the parties,[74] even though this may vary or add to the written instrument.[75] Thus a conveyance may be shown to be merely a mortgage,[76] a sale and hire-purchase agreement to be an unregistered bill of sale,[77] and a sale of property to be a loan on security.[78]

---

[61] *Jayne v. Hughes* (1854) 10 Exch. 430.

[62] *Hall v. Cazenove* (1804) 4 East 477; *Pasmore v. North* (1811) 13 East 517; *Armfield v. Allport* (1857) 27 L.J.Ex. 42; Bills of Exchange Act 1882, s.13(1).

[63] *Davis v. Jones* (1856) 17 C.B. 625; Bills of Exchange Act 1882, ss.12, 20.

[64] *Goss v. Lord Nugent* (1833) 5 B. & Ad. 58, 64. But a contract required by law to be in or evidenced by writing can in principle only be varied by writing: see *post*, § 23–033.

[65] *Morris v. Baron & Co. Ltd* [1918] A.C. 1; *post*, § 23–030.

[66] *Pickering v. Dowson* (1813) 4 Taunt. 779; *Dobell v. Stevens* (1825) 3 B. & C. 623.

[67] *Collins v. Blantern* (1767) 2 Wils. 347; *Doe d. Chandler v. Ford* (1853) 3 A. & E. 649; *Reynell v. Sprye* (1852) 1 De G.M. & G. 660, 672; *Madell v. Thomas & Co.* [1891] 1 Q.B. 230. See also *Woods v. Wise* [1955] 2 Q.B. 29 (evidence to support legality).

[68] *Pennsylvania Shipping Co. v. Compagnie Nationale de Navigation* [1936] 2 All E.R. 1167.

[69] See *ante*, § 5–001.

[70] See *ante*, § 7–001.

[71] *Martin v. Pycroft* (1852) D.M. & G. 785; *Webster v. Cecil* (1861) 30 Beav. 62. But see *ante*, § 5–063.

[72] *Druiff v. Parker* (1868) L.R. 5 Eq. 131; *Olley v. Fisher* (1887) 34 Ch.D. 367; *Henderson v. Arthur* [1907] 1 K.B. 10, 13; *Lovell and Christmas Ltd v. Wall* (1911) 104 L.T. 85; *Craddock Bros. v. Hunt* [1923] 2 Ch. 136, 151; *Hamed El Chiaty & Co. v. Thomas Cook Group Ltd* [1992] 2 Lloyd's Rep. 399, 407, 408.

[73] *Paget v. Marshall* (1884) 28 Ch.D. 255.

[74] *Steele v. M'Kinlay* (1880) 5 App.Cas. 754, 778–779; *Macdonald v. Whitfield* (1883) 8 App.Cas. 733, 745; *National Sales Cpn. Ltd v. Bernardi* [1931] 2 K.B. 188; *McCall Bros. Ltd v. Hargreaves* [1932] 2 K.B. 423; *Yeoman Credit Ltd v. Gregory* [1963] 1 W.L.R. 343; and see *post*, § 12–114.

[75] Including direct evidence of intention.

[76] *Re Duke of Marlborough* [1894] 2 Ch. 133.

[77] *Madell v. Thomas & Co.* [1891] 1 Q.B. 230; *Polsky v. S. & A. Services* [1951] 1 All E.R. 1062.

[78] *Maas v. Pepper* [1905] A.C. 102.

Evidence of agency. Extrinsic evidence may also be adduced to show that   **12–112**
one or both of the contracting parties to an agreement were agents for other
persons and acted as such in making the contract so as to give the benefit or the
burden of the contract to their undisclosed principals.[79] Such evidence relates to
the *factum* of the written instrument.[80] It is therefore a moot point whether
evidence can be given which is inconsistent with the written agreement. There is
authority for the view that, where an action is brought against a party who has
contracted in terms indicating that he is the real and only principal, evidence
cannot be given that he contracted merely as agent as this would contradict the
written agreement.[81] Thus where a party was described as "owner" of a ship[82] or
as "proprietor" of a building site,[83] he being, in fact, merely the agent of an
undisclosed principal, it was held, in an action by the principal on the contract,
that evidence could not be received to show the fact of the agency so as to give
the principal a right to sue on the contract. On the other hand, these cases may
be explained as cases in which the personality of the contracting party was of
sufficient importance to have become a term of the contract[84] or simply that they
were wrongly decided.[85] The issue is still an open one.[86]

Where a person describes himself in a contract as agent of an unnamed   **12–113**
principal, either he or the other contracting party may bring evidence to show
that, although described as agent, he is in fact the principal.[87]

Evidence of suretyship. Evidence is admissible to show that a person who   **12–114**
signed a document did so as surety, even though it might appear that he entered
into the agreement as principal debtor or on behalf of another or in some other
capacity.[88]

---

[79] *Bateman v. Phillips* (1812) 15 East 272; *Wake v. Harrop* (1861) 30 L.J.Ex. 273; *McCollin v. Gilpin* (1881) 29 W.R. 408; *Fred Drughorn Ltd v. Rederiaktiebolaget Transatlantic* [1919] A.C. 203; *Danziger v. Thompson* [1944] K.B. 654; *Epps v. Rothnie* [1945] K.B. 562; *Finzel, Berry & Co. v. Eastcheap Dried Fruit Co.* [1962] 1 Lloyd's Rep. 370; affd. [1962] 2 Lloyd's Rep. 11. See Vol. II, § 32–069.

[80] *Young v. Schuler* (1883) 11 Q.B.D. 651.

[81] *Magee v. Atkinson* (1837) 2 M. & W. 440; *Higgins v. Senior* (1841) 8 M. & W. 834; *Humble v. Hunter* (1848) 12 Q.B. 310; *Formby Bros. v. Formby* (1910) 102 L.T. 116. See Vol. II, § 32–065.

[82] *Humble v. Hunter, supra.*

[83] *Formby Bros. v. Formby, supra.*

[84] *Fred Drughorn Ltd v. Rederiaktiebolaget Transatlantic, supra*, at 210; *Rederiaktiebolaget Argonaut v. Hani* [1918] 2 K.B. 247; *Collins v. Associated Greyhound Racecourses Ltd* [1930] 1 Ch. 1. See Vol. II, § 32–065.

[85] *Killick & Co. v. Price & Co.* (1896) 12 T.L.R. 263, 274; *Fred Drughorn Ltd v. Rederiaktiebolaget Transatlantic, supra*, at 209; *Epps v. Rothnie* [1945] K.B. 562, 565 (cases where the description was equivocal).

[86] *Siu Yin Kwan v. Eastern Insurance Co. Ltd* [1994] 2 A.C. 199. See also *Crescent Oil and Shipping Services Ltd v. Importang UEE* [1998] 1 W.L.R. 919, 931.

[87] *Schmaltz v. Avery* (1851) 16 Q.B. 655; *Carr v. Jackson* (1852) 7 Exch. 392; *Adams v. Hall* (1877) 37 L.T. 70; *Harper v. Vigers* [1909] 2 K.B. 549. *cf. Fairlie v. Fenton* (1870) L.R. 5 Ex. 169; *Sharman v. Brandt* (1871) L.R. 6 Q.B. 720. See Vol. II, §§ 32–094, 32–095.

[88] *Hill v. Wilcox* (1831) 1 M. & Rob. 58; *Ewin v. Lancaster* (1865) 6 B. & S. 571; *Overend Gurney & Co. v. Oriental Finance Co.* (1874) L.R. 7 H.L. 348; *Macdonald v. Whitfield* (1883) 8 App.Cas. 733; *Young v. Schuler* (1883) 11 Q.B.D. 651; *Gerald McDonald & Co. v. Nash & Co.* [1924] A.C. 625; *V.H.S. Ltd and B.K.S. Air Transport Ltd v. Stephens* [1964] 1 Lloyd's Rep. 460; *Sun Alliance Pensions Life & Investments Services Ltd v. Webster* [1991] 1 Lloyd's Rep. 410.

(d) *Evidence to Interpret or Explain the Written Agreement*

12–115   **Evidence in aid of interpretation.** Different considerations apply to the admissibility of extrinsic evidence to interpret or explain a written agreement.[89] Extrinsic evidence of this sort does not usurp the authority of the written document or contradict, vary, add to or subtract from its terms. It is the writing which operates. The extrinsic evidence does no more than assist in its operation by assigning a definite meaning to terms capable of such explanation or by pointing out and connecting them with the proper subject-matter.[90] Accordingly, no "parol evidence rule" (in the sense referred to above) will apply to such a situation.[91] However, the nature of the evidence that may be adduced, and the purposes for which it may be used, are subject to certain restrictions imposed by the law.

12–116   **Evidence of surrounding circumstances.** The willingness of the courts to admit extrinsic evidence as an aid to the interpretation of a written contract was established as long ago as 1842 by Tindal C.J. in *Shore v. Wilson*,[92] when he said:

> "The general rule I take to be, that where the words of any written instrument are free from ambiguity in themselves, and where external circumstances do not create any doubt or difficulty as to the proper application of those words to claimants under the instrument, or the subject-matter to which the instrument relates, such instrument is always to be construed according to the strict, plain, common meaning of the words themselves; and that in such case evidence *dehors* the instrument, for the purpose of explaining it according to the surmised or alleged intention of the parties to the instrument, is utterly inadmissible. . . . The true interpretation, however, of every instrument being manifestly that which will make the instrument speak the intention of the party at the time it was made, it has always been considered an exception, or perhaps, to speak more precisely, not so much an exception from, as a corollary to, the general rule above stated, that where any doubt arises upon the true sense and meaning of the words themselves, or any difficulty as to their application under the surrounding circumstances, the sense and meaning of the language may be investigated and ascertained by evidence *dehors* the instrument itself; for both reason and common sense agree that by no other means can the language of the instrument be made to speak the real mind of the party."

But under the older restrictive view expressed in this statement, and endorsed in a number of subsequent cases, extrinsic evidence is admissible only where the sense and meaning of the words of the written instrument is doubtful or difficulty arises when it is sought to apply the language of the instrument to the circumstances under consideration. If the words have a clear and fixed meaning, not capable of explanation, extrinsic evidence would not be admissible to show that

---

[89] See Law Com. No. 154, Cmnd. 9700 (1986), para. 1.2; referred to with approval in *Youell v. Bland Welch & Co. Ltd* [1992] 2 Lloyd's Rep. 127, 140.

[90] *Thorpe v. Brumfitt* (1873) L.R. 8 Ch.App. 650; *Johnstone v. Holdway* [1963] 1 Q.B. 601; *The Shannon Ltd v. Venner Ltd* [1965] Ch. 682; *Perrylease Ltd v. Imecar A.G.* [1988] 1 W.L.R. 463.

[91] *Colpoys v. Colpoys* (1822) Jac. 451.

[92] (1842) 9 Cl. & Fin. 355, 565.

the parties meant something different from what they have written.[93] The more modern view, however, is that the words do not have to be vague, ambiguous or otherwise uncertain before extrinsic evidence will be admitted. Since the purpose of the inquiry is to ascertain the meaning which the words would convey to a reasonable man against the background of the transaction in question, the court is free (subject to certain exceptions) to look to all the relevant circumstances surrounding the transaction, not merely in order to choose between the possible meanings of words which are ambiguous but even to conclude that the parties must, for whatever reason, have used the wrong words or syntax.[94] So the court is entitled (and, indeed, bound) to enquire beyond the language of the document and see what the circumstances were with reference to which words were used, and the object appearing from those circumstances which the person using them had in view.[95] The court must place itself in the same "factual matrix" as that in which the parties were.[96] In *Reardon Smith Line Ltd v. Yngvar Hansen-Tangen*,[97] Lord Wilberforce said:

"No contracts are made in a vacuum; there is always a setting in which they have to be placed. The nature of what is legitimate to have regard to is usually described as 'the

---

[93] *Bank of New Zealand v. Simpson* [1900] A.C. 182, 188. See also *Blackett v. Royal Exchange Co.* (1832) 2 C. & J. 244; *Inglis v. Buttery* (1878) 3 App.Cas. 552; *Edward Lloyd Ltd v. Sturgeon Falls Pulp Co.* (1901) 85 L.T. 162; *Lovell & Christmas Ltd v. Wall* (1911) 104 L.T. 85; *Kinlen v. Ennis* [1916] 2 Ir.R. 299; *G.W. Ry. v. Bristol Corp.* (1918) 87 L.J.Ch. 414; *London County Council v. Henry Boot & Sons Ltd* [1959] 1 W.L.R. 133, 1069; *Codelfa Construction Pty. Ltd v. State Railway Authority of New South Wales* (1982) 149 C.L.R. 337, 352; *Shearson Lehman Hutton Inc. v. Maclaine Watson & Co. Ltd* [1989] 2 Lloyd's Rep. 570, 591; *Hamed El Chiaty & Co. v. Thomas Cook Group Ltd* [1992] 2 Lloyd's Rep. 399, 407; *Adams v. British Airways plc* [1995] I.R.L.R. 577.

[94] *Mannai Investment Co. Ltd v. Eagle Star Life Assurance Ltd* [1997] A.C. 749, 774; *Investors Compensation Scheme Ltd v. West Bromwich Building Society* [1998] 1 W.L.R. 896, 913; *Simon Container Machinery Ltd v. Emba Machinery Ltd* [1998] 2 Lloyd's Rep. 429, 433. cf., *L.G. Schuler A.G. v. Wickman Machine Tool Sales Ltd* [1974] A.C. 235, 261.

[95] *Smith v. Thompson* (1849) 8 C.B. 44; *Burges v. Wickham* (1863) B. & S. 669; *The Curfew* [1891] P. 131; *River Wear Commissioners v. Adamson* (1877) 2 App.Cas. 743, 763; *Mackill v. Wright* (1888) 14 App.Cas. 106, 114, 116, 120; *Bank of New Zealand v. Simpson* [1900] A.C. 182; *Charrington & Co. Ltd v. Wooder* [1914] A.C. 71, 77, 80, 82; *A/S Tankexpress v. Compagnie Financière Belge des Petroles SA* [1949] A.C. 76; *Prenn v. Simmonds* [1971] 1 W.L.R. 1381, 1383; 1384; *Moschi v. Lep Air Services Ltd* [1973] A.C. 351, 354; *Reardon Smith Line Ltd v. Yngvar Hansen-Tangen* [1976] 1 W.L.R. 989, 995, 997; *Bunge v. Kruse* [1977] 1 Lloyd's Rep. 492, 495, 497, 498; *Harmony Shipping Co. SA v. Saudi-Europe Line Ltd* [1981] 1 Lloyd's Rep. 377, 417; *Shell Tankers (U.K.) Ltd v. Astro Comino Armadora SA* [1981] 2 Lloyd's Rep. 40, 44, 45; *Wace v. Pan Atlantic Group Inc.* [1981] 2 Lloyd's Rep. 339, 343; *Perrylease Ltd v. Imecar A.G.* [1988] 1 W.L.R. 463, 470; *Vitol BV v. Compagnie Europeenne des Petroles* [1988] 1 Lloyd's Rep. 574, 576; *Shearson Lehman Hutton Inc. v. Maclaine Watson & Co. Ltd* [1989] 2 Lloyd's Rep. 570, 590; *Forsikringsaktieselskapet Vesta v. J.N.E. Butcher, Bain Dawes Ltd* [1989] 1 Lloyd's Rep. 330, 345; *Anangel Atlas Compania Naviera SA v. I.H.I. Co. Ltd* [1990] 2 Lloyd's Rep. 526, 552; *Bankers Trust Co. v. State Bank of India* [1991] 2 Lloyd's Rep. 443, 456; *Levett v. Barclays Bank* [1995] 1 W.L.R. 1260; *International Fina Services AG v. Katrina Shipping Ltd* [1995] 2 Lloyd's Rep. 344, 350; *Cresspark Ltd v. Wymering Mansions Ltd* [1996] E.G.C.S. 63; *Mannai Investment Co. Ltd v. Eagle Star Life Assurance Ltd* [1997] A.C. 749, 775; *Investors Compensation Scheme Ltd v. West Bromwich Building Society* [1998] 1 W.L.R. 896, 912; *Don King Productions Ltd v. Warren* [1998] 2 Lloyd's Rep. 176, 189; *NLA Group Ltd v. Bowers* [1999] 1 Lloyd's Rep. 109, 110.

[96] *Reardon Smith Line Ltd v. Yngvar Hansen-Tangen, supra*, at 997; *Thoresen Car Ferries Ltd v. Weymouth Portland B.C.* [1977] 2 Lloyd's Rep. 156; *Staffordshire A.H.A. v. South Staffordshire Waterworks Co.* [1978] 1 W.L.R. 1387, 1395; *Hyundai Shipbuilding & Heavy Industries Co. Ltd v. Pournaras* [1978] 2 Lloyd's Rep. 502, 506; *Earl of Lonsdale v. Att.-Gen.* [1982] 1 W.L.R. 887, 900; *Gill & Duffus SA v. Société pour l'Exportation des Sucres SA* [1986] 1 Lloyd's Rep. 322, 325; *Investors Compensation Scheme Ltd v. West Bromwich Building Society, supra* at 912.

[97] [1976] 1 W.L.R. 989, 995–996.

surrounding circumstances' but this phrase is imprecise: it can be illustrated but hardly defined. In a commercial contract it is certainly right that the court should know the commercial purpose of the contract and this in turn presupposes knowledge of the genesis of the transaction, the background, the context, the market in which the parties are operating."

He further stated[98] that, just as the intention of the parties is to be ascertained objectively, so also "when one is speaking of aim, or object, or commercial purpose, one is speaking objectively of what reasonable persons would have in mind in the situation of the parties."

12–117   On the other hand, although evidence of the facts about which the parties were negotiating is admissible to explain what meaning was intended, the court is not entitled to look at what the parties to the contract said or did whilst the matter was in negotiation[99] nor are drafts or preliminary agreements admissible in aid of its interpretation,[1] except where it is sought to rectify the document[2] or to show that the parties negotiated on an agreed basis that the words used bore a particular meaning.[3] Evidence will also not be admitted to show what were the parties' subjective intentions with respect to the words used.[4] "The general rule seems to be that all facts are admissible which tend to show the sense which the words bear with reference to the surrounding circumstances of and concerning which the words were used, but that such facts as only tend to show that the writer intended to use words bearing a particular sense are to be rejected."[5] In *Prenn v. Simmonds*,[6] Lord Wilberforce summed up the position as follows:

> "In my opinion, then, evidence of negotiations, or of the parties' intentions, and *a fortiori* of [the plaintiff's] intentions, ought not to be received, and evidence should be restricted to evidence of the factual background known to the parties at or before the date of the contract, including evidence of the 'genesis' and objectively the 'aim' of the transaction."

---

[98] At 996. See also *Hvalfangerselskapet Polaris Aktieselskap Ltd v. Unilever Ltd* (1933) 39 Com.Cas. 1, 3, 19, 25; *Anangel Atlas Compania Naviera SA v. I.H.I. Co. Ltd* [1990] 2 Lloyd's Rep. 526, 553.

[99] *Inglis v. Buttery* (1878) 3 App.Cas. 552, 558; *Leggott v. Barrett* (1880) 15 Ch.D. 306, 311; *Millbourn v. Lyons* [1914] 2 Ch. 231, 240; *Davis Contractors Ltd v. Fareham U.D.C.* [1956] A.C. 696; *Prenn v. Simmonds* [1971] 1 W.L.R. 1381, 1385; *Moschi v. Lep Air Services Ltd* [1973] A.C. 331, 354; *L.G. Schuler A.G. v. Wickman Machine Tools Ltd* [1974] A.C. 235; *Arrale v. Costain Civil Engineering Ltd* [1976] 1 Lloyd's Rep. 98, 101, 103, 105; *The Raven* [1980] 2 Lloyd's Rep. 266, 270; *Sudatlantica Navegacion SA v. Devamar Shipping Corpn.* [1985] 2 Lloyd's Rep. 271, 274; *Investors Compensation Scheme Ltd v. West Bromwich Building Society* [1998] 1 W.L.R. 896, 913.

[1] *Inglis v. Buttery, supra*; *National Bank of Australasia v. Falkingham* [1902] A.C. 585, 591; *Youell v. Bland Welch & Co. Ltd* [1992] 2 Lloyd's Rep. 127.

[2] See *ante*, § 5–065.

[3] *Partenreederei M.S. Karen Oltmann v. Scarsdale Shipping Co. Ltd* [1976] 2 Lloyd's Rep. 708, 712.

[4] *I.R.C. v. Raphael* [1935] A.C. 96, 142; *Prenn v. Simmonds* [1971] 1 W.L.R. 1381, 1385; *Reardon Smith Line Ltd v. Yngvar Hansen-Tangen* [1976] 1 W.L.R. 989, 996; *Harmony Shipping Co. SA v. Saudi-Europe Line Ltd* [1981] 1 Lloyd's Rep. 377, 416. In *Rabin v. Gerson Berger Assn. Ltd* [1986] 1 W.L.R. 526, opinions of tax counsel given shortly before or at the time of execution of certain trust deeds were held inadmissible.

[5] *Grant v. Grant* (1870) L.R. 5 C.P. 727, 728; approved in *London County Council v. Henry Boot & Sons Ltd* [1959] 1 W.L.R. 133, 138, CA and [1959] 1 W.L.R. 1069, 1075.

[6] [1971] 1 W.L.R. 1381.

More difficulty may perhaps be encountered in determining the extent of the   **12–118**
surrounding circumstances which may properly be admitted as an aid to interpretation. In *Investors Compensation Scheme Ltd v. West Bromwich Building
Society*[7] Lord Hoffmann, referring to the matrix of fact, said: "Subject to the
requirement that it should have been reasonably available to the parties . . . it
includes absolutely anything which would have affected the way in which the
language of the document would have been understood by a reasonable man".[8]
However, in *Scottish Power plc v. Britoil (Exploration) Ltd*[9] in the Court of
Appeal, Staughton L.J. cast doubt on this proposition and complained that often
a great deal of evidence was produced under the heading of surrounding circumstances, background or factual matrix which contributed little or nothing to the
understanding of the parties' contract and so increased the cost of litigation. In
his view "surrounding circumstances" should be confined to what the parties had
in mind, and what was going on around them at the time when they were making
the contract. The main problem seems to be one of relevance. It may, therefore,
be, as Lord Steyn pointed out in *Mannai Investment Co. Ltd v. Eagle Star Life
Assurance Co. Ltd*,[10] that "admissibility is not the decisive matter. The real
question is what evidence of surrounding circumstances may ultimately be
allowed to influence the question of interpretation. That depends on what meanings the language read against the objective contextual scene will let in".

Special meaning of words. It has already been stated that words must be   **12–119**
understood in their plain and ordinary sense.[11] In those cases where they are to
be understood in a special sense[12] extrinsic evidence is admissible to prove that
special sense. Thus evidence may be called to explain technical terms of science
or art,[13] to explain contemporary meanings of the words of an ancient document[14] and to translate a document in a foreign language.[15] Extrinsic evidence is
also admissible to show that words have by custom or usage a peculiar
sense.[16]

Identity of parties. The identity of parties may be established by extrinsic   **12–120**
evidence where it is not clear from the written instrument to whom it refers.[17] So,
where a landlord handed to his tenant a letter addressed "Dear Sir" in which he
promised to renew a lease, extrinsic evidence was admitted to identify the
proposed lessee, even though no mention of his name appeared in the agreement.[18] Extrinsic evidence will also be admitted to show in what capacity the

---

[7] [1998] 1 W.L.R. 896.
[8] At 912–913.
[9] *The Times*, Dec. 2, 1997. See also *NLA Group Ltd v. Bowers* [1999] 1 Lloyd's Rep. 109, 112.
[10] [1997] A.C. 749, 768.
[11] See *ante*, § 12–050.
[12] See *ante*, §§ 12–051, 12–058.
[13] *Shore v. Wilson* (1842) 9 Cl. & Fin. 355, 511. See also *L.G. Schuler A.G. v. Wickman Machine
Tools Sales Ltd* [1974] A.C. 235, 261 ("technical expressions").
[14] *Shore v. Wilson, supra*, at 501, 527, 545, 555–556; *Earl of Lonsdale v. Att.-Gen.* [1982] 1 W.L.R.
887.
[15] *Shore v. Wilson, supra*, at 555–556; *Di Sora v. Phillips* (1863) 10 H.L.C. 624, 633, 638.
[16] See *post*, §§ 12–125—12–131.
[17] *Rossiter v. Miller* (1878) 3 App.Cas. 1124; *Chapman v. Smith* [1907] 2 Ch. 97; *Stokes v. Whicher*
[1920] 1 Ch. 411. *cf. Jarrett v. Hunter* (1887) 34 Ch.D. 182.
[18] *Carr v. Lynch* [1900] 1 Ch. 613.

parties contracted, *e.g.* to show which party was the buyer and which the seller,[19] or to correct a misnomer.[20]

12–121   **Subject-matter.** The subject-matter of the contract may similarly be identified by extrinsic evidence.[21] Thus evidence was admitted as to the quality and quantity of wool described in the written contract as "your wool,"[22] as to the identity of the property which was the subject-matter of a contract of sale[23] and as to its exact area,[24] as to the items of furniture assigned by a deed to which no schedule was attached[25] and as to the liability comprehended by a guarantee.[26] Extrinsic evidence is also admissible where it is sought to restrict the generality of an obligation by reference to the circumstances or the person.[27]

12–122   **Equivocations.** An equivocation arises when the words of the written contract are intended to refer to one person or thing only, and in fact refer to more than one person. In such a case, if it cannot be ascertained from the document itself which was intended, extrinsic evidence is admissible to resolve the ambiguity. Direct evidence of the party's intention is this time admissible. Thus if a person buys goods "ex Peerless from Bombay," and it is shown that there are two vessels of that name sailing from the port of Bombay, the parties may give evidence to show which vessel they themselves intended.[28] Likewise in the case of a bill or note, where there are two payees of the same name, the drawer or maker may give evidence to identify the intended payee.[29]

12–123   **Patent ambiguity.** In the case of a patent ambiguity, that is to say, a defect or ambiguity appearing on the face of the document which renders the words used unintelligible or meaningless, a rule is said to exist that any reference to matter *dehors* the document is forbidden.[30] It is doubtful, however, whether such a rule applies today in respect of written contracts, except possibly in the case of total blanks in a document,[31] although evidence will not be admitted to show what the

---

[19] *Newell v. Radford* (1867) L.R. 3 C.P. 52. See also *ante*, § 12–112 (agency).

[20] *Willis v. Barrett* (1816) 2 Stark. 29; *Dermatine Co. Ltd v. Ashworth* (1905) 21 T.L.R. 510; *Bird & Co. v. Thomas Cook & Son* [1937] 2 All E.R. 227, 230–231.

[21] *L.G. Schuler A.G. v. Wickman Machine Tools Sales Ltd* [1974] A.C. 235, 261.

[22] *Macdonald v. Longbottom* (1860) 1 E. & E. 977, 987.

[23] *Ogilvie v. Foljambe* (1817) 3 Mer. 53, 61; *Owen v. Thomas* (1834) My. & K. 353; *Bleakley v. Smith* (1840) 11 Sim. 150; *Cowley v. Watts* (1853) 17 Jur. 172; *Wood v. Scarth* (1855) 2 K. & J. 33; *Shardlow v. Cotterell* (1881) 20 Ch.D. 90; *Plant v. Bourne* [1897] 2 Ch. 281; *Harewood v. Retese* [1990] 1 W.L.R. 333; *Freeguard v. Rogers* [1999] 1 W.L.R. 375. *cf. Doe d. Norton v. Webster* (1840) 12 A. & E. 442.

[24] *Scarfe v. Adams* [1981] 1 All E.R. 843.

[25] *England v. Downs* (1840) 2 Beav. 522; *McCollin v. Gilpin* (1881) 6 Q.B.D. 516. See also *Burges v. Wickham* (1863) 3 B. & S. 669, 698; *Savory v. World of Golf* [1914] 2 Ch. 566; *Auerbach v. Nelson* [1919] 2 Ch. 383; *L.G. Schuler v. Wickman Machine Tool Sales Ltd* [1974] A.C. 235, 261. *cf. Caddick v. Skidmore* (1857) 2 De G. & J. 52.

[26] *Heffield v. Meadows* (1869) L.R. 4 C.P. 595; *Perrylease Ltd v. Imecar A.G.* [1988] 1 W.L.R. 463. *cf. Holmes v. Mitchell* (1859) 7 C.B.N.S. 361.

[27] See *ante*, § 12–060.

[28] *Raffles v. Wichelhaus* (1864) 2 H. & C. 906.

[29] *Sweeting v. Fowler* (1815) 1 Stark. 106; *Stebbing v. Spicer* (1849) 8 C.B. 827.

[30] Bacon's *Law Tracts*, 99; *Colpoys v. Colpoys* (1822) Jacob 451; *Great Western Ry. v. Bristol Cpn.* (1918) 87 L.J.Ch. 414, 429. *cf. Watcham v. Att.-Gen. of East African Protectorate* [1919] A.C. 533 (but see *post*, § 12–124, n. 36).

[31] *R. v. Ryan* (1811) Russ. & Ry. 195; *In the Goods of De Rosaz* (1877) 2 P.D. 66, 69. *cf.* Bills of Exchange Act 1882, s.20.

author himself intended to say.[32] The language employed may, of course, be so vague or contradictory as to be incurable.

Subsequent acts. The admissibility of evidence to show that the parties have **12–124** acted upon an instrument in a particular sense is probably confined to ancient documents.[33] Evidence of user, and of acts done in pursuance of an instrument, has been admitted to explain old, or obsolete, or even imperfect expressions to be found in ancient documents.[34] Attempts were, however made to extend the rule to cases where the document was modern and the ambiguity patent.[35] The acts and conduct of the parties under the agreement were admitted to show the sense in which the parties to it used the language they employed, and their intention in executing the instrument as revealed by their language interpreted in this sense.[36] The House of Lords has now decisively rejected this extension and has held that "it is not legitimate to use as an aid in the construction of the contract anything which the parties said or did after it was made."[37] Subsequent actions are therefore inadmissible to interpret a written agreement, although they are admissible to show whether there was a contract and what the terms of the contract were, either originally or by variation, or as the basis for an estoppel.[38]

(e) *Evidence of Custom or Mercantile Usage*

Generally. Extrinsic evidence is also admissible to show the custom of a **12–125** particular locality or the usage of a particular trade. Evidence may therefore be adduced (1) to prove that the words of a contract are used in a peculiar sense and different from the sense which they ordinarily bear,[39] and (2) to annex incidents

---

[32] *Clayton v. Lord Nugent* (1844) 13 M. & W. 200 (will).

[33] *Att.-Gen. v. Parker* (1747) 3 Atk. 576, 577; *Lord Waterpark v. Fennell* (1859) 7 H.L.C. 650; *North Eastern Ry. v. Lord Hastings* [1900] A.C. 260, 269; *L.G. Schuler A.G. v. Wickman Machine Tool Sales Ltd* [1974] A.C. 235, 261, 270 (but see *ibid.* at 252, 261, 269, 272, questions of title to land).

[34] *Duke of Beaufort v. Swansea Corp.* (1849) 3 Exch. 413, 425; *Earl de la Warr v. Miles* (1880) 17 Ch.D. 535, 573; *Neill v. Duke of Devonshire* (1882) 8 App.Cas. 135, 156.

[35] *Doe d. Pearson v. Ries* (1832) 8 Bing. 178, 184; *Chapman v. Bluck* (1838) 4 Bing.N.C. 187; *Van Diemen's Land Co. v. Table Cape Marine Board* [1906] A.C. 92, 96, 98; *Watcham v. Att.-Gen. of East African Protectorate* [1919] A.C. 533.

[36] *Watcham v. Att.-Gen. of East African Protectorate, supra,* at 538. The authority of this case is now extremely fragile: *Gaisberg v. Storr* [1950] 1 K.B. 107, 114; *Sussex Caravan Parks Ltd v. Richardson* [1961] 1 W.L.R. 561, 568; *L.G. Schuler A.G. v. Wickman Machine Tool Sales Ltd* [1974] A.C. 235, 261, 272.

[37] *James Miller & Partners Ltd v. Whitworth Street Estates (Manchester) Ltd* [1970] A.C. 572, 603. See also *ibid.* at 606, 611, 614; *Prenn v. Simmonds* [1971] 1 W.L.R. 1381; *English Industrial Estates Corp. v. George Wimpey & Co. Ltd* [1973] 1 Lloyd's Rep. 118; *Trollope & Colls Ltd v. N.W. Metropolitan Regional Hospital Board* [1973] 1 W.L.R. 601, 611; *L.G. Schuler A.G. v. Wickman Machine Tool Sales Ltd, ante,* at 252, 260, 265–270, 272; *Bushwall Properties Ltd v. Vortex Properties Ltd* [1976] 1 W.L.R. 591, 603; *Arrale v. Costain Civil Engineering Ltd* [1976] 1 Lloyd's Rep. 98; *Harmony Shipping Co. SA v. Saudi-Europe Line Ltd* [1981] 1 Lloyd's Rep. 409, 416; *Haydon v. Lo & Lo* [1997] 1 W.L.R. 198, 205.

[38] *James Miller & Partners Ltd v. Whitworth Street Estates (Manchester) Ltd, supra,* at 615; *L.G. Schuler A.G. v. Wickman Machine Tool Sales Ltd, supra,* at 261; *Liverpool City Council v. Irwin* [1977] A.C. 239, 253; *Wilson v. Maynard Shipbuilding Consultants A.B.* [1978] Q.B. 665; *Todd v. British Midland Airways Ltd* [1978] I.C.R. 959, 964, 967; *Mears v. Safecar Security Ltd* [1983] Q.B. 54, 77. *cf. Port Sudan Cotton Co. v. Govindaswamy Chettiar & Sons* [1977] 2 Lloyd's Rep. 5, 10 (admission); *Amalgamated Investment & Property Co. Ltd v. Texas Commerce International Bank Ltd* [1982] 2 Q.B. 84, 119 (estoppel by convention).

[39] See *ante,* §§ 12–055—12–056.

to the contract upon which the contract is silent.[40] The former is admitted on the ground that "the intention of the parties, though perfectly well known to themselves, would often be defeated if the language were construed according to its ordinary import in the world"[41]; the latter because the parties commonly reduce into writing the special particulars of their agreement, but omit to specify the custom or usage, which is included, however, as of course by mutual understanding: "The contract in truth is partly express and in writing, partly implied or understood and unwritten."[42]

12–126   **Conflict with written instrument.** It has frequently been stated[43] that both of these rules are subject to the qualification that the peculiar sense or incident which it is proposed by the evidence to attach to the terms of the contract must not vary or contradict the terms of the written instrument. But the principle as to whether evidence is admitted to vary a written instrument is perhaps easier to state than to apply, because in a sense any such evidence varies the written agreement. "The contract construed without the custom will be different from what it is if construed with the custom, and in that sense every admission of custom varies the written contract."[44] Yet in interpretation, the custom or usage is being used merely as "a dictionary to explain what words in the contract mean"[45]; in annexing incidents, it is being used to imply a term as to which the contract is silent. Perhaps the best test is still that suggested by Lord Campbell C.J.[46]: "To fall within the exception of repugnancy, the incident must be such as if expressed in the written contract would make it insensible or inconsistent." Nevertheless the distinction is by no means always easy to draw in practice.[47]

12–127   **Requirements.** No custom or usage will be considered by the court on the construction of a contract, unless it is notorious, certain and reasonable[48] and does not offend against the intention of any legislative enactment.[49] The notoriety of a custom or usage is a matter to be proved in evidence; but there are certain usages, which are so well known that judicial notice will be taken of them.[50] Mere trade practice is insufficient.[51]

---

[40] See *post*, §§ 12–129, 12–131, 13–018.

[41] *Brown v. Byrne* (1854) 3 E. & B. 703, 715.

[42] *ibid.*

[43] See, *e.g. Yates v. Pym* (1816) 6 Taunt. 446; *Roberts v. Barker* (1833) 1 Cr. & M. 808; *Cockburn v. Alexander* (1848) 6 C.B. 791; *Spartali v. Benecke* (1850) 10 C.B. 212, 223; *Brown v. Byrne, supra,* at 715; *Re L. Sutro & Co. and Heilbut, Symons & Co.* [1917] 2 K.B. 348; *Westcott v. Hahn* [1918] 1 K.B. 495; *London Export Corp. Ltd v. Jubilee Coffee Roasting Co. Ltd* [1958] 1 W.L.R. 661, 675; *Danowski v. Henry Moore Foundation, The Times,* March 19, 1996. See *post,* § 13–022.

[44] *Produce Brokers Co. Ltd v. Olympia Oil and Cake Co. Ltd* [1917] 1 K.B. 320, 330; *Humfrey v. Dale* (1857) 7 E. & B. 266, 275.

[45] [1917] 1 K.B. 320, 330.

[46] *Humfrey v. Dale, supra,* at 275.

[47] Contrast *Palgrave, Brown & Sons v. SS. Turid* [1922] 1 A.C. 397, with *Smith, Hogg & Co. v. Louis Bamberger & Sons* [1929] 1 K.B. 150.

[48] *Devonald v. Rosser & Sons* [1906] 2 K.B. 728, 743; *Three Rivers Trading Co. v. Gwinear and District Farmers* (1967) 111 S.J. 831. See also the cases cited in § 13–018, *post.*

[49] *Daun v. City of London Brewery Co.* (1869) L.R. 8 Eq. 155, 161.

[50] *George v. Davies* [1911] 2 K.B. 445.

[51] *Cunliffe-Owen v. Teather and Greenwood* [1967] 1 W.L.R. 1421, 1438; *Vitol SA v. Phibro Energy A.G.* [1990] 2 Lloyd's Rep. 84, 90; *Pryke v. Gibbs Hartley Cooper Ltd* [1991] 1 Lloyd's Rep. 602, 615; *Sucre Exports SA v. Northern Shipping Ltd,* [1994] 2 Lloyd's Rep. 266.

Custom to interpret instrument. Evidence of the custom prevailing in a   **12–128**
particular place or locality has therefore been admitted to show that, in Suffolk,
"one thousand" rabbits meant 1,200[52] and what was meant by "regular turns of
loading" according to the usage of the ports of the Tyne.[53] Evidence was also
held to be admissible for the purpose of proving at what time, according to the
custom of the port of Liverpool, a ship chartered to that port with a cargo of
timber, should be deemed to have arrived at her place of discharge within the
meaning of the charterparty[54] and to show, for example, the meaning of "alongside" and "delivery,"[55] "discharge"[56] or "working day"[57] at a particular port.

Custom to annex terms. Terms have also been annexed by custom,[58] a   **12–129**
common case being the "customs of the country" which relate to a tenant's rights
at the end of his tenancy.[59] Evidence of these is admissible.

Usage to interpret instrument. The invariable, certain and general usage of   **12–130**
a particular trade has frequently been admitted to interpret the terms of a written
contract.[60] Thus, where a contract was in these words, "sold eighteen pockets
Kent hops at 100s.," and it appeared that a pocket contained more than a hundred
weight, evidence was admitted to show that by the usage of the trade a contract
so worded was understood to mean £5 per cwt.[61] Where a theatrical manager
contracted with an actress to engage her for "three years" at a certain salary, it
was held that extrinsic evidence might be given to show that, according to the
uniform usage of that profession, the plaintiff was to be paid only during the
theatrical season of each of those years.[62] Evidence of usage has similarly been
admitted to resolve ambiguities.[63]

Usage to annex terms. Usage has also been employed to annex terms to the   **12–131**
contract.[64] So, where goods are sold by sample, evidence of a custom of the trade
as to returning or making an allowance for such of the goods as do not answer
the sample is admissible.[65] In particular, evidence may be adduced to show that
where a broker sells or buys goods without disclosing his principals, he is,
according to the usage of the trade, himself liable as vendor or purchaser.[66]

---

[52] *Smith v. Wilson* (1832) 3 B. & Ad. 728. See *ante*, § 12–056.
[53] *Leidemann v. Schultz* (1853) 14 C.B. 38.
[54] *Norden SS. Co. v. Dempsey* (1876) 1 C.P.D. 654.
[55] *Aktieselskab Helios v. Ekman* (1872) 2 Q.B.D. 83.
[56] *Petersen v. Freebody* [1895] 2 Q.B. 294.
[57] *British and Mexican Shipping Co. Ltd v. Lockett Brothers & Co. Ltd* [1911] 1 K.B. 264; *Reardon Smith Line Ltd v. Ministry of Agriculture, Fisheries and Food* [1963] A.C. 691, 726.
[58] See *post*, § 13–018.
[59] *Hutton v. Warren* (1836) 1 M. & W. 466; *Dashwood v. Magniac* [1891] 3 Ch. 306.
[60] See *ante*, § 12–056.
[61] *Spicer v. Cooper* (1841) 1 Q.B. 424.
[62] *Grant v. Maddox* (1846) 15 M. & W. 737. See also *Hutchinson v. Bowker* (1839) 5 M. & W. 535; *Myers v. Sarl* (1860) 3 E. & E. 306; *Davis v. Temco* [1992] 11 C.L. 208.
[63] *Bold v. Rayner* (1836) 1 M. & W. 343.
[64] *R. v. Inhabitants of Stoke-on-Trent* (1843) 8 Q.B. 303; *Syers v. Jonas* (1848) 2 Exch. 111; *Re Walkers, Winser & Hamm and Shaw, Son & Co.* [1904] 2 K.B. 152; *Produce Brokers Co. Ltd v. Olympic Oil & Cake Co. Ltd* [1916] 1 A.C. 314. See *post*, § 13–018.
[65] *Cooke v. Riddelien* (1844) 1 C. & K. 561.
[66] *Humfrey v. Dale* (1858) E.B. & E. 1004; *Fleet v. Murton* (1871) L.R. 7 Q.B. 126; *Hutchinson v. Thatham* (1873) L.R. 8 C.P. 482; *Pike v. Ongley* (1887) 18 Q.B.D. 708. Contrast *Trueman v. Loder* (1840) 11 A. & E. 589; *Robinson v. Mollett* (1875) L.R. 7 H.L. 802; *Miller, Gibb & Co. v. Smith & Tyrer* [1917] 2 K.B. 141.

CHAPTER 13

IMPLIED TERMS

Nature of implied terms. So far, only express terms have been discussed, **13–001** that is to say, those terms which are actually recorded in a written contract or openly expressed at the time the contract is made. But there are cases in which the law implies a term in a contract although it is not expressly included therein by the parties.

Implication of terms. The problem of the implication of terms is one which **13–002** frequently arises in the law of contract. In certain instances, the parties to a contract may have been content to express only the most important terms of their agreement, leaving the remaining details to be understood. The court will then be asked to imply a term or terms to remedy the deficiency. More often, however, a subsequent disagreement reveals that there are contingencies for which the parties have not provided in their express contract. The question is then whether the court can imply a term to cover the contingency which has unexpectedly emerged.

Terms implied by law. The implication of a term is a matter of law for **13–003** the court,[1] and whether or not a term is implied is usually said to depend upon the intention of the parties as collected from the words of the agreement and the surrounding circumstances.[2] In many classes of contract, however, implied terms have become standardised, and it is somewhat artificial to attribute such terms to the unexpressed intention of the parties. The court is, in fact, laying down a general rule of law that in all contracts of a defined type—for example, sale of goods, landlord and tenant, employment, the carriage of goods by land or sea—certain terms will be implied, unless the implication of such a term would be contrary to the express words of the agreement.[3] Such implications do not depend on the intentions of the parties, actual or presumed, but on more general considerations.[4]

---

[1] *Re Comptoir Commercial Anversois and Power, Son & Co.* [1920] 1 K.B. 868, 899; *O'Brien v. Associated Fire Alarms Ltd* [1968] 1 W.L.R. 1916, 1923, 1925.
[2] *Insurance Co. of Africa v. Scor (U.K.) Reinsurance Co. Ltd* [1983] 1 Lloyd's Rep. 551, 558.
[3] *cf., Johnstone v. Bloomsbury H.A.* [1992] Q.B. 333.
[4] *Lister v. Romford Ice and Cold Storage Co. Ltd* [1957] A.C. 555, 576, 579, 594; *Greaves & Co. (Contractors) Ltd v. Baynham Meikle and Partners* [1975] 1 W.L.R. 1095, 1099, 1100; *Shell U.K. Ltd v. Lostock Garage Ltd* [1976] 1 W.L.R. 1187, 1196; *Liverpool City Council v. Irwin* [1977] A.C. 239, 255, 258; *Scally v. Southern Health and Social Services Board* [1992] 1 A.C. 294, 307; *Ali Shipping Corpn. v. Shipyard Trogir* [1998] 1 Lloyd's Rep. 643, 651; *Mahmud v. Bank of Credit and Commerce International SA* [1998] A.C. 20, 34, 45. Contrast *National Bank of Greece SA v. Pinios Shipping Co.* [1990] 1 A.C. 637; *Reid v. Rush & Tompkins Group plc* [1990] 1 W.L.R. 212, 233; *Industrie Chimiche Italia Centrale and Cerealfin SA v. Alexander G. Tsavliris & Sons Maritime Co.* [1990] 1 Lloyd's Rep. 517, 526; *Ashmore v. Corporation of Lloyd's (No. 2)* [1992] 2 Lloyd's Rep. 620, 631 (one-off or *sui generis* contracts).

13–004   **Intention of parties.** In many cases, however, one or other of the parties will seek to imply a term from the wording of a particular contract and the facts and circumstances surrounding it. The court will be prepared to imply a term if there arises from the language of the contract itself, and the circumstances under which it is entered into, an inference that the parties must have intended the stipulation in question.[5] An implication of this nature may be made in two situations: first, where it is necessary to give business efficacy to the contract, and, secondly, where the term implied represents the obvious, but unexpressed, intention of the parties. These two criteria often overlap[6] and, in many cases, have been applied cumulatively,[7] although it is submitted that they are, in fact, alternative grounds.[8] Both, however, depend on the presumed intention of the parties.

13–005   **Efficacy to contract.** A term will be implied if it is necessary, in the business sense, to give efficacy to the contract. The general principle of law was thus stated by Bowen L.J. in *The Moorcock*[9]:

> "Now, an implied warranty, or, as it is called, a covenant in law, as distinguished from an express contract or express warranty, really is in all cases founded upon the presumed intention of the parties, and upon reason. The implication which the law draws from what must obviously have been the intention of the parties, the law draws with the object of giving efficacy to the transaction and preventing such a failure of consideration as cannot have been within the contemplation of either side; and I believe if one were to take all the cases, and there are many, of implied warranties or covenants in law, it will be found that in all of them the law is raising an implication from the presumed intention of the parties with the object of giving to the transaction such efficacy as both parties must have intended that at all events it should have."

In this situation, although there is an apparently complete bargain, the courts are willing to add a term on the ground that without it the contract will not work.[10]

13–006   The principle laid down in *The Moorcock* has been approved and applied many times. For example, a term has been implied into a contract for the use of a wharf

---

[5] *Hamlyn & Co. v. Wood & Co.* [1891] 2 Q.B. 488, 494.

[6] See, *e.g. Alpha Trading Ltd v. Dunnshaw-Patten Ltd* [1981] 1 Lloyd's Rep. 122, 128, 131.

[7] *e.g.* by Scrutton L.J. in *Reigate v. Union Manufacturing Co. (Ramsbottom) Ltd* [1918] 1 K.B. 592, 598, by Lord Tucker in *Lister v. Romford Ice and Cold Storage Co. Ltd* [1957] A.C. 555, 594, and by Lord Cross in *Liverpool City Council v. Irwin* [1977] A.C. 239, 258. See also *B.P. Refinery (Westenport) Pty. Ltd v. Shire of Hastings* (1977) 52 A.L.J.R. 20, 26, PC; *Codelfa Construction Pty. Ltd v. State Railway Authority of New South Wales* (1982) 149 C.L.R. 337, 347 (High Ct. of Australia).

[8] *Mosvolds Rederi A/S v. Food Corpn. of India* [1986] 2 Lloyd's Rep. 68; *Associated Japanese Bank (International) Ltd v. Crédit du Nord SA* [1989] 1 W.L.R. 255, 263; *Barclays Bank plc v. Taylor* [1989] 1 W.L.R. 1066, 1076; *Marcan Shipping (London) Ltd v. Polish Steamship Co.* [1989] 2 Lloyd's Rep. 138, 144; *Lauritzen (J.) A/S v. Wijsmuller B.V.* [1990] 1 Lloyd's Rep. 1, 6; *Industrie Chimiche Italia Centrale and Cerealfin SA v. Alexander Tsavliris & Sons Maritime Co. (The Choko Star)* [1990] 1 Lloyd's Rep. 517, 524, 526; *Ashmore v. Corporation of Lloyds (No. 2)* [1992] 2 Lloyd's Rep. 620, 627; *Aspden v. Webbs Poultry & Meat Group (Holdings) Ltd* [1996] I.R.L.R. 521.

[9] (1889) 14 P.D. 64, 68.

[10] *Liverpool City Council v. Irwin* [1977] A.C. 239, 254, 262; *Tai Hing Cotton Mill Ltd v. Liu Chong Hing Bank Ltd* [1986] A.C. 80, 106.

that it was safe for a ship to lie at the wharf[11]; into a contract for a Turkish bath that the couches for reclining on were free from vermin[12]; into a charterparty that the charterer would not order the ship to proceed to a port impossible of access[13] and would indemnify the shipowner against loss incurred in complying with the charterer's orders[14]; into a contract of bailment, the purpose of which was the use of the goods by the bailee, an authority to do in relation to the goods all things reasonably incidental to their reasonable use[15]; into a contract for the printing of banknotes that the plates should not be allowed to get into the hands of unauthorised persons[16]; into a father's contract to pay such school bills of his son as should be approved by him, that such consent should not be unreasonably withheld[17]; into a contract between a "pop group" and their personal manager, that the latter would not do anything which he could reasonably foresee would destroy the mutual confidence which was required to exist between them[18]; into a contract to provide a package holiday that reasonable care and skill would be used in rendering the services which the tour operator had contracted to provide, whether these were carried out by the tour organiser or others[19]; into a contract for driving lessons that the vehicle provided would be covered by insurance[20]; and into a contract of agency that the principal would not deprive the agent of his commission by committing a breach of the contract between himself and a purchaser which released the purchaser from his obligation to pay the purchase price.[21]

Obvious inference from agreement. A term which has not been expressed **13–007** may also be implied if it was so obviously a stipulation in the agreement that the parties must have intended it to form part of their contract.[22] "Prima facie that which in any contract is left to be implied and need not be expressed is something so obvious that it goes without saying; so that, if while the parties were making their bargain, an officious bystander were to suggest some express provision for it in the agreement, they would testily suppress him with a common, "oh, of course.' "[23] A term will not, however, thus be implied unless the court is satisfied that *both* parties would, as reasonable men, have agreed to it had it been

---

[11] *The Moorcock* (1889) 14 P.D. 64.

[12] *Silverman v. Imperial London Hotels Ltd* (1927) 137 L.T. 57.

[13] *Aktieselskabet Olivebank v. Dansk Svolsyre Fabrik* [1919] 2 K.B. 162. Contrast *Eurico Spa v. Philipp Brothers* [1987] 2 Lloyd's Rep. 215.

[14] *Triad Shipping Co. v. Stellar Chartering & Brokerage Inc.* [1994] 2 Lloyd's Rep. 227.

[15] *Tappenden v. Artus* [1964] 2 Q.B. 185.

[16] *Banco de Portugal v. Waterlow & Sons Ltd* [1932] A.C. 452.

[17] *Addison v. Brown* [1954] 1 W.L.R. 779.

[18] *Page One Records Ltd v. Britton* [1968] 1 W.L.R. 157; *Denmark Productions Ltd v. Boscobel Productions Ltd* [1969] 1 Q.B. 699.

[19] *Wong Mee Wan v. Kwan Kin Travel Services* [1996] 1 W.L.R. 38; see also *post*, § 13–033.

[20] *British School of Motoring Ltd v. Simms* [1971] 1 All E.R. 317.

[21] *Alpha Trading Ltd v. Dunnshaw-Patten Ltd* [1981] 1 Lloyd's Rep. 122. But see *Marcan Shipping (London) Ltd v. Polish Steamship Co.* [1989] 2 Lloyd's Rep. 138, and Vol. II, § 32–136.

[22] *Reigate v. Union Manufacturing Co. (Ramsbottom) Ltd* [1918] 1 K.B. 592, 605; *Weg Motors Ltd v. Hales* [1961] Ch. 176, 192; *Bronester Ltd v. Priddle* [1961] 1 W.L.R. 1294, 1304; *Hongkong Fir Shipping Co. Ltd v. Kawasaki Kisen Kaisha Ltd* [1962] 2 Q.B. 26, 69; *Gardiner v. Moore* [1969] 1 Q.B. 55, 61; *Alpha Trading Ltd v. Dunnshaw-Patten Ltd* [1981] 1 Lloyd's Rep. 122, 128; *K/S Stamar v. Seabow Shipping Ltd* [1994] 2 Lloyd's Rep. 183, 191; *Fletamentos Maritimos SA v. Effjohn International BV* [1995] 1 Lloyd's Rep. 311, 345; *Cargill International SA v. Bangladesh Sugar & Food Industries Corpn.* [1996] 2 Lloyd's Rep. 524, 531.

[23] *Shirlaw v. Southern Foundries (1926) Ltd* [1939] 2 K.B. 206, 227 (affd. [1940] A.C. 701).

suggested to them.[24] The knowledge or ignorance of each party of the matter to be implied, or of the facts on which the implication is based, is therefore a relevant factor.[25] Further, since "the general presumption is that the parties have expressed every material term which they intended should govern their contract, whether oral or in writing,"[26] the court will only imply a term if it is one which must necessarily have been intended by them,[27] and in particular will be reluctant to make any implication "where the parties have entered into a carefully drafted written contract containing detailed terms agreed between them."[28]

13–008   **Incomplete contract.** There is yet another situation where a term may be implied. This is where the court is simply concerned to establish what the contract is, the parties not having themselves fully stated the terms. "In this sense the court is searching for what must be implied."[29] In *Liverpool City Council v. Irwin*[30] the contract by which dwelling units in a Council block were let to tenants consisted of "conditions of tenancy" which imposed obligations upon the tenants, but which were silent as to the contractual obligations of the landlord. The House of Lords implied an obligation on the part of the landlord to take reasonable care to keep the essential means of access and other communal facilities in reasonable repair. In *Sim v. Rotherham Metropolitan Borough Council*[31] the contracts under which secondary school teachers were employed were in general silent as to the extent of the teachers' obligations as teachers. The court implied an obligation on their part to cover for absent colleagues during non-teaching periods if requested to do so. And in *Scally v. Southern Health and Social Services Board*[32] contracts of employment of public health service employees contained a term, derived from a collective agreement reached between representatives of the employers and of the employees, whereby a valuable pension benefit was conferred upon an employee contingent upon action being taken by him to avail himself of the benefit. An employee could not, in all the circumstances, reasonably be expected to be aware of the term unless it was

---

[24] *Luxor (Eastbourne) Ltd v. Cooper*; [1941] A.C. 108; *Attica Sea Carriers Corpn. v. Ferrostaal Poseidon Bulk Rederei GmbH* [1976] 1 Lloyd's Rep. 250; *Liverpool City Council v. Irwin* [1977] A.C. 239, 258, 266; *Federal Commerce and Navigation Co. Ltd v. Tradax Export SA* [1977] 1 Lloyd's Rep. 217, 229 (affd. [1977] 2 Lloyd's Rep. 301, 309); *Frobisher (Second Investments) Ltd v. Kiloran Trust Co. Ltd* [1980] 1 W.L.R. 425. *cf.* the misgivings felt by May L.J. in *Marcan Shipping (London) Ltd v. Polish Steamship Co.* [1989] 2 Lloyd's Rep. 138, 142.

[25] *The Moorcock* (1889) 14 P.D. 64, 68; *Partabmull Rameshwar v. K.C. Sethia (1944) Ltd* [1950] 1 All E.R. 55 (affd. [1951] 2 All E.R. 352n); *Spring v. National Amalgamated Stevedores and Dockers Socy.* [1956] 1 W.L.R. 585; *Compagnie Algerienne de Meunerie v. Katana Societa di Navigatione Marittima SpA* [1960] 2 Q.B. 115; *Jamil Line for Trading and Shipping Ltd v. Atlanta Handelsgesellschaft Harder & Co.* [1982] 1 Lloyd's Rep. 481.

[26] *Luxor (Eastbourne) Ltd v. Cooper* [1941] A.C. 108, 137; *Kelly v. Battershell* [1949] 2 All E.R. 830.

[27] *L. French & Co. v. Leeston Shipping Co.* [1922] 1 A.C. 451, 455; *Trollope & Colls Ltd v. N.W. Metropolitan Regional Hospital Board* [1973] 1 W.L.R. 601, 609; *Liverpool City Council v. Irwin* [1977] A.C. 239; *Federal Commerce and Navigation Co. Ltd v. Tradax Export SA* [1977] 1 Lloyd's Rep. 217, 228–229 (affd. [1977] 2 Lloyd's Rep. 301, 309).

[28] *Jones v. St. John's College, Oxford* (1970) L.R. 6 Q.B. 115, 126; *Lynch v. Thorne* [1956] 1 W.L.R. 303; *Shell U.K. Ltd v. Lostock Garage Ltd* [1976] 1 W.L.R. 1187, 1200; *J. Lauritzen A/S v. Wijsmuller B.V.* [1990] 1 Lloyd's Rep. 1, 6; *Flamar Interocean Ltd v. Denmac Ltd* [1990] 1 Lloyd's Rep. 434, 437.

[29] *Liverpool City Council v. Irwin* [1977] A.C. 239, 254.

[30] [1977] A.C. 239.

[31] [1987] Ch. 216.

[32] [1992] 1 A.C. 294.

drawn to his attention. The House of Lords implied an obligation on the employer to take reasonable steps to bring the term in question to the employee's attention so that he might be in a position to enjoy the benefit. In this type of case, the implication does not appear so much to depend on the intentions of the parties, but resembles more closely an implication of law,[33] since the term is implied as a "legal incident"[34] of a definable category of contract, though only where certain circumstances exist.

Where term not implied. A term ought not to be implied unless it is in all the   **13–009** circumstances equitable and reasonable.[35] But this does not mean that a term will be implied merely because in all the circumstances it would be reasonable to do so[36] or because it would improve the contract[37] or make its carrying out more convenient.[38] "The touchstone is always *necessity* and not merely *reasonableness*."[39] The term to be implied must also be capable of being formulated with sufficient clarity and precision.[40] But it may be that lack of precision in the criterion to be embodied in the term is not fatal to any implication, since "it is no novelty in the common law to find that a criterion on which some important question of liability is to depend can only be defined in imprecise terms which leave a difficult question for decision as to how the criterion applies to the facts of a particular case."[41] A term will not be implied if it would be inconsistent with the express wording of the contract.[42]

---

[33] But it is still subject to the test of necessity; *Liverpool City Council v. Irwin, supra*, at 254, 262, 266; *Scally v. Southern Health and Social Services Board* [1992] 1 A.C. 294.

[34] *Liverpool City Council v. Irwin, supra*, at 255, 270.

[35] *Young & Marten v. McManus Childs Ltd* [1969] 1 A.C. 454, 465; *Liverpool City Council v. Irwin, supra*, at 262; *BP Refinery (Westenport) Pty. Ltd v. Shire of Hastings* (1977) 52 A.L.J.R. 20, 26, PC.

[36] *Hamlyn & Co. v. Wood & Co.* [1891] 2 Q.B. 488, 491; *Reigate v. Union Manufacturing Co. (Ramsbottom) Ltd* [1918] 1 K.B. 592, 598; *Re Comptoir Commercial Anversois v. Power, Son and Co.* [1920] 1 K.B. 868, 899; *George Trollope & Son v. Martyn Brothers* [1934] 2 K.B. 437, 443; *R. v. Paddington and St. Marylebone Rent Tribunal* [1947] K.B. 984, 990; *British Movietonews v. London and District Cinemas Ltd* [1952] A.C. 166; *Bundar Property Holdings Ltd v. J. S. Darwen (Successors) Ltd* [1968] 2 All E.R. 305; *Lupton v. Potts* [1969] 1 W.L.R. 1749; *Trollope & Colls Ltd v. N.W. Metropolitan Regional Hospital Board* [1973] 1 W.L.R. 601; *Liverpool City Council v. Irwin, supra*; *Duke of Westminster v. Guild* [1985] Q.B. 688.

[37] *Trollope & Colls Ltd v. N.W. Metropolitan Regional Hospital Board, supra*, at 609; *Express Newspapers v. Silverstone Circuits, The Independent*, June 16, 1989, CA.

[38] *Russell v. Duke of Norfolk* [1949] 1 All E.R. 109.

[39] *Liverpool City Council v. Irwin, supra*, at 266; *BP Refinery (Westenport) Pty. Ltd v. Shire of Hastings, supra*, at 26; *Harmony Shipping Co. SA v. Saudi Europe Line Ltd* [1980] 1 Lloyd's Rep. 44; *Tai Hing Cotton Mill Ltd v. Liu Chong Hing Bank Ltd* [1986] A.C. 80, 104; *Scally v. Southern Health and Social Services Board* [1992] 1 A.C. 294.

[40] *Shell U.K. Ltd v. Lostock Garage Ltd* [1976] 1 W.L.R. 1187, 1197, 1201. See also *R. v. Paddington and St. Marylebone Rent Tribunal* [1947] K.B. 984, 990; *Lister v. Romford Ice and Cold Storage Co. Ltd* [1957] A.C. 555, 574; *Trollope & Colls Ltd v. N.W. Metropolitan Regional Hospital Board, supra*, at 610, 614; *BP Refinery (Westenport) Pty. Ltd v. Shire of Hastings, supra*, at 26; *Terkol Rederierne v. Petroleo Brasilero SA* [1985] 1 Lloyd's Rep. 395, 401; *Ashmore v. Corporation of Lloyds (No. 2)* [1992] 2 Lloyd's Rep. 620, 628.

[41] *Shell U.K. Ltd v. Lostock Garage Ltd, supra*, at 1204.

[42] *BP Refinery (Westenport) Pty. Ltd v. Shire of Hastings, supra*, at 26; *Duke of Westminster v. Guild* [1985] Q.B. 688, 700; *Eurico Spa v. Philipp Brothers* [1987] 2 Lloyd's Rep. 215, 219; *Gyllenhammar & Partners International Ltd v. Sour Brodogradevna Industrija* [1989] 2 Lloyd's Rep. 403, 415; *Yorkshire Water Services Ltd v. Sun Alliance & London Insurance plc* [1997] 2 Lloyd's Rep. 21, 33.

13–010   No term was implied into a contract of employment that the employee was to be paid overtime for excess hours worked[43] or that he was not to be paid during absence owing to illness[44]; into a contract for the hire of a private detective that employees of the detective agency would not divulge confidential information[45]; into a contract for the sale and purchase of all grains manufactured over a certain period that the seller would retain his business[46]; into a contract of employment that the employer would take reasonable care to ensure that his employee's effects were not stolen[47] or that he would insure the employee when abroad against accidental injury or advise the employee to obtain such insurance for himself[48]; into a contract for the sale of a patent to a company that the company would keep the patent alive[49]; into a contract for the exchange of two incomplete housing estates that the building work was of good quality[50]; into a contract for the building of a school that the builder should have uninterrupted possession of, and access to, the site[51]; into a lease that the lessor would keep a drain in repair[52]; into a contract for the services of a handwriting expert that he should not voluntarily give assistance to the other side[53]; into a voyage charterparty that the charterers would indemnify the shipowners against claims made by the cargo-owners[54]; into a contract for the carriage of goods by sea that the master was authorised to contract on behalf of the cargo-owners with third parties other than as agent of necessity[55]; into a contract between banker and customer that the customer would take reasonable precautions in his business to prevent forgeries by his employees[56] or that the banker would advise the customer of a new type of interest-bearing account[56a]; into a debenture that the debenture holder could appoint a receiver if his security was in jeopardy[57]; into a contract of insurance that the insurers would indemnify the insured in respect of expenditure incurred by him in preventing or minimising a loss which might fall to them under the policy[58]; into a contract between insurers and the assignee of the policy to inform him that the insured was dishonestly jeopardising the cover provided by the insurers[59]; into a contract between insurers and a reinsurer that they could recover a pro rata share of their costs of investigating, settling or defending

---

[43] *Ali v. Christian Salvesen Food Services Ltd* [1997] 1 All E.R. 721.
[44] *Orman v. Saville Sportswear Ltd* [1960] 1 W.L.R. 1055.
[45] *Easton v. Hitchcock* [1912] 1 K.B. 535.
[46] *Hamlyn & Co. v. Wood* [1891] 2 Q.B. 488. See also *Rhodes v. Forwood* (1876) 1 App.Cas. 256; But see Vol. II, § 32–145.
[47] *Deyong v. Shenburn* [1946] K.B. 277; *Edwards v. West Herts Group Hospital Committee* [1957] 1 W.L.R. 415.
[48] *Reid v. Rush & Tompkins Group plc* [1990] 1 W.L.R. 212; *cf.* Employers' Liability (Compulsory Insurance) Act 1969; Vol. II, § 41–086.
[49] *Re Railway and Electric Appliances Co.* (1888) 38 Ch.D. 597.
[50] *Barratt Southampton Ltd v. Fairclough Building Ltd* (1988) 27 Const.L.R. 623.
[51] *Porter v. Tottenham U.D.C.* [1915] 1 K.B. 776.
[52] *Duke of Westminster v. Guild* [1985] Q.B. 688.
[53] *Harmony Shipping Co. SA v. Saudi Europe Line Ltd* [1980] 1 Lloyd's Rep. 44.
[54] *Ben Shipping Co. (Pte.) Ltd v. An-Board Bainne* [1986] 2 Lloyd's Rep. 285.
[55] *Industrie Chimiche Italia Centrale and Cerealfin SA v. Alexander G. Tsavliris & Sons Maritime Co.* [1990] 1 W.L.R. 576.
[56] *Tai Hing Cotton Mill Ltd v. Liu Chong Hing Bank Ltd* [1986] A.C. 80.
[56a] *Suriya & Douglas v. Midland Bank plc, The Times,* March 29, 1999.
[57] *Cryne v. Barclays Bank* [1987] B.C.L.C. 548, CA.
[58] *Yorkshire Water Services Ltd v. Sun Alliance and London Insurance plc* [1997] 2 Lloyd's Rep. 21.
[59] *Bank of Nova Scotia v. Hellenic Mutual War Risks Assn. (Bermuda) Ltd* [1990] 1 Q.B. 818 (revd. on other grounds [1992] 1 A.C. 283).

claims on the underlying policies[60]; and into an agreement to submit disputes to arbitration that the claimant would proceed with the arbitration without undue delay.[61]

Co-operation. The court may be willing to imply a term that the parties shall **13–011** co-operate to ensure the performance of their bargain.[62] Thus "where in a written contract it appears that both parties have agreed that something shall be done, which cannot effectively be done unless both concur in doing it, the construction of the contract is that each agrees to do all that is necessary to be done on his part for the carrying out of that thing, though there may be no express words to that effect."[63] However, the conditions for the implication of a term mentioned above must be satisfied.[64] Also the duty to co-operate and the degree of co-operation required is to be determined, not by what is reasonable, but by the obligations imposed—whether expressly or impliedly—upon each party by the agreement itself, and the surrounding circumstances.[65]

Prevention of performance. By the same token, "if a party enters into an **13–012** arrangement which can only take effect by the continuance of a certain existing state of circumstances, there is an implied engagement on his part that he shall do nothing of his own motion to put an end to that state of circumstances under which alone the arrangement can become operative."[66] Also where a binding contract is subject to a condition precedent,[67] a term may be implied that a party

---

[60] *Baker v. Black Sea & Baltic General Insurance Co. Ltd* [1998] 1 W.L.R. 974.

[61] *Bremer Vulkan Schiffbau und Maschinenfabrik v. South India Shipping Cpn. Ltd* [1981] A.C. 909.

[62] See Bateson [1960] J.B.L. 187; Burrows (1968) 31 M.L.R. 390, 402.

[63] *Mackay v. Dick* (1881) 6 App.Cas. 251, 263. See also *Hunt v. Bishop* (1853) 8 Exch. 675; *Roberts v. Bury Commissioners* (1870) L.R. 5 C.P. 310, 325; *Nelson v. Dahl* (1879) 12 Ch.D. 568, 592 (affd. (1881) 6 App.Cas. 38); *Sprague v. Booth* [1909] A.C. 576, 580; *Kleinert v. Abosso Gold Mining Co.* (1913) 58 S.J. (PC) 45; *Harrison v. Walker* [1919] 2 K.B. 453; *Colley v. Overseas Exporters* [1921] 3 K.B. 302, 309; *Panamena Europa Navegacion v. Frederick Leyland & Co. Ltd* [1947] A.C. 428, 436; *Luxor (Eastbourne) Ltd v. Cooper* [1941] A.C. 108, 118; *A. V. Pound & Co. Ltd v. M. W. Hardy & Co. Inc.* [1956] A.C. 588, 608, 611; *Sociedad Financiera de Bienes Raices v. Agrimpex* [1961] A.C. 135; *Sunbeam Shipping Co. Ltd v. President of India* [1973] 1 Lloyd's Rep. 482, 486; *Schindler v. Pigault* [1975] 1 C.L. 401; *Metro Meat Ltd v. Fares Rural Co. Pty. Ltd* [1985] 2 Lloyd's Rep. 13, 14; *Merton London B.C. v. Hugh Leach Ltd* (1985) 32 Build.L.R. 51; *Kurt A. Becher GmbH & Co. K.G. v. Roplak Enterprises SA* [1991] 2 Lloyd's Rep. 23, 30, 34; *Davy Offshore Ltd v. Emerald Field Contracting Ltd* (1991) 27 Const.L.R. 138; *Nissho Iwai Petroleum Inc. v. Cargill International SA* [1993] 1 Lloyd's Rep. 80, 84. See also *post*, § 25–031, Vol. II, § 37–068.

[64] *Siporex Trade SA v. Banque Indosuez* [1986] 2 Lloyd's Rep. 146, 161; *North Sea Energy Holdings NV v. Petroleum Authority of Thailand* [1997] 2 Lloyd's Rep. 418.

[65] *Mackay v. Dick, supra*, at 263; *Mona Oil Equipment and Supply Co. Ltd v. Rhodesia Rys. Ltd* [1949] 2 All E.R. 1014; *Hargreaves Transport Ltd v. Lynch* [1969] 1 W.L.R. 215; *Liverpool City Council v. Irwin* [1977] A.C. 239; *Kurt A. Becher GmbH & Co. K.G. v. Roplak Enterprises SA (The World Navigator), supra*, at 30, 31, 34; *North Sea Energy Holdings NV v. Petroleum Authority of Thailand* [1999] 1 Lloyd's Rep. 482, 492.

[66] *Stirling v. Maitland* (1864) 5 B. & S. 840, 852. See also *Rhodes v. Forwood* (1876) 1 App.Cas. 256, 272, 274; *Turner v. Goldsmith* [1891] 1 Q.B. 544; *Ogdens Ltd v. Nelson* [1905] A.C. 109; *Warren v. Agdeshman* (1922) 38 T.L.R. 588; *C. French & Co. Ltd v. Leeston Shipping Co. Ltd* [1922] 1 A.C. 451; *Southern Foundries (1926) Ltd v. Shirlaw* [1940] A.C. 701; *William Cory & Son Ltd v. City of London Corpn.* [1951] 2 K.B. 476, 484; *A. Hamson & Son (London) Ltd v. S. Martin Johnson & Co. Ltd* [1953] 1 Lloyd's Rep. 553; *Shindler v. Northern Raincoat Ltd* [1960] 1 W.L.R. 1038; *The Unique Mariner (No. 2)* [1979] 1 Lloyd's Rep. 37; *Merton L.B.C. v. Hugh Leach Ltd* (1985) 32 Build.L.R. 51. See also Bateson [1960] J.B.L. 187; Burrows (1968) 31 M.L.R. 390; Vol. II, § 37–067.

[67] See *ante*, § 12–028.

will not do an act which, if done, would prevent fulfilment of the condition.[68] But these implications are not inevitable: the alleged term may be unreasonably wide[69] or the nature of the contract may indicate otherwise.[70] A term may also be implied that a right, remedy or benefit expressly conferred upon one party to a contract or to which he may be entitled shall not be available if that party relies on his own breach of the contract, to establish his claim.[71]

13–013   **Export and import licences.** In international trade, contracts of sale of goods are frequently the subject of governmental restrictions and a licence may have to be obtained for the import or export of goods from one country to another. The parties will normally provide expressly who is to assume this responsibility, but, in the absence of any express provision, it will be necessary to imply a term as to whether the duty to obtain a licence rests upon the buyer or the seller.[72] Once the incidence of this duty has been determined, the court will then have to consider whether the party placed under the duty impliedly undertook to use his best endeavours to obtain a licence[73] or whether he undertook absolutely that a licence would be obtained.[74] In any event, both parties are under an obligation to co-operate with each other to the extent that is necessary for the obtaining of a licence.[75]

13–014   **Occupiers of premises.** Where persons enter or use, or bring or send goods to, any premises in exercise of a right conferred by contract with a person occupying or having control of the premises, the duty he owes them in respect of

---

[68] *Inchbald v. Western Neilgherry Coffee, etc., Co.* (1864) 17 C.B.(N.S.) 733; *Roberts v. Bury Improvements Commrs.* (1870) L.R. 5 C.P. 310, 316; *Mackay v. Dick* (1881) 6 App.Cas. 251; *Barque Quilpué Ltd v. Brown* [1904] 2 K.B. 264, 271; *Hickman & Co. v. Roberts* [1913] A.C. 229; *Trollope v. Martyn* [1934] 2 K.B. 436; *Amalgamated Building Contractors Ltd v. Waltham Holy Cross U.D.C.* [1952] 2 All E.R. 452, 455; *Jebco Properties v. Mastforce* [1992] N.P.C. 42; *Nissho Iwai Petroleum Co. Inc. v. Cargill International SA* [1993] 1 Lloyd's Rep. 80. See also *post*, § 25–031.

[69] *Philips Electronique Grand Public SA v. British Sky Broadcasting Ltd* [1995] E.M.L.R. 472.

[70] *Aspdin v. Austin* (1844) 5 Q.B. 671; *European, etc., Mail Co. v. Royal Mail Steam Packet Co.* (1861) 30 L.J.C.P. 247; *Rhodes v. Forwood, supra; Hamlyn v. Wood* [1891] 2 Q.B. 488; *Luxor (Eastbourne) Ltd v. Cooper* [1941] A.C. 108; *William Cory & Son Ltd v. City of London Corpn., supra; Farr v. Admiralty* [1953] 1 W.L.R. 565; *Thompson v. Asda-MFI Group plc* [1988] Ch. 241; *Davy Offshore Ltd v. Emerald Field Contracting Ltd* (1991) 27 Const.L.R. 138; *Philips Electronique Grand Public SA v. British Sky Broadcasting Ltd, supra;* see Vol. II, § 32–136.

[71] See *ante*, § 12–086. *cf. Richco International Ltd v. Alfred C. Toepfer International GmbH* [1991] 1 Lloyd's Rep. 136, 144; *Bulk Shipping A.G. v. Ipco Trading SA* [1992] 1 Lloyd's Rep. 39, 43.

[72] *H.O. Brandt & Co. v. H.N. Morris & Co.* [1917] 2 K.B. 784; *J.W. Taylor & Co. v. Landauer & Co.* [1940] 4 All E.R. 335; *Mitchell Cotts & Co. (Middle East) Ltd v. Hairco Ltd* [1943] 2 All E.R. 552; *A.V. Pound & Co. Ltd v. M.W. Hardy & Co. Inc.* [1956] A.C. 588; *Congimex Companhia Geral, etc., SARL v. Tradax Export SA* [1983] 1 Lloyd's Rep. 250. See *Benjamin's Sale of Goods* (5th ed., 1997), §§ 18–248—18–250.

[73] *Re Anglo-Russian Merchant Traders Ltd and John Batt & Co. (London) Ltd* [1917] 2 K.B. 679; *Brauer & Co. (G.B.) Ltd v. James Clark (Brush Materials) Ltd* [1952] 2 All E.R. 497. See also *Windschuegl Ltd v. Pickering & Co. Ltd* (1950) 84 Lloyd's Rep. 89, 93; *Société D'Avances Commerciales (London) Ltd v. A. Besse & Co. (London) Ltd* [1952] 1 T.L.R. 644, 646; *Compagnie Algerienne de Meunerie v. Katana Societa de Navigatione Marittima SpA* [1959] 1 Q.B. 527; *Provimi Hellas A.E. v. Warinco A.G.* [1978] 1 Lloyd's Rep. 373; *Coloniale Import-Export v. Loumidis Sons* [1978] 2 Lloyd's Rep. 560, 562; *Benjamin's Sale of Goods* (5th ed., 1997), §§ 18–252—18–261.

[74] *Mitchell Cotts & Co. (Middle East) Ltd v. Hairco Ltd, supra; Partabmull Rameshwar v. Sethia (K.C.) (1944) Ltd* [1950] 1 All E.R. 51 (affd. [1951] 2 All E.R. 352n.); *Peter Cassidy Seed Co. Ltd v. Osuustukkukauppa I.L.* [1957] 1 W.L.R. 273; *Congimex Companhia Geral, etc., SARL v. Tradax Export SA, supra.*

[75] *A.V. Pound & Co. Ltd v. M.W. Hardy & Co. Inc., supra,* at 608, 611; *Kyprianou v. Cyprus Textiles Ltd* [1958] 2 Lloyd's Rep. 60.

dangers due to the state of the premises or to things done or omitted to be done on them in so far as the duty depends on a term to be implied in the contract by reason of its conferring that right, is the "common duty of care."[76] The common duty of care is a duty to take such care as in all the circumstances of the case is reasonable to see that the visitor will be reasonably safe in using the premises for the purposes for which he is invited or permitted by the occupier to be there,[77] except in so far as the occupier is free to[78] and does extend, restrict modify or exclude that duty by agreement or otherwise.[79] However, the duty cannot be restricted or excluded by the contract so as to diminish the rights of third parties who are entitled to enter by virtue of its provisions.[80] The same duty applies in relation to fixed and movable structures as it does to premises[81] but does not extend to the obligations imposed by any contract for the hire of, or for the carriage for reward of persons or goods in, any means of transport, or by any contract of bailment.[82]

Fitness for habitation: sale of land. It is well established that prima facie **13–015** upon a contract for sale of a piece of land with a house on it, there is no warranty as to the habitability of the house.[83] The same rule would apply in the case of an uncompleted house, which is the subject-matter of a sale, where the structure stands at the time of the sale. But where the vendor sells a piece of land and covenants to build or complete a house on it, there is, at common law, an implied term (i) that the work will be done in a good and workmanlike manner, (ii) that he will supply good and proper materials, and (iii) that the house will be reasonably fit for human habitation when built or completed.[84] This implication may, however, be rebutted where the purchaser has himself expressly prescribed the way in which the work is to be done, and the work has been completed in accordance with his instructions.[85] The Defective Premises Act 1972[86] in addition, imposes on every person who takes on work for or in connection with the provision of a dwelling a similar statutory duty[87] (which cannot be excluded or restricted by any term of an agreement), subject to certain exceptions provided for in the Act. This statutory duty is owed to any person to whose order the dwelling is provided and also to every person who acquires an interest (whether legal or equitable) in the dwelling.[88]

---

[76] Occupiers' Liability Act 1957, s.5(1), superseding the rule in *Francis v. Cockrell* (1870) L.R. 5 Q.B. 501.

[77] *ibid.* s.2(2).

[78] See the Unfair Contract Terms Act 1977, ss.1, 2, 3 (*post*) and *Monarch Airlines Ltd v. London Luton Airport Ltd* [1998] 1 Lloyd's Rep. 403.

[79] Occupiers' Liability Act 1957, s.2(1). See also *Ashdown v. Samuel Williams & Sons Ltd* [1957] 1 Q.B. 409; *White v. Blackmore* [1972] 2 Q.B. 651 (notices).

[80] *ibid.* s.3(1)–(4).

[81] *ibid.* s.5(2).

[82] *ibid.* s.5(3).

[83] *Hoskins v. Woodham* [1938] 1 All E.R. 692; *Lynch v. Thorne* [1956] 1 W.L.R. 303, 305.

[84] *Lawrence v. Cassell* [1930] 2 K.B. 83; *Miller v. Cannon Hill Estates Ltd* [1931] 2 K.B. 113; *Jennings v. Taverner* [1955] 1 W.L.R. 932; *Hancock v. B.W. Brazier (Anerley) Ltd* [1966] 1 W.L.R. 1317; *Billyack v. Leyland Construction Co. Ltd* [1968] 1 W.L.R. 471; *King v. Victor Parsons & Co.* [1972] 1 W.L.R. 801. See also *post*, § 13–028 and Vol. II, § 37–072.

[85] *Perry v. Sharon Development Co. Ltd* [1937] 4 All E.R. 390, 394; *Lynch v. Thorne, supra; cf. King v. Victor Parsons & Co., supra.*

[86] ss.1, 2, 6. See also s.3 and Vol. II, § 37–075.

[87] *Alexander v. Mercouris* [1979] 1 W.L.R. 1270; *Andrews v. Schooling* [1991] 1 W.L.R. 783.

[88] s.1.

13–016   **Fitness for habitation: leases.** In general, a landlord gives no implied under-taking that leased premises are or will be fit for habitation or for any particular use,[89] or that the premises can lawfully be used for any particular purpose.[90] But where a house or flat is let furnished, there is an implied covenant or warranty that it is reasonably fit for human habitation when let,[91] although there is no obligation at common law to keep furnished or unfurnished premises in that condition or to repair them during the tenancy.[92] However, covenants on the part of the landlord are implied in the cases of houses let at a low rent[93] or for a short term.[94]

13–017   **Buildings in multiple occupation.** Where an essential means of access to units in a building in multiple occupation is retained by the landlord, a covenant may be implied on his part to use reasonable care to keep the essential means of access in reasonable repair and fit for use.[95]

13–018   **When implied from usage or custom.** If there is an invariable, certain and general usage or custom of any particular trade or place, the law will imply on the part of one who contracts or employs another to contract for him upon a matter to which such usage or custom has reference a promise for the benefit of the other party in conformity with such usage or custom[96]; provided there is no inconsistency between the usage and the terms of the contract.[97] To be binding, however, the usage must be notorious, certain and reasonable, and not contrary to law[98]; and it must also be something more than a mere trade practice.[99] But when such usage is proved, it will form the basis of the contract between the

---

[89] *Hart v. Windsor* (1843) 12 M. & W. 68; *Sutton v. Temple* (1843) 12 M. & W. 52; *Robbins v. Jones* (1863) 12 M. & W. 68, 87; *Manchester Bonded Warehouse Co. Ltd v. Carr* (1880) 5 C.P.D. 507; *Bottomley v. Bannister* [1932] 1 K.B. 458, 468. Contrast *Western Electric Ltd v. Welsh Development Agency* [1983] Q.B. 796 (licence).

[90] *Edler v. Auerbach* [1950] 1 K.B. 359; *Hills v. Harris* [1965] 2 Q.B. 601.

[91] *Smith v. Marrable* (1843) 11 M. & W. 5; *Collins v. Hopkins* [1923] 2 K.B. 617.

[92] *Sarson v. Roberts* [1895] 2 Q.B. 395; *Sleafer v. Lambeth B.C.* [1960] 1 Q.B. 43, 56–57; *Duke of Westminster v. Guild* [1985] Q.B. 688; *Adami v. Lincoln Grange Management Ltd* [1998] I.C.L. 379. See also *Warren v. Keen* [1954] 1 Q.B. 15. Contrast *Mint v. Good* [1951] 1 K.B. 517, 522; *Edmonton Corpn. v. Knowles & Son Ltd* (1961) 60 L.G.R. 124; Defective Premises Act 1972, s.4(4).

[93] Landlord and Tenant Act 1985, ss.8, 9, 10.

[94] *ibid.* ss.11–17 (term less than seven years) as amended by s.116 of the Housing Act 1988.

[95] *Miller v. Hancock* [1893] 2 Q.B. 177; *Liverpool City Council v. Irwin* [1977] A.C. 239. See also Occupiers' Liability Act 1957, s.3(4) and Landlord and Tenant Act 1987, Pt. IV.

[96] *Hutton v. Warren* (1836) 1 M. & W. 466; *Dale v. Humfrey* (1858) E.B. & E. 1004; *Tucker v. Linger* (1882) 21 Ch.D. 18, 33, 34 (affd. (1883) 8 App.Cas. 508); *Pike, Sons & Co. v. Ongley & Thornton* (1887) 18 QBD 708; *Fox-Bourne v. Vernon & Co. Ltd* (1894) 10 T.L.R. 647; *Lord Eldon v. Hedley Bros.* [1935] 2 K.B. 1; *E.E. & Brian Smith (1928) Ltd v. Wheatsheaf Mills Ltd* [1939] 2 K.B. 302; *Mount v. Oldham Corpn.* [1973] 1 Q.B. 309; *British Crane Hire Corp. Ltd v. Ipswich Plant Hire Ltd* [1975] Q.B. 303; *Novorossisk Shipping Co. v. Neopetro Co. Ltd* [1990] 1 Lloyd's Rep. 425, 431; *Tony Cox (Dismantlers) Ltd v. Jim 5 Ltd* (1997) 13 Const.L.J. 209. See ante, §§ 12–125—12–131.

[97] See ante, § 12–126; post, § 13–022.

[98] *Yates v. Pym* (1816) 6 Taunt. 446; *Nelson v. Dahl* (1879) 12 Ch.D. 568, 575 (affd. (1881) 6 App.Cas. 38); *Re Walkers, Winser & Hamm and Shaw, Son & Co.* [1904] 2 K.B. 152; *Ropner v. Stoate Hosegood & Co.* (1905) 10 Com.Cas. 73; *Cunliffe-Owen v. Teather and Greenwood* [1967] 1 W.L.R. 1421, 1438, 1439; *Constan Industries of Australia Pty. Ltd v. Norwich Winterthur Insurance (Aust.) Ltd* (1986) 160 C.L.R. 226; *Pryke v. Gibbs Hartley Cooper Ltd* [1991] 1 Lloyd's Rep. 602, 615; *Danowski v. Henry Moore Foundation, The Times*, March 19, 1996, CA.

[99] *Cunliffe-Owen v. Teather and Greenwood, supra,* at 1438; *Pryke v. Gibbs Hartley Cooper Ltd, supra,* at 615; *Vitol SA v. Phibro Energy A.G.* [1990] 2 Lloyd's Rep. 84, 90; *Sucre Export SA v. Northern Shipping Ltd,* [1994] 2 Lloyd's Rep. 266.

parties, and "their respective rights and liabilities are precisely the same as if without any usage they had entered into a special agreement to the like effect."[1] These usages are incorporated on the presumption that "the parties did not mean to express in writing the whole of the contract by which they intended to be bound, but a contract with reference to those known usages"[2] or on the ground that "the courts are spelling out what both parties know and would, if asked, unhesitatingly agree to be part of the bargain."[3] However, even in cases where the party alleged to be liable upon an implied promise, arising solely from the usage of a particular trade, is not shown to have been cognisant of the usage, he can still be held to be liable by virtue of it.[4]

Incorporation of collective employment agreements. In relation to con-   **13–019**
tracts of employment, particular problems arise as to whether the terms of collective agreements between trade unions and employers concerning industrial conditions in a particular trade can be impliedly incorporated by usage into an individual worker's contract of employment[5] as they can be by express reference.[6]

Usage employed by one of the parties. Where the usage is one which merely   **13–020**
applies to the mode of dealing of a particular firm, a party cannot be bound thereby, unless he is shown to have had actual notice of it. To establish a usage it must be proved that a course of dealing has acquired such a notoriety, has been so well established and has become so universal in the particular trade, that it must be taken to be incorporated into any contract that is entered into by the parties dealing in this particular business.[7]

When implied from previous course of dealing. It is, however, clear that a   **13–021**
term may be implied in any given case from the circumstances of the parties having consistently on former and similar occasions adopted a particular course of dealing. Thus, a covenant to pay interest or to allow interest to be added to principal at stated periods and to pay interest on the whole, has been held to be implied from the fact that on former occasions the accounts between the parties have been stated and settled on that footing.[8] And it has been held that an oral contract between the buyer and seller of goods incorporated by a long course of dealing conditions printed on the back of "sold notes" as conditions of sale, in so far as a condition was appropriate to the oral contract.[9]

---

[1] *Raitt v. Mitchell* (1815) 4 Camp. 146, 149; *Produce Brokers Co. Ltd v. Olympia Oil and Cake Co. Ltd* [1916] 1 A.C. 314, 324.

[2] *Hutton v. Warren* (1836) 1 M. & W. 466, 475; *Gibson v. Small* (1853) 4 H.L.C. 353, 397.

[3] *Liverpool City Council v. Irwin* [1977] A.C. 239, 253; *Baker v. Black Sea & Baltic General Insurance Co. Ltd* [1998] 1 W.L.R. 974, 979.

[4] *Sutton v. Tatham* (1839) 10 A. & E. 27; *Bayliffe v. Butterworth* (1847) 1 Exch. 425; *Reynolds v. Smith* (1893) 9 T.L.R. 494; *Hunt v. Chamberlain* (1896) 12 T.L.R. 186.

[5] See Vol. II, § 39–044.

[6] See Vol. II, § 39–043.

[7] *Houlder v. General Steam Navigation Co.* (1862) 3 F. & F. 170; *Salsi v. Jetspeed Air Services Ltd* [1977] 2 Lloyd's Rep. 57.

[8] *Calton v. Bragg* (1812) 15 East 223, 228; *Bruce v. Hunter* (1813) 3 Camp. 467; *Newal v. Jones* (1830) 1 Moo. & M. 449; *Re Marquis of Anglesey* [1901] 2 Ch. 548; *cf. Re Lloyd Edwards* (1891) 65 L.T. 453. But see Vol. II, § 38–246.

[9] *Henry Kendall & Sons v. William Lillico & Sons Ltd* [1969] 2 A.C. 31, 90, 91, 104, 105, 130. See also *J. Spurling Ltd v. Bradshaw* [1956] 1 W.L.R. 461; *Cockerton v. Naviera Aznar SA* [1960] 2 Lloyd's Rep. 451; *Transmotors Ltd v. Robertson Buckley & Co. Ltd* [1970] 1 Lloyd's Rep. 224; *Eastman Chemical International A.G. v. N.M.T. Trading Ltd* [1972] 2 Lloyd's Rep. 25; *Roberts v.*

13–022   **Express terms prevail.** A custom or usage can only be incorporated into a contract if there is nothing in the express or necessarily implied terms of the contract to prevent such inclusion, and it can only be incorporated if it is not inconsistent with the tenor of the contract as a whole.[10] Thus a custom that commission was only payable to the broker who had negotiated a charterparty when freight was actually earned was ousted by an express term that commission was to be paid on the signing of the charter.[11] And a contract to ship rubber from the East to New York "direct and/or indirect" was alleged to have been duly carried out by shipping goods to the American Pacific seaboard and across the American continent to New York by train. Evidence of such a practice, said to have been common in the First World War, was disallowed as being contrary to the contract.[12]

13–023   **Implication from words of recital.** Where words of recital or reference manifest a clear intention that the parties should do certain acts, the courts will from these infer a covenant to do such acts, just as if the instrument had contained an express agreement to that effect.[13] So a recital in a separation deed that a wife had agreed to live apart from her husband implied a covenant by the wife to live apart.[14] Also where by charterparty it was agreed that the ship C, "expected to be at A about December 15," should with all convenient speed sail and proceed to that port and there receive a cargo, it was held that the words "expected, etc," amounted to a warranty that the ship was then in such a position that she might reasonably be expected to arrive by the day named.[15]

13–024   In contrast with the use of words of recital in order to ascertain the construction of a deed,[16] the courts are reluctant to imply such a covenant in the absence of a manifest intention. "It is one thing for the court to effectuate the intention of the parties to the extent to which they may have, even imperfectly, expressed themselves, and another to add to the instrument all such covenants as upon a full consideration the court may deem fitting for completing the intentions of the parties, but which they, either purposely or unintentionally, have omitted."[17] So the recital of an agreement does not create a covenant where there is an express

---

Elwells Engineers Ltd [1972] 2 Q.B. 586, 593; *Gillespie Bros. & Co. Ltd v. Roy Bowles Transport Ltd* [1973] Q.B. 400; *S.I.A.T. di del Ferro v. Tradax Overseas SA* [1928] 2 Lloyd's Rep. 470; *Lamport & Holt Lines Ltd v. Coubro & M. & I. Scrutton Ltd* [1981] 2 Lloyd's Rep. 659 (affd. [1982] 2 Lloyd's Rep. 42). *cf. McCutcheon v. David MacBrayne Ltd* [1964] 1 W.L.R. 125, HL; *Hollier v. Rambler Motors (A.M.C.) Ltd* [1972] 2 Q.B. 71. See Hoggett (1970) 33 M.L.R. 518 and *ante*, § 12–011.

[10] *London Export Corpn. Ltd v. Jubilee Coffee Roasting Co. Ltd* [1958] 1 W.L.R. 661, 675; *Kum v. Wah Tat Bank Ltd* [1971] 1 Lloyd's Rep. 439, 445.

[11] *Les Affréteurs Réunis Société Anonyme v. Walford* [1919] A.C. 801. See generally on this point, *ante*, §§ 12–126, 13–018.

[12] *Re L. Sutro & Co. v. Heilbut, Symons & Co.* [1927] 2 K.B. 348. See also *Humfrey v. Dale* (1857) 7 E. & B. 266, 274; *Tucker v. Linger* (1883) 8 App.Cas. 508, 511; *Westacott v. Hahn* [1918] 1 K.B. 495; *Palgrave, Brown & Son Ltd v. SS. Turid* [1922] 1 A.C. 397.

[13] *Saltoun v. Houston* (1824) 1 Bing. 433; *Easterby v. Sampson* (1830) 6 Bing. 644; *Courtney v. Taylor* (1843) 6 M. & G. 851; *Great Northern Ry. v. Harrison* (1852) 12 C.B.(N.S.) 576, 609; *Knight v. Gravesend, etc., Waterworks Co.* (1857) 2 H. & N. 6; *Farrall v. Hilditch* (1859) 5 C.B.(N.S.) 840; *Jackson v. North Eastern Ry.* (1877) 7 Ch.D. 573; *Mackenzie v. Childers* (1889) 43 Ch.D. 265.

[14] *Re Weston* [1900] 2 Ch. 164.

[15] *Corkling v. Massey* (1873) L.R. 8 C.P. 395.

[16] See *ante*, § 12–064.

[17] *Aspdin v. Austin* (1844) 5 Q.B. 671, 684.

covenant to be found in the witnessing part relating to the same subject-matter.[18]

Implied term as to duration of contract. A contract which contains no **13–025** express provision for its determination may yet be determined by reasonable notice on the part of one or both of the parties. The question whether a contract can be determined in this way is often said to depend upon the implication of a term, although it is probably better to regard it as depending upon the true construction of the agreement.[19] Nevertheless, since *ex hypothesi*, the agreement contains no provisions expressly dealing with determination, the question is not one of construction in the narrow sense of putting a meaning on language which the parties have used, but in the wider sense of ascertaining, in the light of all the admissible evidence and in the light of what the parties have said or omitted to say in the agreement, what the common intention of the parties was in the relevant respect when they entered into the agreement.[20] Thus a contract to supply gas to a public authority in such quantities as it should require has been held determinable by either party on reasonable notice,[21] and a licence to occupy a theatre and to produce there stage plays, which gave to the licensee an option to extend the licence at stated intervals, but which contained no provisions for determination by the licensor, was held to be determinable by the licensor upon giving reasonable notice.[22] Similar constructions have been adopted in the case of contracts between employer and employee,[23] between principal and agent,[24] and between solicitor and client in respect of an indefinite retainer.[25]

Contractual licences. A licence coupled with the grant of an interest in land **13–026** cannot be revoked so as to defeat the grant to which it is appurtenant.[26] Since the Judicature Act 1873 such a licence may be made either by deed or by a specifically enforceable agreement in writing.[27] On the other hand a "bare licence" is revocable at any time upon the licensor giving clear[28] and adequate[29] notice to the licensee. The position of a contractual licensee is that, if a licence

---

[18] *Dawes v. Tredwell* (1881) 18 Ch.D. 354, 359.

[19] *Winter Garden Theatre (London) Ltd v. Millennium Productions Ltd* [1948] A.C. 173, 195, 203; *Martin-Baker Aircraft Co. Ltd v. Canadian Flight Equipment Ltd* [1955] 2 Q.B. 556, 578; *Staffordshire A.H.A. v. South Staffordshire Waterworks Co.* [1978] 1 W.L.R. 1387, 1399–1403, 1405.

[20] *Re Spenborough U.D.C.'s Agreement* [1968] Ch. 139, 147. See also *Llanelly Rail and Dock Co. v. L. & N.W. Ry.* (1873) L.R. 8 Ch.App. 942; (1875) L.R. 7 H.L. 550. *cf.* Carnegie (1969) 85 L.Q.R. 392.

[21] *Crediton Gas Co. v. Crediton Urban Council* [1928] Ch. 174, 447. See also *Beverley Corpn. v. Richard Hodgson & Sons Ltd* (1972) 225 E.G. 799; *Staffordshire A.H.A. v. South Staffordshire Waterworks Co., supra*; *Tower Hamlets L.B.C. v. British Gas Corpn., The Times*, March 23, 1982. Contrast *Kirklees Metropolitan B.C. v. Yorkshire Woollen District Transport Co.* (1978) 77 L.G.R. 448; *Power Co. Ltd v. Gore District Council* [1997] N.Z.L.R. 537.

[22] *Winter Garden Theatre (London) Ltd v. Millennium Productions Ltd, supra*; *cf. Australian Blue Metal Ltd v. Hughes* [1963] A.C. 74.

[23] See Vol. II, §§ 39–137, 39–141. Contrast *McClelland v. Northern Ireland General Health Services Board* [1957] 1 W.L.R. 594 where express terms prevented such implication.

[24] *Martin-Baker Aircraft Co. Ltd v. Canadian Flight Equipment Ltd, supra*. See Vol. II, § 32–146.

[25] *Milner & Son v. Percy Bilton Ltd* [1966] 1 W.L.R. 1582.

[26] *Thomas v. Sorrell* (1673) Vaughan 330; *Jones v. Earl of Tankerville* [1909] 2 Ch. 440.

[27] *Walsh v. Lonsdale* (1882) 21 Ch.D. 9 (or sufficient act of part performance.)

[28] *Mellor v. Watkins* (1874) L.R. 9 Q.B. 400.

[29] *Minister of Health v. Bellotti* [1944] 1 K.B. 298; *Tool Metal Manufacturing Co. Ltd v. Tungsten Electric Co. Ltd* [1955] 1 W.L.R. 761; *Australian Blue Metal Ltd v. Hughes* [1963] A.C. 74.

is given for consideration and coupled with an agreement, whether express or implied, that it will not be revoked until the effluxion of a specified period of time or the happening of a particular event, it is irrevocable until the expiration of the period or the happening of the event.[30] An injunction will be granted to restrain the licensor from revoking the licence, or from acting in pursuance of the purported revocation,[31] and the licensee may also claim damages for breach of contract[32] and for assault should he be forcibly ejected by the licensor.[33]

13–027   **Sale of goods, hire-purchase and hire.** Undertakings as to title, quality, fitness for purpose and correspondence with description or sample are implied into contracts of sale of goods by sections 12 to 15 of the Sale of Goods Act 1979,[34] into contracts of hire-purchase by sections 8 to 11 of the Supply of Goods (Implied Terms) Act 1973,[35] and into contracts for the hire of goods by sections 7 to 10 of the Supply of Goods and Services Act 1982.[36]

13–028   **Supply of goods.** Undertakings in respect of the goods similar to those implied in the case of sale, hire-purchase and hire are implied into contracts for the transfer of goods, *e.g.* for work and materials, by sections 2 to 5 of the Supply of Goods and Services Act 1982.[37] These replace and extend[38] the undertakings previously implied by the common law, for example, into a contract for the manufacture of a set of false teeth,[39] for the repair of a motor car,[40] for the dyeing

---

[30] *Winter Garden Theatre (London) Ltd v. Millennium Productions Ltd* [1948] A.C. 173; *Bannister v. Bannister* [1948] 2 All E.R. 133; *Errington v. Errington* [1952] 1 K.B. 290; *Hounslow L.B.C. v. Twickenham Gardens Development Ltd* [1971] Ch. 233 (not followed in *Mayfield Holdings Ltd v. Moana Reef Ltd* [1973] 1 N.Z.L.R. 309); *Tanner v. Tanner* [1975] 1 W.L.R. 1346; *Verrall v. Great Yarmouth B.C.* [1981] Q.B. 202. *cf. Chandler v. Kerley* [1978] 1 W.L.R. 693 (contractual licence impliedly revocable on reasonable notice). A licence may also be created by estoppel, or its revocation restrained in equity: see *Inwards v. Baker* [1965] 2 Q.B. 29; *E.R. Ives Investment Ltd v. High* [1967] 2 Q.B. 379; *Binions v. Evans* [1972] Ch. 359; *D.H.N. Food Distributors Ltd v. Tower Hamlets L.B.C.* [1976] 1 W.L.R. 852; *Hardwick v. Johnson* [1978] 1 W.L.R. 683; *Pascoe v. Turner* [1979] 1 W.L.R. 431; *Williams v. Staite* [1979] Ch. 291; *Re Sharpe* [1980] 1 W.L.R. 219; *Greasley v. Cooke* [1980] 1 W.L.R. 1306; *Grant v. Edwards* [1986] Ch. 638; *Lloyds Bank plc v. Rosset* [1991] 1 A.C. 107; *Hammond v. Mitchell* [1991] 1 W.L.R. 1127; *Matharu v. Matharu, The Times,* May 13, 1994, CA. *cf. Coombes v. Smith* [1986] 1 W.L.R. 808. See also Moriarty (1984) 100 L.Q.R. 346 and *ante,* § 3–129.
[31] *Winter Garden Theatre (London) Ltd v. Millennium Productions Ltd, supra*; *Foster v. Robinson* [1915] 1 K.B. 149, 156. See also *Verral v. Great Yarmouth B.C., supra* (specific performance), and the cases in equity cited in n. 30, *supra.*
[32] *Kerrison v. Smith* [1897] 2 Q.B. 445.
[33] *Hurst v. Picture Theatres Ltd* [1915] 1 K.B. 1. Contrast *Wood v. Leadbitter* (1845) 13 M. & W. 838; *Thompson v. Park* [1944] K.B. 408; *Cowell v. Rosehill Racecourse Ltd* (1936) 56 C.L.R. 605, but these cases are of doubtful authority: see *Verrall v. Great Yarmouth B.C., supra.*
[34] See Vol. II, §§ 43–059 *et seq.* See also (on exclusion or restriction of liability) *post,* § 14–075.
[35] See Vol. II, §§ 38–277, 38–343 *et seq.* See also (on exclusion or restriction of liability) *post,* § 14–075.
[36] See Vol. II, § 33–062. See also (on exclusion or restriction of liability), *post,* § 14–076.
[37] As amended by Sched. 2, para. 6, of the Sale and Supply of Goods Act 1994. See *Charlotte Thirty Ltd v. Croker Ltd* (1990) 24 Const.L.R. 46. See also (on exclusion or restriction of liability), *post,* § 14–076.
[38] See *Young and Marten Ltd v. McManus Childs Ltd* [1969] 1 A.C. 454; *Gloucestershire C.C. v. Richardson* [1969] 1 A.C. 480.
[39] *Samuels v. Davis* [1943] K.B. 526.
[40] *G.H. Myers & Co. v. Brent Cross Service Co.* [1934] 1 K.B. 46; *Herschtal v. Stewart and Ardern Ltd* [1940] 1 K.B. 155; *Stewart v. Reavell's Garage* [1952] 2 Q.B. 545.

of a woman's hair,[41] for the supply and installation of a burglar-proof door,[42] for the inoculation of cattle,[43] and for the roofing[44] and erection[45] of a building.

Trading stamps. Warranties as to title and quality analogous to those implied by the Sale of Goods Act 1979 are implied on the part of a promoter of a trading stamp scheme in every redemption of trading stamps for goods.[46]   **13-029**

Disposition of property. The covenants for title that are implied on a disposition of property are those set out in Part I of the Law of Property (Miscellaneous Provisions) Act 1994. "Property" is defined[47] in the same terms as in the Law of Property Act 1925, *i.e.* to include "a thing in action, and any interest in real or personal property."   **13-030**

Supply of services. In the case of a contract under which a person agrees to carry out a service, other than a contract of service or apprenticeship[48] and certain other excepted contracts,[49] where the supplier is acting in the course of a business,[50] there is an implied term that the supplier will carry out the service with reasonable care and skill. This term is implied by section 13 of the Supply of Goods and Services Act 1982.[51] If the contract is one for the supply of professional services, the degree of care and skill required of a professional man is that which is to be expected of a member of his profession (in the appropriate speciality, if he be a specialist) of ordinary competence and experience.[52] If the service is to be carried out by an artisan, then the work should be done in a good and workmanlike manner.[53] However, the special circumstances of the case may show that the supplier impliedly warrants that his services will produce a   **13-031**

---

[41] *Ingham v. Emes* [1955] 2 Q.B. 366.

[42] *Reg. Glass Pty. v. Rivers Locking System Pty.* (1968) 120 C.L.R. 516. *cf. Davis & Co. (Wires) v. Afa-Minerva (E.M.I.)* [1974] 2 Lloyd's Rep. 27.

[43] *Dodd and Dodd v. Wilson and McWilliam* [1946] 2 All E.R. 691.

[44] *Young and Marten Ltd v. McManus Childs Ltd, supra,* n. 38.

[45] *Gloucestershire C.C. v. Richardson, supra.*

[46] Trading Stamps Act 1964, s.4, substituted by s.16(1) of the Supply of Goods (Implied Terms) Act 1973. But see the amendments to the 1964 Act effected by s.192 of and Sched. 4, paras. 24–26 to the Consumer Credit Act 1974 from October 6, 1980 (S.I. 1980 No. 50 (C.3)) and the amendments made by the Sale and Supply of Goods Act 1994, Sched. 2.

[47] s.1(4).

[48] s.12(2).

[49] s.12(4). The following orders have been made: Supply of Services (Exclusion of Implied Terms) Order 1982 (S.I. 1982 No. 1771); Supply of Services (Exclusion of Implied Terms) Order 1983 (S.I. 1983 No. 902); Supply of Services (Exclusion of Implied Terms) Order 1985 (S.I. 1985 No. 1).

[50] By s.18(1), "business" includes a profession and the activities of any government department or local or public authority.

[51] Unless excluded (s.16): *Eagle Star Life Assurance Co. Ltd v. Griggs* [1997] C.L.Y. 991. See also (on exclusion or restriction of liability), *post,* §§ 14–069, 14–076; and see Vol. II, §§ 33–086, 37–074.

[52] *Bolam v. Friern Hospital Management Committee* [1957] 1 W.L.R. 582, 586; *Chin Keow v. Govt. of Malaysia* [1967] 1 W.L.R. 813; *Greaves & Co. (Contractors) Ltd v. Baynham Meikle and Partners* [1975] 1 W.L.R. 1095, 1100, 1102; *Saif Ali v. Sidney Mitchell & Co.* [1980] A.C. 198, 218, 220; *Whitehouse v. Jordan* [1981] 1 W.L.R. 246, 263; *Maynard v. West Midlands Regional Health Authority* [1984] 1 W.L.R. 634, 639; *Thake v. Maurice* [1986] Q.B. 644; *Matrix-securities Ltd v. Theodore Goddard* [1998] 2 C.L. 486; *Bolitho v. City and Hackney Health Authority* [1998] A.C. 232.

[53] *Kimber v. W. Willett Ltd* [1947] K.B. 570. See also Vol. II, § 37–069, 37–074.

specified result or that the product of his service will be reasonably fit for the purpose for which it is required.[54]

13–032   By sections 14 and 15 of the 1982 Act, where, under a contract for the supply of a service by a supplier acting in the course of a business,[55] the time for the service to be carried out, or the consideration for the service, is not fixed or determined by the contract, left to be fixed or determined in a manner agreed by the contract or determined by the course of dealing between the parties, there are respectively implied terms that the supplier will carry out the service within a reasonable time and that the party contracting with the supplier will pay a reasonable charge.

13–033   **Package travel etc.** By the Package Travel, Package Holiday and Package Tours Regulations 1992[56] a number of terms are implied in favour of the consumer in contracts for the sale of package travel, package holidays and package tours. These include implied terms: that the contract contains certain elements specified in the Regulations and that these are communicated in writing to the consumer before the contract is made and a copy of them is supplied to him[57]; that the consumer may transfer his booking where he is prevented from proceeding with the package[58]; that if the organiser is constrained before departure to alter significantly an essential term of the contract, such as the price, he will notify the consumer as soon as possible in order to enable the consumer to take appropriate action and in particular to withdraw from the contract without penalty[59]; that if for that reason the consumer withdraws from the contract or if the organiser cancels the package, the consumer will be entitled to take a substitute package or to have repaid to him all moneys paid by him under the contract[60]; and that if a significant proportion of the services contracted for is not provided, the organiser will make suitable alternative arrangements at no extra cost and compensate the consumer for the difference between the services provided and those contracted for.[61] The Regulations also impose (subject to certain exceptions) a strict liability on the other party to the contract for the proper performance of the obligations under the contract, irrespective of whether such obligations are to be performed by that party or by other suppliers of services.[62]

13–034   **Interest on commercial debts.** A term is implied into contracts for the supply of goods and services[63] by the Late Payment of Commercial Debts (Interest) Act

---

[54] *Samuels v. Davis* [1943] K.B. 526; *Greaves & Co. (Contractors) Ltd v. Baynham Meikle and Partners, supra.*; *St. Alban's City and District Council v. International Computers Ltd* [1996] 4 All E.R. 481. Contrast *Lynch v. Thorne* [1956] 1 W.L.R. 303; *Thake v. Maurice, supra.* See Vol. II, § 37–071.

[55] See n. 50, *supra.*

[56] S.I. 1992 No. 3288, implementing Council Directive 90/314/EEC ([1990] O.J. L158/59), and amended by S.I. 1998 No. 1208.

[57] Reg. 9.

[58] Reg. 10.

[59] Reg. 12.

[60] Reg. 13.

[61] Reg. 14.

[62] Reg. 15.

[63] Other than excepted contracts: s.2(5).

1998 whereby any qualifying debt[64] created by the contract is to carry statutory interest subject to and in accordance with the Act.[65]

---

[64] Defined in s.3.
[65] s.1(1). See *post*, § 27–140.

CHAPTER 14

EXEMPTION CLAUSES[1]

1. IN GENERAL

Generally. It is a common feature of written contracts at the present day (and **14–001** in particular of those in standard form) that the person tendering the document will seek to absolve himself either wholly or in part from liability under the contract or from liability for a tort connected with the contract. In a contract for the sale of goods, for instance, the seller may require the buyer to agree that all conditions and warranties, whether express or implied, statutory or otherwise, in respect of the goods sold are to be excluded.[2] In other contracts, such as a contract for the supply of services, the supplier may seek to protect himself, his employees and sub-contractors, against liability, for example, for negligence. It can reasonably be argued that, in many commercial contracts where both parties are of equal bargaining power, such exclusion or restriction of liability does no more than apportion the risk between the parties, in respect of which one party will be expected to insure. Very often, however, the party imposing the condition is in an economically superior position and can dictate his own terms to the other. So, acting within the general limits prescribed by the doctrine of freedom of contract, the courts have attempted to correct the imbalance by adopting rules of construction which require the party seeking to exclude or restrict his liability to do so in clear and unequivocal terms.[3] Inequality of bargaining power, however, in itself, is not a ground for invalidating such a clause at common law.[4]

---

[1] See Lawson, *Exclusion Clauses and Unfair Contract Terms* (1995); Yates, *Exclusion Clauses in Contracts* (2nd ed.); Yates and Hawkins, *Standard Business Contracts: Exclusions and Related Devices* (1986); Jacobs, *Effective Exclusion Clauses* (1990).

[2] *L'Estrange v. Graucob* [1934] 2 K.B. 394.

[3] See Sales (1953) 16 M.L.R. 318; Gower (1954) 17 M.L.R. 155; Turpin (1956) 73 S.A.L.J. 144.

[4] See *post*, § 14–124.

Incorporation of exemption clauses. The question whether an exemption clause contained in a written document or notice has been incorporated as a term of the contract is dealt with in the chapter on Express Terms.[5] The normal rule (where the document is not signed) is that the party affected by the clause will be bound if the party delivering the document has done what may reasonably be considered sufficient to give notice of the clause to persons of the class to which he belongs.[6] But a clause may be incorporated by course of dealing between the parties or because both parties are aware that it is the practice of the particular trade to contract subject to exempting conditions.[7]

14–003   **Types of exemption clause.** Exemption clauses may broadly be divided into three categories.[8] First, there are clauses which purport to limit or reduce what would otherwise be the defendant's duty, *i.e.* the substantive obligations to which he would otherwise be subject under the contract, for example, by excluding express or implied terms, by limiting liability to cases of wilful neglect or default, or by binding a buyer of land or goods to accept the property sold subject to "faults," "defects" or "errors of description." Secondly, there are clauses which purport to exclude or restrict the liability which would otherwise attach to a breach of contract, such as the liability to be sued for breach or to be liable in damages, or which take away from the other party the right to treat as repudiated or rescind the agreement. Thirdly, there are clauses which purport to exclude or restrict the duty of the party in default fully to indemnify the other party, for example, by limiting the amount of damages recoverable against him, or by providing a time-limit within which claims must be made. Traditionally, the approach of English judges has in all cases been to ascertain the liability of the defendant apart from the exemption clause, and then to consider whether or not the clause is sufficient to constitute a defence to that liability.[9] It has, however, been argued[10] that such an approach tends to be misleading, at any rate if applied to exemption clauses which fall within the first two categories. These directly limit the substantive contractual content of the promise and circumscribe the liability of the party in default. The whole contract ought therefore initially to be construed together with the exemption clause. There is considerable logical force in this contention. More recent dicta have tended to support it.[11] The task of the courts has been said to be[12]: "to look at the event [resulting from the breach], and to ascertain from the words and conduct of the parties which created the contract between them what their presumed intention was as to what should be their legal rights and liabilities either original or substituted upon the occurrence of an event

---

[5] See *ante*, §§ 12–013 *et seq.*

[6] *Parker v. South Eastern Ry.* (1877) 2 C.P.D. 416; *Richardson, Spence & Co. v. Rowntree* [1894] A.C. 217; *Hood v. Anchor Line (Henderson Bros.) Ltd* [1918] A.C. 837; *McCutcheon v. David Macbrayne Ltd* [1964] 1 W.L.R. 125, HL; *Thornton v. Shoe Lane Parking Ltd* [1971] 2 Q.B. 163.

[7] See *ante*, §§ 12–011, 12–012.

[8] *Kenyon, Sons & Craven Ltd v. Baxter Hoare & Co. Ltd* [1971] 1 W.L.R. 519, 522; *Trade and Transport Inc. v. Iino Kaiun Kaisha Ltd* [1973] 1 W.L.R. 210, 230. See also Dawson (1975) 91 L.Q.R. 380.

[9] *Rutter v. Palmer* [1922] 2 K.B. 87, 92.

[10] Coote, *Exception Clauses* (1964).

[11] *Suisse Atlantique Société d'Armement Maritime SA v. N.V. Rotterdamsche Kolen Centrale* [1967] 1 A.C. 361, 431; *Photo Production Ltd v. Securicor Transport Ltd* [1980] A.C. 827, 851.

[12] *Hardwick Game Farm v. Suffolk Agricultural Poultry Producers' Assn.* [1966] 1 W.L.R. 287, 309, 333, 343 (affd. *sub nom. Henry Kendall & Sons v. William Lillico & Sons Ltd* [1969] 2 A.C. 31, HL).

of this kind." The traditional approach has for the most part, however, been adopted in the Unfair Contract Terms Act 1977.[13]

Exemption clauses distinguished from other similar clauses. Agreed damages clauses, by which the parties liquidate the damages payable upon breach, are not to be classified as exemption clauses, at least where the liquidated damages provision is a genuine pre-estimate of the loss likely to be suffered in the event of breach.[14] It has also been said that *force majeure* clauses are not exemption clauses.[15] Likewise ordinary arbitration clauses are "in essence mere machinery"[16] and so distinct from exemption clauses, being governed by separate rules.[17] But it is possible that a clause which bars one party's claim unless arbitration is begun within a specified time may be treated as an exemption clause in so far as it may be construed not to extend to cover a fundamental breach of contract.[18]

14–004

2. RULES OF CONSTRUCTION

General principles. Exemption clauses must be expressed clearly and without ambiguity or they will be ineffective.[19] The clause must clearly express what its intention is. In *J. Gordon Alison & Co. Ltd v. Wallsend Shipway and Engineering Co. Ltd*,[20] a cylinder was sold by the defendants to the plaintiffs "subject to our usual guarantee clauses." The clause relied on by the defendants "guaranteed" the purchaser against defects of material or workmanship for six months, but excluded liability for consequential damage. The question arose whether the guarantee clause was applicable to this particular contract, and the Court of Appeal held that it was not: "if a person was under a legal liability and wished to get rid of it he could only do so by using clear words."[21] Exemption clauses will therefore be construed strictly, and the degree of strictness appropriate to their construction may properly depend upon the extent to which they

14–005

---

[13] See *Phillips Products Ltd v. Hyland* [1987] 1 W.L.R. 659, 664; *Smith v. Eric S. Bush* and *Harris v. Wyre Forest DC* [1990] 1 A.C. 831, 857, 873; Coote (1978) 41 M.L.R. 312; Palmer and Yates [1981] C.L.J. 108; *post*, § 14–061.

[14] *Suisse Atlantique Société d'Armement Maritime SA v. N.V. Rotterdamsche Kolen Centrale*, *supra*, at 395, 411, 420, 436. *cf*. 406. See also *post*, § 14–021.

[15] *Fairclough Dodd & Jones Ltd v. J.H. Vantol Ltd* [1957] 1 W.L.R. 136, 143. But in practice they may have the same effect and be as strictly construed: see also *post*, §§ 14–126—14–142.

[16] *Woolf v. Collis Removal Service* [1948] 1 K.B. 11. See also *Atlantic Shipping Co. Ltd v. Louis Dreyfus & Co.* [1922] 2 A.C. 250, 258; *Heyman v. Darwins Ltd* [1942] A.C. 356, 373–375, 400. See also Unfair Contract Terms Act 1977, s.13(2); *post*, § 14–060. But see the Unfair Terms in Consumer Contracts Regulations 1994, S.I. 1994 No. 3159 and s.89 of the Arbitration Act 1996; *post*, § 16–013.

[17] See *post*, § 16–154.

[18] *Atlantic Shipping Co. Ltd v. Louis Dreyfus & Co.*, *supra*, at p. 258; *Ford & Co. Ltd v. Cie Furness* [1922] 2 K.B. 797; *Smeaton Hanscomb & Co. Ltd v. Sasson I. Setty Son & Co. (No. 1)* [1953] 1 W.L.R. 1468. *Sed quaere*?

[19] *Ailsa Craig Fishing Co. Ltd v. Malvern Fishing Co. Ltd* [1983] 1 W.L.R. 964, 966, 970. See also *Photo Production Ltd v. Securicor Transport Ltd* [1980] A.C. 827, 846, 850.

[20] (1927) 43 T.L.R. 323.

[21] At 324.

involve departure from the implied obligations ordinarily accepted by the parties in entering into a contract of a particular kind[22] and whether the clause purports entirely to exclude an obligation or liability or merely to limit the compensation recoverable from the party in default.[23] However, the rules of construction applicable to written contracts[24] apply equally to exemption clauses to ascertain what meaning the words were intended to bear.[25] If the clause is expressed clearly and unambiguously, there is no justification for placing upon the language of the clause a strained and artificial meaning so as to avoid the exclusion or restriction of liability contained in it.[26]

14–006   **Clause must extend to event.** Each clause must be considered according to its actual wording, but it must clearly extend to the exact contingency or loss which has occurred if it is to protect the party relying on it. Thus in a contract for the sale of goods, a stipulation that the goods are bought "as seen"[27] or the exclusion of liability for "latent defects"[28] will not exclude terms as to quality and fitness for purpose implied by the Sale of Goods Act, the exclusion of warranties will not necessarily exclude conditions,[29] and the exclusion of implied terms will not exclude those which are actually expressed.[30] The exclusion of liability for "consequential loss or damage" will not cover loss which directly and naturally results in the ordinary course of events from the breach, but only loss which is less direct or more remote.[31] And a clause which provided that "the goods delivered shall be deemed to be in all respects in accordance with the contract" unless the buyer gave notice to the contrary within 14 days of the arrival of the goods, was held not to apply to a claim for damages for short delivery, *i.e.* in respect of goods not delivered.[32] A clause in a contract of sale or hire-purchase which merely excludes all conditions and warranties, express or implied, will not necessarily extend to the delivery of goods wholly different from the agreed contract goods.[33] A clause may therefore be too narrow in its terms to cover the obligation or liability which it is sought to exclude or restrict.

---

[22] *Photo Production Ltd v. Securicor Transport Ltd, supra,* at 850. See also *Suisse Atlantique Société d'Armement Maritime SA v. N.V. Rotterdamsche Kolen Centrale* [1967] 1 A.C. 361, 482.

[23] *Ailsa Craig Fishing Co. Ltd v. Malvern Fishing Co. Ltd, supra,* at 966, 970; *George Mitchell (Chesterhall) Ltd v. Finney Lock Seeds Ltd* [1983] 2 A.C. 803, 814. Contrast *Darlington Futures Ltd v. Delco Australia Pty. Ltd* (1987) 68 A.L.R. 385.

[24] See *ante,* § 12–041.

[25] *Sydney City Council v. West* (1965) 114 C.L.R. 481.

[26] *Photo Production Ltd v. Securicor Transport Ltd, supra,* at 846, 851; *George Mitchell (Chesterhall) Ltd v. Finney Lock Seeds Ltd, supra; Darlington Futures Ltd v. Delco Australia Pty. Ltd, supra.*

[27] *Cavendish-Woodhouse v. Mancey* (1984) 82 L.G.R. 376.

[28] *Henry Kendall & Sons v. William Lillico & Sons Ltd* [1969] 2 A.C. 31.

[29] *Baldry v. Marshall* [1925] 1 K.B. 260; *Wallis, Son & Wells v. Pratt & Haynes* [1911] A.C. 394.

[30] *Andrews Bros. Ltd v. Singer & Co. Ltd* [1934] 1 K.B. 17. See *Benjamin's Sale of Goods* (5th ed., 1997), §§ 13–025 *et seq.*

[31] *Croudace Construction Ltd v. Cawood's Concrete Products Ltd* [1978] 2 Lloyd's Rep. 55; *British Sugar plc v. NEI Power Projects Ltd* [1997] C.L.Y. 1751; *Deepak Fertilisers and Petrochemicals Corpn v. ICI* [1999] 1 Lloyd's Rep. 387, 402–403.

[32] *Beck & Co v. Szymanowski & Co.* [1924] A.C. 43.

[33] See *post,* §§ 14–027—14–028. But contrast *George Mitchell (Chesterhall) Ltd v. Finney Lock Seeds Ltd* [1983] A.C. 803; *post,* § 14–023.

Inconsistency with main purpose of contract. Conversely, an exemption **14–007** clause may be so broad and general in scope that to apply it literally would create an absurdity or defeat the main purpose of the contract which the parties had in mind.[34] It is the duty of the courts to give effect to the intentions of the parties as exhibited in their agreement.[35] If, therefore, looking at the whole of the contract, its main purpose and intent is clear, the court will be justified in attributing to the clause a construction which is not inconsistent with that main purpose and intent.[36] Thus a wide deviation clause in a bill of lading was restrictively construed so as not to cover a deviation by the carrier inconsistent with the contract voyage,[37] and a clause in a bill of lading which provided that "the responsibility of the carrier shall be deemed to cease absolutely after the goods are discharged from the ship" was held not to cover a release of the goods to the consignees without production of the bill, as the bill expressly required the goods to be delivered "unto order or assigns."[38] Likewise the court will be reluctant to ascribe to an exemption clause a meaning which effectively absolves one party from all duties and liabilities. "One may safely say that the parties cannot, in a contract, have contemplated that the clause should have so wide an ambit as in effect to deprive one party's stipulations of all contractual force: to do so would be to reduce the contract to a mere declaration of intent."[39] In *Tor Line A.B. v. Alltrans Group of Canada Ltd*,[40] in a contract of charterparty, shipowners expressly accepted responsibility for delay in delivery of the vessel or for delay during the currency of the charter and for loss or damage to goods on board, if these were caused by unseaworthiness or other personal act or omission or default of the owners or their manager, but stated that they were "not to be responsible in any other case nor for damage or delay whatsoever and howsoever caused even if caused by the neglect or default of their servants." In breach of an express warranty, the ship was not of the dimensions specified in the charter. On the charterers' claim for financial loss consequent upon the breach of this warranty, the shipowners relied upon the exemption clause. The House of Lords held that the loss was not covered by the clause. One of the reasons put forward by Lord Roskill[41] in his judgment was that, if the clause were to be construed so as to allow a breach of the warranty to be committed or a failure to deliver the vessel at all to take place without financial redress to the charterers:

"the charter virtually ceases to be a contract for the letting of the vessel and the performance of services by the owners . . . and becomes no more than a statement of intent by the owners in return for which the charterers are obliged to pay large sums by

---

[34] *Suisse Atlantique Société d'Armement Maritime SA v. N.V. Rotterdamsche Kolen Centrale* [1967] 1 A.C. 361, 398.

[35] See *ante*, § 12–070.

[36] *Glynn v. Margetson & Co.* [1893] A.C. 351, 357.

[37] *Leduc v. Ward* (1888) 20 Q.B.D. 475; *Glynn v. Margetson & Co., supra*; *Connolly Shaw Ltd v. A/S Det Nordenfjeldske D/S* (1934) 49 Ll.L.Rep. 183.

[38] *Sze Hai Tong Bank Ltd v. Rambler Cycle Co. Ltd* [1959] A.C. 576. Contrast *Glebe Island Terminals Pty. Ltd v. Continental Seagram Pty. Ltd* [1994] 1 Lloyd's Rep. 213.

[39] *Suisse Atlantique Société d'Armement Maritime SA v. N.V. Rotterdamsche Kolen Centrale, supra*, at 482.

[40] [1984] 1 W.L.R. 48.

[41] At 58–59 (with whom all other members of the House of Lords agreed).

way of hire, though if the owners fail to carry out their promises as to description or delivery, are entitled to nothing in lieu."

He found it difficult to believe that this conclusion would accord with the "true common intention" of the parties. Nevertheless the intent of the clause may be to qualify the main purpose of the contract, so that there is no inconsistency.[42] And if the clause does not entirely exclude the liability of one party, but merely limits or reduces his liability, it does not render his contractual promises illusory.[43] Further, if in the context of the contract as a whole and of the business relationship between the parties the words of the clause are clear and fairly susceptible of one meaning only, then effect must in any event be given to the clause.[44]

14–008   **"Four corners" rule.** There is some authority for the view that any damage or liability sought to be covered by an exemption clause must fall within the "four corners" of the contract and not outside of it.[45] This principle could be said to derive support from cases which have held an exemption clause to be inapplicable where a carrier deviated without justification from the agreed or usual route,[46] or carried goods above deck in breach of his obligation to carry them under deck,[47] where a bailee stored goods in a place other than that agreed,[48] and where a carrier or bailee in breach of contract parted with possession of the goods to an unauthorised sub-contractor.[49] Such cases, however, may be *sui generis*.[50] They are better explained as cases where the exemption clause in question was, on its true construction, not intended to cover the breach which occurred[51] and not as establishing any general principle that an exemption clause will be construed to extend only to acts of a party or his servants which fall within the four corners of the contract.[52] In any event, the clause itself may redefine a party's obligations with respect to performance[53] or in its terms be

---

[42] See, *e.g. G.H. Renton & Co. Ltd v. Palmyra Trading Corpn. of Panama* [1957] A.C. 149.

[43] See, *e.g. Ailsa Craig Fishing Co. Ltd v. Malvern Fishing Co. Ltd* [1983] A.C. 964, 971; *Swiss Bank Corpn. v. Brink's Mat Ltd* [1986] 2 Lloyd's Rep. 79, 92–93.

[44] *Swiss Bank Corpn. v. Brink's Mat Ltd, ibid.* at 93; *Darlington Futures Ltd v. Delco Australia Pty. Ltd* (1987) 68 A.L.R. 385.

[45] *Alderslade v. Hendon Laundry Ltd* [1945] K.B. 189, 192; *J. Spurling Ltd v. Bradshaw* [1956] 1 W.L.R. 461, 465, 469; *Thomas National Transport (Melbourne) Pty. Ltd v. May & Baker (Australia) Pty. Ltd* (1966) 115 C.L.R. 353, 376; *Suisse Atlantique Société d'Armement Maritime SA v. Rotterdamsche Kolen Centrale* [1967] 1 A.C. 361, 412, 424, 434; *Levison v. Patent Steam Carpet Cleaning Co. Ltd* [1978] Q.B. 69, 85.

[46] *London & North Western Ry. v. Neilson* [1922] 2 A.C. 263, 272; see also *post*, § 14–029.

[47] *Royal Exchange Shipping Co. Ltd v. Dixon* (1886) 12 App. Cas. 11, 16, 19; *J. Evans & Sons (Portsmouth) Ltd v. Andrea Merzario Ltd* [1976] 1 W.L.R. 1078, 1082, 1084, 1085; *Wibau Maschinenfabric Hartman SA v. Mackinnon Mackenzie & Co.* [1989] 2 Lloyd's Rep. 494.

[48] *Lilley v. Doubleday* (1881) 7 Q.B.D. 510; *Gibaud v. G.E. Ry.* [1921] 2 K.B. 426, 435; *Woolf v. Collis Removal Service* [1948] 1 K.B. 11; see *post*, § 14–035.

[49] *Davies v. Collins* [1945] 1 All E.R. 247; *Garnham, Harris & Elton Ltd v. Ellis (Transport) Ltd* [1967] 1 W.L.R. 940; see *post*, § 14–038.

[50] *Photo Production Ltd v. Securicor Transport Ltd* [1980] A.C. 827, 845. See also *Kenya Railways v. Antares Co. Pte. Ltd* [1987] 1 Lloyd's Rep. 424, 430; and *post*, § 14–029.

[51] *ibid; Wibau Maschinenfabric Hartman SA v. Mackinnon Mackenzie & Co.* [1989] 2 Lloyd's Rep. 494, 505. See also *Compania Portorafti Commerciale SA v. Ultramar Panama Inc.* [1990] 1 Lloyd's Rep. 310 (Hague-Visby Rules).

[52] See *Raymond Burke Motors Ltd v. Mersey Docks and Harbour Co.* [1986] 1 Lloyd's Rep. 155, 162 ("collateral" negligence); *Darlington Futures Ltd v. Delco Australia Pty. Ltd* (1987) 68 A.L.R. 385.

[53] *Photo Production Ltd v. Securicor Transport Ltd, supra,* at 851.

intended to cover even a radical departure from the performance contemplated by the contract.[54]

Construction contra proferentem. This rule of construction embraces two 14-009 differing, but closely related, principles.[55] First, since the party seeking to rely upon an exemption clause bears the burden of proving that the case falls within its provisions,[56] any doubt or ambiguity will be resolved against him and in favour of the other party.[57] Secondly, as in the case of any other written document,[58] in situations of ambiguity the words of the document are to be construed more strongly against the party who made the document and who now seeks to rely on them. In *John Lee (Grantham) Ltd v. Railway Executive*[59] a railway warehouse was leased by the defendants to the plaintiffs. A clause in the lease exempted the defendants from liability for "loss or damage (whether by act or neglect of the company or their servants or agents or not) which but for the tenancy hereby created would not have arisen." Owing to a fire caused by the negligence of the defendants in allowing a spark to escape from a railway engine, goods in the warehouse were damaged. It was held that the words "which but for the tenancy hereby created would not have arisen" confined the exemption to liabilities created by the relationship of landlord and tenant. Although the clause was capable of a wider construction, it was ambiguous and would be construed more strongly against the defendants, the makers of the document.

Liability for negligence. Liability for negligence may be excluded or 14-010 restricted if words are used which sufficiently indicate that the parties intended, in the context of their agreement, that such should be the case. Where a clause purports merely to limit the compensation payable by one party for loss or damage caused by his negligence, it is enough that the wording of the clause, when read as a whole, clearly and unambiguously has that effect.[60] But since it is inherently improbable that one party to the contract would intend to absolve the other party entirely from the consequences of the latter's own negligence,[61] more exacting standards are applied to clauses which are alleged to exclude altogether liability for negligence. The duty of a court in approaching the consideration of such clauses was summarised in the form of three propositions

---

[54] *George Mitchell (Chesterhall) Ltd v. Finney Lock Seeds Ltd* [1983] 2 A.C. 803 (*post*, 14-023); *Glebe Island Terminals Pty Ltd v. Continental Seagram Pty. Ltd* [1994] 1 Lloyd's Rep. 213.

[55] *Pera Shipping Corpn. v. Petroship SA* [1984] 2 Lloyd's Rep. 363, 365; *Youell v. Bland Welch & Co. Ltd* [1992] 2 Lloyd's Rep. 127, 134.

[56] See *post*, § 14-018.

[57] This appears to be the sense in which the rule was referred to in *Photo Production Ltd v. Securicor Transport Ltd, supra*, at 847; *Ailsa Craig Fishing Co. Ltd v. Malvern Fishing Co. Ltd* [1983] 1 W.L.R. 964, 969, 970; *George Mitchell (Chesterhall) Ltd v. Finney Lock Seeds Ltd, supra*, at 814.

[58] See *ante*, § 12-081.

[59] [1949] 2 All E.R. 581. See also *Webster v. Higgin* [1948] 2 All E.R. 127; *Houghton v. Trafalgar Insurance Co. Ltd* [1954] 1 Q.B. 247; *Billyack v. Leyland Construction Co. Ltd* [1968] 1 W.L.R. 471; *Adams v. Richardson & Starling Ltd* [1969] 1 W.L.R. 1645, 1653; *Pera Shipping Corpn. v. Petroship SA, supra*, at 366, [1985] 2 Lloyd's Rep. 103.

[60] *Ailsa Craig Fishing Co. Ltd v. Malvern Fishing Co. Ltd* [1983] 1 W.L.R. 964, 966, 970; *George Mitchell (Chesterhall) Ltd v. Finney Lock Seeds Ltd* [1983] 2 A.C. 803, 814. See also *Continental Illinois National Bank & Trust Co. of Chicago v. Papanicolau* [1986] 2 Lloyd's Rep. 441, 444, and *Skipskredittforeningen v. Emperor Navigation* [1998] 1 Lloyd's Rep. 66, 76 ("no set-off" clause).

[61] *Gillespie Bros. Ltd v. Roy Bowles Transport Ltd* [1973] Q.B. 400, 419; *Ailsa Craig Fishing Co. Ltd v. Malvern Fishing Co. Ltd, supra*, at 970; *Sonat Offshore SA v. Amerada Hess Development Ltd* [1988] 1 Lloyd's Rep. 145, 157.

in the opinion of the Privy Council delivered by Lord Morton in *Canada Steamship Lines Ltd v. The King*.[62] These tests, or guidelines,[63] have been subsequently approved and applied both by the Court of Appeal[64] and the House of Lords[65]:

> "(1) If the clause contains language which expressly exempts the person in whose favour it is made (hereafter called 'the proferens') from the consequences of the negligence of his own servants, effect must be given to that provision . . . (2) If there is no express reference to negligence, the court must consider whether the words used are wide enough, in their ordinary meaning, to cover negligence on the part of the servants of the proferens. If a doubt arises at this point, it must be resolved against the proferens . . . (3) If the words used are wide enough for the above purpose, the court must then consider whether 'the head of damage may be based on some ground other than that of negligence' . . . The 'other ground' must not be so fanciful or remote that the proferens cannot be supposed to have desired protection against it; but subject to this qualification . . . the existence of a possible head of damage other than that of negligence is fatal to the proferens even if the words used are prima facie wide enough to cover negligence on the part of his servants."

14–011   **Words wide enough to cover negligence.** To satisfy the first test, there must be a clear and unmistakable reference to negligence or to a synonym for it.[66] In the absence of any such express reference, it is necessary to proceed to the second test. Words such as "at sole risk,"[67] "at customers' sole risk,"[68] "at owner's risk"[69] and "at their own risk"[70] will normally cover negligence, as will words which clearly indicate an intention to exclude all liability without exception, for example, "no liability whatever"[71] or "under no circumstances,"[72] or all

---

[62] [1952] A.C. 192, 208. For a criticism of these propositions, see Palmer [1983] L.M.C.L.Q. 557.

[63] *Smith v. South Wales Switchgear Co. Ltd* [1978] 1 W.L.R. 165, 168, 178; *Lamport & Holt Lines Ltd v. Coubro & Scrutton (M. & I.) Ltd* [1982] 2 Lloyd's Rep. 42, 45, 48–49, 51.

[64] *Gillespie Bros. Ltd v. Roy Bowles Transport Ltd, supra; Lamport & Holt Lines Ltd v. Coubro & Scrutton (M. & I.) Ltd, supra.*

[65] *Smith v. South Wales Switchgear Co. Ltd, supra.*

[66] *Clark v. Sir William Arrol & Co. Ltd*, 1974 S.L.T. 90, 92; *Smith v. South Wales Switchgear Co. Ltd* [1978] 1 W.L.R. 165, 169, 173; *Lamport & Holt Lines Ltd v. Coubro & Scrutton (M. & I.) Ltd* [1982] 2 Lloyd's Rep. 42, 45, 47, 51; *Spriggs v. Sotheby Parke Bernet & Co.* [1986] 1 Lloyd's Rep. 487; *Shell Chemicals Ltd v. P.&O. Roadtanks Ltd* [1995] 1 Lloyd's Rep. 297.

[67] *Forbes, Abbott & Lennard Ltd v. G.W. Ry.* (1927) 44 T.L.R. 97; *The Jessmore* [1951] 2 Lloyd's Rep. 512; *James Archdale & Co. Ltd v. Comservices Ltd* [1954] 1 W.L.R. 459; *Scottish Special Housing Assn. v. Wimpey Construction U.K. Ltd* [1986] 1 W.L.R. 995; *Norwich City Council v. Harvey* [1989] 1 W.L.R. 828.

[68] *Rutter v. Palmer* [1922] 2 K.B. 87.

[69] *Burton & Co. v. English & Co.* (1883) 12 Q.B.D. 218, 223; *Levison v. Patent Steam Carpet Cleaning Co. Ltd* [1978] Q.B. 69; *cf. Allan Bros. and Co. v. James Bros. & Co.* (1897) 3 Com.Cas. 10, 12; *Svenssons Travaruaktiebolag v. Cliffe Steamship Co.* [1932] 1 K.B. 490, 496; *Exercise Shipping Co. Ltd v. Bay Maritime Lines Ltd* [1991] 2 Lloyd's Rep. 391.

[70] *Reynolds v. Boston Deep Sea Fishing & Ice Co. Ltd* (1921) 38 T.L.R. 22, 429; *Pyman SS. Co. v. Hull and Barnsley Ry.* [1915] 2 K.B. 729. Contrast *Woolmer v. Delmer Price Ltd* [1955] 1 Q.B. 291.

[71] *Reynolds v. Boston Deep Sea Fishing & Ice Co. Ltd, supra; Gibaud v. G.E. Ry.* [1921] 2 K.B. 426; *Swiss Bank Corpn. v. Brink's Mat Ltd* [1986] 2 Lloyd's Rep. 79.

[72] *Haigh v. Royal Mail Steam Packet Co.* (1883) 52 L.J.Q.B. 640; *Akerib v. Booth* [1960] 1 W.L.R. 454 (revd. on other grounds [1961] 1 W.L.R. 367); *Harris Ltd v. Continental Express Ltd* [1961] 1 Lloyd's Rep. 251; *J. Carter (Fine Worsteds) Ltd v. Hanson Haulage (Leeds) Ltd* [1965] 2 Q.B. 495; *Photo Production Ltd v. Securicor Transport Ltd* [1980] A.C. 827, 846. *cf. Taubman v. Pacific Steam Navigation Co.* (1872) 26 L.T. 704.

liability save that specified in the clause.[73] If the defendant merely disclaims liability for "any loss," he may be directing attention to the kinds of losses, and not to their cause or origin; so liability for negligence will not necessarily be excluded.[74] But if he says "however arising" or "any cause whatever," these words can cover losses by negligence.[75] Thus the words "howsoever caused,"[76] "from whatever other cause arising,"[77] "howsoever arising,"[78] "arising from any cause whatsoever,"[79] "relieves from all responsibility for any injury, delay, loss or damage, however caused"[80] have been held to be effective. Likewise a clause which excluded liability for any damage "which may arise from or be in any way connected with any act or omission of any person . . . employed by [the defendant]" has been held to be wide enough to cover negligence on the part of the defendant's servants.[81] However, the intention of the parties must be collected from the entire wording of the clause, and in construing the clause other parts of the contract which throw light on the meaning to be given to it are not to be ignored.[82] So, for instance, even such comprehensive words as "any liability . . . whatsoever"[83] "howsoever caused"[84] "any loss howsoever arising"[85] and "at charterers' risk"[86] may be limited by their context and thus not extend to the negligence of the defendant which it is sought to exclude. On the other hand, where a clause in a charterparty expressly accepted liability for negligence *only* in certain specified respects, it was held that it necessarily followed that it excluded negligence in all other respects.[87]

Liable only if negligent. There is no longer any rule of law that, if the only **14–012** liability of the *proferens* is for negligence, the clause *must* be construed so as to

---

[73] *George Mitchell (Chesterhall) Ltd v. Finney Lock Seeds Ltd* [1983] 2 A.C. 803; *Swiss Bank Corpn. v. Brink's Mat Ltd, supra.*

[74] *Price v. Union Lighterage Co.* [1904] 1 K.B. 412 ("any loss of or damage to goods which can be covered by insurance").

[75] *Joseph Travers & Sons Ltd v. Cooper* [1915] 1 K.B. 73, 101; *Gibaud v. G.E. Ry.* [1921] 2 K.B. 426, 437; *Rutter v. Palmer* [1922] 2 K.B. 87, 94.

[76] *Austin v. Manchester, Sheffield & Lincs. Ry.* (1852) 10 C.B. 454; *The Stella* [1900] P. 161; *Joseph Travers & Sons Ltd v. Cooper, supra*; *Ashby v. Tolhurst* [1937] 2 K.B. 242; *Harris Ltd v. Continental Express Ltd, supra*; *White v. Blackmore* [1972] 2 Q.B. 651. *Stag Line Ltd v. Tyne Shiprepair Group Ltd* [1984] 2 Lloyd's Rep. 211, 222; see also *Hunt & Winterbotham (West of England) Ltd v. B.R.S. (Parcels) Ltd* [1962] 1 Q.B. 617 ("however sustained").

[77] *Ashenden v. L.B. & S.C. Ry.* (1880) 5 Ex.D. 190; *Manchester, Sheffield & Lincs. Ry. v. Brown* (1883) 8 App.Cas. 703.

[78] *Pyman Steamship Co. v. Hull & Barnsley Ry.* [1915] 2 K.B. 729; *Swiss Bank Corpn. v. Brink's Mat Ltd* [1986] 2 Lloyd's Rep. 79. *cf. Bishop v. Bonham* [1988] 1 W.L.R. 742.

[79] *A.E. Farr Ltd v. Admiralty* [1953] 1 W.L.R. 965.

[80] *The Stella* [1900] P. 161.

[81] *Lamport & Holt Lines Ltd v. Coubro & Scrutton (M. & I.) Ltd* [1982] 2 Lloyd's Rep. 42. See also *Monarch Airlines Ltd v. London Luton Airport Ltd* [1998] 1 Lloyd's Rep. 403 ("act, omission, neglect or default").

[82] *Smith v. South Wales Switchgear Co. Ltd* [1978] 1 W.L.R. 165, 168.

[83] *Smith v. South Wales Switchgear Co. Ltd, supra.*

[84] *Raymond Burke Motors Ltd v. Mersey Docks and Harbour Co.* [1986] 1 Lloyd's Rep. 155.

[85] *Bishop v. Bonham* [1988] 1 W.L.R. 742. See also *Sonat Offshore SA v. Amerada Hess Development Ltd* [1988] 2 Lloyd's Rep. 145 ("any damage whatsoever").

[86] *Svenssons Travaruaktiebolag v. Cliffe Steamship Co.* [1932] 1 K.B. 490, 496; *Exercise Shipping Co. Ltd v. Bay Maritime Lines Ltd* [1991] 2 Lloyd's Rep. 391.

[87] *Mineralimportexport v. Eastern Mediterranean Maritime Ltd* [1980] 2 Lloyd's Rep. 572. But contrast *Tor Line A.B. v. Alltrans Group of Canada Ltd* [1984] 1 W.L.R. 48; *Airline Engineering v. Intercon Cattle Meat*, unreported, January 24, 1983, CA; *Caledonia Ltd v. Orbit Value Co. Europe* [1994] 1 W.L.R. 221, 229 (affd. [1994] 1 W.L.R. 1515).

cover negligence otherwise it would lack subject-matter[88]: the duty of the court is always to construe the wording of the clause in question to see what it means.[89]

14–013　　　**Words applicable only to another ground of liability.** Lord Morton's third test is more problematical. It derives from a rule of construction enunciated by Lord Greene M.R. in *Alderslade v. Hendon Laundry Ltd*[90] that "Where . . . the head of damage [liability for which is sought to be excluded] may be based on some other ground than that of negligence, the general principle is that the clause must be confined in its application to loss, occurring through that other cause, to the exclusion of loss arising through negligence." To this statement Lord Morton added the qualification that the "other ground" must not be so fanciful or remote that the *proferens* cannot be supposed to have desired protection against it. Even with this important qualification, however, the Court of Appeal has subsequently cautioned against a too literal or over-legalistic approach.[91] In *Lamport & Holt Lines Ltd v. Coubro & Scrutton (M. & I.) Ltd*, May L.J. said[92]:

> "In seeking to apply Lord Morton's third test, we should not ask now whether there is or might be a technical alternative head of legal liability which the relevant exemption clause might cover and, if there is, immediately construe the clause as inapplicable to negligence. We should look at the facts and realities of the situation as they did or must be deemed to have presented themselves to the contracting parties at the time the contract was made, and ask to what potential liabilities the one to the other did the parties apply their minds, or must they be deemed to have done so."

It is difficult to find many examples[93] of the application of this third test, although it has been illustrated[94] by reference to a common carrier whose liability for loss of or damage to the goods carried may be based on a ground, *i.e.* strict liability, independent of negligence.[95] And, where there were mutual exceptions in a charterparty in certain specified events including "errors of navigation," one of the reasons advanced for holding that negligent errors of navigation were not covered was that the clause was based on the assumption that a shipowner would

---

[88] *Alderslade v. Hendon Laundry Ltd* [1945] 1 K.B. 189, 192. See also *Rutter v. Palmer* [1922] 2 K.B. 87, 92; *Forbes Abbott & Lennard Ltd v. G.W. Ry.* (1927) 44 T.L.R. 97, 98.

[89] *Hollier v. Rambler Motors (A.M.C.) Ltd* [1972] 2 Q.B. 71, 80 (disapproving *Turner v. Civil Service Supply Association* [1926] 1 K.B. 50; *Fagan v. Green & Edwards Ltd* [1926] 1 K.B. 102); *Gillespie Bros. Ltd v. Roy Bowles Transport Ltd* [1973] Q.B. 400, 414; *Smith v. South Wales Switchgear Co. Ltd, supra,* at 108; *Lamport & Holt Lines Ltd v. Coubro & Scrutton (M. & I.) Ltd* [1982] 2 Lloyd's Rep. 42, 49, 51.

[90] [1945] 1 K.B. 189, 192.

[91] *Lamport & Holt Lines Ltd v. Coubro & Scrutton (M. & I.) Ltd* [1982] 2 Lloyd's Rep. 42, 45, 50, 51.

[92] [1982] 2 Lloyd's Rep. 42, 50.

[93] An example often cited is that of *White v. John Warwick & Co. Ltd* [1953] 1 W.L.R. 1285; but see *Lamport & Holt Lines Ltd v. Coubro & Scrutton (M. & I.) Ltd, supra,* at 46. See also *Canada Steamship Lines Ltd v. The King* [1952] A.C. 192, 210; *Re Polemis, Furness, Withy & Co. Ltd* [1912] 3 K.B. 560; *Olley v. Marlborough Court Ltd* [1949] 1 K.B. 532; *A.M.F. International Ltd v. Magnet Bowling Ltd* [1968] 1 W.L.R. 1028; *Smith v. South Wales Switchgear Co. Ltd* [1978] 1 W.L.R. 165, 169, 174, 179; *Caledonia Ltd v. Orbit Valve Co. Europe* [1994] 1 W.L.R. 221, 228 (affd. [1994] 1 W.L.R. 1515); *Shell Chemicals Ltd v. P.&O. Roadtanks Ltd* [1995] 1 Lloyd's Rep. 297.

[94] *Rutter v. Palmer* [1922] 2 K.B. 87, 90.

[95] See Vol. II, § 36–018.

be liable without negligence.[96] Lord Morton's third test was also applied in somewhat different circumstances in *Dorset County Council v. Southern Felt Roofing Co.*[97] where a term in a building contract provided that the employer should bear the risk of "loss or damage in respect of the works by fire, lightning, explosion, aircraft and other aerial devices dropped therefrom." The Court of Appeal held that the term did not apply to fire caused by the contractor's negligence since, by the inclusion of events other than fire which might occur without the fault of any human agent, there were risks not fanciful or remote to which the term could relate other than negligence.

Non-contractual notices. In the absence of a contract, the effect of a notice **14–014** excluding liability may be to defeat a plaintiff's claim for damages for negligence on the basis of *volenti non fit injuria.*[98]

Indemnity clauses. It is not unusual to find clauses by which one party does **14–015** not merely exclude his liability in negligence to the other party but further requires the other party to indemnify him against his liability in negligence to third parties. The law presumes that a party will not readily be granted an indemnity against a loss caused by his own negligence.[99] Nevertheless there is no doubt that a party is entitled to an indemnity against even the consequences of his own negligence if the clause so provides either expressly or by necessary implication.[1] The three tests laid down by Lord Morton in *Canada Steamship Co. Ltd v. The King*[2] normally apply to indemnity clauses as well as exemption clauses.[3] If there is no express reference to negligence, the question is whether the words used are wide enough in their ordinary meaning to cover negligence on the part of the person seeking to be indemnified or his servants.[4] Even if the words used are wide enough for this purpose, the court must consider whether liability for the loss or damage mentioned in the clause may arise on some ground other than such negligence, which ground is not so fanciful or remote that the

---

[96] *Seven Seas Transportation Ltd v. Pacifico Union Marina Corpn.* [1982] 2 Lloyd's Rep. 465, 475 (affd. [1948] 1 Lloyd's Rep. 488). *cf. Industrie Chimiche Italia Centrale SpA v. Nea Ninemia Shipping Co. SA* [1983] 1 Lloyd's Rep. 310, 314.

[97] (1990) 6 Const.L.J. 37. See also *Sonat Offshore SA v. Amerada Hess Development Ltd* [1988] 1 Lloyd's Rep. 145.

[98] *McCawley Ry. v. Furness* (1872) L.R. 8 Q.B. 57; *Buckpitt v. Oates* [1968] 1 All E.R. 1145; *Bennett v. Tugwell* [1971] 2 Q.B. 267; *Birch v. Thomas* [1972] 1 W.L.R. 294. But contrast *Burnett v. British Waterways Board Ltd* [1973] 1 W.L.R. 700 (employee acting under orders of his employer), s.149(3) of the Road Traffic Act 1988 and s.2(3) of the Unfair Contract Terms Act 1977. See also *post,* §§ 14–047, 14–080.

[99] *Walters v. Whessoe* [1968] 1 W.L.R. 1056, 1057; *Smith v. South Wales Switchgear Co. Ltd* [1978] 1 W.L.R. 165, 168.

[1] But see Unfair Contract Terms Act 1977, s.2 (exclusion or restriction of liabililty for negligence), s.4 (unreasonable consumer indemnities); *post,* §§ 14–068, 14–072.

[2] [1952] A.C. 192, 208; see *ante,* §§ 14–010—14–013.

[3] *Smith v. South Wales Switchgear Co. Ltd* [1978] 1 W.L.R. 165, HL; *Shell Chemicals Ltd v. P.&O. Roadtanks Ltd* [1995] 1 Lloyd's Rep. 297; *Deepak Fertilisers and Petrochemicals Corpn. v. ICI* [1999] 1 Lloyd's Rep. 387, 396. See also *Sonat Offshore SA v. Amerada Hess Development Ltd* [1988] 1 Lloyd's Rep. 145 (off-hire payment clause). But see *Morris v. Breaveglen Ltd* [1997] C.L.Y. 937 (clear intention).

[4] *Smith v. South Wales Switchgear Co. Ltd, supra; Deepak Fertilisers and Petrochemicals Corpn. v. I.C.I. supra.*

parties cannot be supposed to have intended the indemnity to apply to it.[5] The scope of the indemnity will therefore depend upon the wording of the particular clause and the intentions of the parties regarding it to be collected from the whole of their agreement.[6]

14–016   **Deliberate breaches.** It has from time to time been suggested that, if the breach by one party evinces "a deliberate disregard of his bounden obligations,"[7] it will not be covered by an exemption clause.[8] But there is no rule of law to prevent the exclusion or restriction of liability arising from even a deliberate act or omission by one party or his servants if the parties so intend.[9] In the *Suisse Atlantique* case,[10] Lord Wilberforce said[11]: "Some deliberate breaches . . . may be, on construction, within an exceptions clause (for example, a deliberate delay for one day in loading.) This is not to say that 'deliberateness' may not be a relevant factor: depending on what the party in breach 'deliberately' intended to do, it may be possible to say that the parties never contemplated that such a breach would be excused or limited." It may therefore be relevant to consider whether an exemption clause was intended by the parties to cover deliberate

---

[5] *Smith v. South Wales Switchgear Co. Ltd, supra* at 169, 174, 179; *Caledonia Ltd v. Orbit Valve Co. Europe* [1994] 1 W.L.R. 221, 228 (affd. [1994] 1 W.L.R. 1515); *Shell Chemicals Ltd v. P.&O. Roadtanks Ltd, supra.*

[6] See (effective indemnities): *A.E. Farr Ltd v. Admiralty* [1953] 1 W.L.R. 965; *Swan Hunter and Wigham Richardson Ltd v. France, Fenwick Tyne & Wear Co. Ltd (The Albion)* [1953] 1 W.L.R. 1026; *James Archdale & Co. Ltd v. Comservices Ltd* [1954] 1 W.L.R. 459; *Harris Ltd v. Continental Express Ltd* [1961] 1 Lloyd's Rep. 251; *Westcott v. J.H. Jenner Plasterers and Bovis* [1962] 1 Lloyd's Rep. 309; *Spalding v. Tarmac Civil Engineering Ltd* [1967] 1 W.L.R. 1508; *Gillespie Brothers & Co. Ltd v. Roy Bowles Transport Ltd* [1973] 1 Q.B. 400; *Blake v. Richards & Wallington Industries* (1974) 16 K.I.R. 151; *Comyn Ching & Co. (London) v. Oriental Tube Co.* [1981] Com.L.R. 67; *Thompson v. T. Lohan (Plant Hire) Ltd* [1987] 1 W.L.R. 649; *Hancock Shipping Co. Ltd v. Deacon & Trysail (Private) Ltd* [1991] 2 Lloyd's Rep. 550; *Nelson v. Atlantic Power and Gas* 1995 S.L.T. 46; *Morris v. Breaveglen Ltd* [1997] C.L.Y. 937; *Smedvig Ltd v. Elf Exploration U.K. plc.* [1998] 2 Lloyd's Rep. 659; *Deepak Fertilisers and Petrochemicals Corpn v. ICI* [1999] 1 Lloyd's Rep. 387. Contrast (ineffective indemnities) *A.M.F. International Ltd v. Magnet Bowling Ltd* [1968] 1 W.L.R. 1028; *Walters v. Whessoe Ltd* [1968] 1 W.L.R. 1056; *British Crane Hire Corp. Ltd v. Ipswich Plant Hire Ltd* [1975] Q.B. 303; *C. Davis Metal Producers Ltd v. Gilyott & Scott Ltd* [1975] 2 Lloyd's Rep. 422; *Smith v. South Wales Switchgear Co. Ltd* [1978] 1 W.L.R. 165; *Actis Co. Ltd v. Sankis Steamship Co. Ltd* [1982] 1 Lloyd's Rep. 7; *Wimpey Construction U.K. Ltd v. Scottish Special Housing Assn.* [1986] 2 All E.R. 951; *Sonat Offshore SA v. Amerada Hess Development Ltd* [1988] 1 Lloyd's Rep. 145; *Dorset County Council v. Southern Felt Roofing Co.* (1990) 6 Const.L.J. 37; *Caledonia Ltd v. Orbit Valve Co. Europe* [1994] 1 W.L.R. 1515; *Glebe Island Terminals Pty. Ltd v. Continental Seagram Pty. Ltd* [1994] 1 Lloyd's Rep. 213. *Shell Chemicals Ltd v. P.&O. Roadtanks Ltd* [1995] 1 Lloyd's Rep. 297; *Stirling v. Norwest* 1997 S.L.T. 974; *Hawkins v. Northern Marine Management Ltd* 1998 S.L.T. 1107.

[7] *Sze Hai Tong Bank Co. Ltd v. Rambler Cycle Co. Ltd* [1959] A.C. 576, 588.

[8] *Alexander v. Railway Executive* [1951] 2 K.B. 882; *Swan Hunter and Wigham Richardson Ltd v. France Tyne & Wear Co. Ltd (The Albion)* [1953] 1 W.L.R. 1026, 1030; *Sze Hai Tong Bank Co. Ltd v. Rambler Cycle Co. Ltd, supra; Colverd & Co. Ltd v. Anglo-Overseas Transport Co. Ltd* [1961] 2 Lloyd's Rep. 352, 363. For a time it was considered that a "deliberate" breach had to be one which could be attributed to the contracting party personally, and not one imputed vicariously through his employees or agents: *Chartered Bank of India v. British India Steam Navigation Ltd* [1909] A.C. 369, as explained in *Sze Hai Tong Bank Co. Ltd v. Rambler Cycle Co. Ltd, supra,* at 588; *John Carter (Fine Worsteds) Ltd v. Harrison Haulage (Leeds) Ltd* [1965] 2 Q.B. 495, but it submitted that this view would no longer be followed. See Guest (1961) 77 L.Q.R. 98, 116.

[9] *Photo Production Ltd v. Securicor Transport Ltd* [1980] A.C. 827; *post,* § 14–022.

[10] [1967] 1 A.C. 361; *post,* § 14–021.

[11] At 435. See also *ibid.* at 394, 414, 415, 429.

misconduct[12] or a deliberate non-performance of the contract,[13] but "to create a special rule for deliberate acts is unnecessary and may lead astray."[14]

Some clauses, however, while disclaiming liability for loss or damage caused **14–017** by negligence, accept liability for loss or damage due to "wilful neglect or default,"[15] "wilful misconduct"[16] or "gross negligence".[17]

Burden of proof. It is for the party seeking to rely on the exemption clause **14–018** to show that the clause, on its true construction, covers the obligation or liability which it purports to restrict or exclude. It would also seem that, in general, it is for that party to prove that the claimant's case is within the clause.[18] If the promise is qualified by an exemption which covers the whole scope of the promise,[19] the claimant must bring himself within the promise as qualified.[20] Further, if there is an exception to the exemption, for example, in the event of wilful neglect or default,[21] then the burden rests upon the claimant to prove that his case falls within the exception.[22] The form is not, however, conclusive, and the matter is in every case a question of construction of the instrument as a whole.[23] In *Firestone Tyre & Rubber Co. Ltd v. Vokins & Co. Ltd*,[24] where a lighterage clause provided that goods were carried only at owner's risk, excepting loss arising from pilferage and theft whilst in the course of transit, Devlin J. held that the onus was still on the lightermen to prove that the loss did not occur by theft or pilferage.

If the party seeking to rely on the clause makes out a prima facie case that the **14–019** facts are such as to bring the case within the clause, then it appears that the

---

[12] *Alexander v. Railway Executive, supra* (but see *post*, § 14–036, n. 9); *Sze Hai Tong Bank Ltd v. Rambler Cycle Co. Ltd, supra*, at 587; *Levison v. Patent Steam Carpet Cleaning Co. Ltd* [1978] Q.B. 69.

[13] *The Cap Palos* [1921] P. 458, 471, 472. Contrast *Compania Portorafti Commerciale SA v. Ultramar Panama Inc.* [1990] 1 Lloyd's Rep. 310 (Hague-Visby Rules).

[14] *Suisse Atlantique* case, *supra*, at 435.

[15] On the meaning of this phrase, see *Re City Equitable Fire Insurance Co. Ltd* [1925] 1 Ch. 407; *Circle Freight International Ltd v. Medeast Gulf Exports Ltd* [1988] 2 Lloyd's Rep. 427; *Bovis International Ltd v. Circle Line Partnerships* [1995] N.P.C. 128.

[16] On the meaning of this phrase, see *Hoare v. G.W. Ry.* (1877) 37 L.T. 186; *Lewis v. G.W. Ry.* (1877) 3 Q.B.D. 195, 206; *Graham v. Belfast & Northern Counties Ry. Co.* [1901] 2 I.R. 13; *Forder v. G.W. Ry.* [1905] 2 K.B. 532; *Horabin v. B.O.A.C.* [1952] 2 Lloyd's Rep 450; *Rustenberg Platinum Mines Ltd v. SAA* [1977] 1 Lloyd's Rep. 564, 569; *National Semiconductors (U.K.) Ltd v. UPS Ltd* [1996] 2 Lloyd's Rep. 212, 214; *Lacey's Footwear v. Bowler International Freight (Wholesale) Ltd* [1997] 2 Lloyd's Rep. 369; *Thomas Cook Group Ltd v. Air Malta Co. Ltd* [1997] 2 Lloyd's Rep 399.

[17] On the meaning of this phrase, see *Red Sea Tankers Ltd v. Papachristidis* [1997] 2 Lloyd's Rep. 547, 586.

[18] *The Glendarroch* [1894] P. 226, 231; *Munro Brice & Co. v. War Risks Association* [1918] 2 K.B. 78 (revd. on other grounds [1920] 3 K.B. 94). Contrast *Hurst v. Evans* [1917] 1 K.B. 352.

[19] See, *e.g. Photo Production Ltd v. Securicor Transport Ltd* [1980] A.C. 827; *post*, § 14–022.

[20] *Munro Brice & Co. v. War Risks Association, supra*, at 88.

[21] See *ante*, § 14–017.

[22] *H.C. Smith Ltd v. G.W. Ry.* [1922] 1 A.C. 178; *Kenyon Son & Craven Ltd v. Baxter Hoare Ltd* [1971] 1 W.L.R. 232; *Johnson Matthey & Co. Ltd v. Constantine Terminals Ltd* [1976] 2 Lloyd's Rep. 215; *Sig Bergesen DY. and Co. v. Mobil Shipping and Transportation Co.* [1993] 2 Lloyd's Rep. 453, 462. *cf. Port Swettenham Port Authority v. T.W. Wu & Co.* [1979] A.C. 580, and n. 30, *infra*, (bailment).

[23] *Munro Brice & Co. v. War Risks Association, supra*, at 89.

[24] [1951] 1 Lloyd's Rep. 32.

claimant must disprove it by showing that the loss or damage was occasioned by an act or omission falling outside the clause.[25] However, in *Levison v. Patent Steam Carpet Cleaning Co. Ltd*,[26] where a clause in a contract of bailment was sufficient to exclude liability for negligence on the part of the bailee but not a "fundamental breach" of the contract, the Court of Appeal held that the onus was on the bailee to show that he was not guilty of a fundamental breach, although the same court had previously decided[27] to the contrary in a case involving a contract of carriage. With the final demise of the doctrine of "fundamental breach,"[28] it is suggested that *Levison's* case deserves reconsideration.[29] A bailor may nevertheless be assisted by the rule that it is for a bailee who is sued in respect of the loss of the goods bailed to prove that the loss occurred without his negligence.[30]

3. Fundamental Breach

14–020   **Supposed rule of law.** It was at one time supposed that a party to a contract would be precluded from relying upon an exemption clause contained in it where he had been guilty of a fundamental breach of contract or the breach of a fundamental term. Statements in certain cases[31] tended to encourage the view that there existed a rule of substantive law preventing a party from relying on an exemption clause in situations of fundamental breach or the breach of a fundamental term, regardless of the wording of the clause. It was predicated that there were certain breaches of contract ("fundamental breaches") which were so totally destructive of the obligations of the party in default that liability for such a breach could in no circumstances be excluded or restricted by means of an exemption clause. Similarly there existed a category of terms ("fundamental terms") which were narrower than a condition of the contract. A fundamental term, so it was said, "underlies the whole contract so that, if it is not complied with, the performance becomes totally different from that which the contract contemplates."[32] It was part of the "core" of the contract,[33] and "however extensive the exception clause may be, it has no application if there has been a

---

[25] *The Glendarroch, supra*, at 231; *Shipping Corpn. of India Ltd v. Gamlen Chemical Co. (Australasia) Pty. Ltd* (1980) 147 C.L.R. 142, 168.

[26] [1978] Q.B. 69. See also *Woolmer v. Delmer Price Ltd* [1955] 1 Q.B. 291.

[27] *Hunt & Winterbotham (West of England) Ltd v. B.R.S. (Parcels) Ltd* [1962] 1 Q.B. 617.

[28] See *post*, § 14–024. *Levison's* case was decided before *Photo Production Ltd v. Securicor Transport Ltd* [1980] A.C. 827 (*post*, § 14–022) but was not doubted in that case.

[29] See *Glebe Island Terminals Pty. Ltd v. Continental Seagram Pty. Ltd* [1994] 1 Lloyd's Rep. 213, 238.

[30] *Joseph Travers & Sons Ltd v. Cooper* [1915] 1 K.B. 73; *Woolmer v. Delmer Price Ltd, supra*; *J. Spurling Ltd v. Bradshaw* [1956] 1 W.L.R. 461, 466; *Houghland v. R.B. Low (Luxury Coaches) Ltd* [1962] 1 Q.B. 694; *Levison v. Patent Steam Carpet Cleaning Co. Ltd* [1978] Q.B. 69, 82; *Port Swettenham Port Authority v. T.W. Wu & Co.* [1979] A.C. 580; *Victoria Fur Traders Ltd v. Roadline (U.K.) Ltd* [1981] 1 Lloyd's Rep. 570; see Vol. II, §§ 33–010, 33–046.

[31] *J. Spurling Ltd v. Bradshaw* [1956] 1 W.L.R. 461, 465; *Karsales (Harrow) Ltd v. Wallis* [1956] 1 W.L.R. 936, 940, 943; *Sze Hai Tong Bank Ltd v. Rambler Cycle Co. Ltd* [1959] A.C. 576, 587, 588, 589; *Yeoman Credit Ltd v. Apps* [1962] 2 Q.B. 508, 520; *Charterhouse Credit Co. Ltd v. Tolly* [1963] 2 Q.B. 683, 710; *Astley Industrial Trust v. Grimley* [1963] 1 W.L.R. 1468, 1470; see also *ante*, § 12–021.

[32] *Smeaton Hanscomb & Co. Ltd v. Sassoon I. Setty, Son & Co.* [1953] 1 W.L.R. 1468, 1470; see *ante*, § 12–021.

[33] See Melville (1956) 19 M.L.R. 26.

breach of a fundamental term."[34] The two expressions "fundamental breach" and "breach of a fundamental term" were used to some extent interchangeably,[35] but formulated in this way they embodied a rule of law to be applied notwithstanding the agreement of the parties as expressed in the exemption clause.

Suisse Atlantique case. The view that the principle of fundamental breach constituted a rule of law was, however, rejected by Pearson L.J. in *U.G.S. Finance Ltd v. National Mortgage Bank of Greece*, where he said[36]:   **14–021**

> "As to the question of 'fundamental breach,' I think there is a rule of construction that normally an exception or exclusion clause or similar provision in a contract should be construed as not applying to a situation created by a fundamental breach of the contract. This is not an independent rule of law imposed by the court on the parties willy-nilly in disregard of their contractual intention. On the contrary it is a rule of construction based on the presumed intention of the contracting parties. . . . This rule of construction is not new in principle but it has become prominent in recent years in consequence of the tendency to have standard forms of contract containing exceptions clauses drawn in extravagantly wide terms, which would produce absurd results if applied literally."

This statement was unanimously approved by the House of Lords in *Suisse Atlantique Société d'Armement Maritime SA v. N.V. Rotterdamsche Kolen Centrale*.[37] In that case, shipowners sued the charterers of a ship for damages for delays in loading and unloading the chartered vessel. The charterers relied on the usual demurrage clause in the charterparty as establishing the full measure of their liability; but the shipowners contended that this clause did not protect the charterers since the breaches of contract which caused the delays amounted to a fundamental breach of contract. They claimed damages at large. The House of Lords rejected this claim. Their Lordships held:

(i) that the demurrage clause was not an exemption clause but an agreed damages provision,[38]

(ii) that, in any event, since the shipowners had not treated the charter as repudiated, they were still bound by its provisions,[39] and

(iii) that, even if the clause were an exemption clause, it plainly covered the breach alleged, whether or not this was "fundamental" in the sense that it would have entitled the shipowners to be discharged.[40]

Their Lordships were clearly of the opinion that any statement of the principle of fundamental breach as a rule of law could not be supported in principle or in the

---

[34] *Karsales (Harrow) Ltd v. Wallis, supra,* at 943.

[35] *cf. Suisse Atlantique Société d'Armement Maritime SA v. N.V. Rotterdamsche Kolen Centrale* [1967] 1 A.C. 361, 393, 421; *Wathes (Western) Ltd v. Austins (Menswear) Ltd* [1976] 1 Lloyd's Rep. 14, 19.

[36] [1964] 1 Lloyd's Rep. 446, 450. See also *Gibaud v. G.E. Ry.* [1921] 2 K.B. 426, 435; *The Cap Palos* [1921] P. 458, 470, 472; *L. & N.W. Ry. v. Neilson* [1922] 2 A.C. 263, 272; *Cunard SS. Co. v. Buerger* [1927] A.C. 1, 13; *Frenkel v. MacAndrews & Co. Ltd* [1929] A.C. 545, 562; *Calico Printers' Assn. v. Barclays Bank* (1931) 36 Com.Cas. 197, 203; *Connolly Shaw v. Nordenfjeldske SS. Co.* (1934) 50 T.L.R. 418.

[37] [1967] 1 A.C. 361; see Treitel (1966) 29 M.L.R. 546.

[38] See *ante,* § 14–004.

[39] [1967] 1 A.C. 361, 395, 407, 413, 426, 437.

[40] *ibid.* at 395, 407, 415, 426, 437.

light of previous authority.[41] So far as the use of the expression "fundamental breach" was concerned, Lord Wilberforce pointed out[42] that it had been used in the cases to denote two quite different things, namely,

    (i) a performance totally different from that which the contract contemplated,

    (ii) a breach of contract more serious than one which would entitle the other party merely to damages and which (at least) would entitle him to refuse further performance of the contract.

There was no necessary coincidence between these two kinds of (so-called) fundamental breach. After giving a series of examples[43] of how the courts had approached the problem of a fundamental breach in the former sense, he concluded[44]: "The conception, therefore, of 'fundamental breach' as one which, through ascertainment of the parties' contractual intentions, falls outside an exceptions clause is well recognised and comprehensible." On the other hand, Lord Reid said[45]: "General use of the term 'fundamental breach' is of recent origin, and I can find nothing to indicate that it means either more or less than the well known type of breach which entitles the innocent party to treat it as repudiatory and to rescind the contract." While, therefore, their Lordships were agreed that the application of an exemption clause to a breach of contract was a matter of construction of the contract, the question whether and to what extent any special rules were applicable to cases of "fundamental breach" (in the sense of "total" as opposed to repudiatory breach), was to some extent left open.

14–022   **Securicor case.** Certain statements in the *Suisse Atlantique* case further suggested (perhaps by way of illustration only) that in particular instances of fundamental breach an exemption clause would or would be presumed to be inapplicable.[46] Moreover, in his speech Lord Reid said[47]: "I do not think that there is generally much difficulty where the innocent party has elected to treat the breach as a repudiation, bring the contract to an end and sue for damages. Then the whole contract has ceased to exist, including the exclusion clause, and I do not see how that clause can then be used to exclude an action for loss which will be suffered by the innocent party after it has ceased to exist . . . ." Lord Reid's statement was taken up and extended by the Court of Appeal in subsequent cases[48] which held that the protection of an exemption clause ceased to be available to a party guilty of a repudiatory breach if the other party accepted the breach as terminating the contract or if the breach was of such a nature as to render the contract impossible of further performance. This departure was, however, condemned by the House of Lords in *Photo Production Ltd v. Securicor*

[41] *ibid.* at 392, 399, 405, 410, 425, 431–432.
[42] At 431.
[43] At 432–435.
[44] At 434. See also Lord Dilhorne at 393.
[45] At 397. See also Lord Hodson at 410; Lord Upjohn at 422.
[46] See Lord Denning M.R. in *Levison v. Patent Steam Carpet Cleaning Co. Ltd* [1978] Q.B. 69; *Photo Production Ltd v. Securicor Transport Ltd* [1978] 1 W.L.R. 856, 863.
[47] [1967] 1 A.C. 361, 398. See also Lord Upjohn at 425.
[48] *Harbutt's "Plasticine" Ltd v. Wayne Tank and Pump Co. Ltd* [1970] 1 Q.B. 447. See also *Farnworth Finance Facilities Ltd v. Attryde* [1970] 1 W.L.R. 1053; *Eastman Chemical International A.G. v. N.M.T. Trading Ltd* [1972] 2 Lloyd's Rep. 25; *Wathes (Western) Ltd v. Austins (Menswear) Ltd* [1976] 1 Lloyd's Rep. 14 (where contract affirmed).

Transport Ltd.[49] In that case, the defendants agreed to provide a visiting patrol service to the plaintiffs' factory at a charge of £8 15s. a week. The contract contained an exemption clause, the most relevant part of which stated: "Under no circumstances shall the company [the defendants] be responsible for any injurious act or default by any employee of the company unless such act or default could have been foreseen and avoided by the exercise of due diligence on the part of the company as his employer." An employee of the defendants deliberately lit a fire in the factory, and a large part of the premises was burned down. The Court of Appeal held[50] that the defendants, having been employed to safeguard the factory, had committed a fundamental breach of their contract with the plaintiffs and that the exemption clause could not be construed to cover the act of their employee in setting the premises on fire. It was further held that the destruction of the factory brought the contract to an end by rendering further performance impossible so that the defendants could not rely on the exemption clause to protect them from the consequences of the breach. The House of Lords reversed the Court of Appeal's decision. Their Lordships unanimously rejected the view that a breach of contract by one party, accepted by the other as discharging him from further performance of his obligations under the contract, brought the contract to an end, and, together with it, any exemption clause.[51] The House further reaffirmed[52] the principle that the question whether an exemption clause protected one party to a contract in the event of breach, or in the event of what would (but for the presence of the exemption clause) have been a breach, depended upon the proper construction of the contract. They held that, as a matter of construction, the exemption clause in question clearly relieved the defendants from liability. The defendants had effectively modified their obligation to one of exercising due diligence in their capacity as employers. The clause apportioned the risk between the parties: the risk of arson not being accepted by the defendants having regard to the nature and cost of the services provided and falling on the plaintiffs who could more economically insure against it.

George Mitchell case. A third leading case is that of *George Mitchell (Chesterhall) Ltd v. Finney Lock Seeds Ltd,*[53] where the respondents ordered from the appellants, who were seed merchants, a quantity of Dutch winter white cabbage seeds. The seeds supplied were invoiced as "Finney's Late Dutch Special." Owing to errors by the appellants' suppliers and employees, the seeds were in fact not of this variety but were autumn cabbage seeds. The resulting crop proved to be worthless and had to be ploughed in. In an action by the respondents for wasted expenditure and loss of anticipated profits, the appellants relied on their standard conditions of sale. These provided: first, that in the event of any seeds sold or agreed to be sold not complying with the express terms of the contract of sale, the limit of the appellants' obligation was to replace the seeds or refund the purchase price; secondly, that the appellants excluded "all liability for any loss or damage arising from use of any seeds . . . supplied by us and for any consequential loss or damage arising out of such use or any failure in the

14–023

---

[49] [1980] A.C. 827. See also *Ailsa Craig Fishing Co. Ltd v. Malvern Fishing Co. Ltd* [1983] 1 W.L.R. 964; *Lifesavers (Australasia) Ltd v. Frigmobile Pty. Ltd* (1983) 1 N.S.W.R. 431.

[50] [1978] 1 W.L.R. 856.

[51] [1980] A.C. 827, 844–845, 847–850, 853. See also s.9(1) of the Unfair Contract Terms Act 1977. An exception may exist in "deviation" cases; see *post,* § 14–029.

[52] *ibid.* at 845, 850–851, 853.

[53] [1983] 2 A.C. 803.

performance of or any defect in any seeds . . . supplied by us or for any other loss or damage whatsoever save for, at our option, liability for any such replacement or refund as aforesaid"; thirdly, that express or implied conditions and warranties not stated in the conditions were excluded. A majority of the Court of Appeal[54] held that, at common law, this wording was insufficient to limit the appellants' liability. Oliver L.J.[55] considered that the first condition applied only to seeds "sold or agreed to be sold" and so could only relate to goods which were actually the subject-matter of the contract between the parties, *i.e.* winter white cabbage seeds. The second condition was merely a supplement to the first and did not cover a case where what had been supplied was wholly different from what had been ordered. The House of Lords, however, unanimously held that, at common law, the limitation was effective.[56] The second condition, read as a whole, unambiguously limited the appellants' liability to replacement of the seeds or a refund of the price. The defective seeds were seeds sold and delivered, just as clearly as they were seeds supplied, by the appellants to the respondents. The judgment of Oliver L.J. came, it was said,[57] "dangerously near to reintroducing by the back door the doctrine of 'fundamental breach' which this House in *Securicor* . . . had so forcibly evicted from the front."

14–024   **Conclusion.** It is clear that there is no longer any rule of law by which exemption clauses are rendered ineffective in the face of a "fundamental breach" or the breach of a "fundamental term." In the *Photo Production* case, Lord Diplock stated[58] that, if the expression "fundamental breach" is to be retained, it should, in the interests of clarity, be confined to the ordinary case of a breach of which the consequences are such as to entitle the innocent party to elect to put an end to all primary obligations of both parties remaining unperformed. No express reference was made by him to the expression "fundamental term," but the inference is that there exists no category of terms which can be said to be in any sense "fundamental" other than conditions.[59] On this basis, it is submitted that there is not now even any presumption that, in inserting a clause of limitation or exclusion into their contract, the parties are not contemplating its application to a fundamental breach or the breach of a fundamental term.[60] The question is in all cases whether the clause, on its true construction, extends to cover the obligation or liability which it is sought to exclude or restrict.

4. Application of Rules of Construction to Particular Contracts

14–025   **Generally.** The rules of construction mentioned in the second section of this chapter may now be illustrated in their application to particular contracts. Certain of the cases cited were, however, decided at a time when the principle of

---

[54] [1983] Q.B. 284 (Oliver and Kerr L.JJ., Lord Denning M.R. dissenting).

[55] Kerr L.J. (with whom Oliver L.J. agreed) also based his decision on the ground that the clause was not sufficiently unambiguous to exclude liability for negligence: see *ante*, § 14–010.

[56] But the clause was, however, held unreasonable under the modified s.55 of the Sale of Goods Act 1979, as set out in para. 11 of Sched. 1 to that Act. See now the Unfair Contract Terms Act 1977; *post*, § 14–087.

[57] [1983] 2 A.C. at 813.

[58] [1980] A.C. 827, 849. See also the *Suisse Atlantique* case [1967] 1 A.C. 361, 397, 410, 422.

[59] [1980] A.C. at 849. See also the *Suisse Atlantique* case, *supra*, at 422; and *ante*, § 14–021.

[60] *cf.* Lord Upjohn in the *Suisse Atlantique* case, *supra*, at 427.

"fundamental breach" was to a greater or less extent recognised by the courts. Such cases should probably now be regarded as instances where an exemption clause was, as a matter of construction, held to be inapplicable.

Contracts of sale of goods: terms about title. Section 6(1) of the Unfair   **14–026**
Contract Terms Act 1977[61] invalidates (except in the case of international sales)[62] any term exempting from the terms about title implied by section 12 of the Sale of Goods Act 1979. Even at common law, however, it is probable that the courts would be reluctant to hold that an exemption clause, framed in general terms, was intended by the parties completely to exclude liability for breach of the implied term on the part of the seller that he has a right to sell the goods, since "the whole object of a sale is to transfer property from one person to another."[63] They would have to be satisfied that the parties intended the transaction to be merely the sale and purchase of a chance (*emptio spei*) that the seller might or might not have a good title to the goods sold.[64]

Sale of goods: terms as to quality, etc. Section 6(2) of the 1977 Act[65] further   **14–027**
invalidates the exclusion of the terms as to quality, fitness for purpose, and correspondence with description and sample, implied by sections 13 to 15 of the Sale of Goods Act 1979, if the buyer "deals as consumer."[66] In any other case, an exemption clause is enforceable only in so far as it satisfies the requirement of reasonableness.[67] But, at common law, if there is a gross disparity between the goods as described in the contract of sale and as delivered, a number of cases have held that an exemption clause, for example, which purports to require the buyer to take the goods "with all faults and imperfections," or to exclude the seller's liability for errors of description, or to take away the buyer's right to reject the goods, may be held not to apply to a failure to supply the contract goods.[68] Even a clause in the familiar form which excludes all conditions and warranties, express or implied by common law, statute or otherwise, may possibly not be construed to cover the delivery of goods which are wholly different

---

[61] See *post*, § 14–075; Vol. II, § 43–068.

[62] See s.26 of the 1977 Act; *post*, § 14–101; Vol. II, § 43–105.

[63] *Rowland v. Divall* [1923] 2 K.B. 500, 507. See also Guest (1961) 77 L.Q.R. 98, 100. Contrast Hudson (1957) 20 M.L.R. 236; (1961) 24 M.L.R. 690; and see Coote, *Exception Clauses* (1964), p. 61.

[64] *Chapman v. Speller* (1850) 14 Q.B. 621; *Eichholz v. Bannister* (1864) 17 C.B.(N.S.) 708; *Bagueley v. Hawley* (1867) L.R. 2 C.P. 625; *Warmings Used Cars v. Tucker* [1956] S.A.S.R. 249. See also s.12(3) of the Sale of Goods Act 1979: Vol. II, § 43–067.

[65] See *post*, § 14–075; Vol. II, § 43–099; But see s.26 (international sales).

[66] Defined in s.12 of the 1977 Act; *post*, § 14–064; Vol. II, § 43–101.

[67] s.6(3). See *post*, § 14–095; Vol. II, § 43–099.

[68] *Shepherd v. Kain* (1821) 5 B. & Ald. 240; *Nichol v. Godts* (1854) 10 Exch. 191; *Wieler v. Schilizzi* (1856) 17 C.B. 619; *Josling v. Kingsford* (1863) 13 C.B.(N.S.) 447; *Azémar v. Casella* (1867) L.R. 2 C.P. 677; *Bowes v. Shand* (1877) 2 App.Cas. 455, 480; *Gorton v. Macintosh* [1883] W.N. 103; *Wallis, Son and Wells v. Pratt and Haynes* [1911] A.C. 394; *Wimble v. Lillico* (1922) 38 T.L.R. 296; *Munro & Co. Ltd v. Meyer* [1930] 2 K.B. 312; *Green v. Arcos Ltd* (1931) 47 T.L.R. 336; *Wilensko v. Fenwick* [1938] 3 All E.R. 429; *Champanhac & Co. Ltd v. Waller & Co. Ltd* [1948] 2 All E.R. 724; *Smeaton Hanscomb & Co. Ltd v. Sassoon I. Setty, Son & Co. (No. 1)* [1953] 1 W.L.R. 1468, 1470; *Boshali v. Allied Commercial Exporters Ltd* (1961) 105 S.J. 987; *Suisse Atlantique Société d'Armement Maritime SA v. N.V. Rotterdamsche Kolen Centrale* [1967] 1 A.C. 361, 404, 410, 427, 433; *Benjamin's Sale of Goods* (5th ed., 1997), §§ 13–026, 13–027, 13–029, 13–030; Vol. II, § 43–107.

from those contracted for.[69] However, there is no rule of law to prevent a seller, who—to use a familiar example—has contracted to deliver peas, from excluding or restricting his liability in the event that he delivers beans,[70] or permits him to substitute beans in their place,[71] provided that the clause is sufficiently unambiguous in its terms to admit of this construction.

14–028   **Hire-purchase.** Section 6 of the Unfair Contract Terms Act 1977[72] contains provisions prohibiting, either absolutely or subject to certain qualifications, exclusion of the terms as to title, quality, fitness for purpose, and correspondence with description or sample implied by sections 8 to 11 of the Supply of Goods (Implied Terms) Act 1973.[73] At common law, principles have been applied to hire-purchase transactions which are similar to those applied to contracts of sale. It has been held, for example, that a clause in such terms as "no condition or warranty as to the condition or fitness for any purpose of the goods is given by the owner or implied herein" will not be construed to extend to the supply of goods which are so defective that what is delivered is totally different from that promised.[74] It is also probable that the courts would not construe a general exemption clause to have so wide an ambit as to negative the implied undertaking on the part of the owner that he has a good title to the goods let on hire, particularly in view of the fact that such terms as "owner" and "option to purchase" appear in the agreement.[75]

14–029   **Carriage of goods: deviation.** Contracts for the carriage of goods are controlled only to a limited extent by the Unfair Contract Terms Act 1977.[76] At common law, in a contract for the carriage of goods, any unnecessary deviation from the agreed or customary route constitutes a breach of the contract of affreightment.[77] Such a breach entitles the owner to treat himself as discharged, and, unless, with knowledge of the facts, he elects to affirm the transaction, the

---

[69] *Pinnock Bros. v. Lewis and Peat* [1923] 1 K.B. 690; *Andrews Bros. (Bournemouth) Ltd v. Singer & Co. Ltd* [1934] 1 K.B. 17, 23; *Suisse Atlantique Société d'Armement Maritime v. N.V. Rotterdamsche Kolen Centrale* [1967] 1 A.C. 361, 404, 413, 432, 433. Contrast *L'Estrange v. Graucob Ltd* [1934] 2 K.B. 394. See also *Beck & Co. v. Szymanowski & Co.* [1924] A.C. 43, 48; *Pollock & Co. v. Macrae*, 1922 S.C.(HL) 192; and *post*, § 14–028, n. 74 (hire-purchase).

[70] *George Mitchell (Chesterhall) Ltd v. Finney Lock Seeds Ltd* [1983] 2 A.C. 803 (although, at 813, Lord Bridge said "In my opinion, this is not a 'peas and beans' case at all.").

[71] See Lord Devlin [1966] C.L.J. at 212.

[72] See *post*, § 14–075; Vol. II, § 38–551.

[73] See Vol. II, §§ 38–277, 38–343.

[74] *Karsales (Harrow) Ltd v. Wallis* [1956] 1 W.L.R. 936; *Yeoman Credit Ltd v. Apps* [1962] 2 Q.B. 508; *Charterhouse Credit Ltd v. Tolly* [1963] 2 Q.B. 683 (which was overruled in *Photo Production Ltd v. Securicor Transport Ltd* [1980] A.C. 827); *Unity Finance Ltd v. Hammond* (1962) 106 S.J. 327; *Suisse Atlantique* case, *ante*, at 402, 404, 425, 433; *Farnworth Finance Facilities Ltd v. Attryde* [1970] 1 W.L.R. 1053; *Guarantee Trust of Jersey v. Gardner* (1973) 117 S.J. 564, CA. Contrast *Handley v. Marston* (1962) 106 S.J. 327; *Astley Industrial Trust Ltd v. Grimley* [1963] 1 W.L.R. 584.

[75] See Vol. II, § 38–277. For the implied undertakings of title at common law, see *Karflex Ltd v. Poole* [1933] 2 K.B. 251; *Mercantile Union Guarantee Corp. v. Wheatley* [1938] 1 K.B. 490; *Warman v. Southern Counties Car Finance Corp. Ltd* [1949] 2 K.B. 576.

[76] See ss.2, 3 and Sched. 1, paras. 2, 3. See *post*, §§ 14–068, 14–069, 14–097, 14–098. *cf.* § 14–102.

[77] *L. & N.W. Ry. v. Neilson* [1922] 2 A.C. 363 (carriage by land); *Hain SS. Co. Ltd v. Tate & Lyle Ltd* (1936) 41 Com.Cas. 350 (carriage by sea). See also *Rotterdamsche Bank N.V. v. B.O.A.C.* [1953] 1 W.L.R. 493, 502–503 (carriage by air); *Suisse Atlantique Société d'Armement Maritime SA v. N.V. Rotterdamsche Kolen Centrale* [1967] 1 A.C. 361, 390, 399, 411, 422, 433; Coote, *Exception Clauses* (1964), p. 80. See Vol. II, § 36–041.

special terms of the contract (including any exemption clause) which are designed to apply to the contract journey are held to have no application to the deviating journey.[78] So strict is this rule that although the deviation has not been the cause of any loss to the owner's goods and is a mere incident in the voyage, nevertheless, once it has taken place the carrier is no longer entitled to rely on clauses of exemption contained in the contract, unless it can be shown that the loss would have happened in any event.[79] But even if the contract is treated as continuing, exemption clauses will be strictly construed, so that, for example, a disclaimer of liability for loss of or damage to goods "in transit" will not extend to cover a deviation.[80] Deviation cases are, however, *sui generis* and not to be extended.[81] Moreover, clauses which confer upon the carrier a liberty to deviate will, if clearly expressed, be upheld[82] although they will be so construed as not substantially to defeat the main purpose of the contract voyage.[83]

Carriage of goods: delay. It is also the duty of the carrier to carry the goods **14-030** with all reasonable dispatch to their destination. An unreasonable and protracted delay may entitle the charterer or consignor to treat the contract as repudiated.[84] Delay will not necessarily lie outside the scope of an exemption clause,[85] but it will do so where the parties cannot be taken to have intended that the clause should extend to the period of the delay[86] or to a risk consequent upon the delay which is wholly at variance with the contract of carriage.[87]

Carriage on deck. Where a carrier of goods by sea undertakes to carry the **14-031** goods under deck, an exemption clause which excludes or restricts his liability

---

[78] See *Davis v. Garrett* (1830) 6 Bing. 716; *Leduc v. Ward* (1888) 20 Q.B.D. 475; *The Dunbeth* [1897] P. 133; *Mallett v. G.E. Ry.* [1899] 1 Q.B. 309; *J. Thorley Ltd v. Orchis SS. Ltd* [1907] 1 K.B. 660; *Internationale Guano, etc. v. Macandreir & Co.* [1909] 2 K.B. 360; *Gunyon v. S.E. & Chatham Ry. Companies' Managing Committee* [1915] 2 K.B. 370; *J. Morrison & Co. Ltd v. Shaw, Savill & Albion Co. Ltd* [1916] 2 K.B. 783; *London & N.W. Ry. v. Neilson, supra*; *U.S. Shipping Board v. Bunge y Born* (1925) 31 Com.Cas. 118; *Cunard SS. Co. Ltd v. Buerger* [1927] A.C. 1; *Stag Line Ltd v. Foscolo, Mango & Co. Ltd* [1932] A.C. 328; *Hain SS. Co. Ltd v. Tate & Lyle Ltd, supra*. On deviation generally, see *Scrutton on Charterparties* (19th ed., 1984), p. 259.

[79] *Suisse Atlantique* case, *supra*, at 442. cf. *Drew Brown v. The Orient Trader* [1973] 2 Lloyd's Rep. 174.

[80] *L. & N.W. Ry. v. Neilson, supra*, at 278.

[81] *Photo Production Ltd v. Securicor Transport Ltd* [1980] A.C. 827, 845. In *Kenya Railways v. Antares Pte Ltd* [1987] 1 Lloyd's Rep. 424, 430 and *State Trading Corpn. of India v. M. Golodetz Ltd* [1989] 2 Lloyd's Rep. 277, 289, Lloyd L.J. stated that "they should now be assimilated into the ordinary law of contract", but this would be difficult to achieve while it remains the case that the protection of the clause goes in the absence of affirmation. See Baughen [1991] L.M.C.L.Q. 70.

[82] *Mayfair Photographic Supplies (London) Ltd v. Baxter Hoare & Co. Ltd* [1972] 1 Lloyd's Rep. 410; *Trade and Transport Inc. v. Iino Kaiun Kaisha Ltd* [1973] 1 W.L.R. 210, 232. See *Scrutton on Charterparties* (19th ed., 1984), p. 264.

[83] *Leduc v. Ward, supra*; *Glynn v. Margetson* [1893] A.C. 351; *Potter v. Burrell* [1897] 1 Q.B. 97, 104; *V.O.S. of Moscow v. Temple SS. Co. Ltd* (1945) 173 L.T. 373, 376; *Suisse Atlantique* case, *supra*, at 393, 412, 427, 430.

[84] *Freeman v. Taylor* (1831) 8 Bing. 124; *Scaramanga v. Stamp* (1880) 5 C.P.D. 295; *Brandt v. Liverpool, Brazil & River Plate Steam Navigation Co.* [1924] 1 K.B. 575; *Cunard SS. Co. Ltd v. Buerger* [1927] A.C. 1. See Vol. II, § 36–042.

[85] *Colverd & Co. Ltd v. Anglo-Overseas Transport Ltd* [1961] 2 Lloyd's Rep. 352. cf. *Marston Excelsior Ltd v. Arbuckle Smith & Co. Ltd* [1971] 1 Lloyd's Rep. 70.

[86] *The Cap Palos* [1921] P. 458 (towage); *Brandt v. Liverpool, Brazil and River Plate S.N. Co. supra*, at 597, 601; *Bontex Knitting Works Ltd v. St. John's Garage* [1943] 2 All E.R. 690; affd. [1944] 1 All E.R. 381n. But see *Suisse Atlantique* case, *supra*, at 435.

[87] *Thomas National Transport (Melbourne) Pty. Ltd v. May & Baker (Australia) Pty. Ltd* [1966] 2 Lloyd's Rep. 347.

for loss or damage to the goods carried may be held to be inapplicable if the goods are carried on deck.[88] No doubt the same will apply if goods carried by land are similarly conveyed in an unauthorised manner.

14-032   **Road and seaworthiness.** A carrier of goods by land probably does not give any implied warranty, in the sense of an absolute undertaking, that he will provide a roadworthy vehicle or a competent and honest driver or crew.[89] At common law, however, a carrier of goods by sea, in the absence of an express stipulation to the contrary,[90] impliedly undertakes that his ship is seaworthy.[91] Although an undertaking of seaworthiness has been said "to underlie the whole contract of affreightment,"[92] its breach will not entitle the shipper to be discharged unless the breach is such as to frustrate the commercial purpose of the contract.[93] Nevertheless, as a matter of construction, exceptions in the charter or bill of lading will not be read as applying to breaches of an obligation to provide a seaworthy ship[94] unless their meaning is clear and unambiguous.[95]

14-033   **Misdelivery by carrier.** Misdelivery of the goods does not, of itself, prevent the application of an exemption clause in a contract of carriage.[96] But where the main object and intent of the contract is that delivery should be made to a certain person or persons, the clause may be limited and modified to the extent necessary to give effect to that object and intent. In *Sze Hai Tong Bank Ltd. v. Rambler Cycle Co. Ltd.*[97] goods carried by sea were to be delivered "unto order or his

---

[88] *Royal Exchange Shipping Co. Ltd v. Dixon* (1886) 12 App. Cas. 11, 16, 19; *J. Evans & Sons (Portsmouth) Ltd v. Andrea Merzario Ltd* [1976] 1 W.L.R. 1078, 1082, 1084, 1085; *Wibau Maschinenfabric Hartman SA v. Mackinnon Mackenzie & Co.* [1989] 2 Lloyd's Rep. 494. Contrast *Kenya Railways v. Antares Co. Pte. Ltd* [1987] 1 Lloyd's Rep. 424 (Hague-Visby Rules).

[89] *Readhead v. Midland Ry.* (1869) L.R. 4 Q.B. 379; *J. Carter (Fine Worsteds) Ltd v. Hanson Haulage (Leeds) Ltd* [1965] 2 Q.B. 495.

[90] Such a stipulation must be expressed in clear words and without ambiguity, or it will be insufficient: *Rathbone v. McIver* [1903] 2 K.B. 378; *Elderslie v. Borthwick* [1905] A.C. 93; *Nelson v. Nelson* [1908] A.C. 16; *Chartered Bank v. British India Steam Navigation Co.* [1909] A.C. 369, 375; *The Rossetti* [1972] 2 Lloyd's Rep. 116.

[91] But under the Carriage of Goods by Sea Act 1971, Sched., art. III(1), the carrier is only bound to exercise due diligence to make the ship seaworthy. See also s.3 of the 1971 Act.

[92] *Atlantic Shipping and Trading Co. Ltd v. Louis Dreyfus & Co.* [1922] 2 A.C. 250, 260.

[93] *The Europa* [1908] P. 84; *Kish v. Taylor* [1912] A.C. 604, 617; *Hongkong Fir Shipping Co. v. Kawasaki Kisen Kaisha* [1962] 2 Q.B. 26; see *post*, § 25–039.

[94] *Tattersall v. National SS. Co. Ltd* (1884) 12 Q.B.D. 297. See also *Steel v. State Line SS. Co.* (1877) 3 App.Cas. 72.

[95] *Kish v. Taylor* [1912] A.C. 604; *Bank of Australasia v. Clan Line* [1916] 1 K.B. 39; *Atlantic Shipping and Trading Co. Ltd v. Louis Dreyfus & Co., supra*, at 257. *Petrofina SA of Brussels v. Compagnie Italiana Transporto Olii Minerali of Genoa* (1937) 63 T.L.R. 650, 653.

[96] *Smackman v. General Steam Navigation Co.* (1908) 98 L.T. 396; *Chartered Bank v. British India Steam Navigation Co.* [1909] A.C. 369; *Pringle of Scotland v. Continental Express* [1962] 2 Lloyd's Rep. 80; *Port Jackson Stevedoring Pty. Ltd v. Salmond and Spraggon (Australia) Pty. Ltd* [1981] 1 W.L.R. 138; *Chellaram & Co. Ltd v. China Ocean Shipping Co.* [1989] 1 Lloyd's Rep. 493. See also *Hollins v. J. Davy Ltd* [1963] 1 Q.B. 844 (bailment), and Vol. II, §§ 36–029, 36–046.

[97] [1959] A.C. 576. See also *Alexander v. Railway Executive* [1951] 2 K.B. 882 (bailment); *Sydney City Council v. West* (1965) 114 C.L.R. 481; *Suisse Atlantique* case [1967] 1 A.C. 361, 411, 434; *Kanematsu (Hong Kong) Ltd v. Eurasia Express Line* [1998] 1 C.L. 472. *cf. Port Jackson Stevedoring Pty. Ltd v. Salmond and Spraggon (Australia) Pty. Ltd, supra; Nissho Iwai Australia Ltd v. Malaysian International Shipping Corpn. Berhad* (1989) 86 A.L.R. 375; *Sucre Export SA v. Northern Shipping Ltd* [1994] 2 Lloyd's Rep. 266; *Pyramid Sound NV v. Briese Schiffahrts GmbH & Co.* [1995] 2 Lloyd's Rep. 144.

assigns," but the contract provided that the responsibility of the carrier should be deemed to cease absolutely after the goods were discharged from the ship. After the goods were discharged from the ship, the carrier's agent released the goods to the consignees without production of the bill of lading. It was held that the exemption clause could not be construed to apply to a deliberate breach by the carrier of his primary obligation under the contract.

Bailment: acts inconsistent with bailment. Contracts of bailment for deposit **14–034** may be controlled in certain situations by the Unfair Contract Terms Act 1977.[98] At common law, any act of a bailee which is basically inconsistent with the terms of the bailment, such as the sale,[99] pledge[1] or offering for sale[2] of the goods bailed, puts an end to the bailment and the immediate right to possession of the goods forthwith revests in the bailor.[3] It is probable that, in the absence of specific authority to do such acts, a court would hold that they were not within the ambit of an exemption clause which simply limited or excluded the bailee's liability for loss of or damage to the goods bailed.[4]

Storage in wrong place. Likewise, under a contract of bailment, "If the **14–035** bailee uses a place other than the agreed one for storing the goods, or otherwise exposes the goods to risks quite different from those contemplated by the contract, he cannot rely on clauses in the contract designed to protect him against liability within the four corners of the contract, and has only such protection as is afforded him by the common law."[5] It should be emphasised, however, that this rule is again one of construction only: the terms of the contract may not require storage in a particular place, and may be otherwise sufficient to exclude liability for negligence, so that the bailee will not be liable.[6]

Misdelivery by bailee. Upon termination of the bailment, a bailee is normally **14–036** under an obligation to return the goods to the bailor or his nominee. If he negligently delivers the goods to a person not entitled to receive them, this will not necessarily preclude him from relying on an exemption clause, which may well be construed to cover the misdelivery in question. In *Hollins v. J. Davy Ltd.*,[7] the plaintiff garaged his motorcar at the defendants' garage under a contract which excluded liability for misdelivery. An employee of the defendants

---

[98] ss.2, 3; see *post*, §§ 14–068, 14–069.

[99] *Fenn v. Bittleston* (1851) 7 Exch. 152.

[1] *Nyberg v. Handelaar* [1892] 2 Q.B. 202.

[2] *North Central Wagon and Finance Co. v. Graham* [1950] 2 K.B. 7.

[3] See Vol. II, §§ 33–012, 33–021, 33–031, 33–039, 33–048, 33–074.

[4] *North Central Wagon and Finance Co. v. Graham, supra*, at 15; *Alexander v. Railway Executive* [1941] 2 K.B. 882, 889; *Garnham, Harris & Elton Ltd v. Ellis (Transport) Ltd* [1967] 1 W.L.R. 940, 946.

[5] *Suisse Atlantique* case [1967] 1 A.C. 361, 412. See also *ibid.* at 392, 424, 434, and *Lilley v. Doubleday* (1881) 7 Q.B.D. 510; *Gibaud v. G.E. Ry.* [1921] 2 K.B. 426, 435; *Alderslade v. Hendon Laundry Ltd* [1945] K.B. 189, 192; *J. Spurling Ltd v. Bradshaw* [1956] 1 W.L.R. 461, 465; *Mendelssohn v. Normand Ltd* [1970] 1 Q.B. 177, 184; Coote, *Exception Clauses* (1964), p. 99.

[6] *Harris v. G.W. Ry.* (1876) 1 Q.B.D. 515; *Gibaud v. G.E. Ry., supra*; *Kenyon Son & Craven Ltd v. Baxter Hoare & Co. Ltd* [1971] 1 W.L.R. 519.

[7] [1963] 1 Q.B. 844. See also *Ashby v. Tolhurst* [1937] 2 K.B. 242; *B.G. Transport Service Ltd v. Marston Motor Co. Ltd* [1970] 1 Lloyd's Rep. 371.

honestly, but mistakenly, delivered the car to a person who fraudulently represented that he had the plaintiff's authority to collect it, and the car was lost. It was held that this act was covered by the exemption clause. On the other hand, in *Alexander v. Railway Executive*,[8] where the officials in charge of a railway cloakroom permitted an unauthorised person to break open and remove the baggage of a depositor without the production of the cloakroom ticket, it was held that an exemption clause limiting liability for loss or misdelivery could not be relied upon to protect the Railway Executive. These cases are not easily distinguishable except on the ground that the former involved an honest, though negligent, error, whereas the latter was concerned with a misdelivery which was known to be unauthorised by the terms of the bailment.[9]

14–037   **Theft or deliberate damage.** A clause which is sufficient to exclude or restrict a bailee's liability for negligence may not in its terms be sufficient to exclude or restrict liability for theft by the bailee's servants, or damage by reckless or wilful misconduct.[10]

14–038   **Sub-contracting.** The terms of a contract of carriage or bailment may expressly or impliedly permit the carrier or bailee to sub-contract his obligations to a third party.[11] If the contract, on its true construction, does not authorise the carrier or bailee to sub-contract, or limits the persons who may properly be employed as sub-contractors, it would appear that the carrier or bailee will not be protected if he exceeds his authority by an exemption clause which is intended to apply only while the goods are in his possession or control.[12]

5. Exemption Clauses and Third Parties

14–039   **Application to third parties.** It not infrequently happens that one of the parties to a contract seeks to extend the burden of its exempting provisions to persons who are not in any direct contractual relationship with him, or endeavours to confer the benefit of those provisions on persons outside the contract, *e.g.* to his employees, agents or sub-contractors. The general rule is that the doctrine of privity of contract[13] prevents the application of an exemption clause to third parties. To this general rule, however, there are a number of exceptions or qualifications.

---

[8] [1951] 2 K.B. 882. See also *Tozer Kemsley & Millbourn (Australasia) Pty. Ltd v. Collier's Interstate Transport Service Ltd* (1956) 94 C.L.R. 384; *Sze Hai Tong Bank Ltd v. Rambler Cycle Co. Ltd* [1959] A.C. 576 (carriage); *Sydney City Council v. West* (1965) 114 C.L.R. 481; *Levison v. Patent Steam Carpet Cleaning Co. Ltd* [1978] Q.B. 69.

[9] In *Suisse Atlantique* case [1967] 1 A.C. 361, 435, Lord Wilberforce rejects the view that there is a separate category of "deliberate breaches" (see *ante*, § 14–016) and explains *Alexander v. Railway Executive* as a case of "total departure" from what was contractually contemplated. *cf. J. Carter (Fine Worsteds) Ltd v. Hanson Haulage (Leeds) Ltd* [1965] 2 Q.B. 495.

[10] *Levison v. Patent Steam Carpet Cleaning Co. Ltd* [1978] Q.B. 69.

[11] See *post*, § 14–050, Vol. II, § 33–024.

[12] *Davies v. Collins* [1945] 1 All E.R. 247; *Garnham, Harris & Elton Ltd v. Ellis (Transport) Ltd* [1967] 1 W.L.R. 940; *The Berkshire* [1974] 1 Lloyd's Rep. 185.

[13] See *ante*, § 3–035, *post*, Chap. 19.

The general rule: burden. Two persons cannot by contract impose the **14–040** burden of an exemption clause on one who is not a party to that contract.[14] In *Haseldine v. C.A. Daw & Son Ltd.*,[15] the owners of a block of flats by contract employed the defendants to maintain a lift in the premises. This contract purported to exempt the defendants from liability for accidents due to their negligence.[16] A third party was injured owing to the negligent repair of the lift by the defendants. It was held that the defendants were not protected against an action in tort by the third party.

The general rule: benefit. Two persons cannot by contract confer the benefit **14–041** of an exemption clause on one who is not a party to that contract.[17] Thus it has been held that an employee of the London Passenger Transport Board, who was sued by a passenger for damages in negligence, was not protected by the terms of a pass given to the passenger by the Board which expressly purported to exempt the employees of the Board from all liability[18]; that the master and boatswain of a ship, who were sued by a passenger alleged to have been injured by their negligence, were not protected by a clause inserted in the passenger's ticket by their employers[19]; that stevedores, who had negligently damaged a drum of chemicals while handling it, were not protected by a clause in the bill of lading which exempted the carriers of the goods from liability in excess of a certain pecuniary limit[20]; and that a licensor of technology and know-how was

---

[14] *Leigh and Sillavan Ltd v. Aliakmon Shipping Co. Ltd* [1986] A.C. 785, 817. See also the cases cited in § 14–053, n. 75, *post* (building contracts) and § 14–059, n. 59, *post*) (carriage of goods and bailment). Contrast *Pyrene Co. Ltd v. Scindia Navigation Co. Ltd* [1954] 2 Q.B. 402, which was said in *Scruttons Ltd v. Midland Silicones Ltd* [1962] A.C. 446, 471 to be supportable only on the ground of an implied contract between the party seeking to rely on the exemption and the third party: see also *The Kapetan Markos (No. 2)* [1987] 2 Lloyd's Rep. 321, 331.

[15] [1941] 2 K.B. 343. Contrast *Fosbroke-Hobbes v. Airwork Ltd* [1937] 1 All E.R. 108, which is explicable (if at all) only on the ground that the contracting party contracted as agent for his guests; *Cockerton v. Naviera Aznar SA* [1960] 2 Lloyd's Rep. 450, 461 (agency for wife).

[16] At 379.

[17] Contrast *London Drugs Ltd v. Kuehne & Nagel International Ltd* (1992) 97 D.L.R. (4th) 261 (Supreme Court of Canada); noted (1993) 109 L.Q.R. 349; (1993) 56 M.L.R. 722.

[18] *Cosgrove v. Horsfall* (1945) 62 T.L.R. 140. See also *Genys v. Matthews* [1966] 1 W.L.R. 758, and *post*, § 14–047; *cf. Gore v. Van der Lann* [1967] 2 Q.B. 31.

[19] *Adler v. Dickson* [1955] 1 Q.B. 158.

[20] *Scruttons Ltd v. Midland Silicones Ltd* [1962] A.C. 446. See also *Wilson v. Darling Island Stevedoring and Lighterage Co. Ltd* [1956] 1 Lloyd's Rep. 346; *Krawill Machinery Corpn. v. Robert C. Head & Co. Ltd* [1959] 1 Lloyd's Rep. 305; *Canadian General Electric Co. Ltd v. The "Lake Bosomtwe"* [1970] 2 Lloyd's Rep. 80; *Herrick v. Leonard and Dingley Ltd* [1975] 2 N.Z.L.R. 566; *The Suleyman Stalskiy* [1976] 2 Lloyd's Rep. 609; *Lummus v. East African Harbours Corpn.* [1978] 1 Lloyd's Rep. 317; *Circle Sales & Import Ltd v. The Tarantel* [1978] 1 F.C. 269 (Canada); *Raymond Burke Motors Ltd v. Mersey Docks and Harbour Co.* [1986] 1 Lloyd's Rep. 155. Contrast *Cabot Corpn. v. John W. McGrath Corpn.* [1971] 2 Lloyd's Rep. 351; *The Mormaclynx* [1971] 2 Lloyd's Rep. 476; *Cable & Montanari Inc. v. American Export Isbrandtsen Lines Ltd* [1968] 1 Lloyd's Rep. 260 (affd. 386 F. 2d 839 (1967); cert. denied 390 U.S. 1013 (1968)); *New Zealand Shipping Co. Ltd v. A.M. Satterthwaite & Co. Ltd (The Eurymedon)* [1975] A.C. 154; *Tessler Bros. (B.C.) Ltd v. Italpacific Line and Matson Terminals Inc.* [1975] 1 Lloyd's Rep. 210; *Eisen und Metall A.G. v. Ceres Stevedoring Co. Ltd* [1977] 1 Lloyd's Rep. 665; *Miles International Cpn. v. Federal Commerce & Navigation Co.* [1978] 1 Lloyd's Rep. 285; *Port Jackson Stevedoring Pty. Ltd v. Salmond and Spraggon (Australia) Pty. Ltd (The New York Star)* [1981] 1 W.L.R. 138; *Godina v. Patrick Operations Pty. Ltd* [1984] 1 Lloyd's Rep. 333 (see also the principles relating to sub-bailments discussed *post*, § 14–050). See now Art. IV *bis* (2) of the Hague-Visby Rules contained in the schedule to the Carriage of Goods by Sea Act 1971.

not protected by a clause in a contract between its licensee and the person to whom the technology and know-how was transferred.[21]

14–042   **Vicarious immunity.** The proposition was at one time advanced that, where a contract contained an exemption clause, any employee or agent who acted under the contract could claim the same exemption as attached to the liability of his employer or principal.[22] This doctrine of "vicarious immunity" was believed to be the result of the decision of the House of Lords in *Elder, Dempster & Co. Ltd v. Paterson, Zochonis & Co. Ltd.*[23] In that case, cargo was shipped by a firm of charterers under bills of lading made between them and the cargo-owners, which purported to exempt both the charterers *and the shipowners* from loss due to bad stowage. The cargo was damaged by bad stowage, and the shipowners (who were not parties to the bill of lading) claimed the benefit of the exemption clause. It was held that they were entitled to do so, but the exact grounds for so holding are by no means clear. Although a number of the speeches[24] appear to support a doctrine of vicarious immunity, the House of Lords has subsequently ruled in *Scruttons Ltd v. Midland Silicones Ltd*[25] that no such principle exists in English law so far as exemption clauses are concerned. If the *Elder, Dempster* case is supportable at all, it would seem that it depends on the inference that the shipowners, when they received the goods, did so as bailees on the terms of the bill of lading[26] or upon agency.[27]

14–043   **Agency.** A third party may be able to take the benefit of an exemption clause by showing that the party imposing the exemption clause was acting as agent in the transaction so as to bring the third party into a direct contractual relationship with the plaintiff.[28] This device was first employed in the nineteenth century in relation to railways. It frequently happened that passengers or goods might be transported over a network of independent railway companies before reaching their destination. The question arose whether the exemption clauses inserted in the contract of carriage with the contracting company could be made to extend to the others with whom there seemed to be no direct contractual relationship. The courts held that the contracting company should be treated either as agent for the passenger or consignor to contract with the other companies[29] or as their agent to contract with him.[30] In more modern times clauses are frequently encountered in standard form contracts whereby one contracting party, *e.g.* a

---

[21] *Deepak Fertilisers and Petrochemicals Corpn. v. ICI* [1998] 2 Lloyd's Rep. 139, 163; [1999] 1 Lloyd's Rep. 387.

[22] *Mersey Shipping and Transport Co. Ltd v. Rea Ltd* (1925) 21 Ll.L.Rep. 375, 378, *per* Scrutton L.J.; *Gilbert Stokes and Kerr Proprietary Ltd v. Dalgety & Co. Ltd* (1948) 81 Ll.L.Rep. 337; *Waters Trading Co. Ltd v. Dalgety & Co. Ltd* [1951] 2 Lloyd's Rep. 385.

[23] [1924] A.C. 522. But see art. IV *bis* (2) of the Hague-Visby Rules, *supra*.

[24] *ibid.* at 534 (Viscount Cave), 548 (Viscount Finlay), 565 (Lord Carson).

[25] [1962] A.C. 446.

[26] *Elder Dempster* case, *supra*, at 548 (Lord Dunedin), 564 (Lord Sumner), 565 (Lord Carson); *Midland Silicones* case, *supra*, at 470, 481, 494. See also *Wilson v. Darling Island Stevedoring and Lighterage Co.* [1956] 1 Lloyd's Rep. 346; *Hispanica de Petroleos SA v. Vencedora Oceanica Navegacion SA (The Kapetan Markos N.L.) (No. 2)* [1987] 2 Lloyd's Rep. 321, 332, 340; *The Pioneer Container* [1994] 2 A.C. 324, 339–340; *The Mahkutai* [1996] A.C. 650, 659–661. For a different explanation, see *Midland Silicones* case, *supra*, at 478, 486–489; *Morris v. C.W. Martin & Sons Ltd* [1966] 1 Q.B. 716, 730.

[27] *Elder Dempster* case, *supra*, at 534; Treitel (1955) 18 M.L.R. 172.

[28] *ibid.*; *Scruttons Ltd v. Midland Silicones Ltd, supra*, at 474, 480.

[29] *Hall v. N.E. Ry.* (1875) L.R. 10 Q.B. 437, 442.

[30] *ibid.* at p. 443; *Barrett v. G.N. Ry.* (1904) 20 T.L.R. 175.

carrier,[31] repairer[32] or building contractor[33] purports to contract on behalf of his employees, agents and the independent contractors employed by him, and to extend to such employees, agents and independent contractors protection from liability. In *Scruttons Ltd v. Midland Silicones Ltd*[34] the House of Lords left open the question whether stevedores could be protected by an exemption clause contained in a contract of carriage to which they were not a party if the carrier contracted as agent on their behalf. Lord Reid said[35]:

> "I can see a possibility of success of the agency argument if (first) the bill of lading makes it clear that the stevedore is intended to be protected by the provisions in it which limit liability, (secondly) the bill of lading makes it clear that the carrier, in addition to contracting for these provisions on his own behalf, is also contracting as agent for the stevedore that these provisions should apply to the stevedore, (thirdly) the carrier has authority from the stevedore to do that, or perhaps later ratification by the stevedore would suffice, and (fourthly) that any difficulties about consideration moving from the stevedore were overcome."

These four propositions were held to have been satisfied in *New Zealand* **14–044** *Shipping Co. Ltd v. A.M. Satterthwaite & Co. Ltd (The Eurymedon)*.[36] In that case, the Judicial Committee, by a majority, held that a stevedore, who had negligently damaged goods in the course of unloading, was protected by a clause in a bill of lading which contained appropriate words exempting him from liability and which was stated to have been made by the carrier acting as agent on his behalf. An action against him by the shipper therefore failed. The Board considered that "the bill of lading brought into existence a bargain initially unilateral but capable of becoming mutual between the shipper and the [stevedore], made through the carrier as agent. This became a full contract when the [stevedore] performed services by discharging the goods. The performance of these services for the benefit of the shipper was the consideration for the agreement by the shipper that the [stevedore] should have the benefit of the exemptions and limitations contained in the bill of lading."[37] This reasoning is, however, somewhat artificial, and the courts of certain Commonwealth jurisdictions have shown a reluctance to follow the *Eurymedon* case or a readiness to find grounds for distinguishing it.[38] It may, perhaps, be justified more on the grounds of policy: that established commercial practice now requires the stevedore, in normal circumstances, to enjoy the benefit of contractual provisions in the bill of lading.[39] In *Port Jackson Stevedoring Pty. Ltd v. Salmond and Spraggon (Australia) Pty. Ltd (The New York Star)*,[40] after goods had been unloaded from a ship

---

[31] See the Railway Board's General Conditions, Vol. II, § 36–052.

[32] *Stag Line Ltd v. Tyne Ship Repair Group Ltd* [1984] 2 Lloyd's Rep. 211, 217.

[33] *Southern Water Authority v. Carey* [1985] 2 All E.R. 1077.

[34] [1962] A.C. 446.

[35] At 474.

[36] [1975] A.C. 154 (noted (1974) 90 L.Q.R. 301).

[37] At 167–168.

[38] *Herrick v. Leonard and Dingley Ltd* [1975] 2 N.Z.L.R. 566; *The Suleyman Stalskiy* [1976] 2 Lloyd's Rep. 609; *Lummus v. East African Harbours Corpn.* [1978] 1 Lloyd's Rep. 317; *Circle Sales and Import Ltd v. The Tarantel* [1978] 1 F.C. 269 (Canada). See Palmer and Rose (1976) 39 M.L.R. 466.

[39] *Port Jackson Stevedoring Pty. Ltd v. Salmond and Spraggon (Australia) Pty. Ltd* [1981] 1 W.L.R. 138, 143.

[40] [1979] 1 Lloyd's Rep. 298; [1981] 1 W.L.R. 138. See also Reynolds (1979) 95 L.Q.R. 183; Reynolds (1980) 96 L.Q.R. 506; Coote [1981] C.L.J. 13; Clarke [1981] C.L.J. 17; Rose (1981) 44 M.L.R. 336, and the cases cited in the latter half of n. 20, § 14–041, *ante*.

and placed in a shed on the wharf under the stevedore's control, a servant of the stevedore negligently delivered the goods to thieves without production of the bill of lading. The High Court of Australia held that the stevedore was not protected by a clause in substantially the same form as that considered in the *Eurymedon* case, since he was no longer acting on behalf of the carrier under the bill of lading. The carrier's responsibilities and immunities under the bill of lading had ceased when the goods were discharged from the ship. On appeal, the Judicial Committee again held that the stevedore was protected on the ground that, whereas the carrier's responsibility as a carrier terminated as soon as the goods left the ship's tackle, his responsibility as bailee under the bill of lading continued until the consignee took delivery of the goods. During this period, both the carrier and the stevedore were entitled to the protection conferred by the bill.

14–045   The technical nature of the *Eurymedon* principle is, however, "all too apparent".[41] In other cases, the courts have rejected its application on the ground that they were compelled to do so by established principles of the law of contract or of agency. Thus, the benefit of an exemption clause has been held not to extend to a third party because the contract did not make it clear that the third party was intended to be protected or that the contracting party contracted as agent for the third party as well as on his own behalf,[42] or because there was no act of the third party which could be identified as constituting acceptance of the offer made to him through the agent,[43] or because no agency could be established since the third party was at all relevant times unascertained,[44] or because the negligence of the third party in respect of which exemption was sought was collateral and not related to the performance of his duties under the contract.[45] It would be preferable to abandon this technical approach in favour of a rule which permitted the benefit of an exemption clause to be extended to third parties.[46]

14–046   **Trust.** Exemption clauses are sometimes found which provide that a party contracts, for the purpose of the clause, as trustee on behalf of third parties, *e.g.* associated companies, or his employees or sub-contractors. It has been doubted whether a trust of the benefit of an exemption clause would be effective,[47] but it is possible that such a trust would be upheld (the contracting party acting as a bare trustee) provided that the identity of the beneficiaries of the trust was sufficiently certain.

---

[41] *The Mahkutai* [1996] A.C. 650, 664.

[42] *Stone Vickers Ltd v. Appledore Ferguson Shipbuilders Ltd* [1992] 2 Lloyd's Rep. 578, 585.

[43] *Raymond Burke Motors Ltd v. Mersey Docks and Harbour Co.* [1986] 1 Lloyd's Rep. 154.

[44] *Southern Water Authority v. Carey* [1985] 2 All E.R. 1077. See also *The Suleyman Stalskiy* [1976] 2 Lloyd's Rep. 609.

[45] *Raymond Burke Motors Ltd v. Mersey Docks and Harbour Co., supra.*

[46] *The Mahkutai* [1996] A.C. 650, 665, citing *London Drugs Ltd v. Kuehne & Nagel International Ltd* (1992) 97 D.L.R. (4th) 261 (Supreme Court of Canada) and *Trident General Insurance Co. Ltd v. McNiece Bros. Pty. Ltd* (1988) 165 C.L.R. 107 (High Court of Australia). See the Contracts (Rights against Third Parties) Bill 1998; *post* 14–055.

[47] *Southern Water Authority v. Carey, supra.* See also *New Zealand Shipping Co. Ltd v. A.M. Satterthwaite & Co. Ltd* [1971] 2 Lloyd's Rep. 389, 408 (at first instance); *Deepak Fertilisers and Petrochemicals Corpn. v. ICI* [1998] 2 Lloyd's Rep. 139, 163; [1999] 1 Lloyd's Rep. 387, and *post,* § 19–072.

Agreement not to sue, etc. An exemption clause which purports to negative   **14–047**
the liability of a third party to a contract cannot be construed as a promise not to
sue that third party.[48] However, the contract may contain an express or implied
provision whereby one party promises the other that he will not institute legal
proceedings against a third party, *e.g.* any employee or sub-contractor of the
promisee.[49] In such a situation, the third party cannot, of course, rely on the
promise as a defence to an action brought against him. But the promisee could,
if he has a sufficient interest in the enforcement of the promise, apply for an order
or claim a declaration that the action be stayed or dismissed.[50]

No voluntary assumption of risk. An exemption clause which purports to   **14–048**
protect a third party cannot ordinarily be construed as a voluntary assumption of
risk by the promisor.[51]

Occupier's liability. It is now provided by statute,[52] that where an occupier of   **14–049**
premises is bound by contract to permit persons who are strangers to the contract
to enter or use the premises, the duty of care which he owes to them as his
visitors cannot be restricted or excluded by that contract, but (subject to any
provisions of the contract to the contrary) shall include the duty to perform his
obligations under the contract, whether undertaken for their protection or not, in
so far as those obligations go beyond the obligations otherwise involved in that
duty. This rule applies to regulate the obligations (*qua* occupier) of a person
occupying or having control over any fixed or movable structure, including any
vessel, vehicle or aircraft; and to the obligations of a person occupying or having
control over any premises or structure in respect of damage to property, including
the property of persons who are not themselves his visitors.[53]

Bailment.[54] A carrier or other bailee of goods may sub-contract to another   **14–050**
performance of the contract between himself and the bailor and for that purpose
deliver possession of the goods to the sub-contractor as sub-bailee. If the sub-
bailee has sufficient notice that the original bailor is interested in the goods, then
he is under a duty to the original bailor, as well as to the bailee, to use reasonable
care to safeguard the goods while in his possession and he will be liable to the

---

[48] *Gore v. Van der Lann* [1967] 2 Q.B. 31.
[49] Such a clause is not subject to ss.2 or 10 of the Unfair Contract Terms Act 1977 (*post*,
§§ 14–068, 14–078): *Neptune Orient Lines Ltd v. J.V.C. (U.K.) Ltd* [1983] 2 Lloyd's Rep. 438.
[50] *Snelling v. John G. Snelling Ltd* [1973] Q.B. 87; *Nippon Yusen Kaisha v. International Import
and Export Co. Ltd* [1978] 1 Lloyd's Rep. 206; *European Asian Bank A.G. v. Punjab & Sind Bank*
[1982] 2 Lloyd's Rep. 356, 359; *Deepak Fertilisers and Petrochemicals Corpn. v. ICI* [1999] 1
Lloyd's Rep. 387, 400–402. *cf. Gore v. Van der Lann, supra; Neptune Orient Lines Ltd v. J.V.C.
(U.K.) Ltd, supra.* See *post*, § 19–057.
[51] *Cosgrove v. Horsfall* (1945) 62 T.L.R. 140; *Scruttons Ltd v. Midland Silicones Ltd* [1962] A.C.
446; *New Zealand Shipping Co. Ltd v. A.M. Satterthwaite & Co. Ltd* [1975] A.C. 154, 168, 173, 182;
Unfair Contract Terms Act 1977, s.2(3). But see *ante*, § 14–014; *post*, § 14–080. Compare also
Norwich City Council v. Harvey [1989] 1 W.L.R. 828, see *post*, §§ 14–052 and 14–054.
[52] Occupiers' Liability Act 1957, s.3(1).
[53] *ibid.* s.1(3).
[54] See Vol. II, §§ 33–024—33–027 (bailment); § 36–056 (carriage). Palmer, *Bailment* (2nd ed.,
1991) 1295, 1631; Palmer and Murdoch (1983) 46 M.L.R. 73; Palmer [1989] L.M.C.L.Q. 466;
Adams and Brownsword (1990) 10 L.S. 12; Swadling [1993] L.M.C.L.Q. 9; Reynolds (1995) 111
L.Q.R., 8; Palmer & McKendrick (eds.), *Interests in Goods* (1993).

original bailor if the goods are lost or damaged[55] through his negligence notwithstanding the absence of any contract between them.[56] Since the sub-bailee is not a party to the contract between the bailee and the original bailor, he cannot rely upon an exemption clause contained in that contract,[57] unless the bailee contracted as agent on his behalf.[58] Nor, in principle, will the original bailor be bound by an exemption clause contained in the sub-contract between the bailee and sub-bailee to which the original bailor is not a party,[59] unless the bailee entered into the sub-contract as his agent.[60] However, it has been held that the original bailor is bound by the terms of the sub-bailment if he has expressly or impliedly consented to the bailee making a sub-bailment containing those terms: the original bailor cannot, despite the lack of any contractual relationship, disregard those terms against the sub-bailee.[61] Thus an exemption clause contained in the sub-contract which excludes or restricts the liability of the sub-bailee may protect the sub-bailee in an action against him by the original bailor. This principle was taken one step further, by Donaldson J. in *Johnson Matthey & Co. Ltd v. Constantine Terminals Ltd*,[62] who stated that the original bailor might

---

[55] Contrast *Bart v. British West Indian Airways Ltd* [1967] 1 Lloyd's Rep. 239; *Mayfair Photographic Supplies (London) Ltd v. Baxter Hoare & Co. Ltd* [1972] 1 Lloyd's Rep. 410, 416; *Mitsui & Co. Ltd v. Novorossiysk Shipping Co. (The Gudermes)* [1993] 1 Lloyd's Rep. 311.

[56] *Meux v. G.E. Ry.* [1895] 2 Q.B. 387; *Harris Ltd v. Continental Express Ltd* [1961] 1 Lloyd's Rep. 251; *Morris v. C.W. Martin & Sons Ltd* [1966] 1 Q.B. 716; *Learoyd Bros & Co. v. Pope and Sons (Dock Carriers) Ltd* [1966] 2 Lloyd's Rep. 142; *Lee Cooper Ltd v. C.H. Jeakins & Sons Ltd* [1967] 2 Q.B. 1; *Moukataff v. B.O.A.C.* [1967] 1 Lloyd's Rep. 396; *Gilchrist Watt & Sanderson Pty. Ltd v. York Products Pty. Ltd* [1970] 1 W.L.R. 1262; *James Buchanan & Co. Ltd v. Hay's Transport Services Ltd* [1972] 2 Lloyd's Rep. 535; *Gillespie Bros. & Co. Ltd v. Roy Bowles Transport Ltd* [1973] Q.B. 406; *C. Davis Metal Brokers Ltd v. Gilyott & Scott Ltd* [1975] 2 Lloyd's Rep. 422; *Johnson Matthey & Co. Ltd v. Constantine Terminals Ltd* [1976] 2 Lloyd's Rep. 215, 220; *Victoria Fur Traders Ltd v. Roadline (U.K.) Ltd* [1981] 1 Lloyd's Rep. 570; *China Pacific SA v. Food Corpn. of India* [1982] A.C. 939, 957; *Hispanica de Petroleos SA v. Vencedora Oceanica Navegacion SA (The Kapetan Markos N.L.) (No. 2)* [1987] 2 Lloyd's Rep. 321, 332, 340; *The Pioneer Container* [1994] 2 A.C. 324; *Spectra International plc v. Hayesoak Ltd* [1997] 1 Lloyd's Rep. 153, [1998] 1 Lloyd's Rep. 162.

[57] *Lee Cooper Ltd v. C.H. Jeakins & Sons Ltd, supra; Moukataff v. B.O.A.C., supra.* But see *post,* § 14–054.

[58] *The Mahkutai* [1996] A.C. 650, 667–668. See *ante,* § 14–043.

[59] *Harris Ltd v. Continental Express Ltd* [1961] 1 Lloyd's Rep. 251; *Learoyd Bros. & Co. v. Pope and Sons (Dock Carriers) Ltd* [1966] 2 Lloyd's Rep. 142; *Lee Cooper Ltd v. C.H. Jeakins & Sons Ltd* [1967] 2 Q.B. 1; *Moukataff v. B.O.A.C.* [1967] 1 Lloyd's Rep. 396; *C. Davis Metal Brokers Ltd v. Gilyott & Scott Ltd* [1975] 2 Lloyd's Rep. 422.

[60] *Morris v. C.W. Martin & Sons Ltd* [1966] 1 Q.B. 716, 731, 741; and see *ante,* § 14–043, n. 30. *cf., Victoria Fur Traders Ltd v. Roadline (U.K.) Ltd* [1981] 1 Lloyd's Rep. 570.

[61] *Elder, Dempster & Co. Ltd v. Paterson, Zochonis & Co. Ltd* [1924] A.C. 522, 564; *The Kite* (1933) 46 Ll.L.Rep. 83; *Morris v. C.W. Martin & Sons Ltd, supra,* at 729–730, 741; *Johnson Matthey & Co. Ltd v. Constantine Terminals Ltd* [1976] 2 Lloyd's Rep. 215, 220; *Hispanica de Petroleos SA v. Vencedora Oceanica Navegacion SA (The Kapetan Markos N.L.) (No. 2)* [1987] 2 Lloyd's Rep. 321, 332, 340; *Singer Co. (U.K.) Ltd v. Tees and Hartlepool Port Authority* [1988] 2 Lloyd's Rep. 164; *Compania Portorafti Commerciale SA v. Ultramar Panama Inc. (The Captain Gregos)* [1990] 2 Lloyd's Rep. 395, 405; *Dresser (U.K.) Ltd v. Falcongate Freight Management Ltd* [1992] Q.B. 502, 511; *The Pioneer Container* [1994] 2 A.C. 324; *Spectra International plc v. Hayesoak Ltd* [1997] 1 Lloyd's Rep. 153, [1998] 1 Lloyd's Rep. 162; *Sonicare International Ltd v. East Anglia Freight Terminal Ltd* [1997] 2 Lloyd's Rep. 48.

[62] [1976] 2 Lloyd's Rep. 215. See also *Singer Co. (U.K.) Ltd v. Tees and Hartlepool Port Authority, supra,* at 168; *Compania Portorafti Commerciale SA v. Ultramar Panama Inc. (The Captain Gregos), supra,* at 406; *Mitsui & Co. Ltd v. Novorossiysk Shipping Co. (The Gudermes)* [1993] 1 Lloyd's Rep. 311, 327. Donaldson J. (at 222) left open the question whether a sub-bailee who himself damages the goods would also be able to rely upon the terms of the sub-contract.

be bound by an exemption clause in the sub-contract irrespective of whether the bailee was authorised to sub-bail the goods on terms to the sub-bailee. But the Judicial Committee of the Privy Council has subsequently held[63] that the sub-bailee can only invoke the terms of a sub-bailment under which he receives the goods from the bailee as qualifying or otherwise affecting his responsibility to the original bailor if the orignal bailor consented to them.

On the other hand, the courts have been reluctant to extend these principles to **14–051** cases where the relationship between the claimant and the defendant who seeks to rely on the exemption clause is not one of bailor and bailee or sub-bailee.[64] So, for example, if it is agreed between the buyer and seller of goods that the seller will enter into a contract for the carriage of the goods to the buyer and for that purpose will bail the goods to a carrier on terms, then, if the goods are lost or damaged by the negligence of the carrier, the buyer will not be bound by an exemption clause contained in the contract of carriage to which he is not a party[65] unless he is or has become the owner of the goods and the carrier is in possession of the goods as his bailee or sub-bailee.[66] In the absence of any such relationship between them, the carrier will have to establish an implied or collateral contract between himself and the buyer[67] or that the seller's rights of suit under the contract of carriage have been transferred to and vested in the buyer[68] or that he has attorned to the buyer by acknowledging that he holds the goods as bailee for the buyer on the terms of the contract of carriage.[69]

Building and construction contracts. Where a contractor is employed to **14–052** carry out building or construction works or works of repair, it may be agreed or understood that the contractor ("the main contractor") will engage a sub-contractor or sub-contractors to execute part of the works. Since there is normally no privity of contract between the employer and the sub-contractors, any action brought by the employer against a sub-contractor in respect of loss or damage caused to him by the sub-contractor must be brought in tort for negligence. As a general rule, no such action will lie in respect of defects in the works which the

---

[63] *The Pioneer Container* [1994] 2 A.C. 324.

[64] *Scruttons Ltd v. Midland Silicones Ltd* [1962] A.C. 446; *Swiss Bank Corpn. v. Brink's Mat Ltd* [1986] 2 Lloyd's Rep. 79, 98; *Leigh and Sillavan Ltd v. Aliakmon Shipping Co. Ltd (The Aliakmon)* [1986] A.C. 785, 818; *Compania Portorafti Commerciale SA v. Ultramar Panama Inc. (The Captain Gregos)* [1990] 2 Lloyd's Rep. 395, at 404, 405; *The Mahkutai* [1996] A.C. 650.

[65] *Leigh and Sillavan Ltd v. Aliakmon Shipping Co. Ltd (The Aliakmon), supra,* at 818; *Compania Portorafti Commerciale SA v. Ultramar Panama Inc. (The Captain Gregos), supra,* at 405.

[66] *Hispanica de Petroleos SA v. Vencedora Oceanica Navegacion SA (The Kapetan Markos N.L.)* (No. 2) [1987] 2 Lloyd's Rep. 321.

[67] *Compania Portorafti Commerciale SA v. Ultramar Panama Inc. (The Captain Gregos), supra* (BP claim). See also the "*Brandt v. Liverpool*" contract (*Brandt v. Liverpool etc. Steam Navigation Co.* [1924] 1 K.B. 575).

[68] By statute under the Bills of Lading Act 1855 or (now) under the Carriage of Goods by Sea Act 1992 (see *Benjamin's Sale of Goods* (5th ed., 1997) §§ 18–058—18–099: a wider liability in tort cannot be asserted) or by assignment: *Britain and Overseas Trading (Bristles) Ltd v. Brooks Wharf Ltd* [1967] 2 Lloyd's Rep. 51. *cf., Compania Portorafti Commerciale SA v. Ultramar Panama Inc. (The Captain Gregos), supra,* at 404.

[69] *Cremer v. General Carriers SA* [1974] 1 W.L.R. 341; and see Vol. II, § 33–027. Contrast *Mitsui & Co. Ltd v. Novorossiysk Shipping Co. (The Gudermes)* [1993] 1 Lloyd's Rep. 311; *Sonicare International Ltd v. East Anglia Freight Terminal Ltd* [1997] 2 Lloyd's Rep. 48.

sub-contractor is engaged to carry out.[70] But the employer is entitled to claim against a sub-contractor damages in tort for negligence if the sub-contractor negligently causes physical damage to the existing structure or to property other than the thing supplied by him.[71] The question, however, arises whether, in such an action, the sub-contractor can rely on an exemption clause contained in (a) the main contract between the employer and the main contractor, or (b) his own sub-contract with the main contractor. The initial contractual arrangements between the employer, the main contractor and the sub-contractor may be such as to give rise to a contract between the employer and the sub-contractor.[72] But, even if no such direct contractual relationship exists between them, the sub-contractor may nevertheless be entitled to rely upon an exemption clause contained in the main contract between the employer and the main contractor. This may be justified either on the ground that the duty in tort owed by the sub-contractor to the employer is negatived or qualified by the clause,[73] or on the ground that, if the clause places a risk in whole or in part on the employer, the circumstances show that the sub-contractor contracted with the main contractor on a like basis.[74]

14–053 **Exemption clause in sub-contract.** Whether the sub-contractor is also entitled to rely upon an exemption clause in his sub-contract with the main contractor is more problematical. Prima facie the employer would not be bound by a clause in a contract to which he was not a party.[75] But, again, the contractual arrangements between the employer, main contractor and sub-contractor may be such as to show that the employer knew of and consented to the clause as, for example, where the sub-contractor is a nominated sub-contractor and the employer is aware of and accepts the terms on which the sub-contractor agrees to carry out the works. In such a case it is submitted that the employer could be held to be bound by the exemption clause.[76]

14–054 **A more general principle?** Apart from the particular instances of bailment and building and construction contracts referred to above, a more general principle may possibly be elicited from the judgments of the Court of Appeal in

---

[70] *Simaan General Contracting Co. v. Pilkington Glass Ltd (No. 2)* [1988] Q.B. 758; *D. & F. Estates Ltd v. Church Commissioners for England* [1989] A.C. 177; *Greater Nottingham Co-operative Society Ltd v. Cementation Piling and Foundations Ltd* [1989] Q.B. 71; *Murphy v. Brentwood DC* [1991] 1 A.C. 398; *Department of the Environment v. Thomas Bates and Son Ltd* [1991] 1 A.C. 499; *Warner v. Basildon Development Corpn.* (1991) 7 Const. L.J. 146; *Nitrigin Eireann Teoranta v. Inco Alloys Ltd* [1992] 1 W.L.R. 598. Contrast *Junior Books Ltd v. Veitchi Co. Ltd* [1983] 1 A.C. 520 (which must now be regarded as an exceptional case) and Vol. II, § 37–086.

[71] *Norwich City Council v. Harvey* [1989] 1 W.L.R. 828; *Nitrigin Eireann Teoranta v. Inco Alloys Ltd, supra.* For the problem of "complex structures," see *D. & F. Estates Ltd v. Church Commissioners for England, supra,* and *Murphy v. Brentwood DC, supra.*

[72] *Welsh Health Technical Services Organisation v. Haden Young* (1987) 37 Build.L.R. 130.

[73] *Southern Water Authority v. Duvivier* [1984] C.I.L.L. 90; *Southern Water Authority v. Carey* [1985] 2 All E.R. 1077; *Welsh Health Technical Services Organisation v. Haden Young, supra; Norwich City Council v. Harvey, supra.* See also *Junior Books Ltd v. Veitchi Co. Ltd* [1983] 1 A.C. 520, 546; *Pacific Associates Inc. v. Baxter* [1990] 1 Q.B. 993, 1022 (§ 14–054, *post*). Contrast *National Trust v. Haden Young Ltd* (1995) 72 Build. L.R. 1.

[74] *Norwich City Council v. Harvey, supra. cf. National Trust v. Haden Young Ltd, supra.*

[75] *Rumbelows Ltd v. AMK* [1980] 19 Build. L.R. 33; *Twins Transport Ltd v. Patrick and Brocklehurst* (1983) 25 Build. L.R. 65. See also *Leigh and Sillavan Ltd v. Aliakmon Shipping Co. Ltd, (The Aliakmon)* [1986] A.C. 785, 817; *Simaan General Contracting Co. v. Pilkington Glass Ltd (No. 2)* [1988] Q.B. 758, 782, 785.

[76] *Morris v. C.W. Martin & Sons Ltd* [1966] 1 Q.B. 716, 729; *Rumbelows Ltd v. AMK, supra,* at 49. See also *Junior Books Ltd v. Veitchi Co. Ltd, supra,* at 534; *Muirhead v. Industrial Tank Specialities Ltd* [1986] Q.B. 507, 525.

Pacific Associates Inc. v. Baxter.[77] In that case the plaintiffs, who were the main contractor and sub-contractor employed to carry out dredging and reclamation work, brought an action in tort for negligence against the defendant, the engineer engaged by the employer to supervise the work. The plaintiffs alleged they had suffered economic loss by the failure of the defendant to certifiy claims made by them and by the rejection of those claims. Since there was no direct contractual relationship between the plaintiffs and the defendant, the question arose whether the defendant owed them in the circumstances any duty of care. The contract between the employer and the main contractor contained a clause ("the disclaimer") by which it was agreed that the defendant engineer was not in any way to be personally liable for the acts or obligations under the contract. The Court of Appeal unanimously held that the circumstances were not such as to impose any duty on the defendant to the plaintiffs to take care to avoid causing them economic loss by the acts complained of. Dealing, however, with the effect of the disclaimer, Purchas L.J.[78] stated that he did not doubt the force of a comment by Lord Brandon in *The Aliakmon*[79] that there was not "any convincing legal basis for qualifying a duty of care owed by A to B by reference to a contract to which A is, but B is not, a party." But he then observed " . . . with great respect to Lord Brandon the absence of a direct contractual nexus between A and B does not necessarily exclude the recognition of a clause limiting liability to be imposed on A in a contract between B and C, when the existence of that contract is the basis of the creation of a duty of care asserted to be owed by A to B." Purchas L.J. continued[80]: "The presence of such an exclusion clause whilst not being directly binding between the parties, cannot be excluded from a general consideration of the contractual structure against which the contractor demonstrates reliance on, and the engineer accepts responsibility for, a duty in tort, if any, arising out of the proximity established between them by the existence of that very contract." Both he and Ralph Gibson and Russell L.JJ.[81] held that the disclaimer, though contained in a contract to which the defendant was not a party, would have negatived any liability of the defendant to the plaintiffs (had such existed), having regard to the relationship of the contractors, employer and engineer in this case. It may therefore be that, where the duty of care owed by A to B is created as the result of a contract between B and C, an exemption clause in that contract excluding or restricting that duty may, in appropriate circumstances,[82] be upheld if that was the intention of all parties to the arrangement.[83]

Contracts (Rights of Third Parties) Bill. The ability of a third party to take advantage of an exemption clause inserted in a contract for his benefit will be greatly enlarged upon the enactment of the Contracts (Rights against Third Parties) Bill 1998. The provisions of this Bill are dealt with more fully in Chapter 19 of this book.[84] Clause 1 of the Bill sets out the circumstances in which a person who is not a party to a contract (a "third party") will be entitled in his own right to enforce a term of a contract if the contract expressly so provides that he **14–055**

---

[77] [1990] 1 Q.B. 993. See Vol. II, § 37–087.
[78] At 1022.
[79] *Leigh and Sillavan Ltd v. Aliakmon Shipping Co. Ltd (The Aliakmon)* [1986] A.C. 785, 817.
[80] At 1022.
[81] At 1022, 1033, 1038.
[82] *i.e.* at least where the claim is for economic loss.
[83] See also the cases cited in § 14–052, *ante* n. 73.
[84] See *post*, § 19–075.

may or if the term purports to confer a benefit on him.[85] The Bill makes it clear that it applies so as to enable a third party to take advantage of an exclusion or limitation clause as well as to enforce "positive" rights such as the right to payment of money or to the performance of some other obligation.[86] However, the third party must be expressly identified in the contract by name, as a member of a class or as answering a particular description but need not be in existence when the contract is entered into.[87] So, for example, when the Bill is enacted, if A (the promisor) enters into a contract with B (the promisee) by which A agrees that B's sub-contractors may avail themselves of a term of the contract which excludes or limits the liability of B to A, and A seeks to hold C, a sub-contractor of B, liable, C may rely on the term as a defence notwithstanding that there is no privity of contract between himself and A. In principle, it appears to be the intention of the draftsman of the Bill that C will enjoy no greater and no less a right to enforce the exemption clause by relying on it than if he had been a party to the contract. Clause 3(6) provides: "Where in any proceedings brought against him a third party seeks in reliance on section 1 to enforce a term of a contract (including, in particular, a term purporting to exclude or limit liability), he may not do so if he could not have done so (whether by reason of any particular circumstances relating to him or otherwise) had he been a party to the contract". Thus if, in the above illustration, the term of the contract which excludes or restricts liability is ineffective because it is caught by section 3 of the Unfair Contract Terms Act 1977[88] and is unreasonable, C will not any more be entitled to rely on it against A than if he (C) had been a party to the contract.[89] The Bill does not in so many words provide that the right of C, the third party, to rely on the term is commensurate with that of B, the promisee, but no doubt this will be the practical effect of the Bill in most cases.

14–056   The Bill does not alter the common law rule that two persons cannot by contract impose the burden of an exemption clause on a person who is not a party to that contract. But where, by virtue of the provisions of the Bill, a contract confers upon a third party a "positive" right to enforce a contractual term, that right may be affected by an exemption clause in the contract which excludes or limits the liability of one of the parties for breach of that term.[90] Suppose that A (the promisor) enters into a contract with B (the promisee) which contains a term under which A is to render certain services to C (a third party), but the contract also contains an exemption clause which effectively excludes or limits the liability of A to B for breach of the term. If A fails to perform the services or fails to perform them satisfactorily, the exemption clause will be available as a defence to A in any proceedings brought by C under the Bill to enforce his right to those services. The reason is that the Bill provides that, where proceedings for enforcement of a term are brought by a third party, the promisor is to have available to him by way of defence any matter that arises from or in connection with the contract and is relevant to the term, and would have been available to him by way of defence if the proceedings had been brought by the promisee.[91]

---

[85] Clause 1(1); see *post*, § 19–076.
[86] Clause 1(6).
[87] Clause 1(3); see *post*, § 19–080.
[88] *Post*, § 14–069.
[89] See *post*, § 19–092.
[90] See *post*, § 19–092.
[91] Clause 3(2).

The question, however, arises whether A can rely on the exemption clause as against C if, by statute, it would not have been available as a defence to A if the proceedings had been brought by B (for example, because it is caught by section 3 of the Unfair Contract Terms Act 1977[92] and is unreasonable). The position appears to be that, in general,[93] A can rely on the exemption clause where C is seeking to enforce against A a contractual liability arising under the contract between A and B notwithstanding the invalidity of the clause between A and B.[94]

6. STATUTORY CONTROL OF EXEMPTION CLAUSES

(a) *Unfair Contract Terms Act 1977*[95]

Unfair Contract Terms Act 1977. This Act derives substantially from rec-   **14–057**
ommendations made by the Law Commission and the Scottish Law Commission in their Second Report on Exemption Clauses.[96] The title of the Act is, however, somewhat misleading. In the first place, the control imposed by the Act is not limited to contract terms, but extends to non-contractual notices which exclude or restrict liability in tort.[97] Secondly, the Act does not seek to control unfair contract terms generally. It applies, for the most part,[98] only to terms that purport to exclude or restrict liability, that is to say, to exemption clauses. The Act does not, in general, affect the basis of liability,[99] so that the first inquiry must normally be whether or not the person seeking to rely on the terms is in fact under any obligation or liability, for example, for breach of contract or negligence, apart from the term.[1] Further, the Act does not affect the preliminary issues as to whether the alleged term is in fact a term of the contract,[2] and, if it is, whether on its true construction it applies to the obligation or liability which it purports to exclude or restrict.[3]

Pattern of control. The control exercised by the Act over exemption clauses   **14–058**
in contracts is complex in nature and by no means comprehensive. There are

---

[92] *Post*, § 14–069.

[93] But see the position with respect to s.2(1) of the Unfair Contract Terms Act 1977, *post*, §§ 14–068, 19–100. Contrast *ibid.* s.2(2) and Clause 7(2) of the Bill, *post*, §§ 14–068, 19–100.

[94] Clause 1(4), 7(4); *post*, § 19–099.

[95] See Thompson, *Unfair Contract Terms Act 1977*; Rogers and Clarke, *The Unfair Contract Terms Act 1977*; Lawson, *Exclusion Clauses and Unfair Contract Terms* (1995); Yates, *Exclusion Clauses in Contracts* (2nd ed.); Coote (1978) 41 M.L.R. 312; Adams (1978) 41 M.L.R. 703; Sealy [1978] C.L.J. 15; Reynolds [1978] L.M.C.L.Q. 201; Palmer and Yates [1981] C.L.J. 108; Adams and Brownsword (1988) 104 L.Q.R. 94; Peel (1993) 56 M.L.R. 98; Brown and Chandler (1993) 109 L.Q.R. 41; Adams (1994) 57 M.L.R. 960.

[96] Law Com. No. 69, Scot. Law Com. No. 39 (1975). Pt. I of the Act applies only to England and Wales and Northern Ireland; Pt. II applies only to Scotland; and Pt. III applies to the whole of the United Kingdom.

[97] Such notices are not dealt with in this chapter.

[98] But see ss.3(2)(b), 4.

[99] But see ss.3(2)(b), 4.

[1] See *ante*, § 14–003; *post*, § 14–061.

[2] See s.11(2) and *ante*, § 12–002.

[3] See s.11(2) and *ante*, §§ 14–005 *et seq.*

three broad divisions of control. First, control over contract terms which exclude or restrict liability for "negligence,"[4] which is defined[5] to mean the breach:

(a) of any obligation, arising from the express or implied terms of a contract, to take reasonable care or exercise reasonable skill in the performance of a contract;

(b) of any common law duty to take reasonable care or exercise reasonable skill (but not any stricter duty); and

(c) of the common duty of care imposed by the Occupier's Liability Act 1957.[6]

Secondly, control over contract terms[7] which exclude or restrict liability for breach of certain terms implied by statute or common law in contracts of sale of goods,[8] hire-purchase[9] and in other contracts for the supply of goods.[10] Thirdly, a more general control in limited circumstances over contract terms which exclude or restrict liability for breach of contract[11] or which purport to entitle one of the parties to render a contractual performance substantially different from that reasonably expected of him or to render no performance at all.[12] However, the provisions of the Act may overlap, so that, in any given situation, it may be necessary to consider whether more than one section is relevant. Further, certain very important contracts are excepted, either wholly or subject to qualifications, from the operation of the Act.[13]

14–059 If the contract term is subject to the control of the Act, that control may assume one of two forms: the exclusion or restriction of liability may be rendered absolutely ineffective,[14] or it may be effective only in so far as the term satisfies the requirement of reasonableness.[15]

14–060 **Varieties of exemption clause.** Subject to certain exceptions,[16] the Act only applies to contract terms which "exclude or restrict" liability. In considering whether a contract term has this effect, the court is concerned with the substance and not the form of the provision.[17] Moreover, by section 13(1), the meaning of these words is extended so as also to prevent:

(a) "making the liability or its enforcement subject to restrictive or onerous conditions" (as, for example, in the case of terms which require a party to

---

[4] ss.2, 5; *post*, §§ 14–068, 14–074. See also s.4; *post*, § 14–072.
[5] s.1(1).
[6] See *Monarch Airlines Ltd v. London Luton Airports Ltd* [1998] 1 Lloyd's Rep. 403.
[7] Whether in the same or in another contract between the same parties. *cf.*, s.10; *post* § 14–078.
[8] s.6; see *post*, § 14–075; Vol. II, §§ 43–068, 43–099.
[9] s.6; see *post*, § 14–075; Vol. II, §§ 38–351.
[10] s.7; see *post*, § 14–076.
[11] s.3(1)(2)(a). See also s.4; *post*, § 14–072.
[12] s.3(1), (2)(b).
[13] See *post*, §§ 14–095—14–104.
[14] ss.2(1), 5, 6(1), (2), 7(2), (3A).
[15] See *post*, § 14–081.
[16] ss.3(2)(b), 4, 10.
[17] *Cremdean Properties Ltd v. Nash* (1977) 244 E.G. 547, 551; *Phillips Products Ltd v. Hyland* [1987] 1 W.L.R. 659, 666; *Johnstone v. Bloomsbury H.A.* [1992] Q.B. 333, 346.

make a claim within a certain time-limit or to commence proceedings within a shorter time-limit than the normal limitation period);

(b) "excluding or restricting any right or remedy in respect of the liability, or subjecting a person to any prejudice in consequence of his pursuing any such right or remedy" (as, for example, in the case of terms which preclude a party from relying on or enforcing a right of set-off[18] or which take away or limit his right to reject defective goods, or require him to pay the expenses of redelivery on rejection);

(c) "excluding or restricting rules of evidence or procedure" (as, for example, terms which state that acceptance of goods or services shall be conclusive evidence that they are in conformity with the contract).[19]

It would seem probable, however, that a genuine liquidated damages clause would not be subject to the Act,[20] and it is specifically provided that an agreement in writing to submit present or future differences to arbitration is not to be treated under Part I of the Act as excluding or restricting any liability.[21]

Certain sections[22] further prevent "excluding or restricting liability by refer-   **14–061** ence to terms which exclude or restrict the relevant obligation or duty."[23] The purpose of this provision appears to be[24] to bring within the control of the Act terms, for example, which state that the seller gives no undertaking with respect to the quality or fitness for purpose of the goods sold or which state that a surveyor accepts no responsibility with respect to the accuracy of a valuation report supplied by him.[25] Exemption clauses of this nature do not purport to exclude to restrict *liability* for breach of an obligation or duty, but purport to exclude the relevant obligation (*e.g.* the conditions implied by section 14 of the Sale of Goods Act 1979) or duty (*e.g.* to use reasonable care and skill in carrying out the valuation). It may be difficult, however, to differentiate between contractual provisions which exclude or restrict the relevant obligation or duty, and those which define the scope of the obligation or which specify the duties of the parties. For example, a seller of kitchen utensils may expressly state that they are suitable to be used only on electric cookers and not with gas,[26] or a surveyor may stipulate that he undertakes to carry out a valuation of the property and not a full

---

[18] *Stewart Gill Ltd v. Horatio Myer & Co. Ltd* [1992] Q.B. 600; *Fastframe Ltd v. Lochinski*, unreported CA, March 3, 1993 (noted (1994) 57 M.L.R. 960); *Esso Petroleum Co. Ltd v. Milton* [1997] 1 W.L.R. 938; *Surzur Overseas Ltd v. Ocean Reliance Shipping Co. Ltd* [1997] C.L.Y. 906; *Skipskredittforeningen v. Emperor Navigation* [1998] 1 Lloyd's Rep. 66; *Schenkers Ltd v. Overland Shoes Ltd* [1998] 1 Lloyd's Rep. 498; *WRM Group Ltd v. Wood* [1998] C.L.C. 189.

[19] See *Howard Marine and Dredging Co. Ltd v. A. Ogden & Sons (Excavations) Ltd* [1978] Q.B. 574; see *post*, § 14–086.

[20] See *ante*, § 14–004, n. 14. But see Law Com. No. 69, Scot. Law Com. No. 39, § 166 (1975).

[21] s.13(2). But see Arbitration Act 1996, ss.89–92; *post*, § 16–013.

[22] ss.2 only.

[23] s.13(1). The contention has been put forward that clauses which "exclude" the relevant obligation or duty *ipso facto* limit the obligation or duty, or prevent its accrual: see Coote, *Exception Clauses* (1964); Coote [1970] C.L.J. 221; Coote (1977) 40 M.L.R. 31; Coote (1978) 41 M.L.R. 312; Palmer and Yates [1981] C.L.J. 108; and *ante*, § 14–003.

[24] For a different view as to its purpose, see *Stewart Gill Ltd v. Horatio Myer & Co. Ltd* [1992] Q.B. 600, 605.

[25] *Smith v. Eric S. Bush* and *Harris v. Wyre Forest DC* [1990] 1 A.C. 831.

[26] See Macleod (1981) 97 L.Q.R. 550.

structural survey.[27] Further, there may be difficulty in distinguishing between provisions which exclude or restrict the relevant obligation or duty, and those which prevent it from arising, such as a clause limiting the ostensible authority of an agent to give undertakings.[28] In *Smith v. Eric S. Bush*,[29] a case concerning the common law duty to take reasonable care and a non-contractual notice disclaiming liability, Lord Griffiths read the relevant provisions of the Act as introducing a "but for" test, that is to say, whether the duty would exist "but for" the notice excluding liability. But it is submitted that this test could not always be satisfactorily applied to contract terms which, in effect, limit the extent of the obligation or duty which one party owes to the other or which even prevent the accrual of the obligation or duty in particular situations.[30]

14–062   It has, however, been stated that the Act "is normally regarded as being aimed at exemption clauses in the strict sense, that is to say, clauses in a contract which aim to cut down prospective liability arising in the course of performance of the contract in which the exemption clause is contained,"[31] and not to liability already accrued.[32]

14–063   **Business liability.** The Act is concerned, for the most part,[33] with terms that exclude or restrict "business liability." This is defined as liability for breach of obligations or duties arising:

    (a) from things done or to be done in the course of a business (whether his own business or another's); or

    (b) from the occupation of premises used for business purposes of the occupier.[34]

"Business" is not defined by the Act, except to the extent that it is stated to include a profession and the activities of any government department or local or public authority.[35] The words "in the course of a business" appear to require that the thing done or to be done is an integral part of the business carried on or that

---

[27] *Gibbs v. Arnold Son & Hockley* (1989) 45 E.G. 156. *cf. Roberts v. J. Hampson & Co.* [1990] 1 W.L.R. 94.

[28] See *Overbrooke Estates Ltd v. Glencombe Properties Ltd* [1974] 1 W.L.R. 1335; *Collins v. Howell-Jones* (1981) 259 E.G. 331; *Museprime Properties Ltd v. Adhill Properties Ltd* [1990] 2 E.G.L.R. 196, 200 (misrepresentation); *ante*, § 6–131. See also *McGrath v. Shah* (1989) 57 P. & C.R. 452; *Thomas Witter Ltd v. TBP Industries Ltd* [1996] 2 All E.R. 573 ("entire agreement" clauses). But see *post*, § 15–063.

[29] [1990] 1 A.C. 831, 857. See also *Phillips Products Ltd v. Hyland* [1987] 1 W.L.R. 659.

[30] *Hurley v. Dyke* [1979] R.T.R. 265, HL (tort). Contrast *ibid.*, 281–282; *Harris v. Wyre Forest DC* [1990] 1 A.C. 831 (revg. the decision of the Court of Appeal [1988] Q.B. 835) (tort); *Cremdean Properties Ltd v. Nash* (1977) 244 E.G. 547 (misrepresentation); *ante*, § 6–133; *Hughes v. Hall* [1981] R.T.R. 430; Macdonald (1992) 12 L.S. 277.

[31] *Tudor Grange Holdings Ltd v. Citibank N.A.* [1992] Ch. 53, 65.

[32] See also s.10; *post*, § 14–078.

[33] Except s.6 (implied terms in contracts of sale of goods and hire-purchase).

[34] s.1(3) (as amended by the Occupiers Liability Act 1984, s.2).

[35] s.14. A business need not necessarily be carried on with a view to profit: see *Roles v. Miller* (1884) 27 Ch.D. 71, 88; *Town Investments Ltd v. Department of Environment* [1978] A.C. 359. Contrast *Smith v. Anderson* (1880) 15 Ch.D. 247, 258.

there is a sufficient degree of regularity about the type of transaction in question.[36] The words "whether his own business or another's" presumably cover the activities of an agent in the course of his principal's business.

Dealing as consumer. A distinction is drawn in the Act between cases where   **14-064**
a party to a contract "deals as consumer" in relation to another party, and cases where he does not so deal. In order that a party should have dealt as consumer, two conditions must be satisfied.[37] First, he must neither make the contract in the course of a business[38] nor hold himself out as doing so.[39] Secondly, the other party must make the contract in the course of a business.[40] In *R. & B. Customs Brokers Co. Ltd v. United Dominions Trust Ltd,*[41] it was held that a freight forwarding and shipping agency company had dealt as consumer when it entered into a conditional sale agreement with a finance company for the purchase of a motor car for personal and business use by one of its directors, on the ground that, to be in the course of a business, the transaction must be an integral part of the business carried on or, if only incidental thereto, be of a type regularly entered into. It was further stated[42] that the company had not "held itself out" as making the contract in the course of a business by submitting a finance application in the corporate name, giving the nature of the company's business, the number of years trading and the number of employees, and giving the names and addresses of the directors.

In addition, in the case of a contract governed by the law of sale of goods or   **14-065**
hire-purchase, or by section 7 of the Act (other contracts under which the ownership or possession of goods passes),[43] a third requirement must be satisfied[44]: the goods passing under or in pursuance of the contract must be of a type ordinarily supplied for private use or consumption.[45]

Agency. On a sale by auction or by competitive tender the buyer is not in any   **14-066**
circumstances to be regarded as dealing as consumer.[46] But the position is otherwise unclear where a private person (the principal) makes a contract through a commercial or professional agent. Under the ordinary principles of agency,[47] if the agency is disclosed,[48] then, whether or not the principal is named, it is the principal who is a party to and makes the contract, and not the agent. The private

---

[36] *Havering L.B.C. v. Stevenson* [1970] 1 W.L.R. 1375; *Davies v. Sumner* [1984] 1 W.L.R. 1301; *R. & B. Customs Brokers Co. Ltd v. United Dominions Trust Ltd* [1988] 1 W.L.R. 321.

[37] s.12(1)(a), (b).

[38] See *ante*, § 14–063, n. 36.

[39] *e.g.*, by producing a trade card or asking for a trade discount in appropriate circumstances. But *cf., infra*, n. 42.

[40] See *ante*, § 14–063, and *R. & B. Customs Brokers Co. Ltd v. United Dominions Trust Ltd, supra,* at p. 336.

[41] [1988] 1 W.L.R. 321. See also *Rasbora Ltd v. J.C.L. Marine Ltd* [1977] 1 Lloyd's Rep. 645 (private buyer of boat substitutes a company owned and controlled by him); *Peter Symmons & Co. v. Cook* (1981) 131 New L.J. 758 (partnership of surveyors purchase Rolls-Royce from car dealer). Contrast *St. Alban's City and District Council v. International Computers Ltd* [1996] 4 All E.R. 481, 490.

[42] At 328–329.

[43] See *post*, § 14–076.

[44] s.12(1)(c).

[45] See Vol. II, § 43–101.

[46] s.12(2). But see *post* § 15–022.

[47] See Vol. II, Chap. 32.

[48] *Aliter* if the agency is not disclosed (the "undisclosed principal"): see Vol. II, § 32–062.

principal does not therefore "make the contract in the course of a business" even though the agent, when entering into the contract on his behalf, acts in the course of a business.[49] So, for example, if a private seller sells goods through a commercial agent to a private buyer, the buyer does not deal as consumer, because the seller does not make the contract in the course of a business. And if a private buyer buys goods through a commercial agent, he may still be held to have dealt as a consumer as he does not make the contract in the course of a business, unless it could be said that, by employing a commercial agent to act for him, he has "held himself out" as making the contract in the course of a business.

14–067   **Burden of proof as to dealing as consumer.** It is for those claiming that a party does not deal as consumer to show that he does not.[50]

14–068   **Negligence liability.** Restrictions are placed by section 2 of the Act on the power of a party to a contract to exempt himself from business liability[51] for negligence.[52] He cannot by reference to any contract term exclude or restrict his liability for death or personal injury[53] resulting from negligence.[54] Any such exclusion or restriction of liability is wholly ineffective. In the case of other loss or damage, he cannot so exclude or restrict his liability, except insofar as the term satisfies the requirement of reasonableness.[55] The words of section 2 are wide enough to include a term which purports to transfer from one contracting party to the other responsibility for injury or damage caused to the latter by negligence on the part of an employee of the former.[56] They do not extend to a term by which one party requires the other to indemnify him against injury or damage caused to third parties by his own negligence or that of his employees,[57] nor to a covenant not to sue a third party.[58]

14–069   **Liability arising in contract.** Section 3 of the Act applies generally to liability arising in contract and (unlike certain later sections) is not limited to contracts of a particular type. However, the section only applies as between contracting parties where one of them deals:

(i) as consumer[59] or

(ii) on the other's written standard terms of business,

and in either case the liability which it is sought to exclude is a business liability.[60] The expression . . . "deals on the other's written standard terms of

---

[49] Contrast Sale of Goods Act 1979, s.14(5).
[50] s.12(3).
[51] See *ante*, § 14–063.
[52] See *ante*, § 14–058.
[53] Defined in s.14.
[54] s.2(1). See also s.2(3) (voluntary acceptance of risk); *Johnstone v. Bloomsbury H.A.* [1992] Q.B. 333, 343, 346.
[55] s.2(2). See also s.2(3) (voluntary acceptance of risk).
[56] *Phillips Products Ltd v. Hyland* [1987] 1 W.L.R. 659. See also *Flamar Interocean Ltd v. Denmac Ltd* [1990] 1 Lloyd's Rep. 434.
[57] *Thompson v. T. Lohan (Plant Hire) Ltd* [1987] 1 W.L.R. 649; *Hancock Shipping Co. Ltd v. Deacon & Trysail (Private) Ltd* [1991] 2 Lloyd's Rep. 550.
[58] *Neptune Orient Lines Ltd v. J.V.C. (U.K.) Ltd* [1983] 2 Lloyd's Rep. 438; see *ante*, § 14–047.
[59] See *ante*, § 14–064.
[60] See *ante*, § 14–063.

business" is not defined or explained by the Act,[61] but it would seem probable that "standard terms of business" would embrace the standard terms of a third party, *e.g.* a trade association, incorporated into the contract by reference or by course of dealing. Since, in any event, no two contracts are likely to be completely identical, but will at least differ as to subject-matter and price, the question arises whether variations or omissions from or additions to standard terms thereby render them "non-standard" and, if they do not, whether all the terms then become standard terms. Where negotiations have taken place around standard terms before the contract is made, and amendments agreed, it is a question of fact whether one party can be said to have dealt on those standard terms.[62] If it is alleged that an ostensibly "one-off" contract is in fact the other's written standard terms of business, extensive discovery may be involved to determine the terms on which contracts have been concluded with others.

In cases falling within section 3, as against the party dealing as consumer or on the other's written standard terms of business, the other party ("the *proferens*") cannot by reference to any contract term,[63] except in so far as the term satisfies the requirement of reasonableness, do either of two things: **14–070**

(a) when himself in breach of contract, exclude or restrict any liability of his in respect of breach[64]; or

(b) claim to be entitled:
    (i) to render a contractual performance substantially different from that which was reasonably expected of him,[65] or
    (ii) in respect of the whole or part of his contractual obligations to render no performance at all.[66]

It would appear to be the intention of (b) that it should apply where there is no breach of contract at all, but where the obligation as to performance has been limited or qualified.[67] An example might be, where one party deals as consumer, of a contract with a holiday tour operator who agrees to provide a holiday at a certain hotel at a certain resort, but who claims to be entitled, by reference to a term of the contract to that effect, in certain circumstances to accommodate the consumer at a different hotel, or to change the resort, or to cancel the holiday in whole or in part. An example in a commercial contract on written standard terms, might be that of a *force majeure* clause[68] by reference to which a seller of goods

---

[61] But see *McCrone v. Boots Farm Sales*, 1981 S.L.T. 103 (on s.17 of the Act in Scotland) and *Flamar Interocean Ltd v. Denmac Ltd* [1990] 1 Lloyd's Rep. 434, at 438.

[62] Compare *St. Alban's City and District Council v. International Computers Ltd* [1996] 4 All E.R. 481, 490–491, with *Salvage Assocation v. Cap Financial Services* [1995] F.S.R. 654. See also *Chester Grosvenor Hotel Co. Ltd v. Alfred McAlpine Management Ltd* (1991) 56 Build.L.R. 115, 131.

[63] Whether in the same or in another contract between the same parties. *cf.* s.10; *post*, § 14–078.

[64] s.3(2)(a). See *Charlotte Thirty Ltd v. Croker Ltd* (1990) 24 Const.L.R. 46; *St. Alban's City and District Council v. International Computers Ltd, supra.*

[65] *i.e.* at the time the contract was made: *Shearson Lehman Hutton Inc. v. Maclaine Watson & Co. Ltd* [1989] 2 Lloyd's Rep. 570, 612. See *Timeload Ltd v. British Telecommunications plc* [1995] E.M.L.R. 459.

[66] s.3(2)(b).

[67] *Shearson Lehman Hutton Inc. v. Maclaine Watson & Co. Ltd* [1989] 2 Lloyd's Rep. 570, 611–612.

[68] See *post*, § 14–126.

claims to be entitled to suspend or postpone delivery of the goods, or to deliver substitute goods, or to cancel the contract, upon the happening of events beyond his control. The argument could, however, be advanced[69] that the effect of clauses such as those mentioned is to define the scope of the obligation of the *proferens* with respect to performance: the contract must be read together with and subject to the clause.[70] The other party could not therefore reasonably expect that the *proferens* would render a contractual performance other than that as qualified by the clause, nor would there be any contractual obligation in respect of which the *proferens* would be claiming to render no performance at all. But it is submitted that a sensible meaning can in most cases only be given to paragraph (b) if one assumes that the contractual performance and contractual obligation referred to is the performance required and the obligation imposed by the contract apart from the contract term relied on.[71]

14–071   Nevertheless it seems unlikely that a contract term entitling one party to terminate the contract in the event of a material breach by the other (*e.g.* failure to pay by the due date) would fall within paragraph (b), or, if it did so, would be adjudged not to satisfy the requirement of reasonableness.[72] Nor, it is submitted, would that provision extend to a contract term which entitled one party, not to alter the performance expected of himself, but to alter the performance required of the other party (*e.g.* a term by which a seller of goods is entitled to increase the price payable by the buyer to the price ruling at the date of delivery, or a term by which a person advancing a loan is entitled to vary the interest payable by the borrower on the loan).[73]

14–072   **Unreasonable indemnity clauses.** A contract may stipulate that, if one party incurs liability (usually to third parties) as the result of the performance of the contract, he shall be entitled to be indemnified by the other party against the liability.[74] Section 4 of the Act provides that a person dealing as consumer[75] cannot by reference to any contract term be made to indemnify another person (whether a party to the contract or not) in respect of liability that may be incurred by the other for negligence[76] or breach of contract, except in so far as the contract term satisfies the requirement of reasonableness.[77] This provision applies whether the liability in question:

(a) is directly that of the person to be indemnified or is incurred by him vicariously; or

(b) is to the person dealing as consumer or someone else.[78]

---

[69] Treitel, *Frustration and Force Majeure*, (1994), § 12–014.

[70] See *ante*, § 14–003.

[71] *Zockoll Group Ltd v. Mercury Communications Ltd (No. 2)* [1998] I.T.C.L.R. 104. See *ante*, § 14–003.

[72] But see *Timeload Ltd v. British Telecommunications plc* [1995] E.M.L.R. 459 (termination not limited to cases where there was a good reason) and *post*, § 15–066.

[73] But such a term in a consumer contract might be unfair and not binding on the consumer under the Unfair Terms in Consumer Contracts Regulations 1994, *post*, Chap. 15.

[74] See *ante*, § 14–015.

[75] See *ante*, § 14–064.

[76] See *ante*, § 14–058.

[77] s.4(1).

[78] s.4(2).

The liability against which indemnity is sought must be a business liability.[79] An example would be a term in a contract for the hire of a motorcar which required the hirer to indemnify the car hire company against third-party claims arising out of the hirer's use of the car.

Indemnities given by persons who do not deal as consumer are not affected by section 4. Although section 2 of the Act inhibits the exclusion or restriction of liability for negligence,[80] nothing in that section will render ineffective a term of a contract by which one party requires the other (who does not deal as consumer) to indemnify him against his liability in negligence to third parties.[81]   **14–073**

"Guarantee" of consumer goods.[82] Section 5 of the Act renders absolutely ineffective the exclusion or restriction of business liability[83] for loss or damage resulting from the negligence[84] of a manufacturer or distributor of goods[85] by reference to any contract term or notice contained in or operating by reference to a guarantee of the goods[86] (such as is often provided by, for example, manufacturers of electrical equipment.) But the goods must be of a type ordinarily supplied for private use or consumption,[87] and the loss or damage must arise from the goods proving defective while "in consumer use," that is, when a person is using them, or has them in possession for use, otherwise than exclusively for the purposes of business.[88] This section does not apply as between parties to a contract under or in pursuance of which possession or ownership of the goods passed.[89]   **14–074**

Sale and hire-purchase. Section 6 of the Act[90] limits the ability of a seller of goods, or of the owner of goods let under a hire-purchase agreement, to exclude or restrict his liability in respect of breach of the terms implied by sections 12 to 15 of the Sale of Goods Act 1979[91] or sections 8 to 11 of the Supply of Goods (Implied Terms) Act 1973.[92] The content of section 6 is discussed in Volume II, Chapter 38 (Credit and Security)[93] and 43 (Sale of Goods),[94] of this work. The liabilities referred to in this section are not confined to business liabilities,[95] but they are confined to those which arise from breach of the statutory *implied* undertakings only.   **14–075**

Miscellaneous contracts under which goods pass. Section 7 of the Act is concerned with contract terms which exclude or restrict business liability for   **14–076**

---

[79] s.1(3); see *ante*, § 14–063.
[80] See *ante*, § 14–068.
[81] *Thompson v. Lohan (Plant Hire) Ltd* [1987] 1 W.L.R. 649; *Hancock Shipping Co. Ltd v. Deacon & Trysail (Private) Ltd* [1991] 2 Lloyd's Rep. 550.
[82] See *post*, § 19–005.
[83] See *ante*, § 14–063.
[84] See *ante*, § 14–058.
[85] Defined in s.14.
[86] Defined in s.5(2)(b).
[87] See Vol. II, § 43–101.
[88] s.5(2)(a).
[89] s.5(2), *e.g.* as between buyer and seller.
[90] As amended by s.63 of, and Sched. 3 to, the Sale of Goods Act 1979.
[91] See Vol. II, §§ 43–068, 43–099 *et seq.*
[92] See Vol. II, §§ 38–279, 38–351.
[93] Vol. II, §§ 38–279, 38–351—38–352.
[94] Vol. II, §§ 43–068, 43–099—43–105.
[95] s.6(4). See *ante*, § 14–063.

breach of an implied obligation in a contract "where the possession or ownership of the goods passes under or in pursuance of" the contract (other than a contract governed by the law of sale of goods or hire-purchase).[96] Examples of such contracts are contracts for the hire of goods or for work and materials. The obligation in the contract must be one which arises "by implication of law from the nature of the contract."[97] In most cases, the obligations to be implied in such contracts are those set out in sections 2 to 5 and 7 to 10 of the Supply of Goods and Services Act 1982.[98] In so far as any liability arises in respect of the goods' correspondence with description or sample, or their quality or fitness for any particular purpose, as against a person dealing as consumer the exclusion or restriction of that liability by reference to any contract term is absolutely ineffective.[99] As against a person dealing otherwise than as consumer, that liability can be excluded or restricted by reference to any contract term, but only in so far as the term satisfies the requirement of reasonableness.[1] Liability for breach of the obligations as to title, etc., arising under section 2 of the 1982 Act (*e.g.* in contracts for work and materials) cannot be excluded or restricted by reference to any contract term.[2] In the case of other contracts (*e.g.* contracts for the hire of goods,) terms excluding or restricting liability in respect of the right to transfer ownership of the goods or give possession, or the assurance of quiet possession to a person taking goods in pursuance of the contract, are subject to the test of reasonableness.[3]

14–077   **Effect of breach.** A term that is required to satisfy the test of reasonableness, and does so, may be given effect to notwithstanding that the contract has been terminated either by breach or by the innocent party electing to treat it as repudiated[4]; and the affirmation of the contract does not of itself exclude the requirement of reasonableness.[5] It would also seem that a term which is rendered wholly ineffective in some respect by the Act is not rendered effective by the fact that the innocent party has affirmed the contract.

14–078   **Anti-avoidance provisions.** Certain anti-avoidance provisions are contained in the Act. Section 10 provides: "A person is not bound by any contract term prejudicing or taking away rights of his which arise under, or in connection with the performance of, another contract, so far as those rights extend to the enforcement of another's liability which this Part of this Act prevents that other from excluding or restricting." The purpose of this provision has been said to be to prevent rights arising in favour of A under a contract between A and B from being affected by the terms of a secondary contract between A and C which take away or inhibit the exercise of those rights,[6] as, for example, where a term in a contract between a manufacturer of goods and the buyer purports to affect the rights of the buyer under the Sale of Goods Act against the retailer from whom

---

[96] Also excluded are goods passing on redemption of trading stamps: s.7(5).
[97] *See ante*, §§ 13–027, 13–028.
[98] ss.2–5 (work and materials); ss.7–10 (bailment for hire). See Vol. II, §§ 33–062, 43–014.
[99] s.7(2). See Vol. II, § 33–072.
[1] s.7(3). See *Charlotte Thirty Ltd v. Croker Ltd* (1990) 24 Const. L.R. 46; *Danka Rentals Ltd v. XI Software Ltd* (1998) 17 Tr.L.R. 74.
[2] s.7(3A), inserted by s.17(2) of the Supply of Goods and Services Act 1982.
[3] s.7(4) (as amended).
[4] s.9(1). See also *ante*, § 14–022.
[5] s.9(2).
[6] *Tudor Grange Holdings Ltd v. Citibank N.A.* [1992] Ch. 53.

he purchases the goods.[7] The scope of the section is, however, enigmatic. It employs the words "prejudicing or taking away rights" instead of the usual "excludes or restricts liability." The extended interpretation of the latter phrase[8] therefore does not apply. Also the reference to "the enforcement of another's *liability*" would preclude the application of section 10 to a case where the terms of the secondary contract purported to entitle a party to another contract to render a performance substantially different from that reasonably expected of him, or to render no performance at all.[9] It has been held that the section does not apply to the compromise or waiver of an existing contractual claim, *e.g.* to the release by a person of rights which have accrued to him as the result of the breach of another contract to which he is a party.[10]

Section 27(2) further prevents evasion of the Act by choice of a foreign law. **14–079** This provision is considered in a later chapter (Conflict of Laws).[11]

Assumption of risk. Section 2(3) of the Act provides that, where a contract **14–080** term (or notice)[12] purports to exclude or restrict liability for negligence a person's agreement to it or awareness of it is not of itself to be taken as indicating his voluntary acceptance of the risk.[13]

Test of reasonableness. Except in those instances where the Act renders **14–081** absolutely ineffective exclusion or restriction of liability, the contract terms controlled by the Act are subject to the requirement of reasonableness. In relation to a contract term, the requirement of reasonableness for the purposes of the Act (and of section 3 of the Misrepresentation Act 1967) is that "the term shall have been a fair and reasonable one to be included having regard to the circumstances which were or ought reasonably to have been, known to or in the contemplation of the parties when the contract was made."[14] The time for determining the reasonableness of the term is the time at which the contract was made. That determination is therefore not affected by the nature or seriousness of the loss or damage caused, or the way in which the term is in fact operated or relied on,[15] except to the extent to which such events were or ought reasonably to have been in the contemplation of the parties at that time. Further, it would appear that circumstances known only to the party seeking to allege that the term is reasonable, for example, the experimental nature of the product or the fact that it had been purchased from a foreign supplier subject to an effective exclusion of liability of his part,[16] are irrelevant if they were not known, and could not

---

[7] See s.55(3),(4) of the Sale of Goods Act 1893, inserted by s.4 of the Supply of Goods (Implied Terms) Act 1973, and repealed by the Unfair Contract Terms Act 1977, s.31(4) and Sched. 4. But in *Neptune Orient Lines Ltd v. J.V.C. (U.K.) Ltd* [1983] 2 Lloyd's Rep. 439, Parker J. held that s.10 had no application to a covenant not to sue a third party (see *ante*,§ 14–047) in tort.

[8] s.13; see *ante*, § 14–060.

[9] s.3(2)(b); *ante*, § 14–070 (there being no breach of contract).

[10] *Tudor Grange Holdings Ltd v. Citibank N.A.*, *supra* (noted (1992) 55 M.L.R. 866). See also Sched. 1, para. 5.

[11] See *post*, § 31–007.

[12] See *ante*, § 14–057.

[13] But see *ante*, § 14–014.

[14] s.11(1). Contrast s.11(3) (notices) and *First National Bank plc v. Loxley* [1996] E.G.C.S. 174.

[15] *Shearson Lehman Hutton Inc. v. Maclaine Watson & Co. Ltd* [1989] 2 Lloyd's Rep. 570, 612. See also *Stewart Gill Ltd v. Horatio Myer & Co. Ltd* [1992] Q.B. 600.

[16] See *post*, § 14–101.

reasonably have been known, to the other party at the time the contract was made.[17]

14–082   **Guidelines.** By section 11(2) of the Act, five guidelines are laid down in Schedule 2[18] and regard is to be had to these in determining whether a contract term satisfies the requirement of reasonableness.[19] The guidelines are only made expressly applicable for the purposes of section 6 (sale of goods and hire-purchase) and section 7 (other contracts for the supply of goods), but they are frequently regarded as being of general application.[20] In any event they are not exhaustive. The guidelines are:

(a) the strength of the bargaining positions of the parties relative to each other, taking account (among other things) alternative means by which the customer's requirements could have been met[21];

(b) whether the customer received an inducement to agree to the term, or in accepting it had an opportunity of entering into a similar contract with other persons, but without having to accept a similar term[22];

(c) whether the customer knew or ought reasonably to have known of the existence and extent of the term (having regard, among other things, to any custom of the trade and any course of dealing between the parties)[23];

(d) where the term excludes or restricts any relevant liability if some condition is not complied with, whether it was reasonable at the time of the contract to expect that compliance with that condition would be practicable[24];

---

[17] See also *Singer Co. (U.K.) Ltd v. Tees and Hartlepool Port Authority* [1988] 2 Lloyd's Rep. 164, 169; *Flamar Interocean Ltd v. Denmac Ltd* [1990] 1 Lloyd's Rep. 434 (actual insurance position at time irrelevant).

[18] The guidelines are similar to those set out in s.55(5) of the Sale of Goods Act 1893 (inserted by s.4 of the Supply of Goods (Implied Terms) Act 1973, and now repealed).

[19] See Vol. II, § 43–102.

[20] *Flamar Interocean Ltd v. Denmac Ltd, supra*, at 438–439; *Stewart Gill Ltd v. Horatio Myer & Co. Ltd, supra*, at 608. See also *Singer Co. (U.K.) Ltd v. Tees and Hartlepool Port Authority* [1988] 2 Lloyd's Rep. 164, 169; *St. Alban's City and District Council v. International Computers Ltd* [1995] F.S.R. 686 (affd. [1996] 4 All E.R. 481).

[21] See *R.W. Green Ltd v. Cade Bros. Farms* [1978] 1 Lloyd's Rep. 602; *George Mitchell (Chesterhall) Ltd v. Finney Lock Seeds Ltd* [1983] 2 A.C. 803; *Singer Co. (U.K.) Ltd v. Tees and Hartlepool Port Authority, supra*; *St. Alban's City and District Council v. International Computers Ltd, supra*; *Schenkers Ltd v. Overland Shoes Ltd* [1998] 1 Lloyd's Rep. 498. In *Denholm Fishselling Ltd v. Anderson*, 1991 S.L.T. (Sh. Ct.) 24, it was held that there was no preponderance of bargaining power where buyers might not be able to purchase except on similar standard conditions but nevertheless had a choice of suppliers. See also Vol. II, § 37–078.

[22] *R.W. Green Ltd v. Cade Bros. Farms, supra*; *George Mitchell (Chesterhall) Ltd v. Finney Lock Seeds Ltd, supra*; *Singer Co. (U.K.) Ltd v. Tees and Hartlepool Port Authority, supra*.

[23] See *George Mitchell (Chesterhall) Ltd v. Finney Lock Seeds Ltd, supra*; *Charlotte Thirty Ltd v. Croker Ltd* (1990) 24 Const.L.R. 46; *AEG (U.K.) Ltd v. Logic Resource Ltd* [1996] C.L.C. 625.

[24] See *R.W. Green Ltd v. Cade Bros. Farms, supra*; *Stag Line Ltd v. Tyne Ship Repair Group Ltd* [1984] 2 Lloyd's Rep. 211; *Rees-Hough Ltd v. Redland Reinforced Plastics Ltd* (1985) 2 Const. L.R. 109; *Sargant v. CIT (England) (t/a Citalia)* [1994] C.L.Y. 566; *Knight Machinery (Holdings) v. Rennie* 1995 S.L.T. 166.

(e) whether the goods were manufactured, processed or adapted to the special order of the customer.[25]

Limits on amount. Exemption clauses in contracts frequently limit the liability in damages of one party to a fixed or determinable sum. Section 11(4) provides: **14–083**

> "Where by reference to a contract term . . . a person seeks to restrict liability to a specified sum of money, and the question arises (under this or any other Act) whether the term or notice satisfies the requirement of reasonableness, regard shall be had in particular (but without prejudice to subsection (2) above[26] in the case of contract terms) to—(a) the resources which he could expect to be available to him for the purpose of meeting the liability should it arise; and (b) how far it was open to him to cover himself by insurance."

This provision was clearly designed to provide some alleviation to the small business, and to professional persons, who may not have the resources available to meet unlimited liability or who may not be able to obtain insurance or who may be exposed to claims in excess of the sums for which insurance cover can be obtained. But it might in some circumstances be construed to operate against those enterprises with such resources or which are able to insure.[27] It seems probable that the words "a specified sum of money" would embrace a determinable sum, *e.g.* the contract price. But it is more questionable whether (b) covers the situation where insurance cover can be obtained, but only on terms which are uneconomic in relation to the margin of profit achieved.[28]

Burden of proof. The onus of proving that it was fair and reasonable to incorporate a term in a contract lies on the party so contending.[29] It is therefore unnecessary for a claimant to indicate in his statement of case that he intends to challenge the reasonableness of a term in a contract relied on by the defendant.[30]   **14–084**

Judicial application of the reasonableness test.[31] There is a growing body of reported cases which illustrate in general terms the way in which the courts may approach the test of reasonableness contained in the Act. However, they are   **14–085**

---

[25] It is uncertain whether the existence of this factor would operate against or in favour of the customer, but it is submitted that it should operate against the customer and in favour of the supplier.

[26] See *ante*, § 14–082.

[27] The availability of insurance is a relevant consideration in applying the test of reasonableness under s.11(1): see *George Mitchell (Chesterhall) Ltd v. Finney Lock Seeds Ltd* [1983] 2 A.C. 803, 817 (*post*, § 14–087); *Rees-Hough Ltd v. Redland Reinforced Plastics Ltd* (1985) 2 Const.L.R. 109; *Phillips Products Ltd v. Hyland* [1987] 1 W.L.R. 659, 666–668; *Singer Co. (U.K.) Ltd v. Tees and Hartlepool Port Authority* [1988] 2 Lloyd's Rep. 164, 169; *Smith v. Eric Bush* [1990] 1 A.C. 831, 858. But the actual insurance position of the parties at the time is normally irrelevant: *Flamar Interocean Ltd v. Denmac Ltd* [1990] 1 Lloyd's Rep. 434; *cf. St. Alban's City and District Council v. International Computers Ltd* [1995] F.S.R. 686 (affd. [1996] 4 All E.R. 481); *Salvage Association v. Cap Financial Services* [1995] F.S.R. 654.

[28] *cf.*, *Smith v. Eric Bush, supra*, at 858 (cost).

[29] s.11(5).

[30] *Sheffield v. Pickfords Ltd* [1997] C.L.C. 648.

[31] See Adams and Brownsword (1988) 104 L.Q.R. 94; Brown and Chandler (1993) 109 L.Q.R. 41; Adams (1994) 57 M.L.R. 960.

of limited value as precedents since the position of the parties and the circumstances surrounding the transaction, and the precise wording of the clause in question, will necessarily differ in each particular situation.

14-086   **Decisions under earlier legislation.** A small number of decisions have been reported with respect to the reasonableness test contained in section 55 of the Sale of Goods Act 1893[32] (now repealed) or section 3 of the Misrepresentation Act 1967 (now amended in its wording by section 8 of the Unfair Contract Terms Act 1977), both of which sections however required the court to determine whether it would be fair and reasonable to allow *reliance* on the term, and not whether it was fair and reasonable to incorporate the term having regard to the circumstances at the time the contract was made.[33] In *Rasbora Ltd v. J.C.L. Marine Ltd*[34] it was held (*obiter*)[35] that it was not fair and reasonable to allow a boatbuilder to rely on a term excluding all liability (other than a warranty to replace defective parts) when the boat was wholly destroyed by a fire, due to defective electrical installations, on the day following its acceptance by the buyer. In *R.W. Green Ltd v. Cade Bros. Farms*[36] a term in a contract for the bulk sale of seed potatoes providing a short time-limit for complaints in respect of latent defects could not be relied on by the seller when the potatoes were infected with a virus; but reliance on a term limiting the liability of the seller to the contract price was allowed, as the term had been in use for many years with the approval of negotiating committees acting on behalf of both buyers and sellers. And in *Howard Marine and Dredging Co. Ltd v. A. Ogden & Sons (Excavations) Ltd*[37] the Court of Appeal by a majority[38] held that it would not have been fair and reasonable to allow reliance on a term in a contract for the hire of barges which provided that acceptance was to be conclusive evidence that the barges were fit for their intended use, even if the clause had been apt (which it was not) to cover a misrepresentation by the owners of the barges as to their deadweight capacity. Lord Denning M.R., however, considered that both the clause itself and reliance on it was fair and reasonable, since the parties were of equal bargaining power, the term was contained in negotiated drafts and it was a familiar term in charterparties and other commercial contracts, such as structural and engineering contracts.

14-087   In *George Mitchell (Chesterhall) Ltd v. Finney Lock Seeds Ltd*[39] the appellant seed merchants, by their standard conditions of sale, limited their liability in respect of seeds that did not comply with the contract of sale to replacement of the seeds or refund of the price, but otherwise excluded all liability for loss or damage arising from the use of seeds supplied by them apart from such replacement or refund. The respondents, who were farmers, purchased from them for £201 a quantity of winter white cabbage seeds. The seeds in fact supplied were autumn cabbage seed; the crop failed; and the respondents claimed damages in excess of £60,000. The House of Lords held that it would not be fair or

---

[32] Inserted by s.4 of the Supply of Goods (Implied Terms) Act 1973.
[33] But see *Howard Marine and Dredging Co. Ltd v. A. Ogden & Sons (Excavations) Ltd* [1978] Q.B. 574, 594.
[34] [1977] 1 Lloyd's Rep. 645.
[35] The sale was held to be a consumer sale: see *ante*, § 14–064, n. 41.
[36] [1978] 1 Lloyd's Rep. 602.
[37] [1978] Q.B. 574; see *ante*, § 6–068.
[38] Bridge and Shaw L.JJ. (but giving no reasons).
[39] [1983] 2 A.C. 803; see *ante*, § 14–023.

reasonable to allow the appellants to rely on the limitation of liability. Lord Bridge said that, in having regard to the various matters to which the relevant statutory provision directs attention,[40] "the court must entertain a whole range of considerations, put them in the scales on one side or the other, and decide at the end of the day on which side the balance comes down."[41] In the instant case, although a similar limitation of liability had for long been embodied without protest in the terms of the trade between seedsmen and farmers,[42] the practice was to negotiate settlements of farmers' claims for damages in excess of the price of the seeds if it was thought that the claims were genuine and justified. This indicated that reliance on the limitation would not be fair or reasonable. Two further facts weighted the scale in favour of the respondents: the error was due to the negligence of the appellants' organisation, and seedsmen could insure[43] against the risk of crop failure resulting from the supply of the wrong variety of seeds without materially increasing the price of seeds.

Reasonableness under Unfair Contract Terms Act 1977. So far as the 1977 **14–088** Act is concerned, in *Walker v. Boyle*,[44] where a vendor in response to preliminary inquiries represented that she was unaware of any boundary dispute connected with the property, although she ought to have known that there was such a dispute, it was held that condition 17 of the National Conditions of Sale, even with a statement that "accuracy is not guaranteed, and [the replies] do not obviate the need to make appropriate searches, inquiries and inspections," did not meet the test of reasonableness required by section 11 of the Act.[45] In *Stag Line Ltd v. Tyne Shiprepair Group Ltd*[46] a term in a ship-repairing contract excluding liability on the part of the repairer for consequential economic loss was held to be reasonable, but not a condition that the shipowner should have no remedy unless he returned the vessel to the repairer's yard for repair, or to such other place as the repairer should direct. In *Phillips Products Ltd v. Hyland*[47] the Court of Appeal held unreasonable in the circumstances[48] a term in a contract for the hire of an excavator and driver which provided that the driver was to be regarded as an employee of the hirer who alone was to be responsible for all claims arising in connection with the operation of the plant by the driver. In *Rees-Hough Ltd v. Redland Reinforced Plastics Ltd*[49] a term in a contract for the supply of piping which excluded all liability of the seller unless notified of complaints within three months of delivery was held unreasonable. In *Smith v. Eric Bush*[50] a non-contractual notice in a report by a building society surveyor disclaiming all liability for negligence in conducting the survey of a modest dwelling-house was held to be unreasonable in view of the fact that the report would be relied on by

---

[40] s.55 of the Sale of Goods Act 1979 (as amended) or s.11 of the Unfair Contract Terms Act 1977.

[41] At 816.

[42] But never negotiated by representative bodies.

[43] See § 14–083, *ante*, n. 27.

[44] [1982] 1 W.L.R. 495. See also *Southwestern General Property Co. Ltd v. Marton* (1982) 263 E.G. 1090 and § 6–130, n. 18, *ante*.

[45] For the purposes of s.3 of the Misrepresentation Act 1967 (as amended).

[46] [1984] 2 Lloyd's Rep. 211.

[47] [1987] 1 W.L.R. 659. But contrast *Thompson v. Lohan (Plant Hire) Ltd* [1987] 1 W.L.R. 649.

[48] The contract was on a "take it or leave it" basis, and the hirer had no control over the way the driver would do the work.

[49] (1985) 2 Const.L.R. 109.

[50] [1990] 1 A.C. 831; see also *Harris v. Wyre Forest DC, ibid.*; *Davies v. Idris Parry* (1988) 20 E.G. 92, 21 E.G. 74; *Beaton v. Nationwide Anglia Building Society* (1991) 31 E.G. 218.

an intending purchaser of the property. In *Charlotte Thirty Ltd v. Croker Ltd*[51] the court held unreasonable a term in a contract to design and build an industrial plant which exonerated the contractor from all liability except as provided in a six-month warranty to replace defective components if these were returned carriage paid to the contractor for adjudication. And in *Stewart Gill Ltd v. Horatio Myer & Co. Ltd*[52] a term in a contract for the supply and installation of a conveyor system, which provided that the purchaser was not to be entitled to withhold payment of any sum due to the supplier under the contract by reason of "any payment, credit, set-off . . . or for any other reason whatsoever," failed to satisfy the requirement of reasonableness.

14–089   In *St. Alban's City and District Council v. International Computers Ltd*[53] a term in a computer software contract made with a local authority limited the liability of the supplier to £100,000, and in *Salvage Association v. Cap Financial Services*[54] a term in a computer accounting contract limited the liability of the supplier to £25,000. Both were held to be unreasonable. In *Edmund Murray Ltd v. BSP International Foundations Ltd*[55] the court held unreasonable a term in a contract for the sale of a drilling rig with detailed requirements for performance, which purported to exclude liability on the part of the seller for breach of both express and implied obligations, and in *AEG (UK) Ltd v. Logic Resource Ltd*[56] a term in a contract for the sale of radar equipment which excluded all warranties and conditions implied by the Sale of Goods Act 1979 was held to be unreasonable despite the giving of an express warranty that the equipment was free of defects caused by faulty materials or bad workmanship. Also in *Timeload Ltd v. British Telecommunications plc*[57] the Court of Appeal held unreasonable a term in BT's standard terms and conditions which permitted BT to terminate the contract on one month's notice since the term was not limited to cases where there was a good reason for the termination.

14–090   On the other hand, in *R. & B. Customs Brokers Co. Ltd v. United Dominions Trust Ltd*,[58] where a finance company purchased a motorcar from a dealer and agreed to sell it under a conditional sale agreement to a commercial company, Dillon L.J. expressed the opinion (*obiter*)[59] that a clause in the conditional sale agreement which excluded all conditions and warranties, express or implied, as to merchantability or fitness for purpose was in the circumstances reasonable, since the director who entered into the agreement on behalf of the buyer company was a man of commercial experience and the finance company never had

---

[51] (1990) 24 Const.L.R. 46. But see Vol. II, § 37–078.

[52] [1992] Q.B. 600. See also *Fastframe Ltd v. Lochinski*, unreported, CA, March 3, 1993 (noted (1994) 57 M.L.R. 960); *Esso Petroleum Co. Ltd v. Milton* [1997] 1 W.L.R. 938, 948, 954. But see the cases cited in § 14–090, nn. 64, 65.

[53] [1995] F.S.R. 686 (affd. [1996] 4 All E.R. 481).

[54] [1995] F.S.R. 654.

[55] (1994) 33 Const. L.R. 1.

[56] [1996] C.L.C. 265.

[57] [1995] E.M.L.R. 459. Contrast *Zockoll Group Ltd v. Mercury Communications Ltd* [1998] I.T.C.L.R. 104.

[58] [1988] 1 W.L.R. 321. See also *W. Photoprint Ltd v. Forward Trust Group Ltd* (1993) 12 Tr.L.R. 146, Q.B.D.

[59] At 331–332. The company was held to be "dealing as consumer": see *ante*, § 14–064.

possession of or inspected the car.[60] In *Singer Co. (U.K.) Ltd v. Tees and Hartlepool Port Authority*,[61] where a machine sub-bailed to a port authority was damaged in the course of loading, Steyn J. held reasonable a clause disclaiming responsibility for damage other than that arising from the proven negligence of the authority and a clause limiting the liability of the authority to a sum of £800 per tonne.[62] In *Sonicare International Ltd v. East Anglia Freight Terminal Ltd*[63] a term in the National Association of Warehouse Keeper's conditions limiting liability to £100 per tonne was similarly held reasonable in the circumstances of that case. A "no set-off" clause in the standard conditions of the British International Freight Association (freight forwarders) was upheld as reasonable in *Schenkers Ltd v. Overland Shoes Ltd*,[64] and "no set-off" clauses in loan and financial agreements have also been upheld.[65] Further, in *Photo Productions Ltd v. Securicor Transport Ltd*[66] (a case which did not involve consideration of any provision of the 1977 Act) Lord Wilberforce stated that, in commercial matters generally, when the parties were not of unequal bargaining power, and when risks were to be borne by insurance, Parliament's intention in the Act seemed to be one of "leaving the parties free to apportion the risks as they think fit . . . and respecting their decisions."[67] This was the approach adopted in *Monarch Airlines Ltd v. London Luton Airport Ltd*[68] where a term in a contract between an airline and an airport operator excluded liability for damage to an aircraft caused by any act, omission, neglect or default on the part of the latter, except if done with intent to cause damage or recklessly with knowledge that damage would probably result. It was held that this term was reasonable on the ground that it was generally accepted in the market, its meaning was clear and both parties could make insurance arrangements on the basis of the term.

Powers of the court. Although the Act uses the words "except in so far as the   **14–091** term satisfies the requirement of reasonableness,"[69] it is the term as a whole that has to be reasonable and not merely some part of it.[70] Thus if the term as a whole is unreasonable, a party cannot be heard to say that the part of the term on which he relies is reasonable.[71] However, where a single provision in a contract consists of several sub-clauses or sentences, it may be difficult to identify what is "the term" for the purposes of the Act.

There is little doubt that the court's powers under the Act are limited to   **14–092** declaring the term either to be reasonable or unreasonable. The court could not

---

[60] But the fact that the finance company had not seen the goods was considered insufficient in *Sovereign Finance Ltd v. Silver Crest Furniture* [1997] C.C.L.R. 76 (hire-purchase) following *Purnell Secretarial Services v. Lease Management Services* [1994] C.C.L.R. 127 (hire).

[61] [1988] 2 Lloyd's Rep. 164.

[62] This figure was below that of the Hague-Visby Rules (£1,210), the CMR convention (£5,195) and the Warsaw Convention (£10,050) at the relevant time.

[63] [1997] 2 Lloyd's Rep. 48.

[64] [1998] 1 Lloyd's Rep. 498.

[65] *Surzur Overseas Ltd v. Ocean Reliance Shipping Co. Ltd* [1997] C.L.Y. 906; *Skipskreditt-foreningen v. Emperor Navigation* [1998] 1 Lloyd's Rep. 66; *WRM Group Ltd v. Wood* [1998] C.L.C. 89.

[66] [1980] A.C. 827.

[67] At 843.

[68] [1998] 1 Lloyd's Rep. 403.

[69] Or, in ss.6(3), 7(3), "only in so far as."

[70] *Stewart Gill Ltd v. Horatio Myer & Co Ltd* [1992] Q.B. 600, 608. But see *R.W. Green Ltd v. Cade Bros. Farms* [1978] 1 Lloyd's Rep. 602; *ante*, § 14–086.

[71] *Stewart Gill Ltd v. Horatio Myer & Co. Ltd*, *supra*, at 607.

rewrite the term by (say) increasing the amount specified in a limitation of liability clause to a sum which it considered to be fair and reasonable.[72] Nor (*semble*) could the court sever words which made the term unreasonable so as to render the term reasonable or limit the application of an unreasonable clause so as to produce a reasonable result.[73]

14–093   If a single term purports to exclude or restrict liability which by the Act cannot in any circumstances be excluded or restricted (for example, liability for death and personal injury resulting from negligence) and also liability which can be excluded or restricted subject to the test of reasonableness (for example, liability in negligence for other loss or damage), it would appear that the term, while being ineffective to exclude or restrict the former liability, could nevertheless be upheld as reasonable in respect of the restriction or exclusion of the latter liability.[74] But it could be argued that the term as a whole is rendered unreasonable by purporting to exclude or restrict the former liability as well as the latter.

14–094   **Appeals.** A decision by the judge of first instance as to whether the term was a fair and reasonable one to be included cannot accurately be described as an exercise of discretion. Nevertheless, since it involves the balancing of various considerations, Lord Bridge has said[75]: "in my view . . . when asked to review such a decision on appeal, the appellate court should treat the original decision with the utmost respect and refrain from interference with it unless satisfied that it proceeded upon some erroneous principle or was plainly and obviously wrong."

14–095   **Specific exceptions.** Some or all of the provisions of the Act do not apply in the case of contracts of a type specified in the Act.

14–096   **Schedule 1.**[76] By paragraph 1 of Schedule 1 to the Act, sections 2 (negligence liability), 3 (liability arising in contract) and 4 (unreasonable indemnity clauses) do not extend to:

> (*a*) any contract of insurance (including a contract to pay an annuity on human life)[76a];
>
> (*b*) any contract so far as it relates to the creation or transfer of an interest in land, or to the termination of such an interest, whether by extinction, merger, surrender, forfeiture or otherwise[77];

---

[72] See *George Mitchell (Chesterhall) Ltd v. Finney Lock Seeds Ltd* [1983] 2 A.C. 803, 816 (on the wording of s.55 of the Sale of Goods Act 1979 (as amended)).

[73] *Stewart Gill Ltd v. Horatio Myer & Co. Ltd, supra.*

[74] The point was left open by Parker J. in *George Mitchell (Chesterhall) Ltd v. Finney Lock Seeds Ltd* [1981] 1 Lloyd's Rep. 476, 480.

[75] *George Mitchell (Chesterhall) Ltd v. Finney Lock Seeds Ltd* [1983] 2 A.C. 803, 810. See also *Edmund Murray Ltd v. BSP International Foundations Ltd* (1994) 33 Const. L.R. 1; *St. Alban's City and District Council v. International Computers Ltd* [1996] 4 All E.R. 481, 491.

[76] See s.1(2).

[76a] But see *post*, § 15–022 (Unfair Terms in Consumer Contracts Regulations 1994).

[77] *Electricity Supply Nominees Ltd v. IAF Group Ltd* [1993] 1 W.L.R. 1059 (no-set-off clause in lease); *Cheltenham and Gloucester B.S. v. Ebbage* [1994] C.L.Y. 3292 (mortgage); *Star Rider Ltd v. Inntrepreneur Pub Co.* [1998] 1 E.G.L.R. 53 (no-set-off clause in draft lease); *Granby Village (Manchester Management Co. Ltd v. Unchained Growth plc* [1998] C.L.Y. 3680 (no set-off clause in lease). But see *post* § 15–012.

(*c*) any contract so far as it relates to the creation of a right or interest in any patent, trade mark, copyright, registered design, technical or commercial information or other intellectual property, or relates to the termination of any such right or interest[78];

(*d*) any contract so far as it relates:

  (i) to the formation or dissolution of a company (which means any body corporate or unincorporated association and includes a partnership), or

  (ii) to its constitution or the rights or obligations of its corporators or members;

(*e*) any contract so far as it relates to the creation or transfer of any right or interest in securities.[79]

Paragraph 2 of Schedule 1 lists three contracts: **14-097**

(*a*) any contract of marine salvage or towage;

(*b*) any charterparty of a ship or hovercraft; and

(*c*) any contract for the carriage of goods by ship[80] or hovercraft.[81]

These contracts are subject to section 2(1) (exclusion or restriction of liability for death or personal injury resulting from negligence), but otherwise sections 2 (negligence liability), 3 (liability arising in contract), 4 (unreasonable indemnity clauses) and 7 (miscellaneous contracts under which goods pass) do not extend to any such contract except in favour of a person dealing as consumer.

Paragraph 3 of Schedule 1 deals with the situation where goods are carried by   **14-098**
ship[82] or hovercraft[83] in pursuance of a contract which either:

(*a*) specifies that as the means of carriage over part of the journey to be covered, or

(*b*) makes provision as to the means of carriage and does not exclude that means.

In such a situation section 2(2) (exclusion or restriction of liability for loss or damage resulting from negligence other than death or personal injury), 3 (liability arising in contract) and 4 (unreasonable indemnity clauses) do not, except in favour of a person dealing as consumer, extend to the contract as it operates for and in relation to the carriage of goods by that means.

By paragraph 4 of Schedule 1, section 2(1) and (2) (negligence liability) do not   **14-099**
extend to a contract of employment, except in favour of the employee.[84]

---

[78] *cf. Salvage Association v. Cap Financial Services* [1995] F.S.R. 654. Contrast Unfair Terms in Consumer Contracts Regulations 1994, *post* § 15–022.

[79] *Micklefield v. S.A.C. Technology Ltd* [1990] 1 W.L.R. 1002.

[80] See Carriage of Goods by Sea Act 1971; Merchant Shipping Act 1981. But see also *post*, § 14–098.

[81] See Hovercraft (Civil Liability) Order 1971 (S.I. 1971 No. 720) made under s.1 of the Hovercraft Act 1968. But see also *post*, § 14–098.

[82] See n. 80 (*supra*).

[83] See n. 81 (*supra*).

[84] See *Johnstone v. Bloomsbury H.A.* [1992] Q.B. 333.

14–100 By paragraph 5 of Schedule 1, section 2(1) (exclusion or restriction of liability for death or personal injury resulting from negligence) does not affect the validity of any discharge and indemnity given by a person, on or in connection with an award to him of compensation for pneumoconiosis attributable to employment in the coal industry, in respect of any further claim arising from his contracting that disease.

14–101 **International supply contracts.** By section 26 of the Act, the limits imposed by the Act on the extent to which a person may exclude or restrict liability by reference to a contract term do not apply to liability arising under an international supply contract (as defined in subsections (3) and (4) of that section),[85] nor are the terms of such a contract subject to any requirement of reasonableness under sections 3 (liability arising in contract) or section 4 (unreasonable indemnity clauses.)

14–102 **Contractual provisions authorised or required by statute or international agreement.** By section 29(1), nothing in the Act removes or restricts the effect of, or prevents reliance upon, any contractual provision which:

(*a*) is authorised or required by the express terms or necessary implication of an enactment[86]; or

(*b*) being made with a view to compliance with an international agreement to which the United Kingdom is a party, does not operate more restrictively than is contemplated by the agreement.

This subsection covers (*inter alia*), provisions in statutes and international conventions relating to the carriage of goods by sea[87] and of passengers, goods and luggage by land and air.[88] A specific temporary provision is made in the Act in respect of the Athens Convention 1974 on the carriage of passengers and their luggage by sea.[89]

14–103 **Contractual provisions approved by a competent authority.** By section 29(2) a contract term is to be taken for the purposes of the Act as satisfying the requirement of reasonableness if it is incorporated or approved by, or incorporated pursuant to a decision or ruling of, a competent authority[90] acting in the exercise of any statutory[91] jurisdiction or function and is not a term in a contract to which the competent authority is itself a party.[92]

14–104 **Choice of English law clauses.** Commercial contracts are frequently, by choice of the parties, made subject to English law, even though having no

---

[85] See Vol. II, § 43–105.
[86] Defined in s.29(3).
[87] Carriage of Goods by Sea Act 1971; Merchant Shipping Act 1981.
[88] See *post*, § 14–107, and Vol. II, Chaps. 35 and 36.
[89] s.28. The Merchant Shipping Act 1995, Sched. 6, now provides that the Athens Convention 1974, as amended by the 1976 protocol, is to have the force of law in the United Kingdom. See also S.I. 1998 No. 2917.
[90] Defined in s.29(3).
[91] Defined in s.29(3).
[92] *cf. Timeload Ltd v. British Telecommunications plc* [1995] E.M.L.R. 459 ("approval" by Director General of Fair Trading not in exercise of statutory function).

substantial connection with England. Section 27(1) of the Act[93] provides that, where the law applicable to a contract is the law of any part of the United Kingdom[94] only by choice of the parties (and apart from that choice would be the law of some country outside the United Kingdom) sections 2 to 7 of the Act do not operate as part of the law applicable to the contract.[95]

(b) *Misrepresentation Act 1967*

Liability for misrepresentation. Section 3 of the Misrepresentation Act   **14–105**
1967, as substituted by section 8 of the Unfair Contract Terms Act 1977, provides that, if a contract contains a term which would exclude or restrict:

(a) any liability to which a party to a contract may be subject by reason of any misrepresentation made by him before the contract was made, or

(b) any remedy available to another party to the contract by reason of such a misrepresentation,

that term shall be of no effect except in so far as it satisfies the requirement of reasonableness as stated in section 11(1) of the 1977 Act; and it is for those claiming that the term satisfies the requirement of reasonableness to show that it does. The implications of this section have been discussed in a previous chapter[96] and it is clear that it applies to a term which excludes or restricts any liability or remedy in respect of misrepresentations which have not become terms of the contract. It seems equally clear that it does not apply to a term which excludes or restricts any liability or remedy in respect of a breach of the terms of a contract, whether statements or promises, if those terms were never communicated as representations before the contract was made. It is, however, probable that section 3 will apply so as to inhibit the exclusion or restriction of the right to rescind a contract where a misrepresentation, first made independently, is subsequently incorporated as a contractual term.[97] But, in so far as a term excludes or restricts any liability or remedy based on an alleged breach of contract, its validity has to be tested by reference to the different scheme in the 1977 Act.[98]

(c) *Other Statutes*

Further statutes. In addition to the Unfair Contract Terms Act 1977 and the   **14–106**
Misrepresentation Act 1967, certain other statutes and statutory instruments currently regulate the right to take advantage of exempting provisions.

---

[93] As amended by s.5 and Sched. 4 of the Contracts (Applicable Law) Act 1990.

[94] "United Kingdom" does not include the Channel Islands or the Isle of Man: Interpretation Act 1978, s.5 and Sched. 1.

[95] See *post*, § 31–007, and *Surzur Overseas Ltd v. Ocean Reliance Shipping Co. Ltd* [1997] C.L.Y. 906.

[96] See *ante*, § 6–130, and see also Atiyah and Treitel (1967) 30 M.L.R. 369, 379–385 and *ante*, § 14–086.

[97] See s.1(a) of the 1967 Act (and, *ibid.* s.2(2)).

[98] *Skipskredittforeningen v. Emperor Navigation* [1998] 1 Lloyd's Rep. 66, 75.

14–107   **Carriage by road or rail.**[99] The Public Passenger Vehicles Act 1981 invalidates a provision contained in a contract for the conveyance of a passenger in a public service vehicle which purports to restrict the liability of a person in respect of a claim which may be made against him in respect of the death of, or bodily injury to, the passenger while being carried in, entering or alighting from the vehicle, or purports to impose any conditions with respect to the enforcement of such liability.[1] The Carriage of Passengers by Road Act 1974[2] regulates the international carriage of passengers and their luggage, and the Carriage of Goods by Road Act 1965[3] regulates the international carriage of goods, by road. The International Transport Conventions Act 1983 gives the force of law to the Convention concerning International Carriage by Rail (COTIF)[4] which regulates the international carriage of passengers and their luggage,[5] and the international carriage of goods,[6] by rail. Each of these "international" instruments contains provisions prohibiting contracting out.

14–108   **Carriage by sea.** The Carriage of Goods by Sea Act 1971,[7] which gives effect to the International Convention for the Unification of certain Rules of Law relating to Bills of Lading signed at Brussels in 1924 (the Hague Rules), as amended by the Protocol signed at Brussels in 1968 (the Hague-Visby Rules) imposes certain duties and obligations upon a carrier who enters into a contract for the carriage of goods by sea to which the Act applies, and invalidates any clause which relieves the carrier or the ship from liability for loss or damage to or in connection with goods arising from negligence, fault or failure in those duties or obligations, or which lessens such liability otherwise than as provided in the Act.[8] The Athens Convention of 1974, and the 1976 Protocol thereto, regulates the carriage of passengers and their luggage by sea[9] and in effect invalidates any contractual provision which seeks to reduce the liability of the carrier contrary to the terms of the Convention.[10]

14–109   **Carriage by air.**[11] The Warsaw Convention regulates the liability of a carrier by air in respect of the carriage of goods, passengers and passengers' luggage. It is given statutory force by the Carriage by Air Act 1961, which was amended by the Carriage by Air (Supplementary Provisions) Act 1962 and by the Carriage by Air and Road Act 1979,[12] and applied with modifications to non-international carriage by the Carriage by Air Acts (Application of Provisions) Order 1967.[13]

---

[99] See *post*, Vol. II, Chap. 36.

[1] See also s.149 of the Road Traffic Act 1988 (agreements between driver and passenger).

[2] (As amended by the Carriage by Air and Road Act 1979: see S.I. 1980 No. 1966 (c. 84)). See Vol. II. § 36–089. This is not yet in force.

[3] (As amended by the Carriage by Air and Road Act 1979: see S.I. 1980 No. 1966 (c. 84)). See Vol. II, § 36–089.

[4] Cmnd. 8535. See Vol. II, § 36–086.

[5] Appendix A (CIV).

[6] Appendix B (CIM).

[7] See the Carriage of Goods by Sea Act 1971 (Commencement) Order 1977 (S.I. 1977 No. 981 (c. 35)).

[8] Art. III, r. 8; *The Hollandia* [1983] 1 A.C. 565. See also Merchant Shipping Act 1981, ss.2–5.

[9] See Merchant Shipping Act 1995, s.183 and Sched. 6; S.I. 1998 No. 2917. See also *R. G. Mayor v. P. & O. Ferries Ltd* [1990] 2 Lloyd's Rep. 144 and Vol. II, § 36–070.

[10] Art. 18.

[11] See *post*, Vol. II, Chap. 35.

[12] See Vol. II, §§ 35–001—35–002.

[13] S.I. 1967 No. 480, and s.4 of Sched. 1; S.I. 1998 No. 1058. See Vol. II, § 35–002, n. 11.

The Convention imposes certain liabilities on the carrier which cannot be excluded or limited by special contract; but, under its provisions, the carrier is prima facie relieved from liability in excess of certain stated pecuniary limits.

Insurance. The Road Traffic Act 1988, s.148, invalidates certain limitations **14–110** on cover and conditions precedent to liability in connection with claims in respect of third-party risks under a compulsory policy of insurance, although these do not affect the position between the insurance company and the insured himself.[14]

Defective premises. The Defective Premises Act 1972, s.6(3), provides that **14–111** any term of an agreement which purports to exclude or restrict, or has the effect of excluding or restricting, the operation of any of the provisions of the Act,[15] or any liability arising by virtue of any such provision, is to be void.

Employment and services. The Law Reform (Personal Injuries) Act 1948, **14–112** s.1(3), invalidates any provision contained in a contract of employment or apprenticeship, or in any agreement collateral thereto, in so far as it would have the effect of excluding or limiting any liability of the employer in respect of personal injuries caused to the person employed or apprenticed by the negligence of persons in common employment with him. Restrictions on contracting out are found in the Employment Rights Act 1996.[16]

The Solicitors Act 1974 regulates the enforcement of agreements between solicitor and client as to remuneration for non-contentious[17] and contentious[18] business, and provides for the determination by the court of fairness and reasonableness of any such agreement.[19] A provision in an agreement with respect to contentious business that a solicitor shall not be liable for negligence, or that he shall be relieved from any responsibility to which he would otherwise be subject as a solicitor, is declared to be void by the Act.[20]

Commodities. The warranty of fitness of animal feeding stuffs implied by the **14–113** Agriculture Act 1970 has effect notwithstanding any contract or notice to the contrary.[21] Likewise the warranties arising from the statutory statements which are required to be given by that Act in relation to fertilisers and feeding stuffs,[22] and by regulations made under the Plant Varieties and Seeds Act 1964 in relation to seeds,[23] cannot be excluded.

Consumer protection. The Unfair Terms in Consumer Contracts Regulations **14–114** 1994[24] are designed to protect the consumer against unfair contract terms. They

---

[14] See Vol. II, § 41–068.

[15] See *ante*, § 13–015.

[16] s.203. See Vol. II, Chap. 39. See also Sex Discrimination Act 1975, s.77; Race Relations Act 1976, s.72; Trade Union and Labour Relations (Consolidation) Act 1992, s.288; Disability Discrimination Act 1995, s.9.

[17] s.140.

[18] s.59–66.

[19] ss.57(5), 61(2).

[20] s.60(5).

[21] Agriculture Act 1970, s.72(3).

[22] *ibid.* s.68(6).

[23] Plant Varieties and Seeds Act 1964, ss.16, 17.

[24] S.I. 1994 No. 3159. See Chap. 15.

implement Council Directive 1993/13/EEC and apply in addition to and separately from the provisions of the Unfair Contract Terms Act 1977. A term which is adjudged to be unfair under the Regulations is not binding on the consumer.[25] For this to occur five conditions must be satisfied. First, the term must be contained in a type of contract which is covered by the Regulations.[26] Secondly, one party (the "seller" or "supplier") may be a natural or legal person but must be acting for purposes relating to his trade, business or profession, whether privately or publicly owned.[27] Thirdly, the other party (the "consumer") must be a natural person who is acting for purposes outside his trade, business or profession.[28] Fourthly the term in question must not have been individually negotiated.[29] Fifthly, the term must be "unfair" as defined in the Regulations.[30] Although the Regulations may undoubtedly operate to invalidate exemption clauses, *i.e.* terms which exclude or restrict liability, they are not so confined and apply to unfair contract terms generally. Accordingly, they have been dealt with in Chapter 15 of this book.[31] It is to be noted that Regulation 8 also imposes certain duties, and confers certain powers, upon the Director General of Fair Trading—distinct from those under the Fair Trading Act 1973[32] in respect of contract terms drawn up for general use which he considers unfair, and the court may on an application of the Director grant an injunction against any person using or recommending the use of such a term in contracts concluded with consumers.[33]

14–115   The liability of a person by virtue of Part I of the Consumer Protection Act 1987 to a person who has suffered damage caused wholly or partly by a defect in a product, or to a dependant or relative of such a person, cannot be limited by any contract term, by any notice or by any other provision.[34] A term contained in a regulated consumer credit or consumer hire agreement, or in an agreement related thereto, is void if, and to the extent that, it is inconsistent with a provision for the protection of the debtor or hirer or his relative or any surety contained in the Consumer Credit Act 1974 or in any regulation made under that Act.[35]

14–116   The terms as to title and quality implied by the Trading Stamps Act 1964 on redemption of trading stamps for goods are implied notwithstanding any terms to the contrary on which the redemption is made.[36]

---

[25] reg. 5.

[26] This is a difficult question: see *post*, § 15–009.

[27] reg. 2(1).

[28] *ibid.*

[29] reg. 3(1)(3)–(5).

[30] reg. 4.

[31] §§ 15–004—15–075.

[32] See *post*, § 14–120.

[33] See *post*, § 15–073.

[34] Consumer Protection Act 1987, s.7.

[35] Consumer Credit Act 1974, s.173(1).

[36] Trading Stamps Act 1964, s.4, as substituted by s.16(1) of the Supply of Goods (Implied Terms) Act 1973 and amended by s.192 and Sched. 4, paras. 24 to 26, of the Consumer Credit Act 1974 and the Sale and Supply of Goods Act 1994, Sched. 2, para. 1.

The terms implied by the Package Travel, Package Holidays and Package   **14–117**
Tours Regulations 1992,[37] and the strict liability to the consumer imposed by
regulation 15 of those Regulations, are mandatory.[38]

Also mandatory are the rights of cancellation conferred by the Consumer   **14–118**
Credit Act 1974,[39] by the Consumer Protection (Contracts concluded away from
Business Premises) Regulations 1987[40] and by the Timeshare Act 1992,[41] as are
the restrictions on the efficacy of consumer arbitration clauses imposed by the
Arbitration Act 1996.[42]

Interest on commercial debts. By section 8 of the Late Payment of Commer-   **14–119**
cial Debts (Interest) Act 1998[43] any contract terms are void to the extent that they
purport to exclude the right to statutory interest conferred by the Act in relation
to a debt for goods or services supplied, unless there is a substantial contractual
remedy for late payment of the debt.[44] The parties may not agree to vary the right
to statutory interest in relation to the debt unless either the right to statutory
interest as varied or the overall remedy for late payment of the debt is a
substantial remedy.[45] Further, any contract terms are void to the extent that they
purport to confer a contractual right to interest that is not a substantial remedy for
late payment of the debt, or vary the right to statutory interest so as to provide
for a right to statutory interest that is not a substantial remedy for late payment
of the debt, unless the overall remedy for late payment of the debt is a substantial
remedy.[46] The meaning of "substantial remedy" is set out in section 9 of the Act.
It requires (*inter alia*) an assessment whether or not it would be fair and
reasonable to allow the remedy to be relied on to oust (or as the case may be) to
vary the right to statutory interest that would otherwise apply in relation to the
debt.[47]

Fair Trading Act 1973. The Fair Trading Act 1973 set up a "Consumer   **14–120**
Protection Advisory Committee."[48] The Director General of Fair Trading, or the
Secretary of State for Prices and Consumer Protection or any Minister, may refer
to the Advisory Committee the question whether a consumer trade practice
specified in the reference adversely affects the economic interests of consumers
in the United Kingdom.[49] The Advisory Committee then considers the reference,
and formulates a report, which may then be followed by legislative action (by
statutory instrument) by the Secretary of State. The Act refers specifically[50] to the
situation where it appears to the Director that "a consumer trade practice has the
effect, or is likely to have the effect . . . of causing the terms or conditions, on or

---

[37] S.I. 1992 No. 3288; *ante*, § 13–033.
[38] r. 15(5).
[39] ss.67, 173(1); see Vol. II, §§ 38–090—38–091.
[40] S.I. 1987 No. 2117 (as amended); Vol. II, §§ 38–092, 43–110.
[41] See Vol. II, § 38–094.
[42] ss.89–92. See *post*, § 16–013.
[43] See *post*, §§ 27–140 *et seq.*
[44] s.8(1).
[45] s.8(3).
[46] s.8(4).
[47] s.9(1)(b).
[48] s.3.
[49] s.14.
[50] s.17(2)(d).

subject to which consumers enter into relevant consumer transactions, to be so adverse to them as to be inequitable." In addition, Part III of the Act[51] enables the Director General to take action against particular persons, firms or companies who persist in a course of conduct which is detrimental to the interests of consumers in the United Kingdom or which is to be regarded as unfair to consumers. If the Director is unable to obtain a satisfactory written assurance that the conduct complained of will cease, he may institute proceedings before the High Court, or another appropriate court (usually the county court),[52] which can make an order against the person, firm or company concerned. The Secretary of State has made a number of Orders under these provisions of the 1973 Act.[53]

7. Common Law Qualifications

14-121   **Misrepresentations as to effect of exemption clause.** A party who misrepresents, whether fraudulently or otherwise, the terms or effect of an exemption clause inserted by him in a contract will not be permitted to rely on it in the face of his misrepresentation. In *Curtis v. Chemical Cleaning and Dyeing Co.*[54] the plaintiff took a dress to the defendants' shop to be cleaned. She was asked to sign a receipt which contained a clause exempting the defendants from all liability for damage to the articles cleaned. When the plaintiff asked why she was required to sign the receipt, the defendants' employee replied that it merely covered risks such as damage to the beads and sequins on the dress. The dress was returned to the plaintiff badly stained. It was held that the defendants were not protected since their employee had represented the effect of the exemption clause to be narrower than was, in fact, the case. If the misrepresentation gives rise to a fundamental mistake as to the character of the document, *non est factum* may also be pleaded.[55]

14-122   **Acknowledgments.** Clauses are often inserted in standard form agreements whereby one party "acknowledges and agrees" that he has "not been induced to enter into the contract by any representation of the other party," or that he has "examined the goods," or that he has "not made known to the other party expressly or by implication the purpose for which the goods are required." In *Lowe v. Lombank Ltd*[56] the Court of Appeal held that such a clause can only give rise to an estoppel, preventing the party making the acknowledgment from asserting the contrary, and cannot operate as a positive contractual obligation. "To call it an agreement as well as an acknowledgment by the plaintiff cannot convert a statement as to past facts, known by both parties to be untrue, into a

---

[51] ss.34–43.

[52] ss.41, 41A (inserted by Sched. 12 to the Competiton Act 1998).

[53] Mail Order Transactions (Information) Order 1976, (S.I. 1976 No. 1812); Consumer Transactions (Restrictions on Statements) Order 1976 (S.I. 1976 No. 1813) (amended by the Consumer Transactions (Restrictions on Statements) Order 1978 (S.I. 1978 No. 127)); Business Advertisements (Disclosure) Order 1977 (S.I. 1977 No. 1918).

[54] [1951] 1 K.B. 805. See also *Jaques v. Lloyd D. George & Partners Ltd* [1968] 1 W.L.R. 625; *Mendelssohn v. Normand Ltd* [1970] 1 Q.B. 177, 183–184, 186; *Charlotte Thirty Ltd v. Croker Ltd* (1990) 24 Const.L.R. 46. *cf. Cockerton v. Naviera Aznar SA* [1960] 2 Lloyd's Rep. 450.

[55] See *ante*, §§ 5-054—5-059.

[56] [1960] 1 W.L.R. 196.

contractual obligation, which is essentially a promise by the promisor to the promisee that acts will be done in the future or that facts exist at the time of the promise or will exist in the future."[57] In order for such an estoppel to be effective, it must further be shown:

(i) that the acknowledgment is clear and unambiguous;

(ii) that the party making it intended it to be acted upon by the other party, or at any rate so conducted himself that a reasonable man in the other party's position would take the acknowledgment to be true and believe that it was meant that he should act on it[58];

(iii) that the other party in fact believed it to be true and was induced by such belief to act on it.[59]

In the particular case, which concerned an acknowledgment by a hirer under a hire-purchase agreement,[60] the court found that none of these requirements was satisfied, and so no estoppel arose.

Oral warranties. A party who would otherwise be entitled to rely on an exempting provision will not be permitted to do so if he gives an express oral warranty which runs counter to the tenor of the written exemption.[61] A warranty given before the agreement is entered into may also be enforced as a collateral contract the consideration of which is the entering into of the written agreement.[62] Thus in *Webster v. Higgin*[63] an oral warranty as to the present condition of a car was enforced as a collateral contract in return for which a contract of hire-purchase, which contained exempting provisions, was signed. **14–123**

Unreasonable provisions. It has been stated on a number of occasions that a clause which excludes or restricts liability should not be given effect if it is unreasonable, or if it would be unreasonable to apply it in the circumstances of the case, at least in contracts in standard form where there is inequality of bargaining power.[64] But it would seem that, except in those situations expressly provided for in the Unfair Contract Terms Act 1977 or (in respect of consumer contracts) by the Unfair Terms in Consumer Contracts Regulations 1994,[65] it is not open to a court to strike down an exemption clause merely on the ground that **14–124**

---

[57] *ibid.* at 204.

[58] *Citizens' Bank of Louisiana v. First National Bank of New Orleans* (1873) L.R. 6 H.L. 352.

[59] *Lowe v. Lombank Ltd, supra*, at 205.

[60] See Vol. II, § 38–354.

[61] *Couchman v. Hill* [1947] K.B. 554; *Harling v. Eddy* [1951] 2 K.B. 739; *Mendelssohn v. Normand Ltd* [1970] 1 Q.B. 177. See also *J. Evans & Sons (Portsmouth) Ltd v. Andrea Merzario Ltd* [1976] 1 W.L.R. 1078.

[62] See *ante*, §§ 12–004, 12–033.

[63] [1948] 2 All E.R. 127.

[64] *Van Toll v. S.E. Ry.* (1862) 12 C.B.(N.S.) 75, 88; *Parker v. S.E. Ry.* (1877) 2 C.P.D. 416, 428; *Watkins v. Rymill* (1883) 10 Q.B.D. 178, 179; *Thompson v. L.M. & S. Ry.* [1930] 1 K.B. 41, 56; *John Lee & Sons (Grantham) Ltd v. Railway Executive* [1949] 2 All E.R. 581, 584; *Gillespie v. Roy Bowles Transport Ltd* [1973] Q.B. 400, 416; *Levison v. Patent Steam Carpet Cleaning Co. Ltd* [1978] Q.B. 69, 79; *Photo Production Ltd v. Securicor Transport Ltd* [1978] 1 W.L.R. 856, 865 (revd. [1980] A.C. 827).

[65] *Post*, Chap. 15.

it is in substance unreasonable or unfair.[66] However, a strong plea for a wider approach, based on a principle of good faith in contracts[67] was made by Brooke L.J. in *Lacey's Footwear (Wholesale) Ltd v. Bowler International Freight Ltd*[68] when he said that he preferred to ask whether it was in all the circumstances fair to hold a party bound by the condition in question rather than "to have resort to interpretative devices of almost Byzantine sophistication to arrive at a result that the words of a contract do not mean what, on the face of it, they clearly do mean".

14–125   **Fraud.** No exemption clause can protect a person from liability for his own fraud[69] or require the other party to assume what he knows to be false.[70]

8. Force Majeure Clauses[71]

14–126   **Force majeure clauses.** The expression *"force majeure* clause" is normally used to describe a contractual term by which one (or both) of the parties is excused from performance of the contract,[72] in whole or in part, or is entitled to suspend performance or to claim an extension of time for performance, upon the happening of a specified event or events beyond his control. Such clauses may assume a variety of forms, and a term "the usual force majeure clauses to apply" has been held void for uncertainty.[73] *Force majeure* clauses have been said not to be exemption clauses,[74] although it is difficult to draw any clear line of demarcation between the two types of clause,[75] since the effect of each may be to relieve a contracting party of an obligation or liability to which he would otherwise be subject, and *force majeure* clauses may nevertheless be affected by the Unfair Contract Terms Act 1977.[76]

---

[66] *Grand Trunk Ry. of Canada v. Robinson* [1915] A.C. 740, 747; *Ludditt v. Ginger Coote Airways Ltd* [1947] A.C. 233, 242; *Photo Production Ltd v. Securicor Transport Ltd* [1980] A.C. 827, 848. But see *ante*, § 12–015 (notice of particularly onerous or unusual terms). See generally Tiplady (1983) 46 M.L.R. 601.

[67] See *post*, § 15–044.

[68] [1997] 2 Lloyd's Rep. 369, 385 (making reference to the judgment of Bingham L.J. in *Interfoto Picture Library Ltd v. Stiletto Visual Programmes* [1989] 1 Q.B. 433, 439 (*ante*, § 12–015).

[69] *S. Pearson & Son Ltd v. Dublin Corpn.* [1907] A.C. 351. See also *Kollerich & Cie. SA v. State Trading Corpn. of India* [1980] 2 Lloyd's Rep. 32 (false certificates). Contrast *Tullis v. Jackson* [1892] 3 Ch. 441 (criticised in *Czarnikow v. Roth, Schmidt & Co.* [1922] 2 K.B. 478, 488); *Compania Portorafti Commerciale SA v. Ultramar Panama Inc.* [1990] 1 Lloyd's Rep. 310 (Hague-Visby Rules); *Armitage v. Nurse* [1998] Ch. 241 (trustees).

[70] *Re Banister* (1879) 12 Ch.D. 131.

[71] See Treitel, *Frustration and Force Majeure* (1994); McKendrick (ed.), *Force Majeure and Frustration of Contract* (2nd ed., 1995).

[72] The contract may even be cancelled automatically: *Continental Grain Export Corpn. v. S.T.M. Grain Ltd* [1979] 2 Lloyd's Rep. 460; *Bremer Handelsgesellschaft mbH v. Finagrain SA* [1981] 2 Lloyd's Rep. 259; *Pagnan SpA v. Tradax Ocean Transportation SA* [1987] 2 Lloyd's Rep. 342.

[73] *British Electrical and Associated Industries (Cardiff) Ltd v. Patley Pressings Ltd* [1953] 1 W.L.R. 280. But such a term could refer to clauses usual in a particular trade.

[74] *Fairclough, Dodd & Jones Ltd v. J.H. Vantol Ltd* [1957] 1 W.L.R. 136, 143. See also *Trade and Transport Inc. v. Iino Kaiun Kaisha Ltd* [1973] 1 W.L.R. 210, 230–231; *The Super Servant Two* [1990] 1 Lloyd's Rep. 1, 7, 12.

[75] See Treitel, *op. cit.*, § 12–014.

[76] See *post*, § 14–141.

Frequently a number of events are specified and then followed by the words **14–127**
"or any other causes beyond our control." Such general words in a commercial
document are prima facie to be construed as having their natural and larger
meaning and are not limited to events *ejusdem generis* with those previously
enumerated.[77] Clauses which excuse performance in general terms may be
construed as *force majeure* clauses. Thus a clause in a contract of sale which
provides that the date of delivery is approximate only, and that the seller is not
to be responsible for any delay or non-delivery, does not confer upon him an
absolute discretion whether to deliver or not and so render the contract nugatory,
but only to excuse him if non-delivery is due to a cause outside his control.[78] In
the absence of a clear indication to the contrary,[79] a *force majeure* clause will not
be construed to cover events brought about by a party's negligence or wilful
default, even though a specified event would in other contexts not be limited to
an event occurring without negligence.[80]

A *force majeure* clause which is prefaced by such words as "while every effort **14–128**
will be made to carry out this contract" will be rendered nugatory unless the
party relying on it has in fact made reasonable efforts to ensure that the contract
is performed.[81]

Burden of proof. It is for a party relying upon a *force majeure* clause to prove **14–129**
the facts bringing the case within the clause.[82] He must therefore prove the
occurrence of one of the events referred to in the clause and that he has been
prevented, hindered or delayed (as the case may be)[83] from performing the
contract by reason of that event.[84] He must further prove[85]:

(i) that his non-performance was due to circumstances beyond his control;
and

---

[77] *Chandris v. Isbrandtsen-Moller Co. Inc.* [1951] 1 K.B. 240, 245–246; *P. J. Vander Zijden Wildhandel N.V. v. Tucker & Cross Ltd* [1975] 2 Lloyd's Rep. 240; *Navrom v. Callitsis Ship Management SA* [1987] 2 Lloyd's Rep. 276, 281 (affd. [1988] 2 Lloyd's Rep. 416). See also *Anderson v. Anderson* [1895] 1 Q.B. 749, 753; *Larsen v. Sylvester* [1908] A.C. 295. Contrast *Thorman v. Dowgate SS. Co.* [1910] 1 K.B. 410; *Jenkins v. Watford* (1918) 87 L.J.K.B. 136; *Sonat Offshore SA v. Amerada Development Ltd* [1988] 1 Lloyd's Rep. 145, 149, 158, 163.
[78] *Barnett v. Ira L. and A.C. Berk Pty. Ltd* (1952) 52 S.R. (N.S.W.) 268. See also *Hartwells of Oxford Ltd v. B.M.T.A.* [1951] Ch. 50; *Monkland v. Jack Barclay Ltd* [1951] 2 K.B. 252.
[79] *Gyllenhammar & Partners International Ltd v. Sour Brodogradevna Industrija* [1989] 2 Lloyd's Rep. 403, 406.
[80] *Sonat Offshore SA v. Amerada Hess Developments Ltd* [1988] 1 Lloyd's Rep. 145; *The Super Servant Two* [1990] 1 Lloyd's Rep. 1.
[81] *B. & S. Contracts and Design Ltd v. Victor Green Publications Ltd* [1984] I.C.R. 419.
[82] *Channel Island Ferries Ltd v. Sealink U.K. Ltd* [1988] 1 Lloyd's Rep. 323, 327.
[83] See *post*, §§ 14–130, 14–132, 14–133.
[84] *P. J. Van der Zijden Wildhandel NV v. Tucker & Cross Ltd* [1975] 2 Lloyd's Rep. 240, 242; *Tradax Export SA v. André et Cie* [1976] 1 Lloyd's Rep. 416, 423, 425; *Bremer Handelsgesellschaft mbH v. Vanden Avenne-Izegem P.V.B.A.* [1978] 2 Lloyd's Rep. 109, 114; *Avimex SA v. Dewulf & Cie* [1979] 2 Lloyd's Rep. 59; *André & Cie SA v. Etablissements Michel Blanc et Fils* [1979] 2 Lloyd's Rep. 427; *Continental Grain Export Cpn. v. S.T.M. Grain Ltd* [1979] 2 Lloyd's Rep. 460; *Toepfer v. Schwarze* [1980] 1 Lloyd's Rep. 385; *Thomas P. Gonzalez Cpn. v. Millers Mühle, Müller GmbH* [1980] 1 Lloyd's Rep. 445; *Raiffeisen Hauptgenossenschaft v. Louis Dreyfus & Co. Ltd* [1981] 1 Lloyd's Rep. 345; *Hoecheong Products Co. Ltd v. Cargill Hong Kong Ltd* [1995] 1 W.L.R. 404, 409.
[85] *B. & S. Contracts and Design Ltd v. Victor Green Publications Ltd* [1984] I.C.R. 419; *Channel Island Ferries Ltd v. Sealink (U.K.) Ltd* [1988] 1 Lloyd's Rep. 323, 327, 328; *Hoecheong Products Co. Ltd v. Cargill Hong Kong Ltd., supra,* at 409.

(ii) that there were no reasonable steps that he could have taken to avoid or mitigate the event or its consequences.

However, in *Trade and Transport Inc. v. Iino Kaiun Kaisha Ltd*[86] where the clause in question referred to "unavoidable hindrances," Kerr J. stated that a party would be debarred from relying upon such a clause if the existence of facts which show that the clause was bound to operate should reasonably have been known to that party prior to the conclusion of the contract, and would have been expected by the other party to be so known. But more recently in *Channel Island Ferries Ltd v. Sealink United Kingdom Ltd*,[87] Parker L.J. expressed doubts[88] whether, because of pre-contract improvidence, a party would be disabled from relying on a *force majeure* clause, even if such clause would otherwise have applied; there was no principle of law that a party who entered into a contract could not rely on its terms because he was improvident in entering into it. It may, nevertheless, be argued that the parties to a contract cannot reasonably have intended that one party should be entitled to rely on a *force majeure* clause which, as the result of facts known to him at the time of entering into the contract, he could reasonably foresee would inevitably come into operation and so affect the performance expected of him by the other party.[89] However, it has been held that there is no justification for limiting the ordinary meaning of words in a *force majeure* clause to events or states of fact not in existence at the date of the contract or to those which are unpredictable at the time it was made.[90]

14-130   **"Prevented" clauses.** Where one party seeks to invoke the protection of a clause which states that he is to be relieved of liability if he is "prevented" from carrying out his obligations under the contract, he must show that performance has become physically or legally impossible, and not merely more difficult or unprofitable.[91] It is not sufficient, for example in a contract of sale of goods, for the seller to show that his intended supplier is unable to supply the goods if he

---

[86] [1973] 1 W.L.R. 210, 224–227. See also *Ciampa v. British India Steam Navigation Co. Ltd* [1915] 2 K.B. 774, 779; *Taylor v. Lewis Ltd* (1927) 28 Ll.L.Rep. 329, 332; *Safadi v. Western Assurance Co.* (1933) 46 Ll.L.Rep. 140, 143. *cf. Steamship "Induna" Co. Ltd v. British Phosphate Commissioners* [1949] 2 K.B. 430, 436.

[87] [1988] 1 Lloyd's Rep. 323.

[88] At 328, with whose judgment Caulfield L.J. agreed. But see the more qualified statements (at 328–329) of Ralph Gibson L.J. See also *Reardon Smith Line Ltd v. Ministry of Agriculture* [1960] 1 Q.B. 493–495, [1962] 1 Q.B. 42, 83, 107, 128 (this point did not arise in the House of Lords [1963] A.C. 691).

[89] See also the Force Majeure (Exemption) Clause of the I.C.C.; (*post*, § 14–136). But see *Hoecheong Products Co. Ltd v. Cargill Hong Kong Ltd* [1995] 1 W.L.R. 404, 408 (where it was pointed out that this proposition was untested.)

[90] *Navrom v. Callitsis Ship Management SA* [1988] 2 Lloyd's Rep. 416, 420. See also *R. Pagnan & Fratelli v. Finagrain Compagnie Commerciale Agricole et Financière SA* [1986] 2 Lloyd's Rep. 395, 401.

[91] *Blythe & Co. v. Richards Turpin & Co.* (1916) 114 L.T. 753; *Tennants (Lancashire) Ltd v. C.S. Wilson & Co. Ltd* [1917] A.C. 495; *Re Comptoir Commercial Anversois and Power Son & Co.* [1920] 1 K.B. 168; *Brauer & Co. (G.B.) Ltd v. James Clark (Brush Materials) Ltd* [1952] 2 All E.R. 497; *Ross T. Smyth & Co. (Liverpool) Ltd v. W.N. Lindsay Ltd* [1953] 2 Lloyd's Rep. 378; *Fairclough, Dodd & Jones Ltd v. J.H. Vantol Ltd* [1957] 1 W.L.R. 136, 143, 144; *Tsakiroglou & Co. v. Noblee Thorl GmbH* [1962] A.C. 93; *Warinco A.G. v. Fritz Mauthner* [1978] 1 Lloyd's Rep. 151; *Exportelisa SA v. Giuseppe & Figli Soc. Coll.* [1978] 1 Lloyd's Rep. 433; *Huilerie l'Abeille v. Société des Huileries du Niger* [1978] 2 Lloyd's Rep. 203; *Channel Islands Ferries Ltd v. Sealink U.K. Ltd* [1988] 1 Lloyd's Rep. 323, 327.

can obtain goods of the contract description from another supplier.[92] But the word "prevented" has always to be interpreted in the context of the particular contract. Thus where the intended method of performance is prohibited by government embargo, but a party is nevertheless able to perform in an alternative manner, it is a question of construction of the clause, and of fact, whether his performance has been effectively "prevented" by the embargo.[93] In particular, c.i.f. sellers in a "circle" or "string" have in some cases been held entitled to rely on a clause of this nature when they or some shipper higher up the "string" were prevented by government embargo from shipping the goods, even though they could have attempted to purchase substitute goods afloat, on the ground that such an attempt would in the circumstances have been impractical and commercially unreasonable.[94] Once a party has discharged the burden of proving that performance has been prevented by the relevant event, he need not normally prove that he could have performed but for the occurrence of the event.[95] An independent state trading organisation may be able to establish that it has been prevented from delivering by "government intervention beyond its control" if an export embargo is imposed by its own government.[96] But, where it is alleged that performance has been prevented by refusal of a licence, the party required to obtain the licence may be obliged to show that he has made reasonable efforts to obtain the licence

---

[92] *Joseph Pyke & Son (Liverpool) Ltd v. Richard Cornelius & Co.* [1955] 2 Lloyd's Rep. 747; *Fairclough Dodd & Jones Ltd v. J. H. Vantol Ltd, supra,* at 146; *Koninklijke Bunge v. Cie Commerciale d'Importation* [1973] 2 Lloyd's Rep. 44; *P. J. van der Zijden Wildhandel N.V. v. Tucker & Cross Ltd* [1975] 2 Lloyd's Rep. 240; *Exportelisa SA v. Giuseppe & Figli Soc. Coll., supra*; *Hoecheong Products Co. Ltd v. Cargill Hong Kong Ltd, supra.*

[93] *Tradax Export SA v. André et Cie* [1976] 1 Lloyd's Rep. 416; *Warinco A.G. v. Fritz Mauthner* [1978] 1 Lloyd's Rep. 151; *Bremer Handelsgesellschaft mbH v. C. Mackprang Jr.*[1979] 1 Lloyd's Rep. 221; *Avimex SA v. Dewulf & Cie.* [1979] 2 Lloyd's Rep. 57; *André et Cie. SA v. Etablissements Michel Blanc et Fils* [1979] 2 Lloyd's Rep. 427; *Bunge SA v. Deutsche Conti Handelsgesellschaft mbH* [1979] 2 Lloyd's Rep. 455; *Continental Grain Export Cpn. v. S.T.M. Grain* [1979] 2 Lloyd's Rep. 460; *Toepfer v. Schwarze* [1980] 1 Lloyd's Rep. 385; *Bremer Handelsgesellschaft mbH v. Westzucker GmbH* [1981] 1 Lloyd's Rep. 207; *Raiffeisen Hauptgenossenschaft v. Louis Dreyfus & Co. Ltd* [1981] 1 Lloyd's Rep. 344; *Bremer Handelsgesellschaft mbH v. C. Mackprang Jnr.* [1981] 1 Lloyd's Rep. 292; *Cook Industries Inc. v. Meunerie Liegeois SA* [1981] 1 Lloyd's Rep. 359; *Tradax Export SA v. Cook Industries Inc.* [1982] 1 Lloyd's Rep. 385; *Bremer Handelsgesellschaft mbH v. Raiffeisen Hauptgenossenschaft* [1982] 1 Lloyd's Rep. 599; *Bremer Handelsgesellschaft mbH v. Continental Grain Co.* [1983] 1 Lloyd's Rep. 269; *Bremer Handelsgesellschaft mbH v. Bunge Cpn.* [1983] 1 Lloyd's Rep. 476; *Pancommerce SA v. Veecheema B.V.* [1983] 2 Lloyd's Rep. 304; *Deutsche Conti-Handelsgesellschaft m.b.H. v. Bremer Handelsgesellschaft mbH* [1984] 1 Lloyd's Rep. 447; *Cook Industries v. Tradax Export SA* [1985] 2 Lloyd's Rep. 454; *Bremer Handelsgesellschaft v. Westzucker GmbH (No. 3)* [1989] 1 Lloyd's Rep. 582. *cf. Koninklijke Bunge v. Compagnie Continentale d'Importation* [1973] 2 Lloyd's Rep. 44; *Tradax Export SA v. Carapelli SpA* [1977] 2 Lloyd's Rep. 157; *Bremer Handelsgesellschaft mbH v. Vanden Avenne-Izegem P.V.B.A.* [1978] 2 Lloyd's Rep. 109; *Sociedad Iberica de Molturacion SA v. Tradax Export SA* [1978] 2 Lloyd's Rep. 545; *Bunge SA v. Kruse* [1979] 1 Lloyd's Rep. 279 (affd. [1980] 2 Lloyd's Rep. 142); *André et Cie SA v. Tradax Export SA* [1983] 1 Lloyd's Rep. 254. See McKendrick (ed.), *Force Majeure and Frustration of Contract* (2nd ed.), Chap. 12; Treitel, *Frustration and Force Majeure* (1994), §§ 12–027—12–030.

[94] *Tradax Export SA v. André et Cie, supra,* at 423; *Bremer Handelsgesellschaft mbH v. Vanden-Avenne Izegem P.V.B.A., supra,* at 115; *Continental Grain Export Corpn. v. S.T.M. Grain, supra,* at 473; *Cook Industries Inc. v. Tradax Export SA* [1983] 1 Lloyd's Rep. 327 (affd. [1985] 2 Lloyd's Rep. 454). See *Benjamin's Sale of Goods* (5th ed., 1997), § 18–288.

[95] *Bremer Handelsgesellschaft mbH v. Vanden Avenne-Izegem P.V.B.A., supra* at 114, 121; *Bremer Handelsgesellschaft mbH v. C. Mackprang Jnr.* [1980] 1 Lloyd's Rep. 210 (affd. [1981] 1 Lloyd's Rep. 292); *Continental Grain Export Cpn. v. S.T.M. Grain, supra. cf. Tradax Export SA v. André et Cie, supra*; *Toepfer v. Schwarze* [1977] 2 Lloyd's Rep. 330 (affd. [1980] 1 Lloyd's Rep. 385); *André et Cie SA v. Etablissements Michel Blanc et Fils,* [1979] 2 Lloyd's Rep. 427.

[96] *C. Czarnikow Ltd v. Centrala Handlu Zagranicznego Rolimpex* [1979] A.C. 351. *cf. Empresa Exportadora de Azucar v. Industria Azucarera Nacional SA* [1983] 2 Lloyd's Rep. 171.

or that a licence would inevitably have been refused[97]; and, if an embargo is not absolute, but subject to certain exceptions, a seller may be obliged to show that he has no goods of the contract description available to him within the "loop-holes" to which the embargo is subject.[98]

14-131   Even though the word "prevented" is not used in the clause, it may be so construed.[99] If the clause provides that one party is to be "excused" or "not to be responsible" upon the occurrence of certain events or any other causes beyond his control, he must show that he has been prevented from fulfilling the contract by one of the specified events or some other cause beyond his control.[1] It has been held that a clause in the form "unforeseen contingencies excepted" will only be effective if performance has become impossible.[2]

14-132   **"Hindered."** A wider scope is, however, given to the word "hindered"[3] and Lord Loreburn said[4]: "to place a merchant in the position of being unable to deliver unless he dislocates his business and breaks his contracts in order to fulfil one surely hinders delivery." Where, due to executive restrictions following a strike, charterers could not load unless they dislocated their businesses and broke other contracts, loading was "hindered."[5] A contract of sale of goods which contemplates the carriage of goods by sea may be hindered by the shortage of ships due to enemy action and an increased risk with resultant rise in freight rates.[6] Normally, however, a mere rise in price rendering the contract more expensive to perform will not constitute "hindrance."[7] The words "impeded", "impaired" and "interfered with" may, in context, be construed as equivalent to "hindered".

14-133   **"Delayed."** If provision is made for an extension of time for performance if "performance" is delayed by circumstances beyond a party's control, the word

---

[97] *Re Anglo-Russian Merchant Traders and John Batt & Co. (London) Ltd* [1917] 2 K.B. 679; *Brauer & Co. (G.B.) Ltd v. James Clarke (Brush Materials) Ltd* [1952] 2 All E.R. 497; *Malik Co. v. Central European Trading Agency Ltd* [1974] 2 Lloyd's Rep. 279; *Provimi Hellas A.E. v. Warinco A.G.* [1978] 1 Lloyd's Rep. 67, 373; *Overseas Buyers Ltd v. Granadex* [1980] 2 Lloyd's Rep. 608.

[98] *Tradax Export SA v. André et Cie, supra; Bremer Handelsgesellschaft mbH v. C. Mackprang Jr.* [1979] 1 Lloyd's Rep. 221; *André et Cie SA v. Etablissements Michel Blanc et Fils, supra; Avimex SA v. Dewulf & Cie., supra; Bunge SA v. Deutsche Conti Handelsgesellschaft mbH, supra; Overseas Buyers Ltd v. Granadex, supra; Raiffeisen Hauptgenossenschaft v. Louis Dreyfus & Co. Ltd, supra; Bremer Handelsgesellschaft mbH v. Westzucker GmbH (No. 2)* [1981] 2 Lloyd's Rep. 130; *Cook Industries Ltd v. Tradax Export SA* [1985] 2 Lloyd's Rep. 454. *cf. Bremer Handelsgesellschaft mbH v. Vanden Avenne-Izegem P.V.B.A., supra.*

[99] *Channel Island Ferries Ltd v. Sealink U.K. Ltd* [1988] 1 Lloyd's Rep. 323, 327.

[1] *P. J. van der Zijden Wildhandel N.V. v. Tucker & Cross Ltd* [1975] 2 Lloyd's Rep. 240. See also *Hong Guan & Co. Ltd v. R. Jumabhoy & Sons Ltd* [1960] A.C. 684 ("subject to").

[2] *George Wills & Sons Ltd v. R.S. Cunningham Son & Co. Ltd* [1924] 2 K.B. 220. *cf. Ashmore & Son v. C.S. Cox & Co.* [1899] 1 Q.B. 436.

[3] *Crawford & Rowat v. Wilson Sons & Co.* (1896) 12 T.L.R. 170; *S. Instone & Co. Ltd v. Speedy Marshall & Co.* (1915) 114 L.T. 370; *Phosphate Mining Co. v. Rankin Gilmour & Co.* (1915) 21 Com.Cas. 248. See also *Navrom v. Callitsis Ship Management SA* [1988] 2 Lloyd's Rep. 416 ("hindrances").

[4] *Tennants (Lancashire) Ltd v. C.S. Wilson & Co. Ltd* [1917] A.C. 495, 510.

[5] *Reardon Smith Line Ltd v. Ministry of Agriculture* [1962] 1 Q.B. 42 (revd. in part [1963] A.C. 691).

[6] *Peter Dixon & Sons Ltd v. Henderson Craig & Co.* [1919] 2 K.B. 778.

[7] *Tennants (Lancashire) Ltd v. C.S. Wilson & Co. Ltd, supra.*

"delayed" is not necessarily to be treated as equivalent to "prevented"[8] and circumstances which merely hinder performance may fall within the provision.[9]

Other expressions. Other, wider expressions may, however, be used, *e.g.* "rendered uneconomic". **14–134**

Specified events. The following words and phrases have been the subject of consideration by the courts: Act of God,[10] storm tempest or flood,[11] fire,[12] perils and dangers or accidents of the sea,[13] war,[14] warlike operations,[15] civil war,[16] riot,[17] civil commotion,[18] strikes,[19] acts of the Queen's enemies,[20] and prohibition of export.[21] However, expressions used in the context of one type of contract, for example, a policy of insurance or a charterparty, may not necessarily be appropriate in the context of another, such as a contract of sale of goods. Moreover, even if the circumstances do not fall precisely within the meaning of **14–135**

---

[8] *Fairclough Dodd & Sons Ltd v. J.H. Vantol Ltd* [1957] 1 W.L.R. 136.

[9] *Re Lockie and Craggs* (1901) 86 L.T. 388. But see also *Matsoukis v. Priestman & Co.* [1915] 1 K.B. 681; *Alfred C. Toepfer v. Peter Cremer* [1975] 2 Lloyd's Rep. 578; *Tradax Export SA v. André et Cie* [1976] 1 Lloyd's Rep. 416; *Bremer Handelsgesellschaft mbH v. Vanden Avenne-Izegem P.V.B.A.* [1978] 2 Lloyd's Rep. 109; *Bremer Handelsgesellschaft mbH v. C. Mackprang Jr.* [1979] 1 Lloyd's Rep. 221; *Avimex SA v. Dewulf & Cie.* [1979] 2 Lloyd's Rep. 57; McKendrick (ed.), *Force Majeure and Frustration of Contract* (1991), Chap. 12.

[10] *Nugent v. Smith* (1876) 1 C.P.D. 423, 437, 438, 441, 444; *Nichols v. Marsland* (1876) 2 Ex.D. 1; *Greenock Corpn. v. Caledonian Ry.* [1917] A.C. 556.

[11] *Oddy v. Phoenix Assurance Co. Ltd* [1966] 1 Lloyd's Rep. 134; *S. & M. Hotels Ltd v. Legal & General Assurance Socy. Ltd* [1972] 1 Lloyd's Rep. 157; *Young v. Sun Alliance Ltd* [1977] 1 W.L.R. 104.

[12] *Thames and Mersey Marine Insurance Co. Ltd v. Hamilton Fraser & Co.* (1887) 12 App.Cas. 484; *The Diamond* [1906] P. 282; *Tempus Shipping v. Louis Dreyfus* [1930] 1 K.B. 699.

[13] *Thames and Mersey Marine Insurance Co. Ltd v. Hamilton Fraser & Co., supra*; *The Xantho, ibid.* at 503; *Hamilton Fraser & Co. v. Pandorf & Co.* (1887) 12 App. Cas. 518; *The Glendarroch* [1894] P. 226; *E.D. Sassoon & Co. v. Western Assurance Co.* [1912] A.C. 561; *Grant Smith & Co. and McDonnell Ltd v. Seattle Construction and Dry Dock Co.* [1920] A.C. 162; *P. Samuel & Co. Ltd v. Dumas* [1924] All E.R. Rep. 66; *Canada Rice Mills Ltd v. Union Marine and General Insurance Co. Ltd* [1941] A.C. 55; *Goodfellow Lumber Sales v. Verrault* [1971] 1 Lloyd's Rep. 185; *The Super Servant Two* [1990] 1 Lloyd's Rep. 1; *Great China Metal Industries Co. Ltd v. Malaysian International Shipping Corpn Bhd.* [1999] 1 Lloyd's Rep. 512.

[14] *Curtis v. Mathews* [1919] 1 K.B. 425; *Pesquieras v. Beer* (1949) 82 Ll.L.Rep. 501, 514; *Kawasaki Kisen Kabushiki Kaisha v. Banham SS Co. Ltd (No. 2)* [1939] 2 K.B. 544. See McKendrick (ed.), *Frustration and Force Majeure* (2nd ed.), Chap. 8.

[15] *Clan Line Steamers Ltd v. Liverpool and London War Risks Insurance Assn. Ltd* [1943] K.B. 209, 221. *cf, Pan American World Airways Inc. v. Aetna Casualty and Surety Co.* [1974] 1 Lloyd's Rep. 207 (affd. [1975] 1 Lloyd's Rep. 77). See McKendrick (ed.), *op.cit.* Chap. 8.

[16] *Spinney's (1948) Ltd v. Royal Insurance Co. Ltd* [1980] 1 Lloyd's Rep. 406.

[17] *London and Lancashire Fire Insurance Ltd v. Bolands Ltd* [1924] A.C. 836.

[18] *Langsdale v. Mason* (1780) 2 Marshall (2nd ed.) 791, 794.

[19] *Re Richardsons & Samuel* [1898] 1 Q.B. 261, 267, 268; *Williams v. Naamlooze* (1915) 21 Com.Cas. 253, 257; *Seeberg v. Russian Wood Agency* (1934) 50 Ll.L.Rep. 146; *Reardon Smith Line Ltd v. Ministry of Agriculture* [1960] 1 Q.B. 439 (affd. [1962] 1 Q.B. 42. This point did not arise in the House of Lords [1963] A.C. 691); *J. Vermaazs Scheepvaartbedrif N.V. v. Association Technique de l'Importation Charbonnière* [1966] 1 Lloyd's Rep. 582; *Tramp Shipping Corpn. v. Greenwich Marine Inc.* [1975] 1 W.L.R. 1042; *B. & S. Contracts and Design Ltd v. Victor Green Publications Ltd* [1984] I.C.R. 419; *Channel Island Ferries Ltd v. Sealink (U.K.) Ltd* [1987] 1 Lloyd's Rep. 559, [1988] 1 Lloyd's Rep. 323. See McKendrick (ed.) *op.cit.*, Chap. 6.

[20] *Russell v. Niemann* (1864) 17 C.B.N.S. 163. *cf. Spence v. Chadwick* (1847) 10 Q.B. 5.

[21] The number of cases is voluminous. See *Benjamin's Sale of Goods* (5th ed., 1997), §§ 18–280 *et seq.*; McKendrick (ed.) *op.cit.*, Chap. 12; Treitel, *op. cit.*, § 12–037.

a particular specified event, they may still be operative by virtue of the addition of more general words in the clause.

14-136　　**"Force majeure."** Sometimes the actual expression *"force majeure"* is employed. *Force majeure* is not a term of art in English law,[22] although it is well known in continental legal systems, for example that of France.[23] The meaning of *force majeure* may nevertheless be ascertained by reference. Thus the incorporation into a contract of sale of the Force Majeure (Exemption) Clause of the International Chamber of Commerce[24] will mean that a party is not liable for failure to perform any of his obligations in so far as he proves:

(1) that the failure was due to an impediment beyond his control; and

(2) that he could not reasonably be expected to have taken the impediment and its effects upon his ability to perform the contract into account at the time of the conclusion of the contract; and

(3) that he could not reasonably have avoided or overcome it or at least its effects.

14-137　　It has rightly been observed that the concept of *force majeure* in English law is wider than that of "Act of God" or *vis major*,[25] as these latter expressions appear to denote events due to natural causes, without any human intervention.[26] In *Lebeaupin v. Crispin & Co.*[27] McCardie J. reviewed the previous authorities on *force majeure*, and it now seems that war,[28] strikes,[29] legislative or administrative interference, for example, an embargo,[30] the refusal of a licence,[31] or seizure,[32] abnormal storm or tempest,[33] flooding which inhibits shipment from

---

[22] *Hackney B.C. v. Doré* [1922] 1 K.B. 431, 437; *Re Podair Trading Ltd* [1949] 2 K.B. 277, 286; *Thomas Borthwick (Glasgow) Ltd v. Faure Fairclough Ltd* [1968] 1 Lloyd's Rep. 16, 28; *Navrom v. Callitsis Ship Management SA* [1987] 2 Lloyd's Rep. 276, 281, 282 (affd. [1988] 2 Lloyd's Rep. 416).

[23] Cod.Civ., § 1148; Carbonnier, *Droit Civil* (19th ed., 1995) IV, no. 1620; Marty and Raynaud, *Droit Civil* (1962), II, Vol. I, p. 527; Mazeaud, *Leçons de Droit Civil* (1962), II, p. 531. But see *Jacobs v. Crédit Lyonnais* (1884) 12 Q.B.D. 589; *Navrom v. Callitsis Ship Management SA, supra*, at pp. 281, 282, for differences between French and English law.

[24] I.C.C. Publication No. 421.

[25] *Matsoukis v. Priestman & Co.* [1915] 1 K.B. 681, 686; *Lebeaupin v. Crispin & Co.* [1920] 2 K.B. 714, 719.

[26] *Nugent v. Smith* (1876) 1 C.P.D. 423, 427, 431, 444.

[27] [1920] 2 K.B. 714.

[28] *Zinc Corporation v. Hirsch* [1916] 1 K.B. 541, 544. *cf.* at 549.

[29] *Matsoukis v. Priestman & Co., supra*; *Torquay Hotel Co. Ltd v. Cousins* [1969] 2 Ch. 106; *cf.* *Hackney B.C. v. Doré* [1922] 1 K.B. 431; *B. & S. Contracts and Design Ltd v. Victor Green Publications Ltd* [1984] I.C.R. 419.

[30] *Lebeaupin v. Crispin & Co., supra*, at 270; *Tradax Export SA v. André et Cie* [1976] 1 Lloyd's Rep. 109. *cf. Re Podar Trading Ltd* [1949] 2 K.B. 277.

[31] *Walton (Grain) Ltd v. British Italian Trading Co.* [1959] 1 Lloyd's Rep. 223; *Coloniale Import-Export v. Loumidis Sons* [1978] 2 Lloyd's Rep. 560. But see *Brauer & Co. (G.B.) Ltd v. James Clark (Brush Materials) Ltd* [1952] 2 All E.R. 497, 501; *Pagnan SpA v. Tradax Ocean Transportation SA* [1987] 3 All E.R. 565.

[32] *Yrazu v. Astral Shipping Co.* (1904) 20 T.L.R. 153, 154–155; *The Turul* [1919] A.C. 515.

[33] *Lebeaupin v. Crispin & Co., supra*, at 720.

river ports,[34] interruption of the supply by rail of raw material,[35] and even the accidental breakdown of machinery[36] can amount to *force majeure*,[37] but not "bad weather, football matches or a funeral,"[38] a failure of performance due to the provision of insufficient financial resources[39] or to a miscalculation,[40] a rise in cost or expense,[41] the failure by a third party to fulfil his contract,[42] or any act, negligence, omission or default on the part of the party seeking to be excused.[43] The words *"force majeure"* are, however, rarely unqualified. The type of circumstance envisaged by the parties will often be set out, so that those circumstances may apply to limit, extend or explain the meaning of *"force majeure."*[44] Further the clause may refer to performance being "prevented," "hindered" or "delayed" by *force majeure*.[45] The expression must therefore be construed with regard to the words which precede and follow it and also with regard to the nature and general terms of the contract.[46]

If the reference to *force majeure* is indeed unqualified, *e.g.* "subject to *force majeure*" or *"force majeure* excepted," then it is submitted that, in English law, performance of the relevant obligation must have been prevented by an event of

14–138

---

[34] *Alfred C. Toepfer v. Peter Cremer* [1975] 2 Lloyd's Rep. 118; *Tradax Export SA v. André et Cie, supra; Bunge GmbH v. Alfred C. Toepfer* [1978] 1 Lloyd's Rep. 506; *Avimex SA v. Dewulf & Cie* [1979] 2 Lloyd's Rep. 57.

[35] *cf. Intertradax SA v. Lesieur-Tourteaux S.A.R.L.* [1978] 2 Lloyd's Rep. 509.

[36] *Matsoukis v. Priestman & Co., supra.; Thomas Borthwick (Glasgow) Ltd v. Faure Fairclough Ltd* [1968] 1 Lloyd's Rep. 16, 28. *Sed quaere? cf. Sonat Offshore SA v. Amerada Hess Development Ltd* [1988] 1 Lloyd's Rep. 145, 158.

[37] See also *Yrazu v. Astral Shipping Co., supra*, at 154–155 (casualty to ship or cargo).

[38] *Matsoukis v. Priestman & Co., supra*, at 687.

[39] *The Concadoro* [1916] 2 A.C. 199.

[40] *Yrazu v. Astral Shipping Co., supra.* See also *Atlantic Paper Stock Ltd v. St Anne Nackawic Pulp and Paper Co. Ltd* (1975) 56 D.L.R. (3d) 409 (lack of business sense).

[41] *Brauer & Co. (G.B.) Ltd v. James Clark (Brush Materials) Ltd* [1952] 2 All E.R. 497.

[42] *Lebeaupin v. Crispin, supra.* See also *Thomas Borthwick (Glasgow) Ltd v. Faure Fairclough Ltd, supra* (failure of Conference to provide vessel). *cf. John Batt & Co. (London) Ltd v. Brooker, Dore & Co. Ltd* (1942) 72 Ll.L.Rep. 149; *Coastal (Bermuda) Petroleum Co. Ltd v. VTT Vulcan Petroleum SA (No. 2)* [1996] 2 Lloyd's Rep. 383.

[43] *New Zealand Shipping Co. v. Société des Ateliers et Chantiers de France* [1919] A.C. 1, 6; *Hong Guan & Co. Ltd v. R. Jumabhoy & Sons Ltd* [1960] A.C. 684, 700; *Sonat Offshore SA v. Amerada Hess Development Ltd, supra; The Super Servant Two* [1990] 1 Lloyd's Rep. 1, 5–8, 11–13.

[44] *Sonat Offshore SA v. Amerada Hess Development Ltd, supra*, at 158.

[45] See *ante*, §§ 14–130, 14–132, 14–133.

[46] *Lebeaupin v. Crispin & Co., supra*, at 702; *Re Podar Trading Ltd, supra*, at 286; see also *Matsoukis v. Priestman & Co.* [1915] 1 K.B. 681 (excepted only the cause of *force majeure* and/or strikes); *Dixon & Sons v. Henderson Craig & Co.* [1919] 2 K.B. 778 (hindered or prevented by *force majeure*); *Brauer & Co. (G.B.) Ltd v. James Clark (Brush Materials) Ltd* [1952] 2 All E.R. 497 (prevented by *force majeure*); *Fairclough Dodd & Jones Ltd v. J.H. Vantol Ltd* [1957] 1 W.L.R. 136 (prohibition of export or any other cause comprehended by *force majeure*); *Hong Guan & Co. Ltd v. R. Jumabhoy & Sons Ltd* [1960] A.C. 684 (subject to *force majeure* and shipment); *Tsakiroglou & Co. Ltd v. Noblee Thorl GmbH* [1962] A.C. 93 (*force majeure* preventing shipment); *Alfred C. Toepfer v. Peter Cremer* [1975] 2 Lloyd's Rep. 118 (delay in shipment occasioned by any cause comprehended in the term *force majeure*); *Tradax Export SA v. André et Cie* [1976] 1 Lloyd's Rep. 109 (*ibid.*); *Bunge GmbH v. Alfred C. Toepfer* [1978] 1 Lloyd's Rep. 506 (*ibid.*); *Bremer Handelsgesellschaft mbH v. Vanden-Avenne Izegem P.V.B.A.* [1978] 2 Lloyd's Rep. 109 (*ibid.*); *Avimex SA v. Dewulf & Cie* [1979] 2 Lloyd's Rep. 57 (*ibid.*); *Marifortuna Naviera SA v. Govt. of Ceylon* [1970] 1 Lloyd's Rep. 247 (*"force majeure* excepted"); *Huilerie l'Abeille v. Société des Huileries du Niger* [1978] 2 Lloyd's Rep. 203 ("strikes . . . or any other cause comprehended by the term *force majeure*"); *The Super Servant Two* [1990] 1 Lloyd's Rep. 1 ("*force majeure,* . . . perils or danger and accidents of the sea").

force majeure and not merely hindered or rendered more onerous.[47] However, there does not appear to be any requirement that the circumstances alleged to constitute *force majeure* should be unforeseeable,[48] although the party seeking to be excused still bears the burden of proving that his non-performance was due to circumstances beyond his control and that there were no reasonable steps that he could have taken to avoid or mitigate the event or its consequences.[49]

14–139   **Conditions precedent.** A clause excusing performance, or permitting one party to postpone or suspend performance, may provide that certain procedures are to be followed or notices given to the other party within a stipulated period of time before he is entitled to rely on the clause. Such measures may be a condition precedent on which the availability of the protection provided by the clause depends,[50] or merely an intermediate term,[51] the non-fulfilment of which does not necessarily deprive him of his right to rely on the clause.[52] The other party may also be held to have waived, or to be estopped from asserting, non-compliance with the measures set out in the clause.[53]

---

[47] But, in the context of E.C. Regulations, the European Court has sometimes held that the expression *force majeure* is not limited to cases where performance is impossible, but extends to unusual circumstances, outside the control of the person concerned, the consequences of which, in spite of the exercise of all due care, could not have been avoided except at the cost of excessive sacrifice: see *Internationale Handelsgesellschaft v. Einfuhr-und-Vorratsstelle* [1970] E.C.R. 1125; *De Jong Verenigde v. V.I.B.* [1985] E.C.R. 2061. Contrast *Schwarzwaldmilch v. Einfuhr-und-Vorratsstelle für Fette* (Case 4/68) [1968] E.C.R. 377; *Valsabbia v. E.C. Commission* [1980] E.C.R. 907. These cases are discussed in McKendrick (ed.), *Force Majeure and Frustration of Contract* (2nd ed.), Chap. 13.

[48] *Navrom v. Callitsis Ship Management SA* [1987] 2 Lloyd's Rep. 276, 281, 282, and see § 14–129, *ante*. Contrast Council Directive 90/314 on package travel, package holidays and package tours ([1993] O.J. L158/59), Art. 4(6), which defines *force majeure* as "unusual and *unforeseeable* circumstances beyond the control of the party by whom it is pleaded, the consequences of which could not have been avoided even if all due care had been exercised": see the Package Travel, Package Holidays and Package Tours Regulations 1992 (S.I. 1992 No. 3288), regs. 13(3)(b), 15(2)(c)(i).

[49] See *ante*, § 14–129.

[50] *Tradax Export SA v. André et Cie* [1976] 1 Lloyd's Rep. 416; *Finagrain SA Geneva v. P. Kruse Hamburg* [1976] 2 Lloyd's Rep. 508; *Berg & Son Ltd v. Vanden Avenne-Izegem P.V.B.A.* [1977] 1 Lloyd's Rep. 499; *Toepfer v. Schwarze* [1977] 2 Lloyd's Rep. 380 (affd. [1980] 1 Lloyd's Rep. 385); *Bunge GmbH v. CCV Landbouwbelang G.A.* [1978] 1 Lloyd's Rep. 217; *Bremer Handelsgesellschaft mbH v. Vanden Avenne-Izegem P.V.B.A.* [1978] 2 Lloyd's Rep. 109; *Intertradax SA v. Lesieur Tourteaux S.A.R.L.* [1978] 2 Lloyd's Rep. 509; *Bremer Handelsgesellschaft mbH v. C. Mackprang Jr.* [1979] 1 Lloyd's Rep. 221; *Bunge GmbH v. Alfred C. Toepfer* [1979] 1 Lloyd's Rep. 554; *Johnson Matthey Bankers Ltd v. State Trading Corpn. of India* [1984] 1 Lloyd's Rep. 427; *Bremer Handelsgesellschaft mbH v. Westzucker GmbH (No. 3)* [1989] 1 Lloyd's Rep. 582. cf. *Hoecheong Products Co. Ltd v. Cargill Hong Kong Ltd* [1995] 1 W.L.R. 404 (certificate required only to attest to occurrence of *force majeure* event).

[51] See § *ante*, § 12–034.

[52] *Bremer Handelsgesellschaft mbH v. Vanden Avenne Izegem P.V.B.A.*, *supra*, at 113. See also *Bunge SA v. Kruse* [1979] 1 Lloyd's Rep. 279 (affd. [1980] 2 Lloyd's Rep. 142). cf. *Tradax Export SA v. André et Cie*, *supra*. See *Benjamin's Sale of Goods* (5th ed., 1997), § 18–295.

[53] *Bremer Handelsgesellschaft mbH v. Vanden Avenne Izegem P.V.B.A.*, *supra*; *Bremer Handelsgesellschaft mbH v. C. Mackprang Jnr.* [1979] 1 Lloyd's Rep. 221 (waiver or estoppel). Contrast *Finagrain SA Geneva v. P. Kruse Hamburg*, *supra*; *Berg & Son Ltd v. Vanden Avenne-Izegem P.V.B.A.*, *supra*; *Toepfer v. Schwarze* [1977] 2 Lloyd's Rep. 380 (affd. [1980] 1 Lloyd's Rep. 385); *Avimex SA v. Dewulf & Cie* [1979] 2 Lloyd's Rep. 57; *Bunge SA v. Kruse* [1979] 1 Lloyd's Rep. 279; *Bremer Handelsgesellschaft mbH v. C. Mackprang Jnr.* [1981] 1 Lloyd's Rep. 292; *Raiffeisen Hauptgenossenschaft v. Louis Dreyfus & Co. Ltd* [1981] 1 Lloyd's Rep. 345; *Tradax Export SA v. Cook Industries Inc.* [1981] 1 Lloyd's Rep. 236 (affd. [1982] 1 Lloyd's Rep. 385); *Bremer Handelsgesellschaft mbH v. Finagrain SA* [1981] 2 Lloyd's Rep. 259; *Bunge SA v. Compagnie Européenne*

Insufficiency of goods. A supplier of goods may as a result of an event of **14–140** *force majeure* have insufficient goods of the contract description to meet all his existing contracts, but nevertheless have at his disposal enough goods to satisfy one or more of those contracts. In such a case he may be entitled to rely upon an appropriately worded *force majeure* clause as an excuse for non-performance of those contracts which are unfulfilled, even though the clause refers to his being "prevented" from delivering the goods and not merely to his being "hindered" from doing so.[54] If he has a number of existing contracts to fulfil, but cannot fulfil all of them, he can rely upon *force majeure* as to the others.[55] He may allocate the available goods in any way which the trade would consider proper and reasonable, whether this is *pro rata*,[56] or in chronological order, or on some other basis.[57] But he cannot make any allocation to those of his customers to whom he has a non-legal moral commitment[58]; nor would it be reasonable to allocate supplies to new contracts in order to take advantage of a resultant rise in price.[59]

Unfair Contract Terms Act 1977. Clauses of the types mentioned above may **14–141** attract the application of section 3 of the Unfair Contract Terms Act 1977.[60] It seems unlikely that a clause which merely permits one party to suspend, postpone or cancel performance upon the happening of events beyond his control would, in a commercial contract, be held to be unreasonable,[61] although there are possibly circumstances where such a clause would be so held, for example, in an exclusive dealing agreement, if the seller was entitled to suspend delivery in such events, but the buyer was nevertheless not entitled, during the suspension, to purchase supplies from elsewhere.

---

des Cereales [1982] 1 Lloyd's Rep. 306; *Bremer Handelsgesellschaft mbH v. Raiffeisen Hauptge-nossenschaft E.G.* [1982] 1 Lloyd's Rep. 599; *Bremer Handelsgesellschaft mbH v. Bunge Cpn.* [1983] 1 Lloyd's Rep. 476; *Bremer Handelsgesellschaft mbH v. Deutsche-Conti Handelsgesellschaft mbH* [1983] 1 Lloyd's Rep. 689; (no waiver or estoppel). See also *Panchaud Frères SA v. Etablissements General Grain Co.* [1970] 1 Lloyd's Rep. 53, 57; *Bunge SA v. Kruse* [1980] 2 Lloyd's Rep. 142; *André et Cie v. Cook Industries Inc.* [1987] 2 Lloyd's Rep. 463. See *Benjamin's Sale of Goods* (5th ed.), § 18–296.

[54] *Bremer Handelsgesellschaft mbH v. Continental Grain Co.* [1983] 1 Lloyd's Rep. 269, 280–281, 291–294. See also *Westfalische Central-Genossenschaft GmbH v. Seabright Chemicals Ltd* (1979), unreported (Robert Goff J.), cited *ibid.*

[55] *Tennants (Lancashire) Ltd v. C.S. Wilson & Co. Ltd* [1917] A.C. 508, 511–512; *Pool Shipping v. London Coal Co. of Gibraltar* [1939] 2 All E.R. 432; *Tradax Export SA v. André et Cie. SA* [1976] 1 Lloyd's Rep. 416, 423; *Kawasaki Steel Corpn. v. Sardol SpA* [1977] 2 Lloyd's Rep. 552, 555; *Bremer Handelsgesellschaft mbH v. Vanden Avenne-Izegem P.V.B.A.* [1978] 2 Lloyd's Rep. 109, 115; *Intertradex SA v. Lesieur Tourteaux S.A.R.L.* [1978] 2 Lloyd's Rep. 509, 513; *Bremer Handelsgesellschaft mbH v. C. Mackprang Jr.* [1979] 2 Lloyd's Rep. 221, 224; *Bremer Handelsgesellschaft v. Continental Grain Co., supra.*

[56] For "pro-rating," see American Uniform Commercial Code, ss. 2–615(b), (c); *Benjamin's Sale of Goods* (5th ed., 1997), §§ 6–047, 8–099, 18–291; Hudson (1968) 31 M.L.R. 535, (1978) 123 S.J. 137.

[57] *Intertradex SA v. Lesieur Tourteaux S.A.R.L., supra*, at p. 512; *Bremer Handelsgesellschaft mbH v. C. Mackprang, supra*, at 224; *Westfalische Central-Genossenschaft GmbH v. Seabright Chemicals Ltd, supra*, at 291–294.

[58] *Pancommerce SA v. Veecheema B.V.* [1983] 2 Lloyd's Rep. 304, 307.

[59] *Westfalische Central-Genossenschaft GmbH v. Seabright Chemicals Ltd, supra.*

[60] s.3(2)(b); *ante*, § 14–070. Contrast Treitel, *Frustration and Force Majeure* (1994), § 12–014.

[61] See *Shearson Lehman Hutton Inc. v. Maclaine Watson & Co. Ltd* [1989] 2 Lloyd's Rep. 570, 612. But see *ante*, § 14–070, n. 72.

14–142   **Unfair Terms in Consumer Contracts Regulations 1994.** These regulations
are discussed in Chapter 15.[62] A *force majeure* clause in a consumer contract may
not be binding on the consumer if, contrary to the requirement of good faith,[63] it
causes a significant imbalance in the parties' rights and obligations arising under
the contract, to the detriment of the consumer[64] or if it is not drafted in plain,
intelligible language.[65] Examples of unfair terms might be *force majeure* clauses
which require the consumer to accept a suspension of performance or delayed or
substitute performance without giving him the opportunity to cancel the contract,
or which deny him a full refund in the event of cancellation of the contract by the
seller or supplier upon the occurrence an event of *force majeure*.[66]

---

[62] See also *ante*, § 14–114.
[63] See *post*, § 15–044.
[64] Reg. 4; *post*, § 15–034.
[65] Reg. 6; *post*, § 15–068.
[66] See, in particular, Sched. 3, para. 1(f)(g)(h)(j)(k), of the Regulations.

UNFAIR TERMS IN CONSUMER CONTRACTS

1. INTRODUCTION

The general position. English law has long taken the view that acceptance of **15–001** the principles of freedom of contract and the binding force of contracts rules out review of the fairness of either the contract as a whole or of particular terms of the contract.[1] As regards the fairness of the contract itself, this general position is expressed in various ways depending on the aspect of contractual unfairness which is in issue. Thus it is said that while a promise is not enforceable without the furnishing of consideration, this "value in the eyes of the law" need not be adequate and may indeed be nominal[2]: substantive inequality of bargain is not a ground for vitiation of a contract. Furthermore, as has already been seen, "unconscionable conduct" or "bad faith" are not without more grounds of vitiation of a contract, whether this unfair behaviour on the part of a party to a contract occurs in the course of its negotiation or the course of its performance or non-performance.[3] As regards the fairness of particular contract terms, this general attitude at common law can be seen most explicitly in its approach to the validity of exemption clauses: for once agreed by the parties to a contract, they are effective to exclude liability both in contract and in tort,[4] even extending to liability for causing death and personal injuries by negligence.[5] However, while these statements remain true as a general statement of the position at common law, they must be qualified to a very considerable extent both as a matter of the

---

[1] See *ante*, § 1–010 *et seq.*

[2] See *ante*, § 3–013.

[3] See *ante*, §§ 1–019 and 7–075.

[4] *Nicholson v. Willan* (1804) 5 East 507.

[5] This is clear *a fortiori* from the effectiveness of non-contractual notices to this effect: *e.g. White v. Blackmore* [1972] 3 All E.R. 158.

common law and as a result of legislative innovation. Of the latter, the Unfair Contract Terms in Consumer Contracts Regulations 1999[6] are the widest in scope and the most distinct in their tests of control. Having noted some other qualifications on the general principle of the effectiveness of contract terms, this chapter will discuss the effect of this very important legislation.

15–002   **Qualifications at common law.** There are two ways in which the effectiveness of particular contract terms has been qualified at common law. First, exceptionally, the courts have held that certain types of contract term are invalid. The clearest example is the penalty clause, the line between this type of clause and its effective relation, the liquidated damages clause, being drawn taking into account a range of considerations.[7] However, the courts have also held other types of clause ineffective, for example, a clause in a mortgage which attempts to fetter a mortgagor's equity of redemption,[8] and they may give relief against the apparent effect of forfeiture clauses in contracts of lease.[9] Other types of term are held ineffective if they are unreasonable in the circumstances, as is the case with covenants in restraint of trade, though this has traditionally been discussed as a matter of illegality rather than "contractual unfairness."[10] Secondly, the courts have become very demanding in the requirement that a particular contract term be agreed by both the parties (the requirement of notice) and that the term be expressed in a way which effectively covers the facts in the way which the party relying on the term seeks to establish (the issue of construction). The demanding approach to the requirement of notice became particularly apparent as regards exemption clauses,[11] but has been applied to other types of particularly surprising or potentially oppressive terms, especially where these are found in the small print of a complex set of standard terms.[12] It has also been in the context of exemption clauses where the courts have been most strict in their attitude to construction, though the orthodox position never went beyond interpretation *contra proferentem*.[13]

15–003   **Legislative control of the fairness of contract terms.** The impact of legislation on the fairness of contract terms has been very considerable and by no means restricted to consumer contracts. This has often been effected by the creation of rights or obligations on the parties to particular types of contracts which are not susceptible of contrary exclusion by agreement, notably as regards contracts of consumer credit,[14] tenancy,[15] and employment.[16] Other than this regulation of particular types of contract, the most important restriction on the effectiveness of contract terms before 1995 was the Unfair Contract Terms Act 1977, which subjected exemption and limitation clauses in both consumer contracts and

---

[6] These regulations revoked and replaced the Unfair Terms in Consumer Contracts Regulations 1994, S.I. 1994 No. 3159 and see *post* §§ 15–004 *et seq.*

[7] See *post*, §§ 27–102—27–126.

[8] Gray, *Elements of Land Law* (2nd. edn., 1993), pp. 949 *et seq.*

[9] Bright and Gilbert, *Landlord and Tenant Law* (1995), pp. 73 *et seq.*

[10] See *post*, §§ 17–075 *et seq.*

[11] See *ante*, §§ 12–013—12–015.

[12] See *Interfoto Picture Library Ltd v. Stiletto Visual Programmes Ltd* [1989] 1 Q.B. 433.

[13] See *ante*, §§ 14–005 *et seq.* (with the exceptions there noted).

[14] See Consumer Credit Act 1974, and Vol. II, §§39–032, 39–089—39–095.

[15] Bright and Gilbert, *op. cit.*, Chap. 6.

[16] See Vol. II, §§ 39–193 *et seq.*

commercial contracts to very considerable restrictions.[17] While this Act also imposed a requirement of reasonableness on the effectiveness of indemnity clauses in consumer contracts,[18] until the Unfair Contract Terms in Consumer Contracts Regulations 1994[19] there was no system of control on the basis of fairness general to all or most other types of contract term. According to a report of the Office of Fair Trading, which was given a policing role in respect of unfair terms by the Regulations,[20] its experience in its first months of operation led it to believe that "the use of unfair terms in consumer contracts is widespread and amounts to a serious problem in the United Kingdom."[21]

2. THE UNFAIR TERMS IN CONSUMER CONTRACTS REGULATIONS 1999

Legislative history. On April 5, 1993 the E.C. Council enacted a directive on **15-004** Unfair Terms in Consumer Contracts ("the Directive").[22] The Directive was implemented into English law first by the Unfair Terms in Consumer Contracts Regulations 1994 ("the 1994 Regulations"), but these were revoked and replaced by the Unfair Terms in Consumer Contracts Regulations 1999 ("the 1999 Regulations"). The main differences between the two sets of regulations are that the 1999 Regulations follow even more closely the terms of the Directive's provisions[23] and they make new provision to enable a number of "qualifying bodies" to apply to the courts for injunctive relief against the use or recommendation for use of unfair terms, whereas under the 1994 Regulations this could be done only by the Director General of Fair Trading.[23a] As regards the effect of these two sets of Regulations on the effectiveness of terms as between the parties to the contract, formally the provisions of the 1994 Regulations apply to contracts made between July 1 1995 and the coming into force of the 1999 Regulations, the provisions of the latter after that date. However, given the position as to the proper interpretation of (at least secondary) legislation implementing E.C. Directives, which will be explained in the following paragraph, it can be argued that there can in law be no difference in the ambit of the two sets of Regulations as properly interpreted, unless either one or other goes beyond the terms of the

---

[17] See *ante*, §§ 14–057 *et seq.*

[18] Unfair Contract Terms Act 1977, s.4 and see *ante*, § 14–072.

[19] S.I. No. 3159. The Regulations came into force on July 1, 1995 but were revoked and replaced by the Unfair Terms in Consumer Contracts Regulations 1999, on which see *post* §§ 15–004 *et seq.*

[20] Reg. 8.

[21] Office of Fair Trading, *Unfair Contract Terms*, Bulletin No. 2 (Sept. 1996), p. 5.

[22] 93/13/E.E.C, O.J. NO. L. 95, 21. For discussion of the Directive or Unfair Contract Terms in Consumer Contracts Regulations 1994, see Dean (1993) 56 M.L.R. 581; Collins (1994) 14 O.J.L.S. 229; Macdonald (1994) J.B.L. 441; Hondius (1994) 7 *Journal of Contract Law* 34; Willett (1994) Con. L.J. 114; Beale in Beatson and Friedmann (eds.), *Good Faith and Fault in Contract Law* (1995), Chap. 9; Bright and Bright (1995) 111 L.Q.R. 655; Weatherill (1995) 3 *Eur. Rev. of Private Law*, 307 esp. at p. 316 *et seq. cf.* Joerges, *ibid.* 175; Collins, *ibid.* 353; de Moor *ibid.* 257; Weatherill, *E.C. Consumer Law and Policy* (1997), p. 78 *et seq.*; Howells and Wilhelmsson, *E.C. Consumer Law* (1997), p. 88 *et seq.*; Beatson, *Anson's Law of Contract* (27th. edn., 1998) pp. 196–198; 291 *et seq.*; Whittaker (2000) 116 L.Q.R. forthcoming.

[23] This may be seen in certain definitional provisions of the 1999 Regulations (see *post*, §§ 15–010, 15–016), in their implementation of Art. 1(2) of the Directive (see *post*, § 15–028) and in their lack of an exclusion of certain types of contract which appears in the preamble to the Directive, but not in its text (see *post*, § 15–021).

[23a] See *post*, §§ 15–073 *et seq.*

Directive in their protection of the position of consumers[23b] (which it is clear that neither set of Regulations have made provision to do). The following discussion will, therefore, describe the position under the 1999 Regulations, though it will note differences (other than insignificant differences of formulation) between their provisions and the 1994 Regulations. Where the text refers simply to "the Regulations", it refers to both the 1994 and 1999 Regulations, unless the context otherwise requires.

15–004A   **The E.C. Directive of 1993.** This Directive was made under what is now Article 95 of the E.C. Treaty, which empowers the Council to issue directives for the approximation of provisions laid down by laws, regulations or administrative action which have as their object the establishment and functioning of the common market, making particularly mention of proposals in the field of consumer protection which must "take as a base a high level of protection."[24] The preamble to the Directive makes clear that its purposes are: (i) to reduce distortions in competition between sellers of goods[25] and suppliers of services caused by differences in rules governing terms in consumer contracts; (ii) to create effective uniform legal protection for consumers from the imposition of unfair contract terms,[26] especially (but not exclusively) where this concerns transactions with suppliers in Member States other than their own[27] and (iii) to enhance the awareness of consumers as to the rules of law which govern consumer contracts in Member States other than their own, for otherwise they may be deterred from entering direct transactions with suppliers in other Member States.[28] It is to be noted at this stage that the Directive was intended only to set minimum requirements for the control of fairness of terms in consumer contracts, it being expressly acknowledged that Member States are free to retain or to introduce systems of control which are more protective of consumers.[29]

15–005   **The nature of directives; "autonomous" versus national interpretations.** As the E.C. Treaty itself makes clear, directives are binding on Member States as to the end to be achieved, leaving to the Member States the choice of form and methods, unlike regulations which are binding in their entirety and directly applicable without more.[30] Use of directives by the institutions therefore allows a Member State a little leeway in terms of the juristic or procedural mechanisms by which it is to be implemented. In this respect, both the 1994 and 1999 Regulations followed a minimalist route, following almost word for word the text of the Directive, an approach being sometimes known as "copy-out."[31]

[23b] Such a greater protection is specifically allowed by Art. 8 of the Directive.

[24] Art. 95(3) E.C.

[25] But see discussion, *post*, §§ 15–010 *et seq.*

[26] Recital 9.

[27] This is clear from recital 2's use of the phrase "*notably,* when [sellers or suppliers] sell or supply in other Member States" (emphasis added) and in recital 7 ("both at home and throughout the internal market").

[28] Recital 5.

[29] Art. 8.

[30] Art. 249 (formerly, Art. 189) E.E.C.

[31] The exception is found in relation to Art. 7's requirement of putting in place "adequate and effective means . . . to prevent the continued use of unfair terms" in consumer contracts, on which see, *post*, §§ 15–073 *et seq.* For criticisms of "copy-out" see Bright and Bright, *op. cit.* and Reynolds (1994) 111 L.Q.R. 1.

However, the Directive remains important even after its implementation into English law by the Regulations. This importance stems from the fact that as a matter of E.C. legal principle and of English judicial practice the Regulations must "as far as possible" be interpreted by English courts so as to give effect not merely to the terms but also as to the purposes of the Directive, this being called the "indirect effect" of E.C. directives.[32] Thus, where the terms of the Directive (on their proper, *i.e.* European Community, interpretation) have one significance, this must wherever possible prevail over any significance which is apparently intended by the words of the United Kingdom's implementing legislation. In this respect, it must be borne in mind that the European Court of Justice takes a less literal and more teleological approach to the interpretation of legislation than is traditional in English law, this meaning that the purposes of the Directive as set out above must be kept in mind in solving any question of interpretation of the Regulations. In the following discussion, therefore, while reference will be made to the terms of the Regulations, it being generally assumed that these reflect the Directive, where necessary reference will be made to the Directive itself.

15–006

In this respect, an important distinction is to be drawn according to whether the European Court of Justice is likely to treat a particular issue as one on which a European view should be taken (giving rise to an "autonomous" or "independent" interpretation) or as one which should be left to the national laws of the Member States. For those issues where a particular legal concept is itself defined (at least in part) by the Directive, it is clear that an "autonomous" interpretation is at least to this extent to be taken.[33] However, for other concepts this choice is much more difficult, this being particularly acute in relationship to the notion of "consumer contract" and even "contract" itself.[34]

15–007

Summary of impact of the 1999 Regulations. The 1999 Regulations subject a very wide range of types of terms in consumer contracts to two requirements: (i) that the terms should be "fair" and (ii) that when in writing they should be written in "plain, intelligible language" (the latter being sometimes referred to as a requirement of "transparency"). There are two levels of effect in respect of any failure to fulfill these requirements. At the level of the relationship between the parties to a contract, a term which fails the requirement of fairness is not binding on the consumer, while a term which fails the requirement of transparency is to be interpreted *contra proferentem* and may be subjected to the test of fairness even if it relates to the contract's price or main subject matter.[35] At a more general level, the 1999 Regulations empower the Director General of Fair Trading and a number of other bodies to bring proceedings for an injunction to prevent a person using a term which they consider is unfair or unclear.[36] Rather than invoking this power to institute proceedings which he possessed under the 1994 Regulations, the Director General of Fair Trading adopted an educative and negotiating strategy, though at times requiring a particular business whose terms offended under the 1994 Regulations to give an undertaking that they will not in future

15–008

---

[32] Case 14/83 *Von Colson and Kammann v. Land Nordrhein-Westfalen* [1984] E.C.R. 1891; Case C–106/89 *Marleasing SA. v. La Comercial Internacionale de Alimentacion SA* [1990] E.C.R. I–4135 and see Craig and De Búrca, *E.U. Law* (2nd. ed., 1998), pp. 198 *et seq.*

[33] *e.g.* "consumer:" Art. 2(b).

[34] See *post*, §§ 15–010 *et seq.*

[35] *Post*, § 16–000.

[36] 1994 Regulations, reg. 8; 1999 Regulations, reg. 12, and see *post*, §§ 15–073 *et seq.*

use offending terms. The Director has also published a series of bulletins reporting on and explaining the work of the Unfair Contract Terms Unit of his Office, these providing invaluable guidance as to the *likely* application of the test of unfairness by the courts.[37]

(a) *The Contracts Governed by the Regulations*

15–009   **Introduction.** It is unfortunate that the Regulations (following the Directive) do not make clear at first sight which types of contract fall within their controls. However, on closer examination a fairly clear picture emerges of the general position, though certain points remain for judicial determination.

15–010   **The 1994 and 1999 Regulations contrasted.** Under the 1994 Regulations, the persons the terms of whose contracts were controlled by their provisions were defined in such a way as to suggest that they applied only to contracts for the sale of goods or for the supply of goods or services to consumers.[38] However, such an apparently simple proposition was capable of being misleading for three reasons: (i) the notion of a contract for the supply of services has to be interpreted very widely indeed for the purposes of the Regulations; (ii) it is most likely that the Directive (and therefore "if possible" its implementing regulations) governs contracts for the sale of land as well as goods and (iii) it is by no means clear that the consumer has to be the "recipient" of the property or services supplied. In this respect, the 1999 Regulations follow even more closely the words of the Directive[39] and thereby avoid appearing to take a view as to the range of consumer contracts governed by their provisions. Thus, the 1999 Regulations define "seller or supplier" for this purpose as "any natural or legal person who, in contracts covered by these Regulations, is acting for purposes relating to his trade, business or profession, whether publicly owned or privately owned."[40] This leaves, however, the question as to the true range of contracts governed by either set of Regulations.

15–011   **All consumer contracts?** The English text of the Directive supports the use by the 1994 Regulations of the terms "seller of goods" and "supplier of services,"[41] and in recital 10 of its preamble states that "whereas more effective protection of the consumer can be achieved by adopting uniform rules of law in the matter of unfair terms; whereas those rules should apply to all contracts concluded between sellers or suppliers and consumers."[42] However, this terminology of sale and supply is not used at the same points in the Directive in a number of its other language versions (all being equally authoritative).[43] So, for example, the second clause of the French text of recital 10 states that "whereas

---

[37] See Office of Fair Trading, bulletins entitled *Unfair Contract Terms* , No. 1 (May 1996); No. 2 (September 1996); No. 3 (March 1997), supplemented by *Home Improvements Guidance* (January 1998); No. 4 (December 1997); No. 5 (October 1998).

[38] 1994 Regualtions, reg. 2(1).

[39] Art. 2(c).

[40] 1999 Regulations, reg. 3(1), "seller or supplier."

[41] See art. 2's definitions and art. 4(1)'s reference to "the nature of the *goods* or services" (emphasis added).

[42] Recital 10.

[43] Brown and Kennedy, *The Court of Justice of the European Communities* (4th. edn., 1994), p. 300.

those rules should apply to *all* contracts between a *professionnel* and a consumer,"[44] and this terminology is followed through into the text of the Directive where the person whose standard terms are to be caught by the Directive is described simply as a *"professionnel"*, this French term referring to someone in business or a profession.[45] This is not to say that other language versions of the Directive do not refer to "sellers of property" and "suppliers of services," but they generally do so in a way which suggests that these phrases are used as a convenient way of describing the contracts which consumers do enter. In all, therefore, even at this formal textual level, these other versions of the Directive suggest that it applies in principle to *all consumer contracts* (as defined) and this is the view taken by some commentators.[46] Certainly it is clear from the terms of the Directive that the notion of "contract for services" in particular has to be understood in a remarkably broad manner. For at other times in the Directive, the assumption is made that types of contracts are included within its ambit which are clearly not "contracts for services" (nor sale) in any traditional English legal sense (for example, as contrasted with contracts of service),[47] notably contracts of insurance and for the supply of financial services.[48]

Contracts for the sale, etc. of an interest in land. If the arguments in the previous paragraph hold good then this suggests that prima facie the Directive was intended to apply to (consumer) contracts for the sale or other disposition of an interest in land, as to all other consumer contracts, but the 1994 Regulations defined "seller" as "seller of goods"[49] and this followed the wording of the English version of the text of and preamble to the Directive.[50] However, there are both textual and more general arguments in favour of the inclusion of contracts for the sale or other disposition (or creation) of an interest in land within in the ambit of the Directive.[51] First, not merely do a number of other language versions of the Directive use a general word for property at the key points at which the English version uses "goods,"[52] but these versions use a different term for "goods" at the beginning of the preamble as regards the classic phrase which in

15–012

---

[44] (Emphasis added): *"que ces règles doivent s'appliquer à tout contrat conclu entre un professionnel et un consommateur."* Similar formulations are found in the Italian, Spanish and German versions of the Directive.

[45] Art. 2. Similarly drafting is found in the Italian, Spanish and German versions of the Directive.

[46] Tenreiro (1993) 7 *Contrats-Concurrence-Consommation* 1; Trochu (1993) *D.S. Chron,* 315 at p. 317; Weatherill, *op. cit.* (1997), p. 83.

[47] See Vol. II, § 39–002.

[48] See recital 19 and Annex, para. 2.

[49] Reg. 2.

[50] See in particular Art. 4(1), which states that "the unfairness of a contractual term shall be assessed, taking into account the nature of the goods or services for which the contract was concluded and by referring . . . " The phrases "sellers of goods" or "sale of goods" are used in recitals 2, 5, 7, 19. The German version of the Directive refers in the preamble to *"Waren "* and Art. 4(1) to *"Güter und Dienstleistungen."* However, recital 10 agrees with the French, Spanish and Italian versions that the Directive applies in principle to "all contracts between a trader and a consumer": see *ante,* § 15–011.

[51] See generally Bright and Bright, *op. cit.,* whose view was cited with approval in *Kindlance v. Murphy* (1997) unreported (N.I. Ch.D.)

[52] Bright and Bright, *op. cit.,* p. 664 who note the French use of *"vendeur de biens."* This is true also of the Italian and Spanish versions of the Directive, which use *"venditori di beni"* and *"vendedor de bens"* respectively.

English appears as "free movement of goods."[53] In these other versions of the Directive there is therefore a contrast with "free movement of goods" and the Directive which applies to "sellers of property." Secondly, and more generally, the broad interpretation given to the phrase "free circulation of goods and services" and the significance of the Directive for the free movement of persons also suggest that the European Court of Justice is likely to include contracts of sale, etc. of land within the scope of the Directive.[54]

15–013   If this view were taken by an English court, it would be obliged as a matter of the doctrine of indirect effect "if possible" to interpret "goods" in the 1994 Regulations so as to include "land"[55] but this difficulty is avoided in the 1999 Regulations which omit reference to "goods" in their defining provision.[55a] As regards "sale of land" itself, given its restriction to consumer contracts, it would govern contracts (including option contracts) made between builders or developers and "consumers." Perhaps even more significant would be the Regulations' application to contracts of lease between a "business landlord" and a "consumer tenant."[56] Moreover, it would be clear beyond all doubt that consumer contracts of mortgage were governed by the Regulations.[57] On the other hand, if the European Court of Justice were to hold that the Directive did not govern contracts involving the creation or the transfer of an interest in land, this would not necessarily mean that contracts of lease were excluded from its ambit: for in the majority of (civilian) Member States these do not give rise to any proprietary interest in the tenant: in principle contracts of lease are contracts of hire, though of a special kind.[58] Thus, the court may well simply include contracts of lease in the Directive as an example of a contract for the provision of services.

15–014   Finally, even if it were held that the Directive does not apply to contracts involving the creation or the transfer of an interest in land, this may not mean that it would not affect any aspect of some of these contracts. So, for example, even

---

[53] Recital 1. The French version uses "*marchandises*," the Italian "*merci*", and the Spanish "*marcadorias*."

[54] Bright and Bright, *op. cit.*, p. 669. *cf.* Kappus, *Neue Juristische Wochenschrift* 1994, p. 1847 (cited with approval by the influential Heinrichs, *Neue Juristische Wochenschrift* 1996, p. 2190) who argues that the Directive does not apply to contracts for the sale of land as these are not to be regarded as part of the common market since they do not involve trans-border transactions (the author is grateful to Dr. N. Jansen of Wolfson College, Cambridge for these references).

[55] See *ante*, § 15–006.

[55a] 1999 Regulations, reg. 3(1).

[56] For an example see *Camden LBC v. McBride* (1999) 1 C.L. 284, Clerkenwell County Court, in which it was assumed that the granting of a tenancy constituted the provision of a service within the meaning of the Regulations.

[57] *cf. Kindlance v. Murphy* (1997) unreported (N.I. Ch.D.) where on a summons for possession of mortgaged property it was held that the Regulations did indeed apply to contracts of mortgage and see similarly, *Falco Finance Ltd v. Gough* (1998), [1999] N.L.J. 7 (Macclesfield Cty. Ct.). There is an argument that mortgages are anyway included within the Regulations as the mortgagee may be said to provide a "financial service," the contract therefore coming within the Regulations' inclusion of contracts for the provision of services.

[58] For, e.g. French law see Bell, Bell and Boyron in Bell, Boyron and Whittaker, *Principles of French Law* (1998), pp. 302–303. The argument would be that the E.C.J. would take an autonomous view of the notion of contracts involving the transfer of interests in land and exclude from it contracts of lease: *cf.* its autonomous view of the notion of rights *in rem* in immovable property for the purposes of Art. 16 (1)(a) of the Brussels Convention in Case 288/82, *Duijnstee v. Goderbauer* [1983] E.C.R. 3663, § 19.

if leases were in general excluded from the ambit of the Regulations, this would not necessarily prevent any service element of the contract being included, for instance, as to service charges for cleaning of the common parts. Certainly, a person who provides such a service to a consumer should not be able to escape the controls of the Regulations simply by including it within another contract which happens to be excluded from their ambit, even though domestic English law would treat such a servicing obligation as accessory.[59]

"Consumer contracts." Clearly, the Regulations do not apply *beyond* "consumer contracts", the "consumer" aspect of this category being defined by them by defining the parties to such a contract. **15–015**

"Sellers or suppliers." Regulation 3(1) of the 1999 Regulations provide that: **15–016**

"'seller or supplier' means any natural or legal person who, in contracts covered by these Regulations, is acting for purposes relating to his trade, business or profession, whether publicly owned or privately owned."[59a]

Restricting consumer protection to situations where the other party is acting "in the course of a business" is familiar to English lawyers from the Unfair Contract Terms Act 1977, many of whose controls are restricted to exemption clauses governing "business liability".[60] Three points in particular arise in relation to these broad, inclusive definitions.

First, it is not enough for the person whose terms are to be caught by the Regulations to be "in business"; he must also be acting for the purposes relating to his business in making the contract.

Secondly, the Regulations make clear that their controls apply to the supply of goods and services by public authorities as well as by private persons. In English law, this clearly includes cases such as the provision of services such as car-parking or use of a swimming pool, where payment is required from the consumer and where English law recognises the existence of a contractual relationship.[61] Another example may be found in the contractual provision of education by publicly owned institutions of higher education.[62] As will be explained below, however, if an autonomous interpretation of "contract" were taken by the European Court, other examples of the provision of public services at present not treated as contractual may well be included.[63]

Thirdly, the question arises whether for this purpose a "business" requires an element of dealing with a view to making a profit. Clearly, most businesses do, but as has been seen in relation to the Unfair Contract Terms Act 1977,[64] English authority suggests that no such additional requirement should be made.[65] This

---

[59] cf. Bright and Bright, *op. cit.*, p. 662.

[59a] cf. 1994 Regulations, reg. 2 "sellers", "suppliers" and "business."

[60] Unfair Contract Terms Act 1977, ss.1(3) (as amended) and 14.

[61] Indeed, the Director General of Fair Trading acting under the Regulations has criticised a term on which a public authority provided a car park to the public: O.F.T., *Unfair Contract Terms* Bulletin No. 1 (May 1996), p. 42.

[62] On the contractual nature of this relationship see *Herring v. Templeman* [1973] 3 All E.R. 569 and Garner (1974) 90 L.Q.R. 6 and Wade, *ibid.* 157.

[63] See *post*, § 15–020.

[64] See *ante*, § 14–063.

[65] *Roles v. Miller* (1884) 27 Ch. D. 71, 88; *Town Investments Ltd v. Department of Environment* [1978] A.C. 359.

may be supported in the context of the Regulations by reference to the inclusion of the contractual provision of public services, which may often be run other than with a view to profit-making and, more generally, by reference to the Directive's purposes of consumer protection and the encouragement of fair competition. For a consumer will not often be in a position to know the aim or aims of the provider of the service which he enjoys (whether for profit or otherwise), and should not be prejudiced in relation to the fairness or transparency of the terms on which the service is provided on such an unknowable basis. Further, if private bodies provide services in the market they should not be able to gain a competitive advantage (by recourse to imposing unfair terms on consumers) simply on the basis that they do not act for profit: charities should deal fairly with their consumers too.[66] If this holds good, it has important implications for those charitable institutions, for example, of higher education which provide services under contracts.

15–017   **"Consumer."** Regulation 3(1) of the 1999 Regulations provides that:

> " 'consumer' means any natural person who, in contracts covered by these Regulations, is acting for purposes which are outside his trade, business or profession."[66a]

This definition of the other party to "consumer contracts" differs somewhat from the familiar definition found in the Unfair Contract Terms Act 1977.[67] First, it restricts consumers to "natural persons" and therefore a company cannot rely on the provisions of the Regulations even if it acts "for purposes which are outside [its] business."[68] Secondly, there is no requirement as regards contracts for the sale of goods that the latter be "of a type ordinarily supplied for use or consumption", so that, for example, hire by a consumer of earth-moving equipment to be used in the hirer's garden would fall within the Regulations.[69] Thirdly, purchase by a consumer at an auction sale or by competitive tender is covered by the Regulations, though it is not by the Unfair Contract Terms Act.[70]

15–018   **"Consumers" as "recipients"?** Does the "supplier of the service" (in the special extended sense) have to be the person in business, the consumer its "recipient?"[71] An example of a person who satisfies the Regulations' definition of a consumer as described above, but who *provides* rather than *receives* a service would be a non-business guarantor guaranteeing the debts of her husband's company to a bank, thereby providing a "financial service."[72] Given the Directive's own provisions defining the parties to the contracts which it governs, it is highly likely that the European Court of Justice would consider it necessary to

---

[66] A charity may not be operated for profit: Hanbury and Martin, *Modern Equity* (15th. edn., 1997), p. 394 in relation to education.

[66a] *cf.* 1994 Regulations, reg. 2, "consumer".

[67] s.12.

[68] An exception is to be found in relation to arbitration clauses in consumer contracts, "consumer" for this purpose having been deemed to include legal as well as natural persons: Arbitration Act 1996, s.90 and see *post*, § 16–013.

[69] Treitel, *The Law of Contract*, (9th edn., 1995), p. 247.

[70] *ibid.* and see s.12(2).

[71] *cf.* the position under the Unfair Contract Terms Act 1977 in relation to which it has been stated that "a person can deal as consumer in disposing of goods, no less than in acquiring goods or services": Treitel, *ibid.* at p. 228.

[72] See for a discussion of this point in the context of suretyship Vol. II, § 44–120.

take an autonomous European view of this question rather than allow the courts of the Member States to answer it according to the understandings of "consumer contract" within the domestic legal systems,[73] and this may be supported by the Court's approach to "consumer contract" for the purposes of the Brussels Convention.[74] In this respect, the English text of Article 1 of the Directive, which describes the business party as the "seller or supplier" may be thought to support an understanding of a consumer as "recipient", though, as has been noted, this formulation is not adopted by all of its other versions.[75] It may also be argued that the assumption found in recital 10 of the Directive that contracts of employment are not "consumer contracts" for its purposes also argues in favour of treating consumers as recipients,[75a] for otherwise an employee (the "consumer") could be said to provide services to his or her employer (the "person in business"). Moreover, the very notion of a "consumer" may be thought to rest on the idea that the relevant person "consumes" another's property or services, rather than supplies them, even if in a non-business capacity. Perhaps most importantly, the concern of the Directive with enhancing the fairness of competition of the supply of property and services may be thought to make sense only where the latter are indeed competing, *i.e.* where their *provision* is by "businesses."[76] In general, moreover, the European Court has taken a restrictive interpretation of the notion of "consumer" even in the context of consumer protection legislation.[77]

An autonomous view of "contract"? So far in this discussion, it has been   **15–019** assumed that the transaction which is (arguably) within the ambit of the Regulations qualifies as a "contract" within the meaning of this notion in English law. However, the question must be raised whether the European Court would indeed rely on the classifications of the domestic laws of the Member States for this purpose, or would instead choose to take an autonomous view of this concept.[78] The European Court would decide between these two positions on the basis of which of them is likely to be most effective in enabling the Directive to achieve its purposes[79] and on the difficulty of constructing a European conception of contract for the purposes of the Directive.[80] As regards the latter, it is to be noted that the Court has already embarked on such an undertaking for the purpose of

---

[73] Leaving it to the laws of the Member States may be difficult, for "consumer" may well be differently defined for different legal purposes even within the law of a particular Member State: such a legal system would not possess a single conception of consumer to be applied for the purposes of the Directive.

[74] Art. 13 and see *Benincasa v. Dentalikit SRL*, Case 2269/95 [1998] All E.R. (E.C.) 135.

[75] *cf. ante*, § 15–011, text at n. 45.

[75a] See *post*, 15–021.

[76] *cf.* also the definition of "consumer contract" for the purposes of Art. 5(1) of the Rome Convention of 19 June 1980 on the law applicable to contractual obligations as "a contract the object of which is the supply of goods or services to a person ('the consumer') for a purpose which can be regarded as being outside his trade or profession, or a contract for the provision of credit for that object."

[77] Reich (1995) 4 *Eur. Rev. of Private Law*, 285, at 292–293 and see *Benincasa v. Dentalikit SRL*, Case 2269/95, *ante*.

[78] For this issue and development of the consequences noted in the following discussion, see Whittaker *op. cit.* (2000).

[79] *cf.* the approach of A.-G. Sir Gordon Slynn in *Arcado SPRL v. Haviland SA* Case 9/87 [1988] E.C.R. 1539, at 1548.

[80] *Tessili v. Dunlop* [1976] E.C.R. 1473.

the Brussels Convention.[81] As regards the purposes of the Directive, both reduction in distortions in competition and the protection of consumers would be enhanced by the Court's taking an autonomous view of "contract" for the purposes of the Directive, for such a view would clearly enhance the harmonising purpose of the Directive and thereby make more effective its policy of consumer protection within the European Union.

15–020   If the European Court were to take such an autonomous view of contract, it is likely that it would do so on the basis of an agreement between the parties.[82] Such a view would require an English court to classify as contractual for the purposes of the Directive a transaction which in English law is considered non-contractual. Three examples may be given. First, the laws of most of the Member States contain no requirement conceptually equivalent to English law's doctrine of consideration.[83] This raises the possibility of including within the ambit of the Directive the terms on which professional services are provided gratuitously. Secondly, the relationship between the beneficiary of a trust and the trustee may sometimes be considered "contractual" for the purposes of the Directive (and therefore the Regulations), even though it is not in the general English law.[84] Thirdly, some provisions of public services, such as water and electricity, may be held to be "contractual" for the purposes of the Regulations even though they are non-contractual under general English law.[85]

15–021   **Contracts specifically excluded from the ambit of the 1994 Regulations.** The 1994 Regulations were expressed as not applying to contracts relating to employment, contracts relating to succession rights, any contract relating to rights under family law and any contract relating to the incorporation and organisation of companies or partnerships.[86] While no similar provision is found in the 1999 Regulations, it is submitted that no substantial change has occurred. The exclusion of these contracts in the 1994 Regulations may be traced to recital 10 of the Directive, according to which "those rules [as to the protection of consumers] should apply to all contracts concluded between sellers or suppliers and consumers; whereas *as a result inter alia* contracts relating to employment, . . . must be excluded from this Directive."[87] It would appear, therefore, that these types of contracts are excluded on the ground that they are not "consumer contracts" within the meaning of the Directive, this being emphasised

---

[81] Art. 5(1) and see *Martin Peters Bauunternehmung GmbH v. Zuid Nederlandse Aannemers Vereniging* Case 34/82 [1983] E.C.R. 987 and *Jakob Handt & Co. GmbH v. Traitements Mécano-chimiques des Surfaces SA* Case 26/91 [1992] E.C.R. 1–3967.

[82] *cf. Jakob Handt & Co. GmbH v. Traitements Mécano-chimiques des Surfaces SA, supra* and see Whittaker, *op. cit.* (2000).

[83] There is no more than a superficial conceptual similarity between *la cause* in French law and the doctrine of consideration and there is no similarity in terms of their respective overall functions: see Whittaker, in Bell, Beyron and Whittaker, *Principles of French Law* (1998). pp. 326–327; H. Kötz and A. Flessner, *European Contract Law*, Vol. I by Kötz (trans. Weir, 1997), pp. 54 *et seq.*

[84] *cf. Gray v. Taylor* [1998] 1 W.L.R. 1093 in which the Court of Appeal held that a person occupying an almshouse under a charitable trust was not a tenant.

[85] For the non-contractual nature of the supply of electricity and water to domestic consumers (even though they pay), see the Electricity Act 1989, ss.16, 22 and *Norweb v. Dixon* [1995] 1 W.L.R. 636 and the Water Industry Act 1991, ss.53–56 and *Read v. Croydon Corpn.* [1938] 4 All E.R. 631. *cf.* the position in relation to gas under the Gas Act 1995, ss.7 and 8 amending Gas Act 1986 ss.7 and 8.

[86] Reg. 3(1) and Sched. 1, (a)–(d).

[87] Emphasis added.

by the list being expressed as a non-exhaustive one.[87a] So, while these types of contracts are indeed excluded from the ambit of the 1999 Regulations, this results simply from the latters' restriction to consumer contracts.

Differences from the ambit of the Unfair Contract Terms Act 1977. It will **15–022** be apparent that the types of contracts governed by the Regulations differ significantly from those governed by the various provisions of the Unfair Contract Terms Act 1977. First, while the ambit of the Regulations is restricted to consumer contracts, a significant number of provisions of the 1977 Act apply to non-consumer contracts, notably, as regards any exclusion of liability for negligence,[88] of contractual liability in general where it arises from breach of a written standard term[89] and as regards the implied terms as to title, quality, etc. in sale of goods.[90] Secondly, on the other hand, as regards consumer contracts, the net of the Regulations is rather wider than the 1977 Act, notably in their inclusion of contracts of insurance,[91] sale at auction and by competitive tender,[92] and contracts which relate to the creation or transfer of a right or interest in intellectual property,[93] the last category in the consumer context including the contractual licenses under which use of computer software is permitted. Furthermore, if contracts for the sale, etc. of land are indeed governed by the Regulations, this marks a significant difference from the 1977 Act.[94] Thirdly, it should be noted that the 1977 Act may apply to non-contractual notices,[95] whereas the Regulations apply only to contract terms, though it has been noted that "contract" may be given for this purpose a meaning different from its general significance in English law.[96]

(b) *Contract Terms Governed by the Regulations*

General. The range of the contract terms caught by the Regulations differs **15–023** according to the two requirements which they impose. Thus, the requirement that the terms be in "plain, intelligible language" applies to *any written term* of the contract,[97] whereas the requirement of fairness applies to any term (whether

---

[87a] The choice of contracts actually mentioned may be explained by the influence on the drafting of the Directive of the German Standard Contracts Act of 1976, a provision of which applies to standard terms in general and from which these very same contracts are excluded: see *Gesetz zur Regelung des Rechts der Allgemeinen Geschäftsbedingungen* § 23 (on which see Markesinis, *The German Law of Obligations*, Vol. I, *The Law of Contract and Restitution: A Comparative Introduction* (1997) by Markesinis, Lorenz and Dannemann, pp. 211 *et seq.*). It may also be argued that the recitals of a directive may not reduce the ambit of provisions in its text: *cf. Denkavit International BV et al. v. Bundesamt fur Finanzen*, Joined Cases 283/94, C–291/94 and C–292/94 [1996] S.T.C. 1445, §§ 24–29.

[88] Unfair Contract Terms Act 1977 Act, s.2.

[89] *ibid.* s.3, *ante*, § 4–069.

[90] *ibid.* s.6, *ante*, § 14–075.

[91] These are excluded from ss.2–4 of the 1977 Act by s.1(2) and Sched. 1 (1)(a).

[92] This is by virtue of the more restricted definition of consumer in this respect in s.12 of the 1977 Act, *ante*, § 14–066.

[93] This type of contract is excluded from ss.2–4 of the 1977 Act by s.1(2), Sched. 1, 1(c). *cf.* Treitel, *op. cit.*, p. 255 who takes the opposite view of the position under the 1994 Regulations on the basis of an interpretation of "goods."

[94] These are excluded from ss.2–4 of the 1977 Act by s.1(2), Sched. 1 (1)(b).

[95] Ss.2, and 14, 1977 Act.

[96] See *ante*, § 15–019.

[97] 1999 Regulations, reg. 7; 1994 Regulations, reg. 6.

written or oral)[98] "which has not been individually negotiated" unless that term defines the subject matter of the contract or its price in a "plain, intelligible" way.[99]

15–024　　"**Where the term has not been individually negotiated.**" The requirement of fairness is restricted to terms of standard form contracts, this being expressed negatively by the exclusion of individually negotiated terms,[1] an exclusion which reflects earlier pressure on the drafters of the Directive based on the need to preserve the contractual freedom of parties even to consumer contracts.[2] There is a technical difference between this test and reference to "written standard terms of business" in section 3 of the Unfair Contract Terms Act 1977[3] in that the former may apply to a non-standard term as long as it was drafted in advance and presented or imposed on the consumer. Moreover, the Regulations weight the issue of individual negotiation firmly in favour of the consumer, providing that:

> "a term shall always be regarded as not having been individually negotiated where it has been drafted in advance and the consumer has therefore not been able to influence the substance of the term."[3a]

The Regulations also place the burden of proof as to the issue of individual negotiation on the person who claims that a term has been so negotiated.[4] Finally, it is also provided that:

> "Notwithstanding that a specific term or certain aspects of it in a contract has been individually negotiated, these Regulations shall apply to the rest of a contract if an overall assessment of it indicates that it is a pre-formulated standard contract."[4a]

Thus, the presence of an individually negotiated term in a consumer contract does not necessarily exclude the application of the Regulations to the rest of the contract. This means that, for example, the general terms of a standard form contract of consumer sale whose delivery date for the goods, price or other particular aspect of the contract has been "individually negotiated" will not escape the requirements of the Regulations altogether.

15–025　　**The partial exclusion of "core terms."** Regulation 6(2) of the 1999 Regulations provides that:

> "In so far as it is in plain intelligible language, the assessment of fairness of a term shall not relate—
> 　(a) to the definition of the main subject matter of the contract, or

---

[98] It is perhaps unusual for an oral term to be other than "not individually negotiated", but it is conceivable, particularly given the rule as to the burden of proof as to this issue (on which see text, *post* 15–024), for example, where a trader simply stipulates orally that a particular non-refundable deposit must be paid for goods or where a trader's standard terms are read by its agents to the consumer over the telephone.

[99] 1999 Regulations, regs 5(1), 6(2); 1994 Regulations, reg. 3.

[1] 1999 Regulations, reg. 5(1); 1994 Regulations, reg. 3.

[2] Howells and Wilhelmsson, *op. cit.*, p. 91 and see Brandner and Ulmer (1991) 29 C.M.L.R. 647.

[3] On which see *ante.* § 14–069.

[3a] 1999 Regulations, reg. 5(2) and see 1994 Regulations, reg. 3(3).

[4] 1999 Regulations, reg. 5(4); 1994 Regulations, reg. 3(5).

[4a] 1999 Regulations, reg. 5(3) and see 1994 Regulations, reg. 3(4).

(b) to the adequacy of the price or remuneration, as against the goods or services supplied in exchange."[4b]

This is an important provision, reflecting the focus of concern of the Directive on unfair *terms*, rather than on unfair *contracts* and so ruling out (in principle) from its ambit any review of contracts on the basis that they represent a bad bargain, from the point of view of the consumer. It excludes from the requirement of fairness terms which define either the subject matter of the contract or the adequacy of the price and these have been conveniently named "core terms",[5] this trying to capture a distinction between the term or terms which express the substance of the bargain and "incidental" (if important) terms which surround them. In many cases it will be clear that the term whose fairness is challenged does not relate to the core of the contract and in this respect the inclusion of a particular type of term in the "grey list" found in the schedules to the Regulations will be particularly helpful,[5a] for as they describe terms which are potentially unfair and thereby assume that these terms are subject to the requirement of fairness and therefore "incidental."[6] However, in some cases the distinction between core and incidental terms will not be straightforward. The Director General of Fair Trading has expressed the view that:

"it would be difficult to claim that any term was a core term unless it was central to how *consumers perceived* the bargain. A supplier would surely find it hard to sustain the argument that a contract's main subject matter was defined by a term which a consumer had been given no real chance to see and read before signing it—in other words if that term had not been properly drawn to the consumer's attention."[7]

Thus, what traditionally would be considered to be the degree of notice needed for incorporation of a term may be relevant to the decision as to whether it forms the "core" of the contract for the purposes of the Regulations.

Examples. The Directive itself recognises the potential difficulty of the distinction between core and incidental terms and attempts to explain it in the context of one particular example, contracts of insurance.[8] So recital 19 states that:

15–026

"it follows [from the exclusion of core terms] *inter alia*, that in insurance contracts, the terms which clearly define or circumscribe the insured risk and the insurer's liability shall not be subject to such assessment since these restrictions are taken into account in calculating the premium paid by the consumer."

It is submitted, therefore, that the type of clause found in a consumer insurance contract which would be subject to the Regulations' requirements would be one which imposes conditions as to the time or other circumstances in which a claim may be brought or one which purports to impose a duty of disclosure on a

---

[4b] And see 1994 Regulations, reg. 3(2).

[5] *e.g.* Office of Fair Trading, *Unfair Contract Terms*, Bulletin No. 2 (September 1996), p. 13.

[5a] 1999 Regulations, Sched. 2; 1994 Regulations, Sched. 3.

[6] See *post*, § 15–051 *et seq.* for the list.

[7] Office of Fair Trading, *Unfair Contract Terms*, Bulletin No. 2 (September 1996) p. 13, § 2.26 (emphasis added).

[8] There is no equivalent explanatory provision in either the 1994 or the 1999 Regulations.

consumer more burdensome than the law of *uberrimae fides*.[9] However, terms governing the price to be paid by a consumer do not necessarily fall outside their requirement of fairness, for the Regulations give as an example of a term which *may* be unfair one which allows the other party to determine the price at the time of delivery of any goods supplied or to increase the price without giving the consumer a right to cancel the contract.[10] Moreover, according to Recital 19 of the Directive, "the main subject matter of the contract and the price/quality ratio may ... be taken into account in assessing the fairness of other [non-core] terms." This idea is not explicitly reflected in the Regulations, but may be included under their injunction to take into account in assessing the fairness of a term "*all* the other terms of the contract."[11] Moreover, the Director General of Fair Trading has taken the view in relation to an agreement which provided for delivery of goods in installments, that a clause which made each delivery a separate contract was potentially unfair because (when combined with another term of the contract) it allowed the seller to increase the price between deliveries[12]: therefore where the parties' dealings in reality form one unitary transaction, a clause which purports to redefine the parties' relations in terms of a series of contracts is to be treated not as going to the subject matter of the contract, but rather as an incidental clause. Finally, it has been suggested that if land contracts fall within the ambit of the Regulations, then terms which define the nature of the interest created, and the amount of rent or service charge would qualify as core terms, but forfeiture clauses and "upwards only" rent review clauses would not and would, therefore, be vulnerable.[13]

15–027   It should be noted that the exclusion of core terms from the fairness requirement of the Regulations is only partial, for all terms including those which define the subject matter or price of the contract are required to be in plain and intelligible language and where they are not they are for this reason subject to the requirement of fairness itself.[14] In this way, an unintelligible or overly complex term which defines the subject matter of the contract may be judged unfair.

15–028   **The exclusion of terms which reflect "mandatory statutory or regulatory provisions" of English law.**[15] The 1999 Regulations are expressed as not applying to:

"contractual terms which reflect ... mandatory statutory or regulatory provisions (including such provisions under the law of any Member State or in Community legislation having effect in the United Kingdom without further enactment)."[16]

---

[9] For example, a clause which makes the accuracy of *all* statements made during the course of negotiations a condition precedent to liability, which on its terms would prevent a consumer from claiming that such a statement was immaterial to the risk: see Vol. II, § 41–055. The French administrative body charged with advising on the fairness of terms under its legislation implementing the Directive (this legislation retaining the exclusion of "core terms": *loi* no. 95–96 of February 1, 1995, Art. 1, new Arts. L.132–1 *et seq. Code de la consommation*) has advised that a clause in a contract of car insurance which makes the indemnity subject to having the damage actually repaired is unfair: *Rapport de la Commission des clauses abusives* (1996), pp. 18–20.

[10] See 1999 Regs, reg. 5(5), Sched. 2(1)(l); 1994 Regs, reg. 4(4), Sched. 3(1)(*l*).

[11] 1999 Regs, reg. 6(1); 1994 Regs, reg. 4(2). Emphasis added.

[12] Office of Fair Trading, *Unfair Contract Terms*, Bulletin No. 2 (Sept. 1996), p. 28.

[13] Bright and Bright, *op. cit.,* pp. 670–671.

[14] 1999 Regs, reg. 6(2); 1994 Regs, reg. 3(2).

[15] For fuller discussion of the questions raised in this paragraph, see Whittaker (2000) *op. cit.* forthcoming.

[16] 1999 Regs, reg. 4(2)(a).

Here, the text of the 1999 Regulations follows more closely the text of the Directive than did the corresponding provision in the 1994 Regulations, for the latter (unlike article 2(1) of the Directive) did not qualify the phrase "statutory or regulatory provisions" by the adjective "mandatory."[16a]

In interpreting this adjective, recourse must be had to the preamble to the Directive, recitals 13 and 14 of which explain that:

"Whereas the statutory or regulatory provisions of the Member States which directly or indirectly determine the terms of consumer contracts are presumed not to contain unfair terms; whereas, therefore, it does not appear to be necessary to subject the terms which reflect mandatory statutory or regulatory provisions . . . ; whereas in that respect the wording 'mandatory statutory or regulatory provisions' in Article 1(2) also covers rules which, according to the law, shall apply between the contracting parties provided that no other arrangements have been established;

Whereas Member States must however ensure that unfair terms are not included, particularly because this Directive also applies to trades, businesses or professions of a public nature."

Recital 13 makes clear that the adjective "mandatory" does not intend to restrict the category of legal rules which impose terms on the parties to a contract to those whose effect is *not* excludable by agreement, rules which are, therefore, "mandatory" in a normal sense, *i.e.* belonging to *ius cogens*.[17] Instead, the term allows the inclusion of rules which simply apply in the absence of any express contractual provision, but which *may* be the subject of contrary contractual exclusion, *i.e.* rules belonging to *ius dispositivum*.[18] However, this leaves open the question as to whether the term "mandatory" adds anything to the phrase "statutory or regulatory provisions." If it does not,[19] as was apparently the view of the drafters of the 1994 Regulations, then this is a very wide category of exclusion of terms from the ambit of the controls of the Regulations, and one of particular importance in the provision of public services, where some or even many of the terms are set by legislation.

However, it has been suggested that use by the Directive of the term "mandatory" refers to the jurisprudence of the European Court on "mandatory provisions" restricting the ambit of freedom of movement of goods associated with the famous *Cassis de Dijon* decision.[20] According to this view, terms ought not to be   **15–029**

[16a] 1994 Regulations, reg. 3(1), Sched. 1(e)(i).

[17] This also rules out any association with the meaning found in private international law: see, for example, the Rome Convention on the law applicable to contractual obligations of June 19, 1980, Art. 7(1).

[18] This is made clear by French jurists for whom the distinction between *ius cogens* (*loi impérative*) and *ius dispositivum* (*loi supplétive*) is traditional: see notably Ghestin and Marchessaux-Van Melle J.C.P. 1995 I.3854 at No. 6.

[19] If it were thought necessary to rescue reference to "mandatory" from redundancy, it could be interpreted as referring to a term which applies whether or not the parties agree *that it should apply.*

[20] Case 120/78 *Rewe-Zentrale AG v. Bundesmonopolverwaltung für Branntwein* [1979] E.C.R. 649. For this view, see Tenreiro, *op. cit,* at p. 2; cited with apparent approval by Trochu, *op. cit.,* p. 315 at p. 317. See also the joint report of the National Consumer Council and the French *Institut National de la Consommation, Rapport sur l'application de la Directive 93/13/1993 du Conseil du 5 avril 1993 concernant les clauses abusives dans les contrats conclus avec les consommateurs aux prestations de service public* (eds. Hall and Tixador), published by the European Commission on the internet (1997), pp. 118–119.

considered "mandatory" unless they are imposed in the general interest of the market and of its users, and not merely in those of the suppliers of the service. The importance of such a view would lie particularly in the context of the provision of public services, where terms are sometimes imposed on consumers in the interests of the public supplier.[21] While this position is clearly attractive as a matter of consumer protection in that it narrows Article 1(2), it is not without difficulty. The *Cassis de Dijon* jurisprudence provides a Member State with grounds of justification for allowing obstacles to the free movement of goods, further to those found in Article 30 of the E.C. Treaty,[22] where these obstacles are necessary to satisfy "mandatory requirements relating in particular to the effectiveness of fiscal supervision, the protection of public health, the fairness of commercial transactions, and the defence of the consumer."[23] This case law therefore allows a Member State to have legal rules which derogate from the principle of freedom of movement of goods if these rules are justified in the interest, for example, of consumer protection or public health. However, this jurisprudence does not altogether fit into the law on unfair contract terms, for the nature of the public interest considerations in the two contexts are going to be very different: for example, in the context of the application of the Directive to the provision of public services, a particular term imposed by law in a contract may be justified as a matter of national law on the basis of the organisation of the public service in question or on an idea such as the importance of the continuity of the public service. It is difficult to see how either a national court or the European Court could weigh this sort of "public interest" with the competing interest of consumer protection as expressed by the Directive's requirements of fairness and transparency. But it is even more difficult to see how an ordinary business supplier of services would be in a position to justify in the *public* interest the terms on which it deals, these terms being imposed on it by a Member State for reasons which may be not at all obvious. In conclusion, it is considered that these difficulties are likely to lead the European Court to adopt the wider view of Article 1(2) of the Directive, with the result that all terms required to be included in a consumer contract by law would be excluded from its scope.[24]

15–030   A second question of interpretation of Article 1(2) concerns what is meant by the word "reflect" in the phrase "contractual terms which reflect mandatory statutory or regulatory provisions." A narrow interpretation would be that this refers only to those contract terms which are required by legislation or regulation to be inserted in the contract in question. However, recital 13 of the Directive's reference to "provisions . . . which directly or indirectly determine the terms of consumer contracts" suggests a broader interpretation. An important category of case which may arguably come within the category of a term which is *indirectly* determined by legislation would be one where the terms of supply of a public service are drawn up by the (commercial) supplier of that service, but then subjected either to a requirement of approval by an administrative body or to a structure of review by a "watchdog" institution. If this approval or review were undertaken under "legislative or regulatory provisions" the latter could be said to "determine indirectly" the content of the contracts. On the other hand, a court

---

[21] National Consumer Council and the French *Institut National de la Consommation, op. cit.*, pp. 117–118.
[22] Formerly, Art. 36 EEC.
[23] See Craig and De Burca, *op. cit,* pp. 627 *et seq.*
[24] This is assumed by Joerges, *op. cit.,* p. 176.

could instead distinguish between those provisions which *determine* and those which *provide for approval* of the terms on which services are provided, only the former being within the terms of Article 1(2).

Terms which reflect "the provisions of international conventions." The Regulations also provide that their requirements do not apply to:

15–031

> "contractual terms which reflect . . . the provisions or principles of international conventions to which the Member States or the Community are party."[25]

As the Directive makes clear, this exclusion is particularly concerned to exclude terms in conventions "in the transport area",[26] notably the Warsaw Convention on international carriage by air.[27] It should be noted that the exception applies to terms which reflect national legislation which uses the *principles* of international conventions to which the Member States or the Community are party, such as in the area of domestic carriage of goods.

(c) *The Requirement of Fairness*

Introduction. It has been noted that the Regulations make two requirements of contract terms, that they be fair and that they be expressed in plain, intelligible language and that the range of terms to which these two requirements apply differs to a degree.[28] In this section, the first of these requirements will be examined.

15–032

A complex test. The Regulations impose a requirement of fairness whose definition for English lawyers contains both familiar and unfamiliar elements. Regulation 5(1) of the 1999 Regulations provides that:

15–033

> "A contractual term which has not been individually negotiated shall be regarded as unfair if, contrary to the requirement of good faith, it causes a significant imbalance in the parties' rights and obligations arising under the contract, to the detriment of the consumer."[28a]

Regulation 6(1) further provides that:

> "Without prejudice to regulation 12,[28b] the unfairness of a contractual term shall be assessed, taking into account the nature of the goods[28c] or services for which the contract was concluded and by referring, at the time of the contract, to all the circumstances attending the conclusion of the contract and to all the other terms of the contract or another contract on which it is dependent."[29]

Furthermore, both the 1994 and 1999 Regulations provide in their schedules (identical) "non-exhaustive lists" of terms which may be regarded as unfair.

---

[25] 1999 Regs, reg. 4(2)(b); 1994 Regs, reg. 3(1), Sched. 1(e)(ii).
[26] Art. 1(2).
[27] See Vol. II, §§ 35–001 *et seq.*
[28] See *ante*, 15–023.
[28a] *cf.* 1994 Regulations, reg. 4(1).
[28b] See *post*, § 15–073 *et seq.*
[28c] On the appropriateness of this limitation to goods, see *ante*, §§ 1–012—1–014.
[29] *cf.* 1994 Regulations, reg. 4(2).

However, there is a difference between the test of fairness enacted by the 1994 Regulations and the 1999 Regulations, as the former but not the latter attempt to explain the significance of the requirement of good faith which forms part of the overall test of fairness. Even without this complication, the elements common to both sets of Regulations form a sophisticated test of unfairness, its complex of different ideas and considerations being clearly aimed at reducing the degree of uncertainty and discretion which is given to a court in requiring it to judge the fairness of a term. This test can be broken down into two elements: (i) the basic test and the range of considerations relevant to its application; and (ii) the significance and contents of the "indicative" or "grey list" of terms, to which may be added other illustrations of potentially unfair terms.

(i) The Basic Test of Unfairness

15–034   **The basic test.** The basic test of unfairness of a term is that "contrary to the requirement of good faith it causes a significant imbalance in the parties' rights and obligations under the contract, to the detriment of the consumer." The significance of this test has given rise to considerable comment,[30] and for some its use of the notion of good faith introduces to English law a new and somewhat alien concept, whose significance is far from clear. In this respect, it is helpful to bear in mind the origins of the reference to good faith, this flowing from its use in the German statute which significantly influenced the Directive.[31] In turn, this German statute can be seen as the legislative recognition of existing judicial controls on unfair contract terms, this law-making being justified by the Civil Code's general provision requiring good faith of parties to contracts[32]: "good faith" in this context can be seen as little more than a convenient legal pigeon hole in which to have placed within the structure of the Civil Code judicial developments which took into account a range of considerations deemed appropriate to the control in hand.[33] For this reason, it can be argued that the reference to "good faith" in the Directive is no more than a bow in the direction of these origins. Indeed, such a very limited significance to the phrase "contrary to the requirement of good faith" is adopted by some French writers[34] and this is reflected in its omission from France's implementing legislation.[35] For a French

---

[30] Collins, *op. cit.*; Beale, *op. cit.*, p. 242 *et seq.*; Weatherill (1995) 3 *Eur. Rev. Private Law* 307; Howells and Willhemson, *op. cit.*, p. 96 *et seq.*; Beatson, *op. cit.* p. 291 *et seq.*

[31] *i.e. Gesetz zur Regelung des Rechts der Allgemeinen Geschäftsbedingungen* ("Standard Contract Terms Act") of 1976, translated in part by Dannemann in Markesinis, Lorenz and Dannemann, *op. cit.*, p. 908 *et seq.* The first draft of the Directive was much closer to the German legislation, applying to commercial as well as to consumer contracts. Apart from the German law, the laws of some other Member States law have used the notion of good faith in their control of unfair contract terms, for example, Spanish law: Paisant, *op. cit.*, p. 100.

[32] § 242 B.G.B. and see Markesinis, Dannemann and Lorenz, *op. cit.*, p. 212.

[33] Whittaker and Zimmermann (eds) *Good Faith in European Contract Law* (forthcoming), Chap. 1. It is noteworthy that the German Standard Terms Act of 1976 did not attempt to explain the requirement of good faith by reference to the already elaborate case law based on § 242 B.G.B., but instead listed the clauses which are either necessarily void or are void if they fail a test of "reasonableness:" see Standard Contract Terms Act 1976 §§ 9–11.

[34] See Larroumet, *Droit Civil, Les obligations*, Tome 3, *Le contrat* (4th. edn., 1998), 401; Paisant, *op. cit.*, p. 100.

[35] *Loi* No. 95/96 of February 1 1995, Art. L.132–1 al. 1 *Code de la consommation*. Again, this reflects French legislative and judicial tradition which preferred to use the notion of the abuse of rights (hence, "*clauses abusives*") rather than the (admittedly closely related) notion of good faith.

lawyer it is unnecessary for two reasons: first, because the French Civil Code already makes a general requirement of the performance of contracts in good faith[36] (an argument of no significance for English law), but, secondly, because a business supplier could not be considered to remain in good faith if he were to seek to enjoy the disproportionate advantages set out in the contract concluded with the consumer.[37] From this perspective, the requirement that the term "causes a significant imbalance in the parties' rights and obligations under the contract to the detriment of the consumer" is sufficient in itself.

It is therefore interesting for this purpose that at least the 1994 Regulations **15-035** clearly interpreted the Directive as creating two distinct elements in the wider judgment that a term is unfair: that it create the imbalance of the requisite kind *and* that this is contrary to the requirements of good faith.[38] This view may be seen in the fact that the 1994 Regulations set out two sets of criteria or factors to be taken into consideration in determining whether these conditions are fulfilled, the first set concerning the assessment of fairness in general, but the second set specifically concerning good faith.[39] As regards good faith, this reflects an attempt by their drafters to "domesticate" the concept of good faith for English law, a process which was presaged by recital 16 of the preamble to the Directive which inspired the considerations used for this purpose by the 1994 Regulations and which is itself an acknowledgement that for common lawyers the Directive's use of good faith lacks resonance in existing legal usage.[40]

"A significant imbalance in the parties' rights and obligations arising **15-036** **under the contract, to the detriment of the consumer."** This phrase encapsulates the key idea of the notion of unfairness for the purposes of both sets of Regulations, requiring that the *term* creates an imbalance in the parties' legal rights and obligations and that this imbalance pass a threshold of significance. Two aspects of this definition have become clear as a result of the Office of Fair Trading's work in policing terms in consumer contracts.[41]

First, a clause will be judged according to its *potential* unfairness: if a clause **15-037** could give rise to a "significant imbalance in the parties' rights", etc. (given the particular and concrete factors to be outlined below), then it is no answer for a seller or supplier wishing to rely on it to say that on the facts it does not do so nor that it was never intended to be relied on so as to do so.[42] So, for example, if a price variation clause gives a supplier an unlimited discretion to vary the price (a term which can for this purpose be assumed to be potentially unfair given

---

[36] Art. 1134 al. 3 C. civ.

[37] Paisant, *op. cit.,* at p. 100.

[38] This view is shared by some English writers: see e.g. Willett, *op. cit.,* p. 114.

[39] See 1994 Regulations, reg. 4 and Sched. 2 respectively and *post,* § 15-044.

[40] Tenreiro, *op. cit.,* p. 2, who notes that this holds good for the Scandinavian legal systems as well.

[41] It is to be noted that the way in which the test of unfairness will apply in disputes between the parties to a contract will differ in certain respects from the way in which it is to be applied by the Director General of Fair Trading (on which, see *post,* § 15-075), but these are not significant for present purposes.

[42] O.F.T., *Unfair Contract Terms,* Bulletin No. 1 (May 1996), §§ 1.2, p. 5; *ibid.,* Bulletin No. 3 (March 1997), p. 7. *cf. Stewart Gill Ltd v. Horatio Myer & Co. Ltd* [1992] Q.B. 600 (in relation to the reasonableness test under the Unfair Contract Terms Act 1977, s. 11) and see *ante,* § 14-081.

its lack of limitation or justification[43]), then it would not be binding on the consumer with the result that even a moderate variation of the price (itself not in the context apparently unfair) would not be effective against the consumer: the unfairness of the term makes it "not binding" on the consumer. This feature of the test of unfairness will require a significant change in thinking behind the drafting of terms for the contracts to which the Regulations apply: no longer should a legal adviser acting for a seller or supplier draw a clause in as wide terms as possible so as to allow the seller or supplier as much room for manoeuvre even if he is unlikely to need it, as such a wide clause is more likely to be held altogether ineffective. Instead, such a legal adviser must in the interest of his own client take into account the legitimate interests of the client's consumer customers as these are reflected in the pattern of considerations gathered under the requirement of fairness (and indeed, of plainness and intelligibility).

15–038   Secondly, the Office of Fair Trading has attached very considerable significance to the notion of balance, so that a term which may look, prima facie, severely prejudicial to the rights of a consumer may yet be considered fair if it is counterbalanced by a corresponding term which could act to the consumer's advantage. Various examples of this thinking are given in the Office's reports, such as a seller's right to increase prices being coupled with a realistic right in the consumer to get out of the contract without penalty.[44] Conversely, the forfeiture of a consumer's deposit where a customer chooses not to go ahead with a contract to supply a fitted kitchen was criticised for the absence of a counterbalancing right in a consumer to receive compensation of an equivalent amount if the supplier decided to cancel the contract.[45] Again, a term in a contract of membership of a fitness club was considered unfair in that it allowed the business to assign the contract to another party without obtaining the consent of the consumers, while they were unable to transfer the benefit of the contract.[46]

15–039   **Factors in fairness.** While it is true that, in principle, the Regulations are concerned with the unfairness of contract terms, rather than with the fairness of the parties' behaviour more generally, certain aspects of their mutual behaviour may be relevant in the assessment of fairness. For, as has been seen,[47] the Regulations require that in assessing the fairness of a term account shall be taken of the nature of the goods or services, all the circumstances attending the conclusion of the contract and all other terms of the contract or of a contract on which it is dependent.[48] While formally this provision requires certain factors to be taken into account (raising the possibility of arguing that only these should be), it is submitted that, quite apart from the inherent openess of the concept of fairness itself, other considerations may be taken into account in assessing fairness by way of application of the requirement of good faith which forms an element within the assessment of fairness.[49]

---

[43] And see Sched. 2(1)(*l*), *post*, § 15–061.
[44] O.F.T., *Unfair Contract Terms*, Bulletin No. 1 (May, 1996), §§ 1.5, p. 6.
[45] *ibid.* p. 45.
[46] O.F.T., *Unfair Contract Terms*, Bulletin No. 4 (December 1997), p. 40.
[47] See *ante*, § 15–033.
[48] 1999 Regs, reg. 6(1); 1994 Regs, reg. 4(1). On the reference to "goods", see *ante*, § 15–012.
[49] See *post*, § 15–044.

"The nature of the goods or services." In certain types of case, the nature **15–040** of the goods or services could argue for the fairness of a term which in other contexts would clearly be unfair. For example, if a consumer hires earthmoving equipment for use in his garden[50] the fact that these goods are normally used in a commercial context by a person with a degree of experience may argue for the fairness of an exemption clause restricting any strict liability of the hirer in respect of any damage to property which the machine may cause while in use.[51] A second example may be found in the context of clauses allowing the forfeiture of a purchaser's disposit in contracts of sale of land. Here, at first sight the loss of ten per cent of the purchase price if the purchaser withdraws from the contract suggests that such a clause is unfair, but it may not be given the need of the seller to cover transaction costs and also to be indemnified for likely loss of profit on the transaction. Indeed, it may be under this heading that a court could properly consider the impact of (good) industry practice in relation to the type of contract in question in assessing a term's fairness.

"All the circumstances attending the conclusion of the contract." This is **15–041** clearly a very inclusive formulation. Here, two possible factors will be mentioned, both of which can be thought of as relating to circumstances relating to the conclusion of the contract. First, the fact that a seller or supplier has put pressure on a consumer to conclude the contract or to do so in haste and without time to think about its significance would point strongly against the fairness of any term which prejudices the consumer, even if this pressure did not amount to either duress or undue influence within the meaning of the general law.[52] Secondly, the degree of genuine opportunity for the consumer to read, understand, consider and decide upon the terms of a contract is also an important factor in their overall fairness. This may be supported by reference to the Schedules' inclusion in the grey list of a term which has the object or effect of "irrevocably binding the consumer to terms with which he had no real opportunity of becoming acquainted before the conclusion of the contract."[52a] Now, a term which irrevocably binds a consumer to the contract is typically to be found in any contract which does not provide for a consumer to withdraw from the contract and so, absent such a provision, the terms of any contract which the consumer did not have a real opportunity of being acquainted are vulnerable to a charge of unfairness. Positively, therefore, a seller or supplier whose explanatory precontractual brochure[53] makes clear the otherwise surprising terms on which he deals or whose staff follow a practice of advising their customers of the terms in a clear and intelligible manner may be more likely to succeed in arguing that the terms in question are fair. This links in with the common law's traditional concern with notice of terms,[54] but it goes further in that a "real opportunity" is referred to and it may be thought that the more theoretical the opportunity, the more likely a term is to be held to be unfair. This approach to fairness also links

---

[50] Such a person being a "consumer" for the purposes of the Regulations, *ante,* §15–017.

[51] Such an exemption clause would escape control by the Unfair Contract Terms Act 1977, s.12(1)(c).

[52] See *ante,* Chap. 7.

[52a] 1999 Regs, Sched. 2(1)(i); 1994 Regs, Sched. 3(1)(i).

[53] O.F.T., *Unfair Contract Terms,* Bulletin No. 2 (September 1996), § 2.22, p. 12 (though considering this to be particularly a matter for the good faith of the trader).

[54] See *ante,* § 12–013 *et seq.*

in with the Regulations' requirement that the contract terms themselves be expressed in plain and intelligible language.[55]

15–042   **"All the other terms of the contract".** The Regulations require courts to take into account the other terms of the contract before them in assessing the fairness of a term. It is to be noticed that *all* the terms should be looked at, this including as has been noted, the contract's "core terms" which relate to its subject matter or price/quality ratio.[56] In the view of the Director General of Fair Trading, an example of "another term" of a contract which may argue for the fairness of a term which by itself looks unfair may be found in a term which provides the consumer with a cooling-off period during which he may decide to cancel the contract without penalty.[57]

15–043   **"The ... terms ... of another contract on which it is dependent."** It would seem from the general formulation of this phrase that there is no requirement that the other contract on which the consumer contract is dependent must itself be a consumer contract within the meaning of the Regulations (though in the vast majority of situations it will be)[58] nor even that the other contract be between the same parties as the one whose term is to be assessed. A situation in the consumer context in which two contracts are related may be found in the context of the financing of a consumer sale. Here, it would seem that whatever controls already exist on the fairness of the terms of either the sale or the financing contract,[59] the terms of the one may go to the fairness of the terms of the other. For example, the fairness of the terms of purchase of a house could be assessed taking into account the terms of a mortgage contract taken out by a consumer mortgagor. However, this example shows the difficulties that would arise in this respect, where the mortgagee is not also the seller, for it may be thought unfair for a mortgagee to be prejudiced by the terms of the sale of which it may know nothing and have even less control. This may lead a court to imply into the phrase "another contract" a requirement that this contract be between the parties to the consumer contract whose terms are to be assessed.

15–044   **Factors in good faith specified by the 1994 Regulations.** Schedule 2 of the 1994 Regulations provided that:

"In making an assessment of good faith, regard shall be had in particular to—
    (a) the strength of the bargaining positions of the parties;
    (b) whether the consumer had an inducement to agree to the term;
    (c) whether the goods or services were sold or supplied to the special order of the consumer, and
    (d) the extent to which the seller or supplier has dealt fairly and equitably with the consumer."[60]

A first important point to notice about this formulation is that it expressly allowed the possibility of recourse to other considerations in making an assessment of

---

[55] See *post,* 15–068.
[56] See *ante,* § 15–025 and Preamble to the Directive, recital 19.
[57] O.F.T., *Unfair Contract Terms,* Bulletin No. 2 (September 1996), p. 12.
[58] For example, even if contracts for the sale of land fall outside the ambit of the Regulations this might not prevent the terms of a purchase of a house being relevant to the fairness of the terms of a mortgage.
[59] Notably, under the Consumer Credit Act 1974 on which see Vol. II, Chap. 38.
[60] Reg. 3(3) and Sched. 2.

good faith. All four of the elements expressly mentioned are found in the preamble to the Directive[61] and all but (d) are very similar indeed to the "guidelines" for the application of the reasonableness test provided by the Unfair Contract Terms Act 1977.[62] This being the case, it is likely that the courts will refer in giving them significance to the existing case law on the 1977 Act, though bearing in mind the differences between the types of term which are subject to control under that Act (exemption clauses and indemnity clauses) and the type of term to be tested before them for assessment under the 1994 Regulations. However, the fourth consideration which Schedule 2 of the 1994 Regulations lists is new and, moreover, seems to invite a very different approach from the one to be taken under the 1977 Act, for " the extent to which the seller or supplier *has* dealt fairly or equitably with the consumer" suggests that the seller's or the supplier's conduct *after* the conclusion of the contract may also form an element within the test of his good faith. It is clear, though, from the text of the Directive that the requirement of good faith is intended to qualify the fairness of the term, not the fairness of a party's *post*-contractual behaviour and this being the case, the fourth consideration becomes redundant, given the general test's reference to "all circumstances attending the conclusion of the contract."[63]

As has been noted, unlike the 1994 Regulations, the 1999 Regulations do not attempt to explain the requirement of good faith. It is submitted, however, that this does not mean that the first three factors previously set out in Schedule 2 of the 1994 Regulations as factors to which regard should be had in the assessment of good faith are irrelevant to the assessment of good faith for the purposes of the 1999 Regulations, for the presence of these factors in the preamble to the Directive make it legitimate to refer to them in the interpretation of article 3(1)'s use of the requirement of good faith and, therefore any national implementing legislation.[64]

Good faith and the provision of public services. Recital 16 of the preamble to the Directive prefaces its explanation of the considerations to which regard shall be had in the assessment of good faith by stating that: **15–045**

> "the assessment . . . of the unfair character of terms, in particular in sale or supply activities of a public nature providing collective services which take account of solidarity among users, must be supplemented by a means of making an overall evaluation of the different interests involved; whereas this constitutes the requirement of good faith . . . "

This reference to taking account of "solidarity among users" does not have any resonance for English lawyers (which is no doubt why it was omitted from the Regulations), but it may allude to the idea to be found, for example, in French administrative law which requires those who use a public service must have equal access to it and be equally treated by it.[65] One result of this is that the

---

[61] Recital 16.

[62] Unfair Contract Terms Act 1977, Sched. 2 (a), (b) and (e) and see *ante*, § 14–082 *et seq.*

[63] 1994 Regulations, reg. 4(2); *cf.* 1999 Regulations, reg. 6(1). *cf.* Treitel, *op. cit.* p. 251 who doubts whether guideline (d) provides any guideline at all, given that it "does little more than rephrase the principal question [whether the term is unfair]."

[64] Recital 16.

[65] Bell in Bell, Boyron and Whittaker, *Principles of French Law* (1998), p. 170 and for details see Chapus, *Droit administratif général*, Tome 1 (9th ed., 1995), p. 542 *et seq.*

public service is not allowed to discriminate between different classes of user of the service (notably as regards any charges to be paid) where to do so is not justified in the public interest.[66] Perhaps, then, this part of recital 16 invites a court to take into account in assessing the fairness of terms on which public services are provided a general principle of equality of treatment. This may even be the case in relation to differential tariffs, for while terms which concern "the adequacy of the price or remuneration, as against the goods or services sold or supplied" are excluded from the requirement of fairness,[67] a term which differentiates unfairly in the charges to be paid for a public service as between different categories of customer may be held not to concern the adequacy of the price *in relation to* the goods or services provided.

15–046 **Other factors in the assessment of good faith or fairness.** Other factors have been suggested as relevant to determining whether the requirement of good faith is satisfied, though most could equally well be thought of simply as going to the issue of fairness in general. A notable example is found in the preamble to the Directive which allows the "price/quality" ratio of the contract to be taken into account.[68] It has also been suggested that E.C. recommendations in the field of consumer protection, for example, as regards payment systems,[69] may be referred to by a court in assessing a term's fairness.[70]

15–047 **The burden of proof as to fairness.** Neither set of Regulations nor the Directive provide a rule for the burden of proof as to the issue of the fairness of a term, oddly perhaps, given their express placing of the burden of proof as to the issue of a term's "individual negotiation" on the seller or supplier.[71] If an English court were to apply the general rule for the placing of burdens of proof in civil cases at common law, then clearly it would rest on the consumer to show that a term is unfair[72] and this would mark an important contrast with the rule found in the Unfair Contract Terms Act 1977 as to the issue of reasonableness of the term, as this provides that "[i]t is for those claiming that a contract term or notice satisfies the requirement of reasonableness to show that it does."[73] However, if the issue of burden of proof were one on which the European Court considered it appropriate to take a European view, the position would be less clear. For while the general rule that it is for a person alleging a fact to prove it is found in many other European legal systems,[74] that court may be inclined rather to concentrate on the purpose of the Directive in protecting consumers and, relying on the

---

[66] Chapus, *ibid.* p. 548. Another significance of the term "solidarity" in E.C. law is to be found in relation to social security schemes "based on the principle of solidarity", *i.e.* where benefits are not based on contributions: see *Decker v. Caisse de Maladie des Employés Privés*, Case C–120/95, [1998] 1 All E.R. (E.C.) 673.

[67] See *ante*, § 15–025.

[68] Recital 19.

[69] Recommendation 94/489/E.C.

[70] Howells and Wilhelmsson, *op. cit.*, at p. 103.

[71] 1999 Regs, reg. 5(4); 1994 Regs, reg. 3(5); Dir. Art. 3(2) § 3.

[72] *Cross and Tapper on Evidence* (8th. ed., 1995), 133–134.

[73] s.11(5) and see *ante*, §§ 14–084.

[74] "*Actori incumbit probatio.*" See, for example, French law, Art. 1315 C. civ. and Ghestin and Goubeaux, *Droit civil, Introduction générale*, (3rd ed., 1990), p. 536; and German law, see Stadler in Ebke and Finkin (eds.), *Introduction to German Law* (1996) Chap. 13, p. 357 at p. 367.

analogies in the consumer legislation of the Member States,[75] reverse the burden of proof on the issue of fairness so as to further this protection.[76] It is, though, by no means clear that the European Court would consider the issue of burden of proof as being appropriate for the development of a European view, given that the very notion of burden of proof has very different significances in the different legal systems of the Member States, this being in part a function of their differing rules of civil procedure and judicial institutions.[77] However, even if the burden of proof as to the issue of fairness were held to lie on the consumer, this may not be an onerous burden to discharge, especially where the term falls within one of the examples of potentially unfair terms found in the schedules to the Regulations.[77a] Moreover, while trade practice may be relevant to the issue of fairness, in the view of the Office of Fair Trading, "in practical terms, mere lack of evidence that the treatment of consumers in relation to a term is any worse than that of competitors is unlikely to satisfy a court as to good faith."[78]

Judicial discretion and appeal. It has been seen that the requirement of **15–048** fairness is a complex one, requiring a range of different considerations to be taken into account by a court, many of which possess a very wide or open content. This being the case, it is likely that the English courts will take a similar view as to the nature of the judicial decision involved as they have taken in relation to the decision on the issue of reasonableness for the purpose of the Unfair Contract Terms Act 1977 and in that context it has been said that while such a decision is not to be merely an exercise of judicial discretion (and therefore one in practice not subject to appeal)[79] there "will sometimes be room for a legitimate difference of judicial opinion,"[80] this indicating a judicial desire to discourage appeals on the issue of reasonableness.[81]

An autonomous European view of fairness or good faith? It has been **15–049** suggested that the concept of good faith is one on which the European Court should take an autonomous European view.[82] However, it is submitted that this is unlikely. First, there is no common meaning or meanings given to the notion of good faith (or its apparent linguistic equivalents) in the laws of those Member States who do in fact use it.[83] Instead, one finds a range of different meanings given to this notion (and its cousin notions of equity or the abuse of rights) according to the legal needs and juristic traditions of the particular legal system

---

[75] *e.g.* the Unfair Contract Terms Act 1977, s.11(5). *cf.* the French legislation which implements the Directive which expressly places the burden of proof as to the issue of fairness on the consumer: *loi* No. 95–96 of February 1, 1995, Art. 1, new Art. L.132–1, al. 3 *Code de la consommation*.

[76] *cf.* Weatherill, (1995) 3 *Eur. Rev. of Private Law* 307 at 317.

[77] See, for example, on French law Whittaker in Bell, Boyron, Whittaker, *op. cit.*, p. 79, at pp. 80–81.

[77a] 1999 Regs, Sched. 2; 1994 Regs, Sched. 3.

[78] Edwards, in O.F.T., *Unfair Contract Terms*, Bulletin No. 4 (December 1997), Part 4, 18 at 23.

[79] See, *e.g.*, the approach of the courts to the exercise of judicial discretion in relation to the award of a "just sum" under the Law Reform (Frustrated Contracts) Act 1943 s.1(3), *post*, §§ 24–088.

[80] *George Mitchell (Chesterhall) Ltd v. Finney Lock Seeds Ltd* [1983] 2 A.C. 803, 816 *per* Lord Bridge.

[81] Treitel, *op. cit.*, p. 239.

[82] Weatherill, 3 *Eur. Rev. Private Law*, 307 (1995); *idem*, *E.C. Consumer Law and Policy* (1997), p. 82; Howells and Wilhelmsson, *E.C. Consumer Law*, (1997), pp. 103–104.

[83] On this and the points made in the following sentences, see Whittaker and Zimmermann, *op. cit.*, esp. Conclusion.

in question, this being a function of a very wide range of factors. Moreover, even where a particular significance of good faith may be established as shared by many or all the Member States (for example, the idea that good faith requires honesty), there may be disagreement as to what this requires on any given set of facts. This being the case, it would be undesirable to attempt to draw out from the laws of the Member States any common significance to good faith in the very particular context of the Directive on unfair contract terms. Secondly, there is no need to develop a European conception of good faith or fairness beyond the one which has already been set out in the Directive, which provides a range of criteria to mould its application by (especially lower) courts. While the European Court may well properly take a view as to the significance of one of these criteria, to go beyond this would be to trespass into the domain of the application of the law rather than its interpretation.[84] Thirdly, and related to this, it may be thought that a value-laden decision such as an assessment of fairness of a term is not one on which it is appropriate for a European view to be taken. As a German jurist has observed, "in assessing the advantages and drawbacks of contractual practices, moral intuition and culturally determined preferences will apply. . . . [D]ifferences among national legal systems in the implementation of the Directive seem inevitable—and it must be 'mutually recognised' that such pluralism is not in itself indicative of inequity."[85]

15–050   **"Fairness" under the Regulations and "Reasonableness" under the Unfair Contract Terms Act 1977.** It has been noted that some of the considerations to be taken into account by a court in assessing the fairness of a term for the purposes of the Regulations (in particular in relation to the requirement of good faith) are the same or very similar to those to be taken into account in assessing the "reasonableness" of a term under the Unfair Contract Terms Act 1977.[86] Moreover, while the specific factors which are to be taken into account may differ somewhat, the "definitions" of the two concepts are both very inclusive, allowing a court to take into account whatever factors it thinks right in judging whether a term should be enforced, as long as these relate to the term (as opposed to post-contractual dealings between the parties).[87] There is, therefore, a profound similarity in the two tests in that they both require a court to decide whether a particular contract term *should* be enforceable according to a range of considerations, some of which relate to the contract itself and some of which relate to the relative positions of the parties to the contract or the circumstances in which the contract was made. All this does not mean, however, that the two tests will have the same significance, but their differences do not stem from use of the language, on the one hand, of "reasonableness" and, on the other, of "fairness" and "good faith." Instead, they flow from the differences in ambit of the two pieces of legislation, in particular as regards the types of term to be tested. For while the Unfair Contract Terms Act 1977 deals (almost exclusively) with exemption clauses, the Regulations deal with any type of contract term as long as it is "incidental"[88] and has not been "individually negotiated."[89] Clearly,

---

[84] Only issues of law can go before the European Court of Justice under the procedure found in Art. 234 (formerly Art. 177) of the E.C. Treaty.

[85] Joerges, (1995) 3 *Eur. Rev. of Private Law* 175, 183–184.

[86] See *ante*, §§ 15–039 *et seq.*

[87] *cf. ante*, §§ 15–044.

[88] *i.e.* not a "core term:" see *ante*, § 15–025.

[89] See *ante*, § 15–024.

the type of considerations which are appropriate in judging the "fairness" of terms other than exemption clauses are likely to differ considerably from those which are appropriate to that context. There are indeed existing parallels for this in English law before the Regulations were issued: so, for example, the factors which are to be taken into account by a court in judging the "reasonableness" of a term of a contract which is in restraint of trade are not the same as those in judging the "reasonableness" of an exemption clause: the terminology of reasonableness is shared but the impact of this requirement differs according to the type of term in question, and the factors in determining reasonableness differ according to the reasons for which the term is viewed with suspicion (whether excluding a person's claim which would otherwise exist or unduly fettering a person's freedom).[90] In a similar way, the application of the requirement of fairness for the purposes of the Regulations will differ according to its context. In the result, therefore, while the application of the test of "fairness" for the purposes of the Regulations to exemption clauses is unlikely to differ from the application of the test of "reasonableness" under the 1977 Act, its application to other clauses will differ appropriately to the context of both the type of term and the type of contract in question.[91]

(ii) *The "Indicative List" of terms*

Introduction. Both the 1994 and the 1999 Regulations contain identical **15–051** "indicative and non-exhaustive list[s] of the terms which may be regarded as unfair."[91a] This list is sometimes termed a "grey list" for the terms which it contains are not necessarily to be held unfair (a "black list"), but they will give rise to a forensic presumption of unfairness (that is to say, in practice it will be very useful in forensic argument for a consumer to be able to point to a term in the list as similar to the one which he challenges). Given its illustrative nature, it is odd that the second paragraphs of the Schedules purport to restrict the scope of particular examples of terms found in the first paragraphs, but this reinforces the importance which was attached by the drafters of the Directive to the illustrative list.[92] Even so, it needs to be emphasised that a type of term included on the list may be held by a court to be fair in the circumstances before it.

The list in paragraph 1 of Schedule 2 of the 1999 Regulations includes a wide **15–052** variety of terms and these not merely illustrate the application of the requirement of fairness, but also the range of types of terms which are subject to the Regulations' controls (in particular in contrast to the limited ambit in this respect of the Unfair Contract Terms Act 1977). In the following paragraphs, these terms will be noted and very briefly discussed, the examples retaining the letter which they bear in the Schedule.

Exclusion or limitation clauses. Terms which have the object or effect of: **15–053**

(a) excluding or limiting the legal liability of a seller or supplier in the event of the death of a consumer or personal injury to the latter resulting from an act or omission of that seller or supplier;

---

[90] *cf. ante*, § 14–081 and *post*, § 17–075 *et seq.*
[91] *cf.* though, the differences in relation to the burden of proof discussed *ante*, § 15–047.
[91a] 1994 Regs, reg. 4(4), Sched. 3, para. 1; 1999 Regulations, reg. 5(5), Sched. 2, para. 1.
[92] This is also shown by the Directive's requirement that the list be included in Member States' implementing legislation: Art. 3(3).

(b) inappropriately excluding or limiting the legal rights of the consumer vis-à-vis the seller or supplier or another party in the event of total or partial non-performance or inadequate performance by the seller or supplier of any of the contractual obligations, including the option of offsetting a debt owed to the seller or supplier against any claim which the consumer may have against him;

. . .

(q) excluding or hindering the consumer's right to take legal action or exercise any other legal remedy, particularly by requiring the consumer to take disputes exclusively to arbitration not covered by legal provisions, unduly restricting the evidence available to him or imposing on him a burden of proof which, according to the applicable law, should lie with another party to the contract.

Many of the terms within these examples would be classed as exemption clauses within the meaning of the Unfair Contract Terms Act 1977,[93] but one difference is that the reference to a term which requires a "consumer to take disputes exclusively to arbitration not covered by legal provisions" may be thought to refer to an arbitration clause, a type of term which when found in a consumer contract[94] has been deemed by the Arbitration Act 1996 to be necessarily unfair within the meaning of the 1994 Regulations if it relates to a claim for a "modest amount", set at the time of writing at £3,000.[95]

15–054   **"Potestative conditions."** Terms which have the object or effect of:

(c) making an agreement binding on the consumer whereas provision of services by the seller or supplier is subject to a condition whose realisation depends on his own will alone;

It may be thought that in English law such a term may render the contract as a whole void for uncertainty or lack of consideration, in that it appears to give the seller or supplier an effective choice whether or not to do anything under the contract,[96] a term which in the Romanist terminology is known as a "potestative condition."[97] This term's presence in the list may be explained by the fact that this result is not uniformly shared throughout the Member States.[98] However, the idea that a term should not enable the seller or supplier to determine in his discretion the rights of a consumer under a contract may be significant for English law. Thus, the Office of Fair Trading has expressed the view that a clause

---

[93] s.12 and see *ante,* §§ 14–060—14–062.

[94] The definition of "consumer contract" is somewhat wider for this purpose than for the purposes of the Regulations in general as it is provided that the consumer may be a legal person as well as a natural one: Arbitration Act 1996, s.90 and *cf. ante,* § 15–017.

[95] Arbitration Act 1996, ss.89, 90; Unfair Arbitration Agreements (Specified Amount) Order 1996 S.I. 1996 No. 3211 of December 19, 1996 (which came into force on January 31, 1997).

[96] de Moor, 3 *Eur. Rev. of Private Law* (1995) 257, 269 at n. 62 and *cf. ante,* § 14–007 and § 15–057.

[97] Thomas, *Textbook of Roman Law,* (1976), p. 237.

[98] For example, while such a term may lead to the annulment of a contract in French law (being termed a *condition potestative,* see art. 1174 C. civ. and Nicholas, *The French Law of Contract* (2nd ed., 1991), p. 159 *et seq.*), it would not necessarily do so in German law (*cf.* German Standard Contract Terms Act 1976 § 10.3).

in a contract between a car manufacturer and the purchaser of one of its cars which subjected a consumer's right to return a car to its manufacturer to a condition that the car had not suffered a particular degree of damage "in the opinion of the [manufacturer's] dealer" is unfair.[99]

Unbalanced forfeiture clauses. Terms which have the object or effect of: **15–055**

(d) permitting the seller or supplier to retain sums paid by the consumer where the latter decides not to conclude or perform the contract, without providing for the consumer to receive compensation of an equivalent amount from the seller or supplier where the latter is the party cancelling the contract;

The type of terms described in this subparagraph include terms under which either a part-payment or deposit paid by a consumer may be forfeited and have proved to be a significant object of the Office of Fair Trading's work. In this respect, important factors in the fairness of such a term are the proportion between the sum to be forfeited and any loss to be suffered by the seller or supplier by the consumer's cancellation[1] and, as subparagraph (d) mentions, the existence of any counter-balancing provision in the contract for the benefit of the consumer.

Penalty clauses. Terms which have the object or effect of: **15–056**

(e) requiring any consumer who fails to fulfil his obligation to pay a disproportionately high sum in compensation;

The type of term described in this subparagraph bears a considerable similarity to the common law understanding of a "penalty clause," since the disproportionately high nature of a sum to be paid on breach is an element within the distinction between a penalty and a (valid) liquidated damages clause. Clearly, though, clauses which are penal in their potential effect may be subjected to the test of fairness under the Regulations, whether or not they count as penalties in the technical common law sense.[2]

Cancellation clauses. Terms which have the object or effect of: **15–057**

(f) authorising the seller or supplier to dissolve the contract on a discretionary basis where the same facility is not granted to the consumer, or permitting the seller or supplier to retain the sums paid for services not yet supplied by him where it is the seller or supplier himself who dissolves the contract;

It could be argued that an executory contract which contains a term permitting either party to "dissolve" it without any prejudicial consequence (such as the

---

[99] O.F.T., *Unfair Contract Terms* Bulletin No. 1 (May 1996), p. 46.
[1] O.F.T., *Unfair Contract Terms*, Bulletin No. 2 (September 1996), p. 26.
[2] *cf. post*, §27–102—27–126. In *Kindlance v. Murphy* (1997) unreported (N.I. Ch.D.) an "interest acceleration clause" in a contract of mortgage was held unfair within the meaning of the 1994 Regulations. For an example of the upholding as fair of a clause requiring a consumer to pay a sum on his own termination of the contract, see *Gosling v. Burrard-Lucas* [1999] 1 C.L. 197.

payment of expenses or the loss of a deposit) is itself void for lack of consideration, for consideration is illusory where it is alleged to consist of a promise the terms of which leave performance entirely to the discretion of the promisor (unless something else of value in the eyes of the law is required instead).[3] However, this is clearly not the assumption of the Regulations (nor indeed of the Unfair Contract Terms Act 1977[4]), which is that such clauses are, in principle, valid. Moreover, from the point of view of consumer protection, it does not help a consumer to say that a clause which allows a seller or supplier to cancel without prejudicial consequence renders the contract as a whole void, for this releases the seller or supplier just the same, whereas a holding that the clause is unfair means merely that the *clause* does not bind the consumer, thereby leaving the *contract* binding for both.

15–058   **Terms relating to notice in contracts of indeterminate duration.** Terms which have the object or effect of:

> (g) enabling the seller or supplier to terminate a contract of indeterminate duration without reasonable notice except where there are serious grounds for doing so.

Terms in a contract of indefinite duration which allow one or other party to terminate it are, in principle, valid in English law, as may be seen from the law governing contracts of employment and partnerships.[5] Subparagraph (g) describes a term which seeks to provide for the termination of a contract of indefinite duration without reasonable notice (a concept familiar to the common law) unless there are serious grounds for doing so. The Office of Fair Trading has applied this example to a contract for the provision of estate agency services which allowed the agency to cancel the contract at any time, preferring its replacement with a term which allowed termination only on 14 days' notice.[6] It is to be noted, though, that paragraph 2 of Schedule 2 of the 1999 Regulations excludes from the scope of subparagraph (g) a range of terms in contracts for the supply of financial services, transactions in transferable securities, etc.[7]

15–059   **"Automatic extension clauses."** Terms which have the object or effect of:

> (h) automatically extending a contract of fixed duration where the consumer does not indicate otherwise, when the deadline fixed for the consumer to express this desire not to extend the contract is unreasonably early;

---

[3] See *ante*, §§ 15–054.

[4] s.3(2) (b)(ii).

[5] See Vol II, §§ 39–141 *et seq.* as regards employment and the Partnership Act 1890, s.26(1) as regards partnerships.

[6] O.F.T., *Unfair Contract Terms*, Bulletin No. 3 (March 1997), p. 26.

[7] Sched. 2, para. 2(a) states that "Subparagraph 1(g) is without hindrance to terms by which a supplier of financial services reserves the right to terminate unilaterally a contract of indeterminate duration without notice where there is a valid reason, provided that the supplier is required to inform the other contracting party or parties thereof immediately. Para. 2(b) provides that subparagraph 1(g) does not apply to "transactions in transferable securities, financial instruments and other products or services where the price is linked to fluctuations in a stock exchange quotation or index or a financial market rate that the seller or supplier does not control; and contracts for the purchase or sale of foreign currency, traveller's cheques or international money orders denominated in foreign currency." Identical provison is contained in the 1994 Regulations, Sched. 3(2).

Thus, for example, a term in a contract for the provision of a vehicle declamping service which stipulated that the annual contract was to be renewed unless the consumer gave notice not less than four weeks before its expiry was considered potentially unfair by the Office of Fair Trading (it being coupled with a clause requiring the payment of a very high percentage of the annual fee if the period for notice was not observed).[8]

Binding terms and the relevance of notice. Terms which have the object or effect of: **15–060**

(i) irrevocably binding the consumer to terms with which he had no real opportunity of becoming acquainted before the conclusion of the contract;

As has already been noted, this example of a possible unfair term is potentially very important in its implications.[9] For the vast majority of consumer contracts made on written standard terms contain a term which binds the consumer irrevocably to the contract, although some rely simply on a requirement of a consumer's signature. Where a contract does contain such a term, then subparagraph (i) suggests that *this term* may be unfair in the absence of a real opportunity of knowing about *other terms* of the contract and if it is, *this term* (and therefore the contract as a whole) will not be binding on the consumer.[10] In this way, the Regulations allow a court to make more onerous requirements of notice than has been the case at common law.[11]

Variation clauses. Terms which have the object or effect of: **15–061**

(j) enabling the seller or supplier to alter the terms of the contract unilaterally without a valid reason which is specified in the contract;

(k) enabling the seller or supplier to alter unilaterally without a valid reason any characteristics of the product or service to be provided;

(l) providing for the price of goods to be determined at the time of delivery or allowing a seller of goods or supplier of services to increase their price;

These three examples of possibly unfair terms are clearly related, each allowing a seller or supplier to vary an aspect of the contract (whether its terms, its subject matter or its price) to the possible prejudice of the consumer. First, paragraph 2(b) of Schedule 2 of the 1999 Regulations provides that subparagraph (j) is:

"without hindrance to terms under which a seller or supplier reserves the right to alter unilaterally the conditions of a contract of indeterminate duration, provide that he is required to inform the consumer with reasonable notice and that the consumer is free to dissolve the contract."[12]

---

[8] O.F.T., *Unfair Contract Terms*, No. 2 (September 1996), p. 18.
[9] See *ante*, § 15–041.
[10] See *post*, § 15–067.
[11] See *ante*, § 12–013 *et seq.*
[12] *cf.* 1994 Regulations, Sched. 3(2)(b).

So, it would seem that a term which allows variations of contract terms under these conditions is likely to be considered to be fair. As to variations in the subject matter, the fact that a term clarifies that any change in, for example, goods to be supplied will be made only if it improves the specification of those goods and that the consumer will bear no extra cost for such improvements argue in favour of its fairness.[13] On the other hand, a term which allows the seller or supplier to pass on any increased costs of the service through price increases to the consumer is likely to be unfair, given that this places "the risk of the contract price proving to have been a bad bargain on the consumer, who would be less likely to be able to anticipate such changes than a business",[14] though this is less likely if another term allows the consumer to cancel the contract if the price is in fact raised.[15] Finally, it is to be noted that subparagraphs (j) and (l) are stated as being limited in their scope in various ways regarding certain terms in contracts for the provision of financial services, transactions in transferable securities, etc.[16]

15–062   **"Supplier's discretion" clauses.** Terms which have the object or effect of:

(m) giving the seller or supplier the right to determine whether the goods or services supplied are in conformity with the contract, or giving him the exclusive right to interpret any term of the contract;

For example, a term in a contract for the repair of computers has been viewed as potentially unfair by the Office of Fair Trading where it gave the repairer the exclusive right to determine whether the goods were faulty, this being exacerbated by the possibility of the repairer being able to impose a fee before the goods were returned.[17]

15–063   **"Entire agreement clauses."** Terms which have the object or effect of:

(n) limiting the seller's or supplier's obligation to respect commitments undertaken by his agents or making his commitments subject to compliance with a particular formality;

The first part of this subparagraph describes an important group of contract terms, which have been the subject of special consideration by the Office of Fair

---

[13] O.F.T., *Unfair Contract Terms*, Bulletin No. 1 (May 1996), p. 36 and see other examples *ibid.* at pp. 17 and 38.

[14] O.F.T., *Unfair Contract Terms*, Bulletin No. 1 (May 1996), p. 44.

[15] O.F.T., *Unfair Contract Terms*, Bulletin No. 2 (September 1996), pp. 21 and 33.

[16] 1999 Regs, Sched. 2, para. 2 and 1994 Regs, Sched. 3, para. 2 states that: "(b) Subparagraph 1(j) is without hindrance to terms under which a supplier of financial services reserves the right to alter the rate of interest payable by the consumer or due to the latter, or the amount of other charges for financial services without notice where there is a valid reason, provided that the supplier is required to inform the other contracting party or parties thereof at the earliest opportunity and that the latter are free to dissolve the contract immediately; . . . (c) Subparagraphs 1(g), (j) and (l) do not apply to: transactions in transferable securities, financial instruments and other products or services where the price is linked to fluctuations in a stock exchange quotation or index or a financial market rate that the seller or supplier does not control; contracts for the purchase or sale of foreign currency, traveller's cheques or international money orders denominated in foreign currency; (d) Subparagraph 1(l) is without hindrance to price indexation clauses, where lawful, provided that the method by which prices vary is explicitly described."

[17] O.F.T., *Unfair Contract Terms*, Bulletin No. 2 (September 1996), p. 23.

Trading and termed "entire agreement clauses."[18] These clauses are those which are aimed at enabling a business to escape liability for promises that conflict with or add to the commitments in the standard written contract (for instance, an agreement to a deadline by which goods will be supplied), to which may be added by analogy those clauses which are aimed at enabling a business to escape liability for misrepresentations (for example, that an item has sold in large quantities and that this is the last one in stock).[19] The Office of Fair Trading gives as a typical example a clause of a mobile telephone airtime contract which provided that:

> "You [the consumer] agree that this Agreement is the complete and exclusive statement between us which supersedes all understandings or prior agreements oral or written and all representations or other communications between us relating to the subject matter of the Agreement."[20]

Another variety of this type of term may be found in a clause which unreasonably restricts or purports to restrict the authority of an agent of the seller or supplier, for example, where the latter is a company by requiring that only representations made in writing and signed by a director of the company shall bind the company.[21] While the Office of Fair Trading concedes that this sort of clause is not always intended to cheat consumers and that their potential effect is "not invariably unfair",[22] in its experience "virtually all entire agreement clauses" drawn to its attention were potentially unfair[23] and it recommends "that traders consider whether they can do without them."[24]

"Unequal opt out clauses." Terms which have the object or effect of: **15–064**

   (o) obliging the consumer to fulfil all his obligations where the seller or supplier does not perform his;

An example of such a term may be found in a contract for the provision of airtime by a mobile telephone service which allowed its provider "from time to time without notice to suspend the Network service . . . ," but further provided that "[n]otwithstanding any suspension of the Network service . . . the Customer shall remain liable for all charges due throughout the period of suspension unless [the supplier] at its sole discretion determines otherwise."[25] Not surprisingly, given its width, the Office of Fair Trading considered that this particular example

---

[18] O.F.T., *Unfair Contract Terms*, Bulletin No. 1 (May 1996), p. 15 *et seq.* An "entire agreement clause" seeks to ensure that a court concludes that it was the intention of the parties that a written document should contain all the terms of the contract, for in the absence of such a finding a court will look at the oral as well as the written agreement of the parties: see *ante*, § 12–102 in relation to the "parol evidence rule."

[19] *ibid.* p. 15.

[20] *ibid.*

[21] O.F.T., *Unfair Contract Terms*, Bulletin No. 2 (September 1996), p. 60. Such a clause attempts to denude the agents of their apparent or ostensible authority: *cf.* Vol. II, §§ 32–057 *et seq.*

[22] O.F.T., *Unfair Contract Terms*, Bulletin No. 1 (May 1996), p. 16 (factors in favour of a clause's fairness are its narrow terms; any balancing equal and opposite burden on the business or grant of an unequal advantage to the consumer; or the fact that it was specifically drawn to the attention of and explained to consumer).

[23] *ibid.* at p. 17.

[24] *ibid.* at p. 19.

[25] O.F.T., *Unfair Contract Terms*, Bulletin No. 3 (March 1997), p. 77.

of an "unequal opt out clause" was potentially unfair, and negotiated its replacement with a clause which advised the consumer to arrange insurance to cover any monthly charges and provided for a refund by the provider of the service if the consumer is unable to use the services in certain circumstances for a continuous period of three days.[26]

15–065   **Assignment clauses.** Terms which have the object or effect of:

(p) giving the seller or supplier the possibility of transferring his rights and obligations under the contract, where this may serve to reduce the guarantees for the consumer, without the latter's agreement.

Such a term is particularly likely to be unfair if the contract prevents the consumer from transferring his own rights under the contract, given the reference in the general test of unfairness to the need for rights to be balanced.[27]

15–066   **Other potentially unfair terms.** The bulletins of the Office of Fair Trading contain a number of types of terms found in consumer contracts which it considers are likely to be considered to be unfair within the meaning of the Regulations. These include terms which put on the consumer the onus to judge technical matters in which the supplier is expert but in which the consumer is not (for example, placing on a consumer the determination whether a driveway was ready for resurfacing with tarmacadam)[28]; terms where the apparent supplier of the service states in small print that he acts only as agent for another person (for example, in the provision of a holiday cottage)[29]; and "unfair enforcement clauses," for example, a term which grants to a seller of goods a right to enter the consumer's home and repossess the goods in certain circumstances without recourse to the court.[30] In the view of the Director General of Fair Trading this last type of clause "could be used to pressure a consumer to give up a legitimate claim to retain part of the contract price, and are entirely inappropriate in consumer contracts."[31]

Apart from these examples, an important type of term which may be thought of as vulnerable under the Regulations is one which allows the seller or supplier to terminate the contract on a minor breach by the consumer, whether this stems from a very slight breach of a significant term or the breach of a very minor term of the contract (notably, where the contract classes the terms in question as "conditions" as opposed to warranties).[32] Other types of clauses which may be thought to be potentially unfair are those which restrict a consumer's legal or equitable rights, such as in relation to discharge of a guarantee on variation of the contract or negligence in relation to the security[33]; a term which imposes on a

---

[26] *ibid.* p. 77.
[27] See *ante*, § 15–033.
[28] O.F.T., *Unfair Contract Terms*, Bulletin No. 3 (March 1997), p. 24.
[29] *ibid*, p. 28.
[30] *e.g.* O.F.T, *Unfair Contract Terms*, Bulletin No. 3 (December 1996), pp. 26, 29.
[31] *ibid.* p. 29.
[32] See *ante*, § 12–019 *et seq.*
[33] This example depends on the wider interpretation being given to "consumer contract" as explained *ante*, § 15–018. (Such a term would not come within Sched. 2, para. 1(b) of the 1999 Regulations as it would not relate to a right in respect of the other party's inadequate *performance*). Another example may be found in a term which attempts to negative an *insurer's* duty of disclosure to the assured (on this duty, see Vol. II, §41–027).

consumer a duty of disclosure of all material facts in a contract where such a duty is not required by law (such as a contract of mortgage), especially where it places the issue of materiality within the decision of the supplier of the service; or a term which imposes on a consumer party to a contract of insurance a duty of disclosure which is more onerous than the law itself requires.[34]

(iii) *The Effect of Failure to Comply with the Requirement of Fairness*

"Not binding on the consumer." Regulation 8 of the 1999 Regulations provides that an unfair term in a consumer contract "shall not be binding on the consumer",[35] but that "[t]he contract shall continue to bind the parties if it is capable of continuing in existence without the unfair term."[36] In the vast majority of cases which concern the unfairness of "incidental terms" the effect is therefore straightforward and unproblematic: the consumer is not bound by the term and is therefore not affected by any purported exercise of any power granted by the term (such as a variation of the price or subject matter of the contract by the seller or supplier); by contrast, in principle, the seller or supplier remains bound by the term, even if it is unlikely that a consumer would wish to hold him to it.   **15–067**

On the other hand, the situation may well be more difficult in relation to a core term which has failed the requirement of plainess and intelligibility[37] and has thereby become subjected to the requirement of fairness.[38] If such a core term were held to be unfair (and not binding on the consumer), it may well be that the contract would be held "incapable of continuing in existence without the unfair term." If this were the case, the Regulations appear to assume that the contract as a whole ceases to bind *both* the parties: this appears to be the force of the phrase "[t]he contract shall continue to bind the *parties* if ... " contained in regulation 8. However, this interpretation of the Regulations has a potentially unattractive result: for if a core term were held not binding on the consumer (since it was both unclear and unfair), it would appear that the seller or supplier could claim that on this ground he was not bound by the contract as a whole. However, this is unlikely to prove a frequent problem as it is unlikely that a consumer would wish to keep the seller or supplier to such a contract.

(d) *The Requirement of Plain and Intelligible Language*

(i) *The Test*

Regulation 7 of the 1999 Regulations provides that: **15–068**

"(1) A seller or supplier shall ensure that any written term of a contract is expressed in plain, intelligible language.
(2) If there is any doubt about the meaning of a written term, the interpretation which is most favourable to the consumer shall prevail except in proceedings brought under regulation 12."[38a]

---

[34] On this duty, see Vol. II, § 41–027.
[35] And see 1994 Regs, reg. 5(1).
[36] 1999 Regs, reg. 8(2); 1994 Regs, reg. 5(2).
[37] See *post*, § 15–068.
[38] See *ante*, § 15–025.
[38a] 1994 Regulations, reg. 6 On proceedings brought under regulation 12, see *post*, §§ 15–073 *et seq*.

It is to be welcomed that this provision is entitled simply "Written contracts", (unlike the 1994 Regulations' equivalent provision, Regulation 6, which was entitled "Construction of written contracts,") for the importance of this requirement runs well beyond this traditional and narrow concern. There are two aspects of this requirement: first, relating to its content and, secondly, relating to its effects.

15–069   **The place of the requirement in the Regulations.** In some ways, the requirement that the terms of written consumer contracts be in plain, intelligible language may be thought of as an expression of their requirement of fairness; indeed, for the Director General of Fair Trading, "it would clearly be difficult to maintain that unintelligible or ambiguous terms were *not* unfair if they had some potential for detriment to the consumer."[39] It is, moreover, linked by the preamble to the Directive to the requirement that the consumer should actually be given an opportunity to examine all the terms before concluding the contract, a requirement which the Directive ties to the fairness of terms.[40] Nevertheless, the requirement in regulation 7 is distinct from these other aspects of the Regulations in that it focusses on the form of drafting of the terms, rather than either their intended legal effect or their accessibility.

The implications of this requirement for the drafting of English consumer contracts are fundamental. The general style of traditional English contractual drafting echoes the general style of English legislative drafting: it is precise, detailed and elaborate, consisting of long clauses (sometimes without punctuation), providing many definitions of the terms or expressions which they use and attempting to leave as little as possible to chance. In its defence, these characteristics may be argued to allow the avoidance of disputes and, therefore, of litigation, but this assumes a degree of understanding of the complexities of the terminology used and its attendant legal implications which is absent in all but the most sophisticated of commercial parties: to a consumer of average intelligence it is incomprehensible. Clearly, there is a need for a sea-change in drafting style if businesses who deal with consumers are not going to fall foul of regulation 7.

In this respect, the work of the Office of Fair Trading in the relatively short time since the 1994 Regulations came into force may indicate the virtues towards which the drafter of a consumer contract should strive.[41] Its starting point has been that the contracts should normally be comprehensible by the consumer without recourse to legal advice.[42] As a result of this, the contract should avoid legal jargon (such as, for example, "representation", "warranty", "consequential

---

[39] O.F.T., *Unfair Contract Terms*, Bulletin No. 2 (September 1996), p. 8.

[40] It does so by giving as an example of a potentially unfair term in the Annex to the Directive (which appears as Schedule 2 to the 1999 Regulations) a term which "irrevocably binding the consumer to terms with which he had no real opportunity of becoming acquainted before the conclusion of the contract:" see *ante*, § 15–041.

[41] See esp. the essay in O.F.T., *Unfair Contract Terms*, Bulletin No. 2 (September 1996), p. 8 *et seq.*

[42] According to the O.F.T., the standard normally to be used is that of an average consumer (see *post*, § 15–075). Perhaps though in certain sectors, a higher degree of sophistication may be expected of a consumer (*e.g.* in relation to a contract for certain types of financial service), but conversely, in other sectors a lower degree of sophistication should be expected. Moreover, it should not be universally assumed that English should be the only language in which the contract should be expressed: for if a particular business targets consumers whose first language is known by it not to be English, to be intelligible a translation of the contract should be appended in that first language.

damages", *"force majeure"*), express itself in direct and ordinary language, notably by using the first and second person rather than by naming and defining the parties to the contract and minimise the number of cross-references. Headings in the contract are helpful, and the size of the print should be large enough to be legible without difficulty.

(ii) *The Effects of Failure to Comply with the Requirement of Plain and Intelligible Language*

Construction *contra proferentem*. Regulation 7 of the 1999 Regulations   **15–070** refers only to one of the effects of a failure in a term to fulfill the requirement of use of plain and intelligible language: that where there is as a result doubt as to its meaning it shall be interpreted in a way most favourable to the consumer. This effect does not seem to add much to the existing position at common law, which has long recognised a rule of construction that an ambiguous written instrument shall be construed more strongly against the person who made it: construction is *contra proferentem*.[43]

Other possible effects. However, there are three other possible consequences   **15–071** of failure of this formal requirement. First, failure of a "core term" to comply with this requirement removes its immunity from challenge on the ground of failure to fulfill the requirement of fairness contained in regulation 5 of the 1999 Regulations.[44] Secondly, although this is not expressly stated in the Regulations, a failure to be intelligible is likely to constitute an important factor in the wider assessment of the fairness of a term, for an unintelligible term does not allow a consumer a "real opportunity of becoming acquainted" with its effect, even if the effect which the court holds it possesses is one most favourable to the consumer. As has been seen, the Regulations do assume that the reality of a consumer's opportunity to get acquainted with a term may be relevant to the issue of the term's fairness[45]: in this way, unintelligibility may form an element within unfairness. Thirdly, and related to this, the Director General of Fair Trading has interpreted his role in policing unfair terms which is imposed on him by the Regulations as including a concern with their formal as well as their substantive fairness,[46] this being justified on terms of the Directive rather than the Regulations themselves.[47]

---

[43] See *ante*, §§ 12–081 *et seq.*
[44] See *ante*, §§ 15–025, 15–033.
[45] *cf. ante*, § 15–038.
[46] O.F.T., *Unfair Contract Terms*, Bulletin No. 2 (September, 1996), p. 9.
[47] Art. 5 (2) of the Directive provides that " the rule on interpretation [*contra proferentem*] shall not apply in the context of the procedures laid down in Article 7(2)." Art. 7(2) imposes on Member States the duty to provide for action to be taken by "persons or organisations, having a legitimate interest under national law in protecting consumers " to prevent the continued use of "unfair terms." The U.K. implemented art. 7 by enacting reg. 8 of the 1994 Regulations, thereby designating the Director General of Fair Trading as the appropriate person for this purpose (though other persons have been added by the 1999 Regulations, regs 10–13, Sched. 1). While Art. 7 refers expressly only to "unfair terms", Art. 5(2)'s exclusion of one aspect of its application under Art. 7 assumes that it will otherwise figure in the role accorded to persons by Member States under Art. 7. In sum, a proper reading of the Directive requires that reg. 8 of the 1994 Regulations be interpreted as imposing on the Director General of Fair Trading duties and powers in respect of terms which fail the plain and intelligible test as much as the fairness test.

(e) *Choice of Law Clauses*

15–072   **Choice of law clauses ineffective.** It is to be noted that, in keeping with the Unfair Contract Terms Act 1977 though subtly differently,[48] the Regulations contain a provision aimed at preventing the avoidance of their provisions by an express choice of law. Regulation 9 of the 1999 Regulations provides that:

> "These Regulations shall apply notwithstanding any contract term which applies or purports to apply the law of a non-Member State, if the contract has a close connection with the territory of the Member States."[48a]

While this provision clearly disallows an express choice of law to avoid the application of the Regulations where the law chosen belongs to a non-Member State, it allows the choice of the law of a Member State, relying in this respect on the effect of the Directive to ensure a minimum protection for consumers throughout the European Union.[49]

(f) *The Prevention of Unfair Terms*

15–073   **Introduction.** The Directive of 1993 required Member States to:

> "ensure that, in the interests of consumers and of competitors, adequate and effective means exist to prevent the continued use of unfair terms in contracts concluded with consumers by sellers or suppliers"

and further provided that these

> "means . . . shall include provisions whereby persons or organizations, having a legitimate interest under national law in protecting consumers, may take action according to the national law concerned before the courts or before the competent administrative bodies for a decision as to whether contractual terms drawn up for general use are unfair, so that they can apply appropriate and effective means to prevent the continued use of such terms."[49a]

These requirements were implemented (or purportedly implemented) into English law by the 1994 Regulations by imposing duties and granting powers in relation to the policing of terms which fail the requirements of fairness or of plainness and intelligibility to the Director General of Fair Trading.[50] While the 1999 Regulations retained this role for the Director General of Fair Trading, they also created similar duties and powers in a number of other bodies ("qualifying bodies"), entrusted with "watch-dog" roles for particular commercial sectors, but one of which—the Consumers' Association—is a private body with a very general concern with the protection of the interests of consumers. One effect of the creation of these powers in other bodies may be to reduce somewhat the role of the Director General of Fair Trading, as other more specialised agencies take

---

[48] s.27.

[48a] 1994 Regulations, reg. 7.

[49] *cf.* the provisions governing express choice of law in consumer contracts in the Rome Convention, Art. 5(2), *post*, § 31–088.

[49a] Dir. art. 7 (1) & (2).

[50] 1994 Regulations, reg. 8. *cf. ante*, § 15–071, n. 47 on the legal basis of the powers in relation to written terms which fail the requirement of plainness and intelligibility.

on the task. A second effect in the extension of the range of persons who may apply for injunctions is likely to be that more proceedings may be brought, as they may not all share the educative and negotiating strategy which the Director has adopted in the exercise of his powers.

The role of the Director General of Fair Trading. Under the 1999 Regulations the Director General of Fair Trading has a duty to consider any complaint made to him that any contract term drawn up for general use is unfair, unless the complaint appears to him to be frivolous or vexatious or unless a "qualifying body" has notified him that it will consider the complaint.[51] The Director may apply for an injunction against any person appearing to him to be using or recommending use of an unfair term drawn up for general use in contracts concluded with consumers,[52] the decision whether or not to do so being subject to a requirement of giving reasons where it has resulted from a complaint.[53] Furthermore, the 1999 Regulations permit the Director to take into account in reaching his decision as to the appropriateness of bringing proceedings any undertaking given to him by or on behalf of any person as to the continued use of such a term in contracts concluded with consumers.[54] The 1999 Regulations empower a court to which the Director has applied to grant an injunction on such terms as it thinks fit, and this may relate not only to use of a particular contract term drawn up for general use but to any similar term or term having like effect used or recommended for use by *any person.*[55] They also give to the Director new powers to obtain documents and information from any person in order to facilitate the consideration of a complaint submitted to him as to an unfair term or to ascertain whether a person has complied with an undertaking or court order as to the continued use of a term in contracts concluded with consumers.[56] Finally, the Regulations require the Director to publish details of any undertakings made to him or to a court or made by a court and empowers him to arrange for the dissemination of information and advice concerning the operation of the Regulations.[57]

15–074

Application of the fairness test by the Director. There are some differences in the way in which the Director has undertaken the assessment of a term put to him under the 1994 Regulations, these reflecting its somewhat more abstract nature than the assessment of a term between parties to a contract. First, as regards the requirement of fairness "the Director General applies the same test [as would a court in relation to a term to be enforced against a consumer], but looking forward rather than back—in other words, considering the circumstances that are generally likely to obtain, not those attending the conclusion of a particular contract."[58] Secondly, in assessing the fairness of a term from the point of view of its clarity and intelligibility, the Director considers that "in order for [article 5 of] the Directive to have its intended effect we should have regard to a term's least favourable meaning, if it is likely to be so understood by the

15–075

---

[51] 1999 Regulations, reg. 10(1). For "qualifying body" see *post*, 15–076.
[52] 1999 Regulations, reg. 12(1).
[53] 1999 Regulations, reg. 10(2).
[54] 1999 Regulations, reg. 10(3).
[55] 1999 Regulations, reg. 12(3) and (4).
[56] 1999 Regulations, reg. 13.
[57] 1999 Regulations, reg. 15(3).
[58] Edwards in O.F.T., *Unfair Contract Terms* Bulletin No. 4 (December 1997), 1 at 21. For the relevance of particular circumstances attending the conclusion of a contract, see *ante*, § 15–041.

average consumer."[59] These differences of approach are equally appropriate to the Director's role under the 1999 Regulations and it is submitted that they are likely to be reflected in future judicial assessments of terms which are the subject of an application for an injunction under the 1999 Regulations.[60]

15–076   **"Qualifying bodies."** Unlike the 1994 Regulations, the 1999 Regulations extend the power to police unfair terms in consumer contracts to a range of bodies other than the Director General of Fair Trading. Rather than providing a general definition or set of criteria by which a body may qualify for the purpose of bringing proceedings for an injunction under the 1999 Regulations, the latter simply list in Schedule 1 those bodies or classes of body which in law do so.[61] Apart from the Consumers' Association, the list includes regulators of former public utilities, such as the Director General of Gas Supply but also, at a local level, every weights and measures authority.[62] Where a qualifying body notifies the Director General of Fair Trading that it agrees to consider a complaint that any contract term drawn up for general use is unfair, it thereby comes under a duty to consider that complaint.[63] A qualifying body is empowered to bring proceedings for an injunction against any person appearing to that body to be using, or recommending for use, an unfair term drawn up for general use in contracts with consumers, subject to a condition of prior notification of the Director.[64] In deciding whether or not to apply for an injunction, a qualifying body may take into account any undertaking given to it as to the continued use of the term and bears a duty to give reasons for its decision.[65] Qualifying bodies enjoy the same powers to obtain documents and information as does the Director General of Fair Trading[66] and the courts' power to grant injunctions is the same as for proceedings brought by the Director.[67]

---

[59] O.F.T., *Unfair Contract Terms*, Bulletin No. 2 (September 1996), p. 9. On the legal justification for the role of the Director General of Fair Trading in respect of terms which fail the "plain, intelligible" requirement, see *ante*, § 15–072, n. 47.

[60] 1999 Regulations, reg. 12.

[61] 1999 Regulations, reg. 1 "qualifying body."

[62] The full list is as follows: the Data Protection Registrar; the Director General of Electricity Supply; the Director General of Gas Supply; the Director General of Electricity Supply, Northern Ireland; the Director General of Gas Supply, Northern Ireland; the Director General of Telecommunications; the Director General of Water Services; the Rail Regulator; every weights and measures authority in Great Britain; the Department of Economic Development in Northern Ireland; the Consumers' Association.

[63] 1999 Regulations, reg. 11(1).

[64] 1999 Regulations, reg. 12(2).

[65] 1999 Regulations, regs 10(2) & (3) and 11(2).

[66] 1999 Regulations, reg. 13(5).

[67] 1999 Regulations, reg. 12(3).

ARBITRATION CLAUSES[1]

Introductory. References to arbitration are of two main kinds, conventional **16–001** and statutory. In the first, the parties agree to refer their present or future disputes to a tribunal of their own choosing, instead of to a court. In the second, such reference is imposed upon them by the terms of a particular statute.[2] This chapter is concerned only with the first kind of arbitration, and in particular with the validity and scope of arbitration agreements, the enforcement of such agreements by the court's power to stay an action brought in breach thereof, the appointment and removal of arbitrators, the conduct of the arbitral proceedings, the extent to which the court can assist the arbitral process, the arbitral award, the powers of the court in relation to the award and the enforcement of the award. These matters are for the most part regulated by statute.

1. Statutory Regulation

Arbitration Act 1996. The current principal statute is the Arbitration Act **16–002** 1996. This Act reproduced, with very few changes, the provisions of a draft Bill formulated by a Departmental Advisory Committee on International Commercial Arbitration Law appointed by the Secretary of State for Trade and Industry and chaired by Saville L.J. The Committee produced a detailed Report on the Bill ("the DAC Report")[3] and this will no doubt be of assistance in construing the provisions of the Act. To a limited extent the Act restated, in different language,

---

[1] For a more detailed account of arbitration, and practice and procedure, the reader should consult: Merkin, *Arbitration Act 1996—An Annotated Guide* (1996); *Russell on Arbitration* (21st ed.) (1997); Rutherford and Sims, *Arbitration Act 1996: A Practical Guide* (1996); Harris, Planterose and Tecks, *Arbitration Act 1996* (1996). Mustill and Boyd, *Commercial Arbitration* (2nd ed.) (1989); Bernstein, Tackaberry and Marriott, *Handbook of Arbitration Practice* (3rd ed.), (1998).

[2] See Arbitration Act 1996, ss.94–98. The County Courts Act 1984, s.64, enabled a county court in such cases as might be prescribed, to order any proceedings to be referred to arbitration. By s.92 of the 1996 Act, nothing in Part I of that Act applies to such county court arbitration. The "small claims track" has now replaced small claims arbitration: CPR, Part 27.

[3] February 1996. See also the 1997 Supplementary Report (January 1997).

the previous legislation on arbitration as set out in the Arbitration Acts 1950, 1975 and 1979, whilst at the same time codifying principles established by case law. But, more importantly, it introduced a number of changes designed to clarify and improve the arbitral process. Its provisions reflect as far as possible those of the United Nations Commission on International Trade Law (UNCITRAL) Model Law on International Commercial Arbitration.[4]

16–003   The Act is unusual in that it sets out, in section 1, certain general principles on which Part I of the Act—which contains its main substantive provisions—is stated to be founded and in accordance with which it is to be construed. These are that

> "(a) the object of arbitration is to obtain the fair resolution of disputes by an impartial tribunal without unnecessary delay or expense;
> (b) the parties should be free to agree how their disputes are resolved, subject only to such safeguards as are necessary in the public interest;
> (c) in matters governed by [Part I] the court should not intervene except as provided in this Part".

Following these general principles, the Act allows considerable flexibility in the way arbitrations are conducted, recognises party autonomy and limits the role of the courts to supporting the arbitral process and intervening only in cases where there is, or is likely to be, a denial of justice. Certain provisions of Part I are mandatory[5] and have effect notwithstanding any agreement to the contrary. But, for the most part, the provisions of Part I are not mandatory: they permit the parties to make their own arrangements by written agreement but provide rules which apply in the absence of such agreement.

16–004   **Commencement.** The Act was brought into force (except for sections 85 to 87) on January 31, 1997,[6] and the provisions of Part I apply to arbitral proceedings commenced on or after that date under an arbitration agreement whenever made. They do not apply to arbitral proceedings commenced before that date,[7] but they do apply to arbitration applications made on or after that date (except those relating to arbitration proceedings commenced before that date).[8]

16–005   Sections 85 to 87 of the Act,[9] which make special provision in relation to domestic arbitration agreements, are unlikely to be brought into force, since there appears to be little support for the maintenance of a distinction between international and domestic agreements and it is arguable that to draw such a distinction is contrary to Article 6 of the Treaty of Rome.[10] Indeed, these sections are likely to be repealed in the not too distant future by an order made under section 88(1).

---

[4] See Hacking (1997) 63 Arbitration 291.

[5] s.4(1) and Sched.1. The sections are: 9–13, 24, 26(1), 28, 29, 31–33, 37(2), 40, 43, 56, 60, 66–68, 70–75.

[6] Arbitration Act 1996 (Commencement No. 1) Order 1996, S.I. 1996 No. 3146.

[7] s.84(1) and art. 4 and Sched. 2(2)(a) to the Commencement No. 1 Order, *supra* see *Great Ormond Street Hospital NHS Trust v. Secretary of State for Health* [1998] C.L.Y. 250.

[8] Art. 4 and Sched. 2 to the Commencement No. 1 Order, *supra*. For applications to the High Court to which the old law applies, see RSC Ord. 73, Part II.

[9] DAC Report, paras. 317–331; Supplementary Report, §§ 47–49.

[10] *Philip Alexander Securities & Futures Ltd v. Bamberger, The Times,* July 22, 1996, CA.

An entirely new RSC Order 73 was also brought into force on January 31, **16–006** 1997.[11] Although the Commercial Court continued to have primary responsibility for the administration and monitoring of the supervisory jurisdiction of the court over arbitrations, provision was made for the allocation of jurisdiction between the High Court and county courts.[12]

Scope of application of the Act: seat of arbitration in England.[13] Section **16–007** 2(1) sets out the basic rule which governs the application of Part I of the Act: it applies where the seat of the arbitration is in England.[14] The "seat of the arbitration" means "the juridical seat of the arbitration which is designated

(a) by the parties to the arbitration agreement, or

(b) by any arbitral or other institution or person vested by the parties with powers in that regard, or

(c) by the arbitral tribunal if so authorised by the parties,

or which, in the absence of any such designation, has been determined having regard to the parties' agreement and all the relevant circumstances."[15] The "seat" is not necessarily the *place* where the arbitration is conducted, but usually the seat of the arbitration and that place will coincide.

Applicants' arbitrations not seated in England. This basic rule is, however, **16–008** subject to a number of exceptions. The effect of these is to enable the English courts to recognise and enforce foreign arbitration agreements and awards and to support, in appropriate cases, foreign arbitral proceedings.[16] First, the provisions relating to a stay of legal proceedings (sections 9 to 11) and to the enforcement of arbitral awards (section 66) apply even if the seat of the arbitration is outside England or no seat has been designated or determined.[17] Secondly, the powers conferred by sections 43 (securing the attendance of witnesses) and section 44 (court powers exercisable in support of arbitral proceedings) likewise apply even if the seat of the arbitration is outside England or no seat has been designated or determined, but the court may refuse to exercise the power if in its opinion the fact that the seat of the arbitration is or is likely to be elsewhere makes it inappropriate to do so.[18] Thirdly, the court may exercise any other power conferred on it by Part I of the Act for the purpose of supporting the arbitral process where no seat of arbitration has been designated or determined and by reason of a connection with England it is satisfied that it is appropriate to do so.[19] Fourthly, the provisions of section 7 (separability of the arbitration agreement) and section 8 (death of a party) apply where the law applicable to the arbitration

---

[11] S.I. 1996 No. 3219 (L.18) rule 6; *Practice Note (Arbitration: New Procedure)* [1997] 1 W.L.R. 391. See now CPR, Part 49.

[12] High Court and County Courts (Allocation of Arbitration Proceedings) Order 1996, S.I. 1996 No. 3215 (L.16), made under s.105 of the 1996 Act, RSC Ord. 73, r. 5; CCR, Ord. 48C, r. 16.

[13] The Act extends to England and Wales but not, in general, to Scotland: s.108.

[14] References in this chapter to England include Wales and Northern ireland.

[15] s.3. See DAC Report, §§ 26, 27; *Sumitomo Heavy Industries v. Oil and Natural Gas Commission* [1994] 1 Lloyd's Rep. 45.

[16] See Blackaby (1997) 3 *Arbitration International* 431.

[17] s.2(2).

[18] s.2(3).

[19] s.2(4).

agreement is the law of England even if the seat of the arbitration is elsewhere or has not been designated or determined.[20] Otherwise it is generally irrelevant that the law applicable to the contract out of which the dispute has arisen is a foreign law.[21]

16–009   **Choice of foreign law.** Nevertheless, the Act does not purport to set out a complete regime concerning all the conflict of laws issues that may arise. In particular, even if the seat of the arbitration is in England, the parties may choose a foreign law to govern any matter provided for in a non-mandatory provision of Part I, such as, for example, the arbitration procedure, and effect must then be given to their choice.[22]

16–010   **Prior legislation.** The previous principal statute was the Arbitration Act 1950 (as amended). Part I of that Act was repealed by the 1996 Act,[23] but Part II, which deals with the enforcement of certain foreign awards and in particular with those to which the Geneva Protocol (1923) applies, remains unrepealed.[24]

16–011   The Arbitration Act 1975, which gave effect in the United Kingdom to the New York Convention on the Recognition and Enforcement of Foreign Arbitral Awards (1958), and the Arbitration Act 1979, which abolished the much-criticised "case stated" procedure, established a new procedure for judicial review of an award and made other amendments to the 1950 Act, were entirely repealed by the 1996 Act.[25] Their provisions were incorporated, though not without changes, into the 1996 Act.

16–012   The 1996 Act also repealed[26] and reproduced[27] the provisions of the 1950 Act[28] and of the Administration of Justice Act 1970[29] which allowed for the appointment of a judge of the Commercial Court or an official referee as sole arbitrator or umpire by or by virtue of an arbitration agreement.

16–013   **Consumer arbitration agreements.** It may be detrimental to the interests of consumers to require them, by contract, to submit disputes to arbitration rather than to have resort to legal proceedings, in particular because of the increased expense involved. The Consumer Arbitration Agreements Act 1988 extended to consumers the right, in certain circumstances, not to be compelled to take a dispute to arbitration. This Act was repealed by the 1996 Act.[30] But the Unfair Terms in Consumer Contracts Regulations 1994 (the scope and effect of which have been discussed in an earlier chapter of this book)[31] include in the "grey list" of the terms that may be regarded as unfair a term which has the object or effect of "excluding or hindering the consumer's right to take legal action or exercise

---

[20] s.2(5).
[21] s.4(4).
[22] s.4(5).
[23] s.107(2) and Sched. 4.
[24] s.99. Its effect has been largely superseded by the New York Convention. See *post*, § 16–149.
[25] s.107(2) and Sched. 4.
[26] *ibid.*
[27] s.93 and Sched. 2.
[28] s.11, as substituted by s.99 of the Courts and Legal Services Act 1990.
[29] s.4 and Sched. 3.
[30] s.107(2) and Sched. 4.
[31] S.I. 1994 No. 3159. See *ante*, Chap. 15.

any other legal remedy, particularly by requiring the consumer to take disputes exclusively to arbitration not covered by legal provisions".[32] Moreover, by section 89 of the 1996 Act, sections 90 and 91 extend the application of the Regulations in relation to a term which constitutes an arbitration agreement. Section 90 provides that the Regulations apply where the consumer is a legal person (for example, a company) as they apply where the consumer is a natural person. And section 91 provides that a term which constitutes an arbitration agreement is unfair for the purposes of the Regulations so far as it relates to a claim for a pecuniary remedy which does not exceed the amount specified by order for the purposes of this section. An amount of £3,000 has been so specified.[33] The result is that an arbitration agreement which is not individually negotiated is not binding on the consumer if it requires him to submit to arbitration a claim which does not exceed £3,000. It is unlikely that section 91 was intended to extend to a term which provides for "voluntary" arbitration, that is to say, a term by which it is agreed that the consumer shall have the option, but not the obligation, to refer such a claim to arbitration. But the drafting of sections 89 to 91 leaves it unclear whether or not such a provision, or the consequent exercise by the consumer of his option to submit the dispute to arbitration, falls outside section 91.

2. THE ARBITRATION AGREEMENT

Definition of "arbitration agreement". The Arbitration Act 1996 defines an **16–014** arbitration agreement to mean "an agreement to submit to arbitration present or future disputes (whether they are contractual or not)"[34] and "dispute" is defined to include any difference.[35] It is clear, therefore, that a claim in tort or a dispute which involves a charge of fraud may be the subject-matter of an arbitration agreement, although the Act expressly preserves any rule of law as to matters which are "not capable of settlement by arbitration".[36] The agreement need be in no particular form, and an arbitration clause even in a most summary form, *e.g.* "arbitration to be settled in London,"[37] "& arbitration . . . in London,"[38] "arbitration, if any, by ICC rules in London"[39] or "suitable arbitration clause"[40] may

---

[32] Sched. 3, para. 1(q).

[33] Unfair Arbitration Agreements (Specified Amount) Order 1996, S.I. 1996 No. 3211. For Northern Ireland, see S.R. 1996 No. 598.

[34] s.6(1).

[35] s.82(1).

[36] s.81(1)(a). In particular, the question has arisen in the United States and elsewhere as to the arbitrability of anti-trust disputes: see *Mitsubishi Motors Corpn. v. Soler Chrysler-Plymouth* 473 U.S. 614 (1985); *Att.-Gen. of New Zealand v. Mobil Oil New Zealand Ltd* [1989] 2 N.Z.L.R. 649; *IBM Australia Ltd v. National Distribution Services Pty. Ltd* (1991) 100 A.L.R. 361 (Australia); Carbonneau (1986) 2 *Arbitration International* 116; Lowenfeld (1986) 2 *Arbitration International* 178; Kühn (1987) 3 *Arbitration International* 226; Park (1989) 63 Tulane L.R. 648; Dalhuisen (1995) 111 *Arbitration International* 151. See also *O'Callaghan v. Coral Racing Ltd* [1998] C.L.Y. 854 (gaming contract).

[37] *Tritonia Shipping inc. v. South Nelson Products Corpn.* [1966] 1 Lloyd's Rep. 114. See also *Naviera Amazonica Peruara v. Compañiá Internacional de Seguros de Peru* [1988] 1 Lloyd's Rep. 116 ("arbitration under the conditions and laws of London"—seat of arbitration London).

[38] *Transamerican Ocean Contractors Inc. v. Transchemical Rotterdam B.V.* [1978] 1 Lloyd's Rep. 238.

[39] *Mangistaumunaigaz Oil Production Association v. United World Trade Inc.* [1995] 1 Lloyd's Rep. 617.

[40] *Hobbs Padgett & Co. (Reinsurance) Ltd v. Kirkland Ltd* [1969] 2 Lloyd's Rep. 547.

be sufficient to amount to an arbitration agreement. There can be a valid arbitration agreement even though the agreement confers on one party alone the right to refer a matter to arbitration, and does not give mutual rights of reference.[41] A clause which provides that "either party may elect to have the dispute referred to arbitration" becomes a binding arbitration agreement once a valid election is made.[42]

16–015   **Agreements to be in writing.** The provisions of Part I of the 1996 Act apply only where the arbitration agreement is in writing.[43] But the concept of an agreement in writing is widely defined.[44] There is an agreement in writing—

    (a) if the agreement is made in writing (whether or not it is signed by the parties),

    (b) if the agreement is made by the exchange of communications in writing, or

    (c) if the agreement is evidenced in writing.[45]

An oral agreement made by reference to terms which are in writing, for example, to a standard form of salvage agreement such as Lloyd's Open Form which contains an arbitration clause, is an agreement "made in writing"[46]; and an oral agreement is "evidenced in writing" if it is recorded by one of the parties to the agreement, or by a third party, with the authority of the parties to the agreement.[47] Further, if in an exchange of written submissions in arbitral or legal proceedings the existence of an oral agreement is alleged by one party against another party and not denied by the latter in his response, this constitutes as between those parties an agreement in writing to the effect alleged.[48] In view of rapidly evolving means of recording, "writing" includes recording by any means.[49]

16–016   Any other agreement between the parties as to any matter provided for in Part I of the 1996 Act is likewise effective only if in writing.[50] Thus any derogation by agreement from the non-mandatory provisions of Part I must be in writing, subject to the broad definition mentioned above.

16–017   **Oral agreements.** An oral agreement to arbitrate is not invalid, since the common law recognises such an agreement and it is expressly saved by section 81(1)(b). But the provisions of Part I do not then apply, including, for example, the right to require a stay of legal proceedings[51] and the right to summary enforcement of the award.[52]

---

[41] *Pittalis v. Sherefettin* [1986] Q.B. 868; *RGE (Group Services) Ltd v. Cleveland Offshore Ltd* (1986) 11 Const. L.R. 77.
[42] *Westfal-Larsen & Co. A/S v. Ikerigi Compañiá Naviera SA* [1983] 1 Lloyd's Rep. 424.
[43] s.5(1).
[44] DAC Report, §§ 31–40.
[45] s.5(2).
[46] s.5(3).
[47] s.5(4).
[48] s.5(5).
[49] s.5(6).
[50] s.5(1).
[51] s.9.
[52] s.66.

Incorporation by reference. An arbitration clause may be incorporated in a **16–018** contract by reference, *e.g.* to the standard terms of a trade association, or by course of dealing between the parties.[53] If this is disputed, the final decision rests with the court, since it goes to the substantive jurisdiction of the arbitral tribunal. By section 6(2) of the 1996 Act, the reference in an agreement to a written form of arbitration clause or to a document containing an arbitration clause constitutes an arbitration agreement if the reference is such as to make that clause part of the agreement. This sub-section does not, however, purport to decide what is required for the effective incorporation of an arbitration clause by reference, *i.e.* whether there must be a specific reference to the arbitration clause or whether a reference to a document containing an arbitration clause will suffice.[54] That is left to be decided by the common law. It is a question of construction in each case whether words in a bill of lading which incorporate some or all of the terms of a charter-party into the bill will have the effect of incorporating into the bill an arbitration clause contained in the charter-party.[55] Where the parties enter into an agreement subsequent to an agreement which contains an arbitration clause, the clause may be incorporated into the subsequent agreement only if that agreement is not a separate and independent contract.[56]

Separability of arbitration agreement.[57] Where parties enter into an ad hoc **16–019** agreement to refer to arbitration an existing or future dispute between them relating to an alleged contract, it is clear that the arbitration agreement is an agreement distinct and separate from the contract in question. But an arbitration clause is often embedded in the substantive contract to which it relates. Section

---

[53] See *ante*, § 12–011.

[54] DAC Report, § 42; *Trygg Hansa Insurance Co. Ltd v. Equitas Ltd* [1998] 2 Lloyd's Rep. 439, 446.

[55] The principles to be derived from previous cases were summarised by Brandon J. at first instance in *The Annefield* [1971] P. 168. See *Hamilton & Co. v. Mackie & Sons* (1889) 5 T.L.R. 677; *T. W. Thomas & Co. Ltd v. Portsea SS. Co. Ltd* [1912] A.C. 1; *The Njegos* [1936] P. 90; *The Merak* [1965] P. 223; *The Phonizien* [1966] 1 Lloyd's Rep. 150; *The Annefield, supra*; *The Rena K* [1978] 1 Lloyd's Rep. 545, 550, [1979] Q.B. 377; *Astro Valiente Compania Naviera SA v. Govt. of Pakistan (No. 2)* [1982] 1 W.L.R. 1096; *The Sevonia Team* [1983] 2 Lloyd's Rep. 640; *Miramar Maritime Corpn. v. Holborn Oil Trading Ltd* [1984] A.C. 676; *Skips A/S Nordheim v. Syrian Petroleum Co. Ltd* [1984] Q.B. 599; *Navigazione Alta Italia SpA v. Svenska Petroleum AB* [1988] 1 Lloyd's Rep. 452; *Federal Bulk Carriers Inc. v. C. Itoh & Co. Ltd* [1989] 1 Lloyd's Rep. 103; *Partenreederei m/s Heidberge and Vega Reederei Friedrich Dauber v. Grosvenor Grain and Feed Co.* [1994] 2 Lloyd's Rep. 287; *Daval Aciers d'Usinor et de Sacilor v. Armare SRL* [1996] 1 Lloyd's Rep. 1. See also (in other contexts) *Pine Top Insurance Co. Ltd v. Unione Italiana Anglo Saxon Reinsurance Co. Ltd* [1987] 1 Lloyd's Rep. 476; *Aughton v. MF Kent Services* (1991) 57 B.L.R. 1; *Barrett v. Henry Boot Management Ltd* [1995] C.I.L.L. 1026; *Co-operative Wholesale Socy. v. Saunders and Taylor* [1995] 11 Const. L.J. 118; *OK Petroleum AB v. Vitol Energy SA* [1995] 2 Lloyd's Rep. 160; *Ceval Alimentos v. Agrimpex Trading Co. Ltd* [1996] 2 Lloyd's Rep. 319; *Extrudakerb (Maltby Engineering) Ltd v. Whitemountain Quarries Ltd, The Times*, July 10, 1996; *Excess Insurance Co. Ltd v. Mander* [1997] 2 Lloyd's Rep. 119; *Roche Products Ltd v. Freeman Process Systems Ltd* (1997) 80 Build. L.R. 802; *Trygg Hansa Insurance Co. Ltd v. Equitas Ltd* [1998] 2 Lloyd's Rep. 439 and see the cases cited in n. 56, *infra*.

[56] *Taylor v. Warden Insurance Co. Ltd* (1933) 45 Ll.L.R. 218; *Kianta Osakeytio v. Britain & Overseas Trading Co. Ltd* [1954] 1 Lloyd's Rep. 247; *Union of India v. E.B. Aaby's Rederi A/S* [1975] A.C. 797; *Faghirzadeh v. Rudolf Wolff (S.A.) Pty. Ltd* [1977] 1 Lloyd's Rep. 630; *Fletamentos Maritimos S.A. v. Effjohn International B.V.* [1996] 2 Lloyd's Rep. 304.

[57] See Schwebel, *International Arbitration: Three Salient Problems* (1987), pp. 1–60; Rogers and Launders (1994) 10 *Arbitration International* 77. Under the Rome Convention (*post*, § 31–016) arbitration agreements are excluded from the scope of the Convention, although the contract in which the agreement is contained is subject to the Convention: see *post*, § 16–037, n. 18.

7 of the 1996 Act maintains the principle established by the common law[58] that, unless otherwise agreed, the arbitration agreement is an agreement distinct from the contract of which it forms part and that its validity or existence or effectiveness is not affected by the fact that that contract is invalid, or did not come into existence or has become ineffective. Two consequences follow. First, since the arbitration clause is separable from the contract in which it is contained, then "the logical question is not whether the issue goes to the validity of the contract but whether it goes to the validity of the arbitration clause".[59] Thus the clause may be valid and binding even if, for example, the contract is void, voidable for fraud or misrepresentation, or if it has been discharged by breach, frustration or supervening illegality. Of course, there will be cases in which a claim that no contract came into existence between the parties necessarily entails a denial that there was any agreement to arbitrate. Cases of *non est factum* and mistake as to the person provide instances. But the initial invalidity or illegality of the contract will not necessarily involve these consequences unless it is such as directly to impeach the arbitration agreement itself.[60] Secondly, if the arbitration agreement is valid and binding and is sufficiently wide in its terms,[61] issues relating to the validity, existence or effectiveness of the contract are within the substantive jurisdiction of the arbitral tribunal and it can decide on those issues. So, for example, it can decide whether an initially valid but voidable contract has been or ought to be rescinded,[62] whether an allegedly illegal contract is unenforceable by one or both of the parties,[63] whether a breach of the contract by one party has brought the contract to an end,[64] whether the contract has been frustrated and the consequences of frustration,[65] and whether one party is entitled to terminate or invalidate the contract by virtue of a term contained in it.[66] An appropriately worded arbitration clause may also be held to confer upon the tribunal jurisdiction to rectify the contract in which the clause is contained.[67]

---

[58] *Harbour Assurance Co. (U.K.) Ltd v. Kansa General International Insurance Co. Ltd* [1993] Q.B. 701. See DAC Report, §§ 43–47.

[59] *Harbour Assurance Co. (U.K.) Ltd v. Kansa General International Insurance Co. Ltd, supra,* at 724.

[60] *ibid.* at 712, 715, 724; *Westacre Investments Inc. v. Jugo-import-SPDR Holding Co. Ltd* [1998] 3 W.L.R. 770; *FAI General Insurance Ltd v. Ocean Marine Mutual Protection and Indemnity Assn* (No. 2) [1998] Lloyd's Rep. IR 24. *cf., Smith, Coney & Barrett v. Becker, Gray & Co.* [1916] 2 Ch. 86, 92 (war); *O'Callaghan v. Coral Racing Ltd* [1998] C.L.Y. 854 (gaming contract); *Soleimany v. Soleimany* [1998] 3 W.L.R. 811 (public policy).

[61] See *post,* § 16–021.

[62] *Mackender v. Feldia AG* [1967] 2 Q.B. 590; *Ashville Investments Ltd v. Elmer Contractors Ltd* [1989] 1 Q.B. 488.

[63] *Harbour Assurance Co. (U.K.) Ltd v. Kansa General International Insurance Co. Ltd, supra*; *Westacre Investments Inc. v. Jugo-import-SDPR Holding Co. Ltd, supra,* at 129. See also *Prodexport State Company for Foreign Trade v. E.D. & F. Man Ltd* [1973] Q.B. 389 (supervening illegality).

[64] *Heyman v. Darwins Ltd* [1942] A.C. 356.

[65] *Heyman v. Darwins Ltd, supra,* at 366, 383, 400–401; *Kruse v. Questier & Co. Ltd* [1953] 1 Q.B. 669; *Government of Gibraltar v. Kenney* [1956] 2 Q.B. 410.

[66] *Stebbing v. Liverpool and London Globe Insurance Co. Ltd* [1917] 2 K.B. 433; *Woodall v. Pearl Assurance* [1919] 1 K.B. 593; *Freshwater v. Western Australian Assurance Co.* [1933] 1 K.B. 515; *Paul Smith Ltd v. H & S. International Holding Inc.* [1991] 2 Lloyd's Rep. 127. See also *De la Garde v. Workshop & Co.* [1928] Ch. 17 (condition precedent).

[67] *Ashville Investments Ltd v. Elmer Contractors Ltd* [1989] Q.B. 488; *Overseas Union Insurance Co. Ltd v. AA Mutual Insurance Co. Ltd* [1988] 2 Lloyd's Rep. 63; *Ethiopian Oil Seeds & Pulses Export Corpn. v. Rio del Mar Foods Inc.* [1990] 1 Lloyd's Rep. 86. Contrast *Printing Machinery Co. Ltd v. Linotype and Machinery Ltd* [1912] 1 Ch. 566; *Crane v. Hegeman-Harris Co. Inc.* [1939] 3 All E.R. 68.

Section 7 applies where the law applicable to the arbitration agreement is the   **16–020**
law of England even if the seat of the arbitration is elsewhere or has not been
designated or determined.[68]

Scope of the arbitration agreement. The scope of an arbitration agreement   **16–021**
is to be determined by reference to the precise wording of the agreement,
construed according to its language and in the light of the circumstances in which
it was made.[69] The words "all disputes or differences" or "all claims" are words
of wide import, but must necessarily be controlled by the subject-matter to which
they relate.[70] The word "differences" is wide enough to embrace a difference
between the parties, *e.g.* as to the price, where the contract provides for this to be
determined by mutual agreement, and the parties fail to agree.[71] There is a
"dispute" between the parties if a claim is made by one party on the other, which
is neither admitted nor disputed, but merely ignored.[72] There is also a "dispute"
even if the claim made by one party on the other is one to which there is no
arguable defence.[73] The words "in connection with" "in relation to" "in respect
of" or "with regard to" (a contract) are clearly wide in scope. A wide meaning
will also be attributed to the words "arising out of".[74] Thus even a claim for
damages in tort[75] or for general average[76] may be within an arbitration clause if
closely connected with the contract, but not a claim on a bill of exchange.[77]
Disputes arising "under" a contract may, however, be more narrowly
construed.[78]

Under a clause submitting to arbitration any dispute arising out of a contract,   **16–022**
an arbitrator has jurisdiction finally to determine the application of a trade custom

---

[68] s.2(5).

[69] *Heyman v. Darwins Ltd* [1942] A.C. 356, 366.

[70] *Re Hohenzollern Act für Locomotivbahn and the City of London Contract Corpn.* (1886) 54 L.T. 596.

[71] *F. & G. Sykes (Wessex) Ltd v. Fine Fare Ltd* [1967] 1 Lloyd's Rep. 53; *Vosper Thorneycroft Ltd v. Ministry of Defence* [1976] 1 Lloyd's Rep. 58; *Queensland Electricity Generating Board v. New Hope Collieries Pty. Ltd* [1989] 1 Lloyd's Rep. 205.

[72] *Tradax Internacional SA v. Cerrahogullari T.A.S.* [1981] 3 All E.R. 344, 350; *Ellerine Bros. (Pty.) Ltd v. Klinger* [1982] 1 W.L.R. 1375; Mann (1982) 98 L.Q.R. 530.

[73] *Halki Shipping Corpn. v. Sopex Oils Ltd* [1998] 1 W.L.R. 726.

[74] *Ethiopian Oil Seeds & Pulses Export Corpn. v. Rio del Mar Foods Inc.* [1990] 1 Lloyd's Rep. 86; *Harbour Assurance Co. (U.K.) Ltd v. Kansa General International Insurance Co. Ltd* [1993] Q.B. 701; Mustill and Boyd, *Commercial Arbitration* (2nd ed.), p. 120. Collateral or even subsequent contracts may, in certain circumstances, be covered: *Faghirzadeh v. Rudolf Wolff (SA) Pty. Ltd* [1977] 1 Lloyd's Rep. 630; *Overseas Union Insurance Ltd v. AA Mutual International Insurance Ltd* [1988] 2 Lloyd's Rep. 63. Contrast *Fillite (Runcorn) Ltd v. Aqua-Lift* (1989) 45 Build. L.R. 27 ("under").

[75] *Astro Vencedor Compañía Naviera SA of Panama v. Mabanaft GmbH* [1971] 2 Q.B. 588; *Lonrho Ltd v. Shell Petroleum Ltd, The Times,* February 1, 1978; *The Playa Larga* [1983] 2 Lloyd's Rep. 171; *Société Commerciale de Réassurance v. Eras International Ltd* [1992] 1 Lloyd's Rep. 570; *Chimimport plc v. G. D'Alesio SAS* [1994] 2 Lloyd's Rep. 366; *Abdullah M. Fahem & Co. v. Mareb Yemen Insurance Co.* [1997] 2 Lloyd's Rep. 738. Contrast *Fillite (Runcorn) Ltd v. Aqua-Lift* (1989) 45 Build. L.R. 27 ("under").

[76] *Union of India v. E.B. Aaby's Rederi A/S* [1975] A.C. 797.

[77] *Nova (Jersey) Knit Ltd v. Kammgarn Spinnerei GmbH* [1977] 1 W.L.R. 713.

[78] *Heyman v. Darwins Ltd* [1942] A.C. 356, 399 (*cf. ibid.* at 393, 394) *Government of Gibraltar v. Kenney* [1956] 2 Q.B. 410, 421; *Fillite (Runcorn) Ltd v. Aqua-Lift, supra.* But see *Union of India v. E. B. Aaby's Rederi A/S, supra,* at 814, 817; *The Playa Larga, supra,* at 183; *Société Commerciale de Reassurance v. Eras International Ltd, supra,* at 607; *Chimimport plc v. G D'Alesio SAS, supra.*

affecting the rights and obligations of the parties,[79] provided that it is not inconsistent with the contract or unreasonable.[80]

16–023 **Substantive jurisdiction for court.** Though the arbitral tribunal may (unless otherwise agreed) rule whether or not the dispute is within the scope of the arbitration agreement,[81] it cannot finally decide this issue: it goes to the substantive jurisdiction of the arbitral tribunal which, if challenged, is a matter for the court to determine.[82]

16–024 A dispute as to whether notices of appeal from an arbitrator's award to an appellate tribunal have been properly served does not arise out of the contract but out of the award and is therefore not within the scope of an arbitration clause.[83]

16–025 **Pre-conditions.** There will normally be no valid reference to arbitration if the arbitration agreement stipulates that certain facts or events shall be a pre-condition of a reference to arbitration and the pre-condition is not fulfilled.[84] Here, too, the arbitral tribunal may rule whether or not facts or events exist which found its jurisdiction,[85] but the final determination of this question rests with the court.[86] A stipulation that the parties should first strive to settle the dispute amicably, or that the dispute should, in the first place, be submitted for conciliation, is not such a pre-condition and does not create an enforceable legal obligation.[87] Where parties agreed that arbitration would be held in London before two arbitrators and an umpire in accordance with ICC rules, the fact that the ICC declined jurisdiction did not frustrate the reference.[88]

16–026 **Parties bound by arbitration agreement: minors.** A minor is bound by an arbitration agreement in a contract of apprenticeship if the contract as a whole is for his benefit.[89]

16–027 **Trustees in bankruptcy.** Where a bankrupt has become party to a contract containing an arbitration agreement before the commencement of his bankruptcy, then, if the trustee in bankruptcy adopts the contract, the arbitration agreement is enforceable by or against the trustee in relation to matters arising from or

---

[79] *Produce Brokers Co. Ltd v. Olympia Oil and Cake Co. Ltd* [1916] 1 A.C. 314.

[80] *Produce Brokers Co. Ltd v. Olympia Oil and Cake Co. Ltd* [1916] 2 K.B. 296; [1917] 1 K.B. 320, described by Scrutton L.J. at 324 as "a terrible example of the disadvantages of combining a commercial arbitration with proceedings in the courts". See *ante*, §§ 12–125—12–131, 13–018.

[81] Arbitration Act 1996, ss.30, 31.

[82] *ibid.*, ss.32, 67, 72.

[83] *Getreide-import GmbH v. Contimar SA Compañía Industrial Commercial y Maritima* [1953] 1 W.L.R. 793. Contrast *Gunter Henck v. André et Cie SA* [1970] 1 Lloyd's Rep. 235.

[84] *Smith v. Martin* [1925] 1 K.B. 745; *Mid-Glamorgan C.C. v. The Land Authority for Wales* (1990) 49 Build. L.R. 61.

[85] Arbitration Act 1996, ss.30, 31.

[86] *ibid.* ss.32, 67, 72.

[87] *Courtney & Fairbairn Ltd v. Tolaini Brothers (Hotels) Ltd* [1975] 1 W.L.R. 297; *Itex Shipping Pte Ltd v. China Ocean Shipping Co.* [1989] 2 Lloyd's Rep. 522, 525; *Paul Smith Ltd v. H. & S. International Holding Inc.* [1991] 2 Lloyd's Rep. 127, 131. But see *Channel Tunnel Group Ltd v. Balfour Beatty Construction Ltd* [1993] A.C. 334; *Halifax Financial Services Ltd v. Intuitive Systems Ltd,* (unreported, 1998) (alternative dispute resolution procedure) and ss.9(2), 12(1)(b) of the 1996 Act.

[88] *Sumitomo Heavy Industries v. Oil and Natural Gas Commission* [1994] 1 Lloyd's Rep. 45.

[89] *Slade v. Metrodent* [1953] 2 Q.B. 112.

connected with the contract.[90] Even if the trustee does not adopt the contract, the court has power, on the application either of the trustee with the consent of the creditors' committee established under section 301 of the Insolvency Act 1986, or of any other party to the arbitration agreement, to make an order that the matter be referred to arbitration.[91] A trustee in bankruptcy may, with the permission of the creditors' committee, refer any dispute to arbitration.[92]

Personal representatives. Unless otherwise agreed by the parties, an arbitration agreement is not discharged by the death of a party and may be enforced by or against the personal representatives of that party.[93] Personal representatives may submit to arbitration any debt or claim relating to the deceased's estate.[94] **16–028**

The Crown. Part I of the Arbitration Act 1996 binds the Crown.[95] **16–029**

Assignees. An assignee of a contract is bound by and may take the benefit of an arbitration clause contained therein,[96] but he cannot continue an arbitration already commenced by the assignor unless and until he gives notice of the assignment to the other party to the dispute and submits to the jurisdiction of the arbitrator.[97] **16–030**

Subrogation. A person subrogated to the rights of an assured under a policy of insurance by virtue of the Third Parties (Rights against Insurers) Act 1930 is bound by an arbitration clause contained in the policy.[98] **16–031**

Award a condition precedent to action. The parties to a contract can agree that the award of an arbitrator shall be a condition precedent to the right to bring **16–032**

---

[90] Insolvency Act 1986, s.349(2) (inserted by s.107(1) and Sched. 3, para. 46, of the Arbitration Act 1996).

[91] Insolvency Act 1986, s.349(3).

[92] Insolvency Act 1986, s.314 and Sched. 5, para. 6.

[93] Arbitration Act 1996, s.8. See also s.2(5) (conflict of laws).

[94] Trustee Act 1925, s.15.

[95] s.106.

[96] *Aspell v. Seymour* [1929] W.N. 152; *Shayler v. Woolf* [1946] 1 Ch. 320; *Rumput (Panama) SA v. Islamic Republic of Iran Shipping Lines* [1984] 2 Lloyd's Rep. 259; *Court Line Ltd v. Aktiebolaget Gotaverken* [1984] 2 Lloyd's Rep. 283, 289; *The Padre Island* [1984] 2 Lloyd's Rep. 408; *Kauko-markkinat O/Y v. "Elbe" Transport Union GmbH* [1985] 2 Lloyd's Rep. 85; *Montedipe SpA v. JTP-Ro Jugotanker* [1990] 2 Lloyd's Rep. 11, 15; *Schiffahrtsgesellschaft Detler von Appen GmbH v. Wiener Allianz Versicherungs AG* [1997] 2 Lloyd's Rep. 279. Contrast *Cottage Club Estates Ltd v. Woodside Estates Co. Ltd* [1928] 2 K.B. 463; *London Steamship Owners Mutual Insurance Association Ltd v. Bombay Trading Co. Ltd* [1990] 2 Lloyd's Rep. 21, 25; Mustill and Boyd *op. cit.* pp. 137–139. See [1992] 8 *Arbitration International* 121. An assignor under an equitable assignment, of which no notice has been given to the respondent, may still commence an arbitration: *Herkules Piling Ltd v. Tilbury Construction Ltd* (1992) 61 Build. L.R. 107.

[97] *Montedipe SpA v. JTP-Ro Jugotanker, supra*; *Baytur SA v. Finagro Holding SA* [1992] Q.B. 610.

[98] *Freshwater v, Western Australia Insurance Co. Ltd* [1933] 1 K.B. 515; *Dennehy v. Bellamy* [1938] 2 All E.R. 262; *Smits v. Pearl Assurance Co. Ltd* [1939] 1 All E.R. 95; *Digby v. General Accident Fire and Life Assurance Corpn. Ltd* [1940] 2 K.B. 226, 236; *The Padre Island* [1984] 2 Lloyd's Rep. 408, 414; *The Padre Island (No. 2)* [1987] 2 Lloyd's Rep. 529, 533; *London Steamship Owners Mutual Insurance Association Ltd v. Bombay Trading Co. Ltd* [1990] 2 Lloyd's Rep. 21, 26. See also *The Fanti and the Padre Island (No. 2)* [1990] 2 Lloyd's Rep. 191. For the position where arbitration proceedings have already commenced, see *London Steamship Owners Mutual Insurance Association v. Bombay Trading Co. Ltd, supra*.

an action on the contract.[99] Such a provision is known as a "*Scott v. Avery* clause". Its effect is that no action shall lie for breach of the contract until the matters in dispute have been submitted to arbitration,[1] unless the condition has been waived by the party relying on the clause,[2] or if his neglect or default has prevented the other party from obtaining an award.[3] However, if an application is made for a stay of legal proceedings under section 9 of the 1996 Act, and the court refuses a stay, the condition is of no effect in relation to those proceedings.[4]

16–033   Since the cause of action under such a clause does not arise until an arbitrator has made his award, it was formerly held that time under the Statutes of Limitation ran from the date of the award and not from the date of the breach.[5] But section 13(3) of the 1996 Act provides that, in determining for the purposes of the Limitation Acts when a cause of action accrued, any provision that an award is a condition precedent to the bringing of legal proceedings in respect of a matter to which an arbitration agreement relates is to be disregarded.

16–034   If an accident insurance policy contains a *Scott v. Avery* clause, and by reason of the insolvency of the insured his rights pass to the injured third party under the Third Parties (Rights against Insurers) Act 1930, the third party is bound by the clause, for he is merely subrogated by the statute to the rights of the insured.[6]

16–035   **Confidentiality.** It is an implied term of an arbitration agreement governed by English law that the parties to an arbitration must keep confidential information acquired by them in the course of the arbitration.[7] This duty extends not only to the award but also to pleadings, written submissions, proofs of witnesses as well as transcripts and notes of the evidence given in the arbitration.[8] The duty is, however, not absolute. It is subject to a number of exceptions, in particular if the other party consents to disclosure, or if disclosure is ordered by the court or if it is reasonably necessary for the protection of the legitimate interests of the arbitrating party or if it is required in the interests of justice.[9] But there may be further exceptions or qualifications since the law in this area has still to be worked out. Breach of this duty of confidentiality will be restrained by injunction unless the objecting party can be shown to be fraudulent or the claim to relief is in the nature of an abuse of process.[10]

---

[99] *Scott v. Avery* (1856) 5 H.L.C. 811.

[1] A claim for damages may, in certain circumstances, lie for breach of the clause, which claim will be a dispute arising out of the contract and subject to the arbitration clause: *Mantovani v. Carapelli SpA* [1980] 1 Lloyd's Rep. 375.

[2] *Toronto Ry. v. National British, etc. Insurance Co.* (1914) 20 Com. Cas. 1.

[3] As to this, see *Hickman & Co. v. Roberts* [1913] A.C. 229; *Neale v. Richardson* [1938] 1 All E.R. 753; *cf. Panamena Europea Navigacion Cia. Lda. v. Frederick Leyland & Co. Ltd* [1947] A.C. 428.

[4] s.9(5). See also s.10(2) (interpleader).

[5] *Board of Trade v. Cayzer, Irvine & Co.* [1927] A.C. 610.

[6] *Dennehy v. Bellamy* [1938] 2 All E.R. 262; *Socony Mobil Oil Co. Inc. v. West of England Shipowners Mutual Assurance (London) Ltd* [1984] 2 Lloyd's Rep. 408.

[7] *Ali Shipping Corpn. v. Shipyard Trogir* [1999] 1 W.L.R. 314. See also *Dolling-Baker v. Merrett* [1990] 1 W.L.R. 1205; *Hassneh Insurance Co. v. Stewart J. Mew* [1993] 2 Lloyd's Rep. 243; *London & Leeds Estates Ltd v. Paribas (No. 2)* [1995] 2 E.G. 134. Contrast *Esso Australia Resources Ltd v. Plowman* (1995) 183 C.L.R. 10 (High Court of Australia).

[8] *Ali Shipping Corpn. v. Shipyard Trogir, supra*, at 327.

[9] *ibid.* at 326.

[10] *ibid.* at 329.

3. STAY OF LEGAL PROCEEDINGS

Resort to legal proceedings. If, contrary to an agreement to refer a matter to 16–036 arbitration, one party resorts to legal proceedings in an English court in respect of that matter, the court has jurisdiction to hear the dispute.[11] The existence of the arbitration agreement, or even the fact that an arbitration is already in progress, affords no defence to the action. The appropriate course is for the other party to apply for a stay of the legal proceedings.[12] Conversely, there is no principle that requires arbitral proceedings to terminate if a party to the arbitration resorts to legal proceedings.[13] Nor does resort to legal proceedings of itself constitute a repudiation of the arbitration agreement,[14] although it might do so if he thereby unequivocally demonstrates an intention to renounce or abandon the agreement.[15] If there are concurrent or overlapping proceedings in respect of the same matter, both in arbitral and legal proceedings, the court may grant an injunction to restrain the continuance of the arbitral proceedings. But it will not necessarily do so and may allow them to continue.[16] However, in such a case, it would seem that an award in concurrent proceedings without the consent of both parties would then have no effect.[17]

Foreign proceedings. The court has power to restrain by injunction the 16–037 institution or continuance of proceedings in a foreign court which are brought in breach of an agreement to arbitrate in England.[18] The courts now appear to be more willing to grant anti-suit injunctions than heretofore,[19] but it is arguable that

---

[11] See also s.43A of the Supreme Court Act 1981, inserted by s.100 of the Courts and Legal Services Act 1990 (specific powers of arbitrator exercisable by High Court).

[12] See *post*, §§ 16–038—16–040.

[13] *Lloyd v. Wright* [1983] Q.B. 1065.

[14] *Rederi Kommanditselskaabet Merc-Scandia IV v. Couniniotis SA* [1980] 2 Lloyd's Rep. 183; *Lloyd v. Wright, supra*; *World Pride Shipping Ltd v. Daiichi Chuo Kisen Kaisha* [1984] 2 Lloyd's Rep. 489.

[15] See Mustill and Boyd, *Commercial Arbitration* (2nd ed.), p. 506.

[16] *Northern Regional H.A. v. Derek Crouch Construction Co. Ltd* [1984] Q.B. 644; *Industrie Chimiche Italia Centrale v. Alexander G. Tsavliris & Sons* [1987] 1 Lloyd's Rep. 508. See also *Lloyd v. Wright, supra. cf., University of Reading v. Miller Construction Ltd* (1995) 11 Const. L.J. 388.

[17] *Doleman & Sons v. Ossett Corpn.* [1912] 3 K.B. 257, as interpreted in *Lloyd v. Wright, supra*.

[18] *Pena Copper Mines Ltd v. Rio Tinto Co. Ltd* (1912) 105 L.T. 846; *Gorthon Invest AB v. Ford Motor Co. Ltd* [1976] 2 Lloyd's Rep. 720; *Marazura Navegacion S.A. v. Oceanus Mutual Underwriting Association* [1977] 1 Lloyd's Rep. 283; *Tracomin SA v. Sudan Oil Seeds Co. Ltd (No. 2)* [1983] 1 W.L.R. 1026; *Sokana Industries Inc. v. Freyre & Co. Inc.* [1994] 2 Lloyd's Rep. 57; *Aggeliki Charis Compania Maritima SA v. Pagnan SpA* [1995] 1 Lloyd's Rep. 877; *Schiffahrtsgesellschaft Detlev von Appen GmbH v. Voest Alpine Intertrading GmbH* [1997] 1 Lloyd's Rep. 179; *Shell International Petroleum Co. v. Coral Oil Co. Ltd* [1999] 1 Lloyd's Rep. 72. Art. 1 of Sched. 1 to the Civil Jurisdiction and Judgments Act 1982 states that the Convention on Jurisdiction and the Enforcement of Judgments in Civil and Commercial Matters (the Brussels Convention) does not apply to arbitrations. See on this point: *Marc Rich & Co. AG v. Societa Italiana Impianti pa (The Atlantic Emperor)* [1989] 1 Lloyd's Rep. 548, CA; [1992] 1 Lloyd's Rep. 342 (Eur. Ct.); *Partenreederei m/s "Heidberg" v. Grosvenor Grain and Feed Ltd* [1994] 2 Lloyd's Rep. 287; *Arab Business Consortium International Finance and Investment Co. v. Banque Franco-Tunisienne* [1996] 1 Lloyd's Rep. 485, [1997] 1 Lloyd's Rep. 288 (Lugano Convention); *Union de Remorquage et de Sauvetage SA v. Lake Avery Inc.* [1997] 1 Lloyd's Rep. 540; *Lexmar Corpn. and Steamship Mutual Underwriting Association (Bermuda) Ltd v. Nordisk Skibsrederiforening* [1997] 1 Lloyd's Rep. 289; *Toepfer International GmbH v. Société Cargill France* [1998] 1 Lloyd's Rep. 379; (1991) 7 *Arbitration International* 179–298; (1993) 9 *Arbitration International* 1–55.

[19] *Aggeliki Charis Compañía Maritima SA v. Pagnan SpA* [1995] 1 Lloyd's Rep. 87.

the appropriate course for the aggrieved party to take may be to apply to the foreign court for a stay or similar relief.[20] A judgment given by a court of an overseas country in any proceedings will not be recognised or enforced in the United Kingdom if the bringing of proceedings in that court was contrary to a valid and effective agreement[21] under which the dispute in question was to be settled otherwise than by proceedings in the courts of that country, and those proceedings were not brought in that court by, or with the agreement of, the person against whom the judgment was given, and that person did not counter-claim or otherwise submit to the jurisdiction[22] of that court.[23]

16–038   **Stay of legal proceedings.** Section 9 of the Arbitration Act 1996 provides for a stay of legal proceedings brought contrary to an arbitration agreement. It is a mandatory provision. By section 9(1):"A party to an arbitration agreement against whom legal proceedings are brought . . . in respect of a matter which under the agreement is to be referred to arbitration may (upon notice to the other parties to the proceedings) apply to the court in which the proceedings have been brought to stay the proceedings so far as they concern that matter".[24] An application can only be made by a party against whom legal proceedings are brought (as opposed to any other party). But "party" is defined to include any person claiming under or through a party to the arbitration agreement,[25] e.g. an assignee.[26] A stay can be sought of a counterclaim as well as of a claim,[27] or of part of the legal proceedings only, and an application may be made notwithstanding that the matter is to be referred to arbitration only after the exhaustion of other dispute resolution procedures.[28] Section 9 applies even if the seat of the arbitration is outside England or no seat has been designated or determined.[29] An appeal lies to the Court of Appeal against the grant or refusal of a stay.[29a]

16–039   **Time for application to stay.** By section 9(2), an application for a stay "may not be made by a person before taking the appropriate procedural step (if any) to acknowledge the legal proceedings against him or after he has taken any step in those proceedings to answer the substantive claim". These conditions reflect to some extent the language of section 4(1) of the Arbitration Act 1950 which stated that an application for a stay might be made "at any time after appearance and before delivering any pleadings or taking any other steps in the proceedings" With respect to the 1950 Act it was said: "The authorities show that a step in the

---

[20] *World Pride Shipping Ltd v. Daiichi Chuo Kisen Kaisha* [1984] 2 Lloyd's Rep. 489, 498. But see the observations on this case in *Aggeliki Charis Compania Maritima SA v. Pagnan SpA, supra.*
[21] Civil Jurisdiction and Judgments Act 1982, s.32(2). But see *ibid.* s.32(3) and n. 18, *supra.*
[22] *ibid.* s.33.
[23] *ibid.* s.32(1),. See *Tracomin SA v. Sudan Oil Seeds Co. Ltd (No. 2)* [1983] 1 W.L.R. 1026.
[24] See RSC Ord. 73, rr. 4, 6 *et seq.* and CPR r. 49.
[25] s.82(2). See *Roussel-Uclaf v. G. D. Searle & Co. Ltd* [1978] 1 Lloyd's Rep. 225; *Rumput (Panama) SA v. Islamic Republic of Iran Shipping Lines* [1984] 2 Lloyd's Rep. 259. But not by a third party: *Eltri Fans Ltd v. NMB (U.K.) Ltd* [1987] 1 W.L.R. 110. A guarantor of a party to a contract containing an arbitration clause is not such a person: *Alfred McAlpine Construction v. Unex Corpn.* [1994] N.P.C. 16, but the court might stay an action against the guarantor under its inherent jurisdiction: *ibid.* and see *Roche Products Ltd v. Freeman Process Systems Ltd* (1997) 80 Build. L.R. 802.
[26] See *ante*, § 16–030.
[27] s.9(1).
[28] s.9(2).
[29] s.2(2).
[29a] *Inco Europe Ltd v. Choice Distribution* [1999] 1 W.L.R. 270.

proceedings means something in the nature of an application to the court, and not mere talk between solicitors and solicitors' clerks nor the writing of letters, but the taking of some step, such as taking out a summons or something of that kind, which is, in the technical sense, a step in the proceedings".[30] Accordingly, any application to the court[31] or attending upon the other side's application to the court[32] (unless expressed to be without prejudice)[33] amounted to a step in the proceedings, if the defendant thereby evinced an intention to abide by the legal proceedings and waived his right to ask for arbitration.[34] But section 9(2) of the 1996 Act adds to the words "after he has taken any step in those proceedings" the words "to answer the substantive claim", which limits still further the types of procedural steps that may be held to bar an application for a stay.[34a]

Mandatory stay. On an application under section 9, section 9(4) provides that **16–040** the court *shall* grant a stay unless satisfied that the arbitration agreement is null and void,[35] inoperative,[36] or incapable of being performed.[37] This provision for a mandatory stay reflects the provisions of the UNCITRAL Model Law and the New York Convention on the Recognition and Enforcement of Foreign Arbitral Awards. It is in the same terms as that of section 1 of the Arbitration Act 1975 but with the significant omission of the further ground for refusing a stay contained in the 1975 Act that "there is not in fact any dispute between the parties with regard to the matter agreed to be referred". The onus of satisfying the court that one or more of the three statutory grounds exist for refusing a stay rests upon the party resisting the stay.[38] A cross-claim by way of legal set-off which is subject to a mandatory stay, cannot be set-off against a claim in legal proceedings for summary judgment.[39]

Discretionary stay. Section 86 of the 1996 Act nevertheless provides that, in **16–041** the case of a "domestic agreement" (as defined in section 85(1)), the court may refuse a stay on the further ground that "there are other sufficient grounds for not

---

[30] *Ives and Barker v. Willans* [1894] 2 Ch. 478, 484. See also *Brighton Marine Palace and Pier Ltd v. Woodhouse* [1893] 2 Ch. 486 (writing for further time to deliver defence).

[31] *Chappell v. North* [1891] 2 Q.B. 252; *Adams v. Catley* (1892) 66 L.T. 687; *Ford's Hotel Co. Ltd v. Bartlett* [1896] A.C. 1; *Pitchers Ltd v. Plaza (Queensbury) Ltd* [1940] 1 All E.R. 151. Contrast (no step in the proceedings): *Zalinoff v. Hammond* [1898] 2 Ch. 92; *Lane v. Herman* [1939] 3 All E.R. 353; *London Sack and Bag Co. v. Dixon and Lugton Ltd* [1943] 2 All E.R. 763; *Eagle Star Insurance Co. Ltd v. Yuval Insurance Co. Ltd* [1978] 1 Lloyd's Rep. 357; *RGE (Group Services) Ltd v. Cleveland Offshore Ltd* (1986) 11 Const. L.R. 77. See Mustill and Boyd *op. cit.* pp. 472–473.

[32] *County Theatres and Hotels Ltd v. Knowles* [1902] 1 K.B. 480; *Richardson v. Le Maitre* [1903] 2 Ch. 222; *Ochs v. Ochs Brothers* [1909] 2 Ch. 121; *Turner & Goudy v. McConnell* [1985] 1 W.L.R. 898.

[33] *Metropolitan Tunnel and Public Works Ltd v. London Electric Ry* [1926] Ch. 371, 384, 393.

[34] *Eagle Star Insurance Co. Ltd v. Yuval Insurance Co. Ltd, supra,* at 361.

[34a] *Patel v. Patel, The Times,* April 9, 1999.

[35] *Willcock v. Pickfords Removals Ltd* [1979] 1 Lloyd's Rep. 244; *A. B. Bofors-UVA v. A. B. Skandia* [1982] 1 Lloyd's Rep. 410; *cf. Cia Maritima Zorroza SA v. Sesostris* [1984] 1 Lloyd's Rep. 652.

[36] *cf. Lonhro v. Shell Petroleum Co., The Times,* February 1, 1978; *The Merak* [1965] P. 223, 229; *Ethiopian Oilseeds & Pulses Export Corpn. v. Rio del Mar Foods Inc.* [1990] 1 Lloyd's Rep. 86, 98.

[37] *cf., The Rena K.* [1979] Q.B. 377 (ability to satisfy award irrelevant); *Paczy v. Haendler & Natermann GmbH* [1981] 1 Lloyd's Rep. 302 (impecuniosity of plaintiff irrelevant).

[38] *Nova (Jersey) Knit Ltd v. Kammgarn Spinnerei GmbH* [1977] 1 W.L.R. 713, 718. But *cf. ibid.* at 732.

[39] *Aectra Refining and Manufacturing Inc. v. Exmar NV* [1994] 1 W.L.R. 1634.

requiring the parties to abide by the arbitration agreement". This section, in effect, confers upon the court a wide discretion to refuse a stay similar to that previously conferred in the case of "domestic arbitration agreements" by section 4(1) of the Arbitration Act 1950. But section 86 of the 1996 Act is unlikely to be brought into force[40] and in consequence a stay will in all cases be mandatory subject to the exceptions set out in section 9.

16–042   **Claims indisputably due.** The additional words, referred to in §16–040 above, which were contained in the 1975 Act but omitted from section 9(4), were a source of some confusion and possible misinterpretation. In particular, they had been held to justify the court, upon an application by a plaintiff for summary judgment under RSC, Order 14,[40a] to refuse a stay and give judgment for the amount claimed where the court was satisfied that the claim was indisputably due, on the ground that the court had then decided that in reality there was not in fact any "dispute" between the parties.[41] The omission of the additional words has taken away from the court the power to refuse a stay and give summary judgment on an indisputable, though nevertheless disputed, claim.[42] Accordingly a claimant will only be entitled to summary judgment without a stay if his claim is admitted. Where part of the claim is admitted, then the court may, on an application for a stay, give summary judgment for that amount, but stay the action in respect of the balance or other matters in dispute.[43] Likewise, if liability is admitted, but there is a dispute as to damages, it would seem that the court could grant a stay on the issue of damages only.[44] The power of the court to give summary judgment on an *admitted* claim appears to derive from the fact that an admission, in effect, amounts to an agreement to pay the claim, so that the legal proceedings are not brought "in respect of a matter which under the agreement is to be referred to arbitration".

16–043   It is arguable that the court has lost a useful power in no longer being able to give summary judgment on an indisputable, but nevertheless disputed, claim, especially in relation to construction disputes where arbitrations may be long drawn out. But, when seised of such a claim, the arbitration tribunal itself could (under and subject to section 33 of the Act)[45] adopt a procedure equivalent to summary judgment to deal with the claim. If, however, it feels that this is too bold a step to take, it could give directions for an early trial of the issue on the merits.[46]

16–044   **Interpleader issues.** Section 10 of the 1996 Act provides[47] that where in legal proceedings relief by way of interpleader is granted and any issue between the claimants is one in respect of which there is an arbitration agreement between

---

[40] See *ante*, § 16–005.

[40a] Now CPR, Part 24.

[41] See the discussion in *Hayter v. Nelson and Home Insurance Co.* [1990] 2 Lloyd's Rep. 265, CA; DAC Report, § 55.

[42] *Halki Shipping Corpn. v. Sopex Oils Ltd* [1998] 1 W.L.R. 726.

[43] *Ellis Mechanical Services Ltd v. Wates Construction Ltd* [1978] 1 Lloyd's Rep. 33. Contrast *Associated Bulk Carriers Ltd v. Koch Shipping Inc.* [1978] 1 Lloyd's Rep. 24.

[44] *Texaco Ltd v. Eurogulf Shipping Ltd* [1987] 2 Lloyd's Rep. 541.

[45] See *post*, § 16–076.

[46] See (1997) 13 *Arbitration International* 403, 424 *cf.*, (1998) 64 *Arbitration* (No. 1, Supplement) 48.

[47] This section is based on s.5 of the 1950 Act. It is mandatory.

them, the court granting the relief is to direct that the issue be determined by arbitration. The court must so direct unless the circumstances are such that proceedings brought by a claimant in respect of the matter would not be stayed.[48]

Admiralty proceedings. Under section 11,[49] where Admiralty proceedings   **16–045**
are stayed on the ground that the dispute in question should be submitted to arbitration, the court granting the stay may, if in those proceedings property has been arrested or bail or other security has been given to prevent or obtain release from arrest, either order that the property arrested be retained as security for the satisfaction of an enforceable[50] award given in the arbitration in respect of that dispute, or order that the stay of those proceedings be conditional on the provision of equivalent security for the satisfaction of any such award.

4. COMMENCEMENT OF ARBITRAL PROCEEDINGS

Conditions as to time. The parties to a contract may lawfully agree that   **16–046**
arbitral proceedings must be commenced, and the claimant's arbitrator appointed, within a shorter time than that allowed by the Limitation Act 1980, and that if this provision is not complied with the claim shall be deemed to be waived and absolutely barred.[51] Such a clause is not contrary to public policy as tending to oust the jurisdiction of the court, however short the time may be.[52] Yet a clause of this nature will be narrowly construed[53] and it may even be that a party who commits a fundamental breach of contract will be unable to take advantage of the clause when sued in the ordinary courts.[54] But if the other party claims arbitration in such a case, he cannot do so after the time has expired[55] unless the court exercises its statutory power to extend the time. A claim will be barred by an arbitrator's award deciding that the claim is out of time,[56] but not by an arbitrator declining jurisdiction.[57]

Power of court to extend time for beginning arbitral proceedings. Section   **16–047**
12 of the 1996 Act confers on the court power to extend a contractual time-limit

---

[48] Subs. (2) deals with the effect of dismissal of the application on a *"Scott v. Avery"* clause.

[49] This section re-enacts s.26 of the Civil Jurisdiction and Judgments Act 1982, but with the omission of subs. (2) of that section. It is mandatory.

[50] *i.e.*, enforceable in England.

[51] *Atlantic Shipping Co. Ltd v. Louis Dreyfus & Co.* [1922] 2 A.C. 250. See Mustill and Boyd *op. cit.* p. 201. A claim may be barred even though the cause of action has not yet arisen when the time limit expired: *The Himmerland* [1965] 2 Lloyd's Rep. 353, 360; *Union of India v. E. B. Aaby's Rederei A/S* [1975] A.C. 797, 810, 813, 817–818; *Comdel Commodities Ltd v. Siporex Trade SA (No. 2)* [1989] 2 Lloyd's Rep. 13 (affd. [1991] 1 A.C. 148). *cf. The M Eregli* [1981] 2 Lloyd's Rep. 169, 173.

[52] *ibid.*

[53] *Board of Trade v. Steel Bros. & Co. Ltd* [1952] 1 Lloyd's Rep. 87; *Alan v. El Nasr Export and Import Co.* [1971] 1 Lloyd's Rep. 401; [1972] 2 Q.B. 189; *Bunge S.A. v. Deutsche Conti-Handelsgesellschaft mbH (No. 2)* [1980] 1 Lloyd's Rep. 352; *Ch. Daudruy van Cauwenberghe & Fils SA v. Tropical Products Sales SA* [1986] 1 Lloyd's Rep. 535.

[54] *Ford & Co. Ltd v. Cie Furness* [1922] 2 K.B. 797, 802; *Smeaton Hanscomb & Co. Ltd v. Sassoon I. Setty, Son & Co. (No. 1)* [1953] 1 W.L.R. 1468, 1471. But contrast *Woolf v. Collis Removal Service* [1948] 1 K.B. 11 and see *post*, § 16–154.

[55] *Ford & Co. Ltd v. Cie Furness, supra.*

[56] *Ayscough v. Sheed, Thomson & Co. Ltd* (1924) 40 T.L.R. 707, HL.

[57] *Pinnock Brothers v. Lewis and Peat Ltd* [1923] 1 K.B. 690.

which would otherwise bar the claim. Where an arbitration agreement to refer future disputes to arbitration provides that a claim shall be barred, or the claimant's right extinguished, unless the claimant takes within a time fixed by the agreement some step to begin arbitral proceedings (or to begin other dispute resolution procedures which must be exhausted before arbitral proceedings can be begun), the court may by order extend the time for taking that step.[58] An application for such an order can be made only after a claim has arisen and after exhausting any available arbitral process for obtaining an extension of time.[59] Previously, under section 27 of the 1950 Act, the court had a wide discretion to extend time "if of opinion that in the circumstances of the case undue hardship would otherwise be caused". But, under section 12(3), a much narrower test is to be applied.[60] The court can make an order only if satisfied

(a) that the circumstances are such as were outside the reasonable contemplation of the parties when they agreed the provision in question, and that it would be just to extend the time, or

(b) that the conduct of one party makes it unjust to hold the other party to the strict terms of the provision in question.

It is to be noted that subsection 3(a) places no limit on the circumstances referred to and that all the circumstances in which the application for an extension arises are potentially relevant.[61] But the court can have regard only to such circumstances as were "outside the reasonable contemplation of the parties when they agreed the provision in question" and this may involve consideration of the relevant transaction, of ordinary practices within that type of transaction and with the reasonable expectation of parties involved in such a transaction.[62] The fact that a party made a mistake as to the operation of the time limitation clause in the contract both in regard to making a claim and appointing an arbitrator has been held not to be something which was outside the reasonable contemplation of the parties.[63] The ground set out in subsection 3(b) would appear to require at least that the failure to comply with the time bar is attributable to the conduct of the party relying on the clause.[64]

16–048   An order extending time is therefore likely to be the exception rather than the rule. It is arguable that time limitation clauses are a beneficial feature in commercial contracts, since they enable the parties to draw a line beneath transactions at a much earlier stage than limitation statutes allow, and the underlying philosophy of the 1996 Act is to respect party autonomy. Nevertheless, a clause barring a claim unless arbitral proceedings or other dispute resolution procedures are begun within a short period of time can operate very harshly in some situations, for example, in "string" contracts where the buyer resells the goods and defects

---

[58] s.12(1).
[59] s.12(2). See RSC, Ord. 73 (and CPR r. 49).
[60] DAC Report, §§ 62–75.
[61] *Vosnoc Ltd v. Trans Global Projects Ltd* [1998] 1 W.L.R. 101, 112.
[62] *Cathiship SA v. Allanasons Ltd* [1998] 2 Lloyd's Rep. 511.
[63] *ibid. Grimaldi Compāgnía di Navigazione Spa v. Sekihyo Lines Ltd,* [1999] 1 W.L.R. 708; *Fox & Widley v. Guram* [1998] 3 E.G. 142 (extension refused). *cf. Vosnoc Ltd v. Trans Global Projects Ltd, supra* (extension granted).
[64] *Fox & Widley v. Guram, supra; Grimaldi Compāgnía di Navigazione Spa v. Sekihyo Lines Ltd, supra* at 725.

therein do not become apparent until time has expired. In consumer contracts, clauses imposing a time-limit for the commencement of arbitral proceedings may well be regarded as unfair and so not binding on the consumer under the Unfair Terms in Consumer Contracts Regulations 1994.[65]

If the conditions are satisfied for the making of an order, the court may extend the period and on such terms as it thinks fit, and may do so whether or not the time previously fixed (by agreement or by a previous order) has expired.[66] The leave of the court is required for any appeal from a decision of the court under section 12.[67] The applicant will normally have to pay the costs of any section 12 application.   **16–049**

The court's power to extend time for beginning arbitral proceedings applies, not only where the effect of a failure to comply with the stipulated time-limit is merely to deprive a claimant of the right to go to arbitration, but also where non-compliance bars or extinguishes the claim itself.[68] But no such power exists if the clause provides that a claim is to be barred or extinguished unless notified to the other party within a limited period of time, except where such notification is a step to begin arbitral proceedings.[69] Nor can such a power be exercised where a statutory time bar applies, e.g., that provided for in the Hague-Visby Rules.[70]   **16–050**

Section 12 is a mandatory provision.[71] Under the corresponding provision in the 1950 Act it was held that the power to extend time could be exercised where the law applicable to the contract containing the arbitration clause (including the time bar) was English law, even though some other law might govern the subsequent arbitration procedure.[72] The effect of the 1996 Act, however, is that the power to extend time can be exercised only where either (a) the seat of the arbitration is in England or (b) no seat has been designated or determined and the court is satisfied that it is appropriate to do so by reason of a connection with England (though such a connection could be that the arbitration agreement was   **16–051**

---

[65] S.I. 1994 No. 3159; see *ante*, §§ 15–001, 16–013.

[66] s.12(4).

[67] s.12(6).

[68] *Consolidated Investment and Contracting Co. v. Saponaria Shipping Co. Ltd* [1978] 2 Lloyd's Rep. 167; *Tradax Export SA v. Italcarbo Societa di Navigazione SpA* [1983] 1 Lloyd's Rep. 514; *Jadranska Slobodna Plovidba v. Oleagine SA* [1984] 1 W.L.R. 300; *The Medusa* [1986] 2 Lloyd's Rep. 328; *The Stephanos* [1989] 1 Lloyd's Rep. 506.

[69] *Smeaton Hanscomb & Co. Ltd v. Sassoon I. Setty, Son & Co. (No. 1)* [1953] 1 W.L.R. 1468; *Metalimex Foreign Trade Corpn. v. Eugenie Maritime Co. Ltd* [1962] 1 Lloyd's Rep. 378; *Babanaft International Co. SA v. Avant Petroleum Inc.* [1982] 1 W.L.R. 871; *Crown Estate Commissioners v. John Mowlem & Co.* [1994] 10 Const. L.J. 311; *Metalfer Corpn. v. Pan Ocean Shipping Co. Ltd* [1998] 2 Lloyd's Rep. 632.

[70] *Kenya Railways v. Antares Co. Pte. Ltd* [1987] 1 Lloyd's Rep. 424. Contrast *Nea Agrex SA v. Baltic Shipping Co. Ltd* [1976] Q.B. 933; *Consolidated Investment & Contracting Co. v. Saponaria Shipping Co. Ltd* [1978] 2 Lloyd's Rep. 167 (Hague Rules incorporated by contract). *cf., Freedom General Shipping SA v. Tokai Shipping Co. Ltd* [1982] 1 Lloyd's Rep. 73; *Government of Sierra Leone v. Marmaro Shipping Co. Ltd* [1989] 2 Lloyd's Rep. 130; Mann (1987) 103 L.Q.R. 523. See also s.12(5) of the 1996 Act.

[71] s.4(1) and Sched. 1.

[72] *International Tank and Pipe S.A.K. v. Kuwait Aviation Fuelling Co. KSC* [1975] Q.B. 224. Contrast *C. M. Van Stillevoldt BV v. El Carriers Inc.* [1983] 1 W.L.R. 207; *Mitsubishi Corpn. v. Castletown Navigation Ltd* [1989] 2 Lloyd's Rep. 383 (foreign applicable law).

governed by English law or that it is extremely likely that, once a seat is designated, the seat will be in England).[73]

16–052 **Commencement of arbitral proceedings.** The parties are free to agree when arbitral proceedings are to be regarded as commenced for the purposes of Part I of the 1996 Act and for the purpose of the Limitation Acts.[74] If there is no such agreement, then section 14[75] provides that arbitral proceedings are commenced in respect of a matter[76] as follows:

(i) where the arbitrator is named or designated in the arbitration agreement, when one party serves on the other party or parties a notice in writing requiring him or them to submit that matter to the person so named or designated[77];

(ii) where the arbitrator or arbitrators are to be appointed by the parties, when one party serves on the other party or parties a notice in writing requiring him or them to appoint an arbitrator or to agree to the appointment of an arbitrator in respect of that matter[78];

(iii) where the arbitrator or arbitrators are to be appointed by a person other than a party to the proceedings, when one party gives notice in writing to that person requesting him to make the appointment in respect of that matter.[79]

5. The Arbitral Tribunal

16–053 **The arbitral tribunal.** The constitution of the arbitral tribunal is primarily a matter for the parties to decide. They are free to agree on the number of arbitrators to form the tribunal and whether there is to be a chairman or an umpire.[80] Unless otherwise agreed by the parties, an agreement that the number of arbitrators shall be two or any other even number is to be understood as

---

[73] s.2(4).

[74] s.14(1). See *Transpetrol Ltd v. Ekali Shipping Co. Ltd* [1989] 1 Lloyd's Rep. 62.

[75] This section replaces s.34(3) of the Limitation Act 1980 and reflects to some extent Art. 21 of the Model law. Since the wording of subs. (3)(4) is similar to that of s.34(3) of the 1980 Act, decisions on the latter may be relevant: *Nea Agrex SA v. Baltic Shipping Co. Ltd* [1976] Q.B. 933; *Surrendra Overseas Ltd v. Government of Sri Lanka* [1977] 1 W.L.R. 565; *Casillo Grani v. Napier Shipping Co.* [1984] 2 Lloyd's Rep. 481; *Leif Hoegh & Co. A/S v. Petrolsea Inc.* [1992] 1 Lloyd's Rep. 45, 49; *Triad Shipping Co. v. Stellar Chartering & Brokerage Inc.* [1993] 2 Lloyd's Rep. 388, 399; [1994] 2 Lloyd's Rep. 227; *Petredec Ltd v. Tokumaru Kaiun Co. Ltd* [1994] 1 Lloyd's Rep. 162; *Vosnoc Ltd v. Trans Global Projects Ltd* [1998] 1 W.L.R. 101. *Charles M. Willie & Co. (Shipping) Ltd v. Ocean Laser Shipping Ltd* [1999] 1 Lloyd's Rep. 225; *Allianz Verischerungsaktiengesellschaft v. Fortuna Co. Inc.* [1999] 1 Lloyd's Rep. 497. On the meaning of "serves", see ss. 76, 77 of the 1996 Act and *Minerals and Metals Trading Corpn. of India Ltd v. Encounter Bay Shipping Co. Ltd* [1986] 2 Lloyd's Rep. 603; *N.V. Stoomy Maats "De Maas" v. Nippon Yusen Kaisha* [1980] 2 Lloyd's Rep. 56.

[76] "Matter" include both disputes and claims: DAC Report, § 76. *cf., Cruden Construction Ltd v. Commission for New Towns* [1995] 2 Lloyd's Rep. 387.

[77] s.14(3).

[78] s.14(4).

[79] s.14(5).

[80] s.15(1).

requiring the appointment of an additional arbitrator as chairman of the tribunal.[81] If there is no agreement as to the number of arbitrators, the tribunal is to consist of a sole arbitrator.[82]

Appointment of arbitrators. No particular form is required for the appointment of an arbitrator, unless the arbitration agreement so requires. As a general rule, however, an arbitrator is fully "appointed" only when (a) the designated person is told of his nomination and is asked whether he is willing to act, (b) he consents so to act, and (c) his name and appointment are communicated to the other side.[83]   **16–054**

Procedures for appointment when parties do not agree. The 1996 Act contains provisions which, in the absence of agreement between the parties, establish procedures for the appointment of arbitrators and which are designed to ensure that the arbitration agreement will not be inoperative merely because one party refuses to make an appointment or if the procedure for the appointment of the arbitral tribunal fails. The parties are free to agree on the procedure for appointing the arbitrator or arbitrators, including the procedure for the appointment of any chairman or umpire.[84] If or to the extent that there is no such agreement, the following provisions apply—[85]   **16–055**

(i) if the tribunal is to consist of a sole arbitrator, the parties are jointly to appoint the arbitrator not later than 28 days after service of a request in writing by either party to do so[86];

(ii) if the tribunal is to consist of two arbitrators, each party is to appoint one arbitrator not later than 14 days after service of a request in writing by either party to do so[87];

(iii) if the tribunal is to consist of three arbitrators, each party is to appoint one arbitrator not later than 14 days after service of a request in writing by either party to do so, and the two so appointed are forthwith to appoint a third arbitrator as the chairman of the tribunal[88];

(iv) if the tribunal is to consist of two arbitrators and an umpire, each party is to appoint one arbitrator not later than 14 days after service of a request in writing by either party to do so, and the two so appointed may appoint an umpire at any time after they themselves are appointed and must do so before any substantive hearing or forthwith if they cannot agree on a matter relating to the arbitration.[89]

---

[81] s.15(2). For the chairman, see s.20; *post*, § 16–060.
[82] s.15(3). See *Villa Denizcilik Sanayi Ve Ticaret AS v. Longen SA* [1998] 1 Lloyd's Rep. 195.
[83] *Tradax SA v. Volkswagenwerk AG* [1970] 1 Q.B. 537. See also *Toepfer v. Cremer* [1975] 2 Lloyd's Rep. 118; *Carras Shipping Co. Ltd v. Food Corpn. of India* [1979] 2 Lloyd's Rep. 179; *Hannaford v. Smallcombe, The Times*, December 30, 1993. *cf. Legumbres S.A.C.I.F.I.A. v. Central de Cooperativas etc. Ltda.* [1986] 1 Lloyd's Rep. 401; *Petredec Ltd v. Tokumaru Kaiun Co. Ltd* [1994] 1 Lloyd's Rep. 162; *Robinson v. Moody, The Times*, February 23, 1994.
[84] s.16(1).
[85] s.16(2). The time limits may be extended by agreement, or by order of the court (s.79).
[86] s.16(3). See *Villa Denizcilik Sanayi Ve Ticaret AS v. Longen SA* [1998] 1 Lloyd's Rep. 195.
[87] s.16(4).
[88] s.16(5).
[89] s.16(6).

In any other case, resort is to be made to section 18 of the Act which provides for the case of a failure of the agreed appointment procedure.[90]

16–056   **Power in case of default to appoint sole arbitrator.** The parties may, for example, have agreed that the reference is to be to two arbitrators, one to be appointed by each party, or that it shall be to three arbitrators, one to be appointed by each party and the third to be appointed by the two appointed by the parties or in some other manner specified in the agreement. Section 17 of the 1996 Act[91] provides a summary procedure which is available in case one party defaults in the appointment of his arbitrator. Unless the parties otherwise agree, where each of two parties to an arbitration agreement is to appoint an arbitrator and one party ("the party in default") refuses to do so, or fails to do so within the time specified,[92] the other party, having duly appointed his arbitrator, may give notice in writing to the party in default that he proposes to appoint his arbitrator to act as sole arbitrator.[93] If the party in default does not within seven clear days of that notice being given (a) make the required appointment, and (b) notify the other party that he has done so, the other party may appoint his arbitrator as sole arbitrator, in which case his award is binding on both parties as if he had been appointed by agreement.[94] Where a sole arbitrator has been thus appointed, the party in default may (upon notice to the appointing party) apply to the court which may set aside the appointment.[95] The Act does not specify the grounds on which the court may so act, but no doubt the court would only set aside the appointment if satisfied that there was real likelihood that the person appointed could not, or would not, fairly determine the issues in the arbitration.

16–057   **Failure of appointment procedure.** The parties are free to agree what is to happen in the event of a failure of the procedure for the appointment of the arbitral tribunal.[96] If and to the extent that there is no such agreement, the court may exercise the powers conferred upon it by section 18 of the Act upon the application of any party to the arbitration agreement (and notice to the other parties).[97] The section does not, however, define what constitutes "a failure of the procedure for the appointment of the arbitral tribunal". But presumably this will embrace (*inter alia*) cases where a person designated as arbitrator or umpire refuses to act, or is incapable of acting, or dies[98]; where the parties or two arbitrators are required or at liberty to appoint an arbitrator or umpire and either cannot agree on the appointment or otherwise fail to appoint; and where an arbitrator or umpire is to be appointed by a third party (*e.g.* an arbitral institution) and the third party refuses or fails to make an appointment. The powers of the court under the section are—[99]

---

[90] s.16(7). See *post*, § 16–057.
[91] This replaces, with changes, s.7(b) of the 1950 Act: see the DAC Report, §§ 83–86.
[92] There is no reference in s.17(1), as there was in s.10(3)(b) of the Arbitration Act 1950, to "or, if no time is specified, within a reasonable time".
[93] s.17(1).
[94] s.17(2). Each stage of the procedure under subs. (1) and (2) must be meticulously complied with.
[95] s.17(3). But all that is set aside is the appointment as *sole* arbitrator. Leave of the court is required for any appeal from a decision of the court under s.17(3): s.17(4).
[96] s.18(1). See *Medov Lines SpA v. Traelandsfos A/S* [1969] 2 Lloyd's Rep. 225. There is no failure if an appointment is duly made under s.17 unless that appointment is set aside.
[97] s.18(2); RSC Ord. 73.
[98] *i.e.* cases previously falling under ss.7, 10 of the Arbitration Act 1950.
[99] s.18(3).

(a) to give directions as to the making of any necessary appointments,

(b) to direct that the tribunal shall be constituted by such appointments (or any one or more of them) as have been made;

(c) to revoke any appointments already made,[1] and

(d) to make any necessary appointments itself.

An appointment made by the court under this section has effect as if made with the agreement of the parties.[2]

The powers conferred upon the court by section 18 are discretionary.[3] If, for example, an application is made for the court to appoint an arbitrator, then it would seem that the court could refuse to appoint on the ground of undue delay by the applicant if in the circumstances justice would not require the making of an appointment.[4] But those powers may be exercised not only where the seat of the arbitration is in England but also where no seat of the arbitration has been designated or determined and by reason of a connection with England the court is satisfied that it is appropriate to do so.[5]   **16–058**

Qualifications of arbitrators. An arbitrator does not have to possess any or any particular qualifications to act as arbitrator, unless the arbitration agreement so requires. Where the appointed arbitrator does not possess the required qualifications, an objection that the arbitral tribunal is improperly constituted may be made under sections 31 and 32 of the 1996 Act.[6] The unqualified arbitrator may also be removed by the court under section 24.[7] In deciding whether to exercise, and in considering how to exercise, any of its powers under section 16 or section 18, the court is to have due regard to any agreement of the parties as to the qualifications required of the arbitrators.[8]   **16–059**

Chairman. The Arbitration Act 1950 made no provision for the office of chairman. But section 20 of the 1996 Act provides for the role of chairman. The parties are free to agree what his functions shall be.[9] In the absence of agreement,[10] decisions, orders and awards are to be made by all or a majority of the arbitrators (including the chairman),[11] but the view of the chairman is to prevail in relation to a decision, order or award in respect of which there is neither   **16–060**

---

[1] See § 88 of the DAC Report.

[2] s.18(4). Leave of the court is required for any appeal from a decision of the court under this section: s.18(5).

[3] *Villa Denizcilik Sanayi Ve Ticaret AS v. Longen SA* [1998] 1 Lloyd's Rep. 195.

[4] *Petredec Ltd v. Tokumaru Kaiun Co. Ltd* [1994] 1 Lloyd's Rep. 162; *Frota Oceanica Brasiliera SA v. Steamship Mutual Underwriting Association (Bermuda) Ltd* [1996] 2 Lloyd's Rep. 461; *West of England Ship Owners Mutual Protection and Indemnity Assn v. Hellenic Industrial Development Bank SA* [1999] 1 Lloyd's Rep. 93 (on s.10 of the 1950 Act).

[5] s.2(4).

[6] *cf., Pan Atlantic Group Inc. v. Hassneh Insurance Co. of Israel Ltd* [1992] 2 Lloyd's Rep. 120.

[7] s.24(1)(b).

[8] s.10. See *Villa Denizcilik Sanayi Ve Ticaret AS v. Longen SA* [1998] 1 Lloyd's Rep. 195.

[9] s.20(1).

[10] s.20(2).

[11] s.20(3).

unanimity nor a majority,[12] for example, if there are three arbitrators and each (including the chairman) has a different view on the amount of the award.

16–061 **Umpire.** Traditionally, an umpire differs from a chairman in that he is not strictly one of the arbitrators but replaces the two party-appointed arbitrators in the event that they are unable to agree. Section 21 of the 1996 Act provides that, where the parties have agreed that there is to be an umpire, they are free to agree what his functions shall be, and in particular whether he is to attend the proceedings and when he is to replace the other arbitrators as the tribunal with power to make decisions, orders and awards.[13] If and to the extent that there is no agreement,[14] he is to attend the proceedings (though not take an active part in them) and be supplied with the same documents and materials as are supplied to the other arbitrators.[15] If and when the arbitrators cannot agree on a matter relating to the arbitration, they must forthwith give notice in writing to the parties and to the umpire, and he then replaces them as the tribunal and with power to make decisions, orders and awards as if he were sole arbitrator.[16] Should one or both of the arbitrators fail to give the necessary notice, any party to the arbitral proceedings can apply to the court for an order that the umpire shall replace the other arbitrators.[17]

16–062 **No chairman or umpire.** In the event that the parties agree not to have a chairman or umpire, they are free to agree how the tribunal is to make decisions, orders and awards. If there is no such agreement, they are to be made by all or a majority of the arbitrators.[18]

16–063 **Revocation of arbitrator's authority.** The parties are free to agree in what circumstances the authority of an arbitrator may be revoked.[19] If and to the extent that there is no such agreement,[20] section 23 of the 1996 Act confirms the long-established rule that it is impossible for one party unilaterally to revoke the authority of an arbitrator.[21] The parties acting jointly may nevertheless do so,[22] but this must be agreed in writing unless the parties also agree (whether or not in writing) to terminate the arbitration agreement.[23] An arbitrator's authority may also be revoked by an arbitral or other institution or person vested by the parties with powers in that regard.[24]

---

[12] s.20(4).
[13] s.21(1).
[14] s.21(2).
[15] s.21(3). cf., *Fletamentos Maritimos S.A. v. Effjohn International BV* [1995] 1 Lloyd's Rep. 311; *Fletamentos Maritimos SA v. Effjohn International BV (No. 2)* [1997] 1 Lloyd's Rep. 295, [1997] 1 Lloyd's Rep. 644 (on 1950 Act).
[16] s.21(4).
[17] s.21(5). Leave of the court is required for any appeal from a decision of the court under this section: s.21(6). See RSC Ord. 73.
[18] s.22(1)(2).
[19] s.23(1).
[20] s.23(2).
[21] Arbitration Act 1950, s.1.
[22] s.23(3)(a).
[23] s.23(4).
[24] s.23(3)(b).

Death of arbitrator. The authority of an arbitrator is personal and ceases on   **16–064**
death.[25] But, unless otherwise agreed by the parties, the death of a person by
whom an arbitrator was appointed does not revoke the arbitrator's authority.[26]

Court's power to revoke appointment. The power conferred on the court   **16–065**
under the 1950 Act[27] to revoke the authority of an arbitrator or umpire where the
dispute involved a charge of fraud was not preserved by the 1996 Act. But the
court may revoke an appointment under section 18 (powers exercisable in case
of failure of appointment procedure)[28] and may remove an arbitrator on the
grounds specified in section 24.[29]

Removal of arbitrator. The court has in certain circumstances the power to   **16–066**
remove an arbitrator. This may be done, under section 24 of the 1996 Act, upon
the application of a party to the arbitral proceedings.[30] The grounds on which
such an application may be made are any of the following—

(a) that circumstances exist which give rise to justifiable doubts as to his
    impartiality[31];

(b) that he does not possess the qualifications required by the arbitration
    agreement[32];

(c) that he is physically or mentally incapable of conducting the proceedings
    or there are justifiable doubts as to his capacity to do so;

(d) that he has refused or failed—

    (i) properly to conduct the proceedings,[33] or
    (ii) to use all reasonable despatch in conducting the proceedings or
         making an award,[34]

---

[25] s.26(1). This sub-section is mandatory.

[26] s.26(2).

[27] Arbitration Act 1950, s.24(2).

[28] s.18(3)(c); see *ante*, § 16–057.

[29] *Post*, § 16–066.

[30] Upon notice to the other parties, to the arbitrator concerned and to any other arbitrator: s.24(1).
See RSC, Ord. 73. Leave of the court is required for any appeal from a decision of the court under
this section: s.24(6).

[31] See (on removal under s.23(1) of the Arbitration Act 1950) *Catalina (Owners) v. Norma
(Owners)* (1938) 61 Ll.L.Rep. 360 (bias expressed against one party's witnesses); *Veritas Shipping
Corpn. v. Anglo-Canadian Cement Ltd* [1996] 1 Lloyd's Rep. 76 (party appoints its managing director
as arbitrator); *Tracomin SA v. Gibbs Nathaniel (Canada) Ltd* [1985] 1 Lloyd's Rep. 586 (arbitrator
sits behind one party's counsel in court). For the test to be applied in cases of alleged bias; see *R .v
Spencer* [1987] A.C. 128; *R. v. Gough* [1993] A.C. 646.

[32] See ante, § 16–059.

[33] See (on removal under s.23(1) of the 1950 Act): *Hagop Ardahalian v. Unifert International SA*
[1984] 2 Lloyd's Rep. 84, 89, and *Modern Engineering (Bristol) Ltd v. C. Miskin & Son Ltd* [1981]
1 Lloyd's Rep. 135 (issue of interim award without hearing submissions on raised point of law); *Fox
v. Wellfair Ltd* [1981] 2 Lloyd's Rep. 514 (arbitrator uses own expert knowledge without giving
parties opportunity to deal with it); *Town and City Properties (Development) Ltd v. Wiltshier Southern
Ltd* (1989) 44 Build. L.R. 109 (procedure akin to valuation adopted rather than arbitration); *Lovell
Partnerships (Northern) Ltd v. A.W. Construction plc* (1997) 81 Build. L.R. 34; Knowles (1996) 62
Arbitration 190.

[34] See (on removal under s.13(3) of the 1950 Act): *Pratt v. Swanmore Builders Ltd* [1980] 2
Lloyd's Rep. 504.

and that substantial injustice has been or will be caused to the applicant.

With respect to ground (a), section 24 omits the reference in the Model Law to "independence" as well as "impartiality": the Departmental Committee concluded that lack of independence, unless it gave rise to justifiable doubts about the impartiality of the arbitrator, was of no significance.[35] With respect to ground (d), the use by a party of this provision to delay or disrupt the arbitral proceedings is discouraged by the requirement that the conduct of the arbitrator must be such that "substantial injustice" has been or will be caused to the applicant,[36] and also by fact that the arbitral tribunal is further empowered to continue the arbitral proceedings while an application to the court is pending.[37] Moreover, section 73(1) provides that a party must object promptly to any impropriety or irregularity in the proceedings,[38] and subsection (2) of section 24 provides that if there is an arbitral or other institution or person vested with the authority to remove an arbitrator, the court is not to exercise its power of removal unless it is satisfied that the applicant has first exhausted his right of recourse to that institution or person. The arbitrator concerned is entitled to appear and be heard by the court before any order is made.[39] If he is removed, this does not affect his immunity, but the court can adjust his entitlement to recover or retain fees or expenses.[40] The filling of the vacancy created is dealt with by section 27.[41] Section 24 is a mandatory provision.[42]

16–067 **Resignation of arbitrator.** An arbitrator will be liable[43] if he resigns in breach of the express or implied terms of his engagement unless the parties agree to release him from his engagement or from liability. Section 25 of the 1996 Act enables him to apply to the court for relief from liability and for an order as to the recovery or retention of his fees and expenses.

16–068 **Filling of vacancy.** Where an arbitrator ceases to hold office, the parties are free to agree whether and if so how the vacancy is to be filled, whether and if so to what extent the previous proceedings should stand, and what effect (if any) his ceasing to hold office has on any appointment made by him (alone or jointly).[44] If or to the extent that there is no such agreement,[45] then—

(a) the provisions of section 16 and 18 apply in relation to the filling of the vacancy as in relation to an original appointment[46];

(b) the tribunal (when reconstituted) is to determine whether and if so to what extent the previous proceedings are to stand[47]; and

---

[35] DAC Report, §§ 101–104.
[36] DAC Report, § 105.
[37] s.24(3). See (1998) 64 *Arbitration* 188.
[38] See *post*, §§ 16–130, 16–139.
[39] s.24(5).
[40] s.24(4).
[41] See *post*, § 16–068.
[42] s.4(1) and Sched. 1.
[43] He is not immune from such liability: s.29(3).
[44] s.27(1).
[45] s.27(2).
[46] s.27(3).
[47] This does not affect any right of a party to challenge those proceedings on any ground which had arisen before the arbitrator ceased to hold office: s.27(4).

(c) his ceasing to hold office does not affect any appointment by him (alone or jointly) of another arbitrator, in particular any appointment of a chairman or umpire.[48]

In contrast with the Arbitration Act 1950,[49] the 1996 Act does not give to the court any initial power to fill a vacancy caused by its removal of an arbitrator: the original appointment procedure is to be used.[50]

Liability for arbitrators' fees and expenses. As a matter of general contract **16–069** law, an arbitrator is entitled to be paid whatever has been agreed between him and any of the parties.[51] This is a several liability which is incurred by the party with whom the agreement was made. However, under section 28 of the Act, all parties are jointly and severally liable to an arbitrator for his fees and expenses, but this joint and several liability is limited to "such reasonable fees and expenses (if any) as are appropriate in the circumstances".[52] The section further enables a party to apply to the court to adjust fees and expenses before they are paid,[53] and, if it is reasonable in the circumstances to do so, to order repayment of fees and expenses after the arbitrator has been paid.[54] The section nevertheless makes it clear that this power to make adjustments and to order repayment does not affect any contractual right of the arbitrator to his fees and expenses.[55] Nor does the section deal with the question which of the parties (as between themselves) are to pay the costs and expenses of the arbitration.[56] It is to be noted that arbitrators' expenses in this section include the fees and expenses of an expert, legal adviser or assessor appointed by the tribunal for which the arbitrators are liable.[57] Section 28 is mandatory.[58]

Difficult problems may arise concerning the liability for fees and expenses of **16–070** a person who successfully challenges the substantive jurisdiction of the tribunal.[59] Section 28 refers to a liability of "the parties" to pay the arbitrators' fees and expenses. If a person has taken no part in the arbitral proceedings, and it is determined that the tribunal has no substantive jurisdiction, it is scarcely arguable that he should be liable for any part of those fees and expenses. But under section 30 the tribunal is empowered to rule on its own jurisdiction and a person may have participated in the proceedings, even though ultimately he establishes that the tribunal lacks jurisdiction. The Act does not answer the question whether such a person is to be considered a "party" for the purposes of liability under this section. But it is submitted that the tribunal would have no jurisdiction to make an award that such a person pay any part of the arbitrators' fees and expenses.

---

[48] s.27(5).
[49] Arbitration Act 1950, s.25(1).
[50] DAC Report, § 117. See *ante*, § 16–055 (s.16).
[51] See DAC Report, § 120; Mustill and Boyd, *op. cit.*, pp. 233. For the difficulties that may arise, see *K/S Norjarl A/S v. Hyundai Heavy Industries Ltd* [1992] Q.B. 863 (commitment fee demanded); *Turner v. Stevenage B.C.* [1998] Ch. 208 (request for interim fee).
[52] s.28(1). See also 28(6) (arbitrator who has ceased to act, and umpire).
[53] s.28(2). See RSC Ord. 73, r. 10(2).
[54] s.28(3). See RSC Ord. 73, r. 10(2).
[55] s.28(5).
[56] *ibid.* See ss. 59–65; *post*, §§ 16–117—16–123.
[57] s.37(2).
[58] s.4(1) and Sched. 1.
[59] DAC Report, § 126.

6. JURISDICTION OF THE ARBITRAL TRIBUNAL

16–071   **Tribunal can rule on its own jurisdiction.** English law has always taken the view that the arbitral tribunal cannot be the final adjudicator of its own jurisdiction. The final decision as to the substantive jurisdiction of the tribunal rests with the court.[60] However, there is no reason why the tribunal should not have the power, subject to review by the court, to rule on its own jurisdiction. Indeed, such a power (often referred to as the principle of *"kompetenz-kompetenz"*) has been generally recognised in other legal systems. It had also been recognised by English law before the 1996 Act,[61] but section 30 of the Act puts this on a statutory basis. Unless otherwise agreed by the parties, the arbitral tribunal may rule on its own substantive jurisdiction, that is, as to (a) whether there is a valid arbitration agreement, (b) whether the tribunal is properly constituted, and (c) what matters have been submitted to arbitration in accordance with the arbitration agreement.[62] Any such ruling may be challenged by any arbitral process of appeal or review or in accordance with the provisions of Part I of the Act,[63] notably by an application under section 32[64] or by a challenge to the award under section 67.[65]

16–072   **Objection to substantive jurisdiction of tribunal.** Section 31 of the 1996 Act (which is a mandatory provision[66]) limits the period within which an objection to the substantive jurisdiction of the arbitral tribunal can be raised and sets out the courses open to the tribunal if such an objection is made. An objection that the tribunal lacks jurisdiction at the outset of the proceedings must be raised by a party not later than the time he takes the first step in the proceedings to contest the merits of any matter[67] in relation to which he challenges the tribunal's jurisdiction.[68] And any objection during the course of the arbitral proceedings that the tribunal is exceeding its jurisdiction must be made as soon as possible after the matter alleged to be beyond its jurisdiction is raised.[69] The tribunal may, however, admit an objection made later if it considers the delay justified.[70] If a party to arbitral proceedings takes part or continues to take part in the proceedings without duly objecting that the tribunal lacks substantive jurisdiction, he cannot raise that objection later, before the tribunal or the court,

---

[60] *May v. Mills* (1914) 30 T.L.R. 287; *Produce Brokers Co. Ltd v. Olympia Oil and Cake Co. Ltd* [1916] 1 A.C. 314, 327; *Heyman v. Darwins Ltd* [1942] A,.C. 356, 393; *Brown v. Genossenschaft Oesterreichischer Waldbesitzer R. GmbH* [1954] 1 Q.B. 8; *Dalmia Dairy Industries Ltd v. National Bank of Pakistan* [1978] 2 Lloyd's Rep. 223, 285–293; *Willcock v. Pickfords Removals Ltd* [1979] 1 Lloyd's Rep. 244, 245.

[61] *Golodetz v. Schrier* (1947) 80 Ll.L.Rep. 647, 650; *Brown v. Genossenschaft Oesterreichischer Waldbesitzer R. GmbH, supra*; *Lucanda Exportadora SARL v. Wahbe Tamari & Sons* [1967] 2 Lloyd's Rep. 353, 364.

[62] s.30(1).

[63] s.30(2).

[64] See *post*, § 16–074.

[65] See *post*, § 16–124.

[66] s.4(1) and Sched. 1.

[67] *cf.*, CPR, Part II.

[68] s.31(1). A party is not precluded from raising such an objection by the fact that he has appointed or participated in the appointment of an arbitrator.

[69] s.31(2).

[70] s.31(3).

unless he shows that he did not then know and could not with reasonable diligence have discovered the grounds for the objection.[71]

Where an objection is duly taken to the tribunal's substantive jurisdiction and the tribunal has power to rule on its own jurisdiction, section 31(4) states that the tribunal may adopt one of two courses: first, it may rule on the matter in an award on jurisdiction; secondly, it may deal with the objection in its award on the merits. It may be presumed that at least the first of these alternatives is open to the tribunal if it rules that it lacks jurisdiction as well as if it rules that it has jurisdiction, although it is somewhat peculiar to categorise the declining of jurisdiction as an "award". If the parties agree which of these two courses the tribunal should take, the tribunal is to proceed accordingly. In either case the award may be challenged in court under section 67 of the Act.[72] But a third way of proceeding is also contemplated, albeit in limited circumstances. This is for an application (under section 32) to be made to the court by a party before any award.[73] In this situation, the tribunal may (and, if the parties agree, must) stay the arbitral proceedings whilst such an application is made.[74] It must, however, be borne in mind that a person who is alleged to be a party to arbitral proceedings but who takes no part in those proceedings because he considers that the tribunal lacks substantive jurisdiction cannot be required to take any positive steps to object to the jurisdiction of the tribunal. He may choose instead to challenge the jurisdiction of the tribunal by proceedings in court for a declaration or injunction or other appropriate relief under section 72[75] or to challenge any award made under section 67.[76] **16–073**

Determination of preliminary point of jurisdiction. Section 32 of the 1996 Act confers upon a party, in limited circumstances, the right to apply to the court to determine any question as to the substantive jurisdiction of the arbitral tribunal.[77] In view of the power given to the tribunal by section 30 to rule on its own jurisdiction, such an application is intended to be made in exceptional cases only.[78] The application cannot be considered unless either it is made with the agreement in writing of all the other parties to the proceedings, or it is made with the permission of the tribunal and the court is satisfied (a) that the determination of the question is likely to produce substantial savings in costs, (b) that the application was made without delay, and (c) that there is good reason why the matter should be decided by the court.[79] Unless otherwise agreed by the parties, the tribunal may continue the arbitral proceedings and make an award while an application to the court is pending.[80] **16–074**

Restrictions are placed by sub-sections (5) and (6) of section 32 on the right of appeal. Unless the court gives leave, no appeal lies from a decision of the court **16–075**

---

[71] s.73(1); *post* §§ 16–126, 16–139.
[72] See *post*, § 16–124.
[73] See *post*, § 16–074.
[74] s.31(5). See (1998) 64 *Arbitration* 188.
[75] See *post*, § 16–125.
[76] See *post*, § 16–124.
[77] s.32(1).
[78] DAC Report, § 147.
[79] s.32(2). Unless made with the agreement of the parties, the application must state the grounds on which it is said that the matter should be decided by the court: s.32(3). See also RSC Ord. 73, esp. r. 19.
[80] s.32(4). See (1998) 64 *Arbitration* 188.

whether the conditions referred to above have been met.[81] So far as the decision of the court on the question of jurisdiction is concerned, this is treated as a judgment of the court for the purposes of an appeal. But no appeal lies without the leave of the court which will not be given unless the court considers that the question involves a point of law which is one of general importance or is one which for some other special reason should be considered by the Court of Appeal.[82] It would appear that no appeal lies against a refusal to give leave. Section 32 is mandatory.[83]

7. THE ARBITRAL PROCEEDINGS

16-076   **Conduct of the reference.** Section 33 of the 1996 Act sets out the general duty of the arbitral tribunal in the conduct of the reference. The tribunal is to act fairly and impartially as between the parties, giving each party a reasonable opportunity of putting his case and dealing with that of his opponent,[83a] and is to adopt procedures suitable to the circumstances of the particular case, avoiding unnecessary delay or expense, so as to provide a fair means for the resolution of the matters falling to be determined.[84] The tribunal must comply with this general duty in conducting the arbitral proceedings, in its decisions on matters of procedure and evidence and in the exercise of all other powers conferred upon it.[85] This is a mandatory provision.[86] Subject to the overriding requirements of fairness, impartiality and even-handedness, it is intended to encourage the tribunal to adapt its procedures to suit the particular case and not slavishly to follow court or other set procedures if these are inappropriate.[87]

16-077   The generality of the wording of section 33 may, nevertheless, invite unsuccessful parties to challenge procedural decisions taken by the tribunal, or the award, on the ground that the tribunal has failed to observe one or more of the duties stipulated by the section, especially since the Departmental Advisory Committee suggested that a proceeding which departed from those duties could not "properly be described as an arbitration".[88] However, the sanctions for breach of duty are narrowly circumscribed. They are, first, that the court should remove the arbitrator under section 24 (but this is subject to the limitations imposed by that section)[89]; secondly, that the court should remit, set aside or invalidate the award under section 68 on the ground of "serious irregularity". But an irregularity is only "serious" if the court considers that it has caused or will cause substantial injustice to the applicant.[90] It is therefore to be expected that the courts will not uphold challenges based on breaches of section 33 which are insubstantial.[91]

---

[81] s.32(5).
[82] s.32(6).
[83] s.4(1) and Sched. 1.
[83a] s.33(1)(b); *Gbangbola v. Smith & Sherriff Ltd* [1998] 3 All E.R. 730.
[84] s.33(1)(b).
[85] s.33(2).
[86] s.4(1) and Sched. 1.
[87] DAC Report, § 151.
[88] *ibid.* § 150.
[89] See *ante*, § 16–066.
[90] See *post*, § 16–127.
[91] DAC Report, § 151.

Procedural and evidential matters. The arbitral tribunal has a general power **16–078** to control the manner in which proceedings are conducted. Section 34(1) of the 1996 Act makes this clear by providing that it is for the tribunal to decide all procedural and evidential matters, subject to the right of the parties to agree any matter. There could be a potential conflict between the mandatory duty of the tribunal under section 33 and the principle of party autonomy contained in section 34,[92] for example, if the parties agreed to adopt a procedure, *e.g.* extended disclosure, which involved unnecessary delay or expense contrary to section 33 (1) (b). But such a conflict is likely to be more theoretical than real. In practice, the parties will be free to agree on any procedural or evidential matter, for example, by agreeing to apply the procedural rules of a particular arbitral institution. In the absence of any effective agreement between the parties in respect of such a matter, the tribunal decides how best to proceed in the circumstances of the case.

Section 34(2) gives an illustrative and non-exhaustive list of the procedural **16–079** and evidential matters referred to. These include:

(a) "when and where any part of the proceedings is to be held"—so empowering the tribunal to decide, for example, when meetings are to be held, or that meetings are to be held elsewhere than at the seat of arbitration[93];

(b) "the language or languages to be used in the proceedings and whether translations of any relevant documents are to be supplied"[94];

(c) "whether any and if so what form of written statements of claim and defences are to be used, when these should be supplied and the extent to which such statements can be later amended"—so empowering the tribunal to determine the form of pleadings (if any), whether to order particulars, and to allow and disallow amendments[95];

(d) "whether any and if so which documents or classes of documents should be disclosed between and produced by the parties and at what stage"—so empowering the tribunal to apply or depart from the rules relating to discovery and inspection applied in court proceedings[96];

(e) "whether any and if so what questions should be put to and answered by the respective parties and when and in what form this should be done"—so empowering the tribunal to control the oral and written examination and interrogation of the parties[97];

(f) "whether to apply strict rules of evidence (or any other rules) as to the admissibility, relevance or weight of any material (oral, written or other) sought to be tendered on any matters of fact or opinion, and the time, manner and form in which such material should be exchanged and presented"—so empowering the tribunal to dispense with technical rules of evidence and, as an incidental result, to put an end to any arguments that

---

[92] *cf.* DAC Report, §§ 154–163. See also *ibid.* § 175 (s.40).
[93] See Hunter (1997) 13 *Arbitration International* 345, 347.
[94] *ibid.*
[95] *ibid.* at 349.
[96] *ibid.*
[97] *ibid.* at 350.

it is a question of law whether there is material to support a finding of fact[98];

(g) "whether and to what extent the tribunal should itself take the initiative in ascertaining the facts and the law"—so empowering the tribunal to discard the rules applicable to an adversarial procedure and adopt an inquisitorial approach, by, for example, itself procuring evidence[99];

(h) "whether and to what extent there should be oral or written evidence or submissions"—so, for example, allowing the tribunal to decide the case on the basis of documents only or to render an award after a very short oral hearing.[1]

Sub-section (3) of section 34 further allows the tribunal to fix time-limits for any directions it gives and to extend time-limits fixed.[2] The tribunal has the power to change its mind about any order made (though it is not desirable for it to do so) and to revise or reverse an earlier decision.[2a]

16–080   **Consolidation of proceedings and concurrent hearings.** The parties are free to agree that their arbitral proceedings are to be consolidated with others or that concurrent hearings shall be held.[3] But all parties to all such proceedings must so agree. Unless the parties agree to confer such power on the tribunal, for example, by adopting institutional rules which provide for consolidation or concurrent hearings,[4] neither the arbitral tribunal nor the court has that power.[5] This may constitute a considerable drawback to arbitration as a method of dispute resolution where a number of parties are involved, particularly in relation to construction and engineering projects.[6] But it seems to follow inevitably from the fact that, unless the parties otherwise agree, only their own disputes arising out of their own agreement can be referred to the agreed tribunal.[7] *A fortiori* there is no power in the tribunal or in the court to order that a person who has never agreed to arbitration should be joined as a party to the proceedings.

16–081   **Legal or other representation.** A party to arbitral proceedings may be represented in the proceedings by a lawyer or other person chosen by him.[8] This right is conferred by section 36 of the 1996 Act, but the parties are free to agree otherwise and the rules of some arbitral institutions preclude legal representation at first-tier hearings. The section does not entitle a party to insist that he be

---

[98] *ibid*. at 351.

[99] *ibid*. at 354 (subject to allowing the parties to comment on the evidence).

[1] *ibid*. at 357.

[2] *ibid*.

[2a] *Charles McWillie & Co. (Shipping) Ltd v. Ocean Laser Shipping Ltd* [1999] 1 Lloyd's Rep. 225, 248.

[3] s.38(1).

[4] See Knowles (1996) 62 *Arbitration* 191; Hanotiau (1998) 14 *Arbitration International* 369.

[5] s.38(2).

[6] There may also be difficulties in the case of "string" or "back-to-back" contracts in other spheres. See also *Sacor Maritima SA v. Repsol Petroleo SA* [1998] 1 Lloyd's Rep. 518 and *Aquator Shipping Ltd v. Kleimar NV* [1998] 2 Lloyd's Rep. 379 (head charter and sub-charter).

[7] DAC Report, § 179. See also *ante*, § 16–035 (confidentiality).

[8] s.36. See *Piper Double Glazing Ltd v. DC Contracts* [1994] 1 All E.R. 117 (costs incurred by unqualified person).

represented by a particular person and to delay the proceedings on the ground of the non-availability of that person.[9]

Power to appoint experts, etc. The arbitral tribunal is empowered to appoint experts or legal advisers to report to it and the parties, or to appoint assessors to assist it on technical matters, and it may allow such persons to attend the proceedings.[10] The parties must be given a reasonable opportunity to comment on any information, opinion or advice offered by them.[11] This power does not require the positive agreement of the parties, but the parties may otherwise agree and it is in any event subject to the general duty of the tribunal set out in section 33. The fees and expenses of an expert, etc. appointed by the tribunal for which the arbitrators are liable are expenses of the arbitrators for which (assuming they are reasonable) the parties are jointly and severally liable.[12] **16–082**

General powers exercisable by tribunal. One of the major objectives of the 1996 Act was to enlarge the powers of the arbitral tribunal in the conduct of the reference and to reduce the occasions on which a party would have to apply to the court to intervene in the proceedings. Section 38 of the Act provides that the parties are free to agree on the powers exercisable by the tribunal for the purposes of and in relation to the proceedings.[13] But it then sets out a number of powers which the tribunal has unless otherwise agreed.[14] **16–083**

Security for costs. Sub-section (3) empowers the tribunal to order a claimant to provide security for the costs of the arbitration. This was a major change from the previous law where only the court could order security for costs. The power is no longer vested in the court[15] but only in the tribunal. It remains to be seen whether arbitrators will exercise this power in the same manner as the court under RSC Order 23.[16] But it is expressly provided the the residence or incorporation of the claimant outside the United Kingdom is not to be a ground for the exercise of the power. When the power was vested in the court it was held that, where an arbitration takes place in England under the rules of the International Chamber of Commerce, an order should not ordinarily be made that the claimant give security for costs.[17] The mere fact, however, that an arbitration was international did not render inappropriate an order for security, especially if the arbitration was of a type regularly conducted in London and the contract was governed by English law.[18] **16–084**

Other directions. The section[19] also empowers the tribunal to give directions in relation to property which is the subject of the proceedings owned by or in the **16–085**

---

[9] DAC Report, § 184.

[10] s.37(1)(a).

[11] s.37(1)(b).

[12] s.37(2). See also s.28; *ante*, § 16–069. This is a mandatory provision.

[13] s.38(1).

[14] s.38(2).

[15] But see s.70(6); *post*, § 16–140.

[16] Preserved by CPR, Sched. 1. See (1997) 63 *Arbitration* 166 (guidelines).

[17] *Bank Mellat v. Helliniki Techniki SA* [1984] Q.B. 291. But contrast *SA Coppée Lavalin NV v. Ken-Ren Chemicals and Fertilisers Ltd* [1995] 1 A.C. 38.

[18] *K/S A/S Bani v. Korea Shipbuilding and Engineering Corpn.* [1987] 2 Lloyd's Rep. 445; *Flender Werft AG v. Aegean Maritime Ltd* [1990] 2 Lloyd's Rep. 27, 29; *Regia Autonoma de Electricitate Revel v. Gulf Petroleum International Ltd* [1996] 1 Lloyd's Rep. 67.

[19] s.38(4). See (1998) 64 *Arbitration* 84 (guidelines), 180; CPR, r. 25.1.

possession of a party,[20] to direct that a party or witness shall be examined on oath or affirmation[21] and to give directions to a party for the preservation of any evidence in his custody or control.[22]

16–086   **Provisional relief with agreement of parties.** An arbitral tribunal is entitled under section 47 of the 1996 Act to make interim awards or awards on different issues in the course of the proceedings. Such awards, however, are to be distinguished from orders for provisional relief, for example, a provisional order for the payment of money[23] which is subject to reversal or adjustment when a decision has been reached on the underlying merits of the dispute. Section 39 provides that the parties are free to agree that the tribunal shall have power to order on a provisional basis any relief which it would have power to grant in a final award.[24] But, unless the parties agree to confer such a power on the tribunal, it has no such power.[25] Conferment of the power to order conservatory measures, for example, or to grant interim injunctive relief, will sometimes be found in institutional rules adopted by the parties in the arbitration agreement and so be available to the tribunal.[26]

16–087   **Duties of parties.** Section 40 of the 1996 Act imposes a general duty on the parties to do all things necessary for the expeditious conduct of the arbitral proceedings This includes prompt compliance with decisions, orders and directions of the arbitral tribunal and taking promptly any steps to obtain a decision of the court on a preliminary question of jurisdiction or law.[27] Section 40 is a mandatory provision.[28]

16–088   **Default.** It is open to the parties to agree what shall be the powers of the tribunal in the event of a party's failure to do something necessary for the proper and expeditious conduct of the arbitration.[29] The rules of arbitral institutions often contain provisions which empower the tribunal to take action in cases of default. But, unless otherwise agreed, section 41 of the 1996 Act confers upon the tribunal certain specific powers which may be exercised in case of a party's default.[30]

16–089   **Want of prosecution.** An arbitrator has, at common law, no inherent power to dismiss a claim for want of prosecution,[31] nor had the court power to do so under the 1950 Act or otherwise.[32] However, sub-section (3) of section 41 re-enacts[33] section 13A of the 1950 Act and enables the arbitral tribunal to make an award

---

[20] Under s.12(6)(g) of the Arbitration Act 1950, this power was previously reserved to the court.

[21] This confirms s.12(1)–(3) of the 1950 Act.

[22] Under s.12(6)(e), (g) of the 1950 Act, this power was previously reserved to the court.

[23] s.39(2)(a).

[24] s.39(1). See also s.39(3) (to be taken into account in the final award); and CPR, Part 25.

[25] s.39(4).

[26] Thomas (1997) 13 *Arbitration International* 405; (1998) 64 *Arbitration* 17 (guidelines).

[27] ss.32, 45; *ante* § 16–074; *post*, § 16–096.

[28] s.4(1) and Sched. 1. For a possible conflict with s.34(1), see DAC Report, §175.

[29] s.41(1).

[30] s.41(2).

[31] *Bremer Vulkan Schiffbau und Maschinenfabrik v. South India Shipping Corpn. Ltd* [1981] A.C. 909.

[32] *ibid.*

[33] But with slight changes of language in s.41(3)(a).

dismissing a claim on the ground of want of prosecution.[34] The conditions which must be satisfied for the making of such an award reflect the current case law relating to the powers of a court to dismiss an action for want of prosecution. These conditions are that there has been inordinate and inexcusable delay on the part of the claimant in pursuing his claim and that the delay (a) gives rise, or is likely to give rise, to a substantial risk that it is not possible to have a fair resolution of the issues in that claim, or (b) has caused, or is likely to cause, serious prejudice to the respondent. It is, however, an error of law for an arbitrator to dismiss a claim for want of prosecution before the expiration of the limitation period, save in exceptional circumstances.[35]

Absence of party or failure to submit evidence. Sub-section (4) of section **16–090** 41 empowers the tribunal to proceed in the absence of a party at an oral hearing or if a party fails after due notice to submit written evidence or make written submissions.

Peremptory orders. If without showing sufficient cause a party fails to **16–091** comply with any order or directions of the arbitral tribunal, the tribunal may make a peremptory order to the same effect as the preceding order which was not complied with, prescribing a time limit for compliance.[36] Sub-sections (6) and (7) of section 41 set out the various powers of the tribunal in the event of non-compliance by a party with that peremptory order. These are that the tribunal may: exclude allegations or material which was the subject matter of the order[37]; draw adverse inferences from the non-compliance[38]; proceed to an award on the basis of the materials provided to the tribunal[39]; and make an order as to the costs of the arbitration incurred as a result of the non-compliance.[40] But the powers conferred do not include a power simply to make an award against the defaulting party. They do, however, include, in the case of non-compliance with a peremptory order to provide security for costs, the power to make an award dismissing the claim.[41]

Powers are also conferred upon the court by section 42 to enforce a per- **16–092** emptory order of the tribunal.[41a] But this is envisaged to be a last resort.[42] An application to the court can only be made where the parties have so agreed or the tribunal permits a party to apply or makes the application itself.[43] The court must also be satisfied that there has been a default in complying with the peremptory order within the time prescribed in the order (or, if no time was prescribed, within

---

[34] *Birkett v. James* [1978] A.C. 297; *Department of Transport v. Chris Smaller (Transport) Ltd* [1989] A.C. 1197; *L'Office Cherifien des Phosphates v. Yamashita—Shinnihon Steamship Co.* [1994] 1 A.C. 486. See also *Trill v. Sacher* [1993] 1 W.L.R. 1379; *Roebuck v. Mungovin* [1994] 2 A.C. 224; Davies (1997) 63 *Arbitration* 286.

[35] *James Lazenby & Co. v. McNicholas Construction Co. Ltd* [1995] 1 W.L.R. 615.

[36] s.41(5).

[37] s.41(7)(a).

[38] s.41(7)(b).

[39] s.41(7)(c).

[40] s.41(7)(d).

[41] s.41(6).

[41a] Unless otherwise agreed by the parties: s.42(1). See also the Scheme for Construction Contracts (England and Wales) Regulations 1998, S.I. 1998 No. 649; *Macob Civil Engineering Ltd v. Morrison Construction Ltd, The Times*, March 11, 1999.

[42] DAC Report, § 212.

[43] s.42(2).

a reasonable time)[44] and that the applicant has exhausted any available arbitral process in respect of failure to comply with the order.[45]

8. Powers of the Court

16–093   **Court powers in support of arbitral proceedings.** There is no inherent jurisdiction in the court to supervise arbitrations.[46] But the aid of the court may be invoked to assist the arbitral process. Section 43 of the 1996 Act[47] provides that a party to arbitral proceedings may use the same court procedures as are available in relation to legal proceedings[48] to secure the attendance before the tribunal of a witness in order to give oral testimony or to produce documents or other material evidence, *i.e.* to obtain a witness summons. But this may only be done with the permission of the tribunal or the agreement of the other parties.[49] Moreover, these particular court procedures may only be used if the witness is in the United Kingdom and the arbitral proceedings are being conducted in England.[50]

16–094   Section 44 of the Act also confers upon the court, unless otherwise agreed between the parties, the same powers on certain matters in relation to arbitral proceedings as it has in relation to legal proceedings.[51] These are: the taking and preservation of evidence, making orders in relation to property, the sale of any goods, and the granting of an interim injunction or the appointment of a receiver.[52] However, these powers may only be used when the tribunal or arbitral institution is unable to act or to act effectively.[53] This limitation is entirely consistent with one of the aims of the Act, which is to restrict the power of the court to intervene in the arbitral process. But it remains to be seen how strictly it will be applied. If the case is one of urgency, the court may, on the application of a party or proposed party to the arbitral proceedings, make such orders as it considers necessary for the purpose of preserving evidence or assets,[54] for instance, it may make a search order or grant a freezing injunction.[54a] But if the case is not one of urgency, then the court can act only upon an application of a

---

[44] s.42(4).
[45] s.42(3). See also RSC, Ord. 73. The leave of the court is required for any appeal from a decision of the court under this section: s.42(5).
[46] *Exormisis Shipping SA v. Oonsoo* [1975] 1 Lloyd's Rep. 432, 434; *Bremer Vulkan Schiffbau und Maschinenfabrik v. South India Shipping Corpn. Ltd* [1981] A.C. 909, 979; *K/S A/S Bill Biakh v. Hyundai Corpn.* [1988] 1 Lloyd's Rep. 187, 189; *Kirkawa Corpn. v. Gatoil Overseas Inc.* [1990] 1 Lloyd's Rep. 154, 157; *Charles McWillie & Co. (Shipping) Ltd v. Ocean Laser Shipping Ltd* [1999] 1 Lloyd's Rep. 225, 248. *cf. Japan Line Ltd v. Aggeliki Charis Compañía Maritima SA* [1980] 1 Lloyd's Rep. 288, 292.
[47] s.43(1). s.43 derives from s.12(4) and (5) of the Arbitration Act 1950. It is mandatory.
[48] CPR, r. 34.2; RSC Ord. 73, r. 16.
[49] s.43(2).
[50] s.43(3), *i.e.* England and Wales, or (as the case may be) Northern Ireland.
[51] s.44(1). See also s.44(6) and RSC Ord. 73, r. 18.
[52] s.44(2). See Thomas (1997) 13 *Arbitration International* 105. *cf. Tsakos Shipping & Trading SA v. Orizon Tanker Co. Ltd* [1998] C.L.C. 1003 (order for inspection and tests set aside).
[53] s.44(5).
[54] s.44(3).
[54a] *Re Q's Estate* [1999] 4 C.L. 36.

party to the arbitral proceedings made with the permission of the tribunal or the agreement in writing of the other parties.[55]

The powers of the court under sections 43 and 44 may be exercised even if the   **16–095**
seat of the arbitration is outside England or no seat has been designated or determined, but the court may refuse to exercise any such power if, in its opinion, the fact that the seat is outside England, or that when designated or determined the seat is likely to be outside England, makes it inappropriate to do so.[56]

Determination of preliminary point of law by the court. Section 2 of the   **16–096**
Arbitration Act 1979 enabled a party to an arbitration to apply to the court to determine a question of law arising in the course of the reference. This "Consultative Case" procedure was useful in certain instances since it enabled a definitive answer to be obtained from the court at an early stage of the arbitral proceedings. Section 45 of the 1996 Act confers a similar power on the court to determine any question of law[57] arising in the course of the proceedings, but the court must be satisfied that the question of law substantially affects the rights of one or more of the parties.[58] Further, in order not to interfere unduly in the arbitral process, the conditions subject to which the court is empowered to consider such an application are also limited: the application must be made with the agreement of all the other parties to the proceedings or with the permission of the tribunal, and, in the latter case, the court must be satisfied that the determination of the question is likely to produce substantial savings in costs[59] and that the application is made without delay.[60] Unless otherwise agreed by the parties, the arbitral tribunal may continue the arbitral proceedings and make an award while an application to the court is pending.[61]

It is open to the parties, by agreement, to exclude the court's jurisdiction under   **16–097**
this section[62] and an agreement to dispense with reasons for the tribunal's award is to be considered as such an exclusion agreement.[63]

No appeal lies to the Court of Appeal from a decision as to whether or not the   **16–098**
conditions have been met to enable the court to consider the application unless

---

[55] s.44(5).

[56] s.2(3). *cf., Channel Tunnel Group Ltd v. Balfour Beatty Construction Ltd* [1993] A.C. 334. The court has power to order "provisional, including protective measures" under art. 24 of Sched. 1 to the Civil Jurisdiction and Judgments Act 1982 (the Brussels Convention) even though the courts of another contracting state have jurisdiction as to the substance of the matter. *cf. Van Uden Maritime BV v. Kommanditgesellschaft in Firma Decoline* (C391/95), *The Times,* December 1, 1998.

[57] See (on s.2 of the 1950 Act) *Chapman v. Charlwood Alliance Properties* (1981) 260 E.G. 1041.

[58] s.45(1). See (on ss.1, 2 of the 1950 Act) *Manders (Property) Estates v. Magnet House Properties* (1989) 42 E.G. 111; *Urban Small Space v. Burford Investments Co.* (1990) 28 E.G. 116. For the form of the application, see s.45(3) and RSC Ord. 73, especially rr. 15, 19.

[59] See (on s.2 of the 1950 Act) *Chapman v. Charlwood Alliance Properties, supra*; *Babanaft International SA v. Avant Petroleum Inc.* [1982] 1 W.L.R. 871, 882.

[60] s.45(2).

[61] s.45(4).

[62] s.45(1). See also s.69(1) and *post,* § 16–135. In the case of a domestic arbitration agreement, s.87 provides that any such exclusion agreement must be made after the commencement of arbitral proceedings. But s.87 is unlikely to be brought into force: see *ante,* § 16–005. The specific exceptions listed in s.4 of the Arbitration Act 1950 have also not been retained.

[63] s.45(1).

the court gives leave to appeal.[64] The decision of the court on the question of law itself is to be treated as a judgment of the court for the purposes of an appeal. But no appeal to the Court of Appeal lies without the leave of the court, which is not to be given unless the court considers that the question is one of general public importance or is one which for some other special reason ought to be considered by the Court of Appeal.[65] It would appear that no appeal lies against a refusal of the court to give leave to appeal.

16–099   **Power of court to extend time limits.** Section 79 of the 1996 Act confers upon the court a general power to extend any time limit agreed by the parties or specified in any provision of Part I of the Act (with the exception of the time limit for beginning arbitral proceedings dealt with in section 12)[66] but only after any available arbitral process has been exhausted and only if a substantial injustice would otherwise be done.[67]

9. THE AWARD

16–100   **Arbitrator's award: legal or other criteria.** Before the enactment of the 1996 Act, it was very doubtful whether an arbitration agreement which expressly authorised an arbitrator to decide *ex aequo et bono* or as *amiable compositeur* or otherwise free from the constraints of law[68] was a valid arbitration agreement in English law, or whether an award so made would be enforceable in England as a valid award.[69] But, if the parties so agree, section 46(1)(b) of the Act now authorises—and indeed requires—the arbitral tribunal to decide the dispute in accordance with such considerations as are agreed by the parties or determined by the tribunal. "Equity clauses" or arbitration *ex aequo et bono, amiable composition* or, indeed, any other type of clause which permits the tribunal to decide in accordance with general considerations of fairness and justice will, if so agreed by the parties, therefore be upheld, although it should be noted that the parties are then in effect excluding any right of appeal to the courts as there will be no "question of law" to appeal. The same provision in the Act would also give validity to clauses which stipulate, for example, that the tribunal is to apply the *lex mercatoria* or "general principles of law".

16–101   In the absence of any such agreement, however, "the duty of an arbitrator is to decide the questions submitted to him according to the legal rights of the parties, and not according to what he may consider fair and reasonable under the circumstances".[70] The arbitral tribunal must therefore apply some fixed and

---

[64] s.45(5).

[65] s.45(6).

[66] See *ante*, § 16–047.

[67] s.79(3). The application may be made a party or by the arbitral tribunal: s.79(2). On the extent of this power, see s.79(4), (5). The leave of the court is required for any appeal from a decision of the court under this section: s.79(6).

[68] *cf. Deutsche Schachtbau-und-Tiefbohr gesellschaft mbH v. R'As al-Khaimah National Oil Co.* [1990] 1 A.C. 295.

[69] *Home and Overseas Insurance (U.K.) Ltd v. Mentor Insurance Co. (U.K.) Ltd* [1990] 1 W.L.R. 153, 161, 166. See also *Czarnikow v. Roth Schmidt & Co.* [1922] 2 K.B. 478; *Orion Compañía Espanola de Seguros v. Belfort Maatschappij voor Algemeine Versekgrungen* [1962] 2 Lloyd's Rep. 257, 264; *Home Insurance Co. v. Administratia Asigurarilor de Stat* [1983] 2 Lloyd's Rep. 674, 677.

[70] *David Taylor & Son Ltd v. Barnett Trading Co.* [1953] 1 W.L.R. 562, 568.

recognisable system of law, whether English or foreign.[71] It cannot make a new contract for the parties,[72] but it must give effect to the usages of the trade applicable to the transaction if so required by the law which governs the contract.[73] It has jurisdiction to decide and is bound to give effect to all legal and equitable defences, including the Statute of Limitations[74] and the fact that the contract was illegal.[75]

Conflict of laws. The tribunal must decide the dispute in accordance with the law chosen by the parties as applicable to the substance of the dispute.[76] An express choice of law clause must therefore, unless the parties otherwise agree, be upheld. In the absence of any such choice or agreement, the tribunal is required to apply "the law determined by the conflict of laws rules which it considers applicable".[77] The arbitral tribunal therefore has a discretion as to which conflict of laws rules it will apply and, though the seat of the arbitration is in England, is not bound to apply English conflict rules.[78] It cannot, however, proceed directly to apply whatever substantive law it considers appropriate, but must arrive at the appropriate law by the application of conflict of law rules. **16–102**

Interim awards. As in the case of the 1950 Act,[79] section 47 of the 1996 Act enables the arbitral tribunal to make an interim award unless otherwise agreed by the parties. The expression "interim award" is, however, something of a misnomer, since such an award is in fact final on the matters dealt with in the award. More accurately, therefore, section 47 states that the tribunal "may make more than one award at different times on different aspects of the matters to be determined"[80] and that it may, in particular, make an award relating to an issue affecting the whole claim or to a part only of the claims or cross-claims submitted to it for decision.[81] Under the 1950 Act it was held that an arbitrator had a complete discretion whether or not to make an interim reward as opposed to dealing with the matter in a final award and that he might impose any proper condition which he thought fit on the making of the interim award.[82] There is little doubt that the 1996 Act will be construed no less widely and that, in practice, arbitrators will feel encouraged to use the power to make interim awards **16–103**

---

[71] *Orion Compañía Espanola de Seguros v. Belfort Maatschappij voor Algemeine Versekgrungen, supra.* See the criticisms of Shackleton (1997) 13 *Arbitration International* 375.

[72] *Hooper & Co. v. Balfour, Williamson & Co.* (1890) 62 L.T. 646; *Jager v. Tolme and Runge* [1916] 1 K.B. 939, 953, 957, 961.

[73] DAC Report, § 222.

[74] *Board of Trade v. Cayzer, Irvine & Co.* [1927] A.C. 610, 614; *Naamlooze, etc., Vulcaan v. A/S Ludwig Mowinckels Rederi* (1938) 43 Com. Cas. 252, H.L.; *Leif Hoegh & Co. A/S v. Petrolsea Inc.* [1992] 1 Lloyd's Rep. 45.

[75] *David Taylor & Son Ltd v. Barnett Trading Co.* [1953] 1 W.L.R. 562. *cf. Harbour Assurance Co. (U.K.) Ltd v. Kansa General International Insurance Co. Ltd* [1993] Q.B. 701.

[76] s.46(1)(a) and (2) (no renvoi).

[77] s.46(3). See Wortmann (1998) 14 *Arbitration International* 97.

[78] DAC Report, § 225.

[79] s.14.

[80] s.47(1), (5), (6).

[81] s.47(2).

[82] See *Japan Line v. Aggeliki Charis Compañía Maritime SA* [1980] 1 Lloyd's Rep. 288; *S. L. Sethia Liners v. Naviagro Maritime Corpn.* [1981] 1 Lloyd's Rep. 18; *Leon Corpn. v. Atlantic Lines and Navigation Co. Inc.* [1985] 2 Lloyd's Rep. 470, 476; *Exmar BV v. National Iranian Tanker Co.* [1992] 1 Lloyd's Rep. 169; *Modern Trading Co. Ltd v. Swale Building and Construction Ltd* (1990) 24 Con. L.R. 59. *cf. Minerals & Metals Trading Corpn. of India Ltd v. Encounter Bay Shipping Co. Ltd* [1988] 1 Lloyd's Rep. 51.

in order to separate out issues for early determination. However, if the tribunal makes an interim award, it must specify in its award the issue, or the claim or part of a claim, which is the subject matter of the award.[83]

16–104   **Remedies.** The parties are free to agree on the powers exercisable by the arbitral tribunal as regards remedies[84] and could therefore, by agreement, empower the tribunal to grant forms of relief that are not available to the courts.[85] Unless otherwise agreed by the parties, the tribunal may order the payment of a sum of money in any currency,[86] whether the claim is for a debt or damages, and it should award damages in the currency which best expresses the claimant's loss.[87] It may also grant declaratory relief,[88] including a declaration that one party is entitled to be indemnified by the other. There is further conferred upon the tribunal the same powers as the court to grant injunctive relief,[89] to order specific performance of a contract (other than a contract relating to land),[90] and to order the rectification, setting aside or cancellation of a deed or other document.[91]

16–105   **Interest.** The parties are free to agree on the powers of the tribunal as regards the award of interest.[92] Section 49 of the 1996 Act provides that, subject to the contrary agreement of the parties,[93] the tribunal may award simple or compound interest at such rates and with such rests as it considers meets the justice of the case in respect of periods both before and after the award.[94] Although the power to award interest is discretionary, interest should ordinarily be awarded in a commercial arbitration.[95] The tribunal's powers to award *compound* interest are wider than those of a court.[96] However, compound interest should only be ordered on a compensatory, and not on a punitive, basis.[97] If an arbitrator misdirects himself in his award as to the principles on which his discretion ought to be exercised, this would, it seems, be a question of law which could be made the subject of an appeal to the court.[98] But otherwise the exercise of his discretion will not be open to appeal or challenge.[99]

16–106   **Extension of time for making award.** There is no statutory time-limit placed on the arbitral tribunal within which it must make an award. But the arbitration

---

[83] s.47(3).
[84] s.48(1) *e.g.* contribution (*Wealands v. CLC Contractors Ltd* [1998] C.L.C. 808).
[85] DAC Report, § 234. But these may be difficult to enforce: see *post*, § 16–147.
[86] s.48(4).
[87] *Services Europe Atlantique Sud (S.E.A.S.) v. Stockholms Rederiaktiebolag* [1979] A.C. 685.
[88] s.48(3).
[89] s.48(5)(a). See Supreme Court Act 1981, s.37; CPR, r. 25.1 (interim injunctions).
[90] s.48(5)(b): CPR, Part 24, 24PD–001.
[91] s.48(5)(c).
[92] s.49(1).
[93] s.49(2).
[94] s.49(3)(4).
[95] *Re Badger* (1819) 2 B. & Ad. 691; *Edwards v. G. W. Ry.* (1851) 11 C.B. 588; *Chandris v. Istrandtsen Moller Co. Inc.* [1951] 1 K.B. 240; *Panchaud Frères SA v. Pagnan & Fratelli* [1974] 1 Lloyd's Rep. 394; *P. J. Van der Zijden Wildhandel NV v. Tucker & Cross Ltd* [1976] 1 Lloyd's Rep. 341; *Nea Tyhi Maritime Co. Ltd v. Compagnie Grainiere SA* [1978] 1 Lloyd's Rep. 16; *Thos. P. Gonzalez Corpn. v. F. R. Waring (International) (Pty.) Ltd* [1978] 1 Lloyd's Rep. 494; [1980] 2 Lloyd's Rep. 160; *Warinco AG v. Andre et Cie SA* [1979] 2 Lloyd's Rep. 298; *Tehno-Impex v. Gebr. van Weelde-Scheepvaartkantoor BV* [1981] Q.B. 648.
[96] *Westdeutsche Landesbank Girozentrale v. Islington L.B.C.* [1996] A.C. 669.
[97] *National Bank of Greece SA v. Pinios Shipping Co. (No. 1)* [1990] 1 A.C. 637.
[98] Under s.69; *post*, § 16–132.
[99] *Amec Building Ltd v. Cadmus Investment Co. Ltd* (1997) 51 Con. L.R. 105.

agreement or institutional rules may impose such a time-limit. The court then has power to extend that time-limit subject to two qualifications: first, arbitral procedures for obtaining an extension must be exhausted before recourse to the court, and, secondly, the court must be satisfied that substantial injustice would be done if the time were not extended.[1]

Settlement in form of agreed award. Section 51 of the 1996 Act enables an **16–107** agreed settlement of the dispute to be given the status of an arbitral award which can then be enforced as such. Unless the parties otherwise agree, such an award need not contain any reasons,[2] nor need it be stated in the award that it is an agreed award. However, the tribunal can refuse to make the award[3] and might well decline to do so if, for example, it was in terms which were designed to mislead third parties, such as Customs and Excise or the Revenue, or if it dealt with matters not arbitrable under the applicable law.

Form of award. The parties are free to agree on the form of an award.[4] If or **16–108** to the extent that there is no agreement,[5] the award must be in writing signed by all the arbitrators or all those assenting to the award[6]; it must contain the reasons for the award[7]; and it must state the seat of the arbitration and the date when the award is made.[8] Failure to comply with these requirements of form is a ground for challenge to the award,[9] but only if it has caused or will cause substantial injustice to the applicant.[10] Where there is a reference to the decision of three arbitrators, all the arbitrators, acting together, must fairly consider all the issues in the case prior to the award.[11] But they may sign the award separately[12] and, if it is a majority award, there is no need for the majority to meet with the dissenting arbitrator to discuss with him the re-drafting of their award.[13]

Place of award. In *Hiscox v. Outhwaite*[14] the House of Lords held that the **16–109** place of signature determined where an award was made. But section 53 of the 1996 Act reverses that decision in part[14a] by providing that the award shall be treated as made at the seat of the arbitration (if in England) regardless of where it was signed despatched or delivered to the parties.

Date of award. The arbitral tribunal is to decide what is the date of the **16–110** award.[15] But, if it does not do so, the date of the award is to be taken to be the date on which it is signed by the arbitrator or, where more than one arbitrator

---

[1] s.50. See RSC, Ord. 73.

[2] s.52(4). But see RSC Ord. 73, r. 31(5).

[3] s.51(2).

[4] s.52(1).

[5] s.52(2).

[6] s.52(3).

[7] s.52(4) (Unless it is an agreed award or the parties have agreed to dispense with reasons).

[8] s.52(5).

[9] s.68(2)(h).

[10] s.68(2); *post*, § 16–127.

[11] *European Grain & Shipping Ltd v. R. Johnston* [1983] Q.B. 520; *Bank Mellat v. GAA Development and Construction Co.* [1988] 1 Lloyd's Rep. 44.

[12] *European Grain & Shipping Ltd v. R. Johnston, supra.*

[13] *Bank Mellat v. GAA Development and Construction Co., supra.*

[14] [1992] 1 A.C. 562.

[14a] See also s.100(2)(b).

[15] s.54. Unless otherwise agreed by the parties.

signs, by the last of them. The date of the award is important since the time-limit for challenge or appeal runs from the date of the award.[16]

16–111   **Notification of and power to withhold award.** Subject to contrary agreement, the award must be notified to the parties without delay after the award is made by service on them of copies of the award.[17] However, the tribunal may refuse to deliver an award to the parties except upon full payment of the fees and expenses of the arbitrators.[18] If it refuses on that ground to deliver an award, then, in the absence of any available arbitral process for appeal or review of the amount demanded, a party may apply to the court for an order that the tribunal shall deliver the award pending determination by the court of the amount properly payable.[19] This is a mandatory provision.[20]

16–112   **Correction of award or additional award.**[21] Section 57 of the 1996 Act allows the arbitral tribunal to correct an award so as to remove any clerical mistake or error arising from an accidental slip or omission or clarify or remove any ambiguity in the award or to make an additional award in respect of any claim (including a claim for interest or costs) which was presented to the tribunal but was not dealt with in the award. This may be done by the tribunal on its own initiative or on the application of a party,[22] but only within certain time-limits.[23]

16–113   **Effect of award.** The rules of a trade association may, for example, provide for a process of appeal or review from the award of an arbitrator to an appellate arbitral tribunal. But subject to this and to any other contrary agreement of the parties, and subject to the powers of the court in relation to the award which are set out in Part I of the 1996 Act, an award made by the tribunal pursuant to an arbitration agreement is final and binding both on the parties and on any persons claiming through or under them.[24]

16–114   **Award as a defence.** Except where it is expressly provided to the contrary in the arbitration agreement, or the award is an interim award only, a valid award of damages duly made in pursuance of a submission to arbitration operates between the parties as a bar to any further action *in personam*[25] by the claimant in respect of the matters referred.[26] This is so even though the damages payable under the award have not been paid,[27] the claimant's remedy being to enforce the

---

[16] See *post*, §§ 16–130, 16–133, 16–139.

[17] s.55.

[18] s.56. This is a mandatory provision.

[19] s.56(2). See RSC Ord. 73, and in particular r. 10(2).

[20] s.4(1) and Sched. 1.

[21] See (previously) Arbitration Act 1950, s.17; *Sutherland and Co. v. Hannevig Bros Ltd* [1921] 1 K.B. 336; *Craske v. Norfolk C.C.* [1991] J.P.L. 760.

[22] s.57(3). For the effect of a failure to apply, see s.70(2)(b) and *Gbangbola v. Smith & Sherriff Ltd* [1998] 3 All E.R. 730.

[23] These time-limits are set out in subs. (4), (5), (6).

[24] s.58 (replacing s.16 of the Arbitration Act 1950).

[25] But not an action *in rem*, see *The Rena K* [1978] 1 Lloyd's Rep. 545, 560. But see *Republic of India v. India Steamship Co. Ltd* [1998] A.C. 878.

[26] Unlike a judgment (see *post*, § 26–007), the cause of action does not technically merge in the award, but the effect is the same. cf., *Doleman & Sons v. Ossett Corpn.* [1912] 3 K.B. 257 (award after action brought, where no application is made to stay the action or a stay is refused).

[27] *Gascoyne v. Edwards* (1826) 1 Y. & J. 19.

award. In contrast an award for payment of a debt does not operate as a bar to further action for the original debt,[28] although the parties are bound by the award as to the amount due.[29]

An award will preclude a claimant from commencing a second arbitration **16–115** against the same party to recover further damages arising from the same cause of action which was the subject of the award.[30] The rule that damages resulting from one and the same cause of action must be assessed and recovered once for all in the same proceedings applies in principle to arbitration[31] as it does to actions.[32] But this rule may be displaced if there is an arbitral practice to the contrary in a particular trade[33] or if certain matters only have been included in the terms of reference in the first arbitration[34] or if the first award is merely declaratory of the claimant's rights.[35] Successive arbitrations may, however, be commenced in respect of different causes of action, even though these arise out of the same contract.[36]

A party may be estopped from raising a second time a cause of action which **16–116** has been conclusively determined by a valid award in previous arbitration proceedings between the same parties or their privies,[37] or an issue raised and determined in such proceedings which it was necessary to determine for the purpose of those proceedings.[38] Moreover the court has an inherent jurisdiction to strike out as an abuse of its process a claim based on factual issues which had been raised, or should with reasonable diligence have been raised, in previous arbitration proceedings that have been adjudicated upon by the arbitral tribunal in those proceedings,[39] and it is possible that a court could restrain a party from asserting such a claim in subsequent arbitration proceedings.

---

[28] *Allen v. Milner* (1831) 2 Cr. & J. 47; *Richard Adler v. Soutos (Hellas) Maritime Corpn.* [1984] 1 Lloyd's Rep. 296.

[29] *Cummings v. Heard* (1869) L.R. 4 Q.B. 669, 673–674.

[30] *Conquer v. Boot* [1928] 2 K.B. 336.

[31] *Dunn v. Murray* (1829) 9 B. & C. 780; *Naamlooze, etc. Vulcaan v. A/S Ludwig Mowinckels Rederi* (1938) 60 Ll.L.Rep. 217, 223; *H. E. Daniels Ltd v. Carmel Exporters and Importers Ltd* [1953] 2 Q.B. 242, 255; *Compagnie Grainière SA v. Fritz Kopp AG* [1978] 1 Lloyd's Rep. 511, 521; *Telfair Shipping Corpn. v. Inersea Carriers SA* [1983] 2 Lloyd's Rep. 351, 353.

[32] See *post*, § 26–008.

[33] *E. E. & Brian Smith (1928) Ltd v. Wheatsheaf Mills Ltd* [1939] 2 K.B. 302; *cf.*, *H. E. Daniel Ltd v. Carmel Exporters and Importers Ltd, supra*.

[34] *Purser & Co. (Hillingdon) Ltd v. Jackson* [1977] Q.B. 166; *Compagnie Grainière SA v. Fritz Kopp AG, supra*; *Excomm Ltd v. Guan Guan Shipping (Pte) Ltd* [1987] 1 Lloyd's Rep. 330, 344.

[35] *F. J. Bloemen Pty. Ltd v. City of Gold Coast Council* [1973] A.C. 115, 126; *Compagnie Grainière SA v. Fritz Kopp AG, supra* at 522.

[36] *Brunsden v. Humphrey* (1884) 14 Q.B. 141; *Telfair Shipping Corpn. v. Insersea Carriers SA, supra*; *Siporex Trade SA v. Comdel Commodities Ltd* [1986] 2 Lloyd's Rep. 428. But see *Dunn v. Murray* (1829) 9 B. & C. 780 and the cases cited in n. 39, *post*.

[37] *Ayscough v. Sheed, Thomson & Co. Ltd* (1924) 40 T.L.R. 707; *Aktiebolaget Legis v. V. Berg & Sons Ltd* [1964] 1 Lloyd's Rep. 203. *cf. Taylor v. Vectapike* (1990) 44 E.G. 75; *Sacor Maritima SA v. Repsol Petroleo SA* [1998] 1 Lloyd's Rep. 518.

[38] *Fidelitas Shipping Co. Ltd v. V/O Exportchleb* [1960] 1 Q.B. 630, 640, 643, discussed in *Carl Zeiss Stiftung v. Rayner & Keeler Ltd (No. 2)* [1967] 1 A.C. 853. See also *Middlemiss & Gould v. Hartlepool Corpn.* [1972] 1 W.L.R. 1643, 1647–1648 and *post*, § 26–010.

[39] *Henderson v. Henderson* (1843) 3 Hare 100, 114; *Fidelitas Shipping Co. Ltd v. V/O Exportchleb, supra*, at 640; *Yat Tung Investment Co. Ltd v. Dao Heng Bank Ltd* [1975] A.C. 581, 590; *Dallal v. Bank Mellat* [1986] Q.B. 441. See also *post*, § 26–012.

10. COSTS OF THE ARBITRATION

16–117   **Costs.** Sections 59 to 65 of the 1996 Act provide a code dealing with how the costs of the arbitration should be allocated as between the parties. The "costs of the arbitration" are defined as the arbitrators' fees and expenses, the fees and expenses of any arbitral institution concerned, and the legal or other costs of the parties.[40] Although it is open to the parties to provide how these costs are to be allocated, an agreement which has the effect that a party is to pay the whole or part of the costs of the arbitration in any event is only valid if made after the dispute in question has arisen.[41] This is a mandatory provision.[42]

16–118   The arbitral tribunal is empowered to make an award as to costs[43] and is required (unless the parties otherwise agree) to award costs on the principle that costs are to follow the event except where it appears to the tribunal that in the circumstances this is not appropriate.[44] The tribunal does not therefore have a complete and unfettered discretion over costs but must follow the general approach of the English courts. The court will not interfere merely because it would have exercised that discretion differently.[45] But if the tribunal fails to exercise judicially[46] its discretion over costs in making its award, the aggrieved party may apply to the court for an order that the award, or that part of the award that deals with costs, be varied, remitted or set aside. Following cases on the Arbitration Act 1979,[47] it would appear that an award as to costs can normally only be challenged through the medium of appeal to the court on a point of law

---

[40] s.59(1). See also s.59(2) (costs of taxation proceedings).

[41] s.60. This is based on s.18(3) of the Arbitration Act 1950. It is mandatory.

[42] s.4(1) and Sched. 1.

[43] s.61(1) (subject to any agreement of the parties).

[44] s.61(2).

[45] *Rosen & Co. Ltd v. Dowley and Selby* [1943] 2 All E.R. 172, 174; *Smeaton Hanscomb & Co. Ltd v. Sassoon I. Setty, Son & Co. (No. 2)* [1953] 1 W.L.R. 1481, 1483; *The Erich Schroeder* [1974] 1 Lloyd's Rep. 192, 194; *Blue Horizon Shipping Co. SA v. E. D. & F. Man Ltd* [1980] 1 Lloyd's Rep. 17; *W. Wilhemsen v. Canadian Transport Co.* [1980] 2 Lloyd's Rep. 204, 209; *Eleftheria Niki Compañía Naviera SA v. Eastern Mediterranean Marine Ltd* [1980] 2 Lloyd's Rep. 252, 260; *President of India v. Jadranska Slobodna Plovidba* [1992] 2 Lloyd's Rep. 274, 280; *Everglade Maritime Inc. v. Schiffahrtsgesellschaft Detlef Von Appen mbH* [1993] 1 W.L.R. 33, 39 (affd. [1993] Q.B. 780).

[46] *i.e.* in the same manner as the High Court: *Lloyd del Pacifico v. Board of Trade* (1930) 35 Com. Cas. 325; *Stotesbury v. Turner* [1940] 3 K.B. 370; *Smeaton Hanscomb & Co. Ltd v. Setty, Son & Co. (No. 2), supra; Lewis v. Haverford West R.D.C.* [1953] 1 W.L.R. 1486; *L. E. Cattan Ltd v. A. Michaelides & Co.* [1958] 1 W.L.R. 717; *Perry v. Stopher* [1959] 1 W.L.R. 415, 419; *Messers Ltd v. Heidner & Co.* [1961] 1 Lloyd's Rep 107; *Matheson & Co. Ltd v. A. Tabah & Sons* [1963] 2 Lloyd's Rep. 270, 273; *The Erich Schroeder, supra,* at p. 193; *Tramountana Armadora SA v. Atlantic Shipping Co. SA* [1978] 2 All E.R. 870; *Patroclos Shipping Co. v. Société Secopa* [1980] 1 Lloyd's Rep. 405; *W. Wilhemsen v. Canadian Transport Co.* [1980] 2 Lloyd's Rep. 204; *Archital Luxfer Ltd v. Henry Boot Construction Ltd* [1981] 1 Lloyd's Rep. 642; *The Catherine L* [1982] 1 Lloyd's Rep. 484; *Argolis Shipping Co. SA v. Midwest Steel and Alloy Corpn.* [1982] 2 Lloyd's Rep. 594; *The Ios I* [1987] 1 Lloyd's Rep. 321; *King v. Thomas McKenna Ltd* [1991] 2 Q.B. 480, 499; *President of India v. Jadranska Slobodna Plovidba, supra,* at 278; *Everglade Maritime Inc. v. Schiffahrtsgesellschaft Detlef Von Appen mbH* [1993] Q.B. 780; *Metro-Cammell Hong Kong Ltd v. FKI Engineering plc* (1996) 77 Build. L.R. 84.

[47] *Blixen Ltd v. G. Percy Trentham Ltd* (1990) 42 E.G. 133, CA; *King v. Thomas McKenna Ltd* [1991] 2 QB 480, 499; *President of India v. Jadranska Slobodna Plovidba* [1992] 2 Lloyd's Rep. 274, 276–280; *Everglade Maritime Inc. v. Schiffahrtsgesellschaft Detlef Von Appen mbH* [1993] Q.B. 780; *Cohen v. Baram* [1994] 2 Lloyd's Rep. 138.

under section 69 of the 1996 Act.[48] If there is an effective exclusion agreement,[49] no such appeal will lie, so that a bona fide error on the part of the arbitral tribunal in the matter of costs will be irremediable.[50] An award will only be susceptible to challenge under section 67 or section 68 of the 1996 Act (which sections cannot be excluded)[51] where some other sufficient ground exists, such as a failure to deal at all with the issue of costs,[52] an excess of jurisdiction, or a serious irregularity in relation to costs,[53] but not simply on the ground of an alleged unjudicial exercise of the tribunal's discretion.

16–119 Section 63 of the 1996 Act provides that the parties may agree what costs of the arbitration are recoverable.[54] If they do not do so,[55] the tribunal may determine by award the recoverable costs of the arbitration (*i.e.* assess the amount) on such basis as it thinks fit, but in so doing must specify the basis on which it has acted and the items of recoverable costs and the amount referable to each.[56] If the tribunal does not determine the recoverable costs, any party may apply to the court.[57] The tribunal therefore has the power, but not the obligation, to deal with the costs of the arbitration.[58] The usual practice is for the tribunal to determine in its award the fees and expenses of the arbitrators.[59] The determination of the recoverable legal or other costs of the parties is better left to the court.

16–120 **Basis of costs.** Unless the tribunal or the court determines otherwise, costs will be awarded on a standard basis.[60]

16–121 **Fees and expenses.** Only the reasonable fees and expenses of the arbitrators are recoverable and what fees and expenses are "reasonable" may, on the application of any party, be determined by the court.[61]

16–122 **Power to limit recoverable costs.** Section 65 of the 1996 Act gives to the arbitral tribunal a new power not found in previous legislation: the power to limit in advance the amount of recoverable costs.[62] The tribunal can put a ceiling on costs. A party can incur costs in excess of this ceiling but the excess will then not be recoverable from the other party. The Departmental Advisory Committee considered that this power, properly used, could prove extremely valuable as an

---

[48] *Post,* § 16–132.

[49] *Post,* § 16–135.

[50] *King v. Thomas McKenna Ltd, supra,* at 499.

[51] *Post,* § 16–124, 16–127.

[52] *Re Becker, Shillan & Co. and Barry Brothers* [1921] 1 K.B. 391.

[53] *Harrison v. Thompson* [1989] 1 W.L.R. 1325; *King v. Thomas McKenna Ltd, supra*; *President of India v. Jadranska Slobodna Plovidba, supra,* at 279, 280; *Gbangbola v. Smith & Sherriff Ltd* [1998] 3 All E.R. 730; *Danae Air Transport SA v. Air Canada, The Times,* March 31, 1999.

[54] s.63(1).

[55] s.63(2).

[56] s.63(3).

[57] s.63(4).

[58] As under s.18(1) of the Arbitration Act 1950.

[59] Including fees and expenses of an expert etc. under s.37(2). See *SN Kurkjian (Commodity Brokers) Ltd v. Marketing Exchange for Africa Ltd* [1986] 2 Lloyd's Rep. 618 (taxation of fees of legal adviser), but *cf.* s.63(7).

[60] CPR, r. 44.4.

[61] s.64.

[62] s.65. Unless otherwise agreed by the parties.

aid to reducing expenditure and would discourage those who wished to employ their financial muscle to intimidate their opponents.[63]

16–123   **Sealed offers.** A sealed offer by the respondent in arbitral proceedings is analogous to, but not identical with,[64] a Part 36 payment.[64a] If the claimant in the end has achieved no more than he would have achieved by accepting the offer, the continuance of the arbitration after that date has been a waste of time and money. Prima facie, the claimant should recover his costs up to the date of the offer and should be ordered to pay the respondent's costs after that date. If he has achieved more by going on, the respondent should pay the costs throughout.[65]

11. POWERS OF THE COURT IN RELATION TO THE AWARD

16–124   **Challenging the award: substantive jurisdiction.** A party to arbitral proceedings may apply to the court under section 67 of the 1996 Act challenging any award of the arbitral tribunal as to its substantive jurisdiction[66] or for an order declaring an award made by the tribunal on the merits to be of no effect, in whole or in part, because the tribunal did not have substantive jurisdiction.[67] Such an application must normally be made within the 28 day time-limit prescribed by section 70(3)[68] and is subject to certain restrictions.[69] Where the arbitral tribunal rules that it has substantive jurisdiction and a party to arbitral proceedings who could have questioned that ruling by an arbitral process of appeal or review, or by challenging the award, does not do so timeously or at all, he may not object later to the tribunal's substantive jurisdiction on any ground which was the subject of that ruling.[70] On the hearing of the application the court may by order confirm the award, vary the award or set aside the award in whole or in part.[71] The hearing may be a full re-hearing (including oral evidence) of matters already raised before the tribunal.[71a] Pending the hearing of the application the arbitral tribunal may continue the arbitral proceedings and make a further award if it wishes to do so.[72] Section 67 is a mandatory provision.[73]

16–125   The same right to challenge the award is given to a person alleged to be a party to arbitral proceedings but who takes no part in the proceedings.[74] Alternatively such a person may question whether there is a valid arbitration agreement, or whether the tribunal is properly constituted, or what matters have been properly

---

[63] DAC Report, § 272. But see Miller (1999) 149 N.L.J. 530.
[64] *Huron Liberian Co. v. Rheinoel GmbH* [1985] 1 Lloyd's Rep. 58n.
[64a] CPR, Part 36.
[65] *Tramountana Armadora SA v. Atlantic Shipping Co. SA* [1978] 1 Lloyd's Rep. 391, 398; *Everglade Maritime Inc. v. Schiffahrtsgesellschaft Detlef Von Appen MbH* [1993] Q.B. 780. *cf., Cadmus Investment Ltd v. Amec Building Ltd* [1997] C.L.Y. 270.
[66] ss.30, 31; *ante*, § 16–071, 16–072.
[67] s.67(1). See RSC Ord. 73, especially r. 22.
[68] *Post*, § 16–139.
[69] s.70(2); *post*, § 16–139. See RSC Ord. 73.
[70] s.73(2).
[71] s.67(3).
[71a] *Azov Shipping Co. v. Baltic Shipping Co.* [1999] 1 Lloyd's Rep. 68.
[72] s.67(2). See (1998) 64 *Arbitration* 188.
[73] s.4(1) and Sched. 1.
[74] s.72(2)(a).

submitted to arbitration in accordance with the arbitration agreement, by proceedings in court for a declaration or injunction or other appropriate relief.[75]

16–126 A party to arbitral proceedings will lose the right to object to the substantive jurisdiction of the tribunal if he fails to object timeously and thereafter takes part, or continues to take part, in the proceedings, unless he did not know and could not with reasonable diligence have discovered the grounds for the objection.[75a] But even where this is not the case, then at common law if the parties appoint or accept the appointment of an arbitrator and thereafter take part in the arbitral proceedings without objection on the mistaken assumption that the tribunal has jurisdiction with respect to the whole or a part of the subject-matter of the dispute, they may be held to have entered into an ad hoc agreement to submit their dispute to the jurisdiction of the tribunal,[76] unless that agreement can be said to be vitiated by a fundamental mistake.[77] In this latter situation, however, even if there is no or no valid ad hoc agreement, each may be estopped by convention[78] from alleging lack of jurisdiction on the part of the tribunal.[79]

16–127 **Challenging the award: serious irregularity.** Prior to the enactment of the 1996 Act the High Court had an unqualified power to remit an award for the reconsideration of the arbitrator,[80] and it could set aside an award where the arbitrator had misconducted himself or the proceedings or the arbitration or award had been improperly procured.[81] "Misconduct" did not necessarily imply any reflection on the competence or integrity of the arbitrator: it covered irregularities or procedural unfairness which was not proper in relation to quasi-judicial proceedings.[82] The concept of misconduct was not retained in the 1996 Act. Section 68 established a different regime which enables a party to arbitral proceedings to apply to the court challenging the award on the ground of serious irregularity affecting the tribunal, the proceedings or the award.[83] This is a mandatory provision.[84] The same right to challenge the award is given to a person alleged to be a party to arbitral proceedings but who takes no part in the proceedings.[85]

16–128 For "serious irregularity" to have occurred there must, first, have been an irregularity of one or more of the following kinds[86]:

---

[75] s.72(1).

[75a] s.73(1); *ante* § 16–072.

[76] *Westminster Chemicals & Produce Ltd v. Eicholz & Loeser* [1954] 1 Lloyd's Rep. 99; *Luanda Exportadora SARL v. Wahbe Tamari & Sons Ltd* [1967] 2 Lloyd's Rep. 353; *Cia Maritima Zorroza SA v. Sesostris SAE* [1984] 1 Lloyd's Rep. 652; *Almare Societa di Navigazione SpA v. Derby & Co. Ltd* [1989] 2 Lloyd's Rep. 376; *Furness Withy (Australia) Pty. Ltd v. Metal Distributors (U.K.) Ltd* [1990] 1 Lloyd's Rep. 236.

[77] *Altco Ltd v. Sutherland* [1971] 2 Lloyd's Rep. 515; *Furness Withy (Australia) Pty. Ltd v. Metal Distributors (U.K.) Ltd, supra.*

[78] See *ante*, § 3–100.

[79] *Furness Withy (Australia) Pty. Ltd v. Metal Distributors (U.K.) Ltd, supra.*

[80] Arbitration Act 1950, s.22.

[81] *ibid.*, s.23(2).

[82] See the 27th edition of this book, Vol. I, § 15–042.

[83] s.68(1). See RSC Ord. 73, especially r. 22.

[84] s.4(1) and Sched. 1.

[85] s.72(2)(b).

[86] s.68(2).

(a) failure by the tribunal to comply with section 33 of the Act (general duty of the tribunal);

(b) the tribunal exceeding its powers (otherwise than by exceeding its substantive jurisdiction: see section 67);

(c) failure of the tribunal to conduct the proceedings in accordance with the procedure agreed by the parties;

(d) failure by the tribunal to deal with all the issues that were put to it;

(e) any arbitral or other institution or person vested by the parties with powers relating to the proceedings or the award exceeding its powers;

(f) uncertainty or ambiguity as to the effect of the award[86a];

(g) the award being obtained by fraud or the award or the way in which it was procured being contrary to public policy;

(h) failure to comply with the requirements as to the form of the award; or

(i) any irregularity in the conduct of the proceedings or in the award which is admitted by the tribunal or by any arbitral or other institution or person vested by the parties with powers in relation to the proceedings or the award.

It will be noted that the list of irregularities is a closed one. Some of the listed elements nevertheless have their origins in the previous law relating to misconduct, "procedural mishaps" and mistakes admitted by the arbitrator.[87] As under the previous law, the award cannot be challenged on the ground that the tribunal has come to an erroneous decision, whether of fact or law, and whether or not its findings of fact are supported by evidence.[88] In a two-tier arbitration, under which there is a right of appeal to an appeal board and the appeal board's award supersedes that of the first tier arbitrator, it is submitted that the award cannot be challenged on the ground of any irregularity in the conduct of the first tier proceedings if no irregularity is alleged in respect of the appeal.[89]

16–129   Secondly, the irregularity must be of a kind which the court considers has caused or will cause substantial injustice to the applicant.[90] In this respect, the DAC Report states that the section was "really designed as a long stop, only available in extreme cases where the tribunal has gone so wrong in its conduct of the arbitration that justice calls out for it to be corrected".[91]

[86a] *Ghangbola v. Smith & Sherriff Ltd* [1998] 3 All E.R. 730.

[87] See the 27th edition of this book, Vol. I, §§ 15–040—15–042.

[88] *Gillespie Bros. & Co. v. Thompson Bros. & Co.* (1922) 13 Ll.L.Rep. 519, 524; *Oleificio Zucchi SpA v. Northern Sales Ltd* [1965] 2 Lloyd's Rep. 496; *Prodexport Company for Foreign Trade v. E. D. & F. Man Ltd* [1973] Q.B. 389; *Moran v. Lloyd's* [1983] Q.B. 542, 549, 550; *Bulk Oil (Zug) AG v. Sun International Ltd (No. 2)* [1984] 1 Lloyd's Rep. 531, 533; *K/S A/S Bill Biakh v. Hyundai Corpn.* [1988] 1 Lloyd's Rep. 187, 189.

[89] *Costa v. British Indian Trading Co. Ltd* [1963] 1 Q.B. 201.

[90] s.68(2); *Egmatra v. Marco Trading Corpn* [1999] 1 Lloyd's Rep. 862. On this point, cases on "procedural mishaps" or misunderstandings decided under the Arbitration Act 1950 may possibly provide some guidance, as remission required that the mishap or misunderstanding should have caused injustice to one of the parties: see, *e.g. Indian Oil Corpn. Ltd v. Coastal (Bermuda) Ltd* [1990] 2 Lloyd's Rep. 407, 414 and the cases cited in the 27th edition of this book, Vol. I, § 15–040, n. 42.

[91] § 280.

The application must normally be made within the 28 day time-limit pre-   **16–130**
scribed by section 70(3)[92] and is subject to certain restrictions.[93] A party may
have lost the right to object to the irregularity if he failed to object timeously and
thereafter took part, or continued to take part, in the proceedings, unless he did
not know and could not with reasonable diligence have discovered the grounds
for the objection.[94] If a serious irregularity is shown to have occurred, the court
may remit the award to the arbitral tribunal for reconsideration, or it may set the
award aside, or it may declare the award to be of no effect. It may exercise these
powers in relation to the whole of the award or only part of it. The court is not
to set the award aside or declare it to be of no effect unless it is satisfied that it
would be inappropriate to remit the matters in question to the tribunal for
reconsideration.[95] A party may be precluded from having an award remitted, set
aside or declared to be of no effect if he has in fact taken the benefit of the award
and so affirmed it.[96]

Section 68 applies only to awards and not to interlocutory directions which are   **16–131**
not made in the form of an award.[97]

Appeal on point of law. Section 69 of the 1996 Act re-states in an amended   **16–132**
form section 1 of the Arbitration Act 1979 and provides that, unless otherwise
agreed by the parties, a party to arbitral proceedings may appeal to the court on
a question of law arising out of an award made in the proceedings.[98] Such an
appeal lies only with the agreement of all other parties to the proceedings[99] or
with leave of the court.[1] By subsection (3) of the section, leave to appeal is not
to be given unless the court is satisfied

(a) that the determination of the question will substantially affect the rights of
one or more of the parties,

(b) that the question is one which the tribunal was asked to determine,

(c) that on the basis of the findings of fact in the award—

    (i) the decision of the tribunal on the question is obviously wrong, or
    (ii) the question is one of general public importance and the decision of
    the tribunal is at least open to serious doubt, and

(d) that, despite the agreement of the parties to resolve the matter by arbitration, it is just and proper in all the circumstances for the court to determine
the question.

---

[92] *Post,* § 16–139.

[93] s.70(2); *post,* § 16–139. See also RSC Ord. 73 and now CPR r. 49.

[94] s.73(1); *post,* § 16–139.

[95] s.68(3).

[96] *Dexters Ltd v. Hill Crest Oil Co. (Bradford) Ltd* [1926] 1 K.B. 348; *AA Amram Ltd v. Bremar Co. Ltd* [1966] 1 Lloyd's Rep. 494; *European Grain & Shipping Ltd v. R. Johnston* [1983] 2 Q.B. 520. Contrast *Lissenden v. CAV Bosch Ltd* [1940] A.C. 412; *Sokratis Rokopoulos v. Esperia SpA* [1978] 1 Lloyd's Rep. 456; *Banner Industrial and Commercial Properties v. Clark Paterson* (1990) 47 E.G. 64.

[97] See (on s.22 of the Arbitration Act 1950) *Fletamentos Maritimos SA v. Effjohn International BV (No. 2)* [1997] 2 Lloyd's Rep. 502.

[98] s.69(1); RSC Ord. 73, especially rr. 15, 20, 22.

[99] *Poseidon Schiffahrt GmbH v. Nomadic Navigation Co. Ltd* [1998] 1 Lloyd's Rep. 57 and *Taylor Woodrow Civil Engineering Ltd v. Hutchinson IDH Development Ltd* [1998] C.L.Y. 228 (consent in advance).

[1] s.69(2).

The subsection reflects the limitations placed on the right of appeal under the 1979 Act by the House of Lords, notably in *Pioneer Shipping Ltd v. B.T.P. Tioxide Ltd (The Nema)*[2] and *Antaios Compânía Naviera SA v. Salen Rederiana A.B. (The Antaios)*,[3] but further limits court intervention by requiring that it must be "just and proper in all the circumstances for the court to determine the question".[4]

16–133   The application for leave to appeal must identify the question of law to be determined and state the grounds on which it is alleged that leave to appeal should be granted.[5] The court will normally determine the application for leave without a hearing.[6] As a general rule, the appeal must be brought within the 28 day time-limit prescribed by section 70(3)[7] and is subject to certain restrictions.[8] Appeals are only permitted on a question of law "arising out of an award" and not in respect of extrinsic matters arising in the course of the arbitral proceedings.[9] The court will no doubt, as under the previous law, continue to set its face against entertaining questions of law framed in the form of a question whether there was any evidence to support a particular finding.[10] The court may make any leave which it gives conditional upon the appellant complying with such conditions as it considers appropriate, and in particular may order security for costs or that money payable under the award is to be brought into court or otherwise secured.[11]

16–134   On an appeal under section 69 the court may confirm, vary or set aside the award or remit the award to the tribunal for reconsideration in the light of the court's determination. It may exercise its powers of setting aside or remission as to the whole of the award or only part of it. The court cannot exercise its power to set aside an award unless it is satisfied that it would be inappropriate to remit the matters in question to the tribunal for reconsideration.[12]

16–135   **Right of appeal: exclusion agreements.** Section 69, unlike sections 67 and 68, is not a mandatory provision and it is open to the parties by agreement to exclude the right of appeal.[13] In the case of a domestic arbitration agreement

---

[2] [1982] A.C. 724.

[3] [1985] A.C. 191.

[4] *Egmatra v. Marco Trading Corpn.* [1999] 1 Lloyd's Rep. 862 (foreign law). See also (on s.1 of the Arbitration Act 1979) *Aden Refinery Co. Ltd v. Ugland Management Co. Ltd* [1987] Q.B. 650; *Petraco (Bermuda) Ltd v. Petromed International Ltd* [1988] 1 W.L.R. 896; *Ipswich B.C. v. Fisons plc* [1990] Ch. 709.

[5] s.69(4).

[6] s.69(5) (unless it appears to the court that a hearing is required).

[7] See *post*, § 16–139.

[8] s.70(2); *post*, § 16–139. See also RSC Ord. 73.

[9] *Universal Petroleum Co. Ltd v. Handels und Transport GmbH* [1987] 1 W.L.R. 1178, 1189.

[10] *Mondial Trading Co. GmbH v. Gill & Duffus Zuckerhandelsgesellschaft mbH* [1980] 2 Lloyd's Rep. 376, 379; *Hayn Roman & Co. SA v. Cominter (U.K.) Ltd* [1982] 2 Lloyd's Rep. 458, 462; *Bulk Oil (Zug) AG v. Sun International Ltd* [1984] 1 Lloyd's Rep. 531, 533; *Athens Cape Naviera SA v. Deutsche Dampfschiffahrtsgesellschaft Hansa AG* [1985] 1 Lloyd's Rep. 528, 531–532; *Universal Petroleum Co. Ltd v. Handels und Transport GmbH, supra*; *Geogas SA v. Trammo Gas Ltd* [1993] 1 Lloyd's Rep. 215, 217. But see *Edwards v. Bairstow* [1956] A.C. 14; *Pioneer Shipping Ltd v. B.T.P. Tioxide Ltd (The Nema)* [1982] A.C. 724, 752.

[11] s.70(6), (7), (8).

[12] s.69(7).

[13] s.69(1).

section 87 of the 1996 Act provides that any agreement to exclude the jurisdiction of the court under section 69 or under section 45 (determination of preliminary point of law) is not to be effective unless entered into after the commencement of the arbitral proceedings in which the award is made. But section 87 is not yet in force and is unlikely to be brought into force.[14] The special categories of disputes mentioned in section 4(1) of the 1979 Act where the efficacy of an exclusion agreement was limited have not been retained in the 1996 Act. The parties are therefore free to exclude the right of appeal either in the original arbitration agreement or by the adoption of institutional rules which exclude that right. An agreement to dispense with reasons for the tribunal's award is to be considered an agreement to exclude the court's jurisdiction under section 69.[15]

Challenge or appeal: reasons for award. The arbitral tribunal is required to   **16–136**
give reasons for the award unless the award is an agreed award or the parties have agreed to dispense with reasons.[16] But, in order that the procedures for challenge or appeal may be effective, section 70(4) of the 1996 Act empowers the court to compel the tribunal to give reasons or further reasons for its award.[17] If on an application or appeal it appears to the court that the award does not contain the tribunal's reasons or does not set out the tribunal's reasons in sufficient detail to enable the court properly to consider the application or appeal, the court may order the tribunal to state the reasons for the award in sufficient detail for that purpose. In relation to the similar power conferred upon the court under section 1(5) of the 1979 Act, it was held that this power should be exercised sparingly[18] and it is probable that the court will have to be satisfied that, if an order were made, the application or appeal would be likely to succeed.[19] Otherwise there would be no point in ordering reasons or further reasons to be stated.

Challenge or appeal: additional costs. Where the court makes the order, it   **16–137**
may make such further order as it thinks fit with respect to any additional costs of the arbitration resulting from the order.[20]

Challenge or appeal: facts on which decision based. The power to order the   **16–138**
tribunal to state reasons for the award extends not only to "reasoning" but also to the relevant facts upon which its decision is based.[21] But the power cannot or

---

[14] See *ante*, § 16–005.

[15] s.69(1).

[16] s.52(4).

[17] This replaced s.1(5) of the Arbitration Act 1979. The proper construction of that sub-section, and its application, were considered by the Court of Appeal in *Universal Petroleum Co. Ltd v. Handles und Transport Gmbh* [1987] 1 W.L.R. 1178. See also the cases cited in the 27th edition of this book, Vol. I, § 15–049, n. 9.

[18] *Universal Petroleum Co. Ltd v. Handels und Transport GmbH, supra*, at 1194; *Granges Aluminium AB v. The Cleveland Bridge and Engineering Co., The Times*, May 15, 1990, CA.

[19] *The Gay Fidelity* [1982] 1 Lloyd's Rep. 469, 470; *Warde v. Feedex International Inc.* [1984] 1 Lloyd's Rep. 310, 314, [1985] 2 Lloyd's Rep. 289; *Trave Schiffahrtsgesellschaft mbH v. Ninemia Maritime Corpn.* [1986] Q.B. 802; *Universal Petroleum Co. Ltd v. Handels und Transport GmbH, supra*, at 1194; *Gebr. Van Weelde Scheepvartkantoor BV v. Société Industrielle d'Acide etc.* [1986] 1 Lloyd's Rep. 435; *Kansa General Insurance Co. Ltd v. Bishopsgate Insurance plc* [1988] 1 Lloyd's Rep. 503, 511.

[20] s.70(5).

[21] *Schiffahrtsagentur Hamburg Middle East Line GmbH v. Virtue Shipping Corpn.* [1981] 1 Lloyd's Rep. 533, 539; *Bulk Oil (Zug) AG v. Sun International Ltd (No. 2)* [1984] 1 Lloyd's Rep. 531, 533.

should not be used to order the tribunal to set out the evidence on which it relied in order to reach its conclusion.[22] There is no power in the court, before an award is made, to order the tribunal to state reasons for pre-award rulings.[23]

16–139   **Challenge or appeal: restrictions and time-limits.** An application or appeal may not be brought if the applicant or appellant has not first exhausted any available process of appeal or review and any available recourse under section 57 (correction of award or additional award).[24] Any application or appeal must be brought within 28 days of the date of the award or, if there has been any arbitral process of appeal or review, of the date when the applicant or appellant was notified of the result of that process.[25] This period may be extended[26] by the court, but only after any arbitral process for an extension has been exhausted and only if a substantial injustice would otherwise be done.[27] The right to object to the tribunal's substantive jurisdiction will be lost if the challenge is not made promptly.[27a] Also a party to arbitral proceedings will be held to have lost the right to object that the tribunal lacks substantive jurisdiction, or that the proceedings have been improperly conducted, or that there has been a failure to comply with the arbitration agreement or any provision of Part I of the Act, or that there has been any other irregularity affecting the tribunal or the proceedings, if he failed to object timeously and thereafter took part or continued to take part in the proceedings, unless he shows that he did not then know and could not with reasonable diligence have discovered the grounds for the objection.[27b]

16–140   **Challenge or appeal: supplementary orders.** The court may order the applicant or appellant to provide security for the costs of the application or appeal[28] and may order that any money payable under the award shall be brought into court or otherwise secured.[29]

16–141   **Challenge or appeal: effect of order of the court.** Where the award is varied by the court, the variation has effect as part of the tribunal's award.[30]

16–142   Where the award is remitted by the court to the tribunal for reconsideration, the tribunal must make a fresh award in respect of the matter remitted within three months of the date of the order or such longer or shorter period as the court

---

[22] *Interbulk Ltd v. Aiden Shipping co. Ltd* [1983] 2 Lloyd's Rep. 424, 429, [1984] 2 Lloyd's Rep. 66; *Mafracht v. Patries Shipping Co. SA* [1986] 2 Lloyd's Rep. 405, 414; *Universal Petroleum Co. Ltd v. Handels und Transport GmbH* [1987] 1 W.L.R. 1178; Mustill and Boyd *op. cit.* p. 541. See also *Hayn Roman & Co. SA v. Cominter (U.K.) Ltd* [1982] 2 Lloyd's Rep. 458, 462; *Bulk Oil (Zug) AG v. Sun International Ltd (No. 2), supra,* at p. 533; *Athens Cape Naviera SA v. Deutsche Dampschiffahrtsgesellschaft Hansa AG* [1985] 1 Lloyd's Rep. 528.
[23] *Three Valleys Water Committee v. Binnie and Partners* (1990) 52 Build. L.R. 42.
[24] s.70(2); RSC Ord. 73, r.22. *cf. Gbangbola v. Smith & Sherriff Ltd* [1998] 3 All E.R. 730 (severance of parts of award).
[25] s.70(3). But an appeal may be struck out for want of prosecution; *Huyton SA v. Jakil Spa* [1998] C.L.C. 937.
[26] s.79(1); RSC Ord. 73, r. 22(3).
[27] s.79(3).
[27a] s.73(2); see ante, § 16–124.
[27b] s.73(1); see also ante § 16–072, 16–126, 16–130.
[28] s.70(5)(6).
[29] s.70(7). *cf.,* Italmare Shipping Co. v. Ocean Tanker Inc. [1981] 2 Lloyd's Rep. 489 (affd. [1982] 1 W.L.R. 158) (security for costs but not security for award).
[30] s.71(2).

directs.[31] The effect of the order is to revive the jurisdiction of the tribunal, but only in so far as is necessary to deal with the matter remitted.[32]

Where the award is set aside by the court or declared to be of no effect, the court may also order that any *Scott v. Avery* clause[33] is to be of no effect.[34]   **16–143**

Challenge or appeal: appeals to the Court of Appeal.[35] An appeal lies to the Court of Appeal from a decision of the court on an application under section 67 or section 68, but such an appeal lies only if the court gives leave.[36]   **16–144**

The leave of the court is required for any appeal to the Court of Appeal from a decision of the court under section 69 to grant or refuse leave to appeal.[37] It is probable that leave to appeal will only be granted in exceptional circumstances.[38] Refusal by the court to grant leave to appeal to the Court of Appeal is unappealable.[39]   **16–145**

The decision of the court on an appeal under section 69 is to be treated as a judgment of the court for the purposes of a further appeal.[40] But no such appeal lies without the leave of the court, which will not be given unless the court considers that the question is one of general importance or is one which for some other special reason should be considered by the Court of Appeal.[41] It would appear that no appeal lies to the Court of Appeal against a refusal by the court to give leave to appeal.   **16–146**

Enforcement of awards. By section 66 of the 1996 Act,[42] an award made by the tribunal pursuant to an arbitration agreement may, by leave of the court, be enforced in the same manner as a judgment or order of the court to the same effect,[43] and where leave is so given, judgment may be entered in terms of the award.[44] Leave to enforce an award cannot be given where, or to the extent that, the person against whom it is sought to be enforced shows that the tribunal lacked substantive jurisdiction to make the award,[45] but any objection must be made timeously.[46] Otherwise, the court has a discretion whether or not to enforce the   **16–147**

---

[31] s.17(3).

[32] *Interbulk Ltd v. Aiden Shipping Co. Ltd* [1985] 2 Lloyd's Rep. 410.

[33] See *ante*, § 16–032.

[34] s.71(4).

[35] See Supreme Court Act 1981, s.18(1)(g), as substituted by s.107(1) and Sched. 3, para. 37, of the Arbitration Act 1996.

[36] ss.67(4), 68(4).

[37] s.69(6).

[38] As under s.1 of the Arbitration Act 1979: *The Antaios* [1985] A.C. 191, 205; *Petraco (Bermuda) Ltd v. Petromed International Ltd* [1988] 1 W.L.R. 896, 899.

[39] *Aden Refinery Co. Ltd v. Ugland Management Co. Ltd* [1987] Q.B. 650.

[40] s.69(8).

[41] *ibid.* See (under s.1 of the Arbitration Act 1979) *Geogas SA v. Trammo Gas Ltd* [1991] 2 Q.B. 139. But under s.69(8) of the 1996 Act, only the court (and not the Court of Appeal) can give leave.

[42] This section replaces s.26 of the Arbitration Act 1950. It is mandatory.

[43] s.66(1). See RSC Ord. 73, Part III, CCR Ord. 48C, r. 16; CPR, r. 10.0.2. Part of an award may be enforced where the remaining balance has been duly satisfied: *Continental Grain Co. v. Bremer Handelsgesellschaft mbH (No. 2)* [1984] 2 Lloyd's Rep. 121, 124.

[44] s.66(2).

[45] s.66(3).

[46] s.73; *ante*, § 16–072, 16–124, 16–126.

award. Leave should be given to enforce the award unless there is a real ground for doubting its validity.[47] But leave might be refused, for example, if the award dealt with matters which are not capable of settlement by arbitration,[48] or on the grounds of public policy,[49] or if it was not in a form in which it could be entered as a judgment.[50] An award made in a foreign currency may be enforced,[51] but not an award which specifically requires payment in a foreign country.[52] An award may be enforced under section 66 even though the seat of the arbitration is outside England or no seat has been designated or determined.[53]

16–148 An award may also be enforced by bringing an action on the award.[54] This will be the only method of enforcement available where the arbitration agreement was not in writing[55] or leave to enforce the award under section 66 is refused. In an action on the award the defendant cannot plead as a defence that the findings of the arbitral tribunal were wrong[56] or that the arbitral proceedings leading to the award were unfair, irregular or unsatisfactory.[57] His remedy is to appeal to the court on a question of law arising out of the award[58] or to apply to the court to set aside the award on the ground of serious irregularity,[59] but in either case within the time-limits and subject to the restrictions prescribed.[60] He can, however, raise the defence that the arbitral tribunal acted without jurisdiction or exceeded its jurisdiction.[61]

16–149 **Foreign awards.** A foreign award may likewise be enforced by action.[62] But certain foreign awards are in certain circumstances capable of summary enforcement. First, an award made,[63] in pursuance of an arbitration agreement, in the territory of a state[64] which is a party to the New York Convention on the Recognition and Enforcement of Foreign Arbitral Awards (1958) may, by leave

---

[47] *Middlemiss & Gould v. Hartlepool Corpn.* [1972] 1 W.L.R. 1643 (not following *Re Boks & Co.* and *Peters Rushton & Co. Ltd* [1919] 1 K.B. 491, 497); *Curacao Trading Co. BV v. Harkisandas & Co.* [1992] 2 Lloyd's Rep. 186, 192.

[48] See *ante*, § 16–014, n. 36.

[49] *Soleimany v. Soleimany,* [1998] 3 W.L.R. 811 (illegality). See (1998) 64 *Arbitration* 210.

[50] *Margulies Brothers Ltd v. Dafaris Thomsides & Co. (U.K.) Ltd* [1958] 1 W.L.R. 398, 404.

[51] *Jugoslovenska Oceanska Plovidba v. Castle Investment Co. Inc.* [1974] Q.B. 292 (approved in *Miliangos v. George Frank Textiles Ltd* [1976] A.C. 443). The date for conversion into sterling for the award was said in the former case to be the date of the award, but in the latter case (at 469) it was suggested that conversion could be made on the date that leave to enforce was given.

[52] *Dalmia Cement Ltd v. National Bank of Pakistan* [1975] Q.B. 9. But see *Dalmia Dairy Industries Ltd v. National Bank of Pakistan* [1978] 2 Lloyd's Rep. 223 (action for damages) and *Bank Mellat v. GAA Development and Construction Co.* [1988] 2 Lloyd's Rep. 44, 55 (requirement not part of award).

[53] s.2(2)(b).

[54] See Mustill and Boyd, *op. cit.* p. 417.

[55] See *ante*, § 16–015.

[56] *Walshaw v. Brighouse Corpn.* [1899] 2 Q.B. 286.

[57] *Thorburn v. Barnes* (1867) L.R. 2 C.P. 384; *Oppenhaim & Co. v. Majomed Janeef* [1922] 1 A.C. 482; *Scrimaglio v. Thornett and Fehr* (1924) 131 L.T. 174.

[58] s.69; *ante*, § 16–132.

[59] s.68; *ante*, § 16–127.

[60] ss.70, 73; *ante*, §§ 16–130, 16–139; *Birtley and District Co-operative Socy. Ltd v. Windy Nook and District Co-operative Socy. Ltd (No. 1)* [1959] 1 W.L.R. 142.

[61] *Brown v. Genossenschaft Oesterreichischer Waldbesitzer R. GmbH* [1954] 1 Q.B. 8.

[62] See Dicey and Morris on the Conflict of Laws (12th ed.), p. 601.

[63] An award is to be treated as made at the seat of the arbitration (see *ante*, § 16–007) regardless of where it was signed, despatched or delivered to any of the parties: s.100(2)(b).

[64] For a list of contracting states, see *The Supreme Court Practice*.

of the court, be enforced in the same manner as a judgment or order of the court to the same effect by virtue of section 101 of the 1996 Act.[65] Secondly, except in so far as an award is a New York Convention award, by virtue of Part II of the Arbitration Act 1950 a foreign award is enforceable in the same manner as an English award if it is made in pursuance of an arbitration agreement to which the Geneva Protocol (1923) applies,[66] and which is made between persons of whom one is subject to the jurisdiction of a state party to the Geneva Convention for the Execution of Foreign Arbitral Awards (1927),[67] and the award is made in such a state.[68] Thirdly, an arbitration award made in a Commonwealth country to which Part II of the Administration of Justice Act 1920 has been extended[69] can be enforced in the same manner as a judgment of a court in that place, *i.e.* by registration under that Act or under the Foreign Judgments (Reciprocal Enforcement) Act 1933.[70] Fourthly, various other statutes permit the enforcement of certain awards upon registration.[71] The conditions for enforcement and the grounds on which enforcement of a foreign award may be refused must be ascertained by reference to the particular statute,[72] but neither at common law nor under the statutes concerned can the merits of the arbitrator's decision be impugned.

Once a foreign award has been converted into an English judgment, the judgment is subject to the same procedural rules and conditions as generally apply to such judgments. So, in principle, the court can grant a stay of execution of the judgment. However, it would rarely if ever be appropriate to order a stay in respect of a foreign award enforceable under the New York Convention when, by definition under the Convention, the time for enforcement had arrived.[73]   **16–150**

Civil Jurisdiction and Judgments Act 1982. The 1982 Act provides a summary procedure for the enforcement by registration of an award which has   **16–151**

---

[65] See ss.66(4), 100–104 and *Government of the State of Kuwait v. Sir Frederick Snow and Partners* [1984] A.C. 426; *Agromet Motoimport v. Maulden Engineering (Beds.) Ltd* [1985] 1 W.L.R. 762, *Bank Mellat v. GAA Development and Construction Co.* [1988] 2 Lloyd's Rep. 44. *cf. Deutsche Schachtbau-und Tiefbohrgesellschaft mbH v. R'as al-Khaimah National Oil Co.* [1990] 1 A.C. 295; *Soleh Boneh International Ltd v. Government of Uganda* [1993] 2 Lloyd's Rep. 208; *Minmetals German GmbH v. Ferco Steel Ltd, The Times,* March 1, 1999; Dicey and Morris *op. cit.* (12th ed.), p. 622; RSC Ord. 73, r. 31; CCR, Ord. 48c, r. 16. The court retains jurisdiction in relation to challenge to or appeal from an award (ss.67–69) if the seat of arbitration is in England (or, as the case may be Northern Ireland): s.2(1) and *Hiscox v. Outhwaite* [1992] 1 A.C. 562.

[66] Arbitration Act 1950, Sched. 1.

[67] Arbitration Act 1950, Sched. 2.

[68] Arbitration Act 1996, ss.66(4), 99. For a list of such states, see *The Supreme Court Practice.* See also Dicey and Morris, *op. cit.* (12th ed.), p. 616; RSC Ord. 73, rr. 30, 31; DAC Report, § 346.

[69] For a list of such countries, see *The Supreme Court Practice.*

[70] Administration of Justice Act 1920, s.12(1); Administration of Justice Act 1956, s.51(a); RSC Ord. 71, Ord. 73, r. 33; Dicey and Morris, *op. cit.* (12th ed.), p. 631.

[71] Arbitration (International Investment Disputes) Act 1966, ss.1, 2; Multilateral Investment Guarantee Agency Act 1988, s.1; Carriage of Goods by Road Act 1965, ss.4(1), 7(1) and Sched.; Arbitration Act 1996, s.66(4) and Sched. 3, paras. 21, 24, 49; RSC Ord. 73, rr. 34, 35; Dicey and Morris, *op. cit.* (12th ed.), pp. 633, 634.

[72] For the closed list of cases in which recognition or enforcement of a New York Convention award can be refused, see s.103 of the 1996 Act and *Rosseel NV v. Oriental Shipping (U.K.) Ltd* [1991] 2 Lloyd's Rep. 625; *Soinco Saci v. Novokuznetsk Aluminium Plant* [1998] 2 Lloyd's Rep. 337; *Westacre Investments Ltd v. Jugoimport-SPDR Holding Co. Ltd* [1998] 3 W.L.R. 770; *Soleimany v. Soleimany* [1998] 3 W.L.R. 811; *Minmetals German GmbH v. Ferco Steel Ltd, The Times,* March 1, 1999.

[73] *Far Eastern Shipping Co. v. AKP Sovcomflot* [1995] 1 Lloyd's Rep. 520.

become enforceable in the part of the United Kingdom in which it was given in the same manner as a judgment given by a court of law in that part.[74] But an award which has been registered as a judgment in a foreign state party to the Brussels Convention cannot be registered as a judgment in England under the Act, since such a judgment falls within the exception in Article 1(4) of that Convention relating to arbitration.[75]

16–152   **Injunction in aid of execution.** A freezing injunction may be granted in aid of execution, whether the award is domestic or foreign,[76] and garnishee proceedings may be brought in appropriate circumstances.[77]

16–153   **Limitation.** An action to enforce an award, where the submission is not by deed, must be brought within six years of the date on which the cause of action accrued,[78] *i.e.* from the date on which the claimant was entitled to enforce the award.[79] Alternatively, if the claim is regarded as being one for damages for breach of an implied promise to pay the award, then it accrues when a reasonable time to pay the award has elapsed.[80]

12. Miscellaneous

16–154   **Arbitration and exemption clauses compared.** An arbitration clause differs from an exemption clause in that it is inserted as machinery for settling disputes and is not a term which excludes or restricts the liability of one or both parties.[81] Accordingly, it is not to be treated as an exemption clause at common law,[82] nor is an agreement in writing to submit present or future disputes to arbitration subject to the control of the Unfair Contract Terms Act 1977.[83] However, arbitration clauses may in some circumstances be detrimental to the interests of consumers in that legal aid is not available for arbitration proceedings, and such proceedings may involve greater expense than, *e.g.* proceedings in the county court. Moreover, the arbitration agreement may provide for the appointment of an arbitrator designated by the supplier of the goods or services to the consumer. In

---

[74] s.18(2)(e) (definition of "judgment") and Scheds. 6 or 7. See Dicey and Morris *op. cit.* (12th ed.), p. 630; RSC Ord. 71.

[75] *Arab Business Consortium International Finance and Investment Co. v. Banque Franco-Tunisienne* [1996] 1 Lloyd's Rep. 485 (affd. [1997] 1 Lloyd's Rep. 531). See Hascher (1996) 12 *Arbitration International* 233.

[76] But see *Rosseel N.V. v. Oriental Commercial Shipping (U.K.) Ltd* [1990] 1 W.L.R. 1387 (worldwide freezing injunction refused where award foreign).

[77] *cf. Deutsche Schachtbau-und Tiefbohrgesellschaft mbH v. R'as al-Khaimah National Oil Co.* [1990] 1 A.C. 295.

[78] Limitation Act 1980, s.7. But see Foreign Limitation Periods Act 1984.

[79] *International Bulk Shipping and Services Ltd v. Minerals and Metals Trading Corpn. of India* [1996] 1 All E.R. 1017.

[80] *ibid.* But see *Agromet Motoimport v. Maulden Engineering Co. (Beds.) Ltd* [1985] 1 W.L.R. 762 (date of defendant's failure to honour award when called upon to do so).

[81] *Heyman v. Darwins Ltd* [1942] A.C. 356, 373–375, 400; *Woolf v. Collis Removal Service* [1948] 1 K.B. 11.

[82] *Woolf v. Collis Removal Service, supra.* But see *ante*, § 16–046, n. 54.

[83] s.13(2).

consequence, the application of the Unfair Terms in Consumer Contracts Regulations 1994 is extended in relation to a term which constitutes an arbitration agreement.[84]

Valuers, experts, etc. An agreement to refer a price to a valuer or a question **16–155** to an expert for decision is, as a general rule,[85] not an arbitration agreement[86] and the provisions of the Arbitration Act 1996 do not apply.[87] A valuation or expert's certificate cannot be challenged or appealed as if it were an award[88] nor can it be enforced as if it were a judgment of a court. Nevertheless the court has, under its inherent jurisdiction, a discretionary power to stay an action brought contrary to a dispute resolution agreement which is nearly an effective agreement to arbitrate, but not quite,[89] or which submits the dispute to the decision of an expert.[90] The court also has jurisdiction to determine an issue of construction before the valuer or expert has made his decision,[91] but (as a rule of procedural convenience) will, save in exceptional circumstances, decline to do so.[92]

The function of an architect in certifying payments due under a building **16–156** contract from the employer to the contractor is not to be equated with that of an arbitrator.[93]

A person appointed in an agreement as "sole judge" of matters of fact is not **16–157** an arbitrator. His decision is binding and not reviewable, provided that he acts fairly and not perversely in making his determination.[94]

Adjudication. The Housing Grants, Construction and Regeneration Act 1996 **16–158** provides that a party to a construction contract[95] has the right to refer a dispute

---

[84] See *ante*, § 16–013.

[85] *cf. Re Carns-Wilson and Greene* (1886) 18 Q.B.D. 7, 9; *Leigh v. English Property Corpn. Ltd* [1976] 2 Lloyd's Rep. 298.

[86] *Re Dawdy and Hartcup* (1885) 15 Q.B.D. 426; *Re Carns-Wilson and Greene, supra.* See also *Leeds v. Burrows* (1810) 12 East 1; *Goodyear v. Simpson* (1845) 15 M. & W. 16; *Re Hammond and Waterton* (1890) 62 L.T. 808; *Campbell v. Edwards* [1976] 1 W.L.R. 403; *Arenson v. Arenson* [1977] A.C. 405.

[87] *Collins v. Collins* (1858) 26 Beav. 306; *Bos v. Helsham* (1866) L.R. 2 Ex. 72; *Turner v. Goulden* (1873) L.R. 9 C.P. 57; *Re Dawdy and Hartcup, supra*; *Re Hammond and Waterton, supra*; *Cott (U.K.) Ltd v. F. E. Barber Ltd* [1997] 3 All E.R. 540.

[88] *Campbell v. Edwards, supra*; *Baber v. Kenwood Manufacturing Co.* [1978] 1 Lloyd's Rep. 175. For the limited grounds, and method of impeaching a valuation or expert's certificate, see, *e.g. Collier v. Mason* (1858) 25 Beav. 200; *Finnegan v. Allen* [1943] K.B. 425; *Dean v. Prince* [1954] Ch. 409; *Frank H. Wright (Construction) Ltd v. Frodoor* [1967] 1 W.L.R. 506; *Smith v. Gale* [1974] 1 W.L.R. 9; *Campbell v. Edwards, supra*; *Baber v. Kenwood Manufacturing Co., supra*; *Burgess v. Purchase & Sons (Farms) Ltd* [1983] Ch. 216; *Jones v. Sherwood Computer Services plc* [1992] 1 W.L.R. 277; *Nikko Hotels (U.K.) v. MEPC* (1991) 28 E.G. 86; *Pontsarn Investments v. Kasallis-Osako-Pankki* (1992) 22 E.G. 103; *Mercury Communications Ltd v. Director General of Communications* [1996] 1 W.L.R. 48, 58; *British Shipbuilders v. VSEL Consortium plc* [1997] 1 Lloyd's Rep. 106, 109.

[89] *Channel Tunnel Group Ltd v. Balfour Beatty Construction Ltd* [1993] A.C. 334. *cf. Halifax Financial Services Ltd v. Intuitive Systems Ltd* (unreported, 1998).

[90] *Cott (U.K.) Ltd v. F. E. Barber Ltd* [1977] 3 All E.R. 540.

[91] *Postal Properties v. Greenwell* (1992) 47 E.G. 106.

[92] *British Shipbuilders v. VSEL Consortium plc, supra*, at 109.

[93] *Sutcliffe v. Thackrah* [1974] A.C. 727. *cf. John Barker Construction Ltd v. London Portman Hotel Ltd* (1996) 12 Const. L.J. 277.

[94] *West of England Ship Owners Mutual Insurance Assn. (Luxembourg) v. Cristal* [1996] 1 Lloyd's Rep. 370.

[95] Defined in s.104(1).

arising under the contract for adjudication under a procedure provided by the Act.[96] The purpose of this measure is to establish, in the construction industry, a procedure for the speedy and inexpensive resolution of disputes on a provisional interim basis, and for enabling the adjudicator's decisions to be enforced pending the final determination of such disputes.[96a] But adjudication differs from arbitration in that it does not involve a final disposal of the dispute between the parties. The adjudicator does not perform an arbitral function[97] and does not make any final award definitive of the parties' rights. His decision is, however, binding until the dispute is finally determined by legal proceedings, by arbitration or by agreement.[98] But it cannot be enforced as if it were an arbitral award[99] and it remains to be seen whether the statutory introduction of this informal interim step will indeed produce practical and beneficial results.[1]

16–159   **Immunity of arbitrators and arbitral institutions, etc.** At common law, the extent of the immunity of an arbitrator was not free from doubt.[2] Section 29 of the 1996 Act resolved that uncertainty.[3] An arbitrator is not liable for anything done or omitted in the discharge or purported discharge of his functions as arbitrator unless the act or omission is shown to have been in bad faith, and the same immunity attaches to his employees or agents.[4] This immunity does not affect any liability incurred by an arbitrator by reason of his resigning.[5]

16–160   A similar immunity attaches to an arbitral institution or person responsible for the appointment or nomination of an arbitrator in the discharge or purported discharge of its function in that respect.[6] Nor is such an institution or person vicariously liable for the acts or omissions of the arbitrator nominated or appointed.[7]

16–161   On the other hand, a valuer, expert or adjudicator enjoys no statutory immunity. A valuation or expert certification which is made negligently may give rise to an action in damages at the suit of the party injured thereby.[8] An adjudicator, however, is under the terms of the construction contract to have immunity (subject to an exception in case of bad faith) in the discharge or purported discharge of his functions.[9]

---

[96] ss.108, 114; Scheme for Construction Contracts (England and Wales) Regulations 1998 (S.I. 1998 No. 649). See Vol. II, § 37–250.

[96a] *Macob Civil Engineering Ltd v. Morrison Construction Ltd, The Times,* March 11, 1999.

[97] *A. Cameron Ltd v. John Mowlem & Co. plc* (1990) 52 Build. L.R. 30; *Drake and Scull Engineering Ltd v. McLaughlin & Harvey plc* (1992) 60 Build. L.R. 107. *cf., Cape Durasteel Ltd v. Rosser & Russell Building Services Ltd* (1996) 46 Const. L.J. 75.

[98] s.108(3). But the parties may agree to accept the decision of the adjudicator as finally determining the dispute.

[99] *A. Cameron Ltd v. John Mowlem & Co. plc, supra.* But it can be enforced under s.42 of the 1996 Act: see para. 24 of Part I of the 1998 Regulations, *supra,* and *Macob Civil Engineering Ltd v. Morrison Construction Ltd, supra.*

[1] Davis (1997) 13 *Arbitration International* 411.

[2] *Arenson v. Arenson* [1977] A.C. 405, 431, 432, 440, 442.

[3] It is a mandatory provision: s.4(1) and Sched. 1.

[4] s.29(1)(2). See (1996) 62 *Arbitration* 202.

[5] s.29(3). But see s.25; *ante,* § 16–067.

[6] s.74(1)(3).

[7] s.74(2)(3).

[8] *Sutcliffe v. Thackrah* [1974] A.C. 727; *Arenson v. Arenson, supra.*

[9] Housing Grants Construction and Regeneration Act 1996, s.108(4).

Part Four
ILLEGALITY AND PUBLIC POLICY

ILLEGALITY AND PUBLIC POLICY

1. INTRODUCTION

Underlying principle. The enforcement of contractual claims is in certain **17–001** circumstances against public policy. The effects of public policy differ considerably depending upon the circumstances; thus, in some instances, one or both parties are prevented from suing upon some particular undertaking contained in the contract (or even, where the doctrine of severance[1] can be applied, upon part

---

[1] See *post*, §§ 17–185, 17–194.

of some particular undertaking), whereas in other cases one or both parties are prevented from suing upon the contract at all. The diversity of the fields with which public policy is concerned, and of the circumstances in which a contractual claim may be affected by it, combine to make this branch of the law of contract inevitably complex—a complexity which has been aggravated by lack of systemisation and by the confusing terminology which has often been adopted. Much difficulty would be avoided, if whenever a plea of illegality or public policy were raised as a defence to a contractual claim, the test were applied: does public policy require that this claimant, in the circumstances which have occurred, should be refused relief to which he would otherwise have been entitled with respect to all or part of his claim?[2] In addition, once the court finds that the contract is illegal and unenforceable, a second question should be posed which would also lead to greater clarity: do the facts justify the granting of some consequential relief (other than enforcement of the contract) to either of the parties to the contract.[3] As will be seen, the courts, although not posing this question directly, have been willing to grant consequential relief to the parties to illegal contracts.[4] Further, much confusion would be avoided if contracts were no longer themselves categorised as being void for illegality or on grounds of public policy in the same kind of way as contracts are categorised as being void on other grounds.

17–002   **Plan of chapter.** It is proposed in this chapter to deal first with the different kinds of situation in which one or both parties to a contract are prevented by reason of public policy from enforcing a contractual claim which they would otherwise have been entitled to enforce; the authorities make it necessary to treat the position at common law and by statute separately; the enforcement of collateral and proprietary rights is dealt with next; and thirdly the doctrine of severance, by which the court may reject the illegal part of an agreement and enforce what remains as unobjectionable, is considered.

2. THE POSITION AT COMMON LAW

(a) *Generally*

17–003   **Public policy.** The seriousness and turpitude of the illegality which renders a contract unenforceable varies considerably[4a]. The illegality can arise either from statute or the common law and, particularly where the latter is involved, the courts are faced squarely with the issue of whether public policy requires that a contract (otherwise valid and enforceable) should not be enforced because it is tainted with illegality. Obviously a doctrine of public policy is somewhat open-textured and flexible, and this flexibility has been the cause of judicial censure of

---

[2] *cf. Imperial Chemical Industries Ltd v. Shatwell* [1965] A.C. 656, 675, 678, 683, 693. On the application of a "public conscience" test in determining whether or not contracts should be enforced, see *Tinsley v. Milligan* [1994] 1 A.C. 340; *post,* § 17–173.

[3] See, for example, the sophisticated approach as to remedies adopted by s.5 of the Financial Services Act 1986 where a person improperly carries on an investment business.

[4] See *post,* § 17–168.

[4a] See generally "Illegal Transactions: The Effect of Illegality On Contracts And Torts" (Law Com., Consultation Paper No. 154, 1999).

the doctrine.[5] On occasions it has been seen by the courts as being vague and unsatisfactory, "a treacherous ground for legal decision," "a very unstable and dangerous foundation on which to build until made safe by decision."[6] It is in the context of this doctrine that the unruly horse metaphor rode into the litany of the English lawyer.[7] However, the doctrine has had its defenders. For Winfield, the "variability of public policy is a stone in the edifice of the doctrine, and not a missile to be flung at it."[8] Lord Denning M.R. also viewed the doctrine with favour[9]: "With a good man in the saddle, the unruly horse can be kept in control. It can jump over obstacles." In many respects the discussions on the nature of the doctrine of public policy is a matter of temperament, and it often appears to be nothing more than a verbal dispute. Although it is not something about which one can be dogmatic, the following seems reasonably clear. First, it is inevitable that some doctrine of public policy would evolve with respect to the validity of contracts. As was stated by Sir William Holdsworth,[10] "In fact, a body of law like the common law, which has grown up gradually with the growth of the nation, necessarily acquires some fixed principles, and if it is to maintain these principles it must be able, on the ground of public policy or some other like ground, to suppress practices which, under ever new disguises, seek to weaken or negative them."

Secondly, public policy is not immutable. "Rules which rest on the foundation **17–004** of public policy, not being rules which belong to the fixed customary law, are capable, on proper occasion, of expansion or modification. Circumstances may change and make a commercial practice expedient which formerly was mischievous to commerce."[11] And vice versa, a practice which was once permissible may be proscribed.[12] Thirdly, there is some doubt as to whether the courts can create new heads of public policy rather than merely apply existing doctrines to new situations. This is an area where the precedents hunt in packs of two. Broadly speaking, there are two conflicting positions, that have been referred to as the "narrow view" and "the broad view."[13] According to the former, the courts cannot create new heads of public policy,[14] whereas the latter countenances judicial law-making in this area.[15] To a large extent this debate is verbal. There is a general agreement that the courts may extend existing public policy to

---

[5] See generally Bell, *Policy Arguments in Judicial Decisions* (1983), particularly Ch. VI dealing with restraint of trade.

[6] *Janson v. Driefontein Consolidated Mines Ltd* [1902] A.C. 484, 500, *per* Lord Davey; and see 507.

[7] "It is a very unruly horse, and when once you get astride it you never know where it will carry you": *Richardson v. Mellish* (1824) 2 Bing. 229, 252, *per* Burrough J.

[8] (1928–29) 42 Harv.L.Rev. 76, 94.

[9] *Enderby Town Football Club Ltd v. The Football Association Ltd* [1971] Ch. 591, 606.

[10] *History of English Law*, Vol. III, p. 55.

[11] *Maxim Nordenfelt Guns and Ammunition Co. v. Nordenfelt* [1893] 1 Ch. 630, 666. See also *Nagle v. Feilden* [1966] 2 Q.B. 633, 650; *Shaw v. Groom* [1970] 2 Q.B. 504, 523; *Multiservice Bookbinding Ltd v. Mardon* [1979] Ch.D. 84 where the court had to determine whether an index-linked money obligation was contrary to public policy and decided it was not.

[12] *Esso Petroleum Co. Ltd v. Harper's Garage (Stourport) Ltd* [1968] A.C. 269, 322–324, 333.

[13] Lloyd, *Public Policy* (1953), pp. 112–117.

[14] *Egerton v. Earl Brownlow* (1853) 4 H.L.C. 1, 106–107, 122–124; *Janson v. Driefontein Consolidated Mines Ltd* [1902] A.C. 484, 491, 500, 507.

[15] *Egerton v. Earl Brownlow* (1853) 4 H.L.C. 1, 149–151; *Wilson v. Carnley* [1908] 1 K.B. 729, 737–738. See also *Initial Services Ltd v. Putterill* [1968] 1 Q.B. 396; *McLoughlin v. O'Brian* [1983] 1 A.C. 410, 426–428, 441–443.

new situations[16] and the difference between extending an existing principle as opposed to creating a new one will often be wafer-thin. There will, however, be an understandable reluctance on the part of the courts to create completely new heads of public policy because of the existence of governmental bodies charged with the specific task of law reform and a more activist legislature. However, where Parliament has clearly articulated a principle of public policy then the courts may be willing to extend it by analogy into the field of contract.[17] Lastly, and most importantly, there is a public policy in favour of upholding contracts freely entered into, a policy which of course the doctrine of illegality completely undermines. The point was made forcefully by Jessel M.R. in *Printing and Numerical Registering Co. v. Sampson*.[18]

"It must not be forgotten that you are not to extend arbitrarily those rules which say that a given contract is void as being against public policy, because if there is one thing which more than another public policy requires, it is that men of full age and competent understanding shall have the utmost liberty of contracting, and that their contracts when entered into freely and voluntarily shall be held sacred and shall be enforced by courts of justice. Therefore, you have this paramount public policy to consider—that you are not likely to interfere with freedom of contract."

17–005   **Scope of public policy.** Objects which on grounds of public policy invalidate contracts may, for convenience, be generally classified into five groups: first, objects which are illegal by common law or by legislation[19]; secondly, objects injurious to good government either in the field of domestic[20] or foreign affairs; thirdly, objects which interfere with the proper working of the machinery of justice; fourthly, objects injurious to marriage and morality; and, fifthly, objects economically against the public interest. This classification is adopted primarily for ease of exposition. Certain cases do not fit clearly into any of these five categories. For example, an agreement was held unenforceable by reason of the undertaking contained in it on the part of one of the parties, a newspaper, not to publish any comment on the activities of a company with which the other party was connected (although this was also held to be injurious to trade and commerce as in restraint of trade).[21] Any undertaking not to disclose matters of legitimate public interest may be insufficient consideration to support a contract,[22] and, if the matters are such that in the public interest they ought to be disclosed, an undertaking not to disclose them certainly will not be enforced.[23]

---

[16] *Egerton v. Earl Brownlow* (1853) 4 H.L.C. 1, 149; *Montefiore v. Menday Motor Components Co.* [1918] 2 K.B. 241, 246.

[17] See, *e.g. Nagle v. Feilden* [1966] 2 Q.B. 633; *cf. Newland v. Simons & Willer (Hairdressers) Ltd* [1981] I.C.R. 521.

[18] (1875) L.R. 19 Eq. 462, 465.

[19] Amongst statutory restrictions should now be included those Articles of the Treaties of the European Economic Community and those regulations and directives made thereunder which, either by virtue of the Treaties themselves or of the case law of the European Court, are directly applicable to the United Kingdom: European Communities Act 1972, ss.2 and 3. On the concept of direct applicability of Community law, see Hartley, *The Foundations of European Community Law* (3rd ed., 1994), Chap. 7.

[20] For an unusual example under this head, see *Amalgamated Society of Ry. Servants v. Osborne* [1910] A.C. 87.

[21] *Neville v. Dominion of Canada News Co.* [1915] 3 K.B. 556.

[22] *Brown v. Brine* (1875) 1 Ex.D. 5; such an undertaking would seem not to render unenforceable an otherwise good contract: see *Jennings v. Brown* (1842) 9 M. & W. 496.

[23] *Initial Services Ltd v. Putterill* [1968] 1 Q.B. 396.

It is against public policy to enforce an agreement which would deprive a party **17–006**
to the contract of his sole means of support.[24] And an agreement by which a
moneylender imposed restrictions on the liberty of a borrower, reducing him to
a position little better than that of a slave, was held void as contrary to public
policy.[25] But where a father and son entered into an agreement for the payment
of an annuity to the son upon conditions fettering the son's liberty, the father's
object being to save him from moral and financial ruin, the agreement was held
good.[26] Again, a contract to use undue influence, *e.g.* to procure a legacy, will be
set aside in equity as contrary to public policy[27]; but a contract between expectant
legatees to divide benefits after the death of a testator and meanwhile to abstain
from using influence is good.[28]

How illegality may affect a contract. Illegality may affect a contract in a **17–007**
number of ways[29] but it is traditional to distinguish between (1) illegality as to
formation and (2) illegality as to performance. Broadly speaking the first refers
to the situation where the contract itself is illegal at the time it is formed, whereas
the latter involves a contract which on its face is legal but which is performed in
a manner which is illegal. In this latter situation it is possible for either both or
only one of the parties to intend illegal performance. Where a contract is illegal
as formed, or it is intended that it should be performed in a legally prohibited
manner, the courts will not enforce the contract, or provide any other remedies
arising out of the contract. The benefit of the public, and not the advantage of the
defendant, being the principle upon which a contract may be impeached on
account of such illegality, the objection may be taken by either of the parties to
the contract. "The principle of public policy," said Lord Mansfield, "is this: *ex
dolo malo non oritur actio*. No court will lend its aid to a man who founds his
cause of action upon an immoral or illegal act. If, from the plaintiff's own stating
or otherwise, the cause of action appears to arise *ex turpi causa*, or the transgression of a positive law of this country, there the court says he has no right to be
assisted. It is upon that ground the court goes; not for the sake of the defendant,
but because they will not lend their aid to such a plaintiff. So if the plaintiff and
the defendant were to change sides, and the defendant were to bring his action
against the plaintiff, the latter would then have the advantage of it; for where both
are equally at fault, *potior est conditio defendentis*."[30] The rules on illegality
have been criticised as being unprincipled but a better way of viewing them, as
the previous dictum from *Holmon v. Johnson* illustrates, is as "being indiscrimi-
nate in their effect and are capable therefore of producing injustice."[31] The
"effect of illegality is not substantive but procedural," it prevents the plaintiff
from enforcing the illegal transaction.[32] The "*ex turpi causa* defence," as was

---

[24] *King v. Michael Faraday & Partners* [1939] 2 K.B. 753.
[25] *Horwood v. Millar's Timber and Trading Co. Ltd* [1917] 1 K.B. 305; *cf. A. Schroeder Music
Publishing Co. Ltd v. Macaulay* [1974] 1 W.L.R. 1308.
[26] *Denny's Trustee v. Denny* [1916] 1 K.B. 583.
[27] *Debenham v. Ox* (1749) 1 Ves.Sen. 276; *Higgins v. Hill* (1887) 56 L.T. 426.
[28] *Higgins v. Hill, supra*; and so is a contract to sell an expected devise: *Cook v. Field* (1850) 15
Q.B. 460.
[29] The principle that a man is not permitted, either directly or through his representatives, to found
a contractual claim on the commission of a crime is discussed at §§ 17–161—17–166, *post.*
[30] *Holman v. Johnson* (1775) 1 Cowp. 341, 343. The maxim is further explained in *Bowmakers Ltd
v. Barnet Instruments Ltd* [1945] K.B. 65, 72.
[31] *Tinsley v. Milligan* [1994] 1 A.C. 340, 362.
[32] *ibid.* at 374.

stated by Kerr L.J. in *Euro-Diam Ltd v. Bathurst*,[33] "rests on a principle of public policy that the courts will not assist a plaintiff who has been guilty of illegal (or immoral) conduct of which the courts should take notice. It applies if in all the circumstances it would be an affront to public conscience to grant the plaintiff the relief which he seeks because the court would thereby appear to assist or encourage the plaintiff in his illegal conduct or to encourage others in similar acts". As will be seen later, illegal contracts are not devoid of legal effect,[34] but the *ex turpi causa* maxim entails that no action on the contract can be maintained.

17–008   **Illegality as to formation.** Contracts may be illegal when entered into because they cannot be performed in accordance with their terms without the commission of an illegal act. Thus the contract may involve a breach of the criminal law, statutory or otherwise, or alternatively it may be a statutory requirement that the parties to the transaction possess a licence and where they do not the contract will be illegal as formed. An example of a contract which was illegal as formed is provided by *Levy v. Yates*,[35] a case concerned with the former statutory rule that no play could be lawfully acted within 20 miles of London without a royal licence, which might be given only in certain circumstances. In that case the contract, between a theatre-owner and an impresario, was itself for the performance of a theatrical production prohibited by the statute. The contract was unenforceable since[36] "the agreement could not be carried into effect without a contravention of the law": the parties had contracted to do the very thing forbidden by the statute and the contract was therefore unenforceable.

17–009   **Illegality as to performance.** The illegality may arise because both or one of the parties may intend to perform the contract in an illegal manner. The court will deny its assistance where both or one[37] of the parties intended to perform the contract in an illegal manner or to effect some illegal purpose. In this situation it is customary to distinguish between the situation where the legally objectionable features were known to both parties and the situation where they are known only to one.

17–010   **Both parties aware of legally objectionable features.** Neither party can sue upon a contract if:

   (a) both knew that its performance necessarily involved the commission of an act which, to their knowledge,[38] is legally objectionable, that it is illegal or otherwise against public policy, or

---

[33] [1990] Q.B. 1 (although the manner in which the court applied the illegality doctrine in this case was disapproved of in *Tinsley v. Milligan* [1993] 3 W.L.R. 126, 141, the dictum quoted in the text must remain true as a general principle).

[34] *Post*, §§ 17–158 *et seq.*

[35] (1838) 8 A. & E. 129; *cf. Dungate v. Lee* [1959] 1 Ch. 545.

[36] *ibid.* at 134. See also *Ewing v. Osbaldiston* (1836) 2 My. & Cr. 53. Occasionally it will be difficult to classify a contract as being illegal as to formation as opposed to being illegal as performed: see *J. M. Allan (Merchandising) Ltd v. Cloke* [1963] 2 Q.B. 340.

[37] Where a party is not aware of the *facts* when the contract is made as a result of which the contract cannot be performed legally, see *post*, §§ 17–011 and 17–168 for his remedies. Ignorance of the law is no excuse; see *post*, § 17–012.

[38] Knowledge of illegality by an agent generally has no less effect than knowledge by the principal: *Apthorp v. Neville* (1907) 23 T.L.R. 575; *cf. Stoneleigh Finance Ltd v. Phillips* [1965] 2 Q.B. 537, 572, 580.

(b) both knew that the contract is intended to be performed in a manner which, to their knowledge[39] is legally objectionable in that sense, or

(c) the purpose of the contract is legally objectionable and that purpose is shared by both parties,[40] or

(d) both participate in performing the contract in a manner which they know to be legally objectionable.[41]

Ashmore, Benson, Pease & Co. Ltd v. A.V. Dawson Ltd[42] provides a good example of a contract which was illegal as to performance so as to bar either party from maintaining an action with respect to it. The defendants agreed to transport two boilers belonging to the plaintiffs and did so by carrying the boilers on lorries which could not lawfully carry the loads in question. The goods were damaged in the course of transit but the claim of the owner for damages was rejected; the owner of the goods not only knew that the goods were being transported in an illegal manner but had actually "participated" in the illegality in the sense of assisting the defendant carrier to perform the contract in an illegal manner. However, that a party commits some illegality in the course of performance does not result in his being unable to enforce the contract.[43]

"The fact that a party has in the course of performing a contract committed an unlawful or immoral act will not by itself prevent him from further enforcing that contract unless the contract was entered into with the purpose of doing that unlawful or immoral act or the contract itself (as opposed to the mode of . . . performance) is prohibited by law."

Thus in *St. John Shipping Corporation v. Joseph Rank Ltd*[44] the carrier was able to enforce its claim for freight even though it had illegally overloaded its vessel. However, the plaintiff company would not have been entitled to recover freight had it intended from the beginning to perform the contract in an illegal manner.

Legally objectionable features unknown to one party. It follows from what **17–011** has been said that, if the performance of a contract necessarily and to the knowledge[45] of the plaintiff involves or has as its object the commission by one or both parties of an act known to be legally objectionable, the plaintiff cannot sue on the contract[46] and this is so irrespective of the state of knowledge of the defendant. But when the contract does not necessarily involve the commission of a legally objectionable act and the legally objectionable intention or purpose of one party is unknown to the other, the latter is not precluded from enforcing the

---

[39] *ibid.*

[40] *Alexander v. Rayson* [1936] 1 K.B. 169, 182; *Edler v. Auerbach* [1950] 1 K.B. 359; *Bigos v. Bousted* [1951] 1 All E.R. 92; *J.M. Allan (Merchandising) Ltd v. Cloke* [1963] 2 Q.B. 340.

[41] *Ashmore, Benson, Pease & Co. Ltd v. A. V. Dawson Ltd* [1973] 1 W.L.R. 828.

[42] [1973] 1 W.L.R. 828.

[43] *Coral Leisure Group Ltd v. Barnett* [1981] I.C.R. 503, 509; see also *Newland v. Simons & Willer (Hairdressers) Ltd* [1981] I.C.R. 521, 530.

[44] [1957] 1 Q.B. 267; see also *post*, § 17–151.

[45] *i.e.* knowledge of fact, not of law; see *post*, § 17–012.

[46] *Edler v. Auerbach* [1950] 1 K.B. 359; *Nash v. Stevenson Transport Ltd* [1935] 2 K.B. 341; *Ashmore, Benson, Pease & Co. Ltd v. A. V. Dawson Ltd* [1973] 1 W.L.R. 828.

contract.[47] Thus in *Archbolds (Freightage) Ltd v. S. Spanglett Ltd*,[48] the A Co. agreed with the B Co. to carry goods in a van which, unknown to the B Co., was not licensed for the purpose. The contract, which was not expressly or impliedly prohibited by statute, involved the commission of a criminal offence by the A Co. in using the van for this purpose. But since the B Co. was unaware of this fact, it was not prevented from suing the A Co. for failure to deliver the goods. And in *Bank für Gemeinwirtschaft Aktiengesellschaft v. City of London Garages Ltd*[49] the A Co. had accepted a bill of exchange drawn upon itself by B Co. who later discounted the bill to C Co., a company resident in Germany. When sued by C Co. for dishonour of the bill, A Co. contended that the discounting of the bill to C Co. amounted to the export of a bill of exchange which was unlawful under Exchange Control regulations without the permission of the Treasury. The Court of Appeal held that, as C Co. did not know of B Co.'s failure to obtain Treasury permission and was entitled to assume that B Co. had complied with the requirement, it was not precluded from suing upon the bill.[50] The justification for this result is that it would be inequitable for a person who enters into an apparently unobjectionable contract to be deprived of his rights thereunder merely because the other party had an unlawful object in mind in entering into the contract. To deprive the innocent party of his rights would merely "injure the innocent, benefit the guilty and put a premium on deceit."[51] But upon learning of the illegal object of the other, the innocent party must refuse to assist him by carrying the contract into effect; the innocent party in such circumstances has a *quantum meruit* for what he has already lawfully done.[52] Similarly in a case where the contract appears legally unobjectionable but the other party later elects to perform the contract in an illegal manner: the innocent party is not thereby deprived of his rights but where he learns of the illegal mode of performance he must not participate in it but should do all reasonably within his power to avoid or prevent such performance.[53] If he goes on with the contract with knowledge of what is objectionable he cannot recover, except where the illegality is merely the breach of a by-law which is subsequently waived by the authority which made it, so that the other party lawfully enjoys benefits under the contract, and can modify the work done so as to comply with the by-law.[54]

---

[47] *Mason v. Clarke* [1955] A.C. 778, 793, 805; *Bank für Gemeinwirtschaft Aktiengesellschaft v. City of London Garages Ltd* [1971] 1 W.L.R. 149.

[48] [1961] 1 Q.B. 374; *Davidson v. Pillay* [1979] I.R.L.R. 275; *Corby v. Morrison* [1980] I.C.R. 564 (the test of knowledge is a subjective one). Where the contract is *ex facie* illegal, no question of knowledge arises: *Newland v. Simons & Willer (Hairdressers) Ltd* [1981] I.C.R. 521.

[49] [1971] 1 W.L.R. 149. See also *Credit Lyonnais v. P.T. Barnard & Associates* [1976] 1 Lloyd's Rep. 557.

[50] Contrast the position where the contract infringes a *foreign* exchange control regulation imposed consistently with the I.M.F. Agreement and will be, if it is an "exchange contract," unenforceable in the United Kingdom under the Bretton Woods Agreement Act 1945, irrespective of the British party's ignorance of the foreign illegality: *Wilson, Smithett & Cope Ltd v. Terruzzi* [1976] Q.B. 683. See *post*, §§ 17–031, n. 56. On the status of the Bretton Woods Agreement, see Dicey & Morris, *The Conflict of Laws* (12th ed., 1993), p. 591, n. 95.

[51] *Archbolds (Freightage) Ltd v. S. Spanglett Ltd* [1961] 1 Q.B. 374, 387.

[52] *Clay v. Yates* (1856) 1 H. & N. 73.

[53] *Ashmore, Benson, Pease & Co. Ltd v. A.V. Dawson Ltd* [1973] 1 W.L.R. 828. A possible way of analysing this situation is that the contract has been varied by the parties and the new agreed contractual performance is illegal. See *Archbolds (Freightage) Ltd v. S. Spanglett Ltd* [1961] 1 Q.B. 374, 393.

[54] *Townsend (Builders) Ltd v. Cinema News & Property Management Ltd* [1959] 1 W.L.R. 119.

Parties' ignorance of the law. "Where a contract is to do a thing which **17–012** cannot be performed without a violation of the law, it is void, whether the parties knew the law or not."[55] Thus, in *Miller v. Karlinski*,[56] an employee, whose mode of payment amounted to a fraud on the Revenue, was held unable to recover arrears of salary, whether or not the parties knew that what they were doing was illegal. Equally, where a statute makes the contract itself illegal, the parties' ignorance of the law does not make it the less so.[57] Even where the contract is capable of lawful performance, if the express purpose for which it was made was to do something unlawful, failure by the parties, through ignorance of the law, to appreciate that the purpose was unlawful is irrelevant.[58] But where the contract is not unlawful on its face and is capable of performance in a lawful way and the parties merely contemplate that it will be performed in a particular way which would be unlawful, the parties, through ignorance of the law, failing to appreciate that fact, the contract may be enforced[59] on the ground that there was never a "fixed intention" to do that which was later discovered to be lawful and that while the parties "contemplated" such unlawful act, they did not "intend" to do it.[60] In other words, knowledge of the law is of evidential significance with respect to the parties' intended mode of performance. It is important in this situation that at least the party seeking to enforce the contract can carry it out in a legal manner.

Compromises of illegal contracts. There is a manifestly obvious public **17–013** policy in favour of encouragement and enforcement of compromises of disputes which the parties themselves have agreed to. Compromises result in a saving of public resources and probably produce an optimum result from the disputants' point of view in that they have agreed to one, and that this has not been imposed by a third-party mediator. However, to enforce compromises of illegal contracts would have the effect of undermining the public policy underlying the illegality doctrine: it would be paradoxical, to say the least, to permit a party to enforce the compromise of an illegal contract but not the illegal contract itself. Whether the compromise of an illegal transaction is itself enforceable depends on the question of whether the courts must give effect to the broad social policy underlying the illegality despite any private arrangement between the parties.[61] Normally this will mean that the compromise, like the illegal contract, is not enforceable. An interesting problem on the compromise of an allegedly illegal contract arose in

---

[55] *Per* Blackburn J. in *Waugh v. Morris* (1873) L.R. 8 Q.B. 202, 208. And see *Re Trepca Mines Ltd (No. 2)* [1963] Ch. 199, 221.

[56] (1945) 62 T.L.R. 85; *Napier v. National Business Agency Ltd* [1951] 2 All E.R. 264; *Tomlinson v. Dick Evans "U" Drive Ltd* [1978] I.C.R. 639 (rule about defrauding Revenue applies even in case of a junior employee who goes along with employer's tax fraud); *Newland v. Simons & Willer (Hairdressers) Ltd* [1981] I.C.R. 521.

[57] *Kiriri Cotton Co. Ltd v. Dewani* [1960] A.C. 192: *Re Mahmoud and Ispahani* [1921] 2 K.B. 716. The court may of course decide that breach of the statute does not render the contract unenforceable: see *Shaw v. Groom* [1970] 2 Q.B. 504 and *post*, § 17–140.

[58] *J.M. Allan (Merchandising) Ltd v. Cloke* [1963] 2 Q.B. 340.

[59] *Waugh v. Morris* (1873) L.R. 8 Q.B. 202. *cf. Nash v. Stevenson Transport Ltd* [1936] 2 K.B. 128.

[60] See *Reynolds v. Kinsey* [1959] (4) S.A. 50 where the authorities are reviewed. *cf. Best v. Glenville* [1960] 1 W.L.R. 1198.

[61] *Kok Hoong v. Leon Cheong Kweng Mines Ltd* [1964] A.C. 993, 1014–1019 (estoppel by way of judgment in default could not operate with respect to illegal moneylending agreement). *cf. A.R. Dennis & Co. Ltd v. Campbell* [1978] Q.B. 365.

Binder v. Alachouzos.[62] A lent a sum of money to B which B refused to repay on the grounds that the transaction was one of moneylending and A was not a registered moneylender. A sued B, and after taking legal advice B compromised the action on the terms that he would repay the loan and not contend that the contract was one of moneylending. B then repudiated the compromise arguing that it, like the illegal contract, was unenforceable. The Court of Appeal upheld the compromise, but it did so on the grounds that the compromise was of a dispute of fact whether the contract was in actual fact an illegal moneylending contract.[63] This was not a case where a clearly illegal contract was compromised, assuming *arguendo* that such a contract could be compromised.[64]

(b) *Objects which are Illegal by Common Law or by Statute*

17–014   **Examples of criminality.** Criminal objects which disentitle a party to contractual relief include doing something forbidden by statute,[65] or delegated legislation,[66] such as infringing food and drug legislation[67] or exchange control legislation,[68] and the commission of offences at common law such as publication of a criminal libel[69] and blasphemy.[70] *A fortiori* the courts will not enforce a contract the object of which is such as to render the contract a criminal conspiracy,[71] *e.g.* to corrupt public morals[72] or to rig the market for shares in a company.[73] Whether an agreement to fight is illegal depends upon whether the infliction of the injury is of such a nature, or is inflicted under such circumstances, that its infliction is injurious to the public, which is a question of fact.[74] Similarly, a contract, even if made abroad, is illegal if its purpose is the infringement of the laws of England.[75] But mere knowledge that goods sold abroad may possibly be smuggled into England will not disentitle the seller to sue for their price.[76]

---

[62] [1972] 2 Q.B. 151.

[63] "In my judgment, a bona fide agreement of compromise such as we have in the present case (which is a dispute as to whether the plaintiff is a moneylender or not) is binding": *ibid.* at 158, *per* Lord Denning M.R.

[64] On compromises see *ante*, §§ 3–049—3–055.

[65] *e.g.* see *post*, §§ 17–615, 17–161 but *cf. post*, § 17–168.

[66] *e.g.* see *Palaniappa Chettiar v. Arunasalam Chettiar* [1962] A.C. 294.

[67] *e.g.* see *Langton v. Hughes* (1813) 1 M. & S. 593; and *Askey v. Golden Wine Co.* [1948] 2 All E.R. 35.

[68] *Bigos v. Bousted* [1951] 1 All E.R. 92; *Shaw v. Shaw* [1965] 1 W.L.R. 537. *cf. Wilson, Smithett & Cope Ltd v. Terruzzi* [1976] Q.B. 783.

[69] *Fores v. Johnes* (1802) 4 Esp. 97; as to civil libels, see *post*, § 17–018.

[70] *Cowan v. Milbourn* (1867) L.R. 2 Ex. 230; but see now *Bowman v. Secular Society* [1917] A.C. 406, as to what constitutes blasphemy.

[71] As to where one or both parties are prohibited by statute from making a contract such as that sued upon, see *post*, §§ 17–140 *et seq.*

[72] *Poplett v. Stockdale* (1825) Ry. & Mood. 337; and see *Shaw v. D.P.P.* [1962] A.C. 220.

[73] *Scott v. Brown, Doering, McNab & Co.* [1892] 2 Q.B. 724; *cf. Harry Parker Ltd v. Mason* [1940] 2 K.B. 590.

[74] *Lane v. Holloway* [1968] 1 Q.B. 379; thus an ordinary boxing match with gloves is not unlawful: *R. v. Coney* (1882) 8 Q.B.D. 534, 539; see also Buller, *Nisi Prius* (7th ed.), p. 16; and *Hunt v. Bell* (1822) 1 Bing. 1.

[75] *Clugas v. Penaluna* (1791) 4 Term Rep. 466; *Waymell v. Reed* (1794) 5 Term Rep. 599.

[76] *Pellecat v. Angell* (1835) 2 Cr.M. & R. 311; and see *Holman v. Johnson* (1775) 1 Cowp. 341.

Evasion of statute. It is now established that it is not a criminal offence for **17–015** any person, whether or not acting in concert with others, to do acts which are neither prohibited by Act of Parliament nor at common law, and do not involve dishonesty or fraud or deception, even though an object which Parliament hoped to achieve by its legislation may be thereby thwarted[77]: nor is it an offence to commit a conspiracy to effect a public mischief.[78] Even though agreements which frustrate the policy of an Act of Parliament are not *per se* criminal conspiracies, it may be uncertain whether such agreements are civilly enforceable. If, *e.g.* to take the facts of *Bhagwan*,[79] the owner of the vessel from which B disembarked in order to avoid immigration control had sued for his fare, could B have contended that the agreement was unenforceable since its purpose was to frustrate the policy of the Immigration Acts? It is submitted that unless the policy of the Act in question is one already recognised by the courts as protected under existing heads of public policy, or the means used by the parties are unlawful or dishonest, the agreement is fully enforceable.[80]

Waiver of statutory rights. Difficult questions can arise where a person **17–016** attempts by contract to waive a right conferred on him by statute. Although there is a general principle that a person may waive any right conferred on him by statute (*quilibet potest renunciare juri pro se introducto*) difficulties arise in determining whether the right is exclusively personal or is designed to serve other more broad public purposes. In the latter situation, public policy would require that the right be treated as mandatory and not be waivable by the party for whose benefit it operates. Whether a statutory right is waivable depends on the overall purpose of the statute and whether this purpose would be frustrated by permitting waiver. Thus in *Johnson v. Moreton*[81] the House of Lords held that a tenant could not contract out of the protection afforded by section 24 of the Agricultural Holdings Act 1948 as this would undermine the overall purpose of the Act in promoting efficient farming in the national interest. A contract between a landlord and a statutorily protected tenant whereby the tenant promises to give up possession in return for the landlord's promise of a sum of money is not illegal as an attempt to contract out of the Rent Acts; and although the landlord cannot obtain possession otherwise than under the Acts,[82] the tenant, if he performs his part, can recover the sum promised.[83]

Fraud. Where the object of a contract is the perpetration of a fraud,[84] *e.g.* **17–017** upon prospective shareholders in a company[85] or upon the Government,[86] or a

---

[77] *D.P.P. v. Bhagwan* [1972] A.C. 60; *cf. Zamir v. Secretary of State for the Home Department* [1980] A.C. 365.

[78] *D.P.P. v. Withers* [1975] A.C. 842.

[79] See n. 77, *supra*.

[80] See *ante*, § 17–003.

[81] [1980] A.C. 37. See generally, Bennion, *Statutory Interpretation* (3rd ed., 1997), pp. 38–41.

[82] *Barton v. Fincham* [1921] 2 K.B. 291; see Megarry, *The Rent Acts* (11th ed.), pp. 26–27.

[83] *Rajbenback v. Mamon* [1955] 1 Q.B. 283; see Megarry *op. cit.* pp. 26–27.

[84] Deliberate deceit, even in the absence of moral turpitude, is sufficient: *Brown Jenkinson & Co. Ltd v. Percy Dalton (London) Ltd* [1957] 2 Q.B. 621. This should be distinguished from contracts induced by fraud which are not necessarily illegal: see Treitel, in Tapper (ed.), *Crime, Proof and Punishment, Essays in Memory of Sir Rupert Cross*, p. 107.

[85] *Begbie v. Phosphate Sewage Co. Ltd* (1875) L.R. 10 Q.B. 491.

[86] *Willis v. Baldwin* (1780) 2 Doug.K.B. 450.

trader[87] the contract is illegal. Such frauds are usually criminal[88] but the rule appears to be general; thus a creditor cannot enforce an agreement with an insolvent debtor under which the latter is to pay him an amount in excess of his share under a composition agreement since the agreement to do so is a fraud upon the other parties to the composition agreement.[89] Likewise it is against public policy to enforce an agreement where the purpose of both parties was to defeat the proper claims of the Commissioners of Inland Revenue[90] or of a rating authority.[91]

17–018   **Other civil wrongs.** If a contract has as its object[92] the deliberate commission of a tort,[93] it would seem that the contract is illegal, even though no criminality or fraud is involved.[94] Thus a printer cannot recover the cost of printing matter which he knew to be libellous[95] and the purchaser cannot recover a sum of money deposited with the printer on account of the cost to be incurred in printing it.[96]

(c) Objects Injurious to Good Government

(i) Domestic Affairs

17–019   **Sale of public offices and contracts.** Contracts for the sale or transfer of public appointments,[97] though they may not be prohibited in particular cases by the statutes relative to the sale of public offices,[98] are nonetheless contrary to public policy.[99] So also is a secret agreement to assign to another, in circumstances amounting to a fraud on the Government, the profits of a public contract, such as for the conveyance of the mails.[1] And where a clerk of the peace, appointed by the corporation of a borough under the Municipal Corporations Act 1882 and having fees attached to his office, entered into an agreement with the corporation to receive a salary and account to them for the fees, it was held that

---

[87] *Berg v. Sadler and Moore* [1937] 2 K.B. 158.

[88] See *R. v. Scott* [1975] A.C. 819; Treitel *op. cit.* at p. 87. *cf.* Fair Trading Act 1973, Pt. XI, brought into operation by Fair Trading Act 1973 (Commencement No. 1) Order 1973 (S.I. 1973 No. 1545) which provides for the regulation of pyramid selling and similar trading schemes.

[89] *Cockshott v. Bennett* (1788) 2 T.R. 763; *Mallalieu v. Hodgson* (1851) 16 Q.B. 689; *cf. ante*, § 3–117.

[90] *Miller v. Karlinski* (1945) 62 T.L.R. 85; *Napier v. National Business Agency* [1951] 2 All E.R. 264.

[91] *Alexander v. Rayson* [1936] 1 K.B. 169; *cf. Saunders v. Edwards* [1987] 1 W.L.R. 1116.

[92] As to whether a man can found a contractual claim on his deliberate commission of a tort, see *post*, § 3–117.

[93] As to where the object is the deliberate procurement of a breach of contract with a third party, see Lauterpacht (1936) 52 L.Q.R. 494.

[94] See Pearce L.J. in *Brown Jenkinson & Co. Ltd v. Percy Dalton (London) Ltd* [1957] 2 Q.B. 621, 638, though the case concerned fraud; *Allen v. Rescous* (1676) 2 Lev. 179.

[95] *Apthorp v. Nevill* (1907) 23 T.L.R. 575; see *ante*, § 17–011 as to the printer's proper course if he first learns of the libellous nature of the material after commencing performance of the contract.

[96] *Apthorp v. Nevill*; as to agreements to indemnify against civil liability for libel, see *post*, § 17–167.

[97] As to directorships in limited liability companies, see Companies Act 1985, s.308.

[98] For the definition of a public officer under s.47(3) of the Solicitors Act 1932 (re-enacted by s.22 of the Solicitors Act 1974 and amended by Administration of Justice Act 1985, s.6), see *Beeston & Stapleford U.D.C. v. Smith* [1949] 1 K.B. 656.

[99] *Blachford v. Preston* (1799) 8 T.R. 89, 94; *Parsons v. Thompson* (1790) 1 H.Bl. 322.

[1] *Osborne v. Williams* (1811) 18 Ves. 379.

the agreement was against public policy, as the acceptor of an office of trust can make no bargain in respect of it, and the presumption is that the fees are required to enable the holder to perform the duties of his office.[2]

Contracts by employees and members of public authorities. It is an offence at common law for a public officer to accept a bribe or show favour[3] and a contract with such an object is undoubtedly unenforceable. It is now provided by statute that any officer with a direct or indirect pecuniary interest in a contract to be entered into by a local authority is to give notice that he is so interested and no officer is to take a fee or reward beyond his ordinary remuneration.[4] Members of local authorities are under a similar duty to disclose their interest if they are present at a meeting of the authority at which the contract is the subject of consideration.[5]   **17–020**

Procurement of honours. Though not exactly the sale of an office, an agreement to pay money in return for the procurement of a knighthood for the payer is against public policy since it gives a third person an immediate interest in procuring the title by means which are likely to be improper.[6] Likewise a will limiting estates to persons who should acquire the title of marquis or duke has been held against public policy,[7] but not, perhaps surprisingly, on condition of acquiring a baronetcy, as that was held not to involve public duties.[8]   **17–021**

Assignment of pay, pensions, etc.[9] An agreement to assign or mortgage the salary of a public officer, *i.e.* one paid from national funds,[10] is against public policy; and the same is true of the pension attached to such an office.[11] For instance, the pay of a naval surgeon on active service cannot be assigned[12] nor can half-pay of an army officer.[13] A clerk of petty sessions cannot assign his salary.[14] But it has been held that there may be a lawful partnership in the profits of an office.[15]   **17–022**

Neglect of duty. An agreement, the natural effect of which is to induce a public officer to neglect his duty or which would influence him to perform it in   **17–023**

---

[2] *Liverpool Corporation v. Wright* (1859) 28 L.J.Ch. 868; and see *McCreery v. Bennett* [1904] 2 Ir.R. 69.

[3] *R. v. Whitaker* [1914] 3 K.B. 1283.

[4] Local Government Act 1972, s.117; *cf. Mellis v. Shirley and Freemantle Local Board of Health* (1885) 16 Q.B.D. 446. See *ante*, § 10–031.

[5] Local Government Act 1972, s.94 (as amended by the Local Government and Housing Act 1989, Sched. 11; Police and Magistrates' Courts Act 1994, Sched. 4).

[6] *Parkinson v. College of Ambulance Ltd* [1925] 2 K.B. 1. Such an agreement would now constitute an offence under the Honours (Prevention of Abuses) Act 1925.

[7] *Egerton v. Earl Brownlow* (1853) 4 H.L.C. 1.

[8] *Re Wallace* [1920] 2 Ch. 274.

[9] See *post*, § 20–045.

[10] *Re Mirams* [1891] 1 Q.B. 594 (involving the assignment of the salary of the chaplain to a workhouse which was held not to be against public policy).

[11] *Grenfell v. The Dean and Canons of Windsor* (1840) 2 Beav. 544. Such assignments may also be avoided by statute: *e.g.* see the Army Act 1955, s.203 (on which see *Roberts v. Roberts* [1986] 1 W.L.R. 437), and the Air Force Act 1955, s.203; see also the Sale of Offices Act 1551 as extended by the Sale of Offices Act 1809 and the cases thereon cited in the 22nd ed. of this work, §§ 856–860. *cf.* Logan (1945) 61 L.Q.R. 240.

[12] *Apthorpe v. Apthorpe* (1887) 12 P.D. 192.

[13] *Flarty v. Odlum* (1790) 3 T.R. 681.

[14] *McCreery v. Bennett* [1904] 2 Ir.R. 69.

[15] *Sterry v. Clifton* (1850) 9 C.B. 110; and see *Collins v. Jackson* (1862) 31 Beav. 645.

a particular way, is against public policy. Thus an agreement between one who held the offices of town clerk and clerk of the peace of a borough and an attorney, that the former would, for reward to him, recommend the latter to parties who might want an attorney to conduct prosecutions arising in the town clerk's office, was held illegal.[16]

17–024   **Procurement of public benefits.** An agreement to induce a person who has access to persons of influence to use his position to procure a benefit from the Government is contrary to public policy.[17] Similarly the sale of a recommendation to be given on an application for a beer-house licence is contrary to public policy. But a contract between the tenant of a beer-house and brewers, one of whom was a magistrate, that, in consideration of their paying the costs of his application to the magistrates for a licence, he would tie the premises to them, was held not to be void although it involved the brewers supporting the application, on the ground, *inter alia*, that the agreement was not void for champerty since an application for a licence is not litigation, licensing sessions not being a court.[18]

17–025   **Withdrawal of opposition to Bill.** At any rate in the absence of any intention to practise a fraud on some individual or on the legislature, bargains between the promoters of a private Parliamentary Bill and a third party under which the promoters agree to purchase property from the third party[19] partly as an inducement for him to withdraw opposition to the proposed Bill, or to amend the Bill and pay the third party a sum of money, appear not to be contrary to public policy.[20] Although the court has jurisdiction to enforce by injunction a contract entered into by a person or corporation that they will not apply to Parliament, or will not oppose an application to Parliament, no such injunction appears ever to have been granted and judges have frequently stated that it is difficult to conceive a case in which such jurisdiction should be exercised.[21]

(ii) *Foreign Affairs*

17–026   **Trading with the enemy.** All trading with the enemy,[22] except with royal licence, is against public policy.[23] On the same principle "it is not competent to

---

[16] *Hughes v. Statham* (1825) 4 B. & C. 187l; *Savill Bros. v. Langman* (1898) 79 L.T. 44. And see *ante*, § 3–056.

[17] *Montefiore v. Menday Motor Components Co.* [1918] 2 K.B. 241.

[18] *Savill Bros. v. Langman* (1898) 79 L.T. 44; *cf. Hughes v. Statham* (1825) 4 B. & C. 187 and Criminal Law Act 1967, ss.13, 14.

[19] *Taylor v. Chichester & Midhurst Ry.* (1870) L.R. 4 H.L. 628.

[20] *Simpson v. Lord Howden* (1842) 9 Cl. & Fin. 61; and see *Shrewsbury and Birmingham Ry. Co. v. London and N.W. Ry. Co.* (1851) 17 Q.B. 652; *Edwards v. Grand Junction Ry. Co.* (1836) My. & Cr. 650. "A landowner cannot be restricted of his rights because he happens to be a Member of Parliament": *Earl of Shrewsbury v. North Staffordshire Ry.* (1865) L.R. 1 Eq. 593, 613. See also, *Standards in Public Life* (First Report of the Committee on Standards in Public Life, Cm. 2850–1), Chap. 2.

[21] *Bilston Corporation v. Wolverhampton Corporation* [1942] Ch. 391; *Ware v. Grand Junction Waterworks Co.* (1831) 2 Russ. & My. 470, 483; *Heathcote v. North Staffordshire Ry. Co.* (1850) 2 Mac. & G. 100, 109; *Re London, Chatham & Dover Ry. Arrangement Act* (1869) L.R. 5 Ch.App. 671.

[22] As to who is an enemy, see *ante*, § 11–020, and *post*, § 17–156.

[23] *Ertel Bieber & Co. v. Rio Tinto Co.* [1918] A.C. 260, 273, 289; and see *The Hoop* (1799) 1 C.Rob. 196; *Ogden v. Peele* (1826) 8 Dow. & Ry. 1; as to illegality by statute, see *post*, §§ 17–140—17–155. See further McNair, *Legal Effects of War* (4th ed.); and see *post*, § 17–156—17–157, as to the frustrating effect of war.

any subject to enter into a contract to do any thing which may be detrimental to the interests of" this country in time of war[24] or involving intercourse with or benefit to the enemy,[25] however insignificant in quantum[26] and notwithstanding the benefit which may accrue to this country from such a contract.[27] Nor may the contract merely be suspended during hostilities.[28] Thus, a contract by a British subject to insure an enemy against loss through capture by British ships is unenforceable *ab initio*, even though it was entered into before the commencement of hostilities.[29] Similarly, a contract of insurance on goods shipped from an enemy's port on board a neutral ship, the goods having been purchased in the enemy's country by the agent of the assured after hostilities had commenced, has been held to be against public policy.[30] An English company found to have enemy character by reason of enemy control[31] does not cease, in the eye of English law, to be an English company subject to this rule.[32]

Illegality under applicable foreign law.[33] Where the contract is governed by a system of law other than English, *i.e.* under the principles of English private international law, as now laid down in the Rome Convention on the law applicable to contractual obligations,[34] the law governing the contract is foreign, and the contract is unenforceable for illegality under the relevant doctrine of the foreign system, the contract is also unenforceable in England,[35] unless the vitiating illegality under the governing law is one that the English court declines to recognise because, *e.g.* it imposes an unfair discrimination upon one or both of the contracting parties.[36]   **17-027**

Performance contrary to public policy in place for performance. Where a contract governed by English law is contrary to the public policy of the state where it is to be performed, this will not necessarily constitute a bar to the contract being enforceable in England.[37] However, in *Lemenda Trading Co. Ltd v. African Middle East Petroleum Co. Ltd*[38] Phillips J. stated that,[39]   **17-028**

---

[24] *Furtado v. Rogers* (1802) 3 Bos. & Pul. 191, 198.

[25] *Kuenigl v. Donnersmarck* [1955] 1 Q.B. 515, 536; *Ertel Bieber & Co. v. Rio Tinto Co.* [1918] A.C. 260, 274.

[26] *Bevan v. Bevan* [1955] 2 Q.B. 277, 240.

[27] *The Hoop* (1799) 1 C.Rob. 196, 199–200.

[28] *Ertel Bieber & Co. v. Rio Tinto Co.* [1918] A.C. 260.

[29] *Furtado v. Rogers* (1802) 3 Bos. & Pul. 191; *Ertel Bieber & Co. v. Rio Tinto Co.* [1918] A.C. 260, 273, 289–290.

[30] *Potts v. Bell* (1800) 8 T.R. 548. As to the validity of insurance against seizure immediately before the outbreak of hostilities, see *Janson v. Driefontein Consolidated Mines Ltd* [1902] A.C. 484, 499.

[31] See *post*, § 17–156.

[32] *Kuenigl v. Donnersmarck* [1955] 1 Q.B. 515; and see, *ibid.* at 539: "Many of the old decisions dating from a more liberal age which suggest that British subjects in enemy territory enjoy a measure of freedom in their dealings with the enemy are of doubtful authority today."

[33] See *post*, §§ 31–155 *et seq.*; *Dicey & Morris on the Conflict of Laws* (12th ed., 1993), pp. 1191–1211.

[34] Applicable by virtue of the Contracts (Applicable Law) Act 1990.

[35] Arts. 8, 10.

[36] Art. 16; *Heriz v. Riera* (1840) 11 Sim. 318; *Kahler v. Midland Bank Ltd* [1950] A.C. 24; *Zivnostenska Banka National Corporation v. Frankman* [1950] A.C. 57; *MacKender v. Feldia A.G.* [1967] 2 Q.B. 590, 601; *Re Lord Cable* [1977] 1 W.L.R. 7. As to meaning of applicable law see *post*, § 31–110.

[37] Collier (1988) C.L.J. 169, 170 and cases there cited.

[38] [1988] Q.B. 448.

[39] *ibid.* at 461.

" . . . the English courts should not enforce an English law contract which falls to be performed abroad where: (i) it relates to an adventure which is contrary to a head of English public policy which is founded on general principles of morality, and (ii) the same public policy applies to the country of performance so that the agreement would not be enforceable under the law of that country.

In such a situation international comity combines with English domestic policy to militate against enforcement."

Presumably condition (i) would be sufficient to prevent the contract from being enforced irrespective of the governing law or where the place of performance of the contract may be.[40] However, not all principles of public policy are necessarily of universal application and where the policy is based on "considerations which are purely domestic"[41] then this would not constitute a bar to enforcement of a contract that has to be performed abroad.

17–029   **Contracts legal under applicable law but not under English law.** Where the contract is, however, valid by its foreign governing law, will it be unenforceable in England because it would be regarded as illegal or contrary to public policy under the rules governing domestic contracts? Article 16 of the Rome Convention provides that the "application of a rule of law of any country specified by this Convention may be refused only if such application is manifestly incompatible with the public policy ('ordre public')of the forum."[42] Under the previous law it was clear that if the contract involved criminality either by statute or at common law, then it might be unenforceable in England despite its validity under the governing law and it may be that this is still so if the criminality is serious enough.[43] Where, however, the contract, though not involving criminality, is alleged to offend against one of the recognised heads of English public policy, great care should be exercised by the courts in determining whether the domestic policy demands the non-enforcement of a contract with substantial or even exclusive foreign elements which is valid under the system of law with which it has the closest connection. It cannot, however, be said that the courts have carefully considered this problem; instead they have usually applied the English heads of public policy and held such contracts unenforceable in England.[44] In *Lemenda Trading Co. Ltd v. African Middle East Petroleum Co. Ltd*[45] the court held that the approach adopted in this paragraph would also "seem apposite in the case of an English law contract to be performed abroad."

17–030   Where again the contract is valid by its foreign governing law, but fails to comply with an English regulatory statute rendering similar domestic contracts void or unenforceable but not illegal, the courts have sometimes enforced the

---

[40] *Lemenda Trading Co.* etc., *ibid.* at 459.

[41] *ibid.*

[42] See generally, *Dicey & Morris on the Conflict of Laws* (12th ed., 1993), pp. 1277–1284.

[43] *Boissevain v. Weil* [1950] A.C. 327.

[44] *Grell v. Levy* (1864) 16 C.B.(N.S.) 73; *Kaufman v. Gerson* [1904] 1 K.B. 591; contrast the narrower and, it is submitted, better approach in *Addison v. Brown* [1954] 1 W.L.R. 779. See also *Attorney-General of New Zealand v. Ortiz* [1984] A.C. 1.

[45] [1988] Q.B. 448, 459.

agreement,[46] sometimes not.[47] It is thought that the proper principle is that such agreements should be enforced unless the social policy expressed in the English statute is of such paramount importance that it must be applied even to a transaction with foreign elements or unless the contract, or its breach, has a substantial contact with England. This seems to accord with Article 16 cited above; and also Article 7.2 which allows the application of "the rules of the law of the forum in a situation where they are mandatory irrespective of the law otherwise applicable to the contract."

Illegality under foreign law applicable to contract. Is a contract unenforce- 17–031 able in England in a case where it is illegal by a foreign law other than the law applicable to the contract? The decisions on this question are somewhat confus- ing, but the following propositions appear to represent the law before the adoption of the Rome Convention. First, the English courts would not enforce any contract the recognition of which might constitute a hostile act against a foreign friendly government. Thus, in *De Wütz v. Hendricks*[48] the plaintiff, in order to raise a loan in support of Greek rebels against their Turkish government, deposited with the defendant certain papers. The loan having fallen through, the purpose of the transaction which encompassed the overthrow of a friendly government prevented the plaintiff recovering the papers. Likewise in *Regazzoni v. K.C. Sethia (1944) Ltd*[49] a contract to export a commodity from India to South Africa contrary to the law of the former country was held unenforceable. And although the English courts have refused to enforce a penal law at the suit of a foreign state,[50] nevertheless they will not enforce a contract which involves the breach of such a law,[51] or grant equitable relief[52] to one whose claim is based on such breach unless the law in question was "repugnant to English conceptions of what may be regarded as within the ordinary field of legislation or administrative order even in this country" or such that its enforcement would be against "morals."[53] English courts have also refused to enforce a contract where the common intention of the parties was to violate the law of a foreign friendly state.[54] The above principle, however, has not been extended to cases where there was a mere sale in England in the knowledge that the goods were to be imported

---

[46] *Quarrier v. Colston* (1842) 1 Ph. 147; *Saxby v. Fulton* [1909] 2 K.B. 208; *Sayers v. International Drilling Co.* [1971] 1 W.L.R. 1176.

[47] *Leroux v. Brown* (1852) 12 C.B. 801; *cf. English v. Donnelly*, 1958 S.C. 494 and *Brodin v. A/R Seljan*, 1973 S.L.T. 198.

[48] (1824) 2 Bing. 314.

[49] [1958] A.C. 301.

[50] *Government of India v. Taylor* [1955] A.C. 491. On what constitutes a penal law see *Attorney-General of New Zealand v. Ortiz* [1984] A.C. 1.

[51] *Regazzoni v. K.C. Sethia Ltd* [1958] A.C. 301; *cf. Pye v. B.G. Transport Service* [1966] 2 Lloyd's Rep. 300; *Fielding & Platt Ltd v. Najjar* [1969] 1 W.L.R. 357.

[52] *Re Emery's Investment Trusts* [1959] Ch. 410.

[53] *Regazzoni v. K.C. Sethia Ltd* [1958] A.C. 301, 327, *per* Lord Keith; see also Lord Somervill at 330; *Brokaw v. Seatrain U.K. Ltd* [1971] 2 Q.B. 476; *Attorney-General of New Zealand v. Ortiz, supra*.

[54] *Foster v. Driscoll* [1929] 1 K.B. 470; *Toprak Mahsullri Ofisi v. Finagrain Compagnie Commerciale Agricole et Financière SA* [1979] 2 Lloyd's Rep. 98, 106–107; *Ispahari v. Bank Melli Iran* (1997) T.L.R. 701; *Soleimany v. Soleimany* (1998) C.L.C. 779, 792: "Nor will it [*i.e.* English law] enforce a contract governed by the law of a foreign and friendly state, or which requires performance in such a country, if performance is illegal by the law of that country". Although the courts will not enforce a contract illegal by the law of the country of performance, where it has been performed the courts may recognise its effect: *Royal Boskalis Westminster NV v. Mountain* [1997] C.L.C. 816, 866.

into a foreign country contrary to the revenue law of that country[55] or where there was the giving of an English cheque as part of an arrangement which, as the parties knew and intended, would involve the doing of acts in a foreign country which were criminal by the laws of that country.[56] Nor has the fact that strict compliance with the contract would cause a party to perform illegal acts contravening exchange control regulations in the country of his residence, or place of business, prevented the English court from upholding the contract and awarding damages in the event of its breach.[57] The explanation of these cases was that performance of the contracts did not "necessarily" involve the doing of an act which was unlawful by the law of the place where it had to be carried out.[58] Difficulties have been encountered in ascertaining whether performance of a contract involves such an illegal act. In making this assessment it was said to be "immaterial whether one party has to equip himself for performance by an illegal act in another country. What matters is whether performance itself necessarily involves such an act."[59] But all these matters may now require reconsideration in the light of the Rome Convention.[60]

17–032   **Contract forbidden in place of performance.** Secondly, it is said that English courts will not enforce a contract where performance of that contract is forbidden by the law of the place where it must be performed.[61] This proposition, for which there is authority,[62] would clearly apply where the English law is the law governing the contract. However, beyond this the proposition has been doubted; the cases supporting it have been considered in the final analysis to turn on other propositions,[63] or to have reflected the application of standard principles of contract law or principles of English public policy.[64] There does not appear to be any overriding requirement of English public policy rendering such contracts unenforceable where they are governed by a foreign system of law and are not regarded as illegal under that system.

17–033   **Foreign laws of extra-territorial application.** Thirdly, certain foreign laws are of extra-territorial application and may purport to make contracts illegal although these contracts do not necessitate any illegal acts within the foreign jurisdiction and although the parties to them do not contemplate such acts.[65] In

---

[55] *Foster v. Driscoll* [1929] 1 K.B. 470, 518.

[56] *Sharif v. Azad* [1967] 1 Q.B. 605; *cf. Mansouri v. Singh* [1986] 1 W.L.R. 1393. The contract in this case involved exchange control legislation, on which see *Dicey & Morris on the Conflict of Laws* (12th ed., 1993), pp. 1595–1602; *United City Merchants (Investments) Ltd v. Royal Bank of Canada* [1983] 1 A.C. 168, 188–191.

[57] *Kleinwort Sons & Co. v. Ungarische Baumwolle Industrie Aktiengesellschaft* [1939] 2 K.B. 678; *Kahler v. Midland Bank Ltd* [1950] A.C. 24, 48; *Rossano v. Manufacturers' Life Assurance Co.* [1963] 2 Q.B. 352. See, however, *Dicey & Morris, op. cit.* pp. 1591 *et seq.*

[58] *Libyan Arab Foreign Bank v. Bankers Trust Co.* [1989] Q.B. 728, 743–746.

[59] *ibid.* at 269.

[60] *Post*, § 31–016 *et seq.* and §§ 31–108—31–110.

[61] *Ralli Brothers v. Compania Naviera Sota y Aznar* [1920] 2 K.B. 287.

[62] *Ralli Bros. v. Compania Naviera Sota y Aznar, supra.; Toprak Mahsulleri Ofisi v. Finagrain Cie Commerciale Agricole et Financière SA* [1979] 2 Lloyd's Rep. 98; *Libyan Arab Foreign Bank v. Bankers Trust Co.* [1989] Q.B. 728.

[63] Reynolds (1992) 109 L.Q.R. 553.

[64] Reynolds, *ibid.*; Collier, *Conflict of Laws* (1988), pp. 174–176; *Dicey & Morris op. cit.* pp. 1243–1247 (discussing, *inter alia*, whether *Ralli Bros.* survives the Rome Convention).

[65] *e.g.* the United States Sherman Act 1890; see the *Report of the Attorney-General's Committee to Study the Antitrust Laws* (1955), pp. 66–67; Brewster, *Antitrust and American Business Abroad* (2nd ed., 1983).

such circumstances there is no authority that the English courts would refuse to enforce the contract solely on account of the extra-territorial application of the foreign law, and there are indications to the contrary.[66]

Knowledge of foreign illegality. Where illegality by foreign law is pleaded, **17–034** it may be that one of the parties is unaware of the illegality of the transaction, or of the illegal purpose intended by the other party. In such circumstances, the principles discussed *ante* at 17–011, 17–012, have been applied, except that, foreign law being regarded by an English court as a matter of fact, ignorance as to the actual content of the foreign rule would appear to be equivalent to a mistake of fact, not of law. Thus in *Fielding & Platt Ltd v. Najjar*[67] English machinery manufacturers contracted with a Lebanese company to make and deliver an aluminium press for £235,000, payment to be made by promissory notes given by N, the company's managing director, and payable at intervals during the progress of the work. The English manufacturers began the work, presented the first note for payment, but it was not honoured. In an action upon the note N pleaded that the whole transaction was illegal and unenforceable in that it was agreed that the manufacturers should render invoices which they knew to be false for the purpose of deceiving the Lebanese authorities into admitting goods into Lebanon under import licences which did not in fact cover these goods. The Court of Appeal held that the English manufacturers were entitled to succeed since, even on the assumption that the foreign illegality was capable of vitiating an English contract, it was not a term that the false invoices be made, so that the contract could be performed lawfully; and even if there were such a term, there was not sufficient evidence to show that the manufacturers appreciated the illegality or intended to participate in it.

(d) *Objects Injurious to the Proper Working of Justice*

(i) *Agreements to Conceal Offences and Compromises*

Concealment of crime generally. A provision in any agreement not to **17–035** disclose misconduct of such a nature that it ought, in the public interest, to be disclosed to others is against public policy.[68] There is no confidence as to the disclosure of iniquity.[69] But it may well be permissible for a person against whom frauds have been, and are intended to be, committed to give a binding promise of secrecy, in order to obtain information relating to those frauds, which will enable him, by taking steps himself, to prevent the commission of future frauds. However such a promise will be against public policy where it extends to frauds committed and contemplated against others to whom the communication of the

---

[66] *British Nylon Spinners Ltd v. Imperial Chemical Industries Ltd* [1953] Ch. 19; *Sharif v. Azad* [1967] 1 Q.B. 605, 617. See also Protection of Trading Interests Act 1980. Under Art. 7(1) effect may be given to the mandatory rules of another country but this, by Art. (2), is not to restrict effect being given to the law of the forum where it is mandatory, irrespective of the law other wise applicable to the contract.

[67] [1969] 1 W.L.R. 257.

[68] *Initial Services Ltd v. Putterill* [1968] 1 Q.B. 396. *cf. Schering Chemicals Ltd v. Falkman Ltd* [1982] Q.B. 1; *Hubbard v. Vosper* [1972] 2 Q.B. 84; *A. v. Hayden* (1985) 59 A.L.J.R. 6. See also *Lion Laboratories Ltd v. Evans* [1985] Q.B. 526; *Att.-Gen. v. Guardian Newspapers Ltd (No. 2)* [1990] 1 A.C. 109, 268–269.

[69] *Gartside v. Outram* (1857) 26 L.J.Ch. 113, 114.

information obtained would be of use in preventing the commission of such frauds.[70]

17–036 **Criminality of agreements to conceal an arrestable offence.** In many cases where there is, in effect, an undertaking not to disclose a crime, the crime amounts also to a civil wrong against the promisor and the undertaking is given as part of an agreement to compromise or settle the civil wrong; the question then arises whether the inclusion of the undertaking not to disclose the information or to instigate a public prosecution renders unenforceable the compromise of the civil wrong. Section 5 of the Criminal Law Act 1967 provides that where an arrestable offence[71] has been committed, anyone who knows or believes:

(i) that an arrestable offence[72] has been committed, and:

(ii) that he has information which might be of material assistance in securing the prosecution or conviction of any offender for it

is guilty of an indictable offence[73] if he accepts, for not disclosing that information, any consideration other than:

(a) the making good of loss or injury occasioned by the offence, or

(b) the making of reasonable compensation for that loss or injury.[74]

Otherwise the compounding of an offence (other than treason) is no longer a criminal offence by English law.[75]

17–037 An agreement, express or implied,[76] which is criminal by virtue of the provisions of section 5 of the Criminal Law Act 1967, is undoubtedly unenforceable civilly.[77] But are compromises of offences[78] other than those which are unlawful under section 5 of the Criminal Law Act 1967 enforceable? Where the consideration or part of it takes the form of a promise not to report the matter to the police, or not to initiate a prosecution, the transaction runs the risk of being considered a stifling of a prosecution and may be considered contrary to public policy. It is in any case clear that where a person has already made a statement

---

[70] *Howard v. Odhams Press* [1938] 1 K.B. 1, 41–42.

[71] As to what is an arrestable offence, see Police and Criminal Evidence Act 1984, s.24(1).

[72] *ibid.*

[73] Not necessarily the offence which has in fact been committed.

[74] Such an offence can be prosecuted only by or with the consent of the Director of Public Prosecutions: Criminal Law Act 1967, s.5(3).

[75] Criminal Law Act 1967, s.5(1); *cf. Flower v. Sadler* (1882) 10 Q.B.D. 572.

[76] As to the implication of an agreement in such circumstances, see *William v. Bayley* (1886) L.R. 1 HL 200; *Brook v. Hook* (1871) L.R. 6 Ex. 89; *Whitmore v. Farley* (1881) 45 L.T. 99; *McClatchie v. Haslam* (1891) 65 L.T. 691; *Jones v. Merionethshire Building Society* [1892] 1 Ch. 173. *cf. Howard v. Odhams Press* [1938] 1 K.B. 1; *Bhowampur Banking Corporation Ltd v. Sreemati Durgesh Nandini Dasi* (1941) 68 L.R.I.A. 144, *per* Lord Atkin at 148. As to the possibility of a plea of duress or undue influence in such cases, see *ante*, §§ 7–034—7–035.

[77] See *ante*, § 17–014.

[78] s.1(1) of the Criminal Law Act 1967 abolished as from January 1, 1968, the distinction between felonies and misdemeanours, and s.1(2) provides that, subject to the provisions of that Act, on all matters on which a distinction was previously made between felonies and misdemeanours, the law and practice is to be the law and practice applicable at the commencement of the Act in relation to misdemeanours. The special rules relating to the stifling of a prosecution of a felony have thus been abrogated.

with a view to the provision of evidence in support of criminal proceedings, even if that person is the victim of the alleged crime, that person becomes a witness and the promise to him of an inducement,[79] even by way of compensation for the loss or injury, to alter or withdraw the statement, constitutes the crime at common law of attempting to pervert the course of justice,[80] and is therefore unenforceable. It is clear that an agreement that would not be offensive to public policy is where the innocent party is seen clearly to be compromising *only* his civil claim, and is not offering either not to report the matter, or not to initiate a prosecution, or to withdraw statements already made. Whether other agreements, for example, one involving a promise not to bring a criminal action, would not be enforceable is not clear. Prior to the 1967 Act, an undertaking not to take action with respect to misdemeanours was binding and enforceable; where the agreement pertained to a crime which was a felony or a misdemeanour of a public nature it was not enforceable. What is left of the old learning in the light of both the abolition of the distinction between misdemeanours and felonies and section 5 of the Criminal Law Act 1967 is not clear. The commentators do not speak with a single voice.[81] Given that the courts appear to have been given an opportunity to reconsider the matter, the preferable solution would be to jettison completely the old rule and only strike down those compromises which were manifestly contrary to the public interest.[82]

Trustees in bankruptcy. The trustee in bankruptcy of one who has paid   **17-038**
money or given security in pursuance of an agreement which is rendered illegal by section 5 of the Criminal Law Act 1967 is probably in no better position than the bankrupt and is therefore unable to recover[83] unless perhaps the payment was an offence against the bankruptcy laws.[84]

(ii) *Other Contracts Affecting the Course of Justice*

Interference with course of justice. Any contract which tends to abuse,   **17-039**
prevent or impede the due course of justice is against public policy. A bond upon consideration that criminal proceedings shall be so conducted that the name of a certain person shall not be mentioned, or shall be mentioned only in such a way as not to damage him, is against public policy,[85] as is an agreement not to appear and give evidence at a criminal trial.[86] Similarly agreements to institute a prosecution as a means of gaining publicity,[87] or to consent to a verdict of not guilty in respect of a public nuisance,[88] have been held to be contrary to public policy. And a contract with one who has stood bail to indemnify him amounts to

---

[79] If part of the consideration is also a promise not to commence a civil action for damages, see *post*, § 17-185 for the principles on the possibility of severing the tainted from the untainted promise.

[80] *R. v. Panayiotou* [1973] 1 W.L.R. 1032.

[81] See Hudson (1980) 43 M.L.R. 532.

[82] *ibid.*

[83] *cf. Re Mapleback* (1876) 4 Ch.D. 150 as to the position at common law before 1968 (the trustee takes the estate subject to its limitations in the hands of the bankrupt).

[84] *cf. Re Campbell* (1884) 14 Q.B.D. 32 as to the position at common law before 1968; and see *post*, § 17-176.

[85] *Lound v. Grimwade* (1888) 39 Ch.D. 605.

[86] *Collins v. Blantern* (1767) 2 Wils. 341; 1 Sm.L.C., 13th ed., p. 406; *cf. Fulham Football Club Ltd v. Cabra Estates plc* [1994] 1 B.C.L.C. 363.

[87] *Dann v. Curzon* (1910) 104 L.T. 66.

[88] *Windhill Local Board v. Vint* (1890) 45 Ch.D. 351.

an indictable offence[89] and is unenforceable.[90] However, there are many circumstances in which parties can agree as to the future course of legal proceedings. Thus, for example, in a commercial agreement relating to the sale of land, it has been held not to be against public policy for one of the parties to agree to support the other party's application for planning permission.[91]

17-040   **Procurement of pardon and withdrawal of election petition.** An agreement to pay money, in consideration of a party using his interest to procure the pardon of a convict, is against public policy.[92] And so is an agreement in consideration of a money payment to withdraw an election petition in which charges of bribery are made,[93] it being in the public interest that the investigation should be carried out.

17-041   **Winding up.** An agreement by a shareholder in a company which is being compulsorily wound up that, in consideration of a sum of money, he would endeavour to postpone the making of a call or would support the claim of a creditor is unenforceable as being contrary to the policy of the insolvency legislation and perhaps also an interference with the course of public justice.[94]

17-042   **Bankruptcy.** All "composition" agreements between a debtor and creditor of a preferential character are unenforceable.[95] In addition the essence of such agreements being equality between the creditors, a creditor who has executed a composition deed is entitled to repudiate it against the other creditors if he afterwards discovers that they have been induced to execute the deed by means of a secret bargain for a payment to them in excess of the composition, even if the bargain was made after his own execution of the deed.[96] Similarly, agreements for the withdrawal of opposition to the discharge of a bankrupt are unenforceable.[97] But a contract by an undischarged bankrupt in consideration of a small loan to pay in full a debt due from him at the commencement of and provable in his bankruptcy is not void as being contrary to public policy or the principles of the law of bankruptcy.[98]

17-043   **Divorce: collusive agreements.** A collusive agreement between the parties[99] to matrimonial proceedings is an agreement or bargain between the parties or

---

[89] *R. v. Porter* [1910] 1 K.B. 369.

[90] *Hermann v. Jeuchner* (1885) 15 Q.B.D. 561 (money actually deposited with a surety was held not to be recoverable); *Consolidated Exploration & Finance Co. v. Musgrave* [1900] 1 Ch. 37; *Re Gurwicz* [1919] 1 K.B. 675.

[91] *Fulham Football Club Ltd v. Cabra Estates plc.* [1994] 1 B.C.L.C. 363.

[92] *Norman v. Cole* (1800) 3 Esp. 253; but see *Lampleigh v. Brathwait* (1615) Hob. 105.

[93] *Coppock v. Bower* (1838) 4 M. & W. 361.

[94] *Elliott v. Richardson* (1870) L.R. 5. C.P. 744.

[95] *Mallalieu v. Hodgson* (1851) 16 Q.B. 689; and see *Staines v. Wainwright* (1839) 6 Bing.N.C. 174. See Insolvency Act 1986, ss.339 and 340 dealing with transactions at an undervalue and preferences; *Muir Hunter on Personal Insolvency*, pp. 3159–3171; *post*, § 21–027 *et seq.*

[96] *Re Milner* (1885) 15 Q.B.D. 605. And see *Re Myers* [1908] 1 K.B. 941; *Farmers' Mart v. Milne* [1915] A.C. 106; *Re Johns* [1928] Ch. 737; *cf. ante*, § 17–017.

[97] See *McKewan v. Sanderson* (1875) L.R. 20 Eq. 65; *Kearley v. Thomson* (1890) 24 Q.B.D. 742.

[98] *Wild v. Tucker* [1914] 3 K.B. 36; and see *Jakeman v. Cook* (1878) 4 Ex.D. 26 where the promisor was a discharged bankrupt.

[99] *cf. Prevost v. Wood* (1905) 21 T.L.R. 694 as to an agreement between a petitioner and a third party with whom sexual relations took place.

their agents whereby the initiation of the suit is procured or its conduct provided for.[1] At one time these were held to be unenforceable. However, in *Sutton* v. *Sutton*[2] the court held that public policy, particularly in the light of section 1(2)(*d*) of the Matrimonial Causes Act 1973 (permitting divorce by agreement after two years' separation), no longer rendered a contract unenforceable on the grounds of collusion. In that case the parties, who had lived apart for three years, agreed to an amicable divorce on the grounds of two years' separation and as part of the arrangement the husband agreed to transfer title to the matrimonial home to the wife. The wife sought specific performance of this promise and, although she was unsuccessful on the grounds that the agreement was unenforceable as an attempt to oust the jurisdiction of the court, the court held that the principle that collusive agreements were void and unenforceable, was no longer the law. If of course the parties fabricate the grounds on which a divorce is sought then this would make any agreement to do this unenforceable as an attempt to pervert the course of justice.[3]

(iii) *Ouster of Jurisdiction*

Maintenance agreements. Any provision by which a wife binds herself not   **17–044**
to apply to the Divorce Court for maintenance is void as an ouster of the jurisdiction of the courts[4]: but one which, by purporting to make maintenance a debt enforceable at law, is now by statute[5] binding on the parties and provides consideration for a counter-promise, although on application to the court it may be varied or revoked.[6] But an agreement is not, even at common law, void as contrary to public policy merely because it limits a husband's right to apply to the courts for a reduction in his liability for maintenance for his wife[7] or because it ousts the jurisdiction of a foreign court.[8]

Arbitration.[9] If the parties seek by agreement to take the law out of the hands   **17–045**
of the courts and into the hands of a private tribunal, except as permitted by the Arbitration Act 1996, then the agreement, to the extent that it deprives recourse to the courts in case of errors of law, is contrary to public policy.[10] In *Leigh* v. *National Union of Railwaymen*,[11] it was held that, since the court's jurisdiction could not be ousted, the court was not bound by an express provision in a trade union's rules that domestic remedies must be exhausted first, though a plaintiff would have to show cause why the court should intervene; in the absence of any such provision, though the court would more readily grant relief, it might first require the plaintiff to resort to the domestic remedies. An arbitration clause *per*

---

[1] *Gosling v. Gosling* [1968] P. 1, 11–12.

[2] [1984] Ch. 184; see Cretney and Masson, *Principles of Family Law* (6th ed., 1997), Chap. 15.

[3] Although there is a provision enabling the parties to refer an agreement to the court for approval, this procedure is now obsolete: see Rayden and Jackson, *Divorce* (16th ed.), p. 508.

[4] *Hyman v. Hyman* [1929] A.C. 601; *Bennett v. Bennett* [1952] 1 K.B. 249; *Sutton v. Sutton* [1984] Ch. 184, 195–198; Matrimonial Causes Act 1973, s.34.

[5] Matrimonial Causes Act 1973, s.34. As to the previous position at common law, see *Bennett v. Bennett*, *supra*, at 262, see also § 17–043. The private ordering of the consequences of divorce raises difficult issues: see Cretney and Masson, *op. cit.*

[6] Matrimonial Causes Act 1973, s.35.

[7] *Russell v. Russell* [1956] P. 283.

[8] *Addison v. Brown* [1954] 1 W.L.R. 779.

[9] See Chap. 16.

[10] *Lee v. Showmen's Guild of Great Britain* [1952] 2 Q.B. 329.

[11] [1970] Ch. 326.

se does not at common law oust the jurisdiction of the court[12] and it was held in *Scott v. Avery*[13] that a provision making an arbitration award a condition precedent to the bringing of an action did not oust the jurisdiction of the court. And it is not against public policy to agree that all claims are to be taken to arbitration and that unless this is done within a certain period (however short) a claim is to be deemed as having been waived.[14] The court will set aside an arbitrator's award if it seeks to give effect to a contract which is illegal or contrary to public policy.[15]

17–046   The Arbitration Act 1996 enables parties to enter into binding arbitration agreements which enable the parties to determine "how their disputes are resolved"[16] and to curtail the jurisdiction of the court to interfere with the arbitral procedure which they have established.[17] In order to oust effectively the jurisdiction of the court and to have the rights of the parties determined by arbitration, the parties must have entered into an arbitration agreement. An arbitration agreement is defined as any agreement by the parties in writing[18] to submit their disputes to arbitration.[19] Where an arbitration agreement within the meaning of the 1986 Act is entered into, certain provisions of the Act, referred to as mandatory provisions, have effect irrespective of any agreement of the parties to the contrary.[20] The effect of these mandatory provisions is to ensure that the dispute is resolved by the terms of the agreement and not by recourse to courts.[21]

17–047   **Questions of fact and expert evaluation.** There is no objection to the parties making a private tribunal the final arbiter on questions of fact.[22] Thus, it often happens that by the rules of a game or a race or competition a stated person is to decide who is the winner and so on and that his decision shall be final. Those questions must be decided by the designated person or persons.[23] Where an agreement provides that in the case of a dispute the services of an expert should be used and that his decision "shall be conclusive and final and binding for all purposes," this will be binding on the parties unless there has been fraud or bias on the part of the expert or he has been guilty of "mistake."[24] Mistake in this

---

[12] *Scott v. Avery* (1856) 5 H.L.C. 811; *Edwards v. Aberayron Mutual Ship Insurance Soc.* (1876) 1 Q.B.D. 563; *Hallen v. Spaeth* [1923] A.C. 684.

[13] (1856) 5 H.L.C. 811.

[14] *Atlantic Shipping & Trading Co. Ltd v. Louis Dreyfus & Co.* [1922] 2 A.C. 250. But under s.12 of the Arbitration Act 1996 the court has power to extend the time: see *ante*, § 16–046.

[15] *David Taylor & Son Ltd v. Barnett Trading Co.* [1953] 1 W.L.R. 562; *cf. Birtley & District Co-operative Soc. Ltd v. Windy Nook & District Industrial Co-operative Soc. Ltd (No. 2)* [1960] 2 Q.B. 1; but see *Bellshill & Mossend Co-operative Soc. Ltd v. Dalziel Co-operative Soc. Ltd* [1960] A.C. 832.

[16] Arbitration Act 1996, s.1(b).

[17] *ibid.* s.1(c).

[18] *ibid.* s.5, note in particular s.5(3) and (6).

[19] *ibid.* s.6 (the dispute does not have to be contractual).

[20] *ibid.* s.4 and Sched. 1.

[21] *ibid.* in particular, ss.9–11.

[22] *Baker v. Jones* [1954] 1 W.L.R. 1005, 1010; *West of England Shipowners Mutual Insurance Association v. Cristal Ltd* [1996] 1 Lloyd's Rep. 370. Such a decision, however, is open to challenge on the grounds of fraud or perversity: *West of England Shipowners' etc., ibid.* at 248–249.

[23] *Brown v. Overbury* (1856) 11 Exch. 715; *Sadler v. Smith* (1869) L.R. 5 Q.B. 40; *Cipriani v. Burnett* [1933] A.C. 83.

[24] *Jones v. Sherwood Computer Service plc* [1989] 1 W.L.R. 277 (noted (1993) 109 L.Q.R. 385).

context requires the expert to have "departed from his instructions in a material respect"[25] for example, an expert who has been employed to value shares values the wrong number of shares or values shares in the wrong company.[26] Accordingly, the determination of the expert will be binding if "he has answered the question in the wrong way" but if "he has answered the wrong question, his decision will be a nullity."[27] However, an attempt to oust completely the jurisdiction of the court in the sense that the parties are precluded from seeking judicial redress even if there is fraud or bias by the expert would be ineffective.[28]

(iv) *Maintenance and Champerty*

Maintenance and champerty formerly crimes. For many centuries prior to 1968 maintenance and champerty were crimes both at common law[29] and by statute.[30] However the Criminal Law Act 1967 now provides[31] that, as from January 1, 1968, "any distinct offence under the common law in England and Wales of maintenance (including champerty ...)" should be abolished; and the Act repealed[32] various old statutes relating to the two crimes. The Act further abolished[33] tortious liability for maintenance and champerty. But section 14(2) of the Act provides that "the abolition of criminal and civil liability under the law of England and Wales for maintenance and champerty shall not affect any rule of that law as to the cases in which a contract is to be treated as contrary to public policy or otherwise illegal."   **17–048**

Public policy today respecting maintenance and champerty. It is thought that the provisions of section 14(2) of the Criminal Law Act 1967 must mean that at least prima facie contracts which under the law before 1968 would have been unenforceable for maintenance[34] or champerty[35] are still to be unenforceable therefor, even though the criminality attaching to such contracts has been removed. In *Trendtex Trading Corporation v. Credit Suisse*,[36] Lord Roskill considered it plain from section 14(2) that "Parliament intended to leave the law as to the effect of maintenance and champerty upon contracts unaffected by the abolition of them as crimes and torts." This is an area where the courts clearly   **17–049**

---

[25] *ibid.* at 287.

[26] *ibid.*

[27] *Nikko Hotels (U.K.) Ltd v. MEPC plc* [1991] 2 E.G.L.R. 103, 108. For other relevant authorities see (1993) 109 L.Q.R. 385.

[28] *ibid.* discussing *Re Davstone Estate's Ltd Leases* [1969] 2 Ch. 378.

[29] Maintenance: *Pechell v. Watson* (1841) 8 M. & W. 691; *Neville v. London Express Newspaper Ltd* [1919] A.C. 368, 383, 386, indicating need to prove want of reasonable or probably cause; champerty: *Re Trepca Mines Ltd (No. 2)* [1963] Ch. 199, 224; *Master v. Miller* (1791) 4 T.R. 320, 340.

[30] See Criminal Law Act 1967, Sched. 4.

[31] s.13(1)(a).

[32] s.13(1)(b) and Sched. 4.

[33] s.14(1).

[34] See *post*, §§ 17–050—17–053.

[35] See *post*, §§ 17–054—17–066.

[36] [1982] A.C. 679, 702. See also the views of Lord Denning M.R. in the Court of Appeal that by striking down both the tort and crime of maintenance the Criminal Law Act 1967 also "struck down our old cases as to what constitutes maintenance, including champerty in so far as they were based on an outdated policy": [1980] 1 Q.B. 629, 653. Lord Denning considered that modern public policy could be found in *British Cash and Parcel Conveyors Ltd v. Lamson Store Service Co. Ltd* [1908] 1 K.B. 1006; *Martell v. Consett Iron Co. Ltd* [1955] Ch. 363; and *Hill v. Archbold* [1968] 1 Q.B. 686.

recognise that public policy is subject to change in the light of, for example, the need to ensure access to civil justice.[37] Thus the recent reforms on "no win no fee" arrangements obviously effect a significant change in public policy with respect to maintenance and champerty.[38]

17–050   **Maintenance.** A person is guilty of maintenance if he supports litigation in which he has no legitimate concern without just cause or excuse.[39] The mischief directed against is wanton and officious intermeddling with the disputes of others in which the defendant has no interest whatever and where the assistance he renders to one or the other party is without justification or excuse.[40] The bounds of justification and excuse for supporting litigation by others have been greatly widened over the past 50 years.[41] In the strict sense of the term, the doctrine of maintenance applies only to litigation[42] actually pending[43]; but unjustified *instigation* of actions by others is treated as "savouring of maintenance."[44] It is not the less maintenance because the maintained action was successful.[45]

17–051   **Justification.** The doctrine of maintenance, being founded on considerations of public policy, "cannot at any time become frozen into immutable respectability"[46] but must be "reappraised in light of current notions of public policy and of international trading practices."[47] As long ago as 1883 it was said that it was unhelpful to go back very far in the authorities relating to justification[48] and the grounds of justification have been further greatly widened over the past 50 years,[49] so that Danckwerts J.'s judgment in *Martell v. Consett Iron Co. Ltd*[50] can now be taken as the foundation of the modern law.[51] In that case an association

---

[37] See *Giles v. Thompson* [1993] 3 All E.R. 321, 348, CA, *per* Bingham M.R.; " . . . the law on maintenance and champerty has not stood still, but has accommodated itself to changing times . . . ", *per* Lord Mustill in the House of Lords at [1994] 1 A.C. 142, 164. See also *Thai Trading Co v. Taylor* [1998] 3 All E.R. 65; *Bevan Ashford v. Geoff Yeandle (Contractors) Ltd* [1998] 3 All E.R. 238; *Camdex International Ltd v. Bank of Zambia* [1996] C.L.C. 1477, 1481: "The modern approach is not to extend the types of involvement in litigation that are considered objectionable. There is a tendency to recognise less specific interests as justifying the support of the litigation of another."
[38] These reforms are set out in the judgment of Steyn L.J. in *Giles v. Thompson, supra.* See also *post,* 17–056.
[39] *Hill v. Archbold* [1968] 1 Q.B. 686; *Trendtex Trading Corpn. v. Credit Suisse* [1980] 1 Q.B. 629, 663. See Winfield (1919) 35 L.Q.R. 50 on the history of maintenance. See also Walters (1996) 112 L.Q.R. 560.
[40] *British Cash and Parcel Conveyors Ltd v. Lamson Store Service Co. Ltd* [1908] 1 K.B. 1006, 1012; *Hill v. Archbold, supra,* at 697; *Giles v. Thompson* [1993] 2 W.L.R. 908, 921.
[41] See §§ 17–051, *post.*
[42] See *Re Trepca Mines Ltd (No. 2)* [1963] Ch. 199; *cf. Moore v. Usher* (1835) 7 Sim. 383, 388; *cf. Pickering v. Sogex Services (U.K.) Ltd* (1982) 262 E.G. 770.
[43] *Flight v. Leman* (1843) 4 Q.B. 883.
[44] *ibid.; Greig v. National Amalgamated Union of Shop Assistants* (1906) 22 T.L.R. 274.
[45] *Neville v. London Express Newspaper Ltd* [1919] A.C. 368.
[46] *Martell v. Consett Iron Co. Ltd* [1955] Ch. 363, 375; *Hill v. Archbold* [1994] 1 A.C. 142, 164.
[47] *Trendtex Trading Corpn. v. Credit Suisse* [1980] 1 Q.B. 629, 663; see also [1982] A.C. 679, 702.
[48] *Bradlaugh v. Newdegate* (1883) 11 Q.B.D. 1, 7; and see *Ellis v. Torrington* [1920] 1 K.B. 399, 412.
[49] *Hill v. Archbold, supra,* at 694, 697; *Trendtex Trading Corpn. v. Credit Suisse* [1982] A.C. 679, 702; see also the Law Commission, *Proposals for the Reform of the Law Relating to Maintenance and Champerty* (1966), pp. 3–4; *Giles v. Thompson* [1993] 3 All E.R. 321, 330, CA.
[50] [1955] Ch. 363.
[51] *Hill v. Archbold, supra,* at 694, 700; *Trendtex Trading Corpn. v. Credit Suisse* [1982] A.C. 679, 702.

for the protection of the rights of owners and occupiers of fisheries and for the prevention of pollution of rivers supported an action by one of its members in respect of alleged pollution of a river flowing through the member's land. Danckwerts J. rejected the defendant's contention that the association was unlawfully maintaining the action, holding that "support of legal proceedings based on a bona fide community of pecuniary interest or religion or principle or problems" did not constitute maintenance.[52] The Court of Appeal, in affirming the decision, held that the defendants had not shown that the association was not acting in defence of the collective interests of its members on the principle of mutual protection.[53]

Examples of justification. It has been said that most of the actions in our courts today "are supported by some association or other, or by the state itself. Comparatively few litigants bring suits, or defend them, at their own expense. Most claims by workmen against their employers are paid for by a trade union. Most defences of motorists are paid for by insurance companies."[54] It is clear that ordinarily none of those cases today constitutes maintenance.[55] Similarly a body is not guilty of maintenance in supporting an action for defamation brought by one of its officers where, if the defamatory words complained of are true, the officer is unfit to continue in the body's employment.[56] It has always been a justification for the maintenance of an action that the maintainer acted solely with a charitable motive, and that is so even though there was no ground for the maintainer's action which he took without reasonable inquiry.[57] There may be evidence of maintenance in a solicitor taking up an action for a poor person[58] though it is probable that he may do so if he acts bona fide and has perhaps satisfied himself that there is a proper cause of action.[59] Blood relationship would seem to be a justification for maintenance.[60] The courts, particularly in commercial cases, have recognised that a sufficient interest does not have to be proprietary in character and in *Trendtex Trading Corporation v. Credit Suisse*[61] Oliver L.J. was willing to go so far as to hold that maintenance would be justified "wherever the maintainer has a genuine pre-existing financial interest in maintaining the solvency of the person whose action he maintains." The interest, however, must be distinct from any benefit which arises under the contract which

17-052

---

[52] [1955] Ch. 363, 387.

[53] [1955] Ch. 363, 389, 420, 430.

[54] *Hill v. Archbold, supra,* at 694–695.

[55] *ibid.; Bourne v. Colodense Ltd* [1985] I.C.R. 291.

[56] *Scott v. National Society for the Prevention of Cruelty to Children* (1909) 25 T.L.R. 789; *Hill v. Archbold, supra,* where the Court of Appeal stated that *Oram v. Hutt* [1914] 1 Ch. 98, CA and *Baker v. Jones* [1854] 1 W.L.R. 1005 (Lynskey J.) would not now be decided as they were; contrast *Martell v. Consett Iron Co. Ltd* [1955] Ch. 363, 389, 414–419, 425.

[57] *Harris v. Brisco* (1886) 17 Q.B.D. 504; *Holden v. Thompson* [1907] 2 K.B. 489; *cf. Cole v. Booker* (1913) 29 T.L.R. 295.

[58] *Wiggins v. Lavy* (1928) 44 T.L.R. 721, but that was before legal aid. See also § 17–056.

[59] *Ladd v. London Road Car Co., The Times,* March 14, 1900.

[60] *Rothewel v. Pewer* (1431) Y.B. 9 Hen. 6, p. 64, pl. 713; *Pomeroy v. Abbot Buckfast* (1443) Y.B. 22 Hen. 6; (1442) Y.B. 21 Hen. 6, p. 15, pl. 30; and see *Harris v. Brisco* (1886) 17 Q.B.D. 504, 512–513; 1 Hawkins P.C. (8th ed.), at 458; *cf. Hutley v. Hutley* (1873) L.R. 8 Q.B. 112.

[61] [1980] 1 Q.B. 629, 668. This view was implicitly endorsed in the House of Lords. There Lord Roskill was willing to hold that a genuine commercial interest was sufficient to enable an assignee of a cause of action to enforce it and on this reasoning the views of Oliver L.J. on what constitutes a sufficient justification for maintaining an action were implictly adopted; see [1982] A.C. 679, 703; see also *Brownton Ltd v. Edward Moore Inbucon Ltd* [1985] 3 All E.R. 499; *post,* § 20–047.

is allegedly illegal as constituting maintenance.[62] It has been held that despite the judgment of the Court of Appeal in *Prudential Assurance Co. Ltd v. Newman Industries Ltd*[63] a majority shareholder in a company possesses a sufficient interest so that an assignment to him of the company's cause of action is not against public policy.[64]

17–053   **Effect of maintenance.** In principle a contract of maintenance should be held to be unenforceable between the parties to it.[65] But even when maintenance was a crime, the illegal maintenance of an action was not a defence to the action, nor did it afford a ground for stay of proceedings.[66] The remedy of the other party to the litigation was before 1968 an action in tort. It would still appear to be the position that the court will not stay proceedings which are being maintained provided the proceedings do not constitute an abuse of the process of the court, that is, an action commenced in bad faith with no genuine belief in its merits but commenced for an ulterior purpose.[67] Also, the court does not have inherent jurisdiction to dismiss a maintained action which is not an abuse of the process of the court because the maintainer declines to give an undertaking as to costs, or to make such an order itself.[68]

17–054   **Champerty.** Champerty has been defined as "an aggravated form of maintenance"[69] and occurs when the person maintaining another stipulates for a share of the proceeds of the action or suit[70] or other contentious proceedings where property is in dispute.[71] For champerty there must not only be interference on the suit but there must be the added factor of a division of the spoils.[72] There is an obvious relationship between maintenance and champerty, you cannot have the latter without the former but "there can still be champerty even if the maintenance is not unlawful".[73] In *Giles v. Thompson*,[74] Lord Mustill was of the opinion that champerty as it related to an agreement by a solicitor to accept payment of his fees measured as a proportion of the damages recovered by his

---

[62] *Giles v. Thompson* [1994] 1 A.C. 142, 163, HL.

[63] [1982] Ch. 204 (sharesholder had no standing to bring action where wrong to the company allegedly reduced the value of his shares) (*cf. Fischer (Great Britain) Ltd v. Multi Construction Ltd* [1995] 1 B.C.L.C. 260).

[64] *Circuit Systems Ltd & Basten v. Zucken Redac (U.K.) Ltd* (1995) 11 Const. L.J. 201, 209 (on appeal this point did not have to be decided: [1996] 3 All E.R. 748).

[65] *Cole v. Booker* (1913) 29 T.L.R. 295, 297; Lord Coleridge C.J.'s *obiter dictum* to the contrary in *Bradlaugh v. Newdegate* (1883) 11 Q.B.D. 1, 4 cannot be taken to represent the law.

[66] *Martell v. Consett Iron Co. Ltd* [1955] Ch. 363.

[67] *Abraham v. Thompson* [1997] 4 All E.R. 362. It is considered that *Grovewood Holdings plc v. James Capel & Co. Ltd* [1995] Ch. 80 (dealing with a champertous agreement) is no longer good law: see note (1998) 114 L.Q.R. 207.

[68] *Abraham v. Thompson* [1997] 4 All E.R. 362. See also *Murphy v. Young & Cos. Brewery Plc* [1997] 1 Lloyd's Rep. 236. It is submitted that *McFarlane v. E.E. Caledonia Ltd (No. 2)* [1995] 1 W.L.R. 366 is no longer good law. The proper way to proceed is to seek an order against the maintainer under s.51 of the Supreme Court Act 1981.

[69] *Giles v. Thompson* [1993] 3 All E.R. 321, 328, CA.

[70] *Trendtex Trading Corpn. v. Credit Suisse* [1980] 1 Q.B. 629, 663; *Re Trepca Mines Ltd (No. 2)* [1963] Ch. 199, 219; *Haseldine v. Hosken* [1933] 1 K.B. 822, 831; and see *Anderson v. Radcliffe* (1858) E.B. & E. 806, 819, 825. Champerty only relates to legal proceedings: *Pickering v. Sogex Services (U.K.) Ltd* (1982) 262 E.G. 770.

[71] *Re Trepca Mines Ltd (No. 2), supra*, at 224; *Master v. Miller* (1791) 4 T.R. 320, 340.

[72] *Giles v. Thompson* [1994] 1 A.C. 142, 161.

[73] *Thai Trading Co. v. Taylor* [1998] 3 All E.R. 65, 69.

[74] [1994] 1 A.C. 142.

client survived largely as a rule of professional conduct.[75] While there undoubtedly have been significant changes in the rules relating to fee arrangements between solicitors and their clients which now permit arrangements which previously would have been champertous,[76] it is suggested that it would be going too far to treat the rule as being merely one of professional conduct. It is no justification for a champertous agreement that the contracting parties are related by blood.[77] The question arises whether the court can enjoin proceedings that are champertous. The reasoning in *Abraham v. Thompson*[78] would suggest not. Where the plaintiff relies on a champertous assignment to sue, the action would be enjoined not, however, because of the champerty as such but because it is not possible to assign a cause of action.

Champertous agreements between solicitor and client. An agreement by a solicitor to provide funds for litigation[79] or without charge to conduct litigation,[80] in this country, in consideration of a share of the proceeds is champertous,[81] and this is so even though the agreement was made abroad.[82] It was argued in *Wallersteiner v. Moir (No. 2)*[83] that considerations of policy demanded an exception to this rule, namely where a shareholder intended to bring an action on behalf of a company against those in control of the company who had allegedly committed wrongs against it, such an action being extremely costly to the individual and, in the event of success, bringing him probably small personal benefit. But a majority[84] of the Court of Appeal refused to create such an exception. It is not champertous for a solicitor acting for a party in litigation to agree to forgo all or part of his fees should he lose[85] but an agreement whereby a solicitor obtained more than his profit costs (unless it was a permitted conditional fee), or a contingent fee, would probably be unenforceable.[86] Where a solicitor enters into a champertous agreement, he cannot recover from his client his own costs[87] or even his out-of-pocket expenses.[88] But the solicitor does not act champertously unless he is a party to the agreement or participates in it by voluntarily doing a positive act to assist the parties in its execution, and the mere fact that the solicitor knows or gets to know of a champertous agreement relating to litigation in which he is engaged does not prevent him from suing on an

17–055

---

[75] *ibid.* at 911–912.

[76] See *post*, § 17–056.

[77] *Hutley v. Hutley* (1873) L.R. 8 Q.B. 112; *cf. ante* § 17–052.

[78] See n. 69, *supra*.

[79] See *ante* § 17–052, text to nn. 43 and 44; as to assignments of rights to solicitors, see *post* § 17–064.

[80] *ibid.*

[81] *Re Masters* (1835) 4 Dowl. 18; *Strange v. Brennan* (1846) 15 Sim. 346; *Hilton v. Woods* (1867) L.R. 4 Eq. 432; *Earle v. Hopwood* (1861) 9 C.B. (N.S.) 566; *Hutley v. Hutley* (1873) L.R. 8 Q.B. 112; *Re A Solicitor* [1912] 1 K.B. 302; *Re A Solicitor* (1913) 29 T.L.R. 354; *Wiggins v. Lavy* (1928) 44 T.L.R. 721. And see Solicitors Act 1974, s.59 (amended by Courts and Legal Services Act 1990, s. 98).

[82] *Grell v. Levy* (1864) 16 C.B. (N.S.) 73.

[83] [1975] Q.B. 373.

[84] Lord Denning was prepared to allow a "contingency fee" in such circumstances. See also *Trendtex Trading Corpn. v. Credit Suisse* [1980] 1 Q.B. 629, 654, 663.

[85] *Thai Trading Co. v. Taylor* [1998] 3 All E.R. 65. See also *British Waterways Board v. Norman* (1993) 26 H.L.R. 753.

[86] *ibid.* A fee splitting agreement may be in breach of the Law Society Rules and unenforceable because it is accordingly illegal: see *Mohamed v. Alaga Co.* [1998] 2 All E.R. 720.

[87] *Wild v. Simpson* [1919] 2 K.B. 544.

[88] *Re Trepca Mines Ltd (No. 2)* [1963] Ch. 199.

otherwise lawful retainer.[89] If a lawful retainer is subsequently varied by a champertous agreement, the solicitor probably cannot disregard the agreement and rely on his ordinary rights under the retainer.[90]

17–056   **Non-champertous agreements between solicitor and client.** Section 59 of the Courts and Legal Services Act 1990 is designed to enable a solicitor and client to enter into a "conditional fee agreement" which has similarities to a contingent fee arrangement. A conditional fee agreement is a written agreement between the client and the person providing litigation or advocacy services whereby the advocate or litigator receives normal fees or normal fees plus an uplift in the event of success.[91] The Lord Chancellor can make regulations as regards the level of the uplift[92] and any agreement in which this level is exceeded shall be unenforceable.[93] In certain proceedings, a conditional fee agreement is not permitted, the most important of these being matrimonial and criminal proceedings.[94] There are other forms of fee agreement between a solicitor and client which are not treated as being champertous. There is no objection to a solicitor agreeing to charge no costs against his client.[95] And a solicitor and client may agree for a fixed remuneration in lieu of costs[96]; such agreement must be in writing and is subject to the proviso that no validity is given to any purchase by a solicitor of his client's interest in any action, suit or other contentious proceeding, or to any agreement by which the solicitor stipulates for payment only in the event of success.[97] Also, as we have seen in the last paragraph, a solicitor may enter into an agreement on a "no win no fee" basis.[98]

17–057   **Agreements savouring of champerty: assignments of the right to litigate.** In *Trendtex Trading Corporation v. Credit Suisse,*[99] the Court of Appeal and House of Lords fundamentally re-examined the law of maintenance and champerty in so far as it applied to the assignment of the right to litigate. Much simplified, the facts in that case were as follows. The plaintiff (T) sold cement, payment to be made by confirmed letter of credit. The issuing bank (CBN) failed to honour the letter of credit and T sued for payment. T was successful in the Court of Appeal but leave was given to CBN to appeal to the House of Lords. At

---

[89] *ibid.* at 220–221.

[90] *Wild v. Simpson* [1919] 2 K.B. 544, 565, disapproving *Grell v. Levy* (1864) 16 C.B. (N.S.) 73; and see *Re Trepca Mines Ltd (No. 2)* [1963] Ch. 199, 222.

[91] s.58(1) and (2). The conditional fee is different from the contingent fee in that the latter normally provides for a percentage of any recoveries being paid to the lawyer.

[92] s.58(5) (the regulations can also specify the proceedings to which the uplift applies; s. 58(4)). Orders have been made under the section: Conditional Fee Order 1995 (S.I. 1995 No. 1674); Conditional Fee Agreement Regulations 1995 (S.I. 1995 No. 1675).

[93] s.58(6). It would appear that the whole agreement is unenforceable. It is unclear whether the advocate or litigator could recover on a *quantum meruit*, but if the effect of subs.58(6) is to bring the rules relating to champerty into play then recovery would not be possible.

[94] s.58(10).

[95] *Jennings v. Johnson* (1873) L.R. 8 C.P. 425. Such an agreement precludes the recovery of costs by the client from the other party to the litigation, as costs are given by way of indemnity: *Gundry v. Sainsbury* [1910] 1 K.B. 645.

[96] Solicitors Act 1974, ss.59–63 (contentious business); *cf.* s.57 (non-contentious business); (certain aspects of s.57, 59, 60 and 61 of the 1974 Act have been amended by s.98 of the Courts and Legal Services Act 1990). See also § 17–064; *Electrical Trades Union v. Tarlo* [1964] Ch. 720.

[97] Solicitors Act 1974, s.59(1); and see *Electrical Trades Union v. Tarlo* [1964] Ch. 720.

[98] n. 85, *supra.*

[99] [1980] Q.B. 629, CA [1982] A.C. 679; *Kaukomarkkinat O/Y v. "Elbe" Transport-Union GmbH (The "Kelo")* [1985] 2 Lloyd's Rep. 85.

this juncture T assigned its right of action against CBN to the defendants, Credit Suisse, to whom T was heavily indebted for financial assistance provided in connection with the cement contract and the litigation arising out of the dis- honouring of the letter of credit. The agreement whereby T assigned its right of action to Credit Suisse also provided that Credit Suisse could assign the right of action to a third party which Credit Suisse eventually did. T subsequently considered that it had been duped by the defendants into making the assignment for what turned out to be a gross undervaluation, and sought to have the assignment set aside on the ground that the whole transaction was champertous.[1] The Court of Appeal upheld the assignment. The defendants had a close commer- cial relationship with the defendants which would have justified them in main- taining an action by the plaintiff or in participating in any proceeds of action and, in light of this, Oliver L.J., could not see why the actual "assignment of the cause of action itself" should not also be valid.[2] Lord Denning M.R. saw no reason why the benefit of the right to sue for damages for breach of contract should not be assignable given that the benefit of the contract before breach was assignable.[3] However, the right to litigate about purely personal claims is not assignable[4] and where a solicitor is involved the courts would not adopt such a tolerant attitude to the validity of the assignment "because an English court will not permit one of its own officers to put himself in a position in which his interest and duty may conflict."[5]

Broadly speaking the House of Lords supported the reasoning of the Court of **17–058** Appeal, although it differed on the application of that reasoning to the facts of the instant case. Lord Roskill considered that Oliver L.J., had not failed[6] to dis- tinguish between the interest "necessary to support an assignment of a cause of action and the interest which would justify the maintenance of an action by a third party." If the assignee has "a genuine commercial interest in taking the assignment and in enforcing it for his own benefit (there was) no reason why the assignment should be struck down as an assignment of a bare cause of action or as savouring of maintenance."[7] Lord Roskill did, however, disapprove[8] of the view of Lord Denning M.R. in the Court of Appeal that "The old saying that you cannot assign a 'bare right of litigate' is gone"; this still remained a fundamental

---

[1] The Criminal Law Act 1967, s.14(2), has a bearing on this issue. As s.14(2) only applies to "cases in which *a contract* is to be treated as contrary to public policy or otherwise illegal," it may therefore be argued that completed assignments, which operate as transfers of property and not as contracts, are no longer to be avoided on grounds of public policy. It is submitted that such an argument would fail. Even before the passing of the Criminal Law Act 1967 such assignments were neither crimes nor tort but, being analogised with maintenance and champerty, were on the grounds of public policy simply treated as ineffective. These grounds of public policy remain unaffected by the Criminal Law Act 1967. See *ante*, § 17–049.

[2] [1980] Q.B. 629, 670.

[3] *ibid.* at 656–657. See also Oliver L.J., at 674: "For my part, I would be prepared to hold that where a cause of action arises out of a right which was itself assignable, the cause of action equally remains assignable. . . . "

[4] *ibid.* at 657 and 674 (referred to by Oliver L.J., as "personal and non-assignable" contracts). Lord Denning also considered that the right to sue with respect to certain torts to property would also be assignable, but not with respect to personal torts (at 656–657). See, *e.g. British Cash and Parcel Conveyors Ltd v. Lamson Store Service Co. Ltd* [1908] 1 K.B. 1006.

[5] *ibid.* at 675, *per* Oliver L.J., citing *Grell v. Levy* (1864) 16 C.B. (N.S.) 73. See also *post*, § 20–047.

[6] [1982] A.C. 679, 703.

[7] *ibid.*

[8] *ibid.*

principle of English law and the assignee needed to demonstrate a commercial interest in the enforcement of the claim for the assignment to be valid.[9] The House of Lords considered that the assignment in this case was void because it was the first step in a transaction whereby the cause of action was to be assigned to a third party who had no legitimate commercial interest in the transaction. If the assignment had merely been to Credit Suisse it would have been valid.[10]

17–059   That the vice in *Trendtex* was that the assignment contemplated the assignee selling the claim to a stranger for a higher price than it had paid for it is clear from *Brownton Ltd v. Edward Moore Inbucon Ltd.*[11] In that case the plaintiffs sought advice from A on the installation of computer equipment and on the basis of that advice purchased equipment from B. The equipment never worked. The plaintiffs sued A for damages who in turn alleged that the defective operation of the equipment was due to the fault of B, whereupon the plaintiffs joined B as second defendants. A paid a sum of money into court in settlement of its liability towards the plaintiffs and the plaintiffs were willing to accept this as full satisfaction of its claim against both A and B provided it could reach a satisfactory arrangement on the costs of the various parties. When B refused to agree to any arrangement, A assigned to the plaintiffs any cause of action it might have against B arising out of installation of the equipment. B's claim that this assignment was champertous failed. The court found that the plaintiffs had a sufficient commercial interest to justify the assignment and this distinguished the case from *Trendtex* where the "contemplated assignment to the anonymous third party was objectionable . . . because he had no genuine pre-existing commercial interest in the outcome of the cause of action."[12] The court also held that for the assignment to be valid it was not necessary that the "assignee's interest applied to every facet of the cause of action,"[13] all that was needed was that the assignee possess a genuine commercial interest which had to be determined on an examination of the transaction as a whole. In addition, it was not fatal to the validity of an assignment that the assignee might be better off as a result of the assignment, or that the assignee might make a profit out of it.[14] However, where the "figures . . . were massively disproportionate," the figures being what the assignee paid and what he was liable to gain, then the agreement would be champertous.[15]

17–060   All previous authorities must now be read in the light of *Trendtex's* greater liberality on assignments of the right to litigate and its rejection of any broad rule supposedly prohibiting the assignment of the right to litigate for damages. What

---

[9] *Giles v. Thompson* [1994] 1 A.C. 142, 153 (a bare right of action is not assignable).

[10] One of the features of the assignment was that the plaintiffs assigned all rights even if the assignee recovered more than the debt owing from the plaintiff to the defendant. Lord Roskill considered this to be an agreement to divide the "spoils" between the defendant and the third party: *ibid.* at 779. *Quaere* what the position would have been if recovery beyond the debt was repayable to the plaintiff.

[11] [1985] 3 All E.R. 499.

[12] *ibid.* at 509, *per* Lloyd L.J.

[13] *ibid.* at 505, *per* Sir John Megaw.

[14] Lloyd L.J. left open the question as to whether any profit would be returnable by the assignee to the assignor (at 509). If the assignment is out and out and not by way of security it is difficult to see why this should be so.

[15] *Advanced Technology Structures Ltd v. Cray Valley Products Ltd* [1993] B.C.L.C. 723, 733–734.

appears in the following paragraphs are examples of recurrent situations involving the assignment of a right to litigate. Of course, where the court permitted assignment before *Trendtex* then obviously it will also be permitted after it. Thus assignments of debts are permissible[16] (even though the assignee's object in taking the assignment was to make the debtor bankrupt),[17] or assignments of the fruits of an action,[18] or assignments of property (even though the property is incapable of being recovered without litigation),[19] or assignments designed "to support or enlarge" a property interest which the assignee already possesses.[20] It may also be that the old distinctions between maintenance, champerty and assignment are being dissolved. As was stated by Lloyd L.J. in *Brownton Ltd v. Edward Moore Inbucon Ltd*[21] there is no difference between the interest "required to justify a share in the proceeds, or the interest required to support an out-and-out assignment." On this reasoning involvement in litigation will be justified if it can be shown that the party in question has sufficient interest in the litigation.

Assignment incidental to transfer of property. An assignment of a right to litigate is good if it is incidental and subsidiary to a transfer of property.[22] The question is whether the subject-matter of the assignment is property with an incidental remedy for its recovery, or a bare right of action.[23] Thus a conveyance of property by a vendor who has previously conveyed that property to another by a deed voidable in equity is good, as the vendor retained an interest which he could dispose of and which carried with it a right of action to have the earlier deed set aside.[24] In *Williams v. Protheroe*[25] the vendor and purchaser of an estate agreed that the purchaser, bearing the expense of certain suits which had been commenced by the vendor against an occupier for bygone rent, should have any rent recovered and also any sum that might be recovered for dilapidations, and that the purchaser might at his own expense use the name of the vendor in any action he might think fit to commence against the occupier for arrears of rent or dilapidations. It was held that this agreement was not illegal as amounting to champerty. In *Ellis v. Torrington*[26] the plaintiff took an assignment of the benefit of certain covenants to repair contained in an expired underlease, having already purchased the fee simple of the property from another person. This assignment was held free from objection on the ground of champerty, the right of action on the covenants being so connected with the enjoyment of property as to be more than a bare right to litigate. It was held to be immaterial that the assignment was made later than the purchase of the property, and by a person other than the vendor. Again, in *Performing Rights Society Ltd v. Thompson*[27] the plaintiff

17–061

---

[16] *Ellis v. Torrington* [1920] 1 K.B. 399; *Defries v. Milne* [1913] 1 Ch. 98.

[17] *Fitzroy v. Cave* [1905] 2 K.B. 364 (see the observations on this case in *Trendtex* [1980] Q.B., at 673). Similarly a person may acquire shares in a company for the express purpose of challenging acts of the directors in litigation: *Bloxham v. Metropolitan Ry.* (1868) L.R. 3 Ch.App. 337, 353.

[18] *Glegg v. Bromley* [1912] 3 K.B. 474.

[19] *Dawson v. Great Northern & City Ry.* [1905] 1 K.B. 260.

[20] *Compania Colombiana de Seguros v. Pacific Steam Navigation Co.* [1965] 1 Q.B. 101.

[21] [1985] 3 All E.R. 499, 509.

[22] *Williams v. Protheroe* (1829) 3 Y. & J. 129.

[23] *Glegg v. Bromley* [1912] 3 K.B. 474, 490.

[24] *Dickinson v. Burrell* (1866) L.R. 1 Eq. 337.

[25] (1829) 3 Y. & J. 129.

[26] [1920] 1 K.B. 399; and see *County Hotel & Wine Co. Ltd v. London & N.W. Ry. Co.* [1918] 2 K.B. 251 (affd. on other grounds [1921] 1 A.C. 85).

[27] (1918) 34 T.L.R. 351.

society had been formed as a company to protect the copyright interests of its members, who assigned their copyrights to the society and by its rules shared in all damages recovered by the society. This was held to be a legitimate business arrangement and not champertous. In *Camdex International Ltd v. Bank of Zambia*[28], the court held that the assignment of a debt in accordance with section 136 of the Law of Property Act 1925, in circumstances where it was contemplated that an action would be necessary in order to obtain payment, did not constitute maintenance. Also, such an assignment would not be contrary to public policy even if the assignor maintained some interest in the debt.

17–062   **Assignment to person beneficially entitled to right.** Where before the Judicature Act 1873 equity would have compelled A to exercise his rights against a contract breaker or tortfeasor for the benefit of B, those rights can validly be assigned by A to B and, subject to due compliance with section 136 of the Law of Property Act 1925, can be enforced by B in his own name at law.[29] Therefore an underwriter, who has indemnified his insured under a policy of insurance and has in consequence been legally assigned the insured's rights of action against third parties, may sue those third parties in his own name to enforce those rights of action.[30]

17–063   **Assignment by trustee in bankruptcy and liquidator.** Rights of action which are the property of a bankrupt and pass to his trustee in bankruptcy may be assigned by the trustee, even though they may be only bare rights of action. These are treated as saleable as being part of the assets for the benefit of creditors.[31] And an agreement between some of the creditors of a bankrupt and the trustee that an action of the bankrupt should be carried on at their private expense, on the terms of receiving a larger share of the fruits of the action, was held not to offend against the law of champerty.[32] It has also been held that an assignment of a cause of action can be made by a liquidator.[33] It is not possible for a company to obtain legal aid.[34] In addition, it is possible for a security for costs order to be made against a company if it appears to the court on the evidence presented to it that the company will be unable to pay the costs of the defendant should it be unsuccessful.[35] The combined effect of these rules has serious consequences for a company that goes into liquidation since it will often find it difficult to fund litigation unless the creditors are willing to put it in funds. To circumvent these rules, the question arises as to whether it is possible for the liquidator to assign a cause of action of the company to an individual with an interest in the litigation, for example, a director or the majority shareholder. The

---

[28] [1998] Q.B. 22.

[29] *Compania Colombiana de Seguros v. Pacific Steam Navigation Co.* [1965] 1 Q.B. 101, 121.

[30] *Compania Colombiana de Seguros v. Pacific Steam Navigation Co., supra*; and see Vol. II, § 41–079.

[31] *Seear v. Lawson* (1880) 15 Ch.D. 426; Insolvency Act 1986, s.314(1); *Weddell v. J. A. Pearce & Major* [1988] Ch. 26. See further *post*, § 21–019.

[32] *Guy v. Churchill* (1888) 40 Ch.D. 481.

[33] *Freightex Ltd v. International Express Co. Ltd* (April 15, 1980, CA). The assignment in this case was made to the managing director of the company who arguably had an interest, but the court considered that the language of the legislation, s.242(2)(a) of the Companies Act 1948, absolved the actions of the liquidator from the taint of maintenance or champerty. See now, Insolvency Act 1986, ss.166, 167, 436 and Sched. 4.

[34] Legal Aid Act 1988, s.2(11); *Wallersteiner v. Moir (No. 2)* [1975] Q.B. 373.

[35] Companies Act 1985, s.726.

reason for such assignment is that the individual, unlike the company, is entitled to legal aid and not subject to a security for costs order. *Norglen Ltd (in liq.) v. Reeds Rains Prudential Ltd*[36] involved such an assignment which, *inter alia*, provided that the fruits of the action would be first used to pay the company's creditors and any balance divided equally between the company and the assignee. The assignment was made under the liquidator's powers to sell the company's property which includes choses in action.[37] The court held that the assignment was valid and on established principles was not subject to the rules relating to maintenance and champerty. It has been held that the rules relating to maintenance and champerty apply to the assignment of the fruits of an action (but not the cause of action itself) where the assignee agrees to fund the action.[38] This decision, without expressing any definite view, has been doubted.[39] It is submitted that these doubts are justified. There are no compelling reasons for placing such a gloss on the power of the liquidator to assign a cause action vested in the company. If an assignment of the fruits of an action where the assignee does not undertake to provide funding for the action is valid,[40] it is difficult to see why an undertaking to provide such funding should make a difference; and similar principles apply to an assignment of a bankrupt's cause of action by the trustee in bankruptcy.[41]

Assignments of rights to solicitors. A solicitor cannot lawfully purchase anything in litigation of which he has had the management,[42] nor can he purchase fruits of such litigation before judgment[43]; but an assignment of an action to a solicitor preceding his employment as such is good unless it would have been unenforceable as between strangers.[44] A solicitor may lawfully take from his client a security upon property which is the subject-matter of an action for advances already incurred in the action,[45] and he may take security from his client for his costs to be ascertained by taxation or otherwise.[46]   **17–064**

Other agreements "savouring of champerty." An agreement merely to communicate information to a person in consideration of receiving a share of property to be recovered thereby is unobjectionable, provided there is no suit pending and no stipulation that one shall be commenced.[47] But if it is a term of   **17–065**

---

[36] [1997] 3 W.L.R. 1177.

[37] In so far as the assignees were eligible for legal aid and the company was not, the House of Lords considered that this was a matter for the Legal Aid Board. Regulations have now been passed to deal with this: see [1997] 3 W.L.R. 1177, 1187.

[38] *Grovewood Holdings plc. v. James Capel & Co. Ltd* [1995] Ch. 80. This case was not followed in *Re Movitor Pty Ltd* (1996) 19 A.C.S.R. 440.

[39] *Re Oasis Merchandising Services Ltd* [1997] 2 W.L.R. 765, 771–772.

[40] *Glegg v. Bromley* [1912] 3 K.B. 474.

[41] *Stein v. Blake* [1996] 1 A.C. 243.

[42] *Hall v. Hallet* (1784) 1 Cox 134; *Simpson v. Lamb* (1857) 7 E. & B. 84; *cf. Strachan v. Brander* (1759) 1 Eden 303.

[43] *Wood v. Downes* (1811) 18 Ves. 120; *Simpson v. Lamb, supra; Pittman v. Prudential Deposit Bank Ltd* (1896) 13 T.L.R. 110. There is also a dictum to the effect that public policy in this area may be more strict where solicitors are involved: *Trendtex Trading Corpn. v. Credit Suisse* [1980] Q.B. 629, 674–675; *ante*, § 17–057; *Giles v. Thompson* [1994] 1 A.C. 142.

[44] *Davis v. Freethy* (1890) 24 Q.B.D. 519.

[45] *Anderson v. Radcliffe* (1858) E.B. 806, 819. *cf.* Turner L.J. in *Knight v. Bowyer* (1858) 2 De G. & J. 421, 445.

[46] Solicitors Act 1974, s.65(1) (contentious business); s.56(6) (non-contentious business); see also S.I. 1994 No. 2616.

[47] *Sprye v. Porter* (1856) 7 E. & B. 58; *Rees v. De Bernardy* [1896] 2 Ch. 437.

the agreement that the person giving the information and who is to share in what may be recovered shall himself recover the property or actively assist in its recovery by procuring evidence or otherwise, the agreement is unenforceable as "savouring of champerty,"[48] and will be set aside in equity,[49] though it may be on terms.[50]

17–066   **Effect of champerty.** A champertous agreement is certainly unenforceable as between the parties,[51] though sums actually advanced to the champertor under the agreement have sometimes been held to be recoverable.[52] In respect of any loss sustained in connection with a champertous agreement, a solicitor cannot maintain a claim on a policy of indemnity.[53] The champertous support of the plaintiff in an action is probably not a defence to the action and probably affords no ground for a stay of proceedings.[54] Where a champertous agreement is entered into, a solicitor who provides services under it cannot recover on the grounds of *quantum meruit* or any other basis for the services that he has rendered. However, where payment has been made to a solicitor under a champertous agreement and he has not behaved unconscionably towards the payer or has not been unjustly enriched, the payee is not entitled to recover the price of those services while retaining the benefit of them: the champertous agreement in this situation is simply unenforceable.[55]

(e) *Objects Injurious to Morality and Marriage*

(i) *Immorality*

17–067   **Cohabitation.**[56] Agreements by unmarried persons to cohabit obviously raise important questions of public policy as these agreements could be treated as being *contra bonos mores*[57] and therefore unenforceable. In a number of earlier authorities the courts adopted this position. Agreements in consideration of future illicit cohabitation, even though made under seal, have been held to be unenforceable.[58] But a promise given in consideration of past illicit cohabitation is good as a voluntary promise, and can be enforced if made under deed,[59] or supported by some other consideration, but not otherwise.[60] A bond given for

---

[48] *Stanley v. Jones* (1831) 7 Bing. 369, 377; *Rees v. De Bernardy* [1896] 2 Ch. 437; *Wedgerfield v. De Bernardy* (1908) 25 T.L.R. 21.

[49] 17–058 *supra.*

[50] *Strachan v. Brander* (1759) 1 Eden 303.

[51] *Hutley v. Hutley* (1873) L.R. 8 Q.B. 112.

[52] *James v. Kerr* (1888) 40 Ch.D. 449.

[53] *Haseldine v. Hosken* [1933] 1 K.B. 822.

[54] *cf. ante*, § 17–053.

[55] *Aratra Potato Co. Ltd v. Taylor Joynson Garrett* [1995] 4 All E.R. 695. This case was disapproved of in *Thai Trading Co. v. Taylor* [1998] 3 All E.R. 65 but it is submitted that this aspect of the judgment remains good law.

[56] See Cretney and Masson, *Principles of Family Law* (6th ed., 1996), pp. 3–5, 106, 110.

[57] "In this branch of the law the word 'immoral' connotes only sexual immorality": *Coral Leisure Group Ltd. v. Barnett* [1981] I.C.R. 503, 506.

[58] *Benyon v. Nettlefold* (1850) 3 Mac. & G. 94; *Ayerst v. Jenkins* (1873) L.R. 16 Eq. 275.

[59] *Per* Lord Selborne L.C. in *Ayerst v. Jenkins* (1873) L.R. 16 Eq. 275, 282; and see *Annandale, Marchioness of v. Harris* (1728) 1 Bro.P.C. 250; 2 P.Wms. 432; *Turner v. Vaughan* (1767) 2 Wils.K.B. 339; *Gray v. Mathias* (1800) 5 Ves. 286; *Nye v. Moseley* (1826) 6 B. & C. 133.

[60] *Beaumont v. Reeve* (1846) 8 Q.B. 483. There is no public policy against enforcing such promises as they do not promote immorality and all that is needed is consideration to make the contract binding.

such consideration is not invalidated by the mere fact that the illicit cohabitation continues after its execution[61]; nor that the parties contemplated its continuance, provided their intention forms no part of the consideration for the bond.[62] An agreement by a man to pay a woman with whom he was cohabiting a sum down and an annuity for life if they should separate and she should continue single and not cohabit with one D.G. or anyone else, has also been held good as being a gift on condition that she remained sole and chaste[63]; and so was an agreement by a reputed father of an illegitimate child to pay the mother an annuity if she would maintain the child and keep their connection secret, the maintenance of the child being a sufficient consideration for the contract.[64]

Extra-marital cohabitation is obviously an area where values change[65] and the older authorities clearly reflect a marriage morality which is out of tune with contemporary mores. Recently the courts have been obliged to deal with legal problems arising out of unmarried persons setting up relatively stable domestic arrangements and when these problems have arisen the issue of illegality does not appear to have been argued. For example, in *Tanner v. Tanner*[66] a married man had twins by his mistress and he provided the mistress and the twins with a house. When the man subsequently attempted to evict the mistress, the court held that there was an implied contract between the parties that the mistress could live in the house, the consideration given by the mistress being her relinquishment of a rent-controlled flat. Although the contract undoubtedly involved sexual relations outside of marriage, no question of illegality was raised and there is little doubt that the court would have been unsympathetic to such a plea.[67] One way of reconciling *Tanner v. Tanner* with previous authority is that "an agreement for an immoral consideration is to be treated as enforceable, if there be any other, lawful consideration to support it."[68] From this it would follow that contractual arrangements involving unmarried parties to a relatively domestic arrangement will be enforceable and the older authorities will only apply to relationships which are wholly related to the provision of sexual services.[69]

17–068

---

[61] *Hall v. Palmer* (1844) 3 Hare 532; *Re Vallance* (1884) 26 Ch.D. 353.

[62] *Re Wootton Isaacson* (1904) 21 T.L.R. 89; *cf. Friend v. Harrison* (1827) 2 Car. & P. 584.

[63] *Gibson v. Dickie* (1815) 3 M. & S. 463.

[64] *Jennings v. Brown* (1842) 9 M. & W. 496; see also *Hicks v. Gregory* (1849) 8 C.B. 378; *Smith v. Roche* (1859) 6 C.B. (N.S.) 223; *Ward v. Byham* [1956] 1 W.L.R. 496; *Horrocks v. Foray* [1976] 1 W.L.R. 230, 299.

[65] See *ante*, § 17–003.

[66] [1975] 1 W.L.R. 1346; see also *Chandler v. Kerley* [1978] 1 W.L.R. 693; *Bernard v. Josephs* [1982] Ch. 391. *cf. Horrocks v. Foray* [1976] 1 W.L.R. 230 (the court found that there was no contract between a man and his mistress, but the issue of illegality was not raised). See also on changing values as regards sexual mores: *Andrews v. Parker* (1973) Qd. R. 93; *Dyson Holdings Ltd v. Fox* [1976] Q.B. 503; *Watson v. Lucas* [1980] 1 W.L.R. 1493. *cf. Carega Properties SA v. Sharratt* [1979] 1 W.L.R. 928; Inheritance (Provision for Family and Dependants) Act 1975, s.1 (particularly s.1(1)(e) and (3)); *Re C.* (1979) 123 S.J. 35; *Malone v. Harrison* [1979] 1 W.L.R. 1353; Domestic Violence and Matrimonial Proceedings Act 1976, s.2(1); *Davis v. Johnson* [1979] A.C. 264: Fatal Accidents Act 1976, s.1(3), as amended by Administration of Justice Act 1982, s.3.

[67] See, *e.g. Cook v. Head* [1972] 1 W.L.R. 518; *Eves v. Eves* [1975] 1 W.L.R. 1338.

[68] Barton, 92 L.Q.R. 168 (1976), at p. 169. See also *Eves v. Eves, supra* at 1345C; *Paul v. Constance* [1977] 1 W.L.R. 527.

[69] See, *e.g. Marvin v. Marvin* (1976) 557 P.2d. 104; *Bernard v. Josephs* [1982] Ch. 391; *Heglibiston Establishment v. Heyman* (1977) 36 P. & C.R. 351, 360–362; *Barclays Bank plc v. O'Brien* [1994] 1 A.C. 180, 188 ("Now that unmarried cohabitation, whether heterosexual or homosexual, is widespread in our society, the law should recognise this."); Dwyer (1977) 93 L.Q.R. 386.

17-069 **Prostitution.** An action is not maintainable to recover the rent of lodgings knowingly let for the purpose of prostitution[70] or to a man's mistress for the purposes of the liaison.[71] And where the landlord, although not aware of the true facts at the time of the letting, permitted the tenant to remain after discovering that she was using the lodgings for prostitution, it was held that he could not recover from her the rent which accrued after this had come to his knowledge and he had failed to take steps to evict her.[72] All covenants in an assignment of a lease of premises which the assignor knows the assignee intends to use as a brothel are similarly unenforceable.[73] But although the tenant of an apartment may be a prostitute, and the landlord is aware of her character, he may recover his rent if she does not use his premises for immoral purposes[74]; and, in the absence of evidence specifically to connect the contract with the prostitution,[75] a contract to sell clothes to a prostitute,[76] or to wash for her,[77] is good. Where a contract of employment requires the employee to procure prostitutes, this would be a contract entered into for an immoral purpose and would be illegal and unenforceable.[78]

(ii) *Interference with Marriage*[79]

17-070 **Promise of marriage by married person.** A promise by a married man to marry one who knew him to be already married was unenforceable as against public policy and as tending to immorality.[80] No action lay for breach of such a promise even after the death of the wife.[81] So also with a similar promise by a married woman to marry after the death of her husband[82] or divorce.[83] A promise of marriage made by a married man in the interval between decree nisi and decree absolute was actionable if broken—since after the decree nisi the normal obligations and conditions of marriage have disappeared and consortium has come to an end.[84] Actions for breach of promise of marriage were abolished by section 1 of the Law Reform (Miscellaneous Provisions) Act 1970, so that the cases just discussed are, strictly speaking, obsolete. However, section 2 of the Act

---

[70] *Girardy v. Richardson* (1793) 1 Esp. 13. Similarly a seller cannot recover the price of clothes furnished specifically to enable the purchaser to carry on her trade as a prostitute, the seller expecting to be paid from the profits thereof: *Bowry v. Bennet* (1808) 1 Camp.348; and see *Pearce v. Brooks* (1866) L.R. 1 Ex. 213, § 17–158, *post*. Contrast *Lloyd v. Johnson* (1798) 1 B. & P. 340 (a contract for the cleaning of a prostitute's clothes, in which it was said that the use to be made of the clothes was irrelevant at least where the clothes were of such a nature that the prostitute would need them anyhow). Generally, *cf. Shaw v. D.P.P.* [1962] A.C. 220.
[71] *Upfill v. Wright* [1911] 1 K.B. 506 (in *Heglibiston Establishment v. Heyman* (1977) 36 P. & C.R. 351, 360–362 it was doubted if this case would today be decided the same way on its facts). *cf.* Vol. II, § 32–049.
[72] *Jennings v. Throgmorton* (1825) R. & M. 251.
[73] *Smith v. White* (1866) L.R. 1 Eq. 626.
[74] *Appleton v. Campbell* (1862) 2 C. & P. 347.
[75] See n. 51, *supra*.
[76] *Bowry v. Bennett* (1808) 1 Camp. 348.
[77] *Lloyd v. Johnson* (1798) 1 B. & P. 340.
[78] *Coral Leisure Group Ltd. v. Barnet* [1981] I.C.R. 503.
[79] As to the invalidity of agreements between husband and wife providing for their future separation, see *Brodie v. Brodie* [1917] P.271.
[80] *Wilson v. Carnley* [1908] 1 K.B. 729; *Spiers v. Hunt* [1908] 1 K.B. 720; *Siveyer v. Allison* [1935] 2 K.B. 403.
[81] *Wilson v. Carnley, supra.*
[82] *Spiers v. Hunt, supra.*
[83] *Prevost v. Wood* (1905) 21 T.L.R. 684.
[84] *Fender v. Mildmay* [1938] A.C. 1; *Psaltis v. Schultz* (1948) 76 C.L.R. 547.

provides that "where an agreement to marry is terminated" the formerly engaged couple are to be treated for the purpose of certain rights in and disputes about property as if they had been married; and these provisions can obviously give rise to difficulty where a man has both a wife and an ex-fiancée. It may be that the difficulty can be mitigated by holding that an "agreement" in section 2 must not be contrary to public policy in the sense of the old law. But the analogy is not perfect, and the courts may take the view that, so long as the interests of the wife (or former wife) are protected, an ex-fiancée may sometimes be allowed to take the benefit of section 2 even though she could not before the Act have claimed damages. However, the Act is of very limited effect because, apart from the right to claim a share or enlarged share in a partner's property by having spent money on improvements to that property,[85] property rights between spouses are determined in accordance with the principles of property and trusts law.[86]

Marriage brokage contract. A marriage brokage contract, that is, an undertaking for reward to produce a marriage between two parties, is against public policy.[87] It has, however, been observed that "it is hard to see what is wrong with these [contracts] in modern times"[88] as many are made by quite respectable marriage bureaux. It may be that this is an area where the public policy embodied in the old cases is in need of reappraisal.   **17–071**

Contracts in restraint of marriage. A contract, the object of which is to restrain or prevent a party from marrying[89] or which is a deterrent to marriage in so far as it makes any person uncertain whether he may marry or not,[90] is against public policy. There appears to be no authority on contracts in partial restraint of marriage. Should such a contract come before the courts, the authorities concerning testamentary conditions in partial restraint of marriage would probably be applied.[91]   **17–072**

Contract not to revoke will. A man may validly bind himself or his estate to make certain dispositions by his will.[92] And a contract not to revoke a will or not to alter its contents is not necessarily against public policy. But probably no action could be brought upon its breach by reason of the covenantor's subsequent marriage, for the will is on that event revoked by operation of law[93] and to that extent the covenant is bad as being in restraint of marriage and against public   **17–073**

---

[85] Matrimonial Proceedings and Property Act 1970, s.37.

[86] *Pettitt v. Pettitt* [1970] A.C. 777; *Mossop v. Mossop* [1989] Fam. 77.

[87] *Hermann v. Charlesworth* [1905] 2 K.B. 123. See also § 17–182.

[88] Atiyah, *The Law of Contract* (5th ed., 1995), p. 323.

[89] *Lowe v. Peers* (1768) 4 Burr. 2225; affd. Wilmot 364; and see *Baker v. White* (1690) 2 Vern. 215; *Cock v. Richards* (1805) 10 Ves. 429, 437; *Hartley v. Rice* (1808) 10 East 22.

[90] *Re Fentem* [1950] 2 All E.R. 1073. In *Cartwright v. Cartwright* (1853) 3 De G.M. & G. 382 it was held that a condition in an ante-nuptial agreement that the wife would forfeit her interest if she and her husband separated was against public policy since it contemplated the separation of husband and wife: see generally, Cretney and Masson, *Principles of Family Law* (6th ed.), pp. 96–97.

[91] See *Theobald on Wills* (15th ed., 1993), pp. 654–657, pp. 637–641.

[92] *Dufour v. Pereira* (1769) Dick. 419; *Hammersley v. Baron De Biel* (1845) 12 Cl. & F. 45; *Re Brookman's Trusts* (1869) L.R. 5 Ch.App. 182.

[93] Wills Act 1837, s.18 (as substituted by the Administration of Justice Act 1982, s.18); *cf. Re Marsland* [1939] Ch. 820. (In this case the covenant not to revoke was only held to apply to revocation under s.20 of the Wills Act 1837, and not to revocation by operation of s.18. Thus the issue of public policy was not directly faced and the court did not feel obliged to express any opinion on it.)

policy; but it is divisible and will be construed as a covenant against revocation by any other mode of revocation.[94]

17–074 **Parental responsibility.** The Children Act 1989 confers automatic parental responsibility on parents of a child who are married to each other and on a child's unmarried mother.[95] The Act stipulates that:

"a person who has parental responsibility for a child shall not surrender or transfer any part of that responsibility to another but may arrange for some or all of it to be met by one or more persons acting on his behalf."[96]

An unmarried father may also acquire parental responsibility by agreement with the child's mother made in prescribed form and recorded in the Principal Registry of the Family Division.[97] Local authorities have a statutory duty to make written agreements with the parent of any child it is looking after.[98] But such agreements cannot transfer parental responsibility to the authority, and are not legally binding.[99] The inherent jurisdiction of the court to make appropriate orders concerning the upbringing of children cannot be ousted by agreement between the parties.[1] Surrogacy agreements have been expressly declared to be unenforceable.[2] Although the courts have power to treat a financial settlement agreed between divorcing couples as final, this does not apply with respect to agreements regarding the maintenance of children.[3] An "absent parent" may be required to pay child support maintenance to a "qualifying child" under the Child Support Act 1991 irrespective of the terms of an existing agreement between the child's parents covering the matter.

(f) *Contracts in Restraint of Trade*[4]

(i) *Scope of the Doctrine*

17–075 **General rule.** All covenants[5] in restraint of trade[6] are prima facie unenforceable at common law[7] and are enforceable only if they are reasonable with

---

[94] *Robinson v. Ommanney* (1883) 23 Ch.D. 285; *Theobald on Wills* (15th ed., 1993), pp. 100–101, pp. 94–95. As to the effects of an actionable breach, see *Synge v. Synge* [1894] 1 Q.B. 466; *Central Trusts & Safe Deposit Co. v. Snider* [1916] 1 A.C. 266.

[95] Children Act 1989, s.2(1), (2).

[96] *ibid.* s.2(9).

[97] *ibid.* s.4(1)(b); Parental Responsibility Agreement Regulations 1991 (S.I. 1991 No. 1478).

[98] Arrangements for Placement of Children (General) Regulations 1991 (S.I. 1991 No. 890).

[99] Children Act 1989, s.20(8).

[1] *A. v. C.* [1985] F.L.R. 4451.

[2] Human Fertilisation and Embryology Act 1990, s.361.

[3] *Minton v. Minton* [1979] A.C. 593, 609.

[4] See Heydon, *The Restraint of Trade Doctrine* (1971).

[5] As to conditions, see *post,* § 17–012; and as to the rules of trade associations and kindred bodies, see *post,* § 17–131, n. 93; *cf.* §§ 17–134—17–137.

[6] If the contract is to be performed in England, the fact that its proper law is foreign will not prevent the application of the English rules of public policy: *Rousillon v. Rousillon* (1880) 14 Ch.D. 351. As to covenants against competition abroad, see § 17–089.

[7] An agreement in restraint of trade is generally not unlawful at common law if the parties choose to abide by it; it is only unenforceable if a party chooses not to abide by it: *Mogul SS. Co. Ltd v. McGregor, Gow & Co.* [1892] A.C. 25; *Esso Petroleum Co. Ltd v. Harper's Garage (Stourport) Ltd* [1968] A.C. 269, 297; *Brekkes Ltd v. Cattel* [1972] Ch. 105; *cf. Cooke v. Football Association* [1972] C.L.Y. 516; *Boddington v. Lawton* [1994] I.C.R. 478. But a third party injured by the operation of an agreement in restraint of trade may, it appears, obtain a declaration (*Eastham v. Newcastle United F.C.*

reference to the interests of the parties concerned and of the public. Unless the unreasonable part can be severed[8] by the removal of either part or the whole of the covenant in question, its inclusion renders the covenant[9] or the entire contract[10] unenforceable. A covenant in restraint of trade (if unreasonable) is void in the sense that courts will not enforce it, but if the parties wish to implement it they would not be acting illegally and the courts would not intervene to prevent them from doing so.[11] It also follows from this that where A and B enter into a contract which contains an unreasonable restraint and they deposit money with T for the purposes of the contract then neither could prevent T from dealing with the money on the terms set out in the contract.[12] The doctrine of restraint of trade is probably one of the oldest applications of the doctrine of public policy; cases go back to the second half of the sixteenth century[13] and as early as 1711 it was laid down in *Mitchel v. Reynolds*[14] that a bond to restrain oneself from trading in a particular place, if made upon a reasonable consideration, is good, though if it be upon no reasonable consideration or to restrain a man from trading at all, it is void.

Competition law. This section concentrates on the common law. It should, however, be kept in mind that contracts in restraint of trade or otherwise having a restrictive impact on trade, particularly horizontal or vertical agreements relating to the supply or acquisition of goods, will often have anti-competitive effects and are therefore potentially subject to domestic and European legislation dealing with this topic.[15] For example, Article 85(1) of the Treaty of Rome[16] may render invalid certain restraints between vendors and purchasers.[17] The potential relevance of domestic and European competition law must therefore always be considered in this context. **17–076**

Definition of restraint of trade. The definition of a covenant in restraint of trade presents peculiar conceptual difficulty. The reason for this is that to some extent all contracts are in restraint of trade by at least preventing the parties to them from trading with others, but there has been no suggestion that all contracts are or should be subject to the doctrine.[18] In the leading House of Lords case, *Esso Petroleum Co. Ltd v. Harper's Garage (Stourport) Ltd*[19] Lord Reid stated[20] that he "would not attempt to define the dividing line between contracts which **17–077**

Ltd [1964] Ch. 413; *Greig v. Insole* [1978] 1 W.L.R. 302) or an injunction (*Nagle v. Feilden* [1966] 2 Q.B. 633).

[8] See *post*, §§ 17–183—17–194.

[9] *e.g.* see *Goldsoll v. Goldman* [1914] 2 Ch. 603; [1915] 1 Ch. 292. See *post*, § 17–188.

[10] *e.g.* see the *Esso* case [1968] A.C. 769. See *post*, § 17–189, n. 90; and see *post*, § 17–185 *et seq.*

[11] *Boddington v. Lawton* [1994] I.C.R. 478. Where the restraint has third party effects, the third party affected may be able to challenge its validity: see § 17–134.

[12] *ibid.*

[13] Holdsworth, *History of English Law*, Vol. III, pp. 56, 57; Wilberforce, Campbell and Elles, *The Law of Restrictive Trade Practices and Monopolies* (2nd ed.), §§ 130, 135, 141–144.

[14] (1711) 1 P.Wms. 181.

[15] See Whish, *Competition Law* (1993), at p. 35; see, for example, *Cutsforth v. Mansfield Inns Ltd* [1986] 1 W.L.R. 558; *post*, § 17–119 and §§ 17–130 *et seq.*

[16] See Bellamy & Child, *Common Market Law of Competition* (4th ed.); Vol. II, Chap. 40.

[17] Bellamy & Child *ibid.* at § 6–088. Art. 85 could also have a bearing on non-competition clauses in mergers, exclusive distribution and purchasing agreements.

[18] See, *e.g.* *British Motor Trade Assoc. v. Gray*, 1951 S.C. 586.

[19] [1968] A.C. 269.

[20] *ibid.* at 298.

are and contracts which are not in restraint of trade"; and Lord Wilberforce said[21] that "no exhaustive test can be stated—probably no non-exhaustive test" but that that was not to be regretted since[22] "the common law has often (if sometimes unconsciously) thrived on ambiguity and it would be mistaken, even if it were possible, to try to crystallise the rules of this or any aspect of public policy into neat propositions. The doctrine of restraint of trade is one to be applied to factual situations with a broad and flexible rule of reason."

In the same case Lord Hodson adopted[23] the test shortly before advanced by Diplock L.J. in the Court of Appeal in *Petrofina (Great Britain) Ltd v. Martin*[24] who stated,[25] "A contract in restraint of trade is one in which a party (the covenantor) agrees with any other party (the covenantee) to restrict his liberty in the future to carry on trade with other persons not parties to the contract in such manner as he chooses." Lord Morris said[26] that that was a "helpful exposition," provided that it was used "rationally and not too literally" and that the same was true of the dicta of Lord Denning M.R. in the *Petrofina* case where he had said,[27]

> "Every member of the community is entitled to carry on any trade or business he chooses and in such manner as he thinks most desirable in his own interests, so long as he does nothing unlawful: with the consequence that any contract which interferes with the free exercise of his trade or business, by restricting him in the work he may do for others, or the arrangements which he may make with others, is a contract in restraint of trade. It is invalid unless it is reasonable as between the parties and not injurious to the public interest."

Finally, in the *Esso* case, Lord Pearce, on the basis that[28] "somewhere there must be a line between those contracts which are in restraint of trade . . . and those contracts which merely regulate the normal commercial relations between the parties," said[29] that the doctrine of restraint of trade

> "does not apply to ordinary commercial contracts for the regulation and promotion of trade during the existence of the contract, provided that any prevention of work outside the contract, viewed as a whole, is directed towards the absorption of the parties' services and not their sterilisation."

17–078   **Criteria for application of doctrine.** The following general principles have, with varying degrees of certainty, been laid down:

---

[21] *ibid.* at 332.

[22] *ibid.* at 331.

[23] *ibid.* at 317.

[24] [1966] Ch. 146.

[25] *ibid.* at 180; Diplock L.J.'s test probably requires a distinction to be drawn between obligations on the part of the covenantor which are in substance "positive," *e.g.* to sell to A 100 tons of cast iron of the covenantor's manufacture, and obligations which are in substance "negative," *e.g.* not to sell his cast iron to anyone other than A or to sell to A some percentage of his production (which is an obligation not to sell to others more than the remaining percentage thereof). The difficulty arises that, if the covenantor's production is unlikely to exceed 100 tons, the positive obligation to sell to A 100 tons may be more restrictive of the covenantor's economic liberty to trade with others than would be a negative obligation to sell to A 50 per cent of his production.

[26] [1968] A.C. 269, 307.

[27] [1966] Ch. 146, 169.

[28] [1968] A.C. 269, 327.

[29] *ibid.* at 328.

(1) It has now long been established that there is no distinction in principle between partial and total restraints.[30]

(2) The doctrine is not confined to a limited number of kinds of contracts[31]; but there are certain categories of covenants to which the doctrine traditionally applies, in particular those by which an employee undertakes not to compete with his employer after leaving the employer's service[32] and those by which a trader who has sold his business agrees not thereafter to compete with the purchaser of the business[33]; and those categories will always be subjected, under the doctrine, to the test of reasonableness.

17–079

(3) The doctrine is capable of applying where the restraint relates to the use of a particular piece of property as well as where it relates to the activities of an individual.[34] Thus restraints in mortgages and leases are subject to the doctrine. The application of the doctrine to *Tulk v. Moxhay*[35] covenants is not, however, without difficulties and this will be dealt with later.

17–080

(4) There is strong authority for the proposition that contracts of a kind which have gained general commercial acceptance and have not been traditionally subject to the doctrine will generally not be subjected to it so as to impose upon a plaintiff the burden of justifying as reasonable their terms, though special features may bring particular contracts of that kind within the ambit of the doctrine.[36] However, public policy is not immutable and no guarantee of absolute immunity for any restraint is possible. As was stated by Lord Wilberforce in *Esso*, "absolute exemption for any restriction or regulation is never obtained."[37] Thus, for example, contracts whereby an employee on the termination of his employment agrees not to recruit former fellow employees is now probably subject to the restraint of trade doctrine.[38]

17–081

(5) The doctrine applies to restraints which operate during the continuance of the contract. This is well illustrated by *A. Schroeder Music Publishing Co. Ltd v. Macaulay*.[39] There the plaintiff, a young songwriter, agreed to work as such exclusively for the defendants, who were music publishers, for five years. He assigned to them full copyright of his existing works and in future works

17–082

---

[30] See *ante*, § 17–075.

[31] *Esso* case [1968] A.C. 269, 295, 306, 337; *Bridge v. Deacons* [1984] A.C. 705.

[32] See *post*, § 17–101.

[33] See *post*, § 17–114.

[34] *Esso* case, *supra*, where the principle was established in the case of land; and it would seem that similar considerations apply to other kinds of property.

[35] (1848) 2 Ph. 774.

[36] *Esso* case *supra, per* Lord Wilberforce at 332–333, to some extent supported by Lord Reid at 295 and by Lord Pearce at 328. There is some authority for the alternative approach under which contracts if they contain restrictive elements are always subject to the doctrine but some are "prima facie" reasonable. See *per* Diplock L.J. in *Petrofina (Great Britain) Ltd v. Martin* [1966] Ch. 146, 185.

[37] *ibid.* at 333.

[38] *Office Angels Ltd v. Rainer-Thomas and O'Connor* [1991] I.R.L.R. 214 (employment agency could protect pool of temporary secretaries); Sales (1988) 104 L.Q.R. 600.

[39] [1974] 1 W.L.R. 1308; see also *Clifford Davis Ltd v. W.E.A. Records Ltd* [1975] 1 W.L.R. 61; Cartwright, *Unequal Bargaining* (1991), pp. 205–206; *Watson v. Prager* [1991] 1 W.L.R. 726 (restraint of trade doctrine applied to contract between a boxer and manager and held to be against public policy because of the unreasonable imbalance between the rights and duties of the parties).

composed during the five years. The five years was extended to 10 years if the plaintiff's royalties exceeded £5,000. The defendants could determine the agreement at any time on one month's notice and could assign the benefit of it. Although the plaintiff's royalties depended upon whether the defendants exploited his compositions, there was no obligation on the defendants to exploit any composition of the plaintiff, and if the defendants failed to do so, the plaintiff could not do so even after the determination of the contract. Lord Reid held that the contract was unduly restrictive, it was not a commercially acceptable one "made freely by parties bargaining on equal terms"[40] "or moulded under the pressures of negotiation, competition and public opinion."[41] Lord Diplock, however, asked simply what was the relative bargaining power between the songwriter and publisher at the time of contracting and whether the publisher had used his superior bargaining power to exact from the songwriter promises that were unfairly onerous to him, *i.e.* "was the bargain fair?" There might be a presumption of fairness in cases of conventional commercial contracts established by long usage between equal bargaining partners, but this was not such a case. Where the restraint operates to protect the legitimate interests of the employer and was not as one sided as that in the *Schroeder* decision, it will normally be upheld.

17–083   (6) There is authority for the proposition that it is not possible to invoke the doctrine where the restraint relates to the use or disposition of property acquired by the covenantor under the very agreement under which he accepted the restraint. This proposition found favour with Lord Reid in the *Esso* case: "Restraint of trade appears to me to imply that a man contracts to give up some freedom which otherwise he would have had. A person buying or leasing land had no previous right to be there at all, let alone to trade there, and when he takes possession of that land subject to a negative restrictive covenant he gives up no right or freedom which he previously had. . . . "[42] This test, however, is not free from difficulty and at least three principal objections can be levelled against it.[43] First, it can be easily evaded: for example, A could lease land to B which B could then lease back to A by means of a lease containing a covenant in restraint of trade. There is, however, authority for the proposition that if the transaction is a sham[44] the court will look at the reality of the transaction even though formally it appears that the covenantor is not curtailing an existing freedom. In *Amoco Australia Pty. Ltd v. Rocca Bros. Motor Engineering Co. Pty. Ltd*[45] the Privy Council applied the restraint of trade doctrine to a transaction somewhat similar to the one previously outlined and treated the lease and underlease as part of a single transaction. A somewhat similar approach was adopted in *Alec Lobb (Garages) Ltd v. Total Oil (Great Britain) Ltd*[46] where a lease by a company of

---

[40] *Per* Lord Pearce in the *Esso* case, at 323.

[41] *Per* Lord Wilberforce, *ibid.* at 332–333.

[42] [1968] A.C. 269, 298. See also at 309 (Lord Morris) and at 325 (Lord Pearce) for somewhat similar views. This principle was adopted in *Cleveland Petroleum Co. Ltd v. Darstone* [1969] 1 W.L.R. 116; see also *Stephens v. Gulf Oil Canada Ltd* (1976) 11 O.L.R. (2d) 229; *Re Ravenseft Properties Ltd's Application* [1978] Q.B. 52, 67.

[43] See Heydon, *The Restraint of Trade Doctrine* (1971), pp. 55–59.

[44] On the nature of sham transactions, see *Chase Manhattan Equities Ltd v. Goodman* [1991] B.C.L.C. 997; *Welsh Development Agency v. Export Finance Co. Ltd* [1992] B.C.L.C. 148, 185–188.

[45] [1975] A.C. 561, PC.

[46] [1985] 1 W.L.R. 173.

its premises to its petrol suppliers who leased them back to the sole shareholders of the company, the lease-back containing a solus agreement, was held to be subject to the restraint of trade doctrine. The second objection to Lord Reid's test that the doctrine only applies where a covenantor curtails an existing freedom is that it is a test based on form rather than substance, as was illustrated by counsel in the course of argument in the *Esso* case.[47] Undoubtedly one of the reasons for the adoption of this test (or something like it) was to insulate *Tulk v. Moxhay*[48] type covenants against the application of the restraint of trade doctrine. In *Quadramain Pty. Ltd v. Sevastapol Investments Pty. Ltd*[49] the Australian High Court adopted the reasoning of Lord Reid and thus avoided having to deal with the application of the restraint of trade doctrine to a restrictive covenant which impinged on the commercial use to which land could be put.[50] Thirdly, even where a covenantor purportedly gives up an existing freedom but is insolvent and the restraint is part of a package enabling him to remain in business it is far from evident how such a constraint curtails in any significant sense an existing freedom.[51] It is submitted that as the restraint of trade doctrine is one founded on public policy its application should not be artificially curtailed. No doubt where the court is dealing with the type of restraint which has obtained widespread acceptance then this will be strong evidence of its reasonableness, but all restraints should be subject to the doctrine.

(7) There is authority for the principle that the doctrine does not apply to **17–084** "ordinary commercial contracts for the regulation and promotion of trade during the existence of the contract."[52] But this would appear to be founded on the theory that the doctrine does not apply during the contract, a theory which has been rejected by the House of Lords.[53]

(8) Whether a particular provision operates in restraint of trade is to be **17–085** determined not by the form the stipulation takes but by its effect in practice.[54] Thus a covenant to share profits, or a levy/remission scheme of the traditional cartel type, may in certain circumstances of the case constitute restraint. Likewise, a provision that a salesman who had left his employment would forfeit the commission due to him if he obtained employment with a competitor of his ex-employer was held to be a restraint.[55–56] In other words, what does or does not operate as a restraint is a matter of substance. It is also important to note that it is *trade* which must be restrained. While the courts have not given an exhaustive

---

[47] [1968] A.C. 269, 289–290.

[48] (1848) 2 Ph. 774 (although many such covenants will not actually restrain trade).

[49] (1976) 8 A.L.R. 555. See also *Aberdeen Varieties Ltd v. James F. Donald (Aberdeen Cinemas) Ltd*, 1940 S.L.T. 58.

[50] See also *Irish Shell Ltd v. Elm Motors Ltd* [1984] I.R. 200. As to whether a restrictive covenant affecting the commercial user of land touches and concerns it see *Newton Abbot Co-operative Society Ltd v. Williamson & Treadgold Ltd* [1952] Ch. 286.

[51] *Alec Lobb (Garages) Ltd v. Total Oil (Great Britain) Ltd* [1983] 1 W.L.R. 87, 164 F (at first instance).

[52] [1968] A.C. 269, 328. Lord Pearce also opined that the doctrine only applies where a restraint is directed towards the "sterilisation" of the covenantor's services. On this see Heydon, *The Restraint of Trade Doctrine* (1971), at 61–63; and *cf. Watson v. Prager* [1991] 1 W.L.R. 726.

[53] *A. Schroeder Music Publishing Co. Ltd v. Macaulay* [1974] 1 W.L.R. 1308.

[54] *Stenhouse Australia Ltd v. Phillips* [1974] A.C. 391; *McIntyre v. Cleveland Petrol Co. Ltd*, 1967 S.L.T. 95, 100.

[55–56] *Sadler v. Imperial Life Insurance Co. of Canada Ltd* [1988] I.R.L.R. 388.

definition of what constitutes a trade, it is clear that it extends to a man's profession or calling.[57]

17-086   **Time of application.** Most authorities favour as the time for testing the validity of a restriction the date when the restriction was imposed.[58] It has also been held that an enforceable restriction may become temporarily unenforceable where it operates unfairly in changed circumstances[59]; this is generally considered not to be correct.

17-087   **Covenants by deed.** A covenant in restraint of trade which is contained in a deed requires justification no less than such a covenant contained in a simple contract.[60]

17-088   **Adequacy of consideration.** Subject to the test of reasonableness of the restraint, the courts will not inquire into the adequacy of the consideration.[61]

17-089   **Covenants against competition abroad.** Doubts have been expressed whether the rule against covenants in restraint of trade applies to covenants against competition outside the United Kingdom.[62] But these doubts appear to be unfounded; the question was fully argued before the Court of Appeal in *Commercial Plastics Ltd v. Vincent*[63] where a covenant was struck down *inter alia* on the ground that it was worldwide, whereas on the facts the plaintiffs did not require protection outside the United Kingdom. Although that decision related to a restraint on an ex-employee taking employment abroad, it is submitted that the same principle applies to covenants between traders since the courts ought to

---

[57] *Hepworth Manufacturing Co. Ltd v. Ryott* [1920] Ch. 1, 29.

[58] *Gledhow Autoparts Ltd v. Delaney* [1965] 1 W.L.R. 1366, 1377; *Home Counties Dairies Ltd v. Skilton* [1970] 1 W.L.R. 526, 533, 536; *Commercial Plastics Ltd v. Vincent* [1965] 1 Q.B. 623, 644; *A. Schroeder Music Publishing Co. Ltd v. Macaulay* [1974] 1 W.L.R. 1308, 1309; *Watson v. Prager, supra,* at 738 ("The question of whether the . . . agreement is unenforceable on restraint of trade grounds must be tested by reference to the state of affairs at the date of the agreement").

[59] *Shell (U.K.) Ltd v. Lostock Garage Ltd* [1976] 1 W.L.R. 1187, 1198 (this was a minority view of Lord Denning M.R.).

[60] *Mallan v. May* (1843) 11 M. & W. 653, 655; *cf. Homer v. Ashford* (1825) 3 Bing. 322.

[61] *Hitchcock v. Coker* (1837) 6 A. & E. 438; *Gravely v. Barnard* (1874) L.R. 18 Eq. 518; *Nordenfelt v. The Maxim Nordenfelt Guns and Ammunition Co. Ltd* [1894] A.C. 535, 565; *Alec Lobb (Garages) Ltd v. Total Oil (Great Britain) Ltd* [1985] 1 W.L.R. 173, 179. *cf. A. Schroeder Music Publishing Co. Ltd v. Macaulay* [1974] 1 W.L.R. 1308.

[62] See *Leather Cloth Co. v. Lorsont* (1869) L.R. 9 Eq. 345, 351; *Maxim Nordenfelt Guns & Ammunition Co. v. Nordenfelt* [1893] 1 Ch. 639, 651; [1894] A.C. 535, 554, 574; contrast *Dowden and Pook Ltd v. Pook* [1904] 1 K.B. 45; and see *Lamson Pneumatic Tube Co. v. Phillips* (1904) 91 L.T. 363 where the Court of Appeal's judgments suggested that the matter was still open; *cf. Goldsoll v. Goldman* [1915] 1 Ch. 292 where the plaintiff was able to succeed without taking the point; and dicta in *Vancouver Malt & Sake Brewing Co. Ltd v. Vancouver Breweries Ltd* [1934] A.C. 181, 191, which were *obiter* since the covenant in question was, it would seem, unreasonable in so far as it related to the whole of Canada, where it had been made so that its world-wide application was irrelevant. See also *Cooke v. Football Association* [1972] C.L.Y. 516.

[63] [1965] 1 Q.B. 623, 630–631, 645. See also the decision of the New Zealand Court of Appeal in *Blackler v. New Zealand Rugby Football League (Incorporated)* [1968] N.Z.L.R. 547, 569, *per* McCarthy J. expressing the views of the majority: "My view of the law . . . is that any restraint on employment, wheresoever, whether it is intended to operate in New Zealand, or only overseas, or both, is *prima facie* void . . . ."

have the power to strike down unreasonable restraints on the British export trade.[64]

The test of reasonableness. While all restraints of trade to which the doctrine   **17–090**
applies are prima facie unenforceable,[65] all, whether partial or total,[66] are enforceable if reasonable. As was said by Lord Macnaghten in *Nordenfelt v. Maxim Nordenfelt & Co.*[67]: "It is a sufficient justification, and indeed it is the only justification, if the restriction is reasonable—reasonable, that is, in reference to the interests of the parties concerned and reasonable in reference to the interests of the public, so framed and so guarded as to afford adequate protection to the party in whose favour it is imposed, while at the same time it is in no way injurious to the public." In determining reasonableness the court "*is* entitled to consider whether or not a covenant of a narrower nature would have sufficed for the convenantee's protection."[68] Even if the restraint is unlimited in time[69] or in space[70] it will be upheld if it is reasonable,[71] although the absence of such a limit "is a remarkable feature prima facie needing justification."[72] Worldwide restrictions have passed muster in the courts, but only where the restrictions to be reasonably effectual had to be worldwide.[73] In determining reasonableness the court does not apply any doctrine of "proportionality," that is, an assessment of whether there is a substantial equivalence between the scope of the restraint and what the covenantor received for entering into it.[74] To introduce such a doctrine would be to revive the now discredited doctrine that in assessing the reasonableness of the restraint the court should also consider the adequacy of the consideration.[75]

---

[64] cf. *Bull v. Pitney-Bowes Ltd* [1967] 1 W.L.R. 273, 276–277. If it produces effects in other member states of the E.C., then it may be subject to Art. 85 of the Treaty: see Vol. II, § 42–003 *et seq.*.

[65] But see also *ante*, § 17–077.

[66] *Nordenfelt v. The Maxim Nordenfelt Guns & Ammunition Co.* [1894] A.C. 535, 565; *Mason v. Provident Clothing & Supply Co.* [1913] A.C. 724; these authorities abolished the old distinction between total and partial restraints to be found in, *e.g.*, *Mills v. Dunham* [1891] 1 Ch. 576, 586; *Haynes v. Doman* [1899] 2 Ch. 13, 30.

[67] [1894] A.C. 535, 565; and see *Esso* case [1968] A.C. 269, 299. Restraints normally operate as to time, area, and activity, and must be reasonable with respect to these factors.

[68] *Office Angels Ltd v. Rainer-Thomas and O'Connor* [1991] I.R.L.R. 214, 220 (emphasis in the original, a master and servant case).

[69] *Hitchcock v. Coker* (1837) 6 A. & E. 438; *Haynes v. Doman* [1899] 2 Ch. 13; *Fitch v. Dewes* [1921] 2 A.C. 158.

[70] *Nordenfelt v. The Maxim Nordenfelt Guns and Ammunition Co.* [1894] A.C. 535; *Lamson Pneumatic Tube Co. v. Phillips* (1904) 91 L.T. 363; *Caribonum Co. Ltd v. Le Couch* (1913) 109 L.T. 385, 587.

[71] *Peters American Delicacy Co. Ltd v. Patricia's Chocolates & Candies Pty. Ltd* (1947) 77 C.L.R. 574.

[72] *Commercial Plastics Ltd v. Vincent* [1965] 1 Q.B. 623, 644. In *Bridge v. Deacons* (dealing with a restraint of five years' duration which was upheld) the court stated that "there appears to be no reported case where a restriction which was otherwise reasonable has been held to be unreasonable solely because of its duration" ([1984] A.C. 705, 717E-F); see, however, *Scully (U.K.) Ltd v. Lee*, [1998] I.R.L.R. 259 where the court held that a non-solicitation clause of two years in an employment contract was unreasonable because of excessive duration. cf. Heydon *op.cit.* at pp. 158–162.

[73] *Vancouver Malt & Sake Brewing Co. Ltd v. Vancouver Breweries Ltd* [1934] A.C. 181, 191.

[74] *Allied Dunbar (Frank Weisenger) Ltd v. Weisinger* [1988] I.R.L.R. 60.

[75] *ibid.* "Proportionality," however, may be a factor in obtaining an *Anton Piller* order against an ex-employee: see *Lock International plc v. Beswick* [1989] 1 W.L.R. 1268, 1281 (" . . . there must be *proportionality* between the perceived threat to the plaintiff's rights and the remedy granted").

17–091   **Legitimate interests of the parties.** In the case of the traditional categories of covenant to which the doctrine relates, the expression "the interest of the covenantee" connotes the proprietary or quasi-proprietary interest of an employer in his trade secrets and trade connections and of a purchaser of a business in the goodwill of the enterprise he has acquired. It is the protection of such interests which furnishes the sole justification for a restraint[76] and the restraint must therefore be no *more* than is reasonably necessary for that protection. Similarly, where an otherwise unreasonable restraint is contained in a mortgage, it can be justified by reference to the mortgage only if reasonably necessary to protect the mortgagee's interest in his security.[77] But with the recognition that the doctrine of restraint of trade applies generally and not only to the traditional categories of covenant, it is clear that a proprietary or quasi-proprietary interest is not in every case necessary to support a covenant and the statement that the covenant must be reasonable in the interests of the parties must be taken to mean that the restraint must be reasonable from their point of view. Thus too, while the well-known phrase that a man is not entitled to protect himself against competition *per se* may be helpful in the context of the traditional categories of covenant, where the justification for the covenant is to be found, if at all, in the protection of the covenantee's "interest," the phrase cannot usefully be applied to other kinds of restrictive covenant.[78] For example, agreements to restrict the production or supply of goods or to fix prices can be justified if, by protecting themselves from competition, the parties are not only acting reasonably from their own point of view but are not injuring[79] or are even benefiting[80] the public, so that there is no ground of public policy for refusing to enforce the agreement.

17–092   Indeed, with the recognition that a "legitimate interest" in the sense of a proprietary or quasi-proprietary interest is not necessary in all cases, it could be argued that such an interest is not necessary even in the traditional categories of restraint; *e.g.* if a worker agreed for a million pounds not to work for the rest of his life it is difficult to see why such an agreement is not "reasonable" between the parties (as distinct from in the public interest) simply because the employer is protecting himself from competition *simpliciter* and not protecting some trade secret or customer connection.[81] Conversely, on present authority, once a "legitimate interest" is shown by the covenantee, the covenant is generally treated as reasonable; but the existence of such an interest need not be a sufficient condition for establishing reasonableness between the parties, since the covenant may in such a case be reasonable from the covenantee's point of view but impose undue hardship upon the covenantor. In recent cases the court has recognised the problem created by elaborate conceptualism in the past, and is tending to insist that the restraint be both reasonably necessary for protection of the legitimate interests of the promisee and also commensurate with the benefits secured to the promisor under the contract.[82] It has been held in an employment contract that,

---

[76] See *British Concrete Co. Ltd v. Schelff* [1921] 2 Ch. 563, 574–575.
[77] See *post*, § 17–120.
[78] See *Esso Petroleum Co. Ltd v. Harper's Garage (Stourport) Ltd* [1968] A.C. 269, 301, 329; *McEllistrim v. Ballymacelligott Co-operative Agriculture and Dairy Society Ltd* [1919] A.C. 548, 563–564; *Daunay Day & Co. Ltd v. D'Alfhen* [1997] T.L.R. 334.
[79] *cf. Att.-Gen. of Commonwealth of Australia v. Adelaide Steamship Co.* [1913] A.C. 781.
[80] *cf.* Vol. II, § 42–089 *et seq.*
[81] *cf. Higgs v. Olivier* [1952] Ch. 311; *Wyatt v. Kreglinger and Fernau* [1933] 1 K.B. 793.
[82] *A. Schroeder Music Publishing Co. Ltd v. Macaulay* [1974] 1 W.L.R. 1308.

where the employer specifically states the interest to be protected, he is not entitled to "seek to justify the contract by reference to some separate and additional interest that has not been specified."[83] The justification for this is that the employee may have sought legal advice and his legal advisers would be entitled to give him that advice on the basis of the stated purpose of the covenant. This reasoning would apply equally to other types of contracts.

Public interest and burden of proof.[84] The onus of establishing that a 17–093 covenant is no more than is reasonable in the interests of the parties is on the person who seeks to rely on it[85]; if he establishes that it is no more than reasonable in the interests of the parties, the onus of proving that it is contrary to the public interest lies on the party attacking it.[86] At least where the restraint relates to the traditional categories of employer-employee or vendor-purchaser restraints, this onus will not be a light one.[87] But once an agreement is before the court it is open to the scrutiny of the court in all its surrounding circumstances as a question of law[88] and a determination of the issue whether the covenant should be enforced requires, as a matter of public policy, that a balance should be struck between freedom of trade and freedom of contract.[89] For long, attention was concentrated predominantly on the question of reasonableness in the interests of the parties so that, for example, in 1913 the Privy Council stated that[90] "their Lordships are not aware of any case in which a restraint, though reasonable in the interests of the parties, has been held unenforceable because it involved some injury to the public." But especially in cases falling outside the traditional categories of covenant to which most of the earlier authorities relate, the emphasis may well now have shifted from the interests of the parties to those of the public on the basis[91] that the doctrine is part of the wider doctrine of public policy and that, at any rate where the contract was freely entered into between traders, they are usually the best judges of their own interest.[92] But what is meant in this context by the public interest?[93] It could be taken to mean "the public welfare" or "general utility" to the public, a meaning which, though compelling the court to secure a difficult balance between this objective of public benefit and the other one of fairness to the individual trader, would be the modern equivalent

---

[83] *Office Angels Ltd v. Rainer-Thomas and O'Connor* [1991] I.R.L.R. 214, 219 (where the contract does not state the interest to be protected, the employer is entitled to look to the contract and the surrounding circumstances for the purpose of ascertaining the purpose which is to be protected: *ibid.*).

[84] See *ante*, § 17–075.

[85] *Morris Ltd v. Saxelby* [1916] 1 A.C. 688, 700, 706; *Attwood v. Lamont* [1920] 3 K.B. 571, 587, 588; *Kores Manufacturing Co. Ltd v. Kolok Manufacturing Co. Ltd* [1959] Ch. 108.

[86] *Morris v. Saxelby* [1916] 1 A.C. 688, 700, 707.

[87] *Att.-Gen. of Commonwealth of Australia v. Adelaide Steamship Co. Ltd* [1913] A.C. 781, 797. See, however, *Sherk v. Horwitz* [1972] 2 O.R. 451, affd. [1973] 1 O.R. 160.

[88] *Esso Petroleum Co. Ltd v. Harper's Garage (Stourport) Ltd* [1968] A.C. 269, *per* Lord Hodson at 319; see *post*, § 17–095.

[89] *Morris v. Saxelby* [1916] 1 A.C. 688, 716; *Esso Petroleum Co. Ltd v. Harper's Garage (Stourport) Ltd, supra*, at 304–305.

[90] *Att.-Gen. of Commonwealth of Australia v. Adelaide Steamship Co.* [1913] A.C. 781, 785.

[91] *Esso Petroleum Co. Ltd v. Harper's Garage (Stourport) Ltd* [1968] A.C. 269; *Bull v. Pitney-Bowes Ltd* [1967] 1 W.L.R. 273.

[92] *Esso Petroleum Co. Ltd v. Harper's Garage (Stourport) Ltd, supra*; and see *North Western Salt Co. v. Electrolytic Alkali Co.* [1914] A.C. 461, 471; *English Hop Growers v. Dering* [1928] 2 K.B. 174, 180.

[93] In the *Alex Lobb* case, Waller L.J. considered it to be in the public interest to save a firm from bankruptcy ([1985] 1 W.L.R. 173, 191E).

of the "pernicious monopoly" of ancient times and would harmonise well with modern statutory philosophy against monopolistic practices that are inconsistent with welfare objectives.[94]

17–094   There is, however, now considerable authority for an alternate theory. Thus according to Ungoed-Thomas J. in *Texaco Ltd v. Mulberry Filling Station Ltd*,[95] reasonableness with reference to the interests of the public "is part of the doctrine of restraint of trade which is based on and directed to securing the liberty of the subject and not the utmost economic advantage" and the

> "question which such reasonableness raises would thus not be whether the restraint might be less in a different organisation of industry or society, or whether the abolition of the restraint might lead to a different organisation of industry or society and thus, on balance of many considerations, to the economic or social advantage of the country, but whether the restraint is, in our industry and society as at present organised and with reference to which our law operates, unreasonable in the public interest as recognised and formulated in such principle or proposition of law. For my part, I prefer to decide that the restraints relied on in our case are reasonable in the interests of the public, not on balance of existing or possible economic advantages and disadvantages to the public but because there is, in conditions as they are, no unreasonable limitation of liberty to trade."[96]

The difficulty with this view is that the requirement of public interest adds nothing to the requirement that the restraint be reasonable in the interests of the parties. Thus, if it is reasonable in their interest, then there is no undue interference with individual liberty and the public interest is satisfied; if it is not reasonable it must be because the liberty of one of the parties is unduly restricted and the agreement is *ipso facto* contrary to the public interest.[97] The two limbs of the traditional formula for assessing restraints are then simply tautologous. There may, however, be arguments of policy in favour of this alternate view: the court is dependent on the parties and their advisers to present the economic evidence on the question of the impact of the restraint upon general welfare; it might be thought that such a wide-ranging inquiry of fact should be subject rather to presentation by a representative of the public or to investigation by a public administrative agency,[98–99] although the American practice of "Brandeis briefs," if accepted by the English courts in this context, might meet the objection. It can

---

[94] *e.g.* Competition Act 1998; Arts. 85 and 86 of the EEC Treaty.

[95] [1972] 1 W.L.R. 814, 827, 828.

[96] *cf. Dickson v. Pharmaceutical Society of Great Britain* [1970] A.C. 403, 441, *per* Lord Wilberforce: "I would ... hold [that the restraints do not survive the test] on the simple ground, which I think is the relevant ground in this connection, that there is nothing here to displace the normal proposition that the public has in the absence of countervailing considerations an interest in men being able to trade freely in the goods which they judge the public wants and that these restraints clearly, severely and arbitrarily restrict this freedom. More special arguments to the effect that the restraints might cause a reduction in the number of pharmacies I would regard as less secure: before I could accept them I should require persuasion, first, that this type of consideration may properly be taken into account in relation to the common law doctrine of restraint of trade (as contrasted with proceedings in the Restrictive Practices Court). ... " See also *A. Schroeder Music Publishing Co. Ltd v. Macaulay* [1974] 1 W.L.R. 1308, *per* Lord Diplock at 1315.

[97] It is not inconceivable that an extremely onerous restraint contractually imposed upon an individual might secure enormous utility to the public. But, on the above theory, the restraint must be contrary to the "public interest." *Sed quaere?*

[98–99] *cf.* the Monopolies and Mergers Commission: and the Commission of the EEC under Arts. 85 and 86 of the EEC Treaty. See *Texaco v. Mulberry Filling Station Ltd* [1972] 1 W.L.R. 814, 826.

also be argued that a common law court is not an appropriate forum for assessing economic evidence, making predictions upon it and balancing the interest of conflicting groups in society.[1] There is also the time and expense of litigation which may make it an inappropriate method for providing an answer to economic issues which may have to be decided expeditiously. The optimal solution may be to assign to a government department, for example, the Office of Fair Trading, the primary responsibility for making economic decisions with a limited review being carried out by the courts.

Construction. Covenants in restraint of trade must be clear and definite.[2] In **17–095** construing a covenant in restraint of trade between partners it has been held that

> "(1) the question of construction should be approached in the first instance without regard to the question of legality or illegality; (2) that the clause should be construed with reference to the object sought to be obtained; (3) that in a restraint of trade case the object is the protection of one of the partners against rivalry in trade; [and] (4) the clause should be construed in its context and in the light of the factual matrix when the agreement was made."[3]

The courts will attempt to construe a covenant so as to achieve the parties' intention where there has been a "mere want of accuracy of expression" with the consequence that the covenant will be upheld as not being too wide.[4] However, for this principle to apply it must be clear from the contract and the surrounding circumstances what exactly are the terms of the more limited covenant.[5] Reasonableness is a question of law,[6] that is, a question of the application by the court of a legal standard to the facts of the particular case. Therefore, although evidence of surrounding circumstances at the time the contract was made, such as the character of the business to be protected by the covenant, is admissible in the consideration of the requirements of that business,[7] evidence of the views, about reasonableness, of persons in the particular trade is inadmissible.[8]

---

[1] See Stevens and Yamey, *The Restrictive Practices Court* (1965), Chap. 3 and *Texaco v. Mulberry Filling Station Ltd, supra,* at 827.

[2] *Davies v. Davies* (1887) 36 Ch.D. 359, where a covenant to retire from business "so far as the law allows" was held to be too vague to be enforceable. *cf. Express Dairy Co. v. Jackson* (1930) 99 L.J.K.B. 181.

[3] *Clarke v. Newland* [1991] 1 All E.R. 397, 402. These principles were put forward in connection with a restraint in the contract of a salaried partner, a status that can often be equated with that of an employee: see *Lindley & Banks on Partnership* (17th ed., 1995), pp. 104–105. However, in the light of the courts' disfavour of restraints in employment contracts, these principles will be applied in that context with greater rigour.

[4] The phrase is that of Lindley M.R. in *Haynes v. Dorman* [1899] 2 Ch. 13, 26. For recent examples of this, see *Business Seating (Renovations) Ltd v. Broad* [1989] I.C.R. 729; *Clarke v. Newland* [1991] 1 All E.R. 397.

[5] *Mont v. Mills* [1993] I.R.L.R. 172. It has been suggested that there is a difference of approach by the Court of Appeal in this case to that of the Court of Appeal in *Littlewoods Organisation Ltd v. Harris* [1978] 1 W.L.R. 1472: see *Hanover Insurance Brokers Ltd v. Schapiro* (unreported, August 20, 1993).

[6] *Dowden & Pook Ltd v. Pook* [1904] 1 K.B. 45; *Mason v. Provident Clothing Co. Ltd* [1913] A.C. 724, 732; *Stenhouse Australia Ltd v. Phillips* [1974] A.C. 391, 402.

[7] *Routh v. Jones* [1947] 1 All E.R. 758; *Jenkins v. Reid* [1948] 1 All E.R. 471; *Lyne-Pirkis v. Jones* [1969] 1 W.L.R. 1293; *Peyton v. Mindham* [1972] 1 W.L.R. 8. *cf. Rogers v. Maddocks* [1892] 3 Ch. 346.

[8] *Haynes v. Dorman* [1899] 2 Ch. 13; *North Western Salt Co. v. Electrolytic Alkali Co.* [1914] A.C. 461, 471; *Mason v. Provident Clothing Co.* [1913] A.C. 724, 732.

17–096   **Factors determining unreasonableness.** The considerations which arise in determining the reasonableness of a covenant in restraint of trade differ according to the nature of the contract in which the covenant occurs.[9] It is therefore convenient to consider separately the question of the validity of such covenants in a number of different situations, although since the doctrine is of general application[10] and the categories of restraint of trade are not closed,[11] such situations are not exhaustive.[12]

17–097   **Covenant assignable.** The benefit of a covenant in restraint of trade is assignable, unless it is clear from the terms of the covenant that it is intended to be personal to the covenantee.[13] Thus the purchaser of the goodwill of a business is entitled to enforce covenants entered into for the protection of that business.[14]

17–098   **Repudiation of contract.** If the party in whose favour a covenant in restraint of trade is entered into wrongly repudiates the agreement in which the covenant is contained, the covenantor is thereby discharged from his obligation. Wrongful dismissal, therefore, puts an end to any restrictive covenant in a contract of employment.[15] But payment of wages in lieu of notice is not a wrongful dismissal amounting to a repudiation of the contract which frees the employee from such a restraint, unless the contract of employment is one which obliges the employer to provide work for the employee.[16] It may also be possible to recover profits made by the covenantor from the breach.[17]

17–099   **Injunctions.** If a covenant in restraint of trade is valid, a breach of it may be restrained by injunction, even though the contract in which the covenant is contained provides an alternative remedy[18]; but the plaintiff must elect which of the two remedies he will enforce.[19] The court, however, will normally not grant an injunction which would have the effect of a decree of specific performance of

---

[9] *Jenkins v. Reid* [1948] 1 All E.R. 471.

[10] See *ante,* § 17–130.

[11] *Esso Petroleum Co. Ltd v. Harper's Garage (Stourport) Ltd* [1968] A.C. 269; *Petrofina (Great Britain) Ltd v. Martin* [1966] Ch. 146, 169.

[12] *e.g.* see *ante,* § 17–004, text to n. 13.

[13] As in *Davies v. Davies* (1887) 36 Ch.D. 359; see also *Berlitz School of Languages Ltd v. Duchêne* (1903) 6 F. 181.

[14] *Elves v. Crofts* (1850) 10 C.B. 241; *Jacoby v. Whitmore* (1883) 49 L.T. 335; *Townsend v. Jarman* [1900] 2 Ch. 698; *Welstead v. Hadley* (1904) 21 T.L.R. 165; *Automobile Carriage Builders Ltd v. Sayers* (1909) 101 L.T. 419.

[15] *General Billposting Co. Ltd v. Atkinson* [1909] A.C. 118; *Measures Bros. v. Measures* [1910] 2 Ch. 248; *S. W. Strange Ltd v. Mann* [1965] 1 W.L.R. 629, 637; *Briggs v. Oates* [1991] 1 W.L.R. 407.

[16] *Konski v. Peet* [1915] 1 Ch. 530, distinguishing *General Billposting Co. Ltd v. Atkinson, ante.* See also § 17–103; *Rock Refrigeration Ltd v. Jones* [1997] 1 All E.R. 1 (noted (1997) 113 L.Q.R. 377).

[17] See Birks [1987] L.M.C.L.Q. 421: *cf.* Gurry, *Breach of Confidence,* Chap. XXII.

[18] *National Provincial Bank v. Marshall* (1888) 40 Ch.D. 112; *Texaco Ltd v. Mulberry Filling Station* [1972] 1 W.L.R. 814.

[19] *General Accident Assurance Corporation v. Noel* [1902] 1 K.B. 377. This was a claim for both an injunction and liquidated damages. Where, however, the damages relate to past breaches there is no reason in principle why the plaintiff should not obtain both damages and an injunction as they clearly relate to different heads of loss.

a contract for personal service[20] although the court will enforce negative covenants, *e.g.* not to perform services elsewhere,[21] but not one which would deprive the defendant of his means of livelihood.[22] A restrictive covenant may be enforceable by injunction even though the covenantor is a minor[23] or the covenant is contained in a deed of apprenticeship.[24] No injunction will be granted to a plaintiff who is unable or unwilling to fulfil his obligations under the contract.[25]

Interlocutory injunction. There are no special rules relating to the granting **17–100** of an interlocutory injunction in connection with covenants in restraint of trade.[26] This can give rise to problems particularly with respect to restraints in employment contracts. Since to be valid the restraint will inevitably be of limited duration, the granting of an interlocutory injunction may have the effect of disposing of the matter in that the delays associated with litigation will entail that a reasonable time will have expired by the time the matter comes on for trial on the merits. To deal with this, the courts have held that matters involving restraint of trade in employment contracts are "singularly appropriate for a speedy trial."[27] Where this is not possible, it is then proper for the judge to go on to consider the chances of the plaintiff succeeding in the action.[28]

(ii) *Employer and Employee*

Employee's activities after determination of employment. The doctrine of **17–101** restraint of trade has always been applied to covenants contained in contracts of employment[29] which limit the freedom of the employee to work after the termination of the employment.[30] In some situations it will be difficult to categorise a restraint as relating to an employment contract as opposed to a

---

[20] See *Whitwood Chemical Co. v. Hardman* [1891] 2 Ch. 416; *Ehrman v. Bartholomew* [1898] 1 Ch. 671; *Rely-a-Bell Burglar and Fire Alarm Co. Ltd v. Eisler* [1926] Ch. 609; *cf. Irani v. Southampton and S.W. Hampshire Area Health Authority* [1985] I.C.R. 590; *Evening Standard Co. Ltd v. Henderson* [1987] I.C.R. 588 where injunctions were granted to prevent breach of employment contracts. See further *post*, §§ 28–055 and 28–056.

[21] *Catt v. Tourle* (1869) L.R. 4 Ch.App. 654; *Warner Bros. v. Nelson* [1937] 1 K.B. 209; *Rely-a-Bell Burglar and Fire Alarm Co. v. Eisler* [1926] Ch. 609. *cf. Lumley v. Wagner* (1852) 1 De G.M. & G. 604, 619; *Page One Records Ltd v. Britton* [1968] 1 W.L.R. 157; *Evening Standard Co. Ltd v. Henderson* [1987] I.C.R. 588; *Warren v. Mendy* [1989] 1 W.L.R. 853.

[22] *Palace Theatre Ltd v. Clensy* (1909) 26 T.L.R. 28 (interim injunction).

[23] *Bromley v. Smith* [1909] 2 K.B. 235; *Trevor André v. Bashford* [1965] C.L.Y. 1984; provided, of course, that the contract is beneficial to the minor; *cf. Corn v. Matthews* [1893] 1 Q.B. 310, 314; see *ante*, §§ 8–021 *et seq.*

[24] *Gadd v. Thompson* [1911] 1 K.B. 304.

[25] *Measures Bros. Ltd v. Measures* [1910] 2 Ch. 248.

[26] *Lawrence David Ltd v. Ashton* [1991] 1 All E.R. 385 (it appears that the profession did consider that the *American Cyanamid* principles did not apply to restraint of trade covenants in employment contracts: *ibid.* at 392).

[27] *ibid.* at 395.

[28] *ibid.* at 396; *Lansing Linde Ltd v. Kerr* [1991] 1 All E.R. 418; *Business Seating (Reservations) Ltd v. Broad* [1987] I.C.R. 729 (in both cases merits were considered and an interlocutory injunction refused).

[29] As to contracts between employers as to whom they will employ and on what terms, see *post*, §§ 17–134 *et seq.* Although agreements "in gross" cannot be justified as reasonable, the doctrine applies in the ordinary way to contracts made on the determination of the employee's employment if the contract was related to a subsisting contract of employment: *Stenhouse Australia Ltd v. Phillips* [1974] A.C. 391.

[30] As to contracts which tie the employee only during the continuance of his employment, see *post*, § 17–113.

contract between a vendor and purchaser of business, and what appears to be an employment contract may in substance be a vendor and purchaser contract. For example, where a company bought out its "sales associates" practices the court held that the covenant in the contract of sale was to be "tested by the principles applicable as between vendor and purchaser" since the covenant had been "taken for the protection of the goodwill of the business sold to the plaintiffs by the defendant, rather than for the protection of the plaintiffs' present and future business as employer."[31] Covenants in employment contracts are viewed by the courts much more jealously than the other of the principal traditional categories of covenant to which the doctrine applies, namely, covenants between the vendor and purchaser of a business.[32] The courts, however, clearly accept the enforceability of such covenants provided they satisfy the test of reasonableness and more recent authorities indicate that they will not adopt extravagant interpretations to render them void. "If a clause is valid in all ordinary circumstances which can have been contemplated by the parties, it is equally valid notwithstanding that it might cover circumstances which are so 'extravagant,' 'fantastical,' 'unlikely or improbable' that they must have been entirely outside the contemplation of the parties."[33] Thus in *Home Counties Dairies Ltd v. Skilton*[34] the defendant employee, a milkman, entered into a covenant whereby he agreed that for a period of one year from the termination of his employment that he would not serve or sell "milk or dairy produce" to any customer of his ex-employer. It was argued that the restraint relating to dairy produce resulted in the covenant being too wide, as it would preclude the employee from working for a grocery shop selling butter and cheese where there was a likelihood that the shop might be patronised by his ex-employer's customers. The Court of Appeal, reversing the trial judge, rejected this interpretation as being commercially unreasonable. From the obvious intentions of the parties, it was clear that the restraint was[35] "intended to restrict the employee's activities only when engaged in the same type of business as the employer's." On this interpretation the clause was valid as being reasonable to protect the customer-connection of the employer. Whether a particular contractual provision operates in restraint of trade is "to be determined not by the form the stipulation wears but . . . by its effect in practice."[36] Thus a provision which provides that an employee will be deprived of a pension if, on the cessation of his employment, he competed with his ex-employer will not be viewed as merely setting out the terms of his entitlement to the pension but will be treated as a provision designed to restrict competition

---

[31] *Allied Dunbar (Frank Weisinger) Ltd v. Weisinger* [1988] I.R.L.R. 60, 64. See also *Systems Reliability Holdings plc v. Smith* [1990] I.R.L.R. 377.

[32] *Nordenfelt v. Maxim Nordenfelt Guns & Ammunition Co.* [1894] A.C. 535, 566; *Morris Ltd v. Saxelby* [1916] 1 A.C. 688, 701; *Attwood v. Lamont* [1920] 3 K.B. 571, 586, 587.

[33] *Home Counties Dairies Ltd v. Skilton* [1970] 1 W.L.R. 526, 536, *per* Salmon L.J. See also Cross L.J. *ibid.* at 537; " . . . the validity of a covenant is not to be tried by the improbabilities that might fall within its wording": *Edwards v. Worboys* [1984] A.C. 724, 727 H, *per* Dillon L.J.; *Scully (U.K.) Ltd v. Lee* [1998] I.R.L.R. 259. See also *post*, § 17–113.

[34] *ibid.* See also *Business Seating (Renovations) Ltd v. Broad* [1989] I.R.L.R. 729.

[35] [1970] 1 W.L.R. 526, 535. In adopting this approach to the construction of the restraint the court followed Lord Lindley M.R. in *Haynes v. Dorman* [1899] 2 Ch. 13, 24–25. See also *Littlewoods Organisation Ltd v. Harris* [1977] 1 W.L.R. 1472 in which Lord Denning M.R. criticised the literalist approach of the court in *Commercial Plastics Ltd v. Vincent* [1965] 1 Q.B. 623. For authorities which would probably not be adhered to in light of the *Skilton* and *Littlewood* cases see Heydon, *The Restraint of Trade Doctrine* (1971), pp. 129–131.

[36] *Stenhouse Australia Ltd v. Phillips* [1974] A.C. 391, 402.

and therefore subject to the restraint of trade doctrine.[37] Also, it is on this basis that a covenant restraining an ex-employee from approaching other members of the employer's workforce would be subject to the restraint of trade doctrine.[38]

It is for the employer who seeks to enforce such a covenant against an **17–102** employee to show that it is reasonable in the interests of the parties and in particular that it is designed for the protection of some proprietary interest owned by the employer for which the restraint is reasonably necessary.[39] It has been said that the restraint must be reasonable not only in the interests of the covenantee but in the interests of both the contracting parties.[40] But provided that the covenant affords adequate, and no more than adequate, protection to the covenantee,[41] it seems that the requirement that the restraint must be reasonable in the interests of the parties is satisfied, for the court will not now inquire into the adequacy of the consideration for the covenant.[42] Yet a restraint which is reasonably necessary for the protection of the employer may be oppressive and fatal to the chance of the employee earning his living in this country. Probably the true view is that such a restraint, whether or not it be reasonable in the interests of the parties, is unreasonable in the interests of the public, which require that a man shall not be prevented from supporting himself by disposing of his labour in this country[43] and that the national economy should not be deprived of the services of experienced men.[44] Thus, in *Wyatt v. Kreglinger & Fernau*[45] a retired employee was granted a pension on condition that after retirement from the employment he should be at liberty to engage in any other trade than the wool trade, otherwise the pension would cease. There was no covenant by the employee not to engage in the wool trade nor any limit of time or space. The Court of Appeal rejected the former employee's claim for arrears of the pension, holding that, assuming a contractual relationship was established, the contract was in restraint of trade and therefore void. The decision has been criticised[46] and is explicable, if at all, only on the ground than an otherwise gratuitous promise is not made enforceable by adding to it a condition, the substance of which is such that, had the promisee covenanted to comply with it, the promisor could not,

---

[37] *Bull v. Pitney-Bowes Ltd* [1967] 1 W.L.R. 273; *Sadler v. Imperial Life Assurance Co. of Canada Ltd* [1988] I.R.L.R. 388 (commission payable to an agent after the termination of his employment ceased to be payable if he competed with his ex-employer held to be an unlawful restraint of trade).

[38] See generally, Sales (1988) 104 L.Q.R. 600.

[39] *Attwood v. Lamont, supra; Morris v. Saxelby, supra*, at 710; *Jenkins v. Reid* [1948] 1 All E.R. 471; *Eastham v. Newcastle United F.C. Ltd* [1964] Ch. 413, 431; *Greig v. Insole* [1978] 1 W.L.R. 302.

[40] *Attwood v. Lamont* [1920] 3 K.B. 571, 589.

[41] *Morris v. Saxelby* [1916] 1 A.C. 688, 707.

[42] *ibid.*

[43] *per* Neville J. in *Leetham & Sons Ltd v. Johnstone-White* [1907] 1 Ch. 189, 194.

[44] *Bull v. Pitney-Bowes Ltd* [1967] 1 W.L.R. 273, 277; *Mont v. Mills* [1993] I.R.L.R. 173, 177 (" . . . public policy clearly has regard too to the public interest in competition and in the proper use of an employee's skills."). It is on this basis that so called "garden leave" arrangements can be challenged. These are arrangements whereby an employee is given paid leave normally ending in the termination of the employment relationship and in this way the employer can protect his interests against the disclosure of confidential information, as during the period of paid leave the employee would be under a contractual duty not to disclose any confidential information relating to his employer's business.

[45] [1933] 1 K.B. 793; applied in *Bull v. Pitney-Bowes Ltd* [1967] 1 W.L.R. 273. See also *Howard F. Hudson Pty. Ltd v. Ronayne* (1971) 46 A.L.J.R. 173.

[46] See (1933) 49 L.Q.R. 465.

on the ground of the covenant's unreasonable restraint of trade, have held him to it. The courts will grant, as a matter of independent relief, a declaration that such a condition is void.[47] A restraint otherwise unreasonable does not become reasonable merely because provision is made that the consent of the employer shall not be unreasonably withheld.[48]

17–103   **Restraints after repudiation by employer.** In a number of recent cases the courts have held that a restraint in an employment contract, which applied no matter how the contract was terminated, was unreasonable in that it could apply even where the employer unlawfully terminated the contract.[49] The Court of Appeal recently held that these cases were misconceived. In *Rock Refrigeration Ltd v. Jones*[50] it held, applying the reasoning in *General Billposting Co. Ltd v. Atkinson*,[51] that the effect of the acceptance by an employee of the repudiatory breach by the employer was to terminate the contract and with it the restraint clause. There therefore could be no question of construing the restraint to determine its reasonableness since it ceased to be binding on the employee. Phillips L.J. doubted whether the *General Billposting* case, decided in 1909, now reflected the law on the effect of repudiatory breach in the light of developments since that date. It is now clear that some clauses can survive the acceptance of a repudiatory breach and regulate the rights of the parties and he considered that in certain circumstances there was no good reason why this could not apply to a restraint of trade clause. Whether this is indeed the case will need to be decided in the future. What is clear, however, contrary to what Phillips L.J. considered,[52] is that the survival of such restraints is not necessary to protect the proprietary interests of the employer as these will be protected by normal common law doctrines.[53]

17–104   **Competition.** Whether the restraint sought to be enforced in a particular case affords more than adequate protection to the business of the employer depends to some extent upon the requirements of that business.[54] Certain principles of general application, however, may be laid down. An employer is not entitled to protect himself against mere competition on the part of a former employee.[55] In the course of his employment the employee may have acquired additional skill in and knowledge of the trade or profession in which he has been engaged, so as to be a more formidable competitor upon the termination of a service; but that additional skill and knowledge belong to him and their exercise cannot lawfully be restrained by the employer.[56] So, where a film actor in the course of his employment acquired a reputation under a pseudonym it was held that a term of his contract of service restraining him from using the pseudonym after the

---

[47] *Bull v. Pitney-Bowes Ltd* [1967] 1 W.L.R. 273. *cf. Howard F. Hudson Pty. Ltd v. Ronayne* (1971) 46 A.L.J.R. 173.

[48] *Chafer Ltd v. Lilley* [1947] L.J.R. 231.

[49] See, *e.g. D. v. M.* [1996] I.R.L.R. 192.

[50] [1997] 1 All E.R. 1, (noted (1997) 113 L.Q.R. 377).

[51] [1909] A.C. 118.

[52] [1997] 1 All E.R. 1, 20.

[53] [1997] 1 All E.R. 1, 14, *per* Morritt L.J.

[54] See *Mason v. Provident Clothing Co.* [1913] A.C. 724, 732.

[55] *Bowler v. Lovegrove* [1921] 1 Ch. 642; *Attwood v. Lamont* [1920] 3 K.B. 571, 589.

[56] *Leng & Co. v. Andrews* [1909] 1 Ch. 763, 773; *Mason v. Provident Clothing Co.* [1913] A.C. 724; *Stevenson Jordan and Harrison Ltd v. Macdonald and Evans* [1952] 1 T.L.R. 101.

termination of his employment was invalid as a partial restraint of trade.[57] Similarly, an employer cannot enforce a covenant requiring an ex-employee to disclose and assign inventions discovered after he has ceased to be an employee.[58]

Protection by general law and by covenant. The general law relating to **17–105** breach of confidence[59] prohibits ex-employees from using information which "can fairly be regarded as a separate part of the employee's stock of knowledge which a man of ordinary honesty and intelligence would recognise to be the property of his old employer and not his own to do as he likes with."[60] An employer can only protect by means of a covenant information that constitutes a trade secret and cannot protect information that is merely confidential and which the employee would be precluded by his duty of fidelity from disclosing during his employment.[61] Thus there is considerable overlap between the protection afforded by the general law and that which can be acquired by a restraint of trade covenant. However, a covenant can afford wider protection than the general law in a number of respects. First, the use of a covenant is evidence of the attitude of the employer that the information is a trade secret. While an employer cannot turn confidential information into a protectable trade secret merely by characterising it as a trade secret, the attitude of an employer towards the information is a factor relevant to the court's determination of whether it is a trade secret.[62] Secondly, even where the employer's interest, for the protection of which a covenant is taken, is in trade secrets, a covenant relieves the employer of the need to prove that the employee subjectively appreciated the confidentiality of the information in question, or that the information was separable from the employee's general stock of trade knowledge or indeed that the employee has actually used the information, it being sufficient to frame the covenant to cover, to a reasonable degree, clearly defined activities in which the employee would be likely to use the information.[63] Thirdly, the courts may be reluctant to imply a term as the employee will have had no opportunity of rejecting it[64] and this may have the effect of making the protection afforded by the law slightly narrower than that which can be acquired by covenant. Fourthly, the protection provided by the law will normally be unlimited as to time whereas that under a covenant is more likely than not to be limited as to time.[65] Lastly, a carefully drafted covenant will make it easier for an employer to obtain injunctive relief since it will facilitate the framing of an order in "sufficient detail to enable the

---

[57] *Hepworth Manufacturing Co. v. Ryott* [1920] 1 Ch. 1.

[58] *Electric Transmission Ltd v. Dannenberg* (1949) 66 R.P.C. 183.

[59] North [1968] J.B.L. 32; Jones (1970) 86 L.Q.R. 463; Gurry, *Breach of Confidence* (1984).

[60] *Printers & Finishers Ltd v. Holloway* [1965] 1 W.L.R. 1, 5; *Under Water Welders & Repairers Ltd v. Street and Longthorne* [1968] R.P.C. 498, 507; *Roger Bullivant Ltd v. Ellis* [1987] I.C.R. 464. cf. *Schering Chemicals Ltd v. Falkman Ltd* [1982] 2 Q.B. 1; *Thomas Marshall (Exports) Ltd v. Guinie* [1979] Ch. 227; *Brooks v. Olyslager Oms (U.K.) Ltd* [1998] I.R.L.R. 590 (information in the public domain not confidential).

[61] *Faccenda Chicken Ltd v. Fowler* [1987] Ch. 117 (this case will be analysed in greater detail *post*, § 17–106). On when information ceases to be confidential by publication, see *Speed Seal Products Ltd v. Paddington* [1985] 1 W.L.R. 1327; and on the measure of damages see *Dawson & Mason Ltd v. Potter* [1986] 1 W.L.R. 1419.

[62] *Faccenda Chicken Ltd v. Fowler ibid.* at 138.

[63] cf. *Printers & Finishers Ltd v. Holloway, supra; Littlewoods Organisation Ltd v. Harris* [1977] 1 W.L.R. 1472.

[64] *Balston Ltd v. Headline Filters Ltd* (1987) 13 F.S.R. 330, 352.

[65] *ibid.* at 347–348.

[employee] to know exactly what information he is not free to use on behalf of his new employer."[66]

17–106   **Trade secrets and connection with customers.** An employer can by covenant lawfully prohibit an employee from accepting, after determination of his employment, a position in which he would be likely to utilise information as to secret processes or other trade secrets which have been acquired in the course of his employment.[67] Depending on the nature of the employment[68] he may also be able by covenant lawfully to prohibit the employee (i) from setting up on his own, or accepting a position with one of the employer's competitors,[69] so as to be likely to destroy the employer's trade connection by a misuse of his acquaintance with the employer's customers or clients,[70] or (ii) at least from soliciting the former employer's customers.[71]

> "In fact the reason, and the only reason, for upholding such a restraint on the part of an employee is that the employer has some proprietary right, whether in the nature of trade connection or in the nature of trade secrets, for the protection of which such a restraint is—having regard to the duties of the employee—reasonably necessary."[72]

In determining whether a particular item of information is capable of protection, the court will take into consideration such matters as the nature of the employment and the information and whether the "employer impressed on the employee the confidentiality of the information."[73] Another factor of importance is the "separability" of the information from other non-confidential information that the employee possesses, although this is not "conclusive."[74] It is important to re-emphasise that it is not all confidential information that an employer can protect but only that which amounts to a "trade secret" or which prevents "some personal influence over customers being abused in order to entice them away."[75]

---

[66] *Lock International plc v. Beswick* [1989] 1 W.L.R. 1268, 1274 (grounds on which an *Anton Piller* order was sought not sufficiently particularised).

[67] *Haynes v. Doman* [1899] 2 Ch. 13; *Caribonum Co. v. Le Couch* (1913) 109 L.T. 385; *Clark v. Electronic Applications (Commercial) Ltd* [1963] R.P.C. 234; *Brunning Group v. Bentley* [1966] C.L.Y. 4489; *Littlewoods Organisation Ltd v. Harris* [1977] 1 W.L.R. 1472. *Voaden v. Voaden* (February 21, 1997, Lindsay J. (unreported)).

[68] See *post*, § 17–108 and see *S. W. Strange Ltd v. Mann* [1965] 1 W.L.R. 629.

[69] *Commercial Plastics Ltd v. Vincent* [1965] 1 Q.B. 623, 640. The presence of an enforceable non-solicitation clause diminishes the need for a wider clause against doing business or, at least, increases the burden of justifying the wider clause: *Stenhouse Australia Ltd v. Phillips* [1974] A.C. 391. But if a non-solicitation clause would clearly suffice it may be as hard to justify a clause against doing business that stands alone as it would be to justify a clause against doing business that stands alongside a non-solicitation clause. See also *Office Angels Ltd v. Rainer-Thomas and O'Connor* [1991] I.R.L.R. 214.

[70] *Baines v. Geary* (1887) 35 Ch.D. 154; *Ropeways v. Hoyle* (1919) 88 L.J.Ch. 446; *Fitch v. Dewes* [1921] 2 A.C. 158; *Marion White Ltd v. Francis* [1972] 1 W.L.R. 1423. Contrast *Lucas & Co. Ltd v. Mitchell* [1974] Ch. 129 (anti-solicitation covenant was severable from a trading covenant and enforceable).

[71] *S. W. Strange Ltd v. Mann* [1965] 1 W.L.R. 629; *Lucas & Co. Ltd v. Mitchell* [1974] Ch. 129. Contrast *Spafax (1965) Ltd v. Dommett* (1972) 116 S.J. 711, where the word "customers" was said to be impossibly vague.

[72] *Morris v. Saxelby* [1916] A.C. 688, 710; *Faccenda Chicken Ltd v. Fowler* [1987] Ch. 117, 137.

[73] *Faccenda Chicken Ltd v. Fowler* [1987] Ch. 117, 137–138.

[74] *ibid.*

[75] *Faccenda Chicken Ltd v. Fowler* [1987] Ch. 117, 137; *Poly Lina Ltd v. Finch* [1996] F.L.R. 75.

In *Faccenda Chicken Ltd v. Fowler*[76] it was held that the duty of fidelity which an employee owes to an employer during the continuance of the employment obliges an employee to maintain confidential information which could not be made the subject of a valid restraint on the termination of the employment relationship.[77] At first glance this appears anomalous as the restraint of trade doctrine applies equally during the continuance of the contract as on its termination, and one would have expected that what was protectible during the contract would also be protectible on its termination. It may be that an employee's duty of fidelity is designed to produce a harmonious working relationship and this may be the justification for a wider restraint as long as the employee remains in employment.[78]

The limitations on the permissible scope of a post-employment restrictive covenant with respect to confidential information put forward in *Faccenda Chicken* were considered "improbable as being the law" by Harman J. in *Systems Reliability Holdings v. Smith*.[79] Although *Faccenda Chicken* is a judgment of the Court of Appeal, there is much to commend the judgment of Harman J. As a matter of public policy it is difficult to see why an employer should not be free by agreement to restrain the disclosure of confidential information. The principle in *Faccenda Chicken* will have a very limited scope if the definition of "trade secret" is extended to include information which might in "common parlance" not be considered trade secrets. Thus if the names of customers and the goods that they buy or other nontechnical information are classified as trade secrets,[80] post-employment restraints could validly embrace a wide category of confidential information. A matter on which the law is undecided is whether an employer is entitled to protection where an employee is not seeking to earn his living but is "selling to a third party information which he acquired in confidence in the course of his former employment."[81] Given that the principal justification for the restraint of trade doctrine as applied to employment contracts is to enable an employee to earn his livelihood, there is much to be said for not permitting an employee to sell confidential information unconnected with the need for him to earn a living. **17–107**

Nature of connection with customers. The validity of restrictive covenants by employees frequently depends upon the question whether their employment is of a confidential nature, so that, for example, the necessity of protecting the employer's trade connection has caused restrictive covenants by canvassers and **17–108**

---

[76] *ibid.*

[77] *ibid.*

[78] *Mont v. Mills* [1993] I.R.L.R. 172, 177 ("Once the employment relationship ceases, there is no continuing occasion for loyalty" *per* Simon Brown L.J.).

[79] [1990] I.R.L.R. 377, 384. Harman J. considered that the dictum was *obiter* in that in *Faccenda Chicken* the court was dealing with implied covenants. His own observation was also strictly *obiter* since he found that the restraint before him related to the sale of a business. See also *Balston Ltd v. Headline Filters Ltd* [1987] F.S.R. 330, 347–348 (Scott J. had reservations about the judgment of Neill L.J. in the *Faccenda Chicken* case). See also *Lock International plc v. Beswick* [1989] 1 W.L.R. 1268. *Faccenda Chicken* was followed in *Roger Bullivant Ltd v. Ellis* [1987] I.C.R. 464 and *Mammet Holdings plc v. Austin* [1991] F.S.R. 538.

[80] As two judges were willing to do in *Lansing Linde Ltd v. Kerr* [1991] 1 W.L.R. 251, 260 (Staughton L.J.), 270 (Butler-Sloss L.J.). See also *TSB Bank plc v. Conmell* 1997 S.L.T. 1254, 1260; *FSS Travel and Leisure Systems Ltd v. Johnson* [1998] I.R.L.R. 382.

[81] *Faccenda Chicken Ltd v. Fowler* [1987] Ch. 117, 139.

travellers generally to be upheld.[82] Each case must be decided upon its own facts.[83] The courts have considered the reasonableness of restraints relating to solicitors and legal executives,[84] medical and dental practitioners,[85] actors,[86] commercial managers and agents,[87] canvassers and travellers,[88] shop assistants and salesmen,[89] bookmaker's assistants,[90] estate agents,[91] designers[92] and technicians.[93]

17-109   **Limits on scope of restraint.** A covenant not to solicit[94] customers is valid even if it extends to people who, although customers at the beginning of the employee's employment, ceased to be so before its determination,[95] though not if it extends to those who become customers after the determination of the employment.[96] It is no objection to a covenant restraining dealings with customers of the employer that the identity of all the employer's customers may not be known to the covenantor, for the court would not grant an injunction against him or commit him for contempt for the breach of any injunction already granted if he could show that what he had done he had done inadvertently and would not

---

[82] Absence of control, by professional rules, over an unqualified employee may go to support the maintenance of a restraint: *Scorer v. Seymour Jones* [1966] 1 W.L.R. 1419.

[83] What is acceptable for a senior manager may be held to be unenforceable against a more junior employee: see *Ginsberg v. Parker* [1988] I.R.L.R. 483.

[84] *Whittaker v. Howe* (1841) 3 Beav. 383; *sed quaere*; contrast *S. Nevanas Ltd v. Walker and Foreman* [1914] 1 Ch. 413, 425; *post*, § 17–109; *Dendy v. Henderson* (1855) 11 Ech. 194; *May v. O'Neill* (1875) 44 L.J.Ch. 660; but see the *Nordenfelt* case [1894] A.C. 535, 563–564, 572–573; *Fitch v. Dewes* [1921] 2 A.C. 158, 167 and the comments thereon in *S. W. Strange Ltd v. Mann* [1965] 1 W.L.R. 629, 640.

[85] *Horner v. Graves* (1831) 7 Bing. 735; *Mallan v. May* (1843) 11 M. & W. 653; *Ballachulish Slate Quarries Co. Ltd v. Grant* (1903) 5 F. 1105; *Eastes v. Russ* [1914] 1 Ch. 468 (pathologist); *Whitehill v. Bradford* [1952] Ch. 236; *Macfarlane v. Kent* [1965] 1 W.L.R. 1019; *Lyne-Pirkis v. Jones* [1969] 1 W.L.R. 1293; *Peyton v. Mindham* [1972] 1 W.L.R. 8.

[86] *Tivoli (Manchester) Ltd v. Colley* (1904) 20 T.L.R. 437.

[87] *Lamson Pneumatic Tube Co. v. Phillips* (1904) 91 L.T. 363; *Millers Ltd v. Steadman* (1915) 84 L.J.K.B. 2057; *S. Nevanas Ltd v. Walker and Foreman* [1914] 1 Ch. 413.

[88] *Rousillon v. Rousillon* (1880) 14 Ch.D. 351 (champagne trade); *Rogers v. Maddocks* [1892] 3 Ch. 346 (malt liquors and, if required by his employer, aerated waters); *Underwood & Son v. Barker* [1899] 1 Ch. 300 (hay and straw merchants); *Haynes v. Dorman* [1899] 2 Ch. 13; *Barr v. Craven* (1904) 89 L.T. 574 (insurance agency); *Continental Tyre Co. v. Heath* (1913) 29 T.L.R. 308; *Mason v. Provident Clothing Co. Ltd* [1913] A.C. 724.

[89] *S. Nevanas Ltd v. Walker and Foreman* [1914] 1 Ch. 413; *cf. Perls v. Saalfeld* [1892] 2 Ch. 149; *Great Western and Metropolitan Dairies Ltd v. Gibbs* (1918) 34 T.L.R. 344; *Whitmore v. King* (1918) 87 L.J.Ch. 647; *Vincents of Reading v. Fogden* (1932) 48 T.L.R. 613; *Attwood v. Lamont* [1920] 3 K.B. 571; *Putsman v. Taylor* [1927] 1 K.B. 741; *Home Counties Dairies Ltd v. Skilton* [1970] 1 W.L.R. 526; *Lucas & Co. Ltd v. Mitchell* [1974] Ch. 129; *Spafax (1965) Ltd v. Dommett* (1972) 116 S.J. 711; *Dairy Crest Ltd v. Pigott* [1989] I.C.R. 92.

[90] *S. W. Strange Ltd v. Mann* [1965] 1 W.L.R. 629.

[91] *Scorer v. Seymour Jones* [1966] 1 W.L.R. 1419.

[92] *John Michael Design plc v. Cooke* [1987] 2 All E.R. 332.

[93] *Commercial Plastics Ltd v. Vincent* [1965] 1 Q.B. 623.

[94] As to the meaning of solicitation see *Cullard v. Taylor* (1887) 3 T.L.R. 698; *cf. Horton v. Mead* [1913] 1 K.B. 154 and cases there cited in argument.

[95] *Plowman & Son Ltd v. Ash* [1964] 1 W.L.R. 568; *Home Counties Dairies Ltd v. Skilton* [1970] 1 W.L.R. 526.

[96] *Konski v. Peet* [1915] 1 Ch. 530; *Express Dairy Co. v. Jackson* (1930) 99 L.J.K.B. 181; *Rayner v. Pegler* (1964) 189 E.G. 967; *Gledhow Autoparts Ltd v. Delaney* [1965] 1 W.L.R. 1366; *Business Seating (Renovations) Ltd v. Broad* [1989] I.C.R. 79; *Austin Knight (U.K.) v. Heinz* [1994] F.S.R. 52; *Anamark plc v. Sommerville* 1995 S.L.T. 749.

be repeated.[97] Similarly a covenant ought not to be held invalid because hypothetical cases can be suggested when it might be unreasonable to apply it, if those circumstances were outside the contemplation of the parties to such an extent that they are to be excluded from its operation.[98] It is no objection to the enforcement of a non-solicitation covenant with respect to a particular customer that that customer has no intention of doing any further business with the employer: this is "the very class of case against which the covenant is designed to give protection . . . the plaintiff does not need protection against customers who are faithful to him."[99]

Type of business in which employee was engaged. The employer is not **17–110** entitled to protect by a restrictive covenant of any description any business except the business in which he employed the covenantor[1] (though a covenant which might appear unduly wide with regard to the business to be protected may, on its proper construction, be subject to an implied limitation as a result of which it is valid[2]). Thus a covenant by a tailor's assistant not to carry on any business within certain limits of space and time is therefore invalid, even though it would be valid were it confined to the business of a tailor.[3] So, too, a covenant by an employee of a company intended to protect not merely the business of that company but also the business of associated or subsidiary companies in which he does not serve is an unreasonable restraint.[4]

Limits of space and time. In considering whether or not a restraint is **17–111** reasonable, limitations of space or time imposed upon it are usually of the greatest relevance.[5] The longer the duration of restriction and the greater the area over which it operates, the more difficult it is to prove that the restriction is reasonable.[6] Area restraints "will always be approached with caution by the courts since such restraints amount to a covenant against competition."[7] It has been said that "to preclude a former servant from carrying on his natural business in any part whatever of the United Kingdom is a very strong step and requires

---

[97] *Gilford Motor Co. v. Horne* [1933] Ch. 935, 964; *Plowman & Son Ltd v. Ash* [1964] 1 W.L.R. 568.

[98] *Clark v. Electronic Applications (Commercial) Ltd* [1963] R.P.C. 234, 237; *Commercial Plastics Ltd v. Vincent* [1965] 1 Q.B. 623, 644; *ante*, § 17–101.

[99] *John Michael Design plc v. Cooke* [1987] 2 All E.R. 332, 334 (the unwillingness of the customer to deal with the employer is something that goes to damages).

[1] *Bromley v. Smith* [1909] 2 K.B. 235; *Vandervell Products Ltd v. McLeod* [1957] R.P.C. 185; *Rayner v. Pegler* (1964) 189 E.G. 967; *Commercial Plastics Ltd v. Vincent* [1965] 1 Q.B. 623, 640. On *Commercial Plastics Ltd v. Vincent* see *Littlewoods Organisation Ltd v. Harris* [1977] 1 W.L.R. 1472, 1480–1482, 1488–1489; *ante*, § 17–101, n. 35.

[2] *Plowman & Son Ltd v. Ash* [1964] 1 W.L.R. 568; *Home Counties Dairies Ltd v. Skilton* [1970] 1 W.L.R. 526. See *ante*, § 17–101.

[3] *Baker v. Hedgecock* (1888) 39 Ch.D. 520; *Perls v. Saalfeld* [1892] 2 Ch. 149; *Ehrman v. Bartholomew* [1898] 1 Ch. 671; *cf. Mills v. Dunham* [1891] 1 Ch. 576.

[4] *Leetham & Sons Ltd v. Johnstone-White* [1907] 1 Ch. 322; *Business Seating (Renovations) Ltd v. Broad* [1989] I.C.R. 729. Contrast *Stenhouse Australia Ltd v. Phillips* [1974] A.C. 391 where the employer's business was to some extent transacted for it by its subsidiaries as its agencies or instrumentalities and a covenant which protected the business so transacted for it was held to be reasonable.

[5] See *ante*, § 17–090.

[6] *Herbert Morris Ltd v. Saxelby* [1916] 1 A.C. 688, 715; *M. & S. Drapers v. Reynolds* [1957] 1 W.L.R. 9; *Lucas & Co. Ltd v. Mitchell* [1974] Ch. 129; *Financial Collection Agencies (U.K.) Ltd v. Batey* (1973) 117 S.J. 416; *Luck v. Davenport-Smith* (1977) 242 E.G. 455.

[7] *Office Angels Ltd v. Rainer-Thomas and O'Connor* [1991] I.R.L.R. 214, 221.

exceptional justification"[8]; *a fortiori* where the restraint is worldwide.[9] It has been held reasonable to impose a worldwide restraint on disclosing confidential information on an employee employed in the United Kingdom, the reasoning of the court being that business has become global and that national boundaries did not constrain the dissemination of confidential information.[10] On the other hand, covenants against solicitation, especially if taken from canvassers and travellers, are generally not invalidated by reason of the absence of any limit of space[11] or even, it would seem, of any limit of space or time.[12] But where the employer's business is exclusively for credit, the customer not dealing directly with an employee, it will often be difficult to establish the reasonableness of any area restriction since a mere covenant not to deal with customers on the books of the employer is likely to be sufficient.[13] In considering whether a particular restraint is reasonable in point of time the limit of space imposed shall be considered, and vice versa.[14] In reckoning a spatial limitation the distance will be measured on the map (as the crow flies)[15] unless the parties have adopted some other measurement.

17–112   **Breach.** In considering whether a particular act constitutes a breach of such a restrictive covenant, it is important to note the exact terms in which the covenant is framed, and this is a question of construction. Thus, a covenant not to practise as a solicitor in a defined area is not broken by writing letters to persons resident in that area,[16] though a covenant not to do acts usually done by a solicitor is.[17] A covenant by a doctor not to practise within an area is broken by attendance on patients in that area, even though he does not solicit such patients,[18] but he does not "set up in practice," though he does "practise," by attending a few patients within the prohibited area at their own request, he having no residence or premises within the area[19]; a similar covenant by a house agent is broken by letting houses in the area, though his office is outside.[20] Nor was a covenant not to carry on business as an auctioneer and estate agent broken by the employee, after the employment had terminated, setting up in business as an "Estate Agent, A.A.I." (Associate of the Auctioneers' Institute). He held himself out as an estate agent only and the addition of "A.A.I." did not mean that he held himself out as

---

[8] *S. Nevanas Ltd v. Walker and Foreman* [1914] 1 Ch. 413, 425; *Spencer v. Marchington* [1988] I.R.L.R. 372. cf. *George Silverman v. Silverman Ltd* (1969) 113 S.J. 563.

[9] See *ante*, § 17–090, n. 72.

[10] *Scully (U.K.) Ltd v. Lee* [1998] I.R.L.R. 259.

[11] *Plowman & Son Ltd v. Ash* [1964] 1 W.L.R. 568, 572; *Home Counties Dairies Ltd v. Skilton* [1970] 1 W.L.R. 526: cf. *Marley Tiles Ltd v. Johnson, The Times*, October 16, 1981 (area restraint held to be unreasonable).

[12] *Dubowski v. Goldstein* [1896] 1 Q.B. 478; *Mason v. Provident Clothing Co.* [1913] A.C. 724, 734, 741.

[13] *S. W. Strange Ltd v. Mann* [1965] 1 W.L.R. 629; cf. *Macfarlane v. Kent* [1965] 1 W.L.R. 1019, 1024; *Scorer v. Seymour Jones* [1966] 1 W.L.R. 1419; *Lucas & Co. Ltd v. Mitchell* [1974] Ch. 129.

[14] *Fitch v. Dewes* [1921] 2 A.C. 158, 163, 168.

[15] *Mouflet v. Cole* (1872) L.R. 8 Ex. 32. See *Atkyns v. Kinnier* (1850) 4 Ex. 776 for a case where the parties adopted their own unit of measurement.

[16] *Woodbridge & Sons v. Bellamy* [1911] 1 Ch. 326; *Freeman v. Fox* (1911) 55 S.J. 650.

[17] *Edmundson v. Render* [1905] 2 Ch. 320.

[18] *Rogers v. Drury* (1887) 57 L.J.Ch. 504.

[19] *Robertson v. Buchanan* (1904) 73 L.J.Ch. 408.

[20] *Hadsley v. Dayer-Smith* [1914] A.C. 979.

an auctioneer.[21] An employee has been held to be concerned in[22] and engaged in the business which he serves[23] but not to carry it on or be concerned in carrying it on.[24] The creditor of a business is not concerned or interested in it.[25] An "interest" in a business means a precuniary or proprietary interest. A covenant by a man not to carry on or be in anywise interested in a business does not prevent the business being carried on by his wife as a separate trader and in which he takes no part,[26] but he will not be allowed to evade his covenant by the device of carrying on business under a title,[27] or by means of the formation of a limited company,[28] which is a mere cloak for his own activities. A covenant not to practise as a solicitor is not broken by acting as managing clerk to a solicitor, the test being whether in the work he does the relationship of solicitor and client is constituted between himself and the person for whom he acts.[29] Generally, however, to act as assistant to a professional man such as a surgeon[30] or an architect[31] amounts to carrying on that profession. Covenants often preclude an employee from "soliciting" the customers of his ex-employer. This prohibition obviously covers direct approaches and probably also extends to advertisements by the employee designed to bring his availability for business to the notice of the customers of his ex-employer.[32] This would be so even where the customers are a sub-group of a larger group of potential customers to whom the advertisement is directed.[33] There is, however, a distinction between soliciting and doing business, and an anti-solicitation clause would not preclude the employee from doing business with customers of his ex-employer who unprompted seek out his services.

The position of a subordinate in a commercial house is very different; and it has therefore been held that a salaried manager to a rag merchant does not carry on that business[34] nor is a salaried assistant to a jeweller interested either directly or indirectly in the jewellery business.[35] A manufacturer of margarine, who sells the margarine which he manufactures, does not carry on the business of provision merchant.[36] A covenant not to solicit the customers of a particular shop does not extend to the customers of the same business at a different shop.[37]

Restraints during currency of employment. It now appears probable that **17–113** even restraints which operate only during the currency of employment are subject to the doctrine of restraint of trade, at any rate if they have as their objects the

[21] *Bowler v. Lovegrove* [1921] 1 Ch. 642.
[22] *Hill & Co. v. Hill* (1886) 55 L.T. 769.
[23] *Pearks Ltd v. Cullen* (1912) 28 T.L.R. 371.
[24] *Ramoneur & Co. Ltd v. Brixey* (1911) 104 L.T. 809.
[25] *Cory & Son v. Harrison* [1906] A.C. 274.
[26] *Smith v. Hancock* [1894] 2 Ch. 377; *cf. Scheckter v. Kolbe*, 1955 (3) S.A. 109.
[27] *ibid.*
[28] *Gilford Motor Co. Ltd v. Horne* [1933] Ch. 935.
[29] *Way v. Bishop* [1928] Ch. 647.
[30] *Palmer v. Mallet* (1887) 36 Ch.D. 411.
[31] *Robertson v. Willmott* (1909) 25 T.L.R. 681.
[32] *Sweeney v. Astle* [1923] N.Z.L.R. 1198, 1204–1205.
[33] *ibid.*
[34] *Allen v. Taylor* (1871) 39 L.J.Ch. 627.
[35] *Gophir Diamond Co. v. Wood* [1902] 1 Ch. 950; *cf. Scheckter v. Kolbe*, 1955 (3) S.A. 109.
[36] *Lovell and Christmas Ltd v. Wall* (1911) 104 L.T. 85; *cf. Automobile Carriage Builders Ltd v. Sayers* (1909) 101 L.T. 419.
[37] *Marshall & Murray Ltd v. Jones* (1913) 29 T.L.R. 351.

sterilising rather than the absorption of a man's capacity for work,[38] or perhaps are such that one of the parties is so unilaterally fettered that the contract loses its character of a contract for the regulation and promotion of trade and acquires the predominant character of a contract in restraint of trade.[39] When a contract ties the parties only during the continuance of the contract and the negative ties are only those which are incidental and normal to the positive commercial arrangements at which the contract aims even though those ties exclude all dealings with others, there is probably no restraint of trade within the meaning of the doctrine and no question of reasonableness arises[40]; indeed in appropriate circumstances the courts will even imply a restraint, for example that employees, engaged in skilled work and having knowledge of their employers' manufacturing data, shall not in their spare time carry out similar work for competitors.[41]

(iii) *Vendor and Purchaser of Business*

17–114   **Vendor and purchaser.**[42] Restrictive covenants between vendor and purchaser are looked on with less disfavour by the court. "I think it is now generally conceded," said Lord Watson in *Nordenfelt v. Maxim Nordenfelt Guns and Ammunition Co. Ltd*,[43]

> "that it is to the advantage of the public to allow a trader who has established a lucrative business to dispose of it to a successor by whom it may be efficiently carried on. That object could not be accomplished if, upon the score of public policy, the law reserved to the seller an absolute and indefeasible right to start a rival concern the day after he sold. Accordingly it has been determined judicially, that in cases where the purchaser, for his own protection, obtains an obligation restraining the seller from competing with him, within bounds which having regard to the nature of the business are reasonable and are limited in respect of space, the obligation is not obnoxious to public policy, and is therefore capable of being enforced."

In the vendor and purchaser situation the covenant is as important for the *vendor* as it is for the purchaser: if the vendor could not enter into a valid covenant in restraint of trade then he could not sell his goodwill as the purchaser would have no assurance that the vendor would not compete against him at some time in the future. In other words, an enforceable covenant is necessary to create a property right (a "vendible asset") in the vendor which he can sell.[44] Also, there may be a disparity of bargaining power between employers and employees which is not

---

[38] *Esso Petroleum Co. Ltd v. Harper's Garage (Stourport) Ltd* [1968] A.C. 269, 328, 336; *Young v. Timmins* (1831) 1 Cr. & J. 331. See also *Lido-Savoy Pty. Ltd v. Paredes* [1972] V.R. 297, distinguishing *Warner Bros. Pictures Inc. v. Nelson* [1937] 1 K.B. 209. See also *ante*, § 17–078.

[39] *Esso Petroleum Co. Ltd v. Harper's Garage (Stourport) Ltd*, *supra*, at 328; *A. Schroeder Music Publishing Co. Ltd v. Macaulay* [1974] 1 W.L.R. 1308 and *Clifford Davies Ltd v. W.E.A. Records Ltd* [1975] 1 W.L.R. 61; *Greig v. Insole* [1978] 1 W.L.R 302, 325–327. In the light of these cases it is submitted that *Warner Bros. Pictures Inc. v. Nelson* [1937] 1 K.B. 209, where onerous restrictions upon a film actress were considered not to be within the doctrine since they related to her period of employment, can no longer be relied upon.

[40] [1968] A.C. 269, 307, 328, 336, contrast at 317.

[41] *Hivac Ltd v. Park Royal Instruments Ltd* [1946] Ch. 169.

[42] Also of relevance are the provisions of article 81 E.C. Treaty (on which see *post*, Vol. II, Chap. 42); as a general proposition, a restrictive covenant which is ancillary to a legitimate transaction such as the sale of business with its associated goodwill and which is appropriately limited in subject-matter, geographical scope and time, would not normally infringe E.C. or domestic competition law: see *Remia and Nutricia v. Commission* [1985] E.C.R. 2545.

[43] [1894] A.C. 535, 552.

[44] Blake (1960) 73 Harv.L.Rev. 625, at 646–648; *Attwood v. Lamont* [1920] 3 K.B. 571; *Ronbar Enterprises Ltd v. Green* [1954] 1 W.L.R. 815, 820–821.

present in vendor and purchaser situations, although the extent to which this is presently the case in light of contemporary industrial relations practices is open to question. Deciding whether a covenant is taken to protect goodwill attached to the sale of a business is a matter of substance and not form. Thus where an employer allowed its retiring sales staff to capitalise the value of the contacts they had built up with customers and to be paid a lump sum for it on the cessation of their employment, this was held to be the sale of goodwill (despite appearances to the contrary) and the restraint had to be evaluated accordingly.[45] The court went on to hold that a two-year anti-competition covenant was enforceable even though such a covenant in the employee-employer context would not have been valid.

The more benign attitude of the courts towards restraints in vendor and **17–115** purchaser contracts is illustrated by *Nordenfelt* itself: in that case the court held that a covenant by a patentee and manufacturer of guns and ammunition with the purchasers of the goodwill of his business not to engage in the business of a manufacturer of guns and ammunition for 25 years was not too wide to be a valid restraint. The covenant must, however, have been taken in connection with a genuine sale of a business.[46] A naked covenant in restraint of trade is void.[47] Where the business sold was that of dealing in imitation jewellery in London, it was held that an agreement covering real jewellery and extending to a number of European countries was too wide.[48] Where the lease and goodwill of a hairdresser and tobacconist were sold, the vendor covenanting not to carry on such a business in a particular town during his life, the covenant was held to be unreasonable and void.[49] Where the sale of a goodwill is concerned, if the restriction as to space is considered to be reasonable, it is seldom that the restriction can be held to be unreasonable because there is no limit as to time.[50] The business sold is the only legitimate subject of protection; the purchaser cannot take a covenant protecting other businesses controlled by him.[51] Thus where a vendor sold business A, a gentlemen's hairdresser, he could not enforce against the purchaser a non-competition covenant protecting business B, a ladies' hairdressing business.[52] On the sale of a business with a covenant that the vendor "would not within ten years . . . directly or indirectly carry on or assist in carrying on or be engaged, concerned, interested or employed in the business of a quarry within seventy-five miles of" the quarry sold, it was held to be a breach of this covenant that the vendor had advanced money to his sons to start a similar

---

[45] *Allied Dunbar (Frank Weisinger) Ltd v. Frank Weisinger* [1988] I.R.L.R. 60.

[46] The vendor of shares in a business may, in certain circumstances, be in the same position as the vendor of the business itself: *Connors Bros. Ltd v. Connors* [1940] 4 All E.R. 179; *Greening Industries Ltd v. Penny* (1965) 53 D.L.R. (2d) 643; *Systems Reliability Holdings plc v. Smith* [1990] I.R.L.R. 377; *ante*, § 17–107.

[47] *Vancouver Malt and Sake Brewing Co. Ltd v. Vancouver Breweries Ltd* [1934] A.C. 181, *post*, § 17–130. *cf. ante*, § 17–093. As to agreements between co-operative societies delimiting their trading areas, see *Bellshill and Mossend Co-operative Society Ltd v. Dalziel Co-operative Society Ltd* [1960] A.C. 832, especially at 842; *cf. Re Doncaster Co-operative Society Ltd's and Retford Co-operative Society Ltd's Agreement* [1960] 1 W.L.R. 1186.

[48] *Goldsoll v. Goldman* [1915] 1 Ch. 292. A covenant limited to the sale of imitation jewellery in the United Kingdom and Isle of Man was held to be severable and valid. See *ante*, § 17–089; *post*, §§ 17–188, 17–189.

[49] *Pellow v. Ivy* (1933) 49 T.L.R. 422.

[50] *Connors Bros. Ltd v. Connors* [1940] 4 All E.R. 179, 195.

[51] *British Reinforced Concrete Engineering Co. Ltd v. Schelff* [1921] 2 Ch. 563; *Vancouver Malt and Sake Brewing Co. Ltd v. Vancouver Breweries Ltd* [1934] A.C. 181.

[52] *Giblin v. Murdoch* 1979 S.L.T. 5.

business within the prohibited area and had given them advice as to how to manage the new business.[53] On the sale of a company, its directors may agree not to compete with the purchaser. Such an agreement may be subject to competition legislation: see Vol. II, Chap. 42.

17–116   **Sale of goodwill without express restraint.** Where the goodwill of a business is sold, there being no express agreement as to the vendor's refraining from future competition, the vendor may set up a rival business, but he is not entitled to canvass the customers of the old firm, and may be restrained by injunction from soliciting any person who was a customer of the old firm prior to the sale to continue to deal with the vendor, or not to deal with the purchaser.[54] The ground of this may be either that a man may not derogate from his own grant, or that the vendor had impliedly contracted not to solicit his former customers, or that it would be fraudulent to do so. "It is not right," observed Lord Macnaghten, "to profess to purport to sell that which you do not mean the purchaser to have; it is not an honest thing to pocket the price and then to recapture the subject of sale, to decoy it away or call it back before the purchaser has had time to attach it to himself and make it his very own."[55] For the same reason the vendor of a business may not represent that he is carrying on business in continuance of, or in succession to, the business carried on by his former firm.[56] The principle of *Trego v. Hunt*[57] extends to the executors of a vendor who are executing a contract for the sale of the goodwill. No such covenant can be implied, however, on the part of a bankrupt where the business is sold by the trustee in bankruptcy, because the alienation is compulsory[58]; this is the case even though the bankrupt agreed to aid in realising the business.[59] A purchaser of a business and goodwill of a bankrupt has therefore no right to restrain the bankrupt from setting up a fresh business or from soliciting customers of the old business, and this even though the bankrupt has joined in the conveyance to the purchaser. This rule applies also to the sale of a debtor's business by a trustee of a deed of arrangement for creditors. This is also regarded as a compulsory alienation.[60]

(iv) *Partners*

17–117   **Covenants on dissolution of partnership.** Upon similar principles, including that of *Trego v. Hunt* just referred to, restrictive covenants which operate upon the dissolution of a partnership are valid,[61] if they impose no wider restraint than the

---

[53] *Batts Combe Quarry Ltd v. Ford* [1943] Ch. 51.

[54] *Trego v. Hunt* [1896] A.C. 7, approving *Labouchere v. Dawson* (1872) L.R. 13 Eq. 322. See also *Jennings v. Jennings* [1898] 1 Ch. 378. Even if goodwill is not expressly mentioned, its sale is implied on the sale of a business: *Shipwright v. Clements* (1871) 19 W.R. 599.

[55] *Trego v. Hunt, supra*, at 25.

[56] *Churton v. Douglas* (1859) Johns. 174.

[57] [1896] A.C. 7. See Muir Hunter, *Personal Insolvency*, § 3–116.

[58] *Cruttwell v. Lye* (1810) 17 Ves. 335; *Walker v. Mottram* (1881) 19 Ch.D. 355. This is because, unlike the situation where there is a voluntary alienation, there is no personal covenant when the alienation is compulsory.

[59] *Farey v. Cooper* [1927] 2 K.B. 384.

[60] *Green & Sons (Northampton) Ltd v. Morris* [1914] 1 Ch. 562; followed in *Farey v. Cooper, supra*, per Atkin L.J. at 398.

[61] As to consideration, see *Leighton v. Wales* (1838) 3 M. & W. 545. See generally *Lindley & Banks on Partnership* (16th ed.), pp. 213–223. Restrictive covenants in partnership agreements are also subject to Article 85 of the EC Treaty: see *Lindley & Banks op.cit.* pp. 220–223.

circumstances reasonably require.[62] In *Bridge v. Deacons*[63] it was considered inappropriate to attempt to categorise covenants in partnership agreements as either falling within the vendor-purchaser or employer-employee categories; the court in such cases simply had to determine whether the covenant was no more than was necessary to protect the interests of the covenantee. *A fortiori*, such restrictive covenants are generally valid during the continuance of the partnership[64]; thus, an agreement by one of the proprietors of a theatre not to write plays for any other theatre is good.[65] In the absence of any express covenant an ex-partner (who has been paid the value of his share including his interest in the goodwill) on dissolution of the partnership may carry on a similar and competing business in his own name and may deal with customers of his former firm and he may advertise himself as having been connected with the business sold.[66] He may not directly or indirectly canvass them or persuade them to deal with himself and not with the old firm,[67] nor may he carry on his business in the name of the old firm or represent his business as still being that of the old firm.[68]

Analogous agreements. It is well established that the categories involving the restraint of trade doctrine are neither rigid not exclusive.[69] The traditional categories for applying the restraint of trade principles are vendor and purchaser and employment contracts. This obviously is a small sub-set of commercial relationships. In *Kall-Kwik (U.K.) Ltd v. Frank Clarence Rush*[70] the court had to deal with the application of the restraint of trade doctrine to a franchise agreement whereby on the termination of the franchise, the franchisee was restrained from competing with the franchisor. The court held that such a restraint was more akin to a restraint in a vendor and purchaser situation. The franchisee had an obligation to transfer the "goodwill" attached to the franchise at the end of the franchise period and this was analogous to the situation where the vendor of property enters into a restraint in order to protect any goodwill transferred to the purchaser. Where a majority shareholder sells his shares and enters into a contract of service with the company which contains a covenant in restraint of trade, this could also be categorised as a vendor and purchaser covenant and not one relating to employment.[71] **17–118**

---

[62] See *Whitehill v. Bradford* [1952] Ch. 236; the National Health Service Act 1977 (as amended) has not altered the position with regard to medical partnerships; *Kerr v. Morris* [1987] Ch. 90. See also *Macfarlane v. Kent* [1965] 1 W.L.R. 1019; and *Ronbar Enterprises v. Green* [1954] 1 W.L.R. 815; *Lyne-Pirkis v. Jones* [1969] 1 W.L.R. 1293; *Peyton v. Mindham* [1972] 1 W.L.R. 8.

[63] [1984] A.C. 705, PC. The court also held that a covenant otherwise reasonable was not against public policy because it prohibited a solicitor from soliciting clients of the firm: see also *Oswald Hickson Collier & Co. v. Carter-Ruck* [1984] A.C. 720; *Edwards v. Worboys* [1984] A.C. 724. *cf. Geraghty v. Minter* (1979–80) 142 C.L.R. 177.

[64] See *ante*, § 17–133.

[65] *Morris v. Colman* (1812) 18 Ves. 437.

[66] *Lindley & Banks on Partnership* (17th ed.), pp. 248–251.

[67] *Churton v. Douglas* (1859) Johns. 174; *Macfarlane v. Kent* [1965] 1 W.L.R. 1019.

[68] *Labouchere v. Dawson* (1872) L.R. 13 Eq. 322; *Trego v. Hunt* [1896] A.C. 7; *cf. Curl Brothers Ltd v. Webster* [1904] 1 Ch. 685. The executors of a deceased partner will be restrained from soliciting the customers of the old firm: *Boorne v. Wicker* [1927] 1 Ch. 667.

[69] *Dawnay Day & Co. v. D'Alphen* [1997] T.L.R. 334 (a joint venturer had a sufficient interest to enforce an anti-competition covenant).

[70] [1996] F.S.R. 114.

[71] *Alliance Paper Group plc. v. Prestwich* [1996] I.R.L.R. 25.

(v) *Supply and Acquisition of Goods: Restraints in Vertical Agreements*

17-119 **Application of doctrine.** The treatment of restraints in vertical agreements dealt with in this part (*i.e.* §§ 17-119—17-129) will concentrate on English common law. However, this is an area in which E.C. law and United Kingdom competition law are of equal if not greater importance and this body of law must also be considered when dealing with these types of restraint.[72] Agreements between a supplier of goods[73] and one to whom he supplies them may be described as "vertical" agreements. Such agreements can usefully be treated separately from agreements between suppliers *inter se* and acquirers *inter se*, which may be termed "horizontal" agreements. Although the doctrine of restraint of trade is capable of applying to vertical agreements, they are, for various reasons, less likely to be rendered unenforceable by the doctrine than are horizontal agreements. A further distinction[74-76] is perhaps to be drawn between

(a) restrictions which relate exclusively to the goods supplied under vertical agreements, *e.g.* that the goods shall not be resold for more or less than a certain price or to certain persons or classes of person or outside a certain area, and

(b) restrictions which relate to goods other than those supplied under the agreement, *e.g.* absolutely or conditionally that the seller shall not supply similar goods to others or that the buyer shall not acquire similar goods from others.

Agreements which contain restrictions relating only to the goods supplied thereunder may well fall outside the scope of the common law doctrine of restraint of trade since before making the agreement the person acquiring the goods had no right to deal with them at all and in making the agreement he therefore gave up no right but, rather, acquired a limited right.[77] The doctrine is certainly capable of applying to agreements which contain restrictions relating to goods other than those supplied under the agreement,[78] though it would seem that unless the agreement contains special, oppressive features, the doctrine will not be applied where the inclusion of such a restriction in such a transaction has gained general commercial acceptance[79] as perhaps, for example, where a wholesaler agrees to

---

[72] See Vol. II, § 42–079.

[73] As to certain special rules relating to patented articles, see *post*, § 17–129.

[74-76] *cf.* However, the E.C. Commission proposes to reform competition policy towards distribution agreements by introducing one broad umbrella Block Exemption Regulation applying to both goods and services with a market share threshold or thresholds and a black list of prohibited clauses: see the E.C. Commission "Communication on the application of the E.C. competition rules to vertical restraints" of September 30, 1988 and accompanying press release (IP/98/853). It is currently proposed that when the Competition Act 1998 comes into force on March 1, 2000, vertical agreements will be excluded from the "Chapter I prohibition" (the domestic analogue of Art. 81), see *post*, Vol. II, § 42–119. In any event, an agreement benefiting from an E.C. block exemption will automatically be exempt from the domestic prohibition: see s.10 of the 1998 Act (parallel exemptions). Many vertical agreements will have an anti-competitive effect and be caught by Art. 81: see Vol. II, § 42–101.

[77] *cf. Esso Petroleum Co. Ltd v. Harper's Garage (Stourport) Ltd* [1968] A.C. 269 (*post*, § 17–127), where such reasoning is applied in the case of restrictions relating to the use of land; and see *Elliman, Sons & Co. v. Carrington & Son Ltd* [1901] 2 Ch. 275; but contrast *British Motor Trade Association v. Gilbert* [1951] 2 All E.R. 641, where however the plaintiffs had not supplied the goods.

[78] See *Palmolive Co. (of England) Ltd v. Freedman* [1928] 2 Ch. 264.

[79] *Ante*, § 17–078.

purchase his requirements of a particular class of goods exclusively from a manufacturer.[80]

Exclusive purchasing[81]: solus petrol agreements. An important application **17-120** of the doctrine has been to solus petrol agreements, *i.e.* agreements between petrol companies and the operators of petrol filling stations under which the latter are bound to acquire all their requirements of petrol, whether for resale at a particular station[82] or generally, from the petrol company. So in *Esso Petroleum Co. Ltd v. Harper's Garage (Stourport) Ltd*[83] the defendants had undertaken to purchase from the plaintiffs for the following four years and five months the plaintiffs' petrol at wholesale schedule prices for all the requirements of a station which the defendants operated and, if they sold the station during that time, to procure the buyer to enter into a similar solus agreement with the plaintiffs; the defendants had further undertaken to keep the garage open at all reasonable hours. The evidence relating to the reasonableness or otherwise of the length of the tie was meagre but in the circumstances, and influenced perhaps by the report of the Monopolies Commission on the Supply of Petrol to Retailers in the United Kingdom,[84] the House of Lords held that the tie, being for less than five years, was reasonable and that the agreement should therefore be upheld. But in the same case the House of Lords held unenforceable restrictions of a similar nature contained in a mortgage relating to another station of the defendants, since the restrictions were for 21 years. This further illustrates that where a covenant in restraint of trade, which would be invalid if contained in a simple contract, is incorporated in a mortgage,[85] it does not thereby become enforceable, unless, as it was in the *Esso* case, the covenant is no more than reasonable to protect the mortgagee's interest in the value of the land as security for his loan.[86]

Reasonableness in circumstances. In determining whether a solus agreement **17-121** is enforceable or not, no simple rule can be applied since the court will have regard to all the terms of the agreement and the surrounding circumstances.[87] The

---

[80] *Esso Petroleum Co. Ltd v. Harper's Garage (Stourport) Ltd* [1968] A.C. 269, 328, 336, 963; *cf. Petrofina (Great Britain) Ltd v. Martin* [1966] 1 Ch. 146, 184–185. See also *A. Schroeder Music Publishing Co. Ltd v. Macaulay* [1974] 1 W.L.R. 1308 and *Clifford Davis Ltd v. W.E.A. Records Ltd* [1975] 1 W.L.R. 61.

[81] As to cases decided before 1967 relating to exclusive purchasing, see generally the cases referred to in *Esso Petroleum Co. Ltd v. Harper's Garage (Stourport) Ltd* [1968] A.C. 269. It is important to note that all exclusive purchasing agreements will be affected by the EEC Treaty, in particular Art. 85. See also the block exemption regulation which deals with solus petrol agreements: Commission Regulation 1984/83.

[82] As to where the station was owned by the petrol company when the agreement was made, see *post,* § 17–127.

[83] [1968] A.C. 269, and see (1966) 82 L.Q.R. 307: (1966) 29 M.L.R. 541; [1967] Camb.L.J. 104; *Texaco Ltd v. Mulberry Filling Station Ltd* [1972] 1 W.L.R. 814; *Amoco Australia Pty. Ltd v. Rocca Bros. Co. Engineering Pty. Ltd* [1975] A.C. 561; *Cleveland Petroleum Ltd v. Darstone Ltd* [1969] 1 W.L.R. 116.

[84] House of Commons Paper 1965 No. 264; see *post,* § 17–122.

[85] Restraints contained in mortgages may also be enforceable after redemption as invalid clogs on the equity of redemption: see Megarry and Wade, *The Law of Real Property* (5th ed.), pp. 965–973.

[86] [1968] A.C. 269 and see [1967] 2 Q.B. 514, 555, 578.

[87] *cf. post,* § 17–124, and *ante,* § 17–093.

importance of evaluating the restraint in the light of all the surrounding circumstances is illustrated by *Alec Lobb (Garages) Ltd v. Total Oil (Great Britain) Ltd*[88] in which the Court of Appeal upheld as reasonable a tie for 21 years. Previous to this it had been thought that, as a result of the *Esso* decision, a tie for longer than five years would not be valid unless perhaps the petrol company produced evidence of economic necessity justifying a longer period, something which the petrol company failed to do in *Alec Lobb*. In that case the plaintiff garage company, which was in financial difficulties, renegotiated its solus agreement with the defendant, its petrol supplier. The outcome was a lease and leaseback arrangement whereby the plaintiff company for a premium of £35,000 leased its garage to the defendant for 51 years at a peppercorn rent and the defendant leased it back for 21 years to the principal shareholders in the plaintiff company. The plaintiff company sought to have the lease set aside on a number of grounds, one of which was that the tie constituted an unreasonable restraint of trade. Despite the fact that the defendant produced no evidence of economic necessity, the Court of Appeal upheld the validity of the restraint. Dillon L.J. found that the company had as a matter of substance received £35,000 for the tie, something which was undoubtedly beneficial. In addition there were a number of other factors which rendered the tie unobjectionable:

    (a) for planning reasons the site could only be used as a garage and it made little difference to the public whether the petrol sold on it came from the defendant or some other company;

    (b) the plaintiff company could terminate the tie after seven years under a break clause;

    (c) the premises had been subject to a tie for four years before the 21-year tie had been entered into.

Dunn and Waller L.JJ. were also influenced by the fact that to uphold the validity of the tie would encourage the rescue of firms on the verge of bankruptcy. The implication of this is that the more perilous a firm's financial condition, the longer the tie that can be extracted as a price of rescue.

17–122   **Solus petrol agreements.**[89] Apart from the common law, all solus petrol agreements in the United Kingdom are now in practice substantially affected by the undertakings (which have been periodically altered) given by the petrol companies to the Secretary of State as a result of the Report of the Monopolies Commission on the Supply of Petrol to Retailers in the United Kingdom in 1965.[90] The Monopolies Commission's recommendations, the undertakings given to the Secretary of State and the explanatory notes issued by the Secretary of State can be obtained from the Office of Fair Trading.[91] The undertakings

---

[88] [1985] 1 W.L.R. 173 (noted (1985) 101 L.Q.R. 306).

[89] See Vol II, § 42–051—42–052.

[90] House of Commons Paper 1965 No. 264; Solus Petrol Order 1966 (S.I. 1966 No. 894) as amended by the Solus Petrol (Amendment) Order 1966 (S.I. 1966 No. 931) and Solus Petrol (No. 2) Order 1966 (S.I. 1966 No. 1314) have lapsed. See also *A Report on the Supply of Petrol in the United Kingdom by Wholesalers*, Cmnd. 7433 (1979); *Supply of Petrol*, Cm. 972 (1990). For the current position on undertakings see The Annual Report of the Director General of Fair Trading, 1994, p. 40 and "Competition in the supply of petrol in the U.K.", OFT, May 1998, § 4.4.

[91] *Undertakings Regarding Retail Petrol Suppliers in the United Kingdom Given in 1966 and Amended in 1968, 1976 and 1994*; see also previous footnote.

relate not only to the enforcement and determination of existing solus ties and the inclusion of solus ties in new agreements, but also to other terms of agreements between petrol companies and operators of petrol filling stations, including ties relating to lubricants and other goods sold by such stations, the making of certain commission and other arrangements, options and rights of pre-emption over petrol filling stations and the terms of leases and licences of company-owned filling stations. An exclusive supply obligation will usually fall within the prohibition in Article 81(1) of the E.C. Treaty but may benefit from the block exemption for such agreements set out in E.C. Regulation 1984/83.[92]

Tied public-houses.[93] Another and much older class of exclusive purchasing   **17–123**
agreements comprises agreements under which breweries lease or sell public-houses on the terms that the publican shall buy his beer exclusively from the brewery.[94] Such agreements have long been enforced at common law[95] and would seem still to lie outside the common law doctrine of restraint of trade, either because of the general commercial acceptance which they have long enjoyed[96] or because the publican accepts the restrictions under the very agreement by which he acquires his interest in the public-house.[97]

Implied obligations and limits to rights of supplier. In considering whether   **17–124**
an exclusive purchasing agreement is of a class which has gained general commercial acceptance and therefore falls outside the common law doctrine of restraint of trade,[98] or whether the agreement, though within the doctrine, is reasonable, it is probably relevant to consider the implied obligations of the supplier. Thus a covenant by a lessee of a public-house to take beer only from a particular brewery is subject to an implied condition that good and wholesome beer shall be supplied.[99] It has been said that this rule applies even though there is no specific agreement by the brewer to supply the publican with beer, apparently on the ground that the existence of the tying covenant amounts to an implied guarantee by the covenantee that he will at times supply liquor of good quality at reasonable prices in requisite quantities. An injunction against the publican will be granted only for so long a time as the brewers are prepared to supply him with beers of a reasonable quality at a reasonable price.[1]

---

[92] Commission Regulation 1984/83. See Vol. II, §§ 42–047—42–050.

[93] See Vol. II, §§ 42–046—42–053.

[94] Monopolies Commission, *Report on the Supply of Beer*, Cm. 651 (1989); Supply of Beer (Tied Estate) Order 1989 (S.I. 1989 No. 2390); Supply of Beer (Loan Ties, Licensed Premises and Wholesale Prices) Order 1989 (S.I. 1989 No. 2258); Supply of Beer (Tied Estate) (Amendment) Order 1997, S.I. 1997, No. 1740; these ties will be governed by E.C. law and subject to the block exemptions referred to in n. 74, *supra*. The E.C. Commission's proposals for reform of competition policy towards disribution agreements do not include the retention of sector-specific rules for the beer sector: see the E.C. Commission "Communication on the application of the E.C. competition rules to vertical restraints" of September 30, 1998, Section V(3).

[95] *Hartley v. Pehall* (1827) 1 Peake 178; *Catt v. Tourle* (1869) L.R. 4 Ch.App. 654; *Clegg v. Hands* (1890) 44 Ch.D. 503; *Esso Petroleum Co. Ltd v. Harper's Garage (Stourport) Ltd* [1968] A.C. 269 especially at 333, 334. See also *Cutsforth v. Mansfield Inns Ltd* [1986] 1 W.L.R. 536. But see *post*, § 17–124.

[96] See *ante*, § 17–078; and see *Esso Petroleum Co. Ltd v. Harper's Garage (Stourport) Ltd* [1968] A.C. 269.

[97] As to covenants contained in conveyances and leases generally, see *post*, § 17–127.

[98] *Thornton v. Sherratt* (1818) 8 Taunt. 529.

[99] *Courage & Co. v. Carpenter* [1910] 1 Ch. 262.

[1] *Catt v. Tourle* (1869) L.R. 4 Ch.App. 654.

17–125   **Exclusive selling agreements and co-operative marketing schemes.**[2] Subject to the consideration that it may be more onerous to require a buyer to take his whole supply from one source than to require a seller to sell his whole output to one buyer,[3] exclusive selling agreements are, it would seem, to be treated in the same way as exclusive buying agreements.[4] Thus an obligation imposed on a farmer to sell all his milk to an agricultural co-operative, with no power on the part of the farmer to terminate his obligation, has been held in restraint of trade and unreasonable[5] because in the circumstances it was an unusual and excessive fetter on the farmer's personal liberty.[6] Where such an obligation was imposed under a marketing scheme which had been accepted by the great majority of producers and contained no unusual features it was, in the circumstances, held to be reasonable and enforceable.[7]

(vi) *Restraints on the Use of Land or Chattels*

17–126   **Restraint affecting commercial use of land.** Where a restraint affecting the commercial use of land is accepted by one who enjoyed his interest in the land before the making of the arrangement under which the restraint was imposed, it is clearly established that the doctrine of restraint of trade applies to the same extent as it otherwise would.[8]

17–127   **Restraint contained in conveyance or lease.** There is authority for the proposition that where a restraint on the use of a particular piece of land, *e.g.* that the land shall not be used for the purposes of trade generally or of particular trades or that all the goods of some kind sold from the land shall be bought from a specified source, is imposed in a conveyance or lease of the land in question, the common law doctrine of restraint of trade does not apply. The purchaser or lessee of the land, before he made the agreement, had no right to use the land at all and in making the agreement he therefore gave up no right but, rather, acquired a limited right.[9] This reasoning is not, however, free from difficulty, as has been pointed out in § 17–078, *ante.*

17–128   **Restraint on use of chattels.** On similar reasoning, restraints on the use of a chattel which are imposed upon a party by the contract under which he acquires

---

[2] See Vol. II, § 40–118.

[3] *Esso Petroleum Co. Ltd v. Harper's Garage (Stourport) Ltd* [1968] A.C. 269, *per* Lord Reid at 298.

[4] See *ante*, §§ 17–120—17–123.

[5] *McEllistrim v. Ballymacelligott Co-operative Society Ltd* [1919] A.C. 548; *Joseph Evans & Co. Ltd v. Heathcote* [1918] 1 K.B. 418, where, however, since the association was a "trade union," the agreement fell within the Trade Union Acts 1871 and 1876 and was therefore sufficient to support an account stated, on which the plaintiffs were able to recover. See now *post*, § 17–129.

[6] See *Esso Petroleum Co. Ltd v. Harper's Garage (Stourport) Ltd* [1968] A.C. 269.

[7] *English Hop Growers Ltd v. Dering* [1928] 2 K.B. 174; *Esso Petroleum Co. Ltd v. Harper's Garage (Stourport) Ltd* [1968] A.C. 269.

[8] *Esso Petroleum Co. Ltd v. Harper's Garage (Stourport) Ltd* [1968] A.C. 269. Such agreements may also be subject to the Competition Act 1998 and Art. 85.

[9] *ibid.* at 298, 308, 309, 325; *cf. ibid.* at 316, 334–335. See also *Cleveland Petroleum Co. Ltd v. Dartstone Ltd* [1969] 1 W.L.R. 116; *Robinson v. Golden Chips (Wholesale) Ltd* [1971] N.Z.L.R. 257; *Amoco Australia Pty. Ltd v. Rocca Bros. Motor Engineering Pty. Ltd* [1975] A.C. 561; *Stephens v. Gulf Oil Canada Ltd* (1976) 110 D.L.R. (2d) 229.

the chattel may well fall outside the common law doctrine of restraint of trade.[10] Where the restraint relates to chattels not acquired under the contract which imposes the restraint, the doctrine ought in principle to apply. And while in *United Shoe Machinery Co. of Canada v. Bruner*[11] the Privy Council upheld a condition in a demise of machines that no other machines of a like kind should be used by the lessee during the continuance of the contract, the reasons given for the decision are unsatisfactory.[12]

Patented articles and patent licences. Section 44 of the Patents Act 1977 **17–129** contained provisions designed to prevent the owner of a patent or an interest in a patent using his patent to extend his patent monopoly beyond the terms of the patent, *e.g.* by requiring purchasers of the patented goods to acquire only from him or his nominees other goods or by prohibiting licensees of the patent from using articles, whether patented or not, which are not supplied by him or his nominees. Section 44 was repealed by Section 70 of the Competition Act 1998. The practices proscribed by section 44, and other terms in licences of intellectual property rights might be caught by Article 81(1) E.C. Treaty or the Chapter I prohibition in the Competition Act.[13] However, many such licences enjoy block exemption by virtue of Regulation 240/96 and would benefit from a so-called "parallel exemption" under domestic law.[14–17]

(vii) *Supply and Acquisition of Goods: Restraints in Horizontal Agreements*

Horizontal agreements classified. The treatment of restraints in horizontal **17–130** agreements dealt with in this part (*i.e.* §§ 17–130—17–132) will concentrate on English common law. However, this is an area in which E.C. law and United Kingdom competition law are of equal if not greater importance and this body of law must also be considered when dealing with these types of restraint.[18] The two most common classes of restrictive agreements between producers or suppliers of goods *inter se* are those between vendor and purchaser of a business under which the vendor accepts restrictions for the protection of the goodwill sold and agreements whereby two or more producers or suppliers accept restrictions as to the prices at which or terms on which they will sell, or as to the quantities or descriptions of goods they will produce or sell or as to the persons to whom or areas in which they will sell.[19] Agreements between vendors and purchasers have already been discussed[20]; where the restraint is reasonably required for the protection of the goodwill sold, the restrictive covenant is usually enforceable, otherwise not. Thus where, on "the sale of the goodwill of a licence" to make beer, which in fact the seller had never made, the seller undertook not to make beer for 15 years thereafter, the undertaking was held unenforceable as a bare covenant against competition.[21]

---

[10] See *ante*, § 17–119.

[11] [1909] A.C. 330. This type of arrangement would now be subject to Arts. 85 and 86 of the E.C. Treaty and in the light of the size of the fines exigible for breach of these articles, the common law has a very limited role to play in this area.

[12] *Esso Petroleum Co. Ltd v. Harper's Garage (Stourport) Ltd* [1968] A.C. 269, 297.

[13] See Vol. II, Chap. 42.

[14–17] See Vol. II, § 42–125.

[18] See Vol. II, §§ 42–015, 42–016 *et seq.*

[19] There are many horizontal agreements where the anti-competitive effect of the restrictions is outweighed by its beneficial effects on technical progress or improved distribution, for example, agreements providing for co-operation on research and development.

[20] *Ante*, §§ 17–114 *et seq.*

[21] *Vancouver Malt and Sake Brewing Co. v. Vancouver Breweries* [1934] A.C. 181. As to co-operative marketing schemes see *ante*, § 17–125.

17–131   **Employer's Association.** Section 128 of the Trade Union and Labour Relations (Consolidation) Act 1992 provides that the purpose of an unincorporated
employers' association and, in so far as they relate to the regulation of relations
between employers and workers or trade unions, the purposes of an employers'
association which is a body corporate, shall not, by reason only that they are in
restraint of trade, be unlawful so as, *inter alia*, to make any agreement or trust
void or voidable. This provision replaces earlier ones[22] and makes clear that such
an association is not illegal as it might otherwise be at common law. The
expression "employers' association" is defined by section 122 of the 1992 Act
to include any organisation (whether permanent or temporary) which consists
wholly or mainly of employers or individual proprietors of one or more descriptions and is an organisation whose principal purposes include the regulation of
relations between employers of that description or those descriptions and workers
or trade unions.[23] The principal purposes of such an organisation may also
include cartel purposes but, if they do so, then, applying the reasoning adopted
in *Faramus v. Film Artistes Association*,[24] it would seem that section 128 of the
1992 Act legalises only such agreements as are relevant or directed to the
purposes of the organisation by virtue of which the organisation is an employers'
association and not agreements which are relevant or directed only to other of the
organisation's purposes. The point, however, is academic since *cartel* agreements
fixing prices and quantities are never illegal at common law and therefore do not
require statutory legitimation. But where "legalised" either under section 128 of
the 1992 Act or at common law, such agreements are not thereby rendered
enforceable in the courts and are enforceable, if at all, only if they would be at
common law. However, section 128 of the 1992 Act further provides that no rule
of an unincorporated employers' association nor, in so far as it relates to the
regulation of relations between employers and workers or trade unions, any rule
of an employers' association which is a body corporate, shall be unlawful or
unenforceable by reason only that it is in restraint of trade. It would seem
therefore that *none* of the *rules* of an *unincorporated* cartel is affected by the
doctrine of restraint of trade, provided that the principal purposes of the cartel
include the regulation of labour relations.[25]

17–132   **Price-fixing agreements.** Agreements between suppliers of goods as to the
price at which they will sell their goods are subject to the common law doctrine
of restraint of trade. This matter would now in all likelihood be dealt with under
the Competition Act 1998 or Article 82; it is difficult to imagine parties wanting
to litigate about the validity at common law of a price-fixing arrangement.[26]

17–133   **Auction rings.** An agreement by which the parties agree not to bid against
each other at an auction and to divide the goods purchased, *i.e.* to establish a ring,

---

[22] See the Trade Union Acts 1871 to 1906, particularly ss.3 and 4 of the Trade Union Act 1871,
repeated and replaced by the Industrial Relations Act 1971, particularly ss.35 and 61; Trade Union
and Labour Relations Act 1974, s.3(5).

[23] See *Greig v. Insole* [1978] 1 W.L.R. 302, 356–362.

[24] [1964] A.C. 925.

[25] The validity of such rules may be affected by the Competition Act 1988 or by the E.C. Treaty.
See *ante*, §§ 17–120, 17–122; Vol. II, § 42–033, 42–095.

[26] For a common law example, see *Att.-Gen. of Commonwealth of Australia v. Adelaide Steamship
Co. Ltd* [1913] A.C. 781; and see *Cade & Sons Ltd v. Daly & Co. Ltd* [1910] 1 I.R. 306; contrast
Urmston v. Whitelegg Bros (1890) 63 L.T. 455 (10-year world-wide price-fixing cartel held unreason-
able). See further *ante*, §§ 17–119 *et seq.*

has been held valid at common law as neither fraudulent nor in restraint of trade[27] but if made by a dealer it is a criminal offence[28] and therefore unenforceable.

(viii) *Labour and Services: Restraints in Horizontal Agreements*[29]

Labour. Section 11 of the Trade Union and Labour Relations (Consolidation) **17–134** Act 1992 provides that the purposes of any trade union shall not, by reason only that they are in restraint of trade, be unlawful so as, *inter alia*, to make any agreement or trust void or voidable. This provision is intended to make clear that the purposes of such an association are not illegal (as they might be at common law), and it does not render agreements made by such an association enforceable[30]; whether the agreement is enforceable still depends on the application of the common law rules relating to restraint of trade discussed below. The expression "trade union" is defined by section 1 of the 1992 Act to include any organisation (whether permanent or temporary) which consists wholly or mainly of workers of one or more descriptions and is an organisation whose principal purposes include the regulation of relations between workers of the description or those descriptions and employers or employers' associations. The wording of section 11 of the Act makes it clear that *none* of the *rules* of trade unions is affected by the doctrine of restraint of trade.[31]

An agreement between traders to regulate the wages and hours of employment **17–135** of their workers for one year in accordance with the decision of the majority has been held to be against public policy and unenforceable at common law.[32] Similarly a rule of a trade protection society that no member should employ an employee who had left the service of another member without the consent in writing of his previous employer till after the expiration of two years was held invalid at common law.[33] Also, an arrangement between the organisers of a professional sport which restricts the way in which the participants in that sport may earn their livelihood may be invalidated if it constitutes an unreasonable restraint.[34] Indeed the validity of a contract of that nature may have to be judged by the same strict standards as would an individual covenant by an employee with his employer directed to the same end[35]; moreover while there may be very good reasons for the agreement from the employer's point of view, it may be against the public interest to interfere in such a way with the freedom of

---

[27] *Rawlings v. General Trading Co.* [1921] 1 K.B. 635; and see *Cohen v. Roche* [1927] 1 K.B. 169.

[28] The Auctions (Bidding Agreements) Act 1927, s.1 as amended by the Auctions (Bidding Agreements) Act 1969, ss.1, 2 and the Criminal Law Act 1977, Sched. 13; s.3 of the 1969 Act entitles the vendor to avoid the contract of sale or alternatively to recover damages.

[29] As to restrictions imposed by an employer on his employees, see *ante*, §§ 17–101—17–113.

[30] See *ante*, § 17–131.

[31] This was designed to nullify the effect of *Edwards v. Society of Graphic and Allied Trades* [1971] Ch. 365. See also *Greig v. Insole* [1978] 1 W.L.R. 302, 365; *Associated Newspaper Group Ltd v. Wade* [1979] 1 W.L.R. 697, 710 (restraint of trade does not mean interference with business).

[32] *Hilton v. Eckersley* (1856) 6 E. & B. 47; and see *Mogul Steamship Co. v. McGregor, Gow & Co.* [1892] A.C. 25, 42; (1889) 23 Q.B.D. 598, 619.

[33] *Mineral Water Bottle, etc., Society v. Booth* (1887) 36 Ch.D. 465 (the members of the association could protect any confidential information); *Davies v. Thomas* [1920] 2 Ch. 189, 195.

[34] *Eastham v. Newcastle United F.C. Ltd* [1964] Ch. 413; *Greig v. Insole* [1978] 1 W.L.R. 302; *Buckley v. Tuttey* (1971) 125 C.L.R. 353.

[35] *Kores Manufacturing Co. Ltd v. Kolok Manufacturing Co. Ltd* [1959] Ch. 108. See also *ante*, § 17–101.

employees.[36] An employee who is injured by the operation of such an agreement between employers or by rules to such an effect of an association of employers, whether or not the terms of that agreement or of those rules are incorporated into the employee's contract of employment, may be granted a declaration against the employers or their association that the agreement or rules, as the case may be, are in unreasonable restraint of trade and therefore unenforceable,[37] and perhaps an injunction restraining the parties enforcing or purporting to enforce them.[38]

17–136   **Supply of services: common law.** Restrictive agreements relating to the supply of services are at common law subject to the doctrine of restraint of trade[39] upon the same principles as are restrictive agreements relating to the supply of goods.[40] Thus where a group of master stevedores agreed to divide among themselves the work at a particular port, it was held that a provision that a member who on the request of a customer did work which was allotted to another member should pay that other member an equivalent was valid at common law, but not a provision which in certain circumstances prevented a particular job from being accepted by any member.[41] Such an agreement would also infringe Article 85 of the E.C. Treaty.

17–137   **Supply of professional services.** The regulation of professional services is as much subject to the common law doctrine of restraint of trade[42] as the regulation of other services,[43] at any rate where the profession engages in trade.[44] Public policy may invalidate rules of a body such as the Stewards of the Jockey Club which prevent a class of people, such as women, from exercising a calling over which the body has control[45] or rules of professional conduct laid down for a profession whether or not those rules are intended to be binding.[46]

17–138   **Supply of labour: common law.** Agreements between workers binding them to regulate their work in accordance with the decision of some outside body or otherwise curtailing the free right to dispose of labour are at common law subject to the doctrine of restraint of trade[47] upon the same principles as agreements between employers to regulate the acquisition of labour.[48] Such contracts have

---

[36] *Esso Petroleum Co. Ltd v. Harper's Garage (Stourport) Ltd* [1968] A.C. 269, 300, 301.

[37] *Eastham v. Newcastle United F.C. Ltd* [1964] Ch. 413; *Cooke v. Football Association* [1972] C.L.Y. 516; *Greig v. Insole* [1978] 1 W.L.R. 302.

[38] See *Nagle v. Feilden* [1966] 2 Q.B. 633. See also *Cooke v. Football Association* [1972] C.L.Y. 516 where a claim for damages for loss of wages was rejected as having no ground in contract or tort.

[39] *Collins v. Locke* (1879) 4 App.Cas. 674; *Budget Rent-a-Car International Inc. v. Mamos Slough Ltd* (1977) 121 S.J. 374.

[40] See *ante*, § 17–132.

[41] *Collins v. Locke, supra.*

[42] See *post*, § 17–139 for statutory provisions.

[43] *Dickson v. Pharmaceutical Society of Great Britain* [1970] A.C. 403.

[44] *ibid.* at 455 but it is to be noted that the traditional categories of covenant in restraint of trade include covenants by doctors, dentists, solicitors, etc., who probably do not engage in trade.

[45] *Nagle v. Feilden* [1966] 2 Q.B. 633.

[46] *Dickson v. Pharmaceutical Society of Great Britain* [1970] A.C. 403. The professional services sector is mainly controlled under the Fair Trading Act 1973.

[47] *Hornby v. Close* (1867) L.R. 2 Q.B. 153; *Mogul Steamship Co. Ltd v. McGregor, Gow & Co.* [1892] A.C. 25, 59, 60; *Cullen v. Elwin* (1904) 90 L.T. 840; *Boddington v. Lawton The Times,* February 4, 1994.

[48] See *ante*, § 17–134.

generally been held to be in unreasonable restraint of trade and therefore unenforceable at common law.[49] Where a union's rules impose unjustifiable restraints on members, others of its rules, *e.g.* for the payment to members of superannuation benefits, have been held also to be unenforceable.[50] Where the rules of a union imposed no restrictive obligations on the members, a rule which provided for the payment of strike pay to those who took part in an authorised strike was held to be enforceable at common law as no more than an insurance of the members against the consequences of a strike.[51]

(ix) *Invalidating and Regulatory Statutory Provisions*

Restrictive trade practices, (goods and services) monopolies. Many prac- **17–139** tices which are in restraint of trade, or which are designed to stifle competition, are dealt with by specific statutes. The legislation cover, *inter alia*, restrictive trading agreements relating to goods and services, restrictive labour practices, resale price maintenance and the anti-competitive impact of monopolies. These statutory controls are dealt with in Vol. II, Chapter 41.

3. CONTRACTS UNENFORCEABLE BY STATUTE

(a) *General Principles*

Unenforceability by statute and common law distinguished. The illegality **17–140** which renders a contract unenforceable at common law may arise by statute.[52] Unenforceability by statute, on the other hand, arises where a statute itself on its true construction deprives one or both of the parties of their civil remedies under the contract in addition to, or instead of, imposing a penalty upon them. If the statute does so, it is irrelevant whether the parties meant to break the law or not. A significant distinction between cases of contracts which are unenforceable at common law because they were entered into with the object of committing an act illegal by statute and of contracts which are rendered illegal by statute is that in the former case one has to look to see what acts the statute prohibits; it does not matter whether or not it prohibits a contract; if a contract is deliberately made to do a prohibited act that contract will be unenforceable. In the latter case one has to consider, not what acts the statute prohibits, but what contracts it prohibits; but one is not concerned at all with the intent of the parties[53]; if the parties enter into

[49] *Russell v. Amalgamated Society of Carpenters and Joiners* [1912] A.C. 421; and see Citrine's *Trade Union Law* (3rd ed.), pp. 44–45; Grunfeld, *Modern Trade Union Law* (1966), pp. 64–71; *Boddington v. Lawton* [1994] I.C.R. 478.
[50] *Miller v. Amalgamated Engineering Union* [1938] Ch. 669.
[51] *Gozney v. Bristol Trade and Provident Society* [1909] 1 K.B. 901.
[52] See *ante*, § 17–005.
[53] But the parties' knowledge may not be entirely irrelevant, since only one party may be expressly penalised by the statute and therefore the statute will normally deprive only him of his civil rights under it (see *post*, § 17–152). But if the other has knowledge of the illegality he may become an aider and abettor and accordingly find himself penalised and disabled from suing on the contract: *Archbolds (Freightage) Ltd v. S. Spanglett Ltd* [1961] 1 Q.B. 374, 385, 393; *Ashmore, Benson, Pease & Co. Ltd v. A. V. Dawson Ltd* [1973] 1 W.L.R. 828.

a prohibited contract that contract is unenforceable[54] and ignorance by the parties of the law does not make it the less so.[55]

17-141   **The distinction illustrated.** The distinction between contracts prohibited by statute and those prohibited at common law is well brought out in *Dungate v. Lee*,[56] where the existence of a partnership of a betting office was called in issue. One of the parties denied the existence of the partnership, contending that the bookmaker's permit required by statute was held by him alone and that any partnership would have been contrary to the provisions of the Betting and Gaming Act 1960. It was held that even if, in the course of the partnership, the unlicensed partner committed offences against the Act, the Act did not render the partnership itself illegal as all it required was that one partner be suitably qualified. Nor was the partnership agreement illegal at common law since it did not, by its terms, require the unlicensed partner to act illegally as a bookmaker in the conduct of the business and it was not entered into with an intention on the part of the partners that the unlicensed partner should so act.

17-142   **Express voidness by statute.** Statutes often provide expressly for the civil consequences of breach of their provisions and this is by far the preferable solution.[57] A contract may, by statute, be void without being illegal, the only penalty being that a contract made in contravention of the statute is entirely ineffective to create rights, as in the case of a contract made in contravention of the Gaming Acts 1845 and 1892; or again a contract may be unenforceable without being either illegal or void, in which case it is effective to alter the rights of the parties, although the altered rights are not enforceable by them.[58] However, if a contract is illegal, the effect is "to avoid the contract *ab initio* . . . if the making of the contract is expressly or impliedly prohibited by statute . . . ."[59]

17-143   **Statute expressly not affecting validity.** A statutory prohibition to which a criminal sanction is attached may also provide that it does not render any contract entered into in breach of its terms void or unenforceable.[60] Whether such a provision has no effect whatsoever on the parties' contractual rights and obligations will depend upon the language used and the statutory purpose underlying the legislation. Thus, although the statute may provide that breach of its prohibition does not render a contract void or unenforceable, the court may nevertheless refuse to enforce the contract because this would be assisting in the furtherance of something that is illegal.[61]

---

[54] See *St. John Shipping Corporation v. Joseph Rank Ltd* [1957] 1 Q.B. 267, 283. In any given situation it may not be easy to determine whether a statute prohibits acts as opposed to contracts.

[55] *Kiriri Cotton Co. Ltd v. Dewani* [1960] A.C. 192.

[56] [1969] 1 Ch. 545; *cf. Langton v. Hughes* (1813) 1 M. & S. 593.

[57] See, *e.g.* Trade Descriptions Act 1968, s.35; Fair Trading Act 1973, s.26.

[58] *Eastern Distributors v. Goldring* [1957] 2 Q.B. 600, 614.

[59] *per* Devlin J., *Archbolds (Freightage) Ltd v. Spanglett Ltd* [1961] 1 QB 374, 388. See also *D. R. Insurance Co. v. Central National Insurance Co. of Omaha* [1996] C.L.C. 64, 68; *Royal Boskalis Westminster NV v. Mountain* [1997] C.L.C. 816.

[60] This was the language used in s.8(3) of the Companies Securities (Insider Dealing) Act 1985 which has now been repealed but it is repeated in the replacement legislation: see Criminal Justice Act 1993, s.63(2).

[61] *Chase Manhattan Equities Ltd v. Goodman* [1991] B.C.L.C. 897, 931–934. See also Vol. II, Chap. 39; *S.C.F. Finance Co. Ltd v. Masri (No. 2)* [1987] Q.B. 1002, 1026.

Statute silent as to civil rights. But where the statute is silent as to the civil rights of the parties but penalises the making or performance of the contract, the courts consider whether the Act, on its true construction,[62] is intended to avoid contracts of the class to which the particular contract belongs or whether it merely prohibits the doing of some particular act.[63] In the following paragraphs certain tests which have been applied by the courts are considered. However, it is important to note that where a contract or its performance is implicated with breach of a statute this does not entail that the contract is avoided. Where the Act does not expressly deprive the plaintiff of his civil remedies under the contract the appropriate question to ask is whether, having regard to the Act and the evils against which it was intended to guard and the circumstances in which the contract was made and to be performed, it would in fact be against public policy to enforce it.[64] **17–144**

Aids to statutory interpretation. (1) Where a statute imposes a penalty on one or both of the parties to a contract, as a result of their entering into the contract or of their manner of performing it, the court will consider whether on the construction and purpose of the statute the doing of the particular act is forbidden as illegal or whether there is merely a charge imposed upon it. If the latter, it is clear that the contract itself is not prohibited. Thus where a tobacco manufacturer sued for the price of tobacco he had sold to the defendant, the fact that he was not licensed to sell tobacco and that his name was not painted on his place of business as required by statute did not prevent him from recovering since there was nothing in the Act to prohibit every sale and its only effect was to impose a penalty for the purpose of the Revenue, on the carrying on of the trade without complying with its requirements.[65] If, on the true construction of the statute, "*the contract* be rendered illegal, it can make no difference, in point of law, whether the statute which makes it so has in mind the protection of the revenue or any other object. The sole question is whether the statute *means to prohibit the contract.*"[66] If, on the other hand, the object of the statute is the protection of the public from possible injury[67] or fraud, or is the promotion of some object of public policy, the inference is that contracts made in contravention of its provisions are prohibited.[68] Thus where by statute it was not lawful "to sell, or to supply . . . a motor-vehicle . . . for delivery in such a condition that the use thereof on a road in that condition would be unlawful. . . . " such a sale was held **17–145**

---

[62] The natural meaning of a penal statute is not to be extended by reasoning based on the substance of the transaction under scrutiny: *Re H.P.C. Productions Ltd* [1962] Ch. 466.

[63] See *Archbolds (Freightage) Ltd v. S. Spanglett Ltd* [1961] 1 Q.B. 374, 389–390.

[64] *Shaw v. Groom* [1970] 2 Q.B. 504; *Ailion v. Spiekermann* [1976] Ch. 158; *Geismar v. Sun Alliance and London Insurance Ltd* [1978] Q.B. 383.

[65] *Smith v. Mawhood* (1845) 14 M. & W. 452; *Johnson v. Hudson* (1809) 11 East 180.

[66] *Cope v. Rowlands* (1836) 2 M. & W. 149, 157; *Smith v. Mawhood* (1845) 14 M. & W. 452, 463; and see *Vita Food Products Inc. v. Unus Shipping Co. Ltd* [1939] A.C. 277, 293; *Yin v. Sam* [1962] A.C. 304. See *post*, §§ 17–148, 17–153, 17–158 as to the extent of the unenforceability of the contract.

[67] *Vinall v. Howard* [1953] 1 W.L.R. 987, see *infra*, n. 50. And see Road Traffic Act 1988, s.18(4) and Sched. 1, which makes it an offence to sell motor-cyclists' protective helmets which do not comply with specifications. Such statutes sometimes create statutory duties enforceable at the suit of the injured party, *e.g.* see Consumer Protection Act 1987 and regulations made thereunder: Vol. II, § 38–400.

[68] *Victorian Daylesford Syndicate Ltd v. Dott* [1905] 2 Ch. 624; *Little v. Poole* (1829) 9 B. & C. 192; *Cope v. Rowlands* (1836) 2 M. & W. 149; *Taylor v. Crowland Gas & Coke Co.* (1854) 10 Exch. 293. See, however, *St. John Shipping Corporation v. Joseph Rank Ltd* [1957] 1 Q.B. 267.

illegal and a cheque given for the price could not be sued on.[69] Similarly, it was by statute illegal to contract as a moneylender without registration; accordingly a moneylender's failure to register invalidated contracts made and securities taken by him the course of his business, since the whole purpose of the Act was the protection of the public.[70] It has also been suggested[71] that "not a bad test to apply is to see whether the penalty in the Act is imposed once for all, or whether it is a recurrent penalty imposed as often as the act is done. If it be the latter, then the act is a prohibited act."

17–146   (2) The courts have also been reluctant to find contracts unenforceable because the illegality doctrine operates in an all or nothing way and there is no proportionality between the loss ensuing from non-enforcement and the breach of statute. This is to be contrasted with fines for criminal acts where some proportionality does pertain. This aspect of the matter caused concern to Devlin J. in *St. John Shipping Corp. v. Joseph Rank Ltd.*[72] In that case the illegality involved the plaintiff overloading its ship and the defendants wished to hold back merely that portion of the freight which was earned by the overloading. But as Devlin J. pointed out the principle of illegality "cares not at all for the element of deliberation, or for the gravity of the infraction, and *does not adjust the penalty to the profits unjustifiably earned.*"[73] Thus, were the doctrine to have applied in that case, it would have entitled the defendants to hold back the full freight which was 40 times the maximum fine for the offence of overloading.[74] Coupled with this, non-enforcement may have the effect of punishing the offender twice where the statute contains its own penalty for breach.

     (3) The courts have also been sensitive to the fact that non-enforcement may also result in unjust enrichment to the party to the contract who has not performed his part of the bargain but who has benefited from the performance by the other party. As was stated by Devlin J., in the *St. John Shipping* case, non-enforcement of the contract may result in the forfeiting of a sum which "will not go into the public purse but into the pockets of someone who is lucky enough to pick up the windfall or astute enough to have contrived to get it."[75]

---

[69] *Vinall v. Howard* [1953] 1 W.L.R. 987, applying Road Traffic Act 1934, s.8 (revd. on the facts [1954] 1 Q.B. 375); by s.75(7) of the Road Traffic Act 1988 it is now expressly provided that the statutory prohibition of the sale of unroadworthy vehicles contained in that section shall not affect the validity of contracts or rights arising under contracts.

[70] *Victorian Daylesford Syndicate Ltd v. Dott* [1905] 2 Ch. 624. See now the Consumer Credit Act 1974, ss.21, 40(1) and Pt. III (as amended): *Menaka v. Lum Kum Chum* [1977] 1 W.L.R. 267. It may be, however, that even though the statute is designed to protect the public, precluding a member of the public from being able to sue on it will cause him prejudice. This was the essence of the problem in the reinsurance cases: see *Bedford Insurance Co. Ltd v. Instituto de Resseguros do Brasil* [1985] Q.B. 966; *Stewart v. Oriental Fire and Marine Ins. Co. Ltd* [1985] 1 Q.B. 988; *Phoenix General Insurance Co. of Greece SA v. Administration Asigurarilor, etc.* [1988] Q.B. 216. It is submitted that the proper policy is to allow the contract to be enforced by the innocent party: see now Financial Services Act 1986, s.132. *Deutsche Ruckversicherung AG v. Walbrook Insurance Co. Ltd* [1996] 1 W.L.R. 1152. Section 132 has been held to be retrospective: see *Bates v. Robert Barrow Ltd* [1995] C.L.C. 207. It is submitted that this is to be preferred to the opposite conclusion in *D. R. Insurance Co. v. Seguros American Banamex* [1993] 1 Lloyd's Rep. 120 which was not followed in the *Bates* decision.

[71] *Victorian Daylesford Syndicate Ltd v. Dott* [1905] 2 Ch. 624, 630.

[72] [1957] 1 Q.B. 267.

[73] *ibid.* at 281 (emphasis added). *cf. Archer v. Brown* [1985] Q.B. 401, 423 F–H.

[74] Treitel, "Contract and Crime" in Tapper (ed.), *Crime, Proof and Punishment*, p. 95.

[75] [1957] 1 Q.B. 267, 288.

(4) The courts have also appreciated that the growth in statutory law (including delegated legislation) can result in the unwitting and quite innocent breach of the statute. In *Shaw v. Groom*[76] the court held that failure to comply with the provision of the Rent Act requiring a landlord to provide a tenant with a rent book did not result in the landlord being unable to obtain the payment of rental arrears. One of the factors obviously influencing the court in reaching this conclusion was the growth in the volume of legislation which could easily result in the innocent transgression of some statutory prohibition.[77]

(5) Although the courts have recognised "the desirability of (their) . . . assisting to enforce a statute,"[78] the consequence of this in driving from the seat of judgment sometimes innocent supplicants has also to be weighed in the balance.[79]

None of the above factors constitutes a litmus test which produces foreordained results. Obviously it would be preferable if the legislature were specifically to provide for the consequences of breach of the statute. Experience indicates that such legislative foresight is not always displayed, and where it is not the court must answer the question: does the "ambit and intent of the particular statute in the light of any other legislation affecting the subject matter . . . preclude the plaintiff recovering on the contract if he had committed the offence?"[80]

Illegality through manner of performance. The question of statutory   **17–147**
illegality in a contract generally arises in connection with its formation, but it may also arise in connection with its performance,[81] since the effect of the statute may be to deprive one or both parties of their rights unless the contract is performed in a particular manner, or, to put the matter another way, the manner in which a contract is performed may turn it into the sort of contract that is prohibited by statute.[82] Thus, the seller of agricultural fertiliser, who omitted to give to the purchaser an invoice showing the composition of the fertiliser, was held unable to recover its price since the seller had not performed the contract in the only way in which the statute allowed it to be performed.[83] In another case[84] statutory regulations required that the seller of utility goods should furnish to the buyer an invoice containing certain particulars. The plaintiff made a contract of sale for non-utility goods, to which the regulations did not apply; but he purported to perform it by delivering to the buyer, without objection, utility

---

[76] [1970] 2 Q.B. 504. *cf. Anderson Ltd v. Daniel* [1924] 1 K.B. 138.

[77] [1970] 2 Q.B. 504, 521–522.

[78] *ibid.* at 521.

[79] *St. John Shipping Corpn. v. Joseph Rank Ltd* [1957] 1 Q.B. 267, 288.

[80] *Shaw v. Groom* [1970] 2 Q.B. 504, 520, *per* Sachs L.J.; see also Harman L.J., at 516. See also *Yango Pastoral Co. Ltd v. First Chicago Australia Ltd* (1978) 139 C.L.R. 410; *Fire and All Risk Ins. v. Powell* [1966] V.R. 513; *Pavey & Mathews Pty. Ltd v. Paul* (1986–87) 162 C.L.R. 221 (allowing a *quantum meruit* claim by a builder with respect to work performed under an oral contract which by statute was made unenforceable by the builder unless it was in writing). See the very helpful guidance for determining whether breach of the statute renders a contract illegal and unenforceable: *Nelson v. Nelson* (1995) 132 A.L.R. 133, 192–193.

[81] *Anderson Ltd v. Daniel* [1924] 1 K.B. 138, 149; *Ashmore, Benson Pease & Co. Ltd v. A. V. Dawson Ltd* [1973] 1 W.L.R. 828.

[82] *St. John Shipping Corporation v. Joseph Rank Ltd* [1957] 1 Q.B. 267, 284.

[83] *Anderson Ltd v. Daniel* [1924] 1 K.B. 138; overruled by the Fertilisers and Feeding Stuffs Act 1926, s.1(2); *Marles v. Philip Trant & Sons Ltd* [1954] 1 Q.B. 29, but see now Agriculture (Miscellaneous Provisions) Act 1954, s.12(1).

[84] *B. & B. Viennese Fashions v. Losane* [1952] 1 All E.R. 909.

garments to which the regulations did apply; and he did not furnish the invoice. The Court of Appeal held that this contract was no less unenforceable than would have been a contract the initial terms of which provided for the sale of utility garments, and which could only have been lawfully performed by the delivery of the requisite invoice.

17–148   **Unlicensed transactions.** Where a statute or statutory instrument prohibits the doing of work otherwise than under a licence,[85] a contract under which unlicensed work is carried out will generally be unenforceable.[86] If there is in existence some licence, the illegality only extends to the excess by which the work exceeds the amount of the licence, unless there is an unseverable agreement to exceed the amount licensed.[87]

17–149   **Unlicensed consumer credit business.** Contracts made in contravention of the licensing provisions of the Moneylenders Acts were illegal and would not be enforced.[88] The latter are now being replaced by the Consumer Credit Act 1974, under section 40(1) of which a regulated agreement with a person who carries on consumer credit business while unlicensed is not illegal but is unenforceable against the debtor unless the Director General of Fair Trading orders otherwise.

17–150   **Omission to register according to statute.** Where a statute imposes an obligation to register contracts of a particular kind and provides penalties for failure to register, the non-registration of such a contract has been held not to render the contract itself unenforceable.[89] Such contracts may be expressly avoided by the statute. Thus, the Companies Act 1985[90] expressly avoids as against the liquidator and any creditor of a limited company mortgages and charges created by the company which have not been registered in accordance with the provisions of the Act.[91]

17–151   **Illegal performance of legal contracts.** The cases cited above might appear to support the proposition that an initially legal contract will be unenforceable on the basis that an illegality was committed in its performance. There is authority that in fact they were decided "on the narrower basis that the way in which the contract was performed turned it into the sort of contract that was prohibited by statute."[92] This would also be in keeping with the general principle that the mere fact that there is an illegality associated with the performance of the contract[93]

---

[85] *cf. Re Mahmoud and Ispahani* [1921] 2 K.B. 716, see *post*, § 17–153 (licence necessary for formation of contract).

[86] *Bostel Brothers Ltd v. Hurlock* [1949] 1 K.B. 74; *Jackson Stansfield & Sons v. Butterworth* [1948] 2 All E.R. 558; *Woolfe v. Wexler* [1951] 2 K.B. 154; *Howell v. Falmouth Boat Construction Co. Ltd* [1951] A.C. 837; *Smith & Son (Bognor Regis) Ltd v. Walker* [1952] 2 Q.B. 319; *Young v. Buckles* [1952] 1 K.B. 220.

[87] *Dennis & Co. Ltd v. Munn* [1949] 2 K.B. 327; *Frank W. Clifford Ltd v. Garth* [1956] 1 W.L.R. 570. See also *post*, § 17–186.

[88] See Vol. II, § 43–015.

[89] *Wright v. Horton* (1887) 12 App.Cas. 371; but see now n. 90, *post*, and text thereto.

[90] s.395(1). See *ante*, § 9–044.

[91] As to the effects of failure to furnish particulars of agreements which are subject to registration under the Competition Act 1998, see §§ 42–121, 42–127.

[92] *St. John Shipping Corporation v. Joseph Rank Ltd* [1957] 1 Q.B. 267, 284.

[93] *Coral Leisure Group Ltd v. Barnett* [1981] I.C.R. 503, 508; see also *ante*, § 17–144.

does not render it illegal and unenforceable. Thus in *St. John Shipping Corporation v. Joseph Rank Ltd*[94] cargo owners resisted a claim for freight on the ground that the carriers had so overloaded their ship with the cargo in respect of which the freight was claimed as to submerge the ship below the load line. Devlin J. held that although this amounted to a statutory offence, the legality of the contract was unaffected, since the statute in question was to be construed as prohibiting merely the act and not the contract under which it was done.

Statute: one party only affected. Statutes which prohibit certain contracts   **17–152** often impliedly recognise, for example by punishing only one of the parties, that the parties are not equally at fault, and therefore on their true construction only one of the parties to the contract is prevented from suing upon it. Accordingly, when

> "the policy of the Act in question is to protect the general public or class of persons by requiring that a contract shall be accompanied by certain formalities or conditions, and a penalty is imposed on the person omitting those formalities or conditions, the contract and its performance without those formalities or conditions is illegal, and cannot be sued upon by the person liable to the penalties."[95]

The other party to the contract is not deprived of his civil remedies because of the criminal default of the guilty party.[96]

Statute affecting both parties. In certain cases a statute may be construed to   **17–153** prohibit both parties from suing on a contract of the sort in question, *e.g.* since it makes them both guilty of a criminal offence in entering into the contract. In such cases, no matter how much more culpable one party is than the other, both are equally unable to sue upon the contract; and this is so even though the party who seeks to sue on the contract was at the time it was made ignorant of the facts which brought the contract within the statutory prohibition.[97] Thus in *Re Mahmoud and Ispahani*[98] the plaintiff agreed to sell and the defendant to buy 150 tons of linseed oil. By a statutory order then in force it was illegal "to buy or sell or otherwise deal in" linseed oil unless both parties had a licence. The defendant did not have a licence. Irrespective of the parties' state of knowledge about the existence of licences the contract was illegal and unenforceable by either, since both were prohibited from making it and the prohibition was for the benefit of the public.[99] Since in this case the plaintiff had a licence and had been told by the defendant, albeit falsely, that he also had one, the plaintiff's failure to recover on

---

[94] [1959] 1 Q.B. 267; and see *Dungate v. Lee* [1969] 1 Ch. 545; *Shaw v. Groom* [1970] 2 Q.B. 504.

[95] *Anderson v. Daniel* [1924] 1 K.B. 138, 147.

[96] *Marles v. Philip Trant & Sons Ltd* [1953] 1 All E.R. 645 (there was no appeal from this party of Lynskey J.'s judgment with which Denning L.J. expressed his agreement [1954] 1 Q.B. 29, 36); *Ailion v. Spiekermann* [1976] Ch. 158; see also cases on reinsurance cited in n. 70 to § 17–145, *ante*.

[97] *Re Mahmoud and Ispahani* [1921] 2 K.B. 716. See also *Wilson, Smithett & Cope Ltd v. Terruzzi* [1976] Q.B. 683; *United City Merchants (Investments) Ltd v. Royal Bank of Canada* [1983] A.C. 168, 188–190; *ante*, § 17–031, n. 56 for the effect of the Bretton Woods Agreement Act 1945 upon "exchange contracts."

[98] [1921] 2 K.B. 716.

[99] *ibid.* at 729. At 730 Scrutton L.J. left open the question of whether the plaintiff would have had a remedy for deceit: on this, see *post*, § 17–168.

the contract may seem rather inequitable. Similarly in *Yin v. Sam*,[1] Malayan Rubber Regulations provided that "no person shall purchase ... rubber ... unless he shall have been duly licensed ... " A sold rubber to B, who, unknown to A, did not hold a licence. The Privy Council, purporting to apply *Re Mahmoud and Ispahani*,[2] held that A could not recover the price. But the decision is to be questioned since, whereas in *Re Mahmoud and Ispahani*[3] the regulations made it illegal "to buy or sell," in *Yin v. Sam*[4] the regulations apparently made it an offence only "to buy"; A was therefore not the subject of a direct statutory prohibition[5] nor himself guilty of a criminal offence[6] and ought therefore not to have been held to be statutorily deprived of his rights; nor should he have been barred at common law since he had no knowledge that the performance of the contract would necessarily involve the commission of a criminal offence by B.[7] It is not possible, however, to go so far as to state that an innocent party to a contract rendered illegal by statute will invariably be entitled to enforce the contract.[7a]

17-154   **Alternative cause of action.** Even where a statute deprives a party of a civil remedy under a contract, he may, if in fact innocent of turpitude, be able to sue upon a collateral warranty or implied term that the requirements of the law had been complied with, or for the deceit, or perhaps the negligence, of the other in misrepresenting that fact. This will be dealt with in § 17–168.

17-155   **Alteration of law pending action.** Where the law is altered by statute while an action is pending, the rights of the parties will be decided according to the law as it existed at the time the action was commenced, unless the statute shows a clear intention to vary such rights by making its action retrospective.[8]

(b) *Statutory Regulation of Trading with the Enemy*

17-156   **Trading with the Enemy Act 1939.** Trading with the enemy is regulated and prohibited by the Trading with the Enemy Act 1939. By section 1 of the Act,[9] a person trading with or attempting to trade with the enemy is liable to a fine or

---

[1] [1962] A.C. 304.

[2] *Supra.*

[3] *ibid.*

[4] *Supra.*

[5] *cf. Re Mahmoud and Ispahani* [1921] 2 K.B. 716, 731–732 where Atkin L.J. expressed the view that a direct statutory prohibition sufficed even if the party prohibited could not be prosecuted because he lacked *mens rea.*

[6] See *Sayce v. Coupe* [1953] 1 Q.B. 1.

[7] See *Archbolds (Freightage) Ltd v. S. Spanglett Ltd* [1961] 1 Q.B. 374 (*ante*, § 17–168), which was not cited.

[7a] *Phoenix General Insurance Co. of Greece SA v. Halvanon Insurance Co. Ltd* [1988] Q.B. 216, "Illegal Transactions: The Effect of Illegality On Contracts And Torts" (Law Com., Consultation Paper No. 154, 1999).

[8] *Hitchcock v. Way* (1837) 6 A. & E. 943; *Lauri v. Renard* [1892] 3 Ch. 402, 421; *Re Athlumney* [1898] 2 Q.B. 547, 551; *Beadling v. Goll* (1922) 39 T.L.R. 128; *Ward v. British Oak Insurance Co. Ltd* [1932] 1 K.B. 392, 397; *Croxford v. Universal Insurance Co. Ltd* [1936] 2 K.B. 253; *Re Nautilus Shipping Co. Ltd* [1936] Ch. 17, 28; *Craxfords (Ramsgate) Ltd v. Williams and Steer Manufacturing Co. Ltd* [1954] 1 W.L.R. 1130; and see *York Estates v. Wareham*, 1950 (1) S.A. 125.

[9] As amended by the Emergency Laws (Miscellaneous Provisions) Act 1953, s.2 and Sched. II, para. 2.

imprisonment. By section 1(2), a person shall be deemed to have traded with the enemy:

> "(a) if he has had any commercial, financial or other intercourse with or of the benefit of an enemy, and, in particular, if he has
>> (i) supplied any goods to or for the benefit of an enemy, or obtained any goods from an enemy or traded in or caused any goods consigned to or from an enemy or destined for or coming from enemy territory, or
>> (ii) paid or transmitted any money, negotiable instrument or security for money to or for the benefit of an enemy or to a place in enemy territory, or
>> (iii) performed any obligation to or discharged any obligation of any enemy whether the obligation was undertaken before or after the commencement of the Act, or
> (b) if he has done anything which, by virtue of the provisions of the Act, is to be treated as trading with the enemy."

Anything done under the authority of a Secretary of State, the Treasury or the Department of Trade does not fall within the Act; nor does the receipt of a payment from an enemy of a sum due in respect of a transaction under which all obligations on the part of the person receiving payment had already been performed when the payment was received and had been performed at a time when the person from whom payment was received was not an enemy.[10]

By section 2(1) of the Act[11] an enemy means:

> "(a) any state, or sovereign of a state, at war with Her Majesty;
> (b) any individual resident in enemy territory[12];
> (c) any body of persons (whether corporate or unincorporate) carrying on business in any place, if and so long as the body is controlled by a person who, under section 2 of the Act, is an enemy;
> (d) any body of persons constituted or incorporated in, or under the laws of, a state at war with Her Majesty; and
> (e) as respects any business carried on in enemy territory, any individual or body of persons (whether corporate or unincorporate) carrying on that business; but the expression does not include any individual by reason only that he is an enemy subject."

By section 15(1) of the Act, enemy territory means any area which is under the sovereignty of, or in the occupation of, a Power with whom Her Majesty is at war, not being an area in the occupation of Her Majesty or of a Power allied with Her Majesty.[13]

---

[10] See *R. & A. Kohnstamm Ltd v. Ludwig Krumm (London) Ltd* [1940] 2 K.B. 359.

[11] As amended by the Emergency Laws (Miscellaneous Provisions) Act 1953, s.2 and Sched. II, para. 3. See also s.2(2) of the Act of 1939.

[12] Resident means *de facto* resident: *Re Hatch* [1948] Ch. 592, distinguishing *Vandyke v. Adams* [1942] Ch. 155, where it was held that a British prisoner of war is not resident in enemy territory for the purposes of the Act; and see *The Atlantic Scout* [1950] P. 266; *Vamvakas v. Custodian of Enemy Property* [1952] 2 Q.B. 183.

[13] See also s.15(1A), added by the Emergency Laws (Miscellaneous Provisions) Act 1953, s.2 and Sched. II, para. 8.

4. ENFORCEMENT OF COLLATERAL AND PROPRIETARY RIGHTS[14]

(a) *The Maxim Ex Turpi Causa Non Oritur Actio and Related Rules*

17–158   **Ex turpi causa non oritur actio.** When a contractual right is said to be unenforceable on the ground that *ex turpi causa non oritur actio*, sometimes all that is meant is that the general principles discussed earlier in this chapter[15] apply to deprive the party of a contractual remedy which he would otherwise have, though the maxim is generally confined to cases involving criminality or immorality. On other occasions the maxim is used with specific reference to unenforceability at common law on the ground that an apparently innocent contract was entered into for an objectionable purpose. Thus in *Pearce v. Brooks*[16] the plaintiff sued the defendant, a prostitute, for the hire of a brougham which he knew was to be used by her in her calling. It was held that he could not recover and Pollock C.B. said,

> "I have always considered it was settled law that any person who contributes to the performance of an illegal act by supplying a thing with the knowledge that it is going to be used for that purpose, cannot recover the price of the thing so supplied. . . . Nor can any distinction be made between an illegal and an immoral purpose; the rule which is applicable to the matter is *ex turpi causa non oritur actio*."

This is, in effect, merely an application of the general common law principle that one who knowingly enters into a contract with an improper object cannot enforce his rights thereunder. Where the *ex turpi* maxim is applicable, it applies to assignees.[17]

17–159   **Tainting.** The maxim *ex turpi causa non oritur actio* is also applied to the case of an apparently innocent contract which is nevertheless vitiated by the illegality of another contract to which it is merely collateral—the illegality of the latter tainting the former.[18] Thus in *Spector v. Ageda*[19] the plaintiff loaned money to the defendant to repay a loan which had been made by a third party to the defendant and which was an illegal moneylending transaction. The plaintiff knew that her loan was to be used to pay off the illegal loan and the issue which

---

[14] See Williams (1942) 8 Camb.L.J. 51; Coote (1972) 35 M.L.R. 38; Merkin (1981) 97 L.Q.R. 420.

[15] See *ante*, §§ 17–010, 17–011; *Euro-Diam Ltd v. Bathurst* [1990] 1 Q.B. 1, 34–37.

[16] (1866) L.R. 1 Ex. 213, 217. See also *K. v. P. and J.* [1993] Ch. 140 (defence of *ex turpi causa* does not preclude a claim for contribution under the Civil Liability (Contribution) Act 1978). For the application of the *ex turpi causa* principle in tort see *Hall v. Herbert* [1993] 2 S.C.R. 159 (noted, (1994) 110 L.Q.R. 357).

[17] *D.R. Insurance Co. v. Central National Insurance Co. of Omaha* [1996] C.L.C. 64, 73; [1996] 1 Lloyd's Rep. 74, 82.

[18] *Fisher v. Bridges* (1854) 3 E. B. 642; *Geere v. Mare* (1863) 2 H. & C. 339; *Clay v. Ray* (1864) 17 C.B. (N.S.) 188; *Taylor v. Chester* (1869) L.R. 4 Q.B. 309; *Bigos v. Bousted* [1951] 1 All E.R. 92; *Hall v. Woolston Hall Leisure Ltd* [1998] I.C.R. 651. See also *ante*, §§ 17–164 *et seq.* on severance.

[19] [1973] Ch. 30; see also *Heald v. O'Connor* [1971] 1 W.L.R. 497 involving the Companies Act 1948, s.54 (now replaced by Companies Act 1985, Chap. VI); *Swan v. Bank of Scotland* (1836) 10 Bli. (N.S.) 627; *Pye Ltd v. B. G. Transport Service Ltd* [1966] 2 Lloyd's Rep. 300; *Geismar v. Sun Alliance and London Insurance Ltd* [1978] Q.B. 383; *Euro-Diam Ltd v. Bathurst* [1990] 1 Q.B. 1; *Saunders v. Edwards* [1987] 1 W.L.R. 1116; *Re Berkeley Applegate (Investment Consultants) Ltd* [1989] Ch. 32, 53.

squarely faced the court was, Megarry J. stated,[20] "whether a loan knowingly[21] made in order to discharge an existing loan that was wholly or partially illegal was itself tainted with illegality." He answered the question in the affirmative; the second transaction was tainted by the illegality of the first and was accordingly unenforceable.

Limits to the maxim. It is not sufficient, in order to bring the claimant within the maxim, that he should merely be obliged to give evidence of an illegal contract as part of his case, as for instance where the illegal purpose has not been carried out; for the rule normally applies only where the action is founded upon the illegal contract, and is brought to enforce it.[22] In *Euro-Diam Ltd v. Bathurst*,[23] Kerr L.J. held that the *ex turpi causa* defence must be "approached pragmatically and with caution." He considered that the defence would not succeed where "some reprehensible conduct on [the claimant's] part is disclosed in the course of the proceedings" but the claimant does not have to found his claim on any illegal act.[24] Where property has passed to a party,[25] his proprietary rights therein will be recognised and enforced notwithstanding that his purpose in taking the transfer was objectionable,[26] or that the transfer was otherwise made in pursuance of a contract which on grounds of public policy could not have been enforced.[27] **17–160**

Benefits resulting from crime. Closely akin to the maxim *ex turpi causa non oritur actio* is the rule that neither a party nor his representative is permitted to found rights upon his deliberate commission of a crime. "It is clear . . . that no person can obtain, or enforce, any rights resulting to him from his own crime; neither can his representative, claiming under him, obtain or enforce any such rights. The human mind revolts at the very idea that any other doctrine could be possible in our system of jurisprudence."[28] The rule only makes unenforceable rights to money or property to which, but for the crime, the plaintiff would have **17–161**

---

[20] *ibid.* at 44.

[21] From Megarry J.'s judgment it would appear that the party to the second transaction must actually know of the illegality or deliberately shut their eyes, and the mere fact that they ought to have known is not enough: *ibid.*

[22] *Taylor v. Bowers* (1876) 1 Q.B.D. 291, 295, 300; *Bowmakers Ltd v. Barnet Instruments Ltd* [1945] K.B. 65; *Belvoir Finance Co. Ltd v. Stapleton* [1971] 1 Q.B. 210; *Euro-Diam Ltd v. Bathurst* [1990] Q.B. 1. It may be, however, that the wrongful conduct is of such a nature (*e.g.*, benefiting by means of a collateral transaction from a crime) that the court will refuse to enforce the tainted transaction: *Geismar v. Sun Alliance and London Insurance Ltd* [1978] Q.B. 383.

[23] [1990] 1 Q.B. 1. Although the "affront to the public conscience" test adopted by Kerr L.J. in *Euro-Diam Ltd v. Bathurst* for determining the effect of illegality was rejected by the House of Lords in *Tinsley v. Milligan* [1994] 1 A.C. 340, it is submitted that this aspect of his judgment remains good law. See *post*, § 17–173.

[24] *ibid.* at 35–36.

[25] See *post*, § 17–070.

[26] *Feret v. Hill* (1854) 15 C.B. 207; *Ayerst v. Jenkins* (1873) L.R. 16 Eq. 275, 283, 284; *Alexander v. Rayson* [1936] 1 K.B. 169, 184; *Edler v. Auerbach* [1950] 1 K.B. 359, 373; *cf. Greenwood v. Bishop of London* (1814) 5 Taunt. 727, 746; *Mason v. Clarke* [1954] 1 Q.B. 460 (revd. on the facts on this point [1955] A.C. 778).

[27] See *post*, § 17–170.

[28] *In the Estate of Crippen* [1911] P. 108, 112; *Re Giles* [1972] Ch. 544; *Geismar v. Sun Alliance and London Insurance Ltd* [1978] Q.B. 383. *cf. Gray v. Barr* [1971] 2 Q.B. 554; *Pitts v. Hunt* [1991] 1 Q.B. 24.

had no right or title[29]; it does not apply where the right on which the plaintiff relies would no less have come into existence when it did, even had the plaintiff committed no crime.[30] And it has been said that,

"in these days there are many statutory offences which are the subject of the criminal law, and in that sense are crimes, but which would, it seems, afford no moral justification to a court to apply the maxim"[31]:

"in each case it is not the label which the law applies to the crime ... but the nature of the crime itself which in the end will dictate whether public policy demands the court to drive the applicant from the seat of justice."[32]

17–162   **Rights resulting from victim's death.** Where a husband insured his life for the benefit of his wife, and his wife was convicted of murdering him, neither the wife nor her assigns could recover the insurance money. It was held, however, that there was a resulting trust in favour of the murdered husband's estate, inasmuch as between his representatives and the insurers no question of public policy arose, and their rights were unaffected by the wife's crime.[33] Similarly when a man insured the life of another for his own benefit and then murdered him for the sake of the insurance money, the murderer's representatives could not recover on the policy.[34] The rule would also apply to a conviction for manslaughter.[35] However, a special verdict that the accused is "not guilty by reason of insanity" is, for this purpose, equivalent to a simple acquittal.[36]

17–163   **The Forfeiture Act 1982.** The Forfeiture Act 1982,[37] which started life as a private member's Bill, is intended to modify the public policy in cases such as *R. v. Chief National Insurance Commissioner*[38] where the court held that a wife who had killed her husband forfeited statutory entitlements accruing because of his death despite the fact that in the circumstances there was little moral blame attached to the wife's conduct. This Act vests in the court a discretion to modify

---

[29] *St. John Shipping Corporation v. Joseph Rank Ltd* [1957] 1 Q.B. 267, 292. It also applies where a person who is injured by his accomplice in crime sues the accomplice or his estate in tort: *Pitts v. Hunt, supra.* See also *Thorne v. Silverleaf* [1994] 1 B.C.L.C. 637, 645.

[30] *Marles v. Philip Trant & Sons Ltd* [1954] 1 Q.B. 29.

[31] Per Lord Wright M.R. in *Beresford v. Royal Insurance Co. Ltd* [1937] 2 K.B. 197, 220 (affd. [1938] A.C. 586); *Marles v. Philip Trant & Sons Ltd* [1954] 1 Q.B. 29, 37; *cf. St. John Shipping Corporation v. Joseph Rank Ltd* [1957] 1 Q.B. 267, 292.

[32] *R. v. Chief National Insurance Commissioner* [1981] Q.B. 758, 765. See also *Thorne v. Silverleaf, supra.*

[33] *Cleaver v. Mutual Reserve Fund Life Association* [1892] 1 Q.B. 147, *per* Fry L.J. at 159 (making it clear, however, that the murderer should never benefit). Where the deceased and the killer held property as joint tenants, the forfeiture rule in all probability operates to "sever the joint tenancy in the proceeds of sale and in the rent and profits until sale" a result which can be achieved by treating the "beneficial interests as vesting in the deceased and survivors as tenants in common": *per* Vinelott J. in *Re K. (decd.)* [1985] Ch. 85, 100H (the judgment of Vinelott J. was upheld on appeal [1986] Ch. 180).

[34] *Prince of Wales, etc., Association Co. v. Palmer* (1858) 25 Beav. 605.

[35] *In the Estate of Hall* [1914] P. 1; *Re Giles* [1972] Ch. 54 (manslaughter by reason of diminished responsibility); *cf. ante,* § 17–161, n. 32; *R. v. Chief National Insurance Commissioner* [1981] Q.B. 758 (wife convicted of manslaughter not entitled to widow's allowance under s.24(1) of the Social Security Act 1975).

[36] *Re Houghton* [1915] 2 Ch. 173, relating to the old verdict of "guilty, but insane" under s.2 of the Trial of Lunatics Act 1883, which is now amended by s.1(1) of the Criminal Procedure (Insanity) Act 1964.

[37] See (1983) 46 M.L.R. 62; Cretney (1990) 10 O.J.L.S. 289.

[38] [1981] Q.B. 758.

the "forfeiture rule" which is defined in section 1(1) as "the rule of public policy which in certain circumstances precludes a person who has unlawfully killed another from acquiring a benefit in consequence of that killing." Thus it only applies to benefits acquired by the person who does the killing and not to a situation where the estate of the deceased benefits.[39] The court can modify the forfeiture rule in whole or in part[40] but only where it is satisfied that "having regard to the conduct of the offender and of the deceased and to such other circumstances as appear to the court to be material, the justice of the case requires the effects of the rule to be so modified in that case."[41] The power to modify the forfeiture rule does not however apply "in the case of a person who stands convicted of murder."[42] In circumstances where a person "stands convicted of an offence of which unlawful killing is an element" the Act contains its own limitation period and an order can only be made where proceedings are commenced within a period of three months commencing with the conviction. In the first reported case applying the Act[43] a widow who had for many years been subjected to violent and unprovoked attacks by her husband accidentally shot him with his shotgun in circumstances where she feared another attack. She was convicted of manslaughter and given a non-custodial sentence. In these circumstances, given the relative lack of moral culpability on the part of the widow, Vinelott J. held that the forfeiture rule should not operate and his decision was upheld on appeal. The Court of Appeal considered it appropriate for the court in exercising its discretion under section 2(2) to take into consideration the widow's loyalty as a wife, the widow's mental distress at the time the accident occurred, the deceased's behaviour, and the deceased's own assessment of how the wife should be treated on his death.[44] The Court of Appeal has also held that in exercising its discretion under section 2(2), it was wrong for the court to consider that it had to do justice as between the parties, rather it had to take into consideration all aspects of the case.[45]

Life insurance and suicide. Until 1961 one who committed suicide when **17–164** sane was guilty of a crime, committing as it were murder on himself, and a claim by his personal representatives on a life policy effected by him could not be enforced since it was treated as equivalent to a claim by a murderer or his representative on a policy effected by the murderer on the life of the person murdered.[46] Even before 1961, public policy was no bar to a claim on such a policy,[47] by assignees for value, at any rate to the extent of their actual interest,[48] or by the representatives of the deceased if he was insane at the time of his

---

[39] See, *e.g. Beresford v. Royal Insurance Co. Ltd* [1937] 2 K.B. 197, CA.

[40] s.5.

[41] s.2(2).

[42] s.5.

[43] *Re K* [1985] Ch. 85, [1986] Ch. 180, CA. See also *Re Royse* [1985] Ch. 22; *Re S. (decd.)* [1996] 1 W.L.R. 235; *Dunbar v. Plant* [1997] 4 All E.R. 289 (in this case Phillips L.J. disapproved of the approach of the judge in *Re S (decd.)*: at 387).

[44] The court's discretion was not to be limited by the principles of the Inheritance (Provision for Family and Dependants) Act 1975.

[45] *Dunbar v. Plant* [1997] 4 All E.R. 289, 302–303, 312–313.

[46] *Horn v. Anglo-Australian, etc., Life Assurance Co.* (1861) 30 L.J.Ch. 511; *Beresford v. Royal Insurance Co. Ltd* [1937] 2 K.B. 197; [1938] A.C. 586.

[47] As to the possibility of a claim by the deceased's personal representatives for return of the premiums, see *St. John Shipping Corporation v. Joseph Rank Ltd* [1957] 1 Q.B. 267, 293.

[48] *Beresford v. Royal Insurance Co. Ltd* [1938] A.C. 586, 600; *Moore v. Woolsey* (1854) 4 E. & B. 243.

suicide.[49] Section 1 of the Suicide Act 1961 abrogated the rule of law whereby it was a crime for a person to commit suicide and it is thought that public policy is no longer a bar to any claim resulting from the suicide of the assured. But there may still be a distinction between suicide when sane and when insane. In the case of insane suicide, in the absence of any special condition that the policy is to be avoided by suicide, the policy continues to be enforceable as under the old law.[50] In the case of sane suicide, in the absence of any special condition, express or implied, that the policy shall not be avoided by suicide, policy moneys may still be irrecoverable by reason of the presumption[51] that the promise to pay on the happening of a specified event does not apply where that event was deliberately caused by the assured.[52] Where, however, the policy contains a promise, express or implied, to pay in the event of suicide, there is no room for that presumption to operate.

17–165 **Assured suffering death at the hands of the law.** In *Amicable Society v. Bolland*[53] where the assured was hanged for forgery, it was held that his assignees could not recover the sum for which his life was insured. The essential feature of the decision was that the court would not allow a claim in contract to be based on the contracting party's crime as a necessary constituent of the cause of action, even though an interval of time and circumstance separated the crime from the resulting death.[54]

17–166 **Indemnity against liability resulting from commission of crime.** An indemnity[55] against civil[56] or criminal,[57] liability resulting from the deliberate commission of a crime by the person to be indemnified generally cannot be enforced by the criminal or his representatives, the reason being that, on grounds of public policy, either the indemnity is subject to an implied exclusion which operates against the criminal and his representatives or they are under a personal disability or ban which prevents their suing on it.[58] Thus, in *Askey v. Golden Wine Co. Ltd*[59] a wholesaler, through his own gross negligence, incurred a fine and costs as a result of breaches of the Food and Drugs Act and had to refund money to his retailers. Denning J. held that it would be against public policy to permit him to recover his loss, by way of damages for conspiracy, from those responsible for the management of the company which supplied him with the goods and

---

[49] See n. 46, *ante*.

[50] *ibid.*

[51] See *MacGillivray on Insurance Law* (9th ed., 1997), § 14–66.

[52] Thus under the old law, though claims by assignees for value were not barred by public policy (see n. 27, *ante*), enforcement of such claims depended upon the insurance policy containing a promise to pay, either generally, or to assignees for value (*White v. British Empire Mutual Life Insurance Co. of New York* (1868) L.R. 7 Eq. 394; *Rowett Leakey & Co. v. Scottish Provident Institution* [1927] 1 Ch. 55; *Royal London Mutual Insurance Society Ltd v. Barrett* [1928] Ch. 411), in the event of sane suicide.

[53] (1830) 2 Dow. & Cl.1, where, however, the assignees were volunteers.

[54] *Beresford v. Royal Insurance Co.* [1937] 2 K.B. 197, 213 (affd. [1938] A.C. 586).

[55] As to the right of contribution as between joint tortfeasors, see Civil Liability Contribution Act 1978.

[56] *Haseldine v. Hosken* [1933] 1 K.B. 822 (indemnity against solicitor's civil liability for champerty held unenforceable): but see now *post*, §§ 16–151, 16–152.

[57] *Colburn v. Patmore* (1834) 1 Cr.M. & R. 73; *Fitzgerald v. Leonard* (1893) 32 L.R.Ir. 675. *cf. Geismar v. Sun Alliance and London Insurance Ltd* [1978] Q.B. 838.

[58] *Hardy v. Motor Insurers' Bureau* [1964] 2 Q.B. 745, 760, 765.

[59] [1948] 2 All E.R. 35. See *ante*, § 17–162, n. 33.

it is clear from the judgment that the learned judge would have held a claim against the company for damages for breach of contract in respect of such loss to be equally unenforceable. But probably, as in the case of the closely related rule that a man may not benefit from his own crime, this rule does not apply to every breach of the criminal law[60]; indeed, it has been said that the courts' refusal to permit a person who has committed an anti-social act to assert a resultant right depends not only on the nature of the anti-social act but also on the nature of the right asserted.[61] Thus, for example, the rule does not apply to every breach of the criminal law. It does not apply, for example, to the innocent commission of an offence of strict liability.[62] It is also clear that policies of insurance relating to motor accidents are enforceable, so that a motorist who has to pay damages for negligence can recover an indemnity from his insurers; and this is so even though the negligence was so gross[63] as to amount to manslaughter.[64] Perhaps this is to be explained on the ground that here the act to be indemnified is one intended by the law that people should insure against,[65] or that the social harm which would be caused by not enforcing such insurance rights outweighs the gravity of the anti-social act committed and the extent to which such acts will be encouraged by the enforcement of such rights.[66] With these cases should be contrasted *Gray v. Barr*[67]; a husband shot and killed his wife's lover; it was held by the Court of Appeal that the husband could not recover under an insurance policy (even if it covered the occurrence) the damages which he had had to pay to the lover's estate. The husband had caused the victim's death in the course of deliberately committing an unlawful and dangerous act (threatening the lover with a loaded shotgun) which in the opinion of the Court of Appeal amounted to the crime of manslaughter, and to allow persons to enforce indemnities against the consequences of their own acts of armed violence would clearly be contrary to public policy. There was no evidence in this case whether the husband could satisfy the judgment without obtaining payment from the insurance company. The failure of the court to advert to this would indicate that it was not a relevant factor although

---

[60] *cf. R. v. Chief National Insurance Commissioner* [1981] Q.B. 758, 765, *per* Lord Lane C.J.

[61] *Hardy v. Motor Insurers' Bureau, supra,* at 767–768.

[62] *Gregory v. Ford* [1951] 1 All E.R. 121; *Osman v. J. Ralph Moss Ltd* [1970] 1 Lloyd's Rep. 313.

[63] As to the distinction between negligence and intention in such cases, see *Hardy v. Motor Insurers' Bureau* [1964] 2 Q.B. 745. The *Hardy* case was approved by the House of Lords in *Gardner v. Moore* [1984] A.C. 548 where an uninsured driver had deliberately driven his car at the plaintiff for which he was convicted.

[64] *Tinline v. White Cross Insurance Association Ltd* [1921] 3 K.B. 327; *James v. British & General Insurance Co. Ltd* [1972] 2 K.B. 311; compare *Crage v. Fry* (1903) 67 J.P. 240; *Cointat v. Mynham & Son* [1913] 2 K.B. 220; revd. on a different point (1914) 30 T.L.R. 282: *R. Leslie Ltd v. Reliable Advertising, etc., Agency Ltd* [1915] 1 K.B. 652; *Simon v. Pawsons & Leafs Ltd* (1932) 38 Com.Cas. 151, with *Fitzgerald v. Leonard* (1893) 32 L.R.Ir. 675 and *Askey v. Golden Wine Co. Ltd* [1948] 2 All E.R. 35.

[65] *Per* Greer L.J. in *Haseldine v. Hosken* [1933] 1 K.B. 822, 838; and see the difference of opinion between Denning and Hodson L.JJ. in *Marles v. Philip Trant & Sons Ltd* [1954] 1 Q.B. 29, 39–40 and 44.

[66] *Hardy v. Motor Insurers' Bureau* [1964] 2 Q.B. 745, 768. In *Hardy v. Motor Insurers' Bureau,* at 769, Diplock L.J. considered that an assured who had discharged his liability to the victim would not be able to enforce his contractual right to indemnity against the insurance company where the damages were connected with an intentional criminal act; *cf.* the case of insurance by employers which covers liability for breach of the Factories Act, where under the law before the Employers' Liability (Compulsory Insurance) Act 1969 the explanation put forward in the text to n. 65 *ante*, would not have applied but which had never been suggested to be unenforceable, however gross the employer's negligence.

[67] [1971] 2 Q.B. 554.

the effect of the judgment might be to deprive an innocent party of compensation.

17–167   **Indemnity against liability resulting from commission of tort.** Where the act to be indemnified is not only a tort but also a crime, the position is that set out in the preceding paragraph. Where the act is a mere tort, the enforceability of an agreement to indemnify against liability resulting from its commission depends upon the nature of the act and the circumstances of its commission.[68] Thus a contract to indemnify a person against liability for an act which constitutes the tort of deceit is unenforceable.[69] So also an agreement to indemnify a person against liability for the publication of what he knows to be a libel is unenforceable.[70] But an indemnity against innocent publication of a libel is enforceable by virtue of the provisions of section 11 of the Defamation Act 1952 which enacts that an agreement for indemnifying any person against civil liability for libel in respect of the publication of any matter shall not be unlawful unless at the time of publication that person knows that the matter is defamatory, and does not reasonably believe that there is a good defence to any action brought upon it. And at common law, where, as a natural consequence of a breach of contract by one party, the other incurs liability for defamation, there is no rule of public policy which prevents the recovery by way of damages of the loss suffered by the first party as a result of his tort, at any rate where the commission of the tort was not deliberate.[71]

(b) *Collateral Transactions*

17–168   **Alternative cause of action.** Although the *ex turpi causa* principle precludes a plaintiff from being able directly to enforce an illegal contract, it does not prevent him from enforcing causes of action which are collateral to the contract. By this means the courts have to some extent mitigated the severity of the illegality doctrine. In *Strongman Ltd v. Sincock*[72] the plaintiff carried out building work for which it did not possess the appropriate licence and thus was unable to bring an action on the contract for the work done. However, the defendant (an architect) had assured the plaintiff that he would obtain the necessary licence and the court held that this gave rise to a collateral contract on which the plaintiff could maintain an action. An action may also lie in fraud as occurred in *Shelley v. Paddock*[73] where the plaintiff was induced to enter into an illegal contract for

---

[68] See the dicta in *Hardy v. Motor Insurers' Bureau* [1964] 2 Q.B. 745, 767–770. *cf. Adamson v. Jarvis* (1827) 4 Bing. 66; *Betts & Drewe v. Gibbins* (1834) 2 A. & E. 57; *Lister v. Romford Ice & Cold Storage Co. Ltd* [1957] A.C. 555; in all of which indemnities have been enforced.

[69] *Brown Jenkinson & Co. Ltd v. Percy Dalton (London) Ltd* [1957] 2 Q.B. 621.

[70] *Smith v. Clinton* (1908) 99 L.T. 840.

[71] *Bradstreets British Ltd v. Mitchell and Carapanayoti & Co. Ltd* [1933] Ch. 190; *Daily Mirror Newspapers Ltd v. Exclusive News Agency* (1937) 81 S.J. 924; *K. v. P.* [1993] Ch. 140 (in an action against the defendant for conspiracy to defraud, the *ex turpi causa* maxim did not preclude the defendant from serving a contribution notice on a third party).

[72] [1955] 2 Q.B. 525.

[73] [1980] Q.B. 348 (Brandon L.J., had serious doubts but he reluctantly agreed with the majority). It is also important to note that in *Shelley v. Paddock* the fraud did not relate to the legality of the transaction, that is, the sale of the house: see (1978) 94 L.Q.R. 484. See also *Burrows v. Rhodes* [1899] 1 Q.B. 816; *Dott v. Brickwell* (1906) 23 T.L.R. 61; *Archbolds (Freightage) Ltd v. S. Spanglett Ltd* [1961] 1 Q.B. 374, 392–393; *Southern Industrial Trust Ltd v. Brooke House Motors Ltd* (1968) 112 S.J. 798.

the sale of a house in Spain by the fraud of the defendant. Also, where the circumstances are appropriate, there is no reason why a plaintiff should not recover damages for negligent misrepresentation. It was once thought that it was essential for the plaintiff to show that he was ignorant of the illegality.[74] This was a point emphasised in both *Strongman Ltd v. Sincock*[75] and *Shelley v Paddock*.[76] However, in *Saunders v. Edwards*[77] the court allowed a plaintiff, who was a knowing party to an illegal contract, to recover damages for the fraud of the defendant. The plaintiff had purchased a flat from the defendant. The purchase price contained an inflated figure for fixtures and fittings which reduced the stamp duty payable by the plaintiff. Despite the fact that the court found that the plaintiff's conduct was tainted by the illegality connected with the evasion of stamp duty, the court allowed the plaintiff to recover damages for the fraud of the defendant in misrepresenting the extent of the property being sold. The court held that the "relative moral culpability" of the parties could be taken into consideration in deciding whether the plaintiff should be given a remedy which did not involve the enforcement of the contract.[78] As the moral culpability of the defendant greatly outweighed that of the plaintiff in the *Saunders* case, the court allowed the plaintiff to recover. In the light of the House of Lords disapproval in *Tinsley v. Milligan*[79] of the approach of the court in the *Saunders* case, it is no longer proper to carry out a balancing exercise as to the relative culpability of the parties. However, the decision in *Saunders v. Edwards*[80] can possibly be explained on the grounds that the plaintiff had "an unassailable claim for damages for fraud which did not involve any reliance on the contract of sale itself."[81] Also, where services are rendered under a contract which is intended to be performed in an illegal manner, or which is illegal at its inception, a *quantum meruit* claim will not lie.[82] Such a claim would circumvent the public policy underlying the making of a contract illegal.

(c) *Recovery of Money Paid or Property Transferred under Illegal Contracts*[83]

Non-recovery of consideration. While cases in which the plaintiff seeks the   **17–169**
enforcement of an illegal contract are governed by the maxim *ex turpi causa non*

---

[74] It was considered that if the plaintiff had knowledge of the illegality he would be *in pari delicto* with the defendant and thus unable to obtain the assistance of the court.

[75] [1955] 2 Q.B. 525, 536–537. Denning L.J., in that case also thought it important that the plaintiff was not negligent with respect to determining the existence of the illegality. *cf.* the degree of knowledge required where a contract is allegedly tainted with the illegality of some other transaction: *ante*, § 17–159, n. 21.

[76] [1980] Q.B. 348, 357.

[77] [1987] 1 W.L.R. 1116; see also *Mitsubishi Corp. v. Alafouzos* [1988] 1 F.T.L.R. 47; *Hughes v. Clewley (The "Siben") (No. 2)* [1996] 1 Lloyd's Rep. 35.

[78] It was on this basis that the court distinguished *Alexander v. Rayson* [1936] 1 K.B. 169. The court left open the issue of what would have happened had the defendant refused to complete and the plaintiff had sued for specific performance or damages (at 1125C). The court also considered that the dictum of Lindley L.J. in *Scott v. Brown, Doering, McNab & Co.* [1892] 2 Q.B. 724, 729 could not be applied literally in every situation (at 1127).

[79] [1993] 3 W.L.R. 126.

[80] *Supra.*

[81] *Tinsley v. Milligan* [1994] 1 A.C. 340, 360. On this reasoning, the point left open by the judge (see n. 78 *supra*) would be answered in the negative.

[82] *Taylor v. Bhail* [1996] C.L.C. 377 (cost of repairs inflated to defraud insurers).

[83] The approach in this section follows that of Treitel, *The Law of Contract* (9th ed., 1995), pp. 438–459. See also Goff and Jones, *The Law of Restitution* (4th ed., 1993), Chap. 22; Burrows, *The Law of Restitution* (1993), pp. 333–344, 461–472.

oritur actio, those in which he seeks some release from its operation fall within the principle *in pari delicto potior est conditio defendentis*. The result of the application of this principle is that where both parties, contracting on an equal footing, are aware of the illegal nature of the contract, whether it be on its face illegal or whether the common intention be to carry out the contract in an illegal manner, neither party can recover anything paid or transferred thereunder. So, in a contract to secure a title for the plaintiff in return for payment, the plaintiff, when he failed to receive his title, could not recover back what he had paid, the contract being *turpis* and the parties *in pari delicto*.[84] *A fortiori* where the defendant had performed his part of the agreement the plaintiff cannot set up the illegal nature of the transaction in order to recover a deposit or part payment. Thus in *Taylor v. Chester*[85] the plaintiff failed to recover the half of a £50 banknote deposited with the defendant to secure payment by the plaintiff of the price of wines and suppers supplied by the defendant in her brothel for the purposes of a debauch and of loans of money by the defendant to the plaintiff for expenditure in riot, debauchery and immoral conduct. The court held that the plaintiff failed, since he could not make out his case "otherwise than through the medium and by the aid of the illegal transaction to which he was himself a party."[86]

17–170   **Transfer of property under illegal transactions.**[87] When property has been delivered in pursuance of an illegal agreement[88] and there is subsequently a dispute about the property between the transferor and the transferee, the question often arises whether the court should give effect to the transferee's interest[89] or disregard it and enforce the transferor's original rights. The fact that by reason of illegality the transferee could not have enforced the agreement under which the transfer was made does not necessarily mean that delivery to him of property thereunder will not pass to him the property or the interest in question. Thus where goods are delivered in pursuance of an illegal contract of sale, the property in them passes to the purchaser who will be entitled to damages against anyone, including the vendor, who thereafter wrongfully deprives him of those goods.[90] Where a person takes a lease of property intending to use it for an immoral purpose, he acquires an interest under the executed lease despite the intention to use the property for an immoral purpose.[91] It is now clear that property may pass under an illegal sale, although the goods have not been delivered to the buyer,[92] so that the buyer may obtain rights against a *third* person. But it would not appear that a buyer to whom property in goods has passed under an illegal contract can

---

[84] *Parkinson v. College of Ambulance Ltd* [1925] 2 K.B. 1; and see *Shaw v. Shaw* [1965] 1 W.L.R. 537.

[85] (1869) L.R. 4 Q.B. 309. See also *Bigos v. Bousted* [1951] 1 All E.R. 92.

[86] (1869) L.R. 4 Q.B. 309, 314.

[87] See Higgins (1962) 25 M.L.R. 149: Grodecki (1955) 71 L.Q.R. 254.

[88] *cf. post*, § 17–171.

[89] The transferor cannot claim to have retained the beneficial interest where, in order to establish the trust in his favour, he must rely on the illegal purpose of the transfer: *Palaniappa Chettiar v. Aranasalam Chettiar* [1962] A.C. 294.

[90] *Singh v. Ali* [1960] A.C. 167. And see *Taylor v. Chester* (1869) L.R. 4 Q.B. 309 ; *Tinsley v. Milligan* [1994] 1 A.C. 340, 374 *per* Lord Browne-Wilkinson: " . . . the effect of illegality is not to prevent a proprietary interest in equity from arising or to produce a forfeiture of such right: the effect is to render the equitable interest unenforceable in certain circumstances."

[91] *Feret v. Hill* (1854) 15 C.B. 207.

[92] *Belvoir Finance Co. Ltd v. Stapleton* [1971] 1 Q.B. 210; *cf. Kingsley v. Sterling Industrial Securities* [1967] 2 Q.B. 747, 783.

claim them, or damages for their conversion, from a *seller* who has never delivered them at all. Such a claim would not differ in substance from a claim for the delivery, or for damages for the non-delivery, of the goods under the illegal contract and its success would defeat the policy of the rule against the enforcement of such a contract.[93] Statutes may avoid not only the agreement in pursuance of which a transfer is made[94] but also the transfer itself so that the transferor can rely on his original title and recover the property from the transferee to whom, because of the statute, no property passed and who therefore cannot set up any interest in the property by way of defence to the claim.[95]

Determination of limited interests created by illegal transactions. Where   **17–171**
the interest created by an illegal transaction was by the provisions of the transaction limited for a term, after the expiry of that term the transferor can probably recover the property. Thus, the owner of a house let to a prostitute could no doubt recover possession by ejectment at the end of the term, though he would be precluded from recovering rent if he knew the purpose to which it was intended to put the premises.[96] Whether an owner could recover possession for non-payment of rent (assuming the lease provides for this) where, for example, he knowingly rents premises for the purposes of prostitution is more problematical. It is difficult to see how the owner could recover without relying on the lease and accordingly he would be denied the assistance of the court. It has been argued that as the lease is illegal neither party can rely on it so that the tenant is a tenant at will and the owner can thereupon take steps to terminate the lease.[97] Although creative as a solution to the problem, it ignores the fact that illegal contracts can operate to transfer title and presumably any other proprietary interest. Accordingly, the tenant would acquire a limited interest under the lease and it would appear that the owner would therefore be unable to recover possession until the limited property interest of the tenant comes to an end.[98] On the other hand, money or property may be paid or transferred by way of security for the performance of an illegal act which is not performed; in such cases it is thought that a claim to recover the money or property, on the ground of the non-performance of the act for which payment was made, would fail. For had the money or property been paid or transferred outright by way of payment a claim based on a total failure of consideration would have failed.[99] Great difficulties arise however in the case where the property has been bailed under a contract which is illegal by common law or statute.

In *Bowmakers Ltd v. Barnet Instruments Ltd*[1] the Court of Appeal formulated   **17–172**
the rule to be applied in cases of bailment of chattels thus: "In our opinion a

---

[93] Treitel, *The Law of Contract* (9th ed., 1995), p. 458.
[94] See *ante*, § 17–153.
[95] *Amar Singh v. Kulubya* [1964] A.C. 142.
[96] *Jajbhay v. Cassim*, 1939 A.D. 537, 557 (S. Africa); *Alexander v. Rayson* [1936] 1 K.B. 169, 186–187.
[97] *Munro v. Morrison* [1980] V.R. 83.
[98] See *Jajbhay v. Cassim* 1939 A.D. 537.
[99] See *ante*, § 17–057. Contrast *Milner v. Staffordshire Congregational Union (Incorporated)* [1956] Ch. 275, where the contract was statutorily unlawful only in the sense of being void and a deposit was therefore recoverable. And see *South Western Mineral Water Co. Ltd v. Ashmore* [1967] 1 W.L.R. 1110; *post*, § 17–192.
[1] [1945] K.B. 65, 71; applied in *Singh v. Ali* [1960] A.C. 167 and also in *Belvoir Finance Co. Ltd v. Harold G. Cole & Co. Ltd* [1969] 1 W.L.R. 1877; *Tinsley v. Milligan* [1993] 3 W.L.R. 126.

man's right to possess his own chattels will as a general rule be enforced as against one who, without any claim or right, is detaining them or has converted them to his own use, even though it may appear either from the pleadings, or in the course of the trial, that the chattels came into the defendant's possession by reason of an illegal contract between himself and the plaintiff, provided that the plaintiff does not seek and is not forced either to found his claim on the illegal contract or to plead its illegality in order to support his claim." In that case, illegal bailments of machinery under hire-purchase agreements were assumed to have been terminated, in some cases by the sale of the machinery by the bailees, and, in one other case, by their refusal to deliver the machinery up to the plaintiffs on demand. The bailments having been terminated, the plaintiffs were held entitled to rely on their proprietary interests in the machinery, and accordingly recovered damages for conversion.[2] The principal difficulty in the case arises with regard to the implicit finding that the latter bailment was terminated by the defendant bailees' refusal to deliver up the machinery on demand. If it were always possible for a bailor to terminate an illegal bailment on breach of its terms by the bailee, merely by demanding the return of the property bailed, little would be left of the general rule of non-recovery so far as bailments are concerned.[3] It has been argued that the hire-purchase agreement in *Bowmakers Ltd v. Barnet Instruments Ltd* probably contained a cesser clause making the agreement determine on the failure of the hirer to pay instalments and thus the owner was entitled to recover the machinery which was still in the possession of the defendants.[4] There may also be special cases where a person is not entitled to recover property although his title to it is clear. An example of this type of case was given by Du Parcq L.J., in *Bowmakers Ltd v. Barnet Instruments Ltd*[5] as occurring where the owner of obscene books attempts to recover them, and a similar result has been suggested where the owner of a weapon to be used to commit a serious crime tries to recover it.[6]

17–173   The principle in *Bowmakers* also applies to equitable interests. In *Tinsley v. Milligan*[7] the plaintiff and the defendant contributed to the purchase of a house which was placed in the sole name of the plaintiff for the purpose of enabling the defendant to make fraudulent claims on the Department of Social Security. The plaintiff and defendant quarrelled and the plaintiff, having moved out of the house, commenced proceedings asserting ownership of the whole of the house. The defendant successfully counterclaimed for, *inter alia*, an order that the plaintiff held the house on trust in equal shares for the defendant and plaintiff. The House of Lords reasoned that the fact that the arrangement involved an illegality did not prevent an equitable interest from arising[8] and, since the fusion of law and equity, the principle in *Bowmakers* extended to equitable interests. As

---

[2] But if the action for conversion is statute-barred and the only cause of action is under the illegal bailment, the action will fail: *Thomas Brown & Sons v. Fazal Deen* (1962) 108 C.L.R. 391 (Australia).
  [3] Contrast *Bigos v. Bousted* [1951] 1 All E.R. 92; *Archbolds (Freightage) Ltd v. S. Spanglett Ltd* [1961] 1 Q.B. 374, 384. And see Hamson (1949) 10 Camb.L.J. 249; Paton, *Bailment in the Common Law* (1972), pp. 34–36; Coote (1972) 35 M.L.R. 38.
  [4] See Treitel, *The Law of Contract* (9th ed., 1995), p. 457.
  [5] [1945] K.B. 65, 72.
  [6] Treitel *op. cit.* at 457. See, however, Lord Goff's terrorist example in *Tinsley v. Milligan* [1994] 1 A.C. 340, 362.
  [7] *Supra*.
  [8] *ibid.* at 373–374.

all that the defendant was seeking was recovery of an equitable proprietary interest which arose under a resulting trust, she could recover it without having to rely on the illegality. The majority of the House in *Tinsley v. Milligan*[9] also rejected the argument that the "clean hands" maxim in equity precluded the plaintiff from recovering on the grounds of title.

Locus poenitentiae: presumption of advancement. In *Tinsley v. Milligan*[10] **17–174** the House of Lords considered that its reasoning would not apply to a situation where there was a presumption of advancement between the plaintiff and the defendant[11] (in that the presumption would negative the resulting trust). This was the issue that was before the court in *Tribe v. Tribe*.[12] In that case, a father transferred to his son shares in a company in order to protect them against the possible claims of his creditors, the shares to be held by his son on trust for him until he had settled the claims. Eventually, he settled with his creditors and sought to recover the shares from his son who refused to re-transfer them. The court held that the father could recover his shares. The court reasoned that provided the "illegal purpose has not been carried into effect in any way",[13] the father could recover his shares on the grounds that he did not intend to confer the beneficial interest on the son and therefore the presumption of advancement would be successfully rebutted. On the facts of the case the court held that as the illegal purpose had not been carried into effect since no deception had been practised on the father's creditors, the father could recover the shares. This decision extends, in a way that is unacceptable, the principles on the right of withdrawal with respect to illegal contracts, in that it enables the tranferor of property to recover it where the illegal purpose for which it was transferred in the first place is no longer needed to protect the transferor's interests.[14] Millett L.J. considered that the policy underlying the *locus poenitentiae* was the discouragement of fraud and therefore it necessarily also encouraged "withdrawal from a proposed fraud before it is implemented."[15] However, Millett L.J. recognised that in *Tribe v. Tribe* recovery by the father would not be necessary to encourage withdrawal since the reason for the withdrawal was not a change of mind but simply that it was no longer needed.[16] This, rather than discouraging illegal contracts, produces the opposite effect since the transferor of property has nothing to lose and everything to gain by entering into the illegal transaction. On these grounds, *Tribe v. Tribe* should be viewed as an extreme, if not wrong, application of the *locus poenitentiae* rule.

The approach in *Tinsley v. Milligan*, depending as it does on proprietary concepts, was not followed in the important decision of the High Court of Australia, *Nelson v. Nelson*.[17] It is not possible to do justice to the subtlety and scholarship of this judgment. *Nelson v. Nelson* involved a contract designed to

---

[9] *ibid.* (Lord Keith and Lord Goff dissenting). All of the law lords disapproved of the approach of the courts in *Thackwell v. Barclays Bank plc* [1986] 1 All E.R. 676, *Saunders v. Edwards* [1987] 1 W.L.R. 1116 and *Euro-Diam Ltd v. Bathurst* [1990] Q.B. 1 which had been followed by the majority of the Court of Appeal in *Tinsley v. Milligan*.
[10] [1994] 1 A.C. 340. See Enonchony (1994) 14 O.J.L.S. 295.
[11] *ibid.*, at 372.
[12] [1996] Ch. 107. See Enonchony [1996] R.L.R. 78.
[13] *ibid.* at 121, *per* Nourse L.J.; see also Millett L.J. at 135.
[14] See Rose (1996) 112 L.Q.R. 386.
[15] [1996] Ch. 107, 134.
[16] *ibid.* at 135.
[17] (1995) 132 A.L.R. 133.

acquire for the transferor of property under the contract a statutory benefit to which she would not have been entitled had the transfer not been effected. Thus it was a situation on all fours with *Tinsley v. Milligan*. Rather than adopt the proprietary based reasoning of *Tinsley v. Milligan*, the approach of the High Court was to determine whether the statutory rule which rendered the contract illegal precluded relief and the court held that it did not. The court cited with approval the views of an American author to the effect: "if illegality consists of the violation of a statute, courts will give or refuse relief depending upon the fundamental purpose of the statute."[18] The majority also held that in granting relief the court could do it on terms; such a power enables the harshness of the illegality doctrine to be tempered in appropriate circumstances.

17-175   The *Bowmakers* principle can, as with the illegality doctrine in general, operate in a capricious way. The capriciousness of its operation was trenchantly criticised in the Australian Higher Court decision, *Nelson v. Nelson*.[19]

"The *Bowmakers* rule has no regard to the legal and equitable rights of the parties, the merits of the case, the effect of the transaction in undermining the policy of the relevant legislation or the question whether the sanctions imposed by the legislation sufficiently protect the purpose of the legislation. Regard is had only to the procedural issue; and it is that issue and not the policy of the legislation or the merits of the parties which determines the outcome. Basing the grant of legal remedies on an essentially procedural criterion which has nothing to do with the equitable positions of the parties or the policy of the legislation is unsatisfactory, particularly when implementing a doctrine that is founded on public policy."

17-176   **Class-protecting statutes.** The action for money had and received will also lie where it is clear from the statute which prohibits the making of the contract or the doing of the act in question that the parties are not to be treated as *in pari delicto*. Thus, as Lord Mansfield said in *Browning v. Morris*,[20]

"But where contracts or transactions are prohibited by positive statutes, for the sake of protecting one set of men from another set of men, the one, from their situation and condition, being liable to be oppressed or imposed upon by the other, there the parties are not *in pari delicto*; and in furtherance of these statutes, the person injured, after the transaction is finished and completed, many bring his action and defeat the contract."

The court will normally grant him relief without putting him on terms, as to impose terms as a condition precedent to the granting of relief would be virtually tantamount to enforcing the illegal contract.[21] For example, the Rent Act 1977 contains provisions[22] entitling a tenant to recover money which he could not lawfully have been required to pay; and in a case decided under an earlier Act it

---

[18] *ibid.* at 149.
[19] *ibid.* at 190.
[20] (1778) 2 Cowp. 790; *Barclay v. Pearson* [1893] 2 Ch. 154; *Bonnard v. Dott* [1906] 1 Ch. 740. In *Lodge v. National Union Investment Co.* [1907] 1 Ch. 300 it was held that the borrower could not recover his securities unless he repaid the money lent to him; but this decision has been distinguished out of existence: *Chapman v. Michaelson* [1908] 2 Ch. 612, [1909] 1 Ch. 238; *Cohen v. J. Lester Ltd* [1939] 1 K.B. 504; *Kasumu v. Baba-Egbe* [1956] A.C. 539; *cf. Barclay v. Prospect Mortgages Ltd* [1974] 1 W.L.R. 837. See also now Consumer Credit Act 1974, s.40(1).
[21] *Kasumu v. Baba-Egbe* [1956] A.C. 539.
[22] *e.g.* ss.119–125; see, *e.g. Steele v. McMahon* [1990] 44 E.G. 65; *Saleh v. Robinson* [1988] 36 E.G. 180. See also Housing Act 1980, s.79; *Ailion v. Spiekermann* [1976] Ch. 158 (illegal premium on assignment); *Farrell v. Alexander* [1977] A.C. 59.

was held that he could recover an illegal premium even though he was a willing party to a fraudulent scheme to evade the Act.[23] It used to be thought that the prevalence of such provisions had made the old class-protecting rules obsolete,[24] until their reaffirmation by the Privy Council in *Kiriri Cotton Co. Ltd v. Dewani*[25]: a tenant paid his landlord a premium for a flat; by accepting the premium, the landlord committed an offence under a Rent Restriction Ordinance which did not expressly say that such premiums could be recovered. Nonetheless the tenant was allowed to recover the premium under the old rules relating to class-protecting statutes.

Oppression and fraud. A person can recover money paid or property trans-   **17-177** ferred under an illegal contract if he was forced by the other party to enter into the illegal contract. "Oppression" is here used in a somewhat broad sense. Thus in *Atkinson v. Denby*[26] the plaintiff was insolvent and offered to pay his creditors a dividend of 5s. in the £. All the creditors were willing to accept the dividend in full settlement of their claims, except the defendants, who said he would only accept it if the plaintiff first paid him £50. The plaintiff did so, but was later allowed to recover the £50 on the ground that he had been forced to agree to defraud the other creditors.[27] Similarly, recovery is possible if the party entered into the contract as a result of the other party's fraudulent misrepresentation that the contract was lawful. Thus in *Hughes v. Liverpool Victoria Legal Friendly Soc.*[28] the plaintiff effected a policy of insurance with the defendants on the life of a person in which he had no insurable interest. The contract was illegal,[29] but the plaintiff was able to recover the premiums he had paid as he had been induced to make the contract by the fraudulent representation of the defendants' agent that the policy was valid. The decisive factor in these cases is the fraud of the defendant and not the innocence of the plaintiff, although if the plaintiff is not innocent there can be no recovery.[30] The plaintiff would have failed if the representation that the policy was valid had been innocently made[31]; if, however, the misrepresentation is one of *fact* rather than law, and no bar to rescission has arisen, then the person who has been induced to enter the contract after the misrepresentation has been made, even *innocently*, would seem to have the right to rescind it and so recover his money or property.[32]

Mistake.[33] There is some authority for the view that money can be recovered   **17-178** if it was paid under an excusable mistake of *fact* affecting the legality of the

---

[23] *Gray v. Southouse* [1949] 2 All E.R. 1019.
[24] See *Green v. Portsmouth Stadium* [1953] 2 Q.B. 190; where the ratio now appears to be that the statute in question was passed, not to protect bookmakers, but to regulate racecourses.
[25] [1960] A.C. 192.
[26] (1862) 7 H. & N. 934; *cf. Smith v. Cuff* (1817) 6 M. & S. 169; *Davies v. London & Provincial Marine Insurance Co.* (1878) 8 Ch.D. 469; *Erwin v. Snelgrove* [1927] 4 D.L.R. 1028.
[27] For a case where the "oppression" was caused by factors other than the other party's conduct see *Kiriri Cotton Co. Ltd v. Dewani* [1960] A.C. 190, 205, *per* Lord Denning; contrast *Bigos v. Bousted* [1951] 1 All E.R. 92 (illness of daughter not sufficient to excuse party in making unlawful foreign exchange transaction).
[28] [1916] 2 K.B. 482; *Reynell v. Sprye* (1852) 1 De G.M. & G. 660.
[29] Life Assurance Act 1774, s.1.
[30] *Parkinson v. College of Ambulance Ltd* [1925] 2 K.B. 1.
[31] *Harse v. Pearl Life Assurance Co.* [1904] 1 K.B. 558.
[32] This was assumed in *Edler v. Auerbach* [1950] 1 K.B. 359 where, however, a bar to rescission had arisen. See Treitel, *The Law of Contract* (9th ed., 1995), pp. 449–450.
[33] See Treitel *op. cit.* p. 450. On mistake of law see *post*, §§ 30–038 *et seq.*

contract. In *Oom v. Bruce*[34] the plaintiff as agent for the Russian owner of goods in Russia took out a policy of insurance with the defendant. Neither party knew (or could have known) that Russia had declared war on this country before the contract was made. It was held that the plaintiff could recover his premium as he was not guilty of any fault or blame in entering the illegal contract.

17–179   **Locus poenitentiae: general.**[35] Another exception to the general rule of non-recovery of money paid or property transferred under an illegal contract arises out of the parties' right to resile from such a contract while it is still executory and to recover anything already paid or transferred under the contract.[36] But:

(1) if the illegal purpose has been wholly or substantially effected, or
(2) if the parties have merely been frustrated in their illegal purpose,

the law allows no *locus poenitentiae*. It would also appear that where the contract involves gross moral turpitude or criminality then this doctrine will not apply.[37]

17–180   **Locus poenitentiae: performance.** The first requirement for the operation of the *locus poenitentiae* rule is that the illegal contract must not have been substantially performed. In *Taylor v. Bowers*[38] A delivered his goods to B to put them out of reach of his creditors. B, by a fictitious bill of sale, without A's assent assigned them to a third party, who was aware of A's illegal purpose. A sought to repudiate the transaction and recover the goods from the third party. It was held he could do so, as the fraudulent purpose had not been carried out, and therefore A was not driven to rely on the illegal transaction between himself and B. C had no better title than B, as he knew how B had come to be possessed of the goods. The court will not allow a party to repudiate a contract merely because his illegal purpose has not yet been wholly performed; substantial performance will preclude his recovering. Thus in *Kearley v. Thomson*[39] it was agreed that a solicitor's costs would be paid if he consented not to appear at a public examination of a bankrupt and not to oppose his discharge. The solicitor did not appear at his examination, and before any application for discharge was made, the plaintiff brought his action to recover back the money he had paid as costs. The contract was illegal and its substantial performance prevented recovery. *Taylor v. Bowers*[40] and *Kearley v. Thomson*[41] are difficult to reconcile. Perhaps *Taylor v. Bowers* is to be explained as a case of bailment in which the plaintiff could disregard the illegal contract and rely on his continuing proprietary interest.[42] Or it may merely be that both are borderline cases, but that, on the view of the facts taken by the courts, whereas in *Taylor v. Bowers* nothing irrevocable had yet been

---

[34] (1810) 12 East 225.

[35] See Beatson (1975) 91 L.Q.R. 313; Merkin (1981) 97 L.Q.R. 420.

[36] *Bone v. Ekless* (1860) 29 L.J.Ex. 438, 440; *Palaniappa Chettiar v. Arunasalam Chettiar* [1962] A.C. 294, 302–303.

[37] See *Tappenden v. Randall* (1801) 2 B. & P. 467.

[38] (1876) 1 Q.B.D. 291; *Symes v. Hughes* (1870) L.R. 9 Eq. 475; *Tribe v. Tribe* [1996] Ch. 107.

[39] (1890) 24 Q.B.D. 742; *Re National Benefit Assurance Co. Ltd* [1931] 1 Ch. 46; *Parker (Harry) Ltd v. Mason* [1940] 2 K.B. 590.

[40] (1876) 1 Q.B.D. 291.

[41] (1890) 24 Q.B.D. 742.

[42] See *ante*, §§ 17–171, 17–172.

done in the performance of the illegal contract, in *Kearley v. Thomson* a substantial part of it had clearly been performed. It has been argued that the "limit of the *locus poenitentiae* may well be at the point whereby recovery will not increase the chances of thwarting the illegal purpose"[43]: thus recovery was needed in *Taylor v. Bowers*[44] to protect the interests of the plaintiff's creditors but no such recovery was required in *Kearley v. Thomson*. Although, if this is adopted as the guiding principle, then arguably the courts should allow recovery up to the point where the contract has been performed.[45] This will provide the parties with the maximum opportunity to resile and thus defeat the carrying out of the illegal purpose, and will also not provide any incentive for the parties to perform in part as a ploy for preventing the operation of the *locus poenitentiae* principle.[46]

Locus poenitentiae: frustration. The second requirement with respect to the **17–181** *locus poenitentiae* principle is that the reason for the plaintiff's repudiation must be voluntary; the plaintiff must genuinely repent and not merely seek recovery because the illegal purpose of the contract has been frustrated. *Bigos v. Bousted*[47] illustrates the operation of this requirement. There one party agreed to supply another party with lira. The agreement was illegal as it violated the prevailing exchange control legislation. The party who agreed to supply the lira failed to do so, and the other party brought an action to recover securities deposited in connection with the illegal agreement. His action was unsuccessful, the court reasoning that he had not repented but rather his reason for repudiating the agreement was merely that the other party had failed to carry it out.[48]

Marriage brokage contracts. For historical reasons the general rule of non- **17–182** recovery after substantial performance does not apply to marriage brokage contracts. In such cases, equity had always allowed relief to the party dealing with the marriage broker owing to the jealousy with which contracts relating to marriage were regarded; and the common law courts adopted this equitable exception. In *Hermann v. Charlesworth*,[49] therefore, although the defendant had taken steps and incurred expense towards carrying out his part of a marriage brokage contract, the plaintiff was allowed to recover back money she had paid thereunder.

Principal and agent. A principal can recover from his agent money which he **17–183** has paid to the agent, albeit for a legally objectionable purpose, provided that he instructs the agent to return it to him before the agent has paid it over under the

---

[43] Beatson (1975) 91 L.Q.R. 313, 316; Treitel, "Contract and Crime" in Tapper (ed.), *Crime, Proof and Punishment*, pp. 103–104.

[44] (1876) 1 Q.B.D. 291, 300, *per* Mellish L.J.: "To hold that the plaintiff is enabled to recover does not carry out the illegal transaction, but the effect is to put everybody in the same situation as they were before the illegal transaction was determined upon, and before the parties took steps to carry it out."

[45] See Burrows, *The Law of Restitution* (1993), p. 340.

[46] See, *e.g. Harry Parker Ltd v. Mason* [1940] 2 K.B. 590; Palmer, *Law of Restitution* (1978), Vol. II, p. 216 dealing with *Hastelow v. Jackson* (1828) 2 B. & C. 221.

[47] [1951] 1 All E.R. 92; *Tribe v. Tribe, supra*. See also Merkin (1981) 97 L.Q.R. 420, 428–431.

[48] It is unclear how far normal bars to rescission apply to withdrawal during the *locus poenitentiae*: see Burrows *op. cit.* pp. 340–341.

[49] [1905] 2 K.B. 123; and see *Roberts v. Roberts* (1730) 3 P.Wms. 66, 75, 76; *Cole v. Gibson* (1750) 1 Ves.Sen. 503. See also § 17–072.

contract,[50] at any rate if the purpose was not grossly criminal or turpitudinous or if the principal still enjoyed a *locus poenitentiae*.[51] Where money is received by an agent for his principal from a third party under an illegal contract it would seem that the principal may recover the money from the agent in an action for money had and received.[52] Where the receipt of the money is itself illegal and part of an illegal transaction in which both the principal and the agent are concerned,[53] or the agency itself is otherwise illegal,[54] the principal cannot recover the money from the agent; similarly in such a case in the absence of a *locus poenitentiae*,[55] the principal cannot recover from the agent money which he has paid to the agent for the purposes of the contract and which the agent has wrongfully appropriated to his own use.[56] Nor can a principal sue his agent for failure to perform a transaction which is, by common law or statute, void or otherwise unenforceable at the principal's suit.[57]

17–184   **Trustees and other fiduciaries.** A trustee who misapplies trust funds for an illegal purpose would, on the principles stated above, be unable to recover the funds thus advanced. The *cestuis que trust*, however, where they do not know of, or acquiesce in, the illegal transaction effected by their trustee, appear to be in a better position than he is to recover the trust property which has been illegally advanced and is traceable in the hands of third parties who would, in the absence of illegality, be bound to restore such property. It is submitted that there is no reason of policy why the beneficiary, if innocent of any illegal purpose, should be precluded from recovering in a proprietary action, provided, of course, a proprietary base to the claim can be shown. In any case it is clear that an innocent beneficiary may bring an action *in personam* against the trustee claiming damages for breach of trust, notwithstanding the latter's unlawful purpose. Thus in *Selangor United Rubber Estates Ltd v. Cradock (No. 3)*[58] the plaintiff company, through its directors, lent money to various persons for the purpose of purchasing shares in itself, contrary to section 54 of the Companies Act 1948.[59] It was held

---

[50] *Hampden v. Walsh* (1876) 1 Q.B.D. 189; *Hastelow v. Jackson* (1828) 8 B. & C. 221, 226; *Burge v. Ashley & Smith Ltd* [1900] 1 Q.B. 744.

[51] *Bone v. Eckles* (1860) 5 H. & N. 925; *Tennant v. Elliott* (1791) 1 B. & P. 3; *Farmer v. Russell* (1798) 1 B. & P. 296. As to *locus poenitentiae*, see *ante*, §§ 17–179, 17–181.

[52] See *Sykes v. Beadon* (1879) 11 Ch.D. 170, 194–195; and see *Bridger v. Savage* (1885) 15 Q.B.D. 363; *De Mattos v. Benjamin* (1894) 63 L.J.Q.B. 248; *cf. Rawlings v. General Trading Corporation* [1921] 1 K.B. 635, 642; *Hill v. William Hill (Park Lane) Ltd* [1949] A.C. 530.

[53] *Nicholson v. Gooch* (1856) 5 E. & B. 999, 1016; *cf. Jubilee Cotton Mills Ltd v. Lewis* [1924] A.C. 958, 978.

[54] See *Harry Parker Ltd v. Mason* [1940] 2 K.B. 590; *Kabel v. Ronald Lyon Espanola S.A.* (1968) 208 E.G. 269. For criticisms of this requirement, see Merkin (1981) 97 L.Q.R. 420, 437–439.

[55] See n. 39, *supra*.

[56] See n. 42, *supra*.

[57] *Cohen v. Kittell* (1889) 22 Q.B.D. 680.

[58] [1968] 1 W.L.R. 1555, 1652–1659.

[59] The Companies Act 1948, s.54, has been repealed by the Companies Act 1981, Sched. 4. On the provision of financial assistance by a company for the purchase or subscription of its shares see Companies Act 1985, ss.151–154 (special rules for private companies are to be found in ss.155–158). Subsequent to *Selangor United Rubber Estates Ltd v. Cradock (No. 3)* [1968] 1 W.L.R. 1555 the courts interpreted the Companies Act 1948, s.54, as being for the protection of the company, despite the fact that criminal sanctions can be imposed on the company for breach of the section (s.54(2)), and thus the company could bring an action to recover any money or property transferred under the section. See *ante*, § 9–035; *Belmont Finance Ltd v. Williams Furniture Ltd (No. 2)* [1980] 1 All E.R. 393; *Armour Hick Northern Ltd v. Whitehouse* [1980] 1 W.L.R. 1520. See also *International Sales and Agencies Ltd v. Marcus* [1982] 2 C.M.L.R. 46, 55.

that the company could claim damages[60] against its directors for breach of their fiduciary duty to the company to apply its funds for authorised purposes only, and against its bankers both for breach of their duty as constructive trustees of the company's accounts and also in contract for negligence in the running of its financial affairs.

5. SEVERANCE

Introductory. Where all the terms of a contract are illegal or against public   **17–185** policy or where the whole contract is prohibited by statute, clearly no action can be brought by the guilty party on the contract; but sometimes, although parts of a contract[61] are unenforceable for such reasons, other parts, were they to stand alone, would be unobjectionable. The question then arises whether the unobjectionable may be enforced and the objectionable disregarded or "severed."[62] The same question arises in relation to bonds where the condition is partly against the law.[63]

Partial statutory invalidity. It was laid down in some of the older cases that   **17–186** there is a distinction between a deed or condition which is void in part by statute and one which is void in part at common law.[64] This distinction must now be understood to apply only to cases where the statute enacts that an agreement or deed made in violation of its provisions shall be wholly void.[65] Unless that is so, then provided the good part is separable from and not dependent on the bad, that part only will be void which contravenes the provisions of the statute. The general rule is that "where you cannot sever the illegal from the legal part of a covenant, the contract is altogether void; but, where you can sever them, whether the illegality be created by statute or by the common law, you may reject the bad

---

[60] Breach of s.54 (repealed and replaced by s.151 of the Companies Act 1985) would give rise to an action for breach of trust against the directors and any person who assisted in that breach: *Selangor United Rubber Estates Ltd v. Cradock (No. 3)* [1968] 1 W.L.R. 1555; *Belmont Finance Corp. Ltd v. Williams Furniture Ltd (No. 2)* [1980] 1 All E.R. 393.

[61] Where one contract is collateral to another and illegal contract, the former may be "tainted" by the illegality of the latter (see the authorities cited in § 17–159, n. 18, *ante*); the courts thus look at the substance of the matter and treat the two transactions as forming a single and unseverable arrangement. In *Spector v. Ageda* [1973] Ch. 30, Megarry J. expressed the view *obiter* that where the original transaction is only partially illegal, *e.g.* by statute, then unless that partial illegality is shown to relate solely to some defined portion of the subsequent transaction, so that only that defined portion is affected, the *whole* of the subsequent transaction will be affected by the illegality. This means that the party to the subsequent transaction is put in a worse position than the party to the original illegal transaction, a view admitted by the judge to be "draconian," but consistent with the court's policy against devising means of preventing those who are implicated from burning their fingers more than to a limited extent. Similarly, individual covenants in a contract may be so closely connected that they stand or fall together, although the remainder of the contract may be severable: *Esso Petroleum Co. Ltd v. Harper's Garage (Stourport) Ltd* [1968] A.C. 269, 314, 321.

[62] See Marsh, (1948) 64 L.Q.R. 230, 347.

[63] See *Baker v. Hedgecock* (1889) 39 Ch.D. 520; *Kearney v. Whitehaven Colliery Co. Ltd* [1893] 1 Q.B. 700; *S. Nevanas & Co. v. Walker and Foreman* [1914] 1 Ch. 413, 423; *British Reinforced Concrete Engineering Co. Ltd v. Schelff* [1921] 2 Ch. 563.

[64] *Maleverer v. Redshaw* (1670) 1 Mod. 35; repudiated in *Collins v. Blantern* (1767) 2 Wils.K.B. 341, 347, 351.

[65] *Doe d. Thompson v. Pitcher* (1815) 6 Taunt. 359, 369.

part and retain the good."⁶⁶ Thus, a covenant in a lease that the tenant should pay "all parliamentary taxes," only included such as he might lawfully pay, and a separate covenant to pay the landlord's property tax, which it was illegal for a tenant to contract to pay, although void, did not affect the validity of the instrument.⁶⁷ In some situations where there is a statutory requirement to obtain a licence for work above a stipulated financial limit but up to that limit no licence is required, the courts will enforce a contract up to that limit.⁶⁸ There is some doubt whether this applies to a lump sum contract "for a single and indivisible work."⁶⁹ Even in this situation if the cost element can be divided into its legal and illegal components, the courts will enforce the former but not the latter.⁷⁰

17–187   **General principles.** Although a number of authorities on the application of the doctrine of severance cannot easily be reconciled, it is submitted that two underlying principles have throughout guided the courts. First, the courts will not make a new contract for the parties, whether by rewriting the existing contract, or by basically altering its nature⁷¹; secondly, the courts will not sever the unenforceable parts of a contract unless it accords with public policy to do so.⁷²

17–188   **Contracts cannot be rewritten.** The first limitation on the courts' power to sever the bad from the good is that they cannot make a new contract for the parties. Examples of one aspect of this limitation are provided by the courts' refusal to rewrite contracts which contain provisions in restraint of trade. The severance of the unreasonable part of the covenants in these cases is effected only where it is possible to do so by merely running a blue pencil through the offending part. For the blue pencil test to apply, it is essential that "the severed parts are independent of one another and can be severed without the severance affecting the meaning of the part remaining."⁷³ Thus, in *Goldsoll v. Goldman*,⁷⁴ the defendant, who was a London dealer in imitation jewellery, on selling his business to the plaintiff, covenanted not to compete with the plaintiff as "a dealer in real or imitation jewellery in . . . any part of the United Kingdom, . . . the

---

⁶⁶ *Pickering v. Ilfracombe Ry.* (1868) L.R. 3 C.P. 235, 250; *Payne v. Brecon Corporation* (1858) 3 H. & N. 572; *Pallister v. Gravesend Corporation* (1850) 9 C.B. 774; *Royal Exchange Assurance Corporation v. Sjorforsakrings Aktiebolaget Vega* [1901] 2 K.B. 567, 573; *Chemidus Wavin Ltd v. Société Pour La Transformation Et L'Exploitation Des Resines Industrielles SA* [1978] 3 C.M.L.R. 514. *cf. Electrical Trades Union v. Tarlo* [1984] Ch. 720, 731.

⁶⁷ *Gaskell v. King* (1809) 11 East 165; and see *Wigg v. Shuttleworth* (1810) 13 East 87; *Howe v. Synge* (1812) 15 East 440; *Greenwood v. Bishop of London* (1814) 5 Taunt. 727; as to personal covenants in deeds where the real security is by statute void see *Mouys v. Leake* (1799) 8 T.R. 411; *Gibbons v. Hooper* (1831) 2 B. & Ad. 734.

⁶⁸ *Frank W. Clifford Ltd v. Garth* [1956] 1 W.L.R. 570.

⁶⁹ *ibid.* at 572.

⁷⁰ *United City Merchants (Investments) Ltd v. Royal Bank of Canada* [1982] Q.B. 208, on appeal [1983] 1 A.C. 168. See also *ante*, § 17–148.

⁷¹ Where a contract contains an ancillary provision which is illegal and which is for the benefit of the plaintiff, the court will normally be disposed to allow the plaintiff to waive it and enforce the contract: *Carney v. Herbert* [1985] A.C. 301, 317A–B, PC.

⁷² For observations on the statement of principle in § 17–187, see *United City Merchants, etc., ibid.* at 229–230, *per* Stephenson L.J.

⁷³ *Business Seating (Renovations) Ltd v. Broad* [1989] I.C.R. 729, 734. Where the covenant contains a number of separate and distinct prohibitions, severance will be more easy to effect: see *Ginsberg v. Parker* [1988] I.R.L.R. 483.

⁷⁴ [1914] 2 Ch. 603; [1915] 1 Ch. 192; followed in *Ronbar Enterprises Ltd v. Green* [1954] 1 W.L.R. 815; and see *Scorer v. Seymour Jones* [1966] 1 W.L.R. 1419; *Francis Delzenne Ltd v. Klee* (1968) 112 S.J. 583.

United States of America, Russia or Spain." The covenant was unreasonable in so far as it extended to real jewellery and to competition outside the United Kingdom, but was otherwise reasonable. It was held that the words "real or" and the listed places outside the United Kingdom could be severed leaving only a reasonable covenant which could be enforced.

Scope of agreement to be left unchanged. Although the courts will never **17–189** effect a severance unless the illegal part can be "blue pencilled," it does not follow that they will always effect a severance when that is so.[75] The court will not strike out words of a contract if to do so would "alter entirely the scope and intention of the agreement,"[76] there being "in truth but one covenant" and not two.[77] The question of what is a single covenant and of what is the scope of an agreement is in each case one as to the proper construction of that particular covenant or agreement.[78] Thus, where the business intended to be protected by a restrictive covenant contained several departments, it was held that a covenant which restricted the covenantor from carrying on any of the sorts of business carried on by those departments, was a single covenant and was not severable in respect of the different sorts of business.[79] Again, a covenant not to engage in a business in any one of several capacities was held to be a single covenant.[80] *Goldsoll v. Goldman*,[81] on the other hand, provides an illustration where certain areas[82] and types of business[83] which a covenant in restraint of trade unreasonably covered were held to be severable. So too, a covenant not to disclose trade secrets may be severable from a covenant not to engage in a business.[84] Where an employee's covenant not to interfere with customers of the employer[85] is so construed that "customers" includes those persons who first become customers after the termination of the service, it will in ordinary circumstances be regarded as a single covenant and will not be severed so as to allow of its enforcement in respect of those who were customers during the service.[86]

Severance of a condition. Many covenants in restraint of trade will be in **17–190** conditional form and provide that X will receive £Y on condition that he refrains

---

[75] *Attwood v. Lamont* [1920] 3 K.B. 571, 578, 593.

[76] *ibid.* at 580; and see *post*, § 17–192.

[77] *Attwood v. Lamont, supra,* at 593; and see *Baker v. Hedgecock* (1888) 39 Ch.D. 520; *Kenyon v. Darwen Cotton Manufacturing Co. Ltd* [1936] 2 K.B. 193.

[78] *Miles v. Durham* [1891] 1 Ch. 576.

[79] *Attwood v. Lamont, supra; British Reinforced Concrete Engineering Co. Ltd v. Schelff* [1921] 2 Ch. 563.

[80] *British Reinforced Concrete Engineering Co. Ltd v. Schelff, supra.*

[81] [1914] 2 Ch. 603; [1915] 1 Ch. 292.

[82] And see *Mallan v. May* (1843) 11 M. & W. 653; *Underwood & Son Ltd v. Barker* [1899] 1 Ch. 300; *Hooper & Ashby v. Willis* (1905) 94 L.T. 624; *Bromley v. Smith* [1909] 2 K.B. 235; *Nevanas & Co. v. Walker and Foreman* [1914] 1 Ch. 413; *Putsman v. Taylor* [1927] 1 K.B. 637, 741.

[83] And see *Hooper v. Willis, supra; Bromley v. Smith, supra.*

[84] *Caribonum Co. Ltd v. Le Couch* (1913) 109 L.T. 385, 587.

[85] A covenant by a managing director against soliciting customers while so employed or afterwards has been upheld as not wider than necessary for the protection of the covenantee's trade: *Gilford Motor Co. Ltd v. Horne* [1933] Ch. 935.

[86] *Konski v. Peet* [1915] 1 Ch. 530; *East Essex Farmers Ltd v. Holder* [1926] W.N. 230; *Express Dairy Co. v. Jackson* (1930) 99 L.J.K.B. 181; in *Baines v. Geary* (1887) 35 Ch.D. 154 and *Dubowski & Sons v. Goldstein* [1896] 1 Q.B. 478, the covenants were held to be severable; but unless distinguishable on the terms of the covenants, these two authorities probably cannot now be relied on: see *Continental Tyre Co. v. Heath* (1913) 29 T.L.R. 308. See also *S. Ivestone Records Ltd v. Mountfield* [1993] E.M.L.R. 152.

from doing a particular act. Assuming that the condition is in restraint of trade, the question arises as to whether the severance of the condition is at all possible in that it will transform a conditional obligation on the part of the covenantor into an absolute one; that is, payment of the £Y will be due even though X does not perform part of the bargain. This was the issue in *Marshall v. N.M. Financial Management Ltd.*[87] The case involved a provision in a contract for the payment of commission to a self-employed sales agent after the contract's termination. Payment of the commision was conditional on the ex-agent not competing with the defendant for a period of one year. The court held that the anti-competition covenant was in restraint of trade. The question before the court was whether the plaintiff as the party "who has been freed from an invalid restraint of trade can enforce the remainder of the contract without it".[88] The court held that he could since the "whole or substantially the whole [of the] consideration[89] was not the restraint but the provision of the services that earned the commission.

Where a mortgage imposed upon the mortgagor an obligation, which was in unreasonable restraint of trade, to buy certain kinds of goods only from the mortgagee for 21 years, the unenforceability of the tie was so closely linked with the provision in the mortgage that it should be irredeemable for the same period, that this provision too was held to be unenforceable, though in other respects the enforceability of the mortgage itself was unaffected.[90]

17–191   **Rules of association in part objectionable.** If the fundamental object of any association, whether it be a combination to fix prices or a trade union, is obnoxious to the law because it is an unreasonable restraint of trade, at common law the association is illegal and the agreement upon which it is founded is wholly unenforceable.[91] So, for instance, where a society with the militant objects of a trade union combined with these the provident purposes of a friendly society and by its rules members might be expelled and their benefits forfeited for non-compliance with the decisions of committees directing the militant operations, it was held that the main object was illegal as being in restraint of trade and that as the provident rules were inseparably connected with that object, they were affected by its illegality and were therefore unenforceable.[92] If the fundamental object of the association is not unlawful, the fact that certain of its rules are in unreasonable restraint of trade does not make the association unlawful though of course those particular rules cannot be enforced.[93]

17–192   **Illegality of part of the consideration.** Many of the older authorities laid down that if a contract was made on several considerations, one of which was illegal, the whole contract was unenforceable and severance was impossible.[94]

---

[87] [1997] 1 W.L.R. 1527.

[88] *ibid.* at 1531.

[89] Citing Denning L.J., *Bennett v. Bennett* [1952] 1 K.B. 249, 261.

[90] *Esso Petroleum Co. Ltd v. Harper's Garage (Stourport) Ltd* [1968] A.C. 269, 314, 321. *cf. Petrofina (Gt. Britain) Ltd v. Martin* [1966] Ch. 146 where there was no mortgage and the unreasonable restraints were so pervasive as to vitiate the entire contract.

[91] *Hilton v. Eckersley* (1856) 6 E. & B. 47. See *ante*, §§ 17–131—17–134 as to statutory position of such associations.

[92] *Russell v. Amalgamated Society of Carpenters* [1912] A.C. 421; *cf. Swaine v. Wilson* (1889) 24 Q.B.D. 252; *Finch v. Oake* [1896] 1 Ch. 409.

[93] *Collins v. Locke* (1879) 4 App.Cas. 674; *Osborne v. Amalgamated Society of Railway Servants* [1911] 1 Ch. 540, 553.

[94] *Shackell v. Rosier* (1836) 3 Scott 59; *Lound v. Grimwade* (1888) 39 Ch.D. 605; *Jones v. Merionethshire Permanent Benefit Bldg. Soc.* [1891] 2 Ch. 587; [1892] 1 Ch. 173.

Such a test is unworkable[95] and, as has been recognised in more modern decisions, the partial illegality, and hence unenforceability, is only relevant in one of two ways. First, the severance of the offending clause may so alter the scope of the whole contract as to make it a new contract. The true test under this head is therefore whether the illegal promise is substantially the whole or main consideration for the promise now sought to be enforced. If it is, then the court will not sever it, leaving only a small part of the consideration to support the promise of the defendant[96]; otherwise it may. Thus, in *Goodinson v. Goodinson*,[97] a husband promised to make regular payments to his wife if she would forbear to bring any matrimonial proceedings against him, would indemnify him against her debts and would not pledge his credit for necessaries. The agreement not to commence matrimonial proceedings was against public policy as an attempt to oust the jurisdiction of the court; but as it did not form the main part of the consideration for the promise to make the payments, the court severed that part of the agreement and enforced the rest in favour of the wife.[98] Similarly an employee can sue for his whole wages notwithstanding that his contract of employment imposes upon him a severable covenant in restraint of trade. An alternative approach is to be found in *South Western Mineral Water Co. Ltd v. Ashmore*[99]; the illegal term of a contract was there severed, but the contract was thereby so altered in scope that it was held to be unenforceable; *restitutio in integrum* was therefore ordered and an order was made for the return of money paid under the contract. Such an order could not have been made but for the severance of the illegal term.[1]

Severance and public policy. The second way in which the partial illegality **17-193** of the consideration is relevant relates to the second of the two general principles mentioned above.[2] This second limitation on the courts' power to sever the bad from the good is that they will not do so unless this accords with public policy. For example, part of the consideration for the promise of either party may be such as so gravely to taint the whole contract that there is no ground of public policy requiring the courts to assist either party by severing the offending parts.[3] "In all the cases a distinction is taken between a merely void and an illegal consideration."[4] In this context illegal means that which amounts to a criminal offence or is *contra bonos mores*,[5] where, on grounds of public policy, the illegality may, though does not invariably, preclude severance. Agreements the object

---

[95] Williston, *Contracts* (3rd ed.), § 1782; Marsh (1948) 64 L.Q.R. 230, 242.

[96] *Bennett v. Bennett* [1952] 1 K.B. 249; see also *Putsman v. Taylor* [1927] 1 K.B. 637, 639, affd. [1927] 1 K.B. 741; *Chemidus Wavin Ltd v. Société Pour La Transformation Et L'Exploitation Des Resines Industrielle SA* [1978] 3 C.M.L.R. 514, CA.

[97] [1954] 2 Q.B. 118; see now Matrimonial Causes Act 1973, s.34.

[98] And see *Kearney v. Whitehaven Colliery Co.* [1893] 1 Q.B. 700; *Furlong v. Burns & Co.* (1964) 43 D.L.R. (2d) 689; *Ailion v. Spiekermann* [1976] Ch. 158.

[99] [1967] 1 W.L.R. 1110. This case involved the application of Companies Act 1948, s.54, on which see *ante*, § 17–184, n. 59.

[1] See *ante*, §§ 17–169, 17–171.

[2] *Ante*, § 17–187.

[3] *Kuenigl v. Donnersmarck* [1955] 1 Q.B. 515, 537 (in this case the conditions for severance were not satisfied).

[4] *Shackell v. Rosier* (1836) 3 Scott 59, 74.

[5] *Bennett v. Bennett* [1952] 1 K.B. 249, 253–254; *Goodinson v. Goodinson* [1954] 2 Q.B. 118, 120.

of which is to defraud the Revenue,[6] or which involve trading with the enemy,[7] have been held to be incapable of severance.[8] On the other hand, examples of mere voidness on grounds of public policy are agreements to oust the jurisdiction of the court[9] and agreements which are merely in restraint of trade.[10]

17–194   **Employer and employee covenants in restraint of trade.** There is authority for saying that, on grounds of public policy, the courts should be reluctant to sever in favour of an employer[11] the unreasonable clauses in a covenant in restraint of trade made between employer and employee. Thus Lord Moulton in *Mason v. Provident Clothing Co. Ltd*[12] expressed the view that parts of such a covenant should only be severed "in cases where the part so enforceable is clearly severable, and even so only in cases where the excess is of trivial importance, or merely technical, and not a part of the main purport and substance of the clause"; on the ground that it would "be *pessimi exempli* if, when an employer had exacted a covenant deliberately framed in unreasonably wide terms, the courts were to come to his assistance and, by employing their ingenuity and knowledge of the law, carve out of this void covenant the maximum of what he might validly have required." "To hold otherwise," it has been said,[13] is,

> "to expose the covenantor to the almost inevitable risk of litigation which in nine cases out of ten he is very ill able to afford, should he venture to act upon his own opinion as to how far the restraint upon him would be held by the court to be reasonable, while it may give the covenantee the full benefit of unreasonable provisions if the covenantor is unable to face litigation."

However, more modern authorities[14] appear to be in favour of applying to covenants in restraint of trade between employer and employee the same rule as to other covenants, that is to say, the rule that where the parts of a covenant really amount to separate and independent covenants they may be severed from one another, but not otherwise.[15]

---

[6] *Miller v. Karlinski* (1945) 62 T.L.R. 85; *Napier v. National Business Agency Ltd* [1951] 2 All E.R. 264.

[7] *Kuenigl v. Donnersmarck* [1955] 1 Q.B. 515.

[8] This passage was cited with approval in *Hyland v. J. H. Barker (North West) Ltd* [1985] I.C.R. 861, 863–864 where the court held that in determining the continuity of an employee's contract of employment the period during which he was paid an illegal tax-free allowance could not be taken into consideration.

[9] *Czarnikow v. Roth, Schmidt & Co.* [1922] 2 K.B. 478; *Goodinson v. Goodinson* [1954] 2 Q.B. 118.

[10] *e.g. Ronbar Enterprises Ltd v. Green* [1954] 1 W.L.R. 815; and see *Mogul SS. Co. Ltd v. McGregor, Gow & Co.* [1892] A.C. 25, 46–47; *R. v. Stainer* (1870) L.R. 1 C.C.R. 230.

[11] But the employee can sever on the ordinary principles so as, *e.g.* to sue for his whole wages during the continuance of his employment despite the fact that he is subject to an unreasonable restraint: see *ante*, §§ 17–185 *et seq.*; and *cf. ante*, § 17–113.

[12] [1913] A.C. 724, 745.

[13] *Goldsoll v. Goldman* [1914] 2 Ch. 603, 613 (affd. [1915] 1 Ch. 292) cited with approval in *Attwood v. Lamont* [1920] 3 K.B. 571, 595.

[14] *Francis Delzene v. Klee* (1968) S.J. 583; *Lucas & Co. Ltd v. Mitchell* [1974] Ch. 129; *Stenhouse Australia Co. Ltd v. Phillips* [1974] A.C. 391. *cf. Ronbar Enterprises v. Green* [1954] 1 W.L.R. 815, 820.

[15] *S. Nevanas & Co. v. Walker and Foreman* [1914] 1 Ch. 413, 423 (where it was said that the remarks of Lord Moulton cited *ante* were not intended to apply where parts of a covenant are clearly severed by the parties themselves so as to amount to separate covenants); *Putsman v. Taylor* [1927] 1 K.B. 637, 641; *Spink (Bournemouth) Ltd v. Spink* [1936] Ch. 544.

6. PLEADING AND PRACTICE

Presumption of legality. The party alleging the illegality of the contract bears   **17-195**
the legal burden of proving this fact[16]; therefore if the contract be reasonably
susceptible of two meanings or two modes of performance, one legal and the
other not the legal burden of proving its illegality is undischarged and that
interpretation is to be put upon the contract which will support it and give it
operation.[17] If the contract on the face of it shows an illegal intention, an
evidential burden lies upon the party supporting the contract to bring evidence
reasonably capable of showing the legality of the intention.[18]

Pleading of illegality. Where a contract is *ex facie* illegal, the court will not   **17-196**
enforce it, whether the illegality is pleaded or not; secondly, where the contract
is not *ex facie* illegal, evidence of extraneous circumstances tending to show that
it has an illegal object should not be admitted unless the circumstances relied on
are pleaded; thirdly, where unpleaded facts, which, taken by themselves, show an
illegal object, have been put in evidence (because, perhaps, no objection was
raised or because they were adduced for some other purpose), the court should
not act on them unless it is satisfied that the whole of the relevant circumstances
are before it; but fourthly, where the court[19] is satisfied that all the relevant facts
are before it and it can clearly see from them that the contract had an illegal
object, it may not enforce the contract, whether the facts were pleaded or not.[20]
It has been said that counsel is not acting improperly in inviting the court to
consider the possible, though unpleaded, illegality of a transaction but that on the
contrary counsel's duty is to prevent the court from enforcing illegal
transactions.[21]

Costs. Where a defendant successfully raises a plea of illegality, the ordinary   **17-197**
rules as to costs apply.[22]

---

[16] *Hire-Purchase Furnishing Co. v. Richens* (1887) 20 Q.B.D. 387, 389.

[17] *R. v. Inhabitants of Haslingfield* (1814) 2 M. & S. 558; *Bennett v. Clough* (1818) 1 B. & Ald.
461; *Lewis v. Davison* (1839) 4 M. & W. 654, 657; *Mittelholzer v. Fullarton* (1842) 6 Q.B. 989; *Edler
v. Auerbach* [1950] 1 K.B. 359, 368; *Archbolds (Freightage) Ltd v. S. Spanglett Ltd* [1961] 1 Q.B.
374, 391-392. See also § 17-007—17-011, *ante*.

[18] *Holland v. Hall* (1817) 1 B. & Ald. 53.

[19] The rule applies to appellate courts as well as to courts of first instance: *Snell v. Unity Finance
Ltd* [1964] 2 Q.B. 203.

[20] *Edler v. Auerbach* [1950] 1 K.B. 359, 371. See *Holman v. Johnson* (1775) 1 Cowp. 341; *Evans
v. Richardson* (1817) 3 Mer. 469; *Scott v. Brown, Doering, McNab & Co.* [1892] 2 Q.B. 724; *Gedge
v. Royal Exchange Assurance Corporation* [1900] 2 Q.B. 214; *North Western Salt Co. v. Electrolytic
Alkali Co. Ltd* [1913] 3 K.B. 422, 424; [1914] A.C. 461, 476, 477; *Montefiore v. Menday Motor
Components Co. Ltd* [1918] 2 K.B. 241; *Alexander v. Rayson* [1936] 1 K.B. 169, 190; *Commercial
Air Hire Ltd v. Wrightways Ltd* [1938] 1 All E.R. 89; *Palaniappa Chettiar v. Arunasalam Chettiar*
[1962] A.C. 294; *Snell v. Unity Finance Co. Ltd* [1964] 2 Q.B. 203; *Mercantile Credit Co. Ltd v.
Hamblin* [1965] 2 Q.B. 242, 261–262, 276; *Crouch and Lees v. Haridas* [1972] 1 Q.B. 158; *U.C.M.
v. Royal Bank of Canada* [1983] 1 A.C. 168, 169; the law is summarised in *Bank of India v. Trans
Continental Commodity Merchants Ltd* [1982] 1 Lloyd's Rep. 427, 429.

[21] *Mercantile Credit Co. Ltd v. Hamblin* [1964] 1 W.L.R. 423 (affd. on other grounds [1965] 2 Q.B.
242).

[22] *Sphinx Export Co. v. Specialist Shippers* [1954] C.L.Y. 1440.

Part Five

JOINT OBLIGATIONS, THIRD PARTIES AND ASSIGNMENT

CHAPTER 18

JOINT OBLIGATIONS[1]

Introductory: definitions. Several liability arises when two or more persons **18–001** make separate promises to another, whether by the same instrument or by different instruments. Thus if A and B covenant with C that they will each pay him £100, each is liable to pay £100[2]; their promises are cumulative and payment by one does not discharge the other.[3]

Joint liability arises when two or more persons jointly promise to do the same **18–002** thing. There is only one obligation,[4] and consequently, performance by one discharges the others. Joint liability is subject to a number of strict and technical rules of law which are discussed in the paragraphs that follow.

Joint and several liability arises when two or more persons in the same **18–003** instrument jointly promise to do the same thing and also severally make separate promises to do the same thing. Joint and several liability gives rise to one joint obligation and to as many several obligations as there are joint and several promisors. It is like joint liability in that the co-promisors are not cumulatively liable, so that performance by one discharges all; but it is free from most of the technical rules governing joint liability.

It should be emphasised that the above definitions—and the treatment in this **18–004** chapter—focus on the standard *contractual* situations where the issues of several, joint, or joint and several liability arise. Particularly in mind is where the contractual liability is to pay an agreed sum (that is, a debt). Cutting across those definitions is joint and several liability in its traditional "tort" sense[5] of wrong-doers acting independently to cause the same damage to the same claimant: and a wrongdoer for these purposes can include a contract-breaker as well as a

---

[1] See, generally, Williams, *Joint Obligations* (1949).

[2] *e.g. Mikeover Ltd v. Brady* [1989] 3 All E.R. 618.

[3] An exception is an original lessee's and a subsequent assignee's covenants to the lessor to pay rent. These are regarded as creating several but non-cumulative liability. Payment by one does discharge the other; and the rules of release for joint and several liability apply so that contractual release of one promisor releases the other. See Williams, *Joint Obligations* (1949), § 5; *Deanplan Ltd v. Mahmoud* [1993] Ch. 151. For leases granted after 1995 the original tenant will generally be released from covenants in the lease once the lease has been assigned: see Landlord and Tenant (Covenants) Act 1995, ss.3 and 5. But under s.16 a tenant may enter into an "authorised guarantee agreement" to guarantee compliance with the covenants by the assignee.

[4] *King v. Hoare* (1844) 13 M. & W. 494; *Kendall v. Hamilton* (1879) 4 App.Cas. 504; *Re Hodgson* (1885) 31 Ch.D. 177, 188.

[5] For the tort definitions of several, joint, and joint and several liability, and the rules applying to them, see *Clerk and Lindsell on Torts* (17th ed., 1995), §§ 4–54—4–67. See also Williams, *Joint Torts and Contributory Negligence* (1951). The tort rules (*e.g.* on release) applicable to joint and several wrongdoers (*e.g.* release of one does not release the others; see *Clerk and Lindsell on Torts*, § 4–55) appear to differ from the contractual rules applicable to joint and several promisors (*e.g.* release of one releases the others: see *post*, § 18–017).

tortfeasor.[6] So if the same loss is caused to P by D1's breach of contract and D2's tort, D1 and D2 are jointly and severally liable to P.[7] This will mean that D1 and D2 are each liable for the whole of P's loss albeit that, if one defendant pays a disproportionate sum to the other, contribution can be recovered from the other defendant under the Civil Liability (Contribution) Act 1978.

18–005   **Creation of joint liability.** The presumption is that a promise made by two or more persons is joint so that express words are necessary to make it joint and several.[8] There are one or two special cases in which equity treats as joint and several an obligation which at law is joint, but they do not cover much ground and are of slight importance in the law of contract.[9] The liability of partners for partnership debts is a good example of joint liability, but it differs from the ordinary case of joint liability in that the estate of a deceased partner is liable for partnership debts (after satisfaction of personal debts) if the firm is unable to satisfy them itself.[10] So also the liability of two or more acceptors, drawers or indorsers of a bill of exchange to the holder thereof is joint.[11] In the case of promissory notes the liability is joint, or joint and several, according to the "tenor" of the note[12]; but if the note runs "I promise to pay" and is signed by two or more persons the liability is joint and several.[13] In the absence of words of severance, the liability of principal debtor and surety on a single promise is joint, but if there is not one single promise the general rule is that the liability is several.[14] Consequently the liability of a principal debtor and surety is prima facie joint and several.[15]

18–006   **Words of severance.** As to what constitute words of severance, the cases run to fine distinctions. Thus if A and B promise for themselves or either of them that they will pay £100, the promise is joint and several. But if they promise for themselves that they or either of them will pay £100 the promise is merely joint.[16]

---

[6] There has recently been considerable debate over whether joint and several liability, in its tort sense, should be replaced by proportionate liability. The case for that reform has particularly been urged by auditors in respect of contractual or tortious liability for negligence. For a rejection of that reform, see *Feasibility Investigation of Joint and Several Liability, by the Common Law Team of the Law Commission* (DTI Consultation Paper, 1996). See generally, R. Wright, "The Logic and Fairness of Joint and Several Liability" (1992) 23 Memphis State L.R. 45; M. Simpson, "Apportionment or Compensation? Joint and Several Liability Reconsidered" [1995] N.Z.L.J. 407; J. Payne, "Limiting the Liability of Professional Partnerships: In Search of this Holy Grail" (1997) 18 Company Lawyer 81; J. Freedman and V. Finch, "Limited Liability Partnerships: Have Accountants Sewn Up the 'Deep Pockets' Debate?" [1997] J.B.L. 387.

[7] This is so even though in relation to other promisors D1 might conceivably have been severally, jointly, or jointly and severally liable, in the standard contractual sense, to P.

[8] *White v. Tyndall* (1888) 13 App.Cas. 263; *The Argo Hellas* [1984] 1 Lloyd's Rep. 296, 300.

[9] Williams *op. cit.* § 12.

[10] Partnership Act 1890, s.9. But by reason of s.12 of the 1890 Act, a partner is jointly and severally liable with his co-partners for wrongs committed in the ordinary course of business of the firm.

[11] *Other v. Iveson* (1855) 3 Drew. 177; *Re Barnard* (1886) 32 Ch.D. 447.

[12] Bills of Exchange Act 1882, s.85(1).

[13] *ibid.* s.85(2).

[14] *Lep Air Services Ltd v. Rolloswin Investments Ltd* [1971] 1 W.L.R. 934, affd. on other grounds *sub nom. Moschi v. Lep Air Services Ltd* [1973] A.C. 331. As to the liability of an agent in cases where he is liable together with his principal, see Vol. II, § 32–093.

[15] *Re E.W.A.* [1901] 2 K.B. 642.

[16] *Wilmer v. Currey* (1848) 2 De G. & Sm. 347; *Levy v. Sale* (1877) 37 L.T. 709; *White v. Tyndall* (1888) 13 App.Cas. 263.

This is so even if they promise for themselves their executors and administrators[17]: for the reference to personal representatives is taken to mean the representatives of the survivor.

Contract by person with himself. At common law a joint contract between **18–007** A and B on the one hand and B (or B and C) on the other was void, because a man cannot contract with himself.[18] This rule was altered (with retrospective effect) by section 82 of the Law of Property Act 1925, which provides that any agreement entered into by a person with himself and one or more other persons shall be construed and be capable of being enforced as if it had been made with the other person or persons alone.

Minors. A joint promise by an adult and a minor is binding on the adult **18–008** though it may be unenforceable against or voidable by the minor.[19] A guarantee given by an adult of an obligation undertaken by a minor is not unenforceable against the adult merely because the principal obligation is unenforceable against or is repudiated by the minor.[20]

Joinder of parties. Since a joint promise creates only one obligation, the **18–009** common law rule was that all the promisors who were still alive had to be joined as defendants to the action.[21] There were a number of exceptions to this rule which are detailed below; and since 1959 it has not applied to actions in the county court.[22] The rule does not appear to have been affected by the Civil Liability (Contribution) Act 1978, although that Act (as noted below, § 18–015) has abolished the related common law rule that an action against a joint contractor served to bar any other proceedings against another joint contractor. But the Civil Procedure Rules have been amended since the commencement of the 1978 Act. By Civil Procedure Rules 1998, Part 19, r. 1, the court may, on its own initiative, or on the application of an existing party or a person who wishes to become a party, order a person to be added as a new party if: "(a) it is desirable to add the new party so that the court can resolve all the matters in dispute in the proceedings: or (b) there is an issue involving the new party and an existing party which is connected to the matters in dispute in the proceedings, and it is desirable to add the new party so that the court can resolve that issue."

Under the modern law, therefore, failure to join a party in the first instance can **18–010** no longer be visited by any sanctions, except as to costs[23]; all that can happen is that the court may direct that he be joined. As stated above, the common law rule was that all joint contractors had to be joined as defendants but there were

---

[17] *ibid.* But *cf. Tippins v. Coates* (1853) 18 Beav. 401.

[18] *Mainwaring v. Newman* (1800) 2 Bos. & P. 120; *Neale v. Turton* (1827) 4 Bing. 149; *Faulkner v. Lowe* (1848) 2 Exch. 595; *Boyce v. Edbrooke* [1903] 1 Ch. 836; *Ellis v. Kerr* [1910] 1 Ch. 529; *Napier v. Williams* [1911] 1 Ch. 361.

[19] *Gibbs v. Merrill* (1810) 3 Taunt. 307; *Burgess v. Merrill* (1812) 4 Taunt. 468; *Lovell and Christmas v. Beauchamp* [1894] A.C. 607.

[20] Minors Contracts Act 1987, s.2, which reverses *Coutts and Co. v. Browne-Lecky* [1947] K.B. 104. See also s.4, which amends Consumer Credit Act 1974, s.113(7).

[21] Williams, *Joint Obligations*, § 15; *Cabell v. Vaughan* (1669) 1 Wms.Saund. 290a; *Kendall v. Hamilton* (1879) 4 App.Cas. 504, 542–544.

[22] County Courts Act 1984, s.48(1).

[23] See especially s.4 of the 1978 Act.

exceptions to this rule. There was no need to join one who was a discharged bankrupt,[24] or a person outside the jurisdiction,[25] or a minor as regards whom the contract was void or voidable,[26] or a person protected by the Limitation Act[27] (now the Act of 1980), or a member of a firm of common carriers,[28] or an undisclosed sleeping partner,[29] or an active partner where the defendant represented himself as being the sole contracting party.[30]

18–011   **Joinder of joint and several promisors.** If the obligation is joint and several the claimant has always been able to sue all the promisors together or such one or more of them separately as he thinks fit.[31] But the court's control over procedural matters now means that even in these cases joinder of another co-defendant may be directed where desirable.[32]

18–012   **Death of a joint contractor.** If one joint contractor dies, his obligation ceases and the whole obligation passes to the survivors or survivor and not to his personal representatives.[33] When the last surviving joint contractor dies, the obligation passes to his personal representatives because once there is only a single debtor, the obligation necessarily becomes several.[34] There is one exception to the rule that the personal representatives of one of a number of joint contractors are not liable: though partners are jointly liable for partnership debts, the estate of a deceased partner is also severally liable, subject however to the prior payment of his separate debts.[35]

18–013   **Death of joint and several contractor.** If one joint and several contractor dies, his several liability passes to his personal representatives.[36]

---

[24] Insolvency Act 1986, s.345(4).

[25] Civil Procedure Act 1833, s.8. This section was repealed by the Statute Law Revision and Civil Procedure Act 1883, s.4, but its principle is still applied by the courts, although under RSC, Ord. 11, r. 1(1)(c), preserved by the Civil Procedure Rules 1998, Sched. 1, leave to serve notice of the writ out of the jurisdiction may be granted where any person is a necessary or proper party to an action properly brought against some other person within the jurisdiction. See *Wilson Sons & Co. v. Balcarres Brook SS. Co.* [1893] 1 Q.B. 422.

[26] *Gibbs v. Merrill* (1810) 3 Taunt. 307; *Burgess v. Merrill* (1812) 4 Taunt. 468.

[27] Jacobs and Goldrein, *Pleadings: Principles and Practice* (1990), pp. 200–201. One joint debtor may be protected by the Limitation Act and the other not where, *e.g.* the other has acknowledged the debt: Limitation Act 1980, s.31(6), *post*, § 18–026.

[28] Carriers Act 1830, s.5.

[29] *Ex p. Hodgkinson* (1815) 19 Ves. 291, 294; *Ex p. Norfolk* (1815) 19 Ves. 455, 458; *Mullett v. Hook* (1827) M. & M. 89; *De Mautort v. Saunders* (1830) 1 B. & Ad. 399; *Kendall v. Hamilton* (1879) 4 App.Cas. 504, 513–514, 541.

[30] *Baldney v. Ritchie* (1816) 1 Stark. 338; *Stansfeld v. Levy* (1820) 3 Stark. 8.

[31] *Cabell v. Vaughan* (1669) 1 Wms.Saund. 291, n. 4; Williams, *Joint Obligations* (1949), § 20; Treitel, *The Law of Contract* (9th ed., 1995), p. 524.

[32] Civil Procedure Rules 1998, Part 19, r. 1.

[33] *White v. Tyndall* (1888) 13 App.Cas. 263. *Quaere* whether this rule has been abolished by s.1(1) of the Law Reform (Miscellaneous Provisions) Act 1934: see Williams *op. cit.* § 25; Treitel *op. cit.* p. 525.

[34] *Calder v. Rutherford* (1882) 3 Brod. & Bing. 302.

[35] Partnership Act 1890, s.9; *cf. Kendall v. Hamilton* (1879) 4 App.Cas. 504, 538–539; *Re Hodgson* (1885) 31 Ch.D. 177.

[36] *Read v. Price* [1909] 1 K.B. 577; Williams *op. cit.* § 30.

Discharge by performance. Payment of the debt by any one of a number of joint or joint and several debtors operates as a discharge of all, for in neither case is the obligation cumulative.[37]

18–014

Judgment against one joint debtor. At common law, the general rule was that a judgment against one joint debtor operated to bar an action against the others, even though the judgment was not satisfied.[38] This was explained on the ground that the debt was merged in the judgment, and also on the ground that joint debtors had a right to be sued together: but neither ground was satisfactory, and the rule was capable of working hardship. The rule applied to a judgment obtained by consent,[39] even if the defendant subsequently consented to the plaintiff's application to set aside the judgment in order that the plaintiff could sue another joint contractor.[40] The rule has now been abrogated by section 3 of the Civil Liability (Contribution) Act 1978.[41] This section applies to joint contractors generally, and is not confined to joint debtors.[42]

18–015

Judgment against one joint and several debtor. When the liability is joint and several, a judgment against one debtor did not, even at common law, bar a several action against another.[43] But satisfaction of the judgment did so, for the obligation was not cumulative; hence payment by one, whether before or after judgment, discharged the others. At common law, it seems that a joint judgment against all the joint and several debtors, if unsatisfied, did not bar a several action against one of them[44]; nor did an unsatisfied several judgment against one bar a joint action against the others.[45] But these rules are of little

18–016

---

[37] Williams *op. cit.* § 42.

[38] *King v. Hoare* (1844) 13 M. & W. 494; *Kendall v. Hamilton* (1879) 4 App.Cas. 504. There were exceptions to the general rule. For example, if the judgment was a foreign one (*Bank of Australasia v. Nias* (1851) 16 Q.B. 717); or if the defendant in the second action agreed that his own liability should survive the judgment in the first action (*Duffner v. Bowyer* (1924) 40 T.L.R. 700); or if the judgment was on an independent cause of action, such as a negotiable instrument given by one joint debtor (*Drake v. Mitchell* (1803) 3 East 251; *Wegg Prosser v. Evans* [1895] 1 Q.B. 108; *Badeley v. Consolidated Bank* (1886) 34 Ch.D. 536, 556; affd. (1888) 36 Ch.D. 238; *Goldrei, Foucard & Son v. Sinclair* [1918] 1 K.B. 180); or, in relation to liquidated demands, where a judgment was signed against one or more joint debtors in default of notice of intention to defend or in default of defence (Rules of the Supreme Court Ord. 13, r. 1, Ord. 19, r. 2; see also, as regards summary judgment, Ord. 14, r. 8; see now Civil Procedure Rules 1998, Part 12, r. 8 and Part 24).

[39] *McLeod v. Power* [1898] 2 Ch. 295.

[40] *Hammond v. Schofield* [1891] 1 Q.B. 453. See Vol. II, § 32–070.

[41] But in *Morris v. Wentworth-Stanley*, [1999] 2 W.L.R. 470, it was held by the Court of Appeal that section 3 of the Civil Liability (Contribution) Act 1978 did not apply to a judgment obtained by consent: that judgment embodied an accord and satisfaction and the applicable rule was that an accord and satisfaction with one joint debtor released other joint debtors.

[42] It has been said that s.3 applies only to judicial determinations and not to arbitral awards: *The Argo Hellas* [1984] 1 Lloyd's Rep. 296, 304. Section 3 of the 1978 Act replaced s.6 of the Law Reform (Married Women and Tortfeasors) Act 1935, which abolished the "merger" doctrine in respect of joint tortfeasors only. By s.4 of the 1978 Act, if more than one action is brought in respect of the same damage, the plaintiff is to be deprived of his costs unless the court is of the opinion that there was reasonable ground for bringing the action.

[43] *Lechmere v. Fletcher* (1833) 1 C. & M. 623; *King v. Hoare* (1844) 13 M. & W. 494, 505; *Blyth v. Fladgate* [1891] 1 Ch. 337, 353.

[44] *Re Davison, ex p. Chandler* (1884) 13 Q.B.D. 50.

[45] *ibid.* at 53.

importance now, having regard to the general words of section 3 of the Act of 1978.

18–017 **Release, accord and satisfaction and covenant not to sue.** The discharge of one joint debtor by release under seal[46] or by accord and satisfaction[47] discharges all, in accordance with the general principle that joint liability creates only one obligation[48]; and the same is true, illogical though it may seem, if one joint and several debtor is so discharged.[49] On the other hand, a covenant not to sue one joint or joint and several debtor does not discharge the others,[50] though it may leave the covenantee liable to pay contribution to the other debtors,[51] and thus deprive the covenant of some of its apparent effect.[52]

18–018 The courts generally construe a release as a covenant not to sue if it contains an indication of intention that the other debtors are not to be discharged.[53] Moreover, even an accord and satisfaction with one joint or joint and several debtor will not discharge the others if the agreement, expressly or impliedly, provides that the creditor's rights against them shall be preserved.[54]

18–019 The distinction between a release and a covenant not to sue rests on the intention of the parties. A release involves total destruction of the debt or claim; a covenant not to sue implies that the creditor undertakes not to take proceedings against the debtor in question (the covenantee) while not necessarily abandoning his rights against any other party liable. In this context the term "covenant" does

---

[46] Williams, *Joint Obligations* (1949), § 50.

[47] *Nicholson v. Revill* (1836) 4 A. & E. 675; *Re E.W.A.* [1901] 2 K.B. 642; *Morris v. Wentworth-Stanley,* [1999] 2 W.L.R. 470; *cf. Cutler v. McPhail* [1962] 2 Q.B. 292 (joint tortfeasors); *contra,* Williams *op. cit.* § 55, citing earlier authorities to the contrary, some of which, however, may be explained on the principle stated below at n. 54.

[48] In *North v. Wakefield* (1849) 13 Q.B. 536, 541, the reason given was that otherwise the debtor released would be liable for contribution to the debtors not released and so the intention of the parties would be frustrated. But this reasoning seems dubious for it assumes what requires to be proved, *viz.* that the creditor intends to protect the debtor released against claims from his co-debtors. See *Ex p. Good, re Armitage* (1877) 5 Ch.D. 46, 57 where Jessel M.R. said: "It is very dangerous for modern judges to endeavour to find modern reasons for these old rules." See also Williams *op. cit.* pp. 111–112. Similar difficulty attends the rules relating to the discharge of a surety as a result of an agreement to discharge a principal debtor, see Vol. II, §§ 44–068—44–073.

[49] *Nicholson v. Revill* (1836) 4 A. & E. 675; *Re E.W.A.* [1901] 2 K.B. 642; *Deanplan Ltd v. Mahmoud* [1993] Ch. 151; Williams *op. cit.* § 63. *cf. Jameson v. Central Electricity Generating Board* [1999] 2 W.L.R. 141 (a settlement, satisfying a claim against one joint and several tortfeasor, on its true interpretation extinguished the cause of action against the other joint and several tortfeasor).

[50] *Lucy Clayton v. Kynaston* (1699) 12 Mod. 221, 415, 548; *Dean v. Newhall* (1799) 8 T.R. 168; *Hutton v. Eyre* (1815) 6 Taunt. 289 (joint tortfeasors).

[51] *Mallet v. Thompson* (1804) 5 Esp. 178; *Hutton v. Eyre* (1815) 6 Taunt. 289; Williams *op. cit.* § 52.

[52] As to the effect of a covenant, or agreement, not to sue a principal debtor on the liability of a surety, see Vol. II, §§ 44–068—44–073.

[53] *Solly v. Forbes* (1820) 2 Brod. & Bing. 38; *North v. Wakefield* (1849) 13 Q.B. 536; *Thompson v. Lack* (1846) 3 C.B. 540; *Price v. Barker* (1855) 4 E. & B. 760; *Willis v. De Castro* (1858) 4 C.B.(N.S.) 216; *Bateson v. Gosling* (1871) L.R. 7 C.P. 9; *cf. Duck v. Mayeu* [1892] 2 Q.B. 511 (joint tortfeasors); *Apley Estates Co. v. De Bernales* [1947] Ch. 217 (joint tortfeasors); *Gardiner v. Moore* [1969] 1 Q.B. 55 (joint tortfeasors); *Bryanston Finance v. de Vries* [1975] 1 Q.B. 703 (joint tortfeasors); *Watts v. Adlington, The Times,* December 16, 1993 (joint tortfeasors).

[54] *Watters v. Smith* (1831) 2 B. & Ad. 889; *Ex p. Good, re Armitage* (1877) 5 Ch.D. 46; *Re Wolmershausen* (1890) 62 L.T. 541; *Re E.W.A.* [1901] 2 K.B. 642, 648–649; *Johnson v. Davies* [1998] 3 W.L.R. 1299; *cf. Watts v. Adlington, The Times,* December 16, 1993 (joint tortfeasors).

not bear its traditional meaning of a promise under seal, but extends to any promise.

In practice the difficulty normally arises from the fact that, in making the agreement, the parties have overlooked the position of co-debtors, and it is not clear whether the creditor intends to reserve his rights against them or not.[55] If the agreement appears from its words to be a release and there are no words reserving rights against the other debtors, nor anything in the circumstances to rebut the prima facie meaning of words used, the agreement will release all the debtors[56]; but it would seem that the courts lean in favour of other debtors not being discharged by construing the agreement as a covenant not to sue or as a release but subject to an implied reservation of rights against other debtors.[57]

18–020

Sureties. Some special rules apply to joint or joint and several debtors who are sureties. For instance, an agreement to give time to a principal debtor without the consent of a surety discharges the surety unless there is an express reservation of rights against the surety[58]; but an agreement to give time to one co-debtor without the consent of the other does not discharge them[59] unless they are sureties. These special rules as to sureties are fully discussed elsewhere in this work.[60]

18–021

Material alteration. As will be seen,[61] if a material alteration is made in a specialty or any other contractual document without the consent of the promisor, whether by the promisee or (possibly) by a stranger, when the document is in the custody of the promisee or his agent, such alteration discharges the promisor from all liability thereon.[62] The same rule applies to a contract entered into by joint or joint and several contractors.[63] There is no authority on the question whether a material alteration which discharges one operates also to discharge them all.

18–022

Debtor becoming executor or administrator. Where a debtor becomes executor or administrator of the estate of his creditor, the debt is extinguished, but the debtor may be accountable for the amount of the debt,[64] unless the creditor intended by appointing him as executor, to discharge the debt.[65] Although this

18–023

---

[55] *Re E.W.A., supra*, at 649.

[56] *Deanplan Ltd v. Mahmoud* [1993] Ch. 151; *Morris v. Wentworth-Stanley*, [1999] 2 W.L.R. 470.

[57] *Watts v. Adlington, The Times*, December 16, 1993 (which concerned joint tortfeasors). The High Court of Australia in *Thompson v. Australian Capital Television Pty. Ltd* (1996) 186 C.L.R. 574 has removed the release rule altogether in respect of joint tortfeasors. See A. D. M. Hewitt, "Compromising With One Joint Tortfeasor" (1998) 72 A.L.J. 73.

[58] See Vol. II, § 44–082.

[59] *Swire v. Redman* (1876) 1 Q.B.D. 536.

[60] See Vol. II, §§ 44–080—44–089.

[61] *Post*, §§ 26–019—26–021.

[62] *Pigot's Case* (1614) 11 Co.Rep. 26b; *Master v. Miller* (1791) 4 T.R. 320; (1793) 5 T.R. 367.

[63] *Perring v. Hone* (1826) 4 Bing. 29; *Gardner v. Walsh* (1855) 5 E. & B. 83.

[64] See s.21A of the Administration of Estates Act 1925 (inserted by s.10 of the Limitation Amendment Act 1980).

[65] *Strong v. Bird* (1874) L.R. 18 Eq. 315; *Re Applebee* [1891] 3 Ch. 422; *Re Bourne* [1906] 1 Ch. 697. The effect of these decisions is preserved by the wording of s.21A(1)(b) of the Administration of Estates Act 1925, but is now extended also to the case of the debtor who is appointed as administrator.

rule is now statutory, previous authorities holding that co-debtors were necessarily discharged in these circumstances seem unaffected.[66] This result, however, does not prevent the executor or administrator from recovering contribution under the principle stated in § 18–027.[67] In the converse case where the creditor becomes executor to his debtor, the debt is not discharged unless the executor proves the will and has assets out of which he can pay the debt by means of his right of retainer.[68]

18–024 **Bankruptcy.** The discharge in bankruptcy of one joint or joint and several debtor does not discharge the others.[69]

18–025 **Voluntary arrangements with creditors.** Whether a voluntary arrangement with creditors entered into by an insolvent co-debtor, pursuant to the Insolvency Act 1986, does or does not discharge other co-debtors, who are not parties to the voluntary arrangement, will depend on the term of the voluntary arrangement.[70]

18–026 **Limitation Act 1980.** An acknowledgment or part payment of a debt or other liquidated pecuniary claim made by one joint debtor does not take a case out of the Limitation Act 1980 as regards the others,[71] unless (1) it is made with their authority as agent for them,[72] or (2) a part payment (not an acknowledgment) is made before the expiration of the limitation period.[73] The reason for the second exception is that a part payment made before the expiration of the period enures for the advantage of all the joint debtors, hence it is thought fair that they should share the disadvantage too.[74] The rules appear to be the same for joint and several debtors as they are for joint debtors.

18–027 **Contribution between joint debtors.** Joint and joint and several debtors have a restitutionary right of contribution among themselves: that is to say, if one has paid more than his share of the debt, he can recover the excess from the others in equal shares, subject to any agreement to the contrary.[75] In the absence of agreement to the contrary each co-debtor is liable for an equal share of the debt or obligation.[76] This right is statutory in cases where a county court judgment

---

[66] *Cheetham v. Ward* (1797) 1 Bos. & P. 630; *Jenkins v. Jenkins* [1928] 2 K.B. 503.

[67] See *Jenkins v. Jenkins, supra*, at 506.

[68] *Lowe v. Peskett* (1856) 16 C.B. 500; *Re Rhoades* [1899] 2 Q.B. 347.

[69] Insolvency Act 1986, s.281(7).

[70] *Johnson v. Davies* [1998] 3 W.L.R. 1299 (on the construction of its terms, the voluntary arrangement was held not to discharge co-debtors).

[71] Limitation Act 1980, s.31(6). See *post*, § 29–106.

[72] s.30(2).

[73] s.31(7).

[74] But the Law Commission has provisionally recommended that acknowledgments and part payments by one co-debtor should only affect the limitation period running against that debtor and not other co-debtors: see *Limitation of Actions*, Consultation Paper No. 151 (1998), §§ 12.168–12.172.

[75] *Deering v. Earl of Winchelsea* (1787) 1 Cox 318; 2 Bos. & P. 270; *Hutton v. Eyre* (1815) 6 Taunt. 289; *Coope v. Twynam* (1823) Turn & R 426; *Pendelbury v. Walker* (1841) 4 Y & C Ex 424; *Boulter v. Peplow* (1850) 9 C.B. 493; *Batard v. Hawes* (1853) 2 E. & B. 287; see Williams, *Joint Obligations* (1949), Chap. 9; Goff and Jones, *The Law of Restitution* (5th ed., 1998), Chap. 14.

[76] For an example of proportionate, rather than equal, contribution, see *Commercial Union Assurance Co. Ltd v. Hayden* [1977] Q.B. 804. A surety has a right of indemnity, not merely contribution: see Vol. II, §§ 44–098 *et seq.*

against one joint debtor has been satisfied.[77] The right of contribution is independent of any present right of the principal creditor. Thus one co-debtor can recover contribution from another although the principal creditor's right to recover from that other debtor has become statute-barred.[78] Again, the right to contribution may be enforced against the personal representatives of a deceased joint debtor,[79] even though (as we have seen)[80] they would not be liable to the creditor. (There is an exception to this rule in the case of lessees who are joint tenants: if one dies, the survivor cannot claim contribution in respect of rent from the personal representatives of the deceased lessee.[81]) If one joint or joint and several debtor is insolvent, the loss resulting from his insolvency is spread equally among the solvent debtors.[82]

It is a condition precedent to the right to recover contribution that the claimant should have been liable to pay the whole debt[83] and should have paid more than his share of it.[84] If he merely pays his share and no more, he has no present right to contribution: but he will acquire such right as soon as anything happens in the future which discharges the debt and thus brings it about that he has paid more than his share, for instance if the debt should become statute-barred.[85] Moreover, a surety against whom the principal creditor has obtained judgment for the full amount of the debt, but who has paid nothing in respect of that judgment, can obtain a prospective order directing a co-surety, on payment by the surety of his own share of the debt, to indemnify him against further liability, or (if the principal creditor is a party to the action) an order directing the co-surety to pay his proportion to the principal creditor.[86] A surety suing his co-sureties for contribution must join as defendants all those who are liable to make contribution, unless one of them is insolvent or there is some other good reason why he should not be joined.[87]   **18-028**

Contribution between persons liable in respect of the same damage. The   **18-029**
rules stated in §§ 18-027—18-028, *ante*, only apply to co-debtors, *i.e.* persons liable in respect of the same *debt*. Where two or more persons are liable in respect of the same *damage*, the position is now regulated by section 1 of the

---

[77] County Courts Act 1984, s.48(2); see *ante*, § 18-009, n. 22.

[78] *Wolmershausen v. Gullick* [1893] 2 Ch. 514; *Gardner v. Brooke* [1897] 2 Ir.R. 6. Time begins to run, in respect of the right to contribution, only when that right crystallises by actual payment. See also Vol. II, §§ 44-102 *et seq.*

[79] *Ashby v. Ashby* (1827) 7 B. & C. 444, 449, 451–452; *Prior v. Hembrow* (1841) 8 M. & W. 873; *Batard v. Hawes* (1853) 2 E. & B. 287, 298.

[80] *Ante*, § 18-012.

[81] *Cunningham-Reid v. Public Trustee* [1944] K.B. 602.

[82] *Peter v. Rich* (1630) 1 Ch.Rep. 34; *Hitchman v. Stewart* (1855) 3 Drew. 271; *Lowe v. Dixon* (1885) 16 Q.B.D. 455. Before the Judicature Act 1873, the rule at law was otherwise. Since that Act, the rule in equity prevails.

[83] A debtor who was liable only for 50 per cent. of the debt but who has paid in full cannot recover contribution: *Legal & General Assurance Society Ltd v. Drake Insurance Co. Ltd* [1992] 1 Q.B. 887.

[84] *Davies v. Humphreys* (1840) 6 M. & W. 153, 168–169; *Re Snowdon* (1881) 17 Ch.D. 44; *Stirling v. Burdett* [1911] 2 Ch. 418.

[85] *Davies v. Humphreys, supra*, at 169.

[86] *Wolmershausen v. Gullick* [1893] 2 Ch. 514.

[87] *Hay v. Carter* [1935] Ch. 397.

Civil Liability (Contribution) Act 1978.[88] Section 1(1) of this Act provides that "any person liable in respect of any damage suffered by another person may recover contribution from any other person liable in respect of the same damage (whether jointly with him or otherwise)." This provision, as is made clear by the words in brackets, applies even where the liability arises out of two separate contracts, for example, where an architect and a builder, each employed under a separate contract, are both guilty of breaches of contract causing damage to the owner of the building.[89] The section would also apply if one person were liable in contract and another in tort.[90] By sections 1(2) and (3) it is immaterial that the original liability of the claimant or the party from whom contribution is sought, has become statute-barred.

18-030   **Amount of contribution.** Section 2(1) of the 1978 Act provides that the amount of the contribution shall be "such as may be found by the court to be just and equitable having regard to the extent of that person's responsibility for the damage in question." In this respect the Act makes a major change to the common law rules which still apply to cases of co-debtors; for under the rule stated in § 18-027, the debt can only be divided equally between the co-debtors. Under the Act, the liability can be apportioned unequally; in both cases, however, a complete indemnity can be awarded where appropriate.

18-031   **Effect of judgment or compromise.** Any judgment of a court is conclusive against the party from whom contribution is sought that the party claiming contribution was in fact liable for the damage in question.[91] A bona fide compromise is likewise conclusive, but in this case only assuming that the factual basis of the claim can be established.[92] The Act does not affect any contractual provision excluding or regulating a right to contribution, nor does it apply where a surety has a right to an indemnity as distinguished from a right to contribution.

18-032   **Contribution from party against whom limitation has run.** The Act, in replacing (as well as extending) the provisions of section 6 of the Law Reform (Married Women and Tortfeasors) Act 1935, has avoided some of the difficulties which arose under that Act where contribution was sought against a party who had been found (or was) not liable under a limitation statute.[93] Under the 1978 Act, it is expressly provided by section 1(3) that contribution can be sought from someone who has "ceased to be liable," and it seems clear that this remains the

---

[88] The Act is based on the *Report on Contribution* of the Law Commission (Law Com. No. 79, 1977); see generally Dugdale (1979) 42 M.L.R. 182; *Clerk and Lindsell on Torts* (17th ed., 1995), §§ 4–58—4–63.

[89] Here the defendants would, in the contractual sense of the term, be severally liable but in the tort sense they would be jointly and severally liable; see *ante*, § 18–004.

[90] It has also been held that liability for the same damage includes a restitutionary liability to repay money (*e.g.* for mistake of fact) as well as a liability in damages for, *e.g.*, a tort or breach of contract: *Friends' Provident Life Office v. Hiller Parker May & Rowden* [1996] 2 W.L.R. 123.

[91] s.1(5).

[92] s.1(4). Where the facts are undisputed, and the compromise has been arrived at because of doubts about the law, the position seems to be that s.1(4) is irrelevant, and that contribution can only be claimed if both parties were "liable," which is explained by s.1(6) to mean "any such liability which has been or could be established in an action brought against him in England and Wales by or on behalf of the person suffering the damage."

[93] *Wimpey & Co. Ltd v. B.O.A.C.* [1955] A.C. 169; *Hart v. Hall and Pickles Ltd* [1969] 1 Q.B. 405.

case even if he has actually been sued and successfully pleaded the Limitation Act.[94]

Assessment of contribution. The method of assessing the contribution under the 1978 Act follows the precedents previously set in section 6 of the 1935 Act and also the Law Reform (Contributory Negligence) Act 1945. In both these Acts the courts were given broad powers of apportioning liability (or responsibility) for damage in accordance with the "just and equitable" formula. In general it is well established that the courts must have regard to considerations of relative causative potency as well as to comparative blameworthiness under these provisions.[95] It is not wholly clear how easily these concepts will be transferable from the tort context, where liability is usually based on negligence, to the contractual context where liability is usually strict, and does not involve "blameworthiness" except in the sense that any breach of contract may be said to be blameworthy.   **18–033**

Limits on right to contribution. It may also be worth noting that although the Act is designed to enable contribution to be obtained from any person liable in respect of the same damage, even though the liability of the parties arises from different legal sources (*e.g.* contract and tort), there will still be circumstances in which contribution will be unobtainable. For instance, a purchaser of defective goods who is held liable in negligence to a third party for damage caused by use of the goods, cannot claim contribution from the person who sold those goods to him if that person was not also liable to the third party; if the seller was guilty of a breach of the terms of the contract of sale, the purchaser may be able to recover a complete indemnity from the seller, depending on whether his own conduct has broken the causal link between the seller's breach and the third party's injury, but there can be no claim under the 1978 Act.[96]   **18–034**

---

[94] Or if he has settled: *Logan v. Uttlesford DC* (1984) (C.A.T. No. 263). Compare, as to the position before the coming into force of the 1978 Act, *Harper v. Gray & Walker* [1985] 2 All E.R. 507.

[95] See, *e.g. Davies v. Swan Motor Co.* [1949] 2 K.B. 291 (contributory negligence); *Downs v. Chappell* [1997] 1 W.L.R. 426 (contribution).

[96] See Hervey (1981) 44 M.L.R. 575, 576. In *Birse Construction Ltd v. Haiste Ltd* [1996] 1 W.L.R. 675 a reservoir was defectively constructed: although D1 was liable to P (who was itself liable to X) and D2 was liable to X, D1 and D2 were not liable for the same damage to the same person and hence contribution could not be recovered by D1 and D2.

THIRD PARTIES[1]

1. Introduction

Preliminary. Our concern in this Chapter is with the extent to which persons can either take the benefit of, or be bound by, contracts to which they are not parties. The law on this topic is at the time of writing in a stage of transition. Under the common law doctrine of privity of contract, the general rule is that contracts cannot be enforced either by or against third parties. The second limb of this rule (under which a contract cannot impose liabilities on anyone except a party to it) is generally regarded as just and sensible.[2] But its first limb (under which a contract cannot confer rights on anyone except a party to it) has been the subject of much criticism, culminating in a Report, issued by the Law Commission in 1996, on *Privity of Contract: Contracts for the Benefit of Third Parties*.[3] A Bill ("the 1998 Bill") has been introduced in the House of Lords to implement the recommendations of this Report (where legislation for this purpose is necessary); this Bill is expected to complete its passage through Parliament in 1999. The 1998 Bill does not precisely follow the wording of the Draft

19–001

---

[1] Finlay, *Contracts for the Benefit of Third Persons* (1939); Dold, *Stipulations for a Third Party* (1948); Corbin (1930) 47 L.Q.R. 12; Dowrick (1956) 19 M.L.R. 374; Furmston (1960) 23 M.L.R. 373; Wilson, 11 Sydney L.Rev. 230 (1987). Flannigan (1989) 105 L.Q.R. 564; Kincaid [1989] C.L.J. 454; Andrews (1988) L.S. 14.

[2] See *post*, § 19–115. The rule that a contract cannot in other respects bind a third party can be inconvenient in cases involving exemption clauses (modified in a number of ways and is therefore discussed in Chapter 14.

[3] Law Com. No. 242 (hereafter "Report"). For an earlier proposal, see Law Revision Committee, 6th Interim Report (Cmnd. 5449) Section D.

Bill attached to the Law Commission's Report, but the changes in the wording do not reflect any major departures from the policy of the recommendations in that Report: their object has rather been to secure the clearer and more effective implementation of that policy. For this reason, it is submitted that reference can appropriately be made to the Report in discussing the provisions of the 1998 Bill; and such references will be made in this Chapter. Any further changes in its wording will, so far as possible, be noted in the Preface to this book.

19–002   **Present structure of the subject.** It is important at the outset to make a point about the nature of the changes to be made by the 1998 Bill, since this determines what will be the structure of the subject. A crucial passage in the Law Commission's Report states that "it is important to emphasise that, while our proposed reform will give some third parties the right to enforce contracts, there will remain many contracts where a third party stands to benefit and yet will not have a right of enforceability. Our proposed statute carves out a general and wide-ranging exception to the third party rule, but it leaves that rule intact for cases not covered by the statute."[4] The rights to be conferred on third parties by the 1998 Bill will therefore have the character of a new statutory exception to the common law doctrine of privity; and the 1998 Bill will be treated as such an exception in the present Chapter, though because of its importance a separate section will be devoted to it.[5] There will, however, be limitations on the scope of the exception, so that it will not cover a significant number of situations in which problems can arise which have in the past been perceived as resulting from the doctrine of privity. Situations which are outside the scope of the new statutory exception will not be affected by the provisions of the 1998 Bill at all: this is, for example, true of many of the cases in which third parties who have suffered loss in consequence of the breach of a contract between others have sought a remedy in tort against the party in breach.[6] The new statutory exception is, moreover, in turn subject under the 1998 Bill to exceptions[7] to which the third party's new statutory rights will not extend; and the effect of this is that in some[8] of these cases the common law doctrine of privity will continue to apply. The 1998 Bill is also not to affect any rights which the third party has apart from its provisions[9]: thus it does not deprive the third party of rights which he has because the case falls either outside the scope of the common law doctrine or within one of the exceptions to it recognised either at common law, or in equity or under other legislation. The scope of the doctrine and these other exceptions therefore continue to call for discussion, particularly because the content of rights available apart from the 1998 Bill in some ways differs from that of the rights available under it.[10] The 1998 Bill also (in accordance with the Law Commission's recommendations[11]) does not affect the common law rule that a contract cannot

---

[4] Report § 5.16; the importance of the point appears from the fact that it is repeated in almost identical terms in § 13.2 of the Report.

[5] *Post*, §§ 19–075 *et seq.*

[6] For further discussion of this point, see *post*, § 19–023 *et seq.*

[7] See Clause 6 of the Bill, discussed in §§ 19–093—19–095, *post*.

[8] *e.g.* subsections 6(2) and 6(3); under some of the other exceptions, the third party will be able to get rights by another legal route: *e.g.* under those stated in subsections 6(1) and (5): see § 19–094, *post*.

[9] Subsection 7(1), *post* § 19–096; Report, § 12.12.

[10] *e.g.*, Clauses 2 and 3 of the 1998 Bill will not apply where the third party has rights apart from the Bill; see further § 19–098, *post*.

[11] Report, §§ 10.32, 7.6.

impose liabilities on a third party or (in general) otherwise bind him, so that this aspect of the common law doctrine, too, continues to call for discussion. Nor does the Bill affect any rights of the promisee to enforce any term of the contract[12]: such questions as whether the promisee can recover damages in respect of the third party's loss will therefore continue to be governed by the rules which have been (and no doubt will further be) developed as a matter of common law. There is finally the point that the 1998 Bill will not have retrospective effect: it is to come into force six months after it has been passed and will not apply to contracts made before the end of that period (except where a contract made within the period expressly provides that the Bill is to apply to it).[13] It is therefore likely that for some time to come the courts will be concerned with contracts subject to the rules of law which were established before the Bill's coming into force. These rules will also, in a significant number of the situations described above, continue to apply even to contracts made after that date. For all these reasons, these rules still require discussion, even though a considerable number of the cases on which they are based will, after the 1998 Bill has come into force, on their actual facts be decided differently (where they had denied the third party the right to enforce a term of the contract) or be decided on different grounds (where they had given the third party such a right). The result of all these points is that the 1998 Bill will no doubt improve, but that it will scarcely simplify, the law on this topic.

2. THE COMMON LAW DOCTRINE

Statement. The common law doctrine of privity of contract may be stated as   19–003
follows: a contract cannot (as a general rule) confer rights or impose obligations arising under it on any person except the parties to it. Two questions arise from this statement: who are the parties to the agreement? and has the claimant provided consideration for the promise which he is seeking to enforce?

(a) *Parties to the Agreement*

Who are the parties? Normally, the answer to this question is obvious   19–004
enough: the parties to the agreement are the persons from whose communications with each other the agreement has resulted. There may, indeed, be factual difficulties in identifying these persons[14]; but such difficulties do not raise any questions of legal principle. Problems as to the legal analysis of clearly established facts can, however, arise in a number of situations in which there is clearly an agreement, while it is doubtful exactly who the parties to it are; and difficulty in deciding who the parties to a particular contract are may also arise when there are several contracts which affect the same subject-matter and involve more than two parties. The rights of all the parties to such contracts arise independently of the Contracts (Rights of Third Parties) Bill 1998 and will not be limited by its provisions. Situations in which such contracts may arise are discussed in the following paragraphs.

---

[12] 1998 Bill, Clause 4.

[13] *ibid.* subsections 8(2) and (3).

[14] *e.g. Stag Line Ltd v. Tyne Ship Repair Group (The Zinnia)* [1984] 2 Lloyd's Rep. 211; *Empresa Lineas Maritimas Argentinas v. The Oceanus Mutual Underwriting Association (Bermuda) Ltd* [1984] 2 Lloyd's Rep. 517.

19–005　　　**Collateral contracts.**[15] A contract between two persons may be accompanied by a collateral contract between one of them and a third person relating to the same subject-matter. In *Shanklin Pier v. Detel Products Ltd*[16] the claimants had employed contractors to paint a pier and instructed them for this purpose to buy paint made by the defendants. This instruction was given in reliance on a statement made by the defendants to the claimants that the paint would last for seven years. In fact it only lasted for three months. Although the main contract for the sale of paint was between the contractors and the defendants, it was held that there was also a collateral contract between the claimants and the defendants that the paint would last for seven years. The same reasoning may apply where a person buys goods from a dealer and is given a "guarantee" in the name of the manufacturer. Here the main contract of sale is between the customer and the dealer, but it seems that the "guarantee" could also be regarded as a collateral contract between the manufacturer and the customer.[17] Again, a contract for the execution of building work between A and B may be performed, wholly or in part, through the instrumentality of a sub-contractor C, nominated by A but engaged by B. Such an arrangement usually gives rise to a contract between A and B and to one between B and C, but not to one between A and C[18]; but it is possible for a collateral contract to arise between these last two parties,[19] making C contractually liable to A.

19–006　　　**Hire-purchase.** The collateral contract device can also be used where a dealer makes a representation to a customer in order to induce him to enter into a hire-purchase contract. The main contract of hire-purchase is usually between the customer and the finance company. Accordingly, a representation by the dealer as to the quality of the goods did not formerly impose any liability on the finance company[20]; but the dealer could be liable on the representation as a collateral contract.[21] If the transaction is a regulated agreement within the Consumer Credit Act 1974[22] a dealer who conducts antecedent negotiations is in certain circumstances deemed to do so as agent of the creditor as well as in his actual capacity.[23] The representation can therefore make the finance company liable under the main

---

[15] Wedderburn [1959] C.L.J. 58.

[16] [1951] 2 K.B. 854; followed in *Wells (Merstham) Ltd v. Buckland Sand & Silica Co. Ltd* [1965] 2 Q.B. 170, even though in that case no specific main contract was contemplated when the collateral undertaking was given. See *ante*, § 12–004. As to sales by auction, see *Chelmsford Auctions Ltd v. Poole* [1973] Q.B. 542, 550; Vol. II, §§ 32–014, 44–447.

[17] For legislative control of exemption clauses in such guarantees, see *ante*, Chap. 14.

[18] *e.g. Simaan General Contracting Co. v. Pilkington Glass Ltd (No. 2)* [1988] Q.B. 758; *National Trust v. Haden & Young* (1994) 72 B.L.R. 1.

[19] *Holland Hannen & Cubitts (Northern) v. Welsh Health Technical Services Ltd* (1987) 7 Con.L.R. 14; *cf. Welsh Health Technical Service Organisation v. Haden Young* (1987) 37 Build.L.R. 130; *Greater Nottingham Co-operative Soc. Ltd v. Cementation Ltd* [1989] Ch. 497; contrast *National Trust v. Haden & Young, supra*, where there was no such collateral contract; for C's possible liability to A in tort, see *post* §§ 19–023—19–038.

[20] *Campbell Discount Co. Ltd v. Gall* [1961] 1 Q.B. 431; revd. on other points in *Branwhite v. Worcester Works Finance Ltd* [1969] 1 A.C. 552 and *United Dominions Trust v. Western* [1976] Q.B. 513.

[21] *Brown v. Sheen & Richmond Car Sales Ltd* [1950] 1 All E.R. 1102; *Andrews v. Hopkinson* [1957] 1 Q.B. 229; Diamond (1957) 21 M.L.R. 177; *cf. Astley, Industrial Trust Ltd v. Grimley* [1963] 1 W.L.R. 584. As to damages, see *Yeoman Credit Ltd v. Odgers* [1962] 1 W.L.R. 215.

[22] Vol. II, §§ 32–002, 38–015.

[23] s.56(2); *cf.* also s.75.

contract, while the dealer may still be liable on the representation as a collateral contract.

Payment by cheque or credit card. Yet a further situation in which a   **19–007**
transaction involves several contracts is that in which a supply of goods is paid
for by the use of a cheque card or credit card. Such a transaction involves three
contracts: one between the supplier and the customer, a second between the
customer and the issuer of the card, and a third between the issuer and the
supplier of the goods.[24] The supplier therefore has a common law right of action
against the issuer on this third contract.

Consideration in collateral contracts. In the cases so far discussed, it is   **19–008**
fairly easy to see what is the consideration for the defendant's promise in the
collateral contract. In the *Shanklin Pier* case it was the instruction given by the
claimants to their contractors[25]; in the building sub-contractor case, it is similarly
the client's nomination of the sub-contractor; in the guarantee case it is the
purchase by the customer of the goods from the dealer[26]; in the hire-purchase
case it is the entering by the customer into a hire-purchase agreement with the
finance company; in the cheque card or credit card case, it is the supply of the
goods by the supplier to the customer, and the discount allowed by the supplier
to the issuer of the credit card.[27] A case in which the problem of consideration
gives rise to more difficulty is *Charnock v. Liverpool Corporation*.[28] A car had
been damaged and was later repaired under a contract between the owner's
insurance company and a garage. It was held that there was also a collateral
contract between the owner and the garage (to do the repairs within a reasonable
time), even though the owner did not pay or promise to pay the garage anything.[29] The consideration for the garage's promise was found in the owner's
"leaving his car with the garage for repair."[30] This might not be a detriment to
the owner, at least in the factual sense.[31] But it was a benefit to the garage in
giving it the opportunity of making a contract for the repair of the car with the
insurance company; and this benefit constituted the consideration for the garage's
promise to the owner.

---

[24] *Re Charge Card Services* [1987] Ch. 150, affd. [1989] Ch. 497; *cf. Customs and Excise Commissioners v. Diners Club Ltd* [1989] 1 W.L.R. 1196; *First Sport Ltd v. Barclays Bank plc* [1993] 1 W.L.R. 1229 (where the card had been stolen and been presented by the thief to the retailer). A different analysis probably applies where the card is issued by the suppliers, as is the practice of some department stores: *Richardson v. Worrall* [1985] S.T.C. 693, 720.

[25] In the *Shanklin Pier* case McNair J. said at 856: "I see no reason why there may not be an enforceable warranty between A [the defendant] and B [the plaintiff] supported by the consideration that B should cause C [the contractors employed by the plaintiffs] to enter into a contract with A [*viz.* to buy the paint from A]."

[26] *cf.*, in another context, *Penn v. Bristol & West Building Society* [1997] 1 W.L.R. 1356, 1363 ("entering into some transaction with a third party").

[27] *Customs and Excise Commissioners v. Diners Club Ltd* [1989] 1 W.L.R. 1196. On consideration in collateral contracts, see also *Brikom Investments Ltd v. Carr* [1979] Q.B. 467 (*ante*, § 3–075), where no third-party problem arose.

[28] [1968] 1 W.L.R. at 1498.

[29] *cf. Godfrey Davies Ltd v. Culling and Hecht* [1962] 2 Lloyd's Rep. 349; *Cooter & Green Ltd v. Tyrell* [1962] 2 Lloyd's Rep. 377; *Brown & Davies v. Galbraith* [1972] 1 W.L.R. 997.

[30] [1968] 1 W.L.R. at 1505.

[31] *Ante*, § 3–006; the transfer of possession might subject the repairer to the obligations of a bailee, but these would not include an obligation to repair. For similar reasoning, see *International Petroleum Refining & Supply Ltd v. Caleb Brett & Son Ltd* [1980] 1 Lloyd's Rep. 569, 594.

19–009   **Contractual intention in collateral contracts.** A collateral contract will be found to exist only on proof of contractual intention[32]; and this is as true in the present context as it is in other situations in which the collateral contract device has been used. In *Alicia Hosiery Ltd v. Brown Shipley Ltd*[33] the owner of goods in a warehouse pledged them to a bank and subsequently sold them. The bank gave the buyer a delivery order addressed to the warehouseman but the latter refused to deliver the goods to the buyer who claimed damages from the bank. It was held that there was a contract between the buyer and the seller, and one between the seller and the bank, but none between the buyer and the bank as no intention to enter into such a contract had been shown.[34] Similarly, in *Independent Broadcasting Authority v. E.M.I. Electronics*[35] A had contracted with B for the erection of a television mast, on the terms that the actual work was to be done by C, a sub-contractor. C, who was not a party to the contract between A and B, wrote to A saying: "We are well satisfied that the structure will not oscillate dangerously." The mast having later collapsed, it was held that C's letter did not have contractual force as there was no *animus contrahendi* (though C was held liable in negligence). And where A acquired shares from B which had previously been brought by B from C on the terms that certain payments were to be made to C in events which later happened, it was held that there was no collateral contract between A and C, obliging A to make the payments.[36] No intention on A's part to enter into such a contract could be inferred, while C did not know of A at the time of the alleged collateral contract and so equally lacked any intention to contract with A.

19–010   **Multilateral contracts.** When a person joins a club or other unincorporated association, he may contract with all the other members although he may be quite unaware of their identity and although he may be in direct communication only with the secretary.[37] Similarly, where an insurance policy was expressed to be between the assured and a syndicate of underwriters at Lloyd's, it was held nevertheless to constitute a number of separate contracts between the assured and each of the participating syndicates.[38]

19–011   **Sporting competitions.** Where a number of persons agree to enter into a competition subject to certain rules, it is often doubtful exactly who the parties to the resulting contract are. In one case it was held that the competitors in a regatta contracted not only with the committee of the organising club, but also with each other.[39] But in another case it was held that persons who had entered

---

[32] *Heilbut, Symons & Co. v. Buckleton* [1913] A.C. 30, 47; *ante*, § 2–152.

[33] [1970] 1 Q.B. 95.

[34] *cf.* also *Hannam v. Bradford C.C.* [1970] 1 W.L.R. 937; *Construction Industry Training Board v. Labour Force Ltd* [1970] 3 All E.R. 220.

[35] (1980) 14 Build.L.R. 1; *cf. Lambert v. Lewis* [1982] A.C. 225; *ante*, § 2–151.

[36] *Law Debenture Trust Corp. v. Ural Caspian Oil Corp. Ltd* [1993] 1 W.L.R. 138, 142; revd., on another point [1995] Ch. 152.

[37] *Hybart v. Packer* (1858) 4 C.B.(N.S.) 209; *Gray v. Pearson* (1870) L.R. 5 C.P. 568; *Evans v. Hooper* (1875) 1 Q.B.D. 45.

[38] *Touche Ross & Co. v. Colin Baker* [1992] 2 Lloyd's Rep. 207.

[39] *The Satanita* [1895] P. 248; affd. *sub nom. Clarke v. Dunraven* [1897] A.C. 59, where only Lord Herschell dealt with the point here discussed; *cf. Meggeson v. Burns* [1972] 1 Lloyd's Rep. 223; *White v. Blackmore* [1972] 2 Q.B. 651 (where there was no contractual intention).

horses for races organised by the Jockey Club had contracted only with the Club and not with each other.[40]

Agency. Where a person negotiates a contract as agent between his principal and a third party, the contract will generally be between the principal and the third party. But it is sometimes doubtful whether a person acted as agent or on his own behalf.[41] In one case, a husband booked tickets on a cross-Channel ferry for himself and his wife and children. It was said that there was a "contract of carriage between the [wife] and the [carriers],"[42] presumably made by the husband as his wife's agent. Where a husband and wife lunched together at a restaurant, it was again held that there was a contract between the wife and the proprietor, though on the different ground that the husband and wife had each made a separate contract with the proprietor.[43] But if there were no such separate contracts and the host on such an occasion did not act as agent, it has been said that there would be a contract only between him and the restaurant proprietor.[44]

19–012

Sub-Agency. Similar problems arise where an agent employs a sub-agent.[45] In some such cases there is privity of contract between principal and sub-agent, while in others the sub-agent is in a contractual relationship only with the agent who employed him. In border-line cases of this kind, it is again clear that there is a contract, but doubtful who the parties to the contract are.[46]

19–013

Mortgage valuations. Problems as to parties can also arise where a house is valued at the instigation of a building society after a prospective purchaser has applied to it for a loan which is to be secured by a mortgage on the house. Where the valuation is carried out by a full-time employee of the building society, there will usually be a contract between the society and its employee, and one between the society and the borrower (under which the society will be vicariously liable for the valuer's negligence) but none between the valuer and the borrower.[47] Where, on the other hand, the valuation is carried out by an independent valuer, there may be a contract between him and the borrower[48] but this is not necessarily the case. If, for example, the independent valuer were appointed and paid by the society and reported directly to it, there is unlikely to be any contractual relationship between borrower and valuer, though the valuer will be liable to the

19–014

---

[40] *Ellesmere v. Wallace* [1929] 2 Ch. 1.

[41] See the authorities cited in nn. 42–45, *infra*.

[42] *Daly v. General Steam Navigation Co. Ltd (The Dragon)* [1979] 1 Lloyd's Rep. 257, 262, affd. [1980] 2 Lloyd's Rep. 415; *cf. Wilson v. Best Travel Ltd* [1993] 1 All E.R. 353, 355; *Bowerman v. Association of British Travel Agents* [1995] N.L.J. 815 (holiday booked for pupil by her teacher).

[43] *Lockett v. A.M. Charles* [1938] 4 All E.R. 170.

[44] *Jackson v. Horizon Holidays Ltd* [1975] 1 W.L.R. 1468, 1473 (where *Lockett v. A. M. Charles Ltd, supra* was not cited).

[45] Similar problems can arise in relation to "forwarding agents" see, *e.g. Jones v. European General Express* (1920) 25 Com.Cas. 296; *Elektronska, etc. v. Transped, etc.* [1986] 1 Lloyd's Rep. 49.

[46] *Henderson v. Merrett Syndicates Ltd* [1995] 2 A.C. 145; see generally, Vol. II, Chap. 32.

[47] *Halifax Building Society v. Edell* [1992] Ch. 436. Nor could the borrower enforce a term of the valuer's employment contract by virtue of the Contracts (Rights of Third Parties) Bill 1998: see subsection 6(3), *post* § 19–095.

[48] *Halifax Building Society v. Edell, supra*, at 454.

borrower in tort if as a result of his negligence his report is inaccurate or incomplete and the borrower suffers loss.[49]

19–015   The reason why there is no separate contract in the first of the above situations is presumably that the valuer has no intention to contract with the borrower since he believes that he is merely carrying out his duties under his contract with the society. The further suggestion that, in this situation, there is "seemingly no consideration for a contract by the valuer as principal"[50] is, with respect, harder to follow. It cannot mean that there is no consideration because the valuer is doing no more than performing his contract of employment, for it is now settled that the performance of a contractual duty owed to a third party can constitute consideration,[51] and in any event the question is whether there is consideration for the valuer's promise, and this consideration must move, not from him, but from the purchaser. Prima facie, such consideration is provided by the payment of the survey fee by the purchaser to the society, or by his entering into the mortgage transaction; and it is immaterial that this consideration does not move (at least directly) to the valuer; for so long as consideration moves from the promisee it need not move to the promisor.[52] Nor would such consideration be past, even if the fee had been paid before the valuer had been engaged; for the test for deciding whether consideration is past is a functional (rather than a strictly chronological) one, which is satisfied in the situation here under discussion since the consideration and the promise given in return are substantially one transaction.[53] Indeed, the assumption that it is so satisfied is supported by the view that there can be a contract between an independent valuer and the purchaser,[54] since the consideration which moves from the purchaser is exactly the same whether the valuer is an employee of the building society or an independent person.

(b) *Parties to the Consideration*

19–016   **Relation to the rule that consideration must move from the promisee.**[55] It is disputed whether the rule that consideration must move from the promisee is the same as or different from the common law rule that only a party to the agreement can sue.[56] In the English cases the two rules have always led to the same result, which the judges have sometimes based on the first rule and sometimes on the second.[57] To be entitled to enforce a promise, a person must (at common law) generally show (1) that it was made to him *and* (2) that consideration for it moved from him. The statement that consideration must move *from the promisee* simply assumes that the first requirement has been satisfied. If the rule were stated to be that consideration must move *from the party seeking to enforce*

---

[49] See *Smith v. Eric S. Bush* [1990] 1 A.C. 831.
[50] *Halifax Building Society v. Edell* [1992] Ch. 436, 454.
[51] *Ante*, § 3–068.
[52] *Ante*, § 3–037.
[53] *Ante*, § 3–026.
[54] *Supra*, at n. 48.
[55] *Ante*, § 3–035.
[56] Furmston (1960) 23 M.L.R. at 383–384.
[57] Thus the judgments in *Tweddle v. Atkinson* (1861) 1 B. & S. 393 are based on the rule that consideration must move from the promisee; while the judgments of Littledale and Patteson JJ. in *Price v. Easton* (1833) 4 B. & Ad. 433 are based on the doctrine of privity.

the promise it would be clearly distinct from the rule that only a party to the agreement can sue. A man might, for example, promise his daughter to pay £1,000 to any man who married her. A person who married the daughter with knowledge of and in reliance on such a promise might provide consideration for it, but could not enforce it, as it was not addressed to him.

In *Kepong Prospecting Ltd v. Schmidt*[58] a third party made a claim to enforce **19–017** a contract under the law of Malaysia, by which consideration need not move from the promisee. In rejecting the claim, the Privy Council said "It is true that section 2(*d*) of the Contracts Ordinance gives a wider definition of 'considera-tion' than that which applies in England particularly in that it enables considera-tion to move from another person than the promisee, but the appellant was unable to show how this affected the law as to enforcement of contracts by third parties."[59] This decision seems therefore to support the view that the doctrine of privity is distinct from the rule that consideration must move from the promisee.

Promises made to more than one person. The doctrine of privity does not **19–018** affect the enforceability by any promisee of promises made to a number of persons, whether jointly or severally or jointly and severally. The question whether one of the promisees can enforce such a promise if he has not provided any part of the consideration for it has been discussed in Chapter 3.[60]

(c) Development of the Common Law Doctrine

The doctrine established. In the early authorities, there was support both for **19–019** the view that a person could not,[61] and for the view that he could,[62] enforce a contract to which he was not a party. The point appeared to have been settled in 1861 by *Tweddle v. Atkinson*,[63] where the fathers of a husband and wife in pursuance of an oral contract between them before the marriage agreed together in writing to pay the husband, the one £200 and the other £100, adding that the husband should have full power to sue them in any court of law for those sums. The husband, who was not a party to this contract, sued the wife's father for the payment promised by him under it; and the claim was dismissed.

This case was usually considered to have established the common law doctrine **19–020** of privity,[64] which was approved by the House of Lords in 1915, when the principle that "only a person who is a party to the contract can sue on it" was said

---

[58] [1968] A.C. 810.
[59] *ibid.* at 826.
[60] *Ante* §§ 3–039—3–042.
[61] *Bourne v. Mason* (1668) 1 Ventris 6; *cf. Crow v. Rogers* (1726) 1 Stra. 592; *Price v. Easton* (1833) 4 B. & Ad. 433. For the history, see Holdsworth, *History of English Law*, VIII, pp. 11–13, 40; E.J.P. (1954) 70 L.Q.R. 467; Scamell (1955) 8 C.L.P. 131; Palmer, 33 Am.Jl. of Legal History 3 (1989); Ibbetson in Barton (ed.), *Towards a History of the Law of Contract*, pp. 67, 96–99; Palmer, *The Paths to Privity: The History of Third Party Beneficiary Contracts in English Law* (1992); Andrews, 69 Tulane L.Rev. 69 (1995).
[62] *Dutton v. Poole* (1677) 2 Lev. 210; affd. T.Raym. 302. *cf. Thomas v. —— (1655) Sty. 461; Martyn v. Hind* (1776) 2 Cowp. 437, 443; *Marchington v. Vernon* (1787) 1 B. & P. 101, note (c).
[63] (1861) 1 B. & S. 393.
[64] *Gandy v. Gandy* (1884) 30 Ch.D. 57, 69.

to be a "fundamental"[65] one in English law. This view was, indeed, judicially doubted in a number of cases[66]; but these doubts appeared to have been set at rest in 1961, when the House of Lords again affirmed the existence of the doctrine of privity of contract in holding that a person could not take the benefit of a limitation of liability clause contained in a contract to which he was not a party.[67] The continued existence of the doctrine is also assumed in many later cases,[68] as well as by the proposals for legislative reform to which reference has already been made.[69]

19–021   **Beswick v. Beswick.** The leading modern authority is *Beswick v. Beswick*.[70] A coal merchant transferred his business to his nephew who promised him (*inter alia*) that he would, after the uncle's death, pay an annuity to the uncle's widow. After the uncle's death, the widow became his administratrix. She brought an action to enforce the nephew's promise, suing both in her own right and as administratrix. In the Court of Appeal it was held, (1) by Lord Denning M.R., that the widow could sue in her own right at common law, notwithstanding the doctrine of privity: this doctrine was "at bottom . . . only a rule of procedure"[71] and could be overcome by simply joining the promisee as a party to the action[72]; (2) by Lord Denning M.R. and by Danckwerts L.J., that the widow could sue in her own right by virtue of section 56(1) of the Law of Property Act 1925[73]; and (3) by Lord Denning M.R. and by Danckwerts and Salmon L.JJ., that the widow could sue in her capacity as administratrix of the promisee and could in that capacity obtain an order of specific performance against the nephew obliging him to pay the annuity to her for her own personal benefit. The House of Lords

---

[65] *Dunlop Pneumatic Tyre Co. Ltd v. Selfridge & Co. Ltd* [1915] A.C. 847, 853; for a similar, earlier, statement see *Keighley Maxsted & Co. v. Durant* [1901] A.C. 240, 246.

[66] *Smith and Snipes Hall Farm Ltd v. River Douglas Catchment Board* [1949] 2 K.B. 500, 514–516; *Drive Yourself Hire Co. (London) Ltd v. Strutt* [1954] 1 Q.B. 250, 272–275. *Pyrene Co. Ltd v. Scindia Steam Navigation Co. Ltd* [1954] 2 Q.B. 402 (explained on other grounds in *Scruttons Ltd v. Midland Silicones Ltd* [1962] A.C. 446, 471); *Rayfield v. Hands* [1960] Ch. 1; Dowrick (1956) 19 M.L.R. 375. *cf.* Flannigan (1987) 103 L.Q.R. 564; Andrews (1988) 8 L.S. 14.

[67] In *Scruttons Ltd v. Midland Silicones Ltd* [1962] A.C. 446; *ante*, § 14–043. The Court of Appeal had taken a similar view of the continued existence of the doctrine in *Green v. Russell* [1959] 2 Q.B. 226.

[68] *Rookes v. Barnard* [1964] A.C. 1129; *Hepburn v. A. Tomlinson (Hauliers) Ltd* [1966] A.C. 451; *New Zealand Shipping Co. Ltd v. A.M. Satterthwaite Ltd (The Eurymedon)* [1975] A.C. 154; *Port Jackson Stevedoring Pty. Ltd v. Salmond & Spraggon (Australia) Pty. Ltd (The New York Star)* [1980] 1 W.L.R. 138; *Woodar Investment Development Ltd v. Wimpey Construction U.K. Ltd* [1980] 1 W.L.R. 277; *Balsamo v. Medici* [1984] 1 W.L.R. 951, 959–960; *Southern Water Authority v. Carey* [1985] 2 All E.R. 1077, 1083; *The Forum Craftsman* [1985] 1 Lloyd's Rep. 291, 295; *Swiss Bank Corp. v. Brink's-Mat Ltd* [1986] 2 Lloyd's Rep. 79; *Singer (U.K.) Ltd v. Tees & Hartlepool Port Authority* [1988] 2 Lloyd's Rep. 164, 167; *J.H. Rayner (Mincing Lane) Ltd v. D.T.I.* [1990] A.C..643, 662; *Cia. Portorafti Commerciale SA v. Panama Inc. (The Captain Gregos)* [1990] 1 Lloyd's Rep. 310, 318; *Law Debenture Trust Corp. v. Ural Caspian Oil Corp. Ltd* [1993] 2 All E.R. 355, 365 (revd. on another point, [1995] Ch. 152; *Siu Yin Kwan v. Eastern Insurance* [1994] 2 A.C. 199, 207; *Rhone v. Stephens* [1994] 2 A.C. 310, 321; *K.H. Enterprise v. Pioneer Container (The Pioneer Container)* [1994] 2 A.C. 324, 355; *White v. Jones* [1995] 2 A.C. 207, 252, 266; *The Mahkutai* [1996] A.C. 650, 658; *Amsprop Trading Ltd v. Harris Distribution Ltd* [1997] 1 W.L.R. 1025, 1028; *The Giannis K* [1998] A.C. 605, 616. The point is perhaps left open in *Esso Petroleum Ltd v. Hall Russell & Co.* [1989] A.C. 643, 662.

[69] See, *ante*, 19–001.

[70] [1968] A.C. 58; affg. [1966] Ch. 538.

[71] [1966] Ch. at 557.

[72] For criticism of this view, see § 9–062, *post.*

[73] *Post*, §§ 19–104—19–107.

affirmed the decision on the third ground,[74] rejected the second[75] and found it unnecessary to express a concluded view on the first. But the speeches all assume the correctness of the generally accepted view that at common law a contract can be enforced only by the parties to it,[76] though the House of Lords has on a number of occasions indicated its willingness to reconsider this position.[77] Such a reconsideration has indeed been undertaken by a majority of the High Court of Australia, but in a decision in which so many divergent views were expressed that it provides no firm guidance for the development of the law.[78] The difficulties of reaching satisfactory results in this area through purely judicial reconsideration are formidable; they arise, in particular, in defining exactly what classes of third parties can acquire rights under the contract, and how these rights might be affected by attempts by the contracting parties to rescind the contract or to vary it, and by defences available between the contracting parties.[79] A satisfactory solution of such difficulties is more likely to be achieved by legislative reform,[80] such as that contained in the Contracts (Rights of Third Parties) Bill, 1998.[81] In a significant number of situations, however, third parties will not acquire rights by virtue of this Bill[82]; and in many such situations the common law doctrine of privity will continue (at least for the time being)[83] to apply.

3. Scope

General. The common law doctrine of privity means, and means only, that a   **19-022** person cannot acquire rights, or be subjected to liabilities, *arising under* a contract to which he is not a party. For example, it means that, if A promises B

---

[74] [1968] A.C. 58; Goodhart (1967) 83 L.Q.R. 465; Fairest [1967] C.L.J. 149; Treitel (1967) 30 M.L.R. 687.

[75] See *post*, §§ 19-106—19-107.

[76] [1968] A.C. 58, 72D, 81G, 92-93, 95G.

[77] *ibid.* at 72; *Woodar Investment Development Ltd v. Wimpey Construction U.K. Ltd* [1980] 1 W.L.R. 277, 291, 297-298, 300; *Swain v. Law Society* [1983] 1 A.C. 598, 611; *cf. Williams v. Natural Life Health Foods Ltd* [1998] 2 All E.R. 577, 584.

[78] *Trident Insurance Co. Ltd v. McNiece Bros. Pty. Ltd* (1988) 165 C.L.R. 107, where a claim under a liability insurance policy by a person who was not a party to it was upheld by a majority of five to two. But one member of the majority (Deane J.) was only prepared to allow the third party's claim under the well established trust exception to the doctrine of privity (*post*, § 19-065—19-073); while another (Gaudron J.) based her decision in favour of the third party, not on contract but on unjust enrichment, and said that this was "not an abrogation of the doctrine of privity of contract (at 177, and see *post*, § 19-040). Only three of the seven members of the court can be said to have countenanced such an abrogation, and even their view may be restricted to the special insurance context with which the case was concerned. See also Edgell [1989] L.M.C.L.Q. 139; Kincaid (1989) 2 J.C.L. 160. For a different judicial approach in Canada, proceeding by means of developing an exception to the doctrine in the context of exemption clauses, see *London Drugs Ltd v. Kuehne & Nagel International Ltd* [1992] 3 S.C.R. 299; Waddams (1993) 109 L.Q.R. 349.

[79] See the discussion of these problems in American law (which in principle recognises the rights of third-party beneficiaries) in *Corbin on Contracts*, Chapters 41-44. The complexity of this discussion indicates that the subject is more suitable for legislative than for judicial reform. See *post*, § 19-075; *cf.* in New Zealand, Contract (Privity) Act 1982.

[80] See Treitel (1966) 29 M.L.R. 657, 665; Reynolds (1989) 105 L.Q.R. 1, 3; *ante*, § 19-001. Judicial reform is favoured by Steyn L.J. in *Darlington B.C. v. Wiltshire Northern Ltd* [1995] 1 W.L.R. 68, 76, discussed in § 19-052 *post*. See also Beale (1995) J.C.L. 103.

[81] *Post*, § 19-075 *et seq.*

[82] *Ante*, § 19-002.

[83] The passing of the 1998 Bill will probably reduce the pressure for judicial reform.

to pay a sum of money to C, then C cannot sue A for that sum.[84] Similarly, if a contract between A and B contains a term purporting to exempt C from tortious liability to A, the doctrine of privity may prevent C from relying on that term in an action in tort brought against him by A.[85] But it does not follow that a contract between A and B cannot affect the legal rights of C indirectly. For example, an agreement between A and B under which A accepts from B part payment of a debt owed by C to A in full settlement of that debt can benefit C by precluding A from suing C for the balance of the debt[86]; and *a fortiori* full performance by B of C's obligation to A can discharge that obligation. Conversely, a building contract between A and B may benefit C by defining his rights: *e.g.* by specifying the time at which payment becomes due to C under a subcontract between B and C for the execution of part of the work.[87] It is also possible for a contract between A and B to affect C adversely[88]: this possibility is more fully discussed later in this Chapter.[89] At this stage, our concern is with a number of further situations in which a contract between A and B can operate to the advantage of C: in particular, with situations in which C may have a right of action against A in tort.

(a) *Liability in Negligence to Third Parties*

19–023   **Duty of care may be owed to third party.** While the primary effect of a contract between A and B is to oblige the parties to perform their promises to each other, the contract may also impose on A a duty of care to C, the breach of which will enable C to sue A in tort for negligence. The contract may, for example, have this effect because it gives rise between A and C to the relationship of passenger (or cargo-owner) and carrier,[90] or bailor and sub-bailee.[91] In a

---

[84] *Tweddle v. Atkinson* (1861) 1 B. & S. 393; *ante*, § 19–019.

[85] *Scruttons Ltd v. Midland Silicones Ltd* [1962] A.C. 446; §§ 14–043, 19–020; but there may be a contract between A and C, as in *New Zealand Shipping Co. Ltd v. A.M. Satterthwaite & Co. Ltd (The Eurymedon)* [1975] A.C. 154; *Port Jackson Stevedoring Pty. Ltd v. Salmond & Spraggon (Australia) Pty. Ltd (The New York Star)* [1980] 1 W.L.R. 138; *ante*, §§ 14–044, 14–045. Contrast, in Canada, *London Drugs Ltd v. Kuehne & Nagel International Ltd* [1992] 3 S.C.R. 299. *cf. The Mahkutai* [1996] A.C. 650, where the actual decision is based, not on the doctrine of privity, but on the fact that an exclusive jurisidiction clause was not, as a matter of construction, one of the "exceptions, limitations, provisions, conditions and liberties" of the contract on which the third party sought to rely. Hence it was not necessary to decide whether the English courts should, in cases of this kind, adopt the Canadian view taken in the *London Drugs* case [1992] 3 S.C.R. 299, but Lord Goff at 665 in *The Mahkutai* left the point open.

[86] *Hirachand Punamchand v. Temple* [1911] 2 K.B. 330; *ante*, § 3–118 (where the effect on such facts of the Contracts (Rights of Third Parties) Bill 1998 is also discussed); *cf. Johnson v. Davies* [1998] 2 All E.R. 649, 658.

[87] *Co-operative Wholesale Society Ltd v. Birse Construction Ltd*, The Times, August 13, 1997.

[88] *e.g. West of England Shipowners Mutual Insurance Association (Luxembourg) v. Cristal Ltd (The Glacier Bay)* [1996] 1 Lloyd's Rep. 370; *Banque Financière de la Cité v. Parc (Battersea) Ltd* [1998] 1 All E.R. 737.

[89] *Post* §§ 19–116—19–128.

[90] *Austin v. G.W. Ry.* (1867) L.R. 2 Q.B. 442; *Sammick Lines Co. v. Owners of the Antonis P. Lemos (The Antonis P. Lemos)* [1985] A.C. 771.

[91] *Moukataff v. B.O.A.C.* [1967] 1 Lloyd's Rep. 396; *Bart v. B.W.I.A.* [1967] 1 Lloyd's Rep. 239 (where the claim failed as the sub-bailee's duty was limited to one to keep safely, and did not extend to transmission of the package); *Hispanica de Petroles SA v. Vencedora Oceanica Navegacion SA (The Kapetan Markos NL) (No. 2)* [1987] 2 Lloyd's Rep. 321. Such a sub-bailment may also operate to the disadvantage of C in that he may be bound by an exemption clause in the contract between A (the head bailee) and B (the sub-bailee): see *Morris v. C.W. Martin Ltd* [1966] 1 Q.B. 716; *K.H. Enterprise v. Pioneer Container (The Pioneer Container)* [1994] 2 A.C. 324; *Spectra International plc v. Hayesoak Ltd* [1997] 1 Lloyd's Rep. 153 (revsd. on another ground [1998] 1 Lloyd's Rep. 162);

number of cases persons providing professional services, such as solicitors,[92] insurance brokers,[93] safety consultants[94] valuers and surveyors[95] have been held liable in tort to persons other than their immediate clients[96] for negligence in the performance of their contracts with these clients. Sometimes the provider of the services is liable in tort because his negligence in performing the contract with his client of itself causes loss to a third party: *e.g.* where a solicitor's negligence in failing duly to carry out his client's testamentary instructions causes an intended gift to a prospective beneficiary to fail.[97] Sometimes the defendant's negligence results in his making a misrepresentation to the third party and the loss is suffered by the latter in consequence of his acting in reliance on that representation: *e.g.* where a valuer employed by A negligently makes a report on the structure of a house and the report is communicated to B and induces him to buy the house for more than its true value[98]; or where an accountant employed by X negligently makes a report on the affairs of a company and the report induces Y to invest money in the company and to suffer loss by reason of the falsity of the report.[99] The types of relationships out of which such liability in tort for misrepresentation can arise are more fully discussed in Chapter 6.[1] The only point to be made here is that such liability is commonly incurred to the claimant

---

Sonicare International Ltd v. EAFT Ltd [1997] 2 Lloyd's Rep. 48. But B cannot take the *benefit* of a term in the contract between A and C: see *The Mahkutai* [1996] A.C. 650; the principle of *The Pioneer Container, supra,* merely enables B to rely on the terms of his *own* contract with A against C where C has authorised the relevant terms of the sub-bailment. No sub-bailment arises merely because a sub-agent has received the proceeds of the sale of the principal's property from the buyer: *Balsamo v. Medici* [1984] 1 W.L.R. 951.

[92] See the authorities cited in n. 97 *infra.*

[93] *Punjab National Bank v. de Boinville* [1992] 1 W.L.R. 1138, 1152; *cf.* [1995] 2 A.C. 145; *Aiken v. Stewart Wrightson Members Agency Ltd* [1995] 1 W.L.R. 1281; Cane in (ed. Rose) *Consensus ad Idem, Essays in the Law of Contract in Honour of Guenter Treitel,* 96.

[94] *Driver v. William Willett (Contractors) Ltd* [1969] 1 All E.R. 665; *cf. Dove v. Banham's Patent Lock Ltd* [1983] 1 W.L.R. 1436; contrast *Marc Rich & Co. A.G. v. Bishop Rock Marine Co. Ltd (The Nicholas H)* [1996] A.C. 211.

[95] *Yianni v. Edwin Evans & Sons* [1982] QB 438; *cf. Bourne v. McEvoy Timber Preservation* (1975) 237 E.G. 496; *Davies v. Pally* [1988] 20 E.G. 74; *Roberts v. J. Hampson & Co.* [1990] 1 W.L.R. 94; *Smith v. Eric S. Bush* [1990] 1 A.C. 831 (where *Yianni's* case is cited with approval at 852–853, 864, 875); contrast *Beaumont v. Humberts* [1989] 29 E.G. 104; *cf. Halifax Building Society v. Edell* [1992] Ch. 436, 454.

[96] See also *Knight v. Lawrence* [1991] 1 E.G.L.R. 143; *Barings plc v. Coopers & Lybrand, The Times,* December 6, 1997; *Medforth v. Blake* [1999] N.L.J. 929.

[97] *Post* § 19–026; *Ross v. Caunters* [1980] Ch. 287; *White v. Jones* [1995] 2 A.C. 207; *cf. Smith v. Clarement Haynes, The Times,* September 3, 1991; *Al Kandari v. J.R. Brown & Co.* [1988] Q.B. 665. Contrast *Clarke v. Bruce Lance & Co.* [1988] 1 W.L.R. 881 (solicitor acting for testator in a different transaction held to owe no duty to beneficiary); *Worby v. Rosser, The Times,* June 9, 1999. For earlier discussion of *Ross v. Caunters, supra,* see *Banque Keyser Ullman SA v. Skandia (U.K.) Insurance Co. Ltd* [1990] Q.B. 659, 794–795, affd. on other grounds [1990] 2 All E.R. 947; *Van Oppen v. Clerk of the Bedford Charity Trustees* [1989] 1 All E.R. 273, 289, affd. [1990] 1 W.L.R. 235; *Caparo Industries plc v. Dickman* [1990] 2 A.C. 605, 635; *Murphy v. Brentwood DC* [1991] 1 A.C. 398, 486.

[98] See the authorities cited in n. 95, *supra;* contrast *Gran Gelato Ltd v. Richcliff Group Ltd* [1992] Ch. 560 (vendor's solicitor not liable to purchaser for negligently representing his client's state of mind).

[99] See the overruling of *Candler v. Crane Christmas & Co.* [1951] 2 K.B. 164 in *Hedley Byrne v. Heller & Partners Ltd* [1964] A.C. 465; *cf. Caparo Industries plc v. Dickman* [1990] 2 A.C. 605, 625; *Morgan Crucible Co. plc v. Hill Samuel Bank plc* [1991] Ch. 295; contrast *James McNaughton Paper Group v. Hicks Anderson & Co.* [1991] 2 Q.B. 113, where the circumstances in which the report was prepared negatived the duty.

[1] *Ante,* §§ 6–078 to 6–086.

even though the misrepresentation giving rise to it is made in the performance of a contract to which he is not a party.

19–024   **The *Junior Books* case.** The most controversial extension of tort liability to a third party was made in *Junior Books Ltd v. Veitchi Co. Ltd*,[2] where B had undertaken to build a factory for C by a contract which entitled C to nominate sub-contractors. C nominated A as flooring sub-contractor; A in consequence entered into a contract with B; but no contract came into existence between A and C.[3] The floor later cracked and, on the assumption that this was due to A's negligence in doing the work, it was held that A was liable to C for the loss suffered by C in consequence of the fact that the work had to be done again. At first sight, this represented a considerable encroachment on the common law doctrine of privity; but the following discussion will show that later decisions have taken a highly restrictive view of the scope of the *Junior Books* case.

19–025   **Tort and contract of liability distinguished.** It is important to emphasise that, in the situations just described, A's liability to C is in tort and not on the contract between A and B as such: both the basis and the standard of liability may differ according to whether A is being sued on the contract by B or in tort by C. Thus in the *Junior Books* case it does not seem that C could have sued A if A had repudiated his contract with B on an untenable ground and done no work under it at all, with the result that completion of the building was delayed and C suffered loss.[4]

19–026   **Ommissions.** In one group of cases, A has indeed been held liable in tort to C for simple failure to take steps in the performance of his contract with B. These are cases, such as *White v. Jones*,[5] which hold that where a solicitor (A) negligently fails to carry out his client's (B's) instructions to make a will in favour of C, then A can, after B's death, be held liable in tort to C for the value of the benefit lost by C as a result of A's failure to act. But one reason for this conclusion was that A's omission made him liable in tort, as well as for breach

---

[2] [1983] 1 A.C. 520; Jaffey [1983] C.L.J. 37; Palmer and Murdoch (1983) 46 M.L.R. 213; Jaffey (1985) 5 L.S. 77; Reynolds (1985) 11 N.Z.U.L.R. 215; Stapleton (1988) 104 L.Q.R. 213, 389; Huxley (1990) 53 M.L.R. 361; Beyleveld and Brownsword (1991) 54 M.L.R. 48. The Contracts (Rights of Third Parties) Bill 1998 would probably not apply on such facts: *post* § 19–079.

[3] In *Greater Nottingham Co-operative Society Ltd v. Cementation Piling & Foundations Ltd* [1989] Q.B. 71 there was such a contract between A and C, and it was held that A's duty to C was governed by that contract alone, and not by the general law relating to the tort of negligence; *cf. Welsh Health Technical Services v. Haden Young* (1987) 37 Build.L.R. 130; *Sonat Offshore SA v. Amerada Hess Development Co.* [1988] 1 Lloyd's Rep. 145, 159; *Red Sea Tankers Ltd v. Papachristidis (The Hellespont Ardent)* [1997] 2 Lloyd's Rep. 547, 593. But it was recognised that breaches of duty arising out of certain contractual relationships may be actionable in tort as well as in contract; see *e.g. Forsikringsaktieselskapet Vesta v. Butcher* [1989] A.C. 852, 860, affd., without reference to this point, *ibid* 880; *cf. Nitrigin Eirann Teoranta v. Inco Alloys Ltd* [1992] 1 All E.R. 854, 856–857; *Saipem SpA v. Dredging VO2 BV (The Volvox Hollandia) (No. 2)* [1993] 2 Lloyd's Rep. 315, 322; *Henderson v. Merrett Syndicates Ltd* [1995] 2 A.C. 145; *Holt v. Payne Skillington, The Times,* December 22, 1995; *Sumitomo Bank Ltd v. Banque Bruxelles Lambert S.A.* [1997] 1 Lloyd's Rep. 487, 512–514; the same is true in the relationships described at nn. 90 and 91 *ante.*

[4] In *G.A.F.L.A.C. v. Tanter (The Zephyr)* [1984] 1 Lloyd's Rep. 58, 85, it was said at first instance that even the law of torts can sometimes impose "positive duties . . . recognised . . . only because a party has voluntarily undertaken them." This suggestion was disapproved on appeal; [1985] 2 Lloyd's Rep. 529: *cf. White v. Jones* [1995] 2 A.C. 207, 261. No issue of privity arose in *The Zephyr*; the dispute was as to contractual intention (*ante*, §§ 2–146, 3–167).

[5] [1995] 2 A.C. 207 (*post*, § 19–037).

of contract, even to his own client B. This would not have been the position if, in the *Junior Books* case,[6] A had wrongfully repudiated his contract with B or had simply failed to do any work under it: such a repudiation or omission would have made A liable to B only for breach of contract (and not in tort). The "disappointed beneficiary" cases are also distinguishable from the building contract cases for other reasons to be discussed in § 18–037 below; and they therefore do not support any general proposition that A's omission to perform his contract with B can give a cause of action in tort to C merely because, as a result of the omission, C suffers loss. Indeed, in *White v. Jones* itself Lord Goff[7] recognised the general principle that in tort there was no liability for pure omissions; but he subjected[8] it to an exception where, as in that case, there had been an "assumption of responsibility" by A towards C. The basis of that assumption seems to have been that A undertook a duty of care in relation to the provision of professional services, making him liable even to B in tort (as well as in contract) for failure to act with due diligence and care. This reasoning would not apply to cases of A's simple failure to take any steps in the performance of his building contract with B, causing loss to C.

Further differences between tort and contract liability. Further differences   **19–027**
between contract and tort liability in cases involving three parties are that the contract between A and B might have made A strictly liable to B,[9] without proof of negligence, while negligence was an essential element of C's cause of action in tort against A; that in contract, B would have a cause of action against A as soon as the defective work was done, while in tort C's cause of action would only accrue when the resulting loss was suffered[10]; and that in B's action on the contract it is only necessary to show that the contract has been made and broken, while in C's action in tort, C must establish that there was a relationship between himself and A by virtue of which A owed him a duty of care.

Restrictions on scope of the duty of care. A relationship giving rise to a duty   **19–028**
of care[11] is not established merely by showing that C has suffered foreseeable loss as a result of A's defective performance of his contract with B. In the *Junior Books* case, there were many special factors giving rise to such a relationship: A were nominated as sub-contractors by C; A were specialists in flooring and knew of C's requirements; C relied on A's special skills in laying floors; and A must have known that defects in the work could necessitate repairs and lead to economic loss.[12] These special factors (and in particular the extent of C's reliance on A's special skills) may have given rise to a "special relationship" and hence

---

[6] [1983] 1 A.C. 520.
[7] at 258.
[8] *ibid.* at 268.
[9] *e.g.* on facts such as those of *Donoghue v. Stevenson* [1932] A.C. 562 liability for breach of contract in respect of defects in the goods sold would be strict, while the tort liability of, or to, a third party would have depended on negligence. This difference between contract and tort liability in such cases is considerably reduced in importance by Part I of the Consumer Protection Act 1987, introducing strict "product liability" to the ultimate consumer. But such liability is subject to important qualifications, so that it does not extend to many of the situations with which the discussion in this chapter is concerned.
[10] *Dove v. Banham's Safety Locks Ltd* [1983] 1 W.L.R. 1463; *cf. Bell v. Peter Browne & Co.* [1990] 2 Q.B. 495.
[11] *Ante,* § 19–023.
[12] [1983] 1 A.C. 520, 546.

to a duty of care.[13] But such factors are unlikely to arise in the ordinary case where C suffers loss as a result of the defective performance by A of his contract with B. Accordingly, later authorities[14] have emphasised the exceptional nature of the circumstances in the *Junior Books* case. It has been said that those circumstances were "unique"[15]; that the case "cannot now be regarded as a useful pointer to the development of the law"[16]; or as "laying down any principle of general application in the law of tort"[17]; that "it is really of no use as an authority on the general duty of care"[18]; and that the statement of principle in Lord Brandon's dissenting speech is to be preferred to the views of the majority.[19] The authority of the case is further undermined by the fact that the reasoning of the majority is to a considerable extent based on earlier decisions[20] which (so far as they hold defendants liable for economic loss)[21] have since been overruled by the House of Lords.[22] In consequence of these developments, the decision in the *Junior Books* case has been described as "discredited"[23] and "virtually extinguished."[24]

19–029   The duty owed by A to C in tort may also be less extensive than that owed by A to the other contracting party. This was, for example, the position where A was employed as solicitor by B who was guarantor of C's mortgage. It was held[25] that, although A might owe a duty of care to C, this duty did not extend to requiring A to explain the implications of the mortgage to C, since the imposition of such an extensive duty might give rise to a conflict between A's duty to his own client (B) and the alleged duty to C.

19–030   **Duty restricted by terms of contracts.** The scope of any duty owed by A to C may, finally, be restricted by the terms of the contracts between A and C and between B and C. These contracts may be relevant for this purpose either in specifying exactly what it is that A is required to do, or in showing that C has

---

[13] *Murphy v. Brentwood DC* [1991] 1 A.C. 398, 466, 481.

[14] *Post*, § 19–036, nn. 63 and 64.

[15] *D. & F. Estates Ltd v. Church Commissioners for England* [1989] A.C. 177, 202; *cf. Van Oppen v. Clerk to the Bedford Charity Trustees* [1989] 1 All E.R. 273, 289, affd. [1990] 1 W.L.R. 235; *Duncan Stevenson MacMillan v. A.W. Knott Becker Scott Ltd* [1990] 1 Lloyd's Rep. 98; *Nitrigin Eirann Teoranta v. Inco Alloys Ltd* [1992] 1 W.L.R. 498, 504.

[16] *Simaan General Contracting Co. v. Pilkington Glass Ltd (No. 2)* [1988] Q.B. 758, 784.

[17] *D. & F. Estates Ltd v. Church Commissioners for England* [1989] A.C. 177, 202.

[18] *ibid.* at 215.

[19] *ibid.* at 202, 215; *Department of the Environment v. Thomas Bates & Son Ltd* [1989] 1 All E.R. 1075, 1084, affd. [1991] 1 A.C. 499; *Islander Trucking Ltd v. Hogg Robinson & Gardner Mountain (Marine) Ltd* [1990] 1 All E.R. 826, 829; *cf. Murphy v. Brentwood DC* [1991] 1 A.C. 398, 466, 469; and, in Scotland, *Strathford East Kilbride Ltd v. Film Design Ltd*, 1997 S.C.L.R. 877.

[20] *i.e. Anns v. Merton L.B.C.* [1978] A.C. 728; *Dutton v. Bognor Regis B. Co. Ltd* [1972] 1 Q.B. 373.

[21] *Stovin v. Wise* [1996] A.C. 923, 949.

[22] *Murphy v. Brentwood DC* [1991] 1 A.C. 398. Contrast in Australia *Bryan v. Maloney* (1995) 182 C.L.R. 609; in New Zealand (as accepted by the Privy Council) *Invercargill City Council v. Hamlin* [1996] A.C. 624; in Canada *Winnipeg Condominium Corp. v. Bird Construction Co. Ltd* (1995) 121 D.L.R. (4th) 193 (where the defect made the building dangerous); and in Singapore *RSP Architects Planners & Engineers v. Ocean Front Ltd* (1998) 14 Const.L.J. 139.

[23] *Societe Commerciale de Reassurance v. ERAS International Ltd* [1992] 1 Lloyd's Rep. 570, 599.

[24] *Saipem SpA v. Dredging VO2 BV (The Volvox Hollandia) (No. 2)* [1993] 2 Lloyd's Rep. 315, 322; *Losinjska Plovidba v. Transco Overseas Ltd (The Orjula)* [1995] 2 Lloyd's Rep. 395, 401.

[25] *Woodward v. Wolfertrans The Times*, April 8, 1997.

assented to an exclusion or restriction of A's liability for defective performance.[26]

Economic loss and physical harm. Except where there is a special relation- **19–031** ship between the parties, such as that which existed in the misrepresentation cases discussed in Chapter 6, and in those in which a claim is based on the defendant's failure to perform a contract with another to perform professional services[27] a claimant cannot rely on the breach of a contract to which he was not a party as giving him a cause of action in tort merely because, as a result of the breach, he has suffered economic loss, that is loss not taking the form either of personal injury or of physical damage to his property.[28] The importance of this point is illustrated by *Simaan General Contracting Co. v. Pilkington Glass Ltd (No. 2),*[29] where the defendants had been nominated as suppliers of glass for incorporation in a building which was being erected by the claimants as main contractors for a client in Abu Dhabi. The glass had been sold by the defendants to a sub-contractor engaged by the claimants, so that there was no contract between claimants and defendants; the glass was perfectly sound but not of the colour specified in the contract of sale or in the main building contract. In consequence of this shortcoming, the claimants were not paid by their client and so suffered financial loss; but it was held that the defendants' breach of their contract with the sub-contractors did not give the claimants any right of action in tort against the defendants merely because that breach had caused the claimants to suffer financial loss. Similarly, it was held in *Balsamo v. Medici*[30] that a sub-agent who negligently paid over the proceeds of the sale of the principal's property to a fraudulent impostor was not liable in tort to the principal for such negligence in handling the money; nor was he liable to the principal in contract as there was no privity of contract between the sub-agent and the principal. To extend the *Junior Books* case to such a situation would, it was said, "come perilously close to abrogating the doctrine of privity altogether."[31] A doctor

---

[26] *Junior Books* case [1983] 1 A.C. 520, 546, applied in *Southern Water Authority v. Carey* [1985] 2 All E.R. 1077; doubted (though in another context) in *Leigh & Sillavan Ltd v. Aliakmon Shipping Co. Ltd (The Aliakmon)* [1986] A.C. 785, 817 (*post* § 19–034); see also *Pacific Associates Inc v. Baxter* [1990] 1 Q.B. 993; *cf. Norwich C.C. v. Harvey* [1989] 1 All E.R. 1180, 1187 and, in Scotland, *British Telecommunications plc v. James Thomson & Sons (Engineers) Ltd* 1997 S.C.L.R. 59. And see *ante* § 14–050.

[27] As, for example, in *Henderson v. Merrett Syndicates Ltd* [1995] 2 A.C. 145 and *White v. Jones* [1995] 2 A.C. 207.

[28] *Tate & Lyle Industries Ltd v. G.L.C.* [1983] 2 A.C. 509, 530–531; *cf. London Congregational Union Inc. v. Harriss* [1988] 1 All E.R. 15, 25; *Simaan General Contracting Co. Ltd v. Pilkington Glass Ltd (No. 2)* [1988] 1 Q.B. 758, 781; *Greater Nottingham Co-operative Society Ltd v. Cementation Piling & Foundation Ltd* [1989] Q.B. 71, 94; *Verderame v. Commercial Union Assurance Co. plc., The Times,* April 2, 1992; *Preston v. Torfaen B.C.* [1993] E.G.C.S. 137; *cf.,* as to the restricted scope of such a duty, *Hill Samuel Bank v. Frederick Brand Partnership* (1994) 10 Const.L.J. 72.

[29] *Supra,* n. 28.

[30] [1984] 1 W.L.R. 951; Whittaker (1985) 48 M.L.R. 86. *cf.* also *Michael Salliss & Co. v. E.C.A. Call* (1984) 4 Const. L.J. 125.

[31] At 959–960. The soundness of the decisions discussed in this paragraph is not questioned in *Henderson v. Merrett Syndicates Ltd* [1995] 2 A.C. 145, where the liability in tort of a subagent to a principal with whom he was in no contractual relationship was said at 195 to be based on the "most unusual" situation in that case. It seems that on facts such as those of *Balsamo v. Medici, supra,* the requirements of subsections 1(1) (2) and (3) of the Contracts (Rights of Third Parties) Bill, 1998, (*post,* §§ 19–076, 19–078, 19–080) would not be satisfied.

employed by a company to assess replies of job applicants to medical questionnaires has likewise been held to owe no duty in tort to those applicants.[32]

19–032   **Requirement of "proximity".** The point that is emphasised in cases such as the *Simaan* and *Balsamo* cases is that the claimants in them suffered no physical harm as a result of the defendants' acts or omissions. It does not follow that the mere fact of the claimant's having suffered foreseeable harm of this kind is a sufficient condition of the defendant's liability in tort. The claimant must, in addition, show that there was a relationship of "proximity" between him and the defendant, so that it is fair, just and reasonable to impose a duty of care on the defendant.[33] This requirement was held not to have been satisfied in *The Nicholas H*,[34] where a ship classification society had, in breach of its contract with shipowners, advised them that their ship could proceed on her current voyage until the cargo which she was then carrying had been discharged. In the course of that voyage the ship sank, and it was held that the owners of the cargo had no cause of action in tort against the society in respect of the loss of their cargo. The main reason given by the House of Lords for this conclusion was that the shipowners were, in turn, in breach of their contract of carriage with the cargo-owners; and that it was not fair, just or reasonable to impose on the classification society a liability to the cargo-owners in tort[35] since this would not be subject to the limitations of liability available to the shipowners under international Conventions[36] which have the force of law. The effect of holding classification societies liable in tort to cargo-owners would be to deprive shipowners of the benefits of these Conventions since the societies would pass this liability on to shipowners; and this would be an undesirable conclusion[37] particularly as loss suffered by cargo-owners in excess of the Convention limits was "readily insurable."[38]

19–033   **Defects in the very thing supplied insufficient.** Even where A's negligence in the performance of his contract with B has resulted in damage to "property," the scope of C's tort remedy is further restricted by the fact that "property" in this context normally refers to property belonging to C *other* than the very thing supplied by A under his contract with B. Thus where A sold goods to B who

---

[32] *Kapfunde v. Abbey National plc*, [1998] I.R.L.R. 583 disapproving *Baker v. Kaye* [1997] I.R.L.R. 219 so far as it holds that a duty was owed by the doctor to the applicant.

[33] For these requirements, see, *inter alia, Caparo Industries plc v. Dickman* [1990] 2 A.C. 605, 617–618 (where it is also said at 632 that "these requirements are, at least in most cases, merely facets of the same thing"); *Murphy v. Brentwood DC* [1991] 1 A.C. 398, 480, 486; *X (Minors) v. Bedfordshire C.C.* [1995] 2 A.C. 633, 739; *W v. Essex C.C.* [1998] 3 All E.R. 111, 127; *British Telecommunications plc v. James Thomas & Sons (Engineering) Ltd* [1999] 2 All E.R. 241, 244.

[34] *Marc Rich & Co. A.G. v. Bishop Rock Marine Co. Ltd (The Nicholas H.)*, [1996] A.C. 211; see also the *X (Minors)* case, *supra*, at 749; *Reeman v. Department of Transport* [1997] 2 Lloyd's Rep. 648.

[35] Nor had there been an "assumption of responsibility" (*ante*, § 6–083) since the cargo-owners were "not even aware of [the classification society's] examination of the ship:" [1996] A.C. 211, 242.

[36] The Convention in question related to tonnage limitations; effect was given to this Convention by Merchant Shipping Act 1979 s.17 and Sched. 4, now superseded by Merchant Shipping Act 1995, s.185 and Sched. 7, Part I. The reasoning of the House of Lords is equally applicable to the contractual limitations and exceptions which protect the carrier by virtue of Carriage of Goods by Sea Act 1971 s.1(2) and Sched: see *Marc Rich & Co. v. Bishop Rock Marine (The Nicholas H)* [1996] A.C. 211, 238. No similar policy reasons for protecting an aircraft inspection authority were said to exist in *Perrett v. Collins, The Times*, June 23, 1998.

[37] *cf.* post § 19–034 at nn. 48 and 49.

[38] *The Nicholas H* [1996] A.C. 211, 242.

resold them to C, it was held that A would not be liable in tort to C merely because those goods disintegrated on account of a defect in them amounting to a breach of A's contract with B.[39] Nor, where goods are bought from a retailer, is the manufacturer liable to the buyer in tort[40] for negligence if the goods are defective and the defect is discovered before any injury, or harm to other property, has resulted. Even if the goods deteriorate by reason of the defect, the buyer's only loss is the financial or economic loss which he suffers because the defect has made them less valuable or because he discards them or incurs the cost of repairing them. Loss of this kind is not generally recoverable in tort,[41] though there may be an exception to this general rule where the defect is a source of danger in respect of which the claimant could become liable to third parties, so that money has to be spent in averting this danger.[42] The *Junior Books* case appears, indeed, to be inconsistent with the general rule; for the only "property" which could be said to have been damaged was the factory floor (which had cracked), and that damage was no more than a defect in the very thing supplied by A. The fact that A was nevertheless held liable in tort to C is now explicable (if at all) only by reference to the same special, or "unique," factors[43] which gave rise to the relationship of proximity in that case.

Claimant having no title to thing damaged. Even where A's breach of his **19–034** contract with B does result in physical damage, the mere fact that the loss so occasioned falls on C will not necessarily give C a right of action in tort against A in respect of that loss. In *The Aliakmon*[44] A, a carrier, had contracted with B for the carriage of a quantity of steel coils which B had sold to C. The goods were damaged, as a result of A's negligent breach of the contract of carriage, after the risk in them had passed to C under the contract of sale, but while B remained owner of them. C had no claim under the contract of carriage as he was not a party to it[45]; and the House of Lords held that he also had no cause of action against A in tort in respect of the loss which he had suffered as a result of remaining liable for the full price of the goods in spite of the fact that they had been damaged in transit. This conclusion was based on a long line of authority[46]

[39] *Aswan Engineering Establishment Co. v. Lupdine Ltd* [1987] 1 W.L.R. 1; *cf. D. & F. Estates Ltd v. Church Commissioners for England* [1989] A.C. 177, 202, 216; *Reid v. Rush & Tompkins Group plc* [1990] 1 W.L.R. 212, 224; *Warner v. Basildon Development Corp.* (1991) 7 Const.L.J. 146.

[40] For possible liability in contract under a manufacturer's guarantee, see *ante*, § 19–005.

[41] *Murphy v. Brentwood DC* [1991] 1 A.C. 398, 469, 475; *cf. Nitrigin Eirann Teoranta v. Inco Alloys Ltd* [1992] 1 W.L.R. 498.

[42] *Losinjska Plovida v. Transco Overseas Ltd (The Orjula)* [1995] 2 Lloyd's Rep. 395, 402, where it was also arguable that the defective thing supplied by the defendant had caused physical harm to *other* property in which the claimant had a prior interest as lessee.

[43] *Ante*, § 19–028 at n. 15.

[44] *Leigh & Sillavan Ltd v. Aliakmon Shipping Co. Ltd (The Aliakmon)* [1986] A.C. 785; Treitel [1986] L.M.C.L.Q. 294; Markesinis (1987) 103 L.Q.R. 354, 384–390; Tettenborn [1987] J.B.L. 12; *cf. Transcontainer Express Ltd v. Custodian Security Ltd* [1988] 1 Lloyd's Rep. 128; *Mitsui & Co. Ltd v. Flota Mercante Grancolombiana SA (The Ciudad de Pasto)* [1988] 1 W.L.R. 1145; *The Hamburg Star* [1994] 1 Lloyd's Rep. 399, 403–405. For a possible qualification, see *Virgo Steamship Co. SA v. Skaarup Shipping Corp. (The Kapetan Georgis)* [1988] 1 Lloyd's Rep. 352.

[45] The benefit of the contract of carriage had not been transferred to C under Bills of Lading Act 1855, s.1 as the property in the goods had not passed to him. On the facts of *The Aliakmon* rights under the contract of carriage would now be transferred to C by virtue of the Carriage of Goods by Sea Act 1992, s.2: see *White v. Jones* [1995] 2 A.C. 207, 265. But cases can still be imagined where this would not be the case: see *Benjamin's Sale of Goods*, 5th ed., § 18–103.

[46] Stretching from *Cattle v. Stockton Waterworks Co.* (1875) L.R. 10 Q.B. 453 to *Candlewood Navigation Corp. v. Mitsui O.S.K. Lines (The Mineral Transporter)* [1986] A.C.1.

which had established "the principle of law that, in order to enable a person to claim in negligence for loss caused to him by reason of loss or damage to property, he must have had either the legal ownership of or a possessory title to the property concerned at the time when the loss or damage occurred, and it is not enough for him to have only had contractual rights in relation to such property when the loss or damage occurred."[47] The House of Lords refused to create an exception to this principle where (as in *The Aliakmon*) the contractual right which C had under his contract of sale with B was one to have property and possession of the goods transferred to him at a later date. The main reason for this refusal was that the contract of carriage between A and B was expressed to be subject to an international Convention[48] which gave A (as carrier) the benefit of certain immunities from, and limitations of, liability; and to have held A liable in tort to C would have produced the undesirable result of depriving A of the protection of that contract,[49] since C (being a stranger to it) was no more bound by its terms than entitled to assert rights under it.

19–035   **Tort and contract damages contrasted.** Where a third party can recover damages in tort for the negligent performance of a contract between two others, the damages in such a tort action will not normally be assessed in the same way as they would be in a contractual action. In particular, certain kinds of loss are generally regarded as being recoverable only in a contractual action. This follows from the general principle that the object of awarding damages in a contractual action is to put the claimant into the same position as that in which he would have been if the contract had been performed, while in an action in tort that object is to put him back into the position in which he was before the tort was committed. The distinction is well illustrated by *Muirhead v. Industrial Tank Specialities Ltd*[50] where the plaintiff, who owned a lobster farm, had entered into a contract for the installation of pumps, which later failed because of a defect in their electric motors. There was no contract between the plaintiff and the supplier of the motors but his claim against that supplier succeeded in tort in respect of the physical damage caused by that failure (*i.e.* the value of the lobsters which had died); and "any financial loss suffered by the plaintiff in consequence of that physical damage."[51] (*i.e.* the loss of profits on the sale of *those* lobsters). But a further claim "in respect of the whole economic loss suffered"[52] by the plaintiff (*i.e.* for loss of profits that he would have made from the installation, had it not been defective) was rejected: such damages might have been recoverable from

---

[47] [1986] A.C. 785, 809. Griew, (1986) 136 N.L.J. 1201 suggests that the principle may have been qualified by Latent Damage Act 1986, s.3; but there is no hint in the legislative history of s.3 that such a qualification was intended. It can, in any event, only apply where the damage was still latent when the claimant became owner; and this was not the position in *The Aliakmon*.

[48] *i.e.* the Hague Rules set out in the Schedule to the Carriage of Goods by Sea Act 1924, now superseded in England by Carriage of Goods by Sea Act 1971.

[49] *cf. Simaan General Contracting Co. v. Pilkington Glass Ltd (No. 2)* [1988] Q.B. 758, 782–783. For the suggestion that the position may be different where the potential tortfeasor has no such protection, see *Triangle Steel & Supply Co. v. Korean United Lines Inc.* (1985) 63 B.C.L.R. 66, 80 (the reasoning of which is in other respects inconsistent with that of *The Aliakmon*). See also *Sidhu v. British Airways plc* [1997] A.C. 430, 450–451 stating that, in a case governed by the Conventions on international carriage of goods by air, the only persons having the right to sue in respect of loss of damage to the goods were those specified in the Conventions for this purpose; in an action by such persons, the carrier would be entitled to the protection of the Conventions.

[50] [1986] Q.B. 507; Whittaker (1986) 49 M.L.R. 469; Oughton [1987] J.B.L. 370.

[51] [1986] Q.B. at 533.

[52] *ibid.*

the installer of the pumps in contract but they could not be claimed from the suppliers of the motors party in tort.

Considerable difficulty again arises in this connection from the *Junior Books*[53] case. The main question discussed in that case was whether any economic or financial loss could be recovered in a tort action in the absence of any allegation that the cracks in the floor were a source of danger to persons or to other property. In the exceptional circumstances of the case, this question was answered in the affirmative and on that basis most of the items of loss, in respect of which damages were said to be recoverable, can be explained in terms of the principles governing the assessment of damages in tort: this is, for example, true of the profits lost and of the wages and overheads wasted while the factory was closed for repairs to the floor. But it was also said that factory owners were entitled to the *cost of replacing the floor*[54]; and such an award would, by putting them into the position in which they would have been if the sub-contractor's promise had been performed, amount to an award of contract damages in spite of the fact that there was no contract between the factory owners and the sub-contractors.[55] On the normal basis of assessment in tort, the damages for this item should not have included the cost of replacing the defective floor with a good one.[56] In the *Junior Books* case, Lord Keith explained this aspect of the case on the ground that, in replacing the floor, the factory owners had simply mitigated the loss of profit resulting from the defects in the floor originally provided[57]; and it is well established that expenses reasonably incurred in mitigation are recoverable.[58] But as this reasoning was not adopted by the other members of the House of Lords, an alternative explanation was given in the *Muirhead* case, namely that the same special (or unique) factors in the *Junior Books* case, which gave rise to the duty of care there,[59] also explain the assessment of damages.[60] This narrow view of the *Junior Books* case is supported by dicta in the *Junior Books* case itself[61]; by the fact that there is no subsequent similar[62] case in which a third party has recovered damages in tort to put him into the position in which he would have been if the contract between two others *had been performed* (as opposed to that

---

[53] [1983] 1 A.C. 520; Grubb [1984] C.L.J. 111; Holyoak (1983) 99 L.Q.R. 591; Smith and Burns (1983) 46 M.L.R. 1 & 7.

[54] This was one of the items claimed; the question whether the claim was proved was not before the House of Lords, which decided only that there was a cause of action in respect of it if negligence were established.

[55] The case was governed by Scots law, which recognises a *jus quaesitum tertio*, but the conditions giving rise to such a right were not satisfied. *cf. British Telecommunications plc v. James Thomson (Engineers) Ltd* [1999] 2 All E.R. 241, 248.

[56] *cf. Murphy v. Brentwood DC* [1991] 2 A.C. 398, 469. Lord Roskill in the *Junior Books* case at 545 discusses (without reaching a definite conclusion) the question whether the pursuer in *Donoghue v. Stevenson* [1932] A.C. 562 could have recovered damages "for the diminished value of the ginger beer"—not for the cost of replacing the contaminated with pure ginger beer. Even the former basis of assessment would seem to be ruled out by the authorities cited in § 19–033, n. 39, *ante*.

[57] [1983] 1 A.C. 520, 536.

[58] *cf. post* § 27–098.

[59] *Ante* § 19–028.

[60] [1986] Q.B. 507, 523, 533–535.

[61] [1983] 1 A.C. 520, 533 (*per* Lord Fraser, who took the same narrow view of the *Junior Books* case in *The Mineral Transporter* [1986] A.C. 1, 24–25); and [1983] 1 A.C. 520, 546 (*per* Lord Roskill).

[62] For the different treatment of the "disappointed beneficiary" cases, see *post*, § 19–037.

in which he was *before it was broken*); and by the fact that many later decisions[63] have made it highly unlikely that such damages will, in a future tort case of this kind be awarded to a third party. On the contrary, two House of Lords decisions have specifically rejected such claims.[64] In each case, a lessee claimed damages in tort for the cost of remedying defects alleged to be due to the negligence of a building contractor in the performance of a contract to which the lessee was not a party. In each case, the contractor was held not liable in tort, even if he was negligent,[65] since the defects had been discovered before they had caused any personal injury, or damage to other property belonging to the lessees. To make the contractor liable for the purely economic loss suffered by the lessee in remedying the defect would "impose upon [the contractor] for the benefit of those with whom he had no contractual relationship the obligation of one who warranted the quality of"[66] his work. Such a result would have been inconsistent with the common law doctrine of privity; and these cases reinforce the view that liability in negligence to third parties has not wholly subverted (though it may have limited the scope of) that doctrine.

19–037   **Damages in "disappointed beneficiary" cases.** The general principle that a third party cannot recover damages in tort to put him into the position in which he would have been if a contract between two others had been performed is, at least at first sight, hard to reconcile with cases such as *White v. Jones*,[67] where A had instructed his solicitor B to draw up a will containing bequests in favour of his daughters C and D, but B negligently and in breach of his contract with A had done nothing to carry out these instructions by the time of A's death. The House of Lords by a majority held that B was liable in tort to C and D, and that the damages to which they were entitled consisted of the amounts which they would have obtained under A's will, if B had duly carried out A's instructions. The case presented certain special features, namely that C had discussed A's testamentary intentions with B, and that the letter setting out A's wishes had been drafted by D's husband. The majority do not seem to restrict the principle of liability to such special circumstances[68] though they accept that there must be "boundaries to the availability of the remedy" which "will have to be worked out . . . as practical

---

[63] *i.e. Tate & Lyle Industries Ltd v. G.L.C.* [1983] 2 A.C. 509; *Balsamo v. Medici* [1984] 1 W.L.R. 951; *Candlewood Navigation Corp. v. Mitsui O.S.K. Lines (The Mineral Transporter)* [1986] A.C. 1; *Muirhead v. Industrial Tank Specialities Ltd* [1986] Q.B. 507; *Leigh & Sillavan Ltd v. Aliakmon Shipping Co. Ltd (The Aliakmon)* [1986] A.C. 785; *Aswan Engineering Establishment Co. v. Lupdine Ltd* [1987] 1 W.L.R. 1; *cf.* also *Smith v. Littlewoods Organisation Ltd* [1987] A.C. 241, 280; *Yuen Kun Yeu v. Att.-Gen. of Hong Kong* [1988] A.C. 175; *Simaan General Contracting Co. v. Pilkington Glass Ltd (No. 2)* [1988] Q.B. 758; *Greater Nottingham Co-operative Society Ltd v. Cementation Piling & Foundation Ltd* [1989] Q.B. 71, 84; *Davies v. Radcliffe* [1990] 1 W.L.R. 821; *Parker-Tweedale v. Dunbar Bank plc* [1991] Ch. 12, 24; *Deloitte Haskins & Sells v. National Mutual Life Nominees* [1993] A.C. 774.

[64] *D. & F. Estates Ltd v. Church Commissioners for England* [1989] A.C. 177; *Department of the Environment v. Thomas Bates & Son Ltd* [1991] 1 A.C. 449.

[65] In the *D. & F. Estates* case, there was no such negligence as the builders had employed competent sub-contractors.

[66] [1989] A.C. 177, 207; *cf. ibid.* at 211–212.

[67] [1995] 2 A.C. 207 (Lords Keith and Mustill dissenting), approving the result (though not the reasoning) in *Ross v. Caunters* [1980] Ch. 287, where B's negligence took the form, not of simply failing to carry out A's instructions, but of carrying them out ineffectively. *cf. Esterhuizen v. Allied Dunbar Assurance plc, The Times* June 10, 1998 and (in Australia) *Hill v. Van Erp* (1997) 142 A.L.R. 687, a case of actual misfeasance by the solicitor.

[68] [1995] 2 A.C. 207, 295.

problems come before the courts."[69] It is, for example, an open question whether such a remedy would be available to a prospective beneficiary who had no previous connection with the testator or knowledge of his intentions; and it has been said that the solicitor would not be liable for the amount of the intended benefit where it would have been reasonable for him to have mitigated his loss by taking proceedings against the estate for rectification of the will and so to have obtained the intended benefit.[70] But where the principle (whatever its precise scope may turn out to be) does apply, its effect is to put C into the position in which he would have been if the contract between A and B had been properly performed. Such cases are, however, distinguishable in several respects from those which hold that building contractors are not liable to third parties in respect of purely economic loss caused by defective work. In the building cases, the third party's complaint is that he has not received the benefit of the contractor's performance. In the disappointed beneficiary cases, the benefit of which the third party is deprived is not that of the solicitor's work: the lost benefit was to be provided, not by the solicitor, but by the testator; it was not to be created by the solicitor's work, but existed independently of it. The third party is not entitled to the cost of curing the defects in the solicitor's work (*e.g.* to the cost of employing another solicitor to give effect to the testator's intention). On the contrary, it has been held that, if the defect is discovered when cure is still possible, the solicitor owes no duty to the beneficiary.[71] There are also the points that, if any duty is to be imposed on the solicitor to the disappointed beneficiary, the only realistic measure of damages is the value of the lost benefit; and that no more than nominal damages could be recovered from the solicitor by the client's estate, since it would have suffered no loss. The negligent solicitor would thus escape all substantial liability if he were not held liable to the disappointed beneficiary for the value of the lost benefit. In the building contract cases, on the other hand, the employer will usually have a substantial remedy against the defaulting builder for damages, amounting either to the cost of curing the defects in the work or to the difference between the value of the work which was done and that which should have been done; and such a remedy may be available to the employer, not only in respect of his own loss, but also (in appropriate circumstances) in respect of loss suffered by the third party.[72] For these reasons, it is submitted that the building contract cases can be distinguished from disappointed beneficiary cases such as *White v. Jones*. The principle of that case was still further extended in *Carr-Glynn v. Frearsons*[73] where the solicitors' negligence took the form, not of failing to secure the proper execution of the will, but of failing to take steps to ensure that property specifically bequeathed to the beneficiary remained within the client's estate after her death.[74] Loss was thus suffered by the estate but the solicitors were nevertheless held liable to the intended legatee since the proceeds of any claim by the estate would have benefited, not that legatee, but the person entitled under the will to the residuary

---

[69] *ibid*, at 269.

[70] On the question whether it would have been reasonable for the beneficiary to take rectification proceedings, contrast *Walker v. Geo. H. Medlicott & Son* [1999] 1 All E.R. 685 with *Horsfall v. Hayward* [1999] N.L.J. 452.

[71] *Hemmens v. Wilson Browne* [1995] Ch. 223.

[72] *Post.* § 19–049 *et seq.*

[73] [1998] 4 All E.R. 225.

[74] The testatrix was joint owner of the property in question and the solicitors had negligently failed to advise her to sever the joint tenancy, so that on her death her share passed to the other co-owner by right of survivorship.

estate, thus defeating the intention of the testatrix. The decision can be explained on the ground that "the estate" is something of a legal abstraction, the loss being in fact suffered by the individual who under the will would, but for the solicitors' negligence, have received the property which was lost to "the estate"; and that the court looked behind that abstraction[75] so as to fashion a remedy for that individual. The alternative possibility that the estate might have had a claim against the solicitors in respect of the intended legatee's loss[76] was not considered, nor was any attempt made to reconcile the result with those building contract cases (discussed above[77]) in which a third party was held to have no remedy in tort against the contractor for pure economic loss. The decision shows that the disappointed beneficiary cases go further than any other group of negligence cases in encroaching on the common law doctrine of privity. Perhaps for this reason, they are best regarded as *sui generis*.[78]

19–038   The view that the "disappointed beneficiary" cases are *sui generis* derives some support from their description as "an unusual class of cases" in *Goodwill v. Pregnancy Advisory Service*.[79] In that case, the defendant had arranged for one M to have a vasectomy and, after the operation had been carried out, told him that it had been successful and that he no longer needed to use any other method of contraception. Some three years later, M formed a sexual relationship with the claimant, to whom he communicated the information given to him by the defendant relating to the vasectomy; she ceased to use any method of contraception after having consulted her own general practitioner who told her that there was only a minute chance of her becoming pregnant. The vasectomy having undergone a spontaneous reversal, the claimant became pregnant by M and one reason for holding that the defendant was not liable to her in damages was that a doctor performing a vasectomy could not realistically be described as having been employed to confer a benefit on his patient's future sexual partners.[80] The case was also said to be unlike the "disappointed beneficiary" cases in that dismissal of the claim would not produce the "rank injustice"[81] that would arise in those cases if in them the only person with a claim against the negligent solicitor were the testator's estate, which would have suffered no loss. In a sterilisation case, a substantial remedy for negligence (if established) would normally be available to the patient him (or her) self.

(b) *Liability to Third Parties for Intimidation*

19–039   **Tort of intimidation.** The tort of intimidation is committed where A induces B to act to the detriment of C by threatening B with some unlawful course of

---

[75] In a way somewhat reminiscent of the process, well known in company law, of "lifting the corporate veil."

[76] See *post*, § 19–048, *et seq.*

[77] *Supra*, n. 64.

[78] *cf.* the description of *White v. Jones* as having been "decided on special facts" in *Williams v. National Life Health Foods* [1998] 2 All E.R. 577, 584.

[79] *Goodwill v. Pregnancy Advisory Service* [1996] 1 W.L.R. 1397, 1403.

[80] For dismissal on other grounds in Scotland of a similar claim by the patient's wife, see *McFarlane v. Tayside Health Board*, *The Times*, November 11, 1996.

[81] [1996] 1 W.L.R. 1397, 1403.

conduct. In *Rookes v. Barnard*[82] the House of Lords decided that a threat by A to break his contract with B is for this purpose a threat to do an unlawful act. Such a threat may therefore entitle C to sue A for intimidation; and in bringing such an action C will to some extent be relying on a contract to which he is not a party. But the suggestion[83] that this position "outflanks" the common law doctrine of privity has been rejected by the House of Lords.[84] In the case put, C does not sue to enforce A's promise to B. "His cause of action is quite different."[85] C's complaint is not that A has broken his contract with B, but that A has coerced B into acting to C's detriment.

(c) *Liability to Third Parties in Restitution?*

Restitution. It has been suggested in Australia that the third party may have   **19-040**
a claim in restitution where the promisor has received payment (or some other performance) from the promisee and has then failed or refused to perform the promise in favour of the third party; and that the measure of recovery on such a claim is the amount promised.[86] The suggestion was made where premiums under a policy of liability insurance for the benefit of a third party had been paid by the promisee to the promisor (the insurance company) which had then refused to pay the third party. The promisor's liability in restitution was said to be based on his unjust enrichment, and to arise in spite of the fact that there was no correlative impoverishment of the third party. But while it is true that liability in restitution is not based on loss to the claimant, it is (in the case put) based on gain to the defendant and it is hard to see what justification there can be for wholly disregarding this *basis* of restitutionary liability in determining its *measure*. And the argument that, to hold the promisor liable to the third party was "not an abrogation of the doctrine of privity of contract,"[87] merely because the liability was said to arise in restitution, is, it is submitted, inconsistent with the practical result of making the promisor so liable. We have seen that, in England, the promisor is not liable in tort where the practical effect of imposing such liability would be to abrogate the common law doctrine of privity[88]; and there seems to be no reason why the position should be different merely because the alleged basis of liability is restitution rather than tort. The suggestion that the promisor is liable in restitution to the third party for the amount promised, merely because the promisor has received performance from the promisee is, moreover, inconsistent with the reasoning of *Beswick v. Beswick*,[89] where it was assumed that the

---

[82] [1964] A.C. 1129. For restrictions on the scope of such liability where the unlawful conduct takes the form of acts done in the contemplation or furtherance of a trade dispute, see Trade Union and Labour Relation (Consolidation) Act 1992, s.219, as amended by Trade Union Reform and Employment Rights Act 1993, s.49(1) and Sched. 8, para. 72; for an extension of the principle in favour of an individual whose expected supply of goods or services is disrupted by unlawful acts inducing industrial action, see Trade Union and Labour Relations (Consolidation) Act 1992, s.235A, as inserted by Trade Union Reform and Employment Rights Act 1993, s.22.

[83] Wedderburn (1961) 24 M.L.R. 572, 577; accepted by Pearson L.J. in *Rookes v. Barnard* [1963] 1 Q.B. 623, 695, but later rejected: *infra* at n. 84.

[84] *Rookes v. Barnard* [1964] A.C. 1129, 1168, 1200, 1208, 1235; Hamson [1961] C.L.J. 189; [1964] C.L.J. 159; Hoffmann (1965) 81 L.Q.R. 116, 124–128.

[85] *Rookes v. Barnard* [1964] A.C. 1129, 1208; if C were suing to enforce the contract, the damages might be quite different.

[86] *Trident Insurance Co. Ltd v. McNiece Bros. Pty. Ltd* (1988) 165 C.L.R. 107, *per* Gaudron J.; this view does not seem to be shared by any other member of the Court; Soh (1989) 105 L.Q.R. 4.

[87] 165 C.L.R. at 177.

[88] *Ante*, §§ 19–031, 19–035.

[89] [1968] A.C. 58; *ante*, § 19–021.

third party had no common law right to sue the promisor in her own name, in spite of the fact that the promisor had received performance in full from the promisee. The view that claims of the kind here discussed fall outside the scope of the doctrine of privity of contract must therefore be viewed with scepticism. The argument based on restitution would in any event be of no avail to the third party where the promisor was willing to pay and the issue was merely whether it should pay the third party or the promisee[90]: in such cases the promisor would not just be unjustly enriched so that there would be no basis for restitutionary liability.

The above discussion is based on the assumption that the promisor would be unjustly enriched if he were allowed to retain a payment received *from the promisee* in spite of his failure to perform his promise to pay the third party. There is the further possibility that the promisor may have received a benefit *from a third party*: for example, where A contracts to grant a development lease to B, a company controlled by C, and C incurs expense in improving A's land in anticipation of the development, which then fails to take place because of A's failure to perform his contract with B. In such a case, it is arguable that C may have a restitution claim against A.[91] To allow such a claim would not be inconsistent with the doctrine of privity since in such a case C's claim is not based on any promise made by A to B for the benefit of C; no such promise has been made. The basis and measure of any restitution claim which C may have against A is more closely analogous to cases in which restitution is granted in respect of benefits conferred under anticipated contracts which fail to come into existence.[92]

4. ATTEMPTS TO CONFER BENEFITS UPON STRANGERS

(a) *Effects of a Contract for the Benefit of a Third Party*

19–041   **General.** Although a contract for the benefit of a third party generally does not, at common law, enable the third party to assert rights arising under it, the contract remains nevertheless binding between promisor and promisee. The fact that the contract was made for the benefit of a third party does, however, give rise to special problems so far as the promisee's remedies against the promisor are concerned. Actual performance of the contract may also lead to disputes between promisee and third party.

(i) *Promisee's Remedies*

19–042   **Specific performance.** The promisee (or those acting for his estate) may seek specific performance of the contract. If, as in *Beswick v. Beswick*[93] such an order is obtained, the third party will in fact receive the benefit contracted for.[94] But the

---

[90] See *post*, § 19–060; *cf.* such cases as *Re Schebsman* [1944] Ch. 83 and *Re Sinclair's Life Policy* [1938] Ch. 799 (*post* § 19–066).

[91] *Brennan v. Brighton B.C.*, *The Times*, May 15, 1997, where B was a company which had been wound up and so could no longer sue A for breach of the contract between them.

[92] *Post*, § 30–185.

[93] [1968] A.C. 58; *ante*, § 19–021.

[94] The third party can enforce the order although he is not a party to the proceedings in which it was obtained: RSC, Ord. 45, r. 9, preserved by CPR, Sched. 1.

scope of the remedy of specific performance is limited in various ways; these limitations, and their applicability to cases involving third parties, will be discussed in detail in Chapter 28.[95] In the following paragraphs we shall therefore consider what other remedies may be available to the promisee if the contract is broken.

Restitution. The promisee might claim restitution of the consideration provided by him. But part performance of the promise in favour of the third party could defeat this remedy,[96] and it might also be unjust to restrict the promisee to this remedy: for example, return of premiums could be a quite inadequate remedy where a policy of life insurance had been taken out for the benefit of a third party and had matured.   **19–043**

Claim for the agreed sum. The promisee might sue for payment of the agreed sum to himself. It may be objected that to allow such a claim would force the promisor to do something which he never contracted to do, *viz.* to pay the promisee when he contracted to pay the third party. The objection loses much of its force if the promisor would not in fact be prejudiced by having to pay the promisee rather than the third party.[97] There is little authority on the question, but the most recent pronouncement supports the view that the promisee cannot sue for the agreed sum,[98] save in exceptional circumstances to be discussed later in this Chapter.[99]   **19–044**

Damages in respect of promisee's loss. The promisee might claim damages where he has suffered loss as a result of the promisor's failure to perform in favour of the third party. But in *Beswick v. Beswick* the majority of the House of Lords[1] evidently thought that no such loss had been or would be suffered, and that accordingly the damages recoverable by the estate for breach of the nephew's promise would be merely nominal. Lord Upjohn explained that this would be the case because the promisee "died *without any assets* save and except the agreement which he hoped would keep him and then his widow for their lives."[2] It seems possible to deduce from this statement that damages might have been substantial if the promisee had had other assets—either because the widow might have had a claim against those assets if the promise was not performed[3] or because the promisee or his estate would in fact, even if not legally obliged to do so, have made some other, wholly voluntary, provision for the widow. The loss suffered by the promisee would be the cost of making an alternative provision, and there is some authority for the view that damages for breach of contract may   **19–045**

---

[95] *Post*, §§ 28–044A—28–048A.

[96] As there would be no "total failure of consideration"; and as "rescission" for breach could probably not be allowed unless the third party was willing to restore any performance received.

[97] cf. *post*, § 19–060.

[98] See *Coulls v. Bagot's Executor and Trustee Co.* [1967] A.L.R. 385, 411, qualifying a dictum in *Lloyd's v. Harper* (1880) 16 Ch.D. 290, 321 by restricting it to cases of trust; the qualification was accepted by Lord Pearce in *Beswick v. Beswick* [1968] A.C. 58, 88. It was denied by Lord Denning M.R. in *Jackson v. Horizon Holidays Ltd* [1975] 1 W.L.R. 1468, 1473, but his approach to the remedies available to the promisee was disapproved in *Woodar Investment Development Co. Ltd v. Wimpey Construction U.K. Ltd* [1980] 1 W.L.R. 277, *post*, § 19–047.

[99] See *Cleaver v. Mutual Reserve Fund Life Association* [1892] 1 Q.B. 14, *post*, § 19–071.

[1] Lord Pearce thought that damages would be substantial: [1968] A.C. 58 at 88.

[2] [1968] A.C. 58 at 102 (italics supplied).

[3] *e.g.* under (at that time) the Inheritance (Family Provision) Act 1938, now Inheritance (Provision for Family and Dependants) Act 1975.

be recovered to compensate for such loss even though the provision is wholly voluntary.[4] *A fortiori* the promisee can recover substantial damages where he is under a legal obligation to make a payment to the third party and where this obligation would have been discharged if the promisor had paid in accordance with the contract.

19–046   **Damages in respect of third party's loss: general rule.** The starting point of the following discussion is the general principle that, in an action for damages, the claimant cannot recover more than the amount required to compensate him for his loss[5]: he cannot, in general, recover damages in respect of loss suffered by a third party.[6] That principle was, indeed, denied by Lord Denning M.R. in *Jackson v. Horizon Holidays Ltd*,[7] where the defendants contracted with the claimant to provide holiday accommodation for the claimant, his wife and their two three-year-old children; and it was assumed that the wife and children were not parties to the contract.[8] The accommodation fell seriously short of the standard required by the contract, and the plaintiff recovered damages including £500 for "mental distress."[9] Lord Denning said that this sum would have been excessive compensation for the claimant's own distress.[10] He nevertheless upheld the award on the ground that the claimant had made a contract for the benefit both of himself and of his wife and children[11]; and that he could recover in respect of their loss as well as in respect of his own. But the authorities cited in support of this conclusion seem to contradict, rather than to favour, it.[12] Moreover, in *Beswick v. Beswick*[13] a majority of the House of Lords said that the promisee's estate could have recovered no more than nominal damages as it had suffered no loss.[14] This is scarcely consistent with the view that the promisee

---

[4] *Admiralty Commissioners v. SS. Amerika* [1917] A.C. 38, 61, where the actual decision was that payments voluntarily made to the victim of an alleged *tort* could not be recovered; on this point, see also *Esso Petroleum Co. Ltd v. Hall Russell & Co. Ltd* [1989] A.C. 643 (where there was no causal link between the voluntary payment and the defendants' wrongdoing). For the possibility of recovering voluntary payments to third parties in a contractual action, see also the rules as to mitigation and especially *Banco de Portugal v. Waterlow & Son Ltd* [1932] A.C. 452, where a bank recovered damages in respect of payments which it was not legally liable to make: *post*, § 28–087. And see the discussion in § 19–049 *post* of *Linden Gardens Trust Ltd v. Lenesta Sludge Disposals Ltd* [1994] A.C. 85.

[5] *Post*, § 27–018; *cf. White v. Jones* [1995] 2 A.C. 207 (*ante*, § 19–037), where the damages recoverable by the estate of the other contracting party would have been no more than nominal.

[6] *Albacruz (Cargo Owners) v. Albazero (Owners) (The Albazero)* [1977] A.C. 774, 846; *Linden Gardens case*, *supra*, n. 4 at 114, Weir [1977] C.L.J. 24.

[7] [1975] 1 W.L.R. 1468; Yates (1975) 39 M.L.R. 202.

[8] Contrast *Daly v. General Steam Navigation Co. Ltd (The Dragon)* [1979] 1 Lloyd's Rep. 257, 262 (affd. [1980] 2 Lloyd's Rep. 415), *ante*, § 19–012.

[9] [1975] 1 W.L.R. 1468 at 1472.

[10] [1975] 1 W.L.R. 1468.

[11] At 1474; *cf. McCall v. Abelesz* [1976] Q.B. 585, 594.

[12] Lord Denning M.R. relied on a dictum of Lush L.J. in *Lloyd's v. Harper* (1880) 16 Ch.D. 290, 331, said to have been quoted by Lord Pearce in *Beswick v. Beswick* "with considerable approval": [1975] 1 W.L.R. 1468 at 1473. In fact, Lord Pearce said that the dictum "cannot be accepted without qualification and regardless of the context": [1968] A.C. 58, 88; *cf. ibid.* at 101; he agreed with the view expressed in *Coulls v. Bagot's Executor & Trustee Co. Ltd* [1967] A.L.R. 385, 411, that Lush L.J.'s dictum must be confined to cases in which the contract creates a trust in favour of the third party: *post*, §§ 19–065—19–073. *Lloyd's v. Harper*, *supra*, was treated as a case of trust by Fry J. at first instance, and by James and Cotton L.JJ in the Court of Appeal. Cases of trust fall within the special exceptions stated in § 19–048, *post* to the general rule that in an action for damages the plaintiff can only recover damages for his *own* loss.

[13] [1968] A.C. 58.

[14] *Ante*, § 19–045.

under a contract for the benefit of a third party is, as a general rule, entitled to damages in respect of the third party's loss. James L.J. in *Jackson's* case seems to have regarded the £500 as compensation for the claimant's own distress.[15] No doubt this was increased by his witnessing the distress suffered by his wife and children; and if the promisee himself suffers loss he should not be prevented from recovering for it in full merely because the contract was partly made for the benefit of third parties, who also suffered loss.[16]

Lord Denning's approach to the question of damages in *Jackson's* case was   **19–047**
disapproved by the House of Lords in *Woodar Investment Development Ltd v. Wimpey Construction Co. Ltd*[17]; though the actual decision in *Jackson's* case was supported on the ground that the damages there were awarded in respect of the claimant's own loss[18]; or alternatively on the ground that cases such as the booking of family holidays or ordering meals in restaurants[19] might "call for special treatment."[20] In the *Woodar* case itself, a contract for the sale of land provided that on completion the purchaser should pay £850,000 to the vendor and also £150,000 to a third party. The vendor claimed damages on the footing that the purchaser had wrongfully repudiated the contract and the actual decision was that there had been no such repudiation,[21] so that the issue of damages did not arise. But the question of what damages would have been recoverable in the *Woodar* case if there had been a wrongful repudiation was described as "one of great doubt and difficulty"[22]; presumably it would turn on such factors as whether the vendor was under a legal obligation to ensure that the third party received the payment, or whether, on the purchaser's failure to make the payment, the vendor had actually made it, or procured it to be made, from other resources available to him.

The assumption underlying *Woodar Investment Development Ltd v. Wimpey Construction U.K. Ltd* thus seems to be that damages for breach of a contract for the benefit of a third party cannot, as a general rule, be recovered by the promisee in respect of a loss suffered only by the third party. At the same time, this position was described as "most unsatisfactory"[23] and said to be in need of reconsideration, either by the legislature or by the House of Lords itself.[24] The general rule was again criticised in *Forster v. Silvermere Golf and Equestrian Centre*,[25] where the claimant transferred land to the defendant who undertook to build a house on

---

[15] [1975] 1 W.L.R. 1468 at 1474.

[16] *cf. Radford v. de Froberville* [1977] 1 W.L.R. 1262 (damages for failure to perform a contract to build a wall not reduced merely because the promisee had entered into the contract not merely for his own benefit, but also for that of his tenants).

[17] [1980] 1 W.L.R. 277.

[18] *ibid.* at 283, 293, 297. Where a contract is made with a company and the breach causes loss to its subsidiary, damages can be recovered by the company since the value of its holding in the subsidiary will be reduced in consequence of the loss: *George Fischer (Great Britain) Ltd v. Multi Construction Ltd* [1995] 1 B.C.L.C. 260.

[19] *cf. Lockett v. A.M. Charles Ltd* [1938] 4 All E.R. 170, where agency reasoning was used in such a situation.

[20] [1980] 1 W.L.R. 277, 283. *cf. Calabar Properties Ltd v. Stitcher* [1984] 1 W.L.R. 287, 290 where it was not disputed that a tenant's damages for her landlord's breach of his covenant to repair should include compensation for ill-health suffered by her husband.

[21] *Post,* § 25–017.

[22] [1980] 1 W.L.R. 277 at 284.

[23] [1980] 1 W.L.R. 277 at 291; *cf.* 297–298; 300–301.

[24] *cf. ante,* § 19–021 at nn. 77–80.

[25] (1981) 125 S.J. 397.

it and to allow the claimant and her children to live in it rent free for life. It was held that the claimant could recover damages in respect of her own loss but not in respect of any rights of occupation which her children might have enjoyed after her death. Dillon J. described this result as "a blot on our law and most unjust." It is submitted (on the basis of the explanation of *Beswick v. Beswick*[26] given above)[27] that any expenses incurred by the claimant in making alternative provisions for the accommodation of her children after her death could have been recovered as forming part of her own loss. On the other hand, it is unlikely that the claimant could have secured the intended benefit for her children by seeking specific performance, for it does not seem that the defendant's obligation to build was defined with sufficient precision to enable the court to enforce it specifically.[28]

19–048   **Damages in respect of third party's loss: exceptions.** Judicial awareness of the unsatisfactory results which can flow from the general rule stated in § 19–047 above has led to the creation of a number of exceptions to that rule. For example a trustee may be able to recover substantial damages for breach of contract even though the loss is suffered by his *cestui que trust*[29]; an agent may be able to recover substantial damages even though the loss is suffered by his undisclosed principal[30]; a local authority may be able to recover substantial damages even though the loss is suffered by its inhabitants[31]; and a shipper of goods may be able to recover substantial damages from the shipowner for breach of the contract of carriage in respect of the loss of the goods, even though that loss is suffered by a person to whom the shipper has sold the goods but who has not himself acquired any rights under the contract of carriage against the shipowner.[32] In all these exceptional cases, a person recovers substantial damages for breach of contract, even though the breach caused no loss to him, but only to a third party. A similar possibility is recognised in the law of tort which, like the law of contract, starts with the principle that the claimant can recover "no more and no less than he has lost."[33] But where a third party voluntarily renders services in caring for a claimant who has suffered personal injury as a result of a tort, the claimant can recover damages in respect of the value of those services; and the "central objective" of such an award has been described as "compensating the voluntary carer,"[34] for whom such damages must be held on trust by the

---

[26] [1968] A.C. 58.

[27] *Ante*, § 19–045.

[28] *Post*, § 28–025.

[29] See, for example, *post* § 19–070. *cf.*; *Pan Atlantic Insurance Co. Ltd v. Pine Top Insurance Co. Ltd* [1988] 2 Lloyd's Rep. 505; *post* § 19–110.

[30] See *Siu Yin Kwan v. Eastern Insurance Co. Ltd* [1994] 2 A.C. 199, 207.

[31] *St. Albans C.C. v. International Computers Ltd* [1996] 4 All E.R. 481.

[32] *Dunlop v. Lambert* (1839) 2 Cl. & F. 626, 627; *cf. Obestain Inc. v. National Mineral Development Corp. Ltd (The Sanix Ace)* [1987] 1 Lloyd's Rep. 465; *Wibau Maschinenfabric Hartman SA v. Mackinnon Mackenzie & Co (The Chanda)* [1989] 2 Lloyd's Rep. 494. The rule was recognised by the House of Lords in *Albacruz (Cargo Owners) v. Albazero (Owners) (The Albazero)* [1977] A.C. 774, but held inapplicable as the buyer had acquired his own contractual rights against the shipowner under Bills of Lading Act 1855, s.1 (now repealed and replaced by Carriage of Goods by Sea Act 1992); Weir [1977] C.L.J. 24. In the case of contracts to which the Carriage of Goods by Sea Act 1992 applies, a special statutory exception is created by s.2(4) of the Act to the general rule that a person can recover damages only in respect of his own loss; for a full discussion of this subsection, see *Benjamin's Sale of Goods*, 5th ed. (1997) §§ 18–083 to 18–086.

[33] *Hunt v. Severs* [1994] 2 A.C. 350, 357.

[34] *ibid.* at 363.

claimant.[35] In substance, though not in form, the claimant in such a case recovers damages in respect of the loss which has been suffered by the third party in (for example) giving up his or her job so as to look after the injured plaintiff.

Further exceptions. The list of exceptions stated in § 19–048 above should   **19–049**
not be regarded as closed and the possibility of creating further exceptions is well illustrated by the decision of the House of Lords in *Linden Gardens Trust v. Lenesta Sludge Disposals Ltd.*[36] The speeches in that case also raise the question (also discussed in a number of later cases[37]) how far the process of extending the development there initiated can be taken in the direction of allowing the promisee to recover damages in respect of the third party's loss merely because the contract which has been broken was one for the benefit of a third party. In the *Linden Gardens* case, a building contract between parties described in it as employer and contractor provided for work to be done by the contractor by way of developing a site owned by the employer as shops, offices and flats. The site (but not the benefit of the contract) was later transferred by the employer to a third party, and it was assumed[38] for the purpose of the proceedings that the third party had suffered financial loss as a result of having to remedy breaches of the building contract committed after the transfer. In an action for breach of the building contract brought by the employer, the contractor argued that no loss had been suffered by the employer as he was no longer owner of the land when the alleged breaches occurred, and that the employer was therefore entitled to no more than nominal damages. In the House of Lords, this argument was rejected, and the employer's claim upheld,[39] on two distinct grounds.

Promisee's expense of curing the breach. Lord Griffiths upheld the employ-   **19–050**
er's claim on the ground that the employer "ha[d] suffered financial loss because he ha[d] to spend money to give him the benefit of the bargain which the defendant had promised but failed to deliver."[40] He added that "the court will of course wish to be satisfied that the repairs have been or are likely to be carried out."[41] This approach is, it is submitted, consistent with the explanation given in *Beswick v. Beswick*[42] of the fact that the damages there were regarded as no more than nominal: the court there could not be satisfied that the substitute provision for the widow was likely to be made, precisely because the promisee lacked the means to make it.[43] The essence of this reasoning is that the promisee recovers damages in respect of the loss which he himself suffers in ensuring that the third

---

[35] *Post* § 19–063; no such damages can be recovered where the voluntary carer is the tortfeasor: *Hunt v. Severs* [1994] 2 A.C. 350; *post* § 19–063, n. 96; nor where no obligation to hold the damages for the third party could be imposed on the claimant: *Dimond v. Lovell* [1999] 3 All E.R. 1.

[36] [1994] 1 A.C. 85.

[37] *Post*, §§ 19–052 to 19–054.

[38] The case is reported on a preliminary issue of law, so that the alleged facts had not been proved.

[39] *cf. IMI Cornelius (U.K.) v. Alan J. Bluor* (1993) 57 B.L.R. 108.

[40] [1994] A.C. 85, 97. In fact the third party had reimbursed the employer in respect of this expenditure: see *ibid.* at 422; but this did not affect the question of liability.

[41] *ibid.* This requirement has been doubted on the ground that, in general, the court is "not concerned with what the plaintiff proposes to do with this damages:" *Darlington B.C. v. Wiltshier Northern Ltd* [1995] 1 W.L.R. 68, 80. But it seems, with respect, that Lord Griffiths' requirement is concerned, not with the question what the plaintiff proposes to do with the damages, but with the question whether he has suffered any loss.

[42] [1968] A.C. 58.

[43] *ibid.* at 102; *ante* § 19–045.

party receives the intended benefit. The requirement that the promisee must suffer such loss is significant, particularly where there is no practical possibility of curing the breach and so of securing the intended benefit to the third party, as in the "family holiday" cases discussed above.

19–051 **Loss suffered by third party to whom the subject-matter was to be transferred.** Although Lord Keith had "much sympathy"[44] with, and Lord Bridge was "much attracted by,"[45] Lord Griffiths' reasoning, they (as well as Lord Ackner) preferred to base their decision on the narrower ground stated by Lord Browne-Wilkinson. This treats the loss as having been suffered by the third party rather than by the employer, but concludes that the employer could nevertheless recover substantial damages as the case fell within the rationale of one of the exceptions (stated in § 19–048 above) to the general rule that a party can recover damages only in respect of his own loss. The exception in question was that which entitled a shipper of goods to substantial damages from the carrier for breach of the contract of carriage between them, causing damage to the goods, even though when that damage was caused property and risk had passed from the shipper to a third party[46] (so long as that third party had not himself acquired contractual rights under the contract of carriage against the carrier[47]). The rationale of this exception was that, since the parties to the contract of carriage must have contemplated that property in the goods might be transferred to third parties after the contract had been made, the shipper must be treated in law as having made the contract of carriage for the benefit of all persons who might after the time of contracting acquire interests in the goods.[48] This rationale applied equally to the facts of the *Linden Gardens* case since the contractor could foresee that parts of the new development were going to be "occupied and possibly purchased by third parties" so that "it could be foreseen that damage caused by a breach would cause loss to a later owner."[49] The contractor could also foresee that a later owner would not have acquired rights under the building contract against the contractor since that contract expressly prohibited assignment by the employer without the contractor's written consent, which had not been sought. The effect of the *Linden Gardens* case was thus to extend the scope of the carriage by sea exception to contracts generally, but it was consistent with two factors which had restricted the scope of that exception: namely that (a) the loss or damage was caused to property which had been transferred by one of the contracting parties to the third party; and (b) the third party had not acquired any rights under the building contract[50] and it was foreseeable (by reason of the prohibition against assignment) that he would not do so. Lord Browne-Wilkinson left open the question whether the *first* of these factors was an essential requirement of the (extended) exception 1,[51] and two later cases, taken together, support the view that the extended exception can operate even though *neither* factor is present.

---

[44] [1994] 1 A.C. 85, 95.
[45] *ibid.* at 96.
[46] *Dunlop v. Lambert* (1839) 2 Cl. & F. 626, 627; *Obestain Inc. v. National Mineral Corp. (The Sanix Ace)* [1987] 1 Lloyd's Rep. 465.
[47] *Albacruz (Cargo Owners) v. Albazero (Owners) (The Alabazero)* [1977] A.C. 774.
[48] *ibid.* at 847.
[49] [1994] 1 A.C. 85, 114.
[50] *cf. ante*, § 19–048 at n. 32.
[51] [1994] 1 A.C. 85, 112.

The *Darlington* case. The first of these cases was *Darlington B.C. v. Wiltshier*   **19–052**
Northern Ltd[52] where a local authority (the council) which wished to develop
land which it already owned. The building work was to be done by the defendant;
finance was to be provided by a bank but this could not be done in the most
obvious way, by a loan from the bank, since such an arrangement would have
violated government restrictions on local authority borrowing. The transaction
was therefore cast in the form of two contracts: (1) a building contract in which
the bank was the employer and the defendant the building contractor, and (2) a
contract between the council and the bank, by which the bank undertook to
procure the erection of the buildings on the site, to pay all sums due under the
building contract and to assign to the council the benefit of any rights against the
defendant to which the bank might be entitled at the time of the assignment.
Clause 4(5) of this second contract provided that the bank was not to be liable to
the council "for any incompleteness or defect in the building work," and it was
this provision which was the principal source of the difficulties in the case. The
bank duly assigned its right against the defendant to the council which claimed
damages as such assignee from the defendant in respect of defects in the work.
Since an assignee cannot recover more that the assignor could have been done,
the question therefore arose what the bank could have recovered; and it was
argued that it could have recovered no more than nominal damages since it had
suffered no loss, having no interest in the land (or buildings) on which the work
had been done and being, by virtue of clause 4(5) of its contract with the council,
not liable for defects in the work to the council.[53] But the Court of Appeal
rejected this argument and held that the bank could have recovered substantial
damages from the defendant in respect of the council's loss and that it was this
right which had been assigned to the council. Dillon L.J. described this result as
a "direct application"[54] of the carriage by sea cases, as extended to building
contracts in the *Linden Gardens* case. But one crucial factor in all these cases was
that the parties to the contracts in question envisaged the *transfer* of the property
in respect of which the contractual services were to be rendered; and another
factor stressed in the *Linden Gardens* case was that the building contract prohibited assignment without the consent of the contractor, who could therefore
foresee that a later owner of the site would not acquire rights against him. Neither
of these factors was present in the *Darlington* case, so that Steyn L.J. was, with
respect, right in saying[55] that Lord Browne-Wilkinson's formulation in the
Linden Gardens case did not "precisely fit the material facts of the present case".
But he added that "only a very limited and conservative extension" of the
principle was required "to apply it by analogy to the present case". He appears
to have been impelled to make this extension by the fear that, if it were not made,
a prima facie meritorious claim would have "disappeared down a legal black
hole".[56] The source of that "black hole", however, appears to have been clause
4(5) of the contract between the council and the bank, rather than any defect in
the law. But for clause 4(5), the bank would have been liable to the council in

---

[52] [1995] 1 W.L.R. 68.

[53] These difficulties are not, it is submitted, removed by Dillon L.J.'s alternative ground for
decision, *viz.* that the bank was constructive trustee for the council of its contractual rights against the
defendant: this reasoning merely pushes the enquiry back to the question what (if anything) the bank
could have recovered from the defendant.

[54] [1995] 1 W.L.R. 68, 75.

[55] *ibid.* at 79. Waite L.J. expressed his agreement with both the other judgments, but his reasoning
seems to be closer to that of Dillon L.J. than to that of Steyn L.J.

[56] [1995] 1 W.L.R. 68, 79.

respect of the defect, and so it would have had a claim over against the defendant.

19–053   **The *Alfred McAlpine* case.** The second case is *Alfred McAlpine Ltd v. Pana-town Ltd,*[57] where the facts resembled those of the *Darlington* case in that a building contract was again made, not between the building contractor and the company which owned the site (the owner), but between that contractor and another company (the employer) associated with the site-owning company; the object of adopting this tripartite structure was to avoid VAT. On the day on which this contract was made, a separate contract (the "Duty of Care Deed") was made between the owner and the contractor; the obligations imposed on the contractor by this deed were not precisely co-terminous with those imposed on him by the building contract and the Deed did not, while the building contract did, contain an arbitration clause. The employer alleged that the building work was seriously defective and in arbitration proceedings claimed damages from the contractor, who argued that the employer should recover no more than nominal damages since any loss resulting from the alleged defects in the work had been suffered, not by the employer, but by the owner. The Court of Appeal held that the fact that the employer had never been owner of the property was no bar to his claim for substantial damages for breach of the building contract. The main reason for this conclusion was what was described as a "contract-based"[58] approach to the question whether breach by A of a contract between A and B can give B a right to substantial damages in respect of loss suffered by C. On this approach, the answer to that question was based on the intention or contemplation of A and B, or, in other words, on the interpretation of the contract between them. The contract in the *Alfred McAlpine* case was said to give B such a right because it provided that B was "not required to pay for defective work. If sued for the price, he could deduct the amount of any damages for which the contractor was liable . . . and if the employer was not entitled to recover damages for defective work . . . the parties' expectations would be defeated."[59] The main difficulty with this reasoning is that the right to deduct damages from the price is not necessarily the same as a free-standing right to damages: so far as the existence of the former right gives rise to any inference as to the intention of the parties, that inference might well be that B's right to damages should extend no further than the contract price and in the *Alfred McAlpine* case the claim appears to have been considerably in excess of this price.[60] Further difficulty arises from the fact that in that case there was a separate contract between A and C; this makes it hard to reconcile the case with the reasoning of the carriage by sea cases, on which the present line of building contract cases is ultimately based. In the carriage by sea cases, B has *no* right to substantial damages against A in respect of C's loss where C has an independent contractual right against A.[61] This was the position in the *Alfred McAlpine* case, where it is not at all clear why no claim was made by C against A under the Duty of Care Deed. No doubt it is true that, applying the "contract-based" approach, the construction of the contract between A and B is not determined by a different contract between A and C. But the fact that the

---

[57] (1998) 58 Const.L.R. 58; *Treitel* (1998) 114 L.Q.R. 527.
[58] (1998) 58 Const.L.R. 58, 94; *cf.* p. 93.
[59] *ibid.* at 96.
[60] This was £10 million while the amount at stake in the litigation was £40 million.
[61] *Albacruz (Cargo-Owners) v. Albazero (Owners) (The Albazero)* [1977] A.C. 774; *ante,* § 19–048.

two contracts were made on the same day does seem to make the second part of the "matrix of facts"[62] relevant to the construction of the first, or relevant for this purpose as part of the "contractual structure"[63] created by the parties.

Present scope of the exception. The *Darlington* and *Alfred McAlpine* cases **19–054** have gone considerably beyond the *Linden Gardens* case in extending the exception (which had originated in the carriage by sea cases) to the general rule that damages cannot be recovered in respect of the third party's loss. Indeed, the *Alfred McAlpine* case can be said to cast doubt on the question whether it is still proper to talk of a general rule[64]: on the "contract-based" approach of that case, the right to recover damages in respect of a third party's loss depends simply on the contemplation of the parties; it does not even depend on the policy argument that, but for the existence of such a right, the party in breach would escape all substantial liability.[65] The reasoning of that case is also hard to reconcile with a number of House of Lords cases in which it was clearly assumed that, where B had not himself suffered loss, he could not recover substantial damages in respect of C's loss[66]: on the "contract-based" approach, these cases can be explained only by a process of *ex post facto* rationalisation. Criticism of the two decisions must no doubt be muted in view of the frequent judicial disapproval of what had hitherto been regarded as the "general rule."[67] But that criticism occurred in cases in which the third party problem was an inescapable consequence of normal commercial factors, such as those which existed also in the *Linden Gardens* case.[68] The pressure for eroding the unpopular general rule is much less strong where the third party problem is, so to speak, manufactured by the parties for an ulterior motive, such as avoiding government restrictions on borrowing, as in the *Darlington* case, or avoiding tax, as in the *Alfred McAlpine* case; and that pressure is still further reduced where, as in that case, the third party has his own remedy under a separate contract with the party in breach.

Relation to third party's right. Even where, on one of the views discussed **19–055** above, the promisee can recover damages in respect of the third party's loss, no right to enforce the contract is conferred directly on the third party, whose only claim will be to the fruits of any action which the promisee may decide to bring.[69] The third party will have a direct right against the promisor only under one of the exceptions to the doctrine of privity. On the facts of some[70] (though not of all)[71] of the cases discussed above, the third party would probably have such a right if

---

[62] *Prenn v. Simmonds* [1971] 1 W.L.R. 1381, 1384.

[63] *Henderson v. Merrett Syndicates Ltd* [1995] 2 A.C. 145, 195 (discussing the faintly analogous question whether a contract between A and B can impose on A a duty of care in tort to C).

[64] See (1998) 58 Const.L.R. 58, 93.

[65] It was this policy argument which weighted with Steyn L.J. in the *Darlington* case; see *supra* at n. 56; and it was also influential in leading the House of Lords to fashion a remedy in tort in *White v. Jones* [1995] 2 A.C. 207.

[66] *Beswick v. Beswick* [1968] A.C. 58; *Woodar Investment Development Ltd v. Wimpey Construction Co. Ltd* [1980] 1 W.L.R. 277; *White v. Jones* [1995] 2 A.C. 207 (where it was assumed that the client's estate could recover no more than nominal damages).

[67] *Ante*, § 19–047.

[68] [1994] 1 A.C. 85.

[69] *Post*, § 19–063.

[70] *e.g.*, the *Woodar* case [1980] 1 W.L.R. 277 (*ante*, 19–03). See Law Com. No. 242, § 7–49; and probably the *Forster* case (1981) 125 S.J. 397 (*ante*, § 19–033).

[71] *e.g.*, probably, the *Linden Gardens* case [1994] 1 A.C. 85 (*ante*, § 19–049): see *post*, § 19–079.

those facts recurred after the coming into force of the Contracts (Rights of Third Parties) Bill 1998.[72] This point may restrict the number of situations in which the promisee can recover damages in respect of the third party's loss[73]; and it will probably reduce the pressure on the courts to extend the range of such situations.[74] But Clause 4 of the 1998 Bill preserves the promisee's rights under the contract.[75] The question of his right to recover damages in respect of the third party's loss will therefore continue to arise and to be of practical importance: *e.g.* where the promisor has a defence against the third party which is not available against the promisee.[76]

19–056 **Negative promises.** In §§ 19–046 to 19–054 it has been assumed that the promise is positive in nature, *e.g.* to pay money, to deliver goods or to do some other act. Where the promise is negative in nature, the promisee's most obvious remedy is an injunction to restrain the promisor's breach. This would certainly be possible where A validly promised B not to compete with C.

19–057 **Promise not to sue a third party.** One type of negative promise which gives rise to special difficulty is a promise by A to B *not to sue* C. If, in breach of such a promise, A nevertheless does sue C, it would not be appropriate for B to start a second action for an injunction to restrain A from proceeding with the first action; for such a step would lead to undesirable multiplicity of legal proceedings.[77] B's remedy is to ask the court to exercise its discretion[78] to stay A's action against C. In *Gore v. Van der Lann*[79] the Court of Appeal held that B could obtain a stay of A's action against C only if two conditions were satisfied; there must be a definite promise by A to B not to sue C, and B must have a sufficient interest in the enforcement of A's promise. This last requirement would not be satisfied unless, as a result of A's breach, B was exposed to legal liability to C: for example where B had contracted with C to procure his release from a debt or liability to A, and would be put in breach of that contract by A's action against C.

19–058 In *Snelling v. John G. Snelling Ltd*[80] the court went even further in giving effect to a promise of this kind. Three brothers had lent money to a family company of which they were directors. They agreed that if one of them resigned he should "forfeit" any money due to him from the company. One of them did resign and sued the company for the amounts due to him. By way of defence the company relied on the agreement between the brothers, and if matters had rested

---

[72] *Post*, §§ 19–075 *et seq.* Subsections 1(1)(a) and (3) will make it possible to draw up contracts on facts similar to those of the *Linden Gardens* case, *supra*, so as to confer a right of enforcement directly on the third party: see *post*, §§ 19–076, 19–080.

[73] On the reasoning of *The Albazero* [1977] A.C. 774, *ante* § 19–048.

[74] The "legal black hole" referred to in the *Darlington* case [1995] 1 W.L.R. 68 at 79 would be much reduced in significance.

[75] See *post*, § 19–101.

[76] 1998 Bill, subsection 3(4), *post*, § 19–092.

[77] Supreme Court Act 1981, s.49(2), replacing Supreme Court of Judicature (Consolidation) Act 1925, s.41.

[78] Under Supreme Court Act 1981, s.49(3).

[79] [1967] 2 Q.B. 31; Davies (1980) 1 L.S. 287; *cf. The Elbe Maru* [1978] 1 Lloyd's Rep. 206; *European Asian Bank A.G. v. Punjab & Sind Bank* [1982] 2 Lloyd's Rep. 356; *Neptune Orient Lines Ltd v. J.V.C. (U.K.) Ltd (The Chevalier Roze)* [1983] 2 Lloyd's Rep. 438; *Deepak Fertilisers and Petrochemicals Corp. v. ICI* [1999] 1 Lloyd's Rep. 387, 401.

[80] [1973] 1 Q.B. 87; Wilkie (1973) 36 M.L.R. 214.

there the defence would have failed as the company was not a party to the agreement.[81] But the other two brothers applied to be joined as defendants to the action, adopted the company's defence and counterclaimed for a declaration that the third brother's loan was forfeited. It was held that they were entitled to such a declaration by virtue of the contract between them and the third brother.[82] Ormrod J. further held that they could obtain a stay of the action against the company and that the most convenient way of disposing of the action against the company was to dismiss it. So far as the granting of the stay is concerned, the judgment is hard to reconcile with the requirement of a sufficient interest as explained in *Gore v. Van der Lann*[83]; but it is submitted that Ormrod J.'s actual decision is consistent with the spirit of *Beswick v. Beswick*.[84] If *the promisee* takes steps specifically to enforce the contract, the court should wherever possible grant such remedy as is most appropriate for that purpose. Normally this will be an order of specific performance or an injunction. The fact that the latter remedy is not appropriate to enforce a promise not to sue should not deter the court from granting other remedies that serve substantially to enforce the promise.

Such a remedy is, again, available only if it is sought *by the promisee*. If, in the *Snelling* case, the two brothers had not applied to be joined to the action, the company could not have relied on the agreement between them and the third brother by way of defence.

(ii) *Position between Promisee and Third Party*

Introduction. The promisor may be willing to perform, and may actually   **19–059** perform, in favour of the third party, *e.g.* by paying him the agreed sum. These possibilities give rise to further problems between the third party and the promisee. In discussing these problems we shall in §§ 19–060 to 19–063 assume that the case does not fall within any of the exceptions to the doctrine of privity which will be considered later in this Chapter.[85]

Promisor pays or is willing to pay. The promisor may actually pay or be   **19–060** willing to pay the third party in accordance with the contract, and the promisee may claim that the third party is not entitled to keep the money for his own benefit but that he must hold it on behalf of the promisee. Such a claim is not likely to be made by the promisee himself, as he generally wants to benefit the third party. But it might be made by the promisee's trustee in bankruptcy, or by his personal representative on death. In *Beswick v. Beswick* the House of Lords held that the third party was entitled to keep the money which the promisor was ordered to pay her, simply because it appeared from the true construction of the contract that this was the intention of the contracting parties.[86] It seems that this rule would apply equally to payments made willingly, *i.e.* without any order of

---

[81] [1973] 1 Q.B. at 95.

[82] *ibid.* at 96.

[83] [1967] 2 Q.B. 31.

[84] [1968] A.C. 58; *ante* § 19–021.

[85] *Post*, §§ 19–064—19–114.

[86] *Beswick v. Beswick* [1968] A.C. 58, 71, 94, 96, on this point overruling *Re Engelbach's Estate* [1924] 2 Ch. 348 and doubting *Re Sinclair's Life Policy* [1938] Ch. 799. Earlier cases supporting the view stated in the text include *Ashby v. Costin* (1888) 21 Q.B.D. 401; *Harris v. United Kingdom, etc., Society* (1889) 87 L.T.J. 272; *Re Davies* [1892] 3 Ch. 63.

the court.[87] Payments actually received by the third party can be claimed by the promisee only if, on the true construction of the contract, they were made to the third party as nominee for the promisee. Where the money has not yet been paid, the promisor and the promisee can agree to rescind or vary the contract; and if they vary it so as to provide for payment to the promisee, the third party has no claim under the contract. But the question whether the promisee can unilaterally (*i.e.* without the consent of the promisor) demand that payment should be made to himself depends once again on the construction of the contract. If the contract can be construed as one to pay the third party "or as the promisee shall direct" then the promisee is entitled to demand payment to himself.[88] But the contract is not likely to be construed in this way where it is a matter of concern to the promisor that payment should be made to the third party, *e.g.* because the third party is a near relative of the promisor and it matters to the promisor that the third party should be provided for.[89]

19–061   **Revocable mandate.** The rules stated in § 19–060 above apply only if there is indeed a promise to pay the third party. In *Coulls v. Bagot's Executor and Trustee Co. Ltd*[90] an agreement between A and B provided for payment of royalties by B to A and concluded: "I [A] authorise . . . [B] to pay all money connected with this agreement to my wife . . . and myself . . . as joint tenants." The document was signed by A, B and A's wife. A majority of the High Court of Australia held that there was no *promise* by B to A to pay A's wife but only a *mandate* by A authorising B to pay A's wife (so that such payment would discharge B). This mandate was revocable and had been revoked by A's death. Consequently, the money (which B was willing to pay) belonged to A's estate and not to his wife. The third party would, *a fortiori*, not be entitled to the money if he were mentioned in the contract as a mere nominee in such a way as to indicate that no beneficial interest was intended to pass to him and that payment to him without the request of the promisee should not discharge the promisor.[91]

19–062   **Promisee refuses to sue.** A further problem arises where the promisee fails or refuses to take any action to enforce the promise. Lord Denning has suggested that, even at common law, the third party could in such a case circumvent the doctrine of privity by suing the promisor and joining the promisee as co-defendant.[92] But Diplock and Salmon L.JJ. have said that the action can (in cases not falling within any of the exceptions to the doctrine of privity) be brought only by the promisee[93]; and it is submitted that this is the correct view. Lord Denning's view is fundamentally inconsistent with the common law doctrine of privity, which was recognised in *Beswick v. Beswick* and in many later cases.[94] It is also inconsistent with the reasoning of the cases on trusts of

---

[87] This appears from the treatment in *Beswick v. Beswick* of *Re Engelbach's Estate, supra*, n. 86, where the money had in fact been paid to the third party: see 93 L.J.Ch. 616, 617.

[88] The same is true where a contract provides for some other performance to be rendered to a third party: *e.g. Mitchell v. Ede* (1840) 11 Ad. & El. 888; *Elder Dempster Lines v. Zaki Ishag (The Lycaon)* [1983] 2 Lloyd's Rep. 548.

[89] As in *Re Stapleton-Bretherton* [1941] Ch. 482.

[90] [1967] A.L.R. 385.

[91] *Thavorn v. Bank of Credit & Commerce SA* [1985] 1 Lloyd's Rep. 259.

[92] *Beswick v. Beswick* [1966] Ch. at 557; *Gurtner v. Circuit* [1968] 2 Q.B. 587, 596.

[93] *Gurtner v. Circuit* [1968] 2 Q.B. at 599, 606.

[94] *Ante*, § 19–021.

promises, to be discussed later in this Chapter[95]; for if the third party could always sue by joining the promisee to the action, it would be pointless to insist that he must in addition show the existence of a trust.

Promisee sues for damages or restitution. A final problem arises where the   19–063
promisee sues but claims some form of relief other than specific performance in favour of the third party: *e.g.* where he claims damages, or recovery of the consideration provided by him. If such a claim succeeded, it would seem to lead to a judgment for payment to the promisee and not to the third party; and the question would arise whether the promisee could keep the payment for his own benefit or whether he would be bound to hold it for the third party. In tort, a person can sometimes recover damages for a loss suffered, not by himself, but by another; *e.g.* a husband may get damages for loss of earnings suffered by his wife in giving up her job to nurse him after an accident; and such damages must then be held on trust for the other person.[96] Similarly, where one person can recover damages for breach of contract in respect of loss suffered by another person in the exceptional cases mentioned in §§ 19–048 to 19–054 above, those damages must be held for that other person.[97] But these exceptions apart, there does not appear (at least as a general rule) to be any similar possibility where the promisee claims damages for breach of a contract merely because the contract was made for the benefit of a third party. The general rule in such a case is that damages will be awarded only to compensate the promisee for his *own* loss,[98] and where that general rule applies it does not seem that he can be under any obligation to pay over those damages (or any part of them) to the third party.[99] There may, however, be cases "calling for special treatment,"[1] such as the booking of family holidays or ordering meals in restaurants. If, in such special cases, the promisee can recover damages in respect of the third party's loss, it may be that those damages, when recovered, would (as in the exceptional situations discussed in § 19–048 to 19–054) be held by the promisee as money had and received for the use of the third party.[2]

---

[95] *Post*, §§ 19–065—19–073.

[96] *Hunt v. Severs* [1994] 2 A.C. 350, 363 following *Cunningham v. Harrison* [1973] Q.B. 942, 952 and rejecting the contrary view in *Donelly v. Joyce* [1974] Q.B. 454, 461–462. *cf. Allen v. Waters* [1935] 1 K.B. 200 and *Dennis v. L.P.T.B.* [1948] 1 All E.R. 779 as explained in (1956) 72 L.Q.R. 187; *Robertson v. Wait* (1853) 8 Exch. 299. For further problems which may arise where the person who provides the nursing or other services in respect of which damages are claimed is also the tortfeasor (*e.g.* where tortfeasor and victim are members of the same family involved in the same motor accident) see *Hayden v. Hayden* [1992] 1 W.L.R. 986 and *Hunt v. Severs* [1994] 2 A.C. 350, holding that in such circumstances the claimant cannot recover damages in respect of the value of services voluntarily rendered the tortfeasor himself.

[97] See, *e.g. Albacruz (Cargo Owners) v. Albazero (Owners) (The Albazero)* [1977] A.C. 774, 842 and other authorities cited in § 19–048, *ante*; and *cf. Conservative Central Office v. Burrell* [1980] 3 All E.R. 43, 63, affd. (without any reference to *Beswick v. Beswick* [1986] A.C. 58) [1982] 1 W.L.R. 522; *O'Sullivan v. Williams* [1992] 3 All E.R. 385, 387, discussing *The Winkfield* [1902] P. 42. *Linden Gardens* case [1994] 1 A.C. 85, *ante*, § 19–049); Carriage of Goods by Sea Act 1992 s.2(4) ("for the benefit of the person who sustained the loss").

[98] See *ante*, §§ 19–046—19–047.

[99] *cf. Coulls v. Bagot's Executor and Trustee Co. Ltd* [1967] A.L.R. 385, 411.

[1] *Woodar Investment Development Ltd v. Wimpey Construction U.K. Ltd* [1980] 1 W.L.R. 277, 283.

[2] This was the view of Lord Denning M.R. in *Jackson v. Horizon Holidays Ltd* [1975] 1 W.L.R. 1468, 1473. The strange result would be that the claimant was under some quasi-contractual liability to his two small children in respect of part of the £500 recovered as damages for distress.

(b) *Exceptions to the Doctrine*

19–064   **In general.** The doctrine of privity of contract is subject to many exceptions. Some of these, such as assignment and agency, are discussed in other parts of this work.[3] Others, such as covenants relating to land, are beyond its scope. In the following paragraphs of this Chapter, we shall discuss a further group of situations in which a third party can acquire rights under a contract by virtue of a number of equitable and statutory exceptions to the doctrine of privity. The most important of these is likely to be the new "general and wide-ranging"[4] one which will be created on the coming into force of the Contracts (Rights of Third Parties) Bill, 1998. This Bill, however preserves any right or remedy which the third party may have under the previously established exceptions[5]; and these still call for discussion since situations may arise in which it will be to the third party's advantage to rely on one of them rather than on the new one to be created by the Bill.[6]

(i) *Equitable Exceptions*

19–065   **Trusts of promises.**[7] It has long been settled that, where A makes a promise to B for the benefit of C, the promise can be enforced by C against A if B has constituted himself trustee of A's promise for C.[8] This exception to the doctrine of privity was approved by the House of Lords in *Walford's* case[9] where C (a broker) negotiated a charterparty in which the shipowner (A) promised the charterer (B) to pay a commission to C. It was held that B was trustee of A's promise for C, who could accordingly enforce the promise against A.

19–066   **Intention to create a trust.** A promisee will not be regarded as a trustee for the third party unless he has the intention to create a trust.[10]

Such an intention is most easily established where the word "trust" or "trustee" has been used[11]: the only[12] problem in such cases is whether the third party claiming to enforce the promise is a person in whose favour the trust has been created.[13] But a trust may be created without using any particular form of

---

[3] See Chaps. 20, 21 and Vol. II, Chap. 32. See also §§ 14–039—14–056 *et seq., ante.*

[4] Law Com. No. 242, § 5.16.

[5] See subsection 7(1) of the 1998 Bill.

[6] See *ante,* § 19–001; *post,* § 19–098.

[7] Corbin, 46 L.Q.R. 12 (1930); *Contracts,* Chap. 46; Jaconelli [1998] Conv. 88.

[8] *Tomlinson v. Gill* (1756) Amb. 330; *cf. Gregory v. Williams* (1817) Mer. 582; *Lloyd's v. Harper* (1880) 16 Ch.D. 290; for recognition of the device at common law (allowing B to recover more than he had lost on the ground that he was bound to hold the surplus for C) see *Lamb v. Vice* (1840) 6 M. & W. 467; *Robertson v. Wait* (1853) 8 Ex. 299; *Prudential Staff Union v. Hall* [1947] K.B. 685. For the effectiveness of a direction (not of a contractual nature) to executors in favour of a third party, see *Crowden v. Aldridge* [1993] 1 W.L.R. 433.

[9] *Les Affréteurs Réunis SA v. Leopold Walford (London) Ltd* [1919] A.C. 801; *cf. Howard Houlder & Partners Ltd v. Marine General Transporters (The Panaghia P)* [1983] 2 Lloyd's Rep. 653, 655; *Atlas Shipping Agency (U.K.) Ltd v. Suisse Atlantique Société d'Armement Maritime S.A.* [1995] 2 Lloyd's Rep. 188. Contrast *Marcan Shipping (London) Ltd v. Polish SS. Co. (The Manifest Lipkowy)* [1989] 2 Lloyd's Rep. 138, where an agreement for the sale of a ship provided for deduction of commission from the price but seems to have contained no *promise* to pay the broker.

[10] *Swain v. Law Society* [1983] 1 A.C. 598, 620; Feltham (1982) 98 L.Q.R. 17.

[11] *Fletcher v. Fletcher* (1844) 4 Hare 67; *Bowskill v. Dawson* [1954] 1 Q.B. 288.

[12] For the purpose of the present discussion, it is assumed that formal requirements, such as that imposed by Law of Property Act 1925, s.53(1)(b), have been satisfied. As to the effect on the rights of third parties of failure to satisfy such requirements, see Feltham (1987) Conv. 246.

[13] See *Gandy v. Gandy* (1844) 34 Ch.D. 57.

words; and where the word "trust" or "trustee" has not been used, the question whether there is an intention to create a trust gives rise to very great difficulty. Thus in some cases[14] a promise to a person to provide for his dependants on his retirement or death has been held to create a trust in their favour, while in other cases[15] such a promise has been held not to have this effect.[16] Similarly, life insurance policies expressed to be for the benefit of third parties have in some cases been held to create trusts in their favour,[17] and in others to confer no enforceable rights on them.[18] And in some cases concerning other types of insurance[19] the courts have held that the third party could take advantage of the policy under the trust device,[20] while in others they have held that the third parties had no rights because of the doctrine of privity.[21] There is no point in trying to reconcile all these cases. They represent different stages in the development of the law. At one time, the courts were very ready to apply the trust device in order to protect the interests of the third party.[22] Later, they became more reluctant to apply the device because, once a contract was held to have created a trust in favour of the third party, the parties to that contract lost the right to vary it by mutual consent.[23] Although there are, therefore, no fixed rules which determine the existence of a trust in cases of this kind, it is possible to point to a number of factors which have influenced the decisions of the courts and which will serve as some guide to the solution of future problems. They are discussed in §§ 19–067 to 19–069 below.

Intention to benefit third party necessary. There must be an intention to   **19–067**
benefit the third party. If the promisee took the promise for his own benefit there

---

[14] *Re Flavell* (1883) 25 Ch.D. 89; *cf. Page v. Cox* (1852) 10 Hare 163; *Re Gordon* [1940] Ch. 851; *Drimmie v. Davies* [1899] 1 I.R. 176.

[15] *Re Schebsman* [1944] Ch. 83; *cf. Re Stapleton-Bretherton* [1941] Ch. 482. In *Re Miller's Agreement* [1947] Ch. 615 and *Beswick v. Beswick* [1968] A.C. 58 it was conceded that there was no trust.

[16] In *Re Schebsman, supra,* the argument that there was a trust was, paradoxically, advanced, not on behalf of the third parties, but on behalf of the promisee's trustee in bankruptcy. The point of the argument was to have the trust set aside under the Bankruptcy Act 1914, s.42 (now superseded by Insolvency Act 1986, s.339): see [1944] Ch. at 86. At 104 the argument is attributed to "Mr. Denning," who appeared for the third parties. But this must be a mistake; the corresponding passage in [1943] 2 All E.R. 768, 779 correctly attributes it to "counsel for the appellant," *i.e.* for the trustee in bankruptcy. As the company was willing to pay, the outcome of holding that there was *no* trust was that the third parties obtained the intended benefit (*cf. ante*, § 19–060). In *Re Flavell, supra* n. 14, the same result followed from the decision that there *was* a trust.

[17] *Re Richardson* (1882) 47 L.T. 514; *Royal Exchange Assurance v. Hope* [1928] Ch. 179; *Re Webb* [1941] Ch. 225; *Re Foster's Policy* [1966] 1 W.L.R. 222.

[18] *Re Burgess' Policy* (1915) 113 L.T. 443; *Re Clay's Policy of Assurance* [1937] 2 All E.R. 548; *Re Foster* [1938] 3 All E.R. 357; *cf. Re Engelbach's Estate* [1924] 2 Ch. 248 and *Re Sinclair's Life Policy* [1938] Ch. 799; these two cases were disapproved or doubted on another ground in *Beswick v. Beswick* [1968] A.C. 58: see *ante*, § 19–060, n. 86.

[19] For statutory exceptions to the doctrine of privity in cases of insurance, see *post*, §§ 19–108 to 19–112.

[20] *Waters v. Monarch Fire and Life Assurance Co.* (1856) 5 E. & B. 870; *Williams v. Baltic Insurance Co.* [1924] 2 K.B. 282; *post*, § 19–109; *Prudential Staff Union v. Hall* [1947] K.B. 685; *cf.* Deane J. in *Trident General Ins. Co. Ltd v. McNiece Bros. Pty Ltd* (1988) 165 C.L.R. 107 (*ante*, § 19–021).

[21] *Vandepitte v. Preferred Accident Insurance Corp.* [1933] A.C. 70; *Green v. Russell* [1959] 2 Q.B. 226.

[22] See *Hill v. Gomme* (1839) 5 My. & Cr. 250; *Page v. Cox* (1852) 10 Hare 163.

[23] *Re Schebsman* [1944] Ch. 83, 104; *Re Sinclair's Life Policy* [1938] Ch. 799.

will be no trust in favour of the third party.[24] The same may be true if it is as consistent with the facts that the promisee took the promise for his own benefit as for the benefit of the third party.[25] Conversely, the fact that the promisee had *not* intended to take the promise for his own benefit can be relied on to support the conclusion that there was a trust in favour of the third party.[26]

19–068   **Irrevocability of intention to benefit third party.** As a general rule,[27] the intention to benefit the third party must be irrevocable; so that a contract will not normally give rise to a trust in favour of the third party if, under the terms of the contract, the promisee is entitled to deprive the third party of the benefit by diverting it to himself or to other beneficiaries not mentioned in the contract.[28] On the other hand, the existence of such a power to divert the benefit will not negative the intention to create a trust where the power is expressed to be exercisable only for a limited period and is not in fact exercised within that period.[29] Nor will the existence of a trust necessarily be negatived where a contract names a group of beneficiaries, but reserves to the promisee a power to redistribute the intended benefits among them in variation of the terms of the original contract.[30] And where a contract *by statute* creates a trust, a general provision purporting to entitle the promisee to divert the benefit to whom he pleases will not defeat the trust: on the contrary, such a power can be used only for the benefit of the objects of the trust.[31] The court may conclude that there was no intention irrevocably to benefit the third party even though the contract contains no express provision entitling the promisee to divert the benefit away from the third party. It may do so on the ground that the contract would, if it were held to give rise to a trust, unduly limit the freedom of action of the parties or of one of them: *e.g.* by restricting the promisee's freedom of movement[32] or by depriving the parties to the contract of their right to vary it by mutual consent.[33]

19–069   **Intention to benefit third party not sufficient.** The intention to benefit the third party is not, without more, sufficient, for the law distinguishes between an

---

[24] *West v. Houghton* (1879) 4 C.P.D. 197; criticised in *Re Flavell* (1883) 25 Ch.D. 89, 98 and in *Lloyd's v. Harper* (1880) 16 Ch.D. 290, 311.

[25] *e.g. Vandepitte v. Preferred Accident Insurance Corp.* [1933] A.C. 70, where one relevant factor was that the insured was under the law governing the policy himself liable for the torts of the third party; contrast *Williams v. Baltic Insurance* [1924] 2 K.B. 282. For the statutory position in such motor insurance cases, see *post* § 19–109.

[26] *Lyus v. Prowsa Development Ltd* [1982] 1 W.L.R. 1044.

[27] For exceptions, see *infra* at nn. 29–31.

[28] *Re Sinclair's Life Policy* [1938] Ch. 799 (criticised on another ground in *Beswick v. Beswick* [1968] A.C. 58, 96); and *cf. Re Schebsman* [1944] Ch. 83; for the earlier view on this matter see *Hill v. Gomme* (1839) 5 My. & Cr. 250; *Page v. Cox* (1852) 10 Hare 163. A provision of the kind here under discussion would not fall within Contracts (Rights of Third Parties) Bill, 1998, Clause 2, since this applies only to rescission or variation *by mutual consent*: see *post*, §§ 19–083, 19–084.

[29] *Re Foster's Policy* [1966] 1 W.L.R. 222.

[30] *Re Webb* [1941] Ch. 225.

[31] *Re a Policy of the Equitable Life Assurance of the United States and Mitchell* (1911) 27 T.L.R. 213; *Re Fleetwood's Policy* [1926] 1 Ch. 48.

[32] *e.g. Re Burgess' Policy* (1915) 113 L.J. 43 (policy to become void if insured went "beyond the boundaries of Europe" without previously notifying insurers).

[33] *e.g. Re Schebsman* [1944] 83, 104 (parties "intended to keep alive their common law right consensually to vary the terms of the obligation"). The existence of such a right would not negative the statutory right of enforcement which third parties will have under the Contracts (Rights of Third Parties) Bill, 1998: this is clear from the provisions of Clause 2 of that Bill.

intention to make a gift and an intention to create a trust.[34] There are many cases in which the courts have refused to apply the trust device although the promisee did quite clearly, irrevocably and without qualification intend to benefit the third party.[35] There must be an intention to create a trust; and it seems that such an intention will readily be found where the contract in favour of the third party is made in pursuance of some contractual[36] or fiduciary[37] obligation owed by the promisee to the third party. But the trust device has not been wholly confined to such cases—probably because the courts did not formerly insist very strictly on proof of intention to create a trust. The fact that they later came to do so accounts for the present more restricted scope of the trust device.

The intention to create a trust may, finally, be negatived on the ground that a trust is not necessary to give rights to the third party because he is entitled to enforce the contract (even in the absence of a trust) under a statutory exception to the doctrine of privity.[38]

Effects of the trust. Two consequences generally flow from a finding that there is a trust in favour of a third party. First, the third party is entitled to sue the promisor for the money or property which the promisor had promised to pay or to transfer to him.[39] He must join the promisee as a party to the action[40] since otherwise the promisor might be sued a second time by the promisee. As this rule as to joinder of parties exists for the benefit of the promisor, it can be waived by him.[41] Secondly, the third party is (as a general rule[42]) beneficially entitled to any money paid or payable under the contract; the promisee has no right to such money.[43] After *Beswick v. Beswick*[44] the third party can generally keep money paid to him even if there is no trust.[45]

19–070

---

[34] See *Richards v. Delbridge* (1874) L.R. 18 Eq. 11; *Swain v. Law Society* [1983] 1 A.C. 598, 620.

[35] *Re Clay's Policy of Assurance* [1937] 2 All E.R. 548; *Re Foster* [1938] 3 All E.R. 357; *Re Stapleton-Bretherton* [1941] Ch. 482; *Green v. Russell* [1959] 1 Q.B. 28; *Re Cook's Settlement Trusts* [1965] Ch. 902. Under the Contracts (Rights of Third Parties) Bill, 1998, subsections 1(1)(b) and (2) it will suffice for the term to purport to confer a benefit on the third party, so long as it is not shown that the contracting parties did not intend the term to be enforceable by the third party. For the reasons given in § 19–001 *ante* and § 19–098 *post*, however, it may be in the third party's interest to establish an intention to create a trust, so that he can rely on the trust exception rather than on the new statutory right.

[36] See *Re Independent Air Travel Ltd, The Times*, May 20, 1961, where counsel, with the approval of the court, conceded this point.

[37] *Harmer v. Armstrong* [1934] Ch. 65.

[38] *Swain v. Law Society* [1983] 1 A.C. 598, esp. at 621.

[39] But where a trustee engages a professional adviser for the purpose of administering the trust, a claim for negligence against that adviser cannot be brought by the beneficiary since such a claim is not part of the trust property (though any damages recovered by the trustee would be): *Bradstock Trustee Services Ltd v. Nabarro Nathanson* [1995] 1 W.L.R. 1405.

[40] cf. *Performing Right Society Ltd v. London Theatre of Varieties* [1924] A.C. 1; *Howard Houlder & Partners v. Marine General Transporters Co. (The Panaghia P)* [1983] 2 Lloyd's Rep. 653, 655; *Atlas Shipping Agency (U.K.) Ltd v. Suisse Atlantique Société d' Armement Maritime S.A.* [1995] 2 Lloyd's Rep. 188, 193.

[41] As in *Les Affréteurs Réunis v. Leopold Walford (London) Ltd* [1919] A.C. 801; cf. *William Brandt's Sons & Co. v. Dunlop Rubber Co.* [1905] A.C. 454.

[42] *i.e.* subject to the exceptions stated in § 19–071, *post*.

[43] *Re Flavell* (1883) 25 Ch.D. 89; *Re Gordon* [1940] Ch. 851; cf. *Paul v. Constance* [1977] 1 W.L.R. 527.

[44] [1968] A.C. 58.

[45] *Ante*, § 19–066.

19-071   **Failure of the trust.** There are exceptional cases in which the promisee may be entitled to the money even though there was a trust. In *Cleaver v. Mutual Reserve Fund Life Association*[46] a husband insured his life for the benefit of his wife by a policy which, by statute, created a trust in her favour.[47] The wife was convicted of murdering the husband and was therefore disqualified from enforcing the trust. It was held that the executors of the husband were entitled to the policy moneys. The decision can be criticised on the ground that the promisor should not have been held liable to pay the promisee when its promise was one to pay the third party.[48] But it seems that the destination of the payments was a matter of indifference to the insurance company and that there was nothing to show that the company would (even if there had been no conviction) have been in any way prejudiced by paying the husband's executors rather than the wife.[49] The actual decision may also turn on the interpretation of the statute creating the trust.[50]

19-072   **Kinds of promises which can be held on trust.** The trust device has so far been applied only to promises to pay money or to transfer property. It is sometimes suggested that it might be applied to other kinds of promises, *e.g.* that an employer might hold the benefit of an exemption clause on trust for his employee.[51] But the present judicial tendency is to confine the trust device within narrow limits; and the suggestion has therefore been rejected on the ground that "the conception of a trust attaching to a benefit under an exclusion clause extends far beyond conventional limits."[52] A number of other techniques have, however, been developed for making the benefit of exemption clauses available to third parties.[53]

19-073   **Relation of trust device to doctrine of privity.** It has been argued[54] that, where the trust device applied and so conferred rights on a third party, there was before 1873 a conflict between the rules of equity and those of common law; that the rules of equity now prevail[55]; and that a third party should now generally be entitled to enforce a contract made for his benefit. But this argument has been rightly rejected[56]; for even in equity a third party could sue on a contract only if that contract created a trust in his favour[57]; and the mere fact that it was

[46] [1892] 1 Q.B. 147.

[47] Married Women's Property Act 1882, s.11; *post*, § 19–108.

[48] Ames, *Lectures*, 320; *Coulls v. Bagot's Executor & Trustee Co. Ltd* [1967] A.L.R. 385, 410–411, *per* Windeyer J. (dissenting); *ante* § 19–044.

[49] *cf. ante*, § 19–060.

[50] See [1892] 1 Q.B. 147, 157.

[51] See the clause in *New Zealand Shipping Co. Ltd v. A. M. Satterthwaite & Co. Ltd (The Eurymedon)* [1975] A.C. 154; *Port Jackson Stevedoring Pty. Ltd v. Salmond & Spraggon (Australia) Pty. Ltd (The New York Star)* [1980] 1 W.L.R. 138, *ante*, § 14–044.

[52] *Southern Water Authority v. Carey* [1985] 2 All E.R. 1077, 1083.

[53] *Ante*, §§ 14–039 to 14–047.

[54] *Drimmie v. Davies* [1899] 1 I.R. 176, 182; Corbin (1930) 46 L.Q.R. 12, 36; *cf.* Langbein, 105 Yale L.J. 625, 646–647 (1997).

[55] Judicature Act 1873, s.25(11); now Supreme Court Act 1981, s.49(1).

[56] *Re Schebsman* [1943] 1 Ch. at 370, approved [1944] Ch. at 104.

[57] *Colyear v. Mulgrave* (1836) 2 Keen 81. The actual decision has been criticised but without impairing the principle stated in the text: see *Page v. Cox* (1852) 10 Hare 163; *Kekewich v. Manning* (1851) 1 D.M. & G. 176.

expressed to have been made for his benefit is not sufficient to produce this result.[58]

Covenants in marriage settlements. In equity a covenant to settle after-acquired property contained in a marriage settlement can be enforced by persons "within the marriage consideration," that is, by husband, wife and the issue of the marriage. But the covenant confers no rights on mere volunteers such as the next-of-kin of the wife, or her children by a previous marriage.[59]   **19–074**

(ii) *Contracts (Rights of Third Parties) Bill 1998*[60]

Third party's right of enforcement. The 1998 Bill will, when it comes into force, create "a general and wide-ranging exception to" the doctrine of privity.[61] Its central purpose is to enable a third party to acquire rights under a contract if, and to the extent that, the parties to the contract so intend. Subsection 1(1) provides that a person who is not a party to the contract may in his own right enforce a term of the contract in the two situations to be described in §§ 19–076 and 19–078 below. In discussing these situations and other provisions of the Bill, it will be convenient to refer to the person who makes the promise which the third party is claiming to enforce (the promisor) as A, to the person to whom that promise is made (the promisee) as B[62] and to the third party as C.   **19–075**

Express provision. Under subsection 1(1)(a) of the 1998 Bill, C can enforce a term of the contract if "the contract expressly provides that he may": *e.g.* where a contract contains a promise by A to B to pay £1,000 to C and goes on to provide that C is to be entitled to enforce the term which contains this promise. If the contract contains such a provision, there is no further requirement (as there is under subsection 1(1)(b), to be discussed in § 19–078 below) that the promise was made for C's own benefit: *e.g.* he can enforce the term even though the payment is to be made to him as trustee for D.[63] Express provisions in contracts of the kind just described, to the effect that C is to be entitled to enforce the term containing the promise made by A to B, have hitherto been rare, presumably because under the doctrine of privity they would at common law have been ineffective. The 1998 Bill will provide a new drafting device to enable the contracting parties to give effect to their intention that C is to acquire an enforceable right against A. Apart from the Bill, a similar result can be achieved by creating a trust of A's promise in favour of C[64] or by making him a co-promisee.[65] There will be a procedural advantage in making use of the machinery of subsection 1(1)(a) in that, if C sues under this provision, he will not   **19–076**

---

[58] See *ante*, § 19–069.

[59] *Hill v. Gomme* (1839) 5 My. & Cr. 250, 254; *Re D'Angibau* (1880) 15 Ch.D. 228; *Green v. Patterson* (1886) 32 Ch.D. 95, 107; *Re Plumptree's Marriage Settlement* [1910] 1 Ch. 609; *Re Cook's Settlement Trust* [1965] Ch. 902. These cases, apart from forming an exception to the doctrine of privity, are also hard to reconcile with the modern definition of consideration: *cf. ante*, § 3–031 and the statement in *Hill v. Gomme*, *ubi supra*, that the children were "quasi-parties" is curiously reminiscent of the reasoning of *Dutton v. Poole*, cited in § 19–028, *ante*.

[60] See *ante*, § 19–001.

[61] Law Commission Report on *Privity of Contract: Contracts for the Benefit of Third Parties*, Law Com. No. 242, (1996), hereafter "Report".

[62] *cf.* the definitions of "promisor" and "promisee" in s.1(7) of the 1998 Bill.

[63] Report, § 7.5.

[64] *Ante*, § 19–065.

[65] See *McEvoy v. Belfast Banking Co.* [1935] A.C. 24, *ante*, § 3–042.

(it seems) need to join B as a party to the action;[66] though the court could order B to be so joined where claims against A were made by both B and C, or where A relied against C on a defence available to A against B,[67] since in such a case B's presence before the court is likely to be "desirable . . . so that the court can resolve all the matters in dispute in the proceedings."[68] If C does have a claim apart from the Bill as the beneficiary of a trust of A's promise or as co-promisee, it may, in spite of the need to join B to the action, be in C's interest to pursue that claim since it would not be subject to other provisions of the Bill which may restrict his rights under it: *e.g.* to those relating to the cancellation or variation of the contract between A and B, or to defences available to A against B.[69]

19–077   Subsection 1(1)(a) is also likely to cover clauses such as *Himalaya* clauses,[70] by which A promises B that any exemptions from or limitations of liability available to B shall also be available for the benefit of C, who typically will be an employee, agent or subcontractor employed by B for the purpose of performing some or all of B's obligations under the contract. This follows from subsection 1(6) of the 1998 Bill, by which references to C's "enforcing" a term which "excludes or limits liability"[71] are to be "construed as references to his availing himself of the exclusion or limitation." Words in the contract to the effect that C is to be protected by the exemption or limitation clause therefore amount in themselves to an express provision that C may enforce the clause[72]; no further words will be necessary.

19–078   **Term conferring benefit on third party.** Under subsection 1(1)(b) of the 1998 Bill, C may enforce a term of the contract if "the term purports to confer a benefit on him"; but his right to do so in such a case is subject to subsection 1(2), by which C has no such right "if on a proper construction of the contract it appear that [A and B] did not intend the term to be enforceable by" C. These will probably be the most significant provisions of the 1998 Bill and their interpretation is likely to give rise to a number of difficulties. It seems that a "benefit" within subsection 1(1)(b) can include any performance due under the contract between A and B: thus it can include a payment of money, a transfer of property, or the rendering of a service; it can also (by virtue of subsection 1(6)) include the benefit of an exemption or limitation clause. The term must, moreover, purport to confer the benefit on C, so that it is not enough for C to show that he would happen to benefit from its performance. The question whether the term purported to confer a benefit on C would be one of construction. If, for example, A were employed by B "to cut my hedge adjoining C's land", performance by A might benefit C, but the term would not "purport to confer a benefit" on C. The question of construction could be particularly hard to answer where A was a

---

[66] This appears to follow from the words "in his own right" in s.1(1); *cf.* Report, § 14.3.

[67] Under clause 3 of the 1998 Bill: see *post*, § 19–092.

[68] CPR, r. 19.1(2)(a).

[69] See clauses 2 and 3 (*post*, §§ 19–083 to 19–091 and 19–092) and subs. 7(1) of the Bill *post*, § 19–096).

[70] *Ante*, § 14–044.

[71] This phrase would not include other terms in the contract on which C might wish to rely: *e.g.* not choice of forum clauses: see Report, § 14.9; *cf.*, at common law, *The Mahkutai* [1996] A.C. 650, where such a clause was held as a matter of construction not to have been covered by the *Himalaya* clause in that case. If, in a future case, a *Himalaya* clause were so drafted as to cover the choice of forum clause, the case would not fall within subs. 1(6) of the 1998 Bill.

[72] Report, § 7.10.

subcontractor employed by B to render services in relation to property owned by C. Assuming that the term does purport to confer a benefit on C, it is then necessary to construe the contract as a whole to determine the nature and extent of C's right to enforce the term. This follows from subsection 1(4), under which "this section does not confer a right on [C] to enforce a term of a contract otherwise than subject to and in accordance with any other relevant terms of the contract." This provision would, for example, apply if the term which C was seeking to enforce provided for the payment to him of £1,000, but another term of the contract provided that claims under the former term must be made within one year. Yet a further and different question of construction would arise under subsection 1(2) (quoted above) and it appears from the wording of this subsection that the burden of proof under it rests on A, or (in other words) that if the term purports to confer a benefit on C, then there is a rebuttable presumption that the term is to be enforceable by C.[73] To rebut the presumption, A must (in the words of subsection 1(2)) show that "the parties" did not intend the term to be enforceable by C. Thus it is not enough for A to show that he did not so intend; he must show that neither he nor B had this intention. Nor is the presumption rebutted merely because in the contract A and B had reserved the right to rescind or vary the contract: this follows from the provisions with regard to such rescission or variation made in clause 2 of the Bill and discussed in § 19–083 to 19–091 below. As the question of intention put in subsection 1(2) is there described as one of construction, it seems that the evidence which A will be allowed to adduce for this purpose will, in general, be limited by the rules which restrict the types of evidence admissible on other questions of construction.[74]

Application to previous decisions? It is tempting to speculate how the   **19–079** provisions discussed in § 19–078 above would apply to some of the leading cases in which the doctrine of privity has been applied before the 1998 Bill. To some extent, indeed, such an exercise is likely to be fruitless since the courts have not in the past directed their attention to the issues which will arise under the Bill. In *Beswick v. Beswick*,[75] for example, the contract no doubt purported to confer a benefit on C; but no finding of fact was made (because such a finding would have been irrelevant) as to the intention of A and B on the issue of legal enforceability by C: it is conceivable that A could succeed on this issue if, for example, he could show that A and B, when making the contract, had agreed not to disclose its existence to C. On the facts of a number of other cases, the position under the 1998 Bill would, it is submitted be clearer. Thus in the "disappointed beneficiary" cases such as *White v. Jones*[76] C would not get a right against A, the negligent solicitor, since the terms of the solicitor's retainer (even if they identified C[77]) would not purport to confer a benefit on C: the intended benefit was to come, not from A, but from B.[78] It is similarly unlikely that cases such as the *Junior Books* case,[79] in which A is a subcontractor employed by B to enable B to perform his contract with C, would be covered, even if the subcontract

---

[73] Report, §§ 7.5, 7.17.
[74] See *ante*, § 12–094; but the rule that evidence is not admissible to ascertain the "parties' intention" (*Prenn v. Simmonds* [1971] 1 W.L.R. 1381, 1385) can scarcely apply in the present context since the very purpose of the enquiry under subs. 1(2) is to determine what the parties intended.
[75] [1968] A.C. 58; *ante*, § 19–021.
[76] [1995] 2 A.C. 207; *ante*, § 19–037.
[77] See *post*, § 19–080.
[78] Report, § 7.25.
[79] *Junior Books Ltd v. Veitchi Co. Ltd* [1983] 1 A.C. 520; *ante*, § 19–024.

named C, since the purpose of such a subcontract would, *prima facie*, be to regulate the relations between A and B rather than to confer a benefit on C.[80] Cases such as the *Linden Garden* case[81] would likewise not be affected by Clause 1 since the mere possibility that land on which work is done by a building contractor might be transferred to purchasers would not be sufficient to show that the term relating to the quality of the work purported to "confer a benefit" on such purchasers; nor would the contract, without more, adequately "identify"[82] such purchasers as third parties for the purpose of subsection 1(1)(b). Nor, it is submitted, would the mere fact that the building contractor (A) knew that the property on which he was working in pursuance of his contract with B belonged to someone other than B[83] suffice to show that the benefit was to be conferred on that person: the answer to the question whether the work was being done for the benefit of that person (C) or B would depend on the contractual relations between B and C, of which A might be wholly unaware. In the "family holiday" cases discussed in § 19–046 above, the present issue would depend on the nature of the transaction. If the person making the booking supplied the names of other members of the family when the contract was made, those other members would probably acquire rights under subsection 1(1); but no such rights are likely to be acquired if a person simply rented a holiday cottage without giving any information as to the number or names of the person with whom he proposed to share the accommodation. In many of the situations which have here been discussed, the question whether the contract purports to confer a benefit on C will be closely related to the question, to be discussed in the following paragraph, whether C is adequately "identified" in the contract between A and B.

19-080   **Identification of third party.** Under subsection 1(3) of the 1998 Bill, it is a requirement of C's right to enforce A's promise that C must have been expressly identified in the contract between A and B by name, as a member of a class or as answering a particular description[84]; and it follows from this requirement that C could not rely for the purpose of subsection 1(1) on the argument that the contract referred to him by implication.[85] So long as C is identified in accordance with these requirements, there is no need for C to be in existence when the contract was made: for example a promise in favour of an unborn child, a future spouse or of an unformed company could be enforced by[86] such a third party when it came into existence. Although it is a necessary condition for the creation of C's rights under subsection 1(1) that he must be expressly identified in the contract between A and B, such identification is not a sufficient condition for this purpose, since a contract which identifies C does not necessarily purport to

---

[80] The case was a Scottish case and no claim was made in contract even though Scots law recognises a *jus quaesitum tertio* arising by way of contract.

[81] *Linden Gardens Trust Ltd v. Lenesta Sludge Disposals Ltd* [1994] 1 A.C. 85; *ante*, § 19–049.

[82] Within subs. 1(3), *post* § 19–080.

[83] As appears to have been the position in *Darlington B.C. v. Wiltshier Northern Ltd* [1995] 1 W.L.R. 68.

[84] subs. 1(3).

[85] Thus cases such as *London Drugs Ltd v. Keuhne & Nagel International Ltd* [1992] 3 S.C.R. 299 would not appear to be covered by the Bill.

[86] A company which did not at the time of the contract exist could, on coming into existence, by virtue of subs. 1(3) enforce a term made for its benefit (within subsection 1(1); but the rules relating to contracts made on behalf of such a company would continue to govern the extent to which such a company could be *bound* by a contract made on its behalf: Report §§ 8.9 to 8.16.

confer a benefit on him. If, for example, a portrait painter (A) were commissioned by a college (B) to paint a portrait of the head of the college (C) for display on its premises, the contract would not purport to confer a benefit on C, nor would A and B intend the contract to be enforceable by C. It would seem that C must be identified in such a way as to indicate that A and B intended to confer rights on C: thus the identification requirement would be satisfied where A promised B not to sue C for negligence but not where A promised B not to sue B for C's negligence.[87] The requirements of subsection 1(3) are, in other words, additional to those of subsection 1(2). Their operation of may be illustrated by reference to the *Midland Silicones* case[88]: on the facts of that case, C would not be able to enforce the limitation clause since the contract between A and B contained no express reference to C (whether by name, by description or as a member of a class). In these circumstances, neither subsection would be satisfied: C would not be identified and this very fact would indicate that the contract did not purport to confer a benefit on him. Where a contract is (as it was in the *Midland Silicones* case) contained in or evidence by a bill of lading, it is now likely to contain a *Himalaya* clause, which would be likely adequately to identify C and confer a right on him to "enforce"[89] the limitation clause under subsection 1(2). The question whether C is identified in such a way as to give him an enforceable right may itself raise a question of construction: *e.g.* where the words of the term are adequate to identify C but it does not purport (or A and B do not intend) to confer a benefit on him.[90]

Remedies. Where C has a right to enforce a term of the contract by virtue of subsection 1(1) of the 1998 Bill, he has this right in spite of the fact that he is not a party to the contract: the Bill does not, in general, adopt the technique of transferring rights from B to C or of treating C as having acquired rights by means of the fiction that he has become a party to the contract.[91] It does, however, make use of such a fiction so far as C's remedies are concerned.[92] Subsection 1(5) provides that "For the purpose of exercising his right to enforce a term of the contract, there shall be available to the third party any remedy that would have been available to him in an action for breach of the contract if he had been a party to the contract (and the rules relating to damages, injunctions, specific performance and other relief shall apply accordingly)." It follows from this provision that C can invoke the same kinds of judicial remedies as would be available to B if no third party were involved, and that C can recover damages for loss of bargain (or "expectation" loss) even though the bargain was made, not with him, but with B. It also follows that the same principles which would limit B's remedies in a two-party case also apply to an action brought by C: for example, the principles of remoteness and mitigation and those which restrict the

19–081

---

[87] As, for example, in *Adler v. Dickson* [1955] 1 QB 158.

[88] *Midland Silicones Ltd v. Scruttons Ltd* [1962] A.C. 446; *ante*, § 14–042.

[89] See subs. 1(6), *ante*, § 19–077.

[90] Such a question could arise on facts such as those in *Elder Dempster & Co. Ltd v. Paterson Zochonis & Co. Ltd* [1924] A.C. 522, where the form of bill of lading used seems to have been based on the assumption that the goods would be carried by B but they were in fact carried by C and the words of the exemption clause in the Bill happened to be apt to refer also to C.

[91] 1998 Bill, subs. 7(5). This refers only to other legislation, but the principle that C is not to be treated as a party to the contract appears also to apply for the purpose of rules of common law: see *post*, § 19–082.

[92] And also for a number of other purposes relating to defences available to A against C: see subsections 3(4) and (6), *post*, § 19–092.

availability of specific relief.[93] The application of these principles may, however, lead to different practical results where the action is brought by C from those which would follow from them in an action brought by B. For example, in an action brought by C, the test of remoteness would be whether it was C's (not B's) loss which A ought reasonably have contemplated; the principles of mitigation would require the court to ask what steps C (not B) ought reasonably have taken to mitigate his loss; and the question whether specific relief should be refused on account of the conduct of the claimant could receive one answer where the action was brought by C and another if it were brought by B.

19–082   **No requirement of consideration moving from third party.** The 1998 Bill does not impose any requirement that consideration for A's promise must move from C. It does not contain any express provision to this effect[94]; the consequence follows from the fact that the Bill gives C the right to enforce the term and is further supported by the general principle that C is not to be treated as a party to the contract between A and B.[95] Since the promise in contracts of the kind in question is made to B, the fact that C need not provide any consideration for it is not strictly an exception to the rule that consideration must move from the promisee, but it can be regarded as a quasi exception to that rule in the sense that C is a person in whose favour a promise is made and who can enforce it even though he may be no more than a gratuitous beneficiary.

19–083   **Right to rescind or vary the contract.** Under the judge-made rules relating to contracts for the benefit of third parties, one objection to the creation of such rights has been that it would deprive the contracting parties of right to rescind or vary the contract by mutual consent.[96] The 1998 Bill deals with this problem by means of a compromise: it specifies the circumstances in which A and B, prima facie, lose this right, while it at the same time enables them so to draw up their contract so as to retain the right or to change the prima facie rules laid down in the Bill which specify when it is lost.

19–084   **General rule: C's consent required.** The general rule, stated in subsection 2(1) of the 1998 Bill, is that, once C has acquired the right to enforce a term of the contract between A and B "under section 1", then, if one of the circumstances to be described in §§ 19–085 and 19–086 below has arisen, A and B may not without C's consent agree to rescind the contract, or vary it so as to "extinguish or alter" C's entitlement. Rescission calls for no further comment here; but with regard to variation it should be noted that A and B are, under the general rule, precluded from varying the contract not only so as to extinguish but also so as to alter C's rights. An alteration may of course operate not only to C's prejudice, but also to his advantage: *e.g.* where it purports to increase payments to be made to C under the term in question. Such a variation is unlikely to give rise to any problems between A and C, since C will presumably consent to it as soon as he hears of it. But the argument that C is entitled to enforce a term of a contract between A and B can also give rise to problems between one of these

---

[93] Report, §§ 3.32, 3.33.

[94] Report, § 6.8 n. 8.

[95] See *ante*, n. 91.

[96] This has been one reason for the restrictions on the scope of the equitable exception to the doctrine of privity by way of trusts of promises: *ante*, § 19–066.

parties and outside interests: *e.g.* creditors of B in the event of B's insolvency.[97] Such persons may seek to invoke subsection 2(1) where the variation increases C's rights but on the crucial date for the assertion of their rights C has either not yet acquired any knowledge of the variation or has not yet made any communication to A or done any other act from which his assent to the variation can be inferred.

Third party's assent to the term. The first of the circumstances in which A   **19–085** and B cannot, without C's consent, rescind the contract, or vary it in the ways described above[98] arises where C has communicated his assent to the term to A[99]; communication to B does not suffice for this purpose.[1] The assent may be by words or conduct[2]; and if it is "sent" to A by post or other means, it is not regarded as communicated to him "until received by him."[3] In other words, the "posting" rule, as developed in cases of contract formation[4] does not apply in the present context. "Sent" here seems to refer to some act done by C in order to communicate words of assent to A. The rule relating to an assent "sent" to A by post or other means is negative in nature: it states that the assent is not communicated to A until received by him. It thus leaves open the question whether an assent which has been so sent can take effect before it has actually come to A's notice: *e.g.* where it has been delivered to his address but not yet been read by him. If the overriding requirement is one of communication, it may not be satisfied in such a case. The expression "sent" also does not seem to be appropriate to refer to an assent by conduct; but it seems that such an assent must come to A's notice: this seems to follow from the general requirement that C's assent must be "communicated"[5] to A. No formality (such as writing) is required even for an assent in words,[6] so that an oral communication suffices.

Third party's reliance. The right to rescind or vary the contract is also barred   **19–086** where A is aware of C's having relied on the term,[7] or where A could reasonably have foreseen such reliance and it has actually taken place.[8] It would seem that, in such cases, C may be entitled, not merely to the promised performance, but also to damages in respect of his reliance loss: *e.g.* where he has travelled to the place specified in the contract for the receipt by him of the promised performance. This follows from the rule laid down by the 1998 Bill with respect to C's remedies[9]; it of course also follows from this rule that C could not claim under both heads to the extent to which such a combination of claims would result in double recovery or in his being placed in a better position than that in which he

---

[97] As, for example, in *Re Schebsman* [1944] Ch. 83, *ante*, § 19–066.
[98] *Ante*, § 19–083.
[99] Subs. 2(1)(a).
[1] This follows from the words "to the promisor" in subs. 2(1)(a).
[2] Subs. 2(2)(a).
[3] Subs. 2(2)(b).
[4] *Ante*, § 2–043.
[5] Subs. 2(1)(a).
[6] Contrast the requirement of Law of Property Act, 1925, s.136(1), requiring written notice of an assignment.
[7] Subs. 2(1)(b).
[8] Subs. 2(1)(c).
[9] Subs. 1(5); *ante*, § 19–081.

would have been if A had performed his promise in accordance with its original terms.[10]

19–087   **Consequences of attempted rescission or variation without C's consent.** The general rule in subsection 2(1) is that A and B "may not" rescind the contract, or vary it in the ways described above, without C's consent. The most obvious consequences of this provision is that a purported rescission or variation without C's consent is simply ineffective, so that C can, in spite of it, enforce the term in question against A. But such enforcement may, because of the rescission, become a practical impossibility (*e.g.* because A has in consequence of the rescission put it out of his power to perform); and it is arguable that the purported rescission is also wrongful, so as to give C a remedy in damages against B, perhaps on the analogy of liability for wrongful interference with contractual rights.[11] This possibility could have practical significance in the event of A's insolvency.

19–088   **Contract conferring choices on promisee.** Subsection 2(1) of the 1998 bill deals with the situation in which C has become entitled to enforce a term of the contract "under section 1" and the contract is then rescinded or varied by the agreement of A and B. This situation must be distinguished from that in which A promises B to perform in favour of C or as B shall direct. If, in such a case, B directs A to perform in favour of D (or of B himself) the contract is not varied. On the contrary, it is to be performed in accordance with its original terms, under which B has a choice as to the person to whom performance is to be rendered. The case therefore does not fall within subsection 2(1), so that the requirement of C's consent, as there stated, does not apply.[12] Another way of explaining this conclusion is to say that, in the case put, the mere making of the promise was not intended to confer an indefeasible right on C; for the fact that B had power to divert the benefit away from C would indicate that A and B did not at this stage intend[13] the term to be enforceable by C if B exercised the choice which the contract gave him. A term of the present kind might, however, also limit B's power to divert the benefit away from C: *e.g.* by providing that this power was to be exercisable only for a specified period. After the end of that period, C could no longer be deprived of the benefit of A's promise by the unilateral act of B since the consent of A and B would then as a matter of common law be necessary to vary the contract; and any such variation would then be subject to the requirement of C's consent under subsection 2(1).

19–089   **Contrary provision in the contract.** The general requirement of C's consent, contained in subsection 2(1) and stated in § 19–084 above, may be displaced by an express term of the contract. Two possibilities are envisaged. The first, stated in subsection 2(3)(a), is for the express term to state that the contract may be rescinded or varied without the consent of C. Under such a term, it is open to A and B to rescind or vary the contract in spite of the fact that C has acquired a right by virtue of subsection 1(1) and in spite of the fact that the circumstances specified in subsection 2(1) have occurred: that is, even after communication of

---

[10] *e.g.* where it would have been necessary for C to incur the reliance expenditure in order to secure the benefit—perhaps by travelling to the place where it was to be conferred.

[11] *Post*, § 19–117.

[12] *cf.* Report, § 10.3.

[13] Within subs. 1(2).

assent by C to A, or after reliance by C of which A is aware or which he could reasonably have been expected to foresee. It is not entirely clear whether it is enough for the express term to provide that A and B may rescind or vary the contract or whether it must go on to say in so many words that they may do so without the consent of C; but to be sure of achieving the desired result, A and B would be well advised to use the latter form of words.

The second possibility, stated in subsection 2(3)(b), is for the express term to **19–090** provide that the consent of C is required in circumstances other than those specified in subsection 2(1). For example, the term might provide that such consent was required only for a specified period or that it must be given in a specified form (*e.g.* by registered letter). Again, effect would be given to such provisions, so that in the first of our two examples C's consent would no longer be needed (even after the circumstances described in subsection 2(1) had occurred) after the end of the period and in the second it would be ineffective if not given in the specified form.

Judicial discretion to dispense with consent. The court has, by virtue of **19–091** subsection 2(4), power, on the application of A and B, to dispense with the requirement of C's consent to a rescission or variation of the contract in two situations: (a) where C's consent cannot be obtained because "his whereabouts cannot reasonably be ascertained"; or (b) where he is mentally incapable of giving his consent. On a similar principle, the court has under subsection 2(5) the same power where it is alleged that C's consent is required because A could reasonably have foreseen that C would rely on the term[14] but it cannot reasonably be ascertained whether he has in fact relied on it. Where the court under these provisions dispenses with C's consent, it may order compensation to be paid to him[15]; such an order may presumably be made against either A or B or both of them.

Promisor's defences against third party. Clause 3 of the 1998 Bill contains **19–092** an elaborate set of provisions which specify matters on which A can rely by way of defence, set-off or counterclaim against C in an action by C for the enforcement, "in reliance on section 1,",[16] of a term of the contract between A and B. The starting principle, stated in subsection 3(2), is that A can rely by way of defence, or set-off on any matter that "arises from or in connection with the contract [between A and B] and is relevant to the term" and would have been available to A if the proceedings (to enforce the term) had been brought by B. Under this principle, A could, for example, rely against C on a valid exemption clause in the contract between A and B[17]; and on the fact that the contract was void for mistake or voidable for misrepresentation, or that it had been frustrated or that A was justified in refusing to perform it on account of B's repudiatory breach. This general principle can, however, be excluded by a contrary provision in the contract: *i.e.* by a term in the contract between A and B that A is not to be entitled to rely on such matters against C[18]; though where the contract between A and B was wholly void such a term would appear to be of no more effect than

---

[14] See subs. 2(1)(c).
[15] Subs. 2(6).
[16] Subs. 3(1).
[17] *cf.* Report, § 10.31.
[18] Subs. 3(5).

the rest of the purported contract. The general principle can, conversely, be extended by an express term in the contract. Subsection 3(3) provides that A can (in addition to the matters referred to in subsection 3(2)) rely by way of defence or set-off against C on any matter if "an express term of the contract provides for it to be available to him in proceedings brought by" C and it would have been so available to A in proceedings brought by B. Under this provision, A could rely against C on debts owed by B to A even though the debts arose out of other transactions, if the contract containing the term which C was seeking to enforce contained an express term that A was to be entitled to rely on those debts also against C. There is a further possibility that A may have defences or counterclaims against C which he would not have against B: *e.g.* where A had been induced to enter into the contract by C's misrepresentation, or where C was indebted to A under another transaction. Subsection 3(4) enables A to rely on such matters against C if they could have been so relied on if C had been a party to the contract; though this rule, like the general principle stated in subsection 3(2), can be modified or excluded by an express term of the contract between A and B.[19] A rule analogous to the general principle of subsection 3(2) applies where the "enforcement" of the term by C takes the form of his availing himself of an exemption or limitation clause in his favour in the contract between A and B.[20] Subsection 3(6) provides that C cannot in this way "enforce" the term if he could not have done so, had he been a party to the contract. This restriction on C's right to enforce the term would, for example, apply if, by reason of the Unfair Contract Terms Act 1977[21] the clause had been invalid or if it had not satisfied the requirement of reasonableness as imposed by that Act; or if C was guilty of a fraud on A and so on could not have relied on the term (even though B might have been able to do so) by reason of the common law rule that an exemption clause does not protect a party from liability for his own fraud.[22]

19–093   **Exceptions to third party's entitlement.** A number of situations which prima facie fall within clause 1 of the 1998 Bill are excepted from the operation of that clause by clause 6. These exceptions fall into two groups. In cases which fall within the first group, C has, or can acquire, rights under the contract between A and B by virtue of some other rule of law; and the purpose of excepting these cases from the operation of clause 1 is to preserve, not only C's rights, but also the conditions under which those rights arise under those other rules of law. In cases which fall within the second group, by contrast, C has, prima facie, no rights under other rules of law; and the purpose of excepting these cases from the operation of clause 1 is to preserve in them the general rule of common law by which C acquires no rights under the contract between A and B. Such cases, in other words, continue to be governed by the common law doctrine of privity, subject to any limitations on its scope and to any exceptions to it that may exist at common law.

19–094   The first of the above group of exceptions includes contracts on bills of exchange, promissory notes and other negotiable instruments[23]: third parties can acquire rights under such contracts under the rules relating to negotiability,

---

[19] Subs. 3(5) applies to subs. 3(4) as well as to subs. 3(2).
[20] See subs. 1(6), *ante* § 19–077.
[21] *Ante*, §§ 14–057 *et seq.*
[22] *Ante*, § 14–125.
[23] Subs. 6(1).

discussed elsewhere in this book.[24] It also includes contracts for the carriage of goods by sea which are governed by the Carriage of Goods by Sea Act 1992, and corresponding electronic transactions to which that Act may be applied by Order.[25] The carefully regulated scheme of the 1992 Act[26] for the acquisition of rights under such contracts by third parties (such as transferees of bills of lading) would be seriously disrupted if such third parties could acquire rights under the 1998 Bill in circumstances in which no such rights would be acquired under the 1992 Act. The same is (*mutatis mutandis*) true of contracts for the international carriage of goods by rail, road and air, which are governed by international conventions having the force of law in the United Kingdom,[27] so that these contracts are likewise excepted from the operation of clause 1 of the 1998 Bill.[28] The exception is, however, in turn, subject to an exception: C is not precluded from taking the benefit of an exemption or limitation clause in a contract for the carriage of goods governed by the 1992 Act or by the international conventions referred to above merely because such legislation applies to the contract. Before the coming into force of the 1998 Bill, C could in many cases, take the benefit of an exemption or limitation clause in the contract of carriage (*e.g.* where the contract contained a *Himalaya* clause).[29] He could do so even against a claimant who was neither an original party to the contract a carriage, nor a person who, having acquired rights under that contract, was to be treated as if he had been a party to it[30]; and even where C was not within the class of persons specified by the applicable international convention as entitled to the benefit of the exemption or limitation provisions.[31] It was not the purpose of the 1998 Bill to reverse any of these positions or to inhibit their further development. The Bill therefore preserves C's right to take the benefit of exclusion or limitation clauses in contracts of carriage which are otherwise excepted[31a] from the operation of Clause 1.

The second of the groups of exceptions described above includes the contract **19–095** which binds a company and its members on the terms of the memorandum and articles of association, when these documents are registered, by virtue of section 14 of the Companies Act 1985. The purpose of this exception is presumably to preserve the established limitations of the scope of this "statutory contract:"[32] *e.g.* the rule that this contract confers no rights on a director of the company as such.[33] The second group also includes contracts of employment and certain analogous contracts to the extent that such a contract will not give the employer's

---

[24] *Post*, Chapter 20.

[25] Subs. 6(5).

[26] For details of this scheme, see *Benjamin's Sale of Goods* (5th ed.), §§ 18–059 *et seq.*

[27] See *post*, Vol. II Chapters 35 and 36.

[28] Subs. 6(5).

[29] *ante*, § 14–044.

[30] *e.g. New Zealand Shipping Co. Ltd v. A.M. Satterthwaite & Co. Ltd (The Eurymedon)* [1975] A.C. 74.

[31] *e.g.* where a bill of lading is governed by the Hague-Visby Rules (which have the force of law by virtue of the Carriage of Goods by Sea Act 1971) servants or agents (but not independent contractors) employed by the carrier can, under Article IV *bis* of those Rules, rely on bill of lading terms exempting the carrier from, or limiting his, liability; but under a *Himalaya* clause the protection of such terms can, on the principle of *The Eurymedon* [1975] A.C. 74 be available to an independent contractor.

[31a] Subss. 6(5).

[32] *Soden v. British & Commonwealth Holdings plc (in administration)* [1998] A.C. 298, 323.

[33] *Beattie v. E. & F. Beattie Ltd* [1938] Ch. 708; *Rayfield v. Hands* [1960] Ch. 1 is hard to reconcile with this principle: L.C.B.G., 21 M.L.R. 401.

customer any right under clause 1 of the 1998 Bill to enforce any term of the contract against the employee.[34]

19–096   **Third party's other rights unaffected.** Subsection 7(1) of the 1998 Bill provides that "Section 1 does not affect any right or remedy of a third party that exists or is available apart from this Act." It follows that C will continue, after the Bill has come into force, to be able to enforce rights and to rely on defences arising under a contract between A and B, if before then he could have done so under exceptions to the doctrine of privity established at common law, in equity or under other legislation, or if he could have done so because the case fell outside the scope of the doctrine of privity of contract: these possibilities are discussed elsewhere in this Chapter.[35] C will, for example, continue to be able to enforce a promise made by A to B if there is a trust of the promise in his favour[36]; he will be able to rely on *Himalaya* clauses and on other common law and statutory rules under which the benefit of an exemption clause in a contract between A and B is available to him[37]; and he will continue to be able to enforce collateral contracts between himself and A.[38] Indeed, in some such cases it is questionable whether the person seeking to enforce the term is truly a "third party" within the meaning of subsection 1(1) of the 1998 Bill. The whole point of the collateral contract device is to establish a direct contractual relationship between the parties that have here been called A and C; and the reasoning on which the enforceability of *Himalaya* clauses is based likewise seeks to establish that there is a contract of some kind between these parties, though this is not necessarily the same as "the contract" (*i.e.* the contract between A and B) containing the term which C is seeking to enforce. Subsection 7(1) also preserves any rights which C may have to sue A in tort in respect of loss suffered by C in consequence of A's breach of his contract with B; we have seen that in such cases C will often have no rights under the 1998 Bill.[39] The subsection also leaves it open to the courts to develop new exceptions at common law to the doctrine of privity of contract.[40]

19–097   Although subsection 7(1) in terms states only that "Section 1" does not affect other rights and remedies available to C, it follows from the structure of the 1998 Bill that many of its other provisions will likewise not apply where C's rights against A arise apart from the Bill. Of particular significance are the points that the rules as to cancellation and variation, contained in clause 2, and the rules as to defences and related matters, contained in clause 3, will not so apply, since clause 2 applies only "where a third party has a right under section 1 to enforce a term of the contract"[41] and clause 3 applies only "where, in reliance on section 1, proceedings for the enforcement of a term of a contract are brought by a third party."[41a]

---

[34] Subss. 6(3), (4).
[35] *Ante*, §§ 19–005, 19–022, 19–064 *et seq*; *post*, §§ 19–103 *et seq.*
[36] *Ante*, §§ 19–065 *et seq.*
[37] *Ante*, §§ 14–039 *et seq.*
[38] *Ante*, §§ 19–005 *et seq.*
[39] *Ante*, §19–079.
[40] See *infra*, at n. 44.
[41] Subs. 2(1).
[41a] Subs. 3(1).

The structure resulting from the above distinctions is therefore a complex one. **19–098** Four types of cases call for consideration. The first is that in which C has rights under the 1998 Bill but none at common law because the case falls within the scope of the doctrine of privity of contract but not within any of the judge-made or other legislative exceptions to it. Here C's rights and remedies are clearly subject to the provisions of the Bill. The second is the case in which C has no rights under the Bill (either because the requirements of its clause 1 are not satisfied or because one of the exceptions listed in its clause 6 applies) but in which he does have rights apart from the Bill, because the case falls either outside the scope of the doctrine of privity of contract or within one of the judge-made or other legislative exceptions to it. Here the rights and remedies to which C is entitled are clearly not subject to the provisions of the Bill.[42] The third is the case in which C has rights both under the Bill and apart from it (because the case falls outside the scope of the doctrine of privity of contract or within one of the judge-made or other legislative exceptions to it). It would seem that in such a case C can choose between making his claim under the Bill (and so subject to its provisions) and apart from the Bill (and so not subject to its provisions). If, for example, C has a cause of action against A in tort at common law, it may be to C's advantage to pursue that claim (rather than one which may also be, prima facie, available to him under clause 1) since in making such a common law claim he would not, in general, be bound by an exemption clause in the contract between A and B, while he would be so bound if he made a claim under the Bill.[43] The fourth is the case in which C has no rights under the Bill and none under the existing rules of common law or under other legislative exceptions to the doctrine of privity of contract. Here, C's only hope is to induce the court to create a new exception to the doctrine of privity[44] or (in the House of Lords) to reject that doctrine altogether. If C's claim were upheld on one of these grounds, it would plainly not be subject to the provisions of the 1998 Bill.

Nature of the third party's rights. Although the 1998 Bill for certain **19–099** specific purposes makes use of the fiction of treating C as if he were a party to the contract, it in general treats C's rights and defences as being *sui generis*. It does not, in other words, except for the purposes specified in the Bill,[45] treat C as if he were to were deemed to be, or to have become, a party to the contract. In particular, subsection 7(5) provides that C is not to be treated as a party to the contract between A and B for the purposes of other legislation. For example, the references to a party or to the parties to a contract in the Law Reform (Frustrated Contracts) Act 1943[46] and in the Misrepresentation Act 1967[47] will not, when the Bill comes into force, include references to C. The same is true of the Unfair Contract Terms Act 1977. The point can be illustrated by supposing that a contract was made between A and B on A's standard terms of business, that a term of this contract conferred a benefit on C, that this term was enforceable by

---

[42] *White v. Jones* [1995] 2 A.C. 207 (*ante*, §§ 19–037, 19–079) illustrates this possibility.

[43] Subs. 3(2), *ante* § 19–092.

[44] *e.g.* perhaps, to follow the Supreme Court of Canada's decision in *London Drugs Ltd v. Kuehne & Nagel International Ltd* [1992] 3 S.C.R. 299 in recognising, at least to a limited extent, the principle of vicarious immunity.

[45] See subs. 1(5), relating to C's remedies: *ante*, § 19–081; subs. 3(4), relating to certain defences and subs. 3(6), relating to restrictions on the availability of exemption clauses: *ante*, § 19–092; and subs. 7(3), relating to limitation of actions.

[46] *Post*, §§ 24–072 *et seq.*

[47] *Ante*, §§ 6–068 *et seq.*

C by virtue of clause 1 of the Bill, and that the contract contained a term excluding or restricting A's liability for defects in the performance rendered to C. The requirement of reasonableness under section 3 of the 1977 Act[48] would not apply in favour of C since he was not one of the parties to the contract between A and B or a party who had dealt on A's standard terms: the requirement would apply only in favour of B.[49] The justification given by the Law Commission for this position is that to apply the 1977 Act in a three-party case would raise complex policy issues going beyond those involved in reforming the doctrine of privity.[50]

19–100   **Effect on Unfair Contract Terms Act 1977, s.2.** The relationship between the 1998 Bill and the Unfair Contract Terms Act 1977 gives rise to the further difficulty that under section 2(1) of that Act[51] contract terms are void if they purport to exclude or restrict liability for death or personal injury resulting from negligence and that under section 2(2)[52] contract terms are subject to the requirement of reasonableness if they purport to exclude liability for negligence in respect of other loss. Negligence here can include breach of a contractual duty of care,[52a] so that a claim by C affected by section 2 of the 1997 Act could be brought either under the Bill or in tort, apart from the Bill. Where it is brought under the Bill, a compromise solution[53] is adopted for cases of the kind here under discussion, *i.e.* for those in which C sues A for breach of a duty of care arising out of the contract between A and B, and A seeks to rely on a term of that contract excluding his liability for negligence. Where C in consequence of the breach suffers death or personal injury, the strong policy considerations against contract terms excluding such harm are to prevail, so that nothing in the 1998 Bill will affect C's right to impugn the validity of a term excluding A's liability for such harm under section 2(1) of the 1977 Act. But where C suffers other loss, the case is regarded as more closely analogous to the situation (described in § 19–097 above) that can arise under section 3 of the 1977 Act. Subsection 7(2) of the 1998 Bill therefore provides that section 2(2) of the 1977 Act is not to apply where A's alleged negligence consists of the breach of an obligation arising from a term of a contract (between A and B) and the claim by C is brought under clause 1 of the Bill. In such an action, therefore, a term in that contract excluding or restricting A's liability for loss other than death or personal injury is not subject to the requirement of reasonableness under the 1977 Act.

19–101   **Promisee's rights.** At common law, the doctrine of privity of contract does not preclude the promisee from enforcing the contract[54] and this position is preserved by clause 4 of the 1998 Bill, by which "Section 1 does not affect any right of the promisee to enforce any term of the contract." The contract between A and B can thus be enforced by B even where the 1998 Bill also gives C the right to enforce one of its terms against A. On A's failure to perform that term in favour of C, B can therefore make any claims for the agreed sum, for other

---

[48] *Ante*, § 14–081.
[49] Report, § 13.10; for B's right of enforcement, see *post*, § 19–101.
[50] Report, § 13.10 (vii) and (viii).
[51] *Ante*, § 14–068.
[52] *Ante*, § 14–068.
[52a] Unfair Contract Terms Act 1977, s.1(1)(a).
[53] See Report, 13.12.
[54] *Ante*, § 19–041.

specific relief or for damages that would have been available to him at common law apart from the Act. There is also nothing in the Bill that affects B's right to restitution[55] against A in the event of the latter's non-performance of the term in favour of C, even though B's right to restitution would not normally be a "right of [B] to enforce a term of the contract" within clause 4: it would have this character only where the contract provided for the return by A of the consideration provided by B to A in the event of A's failure to perform in favour of C. The 1998 Bill also contains nothing to affect the common law rules which govern the relative rights of B and C where A has performed, or is willing to perform, in favour of C.[56]

Provision against double liability. At common law, A's failure to perform in favour of C may, in circumstances discussed earlier in this Chapter,[57] give B a right to recover damages in respect of C's loss or in respect of expenses incurred by B in making good A's default: *e.g.* in completing A's unfinished, or in repairing A's defective, work. If, after B had recovered such damages, C were to make a claim against A under clause 1 of the 1998 Bill, there would be a risk of A's being made liable twice over for the same loss. Clause 5 of the Bill therefore directs the court in such circumstances "to reduce any award to [C] to such extent as it thinks appropriate to take account of the sum recovered by" B. Such a reduction would not prejudice C since, where damages had been recovered by B in respect of C's loss, these would have to be held by B for C[58]; and where B had incurred expense in curing A's breach, C's loss would be reduced in fact by his receipt of the intended benefit, though by a route other than that envisaged by the contract. It should be noted that clause 5 of the Bill applies only where B has recovered "a sum" (*i.e.* of money) in respect of C's loss or B's expense in making good A's default. Thus it will normally apply where B has recovered damages, though the possibilities of its also applying where B has recovered the agreed sum or where he has made a successful claim for restitution do not appear to be excluded. It will not, however, apply where B has obtained an order for the specific performance of an obligation by A to render some performance to C other than the payment of money, or where B has obtained an injunction to enforce a negative promise made by A for the benefit of C. In such cases, C will obtain the performance due to him under the term made enforceable by him by virtue of clause 1 and so will not have any right to damages for its non-performance. But C might, in addition to the receipt of the performance, claim damages from A, *e.g.* in respect of delay in rendering the performance. Such a claim is not, and should not be, affected by clause 5 of the 1998 Bill since its success would not make A liable twice over for the same loss.

19–102

(iii) *Other Statutory Exceptions*

A number of other exceptions to the doctrine of privity of contract were created by statute before the 1998 Bill and will continue to be available to the third party after that Bill comes into force.[59] The most important of these exceptions are discussed in the paragraphs that follow.

19–103

---

[55] *Ante*, § 19–043.
[56] *Ante*, § 19–059.
[57] *Ante*, § 19–046—19–054.
[58] *Ante*, § 19–064.
[59] See subsection 7(1) of the 1998 Bill.

19–104   **Law of Property Act, s.56(1).**[60] At common law a person could not take an immediate interest in property, or the benefit of any covenant, under an indenture purporting to be *inter partes*, unless he was named as a party to the indenture.[61] The rule did not apply to deeds poll[62] or to indentures not *inter partes*.[63] In the case of such deeds, the grantee or covenantee never had to be named *as a party*, and it was eventually settled that he need not be named at all, so long as he was sufficiently designated.[64] Deeds no longer have to be indented for any purpose[65]; but the law still distinguishes between deeds *inter partes* and other deeds, and the old rule relating to indentures *inter partes*[66] still appears to apply to deeds *inter partes* which do not fall within the provisions (to be discussed below) of section 56(1) of the Law of Property Act 1925.

19–105   The common law rule with regard to indentures *inter partes* was modified by section 5 of the Real Property Act 1845,[67] which provided that "under an indenture executed after the first day of October 1845 an immediate estate or interest in any tenements or hereditaments and the benefit of a condition or covenant respecting any tenements or hereditaments may be taken although the taker thereof be not named a party to the said indenture." This enactment was limited to estates or interests in, and to conditions or covenants respecting, tenements or hereditaments, *i.e.* to real property.[68] It was later held that the enactment was further limited, in the case of covenants, to those which ran with the land.[69]

19–106   Section 5 of the 1845 Act was replaced by section 56 of the Law of Property Act 1925, subsection (1) of which provides: "A person may take an immediate or other interest in land or other property, or the benefit of any condition, right of entry, covenant or agreement over or respecting land or other property, although he may not be named as a party to the conveyance or other instrument." The 1925 Act further defines "property" to include "any thing in action."[70] In

---

[60] Elliott (1956) 20 Conv. 43, 114; Andrews (1959) 23 Conv. 179; Wade [1964] C.L.J. 66; Furmston (1960) 23 M.L.R. 380–385; Ellinger (1963) 26 M.L.R. 396; all these comments on s.56(1) must now be read in the light of the decision of the House of Lords in *Beswick v. Beswick* [1968] A.C. 58.

[61] *Scudamore v. Vanderstene* (1587) 2 Co.Inst. 673; *Storer v. Gordon* (1814) 3 M. & S. 308; *Berkeley v. Hardy* (1826) 5 B. & C. 355; *Southampton v. Brown* (1827) 6 B. & C. 718; *Gardner v. Lachlan* (1836) 8 Sim. 123. The rule was also applied to composition deeds; the cases on this subject are impossible to reconcile (see *Isaacs v. Green* (1867) L.R. 2 Ex. 352, 355) but have become obsolete in view of the Deeds of Arrangement Act 1914, repealed in part by Insolvency Act 1985, s.235 and Sched. 10, Pt. III and amended by Insolvency Act 1986, s.439(2).

[62] *cf. ante* § 1–053.

[63] *Cooker v. Child* (1763) 2 Lev. 74; *Chelsea & Waldham Green Building Soc. v. Armstrong* [1951] Ch. 853.

[64] *Sunderland Marine Insurance Co. v. Kearney* (1851) 16 Q.B. 925, qualifying *Green v. Horn* (1694) 1 Salk. 197.

[65] Law of Property Act 1925, s.56(2).

[66] *Beswick v. Beswick* [1968] A.C. 58, 104B.

[67] Replacing s.11 of the Transfer of Property Act 1844, which was not restricted to real property. For the history of this change see Davidson's *Concise Precedents in Conveyancing* (2nd ed., 1845), pp. 10 *et seq. cf.* Treitel (1967) 30 M.L.R. 687, 688–689.

[68] It is generally agreed that s.5 of the 1845 Act was confined to real property: see *Beswick v. Beswick* [1968] A.C. 58, 87D, 104E.

[69] *Forster v. Elvett Colliery Co. Ltd* [1908] 1 K.B. 629 (in the House of Lords, Lord Macnaghten reserved the point: *Dyson v. Forster* [1909] A.C. 98, 102); *Grant v. Edmonson* [1931] 1 Ch. 1.

[70] s.205(1)(xx).

Beswick v. Beswick Lord Denning M.R. and Danckwerts L.J. held that a promise in writing by A to B to pay a sum of money to C would, by virtue of this definition of "property," be within section 56(1) and so give C a right to sue A.[71] But the House of Lords rejected this view, principally on the ground that the definition of "property" in the Act was stated to apply "unless the context otherwise requires." The context in section 56(1) did otherwise require, since section 56(1) was part of a consolidating Act and was designed to reproduce section 5 of the 1845 Act, which admittedly did not have the wide effect suggested for section 56(1).[72] There was, moreover, nothing in the legislative history of section 56(1) to support the view that the subsection was intended to abolish the doctrine of privity in relation to written contracts[73]; indeed, the legislative history gives some support to the view that no such change was intended.[74] The enacting words[75] of section 56(1) also give some support to this view. They refer to the case in which a person is not *named as* a party: not to the case in which he *is not* a party.[76]

Section 56(1) therefore does not apply to a bare promise in writing by A to B   **19–107** to pay a sum of money to C; and the correctness of a number of previous decisions to this effect[77] is reaffirmed by *Beswick v. Beswick*. But the question, to what other cases the subsection does apply, remains one of great difficulty. There is support in the speeches in *Beswick v. Beswick* for the following limitations on the scope of section 56(1): namely, that it applies only (1) to real property[78] (2) to covenants running with the land[79]; (3) to cases where the instrument is not merely for the benefit of the third party but purports to contain a grant to or covenant with him[80]; and (4) to deeds strictly *inter partes*.[81] But

---

[71] [1966] Ch. 538 (*ante*, § 19–021), and see *Drive Yourself Hire Co. (London) Ltd v. Strutt* [1954] 1 Q.B. 250; criticised on this point by Wade [1954] C.L.J. 66.

[72] [1968] A.C. 58, 77C, 81C, 87C.

[73] [1968] A.C. 58, 73F, 84G, 104F; *cf.* Treitel (1966) 29 M.L.R. 657, 661.

[74] Before the passing of the 1925 Act, a number of reforming measures had been enacted. None of these contained any provisions from which the present s.56(1) is derived. In introducing one of the reforming Bills, which were consolidated, together with earlier Acts, in the 1925 Legislation, Lord Haldane L.C. said that no Parliamentary time would be needed for the consolidating bills "because they do not change what will then be the law": (1924) 59 H.L. Deb. 125. In view of his speech in *Dunlop Pneumatic Tyre Co. Ltd v. Selfridge & Co. Ltd* [1915] A.C. 847, 853, Lord Haldane could hardly have taken this view of the 1925 legislation if the effect of s.56(1) had been to create a *jus quaesitum tertio* arising by way of contract.

[75] But not the side-note, which reads in part "persons taking who are not parties . . . ".

[76] *cf. infra* at nn. 80 and 84.

[77] *Re Sinclair's Life Policy* [1938] Ch. 799; *Re Foster* [1938] 3 All E.R. 357; *Re Miller's Agreement* [1947] Ch. 615. A dictum in the last-mentioned case is doubted in *Beswick v. Beswick* [1968] A.C. at 75F, but the actual decision is several times referred to with approval or at least without disapproval: at 76A, 80B, 86C, 106E.

[78] This view is stated by Lord Guest (at 87F) and perhaps shared by Lord Reid (at 76B) but doubted by Lord Upjohn (at 105F) with whom Lord Pearce agreed (at 94D). Lord Hodson says that "property" must be given "a limited meaning" (at 81C), but he does not say what that meaning is. *cf.* also *Southern Water Authority v. Carey* [1985] 2 All E.R. 1077, 1083.

[79] This follows from Lord Guest's view in *Beswick v. Beswick* [1968] A.C. 58 at 87A that s.56(1) has made no change at all in the law. Contrast Lord Reid's view that s.56(1) has not "substantially" (at 77C) altered the law; and *cf.* Lord Pearce's view of s.56(1) as an "enlargement" of its predecessor (at 93B) making no "substantial innovation"; and *cf.* Lord Upjohn at 105F.

[80] This view is regarded as a possible (though unsatisfactory) one by Lord Pearce (at 94D) and approved by Lord Upjohn (at 106D–F). It is rejected by Lord Guest (at 87B) and mentioned without comment by Lord Reid (at 74–75) and Hodson (at 81A).

[81] This view is stated by Lord Upjohn (at 107A), with whom Lord Pearce agreed (at 94D). It is also mentioned without comment by Lord Reid (at 76–77).

there is no clear majority in the speeches in favour of the imposition of all, some or even one of these restrictions, so that the precise scope of the subsection has not been clarified. There appear to be only two cases in which section 56(1) has actually been applied. The first case[82] is consistent with all four of the above limitations, while the second[83] case is consistent only with the last two. The third limitation was regarded as the operative one both in these cases and in a number of other cases in which the courts have refused to apply the subsection[84]; and as it was, at any rate, not decisively rejected in *Beswick v. Beswick*, it is probable that the subsection will be applied only where the requirements of this limitation are satisfied. There is also much to be said on historical grounds for the fourth limitation, which is consistent with all the cases, though it does not form a ground of decision in any of them. The scope of section 56(1) is further limited by a rule which it was not necessary to consider in *Beswick v. Beswick*, namely, that a person cannot take the benefit of a covenant under the subsection unless he, or his predecessor in title, was in existence[85] and identifiable in accordance with the terms of the instrument at the time when it was made.[86]

19–108   **Life insurance.**[87] Section 11 of the Married Women's Property Act 1882 provides that where a man insures his life for the benefit of his wife or children, or where a woman insures her life for the benefit of her husband or children,[88] the policy "shall create a trust in favour of the objects therein named." This provision applies only where a person insures his or her own life and not where the policy is on the life of the beneficiary[89]; and it is restricted to policies for the benefit of spouses and children and so does not apply in favour of other dependants.[90] These restrictions will not be affected by the coming into force of the Contracts (Rights of Third Parties) Bill, 1998[91]; but persons who have no rights under section 11 of the 1882 Act may, if the requirements of the 1998 Bill are satisfied, acquire the more restricted[92] rights to be conferred on third parties by that Bill. They may also have enforceable rights under the trust device discussed in § 19–066 above.[93]

---

[82] *Re Ecclesiastical Commissioners' Conveyance* [1936] Ch. 430; *cf.* a dictum in *Re Windle* [1975] 1 W.L.R. 1628, 1631 (not affected on this point by the doubts expressed in *Re Kumar* [1993] 1 W.L.R. 224, 235).

[83] *Stromdale and Ball Ltd v. Burden* [1952] Ch. 223.

[84] See *White v. Bijou Mansions* [1937] Ch. 610; affd. [1938] Ch. 351; *Lyus v. Prowse Developments* [1982] 1 W.L.R. 1044, 1049; *Amsprop Trading Ltd v. Harris Distribution Ltd* [1997] 1 W.L.R. 1025. This is a more stringent requirement than those contained in subsections 1(1) and (2) of the Contracts (Rights of Third Parties) Bill 1998.

[85] There is to be no such requirement under the Contracts (Rights of Third Parties) Bill: see subsection 1(3).

[86] *Kelsey v. Dodd* (1883) 52 L.J.Ch. 34; *Westhoughton U.D.C. v. Wigan Coal Co.* [1919] 1 Ch. 159 (both these cases were decided under s.5 of the Real Property Act 1845, but the position under s.56(1) of the 1925 Act seems to be the same): *White v. Bijou Mansions, supra.*

[87] For details of the exceptions discussed in this and the next five paragraphs, see Vol. II, Chap. 41.

[88] Including illegitimate children: Family Law Reform Act 1969, s.19(1).

[89] See *Re Engelbach's Estate* [1924] 2 Ch. 348 which is still good law on this point, although it has, on another point, been overruled (see *ante*, § 19–060, n. 86).

[90] *Re Clay's Policy of Assurance* [1937] 2 All E.R. 548.

[91] Law Com. No. 242, § 12–27.

[92] *e.g.* powers of cancellation or variation under Clause 2 of the 1998 Bill do not apply where a trust has arisen under s.11 of the 1882 Act; *cf. ante*, § 19–098.

[93] *Re Foster's Policy* [1966] 1 W.L.R. 222.

Motor insurance. A person driving a motor vehicle with the consent of the   **19–109**
owner can, by statute, take the benefit of a provision in his favour in the owner's
insurance policy without having to prove that the owner intended to constitute
himself trustee.[94]

Insurance by persons with limited interests. If a person insures for its full   **19–110**
value property in which he has only a limited interest, he may be able to recover
in full from the insurer but be liable to pay over to the other person interested any
sum exceeding his own loss.[95] A number of real or supposed common law
limitations on this principle have been removed by statute. Thus it has been
provided that any person who has an interest in the subject-matter of a policy of
marine insurance can insure "on behalf of and for the benefit of other persons
interested as well as for his own benefit."[96] On a somewhat similar principle,
where property is sold and suffers damage before the sale is completed, any
insurance money to which the vendor is entitled in respect of the damage must
be held by him for the purchaser, and be paid over to the purchaser on
completion.[97]

Fire insurance. Where an insured house is destroyed by fire, "any person . . .   **19–111**
interested" may require the insurance money to be laid out towards reinstating
the house.[98] Thus a tenant may claim under his landlord's insurance; and vice
versa.[99]

Solicitors' indemnity insurance. Under section 37 of the Solicitors Act   **19–112**
1974, a scheme has been established by the Law Society for the compulsory
insurance of solicitors against liability for professional negligence or breach of
duty. The scheme takes the form of a contract between the Society and insurers,

---

[94] Road Traffic Act 1988, s.148(7), replacing Road Traffic Act 1930, s.36(4); discussed in
Tattersall v. Drysdale [1935] 2 K.B. 174 and *Austin v. Zurich, etc., Insurance* [1944] 2 All E.R. 243,
248. *cf.* also Transport Act 1980, s.61.

[95] *Waters v. Monarch Insurance Co.* (1856) 5 E. & B. 870; *Hepburn v. A. Tomlinson (Hauliers) Ltd*
[1966] A.C. 451; *cf. Petrofina (U.K.) Ltd v. Magnaload Ltd* [1984] Q.B. 127 (head contractor insuring
for benefit of himself and sub-contractors); *Pan Atlantic Insurance Co. Ltd v. Pine Top Insurance Co.
Ltd* [1988] 2 Lloyd's Rep. 505 (same principle applied to reinsurance); *Sumitomo Bank Ltd v. Banque
Bruxelles Lambert S.A.* [1997] 1 Lloyd's Rep. 487, 495; *Glengate Properties Ltd v. Norwich Union
Fire Insurance Society* [1996] 2 All E.R. 487, 497. Contrast *Stone Vickers Ltd v. Appledone Ferguson
Shipbuilders Ltd* [1992] 2 Lloyd's Rep. 578, where the main contractors' insurance did not cover the
subcontractors since the main contractors had no authority or intention to contract on behalf of the
subcontractors; for similar reasoning, see *Colonia Versicherung A.G. v. Amoco Oil Co.* [1997] 1
Lloyd's Rep. 261, 270–272. The loss of the insured may exceed the value of his interest, and even
be suffered in spite of his having parted with that interest, by reason of his having undertaken a
contractual obligation with respect to the property: *e.g.* an obligation to reinstate it in the event of
damage by a peril covered by the insurance: *Lonsdale & Thompson Ltd v. Black Arrow Group plc*
[1993] Ch. 361.

[96] Marine Insurance Act 1906, s.14(2).

[97] Law of Property Act 1925, s.47; for the definition of "property" see *ibid.* s.205(1)(xx). In
contracts for the sale of land, s.47 is now commonly excluded: see Law Com. 191 (1990), para. 3.2.
cf. also Law of Property Act 1925, s.108 as to the application of insurance money where property is
mortgaged.

[98] Fires Prevention (Metropolis) Act 1774, s.83.

[99] *Portavon Cinema Co. v. Price & Century Insurance Co.* [1939] 4 All E.R. 601; *Mark Rowlands
Ltd v. Berni Inns Ltd* [1986] Q.B. 211; *Lonsdale & Thompson Ltd v. Black Arrow Group plc* [1993]
Ch. 361. *MacGillivray on Insurance Law* (9th ed., 1998), §§ 20–44, 20–45.

whereby the insurers undertake, on being paid the appropriate premiums, to provide indemnity insurance to solicitors. It has been held that the scheme gives rise to reciprocal rights and duties between the insurers and solicitors.[1] This result follows "by virtue of public law, not the ordinary English private law of contract"[2] for in operating the scheme the Society acts, not in its private capacity as a professional association, but in its public capacity, as a body one of whose functions is to protect members of the public against loss which they may suffer from dealings with solicitors.

19–113   **Third parties' rights against insurers.** Our concern here is not with insurance contracts which purport to confer benefits on third parties, but with those which insure the promisee against liability to third parties. By statute, a third party may in certain circumstances enforce the rights of the insured under the policy[3] by proceeding against the insurance company.[4] In the case of victims of motor accidents, these statutory rights are supplemented by an agreement originally made between the Motor Insurers' Bureau and the Minister of Transport.[5] This provides that the Bureau will pay any judgment (to the extent to which it remains unsatisfied) in respect of any liability which is required to be covered by a policy of insurance under the statutory scheme of compulsory motor insurance. A person who is injured in a road accident cannot technically sue on the agreement as he is not a party to it.[6] But the agreement may be specifically enforced by the appropriate Minister[7]; and although "the foundations in jurisprudence" of the agreement "are better not questioned,"[8] the Bureau's policy is not

---

[1] *Swain v. Law Society* [1983] 1 A.C. 598.

[2] *ibid.* at 611.

[3] See *Socony Mobil Oil Co. Inc. v. West of England Shipowners' Mutual Insurance Association (The Padre Island)* [1984] 2 Lloyd's Rep. 408; *Normid Housing Association Ltd v. R. John Ralphs* [1989] 1 Lloyd's Rep. 265; *Bradley v. Eagle Star Insurance Co. Ltd* [1989] A.C. 957 (third party unable to sue insurer where insured had gone into liquidation before liability was established); *Duncan Stevenson MacMillan v. A.W. Knott Becker Scott Ltd* [1990] 1 Lloyd's Rep. 98; *Lefevrre v. White* [1990] 1 Lloyd's Rep. 569, 577; *Firma C-Trade SA v. Newcastle Protection and Indemnity Association (The Fanti and The Padre Island)* [1991] 2 A.C. 1; *Cox v. Bankside* [1995] 2 Lloyd's Rep. 437, 457, 466–467; *Schiffahrtsgesellschaft Detlev von Appen v. Voest Alpine Intertrading G.m.b.H.* [1997] 1 Lloyd's Rep. 179, 187; *Total Graphics Ltd v. A.G.F. Insurance Ltd* [1997] 1 Lloyd's Rep. 599. *cf. Eagle Star Insurance Co. Ltd v. Provincial Insurance plc* [1994] A.C. 130, where the issue of contribution between insurers arose under legislation in force in the Bahamas giving third parties direct rights against insurers; *Nigel Upchurch Associates v. Aldridge Estates Investment Co. Ltd* [1993] 1 Lloyd's Rep. 533 (third party held to have no right against insurer until the latter's liability to insured had been established). This topic is not to be covered by the Contracts (Rights of Third Parties) Bill 1998: see Law Com. No. 242 § 12–21.

[4] Third Parties (Rights against Insurers) Act 1930; *Bradley v. Eagle Star Insurance Co. Ltd* [1989] A.C. 957; Road Traffic Act 1988 ss.151–153 as amended by Road Traffic Act 1991 s.48 and Sched. 4, para. 66, s.83 and Sched. 8; Michel [1987] L.M.C.L.Q. 228; and see Policyholders Protection Act 1975, s.7 for the rights of such persons where the company is in liquidation. For provisional proposals for reform, see [1998] N.L.J. 42.

[5] See *Hardy v. M.I.B.* [1964] 2 Q.B. 745, 770 and *White v. London Transport Executive* [1971] 2 QB 721, 729 for the text of the agreement and of a supplementary agreement. The current agreements are between the Bureau and the Secretary of State for the Environment and are published by HMSO under the titles *Motor Insurers' Bureau (Compensation of Victims of Untraced Drivers)*, 1972 (discussed in *Evans v. M.I.B.*, *The Times*, November 10, 1997) and *Motor Insurers' Bureau (Compensation of Victims of Uninsured Drivers)*, 1988.

[6] See *Gurtner v. Circuit* [1968] 2 Q.B. 587.

[7] *ibid.*

[8] *Gardner v. Moore* [1984] A.C. 548, 556.

to rely on the doctrine of privity as a defence to claims by the injured parties themselves.[9]

Defective premises. Under the Occupiers' Liability Act 1957, an occupier of premises who is bound by contract to permit persons who are strangers to the contract to enter or use the premises owes them (subject to any contrary provision in the contract) not only the common duty of care but also any stricter obligation he may undertake towards the other contracting party.[10] The Defective Premises Act 1972 imposes certain duties on a person who takes on work for or in connection with the provision of a dwelling. These duties are owed not only to the person to whose order[11] the dwelling is provided but also to any person who acquires an interest (whether legal or equitable) in the dwelling.[12] The Act also deals with the case where premises are let under a tenancy which puts on the landlord an obligation[13] to the tenant for the maintenance or repair of the premises. The landlord in such a case owes a duty to all persons, who might reasonably be expected to be affected by defects in the state of the premises, to take reasonable care to see that such persons are reasonably safe from personal injury or damage to their property caused by a relevant defect.[14] **19–114**

5. ATTEMPTS TO IMPOSE LIABILITIES UPON STRANGERS

Strangers generally not bound by the contract. The general rule is that a contract binds only the parties to it. This rule is regarded as an aspect of the doctrine of privity[15]; and in so far as A and B cannot by a contract between them impose an obligation to perform duties arising under that contract on C, the rule may seem to be so obvious that it scarcely needs to be stated. But the rule equally applies where the contract between A and B merely purports to deprive C of some right or to restrict his freedom of action, without imposing any obligation of performance on him: for example, a person is not bound by an exclusion clause contained in a contract to which he is not a party, unless one of the exceptions to the doctrine of privity can be invoked against him.[16] **19–115**

Exceptions to the rule. The exceptions to the doctrine of privity discussed in §§ 19–065 to 19–114 above all concern situations in which a person can acquire *rights* under a contract to which he is not a party. They do not deal with the **19–116**

---

[9] *Hardy v. M.I.B., supra*, at 757; *Randall v. M.I.B.* [1968] 1 W.L.R. 1900; *Persson v. London County Buses* [1974] 1 W.L.R. 569; *Porter v. Addo* [1975] R.T.R. 503. As the Bureau is interested in the outcome of the litigation between the injured party and the driver it may, at the court's discretion, be added as a party to such litigation: see *Gurtner v. Circuit, supra*, and contrast *White v. London Transport Executive, supra* n. 5. Notice of proceedings against the driver must be served on the Bureau: *Cambridge v. Callaghan, The Times*, March 21, 1997.

[10] Occupiers' Liability Act 1957, s.3(1).

[11] This will generally amount to a contract but the duty is imposed even where this is not the case.

[12] Defective Premises Act 1972, s.1.

[13] This will generally be contractual but might also be imposed (for example) by statute.

[14] Defective Premises Act 1972, s.4.

[15] This aspect of the doctrine will not be affected by the coming into force of the Contracts (Rights of Third Parties) Bill 1998: see *ante* § 19–002.

[16] *Ante*, § 14–040; *cf. Herd v. Clyde Helicopters Ltd* [1997] A.C. 473, where legislation limiting the liability of a party to the contract was held to be effective as against a third party.

converse problem, whether *duties* can be imposed by such a contract on a third party. This possibility can, however, arise, under some of the exceptions to the doctrine which have been referred to in § 19–064, but which (for reasons there stated) are not discussed in this chapter; *e.g.* under the law of agency and under the law as to covenants relating to land.

19–117 **Scope of the rule.** Although a contract cannot generally impose duties on a third party, it can affect the rights of such a person in various ways. For example, it may create a lien,[17] or a lease,[18] or an equitable interest, or give rise to a constructive trust affecting property,[19] and such interests can affect the rights of third parties who later acquire the property. Moreover, although a contract primarily creates rights and duties enforceable by the contracting parties against each other, it also incidentally imposes on third parties a duty not to interfere with the contracting parties in the performance of the contract. In *Lumley v. Gye*[20] the claimant had employed Johanna Wagner as an opera singer. The defendant, knowing of this contract, "maliciously"[21] induced her to refuse to perform it. He was held liable to the claimant for what has since become known as the tort of wrongful interference with contractual or legal rights.[22] The effect of this tort may be not only to restrict the activities of the person guilty of the wrongful interference but also adversely to affect other third parties. For example, where a former employee disclosed trade secrets to a company which he controlled, and which used those trade secrets to secure an order from one of the employer's old customers, an injunction was granted not only to restrain the employee from using the trade secrets, but also to restrain the company from fulfilling its contract with the customer, whose remedy would have been in damages against the company.[23]

---

[17] See *Faith v. E.I.C.* (1821) 4 B. & Ald. 630; *Tappenden v. Artus* [1964] 2 Q.B. 185. Contrast *Chellaram & Sons Ltd v. Butler's Warehousing and Distributing Ltd* [1978] 2 Lloyd's Rep. 142 (third party not bound by agreement purporting to confer on sub-bailee a lien more extensive than that which would, but for such agreement, arise at common law).

[18] As in *Ashburn Anstalt v. Arnold* [1989] Ch. 1 (overruled on another ground in *Prudential Assurance Co. Ltd v. London Residuary Body* [1992] A.C. 386).

[19] See *Ashburn Anstalt v. Arnold, supra,* where the mere fact that C had notice of an earlier contract between A and B was said at 167 to be insufficient to give rise to a constructive trust on C's acquisition of the land affected by that contract; and where Fox L.J. (delivering the judgment of the court) at 160 disapproved dicta in *Errington v. Errington* [1952] 1 K.B. 290, to the effect that a contractual licence to occupy land granted by A to B gave rise to an equitable interest binding third parties; Hill (1988) 51 M.L.R. 226; Oakley [1988] C.L.J. 353. *cf.* also *Binions v. Evans* [1972] Ch. 359; Smith [1973] C.L.J. 81; *Re Sharpe* [1980] 1 W.L.R. 219; *Pritchard v. Briggs* [1980] Ch. 338 (option to purchase); *Lyus v. Prowsa Developments* [1982] 1 W.L.R. 1044.

[20] (1853) 2 E. & B. 216.

[21] *i.e.* deliberately and with knowledge of the existence of the contract: *British Homophone Ltd v. Kunz* (1935) 152 L.T. 589; *D.C. Thompson & Co. v. Deakin* [1952] Ch. 646, 694; *Jones Bros. (Hunstanton) Ltd v. Stevens* [1955] 1 Q.B. 275, 280. Such knowledge may be inferred from surrounding circumstances: *Merkur Island Shipping Corpn. v. Laughton* [1983] 2 A.C. 570. Dicta in *British Industrial Plastics Ltd v. Ferguson* [1940] 1 All E.R. 479, 483, suggesting that liability may be based on constructive notice were not necessary for the decision. See further *post* § 19–122, n. 45. There is no tortious liability for inducing *unfair* dismissal (which is not a breach of contract): *Wilson v. Housing Corporation,* [1997] I.R.L.R. 346.

[22] See *Law Debenture Trust Corp. v. Ural Caspian Oil Corp.* [1995] Ch. 152, 165; *cf. Royal Brunei Airlines Sdn. Bhd. v. Tan* [1995] 2 A.C. 378, 386, where an analogous principle was applied to dishonest interference with a relationship arising by way of trust.

[23] *PSM International v. Whitehouse* [1992] I.R.L.R. 279.

Contracts affecting chattels.[24] The rule in *Lumley v. Gye*[25] may help to solve   **19–118**
the problem: to what extent can a person who acquires a chattel be affected by
a contract concerning it, previously made between two other persons? Such
contracts may take the form of restricting the use or disposition of goods, *e.g.* by
providing that the goods shall only be used along with others made by the same
manufacturer, or that they shall only be sold in packets sealed by the manufacturer, or at fixed prices, or within specified limits of time or territory. Or they
may require the use of some *particular* chattel for their performance, without
creating any proprietary or possessory interest in the chattel: for example, in the
case of a contract to carry cargo in a particular ship. Or they may provide for the
hire of a chattel, or confer an option to purchase it, or do both these things, as in
the case of hire-purchase agreements.

Protection in special cases. In a number of special cases the law protects   **19–119**
such contractual rights against strangers who acquire the chattel in question with
notice of the contractual rights. Thus where an option to purchase a chattel is
specifically enforceable, it may be enforced against third parties who acquire the
chattel with notice of the option.[26] The same would be true where a debtor gave
an undertaking to his creditor that he would repay a loan of money out of specific
property, and later created a charge over the property in favour of a third party.
Since such an undertaking to repay is specifically enforceable, it would create a
charge in equity over the property in favour of the creditor, and this would prevail
against the third party unless he was a bona fide purchaser for value without
notice.[27] This principle can, however, apply only where the contract is one which
relates to specific property. It therefore did not apply where a property developer
undertook in its contract with a builder to set up a retention fund and then
charged its assets to a bank. Although the bank had express notice of the terms
of the building contract, its charge was held not to be subject to the promise to
create the retention fund since there was no specific property to which that
promise could be said to relate.[28]

More general principle rejected. An attempt to establish a more general   **19–120**
principle was made in *De Mattos v. Gibson*, where Knight Bruce L.J. said:

> "Reason and justice seem to prescribe that, at least as a general rule, where a man, by
> gift or purchase, acquires property from another, with knowledge of a previous contract,
> lawfully and for valuable consideration made by him with a third person, to use and
> employ the property for a particular purpose in a specified manner, the acquirer shall
> not, to the material damage of the third person, in opposition to the contract and

---

[24] Chafee (1928) 41 Harv.L.Rev. 945; Wade (1928) 44 L.Q.R. 51.

[25] (1853) 2 E. & B. 216; *ante*, § 19–117.

[26] *Falcke v. Gray* (1859) 4 Drew. 651, as explained in *Erskine Macdonald Ltd v. Eyles* [1921] 1 Ch.
631, 641.

[27] *Swiss Bank Corpn. v. Lloyd's Bank Ltd* [1982] A.C. 584, 598, 613, *post*, § 28–008; the actual
decision was that the contract of loan did *not* create an obligation to repay out of specific property
and hence was not specifically enforceable. *cf.* also *C.N. Marine Inc. v. Stena Line A/B (The Stena
Nautica) (No. 2)* [1982] 2 Lloyd's Rep. 336 (where specific performance was denied). For the special
position of mortgages of ships, see *The Shizelle* [1992] 2 Lloyd's Rep. 444.

[28] *MacJordan Construction Ltd v. Brookmount Erostin Ltd, The Times*, October 29, 1991.

inconsistently with it, use and employ the property in a manner not allowable to the giver or seller."[29]

This principle came to be associated with the rule in *Tulk v. Moxhay*,[30] relating to restrictive covenants concerning land. That rule was later confined to cases in which the claimant's interest in enforcing the covenant consisted in the ownership of land capable of being benefited.[31] This usually meant adjacent land, and since adjacency cannot be a satisfactory criterion of interest in the case of things that can be moved, the tendency of this development of the rule in *Tulk v. Moxhay*, was to undermine the principle stated by Knight Bruce L.J. in *De Mattos v. Gibson*.[32] Nevertheless, in *Lord Strathcona SS. Co. v. Dominion Coal Co.*[33] the Privy Council relied on that principle to hold that a time charterer of a ship had an interest[34] in the ship which he could enforce against a purchaser of the ship with notice of the charterparty: that purchaser was said to be "plainly in the position of a constructive trustee, with obligations which a court of equity will not allow him to violate."[35] The decision provoked much adverse criticism,[36] particularly because the land law analogies and the constructive trust reasoning on which it was based might lead to the third party's being made liable where he had only constructive notice of the earlier contract. Where that contract concerned the use or disposition of a chattel, such a conclusion was open to the objection that it might have the undesirable effect[37] of introducing the doctrine of constructive notice into commercial affairs. When a similar problem arose in *Port Line Ltd v. Ben Line Steamers Ltd*,[38] Diplock J. therefore refused to follow the Privy Council's decision. Alternatively, he was prepared to distinguish that decision on the ground that the purchaser of the ship in the *Port Line* case merely knew the ship was subject to a time charter, but did not have actual notice of the precise extent of the claimants' rights under the charterparty.[39] Thus while the *Port Line* case rejects the general principle stated by Knight Bruce L.J. so far as it relates to contracts concerning chattels, it does not decide that a third party can always disregard such a contract when he acquires the chattel in question. Possible limitations on his freedom to do so are considered in the next nine paragraphs.

19–121   **Remedy.** Later authorities have restricted the principle of *De Mattos v. Gibson*[40] by emphasising that the remedy there sought was simply an injunction to

---

[29] (1858) 4 D. & J. 276, 282.
[30] (1848) 2 Ph. 774.
[31] *L.C.C. v. Allen* [1914] 3 K.B. 642; the actual decision has been reversed by statute (see now Housing Act 1985, s.609) but the principle stated in the text remains unimpaired.
[32] See *Greenhalgh v. Mallard* [1943] 2 All E.R. 234, 249.
[33] [1926] A.C. 108.
[34] *ibid.* at 123.
[35] *ibid.* at 125.
[36] *Clore v. Theatrical Properties* [1936] 2 All E.R. 483, 490; *Greenhalgh v. Mallard* [1943] 2 All E.R. 234; *cf.* the earlier criticisms of Knight Bruce L.J.'s principle in *Barker v. Stickney* [1919] 1 K.B. 121, 132 (as to which see *Tito v. Waddell (No. 2)* [1977] Ch. 106, 300).
[37] See *Manchester Trust Ltd v. Furness* [1895] 2 Q.B. 539, 545; *Westdeutsche Landesbank Girozentrale v. Islington B.C.* [1996] A.C. 669, 704.
[38] [1958] Q.B. 146. The cases cited in § 19–117, n. 19 all apply the constructive trust reasoning to contracts concerning land and do not, it is submitted, undermine the rejection of that reasoning in the *Port Line* case so far as contracts affecting the use or disposition of chattels are concerned.
[39] Hence the purchaser could not be held liable in tort: see *post* § 19–122, n. 45.
[40] *Ante*, § 19–120, n. 29.

restrain the acquirer, C, from using the property inconsistently with the terms of the contract between A and B, known to C.[41] The principle therefore cannot impose any positive obligation on C to perform the terms of the contract between A and B. Thus where A acquired shares from B, promising to make payments to B on the occurrence of specified events, which later happened, it was held that that promise could not be enforced against C who later acquired the shares from A with knowledge of the contract between A and B, nor against D who acquired them from C with such knowledge.[42] An injunction on the principle of *De Mattos v. Gibson* was not available against C or D as they were not proposing to act inconsistently with the contract between A and B: "they are merely proposing . . . to do nothing whatever."[43]

Third party's liability in tort.[44] Where a person acquires a chattel with **19–122** actual knowledge[45] of the terms of a contract affecting it, he may, if his acquisition or use of the chattel is inconsistent with that contract, be liable in tort for wrongful interference with contractual rights.[46] Thus in *British Motor Trade Association v. Salvadori*[47] A bought a car and covenanted with B that he would not resell it for one year without first offering it to B. C bought the car from A within the year with notice of the covenant and was held liable to B for wrongfully interfering with B's contractual rights against A. It has been suggested that the decision of the Privy Council in the *Lord Strathcona* case[48] can be explained on the ground that the purchaser of the ship had committed this tort against the charterer.[49] The tort may be committed even though A was quite willing to break his contract with B. Thus in a case like *Salvadori's* it would be immaterial whether A or C began the negotiations for the sale of the car.[50] Indeed, C's tort liability may arise precisely where he and A collude in order to

---

[41] *Swiss Bank Corpn. v. Lloyds Bank Ltd* [1979] Ch. 574, 581 (as to which see also *infra*, n. 49).

[42] *Law Debenture Trust Corp. v. Ural Caspian Oil Corp. Ltd* [1993] 1 W.L.R. 138; revd., on another point, [1995] Ch. 152.

[43] [1993] 1 W.L.R. 138, 146.

[44] Wade (1926) 42 L.Q.R. 139.

[45] Precise knowledge of the terms of the contract is not generally necessary to make the defendant liable in tort: see *J.T. Stratford & Son Ltd v. Lindley* [1965] A.C. 269, 322; *Emerald Construction Co. Ltd v. Lowthian* [1966] 1 W.L.R. 691; *Daily Mirror Newspapers Ltd v. Gardner* [1968] 2 Q.B. 762; *Greig v. Insole* [1978] 1 W.L.R. 302, 336; and *cf. Distillers Co. (Biochemicals) Ltd v. Times Newspapers* [1975] Q.B. 613; *Merkur Island Shipping Corpn. v. Laughton* [1983] A.C. 570. But in the *Port Line* case (*ante*, § 19–120) the third party assumed that the charterparty with which he was alleged to have interfered contained certain crucial terms to the same effect as those of another charterparty which he had made with one of the parties to the original contract. This assumption was mistaken but not, in the circumstances, unreasonable.

[46] *Ante*, § 19–117.

[47] [1949] Ch. 556; *semble*, that in circumstances the agreement would now be likely to be exempted under Competition Act 1998, s.4 from potential invalidity under s.2 of that Act; *Rickless v. United Artists Corpn.* [1988] Q.B. 40, 58–59; *cf. Law Debenture Corp. v. Ural Caspian Oil Corp. Ltd* [1993] 1 W.L.R. 138 (where the fifth defendant admitted liability on this ground); revsd. on another point [1995] Ch. 152.

[48] [1926] A.C. 108, *ante*, § 19–120.

[49] *Swiss Bank Corpn. v. Lloyds Bank Ltd* [1979] Ch. 581, 574; in the Court of Appeal it was conceded that there was "no substance" in the point: see [1982] A.C. 584, 598 and § 19–126, *post*, at n. 63.

[50] *Sefton v. Tophams* [1965] Ch. 1140, 1161, 1187; revd. without reference to this point [1967] A.C. 50.

get rid (if they can) of a restriction imposed by the contract between A and B.[51]

19–123   The merit of this approach to the problem through the law of tort is that it avoids the danger of importing the doctrine of constructive notice into this branch of the law. On the other hand, it is subject to two limitations.

19–124   First, the tort is not committed if the defendant's interference was not the cause of the claimant's loss. Thus in the *Lord Strathcona* case the shipowners, who were the defendants in the Privy Council proceedings,[52] had mortgaged the ship, after the conclusion of the charterparty. The mortgage gave the mortgagees a power to sell the ship, and it was held in other proceedings[53] that they were entitled to sell her free from the charterers' rights even though they knew of those rights. The reason for this decision was that the shipowners could not have performed the charterparty, even if the ship had not been sold, because they were too poor to put her to sea. It was the poverty of the shipowners, and not the mortgagees' sale of the ship, which was the cause of the charterers' loss. Similarly, where breach of the contract has already been induced by C's acquisition of the property from A, there will be no tort liability for inducing breach of contract on D, who subsequently buys the property from C, even with knowledge of the contract between A and B, for D's conduct will not have played any part in inducing the original breach.[54] Nor will D in such a case be liable for interference with the remedies arising out of the broken contract[55] between A and B.

19–125   Secondly, liability for interference with contractual rights is based on intentional wrongdoing. It follows that, if a defendant negligently damaged a ship that was subject to a time charterparty, he would not commit this tort against the charterer; nor would he be liable to the charterer in negligence for pecuniary loss, such as hire wasted or profits lost while the ship was, by reason of the damage, out of service.[56]

19–126   **Third party's state of mind.** So far, in discussing the third party liability in tort for interference with contractual rights, it has been assumed that C either knew or did not know of the contract between A and B. In the former situation, he could, but in the latter he could not, be liable for this tort.[57] There is also an intermediate situation, in which C at the time of his contract with A had no more than constructive notice of A's earlier contract with B, but then acquired actual

---

[51] *Esso Petroleum Co. Ltd v. Kingswood Motors (Addlestone) Ltd* [1974] Q.B. 142.

[52] [1926] A.C. 108; *ante*, § 19–120.

[53] *The Lord Strathcona* [1925] P. 143; judgment in these proceedings was given four months earlier than that in the Privy Council proceedings. *cf.* also *De Mattos v. Gibson* (1858) 4 D. & J. 276 where the charterer's claim eventually failed on a similar ground; and *The Myrto* [1977] 2 Lloyd's Rep. 243; *Lyus v. Prowsa Developments Ltd* [1982] 1 W.L.R. 1044, 1049 (as to which see also *ante* § 19–067).

[54] *Law Debenture Trust Corp. v. Ural Caspian Oil Corp. Ltd* [1993] 1 W.L.R. 138, and see next note.

[55] *Law Debenture Trust Corp. v. Ural Caspian Oil Corp.*, [1995] Ch. 152, reversing the decision at first instance (*supra*, n. 54) on this point.

[56] *Candlewood Navigation Corpn. v. Mitsui O.S.K. Lines (The Mineral Transporter)* [1986] A.C. 1.

[57] *Ante*, § 19–122.

knowledge of that contract before calling for (or receiving) performance of his own contract with A.[58] On such facts, the question arises whether C is liable to B for the tort of interference with contractual rights. That tort is subject to the defence of "justification,"[59] which is certainly available to C where he had contracted with A *before* B had done so.[60] But the defence is a flexible one,[61] and the principle on which it is based appears to be equally applicable where C's contract with A was made *after* B's but in ignorance of it. The exercise by C of rights thus acquired in good faith against A should not, it is submitted, make C liable in tort to B.[62] Even in such a situation, however, C may be liable to B under the rules stated in § 19–120 above if B's contract with A is specifically enforceable. Where the specific enforceability of this contract gives rise to an equitable interest, this can be asserted against C even though he had, when he contracted with A, only constructive notice of A's contract with B. In such a case, the tort claim would be "of no value"[63] if, as has been submitted above, it only arises where C, when he contracted with A, had actual knowledge of B's rights; but it would equally be unnecessary,[64] since B could succeed against C on the different ground that B's contract with A was specifically enforceable and therefore conferred an equitable interest on B.

Protection of "possessory rights." The possibility of such protection arises **19–127** where the contract is one under which possession of a chattel is, or is to be, transferred. The contracts in the *Strathcona* and *Port Line* cases were not of this kind: they were time charters, *i.e.* contracts under which a shipowner undertakes to render services by the use of a particular ship which remains in his possession.[65] Such charters may be contrasted with demise charters, which are contracts for the hire of a ship under which the shipowner does transfer, or undertake to transfer, possession of the ship to the charterer.[66] The nearest analogy in the land law to contracts for the hire of a chattel is a lease, and not a restrictive covenant. Hence the development of the doctrine of *Tulk v. Moxhay*, discussed in § 19–120 above, need not affect cases concerning such contracts. One reason given by Diplock J. for his decision in the *Port Line* case was that a time charterer had "no

---

[58] This was the position in *Swiss Bank Corpn. v. Lloyds Bank Ltd* [1982] A.C. 854; see [1979] Ch. 548, 568–596 and *infra*, n. 63.

[59] See *Salmond and Heuston on the Law of Torts* (21st ed.), pp. 353–355.

[60] *Smithies v. National Association of Operative Plasterers* [1909] 1 K.B. 310, 337; *Edwin Hill & Partners v. First National Finance Corp. plc* [1989] 1 W.L.R. 225, 230. Even in such a case the court may, in granting injunctive relief to C against A, require C to give undertakings to indemnify B against loss resulting from A's inability (in consequence of the injunction) to perform his contract with B: *Guiness Peat Aviation (Belgium) N.V. v. Hispania Lineas Aereas SA* [1992] 1 Lloyd's Rep. 190.

[61] *Glamorgan Coal Co. v. South Wales Miners' Federation* [1903] 2 K.B. 545, 574–575.

[62] This was admitted in *Swiss Bank Corpn. v. Lloyds Bank Ltd, supra*, n. 58: see [1979] Ch. 548, 569–573.

[63] *Swiss Bank Corpn. v. Lloyds Bank Ltd* [1982] A.C. 584, 598, where it was held, on construction, that the contract did *not* impose an obligation to use the specific property for its performance and was *not* specifically enforceable: see *post*, § 28–008, n. 27.

[64] [1982] A.C. 584, 598.

[65] *Ellerman Lines v. Lancaster Maritime Co. (The Lancaster)* [1980] 2 Lloyd's Rep. 497, 500; *Scandinavian Trading Co. A.B. v. Flota Petrolera Ecuatoriana (The Scaptrade)* [1983] A.C. 694, 702; *Hyundai Merchant Marine Co. Ltd v. Karander Maritime Co. Ltd (The Niizura)* [1996] 2 Lloyd's Rep. 66, 72.

[66] *Baumwoll Manufacturer v. Furness* [1893] A.C. 8; *The Guiseppe di Vittorio* [1998] 1 Lloyd's Rep. 136, 156.

proprietary *or possessory* rights in the ship."[67] It can be inferred that a "possessory right" might have been protected. Where the hirer of a chattel is in actual possession of it, he should certainly be protected against a third party who acquires the chattel with notice of the hirer's interest.

19–128   **Rights to future possession.** It is less clear whether, in this context, the words "possessory right" refer only to the right *of* possession or extend also to a right *to* possession, *i.e.* whether a person who has a contractual right to the *future* possession of a chattel would similarly be protected against the third party. In *The Stena Nautica (No. 2)*[68] A had demise-chartered his ship to B under a contract which also gave B an option to purchase her. Later, while A was in possession of the ship, he granted a second demise charter of her to C who had no knowledge of the earlier contract. B exercised his option to purchase and it was held that his only remedy was by way of damages against A: since B's option to purchase was not specifically enforceable,[69] B could not assert rights to the ship against C. The question whether B could assert his *right to possession as demise charterer* against C did not, strictly speaking, arise since B was suing, not to enforce that right, but rather his right as a person who had exercised an option to purchase. But it seems from the reasoning of the Court of Appeal that B's right to possession as demise charterer would have been protected only if the contract under which the right arose was one in respect of which the court was willing to make an order of specific performance.[70] The argument of commercial convenience which justified the decision in the *Port Line* case would seem to apply as much where a contract creates a right to the future possession of a chattel as where it creates the right to have some particular use made of the chattel. In each case the right is hard to discover and should not be enforced against a third party without actual knowledge of it; and adequate protection against a third party with such knowledge is provided by the rules relating to the tort of wrongful interference with contractual rights.

---

[67] [1958] 2 Q.B. 146, 166 (italics supplied).
[68] *C.N. Marine Inc. v. Stena Line A/B (The Stena Nautica) (No. 2)* [1982] 2 Lloyd's Rep. 336.
[69] *Post*, § 28–014, n. 50.
[70] *Ante*, § 19–119.

CHAPTER 20

ASSIGNMENT

1. ASSIGNMENT[1]

Assignment of choses in action: at common law. The term "things in action" or, as they are still called, choses in action, is used to describe "all personal rights of property which can only be claimed or enforced by action, and not by taking physical possession."[2] Contractual rights, being things in action as opposed to things in possession, were not assignable at common law without the consent of both contracting parties. This rule seems to have been based initially on the difficulty of conceiving of the transfer of an intangible, at any rate one of such a personal nature, and later on the desire to avoid maintenance, *viz.* officious intermeddling in litigation. It was subject to two exceptions: (1) the benefit of a contract could be assigned to or by the Crown; (2) the holder of a bill of exchange could assign it by the law merchant.[3] Further, there were certain assignments by operation of law, *e.g.* on the death or bankruptcy of a contracting party.[4] Before 1875, the only methods of assigning contractual rights at law were by novation,[5] and by procuring the debtor's acknowledgment that he held for the assignee[6]: both of these required the consent of the debtor. Powers of attorney could also be used to effect assignments, but these had considerable disadvantages, being normally revocable.[7]

20–001

---

[1] See Marshall, *The Assignment of Choses in Action* (1950); Biscoe, *Credit Factoring* (1975); Goode, *Legal Problems of Credit and Security* (2nd ed., 1988), Chap. 5; Salinger, *Factoring Law and Practice* (2nd ed., 1995). See also Starke, *Assignments of Choses in Action in Australia* (1972).

[2] *Torkington v. Magee* [1902] 2 K.B. 427, 430; revd. [1903] 1 K.B. 644.

[3] See Milnes Holden, *The History of Negotiable Instruments in English Law* (1955).

[4] See *post*, Chap. 21.

[5] *Post*, § 20–084.

[6] *Post*, § 20–087.

[7] See Marshall, *op. cit.* pp. 67–69.

20–002   **Assignment in equity.** The rule of equity, on the other hand, was to permit the assignment of contractual rights whether such rights were legal or equitable. If the rights were equitable (*e.g.* a legacy or a share in a trust fund), the assignee could sue in his own name, but it was necessary to make the assignor a party to the suit if he retained any interest in the subject-matter, for instance if the assignment was not absolute but conditional or by way of charge. If the right was a legal right, equity could compel the assignor to allow the assignee to use his name in a common law action.[8] The assignor had to be a party to such an action in order to bind him at law.

20–003   **Assignment under particular statutes.** The assignment of certain kinds of choses in action is now regulated by particular statutes. Examples are: bills of lading[9]; policies of life insurance[10]; policies of marine insurance[11]; shares in a company[12]; negotiable instruments[13]; patents[14]; and copyright.[15] Furthermore, to protect the creditors of insolvent assignors, provision has been made for the registration of certain assignments.[16]

20–004   **Statutory and equitable assignments.** General statutory provision for the assignment of choses in action was first made by section 25(6) of the Judicature Act 1873, which is now repealed and substantially re-enacted by section 136 of the Law of Property Act 1925. But an assignment which fails to comply with the statutory requirements is not necessarily invalid, for it may take effect as a perfectly good equitable assignment. "The statute does not forbid or destroy equitable assignments or impair their efficacy in the slightest degree."[17] Indeed, it appears that for the purpose of the substantive law, there is often little (if any) advantage in a statutory assignment over an equitable assignment. To a considerable extent the rules governing them are identical, *e.g.* the rules relating to the question whether a particular right is assignable,[18] to priorities between successive assignees (at any rate in most cases)[19] and to the principle that assignments are "subject to equities."[20] Sometimes, as, *e.g.* with regard to consideration, the rules may be formulated differently, but appear to be substantially identical in result.[21] And even where the rules governing statutory and equitable assignments are different, *e.g.* with regard to the necessity for writing[22] and to assignments by way of charge,[23] the distinction is usually of little importance so far as the substantive law is concerned, because the rules of equity are often wider, but never narrower, than the rules governing statutory assignments.

---

[8] *Hammond v. Messenger* (1838) 9 Sim. 327.
[9] Carriage of Goods by Sea Act 1992.
[10] Policies of Assurance Act 1867, s.1.
[11] Marine Insurance Act 1906, s.50(2).
[12] Companies Act 1985, s.182(1); Stock Transfer Act 1963.
[13] Bills of Exchange Act 1882.
[14] Patents Act 1977, ss.30, 32.
[15] Copyright Designs and Patents Act 1988, ss.90, 94.
[16] Insolvency Act 1986, s.344; Companies Act 1985, ss.395–398; *post,* §§ 20–058—20–064.
[17] *Brandt's Sons & Co. v. Dunlop Rubber Co.* [1905] A.C. 454, 462.
[18] *Post,* § 20–041.
[19] *Post,* § 20–066.
[20] *Post,* § 20–068.
[21] *Post,* §§ 20–019 and 20–027 *et seq.*
[22] *Post,* § 20–016.
[23] *Post,* § 20–012.

Difference between statutory and equitable assignments. However, there is   **20–005**
one very important procedural consequence which attaches to the distinction
between statutory and equitable assignments. A statutory assignee can sue the
debtor without joining the assignor as a party to the action,[24] whereas an
equitable assignee often cannot do this.[25] Furthermore, it must be observed that
whereas a statutory assignment passes a legal right to the assignee, an equitable
assignment passes only an equitable right. In practice, as already observed, this
usually makes little difference as a matter of substantive law to the efficacy of the
assignment; but there are some situations where the distinction can prove of
practical importance. For example, it has been held that an assignee of an option
to renew a contract for services who had not given notice of his assignment to the
other contracting party could not exercise the option: the reasoning is based on
the fact that the assignment was equitable only.[26]

(a) *Statutory Assignments*

Law of Property Act 1925, s.136. This section provides as follows: **20–006**

(1) Any absolute assignment by writing under the hand of the assignor[27] (not
purporting to be by way of charge only) of any debt or other legal thing in action, of
which express notice in writing has been given to the debtor, trustee or other person
from whom the assignor would have been entitled to claim such debt or thing in action,
is effectual in law (subject to equities having priority over the right of the assignee) to
pass and transfer from the date of such notice—

   (*a*) the legal right to such debt or thing in action;
   (*b*) all legal and other remedies for the same; and
   (*c*) the power to give a good discharge for the same without the concurrence of the
   assignor:

Provided that, if the debtor, trustee or other person liable in respect of such debt or
thing in action has notice—

   (*a*) that the assignment is disputed by the assignor or any person claiming under him;
   or
   (*b*) of any other opposing or conflicting claims to such debt or thing in action;

he may, if he thinks fit, either call upon the persons making claim thereto to interplead
concerning the same, or pay the debt or other thing in action into court under the
provisions of the Trustee Act 1925.

---

[24] *Post*, § 20–006.
[25] *Post*, §§ 20–037—20–040.
[26] *Warner Bros. Records Inc. v. Rollgreen Investments Ltd* [1976] Q.B. 430 (see Kloss (1975) 39
Conv.(N.S.) 261). But the authority of the case is somewhat distorted by the formulation of the
question to which the Court of Appeal gave an answer, and some of the dicta may go further than was
necessary for the decision of the case, which should perhaps be regarded as authority only upon the
equitable assignment of options; *quaere* whether the result would have been the same had the
assignment been oral, and so still equitable, but the assignee *had* given notice (even in the same
letter). Note also that some aspects of the reasoning in this case were disapproved by a majority of
the Court of Appeal (Peter Gibson L.J., with whom Waite L.J. agreed) in *Three Rivers D.C. v. Bank
of England* [1996] Q.B. 292.
[27] In view of the specific references to signature by an agent in ss.40 and 53 of the same Act, it
would seem that signature by an agent is here insufficient, at any rate if he signs his own name: see
Wilson v. Wallani (1880) 5 Ex.D. 155; but *cf. Re Diptford Parish Lands* [1934] Ch. 151; Partnership
Act 1890, s.6. See also *Bowstead & Reynolds on Agency* (16th ed., 1996), Art. 6.

(2) This section does not affect the provisions of the Policies of Assurance Act 1867.[28]

20–007   It will be seen that, in order that the section may apply, three conditions must be fulfilled:

(1) the assignment must be absolute and not purport to be by way of charge only;

(2) it must be in writing under the hand of the assignor;

(3) express notice in writing thereof must be given to the debtor or trustee.

The general effect of the section is to allow the assignee to sue the debtor in his own name instead of, as previously, having to sue in the name of the assignor and perhaps having to go to a court of equity to compel his joinder in the action. The section "is merely machinery: . . . it enables an action to be brought by the assignee in his own name in cases where previously he would have sued in the assignor's name, but only where he could so sue."[29]

20–008   **"Debt or other legal thing in action."** The phrase has been held to include the benefit of a contract for the sale of a reversionary interest,[30] and rights to claim indefinite sums of money, as for compensation under statute for the injurious affecting of land by a railway,[31] or for damages for loss in respect of which the assignee was the assignor's insurer.[32] A debt arising out of an existing contract, but payable at a future time, is capable of assignment under section 136.[33] Examples are future instalments of rent, future instalments of money due under an instalment contract, retention moneys under a building contract, future instalments of salary. A future chose in action in the strict sense is incapable of actual assignment, though it may be the subject of an agreement to assign, which will operate in equity in very much the same way as an actual assignment.[34]

20–009   In *Stein v. Blake*[35] it was held by the House of Lords that, if A and B have mutual claims against each other and A becomes bankrupt, the effect of section 323 of the Insolvency Act 1986 is that the debt due to A ceases, on A's bankruptcy, to exist as a chose in action and is replaced by a new chose in action,

---

[28] This Act makes provision for the assignment of life insurance policies. See Vol. II, Chap. 41.

[29] *Torkington v. Magee* [1902] 2 K.B. 427, 435; revd. [1903] 1 K.B. 644.

[30] *Torkington v. Magee, supra.*

[31] *Dawson v. G.N. & City Ry.* [1905] 1 K.B. 260.

[32] *King v. Victoria Insurance Co. Ltd* [1896] A.C. 250; *Compania Colombiana de Seguros v. Pacific S.N. Co.* [1965] 1 Q.B. 101. See also *Re Battle's Feed Mill Ltd* (1975) 59 D.L.R. (3d) 488 (bankruptcy dividend).

[33] *Brice v. Bannister* (1878) 3 Q.B.D. 569 (though the assignment in this case seems to have been treated as equitable); *Buck v. Robson* (1878) 3 Q.B.D. 686; *Walker v. Bradford Old Bank* (1884) 12 Q.B.D. 511; *Jones v. Humphreys* [1902] 1 K.B. 10; *G. & T. Earle Ltd v. Hemsworth R.D.C.* (1928) 44 T.L.R. 605, 758. Contrast *Law v. Coburn* [1972] 1 W.L.R. 1238. See further, *post*, § 20–028.

[34] *Post*, §§ 20–031—20–032.

[35] [1996] A.C. 243.

namely the claim to the net balance owing.[36] Their Lordships went on to decide that, like any other chose in action, that right to the net balance (if any) can be assigned by the trustee in bankruptcy before it has been ascertained by the taking of an account between the trustee and B.

In *Investors Compensation Scheme Ltd v. West Bromwich Building Society*,[37] **20–010** the House of Lords clarified that a right to rescind a mortgage is not a chose in action or part of a chose in action and an owner cannot therefore assign a right to rescission separately from his property. On the other hand, a right to damages is a chose in action which can be assigned. It followed that there was no objection to a clause in the Investors Compensation Scheme claim form by which investors assigned a right to damages against a building society to the Investors Compensation Scheme Ltd but which did not assign (because legally impossible) a right to rescission of the investors' mortgages with the building society.

It might at first sight have been supposed that the expression "debt or other **20–011** *legal* thing in action" was confined to legal choses in action; but the reference to a "trustee" militates against this and there is authority that the phrase includes equitable choses, or, as they are sometimes called, choses in equity.[38] The point seems, however, to be of no importance, for the principal effect of the section is to enable an assignee of a *legal* chose in action to sue alone in certain cases where he could not otherwise do so; the section seems to make no difference to the assignee of an equitable chose in action who can probably sue alone under the Act only in circumstances where he could do so in equity.[39]

"Absolute . . . and not by way of charge." The assignment must be absolute **20–012** and not purport to be by way of charge only. An assignment by way of mortgage may, however, be absolute within the meaning of the section, if there is an express[40] or implied[41] proviso for reassignment on repayment of the loan: for the reassignment would involve fresh notice to the debtor, who would thus be in no doubt as to whom he ought to pay the debt.[42] An assignment of all moneys due or to become due from the debtor, which was expressed to be by way of continuing security for all moneys due from the assignor to the assignee, has been held to be absolute.[43] On the other hand, where the assignor charged a sum which would become due to him from the debtor as security for advances made to him by the assignee, and assigned his interest in that sum until the advances were repaid to the assignee with interest, this was held to be by way of charge and not within the section.[44] The fact that the assignment is expressed to be by way

---

[36] The reasoning on this in *Farley v. Housing and Commercial Developments Ltd* [1984] B.C.L.C. 442 was approved.

[37] [1998] 1 W.L.R. 896.

[38] *Torkington v. Magee* [1902] 2 K.B. 427, 430–431; revd. [1903] 1 K.B. 644; *cf. King v. Victoria Insurance Co.* [1896] A.C. 250, 254; *Manchester Brewery v. Coombs* [1901] 2 Ch. 608, 619; *Re Pain* [1919] 1 Ch. 38, 44–45.

[39] *i.e.* where the assignment is absolute: *post*, § 20–040.

[40] *Tancred v. Delagoa Bay Co.* (1889) 23 Q.B.D. 239.

[41] *Durham Brothers v. Robertson* [1898] 1 Q.B. 765, 772.

[42] *ibid.*

[43] *Hughes v. Pump House Hotel Co.* [1902] 2 K.B. 190.

[44] *Durham Brothers v. Robertson, supra.*

of security for a loan does not by itself prevent it from being absolute,[45] though combined with other factors such expressions may have this effect.[46] Thus, a provision that the assignor was entitled to exercise all its rights over the property until in default under the loan agreement has prevented an assignment from being absolute.[47] The test seems to be, has the assignor unconditionally transferred to the assignee for the time being the sole right to the debt in question *as against the debtor*? If so, the assignment will be absolute; but if the debtor cannot tell whether to pay the assignor or the assignee without examining the state of accounts between them, it will be held to be by way of charge only. Much may depend on the language of the particular instrument; in construing it, the court will look at the whole of its language. The words italicised above are of crucial importance, for it is no concern of the debtor whether the assignor and assignee have some private arrangement for the disposal of the debt after it has been paid by the debtor. Thus the fact that the assignee is to hold the proceeds of the debt,[48] or the surplus proceeds beyond a stated amount,[49] on trust for the assignor does not prevent the assignment from being absolute.

20–013   **Absolute and conditional assignments.** Some cases distinguish between absolute and conditional assignments.[50] To conditional assignments similar criteria will be applied: if the assignor retains, by virtue of the condition, some interest in the debt, it is desirable that he be joined in proceedings regarding it, and the assignment is not absolute.

20–014   **Part of a debt.** An assignment of an unascertained part of a debt, *e.g.* of "so much of my salary" as amounts to a fixed sum and "any further sums in which I may hereafter become indebted to you," is not an absolute assignment.[51] And it is settled, though there were formerly doubts,[52] that an assignment of a definite part of a debt is not within the section.[53] This is because it would increase the burden on the debtor if the creditor were allowed to split up the debt into as many separate causes of action as he thought fit[54]; and also because conflicting decisions might result if the existence or amount of the debt was in dispute.[55] It

---

[45] *Hughes v. Pump House Hotel Co., supra.* See also *Care Shipping Corp. v. Latin American Shipping Corp.* [1983] Q.B. 1005, 1016.

[46] *Mercantile Bank of London Ltd v. Evans* [1899] 2 Q.B. 613.

[47] *The Halcyon the Great* [1984] 1 Lloyd's Rep. 283. See similarly *The Balder London* [1980] 2 Lloyd's Rep. 489.

[48] *Comfort v. Betts* [1891] 1 Q.B. 737; *Fitzroy v. Cave* [1905] 2 K.B. 364.

[49] *Burlinson v. Hall* (1884) 12 Q.B.D. 347; *Bank of Liverpool and Martins Ltd v. Holland* (1926) 43 T.L.R. 29.

[50] *e.g. Durham Brothers v. Robertson* [1898] 1 Q.B. 765, 773; *Grey v. Australian Motorists & General Insurance Co. Pty. Ltd* [1976] 1 N.S.W.L.R. 669. *cf. The Balder London* [1980] 2 Lloyd's Rep. 489, in which Mocatta J. spoke of the assignment being put "in suspense."

[51] *Jones v. Humphreys* [1902] 1 K.B. 10.

[52] See *Brice v. Bannister* (1878) 3 Q.B.D. 569; but the point was not argued, and in the Court of Appeal the assignment seems to have been treated as equitable. See also *Skipper v. Holloway* [1910] 2 K.B. 630.

[53] *Forster v. Baker* [1910] 2 K.B. 636; *Conlan v. Carlow County Council* [1912] 2 I.R. 535; *Re Steel Wing Co.* [1921] 1 Ch. 349; *G. & T. Earle Ltd v. Hemsworth R.D.C.* (1928) 44 T.L.R. 605, 758; *Williams v. Atlantic Assurance Co.* [1933] 1 K.B. 81, 100; *Walter and Sullivan Ltd v. Murphy & Sons Ltd* [1955] 2 Q.B. 584.

[54] *Durham Brothers v. Robertson* [1898] 1 Q.B. 765, 774.

[55] *Re Steel Wing Co.* [1921] 1 Ch. 349, 357.

will be seen that neither of these reasons holds good if the assignor and the assignees are all made parties to the action: and it must be remembered that an assignment which is not within the section because it is not absolute may nevertheless be a valid equitable assignment. The result is that if part of a debt is assigned, the assignee cannot sue for that part without joining the assignor, nor can the assignor sue for the balance without joining the assignee.[56]

Written assignment. The assignment must be in writing under the hand of the assignor. No particular form is however necessary: the writing can be quite informal.[57] A direction in writing by a creditor to his debtor to pay the assignee, handed to the assignee, may amount to an assignment,[58] but such a direction handed to the *debtor* will not by itself constitute an assignment unless there is evidence that the assignee has requested or consented to it[59]; and even if he has, the direction may constitute no more than authority to pay, and gives the assignee no rights. Thus the drawing of a cheque in favour of a third party does not constitute a statutory assignment of a bank balance or part of it.[60]   20–015

Written notice to the debtor. Under the statute notice in writing to the debtor is necessary. It is "wrong to suppose that a separate document purposely prepared as a notice, and described as such, is necessary in order to satisfy the statute. The statute only requires that information relative to the assignment shall be conveyed to the debtor, and that it shall be conveyed in writing."[61] Thus a written demand for payment sent by the assignee to the debtor has been held sufficient.[62] Beyond this, however, the statute has been strictly construed, and it has been held that the notice must be unconditional,[63] and that written notice must be given, even though the debtor cannot read.[64] So also it is essential that the notice be given to the debtor himself: thus, where an insured assigned the proceeds of a policy and notice was given to the broker through whom the proceeds were collected, it was held that the notice was insufficient.[65] The notice is apparently   20–016

---

[56] *Walter and Sullivan Ltd v. Murphy & Sons Ltd* [1955] 2 Q.B. 584.

[57] *Re Westerton* [1919] 2 Ch. 104; *The Kelo* [1985] 2 Lloyd's Rep. 85, 89.

[58] *Brice v. Bannister* (1878) 3 Q.B.D. 569; *Harding v. Harding* (1886) 17 Q.B.D. 442; *Grey v. Australian Motorists & General Insurance Co. Pty. Ltd* [1976] 1 N.S.W.L.R. 669.

[59] *Curran v. Newpark Cinemas Ltd* [1951] 1 All E.R. 295. *cf. post*, § 20–020; *Grey v. Australian Motorists and General Insurance Co. Pty. Ltd, supra.*

[60] *Schroeder v. Central Bank of London Ltd* (1876) 34 L.T. 735, 736; Bills of Exchange Act 1882, s.53(1). *cf. post*, § 20–020. For the different position in Scotland see s.53(2); *Williams v. Williams*, 1980 S.L.T. 25.

[61] *Van Lynn Developments Ltd v. Pelias Construction Co. Ltd* [1969] 1 Q.B. 607, 615. See also *Denney, Gasquet and Metcalfe v. Conklin* [1913] 3 K.B. 177. *cf. James Talcott Ltd v. John Lewis & Co. Ltd* [1940] 3 All E.R. 592 (equitable assignment); see also *Herkules Piling Ltd v. Tilbury Construction Ltd* (1992) 61 Build L.R. 107 (the disclosure to the debtor of a document of assignment on discovery in an action by the assignor held to be insufficient notice for a legal or equitable assignment).

[62] *Van Lynn Developments Ltd v. Pelias Construction Co. Ltd, supra.* But *cf. Warner Bros. Records Inc. v. Rollgreen Investments Ltd* [1976] Q.B. 430 (exercise of option).

[63] *The Balder London* [1980] 2 Lloyd's Rep. 489, 495.

[64] *Hockley and Papworth v. Goldstein* (1920) 90 L.J.K.B. 111.

[65] *Amalgamated General Finance Co. Ltd v. C.E. Golding & Co. Ltd* [1964] 2 Lloyd's Rep. 163; *Magee v. U.D.C. Finance Ltd* [1983] N.Z.L.R. 438. But *cf.* the position of an equitable assignment, *post*, § 20–020, n. 84.

invalid if it purports to identify the assignment by giving its date and that date is a wrong date[66]; though there is nothing in the section which requires the assignment to be dated at all, and it has been held that a notice is valid though it wrongly states that another notice has already been given.[67] On the other hand, the statute does not prescribe any limit of time within which notice must be given,[68] nor does it lay down that the notice must be given by any particular person.[69] It may consequently be given after the death of either the assignor or the assignee.[70] Notice must be given before the assignee issues his writ,[71] though failure to do this will not prevent the assignee from proceeding with his action on the footing that he is an equitable assignee. In this event, however, the court may require the assignor to be made a party to the proceedings.[72]

20–017 "The date of such notice" in the section means the date when it is received by or on behalf of the debtor, at any rate where the issue arises between assignee and debtor.[73] A debtor with notice of an absolute assignment is entitled, and indeed bound, to treat the debt as transferred to the assignee. Payment by the debtor to the assignor will therefore not give him a good discharge, and he will remain liable to pay the debt again to the assignee.[74] If notice is given late, equities which may come into existence prior thereto may be let in, *e.g.* the assignee must give credit for any payments made to the assignor by the debtor while the latter was in ignorance of the assignment. If there are more assignees than one, their priority is determined according to the dates on which they gave notice to the debtor.[75] It has been held that if the debtor pays his debt by cheque, he may disregard a subsequent notice that the debt has been assigned: he is under no duty to stop the cheque.[76]

20–018 Since a creditor can assign by directing his debtor to pay the assignee it seems that a single written document could suffice to constitute both the assignment itself and the notice required by the section.[77]

---

[66] *Stanley v. English Fibres Industries Ltd* (1899) 68 L.J.Q.B. 839; *W. F. Harrison & Co. Ltd v. Burke* [1956] 1 W.L.R. 419; criticised in (1956) 72 L.Q.R. 321 and explained in *Van Lynn Developments Ltd v. Pelias Construction Co. Ltd, supra,* at 612. The *Harrison* case contains (at 421) a suggestion that a misstatement of the amount of the debt might also vitiate the notice.

[67] *Van Lynn Developments Ltd v. Pelias Construction Ltd, supra; Grey v. Australian Motorists & General Insurance Co. Pty. Ltd* [1976] 1 N.S.W.L.R. 669 (date referred to but no date inserted).

[68] There appears to be no authority on the question of whether notice can be given before the assignment takes place.

[69] *Bateman v. Hunt* [1904] 2 K.B. 530, 538.

[70] *Walker v. Bradford Old Bank* (1884) 12 Q.B.D. 511; *Bateman v. Hunt, supra; Re Westerton* [1919] 2 Ch. 104.

[71] *Compania Colombiana de Seguros v. Pacific Steam Navigation Co.* [1965] 1 Q.B. 101, 128–129.

[72] *Post,* §§ 20–037—20–040.

[73] *Holt v. Heatherfield Trust Ltd* [1942] 2 K.B. 1. *Quaere* as to the position between successive assignees: see Treitel, *The Law of Contract* (9th ed., 1995), p. 599.

[74] *Jones v. Farrell* (1857) 1 D & J 208; *Brice v. Bannister* (1878) 3 Q.B.D. 569; Law of Property Act 1925, s.136; *The Halcyon the Great* [1984] 1 Lloyd's Rep. 283, 289. The debtor could prima facie recover the money paid to the assignor if paid under a mistake; *post,* § 30–026—30–047.

[75] *Post,* § 20–066.

[76] *Bence v. Shearman* [1898] 2 Ch. 582.

[77] See *Curran v. Newpark Cinemas Ltd, supra; Cossill v. Strangman* [1963] N.S.W.R. 1695.

Consideration. Consideration is not required for a statutory assignment.[78] **20–019**

(b) *Equitable Assignments*

Essential requirements of equitable assignment. As has been seen above, **20–020** an assignment cannot be effective under the statute unless written notice is given to the debtor, but an assignment may be perfectly valid in equity without any such notice.[79] Notice is, however, obviously desirable, since, as in the case of statutory assignments, until he receives it the debtor is entitled to treat the assignor as his creditor and to discharge his debt by payment to him[80]; the giving of notice may prevent further equities attaching to the debt[81]; and may affect priorities.[82] From the debtor's perspective it seems that, if the debtor ignores a notice and pays the assignor, he is not discharged[83]: unless the debtor can secure the agreement of the assignor and assignee as to the amounts of their respective interests, it would certainly be unsafe for him to settle alone with either, the only safe course being to interplead. Where the assignment concerns a transaction in which an agent, such as a solicitor, was engaged on behalf of the debtor, notice to the agent will constitute notice to the debtor.[84]

Means of assignment. An assignor can assign a contractual right in equity in **20–021** one of two ways. He can inform the assignee that he transfers the chose to him[85]; or he can instruct the debtor to discharge the obligation by payment to, or performance for, the assignee.[86] Thus an agreement by merchants with a bank that payment for goods sold by the merchants should be remitted direct by the purchasers to the bank has been held to constitute a valid equitable assignment of the amounts to the bank.[87]

---

[78] *Harding v. Harding* (1886) 17 Q.B.D. 442; *Re Westerton* [1919] 2 Ch. 104; *Holt v. Heatherfield Trust Ltd* [1942] 2 K.B. 1, 5.

[79] *Gorringe v. Irwell India Rubber Works* (1886) 34 Ch.D. 128; *Re Patrick* [1891] 1 Ch. 82, 87; *Re Westerton* [1919] 2 Ch. 104; *Re City Life Assurance Co. (Stephenson's Case)* [1926] Ch. 191; *Re Trytel* [1952] 2 T.L.R. 32; *Weddell v. J. A. Pearce* [1988] Ch. 26. But as to options see *Warner Bros. Records Inc. v. Rollgreen Investments Ltd* [1976] 2 Q.B. 430, *ante*, § 20–005.

[80] *Stocks v. Dobson* (1853) 4 De G.M. & G. 11.

[81] *Post*, § 20–068.

[82] *Post*, § 20–066.

[83] *Jones v. Farrell* (1857) 1 D. & J. 208; *Brice v. Bannister* (1878) 3 Q.B.D. 569; *Deposit Protection Board v. Dalia* [1994] 2 A.C. 367, CA (Simon Brown L.J. dissented, reasoning, with respect incorrectly, that even after notice the debtor remains liable to the equitable assignor: the question did not arise in the House of Lords, [1994] 2 A.C. 391, which reversed the decision of the Court of Appeal in holding that, as a matter of statutory interpretation, only the original deposit maker, and not an assignee, was a "depositor" entitled to protection under s.58 of the Banking Act 1987); Treitel, *The Law of Contract* (9th ed., 1995), p. 598. See also *ante* § 20–017, n. 74.

[84] *Magee v. U.D.C. Finance Ltd* [1983] N.Z.L.R. 438.

[85] In *Kijowski v. New Capital Properties Ltd* (1990) 15 Con.L.R. 1 this method of assignment was held not to be made out by an answer to enquires before contract.

[86] These are ways of effecting a transfer. It is sometimes said that an assignment can also be effected by the assignor declaring himself trustee of the chose in action. It is not, however, clear that this should in all ways be equated with a transfer; and the effect of the rule in *Milroy v. Lord* (1862) 4 De G.F. & J. 264, that equity will not perfect an imperfect gift, is that the implication of such a trust will be rare. See, however, *G.E. Crane Sales Pty. Ltd v. Commissioner of Taxation* (1971) 126 C.L.R. 177 (factoring arrangement); *Re Turcan* (1888) 40 Ch.D. 5.

[87] *Brandt's Sons & Co. v. Dunlop Rubber Co.* [1905] A.C. 454. See further cases cited at § 20–033, *post*.

20-022   **Assignment or mandate.** On the other hand, a mere direction by a creditor to his debtor to pay money to a third person is not necessarily an assignment, for such a direction may be nothing more than a revocable mandate to the debtor.[88] So, where a person who was overdrawn at his bank directed his debtor to pay sums due to him directly to the credit of his account at the bank, this was held not to be an assignment, but a mere revocable mandate.[89] Where similar instructions were given in another case, but were expressly declared to be irrevocable save with the consent of the bank, it was held that an assignment had been made,[90] but it has also been held in connection with statutory assignment that even an express provision of this nature did not make the instructions irrevocable unless the assignee had prior or subsequent knowledge of them.[91]

20-023   **Known to assignee.** Where an assignment is made by instructions to the debtor it is not clear whether it can have any effect at all before the assignee knows of the instructions and therefore has a chance to accept or decline the assignment. The cases cited above establish that the assignment is not effective as against the creditors of the assignor before the assignee knows of it, so that a creditor who serves a garnishee order on the assignor before the assignee gets to know of the purported assignment will have priority over the assignee.[92] It may be that such an assignment would be valid as against the assignor himself even before the assignee knows of the instructions to the debtor.[93] It has been held that an assignment made by letter is complete as soon as the letter is posted to the assignee,[94] but the proposition seems doubtful unless postal communication was in some way authorised or anticipated, as in the rules regarding the acceptance of contractual offers.[95]

20-024   **Bill of exchange or cheque.** As in the case of statutory assignments, a bill of exchange or cheque drawn on a banker or other fund holder is not an assignment of the amount for which the bill or cheque is drawn even if it is drawn for the precise amount of the debt due to the drawer.[96]

---

[88] *Percival v. Dunn* (1885) 29 Ch.D. 128; *Re Gunsbourg* (1919) 88 L.J.K.B. 479; *Re Williams* [1917] 1 Ch. 1; *Rekstin v. Severo, etc., and Bank for Russian Trade* [1933] 1 K.B. 47; *James Talcott Ltd v. John Lewis & Co. Ltd* [1940] 3 All E.R. 592; *Curran v. Newpark Cinemas Ltd* [1951] 1 All E.R. 295; *Re Danish Bacon Co. Ltd Staff Pension Fund Trusts* [1971] 1 W.L.R. 248.

[89] *Bell v. London and North Western Ry.* (1852) 15 Beav. 548; *Ex p. Hall* (1878) 10 Ch.D. 615.

[90] *Re Kent and Sussex Sawmills Ltd* [1947] Ch. 177. See also *British Eagle International Airlines Ltd v. Cie Nationale Air France* [1973] 1 Lloyd's Rep. 414, 427; affd. [1974] 1 Lloyd's Rep. 429.

[91] *Curran v. Newpark Cinemas Ltd* [1951] 1 All E.R. 295. See also *Coulls v. Bagot's Executor and Trustee Co. Ltd* (1967) 119 C.L.R. 460, where some members of the High Court of Australia appear to have treated a direction as a revocable mandate even though it was intended to be irrevocable, and the payee knew of it.

[92] *Curran v. Newpark Cinemas Ltd, supra*; see also *Rekstin v. Severo, etc., supra*; *Re Hamilton* (1921) 124 L.T. 737.

[93] *cf. Standing v. Bowring* (1885) 31 Ch.D. 282. An assignment made by declaration of trust probably requires no notice: see *Middleton v. Pollock* (1876) 2 Ch.D. 104.

[94] *Alexander v. Steinhardt, Walker & Co.* [1903] 2 K.B. 208; *sed quaere* as the debt had arguably not yet arisen.

[95] *Timpson's Executors v. Yerbury* [1936] 1 K.B. 645, 657.

[96] *Shand v. Du Boisson* (1874) L.R. 18 Eq. 283; *Hopkinson v. Forster* (1874) L.R. 19 Eq. 74; *Brown, Shipley & Co. v. Kough* (1885) 29 Ch.D. 848; Bills of Exchange Act 1882, s.53(1); *cf. ante*, § 20-015.

Formalities for equitable assignments. An equitable assignment of a legal   **20–025**
chose in action need not be in writing, nor in any particular form.[97] On the other
hand, an equitable assignment of an equitable chose in action must be in writing[98]
if it is caught by section 53(1)(c) of the Law of Property Act 1925, which
provides: "A disposition of an equitable interest or trust subsisting at the time of
the disposition must be in writing signed by the person disposing of the same, or
by his agent thereunto lawfully authorised in writing or by will."[99] It has been
held that the word "disposition" in this paragraph must be given a wide meaning,
and that it is apt to cover a direction by the holder of an equitable interest to the
trustee to hold the property on trust for a third party, whether or not this is strictly
an assignment of the equitable interest.[1] A fortiori a direct assignment should do
the same. The paragraph does not prevent the holder of a beneficial interest in a
trust fund from himself making an oral declaration of trust, and so constituting
himself trustee of his own beneficial interest, for this is neither an assignment nor
a "disposition" of his own interest.[2] Nor (it seems) does the provision apply
where a person assigns the legal title to a chose in action together with an option
to acquire the beneficial interest, and the transferee subsequently exercises this
option orally. For in this case the beneficial interest passes not by virtue of any
assignment or disposition to the transferor, but by virtue of the exercise of the
option.[3]

Disposition of legal and equitable interests. Nor again does the paragraph   **20–026**
apply where a person disposes of the entire interest, both legal and equitable, in
a chose in action, for if it did, writing would be required in every case where a
legal chose in action is assigned, unless the legal title were transferred without

---

[97] *Brandt's Sons & Co. v. Dunlop Rubber Co.* [1905] A.C. 454, 462; *Re Wale* [1956] 1 W.L.R.
1346, 1350; *Kijowski v. New Capital Properties Ltd* (1990) 15 Con.L.R. 1, 8. See, *e.g. Re Westerton*
[1919] 2 Ch. 104 (bank deposit receipt); *Cotton v. Heyl* [1930] 1 Ch. 510 (proprietary interest in
invention); *Re Wheeler* [1938] Ch. 725 (money due under building contract); *Thomas v. Harris*
[1947] 1 All E.R. 444 (insurance policy); *Re Tout & Finch Ltd* [1954] 1 W.L.R. 178 (retention money
under building contract); *Letts v. I.R.C.* [1957] 1 W.L.R. 201 (shares); *cf. Re Williams* [1917] 1 Ch.
1 (insurance policy); *James Talcott Ltd v. John Lewis & Co. Ltd* [1940] 3 All E.R. 592 (invoice);
Spellman v. Spellman [1961] 1 W.L.R. 921 (hire-purchase agreement); *E. Pfeiffer Weinkellerei-
Weineinkauf GmbH v. Arbuthnot Factors Ltd* [1988] 1 W.L.R. 150 (reservation of title clause);
Colonial Mutual General Insurance Co. Ltd v. A.N.Z. Banking Group (New Zealand) Ltd [1995] 1
W.L.R. 1140, PC (insurance policy). On the question of whether the requirement of writing in the
Copyright, Designs and Patents Act 1988, s.90(3) applies to an oral contract for the transmission of
a legal interest in copyright, see *Western Front Ltd v. Vestron Inc.* [1987] F.S.R. 66, 76–78. But *cf.
post*, § 20–035.
[98] Perhaps because of the difference in wording with s.53(1)(b), which requires trusts of land to be
manifested and proved by writing, it appears always to have been assumed that an oral disposition is
void and not merely unenforceable.
[99] *Quaere* whether an equitable chose in action is necessarily an "equitable interest or trust." By
s.53(2) it is expressly provided that the section does not affect the creation or operation of resulting,
implied or constructive trusts, and in *Neville v. Wilson* [1997] Ch. 144 the Court of Appeal held that
an oral agreement to assign an equitable interest in shares constituted the promisor an implied or
constructive trustee for the promisee, so that the requirement for writing contained in s.53(1)(c) was
dispensed with by s.53(2). See further Hanbury and Martin, *Modern Equity* (15th ed., 1997),
pp. 75–89.
[1] *Grey v. I.R.C.* [1960] A.C. 1.
[2] *Grey v. I.R.C.* [1958] Ch. 690, 719; affd. [1960] A.C. 1. Perhaps this should be regarded as a
"sub-trust": see (1958) 74 L.Q.R. 180, 182. But see Pettit, *Equity and the Law of Trusts* (8th ed.,
1997), p. 82; [1960] A.C. at 16; *ante*, § 20–021, n. 86.
[3] This seems to follow from *William Cory & Son Ltd v. I.R.C.* [1965] A.C. 1088 though strictly
speaking the decision is not inconsistent with the possibility that the exercise of the option to purchase
in that case was invalidated by s.53(1)(c).

the beneficial interest.[4] So where the holder of the beneficial interest in some shares held on trust absolutely for him directed the trustees to transfer the legal title to the shares to a transferee with the intention that the transferee should also obtain the full beneficial interest, this was held not to be a disposition requiring writing under section 53(1)(c).[5]

20–027   **Consideration needed for agreements to assign.** The extent to which consideration is required for an equitable assignment is one of some difficulty.[6] It should first be observed that the question can only arise as between an assignor (or his successors in title) and assignee. So far as the debtor is concerned, the presence or absence of consideration appears to be immaterial. He cannot refuse to pay the assignee merely on the ground that there was no consideration for the assignment,[7] and, conversely, if he does pay the assignee after due notice has been given to him, it seems clear that the assignor cannot make him pay again. As between the assignor and the assignee the position broadly appears to be that consideration is required for an agreement to assign a chose in action, but is not required for an actual assignment of a chose in action.[8] Since a future chose in action is incapable of assignment in the strict sense, it follows that a purported assignment of a future chose can only operate as an agreement to assign, and as such requires consideration. There is no doubt however that dicta can be produced which suggest that consideration is always required.[9]

20–028   **Distinction between existing and future choses in action.** The distinction between an existing chose in action which is capable of immediate assignment, and a future chose in action which is only capable of being the subject of an agreement to assign, is one of difficulty. On the one hand, it is clear that a mere expectancy, not based on any existing legal right, can be nothing more than a future chose in action, and cannot, therefore, be transferred without consideration. Thus there cannot be an actual assignment of property which the assignor hopes to inherit from a person still alive at the date of the assignment[10] or of sums which the assignor hopes to receive under a contract not yet made.[11] On the other hand, sums which are certain to become payable in the future under an existing contract or other legal obligation are not treated for this purpose as future choses in action, but as existing choses in action. So, for instance, a loan repayable at a

---

[4] *Vandervell v. I.R.C.* [1967] 2 A.C. 291. See also *Re Vandervell's Trusts (No. 2)* [1974] Ch. 269; Harris (1974) 38 M.L.R. 557.

[5] *Vandervell v. I.R.C.*, *supra*. See also *Re Danish Bacon Co. Ltd Staff Pension Fund Trusts* [1972] 1 W.L.R. 248.

[6] See Megarry (1943) 59 L.Q.R. 58; Hollond (1943) 59 L.Q.R. 129; Marshall, *The Assignment of Choses in Action* (1950), Chap. 4; Sheridan (1955) 33 Can. Bar Rev. 284; Hall [1959] C.L.J. 99. See *post*, §§ 20–028—20–034.

[7] *Walker v. Bradford Old Bank* (1884) 12 Q.B.D. 511; *cf. Harding v. Harding* (1886) 17 Q.B.D. 442, but in this case the point was not taken, and in any event consideration was held to be unnecessary.

[8] *Post*, §§ 20–028—20–034.

[9] *e.g.* "For every equitable assignment . . . there must be consideration. If there be no consideration, there can be no equitable assignment": *Glegg v. Bromley* [1912] 3 K.B. 474, 491.

[10] *Meek v. Kettlewell* (1843) 1 Ph. 342; *Re Tilt* (1896) 74 L.T. 163; *Re Ellenborough* [1903] 1 Ch. 697; *cf. Kekewich v. Manning* (1851) 1 De G.M. & G. 176; Hanbury and Martin, *Modern Equity* (15th ed., 1997), pp. 133–135.

[11] *E. Pfeiffer Weinkellerei-Weineinkauf GmbH & Co. v. Arbuthnot Factors Ltd* [1988] 1 W.L.R. 150, 161.

fixed future date, or rent payable in the future under an existing lease, is an existing chose in action, and is capable of actual assignment without consideration. So also the right to be paid sums in the future under an existing contract is an existing chose in action even though the precise amounts which will become payable are as yet unascertained, *e.g.* royalties payable under a patent licensing agreement already made.[12]

The most difficult cases concern those in which there is an existing legal   **20–029** obligation, by way of contract or otherwise, but it is uncertain whether anything will become due under it in the future, either because the obligation is conditional or because it may be terminated. On the one hand, it has been held that sums payable to a builder under an existing contract are an existing chose in action, even though the sums may never become payable if the builder fails to perform the contract.[13] It has even been held that an assignment by a person of sums which will be standing to his credit at his bank at his death is an assignment of an existing chose in action, and therefore needs no consideration, since it is a sum which will become payable under the existing contract between the assignor and his bank.[14] On the other hand, in *Norman v. Federal Commissioner of Taxation*,[15] it was held by a majority of the Australian High Court that interest payable in the future on an existing loan was a mere expectancy, because the loan (not being made for a fixed period) might have been repaid before the interest became due.[16] It was also held (unanimously) in the same case that dividends which may become due in the future on shares already held in a company also constitute nothing more than an expectancy, and cannot therefore be assigned without consideration.

Proceeds of existing obligation uncertain. It is also to be noted that even   **20–030** where there is an existing chose in action which is capable of actual assignment, the *proceeds* of that chose in action may constitute only an expectancy, assignment of which requires consideration. So in *Glegg v. Bromley*,[17] where the proceeds of an action for defamation being brought by the assignor were "assigned" by her, it was assumed that this was a mere expectancy incapable of actual assignment. Again, in a New Zealand case[18] it was held that a purported assignment of "the first £500 of the net income which shall accrue to the assignor" from a certain trust fund in which he had a life interest was nothing more than an agreement to assign an expectancy and required consideration even though the assignment was under seal. Although the assignor's life interest was undoubtedly an existing chose in action and could have itself been assigned without consideration, the assignor had not in fact purported to assign the whole

---

[12] *Shepherd v. Federal Commissioner of Taxation* (1965) 113 C.L.R. 385.

[13] *Hughes v. Pump House Hotel Co. Ltd* [1902] 2 K.B. 190.

[14] *Walker v. Bradford Old Bank* (1884) 12 Q.B.D. 511.

[15] (1963) 109 C.L.R. 9. This case contains lengthy discussion of the principles relating to voluntary assignment of future property. There are many Australian cases on assignment: see Starke, *Assignments of Choses in Action in Australia* (1972).

[16] This is the explanation of the case given by the High Court itself in *Shepherd v. Federal Commissioner of Taxation, supra.*

[17] [1912] 3 K.B. 474.

[18] *Williams v. Commissioner of Inland Revenue* [1965] N.Z.L.R. 395.

or even part of his actual life interest, but merely sums which he had expected to receive by virtue of that interest.

20–031   **Agreement to assign existing chose in action in the future.** It also seems that an agreement to assign an existing chose in action in the future (as distinguished from an actual assignment intended to operate forthwith) requires consideration. Thus, in *Re McArdle*,[19] five brothers and sisters were entitled to a testator's residuary estate subject to a life interest. The wife of one of the brothers executed and paid for certain improvements to a house which formed part of the estate. Subsequently the five brothers and sisters signed a document addressed to her which read: "in consideration of your carrying out certain alterations and improvements to the property we agree that the executors shall repay to you from the estate when distributed £488 in settlement of the amount." The Court of Appeal held that this document could not be construed as an equitable assignment[20] because it purported to be a contract to assign, and not an actual assignment. As such it required consideration, and the only consideration being past, it was not enforceable.

20–032   **Agreement to assign expectancy supported by consideration.** Although a mere expectancy is thus incapable of actual assignment, an agreement for valuable consideration to assign such an expectancy operates in equity to transfer the right to the chose in action as soon as it comes into existence provided only that it is sufficiently identifiable under the agreement.[21] No further action on the part of the assignor is necessary to convert an agreement to assign into an actual assignment. The effect of this equitable principle is that the assignee's interest is more than a mere matter of contract, even before the chose in action comes into existence. So, for instance, in *Re Lind*,[22] a person agreed to assign, for valuable consideration, property which he expected to inherit on his mother's death, at that time his mother being still alive. The assignor became bankrupt, but secured his discharge before his mother's death. It was held that the assignees were entitled to the property inherited by the bankrupt from his mother since they had a valid equitable interest in it even before it became an existing chose in action. Had their interest been merely contractual the assignor's liability would have been discharged when he secured his discharge in bankruptcy.

20–033   **Consideration not needed for actual assignment of existing chose.** The better view seems to be that an actual assignment of an existing chose in action does not require consideration provided that the assignor has done everything which is necessary according to the nature of the property to transfer the title to

---

[19] [1951] Ch. 669; criticised in (1951) 67 L.Q.R. 295.

[20] If it could, the fact that the consideration was past would not have made it invalid.

[21] *Tailby v. Official Receiver* (1888) 13 App.Cas. 523; *Glegg v. Bromley* [1912] 3 K.B. 474; *Cotton v. Heyl* [1930] 1 Ch. 510. But, without consideration, the mere fact that the assignment is by deed is insufficient.

[22] [1915] 2 Ch. 345. See also *Joseph v. Lyons* (1885) 15 Q.B.D. 280 (after-acquired stock-in-trade); *Re Gillott's Settlement* [1934] Ch. 97 (future trust income); *Re Trytel* (1952) 2 T.L.R. 32 (royalties); *Syrett v. Egerton* [1957] 1 W.L.R. 1130 (future income); *Campbell, Connelly & Co. Ltd v. Noble* [1963] 1 W.L.R. 252 (copyright); *The Ugland Trailer* [1985] 2 Lloyd's Rep. 372, 374; *The Annangel Glory* [1988] 1 Lloyd's Rep. 45 (future sub-freights under a charter).

it.[23] It is true that equity will not perfect an imperfect gift, and also that equity will not assist a volunteer; but it is also true that a person can make a gift of a chose in action no less than a chose in possession.[24] Failure to distinguish an actual transfer from the specifically enforceable contract to transfer referred to in the previous paragraph has however led to difficult and confusing dicta.[25] The better view is exemplified by *Holt v. Heatherfield Trust Ltd.*[26] X, being indebted to the plaintiff, assigned to him a debt due from Y. The assignment was in writing and absolute, but before Y received notice of the assignment, the defendants served a garnishee order nisi on Y. The assignment was therefore not statutory but equitable. Atkinson J., having grave doubts whether the antecedent debt constituted sufficient consideration for the assignment in the absence of a forbearance to sue,[27] held that consideration was unnecessary.

"Everything which is necessary." The meaning of the requirement that the **20–034** assignor must have done everything which is necessary according to the nature of the property to transfer the title to it to the assignee has been elucidated by certain cases on the assignment of shares in companies. If the assignor uses a transfer which is not in the appropriate form,[28] or if Treasury consent to the transfer is required but the assignor dies before it is forthcoming,[29] he has not done everything which is necessary according to the nature of the property to transfer the title to the shares, and the assignment is inoperative unless made for value. On the other hand, if the assignor uses the right form of transfer but dies before the directors have registered the shares in the assignee's name, then the assignor has done everything in his power to transfer the title to the shares, and the assignment will operate in equity as from its date (and not from the date of registration), even if there is no consideration.[30] So if the assignor voluntarily assigns a debt to the assignee, but dies before notice is given to the debtor, it would seem that, as between the assignor's estate and the assignee, the assignment would take effect in equity as from its date: for notice to the debtor need not be, and is not usually, given by the assignor. If the assignment was in writing and absolute, it would be converted into a good statutory assignment if the

---

[23] See *Kekewich v. Manning* (1851) 1 De G.M. & G. 176; *Harding v. Harding* (1886) 17 Q.B.D. 442; *Re Griffin* [1899] 1 Ch. 408; *German v. Yates* (1915) 32 T.L.R. 52; *Re Williams* [1917] 1 Ch. 1; *Holt v. Heatherfield Trust Ltd* [1942] 2 K.B. 1; *Re Rose* [1949] Ch. 78; *Re McArdle* [1951] Ch. 669, 676–677; *Re Rose* [1952] Ch. 499, *post*, § 20–034; *Re Wale* [1956] 1 W.L.R. 1346; *Pulley v. Public Trustee* [1956] N.Z.L.R. 771; *Letts v. I.R.C.* [1957] 1 W.L.R. 201; *Norman v. Federal Commissioner of Taxation* (1963) 109 C.L.R. 9; *Shepherd v. Federal Commissioner of Taxation* (1965) 113 C.L.R. 385. See also *Mascall v. Mascall* (1984) 50 P. & C.R. 119 (voluntary conveyance of real property).

[24] Compare *Kekewich v. Manning, supra*, with *Milroy v. Lord* (1862) 4 De G.F. & J. 264. See also *Fortescue v. Barnett* (1834) 3 My. & K. 36; *Voyle v. Hughes* (1854) 2 Sm. & G. 18; *Re Patrick* [1891] 1 Ch. 82. But see *Olsson v. Dyson* (1969) 120 C.L.R. 365, *post*, § 20–035, where a different view was taken by the High Court of Australia.

[25] See the dicta from *Glegg v. Bromley* [1912] 3 K.B. 474, cited *ante*, § 20–027, n. 9; see also *Re Westerton* [1919] 2 Ch. 104, 111.

[26] [1942] 2 K.B. 1.

[27] On this point see the judgment of Windeyer J. in *Norman v. Federal Commissioner of Taxation, supra*, and (1943) 59 L.Q.R. 129, 208.

[28] *Milroy v. Lord* (1862) 4 De G.F. & J. 264.

[29] *Re Fry* [1946] Ch. 312.

[30] *Re Rose* [1949] Ch. 78; *Re Rose* [1952] Ch. 499; *Letts v. I.R.C.* [1957] 1 W.L.R. 201.

assignee were to give written notice to the debtor after the death of the assignor.[31]

20–035   **Defective statutory assignments.** Difficult problems arise where a statutory assignment could have been used but the full requirements were not complied with. Where the defect is that no notice has been given to the debtor, it has been held that the assignment may be valid in equity without consideration, for the assignor has done all that he needed to do to transfer the chose, and notice can be given by the assignee.[32] Where the assignment was not made in writing, *i.e.* is oral, it will be void by statute if it ranks as a disposition of an equitable interest or trust.[33] If the subject-matter is a *legal* chose in action, it can still be argued that an assignor who has not made a statutory assignment has not done all that he can to transfer the chose; hence the transaction can at best be regarded as an agreement to assign and requires consideration. This view has been adopted in the High Court of Australia,[34] and must in fact (despite dicta to the contrary[35]) cast some doubt on the first proposition above regarding notice to the debtor. An argument at the other extreme is, however, that before 1875 an assignee of a legal chose in action could not sue in his own name and only had a right to compel the assignor in accordance with the agreement to allow his name to be used and that this agreement required consideration; but that since 1875 the assignee can sue in his own name, joining the assignor if necessary as co-defendant, so that consideration is no longer necessary for any assignment. This argument seems to go too far[36] and to be based on an imperfect understanding of the old cases.[37] Those cases do not in fact indicate a settled view, and on principle the better approach seems to be that the question whether an oral transaction is an assignment or an agreement to assign is to be collected from its terms and not prejudged by the application of supposed rules.[38]

20–036   Where the defect is that the assignment is non-absolute, it should be borne in mind that the distinction between absolute and non-absolute assignments is not the same as that between assignments and agreements to assign. The former distinction has the purpose of isolating those cases where, whether because the assignor may still have some interest in the debt assigned or because the debtor should not be subjected to successive actions on the same debt, it is desirable that all those involved be parties to litigation.[39] It would seem that whereas an assignment by way of charge shall normally be regarded as an agreement to assign, and so require consideration (which it would normally have in any case[40])

---

[31] As in *Re Westerton* [1919] 2 Ch. 104.

[32] *Holt v. Heatherfield Trust Ltd* [1942] 2 K.B. 1, *ante*, § 20–033; *Magee v. U.D.T. Finance Ltd* [1983] N.Z.L.R. 438. But as to options *cf. Warner Bros. Records Inc. v. Rollgreen Ltd* [1976] QB 30, *ante*, § 20–005.

[33] *Ante*, § 20–025.

[34] *Olsson v. Dyson* (1969) 120 C.L.R. 365. See also *Anning v. Anning* (1907) 4 C.L.R. 1049.

[35] *Olsson v. Dyson, supra*, at 386–387.

[36] See Treitel, *The Law of Contract* (9th ed., 1995), pp. 603–605.

[37] See *Re Westerton* [1919] 2 Ch. 104; Treitel *op. cit.* pp. 601–602; *post*, §§ 20–037—20–040.

[38] See *German v. Yates* (1915) 32 T.L.R. 52 (discussed (1955) 33 Can. Bar Rev. 284, 294–296).

[39] *Ante*, §§ 20–012—20–014; *post*, §§ 20–037—20–040.

[40] See *Matthews v. Goodday* (1861) 31 L.J.Ch. 282; *Re Earl of Lucan* (1890) 45 Ch.D. 470; *cf. ante*, §§ 20–012—20–014.

the assignment of part of a debt may rank as a completed assignment.[41] As before, the effect of a conditional assignment would depend on the interpretation of the condition.[42]

Enforcement of legal chose in action equitably assigned. Before the Judi- 20–037 cature Act 1873, an assignment of a legal chose in action could not usually have been enforced except in the name of the assignor because a legal chose in action had to be enforced in the common law courts, which would only recognise the assignor as entitled to sue. After the passing of the Judicature Act, it has been held that, although assignments of legal choses not complying with the statute remain valid in equity,[43] and the assignee is entitled to sue in his own name, it also remains the position that, as a matter of practice, the assignee is normally required to join the assignor.[44] Where the assignment fails to be statutory because the assignor has not wholly disposed of his interest (*e.g.* where it is by way of charge only, or is of part of a debt only), or where there is a dispute as to whether the documents constitute an assignment,[45] joining the assignor serves a useful purpose. It ensures that all parties with an interest in the chose are brought before the court and that the debtor, if he is adjudged liable, obtains a complete discharge from his liability. But where the assignor retains no interest in the chose in action and the assignment only fails to be statutory, *e.g.* because it was not in writing or because no notice has been given, a requirement that the assignor be made a party to the proceedings would seem to serve no useful purpose and may be dispensed with.[46]

As the requirement that an equitable assignor be a party to a suit is procedural 20–038 and not substantive, an action commenced by an equitable assignee is not a nullity and is effective to stop time running for the purposes of statutes of limitation[47] or a contractual limitation period.[48] The debtor may also waive the requirement that the assignor be joined.[49] In any event the Civil Procedure Rules 1998[50] provide that a court may order a person to be added as a new party either if this is desirable in order that the court can resolve all the matters in dispute in the proceedings; or if there is an issue involving the new party and an existing

---

[41] *Shepherd v. Federal Commissioner of Taxation* (1965) 113 C.L.R. 385; see also *Re McArdle* [1951] Ch. 669, where the court appears to have been willing to construe a gift of part of a debt as an assignment had the circumstances been appropriate. Since part of a debt cannot be statutorily assigned, the reasoning in *Olsson v. Dyson, supra*, n. 34, is inapplicable: see *Re Smyth* [1970] Argus L.R. 919.

[42] *Ante*, § 20–012—20–013.

[43] *Brandt's Sons & Co. v. Dunlop Rubber Co.* [1905] A.C. 454.

[44] *ibid.*; and see also *Performing Right Society Ltd v. London Theatre of Varieties Ltd* [1924] A.C. 1; *Williams v. Atlantic Assurance Co.* [1933] 1 K.B. 81; *Holt v. Heatherfield Trust Ltd* [1942] 2 K.B. 1, 5; *The Aiolos* [1983] 2 Lloyd's Rep. 25; *Weddell v. J.A. Pearce & Major* [1988] Ch. 26; *Three Rivers D.C. v. Bank of England* [1996] Q.B. 292; *Hendry v. Chartsearch Ltd, The Times*, September 16, 1998. In the rare converse case, an assignor wishing to recover for himself must join the assignee: *Walter and Sullivan Ltd v. Murphy & Sons Ltd* [1955] 2 Q.B. 584; *Three Rivers D.C. v. Bank of England* [1996] Q.B. 292.

[45] *The Aiolos, supra*.

[46] *The Aiolos* [1983] 2 Lloyd's Rep. 25, 33–34; *Weddell v. J.A. Pearce & Major* [1988] Ch. 26, 40–41.

[47] *Weddell v. J.A. Pearce & Major* [1988] Ch. 26. *cf. Compania Colombiana de Seguros v. Pacific Steam Navigation Co.* [1965] 1 Q.B. 101, 127–129.

[48] *The Aiolos* [1983] 2 Lloyd's Rep. 25.

[49] *Brandt's Sons & Co. v. Dunlop Rubber Co., supra*.

[50] CPR, Part 19, rr. 1–2.

party, which is connected to the matters in dispute in the proceedings, and it is desirable to add the new party so that the court can resolve that issue. Where a claimant claims a remedy to which some other person is jointly entitled with him, all persons jointly entitled to the remedy must be parties unless the court orders otherwise; but if any such person does not agree to be a claimant, he must be made a defendant, unless the court orders otherwise.

20-039 **Enforcement of equitable chose in action equitably assigned.** Even before the Judicature Act, an assignee of an equitable chose could sue alone to enforce his rights in the Court of Chancery if the assignment was absolute,[51] and this remains the position today, since there is nothing in the Judicature Act to impair this right.

20-040 Although there is no precise authority on the point, it seems that an equitable assignee of an equitable chose must join the assignor wherever the assignor retains an interest in the chose in question. It has already been seen that the reasoning underlying the decisions of the courts on the construction of section 136 of the Law of Property Act 1925 has been founded on the desirability of requiring all interested persons to be made parties to the proceedings; or, where part only of a debt has been assigned, of requiring the debt to be sued for in one action and not in several.[52] These considerations have prompted some of the decisions in which assignments have been held not to be statutory, since (as already seen) a statutory assignee can always sue alone. It would seem, therefore, that even an assignee of an equitable chose cannot sue alone without joining the assignor, wherever the assignor retains an interest in the chose; and, furthermore, that any other party (such as another assignee) who has an interest in it should also be joined.

(c) *Principles Applicable to Statutory and Equitable Assignments*

(i) *What Rights are Assignable*

20-041 **In general.** Despite the existence of the statutory form of assignment under section 136 of the Law of Property Act 1925, the assignability of a contractual right[53] in any given case is generally governed by the rules of equity existing before the Judicature Acts, and these rules now apply to statutory and equitable assignments alike.[54] There is also a number of particular statutory provisions prohibiting assignment in certain cases.[55]

---

[51] *Cator v. Croydon Canal Co.* (1841) 4 Y. & C.Ex. 405, 593; *Donaldson v. Donaldson* (1854) Kay 711.

[52] *Ante*, §§ 20–012—20–014, 20–035.

[53] It seems that an irrevocable offer is assignable in the same way and subject to the same conditions as a contractual right: see *Whiteley v. Hilt* [1918] 2 K.B. 808, 818; *R.A. Brierley Investments Ltd v. Landmark Corpn. Ltd* (1966) 40 A.L.J.R. 425; *Warner Bros. Records Inc. v. Rollgreen Investments Ltd* [1976] Q.B. 430. But this is an instance where an equitable assignment may be less effective than a legal assignment: *ante*, § 20–005.

[54] *Tolhurst v. Associated Portland Cement Manufacturers Ltd* [1902] 2 K.B. 660, 676; *Torkington v. Magee* [1902] 2 K.B. 427, 430–431; revd. [1903] 1 K.B. 644.

[55] *Post*, § 20–045.

Rights declared by contract to be incapable of assignment.[56] If rights   **20–042**
arising under a contract are declared by the contract to be incapable of assignment, a purported assignment will be invalid as against the debtor. In the leading
case of *Linden Gardens Trust Ltd v. Lenesta Sludge Disposals Ltd*[57] the benefits
of building contracts were purportedly assigned by lessees of the properties on
which the building work was being carried out to assignees of the leases. Under
the building contracts there was to be no assignment of the contract by either
party without the other's consent. No such consent for the assignments was
obtained.[58] It was held by the House of Lords that, on the true construction of the
prohibition clause, the assignment of the benefit of the contract, rather than
merely vicarious performance, was barred; and that no distinction was here being
drawn by the parties between barring an assignment of the right to future
performance, as opposed to the fruits, of the contract nor between barring an
assignment of unaccrued, as opposed to accrued, causes of action.[59] Moreover
there was no reason of public policy not to give effect to the prohibition clause,
the legitimate commercial purpose of which was to ensure that the original
parties to the contract were not brought into direct contractual relations with third
parties.[60]

In *Hendry v. Chartsearch Ltd*[61] the majority of the Court of Appeal (Millett   **20–043**
and Henry L.JJ., Evans L.J. preferring to leave the point open) held that, where
there is a clause requiring consent, consent not to be unreasonably withheld,[62] it
is fatal to the validity of the assignment that the debtor's consent was not sought;
it is irrelevant that, on the facts, consent could not have been reasonably
withheld.

---

[56] See generally Allcock (1983) C.L.J. 328.

[57] [1994] 1 A.C. 85; Cartwright (1993) 9 Const.L.J. 281; Duncan Wallace (1994) 110 L.Q.R. 42;
Tettenborn (1994) 53 C.L.J. 24. See also, following *Linden Gardens, Circuit Systems Ltd v. Zuken-
Redac (U.K.) Ltd* [1996] 3 All E.R. 748, CA. See also, prior to *Linden Gardens, Helstan Securities
Ltd v. Hertfordshire CC* [1978] 3 All E.R. 262; noted by Goode (1979) 42 M.L.R. 553. See further
United Dominions Trust Ltd v. Parkway Motors [1955] 1 W.L.R. 719 (benefits of hire-purchase
agreement not assignable where agreement so states): the decision on the measure of damages in that
case has been overruled by *Wickham Holdings Ltd v. Brooke House Motors Ltd* [1967] 1 W.L.R. 295
but without affecting the assignment point (indeed the latter case proceeded on the assumption that
either the benefit of the hire-purchase agreement was not assignable or that the prohibition against
assignment was waived).

[58] In *Orion Finance Ltd v. Crown Financial Management Ltd* [1994] 2 B.C.L.C. 607, although the
defendant had not given its consent, the assignment was held valid because in the circumstances the
defendant was estopped from denying that the assignment was valid.

[59] cf. *Flood v. Shand Construction Ltd, The Times*, January 8, 1997, where a clause prohibiting
assignment, without consent, of a building sub-contract but permitting the assignment of "any sum
which is or may become due and payable under this sub-contract" was construed as permitting
assignment of the right to recover sums already due, but not the right to claim damages or other sums
that needed to be established as due and payable by litigation or arbitration or contractual
machinery.

[60] See also *Oakdale (Richmond) Ltd v. National Westminster Bank plc* [1997] 1 B.C.L.C. 63, where
a clause prohibiting a company from factoring, discounting, charging or assigning its book or other
debts without the bank's consent was held to be necessary if banks were to lend on the security of
book debts and, far from being anti-competitive under Art. 85 of the E.C. Treaty, it promoted
competition because it enabled a company to obtain additional finance from its bank.

[61] *The Times*, September 16, 1998, CA.

[62] See *British Gas Trading Ltd v. Eastern Electricity plc*, unreported, December 18, 1996, CA,
where it was held, upholding Colman J., *The Times*, November 29, 1996, that Eastern had unreasonably withheld its consent to an assignment.

20–044   However, it seems that a prohibited assignment can be effective as between assignor and assignee. It appears to have been in that context that Darling J. uttered his famous dictum that a prohibition "could no more operate to invalidate the assignment than it could interfere with the laws of gravitation."[63] In the *Linden Gardens* case Lord Browne-Wilkinson, giving the leading judgment, said: "[A] prohibition on assignment normally only invalidates the assignment as against the other party to the contract so as to prevent a transfer of the chose in action: in the absence of the clearest words it cannot operate to invalidate the contract as between the assignor and assignee and even then it may be ineffective on the grounds of public policy."[64] It has been held that a covenant in a marriage settlement to settle after-acquired property could be enforced by the beneficiaries with respect to the proceeds of a life insurance policy that had been paid to the covenantor's executor, although the policy was expressed to be not assignable.[65] It has also been held that a purported assignment of a contract relating to the promotion and management of boxing that was ineffective at law, because the contract prohibited assignment and involved personal services, was effective in equity as a declaration of trust of the benefit of the contract.[66] On the facts, this ensured that the parties' commercial intentions were effected.

20–045   **Assignment prohibited by statute or public policy.** Assignment of certain rights is prohibited by statute; for example, benefits under social security legislation are not assignable.[67] And in other cases an assignment may be void on grounds of public policy, *e.g.* an assignment of the salary of a public officer has been held to be void,[68] and the same may be true of an assignment by a wife of her right to maintenance.[69]

20–046   The assignment of a right of action by a party not entitled to legal aid (for example, because a corporate plaintiff) to a party so entitled (for example, the directors and shareholders of a company), where the object and effect of the assignment was to enable the assignee to obtain legal aid that would not have been available to the assignor, was not contrary to public policy or unlawful.[70] The same applied where the object, in effect, of the assignment was to enable the

---

[63] *Tom Shaw & Co. v. Moss Empires Ltd* (1908) 25 T.L.R. 190, 191.

[64] [1994] 1 A.C. 85, 108. See also *Hendry v. Chartsearch Ltd, The Times*, September 16, 1998.

[65] *Re Turcan* (1888) 40 Ch.D. 5. See also *Re Griffin* [1899] 1 Ch. 408 and *Re Westerton* [1919] 2 Ch. 104, where it was held that bank deposits had been validly assigned though the deposit receipts were expressed to be not transferable in both cases; and *Spellman v. Spellman* [1961] 1 W.L.R. 921, 925 (*per* Danckwerts L.J.).

[66] *Don King Productions Inc. v. Warren* [1999] 2 All E.R. 218: (it was also held that the benefit of the contract could be partnership property even though non-assignable).

[67] Social Security Administration Act 1992, s.187. See also, *e.g.* Superannuation Act 1972, s.5(1); Pensions Act 1995, s.91 (the right to a pension under an occupational pension scheme cannot be assigned other than in favour of one's widow, widower or dependant). The Unfair Terms in Consumer Contracts Regulations 1994, in para. 1(p) of Sched. 3, list as a possible unfair term one which has the object or effect of "giving the seller or supplier the possibility of transferring his rights and obligations under the contract, where this may serve to reduce the guarantees for the consumer without the latter's agreement."

[68] See *Re Mirams* [1891] 1 Q.B. 594; *ante,* § 17–022.

[69] *Re Robinson* (1884) 27 Ch.D. 160; *Watkins v. Watkins* [1896] P. 222; *Clark v. Clark* [1906] P. 331; *Pacquine v. Snary* [1909] 1 K.B. 688.

[70] *Norglen Ltd v. Reed Rains Provincial Ltd* [1997] 3 W.L.R. 1177, HL (but in such circumstances the Legal Aid Board, in the exercise of its discretion, might refuse legal aid to the assignee).

action to be brought by an assignee who, unlike the assignor, did not have to provide security for costs.

Assignments savouring of maintenance.[71] A chose in action is not assignable if the assignment savours of maintenance or champerty.[72] For this reason it has often been asserted that a bare right to litigate is not assignable.[73] The principle has, however, been qualified in many important respects, and although in *Trendtex Trading Corporation v. Crédit Suisse*[74] it was said to remain a fundamental principle of our law, the House of Lords in that case recognised that it has limited scope in the modern law. Lord Roskill said,

> "If the assignment is of a property right or interest and the cause of action is ancillary to that right or interest, or if the assignee had a genuine commercial interest in taking the assignment and in enforcing it for his own benefit, I see no reason why the assignment should be struck down as an assignment of a bare cause of action or as savouring of maintenance."[75]

So it has been held that rights of action (even in tort) which are incidental and subsidiary to property may be validly assigned when the property is transferred.[76] Again, it has been held that an assignment of rights of action to an insurer who has paid a loss and would, apart from the assignment, have been able to sue the tortfeasor under the doctrine of subrogation in the name of the insured, may be effective to enable the insurer to sue in his own name.[77] It is also well established that a claim to a simple debt is assignable even if the debtor has refused to pay,[78] and even though this may be said in a sense to be an assignment of a "bare right to litigate."[79] The practice of assigning or "selling" debts to debt-collecting

---

[71] This subject is dealt with in more detail *ante*, §§ 17–048 *et seq.*

[72] *Rees v. De Bernardy* [1896] 2 Ch. 437; *Laurent v. Sale & Co.* [1963] 1 W.L.R. 829.

[73] *Prosser v. Edmunds* (1835) 1 Y. & C. Ex. 481; *Dawson v. Great Northern & City Ry.* [1905] 1 K.B. 260, 271; *Glegg v. Bromley* [1912] 3 K.B. 474, 489–490; *Defries v. Milne* [1913] 1 Ch. 98; *Torkington v. Magee* [1902] 2 K.B. 427, 433–434 (decision revd. [1903] 1 K.B. 644); *Trendtex Trading Corpn. v. Credit Suisse* [1982] A.C. 679; *Giles v. Thompson* [1994] 1 A.C. 142. Trustees in bankruptcy and liquidators, however, are to some extent permitted by statute to make such assignments: Insolvency Act 1986, ss.167, 314, 436, Scheds. 4 and 5; *Guy v. Churchill* (1888) 40 Ch.D. 481; *Re Park Gate Waggon Works* (1881) 17 Ch.D. 234; *Ogdens Ltd v. Weinberg* (1906) 95 L.T. 567; *Ramsey v. Hartley* [1977] 1 W.L.R. 686; *Freightex Ltd v. International Express Co. Ltd* unreported, April 15, 1980, CA; *Grovewood Holdings plc v. James Capel & Co. Ltd* [1995] Ch. 80; *Re Oasis Merchandising Services Ltd* [1998] Ch. 170; *Norglen Ltd v. Reed Rains Prudential Ltd* [1997] 3 W.L.R. 1177, 1184–1185, HL.

[74] [1982] A.C. 679, discussed more fully, *ante*, § 17–057.

[75] *ibid.* at 703.

[76] *Dickinson v. Burrell* (1866) L.R. 1 Eq. 337, 342 (right to rescind earlier conveyance); *Dawson v. Great Northern & City Ry., supra* (right to compensation for injurious affecting of land); *Ellis v. Torrington* [1920] 1 K.B. 399 (breach of covenant relating to land); *G.U.S. Property Management Ltd v. Littlewoods Mail Order Stores Ltd*, 1982 S.L.T. 533 (delictual action for damage to building) noted by Street (1983) Conv. 404. But an order for possession is probably not assignable: *Chung Kwok Hotel Co. v. Field* [1960] 1 W.L.R. 1112. See generally *ante*, § 17–061.

[77] *King v. Victoria Insurance Co. Ltd* [1896] A.C. 250; *Compania Colombiana de Seguros v. Pacific Steam Navigation Co.* [1965] 1 Q.B. 101; *ante*, § 17–062. Even, probably, if the amount recoverable exceeds the loss suffered by the insurer: see *Compania Colombiana* case at 121; *Trendtex Trading Corpn. v. Credit Suisse* [1980] Q.B. 629, 656.

[78] *County Hotel and Wine Co. Ltd v. London & North Western Ry.* [1918] 2 K.B. 251, 258–262; affd. on other grounds [1919] 2 K.B. 29; [1921] 1 A.C. 85. See also *Ellis v. Torrington, supra.*

[79] *Fitzroy v. Cave* [1905] 2 K.B. 364.

agencies and credit factors could hardly be carried on if the law were otherwise.[80]

20–048   In the *Trendtex* case itself it was accepted that a creditor who has financed the transaction giving rise to the right of action will have a legitimate commercial interest in it and an assignment to him will be valid[81] unless it appears that the object of the assignment was not to protect that interest. On the facts the assignment was held void because it was a "step towards the sale of a bare cause of action to a third party who had no genuine commercial interest in the claim."[82] However, the mere fact that the assignee seeks to enforce the assigned rights for another is not fatal where this is a legitimate part of its business activity.[83] So also the fact that the assignee might make a profit out of the assignment does not of itself render the agreement to assign champertous although the prospect of excessive profit can be taken into account in deciding whether the commercial interest is genuine.[84]

20–049   It appears, however, that a purported assignee has no legitimate commercial interest in a purely personal claim so that such a claim is non-assignable.[85] The most obvious example is the right to damages for a personal, as opposed to a proprietary, tort such as assault, defamation, or a tort causing personal injury.

20–050   It is also to be noted that even where a right of action is not assignable on the ground that it amounts to a "bare right to litigate" there is no objection to an agreement to assign the proceeds of an action.[86] In such a case no question of maintenance need arise, for the assignee is not himself given any right to sue the tortfeasor or debtor on the original cause of action.

20–051   The torts and crimes of maintenance and champerty were abolished by the Criminal Law Act 1967, but section 14(2) of that Act expressly provides that this is not to affect "any rule of law as to the cases in which a contract is to be treated as contrary to public policy or otherwise illegal." It is submitted that this phraseology should be interpreted to cover assignments as well as contracts to assign. In *Trendtex* Lord Roskill said that it "seems plain that Parliament intended to leave the law as to the effect of maintenance and champerty upon contracts unaffected by the abolition of them as crimes and torts."[87]

---

[80] *Comfort v. Betts* [1891] 1 Q.B. 737, 739; *Camdex International Ltd v. Bank of Zambia* [1998] Q.B. 22. For an example of "factoring" see *G.E. Crane Sales Pty. Ltd v. Federal Commissioner of Taxation* (1971) 126 C.L.R. 177.

[81] *Trendtex Trading Corpn. v. Credit Suisse, ante,* § 17–057. Assignments have been held valid, applying the *Trendtex* test of a "legitimate commercial interest" in, *e.g. The Kelo* [1985] 2 Lloyd's Rep. 85; *Bourne v. Coloderise Ltd* [1985] I.C.R. 291; *Brownton Ltd v. Edward Moore Inbucon Ltd* [1985] 3 All E.R. 499; *South East Thames Regional H.A. v. Lovell* (1985) 32 Build. L.R. 127. For the assignment of rights to solicitors, see *ante,* § 17–064.

[82] *ibid.* at 704.

[83] *The Kelo* [1985] 2 Lloyd's Rep. 85.

[84] *Brownton Ltd v. Edward Moore Inbucon Ltd* [1985] 3 All E.R. 499. *Quaere* whether, if the assignee did make a profit, he is answerable to the assignor.

[85] *Trendtex Trading Corpn. v. Credit Suisse* [1980] Q.B. 629, 656 (*per* Lord Denning M.R.), 671, 674 (*per* Oliver L.J.); [1982] A.C. 679, 702.

[86] *Glegg v. Bromley* [1912] 3 K.B. 474; *Gould v. Skinner* [1983] Qd. 377.

[87] [1982] A.C. 679, 702; *Pickering v. Soget Services (U.K.) Ltd* (1982) 262 E.G. 770; *ante,* § 16–044.

Personal contracts. The benefit of a contract is only assignable in "cases 20–052 where it can make no difference to the person on whom the obligation lies to which of two persons he is to discharge it."[88] It is to be noted that the question whether an assignment makes any difference to the debtor must be decided by the court on objective grounds, having regard to the nature of the contract and of the subject-matter of the rights assigned. It may in some circumstances make a great deal of difference to a debtor whether his creditor is of an indulgent character, or whether he is likely to enforce his legal rights ruthlessly, but considerations of this kind are ignored by the courts in determining whether a right is assignable or not.[89]

Prima facie contractual rights to, for example, the payment of money, and to 20–053 the sale or occupation or use[90] of land, or to building work,[91] do not involve personal considerations and are capable of assignment. A right to be indemnified against a monetary liability may in some circumstances be assignable,[92] but the benefit of a motor vehicle insurance policy involves personal considerations and is not assignable.[93] Indeed, any contractual right involving personal skill on the part of the creditor, or other personal qualifications (such as his credit),[94] is incapable of assignment. Hence neither an author nor his publisher may assign the right to performance of the other's obligations under a publishing agreement, although an author's right to be paid royalties may be assigned[95]; and if the author has actually transferred the copyright in the work to the publisher, he can of course assign that as an item of property.[96] The right to employ a person under a contract of employment is clearly not assignable,[97] though wages or salary due to the employee are normally assignable by him.[98] The mere presence of an arbitration clause in a contract does not as a general rule render the contract incapable of assignment.[99]

---

[88] *Tolhurst v. Associated Portland Cement Manufacturers Ltd* [1902] 2 K.B. 660, 668; affd. [1903] A.C. 414.

[89] *Fitzroy v. Cave* [1905] 2 K.B. 364 (where the purpose of the assignment was to procure the debtor's bankruptcy).

[90] *J. Miller Ltd v. Laurence & Bardsley* [1966] 1 Lloyd's Rep. 90.

[91] *Charlotte Thirty Ltd and Bison Ltd v. Croker Ltd* (1990) 24 Con.L.R. 46.

[92] *British Union and National Insurance Co. v. Rawson* [1916] 2 Ch. 476.

[93] *Peters v. General Accident, etc., Ltd* [1938] 2 All E.R. 267.

[94] *Cooper v. Micklefield Coal and Lime Co.* (1912) 107 L.T. 457; *Cole v. Wellington Dairy Farmers' Co-op Association* [1917] N.Z.U.L.R. 372.

[95] *Stevens v. Benning* (1855) 6 De G.M. & G. 223; *Hole v. Bradbury* (1879) 12 Ch.D. 886; *Griffiths v. Tower Publishing Co.* [1897] 1 Ch. 21; *Don King Productions Inc. v. Warren* [1998] 2 All E.R. 608, 632 (*per* Lightman J.; decision affd. [1999] 2 All E.R. 218, CA).

[96] Copyright, Designs and Patents Act 1988, s.90.

[97] *Nokes v. Doncaster Amalgamated Collieries Ltd* [1940] A.C. 1014, 1026; *Denham v. Midland Employers' Mutual Assurance Ltd* [1955] 2 Q.B. 437, 443; *cf. I.T. O'Brien v. Benson's Hosiery (Holdings) Ltd* [1980] A.C. 562, 572. See also Transfer of Undertakings (Protection of Employment) Regulations 1981, S.I. 1981 No. 1794, Reg. 5(1), as amended by Trade Union Reform and Employment Rights Act 1993, s.33.

[98] *Shaw v. Moss' Empires and Boston* (1909) 25 T.L.R. 191; *Russell & Co. v. Austin Fryers* (1909) 25 T.L.R. 414. Subject to the rules as to public policy (*ante*, § 17–003) and to statute (*e.g.* Merchant Shipping Act 1995, s.34(1)(c)).

[99] *Shayler v. Woolf* [1946] Ch. 320, explaining *Cottage Club Estates Ltd v. Woodside Estates Co. Ltd* [1928] 2 K.B. 463; *The Halcyon the Great* [1984] 1 Lloyd's Rep. 283, 289; *Montedipe SpA v. JTP-Ro Jugotanker* [1990] 2 Lloyd's Rep. 11; *Baytur SA v. Finagro Holding SA* [1992] 1 Q.B. 610; see *supra* § 16–030.

20–054 **Commercial contracts.** Rights arising under ordinary commercial contracts (*e.g.* for the sale of goods) are prima facie readily assignable, at least if there is no question of credit being granted to the assignee. But commercial contracts may sometimes be drafted so as to make the requirements of one of the parties a material consideration in determining the obligations of the other. In such circumstances there is often difficulty in deciding whether the benefit of the contract is assignable. In *Tolhurst v. Associated Portland Cement Manufacturers Ltd,*[1] the defendant was the owner of certain land upon which there were chalk quarries. He sold part of this land to a company in order to enable the company to carry on there the business of manufacturing Portland Cement. He contracted to supply the company, which was in a small way of business, with 750 tons of chalk per week for 50 years "and so much more as the company shall require for the manufacture of Portland cement upon their said land." The company subsequently assigned the contract, sold its undertaking to the plaintiff company, which was in a large way of business, and went into voluntary liquidation. The House of Lords held that the new company was entitled to the benefit of the contract and could maintain an action against the defendant in its own name. There were two grounds for this decision. (1) The defendant's liability was measured by the capacity of the original company's land: "the [original] company were not entitled to an unlimited supply of chalk, but only to so much as they might want for making cement on their own piece of land."[2] Consequently the effect of the assignment was not to increase the burden on the defendant, for the original company might have increased its capital and worked its land more intensively. (2) By entering into a long-term contract the defendant must have contemplated that the benefit of it might be assigned.[3] The contract should therefore be construed as if it had been made between the defendant and his successors and assignees owners and occupiers of the quarries and the company, its successors and assignees owners and occupiers of the cement works.[4] On the other hand, in *Kemp v. Baerselman*[5] the defendant contracted to supply X, a cake manufacturer, with all the eggs that he should require for manufacturing purposes for one year: and X undertook not to purchase eggs elsewhere. X transferred his business to a company, and it was held that the contract was not assignable, because the defendant's liability was not limited to the capacity of a particular piece of land, and because X's contract not to purchase eggs elsewhere introduced a personal element inasmuch as this obligation would not have been binding on the assignee.[6]

20–055 **Contracts with companies.** It has been said that the fact that one of the parties to a contract is a limited company is no ground for assuming that the

---

[1] [1902] 2 K.B. 660; [1903] A.C. 414.
[2] [1903] A.C. at 423; in CA at 673.
[3] *ibid.* at 419; in Court of Appeal at 674–675.
[4] *ibid.* at 420, 421, 423; *Nokes v. Doncaster Amalgamated Collieries Ltd* [1940] A.C. 1014, 1020.
[5] [1906] 2 K.B. 609.
[6] Yet in *Tolhurst's* case the assignor company was also bound to take all its chalk from Tolhurst, a point totally ignored in the House of Lords. The result of the decision seems to be that although the assignee was not bound by the duty to take chalk from the defendant, if it did take any, it was bound to take all its requirements of chalk for the manufacture of cement on that piece of land from him. See *post*, § 20–077. See also *National Carbonising Co. Ltd v. British Coal Distillation Ltd* (1936) 54 R.P.C. 41, 57.

personality of that party is immaterial to the other party.[7] There is an element of unreality about this in the modern world, for the personality of a company may change without any formal change in the legal identity of the company as, for example, where the ownership and management of the company pass into new hands, or where direction passes into the hands of a receiver or liquidator.[8] Thus persons carrying on business in the form of a company may effectively (though not technically) assign all the company's contracts on a transfer of the business, provided that they transfer the company's shares, and not simply the company's assets, to the assignee. Had this course been adopted in, for example, *Tolhurst's case*[9] no difficulties would have arisen.

(ii) *Validity of Assignments against Assignor's Creditors and Successors in Title*

General. Even where an assignment is valid against the assignor, the position 20–056 may be different between persons deriving title through the assignor on the one hand and the assignee on the other. Four different cases must be considered: the validity of an assignment against the assignor's personal representatives; the validity of an assignment against a trustee in bankruptcy of the assignor; the validity of an assignment against the liquidator or creditors of a company assignor; and the validity of an assignment against creditors generally. These four cases do not necessarily exhaust the cases in which some outside party may wish to dispute the validity of an assignment. For example, tax liability may in some cases turn on the validity of an assignment; in such circumstances it has been assumed that the question must be determined by inquiring whether the assignment is valid against the assignor.[10]

Personal representatives. It never seems to have been doubted that an 20–057 assignor's personal representatives are bound by an assignment which was binding on the assignor,[11] even where the assignment was not intended to operate until the death of the assignor.[12] It has been suggested that an assignment not binding on the assignor may become binding on his death, inasmuch as an assignment without consideration may be revocable by the assignor but will not be revocable by his personal representatives.[13] This seems questionable, however, for if the "assignment" is truly revocable, then it seems that it cannot be an assignment in the strict sense at all[14]; and on the other hand, an actual assignment (as distinct from an agreement to assign) is not revocable merely because of want of consideration.[15]

---

[7] *Griffith v. Tower Publishing Co.* [1897] 1 Ch. 21.
[8] See *Griffiths v. Secretary of State for Social Services* [1974] Q.B. 468 (managing director's contract).
[9] *Supra.*
[10] See, *e.g. Vandervell v. I.R.C.* [1967] 2 A.C. 291 (surtax); *Re Rose* [1952] Ch. 499; *Letts v. I.R.C.* [1957] 1 W.L.R. 201; *Dalton v. I.R.C.* [1958] T.R. 45 (estate duty); and the cases cited *ante*, § 20–025, nn. 2–3, which concerned stamp duty.
[11] *Re Westerton* [1919] 2 Ch. 104; *Re Rose, supra.* Moreover, notice after the death of the assignor is sufficient to comply with s.136 of the Law of Property Act 1925: see *Walker v. Bradford Old Bank* (1884) 12 Q.B.D. 511; *Bateman v. Hunt* [1904] 2 K.B. 530; *Re Westerton, supra.*
[12] *Re Westerton, supra.*
[13] *German v. Yates* (1915) 32 T.L.R. 52; *cf. Errington v. Errington* [1952] 1 K.B. 290, as explained in *National Provincial Bank Ltd v. Hastings Car Mart Ltd* [1975] A.C. 1175, 1252.
[14] See *ante*, § 20–022.
[15] *Ante*, §§ 20–019, 20–033.

20–058   **Trustee in bankruptcy.**[16] Prima facie the position of a trustee in bankruptcy is the same as that of the assignor himself, *i.e.* an assignment valid against the assignor will be equally valid against his trustee in bankruptcy. This could clearly cause grave injustice to creditors, especially in view of the effectiveness in equity of an agreement to assign future choses in action, and there are two important limitations on the principle that a trustee in bankruptcy is bound by assignments binding on the assignor.

20–059   First, an assignment of rights which cannot be *earned* by the assignor until after he has become bankrupt, in the sense that the consideration for the rights is not yet wholly executed by the assignor, is void as against the trustee in bankruptcy.[17] Thus, an assignment of sums already due to the assignor, or of sums which will become due to him without the need for any further action on his part, will be good against the trustee in bankruptcy; but an assignment of sums to be earned by the assignor in the future (that is, after the commencement of the bankruptcy) will be void as against the trustee from the commencement of the bankruptcy.

20–060   Secondly, section 344 of the Insolvency Act 1986 provides that a *general* assignment of existing or future book debts (or any class thereof) by a person engaged in trade or business is void against the assignor's trustee in bankruptcy as regards any debts not paid at the commencement of the bankruptcy unless the assignment has been registered as a bill of sale. This provision, however, does not apply to an assignment of debts due from specified creditors or under specified contracts, nor to an assignment made on a bona fide transfer for value of the assignor's business, nor to an assignment made for the benefit of creditors generally.[18]

20–061   Apart from these particular cases, there are also other more general statutory provisions enabling an assignment to be set aside, by a trustee in bankruptcy, as a transaction at an undervalue, a preference, an extortionate credit transaction, or as a transaction defrauding creditors.[19]

20–062   An assignment made between the date of the petition and the making of the bankruptcy order will bind the trustee in bankruptcy against a bona fide purchaser for value without notice that the petition had been presented[20] but will otherwise be void unless the court has given its consent or has subsequently ratified the transaction.[21]

20–063   **Company liquidator or creditors.** The position of a liquidator of a company which, prior to the commencement of the winding up, has assigned any of its rights is basically the same as that of a trustee in bankruptcy; that is, apart from assignments of future earnings, and from particular statutory provisions, a liquidator is bound by an assignment which would be binding on the company itself.

---

[16] See *post*, §§ 20–024—20–038.
[17] *Ex p. Nichols* (1883) 22 Ch.D. 782; *Wilmot v. Alton* [1897] 1 Q.B. 17; *Re Collins* [1925] Ch. 556; *Re Trytel* (1952) 2 T.L.R. 32; *cf. Drew & Co. v. Josolyne* (1887) 18 Q.B.D. 590.
[18] See Insolvency Act 1986, s.344(3)(b).
[19] Insolvency Act 1986, ss.339–349, 423–425. See *post* §§ 21–027—21–031.
[20] Insolvency Act 1986, s.284(4).
[21] *ibid.* s.284(1).

But the statutory provisions relating to companies differ markedly from those relating to individual bankrupts in this particular respect. Apart from the general provisions relating to preferences, extortionate credit transactions, and transactions at an undervalue,[22] which are similar to those applying to individual bankrupts, the requirements of the Companies Act 1985 only apply to assignments by way of charge, normally but not necessarily a floating charge. By sections 395–398 of the 1985 Act[23] a company is required to register, *inter alia*, a charge on book debts, and failure to comply with the Act renders the charge void against a liquidator[24] or any creditor.[25] On the other hand, this section, unlike section 344 of the Insolvency Act 1986, applies to any charge over book debts, and not merely to a general charge or assignment. Further, failure to comply with the requirements of the Companies Act renders the charge void against any creditor of the company as well as against the liquidator.

An assignment which is absolute under section 136 of the Law of Property Act **20–064** 1925 may sometimes nevertheless be an assignment by way of charge within the meaning of sections 395–398 of the Companies Act 1985. Under section 136, as already seen,[26] the question is whether the assignor has unconditionally transferred to the assignee for the time being the sole right to the debt in question as against the debtor. But under the Companies Act, the question is whether the assignor retains any interest in the nature of an equity of redemption as against the assignee. Thus an assignment intended to operate by way of security, under which the right is vested in the assignee unless and until reassigned to the assignor, would be absolute under section 136 of the Law of Property Act,[27] but registrable as a charge under sections 395–398 of the Companies Act.[28] By section 409 of the Companies Act 1985 the registration requirements of sections 395–398 apply to charges made by a foreign company with a place of business

---

[22] Insolvency Act 1986, ss.238–246. The provisions governing transactions defrauding creditors (ss.423–425 of the 1986 Act) are the same as those for individual bankrupts.

[23] As from a day to be appointed, new ss.395–420 are inserted into the 1985 Act in place of the original ss.395–408 by the Companies Act 1989, ss.93–104.

[24] See, *e.g. Orion Finance Ltd v. Crown Financial Management Ltd* [1996] 2 B.C.L.C. 78, CA; *Orion Finance Ltd v. Crown Financial Management Ltd (No. 2)* [1996] 2 B.C.L.C. 382, CA. A liquidator includes, in certain circumstances, a person appointed in foreign proceedings in the nature of a winding-up: *N.V. Slavenburg's Bank v. Intercontinental Natural Resources* [1980] 1 W.L.R. 1076, 1086–1087.

[25] On the meaning of creditor see Gough, *Company Charges*, (2nd ed., 1998), pp. 740–741; Goode, *Commercial Law*, (2nd ed., 1995), pp. 720–721; *Re Ehrmann Bros. Ltd* [1906] 2 Ch. 697.

[26] *Ante*, §§ 20–012—20–014.

[27] *Ante*, § 20–012.

[28] See *Re Kent and Sussex Sawmills Ltd* [1947] Ch. 177; *Re Miller, Gibb & Co.* [1957] 1 W.L.R. 703; and *Paul and Frank Ltd v. Discount (Overseas) Ltd* [1967] Ch. 348, in all of which assignments which were probably absolute under s.136 of the Law of Property Act were held to be registrable under the Companies Act. Certain reservations of title, commonly known as *Romalpa* clauses, may create a registrable charge (*Re Bond Worth Ltd* [1980] Ch. 228; *Borden (U.K.) Ltd v. Scottish Timber Products Ltd* [1981] Ch. 25; *E. Pfeiffer Weinkellerei-Weineinkauf GmbH & Co. v. Arbuthnot Factors Ltd* [1988] 1 W.L.R. 150; *Tatung (U.K.) Ltd v. Galex Telesure Ltd* (1989) 5 B.C.C. 325; *Re Weldtech Equipment Ltd* [1991] B.C.C. 16; Vol. II, §§ 43–176—43–187. So also certain liens, see *The Ugland Trailer* [1985] 2 Lloyd's Rep. 372; *The Annangel Glory* [1988] 1 Lloyd's Rep. 45. *cf.* a "block discount" agreement which constitutes an absolute assignment of debts and does not create a registrable charge: *Lloyds & Scottish Finance Ltd v. Cyril Lord Carpets Sales Ltd* [1992] B.C.L.C. 609, HL.

in England.[29] This may be so even where the assignment is made abroad and the assignee is also a foreign company.[30]

20–065   **Creditors.** Except in the cases mentioned in the last two paragraphs, an assignment which is valid against an assignor will generally be valid against the assignor's creditors. Thus, except in those cases, a creditor cannot generally attach any debt already assigned by the assignor.[31] There is, however, one other possible case in which an assignment may be valid against an assignor but void against creditors. It has already been seen[32] that an assignment may be constituted by instructions given by the assignor to the debtor to pay the assignee. Where the assignee has no notice of the instructions, and has therefore had no chance to accept or decline the assignment, it has been held that the assignment is not binding on creditors of the assignor since it is incomplete.[33] It is thought that the assignment may be binding on the assignor himself in these circumstances.[34]

(iii) *Priorities between Successive Assignees*

20–066   **Priorities.** As seen above, notice to the debtor is not necessary to perfect an equitable assignment as between assignor and assignee, but where there are successive assignments (whether statutory or equitable), the rule in *Dearle v. Hall*,[35] which originally related to equitable interests in pure personalty, regulates priorities. Under this rule the assignee who first gives notice to the debtor has the prior right, unless he knew of the earlier assignment when he took his assignment.[36] The fact that he knew of the earlier assignment when he gave notice is irrelevant.[37] Thus where a debt due to a firm was assigned by one partner to the defendants by writing and afterwards by the other partner to the plaintiff by deed, and the plaintiff gave notice to the debtor before the defendants, it was held that there was a valid equitable assignment to the plaintiff in priority to the defendants.[38] And a second statutory assignment will not prevail over an earlier

[29] As from a day to be appointed, new ss.703A–703N are inserted into the 1985 Act in place of the original s.409 by the Companies Act 1989, s.105 and Sched. 15.

[30] *N.V. Slavenburg's Bank v. Intercontinental Natural Resources Ltd* [1980] 1 W.L.R. 1076; *Re Oriel Ltd* [1984] B.C.L.C. 241.

[31] *Holt v. Heatherfield Trust Ltd* [1942] 2 K.B. 1.

[32] *Ante,* § 20–021—20–023.

[33] *Rekstin v. Severo, etc., and Bank for Russian Trade* [1933] 1 K.B. 47.

[34] *Ante,* § 20–023.

[35] (1823) 3 Russ. 1.

[36] *Dearle v. Hall* (1823) 3 Russ. 1; see also *Lloyd v. Banks* (1868) L.R. 3 Ch.App. 488; *Re Holmes* (1885) 29 Ch.D. 796; *Ward v. Duncombe* [1893] A.C. 369; *Kelly v. Selwyn* [1905] 2 Ch. 117; *Ellerman Lines Ltd v. Lancaster Maritime Co. Ltd* [1980] 2 Lloyd's Rep. 497; *The Attika Hope* [1988] 1 Lloyd's Rep. 439; *Compaq Computer Ltd v. Abercorn Group Ltd* [1991] B.C.C. 484; *E. Pfeiffer Weinkellerei-Weinenkauf GmbH & Co. v. Arbuthnot Factors Ltd* [1988] 1 W.L.R. 150. The principle does not however apply in favour of a trustee in bankruptcy (*Re Anderson* [1911] 1 K.B. 896); a judgment creditor (*Scott v. Lord Hastings* (1858) 4 K. & J. 633); nor a volunteer (*Justice v. Wynne* (1861) 12 Ir.Ch.Rep. 289). For further discussion of this difficult topic see Snell, *Equity* (29th ed., 1990), pp. 64–70. See also Goode (1976) 92 L.Q.R. 554–559; Donaldson (1977) 93 L.Q.R. 324; Goode (1977) 93 L.Q.R. 487; McLauchlan (1980) 96 L.Q.R. 90; Oditah (1989) 9 O.J.L.S. 513.

[37] *Mutual Life Assurance Society v. Langley* (1886) 32 Ch.D. 460.

[38] *Marchant v. Morton, Down & Co.* [1901] 2 K.B. 829. *Joseph v. Lyons* (1884) 15 Q.B.D. 280; *E. Pfeiffer Weinkellerei-Weinenkauf GmbH v. Arbuthnot Factors Ltd, supra.*

equitable one merely because it confers a legal right upon the assignee[39]: in Phillips J.'s words in the *Pfeiffer* case, " . . . even if the [statutory] assignment is effected for value without notice of a prior equity, priorities fall to be determined as if the assignment had been effected in equity, not in law."[40] The issue of priority must be distinguished from the rule that an assignee takes "subject to equities."[41] Such equities are independent of the assignments and prevail over all assignees.

Nature of notice required. In general, notice need not be formal for the **20–067** purpose of conferring priority over a subsequent assignee: any kind of notice will suffice so long as the fact that assignment has taken place is brought to the notice of the debtor. A letter stating that the writers had authority to collect freight "against which we have made payments" was held a good notice.[42] And oral notice acquired in the ordinary course of business has been held sufficient, even though no notice was given by the assignee.[43] But as regards the assignment of an equitable interest in real or personal property, section 137(3) of the Law of Property Act 1925 lays down that oral notice of the assignment to a trustee does not affect the priority of competing claims of purchasers in that equitable interest.

(iv) *Assignments "subject to equities"*

Assignments "subject to equities."[44] Assignments normally take effect **20–068** "subject to equities." This was always so in equity,[45] and is also the position with a statutory assignment, for section 136 of the Law of Property Act 1925 lays down that an assignment takes effect "subject to equities having priority over the right of the assignee."[46] Thus, where a claim arises out of the contract under which the debt itself arises, and the claim affects the value or amount of the debt which one of the parties purported to assign for value, then if the assignee subsequently sues, the other party to the contract may set up that claim (including the right to set the contract aside[47]) by way of defence against the assignee as cancelling or diminishing the amount to which the assignee asserts his rights under the assignment.[48] Many of the cases have arisen in the context of receivership. The appointment of a receiver by a debenture-holder converts the incomplete assignment constituted by the debenture into a completed equitable

---

[39] *E. Pfeiffer Weinkellerei-Weinenkauf GmbH v. Arbuthnot Factors Ltd* [1988] 1 W.L.R. 150, 161–163. For a contrary approach, see Thomas (1951) 1 J.S.P.T.L. 480; Oditah (1989) 9 O.J.L.S. 513.

[40] [1988] 1 W.L.R. 150, 162. It was left open, at 163, whether a statutory assignee, who has actually been paid the debt, can claim priority as a bona fide purchaser for value of the legal title to the payments received. This was conceded in favour of the assignee in *Compaq Computers Ltd v. Abercorn Group Ltd* [1991] B.C.C. 484, 500. See also *Taylor v. Blakelock* (1886) 32 Ch.D. 560.

[41] *Post*, §§ 20–068—20–074.

[42] *Smith v. SS. Zigurds (Owners)* [1934] A.C. 209.

[43] *Re Worcester* (1868) L.R. 3 Ch.App. 555; *Lloyd v. Banks* (1868) L.R. 3 Ch.App. 488; *Re Dallas* [1904] 2 Ch. 385, 399.

[44] See in general Derham, *Set-off* (2nd ed., 1996), Chap. 13. See also Derham (1991) 107 L.Q.R. 126.

[45] *Mangles v. Dixon* (1852) 3 H.L.C. 702, 731; *Phipps v. Lovegrove* (1873) L.R. 16 Eq. 80, 88.

[46] *Ante*, § 20–006.

[47] *Stoddart v. Union-Trust* [1912] K.B. 181, 189.

[48] *Young v. Kitchin* (1878) 3 Ex.D. 127; *Newfoundland Government v. Newfoundland Ry.* (1883) 13 App.Cas. 199; *Lawrence v. Hayes* [1927] 2 K.B. 111.

assignment of the assets charged by it.[49] The authorities were reviewed in *Business Computers Ltd v. Anglo-African Leasing Ltd*[50] and it was said that the result "is that a debt which accrues due before notice of an assignment is received, whether or not it is payable before that date,[51] or a debt which arises out of the same contract as that which gives rise to the assigned debt, or is closely connected with that contract,[52] may be set off against the assignee. A debt which is neither accrued nor connected may not be set off even though it arises from a contract made before the assignment."[53] The rationale for this is that, after notice of the assignment, the debtor cannot "do anything to take away or diminish the rights of the assignee as they stood at the time of the notice."[54] A direct claim by the debtor against the assignee may, however, be the subject of a set-off although it would not have been available against the assignor.[55]

20–069   **Claims for damages.** It is clear that provided a claim for unliquidated damages can be set off against the assignor,[56] it can also be set off against the assignee if it arises out of the transaction giving rise to the assigned debt, irrespective of whether the claim itself could have been assigned.[57] But in *Stoddart v. Union Trust*[58] it was held that a claim for damages for fraudulently inducing the debtor to enter into the contract with the assignor could not be set up against the assignee unless the debtor rescinded the whole agreement. It is not easy to justify this decision which appears to draw a distinction between a claim for damages for fraud and a similar claim for breach of a term of the contract, and the case is perhaps explicable on a procedural point.[59] In the somewhat analogous case where the fraudulent party becomes bankrupt (instead of assigning his rights) it has been held that the fraud may be set up as a defence against the trustee in bankruptcy.[60]

---

[49] *George Barker (Transport) Ltd v. Eynon* [1974] 1 W.L.R. 462, 467. See also *Watson v. Duff, Morgan & Vermont (Holdings) Ltd* [1974] 1 W.L.R. 450, 456.

[50] [1977] 1 W.L.R. 578.

[51] *Rother Iron Works Ltd v. Canterbury Precision Engineers Ltd* [1974] Q.B. 1; *Biggerstaff v. Rowatts Wharf Ltd* [1896] 2 Ch. 93.

[52] *Newfoundland Government v. Newfoundland Ry.* (1888) 13 App.Cas. 199, 213 (claims "flowing out of and inseparably connected with . . . the transactions which also give use to the subject of the assignment"); *William Pickersgill & Sons Ltd v. London & Provincial, etc., Ins. Co. Ltd* [1912] 3 K.B. 614; *The Raven* [1980] 2 Lloyd's Rep. 266; *cf. Provident Finance Corpn. Pty. Ltd v. Hammond* [1978] V.R. 312; *The Evelpidis Era* [1981] 1 Lloyd's Rep. 54, 66; *The Dominique* [1989] A.C. 1056.

[53] [1977] 1 W.L.R. 578, 585 (Templeman J.). See also *Re Taunton, Delmard Lane & Co. Ltd* [1893] 2 Ch. 175, 183; *Re Pinto Leite & Nephews* [1929] 1 Ch. 221; *Jeffryes v. Agra & Mastermans Bank* (1866) L.R. 2 Eq. 674; *Watson v. Mid-Wales Ry.* (1867) L.R. 2 C.P. 593; *Re Pain* [1919] 1 Ch. 38; *The Khian Captain (No. 2)* [1996] 1 Lloyd's Rep. 429; *Marathon Electrical Manufacturing Corp. v. Mashreqbank P.S.C.* [1997] 2 B.C.L.C. 460.

[54] *Roxburghe v. Cox* (1881) 17 Ch.D. 520, 526.

[55] *The Raven* [1980] 2 Lloyd's Rep. 266.

[56] *The Dominique* [1989] A.C. 1056.

[57] *Young v. Kitchin, supra; Newfoundland Government v. Newfoundland Ry., supra.*

[58] [1912] 1 K.B. 181. For criticism of this decision, see Treitel, *The Law of Contract* (9th ed., 1995), p. 607.

[59] *viz.* that the debtor had "counterclaimed" for damages for the fraud against the assignee instead of merely setting the fraud up by way of defence; *cf. ante,* § 6–107. See also *Lawrence v. Hayes* [1927] 2 K.B. 111. The case was, however, followed in *Provident Finance Corpn. Pty. Ltd v. Hammond* [1978] V.R. 312.

[60] *Jack v. Kipping* (1882) 9 Q.B.D. 113; *Tilley v. Bowman* [1910] 1 K.B. 745; *cf. Kitchen's Trustee v. Madders* [1950] Ch. 134; see *post,* § 21–041. In none of these cases was there, or indeed could there have been, a counterclaim for damages for fraud, for this would have been a provable debt in the bankruptcy.

Modification of "equities" rule. Sometimes the rule that an assignee takes subject to equities is excluded or modified by statute,[61] or by the terms of the contract between the debtor and the assignor.[62]　　**20–070**

Successive assignments. Where there have been several assignments, there is authority for the view that the rule that an assignee takes subject to equities does not include claims available against an intermediate assignee and that a claim or defence against the intermediate assignee could not be set-off in a claim by a subsequent assignee.[63] It has, however, been argued that where the claim or defence against the intermediate assignee arose after the first assignment it should be available in a claim by a subsequent assignee.[64] Moreover, where the assignment is statutory, as "the debt is transferred to the assignee and becomes as though it had been his from the beginning,"[65] it is possible that the subsequent assignee would be required to sue in the name of the intermediate assignee and therefore be subject to such equities available against the intermediate assignee as arose before the subsequent assignee gave notice of the assignment to the debtor.[66]　　**20–071**

Assignee cannot recover more than assignor. A further aspect of the idea that an assignee takes an assignment "subject to equities" is the principle that an assignee cannot recover more from the debtor than the assignor could have done had there been no assignment. For example, in *Dawson v. Great Northern & City Railway Co.*[67] the assignment of a statutory claim for compensation for damage to land did not entitle the assignee to recover extra loss suffered by reason of a trade carried on by him, but not the assignor, that the assignor would not have suffered.　　**20–072**

The application of this principle has given rise to particular difficulty in relation to building contracts or tort claims for damage to buildings. Say, for example, a building is sold at full value along with an assignment to the purchaser of claims in contract or tort in relation to the building. The building turns out to need repairs as a result of a breach of the builder's contract with the assignor (whether that breach is prior, or subsequent, to the sale to the assignee) or of a tort (damaging the building prior to the sale). The assignee pays for the repairs. It might be argued that the assignor in that situation has suffered no loss so that, applying the governing principle that the assignee cannot recover more than the assignor, the assignee has no substantial claim. If correct, " ... the claim to damages would disappear ... into some legal black hole, so that the　　**20–073**

---

[61] *e.g.* Marine Insurance Act 1906, s.50(2); Bills of Exchange Act 1882, s.38(2). On s.50, see *The Evelpidis Era* [1981] 1 Lloyd's Rep. 54.

[62] *Re Agra and Masterman's Bank* (1867) L.R. 2 Ch.App. 391, 397; *Re Blakely Ordinance Co.* (1867) 3 Ch.App. 154, 159–160. Such provisions are often inserted into debentures. See also *William Pickersgill & Sons Ltd v. London & Provincial etc., Ins. Co. Ltd, supra.* As to equities attaching to the debt in the hands of an intermediate assignor, see *Southern British National Trust Ltd v. Pither* (1937) 57 C.L.R. 89. If the assignee in a notice of assignment to the debtor says "no set-off," it is an interesting question, on which there appears to be no authority, whether the debtor is estopped from a set-off if *e.g.* he continues to order goods from the assignor.

[63] *The Raven* [1980] 2 Lloyd's Rep. 266, 273; *Re Milan Railways Co.* (1884) 25 Ch.D. 587, 593.

[64] Treitel, *The Law of Contract*, (9th ed., 1995), p. 608.

[65] *Read v. Brown* (1888) 22 Q.B.D. 128, 132.

[66] Derham, *Set-off* (2nd ed., 1996), p. 591.

[67] [1905] 1 K.B. 260.

wrongdoer escaped scot-free."[68] Acceptance of the argument would also nullify the purpose of the governing principle which is to avoid prejudice to the debtor and not to allow the debtor to escape liability.

20–074   Perhaps not surprisingly, therefore, that argument was rejected by the House of Lords in a Scottish delict case.[69] And the problem has been circumvented in England by the courts' recognition that, where a third party is, or will become, owner of the defective or damaged property, there is an exception to the general rule that a contracting party can recover damages only for its own loss and not the loss of the third party.[70] Where the exception applies, the contracting party (the assignor) is entitled to substantial damages for the loss suffered by the third party (the assignee): by the same token, an award of substantial damages to the assignee does not infringe the principle that the assignee cannot recover more than the assignor.

(v) No Assignment of Liabilities

20–075   **Consent of other party required for release of contracting party.** Everybody has a right to choose with whom he will contract and no-one is obliged without his consent to accept the liability of a person other than him with whom he made his contract. Consequently, the burden of a contract cannot in principle be transferred without the consent of the other party, so as to discharge the original contractor. As Sir R. Collins M.R. said in *Tolhurst* v. *Associated Portland Cement Manufacturers Ltd*,[71] "Neither at law nor in equity could the burden of a contract be shifted off the shoulders of a contractor on to those of another without the consent of the contractee."

20–076   **Benefit and burden.** The principle that the burden of a contract cannot be transferred so as to discharge the original contractor without the consent of the other party means that, as a general rule, the assignee of the benefit of a contract involving mutual rights and obligations does not acquire the assignor's contractual obligations. Thus, where goods are purchased, and the seller assigns the right to the price to a credit factor, the factor is under no liability to the purchaser if the goods are defective although, in an action by the factor, the principle that assignments are subject to equities means that the purchaser will generally be able to rely on any defence or claim which he could raise against the seller.[72] Similarly in *Pan Ocean Shipping Ltd* v. *Creditcorp Ltd*[73] it was held by the House of Lords that an assignee of the payment of hire under a charterparty is not liable

---

[68] *G.U.S. Property Management Ltd* v. *Littlewoods Mail Order Stores Ltd*, 1982 S.L.T. 533, 538 (*per* Lord Keith).

[69] *ibid.*

[70] *Linden Gardens Trust Ltd* v. *Lenesta Sludge Disposals Ltd* [1994] 1 A.C. 85 (see also *ante*, § 20–044); *Darlington B.C.* v. *Wiltshier Northern Ltd* [1995] 1 W.L.R. 68; *Alfred McAlpine Construction Ltd* v. *Panatown Ltd* (1998) 58 Const. L.R. 58. The exception is based on *Dunlop* v. *Lambert* (1839) 6 Cl & F 600 and *The Albazero* [1977] A.C. 774. For detailed discussion, see *ante*, §§ 19–046—19–054. See also Cartwright (1993) 9 Const.L.J. 281; Duncan Wallace (1994) 110 L.Q.R. 42; Tettenborn (1994) 53 C.L.J. 24; Treitel (1998) 114 L.Q.R. 527.

[71] [1902] 2 K.B. 660, 668, CA; *C.B. Peacock Land Co. Ltd* v. *Hamilton Milk Products Co. Ltd* [1963] N.Z.L.R. 576; *Hirachand Punamchand* v. *Temple* [1911] 2 K.B. 330, 80 L.J.K.B. 1155; *Linden Gardens Trust Ltd* v. *Lenesta Sludge Disposals Ltd* [1994] 1 A.C. 85, 103. See also Birks and Beatson (1976) 92 L.Q.R. 188–202.

[72] *Ante*, §§ 20–068—20–069.

[73] [1994] 1 W.L.R. 161.

to the debtor (the charterer), whether in contract or restitution, to repay the hire paid for a period when the ship turned out to be off-hire: rather the liability to repay the unearned hire, which on the facts was contained in an express term of the charterparty, remained exclusively with the assignor. This was so irrespective of whether the debtor would have had a defence to an action for non-payment of hire by the assignee.

Conditional benefits. However, where contractual rights are assigned, the 20-077 extent of those rights will be defined by the original contract. This means that (for example) an exemption clause in the original contract may be binding on the assignee.[74] Again, a patentee who assigned his patent by a contract which provided that certain payments were to be made to him was permitted to sue a company to which the assignees had later assigned their rights.[75] In *Tolhurst's* case,[76] the assignee acquired the benefit of a contract to supply chalk for the manufacture of Portland cement on a particular piece of land. The assignee was not bound by the duty to take chalk from Tolhurst,[77] but if it did take chalk, it was bound to obtain all its requirements for the manufacture of cement on that piece of land from him. Although these cases have sometimes been seen as applications of the principle that he who takes the benefit of a transaction must also bear the burden, it appears that they are examples of another principle; the conditional benefit principle.[78] The conditional benefit principle arises where the right assigned is only conditional or qualified, the condition being that certain restrictions shall be observed or certain burdens assumed. The restrictions or qualifications are an intrinsic part of the right which the assignee has to take as it stands.[79] The question whether a contract creates a conditional benefit is one of construction.[80]

"Pure" benefit and burden principle. In *Tito v. Waddell (No. 2)* Megarry 20-078 V.-C. distinguished the conditional benefit principle from what he termed the "pure principle of benefit and burden."[81] By a series of contracts, a mining company acquired the right to extract phosphates on a Pacific island on the condition that it would "return all worked out lands to the original owners and . . . replant such lands." In 1920 the rights were transferred to government commissioners "subject to . . . the covenants and conditions therein contained." Megarry V.-C. held that the right to extract phosphates given in the contracts between the owners and the company was not qualified by or conditional on the replanting obligations but that the "pure principle" of benefit and burden rendered the present commissioners liable to the owners for breach of the covenant to replant. But in *Rhone v. Stephens*[82] the House of Lords cast doubt on Megarry V.-C.'s views to the extent that he was recognising a "pure principle" that any

---

[74] See *Britain & Overseas Trading Ltd v. Brooks Wharf Ltd* [1967] 2 Lloyd's Rep. 51; *National Carbonising Co. Ltd v. British Coal Distillation Ltd* (1936) 54 R.P.C. 41, 57 *et seq.* See also *Aspden v. Seddon (No. 2)* (1876) 1 Ex.D. 496, 509.

[75] *Werdman v. Société Générale d'Electricité* (1881) 19 Ch.D. 246.

[76] [1903] A.C. 414. *Ante*, § 20–054.

[77] *National Carbonising Co. Ltd v. British Coal Distillation Ltd, ante.*

[78] See generally *Tito v. Waddell (No. 2)* [1977] Ch. 106, 290 *et seq.* See also *Pan Ocean Shipping Co. Ltd v. Creditcorp Ltd, The Trident Beauty* [1994] 1 W.L.R. 161, 171.

[79] [1977] Ch. 106, at 290, 302.

[80] *ibid.* at 302.

[81] [1977] Ch. 106, at 290, 302.

[82] [1994] 2 A.C. 310. See also *Thamesmead Town Ltd v. Allotey* [1998] 37 E.G. 161.

party deriving any benefit from a conveyance must accept any burden in the same conveyance. Lord Templeman instead said that the condition must be relevant to the exercise of the right. On that basis, it was held that the fact that the roof of D's house was supported by P's cottage did not mean that P could enforce against D a covenant made by D's predecessor in title with P's to repair the roof.

2. VICARIOUS PERFORMANCE

20–079   **Vicarious performance.** A contracting party can in the case of many contracts enter into an arrangement by which some other person may perform for him, as far as he is concerned, the obligations of the contract, and the other contracting party will be obliged to accept that performance if it is performance in accordance with the terms of the contract. The contracting party will, however, be liable for any breach that may happen, and the other contracting party is not bound or, indeed, entitled to sue the substituted person for breach of contract,[83] although there may, of course, be a remedy in tort, *e.g.* where the substituted person negligently damages or causes the loss of goods entrusted to him. This is technically known as vicarious performance, and it is "quite a mistake to regard that as an assignment of the contract: it is not."[84]

20–080   It has been said that, "Whether or not in any given contract performance can properly be carried out by the employment of a subcontractor must depend on the proper inference to be drawn from the contract itself, the subject-matter of it, and other material surrounding circumstances."[85] Some contractual obligations are obviously too personal to admit to performance by anyone other than the original contracting parties: for example, a contract to paint a picture, or to write a play or a book.[86] A contractual obligation to store furniture[87] and to carry out building work,[88] has been held to be incapable of vicarious performance, because of the personal confidence reposed by the customer in the original contracting party. And in *Johnson v. Raylton*[89] it was held that where a manufacturer of goods contracts to supply specific goods to a buyer, there is an implied term in the contract that the goods shall be those of the seller's own manufacture.[90] The case should, however, probably not be regarded as laying down a general rule still applicable in modern conditions, for clearly much must depend on the nature of

---

[83] *Stewart v. Reavell's Garage* [1952] 2 Q.B. 545. *cf. John Rigby (Haulage) Ltd v. Reliance Marine Insurance Co. Ltd* [1956] 2 Q.B. 468. It has been suggested that this rule is qualified and the debtor will not be responsible where performance requires specialist skills which he cannot reasonably be expected to possess, see Treitel, *The Law of Contract* (9th ed., 1995), p. 673, n. 46, but the statement in *Investors in Industry Commercial Property Ltd v. Bedfordshire D.C.* [1986] 1 All E.R. 787, 807, upon which the qualification is based, assumes that the other contracting party appoints the specialist to perform the task.

[84] *Davies v. Collins* [1945] 1 All E.R. 247, 249. *cf. Nokes v. Doncaster Amalgamated Collieries Ltd* [1940] A.C. 1014, 1019.

[85] *Davies v. Collins* [1945] 1 All E.R. 247, 250. *Kollerich & Cie SA v. The State Trading Corp. of India* [1980] 2 Lloyd's Rep. 32.

[86] *Tolhurst v. Associated Portland Cement Manufacturers Ltd* [1902] 2 K.B. 660, 669 (*per* Sir R. Collins M.R.); *Fratelli Sorrentino v. Buerger* [1915] 1 K.B. 307, 313; *Southway Group Ltd v. Wolff & Wolff* (1991) 57 B.L.R. 33, 52.

[87] *Edwards v. Newland & Co.* [1950] 2 K.B. 534.

[88] *Southway Group Ltd v. Wolff & Wolff* (1991) 57 B.L.R. 33.

[89] (1881) 7 Q.B.D. 438.

[90] A clause to this effect was originally included in the Sale of Goods Bill 1889.

the goods and the customs of the trade.[91] The terms of the contract may also throw light on the question whether it can be vicariously performed, the test being: Did the contracting party promise personal performance, or did he merely promise a result? In *Davies v. Collins*,[92] the Court of Appeal hesitated to say that a contract to clean clothes was incapable of vicarious performance. They reached the conclusion that the particular contract in that case was not so capable because of the language of an exemption clause.

In *Robson and Sharpe v. Drummond*,[93] the defendant hired a chariot from   **20–081** Sharpe for five years at a yearly rent, payable in advance each year, the chariot to be kept in repair and painted once a year by Sharpe. After three years Sharpe retired from business and purported to delegate performance of the contract to his partner Robson. It was held that the defendant was entitled to repudiate the contract and was not liable to pay the rent for the last two years. Lord Tenterden based his judgment on the ground that the defendant might have been induced to enter into the contract by reason of the personal confidence which he reposed in Sharpe, and therefore might have agreed to pay rent in advance. Littledale and Parke JJ. also said that the defendant had a right to the personal services of Sharpe, and to the benefit of his judgment and taste. On the other hand, in *British Waggon Co. and Parkgate Waggon Co. v. Lea*,[94] the defendant hired 100 railway wagons from the Parkgate Waggon Company for seven years at a yearly rent payable quarterly, the wagons to be kept in repair by the company. After four years the Parkgate Company, which had gone into voluntary liquidation, assigned the benefit of the contract to the British Waggon Company and delegated performance of its obligations to the assignees. It was held that the defendant was not entitled to repudiate the contract. Cockburn C.J. laid down the general principle,

> "that where a person contracts with another to do work or perform service, and it can be inferred that the person employed has been selected with reference to his individual skill, competency or other personal qualification, the inability or unwillingness of the party so employed to execute the work or perform the service is a sufficient answer to any demand by a stranger to the original contract for the performance of it by the other party, and entitles the latter to treat the contract as at an end, notwithstanding that the person tendered to take the place of the contracting party may be equally well qualified to do the service."[95]

He held that the principle did not apply to a contract for the repair of railway wagons—"a rough description of work which ordinary workmen conversant with the business would be perfectly able to execute"; and that the defendant could not have attached any importance to whether the repairs were done by the Parkgate Company or by a sub-contractor.

Vicarious performance and agency. As already seen, in a case of vicarious   **20–082** performance the original contracting party remains liable on the contract. There

---

[91] The dissent of Bramwell L.J. puts strong arguments against the majority decision.

[92] [1945] 1 All E.R. 247.

[93] (1831) 2 B. & Ad. 303, a much criticised case. *cf. Boulton v. Jones* (1857) 2 H. & N. 564; *Jaeger's Sanitary Woollen System Co. v. Walker & Sons* (1897) 77 L.T. 180.

[94] (1880) 5 Q.B.D. 149. See also *C.B. Peacocke Land Co. Ltd v. Hamilton Milk Producers Co. Ltd* [1963] N.Z.L.R. 576.

[95] (1880) 5 Q.B.D. at 153. *cf. Fratelli Sorrentino v. Buerger* [1915] 3 K.B. 367, 370.

is nothing to prevent a person contracting on such terms that he is entitled either to perform the contract himself, or to secure performance by making a new contract with a third party as agent of the other contracting party. If such a new contract is in fact made the original contracting party may be subject to no further liability on the contract. Such an arrangement is not unusual in certain types of business,[96] though difficulty may sometimes arise in deciding whether the case is one of agency or of vicarious performance.[97] Whether it is the one or the other depends on the intention of the parties objectively ascertained.

3. Assignment and Negotiability

20–083 **Assignment and negotiability.** Negotiable instruments, governed formerly by the law of merchants, differ in several ways from contracts which are assignable under the law as explained in the foregoing pages. In particular:

(a) They are transferable by delivery (or in some cases by delivery and indorsement) though it would be more accurate to say that the contract contained in them is transferred.

(b) No notice need be given to the debtor.

(c) The right or contract embodied in them cannot be transferred without the instrument. Thus the rule in *Dearle* v. *Hall*[98] as to priority of notice to the debtor has no application to negotiable instruments.[99]

(d) A bona fide transferee for value may obtain a good title even though the title of his transferor was defective. Thus the transferor of a negotiable instrument can give a better title than he himself has.[1]

4. Assignment, Novation and Acknowledgment

20–084 **Novation.** There is no doubt that with the consent of *both* contracting parties all contracts of any kind may be transferred, and the term "novation" has been introduced from Roman law to describe this species of transfer. Novation takes place where the two contracting parties agree that a third, who also agrees, shall stand in the relation of either of them to the other. There is a new contract and it is therefore essential that the consent of all parties shall be obtained[2]: in this

---

[96] Bills of lading, for example, may contain clauses permitting transhipment without further liability on the original contracting carrier. See also *Investors in Industry Commercial Property Ltd v. Bedfordshire D.C.* [1986] 1 All E.R. 787, 807, *ante*, § 20–079, n. 83.

[97] *e.g.* if a person takes some article to a shop for repair and the shopkeeper sends it on to the manufacturer with the consent of the customer; *cf. Stewart v. Reavell's Garage* [1952] 2 Q.B. 545; *Morris v. C.W. Martin & Sons Ltd* [1966] 1 Q.B. 716; *The Pioneer Container* [1994] 3 W.L.R. 1. Problems can arise in transhipment situations such as those referred to above; see *Scrutton on Charterparties* (20th ed., 1996), Art. 131.

[98] (1823) 3 Russ. 1, *ante*, § 20–066.

[99] See *Bence v. Shearman* [1898] 2 Ch. 582.

[1] Bills of Exchange Act 1882, ss.29, 30, 38. But not if the bill is overdue: s.36(2). See also Consumer Credit Act 1974, s.125. See further Vol. II, Chap. 34.

[2] *e.g. Rasbora Ltd v. J.C.L. Marine Ltd* [1977] 1 Lloyd's Rep. 645; *The Blankenstein* [1985] 1 W.L.R. 435; *The Aktion* [1987] 1 Lloyd's Rep. 283, 310–311.

necessity for consent lies the most important difference between novation and assignment.

Most of the reported cases in English law have arisen either out of the amalgamation of companies, or of changes in partnership firms, the question being whether as a matter of fact the party contracting with the company or the firm accepted the new company or the new firm as his debtor in the place of the old company or the old firm.[3] That acceptance may be inferred from acts and conduct, but ordinarily it is not to be inferred from conduct without some distinct request.[4] Thus where a banking firm consisted of two partners and one died, the acceptance by a customer from the surviving partner of a fresh deposit note for a balance of a debt due was held sufficient evidence of novation to discharge the estate of the deceased partner, as the customer took the money out of a current account and placed it on deposit at the request of the surviving partner.[5]

It should, however, be noted that the effect of a novation is not to assign or transfer a right or liability, but rather to extinguish the original contract and replace it by another. It is therefore necessary that consideration should be provided for the new contract.[6] If A owes B money and both parties agree with C that C, not A, is to pay the money to B, B provides consideration for C's promise to pay him by agreeing to release A; while A provides consideration for B's promise to release him by providing the new debtor, C.

Acknowledgment.[7] There is a distinct line of mainly nineteenth-century cases holding that where a person holds a fund for another and is directed by that other to pay it to a third party, and notifies the third party that he is willing to do so, the third party acquires a right of action for the money (even though the third party has provided no consideration). Such a transaction can obviously be said to be similar to an assignment. The proper assessment of these cases for the present day is however a matter of difficulty, for they antedate the formulation of the rules of privity of contract, trust, assignment and agency that are now accepted. The best explanation of the cases may rest on the idea of attornment of money. If this is so, it would seem essential that the doctrine is confined to funds and not extended to debts: yet in *Shamia v. Joory*,[8] the only recent case in which the doctrine has been invoked, the full complexities were apparently not cited to Barry J. and he applied the doctrine to a mere debt. The extent to which this line of cases survives in view of the development of methods of assignment, and the significance to be attached to the individual cases, are highly doubtful.

---

[3] *Wilson v. Lloyd* (1873) L.R. 16 Eq. 60, 73; *Miller's Case* (1877) 3 Ch.D. 391; *Perry v. National Provincial Bank* [1910] 1 Ch. 464; *Meek v. Port of London Authority* [1918] 2 Ch. 96. For the use of novation or "quasi-novation" in analysing certain credit card transactions, see *Re Charge Card Services* [1989] Ch. 497, 513.

[4] *Re European Assurance Association Society Arbitration Acts, Conquest's Case* (1875) 1 Ch.D. 334; *Chatsworth Investments Ltd v. Cussins (Contractors) Ltd* [1969] 1 W.L.R. 1. See also *Scarf v. Jardine* (1882) 7 App.Cas. 345; *British Homes Assurance Corpn. v. Paterson* [1902] 2 Ch. 404.

[5] *Re Head* [1894] 2 Ch. 236.

[6] *Tatlock v. Harris* (1789) 3 T.R. 174, 180. See also *Cuxon v. Chadley* (1824) 3 B. & C. 591; *Wharton v. Walker* (1825) 4 B. & C. 163. But there can be difficulty in seeing how consideration moves from the promisee: see *Olsson v. Dyson* (1969) 120 C.L.R. 365, 390.

[7] Davies (1959) 75 L.Q.R. 220; Yates (1977) 41 Conv.(N.S.) 49; Goff and Jones, *The Law of Restitution* (5th ed., 1998), Chap. 28; *post*, §§ 30–167—30–169.

[8] [1958] 1 Q.B. 448; criticised by Goff and Jones *op. cit.* pp. 691–693.

CHAPTER 21

DEATH AND BANKRUPTCY

1. DEATH

Introductory. The general rule at common law was that the maxim *actio* **21–001** *personalis moritur cum persona* had no application to any breach of contract, except breach of a promise to marry.[1] Hence the personal representatives of a deceased contracting party could generally sue and be sued on contracts made by him in his lifetime. However, the operation of the maxim quoted above has been greatly circumscribed by the Law Reform (Miscellaneous Provisions) Act 1934, s.1(1) of which provides that on the death of any person after the commencement of the Act, all causes of action (with certain exceptions in tort) subsisting against or vested in him shall survive against or for the benefit of his estate.

Actions by personal representatives. Wherever money due on a contract **21–002** made with the deceased will, when recovered, be assets, the executor or administrator may sue for it in his representative capacity.[2] Therefore, when the defendant ordered a coat of one T, a tailor, but before the coat was finished T died, and the coat was afterwards finished and delivered by his administratrix, it was held that the value of the coat was recoverable in an action for goods sold and delivered by her as administratrix.[3] Again, where a person agreed to do certain work and died before it was begun and his executors did the work, using his materials, it was held that the executors might sue in that capacity for the value of the materials[4]; and in such a case they might also sue for work and labour as executors.[5] An executor may also sue in that capacity for goods sold by

---

[1] *Pinchon's Case* (1611) 9 Co.Rep. 86b; *Hambly v. Trott* (1775) 1 Cowp. 371, 375; *Raymond v. Fitch* (1835) 2 Cr. M. & R. 588; *Phillips v. Homfray* (1883) 24 Ch.D. 439, 456–457.

[2] *Marshall v. Broadhurst* (1831) 1 Cr. & J. 403, 405; *Heath v. Chilton* (1844) 12 M. & W. 632, 637; *Moseley v. Rendell* (1871) L.R. 6 Q.B. 338; *Abbott v. Parfitt* (1871) L.R. 6 Q.B. 346.

[3] *Werner v. Humphreys* (1841) 2 M. & G. 853.

[4] *Marshall v. Broadhurst, supra.*

[5] *ibid.; Edwards v. Grace* (1836) 2 M. & W. 190.

him in the course of carrying on and continuing as executor the testator's business, although the goods were acquired by the executor after the testator's death, provided they formed part of the assets.[6]

21–003   **Recovery of damages by personal representatives.** There is no rule of law which prevents a personal representative from recovering larger damages than the deceased could have recovered had he survived. Accordingly, where solicitors in breach of contract negligently advised a young man that he was tenant in fee simple of certain property and that he need take no steps to reduce it into possession, whereas in fact he was tenant in tail, and he died before barring the entail, his personal representatives recovered substantial damages, although if the deceased had lived he could only have recovered nominal damages, since the mistake could easily have been rectified.[7]

21–004   **When right of action arises.** An executor's title to the property of his testator is derived from the will and not from the grant of probate. He may therefore begin an action as executor before probate, but cannot complete his case without proving his title, and must accordingly obtain probate before the hearing.[8] An administrator's title is derived from the grant of administration, but upon the grant being made, his title relates back to the date of the intestate's death[9]; however, a subsequent grant of letters of administration cannot operate retrospectively to validate a writ which from the beginning was a nullity, *e.g.* as being issued in a representative capacity not possessed by the person issuing the writ.[10]

21–005   **Actions against personal representatives.** Similarly, in principle, the personal representatives of a contracting party are bound, so far as his assets will extend, to perform all his contracts although not named therein.[11] Special pro-

---

[6] *Aspinall v. Wake* (1833) 10 Bing. 51; *Abbott v. Parfitt* (1871) L.R. 6 Q.B. 346.

[7] *Otter v. Church, Adams, Tatham & Co.* [1953] Ch. 280. See also *Ross v. Caunters* [1980] Ch. 297 *Clarke v. Bruce Lance & Co. (A Firm)* [1988] 1 W.L.R. 881; *White v. Jones* [1995] 2 A.C. 207 *Hemmens v. Wilson Browne* [1995] Ch. 223.

[8] *Thompson v. Reynolds* (1872) 3 C. & P. 123; *Re Masonic, etc. Assurance Co.* (1885) 32 Ch.D. 373. As to staying executor's action where the defendant admits the claim, but requires production of the probate, see *Webb v. Adkins* (1854) 14 C.B. 401; *Tarn v. Commercial Bank of Sydney* (1884) 12 Q.B.D. 294.

[9] *Wooley v. Clarke* (1822) 5 B. & Ald. 744; *Foster v. Bates* (1843) 12 M. & W. 226. Administrators now have the same rights and liabilities and are accountable in the same manner as executors: Administration of Estates Act 1925, s.21.

[10] *Ingall v. Moran* [1944] K.B. 160; *Hilton v. Sutton Steam Laundry* [1946] K.B. 65; *Burns v. Campbell* [1952] 1 K.B. 15; *Finnegan v. Cementation Co. Ltd* [1953] 1 Q.B. 688. See also *Re Crowhurst Park* [1974] 1 W.L.R. 583. But *cf.* the different rule in actions for the recovery of land: Limitation Act 1980, s.26. The statement in the text appears to be unaffected CPR, r. 17.4, which gives the court power in certain specified cases to allow amendments to the writ or pleadings, notwithstanding that the effect may be to deprive a party of a defence under the Limitation Act 1980: *Dawson (Bradford) v. Dove* [1971] 1 Q.B. 330 (see n. 12). On limitation, see *post,* § 21–119. As to the effect of RSC Ord. 20, r. 5, the predecessor to CPR, r. 17.4, generally, see *Beck v. Value Capital Ltd (No. 2)* [1975] 1 W.L.R. 6; [1976] 1 W.L.R. 572; *Hancock Shipping Co. Ltd v. Kawasaki Heavy Industries Ltd* [1992] 1 W.L.R. 1025. See *post,* § 21–120.

[11] *Williams v. Burrell* (1845) 1 C.B. 402; *Wills v. Murray* (1850) 4 Exch. 843, 865; *Kennewell v. Dye* [1949] Ch. 517, 521–522; *Youngmin v. Heath* [1974] 1 W.L.R. 135. For the position of options see *Longbutt v. Amoco Australia Pty. Ltd* (1974) 4 A.L.R. 482.

vision now exists enabling proceedings to be brought against a deceased person's estate prior to a grant of probate or administration.[12]

Personal contracts. The Law Reform (Miscellaneous Provisions) Act 1934 **21–006** contains no exception for contracts involving personal skill, taste or confidence, such as a contract of service,[13] a contract to perform at a concert,[14] to paint a picture, to write a book, or to act as professional jockey to the owner of racehorses.[15] In such contracts, however, there is probably no cause of action to survive, as the contract is frustrated by the death of the party whose skill or other personal qualifications were relied upon.[16] The personal representatives are, however, entitled to sue for any money actually earned by the deceased under his contract, which has become due during his lifetime.[17] Further, where the contract is in such terms that the remuneration should continue after the service has ceased, the personal representatives may sue for remuneration accrued due after death.[18] And of course if a personal contract is broken by a contracting party during his lifetime, and one party subsequently dies, the cause of action survives the death and his personal representatives can sue or be sued for breach.[19]

It is thought that the question whether a contract is personal for this purpose **21–007** is generally the same as whether the contract is personal for the purposes of the law relating to voluntary assignments and vicarious performance[20]; that is, the benefit of a contract which can be voluntarily assigned, and the burden of a contract which can be vicariously performed, will (subject to the terms of the contract itself) be transmissible to the personal representatives of the contracting parties.[21] It appears, however, that there are some cases in which the benefit of a contract will pass on the death of a party to his personal representatives, although it may not be assignable *inter vivos*, *e.g.* in the case of third-party road traffic insurance policies.[22]

Personal liability of personal representatives. The general rule is that a **21–008** personal representative is not personally liable on the contracts of the deceased: he is liable only to the extent of the assets of the estate. There is, however, a singular exception in the case of the covenants in a lease. Before entry and taking

---

[12] See RSC Ord. 15, r. 6A, para. 3, preserved by CPR, Sched. 1, which negatives *Dawson (Bradford) v. Dove, supra*. As regards bankruptcy see Insolvency Act 1986, s.421; Administration of Insolvent Estates Deceased Persons Order 1986 (S.I. 1986 No. 1999).

[13] *Farrow v. Wilson* (1869) L.R. 4 C.P. 744.

[14] *cf. Robinson v. Davison* (1871) L.R. 6 Ex. 269.

[15] *Graves v. Cohen* (1829) 46 T.L.R. 121. *cf. Phillips v. Alhambra Palace Co.* [1901] 1 Q.B. 59 (surviving partners who owned a music hall liable on contract with troupe of music hall performers); *Harvey v. Tivoli (Manchester) Ltd* (1907) 23 T.L.R. 592 (surviving members of a troupe of music hall artistes cannot enforce contract against owner of music hall).

[16] *Stubbs v. Holywell Ry.* (1867) L.R. 2 Ex. 311, 314; *post*, §§ 24–036—24–039.

[17] *Stubbs v. Holywell Ry., supra.*

[18] *Wilson v. Harper* [1908] 2 Ch. 370.

[19] *Shaw v. Shaw* [1954] 2 Q.B. 429.

[20] As to personal contracts which cannot be voluntarily assigned or vicariously performed, see *ante*, §§ 20–052—20–053, 20–079—20–082. As to personal contracts the benefit of which do not pass to a debtor's trustee in bankruptcy, see *post*, § 21–034.

[21] See, *e.g. Warner Engineering Co. Ltd v. Brennan* (1913) 30 T.L.R. 191; *Re Worthington* [1914] 2 K.B. 299; *cf. Collins v. Associated Greyhound Racecourses* [1930] 1 Ch. 1.

[22] See *Peters v. General Accident, etc., Ltd* [1938] 2 All E.R. 267 and *Kelly v. Cornhill Insurance Co.* [1964] 1 W.L.R. 158. It is implicit in this latter case that such a policy does not, in the absence of some express stipulation, come to an end on the death of the insured.

possession, the personal representatives of a tenant cannot be made personally liable as assignees of the term,[23] though they are liable to the extent of assets.[24] If they do enter, then they may be personally liable. Yet they may, by proper pleading, limit their liability for rent to the yearly value the premises might have yielded.[25] No such defence is, however, apparently allowed if the personal representative is sued after entry for a breach of the covenant to repair.[26]

21–009   **Confirmation of deceased's contract.** An administrator will generally be liable upon contracts which he confirms whether the contracts are made by the deceased or by an agent of the deceased: this is sometimes referred to as ratification, but does not seem to be a true application of agency principles.[27] However, confirmation of a contract made by an agent and a third party does not necessarily involve confirmation of a contract between the deceased and the agent of which the administrator may have been ignorant. Thus, where an agent, after the death of his principal, in pursuance of a contract made with him before the death sold the principal's goods, it was held that the principal's agreement to remunerate the agent was discharged by the death, and that confirmation of the sale by the administrator did not render him liable to remunerate the agent.[28]

21–010   **Executor carrying on business of testator.** Unless empowered to do so by the testator's will, an executor is not entitled to carry on the testator's business, except for the purpose of winding it up. If he does carry it on, whether with or without authority, he is personally liable upon the contracts he makes, and persons contracting with him have no remedy against the testator's assets.[29] The executor, if he has carried on the business in accordance with his duty, has a right to be indemnified out of the estate, and any profits made belong to the estate. He is not, however, entitled to be indemnified out of the estate in priority to the testator's creditors, even when empowered by the will to carry on the business, unless they consent to its being carried on.[30] The fact that the creditors stand by with knowledge that it is being carried on and without interference is not of itself sufficient to show consent.[31] Executors who carried on their testator's business under the powers of his will in the same firm name as before were held not to be partners, though no doubt joint debtors.[32] An administrator only has power to continue the intestate's business with a view to realising its assets. The statutory power[33] to postpone sale for such period as he may think proper may justify

---

[23] *Wollaston v. Hakewill* (1841) 3 M. & G. 297; *Rendall v. Andreae* (1892) 61 L.J.Q.B. 630.

[24] *Youngmin v. Heath* [1974] 1 W.L.R. 135.

[25] *Rendall v. Andreae, supra; Whitehead v. Palmer* [1908] 1 K.B. 151.

[26] *Tremeere v. Morrison* (1834) 1 Bing.N.C. 89; followed in *Sleap v. Newman* (1862) 12 C.B.(N.S.) 116; *Rendall v. Andreae, supra; Woodfall's Law of Landlord and Tenant* Vol. I, § 17–168 and, more fully, 27th ed., § 1840.

[27] See *Foster v. Bates* (1843) 12 M. & W. 226; Vol. II, § 32–026; Powell, *Law of Agency* (2nd ed.), p. 388, n. 7; *cf. Greenwood v. Martins Bank Ltd* [1933] A.C. 51 (adoption of a forgery).

[28] *Campanari v. Woodburn* (1854) 15 C.B. 400. A *quantum meruit* might have been available. As to this remedy, see *post*, §§ 30–177 *et seq.* But *cf. Ex p. Phillips* (1887) 19 Q.B.D. 234.

[29] *Re Morgan* (1881) 18 Ch.D. 93; *Re Evans* (1887) 34 Ch.D. 597.

[30] *Dowse v. Gorton* (1891) A.C. 190. Except where he has carried on only for such reasonable time as is necessary for selling the business as a going concern: *ibid.* at 199.

[31] *Re Oxley* [1914] 1 Ch. 604; *Re East* (1914) 111 L.T. 101.

[32] *Re Fisher & Sons* [1912] 2 K.B. 491.

[33] Administration of Estates Act 1925, s.33(1).

trading for purposes other than realisation especially in view of the duty of a personal representative to preserve the business as an asset.[34]

Liability on bills or notes. Where a person such as an executor is under an obligation to indorse a bill of exchange in a representative capacity, he may do so in such terms as to negative personal liability.[35] If he fails to do so he is personally liable.[36] **21–011**

Executor de son tort. An executor *de son tort* is one who assumes the office of executor or interferes with the assets without having been appointed executor or having obtained a grant of administration.[37] He is liable in the same manner as a rightful executor[38]; and this rule includes the executor *de son tort* of an original rightful executor. But the executor of an executor *de son tort* is not liable for a breach of contract committed by the person with whose estate the executor *de son tort* has intermeddled, and similarly there is no such liability in the case of an executor of an administrator *de son tort*.[39] **21–012**

Protection of representative on distribution of estate. A personal representative who has protected himself by advertisements[40] in accordance with section 27 of the Trustee Act 1925 may, at the expiration of the time fixed in the notice, distribute the property to which the notice relates, having regard only to the claims of which he has notice[41] and is not liable to any person of whose claim he has not had notice at the time of distribution. A creditor may, however, in spite of the distribution, follow the property or any property representing it into the hands of any person (other than a purchaser) who may have received it, in order to satisfy his claim,[42] and he need not join the representative in any such proceedings.[43] **21–013**

Payment and compounding of debts by executor. By section 15 of the Trustee Act 1925, a personal representative may pay or allow any debt or claim[44] on any evidence that he thinks sufficient, and may accept any composition or any security for any debt and allow any time of payment of any debt, and may compromise, compound, abandon, submit to arbitration, or otherwise settle any debt, account, claim, or thing whatever relating to the testator's or intestate's estate. He is not bound to avail himself of the Limitation Act 1980 in an action brought against him by a creditor of his testator,[45] but he may not pay such a debt **21–014**

---

[34] *Strickland v. Symons* (1883) 22 Ch.D. 666, 671 (1884) 26 Ch.D. 245, see also *Garrett v. Noble* (1834) 6 Sim. 504 (defence to action for breach of trust in continuing business).

[35] Bills of Exchange Act 1882, ss.31(5), 26(1).

[36] *King v. Thom* (1789) 1 T.R. 487. cf. *Childs v. Monins* (1821) 2 B. & B. 460; *Liverpool Borough Bank v. Walker* (1859) 4 De G. & J. 24. See Vol. II, § 34–042.

[37] See, *e.g. Williams v. Heales* (1874) L.R. 9 C.P. 177; *Stratford-upon-Avon Corporation v. Parker* [1914] 2 K.B. 562; Administration of Estates Act 1925, s.28.

[38] *Meyrick v. Anderson* (1850) 14 Q.B. 719.

[39] *Wilson v. Hodson* (1872) L.R. 7 Ex. 84.

[40] Or has been excused from the need to advertise by an order of the court: *Re Gess* [1942] Ch. 37. As to the form of such advertisements, see *Re Aldhous* [1955] 1 W.L.R. 459.

[41] *Guardian Trust and Executors Co. Ltd v. Public Trustee of New Zealand* [1942] A.C. 115.

[42] Trustee Act 1925, s.27(2); Administration of Estates Act 1925, s.38.

[43] *Hunter v. Young* (1879) 4 Ex.D. 256; *Re Frewen* (1889) 60 L.T. 953.

[44] Including a claim by a co-executor: *Re Houghton* [1904] 1 Ch. 622.

[45] *Stahlschmidt v. Lett* (1853) 1 Sm. & G. 415; *Hill v. Walker* (1854) 4 K. & J. 166; *Lowis v. Rumney* (1867) L.R. 4 Eq. 451; *Midgley v. Midgley* [1893] 3 Ch. 282, 297.

after it has been judicially declared by a court of competent jurisdiction to be statute-barred,[46] nor may he pay a debt which is unenforceable under the Statute of Frauds.[47]

2. BANKRUPTCY[48]

21–015   **Preliminary.** The bankruptcy of one or both parties to a contract may have a considerable effect upon their contractual obligations. Technically a debtor only becomes bankrupt on the making of a bankruptcy order,[49] which may take place some time after the commencement of bankruptcy proceedings, but the insolvency of a party to a contract prior to his bankruptcy may materially affect the obligations of the other party.

21–016   The property of a person adjudicated bankrupt vests in the trustee in bankruptcy and, for this purpose, the bankrupt's property includes choses in action. Thus the benefit of a contract made by a person later adjudicated bankrupt passes to his trustee.[50] Broadly speaking, the trustee in bankruptcy steps into the shoes of the bankrupt and, so far as the law of contract is concerned, the result of adjudication is to effect a form of assignment by operation of law. In addition, rights may sometimes pass to the trustee even though they did not belong to the bankrupt.[51] Rights of a personal nature do not pass to the trustee,[52] and he may sometimes disclaim the burden of onerous contracts.[53] Where contracts vest in the trustee, he normally takes them "subject to equities" in the sense that the other contracting party may set up defences against him which would have been available against the bankrupt himself.[54] Purely personal defences cannot, however, be set up against the trustee,[55] and there are special statutory provisions relating to set-off.[56]

21–017   Once a bankruptcy order is made against a person, normal legal remedies cease to be available against him, so that he can no longer be sued for (*inter alia*) breach of contract. The remedy of the other contracting party is to prove for his loss or damage in the bankruptcy,[57] and once the bankrupt has been discharged all liabilities which could have been proved are finally discharged.[58] A bankrupt remains personally liable on contracts entered into by him *after* adjudication,[59]

---

[46] *Midgley v. Midgley, supra.*
[47] *Re Rownson* (1885) 29 Ch.D. 358.
[48] This section does not profess to be a summary of the whole of the law of bankruptcy, but only of the effect of bankruptcy on contracts. See generally *Muir Hunter on Personal Insolvency.* (Bankruptcy is now dealt with in the Insolvency Act 1986. The second group of parts of the Act which deal with individual insolvency is entitled "Insolvency of Individuals; Bankruptcy.")
[49] Insolvency Act 1986, s.278(a).
[50] *Post,* § 21–019.
[51] *Post,* §§ 21–024 *et seq.*
[52] *Post,* § 21–034.
[53] *Post,* § 21–035.
[54] *Post,* § 21–039.
[55] *Post,* §§ 21–034, 21–039 *et seq.*
[56] *Post,* § 21–039.
[57] *Post,* § 21–037.
[58] *Post,* § 21–046.
[59] *Post,* § 21–053.

but since the bankrupt's property can on the application of his trustee in bankruptcy be made to vest in the trustee even where it is acquired after adjudication, the other contracting party may find that the bankrupt has no assets with which to meet any such liability.[60] In these circumstances it is possible to take new bankruptcy proceedings in which property acquired after the previous adjudication and still undistributed will pass to the second trustee.[61]

(a) *Contracts made Prior to Bankruptcy*

Grounds for creditor's bankruptcy petition. A creditor may present a **21–018** bankruptcy petition against a debtor where the debtor owes him a debt for a liquidated sum which is unsecured[62] and which exceeds the "bankruptcy level"[63] and "the debtor either appears to be unable to pay or to have no reasonable prospect of being able to pay" the debt.[64] A creditor can satisfy the requirement of showing that the debtor is unable to pay his debt by serving a statutory demand which the debtor fails to comply with within a three-week period or to have set aside.[65]

Effect of presenting a bankruptcy petition. The bankruptcy of an individual **21–019** commences on the day on which a bankruptcy order is made.[66] The property comprised in the bankrupt's estate is defined by section 283 of the Insolvency Act 1986; broadly it is "all property belonging to or vested in the bankrupt at the commencement of the bankruptcy." The general principle of insolvency law is that the trustee in bankruptcy takes no better title to property than was possessed by the debtor and therefore excluded from the bankrupt's available property is any property held on trust by the bankrupt.[67] Property is given a very wide definition and includes "things in action" and "every description of property wherever situated."[68] In *Heath v. Tang*[69] it was held that a bankrupt could not appeal against the judgment on which the bankruptcy order was based since this

---

[60] Insolvency Act 1986, s.305; § 21–024 *et seq.* In special cases the other contracting party may be able to invoke the rule in *Ex p. James* (1874) L.R. 9 Ch.App. 609, *infra*, § 21–020.

[61] *Post*, § 21–057.

[62] Where the debt is secured, the creditor may waive the security and present a bankruptcy petition: see s.269.

[63] The bankruptcy level is £750 and it can be altered by statutory instrument: s.267. This must be owing at the time the petition is presented: see *Re Patel (A Debtor)* [1986] 1 W.L.R. 221.

[64] s.267(2). The debtor may also present a petition: see s.272.

[65] s.268(1). As regards inability to pay debts not yet due, see s.268(2). A document which purports to be a statutory demand is a statutory demand even though defective: *Re A Debtor (No. 1 of 1987)* [1989] 1 W.L.R. 271; see also *Re A Debtor (No. 1 of 1987)* [1989] 1 W.L.R. 461; *Practice Note (Bankruptcy: Service Abroad) (No. 1 of 88)* [1988] 1 W.L.R. 461; *Practice Note (Bankruptcy: Prescribed Forms) (No. 2 of 88)* [1988] 1 W.L.R. 557; *Re A Debtor (No. 415–5D–1993) The Times*, December 8, 1993 (debtor faced with statutory demand not entitled to have it set aside because he offered security).

[66] Insolvency Act 1986, s.278(a); the bankruptcy continues until the debtor is discharged or the bankruptcy order is annulled: s.278(b). The 1986 Act does not make use of the doctrine of relation back formerly contained in s.37 of the Bankruptcy Act 1914.

[67] s.283(3)(a); see generally, Cork Report, Cmnd. 8558 (1982), Chap. 22.

[68] s.436. It also can include after acquired property: see § 20–040. On the effect of bankruptcy on joint tenancies: see *Re Dennis (A Bankrupt)* [1993] Ch. 72; *Re Palmer (Deceased) (A Debtor)* [1993] 4 All E.R. 812; *Re Pavlou (A Bankrupt)* [1993] 1 W.L.R. 1046, 1048.

[69] [1993] 1 W.L.R. 1421.

right of action was vested in the trustee.[70] Certain property is excluded from the estate of the bankrupt, the major categories being tools and equipment necessary to enable the bankrupt to carry on business and personal belongings.[71] Also certain actions which are personal to the bankrupt, for example, actions for damages for pain and suffering, do not vest in the trustee.[72] Where a person is adjudged bankrupt any disposition of property, if made between the day on which the petition is presented and the vesting of the estate in the trustee, is void except to the extent that it is made with the consent of the court or is ratified by it.[73] This section could obviously affect the validity of a contract involving a disposition or anything done under a contract entered into by the bankrupt after the presentation of a petition. It is important to note that it is only dispositions by the bankrupt that are affected and not dispositions made to him; it is thus possible for a person to make payment to the bankrupt and to obtain a good discharge until the estate is vested in the trustee.[74] A person who deals with the bankrupt in good faith before the commencement of the bankruptcy,[75] who gives value and who has no notice of the presentation of the petition,[76] is protected.[77]

21-020   **Proof of notice.** It is probably for the person supporting the transaction to show that it was entered into without notice of the presentation of the bankruptcy petition.[78] He will probably have to establish that he had no knowledge or notice of any facts which would reasonably lead an ordinary man of business to conclude that a bankruptcy petition had been presented.[79] A statement by a creditor that he intends to present a bankruptcy petition would not be notice for the purpose of the section.[80] Notice to an agent is not necessarily notice to his principal, for example, notice to a sheriff's officer is not notice to the creditor,[81]

---

[70] A bankrupt who is dissatisfied with the conduct of the trustee can seek relief under s.303 of the 1986 Act.

[71] s.283(2); business is defined in s.436 to mean "trade or profession." Where the excluded property exceeds the cost of a reasonable replacement, it can be recovered from the bankrupt and a replacement provided: s.308. The matrimonial home will be dealt with in § 21–036.

[72] *Heath v. Tang* [1993] 1 W.L.R. 1421, 1423.

[73] s.284(1). Section 284(2) extends the section to a "payment" whether in cash or otherwise. No indication is given as to how the court should exercise its discretion but presumably the court will follow the principles developed with respect to similar provision dealing with corporate insolvency: see s.127. Section 284(5) provides special rules with respect to banks.

[74] s.306.

[75] Bankruptcy commences on the date on which the bankruptcy order is made: s.278(a).

[76] It is important to note that it is notice of the petition and not the making of a statutory demand that is important. Notice of the making of a statutory demand may affect the question of good faith: *Muir Hunter on Personal Insolvency*, §§ 3–153—3–154. On the meaning of good faith under s.46 of the Bankruptcy Act 1914, see *Re Simms* [1930] 2 Ch. 22; *Re Dalton* [1963] Ch. 336.

[77] s.284(4); enhanced protection is given to a bank where the bankrupt incurs a debt after the commencement of his bankruptcy: s.284(5); see generally *Muir Hunter on Personal Insolvency*, at p. 3079 (§ 3–154). As regards actions against a debtor once bankruptcy proceedings have begun or an order made, see, s.285; *Realisations Industrielles et Commerciales SA v. Loescher* [1957] 1 W.L.R. 1026.

[78] *Re Dalton* [1963] Ch. 336, 351 (dealing with position under the Bankruptcy Act 1914).

[79] For the position under the Bankruptcy Act 1914, see *Smith v. Osborn* (1858) 1 F. & F. 267; *Ex p. Snowball* (1872) L.R. 7 Ch.App. 534; *Ex p. Dawes* (1875) L.R. 19 Eq. 438; *Herbert's Trustee v. Higgins* [1926] Ch. 794, 800.

[80] *Herbert's Trustee v. Higgins* [1926] Ch. 794.

[81] *Ex p. Schulte* (1874) L.R. 9 Ch.App. 409. Strictly speaking a sheriff's officer is not the agent of the party on whose behalf he acts: *Hooper v. Lane* (1857) 6 H.L.C. 443; *Barclays Bank v. Roberts* [1954] 1 W.L.R. 1212.

but notice to a creditor's solicitor in the course of a particular matter in respect of which a solicitor has usual authority will be sufficient to fix the creditor with notice.[82]

Assignments by bankrupt. Since section 284(4) has the effect of validating assignments of debts made by the bankrupt, it follows that payment by the debtor to the assignee is also validated. In such circumstances it is immaterial that the debtor had notice of an act of bankruptcy, provided only that the assignee had no such notice at the date of the assignment.[83] Moreover, even where there has been no assignment, a payment by a debtor to a third party at the request of the creditor (later made bankrupt) is within the protection of the section though in this case it is essential that the payer has no notice of an act of bankruptcy.[84]
21–021

The rule in _Ex p. James_. The rule in _Ex p. James_,[85] governs situations in which, though in law the money or property belongs to the trustee for the creditors, the trustee is restrained from enforcing his claim to it or retaining it. The court will restrain the trustee whenever it would not be honourable or high minded for the trustee to assert his title.[86] The fact that the applicability of the rule depends upon a finding that the trustee has not met a high standard of moral, as distinct from legal, honesty has led to uncertainty and has been criticised.[87]
21–022

Conditions of application of rule. There are, however, other, more certain, prerequisites to the application of the rule. First, there must be some form of enrichment of the assets of the bankrupt by the person seeking to invoke the rule.[88] Secondly, the claimant must not normally be in a position to submit a proof of the claim in the bankruptcy: the rule should not give a creditor preference but should give relief where there would otherwise be none.[89] Finally, when the rule does apply, it applies only to the extent necessary to nullify the enrichment and not so as to restore the claimant to the _status quo ante_ by compensating him for his full loss.[90] So, the court has allowed an execution
21–023

---

[82] _Brewin v. Briscoe_ (1859) 28 L.J.Q.B. 329. See also _Re Dalton_ [1963] Ch. 336 (notice to debtor's solicitor); see generally _Bowstead and Reynolds on the Law of Agency_ (16th ed., 1996), §§ 8–204—8–213.

[83] _Re Dalton_ [1963] Ch. 336. It is also immaterial that the assignee does not actually claim payment from the debtor until after the receiving order, so long as he had no notice of an act of bankruptcy at the date of the assignment: _Re Seaman_ [1896] 1 Q.B. 412.

[84] _Re Dalton, supra._

[85] [1874] L.R. 9 Ch.App. 609. See also _Re Byfield_ [1982] Ch. 268; _Re Multi Guarantee Co. Ltd_ [1987] B.C.L.C. 257; _Commrs. of Customs & Excise v. T.H. Knitwear Ltd_ [1986] B.C.L.C. 195; _Hartgarten Ltd v. Australian Gas Light Co. Ltd_ (1992) 8 A.C.S.R. 277; Goff and Jones, _The Law of Restitution_ (4th ed., 1993), pp. 156–160.

[86] _Re Wigzell_ [1921] 2 K.B. 835, 850, 858; _Re Tyler_ [1907] 1 K.B. 865; _Re Clark (A Bankrupt)_ [1975] 1 W.L.R. 559, 564. A number of different phrases, all indicating moral opprobrium, have been used to describe the trustee's conduct.

[87] _Re Wigzell_ [1921] 2 K.B. 835, 845, 850, 858; _Re Byfield_ [1982] Ch. 268.

[88] _Government of India v. Taylor_ [1955] A.C. 491, 512–513; _Re Clark (A Bankrupt)_ [1975] 1 W.L.R. 559, 563.

[89] _Re Clark (A Bankrupt), supra_ 564, 566; _Re Gozzett_ [1936] 1 All E.R. 79; _Re Multi Guarantee Co. Ltd_ [1987] B.C.L.C. 257, 270. This may explain the willingness of the court to intervene in _Re Thellusson_ [1919] 2 K.B. 735. But _cf. Re Cushla Ltd_ [1979] 3 All E.R. 415, 423.

[90] _Re Clark (A Bankrupt), supra_, at 564.

creditor to recover money paid to the trustee under a mistake of law,[91] a wife to recover premiums paid (with the knowledge of the official receiver) in respect of her bankrupt husband's life policy,[92] a lender to recover a loan made to the bankrupt the day after the receiving order had been made,[93] agents to retain sums paid to them after the receiving order with the knowledge and approval of the official receiver,[94] a seller to retain the price of goods sold and delivered shortly after, but in ignorance of the making of a receiving order,[95] and executors to retain sums for funeral expenses and creditors for payment for necessaries supplied to the debtor out of money earned by him after the adjudication.[96] On the other hand, premiums paid in respect of life policies have in varying circumstances been held not to be protected,[97] builders who had erected buildings on the debtor's land immediately prior to bankruptcy could not recover because they had omitted to take a charge,[98] and counsel could not recover his fees where they had been paid to a deceased insolvent solicitor.[99]

(b) Vesting of Property in Trustee

21–024 **Appointment of trustee.** Between the making of a bankruptcy order and the vesting of the bankrupt's estate in the trustee, the official receiver is under a duty to act as the receiver and manager of the bankrupt's estate.[1] Once a bankruptcy order has been made it is normally the creditors in general meeting who will appoint the trustee of the bankrupt's estate.[2] No person can be appointed a trustee unless qualified to act as an insolvency practitioner in relation to the bankrupt.[3] The bankrupt's property vests immediately on the appointment of the trustee taking effect and there is no need for a conveyance, assignment or transfer.[4]

21–025 **Vesting provisions mandatory.** The vesting provisions of the Insolvency Act are, it would appear, mandatory, and contracting out is not permissible.[5] Thus a contract is invalid in so far as it provides that on the bankruptcy of one of the

---

[91] *Ex p. James, supra.* Although a trustee who deals with a creditor will not be allowed to take advantage of a technical mistake bona fide committed by the creditor (*Re Tricks* (1885) 3 Morr. 15) the rule will probably not protect a creditor who makes such a mistake in his dealings with other creditors or the debtor: *Re Tyler* [1907] 1 K.B. 865; *Re Gozzett* [1936] 1 All E.R. 79. See also *Re Byfield, supra* (good faith payment by debtor's bank used to pay certain creditors not protected by the rule.)
[92] *Re Tyler, supra.*
[93] *Re Thellusson* [1919] 2 K.B. 735 (breadth of dicta questioned in *Re Wigzell, supra,* but see n. 89, ante).
[94] *Re Wilson, ex p. Salaman* [1926] Ch. 21.
[95] *Re Clark (A Bankrupt), supra.*
[96] *Re Walter* [1929] 1 Ch. 647.
[97] *Tapster v. Ward* (1909) 101 L.T. 503; *Re Phillips* [1914] 2 K.B. 689; *Re Stokes* [1919] 2 K.B. 256. The distinction between these cases and *Re Tyler, supra,* may lie in the fact that in *Re Tyler* the trustee was aware of the existence of the policy and the payments.
[98] *Re Gozzett* [1936] 1 All E.R. 79.
[99] *Re Sandiford (No. 2)* [1935] Ch. 681.
[1] s.287; an interim receiver can be appointed under s.286 and a special manager under s.370.
[2] ss.292–294.
[3] s.292(2). As to who is qualified to act as an insolvency practitioner, see s.388 and s.390.
[4] s.306; *Weddell v. J.A. Pearce & Major* [1988] Ch. 26. For the definition of the bankrupt's estate see § 21–015. On the vesting of after-acquired property, see s.307 and § 21–026—21–027.
[5] This was the position under previous bankruptcy legislation: *Ex p. Mackay* (1873) L.R. 8 Ch.App. 643.

parties debts then due to him are not to pass to the trustee but are (for instance) to be offset or "cleared" against liabilities of the bankrupt to a third party.[6]

Choses in action. Prima facie all choses in action belonging to the bankrupt **21–026** at the commencement of the bankruptcy pass to the trustee as part of the bankrupt's property.[7] There is, however, nothing to prevent the trustee from reassigning a chose in action to the debtor.[8] Difficulties may arise where the bankrupt has purported to assign such a chose in action prior to the commencement of the bankruptcy. Generally such an assignment is valid and binding on the trustee as the successor in title of the assignor, but the trustee can upset such an assignment in two main cases.[9] First, an assignment of future choses in action which are not actually earned (in the sense that the whole consideration is not supplied) until after the commencement of the bankruptcy is void against the trustee.[10] Secondly, a general assignment of existing or future book debts (or any class thereof) by a trader is void against the trustee unless it has been registered as if it were a bill of sale.[11]

Adjustment of prior transactions. There are certain transactions entered **21–027** into by a bankrupt prior to his bankruptcy which can be challenged by his trustee. If these transactions are successfully challenged they will be unenforceable against the estate of the bankrupt and the trustee may be able to recover with respect to them with the consequence that the bankrupt's estate will be increased for the benefit of his creditors. The transactions that may be challenged are (i) transactions at an undervalue, (ii) preferences, (iii) extortionate credit transactions, and (iv) transactions defrauding creditors.

Transactions at an undervalue. A transaction at an undervalue is defined in **21–028** section 339: it is a transaction in which a bankrupt makes a gift or otherwise receives no consideration, enters into a transaction in consideration of marriage,

---

[6] *British Eagle International Airliner Ltd v. Compagnie Nationale Air France* [1975] 1 W.L.R. 758; cf. *Horne v. Chester and Fein Property Developments Pty. Ltd* (1986) 11 A.C.L.R. 485. As regards companies, debt subordination agreements have been upheld: *Re British and Commonwealth Holdings plc (No. 3)* [1992] B.C.L.C. 322; *Re Maxwell Communications Corp. plc* [1993] 1 W.L.R. 1402.

[7] ss.283 and 436(4) ("property includes . . . things in action"). This includes most rights of action but not those arising from contracts for personal service to be performed, defamation, breach of confidence, or an action for damages for pain and suffering: *Bailey v. Thurston & Co.* [1903] 1 K.B. 137; *Wilson v. United Counties Bank Ltd* [1920] A.C. 102; *Re Kavanagh* [1949] 2 All E.R. 264; [1950] 1 All E.R. 39n; *Heath v. Tang* [1993] 1 W.L.R. 1421; *Re Landau (A Bankrupt)* [1998] Ch. 223.

[8] *Ramsay v. Hartley* [1977] 1 W.L.R. 686, 692–694; *Stein v. Blake* [1996] A.C. 243. On the powers of a trustee in bankruptcy, see s.314 and Sched. V.

[9] There are also provisions relating to transactions which can be set aside: see §§ 21–028—21–031.

[10] *Wilmot v. Alton* [1897] 1 Q.B. 17; *Re Collins* [1925] Ch. 556; *Re de Marney* [1943] Ch. 126 (the basis of the reasoning in these cases is that a bankrupt cannot create greater rights in an assignee than those which the bankrupt actually possesses); cf. *Re Davis & Co., ex p. Rawlings* (1888) 22 Q.B.D. 193; *Re Trytel* [1952] 2 T.L.R. 32.

[11] s.344, re-enacting the substance of s.43 of the Bankruptcy Act 1914. This prohibition does not apply to assignments from a specified debtor or under specified contracts, nor to assignments made on a bona fide transfer of an assignor's business, nor to an assignment made for the benefit of creditors generally: s.344(3)(b). As to the meaning of "book debts," see *Shipley v. Marshall* (1863) 14 C.B.(N.S.) 566; *Paul & Frank Ltd v. Discount Bank (Overseas) Ltd* [1967] Ch. 348; *Re Brightlife Ltd* [1987] Ch. 200, 208–209.

or enters into a transaction where the consideration provided by the other person to the contract is "significantly less, in money or money's worth," than the consideration provided by the bankrupt.[12] A transaction at an undervalue can only be challenged by the trustee if it is entered into at the "relevant time" which is defined as a period of five years prior to the presentation of the bankruptcy petition and, provided the transaction was not entered into less than two years before the presentation of the bankruptcy petition, the bankrupt was insolvent or rendered insolvent[13] by the transaction.[14] The onus of showing insolvency is on the trustee but there is a presumption that the bankrupt was insolvent where the transaction is with an associate.[15] Where a transaction at an undervalue is shown to have taken place, the court can "make such order as it thinks fit for restoring the position to what it would have been if that individual had not entered into that transaction."[16] No order can be made against a third party who is a bona fide purchaser for value unless he has notice of certain statutory prescribed circumstances which would allow the transaction to be set aside.[17]

21–029　　**Preferences.** A preference occurs where a person does something which puts one of his creditors, or a surety or guarantor of his debts, in a better position than he would have been in the event of the person's bankruptcy had that thing not been done and the person providing the preference was influenced by a desire to put the other person in such a better position.[18] Such a transaction can only be challenged if the transaction was entered into within the six-month period before the presentation of the petition[19] and the individual is insolvent or rendered insolvent by the transaction.[20] As with transactions at an undervalue, the courts are given very wide remedial powers.[21] The relevant time for determining whether there is an intention to prefer is when the transaction is entered into and the fact that the debtor believes that he will be in a position to pay all his debts will not negative a preference.[22]

21–030　　**Extortionate credit transactions.** The provision on extortionate credit transactions is modelled on sections 137 to 139 of the Consumer Credit Act 1974.[23] A transaction is an extortionate credit transaction if, having regard to the risk accepted by the person providing the credit, it requires the debtor to make grossly

---

[12] s.339(3): see *Re Kumar (A Bankrupt), ex p. Lewis v. Kumar* [1993] 1 W.L.R. 224.

[13] s.341(3) defines insolvency as an inability to pay debts as they fall due or the value of liabilities exceeds assets.

[14] s.341(1) and (2).

[15] s.341(2); associate is defined in s.435 and is qualified by s.341(2) to exclude a bankrupt's employee.

[16] s.339(2); the more specific powers of the court are spelled out in s.342.

[17] s.342(2)(b) and (4) as amended by the Insolvency (No. 2) Act 1994.

[18] s.340(3). There is a rebuttable presumption that such was intended where the transaction was with an associate: see s.340(5). Also the fact that something is done in pursuance to a court order does not prevent it from being a preference: see s.340(6).

[19] s.341(1)(c); where the transaction is entered into with an associate then it can be challenged within a two-year period: s.341(1)(b).

[20] For the definition of insolvency, see s.341(3).

[21] s.342.

[22] *Re F.P. & C.H. Mathews Ltd* [1982] Ch. 257 (dealing with a preference by a company under the previous insolvency legislation); *Re M.C. Bacon Ltd* [1990] B.C.L.C. 324 (dealing with preferences by a company under current legislation).

[23] See Vol. II, §§ 38–191—38–205. The trustee in bankruptcy is precluded from making an application for relief under s.139(1)(a) of the Consumer Credit Act 1974 but must rely on his rights under the Insolvency Act: s.343(6).

exorbitant payment or otherwise grossly contravenes "ordinary principles of fair dealing."[24] A transaction can only be challenged if entered into within three years before the commencement of the bankruptcy.[25] Where the court finds that a bankrupt has entered into an extortionate credit transaction, it is given very wide remedial powers to deal with the issue.[26]

Transactions defrauding creditors. The definition of a transaction defraud- **21–031**
ing creditors in section 423[27] of the Insolvency Act 1986 (which applied to both individual bankruptcy and corporate insolvency[28]) is not unlike a transaction at an undervalue. Thus it applies to gifts, transactions in which a person receives no consideration, or where the consideration received is significantly less than the consideration provided.[29] For such a transaction to be caught, it must have been entered into for the purpose of putting the assets beyond the reach of those who would have a claim against the transferor, or otherwise prejudicing the interests of the transferor's creditors.[30] The advantage of this section over that relating to transactions at an undervalue is that no time limit for avoidance is fixed. In addition, the victim of the transaction may apply to have it set aside and not just the trustee in bankruptcy.[31]

Contracts not terminated by bankruptcy. A contract is not determined by **21–032**
the bankruptcy of one of the parties thereto.[32] Ordinarily the benefit of any contract made by the debtor passes to his trustee in bankruptcy as part of his property, subject to the trustee's right to disclaim unprofitable contracts,[33] and, if it is an executory contract, the trustee may complete it and receive the benefit for the estate[34]; he may give receipts[35] and, with the permission of the creditors' committee,[36] exercise various powers, *e.g.* he may sue on the contract, assign the right of action to creditors[37] or even to the bankrupt,[38] sell the bankrupt's

---

[24] s.343(3). Where a trustee applies to have a transaction set aside under s.343 there is a presumption that it was extortionate: see s.343(3).

[25] s.343(2); on commencement of the bankruptcy, see s.278 and § 21–019.

[26] s.343(4).

[27] See *Arbuthnot Leasing International Ltd v. Havelet Leasing Ltd & others (No. 2)* [1990] B.C.C. 636; *Choan v. Sagar* [1993] B.C.L.C. 661; *Re Ayala Holdings Ltd* [1993] B.C.L.C. 256; *Agricultural Mortgage Corporation plc. v. Woodward* [1995] 1 B.C.L.C. 1; *Barclays Bank plc v. Eustice* [1995] 2 B.C.L.C. 630.

[28] *Re Shilena Hosiery Ltd* [1980] Ch. 219.

[29] s.423(1).

[30] s.423(3).

[31] s.424.

[32] *Ex p. Chalmers* (1873) L.R. 8 Ch.App. 289; *Morgan v. Bain* (1874) L.R. 10 C.P. 15; *Re Sneezum* (1876) 3 Ch.D. 463; *Jennings' Trustees v. King* [1952] Ch. 899. The case of the bankrupt's apprentices or articled clerks is dealt with by s.348 (previously s.34 of the Bankruptcy Act 1914), which provides that if either party gives notice in writing to the trustee to that effect the agreement shall be discharged by the order and a part of any premium may be returned. See also Employment Protection (Consolidation) Act 1978, s.122(1), (3)(e) for payments out of the Redundancy Fund: *post*, § 21–038.

[33] *Post*, § 21–049.

[34] *Ex p. Stapleton* (1879) 10 Ch.D. 586.

[35] s.314, Sched. V, Pt. II, para. 10.

[36] s.314.

[37] s.314, Sched. V, Pt. I; *Guy v. Churchill* (1888) 40 Ch.D. 481; *Seear v. Lawson* (1880) 15 Ch.D. 426. These cases and those in the next three footnotes were decided under previous bankruptcy legislation but probably still reflect the law.

[38] *ibid.*; *Ramsay v. Hartley* [1977] 1 W.L.R. 686; *Stein v. Blake* [1996] A.C. 243.

business (in a proper case even to a company promoted by himself and the creditors' committee[39]), or make any compromise of an action or claim.[40]

21–033 **Effect on contractual rights.** In some cases the rights of the trustee in respect of the bankrupt's contracts differ from the rights which the bankrupt would himself have had if he had remained solvent. Thus, in the case of the sale of goods, if a buyer becomes insolvent before the goods are delivered the seller may refuse to deliver them until paid in cash: " . . . when the insolvency of the purchaser had been declared the vendor [was] . . . not bound to deliver any more goods until the price of the goods delivered . . . as well as those which were to be delivered . . . had been tendered to him."[41] The vendor may also exercise the right of lien[42] even though he has agreed to give the buyer credit, and would not therefore have had any lien in the absence of insolvency of the buyer. So also, the seller's right of stoppage in transit only arises if the buyer is insolvent.[43] Where a person who has entered into a contract is subsequently adjudged bankrupt, the other party to the contract may apply to the court to be discharged. The court may discharge the contract on such terms as it thinks just and equitable and any damages payable by the bankrupt are provable as a bankruptcy debt.[44]

21–034 **Contracts which do not pass.** From the nature of certain contracts it follows that the benefit of them does not pass to the trustee. Contracts in which the personal skill of the bankrupt forms an essential part of the consideration are instances of these.[45] A right of action for the wrongful dismissal of the bankrupt before his bankruptcy passes to his trustee.[46] Rights of action in respect of injury to credit and reputation, or of personal injury, as opposed to injury to property, do not pass to the trustee in bankruptcy,[47] and in this type of case it seems that the trustee cannot even recover the fruits of the action received by the bankrupt[48]; unless perhaps the trustee obtains an order relating to the bankrupt's after-acquired property.[49]

21–035 **Disclaimer.** Section 315 of the Insolvency Act 1986 enables the trustee to disclaim onerous property and for this purpose onerous property is "any unprofit-

---

[39] *ibid.*; *Re Spink* (1913) 108 L.T. 572

[40] *ibid.*; *Re Ridgway* (1889) 6 Morr. 277; *Re A. & T. G. Ridgway* (1891) 8 Morr. 289; *Re Pilling* [1906] 2 K.B. 644.

[41] *Ex p. Chalmers* (1873) L.R. 8 Ch.App. 289, 293; this preceded what is now s.41(1)(c) of the Sale of Goods Act 1979. See *Benjamin's Sale of Goods* (5th ed., 1997), § 15–037; see also *Re Eastgate* [1905] 1 K.B. 465; *Tilley v. Bowman Ltd* [1910] 1 K.B. 745 (right to repossess goods) but *cf. Re Wait* [1927] 1 Ch. 606 and Vol. II. § 43–315.

[42] Sale of Goods Act 1979, s.41(1)(c).

[43] Sale of Goods Act 1979, ss.44–46; Vol. II, §§ 43–324 *et seq.*

[44] s.345.

[45] *Gibson v. Carruthers* (1841) 8 M. & W. 321, 333; *Knight v. Burgess* (1864) 33 L.J.Ch. 727; *Re Collins* [1925] Ch. 556. See also *ante*, § 20–052—20–053 (voluntary assignment of personal contracts) and § 21–006 (transmission of personal contracts on death). *cf. Re Worthington* [1914] 2 K.B. 299.

[46] *Beckham v. Drake* (1849) 2 H.L.C. 579, 596, 627. *cf. Wenlock v. Moloney* (1967) 111 S.J. 437. As to the sale of such rights of action by the trustee, see *ante*, § 17–063. For the position where the contract is unexecuted at the date of the bankruptcy and the breach occurs thereafter see: *Bailey v. Thurston & Co. Ltd* [1903] 1 K.B. 137; *post*, § 21–055.

[47] *Wilson v. United Counties Bank* [1920] A.C. 102, 120, 129–130; *Rose v. Buckett* [1901] 2 K.B. 449. *Heath v. Tang* [1993] 1 W.L.R. 1421.

[48] *Re Kavanagh* [1949] 2 All E.R. 264; [1950] 1 All E.R. 39n.

[49] See § 21–053.

able contract," property which is not saleable or readily saleable, or property that"may give rise to a liability to pay money or perform some other onerous act."[50] The disclaimer operates from the date on which the prescribed notice, which has to be filed in court, is indorsed by the court.[51] Any person who suffers loss or damage in consequence of the disclaimer may prove in the bankruptcy.[52] A notice of disclaimer with respect to property may not be given if the person interested in property had applied in writing to the trustee to decide whether to disclaim or not and 28 days have expired since that notice was given.[53] The trustee is deemed to have adopted any contract which he cannot disclaim by virtue of this section.[54] Disclaimer is the right to get rid of property or contracts which are onerous, any contract which is unprofitable, any property which is unsaleable or not readily saleable, or which gives rise to a liability to pay money or to perform any other contract.[55] Disclaimer is intended to affect the rights of third parties as little as possible; section 315(3) provides that disclaimer only operates to the extent that is necessary "for the purpose of releasing the bankrupt, the bankrupt's estate and the trustee from any liability."[56]

Matrimonial home. Special provision is made to protect the interests of the   **21–036**
bankrupt and his spouse in the matrimonial home. Where a spouse registers an interest under the Matrimonial Homes Act 1983, the interest binds the trustee in bankruptcy of the other spouse.[57] On any application under section 1 of the 1983 Act, or under section 30 of the Law of Property Act 1925,[58] the court has to take into consideration the needs and financial resources of the spouse[59] and the needs of any children as well as the interests of the creditors.[60] Also of relevance is the conduct of the spouse in contributing to the bankruptcy. The bankrupt is also given the right to occupy the dwelling-house provided he has a beneficial interest in it and there is someone under the age of 18 with whom the bankrupt shared the

---

[50] s.315. Special provision is made for the disclaimer of leases (s.317) and land subject to a rentcharge (s.318). Also leave of the court is required to disclaim property acquired under s.307 or s.308 (s.315(4)); *Re Hans Place Ltd* [1993] B.C.L.C. 768; *Re Park Air Services Plc* [1999] 2 W.L.R. 396 (dealing with the equivalent provision for companies).

[51] s.315(3)(a) and Winding Up Rules 1986, r. 6.178(4).

[52] s.315(5).

[53] s.316. This time period can be extended: s.376; *Re Richardson* (1880) 16 Ch.D. 613.

[54] *ibid.*

[55] s.315(2). It is important to note that the lack of profitability of the contract does not have to flow from the onerous nature of the contract: *cf. Re Potters Oils Co. Ltd* [1986] 1 W.L.R. 201. *Re Bastable Ltd* [1901] 2 K.B. 518 would probably be decided in the same way today but the reasoning would not be followed; there could be no disclaimer in that case because it would be depriving a purchaser of an interest and not merely relieving the bankrupt of an onerous obligation.

[56] *Stacey v. Hill* (1900) 69 L.J.Q.B. 796, affd. [1901] 1 K.B. 660. For disclaimer on the part of a company in liquidation see: *Re Potters Oils Ltd* [1986] 1 W.L.R. 201; *Re Distributors and Warehousing Ltd* [1986] B.C.L.C. 129; *Re A.E. (Realisations) Ltd* [1981] B.C.L.C. 486; *Re Hans Place Ltd* [1993] B.C.L.C. 768; *Re Park Air Services Plc* [1999] 2 W.L.R. 396

[57] s.336(2).

[58] The normal position will be that the property will be in the joint names of the bankrupt and his spouse and the trustee will have to seek an order under s.30 of the Law of Property Act 1925. For the principles on which the court will exercise its jurisdiction, see *Re Citro Dominico (A Bankrupt)* [1991] Ch. 142 (noted (1991) 107 L.Q.R. 177). The facts in this case pre-dated the Insolvency Act 1986.

[59] The same consideration must be given to the interests of a former spouse.

[60] s.336. There is a presumption that the interests of the creditors should prevail if the application is made one year after the bankruptcy unless there are exceptional circumstances indicating otherwise: s.336(5). As to what may constitute exceptional circumstances, see *Re Citro Dominico (A Bankrupt)* [1991] Ch. 142, 159, 161.

home at the time the bankruptcy petition was presented.[61] In this situation the bankrupt cannot be evicted except under a court order.[62] The right of occupation is treated as a charge under the Matrimonial Homes Act 1983 and on an application to have the bankrupt evicted the court shall take into consideration not only the interests of the creditors but also the interests of the children but not "the needs of the bankrupt."[63] Where a bankrupt for whatever reason occupies the matrimonial home on condition that he makes payments to satisfy mortgage obligations or to satisfy other outgoings, he does not acquire any interest in the premises by reason of making the payments. If a dwelling-house forms part of the trustee's property and for any reason the trustee is unable to realise it, he may apply to the court for an order imposing a charge on the property for the benefit of the bankrupt's estate.[64]

21–037   **Remedies of contracting party against bankrupt.** A person who has entered into a contract with one who subsequently becomes bankrupt cannot generally sue either the bankrupt or the trustee; but an obligation under a contract is a "liability"[65] provable in the bankruptcy. All such debts and liabilities, except such wages or salary or other debts as are entitled to preferential payment,[66] are payable *pari passu* out of the estate.[67] The right of a creditor to prove in the debtor's bankruptcy is dealt with more fully in a subsequent part of this chapter.[68]

21–038   **Remedies of employee against bankrupt employer.** The Insolvency Act 1986 confers a limited preference on employees for unpaid wages and certain other entitlements.[69] To the extent that a claim falls outside the statutory limits it ranks as an ordinary debt. In practice the right of an employee to recover sums owing to him by an insolvent employer from the Redundancy Fund[70] may be more valuable. This right, governed by section 122 of the Employment Protection (Consolidation) Act 1978, applies in respect of up to eight weeks' arrears of pay, up to six weeks' arrears of holiday pay, pay for the minimum period of notice required for the termination of a contract of employment[71] and any basic compensation for unfair dismissal.[72] Where the Secretary of State makes a

---

[61] s.337.

[62] s.337(2)(a). Where the bankrupt is out of possession, then he can only regain it with a court order.

[63] s.337(5); where the application is made one year after the commencement of the bankruptcy it is presumed that the interests of the creditors prevail unless there are exceptional circumstances indicating otherwise.

[64] s.313.

[65] ss.322 and 382(4).

[66] *Post*, § 21–038.

[67] s.328(3). Debts owed to a spouse are deferred to the claims of ordinary creditors: s.322.

[68] See *post*, § 21–049.

[69] ss.328, 386 and Sched. 6; Employment Protection (Consolidation) Act 1978, s.121.

[70] See Vol. II, §§ 39–227 *et seq.*; *Westwood v. Secretary of State for Employment* [1983] I.R.L.R. 419.

[71] s.122(3)(b) (as amended by the Employment Act 1989, s.18; Employment Act 1990, Sched. 2; Social Security (Consequential Provisions) Act 1992, Sched. 2); *Secretary of State for Employment v. Jobling* [1980] I.C.R. 380. For the application of s.122 to apprentices, see *ante*, n. 32.

[72] s.122(3)(d). This is the sum calculated in accordance with Employment Protection (Consolidation) Act 1978, s.73, but not any "additional" sum under s.71(2)(b). Compensatory awards are covered by s.122(3)(a)–(c). See Vol. II, §§ 39–227 *et seq.*

payment from the Fund he is subrogated to the rights of the employee against the bankrupt employer, including any preferential claims.[73]

(c) *Trustee takes "Subject to Equities"*

General. Broadly speaking, a trustee in bankruptcy (like a voluntary assignee) acquires the property of the bankrupt "subject to equities." Thus a person who has been induced by fraud to sell property to a buyer who subsequently becomes bankrupt does not lose his right to rescind the contract and recover his property merely because it has passed to the trustee in bankruptcy.[74] So also where contractual rights have been validly assigned by the bankrupt before the commencement of the bankruptcy, the trustee takes the benefit of the contract subject to the rights of the assignee.[75] Exceptions to this principle have been discussed above.[76] On the other hand, the trustee in bankruptcy takes the property of the bankrupt free from purely personal claims binding on the bankrupt. **21–039**

Set-off and mutual dealings. The right of set-off in bankruptcy does not rest on the same principle as the right of set-off between solvent parties (which is designed to prevent cross-actions) but is governed by section 323 of the Insolvency Act 1986. The section applies where before the commencement of the bankruptcy "there have been mutual credits, mutual debts or other mutual dealings between the bankrupt and any creditor of the bankrupt proving or claiming for a bankruptcy debt."[77] Where such mutual dealings exist, an account is to be taken of what each party owes and the sums due from one party to the other with respect to mutual dealings between the parties shall be set off against each other.[78] Section 323(3) provides that sums due from the bankrupt shall not be included in any set-off if the other party "had notice at the time they became due" that a bankruptcy petition relating to the bankrupt was pending.[79] Were this provision to be applied literally, it would mean that a creditor could not set off sums due on a contract entered into before a bankruptcy petition was presented but which become due after the presentation of the petition. If such an interpretation were valid, this would severely curtail the right of set-off in a way that was probably not intended by the legislature. To deal with the alleged problem, a reform of section 323 was proposed in the Companies Bill 1989.[80] This was intended to make it clear that no debt or liability could be set-off which arose after the date on which the creditor had notice that a bankruptcy notice relating to the bankrupt was pending; thus debts incurred before but falling due after the debtor's bankruptcy could be set-off. However, it was decided that such a reform was not needed and it was abandoned. Section 323(1) sets out the debts that are **21–040**

---

[73] Employment Protection (Consolidation) Act 1978, s.125 (as amended by the Employment Act 1989, s.19; Employment Act 1990, Sched. 2); *Re T.H. Knitwear (Wholesale) Ltd* [1988] Ch. 275; *Re Urethane Engineering Products Ltd* [1991] B.C.L.C. 48.

[74] *Re Eastgate* [1905] 1 K.B. 465; *Tilley v. Bowman* [1910] 1 K.B. 745; *A.W. Gamage Ltd v. Charlesworth's Trustee* [1910] S.C. 257.

[75] *National Provincial Bank Ltd v. Ainsworth* [1965] A.C. 1175, 1256–1258.

[76] *Ante*, § 21–026.

[77] s.323(1); *Stein v. Blake* [1996] A.C. 243.

[78] s.323(2).

[79] A petition would appear to be pending even though no order has been made on it: Derham, *Set-Off* (2nd. ed., 1996), p. 171.

[80] Clause 161.

capable of being set-off and this refers to all "mutual credits, mutual debts and other mutual dealings." The requirement of being "due" is imposed by section 323(2), but this deals only with the time for the taking of an account and it is clear that unless a debt is due at the time of taking an account it cannot be the subject of set-off.[81]

21–041   The right of set-off under section 323 is mandatory and no contracting out of it is permissible.[82] The question whether there are sufficient mutual credits, debts or other dealings is determined at the date of the bankruptcy order.[83] As the object of the section is to do substantial justice between the parties[84] it has not been restrictively interpreted. Thus, it is not necessary that at the date of the order there should be mutual debts existing. If there are claims for the breach of contractual obligations[85] or other mutual demands which do not arise out of the contract[86] which will result in pecuniary liabilities they may be set off provided, in both cases, that the claims are provable in the bankruptcy. It has also been held that contingent debts and liabilities may be set off in bankruptcy.[87] Whether the debt is a legal or an equitable debt is immaterial, for the bankruptcy jurisdiction proceeds upon equitable principles.[88] The claims on each side must be such as result in pecuniary liabilities. A debt cannot therefore be set off against a claim for the return of goods wrongfully detained, for the judgment in the latter case is for the return of the goods *in specie* and only in the alternative for their value.[89] On the other hand, where property is entrusted to a person for sale, this is a giving of credit.[90] So where a company employed a commission agent to sell its property, and the company owed the agent money by way of commission on earlier sales, it was held that, on the company going into liquidation, the agent was entitled to set off the sum due to him against the value of the property in his possession and still unsold.[91] There was, however, no set-off in respect of other

---

[81] See Goode, *Legal Problems of Credit and Security* (2nd ed.), pp. 184–185; Derham, *Set-Off* (2nd ed., 1996), p. 171. A debtor of a bankrupt cannot gain an advantage by acquiring the bankrupt's liabilities after the making of a bankruptcy order, but this in no way affects the interpretation being put forward in the text: see *Re Charge Card Services Ltd* [1987] Ch. 150, 190 (affd. [1989] Ch. 497). *cf. Stein v. Blake* [1996] A.C. 243.

[82] *National Westminster Bank Ltd v. Halesowen Presswork & Assemblies Ltd* [1972] A.C. 785; *Re Cushla Ltd* [1979] 3 All E.R. 415. See also *Hong Kong and Shanghai Banking Corporation v. Kloeckner & Co. A.G.* [1990] 2 Q.B. 514 (right of party to exclude contractual set-off).

[83] *Re Taylor* [1910] 1 K.B. 562; *Tilley v. Bowman* [1910] 1 K.B. 745, 751; *Re a Debtor* [1927] 1 Ch. 410; *Re a Debtor* [1956] 1 W.L.R. 1226; *cf. Re Charge Card Services Ltd* [1987] 1 Ch. 150; [1989] Ch. 497.

[84] *Foster v. Wilson, supra,* at 203–204; *Re Davies* (1867) L.R. 2 Ch.App. 808; *Re City Life Assurance Co. Ltd* [1926] Ch. 191.

[85] *Re National Benefit Assurance Co.* [1924] 2 Ch. 339; *Re City Life Assurance Co. (Grandfield's Case)* [1926] Ch. 191.

[86] *Re D.H. Curtis (Builders) Ltd* [1978] Ch. 162; *Re Cushla Ltd* [1979] 3 All E.R. 415.

[87] *Re Charge Card Services Ltd* [1987] Ch. 150, [1989] Ch. 497; *Day & Dent Constructions Pty. Ltd (In Liquidation) v. North Australian Properties Pty. Ltd (Provisional Liquidator Appointed)* (1982) 40 A.L.R. 399; Derham *op. cit.* pp. 86–93.

[88] *Bailey v. Finch* (1871) L.R. 7 Q.B. 34; *Mathieson's Trustee v. Burrup, Mathieson & Co.* [1927] 1 Ch. 562.

[89] *Re Winter* (1878) 8 Ch.D. 225; *Eberle's Hotels & Restaurant Co. v. Jonas* (1887) 18 Q.B.D. 459; *cf. Re Thorne* [1914] 2 Ch. 438; *Ellis & Co.'s Trustee v. Dixon-Johnson* [1925] A.C. 489; and contrast *Naoroji v. Chartered Bank of India* (1868) L.R 3 C.P. 444; *Rolls Razor Ltd v. Cox* [1967] 1 Q.B. 552.

[90] *Astley v. Gurney* (1869) L.R. 4 C.P. 714; *Palmer v. Day* [1895] 2 Q.B. 618.

[91] *Rolls Razor Ltd v. Cox* [1967] 1 Q.B. 552. For criticisms of this case see Goode, *Principles of Corporate Insolvency* (2nd ed. 1997), pp. 192–193.

property of the company in the agent's possession which had not been entrusted to him for sale.[92] A debt cannot be set off against a sum of money deposited for a specific purpose which failed owing to the bankruptcy,[93] at least where it would amount to a misappropriation for that money to be used for any other purpose.[94] The right of set-off may exist although one of the debts is secured[95]; to the extent that there is set-off the security is released.[96]

Set-off of unliquidated damages. A claim for unliquidated damages may be set off against a debt under the section.[97] Thus a claim for damages for fraudulent misrepresentation on the sale of a chattel was set off in an action by the bankrupt's trustee for the unpaid price, the fraudulent representation being not merely a personal tort but a breach of the obligation arising out of the contract of sale.[98] **21–042**

Debts must be mutual. In order that debts may be set off they must be mutual. For debts and credits to be mutual they must be between the same parties, in the same right and must be commensurable in the sense that at the relevant time both can be reduced to monetary terms.[99] This may be illustrated by *Re City Life Assurance Co. Ltd (Stephenson's Case)*[1] where a policy holder mortgaged his policy to the company and the deed contained an absolute covenant to pay, but provided that so long as the premiums and interest and other obligations were paid the debt should not be called in. The company equitably assigned the mortgage to trustees for another class of policy holders, no notice of this being given to the mortgagor. The whole mortgage debt was outstanding at the time of the winding up of the company. The policy holder claimed to set off the amount due to him on his policy against his mortgage debt. It was held that as the equitable assignment was complete as between the company and their assignees without notice to the mortgagor, there was no mutual credit or mutual debt between the company and the policy holder within section 31, and the latter had no right of set-off in spite of the provisions of the mortgage deed. Warrington L.J.[2] observed that there was no mutuality because at the date of the winding up there was a debt due from the company to the policy holder, but no debt due from the policy holder to the company because the debt which had been so due had been effectively transferred to certain trustees. Therefore, at the date of the winding up there was no mutual credit or mutual debt which could come within the provisions of section 31 and be set off the one against the other. **21–043**

A debt due to or from the trustee in bankruptcy as such cannot be set off against a debt due from or to the bankrupt. Therefore a person who has received money from the bankrupt under a transaction which is void as against the trustee **21–044**

---

[92] *ibid.*

[93] *Re Pollitt* [1893] 1 QB 455; *Re Mid-Kent Fruit Factory* [1896] 1 Ch. 567; *Re City Equitable Fire Insurance Co.* [1930] 2 Ch. 293; Derham *op. cit.* pp. 123–135.

[94] *National Westminster Bank Ltd v. Halesowen Presswork & Assemblies Ltd* [1972] A.C. 785.

[95] *Ex p. Barnett* (1874) L.R. 9 Ch.App. 293; *Baker v. Lloyds Bank Ltd* [1920] 2 K.B. 322.

[96] *M.S. Fashions Ltd v. Bank of Credit and Commerce International SA* [1993] 3 W.L.R. 220.

[97] *Peat v. Jones & Co.* (1881) 8 Q.B.D. 147.

[98] *Jack v. Kipping* (1882) 9 Q.B.D. 113; *Tilley v. Bowman* [1910] 1 K.B. 745; *cf. Kitchen's Trustee v. Madders* [1950] Ch. 134.

[99] *Re Cushla Ltd* [1979] 3 All E.R. 415, 420–421. See Derham *op. cit.* Chap. 5.

[1] [1926] Ch. 191 (this dealt with s.31 of the Bankruptcy Act 1914).

[2] *ibid.* at 218.

(*e.g.* as a preference) cannot set off a debt due to him from the bankrupt against a claim by the trustee for that money.[3] Similarly a joint debt cannot be set off against a separate debt[4] nor can a debt due to an executor personally be set off against a debt due to him as personal representative of his testator.[5] Debts due in the same right in equity may be set off although they are not due in the same right at law,[6] and a debt due to an agent not known by the other party to have been acting as such may be set off against a debt due from him personally.[7]

(d) *Discharge of Bankrupt*

21–045   **Discharge.** The bankruptcy of an individual continues until the individual is discharged under the provisions of the Insolvency Act 1986. The normal rule is that a person who has been adjudicated bankrupt for the first time will be automatically discharged after the elapse of three years from the commencement of his bankruptcy.[8] This period can be extended by the court where on the application of the official receiver the court is satisfied that the bankrupt is not complying with his obligations under the Insolvency Act 1986.[9] Where an order of criminal bankruptcy[10] has been made against the bankrupt, or where he has "been an undischarged bankrupt at any time in the period of 15 years ending with the commencement of the bankruptcy,"[11] an order of the court under section 280 is necessary to discharge the bankrupt. An application under section 280 may not be made until after the end of a five-year period beginning with the commencement of the bankruptcy.[12] The court possesses the widest of discretions under section 280 to make whatever order it considers proper.[13]

21–046   **Effect of discharge.** Where a bankrupt is discharged, it releases him from all bankruptcy debts except:

(a) from any bankruptcy debt which was incurred in connection with any fraud or fraudulent breach of trust[14];

(b) from any liability in respect of a fine[15];

(c) from any liability relating to damages for personal injuries[16];

---

[3] *Lister v. Hooson* [1908] 1 K.B. 174.
[4] *Tyso v. Petitt* (1879) 40 L.T. 132. *cf. Re Pennington and Owen Ltd* [1925] Ch. 825 (debt owed by a company could not be set off against debt owed to company by a firm of which the creditor was a member; also the principle in *Cherry v. Boultbee* (1839) 4 My. & Cr. 442 did not apply in this situation).
[5] *Bishop v. Church* (1748) 3 Atk. 691; *Nelson v. Roberts* (1893) 69 L.T. 352.
[6] *Bailey v. Finch* (1871) L.R. 7 Q.B. 34; for a criticism of this case see Derham *op. cit.* pp. 211–212; *Re Willis, Percival & Co., ex p. Morier* (1879) 12 Ch.D. 491.
[7] *Lee v. Bullen* (1858) 27 L.J.Q.B. 161 (note the brokers acted "and/or as agents").
[8] s.279(2)(b). Where a certificate for the summary administration of the bankrupt's estate has been issued, the period is shortened to two years: s.279(2)(a).
[9] s.279(3).
[10] See s.264(1)(d).
[11] s.279(1)(a).
[12] s.280(1).
[13] s.280(2).
[14] s.281(3).
[15] s.281(4); in the case of a fine in connection with an offence concerning the public revenue, the Treasury can consent to its discharge.
[16] s.281(5)(a); the court has a discretion to order that the bankrupt be discharged to whatever extent it considers appropriate from these debts.

(d) from any liability with respect to an order made in family or domestic proceedings[17];

(e) from any other bankruptcy debts as may be prescribed.[18]

It is important to note that discharge only releases a bankrupt from "bankruptcy debts" and therefore a debt which is not so classified is not released.[19]

An order of discharge does not release any person who at the date of the **21-047** receiving order was a partner or co-trustee with the bankrupt, or was jointly bound or had made any joint contract with him, or any person who was surety or in the nature of surety for him.[20] It does, however, release the bankrupt from his liability, whether the debt was owed by him alone or jointly with others.[21] As an order of discharge releases the bankrupt from the debt, so it releases him from the operation of a collateral remedy for that debt, such as a licence to seize after-acquired goods.[22] It does not release him where the real effect of the transaction providing the collateral remedy is to assign after-acquired property. Such a transaction gives the assignee a right *in rem* against the property, which is not barred by the bankruptcy.[23] An order of discharge also releases the bankrupt from any liability for consequential damages which may result or arise from the non-payment of the debt.[24]

After the making of a bankruptcy order, no person who is a creditor of the **21-048** bankrupt with respect to a provable debt can enforce any remedy with respect to that debt.[25] However, a promise to pay such a debt binds the bankrupt if made for a fresh consideration or otherwise by means binding in law,[26] and this will apply although the promise and consideration was made or given during the bankruptcy.[27] It may be added that although a discharge releases the debtor from provable debts, it does not necessarily extinguish the obligation for all purposes.[28]

Debts provable. The debts provable in a bankruptcy are defined in the **21-049** broadest possible terms in section 382 of the Insolvency Act 1986.[29] These

---

[17] s.281(5)(b).

[18] s.281(6); see the Insolvency Rules 1986, r. 6.223 (liability under s.1 of the Drug Trafficking Offences Act 1986 not discharged). For what constitutes a prescribed debt, see s.384(1).

[19] See s.382 on the definition of bankruptcy debt. See § 21-049.

[20] s.281(7).

[21] *Ex p. Hammond* (1873) L.R. 16 Eq. 614.

[22] *Thompson v. Cohen* (1872) L.R. 7 Q.B. 527; *Cole v. Kernot* (1872) L.R. 7 Q.B. 534n; *Collyer v. Isaacs* (1881) 19 Ch.D. 342 (in these cases the court held that the committee merely had a personal right and not a proprietary interest).

[23] *Re Reis* [1904] 2 K.B. 769; (affd. [1905] A.C. 442); *Re Lind* [1915] 2 Ch. 345. But if the agreement concerns chattels it may be void unless registered as a bill of sale.

[24] *Van Sandau v. Corsbie* (1819) 3 B. & Ald. 13.

[25] s.285(3). A secured creditor can still enforce his security: s.284(5).

[26] *Jakeman v. Cook* (1878) 4 Ex.D. 26; *Re Aylmer* (1894) 70 L.T. 244; *Re Bonacine* [1912] 2 Ch. 394. See also *Wild v. Tucker* [1914] 3 K.B. 36. *cf. John v. Mendoza* [1939] 1 K.B. 141.

[27] *Wild v. Tucker* [1914] 3 K.B. 36 (contract by undischarged bankrupt to pay in full a larger debt in consideration of smaller loan held a good contract).

[28] *e.g. Re Ainsworth* [1922] 1 Ch. 22 (gift by will to children equally, subject to proviso that one child must account for debt due to testator; bankrupt child must account for balance due after discharge). Also, of course, it does not release the bankrupt from debts which for whatever reason are not provable.

[29] See also the Insolvency Rules 1986, r. 12.3.

include any debt or liability to which the bankrupt is subject at the commencement of the bankruptcy or to which he may be subject.[30] Liability means a liability to pay money or money's worth and it includes "any liability for breach of trust, any liability in contract, tort or bailment and any liability arising out of an obligation to make restitution."[31] It is irrelevant that the debt or liability is present or future "whether it is certain or contingent or whether its amount is fixed or liquidated, or is capable of being ascertained by fixed rules or as matter of opinion."[32] Where a bankruptcy debt bears interest, such interest is provable except in so far as it relates to interest accruing after the commencement of the bankruptcy.[33] Interest with respect to the period after the commencement of the bankruptcy is payable only if there is a surplus after the satisfaction of all of the bankruptcy debts.[34] Certain debts are not provable.[35] Thus a fine imposed for an offence and any obligation "arising under an order made in family or domestic proceedings"[36] are not provable. As well as these statutory exceptions, there are other debts which are not provable in the bankruptcy because they are such that the policy of the law will not allow the creditor to sue and consequently will not give the creditor a remedy in bankruptcy. Such debts are, for example, those given for an illegal or immoral consideration,[37] and in bankruptcy the existence of lawful consideration can be scrutinised even after judgment has been given against the bankrupt so that, as against him, the matter would be *res judicata*.[38] It is also important to keep in mind that the definition of bankruptcy debt has important implications for discharge as it is with respect to these debts that the bankrupt is discharged so that he can have a fresh start.[39]

(e) *Schemes of Arrangement*

21–050   **Voluntary arrangement.** Part VIII of the Insolvency Act 1986 establishes a procedure for enabling a debtor to make what is referred to as a "voluntary arrangement"[40] with his creditors. A debtor intending to enter into a voluntary

---

[30] s.382(1)(a) and (b).

[31] s.382(4).

[32] s.382(3).

[33] s.322(2); for criticisms of the old law see Cork Report, Cmnd. 8558 (1982), Chap. 31.

[34] s.328(4); the rate of applicable interest is set out in s.328(5).

[35] See also § 21–046 on the effect of discharge.

[36] Insolvency Rules 1986, r. 12.3(2); s.281(5)(b). This probably effects a change in law by reversing the decision in *Curtis v. Curtis* [1969] 1 W.L.R. 44; see *Muir Hunter on Personal Insolvency* at p. 3222 (§ 3–388).

[37] See *ante*, Chap. 16. Rule 12.3 of the Insolvency Rules 1986, which deals with provable debts, provides that "Nothing in this Rule prejudices any enactment or rule of law under which a particular kind of debt is not provable, whether on the grounds of public policy or otherwise."

[38] *Ex p. Kibble* (1875) L.R. 10 Ch.App. 373; *Ex p. Banner* (1881) 17 Ch.D. 480; *Re Beauchamp* [1904] 1 K.B. 572; *Re Van Laun* [1907] 1 K.B. 155; [1907] 2 K.B. 23; *Re Mead* 2 Ir.R. 285; *Re a Debtor* [1927] 2 Ch. 367.

[39] The object (as was stated with respect to previous bankruptcy legislation) is that "the bankrupt is to be a freed man—freed not only from debts but from contracts, liabilities, engagements, and contingencies of every kind": *Ex p. Llynvi Coal and Iron Co.* (1871) L.R. 7 Ch.App. 28, 32; and see *Ex p. Waters* (1873) L.R. 8 Ch.App. 562; *Flint v. Barnard* (1888) 22 Q.B.D. 90.

[40] s.253(1). See also County Courts Act 1984, ss.112–117(as amended by the Courts and Legal Services Act 1990, s.13); *Practice Direction (Bankruptcy: Voluntary Arrangements (No. 1/91)* [1992] 1 W.L.R. 120), (making of an administration order.)

arrangement with his creditors can apply to the court for an interim order which precludes a bankruptcy petition from being presented against him and no other proceedings may be commenced against him.[41] The debtor's proposal must provide for a person—"the nominee"—to act in relation to the voluntary arrangement for the purpose of implementing its realisation. The court has a discretion as to whether to make an interim order.[42] If the court makes an interim order, the nominee has to report to the court as to whether a meeting of the debtor's creditors should be summoned to consider the debtor's proposal. If a creditors' meeting is called and it approves the voluntary arrangement (with or without modifications)[43] then broadly speaking it becomes binding on all persons who under the rules were entitled to notice of and to vote at the meeting of creditors held to approve the arrangement.[44] Provision is made for the implementation of the arrangement[45] and a creditor who is aggrieved by the arrangement can petition the court for relief.[46]

Deeds of arrangement.[47] Apart from proceedings in bankruptcy the creditors **21–051** may agree to a voluntary deed of arrangement on the part of the debtor, though such a deed will not have the same effect in favour of a debtor as a discharge in bankruptcy. Section 2 of the Deeds of Arrangement Act 1914[48] provides that deeds of arrangement to which the Act applies[49] shall be void unless registered under the Act.

Deed of arrangement and surety. A deed of arrangement with creditors **21–052** contained a proviso that the deed was not to affect the rights and remedies of the creditors against any surety. The executors of a surety for the debtor sued the latter to recover sums paid on her behalf under the deed. It was held that the covenant by creditors not to sue, as limited by the proviso, imported not only that the deed did not affect any creditors' rights against the surety but also that a surety's consequential rights against the debtor were not to be affected.[50]

---

[41] s.252. As to who may make an application, see s.253.

[42] s.255. The grounds on which the court's jurisdiction is to be exercised are designed to prevent a debtor from misusing the procedure.

[43] No modification may affect the rights of a secured creditor without that creditor's consent: s.258(4). The proposal is treated as being made to creditors as a class and not to each creditor individually: *Re A Debtor (No. 2389 of 1989)* [1991] 2 W.L.R. 578.

[44] s.260. The arrangement only affects creditors' rights as creditors and does not affect proprietory rights such as a landlord's right to forfeit a lease: *Re Mohammed Naeem (A Bankrupt) (No. 18 of 1988)* [1990] 1 W.L.R. 48.

[45] s.263.

[46] s.262; *Re A Debtor (No. 259 of 1990)* 1 W.L.R. 226 (the prejudice must be brought about by the unfairness stemming from the terms of the scheme).

[47] The Cork Committee recommended that the Deeds of Arrangement Act 1914 be repealed (paras. 350–399), but this was not implemented. The relationship between the Insolvency Act 1986 and the Deeds of Arrangement Act 1914 is complex: see Muir Hunter *op. cit.* pp. 2005–2007 (§§ 21–001 *et seq.*).

[48] See also Insolvency Act 1986, s.260(3) and s.388(2)(b).

[49] *i.e.* assignments of property, deeds or agreements for composition, deeds of inspectorship, letters of licence or other agreements for the purpose of carrying on or winding up a debtor's business; see s.1.

[50] *Cole v. Lynn* [1942] 1 K.B. 142; following *Kearsley v. Cole* (1846) 16 M. & W. 128, and *Close v. Close* (1853) 4 De G.M. & G. 176. See further Vol. II, § 44–074—44–075, as to the effect of a scheme or deed of arrangement on the liability of a surety.

(f) Contracts made after Adjudication

21–053   **Bankrupt's liability on contracts.** A bankrupt is clearly responsible upon any contract which he makes *after* he has been adjudicated bankrupt.

21–054   **After-acquired property.** As has been said above,[51] the effect of an adjudication in bankruptcy is to transfer to the trustee only such property as belongs to the bankrupt at the time of adjudication. A trustee can also obtain for the bankrupt's estate any "after-acquired" property, that is property which has devolved upon or which has been acquired by the bankrupt since the commencement of the bankruptcy.[52] Such property does not automatically vest in a trustee; before it does so the trustee must serve notice on the bankrupt and the trustee's title will be deemed to relate back to the time when the property was acquired by the bankrupt.[53] Certain types of after-acquired property are excluded.[54] Protection is provided for the bona fide purchaser for value who deals with the bankrupt without notice of the bankruptcy,[55] it is important to note that it is notice of the bankruptcy that is the determinative factor. The trustee's ability to obtain after-acquired property is subject to a time limit: by section 309 no notice (except with leave of the court) relating to after-acquired property may be served on the bankrupt after the end of a period of 42 days beginning with the day on which "it first came to the knowledge of the trustee" that the property had vested in the bankrupt.[56] The trustee can also seek an order ("an income payments order") requiring the bankrupt to pay over to the trustee part of his income.[57] The court cannot make such an order where this would have the effect of reducing the income of the bankrupt below what is required to meet the reasonable domestic needs of the bankrupt and his family.[58]

21–055   **Action by bankrupt.** An undischarged bankrupt may sue on a contract made by him after his adjudication, unless his trustee intervenes.[59] Thus he may sue on a bill of exchange indorsed to him after adjudication,[60] or for rent in respect of premises let by him,[61] or for work and labour done,[62] or for goods sold,[63] or for specific performance of a contract for the sale of land.[64] And he may sue for wrongful dismissal, occurring after his adjudication, from employment under a

---

[51] *Ante,* § 21–019.

[52] s.307.

[53] s.307(3). This involves a reversal of the decision in *Re Pascoe* [1944] Ch. 219 as was proposed by the Cork Report: see Cmnd. 8558 (1982), Chap. 26.

[54] This is property which does not form part of the bankrupt's estate: see s.307(2).

[55] s.307(4). This protection applies whether or not a notice relating to after-acquired property has been served. For authorities dealing with the concept of value and bona fides in previous bankruptcy legislation: see *Re Bennett* [1907] 1 K.B. 149; *Hunt v. Fripp* [1898] 1 Ch. 675; *Re Stokes* [1919] 2 K.B. 256; *Re Behrend's Trust* [1911] 1 Ch. 687 (marriage consideration); *Hosack v. Robins (No. 2)* [1918] 2 Ch. 339.

[56] s.309(1).

[57] s.310; see Cork Report, Cmnd. 8558 (1982), paras. 1158–1163.

[58] s.310(2).

[59] See *ante,* § 21–053, dealing with after-acquired property.

[60] *Herbert v. Sayer* (1844) 5 Q.B. 965: *cf. Drayton v. Dale* (1823) 2 B. & C. 293; *Fyson v. Chambers* (1842) 9 M. & W. 460.

[61] *Cook v. Wellock* (1890) 24 Q.B.D. 658.

[62] *Jameson v. Brick and Stone Co.* (1878) 4 Q.B.D. 208: *Affleck v. Hammond* [1912] 3 K.B. 162.

[63] *Cumming v. Roebuck* (1816) Holt N.P.C. 172.

[64] *Dyster v. Randall & Sons* [1926] Ch. 932.

contract made before it.[65] Once intervention is made by the trustee he cannot withdraw his intervention nor can the bankrupt deal in any way with the property.[66]

Carrying on business of bankrupt. By section 314 of and Schedule 5 to the 1986 Act, the trustee is given extensive powers to carry on the business of the bankrupt. Some of these powers can only be exercised with the consent of the creditors' committee, if there is one, and if one does not exist with the consent of the court. In certain circumstances a trustee in bankruptcy[67] can compel the suppliers of utilities[68] to continue to supply the business of a bankrupt. This power was introduced on the recommendations of the Cork Committee to deal with the practice of utilities insisting on the payment of old debts as a condition of future supply thus for all intents and purposes putting themselves in a preferential position.[69] If the trustee makes such a request to a utility covered by section 372, the utility may continue to supply the bankrupt but it cannot make it a condition of the continued supply that any outstanding charges owing by the bankrupt and arising before the bankruptcy order are paid.[70] However, as a condition of continuing the supply the utility can make it a condition that the trustee guarantees the payment of any charges.[71]   **21-056**

(g) *Second Bankruptcies*

Second bankruptcies. Sections 334 and 335 deal with the special situation where a bankruptcy order is made against a person who is an undischarged bankrupt. These sections are designed to introduce the principle, indorsed by the Cork Committee, that "in most second and subsequent failures, the assets available are in the main the proceeds of the credit given to the bankrupt by his later creditors and that, in effect, goods supplied by them constitute the assets, and the proceeds thereof should not be shared by them with the creditors in some prior bankruptcy."[72] In other words, assets acquired subsequent to an earlier bankruptcy should be used to meet the claims of creditors in a later bankruptcy. Where a bankruptcy petition is presented against a person already subject to a bankruptcy order which has not been discharged, a prescribed notice may be served on the trustee of the earlier bankruptcy which renders void the disposition of certain assets in the bankrupt's estate unless a court order validating the disposition is obtained.[73] Broadly speaking the assets covered are those assets acquired by the trustee of the first bankruptcy since the commencement of the first bankruptcy which are new assets: these are (i) after-acquired property,[74]   **21-057**

---

[65] *Bailey v. Thurston & Co. Ltd* [1903] 1 K.B. 137. Where the wrongful dismissal occurred before the bankruptcy, the cause of the action passes to the trustee: *Beckham v. Drake* (1849) 2 H.L.C. 579, 627. *Ante*, §§ 21-032—21-033.

[66] *Hill v. Settle* [1917] 1 Ch. 319.

[67] Other office holders also have this right: see s.372(1); for the equivalent in relation to companies see s.233.

[68] Gas, electricity and telecommunications: see s.372(5).

[69] Cmnd. 8558 (1982), Chap. 33; on the legality of this practice see *Wellworth Cash & Carry (North Shields) Ltd v. North Eastern Electricity Board* (1986) 2 B.C.C. 99, 265.

[70] s.372(2)(b).

[71] s.372(2)(a).

[72] Cmnd. 8558 (1982), para. 1166.

[73] The court can also ratify such a disposition: see s.334(2).

[74] See *ante*, § 20-053.

(ii) money derived from an order under section 310 (income payments),[75] and (iii) property derived from either of the above.[76] These assets are also deemed to form part of the bankrupt's estate in the second bankruptcy.[77] The trustee of the first bankruptcy can prove in the second bankruptcy for any unsatisfied balance of debts provable in the first bankruptcy but is not entitled to any dividend on them until the creditors in the second bankruptcy have been satisfied in full.[78]

---

[75] See *ante*, § 20–053.

[76] See s.334(3).

[77] s.335(1). They are however subject to a charge in favour of the trustee of the first bankruptcy for his bankruptcy expenses: see s.335(3).

[78] s.335(5) and (6).

Part Six
PERFORMANCE AND DISCHARGE

PERFORMANCE

1. IN GENERAL

Introduction. The general rule is that a party to a contract must perform **22–001**
exactly[1] what he undertook to do.[2] When an issue arises as to whether performance is sufficient, the court must first construe[3] the contract in order to ascertain
the nature of the obligation (which is a question of law[4]); the next question is to
see whether the actual performance measures up to that obligation (which is a
question of "mixed fact and law" in that the court decides whether the facts of
the actual performance satisfy the standard prescribed by the contractual provisions defining the obligation[5]). This means that although an appellate court, or a

---

[1] On the doctrine of substantial performance, see *post*, § 22–032; on the doctrine of waiver, see
post, §§ 23–039, *et seq.*

[2] See *post*, §§ 22–004, 22–032. *cf.* s.30 of the Sale of Goods Act 1979 (Vol. II, § 43–253). A party
may be held to have failed to perform his contractual obligation, despite the existence of an
exemption clause purporting to cover the matter, if as a matter of construction, the clause is held not
to cover the loss which has been suffered: see *ante*, §§ 14–005 *et seq.* Under s.3(2)(b) of the Unfair
Contract Terms Act 1977, two types of terms are ineffective unless they satisfy the test of reasonableness (as defined in s.11): they are terms under which a person acting in the course of a business and
dealing either with a "consumer" (s.12) or on his "written standard terms of business" claims to be
entitled either "(i) to render a contractual performance substantially different from that which was
reasonably expected of him, or (ii) in respect of the whole or any part of his contractual obligation
to render no performance at all." (See further *ante*, §§ 14–057 *et seq.*). A wide range of clauses may
also be affected by the Unfair Terms in Consumer Contracts Regulations 1994 (see *ante*, Chap.
15).

[3] See also *post*, §§ 22–027, 22–032, 22–037. On the construction of the terms of a contract, see
ante, §§ 12–041 *et seq.*; on the question of the *order* in which the different promises of the parties
have to be performed, see *post*, §§ 22–027, 25–034—25–036.

[4] In addition to the cases cited in nn. 17 and 18, *post* see *ante*, § 12–046, and *Dixon v. Holdroyd*
(1857) 7 E. & B. 903; *Parry v. Great Ship Co. Ltd* (1864) 4 B. & S. 556; *Edmundson v. Longton Corp.*
(1902) 19 T.L.R. 15; *Vigers v. Cook* [1919] 2 K.B. 475. *cf. Herbert Clayton and Jack Waller Ltd v.
Oliver* [1930] A.C. 209 (obligation to give actor "one of the three leading comedy parts in a musical
play").

[5] *Margaronis Navigation Agency Ltd v. Henry W. Peabody & Co. of London Ltd* [1965] 1 Q.B. 300,
318. *cf. post*, §§ 24–015—24–016.

court reviewing the decision of an arbitrator, may not normally question a finding of pure fact by the lower court or arbitrator, it may review the construction of the contract and draw its own conclusion as to whether or not the facts amount to performance.[6]

22–002   The fact that a party to a contract has, in purported performance, acted in a way which may appear, in a commercial sense, to be just as valuable to the other party as the way specified in the contract does not amount to performance in law.[7] Thus, a contract to carry goods by sea from Singapore to New York with liberty to tranship at other ports was held not to be performed by their carriage partly by sea and partly by rail.[8]

22–003   **Promisor need not perform stipulation for his own benefit.** A party to a contract need not carry out a stipulation inserted solely for his own benefit.[9] Thus a covenant by a lessee to insure in the names of the lessors is not performed by insuring in their names and his own jointly[10]; nor a covenant by a lessee to insure in the joint names of the lessor and himself by the lessee insuring in his own name only[11]; but a covenant by a lessee to insure in the joint names of the lessor and himself is well performed by his insuring in the name of the lessor only.[12]

22–004   **Substituted or vicarious performance.** The promisor, in the absence of waiver[13] or subsequent variation by agreement,[14] cannot substitute for the agreed performance anything different, even though the substituted performance might appear to be better than, or at least equivalent to, the agreed performance.[15] If no personal skill of or supervision by the promisor is envisaged by the contract, the promisor may arrange for performance by another person on his behalf[16]; but where the contract expressly or impliedly requires personal performance by the promisor, he may not delegate performance to any other person.[17]

22–005   **Place of performance.** If the contract does not specify where performance is to take place, the place of performance depends upon the implied intention of the parties, to be judged from the nature of the contract and all the surrounding

---

[6] *ibid. cf. Tsakiroglou & Co. Ltd v. Noblee Thorl GmbH* [1962] A.C. 93 (a frustration case: see *post*, § 24–015); *Pioneer Shipping Ltd v. B.T.P. Tioxide Ltd* [1982] A.C. 724 (see *post*, § 24–095, n. 4).

[7] *Arcos Ltd v. E.A. Ronaasen & Son* [1933] A.C. 470. The courts may, however, ignore a trivial failure to perform, under the *de minimis* principle: *Bremer Handelsgesellschaft mbH v. Vanden Avenne-Izegem P.V.B.A.* [1978] 2 Lloyd's Rep. 109; *Margaronis Navigation Agency Ltd v. Henry W. Peabody & Co. of London Ltd, supra*, at 316; see also Vol. II, § 43–252.

[8] *Re L. Sutro & Co. and Heilbut, Symons & Co.* [1917] 2 K.B. 348. *cf. Tsakiroglou & Co. Ltd v. Noblee Thorl GmbH, supra*, at 113.

[9] *Beswick v. Beswick* [1968] A.C. 58, 92.

[10] *Penniall v. Harborne* (1848) 11 Q.B. 368.

[11] *Doe d. Muston v. Gladwin* (1845) 6 Q.B. 953. As to severable contracts in such cases, see *Green v. Low* (1856) 22 Beav. 625.

[12] *Havens v. Middleton* (1853) 22 L.J.Ch. 746. (The lessor was in no way prejudiced by the departure from the contractual undertaking.)

[13] *Post*, §§ 23–039 *et seq.*

[14] *Post*, §§ 23–032 *et seq.*

[15] *Legh v. Lillie* (1860) 6 H. & N. 165; *Forman & Co. Proprietary Ltd v. The Liddesdale* [1900] A.C. 190; *Re L. Sutro & Co. and Heilbut, Symons & Co. supra* (see § 22–002); *Arcos Ltd v. E.A. Ronaasen & Son* [1933] A.C. 470 (*ante*, § 22–002).

[16] On such vicarious performance, see *ante*, §§ 20–079—20–082.

[17] *Davies v. Collins* [1945] 1 All E.R. 247; *Martin v. N. Negin Ltd* (1945) 172 L.T. 275; *Edwards v. Newlands & Co.* [1950] 2 K.B. 534.

circumstances.[18] If no place of performance is specified even by implication, but performance requires the concurrence of the promisee, the general rule is that the promisor must seek out the promisee and perform his promise wherever the promisee may be.[19]

Promises in the alternative. Where a contractual promise is in the alter- **22–006** native, in that the promisor agrees to do one of two or more things, the legal effect of the promise depends on the kind of alternative involved: there may be a promise to perform in one of two or more alternative ways, where the form of the promise *requires* an election to be made; or there may be a primary or basic obligation to perform in one way *unless* the party who holds the "option" chooses to substitute another way.[20] Under the first kind of alternative promise, there is no primary or basic obligation and there must be an election of an alternative by one of the parties. The contract may provide which party may choose the alternative to be performed[21]; in the absence of such a provision, the right to elect the alternative is impliedly vested in the promisor, the rule being that the party who is obliged to perform the first act may choose which alternative he wishes to perform.[22] If the promisee is entitled to elect between the alternatives, he must give notice of his election, and until such notice has been given the liability of the other party does not arise.[23] Once the person entitled to elect chooses the alternative to be performed,[24] he is absolutely bound by his choice[25] even though the chosen mode of performance afterwards becomes impossible to carry out.[26]

In the absence of any such election, if it becomes impossible to perform one **22–007** alternative, it depends on the construction of the contract, in the particular circumstances, whether the promisor is still obliged to perform the remaining

---

[18] *Reynolds v. Coleman* (1887) 36 Ch.D. 453; *Mutzenbecher v. La Aseguradora Espanola* [1906] 1 K.B. 254. See also the cases on the place of payment, *post*, § 22–054. *cf. Comber v. Leyland & Bullins* [1898] A.C. 524; *Re Parana Plantations Ltd* [1946] 2 All E.R. 214. On the place of delivery in a contract for the sale of goods, see s.29(1) and (2) of the Sale of Goods Act 1979; Vol. II, §§ 43–241 *et seq.*

[19] This is the general rule in promises to pay money (see *post*, § 22–054), but it applies to other promises where the promisee must concur in performance: *Rippinghall v. Lloyd* (1833) 5 B. & Ad. 742. *cf. Cranley v. Hillary* (1813) 2 M. & S. 120.

[20] The second kind of alternative is discussed *post* in § 22–008.

[21] *Chippendale v. Thurston* (1829) 4 C. & P. 98 (contract provided for notice to be given by one party). On the assessment of damages where the promisor could choose the method or extent of performance, see *Paula Lee Ltd v. Robert Zehil & Co. Ltd* [1983] 2 All E.R. 390 (*post*, § 27–001).

[22] *Layton v. Pearce* (1778) 1 Dougl. 15; *Re Brookman's Trusts* (1869) L.R. 5 Ch.App. 182; *Reed v. Kilburn Co-operative Society* (1875) L.R. 10 Q.B. 264; *Christie v. Wilson* 1915 S.C. 645.

[23] *Vyse v. Wakefield* (1840) 6 M. & W. 442; (affd. 7 M. & W. 126); *Thorn v. City Rice Mills* (1889) 40 Ch.D. 357; *Narbeth v. James* [1967] 1 Lloyd's Rep. 591, 598; (affd. on appeal [1968] 1 Lloyd's Rep. 168). See also *Rippinghall v. Lloyd* (1833) 5 B. & Ad. 742; *Calaminus v. Dowlais Iron Co. Ltd* (1878) 47 L.J.Q.B. 575.

[24] On the time by which a selection must be made among "alternative cargoes," see *Brightman & Co. v. Bunge y Born Limitada Sociedad* [1924] 2 K.B. 619 (affd. on other grounds [1925] A.C. 799); *Reardon Smith Line Ltd v. Ministry of Agriculture* [1963] A.C. 691, 717, 720.

[25] *Schneider v. Foster* (1857) 2 H. & N. 4; *Rugg v. Weir* (1864) 16 C.B.(N.S.) 471; *Gath v. Lees* (1865) 3 H. & C. 558; *cf. Mallam v. Arden* (1833) 10 Bing. 299. A tender of performance which is not up to the contractual requirements may, however, be withdrawn, and a proper tender substituted within the time fixed for performance (see *post*, § 22–090, n. 77).

[26] *Brown v. Royal Insurance Society* (1859) 1 E. & E. 853.

alternative, or whether he is discharged from his obligation[27]; normally, however, the promisor is still bound to perform another alternative[28]: "if the court is satisfied that the clear intention of the parties was, that one of them should do a certain thing, but he is allowed at his option to do it in one or other of two modes, and one of the modes becomes impossible by the act of God, he is still bound to perform it in the other mode."[29] In *Anderson v. Commercial Union Assurance Co.*[30] an insurance policy contained a condition giving the insurers the option "to reinstate or replace property damaged or destroyed instead of paying the amount of the loss or damage." The defendants argued that they would be discharged from performing either alternative if what had happened made it impossible for them to reinstate the property, but Bowen L.J. said: "It is clear law that if one of two things which have been contracted for subsequently becomes impossible, it becomes a question of construction whether, according to the true intention of the document, the obligor is bound to perform the alternative or is discharged altogether."[31] If, however, the promisor puts it out of his power to perform one alternative, he is bound to perform the other alternative.[32]

22–008 **"Business" options.** The second type of alternative promise is a "true" or "business" option, and it must be contrasted with a contractual obligation which may be performed in different ways (as discussed in the preceding paragraphs). In a "business" option, the contract specifies a single, primary or basic obligation to be performed in one way, unless the holder of the option chooses to substitute another way, and does so by the effective exercise of his option[33]; this power of choice is conferred by the contract on the option-holder "solely for his own advantage" and "in exercising the option . . . the holder is not bound to consider the convenience or the interest of the other party."[34] Hence, if performance of the primary obligation is impeded or frustrated, the option-holder is not obliged to exercise his choice so as to permit performance in the substituted way.[35]

22–009 **When notice to perform is required.** Some promises may be made conditional upon the happening of a particular event; the contract may stipulate that notice of the happening of the event must be given to the promisor by the other party, but in the absence of such a provision, the general rule is that where the

---

[27] *Da Costa v. Davis* (1798) 1 B. & P. 242; *Stevens v. Webb* (1835) 7 C. & P. 60; *Marquis of Bute v. Thompson* (1844) 13 M. & W. 487; *Barkworth v. Young* (1856) 26 L.J.Ch. 153, 163; *Anderson v. Commercial Union Assurance Co.* (1885) 55 L.J.Q.B. 146, 150 (quoted *post*); *McIlquham v. Taylor* [1895] 1 Ch. 53.

[28] *Barkworth v. Young, supra*; *Brightman & Co. v. Bunge y Born Limitada Sociedad* [1924] 2 K.B. 619; *Reardon Smith Line Ltd v. Ministry of Agriculture* [1963] A.C. 691, 717, 730. *cf. post*, § 22–008.

[29] *Barkworth v. Young, supra*, at 163.

[30] *Supra.*

[31] *ibid.* at 150.

[32] *McIlquham v. Taylor, supra* (following *Studholme v. Mandell* (1698) 1 Ld.Raym. 279). *cf. Honck v. Muller* (1881) 7 Q.B.D. 92. See also, in the context of "self-induced" frustration, the case of *J. Lauritzen A.S. v. Wijsmuller B.V. (The Super Servant Two)* [1990] 1 Lloyd's Rep. 1 (*post*, §§ 24–061—24–067).

[33] "There must, therefore, be some provision, express or implied, for its exercise within a reasonable time and for the communication of the election to the other party": *Reardon Smith Line Ltd v. Ministry of Agriculture, supra*, at 731; *Libyan Arab Foreign Bank v. Bankers Trust Co.* [1989] Q.B. 728, 766.

[34] *ibid.* at 730. Such a contractual provision will, however, in some circumstances fall within s.3 of the Unfair Contract Terms Act 1977: see *ante*, § 22–001, n. 2; and §§ 14–057 *et seq.*

[35] The *Reardon Smith Line* case, *supra*, at 730. See also *ibid.* at 719–720.

matter does not lie more properly within the knowledge of the other party than of the promisor, such notice is not required.[36] So where houses were let on the understanding that the landlord was to repair a sea-wall necessary to preserve the houses, no notice to the landlord of want of repair was required.[37] Again, if A agrees to indemnify B against the acts of a third person, the liability attaches without B giving notice of such acts to A.[38]

In certain circumstances, however, notice requiring performance is necessary despite the absence of a clause in the contract requiring such notice. "The general rule is, that a party is not entitled to notice unless he has stipulated for it; but there are certain cases where, from the very nature of the transaction, the law requires notice to be given, though not expressly stipulated for."[39] Thus, where only one party has knowledge of the relevant facts, notice is necessary[40]; so, if a landlord agrees to repair the inside of a house[41] or to keep drains in repair,[42] the tenant must give notice of the disrepair,[43] since "the landlord is not the occupier of the premises and has no means of knowing what is the condition of the premises unless he is told."[44] Notice to the landlord of the need for repair is also required where the covenant to repair is inserted by statute into the contract of letting[45]; this rule applies whether the defect is latent or patent.[46] But notice of disrepair is not necessary where the landlord retains in his own control that part of the premises whose defective condition causes the damage.[47]

When request to perform is necessary. Normally, no request or demand for   **22–010** performance is necessary[48] and the promisor is bound to perform his contractual obligation without being requested to do so; an illustration is the common case of a promise to pay a sum of money, either in general terms or on a specified

---

[36] *Vyse v. Wakefield* (1840) 6 M. & W. 442, especially at 453–454; 7 M. & W. 126; *Dawson v. Wrench* (1849) 3 Exch. 359, 362; *Murphy v. Hurly* [1922] 1 A.C. 369 (distinguishing *Makin v. Watkinson* (1870) L.R. 6 Ex. 25, *infra*). As to the requirement of notice when one party has the right to choose the mode of performance in an alternative promise, see *ante*, § 22–006; as to notice of dishonour of a bill, see the Bills of Exchange Act 1882, ss.48 and 49 (considered in Vol. II, § 34–112).

[37] *Murphy v. Hurley, supra*. (The sea-wall was not in the exclusive occupation of any tenant.)

[38] *Cutler v. Southern* (1668) 1 Wms.Saund. 116; *Lilley v. Hewitt* (1822) 11 Price 494. See Vol. II, § 44–059. But a demand is necessary where the surety promises "to pay on demand" if the principal debtor defaults: *Sicklemore v. Thistleton* (1817) 6 M. & S. 9.

[39] *Vyse v. Wakefield, supra*, at 453. See also *Davies v. McLean* (1873) 21 W.R. 264.

[40] *Makin v. Watkinson, supra*; *London and South Western Ry. v. Flower* (1875) 1 C.P.D. 77, 85; *Manchester Bonded Warehouse Co. v. Carr* (1880) 5 C.P.D. 507.

[41] *Makin v. Watkinson, supra*; *Broggi v. Robins* (1899) 15 T.L.R. 224; *Tredway v. Machin* (1904) 91 L.T. 310. See also n. 45, *post*.

[42] *Hugall v. M'Lean* (1885) 53 L.T. 94; *Torrens v. Walker* [1906] 2 Ch. 166.

[43] Knowledge of the want of repair may come from a source other than the tenant: *Griffin v. Pillet* [1926] 1 K.B. 17; *Uniproducts (Manchester) Ltd v. Rose Furnishers Ltd* [1956] 1 W.L.R. 45; *O'Brien v. Robinson* [1973] A.C. 912, 926.

[44] *Tredway v. Machin, supra*, at 311.

[45] *O'Brien v. Robinson, supra* (Housing Act 1961, s.32; see now Landlord and Tenant Act 1985, s. 11); *McCarrick v. Liverpool Corpn.* [1947] A.C. 219. The landlord's right to enter and inspect the premises does not excuse the tenant from giving notice: *McCarrick v. Liverpool Corpn., supra*.

[46] *O'Brien v. Robinson, supra* (following *Morgan v. Liverpool Corpn.* [1927] 2 K.B. 131).

[47] *Melles & Co. v. Holme* [1918] 2 K.B. 100; *Bishop v. Consolidated London Properties Ltd* (1933) 102 L.J.K.B. 257; *British Telecommunications plc v. Sun Life Assurance Society plc* [1996] Ch. 69 (although the court refrained from expressing a concluded view on the case where the defect is caused by an occurrence which is wholly outside the landlord's control). *cf.* also s.4(2) of the Defective Premises Act 1972.

[48] *Brown v. Dean* (1833) 5 B. & Ad. 848; *Radford v. Smith* (1838) 3 M. & W. 254, 258; *Hooper v. Woolmer* (1850) 10 C.B. 370.

day.[49] A request to perform is essential to complete the promisee's cause of action only if the contract expressly requires such a request,[50] or the nature of the contract shows that it is an implied condition precedent to the promisor's liability that a request for performance should be made. Thus, where the amount of a debt is uncertain and depends on facts known to the creditor, he must make a demand for a specific sum.[51] Similarly, no right of action against the drawer or indorser accrues on a bill of exchange or promissory note until a demand has been made[52]; a bank balance is not due until the depositor claims to withdraw it[53]; a bailor of chattels at will cannot sue for their return until there has been a demand and a refusal to return[54]; and where goods are consigned to an agent for sale on commission, an action will not lie against the agent for failure to account until such an account has been demanded from him.[55] Obviously, where a man has disabled himself from performing his contract, it is unnecessary to make any request or demand of performance.[56]

2. TIME OF PERFORMANCE[57]

22–011   **Time "of the essence of the contract."** A number of difficulties surround the law relating to time stipulations in contracts. The first is that the phrase which is commonly employed, namely "time is of the essence of the contract," is potentially misleading in that the question in each case is whether time is of the essence of the particular term which has been broken, not whether time is of the essence of the contract as a whole.[58] The second is that, historically, common law and equity adopted a divergent approach to time stipulations in contracts. At common law a strict approach was taken so that, as was once stated by Sir John Romilly M.R., "at law time is always of the essence of the contract. When any time is fixed for the completion of it, the contract must be completed on the day

---

[49] *Gibbs v. Southam* (1834) 5 B. & Ad. 911; *Walton v. Mascall* (1844) 13 M. & W. 452; *Bell & Co. v. Antwerp, London & Brazil Line* [1891] 1 Q.B. 103, 107. On payment, see *post*, §§ 22–039 *et seq.* It is a criminal offence for a creditor to "harass" his debtor with the object of coercing him to pay the debt: Administration of Justice Act 1970, s.40.

[50] *e.g. Rawson v. Johnson* (1801) 1 East 203 (contract to deliver goods on request: if the buyer sues for non-delivery, he need only prove a request to deliver and his readiness to pay the price).

[51] *Brown v. Great Eastern Ry.* (1877) 2 Q.B.D. 406.

[52] Bills of Exchange Act 1882, s.45. (The acceptor is liable even where the bill has not been presented for payment: s.52(1).) *cf.* s.87. (See Vol. II, §§ 34–108—34–109, 34–153, 34–192.)

[53] *Joachimson v. Swiss Bank Corporation* [1921] 3 K.B. 110; *Bagley v. Winsome and National Provincial Bank Ltd* [1952] 2 Q.B. 236; *Arab Bank Ltd v. Barclays Bank (Dominion, Colonial and Overseas)* [1954] A.C. 495; *Libyan Arab Foreign Bank v. Bankers Trust Co.* [1989] Q.B. 728, 748–749.

[54] *Cullen v. Barclay* (1881) 10 L.R.Ir. 224; *Miller v. Dell* [1891] 1 Q.B. 468. See Vol. II, § 33–010.

[55] *Topham v. Braddick* (1809) 1 Taunt. 572.

[56] *Lovelock v. Franklyn* (1846) 8 Q.B. 371; *Caines v. Smith* (1846) 15 M. & W. 189, 190. An old illustration is *Short v. Stone* (1846) 8 Q.B. 358, where A, who had promised to marry B, later married C instead. (Such promises no longer have legal effect: see *post*, § 27–017, n. 86.)

[57] Stoljar (1955) 71 L.Q.R. 527; Lindgren, *Time in the Performance of Contracts—Especially for the Sale of Land* (2nd ed.) (Australia); Treitel, *The Law of Contract* (9th ed., 1995), pp. 739–745; Carter, *Breach of Contract* (2nd ed., 1991), §§ 538–568.

[58] *British and Commonwealth Holdings plc v. Quadrex Holdings Inc.* [1989] Q.B. 842, 856–857.

specified, or an action will lie for breach of it."[59] However even at common law there were exceptional cases where time was held not to be of the essence of the contract.[60] But the thrust of the approach of the courts at common law was clear: stipulations as to time were generally of the essence of the contract, so that a party could treat the contract as repudiated if the other party's performance was not completed on the date stipulated by the contract. A different set of rules, however, evolved in equity where time was not of the essence of the contract, except in the three cases considered below. "The court of equity was accustomed to relieve against a failure to keep the date assigned ... if it could do justice between the parties"[61]; "relief is given against mere lapse of time where lapse of time is not essential to the substance of the contract."[62]

Law of Property Act 1925, s.41. Section 41 of the Law of Property Act **22-012** 1925,[63] provides that:

> "Stipulations in a contract, as to time or otherwise, which according to the rules of equity are not deemed to be or to have become of the essence of the contract, are also construed and have effect at law in accordance with the same rules."

Thus the rules at law are now the same as those in equity: the effect of section 41 is that "contractual stipulations as to time ... shall not be construed as essential, except where equity would before 1875 have so construed them—*i.e.* only when the strict observance of the stipulated time for performance was a matter of express agreement or of necessary implication"[64]; or, in other words, section 41 "does not negative the existence of a breach of contract where one has occurred,[65] but in certain circumstances it bars any assertion that the breach has amounted to a repudiation of the contract"[66] which entitles the innocent party to treat the contract as terminated. Following the enactment of section 41, it is only in the three cases set out in the next two paragraphs that time is of the essence of a contract.[67]

Time made expressly or implicitly "of the essence." Time is of the essence: **22-013** (1) Where the parties have expressly stipulated in their contract that the time

---

[59] *Parkin v. Thorold* (1852) 16 Beav. 59, 65.

[60] See, *e.g. Martindale v. Smith* (1841) 1 Q.B. 389, 395 (although note the criticism levelled against the case by Lord Simon in *United Scientific Holdings Ltd v. Burnley B.C.* [1978] A.C. 904, 941); Sale of Goods Act 1979, s.10(1); *Woolfe v. Horne* (1877) 2 Q.B.D. 355; *Re Olympia & York Canary Wharf Ltd (No. 2)* [1993] B.C.C. 159, 172.

[61] *Lock v. Bell* [1931] 1 Ch. 35, 43. The equitable rule was developed in cases of the sale of land: see *Stickney v. Keeble* [1915] A.C. 386, 415–416; *Williams v. Greatrex* [1957] 1 W.L.R. 31. For the history of the law on stipulations as to time, see *United Scientific Holdings Ltd v. Burnley B.C.* [1978] A.C. 904, 924–929, 940–945; *Raineri v. Miles* [1981] A.C. 1050.

[62] *Lennon v. Napper* (1802) 2 Sch. & Lef. 682, 684–685.

[63] Re-enacting s.25(7) of the Judicature Act 1873.

[64] *United Scientific Holdings Ltd v. Burnley B.C., supra,* at 943–944 (*per* Lord Simon).

[65] This means that damages may be recovered for any loss caused by the breach: *Raineri v. Miles, supra* (*post*, § 22–018).

[66] *Raineri v. Miles, supra,* at 1059 (*per* Buckley L.J., approved by the House of Lords in the same case: *ibid.* at 1085).

[67] *United Scientific Holdings Ltd v. Burnley B.C., supra.*; *British and Commonwealth Holdings plc v. Quadrex Holdings Inc.* [1989] Q.B. 842, 857; *Hammond v. Allen* [1994] 1 All E.R. 307, 311.

fixed for performance must be exactly complied with,[68] or that time is to be "of the essence."[69] (2) Where the circumstances of the contract or the nature of the subject-matter indicate that the fixed date must be exactly complied with, *e.g.* the purchase of a leasehold house required for immediate occupation[70]; the sale of business land or premises,[71] such as a public-house as a going concern[72]; the sale of a reversionary interest[73]; the exercise of an option for the purchase or repurchase of property,[74] or for determining a lease under a "break" clause[75] or an option to acquire a leasehold interest *in futuro*[76] (since in these cases, "the parties on the exercise of the option, are brought into a new legal relationship"[77]); "mercantile contracts,"[78] such as a contract for the sale of goods where a time is fixed for delivery,[79] or for the sale of shares liable to fluctuate in value (where the contract stipulated a time for payment),[80] or a charterparty under which the owner is given the right to withdraw the vessel in default of "punctual payment" of hire.[81] However, the mere fact that the contract can be labelled "mercantile" or "commercial" does not determine the issue.[82] The question is whether the time specified in the particular clause was (expressly or by necessary

---

[68] *Hudson v. Temple* (1860) 29 Beav. 536; *Steedman v. Drinkle* [1916] 1 A.C. 275; *Brickles v. Snell* [1916] 2 A.C. 599; *Mussen v. Van Diemen's Land Co.* [1938] Ch. 253; *Harold Wood Brick Co. Ltd v. Ferris* [1935] 2 K.B. 198. The same result follows if the contract provides that the provision is to be a "condition" in this sense, or that any breach of the clause shall entitle the innocent party to "rescind" or terminate. See also *post*, § 22–019, n. 24.

[69] *Lombard North Central plc v. Butterworth* [1987] Q.B. 527 (*post*, § 22–015).

[70] *Tilley v. Thomas* (1867) L.R. 3 Ch.App. 61; *Hudson v. Temple, supra*, at 543.

[71] *Macbryde v. Weekes* (1856) 22 Beav. 533; *Harold Wood Brick Co. Ltd v. Ferris, supra*.

[72] *Tadcaster Tower Brewery Co. v. Wilson* [1897] 1 Ch. 705, 711; *Lock v. Bell* [1931] 1 Ch. 35.

[73] *Newman v. Rogers* (1793) 4 Bro.C.C. 391.

[74] *Dibbins v. Dibbins* [1896] 2 Ch. 348; *Hare v. Nicoll* [1966] 2 Q.B. 130. *cf. Millichamp v. Jones* [1982] 1 W.L.R. 1422.

[75] *United Scientific Holdings Ltd v. Burnley Borough Council, supra*, at 929; *Coventry City Council v. J. Hepworth & Son Ltd* (1982) 46 P. & C.R. 170; *Metrolands Investments Ltd v. J.H. Dewhurst Ltd* [1986] 3 All E.R. 659.

[76] Whether or not it is an option to renew an existing lease: *United Scientific Holdings Ltd v. Burnley B.C., supra*, at 929, 945, 961. An option to a tenant to determine his interest under a "break clause" must also be strictly complied with: *ibid*.

[77] *ibid.* at 945 (see also at 951, 961). *cf.* a rent review clause: *post*, § 22–018.

[78] *Reuter Hufeland & Co. v. Sala & Co.* (1879) 4 C.P.D. 239, 249; *Bunge Corporation, New York v. Tradax Export SA, Panama* [1981] 1 W.L.R. 711, 716. See further *ante*, §§ 12–037 *et seq.*

[79] *Bowes v. Shand* (1877) 2 App.Cas. 455, 463, 464; *Sharp v. Christmas* (1892) 8 T.L.R. 687 (perishable goods); *Hartley v. Hymans* [1920] 3 K.B. 475, 484. See *post*, Vol. II, § 43–243.

[80] *Hare v. Nicoll, supra*. See also *Re Schwabacher* (1908) 98 L.T. 127, 129; *Sprague v. Booth* [1909] A.C. 576, 579–580; *British and Commonwealth Holdings plc v. Quadrex Holdings Inc.* [1989] Q.B. 842, 857; *Grant v. Cigman* [1996] 2 B.C.L.C. 24, 31 (although Judge Weeks Q.C. stated that the dicta in *Re Schwabacher* and *Hare v. Nicoll* "may be too wide" and that "a property company may be different from a trading company, and a company in one line of business may be different from a company trading in another less dynamic market."

[81] *Mardorf Peach & Co. Ltd v. Attica Sea Carriers Corporation of Liberia* [1977] A.C. 850 (approving *Tenax Steamship Co. Ltd v. Brimnes (Owners) (The Brimnes)* [1975] Q.B. 929). Time charters may now contain an "anti-technicality" clause requiring the owner to give notice before withdrawing the vessel: *Italmare Shipping Co. v. Ocean Tanker Co. Inc. (The Rio Sun) (No. 2)* [1982] 3 All E.R. 273; *Afovos Shipping Co. SA v. Romano Pagnan and Pietro Pagnan* [1983] 1 W.L.R. 195. An anti-technicality clause must state that the hire has not been punctually paid and that charterers have a given period of time in which to pay up or risk losing the ship: *Schelde Delta Shipping B.V. v. Astarte Shipping Ltd (The Pamela)* [1995] 2 Lloyd's Rep. 249.

[82] *Bunge Corporation, New York v. Tradax Export SA, Panama* [1981] 1 W.L.R. 711, 729 (*cf.* at 716); *United Scientific Holdings Ltd v. Burnley B.C., supra*, at 924, 938, 950; *Torvald Klaveness A/S v. Arni Maritime Corporation* [1994] 1 W.L.R. 1465 (obligation to make timely redelivery in time charterparty held not to be a condition).

implication) intended by the parties to be essential, *e.g.* because they needed to know precisely what were their respective obligations.[83] Thus, where the buyers were required to give 15 days' notice of readiness of the vessel so that the sellers could then nominate the port for loading, the House of Lords held time to be of the essence: performance by the buyer was a condition precedent to the seller's ability to perform his obligation.[84] (However, under the Sale of Goods Act 1979, s.10, unless a different intention appears from the terms of the contract, stipulations as to time of *payment* are not deemed to be of the essence of the contract of sale.[85])

Notice making time "of the essence." (3) Where time was not originally of the essence of the contract, but one party has been guilty of undue delay, the other party may give notice[86] requiring the contract to be performed within a reasonable time.[87] Notice can be served at the moment of breach: it is not necessary to wait until there has been an unreasonable delay by the party in breach before serving the notice.[88] The period of notice given must, however, be reasonable and what is reasonable will depend upon all the facts and circumstances of the case.[89]

22–014

---

[83] The *Bunge Corporation* case, *supra*. See also *Scandinavian Trading Tanker Co. A.B. v. Flota Petrolera Ecuatoriana* [1983] 2 A.C. 694, 703–704; *Sport Internationaal Bussum B.V. v. Inter-Footwear Ltd* [1984] 1 W.L.R. 776, 783, 793; *Hyundai Merchant Marine Co. Ltd v. Karander Maritime Inc. (The Niizuru)* [1996] 2 Lloyd's Rep. 66, 71.

[84] The *Bunge Corporation* case, *supra*. Other illustrations given in this case of time being of the essence in mercantile contracts include the date fixed for the sailing of a ship, for the opening of a banker's credit, or for payment against documents. See also *Toepfer v. Lenersan-Poortmann N.V.* [1980] 1 Lloyd's Rep. 143 (seller's obligation to tender documents by a specified time); *Société Italo-Belge pour le Commerce et Industrie SA v. Palm and Vegetable Oils (Malaysia) Sdn. Bhd.* [1982] 1 All E.R. 19 (seller's obligation to provide declaration of ship); *Gill & Duffus SA v. Société pour l'Exportation des Sucres SA* [1985] 1 Lloyd's Rep. 621 ("at latest").

[85] See Vol. II, § 43–108. *cf.* s.48(3) of the Act: (Vol. II, § 43–349). Similarly, the times of payment of bills of exchange regularly given under the terms of a long-term distributorship were not treated as of the essence: *Decro-Wall International SA v. Practitioners in Marketing Ltd* [1971] 1 W.L.R. 361. *cf.* however, the time for payment of a deposit: *Portaria Shipping Co. v. Gulf Pacific Navigation Co. Ltd* [1981] 2 Lloyd's Rep. 180.

[86] No notice need be given if it is clear that the party in default does not intend to proceed: *Re Stone and Saville's Contract* [1963] 1 W.L.R. 163, 171. The inclusion in the contract of express provision for the service of a notice requiring performance within a specified time (where the recipient of the notice has failed to complete performance on the due date) does not exclude the rights and remedies at law or in equity which subsist apart from such notice: *Woods v. Mackenzie Hill Ltd* [1975] 1 W.L.R. 613 (approved by the House of Lords in *Raineri v. Miles* [1981] A.C. 1050, 1085–1086). (Such a notice does not waive or expunge the previous breach of contract in failing to complete at the due date: *ibid.*)

[87] *Parkin v. Thorold* (1852) 16 Beav. 59; *Green v. Sevin* (1879) 13 Ch.D. 589; *Compton v. Bagley* [1892] 1 Ch. 313; *Stickney v. Keeble* [1915] A.C. 386; *Re Bagley and Shoesmith's Contract* (1918) 87 L.J.Ch. 626; *Hartley v. Hymans* [1920] 3 K.B. 475; *Charles Rickards Ltd v. Oppenhaim* [1950] 1 K.B. 616 (sale of goods); *United Scientific Holdings Ltd v. Burnley B.C., supra*, at 934, 946–947. *cf. Finkielkraut v. Monohan* [1949] 2 All E.R. 234; *Thorpe v. Fasey* [1949] Ch. 649; *Ajit v. Sammy* [1967] 1 A.C. 255. *cf.* s.48(3) of the Sale of Goods Act 1979.

[88] *Behzadi v. Shaftesbury Hotels Ltd* [1992] Ch. 1, in this respect overruling *Smith v. Hamilton* [1951] Ch. 174 where Harman J. held that it was necessary to wait until there has been an unreasonable delay before serving the notice. Where the contract does not specify a date for completion it remains necessary to wait for a reasonable time before serving the notice but that is because it is only where there has been an unreasonable delay by the other party that there will be a breach of contract which justifies the serving of the notice.

[89] *Stickney v. Keeble* [1915] A.C. 386; *Re Barr's Contract* [1956] Ch. 551; *Ajit v. Sammy* [1967] 1 A.C. 255; *Behzadi v. Shaftesbury Hotels Ltd* [1992] Ch. 1, 27; *Bidaisee v. Sampath* (1995) 46 W.I.R. 461, PC; *Bedfordshire County Council v. Fitzpatrick Contractors Ltd*, unreported, Technology and Construction Court, October 16, 1998.

Factors to which the courts will have regard in assessing the reasonableness of the period of notice include what remains to be done at the date of the notice; the fact that the party giving the notice has continually pressed for completion, or has before given similar notices which he has waived[90]; or that it is especially important for him to obtain early completion.[91] A party who elects to give notice immediately upon the breach of contract would be well advised to be "cautious" in his selection of the period to be included in the notice.[92] Notice making time of the essence of the contract can be given in relation to any term of the contract: entitlement to give notice is not confined to essential terms of the contract.[93] Once notice has been given, both parties are bound by it so that, if the party giving the notice is not ready to perform on the expiry of the notice, the other party may be entitled to terminate.[94] If, by notice, a party has made time of the essence, but later allows a further extension to another fixed date, time remains of the essence.[95] The notice procedure laid down in the contract may be held to be exhaustive of the rights of the parties so that it will not be open to them to serve a notice (for example, of shorter duration) under the general law rather than the contract.[96]

22–015   **Consequences of time being "of the essence."** In determining the consequences of a stipulation that time is to be "of the essence" of an obligation, it is vital to distinguish between the case where both parties agree that time is to be of the essence of the obligation and the case where, following a breach of a non-essential term of the contract, the innocent party serves a notice on the other stating that time is to be of the essence.[97] In the former case the effect of declaring time to be of the essence is to elevate the term to the status of a "condition"[98] with the consequences that a failure to perform by the stipulated time will entitle the innocent party to (a) terminate performance of the contract and thereby put an end to all the primary obligations of both parties remaining unperformed[99]; and (b) claim damages from the contract-breaker on the basis that he has committed a fundamental breach of the contract ("a breach going to the root of the contract") depriving the innocent party of the benefit of the contract ("damages for loss of the whole transaction").[1]

---

[90] *Luck v. White* (1973) 26 P. & C.R. 89 (the notice may be waived by the party who gave it re-opening negotiations, while failing to act upon the other party's neglect to comply with the notice). *cf. Buckland v. Farmar & Moody* [1979] 1 W.L.R. 221.

[91] *Charles Richards Ltd v. Oppenhaim* [1950] 1 K.B. 616.

[92] *Behzadi v. Shaftesbury Hotels Ltd* [1992] Ch. 1, 24.

[93] *Re Olympia & York Canary Wharf Ltd (No. 2)* [1993] B.C.C. 159, 171.

[94] *Finkielkraut v. Monohan* [1949] 2 All E.R. 234; *Quadrangle Development and Construction Co. Ltd v. Jenner* [1974] 1 W.L.R. 68; *Oakdown Ltd v. Bernstein & Co.* (1984) 49 P. & C.R. 282.

[95] *Buckland v. Farmar & Moody* [1979] 1 W.L.R. 221, citing *Howe v. Smith* (1884) 27 Ch. D. 89 and *Lock v. Bell* [1931] 1 Ch. 35.

[96] *Rightside Properties Ltd v. Gray* [1975] Ch. 72; *Country and Metropolitan Homes Ltd v. Topclaim Ltd* [1996] Ch. 307, 314–315. The position is, of course, otherwise where the parties expressly reserve "any other right or remedy" available: *Dimsdale Developments (South East) Ltd v. De Haan* (1983) 47 P. & C.R. 1.

[97] *Ocular Sciences Ltd v. Aspect Vision Care Ltd* [1997] R.P.C. 289, 432–433.

[98] In the sense examined *ante*, §§ 12–025 *et seq.*

[99] The first consequence was the only one mentioned by Lord Diplock in *Scandinavian Trading Tanker Co. AB v. Flota Petrolera Ecuatoriana* [1983] 2 A.C. 694, 703, when he referred to the effect of making time of the essence of an obligation. See also *post*, § 25–046 *et seq.*

[1] *Lombard North Central plc v. Butterworth* [1987] Q.B. 527, 545, 546.

Loss of right to terminate: relief. The right to terminate may, of course, be   **22–016**
lost where the innocent party affirms the contract[2] or is held to have waived (or
to be estopped from exercising) the right to terminate.[3] Additionally, equity may
intervene to grant relief in cases of late payment of money due under a mortgage
or rent due under a lease.[4] but equity will not intervene at the request of a
purchaser who has failed to comply with an essential time stipulation in a
contract for the sale of land.[5] The need for certainty in such cases is paramount
and the very existence of a jurisdiction to grant relief in cases where it would be
unconscionable[6] for the vendor to exercise his right to terminate would detract
from that need for a certain rule. The harshness of this general rule may, however,
be tempered by the prospect of relief being granted in extreme cases. Where, for
example, the vendor has been unjustly enriched by improvements made at the
purchaser's expense, then the court may either relax the principle that specific
performance will not be granted to a purchaser who has broken an essential
condition as to time[7] or, preferably, recognise that the purchaser has a personal
restitutionary claim against the vendor.[8]

Consequences of "time being made of essence." Where, however, notice is   **22–017**
given by one party purporting to make "time of the essence" in respect of a
breach of a non-essential term of the contract, the consequences are altogether
different. Such a notice does not serve to make time of the essence so far as the
obligations in the original contract are concerned, because one party cannot
unilaterally vary the terms of a contract by turning what was previously a non-
essential term of the contract into an essential term[9]: the notice "has in law no
contractual import."[10] The effect of the notice is rather to bring to an end the
interference of equity with the legal rights of the parties[11] so that the entitlement
of the innocent party to terminate future performance of the contract is then
governed solely by ordinary common law rules. Given that the notice cannot

---

[2] See *post*, §§ 25–002—25–003.
[3] See *post*, §§ 25–006—25–008.
[4] *G. and C. Kreglinger v. New Patagonia Meat and Cold Storage Co. Ltd* [1914] A.C. 25, 35;
Shiloh Spinners Ltd v. Harding [1973] A.C. 691, 722.
[5] *Union Eagle Ltd v. Golden Achievement Ltd* [1997] A.C. 514.
[6] Such a jurisdiction has been developed in Australia: see, for example, *Legione v. Hateley* (1983)
152 C.L.R. 406 and *Stern v. McArthur* (1988) 165 C.L.R. 489. These developments generate too
much uncertainty for English tastes.
[7] As has been done in Australia (see n. 6). The occasional English example can also be found (see
In re Dagenham (Thames) Dock Co., ex p. Hulse (1873) L.R. 8 Ch. App. 1022) but the authorities
are generally hostile to such an approach (see *Steedman v. Drinkle* [1916] 1 A.C. 275). The English
courts may "on some future occasion" have to consider whether to "relax" the principle in *Steedman
v. Drinkle* (see *Union Eagle Ltd v. Golden Achievement Ltd* [1997] A.C. 514, 523B and see also
Bidaisee v. Sampath (1995) 46 W.I.R. 461, 466–467 where the point was left open by the Privy
Council).
[8] It seems clear that Lord Hoffmann's preference in *Union Eagle Ltd v. Golden Achievement Ltd*
[1997] A.C. 514, 523 was for the development of an appropriate restitutionary remedy. There is much
to be said for this view. It avoids the land being sterilised while the courts sort out whether or not the
vendor is entitled to terminate, but at the same time it gives to the court a jurisdiction to remove any
unjust enrichment which a vendor has obtained as a result of the termination. A further approach
would be to develop the law of estoppel to deal with the case of the vendor who leads the purchaser
to believe that the contractual time-scale will not be enforced.
[9] *Behzadi v. Shaftesbury Hotels Ltd* [1992] Ch. 1, 12, 24; *Re Olympia & York Canary Wharf Ltd
(No. 2)* [1993] B.C.C. 159, 171–173; *Ocular Sciences Ltd v. Aspect Vision Care Ltd* [1997] R.P.C.
289, 432–433.
[10] *Behzadi v. Shaftesbury Hotels Ltd* [1992] Ch. 1, 24.
[11] *ibid.* at 12; *Re Olympia & York Canary Wharf Ltd (No. 2)* [1993] B.C.C. 159, 173.

have the effect of turning the non-essential term of the contract into a condition, the party giving the notice can only terminate where the failure of the other party to comply with the terms of the notice goes to the root of the contract so as to deprive that party of a substantial part of the benefit to which he was entitled under the terms of the contract.[12] Failure to comply with the terms of the notice can therefore only be used as evidence of a repudiatory breach; it is not a repudiatory breach *per se*.[13]

22–018   **Where time is not of the essence.** Where none of the three exceptions mentioned in the preceding paragraphs applies, the effect of section 41 of the Law of Property Act 1925 (*ante*) is that the breach of a stipulation as to time is not of itself a repudiatory breach[14] which entitles the innocent party to terminate further performance of the contract. Thus, in a contract for the sale and purchase of land, if the purchaser fails to complete on the date fixed for completion, the effect of section 41 is that the purchaser does not commit a repudiatory breach of contract (entitling the vendor to terminate the contract)[15] provided he either completes, or is ready to complete, within a reasonable time thereafter[16]: it is not essential for the purchaser to prove that he was ready and willing to complete on the date fixed for completion.[17] Even where time is not (or has not subsequently been made) of the essence in a contract for the sale and purchase of land, a failure to complete the contract on or before the date stipulated for completion is still a breach leading to liability to pay damages for any loss[18] caused by the delay in completion.[19] A further example comes from leases. The presumption is that time is not of the essence in the timetable specified in a rent review clause in a lease, under which various steps must be taken to determine the rent payable during the period following the review date[20]; strict adherence to the timetable will be necessary only if that is expressly stated, or if it is a "necessary implication" from the surrounding circumstances[21] (*e.g.* in the inter-relation between the rent review clause and other clauses).[22] The fact that the time specified in a rent review clause is held not to be of the essence does not itself mean that there is

---

[12] *ibid Ocular Sciences Ltd v. Aspect Vision Care Ltd* [1997] R.P.C. 289, 432–433.

[13] *ibid. cf. United Scientific Holdings Ltd v. Burnley B.C.* [1978] A.C. 904, 946–947; *Louinder v. Leis* (1982) 149 C.L.R. 509, 526.

[14] See *post*, §§ 25–001, *et seq.* It would become such a breach only if it amounted to a substantial failure of performance.

[15] *cf.* the failure to pay the deposit: *Millichamp v. Jones* [1982] 1 W.L.R. 1422; *John Willmott Homes Ltd v. Read* (1985) 51 P. & C.R. 90.

[16] *Rightside Properties Ltd v. Gray* [1975] Ch. 72, 83.

[17] *ibid.* at 82 (following *Howe v. Smith. supra*, at 103, and *Stickney v. Keeble* [1915] A.C. 386, 404).

[18] It should be noted in this context that the rule in *Bain v. Fothergill* (1874) L.R. 7 H.L. 158 has been abolished by s.3 of the Law of Property (Miscellaneous Provisions) Act 1989. (*post* § 27–075.)

[19] *Raineri v. Miles* [1981] A.C. 1050 (following *Stickney v. Keeble, supra*, at 415–416; *Phillips v. Lamdin* [1949] 2 K.B. 33, 42). (Sometimes, however, the date for completion is "only a target": *Williams v. Greatrex* [1957] 1 W.L.R. 31, 35.)

[20] *United Scientific Holdings Ltd v. Burnley B.C.* [1978] A.C. 904; *Amherst v. James Walker Goldsmith & Silversmith Ltd* [1983] Ch. 305 (mere delay, however lengthy, does not destroy the landlord's right to have the rent reviewed: the tenant can always serve notice on the landlord making time of the essence: *ante* § 22–014).

[21] The *United Scientific* case, *supra*. (No question of damages was involved in this decision, but the failure to adhere to the timetable was clearly a breach of contract: *Raineri v. Miles, supra*.)

[22] On the inter-relation between the timetable in a rent review clause and that in a "break" clause, see *Metrolands Investments Ltd v. J.H. Dewhurst Ltd* [1986] 3 All E.R. 659.

an implied term that the right to a review must be exercised within a reasonable time.[23]

Other principles affecting the time fixed for performance. Apart from the rules considered in the preceding paragraphs, the time fixed for performance may be postponed by waiver[24] or subsequent variation by agreement.[25] On the other hand, where, before the time fixed for performance, the party obliged to perform renounces his obligation, or puts it out of his power to perform, the other party may, at his option, treat this as an "anticipatory breach" without waiting for the time fixed for performance.[26]   **22–019**

Where no precise time for performance is specified.[27] Where a party to a contract undertakes to do an act, the performance of which depends entirely on himself, and the contract is silent as to the time of performance (or merely uses indefinite words such as "with all dispatch") the law implies an obligation to perform the act within a reasonable time having regard to all the circumstances of the case.[28] Thus, where, by the terms of a charterparty, the cargo was "to be discharged with all dispatch according to the custom of the port" of discharge, it was held by the House of Lords that this bound the charterer to discharge the cargo within a reasonable time, regard being had to every impediment arising out of the custom or practice of the particular port, which the charterer could not have overcome by the use of reasonable diligence.[29] Where the act to be done is one in which both parties to the contract are to concur, the implied engagement is not that the act shall be done within either a fixed or a reasonable time, or within the time usually taken, but that each shall use reasonable diligence in performing his part.[30]   **22–020**

Meanings of general terms relating to time. Where a contract is to be performed "directly," this does not mean "within a reasonable time," but "speedily," or "as soon as possible,"[31] which is a more stringent obligation, like "immediately."[32] A contract by a manufacturer to supply certain specified goods "as soon as possible" means that he is to supply them, not within a time which   **22–021**

---

[23] *Amherst v. James Walker Goldsmith & Silversmith Ltd, supra.*

[24] *Post*, §§ 23–039 *et seq.* But, in a contract requiring payment by instalments, time may continue to be of the essence despite a waiver of strict compliance with a fixed date for payment of earlier instalments: *Tropical Traders Ltd v. Goonan* (1964) 111 C.L.R. 41, 52–55. See also *Bird v. Hildage* [1948] 1 K.B. 91, 94–96; *Barclay v. Messenger* (1874) 43 L.J. Ch. 449, 456.

[25] *Post*, §§ 23–032 *et seq.*

[26] *Post*, §§ 25–020, 25–029 *et seq.*

[27] On the time for repayment of a loan, see Vol. II, Chap. 38.

[28] *Postlethwaite v. Freeland* (1880) 5 App.Cas. 599; *Castlegate Shipping Co. Ltd v. Dempsey* [1892] 1 Q.B. 854; *Hick v. Raymond* [1893] A.C. 22; *Carlton Steamship Co. Ltd v. Castle Mail Packet Co. Ltd* [1898] A.C. 486; *Lyle Shipping Co. Ltd v. Cardiff Corporation* [1900] 2 Q.B. 638; *Hulthen v. Stewart & Co.* [1903] A.C. 389; *Barque Quilpué Ltd v. Brown* [1904] 2 K.B. 264; *Monkland v. Jack Barclay Ltd* [1951] 2 K.B. 252; *Re Longlands Farm* [1968] 3 All E.R. 552; *cf. Hartwells of Oxford Ltd v. British Motor Trade Association* [1951] Ch. 50. See also s.29(3) of the Sale of Goods Act 1979 (Vol. II, § 43–244); and *Charnock v. Liverpool Corporation* [1968] 1 W.L.R. 1498 ("reasonable time").

[29] *Postlethwaite v. Freeland, supra.* If performance is to be "in a customary manner," the manner is to be judged as at the time when performance is due: *Reardon Smith Line Ltd v. Black Sea and Baltic General Insurance Co. Ltd* [1939] A.C. 562; *Tsakiroglou & Co. Ltd v. Noblee Thorl GmbH* [1960] 2 Q.B. 318; (affd. [1962] A.C. 93, 113–114).

[30] *Ford v. Cotesworth* (1868) L.R. 4 Q.B. 127; (1870) L.R. 5 Q.B. 544.

[31] *Duncan v. Topham* (1849) 8 C.B. 225.

[32] *Alexiadi v. Robinson* (1861) 2 F. & F. 679. See also *ante*, § 12–053.

he thinks reasonable, but within such a time as would be sufficient to enable a person, who had all the necessary appliances, to execute the contract, regard being had to the other contracts he may already have in hand.[33] Where under a policy of insurance notice of an accident was to be given "as soon as possible," it was held that all existing circumstances must be taken into account, including the available means of knowledge of the insured's personal representative of the existence of the policy.[34] The meaning of words referring to time may sometimes be explained by other terms of the contract. Thus, where the contract was to sell certain goods to the defendants, "the said goods to be delivered forthwith, and the price to be paid by the defendants in cash in 14 days from the time of the making of the said contract," it was held that, by the use of the word "forthwith" in connection with the payment in 14 days, it was manifest that the parties intended the goods to be delivered at some time within 14 days.[35] Otherwise, "forthwith" means "without delay or loss of time."[36]

22–022   **Meaning of "day."**[37] The exact meaning of the word "day" in contracts, particularly in charterparties where the charterer is allowed so many days, has given rise to much litigation. Though every case must turn on the words of the particular contract, certain general rules of interpretation can be given. Usually, "days" include Sundays and holidays, unless there is a custom to the contrary, and this is the meaning of the words "running days"[38]; on the other hand, the phrase "working days" excludes days when work is not ordinarily done, and the terms of a contract may show that the word "day" has this meaning.[39] A day is a period of time as from midnight to midnight, and not a period of 24 consecutive hours,[40] unless it is clear that the latter was intended.[41] Where a person under an obligation to do an act has to do it on or before a specified day, he has the whole of that day to fulfil that obligation, *viz.* until midnight.[42] It is a general rule that a day is indivisible; so in shipping contracts part of a day counts as a day,[43] but this is inapplicable where the day referred to is not a natural day, but an artificial period to be computed in accordance with the provisions of the contract.[44] The law will take account of parts of a day whenever that is intended by Parliament

---

[33] *Hydraulic Engineering Co. Ltd v. McHaffie* (1879) 4 Q.B.D. 670, 673; *Attwood v. Emery* (1856) 1 C.B.(N.S.) 110, 115.

[34] *Verlest v. Motor Union Insurance Co. Ltd* [1925] 2 K.B. 137. As to these expressions of time, *cf.* Odgers, *Construction of Deeds and Statutes* (5th ed.), pp. 126–140.

[35] *Staunton v. Wood* (1851) 16 Q.B. 638; *cf. Hyde v. Watts* (1843) 12 M. & W. 254.

[36] *Roberts v. Brett* (1865) 11 H.L.C. 337, 355; *Hudson v. Hill* (1874) 43 L.J.C.P. 273.

[37] See Odgers *op. cit.* pp. 128–134.

[38] *Nielsen & Co. v. Wait, James & Co.* (1885) 16 Q.B.D. 67, 71–73.

[39] *Commercial SS. Co. v. Boulton* (1875) L.R. 10 Q.B. 346; *Nielsen v. Waite, supra*; *Reardon Smith Line Ltd v. Ministry of Agriculture* [1963] A.C. 691 ("weather working days" in a charterparty).

[40] *The Katy* [1895] P. 56; *Cartwright v. MacCormack* [1963] 1 W.L.R. 18 (*ante*, § 12–091). When payment has to be made on a specified day, it can (in the absence of any custom to the contrary) be made at any time up to midnight on that day: *Afovos Shipping Co. SA v. Romano Pagnan and Pietro Pagnan* [1983] 1 W.L.R. 195.

[41] *Cornfoot v. Royal Exchange Assurance Corpn.* [1904] 1 K.B. 40; *Leonis SS. Co. v. Rank (No. 2)* (1908) 13 Com.Cas. 161, 295; *Momm v. Barclays Bank International Ltd* [1977] Q.B. 790, 803 ("For banking purposes [a day] ends at the close of working hours . . . ").

[42] The *Afovos Shipping* case, *supra*, at 201; *Schelde Delta Shipping B.V. v. Astarte Shipping Ltd (The Pamela)* [1995] 2 Lloyd's Rep. 249.

[43] *Commercial SS. Co. v. Boulton, supra*; *The Katy, supra*; *Houlder v. Weir* [1905] 2 K.B. 267; *L. & Y Ry. v. Swann* [1916] 1 K.B. 263.

[44] *Verren v. Anglo-Dutch Brick Co. (1927) Ltd* (1929) 45 T.L.R. 404, 556; *Carver's Carriage by Sea* (13th ed., 1982), Vols. 1 and 2, §§ 640, 1839–1859.

(or by the parties to a contract), as where the question concerns the sequence of events happening on the same day.[45] If a notice must be received by a specified person by a prescribed day, it must be received at a time when, as an ordinary matter of routine, it will convey the relevant information to that person or his agent, *e.g.* in the case of an office address, during normal business hours.[46]

Computation of time.[47] Expressions relating to time, in deeds and other instruments and documents, are (by the Interpretation Act 1978)[48] to be held to refer to Greenwich mean time, or, in the summer time period, to summer time.[49]   **22–023**

Period from a date or event. Where the time is to be computed *from* a certain date, or an act to be done on the happening of an event, the mode of calculating the time must depend on the circumstances of the particular contract.[50] The general rule is now well established that where a particular time is given from a certain date, within which an act is to be done, the day of the date is to be excluded,[51] but "there is no absolute rule with regard to the inclusion or exclusion of the day on which a particular event takes place," and the court has to decide the meaning of the particular contract.[52] The mode of calculation must therefore depend on the wording of the contract, and where the act done is one to which the party against whom time runs is privy the computation may be inclusive as he has had the benefit of some portion of the day included, but where this is not so and the event is foreign to the party against whom time runs, the general rule will be adopted. So it has been held that the words " . . . not later than 21 days before . . . " mean 21 full or clear days between, not counting the day from which the calculation is to be made.[53]   **22–024**

Period within which to act. Where a contract gives the first party a certain period of time in which to do some act, which period is between two other acts to be done by the second party, both the days for doing the second party's acts should be excluded from the computation of the period, so that the first party has the whole of the period of time in which to do his act.[54] But a notice to quit   **22–025**

---

[45] *Eaglehill Ltd v. J. Needham Builders Ltd* [1973] A.C. 992, 1006, 1010.

[46] *Rightside Properties Ltd v. Gray* [1975] Ch. 72, 78–80; *The Brimnes (Tenax Steamship Co. Ltd v. The Brimnes (Owners))* [1975] Q.B. 929, 945–946, 967, 970. *cf. Eaglehill Ltd v. J. Needham Builders Ltd, supra,* at 1011. *cf.* The *Afovos Shipping* case, *supra,* n. 40.

[47] See *ante,* § 12–091; *post,* § 22–026; on the computation of time for a period of limitation, see *post,* §§ 29–063—29–064; and in a bill of exchange, see Vol. II, §§ 34–014, 34–019.

[48] ss.9, 23(3).

[49] Summer Time Act 1972. (By s.3(1), any reference to time in (*inter alia*) any "deed, notice or other document whatsoever" is to be taken as a reference to summer time during the period of summer time fixed by or under the Act.)

[50] *Re North* [1895] 2 Q.B. 264, 269; *Lester v. Garland* (1808) 15 Ves. 248. See *ante,* § 12–091.

[51] *Goldsmiths' Company v. West Metropolitan Ry.* [1904] 1 K.B. 1, 5 (distinguished in *Hare v. Gocher* [1962] 2 Q.B. 641 ("beginning with the commencement" of a statute); and in *Trow v. Ind Coope (West Midlands) Ltd* [1967] 2 Q.B. 899 ("beginning with the date of . . . " in RSC, Ord. 6, r. 8(1)); *Dodds v. Walker* [1981] 1 W.L.R. 1027, *post,* § 12–091. See also *Radcliffe v. Bartholomew* [1892] 1 Q.B. 161; *Stewart v. Chapman* [1951] 2 K.B. 792; *Cartwright v. MacCormack* [1963] 1 W.L.R. 18 ("15 days from the commencement date").

[52] *English v. Cliff* [1914] 2 Ch. 376, 383. See *ante,* § 12–091.

[53] *Carapanayoti & Co. Ltd v. Comptoir Commercial André & Cie SA* [1972] 1 Lloyd's Rep. 139. See also *post,* § 22–026.

[54] *Young v. Higgon* (1840) 6 M. & W. 49, 54; *Re Railway Sleepers Supply Co.* (1885) 29 Ch.D. 204; *Rightside Properties Ltd v. Gray* [1975] Ch. 72, 80 (a period of "at least 21 days" between serving a notice and forfeiting a deposit).

"within" a period of three months can mean "during" or "before or at the expiry of" the period, thus including the final moment of the period so as to amount to a full three months' notice.[55]

22–026   **Meaning and computation of "month."** By section 61 of the Law of Property Act 1925, in all deeds, contracts, wills, orders and other instruments executed, made or coming into operation after the commencement of the Act, unless the context otherwise requires, "month" means calendar month.[56] In the computation of a calendar "month," the House of Lords has upheld[57] the "corresponding date" rule, viz., that if a period of time in "months" is to be computed *from* or *after* a given date, that day is excluded from the computation,[58] and the period elapses at midnight on the corresponding day of the month of expiry.[59] Thus where under a statute, a tenant's application had to be made " . . . not more than four months after the giving of the landlord's notice,"[60] which was given on September 30, time began to run from midnight on that day (September 30/October 1) and ended at midnight on January 30/31.[61] No account is taken of the fact that some months have more days than others.[62] In the same enactment, the phrase permitting the application only if it was made *not less* than . . . two months after . . . " the landlord's notice has been interpreted to allow the application to be made on the corresponding date itself.[63] "If the application is made on the corresponding date, it cannot be said to be either before or after the corresponding date."[64]

3. PARTIAL PERFORMANCE OF AN ENTIRE OBLIGATION[65]

22–027   **Entire and divisible obligations.** A contract is said to be "entire" when complete performance by one party is a condition precedent to the liability of the other[66]; in such a contract the consideration is usually a lump sum which is

---

[55] *Manorlike Ltd v. Le Vitas Travel Agency, etc., Ltd* [1986] 1 All E.R. 573.

[56] See *ante*, § 12–059. For similar provisions in other statutes, see s.10(3) of the Sale of Goods Act 1979; s.14(4) of the Bills of Exchange Act 1882; Interpretation Act 1978, Sched. 1. (For the former rule, see *P. Phipps & Co. Ltd v. Rogers* [1925] 1 K.B. 14.)

[57] *Dodds v. Walker* [1981] 1 W.L.R. 1027.

[58] See *ante*, § 22–024.

[59] *South Staffordshire Tramways Co. Ltd v. Sickness and Accident Assurance Association Ltd* [1891] 1 Q.B. 402. See also *Webb v. Fairmaner* (1838) 3 M. & W. 473; *Freeman v. Read* (1863) 4 B. & S. 174. *cf. Cartwright v. MacCormack* [1963] 1 W.L.R. 18 ("15 days from . . . ").

[60] Under s.29(3) of the Landlord and Tenant Act 1954.

[61] *Dodds v. Walker, supra.*

[62] *ibid.* If the relevant calendar month in which a period expires is too short to provide a corresponding date, the period expires on the last day of that month: *ibid. Migotti v. Colvill* (1879) 4 C.P.D. 233.

[63] *E.J. Riley Investments Ltd v. Eurostile Holdings Ltd* [1985] 1 W.L.R. 1139, CA.

[64] *ibid.* at 1141.

[65] The law on "entire contracts" or, more accurately, entire obligations is reviewed in the Law Commission's Report (No. 121 (1983)), paras. 2.1–2.88 and Note of Dissent (pp. 36–37). (This report is not to be implemented: see the 19th Annual Report of the Commission, para. 2.11.) See also Treitel, *The Law of Contract* (9th ed., 1991), pp. 697–703, Carter, *Breach of Contract* (2nd ed., 1991), paras 685–695; Williams (1941) 57 L.Q.R. 373, 490. (The enactment of the Law Reform (Frustrated Contracts) Act 1943 (*post*, § 24–072) has rendered obsolete some of the common law discussed in this article.)

[66] *Hoenig v. Isaacs* [1952] 2 All E.R. 176, 180–181. See also the authorities cited in n. 69, *post.*

payable only upon complete performance by the other party (hence, the reference is sometimes to a "lump sum contract"). The opposite of an "entire contract" is a "divisible contract," which is separable into parts, so that different parts of the consideration may be assigned to severable parts of the performance, *e.g.* an agreement for payment *pro rata*.[67]

Yet the phrase "entire contract" is a misleading one in that the real issue in the cases is whether the "obligation" of the party in default is "entire," not whether the contract itself is entire. Of course, the contract may state that one party can only recover on the contract when he has completed his performance under the contract. In such a case it can be said that, from the perspective of such a party, there is no real point of distinction between an entire contract and an entire obligation because the contract may be said to be "entire" from his point of view. But in other cases the distinction may be clear. Where a contract makes provision for payment upon the completion of distinct stages of a construction contract, the completion of each stage being a condition precedent to the obligation to make a stage payment, the obligation to complete each stage may be said to be entire, even though the contract itself is clearly not entire. It is for this reason that the phrase "entire obligation" will be used in preference to "entire contract" in the following paragraphs.   **22–028**

A matter of construction. It is a question of construction whether the obligation is entire or divisible,[68] but in the reported cases the courts have tended to the view that in every lump-sum contract there is an implied term that no part of the price is to be recovered without complete performance.[69] In most modern contracts of any size, however, payments by instalments are specified, so that the law on entire obligations is not relevant to any obligation which has been completely performed.   **22–029**

Partial performance of entire obligations. Where a party has performed only part of an entire obligation[70] he can normally[71] recover nothing, neither the agreed price, since it is not due under the terms of the contract, nor any smaller sum for the value of his partial performance, since the court has no power to   **22–030**

---

[67] See *post*, §§ 22–037, 24–089. *cf.* ss.28 and 31 of the Sale of Goods Act 1979 (sale of goods to be delivered by instalments).

[68] *Appleby v. Myers* (1867) L.R. 2 C.P. 651, 658; *Hoenig v. Isaacs, supra*, at 178, 180; *Regent OHG Aisenstadt und Barig v. Francesco of Jermyn Street Ltd* [1981] 3 All E.R. 327, 333–334. See *post*, § 22–037.

[69] *Appleby v. Myers, supra*, at 660–661 (where the court relied on *Cutter v. Powell* (1795) 6 T.R. 320; *Jesse v. Roy* (1834) 1 Cr.M. & R. 316; *Munroe v. Butt* (1858) 8 E. & B. 738; *Sinclair v. Bowles* (1829) 9 B. & C. 92, which were cases where particular terms in the contract supported such a conclusion: see the criticism in Williams (1941) 57 L.Q.R. 373, 389 *et seq.*); *The Madras* [1898] P. 90; *Sumpter v. Hedges* [1898] 1 Q.B. 673; *Forman & Co. Proprietary Ltd v. Liddesdale* [1900] A.C. 190; *Small & Sons Ltd v. Middlesex Real Estates Ltd* [1921] W.N. 245; *Heywood v. Wellers* [1976] 1 Q.B. 446, 458.

[70] The failure to complete need not be a breach of contract: *Cutter v. Powell, supra*. The contract in effect provides that the risk of non-completion is to be borne by the party undertaking the relevant obligation.

[71] For exceptions, see the doctrines of frustration (*post*, §§ 24–083—24–085), acceptance of partial performance (*post*, § 22–035) and where the defendant prevents complete performance (*post*, § 22–036).

apportion the consideration.[72] The refusal of *pro rata* payment is based on the inability of the court, as a matter of construction, to add such a provision to the contract, and also upon the rule that the mere acceptance of acts of part performance under an express contract cannot, taken alone, justify the imposition of a restitutionary obligation to pay on a *quantum meruit* basis.[73] Thus where an employee is engaged for a fixed period for a lump sum, but fails to complete the term for a reason other than breach of contract by the employer, *e.g.* frustration,[74] the common law rule is that he can recover nothing.[75] In the famous case of *Cutter v. Powell*[76] a seaman was to be paid a lump sum when he completed the voyage; he died before completion of the voyage and it was held that his executor could not recover *pro tanto* wages because it was an entire contract.[77] This was a case of non-feasance, but in a case of misfeasance, as where an employee completes a period of service but does bad work, the employee may recover his wages, subject to a deduction in respect of the bad work.[78] In contracts where wages or salaries are payable, however, the Apportionment Act 1870 has altered the common law rule, for by section 2 "all rents, annuities, dividends, and other periodical payments in the nature of income . . . shall . . . be considered as accruing from day to day,[79] and shall be apportionable in respect of time accordingly." By section 5, "annuities" include salaries and pensions, and it has been held that it also includes wages.[80]

22–031 Although nowadays building contracts of any size normally provide for payments by instalments, the common law rule on entire obligations was developed in cases concerning building contracts, or contracts for work and materials. Where the builder under a lump-sum contract fails to perform some of the agreed work, then, subject to the so-called doctrine of substantial performance,[81] he can recover nothing for the work which was actually completed,[82] despite the fact

---

[72] *Cutter v. Powell, supra; Bates v. Hudson* (1825) 6 Dow. & Ry.K.B. 3; *Sinclair v. Bowles, supra; Adlard v. Booth* (1835) 7 C. & P. 108; *Chanter v. Leese* (1839) 5 M. & W. 698; *Appleby v. Myers, supra* at 660; *The Madras, supra; Sumpter v. Hedges, supra; Vigers v. Cook* [1919] 2 K.B. 475; *Eshelby v. Federated European Bank Ltd* [1932] 1 K.B. 423; *Bolton v. Mahadeva* [1972] 1 W.L.R. 1009.

[73] See *post*, § 22–035.

[74] See *post*, §§ 24–036—24–038.

[75] *Spain v. Arnott* (1817) 2 Stark.M.P.C. 256; *Huttman v. Boulnois* (1826) 2 C. & P. 510; *Turner v. Robinson* (1833) 5 B. & Ad. 789; *Lowndes v. Stamford* (1852) 18 Q.B. 425; *Ridgway v. Hungerford Market Co.* (1853) 3 A. & E. 171; *Lilley v. Elwin* (1848) 11 Q.B. 742; *Boston Deep Sea Fishing and Ice Co. v. Ansell* (1888) 39 Ch.D. 339, 360, 364–365.

[76] (1795) 6 T.R. 320. *cf.* Merchant Shipping Act 1995, s.38.

[77] On the facts, however, the decision could be based on a specific provision in the contract whereby complete performance was a condition precedent to recovery of any wages at all: similarly in *Appleby v. Dods* (1807) 8 East 300 and *Jesse v. Roy* (1834) 1 Cr.M. & R. 316. Particular terms of the contract affected the decisions in *Mapleson v. Sears* (1911) 105 L.T. 639 and *Moriarty v. Regent's Garage Co. Ltd* [1921] 2 K.B. 766.

[78] *Sagar v. H. Ridehalgh & Son Ltd* [1931] 1 Ch. 310, 324–326.

[79] A "day" means a calendar day and not a working day: *Re B.C.C.I. SA* [1994] I.R.L.R. 282 and *Thames Water Utilities v. Reynolds* [1996] I.R.L.R. 186.

[80] *Moriarty v. Regent's Garage Co. Ltd* [1921] 1 K.B. 423 (held, Act applies to wages); reversed on another point: [1921] 2 K.B. 766; *Re William Porter & Co. Ltd* [1937] 2 All E.R. 361, 363; Williams (1941) 57 L.Q.R. 373, 382–383; Matthews (1982) 2 L.S. 302; Vol. II, § 39–176.

[81] See *post*, § 22–032.

[82] *Sumpter v. Hedges* [1898] 1 Q.B. 673; *Forman & Co. Proprietary v. Liddesdale* [1900] A.C. 190; *cf. Sinclair v. Bowles* (1829) 9 B. & C. 92; *Munro v. Butt* (1858) 8 E. & B. 738; *Appleby v. Myers* (1867) L.R. 2 C.P. 651 (the actual decision would probably be the same under the Law Reform (Frustrated Contracts) Act 1943: see *post*, § 24–084, n. 76); *Bolton v. Mahadeva* [1972] 1 W.L.R. 1009.

that the other party may have received substantial benefit therefrom.[83] The building cases take the distinction between substantial non-feasance where recovery is denied, and misfeasance,[84] where recovery is permitted subject to a cross-action for damages.[85] If, however, under such a lump-sum contract the builder is guilty of a serious misfeasance, so that the work is substantially deficient, he can recover nothing.[86]

Substantial performance.[87] Considerable difficulty arises in the case where   **22–032** the part performer has substantially performed or substantially completed an entire obligation but has not completed full performance. In such a case there is some authority for the proposition that a doctrine of "substantial performance" can be applied so that the part performer is entitled to bring an action to recover the price, subject to a counterclaim for damages which will go in diminution of the price.[88] This "doctrine of substantial performance" has, however, been criticised on the ground that "it is based on the error that *contracts*, as opposed to particular *obligations*, can be entire. . . . To say that an obligation is entire *means* that it must be completely performed before payment becomes due. . . . In relation to 'entire' obligations, there is no scope for any doctrine of 'substantial performance.' "[89] On the latter view a court is required to identify with some care the obligation which is alleged to be entire; for example, in *Hoenig v. Isaac*[90] the obligation of the contractor to complete performance of the contract was entire, but the obligation to do so in a workmanlike manner was not, so that the presence of defects in his work did not act as a barrier to a claim under the contract. The obligation to do the work in a workmanlike manner not being entire, there was therefore no need to employ any doctrine of substantial performance. The same analysis can be applied to *Cutter v. Powell*[91] because it has been pointed out that the court "did not decide that if [the seaman] had completed the main purpose of the contract, namely, serving as mate for the whole voyage, the defendant could have repudiated his liability by establishing that in the course of the voyage the sailor had, possibly through inadvertence, failed on some occasion in his duty as mate whereby some damage had been caused."[92] Once again there is no need to resort to any notion of substantial performance because, only the obligation to complete performance being entire, the fact that a minor breach of contract had occurred would not have been sufficient to discharge the defendant from his obligation to pay.

---

[83] See the criticisms in Goff and Jones, *The Law of Restitution* (5th ed., 1998), pp. 552–555.

[84] Some small non-feasance would also fall within the so-called doctrine of substantial performance (*post*, § 22–032): see *H. Dakin & Co. Ltd v. Lee* [1916] 1 K.B. 566, 578–579, 580.

[85] *Post*, § 22–032, n. 99.

[86] *Eshelby v. Federated European Bank Ltd, supra; Bolton v. Mahadeva, supra*. See also the cases cited in n. 82, *ante. cf. Vigers v. Cook* [1919] 2 K.B. 475 (serious misfeasance by undertaker, who was held to be entitled to no remuneration at all under the contract).

[87] See generally Beck (1975) 38 M.L.R. 413.

[88] *Dakin v. Oxley* (1864) 15 C.B.(N.S.) 646, 664–665; *Dakin v. Lee* [1916] 1 K.B. 566; *Bolton v. Mahadeva* [1972] 1 W.L.R. 1009; *Sim v. Rotherham Metropolitan Borough Council* [1987] Ch. 216, 253; *Wiluszynski v. Tower Hamlets L.B.C.* [1989] I.C.R. 493, 499; *Williams v. Roffey Bros. & Nicholls (Contractors) Ltd* [1991] 1 Q.B. 1, 8–10, 17.

[89] Treitel, *The Law of Contract*, (9th ed., 1995), p. 703.

[90] *Hoenig v. Isaacs* [1952] 2 All E.R. 176.

[91] (1795) 6 T.R. 320 (see *supra*. § 22–030).

[92] *Hoenig v. Isaacs* [1952] 2 All E.R. 176, 178.

22–033   On the other hand, it must be conceded that there is some authority which supports the existence of a doctrine of substantial performance in relation to entire contracts.[93] On this view, upon completion of substantial performance, the part performer will be entitled to claim the price, subject to a counterclaim for damages. This so-called doctrine of substantial performance may be excluded by an express provision of the contract[94]; "each case turns on the construction of the contract,"[95] and "it is always open to the parties by express words to make entire performance a condition precedent" (to payment).[96] What is "substantial performance" will depend upon the nature of the contract and all the circumstances; if the contractor abandons performance, or does work entirely different in kind from that contracted for, it is clearly a case of substantial non-feasance and he may recover nothing.[97] Similarly, a builder who abandons work under a lump-sum contract can recover nothing[98]; but if the work is substantially completed, and it is only in some minor details that the workmanship falls below the contractual specifications, the builder may recover the agreed price, less a deduction based on the cost of making good the defects or omissions.[99] "In considering whether there was substantial performance . . . it is relevant to take into account both the nature of the defects and the proportion between the cost of rectifying them and the contract price."[1] The rule applies to unimportant matters of non-feasance as well as to unimportant matters of misfeasance.[2] Notwithstanding these dicta it is suggested that there ought to be no room in English law for a doctrine of substantial performance: rather the court should inquire whether the particular obligation which is the subject matter of the litigation is entire. If it is not, non-performance of a part of that obligation should not, of itself, be a bar to an action to recover the price; but if it is, and the obligation has not been completely performed, it should not be possible for the part performer to bring an action on the contract to recover the price.

22–034   **Application to carriage of goods by sea.** A shipowner normally cannot recover freight unless the goods are carried to the agreed destination. If the goods are carried there, the fact that some breach of the shipowner's contract has caused damage to the goods in transit does not prevent recovery of the freight, subject to a cross-action for the damage.[3] In one case[4] a charterparty provided for payment of lump-sum freight; two-thirds of the cargo was delivered by the shipowner to its destination, despite the loss of the ship outside the port of discharge, and the House of Lords permitted recovery of the whole of the freight,

---

[93] See the authorities cited at n. 88, *ante*.

[94] *Cutter v. Powell* (1795) 6 T.R. 320; *Appleby v. Myers* (1867) L.R. 2 C.P. 651, 660; *Hoenig v. Isaacs* [1952] 2 All E.R. 176, 180–181.

[95] *Hoenig v. Isaacs* [1952] 2 All E.R. 176, 178.

[96] *ibid.* at 181.

[97] See the cases cited in nn. 82 and 94, *ante*.

[98] *Sumpter v. Hedges* [1898] 1 Q.B. 673. (Although the builder had in fact been paid part of the price, the Court of Appeal dealt with the case as a lump-sum contract.)

[99] *H. Dakin & Co. Ltd v. Lee* [1916] 1 K.B. 566; *Hoenig v. Isaacs, supra; Kiely & Sons v. Medcraft* (1965) 109 S.J. 829; *Bolton v. Mahadeva* [1972] 1 W.L.R. 1009. See also *Boone v. Eyre* (1779) 1 Hy. Bl. 273n; *Broom v. Davis* (1794) 7 East 480n; *Basten v. Butter* (1806) 7 East 479; *Mondel v. Steel* (1841) 8 M. & W. 858 at 870–871.

[1] *Bolton v. Mahadeva, supra*, at 1013.

[2] *Boone v. Eyre, supra; H. Dakin & Co. Ltd v. Lee, supra*.

[3] *Dakin v. Oxley* (1864) 15 C.B.(N.S.) 646; *Henriksens Rederi A/S v. T. H. Z. Rolimpex* [1974] Q.B. 233.

[4] *William Thomas & Sons v. Harrowing SS. Co.* [1915] A.C. 58.

on the ground (*inter alia*) that "a substantial part of the cargo"[5] had been delivered.[6]

Acceptance of partial performance. If the circumstances justify the infer- **22–035**
ence that the parties have made a fresh contract, under which the original promisee agrees to accept and pay for partial performance of the original promise, or the requirements of a restitutionary claim have been made out, the recipient will be liable upon a *quantum meruit*[7] to pay a reasonable price for the work actually done, or the goods actually supplied.[8] The mere receipt of a benefit under the original contract is insufficient to justify the inference of such a promise or to establish a restitutionary claim, unless the party receiving the benefit had an opportunity to accept or reject it.[9] Sale of goods is an example where the buyer need not accept goods which are defective or insufficient in quantity; if, however, the buyer does accept delivery, he must pay for them at the agreed rate.[10] Where a builder has abandoned a partially completed erection on the defendant's land, the mere fact that the defendant completes the building does not create a restitutionary obligation to pay for the value of the work already done by the builder under an "entire contract"[11]; the defendant is in possession of his own land, and he cannot be expected to abandon it or to keep the building unfinished.[12] Similarly, where repairs were agreed to be made to the defendant's chattel, the mere fact that he accepted the return of the chattel and used it does not of itself raise the implication that he agreed to pay for the actual repairs done to it despite the fact that the contractual obligation of the repairer had been only partially completed.[13] However, where a builder abandoned work under an "entire contract", but left materials on the site, it was held that he could recover a reasonable sum for the value of these materials when the owner used them to complete the building.[14] The owner had a choice whether or not to use the materials, which could have been returned to the builder.

Defendant preventing complete performance. If the other party to the **22–036**
contract wrongfully prevents the claimant from completing his performance, the claimant may either recover damages for breach of contract, or alternatively sue upon a *quantum meruit* to recover a reasonable remuneration for his partial performance.[15]

---

[5] *ibid.* at 66. *cf.* in the Court of Appeal [1913] 2 K.B. 171, 192; *Leiston Gas Co. v. Leiston U.C.* [1916] K.B. 428. See *Carver's Carriage by Sea* (13th ed., 1982), Vols 1 and 2, §§ 1243, 1676.

[6] On the effect of an "expected peril" in the charterparty, which excused delivery of the balance of the cargo, see Williams (1941) 57 L.Q.R. 490, 500–501; Carver, *op. cit.* §§ 1667 *et seq.*

[7] On *quantum meruit*, see *post*, §§ 30–177—30–189.

[8] *Christy v. Row* (1808) 1 Taunt. 300; *Sumpter v. Hedges, supra*, at 674. See also, in addition to the cases cited in n. 9, *infra*, *Wheeler v. Stratton* (1911) 105 L.T. 786; *Small & Sons Ltd v. Middlesex Real Estates Ltd* [1921] W.N. 245.

[9] *Munro v. Butt* (1858) 8 E. & B. 738; *Sumpter v. Hedges, supra*; *Forman & Co. Proprietary Ltd v. Liddesdale* [1900] A.C. 190; *cf. Shipton v. Casson* (1826) 5 B. & C. 378.

[10] s.30(1) of the Sale of Goods Act 1979 (see Vol. II, § 42–253). *cf. Hoenig v. Isaacs* [1952] 2 All E.R. 176, 179–180, 181 (defendant used defective furniture made by plaintiff).

[11] *Sumpter v. Hedges, supra.*

[12] *ibid.* at 676.

[13] *Forman & Co. Proprietary Ltd v. Liddesdale, supra.*

[14] *Sumpter v. Hedges, supra.*

[15] *Planché v. Colburn* (1831) 8 Bing. 14 (discussed *post*, § 30–178, where other authorities are cited).

22–037   **Divisible (or severable) obligations.** The question whether an obligation is entire or divisible depends on its construction in the light of all the circumstances.[16] In a divisible or severable obligation there is an express or implied agreement that payment will be made in proportion to the extent of performance. If the obligation is held to be divisible (as in the case of a contract to deliver goods by instalments at stated intervals, the price being fixed per item), the obligation to pay for a divisible part of the performance[17] is independent of the performance of other parts of the contract.[18] Blackburn J., speaking of a contract to work other materials into the defendant's property, said[19]:

> "Bricks built into a wall become part of the house; thread stitched into a coat which is under repair, or planks and nails and pitch worked into a ship under repair, become part of the coat or the ship; and therefore, generally and in the absence of something to show a contrary intention, the bricklayer, or tailor or shipwright is to be paid for the work and materials he has done and provided, although the whole work is not complete. It is not material whether in such a case the non-completion is because the shipwright did not choose to go on with the work. . . . "[20]

22–038   **Independent promises.** Analogous to "divisible obligations" are the "independent promises" to be found mainly in the law of landlord and tenant, *e.g.* the rule that the tenant's promise to pay rent is independent of the landlord's promise to repair, so that at law the tenant cannot rely on the landlord's failure to repair as a justification for refusing to pay the rent.[21] However, under a bona fide cross-claim for damages against his landlord, the lessee may be entitled to an equitable set-off against his liability for the rent, provided the cross-claim has a sufficiently close connection with the claim for the rent.[22]

4. PAYMENT

(a) *In General*

22–039   **Payment.** All questions relating to payment of a sum of money in pursuance of a contract depend on the construction of the terms of the contract.[23] The

---

[16] See *ante*, §§ 22–001, 22–027; *post* §§ 24–089, 24–042—25–043.

[17] The "entire obligation" rule applies to each part *viz.* the payment for each part is due only from completed performance of that part of the payee's obligations.

[18] *Roberts v. Havelock* (1832) 3 B. & Ad. 404; *Taylor v. Laird* (1856) 1 H. & N. 266. *cf. Rosenthal & Sons Ltd v. Esmail* [1965] 1 W.L.R. 1117; Vol. II, § 43–260. See also Smith's *Leading Cases* (13th ed.), pp. 1, 9 *et seq.*

[19] *Appleby v. Myers* (1867) L.R. 2 C.P. 651, 660–661.

[20] Citing *Roberts v. Havelock, supra.*

[21] *Taylor v. Webb* [1937] 2 K.B. 283 (this decision was questioned, but on different grounds, by the House of Lords in *Regis Property Co. Ltd v. Dudley* [1959] A.C. 370). On the remedies of the tenant who has expended money on the repairs, see *Taylor v. Beal* (1591) Cro.Eliz. 222; *Granada Theatres Ltd v. Freehold Investment (Leytonstone) Ltd* [1959] Ch. 592; *Lee-Parker v. Izzet* [1971] 1 W.L.R. 1688.

[22] *British Anzani (Felixstowe) Ltd v. International Marine Management (U.K.) Ltd* [1980] Q.B. 137. See also *Melville v. Grapelodge Developments Ltd* (1978) 39 P. & C.R. 179; *B.I.C.C. plc v. Burndy Corporation* [1985] Ch. 232.

[23] *Re Charge Card Services Ltd* [1989] Ch. 497. See Goode, *Payment Obligations in Commercial and Financial Transactions* (1983). On questions of payment due in a foreign currency, see *post* §§ 31–132, 31–163—31–172.

creditor is entitled to require the payment to be made in legal currency.[24] The parties, however, may by subsequent variation,[25] waiver[26] or novation[27] substitute a different obligation from that originally undertaken, so that the original obligation of the debtor to make payment is varied or discharged. An illustration of such a discharge is a settlement of accounts, by which items on one side are agreed to be set off against items on the other side: if the two sides then balance, this is equivalent to payment on both sides[28]; if there is a balance on one side, which is paid in cash, this is likewise equivalent to payment of all sums on both sides.[29] Similarly, payment of a debt may be satisfied by the creditor agreeing to take goods in lieu of cash,[30] or to accept the method of charging the debt to a third party through the debtor's credit card,[31] or by both parties agreeing that a transfer in a banker's books from the debtor's account to the creditor's account shall amount to payment.[32] Payment of wages to a workman, however, must either be in current coin of the realm, or comply with statutory provisions.[33] An obligation to pay money can be frustrated.[34] Payment by negotiable instrument is examined below.[35]

Distinction between claims for payment of a debt and claims for damages.[36] There is an important distinction between a claim for payment of a debt and a claim for damages for breach of contract. A debt is a definite sum of money fixed by the agreement of the parties as payable by one party in return for the performance of a specified obligation by the other party or on the occurrence of some specified event or condition[37]; whereas, damages may be claimed from a party who has broken his primary contractual obligation in some way other than by failure to pay such a debt. (It is also possible that, in addition to a claim for a debt, there may be a claim for damages in respect of consequential loss caused by the failure to pay the debt at the due date.)[38] The relevance of this distinction is that rules on damages do not apply to a claim for a debt,[39] *e.g.* the claimant **22–040**

---

[24] See *post*, § 22–086.
[25] See *post*, §§ 23–032 *et seq.*
[26] See *post*, §§ 23–039 *et seq.*
[27] See *post*, § 23–031.
[28] *Re Harmony and Montague Tin and Copper Mining Co.* (1873) L.R. 8 Ch.App. 407, 414. See also *Livingstone v. Whiting* (1850) 15 Q.B. 722.
[29] *Callander v. Howard* (1850) 10 C.B. 290; *Re Harmony and Montague Tin and Copper Mining Co., supra*; *Larocque v. Beauchemin* [1897] A.C. 358; *North Sydney Investment and Tramway Co. Ltd v. Higgins* [1899] A.C. 263. Where items are on one side only there is no such settlement of accounts: *Perry v. Attwood* (1856) 6 E. & B. 691.
[30] *Hands v. Burton* (1808) 9 East 349; *Saxty v. Wilkin* (1843) 11 M. & W. 622; *Smith v. Battams* (1857) 26 L.J.Ex. 232.
[31] See *post*, § 22–082.
[32] *Bodenham v. Purchas* (1818) 2 B. & Ald. 39. See the discussion, *post*, § 22–045.
[33] See Vol. II, §§ 39–086—39–087.
[34] *Libyan Arab Foreign Bank v. Bankers Trust Co.* [1989] Q.B. 728, 749 but note the criticisms levelled against this proposition by Mann, *The Legal Aspect of Money* (5th ed.), pp. 68 and 418.
[35] See *post*, §§ 22–073 *et seq.*
[36] See *post*, §§ 27–008, 27–111; *Jervis v. Harris* [1996] Ch. 195, 206–207. Payment in full of a debt extinguishes the creditor's cause of action: *Edmunds v. Lloyd's Italic, etc. SpA* [1986] 1 W.L.R. 492, 495. (On interest, see *post* §§ 27–137—27–151.)
[37] See *post*, § 27–008, n. 38.
[38] See *Trans Trust S.P.R.L. v. Danubian Trading Co. Ltd* [1952] 2 Q.B. 297; *Wadsworth v. Lydall* [1981] 1 W.L.R. 598; see generally, *post*, §§ 27–082—27–083.
[39] See *post*, §§ 27–008, 27–111, for a fuller discussion of these and other distinctions.

who claims payment of a debt need not prove anything more than his performance or the occurrence of the event or condition; there is no need for him to prove any actual loss suffered by him[40] as a result[41] of the defendant's failure to pay; the whole concept of the remoteness of damage[42] is therefore irrelevant; the law on penalties does not apply to the agreed sum[43]; and the claimant's duty to mitigate his loss does not generally apply.[44]

22–041 **Payment by agent or third party.** Where payment of a debt is made by a third person who is not jointly[45] liable (*e.g.* as co-contractor), the debt is not discharged unless the payment is made by the third person as agent for and on account of the debtor, and with his prior authority or subsequent ratification.[46] Even after the creditor has sued for the debt, the debtor can ratify such a payment by pleading payment.[47] Where payment is made by a third person on behalf of the debtor but without his authority, the creditor and the person who made the payment may together rescind the transaction at any time before the debtor has ratified the payment; the creditor may repay the money to the third person and thereupon the payment is at an end, so that the debtor cannot later purport to ratify the payment; the debtor therefore becomes again responsible.[48] The payment of a debt by one of a number of joint (or joint and several) debtors discharges all the debtors.[49]

22–042 **Payment to a third party.** If the creditor requests the debtor to pay the debt to a third party, such a payment is equivalent to payment direct to the creditor, and is a good discharge of the debt.[50]

22–043 **Payment to agent.** If payment is made to an agent of the creditor, this discharges the debt if it is made in the ordinary course of business, before the creditor demands payment to himself,[51] and while the agent has actual or ostensible authority from the creditor to receive the payment.[52] Payment to an ostensible agent, who is in fact without actual authority to receive the payment,

---

[40] See *post*, §§ 27–001, 27–007.

[41] On causation, see *post*, §§ 27–024 *et seq.*

[42] See *post*, §§ 27–039 *et seq.*

[43] See *post*, § 27–111.

[44] See *post*, § 27–100.

[45] Or jointly and severally liable. On joint liability, see *ante* §§ 18–001 *et seq.*

[46] *James v. Isaacs* (1852) 12 C.B. 791; *Simpson v. Eggington* (1855) 10 Exch. 845, 847; *Lucas v. Wilkinson* (1856) 1 H. & N. 420; *Walter v. James* (1871) L.R. 6 Ex. 124; *Purcell v. Henderson* (1885) 16 L.R.Ir. 213, 223, 224; *Keighley, Maxsted & Co. v. Durant* [1901] A.C. 240; *Re Rowe* [1904] 2 K.B. 483; *Smith v. Cox* [1940] 2 K.B. 558; *Owen v. Tate* [1976] 1 Q.B. 402. *Pacific Associates Inc. v. Baxter* [1990] 1 Q.B. 993, 1033–1034; *Pacific and General Insurance Co. Ltd v. Hazell* [1997] L.R.L.R. 65, 79–80. See *post*, § 30–141, and Vol. II, §§ 32–026—32–033, especially § 32–033; and Goff and Jones, *The Law of Restitution* (5th ed., 1998), p. 17, n. 2; Birks and Beatson (1976) 92 L.Q.R. 188. *cf.* Burrows, *The Law of Restitution* (1993), pp. 222–230 and Friedman (1983) 99 L.Q.R. 534. The authority of the debtor will often be presumed: see *Bennett v. Griffin Finance* [1967] 2 QB 46 (Vol. II, § 38–290) and *post*, §§ 30–139—30–145.

[47] *Belshaw v. Bush* (1851) 11 C.B. 191.

[48] *Walter v. James, supra,* at 128.

[49] See *ante*, § 18–014.

[50] *Roper v. Bunford* (1810) 3 Taunt. 76; *Page v. Meek* (1862) 32 L.J.Q.B. 4; *cf. Commercial Bank of Australia Ltd v. Wilson & Co.'s Estate* [1893] A.C. 181. On payment into the creditor's bank account, see *post*, § 22–045; on payment by credit or charge card, see *post*, § 22–082.

[51] *Sanderson v. Bell* (1834) 2 C. & M. 304.

[52] See Vol. II, §§ 32–042—32–049.

is a valid discharge of the debt, *e.g.* where money is paid to a person apparently entrusted with the conduct of the creditor's business.[53] There is no general rule that an agent who is authorised to sell on behalf of his principal is also authorised to receive the purchase-money.[54] A solicitor has implied authority to receive payment of a debt for which he is instructed to sue[55]; he also has authority to receive the consideration money for a deed when he produces it, if it contains a receipt for such money and is duly executed by the person entitled to give a receipt for the money.[56]

Payment to agent otherwise than in cash. The creditor's right to payment **22–044** is not affected by a set-off which his debtor may have against the creditor's agent[57] unless this mode of dealing is sanctioned by a usage known to the creditor,[58] or the creditor allowed his agent to sell as apparent principal.[59] Nor can the debtor discharge his debt to the creditor by writing off a debt due to the debtor from the creditor's agent.[60] Prima facie, an agent who is authorised to receive payment (*e.g.* an auctioneer) has authority only to receive it in cash[61]; such an agent cannot bind his principal by accepting a bill of exchange without the express authority of the principal.[62] If such an agent in fact accepts a cheque and cashes it, or the proceeds are collected by his bank, that amounts to a payment in cash.[63] On the other hand, a principal who desires to authorise an agent to receive payment by cheque only and not in cash must plainly notify third parties dealing with his agent of the exact extent of the agent's authority; thus a notification that cheques drawn in payment must be drawn in a particular form

---

[53] *Barrett v. Deere* (1828) Moo. & M. 200; *Wilmott v. Smith* (1828) Moo. & M. 238; *Bocking Garage v. Mazurk* [1954] C.L.Y. 14. The plaintiff's wife may be so authorised: *Offley v. Clay* (1840) 2 M. & G. 172. *cf. Galbraith and Grant Ltd v. Block* [1922] 2 K.B. 155 (delivery of goods at buyer's premises to a person having ostensible authority to receive them).

[54] *Drakeford v. Piercy* (1866) 7 B. & S. 515; *International Sponge Importers Ltd v. Andrew Watt & Sons* [1911] A.C. 279; *Linck, Moeller & Co. v. Jameson & Co.* (1885) 2 T.L.R. 206; *Butwick v. Grant* [1924] 2 K.B. 483. Custom, however, may affect the agent's authority: *Catterall v. Hindle* (1867) L.R. 2 C.P. 368 (broker).

[55] *Yates v. Freckleton* (1781) 2 Dougl. 623; *Weary v. Alderson* (1837) 2 M. & Rob. 127 (implied authority to receive payment extends to solicitor's London agent who issues the writ).

[56] Law of Property Act 1925, s.69; *King v. Smith* [1900] 2 Ch. 425. See also Trustee Act 1925, s.23(3)(a). On a solicitor's authority in general, see Cordery, *Solicitors* (9th ed.), Division F, Section 1.

[57] *Bartlett v. Pentland* (1830) 10 B. & C. 760; *Barker v. Greenwood* (1837) 2 Y. & C. Ex. 414; *Pearson v. Scott* (1878) 9 Ch.D. 198; *Anderson v. Sutherland* (1897) 2 Com.Cas. 65; *Matvieff v. Crossfield* (1903) 8 Com.Cas. 120.

[58] *Scott v. Irving* (1830) 1 B. & Ad. 605; *Stewart v. Aberdein* (1838) 4 M. & W. 211; *Sweeting v. Pearce* (1861) 9 C.B.(N.S.) 534; *Catterall v. Hindle* (1867) L.R. 2 C.P. 368.

[59] *Cooke & Sons v. Eshelby* (1887) 12 App.Cas. 271; *Ex p. Dixon* (1876) 4 Ch.D. 133 (factor selling in his own name); *Borries v. Imperial Ottoman Bank* (1873) L.R. 9 C.P. 38; see Vol. II, § 32–069; *cf. Greer v. Downs Supply Co.* [1927] 2 K.B. 28.

[60] *Underwood v. Nicholls* (1855) 17 C.B. 239; *Pearson v. Scott* (1878) 9 Ch.D. 198.

[61] *Sweeting v. Pearce, supra,* at 540; *Blumberg v. Life Interests and Reversionary Securities Corporation* [1897] 1 Ch. 171; [1898] 1 Ch. 27. Such an agent has no authority to receive payment in other goods: *Howard v. Chapman* (1831) 4 C. & P. 508; nor is a credit to the agent payment to his principal: *Crossley v. Magnac* [1893] 1 Ch. 594. See also Vol. II, § 32–050.

[62] *Sykes v. Giles* (1839) 5 M. & W. 645; *Williams v. Evans* (1866) L.R. 1 Q.B. 352; *Hogarth v. Wherley* (1875) L.R. 10 C.P. 630.

[63] *Bridges v. Garrett* (1870) L.R. 5 C.P. 451; *Charles v. Blackwell* (1877) 2 C.P.D. 151; *Walker v. Barker* (1900) 16 T.L.R. 393; *Robinson v. Marsh* [1921] 2 K.B. 640, 644; *Clay Hill Brick & Tile Co. Ltd v. Rawlings* [1938] 4 All E.R. 100; *cf. Pape v. Westacott* [1894] 1 Q.B. 272 (cheque dishonoured).

does not exclude the presumption that payment may lawfully be made to the agent in cash and not by cheque at all.[64]

22–045   **Payment or transfer into a bank account.**[65] Where the creditor instructs the debtor to pay a sum due to him by making a payment to the credit of a specified bank account, the creditor has made the bank his agent to receive the payment, which is made as soon as the bank receives payment in cash, or by means of a banker's cheque,[66] draft, payment order or transfer which is treated by banks as equivalent to cash.[67] When the contract requires "payment in cash" to be made into the payee's bank account, but the parties obviously do not expect the payment to be literally in cash (*i.e.* in pounds sterling, dollar bills or other legal tender), the payment or credit to the payee's account must be "the equivalent of cash, or as good as cash,"[68] that is, by "any commercially recognised method of transferring funds the result of which is to give the transferee the [unfettered or unrestricted] right to the immediate use of the funds transferred."[69] Thus, where a Telex credit transfer was made to the payee's bank account, and was treated as irrevocable under an Italian inter-bank scheme, but interest on the funds credited would not begin to run in favour of the payee until four days later, the House of Lords held[70] that "payment in cash" had not been made by the book entry of the receiving bank. "Payment in cash" meant that the payee whose account was credited must be able to use it immediately, *e.g.* by immediate transfer to a deposit account where it would earn interest; the fact that the receiving bank would allow the payee immediately to draw on the credit, but subject to his paying interest during the four days, did not make it equivalent to cash, since that arrangement was merely the equivalent of an overdraft facility.[71]

22–046   The point of time at which a transfer or credit payment into a bank account is "made" has been discussed, but not finally decided, in another House of Lords case,[72] where "payment in cash" was required by the contract. The payment was made by a payment order from another bank, under the provisions of an inter-bank settlement scheme, where the system of processing might have taken 24 hours before the payee's account was credited. Lord Salmon, without deciding the point, "inclined to think that . . . there is no real difference between a payment in dollar bills and a payment by payment orders which in the banking world are generally regarded and accepted as cash"[73] (which view Lord Russell

---

[64] *International Sponge Importers Ltd v. Watt & Sons* [1911] A.C. 279; *cf. Bradford & Sons v. Price Bros.* (1923) 92 L.J.K.B. 871.

[65] Goode, *Payment Obligations in Commercial and Financial Transactions* (1983) pp. 90 *et seq.* See also King (1982) 45 M.L.R. 369; and *post,* Vol. II, §§ 34–368 *et seq.*

[66] On receipt of the debtor's own cheque, or other negotiable instrument, as conditional payment, see *post,* § 22–074.

[67] *A/S Awilco of Oslo v. Fulvia SpA Di Navigazione of Cagliari (The Chikuma)* [1981] 1 W.L.R. 314 (see Vol. II, § 34–373); *The Brimnes (Tenax Steamship Co. Ltd v. The Brimnes (Owners))* [1975] Q.B. 929, 948, 964–965, 968–969.

[68] *The Chikuma, supra,* at 320.

[69] *The Brimnes* [1973] 1 W.L.R. 386, 400 (approved by the House of Lords in *The Chikuma, supra,* at 318–320, with the substitution of "unfettered or unrestricted" for "unconditional" as the adjective before "right"). The decision of the Court of Appeal in *The Brimnes* is reported at [1975] Q.B. 929.

[70] *The Chikuma, supra.*

[71] *ibid.* (But see the criticism by Mann (1981) 97 L.Q.R. 379.)

[72] *Mardorf Peach & Co. Ltd v. Attica Sea Carriers Corporation of Liberia* [1977] A.C. 850.

[73] *ibid.* at 880.

was also inclined to accept[74]); but Lord Fraser thought that the payment must be made "in sufficient time to allow for the period of processing normally required for the method of payment they had chosen."[75]

Payment by "in-house" transfer. In the case of "in-house" payments (*viz.*,   **22–047**
a transfer from one customer's account to another's within the same bank), the payment is made as soon as the bank accepts the payer's instructions and credits the payee's account; in other words, the payment is "made" as soon as the bank has set in motion the bank's internal process for crediting the payee's account (*e.g.* by preparing the instructions for the bank's computer) and before the payee receives any notice that this has been done.[76] Thus, where a bank received a Telex instruction (or "transfer order") from a customer to debit his account and to credit another customer's account, the payment was made when the staff of the bank accepted the instruction and marked the appropriate documents in the bank.[77]

Where payment must be to agent. There may be cases where payment must   **22–048**
be made to the agent, and cannot validly be made to the principal, *e.g.* where an auctioneer has an unsatisfied lien on the proceeds of goods sold by him, it is no defence to an action by him for the price[78] that the buyer had paid the principal, unless the contract of sale permitted payment direct to the principal.[79] The same rule applies where the auctioneer has acted on the faith of an agreement between himself and the principal that the proceeds of the sale shall be disposed of in a particular way.[80] The buyer may rely upon any defence or set-off that he may have against the principal in respect of that part of the amount claimed by the auctioneer which, if recovered, he would be bound to hand over to the principal.[81]

Payment to joint creditors, partners, trustees, etc. The payment of a debt   **22–049**
to one of a number of joint creditors discharges a debt owed to them jointly.[82] Similarly, as partnership is founded on agency, payment to one of a number of partners to whom a debt is jointly owed binds them all, even after a dissolution of the partnership: this position holds even where the debtor had notice before payment that the partners had appointed a third person to collect the debts due to

---

[74] *ibid.* at 889.

[75] *ibid.* at 885. (The other Lords did not deal with this point.) See also *Afovos Shipping Co. SA v. Romano Pagnan and Pietro Pagnan* [1983] 1 W.L.R. 195, 202, 204.

[76] *Momm v. Barclays Bank International Ltd* [1977] Q.B. 790 (following *The Brimnes, supra*; and *Eyles v. Ellis* (1827) 4 Bing. 112); *Royal Products Ltd v. Midland Bank Ltd* [1981] 2 Lloyd's Rep. 194.

[77] *The Brimnes, supra,* at 948–951, 963–966, 969. (The mere receipt of the Telex message does not constitute payment, since it is not a negotiable instrument: *ibid.* at 949, 965, 969.)

[78] An auctioneer's special property in the goods entrusted to him entitles him to sue in his own name for the price of the goods: *Williams v. Millington* (1788) 1 H.Bl. 81; *Benton v. Campbell, Parker & Co. Ltd* [1925] 2 K.B. 410, 416.

[79] *Robinson v. Rutter* (1855) 4 E. & B. 954. See Macintyre, *The Law relating to Auctioneers and Estate Agents* (1957), pp. 180–184; Harvey and Meisel, *Auctions Law and Practice* (2nd ed., 1995), pp. 56–62.

[80] *Manley & Sons Ltd v. Berkett* [1912] 2 K.B. 329.

[81] *Grice v. Kenrick* (1870) L.R. 5 Q.B. 340; *Manley & Sons Ltd v. Berkett, supra.*

[82] *Wallace v. Kelsall* (1840) 7 M. & W. 264; *Husband v. Davis* (1851) 10 C.B. 645; *Powell v. Brodhurst* [1901] 2 Ch. 160.

the firm, unless there is something in the notice which expressly takes away the right of the one partner to receive the money.[83] Payment of a debt to one of two trustees is a good discharge as to both.[84] But where bankers pay to one of several trustees money which should be held in their joint account, the bankers are not discharged as against the other trustees unless they authorised such payment[85]; for where money is paid into a bank on the joint account of persons who are not partners, the bankers are not discharged by payment to one of those persons without the authority of the others.[86] Payment of a debt to one of several executors or administrators is a good discharge[87]; and by the Administration of Estates Act 1925, s.27(2), where a representation[88] is revoked all payments and dispositions made in good faith to a personal representative[89] before the revocation are a valid discharge to the person making the same.[90]

22–050   **Bankruptcy.** Payments made to a bankrupt before the date of the bankruptcy order are considered in Chapter 21.[91] The trustee in bankruptcy is empowered to give receipts for any money received by him, which receipts "effectually discharge the person paying the money from all responsibility in respect of its application."[92]

22–051   **Payment under garnishee order.** Under CPR, Sched. 1, R. 49, the court may, upon the application of any person who has obtained a judgment or order for the recovery or payment of money, order that all debts owing or accruing from some third person (known as the garnishee) to the judgment debtor shall be attached to answer the judgment or order.[93] By CPR, Sched. 1, R. 49.8, it is provided that payment made by or execution levied upon the garnishee under any garnishee order absolute[94] shall be a valid discharge to him as against the judgment debtor to the extent of the amount paid or levied, notwithstanding that the garnishee proceedings are subsequently set aside or the judgment or order reversed. Moreover, this is not a mere rule of procedure. Payment under a garnishee order issued by a competent court discharges the garnishee from any further liability

---

[83] *Porter & Bristow v. Taylor* (1817) 6 M. & S. 156. But payment to the firm of a separate debt due to one partner is not payment of the debt unless the firm was authorised to receive it: *Powell v. Brodhurst, supra.* See further *Lindley and Banks on Partnership* (17th ed., 1995), §§ 12–53—12–55.

[84] *Husband v. Davis, supra.*

[85] *Stone v. Marsh* (1826) Ry. & M. 364, 369.

[86] *Innes v. Stephenson* (1831) 1 Moo. & Rob. 145. *cf.* the similar rule in the case of Bank of England stock: *Welch v. The Bank of England* [1955] Ch. 508.

[87] *Can v. Read* (1749) 3 Atk. 695; *Jacomb v. Harwood* (1751) 2 Ves. Sen. 265, 267; *Charlton v. Durham* (1869) L.R. 4 Ch.App. 433.

[88] "Representation" and "personal representative" mean probate or administration and executor or administrator: *ibid.* s.55(1)(xi) and (xx).

[89] *ibid.*

[90] *cf.* cases before statutory provision: *Allen v. Dundas* (1789) 3 T.R. 125; *Prosser v. Wagner* (1856) 1 C.B.(N.S.) 289.

[91] *Ante,* §§ 21–018 *et seq.*.

[92] Para. 10 of Pt. II of Sched. 5 of the Insolvency Act 1986 (by virtue of s.314). Section 306 provides for the bankrupt's estate to vest in the trustee.

[93] Similar provisions are in CPR Ord. 30.

[94] *cf.* a payment made under a private arrangement: *Turner v. Jones* (1857) 1 H. & N. 878; or a payment made on an order nisi: *Re Webster* [1907] 1 K.B. 623.

anywhere,[95] provided that it is shown that payment was made under the compulsion of that order.[96] No garnishee order will be made where there is a substantial risk that the garnishee will be called on to pay the debt over again, *e.g.* by the court of a foreign country.[97]

Amount to be paid. Apart from subsequent variation by agreement,[98] accord **22–052** and satisfaction[99] or the operation of promissory estoppel,[1] the payment of part of a liquidated sum of money due to the creditor is not a discharge of the whole debt,[2] even though the creditor purports to release the remaining obligation, since there is no consideration for the release.[3] If there is no liquidated sum due, and the amount is uncertain or disputed, payment of any sum subsequently agreed upon by the parties will constitute an accord and satisfaction.[4]

Time of payment. The time when payment is due to be made is a question of **22–053** construction of the contractual terms.[5] Sometimes the time for payment must be implied from the circumstances of the contract: thus, where the claimant contracts to work upon the defendant's materials, and no time is fixed for payment of the agreed cost, the defendant must pay as soon as the claimant has completed the work and given the defendant a reasonable opportunity of seeing that the work has been properly done.[6] Money which is repayable on demand must be ready to be handed over to the creditor as soon as he demands it from the debtor: the only time which the creditor needs to give the debtor is time to get the money from some convenient place,[7] not time in which to negotiate a deal or a loan which he hopes will produce the money.[8] The rules discussed above[9] as to exact compliance with the time fixed for performance of the contract apply to the time

---

[95] *Swiss Bank Corporation v. Boemische Industrial Bank* [1923] 1 K.B. 673 (distinguishing *Martin v. Nadel, infra*). See also *Westoby v. Day* (1853) 2 E. & B. 605; *cf. Turnbull v. Robertson* (1878) 47 L.J.C.P. 294.

[96] *Gould v. Webb* (1855) 4 E. & B. 933; *Turner v. Jones, supra*; *Wood v. Dunn* (1866) L.R. 2 Q.B. 73.

[97] *Martin v. Nadel* [1906] 2 K.B. 26; *Employers' Liability Assurance Corporation Ltd v. Sedgwick Collins & Co. Ltd* [1927] A.C. 95.

[98] *Post*, §§ 23–032 *et seq.*

[99] *Post*, §§ 23–012 *et seq.*

[1] *Ante*, §§ 3–080—3–106; *cf. post*, §§ 23–038 *et seq.*

[2] *Post*, §§ 23–016—23–018.

[3] *Ante*, §§ 3–107 *et seq.*

[4] *Post*, § 23–012; *ante*, §§ 3–044 *et seq.*

[5] See *ante*, §§ 12–042 *et seq.*, 22–011 *et seq*; *post*, § 22–089. In *Mardorf Peach & Co. Ltd v. Attica Sea Carriers Corporation of Liberia* [1977] A.C. 850 it was assumed that payment due to be made into a banking account on a date which turned out to be a non-banking day must be made not later than the previous banking day. See also *ante*, § 22–022, n. 40.

[6] *Hughes v. Lenny* (1839) 5 M. & W. 183. In the case of a divisible obligation (*ante*, § 22–037) where no time for payment has been fixed, the person performing the work may be entitled to claim payment for parts of the work already completed: *Roberts v. Havelock* (1832) 3 B. & Ad. 404; *The Tergeste* [1903] P. 26.

[7] *Toms v. Wilson* (1862) 4 B. & S. 442, 453 (" . . . he must have a reasonable time to get it from some convenient place. For instance, he might require time to get it from his desk, or to go across the street or to his bankers for it") (approved in *Moore v. Shelley* (1883) 8 App.Cas. 285, 293). The reasonableness of the opportunity given to a debtor (who is required to pay on demand) may depend on the debtor's knowledge (or means of knowledge) of the amount due, and on the information supplied by the creditor: *Bunbury Foods Pty. Ltd v. National Bank of Australia Ltd* (1984) 153 C.L.R. 491 (High Ct. of Aust.)

[8] *R.A. Cripps & Son Ltd v. Wickenden* [1973] 1 W.L.R. 944, 955. See also *Brighty v. Norton* (1862) 3 B. & S. 305, 312; *Toms v. Wilson, supra*.

[9] *Ante*, §§ 22–011 *et seq.*

fixed for payment. It is therefore only in three cases recognised by equity[10] that a failure to make the payment on the fixed date amounts to a repudiatory breach of contract entitling the other party to terminate the contract. By section 10(1) of the Sale of Goods Act 1979, it is expressly enacted that unless a different intention appears from the terms of a contract for the sale of goods, stipulations as to time of payment are not of the essence of the contract.[11]

22–054   **Place of payment.** Where the place of payment is specified by the contract, the debtor must tender payment at that place in order to discharge his obligation.[12] Where no place of payment is expressly or impliedly specified by the contract, the general rule is that it is the debtor's duty to seek the creditor in order to pay him at his place of business or residence, if it is in England[13]; but the rule is not applicable to large employers of labour who maintain a regular pay-day and pay office.[14] Unless there is evidence of a contrary intention, the place for payment of a debt is the business place or residence of the creditor at the date when the debt was contracted.[15] If the contract specifies alternative places for payment, it is the duty of the party entitled to select the place to notify the other party; if it is for the creditor to select, there is no default in payment until he notifies the debtor which place of payment he selects.[16]

22–055   **Mode of payment.** Except where he has expressly or impliedly agreed to do so, the creditor is under no obligation to accept a negotiable instrument (such as a bill, note or cheque) in payment of the debt.[17] If the creditor does accept payment in this way, the effect upon the existence of the debt depends on the circumstances, and is discussed in detail in a separate section.[18]

22–056   **Loss in post.** Where a banknote, a cheque or other negotiable instrument is sent to the creditor by post, this does not normally amount to payment if it is lost in the post.[19] Where, however, a creditor expressly or impliedly authorises his debtor to transmit the amount of the debt by cheque through the post, the debtor is discharged if he complies with the authority by sending the cheque in a letter

---

[10] *Ante*, §§ 22–011—22–017.

[11] Contrast stipulations as to the time of delivery, *ante*, § 22–013, n. 79.

[12] Except where there is waiver or variation of the obligation to pay at the specified place: see *post*, §§ 23–032—23–045; *Gyles v. Hall* (1726) 2 P.Wms. 378 (debtor gave creditor notice of his intention to pay at a specified time and place; creditor made no objection, and therefore waived personal tender anywhere else).

[13] *Robey & Co. v. Snaefell Mining Co. Ltd* (1887) 20 Q.B.D. 152; *The Eider* [1893] P. 119, 128; *Thompson v. Palmer* [1893] 2 Q.B. 80; *Charles Duval & Co. Ltd v. Gans* [1904] 2 K.B. 685; *Fowler v. Midland Electric Corporation for Power Distribution Ltd* [1917] 1 Ch. 656. The general rule applies to a tenant: *Haldane v. Johnson* (1853) 8 Exch. 689; also where the creditor was out of England when the contract was made, but not where the creditor left England after the date: *Fessard v. Mugnier* (1865) 18 C.B.(N.S.) 286.

[14] *Riley v. William Holland & Sons Ltd* [1911] 1 K.B. 1029, 1031.

[15] *Rein v. Stein* [1892] 1 Q.B. 753, 758; *Charles Duval & Co. Ltd v. Gans, supra; Drexel v. Drexel* [1916] 1 Ch. 251, 259, 260.

[16] *Thorn v. City Rice Mills* (1889) 40 Ch.D. 357; *cf. Re Escalera Silver Lead Mining Co.* (1908) 25 T.L.R. 87; *Re Harris Calculating Machine Co.* [1914] 1 Ch. 920.

[17] See *post*, § 22–087. On payment by bankers' commercial credit, see Vol. II, §§ 34–388 *et seq.*, § 43–238. On payment into the creditor's bank account, see *ante*, § 22–045.

[18] *Post*, §§ 22–073—22–081.

[19] *Luttges v. Sherwood* (1895) 11 T.L.R. 233; *Pennington v. Crossley & Son* (1897) 77 L.T. 43; *Baker v. Lipton Ltd* (1899) 15 T.L.R. 435.

properly addressed to the creditor, even though it does not reach him.[20] The necessary authority is not to be implied from the mere fact that the previous course of dealing between the parties has been to send cheques by post,[21] though very little evidence of authority is required in addition to evidence of such a course of dealing. A request for a remittance by post amounts to an authority to send the sum in question by post in such a form as is appropriate to its amount. To send (in 1916) a sum as large as £48 in banknotes, even in a registered letter, was held to be unusual and inappropriate[22] and so was the sending by post of an uncrossed bearer cheque.[23]

Expressly or impliedly authorised mode. A particular mode of payment **22–057** may be expressly or impliedly authorised by the contract[24]: thus where there is an automatic slot gas meter, payment is effectively made when coins are placed in the meter, as this is the mode of payment authorised by the supplier of the gas; if the money is subsequently stolen without the negligence of the payer, he is not liable.[25] Similarly, payment by credit or charge card may be a method of payment accepted by the creditor.[26] In a contract for the self-service supply of petrol, the garage undertakes to accept a particular charge card in payment if it displays a notice of its willingness to do so.[27]

Proof of payment: receipts. A payment may be proved by any evidence[28] but **22–058** the usual method of proof is the production of a receipt[29] signed by the creditor or his agent. A receipt is not conclusive but only prima facie evidence that the money has been paid.[30] Evidence may be given of the intention with which it was handed over[31] and of the circumstances generally[32]: thus a receipt given "in full discharge" does not exclude an implied agreement to pay interest not covered by

---

[20] *Norman v. Ricketts* (1886) 3 T.L.R. 182 (the cheque reached the hands of a third person who received payment); *Thairlwall v. Great Northern Ry.* [1910] 2 K.B. 509 (dividend warrant lost in the post; the stockholder would probably have been able to obtain another warrant under s.69 of the Bills of Exchange Act 1882 (see Vol. II, § 34–147) or to have brought an action on the warrant); but *cf. Tankexpress A/S v. Compagnie Financière Belges des Petroles SA* [1949] A.C. 76 (letter delayed in the post); *Zim Israel Navigation Co. Ltd v. Effy Shipping Corporation* [1972] 1 Lloyd's Rep 18 (affd. [1972] 2 Lloyd's Rep. 91). *cf.* posting a letter giving notice of dishonour of a bill: *Walter v. Haynes* (1824) Ry. & M. 149; *Berridge v. Fitzgerald* (1869) L.R. 4 Q.B. 639.

[21] *Pennington v. Crossley & Son, supra.*

[22] *Mitchell-Henry v. Norwich Union Life Insurance Society* [1918] 2 K.B. 67.

[23] *Robb v. Gow* (1905) 8 F. 90 (Ct. of Sess.).

[24] See *ante*, § 22–045.

[25] *Edmundson v. Longton Corporation* (1902) 19 T.L.R. 15.

[26] See *post*, § 22–082.

[27] *Re Charge Card Services Ltd* [1989] Ch. 497.

[28] *Eyles v. Ellis* (1827) 4 Bing. 112; *Mountford v. Harper* (1847) 16 L.J.Ex. 184 (proceeds of cheque drawn by debtor received by creditor); *Gadderer v. Dawes* (1847) 10 L.T.(o.s.) 109; *Douglas v. Lloyds Bank Ltd* (1929) 34 Com.Cas. 263 (payment presumed from lapse of time where no explanation given for the delay: *cf. Cooper v. Turner* (1819) 2 Stark. 497).

[29] The practice of giving receipts for ordinary debts paid by cheque has been largely discontinued since the enactment of s.3 of the Cheques Act 1957 which provides "An unindorsed cheque which appears to have been paid by the banker on whom it is drawn is evidence of the receipt by the payee of the sum payable by the cheque."

[30] *Straton v. Rastall* (1788) 2 T.R. 366; *Hawkins v. Gardiner* (1854) 2 Sm. & G. 441; *Wilson v. Keating* (1859) 27 Beav. 121.

[31] *e.g.* in full satisfaction of all claims: *Lee v. Lancashire & Yorkshire Ry.* (1871) L.R. 6 Ch.App. 527; *Ellen v. G. N. Ry.* (1901) 17 T.L.R. 453; *cf. Oliver v. Nautilus Steam Shipping Co. Ltd* [1903] 2 K.B. 639.

[32] *e.g. Graves v. Key* (1832) 3 B. & Ad. 313.

the receipt.[33] Again, the effect of a receipt may be destroyed by proof that it was obtained by fraud or under a mistake of fact,[34] or that it formed part of a transaction which was merely colourable, because no money had in fact been paid.[35] Where, however, a document containing a receipt clause is relied on by third parties, different considerations prevail, and the person signing the document may be estopped, as against third parties, from denying receipt of the money.[36] A receipt may be in any form so long as the words are express.[37] A receipt for consideration money or securities in the body of a deed is a sufficient discharge for the same, without any further receipt being indorsed on the deed.[38] It is no longer necessary for a receipt to be stamped.[39]

(b) Appropriation of Payments

22–059   **Rights to appropriate payments.** Where several separate debts are due from the debtor to the creditor, the debtor may, when making a payment, appropriate the money paid to a particular debt or debts, and if the creditor accepts the payment so appropriated, he must apply it in the manner directed by the debtor; if, however, the debtor makes no appropriation when making the payment, the creditor may do so.[40]

22–060   **Debtor's right to appropriate.** It is essential that an appropriation by the debtor should take the form of a communication, express or implied, to the creditor of the debtor's intention to appropriate the payment to a specified debt (or debts), so that the creditor may know that his rights of appropriation as creditor cannot arise.[41] It is not essential that the debtor should expressly specify at the time of the payment, which debt or account he intended the payment to be applied to. His intention may be collected from other circumstances showing that he intended at the time of the payment to appropriate it to a specific debt or account.[42] Thus, where at the date of the payment some of his debts are statute-barred and others are not, it will be inferred (in the absence of evidence to the

---

[33] *Re W.W. Duncan & Co.* [1905] 1 Ch. 307; *cf. Nathan v. Ogdens Ltd* (1905) 94 L.T. 126.

[34] *Skaife v. Jackson* (1824) 3 B. & C. 421; *Farrar v. Hutchinson* (1839) 9 A. & E. 641; *Cesarini v. Ronzani* (1858) 1 F. & F. 339; *Ward & Co. v. Wallis* [1900] 1 Q.B. 675.

[35] *Bowes v. Foster* (1858) 2 H. & N. 779.

[36] *Rimmer v. Webster* [1902] 2 Ch. 163; *Powell v. Browne* [1907] W.N. 228; *Tsang Chuen v. Li Po Kwai* [1932] A.C. 715.

[37] Sometimes the form is statutory as in the Bills of Sale Act (1878) Amendment Act 1882, s.9. See *Burchell v. Thompson* [1920] 2 K.B. 80.

[38] Law of Property Act 1925, s.67.

[39] As from February 1, 1971, the former stamp duty of 2d. on a receipt for £2 or more was abolished by the Finance Act 1970, s.32 and Sched. 7, para. 2. (For the position when an unstamped receipt dated before that date is tendered in evidence, see s.14 of the Stamp Act 1891; *Sergeant and Sims on Stamp Duties*, (12th ed. 1998), pp. 201 *et seq.*)

[40] *Peters v. Anderson* (1814) 5 Taunt. 596; *Simson v. Ingham* (1823) 2 B. & C. 65; *Cory Bros. & Co. Ltd v. Owners of Turkish Steamship "Mecca"* [1897] A.C. 286. On the appropriation of payments made under a regulated hire-purchase agreement or a conditional sale agreement, see Consumer Credit Act 1974, s.81 (see Vol. II, § 38–136).

[41] *Leeson v. Leeson* [1936] 2 K.B. 156, 161; *Stepney Corporation v. Osofsky* [1937] 3 All E.R. 289.

[42] *Newmarch v. Clay* (1811) 14 East 239, 244; *Shaw v. Picton* (1825) 4 B. & C. 715; *Young v. English* (1843) 7 Beav. 10; *Nash v. Hodgson* (1855) 6 De G.M. & G. 474; *R. v. Miskin Lower Justices* [1953] 1 Q.B. 533.

contrary) that the debtor appropriated the payment to the debts that were not so barred.[43]

Creditor's right to appropriate.[44] Where the debtor has not exercised his   **22–061**
option, and the right to appropriate has therefore devolved upon the creditor,[45] he
may exercise it at any time "up to the very last moment"[46] or until something
happens which makes it inequitable for him to exercise it. What is "the very last
moment" depends on the circumstances of each case. In one instance the creditor
was held entitled, in the witness-box during the course of his action, to exercise
his right to appropriate a payment by his debtor, as nothing had previously
happened to determine his right of election.[47] The creditor need not make his
election in express terms. He may declare it by bringing an action or in any other
way that makes his meaning and intention plain.[48] An entry in the creditor's
books applying a payment to a particular debt does not constitute an election
which will preclude the creditor from afterwards applying it to another debt,
unless the entry has been communicated to the debtor.[49] Once, however, the
election is made and communicated to the debtor, it is irrevocable.[50]

Creditor may not appropriate to an illegal or irrecoverable demand. The   **22–062**
doctrine of appropriation does not entitle a creditor who receives money on
account from his debtor to apply it towards the satisfaction of a debt due under
an illegal contract, or to a claim which does not constitute any legal or equitable
demand against the debtor. Thus where the creditor makes two demands on his
debtor, one arising out of a lawful contract, and the other out of an illegal
contract, any payment by the debtor which is not specifically appropriated by the
debtor must be applied to the lawful demand.[51]

Appropriation to statute-barred debt. A creditor may appropriate a pay-   **22–063**
ment to a debt barred by the Limitation Act 1980,[52] or to a debt which is
unenforceable because of some formal defect in the contract.[53] But a creditor
cannot appropriate a payment to a statute-barred debt after a judgment is given

---

[43] *Nash v. Hodgson, supra. cf.* a balance owing on a current account: *Re Footman Bower & Co. Ltd* [1961] Ch. 443 (and see *post*, § 22–066).

[44] On the right of a secured creditor to appropriate the proceeds of sale of the security, see *Re William Hall (Contractors) Ltd* [1967] 1 W.L.R. 948.

[45] *Lowther v. Heaver* (1889) 41 Ch.D. 248. In the case of hire-purchase payments, see n. 40, *ante.*

[46] *Cory Bros. & Co. v. Owners of Turkish Steamship "Mecca", supra,* at 294.

[47] *Seymour v. Pickett* [1905] 1 K.B. 715. See also *Smith v. Betty* [1903] 2 K.B. 317.

[48] *Cory Bros. & Co. Ltd v. Owners of Turkish Steamship "Mecca", supra,* at 294.

[49] *Simson v. Ingham* (1823) 2 B. & C. 65; *cf. Deeley v. Lloyds Bank Ltd* [1912] A.C. 756, 783, 784.

[50] *Smith v. Betty, supra; Seymour v. Pickett, supra; Albermarle Supply Co. Ltd v. Hind & Co.* [1928] 1 K.B. 307.

[51] *Wright v. Laing* (1824) 3 B. & C. 165; *Keeping v. Broom* (1895) 11 T.L.R. 595; *A. Smith & Son (Bognor Regis) Ltd v. Walker* [1952] 2 Q.B. 319 (instalments paid to builder where part of the work was illegal because no licence had been granted); *cf. Lamprell v. Billericay Union* (1849) 3 Exch. 283.

[52] *Mills v. Fowkes* (1839) 5 Bing.N.C. 455; *Stepney Corporation v. Osofsky* [1937] 3 All E.R. 289. See *post*, § 29–131.

[53] *Cruikshanks v. Rose* (1831) 1 Moo. & Rob. 100; *Philpott v. Jones* (1834) 2 A. & E. 41; *Arnold v. Poole Corporation* (1842) 4 M. & G. 860; *Seymour v. Pickett, supra.*

directing the ascertainment of the amount due from the debtor, excluding items which are statute-barred.[54]

22–064   **Guaranteed debt.** Where one of the debts is guaranteed by a surety, but the other is not, the ordinary rules as to appropriation apply; hence a payment by the debtor will not be appropriated to the guaranteed debt[55] unless there is evidence to show that the debtor (or failing him, the creditor) so appropriated it.[56] Thus a creditor receiving payments on account by the debtor is at liberty to appropriate them to a debt not covered by the guarantee; he is not bound by any implied contract with the surety to apply such payments in reduction of the guaranteed debt.[57]

22–065   **Instalments paid under a composition.** Where a debtor has made a composition with his creditors, and a creditor receives dividends upon a debt partly guaranteed by a third person, the dividends must not be appropriated to the excess of the debt above the sum guaranteed, but must be applied rateably to the whole debt, so that the surety is relieved from liability by the amount of the dividend on the part which is guaranteed.[58] Similarly, where the debtor has made a composition with his creditors, under which instalments are payable in discharge of several debts, an instalment must be appropriated to all the debts rateably.[59] Where the creditor receives from the estate of the principal debtor a dividend on the whole of a debt payable by instalments, the surety is not entitled to have the whole of the dividend applied in discharge of any one instalment, but only rateably in part payment of each instalment as it becomes due.[60]

22–066   **Current account: Clayton's Case.** In the case of a current account, the normal presumption is that the creditor has not appropriated payments to particular items. In a current account there is "one blended fund"[61] into which all receipts and payments are carried in order of their respective dates:

> "In such a case, there is no room for any other appropriation than that which arises from the order in which the receipts and payments take place, and are carried into the account. Presumably, it is the sum first paid in, that is first drawn out. It is the first item on the debit side of the account, that is discharged, or reduced, by the first item on the credit side. The appropriation is made by the very act of setting the two items against each other."[62]

---

[54] *Smith v. Betty, supra.*

[55] *Kirby v. Duke of Marlborough* (1813) 2 M. & S. 18; *Plomer v. Long* (1816) 1 Stark. 153; *Williams v. Rawlinson* (1825) 3 Bing. 71; *Re Sherry* (1884) 25 Ch.D. 692.

[56] *Kinnaird v. Webster* (1878) 10 Ch.D. 139; *Browning v. Baldwin* (1879) 40 L.T. 248; *cf. Marryatts v. White* (1817) 2 Stark. 101; *Pearl v. Deacon* (1857) 1 De G. & J. 461.

[57] *Re Sherry, supra.*

[58] *Raikes v. Todd* (1838) 8 A. & E. 846. See also *Bardwell v. Lydall* (1831) 7 Bing. 489; *cf. Ellis v. Emmanuel* (1876) 1 Ex.D. 157. *cf.* also the position in bankruptcy where the surety guarantees the whole debt, but the creditor received some payments: *Re Houlder* [1929] 1 Ch. 205 (following *Midland Banking Co. v. Chambers* (1869) L.R. 4 Ch.App. 398; *Re Sass* [1896] 2 Q.B. 12).

[59] *Thompson v. Hudson* (1871) L.R. 6 Ch.App. 320.

[60] *Martin v. Brecknell* (1813) 2 M. & S. 39.

[61] *Clayton's Case* (1816) 1 Mer. 572, 608. See also *Bodenham v. Purchas* (1818) 2 B. & Ald. 39; *Simson v. Ingham* (1823) 2 B. & C. 65; *Field v. Carr* (1828) 5 Bing. 13; *Hooper v. Keay* (1875) 1 Q.B.D. 178; *London and County Banking Co. Ltd v. Ratcliffe* (1881) 6 App.Cas. 722; *Re Sherry* (1884) 25 Ch.D. 692, 702; *Egg v. Craig* (1903) 89 L.T. 41; *Deeley v. Lloyds Bank Ltd* [1912] A.C. 756; *Re Primrose (Builders) Ltd* [1950] Ch. 561; *Re Footman Bower & Co. Ltd* [1961] Ch. 443; *Re Yeovil Glove Co. Ltd* [1965] Ch. 148; *Re James R. Rutherford & Sons Ltd* [1964] 1 W.L.R. 1211.

[62] *Clayton's Case, supra*, at 608.

This presumption may be rebutted if a different intention can be inferred from the circumstances, *e.g.* by a particular mode of dealing, such as keeping separate accounts or the creation of a common fund, or by a stipulation between the parties.[63] It has also been stated that the rule is one of convenience rather than presumed intent so that it might not be applied when to do so would result in injustice or otherwise produce a solution which would be impracticable.[64]

Appropriation as between principal and interest. Where there is no appro-   22–067
priation by either debtor or creditor in the case of a debt bearing interest, the law will (unless a contrary intention appears) apply the payment to discharge any interest due before applying it to the earliest items of principal.[65]

(c) *Revalorisation: Gold Clauses and Index-linking*[66]

The nominalistic principle. It has been a principle of English law since the   22–068
seventeenth century that a debt payable at a future time involves an obligation to pay the nominal amount of the debt at the date of payment in whatever is legal tender for that currency at that date, irrespective of any fluctuations in the currency in which the debt is expressed between the date of the contract and the date of payment.[67] Thus, where English law is the law applicable to the contract,[68] a debt expressed in "pounds" may be discharged in whatever are "pounds" according to English law at the date fixed for payment,[69] and a debt expressed in a foreign currency, *e.g.* marks, may be discharged by the same nominal amount of marks at the date of payment, despite changes in the real value of the mark.[70] The creditor runs the risk of depreciation of the currency, while the debtor runs the risk of its appreciation. If the law applicable to the

---

[63] *Henniker v. Wigg* (1843) 4 Q.B. 792; *City Discount Co. v. McLean* (1874) L.R. 9 C.P. 692; *Browning v. Baldwin* (1879) 40 L.T. 248; *Cory Bros. & Co. Ltd v. Owners of Turkish Steamship "Mecca"* [1897] A.C. 286; *Re British Red Cross Balkan Fund* [1914] 2 Ch. 419; *Bradford Old Bank v. Sutcliffe* [1918] 2 K.B. 833 (current account and loan account kept separate); *Re Hodgson's Trusts* [1919] 2 Ch. 189; *Barlow Clowes International Ltd v. Vaughan* [1992] 4 All E.R. 22.

[64] *Barlow Clowes International Ltd v. Vaughan* [1992] 4 All E.R. 22, 42.

[65] *Income Tax Commissioner v. Maharajadhiraja of Darbhanga* (1933) L.R. 60 I.A. 146, 157; *cf. Smith v. Law Guarantee and Trust Society Ltd* [1904] 2 Ch. 569.

[66] See, in general, Mann, *The Legal Aspect of Money* (5th ed., 1992); Downes (1985) 101 L.Q.R. 98; on American law, with discussion of English authorities, see Nussbaum, *Money in the Law, National and International* (1950).

[67] *Gilbert v. Brett* (*le case de Mixt Moneys*) (1604) Davis 18; *British Bank for Foreign Trade v. Russian Commercial and Industrial Bank (No. 2)* (1921) 38 T.L.R. 65; *Ottoman Bank v. Chakarian (No. 2)* [1938] A.C. 260; *Sforza v. Ottoman Bank of Nicosia* [1938] A.C. 282; *Pyrmont Ltd v. Schott* [1939] A.C. 145; *Marrache v. Ashton* [1943] A.C. 311; *Bonython v. Commonwealth of Australia* [1951] A.C. 201; *Treseder-Griffin v. Co-operative Insurance Ltd* [1956] 2 Q.B. 127. The rule is similar in all foreign systems of law: see *Dicey and Morris on the Conflict of Laws* (12th ed., 1993), pp. 1550 *et seq.*; Mann *op. cit.* pp. 86 *et seq.*, 271 *et seq.*; Nussbaum *op. cit.* pp. 171 *et seq.*, 348 *et seq.*; Hauser (1959) 33 Tulane L. Rev. 307; Report on Foreign Money Liabilities, Law Commission Report No. 124 (1983).

[68] On the law applicable to the contract, see *post*, §§ 31–003, 31–110 *et seq.*

[69] *Treseder-Griffin v. Co-operative Insurance Ltd, supra,* at p. 144. *cf. Bonython v. Commonwealth of Australia, supra,* at 222. (On the problems which arise where the currency expression chosen may refer to two or more different currencies (*e.g.* "pound," "dollar" or "franc") see *Dicey and Morris, op. cit.* pp. 1566 *et seq.*) See also §§ 27–066—27–067, *post.*

[70] *Re Chesterman's Trusts* [1923] 2 Ch. 466; *Pyrmont Ltd v. Schott, supra; cf. Addison v. Brown* [1954] 1 W.L.R. 779, 785. In an action in England, the court may give a judgment in a foreign currency: see *post,* § 31–170.

contract is foreign, that law governs the obligations arising under the contract,[71] but such a foreign law will invariably adopt the nominalistic principle[72]; hence, it is for the law of the country in whose currency the debt is expressed to define what is legal tender for the purpose of discharging that debt.[73]

22–069　　**Gold clauses.** In an attempt to avoid the operation of the nominalistic principle (*ante*), creditors have adopted various clauses to protect themselves against the risk of depreciation of the currency.[74] The most popular device used by creditors today is a cost-of-living or other index.[75] But in the earlier part of the century and the post-war years the most usual type of protective clause was a so-called "gold clause"[76]; the validity, meaning, and effect of such a clause are determined by the law applicable to the contract.[77] In an ordinary domestic English case, or a conflicts case where English law is the law applicable to the contract, a clause referring to payment in gold of a specified standard of weight and fineness is presumed to be a gold value clause: it does not impose an obligation to pay gold or gold coins, but is used to ascertain or measure the amount of the debt, so that the debtor is obliged to pay in legal tender of the chosen currency the amount necessary at the date of payment to purchase gold or gold coins to the nominal amount of the debt.[78] This construction imports a special standard or measure of value which may be described sufficiently, though not with precise accuracy, as being the value which the specified unit of account would have if the currency were on a gold basis.[79]

22–070　　The construction of a gold clause as a gold value clause is known as the *Feist* construction, following the decision of the House of Lords in *Feist v. Société Intercommunale Belge d'Electricité*.[80] In this case a bond for £100 was issued in 1928 by the Belgian company bearing interest payable on March 1 and September 1 each year at $5\frac{1}{2}$ per cent. and repayable in 1963 or earlier "in sterling in gold coin of the United Kingdom of or equal to the standard of weight and fineness existing on September 1, 1928." The company claimed the right to pay the sum due on an interest coupon in whatever might be legal tender in England

---

[71] See Chap. 31, *post*.

[72] *Dicey and Morris, op. cit.* pp. 1552 *et seq.* See also *ante*, n. 67.

[73] See n. 67, *ante*, and for illustrations, *R. v. International Trustee* [1937] A.C. 500; *Pyrmont Ltd v. Schott* [1939] A.C. 145; *Miliangos v. George Frank (Textiles) Ltd* [1976] A.C. 443. The law applicable to the contract also determines whether the debtor is liable to make an additional payment by way of "revalorisation" where the currency has depreciated: *Dicey and Morris op. cit.* pp. 1556 *et seq.* (English domestic law knows no such principle.)

[74] A "gold value" clause, *post*, will also protect a debtor against appreciation of the currency.

[75] See *post*, § 22–072.

[76] No legislation in the U.K. has invalidated such a clause. (*cf.* the Joint Resolution of the United States Congress of June 5, 1933, and the Canadian Gold Clauses Act 1937, applied respectively in *R. v. International Trustee, supra*, and *New Brunswick Ry. v. British and French Corporation Ltd* [1939] A.C. 1. Both provisions have now been repealed: *Dicey and Morris, op. cit.*, pp. 1563–1564.).

[77] *Dicey and Morris, op. cit.* pp. 1558 *et seq.*; Arts. 8(1), 10(1)(a) and (b) of the Rome Convention on the Law Applicable to Contractual Obligations (Contracts (Applicable Law) Act 1990, Sched. 1); *R. v. International Trustee* [1937] A.C. 500; *post*, §§ 31–128—31–136.

[78] *Dicey and Morris, ibid.*; *Feist v. Société Intercommunale Belge d'Electricité* [1934] A.C. 161.

[79] *Syndic in Bankruptcy of Khoury v. Khayat* [1943] A.C. 507, 511, 512; *Feist v. Société Intercommunale Belge d'Electricité, supra*, at 172. Another formulation of the principle is that the debtor has to provide at the time of payment such an amount of currency as will buy the same amount of gold as could have been bought with the sum promised at the time of making the contract.

[80] *Supra*. See Mann, *op. cit.* pp. 147 *et seq.*

at the date of payment.[81] The House of Lords held that the proper law of the contract was that of England and that the holder was entitled to receive such a sum in sterling (*i.e.* English legal tender) as should represent the gold value of the nominal amount of each respective payment, such gold value to be ascertained in accordance with the standard of weight and fineness existing on September 1, 1928. Therefore, after the devaluation of the pound in 1931, the clause imposed an obligation to pay in depreciated pounds the amount necessary to purchase 100 gold pounds. Lord Russell of Killowen said[82]: "The parties are referring to gold coin of the United Kingdom of a specific standard of weight and fineness not as the mode in which the company's indebtedness is to be discharged, but as being the means by which the amount of the indebtedness is to be measured and ascertained." The *Feist* construction has been followed in conflict of laws cases where the applicable law was foreign[83] and when interpreting international conventions[84] but it has not yet been applied to any reported case dealing with a domestic English contract.[85] Although the statutes of many foreign countries have declared gold clauses to be illegal, some have now been repealed.[86]

Other possible constructions of gold clauses. Other constructions than the   **22–071**
Feist construction are possible of particular gold clauses, since each clause depends on its own wording and context. First, the clause may show that the parties intended a sale of actual gold or bullion as a commodity, so that no monetary obligation was undertaken.[87] Secondly, the clause may refer to the actual medium in which the debt is to be discharged, *e.g.* a "gold coin" clause whereby the debtor agrees to pay actual gold coins. Thirdly, it may be a descriptive clause, which merely repeats the statutory definition of the legal unit of currency.[88] This third construction was adopted by a majority of the Court of Appeal in 1956[89] where the lessee under a domestic English lease covenanted to pay a rent of £1,900 "yearly during the said term either in gold sterling or in Bank of England notes to the equivalent value in gold sterling"; it was held that

---

[81] On legal tender, see *post*, § 22–086.

[82] [1934] A.C. 161, 172 *et seq.*

[83] *New Brunswick Ry. v. British and French Trust Corporation Ltd* [1939] A.C. 1; *Syndic in Bankruptcy of Khoury v. Khayat* [1943] A.C. 507 (the law of Palestine was the same as English law on this point). *cf. R. v. International Trustee* [1937] A.C. 500 (reversing the decision of the Court of Appeal [1936] 3 All E.R. 407, but approving the Court of Appeal's view that the clause was a gold value clause).

[84] *The Rosa S.* [1989] Q.B. 419; *Brown Boveri (Australia) Pty. Ltd v. Baltic Shipping Co. (The Nadezhda Krupskaya)* [1989] 1 Lloyd's Rep. 518 (New South Wales Court of Appeal).

[85] In *New Brunswick Ry. v. British and French Trust Corporation Ltd, supra,* the law of New Brunswick was probably the applicable law, though the point was left open; in *Treseder-Griffin v. Co-operative Insurance Society Ltd* [1956] 2 Q.B. 127 (discussed *post*, § 22–071) and in *Campos v. Kentucky & Indiana Terminal Railroad Co.* [1962] 2 Lloyd's Rep. 459 (decisions on domestic English law), the *Feist* case, *supra*, was distinguished. See now *post*, § 22–072.

[86] *Dicey and Morris, op. cit.* pp. 1558–1566; Nussbaum, *op. cit.* pp. 280 *et seq.*

[87] *British and French Trust Corporation v. New Brunswick Ry.* [1936] 1 All E.R. 13, 16. But the courts will lean against this construction unless this meaning is clearly expressed, since payment in gold, or export in gold, has been made subject to controls in many countries.

[88] *e.g. St. Pierre v. South American Stores (Gath and Chaves) Ltd* [1937] 3 All E.R. 349 (Chilean law); *Treseder-Griffin v. Co-operative Insurance Ltd* [1956] 2 Q.B. 127 (discussed *post*); *Campos v. Kentucky & Indiana Terminal Railroad Co.* [1962] 2 Lloyd's Rep. 459 (*post*, § 31–132; see Mann (1963) 12 I.C.L.Q. 1005); *cf. Modiano Bros. & Sons v. Bailey & Sons* (1933) 47 Ll.L.Rep. 134, 141.

[89] *Treseder-Griffin v. Co-operative Insurance Ltd, supra.*

this clause merely imposed an obligation to pay £1,900 in current legal tender, *i.e.* pound notes, since a gold sovereign was worth no more than a pound note for the purposes of legal tender. It may be that this decision should have been based on the uncertainty of the intention of the parties, in that the words they used did not definitely indicate that the amount of indebtedness was to be fixed by the current value of gold.[90] The words were obviously chosen by the parties for some purpose, yet the majority of the Court of Appeal treated them as a surplusage; the decision can only be reconciled with that of the House of Lords in *Feist* if the absence of any reference to the weight and fineness of the gold in the former case is treated as crucial.[91]

22–072 **Index-linking clauses in domestic contracts.** In modern times, contracting parties (particularly lenders) have sought other methods to safeguard themselves against a decline in the purchasing power of the pound sterling.[92] In 1977, a court of first instance[93] upheld the validity of an English mortgage (made between businessmen who received separate legal advice) under which both the principal debt and interest were "index-related" to a foreign currency; although payments were due in pounds sterling, their amounts were to vary proportionately to the variation in the rate of exchange between the pound and the Swiss franc.[94] The lender had advanced £36,000 as the capital loan in 1966, and under "the Swiss franc uplift" he became entitled to capital repayments of £87,588 by 1976.[95] It has been pointed out,[96] however, that protection against decline in the domestic purchasing power of sterling would come from index-linking to a domestic index, such as the retail price index[97]; whereas the linking of a domestic debt to a foreign currency is less justifiable, since it could lead to drastic revalorisation as a result of international fluctuations which bear little relation to domestic events.

---

[90] Nor did the clause fix any exact gold standard, such as the selling or buying price of gold coins, or of the content of gold coins, or of bullion. On this, see *Campos v. Kentucky & Indiana Terminal Railroad Co., supra*, at 469. See also *The Rosa S.* [1989] Q.B. 419, 426.

[91] See the criticisms of the decision in *Dicey and Morris, op. cit.* pp. 1562–1564; Mann (1957) 73 L.Q.R. 181; Yale [1956] C.L.J. 169; Unger (1957) 20 M.L.R. 266. (Leave to appeal to the House of Lords was granted, but the appeal was compromised before hearing.)

[92] Rents under leases have, for centuries, been made dependent on the price of corn. See also Nussbaum, *op. cit.* pp. 299 *et seq.*

[93] *Multiservice Bookbinding Ltd v. Marden* [1979] Ch. 84. See Bishop and Hindley (1979) 42 M.L.R. 338. The High Court of Australia has upheld the index-linking of an obligation to a retail price index: *Stanwell Park Hotel Co. Ltd v. Leslie* (1952) 85 C.L.R. 189. The *Multiservice* decision has been followed in a case concerned with the interpretation of the Building Societies Act 1962: *Nationwide Building Society v. Registry of Friendly Societies* [1983] 1 W.L.R. 1226. See also Downes (1985) 101 L.Q.R. 98.

[94] *cf. Howard Houlder and Partners Ltd v. Union Marine Insurance Co.* (1922) 10 Ll.L.Rep. 627.

[95] During the same period, however, the borrower's business in the new premises purchased with the loan had prospered considerably, and the value of the premises had also inflated substantially: [1979] Ch. 84, 102. The judge also held that the terms of the mortgage were not unfair, oppressive or morally reprehensible so as to entitle the court to relieve the borrower under equitable principles applicable to mortgages: *ibid.* at 105–113.

[96] Bowles (1981) 131 New L.J. 4, 5.

[97] On "cost-of-living index" clauses, and other similar clauses, see Nussbaum, *op. cit.* pp. 299 *et seq. cf.* Mann, *op. cit.* pp. 146–147, 164, 180–182. A cost-of-living index clause is of the same nature as a gold value clause, *ante*, § 22–069.

(d) *Payment by Negotiable Instrument or Documentary Credit*

Payment by negotiable instrument.[98] Apart from express agreement,[99] a 22–073
creditor is not bound to accept payment in any way except cash, *i.e.* legal tender.[1]
If, however, he accepts a negotiable instrument,[2] such as a bill of exchange,
promissory note or cheque, it is a question of fact[3] depending on the intention of
the parties, whether it is taken in absolute satisfaction of the debt, or only in
conditional satisfaction. In either event, the acceptance of the instrument gives
the debtor a good defence to an action for the debt, at least until the instrument
matures.[4]

Conditional payment. Normally where a creditor accepts a negotiable instru- 22–074
ment for his debt it is presumed[5] to be taken by him as a qualified or conditional
payment, and, accordingly, although the original debt is still due during the
currency of the instrument, the creditor's remedy is suspended until it is due.[6] If
it is then paid, this amounts to payment of the debt;[7] if it is dishonoured when it
is presented for payment in the ordinary way,[8] the right to sue upon the original
debt revives as if no negotiable instrument had been taken.[9] Hence, if interest was

---

[98] The previous restrictions on payment of wages by cheque have been repealed: see Vol. II,
§ 39–087.

[99] On payment by bankers' commercial credit, see Vol. II, §§ 34–388 *et seq.*, 43–238. On payment
by credit or charge card, see *post*, § 22–082.

[1] *e.g.* where the debtor, in answer to a demand for payment, sent to the creditor a post office order
which was in fact defective, but could easily have been rendered effective by the creditor, it was held
that this was no evidence of payment as the debtor had no right to put his creditor to the trouble of
either correcting the mistake or of returning the defective post office order: *Gordon v. Strange* (1847)
1 Exch. 477.

[2] *cf. Plimley v. Westley* (1835) 2 Bing.N.C. 249 (note endorsed by debtor to creditor, but it was not
negotiable).

[3] *Goldshede v. Cottrell* (1836) 2 M. & W. 20; *Re Boys* (1870) L.R. 10 Eq. 467; *Re Romer and
Haslam* [1893] 2 Q.B. 286; *Palmer v. Bramley* [1895] 2 Q.B. 405. *cf. Re Charge Card Services Ltd*
[1989] Ch. 497.

[4] The same result follows (i) where the bill or note for the debt is given to the creditor by a third
party: *Allen v. Royal Bank of Canada* (1925) 95 L.J.P.C. 17 (see also *Belshaw v. Bush* (1851) 11 C.B.
191, and *cf.* on the need for consideration in such circumstances: *Oliver v. Davis* [1949] 2 K.B. 727);
(ii) where the bill or note is, at the creditor's request, payable to a third person: *Price v. Price* (1847)
16 M. & W. 232, 241; *National Savings Bank Association Ltd v. Tranah* (1867) L.R. 2 C.P. 556.

[5] This presumption is not displaced merely because the cheque was handed over with a bank card:
Re Charge Card Services Ltd [1987] Ch. 150, 166. The Court of Appeal reserved its view on this
point: [1989] Ch. 497, 517.

[6] *Sayer v. Wagstaff* (1844) 5 Beav. 415; *Belshaw v. Bush* (1851) 11 C.B. 191; *Currie v. Misa* (1875)
L.R. 10 Ex. 153 (affd. (1876) 1 App.Cas. 554); *Ex p. Matthew* (1884) 12 Q.B.D. 506; *Re Romer &
Haslam, supra*, at 296; *Felix Hadley & Co. Ltd v. Hadley* [1893] 2 Ch. 680; *Allen v. Royal Bank of
Canada, supra; Re Charge Card Services Ltd, supra*, at 511. See also *Griffiths v. Owen* (1844) 13 M.
& W. 58, 64.

[7] *Thorne v. Smith* (1851) 10 C.B. 659; *Felix Hadley & Co. Ltd v. Hadley, supra; Re Home* [1951]
Ch. 85, 89. Payment in part is *pro tanto* discharge: *Bottomley v. Nuttall* (1858) 5 C.B.(N.S.) 122.

[8] *Re Raatz* [1897] 2 Q.B. 80 (debtor's commission of an available act of bankruptcy amounts to
dishonour of negotiable instrument given to creditor).

[9] *Gunn v. Bolckow, Vaughan & Co.* (1875) L.R. 10 Ch.App. 491; *Cohen v. Hale* (1878) 3 Q.B.D.
371; *Re Romer & Haslam, supra*, at 296; *D.P.P. v. Turner* [1974] A.C. 357, 367–368, 369. Where the
bill has been negotiated and is outstanding in the hands of a third party, the creditor's remedy is still
suspended: *Davis v. Reilly* [1898] 1 Q.B. 1; *Re A Debtor* [1908] 1 K.B. 344 (except where the third
party is a trustee for the plaintiff: *National Savings Bank Association Ltd v. Tranah* (1867) L.R. 2 C.P.
556; or agent for the plaintiff: *Hadwen v. Mendisabal* (1825) 10 Moore C.P. 477). If, though the
dishonoured bill has been negotiated, it has again been transferred to the creditor, the latter may sue
on the original demand: *Tarleton v. Allhusen* (1834) 2 A. & E. 32.

due on the debt, it continues to accrue after the date of acceptance of a cheque which is subsequently dishonoured.[10] It has been held that a plaintiff who accepts a cheque for part of the debt claimed by him cannot sign judgment in default of appearance for the full amount claimed unless the cheque is dishonoured.[11] Similarly, acceptance of an irrevocable documentary credit does not constitute absolute payment to the seller so as to release the buyer; if the credit is not honoured, the seller may sue the buyer.[12]

22–075   **Bill or note from debtor's agent.** A creditor does not lose his remedy against his debtor merely by taking for the debt a bill or note of the debtor's agent, even without the debtor's consent.[13] The debtor will be discharged if the creditor has the opportunity of receiving payment in cash from the debtor's agent, but, for his own convenience, elects to take the agent's (or a third party's) bill or note.[14]

22–076   **Collateral security.** A negotiable instrument may be given to the creditor as collateral security for the debt, so that the existing remedies for the debt are unaffected.[15] This was frequently held to be the intention of the parties when the debt was due under a deed, or another remedy (*e.g.* distress) was also available.[16] Thus, where a cheque was given for interest due on a debenture, there was not a conditional payment so as to release the security; where the cheque was not met and the company went into liquidation, the debenture-holder could still claim to be a secured creditor in respect of the interest.[17] Even where the debt is secured, the acceptance of a negotiable instrument may, in the circumstances, be evidence of an agreement to suspend the remedy under the security.[18]

22–077   **Absolute payment.** If the creditor accepts a negotiable instrument in absolute satisfaction of the original debt, agreeing expressly or impliedly to take upon himself the risk of the instrument not being paid, the effect is to extinguish his right of action for the debt and to leave him without remedy except upon the

---

[10] *D.P.P. v. Turner, supra,* at 368.

[11] *Bolt & Nut Co. (Tipton) Ltd v. Rowlands, Nicholls & Co. Ltd* [1964] 2 Q.B. 10.

[12] *W.J. Alan & Co. Ltd v. El Nasr Export and Import Co.* [1972] 2 Q.B. 189, 209–212, 221; *Maran Road Saw Mill v. Austin Taylor & Co. Ltd* [1975] 1 Lloyd's Rep. 156; *E.D. & F. Man Ltd v. Nigerian Sweets and Confectionery Co. Ltd*; [1977] 2 Lloyd's Rep. 50; *Re Charge Card Services Ltd* [1989] Ch. 497, 511 (*ante,* § 22–082). See Vol. II, §§ 34–423—34–425.

[13] *Robinson v. Read* (1829) 9 B. & C. 449.

[14] *Marsh v. Pedder* (1815) 4 Camp. 257; *Smith v. Ferrand* (1827) 7 B. & C. 19; *Strong v. Hart* (1827) 6 B. & C. 160; *Robinson v. Read, supra,* at 455; *Anderson v. Hillies* (1852) 12 C.B. 499; *Litchfield Union v. Greene* (1857) 1 H. & N. 884, 892. Other rules on agency may also apply to this situation: see Vol. II, §§ 32–069—32–072. *cf. Everett v. Collins* (1810) 2 Camp. 515 (cheque of debtor's "servants" rather than of his "agents").

[15] *Drake v. Mitchell* (1803) 3 East 251; *Pring v. Clarkson* (1822) 1 B. & C. 14; *Peacock v. Pursell* (1863) 14 C.B.(N.S.) 728; *Re London, Birmingham and South Staffordshire Bank* (1865) 34 L.J.Ch. 418; *Modern Light Cars Ltd v. Seals* [1934] 1 K.B. 32 (following *Re Rankin and Shiliday* [1927] N.I. 162).

[16] *Davis v. Gyde* (1835) 2 A. & E. 623; *Worthington v. Wigley* (1837) 3 Bing.N.C. 454; *Belshaw v. Bush* (1851) 11 C.B. 191, 206; *Henderson v. Arthur* [1907] 1 K.B. 10, 13–14; *Re J. Defries & Sons Ltd* [1909] 2 Ch. 423, 428 ("the mere giving of a cheque is not conditional payment of a secured debt so as to release the security"). *cf. Bolt & Nut Co. (Tipton) Ltd v. Rowlands Nicholls & Co. Ltd* [1964] 2 Q.B. 10.

[17] *Re J. Defries & Sons Ltd, supra.*

[18] *Baker v. Walker* (1845) 14 M. & W. 465; *Palmer v. Bramley* [1895] 2 Q.B. 405.

instrument.[19] It is a question of fact in each case whether the instrument was accepted as absolute payment or not.[20]

Invalid or forged instrument. If the instrument given in payment is invalid[21]   **22–078**
or forged,[22] the creditor may treat it as a nullity and sue to recover the debt immediately.[23]

Duties of creditor holding a negotiable instrument. Where a negotiable   **22–079**
instrument, upon which the debtor is not primarily liable, is accepted by the creditor as conditional payment, he is bound to do all that a holder of such an instrument may do in order to get payment[24]; thus it is his duty to present a cheque within a reasonable time, and if he fails to do so, and the debtor is thereby prejudiced, the creditor is guilty of laches and makes the cheque his own, so that it amounts to payment of the debt.[25] Similarly, the creditor must give due notice of dishonour and take other necessary steps to preserve his remedy against the other parties secondarily liable.[26] It is necessary to give notice of dishonour to the debtor only where he is a party to the negotiable instrument to whom such notice is required to be given.[27] The creditor, however, is not under such strict duties if it is the debtor who is primarily liable on the negotiable instrument given as conditional payment; in this case the onus is on the debtor to show a sufficient reason for failing to pay when it fell due.[28]

Loss of instrument. If the creditor loses the bill or note, he may rely on   **22–080**
section 70 of the Bills of Exchange Act 1882: in any action or proceeding upon a bill the court may order that the loss of the instrument shall not be set up, provided an indemnity be given against the claims of any other person upon the instrument in question.[29]

---

[19] *Smith v. Ferrand* (1827) 7 B. & C. 19; *Sard v. Rhodes* (1836) 1 M. & W. 153; *Sayer v. Wagstaff* (1844) 5 Beav. 415; *Sibree v. Tripp* (1846) 15 M. & W. 23 (distinguished on another point: *D. & C. Builders Ltd v. Rees* [1966] 2 Q.B. 617 (*ante*, § 3–108)); *Caine v. Coulton* (1863) 1 H. & C. 764. It does not appear to be essential in such a case that the instrument should be negotiable: *Lewis v. Lyster* (1835) 2 Cr.M. & R. 704, 706.

[20] *cf.* the position with payment by credit or charge card: *post*, § 22–082. *cf.* also where the creditor of a partnership, upon its dissolution, takes the bill or note of the continuing partners for the debt: *Thompson v. Percival* (1834) 5 B. & Ad. 925; *Lyth v. Ault* (1852) 7 Exch. 669.

[21] Older cases concern invalidity caused by an insufficient stamp: *Brown v. Watts* (1808) 1 Taunt. 353; *Wilson v. Vysar* (1812) 4 Taunt. 288; *Cundy v. Marriott* (1831) 1 B. & Ad. 696. The stamp duty on bills of exchange and promissory notes was abolished as from February 1, 1971 (Finance Act 1970, s.32 and Sched. 7, para. 2).

[22] *Camidge v. Allenby* (1827) 6 B. & C. 373, 385. As to the forged renewal of an existing bill, see *Bell v. Buckley* (1856) 11 Exch. 631.

[23] Similarly where the debtor acted fraudulently: *Camidge v. Allenby, supra*, at 382.

[24] *Bridges v. Berry* (1810) 3 Taunt. 130; *Soward v. Palmer* (1818) 8 Taunt. 277; *Peacock v. Pursell* (1863) 14 C.B.(N.S.) 728.

[25] *Camidge v. Allenby, supra*; *Hopkins v. Ware* (1869) L.R. 4 Ex. 268. *cf. Robson v. Oliver* (1847) 10 Q.B. 704.

[26] *Holbrow v. Wilkins* (1822) 1 B. & C. 10; *Bridges v. Berry, supra*; *cf. Goodwin v. Coates* (1832) 1 M. & Rob. 221, 222, note (a).

[27] *Swinyard v. Bowes* (1816) 5 M. & S. 62; *cf. Smith v. Mercer* (1867) L.R. 3 Ex. 51 (notice of dishonour required to be given to the debtor in the particular circumstances).

[28] *National Savings Bank Association Ltd v. Tranah* (1867) L.R. 2 C.P. 556.

[29] *King v. Zimmerman* (1871) L.R. 6 C.P. 466. For the previous position at common law, see *Crowe v. Clay* (1854) 9 Exch. 604; *cf.* also s.69 of the Bills of Exchange Act 1882, as to the holder's rights to a duplicate of a lost bill.

22–081   **Alteration of instrument.** If the creditor alters, in a material particular, a bill drawn upon a third party, he makes the bill his own, and although it may be dishonoured, it operates as payment by the debtor if the debtor's rights are affected by the alteration.[30] If the creditor alters a bill accepted by the debtor, he may, in the absence of fraud, still sue for the original debt where the debtor has not been prejudiced.[31]

(e) *Payment by Credit or Charge Card*

22–082   **Credit or charge card schemes.** A finance company issuing credit or charge cards to approved cardholders sets up a scheme under which it agrees with various retailers in the scheme that the cardholders may charge purchases to the company, which undertakes (in its contract with each retailer) to pay the retailer the total amounts so charged. When a retailer agrees that a cardholder may pay for a purchase by having the price charged in this way, he accepts payment by this method as an unconditional, absolute payment of the price under the contract of sale between himself and the cardholder (unless that contract provides otherwise).[32] The result is that if the finance company fails to pay the retailer the amount[33] so charged, the seller has no recourse against the cardholder for payment of the price in cash.[34] In its decision on this situation the Court of Appeal held that there is no general presumption that whenever payment is agreed to be made through a third party, by a method which involved the risk that the third party may not pay, the acceptance by the seller of that method of payment is conditional upon the third party actually making the payment to the creditor.[35] When a new form of payment is introduced, the question whether it should be treated as absolute or conditional depends on its own circumstances.[36]

5. TENDER

22–083   **The principle of tender.** In many cases a party to a contract cannot complete his obligations without the concurrence of the other party, *e.g.* without his acceptance of goods when delivered, or his acceptance of money paid over. If the other party refuses to accept performance in such cases, he is preventing the promisor from fulfilling his contractual obligations, and the plea of tender is available to the promisor as a defence to a subsequent action against him for failure to perform. The plea is that the defendant has always been willing to complete his side of the contract, and has in fact done so as far as is possible

---

[30] *Alderson v. Langdale* (1832) 3 B. & Ad. 660 (the alteration deprived the debtor of his remedy on the bill against the third party); *cf.* Bills of Exchange Act 1882, s.64. See also *post*, §§ 26–019, 26–022; *Byles on Bills of Exchange* (26th ed.), pp. 267–273.

[31] *Atkinson v. Hawdon* (1835) 2 A. & E. 628; and see *M'Dowall v. Boyd* (1848) 12 Jur. 980.

[32] *Re Charge Card Services Ltd* [1989] Ch. 497.

[33] Less any discount agreed in the contract between the company and the retailer.

[34] *Re Charge Card Services Ltd, supra.* (There are three contracts: one between the company and the cardholder (who undertakes to pay the company the amounts charged to his card); the second between the company and the retailer; and the third the contract of sale between the retailer and the cardholder.)

[35] *ibid.* at 511–512.

[36] *ibid.*

without the concurrence of the other party. A plea of tender must be established by showing that the promisor made an unconditional offer to perform his promise in terms of the contract but that the promisee refused to accept performance.[37] The authorities deal mainly with tender of money due under a contract, but the principle may extend to other cases, such as delivery of goods under a contract of sale[38]: if the buyer refuses to accept the goods, but has had a reasonable opportunity to examine the goods to see that they comply with the contract, the seller is, by his tender, relieved of liability to deliver under the contract.[39]

Tender of money. Where a debtor is obliged to pay a specific sum of money   **22–084**
to a creditor a successful plea of tender does not discharge the debt, but if the creditor subsequently sues for the debt, the debtor may, by paying the money into court[40] and by proving the tender and his continued willingness to pay the debt since the tender,[41] bar any claim for interest[42] or damages after the tender[43]; the creditor will also be liable to pay the debtor his costs of the action, on the ground that the action should not have been brought.[44] A claim for unliquidated damages, not being a claim for a specific sum of money, cannot be met by a plea of tender.[45]

Amount to be tendered. The debtor must tender the full amount of the debt,   **22–085**
since a creditor is not bound to accept less than the whole of his demand; hence, a tender of part of an entire demand is invalid.[46] If there are separate items in a claim, the debtor may make a valid tender in respect of particular items, if he appropriates his tender to such items.[47] A tender of more than is due is a valid tender of the amount due if the debtor does not require change[48]; but if the debtor does ask for change out of the larger sum, this is not a valid tender of the amount

---

[37] *Dixon v. Clark* (1848) 5 C.B. 365, 377 *et seq.*

[38] See Vol. II, §§ 43–239 *et seq.*, especially §§ 43–272–43–289.

[39] *Startup v. Macdonald* (1843) 6 M. & G. 593, 610; *Isherwood v. Whitmore* (1843) 11 M. & W. 347. See Vol. II, §§ 43–272, 43–289.

[40] CPR, Part 36 (There are similar provisions in the County Court Rules.) Payment into court is essential for a successful defence of tender of money: CPR, Part 37, r. 3; *Kinnaird v. Trollope* (1889) 42 Ch.D. 610.

[41] *Dixon v. Clark, supra,* at 377.

[42] But where a *borrower* of money tenders the amount due for principal and interest, the tender does not stop interest running after the date of the tender unless there is evidence that the sum has been set aside and is available for payment at any time: *Barratt v. Gough-Thomas* [1951] 2 All E.R. 48 (following *Edmondson v. Copland* [1911] 2 Ch. 301).

[43] *Norton v. Ellam* (1837) 2 M. & W. 461; *Graham v. Seal* (1918) 88 L.J.Ch. 31. See also Vol. II, § 38–252.

[44] *Griffith v. Ystradyfodwg School Board* (1890) 24 Q.B.D. 307. See also *Dixon v. Clark, supra,* at 377. *cf. Graham v. Seal, supra* (after valid tender by mortgagor the mortgagee will be liable to pay the costs of an action to redeem).

[45] *Greenwood v. Sutcliffe* [1892] 1 Ch. 1, 10.

[46] *Dixon v. Clark, supra*; *James v. Vane* (1860) 29 L.J.Q.B. 169; *Read's Trustee in Bankruptcy v. Smith* [1951] Ch. 439. A tender of part of a debt, after deduction of a set-off, is not strictly a legal tender: *Searles v. Sadgrave* (1855) 5 E. & B. 639; *Phillpotts v. Clifton* (1861) 10 W.R. 135; but such a tender may be relevant when the court exercises its discretion as to costs. A set-off accruing after the date of a tender of part does not validate the tender: *Cotton v. Godwin* (1840) 7 M. & W. 147.

[47] *James v. Vane, supra. cf. Hardingham v. Allen* (1848) 5 C.B. 793 (debtor failed to assign his tender of part to any particular item); *Strong v. Harvey* (1825) 3 Bing. 304, 313. On appropriation, see *ante,* §§ 22–059 *et seq.*

[48] *Dean v. James* (1833) 4 B. & Ad. 546. See also *Wade's Case* (1601) 5 Co.Rep. 114a; *Douglas v. Patrick* (1790) 3 T.R. 683.

due, since a creditor is not obliged to give change.[49] If, however, the creditor does not object to the tender on this ground, but makes some other objection, or demands a larger sum,[50] the tender will be valid, because the creditor will be taken to have waived any objection as to change.[51]

22–086   **Tender must be in legal currency.** A payment or tender must be in legal currency[52]; what amounts to legal tender is specified by section 2 of the Coinage Act 1971 (as amended[53]). Coins made by the Mint are legal tender as follows: gold coins, for payment of any amount[54]; coins of cupro-nickel or silver of denominations of more than 10 pence, for payment of any amount not exceeding £10; coins of cupro-nickel or silver of denominations of not more than 10 pence, for payment of any amount not exceeding £5; coins of bronze, for payment of any amount not exceeding 20 pence. There is power by proclamation to "call in" coins[55] (which then cease to be legal tender) or to make other coins legal tender.[56] By section 1(2) and (6) of the Currency and Bank Notes Act 1954, a tender of a note or notes of the Bank of England expressed to be payable to bearer on demand is legal tender for the payment of any amount. A tender of notes of a bank other than the Bank of England is not a legal tender,[57] but the creditor may waive his objection to the tender on that ground.[58]

22–087   **Tender by negotiable instrument.** A tender by negotiable instrument, such as a bill of exchange or cheque, is not a valid tender[59]; but the creditor may waive an objection to the form of the tender,[60] *e.g.* if he asks for payment by cheque[61] or objects to the tender only on another ground, such as the amount of the tender.[62] There is no custom obliging a vendor to accept a cheque for the payment of a deposit on a sale by auction.[63] Nor is a solicitor, who is authorised to accept a tender of money due on a mortgage, at liberty to accept a cheque: thus a tender of a cheque to him is insufficient.[64]

---

[49] *Betterbee v. Davis* (1811) 3 Camp. 70; *Robinson v. Cook* (1815) 6 Taunt. 336; *cf. Blow v. Russell* (1824) 1 C. & P. 365.

[50] *Black v. Smith* (1791) Peake 121.

[51] *Bevans v. Rees* (1839) 5 M. & W. 306, 308. See also *Saunders v. Graham* (1819) Gow 121; *Atkin v. Acton* (1830) 4 C. & P. 208, 210.

[52] The common law requires that a tender shall be made in the current coin of the realm or in foreign money legally made current by proclamation. See Bac.Abr. *Tender* (B.2). As to tender of foreign money in discharge of a debt due in that foreign currency, see *Société des Hôtels Le Touquet Paris-Plage v. Cummings* [1922] 1 K.B. 451. See also *post*, §§ 31–163—31–169).

[53] By s.1(3) of the Currency Act 1983.

[54] Provided their weight has not become less than that specified: s.2(1) (as amended).

[55] s.3(e) of the Coinage Act 1971.

[56] ss.2(1B), 3(EE) of the Coinage Act 1971 (as amended).

[57] Unless, of course, the contract provides that a sum of money expressed in a foreign currency is to be paid in England: see *Dicey and Morris on the Conflict of Laws* (12th ed., 1993), pp. 1579–1582.

[58] *Polglass v. Oliver* (1831) 2 C. & J. 15.

[59] *Re Steam Stoker Co.* (1875) L.R. 19 Eq. 416; *Blumberg v. Life Interests and Reversionary Securities Corporation* [1897] 1 Ch. 171; [1898] 1 Ch. 27; *Johnson v. Boyes* [1899] 2 Ch. 73.

[60] See *Re Quebrada Co. Ltd* (1873) 42 L.J.Ch. 277; *Cohen v. Roche* [1927] 1 K.B. 169.

[61] *Cubitt v. Gamble* (1919) 35 T.L.R. 223.

[62] *Jones v. Arthur* (1840) 8 Dowl. 442; see also *Lockyer v. Jones* (1796) Peake 239n.; *Cohen v. Roche, supra*, at 180.

[63] *Johnston v. Boyes, supra.* See also *Pollway Ltd v. Abdullah* [1974] 1 W.L.R. 493.

[64] *Blumberg v. Life Interests and Reversionary Securities Corporation, supra.*

Actual production of the money. To constitute a valid tender there must **22–088**
either be an actual production of the money, or its production must be expressly
or impliedly dispensed with by the creditor.[65] Issues as to what constitutes actual
production of the money[66] and to whether the creditor dispensed with actual
production of the money will depend on all the circumstances.[67] In one case,[68]
where the debtor was obliged to make "payment in cash," the Court of Appeal
held that such payment was not made until the creditor either received cash or
what he was prepared to treat as the equivalent of cash, or had a credit available
on which, in the normal course of business or banking practice, he could draw in
the form of cash.[69]

Time of tender. Where by the terms of the contract the money is to be paid **22–089**
on a particular day, the tender to be valid must be made on that day.[70] Although
a tender cannot be effectually made after the actual commencement of an action
for the recovery of the debt, that is, after the issue of the writ,[71] nevertheless,
before the issue of a writ, a late tender of the amount due will normally have the
same effect, in regard to interest and costs,[72] as would a valid tender on the due
day.[73] Where a charterparty gave the owner an express power to withdraw the
vessel on default in payment of hire, late payment made before the owner
exercised his right to withdraw was held not to deprive the owner of that
right.[74]

The acceptor of a bill payable at a future day cannot make a valid tender after **22–090**
the due day, although he pleads a tender of the amount of the bill with interest
from the day it became due up to the day of the tender.[75] Where a bill or note is
payable on demand, a valid tender may be made, at any time before an action has
been brought, by tendering the amount due with interest up to the time of the
tender.[76] In a contract for sale of goods an earlier invalid tender may be

[65] *Finch v. Brook* (1834) 1 Bing.N.C. 253, 257; *The Norway (Owners of) v. Ashburner* (1865) 3
Moo.P.C.(N.S.) 245; *Farquharson v. Pearl Assurance Co. Ltd* [1937] 3 All E.R. 124. See also
Dickinson v. Shee (1801) 4 Esp. 67; *Thomas v. Evans* (1808) 10 East 101.
[66] *e.g. Alexander v. Brown* (1824) 1 C. & P. 288; *Leatherdale v. Sweepstone* (1828) 3 C. & P. 342;
Liddiard v. Skelton (1843) 1 L.T.(O.S.) 143; *Bishop v. Smedley* (1846) 2 C.B. 90; *Humphrey v.
Chapman* (1846) 6 L.T.(O.S.) 413.
[67] *Douglas v. Patrick* (1790) 3 T.R. 683; *Read v. Goldring* (1813) 2 M. & S. 86; *Harding v. Davis*
(1825) 2 C. & P. 77; *Re Farley* (1852) 2 De G.M. & G. 936; *cf. Ryder v. Townsend* (1825) 7 D. &
Ry. 119; *Empresa Cubana De Fletes v. Lagonisi Shipping Co. Ltd* [1971] 1 Q.B. 488, 505 (tender of
a banker's payment slip may be "treated in commercial circles as cash"): the case has been overruled
on another point: see the *Mardorf Peach* case, *infra*, n. 69, and *post*, § 22–089.
[68] *The Brimnes (Tenax Steamship Co. Ltd v. The Brimnes (Owners))* [1975] Q.B. 929.
[69] *ibid.* at 963. See further the discussion in *Mardorf Peach & Co. Ltd v. Attica Sea Carriers
Corporation of Liberia* [1977] A.C. 850, 880, 885, 889 (referred to *ante*, § 22–046).
[70] *Dixon v. Clark* (1848) 5 C.B. 365, 378–379.
[71] The defendant may of course pay the amount into court: CPR Part 36.
[72] See *ante*, § 22–084.
[73] *Briggs v. Calverly* (1800) 8 T.R. 629; *Moffat v. Parsons* (1814) 5 Taunt. 307 (tenders valid,
though made after creditors had instructed their solicitors to act). See also *Johnson v. Clay* (1817) 7
Taunt. 486, and the comment thereon in *Poole v. Tumbridge* (1837) 2 M. & W. 223, 226; *Dixon v.
Clark, supra*, at 378 (if creditor validly demands payment, and the debtor refuses, a subsequent tender
is invalid); *Bennett v. Parker* (1867) Ir. 2 C.L. 89, 95.
[74] *Mardorf Peach & Co. Ltd v. Attica Sea Carriers Corporation of Liberia, supra*.
[75] *Dobie v. Larkam* (1855) 10 Exch. 776 (following *Poole v. Tumbridge, supra*; *Hume v. Peploe*
(1807) 8 East 168). See also *Dixon v. Clark, supra*, at 379.
[76] *Norton v. Ellam* (1837) 2 M. & W. 461, 463.

disregarded if the seller, within the time fixed for delivery, makes a subsequent valid tender.[77]

22–091   **Tender must be unconditional.** A tender, to be valid, must not be made upon any condition to which the creditor has a right to object.[78] The debtor cannot force the creditor to make an admission by accepting the money tendered on terms which the creditor is unwilling to accept. Thus, although a debtor tendering money may exclude any presumption against himself that the sum tendered is only in part payment of the debt, his tender will be invalid if it is made on condition that the creditor acknowledges that nothing more is due from the debtor.[79] So tenders of money "in full of the plaintiff's claims,"[80] as "all that is due,"[81] "as a settlement,"[82] or "in payment of the half-year's rent due at Lady Day last,"[83] have all been held invalid.

22–092   **Tender under protest, or subject to valid condition.** A tender of a sum of money "under protest,"[84] or where the debtor states that he considers the amount tendered to be all that is due, or where the debtor reserves the right to dispute the amount due,[85] is not a conditional tender and is therefore valid; no condition has been imposed that the creditor must make an admission when accepting the money. Where a tender of a mortgage debt is made upon the condition that the mortgagee should immediately execute a re-conveyance (previously seen and approved) of the mortgaged premises, the tender is valid, since the mortgagor is merely insisting on his contractual rights[86]; the tender therefore stops interest running, and renders the mortgagee liable to pay the costs of an action to redeem.[87] The fact that the creditor disputes the amount due and refuses to receive the amount tendered by the debtor does not affect the validity of the tender or render it a conditional tender.[88]

22–093   **Request for receipt.** Since the stamp duty on receipts has been abolished,[89] it is no longer an offence to refuse to give a stamped receipt.[90] It is probably a conditional tender if the debtor demands a receipt as a condition of payment,[91]

---

[77] *Borrowman Phillips & Co. v. Free & Hollis* (1878) 4 Q.B.D. 500. See *Benjamin's Sale of Goods* (5th ed., 1997), § 12–031 and Apps [1994] L.M.C.L.Q. 525.

[78] *Re Steam Stoker Co.* (1875) L.R. 19 Eq. 416; *Bevans v. Rees* (1839) 5 M. & W. 306, 309.

[79] See the cases cited in nn. 80–83, *post.*

[80] *Strong v. Harvey* (1825) 3 Bing. 304, 313. *cf. Evans v. Judkins* (1815) 4 Camp. 156; *Cheminant v. Thornton* (1825) 2 C. & P. 50; *Gordon v. Cox* (1835) 7 C. & P. 172.

[81] *Sutton v. Hawkins* (1838) 8 C. & P. 259; *Field v. Newport, etc., Ry.* (1858) 3 H. & N. 409.

[82] *Mitchell v. King* (1833) 6 C. & P. 237; *cf. Hough v. May* (1836) 4 A. & E. 954 ("balance account").

[83] *Marquis of Hastings v. Thorley* (1838) 8 C. & P. 573. See also *Foord v. Noll* (1842) 2 Dowl.(N.S.) 617; *Finch v. Miller* (1848) 5 C.B. 428.

[84] *Manning v. Lunn* (1845) 2 C. & K. 13; *Scott v. Uxbridge and Rickmansworth Ry.* (1866) L.R. 1 C.P. 596; *Greenwood v. Sutcliffe* [1892] 1 Ch. 1.

[85] *Greenwood v. Sutcliffe, supra.*

[86] *Graham v. Seal* (1918) 88 L.J.Ch. 31.

[87] *ibid.*

[88] *Robinson v. Ferreday* (1839) 8 C. & P. 752; *Henwood v. Oliver* (1841) 1 QB 409; *Bowen v. Owen* (1847) 11 Q.B. 130.

[89] See *ante*, § 22–058, n. 39.

[90] As was provided by s.103 of the Stamp Act 1891 for payment of a sum of £2 or more.

[91] *Laing v. Meader* (1824) 1 C. & P. 257; *cf. Richardson v. Jackson* (1841) 8 M. & W. 298. If the creditor refuses to accept the tender on some other ground, he cannot later maintain that a demand for a receipt invalidated the tender: *Jones v. Arthur* (1840) 8 Dowl. 442; *Richardson v. Jackson, supra.*

but not if he merely asks for a receipt without making it a condition of payment.[92]

Tender to an agent. A tender need not be made to the creditor personally, but **22–094** may be made to an agent who has actual or ostensible authority from the creditor to receive the money.[93] Thus, where a landlord authorises his bailiff to distrain for rent, he gives him implied authority to receive a tender of rent and expenses.[94] After a solicitor has been instructed by the creditor to apply for payment of a debt and has written demanding payment to himself, a tender to the solicitor is valid.[95] So, where the solicitor demands payment at his office, a tender to any person who is in the office carrying on the business is sufficient.[96] The fact that the creditor has instructed his solicitor to commence proceedings to recover the debt does not affect the validity of a tender to the creditor's clerk, who was previously authorised to receive the money, and later told not to receive it because the matter was in the solicitor's hands.[97] If an apparent agent of the creditor, at the time of the tender, disclaimed authority to receive the money, the tender is invalid if in fact the apparent agent had no such authority.[98] If the money is due to a number of creditors jointly, a tender to any one of the joint creditors is valid, though the tender should be pleaded as a tender to the one on behalf of all the creditors.[99]

Tender by an agent. A tender need not be made by the debtor personally, but **22–095** may be made on his behalf by his agent,[1] whether the agent is previously authorised by the debtor, or his unauthorised tender has been subsequently ratified by the debtor. So where an agent was authorised to tender part of a sum, but he tendered at his own risk the whole sum, the tender was held valid after it had been ratified by the debtor.[2]

Failure to comply with valid demand. Since the principle of the defence of **22–096** tender is that the defendant has always been ready to perform the contract,[3] if the

---

[92] *Jones v. Arthur, supra.*

[93] *Kirton v. Braithwaite* (1836) 1 M. & W. 310, 313; *Finch v. Boning* (1879) 4 C.P.D. 143. See also the cases cited *post*, and compare the cases on payment to an agent, *ante*, §§ 22–043—22–048.

[94] *Hatch v. Hale* (1850) 15 Q.B. 10. *cf. Boulton v. Reynolds* (1859) 29 L.J.Q.B. 11 (a man left in charge of premises by the bailiff has no authority to receive rent). But where no place for payment of the rent is fixed, mere readiness to pay the money on the land is insufficient: *Haldane v. Johnson* (1853) 8 Exch. 689.

[95] *Watson v. Hetherington* (1843) 1 C. & K. 36. See also *Crozer v. Pilling* (1825) 4 B. & C. 26 (valid tender of judgment debt and costs to plaintiff's solicitor on the record).

[96] *Watson v. Hetherington, supra.* See also *Wilmott v. Smith* (1828) Moo. & M. 238; *Kirton v. Braithwaite, supra.*

[97] *Moffat v. Parsons* (1814) 5 Taunt. 307; *Caine v. Coulton* (1863) 1 H. & C. 764; *Finch v. Boning, supra*, at 146; *cf. Smith v. Goodwin* (1833) 4 B. & Ad. 413 (a tender to the landlord is valid even after his broker has distrained for rent).

[98] *Bingham v. Allport* (1833) 1 Nev. & M. 398; *Finch v. Boning, supra.*

[99] *Douglas v. Patrick* (1790) 3 T.R. 683. *cf.* payment to a joint creditor: *ante*, § 22–049.

[1] *Finch v. Brook* (1834) 1 Bing.N.C. 253; *Farquharson v. Pearl Assurance Co. Ltd* [1937] 3 All E.R. 124 (mortgagee of insurance policy made valid tender of premium). See also *Cropp v. Hambleton* (1586) Cro.Eliz. 48; and *cf.* payment by an agent: *ante*, § 22–041.

[2] *Read v. Goldring* (1813) 2 M. & S. 86.

[3] See *ante*, § 22–083.

claimant can show that performance of the contract was demanded[4] and refused at any time when by the terms of the contract he had a right to make such a demand, the plea of tender will fail, whether such demand and refusal took place before or after the tender.[5] An application to and refusal by one of two joint debtors is sufficient for this purpose.[6]

---

[4] The demand may be made by an authorised agent, but an unauthorised demand cannot be subsequently ratified: *Coore v. Calloway* (1794) 1 Esp. 115.

[5] *Poole v. Tumbridge* (1837) 2 M. & W. 223; *Cotton v. Godwin* (1840) 7 M. & W. 147; *Brandon v. Newington* (1842) 3 Q.B. 915; *Hesketh v. Fawcett* (1843) 11 M. & W. 356; *Dixon v. Clark* (1848) 5 C.B. 365, 378. *Semble*, that the effect of a tender cannot be defeated by the creditor showing a demand for payment by letter, since a personal demand should be made on the debtor so as to give him at the time of the demand an opportunity of paying the debt: *Edwards v. Yeates* (1826) Ry. & M. 360, 361.

[6] *Peirse v. Bowles and Spibey* (1816) 1 Stark. 323.

DISCHARGE BY AGREEMENT

1. IN GENERAL

Generally. The discharge of a contract by agreement is a subject of **23–001** considerable artificiality and refinement. The niceties of legal reasoning which appear in this branch of the law are not easy to justify, but are attributable in the main to two causes. In the first place, the doctrine of consideration, which plays so important a role in the formation of a binding contract, has also been applied to its discharge.[1] Thus a distinction has to be drawn between those contracts which have been wholly executed on one side (*i.e.* where one party has performed all his obligations under the agreement) and those which are executory on both sides (*i.e.* where both parties still have some obligations to perform). In the former case, the party seeking to be discharged must prove either a release by deed or some consideration agreed by the other party ("accord and satisfaction") in place of his existing obligation or in addition to it.[2] In the latter case, consideration can usually be found in the mutual release by each party of his rights under the contract.[3] Secondly, the evidentiary requirements of the Statute of Frauds 1677 which required certain important classes of contract to be evidenced by writing,[4] were capable of producing even more serious instances of injustice than those which the statute was designed to prevent. Within the limits available to them, the judges endeavoured to circumvent the statute in order that it should not be made a cloak for fraud. Thus, although the variation of the term of a contract required to be evidenced by writing has to be proved by writing,[5] the discharge of the entire agreement[6] and the waiver of contractual terms[7] can be effected by parol. These distinctions have declined greatly in importance since

---

[1] This was criticised by Sir Frederick Pollock, *Principles of Contract* (13th ed.), p. 150, as an unwarrantable extension. See *ante*, § 3–071.

[2] See *post*, §§ 23–003, 23–012; see also "Waiver," *post*, §§ 23–043 *et seq.*

[3] See *post*, §§ 23–025 *et seq.*

[4] See *ante*, §§ 4–004 *et seq.*

[5] See *post*, § 23–033.

[6] See *post*, § 23–030.

[7] See *post*, § 23–040.

the almost total repeal of the Statute of Frauds by the Law Reform (Enforcement of Contracts) Act 1954.[8]

23–002 **Discharge of right of action arising from breach.** It will be convenient also to deal in this chapter with the discharge by agreement of a right of action arising from a breach of contract.

2. RELEASE

23–003 **Release by deed.** Where a contract has been executed by one party only, that is to say, where only one party has fully performed his obligations under the contract and the other party has some obligations still outstanding, the contract may be discharged at any time before breach by release by deed.[9] Also, where one party has committed a breach of the contract, it will be a defence for him to show that the other party has by deed released the cause of action accruing from such breach.[10] The employment of a deed dispenses with the necessity for consideration.[11]

23–004 **Parol release.** A mere parol release, whether oral or in writing, without valuable consideration amounts to *nudum pactum* and is normally insufficient to effect a discharge either at law[12] or in equity.[13] A parol release given in return for valuable consideration amounts to accord and satisfaction.[14]

23–005 **Construction of release.** No particular form of words is necessary to constitute a valid release, and any words which show an evident intention to renounce a claim or discharge the obligation are sufficient.[15] The normal rules relating to the construction of a written contract also apply to a release,[16] and so a release in general terms is to be construed according to the particular purpose for which it was made.[17] The court will construe a release which is general in its

---

[8] See *ante*, § 4–004.

[9] *Foster v. Dawber* (1851) 6 Exch. 839, 851. The need for a seal for the valid execution of an instrument as a deed by an individual was abolished when s.1 of the Law of Property (Miscellaneous Provisions) Act 1989 came into force.

[10] *Tetley v. Wanless* (1867) L.R. 2 Ex. 275. See also *Barker v. St. Quintin* (1844) 12 M. & W. 441 (debt of record).

[11] *Preston v. Christmas* (1759) 2 Wils.K.B. 86.

[12] *Pinnel's Case* (1602) 5 Co.Rep. 117a; *Fitch v. Sutton* (1804) 5 East 230; *Harris v. Goodwyn* (1841) 2 M. & G. 405; *Foster v. Dawber, supra*, at 851; *De Bussche v. Alt* (1878) 8 Ch.D. 286; *Foakes v. Beer* (1884) 9 App.Cas. 605 (see *ante*, § 3–107). If a receipt is given, expressing that money has been received in satisfaction of all demands, it is open to the parties to contradict such a receipt: *Foster v. Dawber, supra*, at 848. For exceptions to this rule, see *ante*, §§ 3–110—3–119; *post*, §§ 23–016—23–018.

[13] *Byrn v. Godfrey* (1798) 4 Ves. 6; *Tufnell v. Constable* (1836) 8 Sim. 69; *Cross v. Sprigg* (1849) 6 Hare 552 (revd. on other grounds: (1850) 2 Mac. & G. 113); *Jorden v. Money* (1854) 5 H.L.C. 185; *Luxmore v. Clifton* (1867) 17 L.T. 460. See also *Stackhouse v. Barnston* (1805) 10 Ves. 453, 466. It is doubtful whether earlier cases in equity culminating in *Flower v. Marten* (1837) 2 My. & Cr. 459, can now be considered good law. But see *ante*, §§ 3–080, 3–120 *et seq.*; *post*, §§ 23–016—23–018, 23–043.

[14] See *post*, § 23–012.

[15] Co.Litt. 264; Com.Dig. *Release* (A.1); Bac.Abr. *Release* (A).

[16] See *ante*, §§ 12–042 *et seq.*, § 12–093.

[17] *L. & S.W. Ry. v. Blackmore* (1870) L.R. 4 H.L. 610, 623; *Solly v. Forbes* (1820) 2 B. & B. 38, 47; *Morley v. Frear* (1830) 6 Bing. 547, 555.

terms in the light of the circumstances existing at the time of its execution, and with reference to its context and recitals, in order to give effect to the intention of the party by whom it was executed.[18] In particular, it will not be construed as applying to facts of which the party making the release had no knowledge at the time of its execution[19] or to objects which must then have been outside his contemplation.[20] But the construction of any individual release will necessarily depend upon its particular wording and phraseology.[21]

Covenants not to sue. A covenant not to sue without any limitation as to **23–006** time is equivalent to a release.[22] The reason for this rule appears to be a desire to avoid the circuity of action which would otherwise arise if the covenantee recovered precisely the same damage that he suffered by reason of the covenantor suing on the original agreement.[23] But, at common law, a covenant, or agreement for valuable consideration, not to sue for a limited time was not equivalent to a release and did not bar the action on the contract.[24] The covenant was construed as giving the covenantee merely a right of action for its breach if the covenantor sued before the expiry of the time so limited. It did not operate as a bar to the original action but gave an action for damages.[25] A court of equity, however, would grant an injunction to restrain the covenantor from suing within that time,[26] and the equitable rule now prevails so as to provide the covenantee with a complete defence in that event.[27]

Joint contractors. The distinction between a release and a covenant not to **23–007** sue can, however, be of importance in relation to the liability of joint contractors. This topic has been dealt with in the chapter on Joint Obligations earlier in this book.[28]

Conditional release. A release will be good although made subject to **23–008** avoidance by the happening of a condition subsequent, as, for example, by the non-fulfilment of a compromise.[29]

---

[18] *Lampon v. Corke* (1822) 5 B. & Ald. 606; *Simons v. Johnson* (1832) 3 B. & Ad. 175; *Lindo v. Lindo* (1839) 1 Beav. 496; *Boyes v. Bluck* (1853) 13 C.B. 652.

[19] *Ecclesiastical Commissioners for England v. N.E. Ry.* (1877) 4 Ch.D. 845.

[20] *Payler v. Homersham* (1815) 4 M. & S. 423; *Lyall v. Edwards* (1861) 6 H. & N. 337; *Re Armitage* (1877) 5 Ch.D. 46; *Turner v. Turner* (1880) 14 Ch.D. 829; *Re Perkins* [1898] 2 Ch. 182; *Re Joint Stock Trust Corp.* (1912) 56 S.J. 272.

[21] Co.Litt. 264B, 291b; *Tynan v. Bridges* (1612) Cro.Jac. 301; *Cutler v. Goodwin* (1721) 11 Mod.R. 344; *Tetley v. Wanless* (1867) L.R. 2 Ex. 275.

[22] *Hodges v. Smith* (1599) Cro.Eliz. 623; *Clayton v. Kynaston* (1699) 12 Mod.R. 221, 222; *Smith v. Mapleback* (1786) 1 T.R. 441, 446; *Ford v. Beech* (1848) 11 Q.B. 852; *Keyes v. Elkins* (1864) 5 B. & S. 240; *Boosey v. Wood* (1865) 3 H. & C. 484.

[23] *Fowell v. Forrest* (1670) 2 Wms.Saund. 47, n. 1; *Ford v. Beech, ante,* at 871.

[24] It was a principle of law that a personal action, once suspended by the act of the parties, was for ever extinct. The courts would not therefore construe the covenant or agreement as a legal suspension of the plaintiff's right to sue since this would have the effect of precluding him from ever suing at all. See Williams, *Joint Obligations*, § 61; *Ford v. Beech, supra,* at 867.

[25] *Deux v. Jefferies* (1594) Cro.Eliz. 352; *Thimbleby v. Barron* (1838) 3 M. & W. 210; *Ford v. Beech, supra*; *Webb v. Spicer* (1849) 13 Q.B. 886, 898; *Ray v. Jones* (1865) 19 C.B.(N.S.) 416. Contrast *Foley v. Fletcher* (1858) 3 H. & N. 769; *Bailey v. Bowen* (1868) L.R. 3 Q.B. 133.

[26] *Beech v. Ford* (1848) 7 Hare 208.

[27] Supreme Court Act 1981, s.49.

[28] See *ante,* §§ 18–017—18–020.

[29] *Newington v. Levy* (1870) L.R. 6 C.P. 180; *Hall v. Levy* (1875) L.R. 10 C.P. 154. See also *Slater v. Jones* (1873) L.R. 8 Ex. 186, 192.

23–009   **Bills of exchange.** The release of a bill of exchange or promissory note[30] need not be effected by deed nor is any consideration required for such discharge.[31] Section 62 of the Bills of Exchange Act 1882 provides that where the holder of a bill at or after its maturity absolutely and unconditionally renounces his rights against the acceptor the bill is discharged. The renunciation must be in writing, unless the bill is delivered up to the acceptor.[32]

23–010   **Effect of misrepresentation.** A release obtained by misrepresentation will be set aside.[33]

23–011   **Pleading of release.** A defence alleging a release must be specifically pleaded.[34]

3. ACCORD AND SATISFACTION

23–012   **Definition.** "Accord and satisfaction is the purchase of a release from an obligation whether arising under contract or tort by means of any valuable consideration, not being the actual performance of the obligation itself. The accord is the agreement by which the obligation is discharged. The satisfaction is the consideration which makes the agreement operative."[35] Thus, although a release not in the form of a deed is normally ineffective to discharge a contract which is executory on one side only,[36] it will operate as a discharge if the other party agrees to accept some other or additional consideration in return for the right which he abandons.[37]

23–013   **Compromise.** Where a claim is asserted by one party which is disputed by the other, they may agree to compromise their dispute on terms mutually agreed between them.[38] Once a valid compromise has been reached, it is not open to the party against whom the claim is made to avoid the compromise on the ground that the claim was in fact invalid, provided that the claim was made in good faith and was reasonably believed to be valid by the party asserting it.[39] Conversely, the claimant cannot avoid the compromise on the ground that there was in fact no defence to the claim, provided that the other party bona fide and reasonably believed that he had a good defence either as to liability or as to amount. In order to establish a valid compromise, it must be shown that there has been an agreement (accord) which is complete[40] and certain in its terms,[41] and that

---

[30] Bills of Exchange Act 1882, s.89.

[31] See *Chalmers and Guest on Bills of Exchange* (15th ed. 1998), p. 523.

[32] The rights of a holder in due course after such release are not affected if he takes without notice of the release: see s.62(2). See Vol. II, § 34–140.

[33] *Wild v. Williams* (1840) 6 M. & W. 490; *Hirschfeld v. L.B. & S.C. Ry.* (1876) 2 Q.B.D. 1.

[34] Although the CPR no longer contain any express reference to a release, it is advisable to continue to plead the defence specifically. The new rules relating to tha contents of the defence are set out in CPR, Part 16.5.

[35] *British Russian Gazette and Trade Outlook Ltd v. Associated Newspapers Ltd* [1933] 2 K.B. 616, 643.

[36] See *ante*, §§ 3–073, 23–004.

[37] *Wilkinson v. Byers* (1834) 1 A. & E. 106; *Steeds v. Steeds* (1889) 22 Q.B.D. 537.

[38] See Foskett, *The Law and Practice of Compromise* (4th ed., 1996).

[39] See *ante*, § 3–049.

[40] See *ante*, § 2–103.

[41] See *ante*, § 2–128.

consideration (satisfaction) has been given or promised[42] in return for the promised or actual forbearance to pursue the claim. It is a good defence to an action for breach of contract to show that the cause of action has been validly compromised.[43]

Form of accord. At common law, accord and satisfaction was no answer to a claim on a specialty, but the rule was otherwise in equity and the latter now prevails.[44] The accord need not be in writing even if the contract which it is sought to discharge, or for the breach of which a claim is made, is required by law to be made or evidenced in writing.[45] An oral accord will suffice, unless the accord itself constitutes a contract or transaction which is required to be made[46] or evidenced[47] in writing. **23–014**

Executory satisfaction. At one time, a number of cases appeared to establish the rule that satisfaction was of no effect unless it was executed. While the satisfaction remained executory, that is to say, so long as the agreement to give satisfaction remained unperformed, the original claim was not discharged, nor would any action lie for breach of the accord.[48] Even a tender of performance of the satisfaction agreed upon was adjudged insufficient.[49] Only executed satisfaction would suffice. This rule, however, was never completely accepted[50] and it is now established that satisfaction may be executory.[51] The question is one of the construction of the accord: whether it was intended that the promise itself or the performance of the promise should discharge the original claim.[52] "The rational distinction seems to be, that if the promise be received in satisfaction, it is a good satisfaction; but if the performance, not the promise, is intended to operate in satisfaction, there will be no satisfaction without performance."[53] In the modern law, therefore, a claimant may still insist upon the performance of some act by the other party in satisfaction of his claim. In that case, there is no satisfaction until performance, and the other party remains liable on the original claim until **23–015**

---

[42] See *post*, § 23–015.

[43] *British Russian Gazette and Trade Outlook Ltd v. Associated Newspapers Ltd* [1933] 2 K.B. 616. See also *Knowles v. Roberts* (1888) 38 Ch.D. 263, 272. Alternatively, the defendant may apply by summons for an order staying the proceedings and the court has jurisdiction to stay under the Supreme Court Act 1981, s.19.

[44] Supreme Court Act 1981, s.49; *Steeds v. Steeds* (1889) 22 Q.B.D. 537.

[45] *Lavery v. Turley* (1860) 6 H. & N. 239. See also *post*, § 23–030.

[46] *e.g.* a legal assignment: see *ante*, § 20–006. See also Law of Property (Miscellaneous Provisions) Act 1989, s.2(1) *ante*, §§ 4–047–4–071.

[47] See *ante*, § 4–004; Vol. II, Chap. 44.

[48] *Peytoe's Case* (1612) 9 Co.Rep. 77b; *James v. David* (1793) 5 T.R. 141; *Reeves v. Hearne* (1836) 1 M. & W. 323; *Bayley v. Homan* (1837) 3 Bing.N.C. 915; *Griffith v. Owen* (1844) 13 M. & W. 58; *Gifford v. Whittaker* (1844) 6 Q.B. 249; *Woods v. Pickersgill* (1859) 1 F. & F. 710; *Edwards v. Hancher* (1875) 1 C.P.D. 111.

[49] *Gabriel v. Dresser* (1855) 15 C.B. 622.

[50] *Goring v. Goring* (1602) Yelv. 11; *Good v. Cheesman* (1831) 2 B. & Ad. 328; *Cartwright v. Cooke* (1832) 3 B. & Ad. 701; *Ford v. Beech* (1848) 11 Q.B. 852; *Crowther v. Farrer* (1850) 15 Q.B. 677; *Henderson v. Stobart* (1850) 5 Exch. 99; *Elton Crop Dyeing Co. Ltd v. Broadbent & Son Ltd* (1919) 89 L.J.K.B. 186; *Morris v. Baron & Co.* [1918] A.C. 1, 35.

[51] *British Russian Gazette and Trade Outlook Ltd v. Associated Newspapers Ltd* [1933] 2 K.B. 616, 643–645; *Jameson v. Central Electricity Generating Board* [1998] Q.B. 323, 335.

[52] *ibid.* at 645, 655; *Green v. Rozen* [1955] 1 W.L.R. 741.

[53] Smith, *Leading Cases* (13th ed.), p. 385.

the satisfaction is executed.[54] More often, however, the claimant will agree to accept the other party's promise of performance in satisfaction of his claim. The original claim is then discharged from the date of the agreement[55] and cannot be revived. The claimant's sole remedy, in the event that the other party fails to perform, is by action for breach of the substituted agreement, and he has no right of resort to the original claim.[56] If he wishes to preserve his right to proceed with the original claim should the other party fail to perform, an express term should be incorporated in the agreement to that effect.[57]

23–016   **Payment of part of a debt.** Where there is a claim for a liquidated sum, the liability for which is not in dispute,[58] the acceptance of a smaller sum in satisfaction does not relieve the debtor for there is no consideration for the creditor's abandonment of the balance.[59] This rule, which is generally known as the rule in *Pinnel's Case*,[60] is nevertheless subject to a number of qualifications' the combined effect of which is substantially to undermine the rule.

23–017   **Payment in different form, at earlier time, in different place.** A debt may be discharged by the acceptance of something different in nature from part payment of the debt, for then there is accord and satisfaction.[61] Even if the satisfaction accepted is much less in value than the debt, it will constitute a good discharge, since the courts will not inquire into the adequacy of consideration.[62] Also payment by a debtor at an earlier time or in a different place from that required by the original contract, if made at the request and for the benefit of the creditor,[63] will effect a discharge.[64]

23–018   **Exceptions.** Other important qualifications relate to part-payment by a third party,[65] compositions with creditors[66] and the *High Trees* principle.[67]

23–019   **Joint obligations.** The effect of accord and satisfaction on joint obligations has been dealt with in the chapter on Joint Obligations earlier in this book.[68]

---

[54] *British Russian Gazette and Trade Outlook Ltd v. Associated Newspapers Ltd, supra*, at 652. But see the statements of Greer L.J. at 655 (counterclaim).

[55] *ibid.* at 644; *Morris v. Baron & Co., supra*, at 35.

[56] *British Russian Gazette and Trade Outlook Ltd v. Associated Newspapers Ltd, supra*, at 644, 654. See also the cases cited in n. 50, *supra*, and *Green v. Rozen, supra*.

[57] For the effect of such a provision, see *Smith v. Shirley and Baylis* (1875) 32 L.T. 234.

[58] For the compromise of disputed claims, see *ante*, § 3–044.

[59] *Richard and Bartlet's Case* (1584) 1 Leon. 19; *Pinnel's Case* (1602) 5 Co.Rep. 117a; *Cumber v. Wane* (1721) 1 Str. 426; *Flitch v. Sutton* (1804) 5 East 230; *Down v. Hatcher* (1839) 10 A. & E. 121; *McManus v. Bark* (1870) L.R. 5 Ex. 65; *Foakes v. Beer* (1884) 9 App.Cas. 605; *Underwood v. Underwood* [1894] P. 204; *Hookham v. Mayle* (1906) 22 T.L.R. 241; *D. & C. Builders v. Rees* [1966] 2 Q.B. 617; *Tiney Engineering v. Amods Knitting Machinery* May 15, 1986 (C.A.T. No. 440); *Re Selectmove* [1995] 1 W.L.R. 474; *Ferguson v. Davies* [1997] 1 All E.R. 315, although Evans L.J. (at 326) expressed no view on this issue. See *ante*, § 3–107.

[60] (1602) 5 Co.Rep. 117a.

[61] See *ante*, § 3–114.

[62] See *ante*, § 3–013.

[63] *cf. Vanbergen v. St. Edmund's Properties Ltd* [1933] 2 K.B. 223.

[64] *Pinnel's Case, ante.*

[65] See *ante*, § 3–118.

[66] See *ante*, § 3–117.

[67] See *ante*, § 3–120.

[68] See *ante*, § 18–017.

Bill of exchange. No satisfaction is required for the discharge of a bill of **23–020**
exchange or promissory note.[69] The holder may renounce his rights in writing, or
by delivery up of the bill to the acceptor.[70]

Ineffective accord. An accord may be vitiated by any circumstance that **23–021**
would render a contract void or voidable, for example, by misrepresentation,[71]
mistake,[72] or duress.[73]

Evidence of accord. The question whether there has been an accord and **23–022**
satisfaction is a question of fact.[74] Thus, retention and use by a creditor of a
cheque sent by a debtor in full and final satisfaction of a larger claim does not,
as a matter of law, constitute an accord and satisfaction.[75] The intention of the
creditor in cashing the cheque must be objectively ascertained. Cashing a cheque
or retention of a cheque without rejection is strong evidence of assent by the
creditor but it is not conclusive evidence so that a creditor who, at the moment
of paying in the cheque, makes clear that he is not assenting to the conditions
imposed by the debtor will not be held to have entered into an accord and
satisfaction.[76] The construction of any correspondence which, it is alleged,
evidences the accord is, however, a question of law.[77]

Pleading. Both the accord and the satisfaction should be specifically **23–023**
pleaded.[78]

Judgment or order. A compromise may by consent be made the subject **23–024**
of a judgment or order of the court. A consent judgment will ordinarily extinguish by merger[79] the contract of compromise, but a consent order will not have
this effect. It does not itself constitute a contract, but it is sufficient evidence of
the contract of compromise on which it is based, and such contract is no less a
contract and subject to the incidents of a contract because there is superadded the
command of a judge.[80] Where an action has been commenced and a compromise
has been reached on agreed terms, the usual form of order sought by consent is

---

[69] See *ante*, § 23–009.
[70] Bills of Exchange Act 1882, ss.62, 89; see Vol. II, § 34–140.
[71] *e.g. Hirschfield v. L.B. & S.C. Ry.* (1876) 2 Q.B.D. 1; *Gilbert v. Endean* (1878) 9 Ch.D. 259; *Re Roberts* [1905] 1 Ch. 704; *Dietz v. Lennig Chemicals Ltd* [1969] 1 A.C. 170. *cf. Wales v. Wadham* [1977] 1 W.L.R. 199. See *ante*, Chap. 6.
[72] *e.g. Huddersfield Banking Co. Ltd v. Henry Lister & Son Ltd* [1895] 2 Ch. 273; *Magee v. Pennine Insurance Co. Ltd* [1969] 2 Q.B. 507. Contrast *Bell v. Lever Bros. Ltd* [1932] A.C. 161. See *ante*, Chap. 5.
[73] *e.g. D. & C. Builders v. Rees* [1966] 2 Q.B. 617. See *ante*, Chap. 7.
[74] *Stour Valley Builders v. Stuart, The Independent*, February 9, 1993, CA; *cf. Pereira v. Inspirations East Ltd* (1992) C.A.T. 1048, discussed in more detail by Foskett, *The Law and Practice of Compromise* (4th ed., 1996), pp. 28–29.
[75] *Day v. McLea* (1889) 22 Q.B. 610; *Auriena Ltd v. Haigh and Ringrose Ltd* (1988) Const. L.J. 200; *Stour Valley Builders v. Stuart*, supra; *Ferguson v. Davies* [1997] 1 All E.R. 315; *cf. Hirachand Punamchand v. Temple* [1911] 2 K.B. 330.
[76] *Stour Valley Builders v. Stuart*, supra; *Budget Rent-A-Car Ltd v. Goodman* [1991] 2 N.Z.L.R. 715.
[77] *Bunge SA v. Kruse* [1977] 1 Lloyd's Rep. 492; *Kitchen Design and Advice Ltd v. Lea Valley Water Co.* [1989] 2 Lloyd's Rep. 221; *Ferguson v. Davies* [1997] 1 All E.R. 315.
[78] *Flockton v. Hall* (1849) 14 Q.B. 380, 386. Although the CPR do not expressly require the defence to be specifically pleaded, it is advisable to continue to plead it specifically. The new rules relating to the contents of the defence are set out in CPR Part 16.5.
[79] See *post*, § 26–007.
[80] *Wentworth v. Bullen* (1829) 9 B. & C. 840, 850; *Lievesley v. Gilmore* (1866) L.R. 1 C.P. 570.

a *Tomlin* order,[81] which provides that all further proceedings in the action be stayed, except for the purpose of carrying such terms into effect, with liberty to apply[82] as to carrying such terms into effect. The court will, if necessary, in appropriate cases enforce the terms of a compromise contained in a *Tomlin* order by specific performance.[83]

4. RESCISSION

23-025   **Rescission by agreement.**   Where a contract is executory on both sides, that is to say, where neither party has performed the whole of his obligations under it, it may be rescinded by mutual agreement, express or implied.[84] A partially executed contract can be rescinded by agreement provided that there are obligations on both sides which remain unperformed. Similarly, a contract which has been fully performed by one party can be rescinded provided that the other party returns the performance which he has received and in turn is released from his own obligation to perform under the contract. The consideration for the discharge in each case is found in the abandonment by each party of his right to performance or his right to damages, as the case may be.[85] A rescission of this nature must be distinguished from a repudiation by one party, which the other party may elect to treat as a discharge of the obligation,[86] and from the right to rescind which is given to one party in cases of fraud, misrepresentation, duress and undue influence, and in certain cases of mistake.[87] It depends upon the consent of both parties, to be gathered from their words or conduct and not upon the intimation by one of them that he does not intend to be bound by the agreement.

23-026   **Effect of rescission.**   A contract which is rescinded by agreement is completely discharged and cannot be revived.[88] The parties will usually make express provision for the restoration of money paid or for payment for services performed under the contract prior to rescission. But in the absence of such provision (express or implied) money paid in pursuance of the abortive contract can be recovered by an action for money had and received,[89] although it is more doubtful whether a claim could be made for payment not yet due in respect of services rendered.[90]

---

[81] *Practice Note* [1927] W.N. 290. See *Chitty and Jacob's Queen's Bench Forms* (21st ed.), §§ 1339, 1350. *cf. McCallum v. Country Residences Ltd* [1965] 1 W.L.R. 657 (no consent).

[82] *Cristel v. Cristel* [1951] 2 K.B. 725.

[83] *Anders Ukhlens Rederi A/S v. O/Y Lovisa Stevedoring Co. A/B* [1985] 2 All E.R. 669.

[84] *Davis v. Street* (1823) 1 C. & P. 18; *Foster v. Dawber* (1851) 6 Exch. 839, 851; *Morris v. Baron & Co.* [1918] A.C. 1; *Rose & Frank Co. v. J.R. Crompton & Bros. Ltd* [1925] A.C. 445.

[85] *Scarf v. Jardine* (1882) 7 App.Cas. 345, 351; *Raggow v. Scougall & Co.* (1915) 31 T.L.R. 564.

[86] See *post,* § 25-046.

[87] See *ante,* Chaps. 5, 6 and 7.

[88] *R. v. Inhabitants of Gresham* (1786) 1 Term Rep. 101; *André et Cie SA v. Marine Transocean Ltd* [1981] Q.B. 694.

[89] *Towers v. Barratt* (1786) 1 Term Rep. 133; *Davis v. Street, supra. cf. Weston v. Downes* (1778) 1 Doug. K.B. 23; *Gompertz v. Denton* (1832) 1 C. & M. 207. See *post,* § 30-048.

[90] *Lamburn v. Cruden* (1841) 2 Man. & G. 253. *cf.* Goff and Jones, *The Law of Restitution* (5th ed.), pp. 530-534.

Abandonment. It is open to the court to infer that the parties have   **23–027**
mutually agreed to abandon their contract where the contract has been followed
by a long period of delay or inactivity on both sides.[91] The party seeking to
establish abandonment of a contract must show that the other party so conducted
himself as to entitle him to assume, and that he did assume, that the contract was
agreed to be abandoned *sub silentio*.[92]

Substituted contract. A rescission of the contract will also be implied   **23–028**
where the parties have effected such an alteration of its terms as to substitute a
new contract in its place.[93] The question whether a rescission has been effected
is frequently one of considerable difficulty, for it is necessary to distinguish a
rescission of the contract from a variation which merely qualifies the existing
rights and obligations.[94] If a rescission is effected the contract is extinguished; if
only a variation, it continues to exist in an altered form. The decision on this
point will depend on the intention of the parties to be gathered from an examination of the terms of the subsequent agreement and from all the surrounding
circumstances.[95] Rescission will be presumed when the parties enter into a new
agreement which is entirely inconsistent with the old, or, if not entirely inconsistent with it, inconsistent with it to an extent that goes to the very root of it.[96]
The change must be fundamental[97] and "the question is whether the common
intention of the parties was to 'abrogate,' 'rescind,' 'supersede' or 'extinguish'
the old contract by a 'substitution' of a 'completely new' or 'self-subsisting'
agreement."[98]

In *Morris v. Baron & Co.*[99] a written contract was entered into for the sale of   **23–029**
some cloth. A dispute arose and legal proceedings were begun. The parties orally
agreed that the action and counterclaim should be withdrawn, that an extension
should be given to the buyer for payment of a sum owed by him under the
contract and that he should have an option to purchase the goods remaining due
to him instead of being bound to take delivery. The House of Lords held that the

---

[91] *André & Cie SA v. Marine Transocean Ltd (The Splendid Sun)* [1981] Q.B. 64; *Tracomin SA v. Anton C. Nielsen A/S* [1984] 2 Lloyd's Rep. 195; *Excomm Ltd v. Guan Guan Shipping (Pte.) Ltd* [1987] 1 Lloyd's Rep. 330 (*ante*, §§ 2–064, 2–070). See also *Tyers v. Rosedale and Ferryhill Iron Co.* (1875) L.R. 10 Ex. 195.

[92] *Paal Wilson & Co A/S v. Partenreederei Hannah Blumenthal* [1983] 1 A.C. 854, 924; *Allied Marine Transport Ltd v. Vale do Rio Doce Navegacao SA (The Leonidas D.)* [1985] 1 W.L.R. 925 (interpreting *Pearle Mill Co. v. Ivy Tannery Co. Ltd* [1919] 1 K.B. 78); *Collin v. Duke of Westminster* [1985] Q.B. 581; *MSC Mediterranean Shipping Co. SA v. B.R.E. Metro-Ltd* [1985] 2 Lloyd's Rep. 239; *Cie. Française d'Importation et Distribution v. Deutsche Continental Handelsgesellschaft* [1985] 2 Lloyd's Rep. 592; *Gebr. van Weelde Scheepvaartkantor B.V. v. Compania Naviera Sea Orient SA* [1987] 2 Lloyd's Rep. 223; *Food Corpn. of India v. Antclizo Shipping Corpn.* [1988] 1 W.L.R. 603; *Tankrederei Ahrenkeil GmbH v. Frahuil SA* [1988] 2 Lloyd's Rep. 486; *Thai-Europe Tapioca Service Ltd v. Seine Navigation Co. Inc.* [1989] 2 Lloyd's Rep. 506.

[93] *Thornhill v. Neats* (1860) 8 C.B.(N.S.) 831; *Hunt v. S.E. Ry.* (1875) 45 L.J.Q.B. 87; *Williams Bros. v. Agius Ltd* [1914] A.C. 510, 527; *Raggow v. Scougall & Co.* (1915) 31 T.L.R. 564; *Morris v. Baron & Co.* [1918] A.C. 1; *British & Beningtons Ltd v. N.W. Cachar Tea Co. Ltd* [1923] A.C. 48, 69; *Rose & Frank Co. v. J.R. Crompton & Bros. Ltd* [1925] A.C. 445.

[94] *British & Beningtons Ltd v. N.W. Cachar Tea Co. Ltd, supra*; *Royal Exchange Assurance v. Hope* [1928] Ch. 179; and see the cases cited in § 23–033, n. 21, *post*.

[95] *United Dominions Trust (Jamaica) Ltd v. Shoucair* [1969] 1 A.C. 340.

[96] *British & Beningtons Ltd v. N.W. Cachar Tea Co. Ltd, supra*, at 62.

[97] *ibid.*

[98] *ibid.* at 67.

[99] [1918] A.C. 1.

original contract of sale was discharged by the substituted agreement. Lord Dunedin commented:

> "The difference between variation and rescission is a real one, and is tested, to my thinking, by this: In the first case there are no such executory clauses in the second arrangement as would enable you to sue upon that alone if the first did not exist; in the second you could sue on the second arrangement alone, and the first contract is got rid of either by express words to that effect, or because, the second dealing with the same subject-matter as the first but in a different way, it is impossible that the two should be both performed."[1]

In order to extinguish the original contract, it is not necessary that the substituted agreement should have been performed; an executory contract is sufficient.[2] Nor is it necessary that it should amount to an enforceable agreement.[3]

23–030   **Form of rescission.** The old rule of the common law was that a contract under seal could only be rescinded by a contract under seal,[4] but in equity a rescission not under seal provided a good defence to an action on the deed. Since the Judicature Act 1873, the equitable rule prevails, so that now a deed can be rescinded by a written or oral agreement.[5] Even if the original contract is one which is required by law to be made in writing, as in the case of a contract for the sale or other disposition of an interest in land,[6] or to be evidenced by writing as in the case of those contracts within the Statute of Frauds 1677,[7] an oral agreement is sufficient to effect its discharge.[8] Nevertheless, the new agreement may itself be unenforceable unless so evidenced. Thus in *Morris v. Baron & Co.*[9] the original contract for the sale of cloth was one which was then required by section 4 of the Sale of Goods Act 1893[10] to be evidenced in writing. The subsequent oral agreement was sufficient to discharge the original contract, but was itself unenforceable for want of writing. In the result, no action could be maintained on the original contract since this had been extinguished, nor on the subsequent agreement since this was unenforceable.[11]

23–031   **Novation.** Novation is a generic term which signifies "that there being a contract in existence, some new contract is substituted for it, either between the same parties (for that might be) or between different parties; the consideration mutually being the discharge of the old contract."[12] In particular, however, it

---

[1] At 25–26.

[2] *Taylor v. Hilary* (1835) 1 Cr.M. & R. 741.

[3] *Morris v. Baron & Co.* [1918] A.C. 1; *Rose & Frank Co. v. J.R. Crompton & Bros. Ltd* [1925] A.C. 445. *cf. Firth v. Midland Ry.* (1875) L.R. 20 Eq. 100. See *post*, § 23–030.

[4] *Kaye v. Waghorn* (1809) 1 Taunt. 428; *West v. Blakeway* (1841) 2 M. & G. 729.

[5] *Berry v. Berry* [1929] 2 K.B. 316; Supreme Court Act 1981, s.49.

[6] Law of Property (Miscellaneous Provisions) Act 1989, s.2(1). See *ante*, § 4–004.

[7] ss.4 and 17, as amended by the Law Reform (Enforcement of Contracts) Act 1954. See *ante*, § 4–004.

[8] s.2(1) of the Law of Property (Miscellaneous Provisions) Act 1989 requires that a contract falling within its scope be "*made* in writing" but does not regulate the discharge or unmaking of such a contract.

[9] [1918] A.C. 1.

[10] Re-enacting s.17 of the Statute of Frauds 1677; repealed by the Law Reform (Enforcement of Contracts) Act 1954. See *ante*, § 4–004.

[11] See also *Williams v. Moss Empires* [1915] 3 K.B. 242; *United Dominions Trust (Jamaica) Ltd v. Shoucair* [1969] 1 A.C. 340.

[12] *Scarf v. Jardine* (1882) 7 App.Cas. 345, 351.

denotes the rescission of one contract and the substitution of another in which the same acts are to be performed by different parties.[13] A novation cannot be forced on a new party without his agreement. So, for example, if there is a contract for the sale and purchase of a ship under which it is agreed that the actual purchaser of the ship will be a company to be nominated by and substituted for the buyer by novation, such substitution must be accepted by the company, either by authorising the nomination or by ratifying it after it has been made.[14]

5. VARIATION[15]

Variation. The parties to a contract may effect a variation of the contract **23–032** by modifying or altering its terms by mutual agreement.[16] In *Berry v. Berry*[17] a husband and wife entered into a separation deed whereby the husband covenanted to pay to the wife a certain sum each year for her support. His earnings proved insufficient to meet this obligation, so they agreed in writing to vary the financial provisions. It was held that this variation was valid and enforceable, and that it could be set up by the husband as a defence to an action against him on the original deed. A mere unilateral notification by one party to the other, in the absence of any agreement, cannot constitute a variation of a contract.[18]

Form of variation. As in the case of a rescission of a contract, the terms **23–033** of a deed or written instrument may be varied by a subsequent agreement, whether oral or written.[19] This may be reconciled with the rule that extrinsic evidence is not admissible to vary or qualify the terms of a written instrument, for that rule only relates to the ascertainment of the original intention of the parties, and not to a subsequent variation.[20] A contract required by law to be made in or evidenced by writing can only be varied by writing,[21] although, as we have seen, it can be rescinded by parol.[22] In *Goss v. Lord Nugent*[23] the plaintiff

---

[13] Partnership Act 1890, s.7(3); *Miller's Case* (1877) 3 Ch.D. 391; *Scarf v. Jardine, supra; Re Head* [1894] 2 Ch. 236; *Re United Railways of Havana and Regla Warehouses Ltd* [1960] Ch. 52, 84; *Chatsworth Investments Ltd v. Cussins (Contractors) Ltd* [1969] 1 W.L.R. 1. *cf. Liversidge v. Broadbent* (1859) 4 H. & N. 603; *Conquest's Case* (1875) 1 Ch.D. 334. see *ante*, §§ 20–084—20–086.

[14] *Damon Compania Naviera SA v. Hapag-Lloyd International SA* [1985] 1 W.L.R. 435; *cf. Aktion Maritime Corpn. of Liberia v. S. Kasmas & Bros. Ltd* [1987] 1 Lloyd's Rep. 283, 311.

[15] See generally Wilken and Villiers, *Waiver, Variation and Estoppel* (1998), Chap. 2.

[16] *Robinson v. Page* (1826) 3 Russ. 114; *Goss v. Lord Nugent* (1833) 5 B. & Ad. 58, 65; *Stead v. Dawber* (1839) 10 A. & E. 57, 65; *Dodd v. Churton* [1897] 1 Q.B. 562; *Fenner v. Blake* [1900] 1 Q.B. 426; *Royal Exchange Assurance v. Hope* [1928] Ch. 179. See Dugdale and Yates (1976) 39 M.L.R. 680.

[17] [1929] 2 K.B. 316.

[18] *Cowey v. Liberian Operations Ltd* [1966] 2 Lloyd's Rep. 45.

[19] *Berry v. Berry, supra.* Statute may, of course, intervene to prescribe a particular form of variation (see, for example, s.82 of the Consumer Credit Act 1974 concerning an agreement to vary or supplement a consumer credit or consumer hire agreement: *post*, Vol. II, § 38–126).

[20] *Goss v. Lord Nugent, supra,* at 64; see *supra,* §§ 12–093 *et seq.*.

[21] *Robinson v. Page, supra; Stead v. Dawber, supra; Marshall v. Lynn* (1840) 6 M. & W. 109; *Noble v. Ward* (1867) L.R. 2 Ex. 135; *Sanderson v. Graves* (1875) L.R. 10 Ex. 234; *Plevins v. Downing* (1876) 1 C.P.D. 220; *British and Beningtons Ltd v. N.W. Cachar Tea Co. Ltd* [1923] A.C. 48; *United Dominions Trust (Jamaica) Ltd v. Shoucair* [1969] 1 A.C. 340; *Richards v. Creighton-Griffiths (Investments) Ltd* (1972) 225 E.G. 2104; *New Hart Builders Ltd v. Brindley* [1975] Ch. 342; *McCausland v. Duncan Lawrie Ltd* [1997] 1 W.L.R. 38.

[22] See *ante*, § 23–030.

[23] (1833) 5 B. & Ad. 58.

agreed in writing to sell to the defendant certain plots of land. In an action by the plaintiff against the defendant for the purchase-money, the defendant pleaded that the title to one of the plots was defective. To this plea the plaintiff replied that the defendant had orally agreed to waive the defect and to accept the existing title. The court held that, since the contract was one which was required by law to be evidenced by writing,[24] the oral variation was not admissible and the defendant was entitled to succeed on the ground that a good title had not been made.

Where the formal requirements apply to a variation but not to a rescission it is obviously important to determine whether there has been a mere variation of terms or a rescission, and this question may not be an easy one to answer. The effect of a subsequent agreement—whether it constitutes a variation or a rescission—will depend upon the extent to which it alters the terms of the original contract. The test suggested by Lord Dunedin in *Morris v. Baron & Co.*[25] has already been referred to,[26] and in the same case Lord Haldane[27] said that, for a rescission, "there should have been made manifest the intention in any event of a complete extinction of the first and formal contract, and not merely the desire of an alteration, however sweeping, in terms which leave it still subsisting." If the changes do not go "to the very root of the contract"[28] there is merely a variation.

23-034   **Consideration.** The agreement which varies the terms of an existing contract must be supported by consideration. In many cases, consideration can be found in the mutual abandonment of existing rights or the conferment of new benefits by each party on the other.[29] For example, an alteration of the money of account in a contract proposed or made by one party and accepted by the other is binding on both parties, since either may benefit from the variation.[30] Alternatively, consideration may be found in the assumption of additional obligations or the incurring of liability to an increased detriment.[31] The position is more difficult in the case of an agreement whereby one party undertakes an additional obligation, but the other party is merely bound to perform his existing obligations, or an agreement whereby one party undertakes an additional obligation, but for the benefit of that party alone. There is a line of authority of respectable antiquity which supports the view that in such a case the agreement will not be effective to vary the contract because no consideration is present.[32] But a more liberal approach has been adopted in some recent cases and the courts have been prepared to find consideration and enforce the agreement where it has conferred a practical benefit upon the promisor.[33] A mere forbearance or concession afforded by one party to the other for the latter's convenience and at his request

---

[24] Statute of Frauds 1677, s.4, re-enacted as s.40(1) of the Law of Property Act 1925, but subsequently repealed by s.2(8) of the Law of Property (Miscellaneous Provisions) Act 1989.

[25] [1918] A.C. 1, 5.

[26] See *ante*, § 23–029.

[27] [1918] A.C. 1, 19.

[28] *British and Beningtons Ltd v. N.W. Cachar Tea Co. Ltd* [1923] A.C. 48, 62, 68.

[29] *Re William Porter & Co. Ltd* [1937] 2 All E.R. 361.

[30] *Woodhouse A.C. Israel Cocoa Ltd SA v. Nigerian Produce Marketing Co.* [1972] A.C. 741, 757; *W.J. Alan & Co. Ltd v. El Nasr Export and Import Co.* [1972] 2 Q.B. 189.

[31] *North Ocean Shipping Co. Ltd v. Hyundai Construction Co. Ltd* [1979] Q.B. 705.

[32] *Stilk v. Myrick* (1809) 2 Camp. 317; *Vanbergen v. St. Edmund's Properties Ltd* [1933] 2 K.B. 233; *Syros Shipping Co. SA v. Elaghill Trading Co.* [1980] 2 Lloyd's Rep. 390; see *ante*, § 3–074—3–075. See also *ante*, §§ 3–107, 23–016—23–018 (payment of part of debt).

[33] *Williams v. Roffey Bros. & Nicholls (Contractors) Ltd* [1991] 1 Q.B. 1; *Anangel Atlas Compania Naviera SA v. Ishikawajima-Harima Heavy Industries Co. Ltd (No. 2)* [1990] 2 Lloyd's Rep. 526.

does not constitute a variation, although it may be effective as a waiver or in equity.[34] Such a forbearance or concession need not be supported by consideration, and can be made orally even when the contract is one which is required to be made or evidenced in writing.[35]

Variation and collateral agreement. A variation of an existing agreement   **23–035**
should be distinguished from a collateral agreement (or collateral warranty)[36] concluded before the main agreement is entered into under which one party agrees not to enforce a term of the main agreement[37] or assumes obligations in addition to or at variance with those contained in the main agreement.[38] Such an agreement may not require to be evidenced by writing even though the main agreement requires to be made or evidenced in writing.[39] There seems to be no reason why such a collateral agreement should not be held to exist even if entered into after the conclusion of the main agreement, provided that there is present (and not merely past) consideration.[40]

Variation and elucidation. A variation should also be distinguished from   **23–036**
the elucidation of a contract by the filling in of details which were agreed before the written contract was signed[41] or by the correction of mistakes which occurred when the contract was reduced to writing.[42]

Effect of extra works. Where, in a contract for the execution of specified   **23–037**
works, it is provided that they shall be completed by a certain day, and that liquidated damages shall be payable by the contractor for non-completion to time, the general rule is that the employer will be unable to recover such liquidated damages if he orders extra work to be done which necessarily delays completion of the works.[43] However, the wording of the contract may be such that the original contract period continues to apply to the completion of the works even though additional work is ordered.[44] Alternatively, the contract may provide that the agreed date for completion shall be extended in the event that delay is caused by the additional work, in which case liquidated damages will be payable from that extended date if the works are not then completed.

---

[34] See *ante*, § 3–080; *post*, § 23–039.
[35] See *post*, § 23–040.
[36] See *ante*, § 12–053.
[37] *City and Westminster Properties (1934) Ltd v. Mudd* [1959] Ch. 129.
[38] *Erskine v. Adeane* (1873) 8 Ch.App. 756; *De Lassalle v. Guildford* [1901] 2 K.B. 215; *Brikom Investments Ltd v. Carr* [1979] Q.B. 467; *Record v. Bell* [1991] 1 W.L.R. 853; see *ante*, §§ 3–074, 12–101, 19–005.
[39] *ibid.*
[40] See *ante*, § 3–074.
[41] *Hudson v. Revett* (1829) 5 Bing. 368; *Rudd v. Bowles* [1912] 2 Ch. 60.
[42] *Bluck v. Gompertz* (1852) 7 Exch. 362; see *ante*, § 5–065.
[43] *Holme v. Guppy* (1838) 3 M. & W. 387; *Russell v. Sada Bandeira* (1862) 13 C.B.(N.S.) 149; *Dodd v. Churton* [1897] 1 Q.B. 562; *Trollope & Colls Ltd v. North West Metropolitan Regional Hospital Board* [1973] 1 W.L.R. 601, 607; *Astilleros Canarios SA v. Cape Hatteras Shipping Co. Inc.* [1982] 1 Lloyd's Rep. 518. See generally *Keating on Building Contracts* (6th ed., 1995), pp. 250–251 and also *Perini Pacific Ltd v. Greater Vancouver Sewerage and Drainage District* (1966) 57 D.L.R. (2d) 307.
[44] *Macintosh v. Midland Counties Ry.* (1845) 14 M. & W. 548; *Legge v. Horlock* (1848) 12 Q.B. 1015; *Jones v. St. John's College, Oxford* (1870) L.R. 6 Q.B. 115; *Tew v. Newbold-on-Avon United District School Board* (1884) 1 Cab. & E. 260.

23–038   **Unilateral power of variation.**   At common law a contract may validly give to one contracting party the power unilaterally to vary the obligations of the parties to the contract. So, for example, in the case of a contract for the sale of goods, it is "a perfectly good contract to say that the price is to be settled by the buyer."[45] The same principle has been applied to consumer credit contracts where the lender is given the power unilaterally and in its absolute discretion to vary the rate of interest subject to notice to the debtor.[46] But where such a provision is contained in a contract concluded between a seller or supplier and a consumer and that contract has not been individually negotiated, it may also fall within the scope of the Unfair Terms in Consumer Contracts Regulations 1994.[47] Thus a contract term which enables the seller or supplier to alter the terms of the contract unilaterally without a valid reason which is specified in the contract,[48] or enables the seller or supplier to alter unilaterally without a valid reason any characteristics of the product or service to be provided,[49] or which provides for the price of the goods to be determined at the time of delivery, or allows a seller of goods or supplier of services to increase their price without in both cases giving the consumer the corresponding right to cancel the contract if the final price is too high in relation to the price agreed when the contract was concluded,[50] may constitute an unfair term which will not be binding upon the consumer.

6. Waiver[51]

23–039   **Waiver or forbearance.**   Where one party voluntarily accedes to a request by the other that he should forbear to insist on the mode of performance fixed by the contract, the court may hold that he has *waived* his right to require that the contract be performed in this respect according to its original tenor.[52] Waiver (in the sense of "waiver by estoppel" rather than "waiver by election"[53]) may also be held to have occurred if, without any request, one party represents to the other that he will forbear to enforce or rely on a term of the contract to be performed or observed by the other party, and the other party acts in reliance on that representation.[54]

---

[45] *May and Butcher v. R.* [1934] 2 K.B. 17, 21.

[46] *Lombard Tricity Finance Ltd v. Paton* [1989] 1 All E.R. 916.

[47] S.I. 1994 No. 3159. See further *ante*, Chap. 15, where the scope of the Regulations and the definition of terms such as "seller or supplier," etc., is discussed in more detail.

[48] See Schedule 3 to the Regulations, para. 1(j), (set out at § 15–061) although note the restricted applicability of this provision to the supply of financial services (para. 2(b)).

[49] See Sched. 3 to the Regulations, para. 1(k).

[50] See Sched. 3 to the Regulations, para. 1(l), although note the restricted applicability of this provision to financial services (para. 2(c)) and that it does not apply to "price-indexation clauses, where lawful, provided that the method by which prices vary is explicitly described" (para. 2(d)).

[51] See generally Wilken and Villiers, *Waiver, Variation and Estoppel* (1998), Chaps. 3–5.

[52] See *ante*, § 3–076.

[53] The distinction between these two types of waiver is discussed, *post* § 25–006. See also *Motor Oil Hellas (Corinth) Refineries SA v. Shipping Corpn. of India* [1990] 1 Lloyd's Rep. 391, 397–399.

[54] See *ante*, 3–076, 3–080.

Form of waiver. A waiver may be oral or written or inferred from **23–040**
conduct[55] even though the provision waived is found in a contract required to be
made in or evidenced by writing. It has been noted that any variation of a contract
required to be made in or evidenced by writing must itself be made in or
evidenced by writing.[56] If it is merely oral, it is of no effect. An oral forbearance
or concession made by one party to the other does not require to be so evidenced,
even if made at the latter's request. Thus, what is ineffective as a variation may
possibly have effect as a waiver. The formal requirements, in relation to such a
contract, of rescission, variation and waiver were thus described by Goddard J.
in *Besseler Waechter Glover & Co. v. South Derwent Coal Co.*[57]:

> "If the parties agree to rescind their original contract and to substitute for it a new one,
> the latter must be evidenced by writing; so, too, if as a matter of contract the parties
> agree that the terms of the original agreement shall be varied, the variation must be in
> writing. But if what happens is a mere voluntary forbearance to insist on delivery or
> acceptance according to the strict terms of the written contract, the original contract
> remains unaffected, and the obligation to deliver and accept the full contract quantity
> still continues. . . . It does not appear to me to matter whether the request comes from
> one side or the other, or whether it is a matter which is convenient to one party or to
> both. What is of importance is whether it is a mere forbearance or a matter of
> contract."

The distinction between variation and waiver is, however, a difficult one to
apply in practice,[58] particularly since a waiver may be consensual and be just as
far reaching in its effect as a variation of the agreement. Fortunately, in respect
of formal requirements,[59] it has become much less important since the almost
total repeal of the Statute of Frauds by the Law Reform (Enforcement of
Contracts) Act 1954.[60]

Effect on party forbearing. The party who forbears will be bound by the **23–041**
waiver and cannot set up the original terms of the agreement. If, by words or
conduct, he has agreed or led the other party to believe that he will accept
performance at a later date than or in a different manner from that provided in the
contract, he will not be able to refuse that performance when tendered.[61] However, in cases of postponement of performance, if the period of postponement is
specified in the waiver, then, if time was originally of the essence, it will remain

---

[55] *Bruner v. Moore* [1904] 1 Ch. 305; *Bremer Handelsgesellschaft mbH v. Vanden Avenne-Izegem P.V.B.A.* [1978] 2 Lloyd's Rep. 109.

[56] See *ante*, § 23–033.

[57] [1938] 1 K.B. 408, 416, 417.

[58] See *Besseler Waechter Glover & Co. v. South Derwent Coal Co.* [1938] 1 K.B. 408; *Watson v. Healy Lands* [1965] N.Z.L.R. 511; Dugdale and Yates (1976) 39 M.L.R. 680.

[59] *cf. ante*, § 3–007.

[60] See *ante*, § 4–004.

[61] *Leather Cloth Co. v. Hieronimus* (1875) L.R. 10 Q.B. 140; *Bruner v. Moore* [1904] 1 Ch. 305; *Panoutsos v. Raymond Hadley Corpn. of New York* [1917] 2 K.B. 473; *Hartley v. Hymans* [1920] 2 K.B. 475; *Besseler Waechter Glover & Co. v. South Derwent Coal Co.* [1938] 1 K.B. 408; *Tankexpress A/S v. Compagnie Financière Belge des Petroles SA* [1949] A.C. 76; *Plasticmoda Societa per Azioni v. Davidsons (Manchester) Ltd* [1952] 1 Lloyd's Rep. 527; *Enrico Furst & Co. v. W.E. Fischer* [1960] 2 Lloyd's Rep. 340; *W.J. Alan & Co. Ltd v. El Nasr Export and Import Co.* [1972] 2 Q.B. 189, 213.

so in respect of the new date.[62] If the period of postponement is not specified in the waiver, the party forbearing is entitled, upon reasonable notice, to impose a new time-limit, which may then become of the essence of the contract.[63] Similarly, in other cases of forbearance, he may be entitled, upon reasonable notice, to require the other party to comply with the original mode of performance,[64] unless in the meantime circumstances have so changed as to render it impossible[65] or inequitable[66] so to do. He cannot treat the waiver as entirely without effect. If a seller of goods withholds delivery of the goods at the purchaser's request (*i.e.* if the seller waives the obligation of the purchaser to accept the goods within a certain time), he will still be under a duty to deliver within a reasonable time if so requested by the purchaser.[67]

23-042   **Effect on party to whom forbearance is extended.** Where one party has induced the other party to accede to his request, the party seeking the forbearance will not be permitted to repudiate the waiver and to rely on the letter of the agreement.[68] Thus in *Levey & Co. v. Goldberg*[69] the defendant agreed in writing to buy from the plaintiffs certain pieces of cloth over the value of £10[70] to be delivered within a certain period. At the oral request of the defendant, the plaintiffs voluntarily withheld delivery during that period. The defendant subsequently refused to accept delivery, and, when sued, contended that the plaintiffs themselves were in breach, as the oral agreement was insufficient to vary the terms of a contract which was required by law to be evidenced by writing. It was held that the forbearance by the plaintiffs at the request of the defendant did not constitute a variation but a waiver, and the plaintiffs were entitled to maintain their action.

23-043   **Consideration for waiver.** A waiver is also distinguishable from a variation of a contract in that there is no consideration for the forbearance moving from the party to whom it is given.[71] It may therefore be more satisfactory to regard this form of waiver, that is "waiver by estoppel", as analogous to, or even identical with, equitable forbearance or "promissory" estoppel.[72] Although consideration need not be proved, certain other requirements must be satisfied for such an estoppel to be effective: first, it must be clear and unequivocal; secondly,

---

[62] *Luck v. White* (1973) 26 P. & C.R. 89; *Buckland v. Farmar & Moody* [1979] 1 W.L.R. 221; *Nichimen Corpn. v. Gatoil Overseas Inc.* [1987] 2 Lloyd's Rep. 46.

[63] *Hartley v. Hymans, supra*; *Charles Rickards Ltd v. Oppenhaim* [1950] 1 K.B. 616; *Jacobson van der Berg & Co. (U.K.) Ltd v. Biba Ltd* (1977) 121 S.J. 333; *State Trading Corpn. of India Ltd v. Compagnie Française d'Importation et de Distribution* [1983] 2 Lloyd's Rep. 679. See also *Ficom SA v. Sociedad Cadex Ltda.* [1980] 2 Lloyd's Rep. 118, 131.

[64] *Panoutsos v. Raymond Hadley Corpn. of New York* [1917] 2 K.B. 473.

[65] *Leather Cloth Co. v. Hieronimus, supra.*

[66] *Toepfer v. Warinco A.G.* [1978] 2 Lloyd's Rep. 569, 576. See also *ante*, § 3–078.

[67] *Tyers v. Rosedale Ferryhill Iron Co.* (1875) L.R. 10 Ex. 195.

[68] *Ogle v. Earl Vane* (1868) L.R. 3 Q.B. 272; *Hickman v. Haynes* (1875) L.R. 10 C.P. 598.

[69] [1922] 1 K.B. 688.

[70] s.17 of the Statute of Frauds 1677 (re-enacted as s.4 of the Sale of Goods Act 1893) required such a contract to be evidenced by writing. Both provisions have now been repealed by the Law Reform (Enforcement of Contracts) Act 1954.

[71] *W.J. Alan & Co. Ltd v. El Nasr Export and Import Co.* [1972] 2 Q.B. 189, 193. See also *ante*, § 3–076.

[72] See *ante*, § 3–080.

the other party must have altered his position in reliance on it, or at least acted on it.[73]

Waiver of condition for benefit of one party. Where the terms of a   **23–044**
contract include a provision which has been inserted solely for the benefit of one
party, he may, without the assent of the other party, waive compliance with that
provision and enforce the contract as if the provision had been omitted.[74] He will
not be permitted to do so where the provision has been inserted for the benefit of
both parties[75] or where there is in reality no concluded agreement.[76]

Waiver of breach. One party may waive his right to terminate a contract   **23–045**
consequent upon a repudiation of the contract by the other party.[77] It is, however,
important to distinguish between the case in which a party waives his right to
treat the contract as repudiated but does not abandon his right to claim damages
for the loss suffered as a result of the breach[78] and the case where the innocent
party waives not only his right to terminate performance of the contract but also
his claim for damages for the breach.[79] The former is an example of waiver by
election,[80] whereas the latter is more properly classified as a species of waiver by
estoppel.[81]

---

[73] *Woodhouse A.C. Israel Cocoa Ltd SA v. Nigerian Produce Marketing Co. Ltd* [1972] A.C. 741,
755, 758, 761, 762, 767–768, 781; *W.J. Alan & Co. Ltd v. El Nasr Export & Import Ltd* [1972] 2 Q.B.
189, 212–214, 215, 217; *Finagrain SA v. P. Kruse* [1976] 2 Lloyd's Rep. 508, 534–535, 540, 546;
Bremer Handelsgesellschaft mbH v. Vanden Avenne-Izegem P.V.B.A. [1978] 2 Lloyd's Rep. 109, 127;
Bunge SA v. Schleswig-Holsteinische Landwirtschaftliche Hauptgenossenschaft Eingetr GmbH
[1978] 1 Lloyd's Rep. 480, 490; *Bremer Handelsgesellschaft mbH v. C. Mackprang* [1979] 1 Lloyd's
Rep. 220, 225–226, 228, 230; *Avimex SA v. Dewulf & Cie* [1979] 2 Lloyd's Rep. 57, 67–68; *Bremer
Handelsgesellschaft mbH v. Westzucker* [1981] 1 Lloyd's Rep. 207, 213; *Cremer v. Granaria B.V.*
[1981] 2 Lloyd's Rep. 583, 587; *Cerealmangimi SpA v. Toepfer* [1981] 3 All E.R. 533; *Cook
Industries Inc. v. Meunerie Liegeois SA* [1981] 1 Lloyd's Rep. 359, 368; *Société Italo-Belge pour le
Commerce et l'Industrie v. Palm and Vegetable Oils (Malaysia) Sdn. Bhd.* [1981] 2 Lloyd's Rep. 695,
700–702; *Bremer Handelsgesellschaft mbH v. Finagrain Compagnie Commerciale, etc. SA* [1981] 2
Lloyd's Rep. 259, 263, 266; *Bremer Handelsgesellschaft mbH v. Raiffeisen Hauptgenossenschaft E/G*
[1982] 1 Lloyd's Rep. 599; *Bremer Handelsgesellschaft mbH v. Deutsche Conti-Handelsgesellschaft
mbH* [1983] 2 Lloyd's Rep. 45; *Allied Marine Transport Ltd v. Vale do Rio Doce Navegacao SA*
[1985] 1 W.L.R. 925; *Motor Oil Hellas (Corinth) Refineries SA v. Shipping Corporation of India*
[1990] 1 Lloyd's Rep. 391. *cf. Scandinavian Trading Tanker Co. A.B. v. Flota Petrolera Ecuatoriana*
[1983] 2 Q.B. 529, [1983] 2 A.C. 694. See *ante*, §§ 3–081—3–090. See also *ante*, § 3–076; *post*,
§§ 25–006—25–008.
[74] *Bennett v. Fowler* (1840) 2 Beav. 302; *Hawksley v. Outram* [1892] 3 Ch. 359; *Morrell v. Studd
and Millington* [1913] 2 Ch. 648; *F.E. Napier v. Dexters Ltd* (1926) 26 Ll.L.R. 62, 63–64, 184,
187–188. See also *North v. Loomes* [1919] 1 Ch. 378 and Sale of Goods Act 1979, s.11(2). Once he
has waived the condition, either expressly or by conduct, he cannot then rely on it to deny his own
liability: *Barrett Bros. (Taxis) Ltd v. Davies* [1966] 1 W.L.R. 1334.
[75] *Lloyd v. Novell* [1895] 2 Ch. 744; *Burgess v. Cox* [1951] Ch. 383; *Heron Garage Properties Ltd
v. Moss* [1974] 1 W.L.R. 148; *Gregory v. Wallace* [1998] I.R.L.R. 387.
[76] *Allsopp v. Orchard* [1923] 1 Ch. 323.
[77] See *post*, § 25–006.
[78] *Motor Oil Hellas (Corinth) Refineries SA v. Shipping Corpn. of India* [1990] 1 Lloyd's Rep. 391,
397–398.
[79] This is sometimes known as "total waiver"; see Sale of Goods Act 1979, s.11(2); *Benjamin's
Sale of Goods* (5th ed., 1997), §§ 12–034—12–036; Treitel, *The Law of Contract* (9th ed., 1995),
p. 726 and *post*, §§ 25–008.
[80] See *post*, § 25–006.
[81] See *post*, § 25–006. There are important differences between the two types of waiver; see *post*,
§ 25–007 and Treitel, *The Law of Contract* (9th ed., 1995), pp. 725–729.

7. PROVISION FOR DISCHARGE IN THE CONTRACT ITSELF

23–046   **Express provision.** The parties may expressly provide in their contract that either or one of them is to have an option to terminate the contract. This right of termination may be exercisable upon a breach of contract by the other party (whether or not the breach would amount to a repudiation of the contract),[82] or upon the occurrence or non-occurrence of a specified event other than breach,[83] or simply at the will of the party upon whom the right is conferred. In principle, since the parties are free to incorporate whatever terms they wish for the termination of their agreement, no question arises at common law whether the provision is reasonable or whether it is reasonable for a party to enforce it,[84] unless the situation is one in which equity would grant relief against forfeiture.[85] However, certain statutes restrict the efficacy of such provisions,[86] and in certain circumstances a term of this nature would have to be shown to be fair and reasonable by virtue of the provisions of the Unfair Contract Terms Act 1977.[87] Where such a provision is contained in a contract concluded between a seller or supplier and a consumer and that contract has not been individually negotiated, it may also fall within the scope of the Unfair Terms in Consumer Contracts Regulations 1994.[88] Thus, a contract term which authorises a seller or supplier to dissolve a contract on a discretionary basis where the same facility is not granted to the consumer may constitute an unfair term which will not be binding upon the consumer.[89]

23–047   The fact that one party is contractually entitled to terminate the agreement in the event of a breach by the other party does not preclude that party from treating the agreement as discharged by reason of the other's repudiation or breach of condition,[90] unless the agreement itself expressly or impliedly provides that it can only be terminated by exercise of the contractual right. Whether the procedure laid down for termination in the contract excludes, expressly or impliedly, the common law right to terminate further performance of the contract in respect of a breach which falls within the scope of the clause is a question of construction

---

[82] See *post*, § 25–001.

[83] See *ante*, § 12–030 (conditions subsequent) and § 14–126 (*force majeure* clauses).

[84] *Financings Ltd v. Baldock* [1963] 2 Q.B. 104, 115; *China National Foreign Trade Transportation Corpn. v. Evlogia Shipping Co. SA* [1979] 1 W.L.R. 1018.

[85] See, *e.g. Stockloser v. Johnson* [1954] 1 Q.B. 476; *Barton Thompson & Co. Ltd v. Stapling Machines Co.* [1966] Ch. 499; *Shiloh Spinners Ltd v. Harding* [1973] A.C. 691; *Starside Properties Ltd v. Mustapha* [1974] 1 W.L.R. 816; *B.I.C.C. plc v. Burndy Corporation* [1985] Ch. 232; *Transag Haulage Ltd v. Leyland DAF Finance plc* [1994] B.C.C. 356 ; *On Demand Information plc v. Michael Gerson (Finance) plc* [1999] 1 All E.R. (Comm.) 512 and *post*, § 27–121. Contrast *Galbraith v. Mitchenall Estates Ltd* [1965] 2 Q.B. 473; *Mardorf Peach & Co. Ltd v. Attica Sea Carriers Corpn. of Liberia* [1977] A.C. 850; *Afovos Shipping Co. SA v. R. Pagnan and Filli* [1983] 1 W.L.R. 195; *Scandinavian Trading Tanker Co. A.B. v. Flota Petrolera Ecuatoriana* [1983] 2 A.C. 694; *Sport Internationaal Bussum B.V. v. Inter-footwear Ltd* [1984] 1 W.L.R. 776; *Union Eagle Ltd v. Golden Achievement Ltd* [1997] A.C. 514.

[86] *e.g.* Law of Property Act 1925, s.146; Consumer Credit Act 1974, ss.76, 86, 87, 98; Housing Act 1996, ss.81 and 82.

[87] s.3(2)(b)(ii); see *ante*, § 14–070.

[88] S.I. 1994 No. 3159. See further *ante*, Chap. 15, where the scope of the Regulations and the definition of terms such as "seller or supplier," etc., is discussed in more detail.

[89] See Sched. 3 to the Regulations, para. 1(f), set out at § 15–057.

[90] *Leslie Shipping Co. v. Welstead* [1921] 3 K.B. 420; *The Mihalis Angelos* [1971] 1 Q.B. 164; *Lombard North Central plc v. Butterworth* [1987] Q.B. 587.

of the contract.[91] Where reliance is placed on the procedure laid down in the contract, it is necessary to comply strictly with the procedure which has been laid down.[92] It can be a matter of some practical importance whether termination has taken place pursuant to a term of the contract or under the general law.[93] A contractual right to terminate can be exercised even if the breach is not repudiatory at common law.[94] On the other hand, a contractual right to terminate, of itself, says nothing about the remedial consequences of termination; that is to say, not every termination pursuant to an express term of the contract will entitle the party terminating the contract to loss of bargain damages. Thus, where a contracting party terminates further performance of the contract pursuant to a term of the contract, and the breach which has caused it to exercise that power is not a repudiatory breach, the party exercising the right to terminate may only be entitled to recover damages in respect of the loss which it has suffered at the date of termination and not for loss of bargain damages.[95] Where, however, the breach is also repudiatory[96] and that repudiatory breach has been accepted,[97] loss of bargain damages can be recovered[98] by relying on the contractual right to do so or by accepting the other party's repudiation of the contract. An example of a case in which the line between the two became distinctly blurred is provided by *Laing Management Ltd v. Aegon Insurance Co. (U.K.) Ltd*[99] where Judge Lloyd Q.C. concluded that reliance on a contractual right to terminate did not amount to an acceptance of a repudiatory breach and that therefore the contract remained alive for the benefit of both parties. The finding that the contract remained alive, notwithstanding the reliance on the express power to terminate, is a difficult one. A simpler analysis would have been to conclude that reliance on the express term in the contract did operate to discharge both parties from their obligation to

---

[91] See, for example, *Lockland Builders Ltd v. Rickwood* (1996) 77 Build L.R. 38 where the contractually agreed procedure for dealing with the consequences of a particular breach was held impliedly to have excluded the common law right to terminate performance of the contract in respect of a breach which fell within the scope of the clause. However, the position would have been otherwise if the party in breach had evinced a clear intention not to be bound by the terms of the contract; in such a case the common law right to terminate and the right contained in the contract would have existed side by side (see Russell L.J. at 46 and Hirst L.J. at 50). A provision to the effect that the contractual right to terminate is "without prejudice to other rights and remedies" will generally suffice to persuade a court that the common law right to terminate has not been excluded.

[92] *The Mihalis Angelos* [1971] 1 Q.B. 164.

[93] Although it can occasionally be difficult to tell whether a party has purported to terminate.

[94] See, for example, *Financings Ltd v. Baldock* [1963] 2 Q.B. 104.

[95] See, for example, *Financings Ltd v. Baldock* [1963] 2 Q.B. 104; *Brady v. St Margaret's Trust* [1963] 2 Q.B. 494; *Anglo-Auto Finance Ltd v. James* [1963] 1 W.L.R. 1042; *United Dominions Trust (Commercial) Ltd v. Ennis* [1968] 1 Q.B. 54. This separation of the right to terminate and the right to claim loss of bargain damages has been rejected by the Supreme Court of Canada in *Keneric Tractor Sales Ltd v. Langille* (1987) 43 D.L.R. (4th) 171 and subjected to academic criticism, see Opeskin (1990) 106 L.Q.R. 293. An attempt to stipulate for a wider right of recovery in the contract in such a case may be invalid as a penalty clause: *Lombard North Central plc v. Butterworth* [1987] Q.B. 527.

[96] This is so whether it is repudiatory under the general law or by virtue of the decision of the parties to treat the term which has been broken as a condition of the contract: *Lombard North Central plc v. Butterworth* [1987] Q.B. 527. *cf.* Treitel [1987] L.M.C.L.Q. 143.

[97] A court may conclude that, having regard to the conduct of the parties, any repudiatory breach committed was not, in fact, accepted so that the contract must be regarded as continuing: see *United Dominions Trust (Commercial) Ltd v. Ennis* [1968] 1 Q.B. 54 and *Laing Management Ltd v. Aegon Insurance Co. (U.K.) Ltd* (1998) 86 Build L.R. 70.

[98] *Yeoman Credit Ltd v. Waragowski* [1961] 1 W.L.R. 1124; *Overstone Ltd v. Shipway* [1962] 1 W.L.R. 117; *Lombard North Central plc v. Butterworth* [1987] Q.B. 527.

[99] (1998) 86 Build L.R. 70.

perform under the contract but that the exercise of the right to terminate did not, of itself, entitle the plaintiff to recover loss of bargain damages.[1]

23-048   **Burden of proof.** It is for the party seeking to terminate the contract to prove the existence of the facts which justify the exercise of his contractual right to terminate.[2]

23-049   **Requirements as to notice.** Where the terms of the contract expressly or impliedly[3] provide that the right of termination is to be exercised only upon notice given to the other party, it is clear that notice must be given for the contract to be terminated pursuant to that provision.[4] Any notice must be sufficiently clear and unambiguous in its terms to constitute a valid notice[5]; but it is a question of construction in each case whether the notice must actually be communicated to the other party and whether it takes effect at the time of dispatch or of receipt.[6] The terms of the contract may further provide that notice can be given only after the occurrence of a specified event[7]; or that a specified period of notice be given; or that the notice is to be in a certain form (*e.g.* in writing); or that it should contain certain specified information; or that it should be given within a certain period of time. Prima facie the validity of the notice depends upon the precise observance of the specified conditions.[8] However, a consideration of the relationship of the notice requirements to the contract as a whole and regard to general considerations of law, may show that a stipulated requirement, for example, that notice be given "without delay,"[9] was intended by the parties to be an intermediate term,[10] the non-observance of which would not invalidate the notice (unless the other party was seriously prejudiced thereby), but would give rise to a claim for damages only.[11]

23-050   **Waiver of defects in notice.** Where the requirements of notice have not been complied with, the party giving the notice may still be entitled to rely on it

---

[1] See *ante*, nn. 96 and 98.

[2] See *Chandris v. Isbrandtsen Moller Co. Inc.* [1951] 1 K.B. 240, 245–246; *P.J. Van der Zijden Wildhandel N.V. v. Tucker & Cross Ltd* [1975] 2 Lloyd's Rep. 240 (*force majeure* clauses). See also *ante*, § 14–129.

[3] See *Mardorf Peach & Co. Ltd v. Attica Sea Carriers Corpn. of Liberia* [1977] A.C. 850 (withdrawal of ship). See also *Abingdon Finance Co. Ltd v. Champion, The Guardian*, November 6, 1961 (seizure of goods let on hire-purchase).

[4] *Reliance Car Facilities Ltd v. Roding Motors* [1952] 2 Q.B. 844. Contrast *Union Transport Finance Ltd v. British Car Auctions* [1978] 2 All E.R. 385.

[5] *Allam & Co. Ltd v. Europa Poster Services Ltd* [1968] 1 W.L.R. 638. See also *May v. Borup* [1915] 1 K.B. 830; *Addis v. Burrows* [1948] 1 K.B. 444; *Aegnoussiotis Shipping Corpn. of Monrovia v. A/S Kristian Jebsens Rederi* [1977] 1 Lloyd's Rep. 268. *cf. P. Phipps & Co. (Northampton and Towcester) Breweries Ltd v. Rogers* [1925] 1 K.B. 14.

[6] *Scarf v. Jardine* (1882) 7 App.Cas. 345, 348; *Re London and Northern Bank* [1900] 1 Ch. 220; *Tenax Steamship Co. Ltd v. The Brimnes* [1973] 1 W.L.R. 386 (affd. [1975] Q.B. 929); *Bremer Handelsgesellschaft mbH v. Vanden Avenne-Izegem P.V.B.A.* [1978] 2 Lloyd's Rep. 109.

[7] *Afovos Shipping Co. SA v. Pagnan & Filli* [1983] 1 W.L.R. 195; *Telfair Shipping Corpn. v. Athos Shipping Co. SA* [1983] 1 Lloyd's Rep. 127.

[8] See *Afovos Shipping Co. SA v. Pagnan & Filli, supra; Tradax Exports SA v. Dorada Compania Naviera SA* [1982] 2 Lloyd's Rep. 140; and the cases cited in n. 12, *post.*

[9] *Bremer Handelsgesellschaft mbH v. Vanden Avenne-Izegem P.V.B.A., supra.*

[10] See *ante*, § 12–039.

[11] *Bremer Handelsgesellschaft mbH v. Vanden Avenne-Izegem P.V.B.A., supra*, at 113. See also *Bunge SA v. Kruse* [1979] 1 Lloyd's Rep. 279 (affd. [1980] 2 Lloyd's Rep. 142).

if the other party has expressly or by conduct waived the defect in the notice.[12]

Waiver of right to terminate. Conversely, if one party is contractually entitled to terminate the agreement on breach by the other, he may be held to have waived his right to terminate.[13]   **23–051**

Implied provision. A contract which appears on its face to be perpetual and irrevocable may nevertheless be construed in the sense that it can be determined upon reasonable notice.[14] This topic has been dealt with in the chapter on Implied Terms earlier in this book.[15] An unlawful repudiation of the contract by one party cannot be relied on by him as a lawful determination upon reasonable notice under an implied term in the contract.[16]   **23–052**

Determination of contract. The parties may expressly provide that the contract shall *ipso facto* determine upon the happening of a certain event.[17] But   **23–053**

---

[12] *Alfred C. Toepfer v. P. Cremer* [1975] 2 Lloyd's Rep. 118; *Bremer Handelsgesellschaft mbH v. Vanden Avenne-Izegem P.V.B.A.* [1978] 2 Lloyd's Rep. 109; *Bremer Handelsgesellschaft mbH v. C. Mackprang* [1979] 1 Lloyd's Rep. 220; *Bunge GmbH v. Alfred C. Toepfer* [1979] 1 Lloyd's Rep. 554. Contrast (no waiver) *V. Berg & Son Ltd v. Vanden Avenne-Izegem P.V.B.A.* [1977] 1 Lloyd's Rep. 499; *Avimex SA v. Dewulf & Cie.* [1979] 2 Lloyd's Rep. 56; *Toepfer v. Schwarze* [1980] 1 Lloyd's Rep. 385; *Bremer Handelsgesellschaft mbH v. C. Mackprang* [1981] 1 Lloyd's Rep. 292; *Tradax Export SA v. Cook Industries Inc.* [1982] 1 Lloyd's Rep. 385; *Raiffeisen Hauptgenossenschaft v. Louis Dreyfus & Co. Ltd* [1981] 1 Lloyd's Rep. 345; *Bremer Handelsgesellschaft mbH v. Westzucker* [1981] 1 Lloyd's Rep. 207; *Cook Industries Inc. v. Meunerie Liegeois SA* [1981] 1 Lloyd's Rep. 359; *Bremer Handelsgesellschaft mbH v. Finagrain Compagnie Commerciale, etc., SA* [1981] 2 Lloyd's Rep. 259; *Bremer Handelsgesellschaft mbH v. Westzucker (No. 2)* [1981] 1 Lloyd's Rep. 130; *Bunge SA v. Compagnie Européenne des Cereales* [1982] 1 Lloyd's Rep. 306; *Bremer Handelsgesellschaft mbH v. Bunge Corpn.* [1983] 1 Lloyd's Rep. 476; *Bremer Handelsgesellschaft mbH v. Deutsche-Conti Handelsgesellschaft mbH* [1983] 2 Lloyd's Rep. 45.

[13] *Keith Prowse & Co. v. National Telephone Co.* [1894] 2 Ch. 147; *Reynolds v. General & Finance Facilities* (1963) 107 S.J. 889. Contrast (no waiver) *Mardorf Peach & Co. Ltd v. Attica Sea Carriers Corpn. of Liberia* [1977] A.C. 850; *China National Foreign Trade Transportation Corpn. v. Evlogia Shipping Co. SA of Panama* [1979] 1 W.L.R. 1018; *Bremer Handelsgesellschaft v. Deutsche-Conti Handelsgesellschaft* [1983] 2 Lloyd's Rep. 45; *Scandinavian Trading Tanker Co. A.B. v. Flota Petrolera Ecuatoriana* [1983] 2 Q.B. 529 (affd. [1983] 2 A.C. 694); *Eximenco Handels A.G. v. Partrederei Oro Chief* [1983] 2 Lloyd's Rep. 509.

[14] *Crediton Gas Co. v. Crediton U.D.C.* [1928] Ch. 174, 178; *Winter Garden Theatre (London) Ltd v. Millenium Productions Ltd* [1948] A.C. 173; *Martin Baker Aircraft Co. Ltd v. Canadian Flight Equipment Ltd* [1955] 2 Q.B. 556; *Re Spenborough U.D.C.'s Agreement* [1968] Ch. 139; *Beverley Corpn. v. Richard Hodgson & Sons Ltd* (1972) 225 E.G. 799; *Staffordshire A.H.A. v. South Staffordshire Waterworks Co.* [1978] 1 W.L.R. 1387. Contrast *Kirklees Metropolitan B.C. v. Yorkshire Woollen District Transport Co.* (1978) 77 L.G.R. 448. See also Carnegie (1969) 85 L.Q.R. 392.

[15] See *ante*, § 13–025.

[16] *Decro-Wall International SA v. Practitioners in Marketing Ltd* [1971] 1 W.L.R. 361. See also *Bridge v. Campbell Discount Co. Ltd* [1962] A.C. 600.

[17] *Jay's Furnishing Co. v. Brand & Co.* [1915] 1 K.B. 458; *Continental Grain Export Corpn. v. S.T.M. Grain Ltd* [1979] 2 Lloyd's Rep. 460; *Bremer Handelsgesellschaft mbH v. Finagrain SA* [1981] 2 Lloyd's Rep. 259. See also *British Leyland U.K. Ltd v. Ashraf* [1978] I.C.R. 979 (employment), subsequently overruled in *Igbo v. Johnson, Matthey Chemicals Ltd* [1986] I.C.R. 505.

such a provision is to be construed subject to the principle that no man can take advantage of his own wrong, so that one party may not be allowed to rely on such a provision where the occurrence of the event is attributable to his own act or default.[18]

---

[18] *Rede v. Farr* (1817) 6 M. & S. 121, 124; *Doe d. Bryan v. Bancks* (1821) 4 B. & Ald. 401, 406; *New Zealand Shipping Co. v. Société des Ateliers et Chantiers de France* [1919] A.C. 1, 6, 8, 9; *Quesnel Forks Gold Mining Co. Ltd v. Ward* [1920] A.C. 222; *Alghussein Establishment v. Eton College* [1988] 1 W.L.R. 587. *cf. Cheall v. Assn. of Professional Executive and Computer Staff* [1988] 2 A.C. 180; *Thompson v. Asda M.F.I. Group plc* [1988] Ch. 241; *Micklefield v. S.A.C. Technology Ltd* [1990] 1 W.L.R. 1002; *Richco International Ltd v. Alfred C. Toepfer International GmbH* [1991] 1 Lloyd's Rep. 136; see *ante*, § 13–012.

CHAPTER 24

DISCHARGE BY FRUSTRATION[1]

1. INTRODUCTION

Introduction. A contract may be discharged on the ground of frustration **24–001**
when something occurs after the formation of the contract which renders it
physically or commercially impossible to fulfil the contract or transforms the
obligation to perform into a radically different obligation from that undertaken at
the moment of entry into the contract.

Frustration and mistake. Although the doctrine of frustration has some **24–002**
affinity with common mistake, in that both doctrines are essentially concerned
with the allocation of risk of an unforeseen event which makes contractual
performance more onerous or even impossible,[2] it is customary to treat the two
doctrines separately on the ground that common mistake is concerned with a
common misapprehension which was present at the date of entry into the

---

[1] Treitel, *Frustration and Force Majeure* (1994); McKendrick (ed.), *Force Majeure and Frustration of Contract* (2nd ed., 1995). See also McElroy and Williams, *Impossibility of Performance*
(1941); Gottschalk, *Impossibility of Performance in Contract* (1945); McNair and Watts, *The Legal
Effects of War* (4th ed.), Chap. 5; Webber, *Effect of War on Contracts* (2nd ed.), especially Parts III
and IV. For an economic analysis of the doctrine of frustration, see Posner and Rosenfield (1977) 6
J.Leg. Stud. 83.
[2] See, *e.g. Amalgamated Investment & Property Co. Ltd v. John Walker & Sons Ltd* [1977] 1
W.L.R. 164; *Associated Japanese Bank (International) Ltd v. Crédit du Nord* [1989] 1 W.L.R. 255,
264; *Jan Albert (H.K.) Ltd v. Shu Kong Garment Factory Ltd* [1990] 1 H.K.L.R. 317.

contract, whereas frustration is solely concerned with events which occur *after* the date of formation of the contract.[3]

24-003   **Narrow scope.** Although the doctrine of frustration is of respectable antiquity, having been established in its present form in 1863 in *Taylor v. Caldwell*,[4] it currently operates within rather narrow confines. This is so for two principal reasons. The first is that the courts do not wish to allow a party to appeal to the doctrine of frustration in an effort to escape from what has proved to be a bad bargain: frustration is "not lightly to be invoked to relieve contracting parties of the normal consequences of imprudent commercial bargains."[5] The second is that parties to commercial contracts commonly make provision within their contract for the impact which various possible catastrophic events may have on their contractual obligations. Thus, *force majeure* clauses[6] and hardship and intervener clauses[7] are frequently inserted into commercial contracts. The effect of these clauses is to reduce the practical significance of the doctrine of frustration because, where express provision has been made in the contract itself for the event which has actually occurred, then the contract is not frustrated.[8] Therefore the wider the ambit of contractual clauses, the narrower is the practical scope of the doctrine of frustration.[9]

24-004   **Historical development.**[10] Prior to the watershed decision of the Court of Queen's Bench in *Taylor v. Caldwell*[11] supervening events were not regarded as an excuse for non-performance because the parties could have provided for such eventualities in their contract.[12] Once a contracting party assumed an obligation he was bound to fulfil it. The classic decision on this rule as to "absolute" contracts is *Paradine v. Jane*,[13] where a lessee who was sued for arrears of rent pleaded that he had been evicted and kept out of possession by an alien enemy; such an event was beyond his control, and had deprived him of the profits of the land from which he expected to receive the money to pay the rent. He was

---

[3] It can sometimes be difficult to decide into which category a particular case falls; see, for example, *Amalgamated Investment & Property Co. Ltd v. John Walker & Sons Ltd* [1977] 1 W.L.R. 164 and *Gamerco SA v. ICM/Fair Warning (Agency) Ltd* [1995] 1 W.L.R. 1226 (it has been argued that the latter case may have been too readily classified as an instance of frustration, see Carter and Tolhurst (1996) 10 J.C.L. 264, 265–266).

[4] (1863) 3 B. & S. 826.

[5] *Pioneer Shipping Ltd v. B.T.P. Tioxide Ltd (The Nema)* [1982] A.C. 724, 752.

[6] See generally *ante*, §§ 14–126—14–142 and McKendrick (ed.), *Force Majeure and Frustration of Contract* (2nd ed., 1995), Chap. 3.

[7] See generally Schmitthoff [1980] J.B.L. 82; Montague (1985) Int. Bus. Lawyer 135.

[8] *Joseph Constantine SS. Line Ltd v. Imperial Smelting Corp. Ltd* [1942] A.C. 154, 163.

[9] In the case of an elaborately drafted contract a court may conclude, as a matter of interpretation, that the parties preferred the "certainty" of termination pursuant to one of the terms of the contract to the uncertainty of possible discharge under the doctrine of frustration: see *Total Gas Marketing Ltd v. Arco British Ltd* [1998] 2 Lloyd's Rep. 209, esp. pp. 221–222.

[10] See generally Treitel, *Frustration and Force Majeure* (1994), Chap. 2 and Ibbetson in Rose (ed.), *Consensus Ad Idem* (1996), Chap. 1.

[11] (1863) 3 B. & S. 826.

[12] (1646) Aleyn 26; *Atkinson v. Ritchie* (1809) 10 East 530; *Barker v. Hodgson* (1814) 3 M. & S. 267 (later held to be wrongly decided by Scrutton L.J. in *Ralli Bros. v. Compagnia Naviera Sota y. Aznar* [1920] 2 K.B. 287, 303); *Bute (Marquis of) v. Thompson* (1844) 13 M. & W. 487; *Hills v. Sughrue* (1846) 15 M. & W. 253; *Jervis v. Tomkinson* (1856) 1 H. & N. 195; *Kirk v. Gibbs* (1857) 1 H. & N. 810; *Brown v. Royal Insurance Society* (1859) 1 E. & E. 853; *Re Arthur* (1880) 14 Ch.D. 603. The same rule was applied in equity: *Leeds v. Cheetham* (1827) 1 Sim. 146, 150.

[13] (1646) Aleyn 26. For fuller analysis of the case and its antecedents see Ibbetson, in Rose (ed.), *Consensus Ad Idem* (1996) Chap. 1.

nevertheless held liable on the ground that "where the law creates a duty or charge and the party is disabled to perform it and hath no remedy over, there the law will excuse him . . . but when the party of his own contract creates a duty or charge upon himself, he is bound to make it good, if he may, notwithstanding any accident by inevitable necessity, because he might have provided against it by his contract."[14]

Physical destruction of the subject-matter. Although this rule was peculiar **24–005** to English law, it continued to be enforced until 1863.[15] However, in 1863, in *Taylor v. Caldwell*[16] the defendants had agreed to permit the plaintiffs to use a music-hall for concerts on four specified nights. After the contract was made, but before the first night arrived, the hall was destroyed by fire. Blackburn J., giving the judgment of the Court of Queen's Bench, held that the defendants were not liable in damages, since the doctrine of the sanctity of contracts applied only to a promise which was positive and absolute, and not subject to any condition express *or implied*. The court employed the concept of an implied condition to introduce the doctrine of frustration into English law, since it might appear from the nature of the contract that the parties must have known from the beginning that the fulfilment of the contract depended on the continuing existence of a particular person or thing. The court held that the particular contract in question was to be construed:

> "as subject to an implied condition that the parties shall be excused in case, before breach, performance becomes impossible from the perishing of the thing, without default of the contractor. . . . [17] The principle seems to us to be that, in contracts in which the performance depends on the continued existence of a given person or thing, a condition is implied that the impossibility of performance arising from the perishing of the person or thing shall excuse the performance. In none of these cases is the promise other than positive, nor is there any express stipulation that the destruction of the person or thing shall excuse the performance; but that excuse is by law implied, because from the nature of the contract it is apparent that the parties contracted on the basis of the continued existence of the particular person or chattel."[18]

The principle of *Taylor v. Caldwell* was soon applied in other cases[19] and was accepted by the legislature in relation to agreements for the sale of goods.[20]

Frustration of the adventure. Though the doctrine of frustration was first **24–006** introduced into English law to cover situations where the physical subject-matter of the contract had perished (as in *Taylor v. Caldwell*[21]), it was quickly extended

---

[14] *ibid.* at 27.

[15] There were some exceptions, *e.g.* no damages could be granted for breach of a promise to marry or of a contract for personal services if one party died (*post*, §§ 24–036 *et seq.*), nor for the breach of a contractual promise when performance of that promise became illegal after the formation of the contract: *Atkinson v. Ritchie, supra*, at pp. 534–535. But the courts still refused to recognise any general principle that a party might be released from liability in the absence of an express condition which operated to release him in the particular events which occurred: *Hall v. Wright* (1858) E.B. & E. 746, 789; *Kearon v. Pearson* (1861) 2 H. & N. 386.

[16] (1863) 3 B. & S. 826.

[17] *ibid.* at 833–834.

[18] *ibid.* at 839.

[19] *e.g. Appleby v. Myers* (1867) L.R. 2 C.P. 651.

[20] s.7 of the Sale of Goods Act 1893. See *post*, § 24–045. (But the legislature did not intend to disturb the rules as to risk: see Vol. II, § 43–034.)

[21] (1863) 3 B. & S. 826.

to cases where, without any such physical destruction, the commercial adventure envisaged by the parties was frustrated. "Frustration of the common venture" first appeared in 1874 in *Jackson v. Union Marine Insurance Co. Ltd*[22] where a ship was required, under a charterparty, to proceed from Liverpool to Newport to load a cargo for San Francisco. On the first day out from Liverpool the ship ran aground, and it took six weeks to refloat her, and another six months to complete repairs. The jury was asked whether the time necessary for getting the ship off and repairing her so as to be a cargo-carrying ship was so long as to put an end in a commercial sense to the commercial speculation entered upon by the shipowner and the charterers. The jury answered in the affirmative, and the Court of Exchequer Chamber held that the charterparty ended upon the mishap. Bramwell B. said that the jury had found that "a voyage undertaken after the ship was sufficiently repaired would have been a different voyage . . . different as a different adventure . . . ."[23] With these decisions, the existence of the doctrine of frustration in English law was firmly established.

2. The Test for Frustration[24]

24–007   **Introduction.** Although the existence of the doctrine of frustration is now firmly established, its juristic basis remains rather uncertain. However in *J. Lauritzen A.S. v. Wijsmuller B.V. (The Super Servant Two),*[25] Bingham L.J. set out the following five propositions which describe the essence of the doctrine. These propositions, he stated, were "established by the highest authority" and were "not open to question."[26] The first proposition was that the doctrine of frustration has evolved "to mitigate the rigour of the common law's insistence on literal performance of absolute promises"[27] and that its object was "to give effect to the demands of justice, to achieve a just and reasonable result, to do what is reasonable and fair, as an expedient to escape from injustice where such would result from enforcement of a contract in its literal terms after a significant change in circumstances."[28] Secondly, frustration operates to "kill the contract and discharge the parties from further liability under it" and that therefore it cannot be "lightly invoked" but must be kept within "very narrow limits and ought not to be extended."[29] Thirdly, frustration brings a contract to an end "forthwith,

---

[22] (1874) L.R. 10 C.P. 125.

[23] *ibid.* at 141.

[24] See Treitel, *Frustration and Force Majeure* (1994), pp. 578–584; Treitel, *The Law of Contract* (9th ed., 1995) pp. 832–836; *Anson's Law of Contract* (J. Beatson) (27th ed., 1998), pp. 513–518; Cheshire, Fifoot and Furmston, *Law of Contract* (13th ed., 1996), pp. 582–586; Webber, *Effect of War on Contracts* (2nd ed.), pp. 404–478; McNair and Watts, *The Legal Effects of War* (4th ed.), pp. 166 *et seq.*, based on (1919) 35 L.Q.R. 84–100 and (1940) 56 L.Q.R. 173–207; Wade (1940) 56 L.Q.R. 519. For a comparison of the theories in different legal systems, see Smit (1958) 58 Col. L.R. 287; for an American assessment of the U.K. cases, see Schlegel (1969) 23 Rutgers L.Rev. 419.

[25] [1990] 1 Lloyd's Rep. 1.

[26] *ibid.* at 8.

[27] Citing *Hirji Mulji v. Cheong Yue Steamship Co. Ltd* [1926] A.C. 497, 510; *Denny, Mott & Dickson Ltd v. James B. Fraser & Co. Ltd* [1944] A.C. 265, 275; *Joseph Constantine Steamship Line Ltd v. Imperial Smelting Corp. Ltd* [1942] A.C. 154, 171.

[28] Citing *Hirji Mulji v. Cheong Yue Steamship Co. Ltd* [1926] A.C. 497, 510; *Joseph Constantine Steamship Line Ltd v. Imperial Smelting Corp. Ltd* [1942] A.C. 154, 183, 193; *National Carriers Ltd v. Panalpina (Northern) Ltd* [1981] A.C. 675, 701.

[29] Citing *Bank Line Ltd v. Arthur Capel & Co.* [1919] A.C. 435, 459; *Davis Contractors Ltd v. Fareham U.D.C.* [1956] A.C. 696, 715, 727; *Pioneer Shipping Ltd v. B.T.P. Tioxide Ltd* [1982] A.C. 724, 752.

without more and automatically."[30] Fourthly, "the essence of frustration is that it should not be due to the act or election of the party seeking to rely on it"[31] and it must be some "outside event or extraneous change of situation."[32] Finally, a frustrating event must take place "without blame or fault on the side of the party seeking to rely on it."[33]

No absolving power. While these propositions establish the essence of the **24–008** doctrine of frustration and provide some guidance as to its limits, they do not explain precisely *why* it is that the courts intervene in these cases, except, at the broadest level, to give effect to the demands of justice. But this appeal to the demands of justice should not be taken to suggest that the court has a broad absolving power to set a contract aside whenever a change of circumstances causes hardship to one of the contracting parties. The proposition that the court has a power to impose a just and reasonable solution to the problem raised by the new circumstances[34] was rejected by the House of Lords in *British Movietonews Ltd v. London and District Cinemas Ltd.*[35] Such a test is too wide, and gives too much discretion to the court; it ignores the limited data for the court's decision, and suggests that attention should be concentrated on the harshness of enforcing the contract in the new situation, without any inquiry whether the original obligation was radically different.[36]

Basis of doctrine. Although a number of judges have considered the basis of **24–009** the doctrine of frustration, it is not clear that the issue gives rise to any practical consequences. The various theories "shade into one another" and a "choice between them is a choice of what is the most appropriate to the particular contract under consideration."[37] The principal theories which have been put forward are set out in the following paragraphs, before further consideration is given to the issue of whether or not any practical consequences flow from this debate.

---

[30] Citing *Hirji Mulji v. Cheong Yue Steamship Co. Ltd* [1926] A.C. 497, 505; *Maritime National Fish Ltd v. Ocean Trawlers Ltd* [1935] A.C. 524, 527; *Joseph Constantine Steamship Line Ltd v. Imperial Smelting Corp. Ltd* [1942] A.C. 154, 163, 170, 171, 187, 200; *Denny Mott & Dickson Ltd v. James B. Fraser & Co. Ltd* [1944] A.C. 265, 274. See also *GF Sharp & Co Ltd v. McMillan* [1998] I.R.L.R. 632.

[31] Citing *Hirji Mulji v. Cheong Yue Steamship Co. Ltd* [1926] A.C. 497, 510; *Maritime National Fish Ltd v. Ocean Trawlers Ltd* [1935] A.C. 524, 530; *Denny, Mott & Dickson Ltd v. James B. Fraser & Co. Ltd* [1944] A.C. 265, 274; *Davis Contractors Ltd v. Fareham U.D.C.* [1956] A.C. 696, 729.

[32] Citing *Paal Wilson & Co. A/S v. Partenreederi Hannah Blumenthal* [1983] 1 A.C. 854, 909.

[33] Citing *Bank Line Ltd v. Arthur Capel & Co.* [1919] A.C. 435, 452; *Joseph Constantine Steamship Line Ltd v. Imperial Smelting Corp. Ltd* [1942] A.C. 154, 171; *Davis Contractors Ltd v. Fareham U.D.C.* [1956] A.C. 696, 729; *Paal Wilson & Co. A/S v. Partenreederei Hannah Blumenthal* [1983] 1 A.C. 854, 882, 909.

[34] *British Movietonews Ltd v. London & District Cinemas Ltd* [1951] 1 K.B. 190, 202; *cf.* Cheshire, Fifoot & Furmston, *Law of Contract* (13th ed., 1996), pp. 585–586 and Lord Denning's modified formulations in *Ocean Tramp Tankers v. V/O Sovfracht (The Eugenia)* [1964] 2 Q.B. 226, 238; and in *Staffordshire A.H.A. v. South Staffordshire Waterworks Co.* [1978] 1 W.L.R. 1387, 1395; (pet. dis.) [1979] 1 W.L.R. 203, HL.

[35] [1952] A.C. 166.

[36] In *Notcutt v. Universal Equipment Co. (London) Ltd* [1986] 1 W.L.R. 641, 646–647 (*post*, § 24–037) the Court of Appeal rejected the suggestion that injustice was an *additional* factor to be considered after the factors which established a radical change in the obligation.

[37] *National Carriers Ltd v. Panalpina (Northern) Ltd* [1981] A.C. 675, 693, *per* Lord Wilberforce.

24–010   **The implied term test.** The test which was originally adopted in *Taylor v. Caldwell*[38] was the implied term test. The classic exposition of the test is to be found in the speech of Lord Loreburn in *F.A. Tamplin SS. Co. Ltd v. Anglo-Mexican Petroleum Products Co. Ltd*[39]:

> "A court can and ought to examine the contract and the circumstances in which it was made, not of course to vary but only to explain it, in order to see whether or not from the nature of it the parties must have made their bargain on the footing that a particular thing or state of things would continue to exist. And if they must have done so, then a term to that effect will be implied, though it be not expressed in the contract.... In most of the cases it is said that there was an implied condition in the contract which operated to release the parties from performing it, and in all of them I think that was at bottom the principle upon which the court proceeded. It is, in my opinion, the true principle, for no court has an absolving power, but it can infer from the nature of the contract and the surrounding circumstances that a condition which was not expressed was a foundation on which the parties contracted.... Were the altered conditions such that, had they thought of them, the parties would have taken their chance of them, or such that as sensible men they would have said, 'if that happens, of course, it is all over between us'?"

So it was by means of this test that the doctrine of frustration was first introduced into English law[40] and it was frequently accepted in later judgments.[41]

24–011   **Objections to the implied term test.** The implied term test has, however, been the subject of considerable criticism and it was finally laid to rest by the House of Lords in *National Carriers Ltd v. Panalpina (Northern) Ltd*.[42] The following objections to it ought to be borne in mind when reading the older decisions. The first objection is that it is artificial and often fictitious in its operation, since there would seldom be a genuine common intention to terminate the contract upon the occurrence of the particular event in question.[43] The parties in the normal case have not foreseen the event, and even if they had, they would probably have "sought to introduce reservations, or qualifications or compensations."[44] Some judges, while paying lip-service to the test, have treated it as an objective one; for instance, in *Dahl v. Nelson, Donkin & Co.*,[45] Lord Watson said: "The meaning of the contract must be taken to be, not what the parties did intend (for they had neither thought nor intention regarding it), but that which the

---

[38] (1863) 3 B. & S. 826.
[39] [1916] 2 A.C. 397, 403–404.
[40] *Taylor v. Caldwell*, supra.
[41] *e.g. Bank Line Ltd v. Arthur Capel & Co.* [1919] A.C. 435, 455 (Lord Sumner); *Joseph Constantine SS. Line Ltd v. Imperial Smelting Corpn. Ltd* [1942] A.C. 154, 163 (Viscount Simon L.C.); *British Movietonews Ltd v. London & District Cinemas Ltd* [1952] A.C. 166, 183 (Viscount Simon) and 187 (Lord Simonds); see also the references collected in McNair and Watts *op. cit.* pp. 167–171.
[42] [1981] A.C. 675, 687, 702, 717 (*cf.* at 693, 694).
[43] *James Scott & Sons Ltd v. Del Sel*, 1922 S.C. 592, 597; *Davis Contractors Ltd v. Fareham U.D.C.* [1956] A.C. 696, 728; *National Carriers Ltd v. Panalpina (Northern) Ltd* [1981] A.C. 675, 687. See also *Horlock v. Beal* [1916] 1 A.C. 486 (*post*, § 24–038).
[44] *Denny, Mott and Dickson Ltd v. James B. Fraser & Co. Ltd* [1944] A.C. 265, 275 (Lord Wright).
[45] (1881) 6 App.Cas. 38, 59.

parties, as fair and reasonable men, would presumably have agreed upon if, having such possibility in view, they had made express provision as to their several rights and liabilities in the event of its occurrence." In *Davis Contractors v. Fareham U.D.C.* Lord Radcliffe said that "the spokesman of the fair and reasonable man, who represents after all no more than the anthropomorphic conception of justice, is and must be the court itself."[46] The implied term approach is also difficult to accept where the parties have actually foreseen the possibility of the event in question, or even inserted in their contract some express provision (short of termination of the contract) for the event which occurred, but the court nevertheless holds that the contract was frustrated by that event.[47]

Test of a radical change in the obligation. The test which found favour with   **24-012** the House of Lords in *Davis Contractors Ltd v. Fareham U.D.C.*[48] and in later cases[49] may be formulated as follows: If the literal words of the contractual promise were to be enforced in the changed circumstances, would performance involve a fundamental or radical change from the obligation originally undertaken?[50] Thus, Lord Radcliffe said:

> " . . . frustration occurs whenever the law recognises that without default of either party a contractual obligation has become incapable of being performed because the circumstances in which performance is called for would render it a thing radically different from that which was undertaken by the contract. *Non haec in foedera veni.* It was not this that I promised to do. . . . There must be . . . such a change in the significance of the obligation that the thing undertaken would, if performed, be a different thing from that contracted for."[51]

Lord Reid put the test for frustration in a similar way. "The question is whether the contract which they did make is, on its true construction, wide enough to apply to the new situation: if it is not, then it is at an end."[52] Later in his speech,[53] he approved the words of Asquith L.J. that the question is whether the events alleged to frustrate the contract were "fundamental enough to transmute the job the contractor had undertaken into a job of a different kind, which the contract

---

[46] [1956] A.C. 696, 728.

[47] See *post*, § 24–057.

[48] [1956] A.C. 696 (for the facts, see *post*, § 24–048).

[49] *National Carriers Ltd v. Panalpina (Northern) Ltd* [1981] A.C. 675; *Pioneer Shipping Ltd v. B.T.P. Tioxide Ltd* [1982] A.C. 724.

[50] This formulation does not cover the special case of supervening illegality (see *post*, § 24–023). With this formulation, compare that in *Williston on Contracts* (3rd ed.), Vol. 18, § 1931, at 8: "The important question is whether an unanticipated circumstance has made performance of the promise vitally different from what should reasonably have been within the contemplation of both parties when they entered into the contract."

[51] [1956] A.C. 696, 729. This statement was explicitly approved by the House of Lords in *National Carriers Ltd v. Panalpina (Northern) Ltd* [1981] A.C. 675, 688, 700, 702, 707, 717 and in *Pioneer Shipping Ltd v. B.T.P. Tioxide Ltd (The Nema)* [1982] A.C. 724, 744, 751–752. Earlier approval was given in *Tsakiroglou & Co. Ltd v. Noblee Thorl GmbH* [1962] A.C. 93. It has also been cited with approval by the Court of Appeal in *William Sindall plc v. Cambridgeshire County Council* [1994] 1 W.L.R. 1016, 1039.

[52] [1956] A.C. 696 at 721. (Lord Somervell agreed with Lord Reid on this issue *ibid.* at 733.)

[53] *ibid.* at 723.

did not contemplate and to which it could not apply."[54] It is submitted that the test put forward by Lord Reid is substantially the same as that of Lord Radcliffe.

24–013   In subsequent cases the House of Lords has expressly upheld the *Davis Contractors* formulation of the test for frustration.[55] In *National Carriers Ltd v. Panalpina (Northern) Ltd*[56] Lord Simon restated the test as follows:

> "Frustration of a contract takes place when there supervenes an event (without default of either party and for which the contract makes no sufficient provision) which so significantly changes the nature (not merely the expense or onerousness) of the outstanding contractual rights and/or obligations from what the parties could reasonably have contemplated at the time of its execution that it would be unjust to hold them to the literal sense of its stipulations in the new circumstances; in such case the law declares both parties to be discharged from further performance."[57]

Yet, at the same time it was said that the doctrine should be flexible and capable of new applications as new circumstances arise.[58]

24–014   **Construction of the contract.** Both Lords Reid and Radcliffe in *Davis Contractors* emphasised that the first step was to construe "the terms which are in the contract read in the light of the nature of the contract, and of the relevant surrounding circumstances when the contract was made."[59] From this construction the court should reach an impression of the scope of the original obligation, that is, the court should ascertain what the parties would be required to do in order to fulfil their literal promises in the original circumstances. This impression will depend on the court's estimate of what performance would have required in time, labour, money and materials, if there had been no change in the circumstances existing at the time the contract was made. The court should then examine the situation existing after the occurrence of the event alleged to have frustrated the contract, and ascertain what would be the obligation of the parties if the words of the contract were enforced in the new circumstances. Having

---

[54] *Sir Lindsay Parkinson & Co. Ltd v. Commissioners of Works* [1949] 2 K.B. 632, 667. See also the words of Lord Sumner in *Bank Line Ltd v. Arthur Capel & Co.* [1919] A.C. 435, 460: "I am of opinion that the requisitioning of the [ship] destroyed the identity of the chartered service and made the charter as a matter of business a *totally different thing*"; also the statement of Lord Simon in *British Movietonews Ltd v. London & District Cinemas Ltd* [1952] A.C. 166, 185: " ... if ... a consideration of the terms of the contract, in the light of the circumstances existing when it was made, shows that they never agreed to be bound *in a fundamentally different situation* which has now unexpectedly emerged, the contract ceases to bind at that point—not because the court in its discretion thinks it just and reasonable to qualify the terms of the contract, but *because on its true construction it does not apply in that situation*"; and that of Lord Dunedin in *Metropolitan Water Board v. Dick, Kerr & Co. Ltd* [1918] A.C. 119, 128: "An interruption may be so long as *to destroy the identity of the work* or service, when resumed, with the work or service interrupted." (Italics supplied.)

[55] *National Carriers Ltd v. Panalpina (Northern) Ltd* [1981] A.C. 675; *Pioneer Shipping Ltd v. B.T.P. Tioxide Ltd (The Nema)* [1982] A.C. 724 (three of their Lordships in the former case referred to it as "the construction test": *ibid.* at 688, 702, 717); *Paal Wilson & Co. A/S v. Partenreederei Hannah Blumenthal* [1983] 1 A.C. 854, 909, 918–919.

[56] [1981] A.C. 675.

[57] *ibid.* at 700. (On the use of the word "unjust," see the use of "injustice," *ibid.* at 701, and *post*, § 24–017.)

[58] *ibid.* at 692, 694, 701, 712.

[59] [1956] A.C. 696, 720–721 (*per* Lord Reid); *cf.* at 729 (*per* Lord Radcliffe).

discovered what was the original "obligation" and what would be the new "obligation" if the contract were still binding in the new circumstances, the last step in the process is for the court to compare the two obligations in order to decide whether the new obligation is a "radical" or "fundamental" change from the original obligation.[60] It is not simply a question whether there has been a radical change in the circumstances, but whether there has been a radical change in the "obligation" or the actual effect of the promises of the parties construed in the light of the new circumstances. Was "performance . . . fundamentally different in a commercial sense?"[61]

Application of the test. Their Lordships also agreed in *Davis Contractors*   **24–015** that it is a matter of law[62] for the court to construe the contract in the light of the facts existing at its formation and then "to determine whether the ultimate situation . . . is or is not within the scope of the contract so construed."[63] It has several times been emphasised in the House of Lords that "that conclusion is almost completely determined by what is ascertained as to mercantile usage and the understanding of mercantile men."[64] Hence, the court should seldom interfere with an arbitrator's application of the test to particular facts:

> "when it is shown on the face of a reasoned award that the appointed tribunal has applied the right legal test, the court should in my view only interfere if on the facts found as applied to that right legal test, no reasonable person could have reached that conclusion. It ought not to interfere merely because the court thinks that upon those facts and applying that test, it would not or might not itself have reached the same conclusion, for to do that would be for the court to usurp what is the sole function of the tribunal of fact."[65]

Objective test. The House of Lords has accepted the view that the test for   **24–016** frustration is objective.[66] It is not a subjective inquiry into the actual or presumed intentions of the parties, as was suggested by the older criterion of the implied term, since the discharge of a contract on the ground of frustration occurs automatically upon the happening of the frustrating event, and does not depend

---

[60] "I turn then to consider the position after the Canal was closed, and to compare the rights and obligations of the parties thereafter, if the contract still bound them, with what their rights and obligations would have been if the Canal had remained open." *Per* Lord Reid, in *Tsakiroglou & Co. Ltd v. Noblee Thorl GmbH* [1962] A.C. 93, 118. "Whether a supervening event is a frustrating event or not, is, in a wide variety of cases, a question of degree . . . " *per* Lord Hailsham, in *National Carriers Ltd v. Panalpina (Northern) Ltd* [1981] A.C. 675, 688.

[61] *Tsakiroglou & Co. Ltd v. Noblee Thorl GmbH* [1962] A.C. 93, 119. See to the same effect *Pioneer Shipping Ltd v. B.T.P. Tioxide Ltd (The Nema)* [1982] A.C. 724, 752.

[62] [1956] A.C. 696, 723; *cf.* 729; *Tsakiroglou & Co. Ltd v. Noblee Thorl GmbH, supra.*

[63] [1956] A.C. 696, 721.

[64] *Tsakiroglou & Co. Ltd v. Noblee Thorl GmbH* [1962] A.C. 93, 124 (*per* Lord Radcliffe) (cited with approval in *Pioneer Shipping Ltd v. B.T.P. Tioxide Ltd (The Nema)* [1982] A.C. 724, 752; see also 738.)

[65] *Pioneer Shipping* case, *supra*, at 752–753, (*per* Lord Roskill, in a speech concurred in by all their Lordships). It is not "open to the court to impose its own view rather than adopt that of the arbitral tribunal" simply because "questions of frustration are ultimately questions of law" (*ibid.* at 753). *cf. International Sea Tankers Inc. v. Hemisphere Shipping Co. Ltd (The Wenjiang)* [1982] 2 All E.R. 437; and *post*, § 24–034, n. 46; and § 24–095, especially n. 4.

[66] *Davis Contractors Ltd v. Fareham U.D.C.* [1956] A.C. 696, at 728 (*per* Lord Radcliffe: " . . . the true action of the court . . . consists in applying an objective rule of the law of contract . . . ").

upon any repudiation or other act of volition on the part of either party.[67] The fact that the parties, at the time of contracting, actually foresaw the possibility of the event or new circumstances in question does not necessarily prevent the doctrine of frustration from applying.[68]

24–017   **Other tests.** Various other theories have been put forward in an attempt to provide a coherent basis for the doctrine of frustration. As we have noted,[69] some judges have maintained that the doctrine seeks to give effect to the demands of justice, but these statements cannot be invoked to justify the conferral upon the courts of a wide-ranging discretion to re-write the parties' bargain in the name of "fairness and reasonableness." Another theory which has been invoked is that both parties have been discharged from further performance of their contractual obligations because of a total failure of consideration; but this rationalisation has been rejected by the House of Lords.[70] The final theory put forward by Lord Haldane in *Tamplin Steamship Co. Ltd v. Anglo-Mexican Petroleum Products Co. Ltd*[71] and Goddard J. in *Tatem Ltd v. Gamboa*[72] is that the doctrine is based on "the disappearance of the foundation of the contract." The difficulty with this theory lies in ascertaining the "foundation" of the contract[73]; the inquiry would appear to be one based on the construction of the contract and, if this is so, it is not easy to see how it differs from the construction theory.

24–018   **Practical differences between the tests.** It is therefore difficult to discern any practical consequence which flows from the different tests because, as Lord Wilberforce has stated, they appear to shade into each other.[74] The courts have regard to the construction of the contract, the effect of the changed circumstances on the parties' contractual obligations, the intentions of the parties (objectively construed) and the demands of justice in deciding whether or not a contract has been frustrated. No one factor is conclusive: the court will balance these different factors in determining whether a contract has been frustrated. On the other hand, it must be conceded that the basis of the doctrine is not unimportant in jurisprudential terms. A test based on a fictitious or artificial assumption (such as the implied term approach) may prevent a proper understanding of the function of the doctrine and of the role of the court in applying it. And the literal application of the one theory might lead to results which are incompatible with the rules which presently make up the doctrine of frustration. For example, the implied term theory, literally applied, may suggest that the question whether a

---

[67] See the statement of Lord Sumner in *Hirji Mulji v. Cheong Yue SS. Co.* [1926] A.C. 497, 510: " . . . its legal effect [*i.e.* of frustration] does not depend on their intention, or their opinions or even knowledge as to the event which has brought this about . . . [Frustration] is irrespective of the individuals concerned, their temperaments and failings, their interests and circumstances." See also *Denny, Mott & Dickson Ltd v. James B. Fraser & Co. Ltd* [1944] A.C. 265, 274; *J. Lauritzen A.S. v. Wijsmuller B.V. (The Super Servant Two)* [1990] 1 Lloyd's Rep. 1, 8. *cf.* the arguments of Goldberg (1972) 88 L.Q.R. 464. *cf.* also the principles on proving that a frustrating event was "self-induced": *post* § 24–063; *F.C. Shepherd & Co. Ltd v. Jerrom* [1987] Q.B. 301, 321–323.
[68] See *post*, § 24–057.
[69] *Ante*, § 24–007.
[70] *National Carriers Ltd v. Panalpina (Northern) Ltd* [1981] A.C. 675, 687, 702.
[71] [1916] 2 A.C. 397, 406–407.
[72] [1939] 1 K.B. 132.
[73] *National Carriers Ltd v. Panalpina (Northern) Ltd* [1981] A.C. 675, 687–688, 703.
[74] *ibid.* at 693.

contract is frustrated is one of fact, based on the intention of the parties, but it is clear law that the question whether a contract has been frustrated is one of law.[75] It is, however, unlikely that a modern court would apply a theory where it led to a result which was incompatible with the present rules and so it is submitted that no practical consequences flow from the debate as to the correct conceptual basis of the doctrine of frustration.[76]

3. ILLUSTRATIONS OF THE DOCTRINE

(a) *General*

Methods of classifying the cases on frustration. Since the doctrine of   **24–019** frustration depends on the construction of the "obligation" created by the particular contract in the light of its own circumstances, reported decisions can be only a rough guide to the future application of the doctrine.[77] Nevertheless, the scope of the doctrine in practice must be gleaned from a study of the decisions in the law reports. The cases may be classified by reference either to the different types of frustrating events (such as a change in the law or subsequent illegality,[78] outbreak of war,[79] cancellation of an expected event[80] or delay[81]), or by reference to particular categories of contracts where frustration has been invoked (such as personal contracts,[82] charterparties,[83] sale and carriage of goods,[84] building contracts,[85] leases,[86] and contracts for the sale of land[87]). The doctrine of executive necessity, according to which the Crown is unable to fetter by contractual undertakings the exercise in the future of its executive discretion, is discussed elsewhere in this Volume[88]; the discharge of contracts by the winding up of a company,[89] or by bankruptcy,[90] is also discussed elsewhere.

In addition to the frustrating events mentioned in the preceding paragraph, the   **24–020** following events may be taken as illustrations of the kind of events which have been held, in the circumstances of particular contracts, to bring the doctrine of frustration into operation: destruction by fire or other cause of the subject-matter

---

[75] *Ante,* § 24–015.
[76] Treitel, *The Law of Contract* (9th ed., 1995), pp. 832–836. Trietel, *Frustration and Force Majeure* (1994), pp. 583–584.
[77] See *ante,* § 24–014, n. 60.
[78] *Post,* §§ 24–021 *et seq.*
[79] *Post,* § 24–029.
[80] *Post,* §§ 24–032—24–033.
[81] *Post,* § 24–034.
[82] *Post,* §§ 24–036—24–039.
[83] *Post,* §§ 24–040—24–044.
[84] *Post,* §§ 24–045—24–046.
[85] *Post,* §§ 24–047—24–049.
[86] *Post,* §§ 24–050—24–054.
[87] *Post,* § 24–055.
[88] See *ante,* §§ 10–007—10–009.
[89] See *ante,* §§ 9–049—9–054.
[90] See *ante,* §§ 21–032 *et seq.*

of the contract,[91] an explosion or stranding disabling a ship,[92] requisitioning of the subject-matter of the contract by the government,[93] seizure of a ship[94] or expropriation of an oil concession[95] by a foreign government, incapacity or death of a person obliged to perform personal services,[96] delay sufficiently long to frustrate the commercial adventure of the parties.[97] On the other hand, mere inconvenience, or hardship, or financial loss involved in performing the contract,[98] or delay which is within the commercial risk undertaken by the parties,[99] has been held insufficient to frustrate particular contracts.

(b) *Common Types of Frustrating Events*

(i) *Subsequent Legal Changes and Supervening Illegality*

24-021   **Subsequent legal changes.** A subsequent change in the law or in the legal position affecting a contract is a well-recognised head of frustration; Parliament or another authority may intervene by legislative action, or the Government may exercise the royal prerogative or administrative powers so as to affect the legal situation of the contracting parties. In the leading case of *Baily v. De Crespigny*[1] a lessor was held not liable for an alleged breach of his covenant that neither he nor his assigns would build on a piece of land adjoining the demised premises, when a railway company, under its powers derived from a subsequent statute, compulsorily acquired the land and erected a station on it. In delivering the judgment of the court, Hannen J. said: "The legislature by compelling him to part with his land to a railway company, whom he could not bind by any stipulation, as he could an assign chosen by himself, has created a new kind of assign, such

---

[91] *Taylor v. Caldwell* (1863) 3 B. & S. 826 (*ante*, § 24–005) (distinguished in *New System Private Telephones (London) Ltd v. Edward Hughes & Co.* [1939] 2 All E.R. 844); *Appleby v. Myers* (1867) L.R. 2 C.P. 651. *cf. Turner v. Goldsmith* [1891] 1 Q.B. 544. *cf.* also *The Maira (No. 2)* [1985] 1 Lloyd's Rep. 300 (contract for management of ship not frustrated by loss of the ship) (affd. on other grounds [1986] 2 Lloyd's Rep. 46).

[92] *Joseph Constantine SS. Line Ltd v. Imperial Smelting Corpn. Ltd* [1942] A.C. 154; *Jackson v. Union Marine Insurance Co. Ltd* (1874) L.R. 10 C.P. 125 (*ante*, § 24–006).

[93] See the cases cited *post*, §§ 24–023—24–025, 24–040—24–042, and *post*, § 24–045, n. 5.

[94] *Tatem v. Gamboa* [1939] 1 K.B. 132 (*post*, § 24–042).

[95] *B.P. Exploration Co. (Libya) Ltd v. Hunt (No. 2)* [1981] 1 W.L.R. 232 (appeal to HL dismissed [1983] 2 A.C. 352).

[96] See the cases cited *post*, §§ 24–036—24–038.

[97] *Post*, § 24–034.

[98] *Davis Contractors Ltd v. Fareham U.D.C.* [1956] A.C. 696, 729 (*post*, § 24–048); *National Carriers Ltd v. Panalpina (Northern) Ltd* [1981] A.C. 675, 707; *Larringa & Co. Ltd v. Société Franco-Americaine des Phosphates de Médulla, Paris* (1923) 30 T.L.R. 316; *Hangkam Kwingtong Woo v. Liu Lan Fong* [1951] A.C. 707; *Palmco Shipping Inc. v. Continental Ore Corpn.* [1970] 2 Lloyd's Rep. 21, 32 (a difference in expense between the expected and the actual performance is not sufficient to produce frustration). See also the cases on Sale and Carriage of Goods cited *post*, §§ 24–045—24–046. The proposition that an increase in expense is not, of itself, sufficient to produce frustration may not be absolute; see Beatson in Rose (ed.) *Consensus Ad Idem* (1996), Chap. 6. On the question whether a term permitting determination upon notice may be implied into a long-term contract, see *Staffordshire A.H.A. v. South Staffordshire Waterworks Co.* [1978] 1 W.L.R. 1387; (pet. dis.) [1979] 1 W.L.R. 203, HL. *cf. Kirklees M.B.C. v. Yorks Woollen District Transport Co.* [1978] L.G.R. 448; *Watford B.C. v. Watford Rural Parish Council* (1988) 86 L.G.R. 524; *Islwyn B.C. v. Newport B.C.* (1994) 6 Admin. L.R. 386. On the judicial response to problems caused by a fall in the value of money, see Downes (1985) 101 L.Q.R. 98; also *ante* § 22–072; *post* §§ 27–066—27–067.

[99] *Post*, § 24–034.

[1] (1869) L.R. 4 Q.B. 180. See also *Islwyn B.C. v. Newport B.C., supra.*

as was not in the contemplation of the parties when the contract was entered into. To hold the defendant responsible for the acts of such an assignee is to make an entirely new contract for the parties."[2] The court also held that it made no difference whether the company was only empowered or was obliged by the statute to build on the land.

Changes affecting employment. Contracts of service may also be frustrated **24–022** by a subsequent change in the law. In *Reilly v. R.,*[3] the appellant was appointed a member of a statutory board in Canada with a specified term of appointment and salary. During the tenure of the appointment the office was abolished by the repeal of the statute establishing the board. By petition of right the appellant claimed damages for breach of contract, but the Judicial Committee held that the contract was discharged, because further performance had become impossible by statute. Similarly, a solicitor's retainer agreement with a gas company was held to be frustrated by the nationalisation effected by the Gas Act 1948.[4]

Supervening illegality.[5] It is now customary to treat supervening illegality as **24–023** an instance of frustration,[6] in that it is similar to frustration by a subsequent change in the law. Apart from the effect of an outbreak of war upon a contract, *e.g.* with a person who thereby becomes an alien enemy,[7] many wartime cases illustrate the power of the Government under statutory authority to forbid, whether temporarily or permanently, the performance of a contract, and so frustrate it. In *Metropolitan Water Board v. Dick, Kerr & Co. Ltd,*[8] under a contract made in July 1914, a reservoir was to be constructed and to be completed in six years from 1914, subject to a proviso that if the contractors should be impeded or obstructed by any cause the engineer should have power to grant an extension of time. Under the powers conferred by the Defence of the Realm Acts and Regulations, the contractors were obliged to cease work on the reservoir by order of the Ministry of Munitions in 1916. The House of Lords held that the contract was frustrated by supervening impossibility, and that the provision for extending the time did not apply to the prohibition by the Ministry. The interruption was of such a character, and likely to last so long, that if the work was to be resumed after the war, it would be a different undertaking altogether. Lord Finlay L.C. said that the interruption was "of such a character and duration that it vitally and fundamentally changed the conditions of the contract, and could not possibly have been in the contemplation of the parties to the contract when it was made."[9] An express provision in the contract cannot exclude frustration by supervening illegality where this would be against public policy.[10]

---

[2] *ibid.* at 186–187.

[3] [1934] A.C. 176.

[4] *Studholme v. South Western Gas Board* [1954] 1 W.L.R. 313. See also *Marshall v. Glanvill* [1917] 2 K.B. 87.

[5] Treitel, *Frustration and Force Majeure* (1994), Chap. 8.

[6] McNair (1944) 60 L.Q.R. 160, 162–163. Supervening illegality is probably included in the term "frustration" in the Law Reform (Frustrated Contracts) Act 1943 (*post*, § 24–072 *et seq.*).

[7] See *post*, § 24–029.

[8] [1918] A.C. 119. *cf. White & Carter Ltd v. Carbis Bay Garage Ltd* [1941] 2 All E.R. 633.

[9] [1918] A.C. 119, 126.

[10] *Ertel Bieber & Co. v. Rio Tinto Co. Ltd* [1918] A.C. 260 (*post*, § 24–029).

24–024   **Other war-time restrictions.** In *Denny, Mott and Dickson Ltd v. James B. Fraser & Co. Ltd*[11] a contract for the sale and purchase of timber contained an option for the appellants to purchase a timber-yard (which was meanwhile let to them) if the contract was terminated on notice given by either party. By the Control of Timber (No. 4) Order 1939 further trading transactions under the contract became illegal, but in 1941 the appellants gave notice to terminate the contract, and also to exercise their option to purchase the timber-yard. The House of Lords held that the option to purchase was dependent on the trading agreement, that the 1939 Order had operated to frustrate the contract, and that, consequently, the option to purchase lapsed upon the frustration since it arose only if the contract was terminated by notice. Temporary, war-time restrictions may not frustrate a long-term lease, which will continue in force for many years after the restrictions are lifted; so long as it exists, the restriction will, however, provide an excuse for not complying with a covenant in the lease.[12]

24–025   **Exercise of statutory power.** The same principle of supervening illegality operates where a statutory power in existence at the time of making the contract is subsequently exercised to render illegal the performance of the contract. Thus in *Re Shipton Anderson & Co. and Harrison Bros. & Co.*[13] wheat was sold upon terms that payment in cash was to be made within seven days against a delivery order. But before delivery and before the property passed to the buyer the government requisitioned the wheat under an Act passed before the date of the contract; the contract was held to be frustrated so that the sellers were excused from performance.

24–026   **Supervening illegality under a foreign law.** Where a contract governed by English law as its applicable law is to be performed abroad, and that performance becomes illegal by the law of the place of performance (*lex loci solutionis*), the contract will not, according to common law rules, be enforced in England.[14] The principle of frustration by supervening illegality operates where the change in the *lex loci solutionis* occurs after the formation of the contract but before its performance. Hence an English court will not enforce a contract governed by English law for the payment in Spain of freight under a charterparty exceeding the maximum amount fixed, after the making of the contract, by Spanish law.[15] A party relying on frustration by the *lex loci solutionis* must show that the illegality covered the whole of the period within which performance was due; thus where a foreign export control regulation prohibited performance of a

---

[11] [1944] A.C. 265.
[12] *Cricklewood Property and Investment Trust Ltd v. Leightons Investment Trust Ltd* [1945] A.C. 221 (*post*, § 24–050). *cf. Eyre v. Johnson* [1946] K.B. 481 (*post*, § 24–064, n. 6).
[13] [1915] 3 K.B. 676. Contrast *Walton Harvey Ltd v. Walker and Homfrays Ltd* [1931] 1 Ch. 274.
[14] *Ralli Bros. v. Compania Naviera Sota y Aznar* [1920] 2 K.B. 287. For an illustration, see *The Nile Co. for the Export of Agricultural Crops v. H. & J.M. Bennett (Commodities) Ltd* [1986] 1 Lloyd's Rep. 555, 581–582. The same result would appear to be reached under Art. 8 of the Rome Convention on the Law Applicable to Contractual Obligations: Contracts (Applicable Law) Act 1990, Sched. 1. See Cheshire and North, *Private International Law* (12th ed.), p. 519; *post*, § 31–155; *Dicey and Morris on the Conflict of Laws* (12th ed., 1993), pp. 1239–1248.
[15] *Ralli Bros. v. Compania Naviera Sota y Aznar, supra; cf. A.V. Pound & Co. Ltd v. M.W. Hardy & Co. Inc.* [1956] A.C. 588 (refusal by foreign authorities to grant export licence for performance of an English contract). On a partial prohibition by the *lex loci solutionis*, see *Benjamin's Sale of Goods* (5th ed., 1997), §§ 18–286—18–293.

contract during only part of the contract period, the exporters were held liable for failure to perform during the time no prohibition existed.[16]

A contract governed by English law is not frustrated where the *lex loci*   **24–027** *solutionis*, without making performance illegal, merely excuses a party from performance in full[17]; nor is an English contract frustrated because the party liable to perform would, by his performance, contravene the law of the place of his residence, or of which he is a national (if that law is neither the applicable law nor the *lex loci solutionis*).[18]

It is uncertain whether illegality by the *lex loci solutionis* as such would have   **24–028** any effect in an English court if the law applicable to the contract was not English but a foreign law, and the place of performance was outside England.[19] In such cases, the effect of illegality by the *lex loci solutionis* would seem to be a matter for the applicable law, subject to the rules of English public policy.[20] The mere fact that performance has become illegal under the law of a foreign country does not of itself amount to frustration of the contract unless the contract expressly or impliedly requires performance in that country.[21]

Outbreak of war. The outbreak of war renders illegal all intercourse between   **24–029** British subjects (or other persons owing temporary allegiance to the Crown) and alien enemies.[22] Consequently, any contract which involves such intercourse is automatically dissolved by the outbreak of war, or by the party thereto becoming an alien enemy,[23] even though it contains a clause suspending its operation during the continuance of a state of war, for this would be void as against public policy.[24] Any contract which, though not actually made with a party who becomes an alien enemy, necessarily involves intercourse with or advantage to

---

[16] *Ross T. Smyth & Co. (Liverpool) Ltd v. W.N. Lindsay (Leith) Ltd* [1953] 1 W.L.R. 1280. *cf. Walton (Grain and Shipping) Ltd v. British Italian Trading Co. Ltd* [1959] 1 Lloyd's Rep. 223.

[17] *Jacobs v. Credit Lyonnais* (1884) 12 Q.B.D. 589 (the headnote of this case is misleading: see *Ralli Bros. v. Compania Naviera Sota y Aznar, supra*, at 292, 297, 301); *Blackburn Bobbin Co. Ltd v. T.W. Allen & Sons Ltd* [1918] 2 K.B. 467.

[18] *Dicey and Morris op. cit.* p. 1244; *Kleinwort Sons & Co. v. Ungarische Baumwolle Industrie Aktien-Gesellschaft* [1939] 2 K.B. 678 (the principle of this case is clearly approved by three members of the House of Lords in *Kahler v. Midland Bank* [1950] A.C. 24).

[19] *Dicey and Morris op. cit.* p. 1245.

[20] For a discussion of the common law rules, see Cheshire and North, *Private International Law* (11th ed.), pp. 485–489; Mann (1937) 18 B.Y.B.I.L. 107. But see dicta to the contrary: *Zivnostenka Banka v. Frankman* [1950] A.C. 57, 78; *Mackender v. Feldia A.G.* [1967] 2 Q.B. 590, 601. The same doubt would appear to exist under the Rome Convention on the Law Applicable to Contractual Obligations. Art. 7(1) of the Convention does not have the force of law in the United Kingdom (Contracts (Applicable Law) Act 1990, s.2(2)) and so cannot be invoked in the present context, although it is arguable that the contract could possibly be invalidated under Arts. 7(2), 10(2) or 16: see further *post*, § 31–155; Cheshire and North, *Private International Law* (12th ed.), pp. 519–520; *Dicey and Morris op. cit.* pp. 1245–1247; Reynolds (1992) 108 L.Q.R. 553.

[21] *Bangladesh Export Import Co. Ltd v. Sucden Kerry S.A.* [1995] 2 Lloyd's Rep. 1, 5–6.

[22] *Robson v. Premier Oil and Pipe Line Co. Ltd* [1915] 2 Ch. 124. See *ante*, § 17–026; McNair and Watts, *Legal Effects of War* (4th ed.), especially Chap. 3; Webber, *Effect of War on Contracts* (2nd ed.); Rogers, *Effect of War on Contracts* (1940); Trotter, *Law of Contract during and after War* (4th ed.). As to who is an alien enemy, see *ante*, §§ 11–020, 17–157; Trading with the Enemy Act 1939, s.2 (as amended); Howard, *Trading with the Enemy* (1943).

[23] *Esposito v. Bowden* (1857) 7 E. & B. 763; *Ertel Bieber & Co. v. Rio Tinto Co. Ltd* [1918] A.C. 260; *Naylor Benzon & Co. Ltd v. Krainische Industrie Gesellschaft* [1918] 2 K.B. 486. On the effect of war on a contract of agency, see Vol. II, § 32–160 (iv).

[24] *Ertel Bieber & Co. v. Rio Tinto Co. Ltd, supra*.

the enemy, is within the rule.[25] In other cases, where the outbreak of war does not itself render one party to the contract an alien enemy, the question whether the contract has been frustrated depends on the effect upon the contract of the acts done in furtherance of the war.[26]

24–030 **Accrued rights.** Accrued rights under a contract which has been frustrated (*e.g.* for a liquidated sum of money already due) are not destroyed,[27] though the right of suing in respect of such rights may be suspended for the duration of the war or so long as the claimant remains an alien enemy.[28] Thus, where a partnership agreement is dissolved by one partner becoming an alien enemy the enemy partner is nevertheless entitled to a share in the profits made thereafter by the English partner with the aid of the enemy partner's share of the capital.[29]

24–031 **Exceptions.** Some executory contracts, whose continuance in force is not against public policy, are not abrogated by one party becoming an alien enemy; for instance, a separation agreement by which a husband agrees to pay regular maintenance to his wife remains in force when she becomes an alien enemy, though during the war payments should be made to the Custodian of Enemy Property.[30]

(ii) *Cancellation of an Expected Event*

24–032 **The "coronation cases."** The cancellation of an expected event can, in exceptional circumstances, operate to frustrate a contract. That this is so can be demonstrated by reference to the "coronation cases," so-called because they arose out of actions brought in consequence of the postponement of the coronation processions in June 1902, owing to the illness of King Edward VII. These cases are important both because they show that the event which is alleged to have frustrated the contract need not result in the physical destruction of the subject-matter of the contract, but may frustrate the "commercial purpose" of the contract and because they also illustrate the narrow confines within which the doctrine of frustration currently operates. The most prominent of these cases is *Krell v. Henry*,[31] where the defendant agreed in writing to hire rooms in the plaintiff's flat in Pall Mall on June 26 and 27 in order to see the coronation processions which had been announced for those days. The written contract made

---

[25] *Re Badische Co. Ltd* [1921] 2 Ch. 331, 373–378. See also the *Fibrosa* case [1943] A.C. 32 (*post*, § 24–070).

[26] *Akties, Nord-Osterso Rederiet v. E.A. Casper, Edgar & Co.* (1923) 14 Ll.L.Rep. 203, 206; *Finelvet A.G. v. Vinava Shipping Co. Ltd* [1983] 1 W.L.R. 1469; *International Sea Tankers Inc. v. Hemisphere Shipping Co. Ltd (The Wenjiang (No. 2))* [1983] 1 Lloyd's Rep. 400, 405–406. On delay, see *post*, § 24–034.

[27] McNair and Watts *op. cit.* pp. 135–144; *Schering Ltd v. Stockholms Enskilda Bank Aktiebolag* [1946] A.C. 219; *Arab Bank Ltd v. Barclays Bank* [1954] A.C. 495; *Re Claim by Helbert Wagg & Co. Ltd* [1956] Ch. 323, 354.

[28] See *ante*, §§ 11–020—11–028.

[29] *Hugh Stevenson and Sons Ltd v. Aktiengesellschaft für Cartonnagen-Industrie* [1918] A.C. 239.

[30] *Bevan v. Bevan* [1955] 2 Q.B. 227.

[31] [1903] 2 K.B. 740. See Treitel, *Frustration and Force Majeure* (1994), §§ 7–005—7–013; McElroy & Williams (1941) 4 M.L.R. 241 and 5 M.L.R. 1.

no express reference to the processions, but it was clear from the circumstances that both parties regarded the viewing of the processions as the sole purpose of the hiring. When the processions were postponed, the defendant declined to pay the balance of the agreed rent, and the Court of Appeal upheld his refusal, on the ground that "the Coronation procession was the foundation of this contract and that the non-happening of it prevented the performance of the contract"[32] within the principle of *Taylor v. Caldwell*.[33] The court also held that parol evidence was admissible to prove what was the subject-matter of the contract.[34] Similarly, in *Chandler v. Webster*[35] another contract to let rooms "to view the first Coronation procession" was held to be frustrated by the postponement; the same result occurred with contracts to take seats on a stand built in order to view the procession.[36]

A different result was reached, however, in *Herne Bay Steamboat Co. v. Hutton*[37] where the plaintiffs' steamboat was engaged by the defendant to take passengers from Herne Bay on June 28 and 29, 1902, "for the purpose of viewing the Naval Review at Spithead and for a day's cruise round the fleet." The hire was £250, of which £50 was paid in advance, the balance to be paid before the vessel left Herne Bay. On June 25 the review was cancelled. The plaintiffs asked the defendant for instructions and for the balance of hire. As the defendant did not reply the plaintiffs used the vessel for their own purposes. In an action for the balance of the £250 the Court of Appeal held that it was payable, as "the purpose of Mr. Hutton, whether of seeing the naval review or of going round the fleet with a party of paying guests, does not lay the foundation of the contract within the authorities,"[38] such as *Taylor v. Caldwell*. The case may also be explicable on another ground, namely, that as the fleet remained anchored in Spithead, it was still possible to use the vessel "for a day's cruise round the fleet," so that there had not been a complete failure of the fundamental purpose of the contract. *Krell v. Henry* and *Herne Bay Steamboat Co. v. Hutton* are not entirely easy to reconcile.[39] But it is clear that it is *Krell* which is the exceptional case: it has been subject to much criticism[40] and as an authority it "is certainly not one to be extended."[41] The vital factor in *Krell* was probably that the flat was hired for the days but not the nights and so the only conceivable purpose of the contract was to view the coronation procession. Thus the case has been kept within very

24–033

---

[32] [1903] 2 K.B. 740, 751.

[33] (1863) 3 B. & S. 826 (*ante*, § 24–005).

[34] [1903] 2 K.B. 740, 754.

[35] [1904] 1 K.B. 493. (That part of the case dealing with the legal consequences of frustration is no longer good law: see *post*, §§ 24–070 *et seq.*)

[36] *Blakeley v. Muller* [1903] 2 K.B. 760n. *cf. Clark v. Lindsay* (1903) 88 L.T. 198; *Griffith v. Brymer* (1903) 19 T.L.R. 434 (although this is a case of common mistake because the "impossibility" was antecedent).

[37] [1903] 2 K.B. 683. See Gottschalk, *Impossibility of Performance in Contract* (1945), pp. 16–18. *cf. Civil Service Co-operative Society v. General Steam Navigation Co.* [1903] 2 K.B. 756.

[38] [1903] 2 K.B. 683, 689.

[39] See the discussion of these cases in Treitel, *The Law of Contract* (9th ed., 1995), pp. 797–799; Cheshire, Fifoot & Furmston, *Law of Contract* (13th ed., 1996), pp. 587–588; McElroy & Williams (references in n. 31, *ante*).

[40] See, for example, *Larringa & Co. Ltd v. Société Franco-Americaine des Phosphates de Médulla, Paris* (1923) 39 T.L.R. 316, 318.

[41] *Maritime National Fish Ltd v. Ocean Trawlers Ltd* [1935] A.C. 524, 529 (Lord Wright).

narrow confines so that it cannot be invoked by a party whose aim is simply to escape from what has proved to be a bad bargain.[42]

(iii) Delay

24–034   **Delay.**[43] It is often a difficult matter to decide whether a contract has been frustrated by an event or change in circumstances which causes unexpected delay in its performance. In *Pioneer Shipping Ltd v. B.T.P. Tioxide Ltd (The Nema)*,[44] Lord Roskill, in a speech concurred in by all their Lordships, said:

> "it is often necessary to wait upon events in order to see whether the delay already suffered and the prospects of further delay from that cause, will make any ultimate performance of the relevant contractual obligations 'radically different' . . . from that which was undertaken by the contract. But, as has often been said, business men must not be required to await events too long. They are entitled to know where they stand. Whether or not the delay is such as to bring about frustration must be a question to be determined by an informed judgment based upon all the evidence of what has occurred and what is likely thereafter to occur.[45] Often it will be a question of degree whether the effect of delay suffered, and likely to be suffered, will be such as to bring about frustration of the particular adventure in question."[46]

For this purpose, causes of delay should not be divided into classes: a strike may cause frustration of a commercial adventure through delay as much as any other cause: "It is not the nature of the cause which matters so much as the effect of that cause upon the performance of the obligations which the parties have assumed one towards the other."[47] To frustrate a contract, the delay must be abnormal, in its cause, its effects, or its expected duration, so that it falls outside what the parties could reasonably contemplate at the time of contracting.[48] The fact that the delay was caused by "a new and unforeseeable factor or event" is a relevant matter.[49] The probable length of the delay must be assessed in relation to the nature of the contract, and to the expected duration of the contract after the

---

[42] *Amalgamated Investment & Property Co. Ltd v. John Walker & Son Ltd* [1977] 1 W.L.R. 164; *Pioneer Shipping Ltd v. B.T.P. Tioxide Ltd (The Nema)* [1982] A.C. 724, 752. See also *Congimex Companhia Geral S.A.R.L. v. Tradax Export SA* [1983] 1 Lloyd's Rep. 250, 253.

[43] Treitel, *Frustration and Force Majeure* (1994), §§ 5–031—5–050; Howard in McKendrick (ed.), *Force Majeure and Frustration of Contract* (2nd ed., 1995) pp. 122–131; Stannard (1983) 46 M.L.R. 738.

[44] [1982] A.C. 724, 752.

[45] "Commercial men must be entitled to act on reasonable commercial probabilities at the time they are called upon to make up their minds": *per* Lord Simon in *National Carriers Ltd v. Panalpina (Northern) Ltd* [1981] A.C. 675, 706 (see also at 688) (following *Embiricos v. Sydney Reid & Co.* [1914] 3 K.B. 45, 54). As to the point of time when prospective delay must be judged, see *Watts, Watts & Co. Ltd v. Mitsui & Co. Ltd* [1917] A.C. 227, 245–246; *Andrew Millar & Co. Ltd v. Taylor & Co. Ltd* [1916] 1 K.B. 402; *Total Gas Marketing Ltd v. Arco British Ltd* [1998] 2 Lloyd's Rep. 209, 222; also *post*, § 24–042, and McNair (1940) 56 L.Q.R. 173, 201–205.

[46] On such a question, an appellate court should be reluctant to interfere with the conclusion of the tribunal of fact: see *ante*, § 24–015; *post*, § 24–095, n. 4. See *Kodros Shipping Corporation v. Empresa Cubana de Fletes (The Evia) (No. 2)* [1983] 1 A.C. 736, 767–768; *cf. International Sea Tankers Inc. v. Hemisphere Shipping Co. (The Wenjiang)* [1982] 2 All E.R. 437; *Adelfamar SA v. Silos E. Mangimi Martini SpA* [1988] 2 Lloyd's Rep. 466, 471.

[47] *Pioneer Shipping Ltd v. B.T.P. Tioxide Ltd (The Nema)* [1982] A.C. 724, 754 (*per* Lord Roskill, citing *The Penelope* [1928] P. 180); *Eridania SpA v. Rudolf A. Oetker (The Fjord Wind)* [1998] C.L.C. 1187.

[48] See the quotation, *post*, in § 24–049.

[49] See *post*, § 24–048, 24–057.

delay is expected to end.[50] There can be no frustration if the delay in question was within the commercial risks undertaken by the parties.[51]

Illustrations. Many illustrations of the effect of delay on particular contracts   **24–035** will be found throughout this chapter: in relation to charterparties, delay caused by the stranding of the ship,[52] the requisitioning of the ship by the Government,[53] its seizure by insurgents,[54] the blocking of the Suez Canal,[55] or strikes[56]; in relation to building contracts, delay caused by war-time restrictions,[57] or by bad weather and unforeseen shortage of labour[58]; in relation to contracts of carriage, delay caused by the blocking of the usual route[59]; and in relation to leases, the prohibition of building,[60] or the closing of vehicular access to the property.[61]

(c) *Application of the Doctrine to Common Types of Contracts*

(i) *Personal Contracts*[62]

Death. The rule is stated by Pollock C.B. in *Hall v. Wright*[63]: "All contracts   **24–036** for personal services which can be performed only during the lifetime of the party contracting are subject to the implied condition that he shall be alive to perform them; and, should he die, his executor is not liable to an action for the breach of contract occasioned by his death." Thus, in *Graves v. Cohen*[64] the court considered the effect upon a jockey's contract for personal services of the death of his employer, a racehorse owner. The court held that death frustrated his jockey's contract with him, since the contract created a relationship involving

---

[50] This is particularly important in leases (*post*, §§ 24–050—24–054); charterparties (*post*, §§ 24–040—24–044); and building contracts (*post*, §§ 24–047—24–049).

[51] *Davis Contractors Ltd v. Fareham U.D.C.* [1956] A.C. 696; *King v. Parker* (1876) 34 L.T. 887 (delay in deliveries of coal due to strike held insufficient to frustrate contract of sale); *Trade and Transport Inc. v. Iino Kaiun Kaisha Ltd* [1973] 1 W.L.R. 210, 221–222; *Intertradex SA v. Lesieur-Tourteaux S.A.R.L.* [1978] 2 Lloyd's Rep. 509, 514, 515–516. (But see the comment of Lord Roskill on the court's imposing its own view on this issue, rather than adopting the view of the arbitral tribunal: *Pioneer Shipping Ltd v. B.T.P. Tioxide Ltd* [1982] A.C. 724, 752–753; and n. 46, *supra*.)

[52] *Ante*, § 24–046.

[53] *Post*, §§ 24–040—24–042.

[54] *Post*, § 24–043.

[55] *Post*, § 24–043.

[56] *Post*, § 24–044.

[57] *Post*, § 24–023.

[58] *Post*, §§ 24–048—24–049.

[59] *Post*, § 24–046.

[60] *Post*, § 24–052.

[61] *Post*, § 24–053.

[62] See *ante*, §§ 21–006, 24–022; Vol. II, §§ 39–153—39–155.

[63] (1858) E.B. & E. 746, 793. (The actual decision in this case, to the effect that supervening illness of the defendant did not frustrate a contract to marry, even though the defendant could not consummate the marriage without danger to his life, might not have been followed, quite apart from the change in the law which now prevents promises to marry from giving rise to legal rights: Law Reform (Miscellaneous Provisions) Act 1970, s.1. The case is discussed in more detail by Treitel, *Frustration and Force Majeure* (1994), § 2–015. For a discussion of the previous law on frustration of a promise to marry, see Powell (1961) 14 C.L.P. 100.) *cf. Stubbs v. Holywell Ry.* (1867) L.R. 2 Ex. 311.

[64] (1930) 46 T.L.R. 121. See also *Morgan v. Manser* [1948] 1 K.B. 184.

mutual confidence. However, in *Phillips v. Alhambra Palace Co. Ltd*[65] one partner in a firm of music-hall proprietors died after the firm had engaged a troupe of performers, but it was held that the contract was not frustrated, since it was not of such a personal character and so could be enforced against the surviving partners. Similarly, it has been held that a tenancy at a weekly rent is not determined by the death of the tenant.[66]

24–037   **Illness or incapacity.** The question whether a contract of employment has been frustrated[67] by the employee's illness or incapacity depends on whether it was of such a nature or likely to continue for such a period, that future performance of his contractual duties would be either impossible or radically different from that envisaged by the contract.[68] In applying this test, the court will treat as relevant factors the terms of the contract (including any sick pay provisions), the nature and expected duration of the employment, the period of past employment, and the prospects of recovery.[69] Thus, permanent illness may frustrate an apprenticeship,[70] while a short period of illness may frustrate a shorter-term contract.[71] A periodic contract of employment which is determinable by the employer by short notice may nevertheless be frustrated by illness or injury which incapacitates the employee[72]: in *Notcutt v. Universal Equipment Co. (London) Ltd*, it was held that the contract was frustrated (by operation of law and thus without notice) as soon as it became clear that the employee's illness would prevent him from ever working again.[73] Illness may also provide an employee with a temporary excuse for non-performance of his contractual obligations without the contract being discharged by operation of the doctrine of frustration.[74]

24–038   **Imprisonment or compulsory service.** A sentence of imprisonment (or of Borstal training) upon an employee (except possibly in the case of a very short

---

[65] [1901] 1 Q.B. 59; for the converse case, *cf. Harvey v. Tivoli (Manchester) Ltd* (1907) 23 T.L.R. 592.

[66] *Youngmin v. Heath* [1974] 1 All E.R. 461 (although the judgments do not discuss the case in terms of the doctrine of frustration).

[67] Even where the contract of employment has not been frustrated, a dismissal of an employee on the grounds of ill-health may not be "unfair" within the relevant statutory provisions: see Vol. II, § 39–202. See Mogridge (1982) 132 New L.J. 795.

[68] *Storey v. Fulham Steel Works* (1907) 24 T.L.R. 89; *Condor v. The Barron Knights Ltd* [1966] 1 W.L.R. 87; *Marshall v. Harland & Wolff Ltd* [1972] 1 W.L.R. 899; *Hebden v. Forsey & Son* [1973] I.C.R. 607; *Hart v. A.R. Marshall & Sons (Bulwell) Ltd* [1977] 1 W.L.R. 1067; *Notcutt v. Universal Equipment Co. (London) Ltd* [1986] 1 W.L.R. 641; *GF Sharp & Co. Ltd v. McMillan* [1998] I.R.L.R. 632. See Howarth [1987] C.L.J. 47; *Harvey on Industrial Relations and Employment Law*, Vol. 1, Div. A, paras. 811–826 and Div. D, paras. 354–368.

[69] *Marshall v. Harland & Wolff Ltd, supra*, at 903–905. See Freedland, *The Contract of Employment* (1976), pp. 301–311. *cf. post*, § 24–042.

[70] *Boast v. Firth* (1868) L.R. 4 C.P. 1. (Temporary illness, however, may give an employee a temporary excuse for failure to work: *post*, § 24–064—24–070, and Vol. II, § 39–155.)

[71] *Egg Stores (Stamford Hill) Ltd v. Leibovici* [1977] I.C.R. 260 ("has the time arrived when the employer can no longer reasonably be expected to keep the absent employee's post open for him?": at 264).

[72] *Notcutt v. Universal Equipment Co. (London) Ltd* [1986] 1 W.L.R. 641.

[73] *ibid.*

[74] This, it is submitted, is the best explanation of the difficult case of *Poussard v. Spiers and Pond* (1876) 1 Q.B.D. 410. The contract there was not automatically discharged as a result of the plaintiff's illness, rather, the defendants were given an option to terminate the contract and they chose to exercise that option. See further § 24–066, n. 13.

sentence) will frustrate his contract of employment or of apprenticeship as from the date of the sentence.[75] Detention during war-time may also frustrate a contract. In *Horlock v. Beal*[76] a British ship was detained in a German port on the outbreak of the First World War and the crew imprisoned. The House of Lords held that the crew were not entitled to wages during their detention, which had rendered it impossible for them to fulfil their contract of employment. Other contracts of employment have been frustrated where a refugee, employed in England, was interned during the war,[77] and where a music-hall artiste was called up for service in the army.[78]

Other events. If an arbitration is restricted to the submission of an identified, **24-039** existing dispute to a named arbitrator, the agreement is frustrated if the arbitrator turns out not to be impartial.[79] But long delay in proceeding with an arbitration does not frustrate the agreement to submit the dispute to arbitration.[80] A separation agreement under which the husband covenants to pay maintenance to his wife is not frustrated by a subsequent decree of divorce obtained by the wife,[81] nor by a subsequent decree of nullity obtained by the husband on the ground of the wife's incapacity.[82] The Court of Appeal has left open the question whether the doctrine of frustration could ever apply to the status of marriage,[83] but it is submitted that it should not, because to frustrate a marriage under a doctrine of

---

[75] *Hare v. Murphy Brothers Ltd* [1974] I.C.R. 603 (12 months' imprisonment); *F.C. Shepherd & Co. Ltd v. Jerrom* [1987] Q.B. 301 (Borstal training, which is for an indefinite period: the sentence would be "a substantial break in the period of training" under the apprenticeship agreement (*ibid.* at 320) which had not yet run for half the period). But see *Chakki v. United Yeast Co. Ltd* [1982] 2 All E.R. 446 (imprisonment may not frustrate the contract immediately upon sentence); *Harvey on Industrial Relations and Employment Law*, Vol. 1, Div. D, paras. 369–400.

[76] [1916] 1 A.C. 486 (distinguished in *Ottoman Bank v. Chakarian* [1930] A.C. 277, where a temporary and limited disability did not frustrate a contract of service).

[77] *Unger v. Preston Corporation* [1942] 1 All E.R. 200. *cf. Nordman v. Rayner & Sturges* (1916) 33 T.L.R. 87.

[78] *Morgan v. Manser* [1948] 1 K.B. 184. See also *Marshall v. Glanvill* [1917] 2 K.B. 87 (*ante* § 24–022). *cf. Hangkam Kwingtong Woo v. Liu Lan Fong* [1951] A.C. 707 (agency not frustrated by agent being in enemy-occupied territory).

[79] *Bremer Vulkan Schiffbau und Maschinenfabrik v. South India Shipping Corporation Ltd* [1981] A.C. 909, 981.

[80] Delay was employed in an unsuccessful attempt to invoke the doctrine of frustration in a line of cases which arose out of agreements to arbitrate which had "gone to sleep" and then one party later attempted to revive the arbitration (the leading example is the decision of the House of Lords in *Paal Wilson & Co. A/S v. Partenreederei Hannah Blumenthal* [1983] 1 A.C. 854, discussed in the 27th edition of this work at 23–025). The problem has now been resolved by statute giving to the arbitrator the power to dismiss any claim in a dispute referred to him if it appears to him that there has been an inordinate and inexcusable delay on the part of the claimant in pursuing the claim and that the delay either will give rise or is likely to give rise to a substantial risk that it is not possible to have a fair resolution of the issues or that it has caused, or is likely to have caused, serious prejudice to the respondent (Arbitration Act 1996, s.41(3)). Regard may be had to delay which occurred before arbitrators were given this statutory power (see *L'Office Cherifien des Phosphates v. Yamashita-Shinnhon Steamship Co. Ltd* [1994] 1 A.C. 486). The intervention of statute has removed the need to invoke the doctrine of frustration in this fact situation.

[81] *May v. May* [1929] 2 K.B. 386. The result is the same if the divorce is obtained by the husband: *Charlesworth v. Holt* (1873) L.R. 9 Ex. 38.

[82] *Adams v. Adams* [1941] 1 K.B. 536. (In this case, as well as in *May v. May, supra*, it was open to either party to apply to the court for a variation of the agreement: see now s.35 of the Matrimonial Causes Act 1973; *Tomkins v. Tomkins* [1948] P. 170.)

[83] *Kenward v. Kenward* [1951] P. 124.

the common law would amount to adding to the grounds for divorce without legislation.

(ii) Charterparties[84]

24–040   **Requisitioning.** The doctrine of frustration has been frequently invoked in disputes concerning charterparties, and the application of the doctrine is well illustrated by such cases. A leading decision of the House of Lords is *Bank Line Ltd v. Arthur Capel & Co.*,[85] where a ship was let on a time charter of 12 months from the time she was delivered to the charterers. Before such delivery, however, the ship was requisitioned by the Government. The charterparty contained a special clause giving the charterers the option of cancelling the charter if the ship was not delivered by a fixed date or if she was commandeered by the Government during the currency of the charter, but the charterers did not exercise their option to cancel. Three months after the requisitioning the owners (who regarded the charterparty as frustrated) sold the ship to third parties subject to her release by the Government, and a month later she was released and the sale completed. The charterers brought an action for non-delivery of the ship, but the House of Lords held that the doctrine of frustration applied to time charters, and that the object of this charterparty had been frustrated by the requisitioning and detention of the ship, since the identity of the chartered service had been destroyed. The House also held that the doctrine of frustration had not been excluded by the special clauses of the charterparty. They merely gave the charterers an express option to cancel in the event of requisition, "without waiting to see or having to show that its object is thereby frustrated."[86] Their function was not to preclude resort to frustration.

24–041   **The Tamplin case.** Three years prior to *Bank Line* the House of Lords decided another case on frustration of a charterparty by requisitioning, namely, *F.A. Tamplin Steamship Co. Ltd v. Anglo-American Petroleum Products Co. Ltd*.[87] In the latter case a ship was chartered under a time charter for five years

---

[84] *Scrutton on Charterparties* (20th ed., 1996), 23–31; Treitel, *Frustration and Force Majeure* (1994) §§ 5–046—5–048; see (in addition to the cases cited *post*) *Geipel v. Smith* (1872) L.R. 7 Q.B. 404 (blockading of port); *Jackson v. Union Marine Insurance Co. Ltd* (1874) L.R. 10 C.P. 125 (stranding; *ante*, § 24–006); *Dahl v. Nelson, Donkin & Co.* (1881) 6 App.Cas. 38 (dock authorities refused to admit ship because dock was full: held, charterer bound to permit unloading at alternative place mentioned in charterparty); *Lloyd Royal Belge SA v. Stathatos* (1917) 34 T.L.R. 70 (ship detained by naval authorities for over two months); *Larrinaga & Co. Ltd v. Société Franco-Americaine des Phosphates de Médulla* (1923) 39 T.L.R. 316; *Hirji Mulji v. Cheong Yue SS. Co. Ltd* [1926] A.C. 497 (requisitioning); *Court Line Ltd v. Dant & Russell Inc.* [1939] 3 All E.R. 314 (boom blocking river during war); *Joseph Constantine SS. Line Ltd v. Imperial Smelting Corporation Ltd* [1942] A.C. 154 (explosion); *Blane SS. Ltd v. Minister of Transport* [1951] 2 K.B. 965 (stranding); *Atlantic Maritime Co. Inc. v. Gibbon* [1954] 1 Q.B. 88 (marine insurance: restraint of princes clause); *cf. Hongkong Fir Shipping Co. Ltd v. Kawasaki Kisen Kaisha Ltd* [1962] 2 Q.B. 26 (delays caused by breakdowns and repairs where shipowners in breach); *Pioneer Shipping Ltd v. B.T.P. Tioxide Ltd (The Nema)* [1982] A.C. 724 (long delay caused by strike at port of loading: see *ante* § 24–034; *Adelfamar SA v. Silos E. Mangimi Martini SpA (The Adelfa)* [1988] 2 Lloyd's Rep. 466 (arrest of vessel by third party). See also the cases cited *ante*, § 24–034, n. 46.

[85] [1919] A.C. 435.
[86] [1919] A.C. 435, 456.
[87] [1916] 2 A.C. 397.

to sail between any safe ports within certain limits as the charterers should direct. After the outbreak of the First World War, when the charter had nearly three years to run, the ship was requisitioned by the Admiralty and converted by structural alterations into a troopship. The owners contended that the charter had been determined by the requisitioning, but this was denied by the charterers, who were willing to continue to pay the agreed freight. The House decided by a majority that the interruption was not sufficient to frustrate the contract. Earl Loreburn said that both parties "would have been considerably surprised to be told that interruption for a few months was to release them both from a time charter that was to last five years . . . I think that they took their chance of lesser interruptions and the condition I should imply goes no further than that they should be excused if substantially the whole contract became impossible of performance, or in other words, impracticable, by some cause for which neither was responsible."[88] The fact that it was the shipowners rather than the charterers who were arguing that the contract was frustrated so that they could obtain the generous rates of compensation paid by the Government undoubtedly weighed with the majority.[89]

The application of the doctrine of frustration will always depend on the **24–042** particular facts of each case, but it is difficult to reconcile these two cases, except on the basis that in *Tamplin* the interruption was of a time charter for five years, while in *Bank Line* the interruption had a more serious effect, since the time charter was for the much shorter period of one year:

> " . . . the main thing to be considered is the probable length of the total deprivation of the use of the chartered ship compared with the unexpired duration of the charter-party. . . . The probabilities as to the length of the deprivation and not the certainty arrived at after the event are also material. The question must be considered at the trial as it had to be considered by the parties, when they came to know of the cause and the probabilities of the delay, and had to decide what to do."[90]

This approach to the problem of requisitioning is supported by the case of *Port Line Ltd v. Ben Line Steamers Ltd*,[91] where Diplock J. held that a time charter-party for 30 months (of which 17 had expired) was not frustrated by a government requisitioning which was expected to last, and did in fact last, only about three months. At the time of derequisition of the vessel there was still 10 months of the charterparty to run and in these circumstances it could not be said that the contract was frustrated. The fact that the ship was requisitioned under the prerogative of the Crown, which meant that the Crown could retain the ship only for such period as was necessary for the defence of the realm was a relevant

---

[88] *ibid.* at 405–406.

[89] Lord Parker of Waddington thought that the doctrine of frustration could not apply to a time charter which "does not contemplate any definite adventure or object to be performed or carried out" (at 425) but this opinion was later rejected by the House of Lords in *Bank Line Ltd v. Arthur Capel & Co.* [1919] A.C. 435, 443.

[90] *Bank Line Ltd v. Arthur Capel & Co* [1919] A.C. 435, 454; *Court Line Ltd v. Dant & Russell Inc. supra*, at 318. See *ante*, § 24–040, n. 84; Howard in McKendrick (ed.), *Force Majeure and Frustration of Contract* (2nd ed., 1995), pp. 129–138.

[91] [1958] 2 Q.B. 146, 161–163.

factor because it indicated that the requisition was "necessarily a temporary taking of possession."[92]

24–043   **Other frustrating events.** In *W.J. Tatem v. Gamboa*[93] a ship was chartered by an agent of the Spanish Republican Government under a time charter for 30 days during the Spanish Civil War, in order to evacuate the civil population from north Spain. The hire of £250 a day (three times the normal rate) was payable until redelivery at a French port, and it was paid in advance for 30 days from July 1, when the charterers took over the ship. On July 14, she was seized by a Nationalist cruiser and detained until September 7. The risk of capture by the insurgents was known to the parties, but there was no provision for this event in the charterparty. The owners claimed hire at £250 a day from August 1 to September 11, the date of redelivery, but Goddard J. held that performance of the charterparty had been frustrated by the seizure. In *The Eugenia*,[94] the Court of Appeal held that a time charterparty, starting at Genoa for a single "trip out to India via Black Sea" (for which the Suez Canal was the customary route) was not frustrated by the blocking of the canal in 1956. Although the voyage around the Cape of Good Hope was longer and more expensive, it was not a "fundamentally different" voyage, since the cargo of metal goods "would not be adversely affected by the longer voyage and there was no special reason for early arrival."[95] On the other hand it was held that charterparties were frustrated when, following the outbreak of the war between Iran and Iraq, vessels were trapped for an indefinite period in the Shatt-al-Arab waterway.[96]

24–044   The reports contain other examples of cases in which an unexpected event has not released a party from his obligation under a charterparty. In *Thiis v. Byers*[97] the master of a ship was obliged, at the place of discharge, to make the cargo of timber into rafts so that the charterer's agents could tow the rafts away. Rough weather prevented this method of unloading for four days, but it was held that when a given number of days is allowed to the charterer for unloading, he must "take the risk of any ordinary vicissitudes" which may delay the operation; hence he was liable for four days' demurrage. Similarly in *Budgett & Co. v. Binnington & Co.*[98] a strike of dock labour did not release the consignees from their obligation to pay demurrage where the clause of the charterparty (incorporated in the bill of lading) fixed the number of lay-days and did not contain any

---

[92] *ibid.* at 161.
[93] [1939] 1 K.B. 132.
[94] *Ocean Tramp Tankers Corporation v. V/O Sovfracht (The Eugenia)* [1964] 2 Q.B. 226.
[95] [1964] 2 Q.B. 226, 240. *The Eugenia* was followed (with reluctance) in *Palmco Shipping Inc. v. Continental Ore Corporation* [1970] 2 Lloyd's Rep. 21. As a result of the 1956 closing of the canal, many later charterparties contained a "Suez Canal clause" which has been held to be intended to apply to a future closing of the canal: see *Achille Lauro Fu Gioacchino & Co. v. Total Societa Italiana Per Azioni* [1969] 2 Lloyd's Rep. 65.
[96] *Kissavos Shipping Co. SA v. Empresa Cubana de Fletes (The Agathon)* [1982] 2 Lloyd's Rep. 211; *Kodros Shipping Corporation of Monrovia v. Empresa Cubana de Fletes (The Evia) (No. 2)* [1983] 1 A.C. 736; *International Sea Tankers Inc. v. Hemisphere Shipping Co. Ltd (The Wenjiang) (No. 2)* [1983] 1 Lloyd's Rep. 400; *Vinava Shipping Co. Ltd v. Fineluet A.G. (The Chrysalis)* [1983] 1 Lloyd's Rep. 503; Howard in McKendrick (ed.), *Force Majeure and Frustration of Contract*, (2nd ed., 1995) pp. 129–138.
[97] (1876) 1 Q.B.D. 244.
[98] [1891] 1 Q.B. 35.

exception for strikes.[99] *Budgett* may be contrasted with *The Penelope*,[1] where the general coal strike of 1926 frustrated a time charter under which the ship was to carry successive cargoes of coal from South Wales over a 12 month period; although the charterparty contained strike provisions, these were held to contemplate only an interruption due to a local withdrawal of labour, and not the total impossibility of any export of coal for more than eight months.

(iii) *Sale and Carriage of Goods*

Sale and carriage of goods. Section 7 of the Sale of Goods Act 1979 **24–045** provides a statutory rule for one instance of frustration: "Where there is an agreement to sell specific goods and subsequently the goods, without any fault on the part of the seller or buyer, perish before the risk passes to the buyer,[2] the agreement is avoided."[3] Where only part of the goods have perished, the court may imply into the contract a term which deals with the resulting situation.[4] Apart from section 7, the normal principles of the common law apply where it is alleged that an agreement to sell goods has been frustrated.[5] Thus, an agreement to sell goods is not frustrated merely because performance of the contract would be commercially unprofitable,[6] at least where performance is still physically and legally possible. On this ground it was once doubted whether a contract for the sale of unascertained goods could ever be frustrated,[7] but it has been held that it can, at all events where the importation of the goods from a particular country was the basis of the contract and where such importation has become impossible.[8] If a government does not place an absolute embargo on dealings in a certain commodity, but permits dealings subject to a licence being obtained, the

---

[99] Charterparties contain many express exceptions known as "excepted perils." See *Scrutton op. cit.* pp. 204 *et seq.* For a case on the construction of an exceptions clause, see *Reardon Smith Line Ltd v. Ministry of Agriculture* [1963] A.C. 691.

[1] [1928] P. 180.

[2] Once the risk has passed to the buyer, he must still pay the price, but the seller is discharged from his obligation to deliver: Vol. II, § 43–188.

[3] See Vol. II, §§ 43–033—43–036; *Benjamin's Sale of Goods* (5th ed., 1997), §§ 6–029 *et seq.*; Atiyah, *The Sale of Goods* (9th ed., 1995), pp. 306–311; Chalmers, *Sale of Goods* (18th ed., pp. 100–101; Fridman, *Sale of Goods in Canada* (4th ed., 1995), pp. 302–307; *Horn v. Minister of Food* [1948] 2 All E.R. 1036. *cf. Elphick v. Barnes* (1880) 5 C.P.D. 321; *Howell v. Coupland* (1876) 1 Q.B.D. 258; *H.R. and S. Sainsbury Ltd v. Street* [1972] 1 W.L.R. 834, 837 (*post*, § 24–066).

[4] See the discussion of *H.R. and S. Sainsbury Ltd v. Street, post*, in §§ 24–066.

[5] *e.g.* (in addition to the cases cited *post*) *Nickoll & Knight v. Ashton, Edridge & Co.* [1901] 2 K.B. 126 (agreement to sell goods to be shipped by specified ship which was stranded before shipment); *Re Shipton, Anderson & Co. and Harrison Bros. & Co.* [1915] 3 K.B. 676 (*ante*, § 24–025; requisition); *Dale SS. Co. Ltd v. Northern SS. Co. Ltd* (1918) 34 T.L.R. 271 (requisition of ship while being built); *Fibrosa Spolka Akcyjna v. Fairbairn Lawson Combe Barbour Ltd* [1943] A.C. 32 (*post*, § 24–070; place of delivery becoming enemy territory); *Denny, Mott & Dickson Ltd v. James B. Fraser & Co. Ltd* [1944] A.C. 265 (*ante*, § 24–024; wartime prohibition). *cf. King v. Parker* (1876) 34 L.T. 887; *Ross T. Smyth & Co. (Liverpool) Ltd v. W.N. Lindsay (Leith) Ltd* [1953] 1 W.L.R. 1280 (*ante*, § 24–026).

[6] *Blackburn Bobbin Co. v. Allen & Sons* [1918] 2 K.B. 467; *Re Comptoir Commercial Anversois & Power, Son & Co.* [1920] 1 K.B. 868; *Beves and Co. Ltd v. Farkas* [1953] 1 Lloyd's Rep. 103. See also *Davis Contractors Ltd v. Fareham U.D.C.* [1956] A.C. 696, 729 (*post*, § 24–048); *Tsakiroglou & Co. Ltd v. Noblee Thorl GmbH* [1962] A.C. 93 (*post*, § 24–046).

[7] *Blackburn Bobbin Co. v. Allen & Sons* [1918] 1 K.B. 540, 550; *Re Thornett and Fehr and Yuills Ltd* [1921] 1 K.B. 219.

[8] *Re Badische Co. Ltd* [1921] 2 Ch. 331, 381–383. (This case concerned frustration from supervening illegality—the outbreak of the war made it illegal to import the goods from Germany: see *ante* § 24–029.)

seller cannot rely on frustration to excuse him from performance unless he actually applies for a licence and is refused.[9]

24–046   **Suez Canal cases.** The closure of the Suez Canal in November 1956 led to a number of cases in which it was argued that c.i.f. contracts for the sale of goods had been frustrated. In *Tsakiroglou & Co. Ltd v. Noblee Thorl GmbH*,[10] the House of Lords heard an appeal concerning a contract whereby the sellers agreed in October 1956 to sell Sudanese groundnuts for shipment during November–December 1956 from Port Sudan c.i.f. Hamburg. On November 2 the Suez Canal was closed to navigation but the goods could have been shipped from Port Sudan round the Cape of Good Hope; this alternative route was three times longer than the route through the canal, and freightage was far more costly. The sellers claimed that the contract had been frustrated by the closure of the canal, but the House of Lords held that although the route via the Cape involved a change in the anticipated[11] method of performance of the contract, it was not such a fundamental change from the obligations undertaken in the contract as to frustrate it. It should be noted that a date had not been fixed for delivery in Europe, and that there was evidence that sufficient shipping was available to carry the goods via the Cape. If the goods had been perishable, or if a definite date for delivery (rather than shipment) had been fixed, or if there had been a shortage of shipping to carry goods from Port Sudan to Europe via the longer route, the contract might well have been frustrated.[12]

(iv) *Building Contracts*

24–047   **Building contracts.**[13] If a builder contracts to do work on an existing building which is destroyed during the progress of the work the contract is frustrated. In *Appleby v. Myers*,[14] the plaintiff contracted to erect certain machinery upon the defendant's premises for a fixed sum, but when the machinery was only partly

---

[9] *J.W. Taylor & Co. v. Landauer & Co.* [1940] 4 All E.R. 335; see *ante*, § 13–013; Vol. II, § 43–237 (export licences). *cf. Société Co-opérative Suisse des Cereales v. La Plata Cereal Co. SA* (1947) 80 Ll.L.Rep. 530 (an effective *de facto* prohibition against export frustrated the contract); *K.C. Sethia (1944) Ltd v. Partabmull Rameshwar* [1950] 1 All E.R. 51; [1951] 2 All E.R. 352; *Pound & Co. Ltd v. Hardy & Co. Inc.* [1956] A.C. 588; *Dalmia Dairy Industries Ltd v. National Bank of Pakistan* [1978] 2 Lloyd's Rep. 223, 253 (affd. on different grounds: *ibid.*); *C. Czarnikow Ltd v. Centrala Handlu Zagranicznego Rolimpex* [1979] A.C. 351. *cf. The Playa Larga* [1983] 2 Lloyd's Rep. 171 (complete breakdown of commercial relations between seller's and buyer's respective countries: contract held frustrated). See *Benjamin's Sale of Goods* (5th ed., 1997), §§ 18–257–18–279 (where a distinction is drawn between cases of supervening imposition of licensing requirements, where the contract may be frustrated, and cases where the contract is stated to be "subject to licence" and one party fails to obtain a licence under a licensing system which was in existence at the moment of formation of the contract. The latter example, it is argued, is not a case of frustration but rather is a case in which a condition is "introduced" into the contract under which neither party is liable to perform unless a licence is obtained; Chalmers, *Sale of Goods* (18th ed.), pp. 39–42; Schmitthoff, *Export Trade* (9th ed.), pp. 192–195.

[10] [1962] A.C. 93. *cf. Ocean Tramp Tankers Corporation v. V/O Sovfracht (The Eugenia)* [1964] 2 Q.B. 226 (*ante*, § 24–043).

[11] The contract may not have been frustrated even if it had *specified* the Suez Canal route: [1962] A.C. 93, 112; see also *Palmco Shipping Co. v. Continental Ore Corporation* [1970] 2 Lloyd's Rep. 21.

[12] *Ocean Tramp Tankers Corporation v. V/O Sovfracht (The Eugenia), supra*, at 240, 243.

[13] *Hudson's Building and Engineering Contracts* (11th ed., 1995), §§ 4–233—4–264; McInnis in McKendrick (ed.), *Force Majeure and Frustration of Contract*, (2nd ed., 1995), Chap. 10; *Keating on Building Contracts* (6th ed., 1995), pp. 143–150.

[14] (1867) L.R. 2 C.P. 651; in 16 L.T. 669 the contract is set out *in extenso*.

erected an accidental fire destroyed the whole of the buildings and the machinery thereon. It was held that since the premises were entirely destroyed without the fault of either party, the contract was frustrated and both parties were excused. Again, government prohibition of, or restrictions on, building operations during wartime have often caused the frustration of building contracts.[15]

The Davis Contractors case. It is in building contracts that the best illustra- **24–048** tion may be found of the principle that "it is not hardship or inconvenience or material loss which calls the principle of frustration into play,"[16] unless there is a radical change in the obligation. In *Davis Contractors Ltd v. Fareham U.D.C.*[17] the plaintiffs agreed to build 78 houses for the defendants at a fixed price, the work to be completed in eight months. Due partly to bad weather, but also to an unforeseen shortage of labour caused by the unexpected lag in the demobilisation of troops after the war, the work took 22 months to complete, and cost the builders some £17,000 more than they anticipated. The builders claimed that the shortage of labour and the delay had frustrated the contract, so that they were entitled to sue for the £17,000 on a *quantum meruit*. The House of Lords unanimously held that the contract had not been frustrated. Viscount Simonds denied that "where, without the default of either party, there has been an unexpected turn of events, which renders the contract more onerous than the parties contemplated, that is by itself a ground for relieving a party of the obligation he has undertaken."[18] Lord Reid said ". . . the delay was greater in degree than was to be expected. It was not caused by any new and unforeseeable factor or event: the job proved to be more onerous but it never became a job of a different kind from that contemplated in the contract."[19] A builder who undertook to perform such work for a definite lump sum undertook the commercial risk that delay would increase his costs.

Abnormal delay. In another case of delay in completing a building contract, **24–049** Asquith L.J. laid down the following principles:

"A contract often provides that in the event of 'delay' through specified causes, the contract is not to be dissolved, but merely suspended, yet such a provision has been held not to apply where the delay was so abnormal, so pre-emptive, as to fall outside what the parties could possibly have contemplated in the suspension clause. In other words 'delay' though literally describing what has occurred, has been read as limited to normal, moderate delay, and as not extending to an interruption so differing in degree and magnitude from anything which could have been contemplated as to differ from it in kind."[20]

---

[15] *Metropolitan Water Board v. Dick, Kerr & Co. Ltd* [1918] A.C. 119 (*ante*, § 24–023); *Federal Steam Navigation Co. Ltd v. Dixon & Co. Ltd* (1919) 64 S.J. 67, HL; *cf. Innholders' Co. v. Wainwright* (1917) 33 T.L.R. 356 (suspension of contract).

[16] *Davis Contractors Ltd v. Fareham U.D.C.* [1956] A.C. 696, 729.

[17] *ibid.* See also *Wates Ltd v. Greater London Council* (1983) 25 Build. L.R. 1; *Dryden Construction Co. Ltd v. Hydro-Electric Power Commission of Ontario* (1957) 10 D.L.R. (2d) 124.

[18] [1956] A.C. 696, 716.

[19] *ibid.* at 724. See *ante*, §§ 24–012—24–016.

[20] *Sir Lindsay Parkinson & Co. Ltd v. Commissioners of Works* [1949] 2 K.B. 632, 665, citing *Metropolitan Water Board v. Dick, Kerr & Co. Ltd* [1918] A.C. 119 (*ante*, § 24–023) as "a good illustration of this."

(v) *Leases and Tenancies*[21]

24–050   **Leases and tenancies.** For many years, there was uncertainty as to whether the doctrine of frustration could ever apply to a lease.[22] In 1945, in *Cricklewood Property and Investment Trust Ltd v. Leightons Investment Trust Ltd*[23] the House of Lords decided unanimously that on the facts there had been no frustration of a long-term building lease by the imposition of building restrictions following the outbreak of war. On the question of principle, the House of Lords was evenly divided.[24] Viscount Simon[25] and Lord Wright[26] thought that on rare occasions a lease may be frustrated, as, for instance, if some vast convulsion of nature swallowed up the property altogether, or buried it in the depths of the sea. Lord Russell[27] and Lord Goddard,[28] however, thought that a lease is more than a contract in that it creates an estate in the land vested in the lessee, and that this estate in the land could never be frustrated, even though some contractual obligations under the lease might be suspended by wartime regulations. In 1980, in *National Carriers Ltd v. Panalpina (Northern) Ltd*,[29] the majority in the House of Lords agreed with the reasoning of Viscount Simon and Lord Wright in the *Cricklewood* case, and thus held that the doctrine of frustration is, in principle, applicable to leases; but several of their Lordships considered that the doctrine would "hardly ever"[30] be applied to a lease.

24–051   **Illustrations of events frustrating leases.** Although there is no reported case in England in which a lease has been held to be frustrated, the reports do contain opinions on the types of situations in which the courts might so hold. The physical disappearance of the demised premises is the most obvious case: a convulsion of nature might "swallow up" the property, or bury it permanently under the sea[31]; or an upper floor flat might be totally destroyed by fire or earthquake.[32] Frustrating events not involving the physical disappearance of the land would include in the case of a building lease, subsequent legislation which

---

[21] Treitel, *Frustration and Force Majeure* (1994), Chap. 11.
[22] But a licence to occupy land could be frustrated: *Krell v. Henry* [1903] 2 K.B. 740 (*ante*, § 24–032); *Taylor v. Caldwell* (1863) 3 B. & S. 826 (*ante*, § 24–005); and a hire-purchase agreement (a lease of chattels) could be frustrated. *cf. British Berna Motor Lorries Ltd v. Inter-Transport Co. Ltd* (1915) 31 T.L.R. 200.
[23] [1945] A.C. 221; *cf.* Walford (1941) 57 L.Q.R. 339.
[24] The fifth member of the House expressed no opinion on the point.
[25] [1945] A.C. 221, 229.
[26] *ibid.* at 241.
[27] *ibid.* at 233–234.
[28] *ibid.* at 243–245.
[29] [1981] A.C. 675.
[30] *ibid.* at 692, 709. (The circumstances in which a lease might be frustrated would be "exceedingly rare": *ibid.* at 692, 697, 715.) *cf.* Lord Wright in *Cricklewood Property and Investment Trusts Ltd v. Leightons and Investment Trust Ltd* [1945] A.C. 221, 241.
[31] *Cricklewood Property and Investment Trusts Ltd v. Leightons and Investment Trust Ltd* [1945] A.C. 221, 229; *National Carriers Ltd v. Panalpina (Northern) Ltd* [1981] A.C. 675, 691, 700–701, 709. These examples were cited in *Holbeck Hall Hotel Ltd v. Scarborough Borough Council* (1998) 57 Con. L.R. 113, 152–153 where the judge was prepared to assume, without deciding the point, that an event of this nature would have operated to discharge the lease by frustration.
[32] *National Carriers Ltd v. Panalpina (Northern) Ltd* [1981] A.C. 675, 690. See Megarry and Wade, *The Law of Real Property* (5th ed.), pp. 691–692; *Woodfall's Law of Landlord and Tenant* 11–042–11–043.

permanently prohibited private building on the site[33]; or a fire which destroyed or seriously damaged the buildings on the demised premises.[34]

Prohibition on intended use. A clause in the lease restricting the use of the demised premises may be an important factor in deciding whether the lease has been frustrated by circumstances affecting that use. In the United States, leases which restricted the use of the premises to the conduct of a liquor saloon were held to have been frustrated by the enactment of provisions prohibiting that use.[35] The following passage in Corbin, *Contracts*[36] was cited with approval in the House of Lords in *National Carriers Ltd v. Panalpina (Northern) Ltd*[37]: "If there was one principal use contemplated by the lessee, known to the lessor, and one that played a large part in fixing rental value, a governmental prohibition or prevention of that use has been held to discharge the lessee from his duty to pay the rent. It is otherwise if other substantial uses, permitted by the lease and in the contemplation of the parties, remain possible to the lessee."

    24–052

Events not frustrating leases. An event which causes an interruption in the expected use of the premises by the lessee will not frustrate the lease unless the interruption is expected to last for the unexpired term of the lease, or, at least, for a long period of that unexpired term. The lease at issue in *National Carriers Ltd v. Panalpina (Northern) Ltd* was a 10-year lease of a warehouse. By a temporary order, the City Council closed the street which gave the only access to the warehouse. The House of Lords held that the lease was not frustrated since the closure was expected to last only for a year or a little longer, which would still allow the lease to run for three more years after the street re-opened. The length of the unexpired term was "a potent factor"[38]: " . . . the likely continuance of the term after the interruption makes it impossible for the lessee to contend that the lease has been brought to an end."[39] In *Cricklewood*,[40] the lessee under a 99-year building lease claimed that wartime building restrictions had frustrated the lease.

    24–053

---

[33] *Cricklewood Property and Investment Trusts Ltd v. Leightons and Investment Trust Ltd* [1945] A.C. 221, 229, 241. In *Rom Securities Ltd v. Rogers (Holdings) Ltd* (1967) 205 E.G. 427, an agreement for a lease was frustrated by refusal of planning permission: see *National Carriers Ltd v. Panalpina (Northern) Ltd* [1981] A.C. 675, 690, 694, 705 (where Lord Simon says that this was a case of frustration, although the judge dealt with it by implying a term), and 715. *cf.* the relevant American authorities: Corbin, *Contracts* (1962), Vol. 6, §§ 1356–1357; Williston, *Contracts* (3rd ed., 1978), Vol. 18, § 1955. (In *Robertson v. Wilson* (1958) 75 W.N. (N.S.W.) 503, a weekly tenancy was held to have been frustrated by the local authority's "closing order.")

[34] *National Carriers Ltd v. Panalpina (Northern) Ltd* [1981] A.C. 675, 701, 713. (The consequences of fire would normally be covered by an express term in the lease.) On the earlier law dealing with the lessee's obligation to pay the rent even when the premises are destroyed, see McElroy and Williams (1941) 4 M.L.R. 241, 256–260. *cf. Taylor v. Caldwell* (1863) 3 B. & S. 826 (a licence to use a hall: *ante* § 24–005).

[35] *Doherty v. Monroe Eckstein Brewing Co.* 191 N.Y.S. 59 (1921); *Industrial Development and Land Co. v. Goldschmidt* 206 P. 134 (1922). These cases are discussed by Treitel, *Frustration and Force Majeure* (1994), §§ 7–021—7–022 and 11–017; Corbin, *Contracts* (1962), Vol. 6, § 1356; Williston, *Contracts* (3rd ed., 1978), Vol. 18, § 1955.

[36] (1962) Vol. 6, pp. 475–476 (Lord Simon quoted the identical passage in (1951) Vol. 6, p. 391).

[37] [1981] A.C. 675, 702 (*per* Lord Simon). (Another similar passage from Corbin was also cited with approval by Lord Wilberforce at 695.)

[38] *ibid.* at 706, *per* Lord Simon.

[39] *ibid.* at 698, *per* Lord Wilberforce.

[40] [1945] A.C. 221. (It was said in this case, however, that frustration might apply to a *covenant* in the lease: see *post*, § 24–064, n. 6.)

The House of Lords held that there had been no frustration, since the lease had over 90 years to run when the war broke out, and it was unlikely that the war would last for more than a small fraction of the whole term. There are also a number of earlier decisions in which the courts, without basing their decisions solely on the then-current doctrine that a lease could never be frustrated, held that specific leases were not frustrated in the particular events which occurred.[41]

24–054   **The consequences of frustration of a lease.** In *National Carriers Ltd v. Panalpina (Northern) Ltd*, it was said that a lease would be "automatically discharged on the happening of a frustrating event."[42] The legal operation of this automatic determination of the lease should be the same as where a lease is prematurely determined by other events, either as specified in the terms of the lease, or by operation of law (*e.g.* forfeiture by denial of title).[43] There is, however, little indication in the cases as to the consequential legal arrangements. If a lease were frustrated, the legal estate would presumably remain vested in the lessee (unless the land itself disappeared), but the lessee could be treated as a trustee for the lessor.[44] Difficulties in regard to land registration are not insuperable, since a trust does not appear on the register, and the court has power, in certain circumstances, to order rectification of the register[45]; even without a court order, the premature determination of a registered lease may be noted on the register.[46] Some legal consequences may be governed by the Law Reform (Frustrated Contracts) Act 1943,[47] which will apply when a lease has been frustrated,[48] but it is clear that the draftsman did not specifically provide for the situation. There should be an obligation on the lessee to pay rent *pro rata* up to the date of the frustration, and for so long thereafter as he retains possession.[49]

---

[41] *London and Northern Estates Co. v. Schlesinger* [1916] 1 K.B. 20 (the actual result in the case was approved by several of their Lordships in *National Carriers Ltd v. Panalpina (Northern) Ltd* [1981] A.C. 675, 689, 694, 696, 715); *Whitehall Court Ltd v. Ettlinger* [1920] 1 K.B. 680 (the actual result in this case was also approved by several of their Lordships in *National Carriers Ltd v. Panalpina (Northern) Ltd*); *Redmond v. Dainton* [1920] 2 K.B. 256; *Matthey v. Curling* [1922] 2 A.C. 180 (Lord Roskill has said that the result in this case depended on its particular facts: *National Carriers Ltd v. Panalpina (Northern) Ltd.* at 696, 715); *Swift v. Macbean* [1942] 1 K.B. 375; *Eyre v. Johnson* [1946] K.B. 481; *Simper v. Coombs* [1948] 1 All E.R. 306; *Denman v. Brise* [1949] 1 K.B. 22; *Yougmin v. Heath* [1974] 1 W.L.R. 135.

[42] [1981] A.C. 675, 702.

[43] *ibid.* at 702.

[44] Interference with property rights has been accepted by the legislature in an analogous field, the rescission of a contract for innocent misrepresentation: the Misrepresentation Act 1967 permits such rescission after a contract has been performed (s.1), and as performance may involve a conveyance or lease of land, rescission of the contract would affect the property rights of the parties. (The Act does not exclude contracts for the sale or lease of an interest in land: *ante*, § 6–128. But the court has a discretion under s.2(2) to award damages in lieu of rescission: *ante*, § 6–095).

[45] The Land Registration Act 1925, s.82. See Ruoff and Roper, *The Law and Practice of Registered Conveyancing*, §§ 40–01 *et seq.*

[46] *Ruoff and Roper, op. cit.* §§ 21–28 *et seq.*

[47] See *post*, §§ 24–072 *et seq.*

[48] This is recognised by Lord Wilberforce in *National Carriers Ltd v. Panalpina (Northern) Ltd* [1981] A.C. 675, 697, and by Lord Simon at 707, who said: "The Act of 1943 seems unlikely to vouchsafe justice in all cases. As often as not there will be an all-or-nothing situation, the entire loss caused by the frustrating event falling exclusively on one party, whereas justice might require the burden to be shared."

[49] For U.S. cases on the point, see Williston, *Contracts* (3rd ed., 1978), Vol. 18, § 1955.

(vi) *Contracts for the Sale of Land*

Contracts for the sale of land. The doctrine of frustration does not apply   **24–055** where a compulsory purchase order has been made relating to land which is the subject of a contract of sale but has not yet been formally conveyed to the purchaser.[50] Similarly, a contract for sale is not frustrated by the subsequent listing of the building as one of architectural or historical interest under planning legislation.[51] Upon the making of the contract, the purchaser is regarded in equity as the owner of the land (subject to payment of the purchase money); hence the purchaser is bound to complete, but will be entitled to the whole of the compensation money payable under the compulsory purchase order. It is doubtful whether the doctrine of frustration could ever apply to a contract for the sale of land,[52] though it has been suggested that it might if the frustrating event prevented the vendor from transferring any estate whatever to the purchaser.[53]

4. THE LIMITS OF FRUSTRATION

Express provision.[54] A clause in the contract which is intended to deal with   **24–056** the event which has occurred will normally preclude the application of the doctrine of frustration.[55] Frustration is concerned with unforeseen, supervening events, not events which have been anticipated and provided for in the contract itself.[56] Thus the effect of a *force majeure* clause or a hardship clause may be to shut out the doctrine of frustration because the contract, on its proper construction, will be held to have covered the event which has occurred.[57] Similarly, the presence of a price-escalation clause in a contract may make a court more reluctant to conclude that a sudden increase in prices has frustrated the contract.[58]

---

[50] *Hillingdon Estates Co. v. Stonefield Estates Ltd* [1952] Ch. 627; *E. Johnson & Co. (Barbados) Ltd v. N.S.R. Ltd* [1997] A.C. 400, 406–407. *cf.* (on frustration of contracts for leases) *Lobb v. Vasey Housing Auxiliary (War Widows Guild)* [1963] V.R. 239 and *Rom Securities Ltd v. Rogers (Holdings) Ltd* (1967) 205 E.G. 427 (*ante*, § 24–051, n. 33); *Denny, Mott and Dickson Ltd v. James B. Fraser & Co. Ltd* [1944] A.C. 265 (A trading contract held frustrated despite the fact that it contained ancillary provisions creating an option to purchase land and an agreement for a lease: see *ante*, § 24–024 and *National Carriers Ltd v. Panalpina (Northern) Ltd* [1981] A.C. 675, 704.)

[51] *Amalgamated Investment & Property Co. v. John Walker & Sons* [1977] 1 W.L.R. 164. (The listing greatly restricted the owner's freedom to develop the property.)

[52] *cf. ante*, §§ 24–050 *et seq.* (But *delay* in building a block of flats, caused by a landslip, may frustrate a contract for sale of a flat: *Wong Lai Ying v. Chinachem Investment Co.* (1979) 13 Build. L.R. 81.)

[53] The latter suggestion is probably an instance of supervening illegality: see *ante*, § 24–023. If, however, the contract entitled the purchaser to vacant possession, the vendor cannot enforce the contract if he is prevented from giving possession (*e.g.* by requisitioning): *Cook v. Taylor* [1942] Ch. 349 (see *post*, § 28–007, n. 26).

[54] Treitel, *Frustration and Force Majeure* (1994), Chap. 12.

[55] *Joseph Constantine SS. Line Ltd v. Imperial Smelting Corp. Ltd* [1942] A.C. 154, 163; *Kuwait Supply Co. v. Oyster Marine Management (The Safeer)* [1994] 1 Lloyd's Rep. 637; *Bangladesh Export Import Co. Ltd v. Sucden Kerry S.A.* [1995] 2 Lloyd's Rep. 1.

[56] The courts may, exceptionally, be able to imply that the contract has made provision for the alleged frustrating event where it is clear from the contract that one party was intended to assume the risk of the alleged frustrating event: *Larringa & Co. Ltd v. Société Franco-Americaine des Phosphates de Médulla, Paris* (1923) 39 T.L.R. 316.

[57] On *force majeure* clauses, see *ante*, §§ 14–126—14–142, *Benjamin's Sale of Goods* (5th ed., 1997), §§ 8–094—8–096, 18–294—18–296, 19–118—19–121; *Schmitthoff's Export Trade: The Law and Practice of International Trade* (9th ed., 1990), pp. 199–203; Cartoon [1978] J.B.L. 230.

[58] *Wates Ltd v. G.L.C.* (1983) 25 Build. L.R. 1.

But the courts are likely to construe such clauses narrowly and insist that the provision for the event be "full and complete"⁵⁹ before the conclusion is reached that frustration is excluded. The more catastrophic the event, the less likely it is that a clause will be held to cover the event which has occurred, unless particularly clear words are used.⁶⁰ Similarly, the fact that a *force majeure* clause makes provision for an extension of time on the occurrence of one of the stipulated events may indicate to the court that the clause was confined in its application to events which are capable of resolution within that particular time-frame: an event which renders further performance of the contract "unthinkable" may therefore not fall within the scope of the clause.⁶¹ Further, the clause may not make complete provision for all the legal issues arising from the event.⁶² For example, a clause may excuse *one* party from the consequences of delay, in the sense that it prevents the delay from constituting a breach of contract, but this does not necessarily exclude the operation of the doctrine of frustration so as to enable that party to hold the other party to the contract when delay occurs.⁶³ An express provision in the contract cannot, however, exclude frustration by supervening illegality where this would be against public policy.⁶⁴

24–057   **Significance of a foreseen event.**⁶⁵ The parties to the contract may not have made express provision for the event which has occurred but they may have foreseen it happening. In such a case, the fact that the parties have foreseen the event but not made any provision for it in their contract will usually,⁶⁶ but not necessarily,⁶⁷ prevent the doctrine of frustration from applying when the event occurs. While an unforeseen event will not necessarily lead to the frustration of a contract,⁶⁸ a foreseen event will generally exclude the operation of the doctrine.

---

⁵⁹ *Bank Line Ltd v. Arthur Capel & Co.* [1919] A.C. 435, 455.

⁶⁰ *Metropolitan Water Board v. Dick Kerr & Co. Ltd* [1918] A.C. 119 (*ante*, § 24–023). See also *Pacific Phosphate Co. Ltd v. Empire Transport Co. Ltd* (1920) 36 T.L.R. 750; *The Penelope* [1928] P. 180 (*ante*, § 24–044); *Fibrosa Spolka Akcyjna v. Fairbairn Lawson Combe Barbour Ltd* [1943] A.C. 32; *Denny, Mott & Dickson Ltd v. James B. Fraser & Co. Ltd* [1944] A.C. 265, 284; *Kodros Shipping Corporation of Monrovia v. Empresa Cubana de Fletes (The Evia) (No. 2)* [1983] 1 A.C. 736; also *ante*, § 24–049.

⁶¹ *Empresa Exportadora De Azucor v. Industria Azucarera Nacional SA (The Playa Larga)* [1983] 2 Lloyd's Rep. 171, 189.

⁶² *Bank Line Ltd v. Arthur Capel & Co.* [1919] A.C. 435, 455–456 (*ante*, § 24–040).

⁶³ *Jackson v. Union Marine Insurance Co. Ltd* (1874) L.R. 10 C.P. 125, 144 (*ante*, § 24–006).

⁶⁴ *Ertel Bieber & Co. v. Rio Tinto Co. Ltd* [1918] A.C. 260 (*ante*, § 24–023). In other cases of supervening illegality (such as export or import restrictions) express provision may exclude the operation of frustration: *Johnson Matthey Bankers Ltd v. State Trading Corp. of India* [1984] 1 Lloyd's Rep. 427.

⁶⁵ Treitel, *Frustration and Force Majeure* (1994), Chap. 13; Treitel, *The Law of Contract* (9th ed., 1995), pp. 813–817; Hall (1984) 4 L.S. 300.

⁶⁶ *Tamplin SS. Co. Ltd v. Anglo-Mexican Petroleum Co.* [1916] 2 A.C. 397, 426; *Bank Line Ltd v. Arthur Capel & Co.* [1919] A.C. 435, 455, 462; *Gulnes (D/S.A/S) v. Imperial Chemical Industries Ltd* [1938] 1 All E.R. 24; *Davis Contractors Ltd v. Fareham U.D.C.* [1956] A.C. 696, 731; *Paal Wilson & Co. A/S v. Partenreederei Hannah Blumenthal* [1983] 1 A.C. 854, 909; *McAlpine Humberoak Ltd v. McDermott International Inc.* (1992) 58 Build. L.R. 1, 18; Treitel, *The Law of Contract* (9th ed., 1995), pp. 813–816.

⁶⁷ *Maritime National Fish Ltd v. Ocean Trawlers Ltd* [1935] A.C. 524, 529; *Tatem Ltd v. Gamboa* [1939] 1 K.B. 132 (*ante*, § 24–043); *Jennings and Chapman Ltd v. Woodman, Matthews & Co.* [1952] 2 T.L.R. 409, 412; *Ocean Tramp Tankers Corporation v. V/O Sovfracht (The Eugenia)* [1964] 2 QB 226, 239; *Nile Co. for the Export of Agricultural Crops v. H. & J.M. Bennett (Commodities) Ltd* [1986] 1 Lloyd's Rep. 555, 582; *Adelfamar SA v. Silos E. Mangimi Martini SpA (The Adelfa)* [1988] 2 Lloyd's Rep. 466, 471.

⁶⁸ *Davis Contractors Ltd v. Fareham U.D.C.* [1956] A.C. 696; *British Movietonews v. London and District Cinemas Ltd* [1952] A.C. 166.

The inference that a foreseen event is not a frustrating event is only a prima facie one and so can be excluded by evidence of contrary intention. Thus, it is a question of construction of the contract whether the parties intended their silence to mean that the contract should continue to bind in that event,[69] or whether they intended the effect of the event, if it occurs, to be determined by any relevant legal rules.[70] If one party foresaw the risk, but the other did not, it will be difficult for the former to claim that the occurrence of the risk frustrates the contract.[71] On the other hand, a contract may be frustrated by supervening illegality, notwithstanding the fact that the war which has brought about the supervening illegality was foreseen.[72]

Event foreseeable but not foreseen. When the event was foreseeable but not **24-058** actually foreseen by the parties, it is less likely that the doctrine of frustration will be held to be inapplicable. Much turns on the extent to which the event was foreseeable. The issue which the court must consider is whether or not one or other party has assumed the risk of the occurrence of the event.[73] The degree of foreseeability required to exclude the doctrine of frustration is, however, a high one: " 'foreseeability' will support the inference of risk-assumption only where the supervening event is one which any person of ordinary intelligence would regard as likely to occur, or . . . the contingency must be 'one which the parties could reasonably be thought to have foreseen as a real possibility.' "[74]

Self-induced frustration.[75] "The essence of frustration is that it should not **24-059** be due to the act or election of the party seeking to rely on it."[76] Thus, a contracting party cannot rely on "self-induced frustration, that is, on frustration due to his own conduct or to the conduct of those for whom he is responsible."[77] Although the concept of self-induced frustration is clearly established as a matter of general principle, the precise limits of the doctrine have not been clearly established. It is merely a "label" which has been used to describe "those situations where one party has been held by the Courts not to be entitled to treat himself as discharged from his contractual obligations."[78] Thus frustration has

---

[69] See, *e.g. Chandler Bros. Ltd v. Boswell* [1936] 3 All E.R. 179.

[70] For example, an intention that if the event were to happen, the parties would "leave the lawyers to sort it out": *Ocean Tramp Tankers Corporation v. V/O Sovfracht (The Eugenia)* [1964] 2 Q.B. 226, 239.

[71] *Walton Harvey Ltd v. Walter and Homfrays Ltd* [1931] 1 Ch. 274; Treitel, *The Law of Contract* (9th ed., 1995), p. 814.

[72] *Ertel Bieber & Co. v. Rio Tinto Co. Ltd* [1918] A.C. 260 (*ante*, § 24–023).

[73] Many events are foreseeable but neither party assumes the risk of their occurrence. Death is the classic example. The death of an employee during the currency of his employment contract is a foreseeable event but it operates to discharge the contract of employment because neither party assumes the risk of its occurrence.

[74] Treitel, *Frustration and Force Majeure* § 13–09. The quote at the end of the citation is taken from the case of *Mishara Construction Company Inc. v. Transit-Mixed Concrete Corp.* 310 N.E. 2d 363, 367 (1974).

[75] Treitel, *Frustration and Force Majeure* (1994), Chap. 14. Swanton (1990) 2 J.C.L. 206.

[76] *J. Lauritzen A.S. v. Wijsmuller B.V. (The Super Servant Two)* [1990] 1 Lloyd's Rep. 1, 8. See also *Bank Line Ltd v. Arthur Capel & Co.* [1919] A.C. 435, 452; *Maritime National Fish Ltd v. Ocean Trawlers Ltd* [1935] A.C. 524, 530; *Joseph Constantine SS. Line Ltd v. Imperial Smelting Corpn. Ltd* [1942] A.C. 154, 170; *Ocean Tramp Tankers Corporation v. V/O Sovfracht (The Eugenia)* [1964] 2 Q.B. 226, 237; *Denmark Productions Ltd v. Bascobel Productions Ltd* [1969] 1 Q.B. 699, 725, 736–737; *National Carriers Ltd v. Panalpina (Northern) Ltd* [1981] A.C. 675, 700.

[77] *Bank Line Ltd v. Arthur Capel & Co.* [1919] A.C. 435, 452.

[78] *J. Lauritzen A.S. v. Wijsmuller B.V. (The Super Servant Two)* [1989] 1 Lloyd's Rep. 148, 154.

been held to be "self-induced" where the alleged frustrating event was caused by a breach[79] or anticipatory breach of contract[80] by the party claiming that the contract has been frustrated, where an act of the party claiming that the contract has been frustrated broke the chain of causation between the alleged frustrating event and the event which made performance of the contract impossible,[81] and where the alleged frustrating event was not a supervening event or "something altogether outside the control of the parties."[82] A party who has been at fault or whose act was deliberate will generally be unable to invoke frustration because of the difficulty which such a party will inevitably face in showing the existence of a supervening event which is outside his control.[83]

24–060   **Allocation of available supplies.** Two leading cases which illustrate the scope of self-induced frustration are *Maritime National Fish Ltd v. Ocean Trawlers Ltd*[84] and *J. Lauritzen A.S. v. Wijsmuller B.V. (The Super Servant Two).*[85] In the former case the appellants chartered a trawler, the *St Cuthbert*, from the respondents. It was fitted with an otter trawl, and both parties knew that under the Canadian Fisheries Act it was forbidden to use an otter trawl without a licence from the Minister of Fisheries. The appellants were operating four otter trawlers besides the *St Cuthbert*, but in reply to their application for five licences, the Minister stated that he would grant only three, leaving it to the appellant to choose three trawlers. They did not include the *St Cuthbert* in the three trawlers they named, but later claimed that the charterparty had been frustrated by the Minister's refusal of a licence. The Privy Council held that they could not rely on frustration, since they had by their own voluntary election prevented the *St. Cuthbert* from being used as an otter trawl. The case is capable of two interpretations. The first is that the critical factor was not that the appellants had a choice as to the allocation of the licences, but that they chose to allocate the licences to their own vessels. The second is that the mere existence of a choice was sufficient to preclude the invocation of frustration.

24–061   In the second case, *J. Lauritzen A.S. v. Wijsmuller B.V. (The Super Servant Two),*[86] the defendants agreed to transport the plaintiffs' rig using one or other of two barges, *Super Servant One* or *Super Servant Two*. The defendants later made an internal decision to allocate the *Super Servant Two* to the performance of the contract with the plaintiffs but, before the time for performance of the contract, the *Super Servant Two* sank while transporting another rig in the Zaire River. The *Super Servant One* having been allocated to the performance of other concluded

---

[79] *Ocean Tramp Tankers Corporation v. V/O Sovfracht (The Eugenia)* [1964] 2 Q.B. 226, 237; *Paal Wilson & Co. A/S v. Partenreederei Hannah Blumenthal* [1983] 1 A.C. 854; *Cheall v. Assn. of Professional Executive and Computer Staff* [1983] 2 A.C. 180, 189.

[80] *New Zealand Shipping Co. Ltd v. Société des Ateliers et Chantiers de France* [1919] A.C. 1, 6.

[81] *Maritime National Fish Ltd v. Ocean Trawlers Ltd* [1935] A.C. 524, (where the fact that the party claiming frustration had a choice as to how to allocate the scarce resources (licences) was held to be sufficient to break the causal link between the alleged frustrating event and the event which made performance impossible, *post* § 24–060).

[82] *Denmark Productions Ltd v. Boscobel Productions Ltd* [1969] 1 Q.B. 699, 736.

[83] *J. Lauritzen A.S. v. Wijsmuller B.V. (The Super Servant Two)* [1990] 1 Lloyd's Rep. 1, 10; *cf. Joseph Constantine SS. Line Ltd v. Imperial Smelting Corpn. Ltd* [1942] A.C. 154, 166–167.

[84] [1935] A.C. 524.

[85] [1990] 1 Lloyd's Rep. 1.

[86] *ibid.* See Treitel, *The Law of Contract* (9th ed., 1995), pp. 819–820; McKendrick [1990] L.M.C.L.Q. 153.

contracts, the defendants sought to argue that the sinking of the *Super Servant Two* had frustrated the contract between the parties. The Court of Appeal held that, whether or not the *Super Servant Two* sank as a result of negligence on the part of the defendants or their employees, the contract was not frustrated. If it sank as a result of negligence then, the court held, the contract was not frustrated because negligence did not constitute a supervening event.[87] Although the House of Lords in *Joseph Constantine SS. Co. v. Imperial Smelting Corp. Ltd*[88] left open the question whether "mere negligence" would justify a finding that frustration was self-induced,[89] subsequent cases have concluded that negligence does exclude a finding of self-induced frustration by asserting that a frustrating event must arise "without blame or fault on the side of the party seeking to rely on it."[90] "Fault" in this context is not confined to a breach of a duty of care owed to the plaintiffs: such an interpretation would have confined the law within "a legalistic strait-jacket" and distracted attention from the real question, which is "whether the frustrating event relied upon is truly an outside event or extraneous change of situation or whether it is an event which the party seeking to rely on it had the means and opportunity to prevent but nevertheless caused or permitted to come about."[91]

If, on the other hand, the *Super Servant Two* sank without negligence on the **24–062** part of the defendants, the contract was still not frustrated because, it was held, the cause of the non-performance of the contract was not the sinking of the *Super Servant Two* but the decision of the defendants not to use the *Super Servant One* in the performance of the contract with the plaintiffs. Yet to have allocated the *Super Servant One* to the contract with the plaintiffs would, doubtless, have exposed the defendants to liability to someone else to whom they had promised to supply either the *Super Servant One* or the *Super Servant Two*. On this analysis, it was the mere fact that the appellants in *Maritime National Fish*[92] had a choice which prevented them from invoking the doctrine of frustration. The effect of the decision of the Court of Appeal is to place a supplier whose source of supply partially fails in a very difficult position. There was some authority, prior to *Super Servant Two*, which appeared to suggest that a supplier in such a case could "prorate," that is to say the supplier would be discharged from further liability if he proportionately rationed the limited supply among his buyers and his regular customers.[93] But in *Super Servant Two* it was held that these cases turned upon the proper interpretation of a *force majeure* clause and were not illustrative of a general common law power to prorate.[94] In the light of the decision in *Super Servant Two*, a supplier would be well advised to include within his contract a *force majeure* clause which allows him to prorate in the

---

[87] [1990] 1 Lloyd's Rep. 1, 10.
[88] [1942] A.C. 154.
[89] *ibid* at 166–167, 179, 195, 202.
[90] *J. Lauritzen A.S. v. Wijsmuller B.V. (The Super Servant Two)* [1990] 1 Lloyd's Rep. 1, 8.
[91] *ibid.* at 10.
[92] *Supra.*
[93] *Tennants (Lancashire) Ltd v. C.S. Wilson & Co. Ltd* [1917] A.C. 495; *Intertradex SA v. Lesieur Torteaux S.A.R.L.* [1978] 2 Lloyd's Rep. 509; *Bremer Handelsgesellschaft mbH v. C. Mackprang Jr.* [1979] 1 Lloyd's Rep. 221; *Continental Grain Export Corp. v. S.T.M. Grain Ltd* [1979] 2 Lloyd's Rep. 460, 473 and *Bremer Handelsgesellschaft mbH v. Continental Grain Co.* [1983] 1 Lloyd's Rep. 269. See generally on this line of cases, Hudson (1968) 31 M.L.R. 535 and (1979) 123 S.J. 137.
[94] *J. Lauritzen A.S. v. Wijsmuller B.V.* [1990] 1 Lloyd's Rep. 1, 9; *Benjamin's Sale of Goods* (5th ed., 1997), § 18–291—18–292.

event of a partial failure of supply. The contract in *Super Servant Two* did in fact contain a *force majeure* clause and this was held to be effective to excuse the defendants provided that the *Super Servant Two* sank without negligence on the part of themselves or their employees.[95]

24-063   **Onus of proof**. The House of Lords in *Joseph Constantine SS. Line Ltd v. Imperial Smelting Corporation Ltd*[96] held that the onus of proving self-induced frustration lies on the party who asserts that this is the case. If A (the party relying on frustration) proves events which prima facie would frustrate the contract, the onus of proving that the frustration was self-induced is on the other party (B) who denies that the contract has been frustrated. B must then prove some default by A which caused the allegedly frustrating event. When A proves and relies on frustration, B cannot prevent its operation by proving that it had been induced by his own (B's) fault.[97] So the fact that it was an employee's (or apprentice's) criminal conduct which led to a sentence of imprisonment[98] or of Borstal training[99] being imposed on him does not amount to "self-induced" conduct so as to prevent frustration of his contract of employment (or apprenticeship) as alleged by his employer.[1] "What matters, however, in the case of self-induced frustration is that the party who is the 'self' cannot treat himself as being discharged."[2]

24-064   **Partial "frustration."** English law has great difficulty in dealing with the case where part of the contract has become impossible of performance. To use the expression partial "frustration" to encompass this situation is not strictly accurate because the effect of frustration is to "kill the contract and discharge the parties from further liability under it."[3] Yet in these cases it is clear that the contract as a whole is not discharged: the argument is the more limited one that the occurrence of some new circumstance may excuse (perhaps temporarily) the performance of a particular contractual obligation without frustrating the whole contract.[4] Thus temporary illness may excuse an employee for his failure to attend for work,[5] while building restrictions imposed during war-time or as a result of the listing of a building may temporarily excuse non-performance of a covenant to build.[6] In some cases supervening illegality may excuse performance

---

[95] [1990] 1 Lloyd's Rep. 1, 6–8; see *ante*, § 24–061.

[96] [1942] A.C. 154.

[97] *F.C. Shepherd & Co. Ltd v. Jerrom* [1987] Q.B. 301. (It is submitted that the dictum at 319C–D is contrary to *Joseph Constantine SS. Line Ltd v. Imperial Smelting Corporation Ltd* [1942] A.C. 154.)

[98] *Hare v. Murphy Brothers Ltd* [1974] I.C.R. 603.

[99] *F.C. Shepherd & Co. Ltd v. Jerrom* [1987] Q.B. 301.

[1] See *ante* § 24–038.

[2] *F.C. Shepherd & Co. Ltd v. Jerrom* [1987] Q.B. 301, 327. A similar statement is that " . . . a party who has been in fault cannot rely on frustration due to his own wrongful act" (*per* Lord Porter in *Joseph Constantine SS. Line Ltd v. Imperial Smelting Corporation Ltd* [1942] A.C. 154, 200).

[3] *J. Lauritzen A.S. v. Wijsmuller B.V. (The Super Servant Two)* [1990] 1 Lloyd's Rep. 1, 8.

[4] *cf.* on the U.S. law, Williston, *Contracts* (3rd ed., 1978), Vol. 18, §§ 1956, 1957; Patterson (1961) 47 Virginia L.Rev. 798; and on South African law, Ramsden (1977) 94 S.A.L.J. 162.

[5] See Vol. II, § 39–155.

[6] *Cricklewood Property and Investment Trust Ltd v. Leightons Investment Trust Ltd* [1945] A.C. 221, 233–234; *John Lewis Properties plc v. Viscount Chelsea* [1993] 2 E.G.L.R. 77, 82. See *ante*, § 24–050.

of a minor contractual obligation without the whole contract becoming frustrated.[7] These cases can be divided into two distinct categories.

Force majeure clauses. The first group concern the construction of clauses,   24–065
such as *force majeure* clauses, which purport to relieve a party from the consequences of a failure to comply with a particular obligation. Thus in *Egham &
Staines Electricity Co. Ltd v. Egham U.D.C.*[8] the council had made a contract
with the electricity company for the supply of current for street lighting. If the
supply failed due to "unavoidable cause over which the company had no
control" payments for current were to abate in proportion. Public street lighting
was forbidden by the Lighting (Restrictions) Order on the outbreak of war in
1939. The company sued to recover the full payments provided for by the
contract, but it was held that the clause providing for abatement of payments had
come into operation; the company was unable to fulfil its contract because it had
become illegal to do so, and this illegality amounted to an "unavoidable cause"
within the meaning of the clause. But this case tells us nothing about any
common law doctrine of "partial frustration"; the court's task was simply to
interpret the clause of the contract which was in issue.

Partial excuse at common law. The second group of cases do not turn on the   24–066
construction of a clause in a contract but rather are based on a general common
law doctrine. An example in this category is provided by the difficult case of *H.
R. & S. Sainsbury Ltd v. Street*.[9] The parties entered into a contract under which
the defendant agreed to sell to the plaintiffs 275 tons of barley from a crop
growing on a farm. Without any fault on the part of the defendant, the yield
turned out to be only 140 tons. The defendant refused to supply the plaintiff with
the 140 tons harvested and so the plaintiff buyers brought a claim for damages.
The defendant claimed that, as a result of the partial failure of the harvest, he was
excused from delivering any of the barley. This argument was rejected by the
court. The plaintiffs did not claim damages for failure to deliver the other 135
tons, conceding that "it was an implied condition of the contract that if the
defendant, through no fault of his, failed to produce the stipulated tonnage of his
growing crop, he should not be required to pay damages."[10] But MacKenna J.
held that the defendant remained bound to deliver the 140 tons of barley
produced.[11] The case could be explained as one of "partial frustration": the
obligation to deliver 135 tons of barley was frustrated by the failure of the crop,
while the obligation to deliver the 140 tons remained valid and enforceable. But
nowhere in the judgment of MacKenna J. is the word frustration used: the focus
of his judgment is upon the implication of terms into a contract. This is not an
altogether satisfactory basis for the decision because it does not explain *why* the

---

[7] *Cricklewood Property and Investment Trust Ltd v. Leightons Investment Trust Ltd* [1945] A.C.
221, 233–234 (see *ante*, § 24–050). *cf. Matthey v. Curling* [1922] 2 A.C. 180; *Eyre v. Johnson* [1946]
K.B. 481, 484; *Innholders Co. v. Wainwright* (1917) 33 T.L.R. 356.
[8] [1944] 1 All E.R. 107; *cf. Williams v. Mercer* [1940] 3 All E.R. 292.
[9] [1972] 1 W.L.R. 834, noted (1972) 88 L.Q.R. 464.
[10] *ibid.* at 835. The basis for this concession would appear to be *Howell v. Coupland* (1874) L.R.
9 Q.B. 462; affd. (1876) 1 Q.B.D. 258; *Barrow, Lane and Ballard Ltd v. Phillip Phillips and Co. Ltd*
[1929] 1 K.B. 574.
[11] Although the plaintiffs were not bound to accept delivery, given that the amount of barley
produced was less than what was contracted for: Sale of Goods Act 1979, s.30(1). In the case of a
non-consumer buyer, the buyer's right to reject is now limited by s. 30(2A) of the Sale of Goods Act
1979.

court saw fit to refuse to imply a term into the contract relieving the defendant from his obligation to deliver the 140 tons. It is suggested that this case is not illustrative of a wider doctrine of "partial frustration" in English law[12] but rather it suggests that English law, in certain circumstances, recognises that a contracting party may have a partial excuse for non-performance of a contractual obligation.[13] It is on this ground that a seller is excused for his failure to deliver 135 tons of barley or an employee who is absent from work through temporary illness is excused for his failure to attend for work. There is no need to invoke "frustration" to explain this rule and it has not been so explained in a number of cases.[14] The use of the word "frustration" is positively misleading in so far as it suggests that the contract as a whole has been terminated when this is clearly not the case.

24–067   Limits of partial excuse. Once the basis of these decisions is recognised, the limits of this "partial excuse for non-performance" must be ascertained. In this respect *Sainsbury Ltd v. Street*[15] presents an odd contrast with *Super Servant Two*.[16] In both cases there was a partial failure of supply: in the former the defendant was excused, in the latter, had it not been for the *force majeure* clause, the defendants would not have been excused. One point of distinction which does emerge is that in *Sainsbury* the defendant had entered into a contract with one buyer, while in *Super Servant Two* the defendants had entered into a number of different contracts with different parties. Yet it is difficult to see why this should be a relevant point of distinction. Rather, *Super Servant Two* illustrates a particularly robust approach on the part of the court, according to which a contracting party who has entered into more contracts than he has supplies, and who later wishes to be excused in the event of a partial failure of supply, "must bargain for the inclusion of a suitable *force majeure* clause in the contract."[17] But on this approach, *Sainsbury v. Street* must be wrong because there the defendant could equally have protected himself by incorporating a carefully drafted *force majeure* clause into the contract. Such an approach would confine the doctrine of frustration within very narrow limits and, taken to its extreme, it could even be applied to cases of total failure of supply. This approach has the potential to "undermine

---

[12] There are dicta which are hostile to the existence of "partial frustration": see *Kawasaki Steel Corp. v. Sardoil SpA (The Zuiho Maru)* [1977] 2 Lloyd's Rep. 552, 555; *cf. Schmitthoff's Export Trade: The Law and Practice of International Trade* (9th ed., 1990), p. 195.

[13] See Treitel, *The Law of Contract* (9th ed., 1995), pp. 749, 802; *Benjamin's Sale of Goods* (5th ed., 1997), § 18–292. See also *Poussard v. Spiers and Pond* (1876) 1 Q.B.D. 410 where illness gave the plaintiff opera singer a temporary excuse for her non-performance of her contract with the defendants. The case has sometimes been viewed as an example of the operation of the doctrine of frustration but this explanation encounters the difficulty of explaining why the defendants had an option whether or not to rescind the contract. If the contract had indeed been frustrated it would have been discharged automatically, whereas, if the defendants had wished to hold the plaintiff to the terms of her contract, it seems clear that they could have done so: see further Treitel, *Frustration and Force Majeure* § 5–053.

[14] See, *e.g. H.R. & S. Sainsbury Ltd v. Street* [1972] 1 W.L.R. 834; *Cricklewood Property and Development Trust Ltd v. Leightons Investment Trust Ltd* [1945] A.C. 221, 233–234; *Libyan Arab Foreign Bank v. Bankers Trust Co.* [1989] Q.B. 728, 772; *John Lewis Properties plc v. Viscount Chelsea* [1993] 2 E.G.L.R. 77, 82. In *Cricklewood* Lord Russell clearly could not have been relying upon the doctrine of frustration because he had just strenuously denied that a lease could be frustrated (at 233); *cf. Sturke v. S.W. Edwards Ltd* (1971) 23 P. & C.R. 185, 190.

[15] *Supra.*

[16] *Supra.*

[17] [1989] 1 Lloyd's Rep. 148, 158. The Court of Appeal (*supra*) did not dissent from the reasoning of Hobhouse J.

the whole basis of the doctrine of frustration"[18] and it is suggested that, while there is much to be said for recognising that frustration operates within narrow confines,[19] this should not prevent the courts from recognising that a contracting party who, without fault on his part has been disabled from performing part of his contractual obligations, may be able to rely on the supervening event as an excuse for that non-performance.

5. THE LEGAL CONSEQUENCES OF FRUSTRATION[20]

Common law. Although the Law Reform (Frustrated Contracts) Act 1943 **24–068** now provides for most of the legal consequences of frustration, it is still necessary to examine the common law on the subject, since some contracts fall outside the scope of the Act, and the interpretation of the Act itself demands a knowledge of the common law.

Contract discharged automatically. At common law frustration does not **24–069** rescind the contract *ab initio*: it brings the contract to an end forthwith, without more and automatically,[21] in the sense that it releases both[22] parties from any further performance of the contract.[23] A court does not have the power at common law to allow the contract to continue and to adjust its terms to the new circumstances.

Recovery of money paid. Having set aside the contract, the initial response **24–070** of the courts at common law was to let the loss lie where it fell. The origins of this rule can be found in the decision of the Court of Appeal in *Chandler v. Webster*[24] where it was held that, while the effect of frustration was to release both parties from their obligations to perform in the future, frustration did not affect the obligations which had accrued prior to the date of frustration. Thus, on

---

[18] Treitel, *The Law of Contract*, (9th ed., 1995), p. 819–820.

[19] *Ante*, § 24–007.

[20] See Treitel, *Frustration and Force Majeure* (1994), Chap. 15; McKendrick (ed.), *Force Majeure and Frustration of Contract* (2nd ed., 1995), Chap. 11; Burrows (ed.), *Essays on the Law of Restitution* (1991), Chap. 6; Stewart and Carter [1992] C.L.J. 66.

[21] *Hirji Mulji v. Cheong Yue SS. Co. Ltd* [1926] A.C. 497, 505; *National Carriers Ltd v. Panalpina (Northern) Ltd* [1981] A.C. 675, 712; *B.P. Exploration Co. (Libya) Ltd v. Hunt (No. 2)* [1981] 1 W.L.R. 232, 241 (the House of Lords upheld the appeal, but without adverting to this point: [1983] 2 A.C. 352); *J. Lauritzen A.S. v. Wijsmuller B.V. (The Super Servant Two)* [1990] 1 Lloyd's Rep. 1, 8.

[22] The theory that one party is discharged by frustration and the other party for failure of consideration resulting from that frustration (see Williams, *Law Reform (Frustrated Contracts) Act 1943*, pp. 21–28; McElroy & Williams, *Impossibility of Performance*, pp. 88–89, 99–100) is not accepted by the Act (" . . . the *parties* thereto have *for that reason* been discharged . . . ": s.1(1)) (italics supplied) nor in various judicial statements (*e.g.* "when 'frustration' occurs . . . it does not merely provide one party with a defence in an action brought by the other. It kills the contract itself and discharges both parties automatically," *per* Viscount Simon in *Joseph Constantine Steamship Line Ltd v. Imperial Smelting Corporation Ltd* [1942] A.C. 154, 163; *National Carriers Ltd v. Panalpina (Northern) Ltd* [1981] A.C. 675, 700.

[23] Some clauses in the contract may, however, be intended by the parties to survive frustration of the contract (*e.g.* an arbitration clause: see *post*, § 24–095: *B.P. Exploration Co. (Libya) Ltd v. Hunt (No. 2)* [1983] 2 A.C. 352, 372 (see also the judgments below: [1981] 1 W.L.R. 232, 240–241; [1979] 1 W.L.R. 783, 829). And see s.2(3) of the 1943 Act (*post*, § 24–090).

[24] [1904] 1 K.B. 493; see also *Blakeley v. Muller & Co.* [1903] 2 K.B. 760n.; *Civil Service Co-operative Society v. General Steam Navigation Co.* [1903] 2 K.B. 756 and *French Marine v. Compagnie Napolitaine d'Eclairage et de Chauffage par le Gaz* [1921] 2 A.C. 494, 523.

the facts of the case, not only was the plaintiff unable to recover the pre-payment which he had made before the frustrating event, but it was held that he remained liable to pay the balance of the sum which he had contracted to pay before that time. Although the Court of Appeal held that money paid was recoverable upon a total failure of consideration, it was held that such a total failure could only arise when the contract was set aside *ab initio*. The harshness of the rule laid down in *Chandler* was often acknowledged but it stood until 1943 when it was overruled by the House of Lords in the case of *Fibrosa Spolka Akcyjna v. Fairbairn Lawson Combe Barbour Ltd*[25] in which English sellers agreed to sell certain machinery to Polish buyers, and to deliver it c.i.f. Gdynia. The contract was made in July 1939, and in that month £1,000 was paid on account of the price. However before the sellers were able to complete the manufacture of the machines the contract was frustrated when Gdynia was occupied by the German army. The buyers sued to recover the £1,000 they had paid on the signing of the agreement. The House of Lords held that they were entitled to recover the money because there had been a total failure of consideration. They overruled *Chandler v. Webster* and rejected the proposition that a total failure of consideration could arise only when a contract was set aside *ab initio*; it arose whenever money[26] was paid on a basis which wholly failed.

24–071   **Defects in the common law.** Although the result in *Fibrosa* represented an improvement upon the rule established in *Chandler*, the common law remained in a less than satisfactory state.[27] Three principal defects were apparent. The first was that the payer could only recover money paid upon a total failure of consideration; a partial failure of consideration did not give rise to a right of recovery.[28] The second was that the House of Lords was of the opinion that the payee could not set off against the money to be repaid any expenditure which had been incurred in the performance of the contract.[29] The third defect arose in relation to a claim by a provider of services. Where the frustrating event destroyed the work which had been done and payment was due only on the completion of the work, then the service provider was not entitled to bring a restitutionary claim to recover payment in respect of the work which he had done prior to the frustration of the contract.[30]

---

[25] [1943] A.C. 32. Although it should be noted that the House of Lords expressly stated that their decision did not affect the law in relation to advance freight. Thus advance freight continues to be governed by a rule "analogous to what we all know as the rule in *Chandler v. Webster*" (*per* Robert Goff J. in *The Lorna I* [1981] 2 Lloyd's Rep. 559, 560 (affd. [1983] 1 Lloyd's Rep. 373); and see also *The Karin Vatis* [1988] 2 Lloyd's Rep. 330. On advance freight see more generally Howard in McKendrick (ed.), *Force Majeure and Frustration of Contract* (2nd ed., 1995), pp. 123–129.

[26] It should apply in the case of goods or services because total failure of consideration is logically applicable both to money claims and to non-money claims; see Birks, *An Introduction to the Law of Restitution*, pp. 230–231.

[27] For a fuller analysis of the decision of the House of Lords in *Fibrosa*, its implications for the common law rules and an assessment of the relevant common law principles, see Burrows (ed.), *Essays on the Law of Restitution* (1991), Chap. 6.

[28] *Whincup v. Hughes* (1871) L.R. 6 C.P. 78.

[29] Although it can be argued that the common law position was not as bleak as their Lordships in *Fibrosa* made it appear; see Burrows *op. cit.* pp. 154–165.

[30] *Appleby v. Myers* (1867) L.R. 2 C.P. 651. The same result is, however, likely to be reached under s.1(3) of the Law Reform (Frustrated Contracts) Act 1943 (post § 24–082). The problem in a case such as *Appleby* lies in showing that the recipient of partial performance has been enriched. If the contract states that he is only required to pay on complete performance, why should the law say that he must pay on receipt of partial performance?

Law Reform (Frustrated Contracts) Act 1943.[31] These remaining defects in   **24–072**
the common law compelled Parliament to intervene in the form of the enactment
of the Law Reform (Frustrated Contracts) Act 1943. The Act applies only to a
contract which is "governed by English law"[32]; that is to say, the crucial question
is whether the law applicable to the contract is English law.[33] A further limiting
factor is that the Act only applies to contracts which have become "impossible
of performance or been otherwise frustrated." The Act does not specify when a
contract is frustrated: it simply alters the legal consequences once the contract is
held to have been frustrated under the rules of the common law. The generic
expression "frustration" in section 1(1) probably includes cases where a contract
is discharged by supervening illegality.[34] The Act does not apply to contracts
which are discharged by subsequent agreement or breach.[35] Nor does it apply to
contracts which are initially impossible of performance or to the discharge of a
contract under an express provision of the contract, which provides for automatic
cancellation of a contract on the occurrence of a specified event.[36]

Principle underlying Act. When seeking to interpret the Act it is important   **24–073**
to have regard to the purpose which it seeks to achieve. In *B.P. Exploration Co.
(Libya) Ltd v. Hunt (No. 2)*[37] Robert Goff J. stated that the "fundamental
principle underlying the Act itself is prevention of the unjust enrichment of either
party to the contract at the other's expense"[38] and that its aim was not to
"apportion the loss between the parties."[39] But the Court of Appeal dismissed
this view, stating that the court got "no help from the use of words which are not
in the statute."[40] The purpose behind the Act therefore remains a matter of some
doubt, although it is suggested that the better view is that the Act does indeed

---

[31] Based on the "Seventh Interim Report (Rule in *Chandler v. Webster*)" of the Law Revision
Committee Cmnd. 6009, (1939). Although the Act is based upon the recommendations of the Law
Revision Committee, it is, in fact, wider in its scope than their recommendations and so in *B.P.
Exploration Co. (Libya) Ltd v. Hunt (No. 2)* [1979] 1 W.L.R. 783, 798, Robert Goff J. held that the
Committee's report should not be used as an aid to the interpretation of the Act. See generally on the
Act, Williams, *Law Reform (Frustrated Contracts) Act 1943*; Goff and Jones, *The Law of Restitution*
(5th ed., 1998), pp. 557 *et seq*; McNair (1944) 60 L.Q.R. 160; Haycroft and Waksman [1984] J.B.L.
207; McKendrick (ed.), *Force Majeure and Frustration of Contract* (2nd ed., 1995), Chap. 11;
Treitel, *Frustration and Force Majeure* (1994) §§15–044—15–075.
[32] s.1(1).
[33] See *post* Chap. 31. See also *B.P. Exploration Co. (Libya) Ltd v. Hunt* [1976] 1 W.L.R. 788 where
there was an argument before Kerr J. as to whether or not the proper law of the contract was English
law. It does, however, seem rather strange that the draftsman has elected to use the proper law of the
contract as the decisive factor when we are here concerned with an independent restitutionary claim
which is, of course, distinct from an action on the contract.
[34] Goff and Jones, *The Law of Restitution* (5th ed., 1998), p. 558; McNair (1944) L.Q.R. 160,
162–163.
[35] It would not therefore apply to the situation in *Sumpter v. Hedges* [1898] 1 Q.B. 673, where the
plaintiff, who abandoned his performance of a lump-sum contract, was unable to recover anything for
his work up to that time. See *ante*, § 22–033.
[36] See McKendrick *op. cit.* pp. 291–297.
[37] [1979] 1 W.L.R. 783.
[38] *ibid.* at 799.
[39] *ibid.* The basic structure of the Act is, first, to identify the benefit which has been obtained by
the defendant at the expense of the plaintiff and then, broadly speaking to allow the plaintiff to
recover so much (not exceeding the value of the benefit) as appears to the court to be just. Loss
apportionment is not explicitly addressed within the Act except to the extent that the court has a
discretion to allow the plaintiff to recover so much of the benefit as appears to the court to be "just".
Contrast the view of Haycroft and Waksman [1984] J.B.L. 207, 225.
[40] [1981] 1 W.L.R. 232, 243.

seek to prevent unjust enrichment and can be analysed in restitutionary terms.[41]

24–074   **Recovery of advance payments.** Section 1(2) of the Act provides that:

> "All sums paid or payable to any party in pursuance of the contract before the time when the parties were so discharged (in this Act referred to as 'the time of discharge') shall, in the case of sums so paid, be recoverable from him as money received by him for the use of the party by whom the sums were paid, and, in the case of sums so payable, cease to be payable:
>
> Provided that, if the party to whom the sums were so paid or payable incurred expenses before the time of discharge in, or for the purpose of, the performance of the contract, the court may, if it considers it just to do so having regard to all the circumstances of the case, allow him to retain or, as the case may be, recover the whole or any part of the sums so paid or payable, not being an amount in excess of the expenses so incurred."

The principal effect of this subsection is to entitle a contracting party to recover money paid to the other contracting party prior to the frustrating event and it also relieves such a party of the obligation to pay any monies which were payable prior to the frustrating event but which had remained unpaid. The court has no discretion over the question whether a sum already paid is recoverable: the only discretion concerns the allowance for expenses.

24–075   **Changes from common law.** Section 1(2) goes beyond the common law rule laid down in *Fibrosa* in two respects. The first is that money paid is recoverable even upon a partial failure of consideration; the common law requirement that the failure be total has therefore been abolished in the case of frustration. One effect of this change may be to rescue a payer from his bad bargain because the prepayment is recoverable irrespective of the consideration which would have been received had the contract been performed.[42] The second respect in which section 1(2) goes beyond the rule in *Fibrosa* is that the payee may be entitled to set off against a claim by the payer "the amount of any expenses incurred before the time of discharge . . . in, or for the purpose of, the performance of the contract." The subsection gives rise to a number of interpretative difficulties.

24–076   **Paid or payable.** Subject to one exception, section 1(2) gives a cause of action to the payer and not to the payee. The one exception arises in the case where money payable by the "payer" to the payee before the time of discharge remains unpaid; in such a case the payee can rely upon section 1(2) to recover so much of his expenses, not exceeding the amount of the prepayment due, as is just.[43] Where no money is either paid[44] or is payable to the payee prior to the frustrating event but the payee nevertheless incurs expenditure in, or for the purpose of, the performance of the contract, the payee cannot recover under

---

[41] See generally Burrows *op. cit.* Chap. 6.

[42] *B.P. Exploration Co. (Libya) Ltd v. Hunt (No. 2)* [1979] 1 W.L.R. 793, 800.

[43] This is because the proviso states that the payee may be able to "recover" in whole or in part any sums which were "payable" to him.

[44] "Paid" would cover a sum actually paid, whether or not there was a contractual obligation to pay before the time of discharge.

section 1(2).[45] Such sums are deemed by section 1(2) to be spent at the risk of the payee. No provision is made in the subsection for any increase in the sum recoverable by the claimant, or in the amount of the expenses to be allowed to the defendant, to take account of the time value of money,[46] although interest[47] may be awarded on a sum in respect of which judgment is given under the Act.[48]

Breaches before discharge. Nor does the subsection expressly release a **24–077** promisor who has failed to perform his promise to do something (other than to pay money) before the time of discharge.[49] In such a case the promisor will be liable to pay damages for his breach of contract but he will not be able to bring the sum so paid into account under section 1(3) of the Act because it is not a benefit which was obtained "before the time of discharge." Where the claimant has, prior to the frustrating event, broken the contract between the parties, the defendant may have an accrued right to damages which may, in turn, be the subject of a set-off or counterclaim. But a prior breach by the claimant has no other impact upon the operation of either section 1(2) or section 1(3).[50]

The time of discharge. Since section 1(2) refers to money paid or payable **24–078** before "the time of discharge" it may be important to fix the exact time of discharge. This will usually be the actual happening of the frustrating event but, if the frustration is caused by the non-occurrence of an expected event, the frustration may take effect when it first becomes generally known that the event will not happen. For instance, where a contract to hire rooms to view a procession is frustrated by the cancellation of the procession two days before it is due to take place, the time of discharge, according to Krell v. Henry,[51] is the time of the official announcement of the cancellation.[52] Where money is paid after the time of discharge the recoverability of the payment will be governed by common law rules.[53] Thus where the payment was made after the time of discharge because the payor was unaware of the occurrence of the frustrating event, then the payment may be recoverable on the ground that it was made under a mistake of fact.[54] Where the payment was made because the payor, although aware of the occurrence of the event, was unaware that it amounted in law to a frustrating

---

[45] Although a claim may be made under s.1(3) where the expenditure results in a valuable benefit being obtained by the other party. See post, § 24–082.

[46] B.P. Exploration Co. (Libya) Ltd v. Hunt (No. 2) [1979] 1 W.L.R. 783, 800: affd. [1981] 1 W.L.R. 232, at 244.

[47] See post, § 24–085.

[48] B.P. Exploration Co. (Libya) Ltd v. Hunt (No. 2) [1979] 1 W.L.R. 783, 835–836; affd. [1983] 2 A.C. 352, 373.

[49] Treitel, The Law of Contract (9th ed., 1995), p. 828.

[50] B.P. Exploration Co. (Libya) Ltd v. Hunt (No. 2) [1979] 1 W.L.R. 783, 808.

[51] [1903] 2 K.B. 740 (ante, § 24–032).

[52] The court will not review the decision of an arbitrator who has, on reasonable grounds, found that the contract was frustrated on a particular date: see Kodros Shipping Corporation of Monrovia v. Empresa Cubana de Fletes (The Evia) (No. 2) [1983] 1 A.C. 736, 767–768, followed in Finelvet A.G. v. Vinava Shipping Co. Ltd [1983] 1 W.L.R. 1469 (the arbitrator's choice of date must be within the permissible range of dates). On arbitration, see post, § 24–095.

[53] See McKendrick (ed.), Force Majeure and Frustration of Contract (2nd ed., 1995), p. 230.

[54] Under the authority of Barclays Bank Ltd v. W.J. Simms Son & Cooke (Southern) Ltd [1980] Q.B. 677, post §§ 30–026 et seq.

event, the payment may now be recoverable as a payment made under a mistake of law.[55]

24-079   **The basis of the proviso.** Although the payee may now be entitled to set off against a claim by the payer "the amount of any expenses incurred before the time of discharge . . . in, or for the purpose of the performance of the contract," it is difficult to establish the basis upon which the payee is entitled to seek to bring his expenditure into account. The consequence of this is that it is difficult, if not impossible, to ascertain with any confidence the amount which the payee will be entitled to retain. Various views have been put forward. First, it has been argued that the loss caused by the frustrating event should be divided equally between the parties on the ground that the "situation with which the Act is concerned is the familiar one in which one of two parties has to suffer loss for which neither is responsible" and that in the "normal case" the just course "would be to order the retention or repayment of half the loss incurred."[56] Secondly, it has been argued that the payee should be entitled to retain the full amount of the expenditure incurred in the performance of the contract; a view supported by the English Law Revision Committee[57] and which also seems to receive some support from the judgment of Robert Goff J. in *B.P. Exploration Co. (Libya) Ltd v. Hunt (No. 2)* who argued that the proviso constituted a "statutory recognition of the defence of change of position"[58] although this rationalisation is controversial.[59] The third view is that the court in deciding what is "just" is exercising a broad discretion, which discretion is not confined to the entitlement to bring expenditure into account but extends to the proportion of the repayment which the payee can retain or recover[60] and that therefore this discretion would be unduly circumscribed by the adoption of either of the other two views. These three views were considered by Garland J. in *Gamerco SA v. I.C.M./Fair Warning (Agency) Ltd*[61] who concluded that he could see "no indication in the Act, the authorities or the relevant literature that the court is obliged to incline towards either total retention or equal division. Its task is to do justice in a situation which the parties had neither contemplated nor provided for, and to mitigate the possible harshness of allowing all loss to lie where it has

---

[55] See generally *Kleinwort Benson Ltd v. Lincoln City Council* [1998] 3 W.L.R. 1095, *post*, §§ 30–041 *et seq.*

[56] *The Law Reform (Frustrated Contracts) Act 1943*, pp. 35–36. Such an approach has been expressly adopted in s.5(3) of the British Columbia Frustrated Contracts Act 1974.

[57] On the ground that it is "reasonable to assume that in stipulating for pre-payment the payee intended to protect himself against loss under the contract" (Cmnd. 6009, (1939)), p. 7. But it is doubtful whether the payee thinks of the possibility of frustration; he probably intends to protect himself against the possibility of the other party's insolvency or default in payment.

[58] [1979] 1 W.L.R. 783, 800.

[59] See further Burrows (ed.), *Essays on the Law of Restitution*, pp. 156–159. One version of the change of position defence requires that the defendant show that he "had materially changed [his] circumstances as a result of the receipt of the money" (*Storthoaks v. Mobil Oil of Canada Ltd* (1975) 55 D.L.R. (3d) 1). But the provison does not require that the payee change his position "as a result of the receipt of the money." The expenditure can be incurred before the receipt of the payment and yet the payee remains entitled to invoke the proviso. The change of position rationalisation must be handled, if at all, with great care and must not be allowed to distort the meaning of the words actually used in the proviso. See further on change of position, *Lipkin Gorman v. Karpnale* [1991] 2 A.C. 508 and §§ 30–114—30–119 *post*.

[60] *cf. National Carriers Ltd v. Panalpina (Northern) Ltd* [1981] A.C. 675, 707 where Lord Simon of Glaisdale did not think that the court was empowered by the Act to engage in loss apportionment and that, in consequence, there would often be an "all-or-nothing" situation.

[61] [1995] 1 W.L.R. 1226.

fallen."[62] The emphasis is thus placed on the "broad nature" of the discretion which the court enjoys and the imperative to do justice on the facts of the case.[63]

Burden of proof. The onus of proof is upon the payee to demonstrate that the **24–080** requirements of the proviso have been satisfied.[64] An illustration of the importance of the location of the onus of proof is provided by *Lobb v. Vasey Housing Auxiliary*,[65] a case decided under the Victorian Frustrated Contracts Act 1959.[66] The defendants were paid £1,250 by Mrs Smith for an exclusive licence to occupy a flat in a block of flats which they were building. Mrs Smith died before her flat was completed. Her death was held to have frustrated the contract between the parties. Her executrix sued to recover the £1,250. The onus of proof was on the defendants to show that it was just in all the circumstances of the case for them to retain any part of the £1,250 and Hudson J. pointed out that, in the normal case they would sell the right to occupy the flat to someone else and so recover their expenses in that way. After an adjournment judgment was entered for the plaintiff for £1,175.[67] On this approach a payee whose expenditure results in a product which he can use in the performance of another contract may find it difficult to discharge the onus of proof.[68] A further consequence of the adoption of this approach may be that, where the payee fails to satisfy the onus, any loss lies on him but that, where he does satisfy the onus, he is entitled to retain or recover all the expenditure incurred in or for the purpose of the performance of the contract.

Allowance for expenses. In identifying the relevant "expenses" to be taken **24–081** into account, it must be noted that expenses includes a reasonable sum for overhead expenses and for work or services personally performed.[69] These expenses must have been incurred "in, or for the purpose of, the performance of the contract." Pre-contract expenditure may not be recoverable on the ground that, at the time of the expenditure, there was no contract for the expenses to be incurred in "the performance of," although it can be argued that such expenditure was incurred "for the purpose of" the performance of the contract and so should be brought into account.[70]

Obligations other than to pay money. Section 1(3) states that: **24–082**

> "Where any party to the contract has, by reason of anything done by any other party thereto in, or for the purpose of, the performance of the contract, obtained a valuable

---

[62] *ibid.* at 1235.

[63] For an attempt to provide a structure for the exercise of this discretion see Burrows *op. cit.* Chap. 6.

[64] *Gamerco SA v. I.C.M./Fair Warning (Agency) Ltd* [1995] 1 W.L.R. 1226, 1235.

[65] [1963] V.R. 239.

[66] An Act which was modelled on the Law Reform (Frustrated Contracts) Act 1943.

[67] The precise basis on which this sum was calculated does not emerge from the judgment.

[68] As was the case in *Davis and Primrose Ltd v. Clyde Shipbuilding and Engineering Co. Ltd*, 1917 1 S.L.T. 297. See also Treitel, *The Law of Contract*, (9th ed., 1995), p. 824 and for a slightly different argument to the same end see Williams *op. cit.* n. 18, p. 39 who argues that expenses in s.1(2) means "expenses after deduction of gains resulting from those expenses."

[69] s.1(4).

[70] It can also be argued that where the expenditure is incurred in the reasonable belief that a contract will be concluded it will be recoverable; see the examples given by Goff and Jones *op. cit.* p. 560.

benefit (other than a payment of money to which the last foregoing subsection applies) before the time of discharge, there shall be recoverable from him by the said other party such sum (if any), not exceeding the value of the said benefit to the party obtaining it, as the court considers just, having regard to all the circumstances of the case and, in particular,—

(a) the amount of any expenses incurred before the time of discharge by the benefited party in, or for the purpose of, the performance of the contract, including any sums paid or payable by him to any other party in pursuance of the contract and retained or recoverable by that party under the last foregoing subsection, and

(b) the effect, in relation to the said benefit, of the circumstances giving rise to the frustration of the contract."

This is the most controversial and difficult provision in the Act, caused in large part by the failure of the draftsman to provide a definition of what constitutes a "benefit" and to identify with sufficient precision the time at which the benefit is to be valued. In *B.P. Exploration Co. (Libya) Ltd v. Hunt (No. 2)*[71] Robert Goff J. held that the proper approach to the construction of the subsection is a three-stage one. At the first stage the valuable benefit must be identified; at the second stage the benefit must be valued; and at the third stage the court must consider the award of a just sum.

24–083   **(1) Identification of the benefit.** The "benefit," which must of course be non-monetary, could consist of either the "end product" of the services or the services themselves. Robert Goff J. concluded, as a matter of construction rather than one of principle,[72] that "in an appropriate case" it was the end product which was to be regarded as the benefit. It is not clear when it would not be "appropriate" to regard the end product as the benefit but there are a number of situations in which it has been argued that the benefit should be identified with the service itself. The general rule is therefore that regard must be had to the end product of the services when identifying the benefit. But there are at least two situations in which it is appropriate to have regard to the services themselves when identifying the benefit. The first case arises where the service, by its very nature, does not result in an end product, for example, "where the services consist of doing such work as surveying, or transporting goods."[73] Where there is no end product the court must simply ascertain the benefit which the defendant has obtained by virtue of the claimant's contractual performance, which benefit can only be measured by reference to the value of the services performed by the claimant under the contract.[74] The second case arises where the services performed result in an end product which has no objective value,[75] in which case the benefit must also be

---

[71] [1979] 1 W.L.R. 783.

[72] As a matter of principle he was of the view that the services themselves should be regarded as the benefit.

[73] [1979] 1 W.L.R. 783, 802.

[74] The conclusion that the existence of an end product was a necessary ingredient of a s.1(3) claim would arguably have led to ridiculous arguments as to what constitutes an "end product": see, for example, Birks, *An Introduction to the Law of Restitution*, p. 252.

[75] Robert Goff J. gave the example of a claimant who commences "the redecoration, to the defendant's execrable taste, of rooms which are in good decorative order": [1979] 1 W.L.R. 783, 803. In such a case, the work of the claimant may even reduce the value of the defendant's property but the services must nevertheless be regarded as a benefit because they were requested by their recipient.

measured by reference to the value of the services provided under the contract.

There is a third situation in which it has been argued that a court should have   **24–084**
regard to the value of the service performed where the frustrating event results in
the destruction of the end product itself. But in *B.P. Exploration Co. (Libya) Ltd
v. Hunt (No. 2)* Robert Goff J. rejected this argument on two principal grounds.[76]
The first was that a distinction is drawn in section 1(3) between the claimant's
performance and the defendant's benefit, thus indicating that the defendant's
benefit cannot be regarded as the value of the claimant's performance. The
second was that "benefit" in section 1(3)(b) clearly refers to the end product of
the services rather than the services themselves.[77] This view has not, however,
commanded universal assent, largely on the basis that section 1(3) applies where
a valuable benefit has been obtained *before* the time of discharge and on the
ground that the words immediately preceeding paragraphs (a) and (b) ("having
regard to all the circumstances of the case, and in particular") appear to be
directed to the assessment of the just sum and not to the identification of the
valuable benefit.[78]

(2) Valuing the benefit. Once the benefit has been identified, the court must   **24–085**
then value it. The conclusion that it is the end product and not the services
themselves which are to be regarded as the benefit gives rise to considerable
difficulties in valuing the benefit because there is no necessary relationship
between the services and the end product. A small service may result in an end
product of great value, while a service of great value may result in an end product
of no or minimal value. If the benefit is only partly attributable to the claimant's
performance, the court should apportion the value of the benefit accordingly.[79]
The wording of the subsection does not permit the court to take account of the
time value of money so that the benefit is valued at the date of the frustrating
event without regard to the money which the defendant may have obtained by
selling the benefit before the date of the frustrating event,[80] although interest[81]
may be awarded on a sum in respect of which judgment is given under the
Act.[82]

Date of valuation. In *B.P. Exploration Co. (Libya) Ltd v. Hunt (No. 2)* Robert   **24–086**
Goff J. held that the benefit must be valued as at the date of the frustrating event.
The difficulty with this proposition is that section 1(3) applies where "a valuable
benefit has been obtained *before* the time of discharge." This suggests that the
date of the valuation should be before the time of discharge and the point may yet
be open for further argument.

---

[76] On this view the result of *Appleby v. Myers* (1867) L.R. 2 C.P. 651 would be unaffected by s.1(3)
of the Act.
[77] Further support for this view can be gleaned from the decision of the Newfoundland Supreme
Court in *Parsons Bros Ltd v. Shea* (1966) 53 D.L.R. (2d.) 86, a case decided under the similarly
worded Newfoundland Frustrated Contracts Act 1956. See also McKendrick (ed.), *Force Majeure
and Frustration of Contract* (2nd ed., 1995), pp. 236–237.
[78] See, *e.g.* Treitel *op. cit.* p. 827.
[79] *B.P. Exploration Co. (Libya) Ltd v. Hunt (No. 2)* [1979] 1 W.L.R. 783, 802.
[80] *ibid.* at 803–804.
[81] See *post* § 27–142, n. 66.
[82] [1979] 1 W.L.R. 783, 836; affd. [1983] 2 A.C. 352, 373.

24–087   **Deduction of expenses.** A further problem arises in relation to the role of section 1(3)(a), namely whether the expenses should be deducted from the benefit or from the just sum. Robert Goff J. held that the expenses were to be deducted from the value of the benefit and not from the just sum.[83] But, as we have already noted, the words immediately preceding paragraph (*a*) suggest that the expenses should be deducted from the just sum and not from the valuable benefit and, once again, the point may yet be open for further argument.[84]

24–088   **(3) The just sum.** The final step is for the court to assess the "just" sum to be awarded to the claimant. Robert Goff J. held that the aim of the court in assessing the just sum ought to be the "prevention of the unjust enrichment of the defendant at the plaintiff's expense"[85] but the Court of Appeal preferred a broader, discretionary approach, stating that "[w]hat is just is what the trial judge thinks is just" and that an appellate court is not entitled to interfere with the assessment of the just sum by the trial judge "unless it is so plainly wrong that it cannot be just."[86] This appears to leave the assessment of the just sum at the complete discretion of the trial judge. There are, however, certain factors which are clearly of relevance in the assessment of the just sum. The first is that the value of the benefit acts as a ceiling on the sum which the court can award so that the "just sum" cannot be greater than the value of the benefit obtained. The second is that the contractual allocation of risk is likely to be an important factor in the assessment of the just sum. It is "likely" that in most cases the claimant's claim will be limited to a rateable proportion of the contract price so that section 1(3) cannot be used to escape the consequences of a bad bargain.[87] The third point is that the process of assessing the just sum may bear some resemblance to the inquiry conducted by the court in an action for a *quantum meruit* or a *quantum valebat*.[88]

24–089   **Severability.** Section 2(4) of the Act provides:

> "Where it appears to the court that a part of any contract to which this Act applies can properly be severed from the remainder of the contract, being a part wholly performed before the time of discharge, or so performed except for the payment in respect of that part of the contract of sums which are or can be ascertained under the contract, the court shall treat that part of the contract as if it were a separate contract and had not been frustrated and shall treat the foregoing section of this Act as only applicable to the remainder of that contract."

Thus, where a contract can be divided into severable and distinct obligations (as opposed to being an "entire contract"[89]) the Act has no application to any obligation which has been completely performed. The Act does, however, apply to those several obligations which have not been completely performed, thus

---

[83] [1979] 1 W.L.R. 783, 804.
[84] See Haycroft and Waksman *op. cit.* p. 220.
[85] [1979] 1 W.L.R. 783, 805.
[86] [1981] 1 W.L.R. 232, 238.
[87] [1979] 1 W.L.R. 783, 806.
[88] *ibid.* at 805 and see also at 825.
[89] See *ante*, § 22–027.

departing from the common law rule which was that no recovery was possible in respect of money paid or benefits conferred in the performance of a severable obligation which had not been completely performed.[90]

Contrary intention. Section 2(3) provides: **24–090**

"Where any contract to which this Act applies contains any provision which, upon the true construction of the contract, is intended to have effect in the event of circumstances arising which operate, or would but for the said provision operate, to frustrate the contract, or is intended to have effect whether such circumstances arise or not, the court, shall give effect to the said provision and shall only give effect to the foregoing section of this Act to such extent, if any, as appears to the court to be consistent with the said provision."[91]

Although it has been stated that, in deciding whether the parties have contracted out of the Act, a court will apply "ordinary principles of construction"[92] it has also been said that "where there is no clear indication that the parties did intend the clause to be applicable in the event of frustration, the court has to be very careful before it draws the inference that the clause was intended to be applicable in such radically changed circumstances."[93] It is for the party who is seeking to rely upon section 2(3) to demonstrate that the clause was intended to operate in the circumstances which have actually happened; where the circumstances which have occurred are so devastating and unusual as to fall outside the ambit of the clause in question, then the Act may not have been excluded.

Implicit provision. A court will be particularly reluctant to imply a term that **24–091** the parties have made provision for the consequences of a frustrating event. But a clause which provides that one contracting party is under an obligation to maintain insurance against the consequences of the frustrating event would appear to be effective to exclude the operation of the Act so that the party upon whom the obligation to insure is imposed cannot bring a claim under the Act.[94] However the fact that a contract is entire and that the contract provides that payment is not due until the work is complete or until a date which is after the date of the frustrating event does not "automatically preclude an award of damages under section 1(3)"[95] and it is only "if upon a true construction of the contract the plaintiff has contracted on the terms that he is to receive no payment

---

[90] *Stubbs v. Holywell Rly. Co.* (1867) L.R. 2 Ex. 311.

[91] It should be noted that we are here concerned with a clause which seeks to regulate the *consequences* of the frustration of a contract and not with a clause which seeks to make provision for an *event* which would otherwise frustrate the contract; where the parties make provision for what would otherwise be a frustrating event the effect of such a clause is to exclude the operation of the doctrine of frustration completely and the Act does not apply to a contract which has not been frustrated.

[92] [1979] 1 W.L.R. 783, 806.

[93] *ibid.* at 829.

[94] *ibid.* at 807A, although it should be noted that s.1(5) provides that "the court shall not take into account any sums which have, by reason of the circumstances giving rise to the frustration of the contract, become payable to that party under any contract of insurance unless there was an obligation to insure imposed by an express term of the frustrated contract or by or under any enactment."

[95] *ibid.* at 807.

in the event which has occurred, will the fact that the contract is 'entire' have the effect of precluding an award under the Act."[96]

24–092 **Effect of contracting out.** It is not, however, enough to contract out of the Act without making alternative provision for the consequences of frustration, because the effect of simply contracting out of the Act would appear to be to re-instate the common law as laid down in *Fibrosa Spolka Akcyjna v. Fairbairn Lawson Combe Barbour Ltd.*[97] Contracting parties who wish to provide a different regime for the remedial consequences of frustration should make express provision to that effect in their contract.

24–093 **Supplementary provisions of the Act.** Section 1(6) of the Act states that the court may allow an action given by subsection (3) to be brought against one party to the contract, though the benefit was conferred on another party to it, or upon a stranger to the contract altogether. Section 2(2) of the Act provides that the Act binds the Crown.

24–094 **Contracts excluded from the Act.** Section 2(5) provides that the Act does not apply to four types of contract: (a) "any charterparty, except a time charterparty or a charterparty by way of demise"; (b) "any contract . . . for the carriage of goods by sea" (since commercial practice has developed well-known rules for insurance against the risks of these contracts[98]); (c) "any contract of insurance" (since there is a well-established principle that no part of a premium is legally recoverable where the subject-matter of the risk ceases to exist before the period of the insurance expires[99]); (d) any contract for the sale of specific goods which perish, whether or not the risk passed to the buyer before the date of perishing.[1] (Any other contract for the sale of goods will be governed by the Act,[2] as will a contract for the sale of specific goods which is frustrated otherwise than by the "perishing" of the goods.)

24–095 **Arbitration.** The paucity of reported decisions on the operation of the Act is possibly due to the fact that the issues arising under the Act are particularly

---

[96] *ibid.*
[97] [1943] A.C. 32.
[98] Williams (1942) 6 M.L.R. 46, 54–55; also *op. cit.* pp. 72–74, 79. This exclusion from the Act preserves two common law rules: freight due in advance is still payable despite the fact that, after payment has fallen due, the voyage specified in the contract is frustrated; and a shipowner cannot recover part of the agreed freight *pro rata itineris peracti* when frustration occurs before completion of the voyage. See *Carver's Carriage by Sea* (13th ed., 1982), Vols. 2 and 3, §§ 779 *et seq.*, 1691 *et seq.*
[99] *Tyrie v. Fletcher* [1777] 2 Cowp. 666, and see *post*, Vol. II, § 41–048.
[1] This formulation of category (d) is an attempt to state the effect of a badly drafted provision of the Act, namely, s.2(5)(c) (as amended by the Sale of Goods Act 1979, s.63 and Sched. 2, para. 2). The provision appears to assume that the rules as to risk adequately cover the situation: see Vol. II, §§ 43–188 *et seq.* Detailed arguments as to the effect of this involved provision may be found elsewhere, *viz.* Williams *op. cit.* pp. 81–90; Goff & Jones *op. cit.* pp. 574–576; Cheshire, Fifoot & Furmston, *Law of Contract* (13th ed.), pp. 604–605; Treitel *op. cit.* pp. 830–832; Atiyah, *The Sale of Goods* (9th ed.), pp. 311–315. Section 7 is discussed in note detail in Vol. II, §§ 43–033—43–036.
[2] Thus, the Act would apply where a contract for the sale of non-specific goods was frustrated, *e.g. Howell v. Coupland* (1876) 1 Q.B.D. 258. *cf. H.R. and S. Sainsbury Ltd v. Street* [1972] 1 W.L.R. 834 (*ante*, § 24–066).

suitable for arbitration.³ The questions whether a contract has been frustrated⁴ and, if so, whether a claim under the Act arises⁵ are within the scope of a wide arbitration clause in a contract, *e.g.* one providing for arbitration "if any dispute or difference shall arise or occur between the parties hereto in relation to any thing or matter arising out of or under this agreement . . . "⁶; the arbitration clause survives the frustration for the purpose of the assessment of any consequential claim under the Act or for the purposes of an independent restitutionary claim.⁷

Services rendered or payments made after frustration. The Law Reform   **24–096** (Frustrated Contracts) Act 1943 has no application to benefits conferred after the date of the frustrating event. Where the parties enter into a fresh contract relating to the post-frustration performance, then that contract will obviously govern the relationship between the parties. Where no such contract is concluded the party who has conferred the benefit on the other party may be able to bring an independent restitutionary claim if he can show that the defendant has freely accepted the benefit of the post-frustration performance, in the sense that the recipient knew that the performance was being rendered non-gratuitously and elected to accept the performance, having had the opportunity to reject it.⁸ In such a case the plaintiff may be able to recover the reasonable value of the services performed.⁹ The only other ground upon which a restitutionary claim could be brought is mistake. Where the benefit has been conferred because the plaintiff was unaware of the occurrence of the frustrating event, then it may be possible to recover the value of the benefit conferred on the ground that it was given under a mistake of fact.¹⁰ Where the benefit was conferred because the plaintiff was unaware that the event, as a matter of law, constituted a frustrating event, then the value of the benefit conferred may now be recovered on the ground that it was given under a mistake of law.¹¹

---

³ *Pioneer Shipping Ltd v. B.T.P. Tioxide Ltd* [1982] A.C. 724, 743–744; *Kodros Shipping Corporation of Monrovia v. Empresa Cubana de Fletes (The Evia) (No. 2)* [1983] 1 A.C. 736. On arbitration clauses, see *ante*, § 16–021.

⁴ *Heyman v. Darwins Ltd* [1942] A.C. 356, 366, 383, 400–401; *Kruse v. Questier & Co. Ltd* [1953] 1 Q.B. 669; *Government of Gibraltar v. Kenney* [1956] 2 Q.B. 410; The *Kodros Shipping* case *supra* (the time of frustration). The House of Lords has held that the court should be reluctant to interfere with the conclusion of an arbitrator that a contract has been frustrated: it must be shown either that the arbitrator misdirected himself in law, or that the decision was such that no reasonable arbitrator could reach: the *Pioneer Shipping* case, *supra*, at 742–744, 752–754. (See *ante*, § 24–015, especially n. 65; and § 24–034, n. 46.) To similar effect see *Kuwait Supply Co. v. Oyster Marine Management (The Safeer)* [1994] 1 Lloyd's Rep. 637.

⁵ *Government of Gibraltar v. Kenney, supra.*

⁶ *ibid.*

⁷ *ibid.*

⁸ See *post*, §§ 30–177 *et seq.* and, more generally, Birks, *An Introduction to the Law of Restitution*, Chap. X.

⁹ *Société Franco-Tunisienne d'Armement v. Sidermar SpA* [1961] 2 Q.B. 278, 313 (overruled on another point: *Ocean Tramp Tankers Corporation v. V/O Sovfracht (The Eugenia)* [1964] 2 Q.B. 226); Furmston (1961) 24 M.L.R. 173; Giles (1964) 27 M.L.R. 351; *Codelfa Construction Pty. Ltd v. State Rail Authority of New South Wales* (1982) 149 C.L.R. 337.

¹⁰ See *post*, §§ 30–026—30–037 and, more generally, Goff and Jones *op. cit.* Chap. 3.

¹¹ See *post*, §§ 30–038—30–047 and *Kleinwort Benson Ltd v. Lincoln City Council* [1998] 3 W.L.R. 1095.

DISCHARGE BY BREACH

1. IN GENERAL[1]

Discharge by breach. One party to a contract may, by reason of the other's **25–001** breach, be entitled to treat himself as discharged from his liability further to perform his own unperformed obligations under the contract and from his obligation to accept performance by the other party if made or tendered.[2] The expression "discharge by breach" is commonly employed to describe the situation where he is entitled to, and does, exercise that right. Nevertheless, the expression is not wholly accurate, at least without further explanation. In the first place, not every breach of contract has this effect. Discharge from liability is not necessarily coincident with a right to sue for damages. The rule is usually stated as follows: "Any breach of contract gives rise to a cause of action; not every breach gives a discharge from liability." Thus the main question discussed in this chapter is whether a party who admittedly has a claim for damages is also relieved from further performance by the other party's breach. Secondly, although sometimes the innocent party is referred to as "rescinding" the contract and the contract as being "terminated" by the breach, it is clear that the contract is not rescinded *ab initio*[3] nor is it extinguished by the breach.[4] The innocent party, or, in some cases, both parties, are excused from further performance of their primary obligations under the contract; but there is then substituted for the

---

[1] See Lord Devlin [1967] Camb.L.J. 192; Reynolds (1963) 79 L.Q.R. 534; Treitel (1967) 30 M.L.R. 139; Shea (1979) 42 M.L.R. 623; Beatson (1981) 97 L.Q.R. 389; Rose (1981) 34 C.L.P. 235; Carter, *Breach of Contract* (2nd ed., 1991).

[2] This principle would appear to apply to leases: see *Hussain v. Mehlman* [1992] 2 E.G.L.R. 87; *Progressive House Pty. Ltd v. Tabali Pty. Ltd* (1985) 157 C.L.R. 17; *Highway Properties Ltd v. Kelly, Douglas & Co.* (1971) 17 D.L.R. (3d) 710; *cf. Total Oil Great Britain Ltd v. Thompson Garages (Biggin Hill) Ltd* [1972] 1 Q.B. 318. See further Pawlowski [1995] Conv. 379.

[3] *Heyman v. Darwins Ltd* [1942] A.C. 356, 373, 399; *Johnson v. Agnew* [1980] A.C. 367, 373; *Photo Production Ltd v. Securicor Transport Ltd* [1980] A.C. 827, 844; *Bank of Boston Connecticut v. European Grain and Shipping Ltd* [1989] A.C. 1056, 1098–1099; *State Trading Corpn. of India Ltd v. M. Golodetz Ltd* [1989] 2 Lloyd's Rep. 277, 286. See *post*, § 25–046.

[4] *Photo Production Ltd v. Securicor Transport Ltd, supra* (overruling *Harbutt's "Plasticine" Ltd v. Wayne Tank and Pump Co. Ltd* [1970] 1 Q.B. 447). See *ante*, § 14–022; *post*, § 25–046.

primary obligations of the party in default a secondary obligation to pay monetary compensation for his non-performance.[5] Thirdly, the innocent party is not ordinarily[6] bound to treat himself as discharged: if the contract is still executory, he may elect instead to treat it as continuing.[7] He may also waive his right of discharge, accept the defective performance of the other party, and content himself with damages, which are his remedy in any event.[8]

25-002   **Affirmation.** Where the innocent party, being entitled to choose whether to treat the contract as continuing or to accept the repudiation and treat himself as discharged, elects to treat the contract as continuing, he is usually said to have "affirmed" the contract.[9] He will not be held to have elected to affirm the contract unless, first, he has knowledge of the facts giving rise to the breach,[10] and, secondly, he has knowledge of his legal right to choose between the alternatives open to him.[11] Affirmation may be express or implied. It will be implied if, with knowledge of the breach and of his right to choose, he does some unequivocal[12] act from which it may be inferred that he intends to go on with the contract regardless of the breach or from which it may be inferred that he will not

---

[5] *R. V. Ward Ltd v. Bignall* [1967] 1 Q.B. 534, 548; *Moschi v. Lep Air Services Ltd* [1973] A.C. 331, 345, 350, 351; *Hyundai Ltd v. Pournouras* [1978] 2 Lloyd's Rep. 502, 507; *Photo Production Ltd v. Securicor Transport Ltd, supra*, at 848–851. See *post*, § 25–051.

[6] On the question of whether the wrongful dismissal of an employee from his contract of employment constitutes an exception to the rule, see Vol. II, § 39–172. See also *Thomas Marshall (Exports) Ltd v. Guinle* [1979] Ch. 227 (repudiation by employee).

[7] *Avery v. Bowden* (1855) 5 E. & B. 714; (1856) 6 E. & B. 953; *Frost v. Knight* (1872) L.R. 7 Ex. 111, 112; *Johnstone v. Milling* (1886) 16 Q.B.D. 460, 470; *Michael v. Hart & Co.* [1902] 1 K.B. 482, 492; *Tredegar Iron and Coal Co. Ltd v. Hawthorn Bros. & Co.* (1902) 18 T.L.R. 716; *Hain SS. Co. Ltd v. Tate & Lyle Ltd* (1936) 41 Com.Cas. 350, 355, 363; *Heyman v. Darwins Ltd* [1942] A.C. 356, 361; *Chandris v. Isbrandtsen Moller Co. Inc.* [1951] 1 K.B. 240, 248; *Howard v. Pickford Tool Co. Inc.* [1951] 1 K.B. 417, 421; *White & Carter (Councils) Ltd v. McGregor* [1962] A.C. 413; *Cranleigh Precision Engineering Ltd v. Bryant* [1965] 1 W.L.R. 1293; *Suisse Atlantique Société d'Armement Maritime SA v. N.V. Rotterdamsche Kolen Centrale* [1967] 1 A.C. 361, 398, 418; *Decro-Wall International SA v. Practitioners in Marketing Ltd* [1971] 1 W.L.R. 361, 368, 375, 381; *Mayfair Photographic Supplies Ltd v. Baxter Hoare & Co. Ltd* [1972] 1 Lloyd's Rep. 410, 417; *Lakshmijit v. Sherani* [1974] A.C. 605; *Thomas Marshall (Exports) Ltd v. Guinle, supra; Tai Hing Cotton Mill Ltd v. Kamsing Knitting Factory* [1979] A.C. 91; *Fercometal S.A.R.L. v. Mediterranean Shipping Co. SA* [1989] A.C. 788; *Vitol SA v. Norelf* [1996] A.C. 800.

[8] *Bentsen v. Taylor, Sons & Co.* [1893] 2 Q.B. 274; *Wallis, Son and Wells v. Pratt and Haynes* [1911] A.C. 394; *Hain SS. Co. Ltd v. Tate & Lyle Ltd, supra; Chandris v. Isbrandtsen Moller Co. Inc., supra; Suisse Atlantique Société d'Armement Maritime SA v. N.V. Rotterdamsche Kolen Centrale, supra*; Sale of Goods Act 1979, s.11(2). See also *post*, § 25–002 (affirmation).

[9] *Suisse Atlantique Société d'Armement Maritime SA v. N.V. Rotterdamsche Kolen Centrale* [1967] 1 A.C. 361, 398; *Peyman v. Lanjani* [1985] Ch. 457.

[10] *Matthews v. Smallwood* [1910] 1 Ch. 777, 786; *U.G.S. Finance Ltd v. National Mortgage Bank of Greece* [1964] 1 Lloyd's Rep. 446, 450; *Suisse Atlantique Société d'Armement Maritime SA v. N.V. Rotterdamsche Kolen Centrale, supra*, at 426; *Panchaud Frères SA v. Etablissements General Grain Co.* [1970] 1 Lloyd's Rep. 53, 57; *Kammins Ballrooms Co. Ltd v. Zenith Investments (Torquay) Ltd* [1971] A.C. 850; *Peyman v. Lanjani, supra; Yukong Line Ltd of Korea v. Rendsberg Investments Corpn. of Liberia* [1996] 2 Lloyd's Rep. 604, 607.

[11] *Kendall v. Hamilton* (1879) 4 App.Cas. 504, 542; *Peyman v. Lanjani, supra. cf. Sea Calm Shipping Co. SA v. Chantiers Navals de L'Esterel* [1986] 2 Lloyd's Rep. 294; *Motor Oil Hellas (Corinth) Refineries SA v. Shipping Corpn. of India* [1990] 1 Lloyd's Rep. 391, 398 where the issue was noted but not resolved; *Yukong Line Ltd of Korea v. Rendsberg Investments Corpn. of Liberia* [1996] 2 Lloyd's Rep. 604, 607.

[12] *China National Foreign Trade Transportation Corpn. v. Evolgia Shipping Co. SA of Panama* [1979] 1 W.L.R. 1018; *Peyman v. Lanjani, supra.*

exercise his right to treat the contract as repudiated.[13] Affirmation must be total: the innocent party cannot approbate and reprobate by affirming part of the contract and disaffirming the rest, for that would be to make a new contract.[14] Mere inactivity after breach does not of itself amount to affirmation,[15] nor (it seems) does the commencement of an action claiming damages for breach.[16] The mere fact that the innocent party has called on the party in breach to change his mind, accept his obligations and perform the contract will not generally, of itself, amount to an affirmation: "the law does not require an injured party to snatch at a repudiation and he does not automatically lose his right to treat the contract as discharged merely by calling on the other to reconsider his position and recognize his obligation."[17] But if the innocent party unreservedly[18] continues to press for performance or accepts performance by the other party after becoming aware of the breach and of his right to elect, he will be held to have affirmed the contract.

Affirmation irrevocable. Once the innocent party has elected to affirm the contract, and this has been communicated to the other party, then the choice becomes irrevocable.[19] There is no need to establish reliance or detriment by the party in default.[20] Thus the innocent party, having affirmed, cannot subsequently **25-003**

---

[13] *Pust v. Dowie* (1863) 5 B. & S. 33; *Bentsen v. Taylor, Sons & Co.* [1893] 2 Q.B. 274; *Matthews v. Smallwood, supra*; *Hain SS. Co. Ltd v. Tate & Lyle Ltd* (1936) 41 Com.Cas. 350, 355, 363; *Temple SS. Co. v. Sovfracht* (1945) 79 Ll.L.Rep. 1, 11; *Chandris v. Isbrandtsen Moller Inc.* [1951] 1 K.B. 240; *Denmark Productions Ltd v. Boscobel Productions Ltd* [1969] 1 Q.B. 699, 731; *Suisse Atlantique Société d'Armement Maritime SA v. N.V. Rotterdamsche Kolen Centrale, supra*; *Sea Calm Shipping Co. SA v. Chantiers Navals de L'Esterel, supra*; *Motor Oil Hellas (Corinth) Refineries SA v. Shipping Corpn. of India, supra* at 398; *Laing Management Ltd v. Aegon Insurance Co. (U.K.) Ltd* (1998) 86 Build L.R. 70, 108 (although the conclusion that the contract remained alive for the benefit of both parties does not sit easily with the fact that the plaintiffs had expressly relied upon an express power to terminate contained in the contract).

[14] *Suisse Atlantique Société d'Armement Maritime SA v. N.V. Rotterdamsche Kolen Centrale, supra*, at 398. See also *Johnstone v. Milling* (1886) 13 Q.B.D. 460.

[15] *Perry v. Davis* (1858) 3 C.B.(N.S.) 769; *Cranleigh Precision Engineering Ltd v. Bryant* [1965] 1 W.L.R. 1293; *Nichimen Corpn. v. Gatoil Overseas Inc.* [1987] 2 Lloyd's Rep. 46. See also *Clough v. L.N.W. Ry.* (1871) 7 Ex. 26; *Allen v. Robles* [1969] 1 W.L.R. 193. But see *Denmark Productions Ltd v. Boscobel Productions Ltd, supra*; *Scandinavian Trader Tanker Co. A.B. v. Flota Petrolea Ecuatoriana* [1981] 2 Lloyd's Rep. 425, 430 (affd. [1983] 2 A.C. 694).

[16] *General Billposting Co. Ltd v. Atkinson* [1909] A.C. 118; *Garnac Grain Co. Ltd v. H.M. Fauré & Fairclough Ltd* [1966] 1 Q.B. 650 (affd. [1968] A.C. 1130n).

[17] *Yukong Line Ltd of Korea v. Rendsberg Investments Corpn. of Liberia* [1996] 2 Lloyd's Rep. 604, 608. Moore-Bick J. added that, in his view, the courts should generally be "slow" to accept that the innocent party has committed itself irrevocably to going on with the contract and then leave it to "the doctrine of estoppel" (*post*, § 25–005) to remedy any potential injustice which may arise in the case where the party in breach has relied upon a representation by the innocent party which suggests that the contract has been affirmed.

[18] *Bremer Handelsgesellschaft mbH v. Deutsche Conti Handelsgesellschaft mbH* [1983] 2 Lloyd's Rep. 45; *Cobec Brazilian Trading & Warehousing Corpn. v. Alfred C. Toepfer* [1983] 2 Lloyd's Rep. 386 (waiver).

[19] *Hain Steamship Co. Ltd v. Tate & Lyle Ltd* (1936) 41 Com.Cas. 350, 355; *Peyman v. Lanjani* [1985] Ch. 457; *Motor Oil Hellas (Corinth) Refineries SA v. Shipping Corpn. of India, supra*; *Yukong Line Ltd of Korea v. Rendsberg Investments Corpn. of Liberia* [1996] 2 Lloyd's Rep. 604, 607; *Laing Management Ltd v. Aegon Insurance Co. (U.K.) Ltd* (1998) 86 Build L.R. 70, 108.

[20] *Edm. J.M. Mertens & Co. P.V.B.A. v. Veevoeder Import Export Vimex B.V.* [1979] 2 Lloyd's Rep. 372, 384; *Telfair Shipping Corpn. v. Athos Shipping Co. SA* [1981] 2 Lloyd's Rep. 74, 87–88 (affd. [1983] 1 Lloyd's Rep. 127); *Peter Cremer v. Granaria B.V.* [1981] 2 Lloyd's Rep. 583, 589; *Peyman v. Lanjani, supra*, at pp. 493, 500; *Sea Calm Shipping Co. SA v. Chantiers Navals de l'Esterel SA* [1986] 2 Lloyd's Rep. 294, 298; *Motor Oil Hellas (Corinth) Refineries SA v. Shipping Corpn. of*

change his mind and rely on the breach to justify treating himself as discharged.[21] Nevertheless, in the case of a breach which is persisted in by the other party, the fact that the innocent party has continued to press for performance will not normally preclude him at a later stage from treating himself as discharged.[22] In such a case the innocent party is not terminating on account of the original repudiation and going back on his election to affirm but rather is "treating the contract as being at an end on account of the continuing repudiation reflected in the other party's behaviour after the affirmation."[23] Nor, in the case of an ongoing contract, will affirmation in respect of one breach preclude the innocent party from treating himself as discharged by reason of further subsequent breaches.[24]

25–004   **Sale of goods.** There are, however, circumstances where the innocent party may be deprived of his right to treat the contract as repudiated notwithstanding that he has no knowledge of the breach or of the right to choose which the law gives to him. A statutory example is provided by section 11(4) of the Sale of Goods Act 1979 whereby a buyer may, in certain circumstances, be deprived of his right to reject the goods and to treat the contract as repudiated by his acceptance of the goods, regardless of his lack of knowledge of the breach.[25]

25–005   **"Inchoate doctrine" of consistency**. The example given in the last paragraph was relied on and extended by the Court of Appeal in *Panchaud Frères SA v. Etablissements General Grain Co.*,[26] a case which concerned a c.i.f. contract for the sale of goods. Buyers of maize to be shipped in June/July 1965 accepted without objection shipping documents which included a bill of lading showing shipment on July 31 and also a certificate of quality which stated that the maize had been loaded in August. On arrival of the vessel the buyers rejected the maize on a ground subsequently found to be inadequate. Some three years later, at the hearing of an arbitration appeal, they became aware of late shipment, and then sought to justify their rejection on this ground. It was held that they were not entitled to do so. The case is best considered to have been decided on the relatively straightforward ground that a buyer under a c.i.f contract who accepts the documents will lose his right to reject the goods on the ground of their late shipment if he fails to notice the late shipment date when he takes up the

---

India, supra, at 398; *Yukong Line Ltd of Korea v. Rendsberg Investments Corpn. of Liberia* [1996] 2 Lloyd's Rep. 604, 607.

[21] *Bentsen v. Taylor Sons & Co.* [1893] 2 Q.B. 274.

[22] *Tai Hing Cotton Mill Ltd v. Kamsing Knitting Factory* [1979] A.C. 91; *Johnson v. Agnew* [1980] A.C. 367.

[23] *Safehaven Investments Inc v. Springbok Ltd* (1996) 71 P. & C.R. 59, 68.

[24] *Segal Securities Ltd v. Thoseby* [1963] 1 Q.B. 887 (lease); *Yukong Line Ltd of Korea v. Rendsberg Investments Corpn. of Liberia* [1996] 2 Lloyd's Rep. 604, 607.

[25] *Wallis Son & Wells v. Pratt and Haynes* [1910] 2 K.B. 1003, 1015 (decision revd. [1911] A.C. 394); *Peyman v. Lanjani* [1985] Ch. 457. See *Benjamin's Sale of Goods* (5th ed., 1997), § 12–038.

[26] [1970] 1 Lloyd's Rep. 53. See also *Woodhouse A.C. Israel Cocoa Ltd SA v. Nigerian Produce Marketing Co. Ltd* [1971] 2 Q.B. 23 (affd. [1972] A.C. 741); *Alma Shipping Corpn. v. Union of India* [1971] 2 Lloyd's Rep. 494; *Alfred C. Toepfer v. Cremer* [1975] 2 Lloyd's Rep. 118; *Waren Import Gesellschaft Krohn & Co. v. Alfred C. Toepfer* [1975] 1 Lloyd's Rep. 322; *Surrey Shipping Co. Ltd v. Cie Continentale (France) SA* [1978] 1 Lloyd's Rep. 191; *Bunge GmbH v. Alfred C. Toepfer* [1978] 1 Lloyd's Rep. 506; *Avimex SA v. Dewulf & Cie* [1979] 2 Lloyd's Rep. 57; *Procter & Gamble Philippine Manufacturing Corp. v. Peter Cremer GmbH & Co.* [1988] 3 All E.R. 843, 848–852; *Glencore Grain Rotterdam BV v. Lebanese Organisation for International Commerce* [1997] 4 All E.R. 514. *cf. V. Berg & Son Ltd v. Vanden Avenne-Izegem P.V.B.A.* [1977] 1 Lloyd's Rep. 499.

documents.[27] Lord Denning M.R., however, stated[28] that the buyers were estopped by their conduct from setting up late shipment as a ground for rejection, in that they had led the sellers to believe that they were not relying on that ground and it would be unjust or unfair to allow them to do so when they had had full opportunity of finding out from the contract documents what the real date of shipment was, but did not trouble to do so. Winn L.J. agreed[29] that, having accepted the documents, the buyers could not properly thereafter turn round and say that the goods tendered were not contract goods. While doubting that there was anything which could be strictly described as an estoppel or quasi-estoppel, he considered that "there may be an inchoate doctrine stemming from the manifest convenience of consistency in pragmatic affairs, negativing any liberty to blow hot and cold in commercial conduct."[30] The difficulty with the estoppel analysis is that there does not appear to have been any reliance by the sellers on any representation which was made by the buyers when they took up the documents. The "inchoate doctrine" referred to by Winn L.J. has received "no support"[31] in subsequent cases and has generally been invoked as an argument of "last resort".[32] In so far as the case can be analysed as an example of estoppel by conduct, it is now clear that there is no "separate doctrine"[33] which can be derived from *Panchaud Frères* alone and the conventional requirements of estoppel by conduct must be satisfied on the facts of any future case.[34]

Waiver and estoppel. Affirmation is sometimes regarded as a species of **25–006** waiver, the innocent party "waiving" his right to treat the contract as repudiated.[35] But the word "waiver" is used in the law in a variety of different senses and so bears "different meanings."[36] Two types of waiver are relevant here. The first type may be called "waiver by election" and waiver is here used to signify the "abandonment of a right which arises by virtue of a party making an election."[37] Thus it arises when a person is entitled to alternative rights inconsistent with one another and that person acts in a manner which is consistent only with his having chosen to rely on one of them.[38] Affirmation is an example of such a waiver, since the innocent party elects or chooses to exercise his right

---

[27] *B.P. Exploration Co. (Libya) Ltd v. Hunt* [1979] 1 W.L.R. 783, 810–811; *Glencore Grain Rotterdam BV v. Lebanese Organisation for International Commerce* [1997] 4 All E.R. 514, 528, 530.

[28] At 57–58. The estoppel explanation was preferred by Hirst J. in *Procter & Gamble Philippine Manufacturing Corp. v. Peter Cremer GmbH & Co.*, *supra*, at 852.

[29] At 60.

[30] At 59.

[31] *Glencore Grain Rotterdam BV v. Lebanese Organisation for International Commerce* [1997] 4 All E.R. 514, 529.

[32] *B.P. Exploration Co. (Libya) Ltd v. Hunt* [1979] 1 W.L.R. 783, 811.

[33] *Glencore Grain Rotterdam BV v. Lebanese Organisation for International Commerce* [1997] 4 All E.R. 514, 530.

[34] *ibid.*

[35] See, *e.g.* Sale of Goods Act 1979, s. 11(2).

[36] *Motor Oil Hellas (Corinth) Refineries SA v. Shipping Corpn. of India*, *supra*, at 397. See also Wilken and Villiers, *Waiver, Variation and Estoppel* (1998), Chap. 3 and *ante*, §§ 3–076, 23–039; *post*, § 25–008.

[37] *Motor Oil Hellas (Corinth) Refineries SA v. Shipping Corpn. of India*, *supra*, at 398.

[38] *Kammins Ballroom & Co. Ltd v. Zenith Investments (Torquay) Ltd* [1971] A.C. 850, 882–883; *China National Foreign Trade Transportation Corpn. v. Evlogia Shipping Co. SA of Panama* [1979] 1 W.L.R. 1018, 1024, 1034–1035; *Telfair Shipping Corpn. v. Athos Shipping Co. SA* [1981] 2 Lloyd's Rep. 74, 87 (affd. [1983] 1 Lloyd's Rep. 127); *Motor Oil Hellas (Corinth) Refineries SA v. Shipping Corpn. of India*, *supra*, at 398.

to treat the contract as continuing and thereby abandons his inconsistent right to treat the contract as repudiated.[39] It is important to appreciate that, in this context, the party who makes the election only abandons his right to treat the contract as repudiated; he does not abandon his right to claim damages for the loss suffered as a result of the breach.[40] A second type of waiver may be called "waiver by estoppel" and it arises when the innocent party agrees with the party in default that he will not exercise his right to treat the contract as repudiated[41] or so conducts himself as to lead the party in default to believe that he will not exercise that right.[42] This type of waiver does not exist as a separate principle[43] but is in fact an application of the principle of equitable estoppel deriving from the classic statement of Lord Cairns in *Hughes v. Metropolitan Railway Co.*[44]

25–007   **Similarities and differences.** Both waiver by election and waiver by estoppel share some common elements. The principal similarity is that both would appear to require that the party seeking to rely on it (i.e. the party in default) must show a clear and unequivocal representation, by words or conduct, by the other party that he will not exercise his strict legal rights to treat the contract as repudiated.[45] But there are also important differences between the two types of waiver. In the case of waiver by election the party who has to make the choice must either know[46] or have obvious means of knowledge[47] of the facts giving rise to the right, and possibly of the existence of the right.[48] But in the case of waiver by

---

[39] *Peyman v. Lanjani* [1985] Ch. 457; *Sea Calm Shipping Co. SA v. Chantiers Navals d'Esterel SA* [1986] 2 Lloyd's Rep. 294; *Motor Oil Hellas (Corinth) Refineries SA v. Shipping Corpn. of India, supra,* at 399; *Yukong Line Ltd of Korea v. Rendsberg Investments Corpn. of Liberia* [1996] 2 Lloyd's Rep. 604, 607.

[40] The latter type of waiver, sometimes called "total waiver," is discussed, *ante,* § 23–045; *post* § 25–008.

[41] See *ante,* § 25–004.

[42] See the cases cited in n. 26, *supra.*

[43] *Glencore Grain Rotterdam BV v. Lebanese Organisation for International Commerce* [1997] 4 All E.R. 514, 530, where the Court of Appeal rejected the argument that any separate doctrine could be derived from the decision of the Court of Appeal in *Panchaud Freres SA v. Etablissements General Grain Co.* [1970] 1 Lloyd's Rep. 53, *ante* § 25–005.

[44] (1877) 2 App. Cas. 439, see *ante,* § 3–080. There would also appear to be a common law species of waiver (sometimes referred to as "forbearance," see *ante,* § 3–076) but the differences between the two appear to be very slight (see *ante,* § 3–097). The equitable variety is most frequently relied upon in the courts.

[45] *Woodhouse A.C. Israel Cocoa Ltd SA v. Nigerian Produce Marketing Co. Ltd* [1972] A.C. 741, 758; *V. Berg & Son Ltd v. Vanden Avenne-Izegem P.V.B.A.* [1977] 1 Lloyd's Rep. 499; *Finagrain SA v. Kruse SA* [1976] 2 Lloyd's Rep. 508; *Bremer Handesgesellschaft mbH v. C. Mackprang Jr.* [1979] 1 Lloyd's Rep. 221, 228; *Avimex SA v. Dewulf & Cie* [1979] 2 Lloyd's Rep. 57, 67; *Peter Cremer v. Granaria B.V.* [1981] 2 Lloyd's Rep. 583; *Telfair Shipping Corpn. v. Athos Shipping Co. SA* [1981] 2 Lloyd's Rep. 74, 87; *Peyman v. Lanjani, supra,* at 501; *Cobec Brazilian Trading and Warehousing Corpn. v. Alfred C. Toepfer* [1983] 2 Lloyd's Rep. 386; *Bremer Handelsgesellschaft mbH v. Deutsche Conti-Handelsgesellschaft mbH* [1983] 2 Lloyd's Rep. 45; *Nichimen Corpn. v. Gatoil Overseas Inc.* [1987] 2 Lloyd's Rep. 46. *cf. Bremer Handelsgesellschaft mbH v. Vanden Avenne-Izegem P.V.B.A.* [1978] 2 Lloyd's Rep. 109, 126; *Yukong Line Ltd of Korea v. Rendsburg Investments Corpn. of Liberia* [1996] 2 Lloyd's Rep. 604, 607. See also *ante,* §§ 3–084—3–087.

[46] *U.G.S. Finance Ltd v. National Mortgage Bank of Greece* [1964] 1 Lloyd's Rep. 446, 450; *Suisse Atlantique Société d'Armement Maritime SA v. N.V. Rotterdamsche Kolen Centrale* [1967] 1 A.C. 361, 425; *Panchaud Frères SA v. Etablissements General Grain Co.* [1970] 1 Lloyd's Rep. 53, 57.

[47] *Bremer Handelsgesellschaft mbH v. C. Mackprang Jr.* [1979] 1 Lloyd's Rep. 221, 228; *Avimex SA v. Dewulf & Cie* [1979] 2 Lloyd's Rep. 57, 67–68.

[48] *Peyman v. Lanjani* [1985] Ch. 457 (affirmation).

estoppel neither knowledge of the circumstances nor of the right is required on the part of the person estopped; the other party is entitled to rely on the apparent election conveyed by the representation.[49] Waiver by election is final and so has permanent effect,[50] whereas the effect of an estoppel may be suspensory only.[51] This difference may not be so marked in the context of waiver of breach because here the waiver may have permanent effect because, in some circumstances, it would be inequitable to allow the innocent party to retract his waiver. For example, in the case where a buyer assures a seller that the goods are in conformity with the contractual specifications, and the seller, in reliance upon these assurances, does not make a fresh conforming tender when he could have done, the buyer will be held to have waived any breach relating to the conformity of the goods and so the waiver will have permanent effect.[52] Finally, waiver by estoppel requires that the party to whom the representation is made rely on that representation so as to make it inequitable for the representor to go back upon his representation.[53] There is, however, no such requirement in the case of waiver by election; once the election has been made it is final whether or not the party has acted in reliance upon the election having been made.[54]

Other waivers. Affirmation must be distinguished from a waiver by one party   25–008
of a term of the contract inserted for his benefit,[55] or a "total" waiver by the innocent party of the breach itself by which he forgoes, not merely his right to treat himself as discharged by the breach, but also any claim for damages for the breach.[56]

Effect of affirmation. Where the innocent party, being entitled to treat him-   25–009
self as discharged by the other's breach, nevertheless elects to affirm the continued existence of the contract, he does not thereby necessarily relinquish his claim for damages for any loss sustained as a result of the breach.[57] Further, he may insist on holding the other party to the bargain and continue to tender due

---

[49] *Panchaud Frères SA v. Etablissements General Grain Co., supra*, at 57, 59 (see *ante*, § 25–005); *Peyman v. Lanjani, supra*, at 501; *Motor Oil Hellas (Corinth) Refineries SA v. Shipping Corpn. of India, supra*, at 399.

[50] *Motor Oil Hellas (Corinth) Refineries SA v. Shipping Corpn. of India, supra*, at 398. See also *ante*, § 25–003.

[51] *Hughes v. Metropolitan Railway Co.* (1877) 2 App. Cas. 439, see *ante* § 3–091.

[52] *Toepfer v. Warinco A.G.* [1978] 2 Lloyd's Rep. 569, 576. See *ante* §§ 3–090, 3–092.

[53] *Finagrain SA v. Kruse SA, supra*, at 535; *Bremer Handelsgesellschaft mbH v. Vanden Avenne-Izegem P.V.B.A., supra*, at 127; *Bunge SA v. Schleswig-Holsteinische Landweretschaftliche Hauptgenossenschaft GmbH* [1978] 1 Lloyd's Rep. 480; *Société Italo-Belge pour le Commerce et l'Industrie SA v. Palm and Vegetable Oils (Malaysia) Sdn.Bhd.* [1982] 1 All E.R. 19; *Peter Cremer v. Granaria B.V., supra; cf. Alfred C. Toepfer v. P. Cremer* [1975] 2 Lloyd's Rep. 118, 123. See also *ante*, §§ 3–088—3–090.

[54] *Moor Oil Hellas (Corinth) Refineries SA v. Shipping Corpn. of India, supra*, at 399; *Yukong Line Ltd of Korea v. Rendsburg Investments Corpn. of Liberia* [1996] 2 Lloyd's Rep. 604, 607.

[55] See *ante*, § 23–044.

[56] Sale of Goods Act 1979, s.11(2); *Benjamin's Sale of Goods* (5th ed., 1997), §§ 12–034—12–036. *cf. European Grain & Shipping Ltd v. Peter Cremer* [1983] 1 Lloyd's Rep. 211.

[57] *Bentsen v. Taylor, Sons & Co.* [1893] 2 Q.B. 274; *Hain SS. Co. Ltd v. Tate & Lyle Ltd* (1936) 41 Com.Cas. 350, 363; *Chandris v. Isbrandtsen Moller Co. Inc.* [1951] 1 K.B. 240, 248; *Suisse Atlantique Société d'Armement Maritime SA v. N.V. Rotterdamsche Kolen Centrale* [1967] 1 A.C. 361, 395.

performance on his part.[58] In *White and Carter (Councils) Ltd v. McGregor*,[59] the appellants, advertising contractors, agreed with the respondent, a garage proprietor, to display advertisements for his garage for three years. On the same day, the respondent repudiated the agreement and requested cancellation, but the appellants refused to cancel and performed their obligations under the contract. They then sued for the full contract price. The House of Lords, by a majority of three to two, upheld the claim. The appellants had elected to treat the contract as continuing and it remained in full effect. The decision in this case has not passed without criticism,[60] and one of the majority (Lord Reid) considered that the right to complete the contract and claim the price would not apply "if it can be shown that a person has no legitimate interest, financial or otherwise, in performing the contract rather than claiming damages."[61] Further, if the innocent party is unable to complete the contract without the co-operation of the other party, his only remedy is to sue for damages and not for the contract sum.[62] So an employee who is wrongfully dismissed can ordinarily only sue for damages[63] and not for his wages or salary.[64] But the fact that the remedies of the innocent party are restricted to damages does not mean that a discharge occurs at the moment of breach[65]; he may (in the case of an anticipatory repudiation) refuse to accept the repudiation and await the time fixed for performance, keeping the contract alive during the interval. In such a case, the innocent party is not required to mitigate his loss before the time for performance arrives.[66]

25–010 **Effect if repudiation not accepted.** If the innocent party elects to treat the contract as continuing, then it remains in existence for the benefit of the wrong-

---

[58] *Heyman v. Darwins Ltd* [1942] A.C. 356, 361.

[59] [1962] A.C. 413. See also *Tredegar Iron and Coal Co. Ltd v. Hawthorn Bros. & Co.* (1902) 18 T.L.R. 716; *International Correspondence Schools v. Ayres* (1912) 106 L.T. 845; *Anglo-African Shipping Co. of New York Inc. v. Mortner* [1962] 1 Lloyd's Rep. 81, 94; *Decro-Wall International SA v. Practitioners in Marketing Ltd* [1971] 1 W.L.R. 373; *Gator Shipping Corpn. v. Trans-Asiatic Oil Ltd SA* [1978] 2 Lloyd's Rep. 357; *Asamera Oil Corpn. Ltd v. Sea Oil and General Corpn.* (1979) 89 D.L.R. (3d) 1, 26.

[60] Goodhart (1962) 78 L.Q.R. 263; Furmston (1962) 25 M.L.R. 364; Scott [1962] Camb.L.J. 12. *cf.* Nienaber [1962] Camb.L.J. 213; Treitel, *The Law of Contract* (9th ed., 1995), pp. 915–918.

[61] [1962] A.C. 413, 431. This dictum was applied or approved in *Attica Sea Carriers Corpn. v. Ferrostaal Poseidon Bulk Reederei GmbH* [1976] 1 Lloyd's Rep. 250, 255; *Gator Shipping Corpn. v. Trans-Asiatic Oil Ltd SA* [1978] 2 Lloyd's Rep. 357, 372–374; *Clea Shipping Corpn. v. Bulk Oil International Ltd* [1983] 2 Lloyd's Rep. 645; *Stocznia Gdanska SA v. Latvian Shipping Co.* [1995] 2 Lloyd's Rep. 592, 600–602 (Clarke J.); [1996] 2 Lloyd's Rep. 132, 138–139, CA. It was unnecessary for the House of Lords to consider this point on appeal ([1998] 1 W.L.R. 574, 581).

[62] [1962] A.C. 413, 430, 432, 439; *Finelli v. Dee* (1968) 67 D.L.R. (2d) 293; *Denmark Productions Ltd v. Boscobel Productions Ltd* [1969] 1 Q.B. 699; *Hounslow L.B.C. v. Twickenham Garden Developments Ltd* [1971] Ch. 233, 251–254; *Attica Sea Carriers Corpn. v. Ferrostaal Poseidon Bulk Reederei GmbH, supra,* at 256; *Telephone Rentals v. Burgess Salmon* [1987] 5 C.L. 52.

[63] In the absence of special circumstances the liability of an employer in damages for wrongful dismissal does not extend beyond the notice period which the employer could lawfully have given under the contract: *Boyo v. Lambeth London Borough Council* [1994] I.C.R. 727.

[64] *Denmark Productions Ltd v. Boscobel Productions Ltd, supra; cf. Boyo v. Lambeth London Borough Council* [1994] I.C.R. 727, 747 where Staughton L.J. inclined to the view that the wrongfully dismissed employee should be able to sue for his wages. See Vol. II, § 39–179.

[65] See (contracts of employment): Vol. II, § 39–172. See also *Heymans v. Darwins Ltd* [1942] A.C. 356, 371.

[66] *Shindler v. Northern Raincoat Co. Ltd* [1960] 1 W.L.R. 1038, 1048. When the time for performance arrives the doctrine of mitigation does come into play. The inapplicability of the doctrine of mitigation to cases of anticipatory breach has been criticised: see Burrows, *Remedies for Torts and Breach of Contract* (2nd ed., 1994) p. 75.

doer as well as of himself.[67] The wrongdoer is entitled to complete the contract and to take advantage of any supervening circumstance which would excuse[68] him from or diminish[69] his liability. The question, however, arises whether the wrongdoer may raise as a defence to liability the fact that the innocent party has failed to perform or is unable to perform his own obligations in some fundamental respect at the time appointed for performance. The answer to this question turns on the difficult case of *Braithwaite v. Foreign Hardwood Co. Ltd.*[70] In that case, it was held that buyers of goods under a c.i.f.[71] contract, who had wrongfully repudiated the contract, could not, in an action by the seller for damages for non-acceptance of a particular consignment of the goods, rely as a defence to liability upon the fact that part of the consignment covered by documents tendered to and refused by them did not answer to the quality specified by the contract. The case has been taken to establish the proposition that, if the innocent party elects to keep the contract alive notwithstanding a prior repudiation by the party in default, then so long as the repudiating party persists in his refusal to perform, he absolves the innocent party from his obligation to perform the contract in accordance with its terms.[72] Such a proposition may be defended on the ground that it would be an empty formality to require the innocent party to carry out his obligations under the contract in the face of a clear refusal by the other party to perform. But it is inconsistent with the principle that, if a repudiation is not accepted, the contract is kept alive for the benefit of *both* parties and the liabilities and obligations of the innocent party continue. In subsequent cases the facts of *Braithwaite* have been the subject of scrutiny,[73] and the opinion has been expressed that the documents covering the defective consignment were never tendered, but only offered to be tendered, and that at this stage the seller in fact accepted the buyers' repudiation and the contract was rescinded.[74] Alternatively, the House of Lords has stated[75] that the proposition sought to be derived from *Braithwaite* is wrong: there is no half-way house between affirmation (in

---

[67] *Frost v. Knight* (1872) L.R. 7 Exch. 111, 112; *Suisse Atlantique Société d'Armement Maritime SA v. N.V. Rotterdamsche Kolen Centrale* [1967] 1 A.C. 361, 395, 419, 437–438; *Fercometal S.A.R.L. v. Mediterranean Shipping Co. SA* [1989] A.C. 788.

[68] *Frost v. Knight, supra,* at 112; *Avery v. Bowden* (1855) 5 E. & B. 714; (1856) 6 E. & B. 953 (*post,* § 25–023); *Heyman v. Darwins Ltd* [1942] A.C. 356, 361; *Fercometal S.A.R.L. v. Mediterranean Shipping Co. SA, supra* (*post,* § 25–024).

[69] *Leigh v. Paterson* (1818) 8 Taunt. 540; *Brown v. Muller* (1872) L.R. 7 Ex. 319; *Tredegar Iron and Coal Co. Ltd v. Hawthorn Bros. & Co.* (1902) 18 T.L.R. 716; *Tai Hing Cotton Mill Ltd v. Kamsing Knitting Factory* [1979] A.C. 91, 104.

[70] [1905] 2 K.B. 543. See Dawson (1980) 96 L.Q.R. 229; Carter [1989] L.M.C.L.Q. 81.

[71] This appears from, *e.g.* the report in (1905) 74 L.J.K.B. 688. On the significance of this fact, see *Benjamin's Sale of Goods* (5th ed., 1997), §§ 19–146—19–149, and see *Gill & Duffus SA v. Berger & Co. Inc.* [1984] A.C. 382.

[72] [1905] 2 K.B. 543, 551. See *Brett v. Schneideman Bros. Ltd* [1923] N.Z.L.R. 938; *Peter Turnbull & Co. Pty. Ltd v. Mundas Trading Co. (Australia) Pty. Ltd* (1954) 90 C.L.R. 235, 246; *Cerealmangimi SpA v. Toepfer* [1981] 1 Lloyd's Rep. 337; *Bunge Corpn. v. Vegetable Vitamin Foods (Private) Ltd* [1985] 1 Lloyd's Rep. 613.

[73] *Benjamin's Sale of Goods* (5th ed., 1997), §§ 9–012—9–020, 19–146—19–149.

[74] *Taylor v. Oakes, Roncoroni & Co.* (1922) 38 T.L.R. 349, 351 (affd. *ibid.* at 517); *Esmail v. J. Rosenthal & Sons Ltd* [1964] 2 Lloyd's Rep. 447, 466 (this point was not discussed on appeal in *J. Rosenthal & Sons Ltd v. Esmail* [1965] 1 W.L.R. 1117, HL); *Fercometal S.A.R.L. v. Mediterranean Shipping Co. SA, supra.*

[75] *Fercometal S.A.R.L. v. Mediterranean Shipping Co. SA, supra.* The correctness of *Braithwaite's Case* had been previously left open by the House of Lords in *J. Rosenthal & Sons Ltd v. Esmail, supra* (Lord Pearson) and in *Gill & Duffus Ltd v. Berger & Co. Inc.* [1984] A.C. 382, 395. See also *Cohen & Co. v. Ockerby & Co. Ltd* (1917) 24 C.L.R. 288; *Taylor v. Oakes, Roncoroni & Co., supra,* at 517; *Bowes v. Chaleyer* (1923) 32 C.L.R. 159, 169, 192, 197–199.

which case the rights and obligations of both parties continue) and acceptance of the repudiation (in which case the rights and obligations of both parties which remain unperformed are discharged).[76]

25-011   Nevertheless, it may be that there are certain circumstances in which the innocent party may be released from performance of one or more of his obligations under the contract, notwithstanding the fact that he has not accepted the wrongdoer's repudiation. The first arises where the repudiating party has, by words or conduct, represented to the innocent party that he will no longer require performance of a particular obligation under the contract, and the innocent party acts upon that representation. In such a case the repudiating party will be estopped from contending that the innocent party still remains bound by that obligation.[77] Secondly, where the repudiating party, by means of a breach of contract or other default, prevents the innocent party from performing his obligations under the contract he cannot rely upon that non-performance to reduce or eliminate his liability.[78] Finally, where the repudiating party stipulates for a mode of performance which is at variance with the terms of the contract and the innocent party attempts to comply with the new stipulation, the repudiating party cannot rely on a failure by the innocent party to perform his original obligations where that failure is attributable to his attempt to comply with the fresh stipulation.[79]

25-012   **Acceptance of repudiation.** Where there is an anticipatory breach, or the breach of an executory contract, and the innocent party wishes to treat himself as discharged, he must "accept the repudiation."[80] An act of acceptance of a repudiation requires no particular form.[81] It is usually done by communicating the decision to terminate to the party in default,[82] although it may be sufficient to lead evidence of an "unequivocal overt act which is inconsistent with the subsistence of the contract . . . without any concurrent manifestation of intent directed to the other party."[83] Unless and until the repudiation is accepted the

---

[76] But in *Segap Garages Ltd v. Gulf Oil (Great Britain) Ltd, The Times*, October 24, 1988; (*post*, § 25–024) the Court of Appeal considered that a breach by the affirming party would be excused if he proved that it had been caused by or was due to the repudiatory breach. *cf. Foran v. Wight* (1989) 168 C.L.R. 385, 409–410, 421–422, 447–449, 459.

[77] *Fercometal S.A.R.L. v. Mediterranean Shipping Co. SA*, *supra*, at 805–806. Estoppel could also arise if the repudiating party represents that he will not exercise a right conferred on him by the contract: *ibid*. A wider role for estoppel was acknowledged by Brennan J. in *Foran v. Wight* (1989) 168 C.L.R. 385, 421–422.

[78] *Bulk Oil (Zug) A.G. v. Sun International Ltd* [1984] 1 Lloyd's Rep. 531.

[79] *B.V. Oliehandel Jonglarid v. Coastal International Ltd* [1983] 2 Lloyd's Rep. 463.

[80] *Heyman v. Darwins Ltd* [1942] A.C. 356, 361. The appropriateness of the word "acceptance" has, however, been questioned: Smith "Anticipatory Breach of Contract" in Lomnicka and Morse (eds.) *Contemporary Issues in Commercial Law: Essays in Honour of A.G. Guest* pp. 175, 184–188.

[81] *Vitol SA v. Norelf Ltd* [1996] A.C. 800, 810–811.

[82] *Heyman v. Darwins Ltd* [1942] A.C. 356, 361; *The Mihalis Angelos* [1971] 1 Q.B. 164, 204. The innocent party need not personally, or by an agent, notify the repudiating party of his election to treat the contract as at an end. It is sufficient that the fact of the election is brought to the attention of the repudiating party, for example, by notification by an unauthorised broker or by another intermediary may be sufficient: *Vitol SA v. Norelf Ltd* [1996] A.C. 800, 811.

[83] *State Trading Corporation of India Ltd v. M. Golodetz Ltd* [1989] 2 Lloyd's Rep. 277, 286; *Holland v. Wiltshire* (1954) 90 C.L.R. 409, 416. See also Dawson [1981] C.L.J. 83, 103. *cf. Vitol SA v. Norelf Ltd (The Santa Clara)* [1993] 2 Lloyd's Rep. 301, 304 where Phillips J. preferred to leave open the question whether "an innocent party can accept an anticipatory repudiation by conduct which is not communicated to the party in anticipatory breach."

contract continues in existence for "an unaccepted repudiation is a thing writ in water."[84] Acceptance of a repudiation must be clear and unequivocal[85] and mere inactivity or acquiescence will generally not be regarded as acceptance for this purpose.[86] But there may be circumstances in which a continuing failure to perform will be sufficiently unequivocal to constitute acceptance of a repudiation. It all depends on "the particular contractual relationship and the particular circumstances of the case".[87] An example of a failure to perform which has been suggested as sufficient to constitute an acceptance is the following:

> "Postulate the case where an employer at the end of the day tells a contractor that he, the employer, is repudiating the contract and that the contractor need not return the next day. The contractor does not return the next day or at all. It seems to me that the contractor's failure to return may, in the absence of any other explanation, convey a decision to treat the contract as at an end."[88]

The requirement that the acceptance be communicated "clearly and unequivocally" is likely to mean that it is only where there has been a failure to carry out an act in relation to the party in breach that silence or inactivity will be sufficiently unequivocal for this purpose. Where the silence or inactivity relates to the performance of a contract to which the party in breach is not privy then it is unlikely that silence will be sufficiently unequivocal.[89] Once a repudiation has been accepted, the acceptance cannot be withdrawn.[90] If the parties thereafter resume performance of the contract, their rights are governed by a new contract, even if the terms remain the same.[91]

No reason or bad reason given. The general rule is well established that, if   25–013
a party refuses to perform a contract, giving therefor a wrong or inadequate
reason or no reason at all, he may yet justify his refusal if there were at the time
facts in existence which would have provided a good reason, even if he did not

---

[84] *Howard v. Pickford Tool Co.* [1951] 1 K.B. 417, 421. See also *Cranleigh Precision Engineering Ltd v. Bryant* [1965] 1 W.L.R. 1293; *Thomas Marshall (Exports) Ltd v. Guinle* [1979] Ch. 227; *Gunton v. Richmond-on-Thames L.B.C.* [1981] Ch. 448; *London Transport Executive v. Clarke* [1981] I.C.R. 355; *State Trading Corporation of India Ltd v. M. Golodetz Ltd* [1989] 2 Lloyd's Rep. 277, 285; *Boyo v. Lambeth London Borough Council* [1994] I.C.R. 727 (although it should be noted that the court was rather reluctant to follow *Gunton*; see in particular the judgment of Staughton L.J. (at 747). *cf. Savage v. Sainsbury Ltd* [1981] I.C.R. 1; and see Vol. II, § 39–172 (contracts of employment).

[85] *Harrison v. Northwest Holt Group Administration* [1985] I.C.R. 668; *Boyo v. Lambeth London Borough Council* [1994] I.C.R. 727; *Vitol SA v. Norelf Ltd* [1996] A.C. 800; *Holland v. Glendale Industries Ltd* [1998] I.C.R. 493.

[86] *Denmark Productions Ltd v. Boscobel Productions Ltd* [1969] 1 Q.B. 699, 732; *State Trading Corporation of India Ltd v. M. Golodetz Ltd* [1989] 2 Lloyd's Rep. 277, 286; *Lefevre v. White* [1990] 1 Lloyd's Rep. 569, 574, 576.

[87] *Vitol SA v. Norelf Ltd* [1996] A.C. 800, 811.

[88] *Vitol SA v. Norelf Ltd* [1996] A.C. 800, 811.

[89] *Jaks (U.K.) Ltd v. Cera Investment Bank SA* [1998] 2 Lloyd's Rep. 89, 96 (where the party alleged to be in breach was the bank under a letter of credit but the inactivity related to the non-performance of the contract of sale).

[90] *Scarf v. Jardine* (1882) 7 App. Cas, 345, 361; *Motor Oil Hellas (Corinth) Refineries SA v. Shipping Corpn. of India, supra*, at 398. *cf.* Vold (1926) 5 Texas L. Rev. 9.

[91] *Aegnoussiotis Shipping Corpn. of Monrovia v. A/S Kristian Jebsens Rederi of Bergen* [1977] 1 Lloyd's Rep. 268, 276.

know of them at the time of his refusal.[92] Thus when an employee brings an action against his employer, alleging that he has been wrongfully dismissed, the employer can rely on information acquired after the dismissal when seeking to justify the dismissal.[93] The general rule is the subject of a number of exceptions. First, a party cannot rely on a ground which he did not specify at the time of his refusal to perform "if the point which was not taken could have been put right."[94] Secondly, a party may be precluded by the operation of the doctrines of waiver or estoppel from relying on a ground which he did not specify at the time of his refusal to perform.[95] Thirdly, a party may be held to have accepted the goods so that he is no longer able to justify his refusal to perform.[96] However there does not appear to be any separate principle which would preclude a party from setting up a different ground simply because it would be unfair or unjust to allow him to do so.[97]

25–014   **Both parties in breach.** Where both parties are alleged to have committed a breach of contract, and it is asserted that each breach (taken independently) gives rise to a right to terminate further performance of the contract, regard must be had to the order in which the breaches occurred. Where one party (A) breaches the contract and that breach is followed by a breach by the other party (B) then, assuming that both breaches are repudiatory, the breach by party A will give party B the right to terminate future performance of the contract. If B exercises

---

[92] *Ridgway v. Hungerford Market Co.* (1835) 3 A. & E. 171, 177, 178, 180; *Baillie v. Kell* (1838) 4 Bing N.C. 638; *Boston Deep Sea Fishing and Ice Co. v. Ansell* (1888) 39 Ch.D. 339, 352, 364; *Taylor v. Oakes Roncoroni & Co.* (1922) 127 L.T. 267, 269; *British & Beningtons Ltd v. N.W. Cachar Tea Co.* [1923] A.C. 48, 71; *Etablissements Chainbaux S.A.R.L. v. Harbormaster Ltd* [1955] 1 Lloyd's Rep. 303, 314; *Universal Cargo Carriers Corpn. v. Citati* [1957] 2 Q.B. 401, 443–445 (affd. in part [1957] 1 W.L.R. 979, and revd. in part [1958] 2 Q.B. 254); *Denmark Productions Ltd v. Boscobel Productions Ltd* [1969] 1 Q.B. 699, 722, 732; *The Mihalis Angelos* [1971] 1 Q.B. 164, 195, 200, 204; *Cyril Leonard & Co. v. Simo Securities Trust* [1972] 1 W.L.R. 80, 85, 87, 89; *Scandinavian Trading Co. A/B v. Zodiac Petroleum SA* [1981] 1 Lloyd's Rep 81, 90; *State Trading Corpn. of India Ltd v. M. Golodetz Ltd* [1988] 2 Lloyd's Rep. 182; *Sheffield v. Conrad* (1988) 22 Con.L.R. 108. The latter case demonstrates that there are limits to the willingness of the courts to speculate about the reaction of the innocent party to the breach of which he was unaware.

[93] *Ridgway v. Hungerford Market Co.* (*supra*); *Baillie v. Kell* (*supra*); *Boston Deep Sea Fishing and Ice Co. v. Ansell* (*supra*); *Cyril Leonard & Co. v. Simo Securities Trust* (*supra*). See also Vol. II, § 39–169. The rule does not apply in cases of *unfair* dismissal: *Earl v. Slater & Wheeler (Airline) Ltd* [1973] 1 W.L.R. 51; *W. Devis & Sons Ltd v. Atkins* [1977] A.C. 931; cf. *Polkey v. A.E. Dayton Services Ltd* [1988] A.C. 344; Vol. II, § 39–204.

[94] *Heisler v. Anglo-Dal Ltd* [1954] 1 W.L.R. 1273, 1278; *Andre et Cie v. Cook Industries Inc.* [1987] 2 Lloyd's Rep. 463, 468–469; *Glencore Grain Rotterdam BV v. Lebanese Organisation for International Commerce* [1997] 4 All E.R. 514, 526–527. But it would appear that the point must be one which could have been taken at the time.

[95] To invoke waiver or estoppel it is, however, necessary to show that there was an unequivocal representation made by one party, by conduct or otherwise, which was acted upon by the other. It may not be easy to establish the existence of such an unequivocal representation: *Glencore Grain Rotterdam BV v. Lebanese Organisation for International Commerce* [1997] 4 All E.R. 514, 527, 530.

[96] This has been held to be the true interpretation of the difficult case of *Panchaud Frères SA v. Etablissements General Grain Co.* [1970] 1 Lloyd's Rep. 53; see *B.P. Exploration Co. (Libya) Ltd v. Hunt* [1979] 1 W.L.R. 783, 811 and *Glencore Grain Rotterdam BV v. Lebanese Organisation for International Commerce* [1997] 4 All E.R. 514, 528.

[97] Support for such a separate principle can be gleaned from dicta of the Court of Appeal in *Panchaud Frères SA v. Établissements General Grain Co.* [1970] 1 Lloyd's Rep. 53, 57, 59 but the proposition that some "separate doctrine" can be derived from *Panchaud Frères* alone has since been decisively rejected by the Court of Appeal: *Glencore Grain Rotterdam BV v. Lebanese Organisation for International Commerce* [1997] 4 All E.R. 514, 528, 530.

that right and accepts the repudiation his subsequent failure to perform his obligations under the contract will not constitute a breach of contract. The position is rather more complex if B does not accept the breach and then himself commits a repudiatory breach of contract. In such a case can A accept the breach and terminate performance of the contract or does the fact that he has previously repudiated the contract prevent him from exercising his option to terminate? It is suggested that, in such a case, the effect of B electing to affirm the contract is to leave the primary obligations of both parties unchanged.[98] The contract therefore remains in existence for the benefit of A as well as for B so that A should be free to elect to terminate performance. Thus in *State Trading Corporation of India v. M. Golodetz Ltd*,[99] Kerr L.J. stated that:

> "[i]f A is entitled to treat B as having wrongfully repudiated the contract between them and does so, then it does not avail B to point to A's past breaches of contract, whatever their nature. A breach by A would only assist B if it was still continuing when A purported to treat B as having repudiated the contract *and* if the effect of A's subsisting breach was such as to preclude A from claiming that B had committed a repudiatory breach. In other words, B would have to show that A, being in breach of an obligation in the nature of a condition precedent, was therefore not entitled to rely on B's breach as a repudiation."[1]

So unless the obligation of A to perform is a condition precedent to B's obligation to perform, the fact that A is in breach of contract should not act as a barrier to A's ability to terminate on the ground of B's breach.

Where both parties are simultaneously in breach of contract, there is authority   **25-015** for the proposition that neither party is entitled to terminate performance of the contract.[2] Thus, it has been held that where both parties agree to submit a dispute to arbitration, and there then follows a substantial period of delay during which neither party seeks to proceed with the reference to arbitration, each party is thereby guilty of a continuing breach of contract with the result that "neither [party] can rely on the other's breach as giving him a right to treat the primary obligations of each to continue with the reference as brought to an end."[3] While a party who has committed a repudiatory breach of contract is not entitled to enforce the contract against a party who is ready and willing to perform his obligations under the contract, it is suggested that it does not follow that the fact that a party has committed a repudiatory breach should preclude him from accepting a repudiatory breach committed by the other party. As has already been stated, until the repudiatory breach has been accepted, the primary obligations of both parties remain unaffected and therefore it is suggested that the proposition that, in such a case, either party is entitled to accept the breach is more consistent with the underlying principles of English law.[4]

---

[98] *Heyman v. Darwins Ltd* [1942] A.C. 356, 361; *Fercometal S.A.R.L. v. Mediterranean Shipping Co. SA* [1989] A.C. 788.

[99] [1989] 2 Lloyd's Rep. 277. See further Treitel (1990) 106 L.Q.R. 185, 188–190.

[1] *ibid.* at 286.

[2] *Bremer Vulkan Schiffbau und Maschinenfabrik v. South India Shipping Corpn. Ltd* [1981] A.C. 909; *Paal Wilson & Co. A/S v. Partenreederei Hannah Blumenthal* [1983] 1 A.C. 854.

[3] *Bremer Vulkan Schiffbau und Maschinenfabrik v. South India Shipping Corpn. Ltd* [1981] A.C. 909, 987–988.

[4] See generally Treitel, *The Law of Contract* (9th ed., 1995), pp. 736–737.

25-016   **Circumstances of discharge.**

"The three sets of circumstances giving rise to a discharge of contract are tabulated by Anson as: (1) renunciation by a party of his liabilities under it; (2) impossibility created by his own act; and (3) total or partial failure of performance. In the case of the first two, the renunciation may occur or the impossibility be created either before or at the time for performance. In the case of the third it can occur only at the time or during the course of performance. Moreover, if the third be partial, the failure must occur in a matter which goes to the root of the contract. All these acts may be compendiously described as repudiation, though that expression is more particularly used of renunciation before the time for performance has arrived."[5]

2. Renunciation

25-017   **Renunciation.** A renunciation of a contract occurs when one party by words or conduct evinces an intention not to perform, or expressly declares that he is or will be unable to perform, his obligations under the contract in some essential respect.[6] The renunciation may occur before or at the time fixed for performance.[7] An absolute refusal by one party to perform his side of the contract will entitle the other party to treat himself as discharged,[8] as will also a clear and unambiguous assertion by one party that he will be unable to perform when the time for performance should arrive.[9] Short of such an express refusal or declaration, however, the test is to ascertain whether the action or actions of the party in default are such as to lead a reasonable person to conclude that he no longer intends to be bound by its provisions.[10] The renunciation is then evidenced by conduct. Also the party in default "may intend in fact to fulfil (the contract) but may be determined to do so only in a manner substantially inconsistent with his obligations"[11] or may refuse to perform the contract unless the other party complies with certain conditions not required by its terms.[12] In such a case, there is little difficulty in holding that the contract has been renounced.[13] Nevertheless, not every intimation of an intention not to perform or of an inability to perform

---

[5] *Heyman v. Darwins Ltd* [1942] A.C. 356, 397; *Universal Cargo Carriers Corpn. v. Citati* [1957] 2 Q.B. 401, 436 (affd. in part [1957] 1 W.L.R. 979, and revd. in part [1958] 2 Q.B. 254).

[6] See also *Martin v. Stout* [1925] A.C. 359; *Brinkibon Ltd v. Stahag Stahl und Stahlwarenhandelgesellschaft mbH* [1980] 2 Lloyd's Rep 556 (affd. [1983] 2 A.C. 34) (place of renunciation).

[7] Where the renunciation takes place before the time fixed for performance, it is known as an anticipatory breach: *post.* § 25–020.

[8] *Freeth v. Burr* (1874) L.R. 6 C.P. 208, 214; *Thompson v. Corroon* (1992) 42 W.I.R. 157.

[9] *Anchor Line Ltd v. Keith Rowell Ltd* [1980] 2 Lloyd's Rep. 351; *The Munster* [1982] 1 Lloyd's Rep. 370; *Texaco Ltd v. Eurogulf Shipping Co. Ltd* [1987] 2 Lloyd's Rep. 541.

[10] *Universal Cargo Carriers Corpn. v. Citati* [1957] 2 Q.B. 401, 436 (affd. in part [1957] 1 W.L.R. 979 and revd. in part [1958] 2 Q.B. 254). See also *Morgan v. Bain* (1874) L.R. 10 C.P. 15; *Bloomer v. Bernstein* (1874) L.R. 9 C.P. 588; *Forslind v. Becheley-Crundall*, 1922, S.C.(HL) 173; *Maple Flock Co. v. Universal Furniture Products (Wembley) Ltd* [1934] 1 K.B. 148, 157; *Laws v. London Chronicle (Indicator Newspapers) Ltd* [1959] 1 W.L.R. 698; *Chilean Nitrate Sale Corpn. v. Marine Transportation Co. Ltd* [1982] 1 Lloyd's Rep. 570, 580; *Re Olympia & York Canary Wharf Ltd (No. 2)* [1993] B.C.C. 159, 168; *Nottingham Building Society v. Eurodynamics plc* [1995] F.S.R. 605, 611–612. *cf. post*, § 25–018.

[11] *Ross T. Smyth & Co. v. Bailey, Son & Co.* [1940] 3 All E.R. 60, 72; *Federal Commerce & Navigation Co. Ltd v. Molena Alpha Inc.* [1979] A.C. 757.

[12] *B.V. Oliehandel Jongkind v. Coastal International Ltd* [1983] 2 Lloyd's Rep. 463.

[13] *Withers v. Reynolds* (1831) 2 B. & Ad. 882; *Booth v. Brown* (1892) 8 T.L.R. 641.

some part of a contract will amount to a renunciation. Even a deliberate breach, actual or threatened, will not necessarily entitle the innocent party to treat himself as discharged, since it may sometimes be that such a breach can appropriately be sanctioned in damages.[14] If the contract is entire and indivisible,[15] that is to say, if it is expressly or impliedly agreed that the obligation of one party is dependent or conditional upon complete performance by the other, then a refusal to perform or declaration of inability to perform any part of the agreement will normally entitle the party in default to treat himself as discharged from further liability.[16] But in any other case: "It is not a mere refusal or omission of one of the contracting parties to do something which he ought to do, that will justify the other in repudiating the contract; but there must be an absolute refusal to perform his side of the contract."[17] If one party evinces an intention not to perform or declares his inability to perform some, but not all, of his obligations under the contract, then the right of the other party to treat himself as discharged depends on whether the non-performance of those obligations will amount to a breach of a condition of the contract[18] or deprive him of substantially the whole benefit which it was the intention of the parties that he should obtain from the obligations of the parties under the contract then remaining unperformed.[19] Words or conduct which do not amount to a renunciation will not justify a discharge.[20]

Unequivocal. The renunciation must be "made quite plain."[21] In particular, **25–018** where there is a genuine dispute as to the construction of a contract, the courts may be unwilling to hold that an expression of an intention by one party to carry out the contract only in accordance with his own erroneous interpretation of it

---

[14] *Suisse Atlantique Société d'Armement Maritime SA v. N.V. Rotterdamsche Kolen Centrale* [1967] 1 A.C. 261, 365. See *post*, § 25–040.

[15] See *ante*, § 22–027; *post*, § 25–042.

[16] *Longbottom & Co. Ltd v. Bass Walker & Co. Ltd* [1922] W.N. 245. See also *Ebbw Vale Steel Co. v. Blaina Iron Co.* (1901) 6 Com.Cas. 33.

[17] *Freeth v. Burr* (1878) L.R. 9 C.P. 208, 213, 214; *Chilean Nitrate Sales Corpn. v. Marine Transportation Co. Ltd, supra,* at p. 572; *Aktion Maritime Corpn. of Liberia v. S. Kasmas & Brothers Ltd* [1987] 1 Lloyd's Rep. 283, 306; *Torvald Klaveness A/S v. Arni Maritime Corpn.* [1994] 1 W.L.R. 1465, 1476.

[18] See *ante*, § 12–025; *post*, § 25–038.

[19] *Federal Commerce & Navigation Co. Ltd v. Molena Alpha Inc.* [1979] A.C. 757; *Afovos Shipping Co. SA v. Pagnan & Filli* [1983] 1 W.L.R. 195, 203; *Weeks v. Bradshaw* [1993] E.G.C.S. 65.

[20] *Franklin v. Miller* (1836) 4 A. & E. 499; *Wilkinson v. Clements* (1872) L.R. 8 Ch.App. 96; *Re Phoenix Bessemer Steel Co.* (1876) 4 Ch.D. 108; *Cornwall v. Henson* [1900] 2 Ch. 298; *Dominion Coal Co. Ltd v. Dominion Iron and Steel Co. Ltd* [1909] A.C. 293; *Household Machines v. Cosmos Exports* [1947] K.B. 217; *Thorpe v. Fasey* [1949] Ch. 649; *Peter Dumenil & Co. Ltd v. James Ruddin Ltd* [1953] 1 W.L.R. 815.

[21] *Spettabile Consorzio Veneziana di Armamento di Navigazione v. Northumberland Shipbuilding Co. Ltd* (1919) 121 L.T. 628, 634, 635; *Woodar Investment Development Ltd v. Wimpey Construction U.K. Ltd* [1980] 1 W.L.R. 277, 287, 288; *Anchor Line Ltd v. Keith Rowell Ltd* [1980] 2 Lloyd's Rep. 351, 353; *Thompson v. Corroon* (1993) 42 W.I.R. 157; *Nottingham Building Society v. Eurodynamics plc* [1995] F.S.R. 605; *Jaks (U.K.) Ltd v. Cera Investment Bank SA* [1998] 2 Lloyd's Rep. 89, 92–93. This proposition applies to words and conduct said to demonstrate that a party is persisting in an earlier repudiation as well as to the earlier repudiation itself (*Safehaven Investments Inc. v. Springbok Ltd* (1996) 71 P. & C.R. 59, 69). See also *Warinco A.G. v. Samor SpA* [1979] 1 Lloyd's Rep. 450; *Metro Meat Ltd v. Fares Rural Co. Pty. Ltd* [1985] 2 Lloyd's Rep. 13; *Sanko Steamship Co. Ltd v. Eacom Timber Sales Ltd* [1987] 1 Lloyd's Rep. 487; *Alfred C. Toepfer International GmbH v. Itex Itagram Export SA* [1993] 1 Lloyd's Rep. 360, 361; *Thompson v. Corroon* (1993) 42 W.I.R. 157.

amounts to a repudiation[22]; and the same is true of a genuine mistake of fact[23] or law.[24] Even the giving of notice of rescission, or the commencement of proceedings by one party claiming rescission of the contract, does not necessarily entitle the other to treat the contract as repudiated, since such action may be taken in order to determine the respective rights of the parties, and so not evince an intention to abandon the contract.[25] On the other hand, it is, generally, no defence for a party who is alleged to have repudiated the contract to show that he acted in good faith.[26] The courts have struggled to reconcile the latter proposition with their reluctance to conclude that a party who has acted in good faith but was mistaken has thereby repudiated the contract. The result of this tension is that the cases in this area are not at all easy to reconcile.[27] The position would appear to be that it may not be a repudiation for one party to put forward his genuine but bona fide interpretation of what the contract requires of him[28] but that where that party performs in a manner which is not consistent with the terms of the contract, it is no defence for that party to show that he acted in good faith.[29]

25–019   **Employer and employee.** In respect of an action for wrongful dismissal at common law, or proceedings for unfair dismissal under statute, the question what acts or omissions amount to or justify such dismissal is dealt within the chapter on Employment in Volume II of this work.[30]

25–020   **Anticipatory breach.** If, before the time arrives at which a party is bound to perform a contract, he expresses an intention to break it, or acts in such a way as to lead a reasonable person to the conclusion that he does not intend to fulfil his part,[31] this constitutes an "anticipatory breach"[32] of the contract and entitles the

---

[22] *James Shaffer Ltd v. Findlay Durham & Brodie* [1953] 1 W.L.R. 106; *Sweet & Maxwell Ltd v. Universal News Services Ltd* [1964] 2 Q.B. 699; *Woodar Investment Development Ltd v. Wimpey Construction U.K. Ltd, supra; Telfair Shipping Corpn. v. Athos Shipping Co. SA* [1983] 1 Lloyd's Rep. 127; *The Design Company v. Elizabeth King*, unreported, July 7, 1992, CA; *Vaswani v. Italian Motors (Sales and Services) Ltd* [1996] 1 W.L.R. 270; *Mitsubishi Heavy Industries Ltd v. Gulf Bank K.S.C.* [1997] 1 Lloyd's Rep. 343, 354; *Orion Finance Ltd v. Heritable Finance Ltd*, unreported, Court of Appeal, March 10, 1997.

[23] *Kent v. Godts* (1855) 26 L.T.(o.s.) 88; *Peter Dumenil & Co. Ltd v. James Ruddin Ltd, supra; Alfred C. Toepfer v. Peter Cremer* [1975] 2 Lloyd's Rep. 118.

[24] *Freeth v. Burr* (1874) L.R. 9 C.P. 208, 214; *Mersey Steel & Iron Co. v. Naylor Benzon & Co.* (1884) 9 App.Cas. 434. Contrast *Federal Commerce & Navigation Co. Ltd v. Molena Alpha Inc.* [1979] A.C. 757.

[25] *Spettabile Consorzio Veneziano di Armamento di Navigazione v. Northumberland Shipbuilding Co. Ltd, supra; Woodar Investment Development Ltd v. Wimpey Construction U.K. Ltd; supra.*

[26] *Federal Commerce & Navigation Co. Ltd v. Molena Alpha Inc.* [1979] A.C. 757.

[27] In particular, the decisions of the House of Lords in *Woodar Investment Development Ltd v. Wimpey Construction U.K. Ltd* [1980] 1 W.L.R. 277 and *Federal Commerce & Navigation Co. Ltd v. Molena Alpha Inc.* [1979] A.C. 757 are not at all easy to reconcile.

[28] *Woodar Investment Development Ltd v. Wimpey Construction U.K. Ltd* [1980] 1 W.L.R. 277; *James Shaffer Ltd v. Findlay Durham and Brodie* [1953] 1 W.L.R. 106; *Sweet and Maxwell Ltd v. Universal News Services Ltd* [1964] 2 Q.B. 699 and *Vaswani v. Italian Motors (Sales) Ltd* [1996] 1 W.L.R. 270.

[29] *Federal Commerce & Navigation Co. Ltd v. Molena Alpha Inc.* [1979] A.C. 757; *Farrant v. The Woodroffe School* [1998] I.C.R. 184.

[30] Vol. II §§ 39–161—39–172 (wrongful dismissal); Vol. II §§ 39–193—39–226 (unfair dismissal).

[31] *Forslind v. Becheley-Crundall*, 1922 S.C.(HL) 173; *Universal Cargo Carriers Corporation v. Citati* [1957] 2 Q.B. 401 (affd. in part [1957] 1 W.L.R. 979 and revd. in part [1958] 2 Q.B. 254); *Greenaway Harrison Ltd v. Wiles* [1994] I.R.L.R. 380.

[32] For a criticism of this expression, see *Bradley v. H. Newsom Sons & Co.* [1919] A.C. 16, 53; Dawson [1981] C.L.J. 83; Mustill, *Butterworth Lectures* 1989–1990, p. 1.

other party to take one of two courses. He may "accept"[33] the renunciation, treat it as discharging him from further performance, and sue for damages forthwith, or he may wait till the time for performance arrives and then sue.

Breach accepted. The first alternative was established by *Hochster v. De la Tour*,[34] where a travelling courier sued his employer who wrote before the time for performance arrived that he would not require his services. The courier sued for damages at once and it was held that he was entitled to do so. In *Johnstone v. Milling*[35] the effect of an anticipatory breach was thus stated by Lord Esher M.R.: **25–021**

> "A renunciation of a contract, or, in other words, a total refusal to perform it by one party before the time for performance arrives, does not, by itself, amount to a breach of contract but may be so acted upon and adopted by the other party as a rescission of the contract as to give an immediate right of action. Where one party assumes to renounce the contract, that is, by anticipation refuses to perform it, he thereby, so far as he is concerned, declares his intention then and there to rescind the contract. . . . The other party may adopt such renunciation of the contract by so acting upon it as in effect to declare that he too treats the contract as at an end, except for the purpose of bringing an action upon it for the damages sustained by him in consequence of such renunciation."[36]

It is nevertheless clear that, in cases of anticipatory breach by renunciation of the contract, the cause of action is not the future breach; it is the renunciation itself.[37] The doctrine is not based on the fiction that the eventual cause of action may, in anticipation, be treated as a cause of action.[38] So, if the anticipatory breach is accepted as a discharge of the contract, it is not open to the party in breach subsequently to tender performance within the time originally fixed.[39] Further, the innocent party can claim damages at once even though his right to future performance of the contract is then only contingent.[40]

If the breach is accepted, the innocent party is relieved from further performance of his obligations under the contract. He is likewise relieved from proving, in any action against the party in default, that he was ready and willing at the date **25–022**

---

[33] See *ante*, § 25–012.

[34] (1853) 2 E. & B. 678; *Xenos v. Danube, etc., Ry.* (1863) 13 C.B.(N.S.) 825; *Frost v. Knight* (1872) L.R. 7 Ex. 111; *Dominion Coal Co. Ltd v. Dominion Iron and Steel Co. Ltd* (1909) 25 T.L.R. 309; *The Mihalis Angelos* [1971] 1 Q.B. 164.

[35] (1886) 16 Q.B.D. 460. For the measure of damages, see *Roper v. Johnson* (1873) L.R. 8 C.P. 167; *Melachrino v. Nickoll and Knight* [1920] 1 K.B. 693; *Millett v. Van Heek & Co.* [1921] 2 K.B. 369; *Wright v. Dean* [1948] Ch. 686; *Sudan Import Co. Ltd v. Société Générale de Compensation* [1958] 1 Lloyd's Rep. 310; *Garnac Grain Co. Inc. v. H.M.F. Faure and Fairclough Ltd* [1966] 1 Q.B. 650 (on appeal [1968] A.C. 1130); *The Mihalis Angelos, supra*; *Tai Hing Cotton Mill Ltd v. Kamsing Knitting Factory* [1979] A.C. 91; and Vol. II, §§ 43–372 *et seq.* §§ 43–392 *et seq.*

[36] At 467. The proposition that a renunciation of the contract before the time for performance has arrived does not amount to a breach until it has been acted upon or adopted has been criticised on the ground that it is inconsistent with *Hochster v. De la Tour* (1853) 2 E. & B. 678 and because whether or not there is a breach must depend on what the promisor does and not on what the promisee does thereafter: see Smith "Anticipatory Breach of Contract" in Lomnicka and Morse (eds.) *Contemporary Issues in Commercial Law: Essays in Honour of A. G. Guest* pp. 175, 178–182.

[37] *The Mihalis Angelos, supra*; *Moschi v. Lep Air Services Ltd* [1973] A.C. 331, 356.

[38] *cf. Frost v. Knight* (1872) L.R. 7 Ex. 111, 114.

[39] *Xenos v. Danube, etc., Ry., supra*

[40] *Frost v. Knight, supra*; *Synge v. Synge* [1894] 1 Q.B. 466.

of the renunciation to perform the contract in accordance with its terms.[41] It follows that it is no defence to liability in such an action to show that, if the contract had not been renounced, the innocent party would not at the time fixed for performance have been able to perform it,[42] although proof of such inability to perform might possibly be material in the assessment of damages.[43]

25–023   **Breach not accepted.** The second alternative[44] is illustrated by *Avery v. Bowden*.[45] In that case there was a contract by charterparty that a ship should sail to Odessa and there take a cargo from the charterer's agent, the cargo to be loaded within a certain number of days. The ship arrived at Odessa and the master demanded a cargo, but the charterer's agent was unable to supply one. The master nevertheless continued to demand a cargo. Before the loading days had expired war broke out between England and Russia and performance became legally impossible. When the charterer was sued for breach of the charterparty, the defence was sustained that there had been no failure of performance before war broke out. Even, however, if the agent's conduct had amounted to an anticipatory renunciation of the contract, so that the shipowner would have been entitled to accept it and claim damages at once, he had lost the right to do so by electing to keep the contract alive, and it continued in force until it was discharged by frustration. In other words, if the second alternative is chosen, the contract subsists at the risk of both parties, and the anticipatory renunciation is ineffective. This is well expressed by Cotton L.J. in *Johnstone v. Milling* where he says[46]:

> "The promisee, if he pleases, may treat the notice of intention as inoperative, and await the time when the contract is to be executed, and then hold the other party responsible for all the consequences of non-performance; but in that case he keeps the contract alive for the benefit of the other party as well as his own; he remains subject to all the obligations and liabilities under it, and enables the other party not only to complete the contract, if so advised, notwithstanding his previous repudiation of it, but also to take advantage of any supervening circumstances which would justify him in declining to complete it. . . . "

---

[41] *Braithwaite v. Foreign Hardwood Co. Ltd* [1905] 2 K.B. 543, 551, 554; *Cooper, Ewing & Co. Ltd v. Hamel and Horley Ltd* (1922) 13 Ll.L.Rep. 466, 590, 593; *Taylor v. Oakes Roncoroni & Co.* (1922) 38 T.L.R. 349, 517; *British and Beningtons Ltd v. North Western Cachar Tea Co. Ltd* [1923] A.C. 48, 66; *Continental Contractors Ltd v. Medway Oil and Storage Co. Ltd* (1925) 23 Ll.L.Rep. 55, 124, 128, 132; *Rightside Property Ltd v. Gray* [1975] Ch. 72, 82; *Gill & Duffus SA v. Berger & Co. Inc.* [1984] A.C. 382, 395–396. *cf.* Dawson (1980) 96 L.Q.R. 239. See also Lloyd (1974) 37 M.L.R. 121.

[42] *Aliter,* if at the time of the renunciation, there was already a breach of contract (albeit unknown) on the part of the innocent party: *Cooper, Ewing & Co. Ltd v. Hamel and Horley Ltd, supra*; *British and Beningtons Ltd v. North Western Cachar Tea Co. Ltd, supra*, at 72. *cf. Gill & Duffus SA v. Berger & Co. Inc., supra.* See also *ante*, § 25–013.

[43] *Braithwaite v. Foreign Hardwood Co. Ltd, supra*, at 552; *Taylor v. Oakes Roncoroni & Co., supra*; *British and Beningtons Ltd v. North Western Cachar Tea Co. Ltd, supra*, at 71, 72; *Continental Contractors Ltd v. Medway Oil and Storage Co. Ltd, supra*, at 132, 133; *Esmail v. Rosenthal & Sons Ltd* [1964] 2 Lloyd's Rep. 447, 466; [1965] 1 W.L.R. 1117; *The Mihalis Angelos* [1971] 1 Q.B. 164; *Gill & Duffus SA v. Berger & Co. Inc., supra*, at 392, 396, 397.

[44] *Michael v. Hart & Co.* [1902] 1 K.B. 482; *Braithwaite v. Foreign Hardwood Co. Ltd* [1905] 2 K.B. 543; *Sinason-Teicher Inter-American Grain Corporation v. Oilcakes and Oilseeds Trading Co. Ltd* [1954] 1 W.L.R. 935, 944 (affd. *ibid.* at 1394).

[45] (1855) 5 E. & B. 714; (1856) 6 E. & B. 953.

[46] (1886) 16 Q.B.D. 470.

Thus in *Fercometal S.A.R.L. v. Mediterranean Shipping Co. SA*,[47] a voyage   **25–024**
charterparty contained a clause entitling the charterers to cancel the charter
should the vessel not be ready to load on or before July 9, 1982. Prior to that date
the charterers prematurely purported to cancel it. This constituted an anticipatory
breach and repudiation of the contract. The repudiation was not accepted by the
shipowners. Nevertheless the nominated vessel was not ready to load by the due
date and the charterers then sent a second notice cancelling the charter. The
House of Lords held that the shipowners, by affirming the contract, had kept it
alive for the benefit of both parties, so that the charterers were entitled, notwithstanding their previous repudiation, to cancel on the ground of the vessel's non-
readiness to load in accordance with the terms of the charterparty. Also in *Segap
Garages Ltd v. Gulf Oil (Great Britain) Ltd*,[48] the defendants, in breach of
contract, failed to supply motor fuel to the plaintiffs. This would have entitled the
plaintiffs, had they chosen to do so, to treat the contract as repudiated, but they
elected to treat it as still continuing. The plaintiffs nevertheless refused to pay for
motor fuel already supplied. This refusal, under the terms of the contract, entitled
the defendants to terminate the contract and they did so terminate it. The Court
of Appeal held that the plaintiffs could recover damages in respect of non-
delivery of motor fuel prior to the termination, but not in respect of the period
following termination. By electing not to accept the defendants' repudiation, the
plaintiffs had kept the contract alive for the benefit of both parties.

Anticipatory breach and actual breach. When establishing whether or not   **25–025**
there has been a renunciation of the contract, there is no distinction between the
tests for what is an anticipatory breach and what is a breach after the time for
performance has arrived.[49] It follows, therefore, that where the conduct of the
promisor is such as to lead a reasonable person to the conclusion that he does not
intend to fulfil his obligations under the contract when the time for performance
arrives, the promisee may treat this as a renunciation of the contract and sue for
damages forthwith. The innocent party is not obliged to wait for the time for
performance because the renunciation, coupled with the acceptance of that
renunciation, renders the breach legally inevitable and the effect of the doctrine
of anticipatory breach is precisely to enable the innocent party to anticipate an
inevitable breach and to commence proceedings immediately.[50]

Renunciation in the course of performance. The law is similar where a   **25–026**
party renounces a contract in the course of its performance, as, for instance,
where the subject-matter is a sale of goods to be delivered by instalments. Thus,
where the purchaser, after accepting some, refuses to take any more of the goods
concerned, the vendor may sue him for damages at once without manufacturing
and tendering the remainder.[51]

---

[47] [1989] A.C. 788.
[48] *The Times*, October 24, 1988, CA
[49] *Thorpe v. Fasey* [1949] Ch. 649, 661; *Universal Cargo Carriers Corporation v. Citati* [1957] 2 Q.B. 401, 438.
[50] *Universal Cargo Carriers Corporation v. Citati, supra*, at 438. The position is otherwise where the mode of anticipatory breach in issue is impossibility created by the act or default of one party. In such a case it is much more difficult to establish that the breach is inevitable, a point which was recognised by Devlin J. in *Citati* at 437. These difficulties are discussed *post* at § 25–028.
[51] *Withers v. Reynolds* (1831) 2 B. & Ad. 882; *Cort v. Ambergate, etc., Ry.* (1851) 17 Q.B. 127.

3. IMPOSSIBILITY CREATED BY ONE PARTY

25–027 **Impossibility.** Where one party has, by his own act or default,[52] disabled himself from performing his contractual obligations in some essential respect, the other party will be entitled to treat himself as discharged.[53] The inability to perform his contractual obligations must be established on the balance of probabilities and the fact that a party has "entered into inconsistent obligations does not in itself necessarily establish such inability, unless these obligations are of such a nature or have such an effect that it can truly be said that the party in question has put it out of his power to perform his obligations."[54] The inability to perform need not be due to a deliberate act. "A party is deemed to have incapacitated himself from performing his side of the contract, not only when he deliberately puts it out of his power to perform the contract, but also when by his own act or default circumstances arise which render him unable to perform his side of the contract or some essential part thereof."[55] So, where a person undertook to transfer certain furniture, but before he could do so a judgment creditor took the furniture in execution and sold it, his inability to perform, though not due to his own deliberate act, constituted a breach of the agreement.[56] However, where part only of one party's obligations are rendered impossible of performance, the other party will not be able to treat himself as discharged unless the resulting non-performance would amount to a breach of condition[57] or would deprive him of substantially the whole benefit of the contract.[58]

25–028 **Impossibility and renunciation.** In most cases where the impossibility created by one party has manifested itself by conduct, the innocent party will rely upon renunciation by conduct rather than impossibility, because renunciation is so much easier to establish.[59] Renunciation is to be preferred because the innocent party need only show that the conduct of the party in default was such as to lead a reasonable man to believe that he did not intend, or was not able, to perform his promise; whereas if the innocent party relies upon impossibility he must show that the contract was *in fact* impossible of performance due to the other party's default.[60] Nevertheless the innocent party would be well advised to rely on both grounds for treating the contract as at an end, because (1) renunciation may not, for some reason,[61] be open to him, and (2) if he has misinterpreted

---

[52] See also *ante*, §§ 24–059—24–063.

[53] *Sir Anthony Main's Case* (1596) 5 Co.Rep. 21a; *Bodwell v. Parsons* (1808) 10 East 359; *Amory v. Brodrick* (1822) 5 B. & A. 712; *Short v. Stone* (1846) 8 Q.B. 358; *Caines v. Smith* (1846) 15 M. & W. 189; *O'Neil v. Armstrong* [1895] 2 Q.B. 418; *Ogdens Ltd v. Nelson* [1905] A.C. 109; *Measures Bros. Ltd v. Measures* [1910] 2 Ch. 248; *British and Beningtons Ltd v. North Western Cachar Tea Co. Ltd* [1923] A.C. 48, 72. See also the cases cited in § 25–029, n. 63, *post*.

[54] *Alfred C. Toepfer International GmbH v. Itex Itagrani Export SA* [1973] 1 Lloyd's Rep. 360, 362.

[55] Smith's *Leading Cases* (13th ed., 1929), Vol. II. p. 40, cited by Devlin J. in *Universal Cargo Carriers Corpn. v. Citati* [1957] 2 Q.B. 401, 441.

[56] *Keys v. Harwood* (1846) 2 C.B. 905; *Powell v. Marshall, Parkes & Co.* [1899] 1 Q.B. 710 (bankruptcy); *cf. Re Agra Bank* (1867) L.R. 5 Eq. 160; *Jennings' Trustees v. King* [1952] Ch. 899.

[57] See *ante*, § 12–025; *post*, § 25–038.

[58] *Afovos Shipping Co. SA v. Pagnan & Filli* [1983] 1 W.L.R. 195, 203; see *post*, § 25–039.

[59] *Universal Cargo Carriers Corporation v. Citati, supra,* at 437; *Sanko Steamship Co. Ltd v. Eacom Timber Sales Ltd* [1987] 1 Lloyd's Rep. 487, 492.

[60] See *post*, § 25–029, n. 65.

[61] *Universal Cargo Carriers Corporation v. Citati, supra,* where Devlin J. held that the erroneous finding of the arbitrator created such a stituation (but see [1958] 2 Q.B. 254).

the conduct of the other party and so rescinded for an inadequate reason he may still fall back on impossibility if it should subsequently appear that the other party was in fact incapable of performing his promise.[62]

Anticipatory breach. Anticipatory breach of contract may be constituted by   **25–029** impossibility as well as by renunciation, and similar principles apply to both. So where a shipowner agreed to charter a ship upon her release from government service, but before the release sold her to another person, it was held that he had put it out of his power to perform the agreement and the charterer was entitled to sue for damages forthwith. It was argued for the shipowner that he might have bought back the ship in time to fulfil the contract, but this was regarded as too speculative a possibility.[63] Also in *Universal Cargo Carriers Corporation v. Citati*,[64] where a charterer of a ship agreed to nominate a berth, to provide a cargo, and to finish loading, all before a certain day, and three days before this day had failed to do any of these things, it was held that the shipowner would be entitled to treat this default as an anticipatory breach of contract if it could prove that the charterer would not have been able to perform its obligations under the charterparty before the point in time at which the delay would have frustrated the commercial object of the venture. In this case it was held that it would not be sufficient for the innocent party to show that he had reasonable grounds for believing that the other party would be unable to perform at the appointed time; he would only be justified in treating himself as discharged if the other party was in fact unable to perform at that time: "An anticipatory breach must be proved in fact and not in supposition."[65]

No anticipation of express right to terminate. Where it is alleged that one   **25–030** party has, by his own act or default, disabled himself from performing his contractual obligations at some future time and the contract also contains an express provision giving to the innocent party the right to terminate the contract in certain circumstances, care must be taken to establish the basis upon which the innocent party seeks to terminate the contract. Where the basis for the decision to terminate is the express right to determine the contract, the requirements of the clause containing the right to terminate must be complied with. On the other hand, where reliance is placed on the inability of the party to perform his obligations under the contract at some future time, it must be demonstrated that the inability to perform relates to some essential aspect of the obligations of the party in breach. To be entitled to terminate, the innocent party must establish that he had a right to terminate on one or other ground. Where he can establish neither ground, he cannot justify his decision to terminate by combining the two grounds so as to apply the doctrine of anticipatory breach to the contractual right to

---

[62] *British & Beningtons Ltd v. N.W. Cachar Tea Co.* [1923] A.C. 48, 70; *Universal Cargo Carriers Corporation v. Citati, supra,* at 443.

[63] *Omnium D'Enterprises v. Sutherland* [1919] 1 K.B. 618; *Lovelock v. Franklyn* (1846) 8 Q.B. 371; *Synge v. Synge* [1894] 1 Q.B. 466; *Guy-Pell v. Foster* [1930] 2 Ch. 169; *cf. Alfred C. Toepfer International GmbH v. Itex Itagrani Export SA, supra,* at 362.

[64] [1957] 2 Q.B. 401 (affd. in part [1957] 1 W.L.R. 979 and revd. in part [1958] 2 Q.B. 254). *cf. Hongkong Fir Shipping Co. Ltd v. Kawasaki Kisen Kaisha Ltd* [1962] 2 Q.B. 26; *Trade and Transport Inc. v. Iino Kaiun Kaisha Ltd* [1973] 1 W.L.R. 210; *F. C. Shepherd & Co. Ltd v. Jerrom* [1987] Q.B. 301, 323, 327–328; Treitel, *Law of Contract* (9th ed., 1995), pp. 770–771.

[65] [1957] 2 Q.B. 401, 449–450. But see *Embiricos v. Sydney Reid & Co.* [1914] 3 K.B. 45, 59 (frustration); *Hongkong Fir Shipping Co. Ltd v. Kawasaki Kisen Kaisha Ltd, supra,* at 57 (failure of performance); Treitel, *The Law of Contract* (9th ed., 1995), p. 775; Carter (1984) 47 M.L.R. 422.

terminate. It is not possible to anticipate a contractual right to terminate.[66] Either the conditions necessary to exercise the right have been satisfied or they have not.

25–031   **Co-operation and prevention of performance.** It has been noted that the court will readily imply a term that each will co-operate with the other to secure performance of the contract[67] and that neither party will, by his own act or default, prevent performance of the contract.[68] If one party is in breach of his duty to co-operate, so that performance of the contract cannot be effected, the other party will be entitled to treat himself as discharged.[69] It has also been said to be a general principle of law that, where performance of a condition precedent[70] is prevented by the act or default of one party, the contract is taken to have been duly performed by the other even though the condition has not been satisfied.[71] Thus, in *Mackay v. Dick*[72] where a contract of sale of goods was subject to a condition precedent to be performed by the buyer, but which he neglected to perform, the seller was held entitled to sue for the price. This principle, however, is by no means always applicable,[73] and the party not in default may be compelled to treat the prevention of performance as a repudiation of the contract and to sue for damages for the breach.

25–032   **Impossibility and frustration.** Similar tests have been applied to determine whether or not a contract has become impossible of performance by reason of the default of one party as have been applied to determine whether there has been a mutual discharge of the contract by reason of the doctrine of frustration.[74]

4. Failure of Performance

25–033   **Failure of performance.** Failure of performance, whether total or partial, may in certain circumstances entitle the other party to the contract to treat the

---

[66] *Afovos Shipping Co. SA v. Pagnan & Filli* [1983] 1 W.L.R. 195. This, it is suggested, is the correct interpretation of Lord Diplock's statement (at 203) that the doctrine of anticipatory breach by conduct which disables a party to a contract from performing one of his primary obligations under the contract has no application to a breach of punctual payment of hire clause in a time charterparty of a ship. In so far as Lord Diplock suggested that the doctrine of anticipatory breach applies only to fundamental breaches, his reasoning cannot be supported: see Treitel, *The Law of Contract* (9th ed., 1995) pp. 773–774 and Carter, *Breach of Contract* (2nd ed., 1991) §§ 744A and 744B.

[67] See *ante*, § 13–011.

[68] See *ante*, § 13–012.

[69] *Kyprianou v. Cyprus Textiles Ltd* [1958] 2 Lloyd's Rep. 60; *Metro Meat Ltd v. Fares Rural Co. Pty. Ltd* [1985] 2 Lloyd's Rep. 13. Contrast *Bremer Vulkan Schiffbau und Maschinenfabrik v. South India Shipping Corpn. Ltd* [1981] A.C. 909 (both parties in breach of duty).

[70] See *ante*, § 12–028.

[71] *Hotham v. East India Co.* (1787) 1 Term Rep. 638, 645; *Smith v. Wilson* (1807) 8 East 437, 443; *Thomas v. Fredricks* (1847) 10 Q.B. 775; *Mackay v. Dick* (1881) 6 App.Cas. 251; *Kleinert v. Abosso Gold Mining Co. Ltd* (1913) 58 S.J.(P.C.) 45.

[72] (1881) 6 App.Cas. 251.

[73] *Colley v. Overseas Exporters* [1921] 3 K.B. 302; *Luxor (Eastbourne) Ltd v. Cooper* [1941] A.C. 108. See also *Benjamin's Sale of Goods* (5th ed., 1997), § 16–020; Vol.II, § 32–145.

[74] *Trade and Transport Inc. v. Iino Kaiun Kaisha Ltd* [1973] 1 W.L.R. 210, 221, citing *Davis Contractors Ltd v. Fareham U.D.C.* [1956] A.C. 696 (*ante*, § 24–048); *Tsakiroglou & Co. Ltd v. Noblee Thorl* [1962] A.C. 93 (*ante*, § 24–046) and *The Eugenia* [1964] 2 Q.B. 226 (*ante*, § 24–043). See also *post*, § 25–045.

contract as discharged. But this is not necessarily the case, and difficult questions of fact and law may arise.

Relation of the promises. In the first place, it is necessary to discover the   **25–034**
relation to one another of the promises which form the contract. They may be either independent or dependent.[75] Promises are said to be independent when the obligation of one party is absolute and not conditional upon the performance by the other of his part of the bargain. They are said to be dependent when the obligation of one party depends upon the performance, or the readiness and willingness to perform, of the other.[76] "The question whether covenants are to be held dependent or independent of each other, is to be determined by the intention and meaning of the parties as it appears on the instrument, and by the application of common sense to each particular case; to which intention, when once discovered, all technical forms of expression must give way."[77]

Independent mutual promises. In the exceptional case of independent   **25–035**
mutual promises, each party has his remedy on the promise made in his favour without performing his part of the contract[78] and conversely neither party can claim to be discharged from liability on the contract by reason of the failure of the other to perform his part. Thus in *Fearon v. Earl of Aylesford*,[79] an action on a separation deed, it was said that a husband would be bound to perform a covenant to pay money to a trustee for his wife, even though the wife might have broken a covenant in the same deed not to molest her husband. But the tendency of the courts is against construing contracts as containing two independent promises. So, in *General Billposting Co. Ltd v. Atkinson*,[80] it was held that a man who had been wrongfully dismissed from his employment was no longer bound by a restrictive covenant contained in his contract of employment as his employers by their action had repudiated the contract. Similarly it has been held that mutual covenants as to draining land by adjoining owners were dependent on each other and not independent promises.[81] On the other hand, it has long been established that a tenant's covenant to pay rent is independent of the landlord's covenant to repair the premises; the tenant is not discharged from his obligation to pay rent merely because his landlord is unwilling to fulfil his obligation.[82] Also in contracts of apprenticeship the covenants of the master and apprentice are normally independent of each other.[83]

Dependent promises. Assuming that the promises are not independent, the   **25–036**
question then arises whether it is any failure by one party to perform a dependent

---

[75] *Pordage v. Cole* (1669) 1 Wms.Saund. 319; *Guy-Pell v. Foster* [1930] 2 Ch. 169.

[76] Cited with approval in *Denmark Productions Ltd v. Boscobel Productions Ltd* [1969] 1 Q.B. 699, 733.

[77] *Stavers v. Curling* (1836) 3 Bing.N.C. 355, 368. cf. *Ritchie v. Atkinson* (1808) 10 East 295, 306; *Huntoon Co. v. Kolynos* [1930] 1 Ch. 528, 558, 559 (where the test is stated in the same terms as the distinction between a condition and a warranty: see *post*, § 25–037).

[78] *Pordage v. Cole, supra*, at 320.

[79] (1884) 14 Q.B.D. 792, 800.

[80] [1909] A.C. 118. In *Rock Refrigeration Ltd v. Jones* [1997] 1 All E.R. 1, 18–20 Phillips L.J. questioned the correctness of *General Billposting*, but the majority of the Court of Appeal were prepared to assume that it had been correctly decided. See further *post*, § 25–047, n. 47.

[81] *Kidner v. Stimpson* (1918) 35 T.L.R. 63.

[82] *Taylor v. Webb* [1937] 2 K.B. 283 (but see *Regis Property Co. Ltd v. Dudley* [1959] A.C. 370).

[83] *Winstone v. Linn* (1823) 1 B. & C. 460; cf. *Ellen v. Topp* (1851) 6 Exch. 424.

promise which entitles the other to treat himself as discharged from further performance. In historical terms, the right of discharge was said to turn upon the non-performance of a "condition precedent" in the contract.[84] Performance by one party of his promise or "covenant" was regarded as a condition precedent to the liability of the other. However, following the case of *Boone v. Eyre*[85] in 1777, it was recognised that precise fulfilment of every promise was not necessarily a condition precedent, and Lord Mansfield said[86]: "Where mutual covenants go to the whole of the consideration on both sides, they are mutual conditions, the one precedent to the other. But where they go only to a part, where a breach may be paid for in damages, there the defendant has a remedy on his covenant, and shall not plead it as a condition precedent." Thus, where one party failed to perform a promise which went to the whole of the consideration, the other party was released from performance as the former had not performed that which was a condition precedent to the latter's liability.[87] For example, in *Cutter v. Powell*,[88] where a seaman undertook to serve as mate on a voyage for an enhanced sum to be paid in a single payment on completion of the voyage and died before that time, his wife was unable to recover *quantum meruit* for work done during that part of the voyage that he lived and served. The seaman's continuing to do his duty as mate during the whole voyage was a condition precedent to his recovering the stipulated sum. On the other hand, where the failure of performance went to part only of the consideration or, as it was later expressed,[89] did not go to the "root" or substantial consideration, the breach did not entitle the innocent party to be discharged from further liability, but to claim damages only. Further there were terms or "warranties," collateral to the main purpose of the contract, the breach of which did not relieve him from liability to perform.[90]

25–037   **Conditions and warranties.** By the end of the nineteenth century, there emerged a strong tendency to classify the terms of a contract as being either *conditions* (any breach of which entitled the innocent party to refuse further performance and treat himself as discharged) or *warranties* (which merely gave him a right to damages). In the Sale of Goods Act 1893, for example, certain implied stipulations were assigned to one or other category by statute.[91] Others were so assigned by virtue of judicial decisions.[92] Numerous cases turned on the question whether or not a particular statement or promise amounted to a condition. In one of these, *Bettini v. Gye*,[93] Blackburn J. stated that, in the absence of an express declaration of intention by the parties, the test was "whether the particular stipulation goes to the root of the matter, so that failure to perform it would render the performance of the rest of the contract a thing different in

---

[84] See *Pordage v. Cole* (1669) 1 Wms.Saund. 319; *Kingston v. Preston* (1773) 2 Doug. 689, 691; *Hongkong Fir Shipping Co. Ltd v. Kawasaki Kisen Kaisha* [1962] 2 Q.B. 26, 65; *Cehave N.V. v. Bremer Handelsgesellschaft* [1976] Q.B. 44, 57, 72; *United Scientific Holdings Ltd v. Burnley B.C.* [1978] A.C. 904, 927; *Dawson* [1981] C.L.J. 83, 87.

[85] (1777) 1 Hy. Bl. 273.

[86] *ibid.* at 273n.

[87] *e.g. Smith v. Wilson* (1807) 8 East. 437.

[88] (1795) 6 Term Rep. 320; see *ante*, § 22–030; *post*, § 25–042.

[89] *Mersey Steel and Iron Co. Ltd v. Naylor, Benzon & Co.* (1884) 9 App.Cas. 434, 444.

[90] Sale of Goods Act 1979, ss.11(3), 61(1); Chalmers, *Sale of Goods* (2nd ed.), p. 164, (18th ed.), p. 373; *ante*, § 12–031.

[91] ss.12–15.

[92] See *ante*, § 12–035.

[93] (1876) 1 Q.B.D. 183.

substance from what the defendant had stipulated for."[94] And in another case[95] Bowen L.J. remarked, "it is often very difficult to decide . . . whether a representation which contains a promise . . . amounts to a condition precedent, or is only a warranty. There is no way of deciding this question except by looking at the contract in the light of the surrounding circumstances"; but he suggested that, "in order to decide this question of construction, one of the first things you would look to is, to what extent the accuracy of the statement—the truth of what is promised—would be likely to affect the substance and foundation of the adventure which the contract is intended to carry out." Such statements as these would suggest that, at that time, the basis for classifying a term as a condition depended on whether its breach would substantially defeat the purpose of the contract.

Failure of performance: breach of condition. The classification of contractual terms has been dealt with in an earlier chapter in this work.[96] It was there noted that, in the modern law, a term of a contract may be held to be a condition if it has been so categorised by statute or by judicial decision, or if the parties have so agreed in their contract, whether expressly or by necessary implication.[97] Any failure of performance which constitutes a breach of condition entitles the innocent party to treat himself as discharged from further liability under the contract.[98] The word condition has therefore broken free from its historical roots and can no longer be confined to an obligation which must be performed as a condition precedent to the liability of the other party. **25-038**

Failure of performance: other situations. Where the failure of performance is not a breach of condition, but of an "intermediate" term,[99] it may still justify the innocent party in treating himself as discharged. But in such a case regard must be had to the nature and consequences of the breach in order to determine whether this right has arisen. A number of expressions have been used to describe the circumstances that warrant discharge, the most common being that the breach must "go to the root of the contract."[1] It has also been said that the breach must "affect the very substance of the contract,"[2] or "frustrate the commercial purpose of the venture,"[3] and, at the present day, a test which is **25-039**

---

[94] At 188, citing Parke B. in *Graves v. Legg* (1854) 9 Exch. 709, 716.

[95] *Bentsen v. Taylor, Sons & Co.* [1893] 2 Q.B. 274, 281.

[96] See *ante*, § 12–019.

[97] See *ante*, § 12–040.

[98] See *ante*, § 12–025.

[99] See *ante*, § 12–034.

[1] *Davidson v. Gwynne* (1810) 12 East 381, 389; *MacAndrew v. Chapple* (1866) L.R. 1 C.P. 643, 648; *Poussard v. Spiers* (1876) 1 Q.B.D. 410, 414; *Honck v. Muller* (1881) 7 Q.B.D. 92, 100; *Mersey Steel and Iron Co. v. Naylor, Benzon & Co.* (1884) 9 App.Cas. 434, 443; *Guy-Pell v. Foster* [1930] 2 Ch. 169, 187; *Heyman v. Darwins Ltd* [1942] A.C. 356, 397; *Suisse Atlantique Société d'Armement Maritime SA v. N.V. Rotterdamsche Kolen Centrale* [1967] 1 A.C. 361, 442; *Decro-Wall International SA v. Practitioners in Marketing Ltd* [1971] 1 W.L.R. 361, 374; *Cehave N.V. v. Bremer Handelsgesellschaft mbH* [1976] Q.B. 44, 60, 73; *Federal Commerce & Navigation Co. Ltd v. Molena Alpha Inc.* [1979] A.C. 757, 779.

[2] *Wallis, Son and Wells v. Pratt and Haynes* [1910] 2 K.B. 1003, 1012.

[3] *Tarrabochcia v. Hickie* (1856) 1 H. & N. 183; *MacAndrew v. Chapple* (1866) L.R. 1 C.P. 643, 647, 648; *Stanton v. Richardson* (1872) L.R. 7 C.P. 421, 433, 437; *Jackson v. Union Marine Insurance Co.* (1874) L.R. 10 C.P. 125, 145, 148; *Inverkip SS. Co. v. Bunge* [1917] 2 K.B. 193, 201; *Astley Industrial Trust Ltd v. Grimley* [1963] 1 W.L.R. 584, 599; *Trade and Transport Incorporated v. Iino Kaiun Kaisha Ltd* [1973] 1 W.L.R. 210, 223.

frequently applied[4] is that stated by Diplock L.J. in *Hongkong Fir Shipping Co. Ltd v. Kawasaki Kisen Kaisha Ltd*[5]: "Does the occurrence of the event deprive the party who has further undertakings to perform of substantially the whole benefit which it was the intention of the parties as expressed in the contract that he should obtain as the consideration for performing those undertakings?" In that case, the charterers of a ship sought to establish that they were discharged from further performance of the charterparty because of repeated break-downs of the ship due to the fact that it was unseaworthy. It was argued on their behalf that the obligation to provide a seaworthy vessel was a condition of the contract, any breach of which entitled them to treat the contract as repudiated. This argument was rejected by the Court of Appeal, which held that regard must be had to the consequences of the breach. On the facts, the delays which had already occurred, and the delay which was likely to occur,[6] as a result of unseaworthiness, and the conduct of the shipowners in taking steps to remedy the same, were not, when taken together, such as to deprive the charterers of substantially the whole benefit which it was the intention of the parties they should obtain from further use of the ship under the charterparty. The charterers were therefore not entitled to treat themselves as discharged.

25–040   **Fundamental breach.** The principle of "fundamental breach" or the breach of a "fundamental term" was developed by the courts with a view to limiting the operation of exemption clauses, the rationale being that no party could exclude or restrict his liability for such a breach.[7] As so conceived, a fundamental breach was more far reaching in its effects (a "total breach")[8] than one which would justify discharge.[9] And a fundamental term was something narrower than a condition: it went to the "core" or substance of the contract.[10] However, in *Suisse Atlantique Société d'Armement Maritime SA v. N.V. Rotterdamsche Kolen Centrale*,[11] the House of Lords expressed the view that the applicability of exemption clauses to particular breaches of a contract was in reality a rule of construction based on the presumed intention of the parties as expressed in the contract.[12] So far as the expression "fundamental breach" is concerned, Lord Reid said[13]: "General use of the term 'fundamental breach' is of recent origin and I can find nothing to indicate that it means more or less than the well-known type of breach

---

[4] *Cehave N.V. v. Bremer Handelsgesellschaft mbH, supra,* at 82; *United Scientific Holdings Ltd v. Burnley B.C.* [1978] A.C. 904, 928; *Photo Production Ltd v. Securicor Transport Ltd* [1980] A.C. 827, 849; *Nitrate Corpn. of Chile Ltd v. Pansuiza Compania de Navigacion* [1980] 1 Lloyd's Rep. 638 (affd. [1982] 1 Lloyd's Rep. 570). See also *Freeman v. Taylor* (1831) 8 Bing. 124, 138; *MacAndrew v. Chapple* (1886) L.R. 1 C.P. 643, 648; *Decro-Wall International SA v. Practitioners in Marketing Ltd, supra,* at 380; *Federal Commerce & Navigation Co. Ltd v. Molena Alpha Inc., supra,* at 783; *Gunatunga v. DeAlwis* (1996) 72 P. & C.R. 161, 171.

[5] [1962] 2 Q.B. 26, 66.

[6] Regard is to be had, not only to the actual consequences which have occurred, but also those which it can reasonably be foreseen will occur as a result of the breach: *ibid.* at 57, 63.

[7] See *ante,* § 14–020.

[8] *Suisse Atlantique Société d'Armement Maritime SA v. N.V. Rotterdamsche Kolen Centrale* [1967] 1 A.C. 361, 431.

[9] See *ante,* §§ 14–020—14–021.

[10] *Smeaton Hanscomb & Co. Ltd v. Sassoon I. Setty, Son & Co.* [1953] 1 W.L.R. 1468, 1470; see *ante,* § 12–021.

[11] [1967] 1 A.C. 361; see *ante,* § 14–021.

[12] See *ante,* § 14–021.

[13] [1967] 1 A.C. 361, 397. See also at 409–410, 421–422, 431.

which entitles the innocent party to treat it as repudiatory and to rescind the contract." Accordingly, the expression would seem to be no more than a restatement, in differing terminology, of the principle that a particular breach or breaches may be such as to go to the root of the contract and entitle the other party to treat such breach or breaches as a repudiation of the whole contract.[14] Likewise, the expression "fundamental term" appears to mean no more than a condition, *i.e.* a stipulation which the parties have agreed (expressly or impliedly) to be, or which the general law regards as, a term which goes to the root of the contract so that any breach of that term may at once and without further reference to the facts and circumstances be regarded by the innocent party as justifying discharge.[15] This view that a fundamental breach was no more than a repudiatory breach was confirmed by Lord Diplock in *Photo Production Ltd v. Securicor Transport Ltd.*[16] In that case, the House of Lords held that discharge consequent upon a fundamental, *i.e.* repudiatory, breach does not disentitle the guilty party from relying on an exemption clause in respect of that breach. It is therefore submitted that there is no separate category of "fundamental" breaches, or terms, producing different effects from those already discussed.[17]

Deliberate breach. The question whether or not a failure of performance is deliberate may be a relevant factor,[18] since it may indicate the attitude of the party in default towards future performance and so be evidence of an intent to renounce the contract.[19] But there is no separate category of "deliberate" breaches and Lord Wilberforce has said[20]: "Some deliberate breaches there may be of a minor character which can be appropriately sanctioned by damages. . . . To create a special rule for deliberate acts is unnecessary and may lead astray." **25–041**

Entire obligations. The rule that the failure of performance must go to the root of the contract to justify discharge suffers an exception when the party in default has undertaken to complete performance of an obligation which is entire and indivisible, and has agreed that this shall be done before his claim to remuneration is due. In such a case, any failure of performance on his part will normally release the innocent party from liability.[21] The innocent party will not be bound to pay anything for the partial performance.[22] But even this exception may to some extent be mitigated by the so-called doctrine of "substantial performance," that is to say, if there is a trivial departure from the exact performance of an entire obligation, the innocent party will not be discharged **25–042**

---

[14] *ibid.* at 422. See also *Thompson v. Corroon* (1993) 42 W.I.R. 157.

[15] *ibid.* at 422.

[16] [1980] A.C. 827, 849; *ante,* § 14–022.

[17] See *ante,* §§ 12–024, 14–024.

[18] *Suisse Atlantique Société d'Armement Maritime SA v. N.V. Rotterdamsche Kolen Centrale* [1967] 1 A.C. 361, 394, 414, 415, 429.

[19] For the coincidence between renunciation and failure of performance, see *Mersey Steel and Iron Co. v. Naylor, Benzon & Co.* (1884) 9 App.Cas. 434, 441, 444.

[20] *Suisse Atlantique* case, *supra,* at 435.

[21] *Ebbw Vale Steel, Iron and Coal Co. v. Blaina Iron and Tinplate Co.* (1901) 6 Com. Cas. 35; *Eshelby v. Federated European Bank Ltd* [1932] 1 K.B. 423; *Bolton v. Mahadeva* [1972] 1 W.L.R. 1009.

[22] See *ante,* §§ 22–027—22–038.

from liability under the agreement, although he will be entitled to a set-off or counterclaim for damages.[23]

25-043   **Divisible or severable obligations.** Contracts for the delivery of goods by instalments will more often be construed as containing divisible (or severable) obligations rather than one entire obligation.[24] A breach relating to one or more instalments must be considered in the light of its effect on the contract as a whole, so that the innocent party will not necessarily be entitled to treat the whole contract as repudiated by such a breach.[25] In the absence of an express renunciation of the contract, he will not be so entitled unless the other party's acts or conduct amount to "an intimation of an intention to abandon and altogether to refuse performance of the contract"[26] (that is to say, an implied renunciation)[27] or the failure of performance is such as to go to "the root or essence of the contract."[28] The most relevant factors have been said to be[29]: "First, the ratio quantitively which the breach bears to the contract as a whole, and secondly the degree of probability or improbability that such a breach will be repeated." Thus the further the parties have proceeded with the performance of the contract, the less likely it is that one party will be entitled to claim that the contract has been discharged by a single breach.[30]

25-044   **Stipulations as to time.** The question whether a stipulation as to the time of performance is or is not "of the essence" and a condition of the contract has been considered in previous chapters.[31]

25-045   **"Frustration by breach" and frustration.** Similar language has been used to describe the seriousness of the interference with performance of the contract that must be shown to have occurred to justify a discharge and to bring about a

---

[23] *H. Dakin & Co. Ltd v. Lee* [1916] 1 K.B. 566; *Hoenig v. Isaacs* [1952] 2 All E.R. 176; *Williams v. Roffey Bros. & Nicholls (Contractors) Ltd* [1991] 1 Q.B. 1, 8–10. *cf. Vigers v. Cook* [1919] 2 K.B. 475; *Eshelby v. Federated European Bank Ltd, supra; Bolton v. Mahadeva, supra. cf.* Beck (1975) 38 M.L.R. 413. See also *ante*, §§ 22–032—22–033, where the existence of a doctrine of substantial performance is doubted.

[24] See *Benjamin's Sale of Goods* (5th ed., 1997), §§ 8–070 *et seq.*.

[25] Sale of Goods Act 1979, s.31(2); see Vol.II, § 43–260.

[26] *Freeth v. Burr* (1874) L.R. 9 C.P. 208, 213. See also *Bloomer v. Bernstein* (1874) L.R. 9 C.P. 588; *Mersey Steel and Iron Co. v. Naylor Benzon & Co.* (1884) 9 App.Cas. 434; *Dominion Coal Co. Ltd v. Dominion Iron and Steel Co. Ltd* [1909] A.C. 293; *Household Machines v. Cosmos Exports* [1947] K.B. 217; *Warinco A.G. v. Samor SpA* [1979] 1 Lloyd's Rep. 450; *Bunge GmbH v. C.C.V. Landbouwbelang G.A.* [1980] 1 Lloyd's Rep. 458.

[27] See *ante*, § 25–017.

[28] *Mersey Steel and Iron Co. v. Naylor Benzon & Co., supra*, at pp. 443–444. See also *Hoare v. Rennie* (1859) 5 H. & N. 19; *Jonassohn v. Young* (1863) 4 B. & S. 296; *Clarke v. Burn* (1866) 14 L.T. 439; *Coddington v. Paleologo* (1867) L.R. 2 Ex. 193; *Simpson v. Crippin* (1872) L.R. 8 Q.B. 14; *Honck v. Muller* (1881) 7 Q.B.D. 92; *Millar's Karri and Jarrah Co. v. Weddel Turner & Co.* (1908) 100 L.T. 128; *Taylor v. Oakes, Roncoroni & Co.* (1922) 127 L.T. 267; *Robert A. Munro Ltd v. Meyer* [1930] 2 K.B. 312; *Maple Flock Co. Ltd v. Universal Furniture Products (Wembley) Ltd* [1934] 1 K.B. 148; *Ross T. Smyth & Co. Ltd v. T.D. Bailey, Son & Co.* [1940] 3 All E.R. 60; *Amos & Wood Ltd v. Kaprow* (1948) 64 T.L.R. 110; *Regent OHG Aisenstadt und Barig v. Francesco of Jermyn Street* [1981] 3 All E.R. 327.

[29] *Maple Flock Co. Ltd v. Universal Furniture Products (Wembley) Ltd, supra*, at 157. See also *Millars Karri and Jarrah Co. v. Weddel Turner & Co., supra*, at 129.

[30] *Cornwall v. Henson* [1900] 2 Ch. 298, 304.

[31] See *ante*, §§ 12–037, 22–011.

discharge of the contract by frustration.[32] Nevertheless, "frustration by breach" must be distinguished from the doctrine of frustration of a contract referred to in Chapter 24.[33] Frustration by breach arises where the failure of performance is due to the act or default of one of the parties, but true frustration will only occur if the frustrating event was not caused by the fault of either party to the contract.[34] Further, where there has been frustration by breach, the innocent party may elect to affirm the contract; but where there is true frustration, the contract is determined automatically, and it cannot be continued by affirmation.[35]

5. CONSEQUENCES OF DISCHARGE[36]

Effect on contract. It has become usual to speak of the exercise by one party **25–046** of his right to treat himself as discharged as a "rescission" of the contract. But, as Lord Porter pointed out in *Heymans v. Darwins Ltd*[37]:

> "To say that the contract is rescinded or has come to an end or has ceased to exist may in individual cases convey the truth with sufficient accuracy, but the fuller expression that the injured party is thereby absolved from future performance of his obligations under the contract is a more exact description of the position. Strictly speaking, to say that on acceptance of the renunciation of a contract the contract is rescinded is incorrect."

This statement was unanimously approved by the House of Lords in *Johnson v. Agnew*,[38] where Lord Wilberforce emphasised[39] that this so-called "rescission" is quite different from rescission *ab initio*, such as may arise for example, in cases of mistake, fraud or lack of consent. It has also become usual to speak of the contract as having been "terminated" or "discharged" by the breach. Again, however, these expressions may be somewhat misleading for they might suggest that the contract ceases for all purposes to exist in that event. Such an approach was indeed adopted by the Court of Appeal in *Harbutt's "Plasticine" Ltd v. Wayne Tank and Pump Co. Ltd*[40] so as to prevent the party in default from relying on an exemption clause inserted in a contract which had been "terminated" by breach. But this case was overruled by the House of Lords in *Photo Production Ltd v. Securicor Transport Ltd*.[41] The true position was there stated to be—where the innocent party elects to terminate the contract, *i.e.* to put an end to all primary obligations of both parties remaining unperformed—that "(a) there is substituted

---

[32] *Jackson v. Union Marine Insurance Co. Ltd* (1874) L.R. 10 C.P. 125, 145, 147; *Trade and Transport Inc. v. Iino Kaiun Kaisha Ltd* [1973] 1 W.L.R. 210, 221; *Nitrate Corpn. of Chile Ltd v. Pansuiza Compania de Navegacion SA* [1980] 1 Lloyd's Rep. 638, 648 (affd. *sub nom. Chilean Nitrate Sale & Corpn. v. Marine Transportation Co. Ltd* [1982] 1 Lloyd's Rep. 570).

[33] See *ante*, §§ 24–001 *et seq.*

[34] See *ante*, §§ 24–059—24–063. For consideration of "mixed causes," see *Nitrate Corpn. of Chile Ltd v. Pansuiza Compania de Navegacion SA, supra*, at 649.

[35] *Hirji Mulji v. Cheong Yue SS. Co. Ltd* [1926] A.C. 497, 509. *cf. B.P. Exploration Co. (Libya) Ltd v. Hunt (No.2)* [1979] 1 W.L.R. 783, affd. [1983] 2 A.C. 352 (waiver).

[36] See Shea (1979) 42 M.L.R. 623; Beatson (1981) 97 L.Q.R. 389; Rose (1981) 34 C.L.P. 235.

[37] [1942] A.C. 356, 399.

[38] [1980] A.C. 367. See also *Bank of Boston Connecticut v. European Grain and Shipping Ltd* [1989] A.C. 1056, 1098–1099.

[39] At 393.

[40] [1970] 1 Q.B. 447.

[41] [1980] A.C. 827; see *ante*, § 14–022.

by implication of law for the primary obligations of the party in default which remain unperformed a secondary obligation to pay money compensation to the other party for the loss sustained by him in consequence of their non-performance in the future and (b) the unperformed primary obligations of that other party are discharged."[42]

25–047   Of course, in assessing damages, the court must have regard to the terms of the contract in order to ascertain the performance promised in it,[43] including performance which would have fallen due after the date of discharge.[44] It must also give effect to terms of the contract which, for example, liquidate the damages recoverable[45] or exclude or restrict the remedies otherwise available for breach.[46] But, from the time of discharge, as a general rule both parties are excused from further performance of the primary obligations of the contract which each has still to perform. However, obligations for the resolution of disputes will remain in full force and effect,[47] "as may other clauses having a contractual function which is ancillary or collateral to the subject-matter of the contract."[48] Arbitration clauses which state without qualification that any difference or dispute which may arise under the contract shall be referred to arbitration will continue to apply notwithstanding the discharge.[49] Moreover, in principle, only those primary obligations falling due after the date of discharge will come to an end; those which have accrued due at the time may still be enforceable as such.[50] Thus, while both parties are discharged from further performance of their primary obligations under the contract, "rights are not divested or discharged which have been unconditionally acquired."[51] The party in breach can therefore enforce against the innocent party such rights as it has "unconditionally acquired" by the date of termination.

---

[42] At 849, *per* Lord Diplock. See also *Moschi v. Lep Air Services Ltd* [1973] A.C. 331, 345, 350, 351; *Thompson v. Corroon* (1993) 42 W.I.R. 157, 172–173.

[43] *Heyman v. Darwins Ltd* [1942] A.C. 356, 373; *F.J. Bloemen Pty. Ltd v. Council of the City of the Gold Coast* [1973] A.C. 115.

[44] *O'Neil v. Armstrong, Mitchell & Co.* [1895] 2 Q.B. 418; *Moschi v. Lep Air Services Ltd, supra*; *The Mihalis Angelos* [1971] 1 Q.B. 164.

[45] See *post,*, § 27–102.

[46] See *ante*, § 14–022.

[47] *Port Jackson Stevedoring Pty. Ltd v. Salmond and Spraggon (Australia) Pty. Ltd* [1981] 1 W.L.R. 138, 145. However, a restrictive covenant in a contract of employment will not generally survive where it is the employer who has repudiated the contract: *General Billposting Co. Ltd v. Atkinson* [1909] A.C. 118, *ante*, § 17–098, although the correctness of this proposition has recently been questioned by Phillips L.J. in *Rock Refrigeration Ltd v. Jones* [1997] 1 All E.R. 1, 18–20 on the basis that "the law in relation to the discharge of contractual obligations by acceptance of a repudiation has been developed and clarified" since *General Billposting* was decided. The employer may, however, be able to protect his property and trade secrets on the basis that his rights of property will survive the termination of the contract as a result of the employee's acceptance of his repudiatory breach (*Rock Refrigeration Ltd v. Jones* [1997] 1 All E.R. 1, 14 and (on rather wider grounds) 20).

[48] *Yasuda Fire & Marine Insurance Co. of Europe Ltd v. Orion Marine Insurance Underwriting Agency Ltd* [1995] Q.B. 174 (principal's contractual right to inspect documents and computer databases relating to transactions entered into by agents held to have survived the termination of the agency agreement).

[49] *Heyman v. Darwins Ltd, supra*; *F.J. Bloemen Pty. Ltd v. Council of the City of the Gold Coast, supra*; *Moschi v. Lep Air Services Ltd, supra*, at 351.

[50] *Bank of Boston Connecticut v. European Grain and Shipping Ltd* [1989] A.C. 1056. See Beatson (1981) 97 L.Q.R. 389; and *post*, §§ 27–121—27–124, 30–048, 30–058.

[51] *McDonald v. Dennys Lascelles Ltd* (1933) 48 C.L.R. 457, 476–477; *Bank of Boston Connecticut v. European Grain and Shipping Ltd* [1989] A.C. 1056, 1098–1099.

Termination of partnership agreement. However, in the case of the termi- **25-048**
nation of a partnership agreement as a result of the acceptance by one partner of
the repudiatory breach of the other partners, the innocent partner's liability to
contribute to the liabilities of the partnership may extend beyond those rights to
contribution which the partners in breach had "unconditionally acquired" before
the date of dissolution of the partnership.[52]

Position of innocent party. Where the innocent party is entitled to, and does, **25-049**
treat himself as discharged by the other's breach, he is thereby released from
future performance of his obligations under the contract.[53] Discharge also
deprives him of any right as against the other party to continue to perform them.[54]
After such discharge he is not bound to accept, or pay for, any further performance by the other party. If he has paid money under the contract to the party in
default, he will be entitled to recover it by an action for money had and
received,[55] but only if the consideration for the payment has totally failed.[56] A
deposit paid by him to secure performance is, however, recoverable.[57]

Rights acquired before discharge. Although both parties are discharged **25-050**
from further performance of the contract, rights are not divested or discharged
which have already been unconditionally acquired. Rights and obligations which
arise from the partial execution of the contract and causes of action which have
accrued from its breach alike continue unaffected.[58] Where, at the time of
discharge, money is due under the contract by the innocent party but that sum
remains unpaid, the innocent party is not required to pay that sum if it would then
be recoverable by him in a restitutionary claim (for example, on the ground that
there had been a (total) failure of consideration). Otherwise, the innocent party
can retain or recover sums paid or due before the time at which the repudiation

---

[52] *Hurst v. Bryk* [1998] [1999] Ch. 1. The exact basis of this more extensive obligation to contribute
is unclear. Peter Gibson L.J. held that the innocent partner could not escape from his share of the
expenses of the winding up of the affairs of the partnership (at 13) and he held that the innocent
partner was also liable to contribute to the rent payable under the lease of the partnership premises
on the ground that he had an equitable interest in the lease which was not determined by the
dissolution of the partnership. The termination of the contract did not thereby divest an "accrued
property right and its concomitant obligation to indemnify the trustees" (at 14). Simon Brown L.J.
took a broader approach and concluded (at 31) that the innocent partner's obligation to contribute to
the various liabilities of the partnership was simply not one of those primary obligations from which
a repudiatory breach discharged him. Hobhouse L.J. dissented on the basis that there was no
justification for departing from the orthodox rules laid down in cases such as *Heyman v. Darwins Ltd*
(*supra*).
[53] *Heyman v. Darwins Ltd* [1942] A.C. 356, 399; *Moschi v. Lep Air Services Ltd* [1973] A.C. 331,
345, 350, 351; *Photo Production Ltd v. Securicor Transport Ltd* [1980] A.C. 827, 844, 848;
Thompson v. Corroon (1993) 42 W.I.R. 157, 173; *cf. Port Jackson Stevedoring Pty. Ltd v. Salmond
and Spraggon (Australia) Pty. Ltd* [1981] 1 W.L.R. 138.
[54] *Moschi v. Lep Air Services Ltd, supra*, at 350, 351; *Photo Production Ltd v. Securicor Transport
Ltd, supra*, at 844.
[55] *Fibrosa Spolka Akcyjna v. Fairbairn Lawson Combe Barbour Ltd* [1943] A.C. 32, 52, 65; *Kwei
Tek Chao v. British Traders and Shippers Ltd* [1954] 2 Q.B. 459, 475; see *post*, § 30–048.
[56] See *post*, §§ 30–048—30–061. The *total* failure requirement may not survive further judicial
scrutiny, see *Goss v. Chilcott* [1996] A.C. 788, 798. For academic criticism of the insistence upon a
total failure see Burrows, *The Law of Restitution* (1993), pp. 259–261.
[57] See *post*, § 30–059.
[58] *McDonald v. Dennys Lascelles Ltd* (1933) 48 C.L.R. 457, 476–477; *Johnson v. Agnew* [1980]
A.C. 367, 396; *Damon Compania Naviera SA v. Hapag-Lloyd International SA* [1985] 1 W.L.R. 435,
450.

is accepted by him[59] and may maintain an action for damages in respect of any cause of action vested in him at that time.[60] If the contract provides for payment of a deposit, which is forfeitable in the event of breach, the acceptance by the innocent party of the repudiation of the contract by the party in default does not preclude him from recovering and forfeiting the deposit if it is at that time due and unpaid.[61] Further in *Damon Compania Naviera SA v. Hapag-Lloyd International SA*[62] the vendor and purchaser of three ships agreed that each would sign a memorandum of agreement within a reasonable time, whereupon the purchaser would be liable to pay a deposit of 10 per cent of the purchase price. The purchaser repudiated the contract by failing to sign the memorandum and this repudiation was accepted by the vendor. The Court of Appeal held that, even though the vendor had acquired no accrued right to the deposit at the time he accepted the repudiation, nevertheless at that time he had a vested right to sue the purchaser for damages for breach of his obligation to sign the memorandum, the measure of such damages being the amount of the deposit. However, in the case of contracts for the sale of land or goods, unless the contract otherwise provides, sums due as part payment of the purchase price from the party in default may be irrecoverable.[63] If the innocent party has expended labour or money under the contract, or delivered goods to the party in default, but payment for these is not yet due, he will be entitled to sue for these on a *quantum meruit* or *quantum valebat*.[64] Otherwise, his remedy is to sue for damages for breach of contract.[65]

25–051   **Position of guilty party.** Upon discharge, the primary obligations of the party in default to perform any of the promises made by him and remaining unperformed come to an end, as does his right to perform them.[66] But for his primary obligations there is substituted by operation of law a secondary obligation to pay to the other party a sum of money to compensate him for the loss he has sustained as a result of the failure to perform the unperformed primary obligations.[67]

---

[59] *Dewar v. Mintoft* [1912] 2 K.B. 373, 387–388; *Damon Compania Naviera SA v. Hapag-Lloyd International SA, supra*, at 451. Contrast *Lowe v. Hope* [1970] Ch. 94.

[60] *Damon Compania Naviera SA v. Hapag-Lloyd International SA, supra*.

[61] *Brooks v. Beirnstein* [1909] 1 K.B. 98; *Leslie Shipping Co. v. Welstead* [1921] 3 K.B. 420; *Chatterton v. Maclean* [1951] 1 All E.R. 761; *Overstone Ltd v. Shipway* [1962] 1 W.L.R. 117; *Galbraith v. Mitchenall Estates Ltd* [1965] 2 Q.B. 473; *Hyundai Shipbuilding & Heavy Industries Co. Ltd v. Pournaras* [1978] 2 Lloyd's Rep. 502; *Hyundai Heavy Industries Co. Ltd v. Papadopoulos* [1980] 1 W.L.R. 1129; *cf. Wehner v. Dene Steam Shipping Co.* [1905] 2 K.B. 929; *China National Foreign Trade Transportation Corpn. v. Evlogia Shipping Co. SA of Panama* [1979] 1 W.L.R. 1018, HL (overpayment); *Thompson v. Corroon* (1993) 42 W.I.R. 157, 173.

[62] [1985] 1 W.L.R. 435.

[63] *Palmer v. Temple* (1839) 9 A. & E. 508; *Dies v. British and International Mining and Finance Corpn. Ltd* [1939] 1 K.B. 724. See also *Mayson v. Clouet* [1924] A. C. 980, 986; *McDonald v. Dennys Lascelles Ltd supra*, at 477; *Hyundai Heavy Industries Co. Ltd v. Papadopoulos, supra*, at 1134, 1142, 1153; Beatson (1981) 97 L.Q.R. 389; and *post*, § 3–061. For the possibility of equitable relief, see *post*, § 27–122.

[64] See *post*, § 30–178.

[65] But see the effect of a buyer's repudiation on the seller's rights in respect of goods: *Benjamin's Sale of Goods* (5th ed., 1997), § 15–107.

[66] *Hurst v. Bryk* [1998] 2 W.L.R. 269, 287.

[67] *Moschi v. Lep Air Services Ltd* [1973] A.C. 331, 345, 350, 351; *Photo Production Ltd v. Securicor Transport Ltd* [1980] A.C. 827, 848–851; *Port Jackson Stevedoring Pty. Ltd v. Salmond and Spraggon (Australia) Pty. Ltd* [1981] 1 W.L.R. 138, 145.

The party in default will not be entitled to recover any deposit paid by him as **25–052** security for the performance of his obligations.[68] In principle, other sums paid by him under the contract before the time of discharge will likewise be irrecoverable.[69] But, unless the contract otherwise provides, he may be permitted to recover money paid as a part-payment of the purchase price where the contract is one for the sale of goods or land,[70] and it is possible that relief in equity may in certain circumstances be available.[71]

Whether he has any claim to be recompensed for partial performance of the **25–053** contract which he has broken will depend on whether the obligation is entire or divisible.[72] If it is entire, he will normally have no claim, unless there is evidence on which to ground the inference of a new contract or an independent restitutionary claim.[73] But if the obligation is not entire but divisible, he may be entitled to claim in respect of a divisible part of the performance completed[74] (subject to a counterclaim by the innocent party in respect of that part of the contract which remains unperformed). Where goods delivered under a contract of sale are not in conformity with the contract, and are rejected by the buyer, the property in the goods revests in the seller.[75]

Effect on guarantor. Where a creditor "accepts" his debtor's wrongful **25–054** repudiation of the contract, and exercises his right to treat himself as discharged, this does not release a guarantor of the debtor from liability in respect of monies payable by the debtor after the date of discharge.[76] Nor is the guarantor released from liability in respect of sums due but unpaid at that time,[77] unless those sums could not have been recovered from the debtor himself[78] and the guarantee does not, on its true construction, require payment by the guarantor in the event of default in payment on the due date.[79]

---

[68] *Palmer v. Temple* (1839) 9 A. & E. 508, 520; *Howe v. Smith* (1884) 27 Ch.D. 87; *Linggi Plantations Ltd v. Jagattheesan* [1972] 1 M.L.J. 89, 91, PC; *Thompson v. Corroon* (1993) 42 W.I.R. 157, 173; and see *post*, § 30–059. But see Law of Property Act 1925, s.49(2).

[69] See *ante*, § 25–050, n. 61, *post*, § 30–059.

[70] see *ante*, § 25–050, n. 63, *post*, § 27–124.

[71] See *post*, § 27–121; Beatson (1981) 97 L.Q.R. 389.

[72] See *ante*, § 25–042; *post*, § 27–121.

[73] See *ante*, §§ 22–030—22–031.

[74] See *ante*, §§ 22–037, 25–043.

[75] *Kwei Tek Chao v. British Traders and Shippers Ltd* [1954] 2 Q.B. 459, 487; *Rosenthal & Sons Ltd v. Esmail* [1965] 1 W.L.R. 1117, 1131.

[76] *Moschi v. Lep Air Services Ltd* [1973] A.C. 331; see Vol. II, Chap. 44.

[77] *Hyundai Shipbuilding and Heavy Industries Co. Ltd v. Pournaras* [1978] 2 Lloyd's Rep. 502; *Hyundai Heavy Industries Co. Ltd v. Papadopoulos* [1980] 1 W.L.R. 1129, HL; see *post*, § 30–061.

[78] See *ante*, § 25–050, n. 63.

[79] *Hyundai Heavy Industries Co. Ltd v. Papadopoulos, supra*; and see Vol. II, Chap. 44.

CHAPTER 26

OTHER MODES OF DISCHARGE

1. MERGER

Merger by taking a higher security. In general, a debt or security by simple **26–001**
contract is extinguished by a specialty security being given for the same if the
remedy on the latter is coextensive with that which the creditor had upon the
former.[1] Thus, if a bond or covenant by the debtor is taken for or to secure a
simple contract debt, the latter is merged in the former, because in contemplation
of law the specialty is an instrument of a higher nature and gives the creditor a
better remedy than he had for the original debt.[2] But in order for this principle to
apply, two conditions must be fulfilled.

First, the later security must be of a higher efficacy than that which it is sought
to replace. Thus, if the securities are of equal degree, as in the case of an earlier
and a later bond,[3] no merger will take place. A negotiable instrument is not a
higher security for the purposes of this rule,[4] although the giving and taking of
a bill or note may act as a discharge of a debt if the parties so intended.[5]

Secondly, the remedy given by the higher security must be coextensive with
the lower security, that is to say, it must secure the same obligation and be made
between the same parties.[6] Thus, if one of two makers of a joint and several
promissory note gives the holder a mortgage to secure the amount with a
covenant to pay it, the other maker is not thereby discharged, for the remedy on
the specialty is not coextensive with the remedy of the note.[7] And where a
specialty is given for payments of amounts due or to become due on a running
account with a bank, the doctrine of merger, if it applies at all, could at most

---

[1] *Acton v. Symon* (1635) Cro.Car. 414; *Twopenny v. Young* (1824) 3 B. & C. 208; *Price v. Moulton*
(1835) 10 C.B. 561.

[2] *Price v. Moulton, supra.*

[3] *Kidd v. Boone* (1871) 40 L.J.Ch. 531. See also *Norwood v. Grype* (1599) Cro.Eliz. 727; *Chetwynd
v. Allen* [1899] 1 Ch. 353.

[4] *Drake v. Mitchell* (1803) 3 East 251.

[5] See *ante,* §§ 22–073—22–075.

[6] *Bell v. Banks* (1841) 3 M. & G. 258; *Ansell v. Baker* (1850) 15 Q.B. 20; *Mowatt v. Lord
Londesburgh* (1854) 3 E. & B. 307; *Chetwynd v. Allen* [1899] 1 Ch. 353; *Lawrence v. Cassel* [1930]
W.N. 137; *Hissett v. Reading Roofing Co. Ltd* [1969] 1 W.L.R. 1757.

[7] *Ansell v. Baker, supra.* Where the remedy is not joint and several, but merely joint, it seems that
merger will operate: *Owen v. Homan* (1850) 3 Mc. & G. 378, 410; *Ex p. Flintoff* (1844) 3 M.D. &
De G. 726; *Ex p. Hernaman* (1848) 12 Jur. 642. Contrast *Sharpe v. Gibbs* (1864) 16 C.B.(N.S.) 527;
Holmes v. Bell (1841) 3 M. & G. 213; *Bell v. Banks* (1841) 3 M. & G. 258. See Williams, *Joint
Obligations,* § 49, and generally on joint obligations, *ante,* Chap. 18.

apply only to the indebtedness which existed at the date when the covenant was taken; for the specialty would otherwise be given in respect of a different future debt.[8]

26–002   **Collateral security.** If it appears on the face of the specialty or from the nature of the transaction that the specialty was intended only as an additional or collateral security, it will not operate as a merger.[9] So, where a banker took from A, his customer, and B, his surety, a bond conditioned for the payment of all sums already advanced or thereafter to be advanced to A, it was held that the bond was evidently intended only as a collateral security, that therefore there was no merger and that A might be sued for the balance of his account as on a simple contract debt.[10]

26–003   **Merger of contract in conveyance.** "It is well settled that, where parties enter into an executory agreement which is to be carried out by a deed afterwards to be executed, the real completed contract is to be found in the deed. The contract is merged in the deed. . . . The most common instance, perhaps, of this merger is a contract for the sale of land followed by conveyance on completion."[11] Merger is not, however, inevitable, but depends upon the intention of the parties.[12] Merger may occur despite the fact that the terms of the conveyance differ from those in the contract; and, where a contract applies to many parcels of land, but the conveyance to only some of them, merger may operate distributively, *i.e. quoad* only the parcels conveyed.[13]

26–004   **Merger of rights and liabilities.** A contract may also be discharged where the rights and liabilities under it become vested, by assignment or otherwise, in the same person in the same right,[14] for a man cannot maintain an action against himself. This type of merger is more often encountered in the law of land,[15] *e.g.* where a tenant for a term of years retains the lease and acquires the reversion. An example in the law of contract is provided by section 61 of the Bills of Exchange Act 1882, which enacts that, when the acceptor of a bill is or becomes the holder of it at or after its maturity, in his own right, the bill is discharged.[16]

26–005   **Debtor becomes creditor's personal representative.** At common law, if a debtor became the personal representative of his creditor, the right of action for

---

[8] *Barclays Bank Ltd v. Beck* [1952] 2 Q.B. 47, 53.
[9] *Twopenny v. Young* (1824) 3 B. & C. 208; *Ex p. Bate* (1838) 3 Deac. 358; *Yates v. Aston* (1843) 4 Q.B. 182; *Norfolk Railway Co. v. M'Namara* (1849) 3 Exch. 628; *Ex p. Hughes* (1872) 4 Ch.D. 34; *Commissioner of Stamps v. Hope* [1891] A.C. 476; *Barclays Bank Ltd v. Beck, supra.*
[10] *Holmes v. Bell, supra.*
[11] *Knight Sugar Co. Ltd v. Alberta Ry. & Irrigation Co.* [1938] 1 All E.R. 266, 269.
[12] *Palmer v. Johnson* (1884) 13 Q.B.D. 351, 357; *Clarke v. Ramuz* [1891] 2 Q.B. 456, 461; *Lawrence v. Cassel* [1930] 2 K.B. 83; *Barclays Bank Ltd v. Beck* [1952] 2 Q.B. 47; *Hancock v. B.W. Brazier (Anerley) Ltd* [1966] 1 W.L.R. 1317; *Hissett v. Reading Roofing Co. Ltd* [1969] 1 W.L.R. 1757; *Tito v. Waddell (No. 2)* [1977] Ch. 107, 284; *Gunatunga v. De Alwis* (1996) 72 P. & C.R. 161, 180.
[13] *Tito v. Waddell (No. 2), supra,* at 284–285.
[14] *e.g.* not as executor or administrator, to which special rules apply, *post.*
[15] See Megarry and Wade, *The Law of Real Property* (5th ed., 1984), p. 685. At common law merger was automatic; but by s.185 of the Law of Property Act 1925, the equitable rule now prevails; that merger depends upon the intention of the person who acquires the two estates. See *Capital and Counties Bank Ltd v. Rhodes* [1903] 1 Ch. 631.
[16] *Harmer v. Steele* (1849) 4 Exch. 1; *Chalmers and Guest on Bills of Exchange* (15th ed., 1998), pp. 519–521. See Vol. II, § 34–139.

the debt was suspended, since he could not maintain an action against himself. But since the suspension of a personal action as the result of the voluntary act of a creditor prevented revival of the action, the result was that, if the creditor appointed the debtor his executor, the debt was extinguished when that appointment became effective on the creditor's death.[17] On the other hand, if the debtor became the administrator of the creditor's estate, this was not the voluntary act of the creditor, and the debt was therefore not extinguished, but was suspended for the duration of the administration.[18] In equity, however, a debtor who was appointed his creditor's executor was treated as having paid the debt to himself, and he was compelled to account for it as assets of the testator held by him[19] unless there was evidence of the testator's settled intention to release him from the debt.[20] But equity did not intervene in the case of a debtor who became administrator. This divergence between the rules applicable to executors and administrators has now been abolished, so that an administrator's debt is likewise extinguished (and not merely suspended), but he is likewise accountable for the amount of the debt as part of the creditor's estate.[21]

Creditor becomes debtor's personal representative. Where a creditor   26–006
becomes the executor or administrator of his debtor's estate, the debt is not extinguished or suspended.[22] He may retain[23] assets of the testator in payment of his debt in priority to other creditors of equal degree.[24]

Merger by judgment recovered. The mere pendency of an action for the   26–007
recovery of a debt or damages is no bar to another action for the same breach of contract on which the claim to such a debt or damages is founded.[25] The defendant's remedy in such a case is either to consolidate the two actions[26] or to have the second action struck out on the basis that there are no reasonable grounds for bringing the claim.[27] But when a prior action has already been successfully brought by the claimant against the defendant in a court of record[28] for the identical demand,[29] and judgment has been recovered thereon, the cause

---

[17] *Wankford v. Wankford* (1704) 1 Salk. 299; *Cheetham v. Ward* (1797) 1 B. & P. 630; *Freakley v. Fox* (1829) 9 B. & C. 130; *Re Applebee* [1891] 3 Ch. 422. See also *Jenkins v. Jenkins* [1928] 2 K.B. 501 and *Williams, Mortimer and Sunnucks on Executors, Administrators and Probate* (17th ed., 1993), p. 649, and *ante*, § 18–023.

[18] *Nedham's Case* (1610) 8 Co.Rep. 135a; *Seagram v. Knight* (1867) L.R. 2 Ch.App. 620.

[19] *Selwin v. Brown* (1735) 3 Brown P.C. 607; *Ingle v. Richards* (1860) 28 Beav. 366; *Re Bourne* [1906] 1 Ch. 697.

[20] *Strong v. Bird* (1874) L.R. 18 Eq. 316; *Re Pink* [1912] 2 Ch. 528; *Re James* [1935] Ch. 449. *cf. Re Freeland* [1952] Ch. 110.

[21] Administration of Estates Act 1925, s.21A (inserted by s.10 of the Limitation Amendment Act 1980).

[22] *Bowring-Hanbury's Trustee v. Bowring-Hanbury* [1942] Ch. 276. See generally *Williams, Mortimer and Sunnucks on Executors, Administrators and Probate* (17th ed., 1993), p. 651; (1943) 59 L.Q.R. 117; (1943) 6 M.L.R. 233.

[23] See *post*, § 29–134.

[24] Administration of Estates Act 1925, s.34(2). But the form of administration bond which a creditor is required to enter into in connection with an application for a grant of administration as creditor prohibits him from using his right of retainer to give himself an advantage over other creditors.

[25] *Harley v. Greenwood* (1821) 5 B. & Ald. 95, 101.

[26] CPR Part 3, r. 1(2)(g).

[27] CPR Part 3, r. 4(2)(a); County Courts Act 1984, s.35.

[28] See *post*, § 26–009.

[29] *Seddon v. Tutop* (1796) 6 T.R. 607; *Hadley v. Green* (1832) 2 Cr. & J. 374; *Wegg Prosser v. Evans* [1895] 1 Q.B. 108; *Economic Life Assurance Socy. v. Usborne* [1902] A.C. 147.

of action is changed or merged into matter of record and the inferior remedy is merged in the higher.[30] In such a case, therefore, if the claimant sues upon the original promise or demand (even although it accrued upon a specialty), it will be a good defence that he has already recovered judgment against the defendant for the same cause of action.[31]

The general rule is that "damages resulting from one and the same cause of action must be assessed and recovered once for all."[32] So in one case[33] the claimant recovered from the defendant in one action as damages for the defendant's breach of contract the damages which a third party had recovered against the claimant. He then brought a second action to recover the costs incurred by him in defending the third party's action. It was held that recovery of judgment in the first action was a bar to the second. But where one contract contains separate promises, or there are separate breaches of the same promise, separate or successive actions may be brought for each breach, and judgment in one will be no bar to the other.[34] However, if a contract contains a single indivisible undertaking, different actions cannot be maintained for different breaches of it. Where, therefore, a builder who had agreed to build a bungalow in a good and workmanlike manner was sued in successive actions by the owner for breach of his contract, inefficiency of workmanship being alleged in the first action and unsuitability of materials in the second, recovery of judgment in the first action was held to be a defence in the second.[35]

26–008   **Interest.** A judgment for interest only is no bar to a claim for the principal money.[36] But where there is a covenant to pay a principal sum, and judgment is obtained upon the covenant for that sum, any covenant to pay interest which is merely incidental to the covenant to pay the principal sum is merged in the judgment.[37] If, however, the covenant to pay interest is expressed in such a manner as to be independent of the covenant to pay the principal sum, it is not merged or extinguished in the judgment.[38]

---

[30] *Greathead v. Bromley* (1798) 7 T.R. 455; *King v. Hoare* (1844) 13 M. & W. 495; *Stewart v. Todd* (1846) 9 Q.B. 759; *Re European Central Ry.* (1876) 4 Ch.D. 33; *Kendall v. Hamilton* (1879) 4 App.Cas. 504; *Aman v. Southern Ry.* [1926] 1 K.B. 59. For the position in regard to judgment against one joint, or joint and several, debtor, see *ante*, § 18–015. For the effect of an arbitration award, see *ante*, §§ 16–114 *et seq.*

[31] But see *Buckland v. Palmer* [1984] 1 W.L.R. 1109, 1115.

[32] *Brunsden v. Humphrey* (1884) 14 Q.B.D. 141, 147; *Darley Main Colliery Co. v. Mitchell* (1886) 11 App.Cas. 127, 132; *Conquer v. Boot* [1928] 2 K.B. 336, 343; *Clark v. Urquhart* [1930] A.C. 28, 54. See also County Courts Act 1984, s.35. The general rule applies also to arbitrations: see Mustill and Boyd, *Commercial Arbitration* (2nd ed.), p. 411.

[33] *Furness, Withy & Co. v. Hall* (1909) 25 T.L.R. 233.

[34] *Bristowe v. Fairclough* (1840) 1 M. & G. 143; *Brunsden v. Humphrey, supra; Ebbetts v. Conquest* (1900) 82 L.T. 560; *Bake v. French* [1907] 1 Ch. 428; *Brooks v. Beirnstein* [1909] 1 K.B. 98; *Isaacs v. Salbstein* [1916] 2 K.B. 139; *South Bedfordshire Electrical Finance Ltd v. Bryant* [1938] 3 All E.R. 580; *National Coal Board v. Galley* [1958] 1 W.L.R. 16; *Overstone Ltd v. Shipway* [1962] 1 W.L.R. 117; *Telfair Shipping Corpn v. Inersea Carriers SA* [1983] 2 Lloyd's Rep. 351. See *post*, §§ 27–012—27–013. But see also *post*, §§ 26–010—26–013 (stay of proceedings where matters could and should have been raised).

[35] *Conquer v. Boot* [1928] 2 K.B. 336. But see (arbitrations), *ante*, § 16–114.

[36] *Morgan v. Rowlands* (1872) 41 L.J.Q.B. 187.

[37] *Ex p. Fewings* (1883) 25 Ch.D. 338. The judgment bears interest: see *post*, § 27–151.

[38] *Popple v. Sylvester* (1882) 22 Ch.D. 98; *Economic Life Assurance Soc. v. Usborne* [1902] A.C. 147.

County court judgments. A county court is a court of record.[39] Judgment **26–009** recovered in a county court is therefore a good defence to an action in the High Court for the same cause,[40] provided that the county court was acting within its jurisdiction.[41]

Estoppel by judgment. Estoppel by judgment, or estoppel *per rem judica-* **26–010** *tam*, is a rule of evidence[42] whereby a party is debarred from relitigating a cause of action which has been conclusively determined by the judgment of a court of competent jurisdiction in previous proceedings between the same parties or their privies, or an issue raised and determined in such proceedings which it was necessary[43] to determine for the purpose of those proceedings.[44] Estoppel *per rem judicatam* has two principal branches: cause of action estoppel and issue estoppel. Cause of action estoppel arises "where the cause of action in the later proceedings is identical to that in the earlier proceedings, the latter having been between the same parties or their privies and having involved the same subject matter. In such a case the bar is absolute in relation to all points decided unless fraud or collusion is alleged such as to justify setting aside the earlier judgment."[45] On the other hand, issue estoppel arises "where a particular issue forming a necessary ingredient in a cause of action has been litigated and decided and in subsequent proceedings between the same parties involving a different cause of action to which the same issue is relevant one of the parties seeks to re-open that issue."[46] Both estoppels are founded "upon the public interest in finality of litigation rather than the achievement of justice as between the individual litigants."[47]

---

[39] County Courts Act 1984, s.1(2).

[40] *Austin v. Mills* (1853) 9 Exch. 288. See also *Vines v. Arnold* (1849) 8 C.B. 632; *Webster v. Armstrong* (1885) 54 L.J.Q.B. 236.

[41] *Briscoe v. Stephens* (1842) 2 Bing. 213.

[42] *Vervaeke v. Smith* [1983] 1 A.C. 145; *Republic of India v. India Steamship Co. Ltd* [1993] A.C. 410, 422.

[43] *Kok Hoong v. Leong Cheong Kweng Mines Ltd* [1964] A.C. 993; *Penn Texas Corpn v. Murat Anstalt (No. 2)* [1964] 2 Q.B. 647; *Fidelitas Shipping Co. Ltd v. V/O Exportchleb* [1966] 1 Q.B. 630, 640; *Mills v. Cooper* [1967] 2 Q.B. 459, 468; *Carl Zeiss Stiftung v. Rayner & Keeler Ltd (No. 3)* [1970] Ch. 506; *Helmville Ltd v. Astilleros Espanoles SA* [1984] 2 Lloyd's Rep. 569; *In re State of Norway's Application (No. 2)* [1990] 1 A.C. 723, 743, 752; *In re B. (Minors) (Care Proceedings: Issue Estoppel)* [1997] Fam. 117, 121–122.

[44] The subject is one of considerable difficulty and refinement: see Halsbury's *Laws of England* (4th ed.), Vol. 16 ("Estoppel"), §§ 974 *et seq.*; *Cross and Tapper on Evidence* (8th ed.), pp. 82 *et seq.* For estoppel by a default judgment, see *Howlett v. Tarte* (1861) 10 C.B.N.S. 813; *New Brunswick Ry. Co. v. British and French Trust Corpn Ltd* [1939] A.C. 1; *Kok Hoong v. Leong Cheong Kweng Mines Ltd, supra.* Neither dismissal for want of prosecution (*Pople v. Evans* [1969] 2 Ch. 255) nor the withdrawal of proceedings (*Owens v. Minoprio* [1942] 1 K.B. 193) is a foundation for *res judicata*.

[45] *Arnold v. National Westminster Bank plc* [1991] 2 A.C. 93, 104.

[46] *ibid.* at 105.

[47] *Republic of India v. India Steamship Co. Ltd* [1993] A.C. 410, 415. See also *Duchess of Kingston's Case* (1776) 20 St.Tr. 573; *R. v. Inhabitants of the Township of Hartington Middle Quarter* (1855) E. & B. 780; *Flittens v. Allfrey* (1874) L.R. 10 C.P. 29; *Hoystead v. Commissioner of Taxation* [1926] A.C. 155, 170; *Fidelitas Shipping Co. Ltd v. V/O Exportchleb, supra*, at 640; *Thoday v. Thoday* [1964] P. 181, 197–198; *Mills v. Cooper* [1967] 2 Q.B. 459, 468; *Carl Zeiss Stiftung v. Rayner & Keeler Ltd (No. 2)* [1967] 1 A.C. 853, 916, 917; *Vervaeke v. Smith* [1983] 1 A.C. 145; *Thrasyvoulou v. Secretary of State for the Environment* [1990] 2 A.C. 273, 289; *Cross and Tapper on Evidence* (8th ed.), pp. 80–81.

26–011   **Requirements.** Three requirements must be satisfied for a plea of estoppel *per rem judicatam* to succeed[48]: first, there must have been a final and conclusive judgment[49] on the merits[50] by a court of competent jurisdiction[51] in the earlier[52] proceedings; secondly, there must be identity of parties in the two sets of proceedings[53] or else the existence of privity between the respective claimants or defendants in the earlier proceedings and those in the later proceedings[54]; thirdly, there must be identity of subject matter in the two proceedings.[55]

---

[48] *Carl Zeiss Stiftung v. Rayner & Keeler Ltd (No. 2), supra*, at 909–910, 935, 943, 967–971; *D.S.V. Silo-und Verwaltungsgesellschaft mbH v. Owners of the Sennar* [1985] 1 W.L.R. 490, 499.

[49] *Marchioness of Huntley v. Gaskell* [1905] 2 Ch. 656; *Carl Zeiss Stiftung v. Rayner & Keeler Ltd (No. 3)* [1970] Ch. 506; *Midland Bank Trust Co. Ltd v. Green* [1980] Ch. 590; *Hines v. Birkbeck College (No. 2)* [1992] Ch. 33; *Buehler AG v. Chronos Richardson Ltd* [1998] 2 All E.R. 960. See also the cases cited in § 26–016, n. 86, *post*.

[50] Where there has been a dismissal on the sole ground that the particular court has no jurisdiction, there has been no decision on the merits which would prevent the plaintiff from commencing proceedings before a court which did have jurisdiction: *Hines v. Birkbeck College (No. 2)* [1992] Ch. 33. Particular difficulties arise in the context of interlocutory rulings (*Carl Zeiss Stiftung v. Rayner & Keeler Ltd (No. 2)* [1967] 1 A.C. 853). A decision on an application to set aside a default judgment is unlikely to give rise to an estoppel in this context (*Mullen v. Conoco Ltd* [1998] Q.B. 382). See *post*, § 26–016, n. 87.

[51] *The European Gateway* [1987] Q.B. 206; *Crown Estates Commissioners v. Dorset C.C.* [1990] Ch. 297. In the case of adjudications subject to a comprehensive statutory code, there is a presumption that, where the statute has created a specific jurisdiction for the determination of any issue which establishes the existence of a legal right, *res judicata* applies unless an intention to exclude the principle can properly be inferred as a matter of construction of the relevant statutory provisions (*Thrasyvoulou v. Secretary of State for the Environment* [1990] 2 A.C. 273, 289). Res judicata has been held to be applicable to arbitral tribunals (*Fidelitas Shipping Co. Ltd v. V/O Exportchleb, supra*; *Dallal v. Bank Mellat* [1986] Q.B. 441) and to industrial tribunals (*Munir v. Jang Publications Ltd* [1989] I.C.R. 1). For the effect of findings of an industrial tribunal on subsequent common law actions, see *Turner v. London Transport Executive* [1977] I.C.R. 952; *Green v. Hampshire C.C.* [1979] I.C.R. 861. See also *post*, §§ 26–015—26–018.

[52] But see *infra*, n. 59.

[53] *Townsend v. Bishop* [1939] 1 All E.R. 805; *Gleeson v. J. Wippell & Co. Ltd* [1977] 1 W.L.R. 510; *Hunter v. Chief Constable of West Midlands* [1982] A.C. 529, 540–541; *C. (A Minor) v. Hackney London Borough Council* [1996] 1 W.L.R. 789; *cf. North West Water Ltd v. Binnie & Partners* [1990] 3 All E.R. 547, where Drake J. rejected the argument that identity of parties was an essential ingredient of an issue estoppel. The parties must have litigated in the same capacity in both actions: *Marginson v. Blackburn B.C.* [1939] 2 K.B. 426; *cf. House of Spring Gardens Ltd v. Waite* [1991] 1 Q.B. 241, 252, where Stuart-Smith L.J. reserved his opinion as to whether the plaintiff's claim in *Marginson* should have been struck out as an abuse of process. See also his rationalisation of *Marginson* in *Talbot v. Berkshire C.C.* [1994] Q.B. 290, 296–297.

[54] *Kinnersley v. Orpe* (1780) 2 Dougl.K.B. 517; *Outram v. Homewood* (1803) 3 East 346, 366; *Mercantile Investment and General Trust Co. v. River Plate Trust, Loan and Agency Co.* [1894] 1 Ch. 578; *Carl Zeiss Stiftung v. Rayner & Keeler Ltd (No. 3), supra*; *Gleeson v. J. Wippell & Co. Ltd, supra*; *Hunter v. Chief Constable of West Midlands* [1982] A.C. 259; *House of Spring Gardens Ltd v. Waite* [1991] 1 Q.B. 241, 252–254.

[55] *Hoystead v. Commissioner of Taxation* [1926] A.C. 155; *Marginson v. Blackburn B.C.* [1939] 2 K.B. 426; *Bell v. Holmes* [1956] 1 W.L.R. 1359; *Society of Medical Officers of Health v. Hope* [1960] A.C. 551; *Randolph v. Tuck* [1962] 1 Q.B. 175; *Wood v. Luscombe* [1966] 1 Q.B. 69; *Re Mantey's Will Trusts (No. 2)* [1976] 1 All E.R. 673. See also *Khan v. Golechha International Ltd.* [1980] 1 W.L.R. 1482; *Taylor v. Vectapike Ltd* [1990] 2 E.G.L.R. 12; *Republic of India v. India Steamship Co. Ltd* [1993] A.C. 410; *Buehler AG v. Chrones Richardson Ltd* [1998] 2 All E.R. 960 and *Cross and Tapper on Evidence* (8th ed.), pp. 88–91. In the case of issue estoppel, the decision on the issue must have been essential for the decision of the court and not merely collateral: see the cases cited in n. 43, *supra*.

Issues not raised previously. Both cause of action[56] and issue estoppel[57] may 26–012
extend to issues which might have been put but were not raised and decided[58] in
the earlier proceedings, although in special circumstances[59] the court may depart
from this rule and permit the parties to raise such an issue. The court also has a
power under rules of court and its inherent jurisdiction to stay or dismiss the
action if a claimant seeks to raise in subsequent proceedings matters which were
or should have been litigated in the earlier proceedings.[60] The court will, unless
there are special circumstances, dismiss or stay such an action on the ground that
it is an abuse of the court.[61] The question whether an action is an abuse of the
court is "closely related"[62] to the question whether or not there is an estoppel *per
rem judicatam* but it is not identical so that an action may be struck out on the
ground that it is an abuse of the court where the plea of estoppel is not strictly
made out.[63] Estoppel *per rem judicatam* may be raised as a defence,[64] but the

---

[56] *Arnold v. National Westminster Bank plc* [1991] 2 A.C. 93, 104, citing *Henderson v. Henderson*
(1843) 3 Hare 100, 114–115; *Hoystead v. Commissioner of Taxation* [1926] A.C. 155, 170; *Yat Tung
Investment Co. Ltd v. Dao Heng Bank Ltd* [1975] A.C. 581, 590.

[57] *Arnold v. National Westminster Bank plc* [1991] 2 A.C. 93, 106, citing *Fidelitas Shipping Co.
Ltd v. V/O Exportchleb* [1966] 1 Q.B. 630, 642; *Brisbane City Council v. Att.-Gen. for Queensland*
[1979] A.C. 411, 425.

[58] The issue should have been decided as well as raised in the earlier proceedings: *Barrow v.
Bankside Agency Ltd* [1996] 1 W.L.R. 257 (plaintiff's claim not barred because it would not have
been decided by the court in the earlier proceedings).

[59] *Henderson v. Henderson* (1843) 3 Hare 100, 115; *Yat Tung Investment Co. Ltd v. Dao Heng Bank
Ltd* [1975] A.C. 581, 590; *Talbot v. Berkshire C.C.* [1994] Q.B. 290, 298–300; *Barrow v. Bankside
Agency Ltd* [1996] 1 W.L.R. 257; *Republic of India v. India Steamship Co. Ltd (No. 2)* [1998] A.C.
878, 897–898; *Hodgkinson & Corby Ltd v. Wards Mobility Services Ltd* [1998] F.S.R. 530.

[60] *Henderson v. Henderson* (1843) 3 Hare 100, 115; *Greenhalgh v. Mallard* [1947] 2 All E.R. 255;
Fidelitas Shipping Co. Ltd v. V/O Exportchleb [1966] 1 Q.B. 630, 640; *Yat Tung Investment Co. Ltd
v. Dao Heng Bank Ltd* [1975] A.C. 581, 590; *L. E. Walwin & Partners Ltd v. West Sussex C.C.* [1975]
3 All E.R. 604; *Brisbane City Council v. Att.-Gen. for Queensland* [1979] A.C. 411, 425; *Green v.
Hampshire C.C.* [1979] I.C.R. 861, 865–866; *Vervaeke v. Smith* [1983] 1 A.C. 145; *Dallal v. Bank
Mellat* [1986] Q.B. 441, 452; *The European Gateway* [1987] Q.B. 206, 212, 221; *S.C.F. Finance Co.
Ltd v. Masri (No. 3)* [1987] Q.B. 1028, 1049; *Talbot v. Berkshire C.C.* [1994] Q.B. 290, 296.

[61] *Fidelitas Shipping Co. Ltd v. V/O Exportchleb* [1966] 1 Q.B. 630, 640; *Yat Tung Investment Co.
Ltd v. Dao Heng Bank Ltd* [1975] A.C. 581, 590; *Bragg v. Oceanus Mutual Underwriting Assn
(Bermuda) Ltd* [1982] 2 Lloyd's Rep. 132; *J.H. Rayner (Mincing Lane) Ltd v. Bank fur Gemein-
wirtschaft A.G.* [1983] 1 Lloyd's Rep. 462; *Siporex Trade SA v. Comdel Commodities Ltd* [1986] 2
Lloyd's Rep. 428, 432–434; *The Mekhanik Evgrafov* [1988] 1 Lloyd's Rep. 330; *Barrow v. Bankside
Agency Ltd* [1996] 1 W.L.R. 257.

[62] *Dallal v. Bank Mellat* [1988] Q.B. 441, 452. The closeness of the link can be seen in the fact that
Henderson v. Henderson, supra, has been explained as an example of the extension of cause of action
estoppel (*Arnold v. National Westminster Bank plc, supra,* at 105) and of the exercise of the inherent
jurisdiction of the court (*Yat Tung Investment Co. Ltd v. Dao Heng Bank Ltd, supra,* at 590). See to
the same effect *Greenhalgh v. Mallard* [1947] 2 All E.R. 255; *Hunter v. Chief Constable of West
Midlands* [1982] A.C. 529, 540; *The European Gateway* [1987] Q.B. 206, 212, 221 and *S.C.F.
Finance Co. Ltd v. Masri (No. 3)* [1987] Q.B. 1028, 1049; *cf. Barrow v. Bankside Agency Ltd* [1996]
1 W.L.R. 257.

[63] *Yat Tung Investment Co. Ltd v. Dao Heng Bank Ltd* [1975] A.C. 581, 590; *Bragg v. Oceanus
Mutual Underwriting Assn (Bermuda) Ltd* [1982] 2 Lloyd's Rep. 132, 137, 138–139; *J. H. Rayner
(Mincing Lane) Ltd v. Bank fur Gemeinwirtschaft A.G.* [1983] 1 Lloyd's Rep. 462, 469; *North West
Water Ltd v. Binnie & Partners* [1990] 3 All E.R. 547, 553; *House of Spring Gardens Ltd v. Waite*
[1991] 1 Q.B. 241, 254–255.

[64] Although the CPR do not expressly require the defence to be specifically pleaded, it is advisable
to continue to plead it specifically. The new rules relating to the contents of the defence are set out
in CPR, Part 16.5. See also *Morrison, Rose and Partners v. Hillman* [1961] 2 Q.B. 266; *Lee v.
Citibank N.A.* [1981] H.K.L.R. 470 (irrelevancy of which proceedings were first commenced).

more usual course is to apply to the court for an order that the statement of claim, or part thereof, be struck out and the action stayed or dismissed.[65]

26–013   **Issue estoppel: exceptional circumstances.** So far as cause of action estoppel is concerned, the rule appears to be absolute[66]: a party cannot relitigate the same cause of action even if new facts or law have subsequently come to light.[67] But there may be circumstances in issue estoppel where the justice of allowing the matter to be relitigated outweighs the hardship to the successful party in the first action in having to relitigate the point.[68] Thus a party may not be estopped if further material which is relevant to the correctness or incorrectness of the assertion and could not by reasonable diligence have been adduced by that party in the previous proceedings has since become available to him[69] or if there has been a change in the law subsequent to the previous proceedings.[70]

26–014   **Ineffective judgments.** A judgment obtained by covin, collusion or fraud is no bar to a subsequent action in respect of the same subject matter.[71] Similarly, a judgment obtained in a court which had no jurisdiction to pronounce it is without legal effect.[72]

26–015   **Foreign judgments.**[73] A judgment of a foreign court (including a court in another part of the United Kingdom) did not at common law operate in England as a merger of the original cause of action in respect of which the judgment was given.[74] However, by section 34 of the Civil Jurisdiction and Judgments Act

---

[65] *Carl Zeiss Stiftung v. Rayner & Keeler Ltd (No. 3)* [1970] Ch. 506.

[66] Subject to cases of covin, collusion and fraud and lack of jurisdiction; *post*, § 26–014.

[67] *Arnold v. National Westminster Bank plc* [1991] 2 A.C. 93, 104.

[68] *Carl Zeiss Stiftung v. Rayner & Keeler Ltd (No. 2)* [1967] 1 A.C. 853, 947; *Yat Tung Investment Co. Ltd v. Dao Heng Bank Ltd* [1975] A.C. 581, 590; *Arnold v. National Westminster Bank plc, supra*, at 108–109.

[69] *Mills v. Cooper* [1967] 2 Q.B. 459, 468. See also *Phosphate Sewage Co. v. Mollison* (1879) 4 App.Cas. 801; *Ladd v. Marshall* [1954] 1 W.L.R. 1489, 1491; *McIlkenny v. Chief Constable of West Midlands* [1980] Q.B. 283, 319–320; *Hunter v. Chief Constable of West Midlands* [1982] A.C. 529, 541.

[70] *Arnold v. National Westminster Bank plc, supra.*

[71] *Duchess of Kingston's Case* (1776) 20 St.Tr. 573; *Girdlestone v. Brighton Aquarium Co.* (1879) 4 Ex.D. 107; *Abouloff v. Oppenheimer & Co.* (1882) 10 Q.B.D. 295; *Vadala v. Lawes* (1890) 25 Q.B.D. 310; *Birch v. Birch* [1902] P.130; *Nixon v. Loundes* [1909] 2 Ir.Rep. 1; *Reg. v. Humphreys* [1977] A.C. 1, 39. In the case of an English judgment, it is impeachable in an English court on the ground that it was obtained by fraud but only by the production and establishment of evidence newly discovered since the trial and not reasonably discoverable before the trial (*Boswell v. Coaks (No. 2)* (1894) 86 L.T. 365n). But in the case of a foreign judgment fresh evidence is not required before it can be attacked on the ground of fraud in an English court (*Abouloff v. Oppenheimer & Co.* (1882) 10 Q.B.D. 295). In *Owens Bank Ltd v. Etoile Commerciale SA* [1995] 1 W.L.R. 44 the Privy Council noted this disparity of treatment in disapproving terms and, while they indicated a preference for the general application of the rule which presently governs English judgments, they stopped short of overruling *Abouloff*. However, the Privy Council went on to hold that the court does have an inherent power to prevent misuse of its process and that that power can be exercised to strike out a defence based on an allegation that a foreign judgment has been obtained by fraud where full particulars of the fraud have not been given. *Abouloff* has since been held to be inapplicable to the enforcement of a foreign arbitration award (*Westacre Investments Inc. v. Jugoimport-SPDR Holding Co. Ltd* [1998] 3 W.L.R. 770).

[72] *Rogers v. Wood* (1831) 2 B. & Ad. 245.

[73] See Dicey and Morris, *The Conflict of Laws* (12th ed., 1993), Chap. 14.

[74] *Smith v. Nicolls* (1839) 5 Bing.N.C. 208; *Bank of Australasia v. Harding* (1850) 9 C.B. 661; *Bank of Australasia v. Nias* (1851) 16 Q.B. 717; *Carl Zeiss Stiftung v. Rayner & Keeler Ltd* [1967] 1 A.C. 853, 917, 927, 938; *Re Flynn (No. 2)* [1969] 2 Ch. 403, 412; *Republic of India v. India Steamship Co. Ltd.* [1993] A.C. 410, 417, 423.

1982, no proceedings may be brought[75] by a person in England on a cause of action[76] in respect of which a judgment[77] has been given in his favour in proceedings between the same parties, or their privies, in a court[78] in another part of the United Kingdom[79] or in a court of an overseas country,[80] unless that judgment is not enforceable or entitled to recognition in England. The effect of section 34 is to reverse the common law rule that a foreign judgment does not of itself extinguish the original cause of action in respect of which the judgment was given.[81] But it does not apply the doctrine of merger in judgment to foreign judgments.[82] So it does not exclude the jurisdiction of the court, but rather it provides a bar against proceedings by the claimant, which bar can be defeated by waiver or estoppel.[83] The claimant need not have been one of the original parties to the foreign proceedings, nor need the proceedings have been exclusively civil in character, provided that the judgment is enforceable or entitled to recognition in England.[84] In deciding whether or not the proceedings are between the same parties, or their privies, the court is likely to take a flexible approach and consider whether the reality is that the claim is between the same parties.[85]

Foreign judgments *in personam*. At common law, a foreign judgment *in personam* which is final and conclusive[86] on the merits[87] will be entitled to   **26–016**

---

[75] Proceedings which are "continued" after judgment has been obtained in other proceedings involving the same parties or their privies fall within the scope of "brought" for this purpose: *Republic of India v. India Steamship Co. Ltd (No. 2)* [1998] A.C. 878, 912.

[76] "Cause of action" is used in the technical sense of every fact which it would be necessary for the claimant to prove, if traversed, to obtain the relief which he claims: *Republic of India v. India Steamship Co. Ltd.* [1993] A.C. 410, 419–421; *Black v. Yates* [1992] Q.B. 526, 543–545.

[77] Defined in s.50.

[78] *ibid.*

[79] *ibid.*

[80] *ibid.*

[81] *Republic of India v. India Steamship Co. Ltd.* [1993] A.C. 410, 418; *Republic of India v. India Steamship Co. Ltd (No. 2)* [1998] A.C. 878, 912; Davenport (1994) 110 L.Q.R. 25.

[82] *ibid.* at 423.

[83] *ibid.* at 423–424; *Showlag v. Mansour* [1995] 1 A.C. 431, 441; *Republic of India v. India Steamship Co. Ltd (No. 2)* [1997] 3 W.L.R. 818.

[84] *Black v. Yates* [1992] Q.B. 526, 546–549, distinguishing *Marginson v. Blackburn B.C.* [1939] 2 K.B. 426 on the ground that it was a case of estoppel and not a case of merger (*quaere*, whether this argument can stand in the light of *Republic of India v. India Steamship Co. Ltd.*, *supra*, n. 81) and on the broader ground that Parliament, when enacting s.34, could not have intended to limit the application of the section to previous proceedings in those countries which have an identical form of action to the English form of action brought by the plaintiff.

[85] *Republic of India v. India Steamship Co. Ltd (No. 2)* [1998] A.C. 878, 896, C.A.

[86] *Plummer v. Woodburne* (1825) 4 B. & C. 625; *Scott v. Pilkington* (1862) 2 B. & S. 11; *Nouvion v. Freeman* (1889) 15 App.Cas. 1; *Beatty v. Beatty* [1924] 1 K.B. 807; *Blohn v. Desser* [1962] 2 Q.B. 116; *Colt Industries Inc. v. Sarlie (No. 2)* [1966] 1 W.L.R. 1287; *Berliner Industriebank A.G. v. Jost* [1971] 2 Q.B. 463; *Helmville Ltd v. Astilleros Espanoles SA* [1984] 2 Lloyd's Rep. 569. *cf. Harrop v. Harrop* [1920] 3 K.B. 386; *Re Macartney* [1921] 1 Ch. 522; *Westfal-Larson & Co. A.S. v. Ikerigi Compania Naviera SA* [1983] 1 Lloyd's Rep. 424. A foreign judgment may be final and conclusive even though it is subject to appeal or is under appeal; but *cf.* Administration of Justice Act 1920, s.9(2)(e); Foreign Judgments (Reciprocal Enforcement) Act 1933, ss.1(3), 5(1).

[87] *Carl-Zeiss Stiftung v. Rayner & Keeler Ltd (No. 2)* [1967] 1 A.C. 853, 917, 925, 967 (estoppel *per rem judicatam*). In the context of issue estoppel, a decision "on the merits" may be procedural in nature: *D.S.V. Silo-und Verwaltungsgesellschaft mbH v. Owners of the Sennar* [1985] 1 W.L.R. 490. *cf. Charm Maritime Inc. v. Kyriakou* [1987] 1 F.T.L.R. 265, CA; *Harris v. Quine* (1869) L.R. 4 Q.B. 653 (limitation); *Black-Clawson International Ltd v. Papierworke-Aschaffenburg A.G.* [1975] A.C. 591 (limitation), but see now the Foreign Limitation Periods Act 1984, s.3; *post*, § 29–151.

recognition in England,[88] provided that it is given by a court having jurisdiction to give the judgment[89] and is not impeachable on grounds of fraud, public policy or breach of natural justice.[90] In the case of a judgment given by a court of a state party to either the Brussels Convention on Jurisdiction and Enforcement of Judgments in Civil and Commercial Matters[91] or the Lugano Convention on Jurisdiction and Enforcement of Judgments in Civil and Commercial Matters[92] and which falls within the scope of either Convention, the judgment will (and must) be recognised in England.[93] Although certain exceptions are provided for in both Conventions,[94] these are very limited in nature and in particular an English court cannot ordinarily question the jurisdiction of the court by which the judgment was given.[95] Where the judgment is that of a court in another part of the United Kingdom, *i.e.* in Scotland or Northern Ireland, it would appear that such a judgment is entitled to recognition, and may be impeached, in accordance with the common law[96]; but the judgment cannot be refused recognition in England solely on the ground that, in relation to that judgment, the court which gave it was not a court of competent jurisdiction according to the rules of private international law in force in England.[97]

26–017   **Estoppel by foreign judgment *in personam*.** A foreign judgment which is entitled to recognition in England may also, if given in favour of the defendant,

---

[88] See Dicey and Morris *op. cit.,* pp. 461–462. See also Administration of Justice Act 1920; Foreign Judgments (Reciprocal Enforcement) Act 1933; Dicey and Morris *op. cit.,* pp. 519–530. Where there are two competing foreign judgments, each of which is pronounced by a court of competent jurisdiction and is final and not open to impeachment on any ground, then the general rule is that the earlier of them in time must be recognised and given effect to, to the exclusion of the latter, although there may be circumstances under which the party holding the earlier judgment may be estopped from relying on it: *Showlag v. Mansour* [1995] 1 A.C. 431.

[89] *i.e.* according to the rules of English private international law: see Dicey and Morris *op. cit.,* pp. 472–494. See also Administration of Justice Act 1920, s.9(2)(a), (b); Foreign Judgments (Reciprocal Enforcement) Act 1933, ss.4(1)(a)(ii), 2(a); Civil Jurisdiction and Judgments Act 1982, s.33 (as amended by Sched. 2, para. 15 to Civil Jurisdiction and Judgments Act 1991).

[90] See Dicey & Morris *op. cit.,* pp. 505–519. By statute, an overseas judgment may also be refused recognition if it is given in proceedings brought in breach of an agreement for settlement of a dispute: see Civil Jurisdiction and Judgments Act 1982, s.32 (as amended by Sched. 2, para. 14 to Civil Jurisdiction and Judgments Act 1991); *Tracomin SA v. Sudan Oil Seeds Co. Ltd (Nos 1 and 2)* [1983] 1 W.L.R. 1026, 1427; Dicey and Morris *op. cit.,* pp. 493–494. See also Administration of Justice Act 1920, s.9(2)(c), (d), (f); Foreign Judgments (Reciprocal Enforcement) Act 1933, ss.4(1)(a)(iv), (v), 8(1), (2); *Owens Bank Ltd v. Bracco* [1992] 2 A.C. 443; *House of Spring Gardens Ltd v. Waite* [1991] 1 Q.B. 241; *Owens Bank Ltd v. Etoile Commerciale SA* [1995] 1 W.L.R. 44.

[91] (1968) together with the 1971 Protocol thereto, both as amended by the Convention on Accession (1978). See the Civil Jurisdiction and Judgments Act 1982, s.2(2) and Scheds. 1, 2, 3. See Dicey & Morris *op. cit.,* pp. 530–542

[92] (1988). See the Civil Jurisdiction and Judgments Act 1982, s.3A and Sched. 3C.

[93] Civil Jurisdiction and Judgments Act 1982, s.2(1) and Sched. 1; Arts. 26, 29, 30 (Brussels Convention) and s.3A(1) and Sched. 3C, Arts. 26, 29, 30 (Lugano Convention). The relationship between the two Conventions is regulated by Art. 54B of the Lugano Convention.

[94] *ibid.* Arts 27, 28 (of both Conventions). An English court should not normally entertain a challenge to a Convention judgment in circumstances in which it would not permit a challenge to an English judgment: *Interdesco SA v. Nullifire Ltd* [1992] 1 Lloyd's Rep. 180, 187–188.

[95] *ibid.* Art. 28 (of both Conventions).

[96] This would appear to be the effect of s.19 of the Civil Jurisdiction and Judgments Act 1982, since the section is negative in its wording. But see s.18 and Scheds 6 and 7 (enforcement).

[97] s.19(1), (2) (subject to s.19(3)) of the Civil Jurisdiction and Judgments Act 1982. For definitions, see *ibid.* s.50.

be relied upon to establish an estoppel *per rem judicatam*[98] and thus afford a good defence to an action in England between the same parties, or their privies, for the same matter.[99] Issue estoppel may arise in respect of an issue determined by previous proceedings in a foreign court.[1]

Foreign judgment *in rem*. A foreign judgment *in rem*, *e.g.* a judgment which   **26–018** determines the right to, or disposition of, some *res*[2] such as a ship or other chattel within the territorial jurisdiction of the foreign court,[3] probably acts as an assignment of the *res*.[4] The adjudication is recognised as binding upon the whole world.

2. ALTERATION OR CANCELLATION OF A WRITTEN INSTRUMENT

Material alteration. If a promisee, without the consent of the promisor,   **26–019** deliberately makes a material[5] alteration in a specialty or other instrument containing words of contract, this will discharge the promisor from all liability thereon, even though the original words of the instrument are still legible.[6] The principle which lies behind this rule has been said to be that "no man shall be permitted to take the chance of committing a fraud, without running any risk of losing by the event, when it is detected."[7] The promisor is therefore not discharged if the alteration is made by accident[8] or by mistake.[9] More difficult to justify, however, is the supposed rule that a material alteration made by a stranger while the instrument is in the custody of the promisee discharges the promisor from his obligation.[10] The reason for this is said to be that the alteration of the

---

[98] See *ante*, §§ 26–010—26–013.

[99] *Ricardo v. Garcias* (1845) 12 Cl. & Fin. 368; *Société Generale de Paris v. Dreyfus Bros.* (1887) 37 Ch.D. 215; *Taylor v. Holland* [1902] 1 K.B. 676, 681; *Jacobson v. Frachon* (1927) 138 L.T. 386; *House of Spring Gardens Ltd v. Waite* [1991] 1 Q.B. 241. See Dicey & Morris *op. cit.*, pp. 466–468, 499–503.

[1] *Carl Zeiss Stiftung v. Rayner & Keeler Ltd (No. 2)* [1967] 1 A.C. 853, 918, 925–927, 966–967 (contrast, *ibid.* at 937–938, 948–949); *Helmville Ltd v. Astilleros Espanoles SA* [1984] 2 Lloyd's Rep. 569; *D.S.V. Silo-und Verwaltungsgesellschaft mbH v. Owners of the Sennar* [1985] 1 W.L.R. 490, 499; *Black v. Yates* [1992] Q.B. 526, 551–552; *Desert Sun Loan Corpn v. Hill* [1996] 2 All E.R. 847 (no issue estoppel arose because not sufficiently clear that the specific issue which arose before the court had been identified and decided against the defendant in the foreign court).

[2] *Fracis, Times & Co. v. Carr* (1900) 82 L.T. 698, 701.

[3] *The Henrich Björn* (1886) 11 App.Cas. 270, 276, 277; *Castrique v. Imrie* (1870) L.R. 4 H.L. 414, 429; *Re Trufort* (1887) 36 Ch.D. 600.

[4] Dicey and Morris *op. cit.*, pp. 495–499.

[5] See *post*, § 26–021.

[6] *Pigot's Case* (1614) 11 Co.Rep. 26b (deed); *Master v. Miller* (1791) 4 Term Rep. 320; *Croockewit v. Fletcher* (1857) 1 H. & N. 893; *Sellin v. Price* (1867) L.R. 2 Ex. 189, and cases cited in n. 20, *post.* cf. *Hamelin v. Bruck* (1846) 9 Q.B. 306; *Pattinson v. Luckley* (1875) L.R. 10 Ex. 330. See generally *Norton on Deeds* (2nd ed.), p. 34; Holmes (1897) 10 Harvard L.R. 457, 473; Williston (1904) 18 Harvard L.R. 105, 165. For the effect of alteration on joint obligations, see *ante*, § 18–002; for negotiable instruments, see *post*, § 26–002.

[7] *Master v. Miller* (1791) 4 Term Rep. 320, 329.

[8] *Hongkong and Shanghai Bank v. Lo Lee Shi* [1928] A.C. 181.

[9] *Henfree v. Bromley* (1805) 6 East 309; *Wilkinson v. Johnson* (1824) 3 B. & C. 428.

[10] *Pigot's Case, supra*, at n. 3; *Davidson v. Cooper* (1844) 13 M. & W. 343; *Crookewit v. Fletcher* (1857) 1 H. & N. 893, 912.

instrument may raise a doubt as to its identity.[11] If this is so, the reason is both illogical and inadequate. It is illogical, because the same doubt would be raised, whether or not the instrument was in the custody of the promisee, and it is inadequate, because extrinsic evidence would be admissible to prove the true words of the agreement.[12] On the other hand, if the reason for the rule is that an alteration made while the document is in the custody of the promisee raises a suspicion that it was made with his connivance or consent, the situation is already adequately covered, since it is incumbent on the party seeking to enforce an altered instrument to show that the alteration was made in such circumstances as not to invalidate it.[13] The acceptance of the rule would mean that an alteration by an officious burglar would discharge the contract.[14] Such a conclusion has rightly been doubted[15] and it is submitted that the rule should be discarded.

26–020   **Burden of proof.** The burden of proving that the promisee has, without the consent of the promisor, deliberately made a material alteration to a written instrument would appear to be on the promisor.[16] But, once it has been proved or it is apparent from the face of the instrument that it has been altered, the burden of proof switches to the promisee to show that the alteration was made in circumstances which were insufficient to discharge the promisee from all liability under the instrument (for example, by proving that the alteration was made before the promisor signed the document).[17] The question whether an alteration is material is a matter of law for the court.[18]

26–021   **Immaterial alteration.** An instrument is not discharged by an immaterial alteration, that is to say, one which does not alter the legal effect of the instrument or impose a greater liability on the promisor.[19] Thus the addition, without the assent of the maker, of the words "on demand" to a promissory note did not vitiate the instrument, since the alteration only expressed the legal effect of the

---

[11] *Sanderson v. Symonds* (1819) 1 B. & B. 426, 430.

[12] See *ante*, § 12–110.

[13] *Johnson v. Duke of Marlborough* (1818) 2 Stark. 313; *Bishop v. Chambre* (1827) Moo. & M. 116.

[14] Williams, *Joint Obligations*, § 67.

[15] *Lowe v. Fox* (1887) 12 App.Cas. 206, 217.

[16] There does not appear to be any authority in English law for this proposition but it flows from the general principle that he who alleges must prove. See generally on alterations *Phipson on Evidence* (14th ed.), §§ 35–28—35–31.

[17] *Johnson v. Duke of Marlborough* (1818) 2 Stark 313, 317; *Bishop v. Chambre* (1827) M. & M. 116; *Henman v. Dickinson* (1828) 5 Bing. 183; *Knight v. Clements* (1838) 8 A. & E. 215, 220; *Cariss v. Tatterswell* (1841) 2 M. & G. 890; *Clifford v. Parker* (1841) 2 M. & G. 909, 911. See also *Halsbury's Laws of England* (4th ed.), Vol. 9, para. 597 and the notes to *Master v. Miller* 1 Smith L.C. (13th ed.), pp. 807, 818. A different rule would appear to apply to deeds because, in the case of a deed, there is a presumption that the alteration was made before the deed was delivered, so that the promisor bears the burden of proving that the alteration was made after the deed was delivered: *Doe d. Tatum v. Catomore* (1851) 16 Q.B. 745, 747; *Halsbury's Laws of England* (4th ed.), Vol. 12, para. 1453.

[18] *Vance v. Lowther* (1876) 1 Ex. D. 176, 178. The burden of proof would appear to be on the promisee to show that the alterations did not alter the liabilities of the parties on the instrument: *Koch v. Dicks* [1933] 1 K.B. 307, 321.

[19] *Pigot's Case, supra*, as qualified in *Aldous v. Cornwell* (1868) L.R. 3 Q.B. 573 and *Bishop of Crediton v. Bishop of Exeter* [1905] 2 Ch. 455. For the test of materiality, see *Gardner v. Walsh* (1855) 5 E. & B. 83, 89; *Suffell v. Bank of England* (1882) 9 Q.B.D. 555, 568, 574, 575; *Koch v. Dicks* [1933] 1 K.B. 307, 320; *Kwei Tek Chao v. British Traders and Shippers Ltd* [1954] 2 Q.B. 459, 475.

note as originally drawn.[20] The alteration in a charterparty of the time of sailing has been held to be material as it altered its legal effect.[21]

Negotiable instruments. By section 64(1) of the Bills of Exchange Act 1882,   26–022
where a bill or acceptance is materially altered[22] without the assent of all parties liable on the bill, the bill is avoided, except as against a party who himself made, authorised or assented to the alteration, and subsequent indorsers[23]; provided that, where a bill has been materially altered, but the alteration is not apparent, and the bill is in the hands of a holder in due course, such holder may avail himself of the bill as if it had not been altered, and may enforce payment of it according to its original tenor.[24]

Bank of England notes. In the case of notes issued by the Bank of England,   26–023
even an alteration which does not affect the contract may be sufficient to avoid the instrument. Thus where such notes had been fraudulently altered by erasing the numbers on them and substituting others with the object of preventing the notes from being traced, the Court of Appeal held that although the alteration did not vary the contract, it was material in the sense of altering the notes in an essential part and that the notes were therefore void.[25]

Cancellation. In early law, the accidental destruction or cancellation of a deed   26–024
or of its seal prevented it being sued upon.[26] Now only the intentional cancellation by the promisee of a bond[27] or bill or promissory note[28] is sufficient.

Loss. The loss of a deed or written instrument does not destroy the obligation,   26–025
but only affects the question of proving the instrument.[29] By section 69 of the Bills of Exchange Act 1882 the holder has the right to a duplicate of a lost bill.[30]

---

[20] *Aldous v. Cornwell, supra.* See also *Waugh v. Bussell* (1814) 5 Taunt. 707; *Sanderson v. Symonds, supra*; *Wood v. Slack* (1868) L.R. 3 Q.B. 379; *Decroix v. Meyer* (1890) 25 Q.B.D. 343; *Re Howgate and Osborne's Contract* [1902] 1 Ch. 451; *Bishop of Crediton v. Bishop of Exeter, supra.*

[21] *Croockewit v. Fletcher* (1857) 1 H. & N. 893. See also *Davidson v. Cooper* (1844) 13 M. & W. 343; *Re United Kingdom Shipowning Co. Ltd* (1865) 2 De G.J. & Sm. 456; *Sellin v. Price* (1867) L.R. 2 Ex. 189; *Suffell v. Bank of England, supra*; *Slingsby v. District Bank* [1932] 1 K.B. 544; *Koch v. Dicks, supra.*

[22] A material alteration is partly defined by s.64(2). See generally *Chalmers and Guest on Bills of Exchange* (15th ed., 1998), pp. 532–534 and Vol. II, §§ 34–142—34–143.

[23] *Master v. Miller* (1791) 4 Term Rep. 320; *Burchfield v. Moore* (1854) 23 L.J.Q.B. 261; *Woollatt v. Stanley* (1928) 138 L.T. 620.

[24] *Scholfield v. Londesborough* [1896] A.C. 514; *Imperial Bank of Canada v. Bank of Hamilton* [1903] A.C. 49; *London Joint Stock Bank v. Macmillan* [1918] A.C. 777.

[25] *Suffell v. Bank of England* (1882) 9 Q.B.D. 555; *Slingsby v. Westminster Bank* [1931] 1 K.B. 173; *Slingsby v. District Bank* [1932] 1 K.B. 544; *Arab Bank v. Ross* [1952] 2 Q.B. 216. *cf. Leeds Bank v. Walker* (1883) 11 Q.B.D. 84; *Hongkong and Shanghai Bank v. Lo Lee Shi* [1928] A.C. 181.

[26] Shep.Touch. 69; *Nichols v. Haywood* (1545) Dyer 59a (seal eaten by mice).

[27] *Bamberger v. Commercial Credit Co.* (1855) 15 C.B. 676, 693; *Perrott v. Perrott* (1811) 14 East 423; *Carew v. White* (1829) 2 Moo. & P. 558.

[28] Bills of Exchange Act 1882, s.63. See Vol. II, § 34–141.

[29] *Read v. Price* [1909] 2 K.B. 724, 737.

[30] See also s.70 of the Act and Vol. II, §§ 34–147, 34–148.

3. Miscellaneous Modes of Discharge

26–026   **Death.** A personal contract is discharged by the death of either party.[31]

26–027   **Bankruptcy.** Proceedings in bankruptcy may act as a discharge of rights and liabilities under a contract.[32]

26–028   **Winding up.** The winding up of a company may result in a stay of proceedings in contract against the company and the discharge of the contract.[33]

26–029   **Set-off and counterclaim.** Where an action is brought for damages for breach of contract, the defendant may claim a set-off or counterclaim in the same action, and judgment may be given for the balance in favour of the claimant or the defendant.[34] This judgment operates to discharge the obligations involved in the claim and set-off or counterclaim. The position is otherwise where the defendant claims a set-off but does not make a counterclaim. In such a case the defendant can later issue fresh proceedings against the claimant even though the claimant has accepted a payment into court made by the defendant in settlement of the claimant's claim against the defendant and the allegations made by the defendant are essentially the same as those pleaded in his defence to the claimant's action.[35]

26–030   **Limitation.** A right of action arising out of a breach of contract may be barred or extinguished by the operation of the Limitation Act 1980 or other limitation enactment.[36]

---

[31] See *ante*, §§ 21–006, 24–036; Vol. II, § 39–154.
[32] See *ante*, §§ 21–032—21–035, 21–037, 21–046—21–048.
[33] See *ante*, §§ 9–049—9–054.
[34] CPR, Part 20, r. 2, Part 16, r. 6.
[35] *Hoppe v. Titman* [1996] 1 W.L.R. 841. The Court of Appeal reached this conclusion with some reluctance but, on the facts, there was no suggestion from the plaintiffs, when the payment in was made, that it was intended to take into account and satisfy their own cause of action for breach of contract.
[36] See *post*, Chap. 29.

Part Seven
REMEDIES FOR BREACH OF CONTRACT

CHAPTER 27

DAMAGES[1]

1. Nature and Kinds of Damages

(a) *In General*

Introduction. Subject to a few controls,[2] the parties to a contract may them-   **27–001**
selves specify in their contract the remedy available to the innocent party
following the other's breach. In the absence of any such "tailor-made" clause on

---

[1] On the whole subject of damages, see *McGregor on Damages* (16th ed., 1997); Harris, *Remedies in Contract and Tort* (1988), Chaps. 1–14; Waddams, *The Law of Damages* (3rd ed.); Ogus, *The Law of Damages* (1973); Burrows, *Remedies for Torts and Breach of Contract* (2nd ed.); Beale, *Remedies for Breach of Contract* (1980); Street, *Principles of the Law of Damages* (1962), especially Chap. 10. For a comparison between common law and civil law, see Treitel, *Remedies for Breach of Contract* (1988), Chaps. IV to VII.

[2] *e.g.* the law on penalties *post,* §§ 27–102 *et seq.*; and statutory controls such as the Unfair Contract Terms Act 1977 (*ante* §§ 14–057 *et seq.*), the Unfair Terms in Consumer Contracts Regulations 1994 (*ante,* §§ 15–001 *et seq.*) and the Consumer Credit Act 1974 (*post,* Vol. II, §§ 38–002 *et seq.*)

the remedy, the law on damages fills the gap with standard-form provisions on the assessment of money compensation which apply to all types of contract.[3] Damages for a breach of contract committed by the defendant are a compensation to the claimant for the damage, loss or injury he has suffered through that breach.[4] He is, as far as money can do it, to be placed in the same position as if the contract had been performed. This implies a "net loss" approach in which the gains made by the claimant as the result of the breach (*e.g.* savings made because he is relieved from performing his side of a contract which has been terminated for breach; savings in taxation; benefits obtained from partial performance; or the salvage value of something left in his hands) must be set off against his losses arising from the breach (after he has taken reasonable steps to minimise those losses).[5] In assessing damages for breach of contract, the court can take account of only strict, legal obligations: it cannot take account of "the expectations, however reasonable, of one contractor that the other will do something that he has assumed no legal obligation to do."[6] Thus, if the contract-breaker had a choice of alternative methods of performance, damages will be assessed on the basis of his minimum legal obligation, *viz.* on the alternative which would have been least onerous, or most beneficial to him.[7] If the claimant cannot establish an actual loss, he is entitled only to nominal damages.[8] Even where the claimant can prove his loss, damages are hardly ever a full recompense, since "it must be remembered that the rules as to damages can in the nature of things only be approximately just."[9] The law on damages places various conditions and restrictions on the principle that the claimant is generally entitled to recover all he has lost by the breach.

27–002 **"Expectation" and "reliance" interests.** A distinction has been drawn[10] between the "expectation interest" and the "reliance interest" of the claimant: the former relates to the gains or benefits[11] which he expected to receive from the completion of the promised performance of the other party's obligation but

---

[3] Harris *op. cit.* pp. 52–57.

[4] *Robinson v. Harman* (1848) 1 Exch. 850, 855; *Lock v. Furze* (1866) L.R. 1 C.P. 441, 450–451, 453; *Livingstone v. Rawyards Coal Co.* (1880) 5 App.Cas. 25, 39; *Wertheim v. Chicoutimi Pulp Co.* [1911] A.C. 301, 307; *British Westinghouse Electric Co. Ltd v. Underground Electric Rys.* [1912] A.C. 673, 689; *Watts & Co. Ltd v. Mitsui & Co. Ltd* [1917] A.C. 227, 241; *Banco de Portugal v. Waterlow & Sons Ltd* [1932] A.C. 452, 474; *Monarch SS. Co. Ltd v. Karlshamns Oljefabriker (A/B)* [1949] A.C. 196, 220–221; *C. Czarnikow Ltd v. Koufos* [1969] 1 A.C. 350, 414; *Johnson v. Agnew* [1980] A.C. 367, 400; *Surrey County Council v. Bredero Homes Ltd* [1993] 1 W.L.R. 1361, 1364.

[5] The language of "balancing" or "setting off" gains and losses is used by the House of Lords in the *British Westinghouse* case, *supra* at 691, and in *Westwood v. Secretary of State for Employment* [1985] A.C. 20, 44.

[6] *Lavarack v. Woods of Colchester Ltd* [1967] 1 Q.B. 278, 294 (distinguished in a case of "unfair dismissal": *York Trailer Ltd v. Sparkes* [1973] I.R.C. 518; *cf. Janciuk v. Winerite Ltd* [1998] I.R.L.R. 63). See also *post*, § 27–036.

[7] See *post*, § 27–036.

[8] See *post*, § 27–007.

[9] *Rodocanachi v. Milburn* (1886) 18 Q.B.D. 67, 78. But see Street *op. cit.* Chap. 5 and *cf.* the use of actuarial calculations approved by the House of Lords in *Wells v. Wells* [1998] 3 W.L.R. 329.

[10] Street *op. cit.* pp. 240–247; Fuller and Perdue (1937) 46 Yale L.J. 52, 373 (on this article, see Friedmann (1995) 111 L.Q.R. 628). (A third interest, the "restitution" interest, is protected by other rules: see *post*, §§ 27–021, 30–048 *et seq.*) In *Surrey County Council v. Bredero Homes Ltd* [1993] 1 W.L.R. 1361, 1369, Steyn L.J. accepted this three-fold division of the interests protected by the award of damages.

[11] "Benefit" may include a personal or subjective, even idiosyncratic, benefit: see *post*, § 27–070. The "performance interest" is another concept used by some writers, *e.g.* Coote [1997] C.L.J. 537.

which were in the event prevented by the breach of contract committed by the latter[12]; the reliance interest relates to the expense or loss which the claimant has himself incurred in reliance on the promised performance[13] and which is wasted by the defendant's breach.[14] Both interests are protected by the law on damages, but it is not yet clear whether English law permits the claimant to recover both his expected profit on the contract and the consequential expense he has incurred in reliance on the defendant's promise.[15] In principle, he should be entitled to recover his expected *net* profit plus any of his incidental expenditure of a type reasonably contemplated by the parties at the time the contract was made, but not his *gross* profit (*e.g.* the full contract price) plus his disbursements which would have been incurred in earning that gross profit.[16]

Damages in lieu of specific performance or injunction. The court is   **27–003** empowered to award damages in addition to, or in substitution for an order for specific performance or an injunction: the assessment of damages under this power is examined in the next chapter.[17]

Concurrent liability. If the claimant is able to sue in tort (*i.e.* there is   **27–004** concurrent liability,[18] which has been considerably widened by *Henderson v. Merrett*[19]) he will be able to take advantage of the more favourable rules on damages in tort, *e.g.* on remoteness of damage.[20] But concurrent liability in tort may benefit the defendant, *e.g.* in regard to contributory negligence.[21]

Kinds of damages: general and special damages. Various types of damages   **27–005** are distinguished for different purposes; the more important types are examined in the succeeding paragraphs. Thus, the distinction between general damages and special damages is mainly a matter of pleading and evidence. General damages are given in respect of such damage as the law presumes to result from the infringement of a legal right or duty[22]: damage must be proved but the claimant cannot quantify exactly any particular items in it.[23] The main meaning[24] of

---

[12] See, *e.g. post*, §§ 27–054—27–057.

[13] Costs incurred by the claimant in attempting to mitigate (see *post*, § 27–098) are incurred as a result of the defendant's breach and are therefore outside this definition.

[14] See, *e.g. post*, §§ 27–058—27–063; Vol. II, §§ 43–417—43–419. See also Owen (1984) 4 O.J.L.S. 393. The reliance interest includes the award of damages in some situations to restore the claimant to the position he would have been in if he had not entered a particular transaction: see *post* § 27–065.

[15] Street *op. cit.* pp. 243–245.

[16] Street *op. cit.* p. 245; Morris L.J. (dissenting) in *Cullinane v. British "Rema" Manufacturing Co.* [1954] 1 Q.B. 292 (the majority of the Court of Appeal in this case held that the plaintiff must elect between claiming reliance expenditure and claiming loss of expected profits: see *post*, § 27–063 and Vol. II, § 43–421.

[17] *Post*, §§ 28–071 *et seq.*

[18] See *ante*, §§ 1–059—1–122.

[19] [1995] 2 A.C. 145.

[20] *Post*, §§ 27–039 *et seq.*

[21] *Post*, § 27–037.

[22] Pollock, *Contracts* (13th ed.), p. 536. *cf.* the cases on dishonouring a cheque, Vol. II, § 34–302.

[23] *Aerial Advertising Co. v. Batchelor's Peas Ltd* [1938] 2 All E.R. 788; and *cf. Sunley & Co. Ltd v. Cunard White Star Ltd* [1940] 1 K.B. 740.

[24] For other meanings, see Street *op. cit.* pp. 18–22. One meaning which has recently been used again is the reference to damages under the second rule in *Hadley v. Baxendale* (1854) 9 Exch. 341 (*post*, §§ 27–049 *et seq.*): see *President of India v. La Pintada Compania Navegacion SA* [1985] A.C. 104, 125–127.

special damages is that precise amount of pecuniary loss which the claimant can prove to have followed from the particular facts set out in his pleadings. Special damage must be specifically pleaded and evidence relevant to it cannot be adduced if only general damages have been pleaded,[25] since the purpose of pleading special damage is to prevent surprise at the trial by giving the defendant prior notice of any item in the claim for which a definite amount can be given in evidence, *e.g.* in a claim for wrongful dismissal, loss of salary during the period of notice required by the contract.[26] A claimant who bases his claim on precise calculations must give the defendant access to the facts on which they are based[27]: thus it was held that where loss of profits was not a necessary consequence of the alleged breach of contract the claim for such loss should be specifically pleaded, in order to give the defendant fair warning of the claim.[28]

27–006   **Difficulty of assessment.** The fact that damages are difficult to assess does not disentitle the plaintiff to compensation for loss resulting from the defendant's breach of contract.[29] Where it is clear that the claimant has suffered substantial loss, but the evidence does not enable it to be precisely quantified, the court will assess damages as best it can on the available evidence.[30] Similarly, the fact that the amount of that loss cannot be precisely ascertained, as, for example, where it depends on a contingency, does not deprive the claimant of a remedy. Where, if the defendant had fully performed his undertaking, there was only a chance that the claimant would acquire a benefit or make a profit, the court will discount the damages to reflect the likelihood that the benefit or profit would have been received.[31] The loss of profits suffered by a claimant as the result of the defendant's breach of contract frequently depends on many speculative factors, but the courts will always attempt to assess the amount of the loss.[32]

(b) *Nominal Damages*

27–007   **Nominal damages.** Wherever the defendant is liable for a breach of contract, the claimant is in general entitled to nominal damages although no actual damage is proved[33]; the violation of a right at common law will usually entitle the claimant to nominal damages without proof of special damage.[34] Normally, this situation arises when the defendant's breach of contract has in fact caused no loss to the claimant, but it may also arise when the claimant, although he has suffered

---

[25] *Hayward v. Pullinger and Partners Ltd* [1950] 1 All E.R. 581; *Anglo-Cyprian Trade Agencies Ltd v. Paphos Wine Industries Ltd* [1951] 1 All E.R. 873. See also *The Susquehanna* [1926] A.C. 655, 661; *National Broach and Machine Co. v. Churchill Gear Machines Ltd* [1965] 1 W.L.R. 1199 (this decision was accepted by the appellants in the House of Lords: [1967] 1 W.L.R. 384).

[26] *Hayward v. Pullinger and Partners Ltd, ante.* See Vol. II, § 39–180.

[27] *Perestrello e Companhia Limitada v. United Paint Co. Ltd* [1969] 1 W.L.R. 570.

[28] *ibid.*

[29] *Chaplin v. Hicks* [1911] 2 K.B. 786 (*post*, § 27–034(b)); *Simpson v. L.N.W. Ry.* (1876) 1 Q.B.D. 274.

[30] *Tai Hing Cotton Mill Ltd v. Kamsing Knitting Factory* [1979] A.C. 91, 106. *cf. post*, § 27–081.

[31] See *post*, §§ 27–034—27–035.

[32] See *post*, §§ 27–054—27–057.

[33] *Marzetti v. Williams* (1830) 1 B. & Ad. 415; *The Mediana* [1900] A.C. 113, 116; *Surrey County Council v. Bredero Homes Ltd* [1993] 1 W.L.R. 1361.

[34] *Ashby v. White* (1704) 2 Ld.Raym. 938; *Constantine v. Imperial Hotels Ltd* [1944] K.B. 693. On nominal damages when a bank wrongly dishonours a customer's cheque, see Vol. II, §§ 34–302.

loss, fails to prove any loss flowing from the breach of contract,[35] or fails to prove the actual amount of his loss.[36] A regular use of nominal damages, however, is to establish the infringement of the claimant's legal right, and sometimes the award of nominal damages is "a mere peg on which to hang costs."[37]

(c) *Claims for an Agreed Sum*

Distinction between claims for payment of an agreed sum and claims for   **27–008**
damages. There is an important distinction between a claim for payment of a debt and a claim for damages for breach of contract. A debt is a definite sum of money fixed by the agreement of the parties as payable by one party in return for the performance of a specified obligation by the other party or upon the occurrence of some specified event or condition[38]; damages may be claimed from a party who has broken his contractual obligation in some way other than failure to pay such a debt. (It is also possible that, in addition to a claim for a debt, there may be a claim for damages in respect of consequential loss caused by the failure to pay such a debt at the due date.[39]) The relevance of this distinction is that rules on damages do not apply to a claim for a debt, *e.g.* the claimant who claims payment of a debt need not prove anything more than his performance[40] or the occurrence of the event or condition[41]; there is no need for him to prove any actual loss suffered by him[42] as a result[43] of the defendant's failure to pay; the whole concept of the remoteness of damage[44] is therefore irrelevant; the law on penalties does not apply to the agreed sum[45]; the claimant's duty to mitigate his loss does not generally apply[46]; and the claimant will usually be able to seek summary judgment.[47] The distinction may also be relevant where a contract provides for payment to be made by instalments; thus, under a hire-purchase agreement, a claim for arrears of instalments already due is a claim in debt quite

---

[35] *Columbus & Co. Ltd v. Clowes* [1903] 1 K.B. 244; *Weld-Blundell v. Stephens* [1920] A.C. 956; *Taylor & Sons Ltd v. Bank of Athens* (1922) 91 L.J.K.B. 776; *James v. Hutton and J. Cook & Sons Ltd* [1950] 1 K.B. 9; *Sykes v. Midland Bank Executor and Trustee Co. Ltd* [1971] 1 Q.B. 113. See *post*, §§ 27–024 *et seq.*

[36] *Erie County Natural Gas and Fuel Co. Ltd v. Carroll* [1911] A.C. 105. *cf. Government of Ceylon v. Chandris* [1965] 3 All E.R. 48. *cf. Tai Hing Cotton Mill Ltd v. Kamsing Knitting Factory* [1979] A.C. 91, 106 (see *ante*, § 27–006, text at n. 30). *cf.* also *Dean v. Ainley* [1987] 1 W.L.R. 1729.

[37] *Beaumont v. Greathead* (1846) 2 C.B. 494, 499. But costs are in the discretion of the court, and sometimes a plaintiff who recovers nominal damages will not receive costs: *Anglo-Cyprian Trade Agencies Ltd v. Paphos Wine Industries Ltd* [1951] 1 All E.R. 873, 874.

[38] *e.g. Alder v. Moore* [1961] 2 Q.B. 57 (*post*, § 27–120); *Hyundai Heavy Industries Co. Ltd v. Papadopoulos* [1980] 1 W.L.R. 1129, HL (guarantee: see Vol. II, Chap. 42); *Damon Compania Naviera SA v. Hapag-Lloyd International SA* [1985] 1 W.L.R. 435, 449 (suing in debt to recover an unpaid deposit); *Jervis v. Harris* [1996] Ch 195. See *post*, § 27–111; Vol. II, Chap. 41 (contracts of insurance).

[39] See *post*, §§ 27–082—27–083.

[40] On the question when an action lies for the price under a contract for the sale of goods, see Vol. II, §§ 43–357 *et seq.*

[41] See n. 38, above.

[42] See *ante*, §§ 27–001, 27–007.

[43] On causation, see *post*, §§ 27–024 *et seq.*

[44] See *post*, §§ 27–039 *et seq.*

[45] See *post*, § 27–111.

[46] *White and Carter (Councils) Ltd v. McGregor* [1962] A.C. 413. (See *post*, § 27–100.)

[47] CPR, Part 24. A debt can be factored, *viz.* sold to a financial institution.

distinct from a claim for damages for breach of the contract as a whole.[48] Under a contract for payment by instalments, no claim in respect of instalments due in the future may be brought as a claim for a debt, but if the party due to pay the instalments has committed a breach of his obligations which entitles the other party to terminate the contract, then, subject to the general rules on damages, an award of damages may be made in respect of the prospective loss of the future instalments, allowance being made for a discount on account of the earlier payment of a lump sum to be received under the judgment instead of the instalments spread over the future period.[49]

(d) *Liquidated and Unliquidated Damages*

27–009   **Liquidated and unliquidated damages.** The term liquidated damages is applied where the damages have been agreed and fixed by the parties (in respect of which the law has developed criteria for their validity[50]), or fixed by statute as in the case of damages against parties to a dishonoured bill of exchange.[51] Unliquidated damages is the term applied where the damages are at large and are to be assessed by a jury or by a judge sitting as a jury; the rules as to remoteness of damage[52] are the main criteria for such damages.

27–010   Often the parties to a contract fix a sum as liquidated damages in the event of one specific breach, and leave the claimant to sue for unliquidated damages in the ordinary way if other types of breach occur.[53] Again, where there is provision for liquidated damages the claimant may, in appropriate cases, nevertheless elect to ask instead for an injunction to restrain a breach.[54]

27–011   **Contract excluding or varying right to damages.** At common law, the right of a contracting party to claim damages for a breach of the contract may be excluded by the express terms of the contract, provided that the language employed to do so is plain.[55] Subject to the law as to penalties[56] and to the general principles of the law of contract, such as illegality, the courts will enforce a contractual provision designed to operate in the event of a breach.[57] But the

---

[48] *Overstone Ltd v. Shipway* [1962] 1 W.L.R. 117, 123, 129. (See Vol. II, § 38–306. *cf.* Vol. II, §§ 38–182—38–185, 38–334.)

[49] *Interoffice Telephones Ltd v. Robert Freeman Co. Ltd* [1958] 1 Q.B. 190; *Robophone Facilities Ltd v. Blank* [1966] 1 W.L.R. 1428; *Lombard North Central plc v. Butterworth* [1987] Q.B. 527 (*post,* § 27–116). *Stoeznia Gdanska SA v. Latvian Shipping Co.* [1998] 1 All E.R. 883, HL. On the question of the discount, see also *Overstone Ltd v. Shipway, supra,* (approved by HL in *Christopher Moran Holdings Ltd v. Bairstow* [1999] 2 W.L.R. 396, 400, 403, 407 and *post,* § 27–128, between n. 89 and n. 90. On damages for prospective loss in general, see *post,* §§ 27–012—27–013.

[50] *Post,* §§ 27–102 *et seq.*

[51] Bills of Exchange Act 1882, s.57 (see Vol. II, § 34–120); *Re Rickett* [1949] 1 All E.R. 737.

[52] *Post,* §§ 27–039 *et seq.*

[53] *e.g. Aktieselskabet Reidar v. Arcos Ltd* [1927] 1 K.B. 352. See *post,* § 27–102.

[54] But the plaintiff cannot have both an injunction and liquidated damages in respect of a single breach: *Sainter v. Ferguson* (1849) 1 Mac. & G. 286; *Carnes v. Nesbitt* (1862) 7 H. & N. 778; *General Accident Insurance Co. v. Noel* [1902] 1 K.B. 377. *cf.* the position if there are different breaches: *Imperial Tobacco Co. v. Parslay* [1936] 2 All E.R. 515; *Elsley v. J. G. Collins Insurance Agencies Ltd* (1978) 83 D.L.R. (3d) 1 (Sup.Ct. of Canada) (injunction granted to restrain future breaches of employee's covenant not to compete, together with damages in respect of past breaches). See also *Upton v. Henderson* (1912) 28 T.L.R. 398.

[55] On such exclusion or exemption clauses, see *ante*, Chap. 14.

[56] See *post,* §§ 27–102 *et seq.*

[57] For illustrations, see *post,* §§ 27–117—27–119.

Unfair Contract Terms Act 1977 and the Unfair Terms in Consumer Contracts Regulations 1994 impose some statutory restrictions on attempts to exclude or limit liability for breach of contract.[58]

(e) *Prospective Loss and Continuing Breaches*

Prospective loss.[59] The general rule, in contract as well as in tort, is that **27–012** damages for all prospective loss flowing from a single cause of action must be recovered once and for all in one action[60]: the claimant cannot recover damages for one part of his loss in one action, and then recover further damages for another part of his loss in a subsequent action.[61] Hence the claimant should claim at the same time damages for all his loss resulting or likely to result from the defendant's breach of contract, whether the loss is past or is reasonably anticipated in the future. Damages for prospective loss should take into account the contingencies of life and other uncertainties affecting the future.[62] The court may, however, defer the assessment of damages for future losses which are very uncertain.[63]

There may be separate breaches of different promises in the same contract, giving rise to separate causes of action, as where there are successive breaches of an instalment contract[64]; in such a case, damages may be awarded for the separate breaches in separate actions.

Continuing breaches of contract. There is, however, a difference between a **27–013** breach of contract which is a continuing one (giving rise to a continuing cause of action) and repeated breaches of recurring obligations.[65] With a continuing wrong, a fresh cause of action arises after recovery of damages in an earlier action, and the claimant may bring a second action to recover damages for loss arising after the earlier action. "Where damages are to be assessed . . . in respect of any continuing cause of action, they shall be assessed down to the time of the assessment."[66] An instance of a continuing breach of contract has been given by the Court of Appeal[67]:

---

[58] See *ante*, §§ 14–057 *et seq.*, 15–001 *et seq.*

[59] On damages for sums of money payable in the future, see *ante*, § 27–008.

[60] *Rowntree & Sons Ltd v. Allen & Sons (Poplar) Ltd* (1936) 41 Com.Cas. 90. See *ante*, § 26–007; s.35 of the County Courts Act 1984. *cf.* the same rule in tort: *Darley Main Colliery Co. v. Mitchell* (1886) 11 App.Cas. 127, 132. See also *Pegler v. Railway Executive* [1948] A.C. 332.

[61] *Furness Withy & Co. v. Hall* (1909) 25 T.L.R. 233. See also *Conquer v. Boot* [1928] 2 K.B. 336 (distinguished in *Purser and Co. (Hillingdon) Ltd v. Jackson* [1977] Q.B. 166 (successive arbitrations over different building defects)); *H. E. Daniels Ltd v. Carmel Exporters and Importers Ltd* [1953] 2 Q.B. 242. Prospective loss falls within the rule: *Clarke v. Yorke* (1882) 47 L.T. 381.

[62] *e.g. Johnston v. G.W. Ry.* [1904] 2 K.B. 250, 259–260. On discounting for contingencies in hypothetical situations, see *post*, §§ 27–034 *et seq.*

[63] *Deeny v. Gooda Walker Ltd (No. 3)* [1995] 4 All E.R. 289 (the plaintiff's future liabilities to policyholders could not be predicted with reasonable confidence; there was also the risk that, having received a substantial sum for future losses, the plaintiff might allow the damages to be dissipated before the policyholders' claims were made).

[64] *H. E. Daniels Ltd v. Carmel Exporters and Importers Ltd, supra*, at 252; *National Coal Board v. Galley* [1958] 1 W.L.R. 16, 26.

[65] *National Coal Board v. Galley, supra* (failure to work Saturday shifts at a colliery amounted to repeated breaches of a recurring obligation).

[66] RSC, Ord. 37, r. 6. See *Hole v. Chard Union* [1894] 1 Ch. 293. *cf.* the award of damages in lieu of an injunction: *post* §§ 28–071 *et seq.*

[67] *National Coal Board v. Galley, supra*, at 26.

"For example, a contract of service for a specified term might contain a stipulation that the employee should not during the period of his service carry on or be concerned in any other business of the same kind as the employer's business. If the employee, in breach of such a stipulation, did proceed to carry out some other business of the kind in question, the breach would, we think, clearly be a continuing one, in that the employee would *de die in diem* be continuously in breach of the stipulation so long as the prohibited business was carried on."

, (f) *Substitute Performance (Cost of Completion or Repairs)*

27–014   **Damages for the cost of completion, reinstatement or repairs.** In appropriate circumstances, damages may be assessed on the basis of what it will cost the claimant to obtain performance (or completion of performance) of the contractual undertaking by a third party.[68] Where the contract was one to transfer property to the claimant, it is assumed that the claimant will obtain performance by purchasing property that conforms to the contractual requirements, and damages will be assessed as the difference between the cost (if reasonable) of the substitute purchase and the price fixed in the original contract (the rules of mitigation apply). In other situations, the damages are assessed as the difference between the market value of the defendant's performance in its defective or incomplete state, and the market value of the performance if it had been properly completed.[69] In a contract to perform services or for work and materials it will be assumed that the claimant will have the incomplete or defective performance completed or corrected and the damages will be assessed by the cost of getting this done; however, if the claimant will not have the work done or it would be unreasonable to do so, the damages will again be measured by the difference in value, which may be less than the cost of having the work done. The claimant is entitled to the reasonable cost of having the remedial work done if, in all the circumstances, it is (or was) reasonable for him to insist on having the work done.[70] Factors which are relevant to the issue of reasonableness include:

(i) the claimant has actually had the work done[71]; or

(ii) he undertakes to have it done[72] (but such an undertaking will not, on its own, make it reasonable for the claimant to have it done[73]); or

---

[68] The advantages of this remedy are reviewed by Harris *op. cit.* pp. 163–166.

[69] *Tito v. Waddell (No. 2) (The Ocean Island case)* [1977] Ch. 106. In appropriate circumstances, damages may be awarded for loss of amenity, even the loss of a personal, subjective value in obtaining the benefit of performance: see *post*, § 27–070. Such a measure will fall between the cost of reinstatement and the diminution in market value.

[70] *Ruxley Electronics and Construction Ltd v. Forsyth* [1996] A.C. 344 (see the comment by Poole, (1996) 59 M.L.R. 272; and Coote [1997] C.L.J. 537); *Harbutt's "Plasticine" Ltd v. Wayne Tank and Pump Co.* [1970] 1 Q.B. 447, 473. On the question of the reasonableness of substitute performance in building contracts, see *East Ham Corporation v. Bernard Sunley & Sons Ltd* [1966] A.C. 406 (repairs carried out promptly when defect discovered); *Radford v. De Froberville* [1971] 1 W.L.R. 1262 (commented on by Wallace in (1980) 96 L.Q.R. 101, 341); *Bevan Investments Ltd v. Blackhall and Struthers (No. 2)* [1973] 2 N.Z.L.R. 45; [1978] 2 N.Z.L.R. 97; *G.W. Atkins Ltd v. Scott* (1980) 7 Construction L.J. 215 (CA).

[71] *Jones v. Herxheimer* [1950] 2 K.B. 106.

[72] The *Ocean Island* case, *supra*, at 333.

[73] The *Ruxley Electronics* case, *supra*, at 373.

(iii) he shows a "sufficient intention" to have the work done if he receives damages on this basis[74]: the claimant's subjective intention is relevant.[75]

In *Ruxley Electronics and Construction Ltd v. Forsyth*,[76] *supra*, the House of **27–015** Lords emphasised the role of reasonableness and held that where the cost of reinstatement was out of all proportion to the advantage to be gained by the plaintiff from reinstatement,[77] it would be unreasonable for the plaintiff to insist on it. In this case, a swimming pool was not built to the depth specified in the contract but was sufficiently deep for diving according to normal standards so that the market value of the property was not reduced. It was held that it was unreasonable for the plaintiff to claim the cost of rebuilding the pool to the contractual specification. (However, the House of Lords did approve the award of £2,500 as damages for loss of amenity or loss of consumer surplus.)[78] But the courts have refused to assess damages at the cost of repairs where a surveyor negligently failed to report defects in a property purchased by the claimant in reliance on the report.[79]

The time at which the cost of repairs should be assessed is when it would have **27–016** been reasonable for the claimant to begin repairs,[80] which may be as late as the date of the hearing if the claimant was acting reasonably in not mitigating earlier.[81]

(g) *Exemplary Damages and Depriving the Defendant of his Profit*

Exemplary damages.[82] Exemplary damages are damages awarded against **27–017** the defendant as a punishment, so that the assessment goes beyond mere compensation of the claimant. Such "punitive" or "vindictive" damages were permitted in some cases of tort until 1964 when the House of Lords in *Rookes v. Barnard*[83] severely restricted their use in such cases by specifying only two categories where they may be awarded at common law. The right to receive

---

[74] The *Ocean Island* case, *supra*, at 333; *Radford v. De Froberville, supra*, at 1269–1270. *cf.* the tort case of *Dodd Properties Ltd v. Canterbury City Council*, [1980] 1 W.L.R. 433.

[75] The *Ruxley Electronics* case, *supra*. at 359, 372–373.

[76] [1996] A.C. 344.

[77] On the question whether the "cost of cure" is disproportionate to the benefit, see *Channel Island Ferries Ltd v. Cenargo Navigation Ltd (The Rozel)* [1994] 2 Lloyd's Rep. 161.

[78] See *post*, § 27–070.

[79] See *post*, § 27–077.

[80] *Radford v. De Froberville, supra*; *London Congregational Union Inc. v. Harriss and Harriss* [1985] 1 All E.R. 335, 344 (the appeal did not deal with this point: [1988] 1 All E.R. 15); *Cormier Enterprises Ltd v. Costello* (1980) 108 D.L.R. (3d) 472. See *post*, § 27–052; and, on the duty to mitigate in general, *post*, § 27–085. *cf.* the tort case of *Dodd Properties Ltd v. Canterbury City Council* [1980] 1 W.L.R. 433.

[81] *Radford v. De Froberville, supra*; *Dodd Properties Ltd v. Canterbury City Council, supra* (a tort case where a building was damaged by defendant's tort; plaintiff reasonably postponed repairs until defendant admitted liability); *Bevan Investments Ltd v. Blackhall and Struthers (No. 2), supra* (commented on by Wallace (1980) 96 L.Q.R. 101, 115, and 341); *Perry v. Sidney Phillips & Son* [1982] 1 W.L.R. 1297 (defendant denied liability).

[82] See the Law Commission Report, Law Com. No. 247 (1997), Part III (paras. 3.33–3.37, 3.45–3.47 refer to breach of contract cases); Smith, (1997) 60 M.L.R. 360.

[83] [1964] A.C. 1129, 1220–1231; the ruling was upheld by the House of Lords in *Cassell & Co. Ltd v. Broome* [1972] A.C. 1027 (libel), but it was not followed by the Privy Council in an appeal from Australia: *Australian Consolidated Press v. Uren* [1969] 1 A.C. 590.

exemplary damages for breach of contract was, for many years before 1964,[84] confined to the single case of damages for breach of promise of marriage,[85] but this cause of action was abolished in 1970.[86] In 1909, the House of Lords in *Addis v. Gramophone Co. Ltd*[87] held that exemplary damages could not be awarded for wrongful dismissal: no compensation should be given for the plaintiff's injured feelings[88] even where the dismissal was carried out in a humiliating manner.[89] The principle of this decision is not confined to cases of wrongful dismissal, and it is submitted that it now prevents the recovery of exemplary[90] damages for any breach of contract.[91] However, in special circumstances, damages may be awarded for mental distress where the parties contemplated it as a not unlikely consequence of breach.[92]

27–018 **Depriving the defendant of profit made through his breach.** The traditional view (recently upheld by the Court of Appeal[93]) is that when assessing damages for breach of contract, the court is "concerned with the [plaintiff's] loss and not with the [defendant's] profit, the latter being wholly irrelevant."[94] The only recognised[95] exceptions to this principle are where the claimant has a remedy in tort or in restitution or can enforce a fiduciary obligation, or has an interest in property used by the defendant without permission. These are briefly reviewed in turn. In tort, damages have often been awarded for unauthorised use of the claimant's land.[96] On a similar principle, damages for retaining goods or

---

[84] In some cases last century, before *Addis v. Gramophone Co. Ltd, infra*, exemplary damages for breach of contract were awarded, *e.g. Lord Sondes v. Fletcher* (1822) 5 B. & Ald. 835; *Maw v. Jones* (1890) 25 Q.B.D. 107.

[85] *Quirk v. Thomas* [1916] 1 K.B. 516, 527, 531, 538.

[86] s.1 of the Law Reform (Miscellaneous Provisions) Act 1970 provides that an engagement to marry shall not have effect as a contract giving rise to legal rights. (See notes in (1971) 87 L.Q.R. 158, 314.)

[87] [1909] A.C. 488 (see further, *post*, § 27–069).

[88] Followed in *Bliss v. S.E. Thames Regional H.A.* [1987] I.C.R. 700.

[89] Some of the general statements in the *Addis* case have been qualified by the House of Lords in *Malik v. Bank of Credit and Commerce International SA* [1998] A.C. 20 (see *post*, §§ 27–069, 27–071). *cf. Dunk v. George Waller & Son Ltd* [1970] 2 Q.B. 163 (employer's breach of contract of apprenticeship: see Vol. II, § 39–182); *Edwards v. Society of Graphical and Allied Trades* [1971] Ch. 354 (damages for wrongful expulsion from a trade union, leading to dismissal from employment, may include damages "for the difficulty the dismissal causes to a plaintiff in getting fresh employment": *ibid.* at 379).

[90] The decision in *Addis*'s case, *supra* is wide enough to mean that aggravated damages (as sometimes available in tort) cannot be awarded in contract: see *Kralj v. McGrath* [1986] 1 All E.R. 54, 61.

[91] *Perera v. Vandiyar* [1953] 1 W.L.R. 672; *Kenny v. Preen* [1963] 1 Q.B. 499 (but both doubted in *McCall v. Abelesz* [1976] Q.B. 585, 594). *cf. Lavender v. Betts* [1942] 2 All E.R. 72 (action in tort in similar circumstances); *cf.* also *Drane v. Evangelou* [1978] 1 W.L.R. 455 (exemplary damages awarded for trespass when landlord wrongfully evicted his tenant). The Supreme Court of Canada has considered the possibility of punitive damages being (rarely) awarded in a contract case: *Vorvis v. Insurance Corp. of British Columbia* (1989) 58 D.L.R. (4th) 193.

[92] See *post*, § 27–069.

[93] *Surrey County Council v. Bredero Homes Ltd* [1993] 1 W.L.R. 1361.

[94] *The Solholt* [1983] 1 Lloyd's Rep. 605, 608.

[95] *Surrey County Council v. Bredero Homes Ltd, supra.*

[96] *e.g.* the wayleave cases, such as *Phillips v. Homfray* (1871) L.R. 6 Ch. App. 770; or where the defendant had trespassed by tipping soil on the plaintiff's land: *Whitwham v. Westminster Brymbo Coal and Coke Co.* [1896] 2 Ch. 538; or where a landlord wrongfully ejected his tenant and the damages for trespass were assessed as a reasonable rent for the entire period of the trespass, whether or not the landlord had derived any benefit from using the property: *Inverugie Investments Ltd v. Hackett* [1995] 1 W.L.R. 713, PC. See Cooke (1994) 110 L.Q.R. 420.

buildings beyond the period of a letting to the defendant are assessed at the ordinary letting value of their use[97]; the same approach has been used in assessing damages against a buyer who refused to remove the goods from the seller's premises.[98] Restitutionary remedies may also be used to deprive the defendant of a profit[99] *e.g.* to deprive an agent of a bribe or secret profit[1] or an employee of profits arising from misuse of confidential information.[2] The equitable remedy of tracing property[3] and the wide use of the remedial device of a constructive trust,[4] have also been used to deprive a defendant of his profit. So the Privy Council held a defendant liable to account for the profits made through the wrongful use of a telegraph wire.[5]

Invasion of property interest. Where a breach of contract also amounts to   **27–019** the invasion of a property interest vested in the claimant, he may obtain a remedy which has the effect of depriving the contract-breaker of some of his profit.[6] So where the defendant built on his land in defiance of a restrictive covenant in favour of the plaintiff, the damages (in lieu of an injunction[7]) were assessed at the price which the plaintiff could reasonably have expected to receive from a negotiated partial release from the covenant; this price could be a proportion of the profits expected to be made by the defendant.[8] Similarly, the infringement of a patent is treated as injury to the claimant's property right, so that damages may be assessed as a royalty for every infringing article.[9]

No general principle that claimant entitled to share of profit. But in 1993   **27–020** the Court of Appeal refused[10] to generalise from these instances so as to allow a remedy in contract damages where the defendant (without infringing any property interest of the claimant) deliberately broke his undertaking in order to

---

[97] *Strand Electric and Engineering Co. Ltd v. Brisford Entertainments Ltd* [1952] 2 Q.B. 246; *Swordheath Properties Ltd v. Tabet* [1979] 1 W.L.R. 285.

[98] *Penarth Dock Engineering Co. Ltd v. Pounds* [1963] 1 Lloyd's Rep. 359 (the reasonable charge for storage facilities was allowed as damages: *post*, § 30–022.

[99] Goff and Jones, *The Law of Restitution* (5th ed., 1998), pp. 734–742; Dawson (1959) 20 Ohio State L.J. 175, 185–188. On the possibility of restitutionary damages, see *post*, § 27–021.

[1] *Post*, § 30–172.

[2] See Vol. II, §§ 32–128, 39–059—39–061.

[3] *Post*, § 30–097.

[4] *Post*, § 30–107. The U.S. Supreme Court has used a remedial constructive trust to deprive a cynical contract-breaker of his profits: *Snepp v. United States* (1980) 444 U.S. 507, but the English Court of Appeal preferred not to use this concept: *Att. Gen. v. Blake* [1998] Ch. 439, 459. See *post*, §§ 30–107 *et seq.* See also Deane J. (dissenting) in *Hospital Products Ltd v. U.S. Surgical Corporation* (1984) 156 C.L.R. 41 (High Ct. of Aust.).

[5] *Reid Newfoundland Co. v. Anglo-American Telegraph Co. Ltd* [1912] A.C. 555 (a promise to account for the profits of breach). See also *Reading v. Attorney-General* [1951] A.C. 507.

[6] *e.g. Lake v. Bayliss* [1974] 1 W.L.R. 1073.

[7] s.50 of the Supreme Court Act 1981 (formerly, Lord Cairns' Act).

[8] *Wrotham Park Estate Co. v. Parkside Homes* [1974] 1 W.L.R. 798 (approved by the Court of Appeal in *Jaggard v. Sawyer* [1995] 1 W.L.R. 269 (the damages could be the amount which the plaintiff "could reasonably have demanded as the price of waiving [his] rights": at 289); followed in *Bracewell v. Appleby* [1975] Ch. 408; *Tito v. Waddell (No. 2)* [1977] Ch. 106, 335; *cf. Carr-Saunders v. Dick McNeil Associates* [1986] 1 W.L.R. 922 (damages in lieu of injunction for interference with right to light); *cf.* also *Stoke on Trent City Council v. W. & J. Wass Ltd* [1988] 1 W.L.R. 1406 (infringement of the right to hold a market).

[9] *Watson, Laidlaw & Co. Ltd v. Pott, Cassels and Williamson* (1914) 31 R.P.C. 104, HL. In cases of interference with intellectual property the plaintiff may choose either damages or an account of profits made by the defendant from his wrongful act *e.g. Lever v. Goodwin* (1887) 36 Ch.D. 1, 7.

[10] *Surrey County Council v. Bredero Homes Ltd, supra.*

make a profit from the breach. It was held that, where the breach deprived the plaintiff of the opportunity to negotiate a price for giving permission to the defendant to act in a way contrary to his undertaking, there was no general power in the court to fix damages at the level of the reasonable price which reasonable parties should have agreed.[11] However, since a claimant who is entitled to an order for specific performance or an injunction is able to negotiate a price for releasing the defendant from the order (thereby depriving him of some of his profits from breach), the Court of Appeal has accepted that, in lieu of making such an order, the court itself may award damages on that basis.[12] The limits to the entitlement to specific relief are thus taken as the limits to the entitlement to deprive the defendant of some of his profits from breach, even though the former limits were obviously not designed to achieve the latter purpose.[13]

27–021   **Restitutionary damages.**[14] Dicta in the Court of Appeal indicate the probability that restitutionary damages may in "exceptional" situations in future be awarded for breach of contract.[15] At least two situations were suggested: (1) skimped performance, where the contract-breaker fails to complete the full performance for which he has already been paid and by his breach he has avoided expense; (2) where the contract-breaker has made a profit by doing the very thing he undertook not to do (*e.g.* in *Blake's* case, he had promised not to disclose official information).[16] In both these situations, the breach directly produced the extra profit, and did not merely provide the opportunity to make it.

(h) Appeals Against the Assessment of Damages

27–022   **Power of appellate court to reassess damages.** When the Court of Appeal hears an appeal[17] against the assessment of damages made by a judge sitting

---

[11] *ibid.* This was a principle arguably derived from the cases cited in n. 8, *supra* and was supported by some writers: Sharpe and Waddams (1982) 2 O.J.L.S. 290; Waddams, *The Law of Damages* (3rd ed.), Chap. 9; Harris, *Remedies in Contract and Tort* (1988), pp. 146–151. 159–161, 186, 351–352, 370–373. See also *Adras Ltd v. Harlow & Jones GmbH* (1988) published in English [1995] R.L.R. 235. (Israeli Supreme Court) discussed in 104 L.Q.R. 383 (1988); *Hickey & Co. Ltd v. Roche Stores (Dublin) Ltd* (1975) reported in [1993] Restitution L. Rev. 196.

[12] *Jaggard v. Sawyer* [1995] 1 W.L.R. 269; *Surrey County Council v. Bredero Homes Ltd, supra,* at 1367, 1368, 1370. No injunction had been sought in *Surrey County Council v. Bredero.*

[13] See (in addition to the references cited in nn. 8 and 11 *supra*) Birks [1987] Lloyds M.C.L.Q. 421; Birks (1993) 109 L.Q.R. 518; Jones (1983) 99 L.Q.R. 443; Goff and Jones, *The Law of Restitution* (5th ed., 1998), pp. 518–522; Friedmann (1980) 80 Col.L.R. 504; Farnsworth (1985) 94 Yale L.J. 1339; O'Dair [1993] 46(2) C.L.P. 113 and [1993] R.L.R. 31; Goodhart [1995] R.L.R. 3.

[14] See also the Law Commission's Report, Law Com. No. 247 (1997), paras. 3.33–3.37, 3.45–3.47. See *post,* § 30–096.

[15] *per* Lord Woolf M.R. in *Att. Gen. v. Blake* [1998] Ch. 439, 456–459, citing a long list of academic articles. (In *Blake's* case, a public law remedy—an injunction—was granted to restrain a criminal from receiving a further benefit (royalties) from his crime.) Leave to appeal has been granted by the House of Lords: [1999] 1 W.L.R. 1279.

[16] *Att. Gen. v. Blake, supra.*

[17] The appeal is by way of rehearing: CPR Sched 1: R.S.C., Ord. 59, r. 3(1) which enables the court to substitute its own view of the assessment of damages: *Flint v. Lovell* [1935] 1 K.B. 354, 360; *Davies v. Powell Duffryn Associated Collieries Ltd* [1942] A.C. 601, 616–617. Hence, the Court of Appeal is more willing to interfere with a judge's award than with a jury's award of damages (*ibid.*); and if it reverses a decision for the defendant on the issue of liability, it will assess the damages itself: *Reaney v. Co-operative Wholesale Society* [1932] W.N. 78. *cf.* the position in the Privy Council: *Ratnasingam v. Kow Ah Dek* [1983] 1 W.L.R. 1235.

alone, without a jury, it applies similar principles to those followed previously in considering appeals against the award of damages by the verdict of a jury.[18] The court will interfere only if it is convinced that the trial judge acted upon some wrong principle of law,[19] or that the amount awarded was so extremely high or so very small as to make it, in the judgment of the Court of Appeal, an entirely erroneous estimate of the damages to which the claimant is entitled.[20] Great attention is paid to the opinion of the trial judge and the appellate court should be slow to reverse the judgment of the judge who saw and heard the witnesses.[21] In special situations, the appellate court may take account of circumstances affecting the assessment of damages which arise after the first instance trial.[22] *e.g.* if the fresh evidence showed that the "basic or fundamental assumption" underlying the judge's assessment had been "falsified by later events."[23]

(i) *Third Party Beneficiaries*

Breach of promises intended to benefit third persons. Chapter 19 of this   **27–023** work[24] includes a full discussion of the situations in which the promisee can recover either the agreed sum[25] due to be paid to a third person who is not a party to the contract[26] or substantial damages for breach of a promise intended to benefit such a person.[27]

---

[18] The verdict of a jury awarding damages can be set aside only if the Court of Appeal upon consideration of all the circumstances comes to the conclusion that the damages awarded were so small or so large that 12 sensible jurors could not reasonably have awarded them: *Mills v. Stanway Coaches Ltd* [1940] 2 K.B. 334, 340; *Phillips v. London & S.W. Ry* (1879) 4 Q.B.D. 406; (1879) 5 QBD 78; or if the court is satisfied that the jury took into consideration matters which they ought not to have considered or had disregarded matters which they ought to have considered: *Smith v. Schilling* [1928] 1 K.B. 429, 440. See also *Praed v. Graham* (1889) 24 Q.B.D. 53; *Johnston v. G.W. Ry* [1904] 2 K.B. 250; *Bocock v. Enfield Rolling Mills Ltd* [1954] 1 W.L.R. 1303; *Nance v. British Columbia Electric Ry* [1951] A.C. 601, 613; *Scott v. Musial* [1959] 2 Q.B. 429; *Cavanagh v. Ulster Weaving Co. Ltd* [1960] A.C. 145; *Ward v. James* [1966] 1 Q.B. 273.

[19] *e.g. Benham v. Gambling* [1941] A.C. 157; *Naylor v. Yorkshire Electricity Board* [1968] A.C. 529; *Dingle v. Associated Newspapers* [1964] A.C. 371; *Lai Wee Lian v. Singapore Bus Service (1978) Ltd* [1984] A.C. 729 (all cases on torts).

[20] *Flint v. Lovell, supra,* at 360 (approved in *Owen v. Sykes* [1936] 1 K.B. 192). See also *Davies v. Powell Duffryn Associated Collieries Ltd, supra,* at 616–617, 623–624; *Nance v. British Columbia Electric Ry.* [1951] A.C. 601, 613; *Warren v. King* [1964] 1 W.L.R. 1, 9; *Morey v. Woodfield (No. 2)* [1964] 1 W.L.R. 16. *cf. Hinz v. Berry* [1970] 2 Q.B. 40; *Bone v. Seale* [1975] 1 W.L.R. 797 (nuisance case). For an appeal from a county court judge, see *Shave v. J. W. Lees (Brewers) Ltd* [1954] 1 W.L.R. 1300.

[21] *Powell v. Streatham Manor Nursing Home* [1935] A.C. 243. See also *Smith v. Schilling* [1928] 1 K.B. 429, 432–433 (similar remarks concerning the opinion of the trial judge who took the verdict of the jury).

[22] *Edwards v. Society of Graphical and Allied Trades* [1971] Ch. 354, 377, 384 (a contract case, following the tort case of *Murphy v. Stone-Wallwork (Charlton) Ltd* [1969] 1 W.L.R. 1023); see also *Mulholland v. Mitchell* [1971] A.C. 666.

[23] *Hunt v. Severs* [1993] Q.B. 815, 838 (a tort case: the House of Lords did not deal with this point: [1994] 2 A.C. 350).

[24] See §§ 19–042—19–058.

[25] See *ante,* § 27–008. (In most "third-party beneficiary" cases it is an agreed sum which is in question.)

[26] On the common law doctrine of privity of contract, see *ante,* §§ 19–003 *et seq.*

[27] See the Law Commission's Report: *Privity of Contract: Contracts for the Benefit of Third Parties,* (1996) Law Com. No. 242; and the Contracts (Rights of Third Parties) Bill 1998.

2. CAUSATION AND CONTRIBUTORY NEGLIGENCE[28]

27–024   **Requirement of a causal connection.** The important issue in remoteness of damage in the law of contract is whether a particular loss was within the reasonable contemplation of the parties,[29] but causation must first be proved: there must be a causal connection between the defendant's breach of contract[30] and the claimant's loss.[31] The claimant may recover damages for a loss only where the breach of contract was the "effective" or "dominant" cause of that loss.[32] The courts have avoided laying down any formal tests for causation: they have relied on common sense to guide decisions as to whether a breach of contract is a sufficiently substantial cause of the claimant's loss.[33] The answer to whether the breach was the cause of the loss or merely the occasion for the loss must "in the end" depend on "the court's commonsense" in interpreting the facts.[34] So where a company continued to trade after a negligent audit by the defendant failed to reveal the true financial position of the company, the Court of Appeal held that the auditor's breach of contract gave the company "the *opportunity* . . . to incur . . . trading losses: it did not *cause* those trading losses".[35] The trading losses flowed from trading, not auditing.

27–025   The problems of causation most likely to arise concern intervening acts of either a third party or of the claimant; but an issue of causation may also arise when the alleged loss is claimed on the basis of a hypothesis as to what the claimant or a third person would have done had the defendant not broken the contract.[36]

27–026   **Intervening act of third party.** Although the voluntary act of a third person intervening between the breach of contract by the defendant and the loss suffered by the claimant will normally "break the chain of causation," this will depend on the court's appraisal of the particular circumstances. Thus, where the negligence of a solicitor (in breach of his contractual duty to his client) creates a risk for the client, an "error of judgment" made subsequently by counsel advising the client

---

[28] This topic has been developed mainly in the law of torts, but may arise in the law of contract (see Hart & Honoré, *Causation in the Law* (2nd ed.), Chap. 11). No doubt the numerous decisions on causation in the law of torts may be used as analogies in the law of contract.

[29] See *post*, §§ 27–039 *et seq.*

[30] The loss must have been caused by the breach itself, since "damages for breach of contract may . . . [not] be awarded . . . for loss caused by the manner of the breach": *per* Lord Steyn in *Malik v. Bank of Credit and Commerce International SA* [1998] A.C. 20, at 51 (citing *Addis v. Gramophone Co.* [1909] A.C. 488 (see *post*, § 27–069).

[31] *Monarch Steamship Co. Ltd v. Karlshamns Oljefabriker (A/B)* [1949] A.C. 196, 225; *Quinn v. Burch Bros. (Builders) Ltd* [1966] 2 Q.B. 370; *Sykes v. Midland Bank Executor and Trustee Co. Ltd* [1971] 1 Q.B. 113.

[32] *Galoo v. Bright Grahame Murray* [1994] 1 W.L.R. 1360, at 1374–1375. The breach of contract need not be the sole cause: *post*, § 27–033.

[33] This sentence was quoted with approval by the CA in *Galoo v. Bright Grahame Murray, supra.*, at 1374–1375.

[34] *ibid.*; *Racing Drivers' Club Ltd v. Hextall Erskine & Co.* [1996] 3 All E.R. 667, 671–672, 681–682. See also *County Ltd v. Girozentrale Securities* [1996] 3 All E.R. 834, CA (causation does not depend on the parties' contemplation).

[35] The *Galoo* case, *supra.*, at 1375. The contrast between the "occasion" (or "opportunity") and the "cause" is also made in *Quinn v. Burch Bros. (Builders) Ltd* [1966] 2 Q.B. 370 (*post*, § 27–029).

[36] See *post*, §§ 27–034—27–035.

may not interrupt the chain of causation resulting from the solicitor's negligence.[37] Similarly, in a case where insurers were held liable to a bank, the mortgagee of a ship, for failing (in breach of contract) to notify the bank that the ship had been trading in a war zone prohibited by the terms of the insurance, the fact that the shipowners lied to the bank when seeking the re-financing of their loan, did not break the chain of causation between the breach of contract and the bank's loss as a result of the re-financing.[38]

If the defendant owes a contractual duty to the claimant to take care to ensure   **27-027**
that an intervening and voluntary act of a third party is not permitted, then the defendant will be liable if he fails to take such care.[39] Thus a customer of a bank owes a duty to the bank to draw his cheques carefully so as not to facilitate fraud; where the customer drew a cheque in such a way that the amount could be readily altered, he was held liable to the bank for the increase forged by a third party, who obtained payment of the increased amount.[40] "The fact that a crime was necessary to bring about the loss does not prevent its being the natural consequence of the carelessness."[41]

There are, however, cases where although the intervening act of a third party   **27-028**
was probably foreseeable, the defendant was held not liable for loss resulting from that act. In *Weld-Blundell v. Stephens*,[42] the defendant, in breach of his contract, negligently left a libellous letter (written by the plaintiff) where it was read by a third party, who was likely to, and did, communicate its contents to the persons libelled; the latter recovered damages for libel from the plaintiff, who thereupon sued the defendant. The House of Lords, by a bare majority, held that the plaintiff could recover only nominal damages for the defendant's breach of contract, and not the damages and costs paid in the libel action, since the act of the third party was a "new and independent" cause.[43]

Intervening act or omission of the claimant. The doctrines of mitigation[44]   **27-029**
and possibly of contributory negligence[45] may, in addition to causation, be relevant where the claimant, following the defendant's breach of contract, has suffered loss through his own voluntary act or omission. In *Quinn v. Burch Bros. (Builders) Ltd*[46] the defendants could have foreseen that their failure (in breach

---

[37] *Cook v. S.* [1966] 1 W.L.R. 635, 642 (the Court of Appeal did not discuss this aspect of the case: [1967] 1 W.L.R. 457; *post*, § 27–069). *cf. East Ham Corporation v. Bernard Sunley & Sons Ltd* [1966] A.C. 406 (failure of architect to notice defective work by builder).

[38] *Bank of Nova Scotia v. Hellenic Mutual War Risks Association (Bermuda) Ltd* [1992] 1 A.C. 233, 266–268.

[39] *London Joint Stock Bank Ltd v. Macmillan* [1918] A.C. 777. See also *De la Bere v. Pearson* [1908] 1 K.B. 280; *Stansbie v. Troman* [1948] 2 K.B. 48; *Marshall v. Rubypoint Ltd* [1997] 25 E.G. 142; *cf. Cobb v. G.W. Ry.* [1894] A.C. 419.

[40] *London Joint Stock Bank Ltd v. Macmillan, supra.*

[41] *ibid.* at 794. See also the cases cited in n. 39, *ante.*

[42] [1920] A.C. 956 (the intervening act was foreseeable: see at 974, 987, 991. But see Treitel, *The Law of Contract* (9th ed.), p. 881.

[43] *Weld-Blundell v. Stephens, supra,* at 986.

[44] See *post*, § 27–085.

[45] See *post*, § 27–037. A similar problem arises when loss is caused by breaches of contract by both the plaintiff and the defendant: *Government of Ceylon v. Chandris* [1965] 3 All E.R. 48.

[46] [1966] 2 Q.B. 370 (followed in *Sole v. W. J. Hallt Ltd* [1973] Q.B. 574 (but it is submitted that this decision is unsatisfactory on this point); see also *O'Connor v. B. D. Kirby & Co.* [1972] 1 Q.B. 90.

of contract) to supply the plaintiff, an independent contractor, with adequate equipment might result in an accident if he used unsuitable equipment. When this actually happened so that the plaintiff was injured, the Court of Appeal held that it was the voluntary choice of the plaintiff following the breach of contract which *caused* the accident; the breach of contract did not cause it but merely gave the plaintiff the opportunity to injure himself by his choice to use the unsuitable equipment, despite his appreciation of the risk involved.[47] Similarly, where a buyer engaged a third party to repair the defect in a machine supplied by the seller, but the buyer then failed to inspect the repairs before using the machine, the Court of Appeal held[48] that the cause[49] of the subsequent explosion was the negligence of the buyer in using the machine without inspecting it to see whether the defect had been adequately repaired.[50]

27–030   Other contract cases dealing with the causal effect of the claimant's intervening act mainly concern the actions of masters of ships in obeying instructions of the charterers. Thus where a charterer was obliged to nominate a safe port of loading, but nominated a port which in fact was unsafe, and the master of the ship acted reasonably in accepting the nomination, the owners of the ship were entitled to recover damages from the charterer for injury sustained by the ship[51]; the master of a ship cannot enter a port which is obviously unsafe and then charge the charterers with damage done, but normally "a man is entitled to act in the faith that the other party to a contract is carrying out his part of it properly."[52] If the claimant is put on the horns of a dilemma by the defendant's breach of contract, the defendant cannot escape liability if the claimant acts in a reasonable way.[53]

27–031   **Apportionment between claimant and defendant.** In one case, the Court of Appeal unusually allowed apportionment of causation between the claimant and the defendant.[54]

---

[47] *cf. Galoo v. Bright Grahame Murray* [1994] 1 W.L.R. 1360 (*ante*, § 27–024). *cf.* also *Young v. Purdy* [1997] P.N.L.R. 130. An analogous situation is dealt with in *Lambert v. Lewis* [1982] A.C. 225 (*post*, § 27–089; Vol. II, § 43–414). This decision indicates that a buyer who negligently fails to discover a defect in the goods may not be able to recover from the seller for breach of his implied undertakings as to the quality of the goods: see Hervey (1981) 44 M.L.R. 575.

[48] *Beoco Ltd v. Alfa Laval Co. Ltd* [1995] Q.B. 137.

[49] It is submitted that mitigation (*post*, §§ 27–085 *et seq.*) would be a more appropriate principle for the decision. The explosion was caused by the original defect (which had not been cured) but the buyer had failed, after discovery of the defect, to take reasonable steps to avoid further loss; instead of saying the buyer *caused* the further loss it would be better to say that he failed to avoid it when he unreasonably decided to use the machine without testing it after the repairs.

[50] Although the seller was liable for the cost of repairing the original defect, and for the loss of the buyer's profit while the original repairs were made, the seller was not liable for the cost of repairing the explosion damage, nor for the further loss of production after the explosion. The need for further repairs to remedy the original defect had been overtaken by the need for more extensive repairs due to the explosion, and the buyer could not recover damages for the loss of production during the notional period which would have been necessary for further repairs even if there had been no explosion.

[51] *Reardon Smith Line Ltd v. Australian Wheat Board* [1956] A.C. 266, 282–283 (PC, approving the judgment of Devlin J. in *Compania Naviera Maropan SA v. Bowaters Lloyd Pulp and Paper Mills Ltd* [1955] 2 Q.B. 68.)

[52] *Compania Naviera Maropan SA v. Bowaters Lloyd Pulp and Paper Mills Ltd, supra,* at 77.

[53] *ibid.* at 88. *cf. Lambert v. Lewis, supra.*

[54] *Tennant Radiant Heat Ltd v. Warrington Development Corporation* [1988] 1 E.G.L.R. 41 (discussed *post* § 27–038, where later doubts in the Court of Appeal are noted).

Intervening events. An intervening event which could reasonably be 27–032
expected will not excuse the defendant for loss caused by the combined operation
of the defendant's breach of contract[55] and the intervening event.[56] Thus in
Monarch Steamship Co. Ltd v. Karlshamns Oljefabriker (A/B)[57] the defendants'
ship was chartered to carry a cargo from Manchuria to Sweden. The ship should
have reached Sweden in July 1939 but the defendants broke their contractual
duty to provide a seaworthy ship and she was delayed till September. By this time
war had broken out, and the vessel was ordered by the British Admiralty to
unload at Glasgow. The plaintiffs (indorsees of the bills of lading) incurred
expenses in forwarding the cargo to Sweden in neutral ships, and the House of
Lords held that these could be recovered from the defendants. Reasonable
business men, knowing of the possibility of war, would have foreseen that a delay
might lead to the risk that the vessel would be diverted by the Admiralty. The
House of Lords held that the cost of transhipment was due to, or caused by, the
breach of contract, and was damage arising as a direct and natural consequence
of the breach.[58]

Two causes. If a breach of contract is one of two causes, both co-operating 27–033
and both of equal efficacy in causing loss to the plaintiff, the party responsible for
the breach is liable to the plaintiff for that loss.[59] The contract-breaker is liable
so long as his breach was "an" effective cause of his loss: the court need not
choose which cause was the most effective.[60]

The claimant's lost opportunities: hypothetical consequences. The claim- 27–034
ant may claim that, in the absence of the defendant's breach of contract, he might
have obtained a benefit or avoided a loss[61]: this consequence was not certain to
follow proper performance of the contract but the breach deprived the claimant
of the opportunity to benefit from it. The question usually arises when the
defendant has failed to do something, but it could arise where his performance
had been inadequate or deficient in some way. The law distinguishes two

---

[55] The defendant will not be liable if his breach did not contribute to the risk of the event occurring:
see *post*, n. 58. *cf.* the cases dealing with a fall in the property market: *post*, § 27–078.

[56] *Monarch Steamship Co. Ltd v. Karlshamns Oljefabriker (A/B)* [1949] A.C. 196. See also *The
Wilhem* (1866) 14 L.T. 636; *cf. Associated Portland Cement Manufacturers (1900) Ltd v. Houlder
Brothers & Co. Ltd* (1917) 86 L.J.K.B. 1495; *Diamond v. Campbell-Jones* [1961] Ch. 22.

[57] *Supra.*

[58] But if during the delayed voyage the ship ran into a typhoon and suffered damage, it could not
be said that the delay caused the damage: [1949] A.C. 196, 215. *cf.* the explosion in *Beoco Ltd v. Alfa
Laval Co. Ltd* [1995] Q.B. 137 (*ante* § 27–029) for which the plaintiff (the buyer) was held
responsible, and which put an end to any continuing liability on the seller for the cost of further
repairs even though the original defect was due to the seller's breach of contract.

[59] *Heskell v. Continental Express Ltd* [1950] 1 All E.R. 1033, 1047–1048; *Banque Keyser Ullmann
SA v. Skandia (U.K.) Insurance Co. Ltd* [1990] Q.B. 665, 813–814 (the decision of the HL did not
deal with this point: [1991] 2 A.C. 249). The defendant may seek contribution from a third party who
contributed to the causation of the loss and who would also have been liable to the claimant: s.1(1)
of the Civil Liability (Contribution) Act 1978.

[60] *County Ltd v. Girozentrale Securities* [1996] 3 All E.R. 834, CA.

[61] The question whether a past event occurred must be decided on the balance of probabilities—
once the claimant proves that it was more likely than not to have occurred, the court treats it as a
definite fact: *Davies v. Taylor* [1974] A.C. 207, 213 (a tort case); it does "not raise any question of
what might have been the situation in a hypothetical state of facts": *Hotson v. East Berkshire A.H.A.*
[1987] A.C. 750, 785; and so "chances" are not legally relevant. See Reece, (1996) 59 M.L.R.
188.

situations: where the hypothetical consequence involves the hypothesis of the claimant's act and where it involves that of a third party.

(a) *A hypothetical action of the claimant.* This situation arises where a particular contingency depends on the hypothetical question whether the claimant himself would have acted in a certain way. It is illustrated by the case where a solicitor failed to give proper advice to his client and the issue is whether the client would have accepted the advice and acted on it in a particular way. The client must prove, on the balance of probabilities, that he would have done so: unless he can prove this, he fails to establish the causal link between the defendant's omission and the loss he would have avoided if he had accepted and acted on the hypothetical advice.[62] But if he can satisfy this burden of proof, it is not a case of loss of a chance, because the claimant has proved what he would have done and damages must be assessed on this basis.[63]

(b) *A hypothetical action of a third party.* This situation arises where a particular contingency depends on whether a third party would have acted in a certain way.[64] Where the claimant claims that, in the absence of the breach of contract by the defendant, a third party would have acted in a particular way, so as to benefit the claimant, he need not prove that hypothetical action on the balance of probabilities. Provided that the claimant can prove that in the absence of the breach there was a "real" or "substantial" (not a speculative) chance of the third party's action, the court must assess the chance of that action resulting (usually as a percentage) and then discount the claimant's damages for his loss by that percentage.[65] In the leading case of *Chaplin v. Hicks*[66] the defendant, by a breach of contract in conducting a contest, deprived the plaintiff, one of 50 finalists, of the opportunity to compete for one of the 12 prizes. Although there could be no precision in calculating the value of her lost chance, she was entitled to substantial damages. Similarly, where the breach of contract caused the claimant to lose his chance of success in litigation, the question is what chance the claimant would have had of a favourable outcome. So where the client's claim became statute-barred because his solicitor failed to bring proceedings within time, the measure of the client's damages recovered from the solicitor was the expected proceeds of the original claim[67]: what he might have recovered in the original claim must be discounted by his chances of success in recovering it.[68] However, "the more the contingencies, the lower the value of the chance or

---

[62] *Allied Maples Group Ltd v. Simmons and Simmons* [1995] 1 W.L.R. 1602, CA; *Brown v. K.M.R. Services Ltd* [1995] 4 All E.R. 598, 617, 638, CA. See also *Sykes v. Midland Bank Executor and Trustee Co.* [1971] 1 Q.B. 113.

[63] The case of *Otter v. Church, Adams Tatham & Co.* [1953] 1 Ch. 280, which decided the contrary, was criticised in the CA in both the *Allied Maples* case, above, at 290; and *Sykes v. Midland Bank Executor and Trustee Co.*, *supra.*, at 130.

[64] This issue could arise in a case where it was also relevant to decide how the claimant himself would have acted: the *Allied Maples* case, *supra.* Loss of profits will always depend on many speculative factors, such as third parties continuing to deal with the claimant: this paragraph, however, deals with the loss of a specific opportunity.

[65] The *Allied Maples* case, *supra.* (CA: a claim in tort, but the facts also amounted to a breach of contract). The chance of the third party's action can be considerably less than 50%. But no discount for contingency is appropriate if it is certain what the third party would have done: see *White v. Jones* [1995] 2 A.C. 207, 228, CA; *Dickinson v. Jones Alexander & Co.* [1993] 2 F.L.R. 321.

[66] [1911] 2 K.B. 786, CA. (This case, and *Kitchen's* case cited in the next note, were cited by the House of Lords in *Hotson v. East Berkshire A.H.A.* [1987] A.C. 750, 782, 792–793 (a tort case).)

[67] *Kitchen v. Royal Air Force Association* [1958] 1 W.L.R. 563, 575–576; *Cook v. Swinfen* [1967] 1 W.L.R. 457; *Malyon v. Lawrence, Messer & Co.* [1968] 2 Lloyd's Rep. 539.

[68] *cf. Yeoman's Executrix v. Ferries* 1967 S.L.T. 332 (the value of an "out-of-court" settlement of the plaintiff's claim).

opportunity of which the plaintiff was deprived".[69] Where one contingency may depend on another, the chance should be evaluated as a percentage of a percentage.[70]

A similar approach to assessing damages is found in other "loss of a chance"   27–035
cases not involving litigation: for instance, where through a solicitor's failure to give proper advice, the client lost the chance to negotiate better terms in a commercial transaction with a third party, who might have accepted such terms[71]; or where an author or actor lost the opportunity to enhance his reputation.[72]

The contract-breaker's opportunity to minimise the cost of perform-   27–036
ance.[73] A contingency may depend on whether the contract-breaker would have acted in a certain way. If the defendant fails to perform, when he had an option to perform the contract in one of several ways,[74] damages are assessed on the basis that he would have performed in the way which would have benefited him most,[75] *e.g.* at the least cost to himself.[76] So damages were assessed against charterers on the basis that they would have used their contractual entitlements to produce the least profitable result for the owners.[77] A similar situation arises where the contract-breaker had an option to terminate the contract: if the claimant accepts the anticipatory breach of the defendant as a ground for terminating the contract,[78] but the defendant could have exercised his option to terminate the contract so as to extinguish or reduce the loss caused by the anticipatory breach, the court will assess the damages for the breach on the assumption that the defendant would have exercised the option.[79]

Contributory negligence.[80] The Law Reform (Contributory Negligence) Act   27–037
1945 permits apportionment of loss by the reduction of the claimant's damages where he "suffers damage as the result partly of his own fault and partly of the fault of any other person."[81] Although the Act was obviously designed for claims

---

[69] *Hall v. Meyrick* [1957] 2 Q.B. 455, 471 (revd. by CA on other grounds).

[70] *Ministry of Defence v. Wheeler* [1998] 1 All E.R. 790, CA.

[71] The *Allied Maples* case, above; *Stovold v. Barlows* [1996] P.N.L.R. 91. *cf. First Interstate Bank of California v. Cohen Arnold* [1996] P.N.L.R. 17, CA (negligence claim against accountants); *Davies v. Taylor* [1974] A.C. 207 (loss of chance of widow's fatal accident claim); *Spring v. Guardian Assurance* [1995] A.C. 296, 327 (tort claim for former employee's loss of reasonable chance of a particular employment).

[72] *Post,* § 27–071.

[73] *cf. Lavarack v. Woods of Colchester Ltd* [1967] 1 Q.B. 278, 294 (*ante* § 27–001).

[74] See *ante,* § 22–006.

[75] But where the defendant had a choice of alternative methods of performance, the damages will be assessed on the basis of the method least onerous to him only where that method was reasonable in all the circumstances: *Paula Lee Ltd v. Robert Zehil & Co. Ltd* [1983] 2 All E.R. 390. *cf. Abrahams v. Herbert Reiach Ltd* [1922] 1 K.B. 477.

[76] *Re Thornett, Fehr and Yuills* [1921] 1 K.B. 219; *Withers v. General Theatre Corpn.* [1933] 2 K.B. 536; *Beach v. Reed Corrugated Cases* [1956] 1 W.L.R. 807, 816–817; *Bunge Corp., New York v. Tradax S.A. Panama* [1981] 1 W.L.R. 711, HL; *Johnson Matthey Banking v. State Trading Corpn. of India* [1984] 1 Lloyd's Rep. 427 (sellers entitled to take advantage of 1.5% tolerance).

[77] *Spiliada Maritime Corpn. v. Louis Dreyfus Corpn.* [1983] Com. L.R. 268. See also *Kaye Steam Navigating Co. v. Barnett* (1932) 48 T.L.R. 440; *Becher v. Koplak Enterprises* [1991] 2 Lloyd's Rep. 23, CA.

[78] See *ante,* §§ 25–020—25–026, 25–029.

[79] *The Mihalis Angelos* [1971] 1 Q.B. 164 (see *ante,* § 25–021). *cf.* the principles on which damages are assessed for wrongful dismissal: Vol. II, § 39–179—39–180.

[80] Proposals to change the law are found in the Law Commission's Report No. 219, *Contributory Negligence as a Defence in Contract* (1993). See the comment by Porat, (1995) 111 L.Q.R. 228.

[81] s.1(1). At common law, the claimant's contributory negligence was a complete defence in an action in tort; the defence had never been applied (*eo nomine*) in an action in contract before 1945:

in tort,[82] the definition of "fault" as (*inter alia*) "negligence" raises the question whether a defendant guilty of a breach of contract can take advantage of this provision if the claimant has himself contributed to causing his loss by some "fault" on his part. In *Vesta v. Butcher*[83] the Court of Appeal accepted that three categories are relevant to this question: category 1, where the defendant is liable only in contract for breach of a strict duty (negligence being irrelevant); category 2, where the defendant is liable only in contract for breach of an obligation to take care (there being no corresponding duty of care in tort); and category 3, where the defendant's liability in contract is the same as his liability in negligence (the tortious duty of care arising independently of the contract). In *Vesta v. Butcher*[84] the Court of Appeal held[85] that the Act of 1945 applied only to category 3 cases,[86] namely those where the breach of contract is co-extensive with the breach of the tortious duty.[87] In this situation it would be anomalous if the claimant could avoid the apportionment provisions of the Act by the simple device of suing only in contract.[88] The decision in *Vesta v. Butcher* means that where the defendant's liability arises only in contract (categories 1[89]; and 2[90]) contributory negligence cannot be relied on to reduce the claimant's damages.

---

see the discussion in Williams, *Joint Torts and Contributory Negligence* (1951), pp. 214–222; and in the Law Commission's Report No. 219, Part. II.

[82] Contributory negligence may be raised in a claim under s. 2(1) of the Misrepresentation Act 1967: *Gran Gelato Ltd v. Richcliff (Group) Ltd* [1992] Ch. 560, 572–575.

[83] *Forsikrings Vesta v. Butcher* [1989] A.C. 852, 860–867, 875, 879 (in the decision of the House of Lords, contributory negligence was not dealt with).

[84] *Supra.*

[85] Following a New Zealand decision, *Rowe v. Turner Hopkins and Partners* [1980] 2 N.Z.L.R. 550. The question had been examined by academic writers: Swanton (1981) 55 A.L.J. 278; Chandler (1989) 40 N.I.L.Q. 152; Anderson [1987] L.M.C.L.Q. 10.

[86] This decision has been followed (*obiter*) by the Court of Appeal in *Bank of Nova Scotia v. Hellenic Mutual War Risks Association (Bermuda) Ltd* [1990] 1 Q.B. 818, 904. (The appeal was allowed by the House of Lords on another issue, with the result that contributory negligence was not considered: [1992] 1 A.C. 233, 266.)

[87] In other words, the claim in contract is founded on an act or omission by the defendant which would also have given rise to liability in tort. Illustrations of category 3 are: *Sayers v. Harlow U.D.C.* [1958] 1 W.L.R. 623 (see the comments on this case in *Vesta v. Butcher, supra,* at 861, 866–867); *Vesta v. Butcher, supra* (insurers' claim against brokers for failing to inform reinsurers that the insured could not comply with a clause in the contract of reinsurance); *Platform Home Loans Ltd v. Oyston Shipways Ltd* [1999] 2 W.L.R. 518, HL (lender suing valuer for negligent over-valuation of the security). The decision in *Vesta v. Butcher* leaves open the question whether the Act of 1945 applies where the plaintiff's claim in tort is not co-extensive with his claim in contract: see the Law Commission's Report No. 219 (1993) para. 3.29.

[88] Category 3 cases will be more frequent after the decision in *Henderson v. Merrett* [1995] 2 A.C. 145 (see *ante*, §§ 1–078 *et seq.*) (especially where clients sue those providing professional services and advice).

[89] Illustrations of category 1 cases are: *Basildon District Council v. J.E. Lesser (Properties) Ltd* [1985] QB 839 (claim for an indemnity under a deed); *Quinn v. Burch Brothers (Builders) Ltd* [1966] 2 QB 370 (the Court of Appeal did not discuss contributory negligence: see *ante*, § 27–029); *Tennant Radiant Heat Ltd v. Warrington Development Corporation* [1988] 1 E.G.L.R. 41 (but see *post* n. 93); *Banque Keyser Ullmann SA v. Skandia (U.K.) Insurance Co. Ltd* [1990] Q.B. 665, 720–721 (neither the Court of Appeal, *ibid.* at 815–817, nor the House of Lords [1991] 2 A.C. 249 dealt with this point); *Bank of Nova Scotia v. Hellenic Mutual War Risks Association (Bermuda) Ltd supra,* at 904; *Barclays Bank plc. v. Fairclough Building Ltd* [1995] Q.B. 214 (strict undertakings by builder that roofing work should be done by specialists, and that the workmanship should be the best of its kind).

[90] Illustrations of category 2 cases are: *A.S. James Pty Ltd v. Duncan* [1970] V.R. 705; *De Meza v. Apple* [1974] 1 Lloyd's Rep. 508 (solicitor's claim for both negligence and breach of contract against auditors: the appeal did not deal with the point: [1975] 1 Lloyd's Rep. 498, 509; it is

Recovery barred on other grounds. But even where the Act does not apply   27–038
to claims founded only on contract, there are many situations where conduct of
the claimant which would have constituted contributory negligence under the Act
will bar his recovery on the ground of his failure to mitigate,[91] or his failure to
prove causation—his own carelessness may be held to be the sole cause of the
loss.[92] In one case, the Court of Appeal, after holding that contributory negligence did not apply to a Category 1 case, nevertheless reached a similar result by
an unusual application of causation: a landlord's damages against his lessees for
breach of a repairing covenant (a strict obligation) were reduced by 90 per cent
because he (the landlord) had negligently failed to keep clear the drainage outlets
of the roof.[93] The landlord's failure was held to be a concurrent cause of the
collapse of the roof, to which 90 per cent of the total causation was assigned.

3. REMOTENESS OF DAMAGE[94]

(a) *General Rules*

Introduction. The term "remoteness of damage" refers to the legal test used   27–039
to decide which types of loss caused by the breach of contract may be compensated by an award of damages.[95] If there is no explicit clause in the contract
dealing with the assessment of damages, the law supplies a standard test which
specifies the extent of responsibility implicitly undertaken by the promisor. There
is a reciprocal allocation of risks; the precise legal test is examined below, but it
can be said in general terms that the promisor implicitly accepts responsibility for

---

submitted that the decision at first instance is not consistent with *Vesta v. Butcher, supra*); *Marintrans (A.B.) v. Comet Shipping Ltd* [1985] 1 W.L.R. 1270.

[91] *Post,* § 27–085 *et seq.* For an illustration, see *Lambert v. Lewis* [1982] A.C. 225 (*post,* § 27–089).

[92] *Ante,* § 27–029.

[93] *Tennant Radiant Heat Ltd v. Warrington Development Corporation* [1988] 1 E.G.L.R. 41 (but the principle applied in this case was doubted by the Court of Appeal in *Bank of Nova Scotia v. Hellenic Mutual War Risks Association (Bermuda) Ltd* [1990] 1 QB 818, 904: the House of Lords did not deal with this point: [1992] 1 A.C. 233, 266). See also Bennett (1984–85) 4 *Litigation* 195, 197; the Law Commission's Report No. 219 (n. 80, *supra*), 3.13 to 3.15; and *Schering Agrochemicals Ltd v. Resibel NVSA* (unreported; noted at (1993) 109 L.Q.R. 175).

[94] The term "remoteness of damage" has been distinguished from the term "measure of damages" (or "quantification"), the former referring to the rules as to which types of consequences or losses may be compensated, the latter to the method of assessing in money the compensation for a particular consequence or loss which has been held to be not too remote: Cheshire and North, *Private International Law* (5th ed.), pp. 708–712 (approved in *D'Almeida Araujo v. Becker* [1953] 2 Q.B. 329; see now 12th ed., pp. 92–96). This distinction, however, is not adopted in this chapter because it has not yet found favour with the courts in a domestic case: see *Handel (N.V.) My. J. Smits Import-Export v. English Exporters Ltd* [1955] 2 Lloyd's Rep. 69, 72 (affd. at 317); *Boys v. Chaplin* [1968] 2 Q.B. 1, 31; but the distinction has been accepted in a conflict of laws problem: *Boys v. Chaplin* [1971] A.C. 356, 378–379, 382–383, 392–393, 394. See *Dicey & Morris on the Conflict of Laws* (12th ed., 1993), pp. 183–184, 1263–1264 (At 1263: "It is probable that, in the field of contractual obligations, the distinction survives the" Contracts (Applicable Law) Act 1990.) *cf. Wroth v. Tyler* [1974] Ch. 30, 60–62 (*post,* § 27–049).

[95] For a comparison between the rules on remoteness in tort and in contract, see Harris *op. cit.* pp. 225–227; and Cartwright [1996] C.L.J. 488.

the usual consequences of a breach of the promise in question, while the promisee implicitly accepts the risk of any other consequences. (In other words, the promisee implicitly agrees not to hold the promisor responsible for unusual consequences.)[96] The test should ultimately depend on the express or implied intention of the parties. Hence, the promisor may be liable for an unusual type of loss where he is made aware of the risk and thus expressly or impliedly accepts responsibility for it.[97]

27-040   **Hadley v. Baxendale.** The classic statement of the rules regarding remoteness of damage in contract (which apply when the damages claimed are unliquidated) is to be found in the judgment of the Court of Exchequer in *Hadley v. Baxendale*,[98] as interpreted in later cases.[99] In this case, the plaintiffs' mill was brought to a standstill by the breakage of their only crankshaft. The defendant carriers failed to deliver the broken shaft to the manufacturer at the time they had promised to do, and the plaintiffs sued to recover the profits they would have made had the mill been started again without the delay. The court rejected the claim on the ground that the facts known to the defendants were insufficient[1] to "show reasonably that the profits of the mill must be stopped by an unreasonable delay in the delivery of the broken shaft by the carriers to the third person."[2]

27-041   The judgment of the court was delivered by Alderson B., who said[3]:

"Where two parties have made a contract which one of them has broken, the damages which the other party ought to receive in respect of such breach of contract should be such as may fairly and reasonably be considered either as arising naturally, *i.e.* according to the usual course of things, from such breach of contract itself, or such as may reasonably be supposed to have been in the contemplation of both parties, at the time they made the contract, as the probable result of the breach of it. Now, if the special circumstances under which the contract was actually made were communicated by the plaintiffs to the defendants, and thus known to both parties, the damages resulting from the breach of such a contract, which they would reasonably contemplate, would be the amount of injury which would ordinarily follow from a breach of contract under these special circumstances so known and communicated. On the other hand, if these special circumstances were wholly unknown to the party breaking the contract, he, at the most, could only be supposed to have had in his contemplation the amount of injury which would arise generally, and in the great multitude of cases not affected by any special circumstances, from such a breach of contract."

27-042   **Modern statement of the rule.** The principles laid down in *Hadley v. Baxendale, supra,* have been interpreted and restated by the Court of Appeal in 1949

---

[96] In an exemption clause (see Chap. 14, *ante*), the promisee expressly accepts that the promisor is not to be liable for specified consequences.

[97] This is the second rule in *Hadley v. Baxendale, post,* § 27–049.

[98] (1854) 9 Exch. 341. (See comments by Simpson (1975) 91 L.Q.R. 247, 273; Pugsley (1976) 126 New L.J. 420; Danzig (1975) 4 J.Leg.Stud. 249; Harris *op. cit.* pp. 55–56.)

[99] See *post,* § 27–042 *et seq.*

[1] *Victoria Laundry (Windsor) Ltd v. Newman Industries Ltd* [1949] 2 K.B. 528, 537–538. (The headnote of *Hadley v. Baxendale, supra,* is misleading.)

[2] (1854) 9 Exch. 341, 355. See also *Collins v. Howard* [1949] 2 All E.R. 324.

[3] (1854) 9 Exch. 341, 354–355.

in *Victoria Laundry (Windsor) Ltd v. Newman Industries Ltd*[4] and by the House of Lords in 1967, in *Koufos v. C. Czarnikow Ltd (The Heron II)*.[5] The combined effect of these cases may be summarised as follows: A type or kind of loss is not too remote a consequence of a breach of contract if, at the time of contracting (and on the assumption that the parties actually foresaw the breach in question), it was within their reasonable contemplation as a not unlikely result of that breach.[6] The following paragraphs expound the different aspects of this summary.

The *Victoria Laundry* case. The three main propositions in the *Victoria*   **27–043**
Laundry case were[7]:

"(2) In cases of breach of contract the aggrieved party is only entitled to recover such part of the loss actually resulting as was at the time of the contract reasonably foreseeable as liable to result from the breach. . . . "

"(3) What was at that time reasonably so foreseeable depends on the knowledge then possessed by the parties or, at all events, by the party who later commits the breach. . . ."

"(4) For this purpose, knowledge 'possessed' is of two kinds; one imputed, the other actual. Everyone, as a reasonable person, is taken to know the 'ordinary course of things' and consequently what loss is liable to result from a breach of contract in that ordinary course. . . . But to this knowledge, which a contract-breaker is assumed to possess whether he actually possesses it or not, there may have to be added in a particular case knowledge which he actually possesses, of special circumstances outside the 'ordinary course of things,' of such a kind that breach in those special circumstances would be liable to cause more loss. . . . "

The *Heron II*. In *The Heron II*[8] their Lordships did not agree upon a common   **27–044**
formulation, but three of their Lordships[9] gave general approval to these and other[10] propositions in the *Victoria Laundry* case. Somewhat different formulations were adopted by Lords Reid and Upjohn: the former said that Alderson B. in *Hadley v. Baxendale, supra,*

---

[4] [1949] 2 K.B. 528. (Some of the propositions in this case were cited with approval in *East Ham Corporation v. Bernard Sunley & Sons Ltd* [1966] A.C. 406, 440, 445, 450–451.) See *post*, § 27–054.

[5] [1969] 1 A.C. 350. The Court of Appeal has further considered these principles in *H. Parsons (Livestock) Ltd v. Uttley Ingham & Co. Ltd* [1978] Q.B. 791. (The two cases cited in the text at the beginning of § 27–042 are not limited in their application to loss of profits: *ibid.* at 804–805, 805–806, 813. *cf.* at 802–804.) See further, *ante*, § 27–032.

[6] This sentence was quoted with approval by Stuart-Smith L.J. in *Brown v. K.M.R. Services Ltd* [1995] 4 All E.R. 598, 621 (see also 642–643). *cf.* the summary of Scarman L.J. in *H. Parsons (Livestock) Ltd v. Uttley Ingham & Co. Ltd, supra,* at p. 807 ("The court's task . . . is to decide what loss to the plaintiff it is reasonable to suppose would have been in the contemplation of the parties as a serious possibility had they had in mind the breach when they made their contract."). The test is not one of "directness": *Ogilvie Builders Ltd v. Glasgow City D.C.*, 1995 S.L.T. 15. As to the judicial discretion involved in applying the test for remoteness, see Cooke [1978] C.L.J. 288.

[7] [1949] 2 K.B. 528, 539–540 (propositions (1), (5) and (6) are omitted for reasons of space). For the facts in the case, see *post*, § 27–054.

[8] [1969] 1 A.C. 350. For the facts see *post*, § 27–073.

[9] [1969] 1 A.C. 350, 399 (Lord Morris), 410–411 (Lord Hodson), 414–417 (Lord Pearce). (But Lord Reid, at 388–391, rejected parts of the *Victoria Laundry* propositions.)

[10] See *post*, § 27–046.

"clearly meant that a result which will happen in the great majority[11] of cases should fairly and reasonably be regarded as having been in the contemplation of the parties, but that a result which, though foreseeable as a substantial possibility, would only happen in a small minority of cases should not be regarded as having been in their contemplation."[12]

Lord Reid continued:

"The crucial question is whether, on the information available to the defendant when the contract was made, he should, or the reasonable man in his position would, have realised that such loss was sufficiently likely to result from the breach of contract to make it proper to hold that the loss flowed naturally from the breach or that loss of that kind should have been within his contemplation."[13]

Lord Upjohn stated "the broad rule as follows: 'What was in the assumed contemplation of both parties acting as reasonable men in the light of the general or special facts (as the case may be) known to both parties in regard to damages as the result of a breach of contract.' "[14] There is no need for the breach itself to be within the contemplation of the parties: "It is clear that one starts from the assumption that the contract-breaker contemplates, at the date of the making of the contract, the occurrence of the particular breach which he, although at the time he may have no notion of it, is thereafter going to commit."[15]

27–045   **The type or kind of loss.**[16] The reference to "the loss" in the formulations of the test for remoteness of damage is to be interpreted as the type or kind of loss in question.[17] The "party who has suffered damage does not have to show that the contract-breaker ought to have contemplated, as being not unlikely, the precise detail of the damage or the precise manner of its happening. It is enough if he should have contemplated that damage *of that kind* is not unlikely."[18] (There is a similar formulation in the test for remoteness of damage in tort: "the essential factor in determining liability is whether the damage is of such a kind as the

---

[11] Lord Hodson [1969] 1 A.C. 350, 411, also adopted the expression used in *Hadley v. Baxendale, ante*: "in the great multitude of cases": (1854) 9 Exch. 341, 355, 356.

[12] [1969] 1 A.C. 350, 384 (see also at 385). Both Lords Reid and Upjohn criticised the words "foreseeable" or "reasonably foreseeable" in the *Victoria Laundry* formulations: *ibid.* at 389, 422–423; Lord Upjohn, at 422–423, expressly preferred "contemplate" or "in contemplation" for cases in contract, and these are the words used by Lord Reid at 384–385.

[13] *ibid.* at 385.

[14] *ibid.* at 424.

[15] *Christopher Hill Ltd v. Ashington Piggeries Ltd* [1969] 3 All E.R. 1496, 1523 (Court of Appeal: the House of Lords reversed the decision on other grounds, without discussing *The Heron II*: [1972] A.C. 441); *H. Parsons (Livestock) Ltd v. Uttley, Ingham & Co. Ltd, supra*, at 802, 807.

[16] This paragraph was quoted with approval by Stuart-Smith L.J. in *Brown v. K.M.R. Services Ltd* [1995] 4 All E.R. 598, 621.

[17] In *The Heron II, supra*, Lord Reid spoke of "type of damage" (at 385–386), "loss of a kind which" (at 382, 383) and "type of loss" (at 385); while Lord Pearce spoke of "type of consequence" (at 417). See also *H. Parsons (Livestock) Ltd v. Uttley, Ingham & Co. Ltd* [1978] Q.B. 791, 801, 805, 806, 813.

[18] *Christopher Hill Ltd v. Ashington Piggeries Ltd, supra*, at 1524; *Brown v. K.M.R. Services Ltd, supra*, at 621; *Kpohraror v. Woolwich Building Society* [1996] 4 All E.R. 119, 126. See *post*, § 27–049 for the corresponding formulation in the second rule in *Hadley v. Baxendale, supra*.

reasonable man should have foreseen."[19]) If the parties ought to have contemplated a particular type of loss ("head of damage") they need not have contemplated the extent of that loss.[20] The application of the test for remoteness to a particular set of facts therefore depends largely on the judicial discretion[21] to categorise losses into broad categories,[22] without requiring any contemplation of the precise manner in which the loss was caused, or of the precise details of the loss.[23]

The degree of probability. What was in the contemplation of reasonable men   **27–046**
obviously depends on the relevant degree of likelihood[24] that a particular kind of loss may occur, and this issue was extensively discussed in *The Heron II*.[25] Lord Reid used "the words 'not unlikely' as denoting a degree of probability considerably less than an even chance but nevertheless not very unusual and easily foreseeable."[26] Although Lord Morris thought it unnecessary to choose any one phrase[27] he used "not unlikely to occur,"[28] with "liable to result" as an alternative[29]; Lord Hodson accepted the latter phrase.[30] Both Lords Pearce[31] and

---

[19] *Overseas Tankship (U.K.) Ltd v. Morts Dock & Engineering Co. Ltd (The Wagon Mound)* [1961] A.C. 388, 426.

[20] *H. Parsons (Livestock) Ltd v. Uttley, Ingham & Co. Ltd, supra,* at 804, 805, 813; *Brown v. K.M.R. Services Ltd, supra,* at 621, 642–643. *cf. Wroth v. Tyler* [1974] Ch. 30, 60–62 (dealing with the corresponding position under the second rule in *Hadley v. Baxendale*). But *cf.* the cases on loss of profits, *post,* § 27–054; Vol. II, §§ 43–406—43–408, where the type of profits expected from the normal use of a profit-earning machine is used to place a cap on a claim for loss of a different type of profit caused by the breach of contract; *Vacwell Engineering Co. Ltd v. B.D.H. Chemicals Ltd* [1971] Q.B. 88; *cf.* also the limitation on the extent of a valuer's liability to a lender for a negligent over-valuation: *South Australia Asset Management Corp. v. York Montague Ltd* [1997] A.C. 191 (*post,* § 27–078).

[21] For recent illustrations, see *Balfour Beatty Construction (Scotland) Ltd v. Scottish Power plc,* 1994 S.L.T. 807 (HL: not contemplated that interruption of electricity supply to a concrete batching plant would result in demolition and rebuilding of a partly-constructed aqueduct); *Kpohraror v. Woolwich Building Society* [1996] 4 All E.R. 119 (CA: not contemplated that one day's delay by a bank in meeting a cheque might cause the plaintiff to lose the transaction in question or incur a trading loss in future).

[22] As is illustrated by cases in later paragraphs of this chapter, *e.g.* loss of profits; physical damage to a chattel or building; illness or death of a person; illness or death of an animal; expenses incurred by the plaintiff in reliance on the contract; personal, subjective loss of amenity; damages and costs paid by the plaintiff to a third party as a result of the breach of contract leading to the plaintiff being held liable to the third party. *cf.* the similar broad interpretation of the "type" or "kind" of loss in the test for remoteness of damage in tort: *Overseas Tankship (U.K.) Ltd v. Morts Dock & Engineering Co. Ltd, supra*; *Hughes v. Lord Advocate* [1963] A.C. 837.

[23] *H. Parsons (Livestock) Ltd v. Uttley, Ingham & Co. Ltd, supra,* at 811 (" . . . contemplation that a hopper unfit for its purpose of storing food in a condition suitable for feeding pigs, might well lead to illness" of the pigs or their "physical injury" (at 805, 813), but not that it might lead to a specific type of serious illness (at 812, 813)). "Loss of profit" is obviously another "type" of loss: *ibid.* at 802–803, 813; see also *post,* §§ 27–054 *et seq.*

[24] *Southern Portland Cement Ltd v. Cooper* [1974] A.C. 623, 640. The contractual test requires a higher degree of probability than the test for remoteness in tort: see Harris *op. cit,* pp. 226–227. Where the loss in question would, apart from the breach of contract, depend on various contingencies, the damages should reflect the appropriate degree of likelihood: see *ante,* § 27–034 *et seq.*

[25] [1969] 1 A.C. 350. For the facts, see *post,* § 27–073.

[26] *ibid.* at 383. (See also his statements at 388: "a very substantial degree of probability.")

[27] *ibid.* at 397, 399.

[28] *ibid.* at 406.

[29] *ibid.* at 406. "Liable to result" was also one of the phrases accepted in the *Victoria Laundry Case* [1949] 2 K.B. 528, 540.

[30] [1969] 1 A.C. 350, 410–411. (Lord Reid, at 389, rejected this phrase.)

[31] *ibid.* at 415.

Upjohn[32] adopted the words "a real danger" or "a serious possibility"[33] which were the phrases used in the House of Lords in 1991.[34] (Four of their Lordships in *The Heron II* agreed that the colloquialism "on the cards" should not be used.[35])

27–047   **Actual and imputed knowledge.** In general, it is necessary to consider the actual knowledge of the defendant (the promisor) only where he would not have been liable without that knowledge; normally the imputed knowledge of the defendant will be at least as great as (if not greater than) his actual knowledge. Actual knowledge may occasionally operate to the advantage of the defendant. For instance, Devlin J. has said:

> "If, however, a sub-sale is within the contemplation of the parties, I think that the damages must be assessed by reference to it, whether the plaintiff likes it or not. . . .
> If it is the plaintiff's liability to the ultimate user that is contemplated as the measure of damages and it is in fact used without injurious results so that no such liability arises, the plaintiff could not claim the difference in market value, and say that the sub-sale must be disregarded."[36]

27–048   The test for imputed knowledge has been said by Lord Wright[37] to be "what reasonable business men must be taken to have contemplated as the natural and probable result if the contract was broken. As reasonable business men, each must be taken to understand the ordinary practices and exigencies of the other's trade or business."[38] The defendant's knowledge of the type of business conducted by the claimant may be a ground for imputing knowledge,[39] but the defendant cannot be expected to know the technical details of the claimant's activity where it involved complicated techniques.[40] Again, in contracts for the sale of goods, the defendant is normally taken to have known that the market price and the supply and demand of the market may change.[41] The kind of consequence which falls within the imputed knowledge of the defendant will be

---

[32] *ibid.* at 425.

[33] These words were rejected by Lord Reid (at 390), who also rejected "foreseeable as a real possibility" (at 385). The *Victoria Laundry* case, *supra*, at 540, also accepted "a real danger" or "a serious possibility." (The latter phrase was used by the Court of Appeal in *H. Parsons (Livestock) Ltd v. Uttley, Ingham & Co. Ltd, supra*, at 802, 805, 807.)

[34] *Bank of Nova Scotia v. Hellenic Mutual War Risks Association (Bermuda) Ltd* [1992] 1 A.C. 233, 267.

[35] [1969] 1 A.C. 350, 390, 399, 415, 425. (It was yet another phrase used in the *Victoria Laundry* case, *supra*, at 540.)

[36] *Biggin & Co. Ltd v. Permanite Ltd* [1951] 1 K.B. 422, 436. (The actual decision in this case was reversed on another ground: [1951] 2 K.B. 314 (see Vol. II, § 43–429).) See also *Bence Graphics International Ltd v. Fasson U.K. Ltd* [1998] Q.B. 87 (*post*, §§ 43–411, 43–413, where criticism by Treitel is noted); *The Heron II* [1969] 1 A.C. 350, 416. *cf. Trans Trust S.P.R.L. v. Danubian Trading Co. Ltd* [1952] 2 K.B. 297, 306; and *post*, § 27–117.

[37] *Monarch Steamship Co. Ltd v. Karlshamns Oljefabriker (A/B)* [1949] A.C. 196, 224 (examined further in *Balfour Beatty Construction (Scotland) Ltd v. Scottish Power plc*, 1994 S.L.T. 807, HL).

[38] See also *Bank of Nova Scotia v. Hellenic Mutual War Risks Association (Bermuda) Ltd* [1992] 1 A.C. 233, 267.

[39] *Victoria Laundry (Windsor) Ltd v. Newman Industries Ltd* [1949] 2 K.B. 528 (*post*, § 27–054); *cf. Diamond v. Campbell-Jones* [1961] Ch. 22.

[40] The *Balfour Beatty* case, *supra*.

[41] *Interoffice Telephones Ltd v. Robert Freeman Co. Ltd* [1958] 1 Q.B. 190, 202 (*post*, § 27–056). The same holds for contracts for the carriage of goods: *post*, § 27–073.

illustrated by cases throughout the rest of this section, and in particular, by cases on damages in contracts for the sale of goods.[42]

Actual knowledge of special circumstances. The so-called second rule in **27–049** *Hadley v. Baxendale*[43] applies when the loss (the "type or kind of loss"[44]) flowing from the breach of a particular contract is greater than, or different from what it would have been in normal circumstances. If actual knowledge of the defendant (the promisor) is relied upon to make him liable for exceptional losses resulting from breach of the contract in the special[45] circumstances, that knowledge must have existed at or before the making of the contract.[46] The second rule covers "heads of damage" not the quantum or extent of loss; thus, it is unnecessary for the parties to have contemplated the quantum of damages, or the extent of the loss, provided it falls within a contemplated type of loss.[47]

Knowledge and assumption of risk. An unsettled point is whether bare **27–050** knowledge of the special circumstances is enough to fix the defendant with liability for an unusual loss if he breaks the contract.[48] In 1868, Willes J. said[49]:

> "The mere fact of knowledge cannot increase the liability. The knowledge must be brought home to the party sought to be charged, under such circumstances that he must know that the person he contracts with reasonably believes that he accepts the contract with the special condition attached to it . . . knowledge on the part of the carrier is only important if it forms part of the contract. It may be that the knowledge is acquired casually from a stranger, the person to whom the goods belong not knowing or caring whether he had such knowledge or not."

It is submitted, however, that it is unnecessary to hold that the defendant's assumption of liability for unusual loss (in the special circumstances made known to him) can be enforced only where there is an express or implied term of the contract to that effect[50]; but that it is sufficient if, on the basis of his

---

[42] *Post*, §§ 27–072, *et seq.*

[43] (1854) 9 Exch. 341 (*ante*, § 27–040).

[44] *Wroth v. Tyler* [1974] Ch. 30, 61.

[45] The facts or circumstances do not have to be "unusual" before the second rule in *Hadley v. Baxendale* may come into play: see *post* § 27–082, text at n. 49.

[46] *Victoria Laundry (Windsor) Ltd v. Newman Industries Ltd* [1949] 2 K.B. 528, 539 (Proposition 3, cited *ante*, § 27–043). See also *Hydraulic Engineering Co. Ltd v. McHaffie Goslett & Co.* (1878) 4 Q.B.D. 670, 676. *cf. Kollman v. Watts* [1963] V.L.R. 396 (knowledge acquired *after* the contract was made).

[47] *Wroth v. Tyler, supra,* at 60–62. *cf. ante*, § 27–045. *cf.,* however, the cases on loss of profits, which show that a loss of profits from one use of a chattel may be treated as different from a loss of profits from another use: see *post*, § 27–054; Vol. II, §§ 43–406, 43–408. *cf.* also *South Australia Asset Management Corp. v. York Montague Ltd* [1997] A.C. 191 (*post* § 27–078).

[48] *Patrick v. Russo-British Grain Export Co. Ltd* [1927] 2 K.B. 535, 540.

[49] *British Columbia, etc., Saw Mill Co. Ltd v. Nettleship* (1868) L.R. 3 C.P. 499, 509. See also *Horne v. Midland Ry.* (1873) L.R. 8 C.P. 136, 139, 141, 145, 146–147 (*cf.* at first instance (1872) L.R. 7 C.P. 583, 591–592); *Elbinger Aktiengesellschaft v. Armstrong* (1874) L.R. 9 Q.B. 473, 478; *Victoria Laundry (Windsor) Ltd v. Newman Industries Ltd* [1949] 2 K.B. 528, 538; *Robophone Facilities Ltd v. Blank* [1966] 1 W.L.R. 1428, 1448.

[50] See *Koufos v. C. Czarnikow Ltd* [1969] 1 A.C. 350, 421–422 (*obiter*); *Satef-Huttenes Albertus SpA v. Paloma Tercera Shipping Co. SA* [1981] 1 Lloyd's Rep. 175, 183–184. Such a rule might create difficulties where the contract was required to be in writing, or evidenced by a memorandum in writing: see *Hydraulic Engineering Co. Ltd v. McHaffie Goslett & Co.* (1878) 4 Q.B.D. 670.

knowledge of the special circumstances, the reasonable man in the defendant's position at the time of contracting would have understood that, by making the promise in those circumstances, he was assuming responsibility for the risk of the type of loss in question.[51] First, a subjective test should be employed: if it is clear from all the circumstances that the defendant—to the knowledge of the plaintiff—did not wish to accept the risk of the unusual loss, then mere knowledge of the special circumstances is insufficient. Secondly, an objective test should be employed: if it is clear from all the circumstances that a reasonable man in the place of the defendant would not, despite his knowledge of the special circumstances, have accepted the risk of the unusual loss, mere knowledge is again insufficient.[52]

27–051   There is no need to elevate these principles into terms of the contract: notice of the special circumstances will make the defendant liable for the unusual loss resulting from a breach of contract in those circumstances, if the reasonable man would consider himself, in all the circumstances of the contract, to have undertaken the risk of such loss when he made the contract. Was it in the contemplation of the parties, as reasonable men, that the defendant was accepting the risk of the unusual loss?[53] In *Hadley v. Baxendale*[54] itself, "communication" was said to be the vital factor, but obviously a casual communication from a stranger is insufficient. It is essential that there should be communication of the special circumstances by or on behalf of the claimant to the defendant or his agent so as to show that the claimant thought it important that the defendant should know what other matters depended on his fulfilment of the contract; these facts may, in appropriate circumstances, lead to the inference that the defendant, as a reasonable man, was accepting the risk of special loss to the claimant.[55]

---

[51] See the formulation of Robert Goff J. in the *Satef-Huttenes* case, *supra*, at 183: "have the facts in question come to the defendant's knowledge in such circumstances that a reasonable person in the shoes of the defendant would, if he had considered the matter at the time of making the contract, have contemplated that, in the event of a breach by him, such facts were to be taken into account when considering his responsibility for loss suffered by the plaintiff as a result of such breach." (At 184, the learned judge used wording similar to that in the text: "assuming responsibility for the risk of such loss in the event of" breach.) See also *Seven Seas Properties Ltd v. Al-Essa (No. 2)* [1993] 1 W.L.R. 1083, 1088.

[52] *cf. Robophone Facilities Ltd v. Blank* [1966] 1 W.L.R. 1428, 1437, 1448; *Koufos v. C. Czarnikow Ltd, supra*, at 385. The rules in *Hadley v. Baxendale* encourage the efficient exchange of information. There is no need for the promisee to inform the promisor about the usual consequences of a breach of his promise, but if he intends the promisor to be responsible for an unusual type of risk he must inform the promisor of that risk, so that, by making the promise with that knowledge, the promisor is implicitly assuming responsibility for it. (The promisor can then increase the "price" he requires in exchange.)

[53] *Muhammad Issa el Sheikh Ahmad v. Ali* [1947] A.C. 414, 427 (impecuniosity of one party in the contemplation of the parties: "damages which, on the facts found by the trial judge, might reasonably be expected to be in the contemplation of the parties"); *Trans Trust S.P.R.L. v. Danubian Trading Co. Ltd* [1952] 2 Q.B. 297. See *post*, §§ 27–082, 27–138.

[54] (1854) 9 Exch. 341, 354 (*ante*, § 27–040).

[55] The cases on sub-sales, considered in Vol. II, §§ 43–399—43–402, 43–413, 43–422, provide a good illustration of this principle. For other illustrations see *Panalpina International Transport Ltd v. Densil Underwear Ltd* [1981] 1 Lloyd's Rep. 187, 191; the *Victoria Laundry* case [1949] 2 K.B. 528 (*post*, § 27–054); *Wadsworth v. Lydall* [1981] 1 W.L.R. 598 (upheld by House of Lords in *President of India v. La Pintada Compania Navegacion SA* [1985] A.C. 104, 125–127) (see *post*, § 27–138); *Kemp v. Intasun Holidays Ltd* [1987] 2 F.T.L.R. 234 and *post*, §§ 27–054, 27–057, 27–082.

(b) *Timing of the Assessment of Damages*

The relevant date for the assessment of damages.[56] The general rule is that   **27–052**
damages for breach of contract should be assessed as at the date when the cause
of action arose, *viz.* the date of the breach[57] (which rule usually applies where
substitute performance is readily available in the market[58]). "But this is not an
absolute rule: if to follow it would give rise to injustice the court has power to
fix such other date as may be appropriate in the circumstances."[59] Thus, if, after
a breach, the innocent party reasonably[60] continues to treat the contract as in
force, damages may be assessed as at the later date "when (otherwise than by his
default) the contract is lost,"[61] *viz.* when performance becomes impossible,[62] or
when the innocent party terminates the contract.[63] (Any further delay in his
receiving compensation should be met by the award of interest.[64]) If the claimant
did not know of the breach of contract at the time it occurred, damages will
usually be assessed as at the time when he should reasonably have discovered the
breach, and was able to act on his knowledge,[65] *e.g.* by attempting to mitigate.[66]
The assessment of damages at the cost of substitute performance[67] or at the cost
of a reasonable attempt to mitigate[68] are other situations where the time for
assessment may be postponed after the date of breach.

Inflation and interest rates. If the date for the assessment of damages is   **27–053**
postponed so that the claimant is protected against inflation until that date, the

---

[56] Waddams (1981) 97 L.Q.R. 445. *cf. post,* §§ 27–066, 27–067.

[57] *Miliangos v. George Frank (Textiles) Ltd* [1976] A.C. 443, 468; *Johnson v. Agnew* [1980] A.C. 367, 400 (see *post,* §§ 27–075—27–076).

[58] See Vol. II, §§ 43–367 *et seq.,* §§ 43–387 *et seq.;* and, on the doctrine of mitigation, *post,* §§ 27–085 *et seq.*

[59] *Johnson v. Agnew, supra,* at 401; *Kennedy v. K. B. Van Emden & Co.* (1997) 74 P. & C.R. 19. For the assessment of damages for anticipatory breach, see *post,* § 27–099; Vol. II, §§ 43–379, 43–392. *cf. post,* § 27–100.

[60] In *Malhotra v. Choudhury* [1980] A.C. 52, 77, 81, delay by the plaintiff led to the date for valuing a property being moved back one year from the date of judgment: see *post,* § 27–075.

[61] *Johnson v. Agnew, supra,* at 401 (see *post,* § 27–075) citing *Ogle v. Earl Vane* (1867) L.R. 2 Q.B. 275 (on appeal, L.R. 3 Q.B. 272) (see Vol. II, § 43–391); *Hickman v. Haynes* (1875) L.R. 10 C.P. 598 (see Vol. II, § 43–375); and *Radford v. De Froberville* [1977] 1 W.L.R. 1262. *cf. post,* § 27–050.

[62] *Johnson v. Agnew, supra,* at 401. If the seller postponed delivery, but later repudiated, damages will be assessed at the date of the repudiation: *Barnett v. Javeri & Co.* [1916] 2 K.B. 390.

[63] For cases decided before *Johnson v. Agnew, supra,* where the damages were assessed at dates later than the original breach of contract, see *post,* § 27–075, n. 14.

[64] See *post,* § 27–142.

[65] *East Ham Corporation v. Bernard Sunley & Sons Ltd* [1966] A.C. 406.

[66] *Van den Hurck v. R. Martens & Co. Ltd* [1920] 1 K.B. 850 (damages assessed as at the time when, after delivery of sealed packages, it was reasonable to expect them to be opened and the contents inspected: see Vol. II, § 43–411); *Cehave N.V. v. Bremer Handelsgesellschaft mbH* [1976] 1 Q.B. 44 (damages assessed as at the date of arrival of the goods).

[67] See *ante,* § 27–014. *cf.* the assessment of damages in tort for the cost of repairs to damaged property: *Dodd Properties Ltd v. Canterbury City Council* [1980] 1 W.L.R. 433 (see *ante,* § 27–016); and the comments of Waddams (1981) 97 L.Q.R. 445, 457–461 on the incentives to the plaintiff to maximise his damages which might arise from permitting postponement of the date for assessing damages.

[68] *County Personnel (Employment Agency) Ltd v. Alan R. Pulver & Co.* [1987] 1 W.L.R. 916, 925–926. See *post* §§ 27–065, 27–098.

full market rate of interest (which largely reflects current expectations of inflation) should not be awarded for any earlier period.[69]

(c) Loss of Profits

27–054   **Seller's liability for loss of profits.** The general principles of remoteness of damage in contract may be illustrated by cases where the claimant has claimed for loss of profits as a result[70] of the defendant's breach of contract.[71] A frequent instance is the delayed delivery of a profit-earning chattel.[72] In *Victoria Laundry (Windsor) Ltd v. Newman Industries Ltd*[73] the plaintiffs agreed to buy a large boiler from the defendants, and a date was fixed for delivery. The plaintiffs sued for damages for delay in delivery, and claimed loss of profits in respect of:

(1) the large number of new customers they could have taken on had the boiler been installed; and

(2) the amount which they could have earned under special dyeing contracts with the Ministry of Supply.

The defendants knew that the plaintiffs were launderers and that they wanted the boiler for immediate use; the Court of Appeal held that with such knowledge the reasonable man could have foreseen that delay in delivery would lead to some loss of profits, though he would not have foreseen the loss of profits under the special contracts with the Ministry, since these were special circumstances not within the defendant's actual knowledge.[74] Hence the plaintiff could not recover all of the actual loss of profits which he had incurred under these contracts, but only the normal loss of business in respect of dyeing contracts to be reasonably expected.[75] Where the defendant contracted to supply a profit-earning chattel, which the plaintiff intended to put to an exceptional use (outside the defendant's reasonable contemplation), the loss of profits expected under its normally contemplated use placed a ceiling on the damages recoverable by the plaintiff for the

---

[69] *Dodd Properties Ltd v. Canterbury City Council, supra.* See Waddams (1981) 97 L.Q.R. 445, 454–455; and 1 O.J.L.S. 134 (1980); Swan (1980) 10 *Real Property Reports* (Canada) 267; Wallace (1980) 96 L.Q.R. 101, 115, 341 and (1982) 98 L.Q.R. 406.

[70] On the question of evaluating contingencies affecting the chance of making a profit, see *ante,* §§ 27–034—27–035.

[71] In *H. Parsons (Livestock) Ltd v. Uttley, Ingham & Co. Ltd* [1978] Q.B. 791, 802–803, Denning M.R. said that in the test for remoteness of damage in contract there is a distinction between loss of profit (or only economic loss) cases, and physical damage (or expense) cases; but this distinction was not accepted by the other members of the Court of Appeal, and lacks supporting authority: see *per* Orr L.J. *ibid.* at 804–805; and *per* Scarman L.J. *ibid.* at 805–806.

[72] *Hadley v. Baxendale* (1854) 9 Exch. 341 (*ante,* § 27–040); *Fletcher v. Tayleur* (1855) 17 C.B. 21; *Wilson v. General Iron Screw Colliery Co. Ltd* (1877) 47 L.J.Q.B. 239; *Hydraulic Engineering Co. Ltd v. McHaffie Goslett & Co.* (1878) 4 Q.B.D. 670; *Saint Lines Ltd v. Richardsons Westgarth & Co.* [1940] 2 K.B. 99; *Victoria Laundry (Windsor) Ltd v. Newman Industries Ltd* [1949] 2 K.B. 528.

[73] *Ante.* See Vol. II, § 43–406.

[74] See *ante,* § 27–049. See *Brown v. K.M.R. Services Ltd* [1995] 4 All E.R. 598, 621; *North Sea Energy Holdings N.V. v. Petroleum Authority of Thailand* [1997] 2 Lloyd's Rep. 418, 438–439.

[75] If the defendant had been told of the special contracts, and should have realised, as a reasonable man, that he was undertaking responsibility for the loss of higher-than-usual profits in the case of breach, he would have been able to demand a higher price, or to cover himself with an exemption.

delay in delivery.[76] The test for remoteness was satisfied, since loss of profits was the contemplated type of loss arising from the breach,[77] and the plaintiff had in fact suffered such a loss to an amount beyond that ceiling.[78] Other cases support the principle that loss of profits may be awarded where there has been delayed delivery by a seller of a profit-earning chattel where it was within his reasonable contemplation that the buyer would use it to make profits[79]; or would have resold it at a profit[80]; or where the profit-earning chattel which was delivered was defective.[81]

Purchaser's intended use of land. In a contract to sell land or a leasehold **27–055** interest in land, "special circumstances are necessary to justify imputing to [the] vendor a knowledge that the purchaser intends to use it in any particular manner" so as to entitle the purchaser to recover damages for loss of the profit he would have made from that use.[82]

Seller's claim for loss of profits. If the defendant, in breach of his contract, **27–056** has refused to accept goods sold[83] or hired[84] to him by a dealer or goods manufactured for him,[85] but the claimant has found a third person who will take the goods by a similar contract (under which the claimant makes a similar profit), the claimant is entitled to recover his loss of profit on the defendant's contract where the supply of such goods exceeds the demand; for in such a case the claimant has lost one profit he would otherwise have made.[86] If however, in similar circumstances, the demand for such goods exceeds the supply, the claimant will recover only nominal damages, since he has received the same profit through the substituted contract as he would have if the defendant had performed his contract.[87] Other cases dealing with loss of profits in sub-contracts and "string" contracts are discussed in Volume II.[88]

---

[76] *Cory v. Thames Ironworks and Shipbuilding Co. Ltd* (1868) L.R. 3 Q.B. 181.

[77] See *ante*, § 27–045.

[78] This explanation is supported by the *Victoria Laundry* case, *supra*.

[79] *Cory v. Thames Ironworks & Shipbuilding Co. Ltd, supra. cf. Re Trent and Humber Co.* (1868) L.R. 4 Ch.App. 112 (delay by a repairer); *Steam Herring Fleet v. Richards* (1901) 17 T.L.R. 731.

[80] See Vol. II, §§ 43–399—43–402, 43–413, 43–422.

[81] *H. Parsons (Livestock) Ltd v. Uttley, Ingham & Co., supra*, at 810, 813; Vol. II, § 43–420. (Loss of "repeat orders" from the buyer's disappointed customers may also be recovered: see Vol. II, § 43–423.)

[82] *Diamond v. Campbell-Jones* [1961] Ch. 22; *Cottrill v. Steyning and Littlehampton Building Society* [1966] 1 W.L.R. 753; *Malhotra v. Choudhury* [1980] Ch. 52. See *post*, §§ 27–075—27–076. *cf. Wright v. Dean* [1948] Ch. 687; *G. & K. Ladenbau (U.K.) Ltd v. Crawley & De Reya* [1978] 1 W.L.R. 266 (solicitors who were negligent in checking title, which delayed completion, held liable for interest for delayed receipt of profits on a resale within their reasonable contemplation).

[83] *W. L. Thompson Ltd v. Robinson (Gunmakers) Ltd* [1955] Ch. 177.

[84] *Interoffice Telephones Ltd v. Robert Freeman Co. Ltd* [1958] 1 Q.B. 190; *Robophone Facilities Ltd v. Blank* [1966] 1 W.L.R. 1428 (*post*, Vol. II, § 38–280). On damages for loss of profits under a hire-purchase agreement, see Vol. II, §§ 38–307—38–309.

[85] *Re Vic Mill Ltd* [1913] 1 Ch. 465.

[86] It is a "lost volume" case.

[87] *Charter v. Sullivan* [1957] 2 Q.B. 117. The plaintiff should also be entitled to recover any extra expenses incurred in making the substituted contract: see *post*, § 27–064. (To a certain extent, this decision and that in *W. L. Thompson Ltd v. Robinson (Gunmakers) Ltd, ante*, depend on the absence of an "available market" where the price fluctuates in accordance with supply and demand: see Vol. II, §§ 43–367—43–377.)

[88] Vol. II, §§ 43–399—43–402, 43–413, 43–422.

27–057   **Carrier's liability for loss of profits.** A carrier who fails to deliver goods within the agreed time may also cause loss of business profits to the consignee.[89] The normal measure of damages for delayed delivery is the difference between the market value of the goods on the due date of arrival and their market value on the actual date of delivery.[90] But "a carrier commonly knows less than a seller about the purposes for which the buyer or consignee needs the goods, or about other 'special circumstances' which may cause exceptional loss if due delivery is withheld."[91] The amount of knowledge imputed to a carrier will therefore be limited in the usual case, and the consignee will be obliged to prove the carrier's actual knowledge of the special circumstances so as to show that the carrier must be taken as a reasonable man to have accepted the risk of unusual loss resulting from breach. In most reported cases, therefore, the carrier has escaped liability for the plaintiff's loss of profits because he lacked sufficient knowledge.[92] Exceptionally, however, the carrier may be liable where it is shown that, at the time of contracting, he knew of the facts which would lead to special loss if he failed to deliver or was late in delivering,[93] *e.g.* where the carrier knew that no substitutes would be available in the market at the place fixed for delivery, he may be liable for loss of "reasonable" resale profits suffered by the consignee.[94]

(d) *Expenditure Wasted or Incurred as a Result of the Breach*[95]

27–058   **Reliance expenditure arising from the claimant's performance.** The claimant may claim damages for wasted expenditure which he incurred in reliance on the contract or as the result of the defendant's breach. The first category is where, before the breach, the claimant had incurred expenditure in reliance on his expectation that the defendant would perform his undertaking, but where the breach results in that expenditure being wasted, at least in part. The first type of this expenditure is that directly related to the claimant's own preparations for his performance, as where he has incurred the cost of labour and

---

[89] On damages for delay in the carriage of passengers, see Vol. II, § 36–072.

[90] See *post*, § 27–073. On special conditions of carriage, see Vol. II, Chap. 36.

[91] *Victoria Laundry (Windsor) Ltd v. Newman Industries Ltd* [1949] 2 K.B. 528, 537. See also *Heskell v. Continental Express Ltd* [1950] 1 All E.R. 1033, 1049, where Devlin J. expressed the view that knowledge of a sub-contract would be more easily imputed to a seller than to a carrier; *André et Cie SA v. J. H. Vantol* [1952] 2 Lloyd's Rep. 282.

[92] *Hadley v. Baxendale* (1854) 9 Exch. 341; *Gee v. Lancs & Yorks Ry.* (1860) 6 H. & N. 211; *British Columbia, etc., Saw Mill Co. Ltd v. Nettleship* (1868) L.R. 3 C.P. 499; *Horne v. Midland Ry.* (1873) L.R. 8 C.P. 131. But the fact that loss of profit under a special contract with a third party is not recoverable, does not prevent the carrier being liable for some damages for delay: *B. Sunley & Co. Ltd v. Cunard White Star Ltd* [1940] 1 K.B. 740 (interest awarded on the value of the goods for the period of the delay); *Koufos v. C. Czarnikow Ltd* [1969] 1 A.C. 350 (damages for reduction in market value at date of late delivery: see *post*, § 27–073).

[93] *Simpson v. L.N.W. Ry.* (1876) 1 Q.B.D. 274; *Jameson v. Midland Ry.* (1884) 50 L.T. 426; *Monte Video Gas and Dry Dock Co. Ltd v. Clan Line Steamers Ltd* (1921) 37 T.L.R. 866; *SS. Ardennes (Cargo Owners) v. SS. Ardennes (Owners)* [1951] 1 K.B. 55 (loss of market); *Satef-Huttenes Albertus SpA v. Paloma Tercera Shipping Co. SA (The Pegase)* [1981] 1 Lloyd's Rep. 175. See also *Schulze & Co. v. G.E. Ry.* (1887) 19 Q.B.D. 30; *cf. Ströms Bruks Aktiebolag v. John & Peter Hutchison* [1905] A.C. 515.

[94] *Satef-Huttenes Albertus SpA v. Paloma Tercera Shipping Co. SA, supra.*

[95] See Owen (1984) 4 O.J.L.S. 393.

materials which will be wasted as a result of the breach.[96] This expenditure is part of the cost of the claimant's performance and if the defendant had fulfilled his side, the claimant would have received the benefit of the expenditure when he received the benefit of the defendant's performance (*e.g.* the price). When the claimant terminates the contract on the ground of the breach, he may claim damages to cover his expenditure towards his own performance, but only to the extent that it has been wasted as a result of the breach.[97]

The ceiling on recovery in an unprofitable contract. If the claimant fully   **27–059**
performed his side of the contract, he would not be entitled to recover from the defendant more than the value of the latter's performance *viz.* the gross return (such as the price) to which the claimant was entitled under the contract. If the claimant is relegated to a claim to damages because he had only partly performed his side by the time the contract was terminated, the amount of the gross return to which he would be entitled upon full performance will be a ceiling on the recovery of damages for the expenditure incurred in his partial performance.[98] By suing for damages for his costs in performing in reliance on the contract, the claimant cannot recover more than he would have been entitled to if the defendant had not broken the contract.[99] The precise arithmetical method of implementing this principle has not yet been decided[1] but it is submitted that the claimant should be entitled to claim his performance expenditure actually incurred to the limit imposed by the gross return (or price) due for full performance.[2] The onus of proof is on the defendant to show (on the balance of probabilities) that the claimant would have made a loss on full performance of both sides of the contract and so would not have recouped all of his own costs in performing his side.[3] In the absence of such proof, the court will assume in the claimant's favour that he would have recouped all the costs incurred in his performance, and so will be willing to award damages to reimburse the claimant.[4] Usually the claimant will seek damages for this reliance expenditure rather than for his loss of expectations (his gross return, less future expenses avoided after the breach) only where he lacks adequate proof of his loss of expectations (*e.g.* profits),[5] or where he feared that it would have been a losing or unprofitable

---

[96] The test of reasonableness in incurring the expenditure would not seem to be relevant (*cf.* the rule in mitigation for post-breach expenditure: *post*, § 27–064). But the expenditure must have been intended by the plaintiff to be part of his performance and must satisfy the remoteness rules.

[97] If the plaintiff can salvage any items of value from his preparations for performance, the rules of mitigation require him to deduct from his claim the amount he obtained from selling the salvageable items to a third party (or the amount he ought reasonably to have obtained from doing so).

[98] This principle is inferred from two cases (*C. & P. Haulage v. Middleton* [1983] 1 W.L.R. 1461; and *C.C.C. Films (London) Ltd v. Impact Quadrant Films Ltd* [1985] Q.B. 16) although they were concerned not with the profitability of the individual contract which the defendant broke, but of the activity of which that contract was an essential part. On this see *post*, § 27–061.

[99] *ibid.*

[1] Harris *op. cit.* pp. 97–100.

[2] This view is found (*obiter*) in the *C.C.C. Films* case, *supra*, at 35. Harris *op. cit.* pp. 97–100, prefers this method to scaling down the plaintiff's damages by reference to the total of his costs incurred to date and the potential costs which (but for the breach) he would thereafter have incurred.

[3] *C.C.C. Films (London) Ltd v. Impact Quadrant Films Ltd, supra.*

[4] *ibid.* at 39–40.

[5] *Molling & Co. v. Dean & Son Ltd* (1902) 18 T.L.R. 216; *Anglia Television v. Reed* [1972] 1 Q.B. 60.

contract so that he would not be able to prove any net loss of expected profit.[6] The courts insist that the claimant has an unfettered choice as to which measure of damages to claim.[7]

27–060 **Reliance expenditure not directed at performance.** Before the breach the claimant may incur expenditure in reliance on the expected performance of the contract by the defendant where the expenditure was not incurred in or towards the performance of his own obligations; this is expenditure from which he expected to benefit, as part of the activity in which he was engaged, after he had received the benefit of the defendant's performance, but which the breach now renders futile. Subject to mitigation,[8] the claimant is entitled to damages to reimburse him for this expenditure, provided it was within the reasonable contemplation of the parties that it was not unlikely that the claimant would incur it in reliance on the contract, and that it would be wasted if the defendant committed the breach in question. (No test of reasonableness in incurring the expenditure has been imposed on the claimant, but if the expenditure was incurred unreasonably, it would not satisfy the remoteness test.) So where the buyer of goods had them repaired before he had to give them up to a third party (because it later emerged that the seller had no title to them), he recovered the cost of the repairs which was wasted from his point of view.[9] Other illustrations of the recovery of wasted expenditure are the cost of painting a machine before it was found to be defective,[10] and the cost of transporting goods to a sub-buyer before they were examined and rejected.[11]

27–061 **Ceiling on recovery if claimant's activity would have been unprofitable.** As with the case of performance expenditure discussed above,[12] the defendant may show[13] that the claimant entered into a contract as part of a commercial or profit-making activity and that he would have made an overall loss on that activity. The defendant must show that, from the gross return which the claimant expected to receive from exploiting or using the subject-matter of his contract with the defendant,[14] he would not have recouped all of the expenditure incurred

---

[6] This statement is probably restricted to a contract where the plaintiff intended to make a profit from his performance of the contract (*viz.* it was not a consumer contract where the plaintiff intended to *use* the subject-matter of the contract).

[7] *Anglia Television v. Reed, supra; C.C.C. Films (London) Ltd v. Impact Quadrant Films, supra,* at 31–32. On the possibility of a "split" claim, see *post,* § 27–063.

[8] See *post,* § 27–085. The plaintiff's damages will be calculated on the basis that he took reasonable steps to realise the salvage value of anything left on his hands after the breach.

[9] *Mason v. Burningham* [1949] 2 K.B. 545. See also *Steam Herring Fleet Ltd v. V. S. Richards & Co. Ltd* (1901) 17 T.L.R. 731 (expenses in preparing for a voyage; delay in delivering ship). See also *Saint Line Ltd v. Richardsons, Westgarth & Co. Ltd* [1940] 2 K.B. 99, 105.

[10] *Cullinane v. British "Rema" Manufacturing Co. Ltd* [1954] 1 Q.B. 292. See also *British Westinghouse Electric and Manufacturing Co. Ltd v. Underground Electric Railways Co. of London Ltd* [1912] A.C. 673, 683 (cost of extra coal used by defective turbines); *Richard Holden Ltd v. Bostock & Co. Ltd* (1902) 18 T.L.R. 317 (beer wasted when ingredient found to be contaminated).

[11] *Molling & Co. v. Dean & Son Ltd* (1901) 18 T.L.R. 217.

[12] *Ante.* § 27–059. (The discussion in that paragraph applies to the present paragraph, subject to the proviso that the latter is not limited to the profitability of the contract in question, but applies to the profitability of the activity in question.)

[13] The onus of proof is on the defendant: *C.C.C. Films (London) Ltd v. Impact Quadrant Films Ltd* [1985] Q.B. 16 (*ante,* § 27–059).

[14] The relevant gross return is that expected from the plaintiff's whole undertaking, of which the contract with the defendant forms an essential part: *C & P Haulage v. Middleton* [1983] 1 W.L.R. 1461. This point is implicitly recognised in *Cullinane v. British "Rema" Manufacturing Co. Ltd* [1954] 1 Q.B. 292.

in reliance on the contract. Where the defendant can prove that, even if he had completely performed that contract, the claimant's gross return from his exploitation would not have covered that expenditure, the claimant's claim for wasted expenditure can succeed only to the extent that it would have been recouped.[15] (The same question as discussed above arises over the method of implementing this principle.[16])

Expenditure incurred before making the contract. The claimant may incur **27–062** expense before entering the contract, but in the expectation that if such a contract is made, the expenditure will be needed to enable him to perform the contract (or to undertake the activity of which the expected contract will form part), and that he will be able to recoup the expenditure from the benefit of the defendant's performance of that contract (*e.g.* the price) or from the profits he expects to make from the activity in question. If, at the time of contracting, it was within the reasonable contemplation of the parties that the claimant would be able to recoup this expenditure in this way, he may recover damages for any wasted[17] part of the expenditure arising from the breach.[18] For instance, the overhead costs (premises, staff, etc.) will often be incurred by the claimant before he makes a particular contract: the defendant, when entering into the contract, can easily contemplate that the claimant will expect to recoup from it a contribution towards overheads.[19]

Claiming for wasted expenditure in addition to net loss of expected **27–063** **profit.** In principle, the claimant should be entitled to claim damages both for his wasted expenditure incurred up to the date of his terminating the contract and also for the net loss of profit[20] which he would have made but for the breach. There can be no valid objection to this, provided the calculations show that there is no overlapping in the claimant's recovery, *viz.* his net loss of profits is calculated by deducting from his expected gross return both the cost of his performance and reliance expenditure to the date of termination[21] and the cost of the further expenditure which he would have incurred after that date if he had completed his performance.[22] However, the Court of Appeal has ruled that the claimant must choose between claiming for his wasted reliance expenditure and claiming for his loss of expected profits, holding that he is not entitled to recover both.[23] This position is correct if it is interpreted to mean that the claimant should not recover both his *gross* return or profits expected under the contract (or from

---

[15] The *C.C.C. Films* case, *supra; C & P Haulage v. Middleton, supra.*

[16] See *ante,* § 27–059.

[17] Under the rules of mitigation, a deduction must be made from the damages in respect of anything with a salvage value arising from the expenditure.

[18] *Anglia Television Ltd v. Reed* [1972] 1 Q.B. 60 (the expenditure was part of the overall activity in which the plaintiff was engaged, the making of a film); *Lloyd v. Stanbury* [1971] 1 W.L.R. 535, 546 (legal costs, and removal expenses: "the costs of performing an act required to be done by the contract"). See Ogus (1972) 35 M.L.R. 423. The question of a ceiling on recovery will be relevant: see *ante,* §§ 27–059, 27–061.

[19] The facts of the *C.C.C. Films* case, *supra,* show that the expenditure in question was incurred before the making of the subsidiary agreement broken by the defendant.

[20] The expected profit will either be from the particular contract (performance expenditure: *ante* § 27–059) or from the profit-making activity of which it forms a part (*ante,* § 27–061).

[21] Allowance must be made for any salvage value.

[22] Macleod [1970] J.B.L. 19; Street, *Principles of the Law of Damages* (1962), pp. 242–245.

[23] *Cullinane v. British "Rema" Manufacturing Co. Ltd* [1954] 1 Q.B. 292, 308. (This case is explored in more detail *post,* Vol. II, §§ 43–420—43–421); *Anglia Television Ltd v. Reed, supra,* at 63–64.

the activity in question)[24] and also the (now wasted) expenditure incurred in reliance on the contract which he had intended to meet from that gross return. But it is submitted that the ruling against a "split" claim cannot be justified if the claimant can show that there is no overlapping between the two claims.[25]

27–064   **Expenditure incurred after, and as a result of the breach.** Subject to the rules on causation and remoteness and to the test of acting reasonably,[26] the claimant may recover as damages the reasonable costs[27] incurred by him in mitigating the loss caused by the breach or in otherwise dealing with the consequences of breach.[28] So where the defendant delayed delivery of a crane sold to the plaintiff whom he knew to be an importer of timber, the plaintiff recovered the extra cost of man-handling timber at his wharf.[29] Other illustrations are the recovery of the cost of substitute performance by a third party[30]; the recovery of the amount of damages and costs paid by the plaintiff to a third party as a consequence of the defendant's breach of contract,[31] as where it was within reasonable contemplation of the parties that the buyer would probably resell the goods, and that the seller's breach in supplying defective goods was not unlikely to result in the buyer being liable to pay damages and costs to a sub-buyer for breach of the sub-contract[32]; the recovery of storage charges after the defendant refused to accept goods[33]; the recovery of the reasonable cost of rebuilding,[34]

---

[24] In both the *Cullinane* and *Anglia Television* cases, *supra*, the relevant profit-making related to the activity in which the plaintiff was engaged (processing clay for sale or making a proposed film) rather than to the individual contract.

[25] See *T.C Industrial Plant Pty. Ltd v. Robert's (Queensland) Pty. Ltd* [1964] A.L.R. 1083; Stoljar [1975] 91 L.Q.R. 68. In *Hydraulic Engineering Co. Ltd v. McHaffie Goslett & Co.* (1878) 4 Q.B.D. 670, both wasted expenses and profits were awarded, but it is not clear whether the latter were *net* profits. See also *Saint Line Ltd v. Richardsons, Westgarth & Co. Ltd* [1940] 2 K.B. 99 which accepted a claim involving both. The distinction between gross and net profits is recognised in the *C.C.C. Films Ltd* case, *supra*, at 32.

[26] The cost of "reasonable" action may be recovered even if it later appears that some other action would have been better: *Gebruder Metelmann GmbH v. NBR (London) Ltd* [1984] 1 Lloyd's Rep. 614, 634. *cf. post.* § 27–098.

[27] See *post*, § 27–098.

[28] *Richard Holden Ltd v. Bostock & Co. Ltd* (1902) 18 T.L.R. 317 (cost of sending notices to customers to minimise loss of business); *Heskell v. Continental Express Ltd* [1950] 1 All E.R. 1033, 1046 (cost of trying to trace goods). On claims for interest charges incurred, see *post*, § 27–138. On mitigation, see *post*, § 27–085.

[29] *John M. Henderson & Co. Ltd v. Montague L. Meyer Ltd* (1941) 46 Com.Cas. 209, 219–220. See also on the costs caused by delay, *Borries v. Hutchinson* (1865) 19 C.B.(N.S.) 445 (extra freight and insurance); *Watson v. Gray* (1900) 16 T.L.R. 308 (increased building costs).

[30] *Ante*, § 27–014.

[31] See Vol. II, § 43–403. The breach of contract may even result in a tortious claim by a third party against the plaintiff, the cost of which is within the remoteness test: *Mowbray v. Merryweather* [1895] 2 Q.B. 640 (see Vol. II, § 43–427.

[32] *e.g. Biggin v. Permanite* [1951] 2 K.B. 314. See Vol. II, §§ 43–429—43–432. If the plaintiff acts reasonably in reaching an out-of-court settlement with the third party, he may be entitled to recover the amount of the settlement: Vol. II, § 43–429. On the recovery of a fine imposed on the plaintiff as the result of the defendant's breach of contract, see Vol. II, § 43–419.

[33] *Harlow & Jones Ltd v. Panex (International) Ltd* [1967] 2 Lloyd's Rep. 509 (there was no available market). See also *SS. Ardennes (Cargo Owners) v. SS. Ardennes (Owners)* [1951] 1 K.B. 55 (increased import duty payable).

[34] *Harbutt's "Plasticine" Ltd v. Wayne Tank and Pump Co. Ltd* [1970] 1 Q.B. 447. See also *Smith v. Johnson* (1899) 15 T.L.R. 179 (mortar supplied by a builder was below standard; it was used for building a wall which the local authority later condemned as unsafe; the owner recovered from the builder the cost of pulling it down and of rebuilding). See also *Calabar Properties Ltd v. Stitcher* [1984] 1 W.L.R. 287 (cost of alternative accommodation during repairs to flat occupied by tenant).

repairing or replacing[35] property of the plaintiff damaged or destroyed through the defendant's breach of contract; the recovery of medical or rehabilitation expenses when the breach causes physical injury to the plaintiff[36]; extra freight and insurance costs arising from late delivery of goods.[37] Unlike in the case of reliance expenditure, there is no question of this category being subject to a ceiling on recovery being fixed by the expected profitability of the contract or activity.[38]

Damages assessed on a "no transaction" basis. In a limited number of   **27–065**
situations, where the claimant claims that he would not have entered into a particular transaction but for the defendant's negligent advice (or failure to advise), his damages have been assessed at the amount needed to restore him to the position he would have been in if he had never entered the transaction. So in *Hayes v. Dodd*[39] a solicitor negligently advised the plaintiff that he had a right of way to give access to the leasehold property he proposed to acquire as a site for his business. There was no legally-enforceable vehicular right of way and the business failed through the lack of adequate access. Damages were assessed on the "no transaction" basis *viz.* all the wasted expenditure incurred by the plaintiff (the initial cost of the lease and goodwill, rent, rates, insurance, bank interest and other expenses wasted until the time he reasonably gave up the business) *less* the amounts recovered by the plaintiff through selling the lease and his plant (the mitigation rules applied). An analogous case is where negligent advice from a solicitor led the client to take a disadvantageous underlease: the damages were the sum paid by the client over five years later to secure its surrender: *County Personnel (Employment Agency) Ltd v. Alan R. Pulver and Co.*[40] In the *South Australia* case[41] the House of Lords said that the distinction between "no transaction" and "successful transaction" cases should be abandoned; but the House approved the two cases just mentioned on the basis of the mitigation or "extrication" principle ("a reasonable attempt to cope with the consequences of the defendant's breach of duty".[42]) However, in *Hayes v. Dodd* the damages went beyond "extrication" and covered *all* the plaintiff's wasted expenditure from the beginning of the transaction. It is clearly established that damages may be assessed on the "no transaction" basis when the defendant fraudulently induced the claimant to enter into the transaction,[43] and it is submitted that the same basis may be appropriate where the breach of contract destroys the whole purpose of the transaction into which the claimant entered in reliance on the defendant's advice.[44] So this basis applied where a lender claimed against a solicitor whose

---

[35] *Bacon v. Cooper (Metals) Ltd* [1982] 1 All E.R. 397.
[36] The decision in *Grant v. Australian Knitting Mills Ltd* [1936] A.C. 85 supports the view that damages for personal injury cased by breach of contract should be assessed on a similar basis to that used in tort.
[37] *Borries v. Hutchinson* (1865) 18 C.B.(N.S.) 445.
[38] See *ante*, §§ 27–059, 27–061.
[39] [1990] 2 All E.R. 815, CA. This case did not involve a fall in the property market after the date of contract, *cf.* the *South Australia* case, *infra*.
[40] [1987] 1 W.L.R. 916, CA.
[41] [1997] A.C. 191 (*post*, § 27–078).
[42] *ibid.* at 218–219.
[43] *Smith New Court Securities Ltd v. Scrimgeour Vickers Ltd* [1997] A.C. 254.
[44] As in *Hayes v. Dodd, supra.* The wasted expenditure must, of course, meet the remoteness test.

negligence did not concern the adequacy of the security[45] but was fundamental in the sense that in the absence of the negligence the lender would have refused to make any loan at all to the particular borrower.[46]

27–066   **Loss in purchasing power of currency; and currency exchange loss.** Debts or damages cannot be increased to take account of a fall in the domestic purchasing power of sterling between the time when the claimant's loss is assessed and the date of judgment.[47] For domestic purposes,[48] sterling[49] is taken by English courts to be constant in value,[50] subject to the award of interest[51]; but this approach has led courts to find grounds for postponing the date when damages are assessed,[52] and to uphold various contractual clauses indexing debts to the value of gold, to a foreign currency, or to a price index.[53]

27–067   **Currency exchange loss.** Where a debt due in a foreign currency is not paid on time, and as a result the creditor suffers a currency loss which was within the reasonable contemplation of the parties, he may recover damages in respect of that loss.[54] The ordinary rules on remoteness of damage apply to a claim to recover a currency exchange loss caused by breach of contract.[55]

(e) Non-pecuniary Losses

27–068   **Physical loss, injury or inconvenience.** Normally, damages for breach of contract relate to financial loss (including loss of expected financial gains), but non-pecuniary losses may be recovered if they were within the contemplation of the parties as not unlikely to result from the breach. If the defendant's breach of

---

[45] The situation covered by analogy with the over-valuation formula in the *South Australia* case [1997] A.C. 191 (*post*, § 27–078).

[46] *Steggles Palmer* case (one of the cases brought by the *Bristol and West Building Society*, and reported in [1997] 4 All E.R. 582.).

[47] *Philips v. Ward* [1956] 1 W.L.R. 471, CA. See *Dicey & Morris on the Conflict of Laws* (12th ed., 1993), pp. 1550 *et seq.*; Mann, *The Legal Aspect of Money* (5th ed., 1992), Chaps. 3, 4, 8. See also *ante*, §§ 22–068 *et seq. cf.* a debt which is calculable in a foreign currency: see *post*, §§ 31–163—31–172.

[48] Sterling is treated as having a fluctuating exchange value in relation to any given foreign currency: *Miliangos v. George Frank (Textiles) Ltd* [1976] A.C. 443 (see *post*, § 30–170).

[49] For the award of debts and damages in a foreign currency, see *post*, § 30–170.

[50] *Philips v. Ward, supra*, at 474 (citing *Di Ferdinando v. Simon Smits & Co.* [1920] 3 K.B. 409, 414; *SS. Celia v. SS. Volturno* [1921] A.C. 544, 563; *Bishop v. Cunard White Star Co.* [1950] P. 240, 246). See also *Treseder-Griffin v. Co-operative Insurance Society Ltd* [1956] 2 Q.B. 127, 144; *Tomkinson v. First Pennsylvania Banking and Trust Co.* [1961] A.C. 1007, 1069–1070; *The Teh Hu* [1970] P. 106.

[51] *Post*, §§ 27–137 *et seq.* If interest is awarded at full market rates, these may often largely compensate the plaintiff for inflation in the sense of loss of domestic purchasing power: see *ante*, § 27–052, text at n. 69.

[52] See *ante*, § 27–052.

[53] See *ante*, §§ 22–068—22–072. A long-term contract which in terms is binding indefinitely may nevertheless be interpreted as permitting determination by reasonable notice; the fact that the contract contains no provision for inflation is relevant: *Staffordshire Area Health Authority v. South Staffordshire Waterworks Co.* [1978] 1 W.L.R. 1387.

[54] See *post*, §§ 31–163 *et seq.* See *Aruna Mills Ltd v. Dhanrajmal Gobindram* [1968] 1 Q.B. 655 (contemplated risk of devaluation) (which was approved by the House of Lords in *President of India v. Lips Maritime Corporation* [1988] A.C. 395, 425).

[55] *President of India v. Lips Maritime Corporation, supra*, at 424.

contract caused physical injury to the claimant himself,[56] or to his property,[57] the claimant may recover damages for that injury, provided the test for remoteness is satisfied. Damages for personal injury caused by breach of contract may include compensation for pain and suffering, disfigurement, loss of faculty, as well as loss of earnings, which are normal heads of damages in the assessment of damages in tort for such injuries.[58] Similarly, where the breach of contract causes the claimant physical inconvenience or discomfort, he may recover damages,[59] as where the claimant suffered physical inconvenience and discomfort as the result of living in a defective house, or of vacating rooms while repairs were carried out.[60] But the quantum of such damages should be "modest".[61] If the remoteness test is satisfied, the claimant's damages for breach of contract may include compensation for loss incurred through the death of a human being, as, *e.g.* for loss of his wife's services, where the cause of action was independent of the death and the death was merely an item of damage.[62]

Mental distress and disappointment; nervous shock.[63] Normally, no damages in contract will be awarded for injury to the claimant's feelings, or for his mental distress, anguish, annoyance, loss of reputation[64] or social discredit caused by the breach of contract[65]; as where an employee is wrongfully dis- **27–069**

---

[56] *Wren v. Holt* [1903] 1 K.B. 610 (defective food sold for human consumption); *Grant v. Australian Knitting Mills Ltd* [1936] A.C. 85 (buyer of defective clothing contracted dermatitis); *Summers v. Salford Corporation* [1943] A.C. 283; *Godley v. Perry* [1960] 1 W.L.R. 9.

[57] *Henry Kendall & Sons v. William Lillico & Sons Ltd* [1969] 2 A.C. 31; *Harbutt's "Plasticine" Ltd v. Wayne Tank and Pump Co. Ltd* [1970] 1 Q.B. 447 (the decision has been overruled on another point: *Photo Productions Ltd v. Securicor Transport Ltd* [1980] A.C. 827); *H. Parsons (Livestock) Ltd v. Uttley, Ingham & Co. Ltd* [1978] Q.B. 791. See also the cases on repair and reinstatement, *ante*, § 27–014.

[58] Often there may be concurrent liability in tort for the personal injury or death, but there may be advantages in suing for breach of contract, *e.g.* in not having to prove the defendant's negligence.

[59] *Burton v. Pinkerton* (1867) L.R. 2 Ex. 340, 349–351; *Hobbs v. L.S.W. Ry.* (1875) L.R. 10 Q.B. 111; *Bailey v. Bullock* [1950] 2 All E.R. 1167; *Stedman v. Swan's Tours* (1951) 95 S.J. 727; *cf. post* § 27–069.

[60] *Perry v. Sidney Phillips & Son* [1982] 1 W.L.R. 1297, CA; *Calabar Properties Ltd v. Stitcher* [1984] 1 W.L.R. 287; *Watts v. Morrow* [1991] 1 W.L.R. 1421, 1439–1443, 1445–1446, CA; damages may also cover the plaintiff's "mental suffering" directly related to the physical inconvenience: at 1445.

[61] *Watts v. Morrow, supra* (the judge's award of £4,000 was reduced by the Court of Appeal to £750: at 1443, 1445). See also Franklin (1988) 4 Const. L.J. 264.

[62] *Jackson v. Watson* [1909] 2 K.B. 193. See also *Priest v. Last* [1903] 2 K.B. 148.

[63] Exemplary damages are not available for breach of contract: *ante*, § 27–017.

[64] See *post*, § 27–071.

[65] *Addis v. Gramophone Co. Ltd* [1909] A.C. 488 (as interpreted by *Malik v. Bank of Credit and Commerce International SA* [1998] A.C. 20). See also *Hamlin v. G.N. Ry* [1856] 1 H. & N. 408; *Groom v. Crocker* [1939] 1 K.B. 194; *Foaminol Laboratories Ltd v. British Artid Plastics Ltd* [1941] 2 All E.R. 393 (loss of co-operation of advertisers); *Bailey v. Bullock* [1950] 2 All E.R. 1167 (no damages for "annoyance or mental distress"); *Last-Harris v. Thompson Bros.* [1956] N.Z.L.R. 995; *Hayes v. Dodd* [1990] 2 All E.R. 815 CA; *Watts v. Morrow* [1991] 1 W.L.R. 1421, CA. Nor are damages recoverable for loss of the society of one's spouse or child; *cf. Jackson v. Watson* [1909] 2 K.B. 193.

missed in a humiliating manner.[66] Although in *Malik's* case[67] the House of Lords created a narrow exception to this principle,[68] it still holds as the general principle: where a breach of an ordinary commercial contract may cause foreseeable anguish and vexation to the plaintiff, no damages are recoverable for that type of loss.[69] However, an exception applies in the enjoyment or "holiday" cases[70]: in the case of a failure, in breach of contract, to provide a holiday of the advertised standard or some other form of entertainment or enjoyment, damages can be awarded for the disappointment and mental distress caused by the breach of contract.[71] (The "loss of amenity" recognised by the House of Lords[72] could be viewed as an extension of the "loss of enjoyment" category.) A further exception arises where the purpose of the contract was to protect the claimant from annoyance or distress, *e.g.* where a woman employed solicitors to protect her from being molested by a former friend, who was causing her mental distress; the damages for the solicitors' failure to obtain protection for her included a sum for the foreseeable annoyance and mental distress which she continued to suffer as a result of their breach of contract.[73] The exception is limited to contracts whose purpose is "to provide peace of mind or freedom from distress,"[74] and does not extend to a contract to survey the condition of a house for a prospective purchaser,[75] or to the breach of a covenant for quiet enjoyment in a tenancy agreement.[76] Damages may also be awarded for nervous shock or an anxiety state (an actual breakdown in health) suffered by the claimant, if that was, at the time the contract was made,[77] within the contemplation of the parties as a not unlikely consequence of the breach of contract.[78]

---

[66] *Addis v. Gramophone Co. Ltd, supra* (see *ante*, § 27–017). The House of Lords later said that " . . . damages for breach of contract may only be awarded for breach of contract, and not for loss caused by the manner of the breach": *Malik v. Bank of Credit and Commerce International SA* [1998] A.C. 20, at 51 (*per* Lord Steyn, interpreting *Addis v. Gramophone Co., supra.*). See also *Bliss v. S.E. Thames Regional Health Authority* [1987] I.C.R. 700; *French v. Barlcays Bank plc* [1998] I.R.L.R. 646, CA; *Johnson v. Unisys Ltd* [1999] 1 All E.R. 854, CA. But *cf.* the damages when a master wrongfully terminates a contract of apprenticeship: Vol. II, § 39–182. On damages for wrongful, or unfair dismissal, see *post*, §§ 39–179 *et seq*, §§ 39–217 *et seq*.

[67] [1998] A.C. 20.

[68] See *post* § 27–071.

[69] *Hayes v. Dodd, supra.*

[70] *Jarvis v. Swans Tours Ltd* [1973] QB 233; *Jackson v. Horizon Holidays Ltd* [1975] 1 W.L.R. 1468; *Jackson v. Chrysler Acceptances Ltd* [1978] R.T.R. 474; *Kemp v. Intasun Holidays Ltd* [1987] 2 F.T.L.R. 234.

[71] *cf. Diesen v. Samson*, 1971 S.L.T. (Sh.Ct.) 49 (failure of photographer to attend a wedding). *cf.* also *Archer v. Brown* [1985] Q.B. 401, 424–426 (deceit).

[72] *Ruxley Electronics and Construction Ltd v. Forsyth* [1996] A.C. 344. See *post*, § 27–070.

[73] *Heywood v. Wellers* [1976] Q.B. 446. *cf.* damages for mental distress awarded against a solicitor whose negligence led to his client's wrongful conviction of a crime: *McLeish v. Amoo-Gottfried & Co.* (1994) 10 Prof. Negligence 102.

[74] *Bliss v. S.E. Thames Regional H.A. supra*, at 718; *Hayes v. Dodd* [1990] 2 All E.R. 815, 824, CA. *French v. Barclays Bank plc* [1998] I.R.L.R. 646, CA.

[75] *Watts v. Morrow, supra*; *Knott v. Bolton* [1995] E.G.C.S. 59 (no damages for distress caused by breach of an architect's contract to design a house). (But damages may be awarded for "mental suffering" directly related to physical inconvenience and discomfort caused by the breach of contract: *Watts v. Morrow, supra*, at 1440–1445 (see *ante* § 27–068).

[76] *Branchett v. Beaney* [1992] 3 All E.R. 910, CA.

[77] See *ante*, § 27–042.

[78] *Cook v. Swinfen* [1967] 1 W.L.R. 457. See also *Walker v. Northumberland C.C.* [1995] 1 I.C.R. 702 (employee's nervous breakdown caused by excessive workload).

Loss of amenity (consumer surplus). In *Ruxley Electronics and Construc-*   27–070
tion Ltd v. Forsyth[79] the House of Lords accepted that damages may be awarded
for the "loss of amenity" suffered by the claimant where the purpose of the
contract was to give him a subjective, even idiosyncratic pleasure or amenity.
The defendant, in breach of contract, built a swimming pool whose depth was
only six feet in the diving area, instead of the specified seven feet six inches.
Despite evidence that a depth of six feet was perfectly safe for diving, and that
the market value of the property was not adversely affected by the breach, the
Court of Appeal[80] had allowed the full cost of re-building the pool. Their
Lordships reversed this decision[81] and appeared to support the trial judge's award
(not appealed) of £2,500 as substantial damages for "loss of amenity" because
the purpose of the contract was "the provision of a pleasurable amenity". Two
Lords agreed with Lord Mustill's speech: he upheld the award as representing the
loss of the "consumer surplus", the personal, subjective gain which the claimant
expected to receive from full performance—an advantage not measured by any
increase in the market value of his property.[82]

Loss of reputation. Damages for loss of reputation as such are not normally   27–071
awarded for breach of contract, since protection of reputation is the role of the
tort of defamation. However, where the breach of contract causes a loss of
reputation which in turn causes foreseeable financial loss to the claimant, he may
recover damages for that financial loss: in *Malik's* case,[83] the House of Lords held
that where, by conducting a dishonest and corrupt business, the employer had
broken his obligation to his employee (under the implied "trust and confidence"
term[84]) the employee could recover damages for the financial loss suffered by
him where his future employment prospects were prejudiced by the stigma of his
former employment. A further exception arises where the contract gave an
opportunity to the claimant to enhance his reputation as an author[85] or an actor[86]:
damages may be awarded for loss flowing from a failure to provide promised
publicity, which loss may include loss to existing reputation.[87] Subject to remoteness, damages are recoverable where the breach of contract causes loss of
commercial reputation involving loss of trade.[88]

---

[79] [1996] A.C. 344 (see the comments by Poole (1996) 59 M.L.R. 272; and Coote [1997] C.L.J.
537).

[80] [1994] 1 W.L.R. 650.

[81] *Ante*, § 27–015.

[82] Lord Mustill cited the article by Harris, Ogus and Phillips (1979) 95 L.Q.R. 581. The "holiday"
cases (*ante*, § 27–069) can be explained on the same basis.

[83] *Malik v. Bank of Credit and Commerce International SA* [1998] A.C. 20. (See the article by
Enonchong, which preceded this decision, (1996) 16 O.J.L.S. 617).

[84] See *post*, § 38–135.

[85] *Tolnay v. Criterion Film Productions Ltd* [1936] 2 All E.R. 1625; *Joseph v. National Magazine
Co. Ltd* [1959] Ch. 14.

[86] *Clayton & Jack Waller Ltd v. Oliver* [1930] A.C. 209; *Marbé v. George Edwardes (Daly's
Theatre) Ltd* [1928] 1 K.B. 269.

[87] *Malik's* case, *supra* (overruling on this point *Withers v. General Theatre Corpn. Ltd* [1933] 2
K.B. 536).

[88] *Malik's* case, *supra*, at 115; *Cointax v. Myham & Son* [1913] 2 K.B. 220 (*post*, § 43–423); *G.K.N.
Centrax Gears Ltd v. Matbro Ltd* [1976] 2 Lloyd's Rep. 555 (*post*, § 43–423).

4. ILLUSTRATIONS OF THE REMOTENESS OF DAMAGE AND THE ASSESSMENT OF DAMAGES[89]

(a) *Sale of Goods*

27–072   **Sale of goods.** Many of the best illustrations of the rules for the remoteness of damage and for the assessment of damages will be found in cases on the sale of goods, which are considered in some detail in Volume II, Chapter 43. Although these cases are often based on the provisions of the Sale of Goods Act 1893 (now consolidated in the 1979 Act), the relevant sections 50, 51, 53 and 54 incorporate former common law decisions on the sale of goods[90] so that cases decided on the Act may be useful analogies for determining the measure of damages for breaches of other types of contract which are still governed by common law rules. The cases discussed in Chapter 43 of Volume II illustrate the types of loss which have been found to be within the contemplation of the parties[91]; the duty to mitigate[92] (especially in cases of anticipatory breach[93]); and the assessment of damages for delay in delivery,[94] and for breaches of terms relating to the quality of the goods.[95]

(b) *Carriage of Goods*

27–073   **Carriage of goods.** If by default of the carrier the goods which he has contracted to deliver are lost or destroyed in transit the normal measure of damages is the market value of the original goods at the time when and place where they ought to have been delivered, less the freight payable under the contract upon safe delivery of the goods.[96] The price in a forward sale made by the consignee is usually irrelevant,[97] but it may be relevant if there is no market for such goods at the place of delivery.[98] Where the carrier delays in delivering the goods, the normal[99] measure of damages is the difference between the market value of the goods at their destination on the date they ought to have been delivered, and the market value at the actual date of delivery[1]; the same rule now

---

[89] Further illustrations will be found in the various chapters of Vol. II of this work.
[90] *Barrow v. Arnaud* (1846) 8 Q.B. 595, 609–610.
[91] *e.g.* loss of profits on sub-contracts: Vol. II, §§ 43–399—43–402, 43–413, 43–422.
[92] Vol. II, § 43–367. See also *post*, §§ 27–085 *et seq.*
[93] Vol. II, §§ 43–379, 43–392.
[94] Vol. II, §§ 43–404 *et seq.*
[95] Vol. II, §§ 43–409 *et seq.*
[96] *Rodocanachi v. Milburn* (1886) 18 Q.B.D. 67, 76. Even where the plaintiff has only a limited interest in the goods, he may recover their full value: *Crouch v. L.N.W. Ry.* (1849) 2 C. & K. 789. (See Vol. II, § 33–127.)
[97] *Rodocanachi v. Milburn, supra.* See also *Slater v. Hoyle and Smith* [1920] 2 K.B. 11 (but on this case see now *Bence Graphics International Ltd v. Fasson U.K. Ltd* [1998] Q.B. 87, which is discussed post, § 43–411, 43–413); *The Arpad* [1934] P.189.
[98] *O'Hanlan v. G.W. Ry.* (1865) 6 B. & S. 484; *The Arpad, supra.*
[99] "Where there is a market it must be assumed to be in the contemplation of the parties as a grave danger that the goods may be sold on arrival so that if there is a delay one of the consequences may be loss of market": *Koufos v. C. Czarnikow Ltd* [1969] 1 A.C. 350, 427.
[1] *Wilson v. Lancs & Yorks Ry.* (1861) 9 C.B.(N.S.) 632; *Collard v. S.E. Ry.* (1861) 7 H. & N. 79; *Schulze v. G.E. Ry.* (1887) 19 Q.B.D. 30; *Heskell v. Continental Express Ltd* [1950] 1 All E.R. 1033, 1046.

applies to carriage of goods by sea.[2] The carrier's liability for loss of profits has already been discussed.[3] Occasionally the carrier may be liable for expenses incurred by the claimant in acquiring the nearest substitute when equivalent goods were not available in the market, and the claimant acted reasonably in incurring the expenses.[4]

If the defendant carries the goods to the wrong place, or completely fails to carry them at all, the claimant may either   **27–074**

(a) engage substitute transport at the market rate and recover from the carrier the difference between that and the contractual rate, together with any difference between the market price of the goods at the actual time of delivery and the agreed time of delivery[5]; or

(b) purchase substitute goods at the agreed place of delivery, and recover from the carrier the difference between the cost of the substituted goods, and the total of the value of the original goods at the place of loading, freight and insurance (or at the wrong place of delivery, as the case may be).[6]

Where the owner of the goods fails to supply the goods for the agreed carriage, but the carrier ought reasonably to have obtained substitute cargo, the normal measure of damages is the difference between the agreed rate of freight, and the market rate (deducting in each case the cost of earning the freight).[7]

(c) Contracts Concerning Land[8]

Contracts for the sale or lease of land.[9] Full details of the damages recover-   **27–075** able for breaches of contracts relating to the sale or lease of land (including breaches of the covenants in a conveyance or lease) should be sought else-where.[10] In respect of contracts made after September 27, 1989 the restrictive rule in *Bain v. Fothergill*[11] (which limited the vendor's liability) no longer

---

[2] *Koufos v. C. Czarnikow Ltd, supra,* (HL, holding that the rule in *The Parana* (1877) 2 P.D. 118 was obsolete).

[3] See *ante,* § 27–057.

[4] *Millen v. Brash* (1882) 10 Q.B.D. 142; cf. *Romulus Films v. William Dempster* [1952] 2 Lloyd's Rep. 535. Other expenses recoverable include the cost of searching for the missing goods: *Hales v. L.N.W. Ry.* (1863) 4 B. & S. 66; *Heskell v. Continental Express Ltd* [1950] 1 All E.R. 1033, 1046.

[5] *Monarch SS. Co. v. Karlshamns Oljefabriker (A/B)* [1949] A.C. 196. The plaintiff must act reasonably in his choice of one of the alternatives (a) or (b): *ibid.* at 217–218, 220; where neither alternative is possible, see *Watts, Watts & Co. Ltd v. Mitsui & Co. Ltd* [1917] A.C. 227.

[6] *Ströms Bruk Aktiebolag v. Hutchison* [1905] A.C. 515 (no substitute transport was available); *Nissho Co. v. Livanos* (1941) 57 T.L.R. 400. Consequential loss is also recoverable: *Heindal A/S v. Questier* (1949) 82 Ll.L.Rep. 452 (perishable goods).

[7] *Smith v. M'Guire* (1858) 3 H. & N. 554; *Aitken Lilburn v. Ernsthausen* [1894] 1 Q.B. 773; *Wallems Rederij A/S v. Muller* [1927] 2 K.B. 99, 105.

[8] On damages for defective building work, see *ante,* § 27–014, n. 70.

[9] The usual remedy of a purchaser under such a contract is specific performance: see *post,* § 28–004.

[10] See *McGregor on Damages* (16th ed., 1997), Chaps. 21 and 22, and the standard textbooks on real property.

[11] (1874) L.R. 7 H.L. 158. The rule provided that where a vendor of land was unable to complete the contract through a defect in his title, no damages could be recovered (in the absence of fraud, misrepresentation, bad faith or default on the part of the vendor) for the loss of the purchaser's bargain. The exceptions to the rule were developed in a line of authorities, which are no longer cited in this work.

applies.[12] Thus, a vendor who breaks his contract by failing to convey the land to the purchaser is liable to damages for the purchaser's loss of bargain and must pay damages calculated in accordance with the ordinary rules, *viz.* the market value of the property at the fixed time for completion (or at a later time so long as it was reasonable[13] for the purchaser to continue to seek performance[14]), less the contract price.[15] The purchaser may claim the loss of profit he intended to make from a particular use of the land (*e.g.* by converting a building into flats and offices) only if the vendor had actual or imputed knowledge of special circumstances showing that the purchaser intended to use the land in that way.[16]

27–076   If the vendor or lessor delays in completion, the normal measure of damages is the value of the use of the land for the period of delay, *viz.* usually its rental value.[17] Where the purchaser of land fails to complete, the normal measure of damages is the contract price less the market price at the time fixed for completion,[18] plus any consequential expenses or loss.[19] Where the vendor reasonably tried to obtain performance by the purchaser, damages were assessed as at the later time when it was reasonable for him to give up seeking performance.[20]

27–077   **Valuer-surveyor's report to a purchaser.** Where, in breach of contract, the defendant surveyor negligently failed to report defects in the property purchased by the claimant in reliance on the report, the claimant's damages[21] should be

---

[12] s.3 of the Law of Property (Miscellaneous Provisions) Act 1989. (The Law Commission proposed the abolition of the rule: Report No. 166.)

[13] *Malhotra v. Choudhury* [1980] Ch. 52,77, 81 (some unnecessary delay by the plaintiff led to the date for assessment being fixed one year before the hearing).

[14] *cf. Johnson v. Agnew* [1980] A.C. 367, 401 (see *post*, §§ 28–073—28–076: breach by purchaser). *cf. Suleman v. Shahsavari* [1988] 1 W.L.R. 1181. In some cases decided before *Johnson v. Agnew*, damages were assessed as at dates later than those originally fixed for completion (*Wroth v. Tyler* [1974] Ch. 30 (as at the date of hearing); *Grant v. Dawkins* [1973] 1 W.L.R. 1406; *Malhotra v. Choudhury, supra*), but the reasoning in these cases cannot now be supported, except to the extent that it is consistent with that in *Johnson v. Agnew*.

[15] *Godwin v. Francis* (1870) L.R. 2 C.P. 295; *Engel v. Fitch* (1869) L.R. 4 Q.B. 659; *Re Daniel* [1917] 2 Ch. 405; *Diamond v. Campbell-Jones* [1961] Ch. 22; *Chitholie v. Nash & Co.* (1973) 229 E.G. 786 (damages for breach of warranty of authority by vendor's agents). An express term in the contract of sale may regulate the rights of the parties in the event of the vendor's title proving to be defective: see the Law Society's General Conditions of Sale (condition 16(1)); and the National Conditions of Sale (condition 10(1)).

[16] *Diamond v. Campbell-Jones, supra; Cottrill v. Steyning and Littlehampton Building Society* [1966] 1 W.L.R. 753; *Malhotra v. Choudhury, supra*, at 80–81. A similar rule applies to claims by a purchaser for losses arising under a sub-contract: *Seven Seas Properties Ltd v. Al-Essa (No. 2)* [1993] 1 W.L.R. 1083; and to expenses incurred by the purchaser: *Lloyd v. Stanbury* [1971] 1 W.L.R. 535, 546–547 (*ante*, § 27–062).

[17] *Royal Bristol Permanent Building Society v. Bomash* (1887) 35 Ch.D. 390. See also *Jones v. Gardiner* [1902] 1 Ch. 191; *Phillips v. Lamdin* [1949] 2 K.B. 33. As to a lessor's delay, see *Jaques v. Millar* (1877) 6 Ch.D. 153 (loss of profits allowed to lessee where lessor knew of his intended trade on the premises).

[18] *Laird v. Pim* (1841) 7 M. & W. 474. A resale price may be evidence of the market price: *Noble v. Edwards* (1877) 5 Ch.D. 378 (reversed on another point: 5 Ch.D. 392); *York Glass Co. v. Jubb* (1926) 134 L.T. 36.

[19] *York Glass Co. v. Jubb, supra*, at 40. (The measure is similar where a lessee refuses to proceed with a contract to take a lease: *Marshall v. Macintosh* (1898) 78 L.T. 750; *cf. Oldershaw v. Holt* (1840) 12 A. & E. 590.)

[20] *Johnson v. Agnew* [1980] A.C. 367, 401 (*post*, §§ 28–073—28–076). See also *Suleman v. Shahsavari* [1988] 1 W.L.R. 1181.

[21] In addition, the plaintiff may be able to recover damages for physical inconvenience: see *ante*, § 27–068.

assessed at the difference between the price paid by him and the market value of the property in its actual (defective) condition at the time of the purchase.[22] Since the surveyor did not contractually warrant that the property was in the condition which he reported, he is not liable to pay the difference between its hypothetical value in the reported condition and its market value in its actual condition.[23] The diminution in value measure does not depend on whether or not the claimant would have bought the property had the surveyor's report been carefully made.[24] But if, on learning of the defects which should have been reported, the claimant had immediately moved out and sold, he might be able to recover (in addition to the diminution in value measure) his wasted costs.[25]

Valuer-surveyor's report to a lender. In the *South Australia* case[26] the   **27–078** House of Lords imposed a limit[27] on the extent of damages payable by a valuer who negligently over-values the intended security and the security turns out to be inadequate through a combination of this and a fall in the value of the property. The lender's "ultimate loss" (*viz.* the difference between (i) the capital of the actual loan and (ii) the net proceeds of realising the security, plus any repayments by the borrower) is caused by, and is not too remote a consequence of, the negligence[28] but the lender's damages for his capital loss may not exceed the extent of the initial deficiency in the supposed value of the security, *viz.* the difference between the amount of the defendant's negligent over-valuation and what would have been a proper[29] valuation at the time of the loan.[30] Within this limit, however, the lender may recover his ultimate loss of capital even though it is due to a fall in the market value of the security since the loan was made. In

---

[22] *Watts v. Morrow* [1991] 1 W.L.R. 1421, CA, following *Phillips v. Ward* [1956] 1 W.L.R. 471, and *Perry v. Sidney Phillips & Son* [1982] 1 W.L.R. 1297. See also *Gardner v. Marsh & Parsons* [1997] 1 W.L.R. 489 (the fact that five years after the purchase the landlord, a third party, remedied the defect at his expense was held to be too remote to be taken into account in assessing the purchaser's damages against a surveyor). (In these cases the courts refused to assess damages at the cost of repairs; see *ante*, §§ 27–014 *et seq.*) In *Watts v. Morrow*, the court left open the question as to *when* the market value should be ascertained: at 1437–1438.

[23] *Watts v. Morrow, supra*, at 1430, 1435. The relevant statement in the headnote is inaccurate; see also *Perry v. Sidney Phillips & Son, supra*, at 1301–1302, 1304.

[24] *Watts v. Morrow, supra*, at 1437–1438. It is submitted that the "excessive price" measure used in a purchaser's claim is not affected by the decision of the House of Lords in the *South Australia* case [1997] A.C. 191 (see *post*, § 27–078) where a lender's claim is based on a negligent over-valuation of the proposed security. The excessive price provides the measure of the purchaser's damages, whereas the initial deficiency in the value of the security provides only a limitation on the lender's damages.

[25] *ibid.* at 1445. *cf.* the "no transaction" measure of damages used in *Hayes v. Dodd* [1990] 2 All E.R. 815, CA (*ante*, § 27–065).

[26] *South Australia Asset Management Corp. v. York Montague Ltd* [1997] A.C. 191 (also known as the *B.B.L.* or *Banque Bruxelles* case). Lord Hoffmann, who gave the only speech, dealt almost exclusively with the scope of the valuer's limited duty of care under the tort of negligence, but he also said that the same result would follow from an implied term in the contract: at 211, 212.

[27] *cf.*, however, the "extrication" or "no transaction" cases recognised by the House of Lords in the *South Australia* case, *supra*, at 218–219 (see *ante*, § 27–065).

[28] *Nykredit Mortgage Bank plc v. Edward Erdman Group Ltd (No. 2)* [1997] 1 W.L.R. 1627, HL, at 1631, 1638. The *Nykredit* case and *Platform Home Loans Ltd v. Oyston Shipways Ltd* [1999] 2 W.L.R. 518, HL, explain the South Australia decision.

[29] See *post*, § 27–081.

[30] The "amount of the loss . . . [is] limited to the extent of the overvaluation": the *Nykredit* case, *supra*, at 1632. The limitation on damages laid down in the *South Australia* case covers both categories previously recognised by *Swingcastle Ltd v. Alastair Gibson* [1991] 2 A.C. 223, *viz.* where, given a proper report, the lender (1) would have lent nothing at all on the proposed security and (2) would have lent a smaller sum.

addition to his claim for loss of capital, the lender may claim (1) his reasonable expenses of realising the security; and (2) interest (see next paragraph).

27–079   **The lender's claim for interest.** In order to decide when interest on the damages should begin, the court must fix the date when the lender first suffers "loss". In a case in which a security has been overvalued, the lender's cause of action may not arise until the security is realised and the difference emerges between its value and the outstanding debt. However, it may be clear long before that date that the security has been overvalued and is inadequate; and if the borrower ceases to pay interest on the loan, the lender is not obliged to wait to bring an action until the security has been realised. According to the *Nykredit* case,[31] the lender first suffers "loss" when the amount of the loan (plus interest) exceeds "the value of the rights acquired, namely the borrower's covenant and the true value of the over-valued property".[32] (This case creates the strange possibility of a fluctuating "loss" because it could be wiped out if the security later increased in value and reinstated if its value fell thereafter.[33]) The rate of interest should be fixed by the court[34] as compensation for the loss of the use of the capital lent to the borrower.[35]

27–080   **Analogous application of the *South Australia* case.** The formula placing a limit on the damages used in the *South Australia* case, *supra*, has been applied by analogy where the negligence of a solicitor resulted in the lender believing it had more adequate security than it in fact had. The solicitor failed to tell the lender of facts which would have led it to doubt the valuation on which it was relying and so to obtain a second valuation: if this showed that the first was an overvaluation the solicitor would be liable only to the extent of the difference between the proper valuation and the overvaluation.[36]

27–081   **Assessing the "proper" valuation of property.** Where the court must fix the "proper" valuation of a property there is normally a range of valuations which might have been made by reasonably careful valuers; the court must choose the figure which it considers to be the most likely outcome of careful assessment: the defendant is not given the benefit of damages being assessed by reference to the highest figure which might have been given without negligence.[37]

---

[31] The *Nykredit* case, *supra*.

[32] *ibid.* at 1631. This "loss" could be suffered by the lender "from the inception of the loan transaction" (at 1632), or before the security is realised: "Realisation of the security does not create the lender's loss, nor does it convert a potential loss into an actual loss. Rather it crystallises the amount of a present loss . . . " (at 1633).

[33] In the *Nykredit* case, at 1631, Lord Nicholls spoke of the lender "currently" having no cause of action.

[34] *Swingcastle Ltd v. Alastair Gibson, supra.* (The House of Lords, however, envisaged the possibility that the lender could produce evidence as to how he would otherwise have used the money; at 239).

[35] The lender cannot recover the contractual (often penal) rate of interest undertaken by the borrower in the loan agreement, because to allow this would be to make the valuer a guarantor of the agreement between the lender and borrower: *ibid.*

[36] *Colin Bishop*, one of the *Bristol and West Building Society* cases reported in [1997] 4 All E.R. 582. Similarly, if the lender obtains a valid title to only half the intended security, the damages should be limited to half of the initial value of the security: *Cooke and Borsay* (*ibid.*).

[37] The *South Australia* case [1997] A.C. 191 (following the Privy Council in *Lion Nathan Ltd v. C-C. Bottlers Ltd* [1996] 1 W.L.R. 1438 (a contractual duty to take reasonable care in making a forecast of likely profits)).

(d) *Contracts to Pay or Lend Money*

Contracts to pay money. Most contracts contain a promise to pay money as **27–082** part of the bargain between the parties. Although the agreed sum itself may be recoverable as a debt,[38] it was for many years uncertain whether at common law the creditor could claim for any other loss resulting from the debtor's failure to pay the agreed sum at the fixed time.[39] Except in the few cases where interest was recoverable at common law,[40] the rule was believed to be that only nominal damages were recoverable for failure to pay money[41]; the House of Lords has now confirmed that at common law interest cannot be awarded by way of *general* damages simply because payment of a debt had been delayed.[42] The court is empowered by statute[43] in its discretion to award interest in an action, whether for debt or for damages. Apart from this statutory power, the House of Lords[44] has approved the decision of the Court of Appeal[45] that, if the test for remoteness based on knowledge of special circumstances is satisfied (the second rule in *Hadley v. Baxendale*),[46] special damages may be awarded for interest paid and other expenses incurred by the claimant[47] in arranging alternative finance as the result of the defendant's breach of his obligation to pay a sum of money on a given date.[48] Later, the Court of Appeal held that it is not necessary

> "to prove that the facts or circumstances were unusual, let alone unique to the particular contract. . . . In drawing inferences as to the parties' actual or imputed knowledge, the court is not obliged to ignore facts or circumstances of which other people doing similar business might have been aware."[49]

In earlier cases the defendant had been held liable for substantial damages where he undertook to maintain the claimant's financial credit.[50] In actions for the

---

[38] See *ante*, §§ 27–008; *post*, § 27–111.

[39] *London, Chatham and Dover Ry. Co. v. South Eastern Ry. Co.* [1893] A.C. 429 (a claim for interest at common law). *cf. Trans Trust S.P.R.L. v. Danubian Trading Co. Ltd* [1952] 2 Q.B. 297; and see the criticism of the rule by Jessel M.R. in *Wallis v. Smith* (1882) 21 Ch.D. 243, 257. On a contract to pay interest, see Vol. II, §§ 38–246 *et seq.*

[40] *e.g.* dishonour of bills of exchange and promissory notes. See *post*, § 27–137; Vol. II, § 34–120.

[41] *London, Chatham and Dover Ry. Co. v. South Eastern Ry. Co., supra.*

[42] *President of India v. La Pintada Compania Navegacion SA* [1985] A.C. 104 (*post*, § 27–137). The High Court of Australia has not followed this rule: *Hungerfords v. Walker* (1989) 171 C.L.R. 125.

[43] See *post*, § 27–140, 27–142 and Vol. II, § 38–256.

[44] The *President of India* case, supra, at 125–127.

[45] *Wadsworth v. Lydall* [1981] 1 W.L.R. 598. See the fuller discussion of this case, *post*, § 27–138.

[46] (1854) 9 Exch. 341. See *ante*, §§ 27–049 *et seq.*; The *President of India* case, *supra*, at 125–127.

[47] A currency loss arising from late payment has been held to fall within this principle: *President of India v. Lips Maritime Corporation* [1988] A.C. 395, 410-412, following *International Minerals and Chemical Corporation v. Karl O. Helm A.G.* [1986] 1 Lloyd's Rep. 81. See also *post*, §§ 31–163 *et seq.*

[48] For other cases on recovery of interest, or interest charges paid, see *post*, § 27–137, 27–138. If the defendant's failure to pay on time entitles the plaintiff to terminate the contract, he may be entitled to recover general damages for the loss he suffers: *Yeoman Credit Ltd v. Waragowski* [1961] 1 W.L.R. 1124; *Lombard North Central plc v. Butterworth* [1987] Q.B. 527 (*post*, § 27–116).

[49] *President of India v. Lips Maritime Corporation*, *ante*, at 411, 412, CA.

[50] *Rolin v. Steward* (1854) 14 C.B. 595; *Wilson v. United Counties Bank* [1920] A.C. 102; *cf. Larios v. Bonany y Gurety* (1873) L.R. 5 PC 346; *Prehn v. Royal Bank of Liverpool* (1870) L.R. 5 Ex. 92.

dishonour of bills of exchange and promissory notes, the measure of damages depends on statutory provisions.[51]

27–083   **Contracts to lend money.** In an action based on a lender's failure to provide the money promised, the normal measure of damages is the difference between the cost of a substitute loan in the market, and the cost of the contracted loan[52]: hence nominal damages will be usual, except where the claimant can obtain a loan elsewhere only "at a higher rate of interest, or for a shorter term of years, or upon other more onerous terms,"[53] or where the claimant cannot raise another loan, and so fails to complete his purchase.[54]

(e) *Sale of Shares*

27–084   **Shares.** In an action for a seller's failure to transfer shares, the buyer may recover the market price of the shares on the day fixed for completion, less the contract price, since the principles of law governing damages in the sale of goods[55] are applied by analogy.[56] A buyer who obtains a decree of specific performance for the delivery of shares may also recover damages equal to the dividends declared by the company between the agreed date of delivery and the actual date (and interest thereon).[57] Where the buyer refuses to accept the shares, the seller may recover the difference between the contract price and the market price on the day fixed for completion.[58]

> "If the seller retains the shares after the breach, the speculation as to the way the market will subsequently go is the speculation of the seller, not of the buyer; the seller cannot recover from the buyer the loss below the market price at the date of the breach if the market falls, nor is he liable to the purchaser for the profit if the market rises."[59]

5. MITIGATION OF DAMAGE

27–085   **Mitigation.** There are three rules often referred to under the comprehensive heading of "mitigation": they will be considered in turn. First, the claimant cannot recover damages for any part of his loss consequent upon the defendant's breach of contract which the claimant could have avoided by taking reasonable steps. Secondly, if the claimant in fact avoids or mitigates his loss consequent upon the defendant's breach, he cannot recover for such avoided loss, even though the steps he took were more than could be reasonably required of him

---

[51] s.57 of the Bills of Exchange Act 1882, considered in Vol. II, § 34–120.
[52] *South African Territories v. Wallington* [1898] A.C. 309; *Astor Properties Ltd v. Tunbridge Wells Equitable Friendly Soc.* [1936] 1 All E.R. 531; *Bahamas Sisal Plantation v. Griffin* (1897) 14 T.L.R. 139. See Vol. II, § 38–228.
[53] *South African Territories v. Wallington* [1897] 1 Q.B. 692, 696–697 (affd. [1898] A.C. 309).
[54] *Manchester and Oldham Bank v. Cook* (1884) 49 L.T. 674, 678 (the lender knew the purpose for which the loan was required). See also *Astor Properties Ltd v. Tunbridge Wells Equitable Friendly Society, supra.*
[55] See Vol. II, §§ 43–366 *et seq.*, §§ 43–386 *et seq.*
[56] *Shaw v. Holland* (1846) 15 M. & W. 136. See also *Tempest v. Kilner* (1845) 3 C.B. 249. *cf. Michael v. Hart & Co.* [1902] 1 K.B. 482.
[57] *Sri Lanka Omnibus Co. v. Perera* [1952] A.C. 76.
[58] *Jamal v. Moolla Dawood & Co.* [1916] 1 A.C. 175.
[59] *ibid.* at 179.

under the first rule. Thirdly, where the claimant incurs loss or expense in the course of taking reasonable steps to mitigate the loss resulting from the defendant's breach, the claimant may recover this further loss or expense from the defendant.

Purpose of mitigation role. The purpose of the rules on mitigation is to **27-086** prevent the waste of resources in society, since they are obviously limited. Wherever the innocent party, following the defendant's breach, is able to find substitute performance from a third party, the mitigation rules give him a strong incentive to accept the substitute. The rules inevitably give some incentive to the defendant deliberately to break his contractual undertaking whenever he finds a better opportunity for the resources he intended to use in performing the contract: if he makes a higher profit on a new contract, he may be better off even after paying damages to compensate the original promisee (because these damages may be relatively low whenever substitute performance is readily available).[60]

Avoidable loss. The first rule "imposes on a plaintiff the duty of taking all **27-087** reasonable steps to mitigate the loss consequent on the breach, and debars him from claiming any part of the damage which is due to his neglect to take such steps."[61] It is not strictly a "duty" to mitigate, but rather a restriction on the damages recoverable, which will be calculated *as if* the claimant had acted reasonably to minimise his loss.[62] Only the claimant's *net* gain from his mitigating effort will be deducted—he may set off against his substitute profits or earnings the reasonable expenses incurred in obtaining them.[63] The position of the claimant under this rule is similar to that of a claimant in tort whose damages are reduced because of his contributory negligence.[64] The onus of proof is on the defendant, who must show that the claimant ought, as a reasonable man, to have taken certain steps to mitigate his loss.[65] Any loss which is directly caused by a failure to meet this standard is not recoverable from the defendant. Thus an employee who has been wrongfully dismissed and unreasonably[66] refuses to accept another equally remunerative post to date from the dismissal is only entitled to nominal damages.[67]

---

[60] This leads many writers on law-and-economics to argue that mitigation supports "efficient" breaches of contract (*viz.* breaches which will leave society as a whole better off, while the original promisee is left no worse off). This "efficiency" argument is reviewed and criticised by Harris *op. cit.*, pp. 6–8; 78–87; 178–186; see also Goetz and Scott (1983) 69 Virg.L.Rev. 967; and Macneil (1982) 68 Virg.L.Rev. 947.

[61] *British Westinghouse Electric Co. Ltd v. Underground Electric Rys.* [1912] A.C. 673, 689. See also *Le Blanche v. L.N.W. Ry.* (1876) 1 C.P.D. 286; *Tucker v. Linger* (1882) 21 Ch.D. 18; *Macrae v. H. G. Swindells (Trading as West View Garage Co.)* [1954] 1 W.L.R. 597.

[62] *Darbishire v. Warran* [1963] 1 W.L.R. 1067, 1075; *The Solholt* [1983] 1 Lloyd's Rep. 605, 608, CA.

[63] *Westwood v. Secretary of State for Employment* [1985] A.C. 20, 44.

[64] See *ante*, § 27–037.

[65] *Roper v. Johnson* (1873) L.R. 8 C.P. 167; *Pilkington v. Wood* [1953] Ch. 770; *Edwards v. Society of Graphical and Allied Trades* [1971] Ch. 354; *Strutt v. Whitnell* [1975] 1 W.L.R. 870.

[66] *Shindler v. Northern Raincoat Co. Ltd* [1960] 1 W.L.R. 1038; *Yetton v. Eastwoods Froy Ltd* [1967] 1 W.L.R. 104. See Vol. II, § 39–179.

[67] *Brace v. Calder* [1895] 2 Q.B. 253. See also *Beckham v. Drake* (1849) 2 H.L.C. 579, 607–608; *cf. Harries v. Edmunds* (1845) 1 Car. & Kir. 686; *British Ticket & Stamp Automatic Delivery Co. v. Haynes* [1921] 1 K.B. 377; *Houndsditch Warehouse Co. v. Waltex Ltd* [1944] K.B. 579. An employee dismissed without the minimum statutory notice must nevertheless seek alternative employment: *Westwood v. Secretary of State for Employment, supra.*

27–088   **"Reasonable steps".** The claimant is not "under any obligation to do any-thing other than in the ordinary course of business"[68]; the standard is not a high one, since the defendant is a wrongdoer.

> "The law is satisfied if the party placed in a difficult situation by reason of the breach of a duty owed to him has acted reasonably in the adoption of remedial measures, and he will not be held disentitled to recover the cost of such measures merely because the party in breach can suggest that other measures less burdensome to him might have been taken."[69]

Questions about the reasonableness of the claimant's steps to mitigate his loss have arisen in cases (discussed elsewhere[70]) where the defendant has failed to complete the contractual work (*e.g.* building or repair work) and the claimant claims damages for the cost of substitute performance by a third party. But the claimant need not take risks with his money[71] in attempting to mitigate, nor need he take a step which might endanger his own commercial reputation, *e.g.* by enforcing sub-contracts.[72] The claimant is under no duty, even under an indem-nity from the defendant, to embark on a complicated and difficult piece of litigation against a third party,[73] nor is the claimant required to sacrifice any of his property or rights in order to mitigate the loss.[74] It has been suggested[75] that the claimant's duty to mitigate does not require him to guard against the effects of inflation *per se, i.e.* it does not apply to the risk of pure price increases which may lead to "inflationary increases in damages" after the date of the breach of contract.[76]

27–089   **The time for mitigating action.** The time when the claimant should have mitigated may depend on when he discovered or ought to have discovered that

---

[68] *Dunkirk Colliery Co. v. Lever* (1878) 9 Ch.D. 20, 25 (approved by Lord Haldane in *British Westinghouse Electric Co. Ltd v. Underground Electric Rys.* [1912] A.C. 673, 689).

[69] *Banco de Portugal v. Waterlow* [1932] A.C. 452, 506. See also *Moore v. DER Ltd* [1971] 1 W.L.R. 1476, 1479.

[70] See *ante*, § 27–014 and the cases cited in n. 70 to that paragraph.

[71] *Jewelowski v. Propp* [1944] K.B. 510; *Lesters Leather & Skin Co. v. Home and Overseas Brokers* (1948) 64 T.L.R. 569. The duty of the buyer to purchase substitute goods if the seller defaults (*post*, § 27–090, and Vol. II, § 43–387) will, of course, involve the buyer in expenditure, but the buyer will normally have available the money with which he intended to pay for the seller's goods. However, in *Robbins of Putney Ltd v. Meek* [1971] R.T.R. 345, when deciding whether the plaintiffs acted reasonably, the court took account of their lack of liquid capital; and in *Bacon v. Cooper (Metals) Ltd* [1982] 1 All E.R. 397, it was held that the plaintiff acted reasonably in incurring a high rate of interest when obtaining a replacement part of a machine on hire-purchase. See *post*, § 27–138.

[72] *Finlay & Co. v. N. V. Kwik Hoo Tong H.M.* [1929] 1 K.B. 400; *Banco de Portugal v. Waterlow* [1932] A.C. 452 (which also, at 471, supports the proposition that the plaintiff need not act so as to injure innocent persons); *Anglo-African Shipping Co. of New York Inc. v. J. Mortner Ltd* [1962] 1 Lloyd's Rep. 81, 94 (on appeal, *ibid.* at 610); *London and South of England Building Society v. Stone* [1983] 1 W.L.R. 1242.

[73] *Pilkington v. Wood* [1953] Ch. 770.

[74] *Elliott Steam Tug Co. v. Shipping Controller* [1922] 1 K.B. 127, 140–141. *cf. Weir (Andrew) & Co. v. Dobell & Co.* [1916] 1 K.B. 722.

[75] Libling and Feldman (1979) 95 L.Q.R. 270, 282. See also *Radford v. De Froberville* [1977] 1 W.L.R. 1262, 1287; and Wallace (1980) 96 L.Q.R. 101, 341.

[76] See *ante*, § 27–052 on the relevant date for the assessment of damages.

the defendant had broken his contractual obligation.[77] So, as soon as the claimant discovers that an item supplied to him by the defendant is unsafe because it is defective (in breach of the contract) he cannot continue to use it at the defendant's risk: he must either make it safe or replace it, since he cannot recover damages from the defendant for any loss which arose after he discovered[78] the defect but which he could reasonably have avoided by taking remedial steps.[79] After he knows (or ought to have known) of the breach, the claimant still has a reasonable time, depending on all the circumstances, before he must decide how to mitigate.[80] In the case of damages for the cost of repairs or reinstatement, it may be reasonable for the claimant to delay getting the repairs or remedial work done so long as there is a reasonable chance that the defendant will repair or cure the defect.[81]

Sale of goods. In contracts for the sale of goods, the normal rule for the measure of damages assumes that the innocent party should act immediately upon the breach, and buy or sell in the market, if there were an available market.[82] Where the claimant does not accept the defendant's anticipatory breach of contract,[83] there is no duty on the claimant to mitigate his loss before the actual breach on the due date for performance.[84]   27–090

Another instance of mitigation arises where the defendant in breach of contract refuses to accept goods which he has agreed to buy,[85] but the claimant is able to sell the goods at the same price to a third person: if the state of the market is such that demand exceeds supply, so that the claimant could always find a purchaser for every article he could get from the manufacturer, he is entitled only to nominal damages from the defendant (and not his loss of profit on the repudiated   27–091

---

[77] *East Ham Corporation v. Bernard Sunley & Sons Ltd* [1966] A.C. 406; *Van den Hurck v. R. Martens & Co. Ltd* [1920] 1 K.B. 850 (see Vol. II, § 43–411). One judge has held that the mitigation rules do not apply until the plaintiff knows of the breach: *Youell v. Bland Welch & Co. Ltd (The "Superhulls Cover"* case) [1990] 2 Lloyd's Rep. 431, 461–462; but another judge has applied the rules when the plaintiff should have known of the breach: *Toepfer v. Warinco* [1978] 2 Lloyd's Rep. 569, 578. *cf.* Treitel, *op. cit.* (9th ed.) p. 881.

[78] It has been argued that the same result should follow as soon as the plaintiff *ought* to have discovered the defect: *Benjamin on Sale of Goods* (5th ed.), paras. 67–056—17–057.

[79] *Lambert v. Lewis* [1982] A.C. 225 (defective trailer coupling: see Vol. II, § 43–428).

[80] *C. Sharpe & Co. Ltd v. Nosawa* [1917] 2 K.B. 814, 821; *Asamera Oil Corpn Ltd v. Sea Oil & General Corpn* (1978) 89 D.L.R. (3d) 1 (Sup.Ct. of Canada). If there is a rising market, the defendant may know that the plaintiff lacks the financial ability to buy a substitute, which may justify him in not attempting to do so: *Wroth v. Tyler* [1974] Ch. 30. See also *ante*, §§ 27–052, 27–076; Vol. II, §§ 43–389, 43–397.

[81] *Radford v. De Froberville* [1977] 1 W.L.R. 1262.

[82] See ss.50(3) and 51(3) of the Sale of Goods Act 1979; *Dunkirk Colliery Co. v. Lever* (1878) 9 Ch.D. 20, 25. A similar rule applies in the case of contracts for the hire of goods (*e.g.* charterparties): where there is an available market in which to hire a substitute, the hirer's damages for breach by the owner in terminating the hire will normally be the difference between the contract rate and the market rate of hire for the remaining period of the contract: *Koch Marine Inc. v. D'Amica Societa di Navigazione A.R.L. (The "Elena D'Amico")* [1980] 1 Lloyd's Rep. 75, 87–90. *cf.* the position of the owner who retakes the goods after the hirer has broken his hire-purchase agreement: see Vol. II, §§ 38–307—38–309.

[83] See *ante*, § 25–023.

[84] *Brown v. Muller* (1872) L.R. 7 Ex. 319; *Roper v. Johnson* (1873) L.R. 8 C.P. 167; *Melachrino v. Nickoll & Knight* [1920] 1 K.B. 693. See *post*, § 27–099; Vol. II, §§ 43–379, 43–392. *cf. White and Carter (Councils) Ltd v. McGregor* [1962] A.C. 413 (*post*, § 27–100).

[85] If the property in the goods has passed to the buyer, the seller is entitled to the price, and no question of mitigation arises. See Vol. II, §§ 43–357 *et seq.*

sale) since he sold the same number of articles and made the same number of fixed profits as he would have done if the defendant had duly performed his contract.[86] If an exact substitute is not available to the buyer in the market, it is not clear whether he should be required to accept a "near equivalent,"[87] but if he does reasonably choose to do so, he can recover damages on the basis of the cost of the nearest available equivalent in quality and price.[88]

27–092   **Offer by defendant.** The opportunity to mitigate the loss may arise through an offer made by the party who committed the breach of contract: if the claimant unreasonably[89] refuses to accept the offer he is in breach of his duty to mitigate his loss.[90] Where a seller in breach of his contract declined to deliver goods on the agreed credit terms but offered to do so on terms of "cash on delivery" the refusal of the buyer to accept that offer, being in the circumstances unreasonable, was taken into account in reduction of the damages.[91] Similarly, where the plaintiff bought a ship from the defendant, who could not deliver her on the agreed date, it was held that it would have been reasonable for the plaintiff to mitigate his loss by accepting her late delivery at the original price.[92] (The plaintiff was, of course, entitled to claim damages for any residual loss arising from the delay.) Where the vendor offered to repurchase a house which he sold with vacant possession but which was in fact occupied by a protected tenant, it was held that the buyer was not obliged by the doctrine of mitigation to accept the offer: his choice to retain the house and to sue for damages for the breach of contract was not to be subjected to the test of reasonableness.[93]

27–093   **Loss which is avoided cannot be recovered.** The second rule of mitigation concerns potential loss which is not actually suffered. If, by taking steps which

---

[86] *Charter v. Sullivan* [1957] 2 Q.B. 117 (see s.50(3) of the Sale of Goods Act 1979). *cf.* the cases cited in Vol. II, §§ 43–367—43–382.

[87] In cases of wrongful dismissal, any alternative employment can obviously be no more than a "near equivalent": see Vol. II, § 39–179.

[88] *Hinde v. Liddell* (1875) L.R. 10 Q.B. 265; *Erie County National Gas and Fuel Co. Ltd v. Carroll* [1911] A.C. 105, 117. The nearest equivalent may be of superior quality and so higher in price: *Diamond Cutting Works v. Treifus* [1956] 1 Lloyd's Rep. 216. The claimant may also recover any extra cost arising from his adapting the nearest substitute to suit his requirements, to the extent that goods of the contractual description would suit these requirements: *Blackburn Bobbin Co. Ltd v. T. W. Allen & Sons Ltd* [1918] 1 K.B. 540, 554 (appeal decided on another ground: [1918] 2 K.B. 467). Similarly, where a seller manufactured goods to the buyer's requirements, but he failed to accept them, the seller may recover as part of his damages the expense incurred in adapting the goods to suit another buyer: *Re Vic Mill Ltd* [1913] 1 Ch. 465, 473, 474.

[89] It is not reasonable for the offer to be on terms that the claimant should relinquish his claim against the defendant for damages: *Shindler v. Northern Raincoat Co. Ltd* [1960] 1 W.L.R. 1038.

[90] *Payzu v. Saunders* [1919] 2 K.B. 581; *Houndsditch Warehouse Co. v. Waltex* [1944] K.B. 579; *Brace v. Calder* [1895] 2 Q.B. 253 (contract of service). *cf. Edwards v. Society of Graphical and Allied Trades* [1971] Ch. 354; *A.B.D. (Metals & Waste) Ltd v. Anglo Chemical & Ore Co. Ltd* [1955] 2 Lloyd's Rep. 456.

[91] *Payzu v. Saunders, supra* (substitute goods could be obtained only at a higher price). But a buyer who rejects goods on the ground of defective quality is not required to accept them if offered by the seller in mitigation since this would undermine the buyer's right to reject: *Heaven & Kesterton Ltd v. Etablissements François Albiac & Cie* [1956] 2 Lloyd's Rep. 316.

[92] *The Solholt* [1983] 1 Lloyd's Rep. 605. (The Court of Appeal held that on the facts it would have been reasonable for the *buyer* to have taken the initiative in making the offer.)

[93] *Strutt v. Whitnell* [1975] 1 W.L.R. 870; *cf. The Solholt, supra. cf.* also *Hussey v. Eels* [1990] 2 Q.B. 227. On the choice between remedies, see *post*, § 27–099.

could not reasonably have been required of him, the claimant has in fact avoided the potential loss resulting from the defendant's breach of contract, he cannot recover damages in respect of such potential loss.[94] "When in the course of his business [the claimant] has taken action arising out of the transaction, which action has diminished his loss, the effect in actual diminution of the loss he has suffered may be taken into account even though there was no duty on him to act."[95] The claimant is entitled to damages only for his actual loss, which is assessed by taking account of all the items in his notional "profit and loss" calculation for the whole transaction.[96] The court is required to decide whether the claimant's actions arose *out of* his attempts to mitigate the potential loss resulting from the breach, or whether his actions were "independent" of his mitigating steps, so that any benefit to him should not be used to reduce the damages payable by the defendant.[97] So where a seller delivers defective goods, and the buyer acquires a substitute through which he gains a consequential benefit, *e.g.* a greater profit, this benefit must be set off against the cost of the substitute when the buyer sues the seller to recover such cost,[98] since the benefit arises directly from the act of mitigation.

Benefits independent of mitigation. Damages will not be reduced where the   **27–094**
benefit received by the claimant is independent of any act of mitigation: thus, where a breach of contract caused the destruction of a building, and the owners acted reasonably both in deciding to rebuild and in choosing the plan for the new building, it was held that the defendants were not entitled to a reduction in damages (which consisted in the actual cost of rebuilding) on account of the "betterment" enjoyed by the claimants in having a new building in place of the old one—the claimants had no effective choice: but a reduction would be made for any extra accommodation or improvement going beyond replacement.[99] Similarly, where, as a result of breach of contract, a partly-used working part of a machine had to be replaced with a new part which would last longer, the plaintiff was nevertheless entitled to the full cost of the replacement.[1] Again, where a seller of goods chooses not to resell upon the date of the buyer's breach

---

[94] *British Westinghouse Electric Co. Ltd v. Underground Electric Rys.* [1912] A.C. 673, 689, 690.

[95] *ibid.* at 689. See also *R. Pagnan & Fratelli v. Corbisa Industrial Agropacuaria Limitada* [1970] 1 W.L.R. 1306 (see Vol. II, § 43–395); and *cf. The World Beauty* [1969] P. 12 (affd. in part [1970] P. 144).

[96] The amount of "avoided loss" to be deducted from his damages will be his *net* gain after deducting his reasonable expenses in earning the gross gain: *Westwood v. Secretary of State for Employment* [1985] A.C. 20, 44.

[97] *Hussey v. Eels* [1990] 2 Q.B. 227, CA, ((pet. dis.) [1990] 1 W.L.R. 414) (induced by defendant's misrepresentation, plaintiff bought and lived in a defective house for over two years, before reselling it at a profit to a developer: held, the resale profit arose from an independent transaction, and should not be taken into account in assessing the damages payable by defendants).

[98] *British Westinghouse* case, *ante* (see Vol. II, § 43–412.) See also *Erie County Natural Gas Co. v. Carroll* [1911] A.C. 105; *Hill v. Showell* (1918) 87 L.J.K.B. 1106; *Nadreph Ltd v. Willmett & Co.* [1978] 1 W.L.R. 1537; *Levison v. Farin* [1978] 2 All E.R. 1149 (the breach of contract resulted in a trading loss, which enabled the innocent party to claim a reduction in tax on subsequent profits: the tax benefit was deducted from the damages). *cf. Bellingham v. Dhillon* [1973] Q.B. 304.

[99] *Harbutt's "Plasticine" Ltd v. Wayne Tank and Pump Co. Ltd* [1970] 1 Q.B. 447. (This case has been overruled by the House of Lords on another point: *Photo Production Ltd v. Securicor Transport Ltd* [1980] A.C. 827 (*ante*, § 14–022).)

[1] *Bacon v. Cooper (Metals) Ltd* [1982] 1 All E.R. 397. (See also *post*, § 27–138.)

(which is the normal date when his duty to mitigate must be tested[2]) but retains the goods for some time and resells at a gain when the market price later rises, the benefit to the claimant does not arise from any act of mitigation[3] and is irrelevant in assessing damages.[4] The seller could not have made the buyer liable for additional loss had the market price fallen after the date of the breach,[5] so he is entitled to the gain when the market price happens to rise after that date. The decision to retain the goods was an independent speculation by the seller.

27–095   Advantages gained by the claimant from wholly independent transactions, especially those entered into before the defendant's breach of contract, as for example, a sum due under an insurance policy,[6] cannot be relied on in mitigation of loss arising from the defendant's breach.[7] So where the claimant, by another contract with a third party entered into before the defendant's breach of his contract with the claimant, has made an arrangement which should or does in fact prevent loss to the claimant from the defendant's breach, the defendant cannot rely on that other contract to reduce his damages[8]; it is *res inter alios acta*, or an extraneous circumstance. Even where a benefit to the claimant arises in the course of his mitigating action, there may not be a sufficient causal connection between the defendant's breach and that benefit to justify taking it into account in assessing the claimant's damages.[9]

27–096   **Release of resources for other uses.**[10] When the claimant terminates his contract with the defendant on the ground of the latter's breach of contract, the resources which the claimant would otherwise have devoted to his performance (whether capital, skill, labour, etc.) are always released for redeployment else-where. Even where there is no substitute or "near equivalent" use to which the

---

[2] s.50(3) of the Sale of Goods Act 1979. See Vol. II, §§ 43–366 *et seq.*

[3] *Jebsen v. East and West India Dock Co.* (1875) L.R. 10 C.P. 300.

[4] *Campbell Mostyn v. Barnett* [1954] 1 Lloyd's Rep. 65 (distinguished in *R. Pagnan & Fratelli v. Corbisa Industrial Agropacuaria Limitada, ante,* where the plaintiff buyer finally accepted the *same* goods at a reduced price) (see Vol. II, § 43–395). See also *Jones v. Just* (1868) L.R. 3 Q.B. 197 (breach by seller but loss avoided by buyer when market price later rose); *Jamal v. Moolla Dawood* [1916] 1 A.C. 175; and *Hussey v. Eels, ante,* § 27–093, n. 97; *Gardner v. Marsh & Parsons* [1997] 1 W.L.R. 489 (see § 27–077, n. 22).

[5] *Koch Marine Inc. v. D'Amico Società di Navigazione A.R.L. (The "Elena D'Amico")* [1980] 1 Lloyd's Rep. 75, 87–90.

[6] *Bradburn v. G.W. Ry.* (1874) L.R. 10 Ex. 1. Similarly, an employee's damages for wrongful dismissal should not be reduced by reference to a pension payable before his normal retirement age to the employee from his employer's pension scheme: *Hopkins v. Norcross plc* [1993] 1 All E. R. 565. (The pension entitlement was "earned" and thus "paid for" by the employee; and the pension scheme should be treated as a form of insurance.) See also Vol. II, § 39–179.

[7] *Lavarack v. Woods of Colchester Ltd* [1967] 1 Q.B. 278. *cf. Brown v. K.M.R. Services Ltd* [1995] 4 All E.R. 598, 640–641.

[8] *Haviland v. Long* [1952] 2 Q.B. 80, especially at 84. See also *Joyner v. Weeks* [1891] 2 Q.B. 31; *Slater v. Hoyle and Smith* [1920] 2 K.B. 11 (buyer of defective goods able to avoid loss on sub-sale; but see *Bence Graphics International Ltd v. Fassoun U.K. Ltd* [1998] Q.B. 87 (discussed *post,* §§ 43–411, 43–413); the contrary decision of the Privy Council in *Wertheim v. Chicoutimi Pulp Co.* [1911] A.C. 301, may be wrong: see Vol. II, § 43–405, n. 63).

[9] *Famosa Shipping Co. Ltd v. Armada Bulk Carriers Ltd (The "Fanis")* [1994] 1 Lloyd's Rep. 633.

[10] The arguments in this paragraph are developed more fully in Harris, *Remedies in Contract and Tort* (1988), pp. 87–93.

claimant can be expected to devote his released resources (under the "avoidable loss" rule) he will always in practice devote them to some other use, which raises the application of the "avoided loss" rule. So an employee who was wrongfully dismissed will have his damages reduced *either* (under the "avoidable loss" rule) by the hypothetical earnings he should reasonably have earned for the relevant period in some similar employment *or* (whether or not the "avoidable loss" rule applied) by his *actual* earnings under another contract which he was able to undertake *only* as the result of the defendant's breach of contract.[11] If the claimant could not have undertaken the second contract but for the defendant's breach, and he deployed substantially the same skills, time and effort as he would have done in working for the defendant,[12] his earnings can legitimately be treated as substitute earnings even when the employment was different. If he is required to employ different skills in his new work, or to put in a greater effort, it is submitted that the courts should make allowance for this greater or different input from the claimant by deducting only a proportion of his substitute earnings.[13]

Except in the extremely rare situation where a resource cannot be redeployed   **27–097**
to any other use at all, the release of resources always confers some benefit on the claimant, because he can find some use for them. But the courts have seldom taken this benefit into account where the alternative use chosen by the claimant was substantially different from his promised performance under the original contract. Where the alternative use has a similar goal (*e.g.* the earning of profits or wages), the courts have been more likely to take it into account in assessing damages. But, since there is nearly always some value to the claimant arising from the release of his resources, it is submitted that some assessment of that value should be made no matter where the redeployment is made.[14] However, it is submitted that the assessment should not deprive someone in the claimant's position of all incentive to redeploy: some incentive would remain if the court did not deduct the whole of the net benefit but left him to enjoy some of it as a reward for his initiative in seeking the alternative use.[15]

Recovery of loss or expense suffered while attempting to mitigate. The   **27–098**
third rule of mitigation is that the claimant may recover damages for loss or

---

[11] *Jackson v. Hayes Candy and Co. Ltd* [1938] 4 All E.R. 587; *Collier v. Sunday Referee Publishing Co.* [1940] 2 K.B. 647, 653; *Lavarack v. Woods of Colchester Ltd* [1967] 1 Q.B. 278.

[12] The causal test should be (1) that the claimant used substantially the same resources as he would have done in the contractual activity, and (2) that the opportunity for the claimant to use them in the new activity would not have arisen *but for* the defendant's breach of contract, that is, it was the breach alone which released them for the alternative use. For instance, in *Hill v. Showell* (1918) 87 L.J.K.B. 1106, 1108, the breach enabled the plaintiff to execute other profitable orders: it led to "the situation in which his machinery was rendered *free by reason of the breach* . . . " (italics supplied).

[13] Some support for this is found in *Lavarack v. Woods of Colchester Ltd, supra.*

[14] For the causal test, see n. 12 *supra.*

[15] In the *Lavarack* case, *supra* (wrongful dismissal), the court took into account only *part* of the profit made by the plaintiff through his personal exertions in enhancing the value of his shares in the company where he took employment after his wrongful dismissal by the defendant. However, in *British Westinghouse Electric Co. v. Underground Electric Railway Co.* [1912] A.C. 673 (see Vol. II, § 43–412) the House of Lords held that the *whole* of the benefit of the mitigating action of the plaintiff could be used to reduce the damages payable by the defendant, even though the plaintiff would not have been obliged under the "avoidable loss" rule to take that action: see Harris *op. cit.* pp. 91–93.

expense incurred by him in reasonably[16] attempting to mitigate his loss following the defendant's breach, even when the mitigating steps were unsuccessful or in fact led to greater loss.[17] As most attempts are successful, it is in the interests of the defendant (as well as of the wider society) that the claimant, who is usually in the better position to minimise his loss, should be encouraged to try to do so: he may recover the cost of his reasonable attempt to "extricate" himself from the disadvantageous position in which he was placed by the breach.[18]

27–099   **Innocent party's choice between remedies.** The rules of mitigation do not apply to the innocent party's choice between different remedies open to him following the other party's breach of contract: he is not bound to act "reasonably" in exercising his choice.[19] Thus, where the buyer commits an anticipatory breach by repudiating his obligation to take delivery of the goods before the date fixed for delivery, the seller has an option: he may either accept the repudiation and so treat it forthwith as a breach, or he may continue to treat the contract as binding and thus not accept the repudiation as a breach.[20] In exercising this choice between these alternative courses of action, the seller is not obliged to act "reasonably."[21] If the seller accepts the buyer's anticipatory repudiation, he is thereupon obliged to take reasonable steps to mitigate his loss[22]; but if the seller does not accept the anticipatory repudiation he does not have any duty to mitigate unless and until the buyer actually commits a breach of contract.[23] After the innocent party has terminated the contract, the rules on mitigation will apply to any claim for damages he makes; it may then be reasonable for him to act in a way which has the effect of nullifying the consequences of that decision, *e.g.* by entering into a new contract with the contract-breaker.[24]

27–100   **Recovery of sum due on performance.** By implication, the House of Lords has decided that the rules on mitigation do not apply to a claim for a debt due

---

[16] For an illustration of unreasonable expenses incurred by the plaintiff, see *Compania Financiera "Soleada" SA v. Hamoor Tanker Corporation Inc. (The Borag)* [1981] 1 W.L.R. 274 (see *post*, § 27–138). *cf.* the tort case of *Dodd Properties Ltd v. Canterbury City Council* [1980] 1 W.L.R. 433 (*ante*, § 27–016, n. 81).

[17] *Wilson v. United Counties Bank* [1920] A.C. 102, 125; *Lloyds and Scottish Finance Ltd v. Modern Cars and Caravans (Kingston) Ltd* [1966] 1 Q.B. 764, 782–783; *The World Beauty* [1970] P. 144, 156; *British Racing Drivers' Club Ltd v. Hextall Erskine & Co.* [1996] 3 All E.R. 667 (legal costs incurred by the plaintiff). See also *Erie County Natural Gas and Fuel Co. Ltd v. Carroll* [1911] A.C. 105, 119. *cf. Le Blanche v. L.N.W. Ry.* (1876) 1 C.P.D. 286; *Quinn v. Burch Bros. (Builders) Ltd* [1966] 2 Q.B. 370 (*ante*, § 27–029); *Westwood v. Secretary of State for Employment* [1985] A.C. 20, 44. *cf.* also the cases on reinstatement damages, *ante*, § 27–014.

[18] *County Personnel (Employment Agency) Ltd v. Alan R. Pulver & Co.* [1987] 1 W.L.R. 916, 926. This "extrication" principle was accepted by the House of Lords in *South Australia Asset Management Corp. v. York Montague Ltd* [1997] A.C. 191, 218–219 (see *ante*, § 27–065).

[19] *Strutt v. Whitnell* [1975] 1 W.L.R. 870 (see *ante*, § 27–092); *The Solholt* [1983] 1 Lloyd's Rep. 605, 608–609, CA; *cf. Lombard North Central plc v. Butterworth* [1987] Q.B. 527 (*post*, § 27–116).

[20] See *ante*, §§ 25–020 *et seq.*; and Vol. II, § 43–379. *cf.* Vol. II, § 43–392—43–393.

[21] *Tredegar Iron and Coal Co. (Ltd) v. Hawthorn Bros & Co.* (1902) 18 T.L.R. 716, 716–717; *White and Carter (Councils) Ltd v. McGregor* [1962] A.C. 413 (*ante*, § 25–009; *post*, § 27–100); *Fercometal S.A.R.L. v. Mediterranean Shipping Co. SA* [1989] A.C. 788.

[22] See Vol. II, § 43–379. *cf.* the situation when it is the seller's anticipatory repudiation: Vol. II, § 43–392.

[23] *ibid.*

[24] *The Solholt, supra,* at 609. (See *ante*, § 27–092.)

under a contract in return for the claimant's performance of his obligation[25]; such a claim is distinct from one for damages for breach of contract.[26] In *White and Carter (Councils) Ltd v. McGregor*[27] the plaintiff refused to accept the defendant's anticipatory repudiation of the contract[28] and was able thereafter to complete the performance of his side of the contract without the co-operation of the defendant[29]; the majority of their Lordships held that the plaintiff could recover the full amount due for his performance: he was under no obligation to terminate the contract on the ground of the defendant's anticipatory breach and sue for damages. The two of their Lordships in the minority thought the plaintiff should have mitigated his loss by discontinuing his performance of the contract, but the majority held (by implication) that in the special circumstances of the case[30] there was no such duty on the plaintiff to act reasonably.

"Legitimate interest" in performing. The difficulty of this situation is that   **27–101** the policy of the mitigation rules (*viz.* to avoid the waste of resources and effort) seems to be contravened if the innocent party, following a repudiation, can elect (despite his knowledge that the expense of performance is now useless to the other party) to *continue* his performance of the contract so as to recover an agreed sum of money greater than the damages which the law would allow if the repudiation were treated at the time as a breach of contract.[31] Lord Reid, one of the majority in the *White and Carter* case, introduced a qualification, to the effect that the plaintiff could not insist on completing performance so as to be able to claim the agreed price as a debt, if he had "no legitimate interest, financial or otherwise, in performing the contract rather than claiming damages. . . . "[32] The Court of Appeal[33] has accepted this qualification, and a judge at first instance[34] has applied it to a shipping dispute, where for seven months the plaintiff shipowner kept a ship at anchor with a full crew ready to sail, despite the fact that the defendant treated the charterparty as ended.

---

[25] *White and Carter (Councils) Ltd v. McGregor* [1962] A.C. 413 (a full statement of facts will be found *ante*, § 25–009); followed in *Anglo-African Shipping Co. of New York Inc. v. J. Mortner Ltd* [1962] 1 Lloyd's Rep. 81, 610; but distinguished in *Attica Sea Carriers Corporation v. Ferrostaal Poseidon Bulk Reederei GmbH (The Puerto Buitrago)* [1976] 1 Lloyd's Rep. 250, 254–256 and in *Clea Shipping Corporation v. Bulk Oil International Ltd (The Alaskan Trader)* [1984] 1 All E.R. 129.

[26] See *ante*, § 27–008.

[27] *Supra.*

[28] On anticipatory breach, see *ante*, §§ 25–020 *et seq.*

[29] *Hounslow London Borough Council v. Twickenham Gardens Developments Ltd* [1971] Ch. 233, 253–254 (plaintiff cannot insist on being given access to the defendant's land to enable him to complete work there). A wrongfully dismissed employee cannot sue for his wages as such, but is relegated to a claim for damages.

[30] The circumstances were unusual, in that there was nothing which the defendant had to do or accept in order to enable the plaintiff to complete his performance. As to whether the principle will extend to the sale of goods, see Lord Keith (dissenting) [1962] A.C. 413, 437; and *Benjamin's Sale of Goods* (5th ed., 1997), §§ 16–019, 16–053.

[31] See [1962] Camb.L.J. 12, 213; (1962) 78 L.Q.R. 263; (1962) 25 M.L.R. 364. *cf.* the American Law Institute's *Restatement of the Law of Contracts*, s.338, especially Comment (c). (See (1962) 78 L.Q.R. 263, 267.)

[32] [1962] A.C. 413, 431. This standard could be interpreted so as to bring it close to the reasonableness standard in the mitigation rules.

[33] *Attica Sea Carriers Corporation v. Ferrostaal, etc., GmbH (The Puerto Buitrago)* [1976] 1 Lloyd's Rep. 250, 254–256.

[34] *Clea Shipping Corporation v. Bulk Oil International Ltd (The Alaskan Trader)* [1984] 1 All E.R. 129.

6. PENALTY OR LIQUIDATED DAMAGES[35]

27-102 **Damages fixed by the parties.** Where the parties to a contract agree that, in the event of a breach, the contract-breaker shall pay to the other a specified sum of money, the sum fixed may be classified by the courts either as a penalty (which is irrecoverable) or as liquidated damages (which are recoverable).[36] The clause is enforceable if it does not exceed a genuine attempt to estimate in advance the loss which the claimant would be likely to suffer from a breach of the obligation in question[37]: it is enforceable irrespective of the loss actually suffered. The purpose[38] of the parties in fixing a sum is to facilitate recovery of damages without the difficulty and expense of proving actual damage[39]; or to avoid the risk of under-compensation, where the rules on remoteness of damage might not cover consequential, indirect or idiosyncratic loss[40]; or to give the promisee an assurance that he may safely rely on the fulfilment of the promise.[41] The Privy Council[42] has recently cited with approval[43] the view of Dickson J. in the Supreme Court of Canada that

" . . . the power to strike down a penalty clause is a blatant interference with freedom of contract and is designed for the sole purpose of providing relief against oppression for the party having to pay the stipulated sum. It has no place where there is no oppression."[44]

Therefore, where there is no suggestion of oppression, "the court should not be astute to decry a 'penalty clause' ."[45] Courts of equity held that if the sum fixed was unenforceable as a penalty to ensure that the promise was not broken, the promisee should nevertheless receive by way of damages the sum which would

---

[35] The Law Commission, in its Working Paper No. 61 (1975), has made proposals for reform of the law on penalty clauses and on forfeiture of moneys paid. For a critique of the law, see Kaplan (1977) 50 S.Calif.L.Rev. 1055. For an empirical study of the use of liquidated damages in the travel industry, see Milner (1979) 42 M.L.R. 508. Some businessmen are reluctant to enforce agreed damages clauses for delay: Beale and Dugdale (1975) 2 Brit.J. Law and Soc. 45, 55.

[36] A valid agreed damages clause is probably not subject to the Unfair Contract Terms Act 1977 (*ante*, §§ 14–057 *et seq.*): see Treitel *op. cit.* (9th ed.), pp. 228, 902. *cf.* however, the Unfair Terms in Consumer Contracts Regulations 1994 (*ante*, §§ 15–001 *et seq.*), *post*, § 27–126).

[37] *cf.* a performance bond, which is *not* an estimate of the damages which might be caused by a breach of contract: *Cargill International SA v. Bangladesh Sugar & Food Industries Corp.* [1996] 4 All E.R. 563; *Comdel Commodities Ltd v. Siporex Trade SA* [1997] 1 Lloyd's Rep. 424, CA.

[38] For an economic analysis of agreed damages clauses, see Goetz and Scott (1977) 77 Col.L.R. 554; Rea (1984) 13 J.Leg.Stud. 147. See also Harris *op. cit.*, Chap. 8.

[39] *Clydebank Engineering and Shipbuilding Co. Ltd v. Don Jose Ramos Yzquierdo y Castaneda* [1905] A.C. 6, 11.

[40] *Robophone Facilities Ltd v. Blank* [1966] 1 W.L.R. 1428, 1447–8. The agreed sum may take account of loss likely to be suffered which may not fall within the normal remoteness test: *Robert Stewart & Sons Ltd v. Carapanayoti & Co. Ltd* [1962] 1 W.L.R. 34, 39; *Philips Hong Kong Ltd v. Att.-Gen. of Hong Kong* (1993) 61 Build. L.R. 49, 60–61 (the agreed sum may be justified by knowledge of "special circumstances").

[41] The clause may also operate as a limitation on liability: *post*, § 27–117. The present legal test, which is restricted to expected *loss*, does not permit the promisee to justify the sum fixed as a reasonable incentive to the promisor to perform his promise, nor as a disincentive to the promisor not to commit a *deliberate* breach: Harris *op. cit.* pp. 109–110.

[42] *Philips Hong Kong Ltd v. Att.-Gen. of Hong Kong, supra*, at 58.

[43] The view was also cited with approval in the High Court of Australia: *Esanda Finance Corporation Ltd v. Plessing* (1989) 166 C.L.R. 131, 140.

[44] *Elsey v. J.G. Collins Insurance Agencies Ltd* (1978) 83 D.L.R. (3d.) 1, 15.

[45] *Robophone Facilities Ltd v. Blank* [1966] 1 W.L.R. 1428, 1447.

compensate him for his actual loss.[46] The Court of Appeal has held that the strict legal position is that the innocent party can sue on the penal clause, but "it will not be enforced . . . beyond the sum which represents [his] actual loss"[47]; and that the law on penalties also applies to a clause which, upon breach, obliges the contract-breaker to transfer some property to the innocent party.[48] The Privy Council has recently treated the forfeiture of money held by the innocent party (for the breaching party) as subject to rules akin to those on penalties,[49] but no English case has yet done so.[50]

Statement of penalty rules. The question whether a sum stipulated for in a **27–103** contract is a penalty or liquidated damages is a question of law.[51] Lord Dunedin in delivering his opinion in *Dunlop Pneumatic Tyre Co. Ltd v. New Garage and Motor Co. Ltd*[52] summed up the law in the following propositions:

"(1) Though the parties to a contract who use the words 'penalty' or 'liquidated damages' may prima facie be supposed to mean what they say, yet the expression used is not conclusive. The court must find out whether the payment stipulated is in truth a penalty or liquidated damages. . . . [53]

(2) The essence of a penalty is a payment of money stipulated as *in terrorem* of the offending party; the essence of liquidated damages is a genuine pre-estimate of damage.[54]

(3) The question whether a sum stipulated is a penalty or liquidated damages is a question of construction to be decided upon the terms and inherent circumstances of

---

[46] Story, *Equitable Jurisprudence*, § 1316. The assessment of damages is according to common law; there is no equitable rule on damages where a clause has been held to be penal: *AMEV-UDC Finance Ltd v. Austin* (1986) 60 A.L.J.R. 741.

[47] *Jobson v. Johnson* [1989] 1 W.L.R. 1026, 1040 (see also at 1038, 1039–1042, 1049). (*cf.*, however, the dictum in *Scandinavian Trading Tanker Co. A.B. v. Flota Petrolera Ecuatoriana (The Scaptrade)* [1983] 2 A.C. 694, 702 ("The classic form of relief against such a penalty clause has been to refuse to give effect to it, but to award the common law measure of damages for the breach of the primary obligation instead.")

[48] *Jobson v. Johnson, supra*, at 1034–1036, 1042, 1049. Such a clause will be penal if the value of the property at the time of transfer exceeds the actual loss of the innocent party: *ibid.* at 1037, 1042, 1047–1048. (*Sed quaere*: if the *Dunlop* case, *infra*, is followed, the test should be whether, at the time of contracting, the parties made a genuine pre-estimate both of the expected value of the property to be transferred and of the loss expected to be caused by breach, and then expected that the two would approximately match.) On the relief granted in *Jobson v. Johnson*, see *post*, § 27–123.

[49] *Workers Trust & Merchant Bank Ltd v. Dojap Investments Ltd* [1993] A.C. 573, 578 (a case on a deposit: see *post*, § 27–123).

[50] See *post*, § 27–123.

[51] *Sainter v. Ferguson* (1849) 7 C.B. 716, 727.

[52] [1915] A.C. 79, 86–88.

[53] "But no case . . . decides that the term used by the parties themselves is to be altogether disregarded, and I should say that, where the parties themselves call the sum made payable a 'penalty,' the onus lies on those who seek to show that it is to be payable as liquidated damages": *Willson v. Love* [1896] 1 Q.B. 626, 630. See *Alder v. Moore* [1961] 2 Q.B. 57, 65; *Robert Stewart & Sons Ltd v. Carapanayoti & Co. Ltd, supra. cf.* the *Workers Trust* case, *supra*, at 579.

[54] *Clydebank Engineering and Shipbuilding Co. Ltd v. Don Jose Ramos Yzquierdo y Castaneda, supra*. See also *Bridge v. Campbell Discount Co. Ltd* [1962] A.C. 600, 622; *Photo Production Ltd v. Securicor Transport Ltd* [1980] A.C. 827, 850; *Cameron-Head v. Cameron & Co.*, 1919 S.C. 627; the *Workers Trust* case, *supra*. It should be noted that by s.24 of the Agricultural Holdings Act 1986 "notwithstanding any provision in a contract of tenancy of an agricultural holding making the tenant liable to pay a higher rent or other liquidated damages" for breach of covenant, etc., the landlord may not recover for any such breach any sum "in excess of the damage actually suffered."

each particular contract, judged of at the time of the making of the contract, not as at the time of the breach.[55]

(4) To assist this task of construction various tests have been suggested which, if applicable to the case under consideration, may prove helpful or even conclusive.[56] Such are:

(a) It will be held to be a penalty if the sum stipulated for is extravagant and unconscionable in amount in comparison with the greatest loss which could conceivably be proved to have followed from the breach.[57]

(b) It will be held to be a penalty if the breach consists only in not paying a sum of money, and the sum stipulated is a sum greater than the sum which ought to have been paid. . . . [58]

(c) There is a presumption (but no more) that it is a penalty when 'a single lump sum is made payable by way of compensation, on the occurrence of one or more or all of several events, some of which may occasion serious and others but trifling damage.'[59]

On the other hand:

(d) It is no obstacle to the sum stipulated being a genuine pre-estimate of damage, that the consequences of the breach are such as to make precise pre-estimation almost an impossibility. On the contrary, that is just the situation when it is probable that pre-estimated damage was the true bargain between the parties."[60]

27–104 The word "genuine" in paragraph (2) of this statement has not been interpreted in a reported case: presumably it means a serious attempt to estimate loss, one made in good faith, however unreasonable it might appear to others. Again, the word "damage" must mean "net loss" after taking account of the claimant's expected ability to mitigate his loss.[61] The fact that the damage is difficult to assess with precision strengthens the presumption that a sum agreed between the parties represents a genuine attempt to estimate it and to overcome the difficulties

---

[55] *Public Works Commissioner v. Hills* [1906] A.C. 368, 376; *Webster v. Bosanquet* [1912] A.C. 394. *cf.*, however, the Unfair Terms in Consumer Contracts Regulations 1994 (*post*, § 27–126).

[56] *Pye v. British Automobile Commercial Syndicate Ltd* [1906] 1 K.B. 425.

[57] *Clydebank Engineering and Shipbuilding Co. Ltd v. Don Jose Ramos Yzquierdo y Castaneda, supra*, at 17; *Webster v. Bosanquet, supra*; *Cooden Engineering Co. Ltd v. Stanford* [1953] 1 Q.B. 86; *cf. Bridge v. Campbell Discount Co. Ltd, supra* (*post*, § 27–111).

[58] *Kemble v. Farren* (1829) 6 Bing. 141. See also *Astley v. Weldon* (1801) 2 B. & P. 346; *Wallis v. Smith* (1882) 21 Ch.D. 243, 256–257. The breach may involve more than a failure to pay: *Thos. P. Gonzales Corp. v. F. R. Waring (International) Pty. Ltd* [1986] 2 Lloyd's Rep. 160, 163. A discount for prompt payment, however, does not make the undiscounted sum a penalty; nor is it a penalty where a loan agreement provides for a modest increase in the rate of interest, which operates only from the date of the borrower's default: *Lordsvale Finance plc v. Bank of Zambia* [1996] Q.B. 752 (a one per cent increase: if, however, the increase operated retrospectively, it might be a penalty: *ibid.*)

[59] *Lord Elphinstone v. Monkland Iron & Coal Co. Ltd* (1886) 11 App.Cas. 332, 342. See *Kemble v. Farren, supra*, at 148; *Magee v. Lavell* (1874) L.R. 9 C.P. 107, 115; *Ford Motor Co. v. Armstrong* (1915) 31 T.L.R. 267 (see *post*, § 27–108); *Michel Habib Raji Ayoub v. Sheikh Suleiman* [1941] 1 All E.R. 507, 510; *Cooden Engineering Co. Ltd v. Stanford, supra*, at 98; *Interoffice Telephones Ltd v. Robert Freeman Co. Ltd* [1958] 1 Q.B. 190, 194. The parties, in such a case, should fix separate sums for the various possible breaches: *Imperial Tobacco Co. v. Parslay* [1936] 2 All E.R. 515.

[60] See *Clydebank Engineering and Shipbuilding Co. Ltd v. Don Jose Ramos Yzquierdo y Castaneda, supra*, at 11; *Webster v. Bosanquet, supra*, at 398; *English Hop Growers Ltd v. Dering* [1928] 2 K.B. 174; *Imperial Tobacco Co. v. Parslay, ante*, at 519; *Philips Hong Kong Ltd v. Att.-Gen. of Hong Kong* (1993) 61 Build. L.R. 49, 60, PC (the impact of delay by one contractor on other contracts).

[61] The question whether the parties may give their own meaning to "loss" is mentioned *post* § 27–111, text at n. 14.

of proof at the trial.[62] Even where the consequences of a breach are precisely ascertainable, a sum reserved by the contract may be intended by the parties as an agreed estimate of damage in order to avoid the expense and difficulty of assessment.[63] Often the parties to a contract fix a sum as liquidated damages in the event of one specific breach, and leave the claimant to sue for unliquidated damages in the ordinary way if other types of breach occur.[64] Where there is provision for liquidated damages, the claimant may nevertheless, in appropriate cases, elect to ask for an injunction instead of enforcing the liquidated damages.[65]

Fluctuating sums. Although a valid agreed damages clause may specify a **27–105** graduated scale of sums payable according to the varying extent of the expected loss,[66] a sum which is liable to fluctuate according to extraneous circumstances will not be classified as liquidated damages.[67] In a railway construction contract it was provided that in the event of a breach by the contractor he should forfeit "as and for liquidated damages" certain percentages retained by the government of money payable for work done as a guarantee fund to answer for defective work, and also certain security money lodged with the government. The Judicial Committee held that this was a penalty, since it was not a definite sum, but was

> "liable to great fluctuation in amount dependent on events not connected with the fulfilment of this contract. It is obvious that the amount of retained money . . . depended entirely on the progress of those contracts, and that further, as those moneys are primarily liable to make good deficiencies in these contract works, the eventual sum available . . . could not in any way be estimated as a fixed sum."[68]

Minimum payment clause. A "minimum payment" clause in a hire-pur- **27–106** chase or hiring agreement will usually be held to be a penalty if it provides for the same total sum to be payable by the hirer irrespective of how long the agreement has been in force[69] or "regardless of the seriousness or triviality of the breach in question."[70] (But the position in regard to the assessment of damages at common law will be different if the parties made the term into a condition, any breach of which entitled the innocent party to terminate the contract.[71])

---

[62] *Dunlop Pneumatic Tyre Co. Ltd v. New Garage Motor Co. Ltd* [1915] A.C. 79; *English Hop Growers Ltd v. Dering, supra; Imperial Tobacco Co. v. Parslay, supra; Robophone Facilities Ltd v. Blank* [1966] 1 W.L.R. 1428, 1447; *Philips Hong Kong Ltd v. Att.-Gen. of Hong Kong, supra* (the loss to a governmental body caused by delay in construction was especially difficult to assess).

[63] *Diestal v. Stevenson* [1906] 2 K.B. 345.

[64] *e.g. Aktieselskabet Reidar v. Arcos Ltd* [1927] 1 K.B. 352.

[65] See the cases cited, *ante*, § 27–010, n. 54. Agreed damages clauses do not bar the remedy of rejection of the goods: *Benjamin's Sale of Goods* (5th ed., 1997), § 13–034.

[66] See *post*, § 27–110, for graduated damages.

[67] *Public Works Commissioner v. Hills* [1906] A.C. 368, 376. In a case concerning a deposit, which was held to be unreasonable in amount, the Privy Council followed this case: *Workers Trust & Merchant Bank Ltd v. Dojap Investments Ltd* [1993] A.C. 573 (*post*, § 27–121).

[68] *Public Works Commissioner v. Hills, supra*, at 376 (followed in *Jobson v. Johnson, supra*, at 1036).

[69] *Lamdon Trust Ltd v. Hurrell* [1955] 1 W.L.R. 391. See also *Anglo-Auto Finance Co. Ltd v. James* [1963] 1 W.L.R. 1042; *United Dominions Trust (Commercial) Ltd v. Ennis* [1968] 1 Q.B. 54.

[70] *cf. Lombard North Central plc v. Butterworth* [1987] Q.B. 527.

[71] *Ante*, § 12–025, *post*, § 27–116.

27–107 **Single sum payable upon different breaches.** The mere fact that the same amount is made payable upon the breach of several undertakings of varying importance is by no means conclusive.[72] It may be that the amount is not disproportionate to the least important of these undertakings, and therefore represents a genuine attempt at an agreed estimate of real damage.[73] In *Dunlop Pneumatic Tyre Co. Ltd v. New Garage and Motor Co. Ltd*,[74] dealers in tyres agreed not to resell any tyres bought from the manufacturers to any private customers at less than the manufacturers' current list prices, not to supply them to persons whose supplies the manufacturers had decided to suspend, not to exhibit or export them without the manufacturers' consent, and to pay £5 by way of liquidated damages for every tyre sold or offered in breach of the agreement. It was held that the £5 was not a penalty and thus was recoverable as liquidated damages.[75]

27–108 In *Ford Motor Co. v. Armstrong*,[76] however, the retailer in a similar case agreed to pay £250 as "the agreed damage which the manufacturer will sustain" upon the breach of any one of several covenants (similar to those in the *Dunlop* case, *supra*), and the Court of Appeal by a majority held that this (in 1915) was a penalty, since it was an arbitrary and substantial sum, and made payable for various breaches differing in kind, some of which might cause only trifling damage. The high amount of the agreed sum in this case showed that it could not be a genuine pre-estimate of loss, as in the *Dunlop* case.

27–109 However, the cases on covenants in restraint of trade[77] have generally treated the sum payable for a breach as a sum stipulated for the breach of a single obligation, although it "is capable of being broken more than once, or in more ways than one."[78] Again, if a sum is payable upon different breaches, it may nevertheless be recoverable as liquidated damages where "the damage caused by each and every one of those events, however varying in importance, may be of such an uncertain nature that it cannot be accurately ascertained"[79] or where the stipulated sum is taken as an average or mean figure of the losses probably incurred in the different events.[80]

27–110 **Graduated damages.** In building contracts and other similar contracts the courts have upheld as liquidated damages a system of graduated sums which

---

[72] See rule 4(c) in Lord Dunedin's proposition, *ante*, § 27–103.

[73] *Wallis v. Smith* (1882) 21 Ch.D. 243; *Pye v. British Automobile Commercial Syndicate Ltd* [1906] 1 K.B. 425; *Dunlop Pneumatic Tyre Co. Ltd v. New Garage and Motor Co. Ltd, supra*; *Philips Hong Kong Ltd v. Att.-Gen of Hong Kong* (1993) 61 Build. L.R. 49, 62–63 (Privy Council refers to "the error of assuming that, because in some hypothetical situation the loss suffered will be less than the sum quantified in accordance with the liquidated damage provision, that provision must be a penalty . . . ").

[74] *Supra.*

[75] The House of Lords took the view that the £5 did not apply to the second and third obligations (not to sell to prohibited person, and not to exhibit without permission).

[76] (1915) 31 T.L.R. 267.

[77] *Crisdee v. Bolton* (1827) 3 C. & P. 240; *Price v. Green* (1847) 16 M. & W. 346, 354; *Reynolds v. Bridge* (1856) 6 E. & B. 528, 541.

[78] *Dunlop Pneumatic Tyre Co. Ltd v. New Garage and Motor Co. Ltd* [1915] A.C. 79, 98 (see also at pp. 92–93); *Law v. Redditch Local Board* [1892] 1 Q.B. 127, 136.

[79] *Dunlop Pneumatic Tyre Co. Ltd v. New Garage and Motor Co. Ltd, supra*, at 95–96. See also *Galsworthy v. Strutt* (1848) 1 Exch. 659, 666–667.

[80] *Dunlop Pneumatic Tyre Co. Ltd v. New Garage and Motor Co. Ltd, supra*, at 99; *English Hop Growers Ltd v. Dering* [1928] 2 K.B. 174, 182.

increase in proportion to the seriousness of the breach, *e.g.* so much per week for delay in performance,[81] or so much according to the number of items in question.[82] If in a building contract there is no such graduation the sum fixed is more likely to be held to be a penalty.[83] The sum must be graduated so that it changes in the right direction. Depreciation obviously increases over time, so a sum said to be compensation for depreciation is not a genuine pre-estimate of loss if it *decreases* over time as a hirer pays more instalments.[84]

The scope of the law on penalties. The law on penalties is not applicable to   **27–111** many sums of money payable under a contract.[85] Thus, it is not relevant where the claimant claims an agreed sum (a debt) which is due from the defendant in return for the claimant's performance of his obligations,[86] or which is due upon the occurrence of an event other than a breach of the defendant's contractual duty owed to the claimant.[87] In *Campbell Discount Co. Ltd v. Bridge*,[88] a hire-purchase agreement permitted the hirer at his option to terminate the hiring during the period of the agreement, and provided that the hirer should thereupon pay a sum by way of agreed compensation for the depreciation of the chattel; the Court of Appeal held that the owner could recover the agreed sum, since being payable upon an event not constituting a breach of the agreement, it fell outside the scope of the law as to penalties. In the House of Lords[89] the decision was based on a different view of the facts,[90] but four of their Lordships expressed *obiter* their views on the ruling of the Court of Appeal; two agreed that the law

---

[81] *Clydebank Engineering Co. v. Don Jose Ramos Yzquierdo y Castaneda* [1905] A.C. 6; *Philips Hong Kong Ltd v. Att.-Gen. of Hong Kong* (1993) 61 Build. L.R. 49, 60, PC. See also *Law v. Redditch Local Board, supra*; *Cellulose Acetate Silk Co. Ltd v. Widnes Foundry (1925) Ltd* [1933] A.C. 20 (*post*, § 27–117). The party entitled to the benefit of a liquidated damages clause in the event of failure to complete on time cannot take advantage of it if the delay is partly due to his own fault: *Peak Construction (Liverpool) Ltd v. McKinney Foundations Ltd* (1971) 69 L.G.R. 1, 11, 16. Demurrage under a charterparty is a case of graduated liquidated damages: *President of India v. Lips Maritime Corporation* [1988] A.C. 395, 422–423.

[82] *Elphinstone v. Monkland Iron and Coal Co.* (1886) 11 App.Cas. 332; *Diestal* v. *Stevenson* [1906] 2 K.B. 345.

[83] *e.g. Public Works Commissioner v. Hills* [1906] A.C. 368 (*ante*, § 27–105, text at nn. 67, 68). See also *Re Newman* (1876) 4 Ch.D. 724.

[84] *Bridge v. Campbell Discount Co. Ltd* [1962] A.C. 600. ("It is a sliding scale of compensation, but a scale that slides in the wrong direction": at 623.) If it slides in the right direction, the clause is more likely to be held valid: *Phonographic Equipment (1958) Ltd v. Muslu* [1961] 1 W.L.R. 1379. *cf. Lombank Ltd v. Excell* [1964] 1 Q.B. 415.

[85] But Bingham L.J. has adverted to the possibility of "a disguised penalty clause": *Interfoto Picture Library Ltd v. Stiletto Visual Programmes Ltd* [1988] 1 All E.R. 348, 358 (see *ante*, § 1–019).

[86] *White and Carter (Councils) Ltd v. McGregor* [1962] A.C. 413 (*ante*, § 27–100). The contrast between a debt and liquidated damages is drawn by the House of Lords in *President of India v. Lips Maritime Corporation* [1988] A.C. 395, 422–423, 424.

[87] *Export Credits Guarantee Dept. v. Universal Oil Products Co.* [1983] 1 W.L.R. 399 (see *post*, § 27–112). See also *Jervis v. Harris* [1996] Ch. 195, 206–207.

[88] [1961] 1 Q.B. 445 (following *Associated Distributors Ltd v. Hall* [1938] 2 K.B. 83); see Vol. II, §§ 38–311—38–315. The decision is based on the non-statutory law. For statutory regulation of hire-purchase agreements, see Vol. II, §§ 38–318 *et seq.*

[89] [1962] A.C. 600.

[90] *viz.* that the hirer had committed a breach. The law on penalties applies to a minimum payment clause if the agreement is in fact terminated on the ground of the hirer's breach: *Cooden Engineering Co. Ltd v. Stanford* [1953] 1 Q.B. 86; *Lamdon Trust Ltd v. Hurrell* [1955] 1 W.L.R. 391. See Vol. II, §§ 38–310—38–315.

as to penalties was inapplicable, but two were prepared to hold that the hirer was entitled to some relief.

27–112   **Sum payable on event other than breach.** However, a later House of Lords case appears to support the restriction upon the scope of the law on penalties. In the *Export Credits Guarantee* case,[91] the House held that the law did not apply to a clause providing for the contract-breaker (the defendant) to pay a specified sum to the plaintiff upon the happening of a certain event which was *not* the breach of a contractual duty owed by the defendant to the plaintiff. So it could not be a penalty where the defendant had agreed to reimburse the plaintiff the amount paid by the plaintiff to third parties under a guarantee (even where the plaintiff's obligation to meet the guarantee arose on the occasion of the defendant's breach of his contractual duties owed to other parties).[92] Although the case concerned a guarantee in a complex commercial arrangement and the plaintiff was claiming only the sum it had actually lost, their Lordships' limitation on the scope of the law on penalties was expressed in such wide terms that it would prevent many other clauses from being subject to that law.[93] Although statutory protection is available in some cases[94] the common law position is unsatisfactory; for instance, an honest hirer, who terminates his hire-purchase agreement when he finds that he cannot keep up the instalments, is in a worse position than the hirer who simply breaks his agreement by failing to pay the instalments.[95] The Privy Council has recently held that the law on penalties applies to a "deposit" which is unreasonable in amount,[96] and, more generally that the law on penalties applies to a clause "forfeiting" money held on behalf of the contract-breaker.[97]

27–113   **Other cases outside the law on penalties.** It is uncertain how far the law applies to a clause which imposes on the contract-breaker adverse consequences other than the payment of money or forfeiture of money already paid, or of proprietary or possessory rights held by him.[98] The law does not apply where one party to the contract is given an option to choose a particular method of performance, subject to his making a stipulated payment to the other[99]; or where a member of a pooling agreement failed to pay his levy to finance litigation and was excluded from sharing in the proceeds of the litigation.[1] The law on penalties may apply to a clause which entitles the innocent party to withhold a payment

---

[91] *Export Credits Guarantee Department v. Universal Oil Products Co.* [1983] 1 W.L.R. 399. It is unfortunate that the short speech in this case made no attempt to discuss the opinions expressed in the *Campbell Discount* case, *supra*.

[92] *ibid.*

[93] The death or bankruptcy of a party might be another event, not constituting a breach, upon which money is to be paid. *cf. Mount v. Oldham Corporation* [1973] Q.B. 309 (claim for a term's school fees in lieu of notice withdrawing a pupil).

[94] *Post*, §§ 27–125—27–126.

[95] See the Law Commission's Working Paper No. 61 (1975), paras 17–26.

[96] *Workers Trust & Merchant Bank Ltd v. Dojap Investments Ltd* [1993] A.C. 573 (See *post*, § 27–121, 27–123).

[97] *ibid.*

[98] This was considered by the High Court of Australia in *Forestry Commission of N.S.W. v. Stefanetto* (1976) 133 C.L.R. 507 (on the contractor's breach, the owner of the land was entitled to use the contractor's plant to complete the work). On clauses requiring the contract-breaker to transfer property to the innocent party, see *ante*, § 27–102; *post*, § 27–123.

[99] *Fratelli Moretti SpA v. Nidera Handelscompagnie B.V.* [1981] 2 Lloyd's Rep. 47, 53.

[1] *Nutting v. Baldwin* [1995] 1 W.L.R. 201.

(which would otherwise be due to the contract-breaker) on the ground that he has failed "to comply with any of the conditions" of the contract.[2]

Incentive payments. The reverse of an agreed damages clause is an incentive   **27–114**
payment such as an extra payment for early completion. The law on penalties does not apply to a clause providing for an *increase* in the price if certain targets in the contract are bettered or if costs are reduced; similarly, the price for a specially-manufactured machine may be graduated according to its efficiency in operation. A Government report has recommended that in building contracts incentive payments should be preferred to agreed damages clauses.[3]

Acceleration clauses. An "acceleration" clause is often found in contracts   **27–115**
providing for payment by instalments: on default in paying one instalment, all future instalments become immediately payable as one sum. Although the operation of these clauses produces results which may be "penal," the courts have usually enforced them on the ground that they do not increase the contract-breaker's overall obligation.[4] The Court of Appeal has held that it is not a penalty for an acceleration clause in a contract of loan to provide that, upon failure to pay an agreed instalment, the whole capital of the loan becomes immediately due and repayable.[5] But it might be held to be a penalty if it provided that, upon such failure, future interest (*viz.* payments not yet due) should be payable immediately.[6]

Damages following termination by the innocent party under an express   **27–116**
term. Where the hirer has neither repudiated the hiring (or hire-purchase) agreement, nor committed a "fundamental breach" of it, but the owner terminates it in the exercise of an express power to do so conferred by the agreement, the owner's damages are limited to loss suffered through any breaches up to the date of the termination.[7] A Court of Appeal case (*Lombard*) holds that this principle does not apply where the contract made the broken term into a condition, any breach of which entitled the innocent party to terminate (*e.g.* a

---

[2] *Gilbert Ash (Northern) Ltd v. Modern Engineering (Bristol) Ltd* [1974] A.C. 689. *cf. The Vainqueur José* [1979] 1 Lloyd's Rep. 557, 577–578.

[3] Banwell Report (Report of the Committee on Placing and Management of Contracts for Building and Civil Engineering Work) (HMSO, 1964), para. 9.22.

[4] *Protector Endowment Loan Co. v. Grice* (1880) 5 Q.B.D. 592 (a loan case); *Wallingford v. Mutual Society* (1880) 5 App.Cas. 685. See Goode [1982] J. Bus. L. 148. *cf. Wadham Stringer Finance Ltd v. Meaney* [1981] 1 W.L.R. 39, 48 (see Vol. II, § 38–235). The High Court of Australia has sometimes upheld acceleration clauses (*I.A.C. (Leasing) Ltd v. Humphrey* (1972) 126 C.L.R. 131 (see also Vol. II, § 38–314)) but sometimes not (holding them to be penalties): *O'Dea v. Allstates Leasing Systems (W.A.) Pty. Ltd* (1983) 152 C.L.R. 359; Muir (1985) 10 Sydney L.R. 503; *AMEV-UDC Finance Ltd v. Austin* (1986) 162 C.L.R. 170. *cf. Esanda Finance Corporation Ltd v. Plessing* (1989) 166 C.L.R. 131.

[5] *The Angelic Star* [1988] 1 Lloyd's Rep. 122, 125, 127.

[6] *ibid. cf. Lordsvale Finance plc v. Bank of Zambia* [1996] Q.B. 752 (see *ante*, § 27–103, n. 58).

[7] *Financings Ltd v. Baldock* [1963] 2 Q.B. 104. (A "minimum payment" clause specifying a larger sum will be held to be a penalty: see *ante*, § 27–103.) The principle stated in the text has been regularly followed by the Court of Appeal: *Brady v. St. Margaret's Trust Ltd* [1963] 2 Q.B. 494; *Charterhouse Credit Co. Ltd v. Tolly* [1963] 2 Q.B. 683; *United Dominions Trust (Commercial) Ltd v. Ennis* [1968] 1 Q.B. 54; *Capital Finance Co. Ltd v. Donati* (1977) 121 S.J. 270; *Lombard North Central plc v. Butterworth* [1987] Q.B. 527. See also the Australian cases cited, *ante*, § 27–115, n. 4.

clause making compliance with time "of the essence"[8]): in this case the innocent party may both terminate the contract and recover damages for the loss of the bargain (*viz.* in respect of all the outstanding obligations of the other party).[9] The Court of Appeal decided that a clause of the latter type is not subject to the law on penalties.[10] The difference between the two types of clause (*viz.* an express power to terminate, and a clause making time of the essence) is "one of drafting form and wholly without substance."[11] It is submitted that such a clause should be interpreted so as to give the innocent party the power to terminate, but not an entitlement to damages for loss of the contract as a whole (unless the clause satisfies the criteria for liquidated damages).[12] If the *Lombard* decision is upheld, the whole law on penalties can be avoided by a simple, small change in the terminology of the contract which makes every term a "condition" in the sense of a term any breach of which entitles the promisee to terminate.[13] If, in the light of such a clause, any sum specified as damages for breach must be tested on the basis that it is a pre-estimate of "the loss to the promisee resulting from the loss of his bargain" as a whole,[14] the law as to penalties can be avoided.[15]

27–117   **Limitation of liability for damages.**[16] The courts have upheld clauses in contracts which fix a limit to the amount of damages recoverable for a breach, and they will also uphold a clause which, though not fixing a limit, is similar in effect because it fixes an exact sum[17]; if both parties could foresee that the actual damage flowing from the breach would or might be greater than the sum fixed as damages for the breach, it is likely that the courts will construe[18] the clause as one placing an agreed limitation on the extent of the liability of the contract-

---

[8] See *ante*, §§ 22–011 *et seq.*

[9] The *Lombard* case, *supra*. See Treitel [1987] L.M.C.L.Q. 143; Beale (1988) 104 L.Q.R. 355.

[10] The *Lombard* case, *supra* at 536–537. But *cf. Gilbert Ash (Northern) Ltd v. Modern Engineering (Bristol) Ltd* [1974] A.C. 689 (*ante*, § 27–113).

[11] The *Lombard* case, *supra*, at 546.

[12] In the *Lombard* case, *supra*, it was held that, according to common law principles, the hirer had not committed a repudiatory breach of the contract: *ibid.* at 543–545. The court nevertheless awarded as damages at common law almost the same sum which it had previously found not to be a genuine pre-estimate of loss (a penalty).

[13] Would the law uphold a clause providing expressly that for any breach, however trivial, the damages shall be assessed on the basis that the whole benefit of the contract has been lost by the other party? *cf.* decisions on mitigation, such as *The Solholt* [1983] 1 Lloyd's Rep. 605 (*ante*, § 27–092).

[14] The *Lombard* case, *supra*, at 537. This means that the tests for liquidated damages are not to be applied to what the law itself holds to be "loss" anticipated to be caused by the *breach*, but rather the "loss" anticipated to result from the promisee's *decision* to terminate.

[15] This type of clause should be directly controlled. *cf.* the recent decision of the Privy Council, which applied the law on penalties to a deposit of an unreasonable amount: *Workers Trust & Merchant Bank Ltd v. Dojap Investments Ltd* [1993] A.C. 573 (*post*, § 27–121).

[16] *cf.* exemption clauses (*ante*, §§ 14–001 *et seq.*). *cf.* also the *South Australia* case [1997] A.C. 191 (*ante*, § 27–078: a "limited" duty of care may operate in a way similar to a limitation of damages provision). See *Benjamin's Sale of Goods* (5th. ed., 1997), § 13–034.

[17] *Cellulose Acetate Silk Co. Ltd v. Widnes Foundry (1925) Ltd* [1933] A.C. 20. The Unfair Contract Terms Act 1977 may now apply to such a clause: *St. Albans City Council v. International Computers Ltd* [1996] 4 All E.R. 481; see *ante*, §§ 14–057 *et seq.*

[18] *cf.* the rule that the effect of an exemption clause depends on the construction of the contract: *Suisse Atlantique Societe d'Armement Maritime v. N.V. Rotterdamsche Kolen Centrale* [1967] 1 A.C. 361; *Photo Production Ltd v. Securicor Transport Ltd* [1980] A.C. 827 (see *ante*, §§ 14–020 *et seq.*).

breaker.[19] These clauses are often the basis of the insurance arrangements to be made by the parties.

Can damages exceed sum fixed in penal clause? However, this principle has   **27–118**
not been applied to the special category of charterparties, where a fixed penalty may be ignored if it is less than the actual damage suffered. Where a charterparty contained the following clause: "Penalty for non-performance of this agreement proved damages, not exceeding estimated amount of freight," it was held that the clause provided a penalty and not a limitation of liability, so that the party complaining of non-performance was entitled to recover damages for his actual loss although it exceeded the estimated amount of freight.[20] It is unsettled whether this principle applies to penalty clauses in other types of contract, so as to entitle the claimant to ignore the sum stipulated as a penalty (where it was clearly not intended to limit liability) and to sue for damages for a greater amount to compensate him for his actual loss.[21]

"Invoicing back" clauses. The express terms of the contract may not only   **27–119**
exclude or limit the innocent party's right to claim damages for breach of contract,[22] but may also provide other provisions intended to apply in the event of a breach. Subject to the law as to penalties,[23] and to the effect of the Unfair Contract Terms Act 1977,[24] the courts will enforce these terms, despite the unexpected results which may occur. In one case,[25] a clause in a contract for the sale of goods provided that if the sellers made default in shipping, the contract should "be closed by invoicing back the goods" at the closing price fixed by the London Corn Trade Association. The sellers failed to ship, and the Association declared a closing price, which, because of a fall in market price, was lower than the contract price, so that a balance was due in favour of the sellers. Nevertheless, the Court of Appeal enforced the clause, despite the fact that the sellers were the

---

[19] *Cellulose Acetate Silk Co. Ltd v. Widnes Foundry (1925) Ltd, supra; Elsley v. J.G. Collins Insurance Agencies Ltd* (1978) 83 D.L.R. (3d) 1, 14–16. *cf. Diestal v. Stevenson, ante; Biggin & Co. Ltd v. Permanite Ltd* [1951] 1 K.B. 422, 436 (quoted *ante*, § 27–047) (revd. on another ground: [1951] 2 K.B. 314); *Elphinstone v. Monkland Iron and Coal Co., supra*, at 346.

[20] *Wall v. Rederiaktiebolaget Luggude* [1915] 3 K.B. 66 (approved by the House of Lords in *Watts, Watts & Co. Ltd v. Mitsui & Co. Ltd* [1917] A.C. 227). But this case may require reconsideration in the light of the *Suisse Atlantique* case, *supra*, n. 18 (where a demurrage clause was held to be an agreed damages clause) and the *Photo Production* case, *supra*, n. 18.

[21] In *Cellulose Acetate Silk Co. Ltd v. Widnes Foundry (1925) Ltd, supra*, at 26, the House left "open the question whether, where a penalty is plainly less in amount than the prospective damages, there is any legal objection to suing on it or, in a suitable case, ignoring it and suing for damages." *cf.* dicta to the effect that the penalty fixes the maximum recoverable: *Wilbeam v. Ashton* (1807) 1 Camp. 78; *Elphinstone v. Monkland Iron & Coal Co., supra*, at 346; *Elsley v. J.G. Collins Insurance Agencies Ltd* (1978) 83 D.L.R. (3d) 1, 14–16; *W. & J. Investments Ltd v. Bunting* [1984] 1 N.S.W.L.R. 331, 335–336. See also Hudson (1974) 90 L.Q.R. 31; Gordon (1974) 90 L.Q.R. 296; Hudson (1975) 91 L.Q.R. 25; Barton (1976) 92 L.Q.R. 20; Hudson (1985) 101 L.Q.R. 480; Treitel *op. cit.* (9th ed.), p. 902.

[22] On exemption clauses, see Chap. 14, *supra*.

[23] *Ante*, §§ 27–102 *et seq.*

[24] See *ante*, §§ 14–057 *et seq.*

[25] *Lancaster v. J. F. Turner & Co. Ltd* [1924] 2 K.B. 222 (Scrutton L.J. dissenting); followed in *J.F. Adair & Co. Ltd v. Birnbaum* [1939] 2 K.B. 149 (and the earlier case noted *ibid.* at 173); *Podar Trading Co. Ltd v. Tagher* [1949] 2 K.B. 277. *cf. Laing, Son & Co. Ltd v. Eastcheap Dried Fruit Co. Ltd* [1961] 2 Lloyd's Rep. 277.

party in default.[26] An "invoicing back" clause may not be interpreted as the exclusive remedy,[27] *e.g.* the clause may not prevent the buyer obtaining damages for his loss of profits,[28] and judges have interpreted such clauses restrictively.[29] An "invoicing back" clause may also allow a percentage of the market price to be added to, or deducted from, the price, which if reasonable, will be upheld as liquidated damages covering items of loss not covered by the price alone.[30]

27-120　　**Reimbursement is not a penalty.** If a contract provides that in a certain event a sum of money paid under the contract is to be repaid to the original payer, the reimbursement cannot be a penalty.[31] So where the defendant received an insurance payment on the basis of his permanent disablement the insurers were able to enforce his undertaking to pay them "a penalty" of the same amount if he took part in a specified sport in future.[32]

27-121　　**Forfeiture: purchase by instalments and pre-payment of price.**[33] This, and the following paragraph, deal with the law apart from the Consumer Credit Act 1974[34]; many situations, however, will be covered by the provisions of that statute. A contract may, instead of fixing a sum to be paid upon breach, provide that a sum already paid shall be forfeited[35] upon breach by the party who paid it.[36] English courts have always treated such a forfeiture clause as different from a sum payable upon breach, but the Privy Council has recently said, in general terms, that the law on penalties applies to "a contractual provision which requires one party in the event of his breach of the contract to pay or forfeit a sum of

---

[26] Some clauses are drafted differently and avoid this difficulty, *e.g.* the clause may apply only to the defaulting buyer, and only if the market price has fallen: *Alexandria Cotton and Trading Co. (Sudan) Ltd v. Cotton Co. of Ethiopia Ltd* [1963] 1 Lloyd's Rep. 576.

[27] *Roth, Schmidt & Co. v. D. Nagase & Co. Ltd* (1920) 2 Ll.L.Rep. 36 (CA: the clause did not expressly exclude the right to reject the goods or to recover damages upon rejection).

[28] *Re Bourgeois and Wilson Holgate & Co.* (1920) 25 Com.Cas. 260 (the Court of Appeal decided in this case that the seller in these circumstances could not enforce the clause against the buyer).

[29] One judge has held that the interpretation of a clause which requires damages to be paid *to* the defaulting party is contrary to "natural justice": *Cassir, Moore & Co. Ltd v. Eastcheap Dried Fruit Co.* [1962] 1 Lloyd's Rep. 400, 402. See also the qualifications suggested in *Lancaster v. J. F. Turner & Co. Ltd, supra,* at 231; *J.F. Adair & Co. Ltd v. Birnbaum, supra,* at 169.

[30] *Robert Stewart & Sons Ltd v. Carapanayoti & Co. Ltd* [1962] 1 W.L.R. 34.

[31] *Alder v. Moore* [1961] 2 Q.B. 57 (approving *Re Apex Supply Co. Ltd* [1942] Ch. 108).

[32] *Alder v. Moore, supra.*

[33] See *ante,* § 27–102, n. 36; Goff and Jones, *The Law of Restitution* (5th ed., 1998), pp. 540–546; *McGregor on Damages* (6th ed., 1997), §§ 544 *et seq.*; the Law Commission, Working Paper No. 61 (1975) ("Penalty Clauses and Forfeiture of Moneys Paid"), §§ 50, 65, 66. *cf. Commissioners of Public Works v. Hills* [1906] A.C. 368 (recovery of amount deposited as "security" in a building contract; *ante,* § 27–105).

[34] See *post,* § 27–125.

[35] The payee "forfeits" the sum where he retains it for his own beneficial use, having freed himself of any further obligations under the contract by terminating the contract on account of the payer's breach. It is then up to the payer to challenge the forfeiture if he has any legal ground for doing so.

[36] If the sum is a deposit paid by the buyer (*viz.* a sum intended to be received by the seller as a security for the completion of the purchase by the buyer) it will be assumed that it is intended to be forfeited to the seller if the buyer defaults: *Howe v. Smith* (1884) 27 Ch.D. 89, 97–98 (*post,* § 30–059); *Stockloser v. Johnson* [1954] 1 Q.B. 476, 490 (" . . . or the money is expressly paid as a deposit (which is equivalent to a forfeiture clause) . . . "). The court has power to order the return of deposit paid under a contract for the sale of land: see *post,* § 30–060.

money to the other party."[37] However, no English court has yet equated the two clauses. (A similar type of clause is one which entitles the innocent party to the re-transfer[38] of property which, under the terms of the contract, he had previously transferred to the contract-breaker.[39]) Traditionally, the courts were willing to grant relief against such "forfeiture" clauses in only two situations: first, in landlord and tenant cases, there has been a long history of equitable relief against forfeiture of leasehold interests *viz.* where a clause in the lease entitled the landlord to repossess the premises if the tenant failed to pay an instalment of the rent.[40] In the second situation, the contract-breaker has been purchasing land by paying the price by instalments: it is clearly established that if, under a contract to purchase land by instalment payments, the purchaser defaults in payment of an instalment of the price, the court has jurisdiction in a proper case to relieve him against a clause providing for forfeiture of the instalments already paid, by granting him an extension of time within which he could pay the instalment now due.[41] It is implicit in these cases that payment within the extended period would preserve the purchaser's contractual rights in the same way as payment by the time originally agreed would have done.

For many years the courts would not treat other "forfeiture" clauses as **27–122** analogous to penalty clauses. It is only recently that the courts have begun to grant a limited type of relief against forfeiture in a wider range of situations. A condition said to be necessary before equitable relief may be granted is that the forfeiture clause was inserted in order "to secure a stated result which can effectively be attained when the matter comes before the court, and where the forfeiture provision is added by way of security for the production of that result."[42] The wider development began in 1954 with *Stockloser v. Johnson*[43]:

---

[37] *Workers Trust & Merchant Bank Ltd v. Dojap Investments Ltd* [1993] A.C. 573, 578. This was a case of a deposit of an amount held to be unreasonable and thus recoverable by the contract-breaker (subject to a cross-claim for any loss suffered by the innocent party). See Beale (1993) 109 L.Q.R. 524.

[38] Although the cases deal with "re-transfers", it is submitted that the principle discussed in this paragraph should apply to a clause which entitles the innocent party to require the contract-breaker to transfer property which he had not received from the innocent party. Support for this may be found in *B.I.C.C. plc v. Burndy Corpn* [1985] Ch. 232 (*infra*) which concerned the right of the innocent party to require the contract-breaker to assign to him all his interests in patent rights held jointly by the two parties.

[39] *Jobson v. Johnson* [1989] 1 W.L.R. 1026; *Re Dagenham (Thames) Dock Company* (1873) L.R. 8 Ch.App. 1022 (vendors entitled to re-enter land if the purchaser failed to pay an instalment of the price). In these cases, the innocent party must seek an order of the court to enforce the re-transfer to him: contrast the "forfeiture" of money already held by him (n. 35, *supra*).

[40] See also s.146 of the Law of Property Act 1925. See also n. 42, *infra*.

[41] *Re Dagenham (Thames) Dock Co. supra*; *John H. Kilmer v. British Columbia Orchard Lands Ltd* [1913] A.C. 319; *Steedman v. Drinkle* [1916] 1 A.C. 275; *Mussen v. Van Diemen's Land Co.* [1938] Ch. 253; *Starside Properties Ltd v. Mustapha* [1974] 1 W.L.R. 816 (Time was not made "of the essence" in this contract: *cf. ante*, § 27–116.) The Privy Council has refused to extend this principle: *Union Eagle Ltd v. Golden Achievement Ltd* [1997] A.C. 514 (see the comments by Heydon, (1997) 113 L.Q.R. 385); and Stevens (1998) 61 M.L.R. 255. See Lang (1984) 100 L.Q.R. 427; Harpum [1984] C.L.J. 134.

[42] *Shiloh Spinners Ltd v. Harding* [1973] A.C. 691, 723. (The case concerned the right to forfeit (re-enter upon) leasehold property for failure to repair fences and to maintain works for the protection of adjoining property.) Relief was not granted to a lessee under a finance lease because possession could no longer be restored to the lessee: *On Demand Information plc v. Michael Gerson (Finance) plc* [1999] 2 All E.R. 811.

[43] [1954] 1 Q.B. 476. (See also Vol. II, § 38–305.)

there was a provision, in a contract to purchase plant and machinery by instalment payments, that upon default by the buyer, the seller might terminate the contract and forfeit the instalments already paid. The majority of the Court of Appeal held that the court has an equitable jurisdiction to relieve against forfeiture of such instalments, even after termination of the contract, if in the actual circumstances of the case the clause was penal and it would be oppressive and unconscionable for the seller to retain all the instalments. In 1983, the House of Lords upheld the jurisdiction to relieve against forfeiture, but limited it to contracts concerning the transfer or creation of proprietary or possessory rights.[44] Thus it did not apply to the facts of the case before the House, where a shipowner withdrew his ship (chartered under a time charter[45]) on the ground of the charterer's failure to make punctual payment of an instalment of hire. Similarly, the House of Lords has refused relief against the forfeiture of "mere contractual licences" to use certain names and trade marks.[46] But the Court of Appeal has granted relief (in the form of an extension of time in which a payment could be made by the defendant) in a commercial contract which provided that his failure to pay a sum on time would entitle the plaintiff to claim an assignment of patent rights held by the defendant.[47] This decision holds that interests in personal property may be given this limited protection against forfeiture.

27–123   **Form of relief.** Under this equitable principle, the courts will seldom do more than give the contract-breaker more time in which to pay the sum he had failed to pay on time. This relief has the effect that the contract-breaker does not forfeit the rights which he had under the contract, provided he pays within the time fixed by the court. Occasionally the contract-breaker has obtained an order that the money he had paid in advance to the innocent party should, despite a forfeiture clause, be repaid to him (subject to his paying damages for the actual loss caused to the innocent party by the breach of contract).[48] This was the relief granted by the Privy Council in the case which treated a clause forfeiting money as subject to the ordinary law on penalties.[49] However, in one case[50] the contract-breaker was granted another type of relief against a clause which required him, upon breach, to re-transfer some property to the innocent party: the relief was given in the form of an option to the innocent party to accept a sale of the relevant property by the court, with his receiving out of the proceeds the amount of his

---

[44] *Scandinavian Trading Tanker Co. A.B. v. Flota Petrolera Ecuatoriana (The Scaptrade)* [1983] 2 A.C. 694 (followed in *Union Eagle Ltd v. Golden Achievement Ltd, supra* (PC, failure by ten minutes to pay balance of purchase price on time, when time was "of the essence": see Heydon, (1997) 113 L.Q.R. 385; Stevens, (1998) 61 M.L.R. 255). See also *The Laconia* [1977] A.C. 850, 869–870, 873–874, 878, 887. *cf.* the High Court of Australia in *Legione v. Hateley* (1983) 46 A.L.R. 1; *Ciavarella v. Balmer* (1983) 153 C.L.R. 438; and in *Stern v. McArthur* (1988) 165 C.L.R. 489.

[45] A charter by demise would have given the charterer a possessory interest in the ship.

[46] *Sport Internationaal Bussum B.V. v. Inter-Footwear Ltd* [1984] 1 W.L.R. 776 (followed in *Crittall Windows Ltd v. Stormseal (UPVC) Window Systems Ltd* [1991] R.P.C. 265).

[47] *B.I.C.C. plc v. Burndy Corporation* [1985] Ch. 232, 251–252. (The line drawn between this and the *Sport Internationaal* case, *supra*, is not justifiable in commercial terms.) Jurisdiction to grant relief can apply to the lessee's interest under a finance lease: *On Demand Information plc v. Michael Gerson (Finance) plc* [1999] 2 All E.R. 811.

[48] *Public Works Commissioner v. Hills* [1906] A.C. 368 (*ante*, § 27–105).

[49] See *The Workers Trust* case cited, *supra*, in n. 37 (which followed the case just cited in n. 48.)

[50] *Jobson v. Johnson* [1989] 1 W.L.R. 1026, 1037, 1045–1046.

actual loss, and the surplus going to the contract-breaker.[51] But in a contract of sale the court will not be easily satisfied that the seller's conduct is unconscionable, especially where the buyer has had the use or benefit of the subject matter of the contract over a period.[52] On the facts of *Stockloser v. Johnson, supra*, although the majority of the court treated the clause as penal, they did not think that the seller's conduct in retaining £4,750 out of the £11,000 price in one contract, and £3,500 out of the £11,000 price on another, was unconscionable, because the buyer had already received substantial benefits in the form of royalties.[53] Previously it was obvious that the courts were more reluctant[54] to allow recovery of money already paid by the contract-breaker (*i.e.* to grant affirmative relief)[55] than to deny recovery of a sum (a penalty) agreed to be payable upon breach by the contract-breaker (*i.e.* to grant negative relief) or to give more time to him to make a payment. It remains to be seen whether English courts will follow the lead of the Privy Council in treating both types of clause in the same way.[56]

Recovery of prepayments. If in a contract of sale there is no express for   **27–124**
feiture clause of the type discussed in the preceding paragraphs, and the seller terminates the contract upon the buyer's default, the buyer may recover any prepayment or instalments paid in part payment of the price, subject to a crossclaim by the seller for damages for the breach of contract.[57] Thus, in *Dies v. British and International Mining and Finance Corpn Ltd*,[58] where a buyer repudiated his contract to purchase goods, he was nevertheless held to be entitled to recover a substantial prepayment (not in the nature of a deposit) made by him, subject to a deduction in respect of the actual damage suffered by the seller through the breach of contract: the court held that if it permitted the whole prepayment to be retained by the seller, it would be permitting the retention of a penalty, not liquidated damages.[59] This decision has been distinguished by two of their Lordships in the House of Lords[60] on the ground that it concerned a sale of existing goods where no expenditure was intended to be incurred by the seller in

---

[51] The other option offered to the innocent party was to accept an order for specific performance, (*i.e.* to compel re-transfer of the property) if a court-directed inquiry showed that the present value of the property did not exceed the innocent party's actual loss: *ibid.* at 1037, 1045–1046.

[52] *Stockloser v. Johnson, supra* ("the forfeiture clause must be of a penal nature, in this sense, that the sum forfeited must be out of all proportion to the damage": at 490 (*cf.* at 484)).

[53] [1954] 1 Q.B. 476, 484, 492.

[54] *Dies v. British and International Mining and Finance Corporation Ltd* [1939] 1 K.B. 724 (sale of goods); *Stockloser v. Johnson, supra*, at 483, 489–490; *Mayson v. Clouet* [1924] A.C. 980 (sale of land); *Galbraith v. Mitchenall Estates Ltd* [1965] 2 Q.B. 473.

[55] *cf. post*, § 27–124.

[56] See *The Workers Trust* case, *supra*, at n. 37.

[57] *Palmer v. Temple* (1839) 9 A. & E. 508; *Mayson v. Clouet, supra*; *Dies v. British and International Mining and Finance Corporation Ltd* [1939] 1 K.B. 724; *Stockloser v. Johnson* [1954] 1 Q.B. 476, 483, 489–490; Williams, *Vendor and Purchaser* (4th ed.), p. 1006.

[58] *Supra* (followed in *Rover International Ltd v. Cannon Film Sales Ltd* [1989] 1 W.L.R. 912.

[59] See also *R. V. Ward Ltd v. Bignall* [1967] 1 Q.B. 534 (Vol. II, § 43–356).

[60] *Hyundai Heavy Industries Co. Ltd v. Papadopoulos* [1980] 1 W.L.R. 1129, 1142–1143, 1147–1148. (The contract in this case was for work and material supplied in the course of building a ship, and so it was treated as analogous to a building contract: see Beatson (1981) 97 L.Q.R. 389, 401–404; *Stocznia Gdanska SA v. Latvian Shipping Co.* [1998] 1 W.L.R. 574, HL.) The *Dies* case was also distinguished in the *Hyundai* case, *supra*, at 1134–1136, on the ground that there was a total failure of consideration in *Dies*: see *post*, § 30–048.

reliance on the advance payment. It has been persuasively argued[61] that the question should depend on the construction of the clause in the contract requiring the advance payment: was the right to retain the payment intended to be conditional upon performance by the payee of his obligations, or was it intended to be a security for performance of the payer's obligations?

27–125 **The Consumer Credit Act 1974.** Some of the problems created by contractual provisions requiring payments on the occurrence of specified events will be governed by the Consumer Credit Act 1974, which is discussed in Volume II of this work.[62] For instance, section 100(1) provides that where a debtor under a regulated hire-purchase (or a regulated conditional sale) agreement[63] has prematurely terminated the agreement, he shall be liable to pay the difference between the sums already paid or payable by him and one-half of the total price; but by section 100(3) the court may order payment of a smaller sum if that would be equal to the loss sustained by the creditor.[64] The court is also empowered to reopen a credit agreement "on the ground that the credit bargain was extortionate,"[65] and may set aside the whole or part of any obligation imposed on the debtor, or may require the creditor to repay the whole or part of any sum paid by the debtor.[66] This Act will therefore cover many of the situations which arise in practice, and the common law and equitable rules will not need to be applied. Thus, it is uncertain how far the principle discussed in § 27–121—27–123, *ante*, applies to hire-purchase[67] or hiring[68] agreements so as to permit the court to grant relief to a hirer against a clause providing for the forfeiture of instalments already paid or for a "minimum payment" by the hirer upon termination of the agreement.[69] When a hire-purchase agreement is terminated by the owner upon the hirer's default, the common law as to penalties[70] and the provisions of the Act will often protect the hirer against clauses requiring further payments, *e.g.* for "depreciation"; the common law rules apply to similar clauses in hiring agreements.[71] The question whether a depreciation clause is a penalty or not depends

---

[61] Beatson *loc. cit.* at 391–401. See also Dixon J. in *McDonald v. Dennys Lascelles Ltd* (1933) 48 C.L.R. 457, 477 (following termination of the contract "rights are not divested or discharged which have already been *unconditionally* acquired" (italics supplied)); and the *Fibrosa* case [1943] A.C. 32, 65 ("The condition of retaining it [the advance payment] is eventual performance"; *cf.* at 75).

[62] §§ 33–079 *et seq.* deal with hiring agreements, while §§ 38–002 *et seq.* deal with the other agreements within the scope of the Act.

[63] Definitions of these agreements are examined in Vol. II, §§ 38–317 *et seq.*

[64] See Vol. II, §§ 38–329—38–330, *cf.* the similar power conferred on the court by s.132 in the case of a regulated consumer hire agreement.

[65] ss.137–140. s.138(1) provides *inter alia* that a credit bargain is extortionate if it requires the debtor to make payments (whether conditionally, or on certain contingencies) which are grossly exorbitant; see Vol. II, § 38–195; and Guest and Lloyd, *Encyclopaedia of Consumer Credit*, § 2–138 *et seq.*

[66] s.139(2).

[67] *Campbell Discount Co. Ltd v. Bridge* [1961] 1 Q.B. 445, CA (on appeal, the case was decided on another point: [1962] A.C. 600); see Vol. II, §§ 38–313—38–314; Diamond (1956) 19 M.L.R. 498 and (1958) 21 M.L.R. 199; Prince (1957) 20 M.L.R. 620.

[68] *Galbraith v. Mitchenall Estates Ltd* [1965] 2 Q.B. 473; *Barton Thompson & Co. Ltd v. Stapling Machines Co.* [1966] Ch. 499.

[69] See the proposals for reform in the Law Commission's Working Paper No. 61, *Penalty Clauses and Forfeiture of Moneys Paid* (1975).

[70] *Bridge v. Campbell Discount Co. Ltd* [1962] A.C. 600, upholding the decision of the Court of Appeal in *Cooden Engineering Co. Ltd v. Stanford* [1953] 1 Q.B. 86; *Anglo Auto Finance Co. Ltd v. James* [1963] 1 W.L.R. 1042, 1049.

[71] *Robophone Facilities Ltd v. Blank* [1966] 1 W.L.R. 1428.

on the construction of the clause in the light of all the circumstances surrounding the particular agreement.[72]

The Unfair Terms in Consumer Contracts Regulations 1994.[73] These **27–126** Regulations provide that in a contract between a business and a consumer an "unfair term" will not be binding on the consumer.[74] The Regulations give illustrations of terms which will, prima facie, be regarded as unfair: relevant to clauses fixing damages is "(e) requiring any consumer who fails to fulfil his obligation to pay a disproportionately high sum in compensation". So a consumer will be able to appeal to this standard, as well as to the common law on penalties.

7. THE TAX ELEMENT IN DAMAGES

The tax element in damages.[75] In *British Transport Commission v. Gour-* **27–127** *ley,*[76] a decision on the assessment of damages for loss of earnings following personal injuries caused by negligence, the House of Lords held that income tax (including the higher rates) must be taken into account in assessing damages for either actual or prospective loss of earnings. The main principle to be applied is that damages are to compensate the claimant only in respect of what he has lost, and in view of the incidence of taxation, he has in such a case lost only his *net* earnings. The rule in *Gourley's* case (*supra*) will apply only where two conditions are satisfied[77]: (1) the money, for the loss of which damages are awarded, would have been subject to tax as income[78]; and (2) the damages awarded to the claimant are not subject to tax[79] in his hands.[80] If these conditions are satisfied, the rule in *Gourley's* case will apply to the assessment of damages in contract.[81]

---

[72] *Lombank Ltd v. Excell* [1964] 1 W.L.R. 415 (interpreting *Phonographic Equipment (1958) Ltd v. Muslu* [1961] 1 W.L.R. 1379).

[73] S.I. 1994 No. 3159 (in force on July 1, 1995).

[74] See *ante*, §§ 15–001 *et seq.*

[75] *Whiteman on Income Tax* (3rd ed., 1988), §§ 25–01 *et seq.*; Simon's *Direct Tax Service* (looseleaf) E4.821—E4.826. See the Seventh Report of the Law Reform Committee, *Effect of Tax Liability on Damages,* Cmnd. 501 (1958); Stevenson and Orr [1956] B.T.R. 1; Dworkin [1967] B.T.R. 315, 373.

[76] [1956] A.C. 185.

[77] The defendant must show that the second condition is satisfied: *Stoke-on-Trent City Council v. Wood Mitchell & Co. Ltd* [1980] 1 W.L.R. 254. (This was not a contract case.) Then the onus of proof is on the plaintiff to prove his damage, and thus to show that the first condition is inapplicable: *Hall v. Pearlberg* [1956] 1 W.L.R. 244.

[78] Thus where the plaintiff is deprived of a capital asset and his damages represent its capital value, no question of income tax arises unless he also claims for loss of profits: *cf. Hall v. Pearlberg, supra*; *Sykes v. Midland Bank Executor and Trustee Co. Ltd* [1969] 2 Q.B. 518, 536–537 (revd. on a different ground: [1971] 1 Q.B. 113). See *post*, § 27–133.

[79] On the position where the damages are subject to capital gains tax (*post*, § 27–136).

[80] See *post*, § 27–133. By s.329 of the Income and Corporation Taxes Act 1988, where the court awards a sum which includes interest on damages in respect of personal injuries or death, that interest is not regarded as income for any income tax purpose. See *Mason v. Harman* [1972] R.T.R. 1.

[81] But see the splitting of the award into taxable and non-taxable elements in cases of wrongful dismissal: *Phipps v. Orthodox Unit Trusts Ltd* [1958] 1 Q.B. 314 (*post*, § 27–129); *Parsons v. B.N.M. Laboratories Ltd* [1964] 1 Q.B. 95 (*post*, § 27–128). *cf. post*, § 27–135, n. 22.

27–128   **Taxation on damages for wrongful dismissal.**[82] By sections 148 and 188 of (and Schedule 11 to) the Income and Corporation Taxes Act 1988 any payments made on a person's retirement or removal from any office or employment are taxable[83]; the terms of the Act are wide enough to cover damages awarded for loss of earnings in an action for wrongful dismissal, although it was no doubt primarily intended to apply to agreed compensation for loss of office.[84] Tax is not chargeable on the first £30,000 of any such payment[85]; and the excess over £30,000 is subject to income tax in the normal way.[86] It has not been held (as might have been expected) that since the taxation rules covered the situation, the rule in *Gourley*'s case was ousted: instead the Court of Appeal has held that the rule in *Gourley*'s case continues to apply to the assessment of damages for wrongful dismissal where the damages are under the exempted amount (at that time, £5,000).[87] Although the court discussed the position where both the lost earnings and the damages are taxable,[88] the position where damages for wrongful dismissal exceed the exempted amount was not finally decided. At first instance it was later held that in this event notional tax should be deducted as if the total award was only for the exempted amount[89]; on the facts of the particular case, the exempted amount of £5,000 represented future earnings of £5,850 over the remaining years of the contract of employment (discounted on the basis of the cost of an annuity) and the tax to be deducted was calculated on this gross sum, after the other income of the plaintiff was taken into account to calculate the rate of tax. A second solution adopted in Scotland[90] was to assess the damages as if the whole award was subject to the *Gourley* principle, and then to add to that sum a further amount which would be sufficient to cover the tax payable by the plaintiff on the excess over the exempted amount (at that time, £5,000). This is the more precise method, since it will meet the claimant's exact loss[91]; but it suffers from the disadvantage that the addition to the award of the amount of tax may cause the amount of tax payable to be increased. The second method has been adopted at first instance in England,[92] and it is submitted that it is the better method.[93]

---

[82] See Powell (1981) 10 I.L.J. 239; *Whiteman on Income Tax* (3rd ed.), Chap. 15.

[83] There are a number of exemptions: see s.188.

[84] s.148(2) refers to any payment made "either directly or indirectly in consideration or in consequence of, or otherwise in connection with, the termination of the holding of the office or employment . . . " On the meaning of "office," see *Inland Revenue Commissioners v. Brander & Cruickshank* [1971] 1 W.L.R. 212, HL.

[85] s.188(4) of the 1988 Act (as amended). This provision applies to payment after April 5, 1988. Top-slicing relief no longer applies: Finance Act 1988, s.74, Sched. 14, Pt. IV repeals Sched. 11, paras 4–7 of the 1988 Act.

[86] On the question whether the first £30,000 might be subject to capital gains tax, see Whiteman *op. cit.* § 15–15.

[87] *Parsons v. B. N. M. Laboratories Ltd* [1964] 1 Q.B. 95 (on the provision now superseded by the 1988 Act).

[88] See *post*, § 27–135.

[89] *Bold v. Brough, Nicholson & Hall Ltd* [1964] 1 W.L.R. 201 (followed in *Basnett v. J. & A. Jackson Ltd* [1976] I.C.R. 63, 74).

[90] *Stewart v. Glentaggart Ltd*, 1963 S.L.T. 119. See Simon's *Direct Tax Service* (looseleaf) E4.823; McGregor *op. cit.* §§ 601–605.

[91] It is possible under this method for the award to be higher than the plaintiff's gross loss: *Shove v. Downs Surgical* [1984] 1 All E.R. 7.

[92] *Shove v. Downs Surgical, supra.*

[93] Whiteman (*op. cit.* § 15–23) also submits that this method should be followed.

Method of calculating tax. Where the damages are calculated in respect of a   **27–129**
number of years, the *Gourley* calculation will spread the payments and the
relevant tax over the same number of years.[94] The House of Lords[95] has
emphasised that the courts cannot make an elaborate assessment of the claimant's
tax liability, but should act on broad lines. The rate of tax to be considered is the
effective rate of tax applicable to the claimant's earnings, and not the standard
rate of tax[96]; moreover, the relevant rates of tax are those in force at the time of
the court's judgment.[97] If the claimant's rate of tax depends partly on unearned
income, the court may pay comparatively little regard to the unearned income in
fixing the deduction for tax on his prospective earned income from the defendants, since the claimant is able to dispose of his private capital at any time, *e.g.*
by settlements, covenants or gifts.[98]

Loss of part of earnings. Where the claimant's claim for loss of earnings   **27–130**
represents only part of his earnings for the relevant tax year, the lost earnings are
treated as the top slice of the claimant's notional total income for that year. In
Lyndale Fashion Manufacturers v. Rich[99] the plaintiff was awarded a sum as
damages for loss of commission following the wrongful termination of his
appointment as a salesman. The Court of Appeal held that the amount of tax to
be deducted under the *Gourley* principle was to be calculated by treating the
gross sum for loss of commission as the top slice of the plaintiff's notional
income for the relevant year. (The notional total comprised his actual receipts in
that year and the gross amount of the damages.) This top slice would therefore
attract to itself all the additional tax applicable to the notional total income for
that year.[1] It was also held that any expenses which would have been incurred in
earning the lost commission should be set against the assumed additional income.
The defendant is entitled to reasonable particulars of the claimant's taxable
income from other sources, and of his tax assessments and allowances, since
these particulars are directly relevant to the assessment of the claimant's net loss
of earnings[2]; elaborate particulars, however, might increase costs, and are unnecessary, since "particulars should be limited to what is really reasonably necessary
to enable the party seeking them to know what case he has to meet."[3]

Foreign tax laws. Foreign tax laws are to be treated in the same way as   **27–131**
United Kingdom tax laws in this connection: if the claimant in a claim for loss

---

[94] *Re Houghton Main Colliery Co. Ltd* [1956] 1 W.L.R. 1219.
[95] *British Transport Commission v. Gourley* [1956] A.C. 185, 203, 207, 215.
[96] *ibid.* at 207.
[97] *ibid.* at 209.
[98] *Beach v. Reed Corrugated Cases Ltd* [1956] 1 W.L.R. 807 (wrongful dismissal).
[99] [1973] 1 W.L.R. 73. (McGregor *op. cit.* § 606, criticises the view taken in this case that the damages would not be taxable in the hands of the plaintiff. In § 607 he relies on the decision of the House of Lords in *Deeny v. Gooda Walker (No. 2)* [1996] 1 W.L.R. 426 (see *post*, § 27–133, n. 8).
[1] The Court of Appeal did not accept the view taken in *Re Houghton Main Colliery Ltd* [1956] 1 W.L.R. 1219 that the partial loss was not to be treated as any particular part of the plaintiff's income, so as to attract a higher or lower rate of tax.
[2] *Phipps v. Orthodox Unit Trusts Ltd* [1958] 1 Q.B. 314 (following *Monk v. Redwing Aircraft Co. Ltd* [1942] 1 K.B. 182, where the plaintiff was compelled to give particulars of other employment he had undertaken since his wrongful dismissal).
[3] *Phipps v. Orthodox Unit Trusts Ltd, supra*, at 321.

of earnings is subject to foreign fiscal laws under which no tax is payable on the damages it would seem that the rule in *Gourley*'s case (*supra*) would apply.[4]

27–132   **National insurance contributions; tax rebates.** On the basis of the approach adopted in *Gourley*'s case, it has been held that in the assessment of damages for wrongful dismissal, a deduction should be made for the employee's national insurance contributions which the employer would have been obliged to deduct from the employee's wages[5]; an income tax rebate received in respect of a period of unemployment should also be taken into account to reduce damages for loss of earnings during that period.[6]

27–133   **Instances where the Gourley principle is irrelevant.** If a sum awarded as damages for loss of profit would be subject to tax in the hands of the claimant, the tax element should be ignored in assessing damages, even though the tax likely to be levied on the damages may be less than that which would have been levied on the income (if it had been received).[7] The general principle is that if the sum paid as damages would have been taxable as income if it had been paid by the defendant without dispute, then the damages themselves are subject to income tax.[8] Thus, in a claim against a vendor for breach of a contract to sell land, the purchaser, a dealer in real estate, was held entitled to a sum equal to the gross amount of his profit (namely, the difference between the purchase price and the market value of the land at the date of the breach) since any damages recovered by the claimant would attract tax as part of the profits of his business.[9] Damages in respect of goods which constitute the claimant's trading stock are treated as a taxable revenue receipt.[10] If the goods would have represented a capital asset in the claimant's hands, and the damages are in respect of their capital value, the first condition in *Gourley* is not satisfied; but where the claimant recovers damages for loss of use of such goods (or for interest on their

---

[4] *Julien Praet et Cie SA v. H. G. Poland Ltd* [1962] 1 Lloyd's Rep. 566 (where damages for breach of contract are subject to foreign taxation, the rule in *Gourley*'s case does not apply). In *John v. James* [1986] S.T.C. 352, a complicated situation created possible tax liabilities in seven foreign countries (as well as the U.K.) over many years, but the judge calculated damages without making any deductions on account of tax.

[5] *Cooper v. Firth Brown Ltd* [1963] 1 W.L.R. 418 (Vol. II, § 39–184). In a personal injury tort case, a deduction has also been made from the plaintiff's lost wages in respect of the contributions he did not have to make to a pension scheme to which he was obliged to belong as one of the terms of his employment: *Dews v. National Coal Board* [1988] A.C. 1. (Any diminution in his ultimate pension should be valued separately: *ibid.* at 14–15, 18.)

[6] *Hartley v. Sandholme Iron Co. Ltd* [1975] Q.B. 600 (a tort case). *cf.* also the question of deducting a redundancy payment from damages for wrongful dismissal: see Vol. II, § 39–185.

[7] *Parsons v. B.N.M. Laboratories Ltd* [1964] 1 Q.B. 95; *Diamond v. Campbell-Jones* [1961] Ch. 22, 37; *Julien Praet et Cie, SA v. H. G. Poland Ltd, supra.* (See, however, the splitting of damages for wrongful dismissal into separate parts—taxable and non-taxable: *ante*, § 27–128.) *cf. Burmah SS. Co. v. I.R.C.* (1931) 16 T.C. 67.

[8] *Whiteman on Income Tax* (3rd ed.), §§ 25–01 *et seq.* See *Deeny v. Gooda Walker (No. 2)* [1996] 1 W.L.R. 426 (HL, " . . . payments in compensation for what would have been revenue items in the trade": at 437).

[9] *Diamond v. Campbell-Jones, supra. cf. Lyndale Fashion Manufacturers v. Rich* [1973] 1 W.L.R. 73 (where the *Gourley* principle was applied to damages for loss of a salesman's commission; but McGregor *op. cit.* (16th ed.) §§ 606–607, argues that the damages should have been treated as taxable).

[10] *Sommerfelds v. Freeman* [1967] 1 W.L.R. 489.

value[11]) the damages will be treated as a trading receipt in the calculation of his trading profits.[12] Other awards held to be taxable in the hands of the recipient were for loss of rent from a tenant who failed to comply with a valid notice to quit[13]; and for damages received by a Lloyd's Name from his agent.[14]

Salvage services. There are conflicting decisions of two judges at first   **27–134** instance on the question whether liability to tax is a relevant factor in assessing an award for salvage services.[15] It is submitted that the better view is that[16] the rule in *Gourley's* case (*supra*) is only applicable to diminish an award for damages for loss of personal earnings where the damages are not subject to tax, and thus not applicable to increase the assessment of a salvage award merely because the profit of the salvor is taxable.[17]

Where both the lost earnings (or profits) and the damages are taxa-   **27–135** **ble.** The Court of Appeal[18] has upheld the practice that in cases where both the lost earnings or profits and the damages to be awarded would be taxable, the incidence of taxation should be ignored. The tax on the damages is left to be set off against the tax on the lost earnings or profits; "rough justice is done and a great expenditure of time and costs is saved by ignoring the tax on both sides"[19] even though the actual amounts of tax, if calculated precisely, might differ widely.[20] However, one judge has considered the incidence of taxation on both sides, in a commercial case where failure to do so would have given the plaintiff substantially more than his actual loss.[21] In some instances the court has divided the award of damages into two separate elements, one being taxable while the other is not.[22]

---

[11] *Riches v. Westminster Bank* [1947] A.C. 390 (interest awarded as damages held to be taxable); *The Norseman* [1957] P. 224 (interest).

[12] *Burmah SS. Co. v. Inland Revenue Commissioners* (1931) 16 T.C. 67 (a Scots case).

[13] *Raja's Commercial College v. Gian Singh & Co. Ltd* [1977] A.C. 312. *cf. Stoke-on-Trent City Council v. Wood Mitchell & Co. Ltd* [1980] 1 W.L.R. 254 (loss of profits as part of statutory compensation for compulsory acquisition); *London and Thames Haven Oil Wharves Ltd v. Attwooll* [1967] Ch. 772 (loss of trading profits: the dictum of Diplock L.J. in this case was discussed by the HL in *Deeny v. Gooda Walker Ltd (No. 2)*, *supra*.)

[14] *Deeny v. Gooda Walker Ltd (No. 2)*, *supra*.

[15] *The Telemachus* [1957] P. 47; *The Makedonia* [1958] 1 Q.B. 365; *cf. The Frisia* [1960] 1 Lloyd's Rep. 90, 94, 95, 96. *McGregor* on *Damages* (16th ed.), § 584, n. 59, submits that the decision in *The Telemachus* was wrong. On salvage, see *post*, § 30–191.

[16] *The Makedonia*, *supra*.

[17] Hall (1957) 73 L.Q.R. 212, 219–220; (1958) 74 L.Q.R. 168; (1958) 21 M.L.R. 301.

[18] *Parsons v. B.N.M. Laboratories Ltd* [1964] 1 Q.B. 95 (" ... it is impossible to maintain that there can be derived from *Gourley's* case any principle requiring taxation to be taken into account in assessing damages in a situation where both the lost earnings or profits and the damages are taxable": *ibid.* at 136). See also *Julien Praet et Cie SA v. H. G. Poland Ltd* [1962] 1 Lloyd's Rep. 566.

[19] *Parsons v. B.N.M. Laboratories Ltd*, *supra*, at 135. It was similarly assumed that the damages would be taxable in *Dickinson v. Jones Alexander & Co.* [1993] 2 F.L.R. 321.

[20] Exceptional cases might justify separate assessments of tax: *Parsons v. B.N.M. Laboratories Ltd, supra* at 137.

[21] *Amstrad plc v. Seagate Technology Inc.* (1997) 86 Build. L.R. 34.

[22] *O'Sullivan v. Management Agency and Music Ltd* [1985] Q.B. 428 (CA: claim for accounting of profits, some of which would not be taxable in the plaintiff's hands, because of the time period in question). *cf.* the contrary opinion at first instance in *John v. James* [1986] S.T.C. 352. See also *ante*, § 27–128 (where awards of damages for wrongful dismissal are discussed: such awards have been split into taxable and non-taxable parts) and the opinion of Lord Hunter in *Stewart v. Glentaggart Ltd*, 1963 S.L.T. 119 (*ante*, § 27–128).

27–136 **Capital gains tax.** Capital gains tax is charged upon gains accruing to a person on the disposal of assets.[23] The list of types of property subject to capital gains tax includes: "21(1)(*a*) options, debts and incorporeal property generally" (which is wide enough to cover rights of action[24]); and "22(1)(*a*) capital sums received by way of compensation for any kind of damage or injury to assets or for the loss, destruction or dissipation of assets or for any depreciation or risk of depreciation of an asset." Many instances of the receipt of damages in contract will therefore be liable to capital gains tax[25] and so the *Gourley* principle will not apply.[26] There is a wider ground, for it seems that whenever the asset lost by the claimant would have been subject to capital gains tax, the damages recovered by him in respect of its value will also be subject to the tax.[27] However, the Act provides[28] that "sums obtained by way of compensation or damages for any wrong or injury suffered by an individual in his person or in his profession or vocation are not chargeable gains" for the purposes of the taxation of capital gains. This provision exempts many heads of damages in tort from the new tax but it is conceivable that the words "any wrong . . . suffered by an individual . . . in his profession or vocation" could apply to some damages in contract, unless it is held that no breach of contract is a "wrong" in this context.[29]

8. INTEREST[30] AND RATE OF EXCHANGE

27–137 **The award of interest at common law.** In 1985, the House of Lords[31] refused to depart from its previous decision in 1893[32] which laid down that the common law does not permit the award of interest by way of general damages for delay in payment of a debt beyond the date when it was contractually due. It has, however, always been open to the parties to make express provision in their

---

[23] Taxation of Chargeable Gains Act 1992, s.1(1). See Simon's *Direct Tax Service* (looseleaf) Cl. 319, Cl.325–Cl.328; Whiteman, *Capital Gains Tax* (4th. ed.); Sumption, *Capital Gains Tax* (looseleaf); McGregor on *Damages* (16th ed.), §§ 14 *et seq.*

[24] *cf.* s.51(2). See also *O'Brien v. Benson's Hosiery* [1979] S.T.C. 735 (payment by employee for release from a contract of employment was an "asset" for the purposes of capital gains tax).

[25] Since the deriving of a capital sum may be a disposal of assets, a seller's damages for the buyer's failure to accept the goods may be subject to capital gains tax.

[26] McGregor *op. cit.* §§ 614–621; Whiteman *op. cit.* §§ 6–29 *et seq.*, 7–73 to 7–74. If damages for breach of contract awarded to a buyer or seller amount to a trading receipt in the hands of the recipient and thus liable to income tax, they will not be liable to capital gains tax: s.37 of the 1992 Act; Sumption *op. cit.* A.18.03.

[27] *cf. Zim Properties v. Procter* [1985] S.T.C. 90 (criticised by McGregor *op. cit.* §§ 616, 621). See also the Extra-Statutory Concession dated December 19, 1988 (see Whiteman *op. cit.* 9th Cum. Supp., §§ 6–29 to 6–36; Sumption *op. cit.* D.33.

[28] s.51(2).

[29] Provision is made for the postponement of the capital gains charge in certain circumstances, *e.g.* if the recipient of damages uses them to repair damaged property: s.23 of the Act. (See also ss.152–154.) If the amount recovered for the damage, destruction or misappropriation of a chattel is less than £6,000, s.262 of the Act exempts it from any capital gains charge.

[30] See also Vol. II, §§ 38–245 *et seq.*; *McGregor on Damages* (16th ed., 1997), Chap. 14; Thompson, *Recovery of Interest: Practice and Precedents* (1985).

[31] *President of India v. La Pintada Compania Navegacion SA* [1985] A.C. 104 (which was further considered by the House of Lords in *President of India v. Lips Maritime Corporation* [1988] A.C. 395. See Mann (1985) 101 L.Q.R. 30.

[32] *London, Chatham and Dover Railway Co. v. South Eastern Railway Co.* [1893] A.C. 429.

contract for the payment of interest, which the courts would enforce[33] (except in situations covered by specific statutory provision[34]). The courts were sometimes prepared to infer an agreement to pay interest where the inference could be based on the course of dealing between the parties[35] or on a relevant trade usage.[36]

Finance charges on particular transaction contemplated. One common law exception to the rule was created by the Court of Appeal in 1981[37] (and was expressly approved by the House of Lords in 1985[38]): provided the second rule in *Hadley v. Baxendale*[39] (the remoteness test where a promisor with notice of special facts had assumed responsibility for a type of loss not normally within contemplation[40]) was satisfied, special damages could be awarded where, as the result of the defendant failing to pay money when it was due, the claimant had actually incurred interest charges[41] in obtaining finance from another source. The defendant knew that the claimant needed the payment to finance a purchase, and that, if the defendant failed to make the payment, the claimant would need to borrow the amount elsewhere. An analogous situation arose where the plaintiff was buying a machine on hire-purchase. The defendant's breach of contract led to the need to replace an expensive part of it; since it was found that the plaintiff acted reasonably in buying the replacement on hire-purchase, the defendant was held liable to pay the finance charges.[42]

27–138

Admiralty—equity jurisdiction. In some jurisdictions outside the common law, interest could be awarded by the court, *e.g.* in the Admiralty Court on a salvage award,[43] or in the equitable jurisdiction of the Chancery Court.[44]

27–139

Interest on commercial debts. Interest is now payable on certain debts under a term implied into contracts by the Late Payment of Commercial Debts (Interest) Act 1998.[45] The Act applies to "a contract for the supply of goods or

27–140

---

[33] See Vol. II, §§ 38–246 *et seq.*

[34] By ss.137–140 of the Consumer Credit Act 1974 the court is empowered to reopen certain transactions where the rate of interest is "grossly exorbitant" (see Vol. II, §§ 38–191 *et seq.*) *cf.* ss.244 and 343 of the Insolvency Act 1986.

[35] *Re Anglesey* [1901] 2 Ch. 548. See also *Great Western Insurance Co. v. Cunliffe* (1874) L.R. 9 Ch. 525; *Re Duncan & Co.* [1905] 1 Ch. 307.

[36] *Ikin v. Bradley* (1818) 8 Taunt. 250; *Page v. Newman* (1829) 9 B. & C. 378, 381. *cf.* the implied term arising under the Late Payment of Commercial Debts (Interest) Act 1998 (*post*, § 27–140; Vol. II. §§ 38–256 *et seq.*).

[37] *Wadsworth v. Lydall* [1981] 1 W.L.R. 598. (See *ante* § 27–082.)

[38] *The President of India* case [1985] A.C. 104, at 125–127.

[39] (1854) 9 Ex. 341.

[40] *Ante*, §§ 27–027—27–028.

[41] *Compania Financiera "Soleada" SA v. Hamoor Tanker Corpn Inc. (The Borag)* [1981] 1 W.L.R. 274 (interest charges held unreasonable).

[42] *Bacon v. Cooper (Metals) Ltd* [1982] 1 All E.R. 397 (see *ante*, § 27–056).

[43] *The Aldora* [1975] Q.B. 748; *The Rilland* [1979] 1 Lloyd's Rep. 455.

[44] *Wallersteiner v. Moir (No. 2)* [1975] Q.B. 373, 388, 406; *O'Sullivan v. Management Agency and Music Ltd* [1985] Q.B. 428 (fiduciary relationship). The award of interest in equity was examined (especially in relation to compound interest) in *Westdeutsche Landesbank Girozentrale v. Islington London B.C.* [1996] A.C. 669 (*post*, § 27–142, n. 67).

[45] The Act came into force on November 1, 1998: S.I. No. 2480 (There is also a draft Directive from the European Union on the same subject: [1998] O.J. C168.)

services"[46] where both parties are acting in the course of a business.[47] It is an implied[48] term in any such contract that any "qualifying debt"[49] created by the contract carries simple interest (called "statutory interest" in the Act).[50] The rate of statutory interest (or the formula for calculating it) is to be prescribed by order of the Secretary of State.[51]

27–141 **Period and rate of statutory interest.** Where the parties agree a date for payment of the debt, statutory interest starts to run on the next day[52]; but when the debt relates to an obligation to make an advance payment,[53] the debt is treated as created on the day when the supplier's obligation is performed.[54] In other cases, statutory interest runs after the period of 30 days from the performance of the obligation to which the debt relates[55]; or from the day when the purchaser has notice of the amount of the debt.[56] Statutory interest ceases to run when the interest would cease to run if it were carried under an express contract term.[57] But statutory interest does not run for any period where "by reason of any conduct of the supplier",[58] "the interests of justice require".[59]

27–142 **Statutory power to award interest.** A statutory provision may empower the court to award interest in particular circumstances, *e.g.* where a bill of exchange

---

[46] Defined by s.2(2), (3) and (4). (Some other relevant definitions are found in s.16). Certain contracts are excepted by s.2(5): consumer credit agreements; mortgages, pledges, charges or other securities; and other contracts specified by the Secretary of State. s.12 makes provision for the conflict of laws: see §§ 31–142—31–145.

[47] s.2(1). The meaning of "business" includes a profession and the activities of any government department or local or public authority (s.2(7)). Initially, only businesses with 50 or fewer employees are entitled to claim under the Act: S.I. 1998 No. 2479, art.2(2); see also S.I. 1998 No. 2481 (on questions of proof of the size of the purchaser). It is expected that the Act will be extended to all businesses by November 1, 2002.

[48] In cases where the contract provides "a substantial remedy" (as defined in s.9) for late payment of the debt, s.1(3) and Part II of the Act (ss.7–10) permit the parties to oust or vary the right to statutory interest conferred by s.1(1).

[49] As defined by s.3(1). s.3(2) and (3) exclude debts where any other enactment or any rule of law confers a right to interest or to charge interest. By s.3(4) the Secretary of State may by order exclude other debts from the Act. By s.13, the Act applies to a qualifying debt despite any assignment of the debt or the transfer of the duty to pay it, or any change in the identity of the parties, whether by assignment, operation of law or otherwise.

[50] s.1(1).

[51] s.6. The initial rate has been fixed at 8% over the official dealing rate of the Bank of England: S.I. 1998 No. 2765.

[52] s.4(3). The agreed date "may depend on the happening of an event or the failure of an event to happen": s.4(3). s.14 extends the application of the Unfair Contract Terms Act 1977 to a contract term postponing the time when a qualifying debt would otherwise arise.

[53] ss.4(4) and 11.

[54] s.11(3). s.11(4) to (7) prescribe detailed rules on advance payments in respect of part performance or the hire of goods.

[55] s.4(5)(a). If the debt arises from a period of hire of goods, the 30 days runs from the last day of that period: s.4(6).

[56] If the amount is unascertained, the 30-day period runs from the day when the purchaser has notice of the sum claimed: s.4(5)(b).

[57] s.4(7).

[58] s.5(1). "Conduct" includes any act or omission (s.5(5)) and may be relevant whether it occurs before or after the time when the debt is created (s.5(4)).

[59] s.5(1) and (2). By s.5(3) a reduced rate of statutory interest may apply if "the interests of justice require". For possible analogies, see *ante* § 15–034 on "unfairness", and *ante*, § 14–081 on "reasonableness".

has been dishonoured.[60] The first general discretionary power was enacted in 1934[61] and is now found in two separate statutes covering the main courts.[62] (It should be noted that those statutes do not confer on the creditor a right to interest[63]). The High Court[64] and the county court[65] are empowered, in proceedings for the recovery of a debt or damages,[66] to include "in any sum for which judgment is given" simple[67] interest[68]; subject to any rules of court,[69] the court is given a discretion to fix the rate of interest,[70] to decide whether the interest should be on "all or any part of" the debt or damages, and for "all or any part of the period between the date when the cause of action arose" and either the date of payment (of any sum paid before judgment) or the date of judgment.[71] The plaintiff[72] is also entitled (subject to a similar[73] judicial discretion as to the rate of interest, the period for which it is payable, and whether it should be on all or only part of the debt or damages) to the award of simple interest where the defendant pays the whole of a debt to the plaintiff after proceedings for its recovery were instituted but before any judgment.[74] Where an action has been brought for damages for breach of contract, payment of the amount claimed prior to the hearing does not extinguish the cause of action[75]: hence, when the payment

---

[60] s.57 of the Bills of Exchange Act 1882 (see Vol. II, § 34–120). In the enactment of general powers to award interest (discussed *infra*), this provision has been preserved: s.3(1)(c) of the Law Reform (Miscellaneous Provisions) Act 1934; s.35A(8) of the Supreme Court Act 1981; and s.69(7) of the County Courts Act 1984. See also s.93 of the Insolvency Act 1986; CPR, Sched. 1 (RSC, Ord. 59, r. 13(2).)

[61] The Law Reform (Miscellaneous Provisions) Act 1934, s.3(1).

[62] The new statutory provisions were the result of the Law Commission's *Report on Interest* No. 88 (Cmnd. 722a (1978)).

[63] *cf. ante*, § 27–140; *post*, § 27–149.

[64] By s.35A of the Supreme Court Act 1981 (which was inserted by s.15 of and Sched. 1 to the Administration of Justice Act 1982). For the power given to arbitrators, see *post*, § 27–150.

[65] By s.69 of the County Courts Act 1984. S.3 of the Law Reform (Miscellaneous Provisions) Act 1934 which is examined in the 25th edition of this work (Vol. I, §§ 1745–1747) remains in force for courts of record other than the High Court and county court.

[66] The House of Lords held that the words "any debt or damages" in s.3(1) of the 1934 Act, *supra*, "are very wide, so that they cover any sum of money which is recoverable by one party from another, either at common law or in equity or under a statute of the kind here concerned" (*viz.* the Law Reform (Frustrated Contracts) Act 1943): *B. P. Exploration Co. (Libya) Ltd v. Hunt (No. 2)* [1983] 2 A.C. 352, 373. This statement should also apply to ss.35A and 69 of the present Acts, *supra*.

[67] *Wentworth v. Wiltshire County Council* [1993] 2 All E.R. 256, 269 (also 263) (not a contract case). s.3 of the 1934 Act explicitly excluded "the giving of interest upon interest": see *Bushwell Properties Ltd v. Vortex Properties Ltd* [1975] 1 W.L.R. 1649 ("the court is not to award interest on such part of the sum claimed as represents contractual interest": at 1660.) (The decision was reversed on another point: [1976] 1 W.L.R. 591.) In equity, compound interest has been awarded for profits made through breach of a fiduciary duty: *Wallersteiner v. Moir (No. 2)* [1975] Q.B. 373. In *Westdeutsche Landesbank Girozentrale v. Islington London B.C.* [1996] A.C. 699, the House of Lords held that in equity compound interest may be awarded only in cases of fraud or against a trustee (or other person in a fiduciary position) in respect of profits improperly made by him. See also *Mathew v. T.M. Sutton Ltd* [1994] 1 W.L.R. 1455, 1463.

[68] For interest on judgment debts and arbitration awards, see *post*, §§ 27–150, 27–151.

[69] See *post*, § 27–147, and nn. 7 and 8.

[70] See *post*, § 27–144.

[71] Subs. (1) of ss.35A and 69 respectively. After the judgment, interest is payable under a different authority: see *post*, § 27–151. On the time of "entering up" a judgment, see *Parsons v. Mather & Platt Ltd* [1977] 1 W.L.R. 855.

[72] Defined as the person seeking the debt or damages: s.35A(7) and s.69(6) respectively.

[73] As in subs. (1) *supra*.

[74] Subs. (3) of ss.35A and 69 respectively. (This provision is wider than s.3 of the 1934 Act.)

[75] *Edmunds v. Lloyd Italico, etc., SpA* [1986] 1 W.L.R. 492, 495. (The payment merely gives rise to an equitable set-off which could be used as a potential cross-claim: *ibid.*)

does not include interest on the amount claimed, the court can still award the damages and interest under the statute.[76] (It should be noted, however, that neither enactment[77] gives the court a discretionary power to award interest on any sum paid late before any proceedings for its recovery have been begun.[78] This applies to late payment of the whole or part of a debt and to a sum paid as damages before the commencement of proceedings.[79] But interest may arise as of *right* under other statutory provisions,[80] such as under the Late Payment of Commercial Debts (Interest) Act 1998[81]). Any claim for interest, whether under the statutory provisions or otherwise, must be specifically pleaded.[82] Special rules apply to the award of interest on damages in respect of death or personal injuries.[83]

27–143   **Exercise of the discretion to award interest.** The basic principle[84] is that the court should award interest wherever the defendant's breach of contract deprived the claimant of the opportunity to put the subject-matter of the claim to work to earn profits or income.[85] So where the buyer failed to pay the price of goods sold and delivered to him, interest has been awarded "on the simple commercial basis that if the money had been paid at the appropriate commercial time, the other side would have had the use of it."[86] Where the seller failed to deliver the goods, the buyer's damages should include interest on the normal measure of the damages, *viz.* the difference between the contract price and the market price for substitute goods available at the date fixed for delivery.[87] Again, where the claimant has reasonably incurred expenditure as the result of the defendant's breach,[88] interest should be awarded as damages in respect of that expenditure.[89] The court should not award interest if that would give the claimant double recovery for the same loss: the use of property, or the receipt of the income arising from its use, is the

---

[76] *ibid.* (The defendant could resist any attempt to levy execution on the judgment which failed to give credit for the amount already paid: *ibid.*)

[77] See nn. 64 and 65, *supra.*

[78] *I.M. Properties plc v. Cape & Dalgleish (a firm)* [1999] Q.B. 297, CA. In *President of India v. La Pintada Compania Navigacion SA* [1985] A.C. 104, 129–131, the House of Lords considered this to be a gap in the law. *cf. Mathew v. T.M. Sutton Ltd, supra.*

[79] *I.M. Properties plc v. Cape & Dalgleish, supra.* (The court also said that the court had no power to award interest on any sum paid by a third party in reduction of the plaintiff's claim against the defendant: at 306, but *cf.* 308).

[80] See *post,* § 27–149.

[81] *Ante,* § 27–140; *post,* §§ 31–142—31–145 *et seq.*

[82] CPR, Part 16.4(2): the claimant must give details of the legal basis of the claim and, where a specified amount of money is claimed, the percentage rate claimed, the date from which it is claimed, the total amount claimed up to the date of calculation, and the daily rate at which interest accrues after that date.

[83] s.35A(2) of the 1981 Act; s.69(2) of the 1984 Act. (In particular the court is required, in the absence of special reasons, to award interest on such damages.) See *McGregor on Damages* (16th ed., 1997), §§ 645–653, 659–662, 679–681; and standard textbooks on tort.

[84] *cf.* the statement in a personal injury (tort) case: *Jefford v. Gee* [1970] 2 Q.B. 130, 146.

[85] Interest should be awarded only on money which has been wrongfully withheld: *Business Computers Ltd v. Anglo-African Leasing Ltd* [1977] 1 W.L.R. 578, 587–8.

[86] *Kemp v. Tolland* [1956] 2 Lloyd's Rep. 681, 691. *cf. Marsh v. Jones* (1889) 40 Ch.D. 563.

[87] *Panchaud Frères v. Pagnan and Fratelli* [1974] 1 Lloyd's Rep. 394, 411, 414. See Vol. II, §§ 43–387 *et seq.*

[88] See *ante,* §§ 27–064, 27–098.

[89] *Harbutt's "Plasticine" v. Wayne Tank and Pump Co.* [1970] 1 Q.B. 447. (Overruled on another point: see *ante,* § 14–022.)

equivalent of interest earned by a sum of money.[90] For instance, if the seller retains income-producing property, which would have been transferred to the buyer had he paid the price, the seller should not be given interest on the price if he is entitled to the income arising from the property during the delay until the price is paid.[91] Where the breach of contract deprives the claimant of the use of land or goods, and the court awards him damages for the loss of that use (*e.g.* loss of rents or profits), he should not also be awarded interest on the value (or price) of the land or goods.

Period of interest. In principle, interest should run only from the date (after   **27–144** accrual of the cause of action) when the claimant incurred the loss in question.[92] The court has a discretion to fix a later date,[93] as where the claimant has unreasonably delayed bringing his action.[94] A question about the relevant dates from which interest should run arises when the claimant was insured against the particular loss. In one case,[95] the Court of Appeal was prepared to award interest on damages for the period after the plaintiffs were in fact indemnified by their insurers in respect of the loss. The court implied a term into the contract of insurance, to the effect that the plaintiffs could retain any interest awarded which accrued before the insurers paid the plaintiffs, but that any interest for a later period must go to the insurers.

No power where interest already running. The relevant statutes provide   **27–145** that interest in respect of a debt must not be awarded "for a period during which, for whatever reason, interest on the debt already runs."[96] Hence, if the contract itself fixes interest, the court can only enforce that provision: its statutory power does not override the contractual provision, *e.g.* the court may not fix a different rate of interest.

Rates of interest. The court is empowered to award interest "at different rates   **27–146** in respect of different periods."[97] In business[98] contexts, the rate of interest

---

[90] *Fletcher v. Tayleur* (1855) 17 C.B. 21, 29 (delay in building a ship); *British Columbia Saw Mill Co. Ltd v. Nettleship* (1868) L.R. 3 C.P. 499, 507 (delay in obtaining replacement for goods lost by carrier); *Jaques v. Millar* (1877) 6 Ch.D. 153 (lease). *cf. Bushwall Properties Ltd v. Vortex Properties Ltd* [1975] 1 W.L.R. 1649 (revd. on another point: [1976] 1 W.L.R. 591).

[91] *cf. Janred Properties Ltd v. Ente Nazionale Italiano per il Turismo* [1989] 2 All E.R. 444, 456–457.

[92] *Harbutt's "Plasticine" v. Wayne Tank and Pump Co., supra*; *Metal Box Co. Ltd v. Currys Ltd* [1988] 1 W.L.R. 175 (tort: damages for value of destroyed chattel). *cf. ante*, § 27–079.

[93] This is illustrated in cases not involving breach of contract: *General Tire and Rubber Co. v. Firestone Tyre and Rubber Co.* [1975] 1 W.L.R. 819 (infringement of patent); *B.P. Exploration Co. (Libya) v. Hunt (No. 2)* [1979] 1 W.L.R. 783 (upheld in [1983] A.C. 353) (restitution following frustration).

[94] *Metal Box Co. Ltd v. Currys Ltd, supra.* Another illustration of a later date is the payment of demurrage: *President of India v. Lips Maritime Corporation* [1988] A.C. 395, 424–425.

[95] *H. Cousins & Co. v. D. and C. Carriers Ltd* [1971] 2 Q.B. 230.

[96] s.35A(4) and s.69(4) respectively. See *post*, § 27–149.

[97] s.35A(6) of the 1981 Act; s.69(5) of the 1984 Act. Delay by the claimant in progressing his claim may be reflected in a reduced rate of interest for the overall period (instead of depriving him of all interest for the period of the delay): *Derby Resources A.G. v. Blue Corinth Marine Co. Ltd (No. 2)* [1998] 2 Lloyd's Rep. 425.

[98] In cases where one party is a private person, the Court of Appeal is reluctant to interfere with the judge's discretion in fixing the rate of interest: *Watts v. Morrow* [1991] 1 W.L.R. 1421, 1443–1444, 1446.

should reflect the current commercial rate.[99] The approach of the Commercial Court is to award interest at a rate which broadly represents the rate at which the successful party would have had to borrow the amount recovered over the period in question.[1] The Court of Appeal has upheld the practice of the Commercial Court to award interest at a borrower's rate of 1 per cent. above the base rate prevailing from time to time,[2] but this is only a presumption which can be displaced if its application would be unfair to either party.[3]

27–147   Rules of court may be made[4] fixing the rate of interest which the court may award by reference to the rate fixed from time to time for judgment debts under the Judgment Act 1838[5] or by reference to a rate for which any other enactment provides. The Civil Procedure Rules 1998 contain provisions about interest when the claimant seeks judgment by default, when the claimant makes an offer or when the defendant makes a payment into court. Where the claimant claims interest on a specified amount of money (under section 35A of the 1981 Act or section 69 of the 1984 Act) at a rate no higher than that payable on judgment debts[6] at the date when the claim form was issued, a default judgment may include the amount of interest to the date of judgment.[7] If the claim is for a different rate of interest, the default judgment must exclude interest but judgment may be entered for interest to be decided by the court.[7a] A claimant's Part 36 offer which offers to accept a sum of money, or a Part 36 payment notice (which accompanies a payment into court) will, unless it indicates to the contrary, be treated as inclusive of all interest until the last date on which it could be accepted without needing the court's permission.[8]

27–148   **Debt or damages in foreign currency.** When the debt or damages are calculated in a foreign currency, the rate of interest should be the commercial borrowing rate in that currency in the relevant country.[9]

27–149   **Interest due as of right.** The general statutory powers to award interest which have been examined in the preceding paragraphs do not apply where interest is

---

[99] cf. *The Mecca* [1968] P. 665, 672.

[1] *Cremer v. General Carriers SA* [1974] 1 W.L.R. 341, 355–358.

[2] *Polish SS. Co. v. Atlantic Maritime Co.* [1985] Q.B. 41, 67 (followed in *Metal Box Co. Ltd v. Currys Ltd* [1988] 1 W.L.R. 175, 182–183 (insurers subrogated to a claim in tort for loss of chattels.)). (Base rate replaces the minimum lending rates and the London Interbank Offered Rate, previously used: see *Cia Banca de Panama SA v. George Wimpey & Co. Ltd* [1980] 1 Lloyd's Rep. 598, 615–617; *Shearson Lehman Hutton Inc. v. Maclaine Watson & Co. Ltd* [1990] 3 All E.R. 723, 732–733.)

[3] The *Shearson Lehman* case, *supra*, at 733. Evidence is admissible as to the rate at which persons with the general attributes of the claimant could have borrowed the money: *ibid.*; *Tate & Lyle Food and Distribution Ltd v. G.L.C.* [1982] 1 W.L.R. 149, 154–155.

[4] Under s.35A(5) of the 1981 Act. See CPR Part 12, r.6, *infra*.

[5] s.17. See *post*, § 27–151.

[6] See *post*, § 27–151.

[7] CPR, Part 12, r.6.

[7a] CPR, Part 12, r.6(2). The procedure for deciding the amount of interest is set out in CPR Part 12, r.7.

[8] CPR, Part 36, r.22. If the offer or notice is expressed not to include interest, it must state whether interest is offered, and, if so, the amount offered, the rate offered and the period for which it is offered: CPR, Part 36, r.22(2).

[9] *Miliangos v. George Frank (Textiles) (No. 2)* [1977] Q.B. 489, 497; *Helmsing Schiffahrts v. Malta Drydocks Corporation* [1977] 2 Lloyd's Rep. 444, 449. See further *post*, §§ 31–163—31–172; and Bowles and Phillips (1976) 39 M.L.R. 196.

payable under the terms of the contract itself[10] or under some other special provision.[11] Thus, the Late Payment of Commercial Debts (Interest) Act 1998 confers on the creditor a right under an implied term to "statutory interest" on "qualifying debts" where both parties are acting in the course of a business.[12] Similarly, where the contract itself[13] entitles the seller to claim interest on the price, the seller is not dependent on the exercise of the court's discretion and the court can award interest only at the rate specified in the contract.[14] A suitably worded contractual clause may fix interest to run beyond judgment for the debt.[15]

Arbitration awards. At common law an arbitrator has no power to award   **27–150** general damages in respect of interest on debts paid late.[16] But section 49 of the Arbitration Act 1996[17] provides that (unless the parties agree otherwise) the arbitral tribunal may award simple or compound interest from such date at such rates and with such rests as it considers meets the justice of the case. Such interest may be awarded on the whole or any part of (a) the amount awarded in respect of any period up to the award[18]; and (b) any amount which was claimed in the arbitration and outstanding at the commencement of the arbitral proceedings, but was paid before the award was made in respect of any period up to the date of payment.[19] This power is similar to that granted to courts[20] but wider in that compound interest may be awarded.[21] But the arbitral tribunal cannot award interest on a debt which was paid late but before the proceedings began.[22]

Interest on judgment debts and arbitration awards. A special enactment   **27–151** prescribes the rate of interest on a High Court judgment debt from the time of

---

[10] For illustrations, see Vol. II, §§ 38–246 et seq.

[11] By s.35A(4) of the Supreme Court Act 1981 and s.69(4) of the County Courts Act 1984 the court must not award interest in respect of a debt "for a period during which, for whatever reason, interest on the debt already runs."

[12] Ante, § 27–140; post, Vol. II, §§ 38–256 et seq.

[13] A course of dealing between the parties, or the custom or usages of a particular trade, may lead to an implied term that interest may be charged: see ante, § 27–137.

[14] ss. 137–140 of the Consumer Credit Act 1974 enable the court to re-open certain transactions where the rate of interest is "grossly exorbitant." (cf. ss.244 and 343 of the Insolvency Act 1986). See Vol. II, §§ 38–191 et seq.

[15] Economic Assurance Society v. Usborne [1902] A.C. 147.

[16] President of India v. La Pintada Compania Navegacion SA [1985] A.C. 104. See ante, § 27–137. (In the same case it was held that the Admiralty jurisdiction does not extend to the award of interest on debts already paid, nor to the award of compound interest.)

[17] The Act came into force on January 1, 1997. Since an arbitration agreement impliedly empowers the arbitrator to decide the dispute according to the law existing at the date of his award, s.49 applies to all arbitration agreements under the Act, whenever made: Food Corporation of India v. Marastro Compania Naviera SA of Panama (The Trade Fortitude) [1987] 1 W.L.R. 134 (decided on the previous Act).

[18] See post, § 27–151 for interest after the date of the award.

[19] s.49(3). By s.49(6) the provisions in s.49(3) do not affect any other power of the tribunal to award interest, e.g. ante, § 27–149.

[20] See ante, §§ 27–142 et seq. The power of the arbitral tribunal applies whether the sum claimed is a debt or damages: Edmunds v. Lloyd Italico, etc. SpA [1986] 1 W.L.R. 492, 495–496 (decided on the preceding Act).

[21] See ante, § 27–142.

[22] See the President of India case, supra. (cf. ante, § 27–142.)

entering up the judgment[23]: the current rate is fixed from time to time by statutory instrument.[24] County Court judgments[25] for £5,000 or more which are given on or after July 1, 1991 also carry interest at the same rate.[26] The rate of interest is fixed at the rate in force at the time the judgment was entered up: it does not fluctuate in accordance with later statutory instruments made before the judgment or award is satisfied.[27] By statute,[28] an arbitrator has discretion to decide whether an award should or should not carry interest.[29] By the Arbitration Act 1996[30] an arbitral tribunal may award simple or compound interest from the date of the award (or any later date) until payment: it has discretion to fix the rates of interest and the rests (if any).

27–152   **Rate of exchange.** The question of the appropriate rate of exchange when the debt or damages for breach of contract are calculable in a foreign currency is examined in Chapter 31.[31]

---

[23] s.17 of the Judgments Act 1838 (as amended by s.44(1) of the Administration of Justice Act 1970 which empowers the making of an order amending the rate of interest in s.17). The interest runs from the time of entering up a judgment, on which see *Parsons v. Mather & Platt Ltd* [1977] 1 W.L.R. 855 (approved by the Court of Appeal in *Erven Warnink B.V. v. J. Townend & Sons (Hull) Ltd* [1982] 3 All E.R. 312).

[24] For judgments entered up after April 1, 1993, the rate is 8 per cent.: see Judgment Debts (Rate of Interest) Order 1993 (S.I. 1993 No. 564). On the time from which interest begins to run, see CPR, Part 40.8. However, a clause in the contract may explicitly fix a rate to run on a judgment for a debt: see *ante*, § 27–149.

[25] By s.74 of the County Courts Act 1984 the Lord Chancellor is empowered to provide by order that county court judgments or orders shall carry interest.

[26] The County Courts (Interest on Judgment Debts) Order 1991 (S.I. 1991 No. 1184). Some judgments are excluded from the provision. By S.I. 1998 No. 2400 (L.9) county court judgments in respect of qualifying debts under the Late Payment of Commercial Debts (Interest) Act 1998 (see *ante* § 27–140) are included in the 1991 Order.

[27] *Rocco Giuseppe & Figli v. Tradax Export SA,* [1984] 1 W.L.R. 742 *cf.* the decision of the Privy Council on a New Zealand provision: *Rowling v. Takaro Properties Ltd* [1988] 1 All E.R. 163.

[28] s.49(4) of the Arbitration Act 1996.

[29] Under the previous statutory power (s.20 of the Arbitration Act 1950) it was held that if the arbitration award was silent on the question, it automatically carried interest: *Continental Grain Co. v. Bremer Handelsgesellschaft mbH (No. 2)* [1984] 1 Lloyd's Rep. 121.

[30] s.49(4).

[31] *Post*, §§ 31–163—31–172.

CHAPTER 28

SPECIFIC PERFORMANCE AND INJUNCTION[1]

1. INTRODUCTION

Generally. The common law did not specifically enforce contractual obliga- **28–001** tions except those to pay money. Specific enforcement of other contractual obligations was available only in equity. For the claimant, this was often a more advantageous remedy than the common law remedy of damages. With reference to this equitable remedy, Fry L.J. in his work on *Specific Performance* wrote:

> "If a contract be made and one party to it make default in performance, there appears to result to the other party a right at his election either to insist on the actual performance of the contract, or to obtain satisfaction for the non-performance of it. It may be suggested from this that it follows . . . that it ought to be assumed that every contract is specifically enforceable until the contrary be shown. But so broad a proposition has never, it is believed, been asserted by the judges of the Court of Chancery or their successors in the High Court of Justice, though if prophecy were the function of a law writer, it might be suggested that they will more and more approximate to such a rule."[2]

This prophecy has not been wholly fulfilled, for the scope of the remedy remains subject to many limitations.

Bases of limitations on the remedy. These limitations are based on a number **28–002** of factors. The first is "the heavy-handed nature of the enforcement mechanism,"[3] by reason of which specific enforcement leads (more readily than an award of damages) to attachment of the defendant's person.[4] But this is an

---

[1] Fry, *Specific Performance* (6th ed.); Jones and Goodhart, *Specific Performance* (2nd ed., 1996); Sharpe, *Injunctions and Specific Performance* (2nd ed.); Spry, *Equitable Remedies* (5th ed.).

[2] See now 6th ed., p. 21; *cf.* Burrows (1984) 4 L.S. 102.

[3] *Co-operative Insurance Society Ltd v. Argyll Stores (Holdings) Ltd* [1998] A.C. 1, 12.

[4] *cf. Enfield L.B.C. v. Mahoney* [1983] 1 W.L.R. 749, where even imprisonment failed to induce compliance with an order for specific restitution. "Lawful arrest or detention of a person for non-compliance with the lawful order of a court" is permitted by Human Rights Act 1998, Sched. 1, Part I, art. 5(1)(b).

important factor only where the contract calls for "personal" performance, by the defendant himself. Where the contract is not of this kind, it can be specifically enforced without personal constraint[5]: *e.g.* by sequestration, the appointment of a receiver[6] or by the execution of a formal document by an officer of the court.[7] The second is that the specific enforcement of certain contracts, especially of those for the sale of goods or shares for which there is a market, could, in effect, conflict with the claimant's duty to mitigate his loss by making a substitute contract where this was reasonably possible.[8] Although certain limitations on the scope of specific enforcement are thus justifiable, others are more open to debate: this is, in particular, true of the limitations which are based on the arguments that in certain situations specific relief is either unnecessary or impracticable.[9] In a number of later authorities, some of these reasons are no longer regarded as entirely convincing, so that these cases support some expansion in the scope of the remedy.[10] The most recent decision of the House of Lords[11] on the point may foreshadow some degree of return to a more restrictive view, though with modern justifications.

28–003   **Foundation and nature of the jurisdiction.** The jurisdiction to order specific performance is based on the existence of a valid, enforceable contract. The scope of the remedy is in one respect wider than that of an action for damages, since specific performance may be ordered before there has been any breach.[12] It will not be ordered if the contract suffers from some defect, such as failure to comply with formal requirements or mistake or illegality, which makes the contract invalid or unenforceable: these matters are discussed elsewhere in this book. But even if the contract is unimpeachable in these respects, specific performance will not necessarily be ordered; and the present chapter is mainly concerned with limitations on the availability of the remedy where the contract is not defective.

28–004   **Meaning of "specific performance".** The term "specific performance" will here be used in its traditional sense, to refer to the remedy available in equity to compel a person actually to perform a contractual obligation. Where a person has under a contract become liable to pay a fixed sum of money, the actual perform-ance of that obligation can be enforced by bringing an action for that sum, *e.g.* where a seller of goods sues for the price or where a person who has done work sues for the agreed remuneration. But such actions are not usually described in

---

[5] *cf.* Corbin, *Contracts*, § 1138.

[6] *Miliangos v. George Frank (Textiles) Ltd* [1976] A.C. 443, 494, 497.

[7] *Astro Exito Navegacion SA v. Southland Enterprise Co. Ltd (The Messiniaki Tolmi)* [1983] 2 A.C. 787.

[8] *Ante*, § 27–087; *Buxton v. Lister* (1746) 3 Atk. 383, 384; *Re Schwabacher* (1908) 98 L.T. 127; *cf. Colt v. Nettervill* (1725) 2 P.Wms. 301 (defendant given option of transferring shares or paying the difference between contract and market price on date fixed for performance). See also *Whiteley Ltd v. Hilt* 1918] 2 K.B. 808.

[9] *e.g. post*, §§ 28–013, 28–023.

[10] *e.g. post*, §§ 28–005, 28–013, 28–020.

[11] *Co-operative Insurance Society Ltd v. Argyll Stores Ltd* [1998] A.C. 1.

[12] *Roy v. Kloepfer Wholesale Hardware and Automotive Corp.* [1951] 3 D.L.R. 122; *Thomas Feather & Co. v. Keighley Corp.* (1953) 52 L.G.Rev. 30; *Hasham v. Zenab* [1960] A.C. 316; (1960) 76 L.Q.R. 200. And see *post*, § 28–072, n. 62

English law as actions for specific performance and are not subject to the limitations on the scope of that remedy which are considered in the present chapter.

2. THE "ADEQUACY" OF DAMAGES

Generally. The historical foundation of the equitable jurisdiction in granting   28–005
a decree for specific performance of a contract is that the party seeking it cannot obtain a sufficient remedy by the common law judgment for damages.[13] Hence the traditional view was that specific performance would not be ordered where damages were an "adequate" remedy.[14] Typically, this would be the case where the claimant could readily make a substitute contract for a performance equivalent to that promised by the defendant: the claimant would then be adequately compensated by damages based on the difference between the cost (or market price) of the substitute, and the contract price. Some of the early authorities[15] approach this problem by asking whether damages would *in fact* adequately compensate the claimant. At a later stage in the development of the subject, the courts tended rather to ask whether damages were *likely* to be an adequate remedy for breach of the particular *type* of contract before the court.[16] But more recently the courts have reverted to the earlier approach, by focusing attention on the appropriateness of the remedy of specific performance in the circumstances of each case.[17] The question is not whether damages are an "adequate" remedy, but whether specific performance will "do more perfect and complete justice than an award of damages."[18] The modern approach to this question was well expressed in a case in which an interim injunction was sought: "The standard question . . . , 'Are damages an adequate remedy?' might perhaps, in the light of the authorities in recent years, be rewritten: 'Is it just, in all the circumstances, that a plaintiff should be confined to his remedy in damages?' "[19]

Where action for agreed sum available. A similar approach has been   28–006
adopted to the analogous question whether specific performance could be ordered where the common law action for the agreed sum is also available. At one time, a negative answer was given to this question, apparently because the common law remedy was regarded as an "adequate" one.[20] But the current view is that

---

[13] *Harnett v. Yielding* (1805) 2 Sch. & Lef. 549, 553.

[14] *Co-operative Insurance Society Ltd v. Argyll Stores (Holdings) Ltd* [1998] A.C. 1, 11.

[15] *e.g. Adderley v. Dixon* (1824) 1 S. & S. 607, 610.

[16] *e.g. Cohen v. Roche* [1927] 1 K.B. 169.

[17] *Beswick v. Beswick* [1968] A.C. 58, 88, 90–91, 102; *cf. Coulls v. Bagot's Executor and Trustee Co.* [1967] A.L.R. 385, 412.

[18] *Tito v. Waddell (No. 2)* [1977] Ch. 106, 322; *Rainbow Estates Ltd v. Tokenhold Ltd* [1998] 2 All E.R. 860, 868.

[19] *Evans Marshall & Co. Ltd v. Bertola SA* [1973] 1 W.L.R. 349, 379 (and see the subsequent proceedings: [1975] 2 Lloyd's Rep. 373). *cf.* in a different but analogous context *Miliangos v. George Frank (Textiles) Ltd* [1976] A.C. 443.

[20] *e.g. Crampton v. Varna Ry.* (1872) L.R. 7 Ch.App. 562, 567 ("a money contract not enforceable in this court").

specific performance can be ordered in cases of this kind, if in all the circumstances it is the most appropriate remedy.[21]

28–007   **Land.** The law takes the view that the purchaser of a particular piece of land or of a particular house (however ordinary) cannot, on the vendor's breach, obtain a satisfactory substitute, so that specific performance is available to him.[22] It seems that this is so even though the purchaser has bought for resale. Even a contractual licence to occupy land, though creating no interest in the land[23] be specifically enforced.[24] A vendor of land, too, can get specific performance[25]; for damages will not adequately compensate him if he cannot easily find another purchaser or if he is anxious to rid himself of burdens attached to the land. It seems to make no difference that the land is readily saleable to a third party; or that after contract but before completion a compulsory purchase order is made in respect of it.[26] Yet in such cases damages (based on the difference between the contract price and the resale price, or the compensation payable on the compulsory acquisition) would seem normally to be an adequate remedy.

28–008   **Difficulty of quantifying damages.** In a number of other cases damages are considered to be an inadequate remedy because of the difficulty of quantifying them. For this reason specific performance may be ordered of a contract to execute a mortgage in consideration of money advanced at or before the time of the contract,[27] and of a term of a contract of loan giving the creditor the right to

---

[21] *e.g. Beswick v. Beswick* [1968] A.C. 58; the burden is on the claimant to show that the common law remedy is not adequate: *C.N. Maritime Inc. v. Stena Line A/B (The Stena Nautica) (No. 2)* [1982] 2 Lloyd's Rep. 336, 348.

[22] Fry, *Specific Performance*, § 62; unless he elects to claim damages, as in *Meng Long Development Pte. Ltd v. Jip Hong Trading Co. Pte. Ltd* [1985] A.C. 511. Damages are, however, an adequate remedy for breach of a "lock-out" agreement relating to land (*ante*, § 2–111) since such an agreement is intended merely to protect the prospective purchaser from wasting costs and does not give him any right to insist on conveyance of the land: *Tye v. House* [1997] 2 E.G.L.R. 171.

[23] See *Ashburn Anstalt v. Arnold* [1989] Ch.1; overruled on another ground in *Prudential Assurance Co. Ltd v. London Residuary Body* [1992] A.C. 386.

[24] *Verrall v. Great Yarmouth B.C.* [1981] Q.B. 202.

[25] *Lewis v. Lechmere* (1722) 10 Mod. 503, 505; *Kenney v. Wexham* (1822) 6 Madd. 355; *Adderley v. Dixon* (1824) 1 S. & S. 607, 622; *Clifford v. Turrell* (1841) 1 Y. & C.C.C. 138; *Walker v. Eastern Counties Ry.* (1848) 6 Hare 594; *Miliangos v. George Frank (Textiles) Ltd* [1976] A.C. 443, 496; *cf. Amec Properties v. Planning Research & Systems* [1992] 1 E.G.L.R.70 (specific performance against prospective lessee). Where the purchaser has been allowed to go into possession and has then failed to complete, and the vendor has not elected between rescission and specific performance, the court may (unless the contract otherwise provides) order the purchaser either to perform or to vacate the premises: see *Greenwood v. Turner* [1891] 2 Ch. 144; *Maskell v. Ivory* [1970] Ch. 502; *Attfield v. D.J. Plant Hire & General Contractors* [1987] Ch. 141.

[26] *Hillingdon Estates Co. v. Stonefield Estates Ltd* [1952] Ch. 627. The actual decision may be explicable on the ground of the purchaser's delay.) But specific performance cannot be ordered where the land is sold with vacant possession and before the time for completion the land is requisitioned and possession of it is taken by the requisitioning authorities, for in that case the vendor will be unable to perform his contractual obligation to give possession: *Cook v. Taylor* [1942] 1 Ch. 349; *cf. James Macara Ltd v. Barclay* [1945] K.B. 148 (action for return of deposit); contrast *Re Winslow Hall Estates Co.* [1941] Ch. 503 (possession not taken.) The contract is not frustrated by the making of the order: but after title to the land has vested in the acquiring authority by virtue of the compulsory purchase, the vendor's remedy is in damages and not by way of specific performance: *E. Johnson & Co (Barbados) v. NSR Ltd* [1997] A.C. 400.

[27] *Ashton v. Corrigan* (1871) L.R. 13 Eq. 76. *cf. Swiss Bank Corpn v. Lloyds Bank Ltd* [1982] A.C. 584, 595, affd. *ibid.* at 610; *ante*, § 19–119; *infra*, n. 28.

have the loan repaid out of specific property[28]: the value to the creditor of obtaining security for a debt cannot be precisely quantified. For the same reason, specific performance can be ordered of a contract to pay (or to sell) an annuity,[29] of a contract to indemnify,[30] and of a sale of debts proved in bankruptcy.[31] Damages may also be an inadequate remedy because the claimant's loss is difficult to prove[32] or because certain items of loss[33] are, or may not be, legally recoverable, or quite simply because the defendant may not be "good for the money."[34]

Damages nominal. In *Beswick v. Beswick*[35] specific performance was ordered   **28–009** of a promise to pay an annuity to a third party. One reason[36] why this form of relief was granted was that damages were an inadequate remedy since (in the view of the majority of the House of Lords) they would be purely nominal, the promisee or his estate having suffered no loss.[37] The point here is not that the promisee would be inadequately compensated by damages. It is rather that the party in breach would be unjustly enriched (if damages were the sole remedy) by being allowed to retain the entire benefit of the promisee's performance, while rendering only a small part of his own.

Other factors. Damages may be regarded as inadequate on grounds uncon-   **28–010** nected with a material or financial loss likely to be suffered by the claimant. Thus specific performance has been ordered of a contract to grant a licence to use a hall

---

[28] *Swiss Bank Corp. v. Lloyd's Bank Ltd* [1979] Ch. 548, revd. [1982] A.C. 584 but on the ground that the contract did not, on its true construction, contain any such term. This was also the position in *Kingcroft Insurance Co. Ltd v. H.S. Weaver (Underwriting) Agencies Ltd* [1993] 1 Lloyd's Rep. 187, 193. cf. *Napier & Ettrick v. Hunter* [1993] 1 A.C. 713 recognising that an insurer's right of subrogation gives him an equitable interest in the insured's rights of action.

[29] *Kenney v. Wexham* (1822) 6 Madd. 355; *Swift v. Swift* (1841) 31 I.R.Eq. 267; *Beswick v. Beswick* [1968] A.C. 58, *post*, § 28–045.

[30] *Ranelaugh Earl v. Hayes* (1683) 1 Vern. 189; *Sporle v. Whayman* (1855) 20 Beav. 607; *Anglo-Australian Life Assurance Co. v. British Provident Life and Fire Society* (1862) 3 Giff. 521; *Ascherson v. Tredegar Dry Dock & Wharf Co. Ltd* [1909] 2 Ch. 401. The terms of the decree in *Earl Ranelaugh v. Hayes, supra,* were disapproved insofar as they related to future contingent liabilities in *Lloyd v. Dimmack* (1877) 7 Ch.D. 398 and in *Hughes-Hallett v. Indian Mammoth Gold Mines Co.* (1882) 22 Ch.D. 561; and see Fry, *Specific Performance* (6th ed.), § 1612. But the court may (it seems) grant a declaration in such a case: *Household Machines Ltd v. Cosmos Exporters Ltd* [1947] K.B. 217.

[31] *Adderley v. Dixon* (1824) 1 S. & S. 607.

[32] *Decro-Wall International SA v. Practitioners in Marketing Ltd SA* [1971] 1 W.L.R. 361; but this factor is not decisive as "such difficulties frequently arise in litigation": *Société des Industries Metallurgiques SA v. Bronx Engineering Co. Ltd* [1975] 1 Lloyd's Rep. 465, 468.

[33] See *Hill v. C.A. Parsons Ltd* [1972] 1 Ch. 305; *Evans Marshall & Co. Ltd v. Bertola SA* [1973] 1 W.L.R. 349 (injury to employment prospects or reputation were formerly regarded as items of loss which could not be recovered by an employee: see now *Mahmud v. B.C.C.I.* [1998] A.C. 20).

[34] *Evans Marshall & Co. Ltd v. Bertola SA, supra,* at 380. cf. *Associated Portland Cement Manufacturers Ltd v. Teigland Shipping A/S (The Oakworth)* [1975] 1 Lloyd's Rep. 581, 583; *Eximenco Handels A.G. v. Partrederiet Oro Chef (The Oro Chef)* [1983] 2 Lloyd's Rep. 509, 521; but not merely because the defendant has no assets in the jurisdiction: *Locobail International Finance Ltd v. Agroexport (The Sea Hawk)* [1986] 1 W.L.R. 657, 665; *Lawrence David Ltd v. Ashton* [1989] I.C.R. 123, 134. See also *Themehelp Ltd v. West* [1996] QB 84; *Kall-Kwik Printing (U.K.) v. Bell* [1994] F.S.R. 674.

[35] [1968] A.C. 58; *ante*, § 19–021; *post*, § 28–045. For the effect on such facts of the Contracts (Rights of Third Parties) Bill 1998, see *ante* § 19–079.

[36] For others, see *ante*, § 28–008, at n. 29; *post*, § 19–079.

[37] [1968] A.C. 58, 81, 102; *cf.* 73, 83; *ante*, § 19–046. Lord Pearce thought that damages would be substantial: [1968] A.C. 58, 88.

for a political meeting; and one reason for making the order was said to be that this form of relief would promote freedom of speech and assembly.[38]

28–011   **Cases where damages are regarded as adequate.** Damages are considered to be an adequate remedy where the claimant can readily get the equivalent of what he contracted for from another source. For this reason specific performance is not generally ordered of contracts for the sale of commodities,[39] or of government stock,[40] or of shares which are readily available in the market.[41] On the other hand, a contract to subscribe for shares in a company is specifically enforceable[42]; and so is a contract to buy shares which are not readily available in the market,[43] even (it seems) although the directors of the company have a discretion to refuse to register the transfer.[44]

28–012   **Loans of money.** A contract to lend money cannot, as a general rule, be specifically enforced at the suit of either party[45]: it is assumed that damages, based on current rates of interest, are an adequate remedy. However, section 195 of the Companies Act 1985 provides that a contract to take up and pay for debentures in a company may be specifically enforced.[46]

28–013   **Sale of goods.** Section 52 of the Sale of Goods Act 1979 enables the court to order specific performance where an action is brought for breach of a contract to deliver "specific or ascertained" goods. Although the section only deals with cases in which this remedy is sought by the buyer, the court also has power to order specific performance at the suit of the seller.[47]

---

[38] *Verrall v. Great Yarmouth B.C.* [1981] Q.B. 202.

[39] *Buxton v. Lister* (1746) 3 Atk. 383, 384; *ante*, § 2–002; *cf. Garden Cottage Foods Ltd v. Milk Marketing Board* [1984] A.C. 130 (no injunction against refusal (in violation of art. 86 of the European Community Treaty) to supply butter to a distributor, as his loss of profits could easily be assessed).

[40] *Cud v. Rutter* (1719) 1 P.Wms. 570.

[41] *Re Schwabacher* (1908) 98 L.T. 127, 128; *Chinn v. Hochstrasser* [1979] Ch. 447 (revd. on other grounds [1981] A.C. 533).

[42] *Odessa Tramways Co. v. Mendel* (1878) 8 Ch.D. 235; *Sri Lanka Omnibus Co. v. Perera* [1952] A.C. 76.

[43] *Duncuft v. Albrecht* (1841) 12 Sim. 189; *Cheale v. Kenward* 1858) 3 De G. & J. 27; *Langen & Wind Ltd v. Bell* [1972] Ch. 685; *Jobson v. Johnson* [1989] 1 W.L.R. 1026. *cf. Pao On v. Lau Yiu Long* [1980] A.C. 614, where this point was conceded; *Harvela Investments Ltd v. Royal Trust Co. of Canada (C.I.) Ltd* [1986] A.C. 207 (shares not available in the market and giving a controlling interest in the company); *Grant v. Cigman* [1996] 2 B.C.L.C. 24.

[44] *Hawkins v. Maltby* (1867) L.R. 3 Ch.App. 188, 194; *Stray v. Russell* (1859) 1 E. & E. 888 but see *Bermingham v. Sheridan, Re Waterloo Life Assurance Co. (No. 4)* (1864) 33 Beav. 660; *Poole v. Middleton* (1861) 29 Beav. 646. Specific performance of a contract to buy shares will not (save in exceptional circumstances) be ordered against a purchaser after an order has been made for the company to be wound up since the transfer of the shares would be void against the company: *Sullivan v. Henderson* [1973] 1 W.L.R. 333.

[45] *Rogers v. Challis* (1859) 27 Beav. 175; *Sichel v. Mosenthal* (1862) 30 Beav. 371. *cf. Handley Page Ltd v. Commissioners of Customs & Excise* [1970] 2 Lloyd's Rep. 459.

[46] Reversing *South African Territories v. Wallington* [1898] A.C. 309.

[47] *Astro Exito Navegacion SA v. Southland Enterprise Co. Ltd (The Messiniaki Tolmi)* [1982] Q.B. 1248, affd. without reference to this point [1983] 2 A.C. 787 (sale of ship.) For earlier authorities on the availability of the remedy to the seller, contrast *Shell-Mex Ltd v. Elton Cop Dyeing Co.* (1928) 34 Com.Cas. 39, 47 with *Elliott v. Pierson* [1948] 1 All E.R. 939, 942. The practical effect of an order of specific performance at the suit of the seller would be to enable the seller to get the price in a case falling outside s.49 of the Sale of Goods Act 1979.

The object of section 52[48] was to enlarge the scope of the remedy, which   **28–014** appeared to have been restricted to cases in which the claimant could not get a satisfactory substitute because the goods were "unique." For the purpose of specific relief, heirlooms and great works of art and rare antiques were regarded as "unique"[49]; and it seems that the courts went some way towards recognising a concept of commercial "uniqueness". Thus a contract to supply a ship, or machinery or other industrial plant which could not readily be obtained elsewhere might be specifically enforced.[50] Another special factor which may induce the court to order specific performance of a contract for the sale of goods is that the goods form the contents of a house which is being sold by the same seller to the same buyer, either by the same contract or by a separate contemporaneous one.[51] The court is particularly ready to order specific performance in such a case if removal of the goods would damage the land, but the remedy is not limited to such circumstances.[52] It has also been suggested that under section 52 the court could specifically enforce a contract for the sale of growing timber (so long as it was ascertained) which was to be severed, whether by the vendor or by the purchaser.[53]

Under section 52, the discretion to order specific performance is no longer   **28–015** limited to cases in which the goods are "unique"; but the courts at one time nevertheless took the view that the discretion should be sparingly exercised. One reason for this view is that the specific enforceability of a contract for the sale of goods might give the buyer an equitable interest in the goods,[54] and this could adversely affect third parties who had only constructive (but no actual) notice of

---

[48] And of its precursor, s.2 of the Mercantile Law Amendment Act 1856, which gave effect to a recommendation in the 2nd Report of the Mercantile Law Commission (1855). See Vol. II, § 43–435.

[49] *Pusey v. Pusey* (1684) 1 Vern. 273; *Somerset v. Cookson* (1735) 3 P.Wms. 390; *Lowther v. Lowther* (1806) 3 Ves. 95; a slightly wider view may be taken by *Falcke v. Gray* (1859) 3 Drew. 651, 658.

[50] See *Nutbrown v. Thornton* (1804) 10 Ves. 159; *North v. G.N. Ry.* (1860) 2 Giff. 64; *Behnke v. Bede Shipping Co.* [1927] 1 K.B. 649 the latter decision might have been, but was not, based on the fact that the subject matter was a ship: see *Bathynay v. Bouch* (1881) 50 L.J.Q.B. 221 and *cf.* Lord Simon's statement in *Mardorf Peach & Co. Ltd v. Attica Sea Carriers Corpn of Liberia (The Laconia)* [1977] A.C. 850, 873–874 that "In some respects the law of contract already treats a ship as if she were a piece of realty." See also *Lingen v. Simpson* (1824) 1 S. & S. 600; contrast *Soc. des Industries Metallurgiques SA v. Bronx Engineering Co. Ltd* [1975] 1 Lloyd's Rep. 465 (machinery available from another source). *cf. C.N. Marine Inc. v. Stena Line A/B (The Stena Nautica) (No. 2)* [1982] 2 Lloyd's Rep. 336, where the Court of Appeal recognised that "specific performance can be made in the case of ship" (at 347) but refused to make such an order as the claimant had failed to show that he had a special need for the ship or that damages would not be an adequate remedy; *Eximento Handels A.G. v. Partrederiet Oro Chef (The Oro Chef)* [1983] 2 Lloyd's Rep. 509, 520–521; *Allseas International Management Ltd v. Panroy Bulk Transport Ltd (The Star Gazer)* [1985] 1 Lloyd's Rep. 370; *Gyllenhammer Partners International v. Sour Brodogradevna* [1989] 2 Lloyd's Rep. 403, 422.

[51] *Record v. Bell* [1991] 1 W.L.R. 853, 862.

[52] *ibid.*

[53] *Jones v. Tankerville* [1909] 2 Ch. 440, 445.

[54] For the view that specific enforceability does not necessarily give rise to an equitable interest, see *Tailby v. Official Receiver* (1888) 13 App.Cas 523, 548; *Re London Wine Co. (Shippers)* [1986] P.C.C. 121, 149. *cf.* also *Leigh & Sillavan Ltd v. Aliakmon Shipping Co. (The Aliakmon)* [1986] A.C. 785, where it was said at 812–813 that equitable "ownership" or "title" did not pass under a contract for the sale of unascertained goods on "appropriation" of particular goods to the contract; but damages for breach of the contract would clearly have been an adequate remedy (*post*, § 28–011) so that the question whether an equitable interest in goods can pass under a specifically enforceable contract for the goods remains an open one.

that interest: *e.g.* it could give the buyer priority over not only unsecured but also secured creditors if he had paid for the goods and the seller had then become insolvent.[55] But a restrictive view of the scope of specific performance in contracts for the sale of goods has been taken even where no such prejudice to third parties was likely to result. For example, in *Cohen v. Roche*[56] the court refused specific performance to the buyer of a set of Heppelwhite chairs, saying that they were "ordinary articles of commerce and of no special value or interest."[57] This seems to amount to a refusal to exercise the discretion under section 52 on the ground that the goods were not "unique" in the sense of the old law.[58]

28–016   **"Specific or ascertained" goods.** The court's discretion under section 52 is, furthermore, confined to cases in which the goods are "specific or ascertained."[59] The section therefore does not apply where the goods are purely generic (*e.g.* where the sale is of "1,000 tons of wheat"). Where the goods form an undifferentiated part of an identified bulk, a distinction must, as a result of amendments to the Sale of Goods Act made in 1995,[60] be drawn between two types of cases. The first consists of cases in which the part sold is expressed as a *fraction or percentage* of the bulk: *e.g.* half the cotton shipped on the *Peerless*. Such a contract is one for the sale of specific goods so long as the bulk was identified and agreed on when the contract was made,[61] and the court therefore has a discretion to order specific performance of it under section 52 of the 1979 Act. The second consist of cases in which the part sold is expressed as a *specified quantity* to be taken from an identified bulk: *e.g.* 5,000 out of 10,000 bales of cotton shipped or to be shipped on board the *Peerless*.[62] In such a case[63] the

---

[55] It was the fear of giving the buyer priority over secured creditors that was the main reason why specific performance was refused in *Re Wait* [1927] 1 Ch. 606: see esp. 640. The buyer's problems in that case arose from the general rule, laid down by Sale of Goods Act 1979 s.16, that property under a contract of sale cannot pass in goods which are unascertained: see *Re Goldcorp Exchange Ltd* [1995] 1 A.C. 74; contrast *Re Stapylton Fletcher* [1994] 1 W.L.R. 1181, where the goods were segregated from the seller's own stock after sale. The buyer's interests are now in turn protected by a statutory exception to the general rule in s.16: see s.20A, discussed after n. 62, *infra*. Insolvency of the defendant is not a ground for refusing specific performance where the remedy is normally available as a matter of course: *Amec Properties v. Planning Research and Systems* [1992] 1 E.G.L.R. 70.

[56] [1927] 1 K.B. 169.

[57] At 181; contrast *Phillips v. Lamdin* [1949] 2 K.B. 33 (Adam style door). And see *Rawlings v. General Trading Co.* [1921] 1 K.B. 635 where specific performance of an undertaking to deliver a quantity of shell cases was ordered without argument as to the remedy. The actual decision in that case has been reversed by the Auctions (Bidding Agreements) Act 1927 on a point unconnected with specific performance.

[58] *i.e.* before its amendment in 1856: see *supra*, n. 48. For criticism see Treitel [1966] J.B.L. 211.

[59] "Specific" refers primarily to goods "identified and agreed on at the time a contract of sale is made:" Sale of Goods Act 1979 s.61(1); for an extension of the definition, see *infra* at n. 61. "Ascertained" is not defined in the Act but seems to mean "identified in accordance with the agreement after the time a contract of sale is made:" *Re Wait* [1927] 1 Ch. 606, 630; or identified in any other way: *Thames Sack & Bug Co. Ltd v. Knowles* (1918) 88 L.J.K.B. 585, 588.

[60] By Sale of Gods (Amendment) Act 1995.

[61] Sale of Goods Act 1979, s.61(1), definition of "specific goods" as amended by s.2(a) of the 1995 Act; the bulk must (as in our example) be identified and agreed on when the contract was made.

[62] As in *Re Wait* [1927] 1 Ch. 606.

[63] Sale of Goods Act 1979 s.20A(1), as inserted by s.1(3) of the 1995 Act.

buyer can become owner in common of the goods to the extent that he has paid for them[64] and so he would have less need[65] to seek specific performance to secure priority over other creditors in the event of the seller's insolvency. He would, however, acquire such ownership, not because the goods were specific or ascertained, but in spite of the fact they remained unascertained.[66] Cases of this kind therefore remain outside the scope of the court's discretion under section 52 to order specific performance of a contract for the sale of "specific or ascertained" goods. It is doubtful whether section 52 applies to a contract for the sale of goods to be manufactured or produced by the seller, since such goods may not be "specific or ascertained." It is, moreover, an open question whether specific performance may be ordered in a case falling outside section 52. The section does not in terms say that specific performance is available to a buyer *only* where the goods are "specific or ascertained"; and, even where the goods are not of this kind it is arguable that the remedy should be available on the general principle governing its scope. It should, in other words, be available where, in the particular case, the buyer cannot in fact obtain a substitute or be adequately compensated by damages. This might, for example, be the case where a person who had agreed to make and supply components for a manufacturer then repudiated his undertaking to do so. In such a case, damages for the manufacturer's loss of profits might not be adequate since they "would be a poor consolation if the failure of supplies forces a trader to lay off staff and disappoint his customers (whose affections may be transferred to others) and ultimately forces him towards insolvency. . . . "[67] The view that specific performance could be ordered on such grounds[68] seemed at one stage to have been abandoned[69]; but some more recent cases give it fresh support. During a steel strike in 1980 a manufacturer of steel obtained an order for the specific delivery of a quantity of steel belonging to him against a rail carrier who (in fear of strike action[70]) had refused to allow it to be moved.[71] Specific delivery was ordered because during the strike "steel [was] available only with great difficulty, if at all."[72] It is submitted that in such circumstances specific performance should similarly be available to a buyer. This view is supported by a case in which, during the petrol shortage in 1973 an interim injunction was granted to stop an oil company from cutting off supplies of petrol to a garage, since alternative sources of supply were

---

[64] *ibid.* s.20A(2).

[65] The buyer's property acquired by virtue of s.20A(2) would not necessarily prevail against a competing interest such as that of the bank to which documents of title representing the goods had been pledged, as in *Re Wait, supra;* and where it did not so prevail the court would be unlikely to order specific performance to disturb this state of affairs: see *Benjamin's Sale of Goods* (5th ed.), §§ 18–239, 19–180.

[66] Sale of Goods Act 1979, s.20A(1) refers to the goods (in a case of the present kind) as "a specified quantity of *unascertained* goods".

[67] *Howard E. Perry & Co. v. British Railways Board* [1980] 1 W.L.R. 1375, 1383.

[68] Supported by some early cases: see *Taylor v. Neville* (unrep.), cited with approval in *Buxton v. Lister* (1746) 3 Atk. 386 and in *Adderley v. Dixon* (1824) 1 S. & S. 607; but disapproved in *Pollard v. Clayton* (1855) 1 K. & J. 462.

[69] See *Fothergill v. Rowland* (1873) L.R. 17 Eq. 137; *Pollard v. Clayton* (1855) 1 K. & J. 462; *Dominion Coal Co. v. Dominion Iron and Steel Co.* [1909] A.C. 293. *Donnell v. Bennett* (1883) 23 Ch.D. 835 takes a more liberal view.

[70] *cf. post,* § 28–028.

[71] *Howard E. Perry & Co. v. British Railways Board* [1980] 1 W.L.R. 1375.

[72] *ibid.* at 1383.

not available.[73] The goods in this case were purely generic and the case supports the view that an obligation to deliver goods may be specifically enforced in a case that is not covered by section 52 because the goods are not "specific or ascertained."[74]

3. Contracts not Specifically Enforceable

28–017 **General.** Specific performance of certain types of contracts may be refused, whether or not damages are an adequate remedy. In these cases the reason for refusing the remedy is not that it is unnecessary, but that it may be undesirable to grant it or impracticable to enforce it.

28–018 **Contracts involving personal service.** It has long been settled that a contract of service (or employment) will not, as a general rule, be specifically enforced at the suit of either party.[75] The principle applies where a company director's service agreement is wrongfully determined by the company[76]; but the court may by injunction restrain one director from interfering with the exercise by another director of his powers as such.[77]

28–019 The reason why specific enforcement is not available against an employee is that such an order is thought to interfere unduly with his personal liberty. Legislative force has been given to this principle by the Trade Union and Labour Relations (Consolidation) Act 1992, s.236 of which provides that no court shall compel an employee to do any work by ordering specific performance of a contract of employment or by restraining the breach of such a contract by injunction. Conversely, an employer could not be forced to employ: it was thought to be difficult or undesirable to enforce the continuance of a "personal" relationship between unwilling parties. This principle is also reflected in the provisions of the Employment Rights Act 1996[78] as to the remedies for "unfair" dismissal (which is not normally a breach of contract at all). Under the Act, a tribunal may order the re-instatement or re-engagement of the employee. Such an order is intended to be the employee's primary remedy; but if it is not complied

---

[73] *Sky Petroleum Ltd v. V.S.P. Petroleum Ltd* [1974] 1 W.L.R. 576; *cf.* also *Total Oil Great Britain Ltd v. Thompson Garages (Biggin Hill) Ltd* [1972] 1 Q.B. 318. *Wake v. Renault, The Times,* August 1, 1996 could be explained on the same ground, though the case gives rise to difficulties discussed in § 28–065, *post.*

[74] This possibility was doubted in *Re London Wine Co. (Shippers)* [1986] P.C.C. 121, 149; but in that case it was not necessary to reach a conclusion on the specific enforceability of a contract for the sale of goods which were not "specific or ascertained" since on the facts damages were clearly an adequate remedy: *cf. ante,* § 28–011.

[75] *Johnson v. Shrewsbury & Birmingham Ry.* (1853) 3 D.M. & G. 914; *Brett v. East India Shipping Co.* (1864) 2 H. & C. 404; *Britain v. Rossiter* (1879) 11 Q.B.D. 123, 127; *Rigby v. Connol* (1880) 14 Ch.D. 482, 487; *cf. Whitwood Chemical Co. v. Hardman* [1891] 2 Ch. 416 (injunction); *Taylor v. N.U.S.* [1967] 1 W.L.R. 532 (declaration); *Chappell v. The Times Newspapers* [1975] 1 W.L.R. 482 (injunction) *Scandinavian Tanker Trading Co. A.B. v. Flota Petrolera Ecuatoriana (The Scaptrade)* [1983] 2 A.C. 694, 700–701; *cf. Wishart v. National Association of Citizens' Advice Bureaux* [1990] I.C.R. 794 (where no employment relationship ever came into existence); *Wilson v. St Helen's BC* [1998] 3 W.L.R. 1070, 1087.

[76] *Bainbridge v. Smith* (1889) 41 Ch.D. 462.

[77] *Pulbrook v. Richmond Consolidated Mining Co.* (1878) 9 Ch.D. 610; *Hayes v. Bristol Plant Hire Ltd* [1957] 1 W.L.R. 49; *cf. British Murac Syndicate v. Alperton Rubber Co.* [1915] 2 Ch. 186.

[78] Part X.

with, the employer can, in the last resort, only be ordered to pay compensation.[79] Where an employee is dismissed in breach of contract, his normal remedy is a claim for damages or a declaration that the dismissal was *wrongful*: not specific enforcement, or a declaration that the dismissal was *invalid*.[80] The statutory "right to return to work"[81] after maternity leave appears likewise not to be specifically enforceable.[82]

Exceptions. The arguments usually advanced in support, of the equitable **28–020** principle are no longer wholly convincing[83] and the principle is subject to a growing list of exceptions. A person who is dismissed from a public office in breach of the terms of his appointment may be entitled to re-instatement[84]; and the Visitor of a University has power to order the reinstatement of a wrongfully dismissed lecturer (even where such a remedy would not be available in the ordinary courts),[85] such a dismissal being, if it amounts to a violation of the

---

[79] Employment Rights Act 1996, ss.113–117. Under ss.129(9) and 130 of the 1996 Act, orders may be made for the continuation of the contract, but these do not give rise to the remedy of specific performance. *cf.* also Sex Discrimination Act 1975, ss.65(1)(*c*), 65(3)(a), 71(1); Race Relations Act 1976, ss.56(1)(c), 56(4); Reserve Forces (Safeguard of Employment) Act 1985, ss.10, 17 and 18; Trade Union and Labour Relations (Consolidation) Act 1992, ss.152–167 (as amended by s.49 and Scheds 7 and 8 of Trade Union Reform and Employment Rights Act 1993) (dismissal on grounds related to trade union membership or activities); Disability Discrimination Act 1995; s.8(5) and Sched. 3, para. 2(1).

[80] *Francis v. Kuala Lumpur Councillors* [1962] 1 W.L.R. 1411; *Vidyodaya University Council v. Silva* [1965] 1 W.L.R. 77; *Gunton v. London Borough of Richmond-upon-Thames* [1981] Ch. 448; *Marsh v. National Autistic Society* [1993] I.C.R. 453. A declaration may also be made that a *decision* by a disciplinary committee leading to dismissal was void for failure to comply with the rules of natural justice: *Stevenson v. United Road Transport Union* [1977] I.C.R. 893; but this does not amount to a declaration that the *contract* remains in operation: *ibid.* at 906; *cf. R. v. Berkshire H.A., ex p. Walsh* [1985] Q.B. 152 (judicial review not available as remedy for allegedly wrongful dismissal of senior nursing officer by Health Authority since no "public law" issue was involved); *R. v. Derbyshire C.C., ex p. Noble* [1990] I.C.R. 808; *McLaren v. Home Office* I.C.R. 824 (claim by prison officer raised no issue of public law); *Roy v. Kensington, etc., Family Practitioner Committee* [1992] 1 A.C. 624 (private law remedy available to general practitioner in respect of practice allowance); contrast *R. v. Secretary of State for the Home Department, ex p. Benwell* [1985] Q.B. 554 (judicial review available as a remedy for allegedly wrongful dimissal of prison officer; not followed on other grounds in *R. v. Secretary of State for the Home Department, ex p. Broom* [1986] Q.B. 198); *R. v. Civil Service Appeal Board, ex p. Bruce* [1989] I.C.R. 171 (judicial review refused to dismissed civil servant as other, preferable, remedies avaliable); *R. v. Crown Prosecution Service, ex p. Hogg, The Times,* April 14, 1994 (no judicial review of dismissal of lawyer employed by Crown Prosecution Service). For exceptions to this aspect of the principle against specific enforceability, see *infra,* after n. 88.

[81] Employment Rights Act 1996, ss.79–85.

[82] ss.79–85 of the 1996 Act contain no provisions as to remedies for infringement of the right.

[83] See Clark (1969) 32 M.L.R. 532.

[84] *Ridge v. Baldwin* [1964] A.C. 40; Ganz (1967) 30 M.L.R. 288; *Malloch v. Aberdeen Corpn.* [1971] 1 W.L.R. 1578; *Chief Constable of the North Wales Police v. Evans* [1982] 1 W.L.R. 1155; *R. v. Secretary of State for the Home Department, ex p. Benwell* [1985] Q.B. 554 (*supra,* n. 80); *cf. Jones v. Lee* (1979) L.G.R. 213 (injunction against dismissal of teacher.) The line between "ordinary" and "public" employment is by no means clear cut: see *Barber v. Manchester Regional Hospital Board* [1958] 1 W.L.R. 181; *Tucker v. Trustees of the British Museum* [1967] C.L.Y. 1430; and criticisms of the *Vidyodaya University* case, *supra,* in *Malloch v. Aberdeen Corpn., supra,* at 1595.

[85] *Thomas v. University of Bradford* [1987] A.C. 795, 824; for subsequent proceedings, see [1992] 1 All E.R. 964, where it was held by the Visitor that the lecturer's removal would have been invalid for procedural irregularities if these had not been waived by the lecturer.

University's Statutes, not merely wrongful but also invalid.[86] The continuance or creation of a "personal" relationship may be enforced where an injunction is granted against expulsion from a social club,[87] or against the refusal of a professional association to admit a person to membership.[88]

More generally, the modern relationship of employer and employee is often much less personal than the old relationship of master and servant was believed to be; and there are signs that the courts are prepared to re-examine or qualify the old equitable principle in the light of this development.[89] Industrial conditions may in fact force an employer to retain an employee whom he would prefer to dismiss or to dismiss one whom he is perfectly willing to retain. For example, in *Hill v. C.A. Parsons Ltd*[90] employers were forced by union pressure to dismiss an employee. The dismissal amounted to a breach of contract and the court issued an injunction to restrain the breach, thus in effect re-instating the employee. As the employers and the employee were perfectly willing to maintain their relationship, the decision does not seem to violate the spirit of the general equitable principle against the specific enforcement of employment contracts. An injunction to restrain dismissal can also be issued in respect of a period during which no services are to be rendered under the contract. Thus where an employee had been suspended on full pay while disciplinary proceedings against him were in progress, it was held that the employers could be restrained from dismissing him before the disciplinary proceedings had run their full course.[91]

28–021   **Scope.** The equitable principle of refusing specific performance extends to contracts involving personal service even though they are not contracts *of* service. Thus it has been held that an agreement to allow an auctioneer to sell a collection of works of art cannot be specifically enforced by either party.[92] Similarly an agreement to enter into a partnership will not be specifically enforced[93] as "it is impossible to make persons who will not concur carry on a business jointly for their common advantage."[94] But a contract for the sale of a

---

[86] *Pearce v. University of Aston (No.2)* [1991] 2 All E.R. 469. The Visitor's decision on the interpretation of the University's statutes is not subject to judicial review: *R. v. Hull University Visitor, ex p. Page* [1993] A.C. 682 (where the Visitor had held the dismissal to be in accordance with those Statutes).

[87] *Young v. Ladies Imperial Club Ltd* [1920] 2 K.B. 522; *post*, § 28–066. See also Sex Discrimination Act 1975, s.71(1) and Race Relations Act 1976, s.62 (injunction against "persistent" discrimination.)

[88] *cf. Nagle v. Feilden* [1966] 2 Q.B. 633; *post*, § 28–069; doubted on the availability of specific relief in *R. v. Disciplinary Committee of the Jockey Club, ex p. Aga Khan* [1993] 1 W.L.R. 909, 933. *cf. R. v. Fernhill Manor School* [1993] FLR 620 (no judicial review of expulsion from private school).

[89] See *C.H. Giles & Co. Ltd v. Morris* [1972] 1 W.L.R. 307.

[90] [1972] 1 Ch. 305; Hepple [1972] C.L.J. 47; *cf. Irani v. Southampton, etc. H.A.* [1985] I.C.R. 590 (where the employers retained confidence in an employee but had dismissed him because of differences between him and another employee); *Powell v. London Borough of Brent* [1988] I.C.R. 176; *Hughes v. Southwark L.B.C.* [1988] I.R.L.R. 55. *Jones v. Gwent C.C.* [1992] I.R.L.R. 521, 526 goes even further and is hard to reconcile with the authorities cited in n. 80, *supra*.

[91] *Robb v. Hammersmith and Fulham B.C.* [1991] I.R.L.R. 72.

[92] *Chinnock v. Sainsbury* (1861) 30 L.J.Ch. 409; *cf. Mortimer v. Beckett* [1920] 1 Ch. 571.

[93] *Scott v. Rayment* (1868) L.R. 7 Eq. 112; *England v. Curling* (1844) 8 Beav. 129, 137.

[94] *England v. Curling, supra*, at 137. On the same principle, specific performance has been refused of a house-sharing arrangement which had been made between members of a family who later quarrelled: *Burrows and Burrows v. Sharp* (1991) 23 H.L.R. 82, where the basis of liability was not contract but proprietary estoppel.

share in a partnership may be specifically enforced where it does not involve personal service or continuing personal relations between the contracting parties.[95] Even where personal service or a continuing personal relationship is involved, the court can order the execution of a formal partnership agreement and leave the parties to their legal remedies on the agreement.[96] Similarly, the court can order the execution of a service contract even though that contract, when made, may not be specifically enforceable.[97]

Specific performance is refused in the above cases because the courts are **28–022** reluctant to force the parties to enter into, or to continue in, a personal relationship against the will of one of the parties. It follows that the refusal of specific performance on this ground is limited to cases in which the services are personal in nature. There is no general rule against the specific enforcement of a contract merely because one party has contracted to provide services.[98] Thus specific performance can be ordered of a contract to publish a piece of music,[99] and sometimes of contracts to build.[1] It has, indeed, been suggested that a time charterparty cannot be specifically enforced against the shipowner because it is a contract for services[2]; but the services that the shipowner undertakes to provide under such a contract will often be no more personal than those to be rendered by a building under a building contract. Denial of specific performance in the case of time charters is best explained on other grounds.[3]

Constant supervision. The court will not specifically enforce a contract **28–023** under which one party is bound by continuous duties, the due performance of which might require constant supervision by the court.[4] In *Ryan v. Mutual Tontine Association*[5] the lease of a service flat gave the tenant the right to the services of a porter who was to be "constantly in attendance." Specific enforcement of this right was refused on the ground that it would have required "that constant superintendence by the court, which the court in such cases has always declined to give."[6] For the same reason the courts have refused specifically to enforce a tenant's undertaking to cultivate a farm in a particular manner[7]; the

---

[95] See *Dodson v. Downey* [1901] 2 Ch. 620.

[96] As in *England v. Curling* (1844) 8 Beav. 129, where the object of obtaining such an order was to prevent one of the contracting parties from competing in business with the other and to procure a judicial determination of the exact terms that had been agreed.

[97] *C.H. Giles & Co. Ltd v. Morris* [1972] 1 W.L.R. 307; *cf. Posner v. Scott-Lewis* [1987] Ch. 25.

[98] *e.g. Regent International Hotels v. Pageguide, The Times,* May 13, 1985 (injunction against preventing claimant company from managing a hotel); *Posner v. Scott-Lewis* [1987] Ch. 25 (*post,* § 28–023.)

[99] *Barrow v. Chappel & Co.* (unreported) cited in *Joseph v. National Magazine Co.* [1959] Ch. 14. It is assumed that it can be clearly shown exactly what is to be published: *cf. post,* § 28–038.

[1] *Post,* § 28–025.

[2] *Scandinavian Tanker Co. A.B. v. Flota Petrolera Ecuatoriana (The Scaptrade)* [1983] 2 A.C. 694, 700–701.

[3] See *post,* § 28–023 at n. 11.

[4] This principle plainly does not apply to continuous obligations to pay money, *e.g.* under an agreement to pay an annuity, for it is well settled that such an agreement can be specifically enforced: *ante,* § 28–008.

[5] [1893] 1 Ch. 116.

[6] *ibid.* at 123.

[7] *Rayner v. Stone* (1762) Eden 128; *Phipps v. Jackson* (1887) 56 L.J.Ch. 550. *cf. Hill v. Barclay* (1810) 16 Ves.Jun. 402 (tenant's covenant to repair); contrast *Jeune v. Queens Cross Properties Ltd* [1974] Ch. 97 (landlord's covenant to repair); *Barrett v. Lounava (1982) Ltd* [1990] 1 Q.B. 348 (landlord's implied covenant to repair).

obligations of a railway company to operate signals and to provide engine power[8]; a contract to keep an airfield in operation[9]; a contract to keep a shop open[10]; the obligations of a shipowner under a voyage charterparty[11]; and a contract to deliver goods by instalments.[12] The difficulty of supervision is also one ground that has been given for the refusal of the courts in some cases specifically to enforce contracts to do building work[13] or to keep buildings in repair.[14] But in such cases specific performance is sometimes ordered and no practical difficulty seems to have arisen in enforcing such orders.[15] This suggests that the "difficulty" of supervision has been somewhat exaggerated; and various devices at the court's disposal can be used to overcome it. The court can, for example, appoint a receiver to perform the acts specified in the order,[16] or appoint an expert to act as officer of the court for the purpose, or it can authorise the plaintiff to appoint a person to act as agent of the defendant for the purpose of performing those acts.[17] Where the acts to be done under the contract are not to be done by the defendant personally, the court can order him simply to enter into a contract to procure those acts to be done. From this point of view, *Ryan v. Mutual Tontine Association*[18] may be contrasted with *Posner v. Scott-Lewis*[19] where the lessor of a block of luxury flats covenanted, so far as lay in his power, to employ a resident porter to perform a number of specified tasks. It was held that the covenant was specifically enforceable in the sense that the lessor could be ordered to appoint a resident porter for the execution of the specified services.

28–024   **Competing factors.** This balancing of arguments for and against ordering specific performance in cases of this kind is well illustrated by *Co-operative Insurance Society Ltd v. Argyll Stores (Holdings) Ltd*[20] where a 31-year lease of premises for use as a food supermarket in a shopping centre contained a covenant by the tenant to keep the premises "open for retail trade during the usual hours

---

[8] *Powell Duffryn Steam Coal Co. v. Taff Vale Ry.* (1874) L.R. 9 Ch.App. 331; *Blackett v. Bates* (1865) L.R. 1 Ch.App. 117.

[9] *Dowty Boulton Paul Ltd v. Wolverhampton Corpn* [1971] 1 W.L.R. 204; for later proceedings in this case, see [1973] Ch. 94.

[10] *Braddon Towers Ltd v. International Stores Ltd* [1987] E.G.L.R. 209 (decided in 1959); *Co-operative Insurance Society Ltd v. Argyll Stores (Holdings) Ltd* [1998] A.C. 1, *post*, § 28–024.

[11] *De Mattos v. Gibson* (1858) 4 D. & J. 276. The view expressed in *Scandinavian Tanker Co. A.B. v. Flota Petrolera Ecuatoriana (The Scaptrade)* [1983] 2 A.C. 694, 700–701, that a time charter cannot be specifically enforced against the shipowner, is best explained on the ground that such enforcement would require too much supervision.

[12] *Dominion Coal Co. v. Dominion Iron & Steel Co.* [1909] A.C. 293. But see *ante*, § 28–016, at n. 73.

[13] *Post*, § 2–025.

[14] *Flint v. Brandon* (1803) 8 Ves. 159; *Wheatley v. Westminster Brymbo Coal Co.* (1869) L.R. 9 Eq. 538; but see *Jeune v. Queens Cross Properties Ltd, supra*, n. 7.

[15] See *Storer v. G.W. Ry.* (1842) 2 Y. & C.C.C. 48 (agreement to construct and "for ever thereafter to maintain one neat archway": specific performance decreed); *Kennard v. Cory Bros.* [1922] 2 Ch. 1 (mandatory injunction to keep a drain open); *Rainbow Estates Ltd v. Tokenhold Ltd* [1998] 2 All E.R. 860.

[16] *cf. Gibbs v. David* (1870) L.R. 20 Eq. 373 (receiver appointed in a rescission action to run a mine.)

[17] *cf.* Law of Property Act 1925, s.101; Insolvency Act 1986, s.44 (as amended by Insolvency Act 1994, s.2).

[18] *Supra* at n. 5.

[19] [1987] Ch. 25; Jones [1987] C.L.J. 21.

[20] [1998] A.C. 1.

of business". Some six years after the commencement of the lease, the super-market was running at a loss and the tenant ceased trading there. The main reason given by the House of Lords for refusing to order specific performance was the difficulty of supervising the enforcement of the order since the question whether it was being complied with might require frequent reference to the court. For this purpose, Lord Hoffmann distinguished between orders (such as that sought here) "to carry on an activity" and orders "to achieve a result." In the latter case, "the court . . . only has to examine the finished work"[21] so that compliance with the order could be judged *ex post facto*: it was on this ground that the cases in which building contracts had been specifically enforced[22] were to be explained. It should, however, be emphasised that difficulty of supervision was not the sole ground for refusing specific performance. Lord Hoffmann referred also to a number of other factors, such as the "heavy-handed nature of the enforcement mechanism"[23] by proceedings for contempt; the injustice of compelling the tenant to carry on business at a loss which might well exceed the loss which the landlord would be likely to suffer if the covenant were broken; and the fact that it was not "in the public interest for the courts to require someone to carry on business at a loss if there is any plausible alternative by which the other party can be given compensation,"[24] *i.e.* by way of damages. Reliance on such factors suggests that, if the court attaches sufficient importance to the claimant's interest in specific enforcement, it will not be deterred from granting such relief merely on the ground that it will require constant supervision. The outcome in each case will depend on the "cumulative effect"[25] of this factor together with any others which favour[26] or (as in the *Co-operative Insurance* case) militate against specific relief.[27]

Building contracts: specific enforcement against builder. The general rule   **28–025**
is that a contract to erect a building cannot be specifically enforced against the builder. There seem to be three reasons for this rule. First, damages may be an adequate remedy if another builder can be engaged to do the work. Secondly, the contract may be too vague to be specifically enforced if it fails to describe the work to be done under it with sufficient certainty.[28] And thirdly, specific enforcement of the contract may require more supervision than the court is willing to provide.[29] But where the first two reasons do not apply, the third has not been

---

[21] *ibid.* at 13; all the other members of the House of Lords agreed with Lord Hoffmann's speech.

[22] *Post,* § 28–025.

[23] [1988] A.C. 1, 12.

[24] *ibid.* at 15.

[25] *ibid.* at 16.

[26] See *Luganda v. Service Hotels* [1969] 2 Ch. 206 (mandatory injunction ordering defendants to allow a protected tenant, who had been wrongfully locked out of a room in a residential hotel, to resume his residence in the hotel); *cf. Films Rover International Ltd v. Cannon Film Sales Ltd* [1987] 1 W.L.R. 670, 682 (for further proceedings, see [1989] 1 W.L.R. 912); *Sutton Housing Trust v. Lawrence* (1987) 19 H.L.R. 520.

[27] *cf. Shiloh Spinners Ltd v. Harding* [1973] A.C. 691, 724 where difficulty of supervision is said to be no longer a bar to relief against forfeiture for breach of a covenant to repair (as it had been in *Hill v. Barclay* (1810) 16 Ves.Jun. 402), but the possibility is recognised that such difficulty sometimes "explains why specific performance cannot be granted." *cf.* also the interpretation of these remarks in *Co-operative Insurance Society Ltd v. Argyll Stores (Holdings) Ltd* [1998] A.C. 1, 14 as relating to relief against forfeiture rather than to the availability of specific performance and doubting their interpretation in *Tito v. Waddel (No. 2)* [1977] Ch. 106, 322.

[28] As in *Mosley v. Virgin* (1796) 3 Ves. 184; *cf. post,* § 28–038.

[29] *Ante,* § 28–023.

allowed to prevail. Specific performance of a contract to erect or to repair buildings can therefore be ordered if (i) the work is precisely defined; (ii) damages will not adequately compensate the claimant; and (iii) the defendant is in possession of the land on which the work is to be done so that the claimant cannot get the work done by another builder.[30]

28–026   **Building contracts: specific enforcement against owner.** The converse question may also arise whether the builder can, in effect, compel the owner to allow him to complete the work. In *Hounslow (London Borough) v. Twickenham Gardens Ltd*[31] a building contract gave a builder a contractual licence to enter the owner's land to execute the agreed work. The licence was held to be irrevocable till the work had been done, but the owner wrongfully purported to terminate it and sought an injunction to restrain the builder from entering the land, and damages for trespass. These claims failed as the purported termination was wrongful and ineffective. It seems, however, that if the licence had not been irrevocable, or if the owner's active co-operation had been required for the completion of the work, the builder's sole remedy would have been in damages.[32]

4. OTHER GROUNDS FOR REFUSING SPECIFIC PERFORMANCE

28–027   **General.** Specific performance is a discretionary remedy.[33] It may be refused although the contract is binding at law and cannot be impeached on some specific equitable ground (such as undue influence); although damages are not an adequate remedy;[34] and although the contract does not fall within the group of contracts, discussed above, which will not be specifically enforced. But the discretion to refuse specific performance is "not an arbitrary . . . discretion but one to be governed as far as possible by fixed rules and principles."[35] In particular, the court may refuse to order specific performance on the grounds to be discussed in the following paragraphs. Its discretion to refuse specific performance on such grounds cannot be excluded by the terms of the contract.[36]

28–028   **Severe hardship to defendant.** Specific performance may be refused on the ground that the order will cause severe hardship to the defendant. Thus in

---

[30] *Wolverhampton Corpn v. Emmons* [1901] 1 Q.B. 515, as modified by *Carpenters Estates Ltd v. Davies* [1940] Ch. 160; *Jeune v. Queens Cross Properties Ltd* [1974] Ch. 97 (landlord ordered to restore collapsed balcony in performance of repairing covenant); *Price v. Strange* [1978] Ch. 337, 357; *cf.* Landlord and Tenant Act 1985, s.17; *Gordon v. Selico* (1986) 278 E.G. 53. *Barrett v. Lounava* [1990] 1 Q.B. 348; *Tustian v. Johnson* [1993] 2 All E.R. 675, 681 (revsd. in part on other grounds [1993] 3 All E.R. 534); *Rainbow Estates Ltd v. Tokenhold Ltd* [1998] 3 All E.R. 860, 864, 870; and see *Channel Tunnel Group Ltd v. Balfour Beatty Construction Ltd* [1993] A.C. 334, where the House of Lords took the view that it had jurisdiction to restrain a building contractor by injunction from stopping work, but refused such relief as a matter of discretion.
[31] [1971] Ch. 233; contrast *Mayfield Holdings v. Moana Reef* [1973] 1 N.Z.L.R. 309.
[32] *cf. Finelli v. Dee* (1968) 67 D.L.R. (2d) 393.
[33] *Scott v. Alvarez* [1895] 2 Ch. 603, 612; *Stickney v. Keeble* [1915] A.C. 386, 419.
[34] *Co-operative Insurance Society Ltd v. Argyll Stores (Holdings) Ltd* [1998] A.C. 1, 12 ("even when damages are not an adequate remedy").
[35] *Lamare v. Dixon* (1873) L.R. 6 H.L. 423; *Holliday v. Lockwood* [1917] 2 Ch. 56, 57; *Co-operative Insurance Society Ltd v. Argyll Stores (Holdings) Ltd* [1998] A.C. 1, 16.
[36] *Quadrant Visual Communications Ltd v. Hutchison Telephone (U.K.) Ltd* [1993] B.C.L.C. 442.

Denne v. Light[37] the court refused specific performance, against the buyer, of a contract to purchase farming land wholly surrounded by land which belonged to others and over which the buyer would have no right of way. Specific performance may also be refused where the cost of performance to the defendant is wholly out of proportion to the benefit which performance will confer on the claimant[38]; and where the defendant can put himself into a position to perform only by taking legal proceedings against a third party (especially if the outcome of such proceedings is in doubt.)[39] Severe hardship may be a ground for refusing specific performance even though it results from circumstances which arise after the conclusion of the contract, which affect the person of the defendant rather than the subject matter of the contract, and for which the claimant is in no way responsible. For example, in *Patel v. Ali*[40] specific performance of a contract for the sale of a house was refused after a four-year delay (for which neither party was responsible), the vendor's circumstances having during this time changed disastrously as a result of her husband's bankruptcy and of an illness which had left her disabled. On the other hand, "mere pecuniary difficulties" would "afford no excuse."[41] Thus the purchaser of a house will not be denied specific performance merely because the vendor finds it difficult, on a rising market, to acquire alternative accommodation with the proceeds of the sale.[42] Nor will specific performance be refused merely because compliance with the order exposes the defendant to the risk of a strike by his employees.[43]

Unfairness and surprise. The court may refuse specific performance of a   **28–029** contract which has been obtained by means that are unfair, even though they do not amount to grounds on which the contract can be invalidated. In *Walters v. Morgan*[44] the defendant agreed to grant the claimant a mining lease over land which the defendant had only just bought. Specific performance was refused on the ground that the defendant was "surprised and was induced to sign the agreement in ignorance of the value of his property."[45] It seems that mere failure by the claimant to disclose factors which affect the value of the property, or the defendant's willingness to contract with him, would not be a ground for refusing specific performance. Something more must be shown: for example, that the claimant has taken unfair advantage of his superior knowledge. In *Walters v. Morgan* the court relied on the fact that the claimant had hurried the defendant into the transaction before he could discover the true value of the property. On the same principle it seems that specific performance may be refused where the

---

[37] (1857) 8 D.M. & G. 774; *cf. Wedgewood v. Adams* (1843) 6 Beav. 600. See also *Sullivan v. Henderson* [1973] 1 W.L.R. 333, *ante*, § 28–011, n. 44; *Jaggard v. Sawyer* [1995] 1 W.L.R. 269 (injunction); *Insurance Co. v. Lloyd's Syndicate* [1995] 1 Lloyd's Rep. 273, 276 (injunction).

[38] *Tito v. Waddell (No. 2)* [1977] Ch. 106, 326; *Morris v. Redland Bricks Ltd* [1970] A.C. 652, and *post*, § 28–045, n. 90.

[39] *Wroth v. Tyler* [1974] Ch. 30 (where an additional ground for refusing specific performance was that the third party against whom the proceedings would have to be taken was the defendant's wife, so that the proceedings would tend to split up the family); *cf. Watts v. Spence* [1976] Ch. 165, 173.

[40] [1984] Ch. 238.

[41] *ibid.* at 288; *cf. Francis v. Cowcliffe* (1977) 33 P. & C.R. 386.

[42] *Mountford v. Scott* [1975] Ch. 258; *cf. Easton v. Brown* [1981] 3 All E.R. 278.

[43] *Howard E. Perry & Co. v. British Railways Board* [1980] 1 W.L.R. 1375.

[44] (1861) 3 D.F. & J. 718; *cf. Evans v. Llewellin* (1781) 1 Cox C.C. 333; *Quadrant Visual Communications v. Hutchison Telephone (U.K.) Ltd* [1993] B.C.L.C. 442; contrast *Mountford v. Scott* [1975] Ch. 258.

[45] (1861) 3 D.F. & J. (1861) 718, 723.

claimant has taken advantage of the defendant's drunkenness, though it was not so extreme as to invalidate the contract at law.[46] The claimant's failure to disclose his own breach of the contract, reducing the value of the subject matter,[47] has also been held to be a ground for refusing specific performance, even though the non-disclosure was not a ground for setting the contract aside at law.

28–030   **Inadequacy of consideration.** The authorities on inadequacy of consideration as a ground for refusing specific performance are not easy to reconcile. On the one hand it is settled that *mere* inadequacy of consideration is not a ground for refusing to grant the remedy.[48] On the other hand the statement that inadequacy of consideration is not a ground for refusing specific performance unless it is "such as shocks the conscience and amounts in itself to conclusive and decisive evidence of fraud"[49] is probably too narrow, even when allowance is made for the possibility that fraud may have had a wider meaning in equity than at law. The best view seems to be that specific performance may be refused where inadequacy of consideration is coupled with some other factor not necessarily amounting to fraud or other invalidating cause at law—for example, mistake that is operative only in equity,[50] surprise[51] or unfair advantage taken by the claimant of his superior knowledge or bargaining position.[52] Specific performance may be refused on the ground of inadequacy of consideration even though the circumstances do not justify rescission of the contract.[53]

28–031   **Lack of consideration.** On the principle that equity will not aid a volunteer, specific performance will not be ordered of a gratuitous promise[54] even though it is binding at law because it is made by deed or supported by a nominal consideration[55] so that an action at law for the agreed sum or for damages can successfully be brought upon it. Where such a promise is made to a trustee for the benefit of a third party, it has been held that the trustee ought not to enforce the promise at law against the promisor[56] unless the promise can be considered to create a trust which is "already perfect."[57] After the coming into force of the Contracts (Rights of Third Parties) Bill 1998, promises for the benefit of a third party will (if the statutory requirements are satisfied) be enforceable not only by the promisee, but also by the third party,[57a] who will then have the right of

---

[46] *Malins v. Freeman* (1837) 2 Keen 25, 34.

[47] *Quadrant Visual Communications v. Hutchison Telephone (U.K.) Ltd, supra,* n. 44.

[48] *Collier v. Brown* (1788) 1 Cox C.C. 428; *Western v. Russell* (1814) 3 V. & B. 187; *Haywood v. Cope* (1858) 25 Beav. 140.

[49] *Coles v. Trecothick* (1804) 9 Ves. 234, 246.

[50] *Webster v. Cecil* (1861) 30 Beav. 62.

[51] *Ante,* § 28–029; *cf. Mortlock v. Buller* (1804) 10 Ves. 292.

[52] *Falcke v. Gray* (1859) 4 Drew. 651.

[53] See *Mortlock v. Buller, supra.*

[54] *Jeffreys v. Jeffreys* (1841) Cr. & Ph. 138.

[55] See *Re Parkin* [1892] 3 Ch. 510; *Cannon v. Hartley* [1949] Ch. 213. Contrast *Gurtner v. Circuit* [1968] 2 Q.B. 587 where the agreement between the Minister and the Motor Insurers' Bureau was said to be specifically enforceable by the Minister. The agreement was made by deed but no consideration seems to have moved from the Minister. *cf. ante,* § 19–113.

[56] *Re Pryce* [1917] 1 Ch. 234; *Re Kay* [1939] Ch. 239; criticised by Elliott (1960) 76 L.Q.R. 100; Hornby (1962) 78 L.Q.R. 228; Matheson (1966) 29 M.L.R. 397; Barton (1975) 91 L.Q.R. 236; Meagher and Lehane (1976) 92 L.Q.R. 427. This rule does not apply where a promise in favour of a third party volunteer is made to a promisee who has provided consideration: *Beswick v. Beswick* [1968] A.C. 58. *Ante,* § 19–021, *post,* §§ 28–045, 28–046.

[57] *Fletcher v. Fletcher* (1844) 4 Hare 67, 74.

[57a] *Ante,* § 19–075 *et seq.*

enforcement even though he has not provided any consideration for the promise.[57b] The third party will, moreover, have available to him any remedy, including specific performance, that "would have been available to him in an action for breach of the contract if he had been a party to the contract.[57c] Nothing in the Bill, however, affects the principle that equity will not aid a volunteer. Hence it is clear that if, between promisor and promisee, the contract is binding at law only because it is contained in a deed or supported by no more than nominal consideration (moving from the promisee), then equity will not order specific performance at the suit of the third party, any more than it will do so at the suit of the promisee. It is less clear what the position would be in the more usual case in which substantial consideration is provided by the promisee but none is provided by the third party. One possible view is that, since the third party is in such a case a volunteer, specific performance will not be ordered in his favour. But this would make the reference to specific performance in the Bill, as one of the remedies available to the third party, largely nugatory. The courts may, therefore, prefer to take the view that the equitable principle applies only to gratuitous promises and that specific performance can be ordered at the suit of the third party, even though he has not provided any consideration for the promise, so long as substantial consideration for it has been provided by the promisee.

The principle that equity will not aid a volunteer does not, moreover, apply where an option to buy land is granted by an instrument for which no substantial consideration is given but which is binding because it is made by deed or supported by a nominal consideration. Such an option has some of the characteristics of an offer coupled with a legally binding promise not to revoke[58]; and it may therefore be exercised notwithstanding an attempted revocation. The resulting contract *of sale* can be specifically enforced[59] so long as that contract is supported by substantial consideration.

Conduct of the claimant. "The conduct of the party applying for relief is   **28-032**
always an important element for consideration."[60] Thus specific performance may be refused if the claimant fails to perform a promise which he made in order to induce the defendant to enter into the contract, but which is neither binding contractually, nor (because it relates to the future) operative as a misrepresentation.[61] Specific performance may also be refused if the claimant's main object in seeking this form of relief is to avoid a set-off that could have been raised against a claim by him for damages.[62]

For the purpose of the principle stated in § 28-032, it may suffice if the   **28-033**
claimant has acted unfairly in performing the contract, even though he has not broken any promise. Specific enforcement of a solus petrol agreement[63] has accordingly been denied to an oil company on the ground that the company had

---

[57b] *Ante,* § 19–082.
[57c] Subsection 1(5) of the 1998 Bill.
[58] See *ante,* § 3–160, n. 79.
[59] *Mountford v. Scott* [1975] Ch. 258.
[60] *Lamare v. Dixon* (1873) L.R. 6 H.L. 414, 413; *Chappell v. The Times Newspapers Ltd* [1975] 1 W.L.R. 482; *Wilton Group v. Abrams* [1990] B.C.C. 310, 317 ("commercially disreputable").
[61] *Lamare v. Dixon, supra.*
[62] *Handley Page Ltd v. Commissioners of Customs and Excise* [1970] 2 Lloyd's Rep. 459.
[63] *Ante,* § 17–120.

given discounts to other garages and had thereby made it impossible for the defendant garage to trade on the terms of the agreement except at a loss.[64]

28–034   An action could formerly be brought on a contract for the sale of land against a party who had provided written evidence of it by one who had not.[65] It had, however, been held that the principle stated in § 28–032 above was a ground for denying specific performance to a purchaser of land if he refused to perform a stipulation to which he had agreed, but which could not be enforced against him for want of written evidence.[66] A contract for the sale of land must now be made (and not merely evidenced) in writing signed by the parties and the writing must incorporate all the terms on which they have expressly agreed.[67] Hence if the stipulation in question was such a term, but was not contained in the documents, specific performance would now be refused on the different ground that no contract had come into existence. An alternative possibility is that the stipulation might have been intended to take effect as a collateral contract.[68] In that event, the main contract would be valid but the reasoning of the cases referred to above might still lead the court to refuse specific performance to the purchaser if it considered that the vendor would not be adequately protected, after being ordered to perform, by his claim for damages for breach of the collateral contract.[69]

28–035   **Contracts expressed to be revocable.** If a contract is expressed to be revocable by the party against whom an order of specific performance is sought, the order will be refused as the defendant could render it nugatory by exercising his power to revoke.[70] On this ground a contract to enter into a partnership at will is not specifically enforceable.[71] The same is true of a contract for a lease which by virtue of the contract itself would contain a stipulation enabling the defendant to determine the lease as soon as it was executed[72]; but a tenancy from year to year, determinable by either party by half a year's notice to quit, is specifically enforceable.[73]

28–036   **Inutility.** The courts will not ordinarily order specific performance of an agreement for a lease, where the term to be granted under the agreement will have expired by the time the order is made.[74] Similarly, specific performance will not be ordered of an agreement for a lease at the suit of a tenant who has so conducted himself that the landlord would have been justified in forfeiting the

---

[64] *Shell U.K. Ltd v. Lostock Garages Ltd* [1977] 1 W.L.R. 1187.

[65] Law of Property Act 1925, s.40, replacing part of Statute of Frauds 1677, s.4, and now repealed by Law of Property (Miscellaneous Provisions) Act 1989, ss.1(8) and 4 and Sched. 2; and see *ante*, § 4–004.

[66] See *Martin v. Pycroft* (1852) 2 D.M. & G. 785, 795; *Scott v. Bradley* [1971] Ch. 850.

[67] Law of Property (Miscellaneous Provisions) Act 1989, s.2(1).

[68] *Ante*, § 4–063.

[69] *i.e.* on the principle of "mutuality" as now understood: *post*, § 28–043.

[70] *Wheeler v. Trotter* (1737) 3 Swan. 174n.

[71] *Hercy v. Birch* (1804) 9 Ves. 357; *Sheffield Gas Co. v. Harrison* (1853) 17 Beav. 294; *cf. Wheeler v. Trotter* (1737) Swan. 174n.; but contrast *Allhusen v. Borrie* (1867) 15 W.R. 739.

[72] See *Lewis v. Bond* (1853) 18 Beav. 85.

[73] *Lever v. Koffler* [1901] 1 Ch. 543; but see *Clayton v. Illingworth* (1853) 10 Hare 451, in which, however, the suit was dismissed merely "in the absence of any authority"; and *cf. Gray v. Spyer* [1922] 2 Ch. 22 (tenancy for year.)

[74] *Walters v. Northern Coal Mining Co.* (1855) 5 De G.M. & G. 629; *cf. Anon. v. White* (1709) 3 Swan. 108n.; *Nesbitt v. Meyer* (1818) 1 Swan. 223.

lease, had it been granted.[75] On a somewhat similar principle, a contract which is subject to a condition precedent not within the control of the party seeking the remedy will not be specifically enforced before the condition has occurred[76]; here too the making of the order could turn out to be nugatory if the condition were not satisfied. The occurrence of the condition will remove this obstacle to specific performance.[77]

Impossibility. Specific performance will not be ordered against a person who   **28–037**
has agreed to sell land which he does not own and cannot compel the owner to convey to him,[78] "because the court does not compel a person to do what is impossible."[79] The position is the same where a person has agreed to assign a lease and the landlord withholds his consent, without which the assignment cannot lawfully be effected.[80] Impossibility of enforcing an order of specific performance (*e.g.* because the defendant is not, and has no assets, within the jurisdiction) may also be a reason for refusing to make such an order.[81]

Vagueness. An agreement may be so vague that it cannot be enforced at all,   **28–038**
even by an action for damages.[82] But although an agreement is definite enough to be enforced in some form of legal proceedings, it may still be too vague to be enforced specifically.[83] Thus specific performance has been refused of a contract to publish an article as to the exact text of which the parties disagreed.[84] The reason for refusing specific performance in these cases appears to be that the court would find it difficult or impossible to state in its order precisely what the defendant was bound to do in obedience to the order; and precision is essential since failure to comply with the court's order may lead to attachment for contempt.[85] An agreement is not, however, too vague to be specifically enforced merely because it is expressed to be subject to such amendments as may reasonably be required by one (or by either) party.[86]

Goodwill. The difficulty of precisely formulating the court's order was at one   **28–039**
time thought to prevent the specific enforcement of contracts for the sale of goodwill alone, without business premises. Thus in one case involving such a contract Sir William Grant M.R. asked rhetorically: "In what way . . . is the court to decree the transfer of such a business? What is it that I am to direct (the

---

[75] *Gregory v. Wilson* (1851) 9 Hare 683.
[76] *Chattey v. Farndale Holdings Inc.,* [1997] 1 E.G.L.R. 153.
[77] *cf. Wu Koon Tai v. Wu Yau Loi* [1997] A.C. 179, 189.
[78] See *Castle v. Wilkinson* (1870) L.R. 5 Ch.App. 534; *Watts v. Spence* [1976] Ch. 165; *cf. Elliott & Elliott (Builders) Ltd v. Pierson* [1948] Ch. 453 (where the vendor sold land owned by a company that he controlled).
[79] *Forrer v. Nash* (1865) 35 Beav. 167, 171.
[80] *Wilmott v. Barber* (1880) 15 Ch.D. 96; *Warmington v. Miller* [1973] Q.B. 877. And see *Sullivan v. Henderson* [1973] 1 W.L.R. 333; *ante,* § 28–011, n. 44.
[81] *Locobail International Finance Ltd v. Agroexport (The Sea Hawk)* [1986] 1 W.L.R. 657, 665.
[82] *Ante,* § 2–128, *Waring & Gillow v. Thompson* (1912) 29 T.L.R. 154.
[83] *Collins v. Plumb* (1810) 16 Ves. 454 as explained in *Catt v. Tourle* (1869) L.R. 4 Ch.App. 654, 658; *Wilson v. Northampton & Banbury Junction Railway Co.* (1874) 9 Ch.App. 279, as explained in *Tito v. Waddell (No. 2)* [1977] Ch. 106, 322–323.
[84] *Joseph v. National Magazine Co.* [1959] Ch. 14; *cf. Slater v. Raw, The Times,* October 15, 1977.
[85] *cf. Lawrence David Ltd v. Ashton* [1989] I.C.R. 123, 132; *Lock International plc v. Beswick* [1989] 1 W.L.R. 1268.
[86] *Sweet & Maxwell Ltd v. Universal News Services Ltd* [1964] 2 Q.B. 699; *Alpenstow Ltd v. Regalia Properties plc* [1985] 1 W.L.R. 721.

vendor) to do?"[87] But in *Beswick v. Beswick*[88] specific performance was ordered of a contract for the sale of goodwill without business premises at the suit of the personal representative of a vendor who had performed his part; and it was said by two members of the House of Lords that specific performance could have been ordered against the vendor, if he had not yet made the transfer.[89] The older, contrary, authorities[90] were not cited; but it seems that they have been made obsolete by the growing legal[91] and commercial precision of the concept of goodwill.

28-040   **Contract specifically enforceable in part only.** In *Ryan v. Mutual Tontine Association*[92] the court refused specifically to enforce a landlord's undertaking to have a porter "constantly in attendance"; and it seems unlikely that the court would, even now, order the landlord to enter into a contract with a porter *on such terms*.[93] A claim that the landlord should be ordered simply to appoint a porter was also rejected on the ground that "when the court cannot grant specific performance of the contract as a whole, it will not interfere to compel specific performance of part of a contract."[94] This does not mean that the court cannot order specific performance of one individual obligation out of a number imposed by a contract[95]: it means only that it will not make such an order in relation to one such obligation if it cannot so enforce the rest of the contract.[96] Even in this restricted sense, the rule is by no means an absolute one. Thus where a monetary adjustment can be made in respect of the unperformable part the court may order specific performance with compensation.[97]

28-041   **Mutuality of remedy.** The court will sometimes refuse to order specific performance at the suit of one party if it cannot order it at the suit of the other. Thus a party who undertakes to render personal services or to perform continuous duties cannot claim specific performance as the remedy is not available against him[98]; and for the same reason a minor cannot claim specific performance.[99] Such cases were explained on the ground that the remedy of specific performance

---

[87] *Bozon v. Farlow* (1816) 1 Mer. 459, 472.

[88] [1968] A.C. 58.

[89] *ibid.* at 89B, 97C.

[90] *Bozon v. Farlow, supra; Baxter v. Connolly* (1820) 1 J. & W. 576; *Coslake v. Till* (1826) 1 Russ. 376; *Thornbury v. Bevill* (1842) 1 Y. & C.C.C. 554, 565; *Darbey v. Whitaker* (1857) 3 Drew. 134, 139.

[91] See *Trego v. Hunt* [1896] A.C. 7.

[92] [1893] 1 Ch. 116; *ante* § 28-023.

[93] An order requiring the landlord to enter into a contract with a porter could be made where the landlord's undertaking specified the tasks to be done by the porter, as in *Posner v. Scott-Lewis* [1988] Ch. 25, *ante* § 28-023.

[94] *Ryan v. Mutual Tontine Association* [1893] 1 Ch. 116, 123.

[95] See *Odessa Tramways Co. v. Mendel* (1878) 8 Ch.D. 235, where such an order was made.

[96] *Rainbow Estates Ltd v. Tokenhold Ltd* [1998] 2 All E.R. 860, 868; *Odessa Tramways Co. v. Mendel* (1878) 8 Ch.D. 235 (where contract is severable, specific performance of each part can be separately ordered).

[97] *Post,* §§ 28-049 to 28-054.

[98] *Blackett v. Bates* (1865) L.R. 1 Ch.App. 117; *cf. Page One Records Ltd v. Britton* [1968] 1 W.L.R. 157 (injunction); a dictum in *Warren v. Mendy* [1989] 1 W.L.R. 853, 866 rejects the requirement of mutuality even in this situation, but the ground for refusing specific relief is that stated in § 28-060 *post.*

[99] *Flight v. Bolland* (1828) 4 Russ. 296; *Lumley v. Ravenscroft* [1895] 1 Q.B. 683.

must be mutual; and it was said that this requirement had to be satisfied at the time when the contract was made.[1]

There are, however, many cases in which specific performance can be obtained   **28–042**
by a party even though it could not at the time of contracting have been ordered against him.[2] If A promises to grant a lease of land to B who in return undertakes to build on the land, B's promise to build may not be specifically enforceable; but if he actually does perform that promise he can get specific performance of A's promise to grant the lease.[3] Specific performance cannot be ordered against a person who sells land which he does not own and cannot force the owner to convey to him[4]; but if he becomes owner before the purchaser repudiates[5] he can get specific performance.[6] Conversely, a vendor with defective title may be compelled to convey at a reduced price although he could not himself have got specific performance.[7] It seems that a person of full age can get specific performance of a voidable contract made during minority even though he could have elected to repudiate the contract.[8] And victim of fraud or innocent misrepresentation can get specific performance although he may be entitled to rescind the contract, so that it could not be enforced against him.[9]

Such cases show that the requirement of mutuality does not have to be satisfied   **28–043**
at the time of contracting: the crucial time is that of the hearing.[10] The rule was reformulated by Buckley L.J. in *Price v. Strange*: the court "will not compel a defendant to perform his obligations specifically if it cannot at the same time ensure that any unperformed obligations of the plaintiff will be specifically performed, unless, perhaps, damages would be an adequate remedy for any default on the plaintiff's part."[11] The defendant in that case had promised to grant an underlease to the plaintiff who had in return undertaken to execute certain internal and external repairs. It was admitted that the plaintiff's undertakings

---

[1] Fry, *Specific Performance* (6th ed.), pp. 219, 386. Here we are concerned with mutuality as a *necessary* requirement. It is also sometimes regarded as a *sufficient* condition when it is said that specific performance can be ordered against a contracting party *merely because* the remedy is available *to* him: this is one reason why specific performance is available *against* a purchaser of land, *ante*, § 28–007. The phrase "lack of mutuality" is also sometimes used to refer to the situation in which a contract purports to be made by an exchange of promises one of which is not binding. In such a case there is no mutuality *of obligation* and accordingly there may be no contract at all; *ante*, §§ 3–153 to 3–157.

[2] This possibility was formerly illustrated by the rule that specific performance of a contract for the sale of land could be enforced against a party who had signed a note or memorandum of the contract by one who had not: see *Seton v. Slade* (1802) 7 Ves. 265; *Martin v. Pycroft* (1852) 2 D.M. & G. 785, 795. Now neither party could sue since no contract would come into existence unless it was in writing signed by both: Law of Property (Miscellaneous Provisions) Act 1989, s.2(1).

[3] *Wilkinson v. Clements* (1872) L.R. 8 Ch.App. 96.

[4] *Ante*, § 28–037.

[5] *Halkett v. Dudley* [1970] 1 Ch. 590, 596; *cf. Cleadon Trust v. Davies* [1940] 1 Ch. 940.

[6] *Hoggart v. Scott* (1830) 1 Russ. & My. 293; *Wylson v. Dunn* (1887) 34 Ch.D. 569.

[7] *Mortlock v. Buller* (1804) 10 Ves. 292, 315; *Wilson v. Williams* (1857) 3 Jur.(N.S.) 810.

[8] *Clayton v. Ashdown* (1714) 9 Vin.Abr. 393 (G. 4) 1.

[9] *Ante*, § 6–101.

[10] *cf. E. Johnson & Co. (Barbados) Ltd v. NSR Ltd* [1997] A.C. 400, 410–411.

[11] [1978] Ch. 337, 367–368; adopting Ames, 3 Col.L.Rev. 1; *Rainbow Estates Ltd v. Tokenhold Ltd* [1998] 2 All E.R. 860, 865, 871. See also *Sutton v. Sutton* [1984] Ch. 184 where the argument of lack of mutuality was rejected because one of the claimant's promises, had been performed, even though another was not binding. Specific performance was refused on grounds of public policy, *ante*, § 17–043.

were not specifically enforceable; and it seems clear that he could not have obtained specific performance of the promise to grant the underlease before any of the repairs had been done. For in that case the only remedy available to the defendant for default on the plaintiff's part might have been in damages, and this might have been inadequate,[12] especially if the plaintiff was of doubtful solvency. But in fact the plaintiff had done the internal repairs and had been wrongfully prevented from doing the external ones by the defendant, who later had these done at her own expense. As by the time of the hearing all the repairs had been completed, specific enforcement, of the defendant's promise to grant the underlease would not expose her to the risk of having no remedy except damages in the event of the plaintiff's default; and specific performance was ordered on the terms that the plaintiff make an allowance in respect of the repairs done by the defendant. The principle that mutuality is judged by reference to the time of the hearing similarly accounts for the rule that a person who has been induced to enter into a contract by misrepresentation can specifically enforce the contract against the other; for by seeking this remedy he affirms the contract[13] and so gives the court power to hold him to it.[14] The court has no such power when specific performance is claimed on behalf of a minor: "the act of filing the bill by his next friend cannot bind him"[15] (*sc.* to perform his side of the bargain.) Similarly, it seems that lack of mutuality would still be good reason for refusing specific performance to A where A agreed to serve B in consideration of B's promise to convey a house to him and B repudiated before A had completed the agreed service.

28–044   **Mistake, misrepresentation and delay.** Specific performance may be refused on the ground of mistake, misrepresentation and delay. The effect of these factors on the availability of specific performance is discussed elsewhere in this book.[16]

5. SPECIFIC PERFORMANCE AND THIRD PARTIES

28–044A   **Introduction.** Where A promises B to render some performance in favour of C, two problems can arise. The first is whether B can specifically enforce the promise against A; the second is whether C can do so.

---

[12] *cf. National Provincial Building Society v. British Waterways Board* [1992] E.G.C.S. 149 where specific performance of a contract for the sale of land was claimed by an assignee of the purchaser's rights and it was held to be a defence that the purchaser's obligation to develop the land remained unperformed and no satisfactory remedy was available to the vendor as the purchaser had been compulsorily wound up without sufficient assets to meet the vendor's claim. If the plaintiff can be ordered to give additional, satisfactory security, he can obtain an order of specific performance even though he has not yet performed and is not ordered immediately to do so: *Langen & Wind Ltd v. Bell* [1972] Ch. 685.

[13] *Ante*, § 6–120.

[14] This reasoning still holds good in the situation described in the text above. It was formerly used to explain the now obsolete rule stated *supra*: see *Martin v. Mitchell* (1820) 2 J. & W. 413, 427; *Flight v. Bolland* (1828) 4 Russ. 298, 301.

[15] *Flight v. Bolland, supra*, at 301.

[16] *Ante*, §§ 5–063, 6–101; *post*, §§ 28–137 *et seq.*

(a) *Claim by Promisee*

Promise seeking specific performance in favour of third party. In *Beswick*   **28–045**
v. Beswick[17] A promised B (in return for B's transfer of his business to A) to pay
an annuity to B's widow, C, after B's death. The House of Lords held that this
promise could be specifically enforced by B's personal representative (who
happened to be C) against A.[18] Thus A was ordered to pay the annuity to C, who
in this way obtained the benefit of a contract to which she was not a party[19] even
though the case did not fall within any exception to the common law doctrine of
privity of contract.[20] After the coming into force of the Contracts (Rights of Third
Parties) Bill 1998,[20a] C will in many such cases be entitled in his or her own right
to enforce against A the term in the contract containing the promise in favour of
C; and where C takes this course, the need for B to seek specific performance in
favour of C will be much reduced. But it will not be altogether eliminated since
there may still be situations in which C will not have any such right against A
because the legislative requirements for its acquisition have not been satisfied.[20b]
The Bill also expressly preserves B's right to enforce any term of the contract
against A even where C has acquited a right of enforcement against A.[20c] The
scope of B's remedy by way of specific performance therefore continues to call
for discussion.

In holding that this remedy was available to B, the House of Lords in *Beswick
v. Beswick* laid stress on three factors: (1) the inadequacy of damages[21] (which,
in the view of the majority of the House, would be merely nominal[22]) as a remedy
for breach of A's promise; (2) the fact that the promisor (A) had received the
entire consideration for his promise[23]; and (3) the fact that the contract could
have been specifically enforced *by* A, had B refused to perform his promise to
transfer the business.[24] Other factors relevant to the issue of specific enforceability, which were also present in *Beswick v. Beswick*, were that A's promise was
one to pay an annuity and so would have been specifically enforceable if it had
been made to B for his own benefit[25]; that, apart from his inadequate remedy by
way of damages, B had no other, more satisfactory, remedy at law[26]; and that, if
the promise had been made to B for his own benefit, specific performance would

---

[17] [1968] A.C. 58; *ante*, §§ 28–009; Goodhart (1967) 83 L.Q.R. 465; Fairest [1967] C.L.J. 149;
Treitel (1967) 30 M.L.R. 687.
[18] Similar orders had been made in *Keenan v. Handley* (1864) 12 W.R. 930, affd. (1864) 2 D.J. &
S.; *Peel v. Peel* (1869) 17 W.R. 586; *Drimmie v. Davies* [1899] 1 I.R. 176 (but in this case there was
probably a trust in favour of the third party); and in *Hohler v. Aston* [1920] 2 Ch. 420.
[19] Under RSC, Ord. 45, r. 9 (preserved by CPR Sched. 1), the order in such cases can be enforced
by the third party in whose favour it is made.
[20] *Ante*, Chap. 19.
[20a] *Ante*, §§ 19–075 *et seq.*
[20b] e.g. because the requirements of subsections 1(1) and (2) are not satisfied; see *ante* § 19–079
for the question whether they would be satisfied on the facts of *Beswick v. Beswick*, supra.
[20c] Clause 4 of the 1998 Bill.
[21] [1968] A.C. 58, 81E, 102C; *cf. ante*, § 28–009.
[22] *ibid.* at 81E, 102A; *cf.* at 73B, 83F. Lord Pearce, alone, thought that damages would be
substantial, *ibid.* at 88F. *cf. ante*, § 19–045.
[23] At 83A, 89B, 97C, 102C; *cf.* at 73C; and see *Hart v. Hart* (1881) 18 Ch.D. 670, 685.
[24] At 89B, 97C; as to the specific enforceability of B's promise, see *ante*, § 28–044A.
[25] *Ante*, § 28–008. The first three cases cited in n. 18, *supra*, were also annuity cases; the contract
in the fourth case was a contract for the disposition of an interest in land and so specifically
enforceable.
[26] Possible remedies are referred to in § 28–048 (examples (e) and (f)).

not have been refused on any of the other grounds (than the availability of satisfactory remedy at law) which have been discussed in this Chapter.[27]

28–046   **Possible limitations on the remedy.** It therefore does not follow from *Beswick v. Beswick* that the promisee can in all cases of contracts for the benefit of a third party obtains an order of specific performance in favour of the third party. In particular, the case is not direct authority for the availability of such a remedy in any of the following cases: (1) where the promisee has a remedy at law other than for nominal damages: *e.g.* for substantial damages,[28] for recovery of the consideration provided by him,[29] or for the agreed sum[30]; (2) where the promisor has not received the whole (or any part of) the consideration for his promise; (3) where the contract, if wholly executory, could not have been specifically enforced by the promisor; and (4) where the promise sued upon would not have been specifically enforceable by the promisee, if it had been made to him for his own benefit. It is submitted that in such cases specific performance should neither be granted merely because the contract provides for performance in favour of a third party, nor refused merely because it would not have been available, had there been no third party in the case. As a general principle, it is submitted that the promisee should be able to obtain specific performance in favour of the third party whenever that is the most appropriate method of enforcing the contract which was actually made.[31] But it should be open to the defendant to resist specific enforcement by showing that this remedy would lead to one of the undesirable results against which the established limitations on the scope of the remedy[32] are meant to provide protection.

28–047   **Examples.** The scope of the promisee's remedy of specific performance in favour of third parties may be illustrated by a series of examples. In discussing these, an attempt will be made to apply the general statement made at the end of the preceding paragraph; but it must be emphasised that in the present state of the authorities some of the solutions which will be put forward can only be tentative.

> (*a*) A promises[33] B to render personal services to C. B should not be able to obtain specific performance in favour of C, because the policy of the rule against the specific enforcement of contracts to render personal services[34] applies equally whether the services are to be rendered to the promisee or to a third party.
>
> (*b*) A promises B to pay £1,000 to C immediately, in return for B's promise (as yet unperformed) to serve A for one year. B should not be able to obtain specific performance in favour of C, because the grant of this

---

[27] *i.e.* in §§ 28–027—28–043 *ante*.

[28] *Ante*, § 19–045.

[29] *Ante*, § 19–043. This remedy was not available in *Beswick v. Beswick*. There was no "total failure of consideration," both by reason of the facts stated in *post*, and because A had made one payment to the widow.

[30] *Ante*, § 19–044. The mere fact that the action for the agreed sum is available to the claimant is no bar to specific performance: see *Miliangos v. George Frank (Textiles) Ltd* [1976] A.C. 443.

[31] See especially [1968] A.C. 58, 88G, 102B and the citation with approval by Lord Pearce at 90–91 of a dictum of Windeyer J. in *Coulls v. Bagot's Executor & Trustee Co. Ltd* (1967) 40 A.L.J.R. 471, 488; and *cf. ante*, § 28–005.

[32] See especially, §§ 28–018—28–024, *ante*.

[33] The "promises" in this and the following examples are assumed to be binding contractually.

[34] *Ante*, § 28–018.

remedy would expose A to the hardship which the requirement of mutuality of remedy[35] is intended to prevent.

(c) The facts are as in (b), except that B has performed the service. Specific performance in favour of C should not be refused merely because A could not, when the contract was made, have obtained specific performance against B. Now that A has got the whole of what he bargained for, he cannot suffer the hardship which the requirement of mutuality is intended to prevent.[36]

(d) A promises B to pay £1,000 per annum to C for 10 years in return for B's promise (as yet unperformed) to transfer to A 100 shares in the X company; the shares are freely available in the market. Specific performance in favour of C should not be refused to B merely because specific performance could not have been ordered against him.[37] The hardship which the mutuality rule is intended to prevent can here be prevented by making the order in favour of C conditional on B's making the agreed transfer. Specific performance in favour of C might, however, be properly refused if the factors mentioned in example (g) below operate so as to cause hardship to A.

(e) Examples (b) and (d) can be varied by supposing part performance by B. It is submitted that this should not generally affect the outcome; but that, by way of exception to this general principle, specific performance in favour of C should, perhaps, be ordered in a case like example (b) if B had substantially (though not completely) performed his part so that the risk of hardship to A as a result of the order was minimal.[38] **28–048**

(f) A (an insurance company) promises B to pay a sum of money to C in 20 years' time. The contract does not fall within any of the exceptions to the doctrine of privity of contract.[39] B has duly paid all premiums. B should be able to obtain specific performance in favour of C though in a two-party case B's remedy would not have been an order for specific performance but an action for the agreed sum.[40] It should make no difference that B might, in the event of A's refusal or failure to pay C have a substantial remedy at common law: e.g. for the recovery of the premiums as paid on a total failure of consideration,[41] or for the agreed sum (if he is named as an alternative payee),[42] or for substantial damages in respect of foreseeable loss arising from A's default.[43] In spite of the availability of such

---

[35] *Ante,* § 28–041.

[36] *Ante,* § 28–043. In *Beswick v. Beswick* itself the contract did in fact provide that B should serve A as consultant for life in return for a payment of £6 10s. per week. This stipulation had been performed and was also held not to destroy "mutuality" because of its minimal importance (see [1968] A.C. at 97C).

[37] *Ante,* § 28–011; damages would be an adequate remedy for A in a two-party case.

[38] *cf.* example (c) at n. 36 *supra.*

[39] *Ante,* §§ 19–064—19–114.

[40] *Ante,* § 28–006. And see *ante,* § 28–046, at n. 28.

[41] *Ante,* § 19–043. To restrict B to such a remedy would obviously be unjust if A's promise took the form of a "with profits" policy.

[42] It seems that in the case of a contract to pay money to a third party an action for the agreed sum cannot normally be brought by the promisee; *ante,* § 19–044.

[43] *e.g.* if B had contracted with C to procure A's payments to C, or was otherwise under a legal obligation to ensure that they (or corresponding payments) were made, or (possibly) if it was foreseeable that B would make a substitute provision for C in the event of A's default, whether or not B was under a legal obligation to do so; *ante,* § 19–045; Treitel (1967) 30 M.L.R. 687.

common law remedies, specific performance in favour of C is here the most appropriate[44] remedy for the enforcement of the contract; and to grant it would not conflict with any of the policies limiting the scope of the remedy in a two-party case.

(g) A promises B that, in return for an immediate payment of £100 by B he will supply 10 tons of coal to C in six months' time. A fails to deliver as agreed; and after breach the market price rises. If the promise had been made to B for his own benefit, B would have been bound to mitigate by taking reasonable steps to procure a substitute (*i.e.* by buying against A in the market where this was possible.) One reason for refusing B specific performance in such a case is that the grant of the remedy would in substance deprive A of the benefit of the mitigation rule.[45] It is not easy to see how this rule can be applied to contracts for the benefit of a third party; for if the promisee's damages are nominal[46] he can hardly mitigate, and it does not seem that there can (at common law[46a]) be any duty to mitigate on the third party. Yet specific performance in favour of C could cause considerable hardship to A in such a case and should probably be refused if such hardship is established.

(b) *Claim by Third Party*

28-048A   **Effect of Contracts (Rights of Third Parties) Bill 1998.** After the coming into force of this Bill, C will in many cases be entitled in his own right to enforce against A the term in the contract between A and B containing A's promise in favour of C.[46b] The Bill expressly lists specific performance as one of the remedies available to C where it would have been available to him "if he had been a party to the contract;" and it states that the rules relating to specific performance "shall apply accordingly."[46c] Some such rules will apply to a claim by C in the same way as they apply to one by B: e.g., it A's promise is one to render personal service to C, it will not be specifically enforceable at the suit of either B or C. Other rules will obviously apply with some modification; e.g., if A promises B to pay a lump sum to C, then the most appropriate remedy for B might be specific performance in equity, while for C it would be a common law action for the agreed sum. The application to claims by C of the limitations on the scope of specific performance will need to be worked out on a case by case basis in the light of the policies which have given rise to these limitations in two-party cases.

6. SPECIFIC PERFORMANCE WITH COMPENSATION[47]

28-049   **Misdescription.** Apart from stipulations relating to errors or misdescription, a vendor of land could not at law sue on an executory contract if the land did not

---

[44] See, *ante*, § 28–005, n. 19. *cf. Gurtner v. Circuit* [1968] 2 Q.B. 587 as to which see *ante*, § 28–031, n. 55; *Sears v. Tanenbaum* [1969] 9 D.L.R. (3d) 425.

[45] *Ante*, § 28–002. This argument would apply even if the case fell within s.52 of the Sale of Goods Act 1979, *e.g.* because the goods were ascertained.

[46] *cf. ante*, § 28–009.

[46a] If C (not B) brings the action under subsection 1(1) of the Contracts (Rights of Third Parties) Bill 1998, he would be required, by virtue of subsection 1(5) to comply with the mitigation rules.

[46b] *Ante*, § 19–075 *et seq.*

[46c] Subsection 1(5) of the 1998 Bill.

[47] Harpum [1981] C.L.J. 108.

correspond with the contractual description. But in such cases equity could order specific performance with "compensation"—*i.e.* with adjustment of the purchase price. This jurisdiction may be exercised where the area of the land sold is less than that stated in the contract,[48] where there is a defect of title,[49] and where there is a physical defect.[50]

A vendor may obtain specific performance with compensation provided that   **28–050**
the misdescription is not fraudulently or wilfully made,[51] that it does not affect the substance of the purchaser's bargain,[52] and that adequate compensation for the defect can be made by a monetary adjustment.[53] A purchaser may succeed in a claim for specific performance with compensation even though the misdescription is of a degree of seriousness that would preclude the grant of the remedy to the vendor.[54] But the remedy will not be granted to a purchaser where it will prejudice third parties,[55] where it will inflict undue hardship on the vendor,[56] where the purchaser knows the true facts at the time of contracting,[57] or where compensation cannot readily be assessed in money.[58] In these cases the purchaser may be entitled to rescind; but if he seeks specific performance he can enforce the contract only without compensation.[59] This rule also applies where there is no misdescription in the contract but only a misrepresentation inducing it[60]; but under section 2(2) of the Misrepresentation Act 1967 the court has in such a case a discretion to declare the contract subsisting and to award "damages" in lieu of rescission.[61] The effect of the exercise of this discretion would probably be similar to that of specific performance with compensation. The main difference between the old equitable and the new statutory powers is that the former was exercisable only before,[62] while the latter can be invoked even after, completion.[63]

Condition against error or misdescription. A contract for the sale of land   **28–051**
may provide that errors and misdescriptions shall not annul the sale but shall give

---

[48] *Aspinalls to Powell and Scholefield* (1889) 60 L.T. 595.

[49] *Burrow v. Scammell* (1881) 19 Ch.D. 175.

[50] *Shepherd v. Croft* [1911] 1 Ch. 521; *cf. Lyons v. Thomas* [1986] I.R. 666 (where the defects arose after contract).

[51] *Price v. Macaulay* (1852) 2 De G.M. & G. 339, 345; *Shepherd v. Croft* [1911] 1 Ch. 521; *Re Belcham & Gawley's Contract* [1930] 1 Ch. 56 (where the vendor knew of the existence of the defect).

[52] *Re Fawcett & Holmes' Contract* (1889) 42 Ch.D. 150; *Jacobs v. Revell* [1900] 2 Ch. 858; *Watson v. Burton* [1957] 1 W.L.R. 19; *cf. Flight v. Booth* (1834) 1 Bing.N.C. 370; *Re Puckett & Smith's Contract* [1902] 2 Ch. 258; *Ridley v. Oster* [1939] 1 All E.R. 618; *Walker v. Boyle* [1982] 1 W.L.R. 495.

[53] *Cato v. Thompson* (1882) 9 Q.B.D. 616, 618.

[54] Williams, *Vendor and Purchaser* (4th ed.), p. 725.

[55] *Willmot v. Barber* (1880) 15 Ch.D. 96 (covenant not to assign lease without licence of lessor).

[56] *Durham v. Legard* (1865) 34 Beav. 611; *Rudd v. Lascelles* [1900] 1 Ch. 815.

[57] *Castle v. Wilkinson* (1870) L.R. 5 Ch. 534.

[58] *Rudd v. Lascelles, supra,* n. 56.

[59] *Durham v. Legard, supra,* n. 56.

[60] *Gilchester Properties Ltd v. Gomm* [1948] 1 All E.R. 493; *cf. Clayton v. Leech* (1889) 41 Ch.D. 103; *Rutherford v. Acton-Adams* [1915] A.C. 866.

[61] *Ante,* §§ 6–095—6–100.

[62] *Joliffe v. Baker* (1883) 11 Q.B.D. 255; *Clayton v. Leech* (1889) 41 Ch.D. 103; the position is different where the contract expressly provides for compensation: *post,* § 28–053 at nn. 81 and 82.

[63] Misrepresentation Act 1967, s.1(b) leads to this result.

rise to a claim for compensation; sometimes the provision may purport to exclude the purchaser's right to compensation for error or misdescription. The first question in such a case is as to the true construction of the provision. Generally it will not apply to defects of title[64]; but it is not invariably restricted to physical defects and may apply where the extent of a restrictive covenant is wrongly stated in the contract.[65]

28–052   A provision of this kind will not help the vendor where the misdescription was wilful or fraudulent,[66] so that in such a case the purchaser can resist a claim for specific performance and rescind the contract. The position was held to be the same[67] where the defect was substantial[68] and where compensation could not readily be assessed in money.[69] These cases seem to be applications of what later became known as the doctrine of fundamental breach[70] and similar cases would now seem to turn on the construction of the provision in question[71] rather than on any substantive rule making it impossible to exclude the court's power to award compensation. Such provisions are not subject to the requirement of reasonableness under sections 2 to 4 of the Unfair Contract Terms Act 1977[72] since those sections do not apply to any contract so far as it relates to the creation or transfer of an interest in land.[73] The point may be important where a developer enters into a contract for the sale of a house on "written standard terms" which would otherwise be subject to the requirement of reasonableness under section 3 of the Act.

28–053   **Effects of misdescription as a misrepresentation.** Further problems as to the effectiveness of a condition against error or misdescription can arise where the misdescription did not form part of the contract but was only a misrepresentation inducing it; or where it originated as such a misrepresentation and was later incorporated in the contract as one of its terms. In such cases, the representee can rescind the contract for misrepresentation,[74] and if the misrepresentation related

---

[64] *Re Beyfus and Master's Contract* (1888) 39 Ch.D. 110; and see *Debenham v. Sawbridge* [1901] 2 Ch. 98, 107, 108.

[65] *Re Courcier and Harrold's Contract* [1923] 1 Ch. 565.

[66] *Duke of Norfolk v. Worthy* (1808) 1 Camp. 337; *Re Terry and White's Contract* (1886) 32 Ch.D. 14, 29; *Shepherd v. Croft* (1911) 1 Ch. 521, 531; see *ante*, §§ 6–129, 14–125.

[67] *Flight v. Booth* (1834) 1 Bing.N.C. 370; *Jacobs v. Revell* [1900] 2 Ch. 858; *Re Puckett and Smith's Contract* [1902] 2 Ch. 258; *Lee v. Rayson* [1971] 1 Ch. 613.

[68] See *Dimmock v. Hallett* (1866) L.R. 2 Ch.App. 21; *Re Terry and White's Contract* (1886) 32 Ch.D. 14, 29; *Re Fawcett and Holmes' Contract* (1889) 42 Ch.D 150; *Re Puckett and Smith's Contract* [1902] 2 Ch. 258; *Lee v. Rayson* [1917] 1 Ch. 613; contrast *Re Courcier and Harrold's Contract* [1923] 1 Ch. 565; *Beyfus v. Lodge* [1925] Ch. 350; *Watson v. Burton* [1957] 1 W.L.R. 19.

[69] *Brooke v. Rounthwaite* (1846) 5 Hare 298; *Rudd v. Lascelles* [1900] 1 Ch. 815; and see Williams, *Vendor and Purchaser* (4th ed.), pp. 728–732.

[70] *Ante*, § 14–020.

[71] *Photo Production Ltd v. Securicor Transport Ltd* [1980] A.C. 827; *George Mitchell (Chesterhall) Ltd v. Finney Lock Seeds Ltd* [1983] 2 A.C. 803; *ante*, §§ 14–022, 14–023.

[72] *Ante*, §§ 14–057 *et seq.*

[73] Unfair Contract Terms Act 1977, Sched. 1, para. 1(c). The E.C. Directive on Unfair Terms in Consumer Contracts (93/13/EEC) seems likewise not to be intended to apply to contracts for the sale of interests in land: see the references to sale "of goods" in Recitals 2, 5, 6 and 7 and the reference in Recital 1 to "goods" which "move freely." The Unfair Terms in Consumer Contracts Regulations 1994 (which implement the Directive in the U.K.) likewise deal with contracts for the sale of goods and the supply of services (Reg. 2(1), definitions of "seller" and "supplier") and seem not to apply to cases of the kind here under discussion.

[74] *Ante*, § 6–103; Misrepresentation Act 1967, s.1(a).

to a matter that was substantial this right to rescind would not normally be affected by the condition.[75] If, on the other hand, the matter misrepresented was *not* substantial, it is likely that the court would, even in the absence of the condition, reject a claim to rescind for misrepresentation; more probably, it would declare the contract as subsisting and award damages in lieu of rescission.[76] The further question then arises, whether a condition against error or misdescription would, in such a situation, be ineffective under section 3 of the Misrepresentation Act 1967.[77] Under this section, a contract term which would exclude or restrict any remedy available to a contracting party by reason of a misrepresentation made before the contract was made is subject to the test of reasonableness. Before the Act, it was held that a condition which excluded the right to rescind *and* the right to compensation entitled the vendor to enforce the contract without compensation.[78] Now, such a condition might well be regarded as unreasonable in so far as it excluded the purchaser's right to compensation, or his right to rescind for a misrepresentation relating to a matter that was of substantial importance.[79] But if the matter misrepresented was of only minor importance, and the condition, while excluding the right to rescind, *provided* for compensation, it is submitted that the requirement of reasonableness would normally be satisfied. For such a condition would not prejudice the purchaser: it would only give contractual effect to the right that the vendor would have had, even in the absence of the condition, to specific performance with compensation, or to the result that the court would be likely to reach under section 2(2) of the Misrepresentation Act 1967.[80] Indeed, in one respect a condition in these terms might even benefit the purchaser; for the equitable rule that compensation could be claimed only *before* completion[81] does not apply where the contract contains such a provision.[82]

Compensation to vendor. A condition which provides for compensation may   **28–054**
also entitle the vendor to compensation for errors to his disadvantage.[83]

7. INJUNCTION

Negative contracts. Where a contract is negative in nature, or contains an   **28–055**
express negative stipulation, breach of it may be restrained by injunction.[84] In such cases an injunction is normally granted as a matter of course, though since it is an equitable, and thus in principle a discretionary remedy, it may be refused on the ground that its award would cause such "particular hardship"[85] to the

---

[75] *Supra*, at n. 68.
[76] Misrepresentation Act 1967, s.2(2); *ante*, § 6–095.
[77] As amended by Unfair Contract Terms Act 1977, s.8; *ante*, §§ 6–130—6–133.
[78] *Re Courcier and Harrold's Contract* [1923] 1 Ch. 565.
[79] *Walker v. Boyle* [1982] 1 W.L.R. 495; *cf. Cremdean Properties Ltd v. Nash* (1877) 244 E.G. 547; *South Western General Property Co. v. Marton* (1982) 263 E.G. 263.
[80] *Ante*, § 6–095.
[81] *Ante*, § 28–049, at n. 62.
[82] *Bos v. Helsham* (1866) L.R. 2 Ex. 72; *Re Turner and Skelton* (1879) 13 Ch.D. 130; *Palmer v. Johnson* (1884) 13 Q.B.D. 351.
[83] *Leslie v. Thompson* (1851) 9 Hare 268.
[84] *Martin v. Nutkin* (1724) 2 P.Wms. 266.
[85] *Insurance Co v. Lloyd's Syndicate* [1985] 1 Lloyd's Rep. 273, 276 (where there was no such hardship). *cf. ante*, § 28–028 (severe hardship).

defendant as to be oppressive to him.[86] An injunction would not be "oppressive" merely because observance of the contract was burdensome to the defendant[87] or because its breach would cause little or no prejudice to the claimant,[88] for, in deciding whether to restrain breach of a negative stipulation, the court is not normally concerned with "'the balance of convenience or inconvenience."[89] This rule, however, applies only to a *prohibitory* injunction restraining a defendant from *future* breaches. If he has already broken his contract (*e.g.* by fencing land that he promised to leave open) he may be ordered by a *mandatory* injunction actually to undo the breach. Such an order *is* subject to a "balance of convenience" test, and may, accordingly, be refused if the prejudice suffered by the defendant in having to restore the original position heavily outweighs the advantage that will be derived from such restoration by the claimant.[90] On the other hand, the court will also, in applying the balance of convenience test, take account of the nature of the breach. Thus where the defendant had in breach of a restrictive covenant erected a building so as to block the claimant's sea view, a mandatory injunction was granted as the breach had been committed deliberately, with full knowledge of the claimant's rights, and as damages would not have been an adequate remedy.[91]

28–056   **Interim injunctions.** Applications for interim injunctions are likewise subject (*inter alia*) to the "balance of convenience" test[92]; except where there is "a plain and uncontested breach of a clear covenant not to do a particular thing."[93] One application of the balance of convenience test is to cases where the injunction is sought for such a period that to grant it would amount in substance to a final resolution of the dispute between the parties. The court will, in considering such a claim for interim relief, take into account the likelihood of the claimant's

---

[86] See *post*, § 28–058.

[87] *cf. ante*, § 27–028.

[88] *Kemp v. Sober* (1851) 1 Sim.(N.S.) 517; *Tipping v. Eckersley* (1855) 2 K. & J. 264; *Marco Productions Ltd v. Pagola* [1945] K.B. 111.

[89] *Doherty v. Allman* (1878) 3 App.Cas. 709, 720; *cf. Warner Bros. Pictures Inc. v. Nelson* [1937] 1 K.B. 209, 217; *Wakeham v. Wood* (1982) 43 P. & C.R. 40; *Att.-Gen. v. Barker* [1990] 3 All E.R. 257, 262.

[90] *Sharp v. Harrison* [1922] 1 Ch. 502; *Shepherd Homes Ltd v. Sandham* [1971] Ch. 340; for subsequent proceedings, see [1971] 1 W.L.R. 1062; *Films Rover International Ltd v. Cannon Film Sales* [1987] 1 W.L.R. 670 (for further proceedings, see [1989] 1 W.L.R. 912); *Sutton Housing Trust v. Lawrence* (1987) 19 H.L.R. 520 (mandatory and prohibitory injunction); *Reed v. Madon* [1989] Ch. 408.

[91] *Wakeham v. Wood* (1982) 43 P. & C.R. 40.

[92] *Texaco Ltd v. Mulberry Filling Station Ltd* [1972] 1 W.L.R. 814; *Evans Marshall & Co. v. Bertola* [1973] 1 W.L.R. 349; *Clifford Davis Management Ltd v. W.E.A. Records Ltd* [1975] 1 W.L.R. 61; *Mike Trading & Transport Ltd v. R. Pagnan & Fratelli* [1980] 2 Lloyd's Rep. 546; *Locobail International Finance v. Agroexport (The Sea Hawk)* [1986] 1 W.L.R. 657; *Kerr v. Morris* [1987] Ch. 90, 112; *Films Rover International v. Cannon Film Sales Ltd* [1987] 1 W.L.R. 670, for further proceedings see [1989] 1 W.L.R. 912; *Evening Standard Co. Ltd v. Henderson* [1987] I.C.R. 588; *Provident Financial Group Ltd v. Hayward* [1989] I.C.R. 160; *Lock International plc v. Beswick* [1989] 1 W.L.R. 1268; *Channel Tunnel Group v. Balfour Beatty Construction Ltd* [1993] A.C. 334; *GFI Group Inc. v. Eaglestone*, [1994] I.R.L.R. 119; *Series 5 Software v. Clarke* [1996] 1 All E.R. 853; *Tate & Lyle Industries v. Cia. Usina Bulhoes* [1997] 1 Lloyd's Rep. 355. For the principles governing such injunctions, see generally *American Cyanamid Co. v. Ethicon Ltd* [1975] A.C. 396; *Fellowes v. Fisher* [1976] Q.B. 122 and *Lawrence David Ltd v. Ashton* [1989] I.C.R. 123 (holding these principles to be applicable in restraint of trade cases).

[93] *Hampstead and Suburban Properties Ltd v. Diomedous* [1969] 1 Ch. 248, 259; *cf. Att.-Gen. v. Barker* [1990] 3 All E.R. 257.

success at the eventual trial.[94] The court can also take into account the financial prejudice which is likely to be suffered either by the claimant if the injunction is refused,[95] or by the defendant if it is granted,[96] and if at the trial the dispute were to be resolved in that party's favour. An award of damages to that party might then be an "inadequate" remedy for reasons discussed earlier in this Chapter[97]: *e.g.* because there was an appreciable risk of the other party's not being able to pay the amount of the award.

Exclusive alternative remedy. An injunction will not be granted to restrain   **28–057** breach of a restrictive covenant affecting land against a body which has acquired the land under statutory powers where the legislation has provided an exclusive remedy by way of statutory compensation.[98]

Oppression. We shall see later in this Chapter[99] that the court has power by   **28–058** statute to award damages in lieu of specific performance or injunction. That power is likely to be exercised if the injury to the claimant is small, if it can readily be estimated in money, if compensation in money would adequately compensate the claimant and if the grant of an injunction would be oppressive to the defendant.[1] These conditions were satisfied, and an injunction was accordingly refused, in *Jaggard v. Sawyer*,[2] where the defendants had built a house on land which could be reached only by committing a breach of covenant and a trespass against neighbouring house-owners, including the plaintiff. An injunction restraining such access would have rendered the new house "landlocked and incapable of beneficial ownership"[3]; and this would have been oppressive as the defendants had acted "openly and in good faith"[4] and not "in blatant disregard of the plaintiff's rights"[5] when they built the house. The test is one of *oppression*,[6] rather than one of *balance of convenience*: if the plaintiff had sought interlocutory relief *before* the house had been built, she "would almost certainly have obtained it"[7]

Express negative promises. Specific performance will not generally be   **28–059** ordered of contracts of personal service[8]; nor will such contracts be indirectly enforced by restraining either party by injunction from committing a breach of

---

[94] *Cambridge Nutrition Ltd v. B.B.C.* [1990] 3 All E.R. 523; *Lansing Linde Ltd v. Kerr* [1991] 1 W.L.R. 251, 258–259.
[95] *Themehelp Ltd v. West* [1996] Q.B. 84, doubted on another point in *Group Josi Re v. Walbrook Ins. Co. Ltd* [1996] 1 W.L.R. 1152, 1162.
[96] *Cambridge Nutrition Ltd v. B.B.C.* [1990] 3 All E.R. 523.
[97] *Ante*, § 28–008 at n. 34.
[98] *Brown v. Heathlands Mental Health N.H. Trust* [1996] 1 All E.R. 133.
[99] See *post*, § 28–071.
[1] See the tort case of *Shelfer v. City of London Electric Light Co.* [1895] 1 Ch. 287, 322–333.
[2] [1995] 1 W.L.R. 269.
[3] *ibid.* at 288.
[4] *ibid.* at 289.
[5] *ibid.* at 283.
[6] *cf. supra* at n. 89.
[7] *ibid.* at 289, *cf.* 283; and see the similar case of *Gafford v. Graham*, (1998) 76 P. & C.R. D18.
[8] *Ante*, § 28–018.

his positive obligation to work or to employ.[9] But such a contract may contain an express negative promise which can be enforced by injunction without indirectly compelling the employee to work for the employer, or the employer to employ the employee. In *Lumley v. Wagner*[10] the defendant had agreed with Mr Lumley to sing at the Drury Lane theatre on two nights a week for a period of three months, and not to use her talents at any other theatre during that period, without the written authority of Mr Lumley. Afterwards she agreed for a larger payment to sing during the three months for Mr Gye at Covent Garden, and to abandon the agreement with Mr Lumley. Lord St. Leonards L.C. granted an injunction, restraining the defendant from singing for Mr Gye. He said: "It is true that I have not the means of compelling her to sing, but she has no cause of complaint if I compel her to abstain from the commission of an act which she has bound herself not to do."[11] On the same principle, breach of negative stipulation against acting for anyone except the employer may be restrained by injunction.[12] Such an injunction may provide an inducement to perform the positive obligation, but it falls short of indirectly compelling the employee to do the agreed work.

28-060   **No indirect specific performance.** An injunction will not, however, be granted where its effect would be to leave the defendant no alternatives except to perform a contract for personal services or to remain idle. If the negative promise which it is sought to enforce would preclude him from working for anyone else in any trade or profession whatsoever, an injunction will be refused.[13] Where the promise is merely one not to work in a *particular* capacity (*e.g.* as a singer or as an actress) for third parties, one view is that the promise may be enforced by injunction because the injunction would not prevent the employee from earning a living by doing other types of work.[14] But it might be quite unreasonable to expect the employee to do this; and more recent cases support the view that an injunction should not be granted except where it leaves the employee with some other *reasonable* means of earning a living.[15] They have arisen where professional entertainers or athletes have entered into long-term exclusive contracts with managers, in whom they then lost confidence. It has been held that the managers could not obtain injunctions either against their clients,[16] or against third parties with whom those clients had entered into substitute management

---

[9] *Whitwood Chemical Co. v. Hardman* [1891] 2 Ch. 416, disapproving *Montagu v. Flockton* (1873) L.R. 16 Eq. 189; *Mortimer v. Beckett* [1920] Ch. 571; *Rely-a-Bell Co. Ltd v. Eisler* [1926] Ch. 609; *Chappell v. The Times Newspapers Ltd* [1975] 1 W.L.R. 482; *cf.* Trade Union and Labour Relations (Consolidation) Act 1992, s.236; *Evans Marshall & Co. v. Bertola SA* [1973] 1 W.L.R. 349; *Scandinavian Tanker Trading Co. A.B. v. Florta Petrolera Ecuatoriana (The Scaptrade)* [1983] A.C. 694, 701; *City & Hackney H.A. v. NUPE* [1985] I.R.L.R. 252; *Alexander v. Standard Telephone and Cables Ltd* [1990] I.C.R. 291. For an exception to the general rule, see *Hill v. C.A. Parsons & Co. Ltd* [1972] 1 Ch. 305, *ante*, § 28–020.

[10] (1852) 1 De G.M. & G. 604.

[11] At 619.

[12] See, *e.g. Grimston v. Cunningham* [1894] 1 Q.B. 125; *Robinson & Co. Ltd v. Heuer* [1898] 2 Ch. 451; *Tivoli (Manchester) v. Colley* (1904) 20 T.L.R. 437; *Warner Bros. v. Nelson* [1937] 1 K.B. 209.

[13] *Ehrman v. Bartholomew* [1898] 1 Ch. 671.

[14] *Warner Bros. Pictures Inc. v. Nelson* [1937] 1 K.B. 209.

[15] Unless this was the position, the grant of an injunction might also be regarded as oppressive: *cf. ante*, § 28–058.

[16] *Page One Records Ltd v. Britton* [1968] 1 W.L.R. 157.

contracts,[17] if the effect of the injunction would "as a practical matter"[18] force the clients to make use of the services of the original manager; and this would commonly be the case since such persons cannot successfully work without a manager.

Injunction imposing undue pressure on employee. The question whether an   **28–061** injunction would put undue pressure on an employee to perform his positive obligation to work can give rise to difficult questions of fact and degree. In one case[19] a newspaper reporter undertook during the term of his contract not to work for others; the contract provided for termination by 12 months' notice. The reporter gave only two months' notice of termination, and it was held that he could be restrained by injunction from breach of the negative stipulation. This was said not to subject him to undue pressure since the employers had undertaken to go on paying him, to allow him to go on working for them for the rest of the contract period, and not to claim damages if he should choose simply to draw his pay without doing such work. But the position might have been different if the employers had merely undertaken to go on paying him, without allowing him to work. A *fortiori*, injunctive relief will be denied to the employer where his refusal to allow the employee to work amounts to a breach of the contract of employment on the employer's part.[20] In such cases, the court can balance the employee's interest in continuing to work (so as to maintain his skill and reputation) against any prejudice likely to be suffered by the employer if the employee works for a third party; and, where the remedy is discretionary,[21] the court may refuse to grant the injunction if it is satisfied that breach of the negative stipulation will not seriously prejudice the employer.[22]

Restraint of trade. Another type of contract containing a negative promise   **28–062** which is often enforced by injunction is that restraining an employee or a purchaser from competition.[23] Such contracts are at common law invalid unless reasonable,[24] while the cases discussed in §§ 28–061 assume that the promise is valid and turn on the question whether an injunction would indirectly compel specific performance of the positive obligations of the contract. Yet it is arguable that the purpose of the negative stipulation in *Lumley v. Wagner*[25] was to restrain competition, as it might have been physically possible for the defendant to sing at Drury Lane for two nights' a week and to sing elsewhere on other nights. It used to be thought that the two lines of cases could be distinguished on the ground that the former concerned the validity of covenants which took effect

---

[17] *Warren v. Mendy* [1989] 1 W.L.R. 853, citing criticism of *Warner Bros. Inc. v. Nelson* (*supra*, n. 14) in *Nichols Advance Vehicle Systems Inc. v. De Angelis* (1979), unreported; McLean [1990] C.L.J. 15.

[18] *Page One Records Ltd v. Britton* [1968] 1 W.L.R. 157, 166. *Lumley v. Wagner* was distinguished at 165 on the ground that Mr. Lumley had no obligation except to pay money; but in fact he also made certain promises which were negative in substance, *viz.* that certain parts were to "belong exclusively" to the defendant.

[19] *Evening Standard Co. Ltd v. Henderson* [1987] I.C.R. 588.

[20] *William Hill Organisation Ltd v. Tucker* [1998] I.R.L.R. 313.

[21] *Ante*, §§ 28–055—28–056 at nn. 90–95; *cf. Delaney v. Staples* [1992] A.C. 687, 692–693 and *William Hill Organisation Ltd v. Tucker* [1998] I.R.L.R. 313, discussing so-called "garden leave."

[22] *Provident Financial Groups plc v. Hayward* [1989] I.C.R. 160.

[23] See *ante*, §§ 17–075 *et seq.*

[24] See *ante*, § 17–090.

[25] (1852) 1 De G.M. & G. 604; *ante* § 28–059.

after employment; while the latter concerned the remedy for breaches of covenants operating *during* employment. But in some cases the distinction may be hard to draw or not obviously relevant, especially where a service contract is a long-term one or gives the employer a series of options to renew it,[26] or where long periods of notice have to be given to terminate the contract.[27] The present position is that stipulations which operate during employment (no less than those which operate thereafter) can sometimes have their validity tested under the restraint of trade doctrine[28]; but even where their *validity* is not subject to these tests, the *remedy* of injunction is likely to be granted only where these tests are satisfied.[29] The employer will be allowed to enforce such a stipulation by injunction only if this remedy will not put the sort of pressure on the employee that was discussed in § 28–061 above: for example, if the employer undertakes to go on paying the employee the agreed remuneration, to allow the employee to go on working till the end of the contract period, and not to claim damages if the employee should choose not to work for the remainder of that period.[30] It is further submitted that, even where a covenant in restraint of trade takes effect after the period of service, and is valid, it may be appropriate not to enforce it by *injunction* (but only by an action for damages) if the grant of an injunction would leave the employee with no other reasonable means of making a living. In such a case, the grant of an injunction might well be regarded as oppressive and refused on that ground.[31]

28–063   **Severance.** A negative stipulation which is too widely expressed to be enforced by injunction as it stands may be severed and enforced in part. Severance is not here governed by the rules relating to severance of promises in illegal contracts. The question is not whether severance alters the nature of the contract but simply whether an injunction to enforce such part of the negative stipulation as the pleader specifies amounts to indirect specific performance of a positive obligation which will not be specifically enforced. In *Warner Brothers Pictures Inc. v. Nelson*[32] a film actress agreed to act for the claimants for a fixed period during which she undertook not only that she would not *act* for third parties, but also that she would not *"engage in any other occupation"* without the claimant's written consent. The claimants applied for an injunction to restrain her from acting for third parties. The court could clearly not restrain her from breach of all the negative undertakings, for that would force her to choose between idleness and performance of the obligation to serve. But this objection was "removed by the restricted form in which the injunction is sought."[33] The defendant was

---

[26] See the terms of the contracts in *Warner Bros. v. Nelson* [1937] 1 K.B. 209 and *cf. Eastham v. Newcastle United Football Club Ltd* [1964] Ch. 413.

[27] *e.g.* in cases of "garden leave".

[28] *Young v. Timmins* (1831) 1 Cr. & J. 331 as explained in *Esso Petroleum Co. Ltd v. Harper's Garage (Stourport) Ltd* [1968] A.C. 269, 328–329; *A. Schroeder Music Publishing Co. Ltd v. Macaulay* [1974] 1 W.L.R. 1308; *Clifford Davis Management Ltd v. W.E.A. Record Ltd* [1975] 1 W.L.R. 61; *ante*, § 17–113.

[29] *William Hill Organisation Ltd v. Tucker* [1998] I.R.L.R. 313.

[30] *Evening Standard v. Henderson* [1987] I.C.R. 588; *cf. ante* § 28–061 at n. 19, and *Delaney v. Staples* [1992] 1 A.C. 687, 692–693.

[31] *cf. ante*, § 28–058.

[32] [1937] 1 K.B. 209.

[33] *ibid.* at 219; *cf. William Robinson & Co. Ltd v. Heuer* [1898] 2 Ch. 451; *Provident Financial Group plc v. Hayward* [1989] I.C.R. 150, 160.

restrained simply from acting for third parties.[34] Of course, if the negative stipulation, though operating during employment, had been as a whole invalid for restraint of trade, the question of severance would have been determined by the principles governing the severance of promises in illegal contracts.[35]

Implied negative promises. An injunction to restrain the breach by an **28–064** employee of a stipulation in a contract of employment will be issued only if the contract contains an *express* negative promise.[36] The remedy has been restricted in this way; because in such cases an injunction may put so much economic pressure on the person who is to render the service that he will in fact be forced to perform the positive part of the contract, and compulsion of this kind is traditionally regarded as undesirable.[37] But where the defendant's obligation is not one to render personal services, there is less objection to an injunction which puts pressure on him to perform his positive undertaking, even though it may not be specifically enforceable; and in cases of this kind the courts have been willing to *imply* negative stipulations and to restrain their breach by injunction. Thus an injunction has been issued to prevent a shipowner from using a ship under charter inconsistently with the charterparty,[38] to restrain breach of a promise to give "first refusal" of purchase of land,[39] and to restrain breaches of various exclusive dealing agreements.[40] And a seller of uncut timber has been restrained from interfering with the right of the buyer to enter the land to cut down the timber and to take it away: this was "not specific performance in the sense of compelling the vendor to do anything. It merely prevents him from breaking his contract."[41]

In the above cases, a negative stipulation, though not express, can readily be **28–065** implied, and its enforcement by injunction does not amount to indirect specific performance. The position would be different where the vagueness of the positive part of the contract made it impossible to say precisely what the defendant had undertaken *not* to do[42]; and also where the only negative stipulation which could be implied was one that would embrace the whole positive obligation. For example, if a seller had simply contracted to deliver a quantity of unascertained

---

[34] See *ante*, § 28–060 for the question whether the injunction, even in these limited terms, left the defendant with a *reasonable* alternative means of earning a living.

[35] Contrast the *Warner Bros.* case, *supra*, n. 32, with *Gledhow Autoparts Ltd v. Delaney* [1965] 1 W.L.R. 1366.

[36] *Mortimer v. Beckett* [1920] 1 Ch. 571. An apparent exception is *Hivac v. Park Royal Scientific Instruments* [1946] Ch. 169 but the injunction was there issued to restrain breach of a duty imposed by law rather than to restrain breach of an implied negative promise. *cf. Printers & Finishers Ltd v. Holloway* [1965] 1 W.L.R. 1; *Cranleigh Precision Engineering Ltd v. Bryant* [1965] 1 W.L.R. 1293.

[37] *Ante*, § 28–060.

[38] *Sevin v. Deslandes* (1860) 30 L.J. (Ch.) 457; *De Mattos v. Gibson* (1859) 4 D. & J. 276; *Lord Strathcona Steamship Co. v. Dominion Coal Co.* [1926] A.C. 108, as to which see *ante*, § 19–120; *Associated Portland Cement Manufacturers Ltd v. Teigland Shipping A/S (The Oakworth)* [1975] 1 Lloyd's Rep. 581.

[39] *Manchester Ship Canal v. Manchester Racecourse Co.* [1901] 2 Ch. 37.

[40] *Donnell v. Bennett* (1883) 22 Ch.D. 835; *Metropolitan Electric Supply Co. v. Ginder* [1901] 2 Ch. 799; *Decro-Wall Internationala SA v. Practitioners in Marketing Ltd* [1971] 1 W.L.R. 361; *Evans Marshall & Co. v. Bertola SA* [1973] 1 W.L.R. 349, and see *ante*, §§ 17–119—17–133. *Fothergill v. Rowland* (1873) L.R. 17 Eq. 132 requires an express negative stipulation even in these cases but has not been followed on this point.

[41] *Jones v. Tankerville* [1909] 2 Ch. 440, 443; *cf. London Borough of Hounslow v. Twickenham Gardens Ltd* [1971] Ch. 223; *ante*, § 28–026; (1971) 87 L.Q.R. 309.

[42] *Bower v. Bantam Investments Ltd* [1972] 1 W.L.R. 1120.

generic goods such as "100 tons of coal" an injunction "not to break the contract" or "not to withhold delivery" would be indistinguishable from a decree of specific performance and would not normally[43] be granted.[44] And the implication of a narrower negative stipulation (*e.g.* not to sell to anyone else) would not fairly arise from the contract. In one case,[45] an injunction was granted against a manufacturer "not to terminate" a distributorship agreement which still had some years to run. The decision is, however, with respect, open to question since the grant of the injunction in these terms amounted to specific enforcement of the manufacturer's positive obligation to keep up the distributor's supplies; and specific performance of such an obligation would not normally be ordered since enforcement of such an order would require "constant supervision."[46]

28–066   **Expulsion from associations.** The rules of a members' club or trade union may have contractual force; and wrongful expulsion from such an association in breach of its rules may be restrained by injunction.[47] Where the expulsion is wrongful because the proper procedure for expulsion has not been followed, the court may nevertheless refuse an injunction on the ground that the procedural defect did not cause any prejudice to the claimant.[48] And where the statutory right of an individual not to be expelled from a trade union is infringed, the only remedies provided by the statute are by way of declaration and compensation.[49]

28–067   **Injunction against refusal to contract.** Generally a person cannot be restrained by injunction from refusing to contract with another; but there are at least three possible exceptions to this rule. These are discussed in the three following paragraphs.

28–068   **Statutory provisions against refusal to contract.** The first exception (or group of exceptions) arises under statutory provisions making it unlawful to refuse to enter into a contract with a person on certain specified grounds, such as that person's race or sex, or the fact that he suffers from a disability. An injunction may similarly be granted (and damages awarded) against persons whose withholding of supplies from distributors amounts to an abuse of a dominant position contrary to European Community[50] or United Kingdom[51]

---

[43] For exceptional cases in which such contracts could be specifically enforced, see *ante*, § 28–016, at n. 73.

[44] *cf.* Fry, *Specific Performance* (6th ed.), § 857; *Whitwood Chemical Co. v. Hardman* [1891] 2 Ch. 416, 426; *Scandinavian Trading Co. A.B. v. Flota Petrolera Ecuatoriana (The Scaptrade)* [1983] 2 A.C. 694, 701.

[45] *Wake v. Renault (U.K.) Ltd, The Times,* August 1, 1996.

[46] *Ante,* §§ 28–023—28–024, the authority of *Wake v. Renault (U.K.) Ltd, supra,* is also undermined to the extent that its reasoning was based on the decision of the Court of Appeal in *Co-operative Insurance Society Ltd v. Argyll Stores (Holdings) Ltd* which was reversed on Appeal: [1998] A.C. 1, *ante,* § 28–024.

[47] *e.g. Young v. Ladies Imperial Club Ltd* [1920] 2 K.B. 523; *Lawlor v. Union of Post Office Workers* [1965] Ch. 712; *R. v. Disciplinary Committee of the Jockey Club, ex p. Aga Khan* [1993] 1 W.L.R. 909, 933; and see *ante,* §§ 9–080—9–090.

[48] *Glynn v. Keele University* [1971] 1 W.L.R. 487; Wade (1971) 87 L.Q.R. 320.

[49] Trade Union and Labour Relations (Consolidation) Act 1992, ss.174 to 177, as substituted by Trade Union Reform and Employment Rights Act 1993, s.14.

[50] European Community Treaty, art. 86 (to be renumbered art. 82 in pursuance of European Communities (Amendment) Act 1998).

[51] Competition Act 1998, s.18.

competition law.[52] Such refusal may in certain circumstances, and subject to the provisions of the relevant statutes, be restrained by injunction.[53] On the other hand, the only remedies provided by statute for infringement of the statutory right not be excluded from a trade union are by way of declaration and compensation.[54]

Rules of associations restricting the right to work. The second exception **28–069** arises where the refusal is based on the rules of an association and unreasonably deprives a person of the right to work in some trade or profession. In *Nagle v. Feilden*[55] the claimant was refused a licence by the stewards of the Jockey Club on the sole ground that she was a woman. It was held that her claim for (*inter alia*) an injunction against the stewards ordering them to grant her a licence ought not to have been struck out as disclosing no cause of action; and it seems that the court was sympathetic to her claims on the merits. On the actual facts of *Nagle v. Feilden* an injunction could now be issued on the ground that the refusal constituted unlawful sex discrimination[56]; but the common law principle recognised in the case could (if still valid[57]) also apply where such a refusal gave effect to a policy of discrimination that was not unlawful by statute. This might be the position where a person was refused admission to an association, and so deprived of the opportunity of exercising a profession, on religious or political grounds that had no bearing on his competence in that profession.[58]

Aiding and abetting breach of an injunction. The third exception is illus- **28–070** trated by *Acrow Automation v. Rex Chainbelt Inc.*[59] The defendant company refused to supply components to a manufacturer in obedience to instructions given by an associated company; these instructions had been given in breach of an injunction against the latter company not to interfere with the manufacturer's business. It was held that the defendant company (which knew of the injunction) could be restrained from obeying the associated company's instructions, and that it could be ordered to make reasonable efforts to supply the manufacturer, since its refusal to supply him amounted to aiding and abetting a breach of the injunction against the associated company. These orders against the defendant company were made even though there was no previous contract between the

---

[52] *Garden Cottage Foods Ltd v. Milk Marketing Board* [1994] A.C. 130.
[53] Race Relations Act 1976, s.62; Sex Discrimination Act 1975, Pts II and III (as amended by Employment Act 1989, ss.1–9); Disability Discrimination Act 1995, ss.4, 5, 12 and 19; Sex Discrimination & Equal Pay (Miscellaneous Amendments) Regulations 1996, S.I. 1996 No. 438; see also the prohibition against discrimination in Human Rights Act 1998, s.1 and Sched. 1, Part I, art. 14; but by virtue of s.6, it is unlawful only for a *public authority* to act inconsistently with the prohibition against discrimination in art. 14. *cf.* also Trade Union and Labour Relations (Consolidation) Act 1992, ss.144, 145, 186 and 187. At common law refusal to contract was sometimes punishable and actionable against persons exercising the "common callings": see *R. v. Ivens* (1835) 7 C. & P. 213; *Constantine v. Imperial Hotels Ltd* [1944] K.B. 593; but there seems to be no reported case in which such a refusal was restrained by injunction.
[54] Trade Union and Labour Relations (Consolidation) Act 1992, ss.174 to 177, as substituted by Trade Union Reform and Employment Rights Act 1993, s.14; *cf.* Disability Discrimination Act 1995, s.13.
[55] [1966] 2 Q.B. 633.
[56] Sex Discrimination Act 1975, s.13.
[57] Its validity was doubted in *R. v. Disciplinary Committee of the Jockey Club, ex p. Aga Khan* [1993] 1 W.L.R. 909, 993.
[58] Some support for this view may be given by Human Rights Act 1998, Sched. 1, Part I, art. 14 (and perhaps art. 9); but see s.6, referred to in n. 53, *supra*.
[59] [1971] 1 W.L.R. 1676.

defendant company and the manufacturer for the supply of the goods in question.

8. Damages and Specific Performance or Injunction

28–071   **Statutory power to award in lieu of specific performance or injunction.** Power to award damages in addition to or "in substitution for" specific performance or injunction was conferred on the Court of Chancery by section 2 of the Chancery Amendment Act 1858 (also known as Lord Cairns' Act). That power is now vested in the High Court by section 50 of the Supreme Court Act 1981.[60] Since claims for specific performance (or injunction) can, by virtue of section 49 of that Act, be combined with claims for damages, it is normally unnecessary to resort to the special power to award damages in lieu of those remedies. But it may still sometimes be to the claimant's advantage to invoke that jurisdiction, and its exercise has also given rise to certain special problems with regard to the assessment of damages.

28–072   **No completed cause of action at law.** Damages may be awarded in lieu of specific performance or injunction even though there is no completed cause of action at law. Thus in *Leeds Industrial Co-operative Society Ltd v. Slack*[61] the House of Lords held that damages could be awarded in lieu of a *quia timet* injunction in respect of a tort which had not yet been committed and which was, therefore, not yet actionable at law. A similar possibility exists where one party to a contract has committed an anticipatory breach by repudiating the contract before performance was due, and the other, instead of "accepting" the repudiation, seeks to uphold the contract and sues for specific performance. In such case the court could make an order for specific performance at once[62] even though performance was not yet due at the time of the action; and it seems that the court can, in its discretion, award damages under the Act even though there was, when the proceedings were commenced, no right to damages at common law.[63] However, a party is not in anticipatory breach of contract merely because the other fears that he will commit a breach of it; and where there is neither a present breach nor a wrongful repudiation, an injunction is not available against the former party,[64] so that there can be no award of damages in lieu. On the principle of *Slack's* case it seems, moreover, that the power to award damages in lieu of an injunction could also be exercised where an injunction is available as a matter of judge-made law against refusal to contract[65]; and that such damages could be awarded even though the refusal gave rise to no claim for damages at common law. Where the refusal is wrongful by statute, the right to damages is commonly

---

[60] See Jolowicz [1975] C.L.J. 224; Pettit [1977] C.L.J. 367; [1978] C.L.J. 51.

[61] [1924] A.C. 851. In this case it was the defendant who asked that damages (rather than an injunction) should be awarded.

[62] *Hasham* v. *Zenab* [1960] A.C. 316, *ante*, § 28–003 (but the order will be for performance on the due day).

[63] cf. *Oakacre Ltd v. Claire Cleaners (Holdings) Ltd* [1982] Ch. 197. For another former illustration of the power (now made obsolete by Law of Property (Miscellaneous Provisions) Act 1989, s.2), see *Price v. Strange* [1978] Ch. 337, 358.

[64] *Veracruz Transportation Inc.* v. *V.C. Shipping Inc. (The Veracruz I)* [1992] 1 Lloyd's Rep. 356; *The P.* [1992] 1 Lloyd's Rep. 470; cf. *Zucker v. Tyndall Holdings plc* [1992] 1 W.L.R. 1127; *Mercantile Group (Europe) A.G.* v. *Aiyela* [1994] Q.B. 366, 375.

[65] *Ante*, §§ 28–067—28–070.

regulated by that statute.[66] An injunction may also be available to a third party where a contract between two others invalid for restraint of trade; and in such cases it is arguable that damages may be awarded in lieu even though the third party has no cause of action for breach of contract against the parties to the contract in question.[67]

Assessment of damages. There was formerly some support for the view that the assessment of damages might be more favourable to the claimant under Lord Cairns' Act than at common law, especially where the value of the subject matter had risen between the time of breach and the time of judgment. This view rested on the assumption that common law damages were necessarily based on the difference between the contract price and the market value of the subject matter *at the time of breach.* On this assumption, any subsequent increase in market value between breach and judgment was, at common law, liable to cause prejudice to the victim of the breach. In *Wroth v. Tyler,*[68] for example, the defendant entered into a contract to sell a house to the claimants for £6,000. The sale was to be completed in October 1971, by which time the value of the house had risen to £7,500. Meanwhile (in July 1971) the defendant had repudiated the contract; but in January 1972 the claimants started proceedings for specific performance and damages. Judgment in the action was given in January 1973, by which time the house was worth £11,500. Megarry J. held that specific performance, though in principle available, should not be ordered[69] and that damages should be awarded in lieu. He assessed these by reference to the value of the house at the time not of breach but of judgment,[70] *i.e.* not at £1,500 but at £5,500. One reason for assessing the damages by reference to the latter time was that they were awarded, not at common law, but under the Act, "in substitution for . . . specific performance." Such damages must, it was said, "constitute a true substitute for specific performance,"[71] and "be a substitute giving as nearly as may be what specific performance would have given."[72] But even at common law the aim of damages is to put the claimant "in the same position . . . *as if* the contract had been *performed*"[73]; and there seems to be no difference in principle between the phrases "as if . . . performed" and "in substitution for . . . specific performance." Both state the same general objective; neither is followed through to its logical conclusion. The judgment in *Wroth v. Tyler* itself appears to recognise the possibility that part of the claimants' loss could have been too remote,[74] and the mitigation rules[75] can also reduce the amount recoverable in lieu of specific

28–073

---

[66] *e.g.* Sex Discrimination Act 1975, ss.65, 66; Race Relations Act 1976, ss.56, 57, as amended by Race Relations (Remedies) Act 1994; Disability Discrimination Act 1995, ss.4, 5, 12 and 19.

[67] According to *Newport Association Football Club v. Football Association of Wales Ltd* [1995] 2 All E.R. 87 the mere availability to the third party of a declaration that the contract is in restraint of trade is a cause of action; but this is hard to reconcile with the reasoning of *Eastham v. Newcastle United Football Club Ltd* [1964] Ch. 413, according to which the court may grant a declaration to the third party even though that party has *no* "cause of action."

[68] [1974] Ch. 30.

[69] See *ante,* § 28–028.

[70] For the possibility of assessment by reference to an even later time, see *Grant v. Dawkins* [1973] 1 W.L.R. 1406.

[71] [1974] Ch. 30, 58.

[72] *ibid.* at 59. *cf. Biggin v. Minton* [1977] 1 W.L.R. 701, 704.

[73] *Robinson v. Harman* (1848) 1 Exch. 850, 855; *ante,* § 27–001.

[74] [1974] Ch. 30, 61; *ante,* §§ 27–039 *et seq.*

[75] *Ante,* § 27–085.

performance.[76] In *Johnson v. Agnew*[77] the House of Lords accordingly expressed the view that the assessment of damages was governed by the same principles whether the damages were awarded under the Act or at common law. Even at common law damages are not invariably assessed by reference to the date of breach. This method of assessment is adopted where it would have been reasonable for the claimant at that date to have mitigated his loss, *e.g.* by making a substitute contract; but if, for some reason, this is not the case, the damages will be assessed by reference to some other date.[78] In *Wroth v. Tyler* the claimants had (as the defendant knew)[79] no financial resources beyond the £6,000 that they had raised for the purpose of completing their contract with the defendant. By the time of breach they therefore could not reasonably have been expected to avoid any part of their loss by making a substitute purchase, since similar houses were financially out of their reach. The decision must now be explained on this ground and not by reference to any supposed distinction between the assessment of damages at common law and under the Act.

The general principle that there is no difference between the assessment of damages at common law and that of damages in lieu of specific performance or injunction is based on the assumption that the damages are claimed in respect of the same breach of contract or other cause of action. The principle obviously cannot apply where there is no cause of action at common law, *e.g.* where specific relief is sought in equity in respect of threatened or future breaches.[80]

28–074   **Damages and specific performance.** Damages may be awarded in addition to specific performance. For example, where a vendor's title is subject to an incumbrance and this amounts to a breach of contract, he can be ordered to convey what title he has and to pay damages based on the cost of discharging the incumbrance.[81] The court may also award damages as to part of a contract and specific performance or injunction as to the rest,[82] and damages for delay in completion in addition to specific performance.[83]

28–075   **Damages after specific performance.** Where an order of specific performance has been made but not been complied with, one course of action open to the injured party is to apply to the court for enforcement of the order. There was formerly some support for the view that this was the only remedy available to him, and that he could not, after having first obtained an order of specific

---

[76] See *Radford v. De Froberville* [1977] 1 W.L.R. 1262, 1286; *cf. Grant v. Dawkins* [1973] 1 W.L.R. 1406.

[77] [1980] A.C. 367, 400. This decision also makes it hard to accept the suggestion that damages under the Act can be based on the defendant's gain (rather than, as at common law, on the claimant's loss): see *Surrey C.C. v. Bredero Homes Ltd* [1993] 1 W.L.R. 1361; *Jaggard v. Sawyer* [1995] 1 W.L.R. 269.

[78] [1980] A.C. 367, at 401; *ante*, § 27–052; *cf. Saleman v. Shasavari* [1988] 1 W.L.R. 1181.

[79] *Wroth v. Tyler* [1974] Ch. 30, 57; but for this fact the loss might well have been (at least in part) too remote: see *ante*, § 27–049.

[80] See *Jaggard v. Sawyer* [1995] 1 W.L.R. 269, 291–292.

[81] *Grant v. Dawkins* [1973] 1 W.L.R. 1406.

[82] *Soames v. Edge* (1860) Johns. 669.

[83] *Ford-Hunt v. Raghbir Singh* [1973] 1 W.L.R. 738; *cf. Oakacre Ltd v. Claire Cleaners (Holdings) Ltd* [1982] Ch. 197 (damages for delay in substitution for specific performance). For the availability of damages for delay, see *Raineri v. Miles* [1981] A.C. 1050 (where no issue as to specific performance arose).

performance, claim damages.[84] But this view was rejected by the House of Lords in *Johnson v. Agnew*.[85] In that case, vendors of land were (as the purchaser knew) relying on the proceeds of sale to pay off a mortgage on the land. The purchaser failed to pay, even after specific performance had been ordered against her, with the result that the land was sold by the mortgagee. It followed that the vendors could no longer convey the land in exchange for the price and that they were therefore not in a position to enforce the order of specific performance. The House of Lords held that the vendors were entitled to damages, not only under the Act,[86] but also at common law. It would seem that the vendors could similarly have obtained damages if the order of specific performance had been obtained, and then not been complied with, by the purchaser.[87]

In *Johnson v. Agnew* the reason why the vendors could not enforce the order **28–076** of specific performance was that they had been disabled, in consequence of the purchaser's default, from performing their side of the bargain. But the reasoning of the House of Lords is not restricted to this type of situation. It is based on the general rules applicable to cases of repudiatory breach, subject only to the qualification that, where an order of specific performance has been made and not complied with, the party injured by such non-compliance must apply to the court for the dissolution of the order "and ask the court to put an end to the contract."[88] The choice between enforcement of the order of specific performance and damages thus seems to be a matter for the injured party; and the reasoning of *Johnson v. Agnew* suggests that damages can be awarded, after failure to comply with an order of specific performance, whenever that party elects to claim damages.

Limits of the court's power. The power to award damages under section 50 **28–077** of the Supreme Court Act 1981 exists only where the court has "jurisdiction to entertain an application for an injunction or specific performance."[89] If the court has such jurisdiction, the power to award damages in lieu can be exercised even though the court in its discretion refuses to order specific relief[90]; but it will not be exercised where no attempt is made to seek specific relief, where any chance of obtaining such relief has been lost by lapse of time, and where the only claim made was one for damages at common law.[91] Under section 49 of the Act, common law damages can be awarded where specific performance or an injunction is claimed, even though the case is not one in which specific relief could have been ordered.[92]

---

[84] See *Capital & Suburban Properties Ltd v. Swycher* [1976] Ch. 319 and the authorities there cited; *infra*, n. 85.

[85] [1980] A.C. 367, disapproving *Capital & Suburban Properties Ltd v. Swycher, supra*, n. 84.

[86] Such damages had been awarded in *Biggin v. Minton* [1977] 1 W.L.R. 701.

[87] The contrary was decided in *Sing v. Nazeer* [1979] Ch. 474. But as that case followed *Capital & Suburban Properties Ltd v. Swycher* (*supra*, n. 84) which is now disapproved (*supra*, n. 85), the claim for damages should now be allowed.

[88] [1980] A.C. 367, 394; *G.K.N. Distributors v. Tyne Tees Fabrication* (1985) 50 P. & C.R. 403.

[89] *Hipgrave v. Case* (1885) 28 Ch.D. 356; *Lavery v. Pursell* (1888) 39 Ch.D. 508; *Price v. Strange* [1978] Ch. 337, 359.

[90] *e.g. Wroth v. Tyler* [1974] Ch. 30 (where specific relief was refused for reasons stated in § 28–028, *ante*); *Jaggard v. Sawyer* [1995] 1 W.L.R. 269 (where specific relief was refused for the reasons stated in § 28–058, *ante*).

[91] *Surrey C.C. v. Bredero Homes Ltd* [1993] 1 W.L.R. 1361.

[92] As in *Dominion Coal Co. Ltd v. Dominion Iron & Steel Co.* [1909] A.C. 293; *cf. Proctor v. Bayley* (1889) 42 Ch.D. 390 (decided under earlier similar legislative provisions).

CHAPTER 29

LIMITATION OF ACTIONS[1]

1. PERIODS OF LIMITATION

Introductory. It is the policy of the law that there should be an end to **29–001** litigation and that "stale demands"[2] should be suppressed. The reasons for this policy have been said to be[3]: first, that defendants should be protected against claims being made on them after a long period during which they may have lost the evidence available to them to rebut those claims; secondly, that claimants should be encouraged not to go to sleep on their rights, but to institute proceedings without unreasonable delay; thirdly, that defendants should be in a position to know that, after a given time, an incident which might have led to a claim against them is finally closed. Accordingly, the legislature has laid down certain periods of limitation after the expiry of which no action can be maintained. The principal statute to which reference must be made for the law of limitation of

---

[1] See generally McGee, *Limitation of Actions* (1990); Prime and Scanlon, *The Modern Law of Limitation* (1993); Merkin, Oughton and Lowry, *Limitation of Actions* (1998). The Law Commission has issued a consultation paper seeking opinions on its provisional proposals to reform the law of limitation of actions which it suggests is complex, outdated and unfair (Law Com. No. 151).

[2] *Cholmondeley v. Clinton* (1820) 2 J. & W. 1; 4 Bli. 1; *A'Court v. Cross* (1825) 3 Bing. 329, 333; *R.B. Policies at Lloyd's v. Butler* [1950] 1 K.B. 76.

[3] *Report of the Committee on Limitation of Actions in Cases of Personal Injury,* Cmnd. 1829 (1962), para. 17; Law Reform Committee, *Twentieth Report*, Cmnd. 5630 (1974), paras 22–23; *Twenty-First Report*, Cmnd. 6923 (1977), paras 1.7–1.14; *Twenty-Fourth Report*, Cmnd. 9390 (1984).

actions is the Limitation Act 1980, which came into force on May 1, 1981.[4] Subject to exceptions which do not affect the law of contract, the Act applies to proceedings by or against the Crown as it applies to proceedings between subjects[5]; but it does not apply to any action or arbitration for which a period of limitation is prescribed by or under any other enactment.[6] The main provisions of the Act so far as it affects the law of contract are discussed in the following pages.

29–002   **Simple contracts.** By section 5 of the 1980 Act, no action[7] founded on simple contract can be brought after the expiration of six years from the date on which the cause of action accrued.[8] The section must also "be taken to cover actions for money had and received, formerly actions on the case . . . though the words used cannot be regarded as felicitous."[9] Restitutionary claims will, therefore, in general be barred after six years,[10] although they may be affected by the special provisions of the Act relating to fraud, concealment or mistake[11] or the fact that they are equitable claims.[12] An action for an account cannot be brought after the expiration of any time limit under the Act which is applicable to the claim which is the basis of the duty to account.[13]

29–003   **Specialties.** By section 8 of the 1980 Act, no action upon a specialty can be brought after the expiration of 12 years from the date when the cause of action accrued[14]: but this does not affect any action for which a shorter period of limitation is prescribed by any other provision of the Act.[15] The words "action upon a specialty" refer to any action to enforce an obligation created or secured by an instrument which is executed as a deed.[16] They extend to an action for

---

[4] s.41(2) (except certain subss. of s.35, *post*, § 29–121). See s.40(1) and Sched. 2 for transitional provisions, also ss.12, 14(3) of the Limitation Amendment Act 1980. The Act has been amended by the Administration of Justice Act 1985, s.57 (defamation actions), by the Latent Damage Act 1986 (*post*, § 29–091), by the Consumer Protection Act 1987 (*post*, § 29–008), and by the Arbitration Act 1996 (*post*, § 29–128). See also the Foreign Limitation Periods Act 1984 (*post*, § 29–151) and the Contracts (Applicable Law) Act 1990 (*post*, § 29–153).

[5] s.37(1).

[6] s.39.

[7] Defined in s.38(1).

[8] But see *post*, §§ 29–004, 29–075, 29–082, 29–095.

[9] *Re Diplock* [1948] Ch. 465, 514, followed in *Kleinwort Benson Ltd v. Sandwell B.C.* (1993) 91 L.G.R. 323, 382–384, and *Kleinwort Benson Ltd v. South Tyneside Metropolitan B.C.,* [1994] 4 All E.R. 972. Contrast (in a different context) *Barclays Bank plc v. Glasgow C.C.* [1993] Q.B. 429, [1994] Q.B. 404.

[10] *Kleinwort Benson Ltd v. Lincoln C.C.* [1998] 3 W.L.R. 1095. See Goff and Jones, *The Law of Restitution* (5th ed., 1998), Chap. 42; McLean [1989] C.L.J. 472.

[11] See *post*, § 29–082.

[12] See *post*, § 29–137.

[13] s.23. *cf. Tito v. Waddell (No. 2)* [1977] Ch. 106, 250–251; *Att.-Gen. v. Cocke* [1988] Ch. 414; *Paragon Finance plc v. Thakerar & Co.* [1991] 1 All E.R. 400, 415.

[14] s.8(1).

[15] s.8(2).

[16] Or under a statute (except where s.9 applies): *Collin v. Duke of Westminster* [1985] Q.B. 581. See (contracts under seal) *Leivers v. Barber, Walker & Co. Ltd* [1943] 1 K.B. 385, 398; *Whittall Builders Co. Ltd v. Chester-le-Street D.C.* (1986) 11 Const.L.R. 40. But the requirement of a seal for a deed executed by an individual was abolished by the Law of Property (Miscellaneous Provisions) Act 1989, and see also (deeds executed by companies) s.36A(4) of the Companies Act 1985; *ante* §§ 1–044, 1–055. It is questionable whether, now, the execution of a document under seal is itself sufficient to make it "clear on its face" that it is intended to be a deed and therefore a specialty: see *ante*, § 1–044. Also in *Re Compania de Electricidad de la Provincia de Buenos Aires Ltd* [1980] Ch.

damages.[17] However, the period of limitation prescribed by the Act to recover arrears of rent[18] or arrears of interest on a mortgage[19] is six years even if the lease or mortgage is by deed.

The Companies Act 1985 provides that the memorandum and articles of association of a company shall, when registered, bind the company and the members thereof to the same extent as if they respectively had been signed and sealed by each member and contained covenants on the part of each member to observe all their provisions.[20] Further, all money payable by any member to the company under the memorandum or articles is a specialty debt due from him to the company.[21] The liability of contributories on a winding-up is also in the nature of a specialty debt.[22] There is little doubt that the obligations between a company incorporated under the Companies Acts and its members arising out of the memorandum and articles are contractual.[23] But judicial opinion is divided as to the appropriate period of limitation to be applied to an action by a member against the company to recover dividends or capital repayable on a reduction of capital. In *Re Artisans' Land and Mortgage Corporation*,[24] Byrne J. applied the period of limitation then applicable to actions upon specialties. But in the later case of *Re Compania de Electricidad de la Provincia de Buenos Aires Ltd*[25] Slade J. held that the six-year period applied, on the ground that, while the Companies Act 1948[26] provided that the deemed contract constituted by the memorandum and articles was to be treated as if executed by the members under seal, and for money payable by members to the company to be specialty debts, it did not make the same provision with respect to the obligations of the company to members or money payable by the company to members under the deemed contract.

Contracts (Rights of Third Parties) Bill. This Bill, when enacted, will   **29–004** enable a person who is not a party to a contract (a "third party") in certain circumstances to enforce a term of the contract.[27] In sections 5 and 8 of the 1980 Act the references to an action founded on a simple contract and an action upon

---

146, it was held that an action to enforce an obligation which was merely acknowledged or evidenced by a sealed instrument was not an "action upon a specialty."

[17] *Aiken v. Stewart Wrightson Members' Agency Ltd* [1995] 1 W.L.R. 1281.

[18] s.19. See also *Romain v. Scuba TV Ltd* [1997] Q.B. 887 (action against guarantor of lessee).

[19] s.20(5). See also *Re Compania de Electricidad de la Provincia de Buenos Aires Ltd, supra* (arrears of interest on bond). But where the mortgagor is seeking to redeem or the mortgagee is accounting to the mortgagor for the surplus, more than six years' interest may be retained by the mortgagee: *Edmunds v. Waugh* (1866) L.R. 1 Eq. 48; *Holmes v. Coucher* [1970] 1 W.L.R. 834; *Ezekiel v. Orakpo* [1997] 1 W.L.R. 340.

[20] s.14(1).

[21] s.14(2).

[22] s.508. See also *Buck v. Robson* (1870) L.R. 10 Eq. 629; *Re Muggeridge* (1870) L.R. 10 Eq. 443 (calls on shares).

[23] *Hickman v. Kent or Romney Marsh Sheep Breeders' Assn.* [1915] 1 Ch. 881. *cf. Rayfield v. Hands* [1960] Ch. 1.

[24] [1904] 1 Ch. 796, following *Smith v. Cork and Bandon Ry.* (1870) I.R. 5 Eq. 65; *Re Drogheda Steam Packet Co.* [1903] 1 Ir.R. 512. Byrne J. also considered whether an action for sums due for repayment of capital under a scheme of arrangement, sanctioned by the court in the exercise of its statutory jurisdiction, would be an action to recover sums "recoverable by virtue of any enactment," for which the period is six years under s.9 of the 1980 Act, but did not decide this point. *cf.* Preston and Newsom, *Limitation of Actions* (3rd ed.), p. 58; Franks, *Limitation of Actions* (1959), p. 84; *Cork and Bandon Ry. v. Goode* (1853) 13 C.B. 826.

[25] [1980] Ch. 146.

[26] s.20(1), now s.14(2) of the Companies Act 1985.

[27] See *ante*, § 19–075.

a specialty will respectively include references to an action brought by the third party relating to a simple contract or to a specialty.[28]

29–005　　**Personal injuries and death.**[29] In the case of any action for breach of duty existing by virtue of a contract where the damages claimed by the claimant consist of or include damages for personal injuries to the claimant or any other person, neither the period applicable to simple contracts[30] nor that applicable to specialties[31] applies, but the limitation period is three years from (a) the date on which the cause of action accrued, or (b) the date of the claimant's knowledge (if later) of certain facts relevant to his right of action against the defendant.[32] "Personal injuries" includes any disease and any impairment of a person's mental or physical condition.[33] But the three-year period applies only to what is popularly referred to as a personal injuries action. It does not extend to an action claiming damages from the defendant in respect of a wrong which consists in causing or permitting the claimant to lose the chance or right to recover compensation for personal injuries from a third party.[34]

29–006　　An action under the Fatal Accidents Act 1976 cannot be brought after the expiration of three years from (a) the date of death, or (b) the date of knowledge of the person for whose benefit the action is brought of certain facts relevant to his right of action against the defendant, whichever is the later.[35]

29–007　　A discretion is, however, vested in the court to override the time limits mentioned above.[36]

29–008　　**Product liability.** In the case of an action for damages by virtue of Part I of the Consumer Protection Act 1987[37] in which the damages claimed by the claimant consist of or include damages for personal injuries to the claimant or any other person or loss of or damage to any property, the limitation period is three years from whichever is the later of (a) the date on which the cause of action accrued, and (b) the date of knowledge of the injured person of certain facts relevant to his right of action against the defendant or, in the case of loss of or damage to property, the date of knowledge of the claimant or (if earlier) of any person in whom his cause of action was previously vested.[38] The normal three-year time limit in respect of Fatal Accident Act claims also applies.[39] The court has a discretion to override these time limits,[40] except where the damages claimed by the claimant are confined to damages for loss of or damage to any property.[41]

---

[28] Clause 7(3).
[29] Todd, *Limitation Periods in Personal Injury Claims* (1982).
[30] s.11(2).
[31] ss.8(2), 11(2).
[32] ss.11, 14. See *Clerk and Lindsell on Torts* (17th ed., 1995), §§ 31–23 *et seq.*
[33] s.38(1).
[34] *Ackbar v. C.F. Green & Co. Ltd* [1975] Q.B. 582.
[35] ss.12, 13, 14. See *Clerk and Lindsell on Torts* (17th ed., 1995), § 31–37.
[36] s.33. *Clerk and Lindsell on Torts* (17th ed., 1995), § 31–31; Davies (1982) 98 L.Q.R. 249.
[37] See Vol. II, § 43–112.
[38] s.11A (inserted by s.6 of and Sched. 1 to the Consumer Protection Act 1987) and s.14 (as so amended). See *Clerk and Lindsell on Torts* (17th ed., 1995), § 31–34.
[39] ss.12, 13, 14 (as so amended); see *ante*, § 29–006.
[40] s.33 (as so amended).
[41] s.33(1A).

However, there is an overall long-stop period of 10 years after which any action for damages by virtue of Part I of the 1987 Act is barred and extinguished.[42] This 10-year period usually begins to run from the time when the defendant[43] supplied the product to another.[44]

Loans. The 1980 Act contains special provisions in respect of the time limit for actions in respect of certain loans.[45] It is not clear, however, whether these provisions apply if the contract of loan is executed as a deed. It is probable that the action is then upon a specialty and subject to the 12-year period.[46]   **29–009**

Contribution. Where under section 1 of the Civil Liability (Contribution) Act 1978 any person becomes entitled to a right to recover contribution in respect of any damage from any other person, no action to recover contribution by virtue of that right is to be brought after the expiration of two years from the date on which that right accrued.[47]   **29–010**

Action on a judgment. An action upon a judgment obtained in England or Wales is barred after the expiration of six years from the date on which the judgment became enforceable,[48] and no arrears of interest in respect of any judgment can be recovered after the expiration of six years from the date on which the interest became due.[49] A foreign judgment of a court of competent jurisdiction gives rise to an implied contract to pay the amount of the judgment,[50] and the six-year period for actions founded on simple contract applies to an action upon such a judgment.[51]   **29–011**

Action on an award. An arbitrator's award is usually enforced by summary procedure under section 66 of the Arbitration Act 1996.[52] But it may also be enforced by bringing an action on the award, and this is the only method available if the submission to arbitration was not in writing, or if the validity of the award is doubtful, or in the case of certain foreign awards.[53] An action to enforce the award of an arbitrator, where the submission was not by deed, cannot   **29–012**

---

[42] s.11A(3). This cannot be overridden: s.33(1A).

[43] Being a person to whom s.2(2) of the 1987 Act applies, *i.e.* the producer or ostensible producer or the importer of the product into a Member State of the E.C.

[44] *i.e.* the "relevant time" within the meaning of s.4 of the 1987 Act. But see s.4(2)(b).

[45] s.6; see *post*, § 29–032.

[46] The action does not appear to be one "for which a shorter period of limitation is prescribed by any other provision of this Act" (s.8(2)) as under s.6(1) only s.5 of the Act is involved.

[47] s.10. See also *post*, § 29–046 (accrual of right).

[48] s.24(1). This does not apply to the enforcement of judgments by execution, as to which see *Lowsley v. Forbes*, [1998] 3 W.L.R. 501. Contrast *Re a Debtor (No. 50A–SD–1995)* [1997] Ch. 310 (bankruptcy proceedings based on a statutory demand for moneys due under a previous judgment are within s.24(1)). See also *E. D. & F. Man (Sugar) v. Haryanto, The Times*, Nov. 24, 1995.

[49] s.24(2). This sub-section does apply to the recovery of interest by way of execution after six years: *Lowsley v. Forbes, supra.*

[50] *Grant v. Easton* (1883) 13 Q.B.D. 302; *Re Flynn (No. 2)* [1969] Ch. 403.

[51] This does not apply to the enforcement of a judgment registered under the Administration of Justice Act 1920, the Foreign Judgments (Reciprocal Enforcement) Act 1933 or Parts I and II of the Civil Jurisdiction and Judgments Act 1982. But certain time limits for registration are imposed by the 1920 and 1933 Acts.

[52] See *ante*, § 16–147.

[53] See *ante*, §§ 16–148—16–149.

be brought after the expiration of six years from the date on which the cause of action accrued.[54]

29–013   **Equitable relief.** The time limits prescribed by sections 5 and 8 of the Act[55] in respect of actions upon simple contracts and specialties do not apply to any claim for specific performance of a contract or for an injunction or for other equitable relief, except in so far as they may be applied by analogy.[56] Such claims may, however, be barred by laches or acquiescence, equitable doctrines which are discussed elsewhere in this chapter.[57]

29–014   **Breach of trust or fiduciary duty.** The limitation period for an action by a beneficiary to recover trust property or in respect of any breach of trust is normally six years from the date on which the right of action accrued.[58] But no period of limitation prescribed by the 1980 Act applies to an action by a beneficiary under a trust in respect of any fraud or fraudulent breach of trust to which the trustee was a party or privy,[58a] or to recover from the trustee trust property or the proceeds of trust property in the possession of the trustee or previously received by the trustee and converted to his use.[59] However, in the case of a claim against a defendant as "constructive trustee" which is based, not upon the assumption by the defendant of the duties of trustee by a lawful transaction not impeached by the claimant, but merely upon the defendant being implicated in a fraud and therefore accountable to the claimant in equity, the court will apply the statute by analogy.[60] The court will similarly apply lthe statute either directly or by analogy to a breach of fiduciary duty unless the defendant is more than a fiduciary and is a trustee of trust property.[61]

29–014A   **Long-stop for negligence actions.** An action for damages for negligence, other than one involving personal injuries to which section 11 of the 1980 Act applies,[62] cannot be brought after the expiration of 15 years from the date (or, if more than one, from the last of the dates) on which there occurred any act or omission (a) which is alleged to constitute negligence, and (b) to which the damage in respect of which damages are claimed is alleged to be attributable (in whole or in part).[63] It is probable that "negligence" is restricted to tortious negligence, and does not extend to breach of a contractual duty to exercise reasonable care and skill.[64] This 15-year long-stop is an absolute bar[65] and

---

[54] Limitation Act 1980, s.7; for accrual of the cause of action, see *post*, § 29–060.

[55] s.7 (actions to enforce arbitral award); s.9 (statute) and s.24 (actions on judgments) are also inapplicable.

[56] s.36(1). As to the application of the statute by analogy, see *post*, § 29–138.

[57] s.36(2); *post*, §§ 29–139, 29–140.

[58] s.21(3).

[58a] s.21(1)(a). See *Armitage v. Nurse* [1998] Ch. 241.

[59] s.21(1)(b). See *Tito v. Waddell (No. 2)* [1977] Ch. 106, 247–249.

[60] *Soar v. Ashwell* [1893] 2 Q.B. 390, 393; *Taylor v. Davies* [1920] A.C. 636, 652; *Paragon Finance plc v. Thakerar & Co.* [1999] 1 All E.R. 400, 407–414. *cf. James v. Williams, The Times,* April 13, 1999. But see s.32(1)(a); *post*, § 29–084.

[61] *Paragon Finance plc v. Thakerar & Co., supra*, at 414–4115 (disapproving *Nelson v. Rye* [1996] 1 W.L.R. 1378); *Coulthard v. Disco Mix Club Ltd., The Times*, March 25, 1999.

[62] See *ante*, § 29–005.

[63] s.14B(1), inserted by s.1 of the Latent Damage Act 1986.

[64] See *post*, § 29–092.

[65] Subject to s.32(5); *post*, § 29–090, n. 76.

operates even though the cause of action has not yet accrued[66] and even though the starting date for the extension available in respect of latent damage[67] has not yet occurred.[68]

Special limitation periods. Certain statutes provide periods of limitation   **29–015** which differ from those provided by the Limitation Act 1980.[69] These, so far as they affect the law of contract, are as follows:

Shipping. Article 23 of the International Convention on Salvage, contained in   **29–016** Schedule 11 to the Merchant Shipping Act 1995, prescribes that any action relating to payment under the Convention is to be time-barred if judicial or arbitral proceedings are not instituted within a period of two years from the day on which the salvage operations are terminated (although the period may be extended by declaration to the claimant). Actions for an indemnity may be instituted within the time allowed by the *forum* where the proceedings are instituted.

Carriage by sea. Where the Hague-Visby Rules are incorporated in a contract   **29–017** of affreightment by the Carriage of Goods by Sea Act 1971,[70] the carrier[71] and the ship are discharged[72] from all liability whatsoever in respect of the goods, unless suit[73] is brought within one year of their delivery[74] or of the date when they should have been delivered.[75] This period may, however, be extended if the parties so agree after the cause of action has arisen.[76] An action for an indemnity against a third person may nevertheless be brought even after the expiration of the year if brought within the time allowed by the law of the court seised of the case,[77] *i.e.*, in an English court, within the six-year period of limitation applicable to simple contracts.[78]

The Athens Convention of 1974 relating to the carriage of Passengers and their   **29–018** Luggage by Sea (as amended by the 1976 Protocol thereto) has the force of law

---

[66] s.14B(2)(a); see *post*, § 29–091.

[67] See *post*, § 29–093.

[68] s.14B(2)(b).

[69] s.39.

[70] See ss.1, 2, 4, 5.

[71] *cf. Freedom General Shipping SA v. Tokai Shipping Co. Ltd* [1982] 1 Lloyd's Rep. 73.

[72] The cause of action is extinguished: see *post*, § 29–129; (Hague Rules) *Aries Tanker Corpn. v. Total Transport Ltd* [1977] 1 W.L.R. 185; *Casillo Grani v. Napier Shipping Co.* [1984] 2 Lloyd's Rep. 481; *Payabi v. Armstel Shipping Corpn.* [1992] Q.B. 907.

[73] "Suit" includes arbitration: *The Merak* [1965] P. 223; *Nea Agrex SA v. Baltic Shipping Co. Ltd* [1976] Q.B. 933; see also *ante*, § 16–050; *post*, § 29–118. The suit may be in another competent jurisdiction: *The Nordglimt* [1988] Q.B. 183, distinguishing *Compania Columbiana de Seguros v. Pacific Steam Navigation Co.* [1965] 1 Q.B. 101. See also *Central Insurance Co. Ltd v. Seacalf Shipping Corpn.* [1983] 2 Lloyd's Rep. 25; *Hispanica de Petroleus SA v. Vencedora Oceania Navegacion SA* [1986] 1 Lloyd's Rep. 211; *Government of Sierra Leone v. Marmaro Shipping Co. Ltd* [1989] 2 Lloyd's Rep. 130; *Transworld Oil (USA) Inc. v. Minos Naviera SA* [1992] 2 Lloyd's Rep. 48; *Mauritius Oil Refineries Ltd v. Stolt-Nielsen Nederlands BV* [1997] 1 Lloyd's Rep. 273.

[74] See *The Beltana* [1967] 1 Lloyd's Rep. 431.

[75] Sched., art. III, r. 6.

[76] See *The Clifford Maersk* [1982] 1 W.L.R. 1292; *Mitsubishi Corpn. v. Castletown Navigation Ltd* [1989] 2 Lloyd's Rep. 383 (Hague Rules). *cf. Alma Shipping Corpn. v. Union of India* [1971] 2 Lloyd's Rep. 494, 502 (after expiry of period new agreement required).

[77] Sched., art. III, r. 6 *bis*.

[78] See *China Ocean Shipping Co. v. Andros* [1987] 1 W.L.R. 1213. *cf.* Limitation Act 1980, s.10 (claims to contribution), *ante*, § 29–010.

in the United Kingdom.[79] It provides[80] for a two-year limitation period in respect of any action for damages arising out of the death of or personal injury to a passenger[81] or for the loss of or damage to luggage. The commencement of the period depends on the nature of the claim made, but in general is not earlier than the date of disembarkation or the date when disembarkation should have taken place. The period may be extended by written declaration of the carrier or by written agreement of the parties after the cause of action has arisen.

29–019   **Carriage by air.** The Carriage by Air Act 1961[82] gives effect to the Warsaw Convention as amended at the Hague 1955, which applies to the international carriage by air of persons, baggage and cargo for reward or gratuitously by an air transport undertaking. The right to damages in respect of the carrier's liability is extinguished if an action[83] is not brought within two years, reckoned from the date of arrival at the destination, or from the date on which the aircraft ought to have arrived, or from the date on which the carriage stopped.[84] Similar provisions are contained in the Carriage by Air Act (Application of Provisions) Order 1967[85] in cases to which the amended convention does not apply, and in the Carriage by Air and Road Act 1979,[86] which gives effect[87] to the protocols signed at Montreal in 1975 further amending the Convention.

29–020   **Carriage by rail.** The International Transport Conventions Act 1983[88] gives the force of law to the Convention concerning International Carriage by Rail (COTIF).[89] Under the Convention, the periods of limitation for actions for damages based on the liability of the railway in case of death of, or personal injury to, passengers are (a) for the passenger, three years from the day after the accident, and (b) in a case where the claimant is not the passenger himself, three years from the day after the death of the passenger, subject to a maximum of five years from the day after the accident.[90] The Convention also contains limitation provisions with respect to other actions arising from a contract for the international carriage of passengers and luggage by rail[91] and for actions arising from a contract for the international carriage of goods by rail,[92] the period of limitation being in general one year with an extension to two years in certain cases. The

---

[79] Merchant Shipping Act 1995, Sched. 6.

[80] Art. 16.

[81] The court's discretion to override the time-limit for such claims contained in s.33 of the 1980 Act (*ante*, § 29–007) does not apply to this two-year period: *Higham v. Stena Sealink Ltd* [1996] 1 W.L.R. 1107.

[82] For the relationship between this Act and the Fatal Accidents Act 1976, s.3, in relation to limitation, see *Clerk and Lindsell on Torts* (17th ed., 1995), § 31–39.

[83] Or arbitration: Carriage by Air Act 1961, s.5(3).

[84] Sched. 1, Pt. 1, art. 29 (see Vol. II, § 35–022). See also s.5 of the Act and s.3(2) of the Carriage by Air (Supplementary Provisions) Act 1962; s.4(4) of the Limitation Act 1963. For the time limits for claims, see Sched. 1, art. 26 to the 1961 Act and Vol. II, §§ 35–061, 35–077, 35–078.

[85] S.I. 1967 No. 480; see Vol. II, § 35–085.

[86] Sched. 1, art. 29. For the time limits for claims, see *ibid.* art. 26.

[87] Vol. II, § 35–002.

[88] ss.1(1)(3), 11(3); S.I. 1985 No. 612.

[89] Cmnd. 8535. See Vol. II, § 36–096.

[90] COTIF, Appendix A (CIV), Art. 55(1); Vol. II, § 36–122. For the time limits for claims, see *ibid.*, Art. 53; Vol. II, § 36–121.

[91] COTIF, Appendix A (CIV), Art. 55(2)(3); Vol. II, § 36–127. For the time limits for claims, in respect of registered luggage, see *ibid.* Art. 54; Vol. II, § 36–127.

[92] COTIF, Appendix B (CIM), Art. 58; Vol. II, § 36–108. For the time limits for claims, see *ibid.*, Art. 57; Vol. II, § 36–107.

starting point of the limitation period varies according to the nature of the claim,[93] but in the case of carriage of goods (a) in actions for compensation for total loss, it runs from the thirtieth day after the expiry of the transit period, and (b) in actions for compensation for partial loss, for damage or for exceeding the transit period, it runs from the day when delivery took place.[94]

Carriage by road. Under the Carriage of Goods by Road Act 1965,[95] which **29–021** gives effect to the Convention on the Contract for the International Carriage of Goods by Road (CMR), the period of limitation is one year, or, in the case of wilful misconduct or equivalent, three years.[96] The period of limitation begins to run: in the case of partial loss, damage or delay in delivery, from the date of delivery; in the case of total loss, from the thirtieth day after the expiry of the agreed time limit or where there is no agreed time limit from the sixtieth day from the date on which the goods were taken over by the carrier; and in all other cases, on the expiry of three months after the making of the contract of carriage.[97]

The Carriage of Passengers by Road Act 1974[98] will (if brought into force) **29–022** give effect to a Convention on the Contract for the International Carriage of Passengers and Luggage by Road (CVR). It provides that the period of limitation for actions arising out of the death or wounding of, or out of any other bodily or mental injury to a passenger, is three years. The period runs from the date on which the person suffering the loss or damage had or should have had knowledge of it, provided that, in any event, the period does not exceed five years from the date of the accident.[99] Otherwise the period of limitation for actions arising out of carriage under the Convention is in all cases one year. The one-year period runs from the date on which the vehicle arrived at the place of destination of the passenger or, in the case of non-arrival, from the date on which the vehicle ought to have arrived at the place of destination of the passenger.[1]

Sale of goods. By the Uniform Laws on International Sales Act 1967, where **29–023** the Uniform Law of International Sales (ULIS) applies,[2] the buyer loses his right to rely on lack of conformity with the contract at the expiration of a period of one year after he has given notice as provided in Article 39.[3] Such notice must be given promptly after he has discovered the lack of conformity or ought to have discovered it, and must in any event be given within a period of two years from

---

[93] COTIF, Appendix A (CIV), Art. 55(3); Appendix B (CIM), art. 58(2).

[94] COTIF, Appendix B (CIM), Art. 58(2)(a), (b).

[95] See Vol. II, § 36–128 and the amendments effected by the Carriage by Air and Road Act 1979, *supra*. See also S.I. 1980 No. 1966 (c. 84).

[96] Carriage of Goods by Road Act 1965, Sched., art. 32(1). For the time limits for claims, see *ibid.* art. 30 and Vol. II, § 36–152.

[97] See Vol. II, § 36–153.

[98] See Vol. II, § 36–158. See also the Carriage by Air and Road Act 1979 and S.I. 1980 No. 1966 (c. 84). For the time limits for claims, see Vol. II, § 36–164. This is not yet in force.

[99] Carriage of Passengers by Road Act 1974, Sched., art. 22(1); Vol. II, § 36–164.

[1] *ibid.* art. 22(2).

[2] See Vol. II, § 43–003.

[3] Uniform Laws on International Sales Act 1967, Sched. 1, art. 49(1) (unless he has been prevented from exercising his right because of fraud on the part of the seller). But see art. 49(2).

the date on which the goods were handed over, unless the lack of conformity constituted a breach of a guarantee covering a longer period.[4]

29–024   **Employment.** Unless the employee has previously made a claim for a redundancy payment by notice in writing given to his employer and in certain other cases, a claim for such a payment cannot be entertained by an employment tribunal after the end of the period of six months beginning with the relevant date (usually the date of termination of his employment).[5] And an employment tribunal cannot consider a complaint of unfair dismissal unless it is presented to the tribunal before the end of the period of three months beginning with the effective date of termination or within such further period as the tribunal considers reasonable in a case where it is satisfied that it was not reasonably practicable for the complaint to be presented within the period of three months.[6] Short periods of limitation are further provided for proceedings where an employer has not provided an employee with a statement of terms of employment[7] and in respect of guarantee payments.[8]

29–025   Legal proceedings by the employer of a worker in retail employment for the recovery from the worker of any amount in respect of a cash shortage or stock deficiency cannot be instituted after the end of a period of 12 months beginning with the date when the employer established the existence of the deficiency or (if earlier) the date when he ought reasonably to have done so, unless he has within that period made a statutory demand for payment in respect of that amount.[9] An employment tribunal cannot entertain a complaint in respect of unauthorised deductions from the wages of a worker or an unlawful payment to an employer unless it is presented within the period of three months from the date of payment of the relevant wages or the date of the receipt of the payment by the employer or within such further period as the tribunal considers reasonable in a case where it is satisfied that it was not reasonably practicable for the complaint to be presented within the period of three months.[10]

29–026   The Equal Pay Act 1970,[11] the Sex Discrimination Act 1975,[12] the Race Relations Act 1976[13] and the Disability Discrimination Act 1995[14] also establish time limits within which complaints must be made.

2. ACCRUAL OF THE CAUSE OF ACTION

29–027   **Meaning of cause of action.** Section 5 of the Limitation Act 1980 provides that the action "shall not be brought after the expiration of six years from the date

---

[4] *ibid.* art. 39(1).
[5] Employment Rights Act 1996, s.164(1). But see s.164(2). See Vol. II, § 39–237.
[6] *ibid.* s.111(2). But see s.111(3)(4). See Vol. II, § 39–221.
[7] *ibid.* s.11(4) (three months); Vol. II, § 39–038.
[8] *ibid.* s.34(2) (three months); Vol II, § 39–081.
[9] *ibid.* s.20(5); see Vol. II, § 39–089.
[10] *ibid.* s.23(2)–(4); see Vol. II, § 39–087.
[11] s. 2(5) (as amended); see Vol. II, § 39–032.
[12] s.76 (as amended) and Sched. 1, Pt. I, para. 6(1) (employment); see Vol. II, § 39–032. See also s.76 of the Act for other instances.
[13] s.68.
[14] Sched. 3, para. 3.

on which the cause of action accrued." The ascertainment of this date is often a question of some difficulty. There is no definition of the term "cause of action" in the Act, and therefore the old law is still applicable. In 1888 it was defined by Lord Esher as "every fact which it would be necessary for the plaintiff to prove, if traversed, in order to support his right to the judgment of the court."[15] In 1891 Lindley L.J. said "it has always been held that the statute runs from the earliest time at which an action could be brought."[16] And in 1927 Lord Dunedin defined cause of action to mean "that which makes action possible."[17] There must also be in existence at this moment a competent claimant and a competent defendant. There is no competent defendant if, *e.g.* he enjoys diplomatic privilege[18] or, being a corporation, it has been dissolved in the country of its incorporation.[19] On the other hand, the mere fact that the defendant cannot be traced, so that in practice the claimant cannot start proceedings, does not prevent the cause of action from accruing.[20] There is no competent claimant or defendant as the case may be in the interval between the death of an intestate and the grant of letters of administration, and the cause of action (*e.g.* for a debt payable at or after the death of the creditor or debtor) cannot accrue until the grant of letters.[21] This is because the title of an administrator is derived from the grant and he cannot sue or be sued until a grant is made. There is also some authority for saying that if at the time when the cause of action would have accrued the potential plaintiff and defendant were one and the same person, so that the hand to pay and the hand to receive were the same, the cause of action does not accrue and time does not begin to run.[22] It should be noted that what is said above about competent parties refers only to the accrual of the cause of action. It does not refer to the suspension of the statute once time has begun to run.[23]

General rule in contract. The general rule in contract is that the cause of   **29–028**
action accrues, not when the damage is suffered, but when the breach takes

---

[15] *Read v. Brown* (1888) 22 Q.B.D. 128, 131. See also *Cooke v. Gill* (1873) L.R. 8 C.P. 107, 116; *Coburn v. Colledge* [1897] 1 Q.B. 702, 706, 707; *Central Electricity Board v. Halifax Corporation* [1963] A.C. 785, 800, 806. *Letang v. Cooper* [1964] 1 Q.B. 232, 242; *Paragon Finance v. Thakerar & Co.* [1999] 1 All E.R. 405.

[16] *Reeves v. Butcher* [1891] 2 Q.B. 509, 511.

[17] *Board of Trade v. Cayzer, Irvine & Co.* [1927] A.C. 610, 617. See also *Letang v. Cooper* [1965] 1 Q.B. 232, 242.

[18] *Musurus Bey v. Gadban* [1894] 2 Q.B. 352.

[19] *Re Russo-Asiatic Bank* [1934] Ch. 720, 738.

[20] *R.B. Policies at Lloyd's v. Butler* [1950] 1 K.B. 76; Goodman (1966) 29 M.L.R. 366. *cf. Clark v. Forbes Stuart (Thames Steel) Ltd* [1964] 1 W.L.R. 836; Limitation Act 1980, ss.14(1)(c), 14(1A)(c), 14A(8)(c).

[21] *Jolliffe v. Pitt* (1715) 2 Vern. 694; *Murray v. East India Co.* (1821) 5 B. & Ald. 204; *Douglas v. Forrest* (1828) 4 Bing. 686, 704; *Pratt v. Swaine* (1828) 8 B. & C. 285; *Burdick v. Garrick* (1870) L.R. 5 Ch.App. 233, 241; *Chan Kit Sam v. Ho Fung Ham* [1902] A.C. 257; *Meyappa Chetty v. Supramanian Chetty* [1916] 1 A.C. 603, 610. This rule does not appear to have been affected by RSC, Ord. 15, r. 6A (made by virtue of s.2 of the Proceedings against Estates Act 1970 and amended by virtue of s.2 of the Administration of Justice Act 1977); but see s.26 of the Limitation Act 1980 (recovery of land), and Administration of Estates Act 1925, ss.9, 55(1)(xv). See now CPR, Sched. 1. For accrual after date of death where there is an executor, see *Webster v. Webster* (1804) 10 Ves.Jun. 93; *Flood v. Patterson* (1861) 29 Beav. 295; *Knox v. Gye* (1871) L.R. 5 H.L. 656; *Lovett v. Ambler* (1876) 3 Ch.D. 198; *Meyappa Chetty v. Supramanian Chetty, supra*, at 608.

[22] *Binns v. Nichols* (1866) L.R. 2 Eq. 256; *Re Pardoe* [1906] 1 Ch. 265.

[23] As to this, see *post*, § 29–066.

place.[24] "In an action of assumpsit, the Statute of Limitations begins to run not from the time when the damage results from breach of the promise, but the time when the breach of promise takes place."[25] The gist of an action for breach of contract is the breach, and not any resulting damage which may be occasioned thereby. Consequently, the Act runs from the time when the contract is broken, and not from the time at which any damage resulting therefrom is sustained by the claimant. Therefore, although such damage may occur within six years before the action is brought, the action will be barred if the contract was broken before that period. For example, in an action for breach of warranty or condition against a seller of goods, the cause of action accrues when the goods are delivered, and not when the defect is discovered.[26]

29–029   **Concurrent liability in tort.** It is, however, well established that in the tort of negligence the cause of action arises when the damage is suffered and not when the act or omission complained of occurs. If, therefore, a claimant has, independently of or in addition to any cause of action in contract, a cause of action in tort for negligence, time will not begin to run in respect of his claim in tort until the damage is sustained. In a number of cases it was held that an action for negligence against, for example, a solicitor[27] or architect[28] was contractual in nature, so that the cause of action accrued when his negligent act or omission took place.[29] But more recent cases have held that the existence of a contractual relationship between the parties does not necessarily exclude a concurrent or independent cause of action in tort.[30] So an action may be brought in tort for negligence in respect of professional services rendered, for example, by a solicitor,[31] insurance broker,[32] architect[33] or engineer[34] within six years of the date when the claimant first sustains damage.[35]

---

[24] *Gould v. Johnson* (1702) 2 Salk. 422; *Battley v. Faulkner* (1820) 3 B. & Ald. 288; *Short v. M'Carthy* (1820) 3 B. & Ald. 626; *Howell v. Young* (1826) 5 B. & C. 259; *Walker v. Milner* (1866) 4 F. & F. 745; *Gibbs v. Guild* (1881) 8 Q.B.D. 296, 302.

[25] *Howell v. Young* (1826) 5 B. & C. 259, 265.

[26] *Battley v. Faulkner, supra*; *Lynn v. Bamber* [1930] 2 K.B. 72, 74.

[27] *Short v. M'Carthy, supra*; *Brown v. Howard* (1820) 2 Brod. & B. 73; *Howell v. Young, supra*; *Bean v. Wade* (1885) 2 T.L.R. 157; *Wood v. Jones* (1889) 61 L.T. 551; *Groom v. Crocker* [1939] 1 K.B. 194; *Somers v. Erskine* [1944] Ir.R. 368; *Clark v. Kirby-Smith* [1964] Ch. 506. See also *Cook v. Swinfen* [1967] 1 W.L.R. 457; *Heywood v. Wellers* [1976] Q.B. 446; *Rowe v. Turner Hopkins & Partners* [1980] N.Z.L.R. 550.

[28] *Bagot v. Stevens Scanlon & Co. Ltd* [1966] 1 Q.B. 197.

[29] *Clark v. Kirby-Smith, supra*; *Bagot v. Stevens Scanlan & Co. Ltd, supra.*

[30] *Henderson v. Merrett Syndicates Ltd* [1995] 2 A.C. 145. See *ante,* §§ 1–068—1–106; *post,* §§ 29–051, 29–053, 29–092.

[31] *Midland Bank Trust Co. Ltd v. Hett, Stubbs & Kemp* [1977] Ch. 384; *Forster v. Outred & Co.* [1982] 1 W.L.R. 86; *D. W. Moore & Co. Ltd v. Ferrier* [1988] 1 W.L.R. 267; *Bell v. Peter Browne & Co.* [1990] Q.B. 495.

[32] *Iron Trades Mutual Insurance Co. Ltd v. Buckenham Ltd* [1989] 2 Lloyd's Rep. 85; *Punjab National Bank v. De Boinville* [1992] 1 W.L.R. 1138. See also *Société Commerciale de Reassurance v. Eras International Ltd* [1992] 1 Lloyd's Rep. 570 (insurance management agreement); *Henderson v. Merrett Syndicates Ltd, supra* (Lloyd's underwriting agents).

[33] *Kensington and Chelsea and Westminster Area Health Authority v. Wettern Composites Ltd* [1985] 1 All E.R. 346; *London Congregational Union Inc. v. Harriss & Harriss* [1988] 1 All E.R. 15; *Wessex Regional Health Authority v. HLM Design* (1994) 10 Const. L.J. 165. *cf. Lancashire and Cheshire Assn. of Baptist Churches v. Howard & Seddon* [1993] 3 All E.R. 467.

[34] *Pirelli General Cable Works Ltd v. Oscar Faber and Partners* [1983] A.C. 1; *Wessex Regional Health Authority v. HLM Design, supra.*

[35] For extension of the period in cases of latent damage, see *post,* § 29–091.

Successive and continuing breaches. Where the innocent party elects to treat   29-030
himself as discharged from further performance consequent upon a breach of the
contract,[36] time begins to run immediately. For instance, if there is an anticipatory breach accepted by him as a repudiation of the contract, his cause of action
accrues at once, and not from the failure of the party in default subsequently to
perform at the time fixed for performance.[37] But if there are one or more breaches
which do not give rise to a discharge either because they are not sufficiently
fundamental or because the innocent party declines to accept them as having that
effect, each will give rise to a separate cause of action.[38] There may also be a
series of breaches of a single covenant. Examples are failure to pay instalments
of interest[39] or rent.[40] Or the breach may be a continuing one, *e.g.* of a covenant
to keep in repair.[41] In such a case the claimant will succeed in respect of so much
of the series of breaches or the continuing breach as occurred within the six (or
12) years before action brought. If the breach consists in a failure to act, it may
be held to continue *die in diem* until the obligation is performed or becomes
impossible of performance or until the innocent party elects to treat the continued
non-performance as a repudiation of the contract. Thus the failure of a solicitor
to register an interest in land or to institute legal proceedings or diligently to
prosecute legal proceedings already instituted will ordinarily constitute a continuing breach of his retainer, and the client's cause of action will not become
barred until six years after registration ceases to be possible or until the proceedings are barred by limitation or are struck out for want of prosecution, as the case
may be.[42]

Misrepresentation. A claim to rescind a contract for misrepresentation will   29-031
normally accrue when the representee enters into the contract in reliance on the
misrepresentation.[43] Where the representee claims damages under section 2(1) of
the Misrepresentation Act 1967,[44] his cause of action will accrue when he
"suffers loss"[45] as a result of entering into the contract. In some cases, at least,
he will suffer loss when the transaction into which he has been induced to enter
is implemented.[46] In other cases, however, he will not suffer loss until even later,
e.g. when he incurs expenditure or sustains other damage in consequence of

---

[36] For discharge by breach, see *ante*, Chap. 25.
[37] *Reeves v. Butcher* [1891] 2 Q.B. 509.
[38] *Arnott v. Holden* (1852) 18 Q.B. 593.
[39] *Bowyer v. Woodman* (1867) L.R. 3 Eq. 313. See s.20(5)(6)(7) of the Act. But *cf. post*, § 29-032.
[40] *Archbold v. Scully* (1861) 9 H.L.C. 360. See s.19 of the 1980 Act.
[41] *Spoor v. Green* (1874) L.R. 9 Ex. 99, 111.
[42] *Midland Bank Trust Co. Ltd v. Hett, Stubbs & Kemp* [1979] Ch. 384; *Doundoulakis v. Sdrinis & Co.* [1989] V.R. 781; *Hopkins v. MacKenzie, The Times*, November 3, 1994, CA; *Carlton v. Fulchers* [1997] P.N.L.R. 337. Contrast *Bean v. Wade* (1885) 2 T.L.R. 157; *Forster v. Outred & Co.* [1982] 1 W.L.R. 86; *Bellway (South East) Ltd v. Holley* (1984) 28 B.L.R. 139; *Bell v. Peter Browne & Co.* [1990] 2 Q.B. 495; Supply of Goods and Services Act 1982, s.14(1). See also *Brickfield Properties Ltd v. Newton* [1971] 3 All E.R. 328.
[43] But the right to rescind may, in equity, be lost long before the expiration of the limitation period: see *post*, § 29-147. Contrast *Lakshmijit v. Sherani* [1974] A.C. 605.
[44] See *ante*, § 6-068.
[45] See *ante*, § 6-069.
[46] See *Forster v. Outred & Co.* [1982] 1 W.L.R. 86; *D. W. Moore & Co. Ltd v. Ferrier* [1988] 1 W.L.R. 267; *Iron Trades Mutual Insurance Co. Ltd v. Buckenham Ltd* [1989] 2 Lloyd's Rep. 85; *Bell v. Peter Browne & Co.* [1990] 2 Q.B. 495; *Islander Trucking Ltd v. Hogg Robinson & Gardner Mountain (Manne) Ltd* [1990] 1 All E.R. 826 (cases on negligence: see *post*, § 29-051).

having entered into the contract and not at the time the contract is entered into.[47] Moreover his cause of action may not be complete until the representation can be shown to be false. So, for example, if there is a contract for the sale of unascertained goods, it may not be possible to show that the representation is false until such time as the goods are delivered[48] and the limitation period will only then start to run.

29–032   **Money lent.** At common law, where no time for repayment was specified in a contract of loan, or where the loan was expressed simply to be repayable "on demand," the lender's cause of action in general[49] accrued when the loan was made and time began to run from that moment.[50] As a result, once the loan was outstanding for more than six years (which not infrequently happens in the case of loans between friends or members of a family)[51] the lender's right to recover the money lent became barred notwithstanding that no demand for repayment had been made. But by section 6 of the Limitation Act 1980, if (a) a contract of loan does not provide for repayment of the debt on or before a fixed or determinable date, and (b) does not effectively (whether or not it purports so to do) make the obligation to repay the debt conditional on demand for repayment made by or on behalf of the creditor or any other matter, then the right of action on the contract of loan is not barred after six years from the date of the loan.[52] Instead, the six-year period does not start to run unless and until a demand *in writing* for repayment of the debt is made by or on behalf of the creditor (or, where there are joint creditors, by or on behalf of any one of them).[53] However, the section establishes an exception in the case where, in connection with taking the loan, the debtor enters into any collateral obligation to pay the amount of the debt or any part of it (as, for example, by delivering a promissory note[54] as security for the debt) on terms which would exclude the application of the section to the contract of loan if they applied directly to repayment of the debt.[55] So, if no time for repayment is specified in the contract of loan, or if it is simply to be repaid "on demand," but the debtor gives to the creditor a post-dated cheque or a promissory note payable on a fixed date, no written or any demand is required to start time running and, it seems, time starts to run from the due date of the note. But if a promissory note is made payable on demand, the cause of action against the maker accrues on the date of the note (or of its issue if later).[56] It is arguable, therefore, that if such a note is given by the debtor to the creditor, but is not acted upon by the creditor until the limitation period has expired, the

---

[47] *Toprak Enerji Sanayi A.S. v. Sale Tilney Technology plc.*, unreported, October 21, 1993 (QBD, Commercial Court). See also *Wardley Australia Ltd. v. State of Western Australia* (1992) 175 C.L.R. 514; *UBAF Ltd v. European American Banking Corpn.* [1984] Q.B. 713, 726.

[48] *Toprak Enerji Sanayi AS v. Sale Tilney Technology plc., supra.*

[49] For exceptions, see *post*, § 29–035 (banker and customer); § 29–042 (guarantees).

[50] *Rumball v. Ball* (1712) 10 Mod. 39; *Garden v. Bruce* (1868) L.R. 3 C.P. 300; *Re Brown's Estate* [1893] 2 Ch. 300, 305; *Bradford Old Bank v. Sutcliffe* [1918] 2 K.B. 833, 840, 845–846, 848, 849; *Tate v. Crowdson* [1938] Ch. 869, 881; *Lloyd's Bank v. Margolis* [1954] 1 W.L.R. 644, 648.

[51] *Twenty-First Report of the Law Reform Committee*, Cmnd. 6923 (1977), §§ 3.19–3.26.

[52] s.6(1)(2). For agreements made by deed, see *ante*, § 29–009.

[53] s.6(3); *Boot v. Boot* [1996] 2 F.C.R. 713.

[54] Defined in s.6(4).

[55] s.6(2). See *Von Goetz v. Rogers*, July 29, 1998, CA.

[56] See *post*, § 29–038.

creditor's remedy will become time-barred; but this does not appear to be the case[57] and time will start to run only from the date of the written demand.

Where the contract of loan does provide for repayment of the debt on or before   **29–033**
a fixed or determinable date, or does effectively make the obligation to repay
conditional upon a demand for repayment[58] or any other matter,[59] it is a question
of construction when the lender's cause of action accrues. Thus where there was
a loan for five years with interest, and the lender was entitled to call in the loan
on any default in the payment of interest, it was held that the lender's cause of
action accrued on the first such default taking place.[60]

Once the right to recover the principal sum is barred, arrears of interest falling   **29–034**
due within six years before the action is brought are also irrecoverable, for the
interest is accessory to the principal.[61]

Banker and customer. The relationship between banker and customer is the   **29–035**
contractual one of debtor and creditor, not that of trustee and *cestui que trust*.[62]
It is well settled that, unless the contrary is agreed, a demand by the customer is
a condition precedent to repayment, whether the money is on current or deposit
account.[63] Accordingly time runs from the date of the demand[63a] and not from the
date when the account was opened or the money paid in, so that banks may be
faced with claims that have lain dormant for years. However, in one case, money
on a deposit account was unclaimed for 60 years, there being no evidence of
repayment or of a demand for repayment, and the court drew the inference from
all the circumstances that the money had at some time been repaid.[64] Where sums
are wrongly debited to the customer's account, time runs from the date on which
the customer demands repayment of the credit balance remaining when those
sums are left out of account.[65] If the relationship of banker and customer is
terminated before a demand is made, *e.g.* by dissolution of the bank, the money
thereupon becomes repayable.[66]

Overdrafts. An overdraft is a loan by the banker to the customer. At common   **29–036**
law, in the case of an overdraft repayable on demand, a demand was in general
not a condition precedent to bringing an action and time ran against the banker
in respect of each advance from the time when it was made.[67] But now, by virtue

---

[57] *Boot v. Boot, supra.*

[58] *Lloyds Bank v. Margolis, supra* (legal charge with covenant to repay on demand given as collateral security); and see *post*, § 29–035 (customer's account with bank).

[59] *Re McHenry* [1894] 3 Ch. 240.

[60] *Reeves v. Butcher* [1891] 2 Q.B. 509.

[61] *Hollis v. Palmer* (1836) 2 Bing.N.C. 73; *Cheang Thye Phin v. Lam Kin Sang* [1929] A.C. 670; *Elder v. Northcott* [1930] 2 Ch. 422.

[62] *Foley v. Hill* (1848) 2 H.L.C. 28.

[63] *Joachimson v. Swiss Bank Corpn.* [1921] 3 K.B. 110; *Arab Bank v. Barclays Bank* [1954] A.C. 495; *Hart v. Sangster* [1957] Ch. 329. See also *Re Dillon* (1890) 44 Ch.D. 76, 81.

[63a] cf. *Mahomed v. Bank of Baroda, The Times,* December 10, 1998 (repeated demands do not start time running afresh).

[64] *Douglass v. Lloyds Bank* (1929) 34 Com.Cas. 263.

[65] *National Bank of Commerce v. National Westminster Bank* [1990] 2 Lloyd's Rep. 514. *cf. ibid.* at 517 (account ultimately in debit).

[66] *Re Russian Commercial Bank* [1955] Ch. 148.

[67] *Parrs Banking Co. v. Yates* [1898] 2 Q.B. 460. Contrast *Lloyds Bank v. Margolis* [1954] 1 W.L.R. 644 (legal charge with covenant to repay on demand given as collateral security).

of section 6 of the 1980 Act, time will not as a normal rule start to run against the banker until a demand in writing is made for repayment of the advance.

29–037 **Negotiable instruments.**[68] The liability to the holder of the acceptor of a bill or the maker of a note payable at a fixed or determinable future time arises upon the maturity of the instrument,[69] unless presentment for payment is necessary to charge the acceptor or maker, in which case the liability arises at the date of presentment.[70] Therefore, on a bill payable on a certain date, or at a certain period after date, the limitation period runs from the time it falls due.[71] In the case of a bill drawn payable after sight, presentment for acceptance is necessary in order to fix the maturity of the instrument.[72] If a bill is payable at a fixed period after sight, the liability of the acceptor arises at the end of the fixed period calculated from the date of acceptance.[73]

29–038 If a bill or note is payable at sight[74] or on demand, the liability of the acceptor or maker to the holder arises on the date of acceptance or, in the case of a note, on the date of the note (or of its issue if later), and no demand is necessary to establish liability.[75] Accordingly, the limitation period will run from that time. It would appear that the cause of action by the holder of a cheque against the drawer, being the party primarily liable on the instrument, likewise accrues on the date of the cheque (or of its issue if later).[76]

29–039 As regards the drawer of a bill and the indorser of a bill or note, time begins to run in his favour when he receives notice of dishonour, or, if notice of dishonour is excused, from the date of dishonour.[77] If a bill is dishonoured by non-acceptance, and afterwards by non-payment, no fresh cause of action accrues to the holder against the drawer by reason of the dishonour by non-payment.[78]

29–040 It would seem that the cause of action of a drawer of a bill, and of the indorser of a bill or note, who has been compelled to pay the instrument accrues against the acceptor or maker on the making of the payment.[79] Likewise, with respect to

---

[68] See *Byles on Bills of Exchange* (26th ed.), pp. 419–427; *Chalmers and Guest on Bills of Exchange* (15th ed.), §§ 1468–1478.

[69] Except where a bill is accepted after maturity, when time runs from the date of acceptance: Bills of Exchange Act 1882, s.10(2).

[70] Bills of Exchange Act 1882, ss.19(2)(c), 52, 87.

[71] *Montague v. Perkins* (1853) 22 L.J.C.P. 187.

[72] Bills of Exchange Act 1882, s.39(1).

[73] *ibid.* ss.11(1), 14(2), (3); *Holmes v. Kerrison* (1810) 2 Taunt. 323.

[74] Bills of Exchange Act 1882, s.10(1)(a).

[75] *Norton v. Ellam* (1837) 2 M. & W. 461; *Re Brown's Estate* [1893] 2 Ch. 300, 304; *Re British Trade Corpn.* [1932] 2 Ch. 1. But see Bills of Exchange Act 1882, ss.19(2)(c), 52(2), 87(1) (presentment for payment). Contrast (instruments payable at a certain period *after* demand): *Thorpe v. Booth* (1826) Ry. & M. 388; *Re Rutherford* (1880) 14 Ch.D. 687.

[76] *Robinson v. Hawksford* (1846) 9 Q.B. 52, 59; *Laws v. Rand* (1857) 3 C.B. (N.S.) 442, 449; *Re Bethell* (1887) 34 Ch.D. 561.

[77] Bills of Exchange Act 1882, ss.43, 47, 48, 50(2), 55, 87(2), (3); *Kennedy v. Thomas* [1894] 2 Q.B. 759.

[78] *Whitehead v. Walker* (1842) 9 M. & W. 506; *Wilkinson v. Verity* (1871) L.R. 6 C.P. 206, 209.

[79] Bills of Exchange Act 1882, ss.57, 59. But since the claim is analogous to that of a surety against the principal debtor (§ 29–043, *post*), it is arguable that the cause of action arises when his liability to pay is ascertained, or even when he receives notice of dishonour.

the claim of an indorser against the drawer of a bill or prior indorsers of a bill or note, it would seem that the cause of action arises when he is compelled to and does pay the instrument.[80]

Securities. In the case of registered securities, time begins to run in respect of   **29–041**
payment of dividends from the date on which the dividend is declared or from the date provided by the declaration for its payment, whichever is the later,[81] and in respect of a scheme or reduction of capital involving an immediate repayment of capital on the date when the scheme or reduction becomes effective.[82] In the case of bearer securities, the question arises whether the document must be presented to the company before the liability of the company accrues, and this is to be determined by reference to the company's articles of association and the terms on which the securities were issued.[83]

Principal and surety. Unless otherwise agreed in the contract of guarantee,   **29–042**
the liability of the surety to the creditor arises on the principal debtor's default, so that time begins to run in favour of both of them at that moment.[84] If the surety undertakes to pay on demand, a demand is a condition precedent to liability and the creditor's cause of action accrues only when a demand is made and not complied with.[85] Where it was agreed that the guarantee should be a continuing one and should apply to the balance that was then or might at any time thereafter be owing, it was held that this was a guarantee of each debit balance as it was constituted, so that the cause of action accrued not when each advance was made to the principal debtor, but when the debit balance in question was constituted.[86]

Unless otherwise agreed, the surety's implied right to an indemnity from the   **29–043**
principal debtor accrues when the surety's liability to the creditor is ascertained, and time runs from that moment.[87] If a surety pays a statute-barred debt, he cannot recover the amount from the principal debtor.[88]

As between co-sureties, the right to contribution of one who has paid more   **29–044**
than his share accrues at the time of such payment,[89] and of one who has been called upon to pay the whole of the debt at the time the claim of the creditor

---

[80] Bills of Exchange Act 1882, s.55(1)(2). But contrast *Webster v. Kirk* (1852) 17 Q.B. 944 (date of receipt of notice of dishonour).

[81] *Bond v. Barrow Haematite Steel* [1902] 1 Ch. 353; *Re Compania de Electricidad de la Provincia de Buenos Aires Ltd* [1980] Ch. 146.

[82] *Re Artisans' Land and Mortgage Corpn.* [1904] 1 Ch. 796; *Re Compania de Electricidad de la Provincia de Buenos Aires Ltd, supra.*

[83] *Re Compania de Electricidad de la Provincia de Buenos Aires Ltd, supra.*

[84] *Parrs Banking Co. v. Yates* [1898] 2 Q.B. 460.

[85] *Re Brown's Estate* [1893] 2 Ch. 300; *Bradford Old Bank v. Sutcliffe* [1918] 2 K.B. 833; *Esso Petroleum Co. Ltd v. Alstonbridge Properties Ltd* [1975] 1 W.L.R. 1474; *Bank of Baroda v. Patel* [1996] 1 Lloyd's Rep. 390.

[86] *Wright v. New Zealand Farmers' Co-operative Association* [1939] A.C. 439. *cf. Hartland v. Jukes* (1863) 1 H. & C. 667.

[87] *Wolmershausen v. Gullick* [1893] 2 Ch. 514; *Re Richardson* [1911] 2 K.B. 705, 709.

[88] *Coneys v. Morris* [1922] 1 Ir.R. 81.

[89] *Davies v. Humphreys* (1840) 6 M. & W. 153; *Re Snowdon* (1881) 17 Ch.D. 44.

against him is established.[90] It is immaterial that, at the time of the action for contribution, time has run out between the creditor and the co-surety.[91]

29–045	**Indemnity and contribution.** At common law, upon a contract to indemnify a person against liability to a third party, the cause of action accrued only when the claimant was actually damnified, *e.g.* by payment to the third party, and not upon the happening of the event which gave rise to his liability[92] or even when that liability had been quantified.[93] In equity, however, it was held that a person entitled to such an indemnity had a right of action to preserve his position as soon as his liability was incurred[94] and could claim on the indemnity when his liability was ascertained or established.[95] The modern authorities are conflicting. It has been held that the limitation period begins to run once the liability is incurred[96] and that it begins to run only when the liability is ascertained or established, for example, by judgment.[97] However, in the case of an express indemnity, the extent of the indemnity and the time at which the cause of action arises will depend on the construction of the contract.[98] Thus the contract may provide that the indemnity is conditional on actual payment,[99] in which case the cause of action will accrue only when such payment has been made.[1]

29–046	In respect of the special two-year period of limitation[2] for claiming contribution under section 1 of the Civil Liability (Contribution) Act 1978, the right of action to recover contribution accrues on the date on which judgment is given or an arbitral award made.[3] In the absence of any judgment or award, if the person entitled to recover contribution in respect of any damage makes or agrees to make any payment to one or more persons in respect of that damage (whether he admits any liability in respect of the damage or not), time begins to run from the

---

[90] *Wolmershausen v. Gullick, supra; cf. Robinson v. Harkin* [1896] 2 Ch. 415 (contribution between co-trustees).

[91] *Wolmershausen v. Gullick, supra.*

[92] *Huntley v. Sanderson* (1833) 1 Cr. & M. 467; *Reynolds v. Doyle* (1840) 1 M. & G. 753.

[93] *Collinge v. Heywood* (1839) 9 A. & E. 633. See also *Re Richardson* [1911] 2 K.B. 705, 709, 713; *McGillivray v. Hope* [1935] A.C. 1, 10.

[94] *Lacey v. Hill* (1874) L.R. 18 Eq. 182, 191; *Johnston v. Salvage Assn.* (1887) 19 Q.B.D. 458, 460; *Ascherson v. Tredegar Dry Dock Co.* [1909] 2 Ch. 401; *Re Richardson, supra; British Union and National Insurance Co. v. Rawson* [1916] 2 Ch. 476, 481.

[95] *Wolmershausen v. Gullick* [1893] 2 Ch. 514; *Robinson v. Harkin* [1896] 2 Ch. 416; *Re Richardson, supra; Littlewood v. Geo. Wimpey & Co. Ltd and B.O.A.C.* [1953] 2 Q.B. 501, 519.

[96] *Bosma v. Larsen* [1966] 1 Lloyd's Rep. 22 (McNair J.).

[97] *County & District Properties Ltd v. C. Jenner & Son Ltd* [1976] 2 Lloyd's Rep. 728 (Swanwick J.); *R.H. Green & Silley Weir v. British Railways Board* [1985] 1 W.L.R. 570 (Dillon J.); *Telfair Shipping Corpn. v. Inersea Carriers SA* [1985] 1 W.L.R. 553 (Neill J., who distinguished an indemnity against liability from a general indemnity, express or implied). See also *Socony Mobil Oil Inc. v. West of England Ship Owners Mutual Insurance Assn. Ltd* [1989] 1 Lloyd's Rep. 239, 255, CA.

[98] *Telfair Shipping Corpn. v. Inersea Carriers SA, supra,* at 566; *Socony Mobil Oil Inc. v. West of England Ship Owners Mutual Insurance Assn., supra,* at 255.

[99] *Wooldridge v. Norris* (1868) L.R. 6 Eq. 410, 414; *Socony Mobil Oil Inc. v. West of England Ship Owners Mutual Insurance Assn., supra.*

[1] *Socony Mobil Oil Inc. v. West of England Ship Owners Mutual Insurance Assn., supra,* at 255, 262, 265.

[2] Limitation Act 1980, s.10(1); *ante,* § 29–010.

[3] s.10(2), (3).

earliest date on which the amount to be paid by him is agreed between him (or his representative) and the person (or each of the persons, as the case may be) to whom the payment is to be made.[4]

Insurance. Under a contract of insurance, unless otherwise agreed, a cause of   29–047
action would appear to accrue, in the case of insurance against loss, when the casualty causing the loss occurs,[5] in the case of life or accident insurance, upon the occurrence of the event which gives rise to the claim,[6] and in the case of liability insurance, when the liability of the assured arises.[7] But in all cases regard must be had to the terms of the policy: the liability of the insurer may not arise unless and until a claim is made or certain other conditions are satisfied.

Sale of goods. In a contract of sale of goods, the property in which has passed   29–048
to the buyer,[8] the seller's right of action for the price accrues at the time for payment specified in the contract or, if no time is specified, when the seller informs the buyer that he is ready and willing to deliver the goods.[9] If the sale is upon credit, the right of action accrues upon the expiry of the period allowed.[10] The buyer's right of action for breach of the implied term as to title accrues at the time of sale or (in the case of an agreement to sell) at the time when the property is to pass,[11] and in the case of a breach of the term as to quiet possession when the buyer's possession is disturbed.[12] Otherwise the buyer's right of action for breach of an express or implied warranty relating to goods accrues when the goods are delivered, and not when the defect is discovered or damage ensues.[13] Where there is a wrongful neglect or refusal to deliver or accept and pay for the goods, the Sale of Goods Act 1979[14] provides that an action may be maintained for damages for non-delivery or non-acceptance. Normally time would appear to run from the time or times when the goods ought to have been delivered or accepted as the case may be,[15] except in the case of an anticipatory breach accepted as a repudiation of the contract, when the limitation period runs from that time.[16] The buyer's right of action for damages for delay in delivery of goods

---

[4] s.10(2), (4).

[5] *Chandris v. Argo Insurance Co. Ltd* [1963] 2 Lloyd's Rep. 65, approved in *Castle Insurance Co. Ltd v. Hong Kong Islands Shipping Co. Ltd* [1984] A.C. 226. See also *Scott Lithgow v. Secretary of State for Defence* (1989) 45 Build.L.R. 1, HL; *Bank of America National Trust and Savings Assn v. Christmas* [1994] 1 All E.R. 401; *Callaghan v. Dominion Insurance Co. Ltd* [1997] 2 Lloyd's Rep. 541.

[6] *Re Haycock's Policy* (1876) 1 Ch.D. 611; *London & Midland Bank v. Mitchell* [1899] 2 Ch. 161.

[7] *Johnston v. Salvage Assn.* (1887) 19 QBD 458; *North Atlantic Insurance Co. Ltd v. Bishopsgate Insurance Ltd* [1998] 1 Lloyd's Rep. 459. Contrast *Socony Mobil Oil Inc. v. West of England Ship Owners Insurance Assn.* [1989] 1 Lloyd's Rep. 239; *Hong Kong Borneo Services Ltd v. Pilcher* [1992] 2 Lloyd's Rep. 593 ("pay to be paid" clauses).

[8] Sale of Goods Act 1979, s.49(1). But see s.49(2).

[9] *ibid.* s.28.

[10] *Helps v. Winterbottom* (1831) 2 B. & Ad. 431.

[11] Sale of Goods Act 1979, s.12(1). But see s.32 of the Limitation Act 1980; *post,* § 29–085.

[12] Sale of Goods Act 1979, s.12(2)(b).

[13] *Battley v. Faulkner* (1820) 3 B. & Ald. 288; *Walker v. Milner* (1866) 4 F. & F. 745.

[14] ss.50(1), 51(1).

[15] Sale of Goods Act 1979, ss.50(3), 51(3).

[16] See *ante,* § 29–030.

which are nevertheless accepted by him would appear to accrue at the time or times when the goods ought to have been delivered.

29-049 **Defects causing injury or damage.** There may, however, be an alternative cause of action against the seller in tort for negligence where defects in the goods cause personal injury or damage to property other than the goods themselves. In such a case, time runs from the date on which the injury or damage is sustained, and not from the date when the goods are delivered; and there is a possibility of an extension where the injury or damage is latent.[17] A claim may also lie against the seller under Part I of the Consumer Protection Act 1987.[18]

29-050 **Conversion of goods.** Once a conversion of goods has occurred, the owner has six years thereafter[19] in which to sue in respect of that and all subsequent acts of conversion whether or not committed by the same person,[20] after which his title to the goods is extinguished.[21] The 1980 Act, however, contains special rules concerning the right of a person from whom goods are stolen[22] to bring an action in respect of the theft.[23]

29-051 **Work and services.** Unless a time for payment is otherwise agreed, the right to claim payment upon an entire contract accrues when the work is completed.[24] This applies to work done by a solicitor, although by statute[25] he cannot bring an action to recover costs until one month after delivery of a proper bill. He is thus deprived of at least one month of the six-year limitation period.[26] Except in cases of fraud or concealment,[27] the contractual cause of action for breach of duty in respect of defective work arises when the breach of duty occurs[28] and not when the defect is discovered or damage ensues.[29] Failure to carry out the work may nevertheless amount to a continuing breach of the contract.[30] However, there may be a separate action in tort for negligence, and the tortious cause of action will not accrue until the plaintiff first suffers relevant loss or damage, *i.e.* loss or damage falling within the measure of damage applicable to the wrong in question.[31] Where a plaintiff received negligent advice from a solicitor[32] or sur-

---

[17] See *ante*, § 29–005; *post*, § 29–091.

[18] See *ante*, § 29–008; Vol. II, § 43–112.

[19] Unless he has recovered possession during the meantime.

[20] s.3(1).

[21] s.3(2). It is submitted that a plaintiff would not be entitled to extend the statutory period by "waiving the tort" (see *post*, 30–084) and bringing an action for money had and received: *Beaman v. A.R.T.S. Ltd* [1948] 2 All E.R. 89, 92–93. Contrast *Chesworth v. Farrar* [1967] 1 Q.B. 407. See Goff and Jones, *Law of Restitution* (5th ed., 1998), p. 790.

[22] Or obtained by deception or by blackmail: s.4(5).

[23] s.4; see Vol. II, § 43–233.

[24] *Emery v. Day* (1834) 1 Cr. M. & R. 245, 248.

[25] Solicitors Act 1974, s.69.

[26] *Coburn v. Colledge* [1897] 1 Q.B. 702.

[27] See *post*, §§ 29–082, 29–086.

[28] *Bagot v. Stevens Scanlan & Co. Ltd* [1966] 1 Q.B. 197. *cf. Brickfield Properties Ltd v. Newton* [1971] 1 W.L.R. 862, 869, 873.

[29] *Bagot v. Stevens Scanlan & Co., supra.* See also the cases cited in § 29–028, *ante.*

[30] See *ante*, § 29–030.

[31] *Nykredit Mortgage Bank plc v. Edward Erdman Group Ltd* [1997] 1 W.L.R. 1627, 1630.

[32] *Forster v. Outred & Co.* [1982] 1 W.L.R. 86; *D.W. Moore & Co. Ltd v. Ferrier* [1988] 1 W.L.R. 267; *Sullivan v. Layton Lougher & Co.* (1995) 49 E.G. 127; *Tabarrok v. E.D.C. Lord & Co., The Times*, February 14, 1997. Contrast the position in Australia: Mullany (1993) 109 L.Q.R. 216.

veyor,[33] it was held that he suffered relevant loss or damage when he entered into a transaction in reliance on that advice. Similarly, where a solicitor[34] or insurance broker[35] negligently failed to protect the plaintiff's interests in respect of a transaction which he was employed to carry out, the plaintiff suffered loss or damage when the transaction was implemented. But more difficulty arises where, as a result of a negligent valuation, property is acquired as security, since relevant loss or damage may not be suffered when the lender enters into the transaction but only later, for example, when the security becomes inadequate[36] or when the borrower defaults. Where negligence on the part of an architect, surveyor or engineer gives rise to a defect which results in physical damage to a building, then as a normal rule[37] time will begin to run when that damage first occurs.[38] In any event, however, the period within which an action in tort for damages for negligence can be brought may be extended if the damage is latent.[39]

Building contracts. There seems to be little doubt that, in building contracts, except in cases of fraud or concealment, any cause of action in contract in respect of defective work accrues when the contractor is in breach of his express or implied obligations under the contract (normally on practical or substantial completion), and not from the time when the defect is discovered or damage occurs. If the contractor delays in completing the works or fails to complete the works in whole or in part, the cause of action presumably accrues when the works ought to have been completed[40] or when the employer elects to treat the failure of performance as a repudiation of the contract.   29–052

Alternative action in tort. There may, however, be an alternative cause of action for negligence against the contractor where the works which he is employed to carry out are defective.[41] No such action will normally lie in respect of economic loss suffered by the employer as a result of the defects or in respect of physical damage caused by the defects to the building or structure which the   29–053

---

[33] *Sec. of State for the Environment v. Essex Goodman & Suggitt* [1986] 1 W.L.R. 1432; *Kitney v. Jones Lang Wootton* (1988) 20 E.G. 88; *Byrne v. Hall Pain & Foster, The Times,* January 8, 1999.

[34] *Bell v. Peter Browne & Co.* [1990] 2 Q.B. 495. See also *Baker v. Ollard & Bentley* (1982), 126 S.J. 593 (C.A.T. No. 155 of 1982). Contrast *Midland Bank Trust Co. Ltd v. Hett, Stubbs & Kemp* [1979] Ch. 384.

[35] *Iron Trades Mutual Insurance Co. Ltd v. Buckenham Ltd* [1989] 2 Lloyd's Rep. 85; *Islander Trucking Ltd v. Hogg Robinson & Gardner Mountain (Marine) Ltd* [1990] 1 All E.R. 826. See also *Société Commerciale de Reassurance v. Eras International Ltd* [1992] 1 Lloyd's Rep. 570, 603; *Knapp v. Ecclesiastical Insurance Group plc., The Times,* Nov. 17, 1997.

[36] *UBAF v. European Banking Corpn.* [1984] Q.B. 713, 726; *First National Commercial Bank v. Humberts* [1995] 2 All E.R. 673; *Nykredit Mortgage Bank plc v. Edward Erdman Group Ltd* [1997] 1 W.L.R. 1627.

[37] See *post,* § 29–053, n. 45. Contrast *Invercargill City Council v. Hamlin* [1996] 1 All E.R. 756; *Clerk and Lindsell on Torts* (17th ed., 1995), § 31–09 (economic loss).

[38] *Pirelli General Cable Works Ltd v. Oscar Faber and Partners* [1983] A.C. 1; *London Congregational Union Inc. v. Harriss & Harriss* [1988] 1 All E.R. 15; *Leicester Wholesale Fruit Market Ltd v. Grundy* [1990] 1 W.L.R. 107, 110. But see O'Dair (1992) 55 M.L.R. 405; Mullany [1993] L.M.C.L.Q. 34; *Clerk and Lindsell on Torts* (17th ed., 1995), § 31–05 *et seq.*

[39] See *post,* § 29–091.

[40] *Kitney v. Jones Lang Wootton* (1988) 20 E.G. 88.

[41] *Dove v. Banhams Patent Locks Ltd* [1983] 1 W.L.R. 1436; *Nitrigen Eireann Teoranta v. Inco Alloys Ltd* [1992] 1 W.L.R. 598.

contractor is employed to erect.[42] But an action will lie in tort for negligence where the defects cause personal injury or physical damage to property other than the building or structure itself.[43] The cause of action arises when the injury or damage is sustained, even though this may be later than the completion of the works.[44]

29–054   A similar cause of action in tort may lie against an architect, surveyor or engineer in respect of injury or damage resulting from defects due to negligent advice, design or supervision of the works, and in this case the cause of action in negligence extends to physical damage caused by the defects to the building or structure itself.[45] In such a case, unless the defects are such that the building or structure is "doomed from the start,"[46] time will not begin to run from the date of completion of the works but from the date on which the damage to the building or structure first came into existence.[47]

29–055   **Latent damage.** At common law, whether the action is in contract or in tort, it is immaterial that the claimant's damage was latent and that it was not discovered and could not with reasonable diligence have been discovered within the limitation period.[48] But the effect of section 14A of the Act[49] is that, in cases of latent damage, the ordinary six-year period of limitation is subject to an extension which permits a claimant to bring an action for damages in tort for

---

[42] *D. & F. Estates Ltd v. Church Commissioners for England* [1989] A.C. 177; *Murphy v. Brentwood D.C.* [1991] 1 A.C. 398; *Department of the Environment v. Thomas Bates and Son Ltd* [1991] 1 A.C. 499; *Nitrigen Eireann Teoranta v. Inco Alloys Ltd, supra.* See also *Simaan General Contracting Co. v. Pilkington Glass Ltd (No. 2)* [1988] Q.B. 758; *Greater Nottingham Co-operative Socy. Ltd v. Cementation Piling and Foundations Ltd* [1989] Q.B. 71; *Warner v. Basildon Development Corpn.* (1991) 7 Const.L.J. 146. Contrast *Junior Books Ltd v. Veitchi Co. Ltd* [1983] 1 A.C. 520 (which must now be regarded as a unique case). For the problem of "complex structures," see the discussion in *D. & F. Estates Ltd v. Church Commissioners for England, supra,* and *Murphy v. Brentwood D.C., supra.* See *ante,* §§ 1–113, 19–024.

[43] *Dove v. Banhams Patent Locks Ltd, supra,* at 206; *Murphy v. Brentwood D.C., supra,* at 470, 478, 497; *Department of the Environment v. Thomas Bates and Son Ltd, supra,* at 519; *Nitrigen Eireann Teoranta v. Inco Alloys Ltd, supra.*

[44] *Dove v. Banhams Patent Locks Ltd, supra; Nitrigen Eireann Teoranta v. Inco Alloys Ltd, supra.*

[45] *Pirelli General Cable Works Ltd v. Oscar Faber and Partners* [1983] A.C. 1; *Bromley B.C. v. Rush and Tomkins* (1985) 4 Const.L.R. 4; *London Congregational Union Inc. v. Harriss & Harriss* [1988] 1 All E.R. 15; *Leicester Wholesale Fruit Market Ltd v. Grundy* [1990] 1 W.L.R. 107. Contrast *Lancashire and Cheshire Assn. of Baptist Churches Inc. v. Howard & Seddon* [1993] 3 All E.R. 467 (no physical damage); *Invercargill City Council v. Hamlin* [1996] 1 All E.R. 756 (negligent supervision by local authority); *Clerk and Lindsell on Torts* (17th ed., 1995), § 31–09 (economic loss).

[46] *Pirelli General Cable Works Ltd v. Oscar Faber and Partners, supra,* at 16; *Chelmsford D.C. v. Evers* (1983) 25 Build.L.R. 99; *Tozer Kemsley and Milbourn Holdings v. J. Jarvis & Sons* (1985) 4 Const.L.R. 24. *cf. Kensington and Chelsea and Westminster Area Health Authority v. Wettern Composites Ltd* [1985] 1 All E.R. 346; *Investors in Industry Commercial Properties Ltd v. South Bedfordshire D.C.* [1986] Q.B. 1034; *Ketteman v. Hansel Properties Ltd* [1987] A.C. 189; *London Congregational Union Inc. v. Harriss & Harriss, supra.*

[47] *Pirelli General Cable Works Ltd v. Oscar Faber and Partners, supra; London Congregational Union Inc. v. Harriss & Harriss, supra; Leicester Wholesale Fruit Market Ltd v. Grundy, supra,* at p. 110. But see O'Dair (1992) 55 M.L.R. 405; Mullany [1993] L.M.C.L.Q. 34.

[48] *Pirelli General Cable Works Ltd v. Oscar Faber and Partners, supra.* Contrast *Invercargill City Council v. Hamlin* [1996] 1 All E.R. 756 and the position in Australia and Canada: see Mullany (1991) 54 M.L.R. 216, 349; (1993) 109 L.Q.R. 215.

[49] Inserted by s.1 of the Latent Damage Act 1986; *post,* § 29–091.

negligence within three years of the date of discovery or reasonable discoverability of facts relevant to the cause of action.

Defective Premises Act 1972. Under section 1 of the Defective Premises Act 1972, any cause of action in respect of duty imposed by the Act (the duty to build dwellings properly) is deemed, for the purposes of limitation, to have accrued at the time the dwelling was completed; but if after that time a person who has done work for or in connection with the provision of a dwelling does further work to rectify the work he has already done, any such cause of action in respect of that further work is deemed for those purposes to have accrued at the time the further work was finished.[50]   **29–056**

Successive owners. Section 3 of the Latent Damage Act 1986 also contains provisions relating to the accrual of a cause of action to successive owners in respect of latent damage to property caused by negligence. Although a fresh cause of action will accrue to each owner on the date on which he acquires his interest in the property, nevertheless the cause of action is deemed for the purposes of section 14A of the 1980 Act to have accrued on the date on which the original cause of action arose.   **29–057**

Breach of trust etc. The right of action by a beneficiary to recover trust property or in respect of any breach of trust normally accrues upon the breach of trust being committed.[51] Time does not normally begin to run between partners in respect of any claim arising out of the partnership until it is dissolved[52] or until an act of ouster occurs.[53] The running of time may further be postponed by reason of fraud or concealment.[54] There is, however, no general principle that the existence of a fiduciary relationship in commercial transactions prevents the running of time. Thus an agent may plead the statute against his principal.[55] But an agent may be a trustee of property entrusted to him, in which case other considerations arise which are outside the scope of this book.[56]   **29–058**

Restitution. The claimant's cause of action will normally accrue when he is damnified, *e.g.* when he pays money to the defendant or to the defendant's use,[57] or when the defendant receives money (or some other benefit) for which he must   **29–059**

---

[50] Defective Premises Act 1972, s.1(5). Since the liability is strict, the extension in respect of latent damage in actions in tort for negligence under s.14A of the 1980 Act (*post*, § 29–092) is not available.

[51] *Re Swain* [1891] 3 Ch. 233; *Re Somerset* [1894] 1 Ch. 231; *Thorne v. Heard* [1895] A.C. 495.

[52] *Knox v. Gye* (1872) L.R. 5 H.L. 656; *Noyes v. Crawley* (1878) 10 Ch.D. 31. *cf. Betjemann v. Betjemann* [1895] 2 Ch. 474; *Gopala Chetty v. Vijayaraghavachariar* [1922] 1 A.C. 488.

[53] *Barton v. North Staffs Ry.* (1888) 38 Ch.D. 458, 463.

[54] *Stainton v. Carron & Co.* (1853) 24 Beav. 346; *Betjemann v. Betjemann, supra.*

[55] *Friend v. Young* [1897] 2 Ch. 421; *Henry v. Hammond* [1913] 2 K.B. 515; *Paragon Finance plc v. Thakerar & Co.* [1999] 1 All E.R. 400, 415.

[56] See ss.21(1)(b), 23 of the Act, and *Bowstead and Reynolds on Agency* (16th ed., 1996) §§ 6–034, 6–042, 6–043, 6–054; *Burdick v. Garrick* (1870) L.R. 5 Ch. App. 233; *North American Land and Timber Co. v. Watkins* [1904] 1 Ch. 242, [1904] 2 Ch. 233.

[57] *Baker v. Courage & Co.* [1910] 1 K.B. 56; *Re Jones* [1914] 1 Ir.R. 188; *Anglo-Scottish Beet Sugar Corpn. Ltd v. Spalding U.D.C.* [1937] 2 K.B. 607, 609, 627; *Re Diplock* [1948] Ch. 465, 513; *Maskell v. Horner* [1915] 3 K.B. 106; *Re Mason* [1928] Ch. 385, 392; [1929] 1 Ch. 1; *Re Blake* [1932] 1 Ch. 54, 60; *Kleinwort Benson Ltd v. Sandwell B.C.* (1993) 91 L.G.R. 323, 382–384; *Kleinwort Benson Ltd v. South Tyneside Metropolitan B.C.*, [1994] 4 All E.R. 972; Limitation Act 1980, ss.5, 23; see *ante*, § 29–002.

account to the claimant.[58] But the running of time may be postponed in the case of fraud, concealment or mistake,[59] or be affected by the fact that the relief claimed is equitable[60] or that the defendant is a constructive trustee.[61]

29–060   **Arbitration and award.** The parties can agree that the award of an arbitrator shall be a condition precedent to a right to bring an action on the contract.[62] This is known as a "*Scott v. Avery*" clause.[63] Since the effect of such a term in an arbitration agreement is that no cause of action accrues in respect of any matter required by the agreement to be referred until an award is made under the agreement, it was formerly held that time ran from the date of the award and not from the date of the original cause of arbitration, and that no limitation period was applicable at all for arbitration proceedings.[64] But section 13(3) of the Arbitration Act 1996 now provides that, in determining for the purposes of the Limitation Acts[65] when a cause of action accrued, any provision that an award is a condition precedent to the bringing of legal proceedings in respect of a matter to which an arbitration agreement applies is to be disregarded.

29–061   The limitation period for the enforcement of an arbitral award accrues when the claimant is entitled to enforce the award.[66] Alternatively, if the claim is for damages for breach of an implied promise to pay the award, then it accrues when a reasonable time to pay the award has elapsed.[67]

29–062   **Burden of proof.**[68] In principle it might be expected that the defendant, having pleaded the statute,[69] would bear the burden of proving that the claimant's cause of action accrued outside the limitation period and was in consequence statute-barred.[70] However, there is weighty authority for the view that, where there is a joinder of issue on the defendant's plea of limitation, the burden of proof is on the claimant to show that his cause of action accrued within the statutory period.[71] In *Cartledge v. E. Jopling and Sons Ltd*[72] the Court of Appeal so held. But in the House of Lords[73] Lord Pearce placed a gloss on this

---

[58] If the basis for restitutionary claims is unjust enrichment (*post*, § 30–016). See McLean [1989] C.L.J. 472 and *Brueton v. Woodward* [1941] 1 K.B. 680.

[59] See *post*, §§ 29–084, 29–085, 29–087.

[60] See *post*, § 29–137, and *Tito v. Waddell (No. 2)* [1977] Ch. 106.

[61] See s.21 of the Act; Goff and Jones, *The Law of Restitution* (5th ed., 1998), p. 857. But see *ante*, § 29–014.

[62] See *ante*, § 16–032.

[63] *Scott v. Avery* (1856) 5 H.L.C. 811.

[64] *Board of Trade v. Cayzer, Irvine & Co.* [1927] A.C. 610.

[65] Defined in s.13(4) of the 1996 Act.

[66] *International Bulk Shipping and Services Ltd v. Minerals and Metals Trading Corpn. of India* [1996] 1 All E.R. 1017.

[67] *Agromet Motoimport v. Maulden Engineering Co. (Beds.) Ltd* [1985] 1 W.L.R. 762; *International Bulk Shipping Ltd v. Minerals and Metals Trading Corpn. of India, supra.*

[68] See Mullany (1993) 109 L.Q.R. 215, 217.

[69] See *post*, § 29–110.

[70] *Lochgelly Iron & Coal Co. Ltd v. McMullen* [1934] A.C. 1, 35.

[71] *Hurst v. Parker* (1817) 1 B. & A. 92; *Beale v. Nind* (1821) 4 B. & A. 566, 571; *Wilby v. Henman* (1834) 2 C. & M. 658; *Darley Main Colliery Co. v. Mitchell* (1886) 111 App.Cas. 127, 135; *O'Connor v. Isaacs* [1956] 2 Q.B. 288, 364; *Arab Monetary Fund v. Hashim* [1996] 1 Lloyd's Rep. 589, 607–608.

[72] [1962] 1 Q.B. 189, 202, 208.

[73] [1963] A.C. 758, 784 (with whom the other members of the House of Lords effectively agreed).

proposition when he stated that, although the initial onus was on the claimant, once he had satisfied that onus, the burden passed to the defendant to show that the apparent accrual of a cause of action was misleading and that in reality the cause of action accrued at an earlier date. Nevertheless it is not sufficient for the claimant to prove, for example, that a breach of contract occurred at some time during the limitation period. In *London Congregational Union Inc. v. Harriss & Harriss*[74] Ralph Gibson L.J. stated that the claimant must show, on the balance of probabilities, that the cause of action accrued, *i.e.* came into existence, on a day within the period of limitation. Only then would the onus shift to the defendant. The burden of proof may less often be of significance in contractual actions than actions in tort, but may still be of importance in certain cases.[75]

3. COMPUTATION OF THE PERIOD

Commencement of the period. The computation of the period may require   **29–063**
the court to determine the precise day on which the period starts running. In the preceding section of this chapter it was pointed out that in actions for breach of contract, the cause of action accrues when the breach takes place and not when the damage is suffered. But does the cause of action accrue on the day of the breach or on the following day? If the breach consists in failure to do something on a particular day, *e.g.* to pay money, and the person who has to do the act has the whole of that day in which to do it,[76] the cause of action is not complete until the commencement of the following day, and it would seem that time begins to run from and is inclusive of the day when the cause of action accrues.[77] On the other hand, if the breach consists in the doing of a positive act, (*e.g.* the delivery of defective goods under a contract of sale) or of an event, no doubt the cause of action accrues on the day when the act is done or the event occurs. Nevertheless, it is now settled law that the day of the act or event is to be excluded from the computation of the period within which the action should be brought, and time begins to run from the following day.[78]

End of the period. If the period of limitation ends on a Sunday or some other   **29–064**
dies non juridicus when the court offices are closed, and the necessary act, (*e.g.* the issue of a claim form) is one which can only be done if the court office is open on the day when time expires, the period is extended until the next day on which the court office is open.[79]

---

[74] [1988] 1 All E.R. 15, 30.

[75] *Chandris v. Argo Insurance Co. Ltd* [1963] 2 Lloyd's Rep. 65, 73; *N.V. Stoomv Maats "De Maas" v. Nippon Yusen Kaisha* [1980] 2 Lloyd's Rep. 56 (overruled on other grounds in *Kodros Shipping Corpn. of Monrovia v. Empresa Cubana de Fletes (No. 2)* [1983] 1 A.C 736); *Arab Monetary Fund v. Hashim, supra.*

[76] See *Afovos Shipping Co. SA v. R. Pagnan & Filli* [1983] 1 W.L.R. 195.

[77] *Gelmini v. Moriggia* [1913] 2 K.B. 549 (failure to pay a promissory note) would appear still to be good law on this point. *cf.* Sale of Goods Act 1979, s.29(5); *Roper v. Johnson* (1873) L.R. 8 C.P. 167, 179; *Bremer Handelsgesellschaft mbH v. Vanden Avenne-Izegem P.V.B.A.* [1978] 2 Lloyd's Rep. 109.

[78] *Radcliffe v. Bartholomew* [1892] 1 Q.B. 161; *Marren v. Dawson Bentley & Co. Ltd* [1961] 2 Q.B. 135; *Pritam Kaur v. S. Russell & Sons Ltd* [1973] Q.B. 336.

[79] *Pritam Kaur v. S. Russell & Sons Ltd* [1973] Q.B. 336, not following *Gelmini v. Moriggia* [1913] 2 K.B. 549 and *Morris v. Richards* (1881) 45 L.T. 210. See also *Hodgson v. Armstrong* [1967] 2 Q.B. 299; CPR, r. 2.8(5); *The Clifford Maersk* [1982] 1 W.L.R. 1292.

4. The Running of Time

29–065   **Introductory.** The general principle is that once time has started to run it continues to do so until proceedings are commenced or the claim is barred.[80] The principle (if any is possible in so technical a matter) is that a claimant who is in a position to commence proceedings, and neglects to do so, accepts the risk that some unexpected subsequent event will prevent him from doing so within the statutory period.[81] The principle is illustrated by a famous group of seventeenth-century cases deciding that the closing of the courts during the Civil War did not suspend the running of time.[82] Thus, if a cause of action has accrued in favour of or against a person who subsequently dies, the fact of his death will not suspend the running of the limitation period even though there may be an interval of time between his death and the grant of letters of administration.[83] However, in the case of a personal injuries action,[84] if the person injured dies before the expiration of the limitation period, the period as respects the cause of action surviving for the benefit of the estate of the deceased by virtue of section 1 of the Law Reform (Miscellaneous Provisions) Act 1934 is extended to three years from the date of death, or the date of the personal representative's knowledge of certain facts relevant to his right of action against the defendant, whichever is the later.[85]

29–066   **Personal representatives.** Before 1980, if a debtor became the administrator of his creditor, the running of time was suspended for the duration of his appointment, because during that time it was impossible for him to sue himself.[86] This rule did not apply when the creditor by will appointed the debtor his executor. In such a case, since the appointment was a voluntary act, the common law held that the appointment extinguished the debt,[87] although equity intervened by treating the debtor-executor as if he had paid the debt to himself, so that he became accountable for the amount of the debt as being an asset of the estate.[88] The two situations have now been assimilated by section 21A of the Administration of Estates Act 1925,[89] and the running of time is no longer suspended if the debtor becomes his creditor's administrator. Instead, if a debtor becomes his deceased creditor's executor (by representation) or administrator, his debt[90] is thereby extinguished, and he is accountable for the amount of the debt as part of

---

[80] *Prideaux v. Webber* (1661) 1 Lev. 31; *Rhodes v. Smethurst* (1840) 6 M. & W. 351; *Homfray v. Scroope* (1849) 13 Q.B. 509; *Fenny v. Brice* (1865) 18 C.B.(N.S.) 393; *Boatwright v. Boatwright* (1873) L.R. 17 Eq. 71; *Re Benzon* [1914] 2 Ch. 68; *Bowring-Hanbury's Trustee v. Bowring-Hanbury* [1943] Ch. 104. But see *post*, § 29–083.

[81] *Re Benzon* [1914] 2 Ch. 68, 76.

[82] *e.g. Prideaux v. Webber, supra.*

[83] *Rhodes v. Smethurst, supra*; *Fergusson v. Fyffe* (1841) 8 Cl. & Fin. 121, 140; *Penny v. Brice, supra*; *Boatwright v. Boatwright, supra*; *Bowring-Hanbury's Trustee v. Bowring-Hanbury, supra*. See also Proceedings against Estates Act 1970, s.2; RSC, Ord. 15, r. 6A (now CPR, Sched. 1).

[84] See *ante*, §§ 29–005—29–007.

[85] Limitation Act 1980, ss.11(5), 11A(3), 14.

[86] *Seagram v. Knight* (1867) L.R. 2 Ch.App. 628, a complicated case which is discussed fully in *Bowring-Hanbury's Trustee v. Bowring-Hanbury, supra.*

[87] *Nedham's Case* (1610) 8 Co.Rep. 135a.

[88] *Re Greg* [1921] 2 Ch. 243.

[89] Inserted by s.10 of the Limitation Amendment Act 1980 and amended by s.40(2) of and Sched. 3 to the Limitation Act 1980. See the *Twenty-First Report of the Law Reform Committee*, Cmnd. 6923, (1977) paras 3.85–3.93.

[90] Or liability: s.21A(3) of the 1925 Act.

the creditor's estate, as if he had been appointed as an executor by the creditor's will.[91]

The running of time is not suspended or otherwise affected in the converse **29–067** case where the creditor becomes executor or administrator of his debtor, since he can satisfy his debt by exercising his right of retainer.[92]

Abrogation of arbitration award or agreement. An exception to the rule **29–068** that, once time has started to run, it runs continuously is provided by section 13(2) of the Arbitration Act 1996. Where the court orders that an arbitration award is to be set aside or to be of no effect (in whole or in part), the court may further order that the period between the commencement of the arbitration and the date of the order of the court shall be excluded in computing the time prescribed by the Limitation Acts[93] for the commencement of proceedings (including arbitral proceedings) with respect to the dispute which is the subject matter of the award.

International carriage. Further exceptions to the rule that time runs con- **29–069** tinuously are contained in certain international conventions relating to carriage by land. Under the Convention on the Contract for the International Carriage of Goods by Road (CMR),[94] the Convention on the Contract for the International Carriage of Passengers and Luggage by Road (CVR)[95] and the Convention concerning International Carriage by Rail (COTIF),[96] a written claim, which has been duly made, suspends the period of limitation until the date on which the carrier rejects the claim by notification in writing and returns any documents accompanying the claim.[97] This principle is familiar in continental law; but in English law it is confined to claims arising under these conventions.

Limitation (Enemies and War Prisoners) Act 1945. The running of any **29–070** limitation period may be suspended by virtue of this Act.[98]

Bankruptcy and winding-up. The presentation of a petition by a petitioning **29–071** creditor is an action within the Limitation Act 1980 and so stops time from running against him.[99] Otherwise, the making of a bankruptcy order stops time running in respect of all claims against the bankrupt which are provable in the

---

[91] s.21A(1), subject to the exception in s.21A(2).
[92] See *post*, § 29–134.
[93] Defined in s.13(4) of the 1996 Act.
[94] Carriage of Goods by Road Act 1965, Sched., art. 32(2); see *ante*, § 29–021; Vol. II, § 36–153.
[95] Carriage of Passengers by Road Act 1974, Sched., art. 22(3); see *ante*, § 29–022; Vol. II, § 36–164.
[96] Appendix A (CIV), Art. 55(4); Appendix B (CIM), Art. 58(3); see *ante*, § 29–020; Vol. II, §§ 36–108, 36–122.
[97] *Microfine Minerals and Chemicals Ltd v. Transferry Shipping Co. Ltd* [1991] 2 Lloyd's Rep. 630.
[98] See *ante*, § 11–027.
[99] Limitation Act 1980, s.38(1) "action"; *Re Karnos Property Co. Ltd* [1989] B.C.L.C. 340; *Re Cases of Taffs Well Ltd* [1992] Ch. 179; *Re a Debtor (No. 50A–SD–1995)* [1997] Ch. 310.

bankruptcy,[1] and the making of a winding-up order against a company has a similar effect.[2]

5. Extension of the Period

29–072   **Extensions.** The Limitation Act 1980 contains a number of provisions, the effect of which will be to extend the time within which an action must be brought beyond that normally applicable. The Act affords such extensions in a number of differing ways.

29–073   It has already been pointed out that, in the case of actions for damages for personal injuries[3] and by virtue of Part I of the Consumer Protection Act 1987,[4] the applicable three-year period of limitation runs from the date on which the cause of action accrued or the date of the claimant's knowledge (if later) of certain facts relevant to his cause of action against the defendant. This "date of knowledge" principle may also serve, in effect, to extend the limitation period where such a cause of action survives for the benefit of the injured person's estate by virtue of section 1 of the Law Reform (Miscellaneous Provisions) Act 1934[5] and where an action is brought under the Fatal Accidents Act 1976.[6]

29–074   Provision is, however, made in the Act for more general extensions in certain contingencies. These statutory extensions are dealt with in the paragraphs which follow, together with the extension of the limitation period by agreement of the parties.

(a) *Disability*

29–075   **Disability.** The Act allows a claimant further time in which to bring proceedings if he was, at the commencement of the limitation period, under a disability, *i.e.* was a minor or a person of unsound mind.[7]

29–076   **Limitation Act 1980, s.28.** If on the date when any right of action accrued for which a period of limitation is prescribed by the Act,[8] the person to whom it accrued was under a disability, the action may be brought at any time before the expiration of six years from the date on which he ceased to be under a disability or died (whichever first occurred) notwithstanding that the period of limitation has expired.[9] This does not apply to actions for which a period of limitation is

---

[1] *Re General Rolling Stock Co.* (1872) L.R. 7 Ch.App. 646, 649; *Re Cullwick* [1918] 1 K.B. 646, 653 (receiving orders). *cf. Re Benzon* [1914] 2 Ch. 68.

[2] *Re General Rolling Stock Co., supra*; *Re Cases of Taffs Well Ltd, supra.* See also *Re Art Reproduction Co. Ltd* [1952] Ch. 89 (passing of resolution for voluntary winding up).

[3] See *ante*, § 29–005.

[4] See *ante*, § 29–008.

[5] Limitation Act 1980, ss.11(5), 11A(3), 14; see *ante*, § 29–005.

[6] See *ante*, §§ 29–005, 29–006.

[7] s.38(2). For the definition of "a person of unsound mind," see s.38(3), (4). See also *Kirby v. Leather* [1965] 2 Q.B. 367.

[8] But see *post*, § 29–081 for exceptions. s.28 also does not apply to any cause of action under s.3 of the Latent Damage Act 1986: see s.3(3) of the 1986 Act.

[9] s.28(1).

prescribed by or under any other enactment.[10] It will be observed that the period allowed after the cesser of disability or death is (subject to the exceptions discussed below)[11] six years, and this is so even though the action is on a specialty. There is no extension of time under this section if the right of action first accrues to some person not under a disability, even if that person is one through whom the person under a disability claims.[12] In other words, the disability must exist when the cause of action accrued: subsequent disability is of no effect.

Successive disabilities. The wording of section 28 ("ceased to be under *a*   **29–077** disability") makes it clear that if the claimant is under successive disabilities with no interval of time between them, *e.g.* is a minor when the cause of action accrues and is of unsound mind at the time of attaining his majority, he will have until the expiration of six years from the cesser of the latter disability in which to bring his action.[13] On the other hand, if a person under a disability dies and is succeeded by a person also under a disability, no further extension of time is allowed by reason of the disability of the second person.[14]

Joint claimants. It was held under the Limitation Act 1623 that if there are   **29–078** a number of joint claimants or creditors, but not all of them under disability when the cause of action accrues, the running of time is not postponed.[15]

Shorter extensions. In the case of the special two-year time limit for claiming   **29–079** contribution under section 1 of the Civil Liability (Contribution) Act 1978,[16] only two years is allowed as an extension of time under section 28 of the 1980 Act[17]; and in the case of the three-year periods prescribed for actions in respect of personal injuries,[18] for actions under Part I of the Consumer Protection Act 1987[19] and for actions under the Fatal Accidents Act 1976,[20] only a three-year extension is allowed.

Limitation Act 1980, s.28A. Similar provision to that contained in section 28   **29–080** is made in section 28A of the 1980 Act for negligence actions in respect of latent damage where the claimant or other relevant person was under a disability on the "starting date" for reckoning the extended period of limitation prescribed by section 14A(4)(b) of the Act.[21] In this case, three years is allowed as an extension of time from the date when he ceased to be under a disability or died.[22]

---

[10] s.39.
[11] *Post*, §§ 29–079, 29–080.
[12] s.28(2). See also s.38(5), (6).
[13] *cf. Borrows v. Ellison* (1871) L.R. 6 Ex. 128 (decided on s.16 of the Real Property Limitation Act 1833).
[14] s.28(3).
[15] *Perry v. Jackson* (1792) 4 T.R. 416.
[16] s.10; see *ante*, § 29–010.
[17] s.28(5).
[18] ss.11, 28(6); see *ante*, § 29–005.
[19] ss.11(A), 28(7)(b) (inserted by s.6 of and Sched. 1 to the Consumer Protection Act 1987); see *ante*, § 29–008.
[20] ss.12(2), 28(6); see *ante*, § 29–006.
[21] See *post*, § 29–093. The s.28A extension applies only where s.28 does not apply to the action.
[22] s.28A(1).

29–081　　**Long-stop periods.** Section 28 does not apply to the 10-year long-stop period for actions under Part I of the Consumer Protection Act 1987,[23] and no action to recover land or money charged on land can be brought by virtue of the section after the expiration of 30 years from the date on which the right of action accrued to the claimant or to some person through whom he claims.[24] Section 28A of the Act does not enable an action to be brought after the end of the 15-year long-stop period for negligence actions not involving personal injuries.[25]

(b) *Fraud, Concealment or Mistake*

29–082　　**Limitation Act 1980, s.32.** Section 32 of the 1980 Act applies if the claimant's action is based on the fraud of the defendant or if a fact relevant to his right of action has been deliberately concealed from him by the defendant or if his action is for relief from the consequences of a mistake. The limitation period does not begin to run until the claimant discovers or with reasonable diligence could have discovered the fraud, concealment or mistake. The section does not, in its terms, extend the period of limitation, but postpones the commencement of the period, although its effect may be to enable an action to be brought more than six years after the date when the cause of action in fact accrued.[26]

29–083　　Where the claimant's action is based on the fraud of the defendant[27] or the action is for relief from the consequences of a mistake,[28] all the relevant circumstances must necessarily be in place when the cause of action accrues. It is therefore apt for section 32(1) to provide that the limitation period "shall not *begin* to run" until discovery or imputed discovery by the claimant of the fraud or mistake. The question, however, arises whether, once the limitation period has started to run, any deliberate *subsequent* concealment[29] will suspend or interrupt its running, or extend the period. In *Tito v. Waddell (No. 2)*[30] Megarry J. expressed the opinion that, if time had already begun to run, a supervening fraudulent concealment[31] would not start time running again. But in *Sheldon v. R.H.M. Outhwaite (Underwriting Agencies) Ltd*[32] Saville J. disagreed with this view and held that a deliberate concealment[33] which occurred after the plaintiff's cause of action accrued nevertheless produced the effect that the period of limitation would not begin to run until the plaintiff discovered, or could with reasonable diligence have discovered, the concealment. The decision of Saville J. was reversed by the Court of Appeal but, on appeal to the House of Lords, his interpretation of section 32 was, by a majority, confirmed.[34] The consequence is that, in the case of a concealment taking place after the accrual of the cause of action, time will start running again and run for the full period from actual or

---

[23] ss.11A(3), 12(1), 28(7)(a) (inserted by s.6 of and Sched. 1 to the Consumer Protection Act 1987); see *ante*, § 29–008.

[24] s.28(4).

[25] ss.14B, 28A(2) (inserted by ss.1, 2 of the Latent Damage Act 1986); see *ante*, § 29–014A.

[26] *Eddis v. Chichester Constable* [1969] 2 Ch. 345, 362.

[27] s.32(1)(a); *post*, § 29–084.

[28] s.32(1)(c); *post*, § 29–087.

[29] s.32(1)(b); *post*, § 29–085.

[30] [1977] Ch. 106, 245.

[31] Under s. 26(b) of the Limitation Act 1939.

[32] *The Times,* December 8, 1993.

[33] Under s.32(1)(b); *post*, § 29–085.

[34] [1996] A.C. 102.

imputed discovery of the concealment. Moreover, it seems that even concealment subsequent to the expiration of the original limitation period will produce this effect. The result seems to be an odd one which is unlikely to have been intended by the legislature.

Fraud. Section 32(1)(a) of the Limitation Act 1980 provides that where the **29–084** action is based upon the fraud of the defendant, the period of limitation shall not begin to run until the claimant has discovered the fraud or could with reasonable diligence have discovered it. This provision is, however, of limited scope because it only covers cases where the cause of action requires the allegation and proof of fraud in the strict sense, *e.g.* as in actions for fraudulent misrepresentation or deceit.[35] It is submitted that an action under section 2(1) of the Misrepresentation Act 1967, though equated for some purposes to an action based on fraud,[36] would not fall within section 32(1)(a).

Concealment. Section 32(1)(b) of the Act provides that where any fact **29–085** relevant to the claimant's right of action[37] has been deliberately concealed from him by the defendant, the period of limitation shall not begin to run until the claimant has discovered the concealment or could with reasonable diligence have discovered it. It is further provided that a deliberate commission of a breach of duty in circumstances in which it is unlikely to be discovered for some time amounts to deliberate concealment of the facts involved in that breach of duty.[38] The use of the word "deliberate" clearly indicates that an unwitting (even if negligent) concealment of a relevant fact or commission of a breach of duty is not enough[39]; but it is more questionable whether recklessness will suffice.[40] It is also clear that no fraud or dishonesty on the part of the defendant need be proved. Where there is a deliberate commission of a breach of duty, *e.g.* a breach of contract, it is unnecessary to show that the defendant took active steps to conceal the breach: all that is required is that it is committed "in circumstances in which it is unlikely to be discovered for some time." These provisions were intended to give effect to a recommendation of the Law Reform Committee[41] that paragraph (b) of section 26 of the Limitation Act 1939 should be reformulated in a way "which reproduces in a more readily intelligible form the construction placed upon that paragraph by the courts."[42] It may therefore be that cases on the 1939 Act will be of some assistance in illustrating the operation of the 1980 Act provisions. Examples are: the furtive and surreptitious taking of coal under ground from the plaintiff's land where the trespass would not be found out "for

---

[35] *Beaman v. A.R.T.S Ltd* [1949] 1 K.B. 550, 558, 567.

[36] *Royscot Trust Ltd v. Rogerson* [1991] 2 Q.B. 297; see *ante,* § 6–069. *cf. UBAF Ltd v. European American Banking Corpn.* [1984] Q.B. 713.

[37] Defined in s.38(9). The recovery of interest by way of execution on a judgment is not a "right of action" within s.32(1)(b): *Lowsley v. Forbes* [1998] 3 W.L.R. 501. Nor (*semble*) is the defendant's concealment of himself or his assets a fact relevant to the claimant's action, *ibid.*

[38] s.32(2).

[39] *Re Coole* [1920] Ch. 536; *King v. Victor Parsons & Co.* [1973] 1 W.L.R. 29, 33, 36; *Kaliszewska v. Clague* [1984] C.I.L.L. 131. *cf. UBAF Ltd v. European American Banking Corpn.* [1984] Q.B. 713.

[40] *cf. Beaman v. A.R.T.S. Ltd* [1949] 1 K.B. 550, 565–566; *King v. Victor Parsons & Co., supra,* at 33.

[41] *Twenty-First Report,* Cmnd. 6923 (1977), paras 2.22–2.25, 2.35. But s.32(1)(b) differs in wording from the reformulation of the Committee.

[42] *ibid.* para. 2.22.

many a long day"[43]; a husband's failure to disclose the true amount of his income, having contracted to pay a proportion of it to his wife under a maintenance agreement[44]; a married man's representing himself as single for the purposes of a subsequent ceremony of marriage with the plaintiff or a subsequent failure to reveal that the second ceremony was bigamous[45]; a reckless sale of bailed goods without communication with the bailor[46]; a solicitor's failure to inform his client that an *ex gratia* payment had been offered by an alleged tortfeasor, which would have revealed the possibility of a cause of action on the part of the client against the solicitor in negligence[47]; the failure of a builder to disclose the deliberate breach by him of a building contract by using defective bricks[48] or inadequate foundations[49]; and the failure to warn the purchaser of a house of a known risk of subsidence due to the fact that the house had been constructed on unsuitable ground.[50] Cases decided under section 32(1)(b) of the 1980 Act have mainly concerned bad work knowingly done by builders, which was subsequently covered up so that the defects were unlikely to be discovered for some time,[51] and allegations in respect of professional negligence by solicitors.[52] The burden of proof rests upon the claimant.[53]

29–086 **Fraud or concealment by agent.** The fraud or concealment may be that of an agent of the defendant or of any person through whom the defendant claims or his agent.[54] In the case of concealment, the word "agent" may include an independent contractor employed by the defendant.[55] The defendant is to be treated as claiming "through" another person if he became entitled by, through, under or by the act of that other person to the right claimed.[56] In the case of property, it has been held that a defendant claims property through another person if he derives his title to the property from that person.[57] And an innocent volunteer claims through a person who fraudulently directs another's money to him.[58]

29–087 **Mistake.** Section 32(1)(c) of the Act provides that where the action is for relief from the consequences of a mistake, the period of limitation shall not begin to run until the claimant has discovered the mistake or could with reasonable diligence have discovered it.[59] The corresponding paragraph in the Limitation

---

[43] *Bulli Coal Mining Co. v. Osborne* [1899] A.C. 351.
[44] *Legh v. Legh* (1930) 143 L.T. 451.
[45] *Beyers v. Green* [1936] 1 All E.R. 613; *Shaw v. Shaw* [1954] 2 Q.B. 429. But see now the Law Reform (Miscellaneous Provisions) Act 1970, ss.1, 6, 7(2) (cause of action abolished).
[46] *Beaman v. A.R.T.S. Ltd* [1949] 1 K.B. 550.
[47] *Kitchen v. R.A.F. Association* [1958] 1 W.L.R. 563.
[48] *Clark v. Woor* [1965] 1 W.L.R. 650.
[49] *Applegate v. Moss* [1971] 1 Q.B. 406.
[50] *King v. Victor Parsons & Co.* [1973] 1 W.L.R. 29.
[51] *Gray v. T P Bennett & Son* (1987) 43 Build L.R. 63; *Kijowski v. New Capital Properties.* (1990) 15 Con.L.R. 1.
[52] *Tunbridge v. Buss Murton & Co., The Times,* April 8, 1997; *Markes v. Coodes* [1997] P.N.L.R. 252.
[53] *Tunbridge v. Buss Murton & Co..*, *supra* (pleading).
[54] s.32(1).
[55] *Applegate v. Moss* [1971] 1 QB 406; *King v. Victor Parsons & Co.* [1973] 1 W.L.R. 29 (but both of these cases were decided on s.26(*b*) of the Limitation Act 1939).
[56] s.38(5).
[57] *Eddis v. Chichester Constable* [1969] 2 Ch. 345, 356–357, 362–363.
[58] *G.L. Baker Ltd v. Medway Building and Supplies Ltd* [1958] 1 W.L.R. 1216.
[59] *Peco Arts Inc. v. Hazlitt Gallery Ltd* [1983] 1 W.L.R. 1315.

Act 1939[60] received a somewhat narrow interpretation in *Phillips-Higgins v. Harper*,[61] where it was said that "it applies only where the mistake is an essential ingredient of the cause of action, so that the statement of claim sets out, or should set out, the mistake and its consequences and pray for relief from those consequences."[62] In that case the defendant employer had underpaid the plaintiff, who had not realised what payments were due to her. Pearson J. held that only six years' arrears were recoverable: the plaintiff's action was to recover moneys due to her under a contract, and was not an action "for relief from the consequences of a mistake." The result seems somewhat anomalous because, if there is an overpayment by mistake, the person paying can claim the benefit of the provision. It is also to be noted that section 32(1)(*c*) does not require that the action be "based upon" a mistake[63]; nor does it require that the mistake should be that of the claimant. A mistake of law is sufficient.[63a]

Reasonable diligence. In cases arising under section 32(1), time begins to run **29–088** when the claimant discovers the fraud, concealment or mistake, or could with reasonable diligence have discovered it. What is "reasonable diligence" must vary with the particular context in which that expression is to be applied.[64] It does not require the claimant to use all means of discovery available to him, but only to do that which an ordinary prudent person, having regard to all the circumstances, would do.[65] The burden of proof rests upon the claimant.[66]

Purchaser for valuable consideration. Section 32(3) of the Act protects **29–089** innocent purchasers for valuable consideration by enacting that nothing in section 32 shall enable any action to recover, or recover the value of,[67] any property, or to enforce any charge against, or set aside any transaction affecting, any property, to be brought against the purchaser of the property or any person claiming through him[68] in any case where the property has been purchased for valuable consideration by an innocent third party since the fraud or concealment or (as the case may be) the transaction in which the mistake took place. A purchaser is an innocent third party for the purposes of the section:

(a) in the case of fraud or concealment of any fact relevant to the plaintiff's right of action, if he was not a party to the fraud or concealment of that fact and did not at the time of the purchase know or have reason to believe that the fraud or concealment had taken place[69]; and

---

[60] s.26(c).

[61] [1954] 1 Q.B. 411 (affd. [1954] 2 All E.R. 51n).

[62] *ibid.* at 419. *cf. Ministry of Health v. Simpson* [1951] A.C. 251, 277.

[63] As in s.32(1)(a) "based upon the fraud" of the defendant. See Franks, *Limitation of Actions* (1959), pp. 206–207 and (in equity) Brunyate, *Limitation of Actions in Equity,* pp. 254–257.

[63a] *Kleinwort Benson Ltd v. Lincoln C.C.* [1998] 3 W.L.R. 1095.

[64] *Peco Arts Inc. v. Hazlitt Gallery Ltd* [1983] 1 W.L.R. 1315, 1322–3.

[65] *ibid.* at 1323. See also *Ecclesiastical Commissioners for England v. N.E. Ry.* (1877) 4 Ch.D. 845, 861; *Rawlins v. Wickham* (1858) 3 De G.L.J. 304; *Chetham v. Hoare* (1870) L.R. 9 Eq. 571; *Vane v. Vane* (1873) L.R. 8 Ch.App. 383, 390n; *Willis v. Howe* [1893] 2 Ch. 545; *Betjemann v. Betjemann* [1895] 2 Ch. 474, 480. *cf., Paragon Finance plc v. Thakerar & Co.* [1999] 1 All E.R. 400, 418.

[66] *Peco Arts Inc. v. Hazlitt Gallery Ltd, supra; Paragon Finance plc v. Thakerar & Co., supra.*

[67] See *Eddis v. Chichester Constable* [1969] 2 Ch. 345, 357 (extension to conversion).

[68] Defined in s.38(5); see § 29–086, n. 56, *ante.*

[69] See *Eddis v. Chichester Constable, supra* (knowledge of agent attributed to principal).

(b) in the case of mistake, if he did not at the time of the purchase know or have reason to believe that the mistake had been made.

29–090　**Application of section 32.** Fraud, concealment and mistake postpone the running of time only in the case of an action for which a period of limitation is prescribed by the Act[70] and do not apply (except to the extent expressly provided therein) to other limitation enactments.[71] The section also does not apply to an action under the Fatal Accidents Act 1976[72] or to the 10-year long-stop period for actions under Part I of the Consumer Protection Act 1987.[73] On the other hand, in the case of an action to which section 32(1)(b) (concealment) applies, neither the three-year extension for negligence actions in respect of latent damage[74] nor the 15-year long-stop period for negligence actions not involving personal injuries[75] will come into operation.[76]

(c) *Latent Damage*[77]

29–091　**Introductory.** Except in the case of actions in respect of personal injuries,[78] under the Fatal Accidents Act 1976[79] or under Part I of the Consumer Protection Act 1987,[80] it is in general[81] no answer to a plea of limitation to say that the claimant was unaware of the existence of his cause of action until after the expiration of the limitation period. Since a cause of action in contract accrues at the date of breach, a claim in contract may become time-barred notwithstanding that the claimant did not discover and could not with reasonable diligence have discovered the facts giving rise to his claim within the six years next following the date of breach.[82] Where a contracting party has an alternative cause of action in tort for negligence,[83] the tortious cause of action will not accrue until he suffers damage. But such a cause of action could nevertheless become time-barred even though the damage was not discovered or discoverable within the limitation period.[84] In particular, considerable hardship could arise in relation to building contracts where damage occurs to a building due to faulty supervision or design. The damage may not manifest itself until long after the building is completed or until long after the damage in fact occurs, by which time any cause

---

[70] s.32(1).

[71] s.39.

[72] s.12(3).

[73] ss.11A(3), 32(4A), inserted by s.6 of and Sched. 1 to the Consumer Protection Act 1987; see *ante*, § 29–008.

[74] s.14A; see *post*, § 29–091.

[75] s.14B; see *ante*, § 29–014A.

[76] s.32(5), inserted by s.2(2) of the Latent Damage Act 1986.

[77] See *Clerk and Lindsell on Torts* (17th ed., 1995), § 31–38; Capper, *Latent Damage Act 1986* (1987); Mullany (1991) 54 M.L.R. 216, 349; [1993] L.C.M.L.Q. 34.

[78] See *ante*, § 29–005.

[79] See *ante*, § 29–006.

[80] See *ante*, § 29–008.

[81] But see s.32; *ante*, § 29–082.

[82] See *ante*, § 29–028.

[83] See *ante*, § 29–029.

[84] *Pirelli General Cable Works Ltd v. Oscar Faber and Partners* [1983] A.C. 1, overruling *Sparham-Souter v. Town & Country Developments (Essex) Ltd* [1976] Q.B. 858.

of action (whether in contract or in tort) could have become barred.[85] In 1984, in its Twenty-Fourth Report,[86] the Law Reform Committee considered the existing law relating to limitation in cases of latent damage and made recommendations for reform. These recommendations were for the most part adopted and embodied in the Latent Damage Act 1986, which amended the Limitation Act 1980 by introducing specific provisions[87] for extension of the limitation period in certain instances of latent damage.

Negligence actions. Section 14A of the Limitation Act 1980[88] prescribes a **29–092** special time limit for negligence actions (other than actions involving personal injuries)[89] where the facts relevant to the cause of action are not known at the date on which the cause of action accrues. It is important to appreciate that this section applies only to an action for damages for *negligence*.[90] Although it might be thought that the word "negligence" was intended to extend to breach of a contractual duty, for example, to use reasonable care and skill,[91] it has been held[92] that the section is restricted to actions in tort for negligence, on the ground (*inter alia*) that it provides[93] that the six-year period of limitation applicable to actions founded on tort[94] is not to apply to actions within its scope, but does not similarly disapply the six-year period applicable to actions founded on simple contract.[95] It follows that the section will only be of assistance to a contracting party who has a concurrent or independent cause of action in tort for negligence.[96] A contractual cause of action continues to accrue at the date of breach and the limitation period is not extended by reason of the fact that the damage caused by the breach is latent. A claimant who sues in contract cannot therefore rely on this section and will have to rely (if at all) on section 32(1)(b) of the Act, *viz.* that a fact relevant to his right of action has been deliberately concealed from him by the defendant.[97]

Extension of the period. In cases to which section 14A of the Act applies, the **29–093** period of limitation is either (a) six years from the date on which the cause of action accrued,[98] that is to say the date on which damage first occurred, or (b) three years from the earliest date (the "starting date") on which the claimant or any person in whom the cause of action was vested before him first had both the knowledge required for bringing an action for damages in respect of the relevant

---

[85] *ibid.* But see *Invercargill City Council v. Hamlin* [1996] 1 All E.R. 756.
[86] Cmnd. 9390 (1984).
[87] s.14A. See also s.14B and s.3 of the Latent Damage Act 1976.
[88] Introduced by s.1 of the Latent Damage Act 1986.
[89] s.11; see *ante*, § 29–005.
[90] s.14A(1). It therefore does not apply to an action for damages for breach of strict duty imposed by statute, *e.g.* under the Defective Premises Act 1972.
[91] See *ante*, § 29–051.
[92] *Iron Trades Mutual Insurance Co. Ltd v. Buckenham Ltd* [1989] 2 Lloyd's Rep. 85; *Société Commerciale de Reassurance v. Eras International Ltd* [1992] 1 Lloyd's Rep. 570, 601–603; *West Bromwich Building Socy. v. Mander Hadley & Co., The Times,* March 9, 1998.
[93] s.14(A)(2). See also s.32(5) (introduced by s.2(2) of the 1986 Act).
[94] s.2.
[95] s.5.
[96] See *ante*, §§ 29–029, 29–049, 29–051, 29–053.
[97] See *ante*, § 29–085. For the relationship between ss.14A and 14B and s.32(1)(b), see s.32(5).
[98] s.14A(4)(a).

damage[99] and a right to bring such an action, if that three-year period expires later than the six-year period.[1] For the purposes of the section, a person's knowledge includes knowledge which he might reasonably have been expected to acquire from facts observable or ascertainable by him or from facts ascertainable by him with the help of appropriate expert advice which it is reasonable for him to seek.[2] Thus if the damage inflicted is latent and is not discovered or discoverable until (say) five, or even seven, years after it first occurred, the claimant will have three years from the starting date in which to bring his action in respect of that damage. But if the damage is discovered or becomes discoverable one year after it first occurs, then the claimant's right of action will not become time-barred until six years from the date on which it first occurred. The burden of establishing that his case falls within the section rests upon the claimant.[3] This may be tried as a preliminary issue.[4]

29–094   **Long-stop.** Actions to which section 14A applies are subject to the 15-year long-stop period for negligence actions not involving personal injuries.[5]

(d) Acknowledgment and Part Payment

29–095   **Origin of the doctrine.** The Jacobean statute of 1623 contained no provision that an acknowledgment of a debt or part payment thereof should extend the period of limitation. At least as early as 1699, however, the judges held that if the defendant made a fresh promise to pay the debt, time began to run anew from the date of the promise.[6] From this it followed that an acknowledgment or part payment had the same effect if, but only if, a fresh promise to pay could thereby be inferred.[7] This judicial process was described by Lord Sumner as "the task of decorously disregarding an Act of Parliament."[8] The judge-made doctrine was recognised by two statutes, one of which required that the acknowledgment should be in writing and signed by the person chargeable,[9] while the other made the signature of his duly authorised agent sufficient.[10] For specialty debts the Civil Procedure Act 1833 abolished the requirement (productive of so much litigation) that there must be an implied promise to pay: but this requirement

---

[99] s.14A(6), (7), (8), (9). See *Iron Trades Mutual Insurance Co. Ltd v. Buckenham Ltd, supra; Horbury v. Craig Hall & Rutley* [1991] E.G.C.S. 81; *Spencer-Ward v. Humberts* [1994] N.P.C. 105; *Campbell v. Meacocks* [1995] N.P.C. 141; *Hallam-Eames v. Merrett Syndicates, The Times,* Jan. 25, 1995; *Bradstock Trustee Services Ltd v. Nabarro Nathanson* [1995] 1 W.L.R. 1405; *Higgins v. Hatch & Fielding* [1995] E.G.C.S. 35; *Wilson v. Le Fevre Wood & Royle* [1996] 1 P.N.L.R. 107; *Hamlin v. Edwin Evans* [1996] P.N.L.R. 398; *Coban v. Allen, The Times,* October 14, 1996; *Finance for Mortgages Ltd v. Farley & Co.* [1996] E.G.C.S. 35; *Henderson v. Merrett Syndicates Ltd (No. 3)* [1997] L.R.L.R. 247; *Perry v. Moysey* [1998] C.L.Y. 540. Ignorance that the known facts might give rise to a claim in law will not postpone the running of time: *HF Pension Trustees Ltd v. Ellison, The Times,* March 5, 1999.
[1] s.14A(4)(b).
[2] s.14A(10), but see the qualification to this subsection.
[3] *Iron Trades Mutual Insurance Co. Ltd v. Buckenham Ltd, supra,* at 98.
[4] *Busby v. Cooper, The Times,* April 2, 1996.
[5] s.14B; *ante,* § 29–014A.
[6] *Hyleing v. Hastings* (1699) 1 Ld.Raym. 389.
[7] *Tanner v. Smart* (1827) 6 B. & C. 603.
[8] *Spencer v. Hemmerde* [1922] 2 A.C. 507, 519.
[9] Statute of Frauds Amendment Act 1828 (Lord Tenterden's Act), s.1.
[10] Mercantile Law Amendment Act 1856, s.13.

continued to exist for simple contract debts until 1940. All these statutes were repealed by the Limitation Act 1939.

Limitation Act 1980, s.29. The 1980 Act lays down a uniform rule for   **29–096**
specialty and simple contract debts by providing that where any right of action has accrued to recover any debt or other liquidated pecuniary claim,[11] and the person liable therefor acknowledges the claim or makes any payment in respect of it, the right is to be treated as having accrued on and not before the date of the acknowledgment or payment.[12] A current period of limitation may be repeatedly extended under this rule by further acknowledgments or payments; but a right of action, once barred by the Act, cannot be revived by any subsequent acknowledgment or payment.[13] However, the Act goes on to provide that payment of a part of the rent or interest due at any time shall not extend the period for claiming the remainder then due, but any payment of interest shall be treated as a payment in respect of the principal debt.[14] The effect of this provision seems to be that part payment of an instalment of rent merely operates as an acknowledgment of the landlord's title, while part payment of an instalment of interest operates (for the purposes of limitation) as part payment of the principal sum.[15]

Form of the acknowledgment. The acknowledgment must be in writing and   **29–097**
signed by the person making it.[16] But extrinsic evidence is admissible to identify the acknowledgment with the debt,[17] to ascertain the amount of the debt,[18] to show the date of execution of the document,[19] or to connect several documents.[20] Extrinsic evidence has also been admitted as secondary evidence of a lost written acknowledgment.[21] As to the requirement of writing, the following (*inter alia*) will qualify: correspondence,[22] an account rendered,[23] a recital in a deed,[24] a company's balance sheet,[25] an affidavit,[26] and a pleading.[27]

---

[11] *Amontilla Ltd v. Telefusion plc* (1987) 9 Con.L.R. 139 (*quantum meruit* held to be liquidated pecuniary claim). *cf.* McLean [1989] C.L.J. 472, 477–479.

[12] s.29(5).

[13] s.29(7). Contrast the position before the Limitation Amendment Act 1980, and see s.40(1) of and Sched. 2, para. 5, to the Limitation Act 1980.

[14] s.29(6).

[15] Franks, *Limitation of Actions* (1959), p. 227.

[16] s.30(1).

[17] *Read v. Price* [1909] 2 K.B. 724, 737, 738; *Jones v. Bellgrove Properties Ltd* [1949] 2 K.B. 700.

[18] *Bird v. Gammon* (1837) 3 Bing.N.C. 883; *Cheslyn v. Dalby* (1840) 4 Y. & C.Ex. 238, 241; *Jones v. Bellgrove Properties Ltd, supra; Dungate v. Dungate* [1965] 1 W.L.R. 1477; *Kamouh v. Associated Electrical Industries International Ltd* [1980] Q.B. 199; *Re Overmark Smith Warden Ltd* [1982] 1 W.L.R. 1195, 1204.

[19] *Edmunds v. Downes* (1834) 1 Cr. & M. 459, 463; *Jayne v. Hughes* (1854) 10 Exch. 430.

[20] *McGuffe v. Burleigh* (1898) 78 L.T. 264.

[21] *Haydon v. Williams* (1830) 7 Bing. 163; *Read v. Price* [1909] 2 K.B. 724.

[22] But not if written "without prejudice," *Re River Steamer Co.* (1871) L.R. 6 Ch.App. 822, 831.

[23] *Hony v. Hony* (1824) 1 Sim. & S. 568.

[24] *Howcutt v. Bonser* (1849) 3 Exch. 491.

[25] *Re Gee & Co. (Woolwich) Ltd* [1975] Ch. 52; see *post*, § 29–104.

[26] *Tristram v. Harte* (1841) 3 Ir.Eq.R. 386. *cf. Bowring-Hanbury's Trustee v. Bowring-Hanbury* [1943] Ch. 104.

[27] *Goode v. Job* (1858) 1 E. & E. 6; *Grindell v. Bass* [1920] 2 Ch. 487; *Wright v. Pepin* [1954] 1 W.L.R. 635, 642. *cf. Re Flynn (No. 2)* [1969] 2 Ch. 403.

29–098 **What constitutes acknowledgment.** What amounts to an acknowledgment is a question of construction and there is a high authority for saying that decided cases are of little value as precedents.[28] A decision on one debtor's words is not much help in construing another's. In reading cases decided under former Statutes of Limitation in regard to simple contracts, it must be remembered that the court was primarily concerned with the question whether a promise to pay could be implied, and not with the question whether there was an acknowledgment. Under the present law, all that is needed is an admission by the debtor that there is a debt or other liquidated pecuniary claim outstanding and of his legal liability to pay it. It is not necessary that the acknowledgment should specify the amount of the debt if it can be ascertained by other means.[29] But it must acknowledge a claim, not merely that there may be a claim,[30] and it must further acknowledge that the claim exists at the date of the acknowledgment or that it existed on a day which falls within the appropriate period of limitation next before action brought.[31] A mere acknowledgment of certain facts which, if taken in isolation, would give rise to liability, but which are alleged by the person who is said to have given an acknowledgment not to give rise to a liability by reason of other surrounding circumstances, is not sufficient.[32] Thus a "confession and avoidance" denying liability on the ground of an alleged set off or cross-claim does not constitute an acknowledgment.[33] The statement relied upon as an acknowledgment must be taken as a whole; the creditor is not entitled to pick out parts and ignore others.[34]

If the creditor stands in a fiduciary relationship to the debtor, he may be unable to rely on an acknowledgment made without independent advice, since he cannot derive any benefit from his position.[35]

29–099 **What constitutes part payment.** Part payment is merely a species of acknowledgment. All that need (and must) be shown is that the part payment constitutes an admission that the balance of the debt remains due,[36] and not that an implied promise to pay the balance can be inferred. Many of the older cases are therefore no longer reliable guides.

29–100 Section 29(5) of the Limitation Act 1980 requires that the payment must be made "in respect of" the claim. A payment cannot acquire this character by any

---

[28] *Spencer v. Hemmerde* [1922] 2 A.C. 507, 519.

[29] *Jones v. Bellgrove Properties Ltd* [1949] 2 K.B. 700; *Dungate v. Dungate* [1965] 1 W.L.R. 1477.

[30] *Good v. Parry* [1963] 2 Q.B. 418; *Kamouh v. Associated Electrical Industries International Ltd* [1980] Q.B. 199.

[31] *Howcutt v. Bonser* (1849) 3 Exch. 491; *Re Gee & Co. (Woolwich) Ltd* [1975] Ch. 52; *Re Overmark Smith Warden Ltd* [1982] 1 W.L.R. 1195. Contrast *Consolidated Agencies Ltd v. Bertram Ltd* [1965] A.C. 470, PC where it was held that an acknowledgment of past liability was ineffective.

[32] *Re Flynn (No. 2)* [1969] 2 Ch. 403, 412.

[33] *ibid.*; *Surrendra Overseas Ltd v. Sri Lanka Government* [1977] 1 W.L.R. 565. If the set off or cross-claim goes to only part of the debt, the statement may amount to an acknowledgment of indebtedness for the balance: *ibid.* at 575.

[34] *Surrendra Overseas Ltd v. Sri Lanka Government, supra,* at 575; *National Westminster Bank plc v. Powney* [1991] Ch. 339.

[35] *Lloyd v. Coote and Ball* [1915] 1 K.B. 242.

[36] *Re Footman Bower & Co. Ltd* [1961] Ch. 443; *Surrendra Overseas Ltd v. Sri Lanka Government, supra.* at 577; *Kleinwort Benson Ltd v. South Tyneside Metropolitan B.C.,* [1994] 4 All E.R. 972.

act of the creditor but only by the act of the debtor or his agent. Hence, if several distinct debts are due, and the debtor makes a part payment without appropriating it to any particular debt, an appropriation by the creditor towards satisfaction of one debt (whether it be statute-barred or not) cannot make the payment one "in respect of" the claim to that debt.[37]

The rule in *Clayton's Case*[38] applies to all current accounts, not merely to **29–101** banking accounts. So if goods are supplied over a period of time and paid for by lump sums bearing no exact relationship to the amount of the buyer's indebtedness at any particular moment, each new credit must prima facie be treated as discharging the earliest outstanding debit. This may be important in ascertaining how far the balance in the account is contributed to by statute-barred items. But it does not affect the true nature of the debt itself, which is a single debt for the amount of the balance due for the time being. Hence a payment "generally on account" is a payment in respect of the whole balance due; it is not a payment in respect of particular items contributing to that balance.[39]

The payment need not necessarily be in money,[40] though this is usually the **29–102** case.

Parties to the acknowledgment or part payment. The acknowledgment or **29–103** payment may be made by the agent of the person liable and must be made to the person or to the agent of the person whose claim is being acknowledged, or in respect of whose claim the payment is being made.[41] An acknowledgment or part payment made by a stranger who is not an agent of the debtor is of no effect.[42] It is clear, however, that the agent need not be expressly authorised to make an acknowledgment: it is sufficient if the making of the acknowledgment is within his general authority.[43] An acknowledgment or part payment made to a stranger who is not an agent of the creditor is likewise ineffective.[44] It has also been said that an acknowledgment must be either delivered to the creditor or his agent by or with the authority of the debtor or his agent or expressly or implicitly addressed to and actually received by the creditor or his agent.[45] In any event, communication of the acknowledgment is required.[46]

A statement in an Inland Revenue affidavit sworn by an executor in order to **29–104** obtain probate was held to be a mere statement of facts and not an acknowledgment of anything to anybody.[47] On the other hand, statements in the balance-sheet of a company (being implicitly addressed to those creditors whose debts are

---

[37] *Re Footman Bower & Co. Ltd supra*, at 449. See also *ante*, § 22–063.
[38] (1816) 1 Mer. 572. See *ante*, § 22–066.
[39] *Re Footman Bower & Co. Ltd, supra.*
[40] *Hart v. Nash* (1835) 2 Cr.M. & R. 337; *Hooper v. Stephens* (1835) 4 A. & E. 71; *Bodger v. Arch* (1854) 10 Exch. 333; *Re Wilson* [1937] Ch. 675.
[41] Limitation Act 1980, s.30(2).
[42] *Newbould v. Smith* (1886) 33 Ch.D. 127; *Re Edwards* [1937] Ch. 553.
[43] *Chinnery v. Evans* (1864) 11 H.L.C. 115; *Wright v. Pepin* [1954] 1 W.L.R. 635; distinguishing *Bowring-Hanbury's Trustee v. Bowring-Hanbury* [1943] Ch. 104 (the solicitor's letter).
[44] *Batchelor v. Middleton* (1848) 6 Hare 75, 83; *Stamford Banking Co. v. Smith* [1892] 1 QB 765.
[45] *Re Compania de Electricidad de la Provincia de Buenos Aires Ltd* [1980] Ch. 146.
[46] *ibid.*; see also *Re Beavan* [1912] 1 Ch. 196; *Lloyd v. Coote* [1915] 1 K.B. 242.
[47] *Bowring-Hanbury's Trustee v. Bowring-Hanbury, supra*, which, however, was decided under the old law under which an implied promise to pay was necessary.

referred to in it) can amount to an acknowledgment if communicated to the creditor or his agent.[48] Thus, a balance-sheet presented to the shareholders at an annual general meeting, signed by chartered accountants as agents of the company and by two directors, was held to be an acknowledgment of a debt owed to a shareholder who was present at the meeting.[49] But a balance-sheet signed by directors showing debts in which they are beneficially interested, e.g. for directors' fees or loans to the company, is not a sufficient acknowledgment by the company[50] unless all the members of the company have agreed to the directors' acknowledgment of the debt.[51]

29–105　　A minor can make an effective acknowledgment or part payment during minority in respect of a contract which is binding on him, e.g. for necessaries.[52]

29–106　　**Effect of acknowledgment and part payment on other persons.** The Act draws an important distinction between acknowledgment and part payment as regards their effect on persons other than the maker or payer. An acknowledgment of a debt or other liquidated pecuniary claim binds the acknowledgor and his successors, but does not bind any other person.[53] By successors are meant the personal representatives of the acknowledgor and any other person on whom the liability in respect of the debt or claim may devolve by reason of death or bankruptcy or otherwise.[54] But a part payment binds all persons liable in respect of the debt or claim (e.g. other joint debtors or sureties).[55] The distinction may be illustrated by the case of joint debtors. If A and B are jointly indebted to C, and A acknowledges the debt, the acknowledgment binds only A and his successors and not B. But if A makes a part payment, this binds B also. The reason for this distinction is that since a part payment operates for the advantage of all the joint debtors, it is only fair that they should share the disadvantage too.[56]

29–107　　**Exclusions.** The rules as to acknowledgment and part payment do not apply to an action to recover contribution under section 1 of the Civil Liability (Contribution) Act 1978[57] nor to an action under the Fatal Accidents Act 1976[58];

---

[48] *Re Atlantic and Pacific Fibre Importing Co. Ltd* [1928] Ch. 836; decided under the Civil Procedure Act 1833, under which such communication was unnecessary; *Jones v. Bellgrove Properties Ltd* [1949] 2 K.B. 700; *Re Gee & Co. (Woolwich) Ltd* [1975] Ch. 52, not following *Consolidated Agencies Ltd v. Bertram Ltd* [1965] A.C. 470 (decided under s.19 of the Indian Limitation Act 1908); *Re Compania de Electricidad de la Provincia de Buenos Aires Ltd, supra; Stage Club v. Millers Hotels Pty.* (1982) 150 C.L.R. 535. *cf. Re Overmark Smith Warden Ltd* [1982] 1 W.L.R. 1195 (statements of affairs made on appointment of receiver and on winding-up).

[49] *Jones v. Bellgrove Properties Ltd, supra.*

[50] *Re Coliseum (Barrow) Ltd* [1930] 2 Ch. 44; *Re Transplanters (Holding Company) Ltd* [1958] 1 W.L.R. 822; contrast *Ledingham v. Bermejo Estancia Co. Ltd* [1947] 1 All E.R. 749.

[51] *Re Gee & Co. (Woolwich) Ltd, supra.*

[52] *Willins v. Smith* (1854) 4 E. & B. 180.

[53] s.31(6).

[54] s.31(9).

[55] s.31(7).

[56] Law Revision Committee's Fifth Interim Report, p. 28.

[57] s.10(5); see *ante*, § 29–010.

[58] s.12(3).

nor do they apply to periods of limitation prescribed by or under any other enactment.[59]

Pleading. As a general rule, the acknowledgment or part payment should be   **29–108** pleaded in the particulars of claim and not in the reply.[60]

(e) *Agreement of the Parties*

Agreement of the parties. The parties may by contract postpone the com-   **29–109** mencement of the limitation period by agreeing that the cause of action shall not accrue until some act or event occurs, *e.g.* service of a written notice of claim.

Pleading the statute. A party is not bound to rely on limitation as a defence   **29–110** if he does not wish to do so. In general, the court will not raise the point *suo officio* even if it appears from the face of the pleading that the relevant period of limitation has expired.[61] A defendant who wishes to rely on limitation must, in his defence, give details of the expiry of any relevant limitation period relied on.[62] Even where the effect of the statute is to extinguish the claimant's title to land[63] or goods,[64] it would not be sufficient simply to deny that title[65] and the statute should be specifically pleaded.[66] Where it is clear that there is a defence of limitation, the defendant can apply to strike out a statute-barred claim on the ground that the statement of case discloses no reasonable grounds for bringing the claim or that the statement of case is an abuse of the court's process.[67]

Agreements not to plead the statute. An express or implied agreement not   **29–111** to plead the statute, whether made before or after the limitation period has expired, is valid if supported by consideration, and will be given effect to by the court.[68] The effect of such an agreement is, however, by no means certain. On one view, the agreement will be enforced by preventing the defendant from relying on the statute.[69] But on another view, the agreement merely enables the claimant to have a separate action (or counterclaim) for damages for breach of the agreement.[70] It is submitted that the former view is preferable.[71] In any event, to constitute an enforceable agreement, there must be consideration for the defendant's promise not to plead limitation as a defence, and this may be found, for example, in mutual promises by each party that accounts between them

---

[59] s.39.
[60] *Busch v. Stevens* [1963] 1 Q.B. 1.
[61] But the court will take the point on behalf of a person under a disability: *Re E.G.* [1914] 1 Ch. 927.
[62] CPR, 16 PD–005, 17.1.
[63] Limitation Act 1980, s.17.
[64] s.3(2); see *ante*, § 29–050, Vol. II, § 43–233.
[65] See also CPR, Part 16, r. 5.
[66] Contrast Franks, *Limitation of Actions* (1959), p. 265.
[67] CPR, Part 3, r. 4. See *Ronex Properties Ltd v. John Laing Construction Ltd* [1983] Q.B. 398, 405–406; *Leicester Wholesale Fruit Market Ltd v. Grundy* [1990] 1 W.L.R. 107.
[68] *Lade v. Trill* (1842) 11 L.J.Ch. 102; *Pearson v. Dublin Corpn.* [1907] A.C. 351, 368; *Lubovsky v. Snelling* [1944] K.B. 44.
[69] *ibid.*
[70] *East India Co. v. Paul* (1850) 7 Moo.P.C. 85, 112.
[71] *i.e.* a form of estoppel by contract.

should be settled without reference to the length of time they have been running[72] or in an express or implied forbearance on the part of the claimant to sue.[73]

29–112   **Estoppel.** In certain cases it has been said that the defendant is estopped from pleading the statute.[74] If the circumstances render it impossible to imply any forbearance to sue on behalf of the claimant, and there is no other consideration for the defendant's promise, this may be the only course available to the claimant to prevent the defendant from raising the defence. It is doubtful, however, whether the ordinary principles of estoppel are applicable, since there is often no representation of existing or past fact. But the claimant might, in appropriate cases, be entitled to rely on estoppel by acquiescence[75] or by convention[76] or upon the principle of equitable forbearance stated in *Hughes v. Metropolitan Ry.*[77] The question has been previously raised and discussed[78] whether, under that principle, the promisee must have suffered some detriment in reliance on the promise or whether it is sufficient that he has in fact relied on it so that it would be inequitable for the promisor to go back on the promise. Where no express extension has been sought and obtained, a claimant may encounter difficulty in establishing that a sufficiently clear and unambiguous representation or promise has been made to him or that he has suffered a detriment or even acted in reliance on the representation or promise if made.[79]

29–113   **Terms of agreement or promise.** Further difficulties may arise in construing the terms of the agreement or promise, *e.g.* whether the defendant undertakes not to plead the statute or merely to suspend the running of time, whether the undertaking is conditional or unconditional and whether it is permanent in effect or merely temporary (the defendant being entitled on reasonable notice to resile from his undertaking or to start time running again), or is for a reasonable time only.[80]

29–114   **Negotiations.** The fact that the parties have entered into negotiations for the settlement of their dispute will not, without more, suspend or otherwise affect the running of time or prevent the defendant from relying on the statute, even though the limitation period may expire before the negotiations are concluded.[81] But in

---

[72] *Lade v. Trill, supra.*

[73] *Lubovsky v. Snelling, supra.* See *ante,* § 3–044.

[74] *Wright v. John Bagnell & Sons Ltd* [1900] 2 Q.B. 240; *Rendall v. Hill's Dry Dock and Engineering Co. Ltd* [1900] 2 Q.B. 245; *Kaliszewska v. Clague* [1984] C.I.L.L. 131; *Commonwealth v. Verwayen* (1990) 64 A.L.J.R. 540.

[75] *cf. K. Lokumal & Sons (London) Ltd v. Lotte Shipping Co. Pte. Ltd* [1984] 1 Lloyd's Rep. 322, [1985] 2 Lloyd's Rep. 28.

[76] *ibid.* See *ante,* § 3–101.

[77] (1877) 2 App.Cas. 439; *ante,* §§ 3–080—3–100.

[78] *Ante,* §§ 3–088—3–089.

[79] *Alma Shipping Corpn. v. Union of India* [1971] 2 Lloyd's Rep. 494, 502; *K. Lokumal & Sons (London) Ltd v. Lotte Shipping Co. Pte. Ltd* [1985] 2 Lloyd's Rep. 28; *Kenya Railways v. Antares Co. Pte. Ltd* [1986] 2 Lloyd's Rep. 633, [1987] 1 Lloyd's Rep. 424; *P.S. Chellaram & Co. Ltd v. China Ocean Shipping Co.* [1991] 1 Lloyd's Rep. 493; *Blaenau Gwent B.C. v. Robinson Jones Design Partnership Ltd* (1997) 53 Const. L.R. 31.

[80] *Waters v. Earl of Thanet* (1842) 2 Q.B. 757.

[81] *Hewlett v. L.C.C.* (1908) 72 J.P. 136.

Wright v. John Bagnall & Sons Ltd,[82] and again in *Lubovsky v. Snelling*,[83] the plaintiff had a claim in tort against the defendant which was subject to a very short limitation period. Before the period had expired, negotiations took place between representatives of the parties in the course of which liability was admitted subject to the question of *quantum*. Soon after the period expired the plaintiff issued a writ and the defendant pleaded the statute. In both cases it was held that the action succeeded: in the former case because the defendant was estopped from pleading the statute, and in the latter case because there was an implied agreement not to plead the statute. Previously, the safest course for a claimant to pursue was to issue a writ within the period but not to serve it until the negotiations broke down. But this practice is now of limited utility, since a claim form must be served within four months, unless the court makes an order extending the period.[84]

6. ABRIDGEMENT OF THE PERIOD

Agreement of the parties. It is open to the parties to a contract to stipulate in **29–115** the contract that legal or arbitral[85] proceedings shall be commenced within a shorter period of time than that provided in the Limitation Act 1980. Such stipulations are not uncommon in commercial agreements and their effect may be (depending on the precise wording of the stipulation) to bar or extinguish any right of action, or to deprive a party of his right to have recourse to particular proceedings, *e.g.* arbitration,[86] after the expiration of the agreed time limit. It is also open to the parties to agree that one party shall be released from liability or the other party's claim shall be extinguished or become barred unless a claim has been presented within a stipulated period of time.[87]

Exemption and other restrictive clauses. Clauses imposing a shorter time **29–116** limit than that allowed by the 1980 Act may, even at common law, be regarded as exemption clauses,[88] so that, for example, they will be strictly construed[89] and be ineffective in the case of claims based on personal fraud.[90] In the case of contracts to which the Unfair Contract Terms Act 1977 applies,[91] to the extent that that Act prevents the exclusion or restriction of any liability, it also prevents (i) making the enforcement of the liability subject to restrictive conditions,[92] and

---

[82] [1900] 2 Q.B. 240; distinguished in *Rendall v. Hill's Dry Dock and Engineering Co. Ltd* [1900] 2 Q.B. 245.

[83] [1944] K.B. 44; distinguished (admittedly on narrow grounds) in *The Sauria and The Trent* [1957] 1 Lloyd's Rep. 396.

[84] See *post*, § 29–119.

[85] *Atlantic Shipping Co. Ltd v. Louis Dreyfus & Co.* [1922] 2 A.C. 250; see *ante*, § 16–046; *post*, § 29–118.

[86] See *ante*, § 16–046.

[87] See *e.g. Metalimex Foreign Trade Corpn. v. Eugenie Maritime Co. Ltd* [1962] 1 Lloyd's Rep. 378; *Babanaft International Co. SA v. Avant Petroleum Inc.* [1982] 1 W.L.R. 871; *Indian Oil Corpn. v. Vanol Inc.* [1991] 2 Lloyd's Rep. 634; *Crown Estate Commissioners v. John Mowlem & Co.* [1994] 10 Const. L.J. 311 *ante*, § 16–050, n. 70.

[88] See *ante*, Chap. 14.

[89] *Bunge SA v. Deutsche Conti-Handelsgesellschaft mbH (No. 2)* [1981] 1 Lloyd's Rep. 352, 358. See *ante*, § 14–005.

[90] See *ante*, § 14–125.

[91] See *ante*, §§ 14–057—14–107.

[92] s.13(1)(a).

(ii) excluding or restricting any right or remedy in respect of the liability.[93] Contract terms which abridge the limitation period may therefore be subject to the control of the 1977 Act. Similar considerations probably apply in respect of remedies for misrepresentation under section 3 of the Misrepresentation Act 1967.[94]

In addition to the statutes referred to above, a number of other statutes regulate exempting provisions[95] and their wording may likewise extend to prevent abridgement of the limitation period.

29–117   **Special limitation periods.** The special limitation periods established by enactments[96] other than the 1980 Act are, in general,[97] mandatory and cannot be shortened by agreement of the parties.

29–118   **Arbitration.** By section 12 of the Arbitration Act 1996, where an arbitration agreement to refer future disputes to arbitration provides that a claim shall be barred, or the claimant's right extinguished, unless the claimant takes within a time fixed by the agreement some step to begin proceedings, or to begin other dispute resolution procedures which must be exhausted before arbitral proceedings can be begun, the court may by order extend the time for taking the step. This section replaced section 27 of the Arbitration Act 1950, though the grounds on which the court may grant an extension of time are now more limited.[98] It is specifically provided that an order under section 12 "does not affect the operation of the Limitation Acts".[99] A similar provision in section 27 of the 1950 Act was interpreted to mean that, where the one-year time bar contained in Article III, rule 6, of the Hague Rules was imported by the parties into their contract, the court had power to grant an extension of time under section 27,[1] but not where the time bar in Article III, rule 6, of the Hague-Visby Rules was rendered applicable by the Carriage of Goods Act 1971.[2] It is probable that the same result would be reached under the 1996 Act since "the Limitation Acts" are defined to mean, in England and Wales, the Limitation Act 1980, the Foreign Limitation Periods Act 1984 and any other enactment (whenever passed) relating to the limitation of actions.[3]

7. Commencement of Proceedings

29–119   **Legal proceedings.** A cause of action will be barred unless legal proceedings[4] in respect of that cause of action are commenced by the claimant within the

---

[93] s.13(1)(b).

[94] As amended by s.8 of the Unfair Contract Terms Act 1977; see *ante*, § 14–105.

[95] See *ante*, § 14–106. In particular, the Unfair Terms in Consumer Contracts Regulations 1994, S.I. 1994 No. 3159; *ante*, Chap. 15.

[96] See *ante*, § 29–015.

[97] But see, *e.g.* the Uniform Laws on International Sales Act 1967, Sched. 1, Art. 3; and *ante*, § 29–023.

[98] See *ante*, § 16–047.

[99] s.12(5).

[1] *The Merak* [1965] P. 223; *Nea Agrex SA v. Baltic Shipping Co. Ltd* [1976] Q.B. 933; *Consolidated Investment & Contracting Co. v. Saponaria Shipping Co. Ltd* [1978] 1 W.L.R. 986.

[2] *Kenya Railways v. Antares Co. Pte. Ltd* [1987] 1 Lloyd's Rep. 424; see *ante*, § 16–050.

[3] s.13(4).

[4] By s.38(1) of the 1980 Act, "action" includes any proceedings in a court of law.

limitation period. Proceedings are started when the court issues a claim form at the claimant's request or on the day on which the form was received by the court office (if earlier).[5] The claim form must normally be served within four months[6] after the date of its issue.[7] But the claimant may apply within that period for an order extending the period within which the form must be served.[8] The court has a discretion whether or not to make the order. Under the old Rules of the Supreme Court, however, the court would not exercise its power to grant an extension if the relevant period of limitation had expired, unless good reason existed for doing so.[9] An application may even be made after the four month period has expired. But the court may then make an order only if the court has been unable to serve the claim form or the claimant has taken all reasonable steps to serve the form but has been unable to do so, and in either case the claimant has acted promptly in making the application.[10] If the claim form is served, but not within the four months or the extended period specified in the court order, the defendant should file an acknowledgment of service and make an application under Part 11 of the Civil Procedure Rules. This must be done within the period for filing a defence.[11]

Proceedings must be commenced by a person properly entitled to bring them.[12] **29–120** An equitable assignee may commence proceedings and so stop time from running even though the assignor has not been joined as a party to the action[13] and even though notice of the assignment has not been given to the defendant until after the claim form has been issued.[14] A claim form issued within the limitation period but without the authority of the norminal claimant is not a nullity. The nominal claimant could subsequently ratify and adopt the claim notwithstanding the expiration of the period.[15]

---

[5] CPR, Part 7, 7PD–002, r. 4.1. For commencement of arbitration proceedings, see *ante*, § 16–052.

[6] Where the claim form has been issued for service outside the jurisdiction, the period is six months. See also *Saris v. Westminster Transport SA* [1994] 1 Lloyd's Rep. 115.

[7] CPR, Part 7, r. 5. Under the old rules, the date of issue of the writ was included in the computation of the four months: *Trow v. Ind Coope (West Midlands) Ltd* [1967] 2 Q.B. 899. If there was more than one defendant, the writ had to be served on the particular defendant within the four months: *Jones v. Jones* [1970] 2 Q.B. 576; *Payabi v. Armstel Shipping Corpn.* [1992] Q.B. 907.

[8] CPR, Part 7, r. 6(1), (2).

[9] *Kleinwort Benson Ltd v. Barbrak Ltd* [1987] A.C. 597. See also *Waddon v. Whitecroft Scovell Ltd* [1988] 1 W.L.R. 309, HL; *Goldenglow Nut Food Co. v. Commodin (Produce) Ltd* [1987] 2 Lloyd's Rep. 569; *Doble v. Haymills (Contractors), The Times*, July 5, 1988, CA; *Baly v. Barrett, The Times,* May 19, 1989, HL; *The Vita* [1990] 1 Lloyd's Rep. 528; *De Pina v. M.S. "Birka" Beutler Schiffahrts K.G.* [1996] 1 Lloyd's Rep. 31. Previous decisions must now be read in the light of these cases, but see *Battersby v. Anglo-American Oil Co. Ltd* [1945] K.B. 23; *E. Ltd v. C.* [1959] 1 W.L.R. 592; *Heaven v. Road and Rail Wagons Ltd* [1965] 2 Q.B. 355; *Baker v. Bowketts Cakes Ltd* [1966] 1 W.L.R. 861; *Stevens v. Services Window and General Cleaning Co. Ltd* [1967] 1 Q.B. 359; *Jones v. Jones* [1970] 2 Q.B. 576; *Stewart-Wrightson Group v. Crocker, The Times*, December 19, 1979, CA; *Chappell v. Cooper* [1980] 1 W.L.R. 958; *Wilkinson v. Ancliff (B.L.T.) Ltd* [1986] 1 W.L.R. 1352. The extension will be for no longer period than is shown to be justified: *Baly v. Barrett, supra.*

[10] CPR, Part 7, r. 6(3).

[11] CPR, Part 15, r. 4.

[12] But see § 29–121, *post* (amendment).

[13] See *ante*, § 20–037.

[14] *Weddell v. J.A. Pearce & Major* [1988] Ch. 26. Contrast *Compania Columbiana de Seguros v. Pacific Steam Navigation Co.* [1965] 1 Q.B. 101, 127, 129.

[15] *Presentaciones Musicales SA v. Secunda* [1994] Ch. 271.

29–121   **Amendments to statement of case after the end of the limitation period.**[16] The Civil Procedure Rules[17] empower the court to allow a party to amend his statement of case in three specific cases where a period of limitation[18] has expired. These cases are as follows:

(1) An amendment to correct a mistake as to the name of a party, but only where the mistake was genuine and not one which would cause reasonable doubt as to the identity of the party in question.[19]

(2) An amendment to alter the capacity in which party claims if the new capacity is one which that party had when the proceedings started or has since acquired.[20]

(3) An amendment whose effect will be to add or substitute a new claim,[21] but only if the new claim arises out of substantially the same facts as a claim in respect of which the party applying for permission to amend has already claimed a remedy in the proceedings.[22]

29–122   In addition, the Civil Procedure Rules[23] provide for a change of parties after the end of a period of limitation.[24] The court may add or substitute a party only

---

[16] See s.35 of the Act (operative May 1, 1981: S.I. 1981 No. 588 (c. 13)) and *Twenty-First Report of the Law Reform Committee*, Cmnd. 6923 (1977), §§ 5.12–5.29. s.35 was repealed in part by s.152(4) of and Sched. 7 to the Supreme Court Act 1981.

[17] CPR, Part 17, r. 4.

[18] Defined to mean a period of limitation under the Limitation Act 1980, the Foreign Limitation Periods Act 1984, section 190 of the Merchant Shipping Act 1995, or any other statutory provision. See also s.39 of the 1980 Act. Contrast (Hague Rules) *Casillo Grani v. Napier Shipping Co.* [1984] 2 Lloyd's Rep. 481, 487; *Payabi v. Armstel Shipping Corpn.* [1982] Q.B. 907; *Transworld Oil (USA) Inc. v. Minos Compania Naviera SA* [1992] 2 Lloyd's Rep. 48; but see *Empresa Cubana Importadora de Alimentos v. Octavia Shipping Co. SA* [1986] 1 Lloyd's Rep. 273; *Katzenstein Adleu Industries (1975) Ltd v. The Borchard Lines Ltd* [1988] 2 Lloyd's Rep. 274.

[19] CPR, Part 17, r. 4.3, formerly RSC Ord. 20, r. 5(3). As to this, see *Rodriguez v. Parker* [1967] 1 Q.B. 116; *Mitchell v. Harris Engineering Co. Ltd* [1967] 2 Q.B. 703; *Kamouh v. A.E.I. International Ltd* [1980] Q.B. 199; *Evans Construction Co. Ltd v. Charrington & Co. Ltd* [1983] Q.B. 810; *Birmingham City DC v. C. Bryant & Son* (1987) 9 Con.L.R. 128; *Katzenstein Adler Industries (1975) Ltd v. The Borchard Lines Ltd* [1988] 2 Lloyd's Rep. 274; *Thistle Hotels Ltd v. Sir Robert McAlpine & Sons Ltd, The Times,* April 11, 1989; *The Sardinia Sulcis* [1991] 1 Lloyd's Rep. 201; *The Lu Shan* [1991] 2 Lloyd's Rep. 386; *Transworld Oil (USA) Inc. v. Minos Compania Naviera Inc.* [1992] 2 Lloyd's Rep. 48; *International Bulk Shipping and Services Ltd v. Minerals and Metals Trading Corpn. of India* [1996] 1 All E.R. 1017.

[20] CPR, Part 17, r. 4.4, formerly RSC Ord. 20, r. 5(4). See also s.35(7), (8) of the Act.

[21] *cf. The Jangmi* [1989] 2 Lloyd's Rep. 1 (change of date).

[22] CPR, Part 17, r. 4.2, formerly RSC Ord. 20, r. 5(5). See also s.35(2)(a), (5)(a), (8) of the Act; *Chatsworth Investments Ltd v. Cussins (Contractors) Ltd* [1969] 1 W.L.R. 1; *Brickfield Properties Ltd v. Newton* [1971] 1 W.L.R. 862; *Beck v. Value Capital Ltd* [1976] 1 W.L.R. 572; *Empresa Cubana Importadora de Alimentos v. Octavia Shipping Co. SA* [1986] 1 Lloyd's Rep. 273; *Steamship Mutual Underwriting Association Ltd v. Trollope & Colls Ltd* (1986) 33 B.L.R. 77; *Fannon v. Backhouse, The Times,* August 22, 1987, CA; *Birmingham City DC v. C. Bryant & Son* (1987) 9 Con.L.R. 128; *Kakkar v. Szelke* [1988] F.S.R. 97; *Hancock Shipping Co. Ltd v. Kawasaki Heavy Industries Ltd* [1992] 1 W.L.R. 1025; *Arab Monetary Fund v. Hashim* [1993] 1 Lloyd's Rep. 543, 593 (reversed on other grounds [1996] 1 Lloyd's Rep. 589); *Sion v. Hampstead Health Authority, The Times,* June 10, 1994, CA; *Clarke (E.) & Sons (Coaches) v. Axtell Yates Hallett* (1994) 30 Const. L.R. 123; *Lloyds Bank plc v. Rogers, The Times,* March 24, 1997; *Paragon Finance plc v. Thakerer & Co.* [1999] 1 All E.R. 400.

[23] CPR, Part 19, r. 4. See also s.35(2)(b), (5)(b), (8) of the Act. (*cf.* s.35(6)). In *Kenya Railways v. Antares Co. Pte. Ltd* [1987] 1 Lloyd's Rep. 424, 432, 433, the Court of Appeal expressed the opinion that s.35 of the Act does not apply to arbitrations in respect of the addition or substitution of a new party.

[24] Defined in the same way as in n. 18, *supra.*

if the relevant limitation period was current when the proceedings were started, and the addition or substitution is necessary. The addition or substitution of a party is necessary only if the court is satisfied that the new party is to be substituted for a party who was named in the claim form in mistake for the new party, or the claim cannot properly be carried on by or against the original party unless the new party is added or substituted as claimant or defendant, or the original party has died or had a bankruptcy order made against him and his interest or liability has passed to the new party.[25]

However, in a claim for personal injuries, the court may in addition add or substitute a party where it directs that section 11 or section 12 of the 1980 Act[26] shall not apply to the claim by or against the new party or where it directs that the issue of whether those sections apply is to be determined.[27]   **29–123**

The court has not otherwise any power to allow a new claim to be made in the course of any action after the expiry of any time limit under the Act which would affect a new action to enforce that claim.[28–33]   **29–124**

Defence, set-off and counterclaim. When a defendant is sued, he can raise any matter which is properly in the nature of a defence, without fear of being met by a plea of limitation.[34] But if he makes a cross-claim, either by way of set-off or counterclaim, he may be time-barred. Section 35 of the Limitation Act 1980[35] provides that, for the purposes of the Act,[36] any claim by way of set-off or counterclaim[37] is deemed to be a separate action and to have been commenced on the same date as the original action.[38] Thus a set-off or counterclaim can be made by an original defendant against an original claimant[39] notwithstanding the expiry of any time limit under the Act, provided that the time limit had not expired on the date of commencement of the original action. However, the court has a discretion to order that it be dealt with separately from the claim of the   **29–125**

---

[25] CPR, Part 19, r. 4.3. See the previous RSC Ord. 15, r. 6(6); *Liff v. Peasley* [1980] 1 W.L.R. 781 (joinder of defendant after claim against him statute-barred disallowed) and *Mitchell v. Harris Engineering Co. Ltd* [1967] 2 Q.B. 703, 717, 721; *Branff v. Holland & Hannen and Cubitts (Southern) Ltd* [1969] 1 W.L.R. 1533; *Lucy v. W.T. Henleys Telegraph Works Co. Ltd* [1970] 1 Q.B. 393; *Marubeni Corpn. v. Pearlstone Shipping Corpn.*, *supra*; *Gawthrop v. Boulton* [1979] 1 W.L.R. 268; *Ketteman v. Hansel Properties Ltd* [1987] A.C. 189; *Birmingham City DC v. C. Bryant & Son*, *supra*; *Hancock Shipping Co. Ltd v. Kawasaki Heavy Industries Ltd*, *supra*; *Payabi v. Armstel Shipping Corpn.*, *supra*; *Bank of America National Trust and Savings Assn. v. Christmas* [1994] 1 All E.R. 401; *Bradstock Trustee Services Ltd v. Nabarro Nathanson* [1995] 1 W.L.R. 1405.
[26] See *ante*, § 29–005.
[27] s.33 of the Act; see *ante* § 29–005.
[28–33] s.35(3). *Kennett v. Brown* [1988] 1 W.L.R. 582 was overruled in *Welsh Development Agency v. Redpath Dorman Long Ltd* [1994] 1 W.L.R. 1409. But an order for the substitution of a party as plaintiff under the previous RSC Ord. 15, r. 7, did not involve the making of a "new claim": *Yorkshire Regional Health Authority v. Fairclough* [1996] 1 W.L.R. 210; *Industrie Chimiche Italia Centrale v. Alexander G. Tsavliris & Sons Maritime Co.* [1996] 1 W.L.R. 774.
[34] *Henriksens Rederi A/S v. T.H.Z. Rolimpex* [1974] Q.B. 233.
[35] Operative May 1, 1981: S.I. 1981 No. 588 (c. 13).
[36] s.35 does not apply to any action or arbitration for which a period of limitation is prescribed by or under any other enactment: s.39. See (on the previous common law) *Walker v. Clements* (1850) 15 Q.B. 1046 (set-off); *Lowe v. Bentley* (1928) 44 T.L.R. 386 (counterclaim); and see s.40(1), Sched. 2, paras. 6, 8(2). See also n. 49, *infra*.
[37] s.35(2).
[38] s.35(1)(b).
[39] s.35(3) ("original set-off or counterclaim"); *JFS (U.K.) Ltd v. DWR Cymru Cyf* [1999] 1 W.L.R. 231.

claimant against the defendant[40] and it may do so notwithstanding that any such action would be barred by limitation.[41]

29–126   A further difficulty which arises is that it is a matter of considerable refinement whether a particular cross-claim is to be treated as a defence or matter of set-off.[42] Section 53(1) of the Sale of Goods Act 1979, for example, provides that the buyer may set up against the seller a breach of warranty in diminution or extinction of the price,[43] and such a claim is therefore to be treated as a defence.[44] Lord Denning M.R. has further put forward the view, in respect of the comparable provision in the Limitation Act 1939,[45] that the word "set-off" meant only a set-off as permitted by the statutes of set-off, and did not apply to an "equitable set-off" pleaded in extinction or diminution of the claim.[46] On this view, if a cross-claim arises out of the same transaction as the claim, or out of a transaction that is closely related to the claim,[47] it is to be treated as an equitable defence[48] and is time-barred only in equity.[49]

29–127   **Part 20 claims.** Section 35(1) of the Limitation Act 1980 provides that, for the purposes of the Act,[50] a new claim made in or by way of third-party proceedings is to be deemed to be a separate action and to have been commenced on the date on which those proceedings were commenced.[51] The result may be (assuming that the situation is not one to which section 1 of the Civil Liability (Contribution) Act 1978 applies)[52] that if a claimant starts proceedings against a defendant at a time when the defendant's cause of action against the third party is, or is on the point of becoming, time-barred, the defendant will have lost or may lose the opportunity of obtaining relief over against the third party. "Third-party proceedings" is defined to mean any proceedings brought in the course of any action against a person not previously a party to the action, other than proceedings brought by joining any such person as defendant to any claim

---

[40] CPR, Part 20, r. 9(1).

[41] *Ernst & Young v. Butte Mining plc* [1997] 1 W.L.R. 1485.

[42] See *Mondel v. Steel* (1841) 8 M. & W. 858; *Henriksens Rederi A/S v. T.H.Z. Rolimpex, supra*; *Aries Tanker Corpn. v. Total Transport Ltd* [1977] 1 W.L.R. 185.

[43] See Vol. II, § 43–409.

[44] s.28.

[45] *Henriksens Rederi A/S v. T.H.Z. Rolimpex, supra*, at 246. But see Cairns and Roskill L.JJ. at 254, 264. Lord Denning's view was followed (*obiter*) by Hobhouse J. in *Kleinwort Benson Ltd v. Sandwell B.C.* (1993) 91 L.G.R. 323, 386.

[46] See, *e.g. Morgan & Son v. S. Martin Johnson & Co.* [1949] 1 K.B. 107; *Hanak v. Green* [1958] 2 Q.B. 9; *Federal Commerce & Navigation Co. Ltd v. Molena Alpha Inc.* [1978] Q.B. 974 (affd. [1979] A.C. 757); *The Raven* [1980] 2 Lloyd's Rep. 266; *British Anzani (Felixstowe) Ltd v. International Marine Management (U.K.) Ltd* [1980] Q.B. 137; CPR, r. 16.6.

[47] See also *Mondel v. Steel* (1841) 8 M. & W. 858.

[48] Supreme Court of Judicature Act 1873, s.24; Supreme Court of Judicature (Consolidation) Act 1925, ss.38, 41; now see the Supreme Court Act 1981, s.49.

[49] s.36(2); *Filross Securities Ltd v. Midgeley* (1998) 43 E.G. 134. Contrast *Aries Tanker Corpn. v. Total Transport Ltd* [1977] 1 W.L.R. 185 (Hague Rules) and, *e.g.* Carriage of Goods by Road Act 1965, Sched., Art. 32(4); *Impex Transport Aktieselskabet v. A.G. Thomas Holdings Ltd* [1981] 1 W.L.R. 1547; *Casillo Grani v. Napier Shipping Co.* [1984] 2 Lloyd's Rep. 481.

[50] The subsection does not apply to any action or arbitration for which a period of limitation is prescribed by or under any other enactment (s.39) and enactments imposing special periods of limitation (see *ante*, § 29–015) may grant an extension of time for third-party proceedings. s.35 became operative on May 1, 1981: see S.I. 1981 No. 588 (c. 13).

[51] s.35(1)(a).

[52] See *ante*, § 29–010.

already made in the original action by the party bringing the proceedings.[53] The rule set out above thus applies to a larger range of proceedings than would usually be considered as "third-party proceedings", and extends to other Part 20 claims for example, a counterclaim by a defendant against an added party.

Arbitral proceedings. The Limitation Acts[54] apply to arbitral proceedings as they apply to legal proceedings,[55] and an arbitrator no less than a judge is bound to give effect to defences based thereon.[56] The arbitration must therefore be commenced before the expiration of the relevant limitation period. The parties are free to agree when arbitral proceedings are to be regarded commenced for the purposes of the Limitation Acts.[57] If there is no such agreement, the rules set out in section 14 of the Arbitration Act 1996 may apply. These have been considered in the chapter on Arbitration Clauses earlier in this book.[58]   **29–128**

8. THE STATUTE BARS THE REMEDY, NOT THE RIGHT

General. Except for the provisions governing extinction of title in relation to land,[59] advowsons[60] and goods,[61] and the 10-year long-stop period for actions under Part I of the Consumer Protection Act 1987,[62] the effect of limitation under the Limitation Act 1980 is merely to bar the claimant's remedy and not to extinguish his right. Limitation is a procedural matter, and not one of substance: the right continues to exist even though it cannot be enforced by action. In contrast, limitation provisions in certain other enactments, such as the Carriage by Air Act 1961[63] and the Carriage of Goods by Sea Act 1971,[64] extinguish the right. Where special statutory periods of limitation are applied, regard must be had to the particular language and intent of the statute in each case. A procedural bar does not go to the jurisdiction of the court or of an arbitral tribunal.[65]   **29–129**

Obtaining payment in other ways. In those cases where the remedy only is barred by the 1980 Act, if a debtor pays a statute-barred debt, he cannot subsequently recover the money on the ground that it was not due.[66] Further,   **29–130**

---

[53] s.35(2).

[54] Defined in s.13(4) of the Arbitration Act 1996.

[55] Arbitration Act 1996, s.13(1).

[56] *Board of Trade v. Cayzer, Irvine & Co.* [1927] A.C. 610, 614; *Naamlooze, etc. Vulcaan v. A/S Ludwig Mowinckel Rederi* (1938) 43 Com.Cas. 252, HL; *Compagnie Europeenne de Cereals SA v. Tradax Export SA* [1986] 2 Lloyd's Rep. 301.

[57] s.14(1). See *Transpetrol Ltd v. Erkali Shipping Co. Ltd* [1989] 1 Lloyd's Rep. 62.

[58] *Ante*, § 16–052. See also Carriage by Air Act 1961, s.5(3); Carriage of Goods by Road Act 1965, s.7(2)(a); Limitation Act 1980, s.40(2) and Sched. 3, paras. 5, 6.

[59] s.17.

[60] s.25.

[61] s.3(2); see Vol. II, § 43–233.

[62] s.11A(3); *ante*, § 29–019.

[63] Sched. 1, Art. 29; see *ante*, § 29–019; Vol. II, §§ 35–022, 35–085.

[64] Sched., Art. 3, r. 6; *Kenya Railways v. Antares Co. Pte. Ltd* [1987] 1 Lloyd's Rep. 424. See also (Hague Rules) *Goulandris Bros. v. Goldman* [1958] 1 Q.B. 74, 105, 106; *Aries Tanker Corporation v. Total Transport Ltd* [1977] 1 W.L.R. 185; *Casillo Grani v. Napier Shipping Co.* [1984] 2 Lloyd's Rep. 481, 487; *Payabi v. Armstel Shipping Corpn.* [1992] Q.B. 907.

[65] *Leif Hoegh & Co. A/S v. Petrolsea Inc.* [1992] 1 Lloyd's Rep. 45, 49.

[66] *Bize v. Dickason* (1786) 1 T.R. 286, 287.

though the creditor cannot recover a statute-barred debt by action, he can obtain satisfaction in a number of other ways.

29–131   **Appropriation.**[67] If a debtor makes a payment without appropriating it to any particular debt, the creditor may at any time before the commencement of proceedings appropriate it to a statute-barred debt.[68] If neither party makes an appropriation, the court will presume that the payment was made in respect of debts which were not statute-barred.[69] But if the debtor has no opportunity of exercising his right of appropriation, then the creditor cannot do so. Thus, he may not appropriate money of the debtor which happens to be in his hands to a statute-barred debt,[70] for that would be not appropriation but set-off.

29–132   **Account stated.** The parties are at liberty to include a statute-barred debt in an account stated and thus render it enforceable by action.[71]

29–133   **Deduction from legacy, etc.** If a legatee owes money to his testator's estate, the personal representatives may deduct the debt from the legacy, even if the debt is statute-barred.[72] The same principle applies to a debt owed by a person entitled on intestacy.[73] But it does not apply to a debt owed by a specific legatee of chattels not represented by money in the hands of the personal representatives,[74] nor where the legatee was not himself the debtor but only the personal representative of a deceased debtor.[75]

29–134   **Executor's right of retainer.** A personal representative may choose to pay a statute-barred debt,[76] unless (perhaps) his fellow personal representative objects,[77] and may therefore exercise his right of retainer in respect of such a debt due to himself.[78] However, this is an anomalous principle which is not to be extended: it does not apply to a debt which has been judicially declared to be statute-barred, for in that case the executor would be failing to rely on the defence of *res judicata* as well as on that of limitation.[79] And the position is different if an order has been made in an administration action. Once such an order has been made, any beneficiary[80] or creditor[81] may insist on the statute

---

[67] See *ante*, § 22–059.

[68] *Mills v. Fowkes* (1839) 5 Bing.N.C. 455; *Nash v. Hodgson* (1855) 6 De G.M. & G. 474, 480–481; *Friend v. Young* [1897] 2 Ch. 421, 433, 437.

[69] *Nash v. Hodgson, supra.*

[70] *Waller v. Lacy* (1840) 1 M. & G. 54; *Coneys v. Morris* [1922] 1 Ir.R. 81, 91–93; *Kleinwort Benson Ltd v. Sandwell B.C.* (1993) 91 L.G.R. 323, 385.

[71] *Ashby v. James* (1843) 11 M. & W. 542.

[72] *Courtenay v. Williams* (1844) 3 Hare 539 (affd. 15 L.J.Ch. 204); *Coates v. Coates* (1864) 33 Beav. 249; *Gee v. Liddell (No. 2)* (1866) 35 Beav. 629; *Poole v. Poole* (1871) L.R. 7 Ch.App. 17; *Re Akerman* [1891] 3 Ch. 212; *Re Taylor* [1894] 1 Ch. 671.

[73] *Re Cordwell's Estate* (1875) L.R. 20 Eq. 644.

[74] *Re Savage* [1918] 2 Ch. 146.

[75] *Re Bruce* [1908] 2 Ch. 682.

[76] *Stahlschmidt v. Lett* (1853) 1 Sm. & G. 415; *Hill v. Walker* (1858) 4 K. & J. 166; *Lowis v. Rumney* (1867) L.R. 4 Eq. 451.

[77] See *Midgley v. Midgley* [1893] 3 Ch. 282, 297; *Astbury v. Astbury* [1898] 2 Ch. 111, 115. The point has never been decided.

[78] *Stahlschmidt v. Lett, supra; Hill v. Walker, supra.*

[79] *Midgley v. Midgley, supra.*

[80] *Shewen v. Vanderhorst* (1831) 1 R. & M. 347; *Moodie v. Bannister* (1859) 4 Drew. 432; *cf. Re Wenham* [1892] 3 Ch. 59, applying the same principle to an originating summons taken out by the executors.

[81] *Fuller v. Redman (No. 2)* (1859) 26 Beav. 614.

being pleaded, except against a creditor who obtained the order and did not have the statute pleaded against him at that earlier stage.[82]

Trustee's right to indemnity for expenses. On similar principles, a trustee **29–135** has been held entitled to recoup himself out of the trust estate in respect of costs and expenses which he had paid, although they were statute-barred.[83]

Creditor's lien. A creditor who has a lien on goods belonging to the debtor **29–136** which are in his possession may exercise it in respect of statute-barred debts.[84]

9. LIMITATION IN EQUITY[85]

Introductory. The earliest Statutes of Limitation applied only to common law **29–137** actions. However, where an equitable remedy was sought in the protection or enforcement of a legal right, a court of equity would act "in obedience" to the statutes,[86] and if an equitable claim was closely analogous to a claim which was covered by the Statutes, the court would apply the same period of limitation "by analogy."[87] But, in cases not covered by any statutory period, equity developed its own doctrines of laches and acquiescence, under which the claimant was barred from equitable relief if he had not shown reasonable diligence in prosecuting his claim or appeared to have waived his rights.[88] "Nothing can call forth this court into activity," said Lord Camden in 1767,[89] "but conscience, good faith and reasonable diligence. Where these are wanting, the court is passive and does nothing. Laches and neglect are always discountenanced and therefore, from the beginning of this jurisdiction, there was always a limitation to suits in this court." These equitable doctrines rest on the same basis as the law of limitation, that stale demands should not be enforced: but with this difference, that while statute ordinarily prescribes a fixed time limit which applies in general irrespective of the conduct of the parties, the equitable doctrines look primarily at the conduct of the plaintiff and its effect on the defendant or on third parties, so that the length of time which will bar the claim varies greatly in accordance with the circumstances and the type of relief sought. The result is, as has been observed,[90] that a certain vagueness is apt to surround the equitable doctrines of delay. From 1833 onwards the Statutes of Limitation tended more and more to encroach on the field in which the equitable doctrines were applied. The Limitation Act 1980 provides

---

[82] *Briggs v. Wilson* (1854) 5 De G.M. & G. 12; *Fuller v. Redman (No. 2), supra.*

[83] *Budgett v. Budgett* [1895] 1 Ch. 202.

[84] *Spears v. Hartly* (1800) 3 Esp. 81; *Higgins v. Scott* (1831) 2 B. & Ad. 413; *Curwin v. Milburn* (1889) 42 Ch.D. 424; *Re Brockman* [1909] 2 Ch. 170.

[85] See Brunyate, *Limitation of Actions in Equity* (1932).

[86] See *Beckford v. Wade* (1805) 17 Ves. 87, 97; *Hovenden v. Annesley* (1806) 2 Sch. & Lef. 607; *Cholmondeley v. Clinton* (1821) 4 Bli. 1, 119; *Knox v. Gye* (1872) L.R. 5 H.L. 656, 674; *Gibbs v. Guild* (1882) 9 Q.B.D. 59, 74–75.

[87] See *e.g. Re Robinson* [1911] 1 Ch. 502; *Re Mason* [1928] Ch. 385, [1929] 1 Ch. 1; *Re Blake* [1932] 1 Ch. 54 (action to recover money paid wrongly by trustee to recipient analogous to common law action for money had and received). But see now *Re Diplock* [1948] Ch. 465, 498, 501, 502, 515, 516.

[88] *Smith v. Clay* (1767) 3 Bro.C.C. 639n.

[89] *ibid.*

[90] *Erlanger v. New Sombrero Phosphate Co.* (1878) 3 App.Cas. 1218, 1231.

expressly for the limitation of certain claims in equity.[91] Nevertheless, the existence of the equitable doctrines continues to be recognised by the Act, since nothing in the Act is to affect any equitable jurisdiction to refuse relief on the ground of acquiescence or otherwise.[92] Further, the Act provides that neither the time limit under section 5 for actions founded on simple contract nor that under section 8 for actions on a specialty are to apply to any claim for specific performance of a contract or for an injunction or for other equitable relief, except in so far as any provision thereof may be applied by the court by analogy.[93] The effect of this "somewhat diffident" language is to limit the analogous application of sections 5 and 8 of the Act to claims of a kind for which no express provision is to be found elsewhere in the statute.[94]

29–138   **The statute applied by analogy.** The statute may be applied to an equitable claim by analogy.[94a] One important example in the modern law of the application of the statute by analogy is afforded by claims for a final injunction to protect a legal right. So long as the right itself is not barred (*i.e.* so long as the claimant could recover damages for its infringement), he retains his right to an injunction,[95] although delay or other circumstances may induce the court to withhold an injunction and award damages in lieu of an injunction.[96] (It is quite different if the claimant seeks an interim remedy. In that case the utmost promptitude is required and a delay of more than a month or two, unless explained, is usually fatal.[97]) There is also some authority for saying that the statute will be applied by analogy to claims for specific performance[98] or rescission[99] of a contract, with the result that the claimant's claim will be barred if his delay exceeds six years (or 12 if the contract was by deed).[1] But, in such a case, even if the statute is applied by analogy, delay short of the statutory period may bar the claim: a claim for specific performance or rescission may be barred on account of acquiescence, laches or affirmation.

29–139   **Acquiescence.**[2]

> "If a person having a right, and seeing another person about to commit, or in course of committing, an act infringing upon that right, stands by in such a manner as really to induce the person committing the act, and who might otherwise have abstained from it,

---

[91] *e.g.* s.16 (claims to redeem mortgaged land), s.20 (claims to recover money secured by a mortgage or the proceeds of sale), s.21 (claims in respect of trust property or for breach of trust), s.22 (claims in respect of personal estate of a deceased person).

[92] s.36(2).

[93] s.36(1). This also applies to s.7 (arbitration awards), s.9 (statutory claims) and s.24 (actions on judgments).

[94] *Re Diplock* [1948] Ch. 465, 515. *cf. Poole Corporation v. Moody* [1945] K.B. 350.

[94a] *Knox v. Gye* (1872) L.R. 5 H.L. 656; *Paragon Finance plc v. Thakerar & Co.* [1999] 1 All E.R. 400; *Coulthard v. Disco Mix Club Ltd, The Times,* March 25, 1999.

[95] *Imperial Gas Light and Coke Co. v. Broadbent* (1859) 7 H.L.C. 600; *Fullwood v. Fullwood* (1878) 9 Ch.D. 176; *Jamieson v. Jamieson* (1898) 15 R.P.C. 169, 179. See *post,* § 29–142.

[96] *Shaw v. Applegate* [1977] 1 W.L.R. 97.

[97] *G.W. Ry. v. Oxford, etc. Ry.* (1853) 3 De G.M. & G. 341.

[98] *Redgrave v. Hurd* (1881) 20 Ch.D. 1, 13; *Firth v. Slingsby* (1888) 58 L.T. 481. Contrast *Williams v. Greatrex* [1957] 1 W.L.R. 31, where a decree was made after 10 years, but there was an explanation of the delay: see *post,* § 29–146.

[99] *Molloy v. Mutual Reserve Life Insurance Co.* (1906) 94 L.T. 756; *Oelkers v. Ellis* [1914] 2 K.B. 139; *Armstrong v. Jackson* [1917] 2 K.B. 822.

[1] Contrast *Tito v. Waddell (No. 2)* [1977] Ch. 106 (account).

[2] See s.36(2).

to believe that he assents to its being committed, he cannot afterwards be heard to complain of the act."[3]

In this sense of the term (which has been described as the only proper one)[4] acquiescence by the claimant amounts to the waiver of his rights and raises a species of estoppel preventing him from subsequently enforcing them. The conduct of the claimant need not necessarily bear any relation to lapse of time, because it may take place before or at the time when his rights are violated. Mere delay by the claimant in seeking relief does not amount to acquiescence.[4a] The essential ingredients of the defence are, however, by no means clear. In *Willmott v. Barber*,[5] Fry J. laid down no less than five requirements, but it has been said[6] that more recent cases indicate:

"a very much broader approach which is directed rather at ascertaining whether, in particular individual circumstances, it would be unconscionable for a party to be permitted to deny that which, knowingly or unknowingly,[7] he has allowed or encouraged another to assume to his detriment than to inquiring whether the circumstances can be fitted within the confines of some preconceived formula serving as a universal yardstick for every form of unconscionable behaviour."[8]

Laches. The term "laches" is sometimes used to denote acquiescence. But, in **29–140** a narrower sense, the essence of the doctrine of laches is that if the claimant has not been reasonably diligent in seeking relief, and in consequence the position of the defendant has been prejudiced or it would now be unjust or unreasonable to grant the relief, the claimant will be debarred from pursuing his remedy on the ground of laches. What amounts to reasonable diligence and what circumstances will render it inequitable to grant the relief will vary with the type of relief sought and the facts of the particular case.

Statements of the doctrine. The most authoritative statement of the doctrine **29–141** is that of Lord Selborne in *Lindsay Petroleum Co. v. Hurd*[9]:

"Now the doctrine of laches in courts of equity is not an arbitrary or a technical doctrine. Where it would be practically unjust to give a remedy, either because the party has, by his conduct, done that which might be fairly regarded as equivalent to a waiver of it, or where by his conduct and neglect he has, though perhaps not waiving that remedy, yet put the other party in a situation in which it would not be reasonable to place him if the remedy were afterwards to be asserted, in either of these cases, lapse

---

[3] *De Bussche v. Alt* (1878) 8 Ch.D. 286, 314. See also *Archbold v. Scully* (1861) 9 H.L.C. 360, 383.

[4] *Duke of Leeds v. Earl of Amherst* (1846) 2 Ph. 117, 123. *cf. Life Association of Scotland v. Siddall* (1861) 3 De G.F. & J. 58, 72.

[4a] *Jones v. Stones, The Times,* June 3, 1999.

[5] (1880) 15 Ch.D. 96, 105–106.

[6] *Taylors Fashions Ltd v. Liverpool Victoria Trustee Co. Ltd* [1982] Q.B. 133n.; *Amalgamated Investment & Property Co. Ltd v. Texas Commerce International Bank Ltd* [1982] Q.B. 84, 103; *Habib Bank Ltd v. Habib Bank A.G.* [1981] 1 W.L.R. 1265, 1285; *Jones v. Stones, supra.* But contrast *The August P. Leonhardt* [1985] 2 Lloyd's Rep. 28; *Att.-Gen. of Hong Kong v. Humphreys Estate (Queen's Gardens) Ltd* [1987] A.C. 114; *Matharu v. Matharu, The Times*, May 13, 1994, CA. See also *ante*, § 3–130.

[7] *cf. Pauling's Settlement Trusts* [1964] Ch. 303 (where it was held that a plaintiff cannot be held to have acquiesced unless he knew, or ought to have known, what his rights were).

[8] See also *Shaw v. Applegate* [1977] 1 W.L.R. 970; *Greasley v. Cooke* [1980] 1 W.L.R. 1306; *Blue Town Investments Ltd v. Higgs and Hill plc* [1990] 1 W.L.R. 696.

[9] (1874) L.R. 5 P.C. 221, 239 (wrongly attributed in the report to Sir Barnes Peacock).

of time and delay are most material. But in every case, if an argument against relief which otherwise would be just, is founded on mere delay, that delay of course not amounting to a bar by any Statute of Limitations, the validity of that defence must be tried upon principles substantially equitable. Two circumstances always important in such cases, are, the length of the delay and the nature of the acts done during the interval, which might affect either party and cause a balance of justice or injustice in taking the one course or the other, so far as relates to the remedy."

In *Erlanger v. New Sombrero Phosphate Co.*[10] Lord Blackburn, after quoting this statement with approval, went on to say:

"I have looked in vain for any authority which gives a more distinct and definite rule than this; and I think, from the nature of the inquiry, it must always be a question of more or less, depending on the degree of diligence which might reasonably be required, and the degree of change which has occurred, whether the balance of justice or injustice is in favour of granting the remedy or withholding it. The determination of such a question must largely depend on the turn of mind of those who have to decide, and must therefore be subject to uncertainty; but that, I think, is inherent in the nature of the inquiry."[11]

29–142   **Delay where statute applies.** Delay short of the statutory period is ordinarily no bar in cases where a statutory limitation provision is applicable either directly or by analogy.[12] In such cases the claimant is entitled to the full statutory period, though the court retains an equitable jurisdiction to refuse relief on the ground of acquiescence or otherwise.[13]

29–143   **Awareness of facts.** The claimant must be aware of the relevant facts[14] (though he need not know of the exact nature of his rights[15]) and therefore there is no question of laches while the claimant is under disability[16] or undue influence.[17] The principle that ignorance negatives laches may account for the fact that delay will not count against the claimant where the existence of the material cause of action has been concealed from him by fraud or unconscionable behaviour on the part of the defendant[18] or where he is under a mistake.[19]

---

[10] (1878) 3 App.Cas. 1218, 1279.

[11] These statements by Lord Selborne and Lord Blackburn have often been cited with approval: see, *e.g. Re Sharpe* [1892] 1 Ch. 154, 168; *Rochefoucald v. Boustead* [1897] 1 Ch. 196, 210–211; *Weld v. Petre* [1929] 1 Ch. 33, 51–52, 63; *Agbeyegbe v. Ikomi* [1953] 1 W.L.R. 263, 266–267; *Nwakobi v. Nzekwu* [1964] 1 W.L.R. 1019, 1025; *Nelson v. Rye* [1996] 1 W.L.R. 1378, 1392.

[12] *Archbold v. Scully* (1861) 9 H.L.C. 360, 383; *Knox v. Gye* (1872) L.R. 5 H.L. 656; *Fullwood v. Fullwood* (1878) 8 Ch.D. 176; *Re Baker* (1881) 20 Ch.D. 230; *Re Maddever* (1884) 27 Ch.D. 523; *Re Pauling's Settlement Trusts (No. 1)* [1964] Ch. 303.

[13] Limitation Act 1980, s.36(2).

[14] *Life Association of Scotland v. Siddall* (1861) 3 De G.F. & J. 58, 74; *Lindsay Petroleum Co. v. Hurd* (1874) L.R. 5 P.C. 221, 241; *Allcard v. Skinner* (1887) 36 Ch.D. 145, 188; *Re Howlett* [1949] Ch. 767, 775. *cf., Nelson v. Rye* [1996] 1 W.L.R. 1378.

[15] *Stafford v. Stafford* (1857) 1 De G. & J. 193, 202; *Molloy v. Mutual Reserve Life Insurance Co.* (1906) 94 L.T. 756.

[16] *Duke of Leeds v. Earl of Amherst* (1846) 2 Ph. 117.

[17] *Allcard v. Skinner* (1887) 36 Ch.D. 145; *Bullock v. Lloyds Bank Ltd* [1955] Ch. 317.

[18] *Booth v. Earl of Warrington* (1714) 4 Bro.P.C. 163; *Gibbs v. Guild* (1882) 9 Q.B.D. 59; *Molloy v. Mutual Reserve Life Insurance Co.* (1906) 94 L.T. 756; *Oelkers v. Ellis* [1914] 2 K.B. 139; *Armstrong v. Jackson* [1917] 2 K.B. 822. See also *ante*, § 29–085.

[19] *Brooksbank v. Smith* (1836) 2 Y. & C.Ex. 58; contrast *Denys v. Shuckburgh* (1840) 4 Y. & C.Ex. 42, where the mistake could have been discovered with reasonable diligence. See also *ante*, § 29–087.

Alternatively it could be said that, in such circumstances, it would not be just or reasonable to deprive the claimant of the relief to which he would otherwise be entitled.[20]

Prejudice to defendant. It is a relevant subject for inquiry whether the **29–144** claimant's delay has prejudiced the defendant, *e.g.* if he has lost the evidence necessary to rebut the claim or has been spending money on the property to the knowledge of the claimant.[21] If the defendant has not been so prejudiced, and no third parties are involved, the court may well treat the claimant's delay as immaterial.[22] In *Nelson v. Rye*[23] Laddie J. left open the question whether a defendant must prove a causal link between the delay and prejudice of which he complains.

Mere delay. Statements may be found suggesting that mere delay will not bar **29–145** the claimant's claim if there is no evidence of acquiescence on his part or of prejudice to the defendant. Thus, in *Life Association of Scotland v. Siddal*[24] Turner L.J. said:

> "Length of time where it does not operate as a statutory or positive bar operates, as I apprehend, simply as evidence of assent or acquiescence. The two propositions of a bar by length of time and by acquiescence are not, as I conceive, distinct propositions. They constitute but one proposition, and that proposition, when applied to a question of this description, is that the *cestui que trust* assented to the breach of trust."

But in the same case Lord Campbell, while expressing his concurrence with Turner L.J.'s statement, was careful to add that "although the rule be that the onus lies on the party relying on acquiescence to prove the facts from which the consent of the *cestui que trust* is to be inferred, it is easy to conceive cases in which from great lapse of time, such facts might and ought to be presumed."[25] It is submitted that the question always is whether, in the circumstances, it would be inequitable to grant relief by reason of the delay,[26] and it may be that if the claimant's delay is very great, his claim will be rejected as a stale demand without further inquiry.[27]

---

[20] *Turner v. General Motors (Australia) Pty. Ltd* (1929) 42 C.L.R. 352, 370.

[21] *Turner v. Collins* (1871) L.R. 7 Ch. 329; *Watts v. Assets Co.* [1905] A.C. 317, 333; *cf. Shaw v. Applegate* [1977] 1 W.L.R. 970; *Nelson v. Rye* [1996] 1 W.L.R. 1395, 1396.

[22] *Gresley v. Mousley* (1859) 4 De G. & J. 78, 95; *Beauchamp v. Winn* (1873) L.R. 6 H.L. 232; *Re Garnett* (1885) 31 Ch.D. 1; *Blake v. Gale* (1886) 32 Ch.D. 571, 578; *Re Sharpe* [1892] 1 Ch. 154, 168; *Re Lacey* [1907] 1 Ch. 330, 350; *Weld v. Petre* [1929] 1 Ch. 33.

[23] [1996] 1 W.L.R. 1378, 1396 (disapproved on other grounds in *Paragon Finance plc v. Thakerar & Co.* [1999] 1 All E.R. 400, 415.

[24] (1861) 3 De G.F. & J. 58, 72–73.

[25] *ibid.* at 77.

[26] *Parkin v. Thorold* (1852) 16 Beav. 59, 73; *Clegg v. Edmonson* (1857) 8 De G.M. & G. 787, 814; *Fitzgerald v. Masters* (1956) 95 C.L.R. 420, 433; *Re Jarvis* [1958] 1 W.L.R. 815; *Lamshed v. Lamshed* (1963) 109 C.L.R. 440, 453.

[27] Contrast *Brooks v. Muckleston* [1909] 2 Ch. 519 (40 years' delay in foreclosing a mortgage of an advowson held to bar the claim) with *Weld v. Petre* [1929] 1 Ch. 33 (18 years' delay in redeeming a mortgage of shares held not to bar the claim). In neither case was a statute of limitations applicable either expressly or by analogy. But see *Re Eustace* [1912] 1 Ch. 561.

29–146   **Specific performance.** A person asking for specific performance of a contract seeks a discretionary remedy and has an option whether to pursue it or claim damages: he must therefore exercise his option promptly and show himself to be "ready, desirous, prompt and eager."[28] Unexplained delay of more than a few months is usually fatal: and this is especially true if the property is speculative or precarious or liable to fluctuate in value, *e.g.* a mine,[29] a public-house,[30] or a short leasehold interest.[31] However, it will be a sufficient explanation of the delay if the purchaser has been let into possession and requires merely to clothe his enjoyment of the property with the legal estate.[32] But this doctrine does not apply if the claimant was in possession under some other title than that of the contract which he seeks to enforce: for instance, if a tenant for years claims to exercise an option to purchase the freehold.[33]

29–147   **Rescission.** A person seeking to rescind a contract which is voidable for misrepresentation or otherwise has an election either to affirm or rescind the contract. He must therefore act promptly if he wishes to rescind[34]: for it is inequitable that he should be allowed to wait and see whether it pays him to rescind or not, for that would be gambling on a certainty at the other party's expense. This is especially true of contracts for the sale or allotment of shares in companies, where the utmost promptness is required.[35] The allottee is not permitted to wait and see whether the company will prosper. Third persons may perhaps deal with the company on the faith of his being a member. Hence a delay of even a few weeks after discovery of the misrepresentation could be fatal. And it has been held that a buyer of goods could not rescind for innocent misrepresentation five years after the making of the contract, although he acted promptly as soon as he discovered the truth.[36]

29–148   **Setting aside voluntary settlements.** A person seeking to set aside a gift or voluntary settlement on the ground of undue influence is in a different position from one who seeks to rescind a commercial contract in that he takes no benefit from the transaction, and is therefore in a less equivocal position. Consequently, he is allowed a longer time in which to exercise his rights after the influence has ceased to operate and he becomes aware of the facts. But a delay of several years

---

[28] *Milward v. Earl of Thanet* (1801) 5 Ves. 720n.; *Eads v. Williams* (1854) 4 D.M. & G. 674; *Oriental Inland Steam Co. Ltd v. Briggs* (1861) 4 De G.F. & J. 191, 194–195.

[29] *Eads v. Williams, supra; cf. Clegg v. Edmondson* (1857) 8 De G.M. & G. 787.

[30] *Mills v. Haywood* (1877) 6 Ch.D. 196.

[31] *Lehmann v. McArthur* (1868) L.R. 3 Ch.App. 496.

[32] *Crofton v. Ormsby* (1806) 2 Sch. & Lef. 583, 603; *Shepheard v. Walker* (1875) L.R. 20 Eq. 659; *Williams v. Greatrex* [1957] 1 W.L.R. 31 (where a delay of 10 years was held to be no bar).

[33] *Mills v. Haywood, supra.*

[34] *Lindsay Petroleum Co. v. Hurd* (1874) L.R. 5 P.C. 221; *Erlanger v. New Sombrero Phosphate Co.* (1878) 2 App.Cas. 1218; *Molloy v. Mutual Reserve Life Insurance Co.* (1906) 94 L.T. 756. See *ante*, § 6–120. But see *Peyman v. Lanjani* [1985] Ch. 457 (knowledge of right to rescind required).

[35] *Taite's Case* (1867) L.R. 3 Eq. 795; *Sharpley v. Louth and East Coast Ry.* (1876) 2 Ch.D. 663; *Re Scottish Petroleum Co.* (1883) 23 Ch.D. 413; *Aaron's Reefs Ltd v. Twiss* [1896] A.C. 273, 294; *Taylor v. Oil and Ozokerite Co.* (1913) 29 T.L.R. 515; *First National Reinsurance Co. Ltd v. Greenfield* [1921] 2 K.B. 260; see *ante*, § 6–123.

[36] *Leaf v. International Galleries* [1950] 2 K.B. 86; see *ante*, § 6–123. See also *Miljus (T/A A & Z Engineering) v. Yamazaki Machinery U.K. Ltd* [1997] C.L.Y. 992 and Misrepresentation Act 1967, s.2(2); *ante*, § 6–095.

will raise an inference of acquiescence sufficient to defeat the claim.[37] Thus, in *Allcard v. Skinner*[38] gifts made under religious influence by an inmate of a convent to the lady superior for the benefit of the sisterhood could not be recalled six years after she left the convent, changed her religion, and received independent advice: for there was not only inactivity but positive evidence of conduct amounting to confirmation of the gift. On the other hand, in *Bullock v. Lloyds Bank*[39] a settlement made under the undue influence of her father by a young lady just of age was successfully impeached four years after the influence ceased and she became aware of her rights, during which time she unsuccessfully tried to persuade the trustee to exercise its power of revocation under the settlement. A longer time may be allowed for setting aside gifts made by mistake.[40]

Rectification. The rectification of deeds and contracts on the ground of **29–149** mistake is subject to the doctrine of laches, but it seems that the claimant is allowed a longer time for claiming rectification than he is for setting aside a voluntary settlement or gift.[41] At any rate this is true if all parties have acted throughout on the claimant's version of what they really intended[42]: for in that case no one is prejudiced by the delay.

10. CONFLICT OF LAWS[43]

Position at common law. Since English law in general treats limitation as a **29–150** matter of procedure,[44] the common law rule was that an English court would apply the provisions of an English limitation statute as the *lex fori* to any action brought in England notwithstanding that the substantive rights in question were governed by a foreign law. No action founded on a contract the proper law of which was not English law could therefore be brought after the expiration of six years from the date on which the cause of action accrued, even though the action was not barred or the right extinguished under the foreign law.[45] Conversely, if an action was barred by a foreign law, but not by an English statute of limitation, it might be brought in England, provided the foreign law in the opinion of the

---

[37] *Wright v. Vanderplank* (1856) 8 De G.M. & G. 133 (10 years' delay a bar); *Turner v. Collins* (1871) L.R. 7 Ch.App. 329 (nine years' delay a bar); *Allcard v. Skinner* (1887) 36 Ch.D. 145 (six years' delay a bar); contrast *Bullock v. Lloyds Bank Ltd* [1955] Ch. 317 (four years' delay not a bar).

[38] (1887) 36 Ch.D. 145.

[39] [1955] Ch. 317.

[40] *Re Garnett* (1885) 31 Ch. D. 1 (20 years); *ante*, § 5–095, n. 51.

[41] *Wolterbeek v. Barrow* (1857) 23 Beav. 423 (rectification allowed 34 years after date of deed and four years after discovery of mistake); *Turner v. Collins* (1871) L.R. 7 Ch.App. 329 (rectification of voluntary settlement allowed though rescission barred).

[42] *M'Cormack v. M'Cormack* (1877) 1 L.R.Ir. 119 (35 years' delay no bar); *Burroughes v. Abbott* [1922] 1 Ch. 86 (12 years' delay no bar).

[43] See *Dicey and Morris on the Conflict of Laws* (12th ed., 1993), pp. 184–189, 1267.

[44] See *ante*, § 29–129, and the exceptions there mentioned.

[45] *British Linen Co. v. Drummond* (1830) 10 B. & C. 903; *Huber v. Steiner* (1835) 2 Bing.N.C. 202, 210; *Don v. Lippmann* (1837) 5 Cl. & Fin. 1; *Fergusson v. Fyfe* (1841) 8 Cl. & Fin. 121; *Ruckmaboye v. Lullaoboy Mottichund* (1853) 8 Moo. P.C. 4, 35–38; *Re Low* [1894] 1 Ch. 147, 162; *Blackburn Corpn. v. Sanderson* [1902] 1 K.B. 794, 807.

English court merely barred the remedy without extinguishing the right.[46] This was so even if a foreign court had declared that the remedy was barred under the foreign law.[47]

29–151   **Foreign Limitation Periods Act 1984.** The common law on this point was altered by the Foreign Limitation Periods Act 1984.[48] Where, in accordance with English conflict of law rules,[49] the law which governs a matter is that of another country, then the law[50] of that other country relating to limitation (whether procedural or substantive)[51] is to be applied[52] to an action or proceedings[53] in respect of the matter in an English court,[54] and the English law of limitation in general does not apply.[55] Questions of limitation in contract are therefore to be decided by reference to the foreign *lex causae*,[56] although English law as the *lex fori* still determines whether, and the time at which, proceedings have been commenced.[57] To this principle there is, however, one important exception. The principle is not to be applied if its application would to any extent conflict with public policy[58]; and it is provided that there is a conflict with public policy to the extent that application of the principle would cause undue hardship to a person who is, or might be made, a party to the action or proceedings.[59] Public policy may, therefore, require the court not to apply a foreign law relating to limitation if undue hardship would be caused to the claimant or to the defendant by the fact that there was a very short or a very long limitation period, or no limitation period at all[60] in the foreign law, or in the circumstances of the particular case.[61] Where the foreign limitation period is thus disapplied by the court (whether on grounds of undue hardship or other conflict with public policy), it will not be

---

[46] *Huber v. Steiner, supra*; *Finch v. Finch* (1876) 45 L.J.Ch. 816; *Alliance Bank of Simla v. Carey* (1880) 5 C.P.D. 429; *S.A. de Prayon v. Koppel* (1933) 77 S.J. 800.

[47] *Harris v. Quine* (1869) L.R. 4 Q.B. 653. cf. *Black-Clawson International Ltd v. Papierwerke Waldhof-Aschaffenburg A.G.* [1975] A.C. 591. Contrast now the present rule in s.3 of the Foreign Limitation Periods Act 1984.

[48] This Act is based on the recommendations of the Law Commission, Law Com. No. 114, Cmnd. 8370 (1982). It was brought into force on October 1, 1985, but does not affect any action commenced in England before that date, nor any matter in respect of which the limitation period would, apart from the Act, have expired before that date: s.7(3). For commentaries on the Act, see Carter (1985) 101 L.Q.R. 68; Stone [1985] L.M.C.L.Q. 497.

[49] See *post*, Chap. 31.

[50] Conflict rules and *renvoi* are excluded: ss.1(5), 4(2).

[51] s.4(2).

[52] For the effect of extension, reduction or interruption of the period under the foreign law, see ss.2(3), 4(1)(a). For discretionary bars, see s.1(4).

[53] For the application of the Act to arbitrations, see s.5.

[54] s.1(1)(a).

[55] s.1(1)(b).

[56] Contrast the position in tort, ss.1(1)(b), (2).

[57] s.1(3), including s.35 of the Limitation Act 1980 (*ante*, § 29–127). See *Arab Monetary Fund v. Hashim* [1993] 1 Lloyd's Rep. 543, 593 (revsd. on other grounds [1996] 1 Lloyd's Rep. 589). See also CPR, r. 17.4, Part 19.

[58] s.2(1).

[59] s.2(2).

[60] See s.4(1)(b).

[61] See *Hellenic Steel Co. v. Svolomar Shipping Co. Ltd* [1990] 1 Lloyd's Rep. 541 (reversed on other grounds [1991] 1 Lloyd's Rep. 370); *Jones v. Trollope & Colls, The Times*, January 26, 1990, CA; *Société Commerciale de Reassurance v. Eras International Ltd* [1992] 1 Lloyd's Rep. 570, 604; *Arab Monetary Fund v. Hashim* [1996] 1 Lloyd's Rep. 589.

reimposed by virtue of the rules of common law.[62] But the effect of disapplication is otherwise uncertain. The probability is that the court would then apply the English limitation period as part of the procedural law of the *forum*.[63]

The Act does not prevent the court, in the exercise of any discretion, from refusing equitable relief on the grounds of acquiescence or otherwise,[64] but does require that, in applying the equitable rules, regard be had in particular to the provisions of the foreign law.[65]   **29–152**

Rome Convention.[66] The Rome Convention on the Law Applicable to Contractual Obligations 1980 has the force of law in the United Kingdom by virtue of the Contracts (Applicable Law) Act 1990. The Convention applies to contracts made after April 1, 1991.[67] Article 10(1)(d) of the Convention provides that the law applicable to a contract by virtue of Articles 3 to 6 and 12 of the Convention is to regulate "prescription and limitation of actions." There is no inconsistency in this respect between the Convention and the Foreign Limitation Periods Act 1984, since both lead to the conclusion that the law relating to limitation (whether procedural or substantive) is the law applicable to the contract as determined in accordance with the Convention.[68] The question, however, arises whether the "public policy" exception contained in the 1984 Act[69] is compatible with the Convention. It is submitted that this exception continues to be applicable, either by reference to Article 7(2) of the Convention (which provides that nothing in the Convention shall restrict the application of the rules of law of the forum in a situation where they are mandatory irrespective of the law otherwise applicable to the contract) or by reference to Article 16 (which provides that the application of a rule of the law of any country specified by the Convention may be refused only if such application is manifestly incompatible with the public policy ("ordre public") of the forum).[70]   **29–153**

The further question which arises is whether the preservation in the 1984 Act[71] of the court's discretion to refuse equitable relief on the grounds of acquiescence or otherwise is compatible with the Convention. This is, perhaps, more doubtful, but it is arguable that the equitable doctrines of acquiescence and laches are not matters of "prescription and limitation of actions" within Article 10(1)(d).[72] They relate to the circumstances in which certain remedies are available in the English courts. As such they are matters of procedure. By Article 1(2)(h) of the   **29–154**

---

[62] *Hellenic Steel Co. v. Svolomar Shipping Co. Ltd* [1991] 1 Lloyd's Rep. 370, 377; (*i.e.* if the foreign law extinguishes the right, *ante,* § 29–150).

[63] *Hellenic Steel Co. v. Svolomar Shipping Co. Ltd* [1991] 1 Lloyd's Rep. 370, 377; *Arab Monetary Fund v. Hashim* [1996] 1 Lloyd's Rep. 589.

[64] *e.g.* on the ground of laches: see *ante*, §§ 29–140—29–144.

[65] s.4(3).

[66] See *post*, § 31–016.

[67] S.I. 1991 No. 707.

[68] With respect to limitation periods imposed by other enactments (§§ 29–015—29–026, *ante*), Art. 21 provides that the Convention is not to prejudice the application of international conventions to which a Contracting State is, or becomes, a party.

[69] s.2; § 29–151, *ante*.

[70] Although Art. 16 is negative in form, it clearly implies that application may be refused if it is manifestly incompatible with the public policy of the forum. On this point, see *Dicey & Morris on the Conflict of Laws* (12th ed., 1993), p. 1267.

[71] s.4(3). See also Limitation Act 1980, s.36(2); § 29–137, *ante*.

[72] Contrast s.36(1) of the 1980 Act (application by analogy); § 29–138, *ante*.

Convention the rules of the Convention do not apply to "procedure." However, by Article 10(1)(c), the law applicable to a contract by virtue of the Convention governs in particular "within the limits of the powers conferred on the court by its procedural law, the consequences of breach, including the assessment of damages in so far as it is governed by rules of law." This would appear to require the English courts to apply a remedy available in the applicable law in consequence of a breach of contract, *e.g.* specific performance, but only within the limits of the powers conferred upon the court by its procedural law. It is submitted that, at least in respect of grant or refusal of the remedies of specific performance and injunction, the equitable doctrines can properly be regarded as limits on the powers conferred upon an English court by its procedural law.

Part Eight
RESTITUTION

CHAPTER 30

RESTITUTION[1]

---

[1] For a full treatment of the subject-matter of this chapter, see Birks, *An Introduction to the Law of Restitution* (1985); Burrows, *The Law of Restitution* (1993); Goff and Jones, *The Law of Restitution* (5th ed., 1998). See also Beatson, *The Use and Abuse of Unjust Enrichment* (1991); Burrows (ed.), *Essays on the Law of Restitution* (1991); Maddaugh and McCamus, *The Law of Restitution* (1990); Mason and Carter, *Restitution Law in Australia* (1995); Palmer, *The Law of Restitution* (1978) (four vols.); Stoljar, *The Law of Quasi-Contract* (2nd ed., 1989); *The American Law Institute's Restatement of the Law of Restitution, Quasi-Contracts and Constructive Trusts* (1937); Winfield, *The Law of Quasi-Contracts* (1952) (also his *Province of the Law of Tort* (1931), Chap. 7).

1. Introduction

(a) *Nature of the Subject*

30–001   **Common law.** Lord Wright[2] has described the nature of restitution or quasi-contract in the following words:

> "It is clear that any civilised system of law is bound to provide remedies for cases of what has been called unjust enrichment or unjust benefit, that is, to prevent a man from retaining the money of, or some benefit derived from, another which it is against conscience that he should keep. Such remedies in English law are generically different from remedies in contract or in tort, and are now recognised to fall within a third category of the common law which has been called quasi-contract or restitution."

Although some statutes[3] do not explicitly envisage restitutionary claims as a third category, others do. Thus the definition of liability in the Insolvency Act 1986, s.382(4), includes liabilities "arising out of an obligation to make restitution" as well as those arising for breach of trust or contract, or in tort and bailment[4] and the Torts (Interference with Goods) Act 1977, s.7(4), imposes liability on a person who is "unjustly enriched."[5]

30–002   The precedents collected under this heading deal with many diverse situations, but their common framework is that they involve a special relationship between two persons where the law imposes a duty on one to pay a sum of money or (exceptionally) to deliver specific property to another. The relationship is based either upon the involuntariness of the payment or transfer, its qualified nature, or the conduct of the transferee. The underlying aim of the precedents seems to be an obligation upon the defendant to make restitution of a benefit which he ought not in justice to retain at the expense of the claimant. A restitutionary or quasi-contractual situation resembles a contractual one in that liability is imposed upon a particular person to pay money to another particular person, yet it differs radically in that restitutionary liability is imposed by the law irrespective of the agreement of the parties. It has been held that a claim for restriction of moneys

---

[2] *Fibrosa Spolka Akcyjna v. Fairbairn Lawson Combe Barbour Ltd* [1943] A.C. 32, 61.

[3] *e.g.* the Limitation Act 1980 (on which see *Kleinwort Benson Ltd v. Lincoln C.C.* [1998] 3 W.L.R. 1095) and the Law Reform (Miscellaneous Provisions) Act 1934, s.1(3) (applied in *Chesworth v. Farrar* [1967] 1 Q.B. 407 but now repealed).

[4] See also the heading to the Minors Contracts Act 1987, s.3 and Financial Services Act 1986, s.6; Pensions Act 1995, s.14.

[5] See *post*, § 30–009.

paid under a purported contract that was void *ab initio* was not one "relating to a contract".[6] On the other hand, restitutionary liability, though like tortious liability in that it is imposed upon the defendant by the law, differs from tortious liability, according to Winfield,[7] in the scope of the defendant's duty: "In tort it is towards persons generally, in quasi-contract it is towards a particular person." But this distinction is doubtful, and the correct one may be that liability in quasi-contract is not necessarily based on any "wrong" (*tort*) committed by the defendant.

Equity. The common law has not been alone in providing a remedy for unjustifiable enrichment. Equity independently developed some principles which are aimed at the same result, *viz.* to force a man to disgorge property in his possession which rightly "belongs" to the claimant. In equity, restitutionary principles have been influential in a number of ways; first in the "constructive" trust, whereby a man was deemed to be a trustee of the property for the claimant, so that many[8] of the remedies of the law of trusts were available to enable the claimant as beneficiary to recover what was due to him.[9] Secondly, there is the mechanism of a tracing order, whereby property in the wrong hands could be "followed" or "traced" by the true owner despite changes in or admixture of the property.[10] Thirdly, the doctrine of acquiescence has enabled relief to be given to a person who has expended money on the property of another.[11] In the United States these different principles of common law and equity have been amalgamated into a single topic in the law called "Restitution," as is evidenced by the volume published in 1937 entitled *The American Law Institute's Restatement of the Law of Restitution, Quasi-Contracts and Constructive Trusts.*[12] English lawyers are now aware of the interrelation of law and equity in the field of quasi-contract and restitution,[13] and it has been said that, in the context of restitution for unjust enrichment, there is no need to treat the action for money had and received and an action for an equitable remedy "as any longer depending upon different concepts of justice."[14] Accordingly, in this chapter some indication will be given of the scope of equitable remedies.

30–003

---

[6] *Kleinwort Benson Ltd v. Glasgow C.C.* [1997] 1 W.L.R. 923.

[7] *Province of the Law of Tort* (1931), p. 188.

[8] *cf.* the concept of a "qualified trusteeship": *Lake v. Bayliss* [1974] 1 W.L.R. 1073, 1074, 1076. See also *English v. Dedham Vale Properties Ltd* [1978] 1 W.L.R. 93.

[9] See *post,* §§ 30–107, 30–175.

[10] See *post,* §§ 30–097 *et seq.*

[11] *Ramsden v. Dyson* (1866) L.R. 1 H.L. 83; *Plimmer v. Wellington Corp.* (1884) 9 App.Cas. 699, 710. See also Birks *op. cit.* pp. 277–279, 290–293. *cf.* Burrows (1988) 104 L.Q.R. 576, 583–586; *op. cit.* p. 123.

[12] Seavey and Scott (1938) 54 L.Q.R. 29; Winfield *op. cit.* at 529; Lord Wright, *Legal Essays and Addresses,* pp. 34 *et seq.*

[13] Winfield (1948) 64 L.Q.R. 46. See also Lord Wright (1936) 6 Camb.L.J. 305 (reprinted in his *Legal Essays and Addresses,* p. 1); Holdsworth (1939) 55 L.Q.R. 37; *Nelson v. Larholt* [1948] 1 K.B. 339, 343 (see also Denning (1949) 65 L.Q.R. 37); *Lipkin Gorman v. Karpnale Ltd* [1991] 2 A.C. 548, 581; *Westdeutsche Landesbank Girozentrale v. Islington L.B.C.* [1994] 4 All E.R. 890 (QB and CA), [1996] A.C. 669; *Tribe v. Tribe* [1996] Ch. 107; Birks *op. cit.* pp. 32–33, 71–72, 81–82, 154–156, 163–164, 277–279, 359–362, 420–423 and Goff and Jones *op. cit.* pp. 4–5, 72–73, Chaps. 3, 7, 11, 33 and 34.

[14] *Westdeutsche Landesbank Girozentrale v. Islington L.B.C.* (1993) 91 L.G.R. 323, 349, see also [1996] A.C. 669.

(b) *Historical Introduction*[15]

30–004   **Writs of assumpsit, debt and account.** Though the origin of the action of assumpsit was some positive act of negligent misfeasance, it had become the regular remedy for breaches of contract at the beginning of the seventeenth century, and so was considered as the main remedy to enforce consensual obligations. However, following *Slade's Case*,[16] *indebitatus assumpsit* became a complete alternative to the old writ of debt, and inherited the wide scope of debt over not only consensual obligations but also some obligations classified in modern law as quasi-contractual. For debt had been the appropriate remedy for some claims which were not based on consent, such as claims for a liquidated sum of money due as a penalty under a statute, as a forfeiture under a by-law, as a customary fine or levy, or as a judgment debt. Debt also lay to recover money which had been paid to the defendant for a specific purpose (*e.g.* to pay to a third person) which the defendant had failed to carry out.[17] The old action of account also embraced some obligations which were not necessarily contractual: in general, it lay to enforce the duty of the guardian, bailiff or receiver to account to the plaintiff for moneys received on his behalf.[18] But by the development of the notion of a "constructive" receiver, account came to be used to recover money paid under a mistake, or money paid for a consideration which had wholly failed.[19] Thus account as well as debt covered some instances of liability to pay money imposed *ab extra* by the law, and not voluntarily assumed under an agreement.

30–005   **Development of indebitatus assumpsit.** The rapid development of *indebitatus assumpsit* in the seventeenth century led to cases where the court permitted the newer and better remedy to replace debt and account for such non-contractual claims, *e.g.* to recover customary dues levied on foreign goods exposed for sale,[20] and to recover a customary fine due to the plaintiff as lord of the manor.[21] In some respects, assumpsit extended the scope of quasi-contractual remedies: it was allowed upon a *quantum meruit* to claim a reasonable remuneration where the plaintiff had rendered services or supplied goods to the defendant at the latter's request, but the parties had not fixed the sum to be paid, although it was obvious in the circumstances that neither party intended the services to be gratuitous, or the goods to be a gift.[22] *Indebitatus assumpsit* soon was employed to remedy many widely differing situations, often under the common formula

---

[15] Jackson, *History of Quasi-Contract* (1936); Winfield, *Quasi-Contracts* (1952), pp. 1–25; Holdsworth, *History of English Law*, Vol. VIII, pp. 88–98; Simpson, *A History of the Common Law of Contract* (1975), pp. 489 *et seq.*; Baker, *An Introduction to English Legal History* (3rd ed.), Chap. 20; Baker and Milsom, *Sources of English Legal History* (1986), pp. 463–481; Birks and McLeod (1986) 6 O.J.L.S. 46.

[16] (1602) 4 Co.Rep. 91a, 92b. See Simpson (1958) 74 L.Q.R. 381; Simpson *op. cit.* pp. 281 *et seq.*, 489 *et seq.*; Baker [1971] C.L.J. 51, 213; Ibbetson (1984) 4 O.J.L.S. 295.

[17] Fifoot *op. cit.* pp. 222–223; Baker *op. cit.* p. 410. (In modern law the term used would be "paid on a consideration which had wholly failed.")

[18] *ibid.* at 268 *et seq.* See Stoljar (1964) 80 L.Q.R. 203.

[19] Fifoot *op. cit.* pp. 272–273; Baker *op. cit.* pp. 410–413.

[20] *City of London v. Goree* (1677) 2 Levinz 174; 3 Keble 677. (The phrase *"quasi ex contractu"* was used in the judgment.)

[21] *Shuttleworth v. Garnett* (1688) 3 Mod. 240; 3 Lev. 261. See also *City of York v. Toun* (1700) 5 Mod. 444; 2 Ld.Raym. 502.

[22] Fifoot *op. cit.* pp. 360–363. *Quantum meruit* was introduced especially to cover services rendered by innkeepers, common carriers, and others exercising a "common calling." See *Warbrook v. Griffin* (1609) 2 Brownlow 254; *Rogers v. Head* (1610) Cro.Jac. 262.

that the sum of money claimed was "had and received to the use of the plaintiff." Thus it lay to recover money paid under a mistake,[23] or extorted from the plaintiff by duress of his goods,[24] or paid to the defendant on a consideration which totally failed,[25] or to recover profits received by the defendant while wrongfully usurping an office belonging to the plaintiff,[26] or as an alternative remedy to trover for the tort of conversion.[27]

Implied promise. It was only by historical accident that all these causes of action were based on the common remedy of *indebitatus assumpsit*, and the courts treated the alleged promise to pay as purely fictitious. The "promise" or obligation to pay was imposed by the law, and any genuine promise was plainly contrary to the facts, especially when the defendant was actually a tortfeasor. Lord Atkin, referring to such a case, said[28]: **30–006**

> " . . . it was necessary to create a fictitious contract: for there was no action possible other than debt or assumpsit on the one side and action for damages for tort on the other. . . . The law, in order to do justice, imputed to the wrongdoer a promise which alone as forms of action then existed could give the injured person a reasonable remedy. . . . These fantastic resemblances of contracts invented in order to meet requirements of the law as to forms of action which have now disappeared should not in these days be allowed to affect actual rights."

(c) *The Principle of Restitution*

Introductory. For many years the theoretical basis of quasi-contractual or restitutionary liability has been controversial. Although in most cases a claimant must bring his claim under a recognised head of liability and not rely on a sweeping generalisation, the underlying theory ought to be examined briefly since it influences the development of the subject, especially when a court is asked to extend or restrict the scope of a specific rule in restitution. Thus, in one case, the fact that no general theory was accepted led the court to reject the relevance of arguments by analogy[29] whereas in another the acceptance of an underlying principle led to the recognition of a new defence.[30] The search is not to discover a precise rule on which liability in restitution can be tested, but to discover a theoretical principle or common factor underlying the categories of restitution which already exist. **30–007**

Two main theories. The two main theories, the principle of unjust enrichment and the implied contract theory, will now be considered. Although the implied contract theory was once influential, it is now discredited as artificial, based on a fiction and misleading and has been rejected by the courts.[31] It should, however, **30–008**

---

[23] *Tomkyns v. Barnet* (1693) Skin. 411.
[24] *Astley v. Reynolds* (1731) 2 Strange 915.
[25] *Martin v. Sitwell* (1690) 1 Show. 156.
[26] *Howard v. Wood* (1680) 2 Levinz 245.
[27] *Lamine v. Dorrell* (1705) 2 Ld.Raym. 1216.
[28] *United Australia Ltd v. Barclays Bank Ltd* [1941] A.C. 1, 27–29.
[29] *Orakpo v. Manson Investments Ltd* [1978] A.C. 95. See *post*, §§ 30–065, 30–176. For criticism of this see (1978) 41 M.L.R. 330, 334. *cf. Spottiswood's* case (1855) 6 De G.M. & G. 345, 371–372, *post*, § 30–177; *Pavey and Matthews Pty. Ltd v. Paul* (1986–1987) 162 C.L.R. 221, 256–257 (Deane J.).
[30] *Lipkin Gorman v. Karpnale Ltd* [1991] 2 A.C. 548. See post, §§ 30–114—30–116.
[31] See *post*, § 30–015.

be noted that the principle of unjust enrichment may in fact only be able to account for all cases in which restitution has been given by similar artificiality, and in particular by an over-broad concept of enrichment.[32] It may be more useful to recognise that the true basis of a number of situations in which restitution is granted is a principle by which the claimant's reasonable reliance on a defendant's words or conduct is protected.[33] Restitution would thus be based either on the principle of unjust enrichment or the protection of the reliance interest.

30–009   **The principle of unjust enrichment.** The American Law Institute's *Restatement of the Law of Restitution, Quasi-Contracts and Constructive Trusts* concisely states that "a person who has been unjustly enriched at the expense of another is required to make restitution to the other."[34] Although there is no general cause of action in English law for unjust enrichment, it has recently been explicitly recognised by the House of Lords in *Lipkin Gorman v. Karpnale Ltd* that the concept of unjust enrichment lies at the heart of and is the principle underlying the individual instances in which the law does give a right of recovery.[35] However, despite the strong support of several judges including Lords Wright,[36] Atkin,[37] Denning,[38] Pearce[39] and Goff[40] and numerous academic writers,[41] the precise shape of English law has until recently been formed against a background of scepticism.[42]

---

[32] *Post*, § 30–018. See also Hedley (1985) 5 L.S. 56.

[33] Fuller & Purdue (1936) 46 Yale L.J. 52; Atiyah, *The Rise and Fall of Freedom of Contract* (1979), pp. 764 *et seq.*; Beatson, *The Use and Abuse of Restitution* (1991), Chap. 2; Stoljar, *The Law of Quasi-Contract* (2nd ed.), pp. 9–10. Goff & Jones recognise that not all the instances of restitution they deal with are based on benefit to or enrichment of the defendant; see pp. 20–22, 26 and Chap. 26.

[34] (1937), para. 1.

[35] [1991] 2 A.C. 548, 559, 578. See also *Woolwich Equitable B.S. v. I.R.C.* [1993] A.C. 70, esp. 196–197; *Westdeutsche Landesbank Girozentrale v. Islington L.B.C.* [1996] A.C. 669, esp. 710. See also *ibid.* at 688, 718, 720, 738; *Kleinwort Benson Ltd v. Lincoln C.C.* [1998] 3 W.L.R. 1095. These built on *Fibrosa Spolka Akcyjna v. Fairbairn Lawson Combe Barbour* [1943] A.C. 32, especially Lord Wright at 61 (quoted at § 30–001 *ante*).

[36] *Brooks Wharf and Bull Wharf Ltd v. Goodman Brothers* [1937] 1 K.B. 534, 545; *Fibrosa Spolka Akcyjna v. Fairbairn Lawson Combe Barbour Ltd* [1943] A.C. 32, 61–64; Lord Wright (1938) 6 Camb.L.J. 305 (reprinted in his *Legal Essays and Addresses*, pp. 1–33).

[37] *United Australia Ltd v. Barclays Bank Ltd* [1941] A.C. 1, 27–29.

[38] *Nelson v. Larholt* [1948] 1 K.B. 339, 343; *Larner v. L.C.C.* [1949] 2 K.B. 683; *Kiriri Cotton Co. Ltd v. Dewani* [1960] A.C. 192, 204–205; (1949) 65 L.Q.R. 37; *Hussey v. Palmer* [1972] 1 W.L.R. 1286.

[39] *Att.-Gen. v. Nissan* [1970] A.C. 179, 228 (approving Winn L.J.'s dicta in [1968] 1 Q.B. 286, 352).

[40] As well as *Lipkin Gorman v. Karpnale Ltd* [1991] 2 A.C. 548 and *Woolwich Equitable B.S. v. I.R.C.* [1993] A.C. 70 see *B.P. (Exploration) Co. (Libya) Ltd v. Hunt (No. 2)* [1979] 1 W.L.R. 788, 799, affd. [1981] 1 W.L.R. 232, CA; [1983] 2 A.C. 352, HL; *British Steel Corp. v. Cleveland Bridge and Engineering Co. Ltd* [1984] 1 All E.R. 504, 511; *R. v. Tower Hamlets L.B.C., ex p. Chetnik Developments Ltd* [1988] A.C. 858, 882; *Whittaker v. Campbell* [1984] Q.B. 318, 327.

[41] *e.g.* Winfield, *Province of the Law of Tort* (1931), pp. 119–141 (also his *Quasi-Contracts* (1952), pp. 9–23; (1937) 53 L.Q.R. 447; (1939) 55 L.Q.R. 161; [1932] *Bell Yard* 32); Munkman (1950), *Quasi-Contracts*, pp. 7–20; Friedmann (1937) 53 L.Q.R. 449; also (1938) 16 Can.Bar Rev. 247, 365; Birks *op. cit.* pp. 34–39.

[42] *Orakpo v. Manson Investments Ltd* [1978] A.C. 95, 104 (Lord Diplock). See also *Bossevain v. Weil* [1950] A.C. 327, 341 (Lord Radcliffe); *Reading v. Att.-Gen.* [1951] A.C. 507, 513 (Lord Porter); *Ministry of Health v. Simpson* [1951] A.C. 251, 275 (Lord Simonds); *Stoke on Trent C.C. v. Wass* [1988] 1 W.L.R. 1406; *Guinness plc v. Saunders* [1990] 2 A.C. 663 (Lord Templeman), and the academic adherents of the implied contract theory); Holdsworth (1939) 55 L.Q.R. 37 (*cf.* Winfield *op. cit.* p. 161); Landon (1937) 53 L.Q.R. 302 (*cf.* Winfield and Friedmann *op. cit.* at pp. 447–449); see

In 1760 Lord Mansfield sought to rationalise the action for money had and **30–010**
received to the use of the claimant in the following well-known passage[43]:

> "This kind of equitable action to recover back money which ought not in justice to be
> kept is very beneficial, and therefore much encouraged. It lies for money which, *ex
> aequo et bono*, the defendant ought to refund; it does not lie for money paid by the
> plaintiff, which is claimed of him as payable in point of honour and honesty, although
> it could not have been recovered from him by any course of law; as in payment of a debt
> barred by the Statute of Limitations, or contracted during his minority, or to the extent
> of principal and legal interest upon a usurious contract, or for money fairly lost at play:
> because in all these cases the defendant may retain it with a safe conscience, though by
> positive law he was debarred from recovering. . . . [T]he gist of this kind of action is
> that the defendant, upon the circumstances of the case, is obliged by the ties of natural
> justice and equity to refund the money."

The equity (*aequum et bonum*) to which Lord Mansfield referred was not the
technical system of equity of the Court of Chancery, but the *jus naturale* of the
Roman law.[44] It was merely a synonym for "natural justice" and has for this
reason often been criticised as vague and uncertain. "Whatever may have been
the case 146 years ago, we are not now free in the twentieth century to administer
that vague jurisprudence which is sometimes attractively styled 'justice as
between man and man.' "[45]

The criticism that the principle of unjust enrichment is too vague to be of any **30–011**
practical use[46] overlooks the fact that there is already a considerable body of case
law dealing with the categories of restitution, so that judges are not called upon
to use their own sense of justice in order to apply or develop the law. The judges
will follow the existing precedents, which cover most of the likely problems of
restitution, and if an extension of the law is sought, the meaning to be attached
to "unjust enrichment" will be gleaned from the precedents. Lord Mansfield's
view of quasi-contractual obligation was accepted by many in the nineteenth
century,[47] though it has been attacked in the first half of this century by judicial[48]

---

also Landon [1931] *Bell Yard* 19; Gutteridge (1934) 5 Camb.L.J. 204, 223–229; Radcliffe (1938) 54
L.Q.R. 24. See also Atiyah, *An Introduction to the Law of Contract*, (5th ed.) pp. 45–6; *Morris v.
Tarrant* [1971] 2 Q.B. 143, 160–162. Allen (1938) 54 L.Q.R. 201 attempted to show that both unjust
enrichment and constructive contract were essential to quasi-contract.

[43] *Moses v. Macferlan* (1760) 2 Burr. 1005, 1012. The actual decision in the case, which set aside
the judgment of a competent court otherwise than by appeal, was not followed later: *Marriott v.
Hampton* (1797) 7 T.R. 269. See Winfield (1944) 60 L.Q.R. 341, 342–343. See also Lord Mansfield
in *Towers v. Barrett* (1786) 1 T.R. 133, 134; *Weston v. Downes* (1778) 1 Dougl. (K.B.) 23, 24.

[44] *Baylis v. Bishop of London* [1913] 1 Ch. 127, 137; *Sinclair v. Brougham* [1914] A.C. 398, 417,
454–456.

[45] *Baylis v. Bishop of London*, ante, at 140, *per* Hamilton L.J. See also *Holt v. Markham* [1923] 1
K.B. 504, 513.

[46] But the similar principles of the reasonable man, and of public policy, which are frequently
employed in the law of torts and contract (and are accepted by the legislature, *e.g.* s.2(2) of the
Occupiers' Liability Act 1957) are not considered too vague. See Winfield (1928) 42 Harv.L.R.
97.

[47] *e.g. Kelly v. Solari* (1841) 9 M. & W. 54; *Edwards v. Bates* (1844) 7 Man. & G. 590; *Freeman
v. Jeffries* (1869) L.R. 4 Ex. 189, 199. See also Bullen & Leake, *Precedents of Pleadings* (3rd ed.,
1868), p. 44.

[48] *e.g.* Lord Sumner in *Sinclair v. Brougham* [1914] A.C. 398, 452–456; Greene M.R. in *Morgan
v. Ashcroft* [1938] 1 K.B. 49, 62–63 (*contra* Scott L.J. at 75–77); *Re Diplock* [1947] 1 Ch. 716, 724
(Wynn-Parry J.); [1948] Ch. 465, 480–481, CA.

and academic[49] adherents of the "implied contract" theory. However, in recent years Lord Mansfield's approach has been strongly supported[50] and was relied on in the decisions of the House of Lords developing the law by recognising the defence of change of position, the liability to make restitution of *ultra vires* receipts of tax, and of money paid in pursuance of an ineffective contract.[51]

30–012   The principle has also been recognised by statute. The Torts (Interference with Goods) Act 1977, s.7(4) imposes a liability to reimburse upon a person who, as a result of enforcement of a double liability in proceedings for wrongful interference with goods, is "unjustly enriched to any extent." Furthermore, the separation in the Insolvency Act 1986, s.382(4), of liabilities arising out of contract, tort, trust and bailment from those "arising out of an obligation to make restitution" may provide implicit support for the principle of unjust enrichment and the statutory power to refund overpayments of rates has been said to create "a statutory remedy of restitution . . . to prevent the unjust enrichment of the rating authority at the expense of the ratepayer."[52] Finally, statutory rights to recover overpaid tax are subject to the *defence* that repayment would unjustly enrich the claimant.[53]

30–013   In conclusion, it does not follow from the absence of a general cause of action in English law for unjust enrichment that the specific remedies provided are not justifiable by reference to the principle of unjust enrichment even if they were originally framed without primary reference to it[54] and the modern cases show an increasing tendency to cut through technicality to perceive and define the underlying principle.[55] The historical development of the subject has affected the way the principle manifests itself; thus English law has not recognised a general action for the recovery of money on the ground that it was not due, a *condictio indebiti*, but, as we shall see, has recognised specific grounds which a plaintiff seeking restitution must establish. English law has now joined United States jurisdictions,[56] Australian law,[57] Canadian law,[58] Scots law,[59] French law[60] and

---

[49] *Ante*, n. 42.
[50] *Ante*, § 30–009.
[51] *Lipkin Gorman v. Karpnale Ltd* [1991] 2 A.C. 548; *Woolwich Equitable B.S. v. I.R.C.* [1993] A.C. 70 and *Westdeutsche Landesbank Girozentrale v. Islington L.B.C.* [1996] A.C. 669 respectively.
[52] *R. v. Tower Hamlets L.B.C., ex p. Chetnik Developments Ltd* [1988] A.C. 858, 882. cf. *BP Exploration Co. (Libya) Ltd v. Hunt (No. 2)* [1981] 1 W.L.R. 232, 243 (CA got "no help from the use of words which are not in the statute"—*re* the Law Reform (Frustrated Contracts) Act 1943, s.1(3)).
[53] Value Added Tax Act 1994, s.80(3) as amended; Sched. 5 to Finance Act 1997. See also *post*, § 30–083.
[54] Dawson, *Unjust Enrichment* (1951), pp. 116–117.
[55] *Woolwich Equitable B.S. v. I.R.C.* [1993] A.C. 70, 166 (Lord Goff).
[56] *e.g. The American Law Institute's Restatement of the Law of Restitution, Quasi-Contracts and Constructive Trusts*, Article 1 (and comment (c) thereon); J. P. Dawson, *Unjust Enrichment* (1951); Palmer, *The Law of Restitution* (1978) (four vols.). For earlier commentary, see *Woodward on Quasi-Contracts* (1913); *Keener on Quasi-Contracts* (1926).
[57] *Pavey and Matthews Pty. Ltd v. Paul* (1987) 69 A.L.R. 57.
[58] *Deglman v. Guaranty Trust Co. of Canada* [1954] S.C.R. 725; *Pettkuss v. Becker* [1980] 2 S.C.R. 834; *Rawluk v. Rawluk* [1990] 1 S.C.R. 70.
[59] *Morgan Guaranty Trust Co. of N.Y. v. Lothian R.C.* (1995) S.C. 151, 229; *Shilliday v. Smith* [1998] S.L.T. 976, 978.
[60] Gutteridge and David (1934) 5 Camb.L.J. 204.

Roman-Dutch law[61] in accepting the principle of unjust enrichment. It is now widely regarded as the correct theoretical principle of restitution since the alternative theory, now to be considered, is obviously inadequate. Where one is concerned with a restitutionary remedy, the appropriate questions are therefore, "first, whether the defendant would be enriched at the claimant's expense; secondly, whether such enrichment would be unjust and thirdly, whether there are nevertheless reasons of policy for denying a remedy."[62] Notwithstanding the acceptance of unjust enrichment as the basis of most restitutionary obligations, as is submitted elsewhere in this chapter,[63] in a number of situations it is preferable to see the basis of liability as the protection of the claimant's reasonable reliance.

The implied contract theory. This theory arises from the fact that for several **30–014** centuries the remedy for quasi-contractual claims at common law was the action of *indebitatus assumpsit*, a contractual remedy. It has been shown in the historical introduction that the allegation of a "promise" in the use of *indebitatus assumpsit* for money had and received to the use of the plaintiff was treated as fictitious by the courts. However, after the abolition of the forms of action some courts considered that the contractual framework of these actions was not merely a matter of procedure, but one of substantive law. The most important statement of this view is in *Sinclair v. Brougham*[64] where Lord Sumner said: "All these causes of action are common species of the genus 'assumpsit.' All now rest, and long have rested, upon a notional or imputed promise to pay."

In *Sinclair v. Brougham* a building society carried on an *ultra vires* banking **30–015** business. On the winding up of the society, the House of Lords held that the depositors could not sue in a common law action for money had and received, since the law could not imply a promise to repay where an actual promise would have been *ultra vires* the society. "The law cannot *de jure* impute promises to repay, whether for money had and received or otherwise, which, if made *de facto*, it would inexorably avoid."[65] But it is clear from the history of quasi-contract that the "notional or imputed promise" mentioned by Lord Sumner was "a legal fiction, intrinsically bound up with the defunct action of assumpsit and expressly abolished by section 49 of the Common Law Procedure Act 1852."[66] Lord Wright has said that Lord Sumner's observation "was not necessary for the decision of the case." He did not understand why or how Lord Sumner's statement "closed the door to any theory of unjust enrichment in English law."

---

[61] *e.g. Hussenabai Hassanally v. Mohamed Muheeth Mohamed Cassim* [1960] A.C. 592; *Willis Faber Enthoven Ltd v. Receiver of Revenue*, 1992 (4) S.A. 202.

[62] *Banque Financière de la Cité v. Parc (Battersea) Ltd* [1998] 2 W.L.R. 475, 485 *per* Lord Hoffmann (subrogation). *Quaere* whether this reformulation will have a similar effect to the recognition of a general principle against unjust enrichment in Canada in *Rathwell v. Rathwell* [1978] 2 S.C.R. 436, 455.

[63] *Ante*, § 30–007, *post*, §§ 30–018, 30–022, 30–026.

[64] [1914] A.C. 398, 452.

[65] *ibid.* at 452 (see also at 415, 417). The House, however, was able to extend the equitable remedy of a tracing order to the case, and to give "a sort of rough justice" by dividing the assets *pari passu* between the shareholders and the depositors in proportion to the sums which they had severally contributed. On this aspect of the case, see *post*, § 30–104, and see generally *ante*, § 9–025.

[66] Munkman *op. cit.* p. 8.

"It would indeed be a *reductio ad absurdum* of the doctrine of precedents. In fact, the common law still employs the action for money had and received as a practical and useful, if not complete or ideally perfect, instrument to prevent unjust enrichment, aided by the various methods of technical equity which are also available, as they were found to be in *Sinclair v. Brougham*."[67]

The "implied contract" theory has found other judicial and academic support since *Sinclair v. Brougham*,[68] but has been severely criticised as artificial by many judges and writers.[69] Such a theory does not elucidate the vital question, which is: "In what circumstances will the law impose restitutionary liability?" Furthermore, not all cases in which an action for money had and received or a *quantum meruit* has succeeded are consistent with the theory.[70] It was "unequivocally and finally" rejected by the House of Lords in *Westdeutsche Landsbank Girozentrale v. Islington L.B.C.*[71]

(d) *The Content of the Principle of Unjust Enrichment*

30–016   The principle of unjust enrichment requires first, that the defendant has been "enriched" by the receipt of a "benefit," secondly, that this enrichment is "at the expense of the claimant," and thirdly that the retention of the enrichment be "unjust." The development of the law of restitution in England has meant that the principle of unjust enrichment has not manifested itself in a general action for the recovery of money paid and other benefits conferred on the ground that they were not due but as a number of specific substantive grounds upon which restitution may be ordered. In *Moses v. Macferlen* Lord Mansfield stated that the action for money had and received "lies for money paid by mistake; or upon a consideration which happens to fail; or for money got through imposition (express or implied); or extortion; or an undue advantage taken of the claimant's situation, contrary to the laws made for the protection of persons under those circumstances."[72] Where a sum has been paid which is not due but the payer cannot establish a ground for recovery it is not recoverable.[73] But the non-recognition of the principle of unjust enrichment in the past has meant that the concepts of "benefit," "at the expense of the claimant" and "unjustness" of retention have tended to develop in a fragmented way within the substantive categories in which relief has been given[74] and sometimes, as in the former rules that only mistakes as to liability gave rise to restitution and that in general a payment under a mistake of law was not recoverable, in an unsatisfactory way.

30–017   Where a ground upon restitution may be granted is established, relief will nevertheless not be granted if it would not be "unjust" to allow the defendant to

---

[67] *Fibrosa Spolka Akcyjna v. Fairbairn Lawson Combe Barbour Ltd* [1943] A.C. 32, 64.

[68] In addition to the authorities cited in nn. 42 and 48, *ante*, § 30–005, see *Transvaal and Delagoa Bay Investment Co. Ltd v. Atkinson* [1944] 1 All E.R. 579.

[69] See the authorities cited in nn. 35–39, *ante*.

[70] *Craven Ellis v. Cannons Ltd* [1936] 2 K.B. 403; *Brook's Wharf and Bull Wharf Ltd v. Goodman Bros.* [1937] 1 K.B. 534; *ante*, § 30–005. See also *Re Rhodes* (1890) 44 Ch.D. 94, 105. But *cf. Guinness plc v. Saunders* [1990] 2 A.C. 663 (Lord Templeman) for apparent acceptance of implied contract as the basis of *quantum meruit* claims.

[71] [1996] A.C. 669, 710. See also at 718, 720, 738. See also *Kleinwort Benson Ltd v. Glasgow C.C.* [1997] 3 W.L.R. 923.

[72] (1760) 2 Burr, 1005, 1007.

[73] *Woolwich Equitable B.S. v. I.R.C.* [1993] A.C. 70, 165, 172 (Lord Goff).

[74] For detailed discussion see the appropriate sections of this chapter, *post*.

retain that received at the claimant's expense.[75] Restitution is denied where the defendant cannot be restored to his original position,[76] is a bona fide purchaser,[77] or where public policy precludes restitution,[78] or the plaintiff is estopped.[79] It is also denied where the benefit was conferred:

(a) as a valid gift;

(b) pursuant to a valid common law, equitable or statutory obligation owed by the claimant to the defendant[80];

(c) by the claimant while performing an obligation owed to a third party[81];

(d) by the claimant acting voluntarily in his own self-interest[82];

(e) in submission to an honest claim, under process of law or a compromise of a disputed claim[83] and;

(f) by the claimant acting "voluntarily" or "officiously."[84]

In practice the most important of these are the requirements that the claimant is not a "volunteer," *i.e.* that he has not acted officiously,[85] and that the defendant can be restored to his original position. There have been difficulties in the development of restitutionary claims in respect of non-monetary benefits.[86] These are, in part, due to the fact that "by their very nature services cannot be restored: nor in many cases can goods be restored, for example where they have been consumed or transferred to another."[87] Furthermore, even where the benefit takes the form of increasing the value of the defendant's property, the increase can only be realised by forcing a sale.[88]

---

[75] See Goff and Jones *op. cit.* pp. 46–47.

[76] This includes change of position by the defendant (*post*, § 30–114) and inability to make *restitution in integrum* of any benefit received by the plaintiff seeking restitution (*ante*, §§ 5–082, 26–112).

[77] On the relationship between bona fide purchase and change of position, see *Lipkin Gorman v. Karpnale Ltd* [1991] 2 A.C. 548; Birks [1991] L.M.C.L.Q. 473; Millett (1991) 107 L.Q.R. 71, 82; Goff and Jones *op. cit.* p. 820.

[78] See *ante*, § 16–150; *post*, §§ 30–038, 30–062, 30–055. See also *R. Leslie Ltd v. Sheill* [1914] 3 K.B. 607; *Boissevain v. Weil* [1950] A.C. 327.

[79] See *ante*, §§ 3–077 *et seq.*; *post*, § 30–111.

[80] *Brittain v. Rossiter* (1879) 11 Q.B.D. 123, 127; *Gilbert & Partners v. Knight* [1968] 2 All E.R. 248, 250; *Pan Ocean Shipping Ltd v. Creditcorp Ltd* [1994] 1 W.L.R. 161, 164, 165; Burrows [1994] Rest. L. Rev. 52; *Portman B.S. v. Hayman Taylor Neck* (1998) 76 P. & C.R. D16. *cf.* where the transaction is void *post*, §§ 30–062, 30–182.

[81] *Brown & Davies Ltd v. Galbraith* [1972] 1 W.L.R. 997; *Pan Ocean Shipping Ltd v. Creditcorp Ltd, ibid* at 166, 170–171; *Esso Petroleum v. Hall Russell & Co.* [1989] A.C. 643.

[82] *Falke v. Scottish Imperial Insurance Co.* (1886) 34 Ch.D. 234; *Ruabon Steamship Co. v. The London Assurance* [1990] A.C. 6, 10.

[83] See *ante*, §§ 3–049, 7–020; *post*, §§ 30–036, 30–038, 30–068, 30–079.

[84] Goff and Jones *op. cit.* pp. 63–65. *cf. G.N.Ry. v. Swaffield* (1874) L.R. 9 Ex. 132; *Matheson v. Smiley* [1932] 2 D.L.R. 787.

[85] See also *Owen v. Tate* [1976] Q.B. 402; *post*, §§ 30–135—30–138.

[86] Birks *op. cit.* pp. 109–128; Jones (1977) 93 L.Q.R. 273.

[87] *B.P. Exploration Co. (Libya) Ltd v. Hunt (No. 2)* [1979] 1 W.L.R. 783, 799, affirmed by the House of Lords [1983] 2 A.C. 352.

[88] In *Greenwood v. Bennett* [1973] 1 Q.B. 195 (*post*, § 30–148) a sale had, in fact, taken place. See also Goff and Jones *op. cit.* pp. 246–251. *Sed quaere* whether their reasons for favouring forced sales of chattels apply to cases where the inventor was not mistaken or acting under necessity.

30–018   **The nature of the enrichment.**[89] This may take the form of a direct addition to the recipient's wealth, such as by the receipt of money,[90] or an indirect one, for instance where an inevitable expense has been saved. The most common example of the second type of benefit is the discharge of an obligation of the defendant, whether by paying his creditor[91] or abating a nuisance[92] or performing some other service[93] for which he is primarily responsible.

30–019   **Services.** In the case of the rendering of services as opposed to the payment of money, "the identity and value of the resulting benefit to the recipient may be debatable."[94] Services may take many forms and while some result in an indirect accretion to the defendant's wealth, for instance by improving his property, other "pure" services do not. The fact that services cannot be restored and the influence of the implied contract theory has meant that they were often not regarded as beneficial so as to give rise to a *quantum meruit* unless the defendant had requested the services or, knowing that they were to be paid for, had freely accepted or acquiesced in them.[95] Many but not all such cases are capable of analysis as a genuine implied contract.[96] These cases do not depend upon the service adding to the defendant's wealth, the service *per se* is treated as a benefit.[97] Thus, recompense has been given in respect of plans prepared in anticipation of the conclusion of a contract by a developer but rendered useless when the landowner decided not to proceed[98] and in respect of work done by a person on his own property at the request of prospective tenants when negotiations for a lease broke down.[99] It is arguable that "if in fact the performance of services has conferred no benefit on the person requesting them, it is pure fiction to base restitution on a benefit conferred"[1] and it is more realistic to see the basis of liability as the protection of the plaintiff's reasonable reliance.[2] Such recompense will not be given if the dealing between the parties shows that the risk is to be borne by the party rendering the services.[3]

---

[89] Goff and Jones *op. cit.* pp. 16–27; Birks *op. cit.* pp. 114–132.

[90] *Kelly v. Solari* (1841) 9 M. & W. 54 (*post,* § 30–026); *Brook's Wharf and Bull Wharf Ltd v. Goodman Bros.* [1937] 1 K.B. 534 (*post,* § 30–128).

[91] *Exall v. Partridge* (1799) 8 T.R. 208 (*post,* § 30–129).

[92] *Gebhardt v. Saunders* [1892] 2 Q.B. 452; (*post,* § 30–133).

[93] *Post,* §§ 30–150 *et seq.,* 30–160.

[94] *B.P. Exploration Co. (Libya) Ltd v. Hunt (No. 2), supra,* at 799.

[95] *Ellis v. Hamlen* (1810) 3 Taunt 52, 53; *Nemes v. Ata Chaglayan,* CA, October 11, 1982; *Marston Construction Co. Ltd v. Kigass Ltd* [1989] 46 B.L.R. 109. *cf. Bookmakers Afternoon Greyhound Services Ltd v. Wilfred Gilbert Staffordshire Ltd* [1994] F.S.R. 723, 742–744.

[96] *Post,* §§ 30–161, 30–167 *et seq.*

[97] *William Lacey (Hounslow) Ltd v. Davis* [1957] 1 W.L.R. 932; *Brewer Street Investments Ltd v. Barclay Woollen Co.* [1954] 1 Q.B. 428, 433–434, 438; *British Steel Corp. v. Cleveland Bridge and Engineering Co. Ltd* [1984] 1 All E.R. 504. *cf. Sumpter v. Hedges* [1898] 1 Q.B. 673; *Wiluszynski v. Tower Hamlets L.B.C.* [1989] I.C.R. 493. See also *Independent Grocers Co-operative Ltd v. Noble Lowndes Superannuation Consultants Ltd* [1993] 60 S.A.S.R. 525. *Post,* §§ 30–167, 30–185.

[98] *William Lacey (Hounslow) Ltd v. Davis* [1957] 1 W.L.R. 932; *Sabemo v. N. Sydney M.C.* [1977] 2 N.S.W.L.R. 880; *Marston Construction Co. Ltd v. Kigass Ltd, supra.*

[99] *Brewer St. Investments Ltd v. Barclays Woollen Co. Ltd* [1954] 1 Q.B. 428.

[1] *Coleman Engineering v. North American Aviation* 420 P2d 713, 729 (1967) (Traynor C.J.). See also Beatson *op. cit.* pp. 21–44; Goff & Jones *op. cit.* pp. 20–21, 667–668; Jones (1980) 18 U.W.Ont.L.R. 447. *cf.* Birks *op. cit.* pp. 44–46, 271, 275.

[2] *Ante,* § 30–007, n. 33.

[3] *Regalian Properties Plc. v. London Dockland Development Corp.* [1995] 1 W.L.R. 212. See also *Bookmakers Afternoon Greyhound Services Ltd v. Wilfred Gilbert Staffordshire Ltd* [1994] F.S.R. 723.

Service resulting in incontrovertible benefit. There is, however, also author- ity that treats a service as beneficial where it results in an "incontrovertible benefit" to the defendant.[4] With the possible exception of necessitous inter- vention to preserve life or health,[5] only services that result in an accretion to the defendant's wealth can constitute an incontrovertible benefit. Goff and Jones state that incontrovertible benefit is established "if a reasonable person would conclude that he has been saved an expense which he otherwise would neces- sarily have incurred or where he has made, in consequence of the claimant's acts, a realisable financial gain."[6]

Receipt of goods. The receipt of goods may, of course, constitute a benefit and although where title has not passed to the recipient the proper claim will be in tort, for wrongful interference to goods,[7] where title has passed it would seem that the principles governing services will apply by analogy and in an appropriate case result in the court awarding a *quantum valebat*.[8]

Enrichment at the claimant's expense.[9] In many cases the increase in the defendant's wealth is the direct result of and matched by a corresponding diminution in the claimant's wealth.[10] However, with the possible exception of waiver of tort,[11] this correspondence between gain and loss does not appear to be necessary and a person may be entitled to relief even where he has suffered no such diminution in his wealth. Thus, dishonest agents have been required to pay over bribes received to their principals[12] and money paid under duress has been recovered even where the payer has been able to pass on the loss, in the form of increased charges, to his customers.[13] The rationale behind such cases may appear to be punitive, *i.e.* to deter certain conduct, and not to fit comfortably within the principle as formulated above.[14] However, although there is no loss to the claimant in the sense of a diminution in his wealth, in some of these cases (typified by cases where the defendant has used the claimant's property to make a gain) he will have lost the opportunity to charge the defendant for permission

---

[4] *Craven-Ellis v. Canons Ltd* [1936] 2 K.B. 403 (*post*, § 30–182); *Greenwood v. Bennett* [1973] 1 Q.B. 195, 202, *post*, § 30–148 (Lord Denning); *Procter & Gamble Corp. v. Peter Cremer GmbH & Co.* [1988] 3 All E.R. 843, 855–856 (Hirst J.); *Re Berkeley Applegate Ltd* [1989] Ch. 32, 50–51.

[5] *Matheson v. Smiley* [1932] 2 D.L.R. 787; *G.N.Ry. v. Swaffield* (1874) L.R. 9 Ex. 132; *post*, §§ 30–161 *et seq.*

[6] *op. cit.* pp. 23, 246–251. cf. Birks *op. cit.* pp. 121–124 (only realised benefits suffice) and see Burrows *op. cit.* pp. 10–11.

[7] Torts (Interference with Goods) Act 1977. But see *post*, §§ 30–084 *et seq.* (waiver of tort).

[8] *Post*, §§ 30–178—30–187. See also Goff and Jones *op. cit.* pp. 26–27.

[9] *Halifax B.S. v. Thomas* [1996] Ch. 217, 227. Goff and Jones *op. cit.* pp. 37–41. cf. Birks *op. cit.* pp. 22–26, Chap. 10 where two senses of "at the expense of," *viz.* "by subtraction from the plaintiff" and "by wrongdoing" are distinguished. See also Beatson *op. cit.* pp. 230–234.

[10] This is so in all cases of money paid; *e.g. Kelly v. Solari* (1841) 9 M. & W. 54 (*post*, § 30–026); *Brook's Wharf and Bull Wharf Ltd* [1937] 1 K.B. 534 (*post*, § 30–128).

[11] *Post*, § 30–088.

[12] *Lister v. Stubbs* (1890) 45 Ch.D. 1; *Reading v. Att.-Gen.* [1951] A.C. 507; *Att.Gen. (Hong Kong) v. Reid* [1994] 1 A.C. 324; *post*, § 30–172, Vol. II, § 32–117. See *Mahesan v. Malaysia Government Officer's Co-operative Housing Society Ltd* [1979] A.C. 374.

[13] *Mason v. New South Wales* (1959) 102 C.L.R. 108, 146.

[14] *Ante*, § 30–009. See also *Chase Manhattan Bank N.A. v. Israel-British Bank (London) Ltd* [1981] Ch. 105, 125.

to carry on the activity which has led to the defendant's enrichment. In these cases the enrichment can be said to be "at the claimant's expense."[15]

(e) *Classification*

30–023   **Classification.** There is no generally accepted method of classifying the instances of restitution. Writers[16] have suggested various methods of classification, in lieu of the old method of classifying by the form of action used, *e.g.* the action for money had and received, or the action for money paid. But in the following pages a pragmatic classification will be used, with some attempt to follow a logical pattern. First, under the heading of "restitution," cases will be examined where the defendant is obliged to restore or pay for a benefit received from the claimant; secondly, under the heading of "reimbursement," cases where the defendant is obliged to repay the claimant in respect of money paid by the plaintiff to a third person; thirdly, cases of "liability to account to the claimant" for money received from a third party; fourthly, cases of "recompense," such as *quantum meruit* claims for services rendered; fifthly, accounts stated.

(f) *Privity*

30–024   **The suggested need for "privity" between the parties.** One consequence of the implied contract theory was the view that the money sought to be recovered by an action for money had and received should have been received by the defendant under such circumstances as to create a privity between him and the claimant. What this "privity" could mean it is difficult to say. It appears that an analogy was sought from the ordinary rules of contract. But the "implied contract" theory is based upon historical fictions which are no longer relevant, and has been rejected. Accordingly, this notion of "privity" is unnecessary in restitution. As Lord Wright said in one case[17]:

> "The obligation [to repay] is imposed by the court simply under the circumstances of the case and on what the court decides is just and reasonable having regard to the relationship of the parties. It is a debt or obligation constituted by the act of the law, apart from any consent or intention of the parties or privity of contract."

The relationship between the parties which in ordinary contract is called "privity of contract" arises by consent, express or implied, of the parties, whereas in

---

[15] *e.g. Strand Electric and Engineering Co. Ltd v. Brisford Entertainments Ltd* [1952] 2 Q.B. 246; *Penarth Dock Engineering Co. v. Pounds* [1963] 1 Lloyd's Rep. 359; *Seager v. Copydex Ltd (No. 2)* [1969] 1 W.L.R. 809; 2 All E.R. 718. The first two were actions in tort in which relief in respect of such enrichment was described as restitutionary. See also *post*, §§ 30–088—30–089. On actions in contract for relief in respect of such enrichment, see *ante*, § 30–018; Beatson *op. cit.* pp. 16–18; Goff and Jones *op. cit.* pp. 518–523; *Surrey C.C. v. Bredero Homes Ltd* [1993] 1 W.L.R. 1361 *cf. Attorney-General v. Blake* [1998] 2 W.L.R. 805; *Jaggard v. Sawyer* [1995] 1 W.L.R. 269. Cases of bribery of agents might be susceptible to this explanation because the principal is presumed to have foregone the opportunity of a higher sale price or a lower purchase price (*Hovenden v. Millhoff* (1900) 83 L.T. 41, 43; *Industries & General Mortgage Co. v. Lewis* [1949] 2 All E.R. 573) but cases of duress are not.
[16] Goff and Jones *op. cit.* pp. 73–75; Winfield, *Province of the Law of Tort* (1931), pp. 148–149 (also *Quasi-Contracts* (1952), pp. 26–27); Clarence Smith (1956) 19 M.L.R. 255; Munkman *op. cit.* pp. 19–20 (on whose classification that adopted *post* is largely based); Birks *op. cit.* pp. 99–108; Burrows *op. cit.* p. 56.
[17] *Brook's Wharf and Bull Wharf Ltd v. Goodman Brothers* [1937] 1 K.B. 534, 545.

restitution (as in the law of torts) the relationship between the parties arises on the facts of the case according to the application of a particular legal rule. For instance, where the claimant, acting under a mistake, pays money to the defendant,[18] the relationship between the parties arises from the fact of payment by the plaintiff, and the fact of its receipt by the defendant.[19]

Winfield concluded[20] that most of the cases cited in support of the privity concept turn upon agency. They in fact lay down the rule of the law of agency that where the principal entrusts his agent with money to be paid to a third party, the latter cannot recover the money from the agent unless, on the facts, the agent has become also the agent of the third party.[21] Thus any mention of the absence of "privity" was unnecessary in these cases, most of which date from a period before the modern development of restitution.[22] The reference to "privity" may mean that a restitutionary remedy will not be granted to a stranger to a contract where that would directly contravene the doctrine of privity of contract or that a benefit to the defendant is, as a general rule, not regarded as "at the claimant's expense" where conferred by a third party (and even this is not universally true).[23] In all other cases, however, the need for "privity" in this context should now be taken to mean simply that on the facts the claimant and defendant must have come into the factual relationship recognised by the appropriate rule of restitution, so that a direct obligation lies upon the defendant to pay money or transfer property to the claimant.[24]

2. RESTITUTION

Under this heading we shall examine cases where the defendant is obliged to restore or pay for a benefit received from the claimant.   **30–025**

(a) *Payment Under a Mistake*[25]

Mistake of fact: "supposed liability" rule. It has long been clear that money   **30–026**
paid under a mistake of the payer as to a material fact is, in certain circumstances,

---

[18] See *post*, § 30–026.

[19] *Colonial Bank v. Exchange Bank of Yarmouth* (1885) 11 App.Cas. 84, 90 ("a payment direct from the plaintiffs to the defendants" enabled the Privy Council to hold that there was "the most direct privity between the two parties").

[20] *Quasi-Contracts* (1952), pp. 14–17 (also his *Province of the Law of Tort* (1931), pp. 134–138). See also Jackson, *History of Quasi-Contract* (1936) *passim*, especially pp. 121–122.

[21] *e.g. Stephens v. Badcock* (1832) 3 B. & Ad. 354; *Howell v. Batt* (1833) 2 Nev. & M. (K.B.) 381; *Cobb v. Beake* (1845) 6 Q.B. 930 (see also the other cases cited by Winfield, *op. cit.* p. 15). The agent may, on the facts, have appropriated the money to the third party: *Williams v. Everett* (1811) 14 East. 582; *Moore v. Bushell* (1827) 27 L.J.Ex. 3 (on this principle, see *post*, §§ 30–167, 30–168).

[22] *e.g Jones v. Carter* (1845) 8 Q.B. 134 (a decision before the Gaming Act 1845 in which a stakeholder was held not liable to return a stake).

[23] See *post*, §§ 30–167, 30–168.

[24] The New Zealand Court of Appeal has denied the need for any special "privity": *Thomas v. Houston Corbett & Co.* [1969] N.Z.L.R. 151.

[25] Although most of the cases concern money payments, there may be restitution of other benefits conferred as the result of a mistake *cf.* a transfer of property made under a mistake: *Gibbon v. Mitchell* [1990] 1 W.L.R. 1304; *Lady Hood of Avalon v. Mackinnon* [1909] 1 Ch. 476; *Re Butlin's S.T.* [1976] 1 Ch. 251; services rendered under a mistake, see *post*, § 30–185; improvements to land and chattels made as a result of a mistake, see *post*, §§ 30–108, 30–146; and recovery of benefits transferred under a contract void for mistake, see *post*, § 30–062.

recoverable. Mistake in this context means lack of knowledge[26] but it is notoriously difficult to make an authoritative statement of the principles upon which recovery is based.[27] Broadly speaking, there are two approaches; one based on the nature of the mistake permitting recovery only for certain types of mistake, the other, which now prevails, based on the effect of the mistake, prima facie permitting recovery whenever the mistake causes the payment. Much of the difficulty seems to be due to the application of dicta, made in the context of particular facts, to quite different facts, as if they established principles of general application.[28] Thus, while the decision of the Court of Exchequer in *Kelly v. Solari*[29] can be seen as the basis of the modern law, the statement of Parke B. can lead to distortion if accepted as a definition of the boundaries of recovery. He said that,

> "where money is paid to another under the influence of a mistake, that is upon the supposition that a specific fact is true, which would entitle the other to the money, but which fact is untrue, and the money would not have been paid if it had been known to the payer that the fact was untrue, an action will lie to recover it back."[30]

In that case a payment was made to the executrix of the assured by an insurance company which had forgotten that the policy had lapsed owing to the non-payment of the premium. Recovery was allowed and, in the context, the reference to "entitlement" is perfectly acceptable. However, together with a dictum of Bramwell B. in *Aiken v. Short*, at one time it was taken to restrict recovery to cases in which the mistake was as to "a fact which, if true, would make the person liable to pay the money; not where, if true, it would merely make it desirable that he should pay the money."[31]

30–027   **Unsatisfactoriness of "supposed liability" rule.** In fact the "supposed liability" rule itself does not explain all the decisions and can have no application to cases of mistaken gifts of money. The true position would appear to be that "liability" mistakes are merely the commonest instance of what suffices to ground recovery, especially where the payment is associated with the performance of contractual obligations.[32] Thus, in *Kerrison v. Glynn Mills, Currie & Co.*[33] the House of Lords permitted recovery of money mistakenly paid in anticipation of a

---

[26] *Kleinwort Benson Ltd v. Lincoln C.C.* [1998] 3 W.L.R. 1095, 1146–1148 (Lord Hope). See also at 1140 (Lord Hoffmann). See also *David Securities Pty Ltd v. Commonwealth Bank of Australia* (1991–1992) 175 C.L.R. 353, 374 (Mason C.J.); *post*, § 30–030.

[27] *Weld-Blundell v. Synott* [1940] 2 K.B. 107, 112; *Commercial Bank of Australia v. Younis* [1979] 1 N.S.W.L.R. 444, 447.

[28] *Commercial Bank of Australia v. Younis, supra; Morgan v. Ashcroft* [1938] 1 K.B. 49, 72.

[29] (1841) 9 M. & W. 54; 11 L.J.Ex. 10. See also *Milnes v. Duncan* (1827) 6 B. & C. 671.

[30] *ibid.* at 58. The report in the *Law Journal* is materially different in omitting any reference to entitlement; 11 L.J.Ex. 10, 13.

[31] (1856) 1 H. & N. 210, 215; 25 L.J.Ex. 321; *post*, § 30–035; *Deutsche Bank v. Beriro & Co. Ltd* (1895) 1 Com.Cas. 255, 259; *Re Bodega Co. Ltd* [1904] 1 Ch. 276, 286; *Steam Saw Mills Co. Ltd v. Baring Bros. & Co. Ltd* [1922] 1 Ch. 244, 250. See also the formulation of the rule in *National Westminster Bank Ltd v. Barclays Bank International Ltd* [1975] Q.B. 654, 675. The most restrictive interpretation of these dicta required the mistake to be "between" payer and payee (*Chambers v. Miller* (1862) 13 C.B.(N.S.) 125, 133); but this has since been rejected (*Colonial Bank v. Exchange Bank of Yarmouth, Nova Scotia* (1885) 11 App.Cas. 84; *Imperial Bank of Canada v. Bank of Hamilton* [1903] A.C. 49; *Barclays Bank Ltd v. W.J. Simms, Son & Cooke (Southern) Ltd* [1980] Q.B. 677).

[32] *Morgan v. Ashcroft, supra*, at 64, 71.

[33] (1911) 81 L.J.K.B. 465.

future liability. Again, in *Sybron Corporation v. Rochem Ltd*[34] a payment of accrued benefits under a pension scheme which provided that in cases of early retirement such benefits were to be dealt with at the discretion of the trustees was made in ignorance of the payee's breach of duty to disclose the fraud of his subordinates with whom he acted. The accrued benefits had been paid under a mistake of fact induced by the payee's breach of duty and the Court of Appeal allowed the payer to recover. Moreover, an agent who pays money to a third party mistakenly believing that he has his principal's authority to make the payment may recover it even where the principal is in fact liable to the third-party payee.[35]

Rejection of "supposed liability" rule. Bramwell B.'s dictum in *Aiken v.*   **30–028** *Short* has been rejected as an exhaustive statement of the law on two occasions by the Court of Appeal. In *Morgan v. Ashcroft* Greene M.R. sought to confine it to "cases where the only mistake is as to the nature of the transaction" which should not, for instance, prevent recovery where a payment is made under a mistake as to the identity of the payee.[36] Scott L.J. went further and was not prepared to accept it as authoritative.[37] Secondly, in *Larner v. L.C.C.*[38] payments made by a local authority in the mistaken belief that it was under a moral obligation to pay were recovered. The authority had voluntarily promised "until further order" to pay all their employees on war service the difference between their service pay and civilian pay. Larner was overpaid because he failed to inform the authority of increases in his service pay but defended the action by alleging that the payments were voluntary and not made in discharge of any legal liability. The Court of Appeal rejected this, saying that, although under no legal obligation to pay, the authority, "for good reasons of national policy, made a promise to the men which they were in honour bound to fulfil. The payments . . . were not mere gratuities. They were made as a matter of duty."[39] These decisions show that it is not necessary for the mistake to induce belief in a legal liability to pay.[40] Although it may be possible to accommodate some of them within Bramwell B.'s dictum by adopting a very broad concept of liability, in such a diluted form it is inadequate as a general principle and attempts have been made to formulate an alternative test.

Personal and proprietary remedies. The normal remedy for the recovery of   **30–029** money paid under mistake is the action for money had and received, a personal remedy. However, it appears that the payer may also have a proprietary tracing remedy. Although a trust could not arise on the mere receipt of money paid under

---

[34] [1984] Ch. 112. *cf. Horcal Ltd v. Gatland* [1984] I.R.L.R. 288 (no breach of duty at relevant date).

[35] *Colonial Bank v. Exchange Bank of Yarmouth, Nova Scotia, supra*; *Anglo-Scottish Beet Sugar Corporation Ltd v. Spalding U.D.C.* [1937] 2 K.B. 607; *Turvey v. Dentons (1923) Ld.* [1953] 1 Q.B. 218. Money mistakenly paid by a third party to an agent for transmission to the principal is also recoverable before the agent has paid the money to the principal: *Buller v. Harrison* (1777) 2 Cowp. 565; *British American Continental Bank v. British Bank for Foreign Trade* [1926] 1 K.B. 328.

[36] [1938] 1 K.B. 49, 66.

[37] *ibid.* at 71.

[38] [1949] 2 K.B. 683. *cf. Lowe v. Wells Fargo & Co. Express*, 96 P. 74 (1908); *Lady Hood of Avalon v. Mackinnon* [1909] 1 Ch. 476; *Re Butlin's S.T.* [1976] 1 Ch. 251; *Barder v. Caluori* [1988] A.C. 20.

[39] *ibid.* at 688.

[40] See also *Rover International Sales Ltd v. Cannon Film Sales Ltd* (No. 3) [1989] 1 W.L.R. 912, 933 (Dillon L.J.); *Australian and New Zealand Banking Group Ltd v. Westpac Banking Corporation* (1988) 78 A.L.R. 157, 161 (High Court of Australia).

a mistake, where the recipient knows of the mistake at that time or learns of it afterwards and retains the money a constructive trust may arise, and, subject to statutory policy, tracing remedies (discussed *post*, § 30–097) may be available.[41] Tracing may also be important in this area when only a personal claim is being made.[42]

The principles discussed in this and the following paragraphs also apply when, instead of money being paid, credit has been given in an account as a result of a mistake as to a material fact.[43]

30–030   **Fundamental mistake.** In *Norwich Union Fire Insurance Society Ltd v. W.H. Price Ltd* Lord Wright stated that it is "essential that the mistake relied on should be of such a nature that it can properly be described as a mistake in respect of the underlying assumption of the contract or transaction or as being fundamental or basic."[44] The use of the term "fundamental" may be misleading because of the danger of confusing the basis upon which mistaken payments are recovered with that upon which a contract is avoided for mistake.[45] It has been said that recovery of mistaken payments can legitimately be granted on a generous basis where there is no contract that would need to be avoided because the policy favouring finality of contract does not apply if there is no transaction to rescind except the payment itself.[46] However, although the policy favouring finality of contract may be stronger than that favouring finality in other transactions, there is no *a priori* reason for this to be the case. In any event, whatever the reason for the difference, it would seem that the test of mistake in restitution is broader than that in contract.[47] Thus, mistakes as to creditworthiness and arithmetical mistakes have sufficed to allow the recovery of payments[48] and the mistake need not be shared by the payee, nor need he know of it.[49] Furthermore, the word "mistake" in this context not only signifies a positive belief in the existence of something which in reality does not exist, but it may also include forgetfulness and sheer ignorance

---

[41] *Westdeutsche Landesbank Girozentrale v. Islington L.B.C.* [1996] A.C. 669, 714–715 doubting *Chase Manhattan Bank N.A. v. Israel-British Bank (London) Ltd* [1981] Ch. 105, 19 but *cf. Banque Financière de la Cité v. Parc (Battersea) Ltd* [1998] 2 W.L.R. 475, HL; *Thavron v. Bank of Credit & Commerce International SA* [1985] 1 Lloyd's Rep. 259; *Re Goldcorp Exchange Ltd (in receivership)* [1995] 1 A.C. 74, 103 and *Friends' Provident Life Office v. Hillier Parker May & Rowden (a firm)* [1997] Q.B. 85, 105–106; *A.G.I.P. (Africa) Ltd v. Jackson* [1990] Ch. 265 (affd. [1991] Ch. 547); Goff and Jones *op. cit.* 200–202. *cf.* Stoljar *op. cit.* pp. 131–132, 138.

[42] *Bank Tejarat v. Hong Kong & Shanghai Banking Corp. (CI) Ltd* [1995] 1 Lloyd's Rep. 239, 245–246; *Boscawen v. Bajwa* [1996] 1 W.L.R. 328, 334.

[43] *Skyring v. Greenwood* (1825) 4 B. & C. 281; *Ward & Co. v. Wallis* [1900] 1 Q.B. 675, 679; *Branwhite v. Worcester Works Finance Ltd* [1969] 1 A.C. 552. Contrast *British and North European Bank Ltd v. Zalzstein* [1927] 2 K.B. 92.

[44] [1934] A.C. 455, 463. See also *Morgan v. Ashcroft* [1938] 1 K.B. 49, 64–67, 77; *Jones v. Waring & Gillow Ltd* [1926] A.C. 670, 696; *Bank of New South Wales v. Murphett* [1983] V.R. 489; *Australia and New Zealand Banking Group Ltd v. Westpac Banking Corporation* (1988) 78 A.L.R. 157, 160–161.

[45] See *ante*, §§ 5–016, 5–028; *post*, § 30–062.

[46] Goff and Jones *op. cit.* p. 179; Palmer *op. cit.* §§ 11.2, 14.1; Palmer, *Mistake and Unjust Enrichment* (1962), pp. 8, 25.

[47] *e.g. Midland Bank plc v. Brown Shipley & Co. Ltd* [1991] 2 All E.R. 690, 700–701.

[48] *Kerrison v. Glyn, Mills, Currie & Co.* (1911) 81 L.J.K.B. 465; *Weld-Blundell v. Synott* [1940] 2 K.B. 107. See also *Re Butlin's S.T.* [1976] 1 Ch. 251 (voluntary settlement).

[49] The mistake may be fraudulently induced by a third person; *R. E. Jones Ltd v. Waring & Gillow Ltd* [1926] A.C. 670.

of something relevant to the transaction.[50] It is possible that the requirement that the mistake be fundamental in fact involves no more than that, without the mistake, the payment would not have been made.[51] A payment made by an agent acting under a mistake of fact is recoverable although the principal himself, or another agent, knows the true facts.[52] If, however, the payment is due under a contract between the payer and the payee the payment cannot be recovered unless the contract itself is held void or is discharged.[53]

Can one recover wherever the mistake causes the payment? The recognition of the principle of unjust enrichment[54] puts into question tests based on the nature of the mistake.[55] In *Barclays Bank Ltd v. W.J. Simms, Son and Cooke (Southern) Ltd* it was stated that "if a person pays money to another under a mistake of fact which causes him to make the payment, he is *prima facie* entitled to recover it."[56] Support for this causation test, which has since been recognised by the High Court of Australia,[57] is found in speeches in several decisions of the House of Lords,[58] most recently in *Kleinwort Benson Ltd v. Lincoln C.C.* where it was stated that the payer "must prove that he would not have made the payment had he known of his mistake at the time when it was made" and that the function of mistake is to show that the benefit which has been received was an unintended benefit.[59]   **30–031**

Burden of proof. It appears that the burden of proof will not be heavy, at any   **30–032** rate if the mistake is serious, and it has been said that it is an "irresistible inference" that a payer who is mistaken about or ignorant of a material fact would not have made the payment had he known the true position.[60] Where, however, the payer would not have appreciated the materiality of a fact recovery

---

[50] See, *e.g. Lucas v. Worswick* (1833) 1 M. & R. 293; *Kelly v. Solari* (1841) M. & W. 54; *Lady Hood of Avalon v. Mackinnon* [1909] 1 Ch. 476; *Home and Colonial Insurance Co. Ltd v. London Guarantee Accident Co.* (1928) 45 T.L.R. 134; *Saronic Shipping Co. Ltd v. Huron Liberian Co. Ltd* [1979] 1 Lloyd's Rep. 341, affd. [1980] 2 Lloyd's Rep. 26; *David Securities Pty. Ltd v. Commonwealth Bank of Australia* (1991–92) 175 C.L.R. 353, 374; *Kleinwort Benson Ltd v. Lincoln C.C.* [1998] 3 W.L.R. 1095, 1147. On the position where the payer is negligent, see *post*, § 30–034.

[51] *David Securities Pty. Ltd v. Commonwealth Bank of Australia* (1992) 66 A.L.J.R. 768, 777; *Bank of New South Wales v. Murphett* [1983] 1 V.R. 489; *Australia and New Zealand Banking Group Ltd v. Westpac Banking Corporation* (1988) 78 A.L.R. 157, 161. *cf.* Birks *op. cit.* pp. 156–159. On the causation test, see *post*, § 30–031.

[52] *Anglo-Scottish Beet Sugar Corporation Ltd v. Spalding U.D.C.* [1937] 2 K.B. 607; *Turvey v. Dentons (1923) Ld.* [1953] 1 Q.B. 218. See also Birks *op. cit.* pp. 159–164.

[53] *Norwich Union v. W.H. Price Ltd* [1934] A.C. 455; *Barclays Bank Ltd v. W.J. Simms, Son & Cooke (Southern) Ltd* [1980] Q.B. 677, 695.

[54] *Ante*, § 30–008.

[55] *Air Canada v. British Columbia* [1989] S.C.R. 1161, 1200; *David Securities v. Commonwealth Bank of Australia* (1992) 66 A.L.J.R. 768, 776, 787; *Woolwich Equitable Building Society v. I.R.C.* [1993] 1 A.C. 70, 192 (Lord Jauncey); *Kleinwort Benson Ltd v. Lincoln C.C.* [1998] 3 W.L.R. 1095, 1113.

[56] [1980] Q.B. 677, 695. See also *Lloyds Bank plc v. Independent Insurance Co. Ltd* [1999] 2 W.L.R. 986. See further Vol. II, § 34–129.

[57] *David Securities Pty. Ltd v. Commonwealth Bank of Australia* (1992) 66 A.L.J.R. 768, 777.

[58] *Kleinwort, Sons and Co. v. Dunlop Rubber Co.* (1907) 97 L.T. 263, 264 (Lord Loreburn); *Kerrison v. Glyn, Mills, Currie and Co.* (1912) 81 L.J.K.B. 465, 470 (Lord Atkinson), 471 (Lord Shaw), 472 (Lord Mersey); *R. E. Jones Ltd v. Waring & Gillow Ltd* [1926] A.C. 670, 679–680 (Viscount Cave L.C.), 686 (Lord Shaw), 691, 692 (Lord Sumner).

[59] [1998] 3 W.L.R. 1095, 1145 (Lord Hope). See also at 1113 (Lord Goff).

[60] *Saronic Shipping Co. Ltd v. Huron Liberian Co. Ltd* [1979] 1 Lloyd's Rep. 341, 362–366 (affd. [1980] 2 Lloyd's Rep. 26).

may be refused on the ground that the payment was made in settlement of a claim.[61] The mistake must be the effective cause of the payment. The position is similar where the payer is aware that there is an issue of law which is relevant but, being in doubt as to what the law is, pays without waiting to resolve that doubt. A person who pays when in doubt takes the risk that he may be wrong.[62]

30–033   **Qualification to causation principle.** This broad principle of recovery is attractive where the payee still has the money for there is then a true superfluity in his assets. But unless the payee has a wide range of defences available, for instance to protect changes of position and security of transactions, it can operate unfairly. This was recognised in *Barclays Bank Ltd v. W.J. Simms, Son and Cooke (Southern) Ltd* by Robert Goff J. who qualified the principle of recovery by stating[63] that a claim may fail if

> "(a) the payer intends that the payee shall have the money at all events, whether the fact be true or false, or is deemed in law so to intend; or (b) the payment is made for good consideration,[64] in particular if the money is paid to discharge and does discharge, a debt owed to the payee (or a principal on whose behalf he is authorised to receive the payment) by the payer or by a third party by whom he is authorised to discharge the debt; or (c) the payee has changed his position in good faith, or is deemed in law to have done so."

The first two did not apply in that case and it was held there was no evidence of any change of position so the judge did not have to consider these questions.[65]

30–034   **Negligence: payer with means of knowledge.** The fact that the person paying money was in a position to discover all the relevant circumstances concerning the payment, may possibly, as a matter of evidence, support the inference that he had actual knowledge of those circumstances or that he has represented that reasonable care was used in making and checking the payment. There is, however, no conclusive rule of law that, because a person has the means of knowledge, he must be taken to have actual knowledge.[66] Thus, a person paying money under a mistake of fact is not prevented from recovering it merely because he was negligent in failing to discover the true facts[67]; Parke B., in *Kelly v. Solari*, said that recovery was possible " . . . however careless the party paying may have been in omitting to use due diligence to inquire into the fact."[68] So the action for money paid under a mistake of fact lies to recover money paid to the

---

[61] *Home and Colonial Insurance Co. Ltd v. London Guarantee Accident Co.* (1928) 45 T.L.R. 134. See *post*, § 30–120.

[62] *Kleinwort Benson Ltd v. Lincoln C.C.* [1998] 3 W.L.R. 1095, 1147 (Lord Hope). See *post*, § 30–121.

[63] [1980] Q.B. 677, 695. See also *Lloyds Bank plc v. Independent Insurance Co. Ltd* [1999] 2 W.L.R. 987, 998–999, 1000, 1002, 1005–1006.

[64] *cf. Commonwealth of Australia v. McCormack* (1982) 69 F.L.R. 9; *post*, § 30–035, n. 78.

[65] For the view that there was in fact a change of position, see Goode (1981) 97 L.Q.R. 254, 259.

[66] *Bell v. Gardiner* (1842) 4 M. & G. 11, 24; *Brownlie v. Campbell* (1880) 5 App.Cas. 925.

[67] *Weld-Blundell v. Synott* [1940] 2 K.B. 107; *Turvey v. Dentons (1923) Ld.* [1953] 1 Q.B. 218, 224; *Chase Manhattan Bank N.A. v. Israel-British Bank (London) Ltd* [1981] Ch. 105. *cf.* s.4(3) of the Cheques Act 1957 (see Vol. II, § 34–341).

[68] (1841) 9 M. & W. 54, 59. The position in Scotland differs since the mistake must be "excusable" and this will be difficult to show where there is negligence: *Taylor v. Wilsons Trustees* (1975) S.C. 146, 148, 156, 159.

defendant by the claimant under bona fide forgetfulness of facts which disentitle the defendant to receive it,[69] or money paid in ignorance of a fact which the claimant could have discovered at the time of payment if he had availed himself of his means of knowledge.[70] Of course, if the claimant pays the money intentionally, waiving any inquiry into the facts, *e.g.* a payment made in submission to an honest claim, it is irrecoverable.[71] Again, if the payer was aware that there was doubt as to whether the payment was due but paid without waiting to resolve that doubt, it will not be recoverable: "a state of doubt is different from that of mistake".[72] Moreover, if parties agree in good faith to compromise a disputed claim, the compromise is binding, even though the claim might in fact be without proper foundation.[73]

Payments made for good consideration. Money paid in discharge of a   **30-035** genuine legal obligation cannot be recovered merely because the payer was induced to fulfil his legal obligation by a mistake. As Lord Hope stated,

> "The payee cannot be said to have been unjustly enriched if he was entitled to receive the sum paid to him".[74]

For example,[75] where the claimant paid money due under a contract to agents of a foreign government in ignorance of the fact that a revolution had broken out which subsequently led to the downfall of the government it was not recoverable even though the claimant would not have made the payment had he known what was happening.[76] "[T]he money was paid, not under a mistake of fact as to the existence of an obligation; it was paid in pursuance of an obligation which in fact existed"[77] and was effective to discharge that obligation. Where, however, the claimant paid money under a contract to agents of the other party in ignorance of the fact that the contract had already been repudiated by the other party, it was held that the payment was recoverable because it did not discharge any legal obligation.[78] *Aiken v. Short*,[79] which was the basis for the view that only

---

[69] *Kelly v. Solari, supra* (approved by PC in *Imperial Bank of Canada v. Bank of Hamilton* [1903] A.C. 49, and by the House Lords in *R. E. Jones Ltd v. Waring & Gillow Ltd* [1926] A.C. 670). See also *Lucas v. Worswick* (1833) 1 Moo. & R. 293; *Commonwealth of Australia v. McCormack, supra*; *R.B.C. Dominion Securities Inc. v. Dawson* (1994) 111 D.L.R. (4th) 230.

[70] *Townsend v. Crowdy* (1860) 8 C.B.(N.S.) 477; *Durrant v. Ecclesiastical Commrs.* (1880) 6 Q.B.D. 234; *Stanley Bros. Ltd v. Nuneaton Corporation* (1913) 108 L.T. 986; *Avon C.C. v. Howlett* [1983] 1 W.L.R. 605, 617–619; *R.B.C. Dominion Securities Inc. v. Dawson* (1994) 111 D.L.R. (4th) 230.

[71] *Beevor v. Marler* (1898) 14 T.L.R. 289. See also *Kelly v. Solari, supra*, at 58, 59; *Woolwich Equitable B.S. v. I.R.C.* [1993] A.C. 70, 98, 165, 174, 200–201; *David Securities Pty. Ltd v. Commonwealth Bank of Australia* (1992) 66 A.L.J.R. 768, 774–776, 788; *Westdeutsche Landesbank Girozentrale v. Islington L.B.C.* (1993) 91 L.G.R 323 (aff'd [1996] A.C. 669).

[72] *Kleinwort Benson Ltd v. Lincoln C.C.* [1998] 3 W.L.R. 1095, 1147 (Lord Hope).

[73] See *ante*, §§ 3–049, 3–050; *Holmes v. Payne* [1930] 2 K.B. 301. *cf. Huddersfield Banking Co. Ltd v. Henry Lister & Son Ltd* [1895] 2 Ch. 273 (*ante*, § 5–090).

[74] *Kleinwort Benson Ltd v. Lincoln C.C.* [1998] 3 W.L.R. 1095, 1145–1146. See also *Lloyds Bank plc v. Independent Insurance Co. Ltd* [1999] 2 W.L.R. 986, 998–999, 1000, 1002, 1005–1006.

[75] *Kerrison v. Glyn, Mills, Currie & Co.* (1910) 15 Com.Cas. 241, 247–248 (revd. on the facts (1911) 81 L.J.K.B. 465; 17 Com.Cas. 41); *Steam Saw Mills Co. Ltd v. Baring Bros. & Co. Ltd* [1922] 1 Ch. 244, 251, 254; *British American Continental Bank v. British Bank for Foreign Trade* [1926] 1 K.B. 328, 336–337, 341, 344.

[76] *Steam Saw Mills Co. Ltd v. Baring Bros. & Co. Ltd* [1922] 1 Ch. 244.

[77] *ibid.* at 254.

[78] *British American Continental Bank v. British Bank for Foreign Trade, ante*; *Commonwealth of Australia v. McCormack, ante* (overpayment of sum due under lease paid having forgotten about previous part payment, recovered).

[79] (1856) 1 H. & N. 210; *ante*, § 30–026.

"liability" mistakes sufficed to permit repayment, is in fact an example of failure to recover a payment which was effective to discharge a debt. The claimant bankers paid a sum of money to the defendant in discharge of a debt owed by one Carter to the defendant which was secured by a mortgage on property which supposedly belonged to Carter. The claimants purchased the property from Carter subject to the defendant's interest on the understanding that they would pay off Carter's debt to the defendant. The claimants paid the defendant because they believed that they were getting rid of the encumbrance on their title and when it transpired that Carter did not in fact own the property, they claimed to recover the sum as having been paid under a mistake of fact. The Court of Exchequer held that the money was irrecoverable. The payment was authorised by Carter[80] and was effective to discharge the debt; the defendant therefore gave consideration for the payment. The operation of this rule is also illustrated by cases in which a bank mistakenly pays a third party who presents a cheque drawn upon it by a customer. The question whether the bank may recover the payment depends whether the payment was with or without mandate.[81] Thus, where the bank pays, having overlooked notice of the customer's death or his instructions counter-manding the cheque, the bank will be able to recover the payment.[82] Because it has paid without mandate the bank cannot debit the customer's account and the payment does not discharge the customer's debt to the payee. Where, however, the bank mistakenly thinks the customer has sufficient funds or overdraft facili-ties to meet the cheque the payment will be irrecoverable.[83] The payment is within the bank's mandate, the bank is therefore entitled to have recourse to the customer and the payment does discharge the customer's debt to the payee.

30–036   **Other bars to recovery.** Payments made in submission to a claim and under compromises are normally irrecoverable.[84] Furthermore, a mistaken payment which is prima facie recoverable might not be recovered on grounds of public policy where granting a remedy would indirectly frustrate the policy of a statutory or common law rule.[85] Thus, in *Morgan v. Ashcroft*[86] a bookmaker, by a clerical mistake, overpaid the defendant on a betting account, and sued to recover the excess. The Court of Appeal rejected his claim primarily because the court could not examine the state of the account between the parties since that would be to recognise wagering transactions as producing legal obligations (contrary to the Gaming Act 1845). The court also held that the money was not in any event recoverable as having been paid under a mistake of fact although the reasons for this are not entirely clear. Greene M.R. stated that "a person who intends to make a voluntary payment and thinks that he is making one kind of

---

[80] *ibid.* at 214, 215. This was said to be a "crucial" fact in the case: *Barclays Bank Ltd v. W.J. Simms, Son & Cooke (Southern) Ltd* [1980] Q.B. 677, 687.

[81] *Barclays Bank Ltd v. W.J. Simms, Son & Cooke (Southern) Ltd* [1980] Q.B. 677, 699–700.

[82] *ibid.* This would appear to be the case whether or not the customer's account was adequate to meet the cheque; Vol. II, § 34–132.

[83] *Pollard v. Bank of England* (1871) L.R. 6 Q.B. 623; *Barclays Bank Ltd v. W.J. Simms, Son & Cooke (Southern) Ltd, supra,* at 699–700.

[84] See generally, *ante*, §§ 3–049—3–050, 4–030, 30–035 and, in the context of mistake; *Kelly v. Solari* (1841) 9 M. & W. 54, 59; *ante*, § 3–034, n. 69; *Grains & Fourrages SA v. Hayton* [1997] 1 Lloyd's Rep. 628 (limits of contractual compromise); Andrews [1989] L.M.C.L.Q. 431; Arrowsmith in Burrows (ed.), *Essays on the Law of Restitution* (1991), Chap. 2; Goff and Jones *op. cit.* pp. 53–54, 234–235.

[85] Goff and Jones *op. cit.* pp. 67–72.

[86] [1938] 1 K.B. 49. See also *Thavron v. Bank of Credit & Commerce SA* [1985] 1 Lloyd's Rep. 259.

voluntary payment whereas upon the true facts he is making another kind of voluntary payment does not make the payment under a mistake of fact which can be described as fundamental or basic"[87] but this has been criticised as too restrictive and the better explanation is to be found in the judgment of Scott L.J. He said that "statutory veto upon the reception of evidence about gaming transactions ... creates a special impediment, and in effect constitutes a special defence to the action for money had and received" by which "the law prevents the plaintiff from saying that he intended anything but a present."[88]

Previous notice and demand. It has been said that in order to entitle a party **30–037** to bring an action to recover money on the ground that it was paid by mistake, notice of the mistake must have been given to the defendant and a demand made for the return of the money.[89] But it is submitted that failure to give notice of the claim before action should be relevant only to the court's discretion in awarding costs.[90] It may be, however, that the giving of notice is a condition precedent to the right to bring an action, but not to the liability to repay. In another case, where the payer and payee were acting under the same mistake, this rule requiring a previous demand was not applied and the period of limitation was held to run from the date of payment.[91]

Mistake of law: formerly not a ground for restitution. Despite a dubious **30–038** legal foundation[92] and the difficulty of drawing any clear dividing line between "law" and "fact"[93] until recently, as a general rule money paid under a mistake as to the general law, or as to the legal effect of the circumstances under which it is paid, but with full knowledge of the facts, was irrecoverable.[94] The rule

---

[87] *ibid.* at 66.

[88] *ibid.* at 71, 77. *cf. Lipkin Gorman v. Karpnale Ltd* [1989] 1 W.L.R. 1340, 1366, 1384; [1991] 2 A.C. 548, 577.

[89] *Kelly v. Solari, supra,* at 58; *Freeman v. Jeffries* (1869) L.R. 4 Ex. 189, 199, 200. In cases of mistaken payment of a forged negotiable instrument notice must be given on the day of the payment: *Cocks v. Masterman* (1829) 9 B. & C. 902; *National Westminster Bank Ltd v. Barclays Bank International Ltd* [1975] 1 Q.B. 654; *Barclays Bank Ltd v. W.J. Simms, Son & Cooke (Southern) Ltd* [1980] Q.B. 677, 701–703. See Vol. II, §§ 34–128—34–133. This may be an example of estoppel: Goff and Jones *op. cit.* pp. 838–841.

[90] In *Colonial Bank v. Exchange Bank of Yarmouth, Nova Scotia* (1885) 11 App.Cas. 84, 90 the Privy Council said that the recipient, when first informed of the mistake in making the payment, would have been justified in not repaying until he had checked the facts.

[91] *Baker v. Courage & Co.* [1910] K.B. 56. See also *Anglo-Scottish Beet Sugar Corporation v. Spalding U.D.C.* [1937] 2 K.B. 607, 609. On the limitation period in such cases, see *ante,* § 29–087.

[92] See Goff and Jones *op. cit.* pp. 213–217; Palmer *op. cit.* § 14.27. Evans, *An Essay on the Action of Money Had & Received* (1802) reprinted [1998] R.L. Rev. 1, 5–8; *Kleinwort Benson Ltd v. Lincoln C.C.* [1998] 3 W.L.R. 1095. See on the whole topic, Winfield (1943) 59 L.Q.R. 327 (summarised in Winfield, *Quasi-Contracts* (1952), pp. 38–51); Law Commission Consultation Paper No. 120 (1991), Part II.

[93] Winfield (1943) 59 L.Q.R. 327. *cf.* Wilson (1963) 26 M.L.R. 609. See also *Eaglesfield v. Marquis of Londonderry* (1875) 4 Ch.D. 693, 703; *West London Commercial Bank v. Kitson* (1884) 13 Q.B.D. 360, 363 (the same problem arises in connection with the rule that, to have legal effect, a representation must be one of fact, not of law: see *ante,* § 6–011.

[94] See *Bilbie v. Lumley* (1802) 2 East 469; *Brisbane v. Dacres* (1813) 5 Taunt. 143; *East India Co. v. Tritton* (1854) 3 B. & C. 280, 290; *Platt v. Bromage* (1854) 24 L.J.Ex. 63; *William Whiteley Ltd v. R.* (1910) 101 L.T. 741, 745; *Sawyer & Vincent v. Window Brace Ltd* [1943] K.B. 32, 34; *Westdeutsche Landesbank Girozentrale v. Islington L.B.C.* (1993) 91 L.G.R. 323, 372 [1996] A.C. 669.

reflected concern to protect security of receipts,[95] especially in the absence of a defence of change of position,[96] but goes beyond this and its width has been criticised.

30–039 **Criticism of the bar to restitution:** The main criticisms of the rule are as follows.[97] First, it allows a payee to retain a payment which would not have been made but the payer's mistake, "whereas justice appears to demand that money so paid should be repaid unless there are special circumstances justifying its retention." Secondly, the distinction between mistakes of fact which can ground liability and mistakes of law which cannot produces results which appear to be capricious. So a payment by an insurer would be irrecoverable where, as in *Bilbie v. Lumlie*,[98] the underwriter had failed to appreciate that he could repudiate the policy for non-disclosure but not where, as in *Kelly v. Solari*,[99] he forgot that the premium had not been paid. Thirdly, the rule became uncertain and unpredictable in its application because of the difficulty of drawing the distinction between mistakes of fact and law and because of the many exceptions and qualifications to which the rule became subject. In practice the scope of the rule was narrowed by the rather artificial distinction made between mistakes of general law and mistakes as to private rights, since the latter grounded recovery.[1] It was also avoided where it was possible to treat the payment as made under some form of compulsion.[2] Many of the cases in which it was applied can in fact be explained as examples of the irrecoverability of payments made in settlement of an honest claim.[3]

30–040 **Rejection of the bar to restitution.** The rule has recently been held not to be part of the law of Scotland.[4] It has also been rejected by the Supreme Court of Canada, the High Court of Australia and the Appellate Division of the Supreme Court of South Africa.[4a] In England the acceptance in 1991 of the principle of unjust enrichment made it difficult to continue to defend a distinction between fact and law, and the recognition of a defence of change of position[5] at the same time has dealt with some of the legitimate concerns about the security of receipts. By 1994, when the Law Commission recommended the abolition of the rule,[6] it

---

[95] See *Mistakes of Law and Ultra Vires Public Authority Receipt and Payments*, Law Com. C.P. No. 120 (1991), paras 2.28–2.35, Law Com. No. 227 (Cm. 2731) paras 2.25–2.38, 5.18.

[96] See *post*, § 30–114.

[97] They are summarised by Lord Goff in *Kleinwort Benson Ltd v. Lincoln City Council* [1998] 3 W.L.R. 1095, 1111–1113. For a fuller account see Law Com. C.P. No. 120 (1991), paras 2.24–2.26 and Law Com. No. 227 (1994), paras 2.5–2.15.

[98] (1802) 2 East 469.

[99] (1841) 9 M. & W. 54, *ante*, § 30–026.

[1] *Cooper v. Phibbs* (1867) L.R. 2 H.L. 149, 170 (Lord Westbury).

[2] The commonest instances of such compulsion are payments to public bodies: *Steele v. Williams* (1853) 8 Ex. 625; *Hooper v. Exeter Corporation* (1887) 56 L.J.Q.B. 457; *Eadie v. Township of Brantford* [1967] S.C.R. 573; 63 D.L.R. (2d) 561; *post*, §§ 30–068, 30–083.

[3] *e.g. Bilbie v. Lumlie* (1802) 2 East 469; *Home & Colonial Insurance Co. Ltd v. London Guarantee Accident Co.* (1928) T.L.R. 135. See further *post*, § 30–120.

[4] *Morgan Guaranty Trust Co. of New York v. Lothian R.C.* (1995) S.C. 151.

[4a] *Air Canada v. British Columbia* [1989] S.C.R. 1161; *David Securities Pty. v. Commonwealth Bank of Australia* (1992) 66 A.L.J.R. 768; *Willis Faber Enthoven (Pty.) Ltd v. Receiver of Revenue* 1992 (4) S.A. 202(A). It has been legislatively modified in New Zealand (Judicature Amendment Act 1958, s.94A) and Western Australia L.R. (Property, Perpetuities and Succession) Act 1962, ss.23, 24.

[5] *Post*, § 30–114.

[6] Law Com. No. 227 (1994).

was clearly "on the turn",[7] and, in 1998 the House of Lords, in *Kleinwort Benson Ltd v. Lincoln City Council*,[8] held that it was not part of English law.

In *Kleinwort Benson Ltd v. Lincoln City Council*[8] the claimants' bank sought to   **30–041**
recover payments made to the defendants under interest rate swaps contracts believed to be binding but subsequently held *ultra vires*.[9] Over half of the payments had been made more than six years before the claim was made, but less than six years after the House of Lords held that the contracts were *ultra vires*. The claim was statute barred unless it was for relief from the consequences of a mistake, in which case section 32(1) of the Limitation Act 1980 provided that the period of limitation only began to run when the bank either discovered the mistake or could with reasonable diligence have discovered it. The bank could not have discovered the true position until it was held that contracts were *ultra vires*. It was held that the rule that the general bar to a restitutionary claim of money paid under a mistake of law should no longer be maintained as part of English law. There is therefore a general right to recover money paid under a mistake, whether of fact or law, subject to the defences available in the law of restitution. Although there was unanimity as to the desirability in principle of abrogating the rule, their Lordships were divided as to whether this should be done judicially. This was due to a difference as to the position where, after a payment has been made, the law changed by judicial decision. The majority held that a payment made under a settled understanding of the law which is subsequently departed from by judicial decision was recoverable in restitution on the ground of mistake of law. The minority considered that such a payment was not made under a mistake of law, and were not prepared to abolish the rule barring restitution in respect of payments made under a mistake of law if that meant that such a payment would be recoverable. This aspect of the decision is considered further below.

Mistake of law: principles governing recovery. It was held that the ques-   **30–042**
tions raised in a claim for restitution of money paid under a mistake of law are the same as those raised in a claim for restitution of money paid under a mistake of fact: was there a mistake, did the mistake cause the payment, and did the payee have a right to receive the sum which was paid to him. Retention of the money is prima facie unjust if the payer paid because he thought he was obliged to do so and it subsequently turns out that he was not. Lord Hope stated that although it may be more difficult to establish that there has been a mistake of law, there is no essential difference in principle with regard to the payer's state of mind or with regard to the state of facts or the law, which must be determined at the time of payment.[10] But his Lordship considered that there was no reason in principle for the mistake to be one that is capable of being discovered at the same time as the time when the payment was made.[11] The prima facie right to recover a mistaken payment is subject to the ordinary defences to restitutionary claims which are concerned to protect the stability of closed transactions; *i.e.* change of position, compromise, and settlement of an honest claim, the last of which may assume an increased importance despite its current somewhat uncertain scope, since many of the cases in which recovery was barred by the mistake of law rule

---

[7] *Friends Provident Life Office v. Hillier Parker* [1997] Q.B. 85, 97.
[8] [1998] 3 W.L.R. 1095, on appeal from [1997] Q.B. 380.
[9] In *Hazell v. Hammersmith & Fulham L.B.C.* [1992] 2 A.C. 1, *ante*, § 10–023.
[10] [1998] 3 W.L.R. 1095, 1147. See *ante*, § 30–031—30–032.
[11] *ibid.* at 1417.

can be explained as examples of such settlements.[12] The House considered, but rejected, a number of other limits to recovery. Thus, the suggestion that restitution is barred where the payee honestly believes that he was entitled to the money, which would exclude recovery in a very large proportion of cases, was rejected.[13] It was also held that restitution is not barred where the transaction under which the money was paid has been fully performed (although this would bar a restitutionary claim based on failure of consideration).[14] Moreover, a bare majority held that a payment made under a settled understanding of the law which is subsequently departed from by judicial decision is made under a mistake of law and is therefore recoverable.[15] Nevertheless Lord Goff left open the possibility that other defences might be developed from judicial decisions in the future.[16]

30–043   **Examples of payments made under a mistake of law.** There are many examples. We first consider cases in which, prior to *Kleinwort Benson Ltd v. Lincoln C.C.*[17] restitution would have been barred. A mistake as to the existence or construction of a statute is clearly one of law,[18] as is a mistaken view of regulations issued under statutory authority.[19] Thus, in *Holt v. Markham*[20] government agents, by mistake, for some time overpaid an officer on the emergency list, who was, by virtue of a certain regulation, entitled to be paid only at a lower rate. The agents sued to recover the overpayments, but it was held that their mistake was one of law and in the state of the law then their claim failed. Mistakes as to the effect of general rules of common law or of equity also fall into this category. Thus, where a tenant paid rent to an equitable mortgagee with notice that the mortgagee claimed it in that capacity the payments were made under a mistake of law.[21] Mistakes in construing a will,[22] such as a mistake as to the technical requisites for the creation of a valid charitable trust[23] are also mistakes of law.

30–044   **Recoverable before the *Kleinwort Benson* case.** Even, before *Kleinwort Benson Ltd v. Lincoln C.C.*[24] there were exceptional cases in which payments made under a mistake of law were recoverable. Some of these were in fact cases in which the payer could establish an alternative ground for restitution, for while

---

[12] *Ante*, § 30–039, n. 3.

[13] [1998] 3 W.L.R. 1095, 1124, 1151. This had been suggested by Brennan J. in *David Securities Pty. Ltd v. Commonwealth Bank of Australia* (1991–92) 175 C.L.R. 353, 398–399.

[14] [1998] 3 W.L.R. 1095, 1125, 1152. *cf.* Birks, (1993) 23 U.W. Aus. L.R. 195.

[15] *Post*, § 30–047.

[16] *Kleinwort Benson Ltd v. Lincoln City Council* [1998] 3 W.L.R. 1095, 1122.

[17] [1998] 3 W.L.R. 1095.

[18] *Sharp Bros. and Knight v. Chant* [1917] 1 K.B. 771; *National Pari-Mutuel Association Ltd v. R.* (1930) 47 T.L.R. 110; *Sawyer & Vincent v. Window Brace Ltd* [1943] K.B. 32. See now Rent Act 1977, s.57. See also *Orphanos v. Queen Mary College* [1985] A.C. 761 (no ground for restitution where contractual meaning given to phrase in mistaken belief that this is statutory meaning).

[19] *Holt v. Markham* [1923] 1 K.B. 504.

[20] *ibid.*

[21] *Finck v. Tranter* [1905] 1 K.B. 427. But *cf. Newsome v. Graham* (1829) 10 B. & C. 234; *Cripps v. Reade* (1796) 6 T.R. 606; *Barber v. Brown* (1856) 1 C.B.(N.S.) 121.

[22] *Rogers v. Ingham* (1876) 3 Ch.D. 351. (Perhaps this case exemplifies the unwillingness of the courts to upset family arrangements: see Winfield *op. cit.* p. 42.)

[23] *cf. Ministry of Health v. Simpson* [1951] A.C. 251 (in the CA, *Re Diplock* [1948] Ch. 465, 480, the mistake was also regarded as one of law, so that the common law remedy for money received was excluded).

[24] [1998] 3 W.L.R. 1095.

mistake of law did not provide a ground for restitution, if a *prima facie* right to recovery on some other ground was established, that was not defeated because of the mistake of law.[25] Thus, where an illegal payment is made under a contract, but the parties are not *in pari delicto*,[26] the payment could be recovered although it was made under a mistake of law in that neither party knew that the contract was illegal.[27] Similarly, recovery has always been permitted where the mistake of law which led to the payment was caused by an *ultra vires* demand by the revenue or possibly any public authority,[28] by fraud, undue influence or breach of a fiduciary obligation on the part of the recipient[29] or where it was caused by oppression[30] and, possibly, practical compulsion.[31] Other exceptions to the rule occured where the payment was made by the court or an officer of the court,[32] and where public funds were disbursed without legal authority.[33]

Equity. Equity has, in certain cases, given relief when a payment has, at least   **30–045** in part, depended on a mistake of law; thus a trustee or personal representative who has overpaid a beneficiary through a mistake of law may deduct the overpayment from future payments due to the beneficiary.[34] Furthermore, the court will not allow one of its officers, such as a trustee in bankruptcy or official receiver, to retain money paid to him under a mistake of law where it would be contrary to fair dealing to do so.[35] The principle in these cases, known as the rule in *Ex parte James*,[36] is not restricted to payments under mistake of law and appears to be based on the need to prevent unjust enrichment.[37]

---

[25] *Westdeutsche Landesbank Girozentrale v. Islington L.B.C.* (1993) 91 L.G.R. 322, 372 (Hobhouse J.) aff'd [1996] A.C. 669.

[26] See *ante*, § 17–176.

[27] *Kiriri Cotton Co. Ltd v. Dewani* [1960] A.C. 192; see *ante*, § 17–176. *cf. Harse v. Pearl Life Assurance Co.* [1904] 1 K.B. 558.

[28] *Woolwich Equitable Building Society v. I.R.C.* [1993] A.C. 70; see *post*, § 30–080.

[29] See *post*, §§ 30–092, 30–079, n. 15; *West London Commercial Bank Ltd v. Kitson* (1884) 13 Q.B.D. 360, 363; *Ward & Co. v. Wallis* [1900] 1 Q.B. 675, 678; *Shelley v. Paddock* [1980] Q.B. 348; *Rogers v. Ingram* (1876) 3 Ch.D. 351, 355–356.

[30] *Smith v. Bromley* (1760) 2 Doug. 696n., 697.

[31] *Ante*, § 17–177; *post*, §§ 30–068, 30–079.

[32] *Re Birkbeck Permanent Benefit Building Society* [1915] 1 Ch. 91.

[33] *Auckland Harbour Board v. R.* [1924] A.C. 318, 326–327. In view of the difficulties in the application of the doctrine of estoppel to *ultra vires* acts of public authorities (*ante*, §§ 10–017, 10–036; *Commonwealth of Australia v. Burns* [1971] V.R. 825, 830) this is potentially a very wide exception to the rule.

[34] *Dibbs v. Goren* (1849) 11 Beav. 439; *Re Musgrave* [1916] 2 Ch. 417; *Gibbon v. Mitchell* [1990] 1 W.L.R. 1304, 1309. *cf. Re Horne* [1905] 1 Ch. 76. See further *Stone v. Godfrey* (1854) 5 De G.M. & G. 76, 90; *Allcard v. Walker* [1896] 2 Ch. 369, 381; Winfield (1943) 59 L.Q.R. 327, 328–333. An equitable tracing order may be available despite a mistake of law: *Sinclair v. Brougham* [1914] A.C. 398, 452 (*post*, § 30–100). See also the discussion in *Minister of Health v. Simpson* [1951] A.C. 251, 269–275. *cf. Re Diplock* [1948] Ch. 465, 479–480. In other contexts deductions have been said to be anomalous and have not been permitted: *R. v. Tower Hamlets L.B.C., ex p. Chetnik Developments Ltd* [1988] A.C. 858, 876–877; *Sharp Bros. & Knight v. Chant* [1917] 1 K.B. 771, CA.

[35] *Ex p. James* (1874) L.R. 9 Ch.App. 609; *Ex p. Simmonds* (1885) 6 Q.B.D. 308; *Re Opera Ltd* [1891] 2 Ch. 154 (revd. on other grounds: [1891] 3 Ch. 260); *Re Tyler* [1907] 1 K.B. 865; *Re Thellusson* [1919] 2 K.B. 735; *Re Wigzell* [1921] 2 K.B. 835, 851; *Re Wyvern Developments Ltd* [1974] 1 W.L.R. 1097, 1105. *cf. Re Sandiford (No. 2)* [1935] Ch. 681; *Taylor v. Wilson's Trustees* (1975) S.C. 146; *Re Multi Guarantee Co. Ltd* [1987] B.C.L.C. 257; *Re T.H. Knitwear (Wholesale) Ltd* [1988] Ch. 275.

[36] (1874) L.R. 9 Ch.App. 609; see *ante*, § 20–022 for a fuller discussion.

[37] *Government of India v. Taylor* [1955] A.C. 491, 513; *cf. Re Clark (a bankrupt)* [1975] 1 W.L.R. 559; *Re Byfield* [1982] Ch. 267; *Re Multi Guarantee Co. Ltd*, *supra*.

30–046   **Mistake as to private rights.** The final example of a payment made under a mistake of law that was recoverable prior to the decision in *Kleinwort Benson v. Lincoln C.C.*[38] is where the mistake can be characterised as one concerning private rights. The House of Lords in *Cooper v. Phibbs*[39] held that ignorance of the existence of a private right of property was a mistake of fact although this ignorance was based on a mistaken interpretation of the law. In that case A agreed to take from B a lease of a fishery, which A in fact already owned as tenant in tail: both parties, however, mistakenly thought that as the result of a private Act of Parliament and a certain deed, B was the owner. The House of Lords set aside the lease on terms, and held that the plaintiff was entitled to repayment of rent.

The principle in *Cooper v. Phibbs*, which was applied in several cases, [40] was difficult to reconcile with the general rule that formerly barred recovery because operative mistake is rarely simply a mistake as to the effect of a general rule of law but is usually a mistake as to its application to particular fact situations; *i.e.* a mistake as to private legal rights.

30–047   **Changes in the law.**[41] Where the law is changed by *legislation* a payment made or service rendered in accordance with the previous law cannot be recovered since there was clearly no mistake when it was made.[42] Where the law is changed by a *judicial decision*, however, the position differs. Such change may either occur by the overruling of an earlier decision, or by changing what had previously been generally regarded as the law. The traditional working assumption upon which the common law proceeds is that judges declare law but do not make it. Thus, where the common law changes, a legal fiction (the declaratory theory) means that the law is regarded as having always been what the post-payment decision has stated it to be. By a bare majority, the House of Lords held that, notwithstanding the common sense notion of a mistake, the consequence of the declaratory theory is that the pre-decision payment must be regarded as mistaken and is therefore recoverable: "common sense does not easily accommodate the concept of retrospectivity."[43] This was so both where the law was established by a judicial decision which is subsequently overruled and where, as in *Kleinwort Benson Ltd v. Lincoln C.C.*, the law was arguably "settled" as a matter of practice but without a decision in point.[44] The position may well differ, however, where the payment was made pursuant to a judgment of the court and

---

[38] [1998] 3 W.L.R. 1095.

[39] (1867) L.R. 2 H.L. 149. The distinction is criticised by Palmer *op. cit.* § 16.4(*c*).

[40] *Anglo-Scottish Beet Sugar Corporation Ltd v. Spalding U.D.C.* [1937] 2 K.B. 607, 615–617; *Meadows v. Grand Junction Waterworks Co.* (1905) 69 J.P. 255; *Stanley Bros. Ltd v. Corporation of Nuneaton* (1912) 107 L.T. 760. See also *Norwich Union Fire Insurance Society Ltd v. Wm. H. Price Ltd* [1934] A.C. 455, 462–463 (Lord Wright found nothing in *Bell v. Lever Bros. Ltd* [1932] A.C. 161 to overrule Lord Westbury's dicta in *Cooper v. Phibbs*); *Sybron Corporation v. Rochem Ltd* [1984] Ch. 112.

[41] See generally Law Com. No. 227 *Restitution: Mistakes of Law and Ultra Vires Public Authority Receipts and Payments* (1994) paras 5.1–5.13.

[42] *Kleinwort Benson Ltd v. Lincoln City Council* [1998] 3 W.L.R. 1095, 1121 (Lord Goff). But the position may be different where the legislation is retrospective; *ibid.* at 1139 (Lord Hoffmann).

[43] *Kleinwort Benson Ltd v. Lincoln City Council* [1998] 3 W.L.R. 1095, 1137 (Lord Hoffmann). See also *ibid.* at 1119 and 1148.

[44] Payments made under public law transactions, such as taxes and similar charges may, because of the large numbers of payments and considerations of the public interest, be treated differently from those under private law transactions: *Kleinwort Benson Ltd v. Lincoln City Council* [1998] 3 W.L.R. 1095, 1121–1122 (Lord Goff).

that judgment is afterwards overruled by a higher court in a different case: "the obligation to pay is to be found in the order which has been made by the court."[45] Lord Browne-Wilkinson and Lord Lloyd took a different view of the general effect of a change in the law or a settled understanding of the law by judicial decision. They considered that such a payment was not made under a mistake because where a decision of a court has in fact changed the law, "retrospectivity cannot falsify history."[46] If at the date of the payment it was the law that the payer was liable, the payer was not labouring under a mistake at that date: the subsequent change in the law could not create a cause of action which, ex hypothesi, did not exist at the relevant time.

(b) *Failure of Consideration*[47]

General principles. Where money has been paid under a transaction that is or **30–048** becomes ineffective the payer may recover the money provided that the consideration for the payment has totally failed. Although the principle is not confined to contracts[48] most of the cases are concerned with ineffective contracts. In that context failure of consideration occurs where the payer has not enjoyed the benefit of any part of what he bargained for.[49] Thus, the failure is judged from the payer's point of view and "when one is considering the law of failure of consideration and of the quasi-contractual right to recover money on that ground, it is generally speaking, not the promise which is referred to as the consideration, but the performance of the promise."[50] The failure has to be total because the consideration is "whole and indivisible," and the courts will not divide or apportion it unless the parties have done so.[51] This is partly because one cannot assume that all parts of the payee's performance are equally valuable and that the

---

[45] [1998] 3 W.L.R. 1095, 1148 (Lord Hope). For Lord Browne-Wilkinson and Lord Lloyd this case is *a fortiori* their view of the general effect of a change in the law or a settled understanding of the law by judicial decision. But *cf.* Lord Goff and Lord Hoffmann, *ibid.* at 1118–1120, 1138.

[46] *Kleinwort Benson Ltd v. Lincoln City Council* [1998] 3 W.L.R. 1095, 1099, 1100, 1132. For support see *Henderson v. Folkestone Waterworks Co.* (1885) 1 T.L.R. 329 and, although less clearly *Derrick v. Williams* [1939] 2 All E.R. 559, 565. But see also *Mercury Machine Importing Corp. v. City of New York* 144 N.E. 2d 400 (1957) (New York); *Julian v. Mayor of Auckland* [1927] N.Z.L.R. 453 (New Zealand); *Torrens Aloha Pty. Co. v. Citybank N.A.* [1997] 72 F.C.R. 581 (Australian).

[47] Stoljar (1959) 75 L.Q.R. 53; Law Commission No. 121 (1983), "Pecuniary Restitution on Breach of Contract," §§ 1.6–1.8, 3.1–3.11.

[48] *Martin v. Andrews* (1856) 7 E. & B. 1 (recovery of conduct money paid to subpoenaed witness when action settled before trial); *Chillingworth v. Esche* [1924] 1 Ch. 97 (recovery of deposit paid under transaction expressed to be "subject to contract" when no contract concluded through actions of payer). See also *post*, § 30–062 (void contracts).

[49] *Fibrosa Spolka Akcyjna v. Fairbairn Lawson Combe Barbour Ltd* [1943] A.C. 32 (*ante*, § 24–070); *Comptoir d'Achat et de Vente du Boerenbond Belge SA v. Luis de Ridder Limitada* [1949] A.C. 293 (*post*, § 30–054); *Branwhite v. Worcester Works Finance Ltd* [1969] 1 A.C. 552; *Rover International Ltd v. Cannon Film Sales Ltd (No. 3)* [1989] 1 W.L.R. 912, noted (1989) 105 L.Q.R. 179; *Stocznia Gdanska SA v. Latvian S.S. Co.* [1998] 1 W.L.R. 574 and cases cited in following footnotes.

[50] *Fibrosa Spolka Akcyjna v. Fairbairn Lawson Combe Barbour Ltd* [1943] A.C. 32, 48 (*per* Viscount Simon). Where, as in certain insurance contracts, the payer bargains for the promise the general rule will not apply: *Tyrie v. Fletcher* (1777) 2 Cowp. 666. See *post*, 30–067. For reconsideration of the requirement of totality, see *Goss v. Chilcott* [1996] A.C. 788 and see *post*, 30–057—30–058.

[51] As where there is a sale at a unit price; *Biggerstaff v. Rowatt's Wharf* [1896] 2 Ch. 93, 100; *Ebrahim Dawood Ltd v. Heath Ltd* [1961] 2 Lloyd's Rep. 512; on which see further *post*, § 30–058.

contract price is earned incrementally,[52] but historically it was also because of the non-recognition in English law of the principle of unjust enrichment until recently.[53] Thus, any performance of the actual thing promised, *as determined by the contract*, is fatal to recovery under this heading.

30-049   **Artificiality of distinctions.** The role of the contractual specification means that it is not true to say that there can be a total failure of consideration only where the payer received no benefit at all in return for the payment. The concept of total failure of consideration can ignore real benefits received by the payer if they are not the benefit bargained for and despite significant detrimental reliance by the payee. Thus, in cases of the sale of a car by a non-owner, the price paid has been recovered despite substantial intermediate enjoyment of the car by the purchaser[54] even where the vendor is subsequently able to perfect his title[55] and where the value of the car has depreciated considerably.[56] Again, if the purchaser of an estate pays the purchase money and enters into possession of the land, but before the conveyance is executed he is evicted in consequence of a defect in the vendor's title, he can recover the purchase-money.[57] Again, an instalment under a film distributorship agreement was said to be recoverable despite the receipt of films because the relevant bargain was the opportunity to earn a share of gross receipts with the certainty of recouping the advance.[58]

30-050   **Contract discharged or ineffective.** Money will only be recoverable on this ground where the contract is discharged.[59] This requirement has practical importance where, as in the case of breach of contract, discharge operates at the election of the innocent party.[60] A contract-breaker will therefore only be able to recover money where the other party has elected to accept the breach as discharging the contract.[61] The requirement is irrelevant where the contract is ineffective

---

[52] *Whincup v. Hughes* (1871) L.R. 6 C.P. 78, 81.

[53] *ibid.* at 82, 84. On this see *ante*, § 30–009.

[54] *Rowland v. Divall* [1923] 2 K.B. 500; 129 L.T. 755. See further *Barber v. N.W.S. Bank* [1996] 1 W.L.R. 641. This rule does not apply where the payer parts with the property for value: *Linz v. Electric Wire Co. of Palestine Ltd* [1948] A.C. 371. See *post*, § 30–054.

[55] *Butterworth v. Kingsway Motors Ltd* [1954] 1 W.L.R. 1286.

[56] *ibid.* The car was bought for £1,275 and used for nearly a year. When it was returned it was worth about £800. For criticisms of this and other similar cases, and proposals for reform, see Law Com. Working Paper No. 65 (1975), Part IV. The same principles apply to hire-purchase: *Karflex Ltd v. Poole* [1933] 2 K.B. 251; *Warman v. Southern Counties Finance Cpn. Ltd* [1949] 2 K.B. 576; Vol. II, § 38–277. *cf. Yeoman Credit Ltd v. Apps* [1962] 2 Q.B. 508, 521, 525; *Kelly v. Lombard Banking Co. Ltd* [1959] 1 W.L.R. 41, *post*, § 30–055, nn. 89–95.

[57] *Johnson v. Johnson* (1802) 3 B. & P. 162. See also *Wright v. Colls* (1849) 8 C.B. 150. *Aliter* if the purchaser negligently fails to discover an error in the title until after completion (*Allen v. Richardson* (1879) 13 Ch.D. 524), or if after the conveyance has been executed the purchaser is evicted by a title to which the covenants in the conveyance do not extend (*Clare v. Lamb* (1875) L.R. 10 C.P. 334, 338; *Clayton v. Leech* (1889) 41 Ch.D. 103; *Debenham v. Sawbridge* [1901] 2 Ch. 98). *cf.* also *Hunt v. Silk* (1804) 5 East. 449.

[58] *Rover International Ltd v. Cannon Film Sales Ltd (No. 3)* [1989] 1 W.L.R. 912, 924–925 (*per* Kerr L.J.). See also *Westdeutsche Landesbank Girozentrale v. Islington L.B.C.* (1993) 91 L.G.R. 323, 367, aff'd [1996] A.C. 669.

[59] *Kwei Tek Chao v. British Traders and Shippers Ltd* [1954] 2 Q.B. 459, 475; *Weston v. Downes* (1778) 1 Doug. 23; *Goodman v. Pocock* (1850) 15 Q.B. 576.

[60] *Ante*, § 30–062.

[61] *Dies v. British and International Mining and Finance Corporation Ltd* [1939] 1 K.B. 724, discussed *post*, § 30–061.

ab initio[62] (*e.g.* for informality or incapacity) or where, as in the case of frustration, it is discharged automatically.[63]

Where the payer has received a benefit from the payee it must, as a general rule, be restored before he can recover his money.[64] Finally, at least in some cases of breach of contract and frustration, recovery is only possible where there is no express or implied term in the contract making the payment irrecoverable.[65]

30–051

Comparison with damages.[66] Where the payee is in breach of contract the quasi-contractual claim is an alternative to an action for damages for breach of contract.[67] This will be an attractive option in cases in which the payer has made a bad bargain[68] or where his damages will be limited or irrecoverable. This may be the result of requirements such as remoteness, the duty to mitigate and restrictions as to the kind of loss that is recoverable.[69] Restitution, therefore, has a clear advantage over a claim for reliance losses since such a claim will not succeed if the defendant shows the reliance loss is greater than the expected profit.[70] Apart from this, the quasi-contractual claim has procedural and evidential advantages in that it is a liquidated claim.[71] It will also be attractive in those exceptional cases in which a total failure of consideration is established despite the receipt of a benefit by the payee. This is because an action for damages, but not an action for the recovery of money, would take account of such benefits.[72]

30–052

---

[62] *Rover International Ltd v. Cannon Film Sales Ltd (No. 3)* [1989] 1 W.L.R. 912; *Westdeutsche Landesbank Girozentrale v. Islington L.B.C.* (1993) 91 L.G.R. 323, 363, [1996] A.C. 669.

[63] *Ante*, § 24–069.

[64] *Towers v. Barratt* (1786) 1 T.R. 133; *Baldry v. Marshall* [1925] 1 Q.B. 260. In certain circumstances, as in the cases of sale by a non-owner, *ante*, n. 56, where the goods have been repossessed by the true owner, the payer is relieved from the duty to restore. *N.B.* that certain benefits, such as use of chattels (but *cf. Rowland v. Divall, supra*), occupation of land or receipt of services, are non-returnable and in such cases the money will be irrecoverable: *Hunt v. Silk* (1804) 5 East. 449; *Harrison v. James* (1862) 7 H. & N. 804.

[65] *Fibrosa Spolka Akcyjna v. Fairbairn Lawson Combe Barbour Ltd* [1943] A.C. 32, 67 (Lord Wright). See also the Law Reform (Frustrated Contracts) Act 1943, s.2(3) and the power to contract out of other rights to restitution; Goff and Jones *op. cit.* p. 50.

[66] Dawson (1959) 20 Ohio St.L.J. 175; Treitel, *The Law of Contract* (9th ed., 199), p. 932; Palmer, *The Law of Restitution* (1978), §§ 4.1 *et seq.*; Birks [1987] L.M.C.L.Q. 421; Goodhart, [1995] Rest. L. Rev. 3; Beale (1996) 112 L.Q.R. 205, 208. For comparison of damages and *quantum meruit*, see *post*, § 30–180 and on availability of restitutionary damages for breach of contract see *ante*, 30–018, *post*, 30–096.

[67] See *ante*, Chap. 26.

[68] *Bush v. Canfield*, 2 Conn. 485 (1818); *B.P. Exploration Co. (Libya) Ltd v. Hunt (No. 2)* [1979] 1 W.L.R. 783, 800 (affd. [1981] 1 W.L.R. 232, CA; [1983] 2 A.C. 352, HL). Although the latter was referring to claims under the Law Reform (Frustrated Contracts) Act 1943, s.1(2) the principle would appear the same. The objection that this reverses the contractual allocation of risks has not apparently been accepted, possibly because the law favours liquidated claims, because the stringency of the requirements needed to establish a total failure of consideration mean that the issue will rarely arise, and because on facts such as those in *Bush v. Canfield, supra*, the payee-seller would otherwise get something for nothing. See also Palmer, *The Law of Restitution* (1978), Vol. 1, pp. 382–383, 392–393.

[69] *e.g.* by a technical rule such as that in *Bain v. Fothergill* (1874) L.R. 7 H.L. 158 (now abolished by Law of Property (Miscellaneous Provisions) Act 1989, s.(3), *ante*, § 27–113.

[70] *C.C.C. Films (London) Ltd v. Impact Quadrant Films Ltd* [1985] Q.B. 16; *ante*, §§ 27–061, 27–059.

[71] *Biggerstaff v. Rowatt's Wharf* [1896] 2 Ch. 93, 105.

[72] *Rowland v. Divall* [1923] 2 K.B. 500; *ante*, § 30–049; but compare *Warman v. Southern Counties Car Finance Corp. Ltd* [1959] 2 K.B. 576, 582–583 (any enrichment at expense of owner not seller). On damages, see *Harling v. Eddy* [1951] 2 K.B. 739.

However, it does have disadvantages. The most obvious is that loss of profits are only recoverable as damages, but there are others. Thus, in cases of sale, where a buyer has paid in advance for goods that he is entitled to reject, in principle he can return the goods and recover the money.[73] But if he has spent money on the goods while they are in his possession, this will be recoverable in an action for damages[74] but not in an action for the return of the price.[75]

30–053   **Total failure of consideration and detrimental reliance.** At common law a total failure of consideration may occur even though the payee has incurred expense in partly performing his side of the contract. "Quasi-contractual redress depends upon benefit conferred, not detriment incurred."[76] However, the line between irrelevant detrimental reliance and benefit may be very fine, and sometimes can appear to turn solely upon the formal classification of the contract in question. Thus, where a contract for the sale of textile machines was later discharged for frustration, the fact that the seller had done a considerable amount of work in manufacturing them did not prevent the buyer recovering a prepayment as having been paid on a total failure of consideration.[77] On the other hand, in a shipbuilding contract, a contract for work and materials, it has been said that work done by the builders in drawing up plans and starting the construction amounted to a contractual benefit which prevented there from being a total failure of consideration.[78] In fact what is relevant is the bargained-for performance and not the formal classification. The classification merely reflects the fact that in contracts for work and materials the purchaser is paying for the work as well as for the end-product while in contracts of sale he is only paying for the end-product.[79] In such cases the reliance in the form of services rendered by the payee is to be regarded as the bargained-for performance. In other cases it is not. Thus, where a prepayment was made under a distributorship agreement it was recoverable despite the fact that, after entering the agreement the licensor-payee had paid a substantial sum to a third party to buy back rights to films subject to the agreement. The bargained-for performance was the opportunity for the licensee to earn a share of gross receipts under the distributorship and thus had wholly failed as a result of the invalidity of the agreement.[80]

30–054   **Illustrations of total failure of consideration.** Where money was paid to brokers to purchase goods in accordance with instructions, but the brokers did not make the contract authorised by their principals, it was held that the money could be recovered by the principals on the basis of a total failure of consideration.[81] So bondholders who had subscribed money for a purpose which failed

---

[73] *e.g. Baldry v. Marshall* [1925] 1 Q.B. 260, *ante*, § 30–050, n. 64.

[74] *Mason v. Burningham* [1949] 2 K.B. 545.

[75] See *post*, § 30–146 for the provisions of s.6(3) of the Torts (Interference with Goods) Act 1977 in relation to actions for the return of the price on the ground of total failure of consideration.

[76] Williams (1942) 6 M.L.R. 46, 53.

[77] *Fibrosa Spolka Akcyjna v. Fairbairn Lawson Combe Barbour Ltd* [1943] A.C. 32, and see [1942] 1 K.B. 12, 14.

[78] *Hyundai Heavy Industries Ltd v. Papadopoulos* [1980] 1 W.L.R. 1129, 1134, 1148 (Viscount Dilhorne and Lord Fraser); *Stocznia Gdanska SA v. Latvian Shipping Co., Latreefers Inc.* [1998] 1 W.L.R. 574; *Association v. C.A.P. Financial Services Ltd* [1995] F.S.R. 654.

[79] Beatson (1981) 97 L.Q.R. 398, 402–403, 407–408, 412–413; Palmer, *The Law of Restitution* (1978), § 4.2.

[80] *Rover International Ltd v. Cannon Film Sales Ltd (No. 3)* [1989] 1 W.L.R. 912, 932, 936–937.

[81] *Bostock v. Jardine* (1865) 3 H. & C. 700.

were entitled to recover their money from the bank which held the subscriptions.[82] In general, where an *ultra vires* issue of shares is made, the subscribers are entitled to recover their money; but if a subscriber to an *ultra vires* issue of shares has sold his shares, he cannot allege that as far as he is concerned there has been a total failure of consideration.[83] In another case sellers were bound to deliver at Antwerp a quantity of rye then in a ship *en route* to Antwerp, and the buyers paid the price against a delivery order directed to the sellers' agents at Antwerp; but the Germans occupied the town and the cargo was sold by the sellers in Lisbon where the ship discharged. The House of Lords held that the consideration had wholly failed so that the buyers were entitled to recover the price.[84] Again, where the names of the drawer and the acceptor were forged to a bill of exchange, and the bill was discounted by the plaintiffs for the defendants (who had indorsed it), it was held that, since the genuineness of the acceptance was of the essence of the description of a bill, there was a total failure of consideration entitling the plaintiffs to recover from the defendants the amount paid to them.[85]

Partial failure of consideration: statute. Under the provisions of the Law 30–055
Reform (Frustrated Contracts) Act 1943,[86] where a contract is frustrated, money paid under the contract may be recovered (subject to a claim or set-off for expenses incurred by the recipient of the payment) even though there has been only a partial failure of consideration.[87] The Act would now apply to a case like *Ferns v. Carr*,[88] where a solicitor had received a premium from an articled clerk, who was to be in his office for five years, but the solicitor died before the five years were completed; under the common law it was held that the clerk could not recover from the solicitor's estate any part of the premium. Where a partnership is prematurely determined, the court has statutory power to order the return of all or part of a premium paid by a partner for admission to the firm.[89]

Partial failure of consideration: common law. Apart from these cases and 30–056
unless the contract is divisible,[90] a claim in restitution to recover money paid

---

[82] *Royal Bank of Canada v. R.* [1913] A.C. 283. See also *National Bolivian Navigation Co. v. Wilson* (1880) 5 App.Cas. 176.

[83] *Linz v. Electric Wire Co. of Palestine Ltd* [1948] A.C. 371 (*quaere*, if subscriber retains the shares, but has received a dividend: *ibid.* at 377). This decision of the Privy Council is criticised in Goff and Jones *op. cit.* p. 503 (n. 23) and may be difficult to reconcile with *Westdeutsche Landesbank Girozentrale v. Islington L.B.C.* [1994] 4 All E.R. 890, 929; *Guiness Mahon & Co. Ltd v. Kensington & Chelsea R.L.B.C.* [1998] 2 All E.R. 272 in relation to closed swap transactions. *cf. Wilkinson v. Lloyd* (1845) 7 Q.B. 27 (recovery of purchase price of shares when directors refused to register the transfer).

[84] *Comptoir d'Achat et de Vente du Boerenbond Belge SA v. Luis de Ridder Limitada* [1949] A.C. 293. (This was really a case of frustration (at 313) but since the facts occurred before 1943, the House of Lords did not refer to the Law Reform (Frustrated Contracts) Act 1943, but followed the common law principles laid down in *Fibrosa Spolka Akcyjna v. Fairbairn Lawson Combe Barbour Ltd* [1943] A.C. 32 (*ante*, § 24–070). Had it been a normal c.i.f. contract the case would have been decided differently: *cf.* the view of the facts taken by the Court of Appeal [1947] 2 All E.R. 443.)

[85] *Gurney v. Womersley* (1854) 4 E. & B. 133.

[86] The Act is fully discussed *ante* in §§ 24–072—24–095.

[87] *B.P. Exploration Co. (Libya) Ltd v. Hunt (No. 2)* [1979] 1 W.L.R. 783, 800 (affirmed [1981] 1 W.L.R. 232, CA); [1983] 2 A.C. 352, HL. The common law rule was limited to total failure of consideration; *Fibrosa Spolka Akcyjna v. Fairbairn Lawson Combe Barbour Ltd* [1943] A.C. 32, *ante*, § 24–070.

[88] (1885) 28 Ch.D. 409; and see *Whincup v. Hughes* (1871) L.R. 6 C.P. 78.

[89] Partnership Act 1890, s.40.

[90] *Post*, § 30–058. On partial performance of an "entire" contract, see *ante*, §§ 22–027—22–036.

does not lie if the contract has been partly performed and the claimant has derived some of the benefit for which he bargained.[91] So, where a vendor sold a patent right, and the purchaser paid the purchase-money and used the patent right and enjoyed a benefit therefrom, but it afterwards appeared that the patent was invalid, it was held that the purchaser could not claim restitution of the purchase-money.[92] Again, a passenger on a cruise ship which sank on the tenth day of a 14 day cruise could not claim restitution of the cruise fare.[93] In another case[94] a hirer paid an initial sum of £186 to a finance company under a hire-purchase agreement "in consideration of the option to purchase" a car. He used the car for over 12 months, paying the monthly instalments under the agreement, but then the finance company validly terminated the agreement because the hirer allowed a judgment creditor to levy execution against him. The hirer claimed recovery of his initial payment on the ground that there had been a total failure of consideration in that he never obtained the option, but the Court of Appeal rejected this contention, holding that the option was an existing right from the moment of signing the contract, notwithstanding that it could not be exercised until certain conditions had been fulfilled. The question whether the retention of all the money received by the finance company amounted to the retention of a penalty and not liquidated damages, was apparently not raised in this case.[95]

30–057   The recognition of the principle of unjust enrichment in English law may lead to reconsideration of the requirement that the failure of consideration be total. Although the Law Commission has recommended that it be maintained[96] this has been criticised[97] as leading to asymmetry between the position of claims for the recovery of money and claims for recompense for services where *quantum meruit* will lie even where some counter-performance has been rendered.[98] It is also inconsistent with the aproach of equity to rescission. In neither situation have the courts regarded the difficulty of placing a value upon the contractual performance rendered which is compatible with the contract itself as insurmountable. We have noted the fine and sometimes artificial distinctions produced by the concept of total failure of consideration[99] and the distinction between entire and divisible contracts.[1] It is also the case that courts are willing to avoid the rule by dividing the contract, sometimes artifically, and holding that there has been a

---

[91] *Hunt v. Silk* (1804) 5 East 449. *cf. Steinberg v. Scala (Leeds) Ltd* [1923] 2 Ch. 452 (*ante,* § 8–039); *Linz v. Electric Wire Co. of Palestine Ltd* [1948] A.C. 371; *Michalinos & Co. Ltd v. Scourfield* (1950) 83 Ll.L.Rep. 494.

[92] *Taylor v. Hare* (1805) 1 B. & P.N.R. 260; and see *Lawes v. Purser* (1856) 6 E. & B. 930; *The Salvage Association v. C.A.P. Financial Services Ltd* [1995] F.S.R. 654.

[93] *Baltic SS. Co. v. Dillon* (1993) 67 A.L.J.R. 228 (High Ct. of Australia).

[94] *Kelly v. Lombard Banking Co. Ltd* [1959] 1 W.L.R. 41. See also *Yeoman Credit Ltd v. Apps* [1962] 2 Q.B. 508, 521, 525. *cf. Warman v. Southern Counties Car Finance Corporation Ltd* [1949] 2 K.B. 576 (*ante,* § 30–049: intermediate enjoyment of a car is not a "benefit" where vendor has no title).

[95] See *Stockloser v. Johnson* [1954] 1 Q.B. 476 (*ante,* § 27–121); *Dies v. British and International Mining and Finance Corporation Ltd* [1939] 1 K.B. 724; *Mayson v. Clouet* [1924] A.C. 980 (*post,* § 30–061). *cf. Galbraith v. Mitchenall Estates Ltd* [1965] 2 Q.B. 473 (Vol. II, § 38–305); *Sport International Poussum B.V. v. Inter-Footwear Ltd* [1984] 1 W.L.R. 776.

[96] "Pecuniary Restitution on Breach of Contract" Law Com. No. 121 (1983).

[97] Birks *op. cit.* pp. 259–264; Burrows (1984) 47 M.L.R. 762 *op. cit.* pp. 259–261; Goff and Jones *op. cit.* pp. 499–506, 516.

[98] *Post,* §§ 30–178—30–180, 30–190.

[99] *Ante,* §§ 30–048, 30–056.

[1] *Ante* § 22–027.

total failure in relation to the parts not performed.[2] Also point to the unsatisfactory state of the law. In the High Court of Australia it has been said that "if counter-restitution is relatively simple . . . , insistance on total failure of consideration can be misleading or confusing"[3] and that "where both parties have impliedly acknowledged that the consideration can be "broken up" or apportioned . . . , any rationale for adhering to the traditional rule requiring *total* failure of consideration disappears."[4] The Privy Council recently has shown support for one of these methods of relaxing the requirement for total failure of consideration, namely apportionment. In *Goss v. Chilcott*, [5] it was suggested that apportionment is not always dependent on the parties' intentions. In that case it was acknowledged that a loan could be apportioned between principal and interest. This is not controversial, but Lord Goff delivering the judgment of the Court suggested that, if required, he would also apportion the principal so that any repayments made of the principal would not prevent there being a restitutionary claim based on failure of consideration but merely reduce the restitutionary claim to the balance of the loan. Moreover, in *Westdeutsche Landesbank Girozentrale v. Islington L.B.C.*,[6] Lord Goff expressed support for the reformulation of the total failure of consideration rule.

Partial failure of consideration in a divisible contract. A claim in restitution **30–058** to recover a definite part of the money already paid to the defendant will sometimes lie where the contract can be regarded as divisible, and some part of the consideration relating to a divisible part of the contract has wholly failed. Lord Porter has said[7]: "If a divisible part of the contract has wholly failed, and part of the consideration can be attributed to that part, that portion of the money so paid can be recovered. . . . " Thus, where the plaintiff ordered and paid for a specified tonnage of goods at a price of "18s. per cwt.," but, on delivery of the goods, it was discovered that less than the specified tonnage had been shipped, it was held that the plaintiff might recover the sum overpaid.[8] The question of divisibility may also arise on contracts where delivery is to be made in instalments.[9] Whether a contract is divisible and whether apportionment can take place has traditionally been an issue of construction based on the presumed intention of the parties. However, in *Goss v. Chilcott* the Privy Council suggested that apportionment is not limited to the intention of the parties and may also occur as a matter of law in those cases in which it can be carried out without difficulty, for instance, where the benefit received by the payer was, as in that case, a monetary one.[10]

---

[2] *Post*, § 30–058.

[3] *David Securities Pty. Ltd v. Commonwealth Bank of Australia* (1992) 66 A.L.J.R. 768, 779.

[4] *ibid.* at 780. Note also *Westdeutsche Landesbank Girozentrale v. Islington L.B.C.* [1996] A.C. 669, 682–683; *DO Ferguson & Associates v. Sohl* (1992) 62 Build. L.R. 92; *White Arrow Express Ltd v. Lamey's Distribution Ltd* (1995) 15 Tr. L.R. 69, CA, noted Beale, (1996) 112 L.Q.R. 205. But *cf. Pan Ocean Shipping Co. Ltd v. Creditcorp Ltd* [1994] 1 W.L.R. 161, 164–166.

[5] [1996] A.C. 788.

[6] [1996] A.C. 669, 682–683. But *cf. Stocznia Gdanska SA v. Latvian S.S.*, [1998] 1 W.L.R. 574, 590.

[7] *Fibrosa Spolka Akcyjna v. Fairbairn Lawson Combe Barbour Ltd* [1943] A.C. 32, 77.

[8] *Deveaux v. Conolly* (1849) 8 C.B. 640. See also *Biggerstaff v. Rowatt's Wharf Ltd* [1896] 2 Ch. 93; *Behrend & Co. Ltd v. Produce Brokers Co. Ltd* [1920] 3 K.B. 530; *Ebrahim Dawood Ltd v. Heath Ltd* [1961] 2 Lloyd's Rep. 512.

[9] See *ante*, §§ 22–030, 22–037, 24–089, 25–042; Vol. II, § 43–288.

[10] [1996] A.C. 788, 798. See *ante* § 30–057.

30–059   **Recovery of deposits.**[11] Where a sum of money is paid under a contract, and the contract is not completed, the right of the payer to claim the return of the money depends on the construction of the particular terms of the contract.[12] If it is called a "deposit" then, if nothing is said expressly about the conditions governing it, it will be taken to be required as a security for the completion of the contract by the payer and will be forfeited to the other party if the payer fails to perform his side of the contract.[13] If only part of the agreed deposit has actually been paid then, the better view is that, provided the obligation to make the payment has accrued, the innocent party can sue to recover the balance of the deposit.[14] A deposit may be recovered in the case of purchase on a condition which is not performed.[15] It is also prima facie recoverable where it is paid during the negotiations for a contract and no binding contract is concluded.[16]

30–060   **Section 49(2) of the Law of Property Act 1925.** This provides:

> "Where the court refuses to grant specific performance of a contract, or in any action for the return of a deposit, the court may, if it thinks fit, order the repayment of any deposit."

This provision is restricted to contracts for the sale or exchange of any interest in land.[17] Apart from this provision, the vendor would be obliged to return the deposit only where he was in breach of contract[18]; the statutory discretion conferred on the court by section 49(2) enables the court to make an order where the justice of the case requires it.[19] It may also be possible to seek equitable relief

---

[11] On recovery of a deposit paid to the other party's agent, see *post*, § 30–172 and Vol. II, § 32–107.

[12] *Howe v. Smith* (1884) 27 Ch.D. 89, 97–98; *Harrison v. Holland* [1922] 1 K.B. 211. See also *Smith v. Butler* [1900] 1 Q.B. 694; *Shuttleworth v. Clews* [1910] 1 Ch. 176. *cf. R. v. Ward Ltd v. Bignall* [1967] 1 Q.B. 534; *Workers' Trust and Merchant Bank Ltd v. Dojap Investments Ltd* [1993] A.C. 573. In the sale of land, the conditions of sale will usually contain express provisions relating to the deposit. See also *post*, §§ 30–170—30–171.

[13] *Howe v. Smith, supra*, at 97–98. But see the proposals of the Law Commission's Working Paper No. 61 (1975), paras. 49–67.

[14] *Hinton v. Sparkes* (1868) L.R. 3 C.P. 161, 166; *The Blankenstein* [1985] 1 W.L.R. 435. *cf. Lowe v. Hope* [1970] 1 Ch. 94; *Johnson v. Jones* [1972] N.Z.L.R. 313, 318. But *Hinton v. Sparkes* was not cited to Pennycuick J. in *Lowe v. Hope* and *Johnson v. Jones* concerned an express forfeiture clause which only applied to "moneys paid." These cases appear inconsistent with the principle that discharge of contract only operates prospectively; applied to moneys due as instalments in *Hyundai Heavy Industries Co. Ltd v. Papadopoulos* [1980] 1 W.L.R. 1129; *Stocznia Gdanska SA v. Latvian S.S.* [1998] 1 W.L.R. 574, *post*, § 30–061. See also Law Com. Working Paper No. 61, para. 59.

[15] *Wright v. Newton* (1835) 2 C.M. & R. 124.

[16] *Chillingworth v. Esche* [1924] 1 Ch. 97.

[17] s.49(3).

[18] *Best v. Hamand* (1879) 12 Ch.D. 1; *Re Scott and Alvarez's Contract* [1895] 2 Ch. 603; *Beyfus v. Lodge* [1925] Ch. 350; *James Macara Ltd v. Barclay* [1945] K.B. 148, 156.

[19] *Finkeilkraut v. Monohan* [1949] 2 All E.R. 235, 237–238. (*cf. James Macara Ltd v. Barclay, supra*, at 156). The enactment "was passed to remove the former hardship which existed where a defendant had a good defence in equity to a claim for specific performance but no defence in law, and, therefore, the deposit was forfeited . . . outside that ambit [the jurisdiction] should only be exercised, if at all, sparingly and with caution": *Michael Richards Properties Ltd v. Corporation of Wardens of St. Saviour's Parish, Southwark* [1975] 3 All E.R. 416, 424. But *cf. Schindler v. Pigault* [1975] 30 P. & C.R. 328; *Universal Corporation v. Five Ways Properties Ltd* [1979] 1 All E.R. 553, for a less restrictive view of the jurisdiction. In the latter, at p. 555, it was said that "repayment must be ordered in any circumstances which make this the fairest course between the two parties." See *County and Metropolitan Homes Survey Ltd v. Topclaim Ltd* [1997] 1 All E.R. 254 (effect of exclusion of Law of Property Act 1925, s.49(2)).

from forfeiture in respect of deposits and other payments required as security for performance where the forfeiture provision is penal[20] and it would be unconscionable for the payee to retain the payment. This jurisdiction, based on *Stockloser v. Johnson*,[21] is fully discussed in the chapter on Damages.[22]

Part payments not intended to be deposits.[23] Different principles apply if there is a substantial prepayment of the purchase price which is not intended to be in the nature of a deposit or earnest. In this situation the payer may still have a claim for recovery, despite the fact that the non-performance of the contract was due to his own fault. Thus, where a buyer repudiated his contract to purchase goods, he was nevertheless held to be entitled to recover a substantial prepayment made by him, subject to a deduction in respect of the actual damage suffered by the seller through the breach of contract.[24] This was because the right to the payment was conditional upon the subsequent completion of the contract.[25] However, where, as in a contract for work and materials, the contractual obligations of the party to whom a part payment or an instalment is made mean that he is bound to incur expenses before completing performance, the right to the payment will be unconditional and the payment will be irrecoverable although it is not required as security for due performance.[26] **30–061**

(c) *Benefits Conferred under a Void, Illegal or Unenforceable Contract*

Benefits conferred under a void contract. Many instances of restitution on the ground of total failure of consideration[27] may be placed under this heading. If a contract is void *ab initio* for mistake[28] any payment or credit received[29] made **30–062**

---

[20] Despite their similar functions clauses requiring payment as security for performance are distinguished from penalty clauses (*ante*, § 27–102) which provide for payment *after* breach. Although *Public Works Commissioners v. Hills* [1906] A.C. 368 supports the application of the rules governing penalty clauses and liquidated damages clauses to stipulations for security for due performance, in the present state of the law, this is doubtful; *Linggi Plantations Ltd v. Jagatheesan* (1972) 1 M.L.J. 89, 91 (*per* Lord Hailsham L.C.) *cf. Workers Trust & Merchant Bank Ltd v. Dojap Investments Ltd* [1995] A.C. 573. See Law Commission Working Paper No. 61 (1975), paras. 57–67.

[21] [1954] 1 Q.B. 476.

[22] See *ante*, §§ 27–121, 27–125. See also Goff and Jones *op. cit.* pp. 540–546.

[23] Beatson (1981) 97 L.Q.R. 389; *op. cit.* Chap. 3; *ante*, § 27–124.

[24] *Dies v. British and International Mining and Finance Corporation Ltd* [1939] 1 K.B. 724. (See *ante*, § 27–124 (distinguished in *Elson v. Prices Tailors Ltd* [1963] 1 W.L.R. 287).) For the same principle in other types of contract, see *Mayson v. Clouet* [1924] A.C. 980; *McDonald v. Dennys Lascelles Ltd* (1933) 48 C.L.R. 457 (contracts for the sale of land); *Rover International Ltd v. Cannon Film Sales Ltd (No. 3)* [1989] 1 W.L.R. 912, 932, 936 (film distribution contract).

[25] *Palmer v. Temple* (1839) 9 A. & E. 508, 521; *McDonald v. Dennys Lascelles Ltd, supra*, at 477; *Fibrosa Spolka Akcyjna v. Fairbairn Lawson Combe Barbour Ltd* [1943] A.C. 32, 65; *Guardian Ocean Cargos Ltd v. Banco de Brasil SA (Nos. 1 & 3)* [1994] 2 Lloyd's Rep. 152.

[26] *Hyundai Heavy Industries Co. Ltd v. Papadopoulos* [1980] 1 W.L.R. 1129. Although that case does not make it entirely clear whether the distinction from *Dies v. British International Mining and Finance Corporation Ltd, supra*, is based on the fact that in *Dies* the consideration for the payment had totally failed or on the need, on facts such as those in *Hyundai* (*ante*, § 30–053), to protect the reliance of the performer (on which, see Beatson *ibid.* at pp. 401–405; *The Use and Abuse of Unjust Enrichment* (1991), pp. 56–61), in *Rover International Ltd v. Cannon Film Sales Ltd, supra*, it was said to be based on total failure of consideration. See also *Stocznia Gdanska SA v. Latvian S.S. Co.* [1998] 1 W.L.R. 574.

[27] See *ante*, §§ 30–048 *et seq.*

[28] See *ante*, §§ 5–003 *et seq.*

[29] A credit received, albeit only in account, is equivalent to payments for this purpose: *Branwhite v. Worcester Works Finance Ltd* [1969] 1 A.C. 552.

under the apparent contract is recoverable,[30] and an action for wrongful interference with property may be brought in respect of goods delivered under the apparent contract.[31]

30–063   Thus, where the claimant paid the purchase-money for an annuity on the life of A, but both parties were ignorant of the fact that A had died some days previously, he was entitled to recover the whole of the money since the contract lacked subject-matter and was therefore void: the consideration had totally failed.[32] Again, where a company paid instalments under a distributorship agreement which had in fact been made before its incorporation it was entitled to recover such instalments as were paid after its incorporation; the agreement was void and the consideration for the instalments had totally failed.[33] Recently, recovery in these cases has been put on a wider basis. It has been held that money paid under void interest rate swap agreements can be recovered because it has been paid for "no consideration" or in the "absence of consideration," even if benefits have been received by the payer-plaintiff and the contract has been fully performed.[34] Where payments have been made both ways restitution is only available to a party on the basis that he gives credit for what he has received[35] and if it is possible to return the parties to their original positions.[36] Where a contract is rendered void by statute, it is a matter of statutory interpretation to discover whether money paid under such an apparent contract is recoverable.[37] For example, if a wagering contract is void under the Gaming Act 1845, money paid to the winner of the wager cannot be recovered by the loser[38]; but money advanced on a bill of sale which is void for want of form or for non-registration may be recovered, with reasonable interest, in restitution.[39] The question whether a *quantum meruit* or a *quantum valebat* will lie where services are rendered or goods supplied under a void contract is discussed *post,* 30–182.

---

[30] *Branwhite v. Worcester Works Finance Ltd, supra.* See the discussion of *Bell v. Lever Brothers* [1932] A.C. 161 (*ante,* § 5–012) between Landon and Tylor: (1935) 51 L.Q.R. 650; (1936) 52 L.Q.R. 27, 478; (1937) 53 L.Q.R. 118.

[31] *Cundy v. Lindsay* (1878) 3 App.Cas. 459 (*ante,* §§ 5–003, 5–048); Torts (Interference with Goods) Act 1977.

[32] *Strickland v. Turner* (1852) 7 Exch. 208; *Kennedy v. Thomassen* [1929] 1 Ch. 426. For a review of the authorities, see *Westdeutsche Landesbank Girozentrale v. Islington L.B.C.* (1993) 91 L.G.R. 323, 358–361. On restitution following "failure of consideration," see *ante,* §§ 30–048 *et seq.*

[33] *Rover International Ltd v. Cannon Film Sales Ltd, supra.*

[34] *Westdeutsche Landesbank Girozentrale v. Islington L.B.C.* [1994] 4 All E.R. 890; affd. [1996] 2 A.C. 669; *Guinness Mahon & Co Ltd v. Kensington & Chelsea R.L.B.C.* [1998] 2 All E.R. 272. See also *Woolwich Equitable B.S. v. I.R.C.* [1993] A.C. 70, 197 (Lord Browne-Wilkinson). On "no consideration" see also *Friends' Provident Life Office v. Hillier Parker May & Rowden (a firm)* [1997] Q.B. 85, 98. *cf. Commissioner of State Revenue (Vic) v. Royal Insurance Australia Ltd* (1994) 182 C.L.R. 51, 67.

[35] *ibid.* at 367; *Guiness Mahon & Co Ltd v. Kensington & Chelsea R.L.B.C.* [1998] 2 All E.R. 272. Where the payer has received a non-monetary benefit, he will probably be liable to a *quantum meruit* or a *quantum valebat, post,* § 30–182.

[36] *Kleinwort Benson Ltd v. S. Tyneside M.B.C.* [1994] 4 All E.R. 972, 987–990.

[37] On restitution of money transferred under an *ultra vires* contract, see *Westdeutsche Landesbank Girozentrale v. Islington L.B.C.* [1996] A.C. 669, *ante,* §§ 9–017—30–015. See also Companies Act 1989, s.108.

[38] *Morgan v. Ashcroft* [1938] 1 K.B. 49, *ante,* § 30–036. *cf. Lipkin Gorman v. Karpnale Ltd* [1991] 2 A.C. 548 (where owner of stolen money recovered it from casino). See Vol. II, § 40–027.

[39] *Davies v. Rees* (1886) 17 Q.B.D. 408; *North Central Wagon Finance Co. Ltd v. Brailsford* [1962] 1 W.L.R. 1288.

Illegal contracts. If money is paid under a contract which is illegal, and not merely void, the general rule is that it cannot be recovered: *in pari delicto potior est conditio defendentis*.[40] Both the general rule and the exceptions are fully discussed in the chapter on Illegality.[41]

30–064

Money paid under unenforceable contract. The mere fact that one party has paid money to another under a contract which he cannot enforce against the latter because of its non-compliance with a statute requiring written evidence or on grounds of public policy, will not entitle the party who has paid the money to recover it as on a failure of consideration, for such a contract is not void, but merely unenforceble.[42] A total failure of consideration[43] must be proved before restitution can be claimed in these circumstances and restitution will not, in any event, be given if it would run counter to the policy of the statute in question.[44]

30–065

Minors' contracts. Money paid by a minor under a contract which is unenforceable against him,[45] will be recoverable provided there has been a total failure of consideration.[46] Where money is paid to a minor, at common law[47] the adult will not be permitted to recover in restitution on the ground of a total failure of consideration if that would "in a roundabout way" contravene the policy of the law and indirectly enforce the unenforceable contract.[48] By section 3(1) of the Minors' Contracts Act 1987 the court is given discretion to require the minor to transfer to the other party "any property" acquired under the contract "or property representing it" if it is just and equitable to do so. Although the matter is not entirely free from doubt, it is possible that "property" will be held to include money since otherwise there would be no power to order the transfer of the proceeds if the minor has resold the goods he bought under the unenforceable contract.[49]

30–066

Recovery of premiums where a policy of insurance is avoided. The premium paid under a policy of insurance may be recovered if the risk insured against does not exist, and this fact was not known to the parties[50]: the consideration has totally failed.[51] Where a policy of marine insurance is avoided by the

30–067

---

[40] *e.g. Parkinson v. College of Ambulance Ltd* [1925] 2 K.B. 1.

[41] See *ante*, Chap. 17.

[42] On requirements of writing, see *Sweet v. Lee* (1841) 3 Man. & G. 452, 467–468. See also *Shaw v. Woodcock* (1827) 7 B. & C. 73, 84; *Thomas v. Brown* (1876) 1 Q.B.D. 714, 723, and see Chap. 4 *ante*. On public policy, see *Aratra Potato Co. Ltd v. Taylor Joynson Garrett (a firm)* [1995] 4 All E.R. 695; Chap. 16 *ante*.

[43] See *ante*, §§ 30–048 *et seq.*

[44] *Orakpo v. Manson Investments Ltd* [1978] A.C. 95.

[45] On the Minors' Contracts Act 1987, see *ante*, Chap. 8.

[46] *Steinberg v. Scala (Leeds) Ltd* [1923] 2 Ch. 452; *Pearce v. Brain* [1929] 2 K.B. 310. *cf. Valentini v. Canali* (1889) 24 Q.B.D. 166 (claim may lie where *restitutio in integrum* is possible). But note that the first case concerned a voidable contract and the other two contracts which were "absolutely void" under the Infants Relief Act 1874, repealed by the Minors' Contracts Act 1987. See further *ante*, § 8–005; Goff and Jones *op. cit.* pp. 641–643.

[47] Common law restitutionary remedies are preserved by the Minors' Contracts Act 1987, s.3(2).

[48] *R. Leslie Ltd v. Shiell* [1914] 3 K.B. 607, 613; *Thavron v. Bank of Credit & Commerce SA* [1985] 1 Lloyd's Rep. 259. *cf. Cowern v. Neild* [1912] 2 K.B. 419 on which see Treitel *op. cit.* pp. 500–501.

[49] Law Com. No. 134 (1984) "Law of Contract Minors' Contracts," para. 4.21; *ante* § 8–050.

[50] *Pritchard v. The Merchant's and Tradesman's Mutual Life Assurance Society* (1858) 3 C.B.(N.S.) 622; *Tyrie v. Fletcher* (1777) 2 Cowp. 666, 668; *Re Cavalier Insurance Co. Ltd* [1989] 2 Lloyd's Rep. 430.

[51] See *ante*, §§ 30–048 *et seq.*

insurer on the ground of the misrepresentation or concealment by the assured of a material fact, the assured, if not guilty of fraud, may recover all premiums which he has paid under the policy.[52]

(d) *Compulsory Payments to the Defendant*[53]

30–068   **Compulsory payments to the defendant.** Where the claimant has paid money to the defendant by wrongful or illegitimate compulsion, or under extortion *colore officii*, the defendant is under an obligation to restore it to the claimant. The principle is very similar where the claimant has been compelled to make a payment to a third person which the defendant was primarily or ultimately liable to pay, but the latter type of compulsory payment is considered later under the heading of "Reimbursement."[54] Under the present heading of "Restitution" will be considered compulsory payments received by the defendant direct from the claimant. The question of what amounts to a voluntary payment (which is irrecoverable) is common to both types of compulsory payments, but is considered in detail later in connection with the second type of compulsory payment.[55]

30–069   **Unlawful or illegitimate compulsion.** The question of what amounts to unlawful or illegitimate compulsion will depend on the circumstances of the particular case. Although the reported cases deal mainly with issues of duress of goods[56] and extortion *colore officii*,[57] duress of the person is obviously included[58] and other forms of pressure to any rights of the person who pays, including economic duress, will be recognised.[59] As a general rule the pressure will be exerted by a threat to commit an unlawful act. However, it has also been said that duress can exist where the threat is of lawful action provided the court regards the demand it is coupled with as illegitimate.[60] Although, in the absence of legis-

---

[52] *Anderson v. Thornton* (1835) 8 Exch. 425, 428; and see Marine Insurance Act 1906, s.84(1). *cf. St John Shipping Corporation v. Joseph Rank Ltd* [1957] 1 Q.B. 267, 293.

[53] Winfield (1944) 60 L.Q.R. 341; Beatson *op. cit.* Chap. 5; Birks *op. cit.* pp. 173 *et seq.* Burrows *op. cit.* Chap. 5; Goff and Jones, *op. cit.* Chap. 10.

[54] See *post*, § 30–625. Authorities on compulsory payments to third persons may be used to elucidate the principles relating to compulsory payments to the defendant, and vice versa.

[55] See *post*, § 30–135. Most of the cases concerning voluntary payments deal with alleged compulsory payments to a third person. See also *ante*, §§ 7–002, 7–038 (duress).

[56] *Post*, §§ 30–071—30–074.

[57] *Post*, § 30–075.

[58] *Post*, § 30–070.

[59] *e.g.* threats of duress to goods will suffice: *Maskell v. Horner* [1915] 3 K.B. 106 (see *post*, § 30–071) as will threats to commit other torts: *Universe Tankships Inc. of Monrovia v. International Transport Workers Federation* [1983] 2 A.C. 366. Threats to commit a breach of contract can amount to duress and a payment in excess of the contract price which is made as the result of a coercive threat by the payee to commit a serious breach of his contractual obligations (unless the excess payment is made) may be recovered in a restitutionary claim: see *North Ocean Shipping Co. Ltd v. Hyundai Construction Co. Ltd* [1979] Q.B. 705; *B. & S. Contracts and Design Ltd v. Victor Green Publications Ltd* [1984] I.C.R. 419; *The Alev* [1989] 1 Lloyd's Rep. 138; *Atlas Express Ltd v. Kafco (Importers and Distributors) Ltd* [1989] Q.B. 833; *C.T.N. Cash and Carry Ltd v. Gallagher Ltd* [1994] 4 All E.R. 714 and the Australian cases of *Nixon v. Furphy* (1925) 25 S.R. (N.S.W.) 151 and *Sundell & Sons v. Emm Yannoulatos (Overseas) Pty. Ltd* (1956) 56 S.R. (N.S.W.) 323; *cf. Crescendo Management Pty Ltd v. Westpac Banking Corp.* (1988) 19 N.S.W.L.R. 40. See also *Pao On v. Lau Yin Long* [1980] A.C. 614. On economic duress see *ante*, § 7–010; *D. & C. Builders Ltd v. Rees* [1966] 2 Q.B. 617 (*ante*, §§3–109, 3–128, 7–010—7–014).

[60] *Universe Tankships Inc. of Monrovia v. International Transport Workers Federation* [1983] 2 A.C. 366, 384, 401; *Dimskal SS. Co. Ltd v. ITWF* [1992] 2 A.C. 152. See also *Thorne v. Motor Trade*

lative guidance,[61] distinguishing legitimate from illegitimate demands is likely to be controversial, the courts may be assisted by drawing on cases of conspiracy where no unlawful means are used[62] and by having regard to usual trade practice. The coercive force[63] of the compulsion will depend on its immediacy,[64] on the ability of the payer to obtain legal advice or legal protection before making the payment,[65] and, in some circumstances, on the availability of an effective alternative remedy or course of action open to the payer.[66] It was sometimes said that economic duress had to coerce the plaintiff's will so as to vitiate his consent,[67] but this approach has been criticised and the better view is to ask whether, where pressure has been applied, that pressure went beyond what the law considers legitimate.[68] If the payment amounts to a genuine compromise of a disputed claim honestly made by the payee,[69] or the payment is made in the course of or under threat of legal proceedings,[70] or the transaction is affirmed,[71] it cannot be recovered.

Duress of the person and undue influence. Duress of the person[72] or undue influence[73] entitles a party to a contract to avoid it[74]; consequently, restitution of benefits conferred under the voidable contract will be ordered by the court,   **30–070**

Association [1937] A.C. 797; *Norreys v. Zeffert* [1939] 2 All E.R. 186; Birks *op. cit.* pp. 177–179; Burrows *op. cit.* pp. 183–188; Goff and Jones *op. cit.* pp. 308–311, 342, 347. *cf. C.T.N. Cash and Carry Ltd v. Gallagher Ltd* [1994] 4 All E.R. 714; *Leyland Daf Ltd v. Automotive Products plc* [1994] 1 B.C.L.R. 244; *Royal Boskalis Westminster N.V. v. Mountain* [1998] 2 W.L.R. 538, 590–591. Beatson *op. cit.* pp. 129–134.

[61] Such as the Trade Union legislation in the *Universe Tankships* case although, note that the threat there was to commit a tort.

[62] *Crofter Hand-Woven Harris Tweed Ltd v. Veitch* [1942] A.C. 435; *Sorrell v. Smith* [1925] A.C. 700, 712.

[63] *Skeate v. Beale* (1841) 11 Ad. & E. 983, 990 ("the fear . . . does not deprive anyone of his free agency who possesses that ordinary degree of firmness which the law requires all to exert"). But see *Barton v. Armstrong* [1976] A.C. 104.

[64] *Maskell v. Horner, supra,* at 118 ("under the compulsion of urgent and pressing necessity"). *cf. Twyford v. Manchester Corporation* [1946] Ch. 236, and *Somes v. British Empire Shipping Co.* (1860) 8 H.L.C. 338.

[65] *Maskell v. Horner, supra,* at 120. See *post,* § 30–071.

[66] The presence of an alternative remedy has been said to be irrelevant in cases involving detention of the payer's property (*Astley v. Reynolds* (1731) 2 Str. 915, *post,* § 30–073; *Kanhaya Lal v. National Bank of India* (1913) 29 T.L.R. 314, 315. *cf. Ashmole v. Wainwright* (1842) 2 Q.B. 837, 845) but would appear to be relevant where there is no such detention (*Knibbs v. Hall* (1794) Peake 276; *Twyford v. Manchester Corporation, ante,* at 241–242; *Pao On v. Lau Yin Long, supra,* at 635); *B. & S. Contracts and Design Ltd v. Victor Green Publications Ltd, supra; The Alev, supra* at 146–147; *Hennessy v. Craigmyle & Co.* [1986] I.C.R. 461. *cf. North Ocean Shipping v. Hyundai Construction Co. Ltd, supra,* at 715, 719.

[67] *The Siboen and The Sibotre* [1976] 1 Lloyd's Rep. 293, 336; *North Ocean Shipping v. Hyundai Construction Co. Ltd, supra,* at 717, 719; *Pao On v. Lau Yin Long, supra,* at 635.

[68] *Universe Tankships Inc. of Monrovia v. I.T.W.F., supra,* at 384, 400; *B. & S. Contracts and Design Ltd v. Victor Green Publications Ltd, supra,* at 426–428; *Dimskal SS. Co. Ltd v. I.T.W.F., supra,* at 165–166.

[69] *Atlee v. Backhouse* (1838) 2 M. & W. 633; *Wakefield v. Newbon* (1844) 6 Q.B. 276, 281; *Callisher v. Bischoffsheim* (1870) L.R. 5 Q.B. 449; *Miles v. New Zealand Alford Estate Co.* (1885) 32 Q.B.D. 266, 291; *The Siboen and the Sibotre* [1976] 1 Lloyd's Rep. 293, 334. See *ante,* §§ 3–049—3–050, 3–070.

[70] See *post,* § 30–079.

[71] *North Ocean Shipping Co. Ltd v. Hyundai Construction Co. Ltd, supra,* at 720–721; *B. & S. Contracts and Design Ltd v. Victor Green Publications Ltd, supra,* at 428.

[72] *Ante,* § 7–008; *cf. ante,* § 30–067.

[73] *Ante,* §§ 7–041—7–074.

[74] *Ante,* §§ 7–039—7–041.

following rescission by the innocent party. Even if there has been no contract, benefits conferred on the defendant as the result of duress or undue influence by him should, in principle, be recoverable from him by a claim in restitution.[75] The duress will usually amount to a tort and recovery will be founded on the principles governing "waiver of tort" considered below.[76]

30–071   **Actual or threatened seizure or distress of the claimant's goods.** Lord Reading C.J. in the leading case of *Maskell v. Horner*[77] said:

> "If a person pays money, which he is not bound to pay, under the compulsion of urgent and pressing necessity or of seizure, actual or threatened, of his goods, he can recover it as money had and received. The money is not paid under duress in the strict sense of the term, as that implies duress of person, but under the pressure of seizure or detention of goods which is analogous to that of duress."

In this case, the defendant owned a market and exacted from the claimant market tolls (to which he was not entitled) by threatening to distrain on the claimant's goods. The plaintiff paid the tolls under protest, but the Court of Appeal later upheld his claim to recover the payments on the ground that they were not voluntary. It would have been unreasonable to expect a man in the claimant's position to forgo the use of his goods while the matter was litigated.[78] Similarly, where the sheriff had seized certain goods, which were claimed by the assignees of a bankrupt as belonging to the bankrupt's estate, and in order to prevent the sheriff from proceeding to a sale, which he threatened to do, the assignees paid the sum claimed under the writ, it was held that they were entitled to recover such sum as money which had been paid by compulsion.[79]

30–072   **Distress for an excessive amount.** Where a distrainor demands an excessive payment before he will return the goods to the owner of the goods there is some doubt whether the distrainee may, without relying on his remedies of replevin or detinue, pay under protest and then sue in restitution to recover the excess.[80]

30–073   **Wrongful demand by defendant detaining goods.**[81] If chattels are wrongfully taken or detained from the claimant by the defendant, and money is paid to

---

[75] In the analogous situation of duress of goods, there is ample authority permitting such recovery: see *post*, §§ 30–071—30–074. *cf. Williams v. Bayley* (1866) L.R. 1 H.L. 200; *Kaufman v. Gerson* [1904] 1 K.B. 591.

[76] *Post*, §§ 30–084—30–095.

[77] [1915] 3 K.B. 106, 118. See *Kanhaya Lal v. National Bank of India* (1913) 29 T.L.R. 314; *Somes v. British Empire Shipping Co.* (1860) 8 H.L.C. 338.

[78] The goods may be merely in the possession of the plaintiff, and not owned by him: *Fell v. Whittaker* (1871) L.R. 7 Q.B. 120. *cf. Scarfe v. Hallifax* (1840) 7 M. & W. 288. Duress of goods is also discussed, *ante*, § 7–009.

[79] *Valpy v. Manley* (1845) 1 C.B. 594. On the position where the money is paid under duress to an agent of a third person, *Oates v. Hudson* (1851) 6 Ex. 346; *Owen & Co. v. Cronk* [1895] 1 Q.B. 265; *T. D. Keegan Ltd v. Palmer* [1961] 2 Lloyd's Rep. 449, 459. See Vol. II, § 32–107. *cf.* the position where the plaintiff is coerced by the defendant to pay money to a third party: *Re Hooper and Grass' Contract* [1949] V.L.R. 269.

[80] See Woodfall, *Landlord and Tenant* (28th ed.), §§ 1–0007 to 1–0008; Bullen, *Distress* (2nd ed.), pp. 223–224 and the discussion in Winfield (1944) 60 L.Q.R. 345–346 of *Glynn v. Thomas* (1856) 11 Exch. 870; *Loring v. Warburton* (1858) E.B. & E. 507; *Fell v. Whittaker* (1871) L.R. 7 Q.B. 120. *cf.* excessive demand on distress damage feasant: *Green v. Duckett* (1883) 11 Q.B.D. 275.

[81] This is another instance of waiver of tort (see *post*, § 30–086) since the defendant would usually be liable in conversion.

the defendant by the claimant simply for the purpose of recovering possession of the chattels, the money can be recovered by the claimant, since it was not a voluntary payment, especially if it was paid under protest.[82] Thus, in *Astley v. Reynolds*,[83] where the claimant had pawned plate with the defendant and the latter would not part with it unless the claimant paid him more than legal interest, it was held that the excess paid to redeem the goods might be recovered, even though the claimant could have brought an action for trover on tendering the sum legally due to the defendant.[84] The same principle applies where a carrier refuses to deliver goods except on payment of excessive charges,[85] or where goods are seized by the sheriff and the owner can redeem them only by paying him an amount in excess of the proper levy.[86]

Wrongful demand by defendant detaining title deeds. Where money was   **30–074**
paid under protest by a mortgagor in order to obtain possession of his title deeds, which were withheld by the solicitor of the mortgagee an unfounded claim of lien, it was held that the money might be recovered by a claim in restitution.[87] Similarly, where the solicitor of a mortgagee who was about to sell, refused to stop the sale or deliver up the title deeds of the mortgaged property, except on payment by the mortgagor of certain expenses with which he was not properly chargeable, it was held that the administratrix of the mortgagor, who had paid the excess under protest, could recover it.[88]

Extortion colore officii.[89] If a public officer demands an illegal fee, or an   **30–075**
excessive fee, for performing duties imposed on him by law, it amounts to extortion *colore officii* and the fee or excess is recoverable by a claim in restitution.[90] It may also be recoverable under the principle laid down in *Woolwich Equitable Building Society v. I.R.C.*[91] discussed below. It is not yet clear

---

[82] *Atlee v. Backhouse* (1838) 3 M. & W. 633, 650. See also *Shaw v. Woodcock* (1827) 7 B. & C. 73; *Green v. Duckett* (1883) 11 Q.B.D. 275 (excessive sum demanded on distress damage feasant); *North v. Walthamstow U.D.C.* (1898) 62 J.P. 836; *T. D. Keegan Ltd v. Palmer* [1961] 2 Lloyd's Rep. 449; *cf. Maskell v. Horner* [1915] 3 K.B. 106 (*ante*, § 30–071).

[83] (1732) 2 Stra. 915.

[84] "The plaintiff might have such an immediate want of his goods, that an action of trover would not do his business" (*ibid.* at 916).

[85] Common Carrier: *Ashmole v. Wainwright* (1842) 2 Q.B. 837; *cf. Skeate v. Beale* (1841) 11 A. & E. 983; *G.W. Ry. v. Sutton* (1869) L.R. 4 H.L. 226 (*post*, § 30–078). See also Vol. II, § 35–024. Other carriers: *The Alev* [1989] 1 Lloyd's Rep. 138.

[86] *Scarfe v. Hallifax* (1840) 7 M. & W. 288, 290.

[87] *Wakefield v. Newbon* (1844) 6 Q.B. 276; *Turner v. Deane* (1849) 3 Exch. 836; and see *Pratt v. Vizard* (1833) 5 B. & Ad. 808; *Smith v. Sleap* (1844) 12 M. & W. 585; *Oates v. Hudson* (1851) 6 Exch. 346. *cf. Re Llewellin* [1891] 3 Ch. 145.

[88] *Close v. Phipps* (1844) 7 M. & G. 586; and see *Fraser v. Pendlebury* (1861) 31 L.J.C.P. 1. The PC has applied a similar rule to detention of land: *Kanhaya Lal v. National Bank of India* (1913) 29 T.L.R. 314.

[89] Birks *op. cit.* pp. 294–299. Burrows *op. cit.* pp. 172–173, 346–348, 353–354; Goff and Jones *op. cit.* pp. 320–327. On recovery of money paid by extortion or oppression, see *post*, § 30–095.

[90] *Morgan v. Palmer* (1824) 2 B. & C. 729; *cf. Traherne v. Gardner* (1856) 5 E. & B. 913; *Hooper v. Exeter Corpn.* (1887) 56 L.J.Q.B. 457 (harbour dues); *Marshall Shipping Co. v. Board of Trade* [1923] 2 K.B. 343; *Brocklebank v. R.* [1925] 1 K.B. 52; *R. & W. Paul Ltd v. The Wheat Commission* [1937] A.C. 139; *Mason v. State of N.S.W.* (1959) 102 C.L.R. 108; *Bell Bros. Pty. Ltd v. Shire of Serpentine-Jarrahdale* (1969) 44 A.L.J.R. 26.

[91] [1993] A.C. 70; *post* § 30–080.

whether that is an additional principle or subsumes *colore officii* cases.[92] A public officer is not on equal terms with a private citizen, who is likely to accept the correctness of an official demand and to believe that, unless he pays, he will suffer some penalty or exclusion from some benefit; it is likely to be held to be a payment under coercion if the official is in a position to prevent the payer from doing an act he wishes to do,[93] or to seize the goods of the payer.[94] But there may be extortion *colore officii* although the officer has not withheld a right or privilege in order to exact the fee,[95] and honestly believed that the fee was properly charged.[96] Thus a fee illegally demanded from a publican as a condition of granting his licence may be recovered[97]; as also may fees charged by a parish clerk, contrary to a statute, for extracts taken from a register book of burials and baptisms[98] or charges by an electricity company, contravening statutory restrictions.[99] Similarly, a party to an arbitration may recover an excessive fee fixed by the arbitrator and paid to him in order to obtain delivery of the award.[1] The fact that the payer was acting under a mistake of law is no defence to an action for extortion *colore officii*, as where a sheriff claimed and was paid a larger fee than he was entitled to by law.[2] But in some circumstances, if no improper pressure or threat is used and the payer has full knowledge of all the facts, fees illegally collected by an official may be irrecoverable on the ground that they were paid voluntarily[3]; the court will assess the possible alternative courses of action open to the payer, such as, how, if at all, would he have suffered if he had refused to pay and, was the only way in which the authority could enforce its demand by suing the payer?[4]

30–076 **Express threat unnecessary.** The requirement, in some cases, that the authority accompany its demand with an express threat does not apply to the restitutionary right in the *Woolwich* case and has been criticised on two grounds. First, that demands made with the weight of an apparently valid governmental authority are far more coercive than demands made by private individuals whether or not there is "any actual threatened withholding of something to which the payer was entitled, or actual threatened impeding of him in the exercise of some right

---

[92] For the view that it does not, see Goff and Jones *op. cit.* pp. 320–323. For the view that it *could*, see Beatson (1993) 109 L.Q.R. 401, 404–410.

[93] *e.g. Morgan v. Palmer, supra; Steele v. Williams* (1853) 8 Exch. 625.

[94] *e.g. Atlee v. Backhouse* (1838) 3 M. & W. 633.

[95] *Steele v. Williams, supra.*

[96] *Morgan v. Palmer, supra.*

[97] *ibid.*

[98] *Steele v. Williams, supra.*

[99] *South of Scotland Electricity Board v. British Oxygen Ltd (No. 2)* [1959] 1 W.L.R. 587 (recovery not directed since facts not found, discussed in *Woolwich Equitable Building Society v. I.R.C.* [1933] A.C. 70, 133–134, 159–160, 165, 187–188.

[1] *Fernley v. Branson* (1851) 20 L.J.Q.B. 178; *Barnes v. Braithwaite* (1857) 2 H. & N. 569; *cf.* Arbitration Act 1950, s.19. See also *North Ocean Shipping Co. Ltd v. Hyundai Construction Co. Ltd* [1979] Q.B. 705, 716.

[2] *Dew v. Parsons* (1819) 2 B. & Ald. 562. On mistake of law, see *ante*, §§ 30–038 *et seq.*

[3] *Twyford v. Manchester Corporation* [1946] Ch. 236 (criticised by Marsh (1946) 62 L.Q.R. 333; Birks *op. cit.* pp. 296–297. On voluntary payments see *post*, §§ 30–135 *et seq.*). *cf. William Whiteley Ltd v. R.* (1909) 101 L.T. 741 (criticised by Munkman *op. cit.* pp. 39–40); *Sebel Products Ltd v. Commissioners of Customs and Excise* [1949] Ch. 409 (*ante*, § 30–044). Note, however, that the plaintiff in *Maskell v. Horner* [1915] 3 K.B. 106 (*ante*, § 30–071) did not bring an action challenging the tolls until he had been paying them for 12 years.

[4] *Twyford v. Manchester Corporation, supra*, at 239, 242; *William Whiteley Ltd v. R., supra.*

or liberty."[5] Secondly, it is contrary to principles of public law for such an authority to keep money obtained in such a manner.[6] Even if there is no need for an express threat under the *colore officii* principle, it is still narrower than the restitutionary right in the *Woolwich* case which is not based on compulsion but on *ultra vires*. On the other hand, insofar as it applies to arbitrators and common carriers, *colore officii* may prove to apply to a wider class of payees.[7]

Compliance with invalid local authority notices. A principle analogous to   **30–077**
extortion *colore officii* allowed recovery of money expended where the claimants were under the impression that they were bound to comply with a notice from the local authority to repair a drain, and did so under pressure practically amounting to compulsion, although the notice was not a statutory one with which they were bound to comply.[8]

Compulsory payment of an excessive amount.[9] In *Great Western Railway v.*   **30–078**
Sutton[10] the railway refused to carry the claimant's goods unless he paid freight at an excessive rate not permitted by law; the House of Lords held that the claimant was entitled to recover the excess on the ground that, since the claimant could not have had his goods carried without meeting the railway's demand, it was a case of compulsion. Willes J. said: "When a man pays more than he is bound to do by law for the performance of a duty which the law says is owed to him for nothing, or for less than he has paid, there is a compulsion . . . in respect of which he is entitled to recover the excess by *condictio indebiti*, or action for money had and received."[11]

Payment made in the course of, or under the threat of, legal proceed-   **30–079**
ings.[12] The general rule is that where a payment has been made in the course of legal proceedings, it is voluntary and irrecoverable; the same rule is generally

---

[5] *Mason v. New South Wales* (1959) 102 C.L.R. 108, 116–117 (Dixon J.). See also, *ibid.* at 126–127, 146; *Steele v. Williams, supra*; *Hooper v. Exeter Corporation* (1887) 56 L.J.Q.B. 457; *Queens of the River SS. Co. Ltd v. Conservators of the River Thames* (1899) 15 T.L.R. 474; *South of Scotland Electricity Board v. British Oxygen Co. Ltd (No. 2)* [1959] 1 W.L.R. 587; *Rogers v. Louth C.C.* [1981] I.R. 265. See further *Woolwich Equitable B.S. v. I.R.C.* [1993] A.C. 70, 173.

[6] *Post*, § 30–080.

[7] *Ante*, n. 99 (arbitrator); *ante*, § 30–060, n. 85, *post*, § 30–078 (carrier). See also Goff and Jones *op. cit.* pp. 320–323.

[8] *North v. Walthamstow U.D.C.* (1898) 67 L.J.Q.B. 972. See also *Gebhardt v. Saunders* [1892] 2 Q.B. 452; *Andrew v. St. Olave's Board of Works* [1898] 1 Q.B. 775; *Ellis v. Bromley R.D.C.* (1899) 81 L.T. 224; *Wilson's Music & General Printing Co. v. Finsbury B.C.* [1908] 1 K.B. 563; *cf. Thompson and Norris Manufacturing Co. Ltd v. Hawes* (1895) 73 L.T. 369; *Oliver v. Camberwell B.C.* (1904) 90 L.T. 285.

[9] Similar principles apply where the payee was legally obliged to act without payment: see Extortion *colore officii, ante*, § 30–075.

[10] (1869) L.R. 4 H.L. 226. *cf. South of Scotland Electricity Board v. British Oxygen Co. Ltd* [1959] 1 W.L.R. 587. On the position of a common carrier, see Vol. II, §§ 36–007 *et seq.*, especially § 36–016.

[11] (1869) L.R. 4 H.L. 226, 249. See also *Parker v. G.W. Ry.* (1844) 7 M. & G. 253; *Denaby Main Colliery Co. Ltd v. M.S. & L. Ry.* (1885) 11 App.Cas. 97; *North Staffs Ry. v. Edge* [1920] A.C. 254. Recovery has been permitted although part of the excess was received by the defendant company as agent for a third party: *Parker v. Bristol and Exeter Ry.* (1851) 6 Exch. 702.

[12] See also the rule permitting the compromise of an invalid claim, *ante*, §§ 3–049—3–055; Beatson [1974] C.L.J. 97, 100–104, *op. cit.* pp. 100–103.

true when legal proceedings are threatened.[13] In such cases legal advice can be taken, and if payment is made without doing so, the payer is deemed to have settled or compromised the dispute. "There must be an end of litigation, otherwise there would be no security for any person."[14] However, if the payee has acted fraudulently or illegally, such a payment may be recoverable[15]; and where money is paid under a void judgment, *e.g.* because an inferior court had no jurisdiction or because the correct procedure was not followed, it may be recovered.[16]

(e) Ultra Vires *Receipts by the Revenue and Public Authorities*

30–080   **Ultra vires demands.** In *Woolwich Equitable Building Society v. I.R.C.*[17] it was held that a payment made pursuant to a demand for tax that was *ultra vires* because of the invalidity of the relevant subordinate legislation was recoverable. Lord Goff stated that "money paid by a citizen to a public authority in the form of taxes or other levies paid pursuant to an *ultra vires* demand by the authority is *prima facie* recoverable by the citizen as of right."[18] In holding this the House consciously reformulated the law which hitherto precluded recovery unless the payment was made under mistake of fact or compulsion.[19] The reasons given for enunciating a new restitutionary right lay in constitutional law and in particular article 4 of the Bill of Rights 1688,[20] the existence of a right to repayment of sums levied by a public body contrary to rules of E.C. law,[21] the unattractive contrast with the position of money paid by the Crown which, if paid without authority, is recoverable,[22] and the fact that demands by the Revenue and other

---

[13] *Marriot v. Hampton* (1797) 7 T.R. 269; *Hamlet v. Richardson* (1833) 9 Bing. 644; *Moore v. Vestry of Fulham* [1895] 1 Q.B. 399; *Self v. Hove Commissioners* [1895] 1 Q.B. 685, 690; *William Whiteley Ltd v. R.* (1910) 101 L.T. 741; *Maskell v. Horner* [1915] 3 K.B. 106, 121–122; *Sawyer and Vincent v. Window Brace Ltd* [1943] K.B. 32; *Woolwich Equitable Building Society v. I.R.C.* [1993] A.C. 70, 98, 121, 135–136, 140, 165, 174, 178, 196, 198, 200–201. *cf. Rogers v. Ingram* (1876) 3 Ch.D. 351; *Caird v. Moss* (1886) 33 Ch.D. 22, 36; *Binder v. Alachouzos* [1972] 2 Q.B. 151. (The rule also applies to payment in the course of foreign litigation: *Clydesdale Bank Ltd v. Schroder & Co.* [1913] 2 K.B. 1.) See generally *ante*, § 7–035.

[14] *Marriot v. Hampton, supra*; *Binder v. Alachouzos, supra.*

[15] *Ward & Co. v. Wallis* [1900] 1 Q.B. 675. *cf. Pitt v. Coomes* (1835) 2 A. & E. 459; *Duke de Cadaval v. Collins* (1836) 4 A. & E. 858.

[16] *Newdigate v. Davy* (1701) 1 Ld.Raym. 742; *Farrow v. Mayes* (1852) 18 Q.B. 516; *Re Smith* (1888) 20 Q.B.D. 321. *cf. O'Connor v. Isaacs* [1956] 2 Q.B. 288.

[17] [1993] 1 A.C. 70; [1989] 1 W.L.R. 137 (Nolan J.). See also Beatson (1993) 109 L.Q.R. 401; Birks [1992] P.L. 580; Burrows *op. cit.* Chap. 12; Goff and Jones *op. cit* Chap. 27.

[18] *ibid.* at 177. See also *ibid.* at 196, 198; *British Steel plc v. Customs and Excise Commissioners* [1997] 2 All E.R. 366.

[19] *ibid.* at 168, 171, 196, 204. See also *Att.-Gen. v. Wilts United Dairies Ltd* (1921) 37 T.L.R. 884, CA; (1922) 127 L.T. 822, HL; *Brocklebank Ltd v. R.* [1925] 1 K.B. 52 (although recovery there was barred by the Indemnity Act 1920); *Congreave v. Home Office* [1976] Q.B. 629, 652; Birks in Finn (ed.), *Essays in Restitution*, pp. 164 *et seq.*; Cornish (1987) 14 Jo. Mal. and Comp. See also *R. v. Tower Hamlets L.B.C., ex. p. Chetnik Developments Ltd* [1988] A.C. 858 (judicial review of refusal to exercise express discretion to repay overpayment of rates).

[20] *ibid.* at 172.

[21] *ibid.* at 177. See case 199/82 *Administrazione delle Finanze dello Stato v. SpA San Giorgio* [1983] E.C.R. 3595.

[22] *ibid.*; *Auckland Harbour Board v. The King* [1924] A.C. 318.

governmental bodies are implicitly backed by the coercive powers of the state and may well entail unpleasant economic and social consequences.

Scope of right. It appears that the *Woolwich* principle applies when the **30–081** money was paid under a mistake of law.[23] It is submitted that it should extend to cases in which the public authority has made no demand for payment, for example where an *ultra vires* tax is paid in reasonable anticipation of a demand.[24] Although Lord Goff and Lord Slynn expressly reserved the question of whether the principle extends to cases in which the tax or other levy has been wrongfully exacted not because the demand was *ultra vires* but for other reasons, for example because the authority has misconstrued the relevant statute or regulation,[25] such misconstruction is an error of law and likely in virtually all cases to be *ultra vires*.[26] It is also not entirely clear whether the principle extends beyond taxation to licence fees or unauthorised charges for the provison of services by statutory utilities, hitherto dealt with under the *colore officii* principle.[27] While explicit guidance was not given on the range of bodies subject to the principle, it is submitted that it should apply to public bodies whose authority to charge is subject to and limited by public law principles, and to other bodies whose authority to charge is solely the product of statute, and thus limited.[28]

Statutory provisions. The restitutionary right is, in the context of taxation, **30–082** limited by statutory provisions for the recovery of overpayments. The broadest is the right to recover any payment of VAT that is not due[29]; the narrowest is the more discretionary remedy in section 33 of the Taxes Management Act 1970 for the recovery of such sum of overpaid income tax, corporation tax, capital gains tax, or petroleum revenue tax by reason of an error or mistaken of tax return as is "reasonable and just."[30] There is no right of recovery where the error reflected "the practice generally prevailing" when the return was made. Where, moreover, a statutory appeal mechanism is applicable to the facts, it appears that the payee will be required to seek its remedy through the statutory framework.[31] Secondly, although the claim is based on the *ultra vires* nature of the receipt, it appears that it is not a precondition to recovery that this be established in judicial review

---

[23] [1993] A.C. 70, 177, 205. See also *Westdeutsche Landesbank Girozentrale v. Islington L.B.C.* (1993) 91 L.G.R. 323; *ante*, § 30–063.

[24] Beatson (1993) 109 L.Q.R. 401, 405; Burrows *op. cit.* p. 356; Law Commission Consultation Paper No. 120, para. 3.90.

[25] *ibid.* at 177, 205.

[26] *Re Racal Communications Ltd* [1981] A.C. 374.

[27] *Steele v. Williams* (1853) 8 Ex Ch. 625; *Hooper v. Exeter Corporation* (1887) 56 L.J.Q.B. 457; *Queens of the River SS. Co. Ltd v. Conservators of the River Thames* (1899) 15 T.L.R. 474 (harbour dues and pier charges); *South of Scotland Electricity Board v. British Oxygen Co. Ltd* [1959] 1 W.L.R. 587 (electricity charges). See *ante*, §§ 30–075—30–078; *Att.-Gen. v. Wilts United Dairies Ltd, supra*; *Brocklebank Ltd v. R.* [1925] 1 K.B. 52; *Mason v. New South Wales* (1959) 102 C.L.R. 108.

[28] [1993] A.C. 70, 79, 138 (Glidewell and Butler-Sloss L.JJ.). See Beatson (1993) 109 L.Q.R. 401, 406–418. *cf. Green v. Portsmouth Stadium Ltd* [1953] 2 Q.B. 190 (where the principle would not apply because, but for the statute, there would have been no limit on the amount the defendant would have been able to charge).

[29] Value Added Tax Act 1994, s.80 as amended.

[30] See also Finance Act 1997, Sched. 5; Inheritance Tax Act 1984, s.241; Stamp Act 1891, s. 13(4); Social Security (Contributions) Regulations 1979 (S.I. 1979 No. 591); Customs and Excise Management Act 1979, s. 127; Council Tax (Administration and Enforcement) Regulations 1992 (S.I. 1992 No. 613).

[31] [1993] A.C. 70, 168–170.

proceedings.[32] The right of recovery is a private law right, albeit one arising out of a background of public law.[33]

30–083   **Defences.** Restitution will not be made where the payment was made to close the transaction.[34] Secondly, the recognition of the defence of change of position means that in principle where a public authority can show that it has so changed its position that it would be inequitable to allow the claim, it should have a defence.[35] Although Lord Goff doubted the advisability of imposing special limits upon recovery in the case of *ultra vires* levies to deal with the problem that a right of recovery might lead to serious disruption of public finances[36] the question of whether a payee who has "passed on" to others, for instance by price increases, the higher cost he has borne because of the overpayment should be precluded from recovery was left open.[37] This defence is permitted by E.C. law[38] and the provision in sections 24 and 29 of the Finance Act 1989 that recovery should not be allowed if the payee can show that the *payer* would be unjustly enriched if he recovered the payment, may reflect its *rationale*. However, it has been criticised[39] and arguments for a similar limit were not accepted by the High Court of Australia or in the context of restitution in respect of money paid under an *ultra vires* contract.[40]

---

[32] [1993] A.C. 70, 200 (Lord Slynn) and see Lord Goff's suggestion (at p. 174) that the right of recovery might need to be limited by strict time limits which implies that the three-month time limit for judicial review proceedings does not apply. In *Woolwich* there had been judicial review proceedings: *R. v. I.R.C., ex. p. Woolwich Equitable Building Society* [1990] 1 W.L.R. 1400, and see [1993] A.C. 70, 169 (Lord Goff).

[33] See *Lonrho plc v. Tebbit* [1992] 4 All E.R. 280, 288; *Roy v. Kensington and Chelsea and Westminster F.P.C.* [1992] 1 A.C. 624 and note that requiring recourse to Ord. 53 would impose two sets of proceedings on a plaintiff since there is no provision for joining a claim for restitution with an application for judicial review: *Wandsworth London Council v. Winder* [1985] A.C. 461, 480.

[34] [1993] A.C. 70, 98 *et seq.*, 121, 135–136, 140, CA; 165, 174, 178, 192, 196, 200–201, HL; *Air Canada v. British Columbia* [1989] S.C.R. 1161, 1200; *David Securities Pty. Ltd v. Commonwealth Bank of Australia* [1992] 66 A.L.J.R. 768, 774–775. See *ante*, § 30–036, *post*, §§30–111—30–124. For the suggestion that only contractual compromise should be a defence see Burrows *op. cit.* p. 357. *cf.* Law Com. No. 227, (1994) paras. 2.25–2.38.

[35] *Post*, §§ 30–114—30–118. *cf.* the narrower defence in *Rural Municipality of Storthoaks v. Mobil Oil Canade Ltd* [1975] 55 D.L.R. (3d) 1, 13.

[36] [1993] A.C. 70, 175–176. See also *Air Canada v. British Columbia* (1989) 59 D.L.R. (4th) 161, 193–197. *cf.* 169 (Wilson J.); *Sargood Bros. v. Commonwealth* (1910–11) 11 C.L.R. 258, 303 (Isaacs J.). See also Law Com. Consultation Paper No. 120, paras. 3.70–3.73; Burrows *op. cit.* pp. 358–360; Jones, *Restitution in Public and Private Law* (1991) pp. 24–28.

[37] [1993] A.C. 70, 177–178.

[38] Case 199–82, *Administrizione delle Finanze dello Stato v. SpA San Giorgio* [1983] E.C.R. 3595.

[39] Rudden and Bishop (1981) 6 E.L.R. 243; Law Commission Consultation Paper No. 120, paras. 3.82–3.85.

[40] *Mason v. New South Wales* (1959) 102 C.L.R. 108, 136, 146; *Kleinwort Benson Ltd v. South Tyneside MBC* [1994] 4 All E.R. 972. See also *Commissioner of State Revenue (Vic) v. Royal Insurance Australia Ltd* (1994) 182 C.L.R. 51 and *Mutual Pools & Staff Pty Ltd v. Commonwealth* (1994) 179 C.L.R. 155. For example outside the field of tax see *Kleinwort Benson Ltd v. Birmingham C.C.* [1997] Q.B. 380. *cf. Allied Air Conditioning v. British Columbia* (1992) 76 B.C.L.R. 2d 218 (distinguishing specific and direct "passing on" of tax and merely treating it as a business cost).

(f) *Wrongdoing*[41]

"Waiver of tort." If a person in the commission of a tort enriches himself by taking or using the property of another, the latter may, if certain conditions are satisfied, instead of suing in tort to recover damages for the injury done, recover the value of that which has been wrongfully taken or used. The remedies in tort and restitution are not concurrent and the claimant is compelled to elect which he will pursue.[42] If he elects to seek restitution, he is said to "waive the tort."[43] Historically, there were a number of advantages of suing in restitution rather than in tort,[44] *e.g.* avoidance of special pleading and of immunity from suit in tort,[45] a different period of limitation, the ability to prove for the claim in the tortfeasor's bankruptcy[46] and circumvention of the rule preventing survival of an action in tort against the estate of a tortfeasor. Some advantages may, however, continue in modern law, such as the avoidance of the necessity to prove the actual loss suffered by the claimant (*e.g.* the exact value of goods lost through conversion) by claiming instead the sum received by the defendant.[47] Furthermore it may be possible to recover more than the loss sustained by claiming any profit made by the defendant which is attributable to the tort.[48] These last two may, however, be less important than they were in view of the relevance, in assessing damages in certain actions in tort, of the defendant's gain.[49]

---

[41] Beatson, *The Use and Abuse of Restitution*, Chap. 8; Birks *op. cit.* pp. 39–44, Ch. X; Birks, *Civil Wrongs: A New World* (1991); Burrows *op. cit.* Chap 14; Goff and Jones *op. cit.* Chap. 36; Winfield, *Province of the Law of Tort* (1931), pp. 168–176 (also *The Law of Quasi-Contracts* (1952), pp. 91–102); Wright (1941) 57 L.Q.R. 184; Fridman (1955) 18 M.L.R. 1; Friedmann (1980) 80 Col.L.Rev. 504; Hedley (1984) 100 L.Q.R. 653. Note also the power of a criminal court, under s.28 of the Theft Act 1968 (as amended by ss.6, 64(1) of and Sched. 5 to the Criminal Justice Act 1972; Sched. 12 to the Criminal Law Act 1977, s.47 and Sched. 1 to the Criminal Procedure and Investigations Act 1996), to order restitution upon conviction: *R. v. Ferguson* [1970] 1 W.L.R. 1246; *R. v. Church* (1970) 55 Cr.App.R. 65; *R. v. Parker* [1970] 2 All E.R. 458. *cf. Malone v. Metropolitan Police Commissioner* [1980] Q.B. 49. See generally *Profits of Crime and their Recovery* (Hodgson Committee) (1984), Chap. 7. The courts are also empowered by s.35 of the Powers of Criminal Courts Act 1973 (amended by s.67 of the Criminal Justice Act 1982, s.104 of the Criminal Justice Act 1988 to make a compensation order against a convicted offender: *R. v. Inwood* (1975) 60 Cr.App.R. 70; *R. v. Kneeshaw* [1975] Q.B. 57; *R. v. Daly* [1974] 1 W.L.R. 133; *R. v. Vivian* [1979] 1 All E.R. 48. Magistrates' courts may also make orders for the delivery of property in the possession of the police to the person appearing to be the owner: Police (Property) Act 1897; *Raymond Lyons & Co. v. Metropolitan Police Commissioner* [1975] Q.B. 321. See further Smith, *The Law of Theft* (7th ed.), paras. 14–06—14–26; Goff and Jones *op. cit.* Chap. 38.

[42] On election, see *post*, § 30–090.

[43] This follows Keener, *A Treatise on the Law of Quasi-Contracts* (1893), p. 159. The principle is fully discussed by the House of Lords in *United Australia Ltd v. Barclays Bank Ltd* [1941] A.C. 1.

[44] Winfield, *Province of the Law of Tort* (1931), pp. 143–146. *cf.* Goff and Jones *op. cit.* pp. 786–792.

[45] *e.g.* the Crown's immunity before the Crown Proceedings Act 1947. See Williams, *Crown Proceedings* (1948), pp. 11–13.

[46] See Law Reform (Miscellaneous Provisions) Act 1934 which was applied in *Chesworth v. Farrar* [1967] 1 Q.B. 407. On the particular point see now, Proceedings Against Estates Act 1970, s.1; Companies Act 1985, ss.611–612. For the present position see, Insolvency Act 1986, s.382 and Insolvency Rules 1986 (S.I. 1986 No. 1925), rr. 13.1, 13.12.

[47] *King v. Leith* (1787) 2 T.R. 141, 145; *Parker v. Norton* (1796) 6 T.R. 695, 700; *Feltham v. Terry* (1772) Lofft. 207, 208. This sum may exceed what could be recovered in tort: *Bavins and Sims v. London and South Western Bank Ltd* [1900] 1 Q.B. 270. See Marshall Evans (1966) 82 L.Q.R. 167–169.

[48] See *post*, § 30–080.

[49] See *post*, § 30–088, nn. 83–,84; § 30–089, n. 92.

30–085 **Nature of obligation to make restitution.** It is not entirely clear whether the restitutionary obligation is a secondary and parasitic obligation, which arises upon the violation of the primary obligation not to commit a tort,[50] or whether the cases are instances of situations in which one set of facts gives rise to two alternative but independent causes of action, one in tort and one in restitution.[51] Although the authorities appear to favour the former[52] (parasitic obligation), on that view it is difficult to see why factors which bar the claim in tort should not also bar the claim in restitution. However, there are cases which are consistent only with the latter view. The scope of the claim in restitution depends on which is adopted. If it is the former (independent obligation) then it is a *sine qua non* of both remedies that a tort has been committed but if it is the latter then one should be available even though the other is not.[53] On this view[54] restitutionary claims in respect of benefits acquired tortiously would be an example of a broader category which includes benefits acquired by criminal acts,[55] breach of equitable duties[56] and, possibly, breach of statutory duties.[57]

30–086 **Which torts may give rise to a restitutionary claim.** Obviously not all torts give rise to an action in restitution, but only those where the tortfeasor receives a definite sum of money, or a definite benefit which can be readily assessed in money, at the expense of the claimant.[58] Restitutionary awards have most commonly been made in cases concerning what have been termed the "proprietary torts."[59] They have been made in the following cases: conversion[60] (as where the defendant tortiously takes the claimant's goods, sells them and

---

[50] *Oughton v. Seppings* (1830) 1 B. & Ad. 241, 243; *Young v. Marshall* (1831) 8 Bing. 43; *Turner v. Camerons Coalbrook Steam Coal Co.* (1850) 5 Ex. 932; *United Australia Ltd v. Barclays Bank Ltd* [1941] A.C. 1, 18, 35; *Commercial Banking Co. of Sydney v. Mann* [1961] A.C. 1, 8. See also *Beaman v. A.R.T.S. Ltd* [1948] 2 All E.R. 89, 92–93; *Redrow Homes Ltd v. Bett Brothers plc* [1998] 2 W.L.R. 198.

[51] See, for instance, *Phillips v. Homfray* (1883) 24 Ch.D. 439, 463; [1892] 1 Ch. 465, 470, 471; *Universe Tankships Inc. of Monrovia v. International Transport Workers Federation* [1983] 1 A.C. 366, 385, 401. See also, *post*, n. 53.

[52] See especially *United Australia Ltd v. Barclays Bank Ltd, supra*, at 18 and 35; *Chesworth v. Farrar* [1969] 1 Q.B. 407, 417 and the cases cited *ante*, n. 50.

[53] *Heilbut & Rocca v. Nevill* (1870) L.R. 5 C.P. 478 (technical requirements of tort not satisfied); *Asher v. Wallis* (1707) 11 Mod. 146 (no action in trover because plaintiff had never possessed the money). See also *Anon* (1700) 12 Mod. 415. The cases on money obtained by fraud, deceit (*post*, § 30–092) and oppression (*post*, § 30–095) support this view because the action for money had and received antedated the development of the torts of deceit (Jackson, *The History of Quasi-Contract in English Law* (1936), pp. 73–75) and intimidation (Beatson *op. cit.* p. 221). See also *Mahesan v. Malaysia Government Officers' Co-operative Housing Society Ltd* [1979] A.C. 374; *Universe Tankships Inc. of Monrovia v. International Transport Workers Federation* [1983] 1 A.C. 366, 385, 401; *National Trust Co. v. Gleason* (1879) 77 N.Y. 400, 403–404.

[54] *Att.-Gen. v. Guardian Newspapers (No. 2)* [1990] 1 A.C. 109, 262, 266, 277, 286.

[55] Goff and Jones *op. cit.* Chap. 38. See *ante*, n. 74 for statutory power to order restitution.

[56] *e.g.* breach of confidence would be included whether or not it is a tort; *post*, § 30–089, n. 91. See also the equitable claims available to a principal whose agent has been bribed; *Reading v. Att.-Gen.* [1948] 1 K.B. 268, 276; [1949] 2 K.B. 232; [1951] A.C. 507; *Mahesan v. Malaysia Government Officers' Co-operative Housing Society Ltd* [1979] A.C. 374; *post*, § 30–172; Vol. II, §§ 32–073, 32–077.

[57] *English v. Dedham Vale Properties Ltd* [1978] 1 W.L.R. 93; Samuel (1978) 94 L.Q.R. 347, 350.

[58] *Hambly v. Trott* (1776) 1 Cowp. 371, 376; *Phillips v. Homfray* (1883) 24 Ch.D. 439; *Morris v. Tarrant* [1971] 2 Q.B. 143, 160–162. See *post*, § 30–088.

[59] *Stoke on Trent C.C. v. W. & J. Wass Ltd* [1988] 1 W.L.R. 1406, 1415 (no restitution where exclusive right to hold a market infringed).

[60] *Re Simms* [1934] Ch. 1 (see *post*, § 30–089).

receives the proceeds,[61] or wrongfully presents and collects the proceeds of his cheque[62]); other wrongful interference or trespass to goods[63] (which the defendant has turned into money,[64] or where the defendant tortiously takes and retains the claimant's money)[65]; trespass to land[66]; fraud or deceit[67]; intimidation[68]; inducing breach of contract[69]; passing off[70]; infringement of intellectual property rights[71]; and some miscellaneous actions.[72]

Effect of statute. If a statute is held to bar actions "in respect of any tortious act," the plaintiff cannot avoid the statute by "waiving" the tort and suing in restitution.[73] Where, however, the statute (or a common law rule) is held only to bar "actions in tort," it is still open to the claimant to sue in restitution[74] unless to allow him to do so would undermine the policy of the statutory (or common law) rule.[75] Moreover, where there is detailed legislation in an area, it has been **30–087**

---

[61] *Lamine v. Dorrell* (1706) 2 Ld. Raym. 1216; *Marsh v. Keating* (1834) 1 Bing.N.C. 198, 215–216; *Phillips v. Homfray, supra,* at 462. *cf. Lake v. Bayliss* [1974] 1 W.L.R. 1073 (see *post,* § 30–175).

[62] *Bavins and Sims v. London and South Western Bank Ltd, supra*; *Morison v. London County and Westminster Bank Ltd* [1914] 3 K.B. 356, 365; *Fenton Textile Association v. Thomas* (1929) 45 T.L.R. 264.

[63] It was also permitted for detinue, now abolished by the Torts (Interference with Goods) Act 1977. Although many aspects of detinue are still actionable under another head (s.2(2)), not all are: Palmer [1981] Conv.(N.S.) 62.

[64] *Oughton v. Seppings* (1830) 1 B. & Ad. 241; *Rodgers v. Maw* (1846) 15 M. & W. 444, 448; *Neate v. Harding* (1851) 6 Exch. 349, 351. *cf.* n. 58, *ante.*

[65] *Neate v. Harding, supra*; *Bavins & Sims v. London and South Western Bank Ltd, supra.*

[66] *Powell v. Rees* (1837) 7 A. & E. 426 (sale of coal extracted from land); *Bracewell v. Appleby* [1975] Ch. 407 (damages in lieu of injunction took into account defendant's profits); *Ministry of Defence v. Ashman* [1993] 2 E.G.L.R. 102; *Ministry of Defence v. Thompson* [1993] 2 E.G.L.R. 107 (claim for *mesne* profit for trespass). See also Cooke (1994) 110 L.Q.R. 420; *Invergugie Investments Ltd v. Hackett* [1995] 1 W.L.R. 713.

[67] *Post,* §§ 30–092—30–094.

[68] *Post,* § 30–095.

[69] *Lightly v. Clouston* (1808) 1 Taunt. 112; *Foster v. Stewart* (1814) 3 M. & S. 191 (see the discussion of these cases in Winfield, *Quasi-Contracts* (1952), pp. 98–99).

[70] *My Kinda Town v. Soll* [1982] F.S.R. 147.

[71] Accounts of profits: *Hogg v. Kirby* (1803) 8 Ves. J. 215, 223; *Colburn v. Simms* (1843) 2 Ha. 543; *My Kinda Town Ltd v. Soll* [1982] F.S.R. 147; *Potton Ltd v. Yorkclase Ltd* [1990] F.S.R. 11. Damages and account of profits: Patents Act 1977, ss.61–62; Copyright, Designs and Patents Act 1988, ss.96, 97, 229. But *cf. Union Carbide Corp. v. B.P. Chemicals Ltd* [1998] F.S.R. 1, 6; *Redrow Homes Ltd v. Bett Bros. plc* [1998] 2 W.L.R. 198.

[72] *e.g.* usurpation of an office (*post,* § 30–174); or where the defendant falsely assumes to act as the plaintiff's agent, and collects rent from his tenants: *Lightly v. Clouston, supra,* at 115; *Asher v. Wallis* (1707) 11 Mod. 146; *Hasser v. Wallis* (1708) 1 Salk. 28. *cf. Kettlewell v. Refuge Assistance Co.* [1908] 1 K.B. 545; [1909] A.C. 243; or for unlawful eviction: Housing Act 1988, ss.27–28. Their appropriateness in nuisance has been recognised: *Carr-Saunders v. Dick McNeill Associates* [1986] 1 W.L.R. 922 (although as there was no evidence of profit no award was made). *cf. Stoke-on-Trent City Council v. W. & J. Wass Ltd* [1988] 1 W.L.R. 1406, 1410.

[73] *Brocklebank Ltd v. R.* [1925] 1 K.B. 52 (Indemnity Act 1920); *Hardie and Lane Ltd v. Chiltern* [1928] 1 K.B. 663, 695 (Trade Disputes Act 1906, s.4). See also *Universe Tankships Inc. of Monrovia v. International Transport Workers Federation* [1983] 1 A.C. 366, HL; [1981] I.C.R. 129, 160–161, CA; Parker J. *ibid.* at 143–144 (Trade Union and Labour Relations Act 1974, s.13(1)).

[74] *Powell v. Rees* (1837) 7 A. & E. 426; *Phillips v. Homfray* (1883) 24 Ch.D. 439 (*actio personalis moritur cum persona*); *Chesworth v. Farrar* [1967] 1 Q.B. 407 (Law Reform (Miscellaneous Provisions) Act 1934, s.1(3) as amended by Law Reform (Limitation of Actions Act 1954, s.4)).

[75] *Universe Tankships Inc. of Monrovia v. International Transport Workers Federation, ante,* at 385, 401; *Dimskal SS. Co. SA v. International Transport Workers Federation* [1992] 2 A.C. 152, 161–162, 166–167; *Union Carbide Corp. v. B.P. Chemicals Ltd* [1998] F.S.R. 1, 6 (restitution cannot supplement patent law).

said that "the courts should not indulge in parallel creativity by the extension of general common law principles."[76]

30–088　　　　**The nature of the benefit.** In *Phillips v. Homfray*[77] a majority of the Court of Appeal held that a trespass to land could only be waived so as to give a restitutionary remedy against the deceased tortfeasor's estate if the "property or the proceeds of property, belonging to another, have been appropriated by the deceased person and added to his own estate or moneys."[78] In that case the tortfeasor had made unauthorised use of roads over, and passages under, the claimant's land and this was held not to give rise to a remedy in restitution. This appropriation or accretion requirement has been criticised as confusing the role of personal and proprietary claims in restitution and as isolating the requirement of benefit from the question of what constitutes benefit in other restitutionary claims.[79] As Baggallay L.J., in a strong dissent, stated, "a gain or acquisition to the wrongdoer by the work and labour of another does not necessarily, if it does at all, imply a diminution of the property of such other person."[80] There are indications in the cases of a broader approach[81] and dicta suggesting that the rule in *Phillips v. Homfray* should be discarded.[82] However, it has recently been followed at first instance.[83] In practice the rule should not prove a serious obstacle to a claimant since it is now possible to use the measure of what the defendant gained (rather than what the claimant lost) in an action in tort in respect of the wrongful use by the defendant of the claimant's land[84] or chat-

---

[76] *Chief Constable of Leicestershire v. M* [1989] 1 W.L.R. 20, 23. See also *Halifax B.S. v. Thomas* [1996] Ch. 217, 229–230; *Att.-Gen. v. Blake* [1998] 2 W.L.R. 805; *Union Carbide Corp. v. B.P. Chemicals Ltd, ante*

[77] (1883) 24 Ch.D. 439. For other stages of this litigation see (1871) 6 Ch.App. 770; (1890) 44 Ch.D. 694, affd. [1892] 1 Ch. 465.

[78] *ibid.* at 454 (Bowen and Cotton L.JJ.). See also *Powell v. Rees* (1837) 7 Ad. & El. 426. *cf. Kirk v. Todd* (1882) 21 Ch.D. 484.

[79] Goff and Jones *op. cit.* pp. 776–780; Beatson *op. cit.* pp. 224–230; Burrows *op. cit.* pp. 390–392. *cf.* Gummow in Finn (ed.), *Essays on Restitution*, 1990, pp. 60–67; *Daniel v. O'Leary* (1976) 14 N.B.R. (2d) 564 (*quantum meruit* awarded against trespasser who hooked his home on to plaintiff's sewage system so that his waste was processed at plaintiff's sewage farm).

[80] (1883) 24 Ch.D. 439, 471–472. Goff and Jones *op. cit.* p. 778, find his views compelling. See also *Restatement of Restitution* (1937), § 1(b).

[81] *Lightly v. Clouston* (1808) 1 Taunt. 112; *Rumsey v. North Eastern Ry.* (1863) 14 C.B.(N.S.) 641, 652. See also the claim of a principal against the person who bribed his agent for the amount of the bribe: *Hovenden & Sons v. Millhoff* (1900) 83 L.T. 41 *post*, §§ 30–070, 30–172; Vol. II, §§ 32–073, 32–117; *Daniel v. O'Leary, supra.*

[82] *Nissan v. Att.-Gen.* [1968] 1 Q.B. 286, 341, 352; [1970] A.C. 179, 228. But *cf. ibid.* at 213, 236, 241. The rule has been rejected in certain jurisdictions in the United States provided the trespass to land was deliberate: *Edwards v. Lee's Administrators* (1936) 265 Ky. 418; 96 S.W. 2d. 1028; *Red Raven Ash Coal Co. v. Bull* (1946) 39 S.E. 2d. 231; *Prosser on Torts* (4th ed.), p. 630.

[83] *Morris v. Tarrant* [1971] 2 Q.B. 143, 158, although Lane J. did recognise that the defendant had been "enriched by his free occupation of property." The case may reflect a policy of protecting spouses in possession of the matrimonial home pending divorce and a property settlement.

[84] *Penarth Dock Engineering Co. v. Pounds* [1963] 1 Lloyd's Rep. 359; *McGregor on Damages* (15th ed., 1988), §§ 1420–1422. See also *Wrotham Park Estate Co. Ltd v. Parkside Homes Ltd* [1974] 1 W.L.R. 798, 812–816 (damages in lieu of injunction for breach of restrictive covenant assessed at 5 per cent. of the profit made by the defendant builder on the basis that this was the sum that might reasonably have been demanded by the plaintiffs as a *quid pro quo* for relaxing the covenant). *Carr-Saunders v. Dick McNeill Associates* [1986] 1 W.L.R. 922; *Anchor Brewhouse Developments Ltd v. Berkeley House (Docklands) Developments Ltd* (1987) 284 E.G. 626; *Jaggard v. Sawyer* [1995] 1 W.L.R. 269. See also Goodhart, [1995] Restitution L.Rev. 3. *cf. Stoke-on-Trent C.C. v. W. & J. Wass Ltd* [1988] 3 All E.R. 394 (nominal damages awarded); *Surrey C.C. v. Bredero Homes Ltd* [1992] 3 All E.R. 302; [1993] 1 W.L.R. 1361, CA

tels.[85] The sum awarded in these cases, the reasonable hiring rate, should not be regarded as compensatory since it is calculated by reference to what the defendant has saved by not having to hire rather than what the claimant had lost. It is irrelevant that the owner suffered no loss because he would not have used the property during the period of use by the defendant or could not have hired it out.[86] The argument that the owner has been deprived of the opportunity of charging a fee and that the remedy is therefore compensatory[87] is only realistic if it is clear that the owner would have been willing to do so.[88]

Profits made by the defendant. Apart from a reasonable hiring fee in respect   **30–089** of wrongful use of land or chattels, there is the question whether further profits[89] may be recoverable by claiming restitution rather than suing in tort. In some cases it will be difficult to attribute profits exclusively to the defendant's tort.[90] This may not be the case where the defendant has committed the tort deliberately,[91] but in such cases it is possible that exemplary damages will be awarded in tort.[92]

Election of remedy. The remedies in tort and in restitution are alternative,   **30–090** and the claimant cannot recover judgment on both, though he may pursue both remedies together.[93] The claimant does not elect one remedy merely by commencing an action in which he claims it[94]; as Lord Atkin said:

---

[85] *Strand Electric & Engineering Co. Ltd v. Brisford Entertainments Ltd* [1952] 2 Q.B. 2465.

[86] *Strand Electric & Engineering Co. Ltd v. Brisford Entertainments Ltd, supra,* at 252, 254, 256–257; *Penarth Dock Engineering Co. v. Pounds, supra,* at 361–362; *Swordheath Properties Ltd v. Tabet* [1979] 1 W.L.R. 285. See the United States cases: *Amatrudi v. Watson* (1952) 88 A. 2d 7 (defendant who benefited innocently from the use by a third party of the plaintiff's equipment liable for its reasonable rental value). See also *Restatement of Restitution* (1937), § 128 (p. 533). *cf. Dilmitis v. Niland,* 1965 (3) S.A. 492 (no proof of extent of defendant's enrichment); *Stoke-on-Trent C.C. v. W. & J. Wass, supra.*

[87] *Strand Electric & Engineering Co. Ltd v. Brisford Entertainments Ltd, supra,* (per Somervell and Romer L.JJ.); *Hillesden Securities Ltd v. Ryjack Ltd* [1983] 1 W.L.R. 959; *Anchor Brewhouse Developments Ltd v. Berkeley House (Docklands) Developments Ltd, supra,* at 633. See Sharpe & Waddams (1982) 2 O.J.L.S. 290. *cf.* Burrows *op. cit.* p. 393.

[88] Hodder (1984) 42 U.Toronto Fac.L.Rev. 105.

[89] As envisaged by *Strand Electric & Engineering Co. Ltd v. Brisford Entertainments, supra,* at 252, 255.

[90] *Re Simms* [1934] Ch. 1; Law Commission No. 110, Cmnd. 8388 (1981) para. 4.86; Birks *op. cit.* pp. 351–355. *cf. My Kinda Town Ltd v. Soll* [1982] F.S.R. 147; [1983] R.P.C. 407; *Colbeam Palmer Ltd v. Stock Affiliates Pty. Ltd* (1968) 122 C.L.R. 25.

[91] *Federal Sugar Refining Co. v. United States Sugar Equalisation Board* 268 F. 575 (1920); *Olwell v. Nye & Nissen Co., supra.* There is apparently no English authority on the question and the rule in *Phillips v. Homfray, supra,* § 30–088, may prevent a restitutionary claim. Goff and Jones, *op. cit.* p. 784, cite the analogy of trade mark and patent cases to suggest that for knowing wrongdoing an account of profits might be allowed. See also breach of confidence: *Peter Pan Manufacturing Corpn. v. Corsets Silhouette Ltd* [1964] 1 W.L.R. 96 (account of profits ordered where product could not have been manufactured without the confidential information). *cf. Seager v. Copydex Ltd* [1967] 1 W.L.R. 923; [1967] 2 All E.R. 415; *No. 2* [1969] 1 W.L.R. 809 (payment for confidential information used innocently but negligently based on market value of information not profits); *Attorney-General v. Guardian Newspapers* [1990] 1 A.C. 109. But see *English v. Dedham Vale Properties Ltd* [1978] 1 W.L.R. 93, 111; *Universal Thermosensors Ltd v. Hibben* [1992] 1 W.L.R. 840, 850–851.

[92] *Rookes v. Barnard* [1964] A.C. 1129, 1220–1231; *Cassell & Co. v. Broome* [1972] A.C. 1027. Such damages have been limited by *A.B. v. S.W. Water Services Ltd* [1993] Q.B. 507 but, where available, are not limited to profits; *McMillan v. Singh* (1985) 17 H.L.R. 120.

[93] *United Australia Ltd v. Barclays Bank Ltd* [1941] A.C. 1; *Halifax B.S. v. Thomas* [1996] Ch. 217; *Personal Representatives of Tang Man Sit v. Capacious Investments Ltd* [1996] A.C. 514.

[94] *ibid.* See also *Rice v. Reed* [1900] 1 Q.B. 54; *Island Records Ltd v. Tring International plc* [1995] 3 All E.R. 444; *cf. Ernest Scragg & Sons Ltd v. Perseverance Banking and Trust Co. Ltd* [1973] 2 Lloyd's Rep. 101, 103.

"I ... think that on a question of alternative remedies no question of election arises until one or other claim has been brought to judgment. Up to that stage the plaintiff may pursue both remedies together, or pursuing one may amend and pursue the other; but he can take judgment only for the one, and his cause of action on both will then be merged in the one."[95]

However, Viscount Simon went further: "What would be necessary to constitute a bar ... would be that, as the result of such judgment or otherwise, the appellant should have received satisfaction"[96] and partial satisfaction may not suffice.[97] The claim in tort may, of course, be waived in other ways, such as by a genuine ratification of an agent's unauthorised act,[98] or by acceptance of the proceeds obtained by the defendant's tortious dealing with the claimant's property,[99] or by affirming a mortgage,[1] and the claimant cannot thereafter sue the wrongdoer in tort.[2] Similarly, where the plaintiff definitely elects in writing to treat the defendant as a wrongdoer, and obtains damages from him on that footing, he cannot also maintain a claim for a further amount in restitution, based on approbation of the defendant's tortious act in using assets to make a profit for himself.[3]

30–091   **Bribery.** It has now been settled that in cases of bribery of an agent the principal's remedies against the agent, one for money had and received and the other for fraud, are not cumulative.[4] However, where a principal rescinds a transaction tainted by a bribe, although the principal has to make restitution of benefits received under the contract he does not have to give credit for the amount of the bribe even where he has recovered it from the agent.[5]

30–092   **Money obtained by fraud or deceit.** An important instance of this use of restitution is where the claimant uses a claim in restitution to recover money obtained from him by fraud or deceit.[6] It has been held that, while restitution is available in respect of money paid by the claimant to the defendant, an account of profits made by the fraudulent defendant does not lie.[7] Thus where the defendant obtained payment of a promissory note payable to the claimant, by

---

[95] *United Australia Ltd v. Barclays Bank Ltd, supra,* at 30 (Lord Wright has discussed the case in (1941) 57 L.Q.R. 184); *Mahesan v. Malaysia Government Officers' Co-operative Housing Society Ltd* [1979] A.C. 374.

[96] *ibid.* at 21 (see also Lord Porter at 50).

[97] *Personal Representatives of Tang Man Sit v. Capacious Investments Ltd* [1996] A.C. 514, 526.

[98] *Verschures Creameries Ltd v. Hull and Netherlands SS. Co. Ltd* [1921] 2 K.B. 608 (tort action against agent barred by unsatisfied judgment against third party in quasi-contract). See also *John v. Dodwell* [1918] A.C. 563, 570–571.

[99] *Lythgoe v. Vernon* (1860) 5 H. & N. 180.

[1] *Halifax B.S. v. Thomas* [1996] Ch. 217.

[2] *Smith v. Baker* (1873) L.R. 8 C.P. 350; *cf. Smith v. Hodson* (1791) 4 T.R. 211; *Roe v. Mutual Loan Fund Ltd* (1887) 19 Q.B.D. 347.

[3] *Re Simms* [1934] Ch. 1, 20, 25–26. See also *Halifax B.S. v. Thomas* [1996] Ch. 217, 227–228.

[4] *Mahesan v. Malaysia Government Officers' Co-operative Housing Society Ltd, supra. cf. Salford Corporation v. Lever* [1891] 1 Q.B. 169. On bribery of agents see *post,* § 30–172; Vol. II, §§ 32–073, 32–117.

[5] *Logicrose Ltd v. Southland United F.C. Ltd* [1988] 1 W.L.R. 1256.

[6] See *Billing v. Ries* (1841) Car. & M. 26; *Bonzi v. Stewart* (1842) 4 M. & G. 295, 325. *cf.* avoidance of conveyances made with intent to defraud creditors: Law of Property Act 1925, ss.172, 173(1).

[7] *Halifax B.S. v. Thomas* [1996] Ch. 217. *Sed quaere.* See *South Australia Asset Management Cpn. v. York Montague Ltd* [1997] A.C. 191, 215; *Attorney-Gen. v. Blake* [1998] 2 W.L.R. 805; Law Com. No. 247 (1997), para. 3.24 *et seq.*

means of a false or forged representation of authority from the claimant, the claimant was entitled to sue the defendant in restitution to recover the money which the defendant had received.[8] The defendant is liable to such an action even where the fraud was committed by his partner and agent, and not by him personally.[9] So where payments of premiums on a policy were continued by the claimant because of false representations by the defendant's agent, it was held that the premiums could be recovered by the claimant in a claim in restitution, although they might also have been recovered in an action of deceit.[10] On the other hand, if the defendant obtains money by fraud from an agent, either the agent or his principal may recover it from him.[11]

Services or property obtained by fraud. If the defendant, without intending   **30–093** to pay for it, fraudulently induces the claimant to perform a service for him, the claimant may sue either for the tort of deceit, or in restitution for reasonable remuneration.[12] Where a sale by auction is advertised or stated by the auctioneer to be "without reserve," the secret employment by the vendor of a puffer to bid for him, without notice, renders the sale void and entitles the purchaser to recover his deposit from the auctioneer by a claim in restitution.[13]

Limits on the right to rescind for fraud. A person induced by fraud to enter   **30–094** into a contract under which he pays money may not rescind the contract and recover the price in restitution[14] if he can no longer restore the parties to the *status quo ante* (*e.g.* if he cannot return what he has received under the contract in the same condition as that in which he received it).[15] His only remedy is a claim for damages in an action for fraud.[16] The right to rescind may also be lost by affirmation.[17] Thus, if a person is induced to purchase an article by the seller's fraudulent misrepresentations about it, and after discovering the fraud he continues to deal with the article as his own, for example by selling it,[18] he cannot recover from the seller the price paid to him for it.[19] Again, if a party, after he has discovered a fraud which induced him to enter into a contract, voluntarily pays a sum of money under it with knowledge of the facts, he cannot claim a return of the money so paid.[20]

---

[8] *Vaughan v. Matthews* (1849) 13 Q.B. 187, 190.

[9] *Crockford v. Winter* (1807) 1 Camp. 124, 127; *Marsh v. Keating* (1834) 1 Bing.N.C. 198, HL (discussed in *Jacobs v. Morris* [1902] 1 Ch. 816).

[10] *Kettlewell v. Refuge Assurance Co.* [1908] 1 K.B. 545; [1909] A.C. 243; but *cf. Salata v. Continental Insurance Co.* [1948] 2 D.L.R. 663, where the agent was only authorised to solicit custom.

[11] *Holt v. Ely* (1853) 1 E. & B. 795.

[12] *Rumsey v. N.E. Ry.* (1863) 14 C.B.(N.S.) 641; *Hill v. Perrott* (1810) 3 Taunt. 274; *Abbotts v. Barry* (1820) 2 Brod. & B. 369.

[13] *Thornett v. Haines* (1846) 15 M. & W. 367; *Green v. Baverstock* (1863) 14 C.B.(N.S.) 204; *Parfitt v. Jepson* (1877) 46 L.J.C.P. 529; and see Sale of Land by Auction Act 1867, ss.4–7. *cf.* solicitor suing, without authority, in the name of a nominal or imaginary plaintiff: *Dupen v. Keeling* (1829) 4 C. & P. 102; see further, Vol. II, § 32–100.

[14] *Whittaker v. Campbell* [1984] Q.B. 318, 327.

[15] *Ante*, §§ 6–113 *et seq.* But *cf. Logicrose Ltd v. Southend United F.C. Ltd* [1988] 1 W.L.R. 1256. See also *Vadasz v. Pioneer Concrete (SA) Pty. Ltd* [1995] 185 C.L.R. 102.

[16] *Clarke v. Dickson* (1858) E.B. & E. 148.

[17] *Ante*, § 6–120.

[18] *Halifax B.S. v. Thomas* [1996] Ch. 217.

[19] *Campbell v. Fleming* (1834) 1 A. & E. 40. See also *Law v. Law* [1905] 1 Ch. 140, CA

[20] *Miles v. Dell* (1821) 3 Stark. 23, 26.

30–095 **Money obtained by oppression or extortion.** Money obtained by illegal oppression or extortion or by taking advantage of the weak and needy may be recovered by a claim in restitution.[21] This is another instance of a restitutionary alternative to an action in tort, since it is, in general, a tort to obtain money by unlawful intimidation.[22] Thus a claim in restitution lies against a broker to recover excessive charges on a distress for rent, paid by the tenant in order to prevent a sale, even although the tenant may have applied for and obtained time in consideration of his promise to pay the charges.[23] But where excessive charges are paid to satisfy a claim purporting to be made by virtue of a statute, but the person paying them is not oppressed or imposed on in any way, it depends on the interpretation of the particular statute whether he is entitled to recover the excess.[24]

30–096 **Breach of contract.**[25] A defendant may make a gain from a breach of contract either by making a larger profit from a third party than he would have made from the other party had he performed[26] or by saving expense from its breach.[27] In general, the gain to a defendant from a breach of contract is irrelevant to the quantification of damages.[28] A claimant who suffers a smaller loss than the defendant's gain or who suffers injury of a non-pecuniary kind from the breach of contract will find a restitutionary award attractive, and, exceptionally, the defendant's gain is relevant to the quantification of damages. The defendant's gain is relevant in sales of land,[29] where there has been a breach of a contractual duty of confidence[30] or a fiduciary duty[31] or where the breach of contract

---

[21] *Lowry v. Bourdieu* (1780) 2 Dougl. 468, 472; *Clarke v. Shee* (1774) 1 Cowp. 197, 200; see also *Astley v. Reynolds* (1732) 2 Stra. 915; *Re Judgment Summons (No. 25 of 1952)* [1953] Ch. 1; *Re Marjory* [1955] Ch. 600 (the threat of the final sanction of bankruptcy, when costs are wrongly demanded, may be extortion). For extortion *colore officii*, see *ante*, § 30–075, for money obtained by wrongful demand, see Compulsory Payments, *ante*, § 30–068 and, for *ultra vires* receipts by tax and other public bodies, see *ante*, § 30–080.

[22] On the tort of intimidation, see *Rookes v. Barnard* [1964] A.C. 1129. But *sed quaere* whether "two party" intimidation is a tort: *J.T. Stratford & Son Ltd v. Lindley* [1965] A.C. 269, 325; Harrison [1964] C.L.J. 159, 168; Hoffmann (1965) 81 L.Q.R. 116, 127–128. But see Beatson *op. cit.* pp. 221 and 118–119. If it is not, these cases provide support for the view (*ante*, § 30–084) that the claims in tort and restitution are entirely independent of each other. See also *Universe Tankships of Monrovia v. International Transport Workers Federation* [1983] A.C. 366; *Dimskal SS. Co. SA v. International Transport Workers Federation* [1992] 2 A.C. 152.

[23] *Hills v. Street* (1828) 5 Bing. 37.

[24] *Green v. Portsmouth Stadium* [1953] 2 Q.B. 190 (a charge contravening the Betting and Lotteries Act 1934, s.13, is not recoverable). On excessive charges paid to public authorities, see *ante*, § 30–080.

[25] See generally, *ante*, §§ 27–018—27–021. See also Friedmann (1980) 80 Col. L.Rev. 504, 513–529; Jones (1983) 99 L.Q.R. 442; Burrows, *Remedies for Torts and Breach of Contract*, 2nd ed. (1994), pp. 308–314; Birks [1987] L.M.C.L.Q. 421; Law Commission No. 247 (1998) *Aggravated, Exemplary and Restitutionary Damages*, Part III.

[26] *Teacher v. Calder* (1899) 1 F. 39, HL.

[27] *Tito v. Waddell (No. 2)* [1977] Ch. 106, *ante*, § 27–014.

[28] *The Siboen* [1976] 1 Lloyd's Rep. 293, at 337 (profits from alternative charter irrelevant); *Tito v. Waddell (No. 2)* [1977] Ch. 106, at 332; *Surrey C.C. v. Bredero Homes Ltd* [1993] 1 W.L.R. 1361. But see Goodhart [1995] Rest. L.Rev. 3; *Jaggard v. Sawyer* [1995] 1 W.L.R. 269. See, generally, *ante*, § 27–020.

[29] *Lake v. Bayliss* [1974] 1 W.L.R. 1073; *Tito v. Waddell (No. 2)* (*supra*), at 332.

[30] *Peter Pan Manufacturing Corporation v. Corsets Silhouette Ltd* [1964] 1 W.L.R. 96. See also *ante*, § 30–089, n.91.

[31] See *Reading v. Attorney-General* [1951] A.C. 507. See also *Hospital Products Ltd v. U.S. Surgical Corp.* (1984) 156 C.L.R. 41 (Australia).

involves the use or interference with the plaintiff's property.[32] These are all cases of specifically enforceable contracts and it is arguable that the defendant's gains should be relevant in all such cases. It has also been suggested that, apart from specifically enforceable contracts, there are two situations in which restitutionary damages[33] for breach of contract may be awarded where compensatory damages would be inadequate and where the defendant's profit is occasioned directly by the breach of contract and attributable to it. The first is the case of skimped performance where the defendant fails to provide the full extent of the services it contracted to provide and for which the claimant has paid.[34] So, a gardening contractor which has agreed to attend to a garden once a week but only does so once a month might be liable to pay the sum it has saved by its breach. Secondly, a defendant who has obtained his profit by doing the very thing which he contracted not to do may be required to pay such profit to the other party.[35]

(g) *Proprietary Remedies for Tracing Property*

Tracing orders.[36] Where the property of the claimant can be identified in the **30–097** hands of the defendant, the claimant as true owner of the property may "follow" or "trace" it and claim its recovery. This proprietary remedy is recognised both at common law[37] and in equity,[38] each with its own limitations[39] but the equitable remedy is likely to prove more useful in practice. The remedy is proprietary rather than personal because it may lie against an innocent recipient of the property, even where no personal claim, whether in tort, restitution, or equity, would lie against him[40]; secondly, if the recipient of the property is insolvent, the true owner by means of a tracing order may, subject to statutory requirements in certain cases,[41]

---

[32] *Penarth Dock Engineering Co. Ltd v. Pound* [1963] 1 Lloyd's Rep. 359; *Wrotham Park Estate Co v. Parkside Homes Ltd* [1974] 1 W.L.R. 798; *Jaggard v. Sawyer (supra).*

[33] *cf. Co-operative Insurance Society Ltd v. Argyll (Holdings) Ltd* [1996] 3 W.L.R. 27, *per* Millett L.J. at 44, disapproving of this term.

[34] *Attorney-General v. Blake* [1998] 2 W.L.R. 805. See also *White Arrow Express Ltd v. Lamey's Distribution Ltd* (1995) 15 Tr. L.R. 69; *City of New Orleans v. Firemen's Charitable Association* 9 So. 486 (1891). See Beale in Birks (ed.) *Wrongs and Remedies in the Twenty-First Century* (1996), pp. 217, 232–238.

[35] *Attorney-General v. Blake* [1998] 2 W.L.R. 805; *Snepp v. United States*, 100 Sup. Ct. 763 (1980).

[36] Snell's *Principles of Equity* (28th ed.), pp. 295–303; Hanbury and Maudsley, *Modern Equity* (13th ed.), pp. 621–644; Goff and Jones *op. cit.* Chap. 2; Birks *op. cit.* pp. 358–375; Lawson, *Remedies of English Law* (2nd ed.), Chap. 6; Smith, *The Law of Tracing* (1997); Wright (1936) 6 Camb.L.J. 305; Lord Denning (1949) 65 L.Q.R. 37; Maudsley (1959) 75 L.Q.R. 234; Babafemi (1971) 34 M.L.R. 12; Goode (1976) 92 L.Q.R. 360, 528; (1987) 103 L.Q.R. 433; Pearce (1976) 40 Conv.(N.S.) 277; *cf. ante,* § 8–076.

[37] *Re Diplock* [1948] Ch. 465, 518 *et seq.*; *Lipkin Gorman v. Karpnale Ltd.* [1991] 2 A.C. 548. *Trustee of the Property of F. C. Jones & Sons v. Jones* [1997] Ch. 159. See also *Scott v. Surman* (1742) Willes 400; *Taylor v. Plumer* (1815) 3 M. & S. 562.

[38] *Sinclair v. Brougham* [1914] A.C. 398; *Re Diplock* [1948] Ch. 465, 520 *et seq.*

[39] In *Nelson v. Larholt* [1948] 1 K.B. 339 at 343, Denning J. considered that common law and equity should be fused into one set of principles on the subject.

[40] *Sinclair v. Brougham* [1914] A.C. 398; *International Sales & Agencies Ltd v. Marcus* (1982) 34 C.M.L.R. 46. But *cf. Thavron v. Bank of Credit & Commerce International SA* [1985] 1 Lloyd's Rep. 259.

[41] *e.g.* the registration requirements of Companies Act 1985, ss.395–399; *Re Bond Worth Ltd* [1980] Ch. 228; *Borden (U.K.) Ltd v. Scottish Timber Products Ltd* [1981] Ch. 25; *Re Peachdart Ltd* [1984] Ch. 131. But *cf. Clough Mill Ltd v. Martin* [1985] 1 W.L.R. 111; *John Snow & Co. Ltd v. D.B.G. Woodcroft Ltd* [1985] B.C.L.C. 54. See further *ante,* § 21–022.

claim specific property[42] in priority to the claims of general creditors[43]; thirdly, if the true owner traces his property into investments bearing interest, he will be entitled to claim the interest in addition.[44] It has been doubted that the possibility of a claim by a third party could be a defence to a tracing claim.[45]

30–098   **Tracing at common law.** At common law a claimant is permitted to trace and claim his property if it has not been mixed with other property but can be identified in a "physical"[46] sense, *e.g.* sovereigns in a bag[47] or an entire chose in action, such as a bank balance[48] or a promissory note.[49] If another asset has been "purchased exclusively"[50] with the claimant's money, it is still identifiable at common law, because common law permits the owner of the original property to assert his title to the product in place of the original property[51] and to profits made from the exchanged property.[52] But in the case of money, identification was held not to be possible if there was "admixture of other money."[53] The remedy at common law may take the form of a claim for wrongful interference with goods,[54] or an action in restitution for money had and received.[55] The scope of the remedy in tort in particular has been considerably widened in order to protect proprietary rights; for instance, an action for conversion is given to the person on whose bank account a cheque belonging to him is drawn without his authority,[56] the common law thus treating him as "owner" of the cheque rather than "owner" of the intangible bank balance. These common law actions are, however, personal although the right

---

[42] At common law it will not be possible, however, to ensure the return of the property *in specie*; *post*, § 30–098. See the discretion to order that a chattel be restored by the Torts (Interference with Goods) Act 1977, s.3.

[43] *cf.* claims for "*Mareva*" injunctions which do not have this effect: *Cretanor Maritime Co. Ltd v. Irish Marine Management Ltd* [1978] 1 W.L.R. 966.

[44] *Re Diplock* [1948] Ch. 465, 517, 557; *Re Tilley's W.T.* [1967] Ch. 1179, 1193.

[45] *El Ajou v. Dollar Land Holdings plc. (No. 1)* [1993] 3 All E.R. 717, 747; *El Ajou v. Dollar Land Holdings plc. (No. 2)* [1995] 2 All E.R. 213, 223. See also *Bank Tejavat v. Hong Kong & Shanghai Banking Corp. (C.I.) Ltd* [1995] 1 Lloyd's Rep. 239, 245–246; *Boscawen v. Bajura* [1996] 1 W.L.R. 328, 334.

[46] *ibid.* at 518. But *cf.* Matthews (1981) 34 C.L.P. 156; *Indian Oil Corporation v. Greenstone Shipping Co. SA* [1988] Q.B. 345.

[47] *ibid.* at 521.

[48] *Banque Belge pour l'Etranger v. Hambrouck* [1921] 1 K.B. 321. *Agip (Africa) Ltd v. Jackson* [1991] 1 Ch. 547; *Lipkin Gorman v. Karpnale Ltd, supra.*

[49] *Scott v. Surman* (1742) Willes 400.

[50] *Re Diplock, supra,* at 519; *Re J. Leslie Engineers Co. Ltd* [1976] 1 W.L.R. 292, 297. See also *Whitecomb v. Jacob* (1710) Salk 160.

[51] *Lipkin Gorman v. Karpnale Ltd, supra,* at 573. This process has been described as "ratification: *Re Diplock, supra,* at 518; *Sinclair v. Brougham, supra,* at 441. This agency fiction is criticised by Lord Denning (1949) 65 L.Q.R. 37, 41–42; it was not accepted in *Taylor v. Plumer, supra,* in *Lipkin Gorman v. Karpnale Ltd supra,* at 574 (Lord Goff). But *cf.* Goode (1976) 92 L.Q.R. 360, 367, n. 27; Khurshid and Matthews (1979) 95 L.Q.R. 78 for criticism of this "exchange product" theory and the view that the plaintiff will acquire no title to the new asset unless it has been transferred to the recipient as agent for him or the recipient appropriates the property to him.

[52] *Trustee of the Property of F. C. Jones & Sons v. Jones* [1992] Ch. 157.

[53] *Re Diplock, supra,* at 518.

[54] *e.g. Miller v. Race* (1758) 1 Burr. 452, 457–458; *Wookey v. Pole* (1820) 4 B. & Ald. 1, 6. See also *Indian Oil Corporation v. Greenstone Shipping Co. SA* [1988] Q.B. 345 (damages for short delivery of wrongfully mixed cargo).

[55] *e.g. Clark v. Shee* (1774) 1 Cowp. 197; *Reid v. Rigby* [1894] 2 Q.B. 40; *Lipkin Gorman v. Karpnale Ltd* [1991] 2 A.C. 548; *Trustee of the Property of F.C. Jones & Sons v. Jones* [1997] Ch. 159.

[56] *Morison v. London County and Westminster Bank Ltd* [1914] 3 K.B. 356; *Lloyds Bank Ltd v. Chartered Bank of India, Australia and China* [1929] 1 K.B. 40; *Midland Bank Ltd v. Reckitt* [1933] A.C. 1; *Lloyds Bank Ltd v. E.B. Savory & Co.* [1933] A.C. 201.

remains proprietary[57] and common law tracing into a substitute "cannot be relied on so as to render an innocent recipient a wrongdoer."[58]

At common law, tracing was mainly used in cases of principal and agent, since **30–099** the right of property normally continues to be vested in the principal. But where the relationship was purely one of debtor and creditor there was no proprietary interest which the creditor could attempt to trace, except in the special case of cheques.

The limitations of the common law remedy[59] are said to be as follows:

(1) common law does not recognise equitable interests in property,[60] so that a beneficial interest under a trust cannot be followed;

(2) at common law it is normally not possible to compel the return of the property *in specie* because the "device of a declaration of charge" is unknown[61];

(3) common law cannot identify the plaintiff's money in a mixed fund.

However, this does not mean that the remedy will be ineffective where the recipient of the property is insolvent since, if it comes into the hands of the trustee in bankruptcy he will be personally liable even where he no longer has it.[62]

Tracing in equity. Tracing in equity is only possible where the claimant can **30–100** establish that the defendant or a third party is in a fiduciary relationship to him which has been broken[63] and that he has an equitable proprietary interest in the relevant property.[64] Once this is established the beneficiary can trace the property into the hands of anyone, until either a bona fide purchaser for value without notice acquires the legal title to the property,[65] or the property ceases to be

---

[57] *Trustee of the Property of F. C. Jones & Sons v. Jones* [1997] Ch. 159, 168. See also Pearce (1976) 40 Conv.(N.S.) 277, 284.

[58] *Lipkin Gorman v. Karpnale Ltd supra*, at pp. 573, 583–588 (in respect of claims funded on conversion). *cf.* Burrows *op. cit.* pp. 66–68.

[59] *Re Diplock* [1948] Ch. 465, 519–520.

[60] *ibid.*

[61] *ibid.* at 519. But see the discretion to order the return of a chattel under the Torts (Interference with Goods) Act 1977, s.3. On chattels, see Goff and Jones *op. cit.* pp. 77–78, see further *Howard E. Perry & Co. Ltd v. British Railways Board* [1980] 1 W.L.R. 1375.

[62] *Giles v. Perkins* (1807) East 12; *Scott v. Surman* (1742) Willes 400; *Trustee of the Property of F.C. Jones & Sons v. Jones* [1997] Ch. 159. See Pearce (1976) 40 Conv.(N.S.) 277, 284.

[63] *Space Investments Ltd v. Canadian Imperial Bank of Commerce Trust Co. (Bahamas) Ltd* [1986] 1 W.L.R. 1072.

[64] *Re Diplock* [1948] Ch. 465, 520–521, 529–530; *Westdeutsche Landesbank Girozentrale v. Islington L.B.C.* [1996] A.C. 669, 714, 716. Lord Denning (in *Nelson v. Larholt* [1948] 1 K.B. 339, 342–343 and (1949) 65 L.Q.R. 37), apparently overlooks the need for a fiduciary relationship, which is an important distinction between tracing at common law and in equity and is required in the recent decisions: *Aluminium Industrie Vassen B.V. v. Romalpa Aluminium Ltd* [1976] 1 W.L.R. 676; *Borden (U.K.) Ltd v. Scottish Timber Products Ltd* [1981] Ch. 25; *Chase Manhattan Bank N.A. v. Israel-British Bank (London) Ltd* [1981] Ch. 105; *Agip (Africa) Ltd. v. Jackson* [1991] Ch. 547; *Re Goldcorp Exchange Ltd* [1995] 1 A.C. 74; *Boscawen v. Bajura* [1996] 1 W.L.R. 328. *Lister v. Stubbs* (1890) 45 Ch.D. 1 which held that a principal could not trace into property purchased by his agent with secret commissions received from third parties has been doubted in *Att.-Gen. (Hong Kong) v. Reid* [1994] 1 A.C. 324.

[65] *Re Diplock, supra*, at 539, 544; *Cowan de Groot Properties Ltd v. Eagle Trust plc* [1994] 4 All E.R. 700, 767. The same limitation apparently applied at common law: *Clarke v. Shee* (1774) 1 Cowp. 197.

identifiable even in equity.[66] Thus, the beneficiary may recover his property from a person who purchases it for value, but with notice of the equitable interest, or from an innocent volunteer who takes the property without notice of the equitable interest but does not give value for it,[67] for in these cases there is no bona fide purchaser for value.[68] But if the trustee or fiduciary agent pays trust money into his private banking account which is overdrawn, and the bank, without notice that it is trust money, uses it to pay off the overdraft, the right to trace is lost.[69]

30–101   **Fiduciary relationship** The authorities requiring that there be a fiduciary relationship have been criticised[70] and courts have, on occasion, been willing to circumvent or manipulate the requirement.[71] Moreover, in some cases the finding that a fiduciary relationship exists has appeared to rest solely on the fact that it would be unconscionable for the recipient or his trustee in bankruptcy to retain the amount by which his assets had been increased.[72] However, the category of fiduciary relationships is broad[73] and the relationship need not originate in a consensual transaction.[74] Nor, apparently, need the property have been the subject of fiduciary obligations before it got into the wrong hands. Although the requirement of a fiduciary relationship appears to have been reaffirmed by the House of Lords recently,[75] it was also stated[76] that stolen moneys are traceable in equity and that an equitable proprietary interest under a resulting or constructive trust will suffice. It therefore appears that the courts will continue to manipulate this requirement where they think it is appropriate.

---

[66] *Re Diplock, supra,* at 521, 546–550; *Borden (U.K.) Ltd v. Scottish Timber Products Ltd, supra,* at 41–42; *R. v. Preddy* [1996] 3 W.L.R. 255, 264.

[67] *Re Diplock, supra,* at 539. See also *Thorndike v. Hunt* (1859) 3 De G. & J. 563; *Taylor v. Blakelock* (1886) 32 Ch.D. 560; *Sinclair v. Brougham* [1914] A.C. 398, 443–447. But *cf. post,* § 30–104 for the refusal to permit a tracing order which would operate unconscionably upon the volunteer.

[68] See Snell *op. cit.* pp. 18 *et seq.;* Babafemi (1971) 34 M.L.R. 12, 22–28.

[69] *Thomson v. Clydeside Bank* [1893] A.C. 282; *Coleman v. Bucks & Oxon Union Bank* [1897] 2 Ch. 243; *Bishopsgate Investment Management Ltd v. Homan* [1995] Ch. 211, 220; *Style Financial Services Ltd v. Bank of Scotland* [1995] B.C.C. 785. See also *Foskelt v. McKeown* [1998] Ch. 265.

[70] Goff and Jones, *op. cit.* pp. 103 *et seq;* Maudsley (1959) 75 L.Q.R. 234, 241–245; (1971) 19 Vanderbilt L.R. 1123, 1136; Babafemi (1971) 34 M.L.R. 12; Oakley (1975) 28 *Current Legal Problems* 64.

[71] *El Ajou v. Dollar Land Holdings plc (No. 1)* [1993] 3 All E.R. 717, 734; *Bristol and West B.S. v. Mothew* [1998] Ch. 1, 23.

[72] *Sinclair v. Brougham, supra,* at pp. 441–444; *Chase Manhattan Bank N.A. v. Israel-British Bank (London) Ltd* [1981] Ch. 105, *supra,* § 29–018; *Clough Mill Ltd v. Martin* [1985] 1 W.L.R. 111; *Re Goldcorp Exchange Ltd* [1995] 1 A.C. 74. See also *English v. Dedham Vale Properties Ltd* [1978] 1 W.L.R. 93 (although the plaintiff there sought a duty to account, not a tracing order). But *cf. Borden (U.K.) Ltd v. Scottish Timber Products Ltd* [1981] Ch. 25 for a more restrictive approach.

[73] Sealy [1962] C.L.J. 69; Goff and Jones *op. cit.,* p. 105, n. 8. For this purpose the relationship between, *inter alia* solicitor and client, bailor and bailee, principal and agent will be regarded as fiduciary. An important factor in determining whether an agent is a fiduciary is whether he is under a duty to keep his own money separate from his principal's money. See also *post,* n. 79 and § 30–102.

[74] *Chase Manhattan Bank N.A. v. Israel-British Bank (London) Ltd* [1981] Ch. 105, 119, discussed, Vol. II, § 34–138. See also *Sinclair v. Brougham, supra; English v. Dedham Vale Properties Ltd, supra,* at 111; *Ex p. James* (1874) L.R. 9 Ch.App. 609, discussed, *ante,* §§ 21–021—21–022, 30–044; see further *Agip (Africa) Ltd v. James* [1991] Ch. 547 but *cf. Re Byfield* [1982] Ch. 267.

[75] *Westdeutsche Landesbank Girozentrale v. Islington L.B.C.* [1996] A.C. 669.

[76] *ibid.* at 716.

Reservation of title clauses: original goods and new products. The ques- **30–102**
tion of entitlement to trace has arisen in a commercial context where sellers of
goods have sought to protect themselves from the consequences of their buyers'
insolvency by including reservation of title clauses in the contract of sale.[77] It has
been held that where the purchaser holds the goods as a bailee an appropriately
drafted clause will entitle the unpaid seller to claim the goods and to trace into
the identifiable proceeds of any further sale of the goods by the buyer.[78] The
reservation of title clause must, however, ensure that the seller retains the
beneficial ownership of the property. Although, for instance, allowing the buyer
to sell the goods or to use them in a manufacturing process may be held to be
inconsistent with this,[79] the seller may be held to have retained beneficial
ownership and the entitlement to trace until the goods are sold or so used.[80]
Where a reservation of title clause applies to the product of a manufacturing
process it will normally be construed as creating a charge on the product by the
buyer in favour of the seller rather than a reservation of title[81] and, as such, is
subject to the registration requirements of the Companies Act 1985.[82] It has,
however, been stated that in principle parties to a contract could provide that title
in new goods created by a manufacturing process could directly vest in the
sellers.[83]

Proceeds of sale. Where it is wished to trace into the proceeds of sale (even **30–103**
where no manufacturing process had occurred), it is necessary to show that the
parties were in a fiduciary relationship.[84] The following factors have been said to
assist in establishing such a relationship:

(a) an obligation to store the goods in a manner manifesting the seller's
ownership;

(b) postponement of the passage of property until payment is made for the
total indebtedness;

(c) provision that the seller obtains the benefit of any claims against a sub-
purchaser;

(d) provision that the buyer act as agent for or on account of the seller and;

---

[77] See Goodhart and Jones (1980) 43 M.L.R. 489, 501–510; Goode (1976) 92 L.Q.R. 528,
547–552, 554–560 (discussion of the effect of such clauses in the context of the assignment of book
debts and other receivables). *Ante*, § 20–042.
[78] *Aluminium Industrie Vaasen B.V. v. Romalpa Aluminium Ltd* [1976] 1 W.L.R. 676. For the
limited nature of this right to trace, see *Borden (U.K.) Ltd v. Scottish Timber Products Ltd* [1981] Ch.
25, 38–41. See also Davies [1984] L.M.C.L.Q. 49.
[79] *Borden (U.K.) Ltd v. Scottish Timber Products Ltd* [1981] Ch. 25. See also *Re Bond Worth Ltd*
[1980] Ch. 228.
[80] *Clough Mill Ltd v. Martin* [1985] 1 W.L.R. 111; *John Snow & Co. v. D.B.G. Woodcroft Ltd*
[1985] BCLC 54; *Re Peachdart Ltd* [1984] Ch. 131, 141; *Hendy Lennox (Industrial Engines) Ltd v.
Grahame Puttick Ltd* [1984] 1 W.L.R. 485, 492. See also *Four Point Garage Ltd v. Carter* [1985] 3
All E.R. 12 (retention of title clause did not preclude implication of term authorising resale and
passage of title to sub-buyer).
[81] *Clough Mill Ltd v. Martin* [1985] 1 W.L.R. 111; *Re Peachdart Ltd* [1984] Ch. 131; *E. Pfeiffer
Weinkellerei-Weinemkauf GmbH & Co. v. Arbuthnot Factors Ltd* [1988] 1 W.L.R. 150; *Re Weldtech
Equipment Ltd* [1991] B.C.L.C. 393.
[82] ss.395–399. See *ante*, §§ 9–048, 20–063—20–064.
[83] *Clough Mill Ltd v. Martin, supra,* at 119–120, 123–124.
[84] *Hendy Lennox (Industrial Engines) Ltd v. Grahame Puttick Ltd* [1984] 1 W.L.R. 485; *Re
Andrabell* [1984] 3 All E.R. 407.

(e) an obligation on the buyer to keep the proceeds of sale separate from his own moneys and not to use them.[85]

30–104   **Identifying property in equity.** Equity may trace property beyond "the verge of actual identification,"[86] into any specific asset purchased with it,[87] or into a bank account even when it is mixed with other moneys[88]; " . . . equity regarded the amalgam as capable, in proper circumstances, of being resolved into its component parts."[89] Accordingly, if the trustee mixes his own money with the trust money, the beneficiary can claim a first charge on the mixed fund, or on any asset purchased with the mixed fund.[90] If the trustee mixes the trust funds of two separate trusts, there is an equal equity in each beneficiary, so that the separate beneficiaries can trace and share *pari passu*, or enjoy *pari passu* any equitable lien or charge on an asset purchased with the mixed fund.[91] (Any equitable charge may be enforced ultimately by sale of the assets.[92]) If the trust money is received by a volunteer who then mixes it with his own money, the beneficiary may again trace his property, claiming a declaration of charge if necessary, but he must share the fund (or any asset purchased therewith) *pari passu* with the volunteer.[93]

30–105   But even equity cannot trace property if its identity is finally lost, *e.g.* by being spent on living expenses such as a dinner,[94] being used to pay off a loan,[95] or by mixing heterogeneous goods in a manufacturing process wherein a wholly new product emerges.[96] It has also been held that the beneficiaries of a trust cannot trace into the proceeds of an insurance policy in respect of which trust moneys had fraudulently been used to pay premiums.[97] Nor will equity permit a tracing order if it would operate in a harsh or unconscionable manner upon the volunteer, *e.g.* if a volunteer who innocently acquires trust property uses it to alter or improve his own land or buildings, the right to trace in equity is lost, since it

---

[85] *ibid.* A fixed credit period has been held to be incompatible with (e).

[86] *Sinclair v. Brougham, supra,* at 459.

[87] *Lane v. Dighton* (1762) Amb. 409; *Hopper v. Conyers* (1866) L.R. 2 Eq. 549.

[88] *Re Diplock, supra,* at 520.

[89] *ibid.* at 520.

[90] *ibid.* at 539; *Re Hallett's Estate* (1880) 13 Ch.D. 696; *Re Pumfrey* (1882) 22 Ch.D. 255; *Re Oatway* [1903] 2 Ch. 356. Where the property purchased by a "mixed" fund has increased in value, the charge will be for a proportionate part of the increased value, as well as for the amount of the trust money: *Scott v. Scott* (1963) 109 C.L.R. 649; *Foskett v. McKeowan* [1998] Ch. 265. *cf. Re Tilley's Will Trusts* [1967] Ch. 1179, 1193. The question whether the rule in *Re Hallett's Estate* applies where money paid under a mistake of fact to a person who is not a trustee was left open in *Chase Manhattan Bank N.A. v. Israel-British Bank (London) Ltd* [1981] Ch. 105, 120 (on which, see Vol. II, § 34–132). It has been applied to such a case in the United States; *Re Berry* 147 F. 208 (1906). See further *Agip (Africa) Ltd v. James* [1991] Ch. 547.

[91] *Re Diplock, supra,* at 533–534, 539; *Sinclair v. Brougham* [1914] A.C. 398, 442 (*ante,* §§ 9–024, 30–014); *Barlow Clowes (International) Ltd v. Vaughan* [1992] 4 All E.R. 22. On the application of this rule to *Sinclair v. Brougham,* where problems of the *ultra vires* doctrine arose, see Stoljar (1959) 22 M.L.R. 21.

[92] *Re Diplock, supra,* at 546–547.

[93] *ibid.* at 534, 539; *Sinclair v. Brougham, supra,* at 442–443.

[94] *Re Diplock, supra,* at 521.

[95] *ibid.* at 548–550. (*Sed quaere,* if the loan was used to acquire a specific, identifiable asset.) See *Re J. Leslie Engineers Co. Ltd* [1976] 1 W.L.R. 292, 300 (payments of debts).

[96] *Borden (U.K.) Ltd v. Scottish Timber Products Ltd* [1981] Ch. 25, 41 but *cf. Clough Mills Ltd v. Martin* [1985] 1 W.L.R. 111, *ante,* § 29–073.

[97] *Foskett v. McKeowan* [1998] Ch. 265. *cf. G & M Motor Co. v. Thompson* 567 P 2d 80 (1977); Smith, [1995] C.L.J. 290; (1997) 113 L.Q.R. 552.

would be inequitable to force the sale of his land.[98] In principle a volunteer should be able to rely on the defence of "change of position."[99]

Withdrawals from a mixed fund in a bank account. In *Clayton's Case*[1] it   **30–106** was held that moneys in a current bank account are presumed to have been paid out in the order in which they were paid in applies in equity where two trust funds, or trust money and a volunteer's own money, have been mixed in the same bank account.[2] Where, however, a fund is intended to be a common investment fund or where the application of the rule in *Clayton's Case* would be impracticable or result in injustice it will not apply if there is a preferable alternative.[3] In such cases the court will incline to rateable division.[4] Moreover, where a trustee mixes his own money with trust money in a bank account, the rule in *Clayton's Case* does not apply, and the trustee is taken to have drawn out first his own money, until his own money in the account is exhausted.[5] If the trustee draws out all the trust money, but later pays in money of his own, the beneficiary cannot trace this money in the account unless he can prove that the trustee intended to replace the trust money.[6] If the trustee or volunteer "unmixes" the trust money by earmarking a particular withdrawal as the trust money, the beneficiary may trace it into another asset purchased with the proceeds of the withdrawal.[7]

(h) *Other Equitable Remedies and Constructive Trusts*

Constructive trusts. Equity has employed the fiction of a trust in order to   **30–107** compel the "trustee" to convey property to the "beneficiary" where, quite apart from the intention of the parties, the rules of equity decide that property is in the wrong hands.[8] This device has been extensively developed in the United States of America,[9] where such a trust is regarded as "purely a remedial institution"[10] and support has been expressed for the development of the remedial constructive

---

[98] *Re Diplock, supra*, at pp. 546–548. (Again, the alteration to the land or buildings may have been to suit the personal needs of the volunteer, so that there was no increase in the market value of the asset.) *cf. ante*, § 29–030.

[99] *Ante*, § 30–114; Goff and Jones *op. cit.* pp. 109–113; Maudsley (1959) 75 L.Q.R. 234, 249–252. *cf. Re Diplock supra*, at 476.

[1] (1816) 1 Mer. 572. See McConville (1963) 79 L.Q.R. 388. It is uncertain whether this rule or the rule in *Re Hallett's Estate, supra*, applies where money has been paid under a mistake of fact; *ante*, n. 90.

[2] *Hancock v. Smith* (1889) 41 Ch.D. 456, 461; *Re Stenning* [1895] 2 Ch. 433; *Re Hallett's Estate* (1880) 13 Ch.D. 696; *Re Diplock, supra*, at 552–554.

[3] *Barlow Clowes (International) Ltd. v. Vaughan* [1992] 4 All E.R. 22. See also *Re British Red Cross Balkan Fund* [1914] 2 Ch. 419.

[4] *ibid.* at 42, 44.

[5] *Re Hallett's Estate, supra*, CA; *James Roscoe (Bolton) Ltd v. Winder* [1915] 1 Ch. 62. But *cf. Re Oatway* [1903] 2 Ch. 356 (money first drawn out and invested held to be traceable where remaining balance later dissipated).

[6] *James Roscoe (Bolton) Ltd v. Winder, supra*; *Bishopsgate Investment Management Ltd v. Homan* [1995] Ch. 211, *Goldcorp Exchange Ltd (in receivership)* [1995] 1 A.C. 74, 107.

[7] *Re Diplock, supra*, at 551–552.

[8] Goff and Jones *op. cit.* pp. 103–119, Chap. 33; Underhill and Hayton, *Law of Trusts and Trustees*, Chap. 7; Snell, *Equity* (28th ed.), Chap. 5; Hanbury and Martin, *Modern Equity* (15th ed.), Chap. 12; Elias, *Explaining Constructive Trusts* (1990); Oakley, *Constructive Trusts* (3rd ed.); Waters, *The Constructive Trust* (1964).

[9] Scott (1955) 71 L.Q.R. 39.

[10] Pound (1920) 33 Harv.L.R. 420, 421.

trust in English law.[11] It has also been called "a constructive quasi-trust"[12] to distinguish it from another type of constructive trust, where the trustee is under the full duties of a trustee, *e.g.* where trust property is conveyed to a purchaser with notice. Under a constructive quasi-trust affecting a "mixed fund"[13] which increases in value, the beneficiary may claim his share in the increased fund.[14] There has been limited development in England of this device; examples must be sought in authorities on trusts.[15]

30–108   **Defendant's acquiescence in improvements to his land.** There are other equitable rules similar to a constructive trust. For instance, where a person in occupation of the land of another expends money on the land (*e.g.* by building) in the expectation, induced or encouraged by the owner of the land, that he will be allowed to remain in occupation, an equity is created under which the court will protect his occupation of the land.[16] The nature of the relief will depend on the circumstances.[17]

30–109   **Equitable doctrine of restitution by fraudulent minors.** Equity has developed a doctrine whereby a minor who has fraudulently obtained property under

---

[11] *Westdeutsche Landesbank Girozentrale v. Islington L.B.C.* [1996] A.C. 669, 716. See also *Re Polly Peck International plc (No. 4) The Times* 18 May, 1998.

[12] Maudsley (1959) 75 L.Q.R. 234, 235, 237.

[13] See *ante*, § 30–104.

[14] *Edinburgh (Lord Provost of, etc.) v. The Lord Advocate* (1879) 4 App.Cas. 823. *cf. ante*, § 30–104, n. 90.

[15] See n. 8, *ante*. For leading cases, see *e.g. Keech v. Sandford* (1726) Cas.t.King 61; *Re Knowles' Will Trusts* [1948] 1 All E.R. 866; *Bannister v. Bannister* [1948] 2 All E.R. 133; *Reading v. Att.-Gen.* [1951] A.C. 507, 516, 517 (*post*, § 30–172); *Re Green* [1951] Ch. 148; *Hepburn v. A. Tomlinson (Hauliers) Ltd* [1966] A.C. 451 (*ante*, § 19–110); *Phipps v. Boardman* [1967] 2 A.C. 46 (*post*, § 30–175) *Guinness plc v. Saunders* [1990] 2 A.C. 663; *Quistclose Investments Ltd v. Rolls Razor Ltd* [1970] A.C. 567; *Selangor United Rubber Estates Ltd v. Cradock* [1968] 1 W.L.R. 1555; *Industrial Development Consultants Ltd v. Cooley* [1972] 1 W.L.R. 443; *Queensland Mines v. Hudson* (1978) 18 A.L.R. 1; *New Zealand Netherland Society "Oranje" Inc. v. Kuys* [1973] 1 W.L.R. 1126 (PC: a special arrangement may displace what would otherwise be a potential fiduciary obligation); *Baden Delvaux & Lecurt v. Soc. Gen. etc.* [1983] B.C.L.C. 325; [1992] 4 All E.R. 161; *Re Montague's S.T.* [1987] Ch. 264; *Agip (Africa) Ltd v. James* [1991] Ch. 547; *Cowan de Groot Properties Ltd v. Eagle Trust plc* [1992] 4 All E.R. 700; *Polly Peck International v. Nadir (No. 2)* [1992] 4 All E.R. 769; *Att.-Gen. (Hong Kong) v. Reid* [1994] 1 A.C. 324 (PC: bribes); *Royal Brunei Airlines S.D.N. B.H.D. v. Phillip Tan Kok Ming* [1995] 2 A.C. 378; *Deutsche Ruckversicherung A.G. v. Walbrook Insurance Co. Ltd* [1994] 4 All E.R. 181, 201–2; *Halifax Building Society v. Thomas* [1996] Ch. 217; *Target Holdings Ltd v. Redferns (a firm)* [1996] A.C. 421; *Re A.M.F. International Ltd* [1996] 1 W.L.R. 77, 83 (a trustee need not compensate a beneficiary for loss arising from a breach of trust if it was inevitable that the beneficiary would suffer that loss anyway). See also *ante*, § 9–015; *post*, § 30–175; Vol. II, §§ 33–022, 41–003—41–009. The concept of a constructive trust has been used to give a remedy to a person who has been led to expect an interest in the "family" home: *Gissing v. Gissing* [1971] A.C. 886, 905; *Binions v. Evans* [1972] Ch. 359; *Cooke v. Head* [1972] 1 W.L.R. 518; *Hussey v. Palmer* [1972] 1 W.L.R. 1286; *Eves v. Eves* [1975] 1 W.L.R. 1338; *Re Sharpe* [1980] 1 W.L.R. 219; *Grant v. Edwards* [1986] Ch. 638.

[16] *Inwards v. Baker* [1965] 2 Q.B. 29; *Chambers v. Pardoe* [1963] 1 W.L.R. 677; *Ward v. Kirkland* [1966] 1 W.L.R. 601, 626–632; *Lee-Parker v. Izzet* [1972] 1 W.L.R. 775, 780–781. *cf. E.R. Ives Investment Ltd v. High* [1967] 2 Q.B. 379; *Siew Soon Wah v. Yong Tong Hong* [1973] A.C. 836; *Dodsworth v. Dodsworth* [1973] E.G. 233; *Crabb v. Arun DC* [1976] Ch. 179 (one landowner encouraged the adjoining owner to act to his prejudice in the belief he would be given a right of way); *Jones v. Jones* [1977] 1 W.L.R. 438; *Pascoe v. Turner* [1979] 1 W.L.R. 431; *Grant v. Edwards* [1986] Ch. 638. For earlier authorities, see *Dillwyn v. Llewelyn* (1862) 4 De G.F. & J. 517; *Ramsden v. Dyson* (1866) L.R. 1 H.L. 129; *Willmot v. Barber* (1880) 15 Ch.D. 96; *Plimmer v. Mayor of Wellington* (1884) 9 App.Cas. 699. See also *ante*, § 9–014; Goff and Jones *op. cit.* pp. 241–245; Allan (1963) 79 L.Q.R. 238; *Van den Berg v. Giles* [1979] 2 N.Z.L.R. 111. *cf.* § 3–129—3–152.

[17] *ibid.*

a void contract may be compelled to restore it if it can be identified and is still in his possession.[18] The doctrine is fully examined in the chapter on Personal Incapacity.[19]

Other equitable remedies. The equitable remedy of rescission[20] of a contract **30–110** on the ground of misrepresentation or mistake[21] may also be viewed as an instance of restitution, since the consequences of rescission include the restitution of benefits transferred by the representee in pursuance of the contract and an indemnity against liabilities necessarily incurred by the representee as a result of the contract.[22] Similarly, rectification[23] of a written document which by a mistake fails to give effect to a prior oral agreement may also lead to restitutionary relief. Full discussion of these remedies will be found in previous chapters.[24] Likewise, equity may permit, as the result of setting aside a transaction, the recovery of benefits conferred on the defendant following undue influence exercised by the defendant over the plaintiff[25]; it may enable restitution of benefits obtained in breach of another's confidence.[26] Equity may also grant relief from certain unconscionable bargains.[27] Finally, where a person seeks to enforce a claim to an equitable interest in property, the court has a discretion to require as a condition of giving effect to that interest that an allowance be made for costs incurred and services rendered in connection with the administration of the property.[28] The factors which will incline a court to make such an allowance include whether the work would in any event have had to be done by the person entitled to the equitable interest or a receiver appointed by the court and, the fact that the work has been of substantial benefit to the property and to the persons entitled to the equitable interest.[29]

(i) *Defences*

Estoppel. In certain circumstances a person making a payment may be pre- **30–111** cluded from recovering it by an estoppel. He may, for instance, be estopped from subsequently alleging that he acted under a mistake of fact.[30] To raise an estoppel

---

[18] *R. Leslie Ltd v. Sheill* [1914] 3 K.B. 607; Atiyah (1959) 22 M.L.R. 273.

[19] *Ante*, §§ 8–048—8–050.

[20] *Whittaker v. Campbell* [1984] Q.B. 318. See *ante*, §§ 7–013 *et seq.*

[21] See *ante*, §§ 5–007—5–091.

[22] See *ante*, §§ 5–065—5–067. *cf.* § 23–026.

[23] See *ante*, §§ 5–065—5–067.

[24] See *ante*, §§ 5–065 *et seq.*, 5–092 *et seq.*, 6–101 *et seq.*

[25] *Allcard v. Skinner* (1887) 36 Ch.D. 145. See *ante*, §§ 7–040 *et seq.*; *cf. ante*, § 30–095.

[26] Jones (1970) 86 L.Q.R. 463.

[27] *Earl of Chesterfield v. Janssen* (1751) 2 Ves.Sen. 125, 157. See *ante*, §§ 7–075—7–088; Vol. II, §§ 38–192 *et seq.*, 38–244; Goff and Jones *op. cit.* Chap. 12.

[28] *Boardman v. Phipps* [1967] 2 A.C. 46; *O'Sullivan v. Management Agency & Music Ltd* [1985] Q.B. 428; *Re Berkeley Applegate Ltd* [1989] Ch. 32. *cf. Guinness plc v. Saunders* [1990] 2 A.C. 663.

[29] *Re Berkeley Applegate Ltd, supra.*

[30] Goff and Jones *op. cit.* pp. 828–841; Spencer-Bower and Turner, *The Law Relating to Estoppel by Representation* (3rd ed., 1991); Jones (1957) 73 L.Q.R. 48, 49–53; Birks *op. cit.* pp. 403, 410, 474.

the payee must satisfy three conditions.[31] First, he must show that either the payer was under a duty to give him accurate information and failed to do so,[32] or that there was an unequivocal[33] misrepresentation made to him for which the payer was responsible.[34] Secondly, he must show that this inaccurate information led him to believe that he was entitled to treat the money as his own[35]; in the case of a mistake as to liability it must have caused him to believe that the payer or a third party was his debtor. Thirdly, he must show that because of his mistaken belief he changed his position in a way which would make it inequitable to require him to repay the money.[36]

30–112 **Fact of payment in itself is insufficient.** The mere fact of payment by itself cannot give rise to an estoppel.[37] However, where there is inequality between the parties, as where the payer is uniquely well placed to know or ascertain the true state of accounts, it may be relatively easy to spell out a representation from the one-sidedness of the means of knowledge. Thus, where, after a computer had been fed with the wrong information by an employer, the employer overpaid one of his employees, it was conceded that, in the circumstances, there was a sufficient representation to found an estoppel.[38] Such situations, exemplified by the "paymaster" cases, are sometimes treated as instances of breach of a duty to inform the payee of the true state of the account rather than as representation cases.[39] In fact neither *Holt v. Markham*[40] nor the old case of *Skyring v. Greenwood*[41] turn on breach of duty. In *Holt v. Markham* the claimant by letter claimed repayment of an excessive gratuity that he had mistakenly paid to the defendant. The defendant replied that the claim was unfounded and heard nothing further from the claimant for over two months. The Court of Appeal held that the mistake was one of law, on which see *ante*, 29–025 but also decided that the claimant was "entitled to assume that his reply was regarded as satisfactory, and that he was at liberty to deal with the money as he pleased."[42] Scrutton L.J.

---

[31] *United Overseas Bank v. Jiwani* [1976] 1 W.L.R. 964, 968.

[32] *Mercantile Bank of India Ltd v. Central Bank of India Ltd* [1938] A.C. 287; *Moorgate Mercantile Co. Ltd v. Twitchings* [1977] A.C. 890, 903 (on facts no duty found); *United Overseas Bank v. Jiwani, ante*. On the question of whether estoppel by negligence is possible in the absence of a special relationship, see *R. E. Jones Ltd v. Waring & Gillow Ltd* [1926] A.C. 670, 693; *Mercantile Credit Co. Ltd v. Hamblin* [1965] 2 Q.B. 242. cf. *Moorgate Mercantile Co. Ltd v. Twitchings, supra*; *Tai Hing Cotton Mill Ltd v. Lin Chong Hing Bank Ltd* [1986] A.C. 80. See also Consumer Credit Act 1974, s.172 which provides that certain statements made by a creditor, owner or trader are to bind him although provision exists for relief from the operation of the section to the extent that it "appears just in an appropriate case"; s.172(3).

[33] *Weld-Blundell v. Synott* [1940] 2 K.B. 107, 114 (see *ante*, § 30–030), *Moorgate Mercantile Co. Ltd v. Twitchings, supra*.

[34] *R.E. Jones Ltd v. Waring & Gillow Ltd* [1926] A.C. 670; *Deutsche Bank v. Beriro & Co.* (1895) 1 Com.Cas. 123, 255; 73 L.T. 669; *United Overseas Bank v. Jiwani, supra*; *Avon C.C. v. Howlett* [1983] 1 W.L.R. 605, 620.

[35] *Holt v. Markham* [1923] 1 K.B. 504, 512; *Transvaal & Delagoa Bay Investment Co. v. Atkinson* [1944] 1 All E.R. 579, 585; *United Overseas Bank v. Jiwani, supra*; *Avon C.C. v. Howlett, supra*, and see Sheldon J. [1981] I.R.L.R. 447.

[36] See *post*, § 30–113.

[37] *R. E. Jones Ltd v. Waring & Gillow Ltd, supra*.

[38] *Avon C.C. v. Howlett, supra*. This approach reflects Birks [1972] C.L.P. 179.

[39] *Weld-Blundell v. Synott, supra*, at 115.

[40] [1923] 1 K.B. 504.

[41] (1825) 4 B. & C. 281.

[42] [1923] 1 K.B. 504, 512.

went further in not relying on the defendant's letter. He stated that "[t]he claimants represented to the defendant that he was entitled to a certain sum of money and paid it, and, after a lapse of time sufficient to enable mistakes to be detected and rectified, the defendant acted on the representation and spent the money."[43] The representation in such cases has never been formulated with precision, but, in view of the need for a lapse of time before it may be acted upon, it is arguably a representation that reasonable care has been used in making and checking the payment.[44]

Reliance by payee. The third requirement of an estoppel, that the payee has **30–113** changed his position so as to make it inequitable[45] to require him to repay the money, is clearly satisfied where he can establish that a particular expenditure has been incurred as a result of the receipt of the money and he is no longer able to recover the money. Examples include investing the money in a company that has since failed,[46] and irretrievably paying it over to a third party to whom the payee thought he was obliged to pay it.[47] However, in certain circumstances, a sufficient change of position to found an estoppel may occur without any obvious change in the payee's style of living. In one case an employee who had been overpaid for a period of some eighteen months and who had spent the money as part of his normal living expenses successfully raised an estoppel.[48] The test is whether, but for the payment the expenditure would have occurred. Thus, there may be circumstances in which even after all the money has been spent it would not be inequitable to require repayment.[49] Conversely, in *Avon County Council v. Howlett*[50] it was stated that, while a plea of estoppel should not enable a profit to be made, a payee who has relied on a representation should not be subjected to the difficult task of having "subsequently to recall and identify retrospectively in complete detail" alterations to his general mode of living, commitments undertaken and other transactions entered into. The operation of estoppel might, therefore, result in the payee returning less than the difference between the amount paid and the precise amount he proved he had irretrievably spent. This was stated to follow from the fact that estoppel by representation is a rule of evidence and does not operate *pro tanto*.[51] However, the finding that the whole of the overpayment had in fact been spent and the recognition by the court that injustice would result if the sum sought to be recovered were so large as to bear no relation to the payee's detriment and that recovery in such circumstances might be unconscionable[52]; suggests that in an appropriate case estoppel may nevertheless operate *pro tanto*.

---

[43] *ibid.* at 514. See also the fuller report on this point in (1923) 128 L.T. 719, 726.

[44] See *ante*, § 30–034; Birks [1972] C.L.P. 179, 194 *et seq.*

[45] *Kleinwort, Sons & Co. v. Dunlop Rubber Co.* (1907) 97 L.T. 263, 264; *United Overseas Bank v. Jiwani, supra.*

[46] *Holt v. Markham* [1923] 1 K.B. 504.

[47] *Deutsche Bank v. Beriro & Co.* (1895) 1 Com.Cas. 123, 255; 73 L.T. 669.

[48] *Avon C.C. v. Howlett* [1981] I.R.L.R. 447, 449–450; [1983] 1 W.L.R. 605. See also *Skyring v. Greenwood* (1825) 4 B. & C. 281, 289 (Abbott C.J.).

[49] *United Overseas Bank v. Jiwani, supra,* at 968–969.

[50] [1983] 1 W.L.R. 605.

[51] *ibid.* at 611, 621–624. For criticism see Burrows *op. cit.* pp. 436–438; Goff and Jones *op. cit.* pp. 831–833. See also *Lipkin Gorman v. Karpnale Ltd* [1991] 2 A.C. 548, 579.

[52] *ibid.* at 612, 624–625.

30–114 **Change of position as a separate defence.** In *Lipkin Gorman v. Karpnale Ltd* the House of Lords recognised a broad defence of change of position. This was said to be "available to a person whose position has so changed that it would be inequitable in all the circumstances to require him to make restitution, or alternatively to make restitution in full."[53] The defence is said to be one of the general principles of the law of restitution[54] and, even before the decision of the House of Lords, its supposed existence was used as a justification for widening the scope of recovery for mistake.[55] Change of position is a wider defence than estoppel because it does not depend on breach of duty of misrepresentation by the payee. In one respect, however, it is narrower than estoppel in not recognising expenditure on everyday expenses.[56] The broad formulation was explicitly chosen by the House of Lords to allow for the development of the defence on a case by case basis. If the basis of the claim is the unjust enrichment of the defendant, in principle any available defences should similarly be based on the extent of any enrichment and should apply where the enrichment has been erased. In the context of mistake, as the ground of recovery is wide and, for instance, does not bar recovery by a negligent payer, it is particularly important to accept a broad defence.

30–115 **Illustrations of change of position.** The mere fact of having spent money or delivered property does not suffice to establish the defence.[57] Nor does the fact that acts have been done in reliance on a void contract where no payments have yet been received.[58] The paradigm case of change of position is where the payee has detrimentally relied on a payment made to him which he has received in good faith. For instance, where the recipient of a mistaken payment, acting in good faith, pays the money or part of it to charity or makes a purchase which he would not have made but for the payment, it is unjust to require him to make restitution to the extent that he has so changed his position.[59] Thus, on the facts of *Lipkin Gorman v. Karpnale Ltd*, where a person who had stolen money used it to gamble, the gaming club was not required to repay the entire amount gambled

---

[53] *Lipkin Gorman v. Karpnale Ltd* [1991] 2 A.C. 548, 580. See also at 558 and 568. This case departed from the previous position on which see *e.g. Durrant v. Ecclesiastical Commissioners* (1880) 6 Q.B.D. 234; *Larner v. L.C.C.* [1949] 2 K.B. 683, 688–689; *Baylis v. Bishop of London* [1913] Ch. 127; *Re Diplock* [1948] Ch. 465, 476 (affd. *sub nom. Minister of Health v. Simpson* [1951] A.C. 251, 276). See also New Zealand Judicature Amendment Act 1958, s.94B; Restatement of Restitution, para. 142.

[54] *R. v. Tower Hamlets L.B.C., ex p. Chetnik Developments Ltd* [1988] A.C. 858.

[55] *Barclays Bank Ltd v. W. J. Simms, Son and Cooke (Southern) Ltd* [1980] Q.B. 677, *ante,* para. 29–020; *Rover International Ltd v. Cannon Film Sales Ltd (No. 3)* [1989] 1 W.L.R. 912; *Midland Bank plc v. Brown Shipley & Co. Ltd* [1991] 2 All E.R. 690, 701–702. See also *Rural Municipality of Storthoaks v. Mobil Oil Canada Ltd* [1975] 55 D.L.R. (3d) 1; *David Securities Pty. Ltd v. Commonwealth of Australia* [1992] 66 A.L.J.R. 768.

[56] *Lipkin Gorman v. Karpnale, supra,* at pp. 559–560, 580.

[57] *Rover International Ltd v. Cannon Films Sales Ltd (No. 3)* [1989] 1 W.L.R. 912. See also *United Overseas Bank v. Jiwani* [1976] 1 W.L.R. 964, 968–969.

[58] *South Tyneside M.B.C. v. Svenska International plc* [1995] 1 All E.R. 545. See also *State Bank of N.S.W. Ltd v. Swiss Bank Corp.* [1997] 6 Bank. L.R. 34. Nolan in Birks (ed.), *Laundering and Tracing* (1995) Chap. 6. See also *Barber v. N.W.S. Bank* [1996] 1 W.L.R. 641.

[59] [1991] 2 A.C. 548, 559, 579. Where the item purchased has a secondhand value there is unjust enrichment to the extent of the secondhand value of that item but where, as where the money is spent on a holiday, the enrichment is erased by the change of position.

but only their net winnings from the thief.[60] In these cases the loss ought to lie where it falls, on the payer who has initiated the loss-causing event, at least where neither party is at fault. But if the payee has used the money to cover expenses which would have been incurred even if he had never received the payment in question, the defence will not be established.[61]

Link between receipt and specific expenditure unnecessary. The broad **30–116** defence as formulated by the House of Lords does not appear to require a link between specific expenditure and specific receipts.[62] This means that deserving cases in which it would be difficult to show a specific link are not necessarily excluded. For instance, where a sick employee is erroneously paid his full salary instead of the reduced sick pay to which he is entitled and as a consequence the employee simply fails to adjust his outgoings in the light of his new income, or where it is difficult to characterise the expenditure as unusual, such as buying "a better cut of meat, maybe, from time to time, or something extra from the grocer,"[63] or where a person with a complicated pattern of expenditure cannot attribute any particular items to the payment[64] provided the payee can satisfy the court that expenditure has increased in line with income it may be possible to establish the defence.[65] The broad test may also be able to deal with situations in which the enrichment is illusory and it would be unjust to order repayment but the payee's loss is not due to his reliance on the payment but to some other factor, such as where the money mistakenly paid has been stolen from him or where its loss is the result of a natural event, such as a fire. While it is likely that hardship unrelated to the payment will be treated as irrelevant and will not establish the defence, in the case where the very notes are stolen or are consumed by fire, it is submitted that the defence should be available.[66]

Similar defences. Prior to the recognition of the broad defence, in certain **30–117** circumstances there were defences which could be rationalised[67] as change of position. Thus, if an agent acting on behalf of a disclosed principal receives money paid under a mistake of fact, and pays the money to his principal before the payer claims recovery, the agent is not liable, since "the person who made the

---

[60] *ibid.* at 559, 579–580. For the reason the provision of gaming services was not regarded as good consideration see *ante,* § 30–062.

[61] *R.B.C. Dominion Securities Inc. v. Dawson* [1994] 111 D.L.R. (4th) 230.

[62] *cf. Rural Municipality of Storthoaks v. Mobile Oil Canada Ltd* [1976] 2 S.C.R. 147 where the defence failed because it was not proved that specific items of expenditure resulted from specific receipts.

[63] *Avon C.C. v. Howlett* [1981] I.R.L.R. 447, 449–450 (Sheldon J.); [1983] 1 W.L.R. 605, 622, CA See *ante,* § 30–113.

[64] *ibid.*

[65] See *Home Office v. Ayres* [1992] I.C.R. 175 (indications by E.A.T. that spending money on normal living expenses, *i.e.* failing to adjust standard of living would probably have qualified as a change of position). See also *David Securities Pty. Ltd v. Commonwealth Bank of Australia* (1992) 66 A.L.J.R. 768, 780–781; *Westdeutsche Landesbank Girozentrale v. Islington L.B.C.* (1993) 91 L.G.R. 325, 390–397 (while no need for link between specific expenditure and specific receipts, losses independent of or prior to the receipt of the benefit cannot be taken into account).

[66] Law Com. No. 227, *Mistakes of Law and Ultra Vires Public Authority Receipts and Payments* (Cm. 2731) (1994), para. 2.21; Burrows *op. cit.* p. 427; Goff and Jones *op. cit.* p. 824, n. 42. *cf.* Birks [1991] L.M.C.L.Q. 473; *Restitution—The Future* (1991), pp. 141–143; Watts, "Judicature Amendment Act 1958—Mistaken Payments" in *Contract Statutes Review* 25 N.Z.L.C. 191 (1993).

[67] *ibid.* 579 (Lord Goff).

mistake is not without redress, but has his remedy over against the principal."[68] Another instance occurs where money is paid under a forged bill of exchange.[69] Furthermore, the need to protect changes of position may well explain the denial of relief in some cases which appear to proceed on other grounds. *Boulton v. Jones*,[70] in which goods mistakenly supplied were consumed by the recipient, but where the recipient was held not to be liable to pay for them is one example. The "paymaster" cases, considered *ante*, 30–028, may be another instance of the indirect operation of the defence in so far as it is difficult to accept them as true cases of estoppel.

30–118   **Fault.** A further question concerns the effect of the relative fault of the parties in failing to avoid the mistaken payment and the reasonableness of the payee's conduct following the payment, for example where he suffers heavy losses as a result of making highly speculative investments, he incurs the expenses after becoming aware of the claimant's claim,[71] or where he pays far over the odds for an item he particularly wants. It is submitted that it is the payee's *real* loss to which the law should look since individuals' perceptions of their own wealth are likely to influence the extent to which they are willing to take risks or are indifferent to price.[72] It is also not clear whether the broad formulation in *Lipkin Gorman v. Karpnale Ltd* would allow the payee's "contributory negligence" to be taken into account in determining the extent to which reliance can be placed on a change of position, as is the law in New Zealand[73] or whether, as appears to be the case under paragraph 142(2) of the Restatement of Restitution, fault is only relevant to exclude the defence where the payee was clearly more at fault than the payer, a "relative fault" approach. The New Zealand approach has been criticised by law reform agencies which have considered this matter on the ground that it goes far beyond what is required to give effect to a change of position defence.[74] The "contributory negligence" approach gives the court a power to split the loss between the two parties rather than simply determining

---

[68] *Buller v. Harrison* (1777) 2 Cowp. 565, 566; *Continental Caoutchoue v. Kleinwort* (1904) 90 L.T. 474, 476; *Gowers v. Lloyds and National Provincial Foreign Bank Ltd* [1938] 1 All E.R. 766; *Agip (Africa) Ltd v. Jackson* [1990] Ch. 265 (affd. [1991] Ch. 547); *Australia and New Zealand Banking Group Ltd v. Westpac Banking Corp.* (1988) 78 A.L.R. 157, 168; *Bank Tejarat v. Hong Kong & Shanghai Banking Corporation (CI) Ltd* [1995] 1 Lloyd's Rep 239. See Vol. II, § 32–109. But see Burrows *op. cit.* pp. 481–482; Goff and Jones *op. cit.* pp. 833–838 for the view that this is a distinct defence applicable under agency law. See also Millett (1991) 107 L.Q.R. 71, 76; Swadling in Birks ed., *Laundering and Tracing*, (1995) Chap. 9. Note that this principle does not apply where the recipient is in the position of a trustee: *Baylis v. Bishop of London, ante*; or received the money as a result of his own wrongdoing, or with knowledge that it resulted from another's wrongdoing: *Oates v. Hudson* (1851) 6 Ex. 346.

[69] *Price v. Neal* (1762) 3 Burr. 1354; *Cocks v. Masterman* (1829) 9 B. & C. 902; *London & River Plate Bank v. Bank of Liverpool* [1896] 1 Q.B. 7; *Imperial Bank of Canada v. Bank of Hamilton* [1903] A.C. 49; *National Westminster Bank Ltd v. Barclays Bank International Ltd* [1975] Q.B. 654; Goff and Jones *op. cit.* pp. 838–841.

[70] (1857) 2 H. & N. 564. See also the requirement of *restitutio in integrum* for rescission for misrepresentation, *ante*, §§ 6–112 *et seq*. The requirement of total failure of consideration, *ante*, § 30–048 *et seq*. has also been justified because of the absence of a defence of change of position; *Whincup v. Hughes* (1871) L.R. 6 C.P. 78, 82, 84. See also the "statutory recognition," of the defence in *B.P. Exploration Co. (Libya) Ltd v. Hunt (No. 2)* [1979] 1 W.L.R. 783, 800.

[71] *Sullivan v. Lee* (1995) 95 B.C.L.R. (2d) 195.

[72] *Skyring v. Greenwood* (1825) 4 B.C. 281, 289; Goff and Jones *op. cit.* p. 825.

[73] *Thomas v. Houston Corbett and Co.* [1969] N.Z.L.R. 151.

[74] Law Commission Consultation Paper No. 120, para. 2.77; Law Reform Commission of British Columbia L.R.C. 51 (1981), p. 79; Law Reform Committee of South Australia (84th Report, 1984), p. 32. Law Reform Commission of New South Wales L.R.C. 53 (1987), para. 5.35.

whether the payee was clearly more at fault than the payer and, if not, simply refusing recovery to the extent of the payee's change of position. It has been argued that "a contributory negligence" approach involves too much uncertainty and complexity and is likely to hamper the settlement of disputes.[75]

Relationship between change of position and estoppel. The flexibility of **30–119** change of position may mean that it will be rare in the future for a defendant who has changed his position to plead that the claimant is estopped.[76] While this may well be the case, the fact that estoppel does not operate *pro tanto*[77] means that defendants may prefer it.[78] But there are indications that the recognition of change of position which operates *pro tanto* means that it should no longer be possible to use estoppel to recover a sum that bears no relation to the payee's detriment.[79] Another reason for a defendant preferring estoppel, at least until change of position is more developed, is that it may be easier to establish the defence where sums from a variety of sources have been spent but no particular item of expenditure can be ascribed to a particular payment or where the payee, erroneously believing his income is higher than it is because of the payments, simply fails to adjust his outgoings to reflect his new income. The importance of estoppel will certainly diminish as the result of the introduction of a broad defence of change of position but it is submitted that it is premature to regard it as redundant.

Settlement of an honest claim.[80] A payment that is made in settlement of or **30–120** submission to an honest claim, or as part of a compromise cannot be recovered. Since greater doubts surround questions of law than questions of fact it is more likely that there will be a settlement or a compromise where the issue is one of law rather than one of fact. Although it has been stated that the precise limits of the settlement defence "have still to be clarified",[81] the current position can be stated in the following way. First, where the payer knows or believes the money is not due but pays in any event, the money will not be recoverable on the ground of mistake.[82] If a claim has been made and disputed but payment eventually made, whether in order to avoid threatened litigation or for some other reason such as to preserve good commercial relations or to secure some advantage, it will either be a compromise or a contractual submission to the claim. If there has been no overt dispute, the reason for irrecoverability may be more difficult to characterise as submission and is better analysed as waiver. In any event in such cases there is no mistake.

---

[75] Burrows *op. cit.* pp. 429–430.

[76] Burrows *op. cit.* pp. 436–439; Goff and Jones *op. cit.* pp. 828–829.

[77] *Ante,* § 30–113.

[78] *Avon C.C. v. Howlett* [1983] 1 W.L.R. 605, 612, 624–625. See *ante,* § 30–113.

[79] *R.B.C. Dominion Securities Inc v. Dawson* (1994) 111 D.L.R. (4th) 230; *Boscawen v. Bajura* [1996] 1 W.L.R. 328. But *cf.* Law Com. No. 227, para. 5.17.

[80] See generally Law Com. No. 227 *Restitution: Mistakes of Law and Ultra Vires Public Authority Receipts and Payments* (1994), paras. 2.25–2.38. See also Andrews, [1989] L.M.C.L.Q. 431; Arrowsmith, in Burrows (ed.) *Essays on the Law of Restitution* (1991).

[81] *Kleinwort Benson Ltd v. Lincoln C.C.* [1998] 3 W.L.R. 1095, 1150 (Lord Hope). See also at p. 1113 (Lord Goff).

[82] *David Securities Pty. Ltd v. Commonwealth Bank of Australia* (1992) 66 A.L.J.R. 768, 775, 778. See also *Kelly v. Solari* (1841) 9 M. & W. 54, 59; *Maskell v. Horner* [1915] 3 K.B. 106, 118; *Mason v. New South Wales* (1959) 102 C.L.R. 108, 143.

30–121   **Payer has doubts but nevertheless pays.** Where the payer has doubts but pays nevertheless, he is unlikely to be able to recover the payment: "a state of doubt is different from that of mistake. A person who pays when in doubt takes the risk that he may be wrong."[83] Three situations must, however, be distinguished. First, if the payee has made a claim accompanied by a threat to sue, recovery will be denied.[84] Secondly, where there has been no overt dispute, if the payer does not care which way that doubt is resolved but consciously makes a decision to pay, there will also be no recovery. In other cases recovery is unlikely, particularly where the payer's doubt concerns a crucial issue,[85] but will depend on the degree of the doubt: while *some* doubt will not prevent recovery,[86] the greater the doubt the less likely it is that recovery will be ordered. In the context of a question of law, a payer who adverted to the issue and nevertheless decided to make the payment is likely to be held to have been indifferent to what the law really was. Thirdly, if the payer would have paid in any event, the mistake of law would not have caused the payment and it would therefore not be recoverable on this ground.[87]

30–122   **Payer has no doubts as to liability.** Where the payer has no doubts as to his liability he is mistaken and will prima facie recover.[88] If, however, the payment is in response to a claim accompanied by a threat to sue, recovery will be denied even if the payer is mistaken.[89] If, moreover, the payer has waived any claim to recover the money or has assumed the risk of any mistake, recovery will be denied. While in the context of mistake of fact it appears that a mistaken payer will only rarely be held to have so waived his right or assumed the risk, it is possible that courts may be more willing to hold that there has been a waiver in the context of mistake of law,[90] perhaps because of the greater prevalence of doubtful questions of law, and particularly where the payer has adverted to the issue but decided to make the payment anyway.[91]

---

[83] *Kleinwort Benson Ltd v. Lincoln C.C.* [1998] 3 W.L.R. 1095, 1147 (Lord Hope).

[84] *Moore v. Vestry of Fulham* [1895] 1 Q.B. 399; *David Securities Pty. Ltd v. Commonwealth Bank of Australia* (1992) 66 A.L.J.R. 768, 788 *per* Dawson J.

[85] *Wason v. Wareing* (1852) 15 Beav. 151; *Cushen v. City of Hamilton* (1902) 4 Ont L.R. 265, 266, 270.

[86] *Charfield v. Paxton* (1799) 2 East 471. See also *Kleinwort Benson Ltd v. Lincoln C.C.* [1988] 3 W.L.R. 1095, 1140, 1150; *Westdeutsche Landesbank Girozentrale v. Islington L.B.C.* [1994] 4 All E.R. 890, 934 *per* Hobhouse J (need for "an actual conscious appreciation" for recovery to be barred); Burrows *The Law of Restitution* (1993), p. 102.

[87] *Home and Colonial Insurance Co. Ltd v. London Guarantee and Accident Co. Ltd* (1928) 45 T.L.R. 134 (regarding the fact that in practice underwriters did not refuse to pay out on unstamped marine insurance policies, although they were not valid). See also *Kelly v. Solari* (1841) 9 M. & W. 54, 59; *Maskell v. Horner* [1915] 3 K.B. 106, 118; *Mason v. New South Wales* (1959) 102 C.L.R. 108, 143.

[88] *Ante*, § 30–026. See also *Woolwich Equitable Building Society v. IRC* [1993] A.C. 70, 192 (Lord Jauncey).

[89] *David Securities Pty. Ltd v. Commonwealth Bank of Australia* (1992) 66 A.L.J.R. 768, 788 *per* Dawson J.; *Moore v. Vestry of Fulham* [1895] 1 Q.B. 399; *cf. Re Roberts* [1905] 1 Ch. 704, 710–711.

[90] See, *e.g. South Australia Cold Stores Ltd v. Electricity Trust of South Australia* (1957) 98 C.L.R. 65, 73–5; Bryan (1993) 15 Syd L.Rev 461, 479–80, 481; *Kleinwort Benson Ltd v. Lincoln C.C.* [1998] 3 W.L.R. 1095, 1140, 1147, 1150.

[91] *Avon C.C. v. Howlett* [1983] 1 W.L.R. 605, 620; *Akt Dampskibbs Steinstad v. William Pearson & Co.* (1927) 137 L.T. 533; *Westdeutsche Landesbank Girozentrale v. Islington L.B.C.* [1994] 4 All E.R. 890.

Compromise. Recovery will also be denied if there has been a compromise of **30–123** the claim. A compromise involves some degree of concession (or consideration) on each side, and this can include the forbearance to sue.[92] Again, it may be binding regardless of the validity of the claim. This, of course, assumes that in cases where the only pressure on the party who makes the payment is the probabilty of being sued, the claimant bona fide believes he has a fair chance of success.[93]

Payment following simple demand. A payment following a simple but **30–124** mistaken demand can be recovered, as there is neither a compromise of or a submission to an honest claim. For example, in *Baylis v. Bishop of London*[94] restitution was granted where the plaintiffs had paid a rentcharge under a mistake of fact to the sequestrator of a benefice, thinking that a lease was in force when in fact it had expired. Money cannot, however, be recovered for mistake if it was paid for reasons other than the mistake as there is no causal link between mistake and payment.[95]

3. REIMBURSEMENT

(a) *Compulsory Payments to a Third Person*[96]

General. In *Moule v. Garrett*,[97] Cockburn C.J. approved the following state- **30–125** ment from *Leake on Contracts*:

"Where the plaintiff has been compelled by law to pay, or, being compellable by law, has paid money which the defendant was ultimately liable to pay, so that the latter obtains the benefit of the payment by the discharge of his liability; under such circumstances the defendant is held indebted to the plaintiff in the amount."

The payment made by the claimant must have discharged a legal liability of the defendant[98]; therefore, it must have been compulsory, since the general rule is that a *stranger* who pays another's debt to the creditor does not thereby obtain a discharge of the debtor's liability to the creditor: a voluntary payment is effective to discharge the debtor's liability only if it was made on his behalf and was subsequently ratified by him.[99] If, however, the claimant is compelled to make

---

[92] *Callisher v. Bischoffsheim* (1870) L.R. 5 Q.B. 449; *Cook v. Wright* (1861) 1 B & S 559; *Atlee v. Backhouse* (1838) 3 M & W 633. See generally, *ante* §§ 3–049—3–052, 4–030.

[93] *Llewellyn v. Llewellyn* (1854) 3 Dow & L 318; 15 L.J.Q.B. 4; 6 L.T.O.S. 158; *Longridge v. Dorville* (1821) 5 B & Ald 117; *Haigh v. Brooks* (1839) 10 Ad & E 309.

[94] [1913] 1 Ch. 127.

[95] *Ante*, §§ 30–031, 30–042.

[96] Goff and Jones *op. cit.* Chap. 15; Winfield (1944) 60 L.Q.R. 341 (also his *Quasi-Contracts* (1952), pp. 62–88). On compulsory payments to the defendant, see *ante*, §§ 30–068 *et seq.* and on duress or undue influence, which renders a contract voidable, see *ante*, §§ 7–001, 7–069, 30–070—30–073.

[97] (1872) L.R. 7 Ex. 101, 104 (which passage was in turn quoted with approval in *Brook's Wharf and Bull Wharf Ltd v. Goodman Brothers* [1937] 1 K.B. 534, 543–544).

[98] See *post*, § 30–128.

[99] *Simpson v. Eggington* (1855) 10 Exch. 845, 847; *Smith v. Cox* [1940] 2 K.B. 558. (These authorities were not considered in *Owen v. Tate* [1976] Q.B. 402 (*post*, § 29–097).) See Goff and Jones *op. cit.* p. 17, n. 2; Birks and Beatson (1976) 92 L.Q.R. 188–202; Beatson *op. cit.* pp. 200–220 and *ante*, § 30–118, *post*, § 30–141. But *cf.* Friedmann (1983) 99 L.Q.R. 534. On voluntary payments, see *post*, §§ 30–135 *et seq.*

the payment to the third person, the cases cited in this section assume that the payment discharges the defendant's liability to the third person.[1] The compulsion may take the form of a secondary legal liability but other forms of practical compulsion have also been recognised. It is sufficient, for instance, that the claimant was faced with the choice of either paying in order to recover possession of his chattel, or being prevented from obtaining possession of it.[2] The payment of a third party's debt in order to release a security and perfect an independent right of reimbursement is a compulsory payment.[3] There are many cases on what amounts to such a compulsory payment, and although the majority of reported cases are grouped under headings in the succeeding paragraphs, there may well be other miscellaneous cases of compulsory payments outside these headings.[4] The liability of a principal debtor to indemnify his surety[5] could be discussed under this heading of compulsory payment, though a distinction might be drawn in that a surety in the first place voluntarily assumes potential liability for the debt.

30–126   **Tortfeasor compelled to pay twice.** Where a tortfeasor is compelled to pay damages to two or more claimants for wrongful interference with the same goods a statutory right to reimbursement arises under the Torts (Interference with Goods) Act 1977. Section 7(4) provides that, "[w]here, as the result of enforcement of a double liability, any claimant is unjustly enriched to any extent, he shall be liable to reimburse the wrongdoer to that extent."[6]

30–127   **The defendant must be under a legal liability to pay the third person.** If the defendant is under no legal liability to pay the money, he is not liable to reimburse the claimant, although it may appear that indirectly the payment by the claimant has benefited the defendant.[7] So where a police authority was under a statutory obligation to pay constables while incapacitated through an injury received in the course of their duty, and a constable was injured by the negligence of the defendant, the Court of Appeal held that the authority could not recover

---

[1] *e.g. Moule v. Garrett, supra; Brook's Wharf and Bull Wharf Ltd v. Goodman Bros.* [1937] 1 K.B. 534, 544.

[2] See *post*, §§ 30–129—30–131.

[3] *Kleinwort Benson Ltd v. Vaughan* [1996] C.L.C. 620.

[4] *e.g. Kendal v. Wood* (1871) L.R. 6 Ex. 243. See also payments made by necessity, *post*, §§ 30–129, 30–138; *Owen v. Tate* [1976] Q.B. 402, 412; *The "Zuhal K"* [1987] 1 Lloyd's Rep. 151. But *cf. Re Gasbourne Pty. Ltd* [1984] V.R. 801, 840–845 (practical commercial compulsion not a ground for restitution). *Quaere* whether this is consistent with the development of economic duress, *ante*, § 7–010. See also *Peel (Regional Municipality v. Canada* [1992] 3 S.C.R. 762 (local authority which was required by ultra vires statute to maintain delinquents not permitted to recover from federal government could not recover because benefit was incidental or collateral).

[5] *Post*, § 30–145. Analogous to this is the surety's right to claim contribution from a co-surety (*post*, § 30–152). Also analogous are other claims to contribution, such as the right of one joint tortfeasor to claim contribution from another (s.1(1) of the Civil Liability (Contribution) Act 1978) (*post*, § 30–150).

[6] The sub-section gives as an example of its operation the case where a converter of goods pays damages first to a finder, and then to the true owner. The finder is unjustly enriched unless he accounts to the true owner who is himself then unjustly enriched and becomes liable to reimburse the converter.

[7] *Receiver for the Metropolitan Police District v. Croydon Corporation* [1957] 2 Q.B. 154 (*Receiver for the Metropolitan Police District v. Tatum* [1948] 2 K.B. 68, though not referred to in this case, must be taken to have been impliedly overruled by it. There is now a statutory "restitutionary" scheme in this context: Social Security Act 1989, Pt. IV. See *Monmouthshire C.C. v. Smith* [1956] 1 W.L.R. 1132 (affd. [1957] 2 Q.B. 154).) See also *Re Nott and Cardiff Corporation* [1918] 2 K.B. 146 (reversed by the House of Lords on a different point: [1919] A.C. 337).

from the defendant the wages paid to the constable during his period of incapacity, although the defendant had not been required to pay anything in respect of loss of earnings to settle the constable's claim for damages for negligence.[8] The defendant had paid to the constable all the damages he was legally liable to pay, and so had not derived an unjust benefit through the authority's payment of wages.[9]

The defendant must be primarily or ultimately liable to pay the third   **30–128**
person. In *Brook's Wharf and Bull Wharf Ltd v. Goodman Bros.*[10] Lord Wright said:

> "The essence of the rule is that there is a liability for the same debt resting on the plaintiff and the defendant and the plaintiff has been legally compelled to pay, but the defendant gets the benefit of the payment, because his debt is discharged either entirely or *pro tanto*, whereas the defendant is primarily liable to pay as between himself and the plaintiff."

In this case the claimants, as bonded warehousemen, were compelled by statute to pay duties on skins stored with them by the defendants; since the defendants were primarily liable to pay these duties, they were required to reimburse the plaintiffs.

Actual seizure of the claimant's goods in respect of the defendant's   **30–129**
debt.

> "Speaking generally, and excluding exceptional cases, where a person's goods are lawfully seized for another's debt, the owner of the goods is entitled to redeem them, and to be reimbursed by the debtor against the money paid to redeem them, and in the event of the goods being sold to satisfy the debt, the owner is entitled to recover the value of them from the debtor. . . . The right to indemnity or contribution in these cases exists, although there may be no agreement to indemnify or contribute and although there may be, in that sense, no privity between the plaintiff and the defendant."[11]

Thus, where the claimant's goods, having been placed on the demised premises with the tenant's consent,[12] were distrained by the landlord for rent due from

---

[8] *Receiver for the Metropolitan Police District v. Croydon Corporation, supra.*

[9] Lord Goddard C.J., *ibid.* at 162, pointed out that the real loss sustained by the police authority was the loss of the constable's services, but that recovery for that loss by an action *per quod servitium amisit* was excluded because a constable was not a "servant" of the authority: *Att.-Gen. for New South Wales v. Perpetual Trustee Co. Ltd* [1955] A.C. 457. See, however, the recommendation of the 11th Report of the Law Reform Committee (Cmd. 2017).

[10] [1937] 1 K.B. 534, 544. This has been taken to mean that the plaintiff and the defendant must have been subject to a *common demand* for money, which the defendant was ultimately liable to pay: *Bonner v. Tottenham and Edmonton Permanent Investment Building Society* [1899] 1 Q.B. 161, 171–174 but the cases on pressure falling short of secondary liability (*post*, §§ 30–129—30–131) show that this is not so; *Whitham v. Bullock* [1939] 2 K.B. 81, 85. See also Goff and Jones *op. cit.* pp. 389–303, 449–453. *Bonner's* case itself can be explained on the ground that no debt was discharged.

[11] *Edmunds v. Wallingford* (1885) 14 Q.B.D. 811, 814–815. See also *Dawson v. Linton* (1822) 5 B. & Ald. 521; *Ex p. Elliot* (1838) 3 Deac. 343; *Johnson v. Skafte* (1869) L.R. 4 Q.B. 700.

[12] If the plaintiff had, as a trespasser, placed his goods there without authority, his payment of rent to the landlord to redeem his goods would give him no right to indemnity from the tenant, since he would have "by his own voluntary act, and without any request of the defendant, express or implied, placed his goods in a position to enable the landlord to seize them": *England v. Marsden* (1866) L.R. 1 C.P. 529, 533. In *Edmunds v. Wallingford, ante*, at 816, the court thought that the decision in *England v. Marsden* was wrong on the facts.

the tenant, and the claimant was obliged to pay the rent to redeem his goods, he was entitled to recover the rent from the tenant.[13] A similar situation arose where the mortgagees of some shares in a vessel paid a claim to redeem the vessel from arrest so that they could take possession under their mortgage; the co-owners of the vessel, who were liable to pay the claim, were compelled to repay the mortgagees.[14]

30–130   **Effect of bankruptcy.** The effect of the debtor's bankruptcy on a claim for reimbursement on this ground has been clarified by the Insolvency Act 1986. Formerly, a payment made to secure the release of goods lawfully distrained for the debt of a person who subsequently became bankrupt was neither provable in the bankruptcy nor barred by an order of discharge since it was not a claim by reason of any contract or promise.[15] However, under the 1986 Act a liability arising out of an obligation to make restitution is a bankruptcy debt and is provable in the bankruptcy.[16] This will be so whether the payment is made before the commencement of the bankruptcy or after that time since the Act provides that it is immaterial whether the liability is present or future, or certain or contingent.[17]

30–131   **Threat to seize the claimant's goods in respect of the defendant's debt-**. The same principle applies where the third person threatens to levy distress on the claimant's goods to satisfy the defendant's debt. Thus if an underlessee, under threat of distress or eviction by the head lessor, pays ground rent due from his immediate lessor to the head lessor, the underlessee may recover it as money paid to the use of his immediate lessor.[18] In these circumstances, the Law of Distress Amendment Act 1908 now enables the underlessee, by adopting a certain procedure, to avoid seizure of his goods. But where one underlessee of part of the premises comprised in the head lease has, under a threat of distress, paid the whole rent due under the head lease, he cannot recover from another underlessee, as money paid to his use, the proportion of rent due from him.[19]

30–132   **Assignees of a lease.** Despite the fact that there have been successive assignments of the term, the original lessee may still be held liable for rent or for breach of covenant under the terms of the lease. In *Moule v. Garrett*[20] it was held that in these circumstances the original lessee may claim an indemnity from a subsequent assignee, even though each assignee may have covenanted expressly to indemnify his own assignor against any breach of covenant committed after

---

[13] *Exall v. Partridge* (1799) 8 T.R. 308. See also *Bevan v. Waters* (1828) 3 C. & P. 520.

[14] *The Orchis* (1890) 15 P.C. 38; *Johnson v. Royal Mail Steam Packet Co.* (1867) L.R. 3 C.P. 38. See also *The Heather Bell* [1901] P. 143 (affd. on another point, *ibid.* at 272).

[15] *Johnson v. Skafte* (1869) L.R. 4 Q.B. 700. *cf. Re Button* [1907] 2 K.B. 180, 188, 190 (in respect of goods bailed to debtor).

[16] s.382(4). See further *ante*, § 30–044.

[17] s.382(3).

[18] *Sapsford v. Fletcher* (1792) 4 T.R. 511; *Jones v. Morris* (1849) 3 Exch. 742, 747; *Underhay v. Read* (1887) 20 Q.B.D. 209. The mere fact that the head lessor grants the underlessee time to pay does not prevent its being a compulsory payment: *Carter v. Carter* (1829) 5 Bing. 406.

[19] *Hunter v. Hunt* (1845) 1 C.B. 300. See also *Johnson v. Wild* (1890) 44 Ch.D. 146 (*post*, § 30–151); Langan (1967) 31 Conv.(n.s.) 38; Goff and Jones *op. cit.* p. 392.

[20] (1872) L.R. 7 Ex. 101 (*ante*, § 30–125). See Megarry and Wade, *The Law of Real Property* (5th ed.), pp. 750–752; Goff and Jones *op. cit.* p. 442. See also Law of Property Act, 1925, s.77 (implied covenant by assignee to indemnify against breach of covenant); *Dickinson U.K. Ltd v. Zwebner* [1989] Q.B. 208; *Re Healing Research Trustee Ltd.* [1992] 2 All E.R. 481.

the assignment to him. The original lessee's right of indemnity from a subsequent assignee will be of less importance in practice since the liability of both the original parties to a lease and of their assignees has been limited in respect of agreements for leases made or leases granted after January 1, 1996 by the Landlord and Tenant (Covenants) Act 1995.

Other illustrations concerning land. Another illustration of the general **30–133** principle concerns a statutory notice served by a sanitary authority on the occupier of premises requiring[21] him to abate a nuisance; if the occupier pays for the required work to abate the nuisance, he may recover the cost from the owner of the premises if, as between the occupier and the owner, the owner is primarily liable.[22] Again, a tenant may obtain reimbursement from his landlord when the tenant is compelled to pay a tax which the landlord is ultimately liable to pay.[23] The same principle of reimbursement of a compulsory payment was applied where land charged with the repair of a bridge was occupied by a lessee; the occupier was, in the first instance, responsible to the public for the repair of the bridge, but he successfully claimed reimbursement from the owner in an action for money paid to the owner's use, since the owner was ultimately liable.[24]

Bills of exchange. If, when the indorser of a bill of exchange is sued by the **30–134** holder, the indorser pays him the whole or part of the amount of the bill, the indorser can recover the amount paid from the acceptor as money paid to his use.[25]

Voluntary payments.[26] If the payment is regarded by the law as voluntary, it **30–135** cannot normally[27] be recovered.[28] In one case Swinfen Eady J. said: "If A voluntarily pays B's debt, B is under no obligation to repay A. There must be a

---

[21] *cf.* a mere recommendation: *Silles v. Fulham B.C.* [1903] 1 K.B. 829.

[22] *Gebhardt v. Saunders* [1892] 2 Q.B. 452, 456, 458 (reimbursement was granted on common law grounds, as well as under the relevant statute). See also the cases cited *ante*, § 30–077, n. 8; *Hackett v. Smith* [1917] 2 I.R. 508.

[23] *Dawson v. Linton* (1822) 5 B. & Ald. 521; *cf. Eastwood v. McNab* [1914] 2 K.B. 361; *Hales v. Freeman* (1819) 1 B. & B. 391. An illustration from a (now repealed) statutory provision was the right of a tenant who paid Schedule A tax to deduct the amount from his next payment of rent: Income Tax Act 1952, s.173; *Hill v. Kirshenstein* [1920] 3 K.B. 556; *cf. Bernard and Shaw Ltd v. Shaw* [1951] 2 All E.R. 267 (employer failed to deduct income tax under PAYE system, and was compelled to pay the same to the Revenue authorities: held, employer had no action to recover the tax paid from the employee). *cf.* the cases cited *ante*, § 30–131, n. 18. See now Income and Corporation Taxes Act 1988, s.23(1)–(8).

[24] *Baker v. Greenhill* (1842) 3 Q.B. 148. *cf. Macclesfield Corporation v. Great Central Ry.* [1911] 2 K.B. 528 (*post*, § 30–135).

[25] *Pownal v. Ferrand* (1827) 6 B. & C. 439; *cf. Ex p. Bishop* (1880) 15 Ch.D. 400. But *cf.* ss.57 and 59(2) of the Bills of Exchange Act 1882 (Vol. II, § 34–126). See also Goff and Jones *op. cit.* pp. 446–448.

[26] *cf.* cases where the request of the defendant to make the payment will be implied: *post*, §§ 30–139—30–145.

[27] For exceptional circumstances in which a voluntary payment may be recovered, see *post*, § 30–138.

[28] See Birks *op. cit.* pp. 102–103; Goff and Jones *op. cit.* pp. 63–65, 444–449; Hope (1929–1930) 15 Cornell L.Q. 25, 205. See, in addition to the cases cited below, *Stokes v. Lewis* (1785) 1 T.R. 20; *Bates v. Townley* (1848) 2 Ex. 152; *Re Cleadon Trust Ltd* [1939] Ch. 286; *Aktieselskabet Dampskibs Steinstad v. William Pearson & Co.* (1927) 137 L.T. 533; *Wilson v. Audio-Visual Equipment Ltd* [1974] 1 Lloyd's Rep. 81. *cf. Pownal v. Ferrand* (1827) 6 B. & C. 439, 443–444; *Owen v. Tate* [1976] Q.B. 402, *post*, n. 64, § 29–020; *Re Gasbourne Pty. Ltd* [1984] V.R. 807; *Esso Petroleum Ltd v. Hall Russell & Co.* [1989] A.C. 643; *Kleinwort Benson Ltd v. Vaughan* [1996] C.L.C. 620.

previous request, express or implied, to raise such an obligation, and in this respect I can see no difference between the discharge of a statutory liability and the discharge of a contractual liability."[29] So where the claimant, drawer of a bill for the accommodation of the defendant, paid the holder a part of the bill after its dishonour, but without notice of dishonour and without any request from the defendant, this was held to be a voluntary payment which could not be recovered.[30] Again, the mere fact that a company promoter pays the fees and stamp duty on the registration of a company does not in itself entitle him to recover them from the company.[31] Where, without any request from the mortgagee, a mortgagor, who is the ultimate owner of the equity of redemption in a life insurance policy, pays a premium due on the policy in order to prevent its lapse, the mortgagor is not entitled to recover the amount from the mortgagee, despite the fact that the latter has benefited from the payment.[32] But a payment made under mistake is not a voluntary payment.[33]

30–136   **Secondary liabilities voluntarily incurred.** The principle of voluntariness applies to secondary liabilities that are voluntarily incurred. In *Owen v. Tate*,[34] Scarman L.J. stated that "[i]f without an antecedent request a person assumes an obligation . . . for the benefit of another, the law will, as a general rule, refuse him a right of indemnity." Thus, where, without consulting the debtor, a person guaranteed a debt in order to release a friend from an earlier guarantee in respect of the same debt, it was held that no action for reimbursement would lie. The principle also applies where the intervener fulfils the defendant's obligation by performing a service. In one case,[35] the defendants were under a statutory duty to repair a road bridge over their canal, but refused to repair it when the claimants, who were the highway authority, called upon them to do so. The claimants then did the work themselves, but they were not able to recover from the defendants the cost incurred by them, since they were under no legal liability to repair the bridge, and accordingly had acted as mere volunteers.

---

[29] *Re National Motor Mail Coach Co. Ltd* [1908] 2 Ch. 515, 520 (approved at 523). See also *ante*, § 28–029.

[30] *Sleigh v. Sleigh* (1850) 5 Exch. 514 (distinguished in *Re Chetwynd's Estate* [1938] Ch. 13). *cf.* payment for honour *supra protest* (s.68(3) and (4) of the Bills of Exchange Act 1882; see Vol. II, § 34–145).

[31] *Re National Motor Mail Coach Co. Ltd, supra* (see *ante*, §§ 9–015—9–016).

[32] *Falcke v. Scottish Imperial Insurance Co.* (1886) 34 Ch.D. 234 (*post*, § 29–093). *cf. Re Leslie* (1883) 23 Ch.D. 552 and note the developing law concerning restitution for interventions in cases of necessity and where an incontrovertible benefit is conferred, *post*, §§ 30–148, 30–160, 30–161—30–165, 30–175, 30–182.

[33] See also *Banque Financière de la Cité v. Parc (Battersea) Ltd* [1998] 2 W.L.R. 475, *post*, § 30–176.

[34] [1976] Q.B. 402, 411–412. The case has been criticised because it assumed, without considering and in the face of the authorities (*ante*, § 30–125, n. 99), that the payment discharged the debt. Had the authorities been considered it is arguable that a claim based on the acquiescence of the debtor (on which see *ante*, § 30–018, *post*, § 30–142) would have succeeded; Birks and Beatson (1976) 92 L.Q.R. 188, 208–212; Beatson *op. cit.* pp. 200–205. *cf.* Friedmann (1983) 99 L.Q.R. 534. There should, moreover, be no objection to the volunteer deriving rights against the debtor by assignment or subrogation. Goff and Jones *op. cit.* pp. 128–129, 444–445; McCamus (1978) 16 Osgoode Hall L.J. 516, 550–559. Subrogation does not appear to have been argued in *Owen v. Tate* on which, see Mercantile Law Amendment Act 1856, s.5; Burrows *op. cit.* pp. 213–216.

[35] *Macclesfield Corporation v. Great Central Ry.* [1911] 2 K.B. 528. *cf. ante*, §§ 30–077, 30–133 and see *Procter & Gamble Phillipine Manufacturing Corp. v. Peter Cremer GmbH & Co.* [1988] 3 All E.R. 843, 854–856 (recognition of incontrovertible benefit although not applicable on facts).

Payment under protest. The fact that a protest is made at the time of   **30–137**
payment may often indicate that a payment is not "voluntary," but the mere
absence of a protest does not necessarily mean that a payment is voluntary. It is
a question of fact whether the protests of the payer amount to no more than
"grumbling acquiescence,"[36] or whether the circumstances indicate a payment
under protest, even where no express words are used.[37] Thus it is not a voluntary
payment which "is made for the purpose of averting a threatened evil, and is
made not with the intention of giving up a right but under an immediate necessity
and with the intention of preserving the right to dispute the legality of the
demand."[38] (But the payments made in the course of, or under threat of, legal
proceedings are not recoverable,[39] since the payer should take legal advice if he
wishes to dispute his liability.) In one case, where a tenant at first protested
against the refusal of his landlord to allow, as a deduction from rent due, land tax
paid by the tenant, yet later during five successive years he paid the land tax
without renewing his objection to the landlord, it was held that he could not
recover any of the sums paid for land tax as money paid to the landlord's use,
since they were voluntary payments.[40]

Exceptional cases where a voluntary payment is recoverable. A voluntary   **30–138**
payment may be recoverable in the following exceptional circumstances:

(1) where the circumstances justify the inference of an implied request by the
     defendant to make the payment[41];

(2) where the doctrines of ratification in agency[42] and of agency of necessity[43]
     apply;

(3) where the special equitable doctrine accepted by the Court of Appeal in *Re
     Cleadon Trust Ltd*[44] applies:

> "Where money is borrowed on behalf of a principal by an agent . . . though it turns out
> that his act has not been authorised, or ratified, or adopted by the principal, then,
> although the principal cannot be sued in law, yet in equity, to the extent to which the
> money borrowed has in fact been applied in paying legal debts and obligations of the
> principal, the lender is entitled to stand in the same position as if the money had
> originally been borrowed by the principal."

(4) where the plaintiff has reasonably intervened on behalf of the defendant in
     an emergency[45];

---

[36] *Maskell v. Horner* [1915] 3 K.B. 106, 119, 127. See also *Twyford v. Manchester Corporation*
[1946] Ch. 236 (*ante*, § 30–075); *William Whiteley Ltd v. R.* (1909) 101 L.T. 741. *Woolwich Equitable
Building Society v. I.R.C.* [1993] A.C. 70, 165, 174, 178, 192, 196, 200.
[37] *Maskell v. Horner, supra*, at 119–120, 126.
[38] *ibid.* at 118.
[39] See *ante*, § 30–073.
[40] *Spragg v. Hammond* (1820) 2 Brod. & B. 59. *cf. Denby v. Moore* (1817) 1 B. & Ald. 123; *ante*,
§ 30–133, n. 23.
[41] See *ante*, § 30–018; *post*, §§ 30–142—30–143.
[42] See Vol. II, §§ 38–024 *et seq.*
[43] See *post*, § 30–160.
[44] [1939] Ch. 286, 302. Discussed in Winfield, *Quasi-Contracts* (1952), pp. 86–88 and Goff and
Jones *op. cit.* See further *post*, § 30–176 (subrogation).
[45] See *post*, § 30–166.

(5) where one person has innocently repaired or improved another's chattel, he may in some circumstances receive reimbursement, directly or indirectly.[46]

(6) although a "voluntary" payment to a third person which in fact benefits the defendant cannot normally create an obligation upon the defendant to indemnify the payer, there are dicta supporting a wider principle in *Owen v. Tate*.[47] Scarman L.J. said[48] that, despite the general rule, if the intervener can show "that in the particular circumstances of the case there was some necessity for the obligation to be assumed, then the law will grant him a right of reimbursement if in all the circumstances it is just and reasonable to do so." In the same case, Stephenson L.J. also assumed that there may be circumstances where a volunteer could recover if "it is obviously unjust that a debtor should be enriched by accepting the benefit."[49] Scarman L.J.'s formulation suggests that cases of necessitous intervention might suffice[50] and it has been followed[51] although Stephenson L.J. preferred not to give instances of the type of situation in which a "volunteer" may recover an indemnity[52] and Ormrod L.J. reserved his opinion on the whole question.[53]

(b) *Payment to a Third Person at the Defendant's Request*

30–139 **Recovery of money paid at the defendant's request.** For many years, restitution has been available (through the action "for money paid") to recover money paid by a person to a third person at the request,[54] express or implied, of the defendant, and with an undertaking, express or implied, on his part to repay it[55]; and it is immaterial whether or not the defendant is relieved from a legal liability by the payment.[56] This type of claim is not obviously contractual, since the implied undertaking to repay is often fictional[57]; furthermore the claimant need not have been under any contractual obligation to make the payment, and the defendant's request may not have referred to a precise sum of money; the ground for recovery is akin to the principle of the law of agency which imposes on the principal an obligation to indemnify his agent against any liability which he may incur in the exercise of his authority.[58] However, although it is treated

---

[46] See *post*, § 30–148. (*cf. ante*, § 30–108.)

[47] [1976] Q.B. 402 (noted (1975) 91 L.Q.R. 308; (1975) 38 M.L.R. 563; [1975] C.L.J. 202). See Birks and Beatson (1976) 92 L.Q.R. 188; *cf. Friedmann* (1983) 99 L.Q.R. 534.

[48] *ibid.* at 411–412.

[49] *ibid.* at 413.

[50] See also Goff and Jones *op. cit.* p. 446.

[51] *The Zuhal K.* [1987] 1 Lloyd's Rep. 151. See also *Re Berkeley Applegate Ltd* [1989] Ch. 32. *cf. Esso Petroleum Ltd v. Hall Russell & Co.* [1989] A.C. 643 (*ante*, § 30–157).

[52] [1976] Q.B. 402, 413.

[53] *ibid.* at 414.

[54] *cf.* compulsory payments, *ante*, §§ 30–068, 30–125.

[55] *Brittain v. Lloyd* (1845) 14 M. & W. 762, 773; approved in *Lewis v. Campbell* (1849) 8 C.B. 541, 547–548 and in *Re a Debtor* [1937] Ch. 156, 163. See also *Re H.P.C. Productions Ltd* [1962] Ch. 466, 487. The transfer of property with a marketable value may be equivalent to the payment of money: *Fahey v. Frawley* (1890) 26 L.R.Ir. 78, 89–90.

[56] *Brittain v. Lloyd, supra.*

[57] *cf. Secretary of State v. Bank of India Ltd* [1938] 2 All E.R. 797, 800 (see *post*, § 30–149).

[58] See Vol. II, § 38–153; also *post*, § 30–143.

here for convenience, it is not restitutionary since the claimant will be entitled to be indemnified even though his payment has conferred no benefit on the defendant.[59]

The payment must be to the use of the defendant. The obligation to **30–140** reimburse the claimant arises only when the money was paid to the use of the defendant. So if A by agreement with B binds himself to pay either to B or to a third party a sum of money which B is primarily liable to pay, and B is afterwards called upon to pay and does pay such sum, his only remedy against A is on the special agreement. For the money so paid by B, having been paid in discharge of his own liability, was not money paid to the use of A.[60]

The payment must be made at the request of the defendant. It is also **30–141** necessary for the claimant to prove the defendant's express or implied request to the claimant to pay the money for his use. It is not sufficient to prove that the defendant was liable to a third person and that the claimant paid the third person: it must be proved that the claimant did so at the instance, either express or implied, of the defendant,[61] or, where the defendant had the option whether or not to ratify the payment, that he exercised his option to ratify it.[62] For no legal right to repayment will be established by the mere voluntary payment of the debt of another person; a man cannot make himself the creditor of another without his knowledge and consent,[63] except by the process of assignment.[64] The words of Bowen L.J. in *Falcke v. Scottish Imperial Insurance Co.*[65] have been frequently quoted:

"The general principle is, beyond all question, that work and labour done or money expended by one man to preserve or benefit the property of another do not according to English law create any lien upon the property saved or benefited, nor, even if standing alone, create any obligation to repay the expenditure. Liabilities are not to be forced upon people behind their backs, any more than you can confer a benefit upon a man against his will . . . .[66] There can, as it seems to me, according to the common law be only one principle upon which a claim for repayment can be based, and that is where

---

[59] *e.g.* by discharging a liability of the defendant; *Brittain v. Lloyd, supra; Warlow v. Harrison* (1858) 1 E. & E. 295, 317. There are, however, cases in which the plaintiff has been given a restitutionary right to reimbursement although there was also a contractual relationship between the parties which could have formed the basis of a claim for indemnity; Goff and Jones *op. cit.* pp. 453–454.

[60] *Spencer v. Parry* (1835) 3 A. & E. 331; *Lubbock v. Tribe* (1838) 3 M. & W. 607.

[61] *Sleigh v. Sleigh* (1850) 5 Exch. 514, 516.

[62] *Leigh v. Dickeson* (1884) 15 Q.B.D. 60, 64–65.

[63] *Stokes v. Lewis* (1785) 1 T.R. 20; *Owen v. Tate* [1976] Q.B. 402 (discussed in (1976) 92 L.Q.R. 188); see also *ante,* § 30–125; but see *Liggett (Liverpool) Ltd v. Barclays Bank* [1928] 1 K.B. 48, for the liability of the defendant in equity, although the meaning, if not the decision, in this case is put into question by *Re Cleadon Trust Ltd* [1939] Ch. 286, 316–318, 326–327.

[64] See *ante,* §§ 20–001 *et seq.*

[65] (1886) 34 Ch.D. 234, 248–249; *The Istros II* [1973] 2 Lloyd's Rep. 152, 157. But see *G.N. Ry. v. Swaffield* (1874) L.R. 9 Ex. 132 (carrier entitled to recover reasonable cost of caring for horse when consignee failed to take delivery of it); *Re Berkeley Applegate Ltd* [1989] Ch. 32 (allowance for expenses of administering trust property to liquidator); *Procter & Gamble Phillipine Manufacturing Corp. v. Peter Cremer GmbH & Co.* [1988] 3 All E.R. 843, 854–855.

[66] *e.g. Sorrell v. Paget* [1950] 1 K.B. 252.

you can find facts from which the law will imply a contract to repay or to give a lien."

30–142   **Implied request by the defendant.** The courts have often inferred from the circumstances an implied request by the defendant to the claimant to make the payment[67] especially where the money paid by the claimant was in discharge of a liability which the claimant had undertaken at the defendant's instance, or by his authority. Lord Greene M.R. has said "if a person knows that the consideration is being rendered for his benefit with an expectation that he will pay for it, then if he acquiesces in its being done, taking the benefit of it when done, he will be taken impliedly to have requested its being done; and that will import a promise to pay for it."[68] In one case[69] the claimant, who had done work for the provisional committee of a projected railway company, had been induced by the defendant, a member of the committee, to sue certain other members of the committee for his bill. The claimant incurred legal costs in bringing those actions, which it was held he could recover from the defendant as money paid at his implied request. The implied request is normally inferred from the circumstances existing at the time of the intervention by the plaintiff who will otherwise be regarded as a volunteer. But even a volunteer, who initially takes the risk of getting no return, may be relieved of that risk by the acquiescence of his beneficiary who, provided he has an opportunity to choose, "is bound by all the rules of honesty not to be quiescent, but actively to dissent, when he knows that others have for his benefit put themselves in a position of disadvantage, from which, if he speaks or acts at once, they can extricate themselves, but from which, after a lapse of time, they can no longer escape."[70] The previous section in the present chapter, on "compulsory payments to a third person,"[71] cites a number of cases which could be regarded as falling within the scope of an implied undertaking to reimburse the claimant for money expended on the defendant's behalf.

30–143   **Payment by agent for principal.** From the relationship of principal and agent the law will imply a promise by which the principal undertakes to indemnify the agent in respect of all liabilities which the agent has properly incurred in the course of the agency.[72] If, by the custom of trade or of the Stock Exchange, an agent is obliged, without any default on his part, to pay money on account of a contract made for his principal, the law will imply a promise on the part of the latter to repay it as money which has been paid to his use; and this will be the case whether or not he was acquainted with the custom by which the agent's

---

[67] cf. cases where the plaintiff has rendered services to the defendant at his implied request (*post*, §§ 30–185), or has salvaged the defendant's ship or its cargo (*post*, §§ 30–192), or has performed services for the defendant in an emergency (*post*, §§ 30–108).

[68] Re Cleadon Trust Ltd [1939] Ch. 286, 299, citing 1 Sm. L.C. (13th ed.), at 156; cf. *Unity Joint Stock Mutual Banking Association v. King* (1858) 25 Beav. 72; cf. also cases where the defendant acquiesces in improvements to his land being made by the plaintiff: *ante*, §§ 30–108.

[69] Bailey v. Haines (1849) 13 Q.B. 815, 832. See also *Brewer Street Investments Ltd v. Barclays Woollen Co. Ltd* [1954] 1 Q.B. 428; *William Lacey (Hounslow) Ltd v. Davis* [1957] 1 W.L.R. 932.

[70] City Bank of Sydney v. McLaughlin (1909) 9 C.L.R. 615, 625 (in the context of agency of necessity). See also *ante*, §§ 3–088, 3–138—3–139, 30–018, 30–108; *Phillips v. Homfray* (1871) L.R. 6 Ch.App. 770, 778; *Brewer Street Investments Ltd v. Barclays Woollen Co. Ltd* [1954] 1 Q.B. 428, 431. See further *Stiles v. Cooper* (1748) 3 Atk. 692; *Van der Berg v. Giles* [1979] 2 N.Z.L.R. 111.

[71] Ante, §§ 30–125 et seq.

[72] See Vol. II, §§ 32–156—32–157.

contracts were governed.[73] But if the expense was incurred by the agent as the result of some default on his own part, there is no such implied promise, although the loss is sustained in a matter connected with his agency.[74]

Tenancy in common. In ordinary circumstances it will be difficult to infer a **30–144** request from one tenant in common to another to expend money upon the property held in common. If one tenant in common chooses to repair a house held in common, he cannot, without a previous express request from the co-owner, recover any part of the expense from him, however much the co-owner may be benefited.[75]

Payment by guarantors.[76] Where one person becomes a guarantor for **30–145** another at his request, the law implies a promise by the latter that he will repay the guarantor whatever the guarantor may be compelled to pay the creditor; the guarantor may recover the amount paid to the creditor as money paid to the use of the debtor.[77] But if the debtor was not consulted before the guarantee was made, the guarantor cannot recover an indemnity from the debtor for the amount paid by the guarantor to the creditor[78] unless the guarantor had acted in a way which was "reasonably necessary" in the interests of the debtor and it was just and reasonable to grant a right of reimbursement.[79]

(c) *Innocent Repairs or Improvements to Another's Goods*

Claims by owner: statutory allowance. The position of a person who, acting **30–146** innocently, has expended money or effort in repairing or improving goods belonging to another is now partly governed by the Torts (Interference with Goods) Act 1977. Section 6(1) of the Act provides that in proceedings for wrongful interference with goods against a person who has improved[80] the goods in the honest but mistaken belief that he had title to them, an allowance shall be made in respect of the improvement to the extent to which the value of the goods

---

[73] *Westropp v. Solomon* (1849) 8 C.B. 345; and see *Duncan v. Hill* (1873) L.R. 8 Ex. 242; *Hartas v. Ribbons* (1889) 22 Q.B.D. 254; *Hunt, Cox & Co. v. Chamberlain* (1896) 12 T.L.R. 186; *Beckhuson and Gibbs v. Hamblet* [1900] 2 Q.B. 18. (The custom must, of course, satisfy the test of reasonableness.)

[74] *Allen v. Wingrove* (1901) 17 T.L.R. 261; *Wilson v. Audio-Visual Equipment Ltd* [1974] 1 Lloyd's Rep. 81. *cf. Bowlby v. Bell* (1846) 3 C.B. 284.

[75] *Leigh v. Dickeson* (1884) 15 Q.B.D. 60; *Re Jones* [1893] 2 Ch. 461, 476 *et seq.*; *Re Cook's Mortgage* [1896] 1 Ch. 923. On a partition, however, equity may take account of expenditure between tenants in common. (This represents the law prior to 1926 as regards tenants in common of land. After 1925 the legal estate will often be vested in the tenants in common as joint tenants on trust for sale and as trustees their liability may have been affected: Law of Property Act 1925, s.34.)

[76] On contracts of guarantee in general, see Vol. II, §§ 44–001 *et seq.* On contribution between sureties, see Vol. II §§ 44–098, 44–106—44–108.

[77] See Vol. II, § 44–098. The surety may also bring a *quia timet* action against the principal debtor: *Watt v. Mortlock* [1964] Ch. 84.

[78] *Owen v. Tate* [1976] Q.B. 402. (The guarantor might, however, obtain from the creditor an *assignment* of the debt: see (1975) 38 M.L.R. 563, 564–565 or, possibly, be *subrogated* to the creditor's rights, a point apparently not taken in the case; *ante*, § 30–135, n. 34.)

[79] *The Zuhal K.* [1987] 1 Lloyd's Rep. 151.

[80] This would appear to include all acts of the defendant which increase the value of the goods, although *cf. McGregor on Damages* (16th ed., 1997), § 1399 (expenses in making goods saleable not improvements) and *Palmer on Bailment* (2nd ed.), p. 257 (maintenance not an improvement). See also Law Reform Committee, Cmnd. 4774, § 89.

is attributable to it.[81] Section 6(2) provides for an equivalent allowance where the action is brought against a bona fide transferee from the improver whether or not the improver was in good faith; but section 6(3) provides that where a transferee who is a purchaser has received this allowance, then in proceedings by him against the seller for recovery of the price on the ground of total failure of consideration,[82] a bona fide seller (who may be the improver) shall be entitled to the allowance. Where the owner seeks an order for delivery to him of the goods under section 3(2) of the Act in circumstances in which an allowance under section 6 would have been made, the court is given discretion to require, as a condition for delivery of the goods, that the allowance be made to the defendant.

30–147   The Act, however, only applies where the improver acts in the honest belief that he had good title[83] to the goods and it has no application where the owner has reacquired the goods without the aid of the court.[84] It would appear that the Act is, in some respects, narrower than the common law which indirectly permitted an allowance in respect of improvements by fixing the damages in actions for conversion as the value of the goods in their unimproved state even where there was no mistake as to title.[85]

30–148   **Claims by the improver.** The position is less easy to state in view of the paucity of authority. Where the owner of the goods has requested, freely accepted or acquiesced in the improvement the improver should, by analogy to the cases on improvements to land, be entitled to claim.[86] The nature of the relief will depend on the circumstances of the case but, in principle, the improver should be entitled to the reasonable value of his services even if this is not reflected in the value of the goods. Apart from cases of acquiescence, the present state of the authorities[87] would seem to preclude the improver having any claim, even one limited to any increase in the value of the goods attributable to the improvement.

---

[81] This would appear to enact the pre-existing common law: *Greenwood v. Bennett* [1973] 1 Q.B. 195 (following *Peruvian Guano Ltd v. Drefus Brothers & Co.* [1892] A.C. 166, 175–176; and *Livingstone v. Raywards Coal Co.* (1880) 5 App.Cas. 25). See [1973] C.L.J. 23 and (1973) 36 M.L.R. 89; Birks (1974) 27 C.L.P. 13, 19 *et seq.*; Matthews [1981] C.L.J. 340; Sutton in Finn (ed.), *Essays on Restitution*, Chap. 7.

[82] See *ante*, § 30–048, s.6(2) refers to the recovery of damages by the transferee but this would seem to be a reference to the action for the price mentioned in s.6(3).

[83] This would not include an improvement done with knowledge that title was disputed. *cf.* at common law, *Reid v. Fairbanks* (1853) 13 C.B. 692.

[84] *Quaere* whether the owner of the goods that have been improved is liable for conversion of the "improvement" unless it has become part of the goods by accession. Accession will occur where the improver has acted wrongfully: *Spence v. Union Marine Insurance Co.* (1868) L.R. 3 C.P. 427, 437–438; *Indian Oil Corp. v. Greenstone Shipping SA (Panama)* [1988] Q.B. 345; Goff and Jones *op. cit.* p. 77.

[85] *Munro v. Willmott* [1949] 1 K.B. 295 (a claim in detinue). *cf. Sachs v. Miklos* [1948] 2 K.B. 23 (value of the goods bailed appreciated over time). Although the Torts (Interference with Goods) Act 1977, s.12 would give a bailee who has taken reasonable steps to communicate with the bailor the right to sell the bailed goods he is obliged to account to the bailor for the proceeds of sale less any costs of sale, but not apparently the value attributable to an improvement unless it can be said to be a cost incurred in the adoption of the best method of sale reasonably available; s.12(5)(a). *cf. McGregor on Damages* (16th ed., 1997), § 1398.

[86] *Ante*, §§ 30–018, 30–108; Goff and Jones *op. cit.* pp. 250–251.

[87] In particular the cases on "voluntariness," *ante*, § 30–135, especially *Falke v. Scottish Imperial Insurance Co.* (1886) 34 Ch.D. 234; (*ante*, § 30–141). See also *Forman & Co. Proprietary Ltd v. Ship "Liddelsdale"* [1900] A.C. 190; *Sumpter v. Hedges* [1898] 1 Q.B. 673.

In *Greenwood v. Bennett*[88] Cairns L.J. doubted that such a claim could be made.[89] However, Lord Denning M.R. was prepared to allow a person who had improved a car honestly believing himself to be its owner a direct claim against the owner.[90]

> "The court will order the plaintiffs, if they recover the car, or its improved value, to recompense the innocent purchaser for the work he has done on it. No matter whether the plaintiffs recover it with the aid of the court, or without it, the innocent purchaser will recover the value of the improvements he has done to it."[91]

In the context of that case, in which the true owner had realised the increased value by selling the car, this may be unexceptionable but it should be noted that where an increase in value has not been realised it is only possible to regard it as a benefit for the purpose of a restitutionary claim if one is willing to force a sale upon the owner.[92]

(d) *Indemnity against Liability incurred when Acting at the Request of Another*

Indemnity against liability incurred when acting at the request of **30–149** **another.** When an act,[93] which is neither manifestly illegal nor illegal to the knowledge of the person doing it, is done by one person at the request of another,[94] and the act turns out to be injurious to the rights of a third person, the person doing the act is entitled to an indemnity (against his liability towards the third person) from the person who requested that the act should be done.[95] Thus, where the transferee under a forged transfer of stock requests the corporation to register the transfer to him, the transferee is obliged to indemnify the corporation against the consequences of the forgery.[96]

---

[88] [1973] 1 Q.B. 195, 203. See also Matthews [1981] C.L.J. 340, 351–358.

[89] *ibid.*

[90] The third member of the court, Phillimore L.J., did not advert to this point.

[91] *ibid.* at 202.

[92] Birks *op. cit.* pp. 121–124. See also *B.P. Exploration Co. (Libya) Ltd v. Hunt (No. 2)* [1979] 1 W.L.R. 783, 799, 803; Beatson (1981) 97 L.Q.R. 389, 410–411, *op. cit.* pp. 66–67; Matthews [1981] C.L.J. 340, 366 for the difficulty in treating this as a benefit. *cf.* Goff and Jones *op. cit.* pp. 175–176, who argue that it would not generally be unreasonable to require the owner to sell the improved chattel to make restitution because most chattels are fungible and point out that the allowance under the Torts (Interference with Goods) Act 1977, s.6 is to be given even where the goods are unique and the owner has no free funds.

[93] One statement of the principle limits it to acts performed in the course of "a statutory or common law duty of a ministerial character": *Sheffield Corporation v. Barclay* [1905] A.C. 392, 399.

[94] The principle may apply even if the person acting was able to deliberate whether he should accede to the request: *Secretary of State v. Bank of India Ltd* [1938] 2 All E.R. 797.

[95] *Sheffield Corporation v. Barclay, ante,* at 397 (citing the argument of Mr. Cave in *Dugdale v. Lovering* (1875) L.R. 10 C.P. 196, 197) and at 399; *Secretary of State v. Bank of India Ltd, supra,* at 800; see also *Stathlorne SS. Co. Ltd v. Andrew Weir & Co.* (1934) 40 Com.Cas. 168. For a similar principle in the law of agency, see Vol. II, § 32–156; *cf. W. Cory & Son Ltd v. Lambton and Hetton Collieries Ltd* (1916) 86 L.J.K.B. 401.

[96] *Sheffield Corporation v. Barclay, supra.* See also *Att.-Gen. v. Odell* [1906] 2 Ch. 47; *Bank of England v. Cutler* [1908] 2 K.B. 208; *Secretary of State v. Bank of India Ltd, supra; Yeung Kai Yung v. Hong Kong and Shanghai Banking Corporation* [1981] A.C. 787.

(e) *Contribution*

30–150   **The right to contribution.** At common law, apart from the cases discussed above,[97] where a right to reimbursement arises in favour of a non-volunteer who discharges the obligation of another, a right to contribution will only arise when a person, who owes with another a duty to a third party and is liable with that other to a common demand, discharges more than his proportionate share of that duty.[98] The amount recoverable is determined by a broad rule of equity:

> "If, as between several persons or properties all equally liable at law to the same demand, it would be equitable that the burden should fall in a certain way, the court will so far as possible, having regard to the solvency of the different parties, see that, if that burden is placed inequitably by the exercise of the legal right, its incidence should be afterwards adjusted."[99]

In general, persons who are liable to the same demand are made to share the burden of that liability equally.[1] This is, of course, subject to contrary agreement since a claim to contribution may be modified or limited by a contractual provision. It will also not apply where the parties undertake a liability in unequal shares or up to differing limits, as for instance occurs in contracts of insurance and guarantee.[2] The above rules still apply in respect of contribution proceedings between persons jointly liable for the same *debt* but the position of parties liable in respect of the same *damage*, whether jointly or otherwise, is now governed by the Civil Liability (Contribution) Act 1978. In a case falling within the statute the rules of equity do not apply and the right to contribution is to be "such as may be found by the court to be just and equitable having regard to the extent of that person's responsibility for the damage in question."[3] By section 6(1),

> "[a] person is liable in respect of any damage for the purposes of this Act if the person who suffered it (or anyone representing his estate or dependants) is entitled to recover compensation from him in respect of that damage (whatever the legal basis of his liability, whether tort, breach of contract, breach of trust or otherwise)."

The Act therefore covers liability arising out of breaches of different contractual obligations,[4] situations in which one person's liability is in contract but the other's is in tort,[5] situations where one person's liability is in either contract or

---

[97] *Ante*, §§ 30–125—30–134. This is referred to as indemnity by the Law Commission: Law Com. No. 79 (1977), para. 16.

[98] Goff and Jones *op. cit.* pp. 389–390, 394–398. See also Law Comm. No. 79 (1977), *Report on Contribution*.

[99] *Whitham v. Bullock* [1939] 2 K.B. 81, 85 (quoting Rowlatt, *Principal and Surety* (3rd ed.), p. 173). *cf.* Goff and Jones *op. cit.* pp. 390–391.

[1] See Williams, *Joint Obligations* (1949), Chap. 9; *ante*, Chap. 17; Law Comm. No. 79 (1977), paras. 13–15, 27–29.

[2] Vol. II, Chap. 41, Chap. 44.

[3] Civil Liability (Contribution) Act 1978, s.2(1). This follows the form of words in the Law Reform (Married Women and Tortfeasors) Act 1935, s.6(2), which it replaces and the principles used in determining what is "just and equitable" under the 1935 Act will be relevant; see Law Commission No. 79 (1977) paras. 68–79. See also *Weaver v. Commercial Process Co. Ltd* (1947) 63 T.L.R. 466; *The Miraflores and The Abadesa* [1967] A.C. 826, 845. *cf. Collins v. Herefordshire C.C.* [1947] K.B. 598.

[4] *e.g.* the facts of *McConnell v. Lynch-Robinson* [1957] N.I. 70.

[5] *e.g. Batty v. Metropolitan Realisations Ltd* [1978] Q.B. 554.

tort and the other's is in restitution,[6] as well as the case, previously governed by an earlier statute,[7] where the liability of both persons is in tort. The Act does not affect any express contractual provision regulating or excluding a right to contribution.[8] The effects of this Act are discussed in the chapter on Joint Obligations earlier in this work.[9]

The common law requirement: liability to a common demand. Apart from   **30–151** the statute, there can be no question of contribution where the parties are not liable to a common demand. In *Johnson v. Wild*[10] a lessee assigned part of the land to the claimant for the residue of the term and gave the defendants an underlease of the other part of the land. In each case the lessee covenanted to pay the rent due to the head lessor, but on the lessee's bankruptcy the head lessor threatened to distrain on the claimant's part of the land, and the claimant paid the whole of the rent due under the head lease. Chitty J. held that the claimant had no right of contribution against the defendant:

> "Now he does not demand contribution from a person liable to a common demand, because the defendants are not liable for the rent; and the defendants are not only not liable for the rent but nobody can sue them in respect of this supposed liability unless it be the plaintiff; whereas, in a common demand for which two persons are liable, if one pays then there is a right of contribution on the part of the other who makes the payment against the one who does not."[11]

The main instances of contribution will now be outlined.[12] The purpose of collecting these instances is to facilitate the use of analogies, since an analogy taken from one category of contribution may well be useful in another category,[13] but it should be noted that the extent of the right to contribution will depend on whether the particular case is governed by the equitable rules or by the statutory discretion.

Guarantees. The leading illustration of contribution comes from the law   **30–152** relating to guarantors or sureties.[14] If several persons become sureties for the same debt, either jointly or severally, and whether by the same or different instruments, and one surety pays more than his proportionate share of the debt, he may recover[15] from his co-sureties proportionate shares of the excess.[16] If, however, a surety has guaranteed the debtor's obligations in respect of matters other than the payment of money, for instance by entering a performance bond, the rules of equity do not apply and the right to contribution is governed by the exercise by the court of the statutory discretion.[17]

---

[6] *Friends' Provident Life Office v. Hillier Parker May and Rowden (a firm)* [1997] Q.B. 85.

[7] Law Reform (Married Women and Tortfeasors) Act 1935, s.6, repealed by the 1978 Act.

[8] Civil Liability (Contribution) Act 1978, s.7(3)(b).

[9] *Ante*, Chap. 17.

[10] (1890) 44 Ch.D. 146.

[11] *ibid.* at 150.

[12] There is no right of contribution between tenants in common: *ante*, § 30–144.

[13] *e.g. Spottiswoode's Case* (1855) 6 De G.M. & G. 345, 371–372.

[14] See Vol. II, §§ 44–001 *et seq.*

[15] In an action for contribution in the Chancery Division, or in a common law action for money paid to the defendant's use.

[16] See *ante*, § 18–027, and Vol. II, §§ 44–106 *et seq.*

[17] Civil Liability (Contribution) Act 1978, s.2(1) (discussed *ante*, § 18–029; *post*, § 30–159).

30–153   **Joint contractors or debtors.** Where two or more persons are joint con-tractors,[18] and one is required to perform more than his proportionate share of a common liability under the contract, he may recover contribution from the other joint contractors.[19] Thus, where several defendants to an action agreed to employ a solicitor to manage their defence on their joint responsibility, the one defendant who paid the solicitor's costs was held entitled to recover contributions from the others.[20] Likewise, when two parties employed an arbitrator and one, in taking up the award, paid the arbitrator's fees, he was entitled to recover half the fees from the other party.[21]

30–154   **Trustees.** Trustees who commit a breach of trust are jointly and severally liable for any resulting loss of the trust property. If one trustee is made responsi-ble for more than his share of the loss, he may recover contribution from the other trustees,[22] but the former rule, which subjected a passive trustee, who allows his co-trustee to administer the trust, to equal liability has now been replaced by the statutory discretion to allow such contribution as is "just and equitable having regard to the extent of responsibility for the damage in question."

30–155   **Directors.** Directors who employ the assets of a company on an *ultra vires* undertaking are liable to indemnify the company in respect of any loss resulting; if one director pays more than his proportionate share of the loss, he may recover contribution from those of his co-directors who are also liable.[23] Again the extent of the right to contribution is governed by the statutory discretion.

30–156   **Partners.** Partners are jointly liable for partnership debts and obligations[24] and one partner who bears more than his own share of a common obligation is entitled to contribution from the other partners,[25] although, if the partnership still subsists, the right to contribution may be enforced only in an action for a general partnership account.[26]

30–157   **Insurers.** Subject to the provisions of any special contribution clause in the relevant insurance policies,[27] one insurer who has paid more than his propor-tionate share of a single loss, where several insurance policies cover the same

---

[18] Or joint and several contractors.

[19] See *ante*, § 18–027.

[20] *Edger v. Knapp* (1843) 5 M. & G. 753.

[21] *Marsack v. Webber* (1860) 6 H. & N. 1.

[22] *Bahin v. Hughes* (1886) 31 Ch.D. 390; *Chillingworth v. Chambers* [1896] 1 Ch. 685; *Robinson v. Harkin* [1896] 2 Ch. 415.

[23] *Spottiswoode's Case* (1855) 6 De G.M. & G. 345, 372; *Ashhurst v. Mason* (1875) L.R. 20 Eq. 225; *Re Alexandra Palace Co.* (1882) 21 Ch.D. 149; *Ramskill v. Edwards* (1885) 31 Ch.D. 100. *cf. Walsh v. Bardsley* (1931) 47 T.L.R. 564 (the breach of duty benefited only the director seeking contribution).

[24] Partnership Act 1890, ss.9–12.

[25] *Re the Royal Bank of Australia, Robinson's Executors* (1856) 6 De G.M. & G. 572, 587–588; *Lindley and Banks on Partnership* (16th ed.), § 20–04 *et seq. cf.* Partnership Act 1890, ss.24(1) and (2), 44.

[26] *Sedgewick v. Daniell* (1857) 2 H. & N. 319.

[27] See *MacGillivray and Parkington on Insurance Law* (8th ed.), §§ 1736, 1738, for a standard form of such a clause.

interest in the same property, may recover contribution from the other insurers.[28]

General average contribution. Parties to a common maritime adventure are required, by the principle of general average contribution, to contribute towards certain extraordinary losses or expenses incurred in time of peril in order to preserve the ship or its cargo.[29] All loss which arises in consequence of extraordinary sacrifices made or expenses incurred for the preservation of the ship and cargo comes within general average, and must be borne proportionately by all those who are interested."[30] **30–158**

Tortfeasors.[31] Where two or more tortfeasors are liable in tort in respect of the same damage, contribution may be recovered by one tortfeasor from another under statutory provisions.[32] The amount of the contribution is to be "such as may be found by the court to be just and equitable having regard to the extent of that person's responsibility for the damage in question."[33] **30–159**

(f) Agency of Necessity

Agency of necessity. Where there is a relationship of principal and agent (or a similar relationship) between the parties, and the agent, in an emergency, has acted reasonably to protect the interests of his principal, the principal is obliged to reimburse the agent his reasonable expenses incurred in so acting, despite the fact that the agent exceeded his authority.[34] The agent must show that it was impracticable at the time of the emergency for him to get instructions from his principal.[35] **30–160**

(g) Benefits Conferred in an Emergency

Necessitous intervention on behalf of the defendant. Except in cases of agency of necessity,[36] or of salvage,[37] English law has usually refused to give a **30–161**

---

[28] *North British and Mercantile Insurance Co. v. London, Liverpool and Globe Insurance Co.* (1876) 5 Ch.D. 569, 581; *Commercial Union Assurance Co. Ltd v. Hayden* [1977] Q.B. 804; *Legal & General Assurance Co. Ltd v. Drake Insurance Co. Ltd* [1992] 1 Q.B. 877. *cf. Eagle Star Insurance Co. Ltd v. Provincial Insurance plc* [1993] 3 All E.R. 1. See also the Marine Insurance Act 1906, s.80; *Arnould on Marine Insurance* (16th ed.), §§ 406–407.

[29] *Lowndes & Rudolf on General Average and York Antwerp Rules* (10th ed.); Arnould *op. cit.* Chap. 26; *Carver on Carriage by Sea* (13th ed.), Chap. 14.

[30] *Birkley v. Presgrave* (1801) 1 East 220, 228–229. *cf.* the Marine Insurance Act 1906, s.66(1). It has been doubted whether general average is a quasi-contractual liability: *cf. Milburn & Co. v. Jamaican Fruit Importing Co.* [1900] 2 Q.B. 540, 548, and Winfield, *Province of the Law of Tort*, p. 182.

[31] See Law Comm. No. 79 (1977).

[32] Civil Liability (Contribution) Act 1978, s.1(1) (replacing Law Reform (Married Women and Tortfeasors) Act 1935, s.6 now repealed). See *Clerk & Lindsell on Torts* (17th ed., 1995), §§ 2–53 *et seq.* Similar provisions permit contribution between vessels responsible for collisions at sea: Merchant Shipping Act 1995, ss.187–189.

[33] Civil Liability (Contribution) Act 1978, s.2(1).

[34] See Vol. II, §§ 32–034—32–036 (*cf. post,* §§ 30–161, 30–193); Goff and Jones *op. cit.* pp.588–589; Merchant Shipping Act 1995, s.40.

[35] Vol. II, § 32–034.

[36] *Ante,* § 30–160.

[37] See *post,* § 30–192. See also Merchant Shipping Act 1995, s.73(2) (obligation to repay expenses in bringing shipwrecked seamen ashore and burial expenses).

remedy to a person who intervenes in the affairs of another, even where the purpose of his intervention is to benefit that other in an emergency or to rescue the other's property from danger.[38] There is, however, support[39] for the emergence of a principle that, in an emergency, provided the claimant has acted reasonably and bona fide in the interests of the defendant, in order to protect the defendant's property, health, or other important interests, the claimant may recover the expenses he incurred and, possibly, reasonable remuneration for his services. It is a condition for recovery that it was impracticable to obtain the defendant's instructions or authority.

30–162 Where the public interest demands that the claimant should have acted, the courts are most likely to permit restitution. For instance, where circumstances make it reasonable that the plaintiff should voluntarily incur expense in burying a person, the executors of the deceased, if they have assets, are liable to repay the expenses incurred by the plaintiff.[40] Where a married woman dies leaving an estate sufficient to pay her funeral expenses, her executors (and not, as formerly, her husband) are now liable to pay them.[41] Similarly, when human life or limb is at risk, the courts are likely to award restitution to a plaintiff who incurred expense or expended effort in a reasonable attempt to preserve life or limb. In a Canadian case,[42] a surgeon who intended to charge for his services was held entitled to recover remuneration for his professional services in his reasonable, but unsuccessful, attempt to revive a person who committed suicide. Legislation[43] in the United Kingdom entitles a hospital or doctor to charge for emergency treatment given after a road accident.

30–163 Although salvage in tidal waters,[44] is restricted to ships and their cargoes, there is some authority for a similar principle applicable to property on land. In an early case, where a person found timber where it had been carried by the tide, and brought it to safety, it was held that he had no lien on the timber for his trouble

---

[38] *Falcke v. Scottish Imperial Insurance Co.* (1886) 34 Ch.D. 234 (*ante*, § 30–138); *Owen v. Tate* [1976] Q.B. 402 (*ante*, § 30–141); *China Pacific SA v. Food Corp. of India* [1982] A.C. 939, 961. See the discussion of "voluntary payments," *ante*, §§ 30–135—30–138.

[39] Birks *op. cit.* pp. 193–203; Hope (1929) 15 Cornell L.R. 25, 42–47; Jones (1977) 93 L.Q.R. 273; Goff and Jones *op. cit.* pp. 467–482; Rose, (1989) 9 O.J.L.S. 167; Stoljar (1989) 10 Int.Encly.Comp. Law Ch. 17; The American Law Institute's *Restatement of the Law of Restitution, Quasi-contracts and Constructive Trusts* (1937), p. 489. See also *Owen v. Tate* [1976] Q.B. 402, 411–412; *The Zuhal K.* [1987] 1 Lloyd's Rep. 151 (*ante*, § 30–135, suggesting that necessity negatives "officiousness" or "voluntariness" in the case of discharge of another's obligation). *cf. The Goring* [1988] A.C. 831.

[40] *Tugwell v. Heyman* (1812) 3 Camp. 298; *Rogers v. Price* (1829) 3 Y. & Jer. 28. See now Public Health (Control of Disease) Act 1984, ss.46–48.

[41] *Rees v. Hughes* [1946] K.B. 517. (*Quaere* whether the husband is still liable, under the old common law rule, if his wife leaves insufficient estate to cover her funeral expenses. Before modern legislation altered the legal position of married women, the common law allowed a stranger who had, without any request from the husband, voluntarily incurred and paid such expenses in burying the wife, to recover them from the husband: see *Ambrose v. Kerrison* (1851) 10 C.B. 776; *Jenkins v. Tucker* (1788) 1 H.Bl. 90; *cf. Bradshaw v. Beard* (1862) 12 C.B.(N.S.) 344 (deceased's brother).)

[42] *Matheson v. Smiley* [1932] 2 D.L.R. 787. (*Quaere* whether services rendered by a non-professional would justify recovery of remuneration for services, *post*, n. 95.)

[43] Road Traffic Act 1988, ss.157–159.

[44] *The Goring* [1988] A.C. 831. *cf.* [1987] Q.B. 687, 693, 707 for criticism of the restriction to tidal waters.

and expense.[45] The decision, however, probably leaves open the possibility that the finder could sue the owner of the timber in *quantum meruit*[46] for the value of his services. A carrier was able to recover reasonable expenses incurred in providing for the safety of the horse he carried when the consignee refused to take delivery of it.[47] In these cases the plaintiff was a bailee of the defendant's property. In such cases (including involuntary bailment[48]) the right to charge the property-owner for reasonable steps to preserve the property can be seen as the correlative of the bailee's duty to the owner in respect of the property.[49] However, recovery is not confined to cases of bailment. Thus, a crane hire firm, called in by the police, recovered a reasonable fee from a lorry owner for freeing the lorry which was stuck under a bridge.[50]

There are a number of other situations where principles analogous to necessitous intervention have been used to justify restitution or reimbursement.[51] Where there is an existing or a previous relationship between the parties, the courts are naturally more willing to allow recovery.[52] Sometimes recovery might be permitted in an indirect way, as has been done in the cases where one person, acting innocently, has expended money or effort in repairing or improving a chattel belonging to another[53] or where an accident victim has recovered the value of nursing services rendered by a relative and holds the money for the relative.[54] For the principle of intervention to apply, there would need to be proof of a real "emergency" or "necessity"[55] to entitle the intervener to sue.[56] If the intervener **30–164**

---

[45] *Nicholson v. Chapman* (1793) 2 H.Bl. 254. (The claim in *Falcke v. Scottish Imperial Insurance Co.*, *supra*, was also for a lien.) *cf.* the position in tort where damages are recoverable by a person injured when trying to rescue property endangered by a fire caused by the defendant's negligence: *Hyett v. G.W. Ry.* [1948] 1 K.B. 345.

[46] See *post*, § 30–185.

[47] *G.N. Ry. v. Swaffield* (1874) L.R. 9 Ex. 132. During the carriage the carrier is under a duty to take reasonable care of the goods, and the case implies a continuation of this duty. It was cited with approval in *China Pacific SA v. Food Corporation of India* [1982] A.C. 939, 960.

[48] See Vol. II, § 33–033.

[49] *China Pacific SA v. Food Corp. of India* [1982] A.C. 939, 960. See also Birks *op. cit.* p. 201.

[50] *J. D. White v. Troups Transport* [1976] C.L.Y. 33. See *Waters v. Weigall* (1795) 2 Anst. 575; Goff and Jones *op. cit.* p. 470, n. 81.

[51] *e.g.* the Bills of Exchange Act 1882, ss.65(1), 66(1) and 68(5) (acceptance of a bill of exchange for the honour of the drawer). See also *Re Berkeley Applegate Ltd* [1989] Ch. 32, *ante*, § 30–110 and see *Procter & Gamble Phillipine Manufacturing Corp. v. Peter Cremer GmbH & Co.* [1988] 3 All E.R. 843, 854–855 for support for the principle of recovery for incontrovertible benefit.

[52] *e.g.* agency of necessity (*ante*, § 30–160; Vol. II, § 32–034); the principle in *Re Cleadon Trust Ltd* [1939] Ch. 286, 302 (*ante*, § 30–138); the supply of necessaries to persons under a disability (*post*, § 30–191); the recovery of expense incurred when the innocent party attempted to mitigate his loss following a breach of contract (*ante*, § 27–098); the relationship of carrier and consignee (*G.N. Ry. v. Swaffield* (1874) L.R. 9 Ex. 132 (*ante*)); and a *quantum meruit* claim when the bailee has acted reasonably in dealing with the goods following frustration of the contract (*ante*, § 24–096).

[53] See *ante*, § 30–146.

[54] *Cunningham v. Harrison* [1973] Q.B. 942, 952; *Donnelly v. Joyce* [1974] Q.B. 454; *Mehmet v. Perry* [1977] 2 All E.R. 529. But not where the carer is the tortfeasor: *Hunt v. Severs* (1994) 2 W.L.R. 602.

[55] *cf.* the concept of "necessity" in agency of necessity: *ante*, § 30–160 and see *Re F. (Mental Patient: Sterilisation)* [1990] 2 A.C. 1, 75; *Re T. (Adult: Medical Treatment)* [1992] 3 W.L.R. 782. In the bailment cases of *Sachs v. Miklos* [1948] 2 K.B. 23 and *Munro v. Willmott* [1949] 1 K.B. 295, there was no real emergency to justify the bailee's sale of goods without communicating with the bailor and obtaining his authority (see *ante*, § 30–147, n. 85).

[56] *cf.* the dicta in *Owen v. Tate* [1976] Q.B. 402, 411–412, 413 (quoted *ante*, § 30–138 which suggest that necessity may negative officiousness).

was officious,[57] or thought that he was protecting his own interests,[58] or did not, at the time of his intervention on behalf of the other, intend to charge for it,[59] no recovery should be allowed.

30–165   The need for the intervention to be reasonable and for the intervener to intend to charge for it will, in many cases, it is submitted, preclude the recovery of remuneration for services rendered in many cases and restrict claims to reimbursement of expenses.[60] Where the intervener is a professional acting as such he will be more likely to recover remuneration.[61]

4. LIABILITY TO ACCOUNT TO THE CLAIMANT

30–166   **Liability to account.** In this group of cases the defendant is under a liability imposed on him to account to the plaintiff in respect of money or property received from a third person; or the plaintiff is entitled to be subrogated to the rights of another against a third person.[62]

(a) Acknowledgment: Defendant holding a Fund for a Third Person at whose Request He Promises to Pay the Claimant

30–167   **General principle.** The principle of a line of cases[63] may be stated as follows[64]: where the defendant holds a fund on behalf of a third person (or acknowledges that he owes a debt to the third person[65]), and the third person directs the defendant to pay the claimant out of the fund or debt, then, if the defendant accepts that direction and promises the claimant to pay him accordingly, the plaintiff may seek restitution from the defendant by an action for money had and received. In the nineteenth century, the emphasis on privity of

---

[57] *cf.* the situations covered by the Unsolicited Goods and Services Act 1971.

[58] In *Falcke v. Scottish Imperial Insurance Co.* (1886) 34 Ch.D. 234 (*ante,* § 30–141) the intervener thought that he was preserving his own property. But *cf. Greenwood v. Bennett* [1973] 1 Q.B. 195, and the other cases cited *ante,* § 30–146.

[59] *Re F. (Mental Patient: Sterilisation)* [1990] 2 A.C. 1, 75. *cf. Re Rhodes* (1890) 44 Ch.D. 94 (necessaries supplied to a lunatic: see *ante,* § 8–071, *post,* § 30–191); *Brown and Davis Ltd v. Galbraith* [1972] 1 W.L.R. 997. *cf.* the Roman law principle that the onus should be on the defendant to show that the intervener intended to make no charge; *Ulpian,* D. 3.5.4; Goff and Jones *op. cit.* p. 472.

[60] *Shallcross v. Wright* (1850) 12 Beav. 558, 561–562. Goff and Jones *op. cit.* pp. 472–473 support this on the ground that, apart from cases of maritime salvage, there is no urgent need to provide a real and positive incentive to take risks for the purpose of saving property. See further, Landes and Posner (1978) 7 J.Leg.Stud. 83.

[61] *Matheson v. Smiley* [1932] 2 D.L.R. 787 (*ante,* n. 42); *J. D. White v. Troups Transport* [1976] C.L.Y. 33 (*ante,* n. 84). See also the burial cases, *ante,* nn. 40–41, from which it would appear that where the intervention takes the form of employing someone else to do the necessary act the two measures will not differ. See in particular *Ambrose v. Kerrison* (1851) 10 C.B. 777.

[62] See *post,* § 30–176.

[63] *e.g. Israel v. Douglas* (1789) 1 H.Bl. 239; *Stevens v. Hill* (1805) 5 Esp. 247; *Williams v. Everett* (1811) 14 East. 582; *Lilly v. Hays* (1836) 5 A. & E. 548; *Hamilton v. Spottiswoode* (1849) 4 Exch. 200; *Griffin v. Weatherby* (1868) L.R. 3 Q.B. 753; *Shamia v. Joory* [1958] 1 Q.B. 448.

[64] Jackson, *History of Quasi-Contract* (1936), pp. 30–34, 92–103; Munkman *op. cit.* pp. 52–61; Davies (1959) 75 L.Q.R. 220; Goff and Jones *op. cit.* Chap. 28. See also *ante,* § 20–087.

[65] *Shamia v. Joory* [1958] 1 Q.B. 448 supports the application of the principle to a defendant who is a debtor and holds no identifiable "fund." See the criticism of Davies *loc. cit.* and *Liversidge v. Broadbent* (1859) 4 H. & N. 603, which was not cited in *Shamia v. Joory.*

contract led to confusion in the judgments on this principle,[66] but Blackburn J. in *Griffin v. Weatherby*[67] laid it down that the claimant's remedy was distinct from contract:

"Ever since the case of *Walker v. Rostron*[68] it has been considered as settled law that where a person transfers to a creditor on account of a debt, whether due or not, a fund actually existing or accruing in the hands of a third person, and notifies the transfer to the holder of the fund, although there is no legal obligation on the holder to pay the amount of the debt to the transferee, yet the holder of the fund may, and if he does promise to pay to the transferee, then that which was merely an equitable right becomes a legal right in the transferee, founded on the promise; and the money becomes a fund received or to be received for and payable to the transferee, and when it has been received an action for money had and received to the use of the transferee lies at his suit against the holder."

Shamia v. Joory. In *Shamia v. Joory*[69] the defendant owed Y some £1,300 as **30–168** remuneration for services rendered, and when Y requested the defendant to pay £500 from this money to the claimant (Y's brother), the defendant agreed to do so and wrote to the claimant promising to send him the money. The claimant later received a cheque for £500 from the defendant, but owing to a technical irregularity the cheque was not met. Although the defendant promised to send the corrected cheque back to the claimant, it was not sent, and the claimant sued to recover the £500 as money had and received by the defendant to the use of the claimant. Barry J. held that although the £500 was to be a gift from Y to the claimant,[70] the plaintiff could recover the money under the principle laid down by Blackburn J., *ante*; there was a "fund" in the defendant's hands when he accepted Y's instructions and promised the claimant to pay him. Barry J. held that there was no need for the third person to hand an identifiable sum of money to the defendant before there could be a "fund" in the hands of the defendant. He said[71]:

" . . . all that the law requires[72] is that there must be in the hands of or accruing to the third person, either a sum of money, or a monetary liability, over which the transferor has a right of disposal. It matters not . . . from what source the liability arises, and I see no reason why it should not include a debt for money lent, or goods sold, or services rendered, or a debt of any kind; nor do I think that the situation can be altered if the debt is of a temporary nature, which in the ordinary course of things would shortly be extinguished by items of contra account, provided, of course, that the debt still exists at the date of the transfer and of the debtor's promise of payment made to the transferee."

It appears from this judgment that the "fund" need not be a specific sum, but may be a general "monetary liability." However, the extension of the principle in

---

[66] Davies *loc. cit.* also shows the confusion which arose from the doctrines of consideration and of novation.

[67] (1868) L.R. 3 Q.B. 753, 758–759.

[68] (1842) 9 M. & W. 411.

[69] [1958] 1 Q.B. 448.

[70] In most of the earlier cases, the plaintiff was a creditor of the third person, and not a donee. But see *Fleet v. Perrins* (1869) L.R. 4 Q.B. 500 (which was a "donee" case not cited in *Shamia v. Joory, supra*).

[71] [1958] 1 Q.B. 448, 459.

[72] But see Davies (1959) 75 L.Q.R. 220, who cites *Liversidge v. Broadbent* (1859) 4 H. & N. 603 as authority for the proposition that where the plaintiff is a creditor of the third party he cannot sue the defendant without furnishing consideration.

Shamia v. Joory has not been applied in any subsequent reported case, and its authority remains in some doubt.

30–169   **Distinct from assignment.** This principle is distinct from the equitable assignment of a chose in action[73] which takes immediate effect as between the assignor and assignee, without any notice to the debtor[74]: the third party in *Shamia v. Joory* did not transfer anything until the defendant accepted his instruction, and the defendant was not bound to accept the third party's instruction, nor to make any promise of payment to the claimant. The consent of the third party or debtor is essential before the principle in *Shamia v. Joory* can apply,[75] whereas in assignment it is irrelevant.[76]

(b) *Stakeholders*

30–170   **Deposit till a claim is ascertained.** A stakeholder is an agent who is entitled, during the continuance of his authority from a party to some arrangement, to make payment, in accordance with that authority, of the money lodged with him by that party. Thus, if A deposits money in the hands of a stakeholder, until the extent of a claim which B has upon A can be ascertained, the stakeholder cannot, before the claim is ascertained, legally pay the amount to B upon his indemnity without the consent of A; if the stakeholder does so, A may maintain an action for money had and received against him without reference to B's claim.[77] Where a stake was deposited with the defendant to abide the result of a sculling race, but there was no proper start and no race as contemplated, it was held that the claimant could recover his stake.[78] The authority of the stakeholder may be withdrawn before he has acted on it: thus, it has been held that the Gaming Act 1892 does not prevent the recovery by the claimant of money deposited with a stakeholder to abide the result of a wager where the claimant demands his deposit back before it has been paid over by the stakeholder to the winner, since, until actual payment, the stakeholder remains the agent of the claimant in regard to the claimant's stake.[79]

30–171   **Auctioneer, solicitor and estate agent as stakeholder.** On a sale of goods an auctioneer has implied authority to receive the sale proceeds[80]; on a sale of an interest in land his only authority is to receive the deposit, unless he is expressly authorised otherwise.[81] Generally he receives the deposit merely as a stakeholder,

---

[73] See *ante*, §§ 20–020 *et seq.* A statutory assignment requires written notice to the debtor: *ante*, § 20–016. The principle is also distinct from novation (see *ante*, §§ 20–084—20–085), and from a completely constituted trust: Davies *loc. cit.*

[74] See *ante*, § 20–020.

[75] The principle seems to be an "attornment" of money, similar to the attornment of a chattel (see Vol. II, § 33–027).

[76] For a discussion of the earlier cases, see Davies *loc. cit.*

[77] *Cowling v. Beachum* (1823) 7 Moore 465; on the deposit of a cheque with a stakeholder, see *Wilkinson v. Godefroy* (1839) 9 A. & E. 536.

[78] *Sadler v. Smith* (1869) L.R. 5 Q.B. 40.

[79] *O'Sullivan v. Thomas* [1895] 1 Q.B. 698; *Burge v. Ashley Ltd* [1900] 1 Q.B. 744, CA. Such recovery was permitted before the Act: *Hampden v. Walsh* (1876) 1 Q.B.D. 189; *Diggle v. Higgs* (1877) 2 Ex.D. 422. See further on the position of a stakeholder in respect of a wager, Vol. II, §§ 41–045—41–048.

[80] *Williams v. Millington* (1788) 1 H.Bl. 81.

[81] *Sykes v. Giles* (1839) 5 M. & W. 645.

in which case he should retain it until the contract is either carried into effect or rescinded and the party entitled to the deposit ascertained.[82]

Where a deposit is paid to an auctioneer as a stakeholder, and the payment to the vendor is to depend on his making a good title to the property sold, the purchaser may, on the vendor failing to make out such title, recover the deposit from the auctioneer without giving him notice that he has rescinded the contract.[83] Where a solicitor acting for a vendor receives the deposit as agent for the vendor, the law will not imply that he receives it as stakeholder (as in the case of an auctioneer); hence he is bound to pay the deposit to the vendor on demand.[84] An estate agent who is authorised to find a purchaser for land is not (in the absence of express or implied authority to do so) authorised as agent for the owner to receive a pre-contract "deposit" from a potential purchaser.[85]

(c) Agent or Employee Receiving a Bribe or Secret Profit

Agent or employee receiving a bribe or secret profit. Where an agent   **30-172** receives from a third party a bribe, secret profit or commission in connection with his principal's affairs his principal is entitled to claim it; the same principle holds in regard to the relationship of employer and employee.[86] Thus the Crown can recover secret bribes received by a police officer,[87] or secret payments received by a soldier for using his uniform illicitly to smuggle goods past civilian police[88]; the employer's right of recovery is not affected by the fact that the money was earned through a criminal act of the employee, nor by the fact that the employer has suffered no loss.[89] In equity, a person in a fiduciary position is held to be a constructive trustee of a profit resulting from that position for the benefit of the person to whom he is accountable.[90]

Where an agent, as the result of a bribe, induces his principal to enter into a   **30-173** contract with the person who paid the bribe, the principal may elect either to recover the bribe or damages for fraud (in respect of any loss he has sustained

---

[82] *Harington v. Hoggart* (1830) 1 B. & Ad. 577, 588–589. *cf. Skinner v. The Trustee of the Property of Reed* [1967] Ch. 1194, and the cases cited in nn. 19, 20, *post.* A stakeholder is not accountable for any interest earned by the deposit while it is in his control, whereas an ordinary agent is so accountable: *Harington v. Hoggart, supra,* at 587; *Potters (A Firm) v. Loppert* [1973] Ch. 399. *cf. Brown v. Inland Revenue Commissioners* [1965] A.C. 244 (followed by the Solicitors Act 1974, s.33 (replacing the Solicitors Act 1965, s.8)).

[83] *Duncan v. Cafe* (1837) 2 M. & W. 244.

[84] *Edgell v. Day* (1865) L.R. 1 C.P. 80.

[85] *Sorrell v. Finch* [1977] A.C. 728. Until a binding contract is made, the estate agent, on demand by the potential purchaser, must repay the "deposit" to him without reference to the vendor: *ibid.* See Vol. II, §§ 32–111, 32–107. See also Estate Agents Act 1979, ss.13, 14.

[86] *Boston Deep Sea Fishing & Ice Co. Ltd v. Ansell* (1888) 39 Ch.D. 339; *Lister v. Stubbs* (1890) 45 Ch.D. 1. See *ante,* §§ 9–058—9–063; Vol. II, §§ 32–072—32–117. *cf. Meadow Schama & Co. v. C. Mitchel & Co.* (1973) 228 E.G. 1511 (arrangement between estate agents after commission earned held not to amount to a secret commission); *Kelly v. Cooper* [1993] A.C. 205.

[87] *Att.-Gen. v. Goddard* (1929) 98 L.J.K.B. 743.

[88] *Reading v. Att.-Gen.* [1951] A.C. 507. See also *A.G. v. Blake* [1998] 2 W.L.R. 805.

[89] *ibid.*

[90] *Regal (Hastings) Ltd v. Gulliver* [1942] 1 All E.R. 378; [1967] 2 A.C. 134n.; *Phipps v. Boardman* [1967] 2 A.C. 46 (the agent or employee may, however, be entitled to some remuneration for his work and skill if he has acted openly: see *post,* § 30–187); *Industrial Development Consultants Ltd v. Cooley* [1972] 1 W.L.R. 443; *Guinness plc v. Saunders* [1990] 2 A.C. 663.

through the contract) from the agent.[91] The person who paid the bribe is similarly liable but double recovery is not permitted and the principal can only recover the amount of the bribe and any additional loss he can prove however he chooses to frame his action and even if he sues both the agent and the briber.[92] Where, however, the principal rescinds the transaction tainted by a bribe he does not have to give credit for the amount of the bribe as part of his duty to make restitution of benefits received under the contract even where he has already recovered the bribe from the agent.[93] A bribe is the payment of a secret commission: proof of corruptness or corrupt motive is not necessary in a civil action.[94]

(d) Usurpation of an Office

30–174 **Usurpation of an office.** A claim in restitution (the action for money had and received) also lies to recover all the fees and profits received by a person who has wrongfully usurped an office belonging to the claimant.[95]

(e) Constructive Trusts

30–175 **Constructive trusts.** The law on constructive trusts, briefly considered above,[96] could be placed under the head of "liability to account to the claimant" when the defendant has received property from a third person. For instance, when a bailee, who has insured the goods bailed to him for their full value, receives payment from the insurers, he may retain so much as would cover his own interest in the goods, and is a trustee for the owner of the goods in respect of the balance.[97] Similarly, where the owner of real property agrees to sell it to a purchaser, he becomes a "qualified trustee" for the purchaser, with the result that if the owner later wrongfully sells the property to a second purchaser and receives the price from him, he is accountable to the first purchaser for the price as trust property to be transferred to the first purchaser upon his completing his obligations under the first contract.[98]

---

[91] *Mahesan v. Malaysia Government Officers' Co-operative Housing Society Ltd* [1979] A.C. 374, applying *United Australia Ltd v. Barclays Bank Ltd* [1941] A.C. 1. On tracing into the proceeds of the bribe, cf. *Lister v. Stubbs* (1890) 45 Ch.D. 1 and *Att.-Gen. (Hong Kong) v. Reid* [1994] 1 A.C. 324; *Att-Gen v. Blake* [1998] 2 W.L.R. 805. See further, Vol. II, §§ 32–072, 32–117; *ante*, § 30–090.

[92] *Mahesan v. Malaysia Government Officers' Co-operative Housing Society Ltd*, *supra*, at 382–383; *Arab Monetary Fund v. Hashim (No. 9)* [1993] 1 Lloyd's Rep. 543. But see Tettenborn (1979) 95 L.Q.R. 68 and cf. Needham (1979) 95 L.Q.R. 536 (1979). See further Vol. II, § 32–072.

[93] *Logicrose Ltd v. Southend United F.C. Ltd* [1988] 1 W.L.R. 1256.

[94] *Industries and General Mortgage Co. Ltd v. Lewis* [1949] 2 All E.R. 573; Vol. II, § 32–072.

[95] *Rowland v. Hall* (1835) 1 Scott 539; *Hall v. Swansea Corporation* (1844) 5 Q.B. 526; *King v. Alston* (1848) 12 Q.B. 971; *Shoubridge v. Clark* (1852) 12 C.B. 335; *Wildes v. Russell* (1866) L.R. 1 C.P. 722; *Osgood v. Nelson* (1872) L.R. 5 H.L. 636. See also *Howard v. Wood* (1679) 2 Lev. 245; *Lamine v. Dorrell* (1705) 2 Ld.Raym. 1216 (after revocation of his grant of administration, an administrator of an estate is accountable for assets received); *Brown & Green Ltd v. Hays* (1920) 36 T.L.R. 330 (*ante*, § 9–061) (recovery of salary as a director paid to defendant whose appointment was not confirmed but see *Craven-Ellis v. Canons Ltd* [1936] 2 K.B. 403 (*post*, § 30–182) for *quantum meruit* in such circumstances); *Re Berkeley Applegate Ltd* [1989] Ch. 32. cf. *ante*, § 30–086, n. 72.

[96] *Ante*, § 30–107.

[97] *Hepburn v. A. Tomlinson (Hauliers) Ltd* [1966] A.C. 451 (*ante*, § 19–110; Vol. II, §§ 33–018, 41–007, 41–008). See also *The Albazero* [1977] A.C. 774.

[98] *Lake v. Bayliss* [1974] 1 W.L.R. 1073. See also *English v. Dedham Vale Properties Ltd* [1978] 1 W.L.R. 93.

(f) Subrogation

Subrogation. By virtue of "subrogation," a person may, in certain situations, **30–176** "step into the shoes" of another so as to enjoy the latter's legal position or his rights against a third person. Subrogation may arise from the express or implied agreement of the parties or by operation of law. The right of an insurer who pays a claim under an indemnity policy in respect of a particular loss to be subrogated to and to enforce the rights of the insured person arising out of that loss against any third person[99] is founded upon contractual intention. So also, in general, is the entitlement of a guarantor who pays the debt of the principal debtor to require the creditor to give him the benefit of any security given by the principal debtor to the creditor[1] and of an indorser of a bill of exchange who pays the bill to claim analogous rights.[2] Where a loan to a minor has been expended on necessaries, the minor will be liable to pay the lender the amount so expended.[3] But in other cases the foundation of a right to be subrogated is based on the principle of unjust enrichment.[4] In such cases the rights are akin to other restitutionary rights, but subject to statute.[5] The two institutions have been said to be "radically different",[6] although the influence of contractual subrogation and of the implied contract theory of restitution has meant that the distinction has not always been maintained. Moreover, some types of transaction[7] may provide examples of both contractual and restitutionary subrogation. Where the right to subrogation is restitutionary, "the appropriate questions are . . . first, whether the defendant would be enriched at the [claimant's] expense; secondly, whether such enrichment would be unjust and thirdly, whether there are nevertheless reasons of policy for denying a remedy."[8] Examples of restitutionary subrogation include *ultra vires* or unauthorised borrowing used to discharge a debt.[9]

Subrogation has also been sought by lenders where, for a variety of reasons, the loan is irrecoverable. Thus, where a loan on mortgage to a minor was void but the money lent was used to buy property, the lender was held to be entitled to a lien over the property by being "subrogated" to the position of the vendor who received the money.[10] Again, where an *ultra vires* loan is made to a company it has been held that the lender may be subrogated to the position of a creditor

---

[99] See Vol. II, § 44–113.

[1] See Vol. II, § 44–114, but see *ante*, § 30–135 for the position of the officious guarantor.

[2] See Vol. II, § 44–114.

[3] See *ante*, § 8–020; *cf. ante*, § 8–071.

[4] *Banque Financière de la Cité v. Parc (Battersea) Ltd* [1998] 2 W.L.R. 475. See also Mitchell, *The Law of Subrogation* (1994); Goff and Jones *op. cit.* Chap. 3; Birks (1971) 34 M.L.R. 207; *Lord Napier and Ettrick v. R. F. Kershaw Ltd* [1993] 2 W.L.R. 42. Thus, a "volunteer" will not be subrogated: *Esso Petroleum Co. Ltd v. Hall Russell & Co. Ltd* [1989] A.C. 643. See further *Boodle Hatfield & Co. v. British Films Ltd* [1986] P.C.C. 176; *Boscawen v. Bajwa* [1996] 1 W.L.R. 328 (subrogation discussed under a restitutionary analysis); Mitchell [1995] L.M.C.L.Q. 451. See also *Kleinwort Benson Ltd v. Vaughan* [1996] C.L.C. 620 CA. But *cf. Orakpo v. Manson Developments Ltd* [1978] A.C. 95, 104, criticised (1978) 41 M.L.R. 330; *Re Byfield* [1982] Ch. 267.

[5] *Re T.H. Knitwear (Wholesale) Ltd* [1988] Ch. 275.

[6] *Banque Financierè de la Cité v. Parc (Battersea) Ltd* [1998] 2 W.L.R. 475, 483 (Lord Hoffmann).

[7] *e.g.* guarantee, see *ante*, § 30–135 (officious guarantor).

[8] *Banque Financierè de la Cité v. Parc (Battersea) Ltd* [1998] 2 W.L.R. 475, 485 (Lord Hoffmann). See also *ibid* at 480, 488, 495–6.

[9] *Ante*, § 9–025 (*ultra vires*); *Bannatyne v. D. & C. MacIver* [1906] 1 K.B. 103 n. 21 (unauthorised borrowing by agent); but *cf.* the unauthorised payment of a debt by a "stranger": *Re Cleadon Trust Ltd* [1939] Ch. 286 (*ante*, §§ 30–125, 30–138).

[10] *Nottingham Permanent Benefit Building Society v. Thurston* [1903] A.C. 6, *ante*, § 8–063.

whose valid debt is discharged with the proceeds of the loan.[11] However, subrogation will not be permitted where it would frustrate the policy of the rule that invalidates the loan. Thus, a moneylender who financed a series of property transactions by loans that were unenforceable for non-compliance with statutory requirements was held not to be able to be subrogated to the security represented by the previously existing charges and unpaid vendors liens that had been discharged by the loans.[12] To give relief by subrogation "would be to enable the court to express a policy of its own in regard to moneylending transactions which would be in direct conflict with the policy of the [statute][13] itself."[14] Where it is allowed, however, this form of subrogation may appear to differ from subrogation in the sense used in the insurance and guarantee cases in so far as the person entitled to be subrogated has, in some cases, only been allowed to succeed to the creditor's personal claim but not to take the benefit of any priority enjoyed by the creditor.[15] Subrogation rights may also be waived.[16]

5. RECOMPENSE

(a) Quantum Meruit *Claims*

30–177   *Quantum meruit.* The development of the *quantum meruit* as a general restitutionary obligation has been impeded by the fact that services cannot be restored and "the identity and value of the resulting benefit to the recipient may be debatable."[17] Furthermore, the term *"quantum meruit"* is used in various contexts, which must be treated separately. As has been said,[18] in some categories the term covers a quasi-contractual or restitutionary obligation based on incontrovertible benefit, in others the obligation is often capable of analysis as a genuine implied contract based on request, free acceptance or acquiescence while in others the basis of liability appears to be the protection of the plaintiff's

---

[11] *Re Cork and Youghal Ry.* (1869) L.R. 4 Ch.App. 748; *Blackburn Benefit Building Society v. Cunliffe, Brookes & Co.* (1882) 22 Ch.D. 61; *Baroness Wenlock v. River Dee Co.* (1887) 19 Q.B.D. 155 (relief given where borrowed money used to pay debts accruing after dates of its receipt). But see *Re Cleadon Trust Ltd* [1939] Ch. 286, 322–344 for the requirement that the debtor must have adopted the benefit of the invalid loan.

[12] *Orakpo v. Manson Investments Ltd* [1978] A.C. 95. See also *Burston Finance Ltd v. Speirway Ltd* [1974] 1 W.L.R. 1648.

[13] Moneylenders Act 1927, s.6 (repealed by the Consumer Credit Act 1974).

[14] *Orakpo v. Manson Investments Ltd, supra,* at 115. See also Megarry (1956) 72 L.Q.R. 480; Goff and Jones *op. cit.* pp. 493–494. This depends on whether a claim to this type of subrogation must be based on the presumed mutual intentions of the borrower and lender for the statute only made a "security given by the borrower" unenforceable. For criticism of the decision in *Orakpo,* see (1978) 41 M.L.R. 330. See also *Re Byfield* [1982] Ch. 267.

[15] *Re Wrexham, Mold and Connah's Quay Ry.* [1899] 1 Ch. 440. See also *Bannatyne v. D. & C. MacIver* [1906] 1 K.B. 108, 109. *cf. Paul v. Speirway Ltd* [1976] 1 Ch. 220 which, by analogy, suggests that if the lender's money is to be used to discharge a secured loan the presumption is that he intended his loan to be secured. See also *Orakpo v. Manson Investments Ltd, supra,* at 105; *McColl's Wholesale Pty. Ltd v. State Bank of N.S.W.* [1984] 3 N.S.W.L.R. 365, 369; Goff and Jones *op. cit.* pp. 122–126, 156–157.

[16] *The Surf City* [1995] 2 Lloyd's Rep. 242.

[17] *B.P. Exploration Co. (Libya) Ltd v. Hunt (No. 2)* [1979] 1 W.L.R. 783, 799 (affirmed by the Court of Appeal [1981] 1 W.L.R. 232 and by the House of Lords [1983] 2 A.C. 352. See also Birks *op. cit.* pp. 109–128, 131–132; Burrows *op. cit.* pp. 8–16; Jones (1977) 93 L.Q.R. 273; Goff and Jones *op. cit.* pp. 18–26, 506; *ante,* § 30–018.

[18] *Ante,* §§ 30–005, 30–018.

reasonable reliance rather than the unjust enrichment of the defendant. For the sake of convenience, however, all categories of *quantum meruit* will be considered in this section.[19]

Quantum meruit for work done where the contract is terminated by **30–178**
breach. According to Winfield[20] there is only one instance of *quantum meruit* which is properly regarded as restitutionary. Alderson B. put it as follows: "Where one party has absolutely refused to perform, or has rendered himself incapable of performing, his part of the contract, he puts it in the power of the other party either to sue for a breach of it, or to rescind the contract and sue on a *quantum meruit* for the work actually done."[21] Thus, in a leading case, *Planché v. Colburn*[22] the defendants engaged Planché to write a volume for publication in the defendant's proposed series of "The Juvenile Library." After Planché had written some of his work, the defendants abandoned the whole publication, and it was held that Planché might, without tendering his completed work, sue to recover reasonable remuneration for his work already done. In *Prickett v. Badger*[23] an agent was employed to sell land at a certain price, but although he found a purchaser, the owner refused to sell and wrongfully revoked the agent's authority. The agent successfully sued for reasonable remuneration for his work and labour up to that date.

Where the innocent party has made a bad bargain the damages for breach may **30–179**
well be less than the reasonable value of the work he has done. It is not clear whether he can secure a better measure by seeking a *quantum meruit* rather than damages or whether any claim for reasonable remuneration will be limited to a rateable proportion of the contract price. The weight of United States authority favours the view that the *quantum meruit* should not be limited in this way[24] but the question does not appear to have been decided authoritatively in England.[25] However, the Privy Council has held that the measure of relief in a *quantum meruit* is the actual value of the work and that the profitability of the contract is

---

[19] *cf.* the liability of minors etc., to pay for necessaries, *post*, § 30–191.

[20] *Province of the Law of Tort* (1931), pp. 157–160; *Quasi-Contracts* (1952), pp. 51–60. See also Winfield (1947) 63 L.Q.R. 35; Birks *op. cit.* pp. 226–234, 239–242; Goff and Jones *op. cit.* pp. 530–534.

[21] *De Bernardy v. Harding* (1853) 8 Exch. 822, 824. See to the same effect *Luxor (Eastbourne) Ltd v. Cooper* [1941] A.C. 108, 140–141. See also Birks *op. cit.* pp. 268–279.

[22] (1831) 8 Bing. 14. At p. 16, Tindal C.J. said: "I agree that when a special contract is in existence and open, the plaintiff cannot sue on a *quantum meruit*," also reported in 5 Car. & P. 58 and 1 M. & S. 51. See, on this point, *Weston v. Downes* (1778) 1 Doug. 23.

[23] (1856) 1 C.B.(N.S.) 296. The position of such an agent employed to effect a sale was fully considered by the House of Lords in *Luxor (Eastbourne) Ltd v. Cooper, supra*. See Vol. II, §§ 31–119 *et seq.*

[24] The most notable instance is *Boomer v. Muir* 24 P. 2d 570 (1933) in which $258,000 was awarded as the value of the work done over and above the price paid although only $20,000 was still due under the contract. See also the authorities cited by Palmer, *The Law of Restitution* (1978), Vol. I, pp. 389–390.

[25] *Inchbold v. Western Neilgherry Coffee, etc.* (1864) 17 C.B.(N.S.) 733 may suggest the use of the contract price as a ceiling but the judgments make no clear distinction between damages and a *quantum meruit*. See also *Burchall v. Gowrie & Blockhouse Collieries* [1910] A.C. 614 (contract price used to value services). *cf. De Bernardy v. Harding* (1853) 8 Ex. 822; *Prickett v. Badger, supra*.

irrelevant[26] and the Law Commission has recommended that a *quantum meruit* granted to an innocent party should not be based on the contract price.[27]

30–180   Although it might be thought wrong to allow the innocent party to "reverse" the contractual allocation of risks[28] and difficult to value the benefit without regard to the contract price,[29] it has also been argued that the contract price was agreed in the context of a contemplated complete performance and that this would not necessarily have been agreed for part performance.[30] The presence of economies of scale may mean that it does not follow that a person who agrees to pave 10 miles of road for a specified price would have agreed to pave 10 yards at a prorated price.[31] Furthermore, to allow a party in breach to reduce the award by reference to the contract price in effect awards him "a portion of his anticipated profit on the contract despite the fact that he was the contract breaker."[32] Finally, the contrast with claims for the recovery of money paid under contracts on the ground that there has been a total failure of consideration should be noted. In those cases the objection that recovery might reverse the contractual allocation of risks does not appear to have been taken.[33] An alternative to prorating the contract price is to limit the *quantum meruit* to the total contract price. This has been justified on the ground that it fully protects the claimant's expectations but avoids giving him a "windfall."[34] However, it does so by awarding the person who has committed a repudiatory breach which has led to the contract being discharged[35] a portion of his contractual expectations and has the consequence of producing disequilibrium between the position of a claimant who has done a small proportion of the work, where the contract price limit would in fact rarely apply, and the position of one who has done the bulk of the work, where the limit would be more likely to apply.[36]

30–181   Normally, the party in breach cannot recover recompense for goods supplied or services rendered, even if the innocent party terminates further performance of the contract[37]; he may, however, be able to claim payment for the performance

---

[26] *Slowey v. Lodder* [1904] A.C. 442, affg. (1900) N.Z.L.R. 321; *Reynard Construction (ME) Pty. Ltd v. Minister of Public Works* (1992) 26 N.S.W.L.R. 234; *Newton Woodhouse v. Trevor Toys Ltd,* December 20, 1991, CA; *Rover International Ltd v. Cannon Film Sales Ltd (No. 3)* [1989] 1 W.L.R. 912 (*post,* § 30–182; see also *ante,* § 30–053) supports this approach although the contract in that case was void.

[27] Law Comm. No. 121, para. 2.52 on which see Birks *op. cit.* pp. 262–263. See in general, Birks [1987] L.M.C.L.Q. 421.

[28] Burrows *op. cit.* pp. 268–270 would restrict the *quantum meruit* to a proration of the contract price unless there is incontrovertible benefit.

[29] *Burchall v. Gowrie & Blockhouse Collieries, supra;* B.P. *Exploration Co. (Libya) Ltd v. Hunt (No. 2)* [1979] 1 W.L.R. 783, 822, 825. See also Law Com. Working Paper No. 65 (1975), paras. 26–32 for other difficulties of valuation. See further Law Com. No. 121, paras. 2.50–2.57.

[30] Palmer (1959) 20 Ohio State L.J. 264; *The Law of Restitution* (1978), Vol. I, pp. 404–406.

[31] *ibid.* This example is taken from the facts of *Kehoe v. Rutherford* 27 A. 912 (1893) in which only a proportionate part of the price was recovered.

[32] Palmer *op. cit.* p. 401. See also *Prickett v. Badger, supra,* at 306.

[33] *Ante,* § 30–052, n. 68.

[34] Goff and Jones *op. cit.* pp. 533–534. Of the various solutions in the U.S. cases, they prefer that in *Wuchter v. Fitzgerald* 163 P. 819 (1917).

[35] On discharge, see *ante* Chaps. 23–25.

[36] Beatson *op. cit.* pp. 14–15. In the road example, if the contract price was £1 million, and the market price was £2 million, the limit would only affect a plaintiff who had completed more than half the work.

[37] *Ante,* §§ 21–023—21–029. See in general, Law Com. No. 121 (1983), *Pecuniary Restitution on Breach of Contract,* Part II.

of a divisible part of a contract which is not an "entire" contract,[38] or in certain special situations.[39]

Work done under a contract which is void. In *Craven-Ellis v. Canons Ltd.*[40] Craven-Ellis was appointed managing director of a company by an agreement under the company's seal, and his remuneration was fixed. But this contract was void, since neither Craven-Ellis, nor the directors who purported to execute the contract, had obtained their qualification shares within two months after appointment (as required by the articles of association). The "directors" could therefore not bind the company, but the Court of Appeal held that the fact that Craven-Ellis had done work under a contract which was void did not disentitle him from recovering on a *quantum meruit*, since the company (either through qualified directors or through its shareholders) had accepted the benefit of his services,[41] knowing that the services were not intended to be gratuitous. Greer L.J. said[42]: "The obligation to pay reasonable remuneration for the work done when there is no binding contract between the parties is imposed by a rule of law, and not by an inference of fact from the acceptance of services or goods." The Lord Justice thus appears to adopt the view that in these circumstances the obligation is purely in restitution. Moreover, there are difficulties with the court's view that liability was imposed on the basis of free acceptance because, at the material time, there was no one with authority to act, acquire knowledge, make a request or enter an agreement for the company.[43] The case is better seen as an early example of liability imposed because of incontrovertible benefit.[44] Greer L.J. pointed out that if the services "had not been performed by the plaintiff, [the company] would have had to get some other agent to carry [them] out."[45] The Court of Appeal in

30–182

---

[38] See by analogy, *Roberts v. Havelock* (1832) 3 B. & Ad. 404; *Taylor v. Laird* (1856) 25 L.J.Ex. 328. See also *Miles v. Wakefield M.B.C.* [1987] A.C. 539 but *cf. Wiluszynski v. Tower Hamlets L.B.C.* [1989] I.C.R. 493.

[39] *Ante*, §§ 22–032—22–037. Note especially the doctrine of substantial performance, *ante*, § 22–032, acceptance of short delivery under an entire contract for the sale of goods, Sale of Goods Act 1979, s.30(1); Vol. II, §§ 44–283 *et seq*, and the position of freight after a deviation, *Hain SS. Co. Ltd v. Tate & Lyle Ltd* (1934) 39 Com.Cas. 259, 271–272; (1936) 41 Com.Cas. 350, 358, 367–368, 373; Goff and Jones *op. cit.* pp. 438–447, but *cf.* Beatson (1981) 97 L.Q.R. 389, 413–414 *op. cit.* pp. 66–69. See also *Miles v. Wakefield M.D.C.* [1987] A.C. 539, but *cf. Wiluszynski v. Tower Hamlets L.B.C., supra.*

[40] [1936] 2 K.B. 403 (distinguished in *Re Richmond Gate Property Co. Ltd* [1965] 1 W.L.R. 335). See Lord Denning (1939) 55 L.Q.R. 54; Evans (1966) 29 M.L.R. 608; Birks *op. cit.* pp. 118–119, 229; [1971] C.L.P. 110, 119–122. See now *Westdeutsche Landesbank Girozentrale v. Islington L.B.C.* [1996] A.C. 669, *ante* § 30–065 (recovery of money). *cf. Guinness plc v. Saunders* [1990] 2 A.C. 663; *Lawford v. Billericay R.D.C.* [1903] 1 K.B. 772; *Société Franco Tunisienne D'Armement v. Sidermar SpA* [1961] 2 Q.B. 278, 313 (*ante*, § 24–096: the continued performance of a contract following frustration); the decision was overruled by the Court of Appeal on the issue of frustration: *Ocean Tramp Tankers Corporation v. V/O Sovfracht (The Eugenia)* [1964] 2 Q.B. 226 (*ante*, § 24–057); (1964) 27 M.L.R. 351; (1961) 24 M.L.R. 173.

[41] It was assumed that the directors had had the opportunity either to accept or reject the plaintiff's services. *cf. Boulton v. Jones* (1857) 27 L.J.Exch. 117 (*ante*, § 5–047) and the cases cited *post*, § 30–186, n. 99.

[42] *Craven-Ellis v. Canons Ltd, supra*, at 412.

[43] [1936] 2 All E.R. 1066, 1069 *per* Croom Johnson K.C. *arguendo.*

[44] Birks [1971] 24 C.L.P. 110, 120 *et seq.* argues convincingly for this explanation. See also Birks *op. cit.* pp. 118–119, 229; Goff and Jones *op. cit.* pp. 587–588. *cf.* Lord Denning (1939) 55 L.Q.R. 54 (acceptance by whole body of shareholders); Lord Templeman in *Guinness plc v. Saunders* [1990] 2 A.C. 663.

[45] [1936] 2 K.B. 403, 412.

Rover International Ltd. v. Cannon Film Sales (No.3)[46] appears to support this view of *Craven-Ellis* in so far as it did not consider whether anything in the nature of an express or implied request was necessary to found a claim for a *quantum meruit* by a company for services rendered after its incorporation but under a pre-incorporation contract. Kerr L.J. said that the task of the court was to carry out a process of equitable restitution. The Court also held that the *quantum meruit* was not to be limited by reference to the claimant's entitlement under the purported contract, primarily because that was irrelevant to a remedy which only arose due to the invalidity of the contract but also by analogy with the position of a valid contract which had been discharged without breach.

30–183   Similarly, when an innocent party learns that the other party to the contract has an illegal object in mind, the innocent party, although he must refuse to continue with the performance of the contract, may sue on a *quantum meruit* for the lawful work he has already done.[47]

30–184   **Work done under an unenforceable contract.** A person who renders services under a contract that is unenforceable will be entitled to a *quantum meruit* if the other party has failed to carry out his part provided the restitutionary claim does not undermine the policy of the statute (or common law rule) rendering the contract unenforceable.[48] Although there is English authority to this effect which shows that the basis of the claim is restitution rather than implied contract,[49] the clearest examples are provided by the decisions of the Supreme Court of Canada and the High Court of Australia. Thus, in *Deglman v. Guaranty Trust Co. of Canada and Constantineau*,[50] a nephew, who rendered services to his aunt under an oral agreement by which she had agreed to bequeath a house to him, was entitled to reasonable remuneration for the services on her failure to do so since she had received the benefits of full performance of the contract. Again, in *Pavey & Matthews Pty. Ltd v. Paul*,[51] a *quantum meruit* was granted to a licensed builder who had renovated a cottage under an unenforceable oral contract. It was held that the claim was an independent restitutionary claim arising from the acceptance of the benefits accruing to the defendant from the plaintiff's execution of the work for which the ineffective contract provided. In these cases it was accepted that the contract had been fully performed.[52] Where it is not, or where performance is alleged to be defective, if the basis of the remedy is the acceptance of performance, it may be arguable that the defendant who has not in fact received the bargained-for performance, should not be deemed to have accepted

---

[46] [1989] 1 W.L.R. 912; (1989) 105 L.Q.R. 179. See also *Cotronic (U.K.) Ltd v. Dezonie* [1991] B.C.L.C. 721.

[47] *Clay v. Yates* (1856) 1 H. & N. 73 (*ante*, § 17–012).

[48] *Pavey & Matthews Pty. Ltd v. Paul* (1987) 69 A.L.R. 577, 584–585, on which see Beatson (1988) 104 L.Q.R. 13; Ibbetson (1988) 8 O.J.L.S. 312.

[49] *Scarisbrick v. Parkinson* (1869) 20 L.T. 175; *Pulbrook v. Lawes* (1876) 1 Q.B.D. 284; *Scott v. Pattison* [1923] 2 K.B. 723 (and see, on the relevance of the local custom, the fuller reports in: 39 T.L.R. 557; 129 L.T. 830; 92 L.J.K.B. 886); *James v. Thomas H. Kent & Co. Ltd* [1951] 1 K.B. 551, 555–556. See further Goff and Jones *op. cit.* Chap. 21; Denning (1925) 41 L.Q.R. 79. These cases concern lack of writing, on which see, *ante*, §§ 4–003, 4–036 *et seq.* 4–062 *et seq.*

[50] [1954] 3 D.L.R. 785.

[51] (1987) 69 A.L.R. 577.

[52] In *Pavey's* case the owner of the cottage denied the reasonableness of the charges claimed by the builder.

non-conforming performance and should not therefore be liable.[53] Alternatively, in the case of a contract unenforceable for lack of writing, where there is an allegation of non-conformity with the promised performance, it is arguable that, if the purpose of the statutory requirement is to avoid disputes as to what was agreed, this would be undermined by a restitutionary *quantum meruit.*

Quantum meruit to fix a price or remuneration. If no price for goods sold has been fixed in the contract of sale, the law will imply that a reasonable price is to be paid, and, in an action for *quantum valebant*, the court will, as "a question of fact dependent on the circumstances of each particular case," decide what is a reasonable price.[54] Similarly, in a contract for work to be done, if no scale of remuneration is fixed, the law imposes an obligation to pay a reasonable sum (*quantum meruit*).[55] The circumstances must clearly show that the work is not to be done gratuitously before the court will, in the absence of an express contract, infer that there was a valid contract with an implied term that a reasonable remuneration would be paid[56]; this principle may extend to services performed in anticipation that negotiations will lead to the conclusion of a contract, provided that the services were requested or acquiesced in by the recipient.[57] In this context, it has been said that *quantum meruit* is not truly restitutionary, since it is only "an incident in assessing the amount due under an ordinary contract where the amount is blank."[58] It is, however, difficult to accept this in the case of services rendered in anticipation that a contract would be entered into later[59] and, in such a case, a *quantum meruit* is not subject to contractual defences such as a claim for late delivery.[60] It has been said that these may be examples of "cases not founded on contract, nor in tort, nor upon the application of any equitable doctrine or principle, where there may be recovery."[61] In *British Steel Corporation v. Cleveland Bridge & Engineering Co. Ltd*[62]

30–185

---

[53] *Sumpter v. Hedges* [1898] 1 Q.B. 673. See also *Wiluszynski v. Tower Hamlets L.B.C., ante.* But *cf.*, albeit in another context, *British Steel Corp. v. Cleveland Bridge & Engineering Ltd* [1984] 1 All E.R. 504 (*post*, § 30–185) where allegedly non-conforming performance gave rise to a *quantum meruit.*

[54] s.8(2) of the Sale of Goods Act 1979; *Foley v. Classique Coaches Ltd* [1934] 2 K.B. 1. (*cf. ante*, §§ 2–128—2–144.)

[55] *e.g. Way v. Latilla* [1937] 3 All E.R. 759, HL; *William Lacey (Hounslow) Ltd v. Davis* [1957] 1 W.L.R. 932; *British Steel Corp. v. Cleveland Bridge & Engineering Co. Ltd* [1984] 1 All E.R. 504. See Ball (1983) 99 L.Q.R. 572; Beatson *op. cit.* pp. 5–8; McKendrick (1988) 8 O.J.L.S. 197. See also *Lagos v. Grunwaldt* [1910] 1 K.B. 41, 48; *Robins v. Power* (1858) 4 C.B.(N.S.) 778. *cf. Re Richmond Gate Property Co. Ltd* [1965] 1 W.L.R. 335. If the person at whose request the work is done subsequently promises a definite sum as remuneration, the so-called rule in *Lampleigh v. Braithwaite* (1615) Hob. 105 may apply: see *ante*, § 3–029.

[56] *ibid.*

[57] *William Lacey (Hounslow) Ltd v. Davis, supra*; *Peter Lind & Co. Ltd v. Mersey Docks and Harbour Board* [1972] 2 Lloyd's Rep. 234; *Sabemo v. N. Sydney Municipal Council* [1977] 2 N.S.W.L.R. 880; *Marston Construction Co. Ltd v. Kigass Ltd* [1989] 46 B.L.R. 109. *cf. Brewer Street Investments Ltd v. Barclays Woollen Co. Ltd* [1954] 1 Q.B. 428; *Regalian Properties plc v. London Dockland Development Corp* [1995] 1 W.L.R. 212.

[58] Winfield, *Quasi-Contracts* (1952), p. 53.

[59] *William Lacey (Hounslow) Ltd v. Davis, supra*, at 939; *Brewer Street Investments Ltd v. Barclays Woollen Co. Ltd, supra* at 435–436. See also Goff and Jones *op. cit.* Chap. 22.

[60] *British Steel Corp. v. Cleveland Bridge & Engineering Co. Ltd, supra.*

[61] *Sabemo v. N. Sydney Municipal Council, ante* at 897, noted (1981) 1 O.J.L.S. 300.

[62] [1984] 1 All E.R. 504, 511.

Robert Goff J. said that the obligation imposed in such cases sounds in quasi-contract or restitution and not in contract.[63]

30–186   The court may infer from the facts a contract to pay for services to be rendered, although this entails disregarding the actual intention of the parties at the time; as, for instance, where both parties, under a mistake of fact, assumed that the defendant was entitled to claim, without charge, the services of the particular fire brigade he had summoned.[64] But no obligation arises unless there is an express or implied request from the defendant to the claimant for the work to be done or the services to be rendered. Apart from the exceptional cases of salvage,[65] agency of necessity,[66] and services or benefits provided in an emergency,[67] or of limited cases where the claimant innocently repairs or improves the defendant's chattels,[68] English law at present appears hostile to claims for services rendered or work done in the absence of a contract (express or implied) between the parties.[69] The mere receipt of a benefit, when the defendant had no real option to accept or reject it, does not justify a claim for *quantum meruit*.[70]

30–187   Where an agent or trustee is liable to account for a profit or commission resulting from his fiduciary position or arising out of his use of his principal's or the trust property,[71] he may, if he has acted openly and honestly (albeit mistakenly), be entitled to some remuneration for his work and skill.[72]

30–188   **Substituted contract.** The term *quantum meruit* is also used where the parties have not performed the terms of their contract, but it can be inferred from their conduct that they have tacitly agreed to substitute another contract for the first one. In *Steven v. Bromley & Son*[73] Bankes L.J. summarised the facts by saying: "When the charterers tendered a cargo which was outside the charterparty, and for which no rate of freight had been agreed, the inference is justified that they made an offer to the owners to pay a reasonable freight if the cargo were accepted for carriage." In the same case Atkin L.J. gave an illustration from the law as to the sale of goods[74]: "If I order from a wine merchant twelve bottles of whisky at so much a bottle and he sends me ten bottles of whisky and two of brandy and

---

[63] See *ante*, §§ 30–007, 30–018—30–020 for doubts as to whether this is always based on unjust enrichment.

[64] *Upton-on-Severn R.D.C. v. Powell* [1942] 1 All E.R. 220.

[65] *Post*, § 30–191. On improvements to land carried out by a limited owner or tenant see Munkman *op. cit.* p. 95, and *cf. ante*, § 30–108.

[66] *Ante*, § 30–160; Vol. II, § 32–034.

[67] *Ante*, § 30–161; *post*, § 30–193.

[68] *Ante*, § 30–161.

[69] *Falcke v. Scottish Imperial Insurance Company* (1887) 34 Ch.D. 234, 248–249. See Goff and Jones *op. cit.* pp. 18–26, 44–50, 404–405.

[70] *Forman & Co. Proprietary Ltd v. Ship "Liddesdale"* [1900] A.C. 190. See also *Taylor v. Laird* (1856) 1 H. & N. 266; *Sumpter v. Hedges* [1898] 1 Q.B. 673 (see *ante*, § 00–000); *Bookmakers Afternoon Greyhound Services Ltd v. Wilfred Gilbert Staffordshire Ltd* [1994] F.S.R. 723. *cf. Owen v. Tate* [1976] Q.B. 402 (see *ante*, §§ 30–135—30–138).

[71] *Ante*, §§ 30–107—30–108; Vol. II, §§ 32–117—32–118.

[72] *Phipps v. Boardman* [1967] 2 A.C. 46, 104, 112 (*ante*, § 22–035).

[73] [1919] 2 K.B. 722, 726; *The Batis* [1990] 1 Lloyd's Rep. 345, 352–353.

[74] *ibid.* at 728. *cf. Chandris v. Isbrandtsen-Moller Co. Inc.* [1951] 1 K.B. 240, 248 *et seq.*, where this principle is discussed in a charterparty case; *Sumpter v. Hedges* [1898] 1 Q.B. 673, where the principle was recognised, although the plaintiff failed on the facts. See also *ante*, § 22–035.

I accept them, I must pay a reasonable price for the brandy." The obligation in such a case is genuinely contractual.

Additional remuneration. The principle of *quantum meruit* may allow **30–189** recovery of a reasonable sum as additional remuneration for extra work by a building contractor, where, although the contract permitted the owner to order extra work, the amount of extra work actually ordered was so great as to go beyond the scope of the contract and entitle the builder to claim that he should not be limited to the maximum profit fixed by the contract.[75] The same principle has been applied to a contract of employment, where, in lieu of an increase of salary, the employer promised to pay a bonus on the net trading profits of the business but the method of assessing the bonus was never agreed.[76]

(b) *Necessaries Supplied to a Minor, Mentally Disordered or Drunken Person*

Necessaries. Analogous to a *quantum meruit* claim is a statutory obligation **30–190** which is usually classified as quasi-contractual or restitutionary, namely, the obligation of a minor or "person who by reason of mental incapacity or drunkenness is incompetent to contract" to pay a reasonable price "where necessaries are sold and delivered" to him.[77]

(c) *Salvage*[78]

Salvage. The obligation of the owner of a ship or its cargo to pay compensa- **30–191** tion to a person who rescues it from peril is a good example of a genuine quasi-contract, as none of the elements of ordinary contract may exist, although in some cases there may be an opportunity for bargaining before the services are rendered.[79] But in many cases this is not so; the services are rendered and the question then is what are the salvors to be paid. In *The Five Steel Barges*[80] Sir James Hannen P. said:

> "The right to salvage may arise out of an actual contract; but it does not necessarily do so. It is a legal liability arising out of the fact that property has been saved, that the owner of the property who has had the benefit of it shall make remuneration to those who have conferred the benefit on him, notwithstanding that he has not entered into any contract on the subject."

In claims for saving life, the shipowner, in the interests of humanity, is compelled to pay for something from which he has derived no personal benefit.[81] In a case[82]

---

[75] *Parkinson (Sir Lindsay) & Co. Ltd v. Commissioners of Works* [1949] 2 K.B. 632. *cf. Gilbert & Partners v. Knight* [1968] 2 All E.R. 248.
[76] *Powell v. Braun* [1954] 1 W.L.R. 401. But *cf. ante*, §§ 1–037, 3–060—3–066; Vol. II, § 39–072.
[77] s.3 of the Sale of Goods Act 1979 (considered *ante*, §§ 8–007 *et seq.*, 8–071, 8–078).
[78] See Kennedy's *Civil Salvage* (5th ed., 1985); Goff and Jones *op. cit.* Chap. 18.
[79] *Semco Salvage & Marine Pte Ltd v. Lancer Navigation Co. Ltd* [1997] A.C. 455. *cf. ante*, §§ 7–030 *et seq.*, 7–076. In *The Troilus* [1950] P. 92, it was pointed out that salvage, an obligation imposed by law irrespective of any contract express or implied, must be distinguished from towage which only arises from an express or implied contract.
[80] (1890) 15 P.D. 142, 146.
[81] Kennedy *op. cit.* pp. 12–13.
[82] *Falcke v. Scottish Imperial Insurance Co.* (1886) 34 Ch.D. 234, 248–249.

where "salvage" was claimed in respect of a policy of life insurance, Bowen L.J. after pointing out that neither a liability nor a benefit could be forced upon a man in order to create a legal obligation at common law, distinguished the law as regards salvage, general average and contribution on the ground that the maritime law differs from the common law; "no similar doctrine applies to things lost upon land, nor to anything except ships or goods in peril at sea."[83] But there is now some authority supporting the view that in some emergencies on land, a claim in restitution may lie.[84]

(d) *Services Performed in an Emergency*

30–192 **Services performed in an emergency.** In a Canadian case,[85] a surgeon, who intended to charge for his services, was held entitled to recover remuneration for his professional services in his reasonable, but unsuccessful, attempt to revive a suicide. There is some English support for the principle underlying this decision, and there are several possible analogies upon which an English court could draw if it wished to follow it.[86]

(e) *Valuable Benefits obtained under a Frustrated Contract*

30–193 **Frustrated contracts.** The court is empowered by the Law Reform (Frustrated Contracts) Act 1943, s.1(3) to order a party to a contract which is subsequently frustrated to pay for a "valuable benefit" obtained by him under the contract.[87] It has been said that "the fundamental principle underlying the Act itself, is prevention of the unjust enrichment of either party to the contract at the other's expense."[88]

6. ACCOUNTS STATED[89]

30–194 **Different meanings of the term "account stated."** The term "account stated" is applied in at least three ways.[90]

(i) To a claim by one party to payment of a definite amount, which is admitted to be correct by the other party. This is merely an admission of a debt out of court[91] and is equivalent to a promise from which the existence of a debt may be

---

[83] See *Sorrell v. Paget* [1950] 1 K.B. 252 (claim for salvage of a heifer).

[84] See *ante*, §§ 30–138, 30–161; *post*, § 30–193.

[85] *Matheson v. Smiley* [1932] 2 D.L.R. 787.

[86] See *ante*, § 30–161, and the references and cases there cited.

[87] For full details, see *ante*, §§ 24–072 *et seq.*

[88] *B.P. Exploration Co. (Libya) Ltd v. Hunt (No. 2)* [1979] 1 W.L.R. 783, 799 (Robert Goff J.), *affd.* [1981] 1 W.L.R. 232, CA; [1982] 2 A.C. 352, HL. In contrast, the Court of Appeal got "no help from the use of words which are not in the statute" [1981] 1 W.L.R. 232, 243.

[89] Accounts stated are for convenience considered in this chapter, although they cannot properly be classified as quasi-contractual or restitutionary. See in general Bullen & Leake and Jacob's *Precedents of Pleadings* (12th ed.), pp. 187–191, 917–919; Atkin's *Encyclopaedia of Court Forms in Civil Proceedings* (2nd ed.), Vol. I, pp. 265–278.

[90] *Camillo Tank SS. Co. Ltd v. Alexandria Engineering Works* (1921) 38 T.L.R. 134, 143; *Siqueira v. Noronha* [1934] A.C. 332, 337.

[91] *ibid.*

inferred.[92] Such an admission is only evidence[93] of a debt, and can be rebutted[94]; an item in an account stated of this type can be challenged or explained,[95] or the admission can be rebutted by evidence that there was no consideration for the promise to pay. In order to have this evidential effect, the admission of liability must be unqualified and must relate to an existing debt.[96]

(ii) The items in an account may have been settled and agreed on the basis of some new valuable consideration received by the party who admitted that he owed the agreed sum, *e.g.* where the repairers of a ship released it to the owners without exercising their lien for the cost of the repairs.[97]

(iii) "A real account stated"[98] is one in which the account includes items on both sides and the parties have agreed that there shall be a set-off and only the balance shall be payable. The " . . . several items of claim are brought into account on either side, and, being set against one another, a balance is struck and the consideration for the payment of the balance is the discharge of the items on each side."[99] Though such an arrangement is frequently regarded as quasi-contractual, it is more properly described as "a promise for good consideration to pay the balance"[1]; and the consideration is valid and the settlement is binding even though some of the debts may be statute-barred,[2] or otherwise unenforceable.[3] Fraud, however, will permit the questioning of an account stated.[4]

> "The essence of an account stated [in this third sense] is not the character of the items on one side or the other, but the fact that there are cross items of account and that the parties mutually agree the several amounts of each and, by treating the items so agreed on the one side as discharging the items on the other side *pro tanto*, go on to agree that the balance only is payable. . . . Nor can it be material . . .whether the balance of indebtedness is throughout, as it must be at the end, in favour of one side."[5]

An account stated in this sense is a new cause of action for the purpose of limitation.[6] But where there are no mutual debits and credits, in that the whole accounting is to be rendered by one party to the other, so that all the items are on one side only, there can be no account stated in this sense.[7] For an account stated in the third sense there must be an "absolute acknowledgment" of the balance

---

[92] *Barker v. Birt* (1842) 10 M. & W. 61; *Perry v. Slade* (1845) 8 Q.B. 115.

[93] It is not evidence unless the defendant clearly acknowledged that a definite sum was due from him: *Hughes v. Thorpe* (1839) 5 M. & W. 656; *Lane v. Hill* (1852) 18 Q.B. 252. See also *Fesenmayer v. Adcock* (1847) 16 M. & W. 449 (an I.O.U.).

[94] *e.g.* by showing that it was made in error. See *Lubbock v. Tribe* (1838) 3 M. & W. 607, 612–613. The admission places on the defendant the burden of proving that it was erroneous: *Camillo Tank SS. Co. Ltd v. Alexandria Engineering Works, supra,* at 141, 143.

[95] *Wilson v. Wilson* (1854) 14 C.B. 616.

[96] *Burgh v. Legge* (1839) 5 M. & W. 418, 421–422. See also *Tucker v. Barrow* (1828) 7 B. & C. 623; *Wayman v. Hilliard* (1830) 7 Bing. 101; *Warwick v. Warwick* (1918) 34 T.L.R. 475.

[97] *Camillo Tank SS. Co. Ltd v. Alexandria Engineering Works, supra* (HL).

[98] *Re Laycock v. Pickles* (1863) 4 B. & S. 497, 506.

[99] *ibid.*

[1] *Siqueira v. Noronha* [1934] A.C. 332, 337.

[2] *ibid.* See also *Ashby v. James* (1843) 11 M. & W. 542 and *ante,* § 29–132.

[3] *Re Laycock v. Pickles, ante.* See also *Dawson v. Remnant* (1806) 6 Esp. 24.

[4] *Vagliano Bros. v. Bank of England* (1888) 22 Q.B.D. 103, 127 (reversed on other grounds: *Bank of England v. Vagliano Bros.* [1891] A.C. 107).

[5] *Bushun Chand (Firm) v. Seth Girdhari Lal* (1934) 50 T.L.R. 465, 468, PC (Accounts between moneylender and borrower can be the subject of an account stated in this sense in the same way as accounts between banker and customer.)

[6] *Bushun Chand (Firm) v. Seth Girdhari Lal, supra.*

[7] *Anglo-American Asphalt Co. Ltd v. Crowley, Russell & Co. Ltd* (1945) 173 L.T. 228.

due to the claimant[8] without any qualification.[9] The debt must also be acknowledged by the defendant in his personal capacity: thus, where the defendants,
directors of a company who were indebted to it, signed a balance-sheet of the
company which showed the amount due by each defendant to the company, the
balance-sheet was held not to be an account stated since the defendants had
signed, not with the intention of contracting, but solely in performance of their
duty as directors.[10] Again, an arbitrator is not the agent of the parties to settle
accounts between them: hence, his award is not an account stated between
them.[11]

30–195   **Illegal or unenforceable debts.** An account stated will not lie if the original
debt is absolutely void because it is based on an illegal[12] or immoral consideration, or is made void by statute.[13] "I do not think that, where a contract from its
nature can give rise to no valid claim, a claim upon it can be used to found an
action upon an account stated."[14] Thus, an account stated will not lie for betting
transactions rendered void by statute,[15] or for items due under a policy of marine
insurance rendered invalid by statute.[16] On the other hand, the fact that a debt
was originally unenforceable through lack of admissible evidence will not invalidate a subsequent account stated based on that debt.[17] Similarly, where by the
Trade Union Act 1871 a contract in restraint of trade between members of a trade
union was not directly enforceable, it could nevertheless be the basis of a
subsequent account stated.[18] But there can be no claim on an account stated
where a statutory condition precedent to recovery has not been fulfilled.[19]

---

[8] *Day v. William Hill (Park Lane) Ltd* [1949] 1 K.B. 632, 641.

[9] *Calvert v. Baker* (1838) 4 M. & W. 417. cf. *Chisman v. Count* (1841) 2 M. & G. 307.

[10] *John Shaw & Sons (Salford) Ltd v. Shaw* [1935] 2 K.B. 113 (the word "Directors" was appended
to their signatures). See also *Petch v. Lyon* (1846) 9 Q.B. 147.

[11] *Bates v. Townley* (1848) 2 Exch. 152.

[12] *Rose v. Savory* (1835) 2 Bing.N.C. 145.

[13] *Cocking v. Ward* (1845) 1 C.B. 858, 870.

[14] *Joseph Evans & Co. Ltd v. Heathcote* [1918] 1 K.B. 418, 427. See also *Kennedy v. Broun* (1863)
13 C.B.(N.S.) 677 (claim for barrister's fees).

[15] *Law v. Dearnley* [1950] 1 K.B. 400; *Alberg v. Chandler* (1948) 64 T.L.R. 394.

[16] *Re Home and Colonial Insurance Co. Ltd* [1930] 1 Ch. 102, 130.

[17] *Cocking v. Ward* (1845) 1 C.B. 858, 868. (This was an account stated of the first type discussed
ante, § 30–195.) But a document which is inadmissible for want of a stamp in one capacity cannot
be relied on as proof of an account stated: Stamp Act 1891, s.14(4).

[18] *Joseph Evans & Co. Ltd v. Heathcote* [1918] 1 K.B. 418.

[19] *Scadding v. Eyles* (1846) 9 Q.B. 858.

Part Nine
CONFLICT OF LAWS

1. Preliminary Considerations

Introduction. A contract may be connected with several territorial jurisdic-   **31–001**
tions because the parties to it reside in different countries, or because the contract
is made in one country but is to be performed in a different country or concerns
subject-matter which is situated in a different country, or for other reasons. In
such cases it may become necessary to determine which legal system is to govern
the contract or a particular aspect of it, *i.e.* to determine what is the law
applicable to the contract.[1]

Sources of the law. This chapter is concerned with the elucidation of the   **31–002**
choice of law rules according to which the law applicable to a contract which is
connected with more than one territorial jurisdiction is determined.[2] Originally,

---

[1] It will also be necessary to decide whether the court of the forum, *i.e.* the English court, has
jurisdiction to entertain an action arising out of such a contract. On the issue of jurisdiction in such
cases, see *Dicey & Morris on the Conflict of Laws* (12th ed., 1993), Chaps. 10–13; Cheshire and
North, *Private International Law* (12th ed., 1992), Chaps. 10–14.

[2] It is not concerned with the rules as to the jurisdiction of English courts: see preceding note. Nor
is it concerned with the rules relating to the recognition of foreign judgments, as to which see *Dicey &
Morris op. cit.* Chaps. 14 and 15; Cheshire and North *op. cit.* Chaps. 15 and 16. The conflict of laws'
aspects of arbitration (as to which see *Dicey & Morris op. cit.* Chap. 16; Cheshire and North *op. cit.*
Chap. 17) are similarly excluded. For the conflict of laws with regard to negotiable instruments see
post, §§ 31–036—31–037 and Vol II, §§ 34–197—34–217. Some contracts for the sale of goods made
on or after August 18, 1972, which are connected with several territorial jurisdictions may be governed
by the provisions of the Uniform Law on International Sales Act 1967 and will not necessitate
examination of the rules of the conflict of laws: Sched. I, Art. 2. See Vol II, § 43–003.

these rules were to be found in the common law as developed by the courts. According to these rules, a contract was governed by its "proper law."[3] These common law rules have been substantially reformulated as a result of the implementation in the United Kingdom of the Rome (E.C.) Convention on the Law Applicable to Contractual Obligations 1980 ("the Rome Convention") in the Contracts (Applicable Law) Act 1990. The rules of that Convention, as implemented in the Act of 1990, will apply to determine the law applicable to a contract which is entered into after April 1, 1991.[4] Since, however, there will be cases involving contracts entered into on or before that date, which will continue to be governed by common law rules, this chapter continues to treat them, albeit in rather briefer form, in Section 2.[5] Section 3, a substantial portion of the chapter, seeks to analyse the provisions of the Rome Convention.[6] Section 4 explores the scope of the applicable law and the relevance of other laws in the context of the incidents of the contract and the various issues which may arise in a contractual context.[7]

31–003   **Terminology.** The Rome Convention does not adopt the familiar terminology of the common law; in particular, it abandons the linguistic usage "proper law of a contract" and replaces that usage with its own terminology. This terminology is variously, "applicable law," "law applicable to the contract," "governing law" or "law governing the contract." This terminology is used interchangeably in Sections 3 and 4 of the chapter. The phrase "proper law of a contract" is, however, retained for the purpose of the discussion of the common law in Section 2.

2. Common Law: The Doctrine of the Proper Law of a Contract[8]

31–004   **Statement of the doctrine.** The modern approach to the problem of determining the proper law of a contract involves the need to examine three possible situations.[9] If the parties have made an express choice of law in the contract

---

[3] See *post*, §§ 31–004—31–015.

[4] The date on which the 1990 Act entered into force: see Rome Convention, Art. 17. *Post*, § 31–016.

[5] See *post*, §§ 31–004—31–015.

[6] See *post*, §§ 31–016—31–109.

[7] See *post*, §§ 31–110—31–172.

[8] For more detailed accounts of the common law position, see the 26th edition of this work, Chap. 30; *Dicey & Morris on the Conflict of Laws* (11th ed., 1987), Chaps. 32 and 33; Cheshire and North, *Private International Law* (11th ed., 1987), Chap. 18.

[9] *Amin Rasheed Shipping Corpn. v. Kuwait Insurance Co.* [1984] A.C. 50, 51. For a short historical account of the development leading to this view, see *Dicey & Morris on the Conflict of Laws* (12th ed., 1993), pp. 1187–1190. The detail may be traced through *Robinson v. Bland* (1760) 2 Burr. 1077; *Lloyd v. Guibert* (1865) L.R. 1 Q.B. 115; *P. & O. SS. Co. v. Shand* (1865) 3 Moo. P.C. (N.S.) 272; *Chartered Mercantile Bank of India v. Netherlands Co.* (1883) 10 Q.B.D. 521; *Jacobs v. Crédit Lyonnais* (1884) 12 Q.B.D. 589; *Re Missouri Steamship Co.* (1889) 42 Ch.D. 321; *Hamlyn v. Talisker Distillery* [1894] A.C. 202; *Spurrier v. La Cloche* [1902] A.C. 446; *N.V. Kwik Hoo Tong Handel Maatschappij v. James Finlay & Co.* [1927] A.C. 604; *R. v. International Trustee for the Protection of Bondholders A.G.* [1937] A.C. 500; *Mount Albert Borough Council v. Australasian, etc, Assurance Building Society Ltd* [1938] A.C. 224; *Vita Food Products Inc. v. Unus Shipping Co. Ltd* [1939] A.C. 277; *Kahler v. Midland Bank Ltd* [1950] A.C. 24; *Bonython v. Commonwealth of Australia* [1951] A.C. 201; *The Assunzione* [1954] P. 150; *Re Helbert Wagg & Co. Ltd's Claim* [1956] Ch. 323; *Re United Railway of the Havana and Regla Warehouses Ltd* [1960] Ch. 52 (affd. *sub nom. Tomkinson v. First Pennsylvania Banking and Trust Co.* [1961] A.C. 1007); *James Miller and Partners Ltd v. Whitworth Street Estates (Manchester) Ltd* [1970] A.C. 583; *Compagnie Tunisienne de Navigation*

itself, then, subject to certain limitations,[10] the law that they have chosen will govern. If there is no express choice, the court must examine all the facts surrounding the contract to determine whether there was an inferred or implied choice of law by the parties. In the absence of any choice, express or implied, the court ceases to look for the intention of the parties (since they are presumed to have no intention on the point) and proceeds, on objective grounds, to determine and apply "the system of law with which the transaction has the closest and most real connection."[11] It is, however, often difficult to distinguish between the second and third approaches, *i.e.* implied choice and no choice, and the same decision may well be justified on either approach.[12] What is clear is that there must be a proper law and that it is not possible to have a contract which is not governed by some system of private law.[13] Furthermore, there must be a proper law from the time that the contract is made.[14] There cannot be a proper law which "floats," *i.e.* is not identified when the contract is made but which is left to be determined later by the unilateral act of one of the parties.[15] In determining the governing law at the time the contract was made, conduct or events subsequent to that date cannot be taken into account.[16] A contract can, however, validly

---

SA v. Compagnie d'Armement Maritime SA [1971] A.C. 572; *Coast Lines Ltd v. Hudig and Veder Chartering N.V.* [1972] 2 Q.B. 34; *Amin Rasheed Shipping Corpn. v. Kuwait Insurance Co.*, *supra*.

[10] *Post*, §§ 31–006—31–007.

[11] *e.g. Bonython v. Commonwealth of Australia, supra*, at 219; *The Assunzione, supra*; *Re United Railways of the Havana and Regla Warehouses Ltd, supra*, at 91–92, 115 (affd. *sub nom. Tomkinson v. First Pennsylvania Banking and Trust Co., supra*, at 1068, 1081–1082); *Philipson-Stow v. Inland Revenue Commissioners* [1961] A.C. 727, 760; *James Miller and Partners Ltd v. Whitworth Street Estates (Manchester) Ltd, supra; Compagnie d'Armement Maritime SA v. Compagnie Tunisienne de Navigation SA, supra; Coast Lines Ltd v. Hudig and Veder Chartering N.V., supra; Amin Rasheed Shipping Corpn. v. Kuwait Insurance Co., supra*. Early decisions tended to express this idea in the language of the presumed intention of the parties rather than as a purely objective test which applied because of an absence of intent as to the applicable law. See, *e.g. Lloyd v. Guibert, supra; Mount Albert Borough Council v. Australasian, etc, Assurance Building Society Ltd, supra; Kahler v. Midland Bank Ltd, supra; The Assunzione, supra.*

[12] See the views of Lord Diplock and Lord Wilberforce in *Amin Rasheed Shipping Corpn. v. Kuwait Insurance Co., supra*. The former (speaking for the majority) treated the case as one of implied choice, the latter as one of no choice. See also *Armadora Occidental SA v. Horace Mann Insurance Co.* [1977] 1 W.L.R. 520 (implied choice) (affd. *ibid.* at 1098 (no choice)).

[13] *Amin Rasheed Shipping Corpn. v. Kuwait Insurance Co., supra*, at 65.

[14] *Armar Shipping Co. Ltd v. Caisse Algérienne* [1981] 1 W.L.R. 207; *Black Clawson International Ltd v. Papierwerke Waldhof-Aschaffenburgh A.G.* [1981] 2 Lloyd's Rep. 446, 456; *The Blue Wave* [1982] 1 Lloyd's Rep. 380, 385; *Cantieri Navali Riuniti S.p.A. v. N.V. Omne Justitia* [1985] 2 Lloyd's Rep. 428, 435; *The Frank Pais* [1986] 1 Lloyd's Rep. 428, 435; *Star Shipping A.S. v. China National Foreign Trade Transportation Corpn.* [1993] 2 Lloyd's Rep. 445.

[15] *Armar Shipping Co. Ltd v. Caisse Algérienne, supra*, at 215–216; *Astro Venturoso Compania Naviera v. Hellenic Shipyards SA* [1983] 1 Lloyd's Rep. 12, 15; *E.I. Du Pont de Nemours v. Agnew* [1987] 2 Lloyd's Rep. 585, 592; *Star Shipping A.S. v. China National Foreign Trade Transportation Corpn., supra* (but there is no objection to an arbitration subject to a "floating" curial law).

[16] *James Miller and Partners Ltd v. Whitworth Street Estates (Manchester) Ltd* [1970] A.C. 583, 603, 611, 614–615; *Compagnie d'Armement Maritime SA v. Compagnie Tunisienne de Navigation SA* [1971] A.C. 572, 593, 595–596, 603; *Armar Shipping Co. Ltd v. Caisse Algérienne* [1981] 1 W.L.R. 207; *Amin Rasheed Shipping Corpn. v. Kuwait Insurance Co.* [1984] A.C. 50, 69. Such subsequent conduct may be relevant in determining whether the parties have entered a new collateral contract (*James Miller and Partners Ltd v. Whitworth Street Estates (Manchester) Ltd, supra*, at 603, 614–615; *Compagnie d'Armement Maritime SA v. Compagnie Tunisienne de Navigation SA, supra*, at 602–608) or as evidence of estoppel (*James Miller and Partners Ltd v. Whitworth Street Estates (Manchester) Ltd, supra* at 611, 614–615). As to the position under the Rome Convention, see *post*, § 31–050. Effect will be given, however, to later changes in a foreign applicable law: see *post*, § 31–008.

provide for two proper laws, the second to be applied if the event on which the application of the first depends is negatived.[17] This would also support the view that the proper law can be changed by the parties during the currency of the contract.[18]

31–005 **Express choice of law.** Determination of the proper law of the contract should not normally involve any difficulty if the parties have stipulated expressly which legal system is to apply to their agreement.[19] Where it is concluded that the choice of law by the parties is meaningless, the express choice will be ignored and the proper law determined by reference to any implied choice or, failing that, the most closely connected system of law.[20] An issue may arise as to the validity of the term which purports to choose the proper law. There is little direct authority on this issue. There is support of the application of English law as the law of the forum to the question,[21] but the better view is to apply the law that would govern if the choice is valid.[22]

31–006 **Limitations on power to choose: common law.** The parties' power to choose the proper law is limited, first, by virtue of an obscure judicial formula which requires that the choice must be "bona fide and legal."[23] The possible effect of this formula (which has never been applied in England to strike down a choice of law) is:

> "that the parties cannot pretend to contract under one law in order to validate an agreement that clearly has its closest connection with another law. If, after having discovered that one particular provision was void under the proper law, they were to try to evade its consequences by claiming that the provision was subject to another legal system, their claim should not be considered as a bona fide expression of their intentions."[24]

---

[17] *Astro Venturoso Compania Naviera v. Hellenic Shipyards SA* [1983] 2 Lloyd's Rep. 12.

[18] *James Miller and Partners Ltd v. Whitworth Street Estates (Manchester) Ltd* [1970] A.C. 583, 603, 614; *Black Clawson International Ltd v. Papierwerke Waldhof-Aschaffenburg A.G.* [1981] 2 Lloyd's Rep. 151, 153; *E.I. du Pont de Nemours v. Agnew* [1987] 2 Lloyd's Rep. 585, 592; *Libyan Arab Foreign Bank v. Bankers Trust Co.* [1989] Q.B. 728, 747. cf. *Armar Shipping Co. Ltd v. Caisse Algérienne* [1981] 1 W.L.R. 207, 216. As to the position under the Rome Convention, see *post*, § 31–054.

[19] See, *e.g. Mackender v. Feldia A.G.* [1967] 2 Q.B. 590; *Compagnie d'Armement Maritime SA v. Compagnie Tunisienne de Navigation SA* [1971] A.C. 572.

[20] *Compagnie d'Armement Maritime SA v. Compagnie Tunisienne de Navigation SA* [1969] 1 W.L.R. 1338 (revd. on a different view of the facts [1971] A.C. 572). Mere difficulty in ascertaining the chosen law will not render the choice ineffective: see, *e.g. The Blue Wave* [1982] 1 Lloyd's Rep. 151; *Star Shipping SA v. China National Foreign Trade Transportation Corpn.* [1993] 2 Lloyd's Rep. 445.

[21] *Mackender v. Feldia A.G.* [1967] 2 Q.B. 590, 598, 603, 605; *Chevron International Oil Co. Ltd v. A/S Sea Team* [1983] 2 Lloyd's Rep. 356, 358–458.

[22] See *Compagnia Naviera Micro SA v. Shipley International Inc.* [1982] 2 Lloyd's Rep. 351. This is the position under the Rome Convention, Arts. 3(4) and 8: see *post*, § 31–055.

[23] *Vita Food Products Inc. v. Unus Shipping Co. Ltd* [1939] A.C. 277, 290.

[24] Cheshire and North, *Private International Law* (11th ed., 1987) p. 454; see also, *Dicey & Morris on the Conflict of Laws* (11th ed., 1987), pp. 1175–1176. And see *Boissevain v. Weil* [1949] 1 K.B. 482, 490 (affd. on other grounds [1950] A.C. 327); *English v. Donnelly*, 1958 S.C. 494; *Kay's Leasing Corporation Pty Ltd v. Fletcher* (1964) 116 C.L.R. 124, 143–144; *Golden Acres Ltd v. Queensland Estates Ltd* [1969] St.R.Qd. 378 (affd. on different grounds *sub nom. Freehold Land Investments Ltd v. Queensland Estates Ltd* (1970) 123 C.L.R. 418); *Nike Information Systems Ltd v. Avac Systems Ltd* (1979) 105 D.L.R. (3d) 455; *Greenshields Inc. v. Johnston* (1981) 119 D.L.R. (3d) 714 (appeal dismissed, (1981) 131 D.L.R. (3d) 234); *Bank of Montreal v. Snoxell* (1982) 143 D.L.R. (3d) 349.

Secondly, it has been said "that there must be no reason for avoiding [the choice] on the ground of public policy,"[25] a limitation which is merely an example of the general principle that a foreign law will not be enforced if it offends English public policy.[26] Thirdly, it has sometimes been suggested that some sort of connection may possibly have to exist between the transaction and the chosen system of law, other than the mere fact that that law has been chosen.[27] The better view appears to be that no such connection need exist, though the absence of such a connection may be evidence that the choice of law is not "bona fide and legal" as described above.[28]

Statutory limitations. The power to choose a proper law may be restricted by statute. Thus, for example, the Unfair Contract Terms Act 1977 makes provision to prevent the use of choice of law clauses to evade the controls on exemption clauses imposed by the Act.[29] The controls cannot be evaded by the choice of the law of a country outside the United Kingdom as the governing law, if it either appears that the choice of law was imposed wholly or mainly to enable the party imposing it to evade the operation of the Act,[30] or where one of the parties dealt as consumer[31] and he was then habitually resident in the United Kingdom and the essential steps for the making of the contract were taken in the United Kingdom.[32] However, the controls in the 1977 Act do not apply where the law applicable to the contract is the law of a part of the United Kingdom only by reason of the choice of the parties,[33] nor do they apply to "international supply contracts."[34] Not all English statutes which express stringent social policy contain (as does the Unfair Contract Terms Act[35]) any indication as to whether their provisions override a choice of a foreign law. Whether any particular

31–007

---

[25] *Vita Food Products Inc. v. Unus Shipping Co. Ltd* [1939] A.C. 277, 290.

[26] See generally *Dicey & Morris on the Conflict of Laws* (12th ed., 1993), pp. 88–96, 1277–1284; Cheshire and North, *Private International Law* (12th ed.), pp. 128–137, 503–504. And see *post*, §§ 31–065, 31–160—31–162.

[27] *Boissevain v. Weil* [1949] 1 K.B. 482, 490 (affd. on other grounds [1950] A.C. 327); *Re Helbert Wagg & Co. Ltd's Claim* [1956] Ch. 323, 341; *The Fehmarn* [1958] 1 W.L.R. 159. See also *The Hollandia* [1983] 1 A.C. 565, 576.

[28] *Vita Food Products Inc. v. Unus Shipping Co. Ltd* [1939] A.C. 277, 290; *British Controlled Oilfields v. Stagg* [1921] W.N. 31. There will often be good commercial grounds for choosing a geographically unconnected system, as, *e.g.* where the parties select a particular system of law because it is neutral: *cf. Steel Authority of India Ltd v. Hind Metals Inc.* [1984] 1 Lloyd's Rep. 405, 409; *Akai Pty. Ltd v. People's Insurance Co. Ltd* [1998] 1 Lloyd's Rep. 90.

[29] For detailed discussion, see *Benjamin's Sale of Goods* (5th ed., 1997), §§ 25–084–25–094, 25–132—25–133; *Dicey & Morris on the Conflict of Laws* (12th ed., 1993), pp. 1296–1297, 1330–1332.

[30] Unfair Contract Terms Act 1977, s.27(2)(a).

[31] *ibid.* s.12.

[32] *ibid,* s.27(2)(b).

[33] *ibid.* s.27(1). See *Surzur Overseas Ltd v. Ocean Reliance Shipping Co. Ltd* [1997] C.L. 318. And see *ante*, §14–104 and *post*, § 31–064. Note a similar provision in the (Australian) Insurance Contracts Act 1984, s.8, as to which see *Akai Pty. Ltd v. The People's Insurance Co. Ltd* (1997) 141 A.L.R. 374 *cf. Akai Pty Ltd v. People's Insurance Co. Ltd* [1998] 1 Lloyd's Rep 90. See also Late Payment of Commercial Debts (Interest) Act 1998, s.12, *post*, §§ 31–142—31–145.

[34] *ibid.* s.26.

[35] See too, Council Directive 93/13/EEC of April 5, 1993 on unfair terms in consumer contracts, [1993] O.J. L 95/29, Art. 6(2), implemented in the United Kingdom in the Unfair Terms in Consumer Contracts Regulations 1994 (S.I. 1994 No. 3159), Reg. 7. See *ante*, § 15–072.

statute, or provision thereof, has such an effect ultimately depends on the construction of the statute.[36]

31–008   **Incorporation by reference.**[37] There is a necessary distinction to be drawn between an express selection by the parties of the proper law to govern the whole contract and the incorporation into the contract of the provisions of some foreign legal system to govern some particular incident of the contract, such as the time at which property or risk should pass under a contract for the sale of goods. In these circumstances the provisions of the foreign law become terms of the contract and the reference to the foreign rules is a shorthand method of incorporating these rules into the contract rather than including a verbatim statement of the rules in the contract.[38] Nevertheless, the question whether a rule of foreign law has been effectively incorporated is a matter for the proper law of the contract. The importance of the distinction between selection of the proper law and incorporation of provisions of a foreign law into the contract by reference is seen most clearly where there is a change in the foreign law between the date of the contract and the time of the proceedings. The proper law selected is normally that of the country in question as existing from time to time with the changes that may befall it,[39] whilst if the provisions of a foreign law are incorporated they become terms of the contract as at the date of incorporation even though such foreign provisions may later be repealed or amended.[40]

31–009   **Implied choice of law.** Where there is no, or no valid, express choice of the proper law in the contract, the court may, nevertheless, be able to conclude that the parties have by implication (or by inference) come to an agreement[41] as to what should be the proper law.[42] Such an implication may be derived from a variety of factors surrounding the contract, the most usual being jurisdiction or

---

[36] See, *e.g. The Hollandia* [1983] A.C. 565 (no freedom to avoid operation of Carriage of Goods by Sea Act 1971 by choice of law clause); *English v. Donnelly*, 1958 S.C. 494 (Scottish hire-purchase legislation mandatory in effect); *Chiron Corpn. v. Organon Teknika (No. 2)* [1993] F.S.R. 567 (Patents Act 1977, s.44 applies to contract governed by foreign law); *D R Insurance Co. v. Central National Insurance Co.* [1996] 1 Lloyd's Rep. 74 (Insurance Companies Act 1982 applies to reinsurance contracts whatever their proper law). As to the application of the Consumer Credit Act 1974 and orders made thereunder, see *Dicey & Morris on the Conflict of Laws* (12th ed., 1993), pp. 1297–1298 and on the general question, *ibid.* pp. 1239–1241; Cheshire and North, *Private International Law* (12th ed., 1992), pp. 499–503.

[37] *Dicey & Morris op. cit.* pp. 1222–1223.

[38] *Ex p. Dever re Suse and Sibeth* (1887) 18 Q.B.D. 660; *Dobell & Co. v. Steamship Rossmore Co.* [1895] 2 Q.B. 408; *Vita Food Products Inc. v. Unus Shipping Co. Ltd* [1939] A.C. 277; *Ocean Steamship Co. Ltd v. Queensland State Wheat Board* [1941] 1 Q.B. 402; *Re Helbert Wagg & Co Ltd's Claim* [1956] Ch. 323; *Amin Rasheed Shipping Corpn. v. Kuwait Insurance Co.* [1984] A.C. 50, 69–70; *D R Insurance Co. v. Central Insurance Co.* [1996] 1 Lloyd's Rep. 74, 81; *The Stolt Sydness* [1996] 1 Lloyd's Rep. 273.

[39] *Re Chesterman's Trusts* [1923] 2 Ch. 466; *R v. International Trustee for the Protection of Bondholders A.G.* [1937] A.C. 500; *Kahler v. Midland Bank Ltd* [1950] A.C. 24; *Zivnostenska Banka v. Frankman* [1950] A.C. 57; *Jabbour v. Custodian of Israeli Absentee Property* [1954] 1 W.L.R. 139; *Re Helbert Wagg & Co. Ltd's Claim* [1956] Ch. 323; *Rossano v. Manufacturers' Life Insurance Co.* [1963] 2 Q.B. 352, 362.

[40] *Vita Food Products Inc. v. Unus Shipping Co. Ltd* [1939] A.C. 277, 286.

[41] There must be actual agreement on the point: *James Miller and Partners Ltd v. Whitworth Street Estates (Manchester) Ltd* [1970] A.C. 583, 603.

[42] *R. v. International Trustee for the Protection of Bondholders A.G.* [1937] A.C. 500, 529–531; *Re United Railways of the Havana and Regla Warehouses* [1960] Ch. 52 (affd. *sub nom. Tomkinson v. First Pennsylvania Banking and Trust Co.* [1961] A.C. 1007); *James Miller and Partners Ltd v. Whitworth Street Estates (Manchester) Ltd* [1970] A.C. 583, 603; *Amin Rasheed Shipping Corpn. v. Kuwait Insurance Co.* [1984] A.C. 50.

arbitration clauses. If the parties agree that the courts of a particular country shall have jurisdiction over any claims made under the contract, that will give rise to a strong implication that the parties have chosen the law of that country as the proper law.[43] Similarly, if the contract contains a clause whereby the parties agree that any disputes shall be submitted to arbitration in a particular country, there is a powerful,[44] though not conclusive,[45] implication that the parties have selected the law of the country of arbitration as the proper law. A variety of other factors may also, in appropriate cases, give rise to an implication that the parties have made a choice of the proper law.

Relevant factors. Such factors have included the nature of the particular transaction,[46] the form of the documents made with respect to the transaction,[47] the style and terminology in which the contract is drafted,[48] the use of a particular language[49] (though this is a factor of minor importance[50]), the currency in which **31–010**

---

[43] *Hamlyn & Co. v. Talisker Distillery* [1894] A.C. 202; *N.V. Kwik Hoo Tong Handel Maatschappij v. James Finlay & Co* [1927] A.C. 604, 608; *Evans Marshall & Co. Ltd v. Bertola SA* [1973] 1 W.L.R. 349, 364; *The Komninos S.* [1991] 1 Lloyd's Rep. 370. The effect of such a clause cannot be by-passed by attempting to formulate a claim in tort rather than in contract: *The Sindh* [1975] 1 Lloyd's Rep. 372.

[44] *Hamlyn & Co. v. Talisker Distillery, supra; Spurrier v. La Cloche* [1902] A.C. 446; *N.V. Kwik Hoo Tong Handel Maatschappij v. James Finlay & Co* [1927] A.C. 604, 608; *Compagnie d'Armement Maritime SA v. Compagnie Tunisienne de Navigation SA* [1971] A.C. 572; *The SLS Everest* [1981] 2 Lloyd's Rep. 389; *Compania Naviera Micro SA v. Shipley International Inc.* [1982] 2 Lloyd's Rep. 351; *Astro Venturoso Compania Naviera v. Hellenic Shipyards SA* [1983] 1 Lloyd's Rep. 12; *Steel Authority of India Ltd v. Hind Metals Inc.* [1984] 1 Lloyd's Rep. 405.

[45] *Compagnie d'Armement Maritime SA v. Compagnie Tunisienne de Navigation SA, supra* (disapproving *Tzortzis v. Monark Link A/B* [1968] 1 W.L.R. 406 where the implication to be derived from an arbitration clause was treated as virtually conclusive); *The Elli 2* [1985] 2 Lloyd's Rep. 107, 117; *Star Shipping A.S. v. China National Trade Transportation Corpn.* [1993] 2 Lloyd's Rep. 445. Where a clause provides for arbitration in a country other than that which is held to be that of the proper law, the curial law of the arbitration proceedings is that of the arbitration forum: *James Miller and Partners Ltd v. Whitworth Street Estates (Manchester) Ltd, supra.* There is no reason why the curial law of an arbitration has to be fixed at the time of the arbitration agreement: *Star Shipping A.S. v. China National Foreign Trade Transportation Corpn., supra.* On conflict of laws' aspects of arbitration see *Dicey & Morris on the Conflict of Laws* (12th ed., 1993), Chap. 16.

[46] *Trade Indemnity plc v. Forsakringsaktiebolaget Njord* [1995] 1 All E.R. 796 (strong presumption that reinsurance contract written on London market is written on the basis of an implied or imputed English proper law); *D R Insurance Co. v. Central National Insurance Co.* [1996] 1 Lloyd's Rep. 74 (when parties enter a particular market in order to transact business they can usually be taken to intend that their relationship will be governed by the system of law in force in that market unless they provide some clear indication to the contrary). *cf. Commercial Union Assurance Co. plc v. N R G Victory Reinsurance Ltd* [1998] 1 Lloyd's Rep. 80, 84–85 affd. [1998] 2 All E.R. 434 (New York arbitration clause and service of suit clause indicated contrary intention).

[47] *Chamberlain v. Napier* (1880) 15 Ch.D. 614; *Re Missouri Steamship Co.* (1889) 42 Ch.D. 321; *Rossano v. Manufacturers' Life Insurance Co.* [1963] 2 Q.B. 352; *James Miller and Partners Ltd v. Whitworth Street Estates (Manchester) Ltd* [1970] A.C. 583; *cf. N.V. Handel My. J. Smits Import-Export v. English Exporters (London) Ltd* [1955] 2 Lloyd's Rep. 69, 72 (affd. [1955] 2 Lloyd's Rep. 317); *Compagnie d'Armement Maritime SA v. Compagnie Tunisienne de Navigation SA* [1971] A.C. 572, 583.

[48] *Chatenay v. Brazilian Submarine Telegraph Co. Ltd* [1891] 1 Q.B. 79, 82; *Rossano v. Manufacturers' Life Insurance Co., supra; James Miller and Partners Ltd v. Whitworth Street Estates (Manchester) Ltd, supra,* at 603, 608, 611–612; *Amin Rasheed Shipping Corpn. v. Kuwait Insurance Co.* [1984] A.C. 50.

[49] *Chatenay v. Brazilian Submarine Telegraph Co. Ltd, supra; St. Pierre v. South American Stores (Gath and Chaves) Ltd* [1937] 2 All E.R. 349.

[50] *Compagnie d'Armement Maritime SA v. Compagnie Tunisienne de Navigation SA, supra,* at 583, 594; *Sayers v. International Drilling Co. N.V.* [1971] 1 W.L.R. 1176, 1183–1184, 1186; *Coast Lines Ltd v. Hudig and Veder Chartering N.V.* [1972] 2 Q.B. 34, 47, 50.

payment is to be made,[51] the use of a "follow London" clause,[52] the nature and location of the subject-matter of the contract,[53] the residence[54] and, occasionally, the nationality[55] of the parties, a connection with a preceding transaction,[56] or, possibly, the fact that one of the parties is a government.[57] If one or more terms of the contract would be valid under one of two possible governing laws but invalid under the other, there is authority in favour of the view that the parties may be taken to have intended that their contract should be governed by the system of law by which it is valid.[58] However, it would seem that the fact that the contract is valid under one system of law is only evidence and not conclusive evidence as to the intention of the parties.[59]

31–011   **No choice of the proper law.** In cases where it is not possible to conclude that the parties have made an express or implied choice of the proper law, then it is necessary to abandon any reference to what the parties intended[60] and look for the law "with which the transaction has the closest and most real connection,"[61]

---

[51] *R. v. International Trustee for the Protection of Bondholders A.G.* [1937] A.C. 500, 553; *The Assunzione* [1954] P. 150; *Rossano v. Manufacturers' Life Insurance Co., supra; Coast Lines Ltd v. Hudig and Veder Chartering N.V.* [1972] 2 Q.B. 34, 47, 50; *cf. Re Helbert Wagg & Co. Ltd's Claim* [1956] Ch. 323; *Sayers v. International Drilling Co. N.V., supra,* at 1183, 1186.

[52] *Armadora Occidental SA v. Horace Mann Insurance Co.* [1977] 1 W.L.R. 1098.

[53] *Lloyd v. Guibert* (1865) L.R. 1 Q.B. 115, 122–123; *British South Africa Co. v. De Beers Consolidated Mines Ltd* [1910] 1 Ch. 354, 383.

[54] *Jacobs v. Crédit Lyonnais* (1884) 12 Q.B.D. 589; *Keiner v. Keiner* [1952] 1 All E.R. 643.

[55] *Re Missouri Steamship Co.* (1889) 42 Ch.D. 321, 328–329; *Sayers v. International Drilling Co. N.V., supra,* at 1183.

[56] *e.g. The Adriatic* [1931] P. 241, 247; *R. v. International Trustee for the Protection of Bondholders A.G.* [1937] A.C. 500, 554, 558; *The Freights Queen* [1977] 1 Lloyd's Rep. 140; *The Broken Hill Pty. Co. Ltd v. Theodore Zenakis* [1982] 2 Lloyd's Rep. 304; *The Elli 2* [1985] 1 Lloyd's Rep. 107; *Turkiye Is Bankasi A.S. v. Bank of China* [1993] 1 Lloyd's Rep. 132; *Wahda Bank v. Arab Bank plc* [1996] 1 Lloyd's Rep. 470; *cf. The Metamorphosis* [1953] 1 W.L.R. 543; *Forsikringsaktieselskapet Vesta v. Butcher* [1989] A.C. 852; *Attock Cement Co. Ltd v. Romanian Bank for Foreign Trade* [1989] 1 W.L.R. 1147.

[57] *R. v. International Trustee for the Protection of Bondholders A.G.* [1937] A.C. 500, 554, 557.

[58] *P. & O. Steam Navigation Co. v. Shand* (1865) 3 Moo. P.C. (N.S.) 272; *Re Missouri Steamship Co.* (1889) 42 Ch.D. 321, 341; *South African Breweries Ltd v. King* [1899] 2 Ch. 173, 180–181; *Coast Lines Ltd v. Hudig and Veder Chartering N.V.* [1972] 2 Q.B. 34, 44, 48; *S.C.F. Finance Co. Ltd v. Masri* [1986] 1 Lloyd's Rep. 293, 304.

[59] *British South Africa Co. v. De Beers Consolidated Mines Ltd* [1910] 2 Ch. 502, 513 (not of "much weight"); *Sayers v. International Drilling Co. N.V.* [1971] 1 W.L.R. 1176, 1184 (a "pointer," the importance of which "must not be exaggerated"); *Coast Lines Ltd v. Hudig and Veder Chartering N.V., supra,* at 50–51; contrast *Monterosso Shipping Co. Ltd v. International Transport Workers Federation* [1982] I.C.R. 675, 683–685 ("irrelevant").

[60] *Amin Rasheed Shipping Corpn. v. Kuwait Insurance Co.* [1984] A.C. 50. Rejection of any reference to the parties' intentions means that the fact that the contract would be valid under one system of law but not another is definitely irrelevant: *Monterosso Shipping Co. Ltd v. International Transport Workers Federation* [1982] I.C.R. 675, 683–685. Opinions may differ as to whether a case presents an example of "implied" choice or "no" choice: compare the contrasting views of Lord Diplock, speaking for the majority in *Amin Rasheed Shipping Corpn. v. Kuwait Insurance Co.* [1984] A.C. 50, 62–65, and Lord Wilberforce, *ibid.* at 69; see also *D R Insurance Co. v. Central National Insurance Co.* [1996] 1 Lloyd's Rep. 74.

[61] *Bonython v. Commonwealth of Australia* [1951] A.C. 201, 219; *Tomkinson v. First Pennsylvania Banking and Trust Co.* [1961] A.C. 1007, 1068, 1081–1082; *James Miller and Partners Ltd v. Whitworth Street Estates (Manchester) Ltd* [1970] A.C. 583; *Compagnie d'Armement Maritime SA v. Compagnie Tunisienne de Navigation SA* [1971] A.C. 572; *Coast Lines Ltd v. Hudig and Veder Chartering N.V., supra; Offshore International SA v. Banco Central SA* [1977] 1 W.L.R. 399; *Power Curber International Ltd v. National Bank of Kuwait* [1981] 1 W.L.R. 1233; *Amin Rasheed Shipping Corpn. v. Kuwait Insurance Co.* [1984] A.C. 50, 61.

on objective grounds.[62] In this regard, all the facts and circumstances of the contract should be examined.[63] Although the weight to be attached to relevant facts and circumstances will vary from case to case, the following may be mentioned as representative. The place where the contract was made,[64] the place where the contract has to be performed,[65] the nature of the legal personality of the parties,[66] the place of residence[67] or business[68] of the parties, the nature, subject-matter[69] and standard terms[70] of the contract, the situation of the funds which are available for the discharge[71] or security of the obligation,[72] the place where a bank must perform its obligation under a letter of credit,[73] or whether the contract

---

[62] Where there is no choice of law by the parties, some older authorities purport to search for the "presumed intention" of the parties: see, *e.g. Lloyd v. Guibert* (1865) L.R. 1 Q.B. 115, 120–123; *R. v. International Trustee for the Protection of Bondholders A.G.* [1937] A.C. 500; *Mount Albert Borough Council v. Australasian Temperance and General Mutual Life Assurance Society* [1938] A.C. 224. In carrying out this exercise there was a tendency to resort to rebuttable presumptions, in favour, depending on the circumstances of the case, of, *e.g.* the law of the place of contracting (*Jacobs v. Crédit Lyonnais* (1884) 12 Q.B.D. 589), the law of the place of performance (*Re Missouri Steamship Co.* (1889) 42 Ch.D. 321; *Benaim & Co. v. Debono* [1924] A.C. 514), the law of the flag (*Lloyd v. Guibert, supra; The Assunzione* [1954] P. 150) or the *lex situs* of an immovable (*British South Africa Co. v. De Beers Consolidated Mines* [1910] 2 Ch. 502). The use of presumptions was rejected in *Coast Lines Ltd v. Hudig and Veder Chartering N.V.* [1972] 2 Q.B. 34, 44, 47, 50. *cf.* the position under the Rome Convention, *post*, §§ 31–066—31–085.

[63] *e.g. The Assunzione* [1954] P. 150; *Coast Lines Ltd v. Hudig and Veder Chartering N.V.* [1972] 2 Q.B. 34.

[64] *P. & O. Steam Navigation Co. v. Shand* (1865) 3 Moo. P.C. (N.S.) 272; *Lloyd v. Guibert* (1865) L.R. 1 Q.B. 115, 122; *Jacobs v. Crédit Lyonnais* (1884) 12 Q.B.D. 589, 596–597, 600; *Re Missouri Steamship Co.* (1889) 42 Ch.D. 321, 326, 338; *British South Africa Co. v. De Beers Consolidated Mines Ltd* [1910] 1 Ch. 354, 381; *Kahler v. Midland Bank Ltd* [1950] A.C. 24; *Zivnostenska Banka v. Frankman* [1950] A.C. 57; *Cantieri Navali Riuniti SpA v. N.V. Omne Justitia* [1985] 2 Lloyd's Rep. 428, 433–435; *cf. Amin Rasheed Shipping Corpn. v. Kuwait Insurance Co.* [1984] A.C. 50, 62.

[65] *e.g. Lloyd v. Guibert, supra*, at 122: *Re Missouri Steamship Co., supra*, at 341; *Chatenay v. Brazilian Submarine Telegraph Co.* [1891] 1 Q.B. 79, 83; *Hamlyn & Co. v. Talisker Distillery* [1894] A.C. 202; *Ralli Bros. v. Compania Naviera Sota y Aznar* [1920] 1 K.B. 614, 630, 631 (affd. [1920] 2 K.B. 287); *Benaim & Co v. Debono* [1924] A.C. 514, 520; *Adelaide Electric Supply Co. Ltd v. Prudential Assurance Co. Ltd* [1934] A.C. 122, 145, 151; *James Miller and Partners Ltd v. Whitworth Street Estates (Manchester) Ltd* [1970] A.C. 583; *cf. Amin Rasheed Shipping Corpn. v. Kuwait Insurance Co., supra*, at 62–63.

[66] *R. v. International Trustee for the Protection of Bondholders A.G.* [1937] A.C. 500, 531, 557, 574; *National Bank of Australia Ltd v. Scottish Union and National Insurance Co.* [1952] A.C. 493; *The Assunzione, supra.*

[67] *Jacobs v. Crédit Lyonnais* (1884) 12 Q.B.D. 589, 600, 602.

[68] *Re Anglo-Austrian Bank* [1920] 1 Ch. 69.

[69] *e.g.* whether it is a contract relating to land (*British South Africa Co. v. De Beers Consolidated Mines Ltd* [1910] 1 Ch. 354, 383) or a contract relating to a marriage settlement (*Re Fitzgerald* [1904] 1 Ch. 573, 587) or a contract of affreightment (*Re Missouri Steamship Co.* (1889) 42 Ch.D. 321, 327); and see *Re United Railways of the Havana and Regla Warehouses Ltd* [1960] Ch. 52, 91.

[70] *Gill and Duffus Landauer Ltd v. London Export Corpn.* [1982] 2 Lloyd's Rep. 627, 629.

[71] *Spurrier v. La Cloche* [1902] A.C. 446, 450.

[72] *Bonython v. Commonwealth of Australia* [1951] A.C. 201, 221 (loan secured on public revenue of self-governing colony).

[73] *Offshore International SA v. Banco Central SA* [1977] 1 W.L.R. 399; *Power Curber International Ltd v. National Bank of Kuwait* [1981] 1 W.L.R. 1233; *Turkiye Is Bankasi A.S. v. Bank of China* [1993] 1 Lloyd's Rep. 132; *Minories Finance Ltd v. Afribank Nigeria Ltd* [1995] 1 Lloyd's Rep. 134; *Bank of Credit and Commerce Hong Kong Ltd v. Sonali Bank* [1995] 1 Lloyd's Rep. 227; *Batstone & Firminger Ltd v. Nasima Enterprises (Nigeria) Ltd* [1996] C.L.C. 1902, 1910. See also *Bank of Bardoa v. Vysya Bank Ltd* [1994] 2 Lloyd's Rep. 87 (a case on the Rome Convention, *post*, § 31–072). *cf. Attock Cement Co. Ltd v. Romanian Bank for Foreign Trade* [1989] 1 W.L.R. 1147; *Wahda Bank v. Arab Bank plc* [1996] 1 Lloyd's Rep. 470.

is closely linked with another contract containing a choice of law clause.[74]

31–012 **Connection of the transaction with a system of law.** The proper law is usually defined as "the system of law with which the transaction has the closest and most real connection."[75] However, it is not wholly clear whether the connection is to be with a "system of law" or with a "country." A number of earlier cases have preferred the latter criterion[76] but the weight of authority supports a connection with a "system of law."[77] The difference may be important when the geographical factors of the contract point to one country, whilst the legal factors point towards the legal system of another country as in the case of a contract to do building work in Scotland, the contractual documents for which were in English form.[78] It may be particularly relevant that one system of law under consideration has no provision dealing with the matter in issue.[79] Indeed, a more recent suggestion is that the two tests should be combined,[80] though this may well be difficult when they point to different solutions.[81]

31–013 **Transaction not contract.** It has been suggested that the connection with the system of law, or country, should be that of the "transaction" contemplated by the contract. This means the connection should be with what is to be done under the contract rather than just with the technical forms of the contract.[82]

31–014 **Splitting of the contract.**[83] Although almost all the incidents of a contract are governed by the proper law,[84] it has to be considered whether that proper law is to be the same for each incident and whether the obligations of both parties to the contract are to be governed by the same proper law, for it has been suggested that: "The fact that one aspect of a contract is to be governed by the law of one country does not necessarily mean that the law is to be the proper law of the contract as a whole."[85] However the basic rule is that there will normally be no

---

[74] *The Njegos* [1936] P. 90; *The Broken Hill Proprietary Co. v. Xenakis* [1982] 2 Lloyd's Rep. 304; *Forsikringsaktieselskapet Vesta v. Butcher* [1988] 3 W.L.R. 565 (affd. on different grounds [1989] A.C. 852); *Mitsubishi Corpn. v. Alafouzos* [1988] 1 Lloyd's Rep. 191.

[75] *Bonython v. Commonwealth of Australia, supra,* at 219.

[76] *Boissevain v. Weil* [1949] 1 K.B. 482, 490; *Tomkinson v. First Pennsylvania Banking and Trust Co.* [1961] A.C. 1007, 1068; *Philipson-Stow v. I.R.C.* [1961] A.C. 727, 760.

[77] *Bonython v. Commonwealth of Australia, supra,* at 219; *Rossano v. Manufacturers' Life Insurance Co.* [1963] 2 Q.B. 352, 361, 368–369; *James Miller and Partners Ltd v. Whitworth Street Estates (Manchester) Ltd* [1970] A.C. 583; *Coast Lines Ltd v. Hudig and Veder Chartering N.V.* [1972] 2 Q.B. 34, 44, 46; *Amin Rasheed Shipping Corpn. v. Kuwait Insurance Co.* [1984] A.C. 50, 60, 71.

[78] *James Miller and Partners Ltd v. Whitworth Street Estates (Manchester) Ltd, supra.*

[79] *Islamic Arab Insurance Co. v. Saudi Egyptian American Reinsurance Co.* [1987] 1 Lloyd's Rep. 315, 320.

[80] *James Miller and Partners Ltd v. Whitworth Street Estates (Manchester) Ltd* [1970] A.C. 583, 603–604, 605–606, 614–616; *Compagnie d'Armement Maritime SA v. Compagnie Tunisienne de Navigation SA* [1971] A.C. 572, 583; *Coast Lines Ltd v. Hudig and Veder Chartering N.V.* [1972] 2 Q.B. 34, 50; *Monterosso Shipping Co. Ltd v. International Transport Workers Federation* [1982] I.C.R. 675. For the position under the Rome Convention, see *post,* § 31–023.

[81] *e.g. James Miller and Partners Ltd v. Whitworth Street Estates (Manchester) Ltd, supra.*

[82] *Coast Lines Ltd v. Hudig and Veder Chartering N.V., supra,* at 46.

[83] See McLachlan (1990) 61 B.Y.I.L. 311. For the position under the Rome Convention, see *post,* §§ 31–052—31–053.

[84] See *post,* §§ 31–110 *et seq.*

[85] *Re United Railways of the Havana and Regla Warehouses* [1960] Ch. 52, 92; and see *Re Helbert Wagg & Co. Ltd's Claim* [1956] Ch. 323, 340.

such "scission," for as Lord MacDermott said [86]: "It is doubtless true to say that the courts of this country will not split the contract in this sense readily or without good reason." Nevertheless, there is some authority in the case of banking accounts of different aspects being governed by different laws[87]; and where a contract of reinsurance (governed by English law) was deemed to be "back to back" with the insurance contract (governed by Norwegian law), a clause in the former was construed as being intended by the parties to have the same effect as under Norwegian law.[88] The parties may, however, agree expressly that different contractual issues shall be governed by different laws.[89] The different obligations of the two parties to a contract will be governed by the same proper law[90] unless they have made an agreement, express or implied, to the contrary.[91]

Renvoi. The doctrine of renvoi[92] has no place in the law of contract.[93] Thus the proper law of the contract means the domestic rules of that law and not its rules of the conflict of laws. **31–015**

3. THE ROME CONVENTION[94]

(a) *In General*

History and purpose.[95] In 1980 the then Member States of the European Community concluded a Convention on the Law Applicable to Contractual **31–016**

---

[86] *Kahler v. Midland Bank Ltd* [1950] A.C. 24, 42.

[87] *Libyan Arab Foreign Bank v. Bankers Trust Co.* [1989] Q.B. 728; *Libyan Arab Foreign Bank v. Manufacturers Hanover Trust Co.* [1988] 2 Lloyd's Rep. 494; and see *Chamberlain v. Napier* (1880) 15 Ch.D. 614; *British South Africa Co. v. De Beers Consolidated Mines Ltd* [1910] 1 Ch. 354, 383; Lord MacDermott, dissenting, in *Kahler v. Midland Bank Ltd* [1950] A.C. 24, 42; *Re Helbert Wagg & Co. Ltd's Claim* [1956] Ch. 323, 340; *Sayers v. International Drilling Co. N.V.* [1971] 1 W.L.R. 1176, 1180–1181.

[88] *Forsikringsaktieselskapet Vesta v. Butcher* [1988] 3 W.L.R. 565 (affd. on different grounds [1989] A.C. 852).

[89] *Hamlyn & Co. v. Talisker Distillery* [1894] A.C. 202; though see *Armar Shipping Co. Ltd v. Caisse Algérienne d'Assurance* [1981] 1 W.L.R. 207, 216. Under the Uniform Laws on International Sales Act 1967, the parties are permitted to choose the uniform law to govern those aspects of their contract covered by that Act: Sched. 1, Arts. 2 and 4. However, other aspects of their contract of sale of goods will be governed by the normal choice of law rules of the conflict of laws.

[90] *Zivnostenska Banka v. Frankman* [1950] A.C. 57, 83.

[91] *Re Helbert Wagg & Co. Ltd's Claim, supra*, at 340.

[92] *Dicey & Morris on the Conflict of Laws* (12th ed., 1993), Chap. 5; Cheshire and North, *Private International Law* (12th ed., 1992), Chap. 5.

[93] *Amin Rasheed Shipping Corpn. v. Kuwait Insurance Co.* [1984] A.C. 50, 61–62; *E.I. du Pont de Nemours v. Agnew* [1987] 2 Lloyd's Rep. 582, 592. See also *Macmillan Inc. v. Bishopsgate Investment Trust plc (No. 3)* [1995] 1 W.L.R. 987, 1008 (Millett J.) affd. on other grounds, [1996] 1 W.L.R. 387, see esp., Staughton L.J., at 405. And see *post*, § 31–027.

[94] *Dicey & Morris on the Conflict of Laws* (12th ed., 1993), Chaps. 32 and 33; Cheshire and North, *Private International Law* (12th ed., 1992), Chap. 18; Kaye, *The New Private International Law of Contract of the European Community* (1993); Plender, *The European Contracts Convention* (1991); Lasok and Stone, *Conflict of Laws in the European Community* (1987), Chap. 9; North (ed.), *Contract Conflicts* (1982); Fletcher, *Conflict of Laws and European Community Law* (1982), Chap. 5; Anton, *Private International Law* (2nd ed., 1990), Chap. 11; Diamond (1986) 216 *Recueil des Cours IV,* 233; North (1990) 220 *Recueil des Cours I,* 3, 176–205; North [1980] J.B.L. 392; Morse (1982) 2 Yb.Eur.L. 107; Jaffey (1984) 33 I.C.L.Q. 531; Williams (1986) 35 I.C.L.Q. 1. Extensive bibliographies will be found in Plender *op. cit.* pp. 337–342 and Kaye, *op cit.*, pp. 507–510.

[95] *Dicey & Morris op. cit.* pp. 1191–1194; Cheshire and North *op. cit.* pp. 459–460; Plender *op. cit.* Chap. 1; North in North (ed.), *Contract Conflicts*, pp. 4–9 reprinted in *Essays in Private International Law* (1993), p. 23; Report on the Convention by Professors Giuliano and Lagarde [1980] O.J. C 282/1, 4–8 (hereafter Giuliano-Lagarde Report), as to which see *post*, § 31–019.

Obligations. This Convention (which is known as the Rome Convention) was ratified by the United Kingdom in 1991 and was implemented in United Kingdom law in the Contracts (Applicable Law) Act 1990.[96] The provisions of the 1990 Act which give the force of law in the United Kingdom to the Rome Convention,[97] entered into force on April 1, 1991.[98] Consequently the rules of the Convention will apply to contracts falling within its scope which are entered into after that date.[99] Schedule 3 to the Act sets out the text of the Brussels Protocol which enables questions concerning the interpretation of the Rome Convention to be referred to the European Court of Justice.[1] The Brussels Protocol is not, as yet, in force.[2]

31–017   The Rome Convention cannot be said to have been received with unequivocal enthusiasm in the United Kingdom.[3] Indeed there was much to be said for the view that the rules for choice of law in contract which had been developed by the common law constituted one of the most satisfactory and acceptable branches of the English conflict of laws.[4] This notwithstanding, the purpose of the Convention is, at a general level, to establish uniform choice of law rules so as to endeavour to achieve two principal aims. First, it was suggested that such uniformity was a necessary step on the route to achieving free movement of goods, services and capital amongst the Member States.[5] Secondly, the Convention was seen as a way of buttressing the work done in the Brussels Convention on Jurisdiction and the Enforcement of Judgments in Civil and Commercial Matters 1968 which is designed to establish uniform rules for the international jurisdiction of courts amongst the Member States.[6] One effect of that Convention is that it "enables the parties, in many matters, to reach agreements assigning jurisdiction and to choose among several courts. The outcome may be that

---

[96] Contracts (Applicable Law) Act 1990, s.2(1). The English text of the Convention is set out in Sched. 1 to the Act "for ease of reference": *ibid.* s.2(4). Each language text is, however, equally authentic: Rome Convention, Art. 33. For the French and German texts, see Plender *op. cit.* pp. 201–237. For French, German, Italian and Dutch texts, see Kaye *op. cit.* pp. 478–505.

[97] Note the power to make reservations to Arts. 7(1) and 10(1)(e) in Art. 22 of the Convention. The U.K. has exercised this power so that Arts. 7(1) and 10(1)(e) do not have the force of law in the United Kingdom: Contracts (Applicable Law) Act 1990, s.2(2). See *post*, §§ 30–059, 31–148.

[98] S.I. 1991 No. 707.

[99] Rome Convention, Art. 17, which provides that the Convention shall apply in a Contracting State to contracts made after the date on which it has entered into force with respect to that State. Accordingly, contracts entered into *on or before* April 1, 1991 will be governed by common law choice of law rules (as to which see *ante*, §§ 31–004—31–015).

[1] See *post*, § 31–018. Sched. 2 to the Act contains the text of the Luxembourg Convention providing for accession to the Rome Convention by Greece. Sched. 3A to the Act contains the text of the Funchal Convention providing for the accession to the Rome Convention by Spain and Portugal (see S.I. 1994 No. 1900) which entered into force for the United Kingdom on December 1, 1997. An Accession Convention for Austria, Finland and Sweden was signed on November 29, 1996 but has not yet entered into force. A consolidated version of the text of the Rome Convention can be found in [1998] O.J. C27/34.

[2] The U.K. has, however, ratified the Protocol.

[3] See F.A. Mann (1983) 32 I.C.L.Q. 265; (1991) 107 L.Q.R. 353; *Hansard*, HL Vol. 515, Cols. 1467–1482; Vol. 517, Cols. 1537–1541. It even provoked correspondence in *The Times*, a rare event in the conflict of laws: see F.A. Mann, *The Times*, December 4, 1989; P.M. North, *The Times*, December 19, 1989.

[4] See *Hansard*, HL Vol. 515, Col. 1482, *per* Lord Goff of Chieveley.

[5] Speech of Director-General of the Internal Market and Approximation of Legislation at the European Commission (Mr. Vogelaar, as to whom see *Hansard*, HL Vol. 515, Col. 1476) quoted in Giuliano-Lagarde Report, p. 5.

[6] [1978] O.J. L 304/77, Cmnd. 7395. See Giuliano-Lagarde Report, p. 5.

preference is given to the court of a State whose law seems to offer a better solution to the proceedings. To prevent this 'forum shopping,' increase legal certainty, and anticipate more easily the law which will be applied, it would be advisable for the rules of conflict to be unified in fields of particular economic importance so that the same law is applied irrespective of the State in which the decision is given."[7] Justification of unification or harmonisation in these terms has not been uncritically accepted.[8] Nevertheless, it cannot be doubted that the Rome Convention has a significant effect in an area of the conflict of laws of great practical importance.

Interpretation: European Court of Justice. As will be seen in what follows, **31–018** virtually all of the difficulties to which the Convention gives rise concern its interpretation. When it enters into force, the Brussels Protocol[9] will confer jurisdiction on the European Court of Justice to give rulings on the interpretation of the Rome Convention, on any conventions for the accession of Member States of the European Communities, and on the Protocol itself.[10] As far as the United Kingdom is concerned, the House of Lords and other courts from which no further appeal is possible[11] and any other United Kingdom court when acting as an appeal court[12] may request a preliminary ruling on a question of interpretation if any of those courts consider that a decision on the question is necessary to enable it to give judgment in a case.[13] No national court is, however, bound to make such a reference.[14] Section 3 of the Contracts (Applicable Law) Act 1990 makes it clear that any question as to the meaning or effect of the Rome Convention shall, if not referred to the European Court in accordance with the Brussels Protocol, be determined in accordance with the principles laid down by, and any relevant decision of, the European Court.[15] There can be little doubt that the European Court will have regard to the objectives and scheme of the Convention in its approach to interpretation and that in so doing it will tend to provide autonomous, uniform meanings for the various terms or concepts used in the Convention.[16] Relevant decisions of the European Court are binding on

---

[7] *ibid.*

[8] Collins (1976) 25 I.C.L.Q. 35, reprinted in Collins *Essays in International Litigation and The Conflict of Laws* (1994), p. 409; Lipstein, in Lipstein (ed.), *Harmonisation of Private International Law by the EEC* (1978), p. 1; Diamond (1986), 216 *Recueil des Cours IV*, 223, 246; Morse (1982) 2 Yb.Eur.L. 107, 108–110.

[9] The U.K. has ratified the Brussels Protocol. A second Protocol (not scheduled to the 1990 Act) is designed to ensure that the European Court has jurisdiction to interpret the Convention even if it is not ratified by all the Member States: for the text, see Plender *op. cit.* pp. 309–310. Both Protocols are the subject of a Report by Professor Tizzano: see [1990] O.J. C 219/1; Plender *op. cit.* pp. 311–331.

[10] Brussels Protocol, Arts. 1 and 2.

[11] *ibid.* Art. 2(a).

[12] *ibid.* Art. 2(b).

[13] *ibid.* Art. 2, Preamble.

[14] *ibid.* Art. 2. *cf.* the position under the Protocol to the Brussels Convention on Jurisdiction and the Enforcement of Judgments in Civil and Commercial Matters 1968, Art. 2(2), by virtue of which an appellate court from which no further appeal is possible is *required* to make a reference to the European Court.

[15] *cf.* Civil Jurisdiction and Judgments Act 1982, s.3(3).

[16] This is the normal practice in cases involving the Brussels Convention, *supra*. See, *e.g. Dicey & Morris op. cit.* pp. 284–288. As to the link between the Brussels Convention and the Rome Convention, see the Preamble to the latter and Case 133/81 *Ivenel v. Schwab* [1982] E.C.R. 1891. See also Forsyth and Moser (1996) 45 I.C.L.Q. 190. It is likely that cases decided by the European Court which do not involve the Rome Convention will provide, where appropriate, persuasive analogies: see Cheshire and North *op. cit.* pp. 465–466. And see *post*, §§ 31–030—31–032.

United Kingdom courts and judicial notice must be taken of any decision of, or expression of opinion by, that court as to the meaning or effect of the Rome Convention in relation to any question that is referred to it.[17]

31–019 **Uniformity of interpretation and application.** Since there is no *obligation* on national courts to refer questions to the European Court, the possibility exists of disparate interpretation amongst those courts. To reduce the likelihood of such a result, Article 18 of the Rome Convention provides that in the interpretation and application of the uniform rules of the Convention, regard shall be had to their international character and to the desirability of achieving uniformity in their interpretation and application.[18] Additionally, if judgments given by the courts of a Contracting State conflict with a judgment as to interpretation given by either the European Court or a court of another Contracting State, power is given, in the Brussels Protocol, to the competent authority of the former Contracting State to request the European Court to give a ruling on the conflict of interpretation.[19] Finally, section 3(3)(a) of the Contracts (Applicable Law) Act 1990 states that the Report on the Convention by Professors Giuliano and Lagarde ("Giuliano-Lagarde Report") may be considered in ascertaining the meaning or effect of any provision of the Convention.[20] The Report will doubtless play a significant role in the interpretation of the Convention if only because it is a document which negotiators representing Member States were able to revise (and into which, it may be noted, the United Kingdom negotiators put revisions[21]).

31–020 **General scope of the Convention.** A number of general questions arise as to the scope of the Convention (as opposed to the specific questions which are included in or excluded from the Convention by the text of the instrument itself[22]).

31–021 **"Laws of different countries".** First, Article 1(1) provides that the rules contained in the Rome Convention "shall apply to contractual obligations in any situation involving a choice between the laws of different countries." According to the Giuliano-Lagarde Report, such situations are those:

---

[17] Contracts (Applicable Law) Act 1990, s.3(2).

[18] See *Egon Oldendorff v. Libera Corp. (No. 2)* [1996] 1 Lloyd's Rep. 380, 387; *Crédit Lyonnais v. New Hampshire Insurance Co.* [1997] 2 Lloyd's Rep. 1, 5, 7. See also Kaye *op. cit.* pp. 355–358.

[19] Art. 3. No competent authority has yet been designated in the U.K. The provision suggests that decisions of courts of other Contracting States may be of, at least, persuasive authority in the U.K. courts which, for this reason, should have regard to them. A joint Declaration to the Brussels Protocol (which does not appear in Sched. 3 to the 1990 Act, but the text of which is reproduced in [1998] O.J. C 27/34, at 50–51 and in Plender *op. cit.* Annex VII) provides a regime whereby Member States agree to exchange information as to decisions by national appellate courts on the Rome Convention through the offices of the European Court.

[20] For the text of the Report, see [1980] O.J. C 282/1; reprinted in North (ed.) *op. cit.* pp. 335–401; Plender *op. cit.* pp. 243–292. The opening words of s.3(3) make it clear that reference to the Report is without prejudice to any other material the court is permitted to look at. Despite the similarities between the Rome Convention and the common law, English courts should not place uncritical reliance on common law decisions in interpreting the Convention: see cases cited *supra*, n. 18; *Dicey & Morris op. cit.* p. 1196; Cheshire and North *op. cit.* pp. 465–466; *cf. Hansard*, HL Vol. 515, Col. 1489.

[21] *Hansard*, HL Vol. 513, Col. 1259.

[22] See *post*, §§ 31–029—31–044.

"which involve one or more elements foreign to the internal social system of a country (for example, the fact that one or all of the parties to the contract are foreign nationals or persons habitually resident abroad, the fact that the contract was made abroad, the fact that one or more of the obligations of the parties are to be performed in a foreign country, etc.), thereby giving the legal systems of several countries claims to apply."[23]

The situation contemplated thus seems to be the presence in a transaction of a foreign element of legal relevance according to customary notions of private international law. Such a relevant foreign element would appear to be present even if the only such element is the fact that a contract otherwise domestic in nature contains a choice of a foreign governing law.[24]

Law specified need not be of a Contracting State. Secondly, Article 2 of the **31–022** Convention provides that any law specified by the Convention shall be applied whether or not it is the law of a Contracting State. Taken with Article 1(1), the effect of this is that it is not necessary that the countries whose laws are implicated in the problem be states which are parties to the Convention or Member States of the E.C. and that the rules of the Convention must be applied even if they point to a governing law which is neither the law of a Contracting State nor the law of a Member State of the E.C. The Convention will thus apply if the choice is between the law of England and the law of Brazil, or between the law of Brazil and the law of India,[25] as it will if the choice is between the law of the Netherlands and the law of Italy. Further, the application of the Convention, in a case where the forum is in the United Kingdom, does not depend on the situation having a factual link with another Contracting State or with another Member State of the E.C. The rules of the Convention will thus apply to all cases[26] brought in United Kingdom courts to which those rules, according to their terms, apply.[27]

Countries with more than one legal system. Thirdly, although Article 1(1) **31–023** refers to situations involving a choice between the law of different *countries*, the rules of the Convention are intended, also, to apply to situations involving a choice between two or more *legal systems* which may not necessarily be the same thing.[28] Article 19(1) of the Convention provides that where a state comprises territorial units, each of which has its own rules of law in respect of contractual obligations, each territorial unit shall be treated as a country for the purposes of identifying the applicable law.[29] Hence the rules of the Convention will apply to

---

[23] Giuliano-Lagarde Report, p. 10.

[24] This would seem to follow from Art. 3(3): see *post*, §§ 31–057—31–058.

[25] *Bank of Baroda v. Vysya Bank Ltd* [1994] 2 Lloyd's Rep. 412; *Egon Oldendorff v. Libera Corp. (No. 2)* [1996] 1 Lloyd's Rep. 380 (law of England and law of Japan).

[26] Including, it seems, cases where it is necessary to determine whether a contract is "by its terms, or by implication, governed by English law" for the purpose of RSC, Ord. 11, r. 1(1)(d)(iii), CPR, Sched. 1, r. 50(3) whereby the court, may, in its discretion, give permission to serve a claim form out of the jurisdiction: see *Bank of Baroda v. Vysya Bank Ltd* [1994] 2 Lloyd's Rep. 87; *Egon Oldendorff v. Libera Corp.* [1995] 2 Lloyd's Rep. 64; *Dicey & Morris op. cit.* p. 1199.

[27] Giuliano-Lagarde Report, p. 13. For criticism of this result by Lords Wilberforce and Goff, see *Hansard*, HL Vol. 515, Cols. 1476–1482, Vol. 517, Cols. 1537–1541.

[28] *cf. James Miller and Partners Ltd v. Whitworth Street Estates (Manchester) Ltd* [1970] A.C. 583; *ante*, § 31–012.

[29] See also Giuliano-Lagarde Report, p. 10.

determine, for example, whether a contract is governed by the law of New York[30] or the law of California, whether a contract is governed by the law of California or the law of British Columbia, whether a contract is governed by the law of England or the law of Luxembourg, or whether a contract is governed by the law of Germany or the law of France.

31–024   **Different parts of U.K.** Fourthly, the Convention rules will apply in the case of conflicts between the laws of the different parts of the United Kingdom. For although Article 19(2) does not require states within which different territorial units have their own rules of law in respect of contractual obligations to apply the Convention to conflicts between the laws of such units, the United Kingdom decided to apply those rules to intra-United Kingdom conflicts.[31] Accordingly, the rules of the Convention will apply to situations involving a choice between the laws of England and Wales, Scotland and Northern Ireland,[32] as the case may be, as well as to situations involving a choice between the laws of England and Germany.[33]

31–025   **Mandatory.** Lastly, it has been suggested that the parties to a contract may be able to exclude the application of the uniform rules contained in the Rome Convention by indicating a choice, in the contract, of "English law excluding the Act of 1990" (*i.e.* the Contracts (Applicable Law) Act 1990) or of English law as it was on the day before the 1990 Act entered into force.[34] This view cannot be accepted,[35] principally because the 1990 Act provides, in unambiguous terms, that the Convention shall have "the force of law" in the United Kingdom[36] and because it is stated in the Convention itself that the Convention "*shall* apply in a Contracting State to contracts made after the date on which this Convention has entered into force with respect to that State."[37] The words of the Act denote the mandatory character of the rules, as a matter of English law,[38] while the words of the Convention clearly indicate a treaty obligation on the United Kingdom to implement the provisions of the Convention, which obligation has, of course, been discharged in the 1990 Act.

31–026   **Relationship with other Conventions and E.C. Law.** Article 21 of the Rome Convention stipulates that the Convention is not "to prejudice the application of international conventions to which a Contracting State is, or becomes, a

---

[30] *cf. The Stolt Sydness* [1997] 1 Lloyd's Rep. 273.

[31] Contracts (Applicable Law) Act 1990, s.2(3).

[32] In such cases it is probable that a U.K. appellate court could make a reference to the European Court under the Brussels Protocol: see *Dicey & Morris op. cit.* p. 1200; Plender *op. cit.* pp. 43–44.

[33] The German Länder would not have to be treated as separate legal systems under Art. 19(1) because German contract law is federal in nature: see *Dicey & Morris op. cit.* p. 1200.

[34] F.A. Mann (1991) 107 L.Q.R. 353, a view perhaps not unconnected with the learned author's general hostility to the Convention. See *ante,* § 31–017, n. 3.

[35] See *Dicey & Morris op. cit.* p. 1205; *Benjamin's Sale of Goods* (5th ed., 1997), § 25–026; Hogan (1992) 108 L.Q.R. 12; North (1992) 3 King's Coll.L.J. 29, 38–40, reprinted in *Essays in Private International Law* (1993), p. 171, at pp. 185–187.

[36] s.2(1) (subject only to s.2(2) and (3)).

[37] Art. 17 (emphasis supplied).

[38] Compare the same treatment of identical wording in the Carriage of Goods by Sea Act 1971, implementing the Hague-Visby Rules, in *The Hollandia* [1982] Q.B. 872 [CA] (affd. [1983] A.C. 565). See also s.5 of and Sched. 4 of the 1990 Act which amend legislation referring to the "proper law of a contract" so as to replace that terminology with words which reflect the Convention usage: and see *ante,* § 31–003.

party."[39] Accordingly, existing and future conventions entered into by Contracting States will apply in those states despite the existence of the Rome Convention.[40] Further, Article 20 seeks to avoid conflicts between the Rome Convention regime and choice of law provisions contained in acts of the institutions of the European Communities or in national law harmonised in accordance with such acts by providing that the latter provisions shall take precedence over the rules contained in the Convention.[41]

No renvoi. Reflecting the common law,[42] Article 15 of the Rome Convention **31–027** excludes the doctrine of renvoi in providing that application of the law of any country specified by the Convention means "the application of the rules of law in force in that country other than its rules of private international law."[43]

Incorporation by reference. At common law, the parties were free to incor- **31–028** porate into the contract provisions of foreign law as part of the terms and conditions of the contract.[44] The Rome Convention does not appear to restrict their power to continue with such a device.[45]

(b) *Exclusions*[46]

Introduction. The specific scope of the provisions of the Rome Convention is **31–029** set out in Article 1. The general purport of Article 1(1) has already been referred to but it is necessary to examine one additional question in relation to that

---

[39] See Plender *op. cit.* pp. 15–18; Kaye *op. cit* pp. 367–370. See also Arts. 23, 24 and 25.

[40] The principal conventions envisaged in this provision would seem to be those concerning matters of private international law: see Art. 24. See, *e.g.* the Hague Convention on the Law Applicable to International Sale of Goods of June 15, 1955 to which Belgium, Denmark, France and Italy, but not the U.K., are parties. Art. 21 is, however, broad enough to enable a State party to the Vienna Convention on the International Sale of Goods 1980 to continue to apply that Convention. A U.K. court *may* be required to apply the Vienna Convention if the law applicable to the contract pursuant to the Rome Convention is that of a country which is a party to the Vienna Convention and which would regard the latter Convention as applicable, but such a conclusion is controversial. It may equally be the case that, because of Art. 21, international conventions are only properly applicable as between Contracting States which are parties thereto, with the consequence that since the U.K. is not a party to the Vienna Convention, it will be the contract law of the country (excluding the Vienna Convention) which will be applicable: this problem is distinct from that of *renvoi*, as to which, see *ante*, § 31–015 and *post*, § 31–027). The power of the parties to a contract of sale to choose the Uniform Law on International Sales to govern the contract would not seem to be prejudiced by the Rome Convention since that power is conferred by statute (Uniform Law on International Sales Act 1967) and ULIS is not the law of a "country" for the purposes of the Rome Convention.

[41] See, *e.g.* the proposed Regulation concerning conflict of laws in employment relationships (1976) Com. (75) Final, which, if implemented, would have had that effect. The proposal was withdrawn in November 1981: see [1981] O.J. C 307/3. As to employment contracts, see *post*, §§ 31–094—31–103.

[42] *Ante*, § 31–015.

[43] Since the exclusion of *renvoi* prevents application of rules of private international law, it has no bearing on the issue concerning the application of the Vienna Convention discussed in n. 40, *supra*, since that Convention establishes rules of substantive law rather than rules of private international law.

[44] *Ante*, § 31–008.

[45] *Dicey & Morris op. cit.* pp. 1222–1223.

[46] *Dicey & Morris on the Conflict of Laws* (12th ed., 1993), pp. 1197–1204; Cheshire and North, *Private International Law* (12th ed., 1992), pp. 467, 469–474; Plender, *The European Contracts Convention* (1991), Chaps. 3 and 4; Kaye, *The New Private International Law of Contract of the European Community* (1993), pp. 98–106, 111–142.

provision, namely the meaning of "contractual obligations." For if an obligation is not a "contractual obligation" for the purposes of that provision, then the Convention does not apply even if the situation involves "a choice between the laws of different countries." Secondly, Article 1(2) excludes certain types of contract and certain issues which are capable of arising in a contractual context from the scope of the Convention. The following paragraphs deal with these two questions.

31–030   **Meaning of "contractual obligations."** At a very general level, it can be said that since the Rome Convention is only concerned with contractual obligations, property rights and intellectual property are not covered by its provisions.[47] This observation, however, does not carry the matter much further and the Giuliano-Lagarde Report provides no additional guidance. Initially, however, it would seem to be generally accepted that an autonomous or Convention interpretation should be given to the expression "contractual obligations"[48] and that, thus, the expression should not necessarily be limited to obligations which the law of the English forum would regard as contractual.[49] But the precise ramifications of this approach will only emerge through decided cases.[50] Additionally, it may be said that the Rome Convention does not apply to tortious obligations. But this observation does not help to resolve the proper classification of an obligation which is contractual under one relevant system of law but tortious under another relevant system of law, and presumably an autonomous or independent concept will have to be developed to deal with this situation as well.[51]

31–031   **Concurrent liability.** A rather different problem is presented when the forum (as is sometimes the case in English law, with employment contracts[52]) allows alternative claims in contract and tort. It is thought,[53] but the matter is by no

---

[47] Giuliano-Lagarde Report, p. 10. Thus, *e.g.*, although the contractual aspects of a sale of goods will be governed by the Rome Convention, the proprietary aspects will not, and thus will be governed by the rules as to proprietary rights developed in the common law. On these rules, see *Benjamin's Sale of Goods* (5th ed., 1997), §§ 25–098—25–126.

[48] See *Dicey & Morris op. cit.* p. 1197; Cheshire and North *op. cit.* p. 467; Plender *op. cit.* pp. 49–52; Kaye *op. cit.* pp. 97–98. And see *ante*, §§1–007, 1–009.

[49] *cf. Re Bonacina* [1912] 2 Ch. 394. See also the decisions of the European Court giving an independent meaning to the phrase "matters relating to contract" in Art. 5(1) of the Brussels Convention on Jurisdiction and the Enforcement of Judgments in Civil and Commercial Matters 1968: Case 34/82 *Peters v. ZNAV* [1983] E.C.R. 987; Case 9/87 *Arcado Sprl v. Haviland SA* [1988] E.C.R 1539; Case C–26/91 *Soc Handte et Cie GmbH v. TMCS* [1992] E.C.R. I–3967. Because of the different language used in Art. 5(1) of the 1968 Convention, such cases are only an approximate guide to the meaning of "contractual obligation" under the Rome Convention. It has been held that where A contracts with B to pay a sum of money to C, an action brought to enforce the obligation by C involves "matters relating to a contract" for the purposes of Art. 5(1) of the Lugano Convention on Jurisdiction and the Enforcement of Judgments in Civil and Commercial Matters 1988 (Civil Jurisdiction and Judgments Act 1982, Sched 3A): see *Atlas Shipping Agency (U.K.) Ltd v. Suisse Atlantique Societe D'Armement Maritime SA* [1995] 2 Lloyd's Rep. 188. Whether the making of a contract was induced by a misrepresentation has also been held to fall within this provision, the relevant "obligation" for the purposes of Art. 5(1) being the obligation to avoid pre-contractual misrepresentation: see *Agnew v. Lansforsakringsbolagens AB* [1997] 4 All E.R. 937, not following on the latter point, *Trade Indemnity plc v. Forsakringsaktiebolaget Njord* [1995] 1 All E.R. 796.

[50] For some speculative views, see Plender *op. cit.* pp. 51–52; Kaye *op. cit.* pp. 98–106. It has been doubted whether "public law" contracts, *e.g.* French administrative law contracts are covered: see Kaye *op. cit.* p. 111; *cf.* Dicey & Morris *op. cit.* p. 1197.

[51] *cf. Soc Handte et Cie GmbH v. TMCS, supra.*

[52] As to which see *post*, §§ 31–094—31–103.

[53] *Dicey & Morris op. cit.* pp. 1198, 1315. *Ante*, § 1–106 and *post*, § 31–103.

means free of doubt,[54] that there is nothing in the Rome Convention which precludes, say, an employee from framing his claim in tort if the tort choice of law rule is more advantageous to him than the rules of the Rome Convention.[55]

Restitution. Finally, it would seem to be the case, in the United Kingdom at any rate, that the Rome Convention will not be applied to claims which are classified, according to English notions, as sounding in restitution (or quasi-contract[56]). This much is suggested by the power to make a reservation to Article 10(1)(e) of the Convention, which refers the "consequences of nullity" of the contract to the law applicable to the contract,[57] which power was exercised by the United Kingdom[58] because such a question is not a matter of contract but one of restitution in United Kingdom legal systems.[59] Consistently with this, a majority of the House of Lords has held that a claim for money paid under a void contract was not a matter "relating to a contract" for the purposes of Article 5(1) of the modified version of the Brussels Convention on Jurisdiction and the Enforcement of Judgments in Civil and Commercial Matters 1968[60] which is applicable as between the component parts of the United Kingdom.[61]

    31–032

Specifically excluded matters. Article 1(2) provides that the rules of the Rome Convention shall not apply to certain specified matters. These are discussed in the following paragraphs.

    31–033

Capacity of natural persons. The Convention is not to apply to "questions involving the status or legal capacity of natural persons" subject to the operation of a special rule relating to the contractual capacity of such persons.[62] This special rule, contained in Article 11, is discussed later in this chapter.[63] The

    31–034

---

[54] See Case 189/87 *Kalfelis v. Schroder* [1988] E.C.R 5565 holding such a claim to be contractual for the purposes of Art. 5(1) of the Brussels Convention, *supra*, n. 49.

[55] cf. *Matthews v. Kuwait Bechtel Corp.* [1959] 2 Q.B. 57; *Coupland v. Arabian Gulf Oil Co.* [1983] 1 W.L.R. 1136 (affd. *ibid.* 1151); *Johnson v. Coventry Churchill International Ltd* [1992] 3 All E.R. 14 (where the claim was made in tort only, the contract not being pleaded). The choice of law rules in tort are now largely to be found in the Private International Law (Miscellaneous Provisions) Act 1995, Part III, (in force from May 1, 1996, S.I. 1996 No. 995). There is nothing in Part III of the Act which precludes an employee from relying on an alternative claim in contract if it is more advantageous to do so: see *Dicey and Morris, op. cit., Fourth Cumulative Supplement*, p. 248. See also *Henderson v. Merrett Syndicates* [1995] 2 A.C. 145, a case not involving the conflict of laws, in which it was confirmed that concurrent duties in contract and tort could co-exist (see *ante*, § 1–068). See also *post*, § 31–103.

[56] See Cheshire and North *op. cit.* p. 467. And *post*, § 31–148.

[57] Rome Convention, Art. 22(1). Even Member States who do not make a reservation will, presumably, not apply the Convention to all aspects of restitution or quasi-contract but only to this aspect since they regard it as contractual. A preliminary draft of the Convention contained (Art. 13) a special provision dealing with quasi-contract which is not contained in the final version: Cheshire and North *op. cit.* p. 467.

[58] Contracts (Applicable Law) Act 1990, s.2(2).

[59] *Hansard*, HL Vol. 513, Cols. 1258–1259. And see *post*, § 31–148.

[60] Civil Jurisdiction and Judgments Act 1982, Sched. 4.

[61] *Kleinwort Benson Ltd v. Glasgow City Council* [1999] 1 A.C. 153, reversing a majority decision of the Court of Appeal to the opposite effect: [1996] Q.B. 678. The European Court of Justice had earlier declined jurisdiction to interpret this version of the Brussels Convention: see Case C–346/93 *Kleinwort Benson Ltd v. Glasgow City Council* [1995] E.C.R. I–5615, [1996] Q.B. 547.

[62] Art. 1(2)(a).

[63] *Post*, § 31–126.

question of the law which determines the capacity of a natural person to enter into a contract will thus, in general, be governed by common law rules.[64] Essentially, this question was excluded because of disagreement between common law and civil law negotiators as to the proper classification of it. A common lawyer usually regards the matter as a contractual issue, whereas the civil lawyer regards it as an issue of status.[65]

31–035 **Wills, succession, etc.** Article 1(2)(b) excludes from the ambit of the Convention contractual obligations relating to wills and succession; rights in property arising out of a matrimonial relationship; rights and duties arising out of a family relationship, parentage, marriage or affinity, including maintenance obligations in respect of children who are not legitimate. The purpose of this is to exclude all matters of family law.[66] In relation to maintenance obligations, the exclusion extends only to contracts which are made by parties under a legal maintenance obligation, in performance of that obligation.[67] All other contractual obligations, even if they provide for maintenance of a member of the family to whom there are no legal maintenance obligations, would fall within the scope of the Convention.[68] The contractual effects of gifts apparently fall within the Convention, even when made within the family, unless they are covered by family law.[69] Contractual effects of gifts would also be excluded if they arise out of the law relating to succession or that relating to matrimonial property rights.[70] Although not specifically mentioned, matters relating to the custody of children are excluded since they fall within the realm of personal status and capacity.[71]

31–036 **Bills of exchange, cheques and promissory notes.** The rules of the Convention do not apply to bills of exchange, cheques and promissory notes.[72] To have included such obligations would have required "rather complicated special rules"[73] which would have been inappropriate in a Convention purporting to deal with contractual obligations in general. Further, many Member States (but not the United Kingdom) are parties to the Geneva Conventions which govern most of these areas.[74] And, in any event, such obligations are regarded as non-contractual in some Member States.[75] Bills, cheques and promissory notes will thus, in England, be dealt with under the relevant statutory and common law rules.[76]

31–037 **Other negotiable instruments.** The exclusion goes further than the obligations just mentioned for, in addition, "other negotiable instruments to the extent

---

[64] *Post*, § 31–126.
[65] North in North (ed.), *Contract Conflicts* (1982), p. 10, reprinted in *Essays in Private International Law* (1993), p. 23.
[66] Giuliano-Lagarde Report, p. 10.
[67] *ibid.*
[68] *ibid.*
[69] *ibid.* See *Dicey & Morris op. cit.* p. 1201.
[70] *ibid.* pp. 10–11.
[71] *ibid.* p. 11.
[72] Art. 1(2)(c).
[73] Giuliano-Lagarde Report, p. 11.
[74] *ibid.*
[75] *ibid.*
[76] See Vol. II, §§ 34–197—34–217.

that the obligations under such other negotiable instruments arise out of their negotiable character"[77] are also excised from the ambit of the uniform rules.[78] Whether a document is to be classified as a negotiable instrument is not, however, a matter for the Convention but one for the law of the forum, including its rules of private international law.[79] But the exclusion only extends to those obligations which arise out of the negotiable character of documents so characterised: it would not, apparently, extend, *e.g.* to contracts pursuant to which such instruments are issued, or contracts for the purchase and sale of such instruments.[80]

Arbitration agreements and agreements on the choice of court. Of considerable practical significance is the exclusion from the scope of the Convention of arbitration agreements and agreements on the choice of court.[81] The exclusion was also a matter of some controversy within the group which negotiated the Convention.[82] As far as arbitration agreements are concerned, the arguments for exclusion were the need to avoid an increase in the number of international conventions in this area, that the concept of closest connection[83] was difficult to apply to arbitration agreements, that the procedural and contractual aspects of such agreements were difficult to separate and that since the Convention permitted "severability,"[84] the arbitration clause could be treated as a distinct entity, apart from the contract, without any difficulty.[85] The result of the exclusion is that not only the procedural aspects but also the formation, validity and effect[86] of an arbitration agreement will have, seemingly, to be determined by common law rules, which is at best inconvenient, whereas the law applicable to the remaining part of the contract will be determined by the rules of the Convention.[87]

Choice of court agreements were excluded because the prevailing view in the negotiating group was that the matter lay within the realm of procedure, that rules of jurisdiction were a matter of public policy, that a court must determine the validity of such an agreement according to its own law rather than the law chosen,[88] that Convention rules would be frustrated if disputes were brought

31–038

---

[77] Art. 1(2)(c).

[78] For discussion, see *Dicey & Morris op. cit.* pp. 1419–1422; Schultsz in North (ed.) *Contract Conflicts* (1982), pp. 188–191; Plender *op. cit.* pp. 64–66; Kaye *op. cit.* pp. 117–118.

[79] Giuliano-Lagarde Report, p. 11. *cf.* Schultsz *op. cit.*

[80] Giuliano-Lagarde Report, *ibid.*

[81] Art. 1(2)(d). For discussion, see *Dicey & Morris op. cit.* pp. 1201–1203; Cheshire and North *op. cit.* pp. 471–472; Plender *op. cit.* pp. 66–70; Kaye *op. cit.* pp. 118–121. An arbitration or choice of court agreement may nonetheless be relevant in determining whether the parties have made a choice of law: see *post*, § 31–049.

[82] Giuliano-Lagarde Report, pp. 11–12. The U.K. argued strenuously for the inclusion of both matters: *ibid.*

[83] See *post*, § 31–066.

[84] See *post*, §§ 31–052—31–053, 31–066.

[85] Giuliano-Lagarde Report, pp. 11–12. In fact only the New York Convention on the recognition and enforcement of foreign arbitral awards touches upon the law applicable to an arbitration agreement (Arbitration Act 1996, s.103(2)(b)), and that only in the context of recognition and enforcement of foreign awards.

[86] Giuliano-Lagarde Report, p. 12.

[87] In practice it may be that the law applicable to the contractual aspects of the arbitration agreement will normally be the same as that which governs the contract of which it forms part: *Dicey & Morris op. cit.* p. 1203; *cf.* Cheshire and North *op. cit.* p. 472.

[88] This is not the case in English law, in which the validity of such an agreement depends on the applicable law: see *Dicey & Morris op. cit.* pp. 422–423.

before courts of non-Contracting States,[89] and, finally, that in relation to cases within the Community most important matters (validity of the clause and form) are governed by Article 17 of the Brussels Convention on Jurisdiction and the Enforcement of Judgments in Civil and Commercial Matters 1968.[90] The result is that this question will again be governed by common law rules.[91]

31-039   **Questions governed by the law of companies, etc.** Questions governed by the law of companies and other bodies corporate or unincorporate such as the creation, by registration or otherwise, legal capacity, internal organisation or winding up of companies and other bodies corporate or unincorporate and the personal liability of officers and members as such for the obligations of the company or body will not fall within the ambit of the Rome Convention.[92] The intention behind the provision is the exclusion of matters of contract which arise in the context of company law,[93] particularly in view of the work being done in the European Community on the harmonisation of company law.[94] Thus, for example, the question of the law applicable to the contractual capacity of a company will be governed by common law rules[95] and not by the Convention. On the other hand, an agreement by promoters to create a company is thought to fall within the scope of the Convention.[96]

31-040   **Power of agent to bind principal, etc.** Further excluded is the question of whether an agent is able to bind a principal, or an organ to bind a company or body corporate or unincorporate, to a third party.[97] The exclusion only affects the question of whether the principal is bound with regard to third parties by the acts of the agent (or organ of a company etc, as the case may be).[98] It is justified because the Convention permits parties a wide freedom to choose the applicable law of a contract,[99] a freedom which it was not thought appropriate to recognise in this context.[1] This matter will, therefore, continue to be governed by common law rules.[2] But the rules of the Convention will apply to determine the law which

---

[89] It is difficult not to regard this reason as incomprehensible, since, presumably, non-Contracting States would not apply the Convention in any event.

[90] Giuliano-Lagarde Report, p. 11. Apparently, according to the view there expressed, "outstanding points, notably those relating to consent, do not arise in practice, having regard to the fact that Art. 17 provides that these agreements shall be in writing." But see *Dicey & Morris op. cit.* pp. 423–424, 578–579, 1202.

[91] *Akai Pty. Ltd v. People's Insurance Co. Ltd* [1998] 1 Lloyd's Rep. 90, 98. However, normally the law applicable to the choice of court agreement will be the same as that applicable to the contract of which it forms part: see n. 87, *ante.*

[92] Art. 1(2)(e). See *Dicey & Morris op. cit.* pp. 1113–1115.

[93] Giuliano-Lagarde Report, p. 12.

[94] On this work, see Dine, *E.C. Company Law* (1991); Andenas and Kenyon-Slade (eds.), *E.C. Financial Market Regulation and Company Law* (1993); Werlauff, *E.C. Company Law* (1993).

[95] See *post,* § 31–127. The exclusion of legal capacity concerns limitations on companies or firms, for example, in respect of acquisition of immovable property, but does not concern "*ultra vires* act by organs of the company or firm" (Giuliano-Lagarde Report, pp. 12–13) which are excluded under Art. 1(2)(f): see *post,* §§ 31–040, 31–127.

[96] Giuliano-Lagarde Report, p. 12.

[97] Art. 1(2)(f).

[98] Giuliano-Lagarde Report, p. 13.

[99] See *post,* §§ 31–045—31–065.

[1] Giuliano-Lagarde Report, p. 13.

[2] As to which, see *Dicey & Morris op. cit.* pp. 1458–1465.

governs the contract (if any) between principal and agent,[3] and also, it would seem, the law which governs the contract (if any) which the agent concludes with a third party.[4] Further excluded by Article 1(2)(f) is the effect of *ultra vires* acts by an organ of a company or firm,[5] but the fact that this is said to be excluded under this provision rather than that dealing with company law (Article 1(2)(e))[6] would appear to be of no practical significance.[7]

Trusts. Article 1(2)(*g*) excludes the constitution of trusts and the relationship   **31–041**
between settlors, trustees and beneficiaries. Trusts in this context, are to be understood in the meaning which they bear in common law countries.[8] This readily explains their exclusion since, in the common law sense, a trust is not a contract.[9] In the civil law systems, however, institutions similar to the trust may fall within the Convention because they are normally contractual in origin.[10] According to the Giuliano-Lagarde Report, it will, nevertheless, be open to the judge to treat these civil law institutions in the same way as the institutions of the common law countries when the former exhibit the same characteristics as the latter.[11]

Evidence and procedure. Article 1(2)(h) of the Convention excludes "evi-   **31–042**
dence and procedure, without prejudice to Article 14," from the scope of the Convention. Article 14 (concerned with the law applicable to presumptions, burden of proof and mode of proof) is discussed at *post*, §§ 31–151—31–154. The Giuliano-Lagarde Report expresses the view that the exclusion of evidence and procedure "seems to require no comment."[12] Presumably it will be for national law to classify an issue as belonging to one or other of these categories.[13] But it must be borne in mind that a matter classified as evidential or procedural will be governed by the law of the forum. The possibility of disparate approaches

---

[3] Giuliano-Lagarde Report, p. 13. For discussion, see *Dicey & Morris op. cit.* pp. 1452–1457. Application of the common law rules on this matter may be affected by the E.C. Directive on Self-employed Commercial Agents ([1986] O.J. L 382/17) implemented in England and Wales and Scotland by the Commercial Agents (Council Directive) Regulations 1993 (S.I. 1993 No. 3053, as amended by S.I. 1993 No. 3173 and S.I. 1998 No. 2868) and in Northern Ireland by the Commercial Agents (Council Directive) Regulations (Northern Ireland) (S.I. 1993 No. 483). The Regulations govern the relations between commercial agents and their principals and apply in respect of the activities of commercial agents in Great Britain (Reg. 1(2)). It is specifically provided that Regulations 3–22, which deal with the mutual rights and obligations of agent and principal, remuneration of the agent, the conclusion and termination of the agency contract and miscellaneous matters such as service of notices, do not apply where the parties have agreed that the agency contract is to be governed by the law of another Member State (Reg. 1(3)(a)). Conversely, Regulations 3–22 will apply where the law of another Member State, corresponding to the Regulations, enables the parties to agree that the agency contract is to be governed by the law of a different Member State and the parties have agreed that it is to be governed by English Law (Reg. 1(3)(b)). For further discussion, see Vol. II, §§ 32–005—32–006; *Bowstead and Reynolds on Agency* (16th ed., 1996) pp. 691–693.
[4] Giuliano-Lagarde Report, p. 13. This conclusion is not free from difficulty: *Dicey & Morris op. cit.* p. 1465. See also *Presentaciones Musicales SA v. Secunda* [1994] Ch. 271.
[5] Giuliano-Lagarde Report, p. 13.
[6] *Ante*, § 31–040.
[7] *Dicey & Morris op. cit.* p. 114.
[8] Giuliano-Lagarde Report, p. 13.
[9] For choice of law rules in trusts, see *Dicey & Morris op. cit.* Chap. 29.
[10] Giuliano-Lagarde Report, p. 13.
[11] *ibid.* See the discussion in Plender *op. cit.* pp. 76–78.
[12] Giuliano-Lagarde Report, p. 13.
[13] See Cheshire and North *op. cit.* p. 474 (stressing that English courts should not necessarily adopt the classifications applied in the common law in the context of the Convention).

to classification amongst the Contracting States may thus constitute an obstacle to the uniformity of choice of law rules which the Convention seeks to achieve.[14]

31–043   **Insurance.** Article 1(3) of the Rome Convention provides that its rules

> "do not apply to contracts of insurance which cover risks situated in the territories of the Member States of the European Economic Community. In order to determine whether a risk is situated in these territories the court shall apply its internal law."

The effect of this provision is as follows. Where the risk covered by the insurance contract is situated outside the territories of the Member States of the European Communities, the rules of the Rome Convention will apply.[15] Additionally, those rules will also apply to determine the law applicable to a contract of reinsurance since such contracts are specifically exempted from the exclusionary rule of Article 1(3), even if the contract of reinsurance covers a risk which is situated in a Member State.[16] Where, however, the risk covered by a contract of insurance is situated in the territories of the Member States of the E.C., the choice of law rules to determine the applicable law are to be found in special legal regimes for, respectively, non-life and life insurance, which regimes are based on Community Directives[17] which have been implemented in United Kingdom law.[18] The detail

---

[14] Cheshire and North *ibid.* suggest that the principles of uniform interpretation (Art. 18, *ante* § 31–019) may be applied to avoid the danger of different states making different classifications. For other matters raising the distinction between substance and procedure, see *post*, §§ 31–118, 31–138—31–139, 31–151—31–154, 31–170—31–172.

[15] See *Crédit Lyonnais v. New Hampshire Insurance Co.* [1997] 2 Lloyd's Rep. 1. For the application of the rules of the Rome Convention in this situation, see *Dicey & Morris op. cit.* Rule 186, pp. 1338–1350.

[16] Rome Convention, Art. 1(4). For application of the Convention rules to reinsurance, see *Dicey & Morris op. cit.* Rule 189, pp. 1376–1384.

[17] Second Council Directive of June 22, 1988 on the co-ordination of laws, regulations and administrative provisions relating to direct insurance other than life insurance and laying down provisions to facilitate the effective exercise of the freedom to provide services: [1988] O.J. L 127/1, amending the First Council Directive of July 24, 1973, [1973] O.J. L 228/3 (the Second Non-Life Insurance Directive); Third Council Directive of June 18, 1992 on the co-ordination of laws, regulations and administrative provisions relating to direct insurance other than life insurance: [1992] O.J. L 228/1, amending the First Council Directive and the Second Non-Life Insurance Directive, *supra* (the Third Non-Life Directive); Second Council Directive of November 8, 1990 on the co-ordination of laws, regulations and administrative provisions relating to direct life assurance, laying down provisions to facilitate the effective exercise of freedom to provide services: [1990] O.J. L 330/50, amending the First Council Directive of March 5, 1979, [1979] O.J. L 63/1 (the Second Life Insurance Directive); Third Council Directive of November 10, 1992 on the co-ordination of laws, regulations and administrative provisions relating to direct life assurance: [1992] O.J. L 360/1, amending the First Council Directive and the Second Life Directive, *supra* (the Third Life Directive). The choice of law rules are to be found respectively in Art. 7 of the Second Non-Life Insurance Directive, as amended by Art. 24 of the Third Non-Life Directive, and Art. 4 of the Second Life Insurance Directive.

[18] The Second Non-Life Insurance Directive was implemented in Insurance Companies (Amendment) Regulations 1990 (S.I. 1990 No. 133), inserting s.94A, now numbered as s.94B (S.I. 1992 No. 2890), Sched. 3A, now Pt. I of Sched. 3A (S.I. 1993 No. 174) and s.96A into the Insurance Companies Act 1982, in force from July 1, 1990. The Third Non-Life Directive was implemented by the Insurance Companies (Third Insurance Directives) Regulations 1994 (S.I. 1994 No. 1696), Reg. 49 of which amends Sched. 3A, Pt. I of the 1982 Act, in force from July 1, 1994. The Second Life Insurance Directive was implemented by the Insurance Companies (Amendment) Regulations 1993 (S.I. 1993 No. 174), inserting Sched. 3A, Pt. II into the Insurance Companies Act 1982, in force from May 20, 1993. The Third Life Directive is implemented by the Insurance Companies (Third Insurance Directives) Regulations 1994, *supra*, but this aspect of the Regulations has no substantial

and complexity of these legal regimes precludes discussion here and the reader is referred to the appropriate source.[19]

Identification of *situs*. One issue which may, however, be appropriately dealt with here is as to the rules which are to be used for identifying the *situs* of a risk. The second sentence of Article 1(3) requires the court to apply its "internal law"[20] to determine whether a risk is situated in the territories of Member States of the E.C. Since, traditionally, the *situs* of a risk had played no role in United Kingdom insurance law, difficulties could have arisen in its identification. These difficulties are resolved by the existence of rules for this purpose in the Second Non-Life Insurance Directive[21] which are incorporated into United Kingdom law in the legislation implementing that Directive,[22] and into the legislation implementing the Second Life Insurance Directive,[23] and by an amendment to the Contracts (Applicable Law) Act 1990 which provides that these rules constitute the relevant internal law in Article 1(3) of the Rome Convention.[24]

(c) *Choice of Law by the Parties*[25]

The general principle. The opening sentence of Article 3(1) of the Rome Convention provides that a "contract shall be governed by the law chosen by the

---

impact on the rules of the conflict of laws. See also the Friendly Societies Act 1992, s.101 and Sched. 20, as amended by the Friendly Societies (Amendment) Regulations 1993, S.I. 1993 No. 2519.

[19] *Dicey & Morris op. cit.* Rule 187, pp. 1350–1368; Rule 188, pp. 1368–1376 and *Fourth Cumulative Supplement* (1997), pp. 197–202; MacNeill (1995) 44 I.C.L.Q. 19. For a case applying Insurance Companies Act 1982, Sched. 3A, Pt. I (see preceding note), see *Crédit Lyonnais v. New Hampshire Insurance Co.* [1997] 1 Lloyd's Rep. 1.

[20] This excludes rules of private international law: Giuliano-Lagarde Report, p. 13.

[21] *Ante*, n. 18.

[22] S.I. 1990 No. 133, inserting a new s.96A into the Insurance Companies Act 1982. The relevant provisions are contained in s.96A(3).

[23] *Ante*, n. 18. The implementing legislation is S.I. 1993 No. 174 inserting a new s.94B(1A) into Insurance Companies Act 1982. Rather than identifying the *situs* of a risk (which is not expressly referred to in the Second Life Insurance Directive) these provisions contain explicit indication as to when the legislation applies.

[24] Contracts (Applicable Law) Act 1990, s.2(1A)(a), inserted by S.I. 1993 No. 2519. As to non-life insurance where the insurance: relates to buildings or to buildings and their contents, in so far as contents are covered by same policy, risk situated in Member State in which property situated (Insurance Companies Act 1982, s.96A(3)(a)); relates to vehicles of any type, risk situated in Member State where vehicle registered (*ibid.* s.96A(3)(b)); relates to a policy of duration of four months or less which covers travel or holiday risks of whatever class, risk situated in Member State where policyholder took out policy (*ibid.* s.96A(3)(c)); relates to cases other than foregoing, if policyholder an individual, risk situated in Member State in which he was habitually resident (*ibid.* s.96A(3)(d)(i)), or if policyholder not an individual in the Member State where the establishment to which the policy relates is situated (*ibid* s.96A(3)(d)(ii)). As to life insurance, the Second Life Insurance Directive, as implemented in the U.K., will apply if the policyholder is an individual who is habitually resident in a Member State (*ibid.* s.94B(1A)(a)), or if the policyholder is not an individual it will apply if the establishment to which the policy relates is situated in a Member State (*ibid.* s.94B(1A)(b)). For some of the difficulties in the application of these rules, see *Dicey & Morris op. cit.* pp. 1343–1344. For the relevant rules in relation to certain insurance contracts with Friendly Societies, see Contracts (Applicable Law) Act 1990, s.2(1A)(b) inserted by S.I. 1993 No. 2519, and Friendly Societies Act 1992, s.101 and Sched. 20, as amended by S.I. 1993 No. 2519.

[25] *Dicey & Morris on the Conflict of Laws* (12th ed., 1993), pp. 1211–1230; Cheshire and North, *Private International Law* (12th ed., 1992), pp. 476–483; Plender, *The European Contracts Convention* (1991), Chap. 5; Kaye, *The New Private International Law of Contract of the European Community* (1993), pp. 147–170. As to the special rules in the Convention for Certain Consumer Contracts (Art. 5) and Individual Employment Contracts (Art. 6), see *post* §§ 31–086—31–103. As to insurance contracts, see *ante*, §§ 31–043—31–044.

parties." The clear intent of this provision is to legitimise, for the purposes of the Convention, the principle of party autonomy.[26] Its effect is that the law chosen by the parties will govern the contract except to the extent that the power to choose is limited or restricted by other provisions of the Convention.[27]

31–046   **Choice must be of law of a country.** By way of introduction, it would first seem that parties may only choose a law of a country to govern the contract. This appears to follow from the terms of Article 1(1) of the Convention.[28] Accordingly, if the parties stipulate that the contract shall be governed by "general principles of law," or by "its own terms" or by the *"lex mercatoria,"* such clauses will not amount to a choice of law.[29] In such cases, the applicable law will have to be determined as if the parties had made no choice of law, *i.e.* according to Article 4 of the Convention[30]: and it will then be for the applicable law, as so identified, to determine whether a clause of this kind is effective.[31]

31–047   **Law neither pleaded nor proved.** Secondly, the question arises as to whether a court faced with a contract containing a choice of law is required to apply that law if that law is neither pleaded nor proved by either party. The use of the word "shall" in the first sentence of Article 3(1) appears to carry a mandatory connotation. However, the English rule that foreign law must be pleaded and proved, failing which English law will be applied,[32] is a rule of evidence[33] or procedure[34] and, as has been pointed out above,[35] such matters are excluded from the scope of the Convention by Article 1(2)(h). It is suggested that the practice of the common law remains unchanged and that the court is not bound to apply a foreign applicable law which is neither pleaded nor proved by the parties.[36] However, this conclusion cannot be free from doubt in the light of the potential lack of harmony which it might introduce into the application of the Convention amongst the Contracting States.[37]

31–048   **Meaning of a "choice" of law: express.** The second sentence of Article 3(1) requires that the "choice must be express or demonstrated with reasonable certainty by the terms of the contract or the circumstances of the case." The first aspect of this formula recognises the efficacy of typical contractual terms such as the contact is to be "governed by"[38] or "construed in accordance with"[39] or

---

[26] Giuliano-Lagarde Report, pp. 15–16. For the background, see *Dicey & Morris op. cit.* pp. 1211–1213.

[27] See *post*, §§ 31–056—31–065.

[28] " . . . Convention shall apply . . . in any situation involving a choice between the *laws of different countries*" [emphasis added]. See *ante*, § 31–021.

[29] *Dicey & Morris op. cit.* pp. 1218–1219; Cheshire and North *op. cit.* p. 482.

[30] *Post*, §§ 31–066—31–085.

[31] See Plender, *op. cit.* p. 55.

[32] *Dicey & Morris op. cit.* Chap. 9; Fentiman, *Foreign Law in English Courts* (1998); Hartley (1996) 45 I.C.L.Q. 271; Fentiman (1992) 108 L.Q.R. 142.

[33] *ibid.*

[34] Giuliano-Lagarde Report, p. 18.

[35] *Ante*, § 31–042.

[36] *Dicey & Morris op. cit.* pp. 299, 1211, 1214; Cheshire and North *op. cit.* pp. 479–480.

[37] See Fentiman, *Foreign Law in English Courts* (1998), at 87–96; Fentiman (1992) 108 L.Q.R. 142.

[38] See, *e.g. Vita Food Products Inc. v. Unus Shipping Co. Ltd* [1939] A.C. 277.

[39] See, *e.g. The Torni* [1932] P. 78.

"subject to"[40] a particular country's law, as apt to make a choice of law.[41]

"Implied choice". More difficulty surrounds the second aspect of the formula.[42] The common law recognised that parties could impliedly choose the law to govern a contract and that an intention on their part to do so could be inferred from the terms and nature of the contract and from the general circumstances of the case.[43] However, Article 3(1) requires that the parties choice be "demonstrated" and further that such demonstration be "with reasonable certainty," which might connote a stricter evidential standard than that involved in drawing an "inference" as to the parties' intentions at common law,[44] particularly when, according to the Giuliano-Lagarde Report, this aspect of the formula is supposed to reveal, in its application, that the parties have made a "real choice of law."[45] Having said that, it is necessary to bear in mind the need for uniform interpretation of the Convention.[46] This means that it is appropriate to adopt a purposive approach to interpretation which does not involve construing the Convention in a narrow, literal fashion.[47] Overall however, the examples given in the Giuliano-Lagarde Report of circumstances which may suffice to demonstrate a choice of law with reasonable certainty, tend to indicate that the relevant factors are broadly similar to those which were capable of indicating an implied choice of law at common law.

> "For example, the contract may be in a standard form which is known to be governed by a particular system of law even though there is no express statement to this effect, such as a Lloyd's policy of marine insurance.[48] In other cases a previous course of dealing between the parties under contracts containing an express choice of law may leave the court in no doubt that the contract in question is to be governed by the law previously chosen where the choice of law clause has been omitted in circumstances which do not indicate a deliberate change of policy by the parties.[49] In some cases the choice of a particular forum may show in no uncertain manner that the parties intend the contract to be governed by the law of that forum, but this must always be subject to the other terms of the contract and all the circumstances of the case.[50] Similarly, references in the contract to specific Articles of the French Civil Code may leave the court in no doubt that the parties have deliberately chosen French law, although there

---

[40] *Dicey & Morris op. cit.* pp. 1217–1218.

[41] *cf. ante,* §§ 31–005, 31–045.

[42] *Dicey & Morris op. cit.* pp. 1223–1227; Cheshire and North *op. cit.* pp. 484–486; Plender *op. cit.* pp. 91–96; Kaye *op. cit.* pp. 150–154; Morse (1982) 2 Ybk. Eur.L. 107, 117.

[43] *Ante,* §§ 31–009—31–010.

[44] See Morse (1982) 2 Ybk.Eur.L. 107, 177. See *ante,* §§ 31–009—31–010.

[45] Giuliano-Lagarde Report, p. 17. See *Egon Oldendorff v. Libera Corp. (No. 2)* [1996] 1 Lloyd's Rep. 380.

[46] Art. 18. *Ante,* § 31–019.

[47] *Egon Oldendorff v. Libera Corp. (No. 2)* [1996] 1 Lloyd's Rep. 380; *Dicey and Morris op. cit.* p. 1218.

[48] *cf. Amin Rasheed Shipping Corpn. v. Kuwait Insurance Co.* [1984] A.C. 50, 62, though an additional factor pointing to an intention to choose English law was the absence of any indigenous code of marine insurance law in Kuwait, the other possible applicable law. *cf. DR Insurance Co. v. Central National Insurance Co.* [1996] 1 Lloyd's Rep. 74. See *ante,* §§ 31–009—31–010.

[49] *cf. ante,* § 31–010, n. 56.

[50] *cf. ante,* §§ 31–009—31–010. In *The Komninos S.* [1991] 1 Lloyd's Rep. 371, the jurisdiction clause referred to "British" courts. This was construed as choice of English courts and English law (" . . . [w]hatever the constitutional niceties, it seems to me altogether far-fetched, in truth a lawyer's point, to suppose that the parties can have intended to embrace the Courts of British dependencies overseas . . . " and "scarcely less far-fetched to suppose that the parties can have meant or intended to embrace" the courts of Scotland or Northern Ireland: *ibid.* at 374, *per* Bingham L.J.).

is no expressly stated choice of law.[51] Other matters that may impel the court to the conclusion that a real choice of law has been made might include an express choice of law in related transactions between the same parties,[52] or the choice of a place where disputes are to be settled by arbitration in circumstances indicating that the arbitrator should apply the law of that place."[53]

In the case of arbitration clauses it appears that the application of Article 3(1) involves a shift of emphasis[54] from the approach which was found in the common law.[55] This results from the fact that, as stated in the extract from the Giuliano-Lagarde Report set out above, the circumstances surrounding the arbitration clause must indicate that it is the intention of the parties that the arbitrator should apply the law of the country in which the arbitration takes place, which is not quite the same test as was adopted in the common law.[56] In practice, however, it is unlikely that any material difference will emerge between the two approaches.[57]

31–050   **Subsequent conduct.** At common law, it was not possible to take into account the conduct of the parties subsequent to the making of the contract in determining their intentions in relation to an implied choice of law.[58] The position under the Rome Convention is not clear. The Giuliano-Lagarde Report recognises that a choice of law may be deduced "in the light of all the facts."[59] It further concludes that where there is no choice of law, so that it is necessary to discover the law of the country with which the contract is most closely connected pursuant to Article 4 of the Convention,[60] "it is also possible to take

---

[51] cf. *The Stensby* (1948) 64 T.L.R. 89; *Keiner v. Keiner* [1952] 1 All E.R. 643. *Ante*, §§ 31–009—31–010.

[52] cf. *Re United Railways of the Havana and Regla Warehouses* [1960] Ch. 52, 94 (affd. [1961] A.C. 1007). See also *Wahda Bank v. Arab Bank plc* [1996] 1 Lloyd's Rep. 470; cf. *Minories Finance Ltd v. Afribank Nigeria Ltd* [1995] 1 Lloyd's Rep. 134; *Bank of Credit and Commerce Hong Kong Ltd v. Sonali Bank* [1995] 1 Lloyd's Rep. 277; *Batstone & Firminger Ltd v. Nasima Enterprises (Nigeria) Ltd* [1996] C.L.C. 1902, 1910.

[53] Giuliano-Lagarde Report, p. 17. cf. *Star Shipping SA v. China National Foreign Trade Transportation Corpn.* [1993] 2 Lloyd's Rep. 445, and see *Dicey & Morris op. cit.* pp. 1225–1227; *ante*, § 31–009. The Report makes no reference to the relevance of an inference *in favorem negotii*: cf. *ante*. § 31–010.

[54] *Dicey and Morris op. cit.*, p. 1226 referred to with approval in *Egon Oldendorff v. Libera Corp. (No. 2)* [1996] 1 Lloyd's Rep. 381. And see *Egon Oldendorff v. Libera Corp. (No. 1)* [1995] 2 Lloyd's Rep. 64.

[55] *Egon Oldendorff v. Libera Corp. (No. 2)* [1996] 1 Lloyd's Rep. 381, 389–390.

[56] Common law decisions did not always stress this additional factor, though there are dicta which refer to it: see, *e.g. Compagnie d'Armement Maritime SA v. Compagnie Tunisienne de Navigation SA* [1971] A.C. 572, 579, 600, 605, 609.

[57] *Egon Oldendorff v. Libera Corp. (No. 2)* [1996] 1 Lloyd's Rep. 381, 390. In this case the parties had agreed to English arbitration by arbitrators conversant with shipping matters in respect of disputes arising out of a well-known English form of charterparty containing standard clauses and terminology with well-known meanings in English law. Although the parties were, respectively, German and Japanese, it was held that all of these factors pointed to an intention to choose English law for the purposes of Art. 3(1) of the Convention. The parties had chosen England as the place of arbitration because it was "neutral". Equally, they must have intended a "neutral" law to apply. The inference to be drawn, in favour of English law, will of course be stronger if the arbitration clause provides for arbitration in England before arbitrators of the London Maritime Arbitrators' Association, or before London brokers, or a London association or exchange: *ibid.* And see *Egon Oldendorff v. Libera Corp. (No. 1)* [1995] 2 Lloyd's Rep. 64.

[58] *James Miller and Partners Ltd v. Whitworth Street Estates (Manchester) Ltd* [1970] A.C. 583. See *ante*, § 31–004.

[59] Giuliano-Lagarde Report, p. 17.

[60] *Post*, §§ 31–066—31–085.

account of factors which supervened after the conclusion of the contract."[61] The better view, it is suggested, is that subsequent conduct may be taken into account in this context also to the extent that it points to the intentions of the parties at the time the contract was made.[62]

"Implied" choice or "no" choice. One difficulty in the common law, which   **31–051** remains under the Convention, is that of distinguishing between a case of "implied" choice of law and a case of "no" choice of law.[63] In the latter case, Article 4 will be used to determine the applicable law.[64] But opinions may legitimately differ on whether a particular case constitutes one in which a choice of law has been demonstrated with reasonable certainty or whether it is, in fact, one in which no choice of law has been made.[65] The obvious solution to this potential uncertainty is to include an express choice of law in the contract.

Partial choice of law. The first sentence of Article 3(1) permits the parties to   **31–052** "select the law applicable to the whole or part only of the contract." The provision introduces into the Convention the notion of the splitting[66] of the contract, or severability[67] thereof, often described in the jargon of the conflict of laws as *dépeçage*,[68] whereby different aspects (or parts) of a contract may be governed by different laws. This notion was also recognised in the common law.[69] Its inclusion in the Convention was not, however, uncontroversial,[70] though ultimately it was accepted that permitting parties, in this way, to choose different laws to govern different parts of the contract or to make a choice of law in relation to one part and no choice in relation to another part or parts of the contract[71] could be justified as the logical conclusion of the principle of party autonomy in choice of law.[72]

The Giuliano-Lagarde Report provides some guidance as to how it is thought   **31–053** the provision is likely to operate. First, it appears that the contract must consist of several parts "which are separable and independent of each other from the legal and economic point of view."[73] Secondly, when the contract can be split in this sense,

> "the choice must be logically consistent, *i.e.* it must relate to elements in the contract which can be governed by different laws without giving rise to contradictions. For

---

[61] Giuliano-Lagarde Report, p. 20.

[62] See *Dicey & Morris op. cit.* pp. 1210–1211; Plender *op. cit* pp. 93–95. This conclusion is supported by the fact that the common law approach is not accepted in other countries: see F.A. Mann (1973) 89 L.Q.R. 464. See also *Egon Oldendorff v. Libera Corp. (No. 2)* [1996] 1 Lloyd's Rep. 380, 382.

[63] See, *e.g.* the views of Lords Diplock and Wilberforce in *Amin Rasheed Shipping Corpn. v. Kuwait Insurance Co.* [1984] A.C. 50. See *ante*, § 31–011, n. 60.

[64] Giuliano-Lagarde Report, p. 17. *Post*, §§ 31–066—31–085.

[65] And compare the use of "reasonable certainty" in the English text with the phrase "*de façon certaine*" in the French text: see Anton, *Private International Law* (2nd ed., 1990), p. 325.

[66] *cf. Kahler v. Midland Bank* [1950] A.C. 24, 42, *per* Lord MacDermott.

[67] Giuliano-Lagarde Report, p. 17.

[68] *ibid.* See generally, *Dicey & Morris op. cit.* pp. 1207–1208; Cheshire and North *op. cit.* pp. 476–477.

[69] *Ante*, § 31–014.

[70] Giuliano-Lagarde Report, p. 17.

[71] *ibid.* and at p. 20.

[72] Giuliano-Lagarde Report, p. 17.

[73] *ibid.*

example, an 'index-linking clause' may be subject to a different law; on the other hand it is unlikely that repudiation of the contract for non-performance would be subjected to two different laws, one for the vendor and the other for the purchaser."[74]

If the chosen laws cannot be reconciled as a matter of logic, then neither choice of law is effective so that the law applicable to the contract will have to be determined according to Article 4 of the Convention, as if the parties had made no choice of law at all.[75] Finally, where parties make a choice of law in relation to one part of the contract but no such choice in relation to the other part or parts, the law applicable to the latter part or parts will also have to be determined according to Article 4 of the Convention.[76]

31–054   **Changing the applicable law.** At common law, it was uncertain whether the parties were free to change the law governing their contract and, if so, what law governed the question of whether they were able to make such change.[77] Support, however, existed for the power to change,[78] such power to change being governed by English law as the law of the forum.[79] Article 3(2) of the Rome Convention provides a specific choice of law rule to deal with the question:

> "The parties may at any time agree to subject the contract to a law other than that which previously governed it, whether as a result of an earlier choice under this Article or of other provisions of this Convention. Any variation by the parties of the law to be applied made after the conclusion of the contract shall not prejudice its formal validity under Article 9 or adversely affect the rights of third parties."

In this formulation, it is necessary to emphasise the proviso as to formal validity of the contract[80] and the need to protect the rights of third parties who may be adversely affected by a change in the applicable law.[81] Subject to these points, however, the provision gives the parties to the contract maximum freedom as to the time when the ultimate choice of law is to be made since it confers on the parties such a wide freedom to change the applicable law.[82] This freedom extends to changing the applicable law when that law was chosen by the parties and to cases where the governing law which is changed was initially applicable by virtue of Article 4 of the Convention.[83] The choice of law which purports to vary or change the original governing law will, however, need to comply with the requirements of Article 3(1) of the Convention.[84] The principle of the common

---

[74] *ibid.*

[75] *ibid.* See *post,* §§ 31–066—31–085.

[76] *ibid.* and at p. 20. See *post,* §§ 31–066—31–085.

[77] *Ante,* § 31–004.

[78] *Ante,* § 31–004.

[79] See *Dicey & Morris op. cit.* p. 1220.

[80] See *post,* §§ 31–117—31–124.

[81] "The preservation of third-party rights appears to be entirely justified. In certain legal systems, a third-party may have acquired rights in consequence of a contract concluded between two other persons. These rights cannot be affected by a subsequent change in the choice of the applicable law": Giuliano-Lagarde Report, p. 18.

[82] *ibid.*

[83] *ibid.*

[84] *ibid.* The power to change the governing law, pursuant to Art. 3(2), would seem to be distinct from any power to change which may exist, as a matter of procedure, in national law. An example in English law would be a case where parties do not rely on an applicable foreign law in their statements of case, in which case English law will apply: see Giuliano-Lagarde Report, p. 18; *ante,* § 31–047.

law which requires that a contract have a governing law from its inception[85] is equally a principle of the Rome Convention which is unaffected by Article 3(2). It would seem, however, that where the contract provides for two governing laws, the second to be applied if the event on which the application of the first depends is negatived,[86] then the applicable law can be said to be changed from the first to the second law, pursuant to Article 3(2), when the relevant event comes about.[87]

Validity of choice of law. Article 3(4) refers the "existence and validity of **31–055** the consent of the parties as to the choice of the applicable law" to the law which the parties purported to choose, *i.e.* the law which would be the chosen law if the choice of law were valid.[88] This so-called "bootstrap" rule would seem to enable one party to choose the law to govern consent to a choice of law.[89] However, it does not provide an answer in cases where there are conflicting standard forms of contract each referring to different applicable laws (or where one standard form contains a choice of law and the other does not). In such cases, it has been suggested that resort should be had to the law which would govern the contract if no choice of law had been made,[90] *i.e.* Article 4 of the Convention. In any event, Article 4 will determine the governing law if, according to the "bootstrap" rule, there is no valid choice of law in the contract itself.[91]

Limitations upon the choice. In general, the provisions of the Rome Conven- **31–056** tion will, in practice, give the parties a comparatively wide freedom to choose the applicable law.[92] There are, however, some provisions which place specific restraints limits upon this freedom. The tendency of these provisions, however, is to limit rather than invalidate *in toto* the choice of law.[93] These specific limitations are discussed in the following paragraphs.

Mandatory rules. The Convention refers to the concept of "mandatory rule" **31–057** in various provisions which will be discussed in this chapter.[94] At this juncture, in connection with the power of the parties to choose the governing law, it is necessary to refer to Article 3(3) which provides as follows:

> "The fact that the parties have chosen a foreign law, whether or not accompanied by the choice of a foreign tribunal, shall not, where all the other elements relevant to the situation at the time of the choice are connected with one country only, prejudice the

---

[85] *Ante*, § 31–004.
[86] *Ante*, § 31–004.
[87] *Dicey & Morris op. cit.* pp. 1220–1222.
[88] Arts. 3(4), 8(1) (*post*, §§ 31–111—31–116), 9(4) (*post*, §§ 31–117—31–124). See *Egon Oldendorff v. Libera Corp. (No. 1)* [1995] 2 Lloyd's Rep. 64; *Egon Oldendorff v. Libera Corp. (No. 2)* [1996] 1 Lloyd's Rep. 380.
[89] Cheshire and North *op. cit.* p. 486.
[90] *Dicey & Morris op. cit.* p. 1229.
[91] *Post*, §§ 31–066—31–085.
[92] For discussion of the more stringent rules in relation to "certain consumer contracts" and "individual employment contracts," see *post*, §§ 31–086—31–103.
[93] A choice of law which is meaningless (*cf. Compagnie D'Armement Maritime SA v. Compagnie Tunisienne de Navigation SA* [1970] A.C. 572, *ante* § 31–005) must be regarded as invalid (or ineffective at any rate) under the Convention. As to a choice which is not that of the law of a country, see *ante*, § 31–046.
[94] See Art. 5 (*post*, §§ 31–087—31–093); Art. 6 (*post*, §§ 31–094—31–103); Art. 7(1) (*post*, § 31–059); Art. 7(2) (*post*, § 31–064); Art. 9(6) (*post*, § 31–121).

application of rules of the law of that country which cannot be derogated from by contract, hereinafter called 'mandatory rules'."[95]

The purpose of this provision would seem, essentially, to be somewhat narrow. It is designed to prevent the evasion of mandatory rules, as defined in the Article, in relation to a contract which, but for a choice of foreign law, would be a purely domestic contract, by the simple device of including in the contract such a choice of foreign law.[96] Such a narrow situation does not appear to have arisen in any reported case at common law,[97] but the narrowness of Article 3(3) is explicable by reference to the desire of the United Kingdom negotiators of the Convention to preserve the possibility of the parties choosing a foreign law although there was no other foreign element in the situation.[98] Such a possibility should only, thus, be restricted by the mandatory rules of the only other country which would otherwise be relevant to the situation.[99]

31–058   **Connection with one country only.** For Article 3(3) to operate it is first necessary that all the elements (other than the choice of law and jurisdiction where present) relevant to the situation (not the contract) at the time of the choice are connected with *one* country only. Accordingly, the provision will not apply where, although at first sight the contract appears to be connected to one country only, there are other elements relevant to the "situation" (which goes beyond the contract itself) which are connected with another country or other countries. Having said that, it is not easy to determine in the abstract whether an element is "relevant" to the "situation." Such a conclusion may be reached if a seller manufactures goods in one country which are then sold in another country under a contract entirely connected with the latter country apart from the choice of the law of yet a different country. It is by no means certain that this is a situation which would not call Article 3(3) into play, though it is suggested that Article 3(3) should not apply here.[1] Secondly, the time at which it must be ascertained whether the relevant elements are connected with one country only is the time at which the choice of law is made so that connections with other countries which materialise after that time must seemingly be ignored. Thirdly, although Article 3(3) speaks literally of a choice of foreign law, it may apply, nonetheless, if parties to a contract have chosen English law if all the other elements relevant to the situation at the time of the choice are connected with a foreign country. Thus if all the other elements relevant to the situation are connected with Germany but the contract contains a choice of English law then the English court would have to apply German mandatory rules.[2] Likewise, if all the other elements relevant to the situation were connected with England, but the contract contains a choice of German law, the English court will have to apply any relevant English mandatory rules.

---

[95] See *Dicey & Morris op. cit.* pp. 1215–1216, 1239–1240; Cheshire and North *op. cit.* pp. 480–482, 496–499; Plender *op. cit.* pp. 100–102; Kaye *op. cit.* pp. 159–168; Philip in North (ed.), *Contract Conflicts* (1982), p. 81, at pp. 95–97; Morse (1982) 2 Ybk.Eur.L. 107, 122–124.

[96] See Giuliano-Lagarde Report, p. 18.

[97] Lasok and Stone, *Conflict of Laws in the European Community* (1987), pp. 377–378.

[98] Giuliano-Lagarde Report, p. 18.

[99] *ibid.*

[1] Lasok and Stone *op. cit.* pp. 377–378; *Dicey & Morris op. cit.* p. 1215.

[2] Presumably, the English court would not apply these rules unless they were pleaded and proved: see *ante*, § 31–047.

"Mandatory rules". The core difficulty with Article 3(3) is, however, the   **31–059**
concept of "mandatory rules." By way of purported definition, the provision
describes them as rules "which cannot be derogated from by contract, hereinafter
called 'mandatory rules'." This wording might be thought to suggest that the
concept of mandatory rules bears this meaning wherever these rules are referred
to in other provisions of this Convention. Reference to such rules appears in
Article 5 (dealing with "certain consumer contracts"),[3] Article 6 (dealing with
"individual employment contracts"),[4] Article 7(1) (which is of broader application) and Article 7(2) (which concerns mandatory rules of the law of the forum[5]).
Article 7(1) does not have the force of law in the United Kingdom[6] which renders
unnecessary a detailed examination of its terms. However, comparison of Articles 3(3) and 7(1) indicates that the Convention contemplates two kinds of
mandatory rule.[7] Article 7(1) gives the courts of a country which implements the
provision a discretion, when applying under the Convention the law of one
country, to give effect to "the mandatory rules of the law of another country with
which the situation has a close connection, if and in so far as, under the law of
the latter country, those rules must be applied whatever the law applicable to the
contract." It appears from this formulation that to be applied under Article 7(1),
a rule must not only be mandatory in the sense of Article 3(3) but must also bear
an additional quality, namely that it must also be a rule which must be applied
whatever the law applicable to the contract. Accordingly, Article 3(3) is concerned with securing the application of mandatory rules of a domestic nature, *i.e.*
rules which cannot be derogated from in a purely domestic transaction, even by
a choice of foreign law, but which can be derogated from in a contract which
bears an international character.[8] On the other hand, Article 7(1) entails the
possibility, for courts of states which implement the provision, to apply mandatory rules of a higher order, namely rules which apply whatever law is
applicable to the contract even when the contract is of an international
character.[9]

Rules not applicable if foreign law chosen. When Article 3(3) applies, its   **31–060**
effect is that the choice of foreign law "shall not . . . prejudice" application of
relevant mandatory rules. On one view, this wording might suggest that a rule is
mandatory for this purpose even if, according to the law of the country of which

---

[3] *Post,* §§ 31–086—31–093.
[4] *Post,* §§ 31–094—31–103.
[5] *Post,* § 31–064. See also Art. 9(6), *post,* § 31–121.
[6] Contracts (Applicable Law) Act 1990, s.2(2). Art. 22 of the Convention permits Contracting
States to make a reservation to the application of this provision, which power the U.K. exercised on
signing the Convention. See *Akai Pty. Ltd v. People's Insurance Co. Ltd* [1998] 1 Lloyd's Rep. 90,
100.
[7] *Dicey & Morris op. cit.* pp. 1239–1243; Cheshire and North *op. cit.* pp. 496–503; Plender *op. cit.*
pp. 100–102, 151–157; Kaye *op. cit.* pp. 160–163, 167–168, 239–267; Philip in North (ed.), *Contract
Conflicts* (1982), Chap. 5; Jackson *ibid.* Chap. 4; Diamond (1986) 216 *Recueil des Cours IV,* 233,
288–298; North (1990) 220 *Recueil des Cours I,* 3, 191–194; Morse (1982) 2 Ybk.Eur.L. 107,
121–124, 142–147.
[8] This view is supported by reference to the French text of the Convention. Mandatory rules in Art.
3(3) are described in that text as *"dispositions imperatives."* Art. 7 is, however, headed by the words
"Lois de Police." The change in terminology reflects a distinction drawn in some Continental legal
systems between the former class of laws from which derogation may be permitted in international
contracts, and the latter class from which no derogation is permitted even in such contracts: Plender
op. cit. p. 101.
[9] For the historical origins of this provision, see F.A. Mann in Lipstein (ed.), *Harmonisation of
Private International Law by the EEC* (1978), pp. 31–32; *Dicey & Morris op. cit.* p. 1242.

it forms part, it is possible to contract out of it by a choice of foreign law. It is submitted, however, that Article 3(3) does not have this effect. If the country of whose law the rule forms part would not apply the rule in the circumstances of the case then the rule is inapplicable in the context of Article 3(3).[10]

31–061   **When is a rule mandatory?** Where an English court is faced with a problem involving Article 3(3) and the possibility arises that foreign mandatory rules may apply, then whether a rule is mandatory for this purpose will depend on the view of it in the law of the country of which it forms part. Where it is alleged that an English mandatory rule is applicable, it will first be necessary to decide whether the particular rule in question does possess a mandatory character. A statute may give an express indication of whether, and to what extent, its provisions are mandatory,[11] but this is not always the case. Further, it may be particularly difficult to determine whether any particular common law rule is mandatory. All that can be said with any degree of certainty is that, in the absence of any express indication, whether any given rule is mandatory will depend on the proper construction of the rule.[12]

31–062   **Mandatory rules of English law.** As far as English law is concerned, it is suggested that most rules possessing a mandatory character will be contained in legislation and these will also be rules which apply whatever the law applicable to the contract.[13] Accordingly, although Article 3(3) is designed to secure application of "domestic" mandatory rules, and, *a fortiori*, internationally mandatory rules, there are unlikely to be many rules of domestic English contract law which will be treated as mandatory for the purposes of Article 3(3). Thus, for example, it would be doubtful whether the requirement of consideration would be treated as mandatory,[14] though it is possible that the English rule against contractual penalties bears that character.[15] In contrast, statutory rules designed to give effect to important social policies, for example rules concerning consumer or employee protection, are more likely to be regarded as being of a mandatory nature.[16]

31–063   **Chosen law governs other issues.** Lastly, it must be emphasised that the application of Article 3(3) does not strike down the choice of law *in toto*. The provision merely restricts application of the chosen law to the extent that the chosen law conflicts with relevant mandatory rules. To the extent that these

---

[10] *Dicey & Morris op. cit.* p. 1216; Morse (1982) 2 Ybk.Eur.L. 107, 123; *cf.* Cheshire and North *op. cit.* p. 497.

[11] See, *e.g.* Unfair Contract Terms Act 1977, s.27(2), *ante*, § 31–007; Unfair Terms in Consumer Contracts Regulations 1994 (*ante*, § 31–007). Reg. 7 provides that the Regulations apply notwithstanding any contract term which applies or purports to apply the law of a non-Member State, if the contract has a close connection with the territories of the Member States: for discussion of this formula, see *Benjamin's Sale of Goods* (5th ed., 1997), § 25–095 and *ante*, § 15–072. See also Knofel (1998) 47 I.C.L.Q. 439. *cf.* Late Payment of Commercial Debts (Interest) Act 1998, s.12(2), discussed *post*, §§ 31–142—31–145.

[12] *cf. The Hollandia* [1983] 1 A.C. 565.

[13] Cheshire and North *op. cit.* p. 497.

[14] *cf. Re Bonacina* [1912] 2 Ch. 394.

[15] *cf. Godard v. Gray* (1870) L.R. 6 Q.B. 139. See *Dicey & Morris op. cit.* p. 1240.

[16] See *post*, §§ 31–089, 31–100.

mandatory rules are not prejudiced, the chosen law will continue to govern issues not covered by mandatory rules.[17]

Mandatory rules of the law of the forum. Article 7(2) of the Rome Convention   **31–064**
tion provides that

> "nothing in this Convention shall restrict the application of the rules of the law of the forum in a situation where they are mandatory irrespective of the law otherwise applicable to the contract."[18]

As far as English courts are concerned, the provision will enable them to give effect to English rules of this nature so as to override the choice of law by the parties.[19] Rules envisaged as applicable through the principle are, notably, rules on cartels, competition and restrictive practices, consumer protection and certain rules concerning carriage.[20] To qualify for application, the relevant mandatory rules must be rules which cannot be derogated from even in an international transaction governed by a foreign law, as opposed to mandatory rules which are the subject-matter of Article 3(3) where what are relevant are rules which are mandatory in a domestic context but which can, nevertheless, be avoided or restricted in application, by a choice of foreign law.[21] Whether any particular rule bears this overriding[22] character will, in the absence of any express indication in the rule itself,[23] depend on the proper construction of the relevant rule.[24]

---

[17] *cf. The Hollandia, supra.*

[18] See *Dicey & Morris op. cit.* pp. 1240–1241; Cheshire and North *op. cit.* pp. 499–503.

[19] Some such rules may completely override the choice of law by the parties: see, *e.g.* Employment Rights Act 1996, s.204, *post*, § 31–098. Others may only restrict the power of the parties to avoid the relevant rules by a mere choice of law where English law would be applicable if there were no such choice: see, *e.g.* Unfair Contract Terms Act 1977, s.27(2), *ante*, § 31–007. Contrast Unfair Contract Terms Act 1977, s.27(1), which provides that the controls on exemption clauses contained in the Act do not apply where the law applicable to the contract is the law of any part of the United Kingdom only by choice of the parties and apart from that choice would be the law of some country outside the United Kingdom. If a contract (other than one excluded from the 1977 Act by s.26) contains a choice of English law, but the contract would be governed by a foreign law were the rules contained in Art. 4 of the Convention (*post*, §§ 31–066—31–085) to be applied, the controls contained in the Act will not form part of the applicable law: *Surzur Overseas Ltd v. Ocean Reliance Shipping Co. Ltd* [1997] C.L. 318. And see Late Payment of Commercial Debts (Interest) Act 1998, s.12(1), discussed post, §§ 31–142—31–145.

[20] Giuliano-Lagarde Report, p. 38. For a discussion of potentially mandatory rules contained in European Union legislation, see Knofel (1998) 47 I.C.L.Q. 439.

[21] See *ante*, §§ 31–059—31–062. *cf.* Art. 7(1), which does not have the force of law in the U.K.: *ante*, § 31–059.

[22] See *Dicey & Morris op. cit.* pp. 21–25.

[23] Employment Rights Act 1996, s.204; Unfair Contract Terms Act 1977, s.27(2); Unfair Terms in Consumer Contracts Regulations 1994, Reg. 7.

[24] *cf. Boissevain v. Weil* [1949] 1 K.B. 482; *Corocraft Ltd v. Pan American Airways Inc.* [1969] 1 Q.B. 616; *The Hollandia* [1982] Q.B. 872 (affd. [1983] 1 A.C. 565); *English v. Donnelly*, 1958 S.C. 494, not followed in *Hong Kong Shanghai (Shipping) Ltd v. The Cavalry* [1987] H.K.L.R. 287; *Chiron Corpn. v. Organon Teknika (No. 2)* [1993] F.S.R. 567; *Kaye's Leasing Corpn. Pty. Ltd v. Fletcher* (1964) 116 C.L.R. 124; *Att.-Gen.'s Reference No. 1 of 1987* (1987) 47 S.A.S.R. 152; *DR Insurance Co. v. Central National Insurance Co.* [1996] 1 Lloyd's Rep. 74. See also *Akai Pty. Ltd v. The People's Insurance Co. Ltd* (1996) 71 A.L.J.R. 156; *cf Akai Pty. Ltd v. People's Insurance Co. Ltd* [1998] 1 Lloyd's Rep. 80. And see *Duncan v. Motherwell Bridge and Engineering Co. Ltd*, 1952 S.C. 131, *post* § 31–089.

31–065   **Public policy.**[25] Article 16 of the Rome Convention contains a general reservation to the application of a foreign law on the basis of public policy (*ordre
public*). "The application of a rule of the law of any country specified by this
Convention may be refused only if such application is manifestly incompatible
with the public policy ('ordre public') of the forum." This provision, although of
general application, may also be resorted to to deny effect to a choice of law by
the parties to the contract.[26] For the purposes of Article 16, public policy includes
"Community public policy."[27] The expression "manifestly" is designed to indicate that there must be special grounds, of an exceptional nature, for the
exclusion to apply.[28] It is also important to stress that the concept of public policy
is not to be applied to a foreign law in the abstract. It may only be resorted to
when a provision of foreign law, if applied to an actual case, would offend
English public policy.[29] The terms of Article 16 clearly warn against an ubiqui-
tous application of the doctrine,[30] although it does not purport to effect any
substantive change in the content of English public policy as such.[31]

(d) *Applicable Law in the Absence of Choice by the Parties*[32]

31–066   **General principle.** Article 4(1) of the Rome Convention provides as follows:
"To the extent that the law applicable to the contract has not been chosen in
accordance with Article 3, the contract shall be governed by the law of the
country with which it is most closely connected."[33] This proposition has a
familiar ring to a common lawyer, since it reflects the general principle of the
common law which was developed to deal with cases where the parties had made
no choice of law in the contract itself.[34] The first general point to note is that
Article 4 envisages the possibility of a contract being governed in part by a law
chosen by the parties and as to another part, by the law applicable through Article
4, since Article 4 operates to "the extent that" the parties have made no choice
of law in the contract itself.[35] This concept of *dépeçage*[36] is extended in the
second sentence of Article 4(1) where it is stated that a "severable part of the
contract" which has a closer connection with another country may, "by way of
exception," be governed by the law of that country though the remaining part or

---

[25] *Dicey & Morris op. cit.* pp. 1277–1284; Cheshire and North *op. cit.* pp. 503–504; Plender *op.
cit.* pp. 157–158; Kaye *op. cit.* pp. 345–350; *post,* §§ 31–160—31–162.
[26] *cf. ante,* § 31–006.
[27] Giuliano-Lagarde Report, p. 38.
[28] *ibid.*
[29] *ibid.*
[30] *ibid.*
[31] Since the doctrine of public policy purports to protect the interests of the forum, it would seem
that the application of Art. 16 to any given case (as opposed to the interpretation of its meaning)
cannot be the subject of a request for a preliminary ruling from the European Court under the Brussels
Protocol (not yet in force). *cf.* Kaye *op. cit.* p. 349.
[32] *Dicey & Morris on the Conflict of Laws* (12th ed., 1993), pp. 1230–1238, 1325–1328,
1345–1349, 1381–1391, 1405–1410, 1455–1456, 1468–1469; Cheshire and North, *Private International Law* (12th ed., 1992), pp. 487–495; Plender, *The European Contracts Convention* (1991),
Chap. 6; Kaye, *The New Private International Law of Contract of the European Community* (1993),
pp. 171–202. As to consumer contracts and employment contracts, see *post,* §§ 31–086—31–103. As
to insurance contracts, see *ante,* §§ 31–043—31–044.
[33] For the meaning of "law of a country," see *ante,* § 31–023.
[34] See *ante,* § 31–011.
[35] Giuliano-Lagarde Report, p. 20. *cf. ante,* §§ 31–052—31–053.
[36] *cf. ante,* §§ 31–052—31–053.

parts of the contract will be governed by the law of the country with which it is, or they are, most closely connected. The Giuliano-Lagarde Report emphasises that the words "by way of exception" are to be interpreted in the sense that the courts must have regard to severability as seldom as possible.[37] Accordingly, it is likely that the second sentence of Article 4(1) will be of limited importance in practice. The second general point to note is the opinion expressed in the Giuliano-Lagarde Report that in order to determine the law of the country with which the contract is most closely connected, it is possible to take account of factors which appear after the conclusion of the contract.[38]

Presumptions. Article 4 departs from the common law in establishing in **31–067** Article 4(2)–(4) a series of presumptions which are to be used to identify the law of the country with which the contract is most closely connected.[39] Specific presumptions are established for certain contracts regarding immovables[40] and contracts for the carriage of goods.[41] Article 4(2) establishes a controversial general presumption which will be applicable in cases involving most other types of contract.[42] However, these presumptions, where applicable, are to be disregarded if it appears from the circumstances as a whole that the contract is more closely connected with another country than it is with the country whose law is indicated by application of the presumption, in which case the law applicable to the contract will be the law of the former country.[43] These various elements of Article 4 are discussed in the following paragraphs.

The general presumption. Article 4(2) provides as follows: **31–068**

"Subject to the provisions of paragraph 5 of this Article, it shall be presumed that the contract is most closely connected with the country where the party who is to effect the performance which is characteristic of the contract has, at the time of the conclusion of the contract, his habitual residence, or, in the case of a body corporate or unincorporate, its central administration. However, if the contract is entered into in the course of that party's trade or profession, that country shall be the country in which the principal place of business is situated or, where under the terms of the contract the performance is to be effected through a place of business other than the principal place of business, the country in which that other place of business is situated."

It can be seen that application of this rule involves, first, the identification of the "characteristic performance" of the contract in question. The law applicable to the contract will then, presumptively, be the law of the habitual residence or central administration (as the case may be) of the party who is to effect that characteristic performance. Secondly, however, if the contract is entered into in the course of the "characteristic performer's" trade or profession, then the applicable law will, presumptively, be the law of the characteristic performer's principal place of business. But where, thirdly, under the terms of the contract

---

[37] Giuliano-Lagarde Report, p. 23.
[38] *ibid. cf. ante*, §§ 31–004, 31–050.
[39] Presumptions, once fashionable in English law, were eventually abandoned: *Coast Lines Ltd v. Hudig & Veder Chartering N.V.* [1972] 2 Q.B. 34. See *ante*, § 31–011.
[40] Art. 4(3). See *post*, §§ 31–077—31–099.
[41] Art. 4(4). See *post*, §§ 31–080—31–083.
[42] See *post*, §§ 31–068—31–076.
[43] Art. 4(5). See *post*, §§ 31–084—31–085.

performance is to be effected through a place of business other than the characteristic performer's principal place of business, the applicable law will be, presumptively, the law of the country in which that other place of business is situated.

31–069 **Characteristic performance.**[44] The central concept of Article 4(2) is that of the "characteristic performance" of a contract. The expression is not defined in the Convention itself and is a novel one for Contracting States,[45] owing its origin to Swiss law.[46] Elucidation of the concept involves identifying specific contracts and then identifying in relation to each such contract the performance which characterises or typifies the relevant contract, in reality identifying the obligation which is peculiar to the contract under consideration.[47] The concept has been much criticised,[48] but is greeted with effusion in the Giuliano-Lagarde Report: "this performance refers to the function which the legal relationship involved fulfils in the economic and social life of any country. The concept of characteristic performance essentially links the contract to the social and economic environment of which it forms part."[49] Whether the reader will be persuaded by such claims remains to be seen.

31–070 **Performance for which payment due "characteristic".** According to the Giuliano-Lagarde Report, which purports to provide guidance to the application of the doctrine, identifying characteristic performance causes no difficulty in the case of unilateral contracts.[50] Presumably, since in such contracts only one party agrees to confer a benefit on another, the characteristic performance will be that of the party agreeing to confer the benefit.[51] More controversy surrounds the analysis of reciprocal or bilateral contracts in which each party has to perform obligations. The Report points out that the performance of

> "one of the parties in a modern economy usually takes the form of the payment of money. This is not, of course, the characteristic performance of the contract. It is the performance for which payment is due, *i.e.* depending on the type of contract, the delivery of goods, the granting of the right to make use of an item of property, the provision of a service, transport, insurance, banking operations, security etc, which usually constitutes the centre of gravity and the socio-economic function of the contractual transaction."[52]

This passage suggests that characteristic performance is a somewhat abstract notion: it is not the payment of money but performance for which such payment is due.

---

[44] *Dicey & Morris op. cit.* pp. 1253–1256; Cheshire and North *op. cit.* pp. 491–494; Plender *op. cit.* pp. 108–113; Kaye *op. cit.* pp. 178–183; Schultsz in North (ed.), *Contract Conflicts* (1982), p. 185; Diamond (1986) 216 *Recueil des Cours IV*, 233, 273–276; Lasok and Stone, *Conflict of Laws in the European Community* (1987), pp. 361–364; Morse (1982) 2 Ybk.Eur.L. 107, 126–131; Lipstein (1981) 3 Northwestern Journal Int'l. L. & Bus. 402; Jessurun d'Oliveira (1977) 25 Am.J.Comp.L. 303.
[45] *cf.* Giuliano-Lagarde Report, p. 20.
[46] See Lipstein *op. cit.*; *Dicey & Morris op. cit.* p. 1233.
[47] Giuliano-Lagarde Report, p. 20.
[48] *e.g.* Lasok and Stone *op. cit.*; Morse *op. cit.*; Jessurun d'Oliveira *op. cit.*
[49] Giuliano-Lagarde Report, p. 20.
[50] *ibid.*
[51] Kaye *op. cit.* p. 181.
[52] Giuliano-Lagarde Report, p. 20.

"Characteristic" performance not determinable. It does not follow from **31–071** this that every contract not specifically dealt with in Article 4(3) and (4) must have a characteristic performance. This is recognised in Article 4(5) which provides that Article 4(2) shall not apply if the characteristic performance cannot be determined.[53] One obvious example is that of a contract of barter or exchange.[54] It has also been suggested that certain kinds of joint venture agreements,[55] certain types of distributorship agreements,[56] and contracts between publisher and author[57] may similarly not have a particular performance which can be said to characterise them. In such cases the most closely connected law will have to be determined without the aid of any presumption.[58]

Specific applications. English courts have so far had relatively few opportu- **31–072** nities to consider the meaning of characteristic performance in the context of particular types of contracts. However, drawing on the few decisions and the passage from the Giuliano-Lagarde Report quoted above, the following conclusions may be reached. In a contract of sale, the characteristic performance is that of the seller[59]; in a contract of hire, the characteristic performance will be that of the party who makes the item available for hire[60]; in a contract of insurance,[61] the characteristic performance is that of the insurer since he provides the service (cover) for which the insured pays his premium[62]; in a contract between an insurance broker and an insurance company seeking reinsurance, the characteristic performance is that of the broker[63]; in a contract between banker and customer, the characteristic performance is that of the bank[64]; in a letter of credit transaction,[65] separation of the various contracts involved reveals that the characteristic performance in the contract between the issuing bank and the buyer is that of the bank,[66] the characteristic performance in the contract between the issuing

---

[53] See, further, *post*, §§ 31–083—31–085.

[54] See, *e.g.* Cheshire and North *op. cit.* pp. 491–492.

[55] Kaye *op. cit.* p. 182.

[56] See Collins in North (ed.), *Contract Conflicts* (1982), pp. 206–210; *Dicey & Morris op. cit.* p. 1235; see Plender *op. cit.* pp. 112–113 who cites a German decision (Dortmund L.G., April 8, 1985 [1989] I Prax 510) to this effect.

[57] Kaye *op. cit.* p. 182.

[58] See *post*, § 31–094.

[59] See, *e.g. Dicey & Morris op. cit.* pp. 1234, 1325; *Benjamin's Sale of Goods* (5th ed., 1997), § 25–054. The Dutch Hoge Raad has held that the characteristic performance of a contract of sale is that of the seller: see *Société Nouvelle des Papeteries de l' Aa S.A. v. B.V. Machinefabrik B.O.A.*, 1992 N.J. 750, discussed by Struycken [1996] L.M.C.L.Q. 18. As to consumer sales see *post*, §§ 31–087—31–094.

[60] *Dicey & Morris op. cit.* pp. 1325–1326.

[61] But see *ante*, §§ 31–043—31–044.

[62] *Crédit Lyonnais v. New Hampshire Insurance Co.* [1997] 2 Lloyd's Rep. 1; Giuliano-Lagarde Report, p. 20; *Dicey & Morris op. cit.* p. 1346. In reinsurance contracts, the characteristic performance will be that of the re-insurer: *ibid* p. 1381. An insurance contract may be a consumer contract: see *post*, §§ 31–087—31–094.

[63] *HIB Ltd v. Guardian Insurance Co. Ltd* [1997] 1 Lloyd's Rep. 412.

[64] *Sierra Leone Telecommunications Co. Ltd v. Barclays Bank plc* [1998] 2 All E.R. 821; Giuliano-Lagarde Report, p. 20; *Dicey & Morris op. cit.* p. 1234. A contract between a bank and a customer may be a consumer contract.

[65] See Morse [1994] L.M.C.L.Q. 560; Davenport and Smith [1994] 9 Butterworths Journal of International Banking and Financial Law 3.

[66] This follows from the authority cited in n. 52, *supra*, since the provision of the credit is a service for the customer (buyer). See also *Bank of Baroda v. Vysya Bank Ltd* [1994] 2 Lloyd's Rep. 87, 92.

bank and the confirming bank is that of the confirming bank,[67] the characteristic performance in the contract between the confirming bank and the beneficiary is that of the confirming bank,[68] while the characteristic performance in the contract between the issuing bank and the beneficiary is that of the issuing bank[69]; in a contract of loan, the characteristic performance is that of the lender (since he provides the "service" for which repayment is due)[70]; in a contract between lawyer and client, the characteristic performance is that of the lawyer[71]; in a contract between principal and agent, the characteristic performance is that of the agent[72]; in a contract of guarantee, the characteristic performance is that of the guarantor[73]; in a contract of pledge, the characteristic performance is that of the pledgor (since he provides the relevant security)[74]; in contract for storage (a bailment), the characteristic performance is that of the bailee[75]; in construction contracts, the characteristic performance is that of the builder[76]; in wagering contracts, the characteristic performance is that of the party who offers the facility for the placing of the wager.[77]

31–073   **Applicable law.** Despite the central importance of characteristic performance, it is not the *place* of such performance which supplies the applicable law. Rather it is either the law of the country where the characteristic performer is habitually

---

[67] *Bank of Baroda v. Vysya Bank Ltd* [1994] 2 Lloyd's Rep. 87, treating the contract as one of agency in which the characteristic performance was the adding of the confirmation to the credit. The same result is likely to ensue if the correspondent bank does not add its confirmation to the credit, since the contract is one of agency and the characteristic performance in such a contract is that of the agent: *ibid.* at 93; Giuliano-Lagarde Report, p. 20. See also *Bank of Credit and Commerce Hong Kong Ltd v. Sonali Bank* [1995] 1 Lloyd's Rep. 223; *Batstone & Firminger Ltd v. Nasima Enterprises (Nigeria) Ltd* [1996] C.L.C. 1902, 1910. *cf. European Asian Bank A.G. v. Punjab and Sind Bank* [1981] 2 Lloyd's Rep. 651.

[68] *Bank of Baroda v. Vysya Bank Ltd* [1994] 2 Lloyd's Rep. 87. This is because either the bank is providing a banking service (Giuliano-Lagarde Report, p. 20) or because it is of the essence of a letter of credit that the confirming bank undertakes to pay the beneficiary (seller) on presentation of conforming documents ([1994] 2 Lloyd's Rep. 87, 92). See also *Bank of Credit and Commerce Hong Kong Ltd v. Sonali Bank* [1995] 1 Lloyd's Rep. 223; *Batstone & Firminger Ltd v. Nasima Enterprises (Nigeria) Ltd* [1996] C.L.C. 1902, 1910.

[69] *Bank of Baroda v. Vysya Bank Ltd* [1994] 2 Lloyd's Rep. 87. It is highly likely that the presumptively applicable law (that of the country in which the issuing bank's principal place of business is situated) will be displaced, pursuant to Art. 4(5), in favour of the law of the country where payment is to be made against presentation of documents, since this is the country where the obligations of the issuing bank towards the beneficiary under the credit are to be performed: *ibid.*; see *post* § 31–085.

[70] *Surzur Overseas Ltd v. Ocean Reliance Shipping Co. Ltd* [1997] C.L. 318 (bank loan); Kaye *op. cit.* p. 182. This conclusion may be questionable: Morse (1982) 2 Ybk.Eur.L. 107, 128. A loan may be a consumer contract: see *post*, §§ 31–087—31–094.

[71] *Dicey & Morris op. cit.* p. 1235, citing a French decision reported in *Clunet* (1984) p. 583. Such a contract may be a consumer contract: see *post*, §§ 31–087—31–094.

[72] Giuliano-Lagarde Report, p. 209; *Dicey & Morris op. cit.* p. 1455; authorities cited in n. 00 *supra*. But *cf. ante*, § 31–071 (distributorship agreements). Such contracts may be consumer contracts: see *post*, §§ 31–087—31–094.

[73] Giuliano-Lagarde Report, p. 20. Such a contract may be a consumer contract: see *post*, §§ 31–087—31–094.

[74] *Dicey & Morris op. cit.* p. 1326, where it is pointed out that this conclusion is not uncontroversial. Such a contract may be a consumer contract: see *post*, §§ 31–087—31–094.

[75] *cf.* Swiss Private International Law Act 1987, Art. 117(3)(d). Such a contract may be a consumer contract: see *post*, §§ 31–087—31–094.

[76] *Dicey & Morris op. cit.* p. 1387. Such a contract may be a consumer contract: see *post*, §§ 31–087—31–094.

[77] *Dicey & Morris op. cit.* p. 1468. Such a contract may be a consumer contract: see *post*, §§ 31–087—31–094.

resident or, where the performer is a body corporate or unincorporate, its central administration. If the contract is, however, entered into in the course of the characteristic performer's trade or profession, then a different set of connecting factors becomes relevant: in such circumstances, the applicable law will be the law of the country where the characteristic performer's principal place of business is situated or where under the terms of the contract the (characteristic) performance is to be effected through a place of business other than the principal place of business, the applicable law will be that of the country in which that other place of business is situated. These various connecting factors are not defined in the Convention. It is likely, however, that they will receive an autonomous interpretation so as to achieve uniformity in the application of Article 4(2). The meaning given to analogous expressions in English case law, discussed below, is, thus, not conclusive as to their meaning under the Convention.[78] The relevant time for identifying each of the relevant connecting factors is the time at which the contract is concluded.

Habitual residence. English case law has not attributed a consistent meaning **31–074** to this concept.[79] Outside the context of commercial law, it has been said that habitual residence refers to a person's abode in a particular country which he has adopted voluntarily and for settled purposes as part of the regular order of his life for the time being whether of short or long duration.[80] It seems possible that, on this basis, a person may have more than one habitual residence, in which case, it has been suggested, the relevant habitual residence should be that of the place having the closest relationship to the contract and its performance, having regard to the circumstances known to, or contemplated by, the parties at any time before or at the conclusion of the contract.[81] It is conceivable, also, that a person may be without any habitual residence.[82] In such circumstances it would seem that the applicable law will have to be determined without reference to the presumption in Article 4(2).

Central administration. Where the characteristic performer is a body corpo- **31–075** rate or unincorporate, the law of the country where that party's "central administration" is situated may apply. This expression is not defined in the Convention, but, presumably, it will be given an autonomous meaning.[83] The nearest analogy in English law is the concept of "central management and control," as used, for example, in the Civil Jurisdiction and Judgments Act 1982,[84] but that Act also fails to supply a definition. Case law suggests that the question is one of fact, to be answered by an examination of the course of business or trading, reference to

---

[78] *Dicey & Morris op. cit.* p. 1236.

[79] *ibid.* pp. 161–163.

[80] *Kapur v. Kapur* [1984] F.L.R. 920; *R. v. Barnet London Borough Council, ex. p. Nilish Shah* [1984] 2 A.C. 309. *See also Re M. (Minors) (Residence Order: Jurisdiction)* [1993] 1 F.L.R. 495; *A. v. A. (Child Abduction)* [1993] 2 F.L.R. 225; *D. v. D. (Custody: Jurisdiction)* [1996] 1 F.L.R. 574.

[81] See Plender *op. cit.* pp. 131–132, relying on Art. 10(a) of the United Nations Convention on the International Sale of Goods 1980. *cf. Cameron v. Cameron*, 1996 S.L.T. 306 (person can only have one habitual residence, a view which is probably confined to the context of The Hague Convention on the Civil Aspects of Child Abduction 1980, implemented in Child Abduction and Custody Act 1985, Pt. I: see *Dicey and Morris op. cit.* p. 163).

[82] *Hack v. Hack* (1976) 6 Fam. Law 177; but *cf. Re. J. (A Minor)(Abduction)* [1990] 2 A.C. 562.

[83] *cf.* Cheshire and North *op. cit.* p. 493.

[84] s.42.

the place where the principal office is, to the place (or places) where the directors and shareholders reside (or meet) and where control over major policy decisions and business operations is actually exercised.[85]

31–076   **Principal place of business and place of business.** In the more likely situation where a body corporate or unincorporate, as characteristic performer, enters into a contract in the course of its trade or profession, the law of the place of central administration will be substituted by either the law of that party's principal place of business at the time of conclusion of the contract, or if that party's performance is to be effected through a place of business other than the principal place of business, the law of the country in which that other place of business is situated. "Principal place of business" and "place of business" are not defined in the Convention. While it is likely that each expression will be given an autonomous meaning, an analogy suggested by English law is with cases dealing with whether a corporation is present in England for the purpose of being subject to the *in personam* jurisdiction of the English courts.[86] These cases established that a place of business constitutes a place that is fixed and definite[87] and that the activity carried on at that place (which must be the business activity[88] of the corporation) must be carried on for a sufficient period of time for it to be characterised as a business.[89] Whether a particular place of business will be regarded as the "principal" such place will be a question of fact and degree.

31–077   **Immovables.**[90] Article 4(3) of the Rome Convention establishes a special presumption with regard to certain contracts concerning immovable property in the following terms:

> "Notwithstanding the provisions of paragraph 2 of this Article, to the extent that the subject matter of the contract is a right in immovable property or a right to use immovable property it shall be presumed that the contract is most closely connected with the country where the immovable property is situated."

It is important to delimit the scope of this provision. It is, first, confined to contracts which have as their subject matter rights in, or rights to use, immovable property. Thus, for example, it will not apply to contracts for the construction or repair of immovable property since "the main purpose of these contracts is the construction or repair rather than the immovable property itself."[91] A contract for

---

[85] *cf. The Rewia* [1991] 2 Lloyd's Rep. 325; see also *The Deichland* [1990] Q.B. 361; *Re Little Olympian Each Ways Ltd* [1995] 1 W.L.R. 560; *Dicey & Morris op. cit.* pp. 1105–1106.

[86] *Dicey & Morris op. cit.* pp. 305–308. See *Adams v. Cape Industries plc* [1990] Ch. 433, 523–531.

[87] *Saccharin Corporation Ltd v. Chemische Fabrik A.G.* [1911] 2 K.B. 516; *The Theodothos* [1977] 2 Lloyd's Rep. 428.

[88] See *South India Shipping Corpn. Ltd v. Export-Import Bank of Korea* [1985] 1 W.L.R. 585.

[89] *Saccharin Corporation Ltd v. Chemische Fabrik A.G., supra*; *South India Shipping Corpn. Ltd v. Export-Import Bank of Korea, supra*; *Okura & Co. Ltd v. Forsbacka Jernverks A/B* [1914] 1 K.B. 715. In the case of a bank account, performance, *i.e.* repayment of the sum deposited, is to be effected through the branch where the relevant account is kept and the country in which the branch is situated will be the relevant place of business: *Sierra Leone Telecommunications Co. Ltd v. Barclays Bank plc* [1998] 2 All E.R. 821.

[90] *Dicey & Morris op. cit.* pp. 1384–1394.

[91] Giuliano-Lagarde Report, p. 21.

the construction or repair of an immovable will thus be subject to the presumption in Article 4(2).[92] Secondly, Article 4(3) is concerned only with the contractual aspects of a transaction relating to immovables. The proprietary aspects will be subject to common law rules, since the Convention does not apply to proprietary matters.[93]

Severance. Since the presumption in favour of the *lex situs* applies "to the extent that" the contract has as its subject matter a right in or a right to use immovable property, a severable part of the contract which has that as its subject matter may be governed by Article 4(3), whereas the remaining part or parts of the contract may be governed by Article 4(2). In view, however, of the view expressed in the Giuliano-Lagarde Report that severance should be resorted to on only the rarest of occasions,[94] cases of this kind are likely to be rare and may, in any event where appropriate, be the kind of cases in which a court will conclude that the presumption is rebutted, pursuant to Article 4(5).   31–078

Types of contracts for immovables. Article 4(3) clearly applies, *inter alios*, to contracts to sell land[95]; agreements to rent premises[96]; and some timeshare arrangements.[97] It also seems to apply to short term tenancies and holiday lettings of apartments.[98]   31–079

Contracts for the carriage of goods.[99]   31–080

"A contract for the carriage of goods shall not be subject to the presumption in paragraph 2. In such a contract if the country in which, at the time the contract is

---

[92] *Ante*, §§ 31–068—31–076.

[93] Giuliano-Lagarde Report, p. 10. The distinction between a contract to transfer land and an actual transfer of land, may, however, become blurred: see *British South Africa Co. v. De Beers Consolidated Mines Ltd* [1910] 2 Ch. 502, 512, 515, 522–524; see also Case C–294/92 *Webb v. Webb* [1994] E.C.R. I–1717, [1994] Q.B. 696; *cf. Re Hayward* [1997] Ch. 45. As to the common law rules relating to the transfer of immovables, see *Dicey & Morris op. cit.* pp. 960–963. Art. 4(3) will not apply where the contractual obligation relating to immovables is excluded from the Convention by virtue of Art. 1: see *ante*, §§ 31–033—31–044. Such cases will be governed by common law rules. At common law the system of law with which a contract with regard to an immovable was most closely connected was sometimes said to be the *lex situs*: see, *e.g. British South Africa Co. v. De Beers Consolidated Mines Ltd*, *supra*, at 523. But, as is shown by that case, this was not an invariable rule. As to formal validity of the contract, see *post*, § 31–121.

[94] Giuliano-Lagarde Report, p. 23.

[95] *cf. Merwin Pastoral Co. Pty. Ltd v. Moolpa Pastoral Co. Pty. Ltd* (1932) 48 C.L.R. 565.

[96] *cf.* Case 73/77 *Sanders v. Van der Putte* [1977] E.C.R. 2383.

[97] *Dicey & Morris op. cit.* pp. 1388–1389; Plender *op. cit.* p. 115; see Timeshare Act 1992, as amended by Timeshare Regulations 1997 (S.I. 1997 No. 1081) which implement in the United Kingdom E.U. Directive 94/97 [1994] O.J. L 280/83 on the protection of purchasers in respect of certain aspects of contracts relating to the purchase of the right to use immovable properties on a timeshare basis. Where the timeshare property is situated in a Contracting State to the Brussels or Lugano Conventions on Jurisdiction and the Enforcement of Judgments in Civil and Commercial Matters, other than the United Kingdom, an English court may have no jurisdiction over a claim for misrepresentation or breach of contract brought by a timeshare purchaser against a timeshare owner since the claim may be one the object of which is a tenancy of immovable property, and such claims are subject to the exclusive jurisdiction of the *situs* of the immovable according to Art. 16(1) of each Convention. Where however the timeshare purchaser has financed the purchase with money lent by a bank, Art. 16(1) does not impose this jurisdictional bar on a claim against the bank pursuant to the provisions of ss.56(2) and 75 of the Consumer Credit Act 1974 ("connected lender" liability, discussed *post* Vol. II, § 38–264); *Jarrett v. Barclays Bank* [1999] Q.B. 1, overruling *Lynch v. Halifax Building Society and Royal Bank of Scotland plc* [1995] C.C.L.R. 42.

[98] *Dicey & Morris op. cit.* p. 1389; *cf.* Plender *op. cit.* p. 115.

[99] *Dicey & Morris op. cit.* pp. 1394–1419.

concluded, the carrier has his principal place of business is also the country in which the place of loading or the place of discharge or the principal place of business of the consignor is situated, it shall be presumed that the contract is most closely connected with that country. In applying this paragraph single voyage charter-parties and other contracts the main purpose of which is the carriage of goods shall be treated as contracts for the carriage of goods."[1]

The effect of this provision is that a contract for the carriage of goods (by whatever mode of transport) will be presumed to be most closely connected with the country in which the principal place of business of the carrier,[2] at the time of the conclusion of the contract, is situated, if that country is also the country in which either the place of loading,[3] or the place of discharge,[4] or the principal place of business of the consignor[5] is situated. Since the provision explicitly excludes the application of Article 4(2) to contracts for the carriage of goods, where there is no relevant grouping of the factors identified in Article 4(4) the applicable law will have to be determined without the aid of any presumption. A contract for the carriage of persons will, however, be subject to the presumption in Article 4(2)[6] and, thus, it is conceivable that where there is a mixed contract for the carriage of goods and persons, the contract may have two different applicable laws.[7]

31–081 **"Other contracts" involving carriage of goods.** It is not clear, however, what is to be included in the expression "contract for the carriage of goods." While Article 4(4) clearly states that a single voyage charter-party is to be treated as such a contract, less clarity surrounds the "other contracts the main purpose of which is the carriage of goods." It is likely (though the matter is controversial) that consecutive voyage charter-parties will fall within the provision,[8] as will contracts of carriage evidenced in a bill of lading,[9] though demise charters will not.[10]

31–082 **International conventions.** It is important to remember that many aspects of international transport are governed by international conventions,[11] which will

---

[1] Rome Convention, Art. 4(4).

[2] Where a party who contracts to carry goods for another does not carry them himself but arranges for a third party to do so, Art. 4(4) will apparently apply, since the term "carrier" means the party who undertakes to carry the goods whether or not he performs the carriage himself: Giuliano-Lagarde Report, p. 22; see *Dicey & Morris op. cit.* pp. 1405–1406. As to the meaning of "principal place of business," see *Dicey & Morris op. cit.* pp. 1406–1407.

[3] The place of loading is that agreed at the time of the conclusion of the contract: Giuliano-Lagarde Report, p. 22; *Dicey & Morris op. cit.* p. 1407.

[4] The place of discharge is that agreed at the time of the conclusion of the contract: see authorities in preceding note.

[5] "Consignor" apparently refers to "any person who consigns goods to the carrier": Giuliano-Lagarde Report, p. 21. See *Dicey & Morris op. cit.* p. 1408. As to the meaning of "principal place of business," see *Dicey & Morris op. cit.* p. 1408 and *ante,* § 31–076.

[6] *Dicey & Morris op. cit.* pp. 1395–1396.

[7] Cheshire and North *op. cit.* p. 494.

[8] See *Dicey & Morris op. cit.* pp. 1403–1404; *cf.* Schultsz in North (ed.), *Contract Conflicts* (1982) pp. 185, 192, 198; Plender *op. cit.* pp. 116–118.

[9] *Dicey & Morris op. cit.* p. 1404.

[10] Giuliano-Lagarde Report, p. 21; *Scrutton on Charterparties* (20th ed., 1996), pp. 14, n. 6, 59–60. Art. 4(2) will apply to such charters: *Dicey & Morris op. cit.* p. 1403.

[11] See Vol. II, §§ 35–001—35–084, 36–091—36–166.

take precedence over the provisions of the Rome Convention when they are applicable.[12]

Non-application of the presumptions. Article 4(5) of the Rome Convention   **31–083**
provides that the presumption in Article 4(2) shall not apply if the characteristic
performance cannot be determined and that each of the three presumptions shall
be disregarded if it appears from the circumstances as a whole that the contract
is more closely connected with another country than it is with the country
indicated by the presumption.

Characteristic performance cannot be determined. Where it is concluded   **31–084**
that the contract is one for which the characteristic performance cannot be
determined,[13] then the law of the country with which the contract is most closely
connected will have to be determined without resort to any presumption. In such
circumstances, the court will have regard to all the facts and circumstances
surrounding the contract and its making: relevant facts and circumstances will be
those treated as relevant in cases decided at common law.[14]

Rebutting the presumptions.[15] Each presumption set out in Article 4 may be   **31–085**
rebutted if it appears from the circumstances as a whole that the contract is more
closely connected with another country than it is with the country whose law is
indicated as applicable by virtue of the presumption.[16] The critical question,
however, is as to the strength that will be attributed to the presumptions. The
Giuliano-Lagarde Report states that paragraphs (2)–(4) of Article 4 are "only
rebuttable presumptions"[17] and that Article 4(5) "obviously leaves the judge a
margin of discretion as to whether a set of circumstances exists in each specific
case justifying the non-application of the presumption,"[18] this being "the inevitable counterpart of a general conflict rule intended to apply to almost all types
of contract,"[19] but such remarks are not particularly revealing as to the weight to
be attributed to the presumptions. In England it has been said, *obiter*, that Article
4(5) means that the presumption is "displaced if the court concludes that it is not
appropriate in the circumstances of any given case. This, formally, makes the
presumption very weak . . . ."[20] Conversely, the Dutch Hoge Raad has decided
that Article 4(5) of the Rome Convention should be applied restrictively. On this
view the presumption in Article 4(2) is the "main rule" which rule should only
be disregarded if, in the special circumstances of the case, the place of business
of the party who is to effect the characteristic performance has "no real significance as a connecting factor."[21]

---

[12] Rome Convention, Art. 21. See *ante*, § 31–026 and *cf. The Hollandia* [1983] 1 A.C 565.
[13] See *ante*, § 31–071.
[14] See *ante*, § 31–011.
[15] *Dicey & Morris op. cit.* pp. 1237–1238, 1327–1328, 1347–1349, 1389–1390, 1409–1410, 1455–1456; Cheshire and North *op. cit.* pp. 494–495; Kaye *op. cit.* pp. 186–191; Lagarde (1981) 22 Virginia J.Int.L. 91.
[16] Rome Convention, Art. 4(5).
[17] Giuliano-Lagarde Report, p. 23.
[18] *ibid.* p. 22.
[19] *ibid.*
[20] *Crédit Lyonnais v. New Hampshire Insurance Co.* [1997] 2 Lloyd's Rep. 1, 5, *per* Hobhouse L.J.
[21] *Société Nouvelle des Papeteries de l'Aa v. B.V. Machinefabriek B.O.A.*, 1992 N.J. 750, discussed by Struycken [1996] L.M.C.L.Q. 18.

Since it is reasonable to conclude that the presumptions were introduced into the Convention with a view to injecting a degree of certainty into the search for the law of the country with which the contract is most closely connected,[22] it would be equally reasonable to conclude that the presumptions are not limited in effect to cases where all the other factors in the case point to an equal balance between two or more countries.[23] In the absence of any clear guidance in the Giuliano-Lagarde Report and the case law to date, all that can be said is that a court will probably apply the presumptively applicable law unless it can be shown by the party making the claim that, on a balance of probabilities (or perhaps even more clearly),[24] having regard to all the circumstances, the contract is more closely connected with another country. Relevant circumstances are likely to include those treated as pointing to a close connection in cases decided at common law[25] and, additionally, factors which supervene after the conclusion of the contract.[26] Accordingly, the application of Article 4(5) will very much depend on the facts and circumstances of individual cases. Having said that, it has been suggested that the presumption in Article 4(2)[27] may most easily be rebutted in cases where the place of performance differs from the place of business of the party who is the characteristic performer.[28] This circumstance is of particular importance in the context of a letter of credit transaction. Here the operation of the presumption in Article 4(2) will almost invariably mean that the contract between the issuing bank and the correspondent bank and that between the correspondent bank and the beneficiary will be governed by the law of the country in which the correspondent bank's principal place of business, or place of business, as the case may be, is situated.[29] However, in relation to the contract between the issuing bank and the beneficiary, the operation of the presumption would lead to application of the law of the country in which the issuing bank's principal place of business, or place of business, as the case may be, is situated, which places will not coincide with those of the correspondent bank.[30] In such a case "application of art. 4(2) would lead to an irregular and subjective position where the governing law of a letter of credit would vary according to whether one was looking at the position of the confirming bank or the issuing bank. It is of great importance to both beneficiaries and banks concerned in the issue and operation of letters of credit that there should be clarity and simplicity in such matters,"[31] which clarity and simplicity could be achieved by invoking Article 4(5) to secure application of the law of the country where the obligation to pay against presentation of conforming documents was to be performed.[32] This may not, of course, be an inevitable outcome in every type of case in view of the fact

---

[22] Giuliano-Lagarde Report, p. 20; North in North (ed.), *Contract Conflicts* (1982), p. 3, at p. 15, reprinted in *Essays in Private International Law* (1993), p. 23.

[23] *Dicey & Morris op. cit.* p. 1236.

[24] *ibid.*

[25] *Ante,* § 31–011.

[26] Giuliano-Lagarde Report, p. 20. See *ante,* § 31–050.

[27] For circumstances in which the presumptions in Art. 4(3) and (4) may be rebutted, see *Dicey & Morris op. cit.* pp. 1389–1390, 1409–1410.

[28] *Dicey & Morris op. cit.* pp. 1236–1237.

[29] *Bank of Baroda v. Vysya Bank Ltd* [1994] 2 Lloyd's Rep. 87; *ante,* § 31–072. See also *Bank of Credit and Commerce Hong Kong Ltd v. Sonali Bank* [1995] 1 Lloyd's Rep. 227; *Batstone & Firminger Ltd v. Nasima Enterprises (Nigeria) Ltd* [1996] C.L.C. 1902, 1910.

[30] *Bank of Baroda v. Vysya Bank Ltd* [1994] 2 Lloyd's Rep. 87.

[31] *ibid.* at 93, *per* Mance J.

[32] *Bank of Baroda v. Vysya Bank Ltd* [1994] 2 Lloyd's Rep. 87; *cf. Offshore International SA v. Banco Central SA* [1977] 1 W.L.R. 399.

that the presumption focuses on the *place of business*, etc., of the characteristic performer rather than on *the place of* the characteristic performance.[33]

(e) *Certain Consumer Contracts and Individual Employment Contracts*

Introduction. Articles 5 and 6 of the Rome Convention contain special rules   **31–086** for determining, respectively, the law applicable to certain consumer contracts and individual employment contracts. The central provisions of these articles are linked by a common underlying philosophy, namely that the consumer and the employee, respectively, are in a weaker position to the other contracting party. As such, the general choice of law rules contained in Articles 3 and 4 of the Convention required modification so as to achieve, respectively, the aim of consumer and employee protection.[34]

"Certain consumer contracts."[35] Article 5 contains the choice of law rules   **31–087** applicable to certain consumer contracts. These rules apply to a contract "the object of which is the supply of goods or services to a person ('the consumer') for a purpose which can be regarded as being outside his trade or profession, or a contract for the provision of credit for that object."[36] A more precise definition was avoided so as not to introduce conflict with definitions which are found in national law,[37] though the European Court, when it obtains jurisdiction to interpret the Rome Convention, is likely to ascribe an autonomous meaning to contracts which fall within the provision.[38] In terms, Article 5 is capable of

---

[33] *Benjamin's Sale of Goods* (5th ed., 1997), §§ 25–059—25–060.

[34] Giuliano-Lagarde Report, pp. 23, 25.

[35] *Dicey & Morris on the Conflict of Laws* (12th ed., 1993), pp. 1285–1302; Plender, *The European Contracts Convention* (1991), Chap. 7; Kaye, *The New Private International Law of Contract of the European Community* (1993), pp. 203–220; Morse in Lomnicka and Morse (eds.) *Contemporary Issues in Commercial Law* (1997), pp. 117–135; Hartley in North (ed.), *Contract Conflicts* (1982), Chap. 6; Morse (1992) 41 I.C.L.Q. 1. As to the formal validity of such contracts, see *post*, § 31–120.

[36] Rome Convention, Art. 5(1). Thus, *e.g.*, Art. 5 will not apply to contracts made by, *e.g.* manufacturers or traders who buy goods or obtain services for business purposes, or to professionals who acquire goods or services for professional purposes: see Giuliano-Lagarde Report, p. 23. For other difficulties in interpreting the language of Art. 5(1), see *Dicey & Morris op. cit.* pp. 1287–1288.

[37] Giuliano-Lagarde Report, p. 23. See the definition in Unfair Contract Terms Act 1977, s.12(1), *ante*, §§ 14–064—14–065.

[38] *cf.* Case 150/77 *Société Bertrand v. Paul Ott K.G.* [1978] E.C.R. 143; Case C–89/91 *Shearson Lehmann Hutton Inc. v. TVB Treuhandgesellschaft für Vermogensverwaltung und Beteiligungen GmbH* [1993] E.C.R. I–139; Case C–318/93 *Brenner v. Dean Witter Reynolds Inc.* [1994] E.C.R. I–4725; Case C–269/95 *Benincasa v. Dentalkit Srl* [1998] All E.R. (E.C.) 135. According to the Giuliano-Lagarde Report, p. 23, the scope of the Article "should be interpreted in the light of its purpose which is to protect the weaker party and in accordance with other international instruments with the same purpose such as the Judgments Convention" (*i.e.* the Brussels Convention of 1968 on Jurisdiction and the Enforcement of Judgments in Civil and Commercial Matters, *ante*, § 31–017). In the abovementioned cases the European Court has consistently stressed that "consumer" in the relevant provisions of the Brussels Convention should be strictly construed as limited to private final consumers who are not engaged in trade or professional activities. This will normally serve to exclude legal persons and traders, unless, possibly, such persons are acting entirely outside their trade or professional activities and can establish that they were in a weaker bargaining position in relation to the supplier. *cf. Chris Hart (Business Sales) Ltd v. Niven*, 1992 S.L.T. (Sh Ct) 53.

applying to a wide variety of contracts including contracts for the sale, hire or pledge of movables[39]; insurance contracts (to the extent that these are not excluded from the Convention)[40]; banking contracts; and wagering contracts. A contract which, for an exclusive price, provides for a combination of travel and accommodation (a so-called "package tour") is specifically made subject to the Article.[41] On the other hand, contracts of carriage are specifically excluded from the operation of Article 5,[42] as are contracts for the supply of services where the services are to be supplied to the consumer exclusively in a country other than that in which he has his habitual residence.[43] Where a contract entered into by a consumer is not within the category of contracts covered by Article 5, or Article 5 is, for some other reason, inapplicable, the governing law will be determined by reference to the general choice of law rules contained in Articles 3 and 4 of the Rome Convention.[44]

31–088   **Choice of law by the parties.** A key element in Article 5 is the restriction on the effect of a choice of law contained in a contract which is subject to that Article. Notwithstanding Article 3, "a choice of law made by the parties shall not have the result of depriving the consumer of the protection afforded to him by the mandatory rules of the law of the country in which he has his habitual residence" if any one of three specified conditions is satisfied.[45] The first condition is where, in the country of the consumer's habitual residence, the contract was preceded by a specific invitation addressed to the consumer, or by advertising, and the consumer had taken in the country of his habitual residence all the steps necessary on his part for the conclusion of the contract.[46] Any invitation must thus be specific to the particular consumer bringing this claim. As to "advertising," the Giuliano-Lagarde Report suggests that the other contracting party must have intended to advertise to the consumer in the latter's country of habitual residence[47]: if this view is accepted, the condition will be extremely restrictive in effect.[48] The provision refers to the "steps" necessary for the conclusion of the contract being taken in the consumer's country so as, apparently, to "avoid the classical problem of determining the place where the contract was concluded."[49] But this does not answer the question whether legal or factual steps are envisaged. To the extent that the Giuliano-Lagarde Report states that "steps" includes writing or any action taken in consequences of an offer or advertisement, the

---

[39] Sales of securities are excluded: Giuliano-Lagarde Report, p. 23.

[40] Art. 1(3). See Giuliano-Lagarde Report, p. 23.

[41] Art. 5(5). In Germany it has been held that a timeshare contract is not a contract the object of which is a supply of services for the purposes of Art. 5(1): BGH NJW 1997, 1697; Knöfel (1998) I.C.L.Q. 439, 443.

[42] Art. 5(4)(a).

[43] Art. 5(4)(b).

[44] *Ante*, §§ 31–045—31–085.

[45] Art. 5(2). See, in particular, *Dicey & Morris op. cit.* pp. 1287–1288; Kaye *op. cit.* pp. 216–218.

[46] Art. 5(2), first indent.

[47] At p. 24.

[48] The Giuliano-Lagarde Report was written before the opportunities for trading over the internet were envisaged. In such a case it is possible that a supplier may be taken to intend to advertise in any country in which the supplier's website can be accessed by a consumer. For a discussion, see Gringras, *Laws of the Internet* (1997), pp. 49–50.

[49] Giuliano-Lagarde Report, p. 24.

implication appears to be that factual steps are those contemplated.[50] According to the second condition, the effect of a choice of law will be limited, as described above, if the other party or his agent[51] received the consumer's order in the country where the consumer was habitually resident.[52] Although this condition overlaps with the first, the overlap is not complete: thus the second condition will apply "where the consumer has addressed himself to a stand of a foreign firm at a fair or exhibition taking place in the consumer's country or to a permanent branch or agency of a foreign firm established in the consumer's country even though the foreign firm has not advertised in the consumer's country in a way covered"[53] by the first condition. The third condition is expressly limited to contracts for the sale of goods. The limits on the effect of a choice of law will also apply, in the case of a sale of goods, if the consumer travelled from the country of his habitual residence to another country and there gave his order, provided the consumer's journey was arranged by the seller for the purpose of inducing the consumer to buy.[54] The provision is intended to catch "cross-border excursion selling" (more common on the European Continent than in the United Kingdom[55]) whereby, for example, the owner of a store in one country arranges one-day bus trips for consumers in a neighbouring country to buy in his store.[56]

Mandatory rules. Provided the relevant contract falls within Article 5 and **31–089** provided one of the conditions discussed in the preceding paragraph applies, the choice of law in the contract shall not have the result of "depriving" the consumer of the protection of the mandatory rules of the law of the country in which he is habitually resident. "Mandatory rules," for these purposes, would seem to be defined by reference to Article 3(3)[57]: they are rules of the law of that country "which cannot be derogated from by contract" and it is not necessary in addition (though it will often be the case) that they are also rules which apply "whatever the law applicable to the contract."[58] In the context of Article 5, such rules will relate to consumer protection.[59]

---

[50] *ibid.* Thus the fact that such factual steps (*e.g.* in relation to offer and acceptance) are deemed, as a matter of law, to occur elsewhere matters not. *cf.* Unfair Contract Terms Act 1977, s.27(2)(b), *ante*, § 31–007. In relation to internet transactions, it is likely that the consumer will be regarded as taking the relevant steps in the country of his habitual residence if that is the country from which he accesses the supplier's website and thereby conducts his part of the transaction: Gringras, *Laws of the Internet* (1997), p. 50.

[51] "Agent" is intended to refer to all persons acting on behalf of the trader: Giuliano-Lagarde Report, p. 24.

[52] Art. 5(2), second indent.

[53] Giuliano-Lagarde Report, p. 24.

[54] Art. 5(2), third indent.

[55] Giuliano-Lagarde Report, p. 24; Plender *op. cit.* p. 130; Kaye *op. cit.* p. 218.

[56] Giuliano-Lagarde Report, p. 24.

[57] *Ante*, §§ 31–057—31–064.

[58] *cf.* Art. 7(1) which does not have the force of law in the U.K.: Contracts (Applicable Law) Act 1990, s.2(2), *ante*, § 31–059.

[59] Examples in English law might include the provisions of the Unfair Contract Terms Act 1977 and some provisions of the Consumer Credit Act 1974: see *Dicey & Morris op. cit.* pp. 1296–1330. See too Unfair Terms in Consumer Contracts Regulations 1994, discussed in *Benjamin's Sale of Goods* (5th ed., 1997), 25–095; Directive 97/7 of the European Parliament and Council of May 20, 1997 on the protection of consumers in respect of distance contracts ([1997] O.J. L144/19), in force from June 4, 1997, but not yet implemented in the United Kingdom. According to Art. 12(2) of the Directive Member States must take measures to ensure that consumers do not lose the protection of the Directive by virtue of the choice of the law of a non-Member State if the contract has a close connection with the territory of one or more Member States.

The relationship between these mandatory rules and the chosen law is, however, somewhat obscure. First, the rules of the chosen law may be more favourable to the consumer than the mandatory rules of the country of his habitual residence. In such circumstances, it cannot reasonably be said that the consumer is "deprived" of the protection of the mandatory rules of the country of his habitual residence since he is better off than he would have been had those rules been applied. Conversely, he would be deprived of the protection of those rules if the chosen law were less favourable to him than the mandatory rules of his habitual residence. Accordingly, the correct interpretation of Article 5(2) is that it enables a consumer to rely on the mandatory rules of the law of his habitual residence if they are more favourable to him than the chosen law or on the chosen law if it is more favourable to him than the mandatory rules of the law of his habitual residence.[60] The law of the habitual residence thus defines the minimum, but not the maximum protection available to the consumer. This solution is, it is suggested, preferable to one which would allow the consumer to rely, cumulatively, on the mandatory rules of both the law of the habitual residence and the chosen law,[61] despite the potential difficulties which may be presented in deciding, in any given case, which set of rules is most favourable to the consumer. There seems to be no obvious justification in giving a consumer "double protection" just because the contract falls within Article 5 of the Convention, and contains a choice of law.

31–090   **Rules which are mandatory irrespective of applicable law.** Independently of Article 5, Article 7(2) enables a court to restrict the scope of the chosen law through the application of English mandatory rules in a situation where those rules apply irrespective of the law applicable to the contract.[62] Unlike the mandatory rules applicable through Article 5(2), these mandatory rules need not relate to consumer protection.

31–091   **Chosen law governs other issues.** Mandatory rules do not apply to strike down the chosen law *in toto*. The chosen law will apply to the extent that it does not conflict with any applicable mandatory rules.

31–092   **Habitual residence.** The meaning of this concept was discussed *ante*, § 31–074 of this chapter.

31–093   **Applicable law in the absence of choice.** Where a consumer contract falling within Article 5 does not contain a choice of law, Article 5(3) provides that notwithstanding Article 4, the contract shall be governed by the law of the country in which the consumer has his habitual residence,[63] if it is entered into in circumstances giving rise to any one of the three conditions described above.[64] If none of those conditions exist or if the contract falls outside Article 5, then the law applicable to the contract will be determined, in the absence of a choice

---

[60] See *Dicey & Morris op. cit.* pp. 1290–1291; Plender *op. cit.* p. 130; Kaye *op. cit.* pp. 212–214; Morse (1992) 41 I.C.L.Q. 1.
[61] *cf.* Philip in North (ed.), *Contract Conflicts* (1982), p. 81, at p. 99.
[62] *cf.* Lasok and Stone, *Conflict of Laws in the European Community* (1987), p. 385.
[63] *Ante*, § 31–074.
[64] *Ante*, § 31–088.

satisfying Article 3, according to the provisions of Article 4 of the Convention.

Individual employment contracts.[65] Article 6 of the Rome Convention con- **31–094** tains special choice of law rules which are expressed to apply to "individual employment contracts." The policy which informs these provisions is the need to secure "more adequate protection for the party who from the socio-economic point of view is regarded as the weaker in the contractual relationship,"[66] *i.e.* the employee. In particular, it was necessary to curb, in this context, the wide freedom to choose the applicable law permitted by Article 3.[67] No doubt, the philosophy of employee protection will be influential in the interpretation and application of Article 6.[68] Very broadly, Article 6 permits the parties to choose the law to govern an employment contract, but provides that the choice of law cannot have the result of depriving the employee of the protection of the mandatory rules of the law which would be applicable were there no choice of law in the contract.[69] In the absence of a choice of law, the applicable law is, in general, that of the country in which the employee habitually carries out his work in performance of the contract even though he is temporarily employed in another country.[70] If he does not habitually carry out his work in any one country the applicable law will be that of the country in which the place of business through which he was engaged is situated.[71] But each of these rules will be displaced if it appears from the circumstances as a whole that the contract is more closely connected with another country, in which case the law of that other country will govern.[72]

Meaning of "employment contract." Article 6 contains no definition of the **31–095** concept of "employment contract." That the Article is expressed to apply to "individual" employment contracts indicates that the provision is not intended to apply to collective agreements but only to contracts entered into by individual employees.[73] Accordingly, the law applicable to a collective agreement will be

---

[65] *Dicey & Morris on the Conflict of Laws* (12th ed., 1993), pp. 1302–1321; Lasok and Stone *Conflict of Laws in the European Community* (1987), pp. 384–385; Plender, *The European Contracts Convention* (1991), Chap. 8; Kaye, *The New Private International Law of Contract of the European Community* (1993), pp. 224–238; Morse in North (ed.), *Contract Conflicts* (1982), Chap. 7; Morse (1992) 41 I.C.L.Q. 1; Smith and Cromack (1993) 22 I.L.J. 1. In 1976 the European Commission published a proposal for a Regulation concerning conflict of laws in employment relationships: see Com. (175) 653 Final, discussed by Hepple in Lipstein (ed.), *Harmonisation of Private International Law by the EEC* (1978), p. 390; Forde (1979) *Legal Issues of European Integration* 85. Had this proposal not been withdrawn in 1981 ([1981] O.J. C307/3) and reached fruition it would have taken precedence over Art. 6 pursuant to Art. 20 of the Rome Convention, *ante*, § 31–026. See also Directive 96/71 concerning the posting of workers in the framework of the provision of services, [1997] O.J. L18/1 which must be implemented in the law of Member States by December 16, 1999. For comment see Smith and Villiers, 1996 Jur. Rev. 167. This Directive will take precedence over the Rome Convention when it is implemented, pursuant to Art. 20 (*ante*, § 31–026).
[66] Giuliano-Lagarde Report, p. 25.
[67] *Ante*, §§ 31–056—31–065.
[68] *cf.* the position with regard to "certain consumer contracts," *ante*, §§ 31–089—31–091.
[69] Art. 6(1).
[70] Art. 6(2)(a).
[71] Art. 6(2)(b).
[72] Art. 6(2), proviso.
[73] Giuliano-Lagarde Report, p. 25.

determined by reference to the general choice of law rules contained in Articles 3 and 4 of the Convention.[74]

31–096   **"Employment": autonomous meaning.** More particularly, different legal systems may have different criteria or principles for determining whether a particular contract is an employment contract.[75] It is thus necessary to formulate an approach to the resolution of this problem for the purposes of Article 6.[76] The obvious approach which suggests itself is the development of an autonomous meaning for the concept so as to secure uniformity of application amongst Contracting States.[77] The danger with such an approach, however, is that the autonomous definition might result in a particular state's employment law being applied to a contract even though that state would not regard the contract as one of employment, or conversely, in a particular state's employment law not being applied to a contract even though that state's law regarded it as being a contract of employment: in either case the applicable law is distorted, a result which is only avoided if the autonomous definition accords with the definition which prevails in the relevant state's law.

31–097   **Alternative "classification" approach.** A different approach could be based in principles of classification. Here, however, the English court should not classify the contract according to the *lex fori*, *i.e.* according to its own criteria for determining whether a contract is one of employment. To do so would again risk the distortion of the applicable law if the forum's conception of a contract of employment did not correspond with that prevailing in the applicable law or *vice versa*. The risk referred to can, however, be minimised if the forum is prepared to classify the relevant contractual relationship according to the *lex causae*. On this view the English court should apply the rules of Article 6 so as to determine the governing law and then decide whether, according to that law, the relevant contract is one of employment. If it is so classified, then the court should apply the rules of the applicable law concerned with employment contracts. If it is not so classified, the court should apply the general choice of law rules contained in Articles 3 and 4 of the Convention to determine the applicable law. Although this approach is open to a considerable objection, *viz.* that it necessitates determining the law applicable under Article 6 before the process of classification has

---

[74] Plender *op. cit.* pp. 134–136. *cf. Monterosso Shipping Corpn. Ltd v. International Transport Workers Federation* [1982] I.C.R. 675; *Dimskal Shipping Co. Ltd v. International Transport Workers Federation* [1992] 2 A.C. 152. This may be an example of a contract for which the characteristic performance cannot be determined so that Art. 4(2) is not applicable. *cf. ante*, §§ 31–071, 31–084.

[75] See Eörsi, "Private and Governmental Liability for the Tort of Employees and Organs" in Tunc (ed.), *International Encyclopedia of Comparative Law*, Vol. XI, Chap. 4, pp. 34–35. For the criteria in English domestic law, see Vol. II, §§ 39–009—39—027.

[76] See *Dicey & Morris op. cit.* pp. 1304–1306; Plender *op. cit.* pp. 136–138; Kaye *op. cit.* pp. 222–223.

[77] See Kaye, *op. cit.*; Anton, *Private International Law* (2nd ed., 1990), p. 347. The Giuliano-Lagarde Report gives little guidance other than to say that Art. 6 covers void contracts and de facto employment relationships "in particular those characterised by failure to respect the contract imposed by law for the protection of employee": pp. 25–26. The "Posted Workers" Directive (*ante*, n. 65), provides that the definition of a worker for the purposes of the Directive is that which applies in the law of the Member State to whose territory the worker is posted: Art. 2(2). In construing Art. 5(1) of the Brussels Convention on Jurisdiction and the Enforcement of Judgments in Civil and Commercial Matters 1968, the European Court has shown itself to be aware of the special problems posed by employment contracts: see, *e.g.* Case 133/81 *Ivenel v. Schwab* [1982] E.C.R. 1891; Case 266/85 *Shenavai v. Kreischer* [1987] E.C.R. 239; Case C–125/92 *Mulox IBC Ltd v. Geels* [1993] E.C.R. I–4075; *Rutten v. Cross Medical Ltd* [1997] I.C.R. 715. And see *ante*, § 1–088.

determined that Article 6 is applicable, it has the merit of avoiding the distortion of the applicable law which is inherent in other situations. Whether a *lex causae* approach[78] or an approach based on autonomous interpretation[79] will eventually be adopted remains to be seen.

Choice of law by the parties and mandatory rules. Although the parties   **31–098** may choose the law to govern an employment contract,[80] the effect of that choice is expressly limited by Article 6(1) which provides that the choice of law shall not have the result of depriving the employee of the protection afforded to him by the mandatory rules of the country the law of which would be applicable to the contract were there no choice of law.[81] For these purposes, a "mandatory rule" bears the meaning given to that expression by Article 3(3) of the Convention, *i.e.* such a rule is one which cannot be derogated from by contract[82] and it is not necessary, in addition, that the rule be a rule which applies irrespective of the law applicable to the contract[83] though some mandatory rules in the employment context may possess this additional characteristic.[84] The Giuliano-Lagarde Report informs that these mandatory rules "consist not only of the provisions relating to the contract of employment itself, but also provisions such as those concerning industrial safety and hygiene which are regarded in certain Member States as being provisions of public law."[85] However, it will fall to the legal system of which the rule forms part to determine whether a rule is mandatory and also the circumstances in which the rule is mandatory.[86] In the English context, modern statutes often indicate, expressly, a mandatory character and the circumstances in which application of the provisions is mandatory.[87] But this is not an invariable legislative habit so that where the statute is silent the question whether a particular rule is mandatory will depend on the construction of the statute.[88]

Chosen law more favourable. Where the chosen law gives less protection to   **31–099** the employee than would the mandatory rules of the law of the country which would have been applicable in the absence of choice, then the mandatory rules of the latter law will prevail over the chosen law. Conversely, where the chosen law is more favourable to the employee than the mandatory rules of the law which would be applicable in the absence of choice, then it can hardly be said that the employee is "deprived" of the protection of mandatory rules since he is

---

[78] Favoured by *Dicey & Morris op. cit.* p. 1306; Plender *op. cit.* pp. 136–138.

[79] Favoured by Anton *op. cit.* p. 347; Kaye *op. cit.* p. 223.

[80] The choice of law must satisfy the requirements of Art. 3(1): see *ante*, §§ 31–045—31–065.

[81] As to which, see *post*, § 31–102.

[82] *Ante*, § 31–059.

[83] *cf.* Art. 7(2), discussed *post*, § 31–100 and Art. 7(1), *ante*, § 31–059 which does not have the force of law in the U.K.: Contracts (Applicable Law) Act 1990, s.2(2).

[84] See statutes referred to in n. 87, *post*.

[85] At p. 25.

[86] See *ante,*, §§ 31–059—31–064.

[87] *e.g.* Equal Pay Act 1970, s.1(1) as amended by Sex Discrimination Act 1975, s.8 and s.1(11) as amended by Contracts (Applicable Law) Act 1990, s.5 and Sched. 4; Trade Union and Labour Relations (Consolidation) Act 1992, ss.285(2), 287, 289; Employment Rights Act 1996, ss.196(2), (3), 203, 204(1), (2). See Vol. II, §§ 39–196—39–223.

[88] *e.g.* Patents Act 1977, ss.39–43 (compensation provisions for employee's inventions probably mandatory; *cf. Chiron Corp. v. Organon Teknika Ltd (No. 2)* [1993] F.S.R. 567 (Patents Act 1977, s.44 applies to contract governed by a foreign law)); Sex Discrimination Act 1975 (mandatory); Race Relations Act 1976 (mandatory); Disability Discrimination Act 1995 (mandatory). See too *Sayers v. International Drilling Co. N.V.* [1971] 1 W.L.R. 1176; Vol. II, §§ 39–222—39–226.

better off under the chosen law, so that the chosen law should prevail.[89] Where, however, the rules of the chosen law and the mandatory rules of the law which would be applicable in the absence of choice are not in direct conflict but offer different rights or remedies to an employee (say compensation for unfair dismissal[90] under the chosen law, in contrast with reinstatement[91] under the law applicable in the absent of choice) more difficulty arises. Article 6(1) merely says that the employee is not to be deprived of the protection of mandatory rules: it does not say he cannot have the benefit of the protective regime of both laws and since he would be deprived of reinstatement if he received only compensation, it could be said that he has been deprived of the protection of applicable mandatory rules. But it is difficult to accept that it was intended to benefit the employee in this way just because his contract contains a choice of law[92] and, therefore, it is suggested that the correct solution in such situations is to apply the law most favourable to the employee despite the fact that it may not always be easy, in any given situation, to determine which law is most favourable.[93]

31–100　　**Rules which are mandatory irrespective of applicable law.** It would seem implicit in Article 6(1) that mandatory rules applicable thereunder should relate to the protection of employees. However, Article 7(2) can also apply to employment contracts[94] to secure the application of English rules in a situation where they are mandatory irrespective of the law applicable to the contract. Such rules need not necessarily relate to employment protection, but many will.[95]

31–101　　**Applicable law in absence of choice.** In effect Article 6(2) supplies two presumptions as to what the applicable law will be in the absence of a choice of law, each presumption being rebuttable according to the proviso to Article 6(2) if it appears from the circumstances as a whole that the contract is more closely connected with another country.[96] Where the employee habitually carries out his work in performance of the contract in a particular country then the law of that country will govern (subject to the proviso) even if the employee is temporarily employed in another country.[97] Article 6(2)(b) provides that if the employee does not habitually carry out his work in any one country then the applicable law will (subject to the proviso) be the law of the country in which the place of business through which he was engaged is situated.[98] Article 6(2)(a) is thus concerned solely with the situation where the employee habitually carries out his work in one country only. Where the work is habitually carried out in more than one country, Article 6(2)(b) applies: this will also be the case where the employee

---

[89] cf. in relation to consumer contracts, *ante*, § 31–089.

[90] See Vol. II, §§ 39–214—39–219.

[91] See Vol. II, §§ 39–214—39–216.

[92] cf. Philip in North (ed.), *Contract Conflicts* (1982), p. 81, at pp. 99–100. The principle of the "more favourable" law is recognised in the "Posted Workers" Directive (*ante*, § 31–094, n. 65): see Preamble, para. (18) and Art. 3(7).

[93] *Dicey & Morris op. cit.* p. 1308; Plender *op. cit.* pp. 140–143; Kaye *op. cit.* pp. 228–229.

[94] cf. Lasok and Stone, *Conflict of Laws in the European Community* (1987), p. 385.

[95] See, *e.g.* statutes referred to in n. 87, *ante*.

[96] Art. 6(2)(a).

[97] As to the meaning of "habitually carries out his work," see *Dicey & Morris op. cit.* pp. 1310–1311; Plender *op. cit.* pp. 143–145; Kaye *op. cit.* pp. 233–235; Morse (1992) 41 I.C.L.Q. 1.

[98] As to the meaning of "place of business through which he was engaged," see *Dicey & Morris op. cit.* pp. 1311–1312; Plender *op. cit.* p. 145; Kaye *op. cit.* pp. 235–236; Morse (1992) 41 I.C.L.Q. 1. cf. *Sayers v. International Drilling Co. N.V.* [1971] 1 W.L.R. 1176.

habitually carries out his work in no particular country or where he habitually carries out his work in a place which is not a country (*e.g.* on a ship or oil rig).[99]

If it appears from the circumstances as a whole that the contract is more   **31–102** closely connected with another country than it is with the country indicated by Article 6(2)(a) or 6(2)(b), as the case may be, then the law of that other country will be the governing law. How easy it will be to displace Article 6(2)(a) and 6(2)(b) will depend on the strength which will be accorded to those presumptive rules. It is possible to speculate (but no more than that) that the court will, in the spirit of Article 6, give more weight to the presumptions if the law applicable through them would be more protective of the employee than would be the law which would govern if the proviso were invoked, and less weight to them if the converse was the case.[1] As to the factors which might serve to trigger the proviso, the law of the residence or centre of business operations of the employer might, in the case of an employer engaging employees of various nationalities in different parts of the world, be regarded as being more closely connected with the contract than the law indicated by the presumption.[2] But each case will depend on its particular facts.[3]

Contract and tort. In English law an employee may elect to sue his   **31–103** employer, for injuries caused by the negligence of the employer, in either contract or tort.[4] There does not appear to be anything in the Rome Convention which excludes this option.[5] The choice of law rules for torts are generally to be found in Part III of the Private International Law (Miscellaneous Provisions) Act 1995.[6] There is nothing in Part III of the 1995 Act which indicates that an employee is not free to frame and pursue a claim in tort rather than contract if the case falls within Part III and it is advantageous to do so. According to the general rule contained in the Act, the law applicable to a tort is the law of the country in which the events constituting the tort in question occur,[7] which rule may be displaced in favour of a different country's law in an appropriate case.[8] Application of these rules might, in particular situations, lead to a law which is more

---

[99] Giuliano-Lagarde Report, p. 26.

[1] See *Dicey & Morris op. cit.* p. 1313. *cf. Sayers v. International Drilling Co. N.V., supra.*

[2] In *Sayers v. International Drilling Co. N.V., supra,* it was held that the contract was most closely connected with Dutch law for this reason.

[3] Other factors suggested as relevant in common law decisions include the residence and domicile of the employee (*South African Breweries v. King* [1899] 2 Ch. 173 (affd. [1990] 1 Ch. 273)) and the language and form of the contract (*South African Breweries v. King, supra; Sayers v. International Drilling Co. N.V., supra; Coupland v. Arabian Gulf Oil Co.* [1983] 1 W.L.R 1136 (affd. [1983] 1 W.L.R. 1151)). If the contract is held to be governed by foreign law according to Art. 6(2), the English court may still apply any English mandatory rules by virtue of Art. 7(2): see *ante,* § 31–064.

[4] *e.g. Matthews v. Kuwait Bechtel Corp.* [1959] 2 Q.B. 57; *Coupland v. Arabian Gulf Oil Co.* [1983] 1 W.L.R. 1136 (affd. [1983] 1 W.L.R. 1151); contrast *Johnson v. Coventry Churchill International Ltd* [1992] 3 All E.R. 14 (action in tort only, case not framed in contract). See *ante,* §§ 1–106, 31–031.

[5] *Dicey & Morris op. cit.* pp. 1198–1199, 1315.

[6] In force from May 1, 1996 (S.I. 1996 No. 995). For discussion, see *Dicey and Morris op. cit., Fourth Cumulative Supplement* (1997), Chap. 35; Harris (1998) 61 M.L.R. 33; Morse (1996) 45 I.C.L.Q. 888; Rodger [1996] Scottish Law and Practice Quarterly 397; Briggs [1995] L.M.C.L.Q. 519.

[7] s.11(1), amplified in s.11(2).

[8] s.12.

favourable to the employee than the law which might govern the contractual claim which he might have against his employer.[9]

(f) *Voluntary Assignments and Subrogation*

31–104   **Voluntary assignments.** Article 12 of the Rome Convention makes a limited excursion into the field of proprietary rights by providing choice of law rules relating to the voluntary assignment of rights. This provision, which is to the same effect as the common law,[10] will apply to assignments made after April 1, 1991[11]: Article 12 will apply even if the contract creating the right assigned was concluded on or before that date (so that the Convention would not apply to that contract).[12]

31–105   **Assignor and assignee.** "The mutual obligations of assignor and assignee under a voluntary assignment of a right against another person ('the debtor') are governed by the law which applies to the contract between assignor and assignee."[13] Although the reference to "voluntary assignment" in this provision is not expressly limited to contractual assignments, the fact that the applicable law is that of the "contract between assignor and assignee" indicates that only contractual voluntary assignments are within Article 12. The law applicable to the contract between assignor and assignee will be determined according to the rules of the Convention discussed earlier in this chapter.[14]

31–106   **Assignability, etc.** Article 12(2) provides that:

> "The law governing the right to which the assignment relates determines its assignability, the relationship between the assignee and the debtor, the conditions under which

---

[9] The common law rule for choice of law in tort which is abolished by s.10(1)(a) of the 1995 Act, except in defamation and related cases (ss.9(3), 10, 13), normally favoured the defendant, because it required that the defendant's conduct be actionable as a tort by English law *and* civilly actionable by the law of the place where the tort was committed, at least as a general rule: see *Dicey and Morris op. cit.* pp. 1198–1199, 1315.

[10] See *Lee v. Abdy* (1886) 17 Q.B.D. 309; *Republic de Guatemala v. Nunez* [1927] 1 K.B. 669; *Re Anziani* [1930] 1 Ch. 407; *Campbell Connelly & Co. Ltd v. Noble* [1963] 1 W.L.R. 252; *Trendtex Trading Corpn. v. Crédit Suisse* [1982] A.C. 679; see also *Macmillan Inc. v. Bishopsgate Investment Trust plc (No. 3)* [1996] 1 W.L.R. 387; 26th ed. of this work, § 2185; *Dicey & Morris on the Conflict of Laws* (11th ed., 1987), pp. 957–965; Cheshire and North *Private International Law* (12th ed., 1992), pp. 809–817; Moshinsky (1992) 109 L.Q.R. 591; Struycken [1998] L.M.C.L.Q. 345. Where the right assigned arises under a contract excluded from the Convention under Art. 1, it is not clear whether Art. 12 or the common law applies, but since Art. 12 applies to voluntary assignments, involuntary assignments will be governed by common law rules: see *Dicey & Morris on the Conflict of Laws* (12th ed., 1993), pp. 984–989; Cheshire and North *op. cit.* pp. 818–819. Although Art. 12 applies to the assignment of non-contractual rights, it may not apply to non-contractual assignments of a voluntary nature (unless by way of gift, see Giuliano-Lagarde Report, p. 10): see *post*, § 31–105. Such non-contractual voluntary assignments will be governed by common law rules (which apply the same principles as Art. 12 in this field). Art. 12 does not apply to the assignment of duties: Giuliano-Lagarde Report, p. 35.

[11] Rome Convention, Art. 17. See *ante*, § 31–016.

[12] *Dicey & Morris op. cit.* p. 979.

[13] Rome Convention, Art. 12(1).

[14] *Ante*, §§ 31–045—31–085. Where Art. 4(2) applies (see *ante*, §§ 31–066—31–085) the characteristic performance appears to be that of the assignor: see *Dicey & Morris op. cit.* p. 981.

the assignment can be invoked against the debtor and any question whether the debtor's obligations have been discharged."[15]

Accordingly, whether a right (which need not be of a contractual nature) is capable of being assigned will be determined by the law which creates the right.[16] That law will also govern the relationship between assignee and debtor.[17] Since that law also governs the conditions under which the assignment can be invoked against the debtor and any question of whether the debtor's obligations have been discharged, it will determine questions of priorities as between competing valid assignments of the same debt (*e.g.* whether notice of the assignment must be given to the debtor).[18]

Subrogation.[19] Article 13 of the Rome Convention contains a choice of law **31–107** rule which is expressed to apply to "subrogation." However, in this context "subrogation" bears a limited meaning: Article 13 is concerned only with cases where a creditor has a claim in *contract* against the debtor and a third person "has a duty to satisfy the creditor, or has in fact satisfied the creditor in discharge of that duty."[20] Thus the provision extends to a contract of guarantee where the guarantor has paid the creditor and is thus subrogated to the latter's rights against the debtor,[21] but not to subrogation by operation of law when the debt to be paid originates in a tort (*e.g.* where the insurer succeeds to the insured's right of action against the tortfeasor).[22] Although the extract from Article 13(1) quoted above suggests that the third party must have a *duty* to satisfy the creditor, the Giuliano-Lagarde Report suggests that the provision may also apply to a situation in which a person has paid without "being obliged so to do by contract or law"[23] but by virtue of having an "economic interest recognised by law" as prevails in some legal systems.[24] But the Report follows this observation, extremely obscurely, by saying that the court "has a discretion in this respect," a comment which does little to clarify the position.

Applicable law. In circumstances falling within Article 13(1), "the law which **31–108** governs the third person's duty to satisfy the creditor shall determine whether the

---

[15] Logically, the question of assignability must be resolved before one reaches the question of the validity of the assignment—dealt with in Art. 12(1). For the reasons for the curious draftsmanship of Art. 12, see Giuliano-Lagarde Report, p. 34.

[16] *cf. Campbell Connelly and Co. Ltd v. Noble* [1963] 1 W.L.R. 252; *Trendtex Trading Corpn v. Crédit Suisse* [1982] A.C. 679, for the same rule at common law. If the right assigned is contractual, the applicable law wil be decided according to the rules of the Convention unless the relevant contract is excluded from the scope of the Convention: see *ante*, §§ 31–033—31–044.

[17] The relations between assignor and debtor (other than the issue of assignability), if a contract exists between them, will be governed by the law applicable to that contract identified by reference to the rules of the Convention: Giuliano-Lagarde Report, p. 35.

[18] This was probably the common law rule: *Dicey & Morris op. cit.* p. 981, n. 98; Cheshire and North *op. cit.* pp. 814–815; *Le Feuvre v. Sullivan* (1855) 100 Moo. P.C. 1; *Kelly v. Selwyn* [1905] Ch. 117; *cf. Republica de Gautemala v. Nunez* [1927] 1 K.B. 669, 695 (*obiter* in favour of *lex fori*); Goode, *Commercial Law* (2nd ed., 1995), pp. 1129–1130; Collier, *Conflict of Laws* (2nd ed., 1994), pp. 256–258 (*lex situs* of debt).

[19] See *Dicey & Morris op. cit.* pp. 1268–1269; Plender, *The European Contracts Convention* (1991), pp. 178–179; Kaye, *The New Private International Law of Contract of the European Community* (1993), pp. 327–330; Morse (1992) 2 Ybk.Eur.L. 107, 158.

[20] Art. 13(1).

[21] Giuliano-Lagarde Report, p. 35.

[22] *ibid.*

[23] *ibid.*

[24] *ibid.*

third person is entitled to exercise against the debtor the rights which the creditor had against the debtor under the law governing their relationship and, if so, whether he may do so in full or only to a limited extent."[25] Thus the law applicable to the relationship between creditor and debtor determines the rights which the former has against the latter. But the law which creates the duty in the third party to satisfy that creditor determines whether and to what extent, the third party is subrogated to those rights.

31–109 **Co-debtors.** The rule described in the previous paragraph applies to cases where several persons (debtors) are subject to the same contractual claim and one of them has satisfied the creditor.[26] Thus, if one debtor satisfies the creditor, it is the law governing the duty which requires him to do this which will determine whether he is subrogated to the creditor's rights against the other debtors.

4. SCOPE OF THE APPLICABLE LAW

31–110 **Introduction.** This section seeks to identify the various issues which may be governed by the applicable law of the contract and to consider the extent to which laws other than the applicable law may be relevant to the determination of any of these issues.[27] In the background, it must be also borne in mind that other laws may impinge upon the scope of the applicable law through the operation, in particular, of Articles 3(3), 5, 6, 7(2) and 16 of the Rome Convention which were considered earlier in this chapter. Formally, only Article 10 is expressed to be concerned with the "scope of the applicable law". However, other provisions, notably Article 8 ("material validity"),[28] Article 9 ("formal validity"),[29] Article 11 ("incapacity")[30] and Article 14 ("burden of proof etc")[31] also raise questions as to the relative competence of the applicable law and other relevant laws and thus are appropriate subjects for discussion in this section.

(a) *Material Validity of the Contract*[32]

31–111 **Provisions of Article 8(1).** Article 8(1) of the Rome Convention which is expressed to apply to the "material validity" of the contract provides as follows: "The existence and validity of a contract, or of any term of a contract, shall be determined by the law which would govern it under this Convention if the

---

[25] Art. 13(1).
[26] Art. 13(2).
[27] Common law principles are referred to where relevant.
[28] *Post*, § 31–111.
[29] *Post*, §§ 31–117—31–124.
[30] *Post*, § 31–126.
[31] *Post*, §§ 31–151—31–154.
[32] *Dicey & Morris on the Conflict of Laws* (12th ed., 1993), pp. 1248–1254; Cheshire and North, *Private International Law* (12th ed., 1992), pp. 505–507; Plender, *The European Contracts Convention* (1991), pp. 162–164; Kaye, *The New Private International Law of Contract of the European Community* (1993), pp. 269–279.

contract or term were valid." Material validity, for these purposes, thus includes[33] the question of whether the contract has come into existence (*i.e.* matters relating to the formation,[34] the validity of the contract and the terms thereof,[35] and the validity of consent to the contract (*e.g.* questions of mistake, misrepresentation, duress or non-disclosure).[36] Since Article 8(1) applies to the validity of the contract and its terms it will also apply to some (but not all) issues of legality of the contract.[37] Where Article 8(1) applies, the relevant applicable law will be the law which would govern the contract under the Convention if the contract or term were valid, the "putative applicable law" or "putative governing law."[38]

Identification of "putative applicable law." Since Article 8(1) stipulates **31–112** that the governing law is the law which would apply, pursuant to the Convention, if the contract or term were valid, the putative governing law will be determined according to the rules for determining the applicable law which are contained in the Convention. Accordingly, where the parties have made a choice of law in the contract and an issue of material validity arises, that chosen law will be the governing law.[39] In the absence of such a choice the putative applicable law will be determined according to Article 4 of the Convention.[40]

Formation of the contract. At common law, it was generally accepted that **31–113** the question as to what minimum acts had to be performed to give rise to a contract was a matter for the "putative proper law" of the contract.[41] This has been the subject of specific decision in relation to offer and acceptance[42] and consideration.[43] Article 8(1) of the Convention thus repeats the common law rule

---

[33] See Cheshire and North *op. cit.* pp. 505–506.
[34] See *post*, §§ 31–113—31–114.
[35] See *post*, § 31–116.
[36] See *post*, § 31–115.
[37] See *post*, §§ 31–155—31–159.
[38] This was very much the approach of the common law: see 26th ed. of this work, § 2175–2177. See *post*, § 31–113. As to consent to choice of the applicable law (Art. 3(4)), see *ante*, § 31–055.
[39] Art. 3(1), *ante*, §§ 31–045—31–065. See *Egon Oldendorff v. Libera Corp. (No. 1)* [1995] 2 Lloyd's Rep. 64; see also *Egon Oldendorff v. Libera Corp. (No. 2)* [1996] 1 Lloyd's Rep. 380; *Merrill Lynch Capital Services Inc. v. Municipality of Piraeus* [1997] C.L.C. 1214.
[40] *Ante*, §§ 31–066—31–085. If the contract is subject to Arts. 5 or 6, the applicable law will be determined according to those provisions: see *ante*, §§ 31–086—31–103. At common law, it was sometimes suggested that the "putative proper law" should be determined without reference to any choice of law made by the parties, *i.e.* on purely objective grounds (see, *e.g.* Cheshire and North, *Private International Law* (12th ed., 1992), pp. 471–477), but this may have rested on a confusion between the putative proper law and the distinct concept of the proper law objectively determined. The weight of authority, however, supported the view that both an express and implied choice of law could constitute the putative proper law: see *The Parouth* [1982] 2 Lloyd's Rep. 351; *The Mariannina* [1983] 1 Lloyd's Rep. 12; *The T.S. Havprins* [1983] 2 Lloyd's Rep. 356; *The Iran Vojdan* [1984] 2 Lloyd's Rep. 380; *Dimskal Shipping Co. SA v. International Transport Workers Federation* [1992] 2 A.C. 152; *The Lake Avery* [1997] 1 Lloyd's Rep. 540. See also *Marc Rich & Co. A.G. v. Soc. Italiana Impianti P.A.* [1989] 1 Lloyd's Rep. 548. *cf. Mackender v. Feldia* [1967] Q.B. 590; *The Heidberg* [1994] 2 Lloyd's Rep. 287; *Oceanic Sun Line Shipping Co. Inc. v. Fay* (1988) 165 C.L.R. 197.
[41] See authorities cited in previous note; Jaffey (1975) 24 I.C.L.Q. 603; Libling (1979) 42 M.L.R. 169; Thomson (1980) 43 M.L.R. 650; Briggs [1990] L.M.C.L.Q. 192.
[42] *Albeko Schumaschinen A.G. v. Kamborian Shoe Machine Co.* [1961] 111 L.J. 519. See also *The Parouth, supra; Union Transport plc v. Continental Lines SA* [1992] 1 W.L.R. 15, 23.
[43] *Re Bonacina* [1912] 2 Ch. 394.

in this regard in so far as it refers such matters to the putative applicable law.[44] Article 8(2), however, creates an exception to this general rule in the following terms:

> "Nevertheless a party may rely upon the law of the country in which he has his habitual residence to establish that he did not consent if it appears from the circumstances that it would not be reasonable to determine the effect of his conduct in accordance with the law specified in [Article 8(1)]."

The purpose of this provision is to "solve the problem of the implications of silence by one party as to the formation of the contract,"[45] but it is not confined to that issue since the "word 'conduct' must be taken to cover both action and failure to act by the party in question."[46] In deciding whether it would not be reasonable to determine the effect of a party's conduct in accordance with the putative applicable law, regard must be had to all the circumstances of the case and not only to the circumstances in which the party claiming not to have consented has acted.[47] In this regard, the court should give particular consideration to the practices followed by the parties *inter se* as well as their previous business relationships.[48] This suggests that Article 8(2) may be relied upon by both natural and legal persons, despite the fact that the concept of habitual residence is normally associated with the former rather than with the latter.[49] It is likely, however, that the provision will be more liberally applied in favour of natural persons than it will be in favour of commercial organisations, if it is eventually decided that both categories of person are covered by it.[50] This much appears from the brief consideration given to the application of Article 8(2) in *Egon Oldendorff v. Libera Corp. (No. 1)*.[51] Here it was assumed, without argument, that the Article could be relied on by a legal person and that the habitual residence of a Japanese corporation was in Japan. It was held that English law should apply to determine whether a clause providing for arbitration in London was incorporated into the contract because the contract was governed by English law. The defendants argued in favour of the application of Article 8(2), contending that Japanese law governed, as the law of their habitual residence, claiming that it would be unreasonable to determine the effects of their conduct in accordance with English law.[52] It was held, however, that it would be unreasonable not to apply English law and unreasonable to apply Japanese law. If the latter law was applied, that would in effect ignore the arbitration clause, a result which would not accord with normal commercial expectations. This supports the sensible conclusion that legal persons engaging in commercial

---

[44] See *Egon Oldendorff v. Libera Corp. (No. 1)* [1995] 2 Lloyd's Rep. 64.

[45] Giuliano-Lagarde Report, p. 28.

[46] *ibid.*

[47] *ibid.*

[48] *ibid.*

[49] *cf.* Art. 4(2) of the Convention (*ante*, § 31–075) which changes the connecting factor of habitual residence into "central administration" when dealing with a body corporate or unincorporate.

[50] Drawing the analogy with Art. 4(2), the definition could involve the application of the notion of "central administration", or "principal place of business", or "place of business", as the case may be.

[51] [1995] 2 Lloyd's Rep. 64.

[52] The onus of establishing that Art. 8(2) applies lies on the party who relies upon it: *ibid.* at 71.

transactions should receive little protection from Article 8(2) in typical commercial situations and that what protection they might receive should be limited to unusual situations where the strict application of Article 8(1) would produce a result which is *commercially unreasonable*.

Article 8(2), it must be emphasised, only has the effect of releasing a party **31–114** from a contract to which he would otherwise be bound under Article 8(1). It cannot have the effect of binding a party to a contract to which he would not be bound under the applicable law.[53]

Validity of consent. The exceptional principle in Article 8(2) seems likely to **31–115** be confined to the existence of consent, as opposed to the question of whether consent, admittedly given, was invalidated by mistake, misrepresentation, duress, undue influence or non-disclosure.[54] Whether these factors vitiate consent would be a matter for the putative applicable law, pursuant to Article 8(1) of the Rome Convention.[55]

Validity of contract or terms. Whether the contract itself is materially (or **31–116** essentially) valid is a matter for the law which would govern it if it were valid. Thus it would seem that Article 8(1) will apply to determine the question, for example, of whether a contract is invalid as being in unreasonable restraint of trade,[56] or invalid as being a wagering contract.[57] If the contract is illegal by its applicable law it will be unenforceable in England.[58] The same principle applies to the material validity of a term of the contract.[59] Thus, the validity of a term purporting to limit or exempt one party from liability will be governed by the law which would apply to the contract assuming the term were valid.[60] In substance, this position is the same as that reached by the common law, though the cases

---

[53] *ibid.*

[54] Though *cf. Dimskal Shipping Co. SA v. International Transport Workers Federation* [1992] 2 A.C. 152, 168, *per* Lord Goff, who appears to regard economic duress as relating both to formation and validity of a contract. *cf. Dicey & Morris op. cit.* p. 1250; Cheshire and North *op. cit.* p. 507.

[55] This was the better view of the position at common law: see *Dimskal Shipping Co. SA v. International Transport Workers Federation, supra*; *Dicey and Morris op. cit.* pp. 1251–1252; 26th ed. of this work, § 2175. Contrast *Mackender v. Feldia* [1967] 2 Q.B. 590. *cf. The Lake Avery* [1997] 1 Lloyd's Rep. 540. As to the existence and validity of consent to a choice of law (Art. 3(4)), see *ante*, § 31–055.

[56] *cf. Roussillon v. Roussillon* (1880) 14 Ch.D. 351. The foreign law upholding or denying the validity of the contract may be refused application on the grounds of public policy: Rome Convention, Art. 16, *post*, §§ 31–160—31–162.

[57] Even if the wagering contract is valid according to the applicable law, it cannot be sued upon in the English courts since such suits are forbidden by Gaming Act 1845, s.18: see *Hill v. William Hill (Park Lane) Ltd* [1949] A.C. 530; *Dicey & Morris op. cit.* pp. 1467–1470.

[58] *cf. Kahler v. Midland Bank Ltd* [1950] A.C. 24. For other aspects of illegality, see *post*, §§ 31–160—31–162.

[59] See *Egon Oldendorff v. Libera Corp. (No. 1)* [1995] 2 Lloyd's Rep. 64.

[60] *Suzur Overseas Ltd v. Ocean Reliance Shipping Co. Ltd* [1997] C.L. 318; *Deepak Fertilisers and Petrochemicals Corp. v. ICI Chemicals & Polymers Ltd* [1998] 2 Lloyd's Rep. 139 reversed in part, but not on this point, [1999] 1 Lloyd's Rep. 387, CA. *cf. P. & O. Steam Navigation Co. v. Shand* (1865) 3 Moo. P.C. (N.S.) 272; *Re Missouri Steamship Co.* (1889) 42 Ch.D. 321; *Jones v. Oceanic Steam Navigation Co.* [1924] 2 K.B. 730; *Sayers v. International Drilling Co. N.V.* [1971] 1 W.L.R. 1176; *Coast Lines Ltd v. Hudig & Veder Chartering N.V.* [1972] 2 Q.B. 34; *Coupland v. Arabian Gulf Oil Co.* [1983] 1 W.L.R. 1136 (affd. [1983] 1 W.L.R. 1153).

tended to speak, in this context, of control by the "proper law" rather than the "putative proper law."[61]

(b) *Formal Validity of the Contract*[62]

31–117   **Introduction.** The position which ultimately came to be accepted at common law[63] was that a contract was formally valid if it complied with the formal requirements of either the law applicable to the contract,[64] or the law of the place where the contract was made.[65] Article 9 of the Rome Convention expresses the same principle as the general rule for formal validity.[66] The Article contains, however, special rules concerning the formal validity of consumer contracts,[67] certain contracts with regard to immovables[68] and the formal validity of acts intended to have legal effect relating to an existing or contemplated contract.[69]

31–118   **Meaning of formal validity.** A difficulty which obtained in the common law and one which persists under the Rome Convention concerns the requirements which are properly to be characterised as affecting formal validity. English common law had relatively few formal requirements and there was also a tendency to regard requirements which appeared, at first sight, to be formal, as questions of procedure to be governed by the *lex fori*,[70] even though, had the requirement been treated as formal, its application would have been determined by the relevant governing law.[71] The Rome Convention does not provide any definition of formal requirements. The Giuliano-Lagarde Report suggests, however, that it is "nevertheless permissible to consider 'form', for the purposes of Article 9, as including every external manifestation required on the part of a person expressing the will to be legally bound, and in the absence of which such expression of will would not be regarded as fully effective."[72] This observation, if accepted, indicates that it is possible that the category of formal requirements

---

[61] See 26th ed. of this work, § 2183; *Dicey & Morris op. cit.* p. 1253.

[62] *Dicey & Morris on the Conflict of Laws* (12th ed., 1993), pp. 1255–1259; Cheshire and North, *Private International Law* (12th ed., 1992), pp. 507–510; Plender, *The European Contracts Convention* (1991), pp. 164–166; Kaye, *The New Private International Law of Contract of the European Community* (1993), pp. 281–295; Lagarde in North (ed.), *Contract Conflicts* (1982), pp. 51–54.

[63] See 26th ed. of this work, §§ 2178–2180; *Dicey & Morris on the Conflict of Laws* (11th ed., 1987), pp. 1207–1213.

[64] *Van Grutten v. Digby* (1862) 31 Beav. 561; *Re Bankes* [1902] 2 Ch. 333; *Viditz* v. *O'Hagan* [1899] 2 Ch. 569, revd. on other grounds [1900] 2 Ch. 87.

[65] *Guépratte v. Young* (1851) 4 De G. & Sm. 217.

[66] Art. 9(1)–(3). See *post*, § 31–119.

[67] Art. 9(5). See *post*, § 31–120.

[68] Art. 9(6). See *post*, § 31–121.

[69] Art. 9(4). See *post*, § 31–122.

[70] See *Leroux v. Brown* (1852) 12 C.B. 801; *G. & H. Montage GmbH v. Irvani* [1990] 1 W.L.R. 667, 684.

[71] As in *Leroux v. Brown, supra* (Statute of Frauds 1677, s.4). This decision has been much criticised: see, *e.g. Monterosso Shipping Co. Ltd v. International Transport Workers Federation* [1982] I.C.R. 675. But it was approved in *G. & H. Montage GmbH v. Irvani, supra.* See too, *post*, n. 73.

[72] At 29. This definition does not include the special requirements which have to be fulfilled where there are persons under a disability to be protected, such as the need in French law for the consent of a family council to an act for the benefit of a minor, or where an act is to be valid against third parties, for example the need in English law for a notice of statutory assignment of a chose in action: *ibid.*

will expand at the expense of the category of procedure and evidence.[73] Where a requirement (*e.g.* of writing) is imposed by the law of the forum with a view to protecting a party to a transaction who is presumed to be in a weaker bargaining position,[74] such a requirement would seem to be neither formal nor procedural but substantive in effect.[75] Under the Rome Convention, such requirements, if not contained in the applicable law, will nonetheless be applicable if they are construed as mandatory rules of the law of the forum, the application of which is required by Article 7(2).[76]

The general rules. Where a contract is concluded between persons who are in the same country, the contract will be formally valid if it satisfies the formal requirements of the law which governs the contract under the Convention or the formal requirements of the law of the country where it is concluded.[77] Where the contract is concluded between persons who are in different countries, the contract will be formally valid if it satisfies the formal requirements either of the law applicable to it under the Convention or the law of one of those different countries.[78] Where the contract is concluded by an agent, the relevant country for the purpose of the foregoing rules is the country where the agent acts.[79] **31–119**

"Certain consumer contracts." The general rules concerning formal validity do not apply to a contract which falls within Article 5 of the Convention if the contract is concluded in any of the circumstances described in Article 5(2).[80] In such circumstances the formal validity of the consumer contract is governed by the law of the country in which the consumer has his habitual residence.[81] **31–120**

Immovables.[82] The formal validity of a contract with regard to an immovable is, in general, governed by the general rules relating to formal validity described above.[83] However, Article 9(6) of the Convention establishes an additional rule, in this respect, for contracts the subject matter of which is a right in or a right to **31–121**

---

[73] The rules in the Rome Convention do not apply to evidence and procedure: Art. 1(2)(h), *ante*, § 31–042. This process might result in a reversal of *Leroux v. Brown, supra*, since s.4 of the Statute of Frauds 1677 could be treated as a formal requirement, the applicability of which depends on Art. 9. A different approach would be to treat s.4 as subject to Art. 14(2) (as to which, see *post*, § 31–154) which permits any act intended to have legal effect to be proved in any manner permitted by the law of the forum or in any manner permitted by the law which renders the contract formally valid under Art. 9, provided the mode of proof can be administered by the forum. If s.4 falls within this provision, *Leroux v. Brown* would be reversed since the contract could have been proved by oral testimony under its French governing law: see *Dicey & Morris on the Conflict of Laws* (12th ed., 1993), p. 1257; Lasok and Stone, *Conflict of Laws in the European Community* (1987), pp. 366–367.

[74] See, *e.g.* Consumer Credit Act 1974, ss.60–65.

[75] *cf. English v. Donnelly*, 1958 S.C. 494, not followed in *Hong Kong Shipping Ltd v. The Cavalry* [1987] H.K.L. Rep. 287; *cf. Kay's Leasing Corpn. Pty. Ltd v. Fletcher* (1964) 116 C.L.R. 124; *Golden Acres Ltd v. Queensland Estates Ltd* [1969] St.R.Qd. 378 (affd. on different ground *sub nom. Freehold Land Investments Ltd v. Queensland Estates Ltd* (1970) 123 C.L.R. 418); *Nike Information Systems Ltd v. Avac Systems Ltd* (1979) 105 D.L.R. (3d) 455; *Greenshields Inc. v. Johnston* (1981) 119 D.L.R. (3d) 714 (appeal dismissed (1981) 131 D.L.R. (3d) 324); *Bank of Montreal v. Snoxell* (1982) 143 D.L.R. (3d) 349.

[76] *Ante*, § 31–064.

[77] Art. 9(1).

[78] Art. 9(2).

[79] Art. 9(3).

[80] Art. 9(5). As to Art. 5, see *ante*, §§ 31–087—31–093.

[81] Art. 9(5). As to the meaning of habitual residence, see *ante*, § 31–074.

[82] See *Dicey & Morris op. cit.* pp. 1391–1393.

[83] See *ante*, § 31–119.

use immovable property.[84] Such a contract "shall be subject to the mandatory requirements of form of the law of the country where the property is situated if by that law those requirements are imposed irrespective of the country where the contract is concluded and irrespective of the law governing the contract."[85] The effect of this provision is to impose the mandatory requirements of form of the *lex situs*, which have the necessary characteristics, on the contract even though the contract is not concluded in the country where the immovable is situated and the law governing the contract is not that of the *lex situs*. Cases in which such rules exist are likely to be "rather rare."[86]

31-122 Acts intended to have legal effect.

"An act intended to have legal effect relating to an existing or contemplated contract is formally valid if it satisfies the formal requirements of the law which under the Convention governs or would govern the contract or of the law of the country where the act was done."[87]

This provision covers unilateral acts, connected with a concluded contract, such as notice of termination, remission of a debt, declaration of rescission or repudiation,[88] or such acts which are connected with a contemplated contract, for example an offer expressed to be open for a specified time.[89]

31-123   Effect of change of applicable law. Article 3(2) of the Rome Convention enables the parties to a contract to change the law which governs it.[90] However, the change in the applicable law shall not prejudice the formal validity of the contract.[91] Thus, the contract is valid in respect of form, if it complies with the formal requirements of either the original governing law or the new governing law or the law of the country or countries where the parties were when they concluded the contract.[92]

31-124   Effect of several applicable laws. Where a contract is subject to several applicable laws (either, *e.g.* because the parties have selected different laws to

---

[84] The scope of the provision is coterminous with that of Art. 4(3), *ante*, § 31–077: see Giuliano-Lagarde Report, p. 32.

[85] *cf.* Plender *op. cit.* p. 166 who appears to maintain that Art. 9(6) is the only rule which deals with the formal validity of contracts the subject matter of which is a right in or a right to use immovable property so that Art. 9(1)–(4) is excluded. This suggestion cannot be accepted for the reasons given in *Dicey & Morris op. cit.* pp. 1392–1393.

[86] Giuliano-Lagarde Report, p. 32. In relation to a contract for the sale or other disposition of English land, the Law of Property (Miscellaneous Provisions) Act 1989, s.2(1) is likely to be regarded as mandatory for the purposes of Art. 9(6): see *Dicey and Morris op. cit.* p. 1393.

[87] Art. 9(4).

[88] Giuliano-Lagarde Report, p. 29. The requirement, in English law, that a contract unsupported by consideration must be by deed, would not seem to be a rule affecting formal validity, but would rather seem to be a rule of substance affecting the material validity of the contract, and would thus be applicable where the contract is, or would be, governed by English law. *cf. Re Bonacina* [1912] 2 Ch. 394. See *ante*, §§ 31–111—31–116.

[89] Lasok and Stone, *Conflict of Laws in the European Community* (1987), p. 305; Kaye *op. cit.* p. 291. Art. 9(4) does not apply to public acts (*e.g.* the act of a notary in authenticating a transaction). The formal validity of such acts is governed by the general rules in Art. 9(1)–(3): Giuliano-Lagarde Report, *ibid.*

[90] *Ante*, § 31–054.

[91] Art. 3(2), second sentence.

[92] Giuliano-Lagarde Report, p. 30; Lagarde in North (ed.), *Contract Conflicts* (1982) p. 49, at pp. 52–53.

govern different parts of the contract pursuant to Article 3(1),[93] or because the court has, by way of exception, severed the contract pursuant to Article 4(1)),[94] the Guiliano-Lagarde Report suggests that, in relation to the issue of formal validity, "it would seem reasonable to apply the law applicable to the part of the contract most closely connected with the disputed condition on which its formal validity depends."[95]

(c) *Capacity*[96]

Introduction. Subject to an exception, discussed below,[97] the uniform rules **31–125** of the Rome Convention do not apply to questions involving the status or legal capacity of natural persons.[98] Nor do the rules apply to the legal capacity of bodies corporate or unincorporate.[99] Accordingly the law applicable to determine the contractual capacity of a natural person will, subject to the exception, be governed by common law rules, and the law governing the contractual capacity of a body corporate or unincorporate will be entirely governed by common law rules.[1]

Natural persons. Despite contrary suggestions in older authorities,[2] it is **31–126** submitted that the contractual capacity of a natural person is governed by the law applicable to the contract.[3] In this context, however, the applicable law means that law objectively ascertained, without taking account of any choice of law in the contract itself.[4] The one intrusion by the Rome Convention on this state of affairs is to be found in Article 11 (entitled "incapacity") which provides as follows:

> "In a contract concluded between persons who are in the same country, a natural person who would have capacity under the law of that country may invoke his incapacity resulting from another law only if the other party to the contract was aware of this incapacity at the time of the conclusion of the contract or was not aware thereof as a result of negligence.[5]

---

[93] *Ante*, §§ 31–052—31–053.

[94] *Ante*, § 31–066.

[95] At p. 30.

[96] See 26th ed. of this work, § 2181; *Dicey & Morris op. cit.* pp. 1111–1112, 1271–1276; Cheshire and North *op. cit.* pp. 510–513; Blaikie, 1984 S.L.T. 161.

[97] *Post*, § 31–126.

[98] Art. 1(2)(a). See *ante*, § 31–034.

[99] Art. 1(2)(e). See *ante*, § 31–039. And see Art. 1(2)(f), *post*, § 31–040.

[1] See authorities cited in n. 96, *supra*.

[2] In favour of the *lex loci contractus*, see *Simonin v. Mallac* (1860) 2 Sw. & Tr. 67, 77; *Sottomayor v. De Barros (No. 2)* (1879) 5 P.D. 94, 100–101; *Baindail v. Baindail* [1946] P. 122, 128; *McFeetridge v. Stewarts and Lloyds Ltd*, 1913 S.C. 773; *Bondholders Securities Corpn. v. Manville* [1933] 4 D.L.R. 609; *cf. Male v. Roberts* (1800) 3 Esp. 163. In favour of the law of the domicile, see *Sottomayor v. De Barros (No. 1)* (1877) 3 P.D. 1, 5; *Re Cooke's Trusts* (1887) 56 L.J. Ch. 637, 639; *Cooper v. Cooper* (1883) 13 App. Cas. 88, 89, 100; *Viditz v. O'Hagan* [1900] 2 Ch. 87.

[3] *Charron v. Montreal Trust Co.* (1958) 15 D.L.R. (2d) 240; see also *The Bodley Head Ltd v. Flegon* [1972] 1 W.L.R. 68 and the authorities cited in n. 96, *supra*. It is possible that the law of the domicile would be applied if it would give capacity but the objective governing law would not: see *Dicey & Morris op. cit.* p. 1274.

[4] See *Cooper v. Cooper* (1883) 13 App. Cas. 88, 108; *Dicey & Morris op. cit.* pp. 1274–1275; Cheshire and North *op. cit.* p. 511.

[5] Such a rule is not uncommon in civil law countries which regard contractual capacity as a matter of status to be governed by the personal law: see Giuliano-Lagarde Report, p. 34.

In terms, this rule is of limited effect. It only applies to contracts concluded between persons who are in the same country, one of whom must be a natural person who has capacity under that country's law, but who seeks to rely on a lack of capacity under the law of another country. That lack of capacity may only successfully be invoked if the other contracting party was aware of it or was unaware of it as a result of negligence.[6]

31–127   **Corporations.** The contractual capacity of a corporation depends both on its constitution and on the law applicable to the contract which is concluded. Thus in so far as a corporation's capacity to enter into a contract depends on its constitution, the law of the country of incorporation is the governing law,[7] though the corporation must also possess capacity under the law applicable to the contract on objective grounds.[8] It may, accordingly, be taken to lack capacity to enter into a contract if the law of the country of incorporation so holds because of a limitation on its powers under its constitution (*e.g.* the doctrine of *ultra vires*)[9] or if the law applicable to the contract so holds on the basis of a principle of capacity which is unrelated to its constitutional powers.[10] According to Article 1(2)(e) of the Rome Convention, as pointed out above,[11] the legal capacity of a corporation is not covered by the Convention. But the Giuliano-Lagarde Report states that this reference is to limitations which may be imposed by law on companies or firms.[12] It does not extend to *ultra vires* acts by organs of the company or firm,[13] which are excluded by Article 1(2)(f) which provides, *inter alia*, that the Convention does not apply to the question whether an organ can bind a body corporate or unincorporate to a third party.[14] Since the combined effect of Article 1(2)(e) and 1(2)(f) is to exclude the contractual capacity of a corporation, however arising, exclusion of *ultra vires* acts under Article 1(2)(f) rather than under Article 1(2)(e) appears to produce no practical consequence, since in either case the common law rules described above will continue to apply.[15]

---

[6] The wording implies that the burden of proof lies on the party lacking capacity to show that the other party knew of the incapacity or should have known of it: Giuliano-Lagarde Report, p. 34.

[7] *Risdon Iron and Locomotive Works Ltd v. Furniss* [1906] 1 K.B. 49, 56–57; *Banque Internationale de Commerce de Petrograd v. Goukassow* [1923] 2 K.B. 682, 690–691; *Janred Properties Ltd v. ENIT* [1989] 2 All E.R. 444; *J.H. Rayner (Mincing Lane) Ltd v. Department of Trade and Industry* [1990] 2 A.C. 418; *Sierra Leone Telecommunications Co. Ltd v. Barclays Bank plc* [1998] 2 All E.R. 821; *Merrill Lynch Capital Services Inc. v. Municipality of Piraeus* [1997] C.L.C. 1214. And see Foreign Corporations Act 1991, s.1; Companies Act 1985, ss.36, 36A and 36C, as substituted and inserted by Companies Act 1989, s.130, as adapted and modified by Foreign Companies (Execution of Documents) Regulations 1994 (S.I. 1994 No. 950), as amended by S.I. 1995 No. 1729, made under Companies Act 1989, s.130(6).

[8] See references in preceding note and: *General Steam Navigation Co. v. Guillou* (1843) 11 M. & W. 877; *Pickering v. Stephenson* (1872) L.R. 14 Eq. 322; *Bateman v. Service* (1881) 6 App. Cas. 386, 389; *Banco de Bilbao v. Sancha and Rey* [1938] 2 K.B. 176; *National Bank of Greece and Athens SA v. Metliss* [1958] A.C. 509; *Carl Zeiss Stiftung v. Rayner & Keeler Ltd (No. 2)* [1967] 1 A.C. 853.

[9] *cf. Janred Properties Ltd v. ENIT, supra.*

[10] There is little likelihood of this happening in practice where English law is the applicable law. The nearest English analogy is the now repealed law of Mortmain: see *Dicey & Morris op. cit.* p. 1112.

[11] *Ante*, §§ 31–039, 31–125.

[12] See Giuliano-Lagarde Report, p. 12 where the example given is a limitation on power to acquire immovable property.

[13] *ibid.* p. 13. See, too, *Dicey & Morris op. cit.* pp. 1113–1115.

[14] *Ante*, § 31–040.

[15] Art. 11 (*ante* § 31–126) only applies to contracts entered into by natural persons.

(d) *Particular Issues: Article 10*[16]

Introduction. Article 10(1) of the Rome Convention, entitled "Scope of the **31–128** applicable law," stipulates that the law applicable to a contract by virtue of Articles 3,[17] 4,[18] 5,[19] 6,[20] and 12[21] of the Convention will govern "in particular" the following matters: interpretation[22]; performance[23]; within the limits of the powers conferred on the court by its procedural law, the consequences of breach, including the assessment of damages in so far as it is governed by rules of law[24]; the various ways of extinguishing obligations, and prescription and limitation of actions[25]; the consequences of nullity of the contract.[26]

Reservation of consequences of nullity. In relation to the last issue it must, **31–129** however, be immediately pointed out that the applicable law will *not* be applied to determine the consequences of nullity of the contract in United Kingdom law. This is because the Convention recognises the power of Contracting States to enter a reservation to this particular provision, which power has been exercised by the United Kingdom.[27] Accordingly, Article 10(1)(e) will not have the force of law in the United Kingdom.[28] In the law of United Kingdom jurisdictions the consequences of nullity of the contract belong to the law of restitution, and, as such, the relevant choice of law rules are those applicable to restitution rather those applicable to contractual obligations.[29]

Overlapping categories. Questions may arise, of course, which overlap the **31–130** particular categories of issue expressly referred to in Article 10(1). For example

---

[16] See *Dicey & Morris on the Conflict of Laws* (12th ed., 1993), pp. 1259–1269; Cheshire and North, *Private International Law* (12th ed., 1992), pp. 513–520; Plender, *The European Contracts Convention* (1991), pp. 169–177; Kaye, *The New Private International Law of Contract of the European Community* (1993), pp. 297–310; Lagarde in North (ed.), *Contract Conflicts* (1982), p. 49, at pp. 54–57.

[17] *Ante*, §§ 31–045—31–065.

[18] *Ante*, §§ 31–066—31–085.

[19] *Ante*, §§ 31–087—31–093.

[20] *Ante*, §§ 31–104—31–106.

[21] *Ante*, §§ 31–134—31–136.

[22] Art. 10(1)(a).

[23] Art. 10(1)(b). As to the "manner of performance," see Art. 10(2).

[24] Art. 10(1)(c).

[25] Art. 10(1)(d).

[26] Art. 10(1)(e).

[27] Art. 22(1)(b).

[28] Contracts (Applicable Law) Act 1990, s.2(2).

[29] See North in North (ed.), *Contract Conflicts* (1982), p. 3, at pp. 16–17; Giuliano-Lagarde Report, p. 33; *Dicey & Morris op. cit.* p. 1268. A majority of the House of Lords has held that a claim for money paid under a void contract was not a matter "relating to a contract" within the meaning of Art. 5(1) of the modified version of the Brussels Convention on Jurisdiction and the Enforcement of Judgments in Civil and Commercial Matters which is applicable within the United Kingdom as Sched. 4 to the Civil Jurisdiction and Judgments Act 1982: see *Kleinwort Benson Ltd v. Glasgow City Council* [1999] A.C. 153; *ante*, § 31–032. For the choice of law rules in restitution, see *Dicey and Morris op. cit.*, Chap. 34; Rose (ed.), *Restitution and the Conflict of Laws* (1995); Dickinson [1996] L.M.C.L.Q. 556. See also *Baring Bros & Co. Ltd v. Cunninghame District Council, The Times,* September 30, 1996 (Outer House of the Court of Session) noted by Stevens (1997) 113 L.Q.R. 249; Bird [1997] L.M.C.L.Q. 182.

whether a contract has been frustrated may relate to interpretation, or performance, or to the extinguishing of obligations.[30] But since the applicable law governs all of these issues, no practical consequence can result from placing frustration (or any other overlapping question) in one category or another.

31–131   **Non-exhaustive list.** The list of issues in Article 10(1) is not intended to be exhaustive,[31] so that in consequence, national courts may refer other issues which may arise in a contractual context to the law which governs the contract. Some of these issues are discussed at a later point.[32]

31–132   **Interpretation.** At common law, a contract was construed and interpreted according to the canons of construction that prevailed in the law applicable to the contract.[33] The same principle is adopted in the Rome Convention.[34] Thus the applicable law will determine the meaning to be given to particular words or phrases in the contract, for example the meaning of payment in "gold,"[35] "pounds"[36] or "shillings."[37]

31–133   **Performance.** Article 10(1)(b) of the Rome Convention provides that the applicable law shall govern "performance" of the contract. The scope of this provision must, initially, be delimited by reference to Article 10(2). The latter provides that in "relation to the manner of performance and the steps to be taken in the event of defective performance regard shall be had to the law of the country in which performance takes place." The distinction between "performance" and "manner of performance" is the distinction, recognised in the common law, between the substance of the obligation to be performed and the mode of performance of that obligation.[38] Whereas the former matter was governed by the law applicable to the contract,[39] the latter question was governed by the law

---

[30] *Dicey & Morris op. cit.* p. 1260. The consequences which flow after it has been determined that the contract has been frustrated according to its applicable law will probably not be determined by the Convention at all, because of the United Kingdom's reservation to Art. 10(1)(e), discussed *ante*, §§ 31–032—31–029 *supra*; and see *post*, § 31–135; *Benjamin's Sale of Goods* (5th ed., 1997), §§ 25–145—25–146.

[31] "The law applicable to a contract . . . shall govern *in particular*" [emphasis added].

[32] *Post*, § 31–149.

[33] *e.g. St Pierre v. South American Stores Ltd* [1937] 3 All E.R. 349; *A.B. Bofors-Uva C.A.V. Ltd v. A.B. Skandia Transport* [1982] 1 Lloyd's Rep. 410.

[34] Art. 10(1)(a).

[35] *cf. St Pierre v. South American Stores Ltd, supra.* See also *Feist v. Société Intercommunale Belge d'Electricité* [1934] A.C. 161; *Treseder-Griffin v. Co-operative Insurance Society Ltd* [1956] 2 Q.B. 127; *The Rosa S.* [1989] Q.B. 419; *SS. Pharmaceutical Co. v. Quantas Airways* [1991] 1 Lloyd's Rep. 288. See *post*, §§ 31–163—31–169.

[36] *cf. Bonython v. Commonwealth of Australia* [1951] A.C. 201. See *post*, §§ 31–163—31–169.

[37] *cf. W.J. Alan & Co. Ltd v. El Nasr Export and Import Co.* [1972] Q.B. 189. If, however, there is no doubt as to the identity of the currency referred to, then it is for the law of the country whose currency is mentioned to determine what is legal tender in that currency: this seems to rest on an "implied" choice of law (Art. 3(1) of the Rome Convention, *ante*, § 31–049 and *post*, §§ 31–164—31–165) which implied choice may be limited to this question alone (*i.e.* the issue is "severed," see *ante*, §§ 31–052—31–053 and *post*, § 31–165) and submitted to its own governing law under Art. 3(1)). *cf. Pyrmont v. Schott* [1939] A.C. 145. See *Dicey & Morris op. cit.* p. 1553. As to currency questions, see further, *post*, §§ 31–163—31–172.

[38] *Jacobs v. Crédit Lyonnais* (1884) 12 Q.B.D. 589; *Mount Albert Borough Council v. Australian Temperance & General Mutual Life Assurance Society* [1938] A.C. 224; *Bonython v. Commonwealth of Australia* [1951] A.C. 201. See the 26th ed. of this work, § 2184.

[39] *ibid.*

of the place of performance[40] which could be a law other than the governing law where the governing law was not that of the country in which the contract was to be performed.[41] As far as "performance" is concerned, the Giuliano-Lagarde Report informs that it "appears to embrace the totality of the conditions, resulting from the law or from the contract, in accordance with which the acts essential for the fulfilment of the obligation must be performed . . . ."[42] This observation lacks clarity but is rendered less difficult by the examples which follow, namely: the diligence with which the obligation must be performed; conditions relating to the place and time of performance; the extent to which the obligation can be performed by a person other than the party liable; the conditions as to performance of the obligation both in general and in relation to certain categories of obligation (joint and several obligations, alternative obligations, divisible and indivisible obligations, pecuniary obligations); where performance consists of the payment of a sum of money, the conditions relating to the discharge of the debtor who has made the payment, the appropriation of the payment, the receipt, etc.[43]

Manner of performance. The foregoing issues must be distinguished from those which merely affect the "manner of performance" which are subject to Article 10(2). The latter expression is not defined in the Convention: no precise meaning is given to it in the various laws of Contracting States, and, indeed, the drafting group was not prepared to provide a strict (or one might add, any) definition of it.[44] In consequence, the Giuliano-Lagarde Report opines that it will be for the *lex fori* to determine what is meant by the expression.[45] This view has, however, been challenged, it being suggested that it would be more appropriate to draw the distinction in a uniform manner on the basis of a Convention interpretation of the distinction.[46]   **31–134**

Examples. However the distinction is ultimately to be drawn (and the suggestion of a uniform interpretation has much to be said for it), the Giuliano-Lagarde Report mentions, as examples of rules affecting the manner of performance, "the rules governing public holidays, the manner in which goods are to be examined, and the steps to be taken if they are refused."[47] Thus, for example, if a contract governed by English law provides that the seller will deliver goods to the buyer in Paris "during usual business hours," it will be for French law to determine what business hours are "usual," since this relates to the manner of performance, but it will be for English law to determine whether performance of the contract is excused by *force majeure*.[48] And if, pursuant to a contract governed by English law, a seller agrees to deliver goods to the buyer in Barcelona for export to Athens, Spanish law will determine whether an export licence is required, though English law will determine whether the seller or the buyer is contractually obliged to obtain a licence and whether, if no licence is obtained, one or other of   **31–135**

---

[40] *e.g. Robertson v. Jackson* (1845) 2 C.B. 412; *Mount Albert Borough Council v. Australian Temperance & General Mutual Life Assurance Society*, *supra*, at 240–241.
[41] *e.g. Bonython v. Commonwealth of Australia, supra.*
[42] At p. 32.
[43] At pp. 32–33.
[44] Giuliano-Lagarde Report, p. 33.
[45] *ibid.*
[46] *Dicey & Morris op. cit.* p. 1261.
[47] At p. 33.
[48] *cf. Jacobs v. Crédit Lyonnais* (1884) 12 Q.B.D. 589; *Dicey & Morris op. cit.* p. 1262.

the parties is in breach of contract.[49] Equally, in a contract of sale, the applicable law will determine matters such as the person other than the buyer (if any) to whom delivery may be made, the identity and quantity of goods to be delivered, the nature of any additional duties of the seller in relation to the goods, and the documents, if any, that must be prepared and tendered by the seller.[50] But questions relating to the mode of delivery such as the usages governing the unloading of goods at a particular port, will be regulated by the law of the place of performance.[51]

31–136   **Discretion.** Although the Convention perpetuates a distinction drawn in the common law between the "substance" of performance and the "manner" of such performance, there may be one difference between Article 10(2) and its common law counterpart. At common law, reference of matters affecting the manner of performance to the law of the place of performance seems to be a choice of law rule the application of which does not depend on any discretionary element. Article 10(2), on the other hand, requires simply that "regard shall be had" to the law of the country in which performance takes place. According to the Giuliano-Lagarde Report, the court "may consider whether such law has any relevance to the manner in which the contract should be performed and has a discretion whether to apply it in whole or in part so as to do justice between the parties."[52] If this view is correct, the role and operation of Article 10(2) becomes somewhat uncertain in scope.

31–137   **Consequences of breach, etc.** According to Article 10(1)(c) of the Rome Convention, the applicable law governs, within the limits of the powers conferred on the court by its procedural law, the consequences of breach including the assessment of damages in so far as it is governed by rules of law. The expression "consequences of breach" is capable of wide interpretation.[53] According to the Giuliano-Lagarde Report, it refers to "the consequences which the law or the contract attaches to the breach of a contractual obligation, whether it is a matter of the liability of the party to whom the breach is attributable or of a claim to terminate the contract for breach. Any requirement of service of notice on the party to assume his liability also comes within this context."[54] The expression would therefore appear to include the question of whether an innocent party has a right to treat the contract as repudiated or rescind the contract.[55] The expression (and the remaining words of Article 10(1)(c)) also raise questions as to the effect

---

[49] cf. *Pound & Co. Ltd v. Hardy & Co. Inc.* [1956] A.C. 588; *Dicey & Morris ibid.*

[50] See *Benjamin's Sale of Goods* (5th ed., 1997), § 25–130.

[51] See *Robertson v. Jackson* (1845) 2 C.B. 412.

[52] At p. 33.

[53] See Kaye *op. cit.* pp. 304–305. See also the Dutch case, *Buenaventura v. Ocean Trade Company* [1984] E.C.C. 183, cited in Cheshire and North *op. cit.* p. 516, where it was said (before the Convention entered into force) that the expression must be construed widely, and could include strikes so that striking crew members on a Saudi Arabian ship lying at a Dutch port could be ordered to return to work on the ground that the strike was illegal under the governing law of the contract, the law of the Philippines: *sed quaere.* As to currency questions, see *post*, §§ 31–163—31–172.

[54] At p. 33. See also Case 9/87 *Arcado v. S.A. Haviland* [1988] E.C.R. 1539, 1555 (Art. 10(1)(c) governs consequences of total or partial failure to comply with obligations under contract and consequently the contractual liability of the party responsible for breach).

[55] *Dicey & Morris op. cit.* p. 1263; Kaye *op. cit.* p. 305; *Benjamin's Sale of Goods* (5th ed., 1997), §§ 25–148—25–172.

of the applicable law on remedies, which questions are discussed in the two paragraphs which follow.

Damages. At common law a distinction is drawn between rules relating to remoteness of damage and heads of damages which are governed by the law applicable to the contract,[56] and rules relating to the measure or quantification of damages which are governed by the *lex fori* since they are treated as a matter of procedure.[57] It would seem incontrovertible that remoteness and heads of damage in contract are matters for the applicable law according to Article 10(1)(c).[58] More doubt surrounds the question of measure or quantification of damages. Article 10(1)(c) states that *assessment* of damages is a matter for the applicable law in so far as it is governed by rules of law. According to the Giuliano-Lagarde Report, this formulation is intended to exclude assessment of damages which is only concerned with questions of fact[59] (*e.g.* arithmetical calculation of loss where the formula for such calculation is not dictated by rules of law). Where, however, a rule of law imposes a limit on compensation,[60] or draws distinctions between penalties and liquidated damages,[61] or provides a principle by which the measure of damages for, say, non-delivery of goods can be calculated,[62] the applicability of the rule will depend on the governing law. In this context (as in other contexts in Article 10(1)(c)) the scope of the applicable law is limited by "the powers conferred on the court by its procedural law." Thus, for example, an English court could refuse to award damages in the form of periodical payments as required by the law governing the contract, because there is no procedural machinery for making such an award.[63]

31–138

Other remedies. Although the matter has received little discussion and is the subject of only scanty authority, it was generally stated that at common law the availability of the equitable remedies of specific performance or injunction was a matter for the *lex fori*.[64] The position appears to be different under the Rome Convention, since the availability of a particular remedy would seem to be a consequence of breach which is referable to the applicable law pursuant to Article 10(1)(c).[65] The applicable law should thus determine the availability of an injunction[66] or a decree of specific performance. Such availability will, of course, be subject to the procedural proviso to Article 10(1)(c), *i.e.* to "the limits of the

31–139

---

[56] *D'Almedia Araujo Lda. v. Sir Frederick Becker & Co. Ltd* [1953] 2 Q.B. 329 (where the question of the existence of a duty to mitigate damage was also said to be governed by the law applicable to the contract); *Livesley v. Clemens Horst Co.* [1925] 1 D.L.R. 159. See also *Boys v. Chaplin* [1971] A.C. 356; *Dicey & Morris op. cit.* pp. 1263–1264; Cheshire and North *op. cit.* pp. 515–517.

[57] *D'Almedia Araujo Lda. v. Sir Frederick Becker & Co. Ltd, supra*, at p. 338; *Livesley v. Clemens Horst Co., supra*; see also *Boys v. Chaplin, supra*, at 378, 381–382, 383, 394 and works cited in preceding note.

[58] As would the existence of a duty to mitigate damage: *cf. supra*, n. 56.

[59] Guiliano-Lagarde Report, p. 33.

[60] *ibid.*

[61] *Dicey & Morris op. cit.* p. 1263.

[62] See, *e.g.* Sale of Goods Act 1979, ss.51(2) and (3); Vol. II, §§ 43–386—43–403.

[63] See Morse (1982) 2 Ybk.Eur.L. 107, 154–155; *cf. The Indian Grace* [1992] 1 Lloyd's Rep. 124, rvsd., on other grounds, *sub nom. Republic of India v. India Steamship Co.* [1993] A.C. 410.

[64] *Baschet v. London Illustrated Standard Co.* [1900] 1 Ch. 73; *Boys v. Chaplin* [1971] A.C. 356, 394; *Dicey & Morris op. cit.* p. 171. See also *Warner Brothers Pictures Incorporated v. Nelson* [1937] 1 K.B. 209 where the point was neither raised nor discussed.

[65] *Dicey & Morris op. cit.* p. 1264; Cheshire and North *op. cit.* pp. 516–517.

[66] This refers to a final injunction. The right to an interlocutory injunction would seem to be a matter of procedure for the *lex fori* as would other forms of interlocutory relief.

powers conferred on the court by its procedural law." Thus the English court could refuse, for example, a decree of specific performance if the order would require constant supervision by the court, according to English principles.[67]

31–140   **Interest.** At common law, liability to pay contractual interest and the rate of interest payable in respect of a contractual debt were determined by the law applicable to the contract under which the debt was incurred.[68] This is also the position under the Rome Convention, though it would seem that this result is reached by reference to Article 10(1)(b) ("performance") since the liability to pay contractual interest and the rate thereof relate to the substance of the obligation to be performed.[69] Where interest was claimed as damages for non-payment of a debt, the better view was that liability at common law similarly depended on the law applicable to the contract.[70] The rate of interest payable as damages was, however, governed by the *lex fori*.[71] Under the Rome Convention, the right to claim interest as damages would seem to be a consequence of breach governed by the applicable law pursuant to Article 10(1)(c) of the Convention.[72] It is also submitted that under the Rome Convention the rate of such interest should continue to be a matter of procedure governed by the *lex fori*, a result which is not at variance with the terms of the Convention since the Convention does not apply to procedure.[73]

31–141   **Exchange losses.** The right to claim contractual interest and interest by way of damages must be distinguished from the question whether a contracting party who has paid a contractual debt after the due date is liable for exchange losses if the currency in which payment is expressed to be paid depreciates in value relative to the currency in which the other contracting party operates. The existence of such liability depended, at common law, on the law applicable to the contract.[74] The same result should follow under the Rome Convention since the

---

[67] See *ante*, § 31–133.

[68] See *e.g. Mount Albert Borough Council v. Australasian Temperance & General Mutual Life Insurance Society* [1938] A.C. 224. As to other currency questions, see *post*, §§ 31–163—31–172.

[69] *Dicey & Morris op. cit.* pp. 1263, 1445.

[70] *Miliangos v. George Frank (Textiles) Ltd (No. 2)* [1977] Q.B. 489, 496–497; *Helmsing Schiffahrts GmbH v. Malta Drydocks Corpn.* [1977] 2 Lloyd's Rep. 444, 449–450. The contrary view, that the question is a matter of procedure governed by the *lex fori* (see *Kuwait Oil Tanker Co. S.A.K. v. Bader, The Independent*, January 11, 1999: *Midland International Trade Services v. Sudairy, Financial Times*, May 2, 1990, not followed by the Court of Appeal of Brunei in *Brunei LNG Sendirian Berhad v. Interbeton BV* (1998) 14 Const. L.J. 117) cannot be accepted: see *Dicey & Morris op. cit.* p. 1447.

[71] This is controversial: in favour, see *Miliangos v. George Frank (Textiles) Ltd (No. 2)* [1977] Q.B. 489; against, see *Helmsing Schiffahrts GmbH v. Malta Drydocks Corpn.* [1977] 2 Lloyd's Rep. 444. Since these decisions the Law Commission has conducted a thorough examination of the question and has concluded that the view expressed in the text should be preferred: see Law Com. No. 124 (1983), paras. 2.32, 3.55 and Law Com. Working Paper No. 80 (1981), paras. 4.22–4.27. See also, *The Pacific Colocotronis* [1981] 2 Lloyd's Rep. 40; *Swiss Bank Corp. v. State of New South Wales* (1993–94) 33 N.S.W.L.R. 63; *Dicey & Morris op cit.* pp. 1448–1451.

[72] Giuliano-Lagarde Report, p. 32; *Dicey & Morris op. cit.* pp. 1446–1447.

[73] Art. 1(2)(h). The reasons for this view are those given by the Law Commission: see references in n. 40, *ante*.

[74] *President of India v. Lips Maritime Corpn.* [1988] A.C. 395; *Ozalid Group (Export) Ltd v. African Continental Bank Ltd* [1979] 2 Lloyd's Rep. 331; *International Minerals and Chemicals Corpn. v. Karl O. Helm A.G.* [1986] 1 Lloyd's Rep. 81; *Isaac Naylor & Sons Ltd v. New Zealand Co-operative Wool Marketing Association Ltd* [1981] 1 N.Z.L.R. 361.

question relates to the consequences of breach, governed by the applicable law by virtue of Article 10(1)(c).[75]

"Statutory interest". The Late Payment of Commercial Debts (Interest) Act 1998[76] makes provision with respect to interest on the late payment of certain debts. By virtue of Part I of the Act, it is an implied term in a contract for the supply of goods or services where the purchaser and the supplier are each acting in the course of a business,[77] other than an "excepted contract",[78] that any "qualifying debt"[79] created by the contract carries simple interest, referred to as "statutory interest",[80] subject to and in accordance with Part I of the Act.[81] Part II of the Act describes the circumstances in which contract terms are permissible to oust or vary this right to statutory interest.[82] Section 12 of the Act contains provisions dealing with the scope of the application of the Act in the context of cases involving the conflict of laws.[83] According to section 12(1), the provisions of the Act do *not* have effect in relation to a contract governed by the law of a part of the United Kingdom by choice of the parties if (a) there is no significant connection between the contract and that part of the United Kingdom; and (b) but for that choice the applicable law would be a foreign law, defined as the law of a country outside the United Kingdom.[84] This would seem to mean that if the parties have chosen, say, English law to govern the contract in accordance with Article 3(1) of the Rome Convention,[85] but there is no significant connection between the contract and England, and, absent the choice of English law, the contract would, according to Article 4 of the Rome Convention,[86] be governed by the law of a country outside the United Kingdom, *e.g.* that of France, the provisions of the 1998 Act will not apply. This would appear to be the case even if the contract did have a significant connection with a part of the United Kingdom other than that whose law had been chosen in the contract, since the provision, in terms, requires the absence of a significant connection with the part whose law has been chosen. Conversely, the Act *will* apply where English law is chosen but, apart from that, the contract would be governed by the law of a country outside the United Kingdom, if there is, nonetheless, a significant connection between the contract and England. Section 12(1) thus envisages that a contract may have a *significant connection* with the part of the United Kingdom whose law has been chosen even though, pursuant to Article 4 of the Rome Convention, it is *most closely connected* with a country outside the United

31–142

---

[75] The cases in the preceding note establish that the question is one of remoteness of damage which is thus governed by the applicable law according to Art. 10(1)(c). See *ante*, § 31–138; *Dicey & Morris op. cit.* pp. 1584–1585.

[76] See *ante*, §§ 27–140—27–141. The Act entered into force to the extent indicated in S.I. 1998 No. 2479 on November 1, 1998. For transitional provisions, see S.I. 1998 No. 2481.

[77] Late Payment of Commercial Debts (Interest) Act 1998, ss.1(1), 2(1), (2), (3), (7), 12(3).

[78] Defined in s.2(5) and (7) as a consumer credit agreement within the meaning of the Consumer Credit Act 1974 (*post*, Vol. II, § 38–014), a contract intended to operate by way of mortgage, pledge, charge or other security and any other contract specified in an order made by the Secretary of State.

[79] *ibid.* ss.1(1), 3(1).

[80] *ibid.* s.1(2).

[81] *ibid.* s.1(1).

[82] *ibid.* ss.7–10.

[83] *cf.* Unfair Contract Terms Act 1977, s.27, *ante*, § 31–007.

[84] 1998 Act, s.12(3). *cf.* Unfair Contract Terms Act 1977, s.27(1), *ante*, § 31–007.

[85] *Ante*, §§ 31–045—31–055.

[86] *Ante*, §§ 31–066—31–085.

Kingdom. The factors which may be taken to constitute a significant connection are not identified in the Act and when such a connection will or will not be held to exist will depend on the circumstances of individual cases. However, by way of example, such a connection may be found to exist, in a contract of sale, where English law is chosen and England is also the place where the purchase price is to be paid, but apart from that choice of law the contract would be governed by the law of France pursuant to Article 4(2) of the Rome Convention[87] since France is the country in which the seller's principal place of business is situated. Further, the provisions of the Act would appear to apply if the law of one part of the United Kingdom is chosen in the contract, but in the absence of that choice the applicable law would be the law of another part of the United Kingdom. This result appears to ensue irrespective of whether a significant connection between the contract and the part of the United Kingdom whose law has been chosen does or does not exist. This is because section 12(1) only applies where in the absence of choice the contract would be governed by a foreign law[88] and that law is, as pointed out above, defined as the law of a country outside the United Kingdom.[89]

31–143   Section 12(2) of the 1998 Act is an anti-avoidance provision.[90] It provides that the Act *has* effect in relation to a contract governed by a foreign law by choice of the parties if (a) but for that choice, the applicable law would be the law of a part of the United Kingdom; *and* (b) there is no significant connection between the contract and any other country other than that part of the United Kingdom. The effect of the provision would seem to be that if, say, a contract contains a choice of French law satisfying Article 3(1) of the Rome Convention,[91] but were it not for that choice, the applicable law would, under Article 4 of the Convention,[92] be English law, the Act *will* apply unless the contract has a significant connection with a country other than England. That significant connection may be with the country whose law has been chosen, France in this example, or with a different foreign country, for example Luxembourg, or even with a part of the United Kingdom other than England, for example Scotland. For although the expression "country" is not defined in the Act, it is tolerably clear that the expression includes the different parts of the United Kingdom in section 12(2) since the subsection expressly refers to "any country other than that *part of the United Kingdom*" whose law has been chosen[93] and that form of words is, in the above example, apt to include Scotland. What will be found to constitute a significant connection for the purposes of the subsection will, as suggested above depend on the circumstances of the individual case, but, as was the case with section 12(1), it is clear that although the contract has its closest connection with the law of a particular part of the United Kingdom, the contract may, nonetheless, have a significant connection with a country other than that part of the United Kingdom.

---

[87] *Ante*, §§ 31–068—31–076.
[88] 1998 Act, s.12(1)(b).
[89] *ibid.* s.12(3).
[90] *cf.* Unfair Contract Terms Act 1977, s.27(2), *ante.* § 31–007.
[91] *Ante*, §§ 31–045—31–055.
[92] *Ante*, §§ 31–066—31–085.
[93] Emphasis added. *cf.* s.12(3), defining foreign law as the law of a country outside the *United Kingdom* (emphasis added). See also *ante*, § 31–023.

Section 12(2) only controls the avoidance of the Act by a choice of foreign **31–144** law, *i.e.* the law of a country outside the United Kingdom.[94] Where, however, an issue arises in English proceedings involving a contract which contains a choice of the law of a different part of the United Kingdom, the Act would appear to apply on general principles,[95] unless it is disapplied because the circumstances of the case fall within section 12(1).[96] The Act also seems to apply where the contract contains no choice of law but, as a result of applying Article 4 of the Rome Convention,[97] the applicable law is the law of a part of the United Kingdom.[98]

The rate of statutory interest under the 1998 Act shall be that prescribed by the **31–145** Secretary of State.[99] It has been set at 8 per cent over the official dealing rate per annum.[1]

Extinguishing obligations, etc. Article 10(1)(d) of the Convention submits **31–146** "ways of extinguishing obligations, and prescription and limitation of actions" to the applicable law. As to the various ways in which an obligation may be extinguished, it is possible that whether a contract has been discharged by performance or by frustration will fall under Article 10(1)(*b*) ("performance") rather than Article 10(1)(d), but this will make no practical difference since in either event the issue will be governed by the applicable law.[2] Discharge (or extinction) by accord and satisfaction,[3] moratorium,[4] outbreak of war[5] or legislation[6] would seem to fall within Article 10(1)(d) of the Convention[7] and, as such, would be determined by the applicable law. Similarly, the question of whether a contractual debt or liability has been discharged by novation would be a matter for the law applicable to the contract which gives rise to the contractual debt or

---

[94] *ibid.*

[95] *Ante*, § 31–024. The Act applies in England and Wales and in Scotland and is expressly stated to extend to Northern Ireland: s.17(5).

[96] *Ante*, § 31–142.

[97] *Ante*, §§ 31–066—31–085.

[98] This is because the Act extends to each part of the United Kingdom.

[99] 1998 Act, s.6. A debt does not carry statutory interest if, or to the extent that it consists of a sum to which a right to interest or to charge interest applies by virtue of a statute other than the 1998 Act: s.3(2).

[1] S.I. 1998 No. 2765.

[2] *Dicey & Morris op. cit.* pp. 1264–1265.

[3] *cf. Ralli v. Denistoun* (1851) 6 Exch. 488.

[4] *cf. Re Helbert Wagg & Co. Ltd's Claim* [1956] Ch. 323; *National Bank of Greece and Athens SA v. Metliss* [1958] A.C. 509; *Adams v. National Bank of Greece SA* [1961] A.C. 509. The distinct question raised in the last two cases as to whether there was a *successio in universum jus* on the amalgamation of the banks would not fall within the Convention rules because of Art. 1(2)(e). That question will be determined according to the law of the place of incorporation: see *Dicey & Morris op cit.* p. 1108.

[5] *cf. Re Anglo-Austrian Bank* [1920] 1 Ch. 69.

[6] *cf. Perry v. Equitable Life Insurance Co.* (1929) 45 T.L.R. 468; *R. v. International Trustee for the Protection of Bondholders A.G.* [1937] A.C. 500; *Mount Albert Borough Council v. Australasian Temperance & General Mutual Life Assurance Society* [1938] A.C. 224; *Re Helbert Wagg & Co. Ltd's Claim* [1956] Ch. 323, 340.

[7] See *Dicey & Morris op. cit.* pp. 1265–1266. The same principle applied at common law: see 26th ed. of this work, § 2192. For the special case of discharge by bankruptcy, see *Dicey & Morris op. cit.* pp. 1180–1183.

liability according to Article 10(1)(d).[8] It would also seem likely that whether a debt has been extinguished by set-off is a matter for the applicable law by virtue of this provision.[9]

31–147   **Prescription and limitation of actions.** Article 10(1)(d) also refers prescription and the limitation of actions to the applicable law. Although, at common law, there was a distinct tendency to classify the rules relating to limitation of actions as procedural and thus as a matter for the *lex fori*,[10] a considerable inroad on this principle was made by the Foreign Limitation Periods Act 1984.[11] Broadly speaking, that Act requires that the rules for the limitation of actions of the *lex causae*[12] are to be applied, which means, in the case of contract, the limitation rules of the governing law[13] and not those of the *lex fori*. The same principle is applied by Article 10(1)(d). Where the Convention applies, the rules as to prescription and limitation of actions will be governed by the applicable law as a result of Article 10(1)(d) rather than as a result of the 1984 Act.[14] Both the Rome Convention and the Foreign Limitation Periods Act 1984 permit a foreign period of limitation to be denied application if its application would infringe public policy.[15] According to section 2(2) of the 1984 Act, application of a foreign period of limitation conflicts with public policy "to the extent that its application would cause undue hardship to a person who is, or might be made, a party to the action or proceedings." Although Article 16 of the Rome Convention requires that the application of a foreign rule must be "manifestly incompatible with the public policy of the forum" it does not seek to define the content of the forum's public policy as such. Accordingly, the "undue hardship" aspect of

---

[8] *cf. Re United Railways of the Havana and Regla Warehouses Ltd* [1960] Ch. 52 (*revd.* on other grounds *sub nom. Tomkinson v. First Pennsylvania Banking and Trust Co.* [1961] A.C. 1007).

[9] *Dicey & Morris op. cit.* pp. 181–182, 1267. A set-off which is merely a claim of a certain kind which the defendant has against the plaintiff and which can be conveniently tried together with the plaintiff's claim against the defendant is procedural and thus a matter for the *lex fori* both at common law and under the Rome Convention: see *Meher v. Dresser* (1864) 16 C.B. (N.S.) 646.

[10] As to the common law position, see *Dicey & Morris op. cit.* pp. 184–185, 189–190; Cheshire and North *op. cit.* pp. 79–80; *ante*, § 29–150.

[11] For comment, see *Dicey & Morris op. cit.* pp. 186–188; Cheshire and North *op. cit.* pp. 80–81; Carter (1985) 101 L.Q.R. 68; Stone [1985] L.M.C.L.Q. 497. The 1984 Act implements recommendations of the Law Commission: see Law Com. No. 114 (1982). For further discussion, see *ante*, §§ 29–151—29–154.

[12] s.1(1).

[13] The foreign *lex causae* is defined to include both procedural and substantive rules in respect to limitation: s.4. But *renvoi* is excluded: ss.1(5), 4(2). A foreign rule under which a limitation period is or may be extended or interrupted, in respect to the absence of a party from any specified jurisdiction or country, must be disregarded: s.2(3). If the *lex causae* confers a discretion, it should be exercised, so far as practicable, in the manner in which it is exercised in comparable cases by the courts of that country: s.2(4). English law will, however, determine the time at which proceedings have been commenced: s.1(3).

[14] See *Dicey & Morris op. cit.* pp. 188, 1269. And see *Crédit Lyonnais v. New Hampshire Insurance Co.* [1997] 2 Lloyd's Rep. 1.

[15] Foreign Limitation Periods Act 1984, s.2(1), (2); Rome Convention, Art. 16. And see *post*, §§ 31–160—31–162. The 1984 Act is not intended to apply to periods of limitation referred to in the contract itself: see Law Com. No. 114 (1982), para. 4.52; *Dicey & Morris, op. cit.* pp. 188–189. At common law such periods were probably substantive and thus referable to the law governing the contract: *Dicey & Morris op. cit.; cf. Allan J. Panozza & Co. Pty Ltd v. Allied Interstate (Queensland) Pty Ltd* [1976] 2 N.S.W.L.R. 192. It is unclear whether such a clause would be regarded as affecting limitation of actions for the purpose of Art. 10(1)(d), but if it does not it would nevertheless be regarded as a way of extinguishing an obligation which is also governed by the applicable law according to Art. 10(1)(d).

public policy referred to in section 2(2) of the 1984 Act can in all probability[16] be applied as part of English public policy through Article 16 of the Convention.[17]

Consequences of nullity of contract. Although, according to Article **31–148** 10(1)(e), the consequences of nullity of the contract are governed by the applicable law, the United Kingdom has entered the permitted reservation to this provision so that Article 10(1)(e) does not have the force of law in the United Kingdom.[18] The consequences of nullity of the contract will be determined according to the choice of law rules applicable to restitutionary claims.[19]

Other unspecified issues. Article 10(1) does not purport to provide a list of **31–149** issues which is exhaustive of those intended to be governed by the applicable law.[20] Courts in Contracting States will thus be free to submit unspecified issues to that law. Amongst unspecified issues are certain aspects of the effects of a contract,[21] *i.e.* aspects of the rights and obligations of the parties under the contract (though some of these are covered by the nominated issues in Article 10(1)). More particularly, the list does not explicitly refer to the extent to which the rights and obligations of the parties to the contract affect third parties. There seems no reason to doubt that this issue is a matter for the applicable law,[22] as it has been held to be at common law.[23] Similarly, whether a defence, *e.g.* that of contributory negligence, to a contractual claim is available should depend on the law applicable to the contract,[24] unless, on proper characterisation, the defence arises out of an aspect of the law which has its own rules of the conflict of laws which are different to the conflict of laws' rules governing contracts.[25]

Two further issues, illegality and public policy, and foreign currency obliga- **31–150** tions, are reserved for special consideration in the concluding sub-sections of this chapter. The former presents special problems in the English conflict of laws while the latter goes beyond pure questions of the conflict of laws.[26]

---

[16] On undue hardship, see *The Komninos S.* [1990] 1 Lloyd's Rep. 541 (revd. but not on this point [1991] 1 Lloyd's Rep. 370 (undue hardship where defendants agreed to an extension of time which turned out to be ineffective under foreign *lex causae*)); *Jones v. Trollope Colls Cementation Overseas Ltd, The Times,* January 26, 1990 (12 months' limitation period caused undue hardship where plaintiff had spent time in hospital and had been led to believe her claim would be met); *Arab Monetary Fund v. Hashim* [1993] 1 Lloyd's Rep. 543 (impossible to hold that application of a three-year limitation period caused undue hardship).

[17] *Dicey & Morris op. cit.* p. 1268.

[18] See *ante*, §§ 31–032, 31–129.

[19] *ibid.*

[20] See *ante*, § 31–131.

[21] See Plender *op. cit.* p. 170; *Dicey & Morris op. cit.* p. 1260. As to set-off, see *Meridien Biao Bank G.m.b.H. v. Bank of New York* [1997] 1 Lloyd's Rep. 437 and *ante*, § 31–146.

[22] Subject to the exclusion of "the question of whether an agent is able to bind a principal, or an organ to bind a body corporate or unincorporate, to a third party": Art. 1(2)(f), *ante*, §§ 31–040, 31–127. *cf. Atlas Shipping Agency (U.K.) Ltd v. Suisse Atlantique Société D'Armement Maritime SA* [1995] 2 Lloyd's Rep. 188; *ante* § 31–030.

[23] *Scott v. Pilkington* (1862) 2 B. & S. 11. See 26th ed. of this work, § 2177.

[24] See *Meridien Biao Bank G.m.b.H. v. Bank of New York* [1997] 1 Lloyd's Rep. 437.

[25] *ibid.* (set-off in insolvency proceedings). See also *Re Bank of Credit and Commerce International SA (No. 10)* [1997] Ch. 213 (English rule on insolvency set-off (Insolvency Rules 1986, r. 4.90) always to be applied in English insolvency proceedings).

[26] *Post*, §§ 31–155—31–172.

(e) Burden of Proof, etc[27]

31–151 **Article 14 of the Rome Convention.** Article 14 of the Rome Convention contains two provisions expressed to be applicable to "Burden of proof etc." One such provision deals, in effect, with the burden of proof and presumptions,[28] the other with "contracts or acts intended to have legal effect."[29]

31–152 **Burden of proof and presumptions.** Article 14(1) of the Convention provides that the law governing the contract pursuant to the rules of the Convention "applies to the extent that it contains, in the law of contract, rules which raise presumptions of law or determine the burden of proof." In relation to the burden of proof, the tendency of the common law was to characterise the burden of proof as a procedural matter to be governed by the *lex fori*.[30] The effect of Article 14(1), however, is that the applicable law will determine the location of the burden of proof provided that the relevant rules for identifying its location are contained *in the law of contract*. The meaning of these italicised words is by no means clear. The Giuliano-Lagarde Report suggests that a rule relating to the burden of proof is a rule contained in the law of contract "to the extent that the law of contract determines it with regard to contractual obligations . . . , that is to say only to the extent to which the rules relating to the burden of proof are in effect rules of substance,"[31] as opposed to rules which are part of procedural law. The example given is Article 1147 of the French Civil Code which provides that a debtor who has failed to fulfil his obligation shall be liable for damages "unless he shows that this failure is due to an extraneous cause outside his control."[32]

31–153 In relation to presumptions, Article 14(1) only applies to presumptions of law.[33] At common law, an irrebuttable presumption of law is regarded as substantive[34]: it is probably the case that rebuttable resumptions of law bear the

---

[27] *Dicey & Morris on the Conflict of Laws* (12th ed., 1993), pp. 179–181, 1208–1209; Cheshire and North, *Private International Law* (12th ed., 1992), pp. 84–85; Kaye, *The New Private International Law of Contract of the European Community* (1993), pp. 331–341; Lasok and Stone, *Conflict of Laws in the European Community* (1987), pp. 354–355; Morse (1982) 2 Ybk.Eur.L. 107, 156–157.

[28] Art. 14(1), *post*, §§ 31–152—31–153.

[29] Art. 14(2), *post*, § 31–154.

[30] *e.g. The Roberta* (1937) 58 Ll.L.Rep. 159. For criticism, see *Dicey & Morris op. cit.* pp. 179–180; Cheshire and North *op. cit.* pp. 84–85.

[31] At p. 36.

[32] *ibid.* For possible examples in English law see *ante*, § 6–045 (Misrepresentation Act 1967, s.2(1)); §§ 14–067, 14–084 (Unfair Contract Terms Act 1977, ss.11(5), 12(3)); § 15–024 (Unfair Terms in Consumer Contracts Regulations 1994, Reg. 3(5); for seller or supplier who claims that a term was individually negotiated to show that it was); § 24–063 (plaintiff has legal burden of proving fault when frustration pleaded as defence to action on contract: *Joseph Constantine Steamship Line Ltd v. Imperial Smelting Corpn. Ltd* [1942] A.C. 154); § 14–129 (burden of proof and *force majeure* clauses); § 26–020 (burden on party seeking to enforce altered instrument to show that alteration made in circumstances such as not to invalidate it); Vol. II, § 33–010 (burden of proving loss not caused by failure to take care rests on bailee); Vol. II, § 38–227 (where money paid by A to B, onus on B to prove his allegation that payment a gift); Vol. II, §§ 41–066—41–067 (insurance).

[33] This is clearly stated in the text of Art. 14(1). In some cases, however, a rule formulated as presumption of law in one legal system may not be so formulated in another. In the Giuliano-Lagarde Report, p. 36, reference is made to a procedural presumption "whereby the claim of a party who appears is deemed to be substantiated if the other party fails to appear, or the rule making silence on the party to an action with regard to the facts alleged by the other party equivalent to an admission of those facts," but neither of these rules involves any "presumption" in English law.

[34] *Dicey & Morris op. cit.* pp. 180–181.

same characteristic.[35] Article 14(1) appears to contemplate the inclusion of both types of presumption under the aegis of the applicable law, subject to the relevant presumption being contained, again, in the law of contract. As far as irrebuttable presumptions of law are concerned, it is not easy to think of pertinent examples in the law of contract. This is because, in effect, an irrebuttable presumption of law is a rule of substantive law and what might, in some legal systems, be formulated as an irrebuttable presumption of law,[36] is more likely, in the English law of contract, to be formulated as a rule of substantive contract law.[37] Examples of rebuttable presumptions spring more readily to mind and might include, in English law, the presumption of undue influence in relation to contracts between persons in a special relationship with one another (*e.g.* parent and child).[38] Although this presumption may arise in other areas of the law, for example the law of trusts, that should not preclude it from being contained in the law of contract for the purposes of Article 14(1).[39]

Contract or act intended to have legal effect. Article 14(2) of the Rome **31–154** Convention provides that a "contract or act intended to have legal effect may be proved by any mode of proof recognised by the law of the forum or by any of the laws referred to in Article 9 under which that contract or act is formally valid, provided that such mode of proof can be administered by the forum." Thus, in English proceedings, a contract, or the terms thereof, may be proved by any method of proof available in English law. If a law applicable by virtue of Article 9[40] would render the contract formally valid, the English court can allow any method of proof permitted by that law to the extent that such method of proof can be administered by the forum.[41] According to the Giuliano-Lagarde Report, this proviso enables the court to disregard modes of proof which its law of procedure cannot generally allow, such as an affidavit, the testimony of a party or common knowledge.[42]

(f) *Illegality and Public Policy*[43]

Illegality. The question of whether a contract is unenforceable or void for **31–155** illegality justifies separate treatment because it involves reference to a number of

---

[35] *ibid.*

[36] It is noteworthy that the Giuliano-Lagarde Report gives no examples.

[37] See, *e.g.* Unfair Contract Terms Act 1977, s.12(2); Unfair Terms in Consumer Contracts Regulations 1994, Reg. 3(3), *ante*, § 15–024.

[38] *Ante*, §§ 7–043, 7–053.

[39] See text at nn.31–32, *ante*.

[40] *Ante*, §§ 31–117—31–124.

[41] For the possible effect of this provision on *Leroux v. Brown* (1852) 12 C.B. 801, see *ante*, § 31–118, n. 73.

[42] See Giuliano-Lagarde Report, pp. 36–37.

[43] *Dicey & Morris on the Conflict of Laws* (12th ed., 1993), pp. 88–92, 1240–1247, 1277–1284; Cheshire and North, *Private International Law* (12th ed., 1992), pp. 128–132, 503–505, 518–520; Plender, *The European Contracts Convention* (1991), Chap. 9; Kaye, *The New Private International Law of Contract of the European Community* (1993), pp. 239–268, 345–350. See *ante*, §§ 17–026—17–034. The separate questions of illegality and public policy in the conflict of laws are, nonetheless, closely linked and not always clearly distinguished: see *Royal Boskalis Westminster NV v. Mountain* [1998] 2 W.L.R. 539; *Soleimany v. Soleimany*, [1998] 3 W.L.R. 811; *Westacre Investments Inc. v. Jugoimport-SDPR Holding Co. Ltd* [1998] 3 W.L.R. 770 affd., *The Times*, May 25, 1999, CA. *cf. Ispahani v. Bank Melli Iran*, [1998] Lloyd's Rep. Bank. 133.

different principles at common law[44] and possible reference to several provisions of the Rome Convention.

31–156 **Illegality under applicable law.** First, a contract is unenforceable for illegality to the extent that it is illegal under its governing law, according to common law rules,[45] or, under the rule of the Rome Convention, illegal by the law which would be applicable to the contract if the contract (or term thereof) was valid.[46]

31–157 **Illegality under English law.** Secondly, at common law, if any party in making or performing the contract commits, or assists another to commit, in England, a criminal offence under English law[47] or commits abroad an act which is a criminal offence under English law by virtue of a statutory provision having extra-territorial operation,[48] then even though the governing law is not English law, the contract is unenforceable in England by the party in question.[49] In cases falling within the Rome Convention, this principle would seem to continue to have effect since the rules applicable by virtue of it appear to be mandatory rules of the law of the English forum which apply irrespective of the law applicable to the contract, so that, accordingly, Article 7(2) may be invoked to secure their application.[50]

31–158 **Act illegal under law of country where to be performed.** Thirdly, in *Ralli Bros. v. Compania Naviera Sota y Aznar*,[51] the Court of Appeal established a common law rule that where an act required by a contract to be performed in a foreign country becomes illegal under that country's law, the contractual obligation to perform that act is discharged. Applying that principle, it was held that where under a contract governed by English law, charterers had agreed to pay freight in Spain to shipowners at a particular rate, and the Spanish government, after the conclusion of the contract, promulgated an order that freight should not exceed a fixed sum which was less than the agreed rate, the charterers were only obliged to pay the fixed rate rather than the agreed rate. The exact scope of this decision is, however, controversial. It has been suggested that the principle of *Ralli Bros.* applies whether or not the contract is governed by English law.[52] But the better view, it is submitted, is that for the principle to apply, the applicable

---

[44] See 26th ed. of this work, §§ 2187–2191.

[45] *Kahler v. Midland Bank Ltd* [1950] A.C. 24; *Zivnostenska Banka v. Frankman* [1950] A.C. 57. The rule rendering the contract illegal under the governing law will not be applied if to do so would infringe English public policy: see *The Playa Larga* [1983] 2 Lloyd's Rep. 171, 189–190; see also *Re Helbert Wagg & Co. Ltd's Claim* [1956] Ch. 323, 345–346, 351–352. See *post*, §§ 31–160—31–162.

[46] Art. 8(1), *ante* §§ 31–111—31–116. This is, again, subject to compliance of the applicable law with English public policy: *post*, §§ 31–160—31–162.

[47] *e.g. Clugas v. Penaluna* (1791) 4 T.R. 466.

[48] *e.g. Boissevain v. Weil* [1950] A.C. 327.

[49] The relevant rule of English law must be one which is intended to affect the validity of contracts: see on this aspect of English domestic law, *ante*, §§ 17–014—17–018.

[50] *Ante*, § 30–064.

[51] [1920] 2 K.B. 287.

[52] *Zivnostenska Banka v. Frankman* [1950] A.C. 57, 78; *Mackender v. Feldia* [1967] 2 Q.B. 590, 601; *R. v. International Trustee for the Protection of Bondholders A.G.* [1937] A.C. 500, 519; *Kleinwort Sons & Co. v. Ungarische Baumwolle Industrie A.G.* [1939] 2 K.B. 678, 697–698.

law must, as it was in *Ralli Bros.* itself, be English law.[53] If the latter view is accepted, it follows that *Ralli Bros.* established a principle of the domestic English law of contract relating to discharge by supervening illegality[54] and does not establish a rule of the conflict of laws.[55] Accordingly, the effect of illegality by the law of the place of performance where a contract is governed by a foreign law is a matter for that foreign law.[56] The question which now arises is as to the status of the principle in *Ralli Bros.* in cases which fall within the Rome Convention. Since the United Kingdom has made a reservation to Article 7(1) of the Convention, that Article cannot be used to give effect, even as a matter of discretion, to the *Ralli Bros.* principle.[57] If the principle only applies, as suggested above and by a dictum in the Court of Appeal which found it unnecessary to express a final view on the point,[58] where the contract is governed by English law, than it will operate, where relevant, if English law is the applicable law of the contract. But if, contrary to this view, it is eventually decided that the principle is of wider import so that it applies irrespective of the law applicable to the contract, it is difficult to accommodate it within the Convention. The first possibility is to argue that it can be applied pursuant to Article 16,[59] as a principle of English public policy, but it is doubtful whether the principle bears the character of a rule of English public policy.[60] Secondly, but more doubtfully, the principle of *Ralli Bros.* could be construed as a mandatory rule of English law, applicable by virtue of Article 7(2) of the Convention. Thirdly, but even more doubtfully, it has been suggested that the principle could be applied by virtue of Article 10(2) of the Convention,[61] but this is most unlikely since Article 10(2) only submits to the law of the place of performance minor matters affecting the detail of performance rather than the substance of the obligation to be performed,[62] and the latter, not the former, was what was at issue in the *Ralli Bros.* case.

Illegality under other foreign law. Illegality under any foreign law, be it the   **31–159**
law of one party's nationality,[63] or of a country where performance may, but need

---

[53] *Kahler v. Midland Bank Ltd* [1950] A.C. 24, 48; *Société Co-operative Suisse des Cereales, etc v. Plata Cereal Co. SA* (1949) 80 Ll.L.Rep. 530, 543–544: *Walton (Grain and Shipping) Ltd v. British Italian Trading Co.* [1959] 1 Lloyd's Rep. 223, 236; *Bangladesh Export Import Co. Ltd v. Sucden Kerry SA* [1995] 2 Lloyd's Rep. 1, 5; *Ispahani v. Bank Melli Iran*, [1998] Lloyd's Rep. Bank. 133; *Dicey & Morris op. cit.* pp. 1245–1247; Cheshire and North *op. cit.* p. 519; F.A. Mann (1937) 18 B.Y.I.L. 97, 107–113; Morris (1953) 6 Vand.L.Rev. 510; Reynolds (1992) 108 L.Q.R. 553.

[54] See *ante*, §§ 24–026—24–028.

[55] See authorities in n. 53, *ante*.

[56] *ibid.*

[57] Contracts (Applicable Law) Act 1990, s.2(2) and Sched. 1, Art. 22, *ante*, § 31–059. See on the status of the *Ralli Bros.* rule in the Convention context, *Dicey & Morris op. cit.* pp. 1245–1247; Reynolds *op. cit.*

[58] See *Ispahani v. Bank Melli Iran*, *supra.* See also *Royal Boskalis Westminster NV v. Mountain* [1998] 2 W.L.R. 538, 593–594.

[59] See *post*, §§ 31–160—31–162.

[60] See *Dicey & Morris op. cit.* p. 1246. If the only remedy provided by the foreign law compelled the defendant to act illegally in the place of performance, as opposed to paying damages elsewhere, this might justify invocation of public policy as a last resort. *cf. Royal Boskalis Westminster NV v. Mountain, supra,* at 593–594.

[61] See Diamond (1986) 216 *Recueil des Cours*, IV, 236, 296.

[62] *Ante*, §§ 31–133—31–136.

[63] *Kleinwort Sons & Co. v. Ungarische Baumwolle Industrie A.G.* [1939] K.B. 678; *Kahler v. Midland Bank Ltd* [1950] A.C. 24, 48; *Toprak Mahsulleri Ofisi v. Finagrain Compagnie Commerciale Agricole et Financière SA* [1979] 2 Lloyd's Rep. 98.

not, take place,[64] or of the place of contracting[65] does not *per se* affect the enforceability of the contract either at common law or, because of the United Kingdom's reservation to Article 7(1) of the Convention,[66] under the provisions of the Rome Convention.

31–160   **Public policy.**[67] It is axiomatic, and a general principle of the conflict of laws, that the forum will not apply a foreign law which is contrary to the public policy of the forum. The public policy principle may have the result of rendering void or unenforceable a contract which is valid under its foreign governing law or it may result in the enforcement of a contract which is invalid by its governing law, if, in either case, the forum regards the public policy principle as applicable. The principle of public policy is recognised in Article 16 of the Rome Convention which provides that the "application of a rule of law of any country specified by this Convention may be refused only if such application is manifestly incompatible with the public policy ('ordre public') of the forum." This provision clearly reflects the common law subject to the expression "manifestly incompatible," an expression designed to indicate that overzealous resort should not be made to the public policy doctrine.[68] It is also important to stress that Article 16 (and the common law) are concerned with public policy in the international sense, rather than the public policy in the domestic sense. Thus, for example, the fact that a contract, valid under its foreign governing law, lacks a requirement (*e.g.* consideration[69]) which is essential to its validity under English law, is insufficient to render the public policy principle applicable.[70] There must be some more fundamental objection to the application of a foreign law before public policy, in the international sense, may be invoked.[71] Further, both at common law and under Article 16, it is the *application* of the foreign law in the circumstances of the case which must infringe English public policy rather than the *content* of the foreign law as such.[72]

---

[64] *Kahler v. Midland Bank Ltd, supra,* at 36, 39, 48. And see *Zivnostenska Banka v. Frankman* [1950] A.C. 57, 79; *Regazzoni v. K.C. Sethia Ltd* [1956] 2 Q.B. 490, 514, 523; *Nile Co. for the Export of Agricultural Crops v. Bennett (Commodities) Ltd* [1986] 1 Lloyd's Rep. 555, 581.

[65] *Vita Foods Products Inc. v. Unus Shipping Co. Ltd* [1939] A.C. 277, 297–300. See *Dicey & Morris op. cit.* pp. 1241–1242; F.A. Mann (1937) 18 B.Y.I.L. 97, 107–113. *cf. The Torni* [1932] P. 78; *Re Missouri Steamship Co. Ltd* (1889) 42 Ch.D. 321, 336; *The Hollandia* [1983] 1 A.C. 565, 576.

[66] See *ante,* n. 57.

[67] See also, *ante,* § 31–065.

[68] Giuliano-Lagarde Report, p. 38.

[69] *Re Bonacina* [1912] 2 Ch. 394.

[70] See, *e.g. Dicey & Morris op. cit.* p. 1279. The distinction is expressed by French jurists as one between *ordre public interne* and *ordre public international*.

[71] Compare the language of Cardozo J. in *Loucks v. Standard Oil Co. of New York* 224 N.Y. 99, 120 N.E. 198 (1918). "If a foreign statute gives the right, the mere fact that we do not give a like right is no reason for refusing the plaintiff what belongs to him. We are not so provincial as to say that every solution of a problem is wrong because we deal with it otherwise at home."

[72] There may be exceptional cases, however, where a foreign law involves such a serious infringement of human rights that it should not be recognised as law at all: see *Oppenheimer v. Cattermole* [1976] A.C. 249. *cf. Kuwait Airways Corp. v. Iraqi Airways Co., The Times,* May 12, 1998 (Iraqi resolution dissolving Kuwait Airways and transferring its assets to Iraqi Airways refused recognition on public policy grounds as representing a clear contravention of international law and the Charter of the United Nations). See also *Royal Boskalis Westminster NV v. Mountain* [1998] 2 W.L.R. 538. It may prove possible to develop the concept of public policy by reference to the European Convention on Human Rights as a result of the incorporation of that Convention into United Kingdom law: see Human Rights Act 1998 (not yet in force), especially Sched. I, Pt. II. But if this is to occur, proper allowance should be made for the fact that the case contains foreign elements

Since the application of the doctrine of public policy must depend very much **31–161** on the circumstances of individual cases, it is not possible to categorise the situations justifying its invocation with any precision. However, in the past, English courts have refused to enforce champertous contracts,[73] contracts in restraint of trade,[74] contracts involving trading with the enemy,[75] and contracts involving collusive arrangements for a divorce.[76] The principle will also apply where the parties make the contract with the intention that its performance should involve the commission in a foreign and friendly country of an act which would violate that country's laws.[77] It has also been held that public policy is infringed where the contract, or circumstances in which it was made, render it incompatible with English ideas of justice and morality.[78] Thus a contract governed by (and valid by) its foreign applicable law may be held unenforceable in England because it was entered into as a result of coercion.[79] And where a contract

---

which are such that the merits of the case should be governed by foreign law according to the normal principles of the conflict of laws.

[73] *Grell v. Levy* (1864) 16 C.B. (N.S.) 73; *cf. Trendtex Trading Corpn. v. Crédit Suisse* [1982] A.C. 679; *Camdex International Ltd v. Bank of Zambia* [1998] Q.B. 22; *Fraser v. Buckle* [1996] 1 I.R. 1. Although champerty has ceased to be a crime or a tort in England, Criminal Law Act 1967, s.14, it will render a contract illegal: see *ante*, §§ 17–048—17–066.

[74] *Rousillon v. Rousillon* (1880) 14 Ch.D. 351, which should be restricted to restraint of trade affecting trade in England.

[75] *Robson v. Premier Oil and Pipe Line Co.* [1915] 2 Ch. 124, 136; *Dynamit A/G v. Rio Tinto Co. Ltd* [1918] A.C. 260. See *ante*, § 17–024.

[76] *Hope v. Hope* (1857) 8 De G.M. & G. 731.

[77] *Regazzoni v. K.C. Sethia Ltd* [1958] A.C. 301. And see *De Wutz v. Hendricks* (1824) 2 Bing. 314; *Foster v. Driscoll* [1929] 1 K.B. 470; *British Nylon Spinners v. I.C.I. Ltd* [1955] Ch. 37, 52; *Euro-Diam Ltd v. Bathurst* [1990] 1 Q.B. 1; *Royal Boskalis Westminster NV v. Mountain* [1998] 2 W.L.R. 538; *Ispahani v. Bank Melli Iran*, [1998] Lloyd's Rep. Bank. 133; *Soleimany v. Soleimany* [1998] 3 W.L.R. 811 (arbitration award based on such a contract unenforceable in England); *Westacre Investments Inc. v. Jugoimport-SDPR Holding Co. Ltd* [1998] 3 W.L.R. 770 affd., *The Times*, May 25, 1999, CA (public policy of sustaining international arbitration awards outweighed public policy of discouraging international commercial corruption). This rule applies, in all probability, to cases where a contract is governed by a foreign law as well as to cases where it is governed by English law (as was the case in *Regazzoni v. K.C. Sethia Ltd, supra*): see *Royal Boskalis Westminster NV v. Mountain* [1998] 2 W.L.R. 538, 552–556, 562–566; *cf. Ispahani v. Bank Melli Iran, supra*. It also applies where the object of the contract is to break the penal or revenue laws of a foreign country (*Regazzoni v. K.C. Sethia Ltd, supra*; *Re Emery's Investment Trusts* [1959] Ch. 410; *Euro-Diam Ltd v. Bathurst, supra*; *Soleimany v. Soleimany, supra*) or foreign exchange control legislation (*Kahler v. Midland Bank Ltd* [1950] A.C. 24, 27; *Zivnostenska Banka v. Frankman* [1950] A.C. 57, 72; *Re Helbert Wagg & Co. Ltd's Claim* [1956] Ch. 323, 349, 351; *Re Lord Cable* [1977] 1 W.L.R. 7, 24; *Ispahani v. Bank Melli Iran, supra*). An English court will not *enforce* the penal or revenue or other public laws of a foreign country: see *Camdex International Ltd v. Bank of Zambia* [1997] C.L.C. 714; *Dicey & Morris op. cit.* pp. 97–103. As to exchange control in the conflict of laws, see *Dicey and Morris op. cit.* pp. 1591–1602.

[78] *Kaufman v. Gerson* [1904] 1 K.B. 591; *Royal Boskalis Westminster NV v. Mountain* [1998] 2 W.L.R. 538. See also *Robinson v. Bland* (1706) 2 Burr. 1077, 1084; *Re Missouri Steamship Co.* (1889) 42 Ch. D. 321, 336. A contract to oust the jurisdiction of the English court (unlike one to oust the jurisdiction of a foreign court) is not contrary to public policy: *cf. Addison v. Brown* [1954] 1 W.L.R. 779.

[79] *Royal Boskalis Westminster NV v. Mountain, supra*; *Kaufman v. Gerson, supra*. In the former case it was stated, at 552, 590, that the degree of coercion exercised in the particular case is relevant, and whether the degree of coercion exercised in the latter case would be regarded as sufficient today was questionable. In *Dimskal Shipping Co. SA v. International Transport Workers Federation* [1992] 2 A.C. 152, 158 it was held that whether a contract was void or voidable for duress depended on the law applicable to the contract, which was English law. However, if the law applicable to the contract is a foreign law and that law would regard the contract as valid despite the presence of duress of an unconscionable degree, the English court will refuse to enforce the contract on the grounds of public policy as happened in *Royal Boskalis Westminster NV v. Mountain, supra*, where a contract governed

governed by English law involved a transaction, to be performed abroad, which was contrary to a head of English public policy based on general principles of morality, the same public policy applying in the country of performance, the contract was similarly unenforceable.[80]

31–162 There is no reason to doubt that similar conclusions to the above may be reached by applying Article 16 of the Rome Convention, subject, possibly, to the requirement that the application of foreign law be "manifestly incompatible" with public policy necessitating a more cautious view of the doctrine than was exhibited in some of the decisions rendered prior to the implementation of the Convention, because the intention behind Article 16 is that it should be used in only exceptional circumstances.[81] On the other hand, Article 16 imports a new dimension into the content of public policy as understood in traditional English conflict of laws, for public policy, in this context, must be understood as including European Community public policy.[82]

(g) Foreign Currency Obligations

31–163 **Scope of discussion.** The remaining paragraphs of this chapter seek to identify and discuss particular problems of practical importance which may arise, in a contractual context, out of what may be loosely described as "foreign currency obligations."[83] The separate treatment of these problems may be justified, first, on the ground that the elucidation of some of these problems involves reference to various different provisions of the Rome Convention which can be most coherently treated together. Secondly, some of these problems require discussion of rules of English domestic law and procedure rather than rules of the conflict of laws in the strict sense.[84]

31–164 **Principle of nominalism.** Where a debt is expressed in the currency of any particular country, the debtor is under an obligation to pay the nominal amount of the debt in whatever is legal tender at the time of payment according to the law of the country in whose currency the debt is expressed, irrespective of any fluctuation in exchange rates which affect that currency.[85] This principle, the

---

and valid by Iraqi law was procured by threats to use personnel as part of the "human shield" in the course of the Iraq-Kuwait conflict. In *Kaufman v. Gerson, supra,* a wife was held to have acted under duress by agreeing to pay sums to her husband's employer under a contract governed and valid by French law, on terms that the employer would refrain from bringing a criminal prosecution against the husband for misappropriation of the employer's funds, hardly duress of the same order.

[80] *Lemenda Trading Co. Ltd v. African Middle East Petroleum Co. Ltd* [1988] Q.B. 448.

[81] Giuliano-Lagarde Report, p. 38. Suspect decisions (at least on their facts) are, in particular, *Kaufman v. Gerson, supra; Addison v. Brown, supra.*

[82] Giuliano-Lagarde Report, p. 38.

[83] See *Dicey & Morris on the Conflict of Laws* (12th ed., 1993), Chap. 36; Cheshire and North, *Private International Law* (12th ed., 1992), pp. 97–105. For an exhaustive and illuminating account of the problems in this area, see F.A. Mann, *The Legal Aspect of Money* (5th ed., 1992). See too, Law Com. No. 124 (1983) and ante, §§ 25–068—25–072.

[84] As to interest, see ante, §§ 31–140—31–144.

[85] The principle goes back to *Gilbert v. Brett* (1604) Davis 18 (also known as the *Case de Mixt Moneys*). See too, *Re Chesterman's Trusts* [1923] 2 Ch. 466; *Ottoman Bank v. Chakarian (No. 2)* [1938] A.C. 260; *Pyrmont Ltd v. Schott* [1939] A.C. 145; *Marrache v. Ashton* [1943] A.C. 311. A party may, of course, be able to recover for exchange losses suffered as a result of late payment by the other party: see ante, § 31–141. If the currency in which the debt is expressed is devalued between the date of the contract and the date when the payment is due, the question of whether the debt should be "revalorised" (*i.e.* whether a party should pay more to compensate for the devaluation) will be

principle of nominalism, applies to claims for unliquidated damages as well as to debts.[86] As a principle of English domestic law, the principle of nominalism applies to debts and contracts governed by English law.[87] Where a debt or contract is governed by a foreign law, it will be for that law to determine whether the principle of nominalism applies[88] but since the principle appears to form "part of the legal systems of all civilised countries"[89] there is little likelihood of its being inapplicable in any given case.

Legal tender. The law of the country in whose currency a contractual debt is   **31–165** expressed will determine what is regarded as legal tender for the purpose of its discharge. This is probably because by referring to a particular country's currency, the parties agree (either impliedly, at common law,[90] or by virtue of Article 3(1) of the Rome Convention[91]) that the law of that country will determine what constitutes the currency of that country. This result will ensue even if the contract as a whole is governed by a different law: the question of what is the legal tender of the currency in which the contractual debt is expressed will be regarded as a severable part of the contract capable of being governed by its own applicable law which will be the law of the country in whose currency the debt is expressed.[92] No other law can rationally determine what is meant by that currency.

Money of account. The "money of account" is the currency in which a debt   **31–166** is expressed or a liability to pay damages is calculated as opposed to the currency in which that debt or liability is to be discharged, described as the "money of payment."[93] The former concept thus describes the currency in which the amount due is to be measured. Where the parties have not indicated in the contract itself the particular currency which is the money of account, the relevant currency must be identified by interpreting or construing the contract, the canons of interpretation or construction being those which prevail in the law which governs the contract.[94] If English law is the applicable law, then in the absence of any

---

governed by the law applicable to the contract: *Anderson v. Equitable Life Assurance Society of the United States* (1929) 45 T.L.R. 468; *Re Schnapper* [1936] 1 All E.R. 322; *Kornatzki v. Oppenheimer* [1937] 4 All E.R. 133; Rome Convention, Art. 10(1)(b) see generally *Dicey and Morris op. cit.* pp. 1556–1558. Parties may seek to guard against fluctuations in exchange rates by inserting a "gold clause" or similar "protective" clause into the contract: see *Dicey & Morris op. cit.* pp. 1558–1566 and *ante*, §§ 25–068—25–072. On the potential implications of the implementation of a single European currency, see Mance [1997] European Business L. Rev. 266; Blair *ibid.* 228.

[86] *The Despina R.* [1979] A.C. 685, 698.

[87] *Re Chesterman's Trusts* [1923] 2 Ch. 466.

[88] *Dicey & Morris op. cit.* pp. 1552–1553. See *Société des Hôtels Le Touquet-Paris-Plage v. Cummings* [1922] 1 K.B. 451.

[89] *Dicey & Morris op. cit.* p. 1552.

[90] *Re Chesterman's Trusts, supra,* at 483; see *ante,* §§ 31–010, 31–132.

[91] *i.e.* this suffices to demonstrate a choice with reasonable certainty for the purposes of Art. 3(1): see *ante,* §§ 31–049—31–050.

[92] Rome Convention, Art. 3(1) which permits parties to select a law applicable to a part only of a contract: see *ante,* §§ 31–052—31–053.

[93] See *Dicey & Morris op. cit.* pp. 1567–1568.

[94] Rome Convention, Art. 10(1)(a): *Adelaide Electric Supply Co. Ltd v. Prudential Assurance Co. Ltd* [1934] A.C. 122; *Auckland Corpn. v. Alliance Assurance Co. Ltd* [1937] A.C. 587; *De Bueger v. Ballantyne & Co.* [1938] A.C. 452; *Bonython v. Commonwealth of Australia* [1951] A.C. 201; *National Bank of Australasia Ltd v. Scottish Union and National Insurance Co. Ltd* [1952] A.C. 493; *National Mutual Life Association of Australasia Ltd v. A.G. for New Zealand* [1956] A.C. 493.

intention emerging from the contract itself when construed according to English law,[95] the parties will be presumed to have intended the currency of the country with which the contract is most closely connected.[96] This may, but need not necessarily, be the country of the applicable law.[97]

31–167   **Currency of damages.** Where damages are claimed for breach of contract, it may be necessary to determine the currency in which such damages are to be calculated, *i.e.* the money of account. In this context, however, the issue is not one of interpretation of the contract but rather one relating to the assessment of damages which, like interpretation, will be governed by the applicable law of the contract.[98] If English law is the applicable law, it has been authoritatively stated that the

> "[first] step must be to see whether, expressly or by implication, the contract provides an answer to the currency question. This may lead to selection of the 'currency of the contract.' If from the terms of the contract it appears that the parties have accepted a currency as the currency of account and payment[99] in respect of all transactions arising under the contract, then it would be proper to give a judgment for damages in that currency.... But there may be cases in which, although obligations under that contract are to be met in a specified currency, or currencies, the right conclusion may be that there is no intention shown that damages for breach of contract should be given in that currency or currencies.... If then the contract fails to provide a decisive interpretation, the damages should be calculated in the currency in which the loss was felt by the plaintiff or 'which most truly expresses his loss.' This is not limited to that in which it first or immediately arose. In ascertaining which this currency is the court must ask what is the currency, payment of which will as nearly as possible compensate the plaintiff in accordance with the principle of restitution, and whether the parties must be taken reasonably to have had this in contemplation."[1]

31–168   **Money of payment.** The "money of payment" is the precise currency in which the debt or damages is actually payable. This, of course, need not

---

[95] See, *e.g. W.J. Alan & Co. Ltd v. El Nasr Export and Import Co.* [1972] 2 Q.B. 189.

[96] *Bonython v. Commonwealth of Australia, supra; National Bank of Australasia Ltd v. Scottish Union and National Insurance Co. Ltd, supra; W.J. Alan & Co. Ltd v. El Nasr Export and Import Co., supra.*

[97] *Adelaide Electric Supply Co. Ltd v. Prudential Assurance Co. Ltd, supra; Bonython v. Commonwealth of Australia, supra.* The process of determining the money of account in English domestic law is similar to, but not, as these cases show, identical with the process of determining the law applicable to the contract according to English conflict rules. See *Dicey & Morris op. cit.* pp. 1571–1572.

[98] Rome Convention, Art. 10(1)(c), see *ante*, § 31–138; *Services Europe Atlantique Sud v. Stockholms Rederaktiebolag Svea* [1979] A.C. 685.

[99] *i.e.* the money of account and the money of payment: see text at n. 93, *ante* and *post*, §§ 31–168—31–169.

[1] *Services Europe Atlantique Sud v. Stockholms Rederaktiebolag Svea* [1979] A.C. 685. See *Bain v. Field* (1920) 5 Ll.L.Rep. 16; *Ottoman Bank v. Chakarian (No. 1)* [1930] A.C. 277; *Kraut A.G. v. Albany Fabrics Ltd* [1977] Q.B. 182; *Société Francaise Bunge SA v. Belcan N.V.* [1985] 3 All E.R. 378; *Metaalhandel J.A. Magnus B.V. v. Ardfields Transport Ltd* [1988] 1 Lloyd's Rep. 471; *The Texaco Melbourne* [1994] 1 Lloyd's Rep. 473 (loss felt in Ghanaian cedis and measured in that currency despite fall in rate of exchange from 2.75 cedis to dollar at date of breach to 375 at date of judgment; criticised by Knott [1994] L.M.C.L.Q. 311). See also *B.P. Exploration Co. (Libya) Ltd v. Hunt (No. 2)* [1981] 1 W.L.R. 232 (affd. [1983] A.C. 352 (restitutionary award under Law Reform (Frustrated Contracts) Act 1943)).

necessarily be the money of account.[2] Where there is no contractual stipulation as to the money of payment, it is, at common law, determined by the law of the country in which payment is made.[3] This is because the question of what money tokens the debtor must tender to the creditor is one concerning the mode of performance which is, thus, referable to the law of the place of performance.[4] Whether this principle continues to apply in cases falling within the Rome Convention depends upon the correct interpretation of Article 10(2).[5] That provision states, so far as relevant, that in relation to the "manner of perform-ance . . . regard shall be had" to the law of the country in which performance takes place. One might reasonably surmise that "manner of performance" can be equated with "mode of performance" in the common law context and it would, on this assumption, appear that the common law rule survives, subject to the possibility that, because of the wording of Article 10(2), the rule is of a discretionary character which did not seem to be the case at common law.[6] One cannot be certain of this conclusion, however, because the Giuliano-Lagarde Report does not include the money of payment among the examples of issues governed by Article 10(2). In contrast the Report suggests that "where perform-ance consists of the payment of a sum of money, the conditions relating to the discharge of the debtor who has made the payment"[7] are governed by Article 10(1)(b).[8] It is likely, however, that this observation is intended only to refer to the money of account. Accordingly, the English courts should interpret Article 10(2) to include this issue.

Where English law is the law of the country of payment, there is a presumption **31–169** that the money of payment is the same as the money of account.[9] If the former currency differs from the latter, the exchange rate between them should, it is submitted be determined by the law applicable to the contract since the relevant rate of exchange is an aspect of the *quantum* of money tokens to be rendered.[10] A sum payable in England under a contract governed by English law may be paid in units of the money of account or in sterling[11]: if payment is tendered in sterling the rate of exchange is the rate at which, on the date when payment is due, units

---

[2] See *ante*, §§ 31–166—31–167. The contract may expressly or impliedly stipulate, or one party may give the other an option to elect, that the money of account and money of payment should be different: see, *e.g. Woodhouse A.C. Israel Cocoa Ltd SA v. Nigerian Produce Marketing Co. Ltd* [1972] A.C. 741 (money of account Nigerian, buyers of goods given option to choose between paying in Nigerian currency or sterling).

[3] *Adelaide Electric Supply Co. Ltd v. Prudential Assurance Co. Ltd* [1934] A.C. 122; *Auckland Corpn. v. Alliance Assurance Co. Ltd* [1937] A.C. 587; *Mount Albert Borough Council v. Australasian etc Life Assurance Society Ltd* [1930] A.C. 224.

[4] *Dicey & Morris op. cit.* pp. 1579–1580.

[5] See *ante*, §§ 31–133—31–136.

[6] *ibid.*

[7] At pp. 42, 43.

[8] *Ante*, §§ 31–133—31–136.

[9] See *Auckland Corpn. v. Alliance Assurance Co. Ltd*, *supra.*

[10] *Dicey & Morris op. cit.* p. 1586: F.A. Mann *op. cit.* pp. 325–326.

[11] *Marrache v. Ashton* [1943] A.C. 311; *Syndic for Khoury v. Khayat* [1943] A.C. 507, 514; *Dicey & Morris op. cit.* pp. 1580–1581; F.A. Mann *op. cit.* pp. 321–322. *cf. National Bank of Australasia Ltd v. Scottish Union and National Insurance Co. Ltd* [1952] A.C. 493; *National Mutual Life Association of Australia Ltd v. A.G. for New Zealand* [1956] A.C. 369. If payment in the foreign currency is impossible, the debtor must pay in sterling: he cannot choose to pay in the foreign currency and then claim that the obligation is discharged or suspended by reason of the impossibility: *Libyan Arab Foreign Bank v. Bankers Trust Co.* [1989] Q.B. 728.

of the money of account can be purchased in London at a recognised and accessible market, irrespective of the official rate of exchange.[12]

31–170   **Judgments in foreign currency.** Until 1975 it had long been accepted that an English court could only order the payment of debts or damages in English currency; this was so whether the judgment stemmed from a breach of a contract whose applicable law was English or foreign.[13] The amount due to the judgment creditor in foreign currency had to be converted into sterling at the appropriate exchange rate when the cause of action arose, for example the date of the breach of contract.[14] This much-criticised[15] rule was abandoned by the House of Lords in *Miliangos v. George Frank (Textiles) Ltd*[16] where the court gave judgment expressed in Swiss francs for the payment of a debt due in that currency. The principle underlying the decision was expressed thus by Lord Wilberforce: "the creditor has no concern with pounds sterling: for him what matters is that a Swiss franc for good or ill should remain a Swiss franc."[17] As a result of the judicial developments which followed that landmark decision, it is now possible to state the law as to judgments in foreign currency with some degree of completeness.[18] The court may give judgment for an amount expressed in foreign currency or its sterling equivalent at the date when the court authorises enforcement of the judgment[19]—this latter being the closest practicable date to the date of actual payment, the ideal date for conversion. This rule applies to contractual actions whether the applicable law of the contract is foreign law[20] or English law.[21] It is

---

[12] *Marrache v. Ashton, supra; Syndic for Khoury v. Khayat, supra; Barclays Bank International Ltd v. Levin Brothers (Bradford) Ltd* [1977] Q.B. 270; *George Veflings Rederi A/S v. President of India* [1979] 1 W.L.R. 59. *Graumann v. Treitel* [1940] 2 All E.R. 188 may be explicable on the ground that German law was the applicable law of the contract (see *Dicey & Morris op. cit.* p. 1581). For a case where there was no recognised and accessible market and no commercial rate of exchange, see *Re Parana Plantations Ltd* [1946] 2 All E.R. 214.

[13] *Manners v. Pearson* [1989] 1 Ch. 581; *Tomkinson v. First Pennsylvania Banking and Trust Co.* [1961] A.C. 1007.

[14] *e.g. Di Ferdinando v. Simon Smits & Co.* [1920] 2 K.B. 409.

[15] *The Teh Hu* [1970] P. 106, 124, 127; *Jugoslavenska Oceanska Plovidba v. Castle Investment Co. Inc.* [1974] Q.B. 292; *Schorsch Meier GmbH v. Hennin* [1975] Q.B. 416.

[16] [1976] A.C. 443.

[17] [1976] A.C. 443, 466.

[18] These developments are not restricted to contractual claims but would appear to apply to all claims made in foreign currency—see, *e.g. The Despina R* [1979] A.C. 685; *Hoffman v. Sofaer* [1982] 1 W.L.R. 1350 (tort); *B.P. Exploration Co. (Libya) Ltd v. Hunt (No. 2)* [1979] 1 W.L.R. 783, 840–841 (affd. [1983] 2 A.C. 352 (restitution)); *Re Dynamics Corporation of America* [1976] 1 W.L.R. 757; *Re Lines Bros. Ltd* [1983] Ch. 1; *Re Lines Bros. Ltd (No. 2)* [1984] Ch. 438 (winding up); *Choice Investments Ltd v. Jeromninon* [1981] 1 Q.B. 149 (garnishee order against English bank); *Re A Debtor (No. 51–SD–1991)* [1992] 1 W.L.R. 1294 (debt in statutory demand under Insolvency Act 1986). See, too, *Re Scandinavian Bank Group plc* [1988] Ch. 87 (s.2(5)(a) of the Companies Act 1985 does not require company to have share capital only denominated in sterling).

[19] *Miliangos v. George Frank (Textiles) Ltd* [1976] A.C. 443; CPR, para. 40.2.3; and see *The Halcyon Skies* [1977] 1 Lloyd's Rep. 22; *George Veflings Rederi A/S v. President of India* [1978] 1 W.L.R. 982 (affd. [1979] 1 W.L.R. 59). For counterclaims, see *The Transoceanica Fransesca* [1987] 2 Lloyd's Rep. 155; *Smit Tak International Zeesleepen Bergingsbedriff B.V. v. Selco Salvage Ltd* [1988] 2 Lloyd's Rep. 398. As to pleading claims in foreign currency, see CPR 1998, PD 16, para. 12.1.

[20] *e.g. Miliangos v. George Frank (Textiles) Ltd* [1976] A.C. 443.

[21] *e.g. Federal Commerce and Navigation Co. Ltd v. Tradax Export SA* [1977] Q.B. 324 (revd. on another ground [1978] A.C. 1); *Barclays Bank International Ltd v. Levin Brothers (Bradford) Ltd* [1977] Q.B. 270; *Services Europe Atlantique Sud v. Stockholms Rederaktiebolag Svea* [1979] A.C. 685.

clear that it is not restricted to claims for payment of debts[22] but extends to claims for damages for breach of contract,[23] whether the claim be for liquidated[24] or unliquidated damages.[25] The rules applicable to judgments are also applicable to arbitration awards,[26] though it may be that conversion is to be effected as at the date of the award,[27] rather than at some date closer to that of payment.

The rule laid down in *Miliangos* is a rule of procedure, to be applied by **31–171** English courts whatever may be the law applicable to the contract in issue.[28] A judgment in foreign currency may be satisfied by payment of the sum due in that currency[29] or by the appropriate sum in sterling converted as at "the date of payment," *i.e.* normally[30] the date when the court authorises enforcement of the judgment in terms of sterling. There are a number of cases where a different conversion date is provided by statute.[31]

The rate of interest on the judgment is a matter for the *lex fori*, even when the **31–172** judgment is expressed in a foreign currency.[32] By statute the English court may order that the rate of interest on foreign currency judgments shall be such rate as the court thinks fit.[33]

---

[22] *Miliangos v. George Frank (Textiles) Ltd* [1976] A.C. 443; *Barclays Bank International Ltd v. Levin Brothers (Bradford) Ltd* [1977] Q.B. 270.

[23] *Services Europe Atlantique Sud v. Stockholms Rederaktiebolag Svea* [1979] A.C. 685; *Société Francais Bunge SA v. Belcan NV* [1985] 3 All E.R. 378.

[24] *Federal Commerce and Navigation Co. Ltd v. Tradax Export SA* [1977] 324, 341–342, 349, 354 (revd. on another point [1978] A.C. 1).

[25] *Services Europe Atlantique Sud v. Stockholms Rederaktiebolag Svea* [1979] A.C. 685; and see *Kraut A.G. v. Albany Fabrics Ltd* [1977] Q.B. 182.

[26] *Jugoslavenska Oceanska Plovidba v. Castle Investment Co. Inc.* [1974] Q.B. 292.

[27] *ibid.* at 305; *cf. Miliangos v. George Frank (Textiles) Ltd* [1976] A.C. 443, 469.

[28] [1976] A.C. 443, 465; and see *The Despina R.* [1979] A.C. 685, 704. As a rule of procedure it is unaffected by the Rome Convention: see *ante*, § 31–042.

[29] See CPR, para. 40.2.3.

[30] The appropriate date in the case of winding-up (both compulsory and voluntary) is that of the winding-up order or resolution: *Re Dynamics Corporation of America, supra; Re Lines Bros. Ltd, supra; Re Lines Bros. (No. 2), supra.* See Insolvency Rules 1986, r. 4.91 and in bankruptcy, where the relevant date is the date of the bankruptcy order, r. 6.111.

[31] See, *e.g.* Carriage by Air Act 1961, Sched. 1, Art. 22(5) (date of judgment); see *Dicey & Morris op. cit.* pp. 1583–1584.

[32] *Dicey and Morris, op. cit.*, p. 1450.

[33] Judgments Act 1838, s.17, as amended by Administration of Justice Act 1970, s.44 and S.I. 1998 No. 2940; Administration of Justice Act 1970, s.44A, inserted by Private International Law (Miscellaneous Provisions) Act 1995, s.1(1). For judgments in the county court, see County Courts Act 1984, s.74(5A), inserted by Private International Law (Miscellaneous Provisions) Act 1995, s.2. The foregoing sections give effect to recommendations of the Law Commission: see Law Com. No. 124 (1983), paras. 4.1–4.15. For arbitral awards, see Arbitration Act 1996, s.49. See *ante* §§ 16–104—16–105.

INDEX

1

Unfair Terms in Consumer Contracts Regulations 1994

arbitration clause, and, 15–053, 16–013
assignment clause, and, 15–065
automatic extension clause, and, 15–059
background, 15–004—15–007
cancellation clause, and, 15–057
choice of law clause, and, 15–072
company incorporation, and contracts relating to, 15–021
consumer contracts
  generally, 15–015
  parties, 15–016—15–018
  types, 15–019—15–022
discharge under contract, and, 23–046
employment contracts, and, 15–021
entire agreement clause, and, 15–063
exclusion clause, and, 15–053
fairness
  generally, 15–032
  relevant terms, 15–023—15–024
  test, 15–033—15–067
fairness criteria
  circumstances of conclusion of contract, 15–041
  dependent contract, terms of, 15–043
  generally, 15–039
  nature of goods and services, 15–040
  other terms of contract, 15–042
fairness test
  appeals, 15–048
  background, 15–034—15–035
  burden of proof, 15–047
  criteria, 15–039—15–043
  ECJ interpretation, 15–049
  generally, 15–033
  good faith, 15–044—15–046
  imbalance in rights, 15–036—15–038
  indicative list, 15–051—15–066
  non-compliance, 15–067
  UK courts' interpretation, 15–050
family rights, and contracts relating to, 15–021
force majeure clauses, and, 14–142
good faith
  ECJ interpretation, 15–049
  generally, 15–044
  other factors, 15–046
  public services, 15–045
indicative list
  assignment clause, 15–065
  automatic extension clause, 15–059
  cancellation clause, 15–057
  entire agreement clause, 15–063
  exclusion clause, 15–053
  generally, 15–051—15–052
  irrevocable binding term, 15–060
  limitation clause, 15–053
  other terms, 15–066
  penalty clause, 15–056

Unfair Terms in Consumer Contracts Regulations 1994—*cont.*

indicative list—*cont.*
  potestative condition, 15–054
  supplier's discretion clause, 15–062
  termination without notice term, 15–058
  unbalanced forfeiture clause, 15–055
  unequal opt out clause, 15–064
  variation clause, 15–061
intelligible language
  non-compliance, 15–070—15–071
  relevant terms, 15–025
  test, 15–068—15–069
limitation clause, and, 15–053
parties
  business, 15–016
  consumer, 15–017—15–018
  generally, 15–015
  recipient, 15–018
  seller, 15–016
  supplier, 15–016
penalty clause, and, 15–056
plain language
  non-compliance, 15–070—15–071
  relevant terms, 15–025
  test, 15–068—15–069
potestative condition, and, 15–054
relevant contracts
  consumer contracts, 15–015—15–022
  generally, 15–009
  sale of goods, 15–010—15–011
  sale of land, 15–012—15–014
  supply of goods, 15–010—15–011
  supply of services, 15–010—15–011
relevant terms
  core terms, 15–025
  examples, 15–026—15–027
  generally, 15–023
  incidental terms, 15–024
  international convention provisions, terms reflecting, 15–031
  regulatory provisions, terms reflecting, 15–028—15–030
  statutory provisions, terms reflecting, 15–028—15–030
remedies, 15–073—15–075
sale of goods, 15–010—15–011
sale of land, 15–012—15–014
standard form contracts, and, 15–024
succession, and contracts relating to, 15–021
summary, 15–008
supplier's discretion clause, and, 15–062
supply of goods, 15–010—15–011
supply of services, 15–010—15–011
suretyship contracts, and, 44–119—44–123
types of contract
  excluded contracts, 15–021
  generally, 15–019—15–020